THE NEW
Southern Living
GARDEN BOOK

THE ULTIMATE GUIDE TO GARDENING

2,000 FULL-COLOR PHOTOS ⚜ **500 GARDEN IDEAS**
8,000 FLOWERS, VEGETABLES, TREES AND MORE

Edited by Steve Bender

Oxmoor House

CONTENTS

WE'RE BACK!

When the first *Southern Living* Garden Book came out in 2004, we were certain we'd produced the most comprehensive guide to Southern gardening ever. But times change and so do gardens. The past decade saw thousands of new superior plants replace tired, old standbys. Gardening practices shifted significantly too. Thus, you hold in your hands a completely revised *The New* Southern Living *Garden Book* that reflects the knowledge and interests of today.

One of the first things you'll notice is the look of the book. We replaced plant illustrations with hundreds of beautiful color photos. We also updated our growing zone map to account for a warming climate and then supplemented our *Southern Living* growing zone ratings for the plants with the United States Department of Agriculture (USDA) hardiness zone ratings to make it easy to determine whether a plant will grow for you. Finally, whenever possible, we recommend natural, organic gardening products to help you succeed in your journey.

This revised book is bigger and showier than its predecessors, but its aim hasn't wavered – to serve a wide range of both beginning and experienced gardeners. Its pages represent *Southern Living's* 50 years of gardening know-how plus the insights of an all-star roster of renowned horticulturists who reviewed its pages for accuracy.

Please enjoy your new book. Then go outside and plant something.

Steve Bender,
Editor

Azaleas, live oaks, Spanish moss, and flowering dogwood create a classic Southern scene at Isle of Hope, Georgia.

THE ESSENTIALS

OF

SOUTHERN GARDENING

At his famous garden at Monticello in Virginia, Thomas Jefferson was among the first in the young United States to grow and promote warm-weather vegetables such as tomatoes, peppers, cucumbers, squash, beans, melons, eggplant, and okra.

PEOPLE VISITING THE SOUTH often note that our gardens and lawns are bigger on average than those found in the Northeast, on the West Coast, or in just about any part of Europe. There's a very good reason for this. In the chunk of the New World that became the United States, the South served as the young nation's first breadbasket. We were farmers and there was room to grow. Neither sea, nor mountains, nor nearby territorial borders hampered our growing efforts.

As farmers, we worked not in offices or factories, but outside in the fields. Time clocks didn't rule the workday; the sun and the moon held that power. Living outdoors became a way of life that's still deeply rooted in our culture. Therefore, it's second nature that we cherish the husbandry of both edible and ornamental plants. As Virginian Thomas Jefferson wrote to Charles Wilson Peale in 1811, "No occupation is so delightful to me as the culture of the earth, and no culture comparable to that of the garden."

Fortunately, our climate smiles upon this pursuit. Yes, it gets so hot in the summer that we argue that air conditioning should be added to the Bill of Rights. But in return we enjoy an extended growing season that makes gardening a year-round activity. Plan wisely and you can have something blooming in your yard in every single month of the year. This fact drives gardeners in other places mad. Email a photo of daffodils blooming in February to a friend snowed under in Montana, and the resulting scream can be heard across two time zones.

Today, the family farm no longer drives the Southern economy. By the middle of the 20th century, big agriculture and burgeoning suburbs were gobbling up small farms faster than a kid with a sack of fresh boiled peanuts. The South eventually transformed into a society of commuters. Wisely anticipating this seismic shift, the *Progressive Farmer* magazine in 1966 published a new special section called *Southern Living,* aimed at suburbanites interested in homes, gardens, food, and travel. After splitting off into a separate publication, *Southern Living* quickly grew into the most successful regional magazine in American history.

In 1998, Birmingham, Alabama-based Oxmoor House published the first truly comprehensive gardening book aimed strictly at Southerners—the *Southern Living Garden Book.* Covering more than 5,000 plants in 500 pages, it earned the title of "the bible of Southern gardening." But because a garden is never finished, a completely revised edition featuring an additional 2,000 plants and 200 pages debuted in 2004.

The newly revised book you're now holding is even bigger and better than that one. It represents how Southern gardening has evolved in both big ways and small over the past ten years. We hope you'll enjoy it and refer to it often.

STEP BY STEP

Luxurious steps of Zoysia grass traverse a gentle slope in the west Georgia garden of Otis and Sandy Scarborough to connect different levels of the garden. Softer and more natural looking than stone or brick, the grass steps add pastoral elegance to the scene. Design: Bill Lincicome and Bruce Jones.

MAKING ROOM

Southerners like nothing more than spending time outdoors entertaining friends. This garden room in Lexington, Kentucky, rests between the house and a detached garage that was turned into a studio. Design by Jon Carloftis

WHAT MAKES A GARDEN SOUTHERN?

G REAT GARDENS AND GARDENERS EXIST ALL OVER THIS COUNTRY. So what key factors coalesce in our region to produce gardens that feel distinctly Southern? You can boil it down to location, plants, style, and people.

Location. For us, the South begins south of the Mason-Dixon Line at the Maryland-Pennsylvania border and extends westward across Kentucky and the bootheel of Missouri to Oklahoma and Texas. Moving south, we cover gardening all the way to the tip of Brownsville, Texas, and Key West, Florida. And although technically the southern counties of Ohio, Indiana, and Illinois don't belong to the South, many folks there identify with our Southern gardens and lifestyle, and we welcome them.

That's a lot of territory to put under one umbrella, but these disparate places share common traits. They enjoy long, warm summers and short, mild winters. Lots of different plants grow here. Because of the strategic location of many old Southern ports such as Baltimore, Charleston, Savannah, Mobile, and New Orleans, exotic plants that would soon be considered classics were imported during colonial times. Historic estates such as Monticello in Virginia and Middleton Place in South Carolina were among the first to display them, and by doing so popularized them across the region.

Of course, not every import liked it here. Iconic plants of New England and northern Europe, such as the common lilac, delphinium, European white birch, and English holly, stewed in our Southern latitudes. However, those that survived often had a bigger impact on Southern gardens than many of our native plants.

A SEA OF SPIDERS

Thousands of spider lilies (*Lycoris radiata*) bloom beneath giant pecan trees at the home of Virginia Sue Barr in Oak Ridge, Louisiana. She divides the lilies every year to make every show bigger than the one before.

IF THERE'S ONE IMAGE of the Southern landscape burned into the minds of people who have never been here, it's the massive live oaks draped in Spanish moss that lined the drive to Twelve Oaks Plantation in *Gone With the Wind.* Thank the stars that these two fabled plants are native to the Southeast, even if most of us don't grow them. Today, environmentalists champion the use of native plants, claiming (not always correctly) that they're hardier, easier to grow, and better for the ecosystem than plants hailing from elsewhere. Isn't it ironic, then, that many of the iconic, ornamental plants that define the look of the Southern garden aren't native to the South or even North America?

Azalea. Camellia. Gardenia. Mimosa. Crepe myrtle. It's harder than leftover fruitcake in January to find a garden anywhere in the South without one of these plants growing in it. We plant them because our neighbors do, and because our mothers did, and because their mothers did before them. We assume because we've seen them since birth that they must be from around here. Not one is.

'Lamarque' Noisette rose

GIFTS FROM ABROAD

Like many of the South's most beloved plants, the saucer magnolia (*Magnolia x soulangiana*) isn't native, but an import from Asia. This doesn't deter us from planting a tree whose outrageously showy spring blooms may stretch 10 inches across.

All arrived aboard merchant ships at the docks of Charleston in the late 1700s. They came from regions in China and Japan with climates very similar to ours. Here they flourished, and as nurseries sprang up, gardeners took them home and cared for them like long-lost family members.

It's the same with edible plants. Except for blueberries, blackberries, muscadines, elderberries, persimmon, and some nuts, practically nothing we consider a Southern staple is native. What we know today as sweet corn not only isn't native to the South, but it really isn't native to anywhere. It originated as a starchy, spiky plant called maize that was first domesticated in southern Mexico more than 9,000 years ago. Tomatoes, peppers, peanuts, and sweet potatoes came from South America. Collards came from southern Europe, figs from the Middle East, citrus and peaches from Asia, and okra from Africa. Even dandelion greens originated in Europe.

That doesn't mean Southerners don't celebrate their native plants. It's hard to find one wildflower that holds a candle to the Texas bluebonnet—or one tree that better expresses a sense of place than South Carolina's cabbage palm. Southerners sing about paw paws, follow trails of dogwoods, search out trilliums, marvel at mountain laurels, grow giddy with the scent of Southern magnolias, and listen to the wind as it whistles through longleaf pines. These indigenous plants are in our blood.

How, then, can you reconcile a region where people put native and exotic plants on equal footing and eventually consider them both essential parts of our heritage? It has little to do with science. It has a lot to do with style.

Texas bluebonnets

HOMEGROWN HARVEST

Backyard vegetable gardens are on the rise as new gardeners seek better flavor, more variety, and more control over the food they eat. As always, tomatoes remain the most popular crop. Many people favor heirloom selections that originated in the South, such as 'Cherokee Purple' and 'Arkansas Traveler'.

TROPICAL PARADISE

Bougainvillea, peace lilies, angel's trumpet,
palms, and lush foliage plants frame a gorgeous
outdoor room in Coral Gables, Florida.
Design: SMI Landscape Architecture;
Owners: Dana & Quentin Nason

MOUNTAIN MAGIC

Hollyhocks grow better at Becky and Ed Savitz's garden in the mountains of western North Carolina than just about any place else. They and many other perennials thrive at higher elevations, where summer days are sunny and the nights are cool.

SOUTHERN STYLE is all about tradition, whether it's food, dress, music, or manners. Our architecture favors traditional styles, such as Greek Revival, Colonial, French Creole, Federal, and Craftsman. So when choosing plants, a Southerner's first instinct is to pick those that have a long history here and also complement traditional styles. Our enthusiasm for "new" plants typically starts with an improved version of a familiar standby—a better crepe myrtle, a better azalea, a better hydrangea, or a better rose. Only then do the true novelty plants appear, such as the purple-leafed loropetalum that's now as common as barbeque and beer.

This hints at a preference for formal design. That's generally true. However, many Southerners opt for a more rustic and funky cottage garden look, where controlled chaos and explosions of color, whimsy, and fun trump straight lines, manicured shrubs, and regimentation.

In this garden, a bottle tree can be just as effective a focal point as a sugar kettle at a plantation house. Other folks eschew the traditional lawn or reduce it to the size of a dining room carpet, devoting the space they save to vegetable gardens, natural areas, or wildflower meadows.

The best Southern gardens express the personalities of their owners. When all is said and done, whether they like it matters more than whether their neighbors do.

'Pride of Mobile' azalea

GRACE AND GARDENIA

If any flower is more fragrant than a gardenia, we haven't
experienced it. Just one cut flower perfumes a room.
While selections with open, starlike blossoms are
common now, the traditional double-flowered forms like
those shown here remain our favorites. One whiff of their
heady, sweet scent says summer is just around the corner.

SHARING PLANTS

At his home in Beach Island, South Carolina, Jenks Farmer preaches the gospel of old Southern plants like crinum lilies that bloomed in our grandparents' gardens.

SOUTHERNERS SHARE. Southern states—specifically, Mississippi, Alabama, Tennessee, and South Carolina—claim four of the top five spots in the nation for percentage of income given to charity. Southerners share recipes, stories, supplies, dialects, and a regional identity like no other group. They also share plants.

It's been this way ever since the South was settled. Poor roads and long distances between neighbors often limited get-togethers to special events like church socials, county fairs, harvest festivals, weddings, and funerals. At such meetings, people might bring a packet of seeds or a sack of bulbs as gifts or for exchange. In time, swapping plants became as ingrained in their nature as swapping tall tales.

Many shared plants were cherished for quirky or valuable traits that made them conversation pieces. For example, naked lady (*Lycoris squamigera*) bloomed without foliage. The flowers of four o'clocks (*Mirabilis jalapa*) perfumed the evening air. Blooms of Confederate rose (*Hibiscus mutabilis*) changed color from white to rose to red. The curved pods of 'Cow Horn' okra remained tender

and spineless up to 10 inches long. 'Arkansas Traveler' tomato produced big crops in hot, dry summers when lesser tomatoes wouldn't.

Today, we call these heirloom plants "passalongs." Passed down from mother to daughter and friend to friend, many are hard to find in nurseries today and survive mainly in the gardens of people who share them. They link us with our past and the people who have gone before. The best part of receiving a passalong plant is that every time you see it in your garden, you instantly remember when you got it and the person who gave it to you.

Swamp Sunflowers

Pots of geraniums, petunias, and blue fan flowers.

WHAT'S NEXT FOR THE SOUTHERN GARDEN

MUCH HAS CHANGED IN GARDENS IN GENERAL OVER THE PAST DECADE. Southern gardens are changing too. One unmistakable trend that continues to pick up steam is gardening in containers. People have discovered that horrible clay soil and too little sun need not prevent you from growing fruits, vegetables, annuals, perennials, shrubs, and even trees. All you need is a suitable container filled with good potting soil that you can place in the proper light and water easily. Most garden plants grow even better in containers than they do in the ground. You'll find lots of good information and ideas for container gardening in these pages.

Succulents, such as these rose-shaped echeverias, are popular additions to containers. They provide terrific texture and need little care.

Also in vogue is the desire to break down the barriers between indoors and outdoors. As mentioned before, Southerners love to spend time outside—whether entertaining, dining, playing, relaxing, or just yammering. Increasingly, they want to create outdoor rooms that not only provide privacy, but also act as extensions of the house. This leads to a search for both attractive screening plants and ornamental and edible plants amenable to growing in smaller spaces. Again, this book will help.

No goal has had a more profound impact on Southern gardens than that of sustainability. People want to enjoy their gardens in an environmentally safe and responsible way, based on the same sound gardening practices our ancestors used—capturing rainwater to hedge against drought; enriching the soil with the free organic matter that naturally falls on the land; composting and using kitchen and garden waste; mulching to conserve moisture and reduce erosion; growing plants that provide food and shelter for wildlife; saving seeds to ensure genetic diversity; choosing plants that resist pests and diseases; and favoring natural fertilizers and pesticides over manufactured ones. Our ancestors knew that only by conserving the soil and returning nutrients to it could we continue to enjoy the land's bounty. Those who ignored this practice paid a heavy price.

Annuals, herbs, and veggies together

RAISING VEGGIES

Old galvanized troughs once used for raising fingerling trout now serve as raised beds for growing a smorgasbord of colorful salad greens.
Design by John McCarley

LEAVES BLAZING

Bathed in early November's late-afternoon sun, trees catch fire around Peter and Jasmin Gentling's rustic home in Asheville, North Carolina. Mountainous locations like this provide the South's most dependable fall color.

COOPED IN COMFORT

No longer confined to the countryside, chickens in the South are moving on up. This handsome coop in the heart of Atlanta houses friendly Buff Orpington hens under the watchful eyes of the Llorens family.

THAT BRINGS US TO the most exciting and welcome trend today—the rebirth of home food gardens. These latter-day victory gardens give us many good things. We enjoy heirloom varieties chosen for their flavor rather than their suitability for shipping. We relish the freshness and nutrition that only comes from homegrown produce. And we appreciate the security of knowing that what we eat contains nothing harmful.

A fascinating corollary to the resurgence of backyard veggies and fruit is the recent enthusiasm for raising backyard chickens. Chicken coops are sprouting everywhere—from the toniest neighborhoods to the heart of the 'burbs—and incorporated into the overall garden. The motivation for this is clear: People want fresh eggs laid by happy chickens raised on a healthy diet—the same thing they want from their tomato, lettuce, and strawberry plants. Beekeeping is another up-and-coming hobby.

Thus, we see that the Southern garden has come full circle. We started off growing crops and raising livestock. Now we've returned. Granted, most of us will never live on a farm, but that won't prevent us from implementing the good lessons our forebears taught us. Be good stewards of the land. Share its bounty. Enjoy its beauty.

For the South, the home garden serves as a bridge between where we've been and where we're headed. Who knows what fantastic new plants lie in our path? One thing is for sure, however. Like the twin-faced Janus of Roman mythology who looked both forward and back, Southerners will pay just as much attention to the gardens we remember as the ones we've yet to see.

Jimmie Henslee, Dallas, Texas

PLANT
FINDER

HOW TO USE THIS PLANT FINDER

On the following pages, you'll find 31 different Plant Selection Guides. They each list dozens of desirable plants that share a common characteristic. Some relate to color (showy flowers, showy foliage, showy fruits and berries), some to classes of common garden plants (trees, vines, vegetables, fruits), and still others to good plants for specific situations (shade, dry soil, container gardens, houseplants). Each plant listing tells you the page number where you can find more information about that plant plus quick keys on how and where to grow the plant using the symbols below.

SUN

☼ Grows best with unobstructed sunlight all day long or almost all day—you can overlook an hour or so of shade at the beginning or end of a summer day

☽ Needs partial shade—that is, shade for half the day or for at least 3 hours during the hottest part of the day

● Prefers little or no direct sunlight—for example, it does best on the north side of a house or beneath a broad, dense tree

WATER

◌ Needs no supplemental watering once it is established—usually 1 or 2 years after planting

◓ Thrives with less than regular moisture—moderate amounts for some plants, little for those with more drought tolerance

◆ Performs well with regular moisture

◆◆ Takes more than regular moisture—includes plants needing constantly moist soil, bog plants, and aquatic plants

CLIMATE

A plant's climate adaptability is shown after the symbol ✎. The letters US, MS, LS, CS, and TS refer to the Southern Living Climate Zones (✎). For more information on these climate zones, and on the corresponding United States Department of Agriculture (USDA) hardiness zones, see pages xxx.

READING THE MAPS

Southern Living divides the South into five broad climate zones: Upper South (US), Middle South (MS), Lower South (LS), Coastal South (CS), and Tropical South (TS). The boundaries of these zones correspond to those of the recently updated United States Department of Agriculture (USDA) Plant Hardiness Zone Map. The Upper South is in USDA Zone 6, the Middle South in Zone 7, the Lower South in Zone 8, the Coastal South in Zone 9, and the Tropical South in Zones 10 and 11. It's important to note that because the USDA map reflects minimum yearly temperatures, it functions solely as a cold-hardiness map. In the South, however, heat is as much a limiting factor as cold. Therefore, when we give a plant a Southern Living climate zone rating, we take into account both summer heat and winter cold. For example, if we recommend astilbe as a permanent plant for your area, we mean that it will not only survive your winters but also endure your summers, and that it will perform satisfactorily for you. We won't recommend astilbe for the Coastal or Tropical South, because although it takes winters there, in summer it melts faster than ice sculptures on a cruise ship.

UPPER SOUTH (US). This region experiences the longest winters and shortest summers in the South, but summers are still hot and sticky. Fortunately, sizzling Southern temperatures rarely last long. Plants that need cool nights and long periods of winter chill do well here. Cold winters bring constraints, however. Frozen soil means that dahlias, cannas, glads, and other summer-flowering bulbs must be dug up in fall and stored over winter. Crepe myrtle, camellias, and figs may not be cold-hardy in all areas. The last frost occurs anywhere from mid-April to the first 10 days of May.

MIDDLE SOUTH (MS). This region forms a transition zone between warm-weather and cool-weather growing zones. Here you often encounter plants from the Northeast, the Midwest, and the Northwest growing alongside Southern natives. Summers are hot and, in most places, humid. The last spring frost generally occurs in the last two weeks of April.

LOWER SOUTH (LS). Spring comes early to the Lower South. Daffodils, flowering quince, and winter daphne open their buds in February. Though summer droughts are common, torrential downpours more than make up the difference. Snow is rare, but ice storms are not. The last frost generally occurs in the last week of March through the first two weeks of April.

COASTAL SOUTH (CS). Two large bodies of water—the Atlantic Ocean and the Gulf of Mexico—rule the Coastal South. Their close proximity ensures that winters are mild and brief but summers are long and humid. The last spring frost usually comes in the last three weeks in February. Spring commences in January, when the Japanese magnolias and common camellias bloom.

TROPICAL SOUTH (TS). Truly its own gardening world, the Tropical South rarely feels frost. In fact, the lowest temperature on record for Miami is 30 degrees. Whereas most of the South deals with dry summers and wet winters, a large portion of the Tropical South reverses that pattern. All sorts of lush, exotic plants with strikingly colorful blooms and foliage flourish. This region can seem like a paradise. But the lack of winter chill comes at a price. Azaleas, forsythia, hosta, hydrangea, and many other temperate plants fail here.

SOUTHERN LIVING PLANTING ZONES

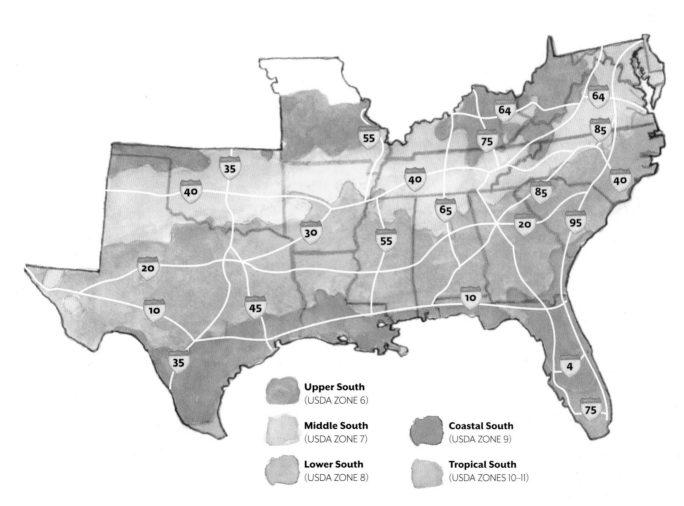

Upper South
(USDA ZONE 6)

Middle South
(USDA ZONE 7)

Coastal South
(USDA ZONE 9)

Lower South
(USDA ZONE 8)

Tropical South
(USDA ZONES 10–11)

Annuals
for Seasonal Color

Flowering annuals provide quick, nonstop color and come in a nearly boundless variety of colors, shapes, and sizes. Yes, most die after one growing season, but that gives you the chance to try something new. Cool-season annuals prefer cool weather, blossoming in spring and fall (and, in mild climates, winter). Warm-season annuals hate frost but love the heat, generally blooming from late spring to fall. Plants marked with the symbol 🌱 are actually tender perennials that may live from year to year in mild-winter areas.

Snapdragon
Antirrhinum majus

California poppy
Eschscholzia californica

Delphinium

Edging lobelia
Lobelia erinus

Flowering cabbage

Carefree spires of larkspur
(*Consolida ajacis*) bloom in spring.

Lupine
Lupinus, Russell hybrid

Bat-faced cuphea
Cuphea llavea

Stock
Matthiola incana

COOL-SEASON ANNUALS

Calendula
☀️💧☀️ ALL
Calendula officinalis — p. 204

California poppy
☀️🌑💧💧☀️ ALL
Eschscholzia californica — p. 302

Delphinium
☀️💧☀️ VARY
— p. 277

Edging lobelia
🌑☀️💧💧☀️ ALL
Lobelia erinus — p. 417

English daisy 🌱
☀️🌑💧☀️ US, MS, LS, TS
Bellis perennis — p. 184

English wallflower
☀️🌑💧☀️ US, MS
Erysimum cheiri — p. 301

Flowering cabbage and kale
☀️🌑💧☀️ ALL
— p. 201

Forget-me-not
🌑💧☀️ US, MS, LS
Myosotis sylvatica — p. 445

Foxglove
🌑💧☀️ US, MS, LS, CS
Digitalis — p. 285

Larkspur
☀️🌑💧☀️ ALL
Consolida ajacis — p. 251

Lupine
☀️🌑💧💧☀️ VARY
Lupinus — p. 420

Monkey flower
☀️🌑💧☀️ ALL
Mimulus x hybridus — p. 438

Nemesia
☀️🌑💧☀️ ALL — p. 449

Pansy, viola, violet
☀️🌑🌑💧☀️ VARY
Viola — p. 641

Poppy (some)
☀️🌑💧☀️ VARY
Papaver — p. 470

Primrose (many)
🌑💧☀️ VARY
Primula — p. 521

Snapdragon
☀️💧☀️ ALL
Antirrhinum majus — p. 153

Stock
☀️🌑💧☀️ ALL
Matthiola incana — p. 433

Sweet William 🌱
☀️🌑💧☀️ ALL
Dianthus barbatus — p. 279

Twinspur
☀️🌑🌑💧☀️ VARY
Diascia — p. 281

WARM-SEASON ANNUALS

Amethyst flower 🌱
🌑💧☀️ ALL
Browallia — p. 195

Angelonia 🌱
☀️💧☀️ ALL
Angelonia angustifolia — p. 151

Annual phlox
☀️💧☀️ ALL
Phlox drummondii — p. 497

Bachelor's button
☀️💧☀️ ALL
Centaurea cyanus — p. 224

For growing symbol explanations, please see page 37.

Bat-faced cuphea ☼ ◐◑⚡ CS, TS, OR ANNUAL
Cuphea llavea   p. 267

Begonia ☼◐◑⚡ ALL
                                             p. 182

Blue daze ☼◐◑◑⚡ TS OR ANNUAL
Evolvulus glomeratus   p. 309

Calibrachoa ☼◐◑⚡ ALL
                                             p. 204

Calliopsis ☼◐◑◑⚡ ALL
Coreopsis tinctoria   p. 254

Cockscomb ☼◐◑⚡ ALL
Celosia argentea   p. 223

Coleus ☼◐◑◑◑⚡ TS OR ANNUAL
Solenostemon scutellariodes   p. 591

Copper leaf ☼◑⚡ TS OR INDOORS
Acalypha wilkesiana   p. 126

Cosmos, common ☼◑⚡ ALL
Cosmos bipinnatus   p. 259

Fan flower ☼◑◑⚡ ALL
Scaevola aemula   p. 578

Floss flower ☼◐◑⚡ ALL
Ageratum houstonianum   p. 139

Flowering tobacco ☼◐◑◑◑⚡ ALL
Nicotiana   p. 453

Geranium ◐◑◑◑⚡ CS, TS OR ANNUAL
Pelargonium   p. 484

Globe amaranth ☼◐◑⚡ ALL
Gomphrena   p. 332

Heliotrope, common ☼◐◑◑◑⚡ TS OR ANNUAL
Heliotropium arborescens   p. 349

Impatiens ☼◑◐◑◑⚡ ALL
                                             p. 373

Indian blanket ☼◐◑◑⚡ ALL
Gaillardia pulchella   p. 322

Lantana ☼◐◑⚡ ALL
                                             p. 400

Madagascar periwinkle
Catharanthus roseus   p. 221

Marigold ☼◐⚡ VARY
Tagetes   p. 611

Mexican sunflower ☼◐⚡ ALL
Tithonia rotundifolia   p. 621

Money plant ☼◐◑◑◑◑⚡ US, MS, LS, CS
Lunaria annua   p. 420

Moss rose ☼◐◑⚡ ALL
Portulaca grandiflora   p. 519

Nasturtium ☼◐◑◑⚡ ALL
Tropaeolum majus   p. 628

Ornamental pepper ☼◐⚡ ALL
                                             p. 489

Perilla ☼◐◑⚡ ALL
Perilla frutescens   p. 489

Petunia ☼◐◑⚡ ALL
Petunia x hybrida   p. 492

Pink (some) ☼◐◑⚡ US, MS, LS, CS
Dianthus   p. 279

Silk flower ☼◐⚡ ALL
Abelmoschus moschatus   p. 124

Spider flower ☼◐⚡ ALL
Cleome hasslerana   p. 244

Star daisy ☼◐◑⚡ ALL
Melampodium paludosum   p. 434

Strawflower ☼◐⚡ ALL
Helichrysum bracteatum   p. 347

Sunflower, common ☼◐◑◑⚡ ALL
Helianthus annuus   p. 345

Swan River daisy ☼◐⚡ ALL
Brachyscome iberidifolia   p. 193

Sweet alyssum ☼◐◑⚡ US, MS, LS, CS
Lobularia maritima   p. 417

Verbena (some) ☼◐⚡ VARY
                                             p. 634

Wishbone flower ◐◑⚡ ALL
Torenia fournieri   p. 625

Zinnia ☼◐⚡ ALL
                                             p. 651

Monkey flower
Mimulus x hybridus

Calibrachoa

Nasturtium
Tropaeolum majus

Silk flower
Abelmoschus moschatus

Spider flower
Cleome hasslerana

Zinnia
Zinnia elegans

Coleus
Coleus x hybridus

Flowering tobacco
Nicotiana sylvestris

Globe amaranth
Gomphrena globosa

Impatiens

For climate zone explanations, please see pages 38–39.

Coral bells
Heuchera x brizoides

Showy Perennials
for Beds and Borders

It's sometimes said that a perennial is any plant that, had it survived, could have come back year after year. Fortunately, most perennials are tougher than this, offering us decades of dazzling flowers and foilage. Among their ranks you'll find an astonishing array of choices, literally something for everyone. Perennials range in size and shape from small mounds to giant towers, and there are choices for every imaginable garden spot. Try out some new plants this year. It's one of the things that makes gardening fun.

Geum, alliums, delphiniums, and verbascum.

Alstroemeria

New England aster
Symphotrichum

Balloon flower
Platycodon grandiflorus

Bee balm
Monarda didyma

Aconite ☼ ◐ ● ◊ ✿ US, MS	
Aconitum	p. 131
Agastache ☼ ◐ ● ◊ ✿ VARY	
	p. 137
Alpinia ☼ ◊ ● ◊ ✿ VARY	
	p. 145
Alstroemeria ☼ ◊ ● ◊ ✿ MS, LS, CS	
	p. 146
Anthemis ☼ ◊ ● ◊ ✿ VARY	
	p. 152
Anthurium ◊ ● ✿ TS	
	p. 152
Asclepias ☼ ◊ ◊ ◊ ● ◊ ✿ VARY	
	p. 168
Aster ☼ ◊ ● ✿ US, MS, LS	
	p. 172
Baby's breath ☼ ◊ ● ✿ US, MS, LS, CS	
Gypsophila paniculata	p. 340
Balloon flower ☼ ◐ ● ◊ ✿ US, MS, LS, CS	
Platycodon grandiflorus	p. 508
Beard tongue ☼ ◊ ◊ ◊ ✿ VARY	
Penstemon (many)	p. 486
Bear's breeches ☼ ◐ ● ◊ ◊ ✿ US, MS, LS, CS	
Acanthus mollis	p. 127
Bee balm ☼ ◐ ● ◊ ◊ ✿ US, MS, LS	
Monarda didyma	p. 440

Bellflower ☼ ◐ ● ◊ ✿ US, MS, LS	
Campanula	p. 213
Bergenia ◐ ● ◊ ✿ US, MS, LS	
	p. 185
Betony ☼ ◐ ● ◊ ✿ US, MS, LS	
Stachys officinalis	p. 599
Bird of Paradise ☼ ◐ ● ✿ CS, TS	
Strelitzia reginae	p. 604
Blanket flower ☼ ◊ ● ✿ ALL	
Gaillardia grandiflora	p. 321
Blazing star ☼ ◊ ◊ ● ◊ ✿ US, MS, LS, CS	
Liatris	p. 409
Bleeding heart, common ◊ ● ◊ ✿ US, MS, LS, CS	
Lamprocapnos	p. 400
Bluestar ☼ ◐ ● ◊ ✿ US, MS, LS, CS	
Amsonia tabernaemontana	p. 149
Bowman's root ☼ ◊ ● ✿ US, MS, LS	
Gillenia trifoliata	p. 329
Bush daisy ☼ ◊ ● ◊ ✿ CS, TS OR ANNUAL	
Euryops pectinatus	p. 309
Butterfly weed ☼ ◊ ● ◊ ✿ US, MS, LS, CS	
Asclepias tuberosa	p. 168
Cardinal flower ◊ ☼ ● ◊ ◊ ✿ US, MS, LS, CS	
Lobelia cardinalis	p. 417
Celandine poppy ◐ ● ◊ ✿ US, MS, LS, CS	
Stylophorum diphyllum	p. 605

Beard tongue
Penstemon

Peach-leafed bluebell
Campanula persicifolia

Bleeding heart, common

For growing symbol explanations, please see page 37.

Columbine
Aquilegia McKana Giants

Crocosmia

Dancing girl ginger
Globba

Coneflower
Rudbeckia

Checkerbloom
☼ ◐ ◢ ✚ US, MS
Sidalcea — p. 588

Chilean avens
☼ ☼ ◐ ◢ ✚ US, MS
Geum chiloense — p. 328

Chinese foxglove
☼ ◐ ◢ ✚ MS, LS, CS, TS
Rehmannia elata — p. 539

Chrysanthemum
☼ ◐ ◢ ✚ VARY
— p. 235

Cinquefoil
☼ ☼ ◐ ◢ ✚ VARY
Potentilla — p. 520

Clinton lily
◐ ◢ ✚ US, MS
Clintonia umbellulata — p. 247

Columbine
☼ ☼ ◐ ◢ ✚ VARY
Aquilegia — p. 160

Coneflower
☼ ◐ ◢ ◢ ✚ US, MS, LS, CS
Rudbeckia — p. 563

Coral bells
☼ ◐ ◢ ◢ ✚ US, MS, LS
Heuchera — p. 354

Coreopsis
☼ ◐ ◢ ◢ ✚ US, MS, LS, CS
— p. 253

Cranesbill
☼ ☼ ◐ ◢ ✚ US, MS, LS
Geranium — p. 326

Crinum
☼ ☼ ◐ ◢ ◢ ✚ VARY
— p. 263

Crocosmia
☼ ☼ ◐ ◢ ✚ US, MS, LS, CS
— p. 264

Cupid's dart
☼ ☼ ◐ ◢ ✚ US, MS, LS
Catananche caerulea — p. 220

Dancing girl ginger
◐ ◢ ◢ ✚ CS, TS
Globba — p. 331

Daylily
☼ ☼ ◐ ◢ ✚ ALL
Hemerocallis — p. 351

Delphinium
☼ ◐ ◢ ✚ VARY
— p. 277

Dicliptera
☼ ☼ ◐ ◢ ◢ ◢ ✚ VARY
— p. 283

Euphorbia
☼ ☼ ◐ ◢ ◢ ◢ ◇ ✚ VARY
— p. 307

Evergreen candytuft
☼ ◐ ◢ ✚ US, MS, CS
Iberis sempervirens — p. 369

False indigo
☼ ◐ ◢ ✚ US, MS, LS, CS
Baptisia — p. 179

False spiraea
☼ ☼ ◐ ◢ ✚ US, MS, LS
Astilbe — p. 172

False sunflower
☼ ◐ ◢ ◢ ◢ ✚ US, MS, LS, CS
Heliopsis helianthoides — p. 348

Fanflower
☼ ◐ ◢ ✚ CS, TS OR ANNUAL
Scaevola aemula — p. 578

Filipendula
☼ ◐ ◢ ◢ ✚ US, MS, LS
— p. 316

Firecracker plant
☼ ☼ ◐ ◢ ✚ CS, TS
Russelia equisetiformis — p. 565

Fortnight lily
☼ ◐ ◢ ◢ ✚ LS, CS, TS
Dietes iridioides — p. 284

Fountain grass
☼ ◐ ◢ ◢ ✚ VARY
Pennisetum — p. 485

Four o'clock
☼ ◐ ◢ ✚ ALL
Mirabilis jalapa — p. 438

Foxtail lily
☼ ◐ ◢ ✚ US, MS, LS
Eremurus — p. 299

Gas plant
☼ ◐ ◢ ◢ ◇ ✚ US, MS, LS
Dictamnus albus — p. 283

Gaura
☼ ◐ ◢ ✚ US, MS, LS, CS
Gaura lindheimeri — p. 324

Geranium
◐ ◢ ◢ ✚ CS, TS OR ANNUAL
Pelargonium — p. 484

Gerbera daisy
☼ ◐ ◢ ◢ ✚ ALL
Gerbera jamesonii — p. 328

Ginger lily
☼ ◐ ◢ ◢ ✚ VARY
Hedychium — p. 344

Globe centaurea
☼ ◐ ◢ ✚ US, MS, LS
Centaurea macrocephala — p. 225

Globeflower
☼ ◐ ◢ ◢ ✚ US, MS
Trollius — p. 628

Globe thistle
☼ ◐ ◢ ✚ US, MS, LS, CS
Echinops — p. 293

Purple fountain grass
Pennisetum setaceum 'Rubrum'

Fortnight lily
Dietes iridioides

Four o'clock
Mirabilis jalapa

Globeflower
Trollius

Delphinium

For climate zone explanations, please see pages 38–39.

Gooseneck loosestrife
Lysimachia clethroides

Hollyhock
Alcea rosea

Bearded iris

Japanese anemone
Anemone x hybrida 'Prinz Heinrich'

Jerusalem sage
Phlomis fruticosa

Goat's beard
☼ ◐ ◑ ⚡ VARY
Aruncus — p. 167

Golden aster
☼ ◐ ⚡ US, MS, LS, CS
Chrysopsis — p. 237

Golden marguerite
☼ ◐ ⚡ US, MS, LS
Anthemis tinctoria — p. 152

Golden ray
◐ ● ◑ ⚡ US, MS, LS
Ligularia — p. 409

Golden star
◐ ◑ ⚡ US, MS, LS, CS
Chrysogonum virginianum — p. 237

Goldenrod
☼ ◐ ◑ ⚡ US, MS, LS, CS
Solidago and Solidaster — p. 593

Gooseneck loosestrife
☼ ◐ ◑ ◑ ⚡ US, MS, LS
Lysimachia clethroides — p. 422

Greek yarrow
☼ ○ ◑ ⚡ US, MS, LS
Achillea ageratifolia — p. 130

Hellebore
◐ ● ◑ ◑ ⚡ ◑ VARY
Helleborus — p. 349

Hesperaloe
☼ ◐ ○ ◑ ⚡ MS, LS, CS, TS
— p. 353

x Heucherella
◐ ◑ ⚡ US, MS, LS
— p. 355

Hollyhock
☼ ◐ ◑ ⚡ US, MS, LS, CS
Alcea rosea — p. 141

Ice plant
☼ ◐ ○ ◑ ⚡ VARY
Delosperma — p. 277

Incarvillea
☼ ◐ ◑ ⚡ VARY
— p. 374

Iris
☼ ◐ ● ◑ ◑ ◑ ⚡ VARY
— p. 377

Ironweed
☼ ◐ ◑ ◑ ● ⚡ US, MS, LS, CS
Vernonia noveboracensis — p. 636

Jacob's ladder
◐ ● ◑ ⚡ US, MS, LS
Polemonium caeruleum — p. 515

Japanese anemone
◐ ◑ ◑ ⚡ US, MS, LS
Anemone x hybrida — p. 150

Jerusalem sage
☼ ◐ ◑ ⚡ MS, LS, CS, TS
Phlomis fruticosa — p. 496

Joe-Pye weed
☼ ◐ ◑ ⚡ US, MS, LS, CS
Eupatorium purpureum — p. 306

Lady bells
☼ ◐ ◑ ◑ ⚡ US, MS
Adenophora — p. 133

Lavender (shrubby perennial)
☼ ◐ ◑ ⚡ VARY
Lavandula — p. 403

Lily
☼ ◐ ◑ ⚡ US, MS, LS, CS
Lilium — p. 411

Lily-of-the-Nile
☼ ◐ ○ ◑ ◑ ⚡ VARY
Agapanthus — p. 136

Lion's tail
☼ ◐ ○ ⚡ VARY
Leonotis — p. 406

Live-forever sedum
☼ ◐ ◑ ⚡ US, MS, LS, CS
Sedum telephium — p. 584

Lobster-claw
☼ ◐ ◑ ● ⚡ TS
Heliconia — p. 348

Lupine
☼ ○ ◑ ◑ ⚡ VARY
Lupinus — p. 420

Marsh marigold
☼ ◐ ● ◑ ◑ ⚡ US, MS, LS, CS
Caltha palustris — p. 207

Meadow rue
◐ ◑ ⚡ VARY
Thalictrum — p. 616

Mexican hat
☼ ◐ ◑ ⚡ US, MS, LS, CS
Ratibida columnifera — p. 539

Muhly grass
☼ ◐ ○ ◑ ◑ ◑ ⚡ MS, LS, CS, TS
Muhlenbergia — p. 442

Mullein
☼ ◐ ⚡ US, MS, LS
Verbascum — p. 634

Nepeta
☼ ◐ ◑ ⚡ VARY
— p. 450

Nerine
☼ ◐ ◑ ⚡ LS, CS, TS
— p. 452

Nodding ladies' tresses
☼ ◐ ◑ ◑ ⚡ US, MS, LS, CS
Spiranthes cernua odorata — p. 597

Obedient plant
☼ ◐ ◑ ⚡ US, MS, LS, CS
Physostegia virginiana — p. 501

Pampas grass
☼ ◐ ◑ ◑ ◑ ⚡ MS, LS, CS, TS
Cortaderia selloana — p. 258

Regal lily
Lilium regale

Showy evening primrose
Oenothera speciosa

Mullein
Verbascum

Obedient plant
Physostegia virginiana

For growing symbol explanations, please see page 37.

Peony
Paeonia

Blue phlox
Phlox divericata

Red-hot poker
Kniphofia uvaria

Blazing star
Liatris sp.

Pearly everlasting
☼◑◔◔◔✂ US, MS, LS
Anaphalis — p. 149

Peony
☼◑◔◔✂ US, MS, LS
Paeonia (herbaceous) — p. 466

Perennial blue flax
☼◔◔✂ US, MS, LS
Linum perenne — p. 414

Perennial hibiscus
☼◔◔✂ ALL
Hibiscus moscheutos — p. 356

Phlox
☼◔◔✂ VARY
— p. 497

Pincushion flower
☼◔◔◔✂ ALL
Scabiosa — p. 578

Pink
☼◔◔◔✂ US, MS, LS, CS
Dianthus — p. 279

Plaintain lily
◑◑◔◔✂ US, MS, LS
Hosta — p. 359

Plume poppy
☼◔◔◔✂ US, MS, LS
Macleaya cordata — p. 423

Porterweed
☼◔◔◔✂ TS
Stachytarpheta — p. 600

Prickly poppy
☼◔✂ ALL
Argemone — p. 163

Primrose
◔◔✂ VARY
Primula — p. 521

Purple coneflower
☼◔◔◔✂ US, MS, LS, CS
Echinacea purpurea — p. 292

Red-hot poker
☼◔◔◔◔✂ US, MS, LS, CS
Kniphofia uvaria — p. 392

Rose campion
☼◔◔◔✂ US, MS, LS
Lychnis coronaria — p. 421

Royal catchfly
☼◔◔◔✂ US, MS, LS, CS
Silene regia — p. 588

Russian sage
☼◔◔◔✂ US, MS, LS, CS
Perovskia atriplicifolia — p. 490

Sage
☼◔◔✂ VARY
Salvia (many) — p. 568

Sea holly
☼◔◔✂ US, MS, LS
Eryngium amethystinum — p. 300

Sedge (some)
☼◑◔◔◔◔✂ US, MS, LS, CS
Carex — p. 216

Showy evening primrose
☼◑◔◔✂ ALL
Oenothera speciosa — p. 457

Showy sedum
☼◑◔◔✂ US, MS, LS, CS
Sedum spectabile — p. 584

Silphium
☼◑◔◔◔✂ US, MS, LS, CS
— p. 588

Sneezeweed
☼◔◔✂✂ US, MS, LS, CS
Helenium autumnale — p. 345

Snow-in-summer
☼◔◔◔✂ US, MS, LS
Cerastium tomentosum — p. 226

Speedwell
☼◔◔◔◔✂ US, MS, LS
Veronica — p. 636

Spiderwort
☼◑◑◔◔◔◔✂ US, MS, LS, CS
Tradescantia virginiana — p. 626

Spiral flag
◔◔◔✂ CS, TS
Costus — p. 260

Statice
☼◔◔✂ VARY
Limonium — p. 413

Stokesia
☼◔◔✂ US, MS, LS, CS
Stokesia laevis — p. 602

Thrift, common
☼◔◔◔✂ US, MS, LS, CS
Armeria maritima — p. 165

Toadflax
☼◔◔◔✂ US, MS, LS, CS
Linaria — p. 413

Toad lily
◑◑◔◔◔✂ US, MS, LS, CS
Tricyrtis — p. 626

Valerian
☼◑◔◔◔✂ US, MS, LS
Centranthus ruber — p. 225

Verbena bonariensis
☼◔◔✂ MS, LS, CS, TS
— p. 635

White turtlehead
☼◑◔◔◔✂ US, MS, LS
Chelone glabra — p. 231

Yarrow
☼◑◔◔✂ US, MS, LS
Achillea — p. 130

Yellow waxbells
◑◔◔✂ US, MS, LS
Kirengeshoma palmata — p. 391

Sneezeweed
Helenium autumnale

Speedwell
Veronica

Valerian
Centranthus ruber

Yarrow, common
Achillea millefolium

Spiderwort
Tradescantia virginiana

For climate zone explanations, please see pages 38–39.

Bulbs
and Bulblike Plants

Because bulbs are often dormant during the most desolate weather, they can survive with little care. That's why many have become heirloom plants, dug and passed along from generation to generation. Some—tulips, hyacinths, and crocuses—need months of winter cold to bloom well. Others can thrill withouth the chill. Bulbs (and corms, tubers, and rhizomes) may flower for only a few weeks each year, but multiplied by scores of blossoms over a lifetime, they make the garden rich with flowers.

Paperwhites (*Narcissus*)

Fancy-leafed caladium
Caladium bicolor 'White Queen'

Crinum

Daffodil
Narcissus 'Peeping Tom'

AUTUMN-PLANTED BULBS

Atamasco lily
☼ ◐ ❀ ⚡ MS, LS, CS, TS
Zephyranthes atamasca   p. 650

Aztec lily
☼ ◐ ❀ ⚡ LS, CS, TS
Sprekelia formosissima   p. 598

Baboon flower
☼ ☼ ◐ ❀ ⚡ LS, CS, TS
Babiana   p. 175

Blackberry lily
☼ ☼ ◐ ❀ ⚡ US, MS, LS, CS
Iris domestica   p. 379

Black calla
☼ ◐ ❀ ◆ ⚡ CS, TS
Arum palaestinum   p. 167

Bloodroot
☼ ◐ ❀ ◆ ⚡ US, MS, LS
Sanguinaria canadensis   p. 573

Blue flag
☼ ☼ ◐ ❀ ⚡ US, MS, LS, CS
Iris versicolor   p. 381

Camass
☼ ☼ ◐ ❀ ⚡ US, MS, LS, CS
Camassia   p. 208

Crested iris
☼ ◐ ❀ ⚡ US, MS, LS, CS
Iris cristata   p. 381

Crinum
☼ ☼ ◐ ❀ ◆ ⚡ VARY
         p. 263

Crocus
☼ ☼ ◐ ❀ ⚡ US, MS, LS
         p. 264

Daffodil
☼ ☼ ◐ ❀ ⚡ US, MS, LS, CS
Narcissus   p. 446

Dog-tooth violet
☼ ◐ ❀ ⚡ US, MS, LS
Erythronium dens-canis   p. 302

English bluebell
☼ ◐ ❀ ⚡ US, MS
Hyacinthoides non-scripta   p. 362

Eucharist lily
● ❀ ⚡ TS OR INDOORS
Eucharis grandiflora   p. 303

Fancy-leafed caladium
☼ ☼ ● ❀ ◆ ⚡ CS, TS
Caladium bicolor   p. 202

Foxtail lily
☼ ◐ ❀ ⚡ US, MS, LS
Eremurus   p. 299

Freesia
☼ ◐ ❀ ⚡ CS, TS
         p. 320

Fritillary
☼ ☼ ◐ ❀ ⚡ US, MS, LS
Fritillaria   p. 320

Globeflower
☼ ☼ ◐ ❀ ◆ ⚡ US, MS
Trollius   p. 628

Glory-of-the-snow
☼ ☼ ◐ ❀ ⚡ US, MS, LS
Chionodoxa   p. 234

Grape hyacinth
☼ ☼ ◐ ❀ ⚡ US, MS, LS
Muscari   p. 443

Greek anemone
☼ ◐ ❀ ⚡ US, MS, LS
Anemone blanda   p. 150

Hidden lily
◐ ❀ ⚡ LS, CS, TS
Curcuma petiolata   p. 268

Hyacinth, common
☼ ☼ ◐ ❀ ◆ ⚡ VARY
Hyacinthus orientalis   p. 363

Freesia

Grape hyacinth
Muscari

Greek anemone
Anemone blanda

For growing symbol explanations, please see page 37.

Oriental lily
Lilium 'Acapulco'

Squill
Scilla

Lily-of-the-Valley
Convallaria majalis

Hymenocallis
☼ ◑ ◐ ◔ ✂ VARY
p. 366

Italian arum
☼ ● ● ◐ ◔ ✂ US, MS, LS, CS
Arum italicum p. 167

Ixiolirion tataricum
☼ ◐ ✂ US, MS, LS, CS
p. 382

Jack-in-the-pulpit
☼ ● ● ◐ ✂ US, MS, LS, CS
Arisaema triphyllum p. 164

Jackson vine
☼ ◑ ◐ ● ◔ ✂ MS, LS, CS
Smilax smallii p. 590

Lily
☼ ◑ ◐ ✂ US, MS, LS, CS
Lilium p. 411

Lily-of-the-Nile
☼ ◑ ◐ ○ ● ◐ ✂ VARY
Agapanthus p. 136

Lily-of-the-Valley
☼ ● ● ◐ ◔ ✂ US, MS, LS
Convallaria majalis p. 251

Ornamental allium
☼ ◑ ◐ ◔ ✂ VARY
Allium p. 142

Oxalis
☼ ◑ ◐ ◔ ✂ ALL
Oxalis rubra p. 464

Oxblood lily
☼ ◐ ✂ MS, LS, CS, TS
Rhodophiala bifida p. 548

Parrot lily
● ◐ ◔ ✂ MS, LS, CS
Alstroemeria psittacina p. 146

Persian ranunculus
☼ ◐ ✂ LS, CS, TS
Ranunculus asiaticus p. 536

Pineapple lily
☼ ◑ ◐ ◔ ✂ MS, LS, CS, TS
Eucomis p. 304

Pregnant onion
☼ ◑ ◐ ◔ ◐ ✂ CS, TS
Ornithogalum longibracteatum p. 462

Rain lily
☼ ◐ ✂ MS, LS, CS, TS
Zephyranthes p. 650

Snowdrop
☼ ◑ ◐ ◔ ✂ US, MS, LS
Galanthus p. 322

Snowflake
☼ ◑ ◐ ◔ ✂ VARY
Leucojum p. 407

Southern spider lily
☼ ◑ ◐ ◔ ◐ ✂ US, MS, LS, CS
Hymenocallis caroliniana p. 366

Spanish bluebell
☼ ◐ ◔ ✂ US, MS, LS, CS
Hyacinthoides hispanica p. 362

Spring star flower
☼ ◑ ◐ ◔ ✂ US, MS, LS, CS
Ipheion uniflorum p. 375

Squill
☼ ◑ ◐ ◔ ✂ US, MS, LS
Scilla p. 580

Star of Bethlehem
☼ ◑ ◐ ◔ ✂ US, MS, LS, CS
Ornithogalum umbellatum p. 462

Star of Persia
☼ ◑ ◐ ✂ US, MS, LS
Allium christophii p. 143

Sternbergia lutea
☼ ◐ ✂ US, MS, LS
p. 601

Summer hyacinth
☼ ◑ ◐ ✂ MS, LS, CS, TS
Galtonia candicans p. 323

Triteleia
☼ ○ ✂ US, MS, LS, CS
p. 627

Tulip
☼ ◑ ◐ ✂ ALL
Tulipa p. 629

Virginia bluebells
☼ ● ◐ ✂ US, MS, LS
Mertensia virginica p. 436

Winter aconite
☼ ◑ ◐ ✂ US, MS
Eranthis hyemalis p. 298

Yellow star grass
☼ ◑ ◐ ◔ ✂ US, MS, LS, CS
Hypoxis hirsuta p. 368

SPRING-PLANTED BULBS

Abyssinian sword lily
☼ ◐ ✂ MS, LS, CS
Gladiolus murielae p. 330

Achimenes
☼ ● ◐ ✂ CS, TS
p. 131

African corn lily
☼ ◐ ✂ LS, CS, TS
Ixia p. 381

x Amarcrinum memoria-corsii
☼ ◑ ◐ ✂ LS, CS, TS
p. 263

Amaryllis
☼ ◑ ◐ ✂ LS, CS, TS
Hippeastrum p. 358

Bolivian sunset
☼ ◐ ✂ LS, CS, TS OR INDOORS
Gloxinia sylvatica p. 332

Snowdrop
Galanthus

Sternbergia
Sternbergia lutea

Lady tulip
Tulipa clusiana

Tulip and hyacinth bulbs

Golden calla
Zantedeschia elliottiana

For climate zone explanations, please see pages 38–39.

Chinese ground orchid
Bletilla striata

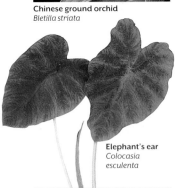

Elephant's ear
Colocasia esculenta

Dahlia

Magic lily
Lycoris squamigera

Rain lily
Habranthus

Calla
☼ ◐ ◑ ⚡ LS, CS, TS
Zantedeschia   p. 649

Canna
☼ ◐ 💧 💧 ⚡ LS, CS, TS
                                      p. 214

Chinese ground orchid
☼ ◐ ◑ ⚡ US, MS, LS, CS
Bletilla striata   p. 189

Crinum
☼ ☼ ◐ ◑ 💧 💧 ⚡ VARY
                                      p. 263

Crimson flag
☼ ◐ ◑ 💧 ⚡ LS, CS
Hesperantha coccinea   p. 353

Crocosmia
☼ ☼ ◐ ◑ ⚡ US, MS, LS, CS
                                      p. 264

Curcuma
☼ ◐ ◑ ⚡ LS, CS, TS
                                      p. 267

Dahlia
☼ ☼ ◐ ◑ ⚡ US, MS, LS
                                      p. 272

Elephant's ear
☼ ◐ ◑ 💧 ⚡ LS, CS, TS
Colocasia esculenta   p. 250

Giant alocasia
☼ ◐ ◑ 💧 ⚡ CS, TS
Alocasia macrorrhiza   p. 144

Ginger lily
☼ ☼ ◐ ◑ ⚡ VARY
Hedychium   p. 344

Gladiolus
☼ ◐ ◑ ⚡ MS, LS, CS
                                      p. 330

Glory lily
☼ ◐ ◑ 💧 ⚡ CS, TS
Gloriosa superba 'Rothschildiana'   p. 331

Jerusalem artichoke
☼ ◐ ◑ 💧 ⚡ US MS LS CS
Helianthus tuberosus   p. 347

Lily
☼ ◐ ◑ ⚡ US, MS, LS, CS
Lilium, Asiatic hybrids   p. 411

Magic lily
☼ ◐ ◑ ⚡ US, MS, LS, CS
Lycoris squamigera   p. 422

Nerine
☼ ◐ ◑ ⚡ LS, CS, TS
                                      p. 452

Rain lily
☼ ◐ ◑ ⚡ MS, LS, CS, TS
Habranthus   p. 341

Society garlic
☼ ◐ ⚡ MS, LS, CS, TS
Tulbaghia violacea   p. 629

Spider lily
☼ ◐ ⚡ VARY
Lycoris   p. 421

Trout lily
☼ ◐ ◑ ⚡ US, MS, LS
Erythronium americanum   p. 302

Tuberose
☼ ◐ ◑ ⚡ MS, LS, CS, TS
Polianthes tuberosa   p. 515

Tuberous begonia
◐ ◑ ⚡ US OR ANNUAL
Begonia   p. 184

Voodoo lily
☼ ◐ ◑ ◑ ⚡ VARY
Amorphophallus   p. 148

Walking iris
☼ ◐ ◑ ⚡ CS, TS
Neomarica gracilis   p. 450

SUMMER-PLANTED BULBS

Amaryllis
☼ ◐ ◑ ⚡ LS, CS, TS
Hippeastrum   p. 358

Crocus (fall-flowering)
☼ ◐ ◑ ⚡ US, MS, LS
                                      p. 264

Cyclamen (except florists' types)
☼ ◐ ◑ ⚡ VARY
                                      p. 268

Meadow saffron
☼ ◐ ◑ ⚡ US, MS, LS
Colchicum   p. 249

PLANT-ANYTIME BULBS

Clivia
◐ ◑ ◑ ⚡ TS
Clivia miniata   p. 247

Daylily
☼ ◐ ◑ ⚡ ALL
Hemerocallis   p. 351

Fortnight lily
☼ ◐ ◑ ◑ ⚡ LS, CS, TS
Dietes   p. 284

Montbretia
☼ ◐ ◑ ⚡ US, MS, LS, CS
Crocosmia crocosmiiflora   p. 264

St. Joseph's lily
☼ ◐ ◑ ⚡ LS CS TS
Hippeastrum x johnsonii   p. 358

Yellow flag
☼ ◐ ◑ ◑ ⚡ US, MS, LS, CS
Iris pseudacorus   p. 380

Daylily
Hemerocallis

Meadow saffron
Colchicum

Clivia
Clivia miniata

Amaryllis
Hippeastrum

For growing symbol explanations, please see page 37.

Azalea
Rhododendron

Landscape Plants
with Showy Flowers

J ust because trees, shrubs, vines, and ground covers form the garden's "backbone" doesn't mean it can't be a colorful back-bone. Many of these plants put on a show every bit as striking as that of annuals and perennials. To help you plan multipe seasons of bloom, we've arranged this list according to the season in which the different plants flower.

French hydrangea
Hydrangea macrophylla

Empress tree
Paulownia tomentosa

Flowering peach
Prunus persica

Beach plum
Prunus maritima

Flowering dogwood
Cornus florida

SPRING
TREES

Black locus
☀◐●●◊⚡ US, MS, LS, CS
Robinia pseudoacacia   p. 550

Bottlebrush
☀●●◊⚡ VARY
Callistemon   p. 206

Catalpa
☀◐●◊⚡ US, MS, LS, CS
                              p. 220

Cleveland select pear
☀●●◊⚡ US, MS, LS, CS
Pyrus calleryana   p. 532

Cornelian cherry
☀◐●◊⚡ US, MS, LS
Cornus mas   p. 256

Dove tree
◐●◊⚡ US, MS
Davidia involucrata   p. 276

Empress tree
☀◐●◊⚡ US, MS, LS, CS
Paulownia tomentosa   p. 474

Epaulette tree
☀●◊⚡ US, MS, LS
Pterostyrax hispida   p. 528

Flowering cherry, peach, plum
☀●◊⚡ VARY
Prunus (many)   p. 522

Flowering crabapple
☀●◊⚡ VARY
Malus   p. 428

Flowering dogwood
☀◐●◊⚡ US, MS, LS, CS
Cornus florida   p. 256

Fringe tree
☀◐●●◊⚡ US, MS, LS, CS
Chionanthus virginicus   p. 234

Goldenchain tree
◐●◊◊⚡ US, MS
Laburnum   p. 394

Hawthorn
☀●◊⚡ VARY
Crataegus   p. 262

Jacaranda
☀●◊⚡ TS
Jacaranda mimosifolia   p. 382

Kousa dogwood
☀●◊⚡ US, MS, LS
Cornus kousa   p. 256

Magnolia (most deciduous)
☀◐●◊⚡ VARY
                              p. 423

Orchid tree
☀●●◊⚡ TS
Bauhinia   p. 179

Redbud
☀◐●●◊⚡ VARY
Cercis   p. 227

Red horsechestnut
☀◐●●◊◊⚡ US, MS, LS
Aesculus x carnea   p. 135

Serviceberry
☀◐●●◊⚡ VARY
Amelanchier   p. 147

Silk-cotton tree
☀●●◊⚡ TS
Ceiba pentandra   p. 222

Silver bell
☀◐●◊⚡ US, MS, LS
Halesia   p. 341

Snowbell
☀◐●◊⚡ VARY
Styrax   p. 605

SPRING
SHRUBS

Acacia (most)
☀◐◊⚡ VARY
                              p. 126

Azalea and rhododendron
◐●●◊◊⚡ VARY
Rhododendron   p. 541

Orchid tree
Bauhinia

Red horsechestnut
Aesculus carnea

Snowbell
Styrax

Rhododendron

For climate zone explanations, please see pages 38–39.

Beauty bush
Kolkwitzia amabilis

Bush daisy
Euryops pectinatus 'Viridis'

Camellia
Camellia japonica 'Elegans Variegated'

Daphne

Banana shrub
☼◐◗✂ LS, CS, TS
Michelia figo   p. 424

Beauty bush
☼◐◗✂ US, MS, LS
Kolkwitzia amabilis   p. 394

Black jetbead
☼◐◗◔✂ US, MS, LS
Rhodotypos scandens   p. 548

Bramble
☼◐◗◔✂ VARY
Rubus   p. 562

Broom
☼◔◗✂ VARY
Genista   p. 326

Bush daisy
☼◔◗◔✂ CS, TS OR ANNUAL
Euryops pectinatus   p. 309

Camellia, common
◐◗◔✂ US, MS, LS, CS
Camellia japonica   p. 209

Chinese fringe tree
☼◐◗◔✂ US, MS, LS, CS
Chionanthus retusus   p. 234

Daphne
◐◗◔✂ VARY
                                     p. 274

Deutzia
☼◐◗◔✂ US, MS, LS
                                     p. 279

Dwarf flowering almond
☼◔◗✂ US, MS, LS
Prunus glandulosa   p. 525

Enkianthus
☼◐◗◔◔ US, MS
                                     p. 295

Firethorn
☼◗✂ VARY
Pyracantha   p. 530

Forsythia
☼◗◔✂ US, MS, LS
                                     p. 317

Fothergilla
☼◐◗✂ US, MS, LS
                                     p. 318

Fragrant abelia
☼◐◗✂ US, MS, LS, CS
Abelia mosanensis   p. 124

Grevillea
☼◐◔◗◔✂ VARY
                                     p. 338

Hardy orange
☼◗◔✂ US, MS, LS, CS
Poncirus trifoliata   p. 518

Honeysuckle
☼◐◗◔✂ VARY
Lonicera   p. 418

Horsechestnut
☼◐◗◔✂ VARY
Aesculus   p. 135

Indian hawthorn
☼◐◔◗◔✂ LS, CS, TS
Rhaphiolepis indica   p. 540

Japanese kerria
◐◗◔✂ US, MS, LS, CS
Kerria japonica   p. 390

Jasmine
☼◐◗◔✂ VARY
Jasminum (some)   p. 382

Leucothoe
◐◗◔◔ US, MS, LS
                                     p. 408

Lilac
☼◐◗✂ VARY
Syringa   p. 609

Mahonia
☼◐◗◔◗✂ VARY
                                     p. 427

Mexican orange
☼◐◗✂ LS, CS, TS
Choisya ternata   p. 235

Mountain laurel
☼◐◗◔✂ US, MS, LS, CS
Kalmia latifolia   p. 390

Myrtle
☼◐◔◗✂ LS, CS, TS
Myrtus communis   p. 445

Paper bush
☼◐◗✂ MS, LS, CS
Edgeworthia chrysantha   p. 293

Pearl bush
☼◐◗✂ US, MS, LS
Exochorda   p. 310

Peony
☼◐◗✂ US, MS, LS
Paeonia   p. 466

Photinia
☼◗◔✂ VARY
                                     p. 500

Pieris
◐◗◔✂ VARY
                                     p. 502

Rose
☼◐◗✂ ALL
Rosa   p. 551

Spiraea
☼◐◗◔✂ VARY
                                     p. 597

Sweet mock orange
☼◐◗◔✂ US, MS, LS, CS
Philadelphus coronarius   p. 495

Texas mountain laurel
☼◐◗◔✂ LS, CS
Sophora secundiflora   p. 594

Indian hawthorn
Rhaphiolepis indica

Japanese kerria
Kerria japonica

Lilac
Syringa vulgaris

Peony
Paeonia

For growing symbol explanations, please see page 37.

Sweet mock orange
Philadelphus coronarius

Texas mountain laurel
Sophora secundiflora

Viburnum

Yellow bells
Tecoma stans

Clematis 'Nelly Moser'

Viburnum (some)
☀☼◗◖⚡ VARY
p. 637

Virginia sweetspire
☀◗◖⚡ US, MS, LS, CS
Itea virginica   p. 381

Weigela florida
☀☼◗◖⚡ US, MS, LS
p. 644

Wild lilac
☀◖⚡ VARY
Ceanothus   p. 222

Winter hazel
☀◖◗◖⚡ US, MS, LS
Corylopsis   p. 258

Yellow bells
☀◗◖◗◖⚡ CS, TS
Tecoma stans   p. 614

SPRING
GROUND COVERS AND VINES

Bougainvillea
☀◗◖⚡ CS, TS
p. 191

Carolina jessamine
☀◗◖◗◖▲◖⚡ MS, LS, CS
Gelsemium sempervirens p. 325

Carpet bugleweed
☀◐●◗⚡ US, MS, LS
Ajuga reptans   p. 140

Cat's claw
☀◗◖◗⚡ LS, CS, TS
Macfadyena unguis-cati p. 423

Cheddar pink
☀◗◖⚡ US, MS, LS, CS
Dianthus gratianopolitanus p. 280

Cherokee rose
☀◗◖⚡ MS, LS, CS, TS
Rosa laevigata   p. 559

Cinquefoil
☀◗◖◗⚡ VARY
Potentilla (some)   p. 520

Clematis
☀◗◖◗⚡ VARY
p. 242

Golden globes
☀◗◖◗◖⚡ MS, LS, CS
Lysimachia congestiflora p. 422

Lady Banks's rose
☀◗◖◗⚡ MS, LS, CS, TS
Rosa banksiae   p. 558

Mazus
☀◗◖◗●◗⚡ US, MS, LS
Mazus reptans   p. 433

Moss pink
☀◗◖◗⚡ US, MS, LS
Phlox subulata   p. 498

Periwinkle
◗●◖◗◖⚡ VARY
Vinca   p. 641

Trumpet honeysuckle
☀☼◗◖◗◖⚡ US, MS, LS, CS
Lonicera sempervirens   p. 419

Wisteria
☀☼◖◗⚡ US, MS, LS, CS
p. 645

SUMMER
TREES

Cassia
☀◖◗◖●◗◖⚡ TS
p. 219

Catalpa
☀☼◗◖◗◖⚡ US, MS, LS, CS
p. 220

Chitalpa
☀◖◗◖⚡ US, MS, LS, CS
x Chitalpa tashkentensis p. 234

Coral tree
☀◖◗◖⚡ VARY
Erythrina (some)   p. 301

Crepe myrtle
☀◖◗⚡ US, MS, LS, CS
Lagerstroemia indica   p. 395

Desert willow
☀◖◗◖⚡ MS, LS, CS
Chilopsis linearis   p. 233

Franklin tree
☀☼◗◖◗⚡ US, MS, LS, CS
Franklinia alatamaha   p. 319

Goldenrain tree
☀◗◖◗◖⚡ US, MS, LS, CS
Koelreuteria paniculata p. 393

Harlequin glorybower
☀◗◖◗⚡ MS, LS, CS, TS
Clerodendrum trichotomum p. 245

Japanese pagoda tree
☀◗◖◗⚡ US, MS, LS
Sophora japonica   p. 605

Jerusalem thorn
☀◖◗◖◗◖⚡ LS, CS, TS
Parkinsonia aculeata   p. 472

Lilac chaste tree
☀◗◖◗⚡ US, MS, LS, CS
Vitex agnus-castus   p. 643

Loblolly bay
☀◗◖◗◖●◗◖⚡ MS, LS, CS, TS
Gordonia lasianthus   p. 333

Pomegranate
☀◗◖⚡ MS, LS, CS, TS
p. 517

Purple trumpet tree
☀◗◖◗◖⚡ TS
Tabebuia impetiginosa   p. 611

Trumpet honeysuckle
Lonicera sempervirens

Wisteria

Cassia

Chitalpa
x Chitalpa tashkentensis

Purple trumpet tree
Tabebuia impetiginosa

For climate zone explanations, please see pages 38–39.

Royal poinciana
Delonix regia

Southern magnolia
Magnolia grandiflora

Angel's trumpet
Brugmansia versicolor 'Ecuador Pink'

Bottlebrush buckeye
Aesculus parviflora

Blue mist
Caryopteris x clandonensis

Royal poinciana
☼ ◗ ⚡ TS
Delonix regia   p. 277

Southern magnolia
☼ ☼ ◗◗ ⚡ US, MS, LS, CS
Magnolia grandiflora   p. 424

Stewartia
☼ ◗◗ ⚡ VARY
                                            p. 601

Sweet bay
☼ ☼ ◗◗ ◗◗ ⚡ US, MS, LS, CS
Magnolia virginiana   p. 425

Yellow poinciana
☼ ☼ ◗ ⚡ TS
Peltophorum pterocarpum   p. 485

SUMMER
SHRUBS AND PERENNIALS

Abelia
☼ ☼ ◗◗ ⚡ VARY
                                            p. 124

Adina
☼ ☼ ◗◗ ◗ ⚡ US, MS, LS, CS
Adina rubella   p. 134

Angel's trumpet
☼ ☼ ◗◗ ◗ ⚡ LS, CS, TS
Brugmansia   p. 195

Bear's breeches
☼ ☼ ◗◗ ◗ ◗◗ ⚡ US, MS, LS, CS
Acanthus mollis   p. 127

Blue mist
☼ ◗◗ ⚡ US, MS, LS, CS
Caryopteris x clandonensis   p. 219

Bottlebrush buckeye
☼ ☼ ◗◗ ◗ ⚡ US, MS, LS, CS
Aesculus parviflora   p. 135

Bouvardia
☼ ◗◗ ◗ ⚡ CS, TS
                                            p. 193

Brazilian plume flower
☼◗ ◗◗ ◗◗ ⚡ CS, TS
Justicia carnea   p. 387

Brunfelsia
☼ ☼ ◗◗ ◗ ⚡ CS, TS
                                            p. 196

Butterfly bush
☼ ☼ ◗◗ ◗ ⚡ VARY
Buddleia   p. 197

Cape plumbago
☼ ☼ ◗◗ ◗ ◗ ⚡ CS, TS
Plumbago auriculata   p. 513

Cat's whiskers
☼ ◗◗ ◗ ◗◗ ⚡ CS, TS
Orthosiphon aristatus   p. 462

Cestrum
☼ ◗◗ ◗ ⚡ TS
                                            p. 228

Cinquefoil
☼ ◗◗ ◗ ⚡ VARY
Potentilla   p. 520

Coral plant
☼ ◗◗ ◗ ◗ ⚡ TS
Jatropha multifida   p. 384

Fairy duster
☼ ◗ ◗ ⚡ CS, TS
Calliandra eriophylla   p. 204

Firecracker plant
☼ ☼ ◗◗ ◗ ⚡ CS, TS
Russelia equisetiformis   p. 565

Flame of the woods
☼ ☼ ◗◗ ◗ ⚡ TS
Ixora coccinea   p. 382

Flowering maple
☼ ☼ ◗◗ ◗ ⚡ CS, TS
Abutilon   p. 125

Frangipani
☼ ☼ ◗◗ ◗ ◗ ⚡ TS
Plumeria   p. 513

Fuchsia
◗◗ ◗ ⚡ VARY
                                            p. 321

Gardenia, common
☼ ☼ ◗◗ ◗ ⚡ LS, CS, TS
Gardenia jasminoides   p. 323

Glorybower
☼ ☼ ◗◗ ◗ ⚡ TS
Clerodendrum   p. 245

Hibiscus
☼ ◗◗ ⚡ VARY
                                            p. 356

Hydrangea
◗◗ ◗ ⚡ VARY
                                            p. 363

Indigo bush
☼ ☼ ◗ ⚡ US, MS, LS, CS
Amorpha fruticosa   p. 148

Jasmine
☼ ☼ ◗◗ ◗ ◗ ⚡ VARY
Jasminum (some)   p. 382

Mexican abelia
☼ ☼ ◗◗ ◗ ⚡ LS, CS
Abelia floribunda   p. 124

Oleander
☼ ◗ ◗ ◗ ◗ ⚡ LS, CS, TS
Nerium oleander   p. 452

Ornamental pomegranate
☼ ☼ ◗◗ ◗ ⚡ MS, LS, CS, TS
Punica granatum   p. 530

Pentas
☼ ◗◗ ⚡ ALL
Pentas lanceolata   p. 487

Peregrina
☼◗ ◗◗ ◗ ⚡ TS
Jatropha integerrima   p. 383

Butterfly bush
Buddleia

Cape plumbago
Plumbago auriculata

Chilean cestrum
Cestrum parqui

Oakleaf hydrangea
Hydrangea quercifolia

For growing symbol explanations, please see page 37.

Pentas
Pentas lanceolata

Chestnut rose
Rosa roxburghii

Mexican bush sage
Salvia leucantha

Baby's breath spiraea
Spiraea thunbergii

Tree mallow
Lavatera thuringiaca 'Barnsley'

Plumleaf azalea
☼ ◗ ● ◐ ◊ ⚡ US, MS, LS
Rhododendron prunifolium   p. 547

Princess flower
☼ ☼ ◗ ● ⚡ TS
Tibouchina urvilleana   p. 620

Rose
☼ ☼ ◗ ● ⚡ ALL
Rosa   p. 551

Rose of Sharon
☼ ◊ ◗ ● ⚡ US, MS, LS, CS
Hibiscus syriacus   p. 357

Sage (several)
☼ ☼ ● ⚡ VARY
Salvia   p. 568

St. Johnswort
☼ ☼ ◗ ● ⚡ VARY
Hypericum   p. 367

Senna
☼ ☼ ◗ ● ⚡ VARY
    p. 586

Spiraea (some)
☼ ☼ ◗ ● ⚡ VARY
    p. 597

Summersweet
☼ ☼ ◗ ● ◐ ⚡ US, MS, LS, CS
Clethra alnifolia   p. 246

Sundrops
☼ ☼ ◗ ◊ ● ⚡ US, MS, LS
Calylophus   p. 208

Texas ranger
☼ ◊ ● ⚡ LS, CS, TS
Leucophyllum frutescens   p. 408

Tree mallow
☼ ● ⚡ VARY
Lavatera   p. 405

Yellow bird of paradise
☼ ◊ ● ◊ ⚡ CS, TS
Caesalpinia gilliesii   p. 201

Yellow shrimp plant
☼ ☼ ◗ ● ⚡ CS, TS
Pachystachys lutea   p. 466

SUMMER
GROUND COVERS AND VINES

Allamanda
☼ ◗ ● ◊ ⚡ TS OR ANNUAL
Allamanda cathartica   p. 142

Aristolochia (some)
☼ ☼ ◗ ● ● ◐ ⚡ VARY
    p. 164

Big blue liriope
☼ ◗ ● ⚡ ALL
Liriope muscari   p. 416

Black-eyed Susan vine
☼ ☼ ◗ ● ⚡ CS, TS
Thunbergia alata   p. 618

Bleeding heart vine
☼ ◗ ● ⚡ TS
Clerodendrum thomsoniae   p. 245

Blue pea vine
☼ ☼ ◗ ● ⚡ TS OR ANNUAL
Clitoria ternatea   p. 247

Bower vine
☼ ◗ ● ⚡ LS, CS, TS
Pandorea jasminoides   p. 469

Clematis (some)
☼ ☼ ◗ ● ⚡ VARY
    p. 242

Confederate jasmine
☼ ☼ ◗ ● ◊ ⚡ MS, LS, CS, TS
Trachelospermum jasminoides   p. 625

Coral vine
☼ ☼ ◗ ● ⚡ LS, CS, TS
Antigonon leptopus   p. 153

Crossvine
☼ ☼ ◗ ◊ ● ⚡ US, MS, LS, CS
Bignonia capreolata   p. 187

Cypress vine
☼ ◗ ● ⚡ ALL
Ipomoea quamoclit   p. 376

Distictis
☼ ☼ ◗ ● ⚡ VARY
    p. 287

Dwarf plumbago
☼ ☼ ◗ ● ⚡ US, MS, LS, CS
Ceratostigma plumbaginoides   p. 226

Firecracker vine
☼ ☼ ◗ ● ⚡ TS OR ANNUAL
Ipomoea lobata   p. 375

Glory lily
☼ ☼ ◗ ● ◊ ⚡ CS, TS
Gloriosa superba 'Rothschildiana'   p. 332

Honeysuckle
☼ ☼ ◗ ● ⚡ VARY
Lonicera   p. 418

Hyacinth bean
☼ ◗ ● ◊ ⚡ LS, CS, TS
Dolichos lablab   p. 288

Jasmine
☼ ☼ ◗ ● ⚡ VARY
Jasminum (some)   p. 382

Lantana, common
☼ ☼ ● ◊ ⚡ LS, CS, TS OR ANNUALS
Lantana camara   p. 401

Mandevilla
☼ ☼ ◗ ● ⚡ VARY
    p. 431

Moonflower
☼ ☼ ◗ ● ⚡ ALL
Ipomoea alba   p. 376

Morning glory, common
☼ ☼ ◗ ● ⚡ ALL
Ipomoea purpurea   p. 376

Princess flower
Tibouchina urvilleana

Coral vine
Antigonon leptopus

Gold flame honeysuckle
Lonicera x heckrottii

Mandevilla

For climate zone explanations, please see pages 38–39.

Rangoon creeper
Quisqualis indica

Rose, climbing
Rosa 'Cl. Cécile Brunner'

Snail vine
Vigna caracalla

King's mantle
Thunbergia erecta

Verbena

Passion vine
☼ ◑ ● ◗ ✗ VARY
Passiflora   p. 473

Pink trumpet vine
☼ ◑ ● ◗ ✗ CS, TS
Podranea ricasoliana   p. 515

Purple allamanda
☼ ● ◗ ✗ TS OR ANNUAL
Allamanda blanchetii   p. 142

Queen's wreath
☼ ● ✗ TS
Petrea volubilis   p. 492

Rangoon creeper
☼ ◑ ● ✗ TS
Quisqualis indica   p. 535

Rose (many climbers)
☼ ◑ ● ✗ ALL
Rosa   p. 551

Snail vine
☼ ● ✗ TS
Vigna caracalla   p. 640

Thunbergia
☼ ◑ ● ✗ TS
                                    p. 618

Trumpet creeper
☼ ◑ ● ◗ ✗ VARY
Campsis   p. 214

Verbena
☼ ● ✗ VARY
                                    p. 634

AUTUMN
TREES AND SHRUBS

Abelia
☼ ◑ ● ✗ VARY
                                    p. 124

Angel's trumpet
☼ ◑ ● ◗ ✗ LS, CS, TS
Brugmansia   p. 195

Autumn flowering cherry
☼ ● ◗ ✗ US, MS, LS
Prunus x subhirtella 'Autumnalis'   p. 523

Butterfly bush
☼ ◑ ● ◗ ✗ VARY
Buddleia   p. 197

Caesalpinia
☼ ◐ ● ◗ ✗ VARY
                                    p. 201

Cat's whiskers
☼ ● ◐ ✗ CS, TS
Orthosiphon aristatus   p. 462

Floss silk tree
☼ ● ✗ TS
Chorisia   p. 235

Fuchsia
◑ ● ✗ VARY
                                    p. 321

Hibiscus (some)
☼ ● ✗ VARY
                                    p. 356

Hong Kong orchid tree
☼ ◑ ● ◗ ✗ TS
Bauhinia x blakeana   p. 179

Mexican bird of paradise
☼ ◐ ● ◗ ✗ TS
Caesalpinia mexicana   p. 201

Mexican bush sage
☼ ● ✗ LS, CS, TS
Salvia leucantha   p. 570

Peregrina
◑ ● ◗ ✗ TS
Jatropha integerrima   p. 383

Pink wild petunia
☼ ◑ ● ◗ ✗ CS, TS
Ruellia macrantha   p. 564

Princess flower
☼ ◑ ● ✗ TS
Tibouchina urvilleana   p. 620

Rose (some)
☼ ◑ ● ◗ ✗ ALL
Rosa   p. 551

Sasanqua camellia
☼ ◑ ● ◗ ✗ US, MS, LS, CS
Camellia sasanqua   p. 211

Shower-of-gold
☼ ● ✗ CS, TS
Galphimia glauca   p. 323

Shrub bush clover
☼ ◐ ● ✗ US, MS, LS
Lespedeza thunbergii   p. 406

'Tardiva' hydrangea
◑ ● ✗ US, MS, LS, CS
Hydrangea paniculata   p. 364

Witch hazel, common
☼ ◑ ● ✗ US, MS, LS, CS
Hamamelis virginiana   p. 342

Yellow bells
☼ ◑ ● ◗ ✗ CS, TS
Tecoma stans   p. 614

AUTUMN
VINES, PERENNIALS

Allamanda
☼ ● ◗ ✗ TS OR AS ANNUAL
Allamanda cathartica   p. 142

Bleeding heart vine
◑ ● ✗ TS
Clerodendrum thomsoniae   p. 245

Cape honeysuckle
☼ ◑ ● ✗ CS, TS
Tecoma capensis   p. 614

Flame vine
☼ ◑ ● ✗ CS, TS
Pyrostegia venusta   p. 531

Chinese abelia
Abelia chinensis

Hibiscus

Shower-of-gold
Galphimia glauca

Shrub bush clover
Lespedeza thunbergii

For growing symbol explanations, please see page 37.

Potato vine
Solanum jasminoides

Sweet autumn clematis
Clematis terniflora

Cornelian cherry
Cornus mas

Japanese flowering apricot
Prunus mume

Yulan magnolia
Magnolia denudata

Glorybower
☼:◑◐◑ ⚡ TS
Clerodendrum (many)   p. 245

Honeysuckle
☼:◑◐◑◐ ⚡ VARY
Lonicera (some)   p. 418

Mandevilla (some)
☼:◑◐◑ ⚡ VARY
     p. 431

Mexican flame vine
☼:◑◐◑ CS, TS
Pseudogynoxys chenopodioides   p. 526

Potato vine
☼:◑◐◑◐◑ ⚡ LS, CS, TS
Solanum jasminoides   p. 591

Rose (some climbers)
☼:◑◐◑ ⚡ ALL
Rosa   p. 551

Silver lace vine
☼:◐◑◐◑ ⚡ US, MS, LS, CS
Fallopia baldschuanica   p. 311

Sneezeweed
☼:◑◐ ◑ ⚡ US, MS, LS, CS
Helenium autumnale   p. 345

Sweet autumn clematis
☼:◑◐ ⚡ US, MS, LS, CS
Clematis terniflora   p. 244

Thunbergia
☼:◑◐◑ ⚡ TS
     — p. 618

WINTER
TREES

African tulip tree
☼:◑◐ ⚡ TS
Spathodea campanulata   p. 595

Bailey acacia
☼:◐ ⚡ CS, TS
Acacia baileyana   p. 126

Cascalote
☼:◐◐◑ ⚡ TS
Caesalpinia cacalaco   p. 201

Cornelian cherry
☼:◑◐◑ ⚡ US, MS, LS
Cornus mas   p. 256

Flowering cherry
☼:◑◐◑ ⚡ US, MS, LS, CS
Prunus 'Okame'   p. 523

Japanese flowering apricot
☼:◑◐◑ ⚡ US, MS, LS, CS
Prunus mume   p. 524

Purple orchid tree
☼:◑◐◑ ⚡ TS
Bauhinia variegata   p. 180

Red maple
☼:◑◐◑◐◑ ⚡ US, MS, LS, CS
Acer rubrum   p. 129

Yulan magnolia
☼:◑◐◑ US, MS, LS, CS
Magnolia denudata   p. 425

WINTER
SHRUBS

Camellia (many)
◑◐◑ ⚡ US, MS, LS, CS
     p. 208

Flowering quince
☼:◑◐◑ ⚡ US, MS, LS, CS
Chaenomeles   p. 228

Heath
☼:◑◐◑ ⚡ VARY
Erica   p. 299

Leatherleaf mahonia
☼:◑◐◑ ⚡ US, MS, LS, CS
Mahonia bealei   p. 427

Stachyurus praecox
☼:◑◐◑ ⚡ US, MS, LS
     p. 600

Winter daphne
:◑◐◑◐◑ ⚡ MS, LS
Daphne odora   p. 274

Winter hazel
☼:◑◐◑ ⚡ US, MS, LS
Corylopsis   p. 258

Winter honeysuckle
☼:◑◐◑◐◑ ⚡ US, MS, LS
Lonicera fragrantissima   p. 418

Wintersweet
☼:◑◐◑ ⚡ US, MS, LS, CS
Chimonanthus praecox   p. 233

Witch hazel
☼:◑◐◑ ⚡ US, MS, LS
Hamamelis (most)   p. 342

WINTER
GROUND COVER AND VINES

Carolina jessamine
☼:◑◐◑◐◑◐◑ ⚡ MS, LS, CS
Gelsemium sempervirens   p. 325

Flame vine
☼:◑◐◑ ⚡ CS, TS
Pyrostegia venusta   p. 531

Lenten rose
◑◐◑◐◑ ⚡ US, MS, LS
Helleborus orientalis   p. 350

Pink jasmine
☼:◑◐◑ ⚡ LS, CS, TS
Jasminum polyanthum   p. 383

Red clerodendrom
☼:◑◐ ⚡ TS
Clerodendrum splendens   p. 245

Winter jasmine
☼:◑◐◑◐ ⚡ US, MS, LS, CS
Jasminum nudiflorum   p. 383

Camellia

Flowering cherry
Prunus 'Okame'

Flowering quince
Chaenomeles 'Cameo'

Wintersweet
Chimonanthus praecox

Winter jasmine
Jasminum nudiflorum

For climate zone explanations, please see pages 38–39.

Freshly picked common camellias.

Larkspur
Consolida ajacis

Flowers
for Cutting

A garden isn't meant to be enjoyed outdoors only. You can cut many different kinds of flowers and bring them indoors. The ones you see here generally last about a week in water. Many of them, indicated by the symbol ⧫, are easy to dry for permanent arrangements. Annuals and biennials must be planted every year; perennials and most bulbs provide flowers year after year. Shrubs are another good source of cut flowers, and some even respond obligingly to cutting by blooming again and again.

Butterfly bush
Buddleia

French hydrangea
Hydrangea macrophylla

Rose
Rosa 'Leander'

SHRUBS

Butterfly bush
☼:◐◐◑◑⧫ VARY
Buddleia   p. 197

Camellia
:◐◐◑⧫ US, MS, LS, CS
                                            p. 208

Flowering quince
☼ ◑◑⧫ US, MS, LS, CS
Chaenomeles sp.   p. 228

Gardenia
☼:◐◐⧫ VARY
                                            p. 323

Hydrangea   ⧫
:◐◑◑⧫ VARY
                                            p. 363

Japanese kerria
:◐◑◑⧫ US, MS, LS, CS
Kerria japonica   p. 390

Lavender   ⧫
☼◑⧫ VARY
Lavandula   p. 403

Lilac
☼:◐◑⧫ VARY
Syringa   p. 609

Rose
☼:◐◑◑⧫ ALL
Rosa   p. 551

Spiraea
☼:◐◑◑◑⧫ VARY
                                            p. 597

ANNUALS

Angelonia
☼◑⧫ ALL
Angelonia angustifolia   p. 151

Annual phlox
☼◑⧫ ALL
Phlox drummondii   p. 497

Bachelor's button   ⧫
☼◑⧫ ALL
Centaurea cyanus   p. 224

Bells-of-Ireland   ⧫
☼◑⧫ ALL
Moluccella laevis   p. 440

Calendula
☼◑⧫ ALL
Calendula officinalis   p. 204

Chinese lantern plant   ⧫
☼◑◑⧫ US, MS, LS, CS
Physalis alkekengi   p. 500

Cockscomb   ⧫
☼◑⧫ ALL
Celosia argentea   p. 223

Cosmos, common   ⧫
☼◑⧫ ALL
Cosmos bipinnatus   p. 259

Globe amaranth   ⧫
☼◑◑⧫ ALL
Gomphrena globosa   p. 332

Gypsophila elegans   ⧫
☼◑⧫ ALL
                                            p. 340

Larkspur   ⧫
☼◑◑⧫ ALL
Consolida ajacis   p. 251

Love-in-a-mist   ⧫
☼◑◑⧫ ALL
Nigella damascena   p. 454

Mexican sunflower   ⧫
☼◑⧫ ALL
Tithonia rotundifolia   p. 621

Money plant   ⧫
☼:◐◐◑◑⧫ US, MS, LS, CS
Lunaria annua   p. 420

Bachelor's button
Centaurea cyanus

Larkspur
Consolida ajacis

Money plant
Lunaria annua

For growing symbol explanations, please see page 37.

Pincushion flower ☼ ○ ● ● ✎ ALL
Scabiosa atropurpurea   p. 578

Safflower ☼ ● ✎ ALL
Carthamus tinctorius   p. 218

Snapdragon ☼ ● ✎ ALL
Antirrhinum majus   p. 153

Spider flower ☼ ○ ● ● ✎ ALL
Cleome hasslerana   p. 244

Statice ☼ ● ✎ ALL
Limonium sinuatum   p. 413

Stock ☼ ○ ● ✎ ALL
Matthiola   p. 433

Strawflower ☼ ● ✎ ALL
Helichrysum bracteatum   p. 347

Sunflower, common ☼ ● ●● ✎ ALL
Helianthus annuus   p. 345

Sweet pea ☼ ● ●● ✎ ALL
Lathyrus odoratus   p. 402

Zinnia ☼ ● ✎ ALL
                                         p. 651

PERENNIALS, BULBS

Alstroemeria ☼ ● ◐ ✎ MS, LS, CS
                                         p. 146

Angel's trumpet ☼ ○ ● ◐ ✎ LS, CS, TS
Brugmansia   p. 195

Artemisia 'Powis Castle' ☼ ○ ● ✎ US, MS, LS
                                         p. 166

Aster ☼ ● ✎ US, MS, LS
                                         p. 172

Baby's breath ☼ ● ✎ US, MS, LS, CS
Gypsophila paniculata   p. 340

Balloon flower ☼ ○ ● ✎ US, MS, LS, CS
Platycodon grandiflorus   p. 508

Beard tongue ☼ ● ● ✎ VARY
Penstemon   p. 486

Bird of paradise ☼ ○ ● ✎ VARY
Strelitzia   p. 604

Spider flower
Cleome hasslerana

Alstroemeria

Strawflower
Helichrysum bracteatum

Black-eyed Susan ☼ ● ● ✎ ALL
Rudbeckia hirta   p. 563

Blazing star ☼ ○ ● ● ✎ US, MS, LS, CS
Liatris   p. 409

Calla ☼ ○ ● ✎ LS, CS, TS
Zantedeschia   p. 649

Centaurea (most) ☼ ● ✎ VARY
                                         p. 224

China aster ☼ ● ✎ ALL
Callistephus chinensis   p. 206

Chrysanthemum (some) ☼ ● ✎ VARY
                                         p. 235

Columbine meadow rue ○ ● ✎ US, MS, LS
Thalictrum aquilegifolium   p. 616

Coneflower ☼ ○ ● ● ✎ US, MS, LS, CS
Rudbeckia   p. 563

Coreopsis (most) ☼ ○ ● ● ✎ US, MS, LS, CS
                                         p. 253

Crinum ☼ ○ ● ●● ✎ VARY
                                         p. 263

Daffodil ☼ ○ ● ✎ US, MS, LS, CS
Narcissus   p. 446

Dahlia ☼ ○ ● ✎ US, MS, LS
                                         p. 272

Delphinium ☼ ● ✎ VARY
                                         p. 277

False sunflower ☼ ○ ● ● ✎ US, MS, LS, CS
Heliopsis helianthoides   p. 348

Fountain grass ☼ ○ ● ● ✎ VARY
Pennisetum   p. 485

Fritillary ☼ ○ ● ✎ US, MS, LS
Fritillaria   p. 320

Gaillardia x grandiflora ☼ ○ ● ✎ ALL
                                         p. 321

Gas plant ☼ ○ ● ● ◐ ✎ US, MS, LS
Dictamnus albus   p. 283

Gerbera daisy ☼ ○ ● ✎ ALL
Gerbera jamesonii   p. 328

Crinum

Dahlia

Delphinium

Checkered lily (Fritillary)
Fritillaria meleagris

For climate zone explanations, please see pages 38–39.

Gerbera daisy
Gerbera jamesonii

Ginger lily, common
Hedychium coronarium

Hollyhock
Alcea rosea

Japanese anemone
Anemone hybrida 'Honorine Jobert'

Geum
☼:◑◐◢ US, MS
p. 328

Ginger lily, common
☼:◑◑◐◢ MS, LS, CS, TS
Hedychium coronarium
p. 344

Gladiolus
☼◐◢ MS, LS, CS
p. 330

Globe thistle
☼◐◢ US, MS, LS, CS
Echinops
p. 293

Golden aster
☼◐◐◢ US, MS, LS, CS
Chrysopsis
p. 237

Goldenrod
☼:◑◐◢ US, MS, LS, CS
Solidago and Solidaster
p. 593

Greek yarrow
☼◯◐◢ US, MS, LS
Achillea ageratifolia
p. 130

Hollyhock
☼:◑◐◢ US, MS, LS, CS
Alcea
p. 141

Iris
☼:◑◐◐◐◐◑◢ VARY
p. 377

Japanese anemone
◑◐◔◢ US, MS, LS
Anemone hybrida
p. 150

Lily
☼:◑◐◢ US, MS, LS, CS
Lilium
p. 411

Lion's ear
☼◯◢ VARY
Leonotis
p. 406

Maiden grass
☼:◑◐◐◢ US, MS, LS, CS
Miscanthus
p. 438

Ornamental allium
☼:◑◐◐◢ VARY
Allium
p. 142

Pampas grass
☼◯◐◐◑◢ MS, LS, CS, TS
Cortaderia selloana
p. 258

Pearly everlasting
☼◐◐◐◢ US, MS, LS
Anaphalis
p. 149

Pentas
☼◐◢ ALL
Pentas lanceolata
p. 487

Peony
☼:◑◐◢ US, MS, LS
Paeonia
p. 466

Persian ranunculus
☼◐◢ LS, CS, TS
Ranunculus asiaticus
p. 536

Phlomis
☼◯◐◢ VARY
p. 496

Pincushion flower
☼◯◐◢ ALL
Scabiosa (some)
p. 578

Pink
☼◐◐◢ US, MS, LS, CS
Dianthus (many)
p. 279

Purple coneflower
☼◐◐◢ US, MS, LS, CS
Echinacea purpurea
p. 291

Reed grass
☼:◑◐◢ US, MS, LS, CS
Calamagrostis
p. 202

Ruby grass
☼◐◐◢ TS OR ANNUAL
Melinis nerviglumis
p. 435

Salvia (many)
☼◐◢ VARY
p. 568

Seashore mallow
☼◐◐◢ ALL
Kosteletzkya virginica
p. 394

Speedwell
☼◐◢ US, MS, LS
Veronica spicata
p. 637

Spike blazing star
☼◯◐◐◢ US, MS, LS, CS
Liatris spicata
p. 409

Star of Bethlehem
☼:◑◐◔◢ LS, CS, TS
Ornithogalum arabicum
p. 462

Statice
☼:◑◐◢ VARY
Limonium (most)
p. 413

Stokesia
☼◐◢ US, MS, LS, CS
Stokesia laevis
p. 602

Summer phlox
☼:◑◐◢ US, MS, LS, CS
Phlox paniculata
p. 498

Sunflower
☼◐◐◢ VARY
Helianthus (most)
p. 345

Tulip
☼:◑◐◢ ALL
Tulipa
p. 629

Verbena bonariensis
☼◐◢ MS, LS, CS, TS OR ANNUAL
p. 635

Viola, violet, pansy
☼:◑◐◐◢ VARY
Viola
p. 641

Giant allium
Allium giganteum

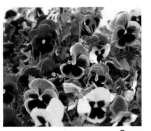

Pansy
Viola

Pearly everlasting
Anaphalis margaritacea

Speedwell
Veronica spicata

For growing symbol explanations, please see page 37.

Peony
Paeonia

Fragrant
Flowering Plants

A garden's fragrance can be as unforgettable as its appearance; the scent of a particular flower can evoke memories of past times and places. You can use fragrant plants in a variety of ways. En masse, they create a bathed-in-scent garden; set out in just a few spots, they provide a mystery perfume from who-knows-where. Plant them in containers to scent a deck or patio; locate them beneath a window to let fragrance waft indoors.

Chinese pink
Dianthus chinensis

Yoshino flowering cherry
Prunus x yedoensis

Harlequin glorybower
Clerodendrum trichotomum

Jerusalem thorn
Parkinsonia aculeata

TREES

Black locust
☀◐💧❄☆ US, MS, LS, CS
Robinia pseudoacacia   p. 550

Citrus
☀💧☆ CS, TS
                              p. 238

Flowering cherry, apricot
☀◐💧☆ VARY
Prunus (some)   p. 522

Flowering crabapple
☀◐💧☆ VARY
Malus (some)   p. 428

Fragrant snowbell
☀◐💧☆ US, MS, LS
Styrax obassia   p. 606

Fringe tree
☀◐💧☆ US, MS, LS, CS
Chionanthus virginicus   p. 234

Harlequin glorybower
☀◐💧☆ MS, LS, CS, TS
Clerodendrum trichotomum   p. 245

Jerusalem thorn
☀◐💧💧☆ LS, CS, TS
Parkinsonia aculeata   p. 472

Magnolia (many)
☀◐💧☆ VARY
                              p. 423

Russian olive
☀◐◐💧💧☆ US, MS
Elaeagnus angustifolia   p. 294

Sweet acacia
☀◐☆ LS, CS, TS
Acacia farnesiana   p. 126

Texas mountain laurel
☀◐💧❄☆ LS, CS
Sophora secundiflora   p. 594

Yellow wood
☀◐💧☆ US, MS, LS
Cladrastis kentukea   p. 242

SHRUBS

Acacia (several)
☀◐☆ VARY
                              p. 126

Adina rubella
☀◐◐💧☆ US, MS, LS, CS
                              p. 134

Alabama azalea
☀◐◐◐💧❄☆ US, MS, LS
Rhododendron alabamense   p. 546

Angel's trumpet
☀◐◐💧❄☆ LS, CS, TS
Brugmansia   p. 195

Anise tree
☀◐◐◐💧❄☆ MS, LS, CS
Illicium   p. 372

Banana shrub
☀◐◐💧☆ LS, CS, TS
Michelia figo   p. 424

Bouvardia longiflora 'Albatross'
☀◐💧☆ CS, TS
                              p. 193

Broom
☀◐💧☆ US, MS, LS
Cytisus   p. 271

Cashmere bouquet
☀◐💧☆ LS, CS, TS
Clerodendrum bungei   p. 245

Cestrum (some)
☀◐💧❄☆ TS
                              p. 228

Daphne (many)
☀◐💧❄☆ VARY
                              p. 274

Elaeagnus
☀◐◐◐💧❄☆ VARY
                              p. 294

Fothergilla
☀◐◐💧☆ US, MS, LS
                              p. 318

Texas mountain laurel
Sophora secundiflora

Angel's trumpet
Brugmansia

Burkwood daphne
Daphne x burkwoodii

For climate zone explanations, please see pages 38–39.

Yulan magnolia
Magnolia denudata

Gardenia, common
Gardenia jasminoides 'Radicans'

Frangipani
Plumeria

Cut-leaf lilac
Syringa x laciniata

Mock orange
Philadelphus

Rose
Rosa

Fragrant snowball
☼◑◐◑✂ US, MS, LS
Viburnum x carlcephalum   p. 638

Frangipani
☼◑◐◑◑♦✂ TS
Plumeria   p. 513

Gardenia
☼◑◐✂ VARY
                                  p. 323

Hardy orange
☼◑◑◐✂ US, MS, LS, CS
Poncirus trifoliata   p. 518

Japanese pittosporum
☼◑◐◑◑✂ LS, CS, TS
Pittosporum tobira   p. 507

Japanese skimmia
☼◑◑◑✂ US, MS
Skimmia japonica   p. 590

Korean spice viburnum
☼◑◐◑✂ US, MS, LS
Viburnum carlesii   p. 638

Lavender
☼◑◑✂ VARY
Lavandula   p. 403

Leatherleaf mahonia
☼◑◐◑✂ US, MS, LS, CS
Mahonia bealei   p. 427

Lilac
☼◑◑◑✂ VARY
Syringa (many)   p. 609

Mexican orange
☼◑◐◑✂ LS, CS, TS
Choisya ternata   p. 235

Mock orange
☼◑◐◑◑✂ VARY
Philadelphus (most)   p. 495

Natal plum
☼◑◐◑◑◑✂ CS, TS
Carissa macrocarpa   p. 217

Orange jessamine
◑◑◑✂ TS
Murraya paniculata   p. 442

Osmanthus (most)
☼◑◐◑◑◑✂ VARY
                                  p. 462

Paper bush
☼◑◐◑◑✂ MS, LS, CS
Edgeworthia chrysantha   p. 293

Rhaphiolepis 'Majestic Beauty'
☼◑◐◑◑◑✂ LS, CS, TS
                                  p. 540

Rhododendron, azalea
◑◐◑◑♦✂ VARY
Rhododendron (some)   p. 541

Rose
☼◑◐◑◑✂ ALL
Rosa (most)   p. 551

Summersweet
☼◑◐◑◑◑✂ US, MS, LS, CS
Clethra alnifolia   p. 246

Sweet box
◑◑◐◑◑✂ US, LS, MS, CS
Sarcococca   p. 576

Sweetshrub, common
☼◑◐◑◑♦✂ US, MS, LS, CS
Calycanthus floridus   p. 207

Sweetspire
☼◑◑◑✂ VARY
Itea   p. 381

Winter hazel
☼◑◐◑✂ US, MS, LS
Corylopsis   p. 258

Winter honeysuckle
☼◑◐◑◑✂ US, MS, LS
Lonicera fragrantissima   p. 418

Wintersweet
☼◑◐◑◑✂ US, MS, LS, CS
Chimonanthus praecox   p. 233

Witch hazel
☼◑◐◑✂ US, MS, LS
Hamamelis   p. 342

VINES

Armand clematis
☼◑◑✂ LS, CS
Clematis armandii   p. 243

Carolina jessamine
☼◑◐◑◑◑♦✂ MS, LS, CS
Gelsemium sempervirens   p. 325

Chilean jasmine
☼◑◐◑✂ CS, TS
Mandevilla laxa   p. 431

Confederate jasmine
☼◑◐◑◑✂ MS, LS, CS, TS
Trachelospermum jasminoides   p. 625

Herald's trumpet
☼◑◐◑◑✂ TS
Beaumontia grandiflora   p. 181

Japanese honeysuckle
☼◑◐◑◑◑✂ ALL
Lonicera japonica   p. 418

Jasmine
☼◑◐◑◑◑✂ VARY
Jasminum   p. 382

Madagascar jasmine
☼◑◐◑◑✂ TS OR INDOORS
Stephanotis floribunda   p. 600

Moonflower
☼◑◐◑◑✂ ALL
Ipomoea alba   p. 376

Passion vine
☼◑◐◑◑◑✂ LS, CS, TS
Passiflora alatocaerulea   p. 473

Summersweet
Clethra alnifolia

Sweetshrub, common
Calycanthus floridus 'Athens'

Winter hazel
Corylopsis

Hybrid witch hazel
Hamamelis

Passion vine
Passiflora alatocaerulea

For growing symbol explanations, please see page 37.

Sweet autumn clematis
Clematis terniflora

Sweet pea
Lathyrus odoratus

English wallflower
Erysimum cheiri

Flowering tobacco
Nicotiana sylvestris

Fragrant plantain lily
Hosta plantaginea

Sweet autumn clematis
☼ ◑ ◆ ✂ US, MS, LS, CS
Clematis terniflora — p. 244

Sweet pea
☼ ◑ ◆ ✂ ALL
Lathyrus odoratus — p. 402

Vanilla trumpet vine
☼ ◑ ◑ ◆ ✂ TS
Distictis laxiflora — p. 287

Wax flower
☼ ◐ ◆ ✂ TS
Hoya carnosa — p. 361

Wisteria
☼ ◐ ◆ ✂ US, MS, LS, CS
— p. 645

PERENNIALS, ANNUALS, BULBS

Angel's trumpet
☼ ◐ ◆ ✂ VARY
Datura — p. 276

Blue corydalis
◐ ◆ ✂ US, MS, LS
Corydalis flexuosa — p. 258

Calanthe
◐ ● ◆ ✂ MS, LS, CS
— p. 203

Chocolate cosmos
☼ ◆ ✂ MS, LS, CS
Cosmos atrosanguineus — p. 259

Crinum
☼ ◑ ◐ ◆ ◑ ✂ VARY
— p. 263

Crocus
☼ ◑ ◐ ◆ ✂ US, MS, LS
Crocus chrysanthus — p. 264

Daffodil
☼ ◑ ◐ ◆ ✂ US, MS, LS, CS
Narcissus (many) — p. 446

Dendrobium (some)
☼ ◐ ◆ ✂ TS OR INDOORS
— p. 278

English bluebell
◐ ◐ ◆ ✂ US, MS
Hyacinthoides non-scripta — p. 362

English primrose
◐ ◐ ✂ US, MS, LS
Primula vulgaris (some) — p. 522

English wallflower
☼ ◑ ◐ ◆ ✂ US, MS
Erysimum cheiri — p. 301

Flowering tobacco
☼ ◑ ◐ ◆ ◑ ✂ ALL
Nicotiana sylvestris — p. 453

Four o'clock
☼ ◐ ◆ ◑ ✂ ALL
Mirabilis jalapa — p. 438

Fragrant plantain lily
☼ ◐ ● ◆ ✂ US, MS, LS, CS
Hosta plantaginea — p. 360

Freesia
☼ ◑ ◐ ✂ CS, TS
— p. 320

Ginger lily
☼ ◑ ◐ ◆ ✂ VARY
Hedychium — p. 344

Heliotrope, common
☼ ◐ ● ◆ ◑ ✂ TS OR ANNUAL
Heliotropium arborescens — p. 349

Hyacinth
☼ ◑ ◐ ◆ ◑ ✂ VARY
Hyacinthus — p. 363

Hymenocallis
☼ ◑ ◐ ◆ ◑ ✂ VARY
— p. 366

Indian lotus
☼ ◑ ◐ ● ✂ ALL
Nelumbo nucifera — p. 449

Iris, bearded (many)
☼ ◑ ◐ ◆ ✂ US, MS, LS, CS
— p. 377

Lady bells
☼ ◑ ◐ ◆ ● ✂ US, MS
Adenophora — p. 133

Lemon daylily
☼ ◑ ◐ ◆ ✂ ALL
Hemerocallis lilioasphodelus — p. 351

Lily
☼ ◑ ◐ ◆ ✂ US, MS, LS, CS
Lilium (many) — p. 411

Lily-of-the-valley
◑ ● ◆ ◆ ✂ US, MS, LS
Convallaria majalis — p. 251

Peony
☼ ◑ ◐ ◆ ✂ US, MS, LS
Paeonia (many) — p. 466

Petunia
☼ ◑ ◆ ◆ ✂ ALL
Petunia x hybrida — p. 492

Pink
☼ ◑ ◆ ◆ ✂ US, MS, LS, CS
Dianthus (many) — p. 279

Stock
☼ ◑ ◐ ◆ ✂ ALL
Matthiola — p. 433

Summer hyacinth
☼ ◑ ◐ ◆ ✂ MS, LS, CS, TS
Galtonia candicans — p. 323

Summer phlox
☼ ◑ ◐ ◆ ✂ US, MS, LS, CS
Phlox paniculata — p. 498

Tuberose
☼ ◑ ◆ ✂ MS, LS, CS, TS
Polianthes tuberosa — p. 515

Hymenocallis 'Sulphur Queen'

Hyacinth, common
Hyacinthus orientalis

Stock
Matthiola incana

Cheddar pink
Dianthus gratianopolitanus
'Bath's Pink'

Indian lotus
Nelumbo nucifera

For climate zone explanations, please see pages 38–39.

Colorful Fruits and Berries

I f you judge a plant solely on the merits of its flowers, you may be doing it a great injustice. Many plants sport showy fruits and berries, principally in the fall and winter, when the garden is often devoid of bright color. Bring in some of the cheery fruits as bouquets. Not only do these fruits catch your eye, but they often attract hungry birds as well. If you'd like to join them for a snack, look for plants with the symbol 🍐 next to their name. This tells you that people can eat the fruit, too, either fresh or in jams and jellies.

Nandina
Nandina domestica

Deciduous possumhaw *(Ilex decidua)* keeps its berries through the winter.

Flowering crabapple
Malus 'Red Jewel'

Harlequin glorybower
Clerodendrum trichotomum

Hawthorn
Crataegus

European mountain ash
Sorbus aucuparia

TREES

Citrus 🍐
☼ ◑ ◐ ✂ CS, TS
p. 238

Dogwood
☼ ☼ ◑ ◐ ✂ VARY
Cornus (several) p. 255

Eastern red cedar
☼ ◑ ○ ◐ ◐ ✂ ALL
Juniperus virginiana p. 385

Flowering crabapple 🍐
☼ ◑ ◐ ◐ ✂ VARY
Malus p. 428

Harlequin glorybower
☼ ◐ ◐ ✂ MS, LS, CS, TS
Clerodendrum trichotomum p. 245

Hawthorn
☼ ◐ ◐ ✂ VARY
Crataegus p. 262

Holly
☼ ◑ ◐ ◐ ✂ VARY
Ilex (many) p. 369

Koelreuteria
☼ ◑ ◐ ◐ ✂ VARY
p. 393

Korean evodia
☼ ◑ ◐ ◐ ✂ US, MS, LS
Tetradium danielii p. 615

Loquat 🍐
☼ ◑ ○ ◐ ◐ ✂ LS, CS, TS
Eriobotrya japonica p. 300

Lychee 🍐
☼ ◑ ◐ ✂ CS, TS
p. 420

Mountain ash
☼ ◑ ◐ ◐ ◐ ✂ VARY
Sorbus p. 594

Persimmon 🍐
☼ ◑ ◐ ◐ ✂ VARY
p. 491

Sea grape 🍐
☼ ◑ ◐ ✂ TS
Coccoloba uvifera p. 248

Serviceberry 🍐
☼ ◑ ◐ ◐ ✂ US, MS, LS, CS
Amelanchier p. 147

Southern magnolia
☼ ◑ ◐ ◐ ✂ US, MS, LS, CS
Magnolia grandiflora p. 424

SHRUBS

Alexandrian laurel
◑ ◐ ◐ ✂ MS, LS, CS
Danae racemosa p. 273

American elderberry 🍐
☼ ◑ ◐ ◐ ✂ US, MS, LS, CS
Sambucus canadensis p. 573

Bayberry
☼ ◑ ◐ ✂ US, MS
Morella pensylvanica p. 441

Beautyberry
☼ ◑ ◐ ◐ ◐ ✂ US, MS, LS
Callicarpa p. 205

Blueberry 🍐
☼ ◑ ○ ◐ ◐ ◐ ✂ VARY
Vaccinium p. 633

Chinese photinia
☼ ◑ ◐ ◐ ✂ US, MS, LS, CS
Photinia serratifolia p. 500

Chokeberry
☼ ◑ ○ ◐ ◐ ◐ ✂ VARY
Aronia p. 165

Cotoneaster
☼ ◑ ○ ◐ ◐ ✂ VARY
p. 260

Persimmon
Diospyros

Southern magnolia
Magnolia grandiflora

American elderberry
Sambucus canadensis

Bearberry
Arctostaphylos uva-ursi 'Wood's Compact'

For growing symbol explanations, please see page 37.

Blueberry 'Coville'

Teton pyracantha (Firethorn)
Pyracantha 'Teton'

Japanese aucuba
Aucuba japonica 'Variegata'

Japanese barberry
Berberis thunbergii

Elaeagnus (several)
☼◐○◑◔◖✂ VARY
p. 294

Eugenia
☼◐◑◖✂ VARY
p. 304

Euonymus
☼◐●◑◔✂ VARY
p. 305

Firethorn
☼◑◖✂ VARY
Pyracantha   p. 530

Golden dewdrop
☼◐○◑◔✂ TS
Duranta erecta   p. 290

Holly
☼◐◑✂ VARY
Ilex (many)   p. 369

Honeysuckle
☼◐○◑◔✂ VARY
Lonicera (most shrubby types)   p. 418

Japanese aucuba
◐●◑◔✂ ALL
Aucuba japonica   p. 174

Japanese barberry
☼◐○◑◔✂ US, MS, LS
Berberis thunbergii   p. 184

Japanese skimmia
◐●◑✂ US, MS
Skimmia japonica   p. 590

Jerusalem cherry
☼◐◑◔◖✂ CS, TS
Solanum pseudocapsicum   p. 591

Mahonia
☼◐●◑◔✂ VARY
p. 427

Marlberry
☼◐●◑◔✂ VARY
Ardisia   p. 163

Nandina
☼◐●◑◔✂ US, MS, LS, CS
Nandina domestica   p. 445

Natal plum   🍐
☼◐○◑◔✂ CS, TS
Carissa macrocarpa   p. 217

Oriental photinia
☼◑◔✂ US, MS
Photinia villosa   p. 500

Ornamental pomegranate (some)   🍐
☼◑◔✂ MS, LS, CS, TS
Punica granatum   p. 530

Prickly pear   🍐
☼○✂ VARY
Opuntia (several)   p. 460

Rose   🍐
☼◐◑✂ ALL
Rosa (especially rugosas)   p. 551, 560

Sapphireberry
☼◐◑✂ US, MS, LS
Symplocos paniculata   p. 609

Snowberry
☼◐●○◑◔✂ US, MS
Symphoricarpos   p. 607

Spicebush
☼◐◑◔✂ US, MS, LS
Lindera benzoin   p. 414

Staghorn sumac
☼○◑◔✂ US, MS, LS
Rhus typhina   p. 549

Turk's cap
◐●○◑◔◖✂ LS, CS, TS
Malvaviscus arboreus drummondii p. 430

Viburnum (many)
☼◐◑✂ VARY
p. 637

Yew
☼◐●◑◔◆✂ US, MS
Taxus   p. 613

PERENNIALS AND VINES

American bittersweet
☼◐◑✂ US, MS, LS
Celastrus scandens   p. 223

Blackberry lily
☼◐◑✂ US, MS, LS, CS
Iris domestica   p. 379

Carolina moonseed
☼◐◑✂ US, MS, LS, CS
Cocculus carolinus   p. 248

Gladwin iris
◐●○◑◔✂ US, MS, LS, CS
Iris foetidissima   p. 380

Honeysuckle
☼◐◑◔✂ VARY
Lonicera (some)   p. 418

Italian arum
◐●◑◔✂ US, MS, LS, CS
Arum italicum   p. 167

Jack-in-the-pulpit
◐●◑✂ US, MS, LS, CS
Arisaema triphyllum   p. 164

Lily of China
◐◑◔✂ MS, LS, CS
Rohdea japonica   p. 551

Mondo grass
◐◑◔✂ MS, LS, CS, TS
Ophiopogon japonicus   p. 460

Partridgeberry
◐●◑◖✂ US, MS, LS, CS
Mitchella repens   p. 439

Porcelain berry
☼◐●◑◔✂ US, MS, LS, CS
Ampelopsis brevipedunculata   p. 148

Japanese ardisia (Marlberry)
Ardesia japonica

Red chokeberry
Aronia arbutifolia

Rose
Rosa

American bittersweet
Celastrus scandens

Porcelain berry
Ampelopsis brevipedunculata

For climate zone explanations, please see pages 38–39.

Plants with Colorful Foliage

A garden isn't meant to be enjoyed outdoors only. You can cut many different kinds of flowers and bring them indoors. The ones you see here generally last about a week in water. Many of them, indicated by the symbol 𝕴, are easy to dry for permanent arrangements. Annuals and biennials must be planted every year; perennials and most bulbs provide flowers year after year. Shrubs are another good source of cut flowers, and some even respond obligingly to cutting by blooming again and again.

Red Japanese barberry and cannas

Fancy-leafed caladium
Caladium bicolor

Agave

GRAY, SILVER
TREES AND SHRUBS

Agave
☼ ◐ ◊ ◊ ✂ CS, TS
p. 137

Aloe
☼ ◐ ◊ ◊ ◊ ✂ TS
p. 144

Arizona cypress
☼ ◊ ◊ ✂ MS, LS, CS
Cupressus arizonica glabra   p. 267

Bush germander
☼ ◊ ✂ US, MS, LS, CS
Teucrium fruticans   p. 616

Eucalyptus (many)
☼ ◊ ✂ VARY
p. 303

Feijoa, Pineapple guava
☼ ◊ ✂ LS, CS, TS
Feijoa sellowiana   p. 312

Juniper
☼ ◐ ◊ ◊ ◊ ✂ VARY
Juniperus (many)   p. 385

Lavender
☼ ◊ ✂ VARY
Lavandula (most)   p. 403

Lavender cotton
☼ ◊ ◊ ✂ US, MS, LS, CS
Santolina chamaecyparissus   p. 575

Red yucca
☼ ◐ ◊ ◊ ✂ ALL
Hesperaloe parviflora   p. 353

Rockrose
☼ ◊ ✂ LS, CS
Cistus   p. 238

Russian olive
☼ ◐ ◊ ◊ ◊ ✂ US, MS
Elaeagnus angustifolia   p. 294

Arizona cypress
Cupressus arizonica glabra

Bush germander
Teucrium fruticans

Silver dollar tree
Eucalyptus cinerea

Plectranthus argentatus
☼ ◐ ◊ ✂ TS OR INDOORS
p. 509

Texas ranger
☼ ◊ ✂ LS, CS, TS
Leucophyllum (most)   p. 408

Thorny elaeagnus
☼ ◐ ◊ ◊ ◊ ✂ US, MS, LS, CS
Elaeagnus pungens   p. 294

GRAY, SILVER
PERENNIALS

Artemisia (many)
☼ ◊ ◊ ✂ VARY
p. 165

'Berggarten' common sage
☼ ◐ ◊ ✂ US, MS, LS
Salvia officinalis   p. 571

'Bowles Mauve' wallflower
☼ ◐ ◊ ◊ ✂ US, MS, LS, CS
Erysimum   p. 301

Dusty miller
☼ ◊ ✂ LS, CS, TS
Centaurea cineraria   p. 224

Dusty miller
☼ ◊ ✂ MS, LS, CS
Senecio cineraria   p. 585

Echeveria (many)
☼ ◐ ◊ ✂ VARY
p. 291

Germander sage
☼ ◊ ◊ ✂ MS, LS, CS, TS
Salvia chamaedryoides   p. 569

Globe thistle
☼ ◊ ✂ US, MS, LS, CS
Echinops   p. 293

Horehound
☼ ◊ ◊ ✂ ALL
Marrubium vulgare   p. 432

Red yucca
Hesperaloe parviflora

Echeveria

Germander sage
Salvia chamaedryoides

For growing symbol explanations, please see page 37.

Lavender cotton
Santolina chamaecyparissus

Rose campion
Lychnis coronaria

Silver sage
Salvia argentea

Woolly thyme
Thymus pseudolanuginosus

Jerusalem sage
☼ ◑◐ ◕◔ ✔ MS, LS, CS, TS
Phlomis fruticosa   p. 496

Lamb's ears
☼ ◑◕◔ ✔ US, MS, LS
Stachys byzantina   p. 599

Licorice plant
☼ ◕✔ TS OR ANNUAL
Helichrysum petiolare   p. 347

Mountain mint
☼ ◑◐ ◕◔ ✔ US, MS, LS
Pycnanthemum incanum   p. 530

Pink
☼ ◕✔ US, MS, LS, CS
Dianthus (many)   p. 279

Red-hot poker
☼ ◑◕ ◔✔ VARY
Kniphofia (some)   p. 392

Rose campion
☼ ◑◕ ◔✔ US, MS, LS
Lychnis coronaria   p. 421

Russian sage
☼ ◐ ◕◔ ✔ US, MS, LS, CS
Perovskia atriplicifolia   p. 490

'Silver Falls' dichondra
☼ ◑ ◕◔ ✔ CS, TS
Dichondra argentea 'Silver Falls'   p. 282

Silver sage
☼ ◕◔ ✔ US, MS, LS
Salvia argentea   p. 568

Snow-in-summer
☼ ◕◔ ✔ US, MS, LS
Cerastium tomentosum   p. 226

Thyme
☼ ◑◕◔ ✔ VARY
Thymus (several)   p. 619

Yarrow
☼ ◑ ◕◔ ✔ US, MS, LS
Achillea (many)   p. 130

BRONZE, RED, PURPLE
TREES AND SHRUBS

Bronze dracaena
☼ ◕◔ ✔ CS, TS OR INDOORS
Cordyline australis 'Atropurpurea'   p. 252

Bronze loquat
☼ ◑◐ ◕◔ ◕◔ ✔ CS, TS
Eriobotrya deflexa   p. 300

Caribbean copper plant
☼ ◕◔ ◕✔ CS, TS
Euphorbia cotinifolia   p. 307

'Crimson King' Norway maple
☼ ◑◕ ◔✔ US, MS
Acer platanoides   p. 129

European beech
☼ ◑◕ ◔✔ US, MS
Fagus sylvatica (some)   p. 310

European filbert
☼ ◕◔ ✔ US, MS, LS
Corylus avellana 'Fuscorubra'   p. 259

Flowering crabapple
☼ ◕◔ ✔ VARY
Malus (some)   p. 428

'Forest Pansy' Eastern redbud
◑◔ ✔ US, MS, LS, CS
Cercis canadensis   p. 227

Japanese barberry
☼ ◑◐ ◕◔ ✔ US, MS, LS, CS
Berberis thunbergii (several)   p. 185

Japanese maple
☼ ◑◐ ◕◔ ✔ US, MS, LS, CS
Acer palmatum (some)   p. 127

Purple-leaf sand cherry
☼ ◑◕ ◔✔ US, MS
Prunus x cistena   p. 525

Smoke tree
☼ ◕◔ ✔ US, MS, LS
Cotinus coggygria (some)   p. 260

Thundercloud plum
☼ ◑◕ ◔✔ US, MS, LS
Prunus cerasifera 'Thundercloud'   p. 524

BRONZE, RED, PURPLE
PERENNIALS

Anthriscus sylvestris 'Ravenswing'
☼ ◑◕◔ ✔ US, MS
                                       p. 152

Bergenia (some)
☼ ◑◕ ◕◔ ✔ US, MS, LS
                                       p. 185

'Black Magic' elephant's ear
◑◕ ◕◔ ◑◔ ✔ VARY OR INDOORS
Alocasia   p. 160

Bronze fennel
☼ ◑◕ ◔✔ US, MS, LS, CS
Foeniculum vulgare 'Purpurascens'   p. 317

Canna (some)
☼ ◕ ◕◔ ✔ LS, CS, TS
                                       p. 214

Carpet bugleweed
☼ ◕ ◕◔ ✔ US, MS, LS
Ajuga (several)   p. 140

Coleus
☼ ◑◕ ◕◔ ◑◔ ✔ TS OR ANNUAL
Coleus x hybridus   p. 256

Coral bells
◑◕ ◕◔ ✔ US, MS, LS
Heuchera micrantha 'Palace Purple'   p. 354

Earth star
◑◕ ◕◔ ✔ TS OR INDOORS
Cryptanthus zonatus   p. 265

'Fanal' false spiraea
☼ ◑◕ ◕◔ ✔ US, MS
Astilbe x arendsii 'Fanal'   p. 172

Caribbean copper plant
Euphorbia cotinifolia

'Forest Pansy' Eastern redbud
Cercis canadensis

Coral bells
Heuchera micrantha 'Palace Purple'

Thundercloud plum
Prunus cerasifera 'Thundercloud'

Canna

For climate zone explanations, please see pages 38–39.

Japanese blood grass
Imperata cylindrica 'Rubra'

New Zealand flax
Phormium tenax 'Purpureum'

Purple fountain grass
Pennisetum setaceum 'Rubrum'

American Arborvitae
Thuja occidentalis

Blue mist
Caryopteris x clandonensis

Japanese blood grass
☼◑◐◆↯ US, MS, LS, CS
Imperata cylindrica 'Rubra'   p. 374

Knotweed
☼◑◐◆↯ VARY
Persicaria (some)   p. 490

Lobelia (some)
☼◑◐◆◗◆↯ VARY
                                           p. 417

New Zealand flax
☼◑◐◑◆◆↯ LS, CS, TS
Phormium tenax (several)   p. 499

'Pele's Smoke' sugar cane
☼◆↯ CS, TS
Saccharum officinarum   p. 566

Pilea
◑◐◆↯ TS OR INDOORS
                                           p. 503

Purple fountain grass
☼◑◐◑◆◆↯ CS, TS OR ANNUAL
Pennisetum setaceum 'Rubrum'   p. 486

Purple heart
☼◑◆◆↯ MS, LS, CS, TS
Tradescantia pallida   p. 626

Purple velvet plant
◑◆◆↯ LS, CS, TS OR INDOORS
Gynura aurantiaca   p. 340

Sweet potato vine
☼◆◆↯ LS, CS, TS
Ipomoea batatas (some)   p. 376

Wood spurge
☼◑◐◆◆↯ US, MS, LS, CS
Euphorbia amygdaloides 'Purpurea' p. 307

YELLOW, GOLD
TREES AND SHRUBS

Arborvitae
☼◑◐◆◆↯ VARY
Thuja (some)   p. 617

Blue mist 'Worcester Gold'
☼◆↯ US, MS, LS, CS
Caryopteris x clandonensis   p. 219

Box honeysuckle
☼◆◆↯ US, MS, LS, CS
Lonicera nitida 'Baggesen's Gold'   p. 418

'Castlewellan' Leyland cypress
☼◑◆◆↯ US, MS, LS, CS
x Cupressocyparis leylandii   p. 267

English yew
☼◑◐◆◆◆↯ US, MS
Taxus baccata (several)   p. 613

European cranberry bush
☼◆◆↯ US, MS, LS
Viburnum opulus 'Aureum'   p. 639

'Frisia' black locust
☼◑◆◆◆↯ US, MS, LS, CS
Robina pseudoacacia   p. 550

Golden fullmoon maple
☼◑◆◆↯ US
Acer shirasawanum 'Aureum'   p. 130

Golden Hinoki false cypress
◑◆◆↯ US, MS, LS
Chamaecyparis obtusa 'Crippsii'   p. 229

Italian cypress 'Swane's Golden'
☼◊◆◆↯ MS, LS, CS
Cupressus sempervirens   p. 267

Japanese aucuba
◑◆◆◆↯ ALL
Aucuba japonica (many)   p. 174

Japanese barberry
☼◑◆◆◆↯ US, MS, LS
Berberis thunbergii (some)   p. 185

Juniper
☼◑◊◊◆◆↯ VARY
Juniperus (several)   p. 385

Spiraea japonica (several)
☼◑◆◆↯ US, MS, LS
                                           p. 597

'Sunburst' honey locust
☼◆◆↯ US, MS
Gleditsia triacanthos   p. 331

'Sundance' Mexican orange
☼◑◆◆↯ LS, CS, TS
Choisya ternata   p. 235

'Vicary' golden privet
☼◑◆◆◆↯ US, MS, LS, CS
Ligustrum 'Vicaryi'   p. 411

YELLOW, GOLD
PERENNIALS

Bleeding heart, common
◑◐◆◆↯ US, MS, LS, CS
Lamprocapnos spectabilis   p. 400

Bowles' golden grass
◑◆◗◆↯ US, MS, LS
Milium effusum 'Aureum'   p. 437

Feverfew 'Aureum'
☼◑◆◆↯ US, MS, LS, CS
Chrysanthemum parthenium   p. 245

Golden moneywort
◐◆◆↯ US, MS, LS
Lysimachia nummularia 'Aurea'   p. 422

Japanese forest grass
◑◐◆◆↯ US, MS, LS
Hakonechloa macra 'Aureola'   p. 341

Japanese sweet flag
◑◐↯ US, MS, LS, CS
Acorus gramineus 'Ogon'   p. 132

'Limelight' licorice plant
☼◑↯ TS OR ANNUAL
Helichrysum petiolare   p. 347

Oregano
☼◊◆↯ VARY
Origanum (several)   p. 460

English yew
Taxus baccata 'Aurea'

Golden Hinoki false cypress
Chamaecyparis obtusa 'Crippsii'

Bleeding heart, common
Dicentra spectabilis

Feverfew
Chrysanthemum parthenium
'Aureum'

Licorice plant
Helichrysum petiolare
'Limelight'

For growing symbol explanations, please see page 37.

Plantain lily
Hosta

Bowles' golden sedge
Carex elata 'Aurea' ('Bowles' Golden')

Bougainvillea
Bougainvillea 'Hawaii'

China fir
Cunninghamia lanceolata 'Glauca'

Colorado blue spruce
Picea pungens

Switch grass
Panicum virgatum 'Heavy Metal'

Plantain lily
US, MS, LS
Hosta (several) p. 359

Sedge
US, MS, LS, CS
Carex (several) p. 216

Thyme
VARY
Thymus (several) p. 619

BLUE
TREES, SHRUBS, AND PERENNIALS

Atlas cedar
US, MS, LS
Cedrus atlantica 'Glauca' p. 222

Blue fescue
US, MS
Festuca glauca p. 312

Blue lyme grass
US, MS, LS, CS
Leymus arenarius p. 409

China fir
MS, LS, CS
Cunninghamia lanceolata 'Glauca' p. 266

Colorado blue spruce
US, MS, LS
Picea pungens (some) p. 502

Eucalyptus (some)
VARY
p. 303

Plantain lily
US, MS, LS
Hosta (several) p. 359

Rue
US, MS, LS, CS
Ruta graveolens p. 565

Switch grass
US, MS, LS, CS
Panicum virgatum (some) p. 469

VARIEGATED
TREES, SHRUBS, VINES

Actinidia kolomikta
US, MS, LS
p. 132

Bougainvillea (some)
CS, TS
p. 191

Caricature plant
TS OR INDOORS
Graptophyllum pictum p. 338

Confederate jasmine 'Variegatum'
MS, LS, CS, TS
Trachelospermum jasminoides p. 625

Drooping leucothoe 'Rainbow'
US, MS, LS
Leucothoe fontanesiana p. 408

Euonymus (some)
VARY
p. 305

Farfugium japonicum (some)
MS, LS, CS, TS OR INDOORS
p. 311

Fiveleaf aralia 'Variegatus'
US, MS, LS
Eleutherococcus sieboldianus p. 295

Flowering dogwood
US, MS, LS, CS
Cornus florida (several) p. 256

Flowering maple
CS, TS
Abutilon (some) p. 125

French hydrangea
US, MS, LS, CS
Hydrangea macrophylla (several) p. 364

Golden elaeagnus
US, MS, LS, CS
Elaeagnus pungens 'Maculata' p. 295

Holly
VARY
Ilex (several) p. 369

Holly osmanthus
US, MS, LS, CS
Osmanthus heterophyllus 'Goshiki' p. 463

Ivy
VARY
Hedera (some) p. 343

Japanese andromeda
US, MS, LS
Pieris japonica 'Variegata' p. 503

Japanese aucuba
ALL
Aucuba japonica (several) p. 174

Japanese pittosporum
LS, CS, TS
Pittosporum tobira (several) p. 507

Juniper
VARY
Juniperus (several) p. 385

Laurustinus
CS, TS
Viburnum tinus 'Bewley's Variegated' p. 640

Mosaic Swedish ivy
TS OR INDOORS
Plectranthus oertendahlii p. 509

Myrtle
LS, CS, TS
Myrtus communis (some) p. 445

Orange-eye butterfly bush
US, MS, LS, CS
Buddleia davidii 'Harlequin' p. 197

Rock cotoneaster
US, MS, LS
Cotoneaster horizontalis 'Variegatus' p. 261

English holly
Ilex aquifolium 'Aurea Marginata'

Wintercreeper euonymus
Euonymus fortunei

English ivy
Hedera helix

Japanese aucuba
Aucuba japonica 'Variegata'

Japanese pittosporum
Pittosporum tobira 'Variegatum'

Juniper
Juniperus horizontalis

For climate zone explanations, please see pages 38–39.

Golden elaeagnus
Elaeagnus pungens 'Maculata'

Weigela
Weigela 'Variegata'

Winter daphne
Daphne odora 'Aureomarginala'

Bishop's weed
Aegopodium podagraria 'Variegata'

Carpet bugleweed
Ajuga reptans

Snow bush
☼ ◐ ♦ ✂ TS OR INDOORS
Breynia nivosa   p. 193

Trailing lantana
☼ ◐ ♦ ✂ LS, CS, TS OR ANNUAL
Lantana montevidensis   p. 400

Tricolor beech
☼ ◐ ♦ ✂ US, MS
Fagus sylvatica   p. 310

Variegated box elder
☼ ◑ ◐ ♦ ✂ US, MS
Acer negundo 'Variegatum'   p. 127

Variegated Chinese privet
☼ ◑ ◐ ♦ ✂ MS, LS, CS, TS
Ligustrum sinense 'Variegatum'   p. 410

Variegated winter daphne
☼ ◐ ♦ ✂ MS, LS
Daphne odora 'Aureomarginata'   p. 274

Weigela hybrid 'Variegata'
☼ ◑ ◐ ♦ ✂ US, MS, LS
                                                 p. 645

VARIEGATED
PERENNIALS

Big blue liriope
☼ ◑ ◐ ● ♦ ✂ ALL
Liriope muscari (some)   p. 416

Bishop's weed
☼ ◑ ◐ ● ♦ ✂ US, MS, LS
Aegopodium podagraria 'Variegatum' p. 134

Calathea
☼ ◐ ♦ ✂ TS OR INDOORS
                                                 p. 203

Calla
☼ ◑ ◐ ♦ ✂ LS, CS, TS
Zantedeschia   p. 649

Carpet bugleweed
☼ ◑ ● ♦ ✂ US, MS, LS
Ajuga reptans (some)   p. 140

Century plant
☼ ◑ ◒ ◐ ♦ ✂ CS, TS
Agave attenuata   p 137

Coleus
☼ ◑ ◐ ● ♦ ◑ ✂ TS OR ANNUAL
Coleus hybridus   p. 256

Coral bells
☼ ◑ ◐ ♦ ✂ US, MS, LS
Heuchera (some)   p. 354

Cranesbill
☼ ◑ ◐ ♦ ✂ US, MS, LS
Geranium (many)   p. 326

Dead nettle
☼ ◐ ● ♦ ✂ US, MS, LS
Lamium (many)   p. 400

Obedient plant
☼ ◑ ◐ ♦ ✂ US, MS, LS, CS
Physostegia virginiana 'Variegata'   p. 501

Fancy-leafed caladium
☼ ◑ ◐ ● ♦ ◑ ✂ CS, TS
Caladium bicolor   p. 202

Gaura (some)
☼ ◐ ♦ ✂ US, MS, LS, CS
Gaura lindheimeri   p. 324

Geranium
☼ ◑ ◐ ♦ ✂ CS, TS OR ANNUAL
Pelargonium (several)   p. 484

Impatiens, New Guinea hybrids
☼ ◑ ◐ ♦ ✂ TS OR ANNUAL
                                                 p. 373

Japanese pachysandra
☼ ◐ ♦ ✂ US, MS, LS
Pachysandra terminalis 'Variegata'   p. 466

Japanese painted fern
☼ ◐ ● ◑ ♦ ✂ US, MS, LS
Athyrium niponicum 'Pictum'   p. 173

Japanese silver grass
☼ ◑ ◐ ♦ ✂ US, MS, LS, CS
Miscanthus sinensis (several)   p. 438

Lungwort
☼ ◐ ● ♦ ✂ US, MS, LS
Pulmonaria (several)   p. 528

Maiden grass
☼ ◑ ◐ ♦ ✂ US, MS, LS, CS
Miscanthus sinensis 'Morning Light' p. 439

Maranta
☼ ◐ ♦ ◑ ✂ VARY
                                                 p. 432

New Zealand flax
☼ ◑ ◒ ◐ ♦ ✂ LS, CS, TS
Phormium tenax (many)   p. 499

Periwinkle
☼ ◐ ● ♦ ♦ ✂ VARY
Vinca (some)   p. 641

Plantain lily
☼ ◐ ● ♦ ✂ US, MS, LS
Hosta (several)   p. 359

Plectranthus (some)
☼ ◐ ♦ ✂ TS OR INDOORS
                                                 p. 509

Sedge
☼ ◑ ◒ ◐ ♦ ◑ ✂ US, MS, LS, CS
Carex (several)   p. 216

Society garlic
☼ ◐ ♦ ✂ MS. LS, CS, TS
Tulbaghia violacea (some)   p. 629

Solomon's seal
☼ ◐ ● ♦ ✂ US, MS, LS
Polygonatum   p. 516

Tricolor common sage
☼ ◑ ◐ ♦ ✂ US, MS, LS
Salvia officinalis   p. 571

Yucca (some)
☼ ◒ ◐ ♦ ✂ VARY
                                                 p 647

Spotted dead nettle
Lamium maculatum

Geranium
Pelargonium x hortorum 'Golden Ears'

New Zealand flax
Phormium tenax

Plantain lily
Hosta

Tricolor common sage
Salvia officinalis 'Tricolor'

For growing symbol explanations, please see page 37.

Red maple
Acer rubrum

Autumn Foliage Color

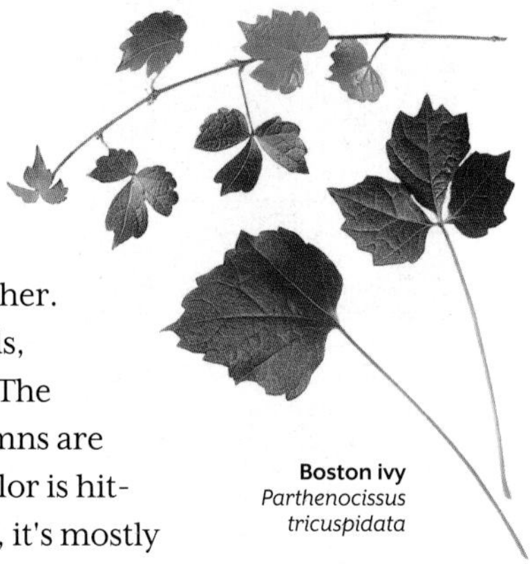

Boston ivy
Parthenocissus tricuspidata

In most places, autumn brings the year's most pleasant weather. Just as welcome is the foliage show that accompanies it—reds, oranges, yellows, burgundies, pinks, and parchment browns. The show is brightest in the Upper and Middle South, where autumns are cooler and fewer pines and cedars dot the countryside. Fall color is hit-or-miss in the Lower South; in the Coastal and Tropical South, it's mostly a theory. But when conditions are right, the following plants take center stage. Because leaf color often varies within a species, shop for plants when they're in color, or buy reliable named selections.

American beech
Fagus grandifolia

Black gum
Nyssa sylvatica

Bald cypress
Taxodium distichum

TREES

American beech
☼ ☼ ◐ ● ◖ ✂ US, MS, LS, CS
Fagus grandifolia — p. 310

Ash
☼ ○ ◐ ● ✂ VARY
Fraxinus — p. 319

Bald cypress
☼ ☼ ◐ ● ◖ ✂ US, MS, LS, CS
Taxodium distichum — p. 613

Birch
☼ ◐ ● ◖ ✂ VARY
Betula — p. 186

Black cherry
☼ ◐ ● ◖ ✂ US, MS, LS, CS
Prunus serotina — p. 525

Black gum
☼ ☼ ◐ ● ✂ US, MS, LS, CS
Nyssa sylvatica — p. 455

Black locust
☼ ○ ◐ ● ◖ ✂ US, MS, LS, CS
Robinia pseudoacacia — p. 550

Callery pear
☼ ◐ ● ◖ ✂ US, MS, LS, CS
Pyrus calleryana — p. 531

Carolina silverbell
☼ ☼ ◐ ● ✂ US, MS, LS
Halesia carolina — p. 341

Chinese parasol tree
☼ ☼ ◐ ● ✂ MS, LS, CS, TS
Firmiana simplex — p. 317

Chinese pistache
☼ ○ ◐ ● ✂ US, MS, LS, CS
Pistacia chinensis — p. 506

Chinese quince
☼ ◐ ● ✂ US, MS, LS
Pseudocydonia sinensis — p. 526

Chinese tallow
☼ ◐ ● ◖ ✂ LS, CS, TS
Triadica sebifera — p. 626

Crepe myrtle
☼ ◐ ● ✂ US, MS, LS, CS
Lagerstroemia indica — p. 395

Dawn redwood
☼ ◐ ● ✂ US, MS, LS, CS
Metasequoia glyptostroboides — p. 437

Fig
☼ ◐ ● ✂ MS, LS, CS, TS
— p. 314

Flowering crabapple
☼ ◐ ● ◖ ✂ VARY
Malus — p. 428

Flowering dogwood
☼ ☼ ◐ ● ✂ US, MS, LS, CS
Cornus florida — p. 255

Franklin tree
☼ ☼ ◐ ● ✂ US, MS, LS, CS
Franklinia alatamaha — p. 319

Fringe tree
☼ ☼ ◐ ● ◖ ✂ US, MS, LS, CS
Chionanthus virginicus — p. 234

Goldenrain tree
☼ ◐ ● ✂ US, MS, LS, CS
Koelreuteria paniculata — p. 393

Hackberry
☼ ☼ ◐ ● ✂ US, MS, LS, CS
Celtis — p. 224

Hawthorn
☼ ◐ ● ✂ VARY
Crataegus (some) — p. 262

Honey locust
☼ ◐ ● ◖ ✂ US, MS, LS
Gleditsia triacanthos — p. 331

Ironwood
☼ ☼ ◐ ● ◖ ✂ US, MS, LS, CS
Carpinus caroliniana — p. 217

Chinese pistache
Pistacia chinensis

Crepe myrtle
Lagerstroemia indica

Fringe tree
Chionanthus virginicus

For climate zone explanations, please see pages 38–39.

Japanese maple
Acer palmatum

Sugar maple
Acer saccharum

Persimmon
Diospyros

Quaking aspen
Populus tremuloides

Sassafras
Sassafras albidum

Katsura tree
US, MS, LS
Cercidiphyllum japonicum — p. 226

Kentucky coffee tree
US, MS, LS
Gymnocladus dioica — p. 339

Larch
VARY
Larix — p. 401

Linden
VARY
Tilia — p. 620

Maidenhair tree
US, MS, LS, CS
Ginkgo biloba — p. 329

Maple
VARY
Acer (many) — p. 127

Mountain ash
VARY
Sorbus — p. 594

Oak
VARY
Quercus (deciduous) — p. 532

Ohio buckeye
US, MS
Aesculus glabra — p. 135

Osage orange
US, MS, LS
Maclura pomifera — p. 423

Pawpaw
US, MS, LS, CS
— p. 475

Persimmon
VARY
— p. 491

Quaking aspen
US, MS
Populus tremuloides — p. 518

Redbud
VARY
Cercis — p. 227

Sassafras
US, MS, LS
Sassafras albidum — p. 577

Sawleaf zelkova
US, MS, LS
Zelkova serrata — p. 649

Serviceberry
US, MS, LS, CS
Amelanchier — p. 147

Shagbark hickory
US, MS, LS, CS
Carya ovata — p. 219

Sourwood
US, MS, LS, CS
Oxydendrum arboreum — p. 465

Southern wild crab
US, MS, LS
Malus angustifolia — p. 429

Stewartia
VARY
— p. 601

Sweet gum, American
US, MS, LS, CS
Liquidambar styraciflua — p. 415

Tulip poplar
US, MS, LS, CS
Liriodendron tulipifera — p. 415

Willow
US, MS, LS
Salix — p. 567

Yellow wood
US, MS, LS
Cladrastis kentukea — p. 242

Yoshino flowering cherry
US, MS, LS
Prunus x yedoensis — p. 523

Yulan magnolia
US, MS, LS, CS
Magnolia denudata — p. 425

SHRUBS

Azalea (deciduous)
VARY
Rhododendron — p. 541

Beautyberry
US, MS, LS
Callicarpa — p. 205

Blueberry
VARY
— p. 190

Bottlebrush buckeye
US, MS, LS, CS
Aesculus parviflora — p. 135

Chokeberry
VARY
Aronia — p. 165

Cotoneaster (most deciduous)
VARY
— p. 260

Disanthus cercidifolius
US, MS, LS
— p. 286

Flame grass
US, MS, LS, CS
Miscanthus 'Purpurascens' — p. 438

Fothergilla
US, MS, LS
— p. 318

Heart's-a-bustin'
US, MS, LS, CS
Euonymus americanus — p. 305

American sweet gum
Liquidambar styraciflua

Sourwood
Oxydendrum arboreum

Azalea, deciduous
Rhododendron

Chokeberry
Aronia

For growing symbol explanations, please see page 37.

Japanese barberry
Berberis thunbergii

Nandina
Nandina domestica

Oakleaf hydrangea
Hydrangea quercifolia

Spicebush
Lindera benzoin

Hercules' club
☼:☼●◖●◢Ⱬ US, MS, LS, CS
Aralia spinosa   p. 161

Japanese barberry
☼:☼●◖●◢Ⱬ US, MS, LS
Berberis thunbergii   p. 185

Japanese kerria
:☼●◖●◢Ⱬ US, MS, LS, CS
Kerria japonica   p. 390

Mahonia
☼:☼●◖●◖◢Ⱬ VARY
                                            p. 427

'Miss Kim' lilac
☼:☼●◖◢Ⱬ US, MS, LS
Syringa patula 'Miss Kim'   p. 610

Nandina
☼:☼●◖●◖◢Ⱬ US, MS, LS, CS
Nandina domestica   p. 445

Oakleaf hydrangea
:☼●◖◢Ⱬ US, MS, LS, CS
Hydrangea quercifolia   p. 364

Oriental photinia
☼:●◖◢Ⱬ US, MS
Photinia villosa   p. 500

Persian parrotia
☼:☼●◖●◢Ⱬ US, MS, LS
Parrotia persica   p. 472

Pomegranate
☼:●◢Ⱬ MS, LS, CS, TS
                                            p. 517

Redvein enkianthus
☼:●◖◐◢Ⱬ US, MS
Enkianthus campanulatus   p. 295

Rose
☼:☼●◖◢Ⱬ ALL
Rosa (some)   p. 551

Shadblow serviceberry
☼:☼●◖●◢Ⱬ US, MS, LS
Amelanchier canadensis   p. 147

Smoke tree
☼:☼●◢Ⱬ US, MS, LS
Cotinus   p. 260

Sparkleberry
☼:☼●◖◢Ⱬ MS, LS, CS
Vaccinium arboreum   p. 633

Spicebush
☼:☼●◖◢Ⱬ US, MS, LS
Lindera benzoin   p. 414

Star magnolia
☼:☼●◖◢Ⱬ US, MS, LS, CS
Magnolia stellata   p. 426

Sumac
☼:◐●◢Ⱬ VARY
Rhus   p. 549

Summersweet
:☼●◐◢Ⱬ US, MS, LS, CS
Clethra alnifolia   p. 246

Sweetshrub, common
☼:☼●◖◑◢Ⱬ US, MS, LS, CS
Calycanthus floridus   p. 207

Sweetbells
:☼●◖◑◢Ⱬ US, MS, LS, CS
Leucothoe racemosa   p. 409

Titi
☼:☼●◖◐◢Ⱬ ALL
Cyrilla racemiflora   p. 270

Van Houtte spiraea
☼:☼●◖◢Ⱬ US, MS, LS
Spiraea vanhouttei   p. 597

Viburnum (many)
☼:☼●◖◢Ⱬ VARY
                                            p. 637

Virginia sweetspire
☼:●◢Ⱬ US, MS, LS, CS
Itea virginica   p. 381

Winged euonymus
☼:☼●◖●◖◢Ⱬ US, MS, LS
Euonymus alatus   p. 305

Winterberry
☼:☼●◖◐◢Ⱬ US, MS, LS, CS
Ilex verticillata   p. 372

Witch hazel, common
☼:☼●◖◢Ⱬ US, MS, LS, CS
Hamamelis virginiana   p. 342

VINES, PERENNIALS

Bittersweet
☼:●◢Ⱬ US, MS, LS
Celastrus   p. 223

Boston ivy
☼:☼●◖●◢Ⱬ US, MS, LS
Parthenocissus tricuspidata   p. 473

Bowman's root
:☼●◢Ⱬ US, MS, LS
Gillenia trifoliata   p. 329

Dwarf plumbago
☼:☼●◖●◢Ⱬ US, MS, LS, CS
Ceratostigma plumbaginoides   p. 226

Grape
☼:●◢Ⱬ VARY
                                            p. 334

Hubricht's bluestar
☼:☼●◖●◢Ⱬ US, MS, LS, CS
Amsonia hubrichtii   p. 149

Royal fern
☼:☼●◖◑Ⱬ US, MS, LS, CS
Osmunda regalis   p. 463

Virginia creeper
☼:☼●◖●◢Ⱬ US, MS, LS, CS
Parthenocissus quinquefolia   p. 473

Wisteria
☼:◐●◢Ⱬ US, MS, LS, CS
                                            p. 645

Sumac
Rhus

Doublefile viburnum
Viburnum plicatum 'Marresii'

Summersweet
Clethra alnifolia

Smoke tree
Cotinus coggygria

Virginia creeper
Parthenocissus quinquefolia

For climate zone explanations, please see pages 38–39.

Deciduous Plants
for Winter Interest

Most Southerners prefer evergreens for their long season of color. Still, deciduous plants offer a special beauty, especially in gardens in the Upper South, where winters can be long. Peeling bark, contorted limbs, and winter fruit cause us to reflect on the subtleties of gardening, those quiet details that make every day outdoors a learning adventure.

Japanese persimmon

American beech
Fagus grandifolia

Chinese elm
Ulmus parvifolia

Crepe myrtle
Lagerstroemia indica

Harry Lauder's walking stick
Corylus avellana 'Contorta'

American beech
US, MS, LS, CS
Fagus grandifolia — p. 310

Birch
VARY
Betula (most) — p. 186

Black walnut
US, MS, LS, CS
Juglans nigra — p. 385

Chinese elm
US, MS, LS, CS
Ulmus parvifolia — p. 632

Coral-bark maple
US, MS, LS, CS
Acer palmatum 'Sango Kaku' — p. 129

Corkscrew willow
US, MS, LS
Salix matsudana 'Tortuosa' — p. 568

Crepe myrtle
US, MS, LS, CS
Lagerstroemia indica — p. 395

Flowering dogwood
US, MS, LS, CS
Cornus florida — p. 256

Harry Lauder's walking stick
US, MS, LS
Corylus avellana 'Contorta' — p. 259

Heart's-a-bustin'
US, MS, LS, CS
Euonymus americanus — p. 305

Ironwood
US, MS, LS, CS
Carpinus caroliniana — p. 217

Japanese flowering cherry
VARY
Prunus serrulata — p. 523

Japanese kerria
US, MS, LS, CS
Kerria japonica — p. 390

Japanese tree lilac
US, MS
Syringa reticulata — p. 610

Kentucky coffee tree
US, MS, LS
Gymnocladus dioica — p. 339

Lacebark pine
US, MS
Pinus bungeana — p. 504

Maidenhair tree
US, MS, LS, CS
Ginkgo biloba — p. 329

Oakleaf hydrangea
US, MS, LS, CS
Hydrangea quercifolia — p. 364

Paperbark maple
US, MS
Acer griseum — p. 127

Persimmon
VARY
— p. 491

Redtwig, yellowtwig dogwood
US, MS
Cornus — p. 257

Saucer magnolia
US, MS, LS, CS
Magnolia soulangeana — p. 426

Shagbark hickory
US, MS, LS, CS
Carya ovata — p. 219

Stewartia
VARY
— p. 601

Sycamore
VARY
Platanus — p. 507

White oak
US, MS, LS, CS
Quercus alba — p. 532

Winged euonymus
US, MS, LS
Euonymus alatus — p. 305

Winterberry
US, MS, LS, CS
Ilex verticillata — p. 372

Yellowtwig dogwood
Cornus sericea 'Flaviramea'

Redtwig dogwood
Cornus sericea

Japanese stewartia
Stewartia pseudocamellia

Sycamore
Platanus

Winterberry
Ilex verticillata

For growing symbol explanations, please see page 37.

Trees

Southern
magnolia

No decision affects your garden more than the numbers and types of trees you plant. So save yourself a lot of time, money, and trouble by selecting trees that are long-lived, strong-wooded, and not pestered by insects and diseases. Lawn trees should cast light, filtered shade and be deep rooted. Trees that shade decks, patios, and parking areas shouldn't drop messy fruits. Always consider a tree's mature size. Here, small trees grow up to 30 feet tall and wide; medium trees grow 30 to 60 feet; large trees grow more than 60 feet—but mature sizes vary somewhat across the South.

Flowering dogwood
Cornus florida

Crepe myrtle
Lagerstroemia indica

Franklin tree
Franklinia alatamaha

English hawthorn
Crataegus laevigata

SMALL TREES
DECIDUOUS

'Acoma' crepe myrtle
☼❍◐ US, MS, LS, CS
Lagerstroemia indica 'Acoma'   p. 395

Amur maple
☼☼◐❍ US, MS, LS
Acer tataricum ginnala   p. 130

Brazilian orchid tree
☼☼◐❍ CS, TS
Bauhinia forficata   p. 180

Carolina silver bell
☼☼◐❍ US, MS, LS
Halesia carolina   p. 341

'Crimson Queen' Japanese maple
☼ ☼◐❍ US, MS, LS, CS   p. 128
Acer palmatum dissectum 'Crimson Queen'

Cry-baby tree
☼◐❍ LS, CS, TS
Erythrina crista-galli   p. 301

Desert willow
☼❍◐ MS, LS, CS
Chilopsis linearis   p. 233

Flowering crabapple
☼◐❍ VARY
Malus   p. 428

Flowering dogwood
☼☼◐❍ US, MS, LS, CS
Cornus florida   p. 256

Franklin tree
☼☼◐❍ US, MS, LS, CS
Franklinia alatamaha   p. 319

Fringe tree
☼☼◐❍ US, MS, LS, CS
Chionanthus   p. 234

Harlequin glorybower
◐❍ MS, LS, CS, TS
Clerodendrum trichotomum   p. 245

Hawthorn
☼◐❍ VARY
Crataegus   p. 262

Hong Kong orchid tree
☼◐◐❍ TS
Bauhinia x blakeana   p. 179

Hop hornbeam
☼☼◐❍ US, MS, LS, CS
Ostrya   p. 464

Japanese flowering apricot
☼☼◐❍ US, MS, LS, CS
Prunus mume   p. 524

Japanese maple
☼☼◐◐❍ US, MS, LS, CS
Acer palmatum   p. 127

Japanese stewartia
◐❍ US, MS
Stewartia pseudocamellia   p. 601

Jerusalem thorn
☼❍◐❍ LS, CS, TS
Parkinsonia aculeata   p. 472

Jujube
☼☼◐❍ US, MS, LS, CS   p. 385

Kousa dogwood
☼☼◐❍ US, MS, LS
Cornus kousa   p. 256

Lilac chaste tree
☼◐◐❍ US, MS, LS, CS
Vitex agnus-castus   p. 643

Mountain ash
☼☼◐◐❍ VARY
Sorbus   p. 594

'Okame' flowering cherry
☼ ◐◐❍ US, MS, LS, CS
Prunus 'Okame'   p. 523

Paperbark maple
☼☼◐❍ US, MS
Acer griseum   p. 127

Persian parrotia
☼☼◐◐❍ US, MS, LS
Parrotia persica   p. 472

Persimmon (Japanese)
☼◐◐❍ MS, LS, CS
Diospyros kaki   p. 491

Japanese maple
Acer palmatum

Kousa dogwood
Cornus kousa

Lilac chaste tree
Vitex agnus-castus

Paperpark maple
Acer griseum

For climate zone explanations, please see pages 38–39.

Redbud
Cercis

Smoke tree
Cotinus coggygria

Orange tree
Citrus

Giant dracaena
Cordyline australis

Purple orchid tree
☀ ◐ ● ◐ ✂ TS
Bauhinia variegata   p. 180

Redbud
☀ ◐ ● ● ◐ ✂ VARY
Cercis   p. 227

Serviceberry
☀ ◐ ● ● ◐ ✂ US, MS, LS, CS
Amelanchier   p. 147

Silky stewartia
☀ ◐ ◐ ✂ MS, LS, CS
Stewartia malacodendron   p. 601

Smoke tree
☀ ◐ ● ◐ ✂ US, MS, LS
Cotinus coggygria   p. 260

Sourwood
☀ ◐ ◐ ● ◐ ✂ US, MS, LS, CS
Oxydendrum arboreum   p. 465

Star magnolia
☀ ◐ ◐ ● ◐ ✂ US, MS, LS, CS
Magnolia stellata   p. 426

Snowbell
☀ ◐ ◐ ● ◐ ✂ VARY
Styrax   p. 605

Sweet acacia
☀ ◐ ✂ LS, CS, TS
Acacia farnesiana   p. 126

Titi
☀ ◐ ◐ ● ● ◐ ✂ ALL
Cyrilla racemiflora   p. 270

Trident maple
☀ ◐ ◐ ● ◐ ✂ US, MS, LS
Acer buergerianum   p. 127

Trumpet tree
☀ ◐ ◐ ● ✂ TS
Tabebuia   p. 611

Yellow wood
☀ ◐ ● ✂ US, MS, LS
Cladrastis kentukea   p. 242

SMALL TREES
EVERGREEN

Bottlebrush
☀ ◐ ● ◐ ✂ VARY
Callistemon   p. 206

Buckwheat tree
☀ ◐ ● ● ◐ ✂ LS, CS
Cliftonia monophylla   p. 247

Citrus
☀ ◐ ✂ CS, TS
                                               p. 238

Dracaena
☀ ◐ ◐ ◐ ✂ TS
                                               p. 288

Fern pine
☀ ◐ ◐ ● ✂ TS
Podocarpus gracilior   p. 514

Giant dracaena
☀ ◐ ● ◐ ✂ CS, TS
Cordyline australis   p. 252

Giant thevetia
☀ ◐ ● ◐ ✂ TS
Thevetia thevetioides   p. 617

Glossy privet
☀ ◐ ◐ ● ◐ ✂ LS, CS, TS
Ligustrum lucidum   p. 410

Gold medallion tree
☀ ◐ ◐ ● ◐ ✂ TS
Cassia leptophylla   p. 219

Hawaiian tree fern
◐ ● ◐ ✂ TS
Cibotium   p. 237

'Little Gem' Southern magnolia
☀ ◐ ◐ ● ◐ ✂ US, MS, LS, CS
Magnolia grandiflora   p. 424

Loquat
☀ ◐ ◐ ◐ ● ● ◐ ✂ LS, CS, TS
Eriobotrya japonica   p. 300

Mango
☀ ◐ ● ◐ ✂ TS
                                               p. 431

Plum yew
☀ ◐ ◐ ● ◐ ✂ VARY
Cephalotaxus   p. 225

Sea grape
☀ ◐ ◐ ✂ TS
Coccoloba   p. 248

Silver dollar tree
☀ ◐ ✂ LS, CS, TS
Eucalyptus cinerea   p. 303

Sweet bay
☀ ◐ ◐ ● ✂ US, MS, LS, CS
Magnolia virginiana   p. 425

Sweet olive
◐ ◐ ◐ ● ◐ ✂ LS, CS, TS
Osmanthus fragrans   p. 463

Texas mountain laurel
☀ ◐ ◐ ● ◐ ✂ LS, CS
Sophora secundiflora   p. 594

Wax myrtle
☀ ◐ ● ◐ ✂ MS, LS, CS, TS
Myrica cerifera   p. 441

MEDIUM TREES
DECIDUOUS

Birch
☀ ◐ ● ● ◐ ✂ VARY
Betula   p. 186

Callery pear
☀ ◐ ● ◐ ✂ US, MS, LS, CS
Pyrus calleryana   p. 531

Chestnut
☀ ◐ ✂ US, MS, LS
                                               p. 232

Glossy privet
Ligustrum lucidum

Star magnolia
Magnolia stellata

Silver dollar tree
Eucalyptus cinerea

Texas mountain laurel
Sophora secundiflora

For growing symbol explanations, please see page 37.

Chinese elm
Ulmus parvifolia

Goldenchain tree
Laburnum

Jacaranda
Jacaranda mimosifolia

Saucer magnolia
Magnolia soulangiana

Chinaberry
☼◑◐◈▨ MS, LS, CS, TS
Melia azedarach   p. 435

Chinese elm
☼◑◐▨ US, MS, LS, CS
Ulmus parvifolia   p. 632

Chinese pistache
☼◐◑◐▨ US, MS, LS, CS
Pistacia chinensis   p. 506

Chinese tallow
☼◑◐◑◐▨ LS, CS, TS
Triadica sebifera   p. 626

Chitalpa
☼◐◑◐▨ US, MS, LS, CS
X Chitalpa tashkentensis   p. 234

Dove tree
◑◐▨ US, MS
Davidia involucrata   p. 276

Floss silk tree
☼◑◐▨ TS
Chorisia   p. 235

Goldenchain tree
◑◐◐◈▨ US, MS
Laburnum   p. 394

Hardy rubber tree
☼◑◐◑▨ US, MS
Eucommia ulmoides   p. 304

Honey locust
☼◑◐◑▨ US, MS, LS
Gleditsia triacanthos   p. 331

Ironwood
☼◐◑◐◐◑▨ US, MS, LS, CS
Carpinus caroliniana   p. 217

Jacaranda
☼◑◐▨ TS
Jacaranda mimosifolia   p. 382

Japanese pagoda tree
☼◐◑◐▨ US, MS, LS
Styphnolobium japonicum   p. 605

Katsura tree
☼◐◑◐▨ US, MS, LS
Cercidiphyllum japonicum p. 226

Koelreuteria
☼◑◐◑▨ VARY
                          p. 393

Korean evodia
☼◑◐◑◐▨ US, MS, LS
Tetradium daniellii   p. 615

Little-leaf linden
☼◑◐▨ US, MS
Tilia cordata   p. 621

Magnolia (some)
☼◐◑◐▨ VARY
                          p. 423

Mesquite
☼◐▨ MS, LS, CS
Prosopis glandulosa   p. 522

'Natchez' crepe myrtle
☼◑◐▨ US, MS, LS, CS
Lagerstroemia   p. 395

Sassafras
☼◑◐◑▨ US, MS, LS
Sassafras albidum   p. 577

Shower of gold
☼◐◑◑▨ TS
Cassia fistula   p. 219

Willow
☼◑◐◑◑▨ US, MS, LS
Salix   p. 567

Yoshino flowering cherry
☼◑◐◑▨ US, MS, LS
Prunus x yedoensis   p. 523

MEDIUM TREES
EVERGREEN

Arborvitae
☼◐◑◐◑▨ VARY
Thuja   p. 617

Bailey acacia
☼◐▨ CS, TS
Acacia baileyana   p. 126

Eastern red cedar
☼◐◑◐◑▨ ALL
Juniperus virginiana   p. 387

Eucalyptus (several)
☼◐▨ VARY
                          p. 303

Hinoki false cypress
◑◐▨ US, MS, LS
Chamaecyparis obtusa   p. 229

Holly (many)
☼◐◑◐▨ VARY
Ilex   p. 369

Loblolly bay
☼◐◑◐◑◑▨ MS, LS, CS, TS
Gordonia lasianthus   p. 333

Lychee
☼◑◐▨ CS, TS
                          p. 420

Queen palm
☼◑◐▨ CS, TS
Syagrus romanzoffiana   p. 607

Southern sweet bay
☼◐◑◐▨ MS, LS, CS, TS
Magnolia virginiana australis p. 425

Windmill palm
☼◐◑◐◑▨ LS, CS, TS
Trachycarpus fortunei   p. 625

LARGE TREES
DECIDUOUS

American beech
☼◐◑◐◑▨ US, MS, LS, CS
Fagus grandifolia   p. 310

Sassafras
Sassafras albidum

Hinoki false cypress
Chamaecyparis obtusa

Eastern red cedar
Juniperus virginiana

Windmill palm
Trachycarpus fortunei

For climate zone explanations, please see pages 38–39.

American beech
Fagus grandifolia

Catalpa, common
Catalpa bignonioides

Sweet gum
Liquidambar

Dawn redwood
Metasequoia glyptostroboides

Norway maple
Acer platanoides

American sycamore
☼ ◑ ✿ US, MS, LS, CS
Platanus occidentalis   p. 508

Ash (white and green)
☼ ◑ ✿ US, MS, LS, CS
Fraxinus   p. 319-320

Bald cypress
☼ ◐ ◑ ◔ ◑ ✿ US, MS, LS, CS
Taxodium distichum   p. 613

Black gum
☼ ◐ ◑ ◔ ◑ ✿ US, MS, LS, CS
Nyssa sylvatica   p. 455

Black locust
☼ ○ ◑ ◔ ✿ US, MS, LS, CS
Robinia pseudoacacia   p. 550

Catalpa
☼ ◐ ◑ ◔ ✿ US, MS, LS, CS
                                          p. 220

Dawn redwood
☼ ◑ ✿ US, MS, LS, CS
Metasequoia glyptostroboides   p. 437

Hackberry
☼ ◐ ◑ ✿ US, MS, LS, CS
Celtis   p. 224

Kentucky coffee tree
☼ ◑ ✿ US, MS, LS
Gymnocladus dioica   p. 339

London plane tree
☼ ◑ ✿ US, MS, LS
Platanus x acerifolia   p. 508

Maidenhair tree
☼ ◑ ◔ ✿ US, MS, LS, CS
Ginkgo biloba   p. 329

Norway maple
☼ ◐ ◑ ◔ ✿ US, MS
Acer platanoides   p. 129

Oak (many)
☼ ◑ ✿ VARY
Quercus   p. 532

Pecan
☼ ◑ ✿ US, MS, LS, CS
                                          p. 483

Red maple
☼ ◐ ◑ ◔ ✿ US, MS, LS, CS
Acer rubrum   p. 129

River birch
☼ ◑ ◔ ✿ US, MS, LS, CS
Betula nigra   p. 186

Sawleaf zelkova
☼ ◑ ✿ US, MS, LS
Zelkova serrata   p. 649

Shagbark hickory
☼ ◑ ◔ ✿ US, MS, LS, CS
Carya ovata   p. 219

Silk-cotton tree
☼ ◑ ◔ ✿ TS
Ceiba pentandra   p. 222

Sugar maple
☼ ◐ ◑ ◔ ✿ US, MS, LS
Acer saccharum   p. 129

Sweet gum
☼ ◑ ◔ ✿ VARY
Liquidambar   p. 415

Tulip poplar
☼ ◑ ✿ US, MS, LS, CS
Liriodendron tulipifera   p. 415

LARGE TREES
EVERGREEN

Cabbage palm
☼ ◐ ◑ ✿ LS, CS, TS
Sabal palmetto   p. 565

Camphor tree
☼ ◐ ◑ ◔ ◑ ✿ LS, CS, TS
Cinnamomum camphora   p. 238

Canadian hemlock
☼ ◐ ◑ ◔ ✿ US, MS
Tsuga canadensis   p. 629

Cedar
☼ ◑ ✿ VARY
Cedrus   p. 222

Cypress
☼ ○ ◑ ✿ VARY
Cupressus   p. 267

Date palm
☼ ◑ ✿ CS, TS
Phoenix   p. 498

Incense cedar
☼ ◐ ◑ ○ ◔ ✿ US, MS, LS
Calocedrus decurrens   p. 207

Japanese cryptomeria
☼ ◐ ◑ ◔ ✿ US, MS, LS
Cryptomeria japonica   p. 265

Laurel oak
☼ ◑ ✿ MS, LS, CS, TS
Quercus laurifolia   p. 533

Live oak
☼ ◑ ✿ LS, CS, TS
Quercus virginiana   p. 535

Pines (most)
☼ ○ ◑ ◔ ✿ VARY
Pinus   p. 504

Royal palm
☼ ◑ ✿ TS
Roystonea   p. 562

Southern magnolia
☼ ◐ ◑ ✿ US, MS, LS, CS
Magnolia grandiflora   p. 424

Spruce
☼ ◐ ◑ ◔ ✿ US, MS
Picea   p. 501

White cedar
☼ ◐ ◑ ◔ ✿ US, MS, LS, CS
Chamaecyparis thyoides   p. 229

Cabbage palm
Sabal palmetto

Camphor tree
Cinnamomum camphora

Blue Atlas cedar
Cedrus atlantica 'Glauca'

Live oak
Quercus virginiana

For growing symbol explanations, please see page 37.

Vines
and Vinelike Plants

Vines are the garden's most flexible members. Unlike trees and shrubs, which have fairly rigid stems, the stems of most vines can be guided to grow where you want them. You can train them to grow upward or outward on a flat, vertical surface; up and around a tree trunk; or up and over an arbor. Many perform alternative duty as ground cover. Some vines climb with tendrils, some use aerial roots, and some employ suction-cuplike holdfasts. Some simply laze about; they only climb if tied to a support. On the following chart, the symbol ✳ indicates vines with showy flowers.

Trumpet honeysuckle
Lonicera sempervirens

Armand clematis
Clematis armandii

Fiveleaf akebia
Akebia quinata

Cape honeysuckle
Tecoma capensis

Bower vine
Pandorea jasminoides

Carolina jessamine
Gelsemium sempervirens

Crossvine
Bignonia capreolata

Madagascar jasmine
Stephanotis floribunda

Mandevilla 'Alice du Pont'

EVERGREEN

Allamanda ✳
☼ ● ◗ ⧖ TS OR ANNUAL
p. 142

Armand clematis ✳
☼ ◗ ⧖ LS, CS
Clematis armandii   p. 243

Bleeding heart vine ✳
☼ ◗ ● ⧖ TS
Clerodendrum thomsoniae   p. 245

Blue pea vine ✳
☼ ◗ ● ◗ ⧖ TS OR ANNUAL
Clitoria ternatea   p. 247

Boston Ivy
☼ ◗ ● ● ◗ ⧖ US, MS, LS
Parthenocissus tricuspidata   p. 473

Bougainvillea ✳
☼ ● ◗ ⧖ CS, TS
p. 191

Cape honeysuckle ✳
☼ ◗ ● ⧖ CS, TS
Tecoma capensis   p. 614

Carolina jessamine ✳
☼ ◗ ● ● ◗ ⧖ MS, LS, CS
Gelsemium sempervirens   p. 325

Cat's claw ✳
☼ ◗ ● ⧖ LS, CS, TS
Macfadyena unguis-cati   p. 423

Confederate jasmine ✳
☼ ◗ ● ◗ ⧖ MS, LS, CS, TS
Trachelospermum jasminoides   p. 625

Creeping fig
☼ ◗ ● ◗ ⧖ LS, CS, TS OR INDOORS
Ficus pumila   p. 314

Crossvine ✳
☼ ◗ ● ◗ ⧖ US, MS, LS, CS
Bignonia capreolata   p. 187

Cup-of-gold vine ✳
☼ ● ◗ ⧖ TS
Solandra maxima   p. 590

x Fatshedera lizei
☼ ● ● ◗ ⧖ LS, CS, TS
p. 311

Fiveleaf akebia ✳
☼ ◗ ● ● ◗ ⧖ US, MS, LS, CS
Akebia quinata   p. 141

Flame vine ✳
☼ ◗ ● ◗ ⧖ CS, TS
Pyrostegia venusta   p. 531

Grape ivy
● ● ◗ ⧖ TS OR INDOORS
Cissus rhombifolia   p. 238

Herald's trumpet ✳
☼ ◗ ● ◗ ⧖ TS
Beaumontia grandiflora   p. 181

Honeysuckle ✳
☼ ◗ ● ● ◗ ⧖ VARY
Lonicera (some)   p. 418

Ivy
☼ ◗ ● ● ◗ ⧖ VARY
Hedera   p. 343

Jackson vine
☼ ◗ ● ◗ ⧖ MS, LS, CS
Smilax smallii   p. 590

Jasmine ✳
☼ ◗ ● ◗ ⧖ VARY
Jasminum (several)   p. 382

Madagascar jasmine ✳
☼ ◗ ● ◗ ⧖ TS, OR INDOORS
Stephanotis floribunda   p. 600

Mandevilla (several) ✳
☼ ◗ ● ◗ ⧖ TS
p. 431

Mexican flame vine ✳
☼ ◗ ● ◗ ⧖ CS, TS
Pseudogynoxys chenopodioides   p. 526

For climate zone explanations, please see pages 38–39.

Passion vine
Passiflora

Queen's wreath
Petrea volubilis

Clematis, large-flow-ered hybrid

Sky flower
Thunbergia grandiflora

Violet trumpet vine
Clytostoma callistegioides

Night-blooming jasmine ✳
☼ ◐ ♦ ✂ TS
Cestrum nocturnum — p. 228

Pandorea ✳
◐ ◐ ♦ ♦ ✂ VARY
— p. 469

Passion vine (most) ✳
☼ ◐ ◐ ♦ ✂ VARY
Passiflora — p. 473

Pink jasmine ✳
☼ ◐ ◐ ♦ ✂ LS, CS, TS
Jasminum polyanthum — p. 383

Pink trumpet vine ✳
☼ ◐ ◐ ♦ ✂ CS, TS
Podranea ricasoliana — p. 515

Potato vine ✳
☼ ◐ ◐ ♦ ♦ ✂ LS, CS, TS
Solanum jasminoides — p. 591

Queen's wreath ✳
☼ ◐ ♦ ✂ TS
Petrea volubilis — p. 492

Sky flower ✳
☼ ◐ ◐ ♦ ✂ TS
Thunbergia grandiflora — p. 618

Violet trumpet vine ✳
☼ ◐ ◐ ♦ ✂ CS, TS
Clytostoma callistegioides — p. 248

Wintercreeper euonymus
☼ ◐ ◐ ♦ ◐ ♦ ✂ US, MS, LS, CS
Euonymus fortunei — p. 305

DECIDUOUS

Bittersweet
☼ ◐ ♦ ✂ US, MS, LS
Celastrus — p. 223

Chilean jasmine ✳
☼ ◐ ◐ ♦ ✂ CS, TS
Mandevilla laxa — p. 431

Clematis (most) ✳
☼ ◐ ♦ ♦ ✂ VARY
— p. 242

Climbing hydrangea ✳
◐ ◐ ♦ ✂ US, MS, LS
Hydrangea anomala petiolaris — p. 363

Coral vine ✳
☼ ◐ ♦ ♦ ✂ LS, CS, TS
Antigonon leptopus — p. 153

Costa Rican nightshade ✳
☼ ◐ ◐ ♦ ♦ ✂ TS
Solanum wendlandii — p. 591

Dutchman's pipe ✳
☼ ◐ ◐ ♦ ◐ ✂ VARY
Aristolochia (several) — p. 164

Grape
☼ ◐ ♦ ✂ VARY
— p. 334

Japanese hydrangea vine ✳
◐ ◐ ✂ US, MS, LS
Schizophragma hydrangeoides — p. 579

Kiwi vine
☼ ◐ ◐ ♦ ✂ US, MS, LS
Actinidia kolomikta — p. 132

Porcelain berry
☼ ◐ ◐ ♦ ♦ ✂ US, MS, LS, CS
Ampelopsis brevipedunculata — p. 148

Rangoon creeper ✳
☼ ◐ ◐ ✂ TS
Quisqualis indica — p. 535

Rose ✳
☼ ◐ ◐ ✂ ALL
Rosa (climbers) — p. 554

Silver lace vine ✳
☼ ◐ ♦ ♦ ✂ US, MS, LS, CS
Fallopia baldshuanica — p. 311

Trumpet creeper, common ✳
☼ ◐ ◐ ♦ ♦ ✂ US, MS, LS, CS
Campsis radicans — p. 214

Virginia creeper
☼ ◐ ◐ ♦ ✂ US, MS, LS, CS
Parthenocissus quinquefolia — p. 473

Wisteria ✳
☼ ◐ ♦ ✂ US, MS, LS, CS
— p. 645

ANNUAL

Bean, scarlet runner ✳
☼ ◐ ✂ ALL
— p. 180

Black-eyed Susan vine ✳
☼ ◐ ◐ ♦ ✂ CS, TS
Thunbergia alata — p. 618

Cup-and-saucer vine ✳
☼ ◐ ✂ ALL
Cobaea scandens — p. 248

Firecracker vine ✳
☼ ◐ ♦ ✂ ALL
Ipomoea lobata — p. 376

Hyacinth bean ✳
☼ ◐ ♦ ✂ LS, CS, TS
Dolichos lablab — p. 288

Moonflower ✳
☼ ◐ ♦ ✂ ALL
Ipomoea alba — p. 376

Morning glory (several) ✳
☼ ◐ ♦ ✂ VARY
Ipomoea — p. 375

Nasturtium ✳
☼ ◐ ◐ ✂ ALL
Tropaeolum majus — p. 628

Sweet pea ✳
☼ ◐ ♦ ◐ ✂ ALL
Lathyrus odoratus — p. 402

Grape 'Swenson Red'

Porcelain berry
Ampelopsis brevipedunculata

American wisteria
Wisteria frutescens

Nasturtium
Tropaeolum majus

For growing symbol explanations, please see page 37.

Plants for
Ground Cover

Dwarf mondo grass
Ophiopogon japonicus 'Nana'

Periwinkle, common
Vinca minor 'La Grave'

While a lawn can be the best ground cover, not every garden is suited to turf. Some sites are too shady, others too steep. Sometimes you just don't feel like mowing. Consider the following plants as options. These low-growing plants shelter the soil, prevent erosion, and may also have striking flowers, foliage, or berries. Some spread by underground runners or root as they grow. Others sprawl over the soil. The symbol ♛ indicates ground cover with showy flowers.

Baby's tears
Soleirolia soleirolii

Bergenia

Carpet bugleweed
Ajuga reptans

Catmint
Nepeta faassenii

Artemisia (several)
☼◖◗▲☀ VARY
p. 165

Asian star jasmine
☼◖◗◆▲☀ MS, LS, CS, TS
Trachelospermum asiaticum   p. 625

Baby's tears
☼◐◗◆☀ CS, TS
Soleirolia soleirolii   p. 591

Bamboo (dwarf types)
☼◖◗◆▲☀ VARY
p. 175-176

Bergenia ♛
☼◐◆☀ US, MS, LS
p. 185

Bishop's weed
☼◖◐◆☀ US, MS, LS
Aegopodium podagraria   p. 134

Blue fescue
☼◖◗◆▲☀ US, MS
Festuca glauca   p. 312

Canada wild ginger
◖◐◗◆▲☀ US, MS, LS
Asarum canadense   p. 168

Carpet bugleweed ♛
☼◐◆☀ US, MS, LS
Ajuga reptans   p. 140

Catmint ♛
☼◖◗◆▲☀ US, MS, LS
Nepeta x faassenii   p. 451

Cinquefoil ♛
☼◖◗◆☀ VARY
Potentilla (several)   p. 520

Cotoneaster (some) ♛
☼◖◆▲☀ VARY
p. 260

Creeping buttercup ♛
☼◖◐◆☀ US, MS, LS, CS
Ranunculus repens pleniflorus   p. 537

Creeping Jenny
◗◆▲☀ US, MS, LS
Lysimachia nummularia   p. 422

Dwarf-eared coreopsis ♛
☼◗▲☀ US, MS, LS, CS
Coreopsis auriculata 'Nana'   p. 253

Dwarf plumbago ♛
☼◖◗◆▲☀ US, MS, LS, CS
Ceratostigma plumbaginoides   p. 226

Epimedium ♛
☼◐◆☀ US, MS, LS
p. 296

Evergreen candytuft ♛
☼◗◆☀ US, MS, CS
Iberis sempervirens   p. 369

Galax
◗◐◆☀ US, MS, LS–
Galax urceolata   p. 322

Germander
☼◗☀ US, MS, LS, CS
Teucrium chamaedrys   p. 615

Golden globes ♛
☼◖◗◆▲☀ MS, LS, CS
Lysimachia congestiflora   p. 422

Golden star ♛
◗◆☀ US, MS, LS, CS
Chrysogonum virginianum   p. 237

Grape ivy
◗◐◆☀ TS
Cissus rhombifolia   p. 238

Holly fern
◗◐◆☀ LS, CS, TS
Cyrtomium falcatum   p. 271

Ice plant ♛
☼◖◆☀ CS, TS
Delosperma   p. 277

Ivy
☼◗◐◆▲☀ VARY
Hedera   p. 343

Japanese ardisia
◗◐◆☀ LS, CS
Ardisia japonica   p. 163

Japanese pachysandra ♛
◗◐◆☀ US, MS, LS
Pachysandra terminalis   p. 466

Dwarf plumbago
Ceratostigma plumbaginoides

Epimedium

Golden star
Chrysogonum virginianum

For climate zone explanations, please see pages 38–39.

Juniper
Juniperus horizontalis 'Prince of Wales'

Lamb's ears
Stachys byzantina

Lady's-mantle
Alchemilla mollis

Lenten rose
Helleborus orientalis

Lungwort
Pulmonaria

Jasmine (some)
☀☀◐●◑⚡ VARY
Jasminum — p. 382

Juniper
☀◐●◑⚡ VARY
Juniperus (low-growing) — p. 385

Knotweed
☀☀◐●⚡ VARY
Persicaria — p. 490

Lady's-mantle
◐● ◑⚡ US, MS, LS
Alchemilla mollis — p. 142

Lamb's ears
☀◐●⚡ US, MS, LS
Stachys byzantina — p. 599

Lavender cotton
☀◐●⚡ US, MS, LS, CS
Santolina chamaecyparissus — p. 576

Lenten rose
◐● ◐◑⚡ US, MS, LS
Helleborus orientalis — p. 350

Lily-of-the-valley
◐● ●◑⚡ US, MS, LS
Convallaria majalis — p. 251

Lungwort
◐● ●⚡ US, MS, LS
Pulmonaria (several) — p. 528

Mazus reptans
☀☀◐● ●⚡ US, MS, LS
— p. 433

Memorial rose
☀☀◐●⚡ US, MS, LS, CS
Rosa wichuraiana — p. 561

Mondo grass
☀◐● ◐⚡ MS, LS, CS, TS
Ophiopogon japonicus — p. 460

Monkey grass (several)
◐● ◑⚡ VARY
Liriope — p. 416

Moss pink
☀☀◐●⚡ US, MS, LS
Phlox subulata — p. 498

Oregano
☀◐●⚡ VARY
Origanum (several) — p. 460

Ornamental strawberry
☀☀◐●⚡ US, MS, LS, CS
Fragaria hybrids — p. 319

Partridgeberry
◐● ●◑⚡ US, MS, LS, CS
Mitchella repens — p. 439

Periwinkle
◐● ●◑⚡ VARY
Vinca — p. 641

Pussy toes
☀◐●⚡ US, MS, LS
Antennaria dioica — p. 152

Rockcress
☀◐●⚡ US, MS, LS
Arabis — p. 160

Rock soapwort
☀◐●⚡ US, MS, LS
Saponaria ocymoides — p. 575

Rosemary
☀◐◐●⚡ US, MS, LS, CS, TS
Rosmarinus officinalis (low) — p. 561

St. Johnswort
☀◐●◐●⚡ VARY
Hypericum (low-growing) — p. 367

Sedge
☀◐●◐●◑⚡ US, MS, LS, CS
Carex (several) — p. 216

'Silver Falls' dichondra
☀☀◐●⚡ CS, TS
Dichondra argentea 'Silver Falls' — p. 282

Snow-in-summer
◐● ●⚡ US, MS, LS
Cerastium tomentosum — p. 226

Southern shield fern
☀◐● ●◑⚡ US, MS, LS, CS
Thelypteris kunthii — p. 616

Spotted dead nettle
◐● ●⚡ US, MS, LS
Lamium maculatum — p. 400

Sprenger asparagus
◐●⚡ CS, TS
Asparagus densiflorus 'Sprengeri' — p. 170

Stonecrop (many)
☀◐◐●⚡ US, MS, LS
Sedum — p. 581

Strawberry geranium
◐● ●⚡ MS, LS, CS
Saxifraga stolonifera — p. 577

Sweet box
◐● ◐●⚡ US, MS, LS, CS
Sarcococca hookeriana humilis — p. 576

Sweet flag
◐◑⚡ US, MS, LS, CS
Acorus — p. 132

Sweet woodruff
◐● ●◐●⚡ US, MS, LS
Galium odoratum — p. 322

Thrift, common
☀◐●⚡ US, MS, LS, CS
Armeria maritima — p. 165

Thyme
☀◐●⚡ VARY
Thymus — p. 619

Sphagneticola trilobata
☀◐●⚡ CS, TS
— p. 596

Wintercreeper euonymus (some)
◐● ●◐●⚡ US, MS, LS, CS
Euonymus fortunei — p. 305

Pussy toes
Antennaria dioica

Rock soapwort
Saponaria ocymoides

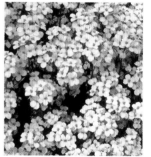

Wall rockcress
Arabis caucasica

Aaron's beard (St. Johnswort)
Hypericum calycinum

Stonecrop
Sedum spathulifolium 'Cape Blanco'

For growing symbol explanations, please see page 37.

Gulf muhly
Muhlenbergia capillaris

Golden bamboo
Phyllostachys aurea

Bowles' golden grass
Milium effusum 'Aureum'

Chinese pennisetum
Pennisetum alopecuroides

Grasses and Grasslike Plants

If you only think of grass as something you mow, it's time you discovered ornamental grasses. The beauty of these denizens of prairie, marsh, seashore, and forest lies in their graceful, fountainlike foliage and remarkable floral displays. As a group, ornamental grasses are easy to grow, free from pests, and simple to divide. Some, such as river oats, palm grass, and silver grass, readily self-sow.

Bamboos	VARY	(Many kinds)	p. 175
Blue fescue	US, MS	Festuca glauca	p. 312
Blue lyme grass	US, MS, LS, CS	Leymus arenarius	p. 409
Blue oat grass	US, MS, LS, CS	Helictotrichon sempervirens	p. 348
Bluestem	US, MS, LS, CS	Andropogon	p. 149
Bowles' golden grass	US, MS, LS	Milium effusum 'Aureum'	p. 437
Feather reed grass	US, MS, LS, CS	Calamagrostis x acutiflora	p. 202
Fountain grass	VARY	Pennisetum	p. 485
Giant reed	ALL	Arundo donax	p. 167
Hair grass	US, MS, LS	Deschampsia	p. 279
Japanese blood grass	US, MS, LS, CS	Imperata cylindrica 'Rubra'	p. 374
Lemon grass	TS OR ANNUAL	Cymbopogon citratus	p. 270
Mexican feather grass	MS, LS, CS, TS	Nassella tenuissima	p. 449
Moor grass	US, MS, LS	Molinia caerulea	p. 440
Muhly grass	MS, LS, CS, TS	Muhlenbergia	p. 442
Natal ruby grass	TS OR ANNUAL	Melinis	p. 435
New Zealand flax	LS, CS, TS	Phormium tenax	p. 499
Palm grass	CS, TS	Setaria palmifolia	p. 587
Pampas grass	MS, LS, CS, TS	Cortaderia selloana	p. 258
Prairie dropseed	US, MS, LS, CS	Sporobolus heterolepsis	p. 598
Rattlesnake grass	ALL	Briza maxima	p. 194
Ravenna grass	ALL	Saccharum ravennae	p. 566
Ribbon grass	US, MS, LS, CS	Phalaris arundinacea picta	p. 494
River oats	US, MS, LS, CS	Chasmanthium latifolium	p. 230
Sedge	US, MS, LS, CS	Carex	p. 216
Silver grass	US, MS, LS, CS	Miscanthus	p. 438
Sweet flag	US, MS, LS, CS	Acorus	p. 132
Switch grass	US, MS, LS, CS	Panicum virgatum	p. 469

Lemon grass
Cymbopogon citratus

Mexican feather grass
Nassella tenuissima

Pampas grass
Cortaderia selloana

Silver grass
Miscanthus

Leather leaf sedge
Carex buchananii

For climate zone explanations, please see pages 38–39.

Vegetables and Fruits

Considering the bounty of fresh produce that's available year-round at the grocery store, why would anyone grow their own? Actually, there are plenty of reasons. Fresh garden vegetables and fruits taste better, and if you grow them organically you won't have to worry about pesticides. You can also grow uncommon varieties not found in supermarkets. Moreover, many edible plants make fine ornamentals—kale, chard, lettuce, persimmons, blueberries, and figs are good examples.

'Sierra' and 'Rosy' Lettuce

Cucumber

Avocado

Snap bean

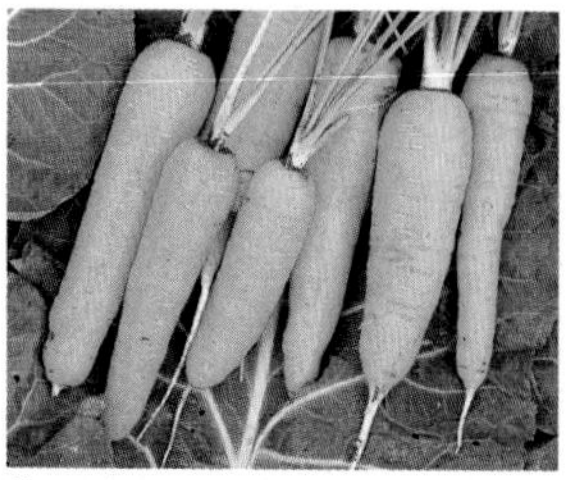

Carrot

VEGETABLES

Asparagus
☼ ● ◿ US, MS, LS
p. 169

Avocado
☼ ● ◿ CS, TS
p. 174

Bean
☼ ● ◿ ALL
p. 180

Beet
☼ ● ◿ ALL
p. 182

Broccoli
☼ ● ◿ ALL
p. 194

Brussels sprouts
☼ ● ◿ ALL
p. 196

Cardoon
☼ ● ◿ LS, CS
p. 216

Carrot
☼ ● ◿ ALL
p. 217

Cauliflower
☼ ● ◿ ALL
p. 221

Celery
☼ ● ◐ ◿ ALL
p. 223

Chayote
☼ ● ◿ CS, TS
p. 231

Common ginger
☼ ● ◐ ◿ LS, CS, TS
Zingiber officinale   p. 650

Corn
☼ ● ◿ ALL
p. 254

Cucumber
☼ ● ◿ ALL
p. 265

Eggplant
☼ ● ◿ ALL
p. 293

Garlic
☼ ● ◿ ALL
p. 324

Gourd
☼ ● ◿ ALL
p. 333

Horseradish
☼ ● ◿ US, MS, LS
p. 358

Jerusalem artichoke
☼ ● ◐ ◿ US, MS, LS, CS
Helianthus tuberosus   p. 347

Jicama
☼ ◐ ◊ ◿ LS, CS, TS
p. 384

Kohlrabi
☼ ● ◿ ALL
p. 393

Leek
☼ ● ◐ ◿ ALL
p. 405

Okra
☼ ● ◿ ALL
p. 457

Onion
☼ ● ◿ ALL
p. 458

Parsnip
☼ ● ◿ US, MS
p. 472

Eggplants

Jicama

Kohlrabi

For growing symbol explanations, please see page 37.

Virginia peanut

Southern pea

Tomatoes

Pea (shelling, snap, or snow)
☼ ◐ ⁄ ALL
p. 476

Peanut
☼ ◐ ⁄ ALL
p. 479

Pepper
☼ ◐ ⁄ ALL
p. 488

Potato
☼ ◐ ◈ ⁄ ALL
p. 519

Pumpkin
☼ ◐ ⁄ ALL
p. 529

Radish
☼ ◑ ◐ ⁄ ALL
p. 536

Rhubarb
☼ ◑ ◐ ◈ ⁄ US, MS, LS
p. 548

Shallot
☼ ◐ ⁄ ALL
p. 587

Southern pea
☼ ◐ ⁄ ALL
p. 595

Squash, summer or winter
☼ ◐ ⁄ ALL
p. 598

Sweet potato
☼ ◐ ⁄ US, MS, LS
p. 606

Tomatillo
☼ ◐ ⁄ ALL
p. 622

Tomato
☼ ◐ ⁄ ALL
p. 622

Turnip and rutabaga
☼ ◐ ⁄ ALL
p. 631

Zucchini (summer squash)
☼ ◐ ⁄ ALL
p. 598

LEAFY VEGETABLES

Asian greens
☼ ◑ ◐ ⁄ ALL
p. 169

Cabbage
☼ ◑ ◐ ⁄ ALL
p. 200

Chicory and radicchio
☼ ◐ ⁄ US, MS, LS
p. 233

Chinese cabbage
☼ ◐ ⁄ ALL
p. 234

Cress, garden
☼ ◑ ◐ ◑ ⁄ ALL
p. 262

Dandelion
☼ ◐ ⁄ US, MS, LS, CS
p. 274

Fennel, common
☼ ◐ ⁄ VARY
p. 317

Garden burnet
☼ ◑ ◐ ⁄ US, MS, LS, CS
Sanguisorba minor
p. 574

Kale and collards
☼ ◑ ◐ ⁄ ALL
p. 389

Lettuce
☼ ◑ ◐ ⁄ ALL
p. 406

Mustard
☼ ◐ ⁄ ALL
p. 444

New Zealand spinach
☼ ◐ ⁄ VARY
Tetragonia
p. 596

Rocket
☼ ◐ ⁄ ALL
Arugula
p. 166

Spinach
☼ ◐ ⁄ VARY
p. 596

Swiss chard
☼ ◑ ◐ ⁄ ALL
p. 607

FRUIT

Apple
☼ ◐ ⁄ VARY
p. 154

Banana
☼ ◑ ◐ ⁄ VARY
p. 178

Blackberry
☼ ◐ ⁄ US, MS, LS, CS
p. 188

Blueberry
☼ ◐ ⁄ VARY
p. 190

Carambola
☼ ◐ ⁄ TS
p. 215

Cherry
☼ ◐ ⁄ VARY
p. 231

Asian greens

Radicchio

Kale

Swiss chard

Blackberry

For climate zone explanations, please see pages 38–39.

Citrus
(Calamondin)

Mandarin orange
Citrus

Muscadine grape

Natal plum
Carissa macrocarpa

Persimmon

Citrus
☼ ◐ ✚ CS, TS
p. 238

Date palm
☼ ◐ ✚ CS, TS
Phoenix
p. 498

Elderberry, American
◆ ☼ ◐ ◐ ✚ US, MS, LS, CS
Sambucus canadensis
p. 573

Fig
☼ ◐ ✚ MS, LS, CS, TS
p. 314

Grape and muscadine
☼ ◐ ✚ VARY
p. 334

Guava
☼ ☼ ◐ ✚ VARY
p. 339

Jujube
☼ ◐ ✚ US, MS, LS, CS
p. 385

Kiwi
☼ ◐ ◐ ✚ VARY
p. 391

Lychee
☼ ◐ ✚ CS, TS
p. 420

Mango
☼ ◐ ◆ ✚ TS
p. 431

Mayhaw
☼ ◐ ✚ MS, LS, CS
Crataegus opaca
p. 262

Melon, cantaloupe, and honeydew
☼ ◐ ✚ ALL
p. 435

Natal plum
☼ ☼ ◐ ◆ ◐ ✚ CS, TS
Carissa macrocarpa
p. 217

Olive
☼ ◐ ◆ ✚ LS, CS
p. 458

Papaya
☼ ◐ ✚ TS
p. 471

Passion fruit
☼ ◐ ✚ TS
p. 474

Pawpaw
☼ ☼ ◐ ✚ US, MS, LS, CS
p. 475

Peach and nectarine
☼ ◐ ✚ VARY
p. 476

Pear, Asian and European
☼ ◐ ✚ VARY
p. 480

Persimmon
☼ ◐ ◆ ✚ VARY
p. 491

Pineapple
☼ ◐ ✚ TS
p. 504

Plum (including prune)
☼ ◐ ◆ ✚ VARY
p. 510

Pomegranate
☼ ◐ ✚ MS, LS, CS, TS
p. 517

Quince
☼ ◐ ✚ US, MS, LS
p. 535

Raspberry
☼ ◐ ✚ US, MS
p. 537

Serviceberry
☼ ◐ ◆ ◐ ✚ VARY
Amelanchier
p. 147

Strawberry
☼ ◐ ✚ ALL
p. 602

Watermelon
☼ ◐ ✚ ALL
p. 644

NUTS

Almond
☼ ◐ ✚ US, MS
p. 143

Chestnut
☼ ◐ ✚ US, MS, LS
p. 232

Coconut palm
☼ ◐ ✚ TS
Cocos nucifera
p. 249

Filbert
☼ ◐ ◆ ✚ US, MS, LS
Corylus
p. 259

Hickory
☼ ◐ ◆ ✚ US, MS, LS, CS
Carya
p. 218

Pecan
☼ ◐ ✚ US, MS, LS, CS
p. 483

Pistachio
☼ ☼ ◐ ◆ ◐ ✚ CS, TS
Pistacia vera
p. 506

Walnut
☼ ◐ ✚ VARY
Juglans
p. 384

'Stanley' Plum

'Wonderful' Pomegranate

Quince

Raspberry

'Chandler' Strawberry

Almond

For growing symbol explanations, please see page 37.

Herbs
for Southern Gardens

The great thing about herbs is that they don't need much space. Most tolerate cramped roots and do just fine in a pot or a small kitchen garden. But two things they do demand are lots of sun and well-drained soil. In addition to their culinary uses, many herbs make excellent ornamentals. For instance, thymes make wonderful ground cover, bay can be clipped into a hedge or topiary, and germander is the standard edging used in formal parterres.

Basil
Ocimum basilicum
'Dark Opal'

Herbs are both colorful and culinary.

Chamomile
Chamaemelum nobile

Dill
Anethum graveolens

Common fennel and chives
Foeniculum vulgare, Allium schoenoprasum

Tricolor sage
Salvia officinalis 'Tricolor'

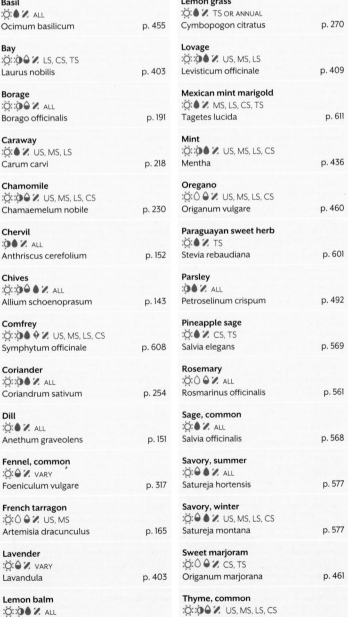

Basil ☼ ALL
Ocimum basilicum — p. 455

Bay LS, CS, TS
Laurus nobilis — p. 403

Borage ALL
Borago officinalis — p. 191

Caraway US, MS, LS
Carum carvi — p. 218

Chamomile US, MS, LS, CS
Chamaemelum nobile — p. 230

Chervil ALL
Anthriscus cerefolium — p. 152

Chives ALL
Allium schoenoprasum — p. 143

Comfrey US, MS, LS, CS
Symphytum officinale — p. 608

Coriander ALL
Coriandrum sativum — p. 254

Dill ALL
Anethum graveolens — p. 151

Fennel, common VARY
Foeniculum vulgare — p. 317

French tarragon US, MS
Artemisia dracunculus — p. 165

Lavender VARY
Lavandula — p. 403

Lemon balm ALL
Melissa officinalis — p. 435

Lemon grass TS OR ANNUAL
Cymbopogon citratus — p. 270

Lovage US, MS, LS
Levisticum officinale — p. 409

Mexican mint marigold MS, LS, CS, TS
Tagetes lucida — p. 611

Mint US, MS, LS, CS
Mentha — p. 436

Oregano US, MS, LS, CS
Origanum vulgare — p. 460

Paraguayan sweet herb TS
Stevia rebaudiana — p. 601

Parsley ALL
Petroselinum crispum — p. 492

Pineapple sage CS, TS
Salvia elegans — p. 569

Rosemary ALL
Rosmarinus officinalis — p. 561

Sage, common ALL
Salvia officinalis — p. 568

Savory, summer ALL
Satureja hortensis — p. 577

Savory, winter US, MS, LS, CS
Satureja montana — p. 577

Sweet marjoram CS, TS
Origanum marjorana — p. 461

Thyme, common US, MS, LS, CS
Thymus vulgaris — p. 620

Lavender
Lavandula

Lovage
Levisticum officinale

Oregano
Origanum vulgare

Rosemary
Rosmarinus officinalis

For climate zone explanations, please see pages 38–39.

Plants that Attract
Songbirds and Hummingbirds

B irds and blossoms seem to go together. Spying a cardinal, goldfinch, or bluebird sitting in a nearby tree can be as exciting as spotting a new rose in bloom. Attracting birds to your garden isn't hard—just provide water, dense plants for nesting and shelter, and food in the form of berries, seeds, and nectar. (But remember to put a bell on your cat's collar.)

Montbretia
Crocosmia crocosmiiflora

American bittersweet
Celastrus scandens

American elderberry
Sambucus canadensis

Purple beautyberry
Callicarpa dichotoma

Chokeberry
Aronia

SONGBIRDS
VINES, SHRUBS

American bittersweet
☼● ✓ US, MS, LS
Celastrus scandens   p. 223

American elderberry
☼:●● ♦ ✓ US, MS, LS, CS
Sambucus canadensis   p. 573

Bayberry
☼●● ✓ US, MS
Morella pensylvanica   p. 441

Beautyberry
☼:●●● ✓ US, MS, LS
Callicarpa   p. 205

Blueberry
☼:●○●○○●● ✓ VARY
Vaccinium   p. 633

Boston ivy
☼:● ●✓ US, MS, LS
Parthenocissus tricuspidata   p. 473

Carolina moonseed
☼:●●✓ US, MS, LS, CS
Cocculus   p. 248

Chokeberry
☼:●●●● ✓ VARY
Aronia   p. 165

Coralberry
☼:●●○●○ ✓ US, MS
Symphoricarpos orbiculatus   p. 607

Cotoneaster
☼:○●●✓ VARY
                                   p. 260

Darwin barberry
☼:●●●✓ MS, LS, CS
Berberis darwinii   p. 184

Elaeagnus
☼:○●○●●✓ VARY
                                   p. 294

Euonymus
☼:●●●●✓ VARY
                                   p. 305

Firethorn
☼:●●✓ VARY
Pyracantha   p. 530

Grape
☼●✓ VARY
                                   p. 334

Holly
☼:●●✓ ♦ VARY
Ilex   p. 369

Honeysuckle
☼:●●●✓ VARY
Lonicera   p. 418

Mahonia
☼:●●●●✓ VARY
                                   p. 427

Photinia
☼:●●●✓ VARY
                                   p. 500

Privet
☼:●●♦✓ VARY
Ligustrum   p. 410

Rose (some)
☼:●●✓ ALL
Rosa   p. 551

Spicebush
☼:●●✓ US, MS, LS
Lindera benzoin   p. 414

Sumac
☼:○●✓ VARY
Rhus   p. 549

Viburnum (deciduous)
☼:●●✓ VARY
                                   p. 637

Virginia creeper
☼:●●✓ US, MS, LS, CS
Parthenocissus quinquefolia   p. 473

Cranberry cotoneaster
Cotoneaster apiculatus

Firethorn
Pyracantha 'Teton'

Japanese holly
Ilex crenata

Mahonia

For growing symbol explanations, please see page 37.

Spicebush
Lindera benzoin

Hawthorn
Crataegus

Serviceberry
Amelanchier

Yaupon
☼ ◐ ◑ ♦ ✿   MS, LS, CS, TS
Ilex vomitoria   p. 372

SONGBIRDS
TREES

American beech
☼ ◐ ◑ ♦ ✿   US, MS, LS, CS
Fagus grandifolia   p. 310

American sweet gum
☼ ◐ ♦ ✿   US, MS, LS, CS
Liquidambar styraciflua   p. 415

Arborvitae
☼ ◐ ♦ ✿   VARY
Thuja   p. 617

Birch
☼ ◐ ♦ ♠ ✿   VARY
Betula   p. 186

Black gum
☼ ◐ ◑ ♦ ✿   US, MS, LS, CS
Nyssa sylvatica   p. 455

Cabbage palm
☼ ◐ ◑ ✿   LS, CS, TS
Sabal palmetto   p. 565

Dogwood
☼ ◐ ♦ ✿   VARY
Cornus   p. 255

Eastern red cedar
☼ ○ ♦ ◑ ✿   ALL
Juniperus virginiana   p. 387

Flowering crabapple
☼ ◐ ♦ ✿   VARY
Malus   p. 428

Glossy privet
☼ ◐ ♦ ✿   LS, CS, TS
Ligustrum lucidum   p. 410

Hackberry, common
☼ ◐ ◑ ♦ ✿   US, MS, LS, CS
Celtis occidentalis   p. 224

Hawthorn
☼ ◐ ♦ ✿   VARY
Crataegus   p. 262

Hemlock
☼ ◐ ♦ ✿   VARY
Tsuga   p. 628

Holly
☼ ◐ ♦ ✿   VARY
Ilex   p. 369

Loquat
☼ ◐ ○ ♦ ♦ ✿   VARY
Eriobotrya   p. 300

Magnolia
☼ ◐ ◑ ✿   VARY
                                            p. 423

Maple
☼ ◐ ◑ ♦ ✿   VARY
Acer   p. 127

Mountain ash
☼ ◐ ♦ ✿   VARY
Sorbus   p. 594

Mulberry
☼ ♦ ✿   VARY
Morus   p. 441

Oak
☼ ♦ ✿   VARY
Quercus   p. 532

Persimmon
☼ ◐ ♦ ✿   VARY
                                            p. 491

Pine
☼ ○ ♦ ✿   VARY
Pinus   p. 504

Sassafras
☼ ◐ ♦ ✿   US, MS, LS, CS
Sassafras albidum   p. 577

Serviceberry
☼ ◐ ♦ ✿   VARY
Amelanchier   p. 147

Spruce
☼ ◐ ♦ ✿   US, MS, LS
Picea   p. 501

Wax myrtle
☼ ♦ ✿   MS, LS, CS, TS
Morella cerifera   p. 441

HUMMINGBIRDS
ANNUALS, PERENNIALS, BULBS

Aloe
☼ ◐ ○ ♦ ♦ ✿   TS
                                            p. 144

Alstroemeria
◐ ♦ ✿   MS, LS, CS
                                            p. 146

Beard tongue
◐ ♦ ✿   VARY
Penstemon   p. 486

Bee balm
☼ ◐ ♦ ♠ ✿   US, MS, LS
Monarda didyma   p. 440

Bird of paradise
☼ ◐ ♦ ✿   CS, TS
Strelitzia reginae   p. 604

Butterfly weed
☼ ○ ♦ ♦ ♠ ♦ ✿   US, MS, LS, CS
Asclepias tuberosa   p. 168

Canna
☼ ♦ ♠ ✿   LS, CS, TS
                                            p. 214

Cape fuchsia
☼ ◐ ♦ ✿   US, MS, LS
Phygelius capensis   p. 500

Cardinal flower
☼ ◐ ♦ ♦ ✿   US, MS, LS, CS
Lobelia cardinalis   p. 417

Oak
Quercus

Bird of paradise
Strelitzia reginae

Canna

Butterfly weed
Asclepias tuberosa

For climate zone explanations, please see pages 38–39.

Delphinium

Geranium
Pelargonium

Firecracker plant
Russelia equisetiformis

Four o'clock
Mirabilis jalapa

Columbine
☼ ◐ � ◿ VARY
Aquilegia   p. 160

Coral bells
◐ � ◿ US, MS, LS
Heuchera sanguinea   p. 354

Cotoneaster
☼ ○ � ◿ VARY
                                             p. 260

Delphinium
☼ ◿ VARY
                                             p. 277

Dicliptera
☼ ◐ ○ ◐ ◐ ◿ VARY
                                             p. 283

Firecracker plant
☼ ◐ ◐ ◿ CS, TS
Russelia equisetiformis   p. 565

Firecracker vine
☼ ◿ TS
Ipomoea lobata   p. 376

Flowering maple
◐ ◐ ◿ CS, TS
Abutilon   p. 125

Four o'clock
☼ ○ ◿ ALL
Mirabilis jalapa   p. 438

Foxglove
◐ ◿ US, MS, LS, CS
Digitalis   p. 285

Fuchsia
◐ ◿ VARY
                                             p. 321

Geranium
◐ ◐ ◿ CS, TS OR ANNUAL
Pelargonium   p. 484

Ginger lily
☼ ◐ ◿ VARY
Hedychium   p. 344

Gladiolus
☼ ◿ MS, LS, CS
                                             p. 330

Hen and chicks
☼ ◐ ◿ CS, TS
Echeveria (several)   p. 291

Hollyhock
☼ ◐ ◿ US, MS, LS, CS
Alcea rosea   p. 141

Impatiens
☼ ◐ ◐ ◿ ALL
                                             p. 373

Indian paintbrush
☼ ◐ ◿ ALL
Castilleja indivisa   p. 220

Iris
☼ ◐ ◐ ◐ ◿ VARY
                                             p. 377

Jatropha
◐ ◐ ◿ TS
                                             p. 383

Montbretia
☼ ◐ ◿ US, MS, LS, CS
Crocosmia crocosmiiflora   p. 264

Penstemon (many)
◐ ◿ VARY
                                             p. 486

Pentas
☼ ◿ ALL
Pentas lanceolata   p. 487

Phlox
☼ ◐ ◿ VARY
                                             p. 497

Porterweed
☼ ◐ ◿ TS
Stachytarpheta   p. 600

Red-hot poker
☼ ◐ ◿ US, MS, LS, CS
Kniphofia uvaria   p. 392

Red yucca
☼ ☼ ○ ◿ ALL
Hesperaloe parviflora   p. 353

Rose campion
☼ ◐ ◿ US, MS, LS
Lychnis coronaria   p. 421

Sage (many)
☼ ◿ VARY
Salvia   p. 568

Snapdragon
☼ ○ ◐ ◿ ALL
Antirrhinum majus   p. 153

Speedwell
☼ ○ ◿ US, MS, LS
Veronica   p. 636

Spider flower
☼ ◿ ALL
Cleome hasslerana   p. 244

Texas tuberose
☼ ◐ ○ ◿ MS, LS, CS
Agave maculosa   p. 138

Zinnia
☼ ◿ ALL
                                             p. 651

HUMMINGBIRDS
VINES

Bean, scarlet runner
☼ ◿ ALL
                                             p. 180

Cape honeysuckle
☼ ◐ ◿ CS, TS
Tecoma capensis   p. 614

Cypress vine
☼ ◿ ALL
Ipomoea quamoclit   p. 376

Ginger lily, common
Hedychium coronarium

Red yucca
Hesperaloe parviflora

Pineapple sage
Salvia elegans

Scarlet runner bean

For growing symbol explanations, please see page 37.

Passion vine
Passiflora alatocaerulea

Flowering quince
Chaenomeles

Bearberry
Arctostaphylos uva-ursi

Cape honeysuckle
Tecoma capensis

'Canberra Gem' grevillea

Flame vine
☼ ◑◐◑ ⚡ CS, TS
Pyrostegia venusta — p. 531

Morning glory, common
☼ ◑◐◑ ⚡ ALL
Ipomoea purpurea — p. 375

Passion vine
☼ ◑◐◑◐ ⚡ VARY
Passiflora — p. 473

Trumpet creeper
☼ ◑◐◑◐ ⚡ VARY
Campsis — p. 214

HUMMINGBIRDS
SHRUBS, TREES, GROUNDCOVERS

Acacia
☼ ◐ ⚡ VARY — p. 126

American elderberry
☼ ◑◐◑ ⚡ US, MS, LS, CS
Sambucus canadensis — p. 573

Beauty bush
◑◐ ⚡ US, MS, LS
Kolkwitzia amabilis — p. 394

Bird of paradise
☼ ◑◐◑ ⚡ CS, TS
Strelitzia reginae — p. 604

Bottlebrush
☼ ◑◐ ⚡ VARY
Callistemon — p. 206

Butterfly bush
☼ ◑◐◑◐ ⚡ VARY
Buddleia — p. 197

Cape honeysuckle
☼ ◑◐◐ ⚡ CS, TS
Tecoma capensis — p. 614

Cestrum
◑◐◑◐ ⚡ TS — p. 228

Citrus
☼ ◑◐ ⚡ CS, TS — p. 238

Coral tree
☼ ◑◐◑◐ ⚡ TS
Erythrina — p. 301

Desert willow
☼ ◐ ◑◐ ⚡ MS, LS, CS
Chilopsis linearis — p. 233

Eucalyptus
☼ ◐ ⚡ VARY — p. 303

Feijoa, Pineapple guava
☼ ◑◐ ⚡ LS, CS, TS
Feijoa sellowiana — p. 312

Firebush
☼ ◑◐◑◐ ⚡ CS, TS
Hamelia patens — p. 343

Flowering quince
☼ ◑◐◑ ⚡ US, MS, LS, CS
Chaenomeles — p. 228

Glossy abelia
☼ ◑◐◑ ⚡ US, MS, LS, CS
Abelia x grandiflora — p. 124

Grevillea
☼ ◑◐ ◑◐◑ ⚡ VARY — p. 338

Hibiscus
☼ ◑◐ ⚡ VARY — p. 356

Honeysuckle
☼ ◑◐◑◐ ⚡ VARY
Lonicera — p. 418

Horsechestnut
☼ ◑◐◑ ◐ ⚡ VARY
Aesculus — p. 135

Lavender (many)
☼ ◑◐ ⚡ VARY
Lavandula — p. 403

Lilac
☼ ◑◐◑ ⚡ VARY
Syringa — p. 609

Mimosa
☼ ◑◐◑ ⚡ US, MS, LS, CS
Albizia julibrissin — p. 141

Orchid tree
☼ ◑◐◑ ⚡ TS
Bauhinia — p. 179

Pink powder puff
☼ ◑◐ ⚡ CS, TS
Calliandra haematocephala — p. 204

Red clerodendrum
☼ ◑◐ ⚡ TS
Clerodendrum splendens — p. 245

Texas ranger
☼ ◐ ◑◐ ⚡ LS, CS, TS
Leucophyllum frutescens — p. 408

Trailing lantana
☼ ◑◐ ◐ ⚡ LS, CS, TS
Lantana montevidensis — p. 401

Trumpet tree
☼ ◑◐◑ ⚡ TS
Tabebuia — p. 611

Weigela
☼ ◑◐◑ ⚡ US, MS, LS
Weigela florida — p. 644

Yellow bird of paradise
☼ ◐ ◑◐ ◐ ⚡ CS, TS
Caesalpinia gilliesii — p. 201

Yellow justicia
◑◐◑ ⚡ CS, TS
Justicia aurea — p. 387

Yellow shrimp plant
☼ ◑◐◑ ⚡ CS, TS
Pachystachys lutea — p. 466

Red horsechestnut
Aesculus carnea

Lavender
Lavandula

Mimosa
Albizia julibrissin

Yellow justicia
Justicia aurea

Trumpet creeper, common
Campsis radicans

For climate zone explanations, please see pages 38–39.

Plants for
Containers

The charm of a garden in the air—whether it is suspended or perched—derives from the choice of plants. You need a full and colorful show with foliage that is lax enough to soften the edges of the arrangement. Here's a selection of proven aerial artists, drawn from a variety of annuals, perennials, and woody plants. Mix and match between them to create your own seasonal effects.

Hybrid fuchsia
Fuchsia x *hybrida*

Coleus
Coleus x hybridus

Dwarf cup flower
Nierembergia caerulea

Dwarf morning glory
Convolvulus tricolor

ANNUALS

Amethyst flower
☼ ◐ ❍ ✿ ALL
Browallia · p. 195

Angelonia
☼ ❍ ✿ ALL
Angelonia angustifolia · p. 151

Bacopa
☼ ◐ ❍ ✿ ALL
Sutera cordata · p. 606

Black-eyed Susan vine
☼ ◐ ❍ ✿ ALL
Thunbergia alata · p. 618

Blue daze
☼ ◐ ❍ ❍ ✿ TS OR ANNUAL
Evolvulus glomeratus · p. 309

Calendula
☼ ❍ ✿ ALL
Calendula officinalis · p. 204

Calibrachoa
☼ ❍ ❍ ✿ ALL
· p. 204

Creeping zinnia
☼ ❍ ❍ ✿ ALL
Sanvitalia procumbens · p. 575

Dwarf cup flower
☼ ❍ ❍ ✿ ALL
Nierembergia caerulea · p. 453

Dwarf morning glory
☼ ◐ ❍ ✿ ALL
Convolvulus tricolor · p. 252

Edging lobelia
☼ ☼ ❍ ❍ ❍ ✿ ALL
Lobelia erinus · p. 417

English daisy
☼ ☼ ❍ ❍ ✿ US, MS, LS, TS
Bellis perennis · p. 184

Floss flower
☼ ◐ ❍ ✿ ALL
Ageratum houstonianum · p. 139

Flowering cabbage and kale
☼ ◐ ❍ ✿ ALL
· p. 201

Flowering tobacco
☼ ◐ ❍ ❍ ✿ ALL
Nicotiana alata · p. 453

Forget-me-not
◐ ❍ ✿ US, MS, LS
Myosotis sylvatica · p. 445

Garden verbena
☼ ❍ ✿ ALL
Verbena x hybrida · p. 635

Geranium, common
◐ ❍ ❍ ✿ CS, TS OR ANNUAL
Pelargonium x hortorum · p. 484

Globe amaranth
☼ ◐ ❍ ✿ ALL
Gomphrena · p. 332

Hyacinth bean
☼ ❍ ❍ ✿ LS, CS, TS
Dolichos lablab · p. 288

Impatiens (many)
☼ ◐ ❍ ❍ ❍ ✿ ALL
· p. 373

Ivy geranium
◐ ❍ ❍ ✿ CS, TS OR ANNUAL
Pelargonium peltatum · p. 484

Monkey flower
◐ ❍ ✿ ALL
Mimulus x hybridus · p. 438

Morning glory
☼ ❍ ❍ ✿ ALL
Ipomoea tricolor · p. 375

Moss rose
☼ ❍ ❍ ✿ ALL
Portulaca grandiflora · p. 519

Hyacinth bean
Dolichos lablab

Ivy geranium
Pelargonium peltatum

Monkey flower
Mimulus x hybridus

Moss rose
Portulaca grandiflora

For growing symbol explanations, please see page 37.

Nasturtium
☼ ◐ ● ◑ ⚡ ALL
Tropaeolum majus   p. 628

Narrow-leaf zinnia
☼ ● ⚡ ALL
Zinnia angustifolia   p. 651

Pentas
☼ ● ⚡ ALL
Pentas lanceolata   p. 487

Persian shield
☼ ◐ ⚡ ALL
Strobilanthes dyeranus   p. 605

Persian violet
☼ ● ◐ ◖ ⚡ ALL OR INDOORS
Exacum affine   p. 309

Petunia
☼ ◐ ● ⚡ ALL
Petunia hybrida   p. 492

Polka-dot plant
☼ ◐ ● ⚡ ALL OR INDOORS
Hypoestes phyllostachya   p. 368

Purple fountain grass
☼ ☼ ● ◖ ● ⚡ CS, TS
Pennisetum setaceum Rubrum   p. 486

Snapdragon
☼ ● ⚡ ALL
Antirrhinum majus   p. 153

Stock
☼ ◐ ● ⚡ ALL
Matthiola incana   p. 433

Swan river daisy
☼ ● ⚡ ALL
Brachyscome iberidifolia   p. 193

Sweet alyssum
☼ ☼ ● ⚡ US, MS, LS, CS
Lobularia maritima   p. 417

Sweet pea
☼ ◊ ◐ ● ⚡ ALL
Lathyrus odoratus   p. 402

Sweet potato vine
☼ ◐ ● ⚡ LS, CS, TS OR INDOORS
Ipomoea batatas   p. 376

Tickseed
☼ ● ◖ ⚡ VARY
Bidens   p. 187

Tuberous begonia
☼ ● ⚡ ALL
                              p. 184

Viola, violet, pansy
☼ ◐ ● ◖ ⚡ VARY
Viola   p. 641

Wishbone flower
◐ ● ⚡ ALL
Torenia fournieri   p. 625

PERENNIALS, BULBS

Achimenes
☼ ● ◖ ⚡ CS, TS OR INDOORS
                              p. 131

Basket-of-gold
☼ ◐ ● ⚡ US, MS, LS, CS
Aurinia saxatilis   p. 174

Billbergia
☼ ● ⚡ ALL
                              p. 188

Cactus
☼ ◐ ◊ ⚡ VARY
Cactaceae (many)   p. 269

Coral bells
☼ ◐ ● ◖ ⚡ US, MS, LS
Heuchera   p. 354

Crassula
☼ ◊ ⚡ TS
                              p. 261

Creeping Jenny
☼ ◐ ● ◖ ⚡ US, MS, LS
Lysimachia nummularia   p. 422

Dendrobium
☼ ● ⚡ TS OR INDOORS
                              p. 278

Donkey tail
☼ ◊ ◊ ● ⚡ TS OR INDOORS
Sedum morganianum   p. 583

Dusty miller
☼ ◊ ● ◖ ⚡ MS, LS, CS
Senecio cineraria   p. 585

Echeveria
☼ ◐ ● ⚡ VARY
                              p. 291

Evergreen candytuft
☼ ● ⚡ US, MS, CS
Iberis sempervirens   p. 369

Fancy-leafed caladium
◐ ☼ ● ◖ ◑ ⚡ CS, TS
Caladium bicolor   p. 202

Flame violet
● ◖ ⚡ TS OR INDOORS
Episcia   p. 297

Fleabane
☼ ◐ ● ⚡ VARY
Erigeron   p. 299

Freesia
☼ ◐ ● ⚡ CS, TS OR INDOORS
                              p. 320

Gazania daisy
☼ ◐ ● ◊ ● ⚡ ALL
Gazania   p. 325

Greater periwinkle
☼ ● ◊ ● ⚡ MS, LS, CS
Vinca major   p. 641

Nasturtium
Tropaeolum majus

Tuberous begonia

Viola
Viola wittrockiana

Billbergia

Gazania daisy
Gazania

Heliotrope, common
Heliotropium arborescens 'Black Beauty'

Creeping Jenny
Lysimachia nummularia 'Aurea'

Donkey tail
Sedum morganianum

For climate zone explanations, please see pages 38–39.

Licorice plant
Helichrysum petiolare 'Limelight'

Himalayan maidenhair
Adiantum venustum

Meyers asparagus
Asparagus densiflorus 'Meyers'

Spotted dead nettle
Lamium maculatum 'Beacon Silver'

Staghorn fern
Platycerium bifurcatum

Heliotrope, common
☼ ◐ ◑ ◆ ⚡ ✄ TS OR ANNUAL
Heliotropium arborescens   p. 349

Hyacinth
☼ ◐ ◑ ◆ ⚡ ✄ VARY
Hyacinthus   p. 363

Ice plant
☼ ◑ ○ ◐ ✄ ALL
Delosperma   p. 277

Japanese forest grass
☼ ● ◆ ✄ US, MS, LS
Hakonechloa macra   p. 341

Jewel orchid
◑ ◆ ✄ TS OR INDOORS
Ludisia discolor   p. 419

Kalanchoe
☼ ◑ ◐ ◆ ✄ TS OR INDOORS
          p. 388

Lantana
☼ ◑ ◆ ⚡ ✄ LS, CS, TS OR ANNUAL
          p. 400

Licorice plant
☼ ◑ ◆ ✄ TS OR ANNUAL
Helichrysum petiolare   p. 347

Maidenhair fern
◑ ● ◐ ✄ VARY
Adiantum   p. 133

Neomarica
☼ ◑ ◐ ✄ ALL
          p. 450

Oregano
☼ ○ ◐ ✄ VARY
Origanum   p. 460

Ornamental asparagus
◑ ◐ ✄ CS, TS OR INDOORS
          p. 170

Ornamental strawberry
☼ ◑ ◐ ◆ ✄ US, MS, LS, CS
Fragaria hybrids   p. 319

Plectranthus (some)
☼ ◐ ✄ TS OR INDOORS
          p. 509

Pocketbook plant
☼ ● ◐ ◆ ✄ ALL
Calceolaria   p. 203

Primrose (some)
☼ ◐ ◆ ✄ VARY
Primula   p. 521

Sedum sieboldii
◐ ☼ ○ ◐ ◆ ✄ US, MS, LS
          p. 583

Spider plant
☼ ◐ ◆ ✄ TS OR INDOORS
Chlorophytum comosum   p. 235

Spotted dead nettle
◐ ● ◐ ◆ ✄ US, MS, LS
Lamium maculatum   p. 400

Staghorn fern
☼ ◐ ◆ ✄ CS, TS
Platycerium bifurcatum   p. 508

Strawberry geranium
☼ ● ◐ ◆ ✄ MS, LS, CS OR INDOORS
Saxifraga stolonifera   p. 577

Sweet flag
☼ ◐◑ ◆ ✄ US, MS, LS, CS
Acorus   p. 132

Threadleaf coreopsis
☼ ○ ◐ ◆ ✄ US, MS, LS, CS
Coreopsis verticillata   p. 254

Tulip
☼ ◐☼ ◐ ◆ ✄ ALL
Tulipa   p. 629

Twinspur
☼ ◐☼ ◐ ◆ ✄ VARY
Diascia   p. 281

Velvet plant
☼ ◐◑ ◐ ◆ ✄ LS, CS, TS OR INDOORS
Gynura   p. 340

Wandering jew
☼ ◐◑ ◐ ◆ ◐ ◆ ✄ CS, TS OR INDOORS
Tradescantia fluminensis   p. 626

SHRUBS, WOODY VINES

SHRUBS, WOODY VINES

Creeping rosemary
☼ ○ ◐ ◆ ✄ ALL
Rosmarinus officinalis 'Prostratus'   p. 562

Dwarf Japanese garden juniper
☼ ◐ ◐ ◆ ✄ US, MS, LS, CS
Juniperus procumbens 'Nana'   p. 386

English ivy
☼ ● ◐ ◆ ✄ ALL
Hedera helix   p. 344

Flowering maple
☼ ◐ ◐ ◆ ✄ ALL
Abutilon   p. 125

Hybrid fuchsia
☼ ◐ ◆ ✄ US OR ANNUAL
Fuchsia x hybrida   p. 321

Japanese ardisia
☼ ◐☼ ● ◐ ◆ ✄ LS, CS
Ardisia japonica   p. 163

Jasmine
☼ ◐☼ ◐ ◆ ✄ VARY
Jasminum   p. 382

Myrtle (dwarf forms)
☼ ◐☼ ◐ ◆ ✄ LS, CS, TS
Myrtus communis   p. 445

Threadleaf coreopsis
Coreopsis verticillata

Tulip
Tulipa saxatilis 'Lilac Wonder'

Flowering maple
Abutilon megapotamicum

English ivy
Hedera helix
'Needlepoint'

For growing symbol explanations, please see page 37.

Bottlebrush
Callistemon

Plants for Tropical Effects

Y ou don't have to fly to Hawaii or Grand Bahama to enjoy the lushness of the tropics. Garden centers carry a surprising number of tropical and tropical-looking plants that offer spectacular blooms and foliage. Some are perfectly winter hardy, while others won't take frost. But you needn't say goodbye to your tropical friends in November. Many can be easily overwintered indoors.

Coral tree
Erythrina

Banana
Musa acuminata

Australian tree fern
Cyathea cooperi

Empress tree
Paulownia tomentosa

TREES

Abyssinian banana
☼:◑◐◔ ⚡ LS, CS, TS
Ensete ventricosum   p. 296

Australian tree fern
:◑◐ ⚡ TS
Cyathea cooperi   p. 268

Banana
☼:◑◑◐◔ ⚡ CS, TS
Musa   p. 442

Bottlebrush
☼:◑◐◔ ⚡ VARY
Callistemon   p. 206

Carambola
☼:◐ ⚡ TS
                                         p. 215

Catalpa
☼:◑◐◑◐◔ ⚡ US, MS, LS, CS
                                         p. 220

Chinese parasol tree
☼:◑◐◔ ⚡ MS, LS, CS, TS
Firmiana simplex   p. 317

Coral tree
☼:◐◔ ◔ ⚡ TS
Erythrina   p. 301

Empress tree
☼:◑◐◑◐◔ ⚡ US, MS, LS, CS
Paulownia tomentosa   p. 474

Fiddleleaf fig
☼:◑◐◑◐◔ ⚡ TS OR INDOORS
Ficus lyrata   p. 313

Fig, edible
☼:◐◔ ⚡ MS, LS, CS, TS
                                         p. 314

Guava
☼:◑◐◔ ⚡ VARY
                                         p. 339

Hawaiian tree fern
:◑◐◔ ⚡ TS
Cibotium glaucum   p. 237

Hercules' club
☼:◑◐◔ ◔ ⚡ US, MS, LS, CS
Aralia spinosa   p. 161

Mexican grass tree
☼:◑◔ ◔ ⚡ CS, TS
Nolina longifolia   p. 454

Mimosa
☼:◑◐◔ ⚡ US, MS, LS, CS
Albizia julibrissin   p. 141

Orchid tree
☼:◐◔ ◔ ⚡ TS
Bauhinia   p. 179

Palms
☼:◐◔ ⚡ VARY
(Many kinds)   p. 498

Papaya
☼:◐◔ ⚡ TS
                                         p. 471

Silk-cotton tree
☼:◐◔ ◔ ⚡ TS
Ceiba pentandra   p. 222

Tasmanian tree fern
:◑◐ ◔ ⚡ TS
Dicksonia antarctica   p. 283

Traveler's tree
☼:◐◔ ⚡ TS
Ravenala madagascariensis   p. 539

Trumpet tree
☼:◑◐◔ ⚡ TS
Tabebuia   p. 611

VINES

Allamanda
☼:◐◔ ◔ ⚡ TS
Allamanda   p. 142

Bougainvillea
☼:◐◔ ◔ ⚡ CS, TS
                                         p. 191

California dutchman's pipe
☼: ☼:◑◐◑◐ ⚡ LS, CS, TS
Aristolochia californica   p. 164

Cry-baby tree
Erythrina crista-galli

Orchid tree
Bauhinia

Pygmy date palm
Phoenix roebelenii

Tasmanian tree fern
Dicksonia antarctica

For climate zone explanations, please see pages 38–39.

Cup-of-gold vine
Solandra maxima

Passion vine
Passiflora x alatocaerulea

Bamboo
Pleioblastus

Copper leaf
Acalypha wilkesiana

Cup-of-gold vine
☼ ● ♦ ✓ TS
Solandra maxima   p. 590

X Fatshedera lizei
☼ ● ♦ ✓ LS, CS, TS
    p. 311

Flame vine
☼ ● ♦ ✓ CS, TS
Pyrostegia venusta   p. 531

Glorybower
☼ ● ● ♦ ✓ TS
Clerodendrum   p. 245

Herald's trumpet
☼ ● ● ♦ ✓ TS
Beaumontia grandiflora   p. 181

Jasmine
☼ ● ● ♦ ✓ VARY
Jasminum   p. 382

Mandevilla
☼ ● ♦ ✓ VARY
    p. 341

Pandorea
☼ ● ♦ ● ✓ CS, TS
    p. 469

Passion vine
☼ ● ● ♦ ● ✓ VARY
Passiflora   p. 473

Rangoon creeper
☼ ● ♦ ✓ TS
Quisqualis indica   p. 535

Sky flower
☼ ● ♦ ✓ TS
Thunbergia grandiflora   p. 618

Split-leaf philodendron
☼ ● ♦ ✓ TS OR INDOORS
Monstera deliciosa   p. 441

Trumpet creeper
☼ ● ● ♦ ● ✓ VARY
Campsis   p. 214

SHRUBS

Angel's trumpet
☼ ● ● ♦ ♦ ✓ LS, CS, TS
Brugmansia   p. 195

Bamboo
☼ ● ● ● ♦ ✓ VARY
    p. 175

Beschorneria
☼ ● ● ♦ ✓ VARY
    p. 186

Caesalpinia
☼ ● ● ♦ ♦ ✓ VARY
    p. 201

Caribbean copper plant
☼ ● ● ♦ ● ♦ ● ✓ CS, TS
Euphorbia cotinifolia   p. 307

Chinese hibiscus
☼ ● ♦ ✓ CS, TS
Hibiscus rosa-sinensis   p. 356

Copper leaf
☼ ● ♦ ✓ TS OR INDOORS
Acalypha wilkesiana   p. 126

Feijoa, Pineapple guava
☼ ● ♦ ✓ LS, CS, TS
    p. 312

Ficus auriculata
☼ ● ♦ ● ♦ ✓ TS
    p. 313

Firespike
☼ ● ♦ ✓ CS, TS
Odontonema strictum   p. 456

Flowering maple
☼ ● ● ♦ ● ✓ CS, TS
Abutilon   p. 125

Frangipani
☼ ● ● ♦ ♦ ✓ TS
Plumeria   p. 513

Grevillea
☼ ● ● ♦ ● ♦ ✓ VARY
    p. 338

Japanese fatsia
☼ ● ● ♦ ✓ LS, CS, TS OR INDOORS
Fatsia japonica   p. 312

New Zealand flax
☼ ● ● ♦ ♦ ✓ LS, CS, TS
Phormium tenax   p. 499

Princess flower
☼ ● ● ♦ ✓ TS
Tibouchina urvilleana   p. 620

Rice paper plant
☼ ● ♦ ✓ LS, CS, TS
Tetrapanax papyriferus   p. 615

Sago palm
☼ ● ● ♦ ✓ CS, TS OR INDOORS
Cycas revoluta   p. 268

Shower-of-gold
☼ ● ♦ ✓ CS, TS
Galphimia glauca   p. 323

Yellow bells
☼ ● ● ♦ ✓ CS, TS
Tecoma stans   p. 614

Yellow shrimp plant
☼ ● ● ♦ ✓ CS, TS
Pachystachys lutea   p. 466

PERENNIALS

Alpinia
☼ ● ● ♦ ✓ VARY
    p. 145

Angelica
☼ ● ● ♦ ✓ US, MS, LS, CS
    p. 151

Flowering maple
Abutilon pictum 'Thompsonii'

Frangipani
Plumeria

Princess flower
Tibouchina urvilleana

Yellow bells
Tecoma stans

Yellow shrimp plant
Pachystachys lutea

For growing symbol explanations, please see page 37.

Bird of paradise
Strelitzia reginae

Calla, common
Zantedeschia aethiopica

Parlor palm
Chamaedorea elegans

Ginger lily
Hedychium

Anthurium hookeri
☼ ◐ ◢ TS OR INDOORS
p. 153

Bear's breeches
☼ ☼◐ ◐◢ US, MS, LS, CS
Acanthus mollis
p. 127

Billbergia
☼◐◢ TS
p. 188

Bird of Paradise
☼ ☼◐◢ VARY
Strelitzia
p. 604

Calathea
☼◐◢ TS OR INDOORS
p. 203

Calla, common
☼ ☼◐◢ LS, CS, TS
Zantedeschia aethiopica
p. 649

Canna
☼ ◐◢ LS, CS, TS
p. 214

Caricature plant
◐◢ TS OR INDOORS
Graptophyllum pictum
p. 338

Cast-iron plant
◐◐ ◐◢ LS, CS, TS OR INDOORS
Aspidistra elatior
p. 171

Cestrum
☼◐◢ TS
p. 228

Chamaedorea
☼◐◢ TS
p. 229

Clivia
☼◐◐◢ TS
Clivia miniata
p. 247

Crinum
☼ ☼◐◐◢ VARY
p. 263

Dancing girl ginger
☼◐◢ CS, TS
Globba
p. 331

Dendrobium
☼◢ TS OR INDOORS
p. 278

Elephant's ear
☼◐◐ ◢ LS, CS, TS
Colocasia esculenta
p. 250

Fancy-leafed caladium
☼☼ ◐◐◢ CS, TS
Caladium bicolor
p. 202

Ginger, common
☼◐◐◢ LS, CS, TS
Zingiber officinale
p. 650

Ginger lily
☼ ☼◐◢ VARY
Hedychium
p. 344

Hidden lily
☼◐◢ LS, CS, TS
Curcuma petiolata
p. 268

Japanese coltsfoot
☼◐◐ ◐◢ US, MS, LS, CS
Petasites japonicus
p. 491

Jatropha
☼◐◐◐◢ TS
p. 383

Joseph's coat
☼◐◢ TS OR ANNUAL
Alternanthera dentata
p. 146

Lobster-claw
☼◐◐◢ TS
Heliconia
p. 348

Orchid cactus
☼◐◐◢ TS OR INDOORS
Epiphyllum
p. 297

Papyrus
☼◐◐ ◐◢ CS, TS
Cyperus papyrus
p. 270

Peace lily
☼◐◐◢ TS OR INDOORS
Spathiphyllum
p. 595

Philodendron
☼◐◐ ◐◢ VARY OR INDOORS
p. 495

Pineapple lily
☼ ☼◐◢ MS, LS, CS, TS
Eucomis
p. 304

Rice paper plant
☼◐◐◢ LS, CS, TS
Tetrapanax papyrifera
p. 615

Shell ginger
☼◐◢ LS, CS, TS
Alpinia zerumbet
p. 146

Shooting stars
☼◐◢ TS
Pseuderanthemum laxiflorum
p. 526

Spiral flag
☼◐◢ CS, TS
Costus
p. 260

Staghorn fern
☼◐◢ TS
Platycerium
p. 508

Udo
☼ ☼◐◐◢ US, MS, LS
Aralia cordata
p. 161

Velvet plant
☼ ☼◐◢ LS, CS, TS OR INDOORS
Gynura
p. 340

Voodoo lily
☼◐ ◐◢ VARY
Amorphophallus
p. 148

Xanthosoma
☼◐◐◢ TS OR INDOORS
p. 646

Canna
'Pretoria'

Lobster-claw
Heliconia

Shell ginger
Alpinia zerumbet

Xanthosoma sagittifolium

For climate zone explanations, please see pages 38–39.

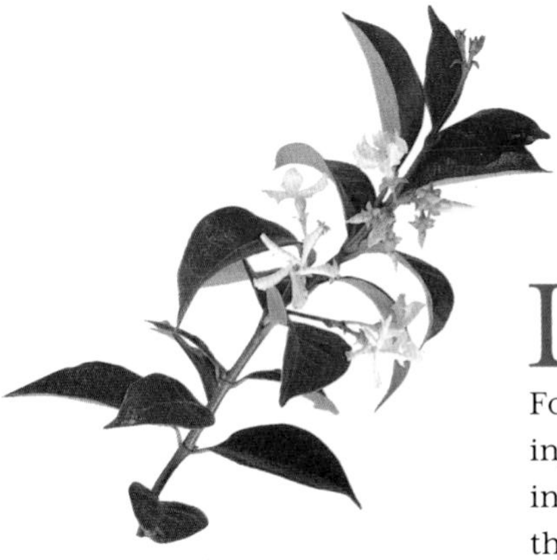

Plants for
Coastal Gardens

Life is no walk on the beach for plants near the coast. They endure constant wind, salt-laden air, and poor, sandy soil. Fortunately, many plants thrive under such conditions. Grouping these plants helps them meet the challenge. And some, indicated by the symbol 👑, are suitable for planting right on the dunes.

Confederate jasmine
Trachelospermum jasminoides

The cabbage palm (*Sabal palmetto*) matches the stature of a coastal home.

Beach plum
Prunus maritima

Japanese cryptomeria
Cryptomeria japonica

Live oak
Quercus virginiana

New Zealand tea tree
Leptospermum scoparium

Southern magnolia
Magnolia grandiflora

Canary Island date palm
Phoenix canariensis

Sea grape
Coccoloba uvifera

TREES

American arborvitae
☼ ◐ 💧 ◑ 💧 ⚡ US, MS
Thuja occidentalis — p. 617

American holly
☼ ◐ 💧 ◐ 💧 ⚡ ALL
Ilex opaca — p. 371

Beach plum
☼ ◐ 💧 ⚡ US, MS
Prunus maritima — p. 525

Chinese elm
☼ ◐ 💧 ⚡ US, MS, LS, CS
Ulmus parvifolia — p. 632

Dahoon
☼ ◐ 💧 ◐ 💧 ⚡ MS, LS, CS, TS
Ilex cassine — p. 370

Eastern red cedar
☼ ○ 💧 ◐ 💧 ⚡ ALL
Juniperus virginiana — p. 387

Glossy privet
☼ ◐ 💧 ◐ 💧 ⚡ LS, CS, TS
Ligustrum lucidum — p. 410

Honey locust
☼ ◐ 💧 ⚡ US, MS, LS
Gleditsia triacanthos — p. 331

Japanese black pine
☼ ○ ◐ 💧 ⚡ US, MS, LS, CS
Pinus thunbergii — p. 506

Japanese cryptomeria
☼ ◐ 💧 ◐ 💧 ⚡ US, MS, LS
Cryptomeria japonica — p. 265

Jerusalem thorn
☼ ○ ◐ 💧 ⚡ LS, CS, TS
Parkinsonia aculeata — p. 472

Live oak
☼ ◐ 💧 ⚡ LS, CS, TS
Quercus virginiana — p. 535

Marlberry
☼ ◐ 💧 ◐ 💧 ⚡ TS
Ardisia paniculata — p. 163

Norfolk Island pine
☼ ◐ 💧 ⚡ TS
Araucaria heterophylla — p. 161

Palms (most)
☼ ◐ 💧 ⚡ VARY
(Many kinds) — p. 498

Sand pine
☼ ○ 💧 ◐ 💧 ⚡ LS, CS, TS
Pinus clausa — p. 504

Sawara false cypress
☼ ◐ 💧 ◐ 💧 ⚡ US, MS, LS
Chamaecyparis pisifera — p. 229

Sea grape 👑
☼ ◐ 💧 ⚡ TS
Coccoloba uvifera — p. 248

Slash pine
☼ ○ 💧 ◐ 💧 ⚡ LS, CS, TS
Pinus elliottii — p. 504

Southern magnolia
☼ ◐ 💧 ◐ 💧 ⚡ US, MS, LS, CS
Magnolia grandiflora — p. 423

Southern red cedar 👑
☼ ◐ 💧 ○ 💧 ◐ 💧 ⚡ LS, CS, TS
Juniperus silicicola — p. 387

Tamarisk
☼ ○ 💧 ◐ 💧 ⚡ VARY
Tamarix — p. 612

Yaupon 👑
☼ ◐ 💧 ◐ 💧 ⚡ MS, LS, CS, TS
Ilex vomitoria — p. 372

SHRUBS

Arrowwood
☼ ◐ 💧 ◐ 💧 ⚡ US, MS, LS, CS
Viburnum dentatum — p. 638

Broom
☼ ◐ 💧 ⚡ US, MS, LS
Cytisus — p. 271

Century plant 👑
☼ ◐ 💧 ○ 💧 ◐ 💧 ⚡ CS, TS
Agave americana — p. 138

For growing symbol explanations, please see page 37.

Century plant
Agave americana

Brightbead cotoneaster
Cotoneaster lacteus

Japanese pittosporum
Pittosporum tobira

Hollywood juniper
Juniperus chinensis 'Kaizuka'

Oleander
Nerium oleander

Coontie
:Ö: ◑ ◕ ✂ CS, TS
Zamia pumila — p. 649

Cotoneaster
:Ö: ◯ ◕ ◔ ✂ VARY
— p. 260

Croton
:Ö: :◑ ◕ ◔◔ ✂ TS
Codiaeum variegatum pictum — p. 249

Dwarf palmetto
:Ö: ◑ ◕ ✂ MS, LS, CS, TS
Sabal minor — p. 565

Dwarf yaupon
:Ö: ◑ ◕ ◔ ✂ MS, LS, CS, TS
Ilex vomitoria 'Stokes' — p. 372

Feijoa, Pineapple guava
:Ö: ◕ ◔ ✂ LS, CS, TS
— p. 312

Flame of the woods
:Ö: :◑ ◕ ✂ TS
Ixora coccinea — p. 382

Indian hawthorn
:Ö: :◑ ◯ ◕ ◔ ✂ LS, CS, TS
Rhaphiolepis indica — p. 540

Inkberry
:Ö: :◑ ◕ ◔ ✂ ALL
Ilex glabra — p. 371

Japanese ardisia
:Ö: :◑ ◕ ◔ ✂ LS, CS
Ardisia japonica — p. 163

Japanese barberry
:Ö: :◑ ◕ ◔ ✂ US, MS, LS
Berberis thunbergii — p. 185

Japanese fatsia
◑ ◕ ◔ ✂ LS, CS, TS
Fatsia japonica — p. 312

Japanese pittosporum
:Ö: :◑ ◕ ◔ ✂ LS, CS, TS
Pittosporum tobira — p. 507

Juniper
:Ö: ◯ ◕ ◔ ✂ VARY
Juniperus — p. 385

Mound-lily yucca
:Ö: ◕ ◔ ✂ US, MS, LS, CS
Yucca gloriosa — p. 647

Myrtle
:Ö: :◑ ◕ ◔ ✂ LS, CS, TS
Myrtus communis — p. 445

Natal plum
:Ö: :◑ ◯ ◕ ◔ ✂ CS, TS
Carissa macrocarpa — p. 217

Oleander
:Ö: ◯ ◕ ◔ ◔ ✂ LS, CS, TS
Nerium oleander — p. 452

Pampas grass
:Ö: ◯ ◕ ◕ ◔◔ ✂ MS, LS, CS, TS
Cortaderia selloana — p. 258

Red chokeberry
:Ö: :◑ ◕ ◔ ◕◔ ✂ US, MS, LS, CS
Aronia arbutifolia — p. 165

Redtwig dogwood
:Ö: :◑ ◕ ✂ US, MS
Cornus sericea — p. 257

Rockrose
:Ö: ◯ ◕ ✂ LS, CS
Cistus — p. 238

Rose of Sharon
:Ö: ◕ ◔ ✂ US, MS, LS, CS
Hibiscus syriacus — p. 357

Rosemary
:Ö: ◕ ◔ ✂ ALL
Rosmarinus officinalis — p. 561

Rugosa rose
:Ö: :◑ ◕ ◔ ✂ US, MS, LS, CS
Rosa rugosa — p. 560

Sago palm
:◑ ◕ ◔ ✂ CS, TS
Cycas revoluta — p. 268

Seashore mallow
:Ö: ◕ ◔ ◕◔ ✂ ALL
Kosteletzkya virginica — p. 394

Southern yew
:Ö: :◑ ◕ ◔ ✂ LS, CS, TS
Podocarpus macrophyllus — p. 514

Sumac
:Ö: ◯ ◕ ◔ ✂ VARY
Rhus — p. 549

Thorny elaeagnus
:Ö: :◑ ◯ ◕ ◔ ✂ US, MS, LS, CS
Elaeagnus pungens — p. 294

Torch aloe
:Ö: :◑ ◕ ◯ ◕ ◔ ◔ ✂ TS
Aloe arborescens — p. 144

Wax myrtle
:Ö: :◑ ◕ ◔ ✂ MS, LS, CS, TS
Myrica cerifera — p. 441

VINES, GROUND COVERS

Allamanda
:Ö: ◕ ◔ ◔ ✂ TS
Allamanda cathartica — p. 142

Beach morning glory
:Ö: ◕ ◔ ✂ CS, TS
Ipomoea pes-caprae — p. 376

Bittersweet
:Ö: ◕ ◔ ✂ US, MS, LS
Celastrus — p. 223

Cape honeysuckle
:Ö: :◑ ◕ ◔ ✂ CS, TS
Tecoma capensis — p. 614

Confederate jasmine
:Ö: :◑ ◕ ◔ ✂ LS, CS, TS
Trachelospermum jasminoides — p. 625

Red chokeberry
Aronia arbutifolia

Redtwig dogwood
Cornus sericea

Rugosa rose
Rosa rugosa

Sumac
Rhus

Allamanda
Allamanda cathartica

For climate zone explanations, please see pages 38–39.

Trumpet creeper, common
Campsis radicans

Cape plumbago
Plumbago auriculata

Daylily
Hemerocallis

Grand crinum
Crinum asiaticum

Silver lace vine
☼ ☽ ● ◐ ● ◊ ✂ US, MS, LS
Fallopia baldschuanica   p. 311

Trumpet creeper, common
☼ ☽ ◊ ● ◊ ✂ US, MS, LS, CS
Campsis radicans   p. 214

Virginia creeper
☼ ● ◐ ✂ US, MS, LS, CS
Parthenocissus quinquefolia   p. 473

Wedelia ♛
☼ ◐ ◊ ✂ CS, TS
Sphagneticola trilobata   p. 646

PERENNIALS, BULBS

Alpine sea holly
☼ ◐ ✂ US, MS, LS
Eryngium alpinum   p. 300

Artemisia (most)
☼ ◊ ◐ ✂ VARY   p. 165

Blue wild indigo
☼ ◐ ✂ US, MS, LS, CS
Baptisia australis   p. 179

Bush daisy
☼ ◊ ◐ ● ◊ ✂ CS, TS OR ANNUAL
Euryops pectinatus   p. 309

Cape plumbago
☼ ☽ ◊ ◐ ● ◊ ✂ CS, TS
Plumbago auriculata   p. 513

Chinese pennisetum
☼ ☽ ◐ ● ✂ US, MS, LS, CS
Pennisetum alopecuroides   p. 485

Crinum
☼ ☽ ● ◐ ◗ ✂ VARY   p. 263

Daylily
☼ ☽ ● ◗ ✂ ALL
Hemerocallis   p. 351

Dusty miller
☼ ☽ ◊ ◐ ● ◗ ✂ MS, LS, CS
Senecio cineraria   p. 585

Euphorbia (most)
☼ ● ◊ ● ◐ ◗ ✂ VARY   p. 307

Evergreen candytuft
☼ ● ◗ ✂ US, MS, CS
Iberis sempervirens   p. 369

Fernleaf yarrow
☼ ◊ ◗ ✂ US, MS, LS
Achillea filipendulina   p. 131

Fleabane
☼ ☽ ◊ ✂ VARY
Erigeron   p. 299

Geranium
☼ ◊ ● ◗ ✂ CS, TS OR ANNUAL
Pelargonium   p. 484

Hen and chickens
☼ ☽ ◊ ◗ ✂ US, MS, LS, CS
Sempervivum   p. 585

Ice plant
☼ ☽ ◊ ◗ ✂ US, MS, LS, CS
Delosperma   p. 277

Indian blanket ♛
☼ ◊ ◗ ✂ ALL
Gaillardia pulchella   p. 322

Jerusalem sage
☼ ◊ ◗ ✂ MS, LS, CS, TS
Phlomis fruticosa   p. 496

Lamb's ears
☼ ◊ ◗ ✂ US, MS, LS
Stachys byzantina   p. 599

Lantana
☼ ● ◗ ✂ LS, CS, TS   p. 400

Lily-of-the-Nile
☼ ☽ ◊ ● ◗ ✂ LS, CS, TS
Agapanthus africanus   p. 136

Lobster-claw
☼ ☽ ◐ ◗ ✂ TS
Heliconia   p. 348

Opuntia
☼ ◊ ✂ VARY   p. 460

Perennial hibiscus
☼ ● ◗ ✂ ALL
Hibiscus moscheutos   p. 356

Pine cone ginger
◊ ● ◐ ✂ LS, CS, TS
Zingiber zerumbet   p. 650

Red-hot poker
☼ ☽ ◊ ● ◗ ✂ US, MS, LS, CS
Kniphofia uvaria   p. 392

River oats
☼ ☽ ● ◗ ✂ US, MS, LS, CS
Chasmanthium latifolium   p. 230

Sandwort
☼ ● ● ◗ ✂ US, MS, LS
Arenaria montana   p. 163

Santolina
☼ ◊ ◗ ✂ US, MS, LS, CS   p. 574

Snow-in-summer
◊ ● ◗ ✂ US, MS, LS
Cerastium tomentosum   p. 226

Spanish bayonet ♛
☼ ◊ ● ◗ ✂ LS, CS, TS
Yucca aloifolia   p. 649

Statice
☼ ◗ ✂ TS
Limonium perezii   p. 413

Stonecrop
☼ ☽ ◊ ● ◗ ✂ US, MS, LS
Sedum   p. 581

Purple ice plant
Delosperma cooperi

Indian blanket
Gaillardia pulchella

Lobster-claw
Heliconia

Red-hot poker
Kniphofia uvaria

Stonecrop
Sedum spathulifolium 'Cape Blanco'

For growing symbol explanations, please see page 37.

Potted geraniums liven up a table.

Houseplants

When it's mild and sunny outside, there's no better place than the garden. But gardens can also grow indoors. Houseplants give us color and fragrance with their blooms, and texture and mass with their foliage. Large ones can balance a room or anchor a corner just like a piece of furniture. Houseplants also humidify dry winter air, and some even absorb air pollutants. But in the end, what makes growing houseplants so rewarding is that it satisfies our desire to see beautiful plants even when it's cold and dreary outside.

Polka-dot plant
Hypoestes phyllostachya

Aechmea (Bromeliad)

Bleeding heart vine
Clerodendrum thomsoniae

Clivia
Clivia miniata

FLOWERING

Aechmea (Bromeliad)	
Aechmea	p. 134
African violet	
Saintpaulia	p. 566
Amaryllis	
Hippeastrum	p. 358
Anthurium	
	p. 152
Begonia (many)	
	p. 182
Bleeding heart vine	
Clerodendrum thomsoniae	p. 245
Cape primrose	
Streptocarpus	p. 604
Cattleya orchids	
	p. 221
Christmas cactus	
Schlumbergera x buckleyi	p. 579
Clivia	
Clivia miniata	p. 247
Coral plant	
Russelia sarmentosa	p. 565
Crinum (some)	
	p. 263
Cymbidium orchids	
	p. 269

Dendrobium orchids	
	p. 278
Desert rose	
Adenium obesum	p. 133
Devil's backbone	
Pedilanthus tithymaloides smallii	p. 483
Earth star	
Cryptanthus zonatus	p. 265
Easter cactus	
Hatiora gaertneri	p. 343
Echeveria (some)	
	p. 291
Eucharist lily	
Eucharis grandiflora	p. 303
Flame violet	
Episcia	p. 297
Florists' cyclamen	
Cyclamen persicum	p. 268
Gardenia, common	
Gardenia jasminoides	p. 326
Geranium	
Pelargonium (many)	p. 484
Ginger lily	
Hedychium	p. 344
Gloxinia	
Sinningia speciosa	p. 589
Hedgehog cactus	
Echinocereus	p. 292

Florists' cyclamen
Cyclamen persicum

Desert rose
Adenium obesum

Gloxinia
Sinningia speciosa

For climate zone explanations, please see pages 38–39.

Hybrid fuchsia
Fuchsia hybrida

Moth orchid
Phalaenopsis

Peace lily
Spathiphyllum

Vriesea

Hybrid fuchsia
☼◐◖
Fuchsia hybrida   p. 321

Lobster-claw
☼ ☼◐◖◖
Heliconia   p. 348

Kalanchoe (most)
☼ ☼◐◖◖
    p. 388

Moth orchid
☼◖◖
Phalaenopsis   p. 494

Nun's orchid
☼◖
Phaius tankervilliae   p. 494

Oncidium orchids
☼◖◖
    p. 458

Peace lily
☼◖◖◖
Spathiphyllum   p. 595

Persian violet
☼◖◖◖
Exacum affine   p. 309

Poinsettia
☼:◖◖
Euphorbia pulcherrima   p. 308

Strawberry geranium
☼◖●◖
Saxifraga stolonifera   p. 577

Vriesea
☼◖◖
    p. 643

Walking iris
☼ ☼◐◖◖
Neomarica gracilis   p. 450

Wax flower
☼◖●◖
Hoya carnosa   p. 361

Yucca (some)
☼○◖◖
    p. 647

FOLIAGE

African mask
☼◐◖◖◖ ◈
Alocasia x amazonica   p. 144

Aglaonema
☼◐◖◖
    p. 139

Arrowhead vine
☼◐◖
Syngonium   p. 609

Asparagus, ornamental
☼◐◖
Asparagus densiflorus   p. 170

Baby rubber plant
☼◐◖
Peperomia obtusifolia   p. 488

Bamboo (several)
☼ ☼◐○◖◖◖
    p. 175

Rabbit's foot fern
☼◐◖
Humata tyermannii   p. 362

Bloodleaf
☼:◖
Iresine   p. 377

Brake
☼◐●◖
Pteris   p. 527

Bunny ears
☼:○
Opuntia microdasys   p. 460

Burmese fishtail palm
☼:◐◖◖ ◈
Caryota mitis   p. 219

Burro tail
☼ ☼○○◖
Sedum morganianum   p. 583

Caricature plant
☼◐◖
Graptophyllum pictum   p. 338

Cast-iron plant
☼◐●◖◖◖
Aspidistra elatior   p. 171

China doll
☼:◐◖
Radermachera sinica   p. 536

Coffee
☼◐◖
Coffea arabica   p. 249

Coontie
☼◐◖
Zamia pumila   p. 649

Corn plant
☼:◐◖◖
Dracaena fragrans   p. 288

Croton
☼:◐●◖ ◖◖
Codiaeum variegatum pictum   p. 249

Dumb cane
☼:◐●◖ ◈ ◈
Dieffenbachia   p. 283

Eternal flame
☼◐◖
Calathea crocata   p. 203

Giant yucca
☼:◐◖
Yucca elephantipes   p. 647

Jade plant
☼:○
Crassula ovata   p. 261

Aglaonema 'Key Lime'

Bloodleaf
Iresine lindenii

China doll
Radermachera sinica

Croton
Codiaeum variegatum pictum

For growing symbol explanations, please see page 37.

Paradise palm
Howea forsteriana

Dumb cane
Dieffenbachia

Nerve plant
Fittonia verschaffeltii

Pilea

Jewel orchid

Ludisia discolor p. 419

Lady palm

Rhapis excelsa p. 540

Madagascar dragon tree

Dracaena marginata p. 288

Madagascar palm

Pachypodium lamerei p. 465

Milkbush

Euphorbia tirucalli p. 308

Moses-in-the-cradle

Tradescantia spathacea p. 626

Neoregelia

  p. 450

Nerve plant

Fittonia verschaffeltii p. 317

Norfolk Island pine

Araucaria heterophylla p. 161

Paradise palm

Howea forsteriana p. 361

Parlor palm

Chamaedorea elegans p. 229

Peacock plant

Calathea makoyana p. 203

Philodendron (many)

  p. 495

Pilea (many)

  p. 503

Polka-dot plant

Hypoestes phyllostachya p. 368

Polypody fern

Polypodium p. 516

Ponytail palm

Beaucarnea recurvata p. 181

Prayer plant

Maranta leuconeura p. 432

Rattlesnake plant

Calathea lancifolia p. 203

Rex begonia

  p. 183

Roundleaf fern

Pellaea rotundifolia p. 485

Rubber plant

Ficus elastica p. 313

Sansevieria

  p. 574

Satin pothos

Scindapsus pictus p. 580

Schefflera

  p. 578

Split-leaf philodendron

Monstera deliciosa p. 441

Swedish ivy

Plectranthus verticillatus p. 509

Sword fern

Nephrolepis exaltata p. 451

Tillandsia

  p. 621

Venus's fly trap

Dionaea muscipula p. 286

Wandering jew

Tradescantia fluminensis p. 626

Weeping fig

Ficus benjamina p. 313

Xanthosoma

  p. 646

Zebra plant

Calathea zebrina p. 203

ZZ plant

Zamioculcas p. 649

Satin pothos
Scindapsus pictus

Rubber plant
Ficus elastica

Venus's fly trap
Dionaea muscipula

Zebra plant
Calathea zebrina

For climate zone explanations, please see pages 38–39.

Southern Natives

Cardinal flower
Lobelia cardinalis

Ask a roomful of gardeners if they like native plants and you'll probably see a lot of raised heads. No wonder—plants indigenous to a region like the South give it a special sense of place. Moreover, native plants are usually less susceptible to pests than introduced ones and are well attuned to the vagaries of local weather. But remember—the South is a big, big place. Just because a plant is native to the Southeast doesn't mean it will thrive in the Southwest. Check the Encyclopedia for each plant listed here to see if it's a good choice for your area.

Bluebonnets and Indian paintbrush

American beech
Fagus grandifolia

TREES

American beech
☼ ◐ ◑ ◆ ✄ US, MS, LS, CS
Fagus grandifolia   p. 310

American holly
☼ ◐ ◆ ◑ ✄ ALL
Ilex opaca   p. 371

American sweet gum
☼ ◆ ◑ ✄ US, MS, LS, CS
Liquidambar styraciflua   p. 415

American sycamore
☼ ◆ ✄ US, MS, LS, CS
Platanus occidentalis   p. 508

Ash
☼ ○ ◆ ◑ ✄ VARY
Fraxinus (most)   p. 319

Bald cypress
☼ ◑ ◆ ◐ ✄ US, MS, LS, CS
Taxodium distichum   p. 613

Black gum
☼ ◐ ◆ ◑ ✄ US, MS, LS, CS
Nyssa sylvatica   p. 455

Cabbage palm
☼ ◐ ◆ ✄ LS, CS, TS
Sabal palmetto   p. 565

Canadian hemlock
☼ ◐ ◆ ✄ US, MS, LS
Tsuga canadensis   p. 629

Carolina silver bell
☼ ◐ ◆ ✄ US, MS, LS
Halesia carolina   p. 341

Eastern red cedar
☼ ○ ◆ ◑ ✄ ALL
Juniperus virginiana   p. 387

Eastern redbud
☼ ◐ ◆ ◑ ✄ US, MS, LS, CS
Cercis canadensis   p. 227

Flowering dogwood
☼ ◐ ◆ ◑ ✄ US, MS, LS, CS
Cornus florida   p. 255

Fringe tree
☼ ◐ ◆ ◑ ✄ US, MS, LS, CS
Chionanthus virginicus   p. 234

Ironwood
☼ ◐ ◆ ◑ ✄ US, MS, LS, CS
Carpinus caroliniana   p. 217

Live oak
☼ ◆ ✄ LS, CS, TS
Quercus virginiana   p. 535

Loblolly bay
☼ ◐ ◆ ◐ ✄ MS, LS, CS, TS
Gordonia lasianthus   p. 333

Loblolly pine
☼ ○ ◆ ◑ ✄ US, MS, LS, CS
Pinus taeda   p. 506

Longleaf pine
☼ ○ ◆ ◑ ✄ MS, LS, CS, TS
Pinus palustris   p. 505

Mesquite
☼ ○ ✄ MS, LS, CS, TS
Prosopis glandulosa   p. 522

Nuttall oak
☼ ◆ ✄ US, MS, LS, CS
Quercus texana   p. 534

Pecan
☼ ◆ ◑ ✄ US, MS, LS, CS
Carya illinoensis   p. 218

Red buckeye
☼ ◐ ◆ ◑ ◆ ✄ US, MS, LS, CS
Aesculus pavia   p. 135

Red maple
☼ ◐ ◆ ◑ ✄ US, MS, LS, CS
Acer rubrum   p. 129

Red oak
☼ ◆ ✄ US, MS, LS
Quercus rubra   p. 534

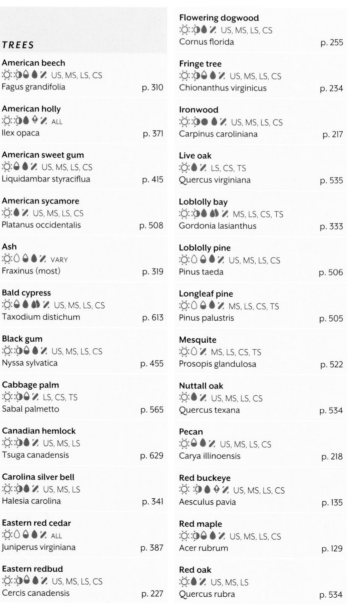

Live oak
Quercus virginiana

Bald cypress
Taxodium distichum

Eastern red cedar
Juniperus virginiana

Red maple
Acer rubrum

Fringe tree
Chionanthus virginicus

River birch
Betula nigra

For growing symbol explanations, please see page 37.

Sugar maple
Acer saccharum

Sweet bay
Magnolia virginiana

Tulip poplar
Liriodendron tulipifera

Bottlebrush buckeye
Aesculus parviflora

River birch
☼ ◐ ◌ ◍ ✂ US, MS, LS, CS
Betula nigra   p. 186

Sassafras
☼ ◐ ◌ ◍ ✂ US, MS, LS, CS
Sassafras albidum   p. 577

Serviceberry
☼ ◐ ◌ ◍ ◍ ✂ US, MS, LS, CS
Amelanchier   p. 147

Shumard red oak
☼ ◐ ◌ ✂ US, MS, LS, CS
Quercus shumardii   p. 534

Sourwood
☼ ◐ ◌ ◍ ✂ US, MS, LS, CS
Oxydendrum arboreum   p. 465

Southern magnolia
☼ ◐ ◌ ✂ US, MS, LS, CS
Magnolia grandiflora   p. 424

Sugar maple
☼ ◐ ◌ ◍ ✂ US, MS, LS
Acer saccharum   p. 129

Sweet bay
☼ ◐ ◌ ◍ ✂ US, MS, LS, CS
Magnolia virginiana   p. 425

Tulip poplar
☼ ◐ ◌ ✂ US, MS, LS, CS
Liriodendron tulipifera   p. 415

Virginia pine
☼ ◌ ◌ ◍ ✂ US, MS, LS
Pinus virginiana   p. 506

Western soapberry
☼ ◌ ◌ ✂ US, MS, LS, CS
Sapindus drummondii   p. 575

White oak
☼ ◐ ◌ ✂ US, MS, LS, CS
Quercus alba   p. 532

Willow oak
☼ ◐ ◌ ✂ US, MS, LS, CS
Quercus phellos   p. 534

Yellow wood
☼ ◐ ◌ ✂ US, MS, LS
Cladrastis kentukea   p. 242

SHRUBS

American beautyberry
☼ ◐ ◌ ◌ ◍ ✂ ALL
Callicarpa americana   p. 205

Bayberry
◌ ◌ ◍ ✂ US, MS
Morella pensylvanica   p. 441

Bottlebrush buckye
☼ ◐ ◌ ◍ ◊ ✂ US, MS, LS, CS
Aesculus parviflora   p. 135

Bush honeysuckle
☼ ◐ ◌ ◍ ✂ US, MS, LS
Diervilla   p. 284

Buttonbush
☼ ◐ ◌ ◌ ◍ ◊ ✂ ALL
Cephalanthus occidentalis   p. 225

Coontie
◐ ◌ ✂ CS, TS OR INDOORS
Zamia pumila   p. 649

Florida flame azalea
◐ ◌ ◍ ◊ ✂ MS, LS, CS
Rhododendron austrinum   p. 546

Fothergilla
☼ ◐ ◌ ✂ US, MS, LS
                                      p. 318

Heart's-a-bustin'
☼ ◐ ◌ ◍ ◌ ✂ US, MS, LS, CS
Euonymus americanus   p. 305

Hop tree
☼ ◐ ◌ ◍ ✂ US, MS, LS, CS
Ptelea trifoliata   p. 527

Indigo bush
☼ ◐ ◌ ✂ US, MS, LS, CS
Amorpha fruticosa   p. 148

Inkberry
☼ ◐ ◌ ◍ ✂ ALL
Ilex glabra   p. 371

Mountain laurel
◐ ◌ ◊ ✂ US, MS, LS
Kalmia latifolia   p. 390

Oakleaf hydrangea
◐ ◌ ✂ US, MS, LS, CS
Hydrangea quercifolia   p. 363

Piedmont azalea
◐ ◌ ◍ ◌ ◊ ✂ US, MS, LS, CS
Rhododendron canescens   p. 546

Pinxterbloom azalea
◐ ◌ ◍ ◊ ✂ US, MS, LS
Rhododendron periclymenoides   p. 54

Plumleaf azalea
◐ ◌ ◍ ◊ ✂ US, MS, LS, CS
Rhododendron prunifolium   p. 547

Possumhaw
☼ ◐ ◌ ◊ ✂ US, MS, LS, CS
Ilex decidua   p. 370

Red chokeberry
☼ ◐ ◌ ◌ ◍ ✂ US, MS, LS, CS
Aronia arbutifolia   p. 165

Sotol
☼ ◐ ◌ ◌ ✂ VARY
Dasylirion   p. 275

Staghorn sumac
☼ ◌ ◌ ✂ US, MS, LS
Rhus typhina   p. 549

Summersweet
◐ ◌ ◍ ✂ US, MS, LS, CS
Clethra alnifolia   p. 246

Texas ranger
☼ ◌ ◌ ✂ LS, CS, TS
Leucophyllum frutescens   p. 408

Heart's-a-bustin'
Euonymus americanus

Mountain laurel
Kalmia latifolia

Possumhaw
Ilex decidua

Summersweet
Clethra alnifolia

For climate zone explanations, please see pages 38–39.

Witch hazel, common
Hamamelis virginiana

Blazing star
Liatris

Bloodroot
Sanguinaria canadensis

Butterfly weed
Asclepias tuberosa

Virginia sweetspire
☼◗♦✂ US, MS, LS, CS
Itea virginica p. 381

Wax myrtle
☼◗♦♦✂ MS, LS, CS, TS
Morella cerifera p. 441

Witch hazel, common
☼◗♦✂ US, MS, LS, CS
Hamamelis virginiana p. 342

Yaupon
☼☼◗♦♀✂ MS, LS, CS, TS
Ilex vomitoria p. 372

PERENNIALS AND ANNUALS

American maidenhair fern
◗●♦♦✂ US, MS
Adiantum pedatum p. 133

Blazing star
☼◐◗♦♦✂ US, MS, LS, CS
Liatris p. 409

Bloodroot
◗●♦♦✂ US, MS, LS
Sanguinaria canadensis p. 573

Blue phlox
☼◗♦✂ US, MS, LS, CS
Phlox divaricata p. 497

Bluebonnet
☼◐◗♦♦✂ MS, LS, CS
Lupinus havardii p. 420

Bluestar
☼☼◐◗♦✂ US, MS, LS, CS
Amsonia tabernaemontana p. 149

Bluestem
☼☼◐◗♦♦♦✂ US, MS, LS, CS
Andropogon p. 149

Bowles' golden grass
☼◗♦♦✂ US, MS, LS
Milium effusum 'Aureum' p. 437

Bowman's root
◗♦✂ US, MS, LS
Gillenia trifoliata p. 329

Butterfly pea
☼☼◗●◐♦♦♦✂ ALL
Clitoria mariana p. 247

Butterfly weed
☼◐♦♦♦♀✂ US, MS, LS, CS
Asclepias tuberosa p. 168

Calliopsis
☼◐♦♦✂ ALL
Coreopsis tinctoria p. 254

Cardinal flower
☼☼◗♦♀✂ US, MS, LS, CS
Lobelia cardinalis p. 417

Carolina bush pea
☼☼◗♦✂ US, MS, LS
Thermopsis villosa p. 617

Clinton lily
●◗♦✂ US, MS
Clintonia umbellulata p. 247

Clustered goldflower
☼◐◗♦✂ US, MS, LS, CS
Tetraneuris scaposa p. 615

Coneflower
☼◗♦✂ VARY
Echinacea p. 291

Dahlberg daisy
☼◗♦✂ CS, TS OR ANNUAL
Thymophylla tenuiloba p. 618

Dropseed
☼◐◗♦✂ US, MS, LS, CS
Sporobolus p. 598

False indigo
☼◗♦✂ US, MS, LS, CS
Baptisia p. 179

Foamflower
◗●♦✂ US, MS, LS
Tiarella p. 620

Galax
◗●♦✂ US, MS, LS
Galax urceolata p. 322

Gaura
☼◗♦✂ US, MS, LS, CS
Gaura lindheimeri p. 324

Golden columbine
☼◗♦✂ US, MS
Aquilegia chrysantha p. 160

Goldenrod
☼◗♦✂ US, MS, LS, CS
Solidago p. 593

Golden star
◗♦✂ US, MS, LS, CS
Chrysogonum virginianum p. 237

Hardy begonia
◗♦✂ ALL
Begonia grandis p. 182

Indian blanket
☼◗♦✂ ALL
Gaillardia pulchella p. 322

Indian paintbrush
☼◗♦✂ ALL
Castilleja indivisa p. 220

Indian pink
◗♦♀✂ US, MS, LS, CS
Spigelia marilandica p. 596

Joe-Pye weed
☼◗♦♦✂ US, MS, LS, CS
Eupatorium purpureum p. 306

Liverwort
◗●♦✂ US, MS, LS, CS
Hepatica p. 352

Louisiana iris
☼☼◗♦♦♦♀✂ US, MS, LS, CS
p. 379

Golden columbine
Aquilegia chrysantha

Purple coneflower
Echinacea purpurea

Goldenrod
Solidago

Hardy begonia
Begonia grandis

For growing symbol explanations, please see page 37.

Lousiana iris

Sundrops
Calylophus

Venus's flytrap
Dionaea muscipula

Virginia bluebells
Mertensia pulmonarioides

Wake robin
Trillium

Mayapple
☼ ● ◐ �💧 ❤ ✂ US, MS, LS, CS
Podophyllum peltatum — p. 514

Mountain mint
☼ ◐◐ �💧 ✂ US, MS, LS
Pycnanthemum incanum — p. 530

New England aster
☼ ◐ ✂ US, MS, LS
Aster novae-angliae — p. 608

Prairie sage
☼ ◐ ✂ ALL
Salvia azurea grandiflora — p. 568

Red yucca
☼ ◐◐ ◐ ✂ ALL
Hesperaloe parviflora — p. 353

River oats
☼ ◐ ◐ ✂ US, MS, LS, CS
Chasmanthium latifolium — p. 230

Royal catchfly
☼ ◐◐ ◐ ✂ US, MS, LS, CS
Silene regia — p. 588

Seashore mallow
☼ ◐ ◐ ✂ ALL
Kosteletzkya virginica — p. 394

Shooting star
☼ ◐ ◐ ✂ US, MS, LS
Dodecatheon — p. 287

Silphium
☼ ◐◐ ◐ ✂ US, MS, LS, CS
— p. 588

Southern maidenhair
☼ ● ◐ ◐ ✂ LS, CS, TS
Adiantum capillus-veneris — p. 133

Sundrops
☼ ◐◐ ◐ ✂ US, MS, LS
Calylophus — p. 208

Swamp milkweed
☼ ◐ ◐ ◐ 💧 ❤ ✂ US, MS, LS, CS
Asclepias incarnata — p. 168

Texas yellow star
☼ ◐ ✂ ALL
Lindheimera texana — p. 414

Twinleaf
☼ ● ◐ ✂ US, MS
Jeffersonia diphylla — p. 384

Venus's flytrap
☼ ◐ ● ◐ ✂ MS, LS OR HOUSEPLANT
Dionaea muscipula — p. 286

Virginia bluebells
☼ ◐ ✂ US, MS, LS
Mertensia virginica — p. 436

Wake robin
☼ ● ◐ ✂ US, MS, LS
Trillium — p. 627

Wild columbine
☼ ◐ ◐ ✂ US, MS, LS
Aquilegia canadensis — p. 160

Wild ginger
☼ ● ◐ ◐ ✂ VARY
Asarum (some) — p. 168

Wine cups
☼ ◐ ✂ US, MS, LS, CS
Callirhoe involucrata — p. 205

VINES

Carolina jessamine
☼ ◐◐ ● ◐ ◐ ❤ ✂ MS, LS, CS
Gelsemium sempervirens — p. 325

Climbing hydrangea
☼ ● ◐ ✂ US, MS, LS, CS
Decumaria barbara — p. 276

Crossvine
☼ ◐◐ ◐ ✂ US, MS, LS, CS
Bignonia capreolata — p. 187

Jackson vine
☼ ◐◐ ◐ ✂ MS, LS, CS
Smilax smallii — p. 590

Jujube
☼ ◐ ✂ US, MS, LS, CS
— p. 385

Maypop
☼ ◐◐ ◐ ✂ US, MS, LS, CS
Passiflora incarnata — p. 473

Trumpet creeper, common
☼ ◐◐ ◐ ✂ US, MS, LS, CS
Campsis radicans — p. 214

Trumpet honeysuckle
☼ ◐◐ ◐ ✂ US, MS, LS, CS
Lonicera sempervirens — p. 419

Virginia creeper
☼ ● ◐ ✂ US, MS, LS, CS
Parthenocissus quinquefolia — p. 473

FRUITS

American persimmon
☼ ◐ ◐ ✂ US, MS, LS, CS
— p. 491

Blackberry
☼ ◐ ✂ US, MS, LS, CS
— p. 188

Blueberry
☼ ◐ ✂ VARY
Vaccinium (some) — p. 190

Mayhaw
☼ ◐ ✂ MS, LS, CS
Crataegus opaca — p. 262

Muscadine grape
☼ ◐ ✂ VARY
— p. 334

Pawpaw
☼ ◐◐ ◐ ✂ US, MS, LS, CS
— p. 447

Trumpet creeper
Campsis radicans

Trumpet honeysuckle
Lonicera sempervirens 'Sulphurea'

Blackberry

Pawpaw

For climate zone explanations, please see pages 38–39.

Plants that
Tolerate Shade

A lot of folks think of shade as a problem. But actually, shade presents a great opportunity to use a wide range of plants that offer stunning flowers, fruits, or foliage in the absence of bright sun. And because fewer weeds plague shady gardens, these leafy retreats usually need less maintenance. The lists below contain trees, shrubs, ground covers, vines, perennials, bulbs, and annuals that prever or accept some degree of shade. The symbol ✳ indicates plants having showy flowers.

Siebold plantain lily
Hosta sieboldiana

Dove tree
Davidia involucrata

Dwarf palmetto
Sabal minor

False aralia
Schefflera elegantissima

TREES

American beech
☼ ◑◐●◗ ✄ US, MS, LS, CS
Fagus grandifolia — p. 310

Black gum
☼ ◑◐●◗ ✄ US, MS, LS, CS
Nyssa sylvatica — p. 455

Dove tree ✳
◑◐● ✄ US, MS
Davidia involucrata — p. 276

Dwarf palmetto
☼ ◑◐ ✄ MS, LS, CS, TS
Sabal minor — p. 565

Eastern redbud ✳
☼ ◑◐●◗ ✄ US, MS, LS, CS
Cercis canadensis — p. 227

False aralia
☼ ◑◐● ✄ TS
Schefflera elegantissima — p. 579

Flowering dogwood ✳
☼ ◑◐● ✄ US, MS, LS, CS
Cornus florida — p. 256

Franklin tree ✳
☼ ◑◐●◗ ✄ US, MS, LS, CS
Franklinia alatamaha — p. 319

Fringe tree ✳
☼ ◑◐●◗ ✄ US, MS, LS, CS
Chionanthus virginicus — p. 234

Hemlock
☼ ◑◐● ✄ VARY
Tsuga — p. 628

Holly
☼ ◑◐● ◗ ✄ VARY
Ilex — p. 369

Ironwood
☼ ◑◐● ◗ ✄ US, MS, LS, CS
Carpinus caroliniana — p. 217

Japanese maple
☼ ◑◐●◗ ✄ US, MS, LS, CS
Acer palmatum — p. 127

Katsura tree
☼ ◑◐◗ ✄ US, MS, LS
Cercidiphyllum japonicum — p. 226

Mountain ash ✳
☼ ◑◐●◗ ✄ VARY
Sorbus — p. 594

Palms (some)
☼ ◑◐● ◑◗ ✄ VARY
(Many kinds) — p. 465, 498, 528

Pawpaw ✳
☼ ◑◐◗ ✄ US, MS, LS, CS
Asimina triloba — p. 475

Podocarpus
☼ ◑◐◗ ✄ VARY
— p. 514

Sassafras
☼ ◑◐◗ ✄ US, MS, LS, CS
Sassafras albidum — p. 577

Serviceberry ✳
☼ ◑◐●◗ ✄ VARY
Amelanchier arborea — p. 147

Silver bell ✳
☼ ◑◐◗ ✄ US, MS, LS
Halesia — p. 341

Snowbell ✳
☼ ◑◐◗ ✄ VARY
Styrax — p. 605

Sourwood ✳
☼ ◑◐◗ ✄ US, MS, LS, CS
Oxydendrum arboreum — p. 465

Stewartia ✳
◑◐◗ ✄ VARY
— p. 601

Sweet bay ✳
☼ ◑◐◗ ✄ US, MS, LS, CS
Magnolia virginiana — p. 425

Canadian hemlock
Tsuga canadensis

Serviceberry
Amelanchier

Sassafras
Sassafras albidum

Snowbell
Styrax

For growing symbol explanations, please see page 37.

Tasmanian tree fern
☼◐◑◮ TS
Dicksonia antarctica   p. 283

Trumpet tree ✳
☼:☼:◐◮ TS
Tabebuia   p. 611

SHRUBS

Alexandrian laurel
☼◐◑◮ MS, LS, CS
Danae racemosa   p. 273

Anise tree
☼◐◭◮◮ MS, LS, CS
Illicium   p. 372

Azalea, native ✳
☼◐◭◮◮ VARY
Rhododendron   p. 541

Banana shrub ✳
☼:☼:◐◮ LS, CS, TS
Michelia figo   p. 424

Bottlebrush buckeye ✳
☼:☼:◐◮◮ US, MS, LS, CS
Aesculus parviflora   p. 135

Boxwood
☼:☼:◐◮◮ VARY
Buxus   p. 199

Bramble ✳
☼:☼:◐◮◮ VARY
Rubus   p. 562

Butcher's broom
☼◐◯◮◮ MS, LS, CS, TS
Ruscus aculeatus   p. 564

Camellia (most) ✳
◐◮◮◮ US, MS, LS, CS
     p. 208

Chinese fringe ✳
☼:☼:◐◮◮ MS, LS, CS
Loropetalum chinense   p. 419

Daphne ✳
☼◐◮◮ VARY
     p. 274

Chinese fringe
Loropetalum chinense

Winter daphne
Daphne odora 'Aureomarginata'

Fiveleaf aralia
☼:☼:◐◮◭◭◮ US, MS, LS
Eleutherococcus sieboldianus   p. 295

Fothergilla ✳
☼:☼:◐◮ US, MS, LS
     p. 318

Gardenia, common ✳
☼:☼:◐◮ LS, CS, TS
Gardenia jasminoides   p. 323

Holly
☼:☼:◐◮◮ VARY
Ilex   p. 369

Hop tree
☼:☼:◐◮◮ US, MS, LS, CS
Ptelea trifoliata   p. 527

Gardenia, common
Gardenia jasminoides

Hybrid fuchsia ✳
☼◐◮ US OR ANNUAL
Fuchsia hybrida   p. 321

Hydrangea ✳
☼◐◮ VARY
     p. 363

Japanese aucuba
☼◐◭◮◮ ALL
Aucuba japonica   p. 174

Japanese cleyera
☼:☼:◐◮ MS, LS, CS, TS
Ternstroemia gymnanthera   p. 614

Japanese fatsia
☼◐◮ LS, CS, TS
Fatsia japonica   p. 312

Japanese kerria ✳
☼:☼:◐◮ US, MS, LS, CS
Kerria japonica   p. 390

Japanese pittosporum ✳
☼:☼:◐◭◮ LS, CS, TS
Pittosporum tobira   p. 507

Japanese skimmia ✳
☼◐◭◮ US
Skimmia japonica   p. 590

Lady palm
☼◐◮ CS, TS
Rhapis   p. 540

Leucothoe ✳
☼◐◭◭◮ US, MS, LS
     p. 408

Mahonia ✳
☼:☼:◐◮◭◮ VARY
     p. 427

Mountain laurel ✳
☼◐◭◮ US, MS, LS, CS
Kalmia latifolia   p. 390

Nandina
☼:☼:◐◮◭◮ US, MS, LS, CS
Nandina domestica   p. 445

Osmanthus
☼:☼:◐◯◭◮ VARY
     p. 462

Philodendron
☼:☼:◐◮ VARY OR INDOORS
     p. 495

Pieris ✳
☼◐◭◮ VARY
     p. 502

Redvein enkianthus ✳
☼:☼:◐◭◮ US, MS
Enkianthus campanulatus   p. 295

Sago palm
☼◐◮◮ CS, TS
Cycas revoluta   p. 268

Snowberry, common
☼:☼:◐◯◮◮ US, MS
Symphoricarpos albus   p. 607

French hydrangea
Hydrangea macrophylla

Japanese skimmia
Skimmia japonica

Mountain laurel
Kalmia latifolia

Holly osmanthus
Osmanthus heterophyllus

Mountain pieris
Pieris floribunda

For climate zone explanations, please see pages 38–39.

Summersweet
Clethra alnifolia

Doublefile viburnum
Viburnum plicatum tomentosum

Bishop's weed
Aegododium podagraria 'Variegatum'

Carolina jessamine
Gelsemium sempervirens

Sparkleberry
☼ ◑ ◐ 🌢 ✶ MS, LS, CS
Vaccinium arboreum   p. 633

Spicebush
☼ ◑ ◐ 🌢 ✶ US, MS, LS
Lindera benzoin   p. 414

Summersweet   ❊
◑ 🌢 ◐ 🌢 ✶ US, MS, LS, CS
Clethra alnifolia   p. 246

Sweet box
☼ ◐ ● 🌢 ✶ US, MS, LS, CS
Sarcococca   p. 576

Viburnum   ❊
☼ ◑ ◐ ✶ VARY
          p. 637

Witch hazel   ❊
☼ ◑ ◐ ✶ US, MS, LS
Hamamelis   p. 342

Yesterday-today-and-tomorrow ❊
☼ ◑ ◐ 🌢 ✶ CS, TS
Brunfelsia pauciflora   p. 196

Yew
☼ ◑ ● ◐ 🌢 🌢 ✶ US, MS
Taxus   p. 613

GROUND COVERS, VINES

Actinidia kolomikta
☼ ◑ ◐ 🌢 ✶ US, MS, LS
          p. 132

Bamboo (some)
☼ ◑ ◐ 🌢 ✶ LS, CS, TS
          p. 175

Bishop's weed   ❊
☼ ● 🌢 ✶ US, MS, LS
Aegopodium podagraria   p. 134

Boston ivy
☼ ◐ ◐ 🌢 ✶ US, MS, LS
Parthenocissus tricuspidata   p. 473

Carolina jessamine   ❊
☼ ◑ ◐ 🌢 ◐ ✶ MS, LS, CS
Gelsemium sempervirens   p. 325

Carpet bugleweed   ❊
☼ ● ◐ ✶ US, MS, LS
Ajuga reptans   p. 140

Confederate jasmine   ❊
☼ ◑ ◐ 🌢 ✶ LS, CS, TS
Trachelospermum jasminoides   p. 625

Creeping buttercup   ❊
☼ ◐ ● 🌢 ✶ US, MS, LS
Ranunculus repens pleniflorus   p. 537

Creeping fig
☼ ◑ ◐ ● 🌢 ✶ LS, CS, TS
Ficus pumila   p. 314

English ivy
☼ ◐ ● 🌢 ◐ ✶ ALL
Hedera helix   p. 344

x Fatshedera lizei
◐ ● 🌢 ✶ LS, CS, TS
          p. 311

Fiveleaf akebia
☼ ● ◐ 🌢 ✶ US, MS, LS, CS
Akebia quinata   p. 141

Forget-me-not   ❊
☼ ◐ 🌢 ✶ US, MS, LS
Myosotis sylvatica   p. 445

Grape ivy
☼ ◐ ● 🌢 ✶ TS
Cissus rhombifolia   p. 238

Hellebore   ❊
☼ ◐ ● 🌢 ◐ ✶ VARY
Helleborus   p. 349

Houttuynia cordata
☼ ◑ ◐ ● 🌢 ◐ ✶ ALL
          p. 361

Japanese ardisia
☼ ◑ ◐ ● 🌢 ✶ LS, CS
Ardisia japonica   p. 163

Japanese pachysandra   ❊
☼ ◐ ● 🌢 ✶ US, MS, LS
Pachysandra terminalis   p. 466

Lily-of-the-valley   ❊
☼ ◐ ● 🌢 ◐ ✶ US, MS, LS
Convallaria majalis   p. 251

Mazus reptans   ❊
☼ ◐ ● 🌢 ✶ US, MS, LS
          p. 433

Mondo grass
☼ ◐ ● 🌢 ◐ ✶ MS, LS, CS, TS
Ophiopogon japonicus   p. 460

Monkey grass   ❊
☼ ◐ ● 🌢 ✶ VARY
Liriope   p. 416

Partridgeberry
☼ ◐ ● 🌢 ✶ US, MS, LS, CS
Mitchella repens   p. 439

Periwinkle   ❊
☼ ◐ ● 🌢 ◐ ✶ VARY
Vinca   p. 641

Split-leaf philodendron
☼ ◐ ✶ TS
Monstera deliciosa   p. 441

Spotted dead nettle   ❊
☼ ◐ ● 🌢 ✶ US, MS, LS
Lamium maculatum   p. 400

Sweet woodruff   ❊
☼ ◐ ● 🌢 ◐ ✶ US, MS, LS
Galium odoratum   p. 322

Virginia creeper
☼ ◐ ● 🌢 ✶ US, MS, LS, CS
Parthenocissus quinquefolia   p. 473

Wintercreeper euonymus
☼ ◐ ● 🌢 ◐ ✶ US, MS, LS, CS
Euonymus fortunei   p. 305

Creeping buttercup
Ranunculus repens pleniflorus

Forget-me-not
Myosotis sylvatica

Lenten rose
Helleborus orientalis

Periwinkle
Vinca

For growing symbol explanations, please see page 37.

False spiraea
Astilbe

Bergenia

Brunnera
Brunnera macrophylla

Chinese foxglove
Rehmannia elata

PERENNIALS, BULBS, ANNUALS

Aconite ✳
☼ ◐ ● ◊ ✿ US, MS
Aconitum — p. 131

African violet ✳
◐ ● INDOORS
Saintpaulia — p. 566

Anemone ✳
☼ ◐ ● ◊ ✿ US, MS, LS
— p. 150

Arum
☼ ◐ ● ◊ ✿ VARY
— p. 167

Bear's breeches ✳
☼ ◐ ● ◊ ✿ US, MS, LS, CS
Acanthus mollis — p. 127

Begonia ✳
◐ ◊ ✿ TS OR ANNUAL
— p. 182

Bergenia ✳
☼ ◐ ● ◊ US, MS, LS
— p. 185

Black snakeroot ✳
☼ ◐ ● ◊ ✿ US, MS, LS, CS
Actaea racemosa — p. 132

Bleeding heart ✳
◐ ● ◊ VARY
Dicentra (most) — p. 282

Bloodroot ✳
◐ ● ◊ ✿ US, MS, LS
Sanguinaria canadensis — p. 573

Bowles' golden grass ✳
◐ ● ◊ ✿ US, MS, LS
Milium effusum 'Aureum' — p. 437

Brunnera ✳
◐ ● ◊ ✿ US, MS
Brunnera macrophylla — p. 196

Calanthe ✳
◐ ● ◊ ✿ MS, LS, CS
— p. 203

Cape primrose ✳
◐ ● ◊ ✿ TS OR INDOORS
Streptocarpus — p. 604

Cardinal flower ✳
☼ ☼ ◐ ● ◊ ✿ US, MS, LS, CS
Lobelia cardinalis — p. 417

Cast-iron plant ✳
◐ ● ◊ ✿ LS, CS, TS
Aspidistra — p. 171

Celandine poppy ✳
◐ ● ◊ ✿ US, MS, LS, CS
Stylophorum diphyllum — p. 605

Chinese foxglove ✳
◐ ◊ ✿ MS, LS, CS, TS
Rehmannia elata — p. 539

Clivia ✳
◐ ● ◊ ✿ TS
Clivia miniata — p. 247

Columbine ✳
☼ ☼ ◐ ◊ ✿ VARY
Aquilegia — p. 160

Coral bells ✳
☼ ◐ ● ◊ ✿ US, MS, LS
Heuchera — p. 354

Corydalis ✳
◐ ◊ ✿ US, MS, LS
— p. 258

Cranesbill ✳
☼ ◐ ● ◊ ✿ US, MS, LS
Geranium — p. 326

Crested iris ✳
◐ ● ◊ ✿ US, MS, LS, CS
Iris cristata — p. 381

Cyclamen ✳
☼ ◐ ● ◊ ✿ VARY
— p. 268

Elephant's ear ✳
◐ ● ◊ ✿ LS, CS, TS
Colocasia esculenta — p. 250

Epimedium ✳
☼ ◐ ● ◊ ✿ US, MS, LS
— p. 296

Erythronium ✳
◐ ● ◊ ✿ VARY
— p. 302

False solomon's seal ✳
◐ ● ◊ ✿ US, MS, LS
Maianthemum racemosa — p. 428

False spiraea ✳
☼ ◐ ● ◊ ✿ US, MS, LS
Astilbe — p. 172

Fancy-leafed caladium ✳
◐ ☼ ● ◊ ✿ CS, TS
Caladium bicolor — p. 202

Ferns ✳
◐ ● ● ◊ ✿ VARY
(Many kinds) — p. 173

Filipendula ✳
☼ ◐ ● ◊ ✿ US, MS, LS
— p. 316

Foamflower ✳
☼ ◐ ● ◊ ✿ US, MS, LS
Tiarella — p. 620

Foxglove ✳
☼ ◐ ● ◊ ✿ US, MS, LS, CS
Digitalis — p. 285

Galax ✳
◐ ● ◊ ✿ US, MS, LS
Galax urceolata — p. 322

Ginger lily ✳
☼ ◐ ● ◊ ✿ VARY
Hedychium — p. 344

Yellow corydalis
Corydalis lutea

Columbine
Aquilegia McKana Giants strain

Crested iris
Iris cristata

Japanese painted fern
Athyrium niponicum 'Pictum'

Foxglove, common
Digitalis purpurea

For climate zone explanations, please see pages 38–39.

Creeping Jacob's ladder
Polemonium reptans

Japanese primrose
Primula japonica

Lady's-mantle
Alchemilla mollis

Oxalis

Globeflower ✳
☼ ◑ ● ◢ ✄ US, MS
Trollius · p. 628

Goat's beard ✳
☼ ◑ ● ◢ ✄ VARY
Aruncus · p. 167

Golden ray ✳
◑ ● ◢ ✄ US, MS, LS
Ligularia · p. 409

Golden seal
◑ ● ◢ ✄ US, MS
Hydrastis canadensis · p. 366

Golden star ✳
◑ ● ◢ ✄ US, MS, LS, CS
Chrysogonum virginianum · p. 237

Greater celandine ✳
◑ ● ◢ ◈ ✄ US, MS, LS
Chelidonium majus · p. 231

Impatiens ✳
☼ ◑ ● ◢ ◈ ✄ ALL
· p. 373

Jack-in-the-pulpit ✳
◑ ● ◢ ✄ US, MS, LS, CS
Arisaema · p. 164

Jacob's ladder ✳
◑ ● ◢ ✄ US, MS, LS
Polemonium · p. 515

Japanese coltsfoot
◑ ● ◢ ✄ US, MS, LS, CS
Petasites japonicus · p. 491

Japanese forest grass
◑ ● ◢ ✄ US, MS, LS
Hakonechloa macra · p. 341

Japanese primrose ✳
◑ ● ◢ ✄ US, MS, LS
Primula japonica · p. 521

Lady's-mantle
◑ ● ◢ ✄ US, MS, LS
Alchemilla mollis · p. 142

Liverwort ✳
◑ ● ◢ ✄ US, MS, LS, CS
Hepatica · p. 352

Lobelia ✳
☼ ◑ ● ◢ ◈ ✄ VARY
· p. 417

Lungwort ✳
◑ ● ◢ ✄ US, MS, LS
Pulmonaria · p. 528

Mayapple
◑ ● ◢ ◈ ✄ US, MS, LS, CS
Podophyllum peltatum · p. 514

Meadow rue ✳
◑ ● ◢ ✄ VARY
Thalictrum · p. 616

Neoregelia
☼ ◯ ◑ ● ◢ ✄ TS OR INDOORS
· p. 450

Oxalis ✳
☼ ◑ ● ◢ ✄ VARY
· p. 464

Palm grass
☼ ◑ ● ◢ ✄ CS, TS
Setaria palmifolia · p. 587

Partridgeberry
◑ ● ◢ ✄ US, MS, LS, CS
Mitchella repens · p. 439

Peace lily ✳
◑ ● ◢ ✄ TS OR INDOORS
Spathiphyllum · p. 595

Peacock ginger ✳
● ◢ ✄ CS, TS
Kaempferia · p. 388

Piggyback plant
◑ ● ◢ ◢ ✄ TS OR INDOORS
Tolmiea menziesii · p. 622

Plantain lily ✳
◑ ● ◢ ✄ US, MS, LS
Hosta · p. 359

River oats
☼ ◑ ● ◢ ✄ US, MS, LS, CS
Chasmanthium latifolium · p. 230

Sedge
☼ ◑ ◯ ◑ ◢ ◢ ◢ ✄ US, MS, LS, CS
Carex · p. 216

Solomon's seal
◑ ● ◢ ✄ US, MS, LS
Polygonatum · p. 516

Strawberry geranium ✳
◑ ● ◢ ✄ MS, LS, CS OR INDOORS
Saxifraga stolonifera · p. 577

Sweet flag
◑ ● ◢ ✄ US, MS, LS, CS
Acorus · p. 132

Toad lily ✳
◑ ● ◢ ◢ ✄ US, MS, LS, CS
Tricyrtis · p. 626

Tradescantia ✳
☼ ◑ ● ◢ ◢ ◢ ✄ VARY
· p. 626

Twinleaf ✳
◑ ● ◢ ✄ US, MS
Jeffersonia diphylla · p. 384

Viola ✳
☼ ◑ ● ◢ ✄ VARY
Viola · p. 641

Virginia bluebells ✳
◑ ● ✄ US, MS, LS
Mertensia virginica · p. 436

Wake robin ✳
◑ ● ◢ ✄ US, MS, LS
Trillium · p. 627

Wild ginger
◑ ● ◢ ◢ ✄ VARY
Asarum · p. 168

River oats
Chasmanthium latifolium

Toad lily
Tricyrtis hirta

Viola

Wake robin
Trillium

For growing symbol explanations, please see page 37.

Plants that Tolerate
Drought

With water conservation becoming a front-page issue in the South, it only makes sense to try to include in your garden plants that sip, rather than guzzle. Fortunately, many plants, once established, grow just fine with infrequent watering. Here are some proven performers. The symbol ✻ indicates plants have showy flowers.

Bougainvillea

Baily acacia
Acacia bailyana

Lilac chaste tree
Vitex agnus-castus

Chitalpa
Chitalpa tashkentensis

Eastern redbud
Cercis canadensis

TREES

Acacia ✻
☀ ◐ ✂ VARY
p. 126

Arizona cypress
☀ ◌ ◗ ✂ MS, LS, CS
Cupressus arizonica p. 267

Ash
☀ ◌ ◐ ◗ ✂ VARY
Fraxinus (most) p. 319

Caddo maple
☀ ◐ ◗ ◗ ✂ US, MS, LS
Acer saccharum 'Caddo' p. 130

Caesalpinia ✻
☀ ◌ ◐ ◗ ✂ VARY
p. 201

Cedar
☀ ◐ ✂ VARY
Cedrus p. 222

Chaste tree ✻
☀ ◐ ◗ ✂ US, MS, LS, CS
Vitex p. 643

Chinese elm
☀ ◗ ✂ US, MS, LS, CS
Ulmus parvifolia p. 632

Chinese pistache
☀ ◗ ✂ US, MS, LS, CS
Pistacia chinensis p. 506

Chitalpa ✻
☀ ◌ ◐ ✂ US, MS, LS, CS
x Chitalpa tashkentensis p. 234

Crepe myrtle ✻
☀ ◌ ◗ ✂ US, MS, LS, CS
Lagerstroemia indica p. 395

Desert willow ✻
☀ ◌ ◗ ✂ MS, LS, CS
Chilopsis linearis p. 233

Eastern redbud ✻
☀ ◐ ◐ ◗ ✂ US, MS, LS, CS
Cercis canadensis p. 227

Eastern red cedar
☀ ◌ ◗ ◗ ✂ ALL
Juniperus virginiana p. 387

Gold medallion tree ✻
☀ ◌ ◗ ✂ TS
Cassia leptophylla p. 219

Goldenrain tree ✻
☀ ◌ ◗ ✂ US, MS, LS, CS
Koelreuteria paniculata p. 393

Hackberry
☀ ◐ ◗ ✂ US, MS, LS, CS
Celtis p. 224

Honey locust
☀ ◗ ◗ ✂ US, MS, LS
Gleditsia triacanthos p. 331

Italian cypress
☀ ◌ ◗ ✂ MS, LS, CS
Cupressus sempervirens p. 267

Japanese pagoda tree ✻
☀ ◐ ◗ ✂ US, MS, LS
Styphnolobium japonicum p. 605

Jerusalem thorn ✻
☀ ◌ ◗ ◗ ✂ LS, CS, TS
Parkinsonia aculeata p. 472

Kentucky coffee tree
☀ ◗ ◗ ✂ US, MS, LS
Gymnocladus dioica p. 339

Locust ✻
☀ ◌ ◗ ◗ ◗ ✂ US, MS, LS, CS
Robinia p. 550

Maidenhair tree
☀ ◗ ◗ ✂ US, MS, LS
s biloba p. 329

Mesquite
☀ ◌ ✂ MS, LS, CS, TS
Prosopis glandulosa p. 522

Oak
☀ ◗ ✂ VARY
Quercus (some) p. 532

Olive
☀ ◌ ◗ ✂ LS, CS
Olea p. 458

Japanese pagoda tree
Sophora japonica

Crepe myrtle
Lagerstroemia indica

Idaho locust
Robinia x ambigua 'Idaho'

Jerusalem thorn
Parkinsonia aculeata

For climate zone explanations, please see pages 38–39.

Sumac
Rhus

Agave

Aloe

Blue mist
Caryopteris x clandonensis

Broom
Cytisus

Pine
:☼: ◐ ● ● 🌢 ⚡ VARY
Pinus (many)   p. 504

Russian olive
:☼: ◐◐ ● ● 🌢 ⚡ US, MS
Elaeagnus angustifolia   p. 294

Strawberry tree
:☼: ◐◐ ● 🌢 ⚡ MS, LS, CS
Arbutus unedo   p. 162

Sumac
:☼: ◐ ● 🌢 ⚡ VARY
Rhus   p. 549

Windmill palm
:☼: ◐ ● 🌢 ⚡ LS, CS, TS
Trachycarpus fortunei   p. 625

SHRUBS AND SHRUBLIKE

Agave   ✳
:☼: ◐◐ ● 🌢 ⚡ CS, TS
                                          p. 137

Aloe   ✳
:☼: ◐◐ ● 🌢 ⚡ TS
                                          p. 144

Barberry
:☼: ◐◐ ● 🌢 ⚡ VARY
Berberis   p. 184

Bay
:☼: ◐◐ 🌢 ⚡ LS, CS, TS
Laurus nobilis   p. 403

Blue mist   ✳
:☼: ● 🌢 ⚡ US, MS, LS, CS
Caryopteris clandonensis   p. 219

Broom   ✳
:☼: ◐ 🌢 ⚡ US, MS, LS
Cytisus   p. 271

Bush daisy   ✳
:☼: ◐ ● 🌢 ⚡ CS, TS OR ANNUAL
Euryops pectinatus   p. 309

Butterfly bush   ✳
:☼: ◐◐ ● 🌢 ⚡ VARY
Buddleia   p. 197

Cape plumbago   ✳
:☼: ◐◐ ● ● 🌢 ⚡ CS, TS
Plumbago auriculata   p. 513

Chinese photinia   ✳
:☼: ● 🌢 ⚡ US, MS, LS, CS
Photinia serratifolia   p. 500

Cotoneaster   ✳
:☼: ◐ ● 🌢 ⚡ VARY
                                          p. 260

Elaeagnus (some)
:☼: ◐◐ ● ● 🌢 ⚡ VARY
                                          p. 294

Feijoa, pineapple guava   ✳
:☼: ● 🌢 ⚡ LS, CS, TS
                                          p. 312

Firethorn   ✳
:☼: ◐ 🌢 ⚡ VARY
Pyracantha   p. 530

Flowering quince   ✳
:☼: ◐ ● 🌢 ⚡ US, MS, LS, CS
Chaenomeles   p. 228

Germander
:☼: ◐ 🌢 ⚡ US, MS, LS, CS
Teucrium chamaedrys   p. 615

Grevillea   ✳
:☼: ◐◐ ● ● 🌢 ⚡ VARY
                                          p. 338

Holly
:☼: ● 🌢 ◢ ⚡ VARY
Ilex   p. 369

Indian hawthorn   ✳
:☼: ◐◐ ● ● 🌢 ⚡ LS, CS, TS
Rhaphiolepis indica   p. 540

Japanese fatsia
◐ ● ● 🌢 ⚡ LS, CS, TS
Fatsia japonica   p. 312

Japanese pittosporum
:☼: ◐◐ ● 🌢 ⚡ LS, CS, TS
Pittosporum tobira   p. 507

Juniper
:☼: ◐ ● 🌢 ⚡ VARY
Juniperus (some)   p. 385

Lemon bottlebrush   ✳
:☼: ● 🌢 ⚡ LS, CS, TS
Callistemon citrinus   p. 206

Mahonia (most)   ✳
:☼: ◐● ● ● 🌢 ⚡ VARY
                                          p. 427

Mediterranean fan palm
:☼: ◐ ● ● 🌢 ⚡ LS, CS, TS
Chamaerops humilis   p. 230

Myrtle   ✳
:☼: ◐◐ ● 🌢 ⚡ LS, CS, TS
Myrtus communis   p. 445

Nandina
:☼: ◐● ● ● 🌢 ⚡ US, MS, LS, CS
Nandina domestica   p. 445

Needle palm
:☼: ● ● ● 🌢 ◐ ⚡ ALL
Rhapidophyllum hystrix   p. 540

Oleander   ✳
:☼: ◐ ● ● 🌢 ◐ ⚡ LS, CS, TS
Nerium oleander   p. 452

Pearl bush   ✳
:☼: ● 🌢 ⚡ US, MS, LS
Exochorda   p. 310

Pomegranate   ✳
:☼: ● 🌢 ⚡ MS, LS, CS, TS
                                          p. 517

Prickly pear cactus   ✳
:☼: ◐ ⚡ VARY
Opuntia   p. 460

Butterfly bush
Buddleia

Strawberry tree
Arbutus unedo

Japanese fatsia
Fatsia japonica

Myrtle
Myrtus communis

New Zealand tea tree
Leptospermum scoparium

For growing symbol explanations, please see page 37.

Pomegranate
Punica granatum

Rockrose
Cistus

Rose of Sharon
Hibiscus syriacus

Rugosa rose
Rosa rugosa

Smoke tree
Cotinus coggygria

Rockrose ☀
☀/◐/💧 LS, CS
Cistus — p. 238

Rose of Sharon ☀
☀◐💧💦 US, MS, LS, CS
Hibiscus syriacus — p. 357

Rosemary ☀
☀◐💧💦 ALL
Rosmarinus officinalis — p. 561

Rugosa rose ☀
☀◐💧💦 US, MS, LS, CS
Rosa rugosa — p. 560

Sago palm
☀💧💦 CS, TS
Cycas revoluta — p. 268

Saltbush
☀ ◐ 💧💦 US, MS, LS, CS
Baccharis halimifolia — p. 175

Senna (some) ☀
☀◐💧💦 VARY
— p. 586

Screw bean
☀◐💦 MS, LS, CS, TS
Prosopis pubescens — p. 522

Smoke tree ☀
☀💧💦 US, MS, LS
Cotinus — p. 260

Sotol
☀◐◐💧💦 VARY
Dasylirion — p. 275

Sumac
☀◐💦 VARY
Rhus — p. 549

Texas ranger ☀
☀◐💧💦 LS, CS, TS
Leucophyllum frutescens — p. 408

Thorny elaeagnus
☀◐◐💧💦 US, MS, LS, CS
Elaeagnus pungens — p. 294

Wax myrtle
☀◐💧💦 MS, LS, CS, TS
Morella cerifera — p. 441

Woadwaxen ☀
☀◐💧💦 VARY
Genista — p. 326

Yellow bells ☀
☀◐💧💦 CS, TS
Tecoma stans — p. 614

VINES AND GROUNDCOVERS

Armand clematis ☀
☀◐💧💦 MS, LS, CS
Clematis armandii — p. 243

Beach morning glory ☀
☀◐💧💦 CS, TS
Ipomoea pes-caprae — p. 376

Bittersweet
☀◐💦 US, MS, LS
Celastrus — p. 223

Boston ivy
☀◐◐💦 US, MS, LS
Parthenocissus tricuspidata — p. 473

Bougainvillea ☀
☀◐💧💦 CS, TS
— p. 191

Carolina jessamine ☀
☀◐◐💧💦◐💦 MS, LS, CS
Gelsemium sempervirens — p. 325

Coral vine ☀
☀◐💧💦 LS, CS, TS
Antigonon leptopus — p. 153

Crossvine ☀
☀◐💧💦 US, MS, LS, CS
Bignonia capreolata — p. 187

Ice plant ☀
☀◐💧💦 US, MS, LS, CS
Delosperma — p. 277

Jackson vine
☀◐💧💦 MS, LS, CS
Smilax smallii — p. 590

Lady Banks's rose ☀
☀◐💧💦 LS, CS, TS
Rosa banksiae — p. 558

Lamb's ears ☀
☀◐💦 US, MS, LS
Stachys byzantina — p. 599

Pink trumpet vine ☀
☀◐💧💦 CS, TS
Podranea ricasoliana — p. 515

Porcelain berry
☀◐💧💦 US, MS, LS, CS
Ampelopsis brevipedunculata — p. 148

Potato vine ☀
☀◐💧💦◐💦 CS, TS
Solanum jasminoides — p. 591

Silver lace vine ☀
☀◐💦 US, MS, LS
Fallopia baldschuanica — p. 311

Snow-in-summer ☀
☀◐💦 US, MS, LS
Cerastium tomentosum — p. 226

Sweet autumn clematis ☀
☀◐💦 US, MS, LS, CS
Clematis terniflora — p. 244

Trumpet creeper, common ☀
☀◐💧💦 US, MS, LS, CS
Campsis radicans — p. 214

Virginia creeper ☀
☀◐💧💦 US, MS, LS, CS
Parthenocissus quinquefolia — p. 473

Wisteria ☀
☀◐💦 US, MS, LS, CS
— p. 645

Bougainvillea

Coral vine
Antignon leptopus

Potato vine
Solanum jasminoides

Trumpet creeper, common
Campsis radicans

For climate zone explanations, please see pages 38–39.

Coreopsis
Coreopsis grandiflora
'Early Sunrise'

Blazing star
Liatris spicata 'Kobold'

Blue fescue
Festuca glauca

EVERGREEN SHRUBS, PERENNIALS, BULBS, ANNUALS

African daisy
☀☀◐◑❀ ALL
Arctotis — p. 162

Agave
☀ ☀◑◑◑❀ CS, TS
— p. 137

Angelonia
☀☀◑❀ ALL
Angelonia angustifolia — p. 151

Apache plume
☀☀◯ ALL
Fallugia paradoxa — p. 311

Artemisia
☀☀◯ ◑❀ VARY
— p. 165

Baby's breath
☀☀◑❀ US, MS, LS, CS
Gypsophila paniculata — p. 340

Bear grass
☀☀◯ ◑❀ LS, CS, TS
Nolinia erumpens — p. 454

Beard tongue
☀◑◑❀ VARY
Penstemon — p. 486

Black-eyed Susan
☀☀◑❀ ALL
Rudbeckia hirta — p. 563

Blackfoot daisy
☀☀◑❀ ALL
Melampodium leucanthum — p. 435

Blanket flower
☀☀◯◑❀ ALL
Gaillardia — p. 321

Blazing star
☀☀◯◑◑❀ US, MS, LS, CS
Liatris — p. 409

Blue fescue
☀☀◑◑◑❀ US, MS
Festuca glauca — p. 312

Broom sedge
☀☀◑◑❀ US, MS, LS, CS
Andropogon virginicus — p. 150

Bouvardia
◑◑◑◑◑❀ CS, TS
— p. 193

Bulbine frutescens
◑◑◑◑❀ CS, TS
— p. 198

Butterfly weed
☀☀◯◑◆❀ US, MS, LS, CS
Asclepias tuberosa — p. 168

California poppy
☀☀◯◑◑❀ ALL
Eschscholzia californica — p. 302

Cockscomb
☀☀◑❀ ALL
Celosia argentea — p. 223

Copper canyon daisy
☀☀◑◆❀ LS, CS
Tagetes lemmonii — p. 611

Coreopsis
☀☀◯◑◑❀ US, MS, LS, CS
— p. 253

Crassula
☀☀◯◑ TS
— p. 261

Daylily
☀☀◑◑❀ ALL
Hemerocallis — p. 351

Dicliptera
☀☀◯◑◑◑◑◑❀ VARY
— p. 283

Dusty miller
☀☀◯◑◑❀ MS LS CS OR ANNUAL
Senecio cineraria — p. 585

Echeveria (most)
☀☀◑◆❀ VARY
— p. 291

Euphorbia (most)
☀☀◑◑◑◑◆❀ VARY
— p. 307

False indigo
☀☀◯◑❀ US, MS, LS, CS
Baptisia — p. 179

False sunflower
☀☀◑◑◑❀ US, MS, LS, CS
Heliopsis helianthoides — p. 348

Feather grass
☀☀◯◑❀ US, MS, LS, CS
Stipa — p. 602

Fortnight lily
☀☀◯◑◑❀ LS, CS, TS
Dietes — p. 284

Fountain grass
☀☀◑◑◑❀ CS, TS
Pennisetum setaceum — p. 485

Gaura
☀☀◑◆❀ US, MS, LS, CS
Gaura lindheimeri — p. 324

Gazania daisy
☀☀ ◑◑◑◑◆❀ ALL
Gazania — p. 325

Geranium
☀◑◑◑◆❀ CS, TS OR ANNUAL
Pelargonium — p. 484

Globe amaranth
☀☀◑◆❀ ALL
Gomphrena globosa — p. 332

Golden aster
☀☀◑◑◆❀ US, MS, LS, CS
Chrysopsis — p. 237

Daylily
Hemerocallis

False sunflower
Heliopsis helianthoides

Feather grass
Stipa gigantea

Gaura
Gaura lindheimeri

Globe amaranth
Gomphrena globosa

For growing symbol explanations, please see page 37.

Iris, bearded

Lion's tail
Leonotis leonorus

Madagascar periwinkle
Catharanthus roseus

Mexican sunflower
Tithonia rotundifolia

Lily-of-the-Nile
Agapanthus
'Peter Pan'

Hedgehog cactus ✳
☼ ◐ ◌ ◓ ✂ VARY
Echinocereus   p. 292

Hummingbird mint ✳
☼ ◐ ◌ ◓ ✂ VARY
Agastache   p. 137

Iris, bearded ✳
☼ ◐ ● ● ◌ ◓ ◓ ◈ ✂ US, MS, LS, CS
   p. 378

Jerusalem sage ✳
☼ ◌ ◓ ✂ MS, LS, CS, TS
Phlomis fruticosa   p. 496

Lantana ✳
☼ ◓ ◈ ✂ LS, CS, TS
   p. 400

Lavender ✳
☼ ◓ ✂ VARY
Lavandula   p. 403

Lavender cotton ✳
☼ ◌ ◓ ✂ US, MS, LS, CS
Santolina chamaecyparissus   p. 575

Lily-of-the-Nile ✳
☼ ◐ ◌ ◌ ◓ ✂ VARY
Agapanthus   p. 136

Lion's tail ✳
☼ ◌ ✂ CS, TS
Leonotis leonorus   p. 406

Madagascar periwinkle ✳
☼ ◐ ◌ ◓ ✂ ALL
Catharanthus roseus   p. 221

Mexican sunflower ✳
☼ ◓ ✂ ALL
Tithonia rotundifolia   p. 621

Mullein ✳
☼ ◓ ✂ US, MS, LS
Verbascum   p. 634

Orange justicia ✳
☼ ◌ ✂ LS, CS, TS
Justicia leonardii   p. 387

Prickly poppy ✳
☼ ◌ ✂ ALL
Argemone   p. 163

Purple coneflower ✳
☼ ◓ ◓ ✂ US, MS, LS, CS
Echinacea purpurea   p. 292

Red-hot poker ✳
☼ ◐ ◓ ◓ ✂ VARY
Kniphofia   p. 392

Red yucca ✳
☼ ◐ ◌ ◓ ◓ ✂ MS, LS, CS, TS
Hesperaloe parviflora   p. 353

Ruby grass ✳
☼ ◓ ◓ ✂ TS
Melinis nerviglumis   p. 435

Ruellia ✳
☼ ◓ ◓ ✂ ALL
   p. 564

Russian sage ✳
☼ ◌ ◓ ✂ US, MS, LS, CS
Perovskia atriplicifolia   p. 490

Sage ✳
☼ ◓ ✂ VARY
Salvia (most)   p. 568

Silphium ✳
☼ ◓ ◓ ◓ ✂ US, MS, LS, CS
   p. 588

Silver grass ✳
☼ ◐ ◓ ◓ ✂ US, MS, LS, CS
Miscanthus   p. 438

Solomon's seal ✳
◓ ◓ ✂ US, MS, LS
Polygonatum   p. 516

Stonecrop ✳
☼ ◐ ◌ ◓ ✂ US, MS, LS
Sedum (many)   p. 581

Sundrops ✳
☼ ◐ ◌ ◓ ✂ US, MS, LS
Calylophus   p. 208

Thrift ✳
☼ ◌ ◓ ✂ VARY
Armeria   p. 165

Valerian ✳
☼ ◌ ◓ ◓ ✂ US, MS, LS
Centranthus ruber   p. 225

Verbena (most) ✳
☼ ◓ ✂ VARY
   p. 634

Wild ageratum ✳
☼ ◐ ◌ ◓ ◓ ◓ ✂ ALL
Eupatorium coelestinum   p. 306

Wild foxglove ✳
◐ ◓ ◓ ✂ US, MS, LS, CS
Penstemon cobaea   p. 486

Wine cups ✳
☼ ◓ ◓ ✂ US, MS, LS, CS
Callirhoe   p. 205

Yarrow ✳
☼ ◌ ◓ ✂ US, MS, LS
Achillea   p. 130

Yellow coneflower ✳
☼ ◓ ◓ ✂ US, MS, LS, CS
Rudbeckia fulgida   p. 563

Yucca (most) ✳
☼ ◌ ◓ ◓ ✂ VARY
   p. 647

Zinnia ✳
☼ ◓ ✂ ALL
   p. 651

Mullein
Verbascum

Ruby grass
Rhynchelytrum nerviglume

Valerian
Centranthus ruber 'Pink Crystals'

Wild foxglove
Penstemon cobaea

For climate zone explanations, please see pages 38–39.

Lupine
Lupinus,
Russell hybrid

Deer-resistant Plants

Appearances to the contrary, deer can be discriminating diners. Some plants are particular favorites; others are more or less left alone. If you live in deer country, it's far simpler to fill the garden with less-favored plants than to protect the more choice morsels. But a word of warning: Although deer generally ignore the plants listed below, their preferences vary in different areas, from year to year, and even from season to season. So don't blame us if Bambi occasionally chomps a plant on the list.

Feather reed grass
Calamagrostis x *acutiflora*
'Karl Foerster'

Arizona cypress
Cupressus arizonica

TREES

Acacia
☼ ◑ ✂ VARY
p. 126

American beech
☼ ◑ ◔ ◔ ✂ US, MS, LS, CS
Fagus grandiflora   p. 310

Ash
☼ ◑ ◔ ✂ VARY
Fraxinus   p. 319

Bald cypress
☼ ◑ ◔ ◔◔ ✂ US, MS, LS, CS
Taxodium distichum   p. 613

Bottlebrush
☼ ◔ ◔ ✂ VARY
Callistemon   p. 206

Cedar
☼ ◔ ◔ ✂ VARY
Cedrus   p. 222

Crepe myrtle
☼ ◔ ◔ ✂ US, MS, LS, CS
Lagerstroemia   p. 395

Cypress
☼ ◑ ◔ ✂ VARY
Cupressus   p. 267

Eucalyptus
☼ ◑ ✂ VARY
p. 303

False cypress
☼ ◑ ◔ ✂ US, MS, LS
Chamaecyparis   p. 229

Fig, edible
☼ ◔ ✂ MS, LS, CS, TS
p. 314

Fir
☼ ◑ ◔ ◔ ◔ ✂ VARY
Abies   p. 124

Flowering dogwood
☼ ◑ ◔ ✂ US, MS, LS, CS
Cornus florida   p. 256

Glossy privet
☼ ◑ ◔ ◊ ✂ LS, CS, TS
Ligustrum lucidum   p. 410

Gold medallion tree
☼ ◑ ◔ ✂ TS
Cassia leptophylla   p. 219

Japanese maple
☼ ◑ ◔ ◔ ✂ US, MS, LS, CS
Acer palmatum   p. 127

Live oak
☼ ◔ ✂ LS, CS, TS
Quercus virginiana   p. 535

Loquat
☼ ◑ ◔ ◔ ◔ ✂ VARY
Eriobotrya   p. 300

Magnolia
☼ ◑ ◔ ✂ VARY
p. 423

Orchid tree
☼ ◔ ◔ ✂ TS
Bauhinia   p. 179

Pine
☼ ◑ ◔ ◔ ✂ VARY
Pinus   p. 504

Palms (many)
☼ ◔ ✂ ZONES VARY
p. 498

Podocarpus
☼ ◑ ◔ ✂ VARY
p. 514

Spruce
☼ ◑ ◔ ◔ ✂ US, MS
Picea   p. 501

Texas mountain laurel
☼ ◑ ◔ ◊ ✂ LS, CS
Sophora secundiflora   p. 594

Saucer magnolia
Magnolia soulangeana

Crepe myrtle
Lagerstroemia indica

Mediterranean fan palm
Chamaerops humilis

Golden Hinoki false cypress
Chamaecyparis obtusa 'Crippsii'

Japanese black pine
Pinus thunbergii

For growing symbol explanations, please see page 37.

Flowering quince
Chaenomeles

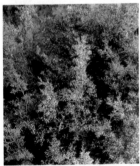

Eastern red cedar
Juniperus virginiana

Japanese kerria
Kerria japonica

SHRUBS

Abelia
☼:◖◗ VARY
p. 124

Angels trumpet
☼:◖◗ LS, CS, TS
Brugmansia
p. 195

Banana shrub
☼:◖◗ LS, CS, TS
Michelia figo
p. 424

Bamboo
☼:◖○◖◗ VARY
p. 175

Barberry
☼:◖◗ VARY
Berberis
p. 184

Bird of Paradise
☼:◖◗ VARY
Strelitzia reginae
p. 604

Butterfly bush
☼:◖◗ VARY
Buddleia
p. 197

Boxwood
☼:◖◗ VARY
Buxus
p. 199

Cape plumbago
☼:◖○◖◗ VARY
Plumbago auriculata
p. 513

Cotoneaster
☼:○◖◗ VARY
p. 260

Daphne
◖◗ VARY
p. 274

Elaeagnus
☼:○◖◗ VARY
p. 294

Feijoa, pineapple guava
☼:◗ LS, CS, TS
p. 312

Flowering quince
☼:◗ US, MS, LS, CS
Chaenomeles
p. 228

Heath
◖◗ VARY
Erica
p. 299

Holly
☼:◖◗ VARY
Ilex
p. 369

Ixora
☼:◖◗ TS
p. 382

Juniper
☼:○◖◗ VARY
Juniperus
p. 385

Japanese kerria
☼◖◗ US, MS, LS, CS
Kerria japonica
p. 390

Lantana species
☼:◖◗ LS, CS, TS
p. 400

Leatherleaf mahonia
☼:◖◗ US, MS, LS, CS
Mahonia bealei
p. 427

Nandina
☼:◖●◖◗ US, MS, LS, CS
p. 445

Natal plum
☼:○◖◗ CS, TS
Carissa macrocarpa
p. 217

Oleander
☼:○◖◗ LS, CS, TS
Nerium oleander
p. 452

Pomegranate
☼:◗ MS, LS, CS, TS
p. 517

Privet
☼:◖◗ VARY
Ligustrum
p. 410

Rockrose
☼:○ LS, CS
Cistus
p. 238

Southern Indica azalea
◖◗ MS, LS, CS
Rhododendron
p. 541

Sweet olive
☼:○◖◗ LS, CS, TS
Osmanthus fragrans
p. 463

Ti
☼: ○◖●◗ TS
Cordyline fruticosa
p. 252

Torch aloe
☼:○◖◗ TS
Aloe arborescens
p. 144

Viburnum
☼:◖◗ VARY
p. 637

Wax myrtle
☼:◖◗ MS, LS, CS, TS
Myrica cerifera
p. 441

Wild lilac
☼:○ VARY
Ceanothus
p. 222

ANNUALS, BULBS, PERENNIALS

Agave
☼:◖○◖◗ CS, TS
p. 137

African daisy
☼:◗ ALL
Dimorphotheca
p. 285

Oleander
Nerium oleander

Privet
Ligustrum japonicum 'Texanum'

Rockrose
Cistus

Tea viburnum
Viburnum setigerum

Tree aloe
Aloe arborescens

For climate zone explanations, please see pages 38–39.

Artemisia

Bear's breech
Acanthus mollis

California poppy
Eschscholzia californica

Cape plumbago
Plumbago auriculata

Coreopsis

Angelonia
☼ ◑ ✂ ALL
Angelonia angustifolia   p. 151

Angel's trumpet
☼ ◑ ✧ ✂ VARY
Datura   p. 276

Artemisia
☼ ◐ ◑ ✂ VARY
                                p. 165

Aster
☼ ◑ ◑ ✂ US, MS, LS
                                p. 172

Beard tongue
☼ ◑ ◑ ◑ ✂ VARY
Penstemon   p. 486

Bear's breeches
☼ ☼ ◑ ● ◑ ✂ US, MS, LS, CS
Acanthus mollis   p. 127

Begonia, tuberous
◑ ◑ ✂ TS OR ANNUAL
                                p. 184

Bleeding heart
◑ ● ◑ ✂ VARY
Dicentra   p. 282

Blue-eyed grass
☼ ☼ ◑ ● ◑ ◑ ✂ VARY
Sisyrinchium   p. 589

Calendula
☼ ◑ ✂ ALL
Calendula officinalis   p. 204

California poppy
☼ ◐ ◑ ◑ ✂ ALL
Eschscholzia californica   p. 302

Calla lily
☼ ☼ ◑ ✂ LS, CS, TS
Zantedeschia   p. 649

Coneflower
☼ ◑ ◑ ✂ VARY
Echinacea   p. 291

Coreopsis
☼ ◐ ◑ ◑ ✂ US, MS, LS, CS
                                p. 253

Cranesbill
☼ ◑ ◑ ✂ US, MS, LS
Geranium   p. 326

Crinum
☼ ◑ ● ◑ ✂ VARY
                                p. 263

Daffodil
☼ ◑ ● ✂ US, MS, LS, CS
Narcissus   p. 446

Dahlia
☼ ◑ ● ✂ US, MS, LS
                                p. 272

Dusty miller
☼ ◐ ◑ ✂ MS, LS, CS
Senecio cineraria   p. 585

Euphorbia
☼ ◑ ● ◑ ◑ ✧ ✂ VARY
                                p. 307

Feather grass
☼ ◑ ● ✂ US, MS, LS, CS
Stipa   p. 602

Fescue
☼ ◐ ◑ ● ✂ US, MS
Festuca   p. 312

Fleabane
☼ ◐ ◑ ✂ VARY
Erigeron   p. 299

Floss flower
☼ ◑ ● ✂ ALL
Ageratum houstonianum   p. 139

Fountain grass
☼ ◑ ● ◑ ✂ VARY
Pennisetum   p. 485

Ginger lily
☼ ◑ ● ◑ ✂ VARY
Hedychium   p. 344

Gloriosa daisy
☼ ◑ ◑ ✂ ALL
Rudbeckia hirta   p. 563

Hellebore
◑ ● ◑ ● ◑ ✧ ✂ VARY
Helleborus   p. 349

Lamb's ears
☼ ◐ ◑ ● ✂ US, MS, LS
Stachys byzantina   p. 599

Lily-of-the-Nile
☼ ◐ ◑ ◑ ◑ ✂ VARY
Agapanthus   p. 136

Lobster claw
☼ ☼ ◑ ● ✂ TS
Heliconia   p. 348

Lupine
☼ ◐ ◑ ◑ ✂ VARY
Lupinus   p. 420

Madagascar periwinkle
☼ ◐ ◑ ● ✂ ALL
Catharanthus roseus   p. 221

Maidenhair fern
◑ ● ◑ ◑ ✂ VARY
Adiantum   p. 133

Mexican mint marigold
☼ ◑ ● ✂ MS, LS, CS, TS
Tagetes lucida   p. 611

Mondo grass
◑ ● ◑ ● ◑ ✂ MS, LS, CS, TS
Ophiopogon japonicus   p. 460

Montbretia
☼ ☼ ◑ ● ✂ US, MS, LS, CS
Crocosmia x crocosmiiflora   p. 264

Opuntia (cactus)
☼ ◐ ◑ ✂ VARY
                                p. 460

Daffodil
Narcissus

Floss flower
Ageratum houstonianum

Lily-of-the-Nile
Agapanthus

Hellebore
Helleborus

Southern maidenhair fern
Adiantum capillus-veneris

For growing symbol explanations, please see page 37.

Madagascar periwinkle
Catharanthus roseus

Shirley poppy
Papaver rhoeas

Whorled clary (sage)
Salvia verticillata

Santolina
Santolina

Oregano
☼◊◐◖ VARY
Origanum   p. 460

Pampas grass
☼◊◖◖◐ VARY MS, LS, CS, TS
Cortaderia selloana   p. 258

Peace lily
◐◖◐ TS
Spathiphyllum   p. 595

Petunia x hybrida
☼◖◐ ALL
                                                  p. 492

Philodendron
☼◐◖ VARY
                                                  p. 495

Polystichum (ferns)
◐◖◐ VARY
                                                  p. 517

Poppy
☼◖◐ VARY
Papaver   p. 470

Reed grass
☼◐◖◐◐ US, MS, LS, CS
Calamagroslis   p. 202

Rosemary
☼◊◖◐ ALL
Rosmarinus officinalis   p. 561

Sage
☼◖◐ VARY
Salvia   p. 568

Santolina
☼◊◖◐ US, MS, LS, CS
                                                  p. 574

Sedge
☼◐◊◖◐◐◐ US, MS, LS, CS
Carex   p. 216

Shasta daisy
☼◐◖◐ US, MS, LS, CS
Chrysanthemum maximum   p. 237

Silver grass
☼◐◖◐ US, MS, LS, CS
Miscanthus   p. 438

Snapdragon
☼◊◖◐◐ ALL
Antirrhinum majus   p. 153

Snow-in-summer
◐◖◐ US, MS, LS
Cerastium tomentosum   p. 226

Society garlic
☼◖◐ MS, LS, CS, TS
Tulbaghia violacea   p. 629

Sweet violet
◐◖◐ US, MS, LS
Viola odorata   p. 642

Sword fern
◐◖◐ TS
Nephrolepis   p. 451

Wake robin
◐◖◐ US, MS, LS
Trillium   p. 627

Thyme
☼◐◖◐ VARY
Thymus   p. 619

Turk's cap
◐◖◊◖◐◐ LS, CS, TS
Malvaviscus arboreus drummondii   p. 430

Valerian
☼◐◖◊◐ US, MS, LS
Centranthus ruber   p. 225

Wallflower
☼◐◖◐◐ VARY
Erysimum   p. 301

Wandering jew
◐◖◐ TS
Tradescantia zebrina   p. 626

Yarrow
☼◊◖◐ US, MS, LS
Achillea   p. 130

Yucca
☼◊◖◐ VARY
                                                  p. 647

VINES

Allamanda
☼◖◐ TS OR ANNUALS
                                                  p. 142

Bougainvillea
☼◖◐ CS, TS
                                                  p. 191

Carolina jassamine
☼◖◐ MS, LS, CS
Gelsemium sepervirens   p. 325

Crossvine
☼◐◖◐ US, MS, LS, CS
Bignonia capreolata   p. 187

English ivy
◐◖◐◐ ALL
Hedera helix   p. 344

Jackson vine
☼◖◐ MS, LS, CS
Smilax smallii   p. 590

Jasmine
☼◐◖◐ VARY
Jasminium   p. 382

Star jasmine
☼◐◖◐ LS, CS, TS
Trachelospermum   p. 625

Trumpet creeper
☼◖◐ VARY
Campsis   p. 214

Wisteria
☼◊◖◐ US, MS, LS, CS
                                                  p. 645

Thyme
Thymus vulgaris

Wallflower
Erysimum 'Bowles Mauve'

Common yarrow
Achillea millefolium

English ivy
Hedera helix

Chinese wisteria
Wisteria sinensis 'Alba'

For climate zone explanations, please see pages 38–39.

THE
SOUTH'S
BEST
PLANTS,
A to Z

THE SOUTHERN PLANT ENCYCLOPEDIA

This section is the heart of our book. It's the most comprehensive guide to what you can grow in the South today, covering both tried-and-true favorites from yesteryear to the latest and greatest of right now. Most of these plants are available in garden centers. Others can be ordered from online nurseries or shared by a friend. And a few are Southern icons not meant to be grown in your garden, but to be admired in nature as evocative symbols of home.

Fruits, nuts, and vegetables, such as apple, pecan, and tomato, are listed at the top of each entry by common name. Ornamental plants and herbs are listed by botanical names, such as *Thymus* (thyme) and *Acer* (maple). Don't sweat the Latin – you'll find both botanical and common names in the index in the back of the book to help you find the right plant.

Each plant mentioned comes with a climate zone rating, telling you where you can grow it. *Southern Living* has traditionally divided our regions into five growing zones – the Upper South, Middle South, Lower South, Coastal South, and Tropical South. In this revision, we've added United States Department of Agriculture (USDA) zones ratings for folks who prefer using them. See our new climate map on pages 38–39 to understand how the two rating systems work together.

A

HOW TO READ A PLANT ENTRY

Each entry begins with the information shown in the example below. Introductory text describes the plant and lists recommended selections, some in chart form. Finally, many entries include a section titled "Care" or "How to Grow," which gives guidelines on everything from soil and fertilizer requirements to dealing with common pests and diseases.

GENUS
COMMON NAME(S)
Family
Plant Type

ACONITUM
ACONITE, MONKSHOOD
Ranunculaceae
Perennials

⚏ **US, MS; USDA 6-7**

☼ ◑ **FULL SUN OR PARTIAL SHADE**

💧 **REGULAR WATER**

⬧ **ALL PARTS ARE POISONOUS IF INGESTED; WEAR GLOVES AND AVOID SKIN CONTACT**

CLIMATE
⚏ *Southern Living* climate zones where the plant grows best (see pages 38–39). USDA Zone equivalents are also provided.

EXPOSURE
☼ Plant grows best with unobstructed sunlight all or almost all day.

◑ Plant needs partial shade (some shade for half the day or at least for 3 hours during the hottest part of the day). Some listings contain qualifications, such as "partial shade in hottest climates."

● Plan needs shade all day.

For more detailed information about sun exposure, see the "Protect" section of "Gardening, Start to Finish."

WATERING
◌ Plant is quite drought-tolerant. Some drough-tolerant plants may need no irrigation once established; others may need a little.

◖ Plant needs less than regular moisture, perhaps a deep soaking every 2 or 3 weeks.

💧 Plant requires regular moisture, perhaps once a week, or more in hot weather; soil shouldn't be too dry or too wet.

💧💧 Plant needs ample moisture at all times.

A range of moisture needs may be indicated for plants that adapt to more or less water. More information on watering may be found in the "How to Grow" and/or "Care" sections.

TOXICITY
⬧ Some part of the plant is known to have toxic or irritant properties.

Aconitum carmichaelii
'Pink Sensation'

Difficult plants to grow in most of the South, as they dislike extended summer heat, drought, and mild winters. Sow seeds in moist, fertile, well-drained soil in late summer or autumn for flowers the following year. Seedlings started in spring may take a year to bloom. Aconite combines effectively with hosta, ferns, meadow rue (*Thalictrum*), and astilbe in lightly shaded gardens; it can also substitute for delphinium in shade. Plants are seldom browsed by deer.

ABELIA

Caprifoliaceae

Evergreen, semievergreen, deciduous shrubs

 ZONES VARY BY SPECIES

☼ ◑ **BEST IN SUN, TOLERATE SOME SHADE, EXCEPT AS NOTED**

💧 **REGULAR WATER**

Abelia

This old-fashioned favorite has renewed popularity due to its more compact selections, deer resistance, and abundant blooms that attract butterflies. The graceful, arching branches are densely set with oval, glossy, ½- to 1½-inch-long leaves that emerge a handsome bronze and then turn green. Tubular or bell-shaped blossoms cluster among the leaves or at ends of branches, typically from spring until fall.

To retain abelia's naturally graceful shape, use hand pruners to cut a few of the main stems to the ground each winter or early spring. This produces more of the vigorous, arching stems that create the plant's pleasing form. Do not shear.

Include abelias in shrub borders, or use them as foundation plantings or informal hedges and screens. Low-growing kinds are useful for slopes and as ground cover. *A. chinensis* is showy enough in flower to be used as a specimen plant, either in the garden or in a large container.

A. chinensis. CHINESE ABELIA. Semievergreen. Zones US, MS, LS; USDA 6-8. Chinese native growing to 5–7 ft. tall and wide, with showy, fragrant, pink-tinted white flowers clustered at the ends of the branches from early summer until frost. 'Ruby Anniversary' has foliage that is darker and thicker.

A. 'Edward Goucher'. Evergreen to semievergreen. Zones US, MS, LS, CS; USDA 6-9. Resembles *A. x grandiflora* but is less hardy, lacier, and more compact, to 3–5 ft. tall and wide. Bears small, lilac-pink flowers with orange throats.

A. floribunda. MEXICAN ABELIA. Evergreen. Zones LS (protected), CS; USDA 8-9. Native to Mexico. Usually 3–6 ft. tall; sometimes up to 10 ft. tall and 12 ft. wide. Arching, reddish, downy or hairy stems. Pendulous reddish purple flowers appear singly or in clusters. Heaviest bloom is in summer, with sporadic bloom during rest of year. Needs partial shade in hottest climates.

A. x grandiflora. GLOSSY ABELIA. Evergreen to semievergreen. Zones US, MS, LS, CS; USDA 6-9. This cross between two Chinese species is the best known and most popular of the abelias. To 8 ft. or taller, spreading to 5 ft. or wider. Flowers white or faintly tinged pink. Leaves may take on bronzy tints in fall. Loses most of its leaves at 15°F. Freezes to the ground at 0°F but usually recovers to bloom the same year, making a graceful border plant 10–15 in. high. The following are among the selections grown.

'Bronze Anniversary'. Mounding form to 3–4 ft. tall and wide. Leaves emerge bronze and then fade to a showy golden lime-green for the remainder of the season. White flowers continue all summer.

'Canyon Creek'. Showy bronze foliage in spring and fall, turning green in summer. Grows 4–6 ft. tall and wide. Fragrant pink flowers.

'Francis Mason'. Compact, to 3–4 ft. high and wide and densely branched, with pink flowers and yellow-variegated leaves.

'Golden Fleece'. Compact mound growing 4–5 ft. tall and wide. Bronze new leaves turn yellow and then light green. Fragrant, pale pink flowers.

'John Creech'. Dense mound to 4 ft. tall and wide, with dark green foliage and white flowers.

'Kaleidoscope'. Compact, 2–3 ft. tall, 3–4 feet wide, with bright red stems. Yellow variegated leaves pick up orange and red tones in fall. White flowers.

'Little Richard'. Dense and compact growth 2–3 ft. high and wide. Shiny dark green leaves that hold on for a long time even in cold winters. White flowers.

'Prostrata'. Low grower, 1–2 ft. tall, spreading 4–5 ft. wide, useful as ground cover, bank planting, or foreground shrub. White flowers.

'Rose Creek'. Compact, growing 2–3 ft. tall and wide with dark green leaves. White flowers.

'Sherwoodii'. Dense, compact, refined growth to 3–4 ft. tall, 5 ft. wide. Pale lavender-pink flowers.

'Sunrise'. Densely branched, 3–6 ft. tall and wide, with gold-edged green leaves that turn red and purple in fall. White flowers.

A. mosanensis. FRAGRANT ABELIA. Deciduous. Zones US, MS, LS, CS; USDA 6-9. Korean native to 5–6 ft. high and wide. Rich pink buds opening to sweet-scented white flowers. Blooms in late spring, early summer. Foliage turns orange-red in autumn.

ABELMOSCHUS

Malvaceae

Perennials grown as annuals

✎ **US, MS, LS, CS, TS; USDA 6-11**

☼ **FULL SUN**

💧 **REGULAR WATER**

Abelmoschus manihot

In bloom, these Asian natives are reminiscent of tropical hibiscus and okra, to which they are related. (In fact, okra—*A. esculentus*—belongs to the same genus; for information, see Okra.) Deeply cut leaves and large,

showy flowers are their hallmarks. Commonly grown as annuals, they thrive in high heat, humidity, and good, fertile soil.

A. manihot. SUNSET MUSKMALLOW. To 6 ft. or taller, 2–3 ft. wide. Large, coarse leaves and 3- to 5-in., cream to deep yellow flowers with maroon central blotch. Cooked leaves are edible and high in Vitamins A and C and iron.

A. moschatus. SILK FLOWER. Bushy plant about 1½ ft. high and wide, with deep green leaves. Five-petaled, 3- to 4-in., cherry-red or deep pink blooms. Can be grown as a houseplant in 6-in. pot; set on a windowsill in bright light.

ABIES

FIR

Pinaceae

Evergreen trees

✎ **ZONES VARY BY SPECIES**

☼ ◑ **FULL SUN OR LIGHT SHADE**

💧 **MODERATE TO REGULAR WATER**

Abies fraseri

Firs are handsome, erect, symmetrical trees with branches in regularly spaced whorls. Needles are short (mostly in the 1- to 2-in. range) and closely set along the branches; they're often banded white on the undersides. Attractive cones of most types grow 2–5 in. long.

Many people confuse firs with spruces (*Picea*), but the two are easily distinguished. Fir needles are typically soft and pull cleanly from the stem; spruce needles have sharp points and pull off with a piece of stalk. Also, fir cones stand upright, while spruce cones hang down.

With the exception of the Appalachian region, the South is generally a difficult environment for firs. They dislike summer heat and drought and heavy, poorly drained soils. Success depends on having rich, deep, well-drained soil, providing light shade in the afternoon, and replenishing mulch regularly to keep roots moist and cool. Firs are popular Christmas trees, both live and cut.

A. balsamea balsamea. BALSAM FIR. Zone US; USDA 6. Native to Northeast. Pyramidal tree to 50 ft. tall and 20 ft. wide; ½- to 1-in.-long, dark green needles. Legendary fragrance makes it a favorite for Christmas trees, wreaths. Use dwarf 'Nana' in rock gardens, containers.

A. balsamea phanerolepis. CANAAN FIR. Zone US; USDA 6. Native to the mountains of Virginia and West Virginia. Medium-size, growing 40–55 ft. tall and 20–25 ft. wide with dark to blue-green foliage, owing to silver line on the ¾- to 1½-in.-long needles. Desirable for its adaptability to seasonally wet soil, but it thrives where soil is moist year-round. Grown for Christmas trees but deserves a place in the garden.

A. concolor. WHITE FIR. Zones US, MS; USDA 6-7. Native to mountain regions of West and Southwest but tolerates hot, humid summers better than most firs. Grows 50–70 ft. tall and 15 ft. wide in gardens. Bluish green, 1- to 2-in.-long needles. 'Candicans' is bluish white.

A. firma. JAPANESE FIR, MOMI FIR. Zones US, MS, LS, CS; USDA 6-9. Native to Japan. Broadly pyramidal to 40–50 ft. tall and about half as wide, with branches held slightly above horizontal. Needles are 1–1½ in. long, dark green above, lighter beneath; unlike needles of other firs, they are very sharp at the tips. Can tolerate hot, moist climates.

A. fraseri. FRASER FIR, SOUTHERN FIR. Zone US; USDA 6. Native to higher, cooler elevations of the Appalachian Mountains. Attractive pyramidal tree resembling *A. balsamea* in both looks and fragrance. Widely grown as a Christmas tree where summers are not too hot.

A. homolepis. NIKKO FIR. Zones US, MS; USDA 6-7. Native to Japan. Broad, dense, rather formal-looking fir to 80 ft. tall and 20 ft. wide. Dark green, ½- to 1-in.

needles are densely arranged and point toward ends of branches. Adapted to warm, moist regions. 'Prostrata' is a low, spreading form that reaches 5–10 ft. tall and wide in 10 years.

ABUTILON
FLOWERING MAPLE
Malvaceae
Evergreen shrubs

🌡 **LS, CS, TS; USDA 8-11, EXCEPT AS NOTED; OR GROW IN POTS**

◑ **PARTIAL SHADE IN HOTTEST CLIMATES**

◌◌ **MODERATE TO REGULAR WATER**

Abutilon hybrid

Long a favorite in Florida gardens, flowering maples continue to win new fans in other regions of the South. This group of semitropical shrubs grows quickly and produces attractive blooms nearly continuously in warm weather. Provide moist, fertile, well-drained soil; watch out for whiteflies and scale insects. Excellent in containers on porch, deck, or patio; in cold-winter areas, bring inside to a sunny window before frost. Easily propagated from cuttings taken from current season's growth. Do not overfeed with nitrogen or you'll get lots of leaves and few flowers. In areas where cold hardiness is questionable, be sure plants have good drainage in winter.

A. hybrids. Also grown as annuals in colder climates. The best-known flowering maples. Upright, arching growth to 4–10 ft. tall, with equal spread. Broad, maple-like leaves can reach 8 in. across; drooping, bell-like, 2- to 3-in. flowers come in white, yel-

low, pink, or red. The following are all good choices.

'Bartley Schwartz'. Arching and weeping, with nearly constant production of orange-yellow, drooping blossoms. Good hanging basket plant or standard.

Bella series. Assorted colors, seed grown. 3-in. flowers on plants 14–18 in. tall.

'Boule de Neige'. Large, vigorous, upright plant with white flowers.

'Canary Bird'. 3-in., clear yellow flowers from early summer to frost.

'Clementine'. Compact. Red-orange bells over a long season.

'Crimson Belle'. Deep red blossoms.

'Dwarf Red'. Compact and free branching, with orange-red flowers.

'Fairy Coral Red'. 12- to 18-in.-tall plants with salmon-pink flowers. Hardy: Middle South.

'Fool's Gold'. Upright to 4 ft.; rust-colored pendant flowers from early summer to frost.

'Kentish Belle'. Trailing habit; yellow-orange flowers.

'Kristen's Pink'. Compact to 2 ft. Pink, 3-in. flowers are ideal for garden or container.

'Linda Vista Peach'. Orange petals protrude from deep pink calyxes.

'Little Imp'. Narrow yellow flowers with red calyxes. Compact plant with arching habit.

Lucky series. Red, tangerine, white, or yellow flowers on compact, 12-in. plants.

'Marion Stewart'. Upright-growing plant producing orange flowers with attractive red veins.

'Mobile Pink'. Upright, compact growth. Large, wide-open flowers in pale pink with deeper pink veining.

'Moonchimes'. Yellow flowers on a compact plant.

'Orange Hot Lava'. Orange and red bells begin early summer on a 4-ft.-tall plant.

'Voodoo'. Upright to 6 ft. Bell-shaped red flowers bloom late summer to fall.

A. megapotamicum. TRAILING ABUTILON. Vine-shrub from Brazil. Vigorous growth to 10 ft. and as wide, with arrowlike, 1½- to 3-in.-long leaves. Red-and-yellow, 1½-in. flowers resembling tiny lanterns gaily decorate the long, rangy branches in spring and summer. Pinch branch tips to control size, force bushier growth.

More graceful in detail than in entirety but can be trained to an interesting pattern. Usually best as loose, informal espalier. Good hanging basket plant. 'Marianne' has better, more intense flower color; 'Variegatum' has leaves mottled with yellow; 'Victory' is compact and floriferous, with small deep yellow flowers.

A. pictum. FLOWERING MAPLE. Maplelike leaves with showy flowers.

'Thompsonii'. Erect grower to 12 ft. tall and 5–12 ft. wide. Mottled yellow and green variegated leaves accent pale orange bells veined with red.

'Souvenir de Bonn'. Upright to 10 ft. tall and 5 ft. wide. Orange flowers with green, cream-edged foliage.

A. vitifolium. CHILEAN TREE MALLOW. From Chile. To 15 ft. tall, 8 ft. wide. Gray-green, maple-like leaves to 6 in. or longer. In summer, lilac-blue to white flowers are borne singly or in clusters on long stalks. Needs high humidity. 'Tennant's White' is a choice form.

THE BLOOMS OF MOST FLOWERING MAPLES RESEMBLE COLORFUL LITTLE BELLS DANGLING FROM THREADLIKE STEMS.

ACACIA
Mimosaceae
Evergreen and deciduous shrubs
or trees

🌡 **ZONES VARY BY SPECIES**

☀ **FULL SUN**

💧 **LITTLE OR NO WATER**

Acacia baileyana

Prized for their feathery foliage and showy blooms, acacia species hail from such warm-weather climes as Central and South America, Australia, Mexico, and the American Southwest. In the South, they are typically shrubs or small trees, most commonly grown in Florida and Texas. They are relatively short lived (20 to 30 years) but grow quickly, suffer from few pests, and tolerate poor and dry soils. Require excellent drainage.

A. baileyana. BAILEY ACACIA (often called mimosa as a cut flower). Evergreen. Zones LS, CS, TS; USDA 8-11. Most widely planted acacia and among the hardiest to cold. Often grown as a multitrunked plant 20–30 ft. high, 20–40 ft. wide. Feathery, finely cut, blue-gray leaves. Starts blooming when young; profuse, fragrant yellow flowers early in the year. Thornless.

'Purpurea'. PURPLE-LEAF ACACIA. Same as *A. baileyana*, except for purple new growth.

A. berlandieri. GUAJILLO. Deciduous. Zones CS, TS; USDA 9-11. Southwestern native planted as a shrub, hedge, or small tree. Thornless growth reaches 15 ft. high and wide. Fernlike foliage. Fragrant white flowers, rich in nectar, bloom winter to spring.

A. farnesiana. SWEET ACACIA, HUISACHE. Deciduous. Zones LS, CS, TS; USDA 8-11. To

20 ft. high and 15–25 ft. wide, with feathery foliage and thorny branches. Fragrant, deep yellow blossoms are borne nearly year-round. In the Lower South, however, cold winters may reduce bloom; flowers may freeze in a cold snap in any area. Garden centers often sell the more cold-tolerant *A. smallii* under this name.

A. schaffneri. TWISTED ACACIA. Deciduous. Zones CS, TS; USDA 9-11. To about 18 ft. tall and a bit wider, with curving branches like green tentacles and finely divided leaves hiding short thorns. Perfumed yellow ball-shaped flowers appear in spring.

A. wrightii. WRIGHT ACACIA, UÑA De GATO. Deciduous. Zones LS, CS, TS; USDA 8-11. Cold-hardy acacia native to Texas; survives winter as far north as Dallas–Fort Worth. Usually grows to 6–10 ft. tall and wide, occasionally to 20 ft. Pale yellow flowers bloom in spring on 2-in. spikes. Delicate foliage sometimes persists through winter. Thorns on branches have sharp hooks. Does best in dry, well-drained soil. Not well adapted to the Southeast.

ACACIAS
ARE PERFECT
FOR QUICK
COVER ON
A ROUGH,
SELDOM-
WATERED
SLOPE.

ACALYPHA
Euphorbiaceae
Evergreen shrubs

🌡 **TS; USDA 10-11, EXCEPT AS NOTED; OR GROWN AS HOUSEPLANTS**

☀ **FULL SUN; BRIGHT LIGHT**

💧 **REGULAR WATER**

Acalypha wilkesiana
'Bronze Pink'

All three species described here are native to Southeast Asia and the Pacific Islands. Beyond their hardiness range, they can be grown indoors; species *A. wilkesiana* and *A. pendula* can be used as annuals in cold-winter areas. All bloom intermittently during the warm months and all must have good drainage. Pinch young plants regularly to encourage bushy growth. Feed houseplants monthly in summer; reduce watering in winter.

A. hispida. CHENILLE PLANT. Can grow to a bulky 10 ft. tall and 6 ft. wide. Heavy, rich green leaves to 8 in. wide. Flowers come in hanging, 1½-ft.-long clusters that look similar to tassels of crimson chenille. Produces heaviest bloom in early summer, with scattered bloom all year. Thrives in semitropical and tropical climates. This shrub can also be grown in a greenhouse or enclosed patio or, with heavy pruning, indoors.

A. reptans (*A. pendula*). FIRETAIL. Resembles *A. hispida* in flower form, but plant is much smaller; shorter tassels droop from trailing branches. Good atop a wall or in a hanging basket. Root hardy in LS, CS; USDA 8-9 with excellent drainage.

A. wilkesiana (*A. tricolor*). COPPERLEAF. Foliage more colorful than many flowers. Often

used as an annual, substituting for flowers from late summer to frost. Leaves to 8 in. long, in color combinations including bronzy green mottled with red and purple; red with crimson and bronze; and green edged with crimson and stippled with orange and red. In a warm, sheltered spot it can grow as a shrub to 6 ft. or taller, nearly as wide. Outdoor potted plants should be kept slightly dry through winter.

Selections worth trying include the following.

'Bronze Pink'. Vivid coral-pink foliage randomly blotched with bronze appears lit from within.

'Ceylon Lime'. Leaves have blotches of cream, lime, and dark green, yet typically glossy.

'Cypress Elf'. Sold under various names, including *A.* 'Mardi Gras' and *A. godseffiana*.

'Heterophylla'. Reaches just 1½–2 ft. high and wide. Narrow, wavy-edged, weeping leaves to 2 in. long are reddish brown with coral margins.

'Macafeeana'. Vigorous plant grows 3–4 ft. high and almost as wide in a single season; tops out at 12–15 ft. in frost-free areas. Giant, (to 1-ft.-long) heart-shaped leaves in red and bronze tones.

'Marginata'. Reaching 3–6 ft. tall and wide, this is the most familiar form with bronze leaves edged in pink.

'Musaica'. Distinguished by large leaves blotched in bright pink, coral, and bronze.

'Obovata'. To 5 ft. tall and about as wide. Oval, 4- to 6-in.-long, slightly weeping leaves are chocolate-brown with hot pink edges.

'Sizzle Scissors'. Growing upright to 2 ft. tall and wide with narrow bronze leaves with ruffled pink edges.

ACANTHUS

BEAR'S BREECHES
Acanthaceae
Perennials

🌿 **US, MS, LS, CS; USDA 6-9**

☼ ◐ ● **SUN OR SHADE**

💧💧 **MODERATE TO REGULAR WATER**

Acanthus mollis

There is nothing subtle about these plants. Bold and coarse textured, they make a grand statement in any garden. Native to southern Europe and the Mediterranean, they feature large, deeply lobed, sometimes spiny leaves in clumps to about 3 ft. wide. The flowers that appear in late spring or summer are a sight to behold—tall spikes of hooded, whitish, rose, or purple blossoms beneath green or purplish bracts.

These tough plants have spreading roots and can be invasive in rich soil, so give them plenty of room or confine their roots with a barrier at least 8 in. deep. Extended drought causes the leaves to yellow and wither in summer; deep watering or rain results in a flush of fresh foliage. Plants do fine in shade gardens, where their foliage and flowers combine well with hostas and ferns. They also thrive in drier, sunny spots in the company of daylilies (*Hemerocallis*), bearded irises, and ornamental grasses. Good drainage is important. Deer resistant.

A. hungaricus (*A. balcanicus*). HUNGARIAN BEAR'S BREECHES. Somewhat smaller than *A. mollis*, with more finely cut and toothed leaves.

A. mollis. BEAR'S BREECHES. Most commonly grown species. To 4–5 ft. high in bloom. Spineless leaves to 2 ft. long are deeply lobed and cut. 'Latifolius' has larger leaves and is hardier. 'Holland's Gold' has the same big, glossy leaves, but golden green. 'Tasmanian Angel' is a variegated form with creamy white edges and some stippling that fades to green in midsummer.

A. spinosus. SPINY BEAR'S BREECHES. Similar to *A. mollis* in size, but leaves are more finely cut and armed with long spines. Foliage is silvery on the true species. Hybrids have bright green leaves and are known as the Spinosissimus Group.

A. 'Summer Beauty'. Thought to be a hybrid between *A. mollis* and *A. spinosus*. It's similar to *A. mollis*, but it has more finely cut foliage and is better suited to hot, humid summers.

ACER

MAPLE
Sapindaceae
Deciduous trees and shrubs

🌿 **ZONES VARY BY SPECIES**

☼ ◐ **FULL SUN OR PARTIAL SHADE, EXCEPT AS NOTED**

💧💧 **MODERATE TO REGULAR WATER**

Acer japonicum

As a group, only oaks rival maples for usefulness in the garden—and there's hardly a place in the South where some kind of maple won't grow. The major limiting factors are extended summer heat or drought and lack of winter cold. Maples come in many shapes and sizes; among them, you'll find large and midsize shade trees, small specimen trees, and dwarf, weeping kinds the size of a shrub. What really sets these trees apart, though, is their spectacular autumn foliage in warm shades of red, orange, and yellow. Color can be quite variable, especially among seedling trees, so shop while the trees are showing their fall color.

Most maples do better when the soil stays moist, though just about all prefer well-drained soil. (*A. rubrum* is an exception, doing fine in boggy soil.) Large maples can be difficult to garden beneath; in addition to casting dense shade, they grow shallow roots that compete with other plants for water and nutrients. The roots can also crack and lift pavement and invade water and sewer lines.

Medium to large maples need little pruning. For smaller types, prune to accentuate the natural form. Avoid pruning in late winter or early spring, as cuts will "bleed" sap. Prune in summer or early winter instead.

A. buergerianum. TRIDENT MAPLE. Deciduous tree. Zones US, MS, LS; USDA 6-8. Native to China and Japan. Grows to 20–25 ft. high and about as wide. Roundish crown of 3-in.-wide, glossy green, three-lobed leaves that are paler green beneath. Fall color usually red, sometimes orange or yellow. Attractive, flaking bark on older wood. Low, spreading growth; stake and prune to make it branch high. A decorative, useful patio tree and favorite bonsai subject.

A. capillipes. SNAKEBARK MAPLE. Deciduous tree. Zones US, MS; USDA 6-7. Native to Japan. Moderate growth rate to 30 ft. tall and wide. Young branches are olive-green with white stripes. Shallowly three-lobed leaves are 3–5 in. long, turn scarlet in fall. Does better in partial shade.

A. griseum. PAPERBARK MAPLE. Deciduous tree. Zones US, MS, LS; USDA 6-8. Native to China. Grows to 25 ft. or higher; may be half to equally as wide as tall. In winter it makes a striking picture with bare branches angling out and up from main trunk and reddish bark peeling away in paper-thin sheets. Late to leaf out in spring. Leaves are divided into three coarsely toothed, 1½- to 2½-in.-long leaflets, dark green above, silvery below. Inconspicuous red flowers in spring develop into showy winged seeds. Foliage turns brilliant red in fall.

A. japonicum. FULLMOON MAPLE. Deciduous shrub or tree. Zones US, MS; USDA 6-7. Native to Japan. To 20–30 ft. high, with equal or greater spread. Nearly round, 2- to 5-in.-long leaves cut into 7 to 11 lobes. Give regular moisture, part shade. For the tree often sold as golden fullmoon maple, see *A. shirasawanum* 'Aureum'.

'Aconitifolium'. FERNLEAF FULLMOON MAPLE is a slow-growing, small selection (to just 10–12 ft. tall and wide) with deeply cut leaves (almost to the leafstalk); each lobe is also cut and toothed. Fine fall color where adapted; nice specimen tree.

'Ed Wood'. Reaches only 20 ft. tall but has larger leaves, big enough to appear tropical. Orange to red fall color.

'Emmit's Pumpkins'. Upright growth to 12 feet. Large green leaves with bronze overlay in early spring. Fall color is orange.

'Green Cascade'. Cascading form that rarely reaches 5 ft. tall. Foliage is very deeply cut. Fall color is orange, yellow, and red.

A. negundo. BOX ELDER. Deciduous tree. Zones US, MS, LS, CS; USDA 6-9. Native to most of U.S. The species is a weed tree of many faults—it seeds readily, hosts box elder bugs, suckers badly, and is subject to breakage. Fast growing to 60 ft. (usually less) and as wide or wider. Leaves divided into three to nine oval, 2- to 5-in.-long leaflets with toothed margins. Yellow in fall. Several selections improve on the species.

'Flamingo'. White and pink leaf markings. Requires some shade in Lower and Coastal South.

'Sensation'. Slower growth (to 30 ft. tall, 25 ft. wide) and better branch structure than the species. Does not sucker. Good deep pink fall color.

'Variegatum'. VARIEGATED BOX ELDER. Best in part shade. Not as large or weedy as the species. Leaf color—a combination of green and creamy white—makes this selection a standout. Prune out growth that reverts to green. Large, pendent clusters of white fruit are spectacular.

A. palmatum. JAPANESE MAPLE. Deciduous shrub or tree. Zones US, MS, LS, CS; USDA 6-9. Native to Japan and Korea. Growing 15–20 ft., with equal or greater spread; normally multiple stemmed, airy, and graceful. Leaves 2–4 in. long, deeply cut into five to nine toothed lobes.

All-year interest—young spring growth is bright green, green with red edges, or glowing red. Summer's leaves are soft green, and fall foliage is scarlet, orange, or yellow. In winter, slender leafless branches in greens and reds provide interest. Japanese maples tend to grow in flat, horizontal planes, so pruning to accentuate this growth habit is easy. Plants fare best in filtered shade, although full sun can be satisfactory in Upper and Middle South, and in some instances even the Lower South.

From simple seedling trees with bold green or red palmate leaves to delicate lacy-leaved selections, these maples have uncommon grace and character. While seedling trees are handsome, they often lack the predictably superior traits of varieties. In recent years, hundreds of grafted forms have become available, meaning new and once-rare selections are now readily available. Here are some of the best ones for the South. Many smaller ones do well in larger pots.

'Beni-otake'. Vase-shaped, small tree to 12 ft. Leaves have long, thin lobes. Red color holds well into summer and turns crimson in fall. Tolerates full sun into Lower South. Name means "Red Bamboo."

'Bihou'. Vigorous, upright growth to 20 ft. Bark on young branches and twigs turns bright yellow or orange in winter.

'Bloodgood'. Vigorous, upright growth to 15 ft., growing wider than tall with age. Foliage is deep red in spring and summer, scarlet in fall. Blackish red bark. Holds red color in summer. Give partial shade in Lower South.

'Butterfly'. Small tree to 10 ft., with small bluish-green leaves edged in white. Cut out growth that reverts to plain green. Best in partial shade.

'Crimson Queen'. Shrubby, 4–6 ft. Finely cut reddish leaves turn bronze in summer, then scarlet in fall. Mushroom-shaped mound with cascading branches. 'Ever Red' and 'Garnet' are similar selections.

'Emperor I'. Upright tree to 15 ft. Buds open late, avoiding late frosts. Dark red foliage in spring, turning green in hot summers and translucent scarlet in fall.

'Fireglow'. Upright tree to 12 ft. Leaves emerge purple-red and hold color well into summer.

Tolerates sun, heat, and humidity. Bright red fall color.

'Garnet'. Upright, cascading branches means a mature plant is about 6–9 ft. tall and 12 ft. wide, although that requires years. Slow growing with burgundy foliage all summer, followed by brilliant red foliage in fall.

'Germaine's Gyration'. Mounding shrub to 6 ft. Large green leaves tolerate full sun. Fall color is yellow and orange.

'Glowing Embers'. Very similar to the species, with small green leaves but tolerates sun, heat, and humidity all the way to the Coastal South. Yellow, orange, and purple fall color.

'Grandma Ghost'. Variegated small tree or shrub to 8 ft. with reticulated leaves (prominent green veins against a white background). Best in partial shade.

'Hogyoku'. Upright growth to 15 ft. Sturdy and easy to grow in most situations. Green leaves turn a deep yellow-orange pumpkin color in fall.

'Inaba-shidare'. Mounding, pendulous shrub to 5 ft. Very dark purple dissected leaves. Fall color is red.

'Kiyohime'. Small shrub to 3 ft. Small, nickel-size leaves emerge green with red edges turning green for summer. Bronze to orange fall color.

'Koto-no-ito'. Small tree to 5 ft. Very thin, straplike, green leaves. Fall color is yellow.

'Nuresagi'. Tall, slender, red-leafed variety to 20 ft. Tolerates full sun. Holds color well. Bright red fall color.

'Orange Dream'. Small tree to 15 ft. Small leaves emerge yellow-orange in spring. Fall color is golden yellow.

'Osakazuki'. Large leaves (to 5 in. wide) turn from a bright green in summer to crimson or deep purple in fall. Grows upright and wider with age, eventually making a 20-ft., round-topped tree. Sun, heat, and drought tolerant.

'Purple Ghost'. Variegated tree to 12 ft., with reticulated leaves (prominent black veins against a purple-red background). Fall color is red or orange.

'Red Dragon'. Ultimately growing 5–10 ft. tall and 5–8 ft. wide, this weeping maple begins with red foliage in spring. Summer brings mature burgundy leaves that hold their color better than

TOP: Acer palmatum 'Crimson Queen'*; A. tataricum ginnala;*
MIDDLE: A. rubrum; BOTTOM: A. p. 'Shaina'*; A. p.* 'Bloodgood'

most. Then in fall they begin to glow with a scarlet flush.

'Ryusen'. This weeping form depends on staking to attain its height. Stems grow straight down. Heat and sun tolerant. Coral-red fall color.

'Sango-Kaku' ('Senkaki'). CORAL-BARK MAPLE. Vigorous, upright growth to 20 ft. Yellow fall foliage. Twigs, branches are a striking coral-red in winter.

'Seiryu'. Upright, green spreading tree to 18 ft. with small green dissected leaves. Tolerates sun, heat, and humidity to the Lower South. In cooler areas fall color is orange or yellow. In hotter areas it is burgundy.

'Shaina'. This dwarf form grows only 3–4 ft. tall and wide, making it ideal for small gardens. Slow growing and maturing into a rounded shrub, the plant features leaves that are showy red in spring, burgundy in summer, and bright orange in fall.

'Shirazz'. Growing 10–14 ft. tall and 7–10 ft. wide, this selection from New Zealand is showier than most flowers. New growth is pink, followed by mature leaves that appear to be a cream-edged green leaf, covered with a rosy pink veil.

'Shishi-gashira'. LION'S HEAD MAPLE. Small, upright tree to 10 ft. Small, crinkled leaves appear clustered tightly around stiff, twiggy branches. Fall color is orange.

'Skeeter's Broom'. Narrow, upright, small maple to 10 ft. tall and 3 ft. wide. Holds dark red color well. Fall color is bright red.

'Tamukeyama'. Leaves open deep crimson-red in spring and turn quickly to dark purple-red; color holds well through summer, even in high heat and humidity. Tolerates full sun. Scarlet fall color. Leaves less lacy than those of 'Crimson Queen', branches more cascading. Fast growing to 7 ft.

'Tsukasa Silhouette'. Growing 18–20 ft. tall, but only 5 ft. wide, this unusual Japanese maple is a living tower in the garden, ideal for screening, accent, or narrow spaces. Bright green in spring, the foliage turns dark red in autumn for a grand finale.

'Viridis'. Small grower to 6 ft. high, 10 ft. wide, with drooping branches, green bark. Pale green, finely divided leaves turn gold in autumn.

'Waterfall'. Very similar to 'Viridis'. Branches cascade. Leaves deeply divided, fernlike, flowing,

and elegant. Brilliant yellow and gold fall color. Takes full sun quite well.

A. platanoides. NORWAY MAPLE. Deciduous tree. Zones US, MS; USDA 6-7. Native to Europe, western Asia. Broad-crowned, densely foliaged tree to 50–60 ft. tall, from two-thirds as wide to equally as wide as high. Leaves five lobed, 3–5 in. wide, deep green above, paler beneath; turn yellow in fall. Showy clusters of small, greenish yellow flowers in early spring. Very adaptable, tolerating many soil and environmental conditions. Once a widely recommended street tree but now less popular because of voracious roots, self-sown seedlings, and aphid-caused honeydew drip and sooty mold. Here are some of the better selections (purple-leafed forms perform poorly in alkaline soils).

'Cleveland' and 'Cleveland II'. Shapely, compact, well-formed trees about 50 ft. tall, 40 ft. wide. Excellent golden yellow fall color. May be sold as 'chanticleer'.

'Columnare'. Slower growing, narrower form than the species (about 20 ft. wide).

'Crimson King'. Maroon-purple foliage from spring through fall. Slower growing than the species.

'Drummondii'. Leaves are edged with silvery white; unusual and striking. Prefers afternoon shade.

'Emerald Queen'. Oval-rounded shape, fast grower. Grows 50 ft. tall, 40 ft. wide. Dark green leaves turn bright yellow in fall.

'Faassen's Black'. Pyramidal in shape, with dark purple leaves. Grows 40–50 ft. tall and wide.

'Green Lace'. Finely cut, dark-green leaves; moderate growth rate to 40 ft.

'Jade Glen'. Vigorous, straight-growing form with bright yellow fall color. Grows 40–50 ft. tall and wide.

'Parkway'. A broader tree than 'Columnare' (about 25 ft. wide), with a dense canopy.

'Royal Red'. A good red- or purple-leafed form. Similar to selection 'Crimson King'.

'Summershade'. Fast-growing, upright, heat-resistant selection. Poor fall color.

A. rubrum. RED MAPLE, SWAMP MAPLE. Deciduous tree. Zones US, MS, LS, CS; USDA 6-9. Native to low, wet areas in eastern North America. Fairly fast

growth to 60 ft. or taller and 40 ft. or wider. Faster growing than *A. platanoides* or *A. saccharum*. Red twigs, branchlets, and buds; quite showy flowers in late winter. Bright red seeds. Leaves 2–4 in. long, with three to five lobes, shiny green above, pale beneath; brilliant scarlet, orange, and yellow fall color in frosty areas. Often among the first trees to color up in fall. Tolerates most soils, but suffers in dry soil. Selected forms include the following.

'Autumn Flame'. Rounded form, 60 ft., excellent early red fall color.

'Bowhall'. Narrow (15 ft. wide), 40 ft., cone shaped, with orange-red color in fall.

'Brandywine.' Seedless male clone. Hybrid of 'October Glory' and 'Autumn Flame'. Moderately columnar; grows about half as wide as tall. Bright red color holds for at least 2 weeks in fall.

'Columnare'. Broadly columnar; 70 ft. tall, 20 ft. wide. Orange-red fall color.

'Florida Flame'. Round and uniform; 45–50 ft. tall and wide. Resistant to leaf spot.

'October Glory'. Round-headed tree; last to turn color in fall. Good scarlet fall color even in the Lower South. Reaches 50–60 ft.

'Red Sunset'. Upright, vigorous, fast growing to 50–60 ft. Early orange-red fall color.

'Schlesingeri'. Broad, fast growing to 60–70 ft., with regular form; orange-red fall color. First red maple to color in fall.

'Shade King'. Very fast grower to 50 ft. tall, 40 ft. wide. Pale green foliage turns bright red in fall.

'Sun Valley'. Slight oval form reaching 40 ft. tall by 35. ft wide. Fall foliage glows coral to red.

A. freemanii. Zones US, MS, LS, CS; USDA 6-9. Hybrid between *A. rubrum* and *A. saccharinum*. Fast growing and resistant to

storm damage.

'Autumn Fantasy'. Oval. 50 ft. tall and 40 ft. wide. Dependable red fall color for warm zones.

'Celebration'. Oval. 50 ft. tall and 35 ft. wide. Yellow to orange in fall.

'Redpointe'. Oval. 45 ft. tall and 30 ft. wide. Red in fall.

'Scarlet Sentinel'. Broadly columnar. 50 ft. tall and half as wide. Yellow-orange fall color.

A. saccharinum. SILVER MAPLE. Deciduous tree. Zones US, MS, LS, CS; USDA 6-9. Native of eastern North America. Grows rapidly to 40–100 ft. with equal spread. Open form, with semi-pendulous branches; casts fairly open shade. Silvery gray bark peels in long strips on old trees. Leaves 3–6 in. wide, five lobed, light green above, silvery beneath. Fall color is usually a poor yellow-green. Aggressive roots are hard on sidewalks, sewers.

You pay a penalty for the advantage of fast growth: Weak wood and narrow crotch angles make this tree break easily. Unusually susceptible to aphids and cottony scale. Suffers from chlorosis in alkaline soils. Many rate it the least desirable of maples, but nonetheless it is often planted for fast growth.

'Silver Queen'. More upright form than the species, seedless. Bright gold fall color.

A. saccharum. SUGAR MAPLE. Deciduous tree. Zones US, MS, LS; USDA 6-8. Native to eastern North America. The source of maple syrup in the Northeast, this tree is renowned for spectacular fall color. Moderate growth to 60 ft. or more, with stout branches and upright, oval to rounded canopy to about 40 ft. wide. Leaves 3–6 in. wide, with three to five lobes, green above, pale below. Brilliant autumn foliage ranges from yellow

A

and orange to deep red and scarlet. Intolerant of road salt; best in acid, moist, well-drained soil. Not well suited to urban conditions.

Commonly available selections include:

'Autumn Splendor'. Grows 45 ft. tall and 40 ft. wide. Heat and drought tolerant.

'Caddo'. CADDO MAPLE. Not a single selection, but a distinct group of heat- and drought-tolerant sugar maples native to Oklahoma. To 50 ft. More tolerant of alkaline soils than eastern maples. Yellow and orange fall color. Good for the Southwest.

'Commemoration'. Heavy leaf texture; yellow, orange, and red fall color. Faster growing than the species; tolerates heat and drought.

'Flashfire'. Grows 45 ft. tall and 40 ft. wide. Early red fall color in spite of heat. Caddo seedling.

'Green Mountain'. Tolerant of heat and drought; autumn leaves are yellow to orange to reddish orange. To 70 ft. Fall color better in Upper South.

'Harvest Moon'. To 50 ft. tall and 35 ft. wide. Orange-red fall

color, heat and drought resistant.

'Legacy'. Fast growing, drought and heat tolerant, multihued in fall; late to leaf out in spring. To 50 ft.

'Monumentale' ('Temple's Upright'). Narrow, erect form to 60 ft. tall, 15 ft. wide. Yellow-orange fall leaves.

'Seneca Chief'. Narrow form, orange to yellow fall color. To 20 ft. wide.

A. saccharum floridanum (*A. barbatum*). SOUTHERN SUGAR MAPLE, FLORIDA MAPLE. Deciduous tree. Zones US, MS, LS, CS; USDA 6-9. Native from Virginia south to Florida and west to Oklahoma and Texas. Grows to 25–30 ft. tall and as wide. Usually turns the same rich yellow and red in autumn as *A. saccharum*, but it is smaller in stature and has smaller leaves, paler bark, and a more open habit. It turns color very late, often in December. It is also better adapted to the hot Coastal Plains of the South. Found in forest understory alongside streams.

A. s. grandidentatum. BIGTOOTH MAPLE. Deciduous

TOP: Acer saccharum; BOTTOM: A. rubrum

tree. Zones US, MS, LS; USDA 6-8. This dense, mid-size tree takes full to partial sun, growing 30–45 ft. tall and 20–25 ft. wide, ideal for landscapes or as a street tree. Three- to five-lobed leaves with large, blunt teeth turn brilliant yellow, orange, or rose red in fall. In nature, this species grows in canyons and on stream banks; in gardens, it requires well-drained soil on the dry side. Good choice for the Southwest. Tolerates alkaline soil. The 'Lost Maple' of the Edwards Plateau in Texas. 'Highland Park' offers classic maple fall color.

A. s. leucoderme (*A. leucoderme*). CHALK MAPLE. Deciduous tree. Zones US, MS, LS, CS; USDA 6-9. Native from North Carolina south to Florida and west to Texas and Oklahoma. Multitrunked tree to 30 ft. tall and almost as wide, with brilliant yellow, orange, and red fall color. Quite similar to *A. barbatum*, but grows faster; prefers drier, upland sites. Its leaves are green on the underside, while those of *A. barbatum* are gray-green beneath. Bark is also ashy gray, hence the common name.

A. s. nigrum (*A. nigrum*). BLACK MAPLE. Deciduous tree. Zones US, MS, LS; USDA 6-8. Native to eastern North America. Similar to *A. saccharum*. Light green leaves with drooping lobes turn yellow in late fall. 'Green column' can reach 65 ft. tall, 25 ft. wide.

A. shirasawanum **'Aureum'** (*A. japonicum* 'Aureum'). SHIRA-SAWA MAPLE, GOLDEN FULL-MOON MAPLE. Deciduous shrub or tree. Zones US, MS; USDA 6-7. Japanese native; grows to 20 ft. tall and wide. Leaves open pale gold in spring and remain pale chartreuse all summer. Partial shade.

A. tataricum ginnala. AMUR MAPLE. Zones US, MS, LS; USDA 6-8. Native to Manchuria, northern China, Japan. Toothed leaves are three lobed, even on mature plants. Clusters of small, fragrant, yellowish flowers bloom in early spring; these are followed by handsome winged seeds in bright red. Striking red fall color. 'Flame', 15–20 ft. high and wide, has especially fiery foliage in autumn. 'Bailey Compact', 10 ft. tall and 15 ft. wide with red fall color.

A. truncatum. PURPLEBLOW MAPLE. Deciduous tree. Zones

US, MS, LS; USDA 6-8. Native to China. Grows fairly rapidly to 25 ft., with equal or slightly smaller spread. Like a small *A. platanoides* with more deeply lobed leaves to 4 in. wide. Leaves emerge purplish red, mature to green by summer, and turn yellow to orange toned in fall. Good lawn or patio tree. Tolerates most well-drained soils and urban conditions.

ACHILLEA
YARROW
Asteraceae (Compositae)
Perennials

◣ **US, MS, LS; USDA 6-8**

☼ **FULL SUN**

◊◖ **LITTLE TO MODERATE WATER**

Achillea millefolium

Mainstays of the summer perennial border, yarrows offer showy blooms and finely cut, aromatic foliage. Their flat-topped flower clusters are excellent for drying. Though often considered carefree, they do require excellent drainage, especially in high-rainfall, high-humidity areas; planting in heavy clay usually results in rot. Once established, they thrive in drought and heat. Seldom browsed by deer. Cut back plants after they finish blooming. Divide and replant clumps every 3 years in late winter.

A. ageratifolia (*A. serbica*). GREEK YARROW. Native to Balkan region. Low, foot-wide mats of silvery leaves, toothed or nearly smooth edged. White, ½- to 1-in.-wide flower clusters are carried on stems 4–10 in. tall.

A. clavennae. SILVERY YARROW. Native to Europe. Silvery gray, silky leaves, lobed somewhat like chrysanthemum leaves, form mats about 8 in. wide. Loose, flat-topped clusters of ½- to ¾-in.-wide, ivory-white flower heads on 5- to 10-in. stems. Often sold as *A. argentea*.

A. filipendulina. FERNLEAF YARROW. From the Caucasus. Tall, erect plants 4–5 ft. high and to 3 ft. wide, with deep green, fernlike leaves. Bright yellow flower heads in large, flat-topped clusters. Dried or fresh, they are good for flower arrangements. Several selections are available. 'Gold Plate' grows up to 5 ft and has flower clusters up to 6 in. wide; hybrid 'Coronation Gold', to about 3 ft. high, also has large flower clusters. 'Cloth of Gold' has large flowers and intermediate height.

A. millefolium. COMMON YARROW. Native to Europe, western Asia. Erect plant with narrow, green or grayish green leaves and flat-topped white flower clusters on 3-ft. stems. Spreads by underground runners. Many selections are available. 'Fanal' ('The Beacon') and 'Rosea' are bright rose-pink; 'Cerise Queen' is deeper pink; 'Lilac Beauty' ('Lavender Beauty') lavender-pink; 'Weser River Sandstone' rose-pink fading to tan; and 'Salmon Beauty' ('Lachs-schönheit') salmon-pink. 'Hoffnung' ('Great Expectations') is pale yellow; 'Fire King', 'Pretty Woman', and 'Paprika' are red (with yellow center) aging to coppery red. 'Feuerland' ('Fireland') is salmon-peach, and 'Peggy Sue' is apricot.

Worthwhile seed-grown garden strains and hybrids include 'Apfelblüte' ('Appleblossom'), 'Martina', 'Terracotta', the Summer Pastels series ('Strawberry Seduction', 'Sunny Seduction', 'Peachy Seduction'), the Summer Berries series, and the Desert Eve series.

A. ptarmica. SNEEZEWORT. From Europe, Asia. Erect plant to 2 ft. high and wide. Narrow leaves with finely toothed edges. White flower heads in rather open, flattish clusters. 'The Pearl' and 'Ballerina' have double flowers.

A. tomentosa. WOOLLY YARROW. From Europe, western Asia. Makes a flat, spreading mat (to about 1½ ft. wide) of fernlike, gray-green, hairy leaves. Golden flower heads in flat clusters top 6- to 10-in. stems. 'King George' has cream blooms. A good edging

and a neat ground cover for small areas with good drainage; used in rock gardens. Shear off dead flowers to leave an attractive gray-green mat.

ACHIMENES
Gesneriaceae
Perennials from rhizomes

🌡 **CS, TS; USDA 9-11, EXCEPT AS NOTED; OR HOUSEPLANTS OR IN GREENHOUSE**

◐ ● **PARTIAL TO FULL SHADE; BRIGHT LIGHT**

💧 **REGULAR WATER**

Achimenes

Native to tropical America. Related to African violet (*Saintpaulia*) and gloxinia (*Sinningia*). Plants 1–2 ft. high, some trailing. Slender stems; roundish, crisp, bright to dark green, hairy leaves. Blooms from summer to autumn, bearing flaring, tubular, 1- to 3-in.-wide flowers in pink, orange, blue, lavender, orchid, or purple.

Sometimes grown in beds as ground cover in Coastal and Tropical South, but more commonly used in containers, either outdoors (protected from direct sun and wind) in window box, on porch or patio, under lath; or indoors (in bright light) or in greenhouse. Plant rhizomes in March or April, placing them ½–1 in. deep in moist peat moss and sand. Keep in light shade at 60°F. When plants are 3 in. high, set 6 to 12 of them in 6- to 7-in. fern pot or hanging basket, in potting mix of equal parts peat moss, perlite, and leaf mold. In fall, dig rhizomes and let dry. Store in cool, dry place over winter; repot in spring.

'Harry Williams' has proven hardy in Zones MS, LS, CS, TS;

USDA 7-11. It may not appear until June, but the crimson flowers are worth the wait.

'Purple King' is unusually hardy and suited to Zones MS, LS, CS, TS; USDA 7-11. Can be brought back from 0°F. Grows to 6 in. tall. Flowers deep purple, 2 in. across, on trailing stems. Breaks dormancy late, not appearing until late May. Blooms intermittently throughout summer.

ACOELORRHAPHE WRIGHTII
PAUROTIS PALM, EVERGLADES PALM
Arecaceae
Palm

🌡 **CS, TS; USDA 9-11; OR HOUSEPLANT**

☀ ◐ **FULL SUN OR PARTIAL SHADE, BRIGHT LIGHT**

💧💧 ◐ **REGULAR TO AMPLE WATER**

Acoelorrhaphe wrightii

Beautiful clumping fan palm; native to the Florida Everglades and West Indies. One of its common names, paurotis palm, refers to its former botanical name, *Paurotis wrightii*. Forms a cluster of slender trunks topped by tufts of fan-shaped, 2- to 3-ft.-wide fronds, green above and silvery beneath. Leafstalks are armed with sharp spines. In Florida, it reaches 30 ft. tall and 20 ft. wide, but it grows considerably smaller in South Texas, where it's somewhat difficult to establish. Hardy to 20°F. Does best in moist, fertile soil but will tolerate many types; good beach plant, as it takes sandy soil and salt spray. Manageable size and attractive shape make this plant a favorite with homeowners and garden

designers. Subject to 'frizzle top' in manganese-deficient soil. Fertilize twice a year with slow-release palm fertilizer.

ACONITUM
ACONITE, MONKSHOOD
Ranunculaceae
Perennials

🌡 **US, MS; USDA 6-7**

☀ ◐ **FULL SUN OR PARTIAL SHADE**

💧 **REGULAR WATER**

◆ **ALL PARTS ARE POISONOUS IF INGESTED; WEAR GLOVES AND AVOID SKIN CONTACT**

Aconitum carmichaelii 'Pink Sensation'

Difficult plants to grow in most of the South, as they dislike extended summer heat, drought, and mild winters. Sow seeds in moist, fertile, well-drained soil in late summer or autumn for flowers the following year. Seedlings started in spring may take a year to bloom. Aconite combines effectively with hosta, ferns, meadow rue (*Thalictrum*), and astilbe in lightly shaded gardens; it can also substitute for delphinium in shade. Plants are seldom browsed by deer.

A. carmichaelii. Native to central China. Densely foliaged plant 2–4 ft. high, nearly as wide. Leathery, dark green leaves are lobed and coarsely toothed. Blooms from late summer into fall; deep purple-blue flowers form dense, branching clusters 4–8 in. long. Selections of the Wilsonii group grow 6–8 ft. high and 1–2 ft. wide, has more open flower clusters 10–18 in. long. 'Arendsii' grows 2-4 ft. high, blooms azure blue, and may be the best for the South.

A. napellus. GARDEN MONKSHOOD. Native to Europe. Upright, leafy plants 2–5 ft. high, up to 1 ft. wide. Leaves 2–5 in. wide, divided into narrow lobes. Spikelike clusters of typically blue or violet flowers in late summer.

A. selections and hybrids. The following grow to about 3½ ft. tall, 1 ft. wide. Leaves are deeply cut.

'Bressingham Spire'. Upright plant with deep violet blossom spikes from midsummer to early fall. Glossy, dark green leaves.

'Eleonara'. White flowers edged in bluish purple; early summer bloom. Glossy, deep green leaves.

'Stainless Steel'. Steel blue flowers in loosely branched spikes bloom in midsummer. Dark grayish green leaves.

ACORUS

SWEET FLAG
Acoraceae
Perennials

🌡 **US, MS, LS, CS; USDA 6-9**

🌓 **LIGHT SHADE**

💧 **AMPLE WATER**

Acorus gramineus 'Ogon'

Sweet flags look like small ornamental grasses, but they're actually related to calla (*Zantedeschia*). Grown for highly attractive foliage. Use in damp borders, at pond edges, in shallow water, or average garden soil. Propagate by dividing clumps in spring or fall.

A. calamus. SWEET FLAG. Native to the Northern Hemisphere. Sword-shaped leaves resembling those of bearded iris are 1½ in. wide, 4–5 ft. long, growing in a clump about 2 ft.

wide. Foliage is fragrant when bruised, as are the thick rhizomes. 'Variegatus' has very showy white-edged leaves. Dies to the ground in winter.

A. gramineus. JAPANESE SWEET FLAG. Native to Japan, China. A trouble-free plant that prefers moist, fertile soil, either boggy or well drained. Fans of narrow, 6- to 12-in.-long semievergreen leaves rise from the ends of slowly creeping rhizomes; the plant eventually forms a rounded clump. Excellent for massing, combining with coarser-leafed plants, or growing in containers. 'Ogon' is especially showy, with arching golden yellow leaves to 10 in. long; it looks great beside dark green, burgundy, or purplish foliage. 'Variegatus' has white-striped green leaves; leaves of 'Licorice' are 1½ ft. long, with fragrance and flavor of licorice. Dwarf *A. g. pusillus*, 3–5 in. high, and lime-green 'Minimus Aureus', 2–3 in. high, spread very slowly and are useful between stepping stones or tucked into niches in a rock garden.

ACTAEA

BANEBERRY, BUGBANE
Ranunculaceae
Perennials

🌡 **ZONES VARY**

🌓 **PARTIAL TO FULL SHADE**

💧 **REGULAR WATER**

💧 **ALL PARTS ARE POISONOUS IF INGESTED**

Actaea simplex
'Black Negligee'

Very desirable woodland plants native to the eastern U.S. and grown chiefly for their showy flowers and berries. To thrive, these plants need moist, rich,

acid, well-drained, woodsy soil and cool roots. In the South, *A. pachypoda* and *A. rubra* do best in the mountainous regions of West Virginia, Virginia, North Carolina, and Tennessee. The genus *Cimicifuga* has recently been incorporated into spring-flowering *Actaea*, expanding the range of the group into warmer regions and including midsummer and fall bloomers.

A. japonica (*Cimicifuga japonica*). JAPANESE BUGBANE. Zones US, MS, LS; USDA 6-8. Native to Japan. White autumn flowers on purplish black, leafless stalks. In bloom, plant is 3–4 ft. tall, 2 ft. wide. Variety *A. j. acerina* has white flowers opening from pink buds.

A. pachypoda (*A. alba*). WHITE BANEBERRY, DOLL'S EYES. Zones US, MS; USDA 6-7. Plant produces showy, ¼-in. berries that are white with a dark spot at the tip; berry stalks are swollen and red. 'Misty Blue' is named for its delicate, blue-green foliage.

A. racemosa (*C. racemosa*). BLACK SNAKEROOT, COHOSH BUGBANE. Zones US, MS, LS; USDA 6-8. Native to eastern North America. Leafy clump to 3–4 ft. tall, 3 ft. wide. Flowering stalks are typically branched and carry dense spikes of white flowers that increase plant height to 7 ft. Blooms between midsummer and early fall.

A. rubra. RED BANEBERRY. Zone US; USDA 6. Similar to *A. pachypoda*, but berries are scarlet, somewhat larger, and borne on slender stems.

A. simplex (*C. simplex*). KAMCHATKA BUGBANE. Zones US, MS, LS; USDA 6-8. Native to Siberia and Japan. Foliage clump to 2 ft. tall and wide, with 3- to 4-ft. flower stalks in fall. 'Atropurpurea' has purplish leaves and pink-tinted flower buds on 5-ft. stems. 'Brunette' and 'Hillside Black Beauty' have even darker foliage and pinkish flowers. 'Black Negligee' has dark purple, finely cut leaves and white flowers tinged with purple. 'Prichard's Giant' (*C. ramosa*) has foliage clumps to 4 ft. tall and wide; erect stems to 7 ft. high carry foot-long, narrow spikes of white flowers.

ACTINIDIA KOLOMIKTA

VARIEGATED KIWI VINE
Actinidiaceae
Deciduous vine

🌡 **US, MS, LS; USDA 6-8**

☀🌓 **FULL SUN OR PARTIAL SHADE**

💧 **MODERATE TO REGULAR WATER**

Actinidia kolomikta

Most kiwi vines are valued for delicious fruit, but this eastern Asian species is grown for its flamboyant foliage. Grows rapidly to 15 ft. or more, producing a marvelous mass of 3- to 5-in.-long leaves with elongated heart shape, some in solid green, others white-splashed green, others green variegated in pink to red. Female selections produce small fruit, but males (which are nonfruiting) typically have better leaf color. Color is best in cool weather and—in warmer regions—in partial shade. 'September Sun' has sweet fruit and the best foliage variegation among female selections. Small, fragrant white flowers appear in early summer. Plants climb by twining; provide sturdy support and train new stems into place. Prune in late dormant season. For information on growing kiwi vines for their fruit, see Kiwi.

ADENIUM OBESUM

DESERT ROSE
Apocynaceae
Succulent shrub

- 🌿 **TS; USDA 10-11; OR HOUSEPLANT**
- ☀️ **FULL SUN; BRIGHT INDIRECT LIGHT**
- 💧 **REGULAR WATER**
- ⚠️ **MILKY SAP IS POISONOUS IF INGESTED**

Adenium obesum

Called desert rose or desert azalea in its native tropical eastern Africa, this odd-looking plant has twisted trunks that emerge from a bulbous, swollen root-stock resembling a giant onion. Leafless for long stretches during dry periods, it redeems itself periodically throughout the growing season with gray-green, 4-in.-long leaves and clusters of deep pink, red, or white, saucer-shaped, 2-in. flowers.

Desert rose will grow outdoors in south Florida and the southernmost parts of Texas, sometimes reaching 9 ft. tall—but it remains primarily a collector's plant, typically topping out at about 5 ft. tall and 3 ft. wide. Because it won't tolerate frost or take less-than-perfect drainage, it's best grown in a pot and moved to a bright, heated room for the winter.

ADENOPHORA

LADY BELLS
Campanulaceae
Perennials

- 🌿 **US, MS; USDA 6-7**
- ☀️ ◐ **FULL SUN OR PARTIAL SHADE**
- 💧💧 **MODERATE TO REGULAR WATER**

Adenophora liliifolia

These showy perennials bear fragrant, bell-shaped flowers on their upper stems. Uncommon in the South and difficult to find at nurseries, they prefer moist, fertile, well-drained soil. Once established, they resent being moved. Not browsed by deer.

A. bulleyana. From western China. Grows to 3 ft. tall, 1 ft. wide. Pale blue bells in autumn.

A. confusa. From western China. To 3 ft. tall, 2 ft. wide. Dark blue flowers in summer.

A. liliifolia. Native from central Europe to Siberia. To 1½ ft. high, 1 ft. wide. Pale blue or white flowers in midsummer.

ADIANTUM

MAIDENHAIR FERN
Pteridaceae
Ferns

- 🌿 **ZONES VARY BY SPECIES**
- ◐ ● **PARTIAL TO FULL SHADE**
- 💧💧 **AMPLE WATER**

Adiantum pedatum

It would be hard to imagine daintier, more graceful ferns than the maidenhairs. Most hail from the tropics, but some originate in North America. Dark, thin, wiry stems hold delicate, finely cut fronds. In most types, the individual leaflets are bright green and fan shaped. Most resist deer.

Maidenhairs typically need rich organic soil, steady moisture, and shade. Tender species are useful as houseplants. Provide bright filtered or indirect light and apply a general-purpose liquid houseplant fertilizer diluted to half strength once a month in spring and summer.

A. capillus-veneris. SOUTHERN MAIDENHAIR. Zones US, MS, LS, CS, TS; USDA 6-11. Native to North America. To 1½ ft. tall and 16 in. wide; fronds twice divided but not forked. Easy to grow. Best in slightly alkaline soil or shaded containers. 'Fan Dance' grows only 6 in. tall, spreading to 2 ft.

A. hispidulum. ROSY MAIDENHAIR. Zone TS; USDA 10-11. Native to tropics of Asia, Africa. To 1 ft. tall and wide. Young fronds rosy brown, turning medium green, shaped somewhat like those of *A. pedatum*. Good indoor or greenhouse plant.

A. pedatum. AMERICAN MAIDENHAIR FERN, NORTHERN MAIDENHAIR. Zones US, MS, LS, CS; USDA 6-8. Native to North America. Fronds fork to make a fingerlike pattern atop slender, 1- to 2½-ft. stems; clumps grow about as wide as high. General effect is airy and fresh. Excellent in containers or shaded beds.

A. peruvianum. SILVER DOLLAR MAIDENHAIR. Zones CS, TS; USDA 9-11. Native to Peru. To 1½ ft. or more tall and about as wide. Leaflets quite large, to 2 in. wide. Good choice for indoors or in greenhouse.

A. raddianum (*A. cuneatum*). Zone TS; USDA 10-11. Native to Brazil. Fronds cut three or four times, 15–18 in. long. There are many named types, differing in texture and compactness. Grow in pots; move outdoors to a sheltered, shaded patio in summer. Selections commonly sold are 'Fritz Lüthi', 'Gracillimum' (most finely cut), and 'Pacific Maid'. Good indoors or in greenhouse.

A. tenerum. WRIGHTII MAIDENHAIR FERN. Zone TS; USDA 10-11. Native to New World tropics. Grows about 2 ft. tall, 3 ft. wide. Long, broad fronds arch gracefully, are finely divided into many deeply cut segments ½-¾ in. wide. In cooler areas, can be grown indoors or in greenhouse.

A. venustum. HIMALAYAN MAIDENHAIR. Zones US, MS, CS, TS; USDA 6-11. Chinese native to 8 in. high. Young fronds are bright bronzy pink, maturing to medium green. Grows slowly but forms a 3-ft.-wide clump in 5 to 10 years.

ADINA RUBELLA

CHINESE BUTTONBUSH
Rubiaceae
Deciduous shrub

US, MS, LS, CS; USDA 6-9

FULL SUN OR PARTIAL SHADE

MODERATE TO REGULAR WATER

Adina rubella

This Chinese native looks much like our native buttonbush (*Cephalanthus*), but it's showier. Fragrant pink flowers that look like little pin cushions appear atop the plant from late spring to late summer. The glossy, bronzy green leaves, similar to those of abelia, persist into late fall. Grows 6–10 ft. tall and wide and needs fertile, acidic, well-drained soil. No serious pests or diseases.

SITE CHINESE BUTTON-BUSH WHERE YOU CAN SEE THE FLOWERS UP CLOSE.

AECHMEA

Bromeliaceae
Perennials

TS; USDA 10-11; OR HOUSE-PLANTS

PARTIAL SHADE; SUNNY WINDOW

UNIQUE WATER NEEDS AND METHODS

Aechmea fasciata

Gardeners in frost-free areas know this genus to be epiphytes, plants that grow on the trunks and branches of trees. All have rigid, strap-shaped leaves (often with spiny margins) that form a funnel of foliage around a central cup that will hold water after a rain. In summer, a plumelike flower arises from the center and is showy for several months.

A. chantinii. AMAZONIAN ZEBRA PLANT. Upright or urnlike rosettes of 1- to 3-ft.-long leaves in green to gray-green or olive-green are banded with silver or darker green. Tall flower clusters have orange, pink, or red bracts, yellow-and-red flowers. Fruit is white or blue.

A. fasciata. SILVER VASE PLANT. Funnel-shaped rosette of handsome gray-green leaves cross-banded with silvery white. From the center grows a cluster of rosy pink flower bracts enclosing pale blue flowers that change to deep rose. The selection 'Silver King' has unusually silvery leaves; 'Marginata' has leaves edged with creamy white bands.

A. fulgens. CORALBERRY. Green leaves dusted with gray, 12–16 in. long, 2–3 in. wide. Flower cluster usually above the leaves; red, blue, or blue-violet blossoms. *A. f. discolor* has brownish red or violet-red leaves, usually faintly striped.

A. hybrids. Dozens of hybrids have been developed from the various species. Among the most readily available are those in the Foster's Favorite group; they have bright, wine-red, lacquered, 1-ft.-long leaves and drooping, spikelike flower clusters in coral-red and blue. Another favorite is 'Royal Wine', which forms an open rosette of somewhat leathery, glossy, light green leaves with burgundy-red undersides; it has drooping clusters of orange-and-blue flowers.

A. pectinata. Stiff rosettes up to 3 ft. wide; leaves to 3 in. wide, strongly marked pink or red at bloom time. Flowers are whitish and green.

A. weilbachii. Shiny leaves to 2 ft. long, green or suffused with red tones, in rosettes 2–3 ft. wide. Dull red, 1½-ft. flower stalk has orange-red berries tipped with lilac.

CARE

These bromeliads can be grown outdoors in light shade in pots or hanging baskets. Just be ready to bring them indoors before a frost. Indoors or out, they require a gritty, fast-draining soil such as orchid mix. Contrary to popular belief, it's not a good idea to keep the central cup of plants grown indoors filled with water; this often causes rot. Instead, water the soil around the plant. Let the soil surface go dry to the touch between waterings; mist the foliage of indoor plants frequently. Soft leaf tips indicate overwatering; hard tips indicate underwatering.

AEGOPODIUM PODAGRARIA

BISHOP'S WEED, GOUT WEED
Apiaceae
Perennial

US, MS, LS; USDA 6-8

SUN OR SHADE

MODERATE WATER

Aegopodium podagraria

Native to Europe and western Asia, this vigorous ground cover has naturalized in much of the South. It spreads by creeping roots and is especially aggressive in rich soil. Confine it behind a concrete, stone, or metal barrier set 8–12 in. deep into the soil. Light green leaves, each with three leaflets, form a dense mass to 6 in. high; flat-topped clusters of white flowers rise above the foliage in summer. Mowing two or three times a year keeps the planting neat. Remove faded flowers promptly to prevent unwanted seedlings. Clumps of bishop's weed are easy to dig and divide, making it a popular passalong plant.

'Variegatum' is the selection most often planted, with white-edged leaflets that create a luminous effect in shade. Set plants 1 ft. apart for quick cover, and pull up any plants that revert to solid green.

AEONIUM

Crassulaceae
Succulent perennials

🌿 **CS, TS; USDA 9-11; OR INDOORS**

☼ ◑ **SUN; PARTIAL SHADE WHERE HOT**

💧 **MODERATE WATER**

Aeonium 'Sunburst'

Most aeoniums are native to the Canary Islands. Their fleshy leaves are held in rosettes at branch tips. After several years, rosettes produce a single large flower stalk in spring or summer; branches that have flowered die. These cool-season growers go dormant in summer to save water. During dormancy, they may appear sick and lose leaves—but when the weather cools and the plants get water, they perk up and regrow leaves.

A. arboreum. Grows 3 ft. tall and wide. Each branch tip carries a 6- to 8-in.-wide rosette of bright green, fleshy leaves. The yellow flowers appear in long clusters. 'Atropurpureum', with magenta-and-green rosettes, is more striking and more widely grown than the species. Hybrid 'Zwartkop', sometimes called black rose, has very dark purple (nearly black) rosettes up to 10 in. across; it can reach 5 ft. tall.

A. 'Blushing Beauty'. Forms a full, tight mound of 8-in.-wide rosettes; the plant reaches 2 ft. tall and wide. Leaves are green with a pronounced red edge. Flowers are yellow.

A. 'Cyclops'. Resembles *A. arboretum* 'Zwartkop', but leaves are deep red rather than black, and each rosette has a green center, or eye. Plants grow 4–5 ft. tall and 3–4 ft. wide, with an open, branching habit.

A. decorum. Bushy, rounded, many-branched plant to 1 ft. high and at least as wide. Each branch ends in a 2-in. rosette. Fleshy, pale green, reddish-tinted leaves have red edges. A neat, compact grower with pink flowers.

A. haworthii. Free branching and shrubby, plants reach 2 ft. tall and 4 ft. wide. Rosettes of blue-green, red-edged leaves are 2–3 in. wide. Cream-colored flowers. Very tough, long-lasting plant that can take more cold than most.

A. 'Kiwi' (*A. decorum* 'Kiwi'). This popular, colorful plant forms a low, tight mound to about 1½–2½ ft. tall and 2 ft. wide. Leaves are tricolored; light green with pale yellow variegation and bright red edges. Pale yellow flowers.

A. nobile. To 2 ft. tall and nearly as wide. An unbranched stem holds a rosette of thick, fleshy green leaves, often tinted reddish with maturity. After several years, rosettes produce a large (to 1 ft. high and wide), flat-topped cluster of red flowers on a thick, red stem. The plant dies after bloom but produces many seedlings.

A. 'Sunburst'. Showy plant with 12-in.-wide rosettes of green leaves variegated in light yellow or creamy white and edged with red. Usually grows 1½–2 ft. high and wide but can mound up to 4 ft high. Flowers are cream colored. Does not respond well to pruning. 'Starburst' is similar, but with less yellow in the leaves.

A. tabuliforme. Unusual species with unbranched stems holds single, nearly flat rosettes just 2–6 in. high and 10–18 in. across; sometimes called 'Dinner Plate'. Light green, hairy-edged leaves radiate from the center in perfect symmetry. After several years, a single 1- to 2-ft.-tall stalk of yellow flowers rises from the center. Plants die after flowering.

A. undulatum. Bright, apple-green leaves are wavy, forming unusual-looking rosettes 10–15 in. wide. Stalks are thick and up to 3–4 ft. tall; makes offsets freely. Yellow flowers.

A. urbicum. Some say this is an *A. undulatum* hybrid. "Dinner plate" rosettes reach 8–15 in. wide. Long, narrow, gray-green leaves loosely arranged, have reddish edges. Forms stems several feet tall, unbranched except for offsets at the base. Does not respond well to pruning. White or pinkish flowers.

AESCULUS

HORSECHESTNUT, BUCKEYE
Sapindaceae
Deciduous trees or shrubs

🌿 **ZONES VARY BY SPECIES**

☼ ◑ **FULL SUN OR LIGHT SHADE**

💧 **REGULAR WATER**

⬦ **SEEDS OF ALL ARE SLIGHTLY TOXIC IF INGESTED**

Aesculus pavia

These trees sport long, showy, typically upright clusters of flowers atop their branches in springtime. Some develop good fall color. Leathery capsules release glossy, dark brown, chestnutlike seeds (buckeyes) in autumn. Prune established horsechestnuts only to remove dead branches. Summer leaf scorch is common when the plants are grown in poor, dry soil; severe cases result in defoliation.

A. x arnoldiana 'Autumn Splendor'. Zones US, MS, LS; USDA 6-8. Very attractive, hybrid of *A. flava*, *A. pavia*, and *A. glabra*. To 35–40 ft. tall and nearly as wide. Glossy, dark green leaves with five (rarely seven) leaflets turn brilliant maroon in autumn and are resistant to leaf scorch. Yellow flowers, each with an orange-red blotch, are borne in clusters to 8 in. long. Best with some shade.

A. x carnea. RED HORSE-CHESTNUT. Zones US, MS, LS; USDA 6-8. Hybrid between *A. hippocastanum* and *A. pavia*. To 40 ft. high and 30 ft. wide—smaller than *A. hippocastanum*, better fit for small gardens. Round headed with large, dark green leaves, each divided into five leaflets; casts dense shade. Bears hundreds of 8-in.-long plumes of soft pink to red flow-

ers. 'Briotii' has rosy crimson flowers; 'Fort McNair' blooms rose-pink, and 'O'Neil's Red' has bright red blooms.

A. flava (*A. octandra*). YELLOW BUCKEYE, SWEET BUCKEYE. Zones US, MS, LS; USDA 6-8. Native to the American South. Most majestic of the North American native species: handsome, round-crowned tree to 90 ft. tall and 50 ft. wide, with dark green leaves divided into five to seven finely toothed, 5- to 8-in.-long leaflets. Yellow flowers form on erect panicles; less showy than those of *A. hippocastanum*. Smooth, brown bark. Orange fall foliage.

A. glabra. OHIO BUCKEYE. Zones US, MS; USDA 6-7. From the central and eastern U.S. Low-branching tree with dense, rounded form; to 40 ft. or possibly taller, to 30 ft. wide. Early to leaf out. Foliage is bright green when new, matures to dark green, turns yellow to orange in fall. Greenish yellow flowers in 4- to 7-in. clusters. Prickly seed capsules enclose shiny brown buckeyes.

A. g. arguta (*A. arguta*). TEXAS BUCKEYE. Zones US, MS, LS; USDA 6-8. Native to southern U.S. Attractive small tree to 15–20 ft. or taller, 12–15 ft. wide. Leaves divided into seven to nine narrow, pointed, 3- to 5-in.-long leaflets. Pale yellow flowers in late spring. Weight of fruit may bend branches in fall.

A. hippocastanum. COMMON HORSECHESTNUT. Zones US, MS; USDA 6-7. Native to Europe. To 60 ft. tall, 40 ft. wide. Bulky and densely foliaged; gives heavy shade. Leaves divided into five to seven toothed, 4- to 10-in.-long leaflets. Spectacular flower show: ivory blooms with pink markings in 1-ft. plumes. Invasive roots can break up sidewalks. 'Baumannii' has double flowers, sets no seed.

A. parviflora. BOTTLEBRUSH BUCKEYE. Zones US, MS, LS, CS: USDA 6-9. Native to southeastern U.S. Shrub to 12–15 ft. tall and wide, spreading by suckers, with dark green leaves divided into five to seven 3- to 8-in.-long leaflets. Very showy white flower clusters (8–12 in. tall, 2–4 in. wide). Bright yellow fall foliage. Good choice for massing, shrub borders, or specimen or understory planting. *A. p. serotina* 'Rogers' has 1½- to 2½-ft.-long flower clusters that are drooping rather than upright and

A

appear about 3 weeks later than those of the species.

A. pavia. RED BUCKEYE. Zones US, MS, LS, CS; USDA 6-9. Native to eastern U.S. Understory shrub or tree grows to 12–20 ft. tall and as wide, with irregular rounded crown. Glossy deep green leaves with five to seven 3- to 6-in.-long leaflets. Bears narrow, erect 10-in. clusters of bright red or orange-red (rarely yellow) flowers. Does best in light shade. Good choice for warm, humid climates.

AGAPANTHUS

LILY-OF-THE-NILE
Agapanthaceae
Perennials from bulbs

✏ **ZONES VARY BY SPECIES**

☼ ◐ **FULL SUN OR PARTIAL SHADE**

◊ ◖ ● **LITTLE TO REGULAR WATER**

Agapanthus

All of these South African natives form handsome, fountainlike clumps of strap-shaped leaves that are evergreen in some species and selections, deciduous in others. In summer, the clumps send up bare stems ending in spherical clusters of funnel-shaped flowers, each cluster like a burst of blue or white fireworks. Some nursery plants are labeled only as "blue" or "white"; if you want a particular shade of blue, choose plants in bloom. Great in containers. Good cut flowers.

A. africanus. Evergreen. Zones LS, CS, TS; USDA 8-11. Shorter, narrower leaves than those of *A. orientalis*; shorter flower stalks (to 1½ ft. high) with fewer flowers (20 to 50 per cluster). Blossoms are deep blue. Often sold as

A. umbellatus.

A. campanulatus. Deciduous. Zones LS, CS, TS; USDA 8-11. To 3 ft. high, with drooping dark blue flowers. 'Albus' is white flowered.

A. inapertus pendulus 'Graskop'. Deciduous. Zones MS, LS, CS, TS; USDA 7-11. A neat clump of light green leaves grows to 2 ft. high, followed by flowering stems that rise another foot above the foliage. The compact, dark violet-blue blossoms droop gracefully.

A. praecox orientalis (*A. orientalis*). Evergreen. Zones CS, TS; USDA 9-11. The most commonly planted species. It forms big clumps with broad, arching leaves, with stems to 4–5 ft. tall bearing up to 100 blue flowers. White ('Albus'), double ('Flore Pleno'), and light to fairly dark blue selections, as well as some with striped leaves, are available. Often sold as *A. africanus, A. umbellatus.*

A. selections and hybrids. Zones MS, LS, CS, TS; USDA 7-11, unless noted. Types sold by selection or hybrid name include the following. All are evergreen, except as noted.

'Baby Blue'. Deciduous. Pale

blue blossoms on 1½-ft. stems.

'Blue Storm'. Growing 2½ ft. tall and in a violet-blue color that blends with anything in the garden, this vigorous, long-blooming selection quickly multiplies into a showy clump with enough blooms to cut for indoor use.

'Bressingham Blue'. Deciduous. Plant is narrow but has 2½-ft. stalks of purple flower clusters 4½ in. across. Good performer.

'Elaine.' Large clusters of nodding bluish purple blossoms borne on 3- to 4-ft.-tall stems. Excellent.

'Ellamae'. Big clusters of large, dark blue flowers on stems to 5 ft. tall. Excellent.

Headbourne hybrids. Deciduous. Flowers in this group come in a range of blues and in white on 2½-ft.-tall stems above fairly narrow, rather upright foliage.

'Henryi'. LS, CS, TS; USDA 8-11. Evergreen. Flowers are white atop a plant 8–12 in. tall and 12–15 in. wide.

'Mood Indigo'. Deciduous. Hybrid involving *A. inapertus,* with deep violet blooms on 3- to 4-ft. stems.

'Peter Pan'. LS, CS, TS; USDA 8-11. Outstanding free-blooming dwarf selection. Foot-high foliage

mass and blue flowers on 1½-ft. stems.

'Queen Anne'. LS, CS, TS; USDA 8-11. Foliage clump to 1½ ft. high; blue blossoms on stems to 2 ft. Excellent.

'Queen Mum'. Deciduous. Grows 1–1½ ft. tall and as wide. Flowers open white with purple base. Excellent.

'Rancho White'. LS, CS, TS; USDA 8-11. Foliage clump grows 1–1½ ft. high; broad leaves. Flower stalks 1½–2 ft. tall carry heavy clusters of white flowers. This selection is also known as 'Dwarf White' and 'Rancho'. 'Peter Pan Albus' is similar or identical.

'Snowstorm'. LS, CS, TS; USDA 8-11. To 2½ ft. tall, with snow-white flowers.

'Stevie's Wonder'. Flower stalks to 2½–3 ft. tall are topped with rich blue-violet blooms. Top performer.

'Storm Cloud'. Growing 2 ft. tall and wide, this plant bears remarkably dark, blue-purple flower clusters.

'Sun Stripe'. Wide, cream-edged variegated foliage makes this agapanthus showy both in and out of bloom. It will reach 1½ ft. tall and 2 ft. wide, topped with blue clusters of flowers.

'Tinkerbell'. LS, CS, TS; USDA 8-11. Grows to 2 ft. tall, with light blue flowers and white-striped leaves.

CARE

Prosper in full sun or light shade. Evergreen types tend to be less hardy, and (despite their description) they may become briefly deciduous in cold weather. Best in loamy soil but will grow in heavy soils. Thrive with regular water, but established plants in the ground year-round can grow and bloom without irrigation during prolonged dry periods in most areas. Mulch for winter protection in Middle and Lower South.

For mass plantings, space plants 1–1½ ft. apart (use the tighter spacing for smaller varieties). Divide every 6 years or so. These are superb container plants. Good near pools. Seldom browsed by deer, but need protection from snails and slugs.

ABOVE: Agapanthus 'Bressingham Blue'

AGARISTA POPULIFOLIA

FLORIDA LEUCOTHOE
Ericaceae
Evergreen shrub

🌿 **US, MS, LS, CS; USDA 6-9**

◐ ● **PARTIAL TO FULL SHADE**

💧 💧 **REGULAR TO AMPLE WATER**

Agarista populifolia 'Leprechaun'

Attractive, upright, arching evergreen shrub native to South Carolina and south to Florida. Grows to 8–12 ft. tall and wide. Oval leaves to 4 in. long are coppery red when new, maturing to a glossy rich green. Cream-colored flowers, borne in early summer, are fragrant but not showy. This plant has an open, multistemmed form that makes it an excellent addition to the woodland garden as a loose, informal screen; it likes shade and moist, acid soil. Good companion for azaleas, rhododendrons, mountain laurel (*Kalmia*), and ferns. Remove old branches at the base periodically to retain the handsome open habit. Avoid shearing. 'Leprechaun' grows only 3–5 ft. tall and 2–3 ft. wide and ne wleaves emerge red. Formerly known as *Leucothoe populifolia*.

AGASTACHE

Lamiaceae
Perennials

🌿 **ZONES VARY BY SPECIES**

☼ ◐ **FULL SUN OR PARTIAL SHADE**

💧 **MODERATE WATER**

Agastache rupestris

Summer-blooming perennials with aromatic foliage and whorls of pink, purple, blue, red, or orange flowers in spikelike clusters. All rebloom if deadheaded. Drought tolerant. Favorites with hummingbirds and butterflies. Species from Mexico and the Southwest need excellent drainage, especially in wet-winter areas.

A. aurantiaca. ORANGE HUMMINGBIRD MINT. Zones MS, LS, CS, TS; USDA 7-11. Native to northern Mexico. To 2½ ft. tall, 2 ft. wide; pink flowers fade to orange. Can be grown as an annual. 'Apricot Sprite' grows 1½ ft. tall. 'Coronado' has yellow blooms suffused with orange.

A. barberi. Zones US, MS, LS, CS, TS; USDA 6-11. From Arizona, New Mexico. To 2 ft. tall and wide, with reddish purple flowers.

A. breviflora. Zones US, MS, LS; USDA 6-8. From Arizona, New Mexico, northern Mexico. To 2 ft. tall, 1½ ft. across; purplish red blossoms.

A. cana. TEXAS HUMMINGBIRD MINT. Zones US, MS, LS, CS, TS; USDA 6-11. Native to Texas, New Mexico. To 2–3 ft. tall, 1½ ft. across. Blooms heavily, bearing reddish pink flowers that smell like bubble gum. A seed-grown selection, 'Heather Queen', blooms the first year if sown early. 'Purple Pygmy' is compact, just 16 in. tall.

A. foeniculum. ANISE HYS-SOP. Zones US, MS, LS, CS; USDA 6-9. From north-central North America. Erect, narrow plant to 3–4 ft. tall and 2 ft. wide, with dense clusters of lilac-blue flowers. Its anise- or licorice-scented leaves make a pleasant tea. Useful and attractive in perennial borders and herb gardens. More tolerant of winter cold and wet than other species. 'Get Riehl' is a hardy selection from the prairie.

A. hybrids. Zones US, MS, LS, CS; USDA 6-9. The following are among the many fine hybrids sold.

'Apricot Sprite'. Grows 2–3 ft. tall, 2 ft. wide. Tubular coral flowers set against rose-pink buds.

'Apricot Sunrise'. To 2½–3 ft. tall, 2–3 ft. wide. Deep orange flowers fade to apricot on opening.

'Black Adder'. Grows 2–3 ft. tall and 1½–2 ft. wide. Red violet flowers may appear black to some.

'Blue Boa'. Grows 2–3 ft. tall and 1½ ft. wide. Blue-violet spikes are remarkably showy.

'Blue Fortune'. To 3 ft. tall, 1½ ft. wide, with powder-blue flower spikes.

'Cotton Candy'. Grows 2 ft. tall and wide, with densely clad spikes of light pink flowers.

'Desert Sunrise'. Tallest of all. Grows to 4 ft. with flowers orange, pink, and lavender.

'Firebird'. To 1½–2 ft. tall, 1½ ft. wide; coppery orange, coral-pink, and red blooms.

'Pink Pop'. 1–1½ ft. tall and about 1 ft. wide. Pink flowers bloom over silver-green leaves.

'Raspberry Summer'. Grows to 2½ ft. tall and 1½–2 ft. wide with large spikes of dark pink flowers.

'Summer Breeze'. To 3 ft. tall, 2 ft. wide. Large, lavender-pink flowers; dark gray-green leaves.

'Summer Glow'. Grows to 2–2½ ft. tall and 1½ ft. wide with pale yellow flowers.

'Tangerine Dreams'. Forms a compact, 1½- to 2-ft.-wide clump; orange flowers, larger and deeper in color than those of 'Apricot Sunrise', top 2- to 3-ft. stems.

'Tutti Frutti'. To 3–4 ft. tall, 1–2 ft. wide, with purplish red blooms set off nicely by gray-green foliage.

A. mexicana. GIANT MEXICAN LEMON HYSSOP. Zones CS, TS; USDA 9-11. Rangy Mexican native to 2–3 ft. (possibly 5 ft.) tall and 1 ft. wide. Bears masses of pink flowers, starting in spring and continuing until late fall. Lemon-scented leaves can be used in tea and as a flavoring. Plants in the Acapulco series bear flowers in salmon-pink, rose-pink, and orange. 'Red Fortune' has red flowers; those of 'Sangria' are reddish purple.

A. rugosa. KOREAN HUMMINGBIRD MINT. Zones US, MS, LS, CS; USDA 6-9. Native to Korea. To 5 ft. tall, 2 ft. wide. Licorice-scented foliage is glossy green with a purple tinge. Flowers are purplish blue. Like *A. foeniculum*, tolerates wet winters. 'Honey Bee Blue' and 'Honey Bee White' are compact growers 2–2½ ft. high. 'Golden Jubilee' grows 1–3 ft. tall and wide with lime-green foliage and violet blooms. The species and its selections will bloom the first year from seed sown early.

A. rupestris. LICORICE MINT, SUNSET HYSSOP. Zones US, MS, LS, CS; USDA 6-9. From southern Arizona, northern Mexico. To 1½–2½ ft. tall and 1½ ft. wide, with threadlike, gray-green leaves and spikes of orange flowers with lavender calyxes. Exceptionally fragrant foliage, with a scent that reminds some of licorice, others of root beer. Outstanding garden performance. Most enduring of these perennials.

AGAVE

Asparagaceae
Succulent perennials

🌿 **CS, TS; USDA 9-11, EXCEPT AS NOTED**

☼ ◐ **FULL SUN OR PARTIAL SHADE, EXCEPT AS NOTED**

◌ 💧 **LITTLE TO MODERATE WATER, EXCEPT AS NOTED**

Agave parryi

Superb as accents, focal points, or in combination with plants of contrasting texture, agaves command attention with their large, fleshy, straplike leaves and tall, unearthly looking blossom spikes. Flowering is sporadic, however, and may not occur for years. The original plant dies after it blooms, leaving offshoots that make new plants.

Gardeners familiar with diverse succulents will note that the former *Manfreda* genus has been merged with *Agave*. These agaves look like crosses between century plant (*Agave*) and tuberose (*Polianthes*). Unlike other agaves, they do not die after blooming. Long, mostly spineless, succulent leaves grow in a rosette from a bulbous base. Flower spikes are tall and sturdy, requiring no staking. The blooms are conversation pieces, good for cut flowers, and appealing to hummingbirds.

The species described here are all easy to grow in well-drained soil. Good in rock gardens and containers.

Like all succulents, agaves tolerate drought but demand excellent drainage. They grow well in containers and are not browsed by deer. Most are tender, but some species withstand freezing weather. Wet soil in winter decreases hardiness. Good plants for coastal gardens.

A. americana. CENTURY PLANT. Zones LS, CS, TS; USDA 8-11. From Mexico. Blue-green leaves to 6 ft. long, with hooked spines along the edges and a wicked spine at the tip. The species is variable but usually makes many offsets. Be sure you really want one before planting it; its bulk (to 8 ft. tall and 12 ft. wide) and spines make it formidable to remove. After 10 years or more, a branched, 15- to 40-ft. flower stalk bearing yellowish green flowers appears. *A. a.* 'Mediopicta Alba' is about half the size of the species, with a cream stripe down the center of each blue-green leaf. The subspecies *A. a. protoamericana* is hardy in the Middle and Lower South.

A. attenuata. FOXTAIL AGAVE. Native to mountains of Jalisco, Mexico. Spineless, fleshy, and somewhat translucent leaves are soft green or gray-green and up to 2½ ft. long. Clumps grow to 6-8 ft. across, and older plants develop a stout trunk to 5 ft. tall. Arching spikes to 12 ft. long are densely set with greenish yellow flowers. This species will take

poor soil but does best in rich soil with regular water. Protect it from frost and hot sun. It makes a statuesque container plant.

A. 'Blue Flame'. Zones CS, TS; USDA 9-11. An elegant, clump-forming hybrid with rosettes of spine-tipped, blue-green leaves to 2½ ft. high and 2 ft. wide. Looks like parent *A. attenuata* but has upward-curving leaf tips that suggest flames. Hardy to about 25°F.

A. 'Blue Glow'. Zones CS, TS; USDA 9-11. This compact, colorful cross between *A. attenuata* and *A. ocahui* grows 1–2 ft. tall and 2–3 ft. wide. It forms a solitary rosette of blue-green leaves edged in red and yellow and tipped with a short red spine; leaves seem to glow when back-lit. Hardy to at least 28°F. In hottest locations, plants grow best with some shade.

A. chrysantha. Zones LS, CS, TS; USDA 8-11. Native to Arizona. Dense rosette to 3 ft. high, 5 ft. wide. Gray-green leaves have hooked spines along the edges and a sharp spine at the tip. Golden yellow flowers are borne on short branches along upper part of a stalk that reaches 12–20 ft. tall.

A. colorata. Zones LS, CS, TS; USDA 8-11. From Mexico. Rosette of broad, flat, spiny-edged, bluish leaves grows slowly to 3 ft. high and wide. Each leaf is tipped with a wickedly sharp 2-in. spine; cut off these spines if you plant this species near a walkway. Reddish orange to yellow flowers on a stalk to 10 ft. tall. Takes heat and cold well.

A. filifera. Zones LS, CS, TS; USDA 8-11. Mexican native. Rosettes are less than 2 ft. wide; leaves are narrow, dark green, lined with white, and edged with long white threads. Spreads fairly quickly to form a clump of tight rosettes. Adapted to very hot, dry sites; hardy to 17°F.

A. guttata 'Jaguar' (*Manfreda guttata* 'Jaguar'). SPOTTED FALSE AGAVE. Zones LS, CS, TS; USDA 8-11. Native to Mexico. Forms a 2-ft.-tall by 3-ft.-wide rosette of lightly toothed, 2-in.-wide, deep green leaves heavily spotted with purple. Tall spikes of spidery, fragrant flowers in summer. Plants form new clumps by offsets.

A. havardiana. Zones US, MS, LS, CS, TS; USDA 6-11. Cold-hardy native of West Texas and New Mexico. Silvery gray leaves

form a sturdy rosette 2 ft. tall and 2½–3 ft. wide. Spines along leaf edges and at tips. Greenish yellow flowers with a reddish tinge are borne on a stalk to 15 ft. tall. Produces the occasional offset but is not really a spreader. Hardy to 0°F in dry gardens.

A. maculosa (*Manfreda maculosa*). TEXAS TUBEROSE. Zones MS, LS, CS; USDA 7-9. Native to southern Texas, northern Mexico. Forms a 1-ft.-tall and 2-ft.-wide rosette of fleshy, narrow, 6- to 12-in.-long leaves in deep green blotched with purple. Dur-

ing summer, 2- to 3-ft.-tall flower stalks bear fragrant, tubular, 2-in.-long blossoms in creamy white aging to purple; long stamens give them a spidery look. Leaves die back in winter but reappear quickly in spring. Plants form new clumps by offsets.

A. mitis (*A. celsii*). Zones CS, TS; USDA 9-11. From the cloud forests of Mexico; tolerates more humidity than other agaves. Apple-green to blue-gray leaves with small, neat teeth form a rosette to 2 ft. tall and wide. Spreads by offsets to form small

TOP: Agave 'Blue Glow'; BOTTOM: A. americana 'Mediopicta Alba'; A. ocahui

colonies. Blossom stalk to 5 ft. tall bears yellowish green to purplish flowers. Provide regular summer water and protection from frost in winter. Needs afternoon shade in hottest areas.

A. ocahui. Zones LS, CS, TS; USDA 8-11. Native to the Sonoran desert. This adaptable species forms a solitary, symmetrical rosette about 2 ft. tall and 3 ft. wide. The straight, narrow, dark green leaves have smooth edges and a sharp but flexible terminal spine. Leaf margins have a thin, dark red, fibrous border that detaches from the mature leaves. Yellow flowers decorate a delicate bloom spike to 10 ft. tall. Plants thrive in sun or shade in any well-drained soil and are hardy to 15°F. Good in pots.

A. parryi. Zones US, MS, LS, CS, TS; USDA 6-11. Native to southwestern U.S. and northern Mexico. Perhaps best known by its two similar botanical varieties, *A. p. parryi* and *A. p. huachucensis*, which produce rosettes resembling giant artichokes 1½–2 ft. high, 2–2½ ft. wide. Both spread by offsets; both have thick blue-green leaves tipped with long spines. *A. p. parryi* is quite cold hardy, and its leaves and spines are smaller than those of *A. p. huachucensis*. When plants are about 20 years old, they produce yellow flowers on a stalk to 15 ft. Both grow well in containers, thrive in partial shade. *A. p. truncata* (Zones MS, LS, CS, TS; USDA 7-11) grows only 1½ ft. tall and wide but multiplies into a clump several feet across.

A. parviflora. Zones MS, LS, CS, TS; USDA 7-11. Native from southeastern Arizona into Mexico. One of the smallest agaves, producing a rosette 6 in. high, 9 in. wide; spreads by offsets. Dark green leaves with white markings; pale yellow flowers on a stalk to about 3 ft. or a little taller.

A. salmiana. Zones LS, CS, TS; USDA 8-11. From Mexico. Rosette to 3–4 ft. high and wide, spreading by offsets. Broad, dark green leaves have smooth edges and spiny tips. Blossom stalk grows 15–25 ft. tall; red buds open to greenish yellow flowers. Dramatic plant for large landscapes. 'Butterfingers' has creamy yellow leaf margins.

A. undulata 'Chocolate Chips' (*Manfreda undulata*

'Chocolate Chips'). Zones MS, LS, CS, TS; USDA 7-11. Native to Mexico. Broad, spreading rosette of deep green, wavy-edged, narrow, cupped leaves covered with purplish brown spots and lightly toothed. Grows about 12 in. tall and twice as wide. Summer flower spikes, up to 3 ft. tall, are lined with dramatic green blooms with long, spidery purple stamens. Great in containers.

A. univittata (*A. lophantha*). Zones LS, CS, TS; USDA 8-11. From Mexico. To 2 ft. high, 4 ft. wide; may spread by offsets to form colonies. Glossy, sword-shaped leaves are dark green with a lighter green stripe (most noticeable in spring and early summer) running down the center. Leaf edges and tips are very spiny. Pale green blossoms on a 6- to 10-ft.-tall stalk. 'Splendida' features a prominent light green stripe down the center of each leaf that endures all season; plant grows 1 ft. tall and 1–2 ft. wide. 'Quadricolor' adds a striking cream edge to the variegated 'Splendida', but is best grown in Coastal South and Tropical South only.

A. variegata (*Manfreda variegata*). Zones LS, CS, TS; USDA 8-11. Native to southern Texas, eastern Mexico. Spreading ground cover for dry soil. Forms a mat to 1 ft. tall and 4 ft. wide. Slender, purple-mottled green leaves to 1½ ft. long. In summer, 4-ft.-tall blossom stalks bear exotic-looking flowers to 1½ in. long that resemble a green-and-maroon version of tuberose blooms.

A. victoriae-reginae. Zones LS, CS, TS; USDA 8-11. Mexican species, forming clumps only a foot or so across. The many stiff, thick leaves are 6 in. long, 2 in. wide, dark green with narrow white lines. Slow growing; will stand in pot or ground 20 years before flowering. Blossoms are greenish, borne on tall stalks. 'Kazo Bana' (Zones CS, TS; USDA 9-11) sports golden edges on the leaves, in addition to the white stripes. Grows slowly to 10 in. tall and 18 in. wide.

A. virginica (*Manfreda virginica*). FALSE ALOE, RATTLESNAKE MASTER. Zones US, MS, LS, CS; USDA 6-9. Native from Maryland to Missouri, south to Texas and Florida. Spreads by rhizomes to form colonies. Dark green leaves may be mottled or striped with red; they grow 2 ft. long and only

2 in. wide. Greenish yellow, spicily fragrant flowers appear atop 6-ft. spikes in summer. Dry seedpods rattle with loose seeds.

AGERATUM HOUSTONIANUM

AGERATUM, FLOSS FLOWER
Asteraceae
Annual

🌿 **US, MS, LS, CS, TS; USDA 6-11**

☀️ ◑ **FULL SUN OR PARTIAL SHADE**

💧 **REGULAR WATER**

Ageratum houstonianum

Reliable favorite for summer and fall color in borders and containers. Native to Central America, West Indies. Hairy, soft green leaves are roundish, usually heart shaped at the base. Tiny, tassel-like flowers in blue, white, or pink come in dense clusters that resemble powder puffs. Most floss flowers form foot-wide clumps, but heights vary. Dwarf kinds (4–6 in. high) with blue flowers include 'Blue Blazer', 'Blue Danube' ('Blue Puffs'), 'Blue Surf', and 'Royal Delft'. Taller (9- to 12-in.) types include 'Blue Mink', 'North Sea', and Patina Delft. Good selections in other colors are 'Pacific Pink', 'Patina Purple', 'Pink Powder-puffs' and 'Summer Snow', all 9–12 in. tall. 'Artist Rose' may grow 8–18 in. tall, and 'Blue Horizon' may reach 1–2½ ft. All are best in rich, moist soil. Easy to transplant even when in bloom. Low growers make excellent edgings or pattern plantings with other annuals of similar size. Taller types provide good cut flowers. Seldom browsed by deer.

AGLAONEMA

Araceae
Perennials

🌿 **TS; USDA 10-11; OR HOUSEPLANTS**

☼ ● **PARTIAL TO FULL SHADE; CAN TAKE VERY LOW LIGHT**

💧 **REGULAR WATER**

Aglaonema 'Key Lime'

Grown for their highly ornamental foliage, these tropical plants are made for low light. In most areas, they are grown strictly indoors. *A. modestum*, the most popular species, will thrive in an interior room lit only by a fluorescent light. In the Tropical South, aglaonemas can be used outdoors in shady plantings.

With the recent arrival of colorful selections from Thailand, aglaonemas have been transformed from the familiar green-and-silver houseplants to specimens splashed with color like a croton, coleus, or caladium. These new spangled plants have the same leathery texture to the leaf and grow well indoors. Look for names such as 'Sparkling Sarah', 'Siam Aurora', 'Valentine', and many more.

Potted plants need rich, well-drained soil mix. Let soil go slightly dry between waterings; in spring and summer, fertilize every other week with general-purpose houseplant fertilizer. Plants growing in dim light will require less frequent watering and feeding. Mealybugs are the most common pests.

A. commutatum. Grows to 2 ft. tall and wide. Deep green leaves to 6 in. long, 2 in. across, with pale green markings on veins. Flowers followed by inch-long clusters of yellow to red berries. *A. c. maculatum*, with many irregular gray-green stripes on leaves, is the most common. 'Pseudobracteatum' grows 1–2 ft. tall, has white leafstalks and deep green leaves marked with pale green and creamy yellow. 'Treubii' has narrow, bluish green leaves heavily marked with silvery gray.

A. costatum. Slow-growing plant to 2½ ft. tall and wide, with leaves to 8 in. long, 4 in. wide. Leaves are bright green, with white spots and a broad white stripe along the midrib. 'Foxii' is similar or identical.

A. crispum. PAINTED DROP-TONGUE. Robust plant to 4 ft. tall and broad. Leathery leaves to 10 in. long, 5 in. wide, dark green with pale green markings. Sometimes sold as *A.* 'Pewter'.

A. 'Key Lime'. Striking leaves marbled with deep green, yellow-green, and gray-green. White leaf stems.

A. modestum. CHINESE EVERGREEN. A tough-as-nails, easily grown plant, in time forming substantial clumps with several stems 2–3 ft. high. Shiny, dark green leaves grow to 1½ ft. long and 5 in. wide. Often sold as *A. simplex*.

A. 'Silver King' and 'Silver Queen'. Both grow to 2 ft. high and wide and are heavy producers of narrow, dark green leaves strongly marked with silver. Leaves of 'Silver King' can reach about 1 ft. long and 4 in. wide; those of 'Silver Queen' are a little smaller.

AGLAONEMA CUTTINGS ARE EASILY ROOTED IN SOIL OR WATER.

AILANTHUS ALTISSIMA

TREE OF HEAVEN
Simaroubaceae
Deciduous tree

US, MS, LS; USDA 6-8

FULL SUN

LITTLE OR NO WATER TO REGULAR WATER

Ailanthus altissima

If any tree could be termed a "garbage tree," this is it. Native to China, it has spread by seed over much of the South. Because it tolerates drought, pollution, wind, and terrible soil (not to mention verbal abuse), it comes up everywhere—alleys, yards, parking lots, roadsides, even cracks in the pavement. Often seen on city streets, thriving where all other trees have failed. Grows very fast to 50 ft. tall and wide. The leaves reach 1–3 ft. long and are divided into many leaflets; they resemble sumac (*Rhus*) foliage. Male trees bear malodorous green flowers; females produce inconspicuous blooms that give rise to showy clusters of reddish winged seedpods. Branches release a sickening smell when cut or broken. Whoever named this plant "tree of heaven" had a dim view of the afterlife.

AJANIA PACIFICA

GOLD AND SILVER CHRYSANTHEMUM

Asteraceae
Perennial

US, MS, LS, CS; USDA 6-9

FULL SUN

REGULAR WATER

Ajania pacifica

Semitrailing and semishrubby perennial from Japan; to 1 ft. tall, 3 ft. wide. Stems densely clad in lobed, dark green leaves with woolly white undersides that show at leaf edges. Broad clusters of yellow, ¾-in. flowers appear in fall; lacking rays, they resemble brass buttons. 'Pink Ice' is pale pink with short rays. Use as bank or ground cover or at front of perennial border. Needs well-drained soil. In Lower and Coastal South, you may cut back after bloom to keep compact form; in Upper and Middle South, wait until strong new growth appears in spring, then cut back partway.

AJUGA

BUGLEWEED
Lamiaceae
Perennials

US, MS, LS; USDA 6-8

SUN OR SHADE

REGULAR WATER

Ajuga reptans 'Black Scallop'

These low-growing ground covers and rock garden plants from Europe offer both handsome foliage and showy flowers; both leaves and blossoms come in several different colors. Bloom runs from spring through early summer. Most types spread quickly to form mats. Easy to divide at any time of year. Good drainage is essential to avoid crown rot. Plants are not browsed by deer.

A. genevensis. GENEVA BUGLEWEED. Rock garden plant 5–14 in. high, 1½ ft. wide; does not spread by runners. Grayish, hairy stems and coarse-toothed leaves to 3 in. long. Blue flowers in spikes. 'Pink Beauty' and 'Alba' offer color choices.

A. pyramidalis. Erect plant 2–10 in. high, 1½ –2 ft. wide; does not spread by runners. Stems have long grayish hairs, are set with many roundish, 2½- to 4-in.-long leaves. Violet-blue flowers are not obvious among the large leaves. 'Metallica Crispa' has reddish brown leaves with a metallic glint.

A. reptans. CARPET BUGLEWEED. This popular form spreads rapidly by runners, making a mat of dark green leaves in the basic species. Each oval to tongue-shaped leaf is 2–3 in. wide in full sun, to 4 in. wide in shade; entire foliage mass tops out at around 4 in. high. Blue flowers in 6-in. spikes appear in spring. Plant

A

l ft. apart in spring or early fall. Subject to root rots and fungal diseases where drainage or air circulation is poor. Mow or trim off old flower spikes.

Many selections are available, and some are sold under several names. The following are among the better choices; all have blue flowers unless otherwise noted. Selections with bronzy or metallic-looking leaves keep their color best in sun.

'Alba'. White-blooming form.

'Black Scallop'. Blackish purple foliage with scalloped edges.

'Blueberry Muffin'. Vigorous ground cover of small, dark leaves and blue flowers on spikes up to 6 in. Comparable to 'Chocolate Chip' but spreads faster. 'Bronze Beauty' has bronze foliage, is a fast spreader.

'Burgundy Glow' ('Burgundy Lace'). Reddish purple foliage variegated with white and pink.

'Catlin's Giant'. Large, bronzy green leaves; flower spikes to 8 in. tall.

'Chocolate Chip' ('Valfredda'). Narrow, chocolate-brown leaves on a slow-growing dwarf plant. 'Toffee Chip' was a mutation and is similar in every way, except leaves are cream and green.

'Jungle Beauty'. Clumps of large, rounded, wavy-edged, bronze-toned leaves; flower spikes to 8–10 in. high.

'Jungle Green'. Large-leafed form with green foliage. Less mounded than 'Jungle Beauty'.

'Linda Applegate'. Bright green form with white flowers that is slow to spread.

'Multicolor' ('Rainbow'). Leaves are green blended with white and pinkish purple.

'Pink Lightning'. Pink blooms, white-edged, gray-green leaves.

'Sparkler'. This variegated form has splotches of white on a green leaf, more striated than others.

AKEBIA QUINATA
FIVELEAF AKEBIA
Lardizabalaceae
Semievergreen to deciduous vine

⚡ **US, MS, LS, CS; USDA 6-9**

☼ ● **SUN OR SHADE**

💧 **REGULAR WATER**

Akebia quinata

The leaves of this native to Japan, China, and Korea are 1½ –3 in. long, each with five oblong leaflets that are notched at the tips. New leaves are tinged purple, then mature to bluish green. Early spring blossoms are fragrant, rosy purple to chocolate-purple, hanging in clusters to 5 in. long. Blooms are mostly hidden by leaves and are not terribly showy. 'Alba' and 'Shirobana' have white flowers; those of 'Rosea' are lavender. 'Variegata' has light pink flowers and leaves splashed with creamy white. Edible fruit, only occasionally produced, resembles a thick purplish sausage 2–4 in. long.

Akebia climbs by twining and will climb as tall as its support. It can easily grow 20 ft. or more in a year, but its stems do not crush lattice or wood or metal supports. Good for quick coverage of arbors, chain-link fences, or large walls (if given attachment for its stems). Can also be used to frame a doorway, though it will require pruning almost weekly to keep it in bounds. In Lower South and Coastal South, the vine is mostly evergreen. It may be deciduous in the Upper and Middle South. Renew or contain plants by pruning to the ground in winter; they rebound quickly. Invasive in moist shade.

A. trifoliata. THREELEAF AKEBIA. Similar to *A. quinata*, but each leaf has three leaflets. It's also less vigorous and less common. 'Deep Purple' boasts blackish purple, extremely fragrant flowers.

ALBIZIA JULIBRISSIN
MIMOSA
Mimosaceae
Deciduous tree

⚡ **US, MS, LS, CS; USDA 6-9**

☼ ◑ **FULL SUN OR PARTIAL SHADE**

💧 **REGULAR WATER**

Albizia julibrissin

Native to Asia from Iran to Japan, mimosa elicits strong opinions in the South. Those who love it point to its soft, ferny foliage, ease of growth, smooth bark for climbing, and showy summer flowers—red, rose, shell-pink, or white powderpuffs that have a light gardenia scent and attract butterflies and hummingbirds. Those who hate mimosa, however, emphasize its susceptibility to webworms and wilt diseases, as well as its weak, brittle branches and invasive roots, its knack for reseeding all over creation, its unattractive appearance in winter, and its relatively short life span.

Mimosa grows rapidly to 40 ft. tall with a wider spread. It tolerates drought, pollution, wind, salt spray, and alkaline soil. 'Rosea' has rich pink flowers and is considered more cold hardy than the species. 'Flame' has rosy red flowers; 'California Red' boasts red blossoms. 'Summer Chocolate' features bronze foliage with pink flowers.

ALCEA
HOLLYHOCK
Malvaceae
Biennials or short-lived perennials

⚡ **US, MS, LS, CS; USDA 6-9**

☼ ◑ **PARTIAL SHADE IN HOTTEST CLIMATES**

💧 **REGULAR WATER**

Alcea rosea

Hollyhocks are cultivated for their big, colorful, funnel-shaped summer flowers. Need rich, well-drained soil.

A. rosea. HOLLYHOCK. This old-fashioned charmer from the Mediterranean region is best against a fence or wall or at the back of a border. Old single selections can reach 9 ft. tall; newer strains and selections are shorter. Big, rough, roundish, heart-shaped leaves, slightly lobed, form a clump to about 3 ft. wide. Flowers are 3–6 in. wide along upright stems; they may be single, semidouble, or double in colors including white, pink, rose, red, purple, creamy yellow, apricot. 'Old Barnyard' mix grows 4–6 ft. tall; 'Happy Lights' are 5–7 ft. tall and rust resistant, 'Spring Celebrities' mix reaches 2½–3 ft. with double flowers, and the 'Indian Spring' mix ranges from dark purple and pink to white. Chater's Double is a fine perennial strain; the 6-ft. spires have 5- to 6-in.-wide flowers. Biennials treated as annuals that bloom the first year from seed include 5- to 6-ft.-tall 'Summer Carnival,' with double flowers; and 2½ -ft.-tall 'Majorette' mix.

A. rugosa. RUSSIAN HOLLYHOCK. Although from southern Russia and Ukraine, this hollyhock is a good perennial for the South. Similar to old single forms of *A. rosea*, the 6- to 7-ft.

stems are topped with single, butter-yellow blossoms. Disease resistant.

CARE

Sow seeds in ground in late summer for next season's bloom; seed annual strains in early spring for bloom that summer. After flowers fade, cut stalks just above the ground; continue to feed and water plants to encourage late-summer or early-fall rebloom. Destroy any rust-infected leaves as soon as disease appears. Look for yellow spots on the leaf surface and orange spots with spores underneath. The spores are carried on the wind and will weaken a plant and destroy new growth. Remove infected leaves from the plant as well as from the mulch below. Also watch for slugs, snails, Japanese beetles.

ALCHEMILLA
LADY'S MANTLE
Rosaceae
Perennials

ZONES VARY BY SPECIES

PARTIAL TO FULL SHADE

REGULAR WATER

Alchemilla mollis

Rounded, pale green, lobed leaves have a silvery look; after rain or watering, they hold beads of water on their surfaces. Summer flowers are yellowish green in large, branched clusters, attractive as a frothy mass. Use for edgings in shady places, as ground cover, and as contrast to brighter flowers. Not browsed by deer.

A. alpina. Zones US, MS; USDA 6-7. Native to northern Europe, Greenland. This mat-

forming plant creeps by runners, with flowering stems 6–8 in. tall. Leaves are divided into five to seven leaflets.

A. ellenbeckii. Zones US, MS; USDA 6-7. Native to mountains of East Africa. Attractive, small-scale ground cover to about 2 in. high, with creeping, rooting stems and leaves less than 1 in. wide.

A. erythropoda. Zones US, MS; USDA 6-7. Native to mountains of Balkans, Turkey. Resembles *A. glaucescens* but has more deeply lobed leaves and red-tinted flowering stems.

A. glaucescens. Zones US, MS; USDA 6-7. Native to Europe. Dense grower, wide spreading in time. Nearly round leaves with seven to nine lobes. Flowering stems to 8 in. high.

A. mollis. Zones US, MS, LS; USDA 6-8. Native to Asia Minor. The most commonly planted lady's mantle. Clump-forming plant to 2 ft. or taller, 2½ ft. wide. Nearly circular, scallop-edged leaves to 6 in. across. To prevent self-sowing, deadhead plants soon after flowering. 'Auslese' bears bright lime-green flowers. 'Thriller' has large, shiny, gray-green leaves and golden-yellow blooms.

A. pectinata. Zones MS, LS; USDA 7-8. Native to Mexico. Miniature, creeping ground cover with inch-wide leaves.

PLANT
LADY'S
MANTLE
ALONG A
SHADY PATH
AND LET IT
RESEED FOR
A CASUAL
LOOK.

ALLAMANDA
Apocynaceae
Evergreen vines or shrubs

TS; USDA 10-11; ANYWHERE AS ANNUALS OR INDOOR/ OUTDOOR PLANTS

FULL SUN

REGULAR WATER

ALL PARTS ARE POISONOUS IF INGESTED

Allamanda cathartica

From Tropical South and Central America. These plants have striking foliage and trumpet-shaped flowers (borne nearly year-round). Plant permanently outdoors only in the mildest climates. Elsewhere, grow as summer-blooming potted plants; keep indoors during cold weather. They tolerate very little frost and need heat for proper growth and bloom; warm nights and warm days are necessary. Remove spent flowers for increased bloom.

A. blanchetii (*A. violacea*). PURPLE ALLAMANDA. Shrubby or with a few vining stems; usually grows 6–10 ft. tall and wide. Leaves are somewhat downy and up to 5 in. long. Rose-purple flowers are 3½ in. across. 'Cherries Jubilee' has brilliant burgundy-red blooms.

A. cathartica. ALLAMANDA, GOLDEN TRUMPET. Can grow to great heights (over 50 ft.) as a vine; it can clamber through trees but must be tied to other supports. Often pinched back to grow as a large, freestanding shrub. Leaves are glossy, leathery, 4–6 in. long. Yellow trumpets are 5 in. wide, 3 in. long. 'Chocolate Swirl' have pinkish-purple flowers with purple-brown throats. 'Flore Pleno' bears double flowers. 'Hendersonii' bears exceptionally

attractive orange-yellow blooms.

A. schottii. BUSH ALLAMANDA. Shrubby growth to 4–6 ft. high and wide; produces occasional climbing stems. Flowers are 3 in. wide, bright yellow, sometimes with throats tinted orange or reddish.

ALLIUM
ORNAMENTAL ALLIUM
Liliaceae
Perennials from bulbs

ZONES VARY BY SPECIES

FULL SUN OR PARTIAL SHADE

REGULAR WATER DURING GROWTH AND BLOOM

Allium 'Globemaster'

About 500 species, all from the Northern Hemisphere. Relatives of the edible onion, peerless as cut flowers (fresh or dried), useful in borders; smaller kinds are effective in rock gardens. Plants bear small flowers in clusters (umbels) atop leafless stems that range from 6 in.–5 ft. tall or more. Umbels may be tightly or loosely arranged; some look like spheres, others like exploding fireworks. Bloom comes in spring or summer with flowers in white and shades of pink, rose, violet, red, blue, and yellow. Most ornamental alliums are hardy, sun loving, easy to grow; they thrive in deep, rich, sandy loam. Plant bulbs in fall. Lift and divide only after they become crowded.

Leaves of most alliums are narrow and upright, varying in form from grassy to strap shaped; they often begin to die back before flowering starts. Small flowers come in roundish, compact or loose clusters. Some

TOP: Allium aflatunense 'Purple Sensation'; BOTTOM: Allium rosenbachianum 'White Empress'

are delightfully fragrant; those with onion odor must be bruised or cut to detect it. All alliums die to the ground after bloom, even in mild climates. Seldom browsed by deer.

A. aflatunense. Zones US, MS, LS; USDA 6-8. Blooms in late spring, bearing tennis ball-size clusters of lilac flowers on stems 2½ –5 ft. tall. Resembles *A. giganteum* but with smaller flower clusters. 'Purple Sensation' has violet-purple blooms.

A. atropurpureum. Zones US, MS, LS; USDA 6-8. Stems to 2½ ft. tall carry 2-in. clusters of dark purple to nearly black flowers in late spring.

A. caeruleum (A. azureum). BLUE ALLIUM. Zones US, MS, LS; USDA 6-8. Cornflower blue flowers in dense, round, 2-in. clusters on 1- to 1½-ft. stems. Late-spring bloom.

A. carinatum pulchellum. Zones US, MS, LS; USDA 6-8. Loose, pendent, 2½-in. clusters of reddish purple flowers on 1- to 2-ft. stems. Blooms in summer.

A. cepa. See Onion

A. christophii. STAR OF PERSIA. Zones US, MS, LS; USDA 6-8. Distinctive. Very large clusters (6–12 in. across) of starlike, lavender to deep lilac flowers with metallic sheen. Late-spring bloom. Stems are 12–15 in. tall. Leaves to 1½ ft. long, white and hairy beneath. Dried flower cluster looks like an elegant holiday ornament.

A. giganteum. GIANT ALLIUM. Zones US, MS, LS; USDA 6-8. Spectacular softball-size clusters of bright lilac flowers on stems to 3–5 ft. or taller. Late-spring bloom. Leaves 1½ ft. long, 2 in. wide.

A. 'Globemaster'. Zones US, MS; USDA 6-7. Popular selection bearing astonishing clusters like a ball on a stick. Clusters are 6–8 in. across and deep violet in late spring. Stalks stand 2½ ft. tall.

A. karataviense. TURKESTAN ALLIUM. Zones US, MS, LS; USDA 6-8. Dense, round, 2- to 3-in. flower clusters in midspring, in colors from pinkish to beige to reddish lilac. Broad, flat, recurved leaves, 2–5 in. across.

A. 'Millenium'. Zones US, MS, LS, CS; USDA 6-9. A reliable perennial summer-blooming onion with 10- to 15-in. tall stems topped with golf ball-size pink blooms.

A. moly. GOLDEN GARLIC. Zones US, MS, LS; USDA 6-8. Stems 9–18 in. tall bear open clusters of flowers in bright, shining yellow. Late-spring bloom.

A. neapolitanum. Zones US, MS, LS, CS; USDA 6-9. Spreading, 2-in. clusters of large, fragrant, white flowers on 1-ft. stems bloom in midspring. Leaves 1 in. wide. 'Grandiflorum' is larger, blooms earlier. A form of 'Grandiflorum' listed as 'Cowanii' is considered superior. Grown commercially as cut flowers.

A. oreophilum (A. ostrowski-anum). Zones US, MS, LS, CS; USDA 6-9. Loose, 1½-in. clusters of rose-colored flowers on 8- to 12-in. stems in late spring; two or three gray-green leaves. Good for rock gardens, cutting.

A. porrum. See Leek

A. rosenbachianum. Zones US, MS, LS; USDA 6-8. Baseball-size clusters of rosy purple blossoms with contrasting white stamens in late spring.

A. sativum. See Garlic

A. schoenoprasum. See Chives.

A. schubertii. Zones MS, LS, CS; USDA 7-9. The mauve starburst of flowers measures 8–10 in. across, yet remains subtle. Blooming in late spring from 12–24 in. tall, it prefers full sun, transitioning to partial shade in warmer areas.

A. scorodoprasum. See Garlic

A. sphaerocephalum. DRUMSTICKS, ROUND-HEADED GARLIC. Zones US, MS, LS, CS; USDA 6-9. Tight, dense, spherical, inch-wide, red-purple flower clusters on 2-ft. stems in early to midsummer. Spreads freely.

A. triquetrum. THREE-CORNERED LEEK. Zones US, MS, LS; USDA 6-8. Heirloom bulb that blooms late spring and early summer when others have finished. A cluster of white bells stand 14–18 in. tall. May naturalize in moist soils.

A. tuberosum. See Garlic Chives

ALMOND
Rosaceae
Deciduous tree

◪ **MS, LS; USDA 7-8**

☼ **FULL SUN**

◖ **MODERATE WATER**

Almonds

In most parts of the South, growing almonds is no joy. Though closely related to the peach, the almond (*Prunus dulcis*) is considerably fussier about its requirements. Nuts develop properly only in regions with long, hot, dry summers, like those in the plant's native Asia Minor and North Africa, and late-spring frosts can spell the end for a developing crop. For these reasons, almost all commercially grown almonds come from Southern California. Some selections, however, can succeed in Texas and Oklahoma.

An almond tree grows 20–30 ft. high, upright when young, and then more rounded with age. Pale pink or white flowers appear in early spring. Fruit looks like a flattened, undersized green peach. In autumn, the pit splits to reveal the nut inside, which is the almond.

ALOCASIA

ELEPHANT'S EAR
Araceae
Perennials

- **ZONES VARY BY SPECIES; OR HOUSEPLANTS**
- **PARTIAL SHADE; BRIGHT INDIRECT LIGHT**
- **REGULAR TO AMPLE WATER**
- **SAP IS POISONOUS IF INGESTED**

Alocasia macrorrhiza

These plants and their big leaves come from the streamsides and marshes of tropical Asia and bring a lush look to gardens. Many fancy-leafed selections have been introduced recently, and more are sure to follow. They can be grown indoors in bright light or outdoors in filtered sunlight. Give them moist, well-drained soil containing lots of organic matter. Provide shelter from wind so leaves don't get tattered. The flowers are like those of calla (*Zantedeschia*)—a spikelike structure (spadix) surrounded by a fleshy, hoodlike bract (spathe). Flowers are followed by reddish fruit, giving spike the look of corn on the cob. Although useful in garden beds and containers, most are sensitive to frost.

A. amazonica. AFRICAN MASK. Zone TS; USDA 10-11. Leathery, deep bronzy green leaves to 16 in. long have wavy edges, heavy white main veins. Plants may grow as tall as 4 ft. and about half as wide. This species is the one most commonly available as a houseplant.

A. cucullata. CHINESE TARO, CHINESE APE. Zones LS, CS, TS; USDA 8-11. Slow-growing, clumping evergreen plant to 3 ft. high. Grown for shiny, deep green, pointed leaves to 15 in. long,

1 ft. wide. Usually massed as a ground cover; plant 1½–2 ft. apart. Requires moist, rich, well-drained soil and protection from wind. Excellent container plant.

A. macrorrhiza. GIANT ALOCASIA, GIANT TARO. Zones CS, TS; USDA 9-11. Evergreen at 29°F; loses leaves at lower temperatures but comes back in spring if frosts are not too severe. Medium to dark green, arrow-shaped leaves grow to 2 ft. or longer on stalks to 5 ft. tall, form a dome-shaped plant 4 ft. across; may grow as large as 12 ft. tall, 10 ft. wide in Tropical South. The foliage of 'Variegata' is blotched with creamy white, gray-green, or darker green. 'Yellow Tail' features thick, twisted, green leaves with irregular yellow blotches.

A. 'Mayan Mask'. Zones LS, CS, TS; USDA 8-11. Hybrid with oversized, arrow-shaped, green leaves with white veins and purple undersides.

A. micholitziana 'Frydek'. Zones CS, TS; USDA 9-11. Velvety, dark green leaves with prominent white veins.

A. 'Morocco'. Zone TS; USDA 10-11. Green leaves have white veins like *A. amazonica*, but the petioles are striking coral-pink.

A. odora. Zones LS, CS, TS; USDA 8-11. Similar to *A. macrorrhiza* but hardier. Fragrant flowers.

A. plumbea. Zones CS, TS; USDA 9-11. This Indonesian species resembles *A. macrorrhiza* but it is not quite as hardy and bears fragrant flowers. Selections with colorful leaves include 'Metallica', with a purple luster; dark green to black 'Nigra'; and red-tinted 'Rubra'.

A. 'Portodora'. Zones LS, CS, TS; USDA 8-11. This hybrid elephant's ear looks much like *A. macrorrhiza* but reaches 8 ft. tall, with giant (4-ft.), wavy, scalloped leaves on purple stems.

A. sanderiana. Zone TS; USDA 10-11. Grows to 6 ft. tall and wide. Arrow-shaped, deeply lobed leaves about 12–16 in. long, metallic dark purplish green with silver veining on surface.

A. 'Sarian'. Zones CS, TS; USDA 9-11. Big, arrow-shaped leaves with prominent white veins reaching 15–36 in. across and 4–8 ft. tall.

A. wentii. Zones LS, CS, TS; USDA 8-11. This is a hardy species, surviving 10°F. Grows in a tight clump. Can reach 4 ft. high and

wide, but may not get bigger than 1½ ft. if grown outdoors in colder part of range. Arrow-shaped leaves to 1 ft. long are bronzy green on top, purplish underneath.

ALOE

Asphodelaceae
Succulent trees, shrubs, and perennials

- **TS; USDA 10-11, EXCEPT AS NOTED**
- **FULL SUN OR LIGHT SHADE, EXCEPT AS NOTED**
- **LITTLE TO MODERATE WATER**
- **SAP BENEATH PLANTS' SKIN IS AN IRRITANT**

Aloe arborescens

Primarily South African natives, the aloes range from 6-in. miniatures to trees; all form clumps of fleshy, pointed leaves and bear branched or unbranched clusters of orange, yellow, cream, or red flowers. Some species bloom nearly every month, but the biggest show comes from midwinter through summer. Leaves may be green or gray-green, often strikingly banded or streaked with contrasting colors. Showy and easy to grow in well-drained soil in reasonably frost-free areas; need little water but can take more. Most tolerate salt spray and are good beach plants. Seldom browsed by deer.

Where winters are too cold for all-year outdoor culture, grow aloes in pots and shelter from frosts. Most kinds make outstanding container plants. Highly valued as ornamentals, in the ground or in pots. The aloes listed here are only a few of the many kinds. Sizes given apply to plants grown outdoors in the ground.

A. arborescens. TORCH ALOE. Zones CS, TS; USDA 9-11. Grows about 10 ft. tall, 6 ft. wide, though older clumps may reach 18 ft. Branching stems carry big clumps of gray-green, spiny-edged leaves. Winter flowers in long, spiky clusters, bright vermilion to clear yellow. Withstands salt spray. Tolerates shade. Foliage damaged at 29°F, but plants have survived 17°F.

A. aristata. Zones LS, CS, TS; USDA 8-11. Dwarf for pots, edging, and ground covers; just 8–12 in. tall and about as wide. Rosettes are packed with 4-in.-long, ¾-in.-wide leaves ending in whiplike threads. Produces orange-red flowers in 1- to 1½-ft.-tall clusters, winter to spring.

A. barberae (*A. bainesii*). Slow-growing tree to 20–30 ft. or taller, with heavy, forking trunk and branches. Rosettes of 2–3 ft. leaves; spikes of rose-pink flowers in winter on 1½- to 2-ft. stalks. Used for stately, sculptural pattern in landscape. Tender to frost.

A. 'Blue Elf'. This dwarf hybrid with 6-in. rosettes of tooth-edged, blue-green foliage eventually forms a dense mound 1–2 ft. high and wide. Orange flowers appear winter to spring. Tolerates light frosts.

A. brevifolia. SHORT-LEAF ALOE. Zones LS, CS, TS; USDA 8-11. Low, spreading clumps of blunt, thick, gray-green, spiny-edged leaves 3 in. long. Clusters of red flowers on 20-in. stalks, intermittent all year. Tolerates light frosts.

A. ciliaris. CLIMBING ALOE. Climbing, sprawling form with pencil-thick stems to 10 ft. long. Small, thick, soft green leaves. Long-stalked, 3- to 6-in. flower clusters with 20–30 green- or yellow-tipped scarlet flowers; intermittent bloom all year. Takes a bit more shade than other species listed here. Tender to frost.

A. distans. JEWELED ALOE. Zones CS, TS; USDA 9-11. Running, rooting, branching stems make clumps of 6-in., fleshy, blue-green leaves with scattered whitish spots and white teeth along edges. Forked flower stems, 1½–2 ft. tall, carry clusters of red flowers in winter. Tolerates light frosts.

A. ferox. CAPE ALOE. Treelike aloe with a large single trunk rising 6–10 ft. high (after 10 years). Trunk is topped by a single crown of gray-green, spiny, red-toothed leaves 3–4 ft. long and 6–8 in. wide. Each branched inflorescence holds hundreds of bright scarlet or orange blossoms in late winter or early spring.

A. maculata (*A. saponaria*). SOAP ALOE. Zones LS, CS, TS; USDA 8-11. Short-stemmed rosettes 1 ft. or more wide feature broad, white-spotted, green leaves to 8 in. long. Multibranched, 1½- to 1½-ft. flower stalks rise in summer, topped with tight heads of nodding blossoms in scarlet, red-orange, salmon-pink, or yellow. May grow as a solitary plant or send out suckers to form dense, expanding colonies. Dig and separate when plants become too crowded. 'Yellow Form' is dense with lemon-yellow flowers that bloom earlier. Among forms with shrimp-pink flowers, the most widely grown is old hybrid 'Commutata'.

A. marlothii. MOUNTAIN ALOE. Large, treelike aloe with a stout trunk to 12 ft. tall, topped by a single, dense foliage rosette. Leaves are green or grayish, 3–4 ft. long and up to 8 in. wide, often spined on both surfaces and margins. Old dried leaves persist on trunk. Winter flower clusters branch horizontally, holding many spikes in yellow, orange, or (rarely) red or bicolors.

A. x nobilis. GOLD-TOOTH ALOE. Dark green leaves edged with small hooked teeth grow in rosettes to 1 ft. wide and high. Suckers freely, forming a spreading, mounded clump. Clustered orange-red flowers on 2-ft. stalks in early summer. Good in pots; takes limited root space.

A. striata. CORAL ALOE. Zones CS, TS; USDA 9-11. Broad, spineless leaves to 20 in. long are gray-green with a narrow pinkish-red edge. They grow in rosettes 2 ft. wide on short trunk. Brilliant coral-pink to orange flowers in branched clusters, midwinter into spring. Handsome, tailored-looking plant.

A. striatula. HARDY ALOE. Zones LS, CS, TS; USDA 8-11. Scrambling shrub has glossy, green leaves, each edged with a thin white margin and minute teeth; distinctly striped leaf bases surround the stem. Multiple stems form a dense mound 5–6 ft. tall and to 15 ft. across, but plant may be kept much more compact with occasional hard pruning. Single spikes of flowers in scarlet, orange, or yellow rise 6–18 in. above the foliage in summer.

A. tenuior. Dense, much-branched, climbing or scrambling shrub to 2–4 ft. tall. Lax stems to 10 ft. long (often horizontal) are tipped with rosettes of 6-in.-long, 1-in.-wide leaves edged with tiny white teeth. In late spring, 6- to 12-in. unbranched spikes of tiny, cylindrical yellow (sometimes red) flowers are held horizontally above the mound. Best given support of a fence or rocks or trained up a palm trunk.

A. variegata. PARTRIDGE-BREAST ALOE, TIGER ALOE. Forms a foot-high, tight rosette of fleshy, triangular, dark green, 5-in.-long leaves strikingly banded and edged with white. Loose clusters of pink to dull red flowers, intermittent all year. Best with some shade; can be grown as a houseplant.

A. vera (*A. barbadensis*). MEDICINAL ALOE, BARBADOS ALOE. Rosettes of narrow, fleshy, upright leaves 1–2 ft. long. Yellow flowers are borne in a dense spike atop 3-ft. stalk, spring and summer. Favorite folk medicine plant used to treat burns, bites, inflammation, and a host of other ills. Needs a moderate amount of water to look good.

ALOYSIA
Verbenaceae
Deciduous or semievergreen shrubs

🌡 **LS, CS, TS; USDA 8-11; OR GROW IN POTS**

☀ **FULL SUN**

💧 **REGULAR WATER**

Aloysia citriodora

With their tiny flowers and leggy stems, these aromatic shrubs from the warmer parts of the Americas aren't grown for their

looks; they're valued for their blossoms and scented leaves, which can be used for seasoning or to flavor iced drinks and teas. Like most herbs, they require good drainage.

A. citriodora (*Lippia citriodora*). LEMON VERBENA. When you read of "the scent of verbena" in novels of the antebellum South, this is the plant being described. Prized for its shiny, aromatic foliage, which fills the air with a citruslike fragrance.

Legginess is the natural state of this shrub. It grows to 6 ft. or taller, sprawling to 6 ft. wide; narrow leaves to 3 in. long are arranged in whorls of three or four along the branches. Plant it among lower plants, or locate it against a wall or fence where you can pinch-prune it to create an interesting tracery. It can also be trained into a standard and tolerates clipping into a hedge. Major pruning is best done late winter and early spring.

Bears open clusters of very small lilac or whitish flowers in summer. Needs well-drained soil. Plants wintered indoors usually lose their leaves and then sprout again in spring.

A. wrightii. OREGANILLO, MEXICAN OREGANO. Native to desert mountains from California to Texas and northern Mexico. This dense grower reaches 5 ft. high and wide, with numerous small stems and small (½-in.) leaves. From spring through fall, produces very sweet-scented white flowers that can be used as a flavoring or for tea. Performs best when it gets lots of heat. Good in natural landscape, herb garden, as informal hedge.

Often confused with *A. lycioides*, a larger plant (to 8 ft. tall and 6 ft. wide) bearing blossoms that have a more vanillalike fragrance and are sometimes tinged with purple. Plants sold under either name may be one or the other—but both are outstanding ornamentals. Both make excellent honey. *A. lycioides* is the Mexican oregano of commerce.

ALPINIA
Zingiberaceae
Perennials

🌡 **ZONES VARY BY SPECIES**

☀ **LIGHT SHADE**

💧 **AMPLE WATER**

Alpinia zerumbet

These tropical beauties grow from rhizomes that produce leafy clumps. Plants are evergreen in the Tropical South, but they are root hardy to about 15°F. They often need to settle in for 2 years after planting before they start to bloom; the clusters of ½- to 2½-in. blossoms typically appear in summer. Give moist, fertile, well-drained soil and a wind-sheltered location. Most form clumps half to fully as wide as they are tall. Each year, cut back to the ground all canes that have finished flowering.

A. formosana. PINSTRIPE GINGER. Zones LS, CS, TS; USDA 8-11. Frost tolerant (to 10°F) species from Taiwan, southern Japan. To 4–5 ft. high. Green leaves have white veins. Small, creamy white flowers are marked with red and yellow.

A. hainanensis (*A. henryi*, *A. katsumadai*). Zones LS, CS. TS; USDA 8-11. From China, growing 4–9 ft. tall. Cream to yellow blossoms marked with dark red lines give off a honeylike perfume in spring. Performs well as a houseplant. 'Pink Perfection' has pink flowers.

A. pumila. DWARF GINGER. Zones LS, CS, TS; USDA 8-11. From China. Silver stripes on dark green leaves make this shade-loving ground cover look more like a Calathea than a ginger. Spreads slowly with leaves 6 in. long and 3 in. wide. Although red, the 1-in. spike of flowers is subtle.

A. purpurata. RED GINGER. Zone TS; USDA 10-11. To 9–12 ft. tall, 2–3 ft. wide. Brilliant inflorescences of red bracts and small white flowers.

A. vittata (*A. sanderae*). VARIEGATED GINGER. Zone TS; USDA 10-11. Native to Solomon Islands. To 3–4 ft. tall, with white-striped leaves. Rarely blooms. A good container plant.

A. zerumbet (*A. nutans*, *A. speciosa*). SHELL GINGER. Zones LS, CS, TS; USDA 8-11. Native to Polynesia and tropical Asia. Grandest of gingers, best all-year appearance. To 8–9 ft. tall. Shiny leaves with distinct parallel veins; maroon leafstalks at maturity. Waxy white or pinkish, shell-like, fragrant flowers marked red, purple, or brown in pendent clusters on arching stems. 'Variegata' has green leaves with yellow bands.

ALSTROEMERIA

Alstroemeriaceae
Perennials from tuberous roots

- ✎ **MS, LS, CS; USDA 7-9, EXCEPT AS NOTED**
- ◐ **PARTIAL SHADE, EXCEPT AS NOTED**
- ⬤ **REGULAR WATER DURING GROWTH AND BLOOM**
- ⬦ **CAN CAUSE DERMATITIS IN ALLERGIC PEOPLE**

Alstroemeria hybrid

There's a good reason why most Southerners see these flashy

perennials only at the florist's: They're difficult to grow in regions with hot, rainy, humid summers and heavy clay soil. They may put on a good show for a while, but they seldom last for more than a year or two. *A. psittacina* and a few new hybrids are exceptions.

A. aurea (*A. aurantiaca*). PERUVIAN LILY. Deciduous species to 3–4 ft. tall, with many leafy, flowering stems topped by yellow, orange, or orange-red blooms sprinkled with dark stripes and flecks. 'Orange King' offers outstanding cut flowers, large, long-lasting, dark-spotted, bright orange blossoms reminiscent of tiger lilies.

A. hybrids. The fanciest alstroemerias, often used for cut flowers, are hybrids. The deciduous Dr. Salter's hybrids feature beautiful flowers in red, orange, peach, shrimp, salmon, and near-white; all are flecked and striped with deeper colors. They produce leafy shoots 2–5 ft. tall in late winter and early spring. As these shoots begin to turn brown, the flowering stems arise, with blooms appearing in early to midsummer. If allowed to set seed, plants will self-sow. They go dormant after blooming. Sow seeds in the garden in fall, winter, or early spring.

Heat-tolerant hybrids (Zones US, MS, LS; USDA 6-8) include 'Freedom,' with peachy red blossoms adorned with yellowish white blotches and carmine specks; grows 2½ ft. tall and forms clumps to about 1 ft. wide. 'Sweet Laura' is mildly fragrant, sporting golden flowers with orange petal tips and cinnamon flecks. Grows 2½ ft. tall; spreads slowly by underground stems. 'Casablanca' graduated from the cut flower trade to Southern gardens with 3½-ft-tall, white summer blooms that are pink on the outside and freckled inside. 'Mauve Majesty' (rose with yellow throat) and 'Tangerine Tango' (golden throat with petals tipped in orange) both grow to a manageable 2½ ft. And for small gardens and containers in the Lower South, 'Princess Mathilde' offers coral blooms on 10-in. stems.

A. psittacina. PARROT LILY. A passalong favorite in the South. Evergreen in mildest areas; elsewhere, mounds of dark green leaves emerge from the ground in winter. Flowering

stalks, separate from the foliage, sprout in summer and rise to 2½–3 ft. Odd-looking red-and-green flowers are marked with purple blotches. Prefers growing in bright, all-day shade; spreads steadily and can be invasive in good soil. 'Variegata' has striking white-edged leaves.

ALTERNANTHERA

JOSEPH'S COAT
Amaranthaceae
Perennials often treated as annuals

- ✎ **TS; USDA 10-11; ANYWHERE AS ANNUAL**
- ☼ **FULL SUN**
- ⬤ **MODERATE WATER**

Alternanthera ficoidea 'Party Time'

These foliage plants grab attention, whether used in large sweeps, in

combination with other plants, or in container gardens. Wonderfully gaudy foliage. Prefer moist, fertile, well-drained soil; easy to root from cuttings. Native from Mexico to Argentina. Thrive in heat.

A. dentata. Upright grower to 1–3 ft. tall and 1–2 ft. wide, with broadly lance-shaped, dark green leaves to 3½ in. long and 2 in. wide. Blooms in late fall and winter, bearing small greenish-white flowers that resemble clover blossoms and are held erect on the stems. 'Rubiginosa' has burgundy stems and leaves. 'Tricolor' offers burgundy foliage edged in deep pink; its new leaves include some green. 'Brazilian Red Hots' glows magenta and burgundy like a burning bush, 'Royal Tapestry' has bronze, narrow foliage and grows 1–2 ft. tall and 2–3 ft. wide, and 'Little Ruby' brings burgundy drama on a plant only 12 in. tall and wide.

A. ficoidea. Sprawling or upright grower ranging from 6 to 20 in. tall, with elliptic to oval or rounded leaves to about 1 in. long. 'Bettzichiana' (*A. bettzichiana*) has spoon-shaped leaves that have red and yellow markings. 'Aurea Nana' grows only 4 in. tall with yellow-splotched foliage. 'Chartreuse' is simply a bright green plant 4–8 in. tall and 6–12 in. wide. 'Crème de Menthe' has green leaves splotched with white. 'Magnifica' is a red-bronze dwarf. 'Parrot Feather' and

ABOVE: *Alternanthera dentata* 'Brazilian Red Hots'

'Versicolor' have broad green leaves with yellow markings and pink veins. In 'Sessilis Alba', leaves are pure white on the upper part of the plant, green closer to the ground. 'Red Threads' is just that, narrow, burgundy leaves in a mound 8 in. tall and 14 in. wide. 'Party Time' grows 1–2 ft. tall and wide, with green leaves heavily marked with bright pink.

A. polygonoides. Sprawling plant with reddish brown, elliptical to oval leaves to 1 in. long. Grows to 4 in. tall and 15 in. wide.

ALYSSUM

Brassicaceae
Perennials

🗡 **US, MS, LS; USDA 6-8**

☀️ ◑ **FULL SUN OR LIGHT SHADE**

💧 **MODERATE WATER**

Alyssum montanum

Mostly native to Mediterranean region. Mounding plants or shrublets that brighten spring borders and rock gardens with their cheerful bloom. They thrive in poor, rocky soil as long as it is well drained.

A. montanum. To 8 in. high, 1½ ft. wide with leaves that are gray and dense, short clusters of fragrant yellow flowers. The compact and heavy-flowering 'Berggold' ('Mountain Gold') is the most commonly sold variety. 'Luna' blooms 2 weeks earlier.

A. saxatile. See *Aurinia saxatilis*

A. wulfenianum. Prostrate and trailing to about 1½ ft. wide, with fleshy, silvery leaves and sheets of pale yellow flowers.

AMARANTHUS

AMARANTH
Amaranthaceae
Annuals

🗡 **US, MS, LS, CS, TS; USDA 6-11**

☀️ ◑ **FULL SUN OR PARTIAL SHADE**

💧 **REGULAR WATER**

Amaranthus caudatus

Sometimes coarse weedy plants, but a few ornamental kinds are grown for colorful foliage or flowers. Sow seed in place in early summer; soil temperature must be above 70°F for germination. When young and tender, leaves and stems of many species (even some of the weedy ones) can be cooked like spinach in hot weather. Blooms appear in late summer and fall. In some species, seeds look like sesame seeds; they are high in protein and can be used as a grain.

A. caudatus. LOVE-LIES-BLEEDING, TASSEL FLOWER. A sturdy, branching plant 3–8 ft. high, 1½–3 ft. wide. The light green leaves reach 10 in. long, 4 in. wide. Red flowers become drooping, tassel-like clusters. More a curiosity than a pretty plant, it does produce grain.

A. hypochondriacus. PRINCE'S FEATHER. To 5 ft. high, 2 ft. wide, usually with reddish leaves 1–6 in. long and ½–3 in. wide. Red or brownish red flowers in many-branched clusters. Some strains are grown as a spinach substitute or for grain.

A. tricolor. JOSEPH'S COAT. Branching plant 1–4 ft. high, 1–1½ ft. wide. Leaves 2½–6 in. long, 2–4 in. wide, blotched in shades of red and green. 'Early Splendor', 'Flaming Fountain', and 'Molten Fire' bear masses of yellow to scarlet foliage at tops of main stems and principal branches. Green-leafed strains are used as a spinach substitute under the name "tampala."

AMELANCHIER

SERVICEBERRY, SHADBLOW
Rosaceae
Deciduous shrubs or small trees

🗡 **ZONES VARY BY SPECIES**

☀️ ◑ **FULL SUN OR PARTIAL SHADE**

💧💧 **MODERATE TO REGULAR WATER**

Amelanchier arborea

Deserving of much wider use in the landscape, these graceful, airy trees and shrubs provide year-round interest. Drooping clusters of white or pinkish flowers, showy but short-lived, appear in early spring, just before or during leaf-out. They are followed in early summer by delicious blueberry-flavored fruit that is excellent for use in pies and jams—if you can beat the birds to it. Leaves are purplish in spring, turning deep green in summer and fiery hues in autumn.

Excellent in woodland gardens, these plants all grow about twice as high as wide. They are easy to garden under due to their noninvasive roots and the light shade they cast. Try planting them against a dark background to better show off the flowers, form, and fall color. All need some winter chill. Rust and fireblight sometimes appear but are seldom serious. Some folks call serviceberries "sarvistrees."

A. arborea. SERVICEBERRY, JUNEBERRY. Zones US, MS, LS, CS; USDA 6-9. Native to eastern and southern U.S. Narrow tree. Similar to *A. canadensis* but is sometimes taller; more often forms a nice round-headed tree; and has larger, pendulous, loose racemes of white flowers that bloom as the leaves unfold. Delicious dark red-purple fruit.

A. canadensis. SHADBLOW SERVICEBERRY. Zones US, MS, LS; USDA 6-8. Narrowish, to 25 ft. tall, with short, erect flower clusters. Plants offered under this name may actually belong to other species. Often suckering and multitrunked.

A. x grandiflora. APPLE SERVICEBERRY. Zones US, MS, LS, CS; USDA 6-9. Hybrid between *A. arborea* and *A. laevis*. Named selections may be sold under any of the three names. Most grow to 25 ft. tall, with drooping clusters of white flowers opening from pinkish buds. Outstanding selections include the following.

'Autumn Brilliance'. Strong stems stand up well to winter storms. Blue-green leaves turn orange-red in fall.

'Cole's Select'. Orange-red autumn color.

'Forest Prince'. Robust selection with especially handsome dark green foliage that turns orange-red in autumn.

'Princess Diana'. Orange-red fall color.

'Prince William'. Shrubby selection to 10 ft. high; orange-red in fall.

'Robin Hill'. Pink buds open to white flowers. Red to yellow fall leaf color.

A. laevis. ALLEGHENY SERVICEBERRY. Zones US, MS, LS; USDA 6-8. Native to eastern North America. Narrow shrub or small tree to 40 ft., with nodding or drooping, 4-in., white flower clusters. Leaves are bronzy purple when new, dark green in summer, yellow to red in autumn. Small black-purple fruit is very sweet. 'Snow Cloud' stands upright, 25 ft. tall and 15 ft. wide, with showy blooms and bright red fall color. 'Spring Flurry' is also upright, 28 ft. tall and 20 ft wide with orange fall color.

AMORPHA

Papilionaceae
Deciduous shrubs

✓ **US, MS, LS, CS; USDA 6-9**

☼ **FULL SUN**

💧 **MODERATE WATER, EXCEPT AS NOTED**

Amorpha canescens

Shrubs with leaves divided featherwise into many leaflets. Spikelike, 3- to 6-in.-long clusters of blue or purple, single-petaled flowers typically bloom in early summer. In cold weather, plants may die back nearly to the ground; in warmer areas, they should be cut back severely to prevent lankiness. Tough and undemanding, withstanding heat and wind. Butterflies love the flowers.

A. canescens. LEAD PLANT. Native to the High Plains from Canada to Texas. About 3 ft. tall and wide, with silvery, downy foliage.

A. fruticosa. INDIGO BUSH, FALSE INDIGO. Native to eastern U.S. Lanky grower reaches 10–15 ft. tall and wide, with light green foliage. Needs hard pruning in winter or early spring to maintain some degree of compactness.

A. texana (*A. roemeriana*). INDIGO BUSH. Native to the Texas Hill Country. Grows to 3–9 ft. high and 3–5 ft. wide, with silvery, downy leaves and spring bloom. This shrub is quite drought tolerant, requiring little supplemental water.

AMORPHOPHAL-LUS

VOODOO LILY
Araceae
Perennials from tubers

✓ **ZONES VARY BY SPECIES**

☼ ● **PART SUN TO SHADE**

💧 **REGULAR WATER**

Amorphophallus bulbifer

Plants don't get much stranger than the voodoo lilies. This large group of aroids, mostly from Asia, grows from huge underground cormlike tubers, some weighing up to 100 pounds. In summer, each produces a single inflorescence that looks like a giant calla (*Zantedeschia*). A large, hoodlike bract called a spathe surrounds a central spike or finger-shaped spadix. The fragrance this emits is unforgettable—the breath of the Devil—but it lasts only for about a day. The carrion stench attracts flies, which are the plant's chief pollinators.

After flowering, voodoo lilies rest for about a month before producing a single giant (to 3 ft. wide) leaf, which lasts for the rest of the summer. Plants need moist, woodsy, well-drained soil. Set the tubers 4 in. deep in late winter or early spring; apply fertilizer monthly for best results. Often grown in pots or tubs; also good for naturalized areas where neighbors aren't too close.

A. bulbifer. Zones LS, CS, TS; USDA 8-11. To 3 ft. high. Stem mottled in various shades of green produces a 1½-ft. spathe—blotched with pink on the outside, red on the inside—surrounding a cream-colored spadix. The flower is followed by a segmented leaf that produces bulbils in its forks

by the end of summer that can be removed and planted.

A. kiusianus. Zones MS, LS, CS, TS; USDA 7-11. To 3 ft. high. Stem speckled with green and white is topped with a 6-in. spathe spotted in the same manner; a dark purple, 8-in. spadix protrudes from the spathe. The leafstalk that follows is topped by an umbrellalike leaf composed of numerous leaflets.

A. konjac. Zones US, MS, LS, CS, TS; USDA 6-11. To 6 ft. tall. Purple-spotted stem holds a similarly mottled 3-ft. spathe from which protrudes a magenta-purple spadix. Leafstalk holds an umbrellalike, deeply lobed leaf. Increases by offsets underground, eventually forming a big clump.

A. paeonifolius. Zones CS, TS; USDA 9-11. Grows to 8 ft. tall. A green marbled stalk that shades to purple at the top carries a ruffled, 1½-ft.-wide, purple-and-green spathe spotted with white. The spathe holds a large, protruding, purple spadix that looks like a bulbous knob or a brain. Leaf is divided into many leaflets and carried atop a green-marbled stalk.

> VOODOO LILIES TRAP POLLINATING INSECTS JUST LONG ENOUGH TO SHOWER THEM WITH POLLEN.

AMPELOPSIS BREVIPEDUNCU-LATA

PORCELAIN BERRY
Vitaceae
Deciduous vine

✓ **US, MS, LS, CS; USDA 6-9**

☼ ● **FULL SUN OR SHADE**

💧 💧 **MODERATE TO REGULAR WATER**

Ampelopsis brevipedunculata

This Asian native is the Dr. Jekyll and Mr. Hyde of ornamental vines. On the one hand, it produces an absolutely stunning display of colorful fruit: clusters of small, grapelike berries that change from greenish ivory to yellowish to metallic blue in late summer and fall, often with several colors present at the same time. On the other hand, it can be extremely invasive. Its rampant stems, clinging by tendrils, can easily grow 15 ft. in a year, and birds eat the fruit and spread the seeds all over. Plant it only where you can contain it; don't let it escape to woods or natural areas. Handsome, dark green leaves to 5 in. across turn red in fall; unfortunately, they are often damaged by Japanese beetles.

In the garden, give porcelain berry the strong support of an arbor, trellis, or wall. 'Elegans' has leaves variegated in white and pink; selection is less vigorous than the species and makes a splendid choice for a hanging basket or container.

AMSONIA

BLUESTAR
Apocynaceae
Perennials

US, MS, LS, CS; USDA 6-9

FULL SUN OR LIGHT SHADE

MODERATE TO REGULAR WATER

Amsonia hubrichtii

These elegant milkweed relatives are native to the South. Plants grow 2–3 ft. high and wide, with narrow leaves and erect stems crowned by clusters of small, star-shaped blue flowers in late spring. They are among the best perennials for fall color—foliage turns bright yellow in autumn. All are tough plants that succeed in ordinary soil. They tolerate some drought and suffer from few pests. Deer don't eat them.

A. ciliata. NARROWLEAF BLUESTAR. From southeastern U.S. Leaves narrower than those of *A. tabernaemontana*, wider than those of *A. hubrichtii*. Rich blue flowers; good fall leaf color.

A. hubrichtii. HUBRICHT'S BLUESTAR. Soft leaves are very narrow, almost needlelike. Discovered in Arkansas in 1942 by Leslie Hubricht and considered by many to be the finest of bluestars. It forms a clump to 3 ft. tall and wide; blossoms are sky-blue. Fall foliage is an exceptionally bright, clear gold.

A. illustris. SHINING BLUESTAR. Native to Texas, Oklahoma, Arkansas, Missouri, and Kansas. Leathery, shiny, willowlike leaves; pale blue blossoms.

A. ludoviciana. LOUISIANA BLUESTAR. Rare bluestar native to Louisiana, Mississippi, Alabama, and Georgia. Backs of leaves are coated with a soft felt. Light blue flowers.

A. rigida. STIFF BLUESTAR. Compact species native to Florida and Georgia. Grows 1½–2 ft. high. Light blue flowers are held atop firm stems. Both leaves and stems are smoky purple when new.

A. tabernaemontana. BLUESTAR. Native to the Southeast, this is the most commercially available species. It has dull, dark green, willowlike leaves and slate-blue flowers. Two selections with deep blue blossoms are 'Blue Ice', a compact grower to 15 in. tall and 2 ft. wide, and 'Louisiana Dwarf', to 1½ ft. tall and 2 ft. wide. 'Purple' has showy purple blooms.

ANAGALLIS ARVENSIS

SCARLET PIMPERNEL
Primulacaeae
Annuals

US, MS, LS, CS, TS; USDA 6-11

FULL SUN OR PARTIAL SHADE

LITTLE TO REGULAR WATER

Anagallis arvensis

Reseeding European annual naturalized throughout the South. Sprawling stems hold bright green leaves and small scarlet-orange blooms. Flowers open and close with the sun. *A. a. caerulea* has deep blue, larger flowers; it tolerates most soils and heat, thrives in dry gardens, and grows well in containers.

ANAPHALIS

PEARLY EVERLASTING
Asteraceae
Perennials

US, MS, LS; USDA 6-8

PARTIAL OR FULL SHADE

MODERATE TO REGULAR WATER

Anaphalis margaritacea

Furry gray foliage is the outstanding characteristic of the pearly everlastings. Most are heat-tolerant, mounding plants with erect, branching stems carrying attractive (though not showy) clusters of papery-textured daisies that may be cut in summer for use in dried arrangements. Since they withstand lower light than most other gray-leafed plants, they're ideal for brightening semishady borders. Not fussy about soil but need reasonably good drainage. Seldom browsed by deer.

A. margaritacea. From many northern climates of the world. To 2–3 ft. high and wide. Leaves, to 6 in. long, are green above, with white and woolly undersides. Pearly white flowers have yellow centers. *A. m. yedoensis* has smaller leaves and brown-tinted flowers; it is less cold hardy than the species.

A. triplinervis. Species from the Himalayas. Slightly smaller in overall size than *A. margaritacea*, with similar flowers but somewhat smaller, silvery leaves.

ANDROPOGON

BLUESTEM
Poaceae
Perennial grasses

US, MS, LS, CS; USDA 6-9

FULL SUN OR LIGHT SHADE

WATER NEEDS VARY BY SPECIES

Andropogon gerardii

Once found in most of the continental U.S., these slender-leafed, upright, clumping native grasses formed a predominant part of old tall- and short-grass prairies. Big bluestem made waves of rippling green, sometimes nearly twice as tall as the settlers. Plant in drifts or masses; for erosion control; as airy vertical accents in flower or shrub borders; or in a natural garden with sunflowers (*Helianthus*), golden rod (*Solidago*), and coreopsis. Be sure to divide clumps every few years when centers start to die; discard the center and replant vigorous young clumps from the edge. Every year, shear dried stems to base before new growth begins in spring.

A. gerardii. BIG BLUESTEM, TURKEYFOOT. Plant has variable growth to 3–7 ft., sometimes reaching to 10 ft. in moist, warm soil. Clumps can spread up to 3 ft. wide. Often tall enough to make a screen or dramatic specimen in large perennial borders. Thin blades are blue-green or silvery in summer, bronze-red in fall. In late summer, smoky purple flower spikes form at stem end in sets of three, like the toes of a turkey foot; these are followed in autumn by purple seed heads. Prefers moisture throughout the growing season; though it takes drought, it grows much less vigorously in dry conditions. Tolerates a wide range of soils, including clay soils and acid or alkaline soils.

A. glomeratus. BUSHY BLUE-STEM, BUSHY BROOM SEDGE. Native to marshy areas in coastal eastern U.S. To 4–6 ft. tall, 2–3 ft. wide. Leaves are bluish green; bushy white flower plumes appear in late summer or early fall. Foliage and blossoms turn coppery orange with autumn's chill; the first heavy frost usually turns the flower plumes into billowing clouds of color that last well into winter. Regular to ample water.

A. virginicus. BROOM SEDGE. Grows to 3–4 ft. tall when in flower and usually less than 1 ft. across. Leaves are light green in summer, changing to a showy orange in fall. Produces silvery white blossom spikes that appear in autumn. Tolerates poor, dry, clay, or rocky soil. Often colonizes abandoned farm fields, roadsides, and disturbed areas such as construction sites. Little water.

ANEMONE
ANEMONE, WINDFLOWER
Ranunculaceae
Perennials

✎ **ZONES VARY BY SPECIES**

☼ ◑ ● **EXPOSURE NEEDS VARY BY SPECIES**

💧 **REGULAR WATER, EXCEPT AS NOTED**

⬦ **ALL PARTS ARE POISONOUS IF INGESTED; SAP CAN IRRITATE SKIN**

Anemone x *hybrida*
'September Charm'

A rich and varied group of plants ranging in size from alpine rock garden miniatures to tall Japanese anemones grown in borders; bloom extends from very early

spring to fall, depending on species. Seldom browsed by deer.

Nontuberous anemones. The types described below have fibrous roots or creeping rhizomes or rootstocks, not tubers.

A. canadensis. MEADOW ANEMONE. Zones US, MS, LS, CS; USDA 6-9. A North American native that grows 1–2 ft. tall and spreads by creeping rhizomes. Its inch-wide, yellow-centered white flowers appear in twos and threes from the upper joints of divided leaves. Blooms profusely from late spring to early summer. Spreads vigorously; too invasive for small gardens. Needs partial shade and more water than most windflowers.

A. x hybrida (*A. japonica*, *A. hupehensis japonica*). JAPA-NESE ANEMONE. Zones US, MS, LS; USDA 6-8. Long-lived, fibrous-rooted perennial indispensable for fall flower color. Graceful, branching stems 2–4 ft. high rise from clump of dark green, three-to five-lobed leaves covered with soft hairs. Single or semidouble flowers in white, silvery pink, or rose. Slow to establish, but once started it spreads readily if roots are not disturbed. Space plants 2 ft. apart. May need staking. Mulch in fall where winters are severe. Increase by divisions in fall or early spring or by root cuttings in spring. Effective in clumps in front of tall shrubbery or under high-branching trees. Partial shade.

Many named selections of Japanese anemone are available, including the following.

'Honorine Jobert'. Single, white flowers on 2- to 3-ft. stems; blooms reliably in Lower South.

'Königin Charlotte' ('Queen Charlotte'). Pink, single flowers bloom on 3-ft. stems.

'Margaret' ('Lady Gilmour'). Semidouble or double rose-pink flowers. 2–3 ft. stems.

'Prinz Heinrich'. Rosy red, semidouble flowers on 1½- to 1-ft. stems.

'September Charm'. Single flowers in silvery pink on 2-ft. stems.

'Whirlwind'. Large semidouble white flowers on 3-ft. stems.

A. nemorosa. WOOD ANEMONE. Zones US, MS, LS; USDA 6-8. European native to 1 ft. high with creeping rhizomes, deeply cut leaves, and inch-wide white (rarely pinkish or blue)

ABOVE: Anemone x *hybrida* 'Honorine Jobert'

spring flowers held above the foliage. Spreads slowly to make an attractive woodland ground cover. Many named selections exist: 'Allenii' has large blue flowers, and there are double forms. Partial or full shade.

A. quinquefolia. AMERICAN WOOD ANEMONE. Zones US, MS, LS; USDA 6-8. American native. Attractive woodland ground cover like *A. nemorosa*; inch-wide, white flowers in spring. *A. q. oregana* is similar but may have blue or pink blooms. Partial shade.

A. sylvestris. SNOWDROP ANEMONE. Zones US, MS, LS; USDA 6-8. European native grows to 1½ ft. tall from a creeping rootstock. Fragrant, 1½- to 3-in, yellow-centered, white flowers in spring, followed by cottony seed heads. Plants spread readily in damp, wooded locations. 'Grandiflora' has larger blossoms; 'Flore Pleno' is double flowered. Partial or full shade.

A. tomentosa. GRAPELEAF ANEMONE. Zones US, MS, LS; USDA 6-8. Vigorous, fibrous-rooted Tibetan native often sold as *A. vitifolia* 'Robustissima'. Foliage resembles grape leaves, grows in a spreading clump that gives rise to branching, 3½-ft.-high stems bearing single, pink flowers in late summer, early fall. Allow 3 ft. between plants. Partial shade.

Tuberous anemones. The

types listed here are native to southern Europe and the Mediterranean; best treated as annuals in rainy-summer or warm-winter climates, where they tend to be short lived. Tuberous anemones make great container plants.

A. blanda. GREEK ANEMONE, GREEK WINDFLOWER. Zones US, MS, LS; USDA 6-8. Tubers produce a spreading mat of finely divided, softly hairy leaves (clumps are wider spreading in colder climates). In spring, each 2- to 8-in. stem bears one sky-blue flower, 1–1½ in. across. Selections with 2-in. flowers on 10- to 12-in. plants include 'Blue Star', 'Pink Star', 'White Splendor', and purplish red 'Radar'. All work well as underplantings for tulips, as ground cover drifts under deciduous shrubs and trees, and naturalized in short grass. Soak tubers in water for several hours before planting. Needs partial shade and winter chill for best performance.

A. coronaria. POPPY-FLOW-ERED ANEMONE. Zones MS, LS, CS, TS; USDA 7-11. This species is rarely seen in gardens; it has been replaced by showy, large-flowered hybrids for cutting and for spectacular spring color. Blooms are 1½–2½ in. across, borne singly on 6- to 18-in. stems above finely divided leaves; come in shades of red and blue, as well as white. Among the most popular strains available are De Caen (single flowers) and St. Brigid (semidouble to double). Full sun or partial shade.

A. x _fulgens_. SCARLET WIND-FLOWER. Zones US, MS; USDA 6-7. Grows 1 ft. tall and 6 in. wide. Spring flowers, to 2½ in. across, are brilliant scarlet with black stamens. St. Bavo strain comes in an unusual color range, including pink and rusty coral. Same uses are for _A. coronaria_. Full sun or partial shade.

CARE

Plant tubers scarred side up (look for depressed scar left by base of last year's stem), setting them 1–2 in. deep and 8–12 in. apart in rich, light, well-drained loam. Or start in flats of damp sand; set out in garden when stems are a few inches tall. Keep soil moist during growth and bloom. Protect from birds until leaves toughen. In high-rainfall areas, excess moisture induces rot. Tuberous types best treated as annuals in much of the South, since they tend to be short lived where summers are rainy or winters are warm. Tuberous anemones make good container plants.

ANEMONELLA THALICTROIDES

RUE ANEMONE
Ranunculaceae
Evergreen and deciduous shrubs

🌿 **US, MS, LS; USDA 6-8**
◐ ● **PARTIAL OR FULL SHADE**
💧 **REGULAR WATER**

Anemonella thalictroides

Delicate woodland plant native to eastern North America. To 9 in.

high and up to 1 ft. wide, with finely divided leaves resembling those of meadow rue (_Thalictrum_). Loose clusters of inch-wide, white (usually) or pink flowers appear in early spring. Attractive for close-up viewing. Selection known as either 'Rosea Plena' or 'Schoaff's Double Pink' has long-lasting, fully double pink flowers like tiny roses. 'Cameo' has double white blooms. Those of 'Betty Blake' are double, light green. Deer resistant.

ANETHUM GRAVEOLENS

DILL
Apiaceae
Annual

🌿 **US, MS, LS, CS, TS; USDA 6-11**
☀ **FULL SUN**
💧 **REGULAR WATER**

Anethum graveolens

Aromatic herb to 3–4 ft. tall. Soft, feathery leaves; umbrellalike, 6-in.-wide clusters of small yellow flowers. The seeds and leaves have a pungent fragrance. Sow seed where the plants are to be grown; for a constant supply, sow several times during spring and summer (germinates and grows better in spring than in summer). Thin seedlings to about 1½ ft. apart. An easy way to grow it in a casual garden is to let a few plants go to seed. Seedlings appear here and there at odd times and can be pulled and chopped for use as seasoning. Use seeds in pickling and vinegar; use fresh or dried leaves in cooked dishes, salads, sauces, as garnish. Caterpillars of black swallowtail butterflies often feed on the foliage.

ANGELICA

ANGELICA
Apiaceae
Biennials

🌿 **US, MS, LS; USDA 6-8**
◐ ● **PARTIAL TO FULL SHADE**
💧 **REGULAR WATER**

Angelica archangelica

Tropical-looking carrot relatives with divided and toothed, yellow-green leaves 2–3 ft. long. In early summer, the plant sends up a thick, hollow stem to 6 ft. tall topped by a 4-ft.-wide, umbrella-shaped cluster of small flowers. Dramatic in a woodland garden. Grow in moist, rich soil. Propagate from seeds as soon as they ripen in fall. Because plants are taprooted and don't transplant well, sow seed in place. To prolong plant's life for a few years, cut out the flowering stem as soon as it forms. Best in Upper South

A. archangelica. Native to northern Europe and western Asia. Green stem topped by greenish yellow flowers. Leaves are a nice addition to salads; the leafstalks can be cooked and eaten like asparagus. Both leafstalks and hollow flower stems can be candied and used to decorate pastries. Seeds are used commercially in flavoring spirits, candies, and cakes.

A. atropurpurea. PURPLE-STEM ANGELICA. Native from Newfoundland to Delaware and the Smoky Mountains. Purple stem capped by greenish white blossoms. This species was used by Native Americans to soothe an upset stomach.

A. gigas (purple or Korean angelica) is similar except all parts are purple.

ANGELONIA ANGUSTIFOLIA

SUMMER SNAPDRAGON
Plantaginaceae
Annual

🌿 **US, MS, LS, CS, TS; USDA 6-11**
☀ **FULL SUN**
💧 **REGULAR WATER**

Angelonia 'Serena Purple'

Native to the tropics of the Americas, angelonia is perennial in the Coastal and Tropical South but grown as an annual in most other places. It looks a bit like a shorter delphinium, but it blooms all summer and loves the heat. Showy spikes of blue, purple, pink, or white blossoms appear atop plants that grow 1–1½ ft. tall and about 1 ft. wide. Periodic deadheading keeps the flowers coming. Excellent both as bedding plants and in containers; provides long-lasting cut flowers. Easy to grow in moist, well-drained soil; not bothered by pests. Deer don't usually eat it.

Many hybrids are offered. The AngelMist series (14–24 in. tall) features a variety of colors, including plum, lavender, and white; some flowers are marked with white, pink, or purple. In the Carita series (18–24 in. tall), stems branch at the base, giving the plant a full look. Blossoms are deep pink, lavender, purple, or white. Carita Purple is a particularly good performer. The Serena series (16–20 in. tall) is compact, and 'Serena Purple' is among the best for the Southern garden. The Serenita series is similar, but shorter—plants grow 6–10 in. tall. The Alonia series features heavily branched plants to 15 in. tall with large, showy flowers. Low-growing, spreading types are ideal for

A

hanging baskets, containers, or in ground cover situations. From the AngelMist Spreading series (4–10 in. tall) Spreading White and Spreading Purple are highly recommended.

ANISACANTHUS QUADRIFIDUS WRIGHTII

FLAME ACANTHUS, TEXAS FIRECRACKER
Acanthaceae
Deciduous shrub

🌿 **MS, LS, CS, TS; USDA 7-11**

☼ ◑ **FULL SUN OR LIGHT SHADE**

◐ ◕ **LITTLE TO MODERATE WATER**

Anisacanthus quadrifidus wrightii

Native to southeastern Texas, northeastern Mexico. This heat-loving shrub grows 3 ft. tall, 4 ft. wide, with dark green leaves 2 in. long and 1 in. wide. Spikes of 2-in.-long, brilliant red-orange flowers appear from early summer to fall. These tubular, nectar-filled blooms have two lobes above the mouth, three on the lower lip. Highly favored by hummingbirds and butterflies. Fairly drought tolerant; for best growth and bloom, water deeply every 2 to 3 weeks in summer. Deer resistant, but rabbits love the new shoots; protect plants with a wire cage until a woody structure is established. For compact shape and prolific bloom, cut back by one half to two thirds before new spring growth commences. 'Mexican Flame' is a superior selection grown from cuttings.

ANTENNARIA DIOICA

PUSSY TOES
Asteraceae
Perennial

🌿 **US, MS; USDA 6-7**

☼ **FULL SUN**

◐ ◕ **MODERATE TO REGULAR WATER**

Antennaria dioica 'Rosea'

Native to Europe, North America. Forms inch-high mats of woolly foliage and slowly spreads among rocks, between paving stones, or at front of border. Furry puffs of flowers are pinkish white in the basic species, deep pink in 'Rubra', and rose-pink in 'Rosea'. Lean, gritty, well-drained soil is essential.

ANTHEMIS

Asteraceae
Perennials

🌿 **ZONES VARY BY SPECIES**

☼ **FULL SUN**

◐ ◕ **MODERATE TO REGULAR WATER**

Anthemis tinctoria

Some species are weedy, but those listed here (from southern

Europe and Turkey) are garden plants with long-lasting daisylike or buttonlike flowers. Many-segmented leaves are aromatic, especially when bruised. Provide good drainage.

A. carpatica (*A. cretica carpatica*). SNOW CARPET. Zones US, MS, LS, CS; USDA 6-9. Forms low, 2-ft.-wide mounds of green to gray-green foliage. Stems about 6 in. high rise from foliage clumps in spring and summer, bearing 1½-in., white daisies with yellow centers.

A. nobilis. See *Chamaemelum nobile*

A. tinctoria. GOLDEN MAR-GUERITE. Zones US, MS, LS; USDA 6-8. Erect, shrubby plant to 2–3 ft. tall and wide, with angular stems, light green leaves, and golden yellow, 2-in. daisies in summer and early fall. Good cut flower. Cut back lightly after first flush of bloom to keep flowers coming. Short lived; start new plants from stem cuttings in spring or divide clumps in spring or fall. Selections include 'Beauty of Grallagh', with flowers in golden orange; 'E. C. Buxton', white with yellow centers; 'Kelwayi', golden yellow; and 'Moonlight', pale yellow.

ANTHRISCUS

Apiaceae
Annuals and perennials or biennials

🌿 **ZONES VARY BY SPECIES**

☼ ◑ **EXPOSURE NEEDS VARY BY SPECIES**

◕ **REGULAR WATER**

Anthriscus cerefolium

Native to Europe, North Africa, and Asia. Though both of these plants produce many umbrella-shaped clusters of tiny flowers, they are valued for their fernlike

foliage. In the first species, the leaves are used in cooking; in the second, the foliage brings deep, striking color to the perennial border.

A. cerefolium. CHERVIL. Annual. Zones US, MS, LS, CS, TS; USDA 6-11. Low foliage mounds about a foot wide; 1- to 2-ft. flower stems topped with white blossoms in summer. The leaves have a parsleylike flavor with overtones of anise. Use like parsley, fresh or dried. Sow seeds in place in early spring (in cold-winter areas) or in fall (where winters are mild). In the following years, volunteer seedlings will keep you supplied with new plants. Goes to seed quickly in hot weather; keep flower clusters cut to encourage leafy growth. Partial shade.

A. sylvestris 'Ravenswing'. Perennial or biennial. Zones US, MS; USDA 6-7. Very attractive purple-black foliage in clump 1½ ft. high, 2½ ft. wide. In late spring or early summer, flowering stems to 3 ft. tall bear white blossoms with purplish pink bracts. Deadhead for best appearance and to prevent self-sowing. Full sun or light shade.

ANTHURIUM

Araceae
Perennials

🌿 **TS; USDA 10-11; OR HOUSE-PLANTS**

☼ **PARTIAL SHADE; BRIGHT INDIRECT LIGHT**

◕ **REGULAR WATER**

Anthurium andraeanum

Native to tropical American rain forests, these exotic-looking plants are prized for their large, often glossy leaves and distinctive "flowers" (a large, flattish bract

often glossy leaves and distinctive "flowers" (a large, flattish bract surrounding a slender, fleshy spike). Among the species listed here, all but *A. hookeri* are usually grown as potted plants, even in tropical climates. Anthuriums, sometimes called flamingo flowers, make unusual houseplants in cooler climates.

A. andraeanum. FLAMING ANTHURIUM. Dark green, oblong leaves to 1 ft. long and 6 in. wide, heart shaped at base. Spreading, heart-shaped, puckered bracts to 6 in. long come in shades of red, rose, pink, or white, and they shine as though lacquered. Spikes are yellow. Bloom more or less continuous—plant may have from four to six flowers during the year. Flowers last 6 weeks on plant, 4 weeks after cutting.

A. crystallinum. Handsome, heart-shaped leaves to 1½ ft. long, 1 ft. wide, deep green with striking white veining. Unexciting flowers with small, narrow, greenish bracts.

A. hookeri. Grown in the tropical landscape for handsome, foot-wide "nest" of leaves that can reach 8 in. long. Excellent as an accent in a wind-sheltered garden or as a potted specimen. Indoors or out, needs high humidity. Grow in well-aerated, rich, moist soil; feed regularly.

A. scherzerianum. Slow-growing, compact plant to 2 ft. Dark green leaves 8 in. long, 2 in. wide. Broad, 3-in.-long bracts in deep red varying to rose, salmon, white. Yellow, spirally coiled flower spikes.

ANTHURIUM FLOWERS CAN LAST UP TO A MONTH IN A VASE.

ANTIGONON LEPTOPUS

CORAL VINE, QUEEN'S WREATH, ROSA DE MONTANA
Polygonaceae
Evergreen or deciduous vine

LS, CS, TS; USDA 8-11; OR ANNUAL

FULL SUN

LITTLE TO REGULAR WATER

Antigonon leptopus

This classic vine of the Deep South is actually native to Mexico and thrives in sweltering summer weather. A rampant grower that climbs by tendrils, it can easily cover 20 ft. in a year. Its handsome, bright green, heart- or arrow-shaped leaves reach 3–5 in. long. From summer to fall, bears a profusion of coral-pink flowers in airy, arching sprays to 6 in. or longer; a vine in full bloom is a magnificent sight. Selections include white 'Album', deep reddish pink 'Baja Red', and near-red 'Rubrum'. Seedlings of these selections vary in flower color.

Coral vine grows from a large tuber and is evergreen in the Tropical South. In regions where winter temperatures drop below 25°F, the plant often dies back to the ground, then resprouts in spring. Mulching in autumn helps to protect the roots during winter in the Lower South. In the Upper and Middle South, treat coral vine as an annual, saving the seeds for next year's plants.

Coral vine is a common sight in Florida, Louisiana, the Gulf Coast, and parts of Central and Southeast Texas. Use it to shade a patio, porch, or terrace, or let its blossoms and foliage adorn fences, walls, railings, and balconies.

ANTIRRHINUM

SNAPDRAGON
Plantaginaceae
Perennial and annual

ZONES VARY BY SPECIES

FULL SUN

WATER NEEDS VARY BY SPECIES

Antirrhinum majus

The two species listed here are prized for their spikes of colorful blooms.

A. hispanicum. SPANISH SNAPDRAGON. Zones US, MS, LS; USDA 6-8. This perennial snapdragon from Spain tops out at about 1 ft. tall and 2 ft wide, blooming pink with a yellow lower lip. The gray, somewhat fuzzy leaves are a clue to its preference for full sun, dry location.

A. majus. SNAPDRAGON. Zones US, MS, LS, CS, TS; USDA 6-11. From southwest Europe and the Mediterranean. Among the best flowers for sunny borders and cutting, reaching greatest perfection in spring and early summer in the Middle and Upper South. In the Lower, Coastal, and Tropical South, will bloom in winter and spring. Individual flower of basic snapdragon has five lobes, which are divided into unequal upper and lower "jaws"; slight pinch at sides of flower will make the dragon open its jaws. Later developments include double flowers; the bell-shaped kind, with round, open flowers; and the azalea-shaped bloom, which is a double bell flower. All are available in many colors. Plants range from 6 in. across for smallest types to 2 ft. wide for the tallest.

Tall and intermediate forms are splendid vertical accents in beds. Dwarf kinds are quite effective as edgings and in rock gardens, in raised beds, and in containers.

Snapping snapdragons in tall (2½- to 3-ft.) range include Rocket and Topper strains (single flowers) and Double Supreme strain. Intermediates (12–20 in.) are Cinderella, Coronette, Liberty, Minaret, Sonnet, Sprite, and Tahiti. Dwarfs (6–8 in.) include Dwarf Bedding Floral Carpet series, Kim, Kolibri, Luminaire, Playful, Royal Carpet, Tahiti, and 'Twinny Peach'. Rose-colored 'Candy Showers' has been developed specifically for baskets and containers.

Bell-flowered strains include Bright Butterflies and Wedding Bells (both 2½ ft.); Little Darling and Liberty Bell (both 15 in.); and Pixie (6–8 in.). Among azalea-flowered strains are Madame Butterfly (2½ ft.) and Sweetheart (1 ft.).

CARE

Sow seed in flats from late summer to early spring for later transplanting; or buy started plants at a garden center. Set out plants in early fall in the Lower, Coastal, and Tropical South, spring in the Upper and Middle South. If snapdragons set out in early fall reach bud stage before night temperatures drop below 50°F, they will start blooming in winter in mild areas and continue until weather gets hot.

To help prevent rust, avoid overhead watering (or do it only in the morning or on sunny days). Feed regularly. If rust persists, change planting locations from one year to the next—or select a different annual.

Snaps can be a challenge for gardeners in the South as a companion for pansies in spring. They do not reach full bloom until the weather is starting to warm up. Meanwhile, the pansies are starting to decline. Planning ahead enables a gardener to replace the pansies with summer annuals while the snaps are flowering. This transition means the bed is never without flowers.

APHELANDRA SQUARROSA

ZEBRA PLANT
Acanthaceae
Evergreen shrub

💧 **TS; USDA 10-11; OR HOUSEPLANT**

☼ **SOME SHADE; BRIGHT INDIRECT LIGHT**

💧 **REGULAR WATER**

Aphelandra squarrosa 'Louisae'

There's little doubt how zebra plant got its name. Its large (8- to 12-in.-long), blackish-green leaves are adorned with striking white stripes along the veins and midribs. As a bonus, the plant blooms for about 6 weeks in fall, when small yellow blossoms peek out from showy, waxy yellow bracts. 'Louisae' is the most common selection, but selections 'Apollo' and 'Dania' are more compact and have more striking venation.

For most Southerners, this native of Mexico and South America is an indoor plant. It prefers filtered sun from a south or west window. Too much sunlight burns the foliage; too little results in leggy growth and small leaves. Let the soil surface dry slightly between waterings, but don't let the plant wilt. Feed with a water-soluble houseplant fertilizer every 2 weeks from spring until fall. Cut back leggy stems after bloom to encourage branching and create a bushier plant.

Gardeners in south Florida can grow zebra plant outdoors, where it blooms in summer and fall. Give it dappled shade and well-drained soil. If an unexpected freeze injures the top, cut the plant to the ground; it will resprout.

APPLE

Rosaceae
Deciduous fruit trees

💧 **ZONES VARY BY SELECTION**

☼ **FULL SUN**

💧 **REGULAR WATER DURING FRUIT DEVELOPMENT**

See chart on page 155

'Cumberland Spur Red Delicious' apple

Our most widely adapted fruit tree, the apple thrives in home gardens and orchards from central Florida all the way north to Canada. The apple blossom is the state flower of Arkansas.

Depending on the selection, apples ripen anywhere from June to early November. To grow and bear fruit properly, most selections require between 900 and 1,200 hours of chilling (hours of temperatures at 45°F or below) each winter. If you live in the Coastal South, be sure you select types with a low chill requirement, such as 'Anna' or 'Dorsett Golden'. Apples won't grow in the Tropical South.

Not all selections require cross-pollination with a different selection to produce fruit, but most do—so unless you already have apples or crabapples growing nearby, you'll need at least two different selections to get fruit. Some selections (such as 'Mutsu', 'Stayman', 'Roxbury Russet', and 'Jonagold') have sterile pollen (called triploids) and cannot pollinate themselves or others. When planting any triploid type apple, always include at least two other selections that can cross-pollinate. Even self-pollinating apples bear heavier crops when cross-pollinated with another selection.

A standard apple tree on seedling rootstock can reach 30 ft. tall or taller. With the introduction of dwarfing and semidwarfing rootstocks after World War II, gardeners gained the advantage in reducing tree size. The smaller trees (5 to 15 ft. tall, depending upon the scion and rootstock combination) are much easier to manage and harvest.

When selecting apple types, always consider those that do well in your area but may not be found in local supermarkets. In general, fruit sold by grocers isn't as flavorful as that grown locally. Usually this is because most store-bought fruit isn't picked fully ripe and is stored for months and shipped hundreds or thousands of miles.

The ideal (if you have space) is to plant several trees to ripen sequentially, providing early, mid-, and late-season fruit. Outstanding dessert apples include 'Ginger Gold', 'Gala', 'Mutsu', Fuji', 'Cumberland Spur Red Delicious', and 'Pink Lady'. For a good baking apple, try 'Rome Beauty', 'Jonathan', 'Granny Smith', or 'Carter's Blue'.

Apple trees are longer lived and easier to grow than most fruit trees, but they still require regular care. Though they'll tolerate heavy clay and even rocky soil, they prefer deep, fertile, well-drained soil. They typically need regular applications of nitrogen; the amount and frequency depend on soil.

Apple selections vary in their adaptability to different locales. Information about the best selections, average hours of chilling in your area, and the care needed is generally available through your local County Extension Office.

To avoid frost damage in spring, plant on slopes rather than in low spots. Supplemental watering during summer dry spells produces juicier fruit. Apples often bear fruit in clusters of three or four; if you let all of them ripen, they'll all be small. Thinning the clusters to one or two in spring results in bigger, juicier fruit spaced 4–6 in. apart.

The main insect pests are apple maggot, codling moth, and plum curculio, all of which infest the fruit. Pheromone traps, *Bacillus thuringiensis* (*Bt*), or horticultural oil may be enough to thwart these pests in most areas,

IN CIDER TRADING

You might think that the colonists who brought apples to the South from Europe raised them for their tasty fruit, but you'd be wrong. In fact, most early apple orchards were primarily planted for cider. Why? Because drinking water was often polluted, whereas the acidity and alcohol in hard cider killed bacteria—and gave the settlers a beverage that was safe to drink. The desire for cider led to the dissemination of many classic heirloom apples, including 'Ashmead's Kernel', 'Grimes Golden', 'Limbertwig', and 'Roxbury Russet'.

but proper timing of controls is critical.

Diseases cause more problems than insects do. Typical diseases include apple scab, which causes hard, corky spots on fruit; cedar-apple rust, which produces orange spots on leaves and fruit; brown rot that causes fruit to rot on the tree; and fireblight, which blackens and kills young twigs and leaves. Applying proper fungicides, as well as dormant oil in winter, can also aid in control.

Dwarf, semidwarf, and spur apples. Dwarf apples (5–8 ft. tall and wide) are good choices if you have limited space or want to grow several types of apples in the space a standard tree would take. Dwarfs bear at a younger age than standard apples, but they have shallow roots and need the support of a post, fence, wall, or sturdy trellis to withstand wind and heavy rain. They also need well-drained soil and extra care in feeding and watering. Genetic dwarf apples, such as 'Garden Delicious', are naturally small and stay that way; even grafting them onto a standard (non-dwarfing) rootstock would not produce a standard-size tree.

Semidwarf trees are larger than dwarfs but smaller than standard trees. They're the best choice for most people, producing a bigger crop than dwarfs in a

APPLE VARIETIES

NAME	ZONES	SEASON	FRUIT	COMMENTS
'Anna'	CS; USDA 9	Early; sometimes a light second crop later in the season	Large; pale green blushed red; crisp, sweet, slightly tangy	Produces at a young age; needs very little winter chill; good annual bearer; use 'Dorsett Golden' as pollenizer
'Arkansas Black'	US, MS, LS; USDA 6-8	Late	Medium size; dark, deep red; hard-crisp; excellent keeper; best flavor after storage for 2 months; good for cooking, fresh eating	Born 1870 in Benton County, Arkansas; 'Arkansas Black Spur' is spurred variation
'Ashmead's Kernel'	US, MS; USDA 6-7	Late	Medium size; red-orange blush over rough yellow-green skin; crisp, juicy, aromatic; a favorite for cider	Good disease resistance; originated in Gloucester, England, around 1700; known as the ugly apple with the sweet, delicious taste
'Black Twig'	US, MS, LS; USDA 6-8	Late	Large to medium; green to yellow blushed with red; tart, fine-grained flesh; good for fresh eating, cooking, and cider; good keeper; best flavor develops in storage	Good disease resistance; originated near Fayetteville, Tennessee, in the early 1800s; favorite of Andrew Jackson
'Carolina Red June'	US, MS, LS; USDA 6-8	Early	Small to medium; pale yellow blushed with purplish red; juicy, aromatic; good for fresh eating, pies, cider	Originated in North Carolina; not a good keeper but ripens fruit over a long period; heavy bearer; thin crop for bigger fruit
'Carter's Blue'	US, MS, LS; USDA 6-8	Early midseason	Medium to large; roundish oblong shape; greenish yellow skin with unique bluish purple bloom; crisp, yellowish white flesh with a sweet-tart flavor	Discovered by Colonel Carter in Mt. Meigs, Alabama, around 1840; not a good keeper
'Cortland'	US, MS; USDA 6-7	Early midseason	Large; dark bluish red skin streaked with yellow; excellent all-purpose fruit; does not turn brown when sliced	Vigorous; bears at a young age; produces annually; holds fruit better than 'McIntosh'; excellent pollinizer; susceptible to disease; self-pollinating
'Cripps Pink' ('Pink Lady')	US, MS, LS; USDA 6-8	Late	Medium; light red; crisp; good keeper; great flavor; good for cooking or fresh eating	Released in Australia in 1973; ripens very late; one of the finest late apples
'Delicious' ('Red Delicious')	US, MS, LS; USDA 6-8	Midseason to late	Medium to large; easily recognized by pointed blossom end with five knobs; color and shape vary with strain and climate; best where days are warm and sunny, nights cool	'Crimson Spur', 'Cumberland Spur Red Delicious', and 'Redchief' are popular home selections; all types susceptible to scab
'Dorsett Golden'	CS; USDA 9	Early	Medium to large; yellow or greenish yellow; sweet flavor; good for eating fresh or cooking; keeps a few weeks	Seedling of 'Golden Delicious' from Bermuda; low winter chill; good pollenizer for 'Tropic Sweet', 'Anna', and 'Ein Shemer'; self-pollinating
'Ein Shemer'	CS; USDA 9	Early	Medium; yellow to greenish yellow; juicy, crisp, mildly tangy	Needs little winter chill; pollinates 'Anna', 'Dorsett Golden', 'Tropic Sweet'; self-pollinating

APPLE VARIETIES (continued)

NAME	ZONES	SEASON	FRUIT	COMMENTS
'Empire'	US, MS, LS; USDA 6-8	Midseason to late	Small to medium; roundish, dark red; creamy white flesh is juicy, crisp, mildly tart; good keeper; good for cider	Cross between 'McIntosh' and 'Delicious'; semispur growth habit; good tree structure; susceptible to spring frost damage
'Enterprise'	US, MS, LS; USDA 6-8	Late	Medium size; firm fruit with red blush; sweet-tart flavor; keeps well; good cooking apple	Disease resistant; subject to preharvest fruit drop
'Freedom'	US, MS, LS, CS; USDA 6-9	Midseason	Medium to large; round red fruit; good for fresh eating and cooking; sweet-tart flavor	Disease resistant; excellent pollenizer for 'Liberty', another disease-resistant selection
'Fuji'	US, MS, LS; USDA 6-8	Midseason to late	Medium to large; yellow-green ground with red stripes; firm, very sweet, excellent flavor; stores exceptionally well	Tends to bear heavy crops in alternate years; a cross between 'Rall's Janet' and 'Delicious' made in Japan in 1939
'Gala'	US, MS, LS; USDA 6-8	Early to midseason	Medium size; beautiful red-on-yellow color; highly aromatic, firm, crisp, juicy, sweet yellow flesh	From New Zealand; vigorous, heavy bearer with long, supple branches that break easily; may need support; susceptible to fireblight
'Garden Delicious'	US, MS, LS; USDA 6-8	Midseason	Medium to large; golden green with red blush	Genetic dwarf growing 5–8 ft. tall and wide
'Ginger Gold'	US, MS, LS; USDA 6-8	Early	Medium to large; yellow, firm, crisp; sweet-tart flavor; resembles 'Golden Delicious'; good keeper; also good for cooking, eating fresh	One of the better early yellow apples; ripens over 2–3 weeks; chance seedling from the orchard of Ginger Harvey in Livingston, Virginia; susceptible to disease
'Golden Delicious' ('Yellow Delicious')	US, MS, LS; USDA 6-8	Midseason to late	Medium to large; clear yellow, may develop skin russeting in some areas; similar in shape to 'Delicious', with less prominent knobs; highly aromatic, crisp; excellent for eating fresh, cooking, cider	Not related to 'Red Delicious'; different flavor, habit; partially self-pollinating; long bloom season, heavy pollen production make it a good pollenizer; strains available: 'Goldspur', 'Smoothie', 'Starspur Golden Delicious', 'Yellowspur'; susceptible to disease
'Golden Russet'	US, MS, LS; USDA 6-8	Late	Medium; greenish yellow to gold, marked with russet; fine-grained yellow flesh; excellent for cider, fresh eating, and cooking	Vigorous; resistant to scab; susceptible to rust, fireblight; partially self-pollinating; good pollenizer for other selections
'Gold Rush'	US, MS, LS; USDA 6-8	Late	Medium; yellow, often with russeting; best after storage; good for pies, fresh eating, cider	Immune to scab; good resistance to mildew; some resistance to fireblight
'Granny Smith'	US, MS, LS, CS; USDA 6-9	Midseason to late	Large; bright to yellowish green; firm and tart; good quality; stores well; good for pies, sauce	Australian favorite before it came to U.S.; good pollinizer; susceptible to disease
'Grimes Golden'	US, MS, LS; USDA 6-8	Midseason	Medium size; round, golden; crisp, spicy-sweet, yellow flesh; good for fresh eating, cider, desserts; stores moderately well	Bears young; discovered in West Virginia by Thomas Grimes around 1804; partially self-pollinating; good pollenizer for other selections
'Jonagold'	US, MS, LS; USDA 6-8	Midseason	Large; heavy red striping over yellow ground; firm and juicy; fine, mildly tart flavor; frequent taste-test favorite; good cooking apple	Productive, medium-size tree; heavy bearer; pollen-sterile; will not pollinate others; not pollinated by 'Golden Delicious'

A

NAME	ZONES	SEASON	FRUIT	COMMENTS
'Jonathan'	US, MS, LS; USDA 6-8	Midseason	Small to medium; roundish oblong; high-colored red; juicy, moderately tart, crackling crisp	All-purpose apple, good keeper; moderately suscep-tible to disease
'Kinnaird's Choice'	US, MS, LS; USDA 6-8	Early midseason	Medium to large; smooth-skinned fruit is yellow flushed with red, deep red in sun; crisp, white flesh; good for fresh eating, cider	Old favorite in north Georgia; originated in Franklin, Tennes-see; will bear heavily one year and lightly the next unless crop is thinned
'Liberty'	US, MS, LS; USDA 6-8	Late midseason	Medium; heavy red blush; crisp flesh with fine, sweet-tart flavor; dessert quality	Productive annual bearer; one of the better disease-resistant selections; immune to scab; re-sists cedar-apple rust, fireblight
'Limbertwig'	US, MS, LS; USDA 6-8	Late	Medium size; greenish yellow blushed red; hard yellow flesh; excellent for cider; good keeper	An old Southern favorite with many regional forms; good disease resistance
'Magnum Bonum'	US, MS, LS; USDA 6-8	Midseason	Medium; greenish yellow streaked with red; crisp, juicy, aromatic flesh; excellent for fresh eating; stores well	North Carolina heirloom originating in Davidson County about 1828; bears at early age; resists diseases except for rust
'Mutsu' ('Crispin')	US, MS, LS, CS; USDA 6-9	Midseason to late	Very large; greenish yellow to yellow blushed red; cream-colored, very crisp flesh with sweet-tart flavor; excellent for dessert or cooking	Exceptionally large and vigor-ous tree; pollen-sterile; long storage life; susceptible to disease
'Newtown Pippin' ('Albemarle Pippin')	US, MS, LS; USDA 6-8	Late	Large; greenish yellow or clear yellow; crisp, firm, juicy, slightly tart; good all-purpose apple; excellent keeper; flavor improves in storage; good for color	Large, vigorous tree; originated in Newtown, Long Island, early 1700s
'Priscilla'	US, MS, LS; USDA 6-8	Early to midsea-son	Red fruit; light, floral flavor; good for dessert, fresh eating, cider; good keeper	Very disease resistant; depend-able bearer
'Paulared'	US, MS; USDA 6-7	Early	Large; red skinned, mild flavored; one of the better early apples	Good branch structure; good disease resistance
'Pristine'	US, MS, LS; USDA 6-8	Early	Medium size; bright yellow; mildly tart white flesh; good for fresh eating, baking, sauce	Immune to scab; resistant to cedar-apple rust; some resis-tance to mildew and fireblight; deer resistant
'Redfree'	US, MS, LS; USDA 6-8	Early	Medium size; glossy red; firm, crisp flesh with good flavor	Heavy bearer; very disease resistant; deer resistant
'Rome Beauty' ('Red Rome')	US, MS, LS; USDA 6-8	Late	Large; smooth, round red apple with greenish white flesh; out-standing baking apple, good for cider, only fair for eating fresh	Bears at an early age; par-tially self-pollinating; several regional strains; moderately susceptible to disease
'Roxbury Russet'	US, MS, LS; USDA 6-8	Late	Large; green fruit with brown russeting; firm, sweet, yellow-ish flesh; good for eating and cooking; superior for cider; good keeper	Blooms late; good disease resistance; pollen sterile; won't pollinate other trees; oldest named American apple, origi-nating in Roxbury, Massachu-setts, in early 1600s

APPLE VARIETIES *(continued)*

NAME	ZONES	SEASON	FRUIT	COMMENTS
'Scarlett O'Hara'	US, MS, LS; USDA 6-8	Midseason	Medium size; red blush over yellow background; mild, slightly spicy, crisp, juicy; stores well	Immune to scab and cedar-apple rust; resistant to scrub and mildew but susceptible to fireblight
'Stayman' (often called 'Winesap')	US, MS, LS; USDA 6-8	Late	Large; 'Stayman' (a 'Winesap' cross) is greenish yellow with red stripes; fine grained, firm, aromatic, with "winey" flavor; good for fresh eating, applesauce, cider, baking; good keeper	Pollinates with 'Golden Delicious', 'Grimes Golden', 'Lodi', 'Golden Russet'; bears at a young age; pollen-sterile; won't pollinate other selections; fruit subject to cracking in wet weather; susceptible to disease
'Tropic Sweet'	CS; USDA 9	Early	Medium to large; green skin blushed with red; very sweet	Low-chill type from Florida; similar to 'Anna' but sweeter; 'Anna', 'Dorsett Golden' are pollenizers
'Williams' Pride'	US, MS, LS; USDA 6-8	Early	Medium size; dark red fruit with spicy-sweet flesh; one of the better early red apples in flavor	Immune to scab; resistant to fireblight; susceptible to mildew
'Yates' ('Jates')	US, MS, LS, CS; USDA 6-9	Late	Small; aromatic fruit; bright red with yellow spots; spicy flavor, best after a frost; keeps well; good for cider	Originated in Georgia in 1813; heavy bearer, vigorous grower; good pollenizer for other selections
'York Imperial'	US, MS; 8-1	Late	Medium to large; yellow or green flushed pink; firm, juicy, yellowish flesh; great for cooking, baking; best flavor if kept till Christmas	One of the best old-time selections for winter keeping; discovered around 1830 by Mr. Johnson in York, Pennsylvania; susceptible to disease.

relatively short period of time.

Spur apples are natural or genetically engineered semi-dwarfs about two-thirds the size of standard apple trees. Their fruiting spurs—short branches that grow from wood 2 years old and older—form earlier than those of nonspur types (within 2 to 3 years of planting) and grow closer together on shorter branches, giving more apples per foot of branch. Among the better spur-type selections are: 'Cumberland Spur Red Delicious', 'Granny Smith Spur', 'Starkspur Golden Delicious', and 'Arkansas Black Spur'.

Garden centers and mail-order nurseries won't generally specify the name of the dwarfing or semidwarfing rootstock they use on the tree they sell you. There are many different rootstocks, however, and not all perform well in the South. Rootstocks such as MM106 and M26 have been cleaned of viruses and are generally sold under the names of EMLA106 and EMLA26, which are virus-free clones of the originals.

HOW TO GROW APPLES

WINTER CHILL Most selections demand 900 to 1,200 hours of temperatures at or below 45°F. In mild-winter areas, look for low-chill selections (100 to 400 hours).

FULL SUN Plenty of sunshine is essential for a good crop—so don't crowd an apple tree into a partially shaded site. To plant more than one selection in a small space, choose dwarf or multiple-selection trees.

WATERING When fruit is developing, make up for any lack of rainfall with periodic deep soakings.

POLLINATION Although some selections are self-pollinating, most need cross-pollination with another selection to bear fruit.

TRAINING AND PRUNING. For most home use, plant dwarf or semidwarf trees for ease in maintenance and harvest. Preferred style is when widely angled branches are encouraged

to grow in spiral placement around the trunk. Prune to develop strong, evenly spaced scaffold branches. Keep narrow-angled crotches from developing; don't let side branches outgrow the leader, or secondary branches outgrow the primary branches.

To prune mature trees (do it late in the dormant season), remove weak, dead, or poorly placed branches and twigs, especially those growing toward the center of the tree (bearing is heaviest when some sun can reach the middle). Also remove any suckers from the base and any water sprouts (unbranched shoots that grow straight up from the main limbs). Removing such growth will encourage development of strong new wood with new fruiting spurs (on apples, spurs may produce for up to 20 years but they tend to weaken after about 3 years) and discourage mildew. If you have inherited an old tree, selective thinning of branches will accomplish the same goal.

If trees growing in 3-gallon pots are planted, 2 to 3 years may be required to begin fruiting. If larger trees (15-gal or larger) are used, only 1 to 2 years are needed to begin harvesting.

THE LOST APPLES OF THE SOUTH

Heirloom apples are back. Celebrate their new golden age with a sweet bite from the past.

Albemarle Pippin
QUEENS, NEW YORK, 1720

This NYC native thrived in the Virginia Piedmont and became a favorite of George Washington and Thomas Jefferson. Today, its sprightly lemon-and-pineapple flavor provides the pizazz in a new wave of Champagne-like ciders.

Yates
FAYETTE COUNTY, GEORGIA, 1840S

Little 'Yates' can take heat and humidity, which is why it became a standard on farms throughout the southernmost states. Sweet and tart with a spicy twang, it makes the perfect small snack all winter long.

Grimes Golden
BROOKS COUNTY, WEST VIRGINIA, 1790

Supersweet with high sugar content and blasts of banana and anise flavors, it became the favorite of moonshiners and children alike. The first 'Golden Delicious' tree sprang from a 'Grimes Golden' seed.

York Imperial
YORK, PENNSYLVANIA, 1820

Comically lopsided with a juicy sweetness and a way of melting into fluffy sauce when cooked, it does best in the states near the Mason-Dixon Line. Find it piled high in Maryland and Virginia markets every Thanksgiving.

Arkansas Black
BENTONVILLE, ARKANSAS, 1870

A stunning 'Winesap' seedling, it was famed for staying power in the root cellar, where its tart and tannic bite mellowed into delightful flavors reminiscent of a glass of iced tea sweetened with orange-blossom honey.

Golden Delicious
CLAY COUNTY, WEST VIRGINIA, 1890

The second-most-successful apple of all time after 'Red Delicious'. The supermarket version is bland, but the honeyed aromas of a tree-ripened one from a Southern farm capture the very essence of apple.

Winesap
MOORESTOWN, NEW JERSEY, LATE 1700S

The most important of all Southern apples, it reigned before the advent of controlled atmosphere storage and the rise of 'Red Delicious'. Tart and foxy, it's equally gifted for fresh eating and in pies or cider.

AQUILEGIA
COLUMBINE
Ranunculaceae
Perennials

🖊 **ZONES VARY BY SPECIES**

☼ ◐ **FULL SUN OR LIGHT SHADE**

💧 **REGULAR WATER**

Aquilegia chrysantha hinckleyana

Lacy foliage and beautifully presented flowers in exquisite pastels, deeper shades, and white give columbines a fairylike, woodland-glen quality. Plants are erect and range in size from 2 in. to 4 ft. high. Divided leaves similar to maidenhair fern (*Adiantum*) may be fresh green, blue-green, or gray-green. Slender, branching stems carry erect or nodding flowers to 3 in. across, often with sepals and petals in contrasting colors; they usually have backward-projecting, nectar-bearing spurs. Some columbines have large flowers and very long spurs; these have an airier look than short-spurred and spurless kinds. Double-flowered types lack the delicacy of the single-flowered sort, but they make a bolder color mass. Blossoms typically appear in spring and early summer.

A. canadensis. WILD COL-UMBINE. Zones US, MS, LS; USDA 6-8. Native to much of eastern and central North America. Grows 1–2 ft. tall (occasionally taller) and about 1 ft. wide. Red-and-yellow, 1½-in., nodding flowers have slightly curved, 1-in. spurs. Red color may wash out to pink in areas with warm night temperatures. Less susceptible to leaf miners than most columbines. 'Corbett' has creamy yellow flowers. Dwarf 'Little Lanterns' grows 10 in. tall.

A. chrysantha. GOLDEN COLUMBINE, GOLDEN-SPURRED COLUMBINE. Zones US, MS, LS, CS; USDA 6-9. Native to Arizona, New Mexico, and adjacent Mexico. One of showiest species. Large, many-branched plant to 3–4 ft. tall, 1–2 ft. wide. Undersides of leaflets densely covered with soft hairs. Upright, clear yellow, 1½- to 3-in. flowers with slender, hooked spurs 2–2½ in. long. 'Yellow Queen' grows 3 ft. tall and produces an abundance of clear yellow, fragrant blossoms.

A. c. hinckleyana. HINCK-LEY'S COLUMBINE. Zones US, MS, LS; USDA 6-8. Native to Big Bend country of Texas. To 1½–2 ft. high and wide, with long-spurred flowers in chartreuse yellow. Blue-gray foliage stays handsome in summer, and leaf miners aren't a big problem.

A. flabellata. FAN COLUM-BINE. Zones US, MS, LS; USDA 6-8. Native to Japan. Stocky plant 8 in.–1½ ft. high, 1 ft. wide, with nodding, 1½-in., two-tone flowers of lilac-blue and creamy white. Hooked spurs to 1 in. long. Differs from most other columbines in having thicker, darker leaves, often with overlapping segments. *A. f. pumila* is a very dwarf form (just 4 in. high). Good rock garden plant. The Cameo series is dwarf (4–8 in.) and comes with two-toned flowers of white and blue, pink, or rose.

A. hybrids. Zones US, MS, LS; USDA 6-8. These include graceful, long-spurred McKana Giants and double-flowering Spring Song (both to 3 ft. tall, 2 ft. wide). Nora Barlow Mixed, reaching 2–2½ ft. high and 2 ft. wide, has double flowers in a wide range of colors (the original 'Nora Barlow' has reddish pink blooms with white margins). About the same size is Vervaeneana Woodside Variegated Mixed, with variegated leaves and various flower colors. Lower-growing strains include Biedermeier and Dragonfly (1 ft. high and wide); early-blooming Spring Magic (14 in. tall and 12 in. wide); long-spurred Music (1½ ft. high and wide); long-blooming Origami (16–18 in. high); and single to double, upward-facing Fairyland (15 in. high and wide).

A. longissima. LONGSPUR COLUMBINE. Zones US, MS, LS, CS; USDA 6-9. Native to Southwest Texas, southern Arizona, and northern Mexico. Grows

2½–3 ft. tall and about 1½–2 ft. wide. This species is quite similar to *A. chrysantha.* Numerous erect, pale yellow blossoms with very narrow, drooping, 4- to 6-in.-long spurs.

A. vulgaris. EUROPEAN COLUMBINE. GRANNY'S BON-NETS. Zones US, MS, LS; USDA 6-8. Native to western, central, and southern Europe; naturalized in eastern U.S. Grows 1–2½ ft. tall, 1 ft. wide. Nodding blue or violet flowers to 2 in. across with short, knobby spurs about ¾ in. long. Many selections and hybrids offer single to fully double blooms, either short spurred or spurless.

CARE

Columbines are not fussy about soil as long as it is well drained. Cut back old stems for second crop of flowers. All kinds attract hummingbirds. Deer tend to leave them alone. Most are not long lived and will need to be replaced every 3 or 4 years. Allow the spent flowers to form seed capsules to ensure a crop of volunteer seedlings. If you're growing hybrids, the seedlings won't necessarily duplicate the parent plants, but seedlings from species (if grown isolated from other columbines) should closely resemble the originals. Leaf miners are a potential pest, especially on hybrids.

ROCK-CRESSES THRIVE AND BLOOM DEPENDABLY EVEN IN HOT, DRY SPOTS WITH INFERTILE SOIL.

ARABIS
ROCKCRESS
Brassicaceae
Perennials

🖊 **US, MS, LS; USDA 6-8, EXCEPT AS NOTED**

☼ **FULL SUN, EXCEPT AS NOTED**

💧 **MODERATE WATER**

Arabis alpina caucasica

Low-growing, spreading plants for edgings, rock gardens, ground covers, pattern plantings. All kinds have attractive year-round foliage and clusters of small, white, pink, or rose-purple flowers in spring. Seldom browsed by deer. Give good drainage.

A. alpina. MOUNTAIN ROCKCRESS. Native to mountain elevations of Europe. Low, tufted, rough-hairy plant 4–10 in. high, 2 ft. wide. Produces white flowers in dense, short clusters. Selection 'Rosea' bears pink flowers; 'Variegata' has yellow-edged green leaves.

A. a. caucasica (*A. albida*). WALL ROCKCRESS. Native from Mediterranean region to Iran. This plant is a dependable old favorite. Forms mat of gray-green leaves to 6 in. high, 1½ ft. wide. White flowers almost cover plant during bloom season. Excellent ground cover and base planting for spring-flowering bulbs such as daffodils and 'Paper White' narcissus. Provide some shade in hot climates. 'Variegata' has gray leaves with creamy white margins; 'Flore Pleno' is double flowered; 'Rosabella' and 'Pink Charm' bear pink blooms.

A. procurrens. WHITE ROCK-CRESS. Zones US, MS; USDA 6-7. Native to southeastern Europe. Creeping plant with 1½-in. leaves and white flowers clustered on 4- to 12-in. stems. Over time, spreads widely.

A. x sturii. Dense, fist-size cushions of small, bright green leaves eventually grow into small mats bearing clusters of white flowers on 2- to 3-in. stems. Some consider this species among the finest rock garden plants.

ARACHNIODES SIMPLICIOR 'VARIEGATA'

VARIEGATED INDIAN HOLLY FERN
Dryopteridaceae
Fern

🌿 **US, MS, LS, CS; USDA 6-9**

☼ ● **PARTIAL OR FULL SHADE**

💧💧 **REGULAR TO AMPLE WATER**

Arachniodes simplicior 'Variegata'

This beautiful fern from Japan and China features shiny, dark green fronds, erect and deeply cut, with a yellow stripe down the center of each segment. It forms a clump 10–18 in. tall and twice as wide. Evergreen in the Lower and Coastal South; deciduous in the Middle and Upper South, where it emerges late in spring. Naturalized in some parts of the Southeast. Showy addition to the shade garden.

ARALIA

Araliaceae
Deciduous shrub-trees

🌿 **ZONES VARY BY SPECIES**

☼ ◐ **FULL SUN OR PARTIAL SHADE**

💧💧 **MODERATE TO REGULAR WATER**

Aralia elata

Most are striking bold-leafed plants that may eventually grow to 25–30 ft. tall under ideal conditions. Not for small gardens. Often shrublike and multi-stemmed (because of suckering habit), especially in colder areas, where they may grow just 10 ft. high. Clumps range from one-half to almost as wide as they are tall. Branches are nearly vertical or slightly spreading, usually very spiny. Huge leaves, clustered at ends of branches and divided into many leaflets, look quite exotic. White mid-summer flowers, small but in such large, branched clusters that they are showy, are followed by berrylike, purplish fruit that is enjoyed by birds.

Grow in well-drained soil. Not good near walkways because of spines; even leafstalks are sometimes prickly. Wind can burn the foliage, so provide a sheltered location. Need minimal pruning; dig out suckers to limit spread of clump.

A. cordata. UDO, JAPANESE SPIKENARD. Zones US, MS, LS; USDA 6-8. From Japan. To 6 ft. tall, half as wide. This species doesn't have spines; forms an attractive foliage mass of oval, unevenly toothed leaflets 2–6 in. long. In Asia, the young spring shoots are blanched and eaten. 'Sun King' (6 ft. tall, 3 ft. wide in partial sun) emerges lime green-gold in spring and remains all summer.

A. elata. ANGELICA TREE. Zones US, MS, LS; USDA 6-8. Native to Asia. Only moderately spiny. Leaves 2–3 ft. long, divided into toothed, stalkless, 2- to 6-in.-long leaflets. 'Variegata' has leaflets strikingly bordered with creamy white.

A. spinosa. HERCULES' CLUB, DEVIL'S WALKING STICK. Zones US, MS, LS, CS; USDA 6-9. Native to eastern U.S. Puts up several spiny, usually unbranched stems to 10–20 ft. tall, each of them crowned by 2- to 6-ft.-long leaves. This is one of the most tropical-looking, hardy plants. Summer flowers and fall fruit are showy. 'Variegata' amplifies the impact with gray-green leaves edged in white.

ARAUCARIA

Araucariaceae
Evergreen trees

🌿 **ZONES VARY BY SPECIES**

☼ **FULL SUN**

💧 **REGULAR WATER**

Araucaria heterophylla

These distinctive conifers are commonly seen in Florida gardens, but some are hardy enough to grow outdoors farther north. Most species bear stiff, closely overlapping, dark to bright green leaves. They accept a wide range of soils with adequate drainage. They thrive in containers for several years.

These trees grow into striking specimens that take up a lot of space. As they age they bear spiny cones that can weigh up to 15 pounds. If one falls on your head from the top of the tree, you'll wander aimlessly for years—should you survive the initial impact.

A. araucana (*A. imbricata*). MONKEY PUZZLE TREE. Zones MS, LS, CS, TS; USDA 8-11. Native to Chile. An arboreal oddity with heavy, spreading branches and ropelike branchlets closely set with sharp-pointed, dark green leaves. Slow growing when young, it eventually reaches 70–90 ft. tall and 30 ft. wide.

A. bidwillii. BUNYA-BUNYA. Zones CS, TS; USDA 9-11. Native to Australia. Moderate growth to 80 ft. tall, 60 ft. wide. Broadly rounded crown casts dense shade. Juvenile leaves are glossy, lance shaped, 1–2 in. long, arranged in two rows; mature leaves are oval, ½ in. long, rather woody, spirally arranged, and overlapping along the branches. Sometimes used as a lawn tree in large yards; grows well in large containers. Tough and tolerant of low light; makes an unusual houseplant.

A. heterophylla (*A. excelsa*). NORFOLK ISLAND PINE. Zone TS; USDA 10-11; or indoors. Native to Norfolk Island, near Australia. Grown outdoors in central and south Florida, where it may reach 80–100 ft. tall and 60 ft. wide. Elsewhere in the South, it's a popular houseplant, prized for its symmetrical shape, evenly spaced whorls of branches, and soft, lush, rich green foliage.

In December, people often bedeck Norfolk Island pines with ribbons, ornaments, and twinkle lights and turn them into indoor Christmas trees. If you want them to last for long indoors, pay attention to their care. Make sure they receive bright light, either natural or artificial; they do well near a south- or west-facing window. Let the soil go slightly dry on the surface between waterings, but don't let it dry out completely—if it does, the lower tiers of branches will die one by one and won't be replaced. Apply a general-purpose liquid houseplant fertilizer twice monthly in spring and summer, monthly in fall and winter. Eventually, your tree will grow tall enough to touch the ceiling—but don't try to give it to a botanical garden. They already have plenty.

A

ARBUTUS

Ericaceae

Evergreen trees or shrubs

◨ **MS, LS, CS, TS; USDA 7-11**

☼ ◑ **EXPOSURE NEEDS VARY BY SPECIES**

◌ ◖ **LITTLE TO REGULAR WATER**

Arbutus unedo

All types have ornamental bark, clusters of little urn-shaped flowers, decorative (and edible) fruit, and handsome foliage. Provide good drainage, especially if plant receives regular water. Best in low-humidity, low-rainfall areas such as West Texas.

A. unedo. STRAWBERRY TREE. Native to southern Europe, Ireland. Slow to moderate growth to 8–35 ft. tall and wide; tends to be a small shrub in Southeast. Trunk and branches have red-brown, shredding bark, become twisted and gnarled in age. Dark green, red-stemmed leaves 2–3 in. long. Small, white or greenish white flowers; red-and-yellow, ¾-in. fruit resembles strawberries but is mealy and bland tasting. Clusters of flowers and fruit often appear simultaneously in fall and winter. Selections include 'Elfin King', a dwarf form (not over 5 ft. tall at 10 years old) that flowers and fruits nearly continuously; 'Compacta', seldom exceeding 10 ft.; and 'Oktoberfest', a 6- to 8-ft. form with deep pink flowers. Give species and selections sun or part shade.

A. xalapensis (*A. texana*). TEXAS MADRONE. Native to Texas, New Mexico, Mexico to Guatemala. Striking multitrunked, small tree to 20–30 ft. tall and wide, with handsome, deep green leaves, clusters of small white or pale pink flowers in spring, raspberrylike fruit in fall. Extremely showy bark changes in color through the year, from cream (when young) to pink and then to brown before it peels, revealing new bark beneath. Requires careful attention to get established. Provide light shade; water consistently for several years but never allow soil to become waterlogged. Grows well in chalky soil.

ARCHONTO-PHOENIX

Arecaceae

Palms

◨ **TS; USDA 10-11; OR GROW IN POTS**

☼ ◑ **FULL SUN OR PART SHADE; BRIGHT INDIRECT LIGHT**

◖ ◖ **MODERATE TO REGULAR WATER**

Archontophoenix alexandrae

Handsome, slender palms native to the rain forests of eastern Australia. Both species described here feature a single narrow trunk and may reach 50 ft. or taller, with a 10- to 15-ft. spread. Their compact, formal shape makes them good lawn and street trees; they tolerate shade and can grow for many years beneath taller trees. Feathery fronds, green above and gray-green beneath, may reach 8–10 ft. long on mature trees. Old fronds shed cleanly, leaving attractive rings on the trunk. Easy to grow in containers, indoors or out. Large specimens are difficult to transplant.

A. alexandrae. ALEXANDRA PALM. Widely planted in south Florida. Very tender to cold; young trees will not survive frost. Trunk is swollen at the base. In summer, clusters of tiny white flowers form beneath the crown. Sometimes confused with *A. cunninghamiana* at nurseries.

A. cunninghamiana (*Seaforthia elegans*). KING PALM. A better, hardier *Archontophoenix* for many Florida gardens. Mature plants may take brief periods of 28°F. Frond leaflets are broader than those of *A. alexandrae*, trunk is less swollen at base. Flowers are lilac.

ARCTOTIS

AFRICAN DAISY

Asteraceae

Annuals and perennials, usually treated as annuals

◨ **US, MS, LS, CS, TS; USDA 6-11**

☼ **FULL SUN**

◖ **MODERATE WATER**

Arctotis hybrid

The name "African daisy" can refer to any of several plants from southern Africa, and identities are often confused, even by many seed companies and nurseries. *Arctotis* species have lobed leaves that are rough, hairy, or woolly; their blossoms usually sport a contrasting ring of color around a central eye. *Dimorphotheca* species have smooth green foliage; their ringless flowers either are white or fall into the yellow-salmon-orange range. Woody, shrubby, white, yellow, or purple African daisies and the trailing types used as ground cover belong to the genus *Osteospermum*.

Seedlings begin blooming about 3 months after germination. They are grown as summer annuals in most of the South but may be used for winter color in Florida and South Texas. The blossoms make good cut flowers, even though they close at night. Plants reseed readily.

A. acaulis. Perennial. Spreading clumps of velvety gray leaves to 1 ft. high are topped by yellow, 3½-in.-wide flowers with purplish black centers. 'Big Magenta' has purplish red flowers.

A. x pubescens (*A. hirsuta*). Masses of 3-in., black-centered, bright orange (or, occasionally, lemon yellow) blossoms on a plant to 1–1½ ft. tall and wide.

A. fastuosa alba (*Venidium fastuosum*). Annual. Bushy growth to 2 ft. tall and 1½ ft. wide, with gray-green, slightly hairy leaves; white, 3-in.-wide daisies with a yellow ring surrounding a deep blue eye. In selection 'Zulu Prince', an inner ring of yellow and darkest purple encircles a black center.

A. hybrids. Most *Arctotis* sold in garden centers are hybrids that grow 1–1½ ft. tall and wide. The 3-in. flowers come in white, pink, purplish, cream, yellow, and orange—usually with a dark ring around a nearly black central eye. Hybrids will self-sow, but the seedlings they produce tend to revert to orange. 'Pink Sugar' features orange-centered pink flowers on silver foliage.

A. venusta. Bushy growth to 2 ft. tall and 1½ ft. wide, with slightly hairy, gray-green leaves. Silvery blue, 3-in.-wide daisies have a yellow ring surrounding a deep blue eye. Tolerates poor, sandy soil.

FOR A HANDSOME CONTRAST, PLANT AFRICAN DAISIES AROUND ORNAMENTAL GRASSES

ARDISIA

MARLBERRY
Primulaceae
Evergreen shrubs

⬛ **ZONES VARY BY SPECIES**

☼ ◐ ● **EXPOSURE NEEDS VARY BY SPECIES**

💧 **REGULAR WATER, EXCEPT AS NOTED**

Ardisia crenata

Of the 150 species of evergreen shrubs in this genus, only the following three are commonly grown. All are valued both for attractive foliage and for their beadlike fruit.

A. crenata CORAL ARDISIA. Zones CS, TS; USDA 9-11; or indoors. Native from Japan to northern India. In Florida, coral ardisia is often grown in the ground on the north side of a house or in planters. As a potted plant, it grows 1½ ft. tall, single-stemmed, with only bright filtered light and routine care, either in shade outdoors or as a houseplant. In a large pot, it can reach 4 ft. with nearly equal spread. In spring, spirelike clusters of ¼-in., white or pinkish flowers are carried above shiny, wavy-edged, 3-in.-long leaves. 'Alba' has reliably white blossoms. Flowers are followed in autumn by brilliant scarlet fruit that usually hangs on through the winter. Outdoors, plant in partial or full shade.

A. japonica. JAPANESE ARDISIA. Zones LS, CS; USDA 8-9. From Japan and China. Prostrate shrub spreads by rhizomes to produce a succession of upright branches that are 5–12 in. high. A high-quality ground cover in partial or full shade. Leathery bright green leaves to 4 in. long are clustered at the branch tips. White, ¼-in. flowers in clusters of two to six

appear in fall; these are followed by small, round, bright red fruit that lasts into winter. 'Chirimen' is an especially cold-hardy selection and may survive even in the Middle South. Selections with colorful foliage include 'Amanoga-wa', with particularly bright red berries and green leaves centered in gold; and 'Hakuokan', bearing green leaves heavily variegated with white on the edges. 'Nishiki' offers gold and pink variegated leaves on new growth.

A. escallonioides (*A. paniculata*). MARLBERRY. Zone TS; USDA 10-11. Slender shrub or small tree to 20–25 ft. high, 10–12 ft. wide. Native to south Florida. Coarse, lance-shaped, dark green leaves to 6 in. long; fragrant, ¼-in., purple-marked white flowers at intervals for much of the year. Small, glossy black fruit. Excellent for coastal gardens; takes salt spray and flourishes in sun or light shade. Tolerates clay and alkaline soils. Needs less water than the above two species.

ARENARIA MONTANA

SANDWORT
Caryophyllaceae
Perennial

⬛ **US, MS, LS; USDA 6-8**

◑ **PARTIAL SHADE**

💧💧 **MODERATE TO REGULAR WATER**

Arenaria montana

Native to the mountains of southwestern Europe, this evergreen plant carpets the ground with mats of mosslike foliage 2–4 in. high. Weak stems to 1 ft. long are set with grayish green, ½- to ¾-in.-long leaves that

are usually coated with soft hairs. In late spring and summer, the plant is covered by a profusion of inch-wide white flowers. Needs well-drained soil. Good for trailing over sunny rocks or tumbling over a low wall; ideal for rock gardens or for planting between stepping stones. Seldom browsed by deer. For the plant sometimes sold as *A. verna* (*A. v. caespitosa* 'Aurea'), see *Sagina subulata glabrata* 'Aurea'.

ARGEMONE

PRICKLY POPPY
Papaveraceae
Annuals or biennials

⬛ **US, MS, LS, CS, TS; USDA 6-11**

☼ **FULL SUN**

◯ **LITTLE OR NO WATER**

Argemone polyanthemos

Prickly-leafed and prickly-stemmed plants to 3 ft. tall, 1½ ft. wide, with large, showy poppies that bloom mainly in summer. Easy to grow from seed sown in place or in pots (transplant gently). Will reseed and colonize. Provide good drainage. Seed specialists may offer additional species.

A. mexicana. MEXICAN POPPY. Annual. Native to West Indies and probably Central America and Florida. Yellow to orange, 1½- to 2½-in. flowers. 'Yellow Lustre' grows 1½–2 ft. tall, has lemony-orange blooms.

A. polyanthemos. Annual or biennial. Western native with white, 2½- to 4-in. flowers.

ARGYRANTHE-MUM FRUTESCENS

MARGUERITE, PARIS DAISY
Asteraceae
Short-lived perennial, annual

⬛ **CS, TS; USDA 9-11**

☼ **FULL SUN**

💧 **REGULAR WATER**

Argyranthemum frutescens

Formerly known as *Chrysanthemum frutescens*, this is a short-lived, shrubby perennial where it is hardy; grown as summer annual elsewhere. Canary Island native has bright green, coarsely divided leaves and abundant daisies 1½–2½ in. across in white, yellow, or pink. Plant reaches about 2½ ft. tall and wide. 'Pink Lady' and 'White Lady' produce buttonlike flower heads; 'Silver Leaf' has gray-green leaves and masses of very small white flowers. 'Snow White', double anemone type, has pure white flowers, more restrained growth habit. Dwarf selections also available. All types are splendid in containers and for quick effects in borders, mass displays in new gardens. For continued bloom, prune lightly at frequent intervals. In Coastal and Tropical South, do not prune severely, since plants seldom produce new growth from hardened wood; replace every 2 to 3 years.

ARISAEMA
JACK-IN-THE-PULPIT,
COBRA LILY
Araceae
Perennials from tubers

✎ US, MS, LS, CS; USDA 6-9

◐ ● PARTIAL OR FULL SHADE

💧 REGULAR WATER DURING GROWTH AND BLOOM

Arisaema triphyllum

Curious rather than beautiful relatives of calla (*Zantedeschia*), attractive both to children and to fanciers of the unusual. Flowers are tiny, crowded on a club-shaped spadix surrounded by an overarching, typically green or dull purple spathe (flower bract) that is often striped in a contrasting color. In late spring, tubers send up one to three leaves, each divided into three or more leaflets. Inflorescences appear on a separate stalk in spring or early summer. As the flowers fade, the spathe withers and the spadix forms orange to red seeds.

These are woodland plants, appreciative of organic material in the soil. Plant in fall, setting tubers 1 ft. apart, 2 in. deep. Plants die to the ground in winter; don't let dormant tubers dry out completely. Species other than those listed below may appear from time to time in specialists' catalogs.

A. fargesii. From China. To 1½ ft. high. Between a pair of big, three-part leaves sits a burgundy-red spathe striped with white; the spathe tip curves over and ends in what looks like a mass of red threads. A dark red spadix peeks from the spathe.

A. kishidae 'Silver Pattern'. Selection of a little-known Japanese species. To 2 ft. high.

Each leafstalk bears two leaves consisting of seven to nine leaflets marked with a central silver band. The spathe is brownish purple, with a hooded extension curving out to one side. A thin, light brown spadix is barely visible.

A. ringens. From China, Japan, Korea. To 2 ft. high. Inflorescence sits on short stalk between two large, three-part leaves. The spathe is striped purple and white; its tip curls and flares to show off a glossy, purple interior. A white spadix is almost hidden by the spathe.

A. serratum mayebarae. Selection of a Japanese species. To 3 ft. high. Each of the two leaves is divided into 7 to 13 leaflets marked down the middle with a silver streak. A thin stem rises slightly above the foliage, bearing a narrow, purple- and white-streaked spathe with a tip that drapes downward. The spadix is yellow-green.

A. sikokianum. From Japan. To 20 in. tall, with 6-in. leaflets. A 4- to 12-in. stalk supports a 6-in. spathe that is erect rather than arching. Spathe is purplish brown on the outside, yellowish white within; pure white spadix is thicker and rounded at the tip.

A. speciosum. Himalayan native. A single leaf grows to 2 ft., with 8- to 16-in leaflets on a stalk marbled with dark purple. Spathe is blackish purple outside, whitish within, up to 8 in. long; spadix has a long, whiplike tip that can reach 2½ ft. in length.

A. tortuosum. Himalayan native. Can reach 4 ft. tall. Leaves have many narrow leaflets. Green or purple spathe to 6 in. long; spadix protrudes from spathe, then curves upward for several inches.

A. triphyllum. JACK-IN-THE-PULPIT. From eastern North America; the common Jack-in-the-pulpit familiar to Easterners. Grows to 2 ft. tall. Both spathe and spadix are green or purple; spathe is striped in white or green.

ARISTOLOCHIA
Aristolochiaceae
Deciduous and evergreen vines

✎ ZONES VARY BY SPECIES

☼ ◐ ● EXPOSURE NEEDS VARY BY SPECIES

💧💧 REGULAR TO AMPLE WATER

Aristolochia gigantea

Twining vines noted for curiously shaped flowers in rather somber colors; the flowers resemble curved pipes with flared bowls or birds with bent necks. Vigorous growers; thin out unwanted growth in late dormant season or wait until after bloom. If plant is too thick and tangled for selective thinning, cut it to the ground before spring growth begins.

A. californica. CALIFORNIA DUTCHMAN'S PIPE. CS, TS; USDA 9-11. Deciduous. Native to Coast Ranges and Sierra Nevada foothills of Northern California. Will cover an 8- by 12-ft. screen with some training or climb by long, thin shoots 10–15 ft. into any nearby tree without harming it. Flower display comes before leaf-out in late winter or early spring; pendulous, 1-in.-long blooms are cream colored with red-purple veins. Bright green, heart-shaped leaves to 5 in. long. Interesting and useful where many less hardy vines would freeze. Sometimes used as a ground cover. Grows from seed. Accepts any soil; best in partial shade.

A. gigantea. GIANT DUTCHMAN'S PIPE. Evergreen. Zones CS, TS; USDA 9-11. From Panama and Brazil. To 30 ft. Triangular to heart-shaped, dark green leaves can reach 4 in. long. Blooms in summer, bearing flowers to 1 ft. long and half as wide; blossoms are burgundy with creamy white

netting and a golden throat. *A. brasiliensis* (*A. g. brasiliensis*) has flowers to 10 in. long and 7 in. wide, in an intricate netted pattern of white and brown. Sun or partial shade.

A. grandiflora. PELICAN FLOWER. Evergreen. Zones CS, TS; USDA 9-11. From Central America and the West Indies. Vigorous grower to 30 ft. or more. Deep green, heart-shaped leaves to 10 in. long. Roundish flowers to 8 in. across bloom in late summer; they are white with burgundy-red veining, a red center, and a slender, foot-long, dangling "tail" (an extension of the blossom's lower lip). Flowers are smelly, so be careful where you plant this one. Give partial shade.

A. littoralis (*A. elegans*). CALICO FLOWER. Evergreen. Zones LS, CS, TS; USDA 8-11; or indoors. Native to Brazil. Grows 15–25 ft. high. Wiry, slender stems; heart-shaped leaves 3 in. long. Blooms in summer; whitish buds shaped like little pelicans open to 3-in.-wide, heart-shaped flowers of deep purple veined in creamy white. Needs rich soil, partial shade.

A. macrophylla (*A. durior*). DUTCHMAN'S PIPE. Deciduous. Zones US, MS, LS, CS; USDA 6-9; short lived in warm-winter areas. From eastern U.S. Easily grown from seed. Large (6- to 14-in.-long), kidney-shaped, deep green leaves are carried in shinglelike pattern to form a dense cloak on a trellis; the vine will cover a 15- by 20-ft. area in a single season and is a longtime favorite for screening porches. Blooms in late spring, early summer. Flowers are almost hidden by leaves; each is a yellowish green, 3-in., curved tube flaring into three brownish purple lobes about 1 in. wide. Thrives in full sun to heavy shade. Give average to good soil and ample water for fastest growth, largest leaves. Will not stand strong winds. Preferred host of the pipevine swallowtail larvae; tropical species may poison them.

A. peruviana. Evergreen. Zones CS, TS; USDA 9-11. From South America. Rare but worth the search. Grows upright to 1–2 ft., with medium green, heart-shaped leaves to 3 in. long. Cup-shaped blooms about 1 in. long and ¾ in. wide may bloom in spring, summer, or fall; they are golden yellow with red edge markings on the inside, mottled chocolate-brown on the outside. Performs well in low light; fine on shaded patio in warmest areas. Interesting houseplant or indoor/ outdoor plant.

ARMERIA
THRIFT, SEA PINK
Plumbaginaceae
Perennials

ZONES VARY BY SPECIES

FULL SUN

LITTLE TO MODERATE WATER

Armeria maritima

Narrow, stiff, evergreen leaves grow in compact tufts or basal rosettes; small white, pink, rose, or red flowers are carried in dense, globular heads. Main bloom period is spring to early summer, but shearing off faded flowers may prolong flowering. Sturdy, dependable plants for edging walks or borders and for tidy mounds in rock gardens or raised beds. Attractive in containers.

Good drainage is essential and permits regular watering, but safest tactic is to water moderately in dry climates, sparingly in moister regions. Tolerate seaside conditions, infertile soil. Seldom browsed by deer. Clumps spread slowly and need dividing only when bare centers show.

A. maritima (*A. vulgaris*). SEA THRIFT. Zones US, MS, LS, CS; USDA 6-11. Native to Europe, North America. Tufted mounds spread to 1 ft.; leaves are 6 in. long. White to rose-pink flowers in tight clusters atop 6- to 10-in. stalks. Bloom is profuse in spring (goes on almost all year in mildest climates). 'Bloodstone' has

rose-red flowers, 'Cotton Tail' white blooms. 'Rubrifolia', with purplish-red foliage and rosy pink blossoms, provides color for much of the year.

A. pseudarmeria. LARGE-FLOWERED THRIFT. Zones US, MS, LS, CS; USDA 6-9. Native to Portugal. Mounded plants grow 8–10 in. tall and wide. Primary bloom in late spring but may rebloom if deadheaded. 'Ballerina Red' offers compact plants 12–14 in. tall.

ARONIA
CHOKEBERRY
Rosaceae
Deciduous shrubs

ZONES VARY BY SPECIES

FULL SUN OR LIGHT SHADE

MODERATE TO AMPLE WATER

Aronia arbutifolia

Native to southern Canada and the eastern U.S., these are tough, undemanding shrubs useful as fillers or background plantings. They tolerate a wide variety of soils. All tend to spread by suckering but are somewhat leggy (good for planting beneath). Small white or pinkish flowers appear in late spring and are followed by showy fruit that lasts well into winter. Fall foliage is brightly colored.

A. arbutifolia. RED CHOKE-BERRY. Zones US, MS, LS, CS; USDA 6-9. Clumping shrub to 6–8 ft. tall and about half as wide, with many erect stems bearing shiny foliage that is rich green above, paler beneath. Fruit is clustered, ¼ in. wide, brilliant red, long lasting. Fall foliage is also bright red, and plants tend to color early. 'Brilliantissima' is a selection with exceptionally fine fall color.

A. melanocarpa. BLACK CHOKEBERRY. Zones US, MS, LS; USDA 6-8. Lower growing than *A. arbutifolia*, to just 3–5 ft. tall, rarely taller; spreads to about 10 ft. Foliage turns purple-red in fall. Shiny black, ½-in. fruit. 'Autumn Magic' has fragrant flowers, reliable fall color, and large, long-lasting fruits.

ARTEMISIA
ASTERACEAE
Perennials and evergreen shrubs

ZONES VARY BY SPECIES

FULL SUN

LITTLE TO MODERATE WATER

Artemisia 'Powis Castle'

Chiefly valued for their ornamental foliage, artemisias offer lacy leaf patterns and aromatic, silvery gray or white leaves. Most of the plants described here have woody stems; however, *A. dracunculus*, *A. lactiflora*, *A. ludoviciana albula*, and *A. stellerana* are herbaceous. Most need excellent drainage. Not the best choice for high-rainfall areas, particularly along the Gulf Coast and in Florida. Plants are seldom browsed by deer.

Most artemisias are excellent in mixed borders, where their white or silvery leaves soften harsh reds and oranges and blend with blues, lavenders, pinks. Flowers are usually insignificant. Divide plants in spring or autumn.

A. abrotanum. SOUTH-ERNWOOD, OLD MAN. Woody perennial. Zones US, MS, LS, CS; USDA 6-9. To 3–5 ft. tall and wide. Native to southern Europe. Beautiful green, feathery, lemon-scented foliage; yellowish white flowers. Use in shrub border for

its fragrant foliage. Hang sprigs in closets to discourage moths. Burn a few leaves in the kitchen to kill cooking odors.

A. absinthium. COMMON WORMWOOD. Woody perennial. Zones US, MS, LS, CS; USDA 6-9. To 2–4 ft. tall, 2 ft. wide. Native to Europe, temperate Asia. Used to flavor the liqueur absinthe. Silvery gray, finely divided leaves with a pungent odor; tiny yellow flowers. Prune for better shape. Divide every 3 years. Use as background shrub; makes a good gray feature in a flower border. Looks particularly fine with delphiniums. 'Lambrook Silver' is a 1½-ft.-tall form with silvery white, especially finely cut leaves.

A. arborescens. Evergreen shrub or woody perennial. Zone CS; USDA 9. Highly attractive Mediterranean native to 3 ft. or a little taller, 2 ft. wide, with silvery white, very finely cut leaves.

A. caucasica. SILVER SPREADER. Evergreen shrublet. Zones US, MS, LS; USDA 6-8. Caucasus native grows just 3–6 in. tall, spreading to 2 ft. wide. Silky foliage in silvery green; small yellow flowers. Use as bank or ground cover; plant 1–2 ft. apart. Needs good drainage. Takes extremes of heat and cold.

A. dracunculus. FRENCH TARRAGON, TRUE TARRAGON. Perennial. Zones US, MS; USDA 6-7. Native to central and eastern Europe and southern Russia. To 1–2 ft. tall; spreads slowly by creeping rhizomes. Shiny, dark green, narrow, very aromatic leaves; greenish white flowers in branched clusters. Attractive container plant. Cut sprigs in early summer to use for seasoning vinegar. Use fresh or dried leaves to season salads, cooked dishes. Divide every 3 or 4 years. Propagate by divisions or cuttings; plants grown from seed are not true culinary tarragon. For warmer areas, Mexican mint marigold (*Tagetes lucida*) is a good substitute.

A. 'Huntington'. Woody perennial. Zones US, MS, LS; USDA 6-8. To 3 ft. tall and 4 ft. wide, with spreading stems covered by a thick dome of very silvery foliage. Resembles *A.* 'Powis Castle' but has bigger, softer leaves.

A. lactiflora. WHITE MUG-WORT. Perennial. Zones US, MS, LS; USDA 6-8. Tall, straight column to 4-5 ft. tall, 2 ft. wide. This native of western China is one of the few artemisias with attractive flowers: in late summer, it bears creamy white blooms in branching, 1½-ft. sprays. Dark green leaves with broad, tooth-edged lobes. Members of the Guizhou group have purple stems and young leaves.

A. ludoviciana mexicana albula. WESTERN MUGWORT. Perennial. Zones US, MS, LS, CS; USDA 6-9. Native to Southwest deserts, adjacent areas of Mexico. Bushy growth to 2–3½ ft. tall, 2 ft. wide, with slender, spreading branches and silvery white, 2-in. leaves. The lower leaves have three to five lobes; the upper ones are narrow and unlobed. Spreads rapidly by rhizomes. Cut foliage is useful in arrangements. Two popular selections are 'Silver Queen', a compact form that grows to 1½–2½ ft. tall with larger foliage; and 'Valerie Finnis', which reaches 2 ft. and has even broader silver leaves that are

slightly lobed toward the tips.

A. pontica. ROMAN WORMWOOD. Evergreen shrub or woody perennial. Zones US, LS, MS, CS; USDA 6-9. Native to southeastern and central Europe; naturalized in eastern North America. Grows 2–4 ft. tall and spreads by rhizomes; makes a good ground cover if given ample room. Silvery gray, feathery leaves can be used in sachets. Heads of nodding, whitish yellow flowers are carried in long, open, branched clusters.

A. 'Powis Castle'. Woody perennial. Zones US, MS, LS; USDA 6-8. Most likely a hybrid of *A. absinthium* and *A. arborescens*. Hybrid grows in a silvery, lacy mound to 3 ft. tall and 6 ft. wide. Unlike most artemisias, does not "melt" during hot, humid summers. It retains its dense shape and is not invasive. Don't prune in fall; instead, wait to cut back until new growth begins to sprout near crown in spring.

A. schmidtiana. ANGEL'S HAIR. Woody perennial. Zones US, MS, LS; USDA 6-8. Japanese native forms a 1- to 2-ft.-high, 1-ft.-wide dome of silvery white, woolly, finely cut leaves. Dies back in winter. Selection 'Silver Mound' is compact, usually under 1½ ft. high and wide. 'Silverado' is somewhat more open and upright than the species; tolerates heat and humidity well.

A. stellerana. BEACH WORM-WOOD, OLD WOMAN, DUSTY MILLER. Perennial. Zones US, MS, LS; USDA 6-8. Native to northeast-ern Asia; naturalized in eastern North America. Dense, silvery gray plant to 2½ ft. tall and 3 ft. wide, with lobed leaves 1–4 in. long. Hardier than *Senecio cineraria* (another dusty miller) and often used in its place in colder cli-mates. Yellow flowers in spikelike clusters. 'Broughton Silver' ('Silver Brocade') is a superior, dense-growing selection.

ARTICHOKE

Asteraceae
Annual or perennial

🌡 **ZONES VARY; SEE BELOW**

☀ ◗ **FULL SUN OR LIGHT SHADE**

💧 **REGULAR WATER**

Artichokes

This attractive Mediterranean native is a big, coarse, ferny-looking plant with an irregular, somewhat fountainlike form to 3–4 ft. high and 4 ft. wide. Large, deeply lobed leaves are silvery green. Big flower buds form at tops of stalks; they are the artichokes you cook and eat. If not cut, the buds will open into spectacular purple-blue, 2- to 5-in., thistlelike flowers that can

be cut for arrangements.

Plants are perennial in Lower South and Coastal South; USDA 8-9. Stalks are cut to the ground after flowering to produce new shoots. If you are growing them in the Tropical South, plant in fall for a winter crop. In colder regions they can be grown as an annual planted in spring. Peren-nial artichokes grow stronger and are more productive. Overwinter your plants by cutting back the stalks near the ground when the leaves begin to yellow. Tie the remaining leaves over the crown and mulch deeply to insulate from cold. In spring, uncover them before growth begins.

Whether plants are newly plant-ed or returning from the previous season, fertilize monthly during the growing season. Water weekly, but if your soil is sandy, they may need water more often.

Harvest just before the flowers begin to open to avoid stringy, tough artichokes. After you cut the big center bud, you will have more from the side shoots. Although not as large, they will be delicious. Use sharp clippers, and cut 2–3 in. below the bud. Handle buds gently.

ARUGULA

ROCKET, ROQUETTE
Brassicaceae
Cool-season annual

🌡 **US, MS, LS, CS, TS; USDA 6-11**

☀ **FULL SUN**

💧 **REGULAR WATER**

Arugula

This Mediterranean native, some-times called rocket, roquette, or rucola coltivata, is grown for its leaves that resemble small

ABOVE: Artemisia stellerana

mustard leaves and lend a peppery zing to green salads. Along with radishes, turnips, and the whole cabbage clan, it's a member of the cress family. Start from seed in winter or spring; grows best in cool weather. In Florida and South Texas, sow seed in fall and winter; elsewhere, sow in early spring or early fall. Thin to about 6 in. apart. Harvest tender young leaves; older, larger ones usually taste too sharp. Sow new seeds every two weeks to always have young plants. Eventually plants will shoot up to 3 ft. tall and bloom. Tender buds and flowers taste like the young leaves. Plants reseed. Easy to grow in containers. Choose a wide bowl at least 6 in. deep. Watch out for cabbage butterflies—their caterpillars find arugula just as tasty as cabbage.

ARUM
LORDS AND LADIES
Araceae
Perennials from tubers

✎ **ZONES VARY BY SPECIES**

◐ ● **PARTIAL OR FULL SHADE**

● **REGULAR WATER DURING GROWTH AND BLOOM**

◊ **SAP IS AN IRRITANT IF INGESTED**

Arum italicum 'Marmoratum'

Attractively veined, arrow-shaped leaves grow from tubers in fall or winter. In spring, short stalks bear curious, often malodorous, callalike blooms featuring a bract (spathe) that half encloses a thick, fleshy spike (spadix) set with tiny flowers. These blossoms are followed by dense clusters of fruit, typically bright red, that look like little ears of corn and persist after leaves have died to the

ground. Use this plant in shady flower borders or as a tropical-looking ground cover.

Plant tubers during late summer or in early autumn (toward the end of their dormancy), setting them 8–12 in. apart and about 2 in. deep. Dormant plantings accept summer water but don't need it. *A. palaestinum* and *A. pictum* are sometimes used as houseplants in colder climates.

A. italicum. ITALIAN ARUM. Zones US, MS, LS, CS; USDA 6-9. Native to southern and western Europe. Foot-long leaves on leafstalks of equal length appear in fall or early winter. Very short stems carry white or greenish white (sometimes purple-spotted) flowers in spring and early summer; the fruit that follows is bright orange-red. Spathe first stands erect, then folds over and conceals short yellow spadix. Leaves die to ground after bloom. In favorable situations, naturalizes by volunteer seedlings. Selection 'Marmoratum' ('Pictum') has white-veined leaves and makes an extremely attractive winter carpet.

A. palaestinum. BLACK CALLA. Zones CS, TS; USDA 9-11. Native to Israel. Leaves emerge in winter; to about 8 in. long, on 1-ft. leafstalks. Spathe is 8 in. long, green outside; opens outward and curls back at tip to reveal purple interior and black spadix. Blooms in spring and early summer; then leaves die back.

A. pictum. Zones LS, CS, TS; USDA 8-10. Native to western Mediterranean. May be called black calla, like *A. palaestinum*, but unlike that species, it has an 8-in. violet spathe with a white base that encloses a dark purple spadix. Flowers appear in fall, sometimes with emerging foliage, sometimes before. Light green leaves with white veins reach 10 in. long and are borne on equally long leafstalks. Foliage dies to ground in hot weather.

ARUNCUS
GOAT'S BEARD
Rosaceae
Perennials

✎ **ZONES VARY BY SPECIES**

☼ ◐ **FULL SUN IN US, MS; LIGHT SHADE ELSEWHERE**

● **REGULAR WATER**

Aruncus dioicus

These perennials resemble astilbe, with slowly spreading clumps of finely divided leaves topped in summer by branching plumes of tiny white or cream flowers. Good in perennial borders or at edge of woodland. Needs moist, rich soil. Slow to establish. Deer resistant.

A. aethusifolius. Zones US, MS; USDA 6-7. Native to Korea. Deep green, finely divided leaves make a mound about 1 ft. tall and wide. White flower plumes reach 16 in. high. Useful in rock garden, as edging, for small-scale ground cover.

A. dioicus (A. sylvestris). Zones US, MS, LS; USDA 6-8. Native to the mountainous south. Grows to 6-7 ft. tall, 4 ft. wide, with foamy plumes of white flowers in 20-in., much-branched clusters. 'Kneiffii' is half the size of the species, with more finely divided leaves. 'Child of Two Worlds' ('Zweiweltenkind') grows to 5 ft. tall, with gracefully drooping flower clusters. 'Misty Lace' grows 1½ ft. tall and 2 ft. wide and has greater heat tolerance and late spring flowers.

ARUNDO DONAX
GIANT REED
Poaceae
Perennial grass

✎ **US, MS, LS, CS, TS; USDA 6-11**

☼ **FULL SUN**

● ◐● **REGULAR TO AMPLE WATER**

Arundo donax versicolor

One of the tallest grasses, often seen in rural gardens throughout the South. A real conversation piece, thanks to strong, woody stems that can tower to 20 ft. or more. Useful as a windbreak, screen, or vertical accent. In most areas, it dies to the ground in winter but regrows quickly in spring. Flat leaves grow to 2 ft. long and 3 in. wide. In summer, the plant is crowned by greenish or purplish blooms in showy panicles that grow up to 2 ft. long.

Spreads quickly by thick rhizomes and can be invasive in moist soil, a quality that has made it a classic passalong plant (it is easy to dig and divide in spring or fall). Seeds can also travel far and wide on the wind, increasing the plant's chances of spreading—so be careful where you plant it, and don't let it escape to the wild. Cut withered stems to the ground in winter; they make good plant stakes.

A. d. versicolor (A. d. 'Variegata') flaunts leaves with creamy or yellowish stripes. It grows about half as tall as the species and is less likely to bloom (but can be invasive nonetheless).

ASARUM

WILD GINGER
Aristolochiaceae
Perennials

- 🖋 **ZONES VARY BY SPECIES**
- ◐ ● **PARTIAL OR FULL SHADE**
- 💧 💧 **REGULAR TO AMPLE WATER**

Asarum caudatum

Roots and leaves of the wild gingers have a scent somewhat like that of culinary ginger (*Zingiber*), but they are not used as seasoning. Low, creeping plants bearing roundish or heart-shaped leaves, they make very attractive woodland ground covers. Their flowers are curious rather than showy, almost hidden among the leaves; they are small (usually less than 2 in. wide) and oddly shaped, with three spreading, leathery lobes that may be brownish, purplish, or greenish. Of the many species that exist, only a few are available to gardeners. Asiatic species with fancy variegated leaves, now grown as connoisseurs' plants in Japan, may eventually make their way here. Deer resistant.

A. arifolium. HEARTLEAF, ARROWLEAF GINGER. Zones US, MS, LS, CS; USDA 6-9. Native from Virginia south to Florida and Alabama. Tough, easy-to-grow evergreen wild ginger with glossy, green (sometimes silver-mottled) leaves to 5 in. long. Flowers are reddish brown. Spreads slowly to form 1½-ft.-wide clumps.

A. campaniflorum. KIWI GINGER. Zones LS, CS; USDA 8-9. From China. Evergreen, deep green leaves grow to 6 in. long and 4 in. wide. Brownish purple flowers are white inside, with a purple ring partway down. Plant is sometimes called kiwi ginger

because the inside of the flower resembles a slice of kiwi fruit.

A. canadense. CANADA WILD GINGER. Zones US, MS, LS; USDA 6-8. Native to eastern North America. Deciduous, kidney-shaped, dark green leaves to 4 in. long, 6 in. wide. Flowers are purplish brown. The hardiest species.

A. caudatum. WESTERN WILD GINGER. Zones US, MS, LS; USDA 6-8. Native to the West Coast. Evergreen in warmest areas of the zones where it will grow. Heart-shaped leaves are 2–7 in. long and wide. Reddish brown flowers have lobes elongated into tails. Where adapted, a valuable, quick-growing ground cover for shady places.

A. europaeum. EUROPEAN WILD GINGER. Zones US, MS, LS; USDA 6-8. Native to Europe. Evergreen, shiny, kidney-shaped, dark green leaves 2–3 in. long and wide. Small brown flowers. Slow spreader.

A. maximum. Zones MS, LS, CS; USDA 7-9. Evergreen Chinese species; sometimes known by the name "panda ginger," thanks to its 2-in.-wide flowers, which are black with a large white eye. Leaves grow to about 6 in. long, 4 in. wide. 'Green Panda' has dark green foliage and particularly showy flowers; 'Ling Ling' bears dark green leaves with light green mottling.

A. shuttleworthii. MOTTLED WILD GINGER. Zones US, MS, LS, CS; USDA 6-9. Native to the Appalachians. Evergreen, 4-in., heart-shaped or roundish leaves, usually variegated with silvery markings. Brown flowers with red spots. Slow growing. 'Callaway' spreads more quickly and has extremely handsome, mottled foliage. The foliage of 'Carolina Silver' is attractively marked with silvery cream. 'Velvet Queen' has silver-mottled leaves and double-size blossoms.

A. speciosum. ALABAMA WILD GINGER. Zones US, MS, LS, CS; USDA 6-9. This Alabama native is a favorite and the showiest of the North American wild ginger species. The plant features large, evergreen, variably mottled leaves and bold black-and-cream flowers. Selection 'Buxom Beauty' is bigger than the species over all: its silver-marbled leaves grow to 10 in. long, and its flowers are about 2 in. across. Like 'Buxom

Beauty', 'Woodlander's Select' also has silver-marked leaves, but they reach just 6 in. long; its flowers are about 1½ in. across.

A. splendens. CHINESE WILD GINGER. Zones US, MS, LS, CS; USDA 6-9. Easy-to-grow Chinese native. Evergreen leaves in dark green heavily mottled with silver are heart shaped with an elongated tip; may reach 7 in. long, 3 in. wide. Large (2-in.-wide) dark purple flowers. Grows quite vigorously in loose, rich soil, forming large colonies. Leaves of 'Quicksilver' are mottled with silver.

A. virginicum. SILVER SPLASH. Zones US, MS, LS; USDA 6-8. Selection of a southeastern U.S. native, with round, evergreen, 2-in. leaves in green boldly marked with silver. Relatively small flowers are reddish brown.

ASCLEPIAS

Apocynaceae
Perennials

- 🖋 **ZONES VARY BY SPECIES**
- ☀ **FULL SUN**
- ◌ 💧 💧 💧 **WATER NEEDS VARY BY SPECIES**
- ❀ **ALL PARTS OF MANY SPECIES ARE POISONOUS IF INGESTED**

Asclepias tuberosa

Though classified as milkweeds (so named for their milky sap), the plants listed here are anything but weeds—they are showy, easy-to-grow garden plants. All bloom in summer, typically bearing many small, starlike flowers in broad, flattened clusters at branch tips. After the flowers fade, silky seeds burst from inflated seedpods and float through the air like dandelion seeds. Among the best plants for attracting butterflies, particularly

monarchs, whose caterpillars feast on the foliage. In fact, gardeners growing milkweed are a lifeline for migrating monarchs. Deer resistant.

A. curassavica. BLOOD FLOWER. Zones CS, TS; USDA 9-11; as annual. Native to South America. Woody-based plant with stiff stems and narrow, 6-in. leaves; grows 3–5 ft. tall, 2 ft. wide. Clusters of vivid red and orange flowers. 'Silky Gold' is similar but bears bright yellow to yellow-orange blooms. Moderate water.

A. humistrata. SANDHILL MILKWEED. Zones MS, LS, CS; USDA 7-9. Herbaceous perennial native to the southeastern U.S. Attractive gray-green leaves with distinct purple veins are widely spaced along 1½- to 2-ft. stems that lean over to form a spreading plant. White flowers may be tinged with lavender. Regular water.

A. incarnata. SWAMP MILKWEED. Zones US, MS, LS, CS; USDA 6-9. Native to U.S. except the west coast. Herbaceous perennial to 2–4 ft. tall, 2 ft. wide. Narrow, pointed leaves to 6 in. long; ball-shaped clusters of pinkish purple flowers. 'Ice Ballet' has pure white blooms. 'Soulmate' blooms deep rose-pink. Regular to ample water.

A. tuberosa. BUTTERFLY WEED. Zones US, MS, LS, CS; USDA 6-9. Native in all but the northwest U.S. From a perennial root, many herbaceous stems rise every year to form a clump about 3 ft. tall, 1 ft. wide. Clusters of bright orange flowers attract swarms of butterflies. Gay Butterflies strain features yellow, red, orange, pink, or bicolored blossoms; selection 'Hello Yellow' has bright yellow blooms. All make long-lasting cut flowers. Provide good drainage, little to moderate water. Does not transplant well due to deep taproot.

ABOVE: *Asclepias tuberosa* 'Hello Yellow'

ASIAN GREENS

Brassicaceae
Cool-season annuals

US, MS, LS, CS, TS; USDA 6-11

☼ ◐ **FULL SUN OR LIGHT SHADE**

💧 **REGULAR WATER**

Bok choy

The annual vegetables in this large group are the mainstays of stir-fry dishes and excellent in salads. Asian greens are primarily quick-maturing, cool-season crops that are planted at the same time as other cool-season vegetables: late winter to early spring for spring-to-summer harvest, late summer to early fall for fall and winter harvest.

Many Asian greens, especially the mustards, are attractive foliage plants that make a colorful addition to the vegetable garden and also look good mixed with flowering annuals and spring bulbs.

Listed here are some of the most common Asian greens; specialty seed catalogs may carry additional kinds. For planting depth and row spacing, follow the instructions on the seed packet.

Bok choy (Chinese white cabbage, pak choi). One of the more familiar Asian greens, bok choy has a mild flavor with a hint of mustard. Tender, crisp, and sweet, it's especially good in soups and stir-fries. Many selections are sold. 'Tatsoi' is similar but more compact. Thin or transplant seedlings to 6–12 in. apart. Harvest approximately 50 days after sowing seed, when plants are loose-headed and 10–12 in. tall.

Broadleaf mustard (dai gai choy). Large green leaves with a pungent, somewhat bitter, mustardlike flavor that gets stronger as the plant matures. Hot weather or inadequate moisture also increases pungency. Best used in soup to tone down the sharp flavor. Thin or transplant seedlings to 10 in. apart. Harvest plants when they are loose headed and 10–14 in. high, about 65 days after sowing.

Chinese broccoli (gai lohn). Similar in flavor and texture to standard broccoli, but with a slight pungency like that of mustard. Thin or transplant seedlings to 10 in. apart. Harvest central stalk and side shoots when stalk is 8–10 in. tall or when flower buds just begin to form, usually about 70 days after sowing.

Chinese mustard greens (gai choy). Milder member of the mustard family. Thin or transplant seedlings to 10 in. apart. Harvest the first greens when the plants are 2 in. high; continue harvesting until leaves turn tough or bitter. It usually takes 45 days after sowing for plants to reach mature height of 6–8 in.

Flowering cabbage (yao choy, choy sum, ching sow sum). Tender, delicate, broccoli-type vegetable. Thin or transplant seedlings to about 6 in. apart. Harvest about 60 days after sowing, when 8–12 in. high.

Mizuna. Mild-flavored, leafy vegetable with finely cut, frilly, white-stemmed leaves. Great in salads. Thin or transplant seedlings to 8–10 in. apart. Start cutting leaves when plants are a few inches tall, or wait until they are mature (8–10 in. high), about 40 days after sowing.

ASPARAGUS, EDIBLE

Asparagaceae
Perennial

US, MS, LS; USDA 6-8

☼ **FULL SUN**

💧 **REGULAR WATER**

Asparagus

One of the most permanent and dependable of home garden vegetables. Plants take 2 to 3 years to come into full production but then furnish

HOW TO GROW ASPARAGUS

PLANTING Seeds grow into strong young plants in one season (sow in spring), but roots are far more widely used. Set out seedlings or roots (not wilted, no smaller than an adult's hand) in fall or winter in mild-winter climates, in early spring in cold-winter areas. Make trenches 1 ft. wide, 8–10 in. deep; space trenches 4–6 ft. apart. Heap loose, manure-enriched soil at bottom of trenches and soak. Space plants 1 ft. apart, setting them so that tops are 6–8 in. below surface; spread roots out evenly. Cover with 2 in. of soil and water again. (Where drainage is poor, plant in raised beds.) As plants grow, gradually fill in the trench; don't cover growing tips.

WATERING Soak deeply whenever the soil begins to dry out at root depth.

HARVESTING Don't harvest spears the first year; let plants build root mass. When plants turn brown in late fall or early winter, cut stems to the ground. In cold-winter areas, permit dead stalks to stand until spring; they will hold snow, which protect root crowns. The following spring, cut your first spears; cut only for 4 to 6 weeks or until appearance of thin spears indicates that roots are nearing exhaustion. Then permit plants to grow. Feed and irrigate heavily. The third year, you should be able to cut spears for 8 to 10 weeks. Spears are ready to cut when they are 5–8 in. long. Thrust knife down at 45° angle to soil; flat cutting may injure adjacent developing spears.

PESTS Clean up debris from asparagus beds in fall to help get rid of overwintering asparagus beetles. Use row covers over beds in spring.

delicious spears every spring for 10 to 15 years or more. They take up considerable space but do so in grand manner: Plants are tall, feathery, graceful, highly ornamental. Use along a sunny fence or as background for flowers or vegetables.

Asparagus seed and roots are sold as "traditional" ('Martha Washington' and others) and "all-male." All-male types include 'UC 157', 'Jersey Giant', and 'Jersey Knight' (the best male for Southern growers). Male hybrids typically produce more and larger spears, because they don't have to put energy into seed production. Such selections still produce an occasional female plant.

'Purple Passion' is an unusual selection that produces deep burgundy spears with a sweet, nutty flavor (the spears turn green when cooked).

HOW TO BLANCH ASPARAGUS

Fresh white asparagus is a delicacy, but it's not a special kind of asparagus; blanching makes it white. To blanch asparagus, do this: In early spring, before spears emerge, mound soil 8 in. high over a row of asparagus. Then, when tips emerge from the mounded soil, push a long-handled knife into the base of the mound to cut each spear well below the surface. Pull cut shoots out by the tips; level mound after the harvest season is over.

ASPARAGUS, ORNAMENTAL

Asparagaceae

Perennials, shrubs, or vines

- ✎ **CS, TS; USDA 9-11, OR HOUSE-PLANTS**
- ☼ **PARTIAL SHADE; BRIGHT FILTERED LIGHT**
- 💧 **REGULAR WATER**

Asparagus densiflorus 'Myersii'

There are about 150 kinds of asparagus besides the edible one—all are members of the lily family. Those described here are native to South Africa. Best known is asparagus fern (*A. setaceus*), which is not a true fern. Although valued mostly for handsome foliage of unusual textural quality, some of the ornamental species have small but fragrant flowers and colorful berries. Green foliage sprays are made up of what look like leaves. Needlelike or broader, these are actually short branches called cladodes. The true leaves are inconspicuous dry scales.

Most ornamental asparagus look greenest in partial shade. Leaves yellow in dense shade. Plant in well-drained soil amended with peat moss or ground bark. Thanks to their fleshy roots, plants can go for some time without water, but they grow better when watered regularly. Feed in spring with complete fertilizer. Trim out old shoots to make room for new growth. Ornamental asparagus will survive light frosts but may be killed to ground by severe cold. After frost, plants often come back from roots.

A. asparagoides. SMILAX ASPARAGUS. Much-branched vine with spineless stems to 20 ft.

or more. Often seen in older gardens. Leaves to 1 in. long, sharp pointed, somewhat stiff, glossy grass-green. Small, fragrant, white flowers in spring followed by blue berries. Fleshy roots are nearly immortal, surviving long drought, then sprouting when rains come. Foliage sprays are prized for table decoration. If it doesn't get much water, plant dies back in summer, revives with fall rains. Becomes a tangled mass unless trained. This asparagus may escape gardens and become an invasive pest, as birds feed on the berries and drop seeds later; plants also self-sow readily. 'Myrtifolius', commonly called baby smilax, is a more graceful form with smaller leaves.

A. crispus. BASKET ASPARAGUS. Airy, graceful plant for hanging baskets. Drooping, zigzag stems have bright green, three-angled leaves in whorls of three. Often sold as *A. scandens* 'Deflexus'.

A. densiflorus. The species is less commonly grown than its cultivated forms; the following are the two most popular. Plants are seldom browsed by deer.

'Myersii'. MYERS ASPARAGUS. Several to many stiffly upright stems to 2 ft. or more, densely clothed with needlelike, deep green leaves that give the plant a fluffy look. Forms a 3- to 4-ft.-wide clump. Good in containers. A little less hardy than 'Sprengeri'. May be sold as *A. meyeri* or *A. myersii*.

'Sprengeri'. SPRENGER ASPARAGUS. Arching or drooping stems 3–6 ft. long. Shiny, bright green, needlelike "leaves," 1 in. long, in bundles. Bright red berries. Popular for hanging baskets or containers, indoors and out. Train on trellis; climbs by means of small hooked prickles. Used as billowy ground cover where temperatures stay above 24°F. Grows in ordinary or even poor soil. Will tolerate dryness of indoors. Sometimes sold as *A. sprengeri*. Form sold as 'Sprengeri Compacta' or *A. sarmentosus* 'Compacta' is denser, with shorter stems.

A. falcatus. SICKLE-THORN ASPARAGUS. Leaves are 2–3 in. long and very narrow, resembling flattened pine needles; they are borne in clusters of three to five at ends of branches. Tiny, fragrant, white flowers in loose clusters are

followed by brown berries. The plant derives its common name from curved thorns along its stems, which it uses to clamber rapidly as high as 40 ft. in its native area (in gardens, it usually reaches about 10 ft.). Makes an excellent foliage mass to cover fence or wall or provide shade for pergola or lathhouse.

A. officinalis. See Asparagus, edible

A. retrofractus. Erect, shrubby, slightly climbing, very tender. Slender, silvery gray stems grow slowly to 8–10 ft. high. Threadlike, inch-long leaves, in fluffy, rich green tufts. Clusters of white flowers. Handsome in containers; useful in flower arrangements. Cut foliage lasts about 10 days out of water, several weeks in water.

A. scandens. BASKET ASPARAGUS. Slender, branching vine climbing to 6 ft. Deep green, needlelike leaves on zigzag, drooping stems. Tiny greenish white flowers; scarlet berries.

A. setaceus (*A. plumosus*). ASPARAGUS FERN. This branching, woody vine climbs by wiry, spiny stems to 10–20 ft. Tiny threadlike leaves form feathery, dark green sprays that resemble fern fronds. Tiny, white flowers; purple-black berries. Forms a dense, fine-textured foliage mass that is useful as screen against walls and fences. Florists use foliage as filler in bouquets; it holds up better than delicate ferns. Dwarf 'Nanus' is good in containers. 'Pyramidalis' has upswept, windblown look, is less vigorous than the species.

MYERS ASPARAGUS LOOKS GREAT IN A LARGE CONTAINER.

ASPIDISTRA
CAST-IRON PLANT
Asparagaceae
Perennials

✂ **LS, CS, TS; USDA 9-11, OR HOUSE-PLANTS**

☼◑● **PARTIAL OR FULL SHADE; BRIGHT TO DIM LIGHT**

◍◍ **MODERATE TO REGULAR WATER**

Aspidistra elatior 'Variegata'

Cast-iron plants were made for brown-thumb gardeners. Sturdy, long-lived, and nearly bulletproof, these evergreen perennials typically form rather open clumps; they tolerate very low light and almost total neglect. Although they don't require well-drained soil enriched with organic matter, they'll be very happy if they get it. If you really want to pamper them, fertilize them occasionally in spring and summer. They make excellent houseplants if placed where they'll get light (4–5 ft. from a sunny, south-facing window, for example). Let the soil surface go dry between waterings. From the Lower South on down, cast-iron plants are also good for deeply shaded areas around the house where few other plants will grow—under a deck, for example. Bright, hot sunlight will burn their leaves. Deer resistant.

A. elatior. Native to Japan and China. The most common cast-iron plant, with upright, arching leaves sporting distinctive parallel veins from base to tip. Leaf blades are 1–2½ ft. long and 4–5 in. wide, carried on grooved, 6–8 in. leaf-stalks. In spring, bears inconspicuous brownish flowers. Selections include the following.

'Akebono'. Leaves to 2½ ft. long flaunt a narrow white streak

ABOVE: Aspidistra elatior

down the center. 'Lennon's Song' is a narrower leaf with similar stripe.

'Asahi'. Deep green leaves reach 20 in. long. As the season progresses, the top third of each leaf turns white. Color holds all winter. Also called 'Morning Sun'. 'Snow Cap' has a larger patch of white that is showy year-round.

'Okame'. Green leaves to 20 in. long, dramatically marked with irregular longitudinal white stripes.

'Variegata'. Rich green leaves are marked from base to tip with streaks of white. Loses variegation if planted in soil that's too rich.

A. hainanensis 'Jade Ribbons'. Selection of a Chinese species. Forms a tight clump; looks a lot like a daylily (*Hemerocallis*) plant. Shiny dark green leaves are 2 ft. long, ½ in. wide.

A. linearifolia 'Leopard'. A bizarre clump-forming selection of a Chinese species; looks like a cross between cast-iron plant and mother-in-law's tongue (*Sansevieria*). Deep green, yellow-speckled leaves are held erect; they grow about 2½ ft. long but just ½ in. wide.

ASPLENIUM
Aspleniaceae
Ferns

✂ **ZONES VARY BY SPECIES**

☼◑● **PARTIAL TO FULL SHADE**

◍◍ **REGULAR TO AMPLE WATER**

Asplenium scolopendrium

Widespread and variable group of rhizomatous ferns, once called spleenwort for their alleged medicinal value. These evergreen species resemble one another only in botanical details and in their need for shade and liberal watering. Unlike many other

ferns, they need a rest period from late fall to early spring when grown indoors; during that time, reduce watering and withhold fertilizer. Indoor plants like bright filtered light; a spot in an east-facing window is ideal. Outdoors, they prefer gritty, well-drained soil.

A. bulbiferum. MOTHER FERN. Zone TS; USDA 10-11; or indoors. From New Zealand. Evergreen or semievergreen. To 4 ft. tall and wide. Graceful, very finely cut, light green fronds produce plantlets that can be removed and planted. Hardy to 26°F. Watch for snails and slugs.

A. x ebenoides. SCOTT'S SPLEENWORT, DRAGON TAIL FERN. Zones US, MS, LS, CS; USDA 6-9. Hybrid of *A. platyneuron* and *A. rhizophyllum*. Small evergreen fern of variable appearance, with deeply indented fronds to 6–12 in. long. Good in rock garden.

A. nidus. BIRD'S NEST FERN. Zone TS; USDA 10-11; or indoors. Evergreen native of Old World tropics. Striking foliage: showy, apple green, undivided fronds 4 ft. long by 8 in. wide, growing upright in a cluster to about 3 ft. wide. Tender; if grown in pots, keep indoors in winter, move to shady patio in summer.

A. platyneuron. EBONY SPLEENWORT. Zones US, MS, LS, CS; USDA 6-9. Native to eastern U.S. Evergreen; 1½ ft. tall and about as wide. Erect, once-divided, dark green fronds have glossy, blackish brown midribs.

A. rhizophyllum (*Camptosorus rhizophyllus*). WALKING FERN. Zones US, MS, LS, CS; USDA 6-9. Native to North America; semievergreen to evergreen. An oddity with 5- to 10-in.-long, undivided fronds that taper to the tips; where they touch soil, tips take root and produce new plantlets. Spreads indefinitely. Needs some lime in the soil.

A. scolopendrium (*Phyllitis scolopendrium*). HART'S TONGUE FERN. Zones US, MS, LS, CS; USDA 6-9. Native to Europe (rare native in eastern U.S.). Strap-shaped, evergreen, 9- to 18-in.-long fronds form a clump about 2 ft. wide. Dwarf, crested, puckered, and forked kinds are collector's items. Plant in soil rich in humus; add limestone chips if soil is acid. Good woodland plant, fine companion for rhododendrons and azaleas; also makes an excellent potted plant.

A. trichomanes. MAID-ENHAIR SPLEENWORT. Zones US, MS, LS, CS; USDA 6-9. Native to much of the Northern Hemisphere. Delicate evergreen fern with narrow, bright green fronds, 4–8 in. long; forms a clump to 8 in. wide. Leaflets are only ½ in. long, round or nearly so. Likes lime. Attractive in shady rock garden or on a wall where it can be seen close up.

ASTER

Asteraceae
Perennials

✎ **US, MS, LS; USDA 6-8, EXCEPT AS NOTED**

☼ **FULL SUN, EXCEPT AS NOTED**

💧💧 **MODERATE TO REGULAR WATER, EXCEPT AS NOTED**

Aster x *frikartii*

Asters range from alpine kinds forming compact, 6-in. mounds to open-branching plants 6 ft. tall. Flowers come in white or shades of blue, red, pink, lavender, or purple, mostly with yellow centers; they bloom in late summer to early fall, except as noted. Taller asters are invaluable for abundant color in large borders or among shrubs. Large sprays are effective in arrangements. Compact dwarf or cushion types make tidy edgings, mounds of color in rock gardens, good container plants. For the common annual or China aster sold at nurseries, see *Callistephus chinensis*. For Stokes' aster, see *Stokesia laevis*. Recent botanical reclassification means new names for many garden asters, as you will see below.

True asters are adapted to most soils, but growth is most luxuriant in fertile soil. Few problems except for mildew on leaves in late fall. Seldom browsed by deer. Divide in late fall or early spring. Replant vigorous young divisions from outside of clump; discard old center.

A. alpinus. ALPINE ASTER. Zones US, MS; USDA 6-7. Native to Alps, Pyrenees. Mounding plant to 1 ft. high, 1½ ft. wide. Leaves ½–5 in. long, mostly in basal tuft. Several stems grow from the leafy clump, each with one violet-blue flower 1½–2 in. across. Late spring to early summer bloom. Best in cold-winter areas. White and pink forms are uncommon.

A. amellus. ITALIAN ASTER. Native to Europe, western Asia. Sturdy, hairy plant grows about 2 ft. tall, 1½ ft. wide. Branching stems bear yellow-centered violet flowers 2 in. across.

A. cordifolius. See *Symphyotrichum cordifolium*

A. divaricatus. See *Eurybia divaricata*

A. ericoides. See *Symphyotrichum ericoides*

A. x frikartii. FRIKART ASTER. One of the finest, most useful and widely adapted perennials. Hybrid between *Symphyotrichum amellus* and *A. thomsonii*, a hairy-leafed, lilac-flowered, 3-ft.-tall species native to the Himalayas. Dark green leaves; abundant clear lavender to violet-blue single flowers about 2½ in. across. Open growth to 2 ft. high and wide. Blooms early summer to fall—almost all year in mild-winter areas if spent flowers are removed regularly. May be short lived. 'Wonder of Staffa' and 'Mönch' are favorites, with blossoms in lavender-blue. 'Flora's Delight', to 1½ ft. high, has gray-green foliage and abundant pale lilac flowers with large yellow centers.

A. fruticosus. See *Felicia fruticosa*

A. laevis. See *Symphyotrichum laeve*

A. lateriflorus. See *Symphyotrichum lateriflorum*

A. novae-angliae. See *Symphyotrichum novae-angliae*

A. novi-belgii. See *Symphyotrichum novi-belgii*

A. oblongifolium. See *Symphyotrichum oblongifolium*

A. patens. See *Symphyotrichum patens*

A. pilosus pringlei (*A. pringlei*). See *Symphyotrichum pilosum pringlei*

A. tataricus. TATARIAN ASTER. US, MS, LS, CS; USDA 6-9. Native to Siberia, China, Japan. Not for small gardens, this giant grows to 5–7 ft. tall and 3 ft. wide, with 2-ft.-long leaves and sheaves of inch-wide blue flowers in flat clusters in fall. Can be invasive. Takes sun or shade. 'Jindai' grows 3–4 ft. tall.

A. tongolensis EAST INDIES ASTER. From China, Himalayas. Dark green leaves in basal tufts; clumps grow to 1½ ft. high and 1 ft. wide. Each stem bears a single lavender-blue, orange-centered, 2½-in. flower in late spring to early summer. 'Napsbury' has dark blue blooms. 'Wartburg Star' forms a dense mound and has violet-blue flowers.

A. Wood's series. 'Wood's Light Blue' is a bushy plant with dark green leaves. It grows 1–1½ ft. high, 1½–2 ft. wide, but it can be severely cut back in early summer and will still flower well at only 6 in. high, bearing an abundance of medium blue, 1-in. blossoms late in the season. 'Wood's Purple', to barely 1 ft. high and wide, has deep purple blooms.

ASTILBE

FALSE SPIREA, MEADOW SWEET
Saxifragaceae
Perennials

✎ **US, MS, LS; USDA 6-8**

☼ ☼ **FULL SUN OR PARTIAL SHADE, EXCEPT AS NOTED**

💧 **REGULAR WATER**

Astilbe x *arendsii* 'Deutschland'

These graceful plants combine showy flowers and handsome, fernlike foliage. Small blossoms in white, pink, peach, rose, red, or purple appear in airy, feathery plumes held by thin, wiry stems ranging in length from 6 in. to 3 ft. or more. Most grow 2–3 ft. wide.

Astilbes are the mainstay of shady borders in the Upper and Middle South but can take some sun in the Upper South if given plenty of water. Combine with columbine (*Aquilegia*), meadow rue (*Thalictrum*), hosta, and epimedium in shady borders, or with peonies (*Paeonia*), delphinium, and irises in sunnier spots. Effective at the edge of ponds, along shady paths, in mass plantings, and in pots. Seldom browsed by deer.

All astilbes need moist, well-drained soil with ample organic matter. Cut off faded flower stems. Divide clumps every 4 to 5 years in autumn or in early spring.

Growing astilbes in the Lower South is challenging, to say the least. Give them rich, well-drained soil, full shade, and plenty of water. If they dry out in summer, the party's over.

A. x arendsii. Most astilbes sold belong to this hybrid group or are sold as such. Parentage is complex, but plants often have *A. japonica, A. chinensis,* and/or *A. thunbergii* in their ancestry. The plants differ chiefly in minor botanical details. Here are some of the many selections in use. Bloom times run from late spring for the early types to late summer for the late-flowering sorts.

'Amethyst'. Late. Lavender, 3–4 ft.

'Beauty of Ernst' (Color Flash). Late season, 1 ft. tall. Pink flowers. Colorful fall foliage.

'Bressingham Beauty'. Late midseason. Drooping pink clusters, 3 ft.

'Bridal Veil' ('Brautschleier'). Midseason to late. Full white plumes, 3 ft.

'Deutschland'. Early. White, 1½ ft.

'Erica'. Midseason. Slender pink plumes, 2½–3 ft.

'Fanal'. Early. Blood red flowers, bronzy foliage, 1½–2½ ft.

'Ostrich Plume' ('Straussenfeder'). Midseason to late. Drooping pink clusters, 3–3½ ft. Heat tolerant.

'Peach Blossom'. Midseason. Light salmon-pink, 2 ft.

'Red Sentinel'. Midseason. Bright red, 2½ ft.

'Rheinland'. Early. Deep pink, 2–2½ ft.

'White Gloria' ('Weisse Gloria'). Early to midseason. Creamy white, 2 ft.

A. chinensis. CHINESE ASTILBE. Resembles the *A.* x *arendsii* hybrids but generally blooms in late summer, grows taller, and tolerates dryness a little better. Varieties and selections include the following:

'Visions'. Upright-growing dwarf to 15 in. high, with raspberry-pink plumes above bronzy green leaves. Blooms a little earlier than other *A. chinensis* selections.

A. c. davidii. Late blooming, with dense, narrow, pink plumes 3 ft. tall. Pink-flowered 'Finale' grows only 18–20 in. tall.

A. c. pumila. Dwarf form with low mats of leaves topped by lilac-pink flower clusters that rise 12–15 in. high.

A. c. taquetii 'Superba'. Bright pinkish purple flowers in spikelike clusters 4–5 ft. tall. 'Purple Candles' is deeper purple, slightly shorter.

A. simplicifolia. JAPANESE ASTILBE. Grows to 16 in., with leaves merely cut or lobed instead of divided into leaflets. Known for its selections. Summer-blooming 'Sprite', the best known, is a low, compact plant with abundant pink, drooping, 1-ft. spires above bronze-tinted foliage. 'Hennie Graafland' is similar but grows a few inches taller and blooms somewhat earlier. 'Key Largo' bears raspberry midsummer flowers at 1½ ft. high. 'Moulin Rouge' has bright magenta flowers on 6-in. stems in midsummer.

ASTRANTIA
MASTERWORT
Apiaceae
Perennials

🌿 **US, MS; USDA 6-7**

☀ ◑ **FULL SUN OR PARTIAL SHADE**

💧 **REGULAR WATER**

Astrantia major 'Roma'

Flowering stems rise from leafy clumps in summer, bearing dense, tight clusters of blossoms surrounded by papery bracts. Flower heads look something like pincushions; they make attractive, long-lasting cut flowers and can also be dried for winter arrangements. Useful plants for woodland or cottage gardens. Native to alpine woods and meadows of Europe. Spread by underground runners. Die back in winter, even in mild climates. Best where summer nights dip below 70°F. Need good drainage. Deer resistant.

A. carniolica. LESSER MASTERWORT. To 1½ ft. tall and wide, with finely divided leaves. Bracts are shorter than in other species. 'Rubra' has dark red flowers with silvery accents.

A. major. GREATER MASTERWORT. Grows to 3 ft. high, 1–2 ft. wide, with inch-wide clusters of white-and-green or white-and-pink blossoms. Good selections with colorful blooms include 'Abbey Road', with reddish purple flowers on black stems; deep red 'Hadspen Blood'; 'Lars', with deep pink blooms opening from maroon buds; 'Rainbow', featuring a range of colors, from white through light pink to rose; 'Roma', with silvery pink blooms; and 'Ruby Wedding', with rosy red flowers on ruby stems. 'Sunningdale Variegated' offers

color in the 2- to 2½-ft.-tall pink flowers and in the splotched green foliage. Selection *A. m. involucrata* 'Shaggy' ('Margery Fish') is a white-flowered form with elongated, green-tipped bracts.

A. maxima. Similar to *A. major* but grows just 2 ft. high and bears pink flowers.

ATHYRIUM

Woodsiaceae
Ferns

🌿 **US, MS, LS; USDA 6-8**

◑ ● **PARTIAL OR FULL SHADE, EXCEPT AS NOTED**

💧💧 **REGULAR TO AMPLE WATER**

Athyrium niponicum pictum 'Silver Falls'

Prized since Victorian times for their beautiful foliage, these ferns are very easy to grow. All species described here prefer rich, moist, well-drained soil containing lots of organic matter. They do not tolerate extended summer drought or heavy root competition from trees. Fronds of most types turn brown after repeated frosts; leave the dead foliage on the plants through winter to provide mulch and to shelter the delicate fronds as they emerge in spring. Propagate by dividing clumps in early spring. Deer resistant.

A. filix-femina. LADY FERN. Native to much of North America. Grows to 4 ft. or taller, 2–3 ft. wide. Rootstock rises up on older plants to make short trunk. Vertical effect; narrow at bottom, spreading at top. Thin, finely divided fronds. Vigorous; can be invasive. Tolerates full sun in constantly moist soil. Specialists stock many selections with oddly cut and feathered fronds.

In 'Frizelliae' (about 8 in. high, 1 ft. wide), frond leaflets are reduced to balls; fronds look like strings of beads. 'Vernoniae Cristatum' (to 2½ ft. high and wide) has crested and feathered fronds. 'Victoriae' has comblike fronds with narrow, noodle-strapped leaflets. It grows 1½ ft. tall and wide.

A. hybrids. Crosses between *A. filix-femina* and *A. niponicum* 'Pictum', combining characteristics of each. These plants are vigorous and easy to grow.

'Branford Beauty'. Upright growth to 2 ft. high, 2½ ft. wide, with silvery-gray fronds and red stalks.

'Ghost'. Rigidly upright to 2–3 ft. high, 1½ ft. wide, with pale silvery gray fronds. A standout in deep shade.

A. niponicum. JAPANESE PAINTED FERN. Arching fronds grow to 1½ ft. long, making a tight, slowly spreading clump 1 ft. high, 1½ ft. wide. Most common is *A. n. pictum*, with fronds that are purplish at base, then lavender, then silvery greenish gray toward the tip. Among its colorful selections are the following. 'Burgundy Lace' has soft burgundy-purple fronds with silver streaking. 'Silver Falls' has long, arching, silver-and-green fronds with purplish red veins; foliage of 'Ursula's Red' is silver flushed with wine-red.

A. otophorum. ENGLISH PAINTED FERN. Actually a native of the Orient. Resembles *A. niponicum* in size and habit; dark green fronds have a reddish or purple midrib.

A. pycnocarpon (*Diplazium pycnocarpon*). GLADE FERN, SILVERY SPLEENWORT. From eastern North America. Attractive, rosette-forming deciduous fern with once-divided fronds to 4 ft. long. New spring fronds are silvery light green; they turn darker in summer, then russet before dying back. Tolerates full sun in constantly moist soil.

AUCUBA JAPONICA

JAPANESE AUCUBA
Garryaceae
Evergreen shrub

US, MS, LS, CS, TS; USDA 6-11; OR INDOORS

PARTIAL OR FULL SHADE; BRIGHT LIGHT

MODERATE TO REGULAR WATER

Aucuba japonica 'Variegata'

Native from the Himalayas to Japan. Seedlings vary in leaf form and variegation; many selections are offered. Standard green-leafed aucuba grows at a moderate rate to 6–10 ft. (sometimes to 15 ft.) high and almost as wide; can be kept lower by pruning. Buxom shrub, densely clothed with polished-looking, tooth-edged, dark green leaves 3–8 in. long, 1½–3 in. wide.

Minute, dark maroon flowers in earliest spring are followed by clusters of bright red, ¾-in. berries in fall and winter. Both sexes must be planted to ensure fruit. 'Rozannie', however, is self-fruitful, producing a heavy crop of berries without a pollinator.

Other green-leafed selections include 'Lance Leaf', with smooth-edged, lance-shaped leaves (male); 'Longifolia' ('Salicifolia'), narrow, willowlike foliage (female); 'Nana', dwarf to about 3 ft. (female); 'Serratifolia', long leaves with coarsely toothed edges (female).

Variegated selections (usually slower growing) include 'Crotonifolia', leaves heavily splashed with white and gold (male); 'Fructualbo', white-variegated leaves and pale pinkish-buff berries (female); 'Picturata' ('Aureo-maculata'), leaves centered with golden yellow, edged with dark green dotted yellow (female); 'Sulphur', green leaves with broad yellow edge (female). 'Variegata', often called gold dust plant, is the best-known aucuba. It has dark green leaves spotted with yellow; plants may be male or female. 'Mr. Gold-strike' (male) and 'Golden King' have heavier gold splashings.

All aucuba selections make choice container plants for shady patio or in the house. Use variegated forms to lighten up dark corners. Plants combine effectively with ferns, hydrangeas.

CARE

Japanese aucuba is tolerant of a wide range of soils but will grow and look better if poor or heavy soils are improved. Requires shade from hot sun, accepts deep shade. Grows well in low light under trees, competes successfully with tree roots. Tolerates sea air. Watch for mealybug and mites. Prune to control height or form by cutting back to a leaf joint.

AURINIA SAXATILIS

BASKET-OF-GOLD
Brassicaceae
Perennial

US, MS, LS; USDA 6-8

FULL SUN OR LIGHT SHADE

MODERATE WATER

Aurinia saxatilis

Mustard relative native to mountains of central and southern Europe, Turkey. Gray, 2- to 5-in.-long leaves form a spreading evergreen mound 8–12 in. high. Dense clusters of tiny golden yellow flowers cover the plant in spring and early summer.

Use as foreground plant in borders, in rock gardens, atop walls; plant about 1½ ft. apart. Poor soils or moderately fertile ones suit the plant perfectly—as long as drainage is good. Shear lightly (don't cut back stems by more than half) right after bloom. Generally hardy but may be killed in extremely cold winters. Short lived in hot, humid climates. Self-sows readily.

Selections include 'Citrina' ('Lutea'), with pale yellow flowers; 'Compacta', a compact grower with lemon-yellow blooms; 'Plena' ('Flore Pleno'), double flowered; 'Silver Queen', compact grower with pale yellow flowers; 'Sunnyborder Apricot', with apricot-shaded flowers; 'Dudley Nevill', similar in flower color to 'Sunnyborder Apricot' but with white-variegated leaves; and dwarf forms 'Goldkugel' ('Gold Ball'), 6 in. high, and 'Tom Thumb', 3 in. high.

AVOCADO

Lauraceae
Evergreen tree

LS (PROTECTED), CS , TS; USDA 8-11

FULL SUN

REGULAR WATER

Avocado

Delicious and popular tropical fruit, native to Mexico and to Central and South America. Three races of avocado (*Persea americana*) are grown, and numerous hybrids among them exist. The Mexican (the hardiest, often surviving to 18°F) is grown in the colder parts of central Florida, while the Guatemalan (hardy to 21–25°F) and the West Indian (the most tropical type, often perishing at temperatures below 25°F) and their hybrids are cultivated southward. Mexican race seedlings are often grown in home gardens across South Texas. For this plant's ornamental relatives, see *Persea*.

Plants bloom in late winter, and pollination is complex. Most types will produce some fruit if grown alone, but production is heavier when two or more selections are planted. Fruit ripens from summer into winter, depending on selection. Guatemalan and West Indian fruit differs from Mexican in generally being larger and having a lower oil content.

When planting an avocado tree in the landscape, consider that most selections will eventually grow quite large (to 40 ft.), produce dense shade, and shed leaves all year. Growth is quite rapid, but plants may be shaped by pinching terminal shoots. Avocado takes well to container culture, and selections in marginal climates can be moved to a protected location during cold spells. 'Day' is especially suited to life in a pot.

Florida selections include hardy 'Brogdon', 'Gainesville', 'Mexicola', and 'Tonnage' (all moderately scab resistant); somewhat less hardy 'Booth', 'Hall', 'Monroe' (all moderately scab resistant), and 'Choquette' (very scab resistant); and least hardy 'Pollock', 'Simmonds', and 'Waldin' (all very scab resistant). Two hardy types that set good crops without cross-pollination are the commercial selections 'Lula' (susceptible to scab) and 'Taylor' (very scab resistant). In Texas, 'Lula' is grown commercially in the lower Rio Grande Valley.

Most avocado trees in home gardens are selections developed from Mexican race seedlings that survived cold winters. For the selections that grow best in your area, check with a local garden center or Cooperative Extension Service office.

Gardeners in warmer coastal selections beyond Florida and Texas are growing and fruiting selections that are more cold hardy. These include 'Brazos Belle' (15°F), 'Joey' (15°F), 'Lila' (15°F), 'Pancho' (15°F), and 'Winter Mexican' (18°F). Naturally, plant hardiness also depends on microclimates and the duration of the cold.

CARE

All avocado trees require good drainage; constantly wet soil encourages fatal root rot. Tree is shallow rooted; do not cultivate deeply. In the absence of rainfall, irrigate lightly and frequently enough to keep soil moist but not wet. A mulch is helpful; the tree's own fallen leaves can provide this. Scab disease can be a problem in Florida; choose resistant selections. *Cercospora* leaf spot and anthracnose are also serious problems there. Anthracnose is a secondary pathogen, usually taking advantage of injury or another disease, such as leaf spot, to gain entry. Both problems can be prevented by applying appropriate fungicides and handling the fruit carefully.

B

BABIANA
BABOON FLOWER
Iridaceae
Perennials from corms

🌱 LS, CS, TS; USDA 8-11; OR DIG AND STORE

☼ ◐ FULL SUN OR LIGHT SHADE

💧 REGULAR WATER DURING GROWTH AND BLOOM

Babiana stricta

These easy-to-grow plants from Africa bear spikes of flowers in jewel-like tones of blue, lavender, purple, or red. Each flowering stem bears six or more 2-in.-wide blooms in mid- to late spring. Ribbed, hairy leaves grow in fans.

Plant corms 4–6 in. deep, 6 in. apart—as edging, in a rock garden, or in pots. In the Lower, Coastal, and Tropical South, plant out in fall; in the Upper and Middle South, plant in spring. In the Upper and Middle South, lift and store corms in fall. Where corms can overwinter in ground, leave them in place; they'll multiply and bloom more profusely each year. Plants get their common name from the fact that baboons like to eat the corms—so don't plant them if baboons are a problem in your neighborhood.

B. rubrocyanea. Ruby-throated royal blue blossoms on 6-in. stems.

B. stricta. Flowers in royal blue, purple, lavender, white, or blue and white appear on stems to 1 ft. tall.

BACCHARIS HALIMIFOLIA
SALTBUSH, GROUNDSEL BUSH
Asteraceae
Deciduous to semievergreen shrub

🌱 US, MS, LS, CS; USDA 6-9

☼ FULL SUN

💧 LITTLE TO REGULAR WATER

Baccharis halimifolia

Saltbush has so much going for it, it's a mystery why it remains largely unknown to Southern gardeners. This upright, multistemmed shrub grows 6–10 ft. tall and wide and features handsome leaves in soft gray-green. What really sets it apart are the fluffy white seed heads that cover it in fall—though it's actually gone to seed, the plant looks as if it's in bloom. It's tough and resilient, needing only

a sunny spot. It tolerates poor, clay, and rocky soil, as well as drought, moisture, wind, salt spray, and browsing deer. Excellent in naturalized areas or at the beach. Female plants are showier than male plants. Cut seed heads look great in arrangements. Self-sows prolifically. 'Orient Point' forms a mound 5–6 ft. tall and wide and features seed heads that are red at the base, creating a bicolor effect. 'White Caps' grows upright to 10 ft. and has especially showy seed heads.

BAMBOO
Poaceae
Giant grasses

🌱 SEE CHART FOR HARDINESS, HEAT TOLERANCE

☼ ◐ FULL SUN OR PARTIAL SHADE

💧 LITTLE TO REGULAR WATER

Phyllostachys nigra

Among Southerners, few plants elicit such strong emotions as bamboo: People seem either to love it or to want desperately to kill it. Though some bamboos grow as tall as trees, all are actually giant grasses. They consist of large, woody stems (culms) divided into sections (internodes) by obvious joints (nodes). Bamboos spread by underground stems (rhizomes) that are jointed and carry buds. The manner in which the rhizomes grow explains the difference between running and clumping bamboos.

In running bamboos, underground stems grow rapidly to varying distances from the parent plant before sending up new vertical shoots. These bamboos

eventually form large patches or groves unless spread is curbed. They are generally fairly hardy plants from temperate regions in China and Japan, and they are tolerant of a wide variety of soils.

In clumping bamboos, underground stems grow only a short distance before sending up new stems. These form clumps that slowly expand around the edges. Most are tropical or subtropical.

Mature bamboos grow phenomenally fast during their brief growth period—culms of giant types may increase in length by several feet a day. Don't expect such quick growth the first year after transplanting, though. In larger types, it may take 3 to 5 years to build up a rhizome system capable of supporting culms that grow several feet a day; aboveground growth during a plant's early years will be much less impressive. To get fast growth and great size, water and feed frequently. Once established, plants tolerate considerable drought, but rhizomes will not spread readily into dry soil and not at all into water.

Culms of all bamboos have already attained their maximum diameter when they poke through ground; in mature plants, they usually reach their maximum height within a month. Many do become increasingly leafy in subsequent years, but not taller. Bamboo plants are evergreen, but there is considerable dropping of older leaves; old plantings develop a nearly weed-proof mulch of dead leaves. Individual culms live for several years but eventually die and should be cut out.

See chart for hardiness. Figures indicate temperatures at which aboveground damage occurs; rhizomes may be considerably hardier. The chart gives maximum heights under ideal growing conditions and warmer zones; in colder zones, plants may be considerably shorter and have smaller culm diameters.

Growth habits. The chart classifies each bamboo by habit of growth, which, of course, determines its use in the garden. In **Group I** are the dwarf or low-growing ground cover types. These running bamboos can be used for erosion control or, in small clumps (carefully confined in a long section of flue tile), in a border or rock garden. **Group II**

BAMBOO

BOTANICAL NAME	COMMON NAME	ZONES + HARDINESS	GROWTH HABIT	MAX. HEIGHT	MAX. STEM DIAMETER	COMMENTS
Bambusa multiplex	HEDGE BAMBOO	CS, TS; USDA 9-11; hardy to 18°F	II	25 ft.	1½ in.	Dense, vase-shaped growth; good for hedges, screens
B. m. 'Alphonse Karr'	ALPHONSE KARR BAMBOO	CS, TS; USDA 9-11; hardy to 18°F	II	25 ft.	1½ in.	Similar to species, but canes are bright yellow with narrow, dark green striping; damaged by cold winds
Fargesia nitida 'Jiuzhaigou'	RED FOUNTAIN BAMBOO	US, MS; USDA 6-7; hardy to -15°F	II	12 ft.	½ in.	Small, narrow leaves on canes that change from green to cinnamon red to yellow; slow growing; more tolerant of heat and humidity than the species
Indocalamus tessellatus	BIG LEAF BAMBOO	US, MS, LS, CS, TS; USDA 6-11; hardy to -10°F	I	7 ft.	½ in.	Largest leaves of any bamboo in cultivation: up to 26 in. long; quite shade tolerant; rapid spreader; excellent choice for large containers
Phyllostachys aureosulcata 'Spectabilis'	YELLOW GROVE BAMBOO	US, MS, LS, CS, TS; USDA 6-11; hardy to -5°F	III	26 ft.	1½ in.	Culms are vibrant yellow with alternating green stripe; lower portions of some stems may have pronounced crooks
P. bissetii	BISSETT BAMBOO	US, MS, LS, CS, TS; USDA 6-11; hardy to -10°F	III	40 ft.	2 in.	Fast grower; makes a dark green privacy screen; vigorous and adaptable
P. edulis	MOSO	MS, LS, CS; USDA 7-9; hardy to 5°F	IV (running)	75 ft.	7 in.	World's largest hardy bamboo, prized for edible shoots and strong culms; leaves are small, contrasting with the massive culms and giving a feathery look
P. nigra	BLACK BAMBOO	US, MS, CS, LS, TS; USDA 6-11; hardy to 5°F	III	30 ft.	2 in.	New culms green, turning black in second year; erect in full sun; may weep attractively in shadier locations
P. nigra 'Henon'	GIANT GRAY BAMBOO	US, MS, CS, LS, TS; USDA 6-11; hardy to 0°F	IV (running)	65 ft.	4½ in.	Dark green leaves make a striking contrast to the whitish green stems; tough and drought-tolerant
P. rubromarginata	RED MARGIN BAMBOO	US, MS, CS, LS, TS; USDA 6-11; hardy to -5°F	IV (running)	60 ft.	3 in.	Aggressive grower with large leaves, long nodes; good for screening; handles salt spray; being evaluated for energy crop and fiber production
P. viridis 'Robert Young'	ROBERT YOUNG BAMBOO	US, MS, CS, LS, TS; USDA 6-11; hardy to 5°F	III	40 ft	3 in.	Very ornamental, with light green foliage and dark yellow culms randomly striped in green
Pseudosasa amabilis	TONKIN CANE	LS, CS; USDA 8-9; hardy to 15°F	III	50 ft.	2½ in.	Erect grower with straight, thick-walled stems; canes used to make fly rods
P. japonica	ARROW BAMBOO	US, MS, CS, LS, TS; USDA 6-11; hardy to 5°F	III	18 ft.	¾ in.	Stiffly erect stems, with one branch at each joint; large, broad leaves; spreads slowly to form a dense, thick hedge
P. j. 'Tsutsumiana'	GREEN ONION BAMBOO	US, MS, LS, CS, TS; USDA 6-11; hardy to 5°F	III	18 ft.	¾ in.	Resembles species, but canes have swollen areas between nodes, giving them the appearance of green onions

BOTANICAL NAME	COMMON NAME	ZONES + HARDINESS	GROWTH HABIT	MAX. HEIGHT	MAX. STEM DIAMETER	COMMENTS
Sasa palmata	BROADLEAF BAMBOO	US, MS, LS, CS, TS; USDA 6-11; hardy to 5°F	III	7 ft.	½ in.	Broad, handsome leaves (to 15 in. long by 2½ in. wide) spread fingerlike from stem and branch tips; prefers shaded sites; good in pots
S. veitchii	KUMA-ZASA	US, MS, LS, CS, TS; USDA 6-11; hardy to 5°F	I	5 ft.	¼ in.	Rampant spreader with large (7- by 1-in.) dark green leaves; edges turn white in cold weather; best with some shade
Sasaella masamuneana 'Albostriata'	WHITE STRIPED BAMBOO	US, MS, LS, CS, TS; USDA 6-11; hardy to 5°F	I	6 ft.	¼ in.	Green leaves heavily striped with cream; makes a thick, colorful ground cover; best with some shade; benefits from yearly mowing in early spring
Semiarundinaria fastuosa	NARIHIRA BAMBOO, TEMPLE BAMBOO	US, MS, LS, CS, TS; USDA 6-11; hardy to 0°F	III	30 ft.	1½ in.	Rigidly upright growth; slow spreader; easily kept to a clump; makes a good tall, narrow, dense hedge or windbreak
Shibataea kumasaca	RUSCUS BAMBOO	US, MS, LS, CS, TS; USDA 6-11; hardy to -5°F	I	7 ft.	¼ in.	Short, wide leaves are closely attached to stems, giving it an unusual look for a bamboo; needs acid soil and some shade; excellent under trees
S. lancifolia	LANCE-LEAF BAMBOO	US, MS, LS, CS, TS; USDA 6-11; hardy to 0°F	I	7 ft.	¼ in.	Lance-shaped leaves reach 8 in. long and 1 in. wide, with a velvety underside; good ground cover for shaded sites

HOW TO GROW BAMBOO

PLANTING AND PROPAGATING Plant container-grown bamboos any time of year. The more crowded a bamboo is in the container, the faster it will grow when planted out. Do not cut or spread the rootball; this may kill some canes. Best time to propagate from existing clumps is just before growth begins in spring; divide hardy kinds in March or early April, tropical ones in May or early June. (Transplanting at other times is possible, but risk of losing divisions is high in summer heat or winter chill and wet soil.) Cut or saw out divisions with roots and at least three connected culms. If divisions are tall, cut back tops to balance loss of roots and rhizomes. Foliage may wilt, but culms will send out new leaves. Rhizome cutting is another means of propagation. In clump bamboos, the cutting consists of the rooted base of a culm; in running bamboos, it is a foot-long length of rhizome with roots and buds. Plant in rich soil mix with ample organic material.

WATERING For best growth, water bamboos frequently and deeply, soaking soil around the plant to at least 12 in. deep. Established plants tolerate considerable drought but look best with regular irrigation.

FERTILIZING Feed in-ground plants once a month, March to October, with a high-nitrogen fertilizer or lawn fertilizer. To restrict size and spread of an established bamboo, cut back on water and fertilizer.

PESTS Scale, mealybugs, and aphids occasionally appear on bamboo but seldom do any harm; if they excrete honeydew in bothersome amounts, spray with insecticidal soap or summer oil. Mites can cause yellow streaking or disfigurement of leaves; they too can be controlled with insecticidal soap.

CONTAINMENT

Running bamboos. Large expanses of concrete or asphalt won't prevent the spread of running bamboos, but it isn't difficult to contain them—provided you understand how they grow. Rhizomes are shallow and spread sideways, not down.

Block them. You can keep the runners from spreading by installing a 30- to 36-in.-deep, 60-mil-thick, continuous polypropylene plastic sheet around the perimeter of the planting; leave a 2-in. lip aboveground to block runners. Never place plastic under roots, as they need excellent drainage. Continuously dry soil extending 10–20 ft. beyond the planting bed also impedes runners. Or contain them by planting in long flue tiles or large plastic plant containers with the bottoms cut out.

Cut them. Equally effective but more labor intensive is to periodically insert a spade down to its full length around the plant, severing the rhizomes and isolating unwanted parts from the main plant. Break off new shoots that rise from the isolated rhizomes; they are unlikely to resprout (if they do, follow instructions for removal in the text).

Surround them with trenches. Another method is to dig an 18-in.-deep, foot-wide trench around plants. You can leave this open and remove any rhizomes that emerge, or fill the trench with loose mulch or sand, then use a spading fork several times a year to search the trench for any roving rhizomes (they're easily severed).

Clumping bamboos. These types grow in an enlarging circle and do not gracefully adjust their shape, although a barrier on just one side is sometimes useful. Plant them well away from fences and sidewalks. Once a clump has expanded to the desired size, keep it in check by breaking off new shoots where you don't want them.

B

includes clump bamboos with a fountainlike habit of growth. They require no more space than the average strong-growing shrub. Clipped, they make hedges or screens that won't spread much into surrounding soil. Unclipped, they create informal screens or grow singly to show off their graceful form. Bamboos in **Group III** are running bamboos of moderate size and more or less vertical growth. Curb them and use as screens, hedges, or alone. **Group IV** includes the giant bamboos. Use running kinds for groves or for oriental effects on a grand scale. Clump kinds have a tropical look, especially if they are used with broad-leafed tropical plants. All may be thinned and clipped to show off the culms. Thin clumps or groves by cutting out old or dead culms at the base.

Some smaller bamboos bloom on some of their stalks every year and continue to grow. Some bloom partially, at erratic intervals. Some have never been known to bloom. Others bloom

heavily, set seed, and die. Some species of *Phyllostachys* bloom at rare intervals of 30 to 100 years, produce flowers for a long period, and become enfeebled. They may recover slowly or die.

Bamboos are not recommended for year-round indoor culture, but container-grown plants can spend extended periods indoors in cool, bright rooms. You can revive plants by taking them outdoors, but it is important to avoid sudden changes in temperature and light.

Should you find yourself with unwanted bamboo, you can use several methods to get rid of it. Digging it out with mattock and spade is the surest tactic, though sometimes difficult. Rhizomes are generally not deep, but they may be widespread. Remove them all, or regrowth will occur. Starve out roots by cutting off all canes and removing any new shoots that emerge. New shoots are fragile and can be mowed easily. Repeat as needed—probably many times over the course of a year for a

well-established grove. Contact herbicide sprays that kill leaves have the same effect as removing culms.

BANANA
Musaceae
Perennials

✎ **FOR ZONES, SEE TEXT**

☼ **FULL SUN**

💧 **AMPLE WATER**

Bananas

Popular symbols of the tropics, lush banana "trees" are not trees at all, but gigantic herbaceous perennials that grow from corms (or pseudobulbs). Thick, fleshy stalks (pseudostems) emerge from the large corms and can increase in height anywhere from 1 to 30 ft. in a year, depending on the selection and location. Each stalk carries spectacular broad, 5- to 9-ft.-long leaves. Each also produces a single flower cluster, which develops fruit; the stalk dies after fruiting, and new stalks then grow from the corm.

Fruiting bananas are often grouped botanically under *Musa acuminata*. To produce a crop, these plants generally need 10 to 15 months of frost-free conditions and a long, warm growing season. They fruit best in the Coastal and Tropical South, but old, established plants growing in protected spots in the Lower South occasionally bear fruit. Drooping clusters of orange-yellow flowers appear in spring, followed by bunches of bananas. The fruit usually ripens by late summer or fall—but whenever you see that the bananas at the top of the bunch have begun to turn yellow, cut off the whole

bunch and let it ripen at room temperature. If left on the plant, the fruit will split and rot. Banana sap permanently stains fabric, so wear old clothes when harvesting or pruning.

Each plant can produce as many as ten suckers, eventually forming a sizable clump. If you want large, high-quality fruit, let just one or two stalks per clump grow; prune out all others as they emerge. After the stalks have bloomed, allow replacement stalks to begin developing for next year's crop. After cutting the bunches of bananas, remove any stalks that have fruited.

Certain types of bananas are grown strictly as ornamentals (see *Ensete ventricosum* and *Musa*), but even fruiting types make bold and striking garden plants. Use them for tropical accents near pools, in sitting areas, at the back of a border, or in large containers. Strong winds tatter the leaves, but some selections have wind-resistant foliage.

Dwarf selections are the best bets for most home gardens. They mature at about 7–15 ft. high and usually ripen fruit 70 to 100 days after blooming. Recommended selections include the following.

'Dwarf Brazilian'. To 8 ft. tall. Excellent fruit. Wind-resistant foliage.

'Dwarf Cavendish'. The most popular dwarf banana, growing only 5 ft. tall. Sweet fruit. Excellent in containers.

'Dwarf Orinoco'. Grows just 5–6 ft. high, yet produces fruit clusters weighing up to 40 pounds. Good cold tolerance and wind resistance.

'Goldfinger'. Grows 12–14 ft. tall. Cold tolerant and disease resistant. Reliable producer of very tasty fruit.

'Grand Nain'. To 6–8 ft. tall. The "Chiquita" banana from Central America. Bears up to 50 pounds of fruit per year. Wind-resistant foliage.

'Ice Cream' ('Blue Java'). Fruit tastes like vanilla custard. Grows 12 ft. tall.

'Mysore'. Sturdy plant, 14–16 ft. tall. Produces large bunches of sweet, thin-skinned fruit.

'Rajapuri'. Cold-hardy selection from India that fruits reliably in Lower South. Sweet fruit. Grows 8 ft. tall, with stout trunk and extra-large leaves.

ABOVE: B. m. 'Alphonse Karr'

B. s. trichophylla. Known as Mexican fire bush or burning bush, is identical to the species, but its foliage turns bright red or purplish red in autumn. Can reseed profusely enough to become a pest; be sure to hoe out any unwanted seedlings when they're still small.

BAUHINIA
ORCHID TREE
Fabaceae
Evergreen, semievergreen, deciduous trees and shrubs

TS; USDA 10-11, EXCEPT AS NOTED

FULL SUN, EXCEPT AS NOTED

MODERATE TO REGULAR WATER

Bauhinia x blakeana

These flamboyant flowering plants have a very special place in central and southern Florida. Common to all garden bauhinias are twin "leaves," actually twin lobes. Not fussy about soil as long as it is reasonably well drained. Not browsed by deer.

B. x blakeana. HONG KONG ORCHID TREE. Partially deciduous tree. Native to southern China. The showiest and most coveted bauhinia; also the least cold hardy. Grows to 20 ft. high and wide; umbrella-type habit. Flowers are much larger (to 6 in. wide) than those of other bauhinias and appear in late fall to spring. They are shaped like some orchids; colors range from cranberry-maroon through purple and rose to orchid-pink, often in the same blossom. Gray-green leaves tend to drop off around bloom time, but the tree does not lose all of its foliage.

BASSIA SCOPARIA
SUMMER CYPRESS
Amaranthaceae
Annual

US, MS, LS, CS, TS; USDA 6-11

FULL SUN

REGULAR WATER

Bassia scoparia trichophylla

Formerly *Kochia scoparia*. Native to Eurasia. To 3 ft. high and 2 ft. wide. Branches are so thickly clothed in soft, narrow, light green leaves that plant is too dense to see through. Grow individually for its gently rounded form; or group plants for low, temporary hedge or edging. Can be sheared into any shape. Grow from seed sown in early spring or (in mild-winter climates) in fall. Seeds need light to germinate, so barely cover them with soil. Tolerates high heat.

reaches 4½ ft. tall and has violet flowers with dark purple centers.

B. sphaerocarpa. YELLOW WILD INDIGO. To 2–3 ft. tall and wide, with clear yellow blossoms.

---

both flowers and pods are interesting in arrangements. Remove spent flowers to encourage repeat bloom. Not usually damaged by deer.

B. alba. WHITE FALSE INDIGO. To 3 ft. tall and wide; clusters of white flowers. Attractive, smoky gray stems. 'Wayne's World' is vigorous and full, to 4 ft. tall and loaded with 18-in.-long flower spikes.

B. australis. BLUE FALSE INDIGO. Grows 3–6 ft. tall, 4 ft. wide; flowers are indigo blue. Several complex hybrids offer improvements on the basic species. 'Blueberry Sundae' is compact and refined at 3 ft. tall and wide, with lavender-blue flowers. 'Cherries Jubilee' is about the same size but sports deep maroon buds that open into bicolored flowers of maroon and yellow. 'Dutch Chocolate', to 2½ ft. tall and 3 ft. wide, has black-purple buds that mature to rich brown. 'Lemon Meringue', 3 ft. tall and wide, produces lemon-yellow blooms. *B. a. minor* is about half the size of the species and comes into bloom earlier.

B. bracteata leucophaea (*B. leucophaea*). PLAINS WILD INDIGO. To 1–1½ ft. high, 2–2½ ft. wide. Creamy white to pale yellow flowers are held nearly horizontally on arching stems. Especially attractive where it can be viewed from below—planted on a hillside or spilling over a wall, for example.

B. 'Carolina Moonlight'. Hybrid between *B. alba* and *B. sphaerocarpa*. To 4–4½ ft. high, 3–4 ft. wide. Profuse clusters of soft yellow flowers. Foliage turns silvery blue in summer heat.

B. 'Purple Smoke'. Hybrid between *B. australis* and *B. alba*,

LEFT: Baptisia 'Purple Smoke'*; RIGHT: B.* 'Carolina Moonlight'

Bananas need moist, fertile, well-drained soil and lots of sun. Feed liberally in spring. They will reliably survive winter outdoors in the Coastal and Tropical South (USDA 9-11); in the Lower South (USDA 8), spread a generous layer of mulch around the plant's base in fall to insulate the corm. Gardeners in the Middle and Upper South (USDA 6-7) can save a banana plant from year to year by cutting off and discarding the top (leafy part) of the plant in fall, then digging up the stalk and corm and storing them for the winter in a cool, dark place such as a basement or garage. No watering is required during the dormant period. Replant after all danger of frost is past.

BAPTISIA
FALSE INDIGO, WILD INDIGO
Fabaceae
Perennials

US, MS, LS, CS; USDA 6-9

FULL SUN

MODERATE WATER

Baptisia australis

Native to eastern and midwestern U.S. The false indigos somewhat resemble lupines (*Lupinus*), but they have deep taproots that enable them to survive difficult conditions. They are long-lived plants that become large clumps with many stems and bloom spikes. They resent transplanting once established. Bluish green leaves are divided into three leaflets. Flower spikes to 1 ft. long top the plants in late spring or early summer. Flowers resemble small sweet peas and are followed by inflated seedpods;

B. forficata (*B. candicans*). BRAZILIAN ORCHID TREE. Evergreen to deciduous large shrub or tree. Zones CS, TS; USDA 9-11. Native to Brazil. From spring through summer, bears narrow-petaled, creamy white flowers to 3 in. wide. Deep green leaves with lobes that are more pointed than those of other species. Grows to 20 ft. tall and broad, often with twisted, leaning trunk, picturesque angled branches. Short, sharp thorns at branch joints. Good canopy for patio. In the Tropical South, give some afternoon shade; when unshaded, blooms tend to shrivel during the day.

B. galpinii (*B. punctata*). RED BAUHINIA. Zones CS, TS; USDA 9-11 Evergreen to semievergreen shrub. Native to tropical and southern Africa. Brick-red to orange, 2½- to 3-in. flowers, as spectacular as those of bougainvillea, spring to fall. Sprawling, half-climbing plant to about 10 ft. tall, spreading to 15 ft. Best as espalier on warm wall. With hard pruning, can make splendid flowering bonsai for large pot or box.

B. lunarioides (*B. congesta*). ANACACHO ORCHID TREE. Evergreen to semievergreen shrub or tree. Zones CS, TS; USDA 9-11. Native from southwestern Texas into northeastern Mexico. To 8–12 ft. high, 4–5 ft. wide, with rounded, very small leaves (½ to ¾ in. long). White- and pink-flowering forms are available. Begins bloom in early spring and repeats many times over spring and summer. Open structured in afternoon shade; bushier in full sun.

B. macranthera. SIERRA ORCHID TREE. Evergreen to semievergreen shrub. Zones CS, TS; USDA 9-11. From eastern Mexico. Grows 8 ft. high and 12 ft. wide; blooms intermittently from spring through autumn, bearing small, exotic-looking flowers that combine tones of lavender and purple. Attractive, glossy green leaves.

B. monandra. BUTTERFLY FLOWER, JERUSALEM DATE. Deciduous shrub or small tree. Native to tropical Asia. Similar to *B. variegata* but 20 ft. tall and wide. Clusters of 4- to 5-in.-wide, pale pink to magenta blossoms, streaked or spotted with purple, come in clusters at ends of branches. Typically flowers in summer, but in Florida bloom time may run from spring through late fall.

B. variegata (*B. purpurea*). PURPLE ORCHID TREE. Partially to wholly deciduous large shrub or tree. Native to India, China. The most frequently planted species. Hardy to 22°F. Spectacular street tree where spring is reliably and steadily warm. Wonderful show of light pink to orchid purple, broad-petaled, 2- to 3-in.-wide flowers, usually blooming January to April. Light green, broad-lobed leaves generally drop in mid-winter. Produces huge crop of messy-looking beans after blooming. Trim beans off if you wish—trimming brings new growth earlier. Inclined to grow as shrub with many stems. Staked and pruned, becomes attractive tree to 25–30 ft. tall and wide. 'Candida' is the same, but with white flowers. Species known to be invasive in Florida.

BEAN

Papilionaceae
Annuals and perennials grown as annuals

✎ US, MS, LS, CS, TS; USDA 6-11
☀ FULL SUN
💧 REGULAR WATER

Pole beans

Gardeners can choose from many types of beans, the most common of which are described below. Except for the soybean (from eastern Asia) and the fava bean (from the Mediterranean region), beans are New World plants belonging to the genus *Phaseolus*. Most are frost-sensitive heat lovers and are easy to grow from seed. Bean flowers are edible.

For information on black-eyed peas and other popular Southern "peas," see Southern Pea.

Dry bean. Grow as you would bush form of snap bean (see below). Leave pods on bush until they dry or begin to shatter; then thresh beans from pods, dry, and store to soak and cook later. 'Pinto', 'Red Kidney', and 'White Marrowfat' belong to this group.

Some types are particularly delicious when harvested at the green shelling stage and cooked like green limas. These include the flageolet bean (a French favorite) and 'French Horticultural Bean', also known as 'October Bean'. Heirloom selections such as 'Aztec Dwarf White', 'Mitla White', and 'New Mexico Appaloosa' were grown by Native Americans of the Southwest and are very well adapted to that region.

Fava bean (broad bean, horse bean). This is a cool-season bean (actually a giant vetch, *Vicia faba*), best known and grown in coastal climates. Cook and eat immature pods like edible-pod peas; prepare immature and mature seeds in same way as green or dry limas. Note that a very few people (mainly of Mediterranean ancestry) have an enzyme deficiency that can cause severe reactions to the beans and even the pollen.

Fava beans require different care than other types described here. In cold-winter areas, plant them as early in spring as soil can be worked; in mild climates, plant in fall for harvest in late winter or early spring. Beans mature in 120 to 150 days. Space rows 1½–2½ ft. apart. Sow seeds 1 in. deep, 4–5 in. apart; thin to 8–10 in. apart. Plants produce busy growth to 2–4 ft. high.

Lima bean. Like snap beans (which they resemble), lima beans come in either bush or vine (pole) form. They develop more slowly than snap beans—bush types need 65 to 75 days from planting to harvest, pole kinds 78 to 95 days—and do not produce as reliably in extremely hot weather. Must be shelled before cooking, a tedious chore but worth it if you like fresh limas. Recommended bush types include 'Fordhook 242', 'Henderson', and 'Jackson Wonder'. Grow all lima beans like snap beans (see below).

Scarlet runner bean. Perennial twining vine (hardy in Coastal and Tropical South) commonly grown as annual. Showy and ornamental, with slender clusters of vivid scarlet flowers and bright green leaves divided into three roundish, 3- to 5-in.-long leaflets. Use it to cover fences, arbors, outbuildings; it provides quick shade on porches. Pink- and white-flowered selections exist.

Flowers are followed by flattened, very dark green pods that are edible and tasty when young but toughen as they reach full size. Beans from older pods can be shelled and cooked like limas. Grow as you would snap beans (see below).

Snap bean (string bean, green bean). The most widely planted bean type. Tender, fleshy pods, not stringy; may be green, yellow (wax beans), or purple (these turn green when cooked). Plants grow as self-supporting bushes (bush beans) or as climbing vines (pole beans). Bush types bear earlier, but vining sorts are more productive. Plants resemble scarlet runner bean, but their white or purple flowers are not as showy. Favorite bush beans include 'Blue Lake', 'Provider', and 'Royal Burgundy'. Among the best pole beans are 'Kentucky Wonder', 'Louisiana Purple Pod', 'Rattlesnake', and 'White Half Runner'.

Pods are ready in 50 to 70 days, depending on selection. Pick every 3 to 5 days; if pods mature, plants will stop bearing.

Soybean. Newcomers to most home gardens, soybeans are an excellent source of protein. Shelled from short, plump, fuzzy pods, the seeds are called "green vegetable soybeans" when harvested green and eaten raw; they are sold in grocery stores as edamame. These are also delicious cooked; prepare them as you would green shelling or lima beans. Dried ground soybeans are used in the preparation of substitutes for flour, nuts, meat, and even milk.

Soybeans grow well in the warm, humid climates of the South and Midwest, forming a bush about the size of a lima bean bush. Treat the seeds with soybean inoculant prior to planting; then plant them 1 in. deep, 4–6 in. apart, in rows spaced 2½ ft. apart. Harvest when the seeds have reached full size but the pods are still green. Before shelling, pour boiling water over the pods to soften them. 'Butterbean' and 'Shironomai'

HOW TO GROW BEANS

INOCULATING For more vigorous beans, buy seeds inoculated with *Rhizobium* bacteria, which helps the plants fix nitrogen from the air and store it in their roots. Or buy the inoculant from a nursery or mail-order seed supplier and treat the seeds yourself.

PLANTING Sow seeds as soon as soil is warm. Plant in loose, open soil that the heavy seed leaves can push their way through; soil needn't be particularly deep, since beans have shallow roots. Plant seeds 1 in. deep and 1–3 in. apart, allowing 2–3 ft. between rows of all kinds of bush beans. Pole beans need something to climb, and this can be provided in one of the following ways: (1) Set three or four 8-ft. poles in the ground and tie them together at the top in tepee fashion; plant four seeds around the base of each pole, thinning to two plants each. (2) Set single poles 3–4 ft. apart and sow six or eight beans around each, thinning to three or four strongest seedlings. (3) Insert poles 1–2 ft. apart in rows and sow seeds as you would bush beans. (4) Sow seeds along a sunny wall, fence, or trellis, and train vines on a web of light string supported by wire or heavy twine.

WATERING & FEEDING Moisten soil thoroughly before planting beans, then do not water again until seedlings have emerged. Once growth starts, keep soil moist. Feed after plants are in active growth and again when pods start to form.

PESTS Control aphids, cucumber beetles, spider mites, and whiteflies if they appear. Row covers help with insect control on bush beans; hosing down helps with aphids; yellow sticky traps work for whiteflies.

ABOVE: Scarlett runner bean

are best eaten fresh, either raw or cooked; 'Envy' is good fresh or dried.

BEAUCARNEA RECURVATA

PONYTAIL PALM, BOTTLE PALM
Asparagaceae
Evergreen shrub or tree

TS; USDA 10-11; OR HOUSEPLANT

FULL SUN; BRIGHT LIGHT

MODERATE WATER

Beaucarnea recurvata

Despite its common name, this Mexican native isn't a palm, but a relative of yucca and agave. Lush, pendulous, bright green leaves sprout from a woody trunk held above a greatly swollen base that the plant uses to store water. Young plants resemble big onions sitting atop the soil (with just a bit of the base below ground); older ones can reach 15 ft. tall and about half as wide, with leaves to 3 ft. or longer. Very old plants may develop several branching trunks and produce large clusters of tiny, creamy white flowers in summer.

Ponytail palms won't tolerate extended cold, so they're indoor plants outside of central and south Florida. Indoors, they need at least 4 hours of sun per day; a south- or west-facing window is a good spot. Make sure the soil is fast draining, and let it go dry between thorough soakings. Overwatering results in soft spots on the plant's base. Feed with a general-purpose liquid houseplant fertilizer every other week in spring and summer, once a month in fall and winter. Use horticultural oil or insecticidal soap to control scale insects and

mealybugs (take plants outdoors to spray them). Prune the woody stem just above a leaf to encourage branching. When repotting, set the plant at the same depth at which it was growing; do not cover the woody base with soil.

Outdoors, plants make striking specimens in the ground or in large containers; they are not browsed by deer. A mature plant can endure 18°F for brief periods—but young plants in pots will quickly freeze to death at even a few degrees higher than this, so bring them indoors when necessary.

BEAUMONTIA GRANDIFLORA

HERALD'S TRUMPET, EASTER LILY VINE
Apocynaceae
Evergreen vine

TS: USDA 10-11

FULL SUN OR PARTIAL SHADE

REGULAR WATER

Beaumontia grandiflora

From the Himalayas. Rampant vine with arching, twining branches; climbs as high as 30 ft. and spreads just as wide. Large (6- to 9-in.), oval to roundish dark green leaves, smooth and shiny above, slightly downy beneath, give lush tropical look. From spring through summer, bears fragrant, trumpet-shaped, 5-in.-long, green-veined white blossoms that look like Easter lilies (*Lilium longiflorum*).

Does best in well-drained soil enriched with organic matter; regular feeding produces most lavish display of foliage and flowers. Prune after bloom to

B

shape or limit size; flowers are produced on wood 2 years old or older, so keep a good proportion of old wood. Hardy to 28°F. Frost kills the vine to the ground, but it usually comes back from the roots. Use as big espalier on warm, wind-sheltered wall or train along eaves of house; sturdy supports are essential, since growth is heavy. Good choice for planting near swimming pools.

BEET

Amaranthaceae
Biennial grown as cool-season annual

- **US, MS, LS, CS, TS; USDA 6-11**
- **FULL SUN**
- **REGULAR WATER**

Beets

This European native, known botanically as *Beta vulgaris*, is grown mainly for its edible roots, but many Southerners also enjoy the tender, fresh greens, which can be cooked or eaten raw in salads. Beets are relatively pest free and make a good crop for small gardens, because they produce a lot in a limited space.

Types with round red roots include old favorites 'Detroit Dark Red' and 'Crosby's Egyptian' as well as newer selections such as 'Early Wonder' and 'Red Ace'. 'Bull's Blood' and 'Big Top' are grown both for roots and for particularly plentiful, tender, tasty greens. Novelties include 'Cylindra' and 'Rodina' (long, cylindrical roots), 'Chioggia' (rings of red and white), and selections with golden yellow, purple, or white roots.

CARE

Grow beets in fertile, well-drained soil without lumps or rocks. They grow best in the cool weather of spring and fall; they become tough and woody in hot weather. Early spring or late summer is the time to sow in most areas, but in the Coastal and Tropical South (USDA 9-11), you can grow beets as a winter crop. Most selections take around 50 days from sowing to harvest. Beet seeds germinate slowly; soaking them in water overnight before planting will speed the process. For spring crops, begin sowing seeds 2 to 4 weeks before the last spring frost; making three sowings spaced 2 to 3 weeks apart will give you a steady supply of roots and greens. For fall and winter crops, make three successive sowings 2 to 3 weeks apart, beginning in late summer.

Beets are light feeders; if you mix plenty of compost into the soil at planting time, a light dose of complete fertilizer after tops are up is sufficient. Sow seeds 1 in. apart and cover with ¼ in. of compost, sand, or vermiculite, and water gently. When seedlings are about an inch tall, thin them to 3 in. apart; the thinnings (both roots and tops) are edible. Early thinning is important, because crowded plants develop small, tough roots. To ensure tender roots, keep soil evenly moist. To thwart insect pests, grow beets under row covers.

Beet greens can be harvested when they are 6 in. tall. Snap off the outer leaves but don't disturb the inner ones; more leaves will grow for future harvests. If you plan to harvest greens regularly, plant beets for this purpose alone, as continual harvesting of greens makes for small roots. Pull roots when they're 1–3 in. wide; larger ones may be tough. In the Upper South (USDA 6), pull roots before the soil freezes in winter.

BEGONIA

Begoniaceae
Perennials

- **AS NOTED; OR INDOORS; OR DIG AND STORE; TS; USDA 10-11; OR TREAT AS ANNUALS**
- **PART SUN TO LIGHT SHADE, EXCEPT AS NOTED**
- **REGULAR WATER, EXCEPT AS NOTED**

Wax begonia

Native to many tropical and subtropical regions worldwide. Begonias are grown for their colorful blooms and textured, multicolored foliage. Outdoors, most grow best in containers in filtered shade. In the ground, they need rich, fast-draining soil; consistent but light feeding; and enough water to keep soil moist but not soggy. Most thrive as indoor plants, in greenhouse, or under a lath. Almost all require at least moderate humidity. (In dry-summer areas or indoors during winter, set pots in saucers filled with wet pebbles.) Most begonias are easy to propagate from leaf, stem, or rhizome cuttings.

Of the many hundreds of species and selections, relatively few are sold widely.

Begonia enthusiasts group or classify the different kinds generally by growth habit, which coincidentally groups them by their care needs.

Cane-type begonias. They get their name from their stems, which are tall and woody, with prominent bamboo-like joints. The group includes so-called angel-wing begonias, named for their folded, often spotted or splotched leaves, which resemble wings.

Cane-type begonias have multiple stems, some reaching 5 ft. or more under the right conditions. Most bear profuse, large clusters of white, pink, orange, or red flowers from early spring through autumn. Some are everblooming. Among the many available selections are 'Bubbles', with spotted foliage and pink flowers with an apple-blossom fragrance; 'Honeysuckle', with plain green foliage and fragrant pink flowers; 'Irene Nuss', with dark red-and-green leaves and huge, drooping clusters of coral-pink flowers; and 'Orange Rubra', with medium green leaves, sometimes spotted with silver, and bright orange flowers.

When roots fill 4-in. pots, plants can be moved to larger containers or planted in the ground. Position plants where they will get plenty of light, some sun, and no wind. They may require staking. Protect them from heavy frosts. Old canes that have grown barren should be pruned to two leaf joints in early spring to stimulate new growth.

Dragon Wing begonias. A hybrid between angel-wing (cane-type) and wax begonias. Shiny green leaves form a foliage mass 1–1½ ft. high and 10–12 in. wide; bright red or pink flowers bloom from spring until frost. Excellent as bedding plants and in containers. Do best with morning sun and light afternoon shade; tend to burn in hot afternoon sun. In shade, plants have a more open habit and bloom less generously. Baby Wing begonias are about the same size but have smaller leaves; white or pink flowers appear earlier than those of Dragon Wing types.

Hardy begonias. Zones US, MS, LS, CS; USDA 6-9. Several begonias are hardy throughout the South, but *B. grandis* (called hardy begonia and sometimes offered as *B. evansiana* or *B. grandis evansiana*) is the best known. It grows from a tuber and reaches 2–3 ft. tall and wide, its branching red stems set with large, smooth, coppery green leaves with red undersides. Pink or white summer flowers are borne in drooping clusters. The plant multiplies readily by bulbils produced in leaf axils; it dies down after a frost. Likes moist, woodsy soil and light shade. Excellent companion for ferns, hostas, and hellebores. The Garden Angel series

TOP: Shrublike begonia 'Bonita Shea'; rex begonia 'Fireworks';
BOTTOM: 'Dragon Wing Red'

includes full, upright plants with small pink blooms and silvery, maplelike leaves highlighted in plum and pink shades; hardy to 0°F. 'Heron's Pirouette' features exceptionally large clusters of hot pink flowers.

B. sinensis has much smaller leaves on a lower-growing plant (to 1 ft. tall and wide). It blooms from summer to fall. The species has pink flowers; 'Shaanxi White' bears pure white blooms.

B. sutherlandii is hardy from the Middle South (USDA 7) southward and grows 1 ft. tall, with wider spread; its weeping form makes it a good choice for hanging baskets and containers. Tooth-edged bright green leaves have red veins and margins. Clusters of creamy orange to bright tangerine blossoms appear in midsummer.

Hiemalis begonias. Usually sold as Rieger begonias. Bushy, compact, to 10–12 in. tall and wide. Profuse bloomers and outstanding outdoor or indoor plants. Flowers average about 2 in. across and appear over a long season that includes winter in frost-free areas. On well-grown plants, green leaves and stems are all but invisible beneath a blanket of bloom. Give indoor plants plenty of light in winter. In summer, keep out of hot noonday sun. Water thoroughly when top inch of soil is dry. Don't mist leaves. Plants may get rangy, an indication of approaching dormancy; if they do, cut stems to 4-in. stubs.

Multiflora begonias. Bushy, compact plants grow to 1–1½ ft. tall and wide. Abundant summer and fall blooms in carmine,

scarlet, orange, yellow, apricot, salmon, and pink. Includes the Nonstop strain. All multifloras are essentially small-flowered, profuse-blooming tuberous begonias; for care, see Tuberous begonias.

Rex begonias. With their bold, multicolored leaves, these probably have the most striking foliage of all begonias. They grow 6–14 in. tall and wide. While many named selections are grown by collectors, easier-to-find unnamed seedling plants are almost as decorative. The leaves grow from a rhizome.

Give rex begonias bright light through a window, and water only when top inch of soil is dry. They also need high humidity (at least 50 percent) to do their best. In dry climates or indoors in winter, provide moisture in the air by misting plants with a spray bottle, placing pots on wet pebbles in a tray, or keeping plants in a greenhouse. When the rhizome grows too far past edge of pot for your taste, either repot into slightly larger container or cut off rhizome end inside pot edge. Old rhizome will branch and grow new leaves. Make rhizome cuttings of the piece you remove and root in mixture of half peat moss, half perlite.

Rhizomatous begonias. Like rex begonias, these grow from a rhizome. Although some have handsome flowers, they are grown primarily for foliage, which varies in color and texture among species and selections. The group includes so-called star begonias, named for their leaf shape. Rhizomatous begonias perform well as houseplants. Plant them in wide, shallow pots. Give them bright light through a window, and water only when the top inch or so of soil is dry. They flower from winter through summer, the season varying among specific plants. White to pink flowers appear in clusters on erect stems above the foliage. Rhizomes will grow over edge of pot, eventually forming a ball-shaped plant; if you wish, cut rhizomes back to pot. (For care of rhizomes, see Rex begonias.)

B. masoniana. IRON CROSS BEGONIA. Large puckered leaves; known for chocolate-brown pattern resembling Maltese cross on green background. Flowers are insignificant.

Shrublike begonias. This large class is marked by multiple stems that are soft and green rather than bamboo-like as in the cane-type group. Grown for both foliage and flowers. Leaves are very interesting. Some are heavily textured, others grow white or red "hairs," and still others develop a soft, feltlike coating. Most begonias in this group grow upright and bushy, but others such as 'Bonita Shea' are less erect and make suitable subjects for hanging baskets. Flowers in shades of pink, red, white, and peach can come any time, depending on species or variety.

Outstanding examples include fern-leaf begonia (*B. foliosa*), with inch-long leaves packed tightly on a twiggy plant for a fernlike look. Its long, drooping stems (to 3 ft.) hold small white flowers nearly year-round in mild weather, or red shades. Fuchsia begonia (sold as *B. fuchsioides* or *B. foliosa miniata*) has delicate stems to 2½ ft. tall, with dangling rose-pink to rose-red flowers that resemble fuchsias. The sturdy, sun- and wind-tolerant 'Richmondensis' can reach 2½ ft. tall and 3 ft. wide, with arching red stems and shiny, deep green leaves with red undersides. Its vivid pink-to-crimson or white flowers develop from darker buds nearly year-round.

Care consists of repotting into larger containers as the plants outgrow their pots. Some shrublike begonias can get very large—as tall as 8 ft. They require ample moisture, but let soil begin to dry on surface between waterings. Prune to shape; pinch tips to encourage branching.

Trailing or climbing begonias. These have stems that trail or climb, depending on how you train them. They are suited to hanging basket culture or planting in the ground where well protected. Growing conditions are similar to those for tuberous begonias, though trailing types are not lifted. Sporadic bloom during warm weather.

Examples include hybrid 'Potpourri', with strongly scented deep pink flowers, and one of its parents, *B. solananthera*, with glossy, light green leaves and fragrant white flowers with red centers. *B. glabra* has trailing stems to 3 ft. long, with heart-shaped, bright green leaves and profuse white flowers in winter and spring.

Tuberous begonias. These magnificent large-flowered hybrids grow from tubers. They range from plants with saucer-size blooms and a few upright stems to multistemmed hanging basket types covered with small flowers. Except for some rare kinds, they bloom in summer and fall, in almost every color except blue.

Strains are sold as hanging or upright. The former bloom more profusely; the latter have larger flowers. Colors are white, red, pink, yellow, and peach; shapes are frilly (carnation), formal double (camellia), and tight-centered (rose). Some flower forms have petal edges in contrasting colors (picotee). Popular strains are Double Trumpet (improved rose form), Prima Donna (improved camellia form), and Hanging Sensation (camellia form). On Top series (camellia form) stands up well to high heat and humidity.

Grow tuberous begonias in filtered shade, such as under lath or in the open with eastern exposure. Tuberous begonias are best in the Upper South and Middle South (USDA 6-7); not suited to areas of extreme heat. In autumn, when leaves begin to yellow and wilt, reduce watering. When stems have fallen off the plants, lift tubers and shake off dirt; then dry tubers in sun for 3 days and store in a cool, dry place, such as a garage, until spring. When little pink growth buds appear, plant the tubers once again. You can also buy tubers from garden centers in spring.

B. boliviensis, to 1 ft. tall and 2 ft. wide, with narrow, pointed leaves and orange flowers, is a parent of many hybrids in the tuberous group. Look for 'Bertini', with deep orange-red blooms; 'Bonfire', with bright orange-red blooms; and 'Bellfire', with dark purple leaves and coral blooms. Heat-tolerant, long-lived 'Santa Cruz Sunset' has rich orange-red flowers.

Wax begonias. Dwarf and taller strains are grown in garden beds or containers as annuals; they bloom from spring through fall, producing lots of small (½–1 in.) flowers in a white through red range. Foliage can be green, red, bronze, or variegated. In mild climates, plants can over-winter and live for years. They thrive in full sun in the Upper South

and Middle South (USDA 6-7); prefer filtered shade elsewhere, but dark-foliaged kinds will take sun if well watered. The popular bronze-leafed Cocktail series, to about 8 in. tall, includes 'Brandy' (light pink flowers), 'Gin' (rose-pink), 'Rum' (pink-edged white), 'Vodka' (scarlet), and 'Whiskey' (white). Super Olympia series is similar in size and flower-color range, but with green foliage. Party series, to 1 ft. tall, is early blooming and heat tolerant; available in green- and bronze-leaf forms. Stara series, 16–20 in. tall, tolerates heat and drought; foliage changes from green to deep bronze as the season progresses.

Plants in the Big series (hybrids between fibrous and angel-wing begonias, sold as *B.* x *benariensis*) are vigorous, bushy, heavy-blooming plants to 20 in. tall and wide, with flowers up to 2½ in. across. Combinations include red flower with green leaf, red with bronze leaf, and rose with bronze leaf. The Whopper series is even larger, to 36 in. tall and wide, with blooms up to 3 in. across. Available in red with green leaf, red with bronze leaf, and rose with green leaf.

BELLIS PERENNIS
ENGLISH DAISY
Asteraceae
Perennial often treated as annual

🌿 **US, MS, LS, TS; USDA 6-11**

☼ ◑ **LIGHT SHADE IN HOTTEST CLIMATES**

● **REGULAR WATER**

Bellis perennis

Native to Europe and Mediterranean region. The original English daisies are the kind you

sometimes see growing in lawns in winter. Plump, fully double ones sold in garden centers are horticultural selections. Dark green leaves 1–2 in. long form rosettes to 8 in. wide. Pink, rose, or white double flowers bloom on 3- to 6-in. stems in spring and early summer. Deadheading prolongs bloom period. Edging or bedding plant; effective with bulbs. In the South, usually a cool-weather annual planted in fall, then allowed to overwinter; blooms in winter or spring.

BERBERIS
BARBERRY
Berberidaceae
Evergreen, semievergreen, deciduous shrubs

🌿 **ZONES VARY BY SPECIES**

☼ ◑ **FULL SUN OR LIGHT SHADE**

●● **MODERATE TO REGULAR WATER**

Berberis thunbergii atropurpurea 'Cherry Bomb'

These dense, spiny-stemmed plants, especially the deciduous species, tolerate climate and soil extremes. They require no more than ordinary garden care and are not browsed by deer. Each year, thin out oldest wood and prune as needed to shape—late in the dormant season for deciduous kinds, after bloom for evergreen and semievergreen types. Barberries make fine hedges. Species grown for their foliage can be sheared, but those grown for their spring flowers and the fruit that follows are best pruned informally, because they bloom on the preceding year's growth. To rejuvenate overgrown or neglected plants, cut them to within a foot of the ground

before new spring growth begins. Flowers are yellow unless otherwise noted.

B. darwinii. DARWIN BARBERRY. Evergreen. Zones MS, LS, CS; USDA 7-9. Hardy to 10°F. Very showy barberry from Chile. Fountainlike growth to 5–10 ft. tall, 4–7 ft. wide. Crisp, dark green, hollylike, 1-in. leaves. Orange-yellow flowers are borne so thickly along branches that foliage is hard to see; these are followed by profuse dark blue berries that are popular with birds. Spreads by underground runners to form a thicket.

B. x *gladwynensis* '**William Penn**'. Evergreen; drops some leaves at 0 to 10°F. Zones US, MS, LS, CS; USDA 6-9. Resembles *B. julianae* in general effect but has broader, glossier leaves and is faster growing, with denser growth. Reaches 4 ft. tall and wide. Good display of spring flowers and bronzy fall color that shades to yellow and purple.

B. x *irwinii.* See *B.* x *stenophylla* 'Irwinii'

B. julianae. WINTERGREEN BARBERRY. Evergreen to semievergreen. Zones US, MS, LS, CS; USDA 6-9. Hardy to 0°F, but foliage is damaged by severe winter cold. Chinese native. Dense, upright, to 6 ft. tall and wide; angled branches. Spiny-toothed, dark green, leathery leaves to 3 in. long; reddish fall color. Blue-black berries. One of the spiniest barberries; good as barrier hedge. Tolerates more shade than most barberries.

B. koreana. KOREAN BARBERRY. Deciduous. Zones US, MS; USDA 6-7. Hardy to –35°F. Korean native grows erect to 4–6 ft. and not quite as wide. Densely foliaged in medium to dark green, 1–3-in. leaves that turn purple in fall. Fragrant flowers in drooping, 3- to 4-in. clusters. Bright red fruit.

B. linearifolia '**Orange King**' (*B. trigona* 'Orange King'). Evergreen. Zones US, MS, LS; USDA 6-8. Hardy to 0 to 10°F. This selection of a Chilean species has an open growth habit to 5 ft. tall and wide, with narrow, glossy, 2-in. leaves. Short clusters of deep orange flowers; bluish black fruit.

B. x *mentorensis.* MENTOR BARBERRY. Evergreen to deciduous hybrid of *B. julianae* and *B. thunbergii.* Zones US, MS, LS; USDA 6-8. Hardy to –20°F but loses some or all leaves below

0°F. Compact growth to 7 ft. tall and wide. Dark green, 1-in. leaves turn a beautiful red in fall where winters are cold. Berries are dull dark red but are rarely seen. Easy to maintain as a hedge. Tolerates hot, dry weather.

B. x stenophylla. ROSEMARY BARBERRY. Evergreen. Zones US, MS, LS; USDA 6-8. Hardy to 0°F. Narrow, ½–1-in.-long leaves with rolled-in edges and spiny tip. Species is 10 ft. tall, 15 ft. wide, but selections are more commonly grown. 'Corallina Compacta', called coral barberry, reaches 1½ ft. high and wide and bears nodding clusters of bright orange flowers and bluish black fruit; effective in rock garden or as foreground plant. 'Irwinii', to 4–5 ft. tall and wide, resembles a compact-growing *B. darwinii.*

B. thunbergii. JAPANESE BARBERRY. Deciduous. Zones US, MS, LS; USDA 6-8. Hardy to –20°F. Graceful habit with slender, arching, spiny branches; if not sheared, usually reaches 4–6 ft. tall with equal spread. Densely covered with roundish, ½- to 1½-in.-long leaves that are deep green above, paler beneath; leaves turn yellow, orange, and red before they fall. Beadlike, bright red berries stud branches in fall and through winter. Use as hedge, barrier planting, or specimen shrub. This species has become invasive in many parts of the South (roughly including Missouri, Tennessee, North Carolina and points north); in these areas, choose low-seed selections and avoid planting near open lands.

The following are among the many attractive selections grown for vivid foliage.

'Aurea'. Bright golden yellow foliage. Best color in full sun (though it can't take it in Coastal South), but plant will tolerate light shade. Slow growing to 2½–3 ft. tall and wide.

'Golden Nugget'. Dwarf selection reaching 1½ ft. tall and wide. Golden leaves may be tinged orange. Sets few or no seeds.

'Kobold'. Extra-dwarf bright green selection. Like 'Crimson Pygmy' in habit but fuller and rounder.

'Sparkle'. To 5 ft. tall and 6 ft. wide, with rich green foliage that turns vivid yellow, orange, and red in fall.

B. t. atropurpurea. RED-LEAF JAPANESE BARBERRY. This group contains plants with leaves in the red to purple-red range. All develop most intense color in sun.

'Bagatelle'. Similar to 'Crimson Pygmy' but with smaller, glossier, deeper red-purple leaves and a narrower shape; 1½–2 ft. tall and wide. Sets few or no seeds.

'Cherry Bomb'. Like 'Crimson Pygmy', but 4 ft. tall, with larger leaves and more open growth. Regular water.

'Concorde'. Grows 18 in. tall and wide, produces maroon-purple leaves that go red in fall; small flowers, red berries.

'Crimson Pygmy' ('Atropurpurea Nana'). The most widely sold Japanese barberry, this selection grows 1½–2 ft. high and 2½–3 ft. wide. New leaves are bright red, mature to bronzy blood red. Sets few or no seeds.

'Golden Ring'. Grows 3 ft. tall and wide. Reddish purple leaves with a thin green or golden green border.

'Golden Ruby'. Dwarf selection reaching 2 ft. high and wide. Leaves open coral, then turn purple-red with golden margins. Sets few or no seeds.

'Helmond Pillar'. Columnar form grows 6 ft. tall, 2 ft. wide, with reddish purple foliage. Sets few or no seeds.

'Pygmy Ruby'. Grows 1½ ft. high, 3 ft. wide, with deep red foliage. Sets few or no seeds.

'Rose Glow'. To 4–6 ft. tall and wide. New foliage marbled bronzy red and pinkish white, deepening to rose and bronze with age. Very popular.

'Royal Cloak'. Compact, mounding to 4 ft. high and at least as wide. Large, dark purple-red leaves.

B. trigona 'Orange King'. See *B. linearifolia* 'Orange King'.

B. verruculosa. WARTY BARBERRY. Evergreen. Zones US, MS; USDA 6-7. Hardy to 0°F. Native to China. Neat, tailored looking. Will reach 4–5 ft. tall and wide but can be kept to 1½ ft. Perky, inch-long leaves are glossy, dark green above, whitish beneath. In fall and winter, the odd red leaf develops as a highlight here and there. Black berries with a purplish bloom. Very choice and effective on banks, in front of leggy rhododendrons or azaleas, in foreground of shrub border. Tolerates poor soils.

B. wilsoniae. WILSON BARBERRY. Deciduous to semi-evergreen. Zones US, MS, LS; USDA 6-8. Hardy to 5°F. Native to China. To 6 ft. tall and wide, but it can be held to 3–4 ft. Light green, roundish, ½- to 1-in. leaves give a fine-textured look. Beautiful coral to salmon-red berries. Makes a handsome barrier hedge.

BERGENIA
Saxifragaceae
Perennials

US, MS, LS; USDA 6-8

PARTIAL OR FULL SHADE

REGULAR WATER

Bergenia cordifolia 'Lunar Glow'

Native to the Himalayas and the mountains of China. Thick rootstocks produce rosettes of ornamental, glossy green leaves to 1 ft. across. Evergreen except in the coldest areas; foliage of many types blushes red in cool weather. Thick, leafless, 1- to 1½-ft.-tall stalks bear graceful, nodding clusters of small white, pink, or rose flowers shaped like funnels or bells; blossoms are typically ½ –1 in. across. Bergenias lend a strong, substantial textural quality to borders and plantings under trees; also make a bold, patterned ground cover. Effective with ferns, hostas, hellebores; good as foreground planting for aucubas, rhododendrons, Japanese yew (*Taxus cuspidata*).

B. ciliata (*B. ligulata*). FRILLY BERGENIA. Choicest, most elegant. To 1 ft. Lustrous light green leaves are smooth on edges but fringed with soft hairs; young leaves bronzy. White, rose, or purplish flowers bloom in late spring, summer. Slightly tender; leaves burn in severe frost.

B. cordifolia. HEARTLEAF BERGENIA. Glossy, roundish leaves are glossy, roundish, heart shaped at base, with wavy, toothed edges. In spring, rose or lilac flowers appear in pendulous clusters partially hidden by leaves. Plant grows to 20 in. tall. Leaves of 'Lunar Glow' emerge creamy yellow and hold their color through much of the summer before turning burgundy in fall; flowers are dark pink. 'Tubby Andrews' has leaves splashed with golden yellow; flowers are pink. 'Winterglut' ('Winter Glow') has bright red flowers and leathery green leaves that turn reddish bronze in cool weather.

B. crassifolia. WINTER-BLOOMING BERGENIA. Dark green leaves, to 8 in. or more across, have wavy, sparsely toothed edges. Rose, lilac, or purple flowers in dense clusters on erect stems that stand well above leaves. Blooms in spring.

B. hybrids. Some of the best are of English or German origin.

'Abendglut' ('Evening Glow'). Dark red flowers and dark reddish leaves with crimped edges.

'Apple Blossom'. Reddish stems hold large (1½-in.-wide), light pink blossoms.

'Bressingham Ruby'. Rose-red blooms rise over green leaves that turn bronzy purple in winter.

'Bressingham White'. White flowers.

'Herbstblute' ('Autumn Glory'). Leaves turn purplish in fall, when it also tends to rebloom.

'Morgenrote'('Morning Red'). Has bronzy-toned leaves, dark red flowers.

'Pink Dragonfly'. Small (10 in. tall), narrow-leafed plant with pink blooms, purple-tinged winter leaves.

'Silberlicht' ('Silver Light'). Large, slightly toothed leaves and white blossoms.

CARE

Bergenias do well in part shade in the Upper and Middle South, full shade in Lower South. Plant about 1½ ft. apart. They do best in good soil with regular watering, good drainage, feeding, and periodic grooming. Cut back yearly to prevent legginess. Divide crowded clumps and replant vigorous divisions in late winter or early spring.

BERLANDIERA
Asteraceae
Perennials

📊 **ZONES VARY BY SPECIES; ANY-WHERE AS ANNUALS**

☀️ **EXPOSURE NEEDS VARY BY SPECIES**

💧 **WATER NEEDS VARY BY SPECIES**

Berlandiera lyrata

Tough and undemanding, these plants decorate the meadows of their native South-west with cheerful yellow daisies. They're also easy to grow out-side their native range, thriving in most soils as long as they have good drainage. Sow seed in fall; or set out small plants in spring.

B. betonicifolia (*B. texana*). TEXAS GREENEYES. Zones US, MS, LS, CS, TS; USDA 6-11. Named for the green center of its yellow blossoms. Grows 1–4 ft. tall; blooms profusely in spring, then again in summer and autumn. Gets by on moderate water but responds well to regular watering and fertilizing. Full sun or dappled shade.

B. lyrata. CHOCOLATE DAISY, CHOCOLATE FLOWER. Zones LS, CS, TS; USDA 8-11. The luscious fragrance of chocolate permeates the morning air wherever this daisy blooms. Rounded, some-what coarse-foliaged plant reaches 1½–3 ft. high and wide. Blooms in spring and summer, sometimes into fall, bearing light yellow daisies with a maroon-and-green center. Native Ameri-cans used the flower heads to flavor foods. Butterflies can't resist the blossoms, which dry well for use in winter bouquets. Give moderate water; plant in full sun.

BESCHORNERIA
Agavaceae
Perennials

📊 **ZONES VARY BY SPECIES**

☀️ **PARTIAL SHADE IN HOTTEST CLIMATES**

💧 **MODERATE TO REGULAR WATER**

Beschorneria yuccoides

Native to Mexico, these striking plants combine handsome, lance-shaped dark green leaves with showy, tubular summer flowers. They are related to yuccas and agaves, but they have spineless leaves and need a bit more water and shade than their cousins. They prefer fertile, well-drained soil, though they will tolerate short periods of drought. Excellent as specimen plants, in lightly shaded borders, or in containers.

B. 'Ding Dong' Zones LS, CS, TS; USDA 8-11. This excellent hybrid between *B. septentrionalis* and *B. yuccoides dekosteriana* forms a rosette 3–4 ft. tall and 2–3 ft. wide; leaves are rough-textured. At maturity, a bright red, 7-ft.-tall flower stalk is topped by bell-shaped red-and-green blossoms.

B. septentrionalis. Zones MS, LS, CS, TS; USDA 7-11. To 3 ft. tall and wide. Lush, pendulous green leaves to about 2 ft. long; fuchsia red flowers atop a glossy red spike. Needs light shade in the Coastal and Tropical South. Tolerates considerable moisture if soil is well drained.

B. yuccoides. Zones CS, TS; USDA 9-11. The most widely avail-able species. Clump slowly grows 3–4 ft. tall and wide; narrow gray-green leaves can reach 2 ft. long and wide. Flowers in early summer, when a thick, branching,

coral-pink, 3- to 7-ft. stalk is hung with pendulous yellowish green blooms with red bracts. Thrives in well-drained garden soil or large container; suffers in cold, wet earth. *B. y. dekosteriana* (Zones LS, CS, TS; USDA 8-11) grows 4 ft. tall and wide, with waxy blue-green leaves and a tall red flower stalk bearing green-and-red blossoms.

BETULA

BIRCH
Betulaceae
Deciduous trees

📊 **ZONES VARY BY SPECIES**

☀️ **FULL SUN**

💧 **REGULAR TO AMPLE WATER**

Betula nigra

No tree has more beautiful bark than a white-barked birch—the tree that comes to mind when most people think of birches. Trouble is, these trees are often difficult to keep alive in most of the South. Native to mountainous areas, where summers are cooler and winters long, they tend to struggle when faced with the hot summers common to our region. And they often succumb to a serious pest: the bronze birch borer, which causes them to die slowly from the top down.

Fortunately, a number of birches that resemble white-barked birches do succeed here; they too have a graceful habit; thin bark that peels in sheets; and small, finely toothed leaves that turn glowing yellow in fall. After the leaves drop, the trees' delicate limbs, handsome bark, and small, conelike fruit provide a striking winter display.

B. lenta. SWEET BIRCH, CHERRY BIRCH. Zone US; USDA 6. Native to eastern U.S. Seldom sold. An attractive tree with shiny reddish to blackish brown bark; grows to 40–50 ft. tall, up to 40 ft. wide. Leaves to 4 in. long; turn rich yellow in fall. Many country children have sampled the bark of this tree, which has a sweet wintergreen flavor and was once routinely used to make a tasty soft drink known as birch beer.

B. maximowicziana. MONARCH BIRCH. Zones US, MS; USDA 6-7. Native to Japan. Fast growing; open growth when young. Can reach 80–100 ft. tall, 40 ft. wide. Flaking, orange-brown bark eventually turns gray or white. Leaves up to 6 in. long. Plants sold under this name are not always the true species.

B. nigra. RIVER BIRCH. Zones US, MS, LS, CS; USDA 6-9. Native to eastern U.S. Very fast growth in first years; eventually reaches 50–90 ft. tall, 40–60 ft. wide. Trunk often forks near ground, but tree can be trained to a single stem. Young bark is apricot to pinkish, very smooth, and shiny; on older trees, bark flakes and curls in cinnamon-brown to blackish sheets. Diamond-shaped leaves, 1–3 in. long, are bright, glossy green above, silvery below. This is the best birch for hot, humid climates. Not a good choice near decks and porches; drops leaves sporadically all summer. Tolerates poor drainage. 'Cully' ('Heritage') is resistant to bronze birch borer and has darker leaves and tan-and-apricot bark; keeps apricot color longer than the species. 'Dura-Heat' is more compact and heat toler-ant than the species. 'Summer Cascade' is the first weeping birch that resists birch borer; grows 15 ft. tall and 20 ft. wide.

B. papyrifera. PAPER BIRCH, CANOE BIRCH. Zone US; USDA 6. Native to northern part of North America. Similar to *B. pendula* but taller (to 100 ft. tall, half as wide), less weeping, with a stouter trunk that is creamy white. Bark peels off in papery layers. Leaves are larger (to 4 in. long), sparser. Excellent fall color. More resistant to bronze birch borer than *B. pendula*. 'Snowy' is a cold-hardy selection with especially hand-some white bark; it is said to be particularly resistant to borers and grows quickly when young.

PLANT BIRCHES AWAY FROM THE HOUSE, AS THEIR ROOTS CAN ENDANGER THE FOUNDATION.

B. pendula. EUROPEAN WHITE BIRCH. Zone US; USDA 6. Native from Europe to Asia Minor. Delicate and lacy. Upright branching with weeping side branches. Average mature tree is 30–40 ft. high and half as wide. Bark on twigs and young branches is golden brown; as tree matures, bark on trunk and main limbs becomes white, marked with black clefts. Oldest bark (at base of tree) is blackish gray. Rich green, glossy leaves to 2½ in. long, diamond shaped with slender, tapered point. Often sold as weeping birch, although trees vary somewhat in habit and young trees show little inclination to weep. Very susceptible to bronze birch borer. The following are some of the hybrids and selections offered.

'Crimson Frost'. Hybrid between *B. pendula* 'Purpurea' and an Asian birch, with burgundy leaf color that persists all summer. Somewhat resistant to borers.

'Fastigiata' PYRAMIDAL WHITE BIRCH. Branches upright; habit somewhat like Lombardy poplar (*Populus nigra* 'Italica'). Excellent screening tree.

'Laciniata' ('Dalecarlica'). CUT-LEAF WEEPING BIRCH. Graceful, open tree with deeply cut leaves, strongly weeping branches. Weeping forms are more affected by dry, hot weather than is the species; foliage will show stress by late summer.

'Purple Rain'. A purple-leafed selection like 'Purpurea', but it holds its color all summer.

'Purpurea' (*B. alba* 'Purpurea') PURPLE BIRCH. Purple-black twigs. Foliage is rich purple-maroon when new, fading to purplish green in summer; looks striking against white bark.

'Youngii'. YOUNG'S WEEPING BIRCH. Slender branches hang straight down. Resembles weeping forms of mulberry (*Morus*) but is more graceful. Decorative tree. Trunk must be staked to desired height. Same climate limitations as those of 'Laciniata'.

CARE

Birches need a steady supply of moisture at all times; drought in summer can cause leaf drop. All fall victim to aphids that drip honeydew; for this reason, they should never be planted near a porch, patio, or parking area. Plant in fertile, slightly acid soil; most prefer good drainage. Prune in summer to remove weak, damaged, or dead branches; trees will bleed sap if pruned in winter. Susceptibility to heat and the bronze birch borer limits most birches to the Upper and Middle South.

BIDENS

TICKSEED
Asteraceae
Annuals and perennials

ZONES VARY BY SPECIES

FULL SUN

REGULAR TO AMPLE WATER

Bidens ferulifolia

These wildflowers are also known as beggar-ticks and stick-tights—references to their barbed seeds, which stick to the clothing or fur of anything that brushes by, allowing the plants to spread by hitchhiking. Many types of tickseed exist; most are out-and-out weeds, but a few offer showy flowers and make fine additions to the border. They prefer full sun and fertile soil that is always moist, be it boggy or well drained. Seeds planted in spring or summer sprout and grow quickly. Once planted, you'll have them forever, as they reseed profusely. Seedlings are nice to share, though, and it's easy to pull out those you don't want.

B. aristosa. Annual. Zones US, MS, LS, CS, TS; USDA 6-11. North American prairie native grows 4–5 ft. tall and 2 ft. wide. Strongly dissected, toothed leaves resemble those of marigold (*Tagetes*). Masses of showy, daisylike yellow flowers to 2 in. wide appear in summer and fall, carried atop the foliage.

B. coronata. Annual. Zones US, MS, LS, CS, TS; USDA 6-11. From bogs and meadows of North America. To 5 ft. tall, 2 ft. wide. Blooms in late summer, bearing golden yellow, daisylike blooms to 3 in. across. Foliage is more deeply dissected than that of *B. aristosa*.

B. ferulifolia. Perennial. Zones CS, TS; USDA 9-11; anywhere as annual. Native to southern U.S., Mexico, Guatemala. The species grows to 3 ft. tall and wide, but the forms most commonly seen are trailing. Bright green leaves are divided into threadlike segments. Flower heads are bright golden yellow, an inch or so wide, with fewer ray flowers than most daisies and a light honey fragrance. Plants bloom almost continuously during mild weather. Extremely heat tolerant. Can be aggressive, clambering into or sprawling over their neighbors; when this happens, cut plants back (they will recover quickly).

Sold under a wide variety of names. Seed-grown kinds include 'Golden Eye', 10–12 in. tall and broad, and 'Golden Goddess', 1½–2 ft. high and wide, with larger (2½-in.) flowers. 'Goldie', 'Gold Marie', and 'Goldilocks Rocks' are cutting-grown plants similar in size to 'Golden Eye'.

BIGNONIA CAPREOLATA

CROSSVINE
Bignoniaceae
Evergreen or semievergreen vine

US, MS, LS, CS; USDA 6-9

FULL SUN OR LIGHT SHADE

MODERATE TO REGULAR WATER

Bignonia capreolata

Vigorous and showy, this woody Southern native can climb to 60 ft. by tendrils and holdfast disks, attaching itself to almost any surface. Each shiny, dark green leaf consists of two 2- to 6-in. leaflets and a branching tendril. Leaves turn purplish in cold weather, and some drop in freezing weather. Clustered, 2-in., trumpet-shaped reddish brown to orange or scarlet flowers appear in midspring, with intermittent summer bloom. 'Atrosanguinea' has reddish purple blooms and longer, narrower leaves than the species. 'Dragon Lady' has rich red blooms. 'Jekyll' has slightly smaller flowers that are yellow on the inside, orange on the outside. Stunning 'Tangerine Beauty' blooms profusely, producing tangerine red blossoms with yellow throats.

CARE

Very easy to grow, with few problems. Prefers acid, moist soil, but tolerates drought. Prune after flowering. Vine is especially pretty when cloaking a sturdy trellis over an entry gate. Or train it over an arbor.

BILLBERGIA
Bromeliaceae
Perennials

- TS; USDA 10-11; OR GROW IN POTS
- FILTERED SUN; BRIGHT INDIRECT LIGHT
- REGULAR WATER

Billbergia nutans

These pineapple relatives are native to Brazil and other parts of the tropics, where they grow as epiphytes on trees. Basal rosettes of stiff, spiny-toothed evergreen leaves produce drooping clusters of showy bracts and tubular flowers. Usually grown in containers for display indoors or on patios. In south Florida, however, they are often planted under trees as an easy ground cover, used in borders, or grown on limbs of trees or bark slabs, with roots wrapped in sphagnum moss and leaf mold. They make excellent cut flowers. Specialists in bromeliads list dozens of selections.

B. nutans. QUEEN'S TEARS. Most commonly grown. Narrow (½-in.-wide), spiny, green leaves to 1½ ft. long. Rosy red bracts in 6- to 12-in. spikes; drooping flowers with green petals edged deep blue. Vigorous. Makes offsets freely; easy to grow and propagate.

B. pyramidalis. Leaves to 3 ft. long, 2½ in. wide, with spiny-toothed margins. Dense flower spikes to 4 in. long; bright red bracts, red petals tipped in violet.

B. sanderiana. Leathery, spiny-toothed, white-dotted leaves grow to 1 ft. long, 2½ in. wide. Produces loose, nodding, 10-in.-long flower clusters with rose-colored bracts, blue-tipped sepals, and blue petals that are yellowish green at the base.

CARE

Need regular moisture during active growth in warm weather; reduce water as weather cools and growth slows. Plants usually hold water in the funnel-like center of the leaf rosette, which acts as a reservoir. Grow in well-drained soil; or pot in a light, porous mixture of sand, ground bark, and leaf mold. Give houseplants warmth and lots of light; mist foliage frequently. To get more plants, cut off suckers from base of plant and pot them up.

BISMARCKIA NOBILIS
BISMARCK PALM
Arecaceae
Palm

- CS (PROTECTED), TS; USDA 9-11
- FULL SUN
- LITTLE TO MODERATE WATER

Bismarckia nobilis

From Madagascar, this striking palm grows 30 to 40 ft. tall; comes in blue and green forms. The fan-shaped fronds are each up to 10 ft. wide, making a round leaf crown about 25 ft. wide. The blue form is better inland because it's more tolerant of heat and cold, while the frost-intolerant green form excels along the coast. Grow where its low, stout trunk and shapely canopy can show off, as in rows along a driveway or as accent in a lawn.

BLACKBERRY
Rosaceae
Berry-producing shrubs

- US, MS, LS, CS; USDA 6-9
- FULL SUN
- REGULAR WATER

Blackberries

Blackberries grow in areas of the South where summers are not too dry and winters not too harsh. They thrive along the eastern coast, as well as in the cool-night areas of the Appalachians, Ozarks, and Blue Ridge Mountains.

Upright (erect) types tend to be hardy and stiff caned; they usually grow 4–6 ft. high. Trailing kinds, known as dewberries or boysenberries, are more lax plants that need support. Crosses between upright and trailing types are termed semierect. Canes of most blackberries are covered with sharp thorns.

All types bear fruit in summer. The fruit clusters of trailing plants ripen earlier and are smaller and more open than those of erect or semierect types. The fruit makes excellent pies, fine jams and jellies, tangy syrups, and even good wines.

The following are some of the top blackberry selections for the South. Plants are deciduous, except as noted.

'Apache'. Erect, thornless canes bear a large crop of large, late-ripening berries with fine flavor. Good vigor and hardiness.

'Arapaho'. Erect, thornless. Large, firm berries ripen 3 weeks before 'Navaho'. Disease resistant. Will grow in north Florida.

'Black Satin'. Semierect, thornless, vigorous. Shiny black, very tart fruit. Does better in Upper and Middle South.

'Boysen' and 'Thornless Boysen'. Most commonly grown trailing types. Large, reddish berries with sweet-tart flavor, delightful aroma.

'Brazos'. Erect. Productive, disease resistant, with large, fairly firm, tart fruit. Good for mild-winter areas such as Texas, Florida, Gulf Coast states.

'Cherokee'. Erect, thorny. Firm berries with excellent flavor. Resists anthracnose. Heat tolerant. Good for Gulf Coast, north Florida.

'Chester'. Semierect, thornless, heavy bearing, and resistant to cane blight. Very cold tolerant. Best in Upper, Middle, and Lower South.

'Cheyenne'. Erect. Vigorous and moderately thorny. Large, firm fruit with very good flavor. Excellent for freezing. Resistant to rust.

'Chickasaw'. Erect, thorny canes. Very productive. Large fruit.

'Choctaw'. Erect. Ripens early, producing berries with excellent flavor and very small seeds. Heat tolerant.

'Darrow'. Erect. A heavy bearer, with large berries ripening over a long season. Best in Upper, Middle, and Lower South.

'Dirksen'. Semierect, thornless selection with large, sweet, glossy black berries. Resistant to anthracnose, leaf spot, and mildew. Good selection for Delaware, Maryland, and Virginia.

'Flordagrand'. Vigorous, thorny evergreen canes are somewhat trailing. Large, tasty berries. Well adapted to hot, humid summers and mild winters. Plant with 'Oklawaha' for best pollination.

'Gem'. Trailing, thorny canes. Excellent berries. Resists rosette.

'Hull'. Erect, thornless. Heavy bearing, with large, glossy black fruit that holds up well in heat. Best in Upper, Middle, and Lower South.

'Illini Hardy'. Erect, very thorny. Cold hardy. Introduced by University of Illinois. Best in southern Midwest and Upper South.

'Kiowa'. Erect, vigorous, very thorny. Extra-large fruit matures over a long season. Performs well in areas where 'Shawnee' succeeds. Resistant to orange rust. Among the best in tolerance to viral diseases.

'Natchez'. Erect, thornless. Early, heavy yield of large, firm berries. Good disease resistance.

'Navaho'. Erect, thornless. Firm, sweet fruit that ripens late. Resistant to rosette but susceptible to orange rust. Heat tolerant. Will grow in north Florida.

'Oklawaha'. Trailing. Vigorous, partially evergreen to evergreen. Developed for Florida and other areas with hot, humid summers and mild winters. Large, good-tasting berries. Best production when planted near 'Flordagrand' for pollination.

'Osage'. Thornless, erect. Firm, glossy fruit with excellent flavor. Lasts well after harvest.

'Ouachita'. Erect, thornless. Large, sweet fruit that lasts well in storage. Resembles 'Apache.'

'Prime Jan'. Erect, thorny. Fruits on new canes in late summer and 2-year-old canes in spring. Very productive. Medium-size, sweet-tart fruit. 'Prime Jim' is similar, but with slightly less sweet fruit on an even more erect plant. Poor performers in Texas. 'Prime-Ark 45' has very sweet fruit that lasts well in storage. 'Prime-Ark Freedom' is erect and thornless, with very large, flavorful berries.

'Rosborough'. Erect. Resembles 'Brazos', but fruit is smaller, sweeter, ripens earlier. Heat tolerant. Good choice for Texas.

'Shawnee'. Erect. Heavy crop ripens late, over a long period. Large, glossy, sweet black berries. Very susceptible to rosette.

'Thornfree'. Semierect, thornless canes bearing large crop of tart berries. Productive from Maryland south to North Carolina and west to Arkansas.

'Triple Crown'. Semierect; late. An improved 'Chester' type with large, very flavorful berries. Vigorous canes. Susceptible to rosette. Best in Upper, Middle, and Lower South.

HOW TO GROW BLACKBERRIES

PLANTING & FEEDING Blackberries need deep, well-drained soil and regular moisture throughout the growing season. They are best located on slight slopes, and a northern exposure helps keep them dormant until spring freezes are past. Don't put plants where they will be in standing water during the dormant season. Rows of all kinds should be about 10 ft. apart. Plant trailing blackberries 5–8 ft. apart, erect blackberries 2–2½ ft. apart, and semierect blackberries 5–6 ft. apart.

Plant bare-root blackberries in late winter to early spring in the Upper and Middle South (USDA 6-7), and in late fall to early winter in the Lower and Coastal South (USDA 8-9). Set new bare-root plants an inch deeper than they grew at the garden center, their crowns covered with an inch of soil. Plant container-grown plants so that the top of the root ball is even with the soil surface.

Feed blackberries with a complete, balanced fertilizer just before new growth begins (rapidly swelling buds will tip you off).

PRUNING & TRAINING Blackberry roots are perennial, but the canes are biennial: They develop and grow one year, flower and fruit the second, then die. Hence the need to distinguish between first- and second-year canes. 'Prime Jan' and 'Prime Jim' are exceptions. They yield two crops per season and have their own pruning regimen.

Trailing and semierect types should be trained fanwise onto a trellis; after harvest, cut to the ground all canes that have fruited, and train remaining canes onto the trellis. Canes of semierect types often become more upright as plants mature.

Erect types don't need support, but tying them to wire helps organize the canes. In midsummer of the first year, cut the canes of all kinds (except 'Prime Jan' and 'Prime Jim') to 2½ ft. to force side growth. Late in the dormant season, cut resulting side branches to 12–15 in. After canes bear fruit in the second year, cut them to the ground. Start the process over with new canes growing from the ground.

'Prime Jan' and 'Prime Jim' produce their first berries in fall on the top third of each first-year cane, and the second crop the following summer on the bottom two-thirds of each second-year cane. Pruning is done in stages. After the fall harvest, cut off the upper (just harvested) portion of each cane; after the subsequent summer harvest, cut out the remainder of each cane that has fruited.

CHALLENGES Blackberries are subject to many pests and diseases, including scale, borers, anthracnose, leaf spot, powdery mildew, rust, and cane blight; for best success, start with healthy plants from a reputable supplier. Also look for disease-resistant selections. Blackberries are also susceptible to verticillium wilt, so don't locate them where potatoes, tomatoes, eggplants, or peppers have grown in the preceding 3 years. To control red-berry mites, spider mites, and whiteflies, apply a dormant spray containing lime sulfur once in winter, then again as buds are about to break.

Rosette (also called double blossom) is a serious fungal disease of blackberries in the South. New growth and blossoms of infected plants are deformed, and fruit fails to set. Most selections are susceptible, though 'Navaho' and 'Gem' have shown some resistance. Good sanitation is the best control. Removal of infected canes after harvest may help, but severely affected plants require removal of all canes at ground level; the resulting new growth will be free of the fungus. Burn or discard prunings. Keep plantings weed free. Wild blackberries can spread the disease, so be sure to plant well away from them.

A new pest, spotted-wing drosophila (a vinegar fly) has found its way into Southern gardens. It makes tiny holes over sunken areas in ripe fruit, including blackberries. So far, the only control is to completely cover plants with fine netting.

BLETILLA STRIATA

CHINESE GROUND ORCHID, HARDY ORCHID
Orchidaceae
Terrestrial orchid from pseudobulb

🌱 US, MS, LS, CS; USDA 6-9

◐ **FILTERED SUN OR PARTIAL SHADE**

💧 **REGULAR WATER DURING GROWTH AND BLOOM**

Bletilla striata

This native of China, Japan, and Tibet is a natural companion to ferns and wildflowers. In late spring to early summer, each 1- to 1½-ft. stem carries up to 12 pinkish purple, 2-in. blossoms resembling cattleya orchids. Bloom lasts for about 6 weeks. Medium to yellowish green leaves, three to six to a plant, remain attractive into early fall. 'Big Bog' is a vigorous, large-flowered selection. 'First Kiss' has white-edged leaves and small white blossoms flushed purple on the lip. 'Murasaki Shikibu' has pale lavender flowers with a bluish-lavender lip. Hybrid 'Kate' can reach 3 ft. tall, with up to 35 light lavender, yellow-lipped flowers per stalk. *B. s. alba* is a white-flowered form. *B. s.* 'Albostriata' bears light pink blossoms above leaves striped in green and white.

CARE

Grow in pots or in ground. Plant pseudobulbs anytime during dormancy (late fall to early spring), 1 ft. apart, with tops 1 in. below soil surface. Plant in humus-rich, well-drained soil; mulch if temperatures will drop below 20°F. Protect from slugs and snails when leaves emerge. Taper off watering when foliage begins to yellow in fall; discontinue when leaves have died

B

back. Plant forms large clumps that can be divided in early spring, before growth starts. (It blooms better, however, when crowded.)

BLUEBERRY

Ericaceae
Deciduous shrub

✎ **ZONES VARY BY TYPE**

☼ **FULL SUN**

💧 **REGULAR WATER**

Blueberries

Native to eastern North America, blueberries thrive in conditions that suit rhododendrons and azaleas, to which they are related. Most blueberries grown for fruit are also handsome plants for hedges or shrub borders—and they grow well in containers. Dark green or blue-green leaves to 3 in. long change to red, orange, or yellow combinations in autumn. Spring flowers are small, white or pinkish, and urn shaped. Summer fruit is very decorative, not to mention delicious. Set plants about 3 ft. apart for an informal hedge; as individual shrubs, space Northern and Southern highbush 4 ft. apart and rabbiteye 6 ft. apart. Grow at least two different selections for better pollination, resulting in larger berries and bigger yields per plant. For a long harvest season, choose types that ripen at different times. Full sun is essential for the sweetest berries. Those grown in partial sun may be tart.

Rabbiteye and Southern highbush blueberries take extended heat better than Northern highbush kinds. Choose the type best suited to your region.

The following are some of the major types of blueberries grown.

(For ornamental relatives, see *Vaccinium*.)

Northern highbush blueberries. Selections of *Vaccinium corymbosum*, these blueberries dislike mild winters and extended summer heat, so they are recommended primarily for the Upper and Middle South (USDA 6-7). Most grow upright to 6 ft. or more; a few are rather spreading and top out at under 5 ft. Most ripen their berries between June and August.

'Berkeley'. Midseason. Open, spreading, tall. Large, light blue berries.

'Bluecrop'. Midseason. Attractive, tall, erect shrub. Large berries with excellent flavor.

'Bluejay'. Early midseason. Very vigorous, tall plant. Large crop of medium-size, mild-flavored fruit that holds well on the bush.

'Bountiful Blue'. Midseason. Compact, attractive plant with bluish leaves. Large, sweet fruit is produced in abundance.

'Coville'. Late. Very attractive, tall, open, spreading shrub with unusually large leaves. Long clusters of very large, light blue berries.

'Darrow'. Late. Vigorous, upright grower. Very large berries, up to the size of a quarter. Heavy producer.

'Duke'. Early. Upright plant. Firm, large fruit. Heavy producer.

'Earliblue'. Early. Tall and erect, with large, heavy-textured leaves. Large berries of excellent flavor.

'Elliott'. Late. Tall and upright plant; medium to large berries with excellent flavor.

'Herbert'. Late. Vigorous, open, spreading plant. Berries are among the largest and best flavored.

'Liberty'. Late. Strong-growing, upright plant with large, firm, flavorful berries that keep for a long time.

'Patriot'. Midseason. Large, firm, tasty berries. Consistently high yields.

'Peach Sorbet'. Mid-season. Compact grower to just 1½–2 ft. tall and wide. Foliage in shades of emerald green, peachy pink, and orange. Large, sweet fruit.

'Pink Lemonade'. Mid- to late season. The first pink blueberry. Attractive plant with medium-size, sweet, mild berries.

'Top Hat'. Late. Dwarf hybrid, just 2 ft. tall and 1½ ft. wide; excellent choice for containers. Showy in bloom; produces firm,

HOW TO GROW BLUEBERRIES

SOIL Blueberries need moist, fertile, well-drained soil that is quite acidic (pH 4.5–5.5) and contains lots of organic matter. Where soil pH isn't acidic enough, create proper conditions by adding sulfur and peat; or grow plants in containers filled with acidic potting mix.

PLANTING & WATERING Blueberries are available bare-root or in containers and are best planted in late fall to early spring. Position crown so that it is ½ in. above the ground. During the first 3 years, give plants a deep soaking—the equivalent of 1 in. of rain—every week during the growing season. In subsequent years, keep them moist (especially during fruiting period) but don't subject them to standing water. Avoid overhead irrigation, which can encourage mildew on leaves and gray mold (botrytis) on fruit.

MULCHING A 4- to 6-in.-thick mulch of pine straw, ground bark, or the like will discourage weeds, protect roots, and help conserve soil moisture. Blueberries have fine roots near the soil surface, so don't cultivate around the plants.

FEEDING Don't fertilize at all the first year, and feed only lightly the second and third years. After that, fertilize once per year in early spring with a slow-release, acid-forming, complete fertilizer.

PRUNING Plants often produce so many fruit buds that berries are undersized and growth of plants slows down. Pruning will prevent overbearing. Keep first-year plants from bearing by stripping off flowers. On older plants, thin out some of the weaker branches each year and reduce the height of upright shoots so that a ladder will not be needed to harvest.

CHALLENGES Netting will keep birds from getting the berries before you do. In home gardens, blueberries don't usually suffer from serious pests or diseases requiring regular controls. Blueberry stem blight, however, can be a severe problem for blueberries in the Southeast. The disease enters plants through wounds in the bark and causes rapid death of some or many stems, which drop their leaves and turn dark brown to black. Young plants may be killed outright. There is no chemical control; prompt pruning of infected stems back to healthy wood is the best way to limit the disease. Stop fertilizing after July to reduce succulent new growth, which is more vulnerable to infection. Avoid the selections 'Bluechip' and 'Bounty', which are very susceptible. Fungicides may be needed to control a fungus called mummyberry that causes berries to shrivel and discolor. Quickly remove and throw away any mummified fruit to prevent further spread.

bright blue berries.

Southern highbush blueberries. These relatively new selections are hybrids of *Vaccinium corymbosum*, *V. ashei*, and *V. darrowi*. They combine the Northern highbush fruit quality with the rabbiteye tolerance for heat and mild winters, and they ripen up to a month earlier than rabbiteye blueberries do. They generally can be grown in the Middle, Lower, and Coastal South (USDA 7-9) and have performed well in southern Georgia and the Florida Panhandle. Some new low-chill selections released by the University of Florida do well as far south as central Florida. Most reach 4–6 ft. tall. Form

varies from upright to spreading. Recommended selections include the following.

'Blue Ridge'. Midseason. Small, dense shrub. Large, high-quality fruit. Performs best in Middle South.

'Blue Suede'. Early. Vigorous grower with large, light blue fruit; very good flavor. Long harvest and dependable red fall color.

'Emerald'. Early. Vigorous, high-yielding bush with large, very tasty berries. Low-chill selection for north and central Florida.

'Georgiagem'. Early. Large and upright. Medium-size fruit with excellent flavor. Does well in Middle and Lower South.

'Jewel'. Early. Large, firm berries

are tart until fully ripe. Low-chill selection good for north Florida.

'Magnolia'. Midseason. Vigorous, spreading plant. Medium-size fruit of fine quality.

'Sharpblue'. Early. Large, fast-growing shrub. Large, light blue berries with sweet-tart flavor.

'Star'. Early. Medium-size bush with spreading habit. Large, deep blue fruit of excellent quality. Low-chill selection good for north Florida.

'Summit'. Midseason to late. Semiupright plant; large, excellent-quality berries.

'Sunshine Blue'. Midseason. Compact, reaching only 3 ft. tall; makes an attractive landscape plant. Large, light blue berries with tangy flavor. Self-fertile. Tolerates a higher soil pH than other blueberries.

Rabbiteye blueberries. Zones MS, LS, CS; USDA 7-9. Like Southern highbush blueberries, these selections of the Southeast native *Vaccinium ashei* are adapted to hot, humid summers and mild winters. They are often taller and wider than highbush plants and ripen their large, light blue berries from May into August, depending on location and selection. They're easier to establish and maintain than Southern highbush in most areas where both can be grown. Can be grown as far south as northern Florida. Foliage has good red fall color. The following list includes some of the most flavorful selections.

'Austin'. Early. Upright, spreading, productive. Large berries with good flavor like that of a huckleberry.

'Baldwin'. Late. Vigorous, upright, and productive. Dark blue, medium-size berries with good flavor. Holds well on the bush.

'Beckyblue'. Early. Tall, upright bush with medium to large berries of excellent quality.

'Brightwell'. Midseason. Large, sweet, light blue berries.

'Briteblue'. Late. Open, spreading form. Large, light blue berries with fair flavor.

'Centurion'. Late, after 'Tifblue'. Vigorous, upright, and productive. Dark blue, medium to large fruit with good flavor.

'Chaucer'. Midseason. Vigorous, tall, and spreading. Medium to large berries with fair to good flavor. Blooms early; not for colder areas.

'Choice'. Late. Vigorous, tall, and productive plant. Dark blue, small to medium-size berries of good quality. Blooms early; not for colder areas.

'Climax'. Early. Upright and spreading. Good pollenizer. Medium-size, dark blue berries.

'Delite'. Midseason to late. Medium-large, light blue fruit. Excellent flavor. Blooms in very early spring; flowers may be killed in areas with late freezes in spring.

'Powderblue'. Midseason to late. Vigorous, tall, and productive. Large, powder-blue berries of excellent quality. Resists cracking after rain.

'Premier'. Early. Large, light blue fruit. Excellent quality; one of the best early selections.

'Tifblue'. Midseason to late. Vigorous, upright. Good commercial selection. Firm, light blue berries with excellent flavor (tart until completely ripe).

'Woodward'. Early. Shorter, more spreading than other rabbiteyes. Rather soft, light blue berries, tart until fully ripe.

BOLTONIA ASTEROIDES
FALSE ASTER
Asteraceae
Perennials

US, MS, LS, CS; USDA 6-9

FULL SUN OR LIGHT SHADE

REGULAR WATER

Boltonia asteroides latisquama 'Jim Crockett'

Native to eastern U.S. Much loved for the masses of showy blooms it bears in late summer and fall. Tall stems bear broad, mounded clusters of yellow-centered, white, pink, or pale to deeper purple flowers about ¾ in. across; blossoms resemble Michaelmas daisies (*Symphyotrichum novi-belgii*). Good for the back of the border, it grows to 6 ft. or taller and about 3 ft. wide; may need support to keep from flopping over after rain or overhead watering. Needs moist, fertile soil containing lots of organic matter and will tolerate very damp soil.

'Pink Beauty' has pink flowers. *B. a. latisquama* has larger flowers than those of the species, up to 1¼ in. across. Its selections include 'Jim Crockett', with violet flowers and bushy growth to about 2 ft. tall; 'Nana', another 2-footer, with lavender-pink blooms; and 'Snowbank', to 5 ft. tall, with pure white flowers.

BORAGO OFFICINALIS
BORAGE
Boraginaceae
Annual

US, MS, LS, CS, TS; USDA 6-11

FULL SUN OR PARTIAL SHADE

MODERATE WATER

Borago officinalis

Delightful sky-blue, star-shaped flowers make this European native a kitchen-garden favorite. Plant forms a rounded clump 2–3 ft. high, 1½–2 ft. wide. Bristly, gray-green leaves to 4–6 in. long are edible, with a cucumber-like flavor; use small, tender leaves in salads, pickle them, or cook them as you would greens. Many people grow the plant simply for its summer flowers: pretty, star-shaped, inch-wide blue blossoms that nod in leafy clusters from branched stems. Cut flowers are attractive in arrangements and can also be used as a decorative garnish for iced drinks, green salads, and fruit compotes.

Tolerates poor soil. Reseeds itself, but deep taproot makes transplanting difficult. In most of the South, the best way to start borage is to sow seeds in place in spring, after the danger of frost is past. In the Coastal and Tropical South (USDA 9-11), sow in fall and grow as a fall-into-spring crop.

BOUGAINVILLEA
Nyctaginaceae
Evergreen shrubby vines

CS, TS; USDA 9-11; OR GROW IN POTS

FULL SUN

MODERATE TO REGULAR WATER

Bougainvillea 'Barbara Karst'

For sheer spectacle and exuberance, no flowering vines surpass bougainvilleas. Native to Central and South America, they're common in Florida, South Texas, and along the Gulf and south Atlantic coasts. And with the advent of low-growing, shrubby types that can be bought in full bloom and grown in containers, more Southerners can enjoy these plants than ever before. Established vines withstand light frosts, but plan to take the plants indoors to a sunny window for the winter if you live where temperatures drop below 20°F.

Bougainvillea's vibrant colors come not from its small, inconspicuous true flowers, but from the three large bracts that surround them. Heaviest bloom

TOP: Bougainvillea 'California Gold'; *B.* 'Purple Queen'; *MIDDLE: B.* 'San Diego Red'; *BOTTOM: B.* 'Orange King'; *B.* 'Mary Palmer Enchantment'

HOW TO GROW BOUGAINVILLEAS

PLANTING Plant in a sunny spot in spring, after the last frost. Provide well-drained, slightly acid soil; alkaline soil can cause chlorosis (yellow leaves with green veins). Roots do not knit soil together in a firm root ball, and they are highly sensitive to disturbance. To minimize shock when planting, cut off container bottom; then set both plant and container in planting hole. Gently slide container up over the plant, filling in with soil as you go. Don't worry about damaging upper part of plant as you do so; stems are pliant, with little horizontal growth. Fasten shoots to a sturdy support so they won't whip in wind. Strong gusts can shred leaves against sharp thorns along stems.

FEEDING & WATERING Fertilize when growing season begins and again in early summer; a 6-8-10 fertilizer high in micronutrients is best. Established plants are quite drought tolerant and need little watering, except if growing in pots. Water thoroughly when foliage wilts, making sure excess water can drain away quickly. Avoid frequent, light watering.

PRUNING Don't be afraid to prune to shape or rejuvenate the plant. Pinch off spent blooms to keep new ones coming. Heavy pruning is best done after the blooming period. Nip back long stems during the growing season to produce more flowering wood. Shrubby forms and heavily pruned plants make good self-supporting container plants for terrace or patio. Without support and with occasional corrective pruning, bougainvillea becomes a broad, sprawling shrub; a bank or ground cover; or an attractive choice for hanging baskets.

comes during the cooler months of spring and fall, when days and nights are nearly equal in length. Plants go dormant in summer. Both single- and double-flowering kinds are sold; double sorts can look messy, as they hold faded blooms for a long time.

These vines are fast, vigorous growers, reaching 15–30 ft., depending on the selection. Stiff stems are armed with long, needlelike thorns and are moderately to densely clothed in medium green, 2½-in., heart-shaped leaves. Bougainvilleas are superb trained against walls or on sturdy fences, trellises, or arbors. They have no means of

attachment (though their thorns help them scramble through shrubs and trees), so you must tie stems to the support while the vine is young.

All of the following are tall-growing vines unless otherwise noted. Most are hybrids produced from *B. glabra* and *B. spectabilis* (from Brazil) and *B. peruviana* (from Colombia and Peru).

'Afterglow'. Heavy bloomer with yellow-orange blossoms. Open growth, sparse foliage.

'Barbara Karst'. Bright red in sun, bluish crimson in shade; blooms young and for a long period. Vigorous growth. Fast

comeback after frost. A popular selection.

'California Gold' ('Sunset'). Deep golden yellow. Blooms young.

'Camarillo Fiesta'. Hot pink to coral to gold blend.

'Cherry Blossom'. Double-flowered rose-pink, with centers of white to pale green.

'Crimson Jewel'. Vigorous, shrubby, sprawling plant. Good in containers, as shrub, or as sunny bank cover. Lower growth, better color than 'Temple Fire'. Heavy bloom, long season.

'Don Mario'. Large and vigorous vine with huge clusters of deep purple-red blooms.

'Jamaica White'. White bracts (sometimes tinged with pink) veined in light green. Blooms young. Moderately vigorous.

'James Walker'. Big, reddish purple bracts on a big vine.

'La Jolla'. Bright red bracts; compact, shrubby habit. Good shrub or container plant.

'Lavender Queen'. An improved *B. spectabilis*, with bigger bracts, heavier bloom.

'Manila Red'. Double, magenta-red blossoms are carried in heavy clusters.

'Mary Palmer's Enchantment'. Bracts are pure white. Quite

vigorous, very large-growing vine.

'Mrs. Butt' ('Crimson Lake'). Old-fashioned type with good crimson color. Needs lots of heat for bloom. Moderately vigorous.

'Oo-La-La'. Vibrant magenta red. Compact, trailing form to 1½ ft. tall, 6–8 ft. wide; good for hanging baskets. Blooms over a long season.

'Orange King'. Bronzy orange. Open growth. Needs long summer; won't take frost.

'Purple Queen'. Deep purple bracts; compact grower. Can reach 15 ft. with support; as a trailer, it grows 1½ ft. tall, 6–8 ft. wide. Very popular.

'Raspberry Ice'. Shrubby, mounding, spreading. Leaves have golden yellow margins. Red-tinged new leaves; cherry-red bracts. Good hanging basket plant. One of the hardiest.

'Rosea'. Large, rose-red bracts on large vine.

'Rosenka'. Gold bracts age to pink. Can be held to shrub proportions if the occasional wild shoot is pruned out.

'San Diego Red' ('San Diego', 'Scarlett O'Hara'). One of the best, with large, deep green leaves that hold well in mild winters and deep red bracts over a long season. Vigorous, hardy, and high climbing. Can be trained to tree form by staking and pruning.

'Singapore Pink' ('Silhouette'). Bright pink. Shrubby and compact; can easily be kept to 3–4 ft. high and wide. Thornless.

'Singapore White'. White bloomer. Shrubby, compact plant; can be held to 3–4 ft. high and wide. Thornless.

'Tahitian Dawn'. Big vine with gold bracts aging to rosy purple.

'Temple Fire'. Shrublike growth to 4 ft. high, 6 ft. wide. Partially deciduous. Bronze-red.

'Texas Dawn'. Choice, vigorous plant. Purplish pink bracts form large sprays of color.

'Torch Glow'. An oddity: an erect, multistemmed plant to 6 ft. high. Needs no support. Reddish pink bracts grow close to the stems and are partially hidden by foliage.

'White Madonna'. Pure white bracts.

B. spectabilis (*B. brasiliensis*). Hardy and vigorous. Blooms well in cool summers. Purple bracts.

BOUVARDIA

Rubiaceae
Evergreen shrubs

CS, TS; USDA 9-11

PARTIAL SHADE

WATER NEEDS VARY BY SPECIES

Bouvardia longiflora

These plants are valued for their showy clusters of tubular flowers; their growth habit is loose, often straggling. One type has fragrant blossoms, but it is also the most tender and looks poorest after flowers are gone. The unscented, red-flowered species are hardier and easier to grow. All appreciate

well-drained soil and midday shade; very heat tolerant. To encourage compact growth, prune lightly after bloom.

B. longiflora. SWEET BOUVARDIA. From Mexico. Jasmine-scented, 3-in., snow-white flowers appear at almost any time; excellent in bouquets. Plant is 2–3 ft. high and 2 ft. wide, with paired, 2-in. leaves. Pinch out stem tips to make bushier. If soil is poor, grow in pots or raised beds in rich, fast-draining soil mix. Provide regular water. 'Albatross' is the form most widely sold; it has larger flowers than the species. 'Stephanie' is more compact and floriferous.

B. ternifolia (*B. jacquinii*). SCARLET BOUVARDIA. Native to Texas, Mexico. To 3 ft. tall, 2½–3 ft. wide, with 2-in. leaves in whorls of three or four. Produces unscented, inch-long, red flowers in loose clusters at branch ends in summer and early autumn. Forms are available with pink, rose, or coral blossoms. Prefers neutral to acid soil. Little water.

BRACHYSCOME

SWAN RIVER DAISY
Asteraceae
Annuals and perennials

US, MS, LS, CS, TS; USDA 6-11

FULL SUN

REGULAR WATER

Brachyscome **hybrid**

Neat, charming Australian daisies bear a profusion of ¾- to 1-in., blue, pink, or white flowers in spring and summer. Finely divided leaves form a mound about 1 ft. tall, 1½ ft. across. Useful at the front of a border, as fillers in pots, and in rock gardens.

B. hybrids. Perennials. 'City Lights' has light lavender-blue flowers. 'New Amethyst' has blooms of dark purple. 'Toucan Tango' flowers are blue with green centers. The Surdaisy series mauve, pink, white, and yellow.

B. iberidifolia. Annual. Flowers are usually blue, but white and pink forms are offered. Sow seeds where plants are to grow—in fall in Florida, in spring elsewhere. 'Blue Star' has blue flowers with unique tubular petals. 'Blue Splendor' features different shades of blue, and central disk varies in color, too—it may be yellow or black. 'Little Missy' has blue flowers with a yellow central disk surrounded by a band of white.

B. multifida. Perennial. Very similar to *B. iberidifolia*, with blooms in blue, pink, purple, soft yellow, or white. Easy to propagate by cuttings.

BRAHEA

Arecaceae
Palms

ZONES VARY BY SPECIES

FULL SUN

LITTLE OR NO WATER

Brahea armata

These fan palms from Mexico resemble *Washingtonia* palms, but are shorter growing and less cold hardy. Fanlike leaves reach 3–6 ft. across. All of the species listed here can tolerate drought.

B. armata. BLUE FAN PALM. Zones LS, CS, TS; USDA 8-11. Hardy to 15°F. Grows slowly to 40 ft. tall, with top spreading to 15–20 ft. Leaves are a silvery blue in color, almost white. Creamy flowers in summer. Takes heat and wind.

B. brandegeei. SAN JOSE HESPER PALM. Zone TS; USDA 10-11. Hardy to 26°F. Slow grower with slender, flexible trunk. Reaches 40 ft. tall and 15 ft. wide. Light gray-green foliage. Trunk sheds oldest leaves.

B. dulcis. MEXICAN CLIFF PALM. Zones LS, CS, TS; USDA 8-11. Hardy to 18°F. To 20 ft. high, 8 ft. wide. Trunk may be solitary or suckering, foliage green or silvery blue. Fronds are smaller and more delicate than those of most fan palms. Tough and drought resistant; often grows right out of rocky cliff sides in its native range.

BREYNIA DISTICHA NIVOSA

SNOW BUSH
Phyllanthaceae
Evergreen shrub

TS; USDA 10-11; OR HOUSEPLANT

FULL SUN OR LIGHT SHADE; BRIGHT INDIRECT LIGHT

REGULAR WATER

Breynia disticha nivosa

Pacific Island native. Delicate, open growth to 3–4 ft. tall and wide, with gracefully arching branches in zigzag pattern. Thin, roundish leaves are rich green variegated with white; they are held nearly opposite each other along the branches. Flowers insignificant. Can naturalize in humid tropical or subtropical regions. Selection 'Roseo Picta', sweet pea bush or calico plant, has leaves that are mottled red, pink, white, and green. Colorful plant, though prone to mites in dry indoor air.

B

BRIZA MAXIMA

RATTLESNAKE GRASS,
QUAKING GRASS
Poaceae
Annual grass

🌿 **US, MS, LS, CS, TS; USDA 6-11**

☼ **FULL SUN**

◌ **NO WATERING NEEDED**

Briza maxima

Native to Mediterranean region. Delicate, graceful ornamental grass; attractive in fresh or dried arrangements. Grows 1–2 ft. high. Leaves are ¼ in. wide, to 6 in. long. Clusters of nodding, ½-in.-long, seed-bearing spikelets (like rattlesnake rattles) can reach 4 in. long. These papery, straw-colored clusters dangle on threadlike stems. Scatter seed where plants are to grow; thin seedlings to 1 ft. apart. *B. media* is similar but perennial; grows 3 ft. tall.

KIDS
LOVE THE
LOOK—AND
SOUND—OF
RATTLE-
SNAKE GRASS
IN BLOOM.

BROCCOLI

Brassicaceae
Biennial grown as cool-season annual

🌿 **US, MS, LS, CS, TS; USDA 6-11**

☼ **FULL SUN**

💧 **REGULAR WATER**

Broccoli

Broccoli is the easiest of the cole crops (cabbage and its close relatives) for the home gardener. Probably a Mediterranean native, this cool-season crop grows 2–3 ft. tall, with a branching habit. Its central stalk bears a cluster of green or purple flower buds; when that cluster is removed, side shoots lengthen and produce smaller clusters. Many Southerners grow two crops each year—one in spring and one in fall. To produce the mammoth heads you admire in seed catalogs or the grocery store, you'd need longer periods of cool weather than we have over most of the South, but you can realistically expect heads to grow to 4–8 in. across.

To get a jump on the growing season, always start broccoli from transplants (you can buy them at the garden center or grow your own from seed in cell-packs). Broccoli doesn't grow well after warm weather arrives in spring, and a hard freeze in fall will kill it. For a spring crop, set out seedlings 4 weeks before the last frost; for a fall crop, plant in late summer or early fall. In the Coastal South (USDA 9), plant between September and March; in the Tropical South (USDA 10-11), plant between September and January.

For spring planting, choose early-maturing types, so the heads will form before hot weather arrives. Try 'Di Ciccio' (50 days from transplanting to harvest), 'Green Comet' (55 days), 'Green Duke' (50 days), 'Green Goliath' (55 days), 'Packman' (57 days), and 'Premium Crop' (58 days). All of these are also good for fall planting. In the Coastal and Tropical South, late-maturing 'Waltham 29' (80 days) is another good selection for fall planting. Production of side shoots is usually more dependable in fall. Selections noted for extended production of side shoots include 'Green Comet', 'Packman', and 'Waltham 29'. For Romanesco, see Cauliflower.

CARE

Broccoli needs fertile, well-drained soil. Set transplants 1–1½ ft. apart in rows 2–3 ft. apart. Feed with water-soluble 20-20-20 fertilizer. Three weeks after planting, sprinkle ½ cup of 10-10-10 fertilizer per 10 ft. of row around plants. Water regularly to maintain steady, rapid growth; don't let the soil dry out. Harvest when the hundreds of tiny flower buds that form the head are still green and tightly closed; a head showing yellow flowers is past its prime. Cut the stem 5–6 in. below the head. Side shoots are usually ready to harvest 2 to 3 weeks after you cut the central head—but if the weather gets too warm, they'll quickly bloom.

A number of pests plague broccoli; they are usually more troublesome in spring than in fall. To prevent a buildup of soil-borne pests, plant in a different site each year. Club root is a serious fungal pest in acid soils; apply lime, if necessary, to raise the pH to at least 6.5. Floating row covers do a good job of controlling insects such as cabbage loopers, cabbageworms, cutworms, and root maggots. You can also control cutworms and root maggots by ringing the base of the plant with a collar made from cardboard. *Bacillus thuringiensis* (*Bt* or spinosad) applied according to label directions controls cabbageworms and loopers.

BROUSSONETIA PAPYRIFERA

PAPER MULBERRY
Moraceae
Deciduous tree

🌿 **US, MS, LS, CS, TS; USDA 6-11**

☼ **FULL SUN**

◌◑● **LITTLE TO REGULAR WATER**

Broussonetia papyrifera 'Laciniata'

Native to China, Korea, and Japan. Common name comes from inner bark, used for making paper and Polynesian tapa cloth. Quite valuable as a shade tree where soil and climate limit choices. Tolerates heat, drought, strong winds, city pollution, and stony, sterile, or alkaline soils.

Moderate to fast growth to 50 ft., with dense, broad crown reaching 40 ft. across; often considerably smaller and more shrublike in gardens. Suckering, weedy habit can be problem in rainy climates and highly culti-vated gardens. Good in rough bank plantings. Smooth gray bark can become ridged and furrowed with age, creating handsome old specimens. Heart-shaped, some-times lobed, 4- to 8-in. leaves are green and rough textured on the upper surface, gray and velvety underneath; edges are toothed. Blooms in spring. Flowers on male trees are catkins; on female trees, rounded flower heads are followed by red fruit if a male tree is growing nearby.

BROWALLIA

AMETHYST FLOWER
Solanaceae
Annuals and perennials

🌿 **US, MS, LS, CS, TS; USDA 6-11**

◐ **PARTIAL SHADE**

💧 **REGULAR WATER**

Browallia 'Endless Illumination'

Choice plants for connoisseurs of blue flowers. Bear one-sided clusters of lobelia-like blooms in brilliant blue, violet, or white; blue and violet flowers are striking because of contrasting white eye or throat. Bloom profusely in warm shade or filtered sunlight. Graceful in hanging baskets or pots. Fine cut flowers. Sow seeds in early spring for summer bloom, in fall for winter color in warmest-winter areas or indoors. You can lift plants in fall, cut back, and pot; new growth will produce flowers through winter in warm spots.

B. americana (*B. elata*). Annual. From Tropical South America. Branching plant, 1–2 ft. high and wide, with roundish leaves. Violet or blue flowers ½ in. long, ½ in. across, are borne among leaves.

B. hybrids. These grow about 1 ft. tall and wide. 'Endless Flirtation' is white; 'Endless Celebration' white with purple flush; 'Endless Illumination' purple; and 'Endless Sensation; lavender-blue.

B. speciosa. Tender perennial usually grown as annual. Sprawling, to 1–2 ft. high, nearly a foot wide. Flowers dark purple above, pale lilac beneath, 1½–2 in. across. 'Blue Bells Improved', with lavender-blue blooms, grows 10 in. tall, needs no pinching to make it branch. 'Marine Bells' has deep indigo blossoms, 'Silver Bells' white flowers.

BRUGMANSIA

ANGEL'S TRUMPET
Solanaceae
Evergreen to semievergreen shrubs

🌿 **LS, CS, TS; USDA 8-11; OR GROW IN POTS**

☼ ◐ **FULL SUN OR LIGHT SHADE**

💧 **REGULAR WATER**

◈ **ALL PARTS ARE POISONOUS IF INGESTED**

Brugmansia x *cubensis*
'Charles Grimaldi'

Thanks to the tropical look of their oversize leaves and huge, exotic blossoms, brugmansias are wildly popular. Related to jimsonweeds, these South American natives are often confused with plants in the genus *Datura*—but brugmansias are large, woody shrubs with typically pendent flowers and bean-shaped seedpods; daturas are lower growing and herbaceous, with upward-pointing flowers and swollen, spiny seedpods. Most brugmansias bloom in summer and autumn. For *Datura*, see page 276.

B. 'Angel's Blushing Beauty'. Strong-growing, upright plant with 9-in.-long, soft-pink flowers with fluted edges. Heavy bloomer.

B. 'Angel's Summer Dream.' Dwarf plant, to about 3 ft. tall, with strong lateral branching pattern. Starts blooming at just 1–2 ft. tall, with orange-yellow, sweetly scented flowers to 6 in. long. Blooms over a long period. Excellent for containers and hanging baskets.

B. x candida. Fast growing to 10–12 ft. tall and wide; dull green leaves to 1 ft. long. Sweet-scented, 8- to 12-in.-long, cream to white trumpets hang straight down

TOP: Brugmansia versicolor 'Ecuador Pink'; *BOTTOM: B.* x *insignis* 'Jamaica Yellow'; *B.* 'Sunset'

from the branches. 'Double White' has creamy white double blossoms, distinctly grayish green foliage. 'Grand Marnier' has large, peachy pink flowers with an especially sweet perfume.

B. 'Cherub'. Seedling from *B.* x *versicolor* 'Ecuador Pink'. To 5–7 ft. tall, with thick, glossy, deep green leaves and a profusion of salmon-pink flowers over a long period.

B. x cubensis 'Charles Grimaldi'. Fast growing to 10–12 ft. tall and 10 ft. wide. Huge (15-in.), golden yellow to golden orange, powerfully fragrant trumpets cover the plant during the bloom season.

B. 'Cypress Gardens'. Grows 5–10 ft. tall and not quite as wide. Blooms heavily even when small, producing 6- to 8-in. white blossoms that age to light pink; they hang straight down from the branches and are fragrant at night and in the morning. Excellent in containers, where it stays 3–6 ft. tall.

B. x insignis. To 10–12 ft. tall and wide. Flowers are large, flaring trumpets that are held at an angle rather than pointing straight down; they have a spicy-sweet fragrance and come in white, pink, yellow, and orange. Size ranges from 8 to 14 in. long, depending on selection. 'Frosty Pink' has salmon pink blooms; 'Jamaica Yellow' has light yellow flowers. 'Jean Pasco' has golden yellow flowers with a lighter yellow throat and a red-orange tinge at the edges. 'Betty Marshall' bears white blossoms on a compact plant 6–8 ft. high.

B. 'Peaches and Cream'. To 5 ft. tall and wide. Flowers over a long spring-into-fall season, producing richly perfumed, light peachy pink blossoms to 8 in. long that open from buds striped in white and green. Blooms profusely, even in small containers. Leaves are dark green, splashed with light green and edged in white and pale yellow.

B. suaveolens. Plants offered as this species are usually *B. x insignis.*

B. 'Sunset' (*B. x candida* 'Variegata'). Grows 5 ft. tall and wide, with foot-long, light golden peach blossoms; its green leaves are attractively edged in white. 'Snowbank' is similar, but leaves are even more heavily variegated with cream and gray-green blotches.

B. versicolor. The most tree-like species, to 15 ft. tall and wide. Huge (15-in.) flowers are a peachy apricot color; they hang straight down from the branches, covering the plant during bloom time. Blossoms are sweetly fragrant at night and in the morning. Pink- and white-flowered selections are also sold. 'Ecuador Pink' has especially fragrant pink trumpets up to 1½ ft. long, with distinctively curled edges; it blooms over a long season, from spring to fall.

CARE

Brugmansias prefer moist, fertile, well-drained soil that contains plenty of organic matter. Boggy soil results in gradual dieback and eventual death. A site providing morning sun and light afternoon shade is ideal. During active growth in spring and summer, water freely and feed every 2 weeks with a balanced water-soluble fertilizer. In fall and winter, reduce watering and cease feeding. Prune only after flowering.

Brugmansias are winter hardy in the Coastal and Tropical South (USDA 9-11). In the Lower South (USDA 8), heavy mulching in late fall is necessary. In the Upper and Middle South (USDA 6-7), treat them as annuals or grow them in containers that you take indoors for winter. Potted plants can spend winters indoors with low light and little water.

BRUNFELSIA

Solanaceae
Evergreen to semievergreen shrubs or small trees

🌿 **CS, TS (USDA 9-11), EXCEPT AS NOTED; OR GROW IN POTS**

☼ ◐ **FULL SUN OR PARTIAL SHADE**

💧 **REGULAR WATER**

⬥ **ALL PARTS ARE POISONOUS IF INGESTED**

Brunsfelsia pauciflora 'Floribunda'

These natives of the American tropics feature clusters of showy flowers during the warmer months. The blossoms are tubular, opening out to flat, round, five-petaled disks; blooms of some species are fragrant, while those of others change color as they age. In central and south Florida, use in large containers, as specimens, or in shrub borders. Elsewhere, grow in a pot that can be brought indoors to a sunny window for the winter.

These are handsome plants that deserve the extra attention they need: grow them in rich, well-drained, slightly acid soil, and give regular feedings throughout the growing season. In alkaline soils, they will develop chlorosis (yellow leaves with green veins). Prune in spring to remove straggly growth and to shape the plants.

B. australis. MORNING-NOON-AND-NIGHT. Large shrub to 12 ft. tall and wide. Elliptical, dark green leaves, 1½–5 in. long. Blooms from spring through fall, bearing sweet-scented, 1½-in.-wide flowers that open rich purple, then fade through lavender shades to white.

B. pauciflora (*B. calycina*). YESTERDAY-TODAY-AND-TOMORROW. The best known of the brunfelsias, this species gets

its common name from clustered spring-to-summer flowers that quickly change from purple to lavender to white as they age; often, all three colors are present on a single plant. Oval to lance-shaped leaves reach 3–6 in. long. Recommended selections include the following three.

'Floribunda'. Flowers to 2 in. wide are borne profusely all over the plant. Oval leaves are dark green above, pale green below, 3–4 in. long. Plant may exceed 10 ft. in height, but it can be held to 3–4 ft. by pruning. Has a rather spreading habit, with several stems from the base; width is nearly equal to height.

'Floribunda Compacta'. Two-thirds the size of the more widely planted 'Floribunda', with slightly smaller flowers but even more profuse bloom.

'Macrantha' ('Magnifica'). Least hardy of the brunfelsias listed here, suitable for planting outdoors only in south Florida. Differs from 'Floribunda' in having fewer but larger flowers, 2–4 in. across. Also has a more slender habit and bigger leaves (to 8 in. long).

BRUNNERA MACROPHYLLA

BRUNNERA, SIBERIAN BUGLOSS
Boraginaceae
Perennial

🌿 **US, MS, LS; USDA 6-8**

◐ ● **PARTIAL TO FULL SHADE**

💧 **REGULAR WATER**

Brunnera macrophylla 'Jack Frost'

This Eastern European woodland plant grows 1½ ft. tall and 2 ft. wide, with dark green, heart-shaped leaves to 4 in. wide. Airy

clusters of tiny, yellow-centered, clear blue flowers reminiscent of forget-me-nots (*Myosotis*) appear in spring—often into summer, especially in shade. Colored-leaf selections, excellent for brightening shady areas, include 'Diane's Gold', with chartreuse leaves; 'Hadspen Cream', with foliage broadly edged in creamy white; 'Jack Frost', silver leaves with green margins and veins; 'Langtrees', with silver-spotted foliage; and 'Looking Glass', whose leaves are nearly white. 'Mr. Morse' resembles 'Jack Frost' but has white flowers.

Brunnera is useful as an informal ground cover under high-branching deciduous trees; among spring-flowering shrubs such as forsythia, deciduous magnolias; and as filler between newly planted evergreen shrubs. Freely self-sows once established. Seeds you plant may not germinate easily (try freezing them before sowing). Needs rich, well-drained, moisture-retentive soil. Increase by dividing clumps in fall.

BRUSSELS SPROUTS

Brassicaceae
Biennial grown as cool-season annual

🌿 **US, MS, LS, CS, TS; USDA 6-11**

☼ **FULL SUN**

💧 **REGULAR WATER**

Brussels sprouts

Raising Brussels sprouts in the South can be challenging—like their relatives broccoli, cabbage, and cauliflower, they need a long, cool growing season to produce firm, tasty, sizable sprouts. But it's well worth the effort, as each

HOW TO GROW BRUSSELS SPROUTS

PLANTING Always start with transplants. You can buy these from garden centers or sow seed yourself in cell-packs. For a spring crop, set out transplants 4 weeks before the last frost. For fall and winter harvests in the Upper, Middle, and Lower South (USDA 6-8), set them out 10 to 14 weeks before the first fall frost; in Florida and the Coastal South, plant in October. Space transplants 1½–2 ft. apart in rows about 2½ ft. apart.

FEEDING Feed at planting time with a water-soluble 20-20-20 fertilizer. Water regularly to keep soil evenly moist. Three to 4 weeks after planting, sprinkle ½ cup of 10-10-10 fertilizer per 10 ft. of row around plants; repeat 3 to 4 weeks later.

PRUNING AND HARVESTING Sprouts develop progressively from the bottom of the plant toward the top, appearing first as tiny buds within the leaf axils. Removing the terminal growth tip when the plants are 15–20 in. tall makes the sprouts grow larger and mature more quickly; this is a particularly useful technique for spring crops. Harvest sprouts when they're 1–1½ in. wide.

CHALLENGES To prevent a buildup of soil-borne pests, plant Brussels sprouts in a different site each year. Club root is a serious fungal pest in acid soils; apply lime, if necessary, to raise the pH to at least 6.5. Control insects such as cabbage loopers, cabbageworms, cutworms, and root maggots by using floating row covers or ringing the base of the plant with a cardboard collar. *Bacillus thuringiensis* (*Bt*) and spinosad also controls cabbageworms and loopers.

plant produces as many as 100 sprouts over a period of 6 to 8 weeks. You can grow both spring and fall crops, but fall crops are much more dependable here. In Florida and the Coastal South, plant in fall for a winter crop. Brussels sprouts can survive occasional hard frosts (the chill even sweetens their flavor), but temperatures below 26°F may kill them. Recommended selections include 'Catskill', 'Diablo', 'Jade Cross', 'Long Island Improved', 'Nautic', 'Prince Marvel', and 'Valiant'.

BUDDLEIA
BUTTERFLY BUSH
Scrophulariaceae
Evergreen, semievergreen, or deciduous shrubs

✎ **ZONES VARY BY SPECIES**

☼ ◑ **FULL SUN OR LIGHT SHADE**

◐ ◑ **MODERATE TO REGULAR WATER**

Buddleia davidii 'Black Knight'

Colorful spring or summer flowers, sweet fragrance, attractiveness to butterflies, and easy care make these shrubs extremely popular. The vast majority sold are selections of *B. davidii*, but many other species are highly ornamental and deserve their fair share of attention. Most types prefer full sun and fertile, moist, well-drained soil. Not browsed by deer. Removing spent flowers extends bloom.

B. alternifolia. FOUNTAIN BUTTERFLY BUSH. Deciduous. Zones US, MS, LS, CS; USDA 6-9. Native to China. Shrub can reach 12 ft. or taller and equally as wide, with arching, willowlike branches rather thinly clothed

with 1- to 4-in.-long leaves, dark dullish green above, gray and hairy beneath. Blooms in spring from the previous year's growth; produces profuse small clusters of mildly fragrant, lilac purple flowers that create sweeping wands of color. Tolerates many soils; does very well in poor, dry gravel. Prune after bloom: remove some of oldest wood down to within a few inches of ground. Or train up into small single- or multiple-trunked tree. So trained, it somewhat resembles a small weeping willow. 'Argentea' has silvery gray foliage.

B. davidii. ORANGE-EYE BUTTERFLY BUSH, SUMMER LILAC. Deciduous or semievergreen. Zones US, MS, LS, CS; USDA 6-9. Native to China, Japan. Fast, rank growth each spring and summer to 5, 6, or even 10 ft. tall and wide. Leaves tapering, 4–12 in. long, dark green above, white and felted beneath. In midsummer, branch ends adorned with small, fragrant flowers in dense, arching, spikelike, slender clusters from 6 to 12 in. or longer. This species and its selections require little more than good drainage and enough water to maintain growth. Cut back plants heavily (nearly to the ground) in late winter to early spring to promote strong new growth for good flowering. In Upper South (USDA 6), plants may freeze to the ground but will regrow each year from the roots. This species is considered invasive in much of the Upper South; gardeners there should consider selections with reduced seed production.

'Black Knight'. Darkest flowers, very deep purple, in 4- to 6-in. spikes. Small leaves. Grows to 6–7 ft.

'Blue Chip'. Dwarf plant grows just 3 ft. tall and wide, with dark green to gray-green leaves and blue-purple flowers. Does not sucker and produces few if any seeds. Part of Lo & Behold series.

'Bonnie'. Attractive gray-green foliage and very fragrant, light lavender blooms in spikes 8–12 in. long. To 10 ft. tall and wide.

'Charming'. Blue-green leaves. Lots of large, lavender-pink flowers in spikes 6–8 in. long. Grows 6–8 ft. tall and wide.

'Dartmoor'. Strongly fragrant, purple flowers in 6- to 8-in., branching spikes with a very full look. To 6-10 ft.

'Ellen's Blue'. Long bloom season, with deep, intense violet-blue flowers in 6- to 10-in. spikes. Silvery green leaves. Grows just 4 ft. tall and wide.

'Empire Blue'. Violet-blue flowers in spikes to 1 ft. long. Silvery green foliage. Vigorous, upright growth to 10–12 ft.

'Harlequin'. Cream variegation on leaves. Reddish purple flowers in 6- to 8-in. spikes. Slower growing than most, and leaves may revert to green. To 7–8 ft.

'Ice Chip'. Compact grower, just 2 ft. tall and twice as wide. White flowers. Virtually seedless. Part of Lo & Behold series.

'Lilac Chip'. Low growing form, at just 1½ ft. tall; spreads to at least 2½ ft. wide. Lilac-colored flowers. Very low seed set. Part of Lo & Behold series.

'Miss Ruby'. To 5–6 ft. tall and wide. Resembles 'Pink Delight' but with more compact growth and brighter pink flowers. Choice.

Nanho series. Plants grow to 4–6 ft. tall and wide, with small, narrow, silvery leaves. 'Nanho Alba' is dense, with white flowers in 8- to 10-in. spikes. 'Nanho Blue' offers profuse blue blooms in 4- to 6-in. spikes. 'Nanho Purple' has dark violet flowers in 4- to 6-in. spikes.

'Opera'. Purple-red spikes are 10–12 in. long. Bushy plant to 5–7 ft.

'Orchid Beauty'. Clusters of lavender flowers up to 20 in. long. To 5–8 ft.

'Pink Delight'. Spikes of clear pink flowers to 1 ft. long. Silvery foliage. To 6–8 ft. Considered by some to be the best pink form.

'Potters Purple'. Violet flower spikes to 10 in. long. Vigorous, upright plant to 7 ft. tall. May be the best purple buddleia.

'Purple Haze'. Low, spreading growth to 2–3 ft. tall and 4–6 ft. wide, with dark green leaves. Medium purple blooms on arching horizontal branches. Produces no seeds.

'Purple Prince'. Very fragrant, violet flowers in spikes 6–14 in. long. Upright growth to 6 ft.

'White Profusion'. The best white selection. To 6–8 ft., with many 8- to 12-in. flower spikes produced over a long period. A magnet for butterflies.

B. lindleyana. WEEPING MARY. Semievergreen. Zones MS, LS, CS; USDA 7-9. Native to China but sometimes found growing wild in the southeastern U.S.

Graceful, open growth to 6–12 ft. tall, not quite as wide. Purplish violet flowers appear in late summer and fall, carried in nodding clusters that may reach 2 ft. long. Deep green, semiglossy foliage; cinnamon-colored, shedding bark. Try removing lower limbs to allow for understory plantings. Blooms on new growth; prune as for *B. davidii*.

B. 'Lochinch'. Deciduous. Zones US, MS, LS, CS; USDA 6-9.

A hybrid between *B. davidii* and another species. To 5–6 ft. tall. Displays woolly white new growth and branching, foot-long clusters of intensely fragrant, lilac blossoms with an orange eye. Produces summer flowers on current year's growth, so prune as for *B. davidii*. Excellent flowers and foliage.

B. x pikei 'Hever' ('Hever Castle'). Deciduous. Zones US, MS, LS, CS; USDA 6-9. Hybrid between *B. alternifolia* and a

Himalayan species. Resembles a smaller *B. alternifolia*, with fragrant, orange-centered lilac flowers in mid- to late spring. Gray-green leaves. Prune as for *B. alternifolia*. Seedless.

B. x weyeriana. Deciduous. Zones MS, LS, CS; USDA 7-9. Hybrid between *B. davidii* and a species from Chile. Produces arching, leafy shoots set with roundish clusters of yellow-orange flowers. To 8–10 ft. tall

and wide. Blooms on old wood, so cut back after flowering as for *B. alternifolia*. (In coldest part of range, however, it freezes to the ground and so blooms on new wood.) 'Honeycomb' is choice, with golden yellow flowers. 'Sungold' has dense clusters of dark orange-yellow flowers.

BULBINE FRUTESCENS

Asphodelaceae
Succulent shrubby perennial

⚡ **CS, TS; USDA 9-11**

◑ **PARTIAL SHADE IN TROPICAL SOUTH**

◌◐● **LITTLE TO REGULAR WATER**

Bulbine frutescens

Native to South Africa. Branching stems of this South African native make a sprawling clump to 1 ft. high, 2–3 ft. wide. Leaves are fleshy, bright green, and shaped like slender, pointed pencils. Blooms through most of the year, producing spikelike, 6- to 12-in. clusters of tubular, bright yellow flowers resembling those of aloe or red-hot poker (*Kniphofia*). 'Hallmark' has orange flowers with fuzzy yellow stamens; it is more compact, less heat tolerant than species. 'Tiny Tangerine' is another compact, orange-flowered selection. All are useful as ground or bank cover in dry, well-drained soil. Leaves are slippery when crushed, so don't locate them where they'll be stepped on.

TOP: Buddleia davidii 'Pink Delight'; *B. x weyeriana; B. d.* 'Empire Blue'; *BOTTOM: Buddleia in landscape*

BUTIA CAPITATA (B. ODORATA)

PINDO PALM, JELLY PALM
Arecaceae
Palm

🌿 **LS, CS, TS; USDA 8-11**

☼ ◑ **FULL SUN OR LIGHT SHADE**

💧 **REGULAR WATER**

Butia capitata

Crowned with 5–10-ft., green or blue-green leaves that curve in toward the trunk, this slow-growing South American native grows 10–20 ft. tall, with a 10–15-ft. head. Long spikes of yellow flowers develop into clusters of yellow to red, edible summer fruit (flavor is sweet-tart, like an apricot-banana-pineapple blend). It is among the hardiest feather palms, taking 15°F. Spent fronds hang down over the stout trunk like a hula dancer's skirt. To show off the patterned trunk, keep all these spent fronds trimmed to the same length.

BUXUS

BOXWOOD, BOX
Buxaceae
Evergreen shrubs

🌿 **ZONES VARY BY SPECIES**

☼ ◑ **FULL SUN OR LIGHT SHADE**

💧💧 **MODERATE TO REGULAR WATER**

Buxus sempervirens 'Suffruticosa'

True garden aristocrats, boxwoods may well be the world's oldest cultivated ornamental plants: They were grown as hedges in ancient Egypt and decorated the gardens of wealthy Romans during the reign of Caesar Augustus. Today, thanks to a wide variety of shapes and sizes, the popularity of boxwoods is rising. They are still widely used as hedges, in formal foundation plantings, and as edgings for walkways and planting beds. In many areas, boxwood is the primary plant in landscapes due to its resistance to damage by deer.

These evergreen shrubs have small (just ¼- to 1-in.), lance-shaped to roundish leaves. All are easy to grow where they are adapted, provided they receive good drainage and a modicum of care. If they're grown in loose, fertile soil that contains plenty of organic matter, heavy fertilizing is seldom necessary. Many of the more recent introductions tolerate pruning well, though most boxwoods have a naturally billowing form that requires little or no pruning. Susceptibility to nematodes limits the use of boxwoods in Florida.

B. Green Series. Zones US, MS, LS, CS; USDA 6-9. Group of Canadian hybrids derived from *B. microphylla koreana* and *B. sempervirens*. Hardy to between –2°F and –30°F. All feature

Trimmed boxwoods form the classic bones of formal gardens at Mount Sharon, Orange, Virginia.

HOW TO GROW BOXWOODS

PLANTING Plant in well-drained soil with lots of organic matter. Soil pH of 6.5–7.2 is optimal. Avoid wet areas to minimize root diseases. Boxwoods generally prefer some shade, though exposure preferences differ by selection. To minimize winter bronzing, avoid sunny southwest exposures.

WATERING Water generously after planting. Avoid overhead watering. For the first year, water weekly during dry periods, less during cool, wet periods. After the first year, only moderate watering is needed; overwatering will cause problems.

PRUNING Lightly hand-prune to maintain natural handsome form. Do any heavy pruning in late winter to early spring before active growth begins. This is also a good time to clean out any dead leaves or other debris that have accumulated in the center of the plant. Thinning cuts that open up the interior to maximize air flow and light penetration will help reduce diseases.

FERTILIZING Feed lightly in late fall with an organic fertilizer such as cottonseed meal or composted manure, or use a granular urea 10-6-4 fertilizer.

CHALLENGES Resistance to boxwood leaf miner varies by selection but is easily controlled with systemic insecticides. Apply in late spring or early summer according to label directions. Check with your local County Extension Office for the best treatment in your area.

handsome, rich green foliage and a naturally attractive shape; need very little pruning. Slight winter bronzing may occur when these are planted in a sunny, southwest-facing location.

'Green Gem'. Slowly forms a mound 2–3 ft. high and wide. Some bronzing of foliage in winter cold.

'Green Mountain'. Forms a dense, rounded cone to 4–5 ft. high, 3 ft. wide. Developed as an alternative to dwarf Alberta spruce (*Picea glauca* 'Conica').

'Green Velvet'. Rounded habit to 2–3 ft. tall and 3 ft. wide. Very popular and widely used.

B. microphylla. LITTLELEAF BOXWOOD. Zones US, MS, LS, CS; USDA 6-9. Hardy to 10°F. Slow-growing species from Japan reaches 3–4 ft. tall and wide. The plain species is rarely planted; the following varieties and selections are much more common.

'Grace Hendrick Phillips'. A wide, mounding plant that matures at 1–2 ft. high and 2–3 ft. wide. Useful as small specimen, foundation plant, or low hedge.

B. m. japonica. JAPANESE BOXWOOD. Zones US, MS, LS, CS; USDA 6-9. Faster growing and taller than the species, to 6 ft. tall and wide. Well suited to the Coastal South; tolerates heat, humidity, and nematodes better than most boxwoods. Round-tipped leaves, ⅓–1 in. long. Foliage may take on a bronzy cast in cold winters. Often used as a clipped hedge in Gulf Coast areas. 'Green Beauty' is a rounded form that matures at 4 ft. tall and wide. Foliage is glossy, deep green and holds its color well through the winter. Responds well to pruning and sunny locations. 'Morris Dwarf' is slow growing and compact (1–2 ft. tall and 2 ft. wide); good for knot gardens and parterres. 'Winter Gem' retains its deep green foliage color through winter.

B. m. koreana. See *B. sinica insularis*

B. sempervirens. COMMON BOXWOOD, AMERICAN BOX-WOOD. Zones US, MS, LS; USDA 6-8. Native to southern Europe, North Africa, western Asia. Hardy to –10°F. Densely foliaged shrub is virtually indispensable in formal garden settings. Takes many years to reach 10–12 ft. tall and wide. Dark green, oval leaves. Can be used in foundation plantings, for hedges, or pruned into a small tree.

'Aureovariegata'. Grows 8–10 ft. tall and wide, with leaves edged in creamy yellow.

'Dee Runk'. Slender pyramidal plant that grows 8–10 ft. tall and just 3 ft. wide. Good accent plant or narrow hedge.

'Suffruticosa'. ENGLISH BOX-WOOD. Dense, compact, very slow growing; takes many years to reach 3 ft. Often used in formal garden settings. Extensively planted but being replaced by newer selections with greater disease resistance.

'Vardar Valley'. Becomes a flat-topped mound, 2–3 ft. tall, nearly twice as wide. New spring foliage is a beautiful powder-blue, shading with maturity to dark blue-green. Hardy to about –15°F.

'Variegata'. Dense and mounded form, eventually to about 5 ft. tall and wide. Leaves are bright green, edged in white.

B. sinica insularis (*B. m. koreana*). KOREAN BOXWOOD. Zones US, MS, LS, CS; USDA 6-9. Slower growing and lower than *B. m. japonica*. Hardy to –25°F. Good choice for severe winters of the Upper South. 'Justin Brouwers' grows to 2–3 ft. tall and wide and is widely used as a replacement for English box-wood (*B. sempervirens* 'Suffruti-cosa'). It responds well to pruning into a small hedge or can be left unpruned for a naturally billowing shape.

BOXWOODS HAVE SHALLOW ROOTS, SO AVOID DISTURBING THE SOIL AROUND THEM.

CABBAGE
Brassicaceae
Biennial grown as cool-season annual

🌿 **US, MS, LS, CS, TS; USDA 6-11**

☼ ◑ **TOLERATES LIGHT SHADE IN HOT CLIMATES**

💧 **REGULAR WATER**

Savoy cabbage

You can grow an amazing assortment of cabbages. Besides the familiar round, light green sorts, you can find types with flat, rounded, or pointed heads in colors ranging from white to dark green to red. Leaves may be packed loosely or tightly; Savoy types have crinkly leaves. Given such an array of choices, gardeners may decide to grow cabbage simply for the opportunity to try something different every year. (For Chinese cabbages, see Asian Greens and Chinese Cabbages; for ornamental relatives, see Cabbage and Kale, Flowering.)

Few vegetable crops can match cabbage in total return per square foot of garden space. To avoid overproduction, set out a few plants every week or two, or plant both early and late kinds. Time your plantings so that heads will form either before or after the hot summer months. In most parts of the South, you can plant both spring and fall crops. For a spring crop, set out transplants 4 to 6 weeks before the last frost.

HOW TO GROW CABBAGE

PLANTING Buy seedlings at garden centers or start your own transplants from seed. Sow seeds about 6 weeks prior to planting-out time. When the seedlings have several sets of leaves, transplant them to rich, moist soil, spacing plants 1½–2 ft. apart in rows 2½ ft. apart. Apply a mulch between plants to keep down weeds, cool the soil, and reduce extremes of soil moisture.

FERTILIZING Cabbage plants are heavy feeders, so be sure to give them a water-soluble 20-20-20 fertilizer weekly for 3 weeks after setting out. Then sprinkle ½ cup of 10-10-10 fertilizer per 10 ft. of row around plants; repeat 3 weeks later. Don't fertilize after heads begin forming—excess nitrogen can cause them to split. Overwatering at this stage can do the same.

HARVESTING Harvest heads anytime after they are firm and solid. Light frosts don't hurt cabbage, but be sure to harvest and store before hard freezes arrive.

CHALLENGES Club root is a serious fungal pest in acid soils; apply lime, if necessary, to raise the pH to at least 6.5. Floating row covers do a good job of controlling insects such as cabbage loopers, cabbage-worms, cutworms, and root maggots. You can also control cutworms and root maggots by ringing the base of the plant with a cardboard collar. *Bacillus thuringiensis* (*Bt*) and spinosad, applied according to label directions, controls cabbage-worms and loopers.

For a fall crop (which may be preferable, because cabbage pests are less numerous then), set out transplants in mid- to late summer, 8 to 14 weeks before the first frost. Gardeners in Florida can plant in fall for a winter crop. To prevent a buildup of soil-borne pests, plant cabbage in a different site each year.

Recommended selections of regular, green-leafed cabbage include 'Dynamo' (70 days from setting out plants until harvest, compact plants, good for small gardens), 'Early Flat Dutch' (85 days, heat tolerant), 'Early Jersey Wakefield' (65 days, frost resistant), 'Emerald Cross' (63 days, easy to grow), 'Megaton' (88 days, 15-pound heads), and 'Stonehead' (60 days, solid heads). For red-leafed cabbage, try 'Red Acre' (76 days, compact plants), 'Red Express' (63 days, compact plants), and 'Super Red 80' (78 days, heat tolerant). Recommended Savoy selections include 'Chieftain Savoy' (83 days, tolerates frost and heat), 'Colorosa' (100 days, red leaves), and 'Savoy Express' (55 days, compact plants).

CABBAGE AND KALE, FLOWERING

Brassicaceae
Biennials grown as cool-season annuals

🌿 **US, MS, LS, CS, TS; USDA 6-11**

☀️ 🌤️ **BEST IN SUN, TOLERATE SOME SHADE**

💧 **REGULAR WATER**

Flowering cabbage

Flowering cabbage and flowering kale are grown for their very

ornamental, highly colored leaf rosettes, which look like giant, deep blue-green peonies marbled and edged with white, cream, rose, or purple. Kale differs from cabbage in that its head is slightly looser and its leaf edges are more heavily fringed. Both are spectacular in the cool-season garden. They appreciate the same soil, care, and timing as conventional cabbage. Plant 15–18 in. apart in open-ground beds, singly in 8-in. pots, or several to a large container. Colors are strongest after first frosts touch plants. A single rosette cut and placed on a spike holder in a bowl makes a striking harvest arrangement. Foliage is edible raw or cooked and is highly decorative as a salad garnish.

If winter does not dip below 15-20 °F, or plants are protected by snow, these low rosettes will survive to bloom in spring. They will bolt, growing 2-4 ft. tall with a flurry of pale yellow flowers. Properly sited, they are lovely. If a tidy, low-growing border is desired, it is time to pull them out when they begin to bloom.

Reliable selections of kale include 'Peacock Red', 'Peacock White', 'Chidori Red', 'Chidori White', and the taller 'Red Bor', 'Winter Bor', 'Lacinato', and 'Red Russian'.

For the edible flowering cabbage typically used in Chinese cooking, see Asian Greens.

IN AUTUMN, PLANT UP A POT WITH FLOWERING CABBAGE SURROUNDED BY PANSIES.

CAESALPINIA

Caesalpiniaceae
Evergreen and deciduous shrubs and trees

🌿 **ZONES VARY BY SPECIES**

☀️ **FULL SUN**

💧💧 **LITTLE TO MODERATE WATER**

🔶 **PODS AND SEEDS ARE POISONOUS IF INGESTED**

Caesalpinia pulcherrima

Ferny-leafed plants grown for their branch-end clusters of colorful blossoms featuring (except *C. platyloba*) protruding stamens. Flowers attract hummingbirds. Plants grow quickly and easily in hot, sunny locations if given light, well-drained soil and infrequent, deep watering. Prune before first flush of spring growth to remove any dead or damaged wood and wayward branches; remove lower limbs for treelike shape in shrubby species.

C. cacalaco. CASCALOTE. Evergreen tree. Zones CS, TS; USDA 9-11. Mexican native grows slowly to 20 ft. tall and wide, with thorny branches and bright green foliage, coarser than that of *C. pulcherrima*. Very showy, large yellow flowers carried well above branches in winter.

C. gilliesii. YELLOW BIRD OF PARADISE. Evergreen to deciduous shrub or tree; drops leaves in cold winters. Zones LS, CS, TS; USDA 8-11. From South America. Tough, fast growing to 10 ft. tall, 8 ft. wide, with finely cut foliage and open, angular branch structure. Blooms all summer, producing clusters of yellow flowers adorned with bright red stamens.

C. mexicana. MEXICAN BIRD OF PARADISE. Evergreen shrub or tree. Zones CS, TS; USDA 9-11. Native to Mexico and the southern tip of Texas. Moderately fast growth to 10–12 ft. tall and wide; can be maintained at 6–8 ft. with pruning. Leaves are coarser than those of *C. pulcherrima*. Blooms throughout year except in coldest months, bearing 6-in. clusters of lemon-yellow flowers.

C. platyloba. CURLY PAELA. Evergreen tree. Zones TS; USDA 10-11. From Mexico. To 20 ft. tall and wide. Narrow, elongated clusters of tiny yellow flowers in spring lack the long, protruding stamens of other caesalpinias. Best feature is airy appearance due to open branching habit and relatively few leaflets. Leaves turn rust red in fall.

C. pulcherrima. RED BIRD OF PARADISE, DWARF POINCIANA. Deciduous shrub; may be evergreen in mild winters. Zones LS, CS, TS; USDA 8-11. Native to tropical America. Fast, dense growth to 10 ft. tall and wide; useful for quick screening. Dark green leaves with many ¾-in. leaflets. Blooms throughout warm weather, bearing clusters of orange or red flowers with red stamens.

Plants freeze to ground in colder part of range but rebound quickly in spring. In milder climates, you can cut them to the ground in early spring to make a more compact shrub. 'Cream Puff' has cream-colored flowers and chartreuse leaves; 'Phoenix Bird' bears bright yellow blooms.

CALADIUM BICOLOR

Araceae

⚘ **CS, TS; USDA 9-11; OR DIG AND STORE; OR GROW IN POTS**

☼ ☼ **SOME SELECTIONS TOLERATE SUN**

💧💧 **REGULAR TO AMPLE WATER**

💧 **SAP CAN CAUSE SWELLING IN MOUTH, THROAT**

Caladium bicolor 'Roseglow'

Few if any plants are more popular than caladiums for brightening shady spots in Southern gardens. These tropical American natives are grown not for their flowers, but for their marvelous foliage: large (to 1½-ft.), long-stalked, heart- or arrow-shaped, often almost translucent leaves colored with spots and blotches of red, rose, pink, white, silver, bronze, and green. Caladiums are excellent both as bedding plants and in containers.

Hybridizing has produced three classes of caladiums: fancy leaf, lance or strap leaf, and dwarf. All caladiums grow best in bright-shade locations, with 2–4 hours of direct sun per day. A number of dwarf hybrids will tolerate full sun.

Most selections sold at garden centers are fancy-leafed types, typically reaching 2 ft. (occasionally to 4 ft.) tall and wide. Popular choices include 'Aaron' (white with green edges); 'Candidum' (white with green veins); 'Carolyn Whorton' and 'Fannie Munson' (pink with crimson veins); and 'Freida Hemple' (red with green border). These and other older selections need shade, but many newer ones have thicker leaves that tolerate part sun; examples

include 'Celebration' (white with red veins and green edge); 'Fire-works' (red with green border); 'Moonlight' ('Florida Moonlight') (white with a very thin green edge); 'Party Punch' (pink with light pink spots and green edges); 'Pink Beauty' (pink with green speckles and edges); 'Rose Glow' (pink with green border); 'Tapestry' (white with pink veins and green edge); and 'White Cap' (white with white veins and green edges). Sun-tolerant selections include 'Raspberry Moon' (light green with red splashes); 'Red Flash' (green with red center and veins and pink spots); and 'White Queen' (white with red veins).

Strap- or lance-leaf caladiums produce large bunches of leaves. Most stay under a foot tall; some grow considerably taller. All tolerate sun and are useful as edging or in mass plantings. Recommended selections include 'Candyland' (green with white veins and heavy splashes of pink); 'Florida Red Ruffles' (intense deep red with a uniform green edge); 'Florida Sweetheart' (rose with green edges); 'Heart's Delight' (red with mottled light and dark green edges); 'Lance Whorton' (pink with red veins and green edges); 'Pink Gem' (salmon pink with dark salmon veins and green edges); 'Red Frill' (red with green edges); and 'White Dynasty' and 'White Wonder' (pure white with green edges).

Dwarf caladiums have small leaves but grow about as tall as fancy-leafed types. Two of the best are 'Gingerland' (white with red spots and green edges) and 'Miss Muffet' (lime green with burgundy spots).

CARE

Caladiums grow best in rich soil, high humidity, and heat. They won't tolerate soil cooler than 60°F and are likely to rot if planted too early in spring. Gardeners wanting to get a jump on the season can start caladiums indoors in pots, then transplant them to the garden. In most winters south of the I-10 corridor, the tubers can remain in the ground all year if provided with a generous layer of mulch (plants die down completely in winter). Elsewhere, dig and store them in fall, or grow the plants in pots and bring them indoors for winter.

To grow in the ground, plant tubers in spring when nighttime temperatures are consistently above 60°F. Plant them knobby-side up, 1–2 in. deep, spaced 6–12 in. apart. Keep well watered and feed lightly with water-soluble fertilizer several times during the growing season, or apply a controlled-release fertilizer once in spring. When foliage begins to look ratty in late summer or fall, cut it back. Where freezes are likely, dig tubers and remove most of the soil from them; then dry them for several days in a shaded, dry location and store in dry peat moss at 55–65°F until planting time in spring.

To grow in pots, start tubers indoors in late winter or outdoors in spring. Plant 2 in. deep in well-drained potting mix to which you've added controlled-release fertilizer; space just an inch apart for the best display. Water thoroughly.

CALAMAGROSTIS

REED GRASS

Poaceae

Perennial grasses

⚘ **US, MS, LS, CS; USDA 6-9**

☼ ☼ **FULL SUN OR PARTIAL SHADE**

💧💧 **REGULAR TO AMPLE WATER**

Calamagrostis x *acutiflora* 'Karl Foerster'

Among the most effective and handsome of ornamental grasses, the reed grasses feature feathery flower plumes that fade from purple-tinted green to yellow to buff. Flowers persist into fall and can be used for fresh or dried arrangements. Cut clumps almost to the ground in late winter, before new growth begins.

Deer-resistant.

C. x acutiflora. FEATHER REED GRASS. Known mainly in the following evergreen to semi-evergreen selections. 'Karl Foerster', with narrow, bright green leaves, forms an erect, somewhat arching clump 2–3 ft. tall and somewhat broader; upright flowering stems increase the height to 5–6 ft. when they first appear in summer. 'Overdam', to 3 ft. tall, is similar but has variegated leaves and prefers afternoon shade. Its young foliage is striped and edged with yellow; as the leaves mature, the yellow ages to white highlighted with pink. Purplish pink tassels bloom in mid- to late summer. 'Stricta' is similar to—and often confused with—'Karl Foerster', but it grows 1–2 ft. taller and blooms slightly later.

C. brachytricha. REED GRASS. Deciduous. Upright, arching clump to 1½ –2½ ft. tall, 2 ft. wide. Broad, rosy purple flower spikes resembling foxtails increase plant height to 4 ft. in late summer or early fall. One of the best grasses for partial shade; great in containers.

CALAMINTHA

CALAMINT

Lamiaceae

Perennials

⚘ **ZONES VARY BY SPECIES**

☼ ☼ **FULL SUN OR LIGHT SHADE**

💧 **MODERATE WATER**

Calamintha grandiflora 'Variegata'

Prized for minty foliage used to make tea, and for long-blooming clusters of two-lipped flowers. Plant near a garden path where you can brush against the leaves and savor their scent. Calamints need well-drained soil.

C. grandiflora. LARGE-FLOWERED CALAMINT. Zones US, MS, LS, CS; USDA 6-9. Native from Mediterranean region to Iran. Creeping rhizomes produce a clump to 2 ft. tall and wide, with slender stems and 1½-in. pink flowers in summer. Better with some shade.

C. nepeta. LESSER CALAMINT. Zones US, MS; USDA 6-7. Native from Mediterranean region to Great Britain. Slow growth to 1½ ft. high, 2½ ft. wide. Many tough, slender stems grow outward, then erect. Upper portion of the plant carries a profusion of ½-in. pale lilac-to-white flowers in late summer and fall. *C. n. nepeta* is a bit larger and more vigorous, with slightly larger flowers. 'Montrose White' grows 12-15 in. tall and wide and blooms nonstop from early summer to fall. 'Blue Cloud' has light blue flowers.

CALANTHE

Orchidaceae
Terrestrial orchids

🗹 **ZONES VARY BY SPECIES**

◐ ● **PARTIAL TO FULL SHADE**

💧 **REGULAR WATER**

Calanthe hybrid

Orchids are reputed to be difficult, but the following hardy terrestrial types from Japan are easy to grow if given moist, woodsy, well-drained soil and partial to full shade. Lush leaves of most types have an attractively pleated look. Their sensational blooms often bear a clovelike scent. Plants may be late to emerge in spring.

C. discolor. Evergreen or semievergreen. Zones US, MS, LS,

CS; USDA 6-9. Dark green, heavily pleated leaves are 6–12 in. long, 2 in. wide and form a clump to 1 ft. across. In midspring, small, fragrant mahogany flowers with a white or pale pink lower lip appear on 1- to 1½-ft.-tall stalks. The Takane hybrids have yellow flowers marked with brown, gold, white, and red.

C. Kozu hybrids. Zones US, MS, LS, CS; USDA 6-9. These hybrids between *C. discolor* and *C. izu-insularis* are largely evergreen. Dark green leaves, 4–6 in. long and 1–2 in. wide, form a foliage clump to about 8 in. tall and wide. In spring, foot-tall flower spikes are covered in clove-scented flowers; blossoms come in red, pink, white, and yellow, in both solid colors and bicolor combinations.

C. reflexa. Evergreen. Zones MS, LS, CS; USDA 7-9. Narrow, pleated leaves to 6–8 in. long, about 1½ in. wide form a clump to 1 ft. tall, 15 in. wide. Unlike most other species, this one blooms in mid- to late summer, when lightly fragrant lavender-and-white flowers appear on 1½-ft.-tall spikes.

C. striata (*C. discolor sieboldii*). Zones MS, LS, CS; USDA 7-9. Resembles *C. discolor* but has clear yellow flowers in even greater profusion.

CALATHEA

Marantaceae
Perennials

🗹 **ZONES VARY BY SPECIES**

◐ **PARTIAL SHADE; BRIGHT INDIRECT LIGHT**

💧 **REGULAR WATER**

Calathea zebrina

Native to tropical Americas and Africa. Ornamental leaves,

beautifully marked in shades of green, white, and pink, arranged in basal tufts. Flowers of most are inconspicuous. Need high humidity and warm air (not under 55°F). Succeed outdoors in south Florida; elsewhere, they are greenhouse or indoor plants that can be brought outdoors in summer. Need porous soil, perfect drainage, frequent misting in dry air. Repot as often as necessary to avoid root-bound condition. Calatheas are often mistakenly called marantas.

C. crocata. ETERNAL FLAME. Zones TS; USDA 10-11. Grows to 10 in. high, 1 ft. wide. Leaves to 6 in. long, 1–1½ in. wide, dark green above, purple beneath. Spikes 2 in. long, consisting of bright orange flower bracts that look like little torches. Clump has several shoots; each shoot dies after blooming, but new ones appear to keep up the show. Variable performance as houseplant; subject to mites in low humidity. Does better in greenhouse.

C. lancifolia (*C. insignis*). RATTLESNAKE PLANT. Zones CS, TS; USDA 9-11; To 1½–2½ ft. tall, 2 ft. wide. Narrow, wavy-edged, 1- to 1½-ft. leaves are yellow-green banded with deep olive green.

C. louisae. Zones LS, CS, TS; USDA 8-11; To 3 ft. tall, 1½ ft. wide. Foot-long dark green leaves heavily feathered with gray-green along midrib. Can be used as a ground cover, but may die back to ground in winter in Lower South.

C. majestica (*C. ornata*). Zones TS; USDA 10-11. Sturdy plant can reach 6 ft. tall and 3 ft. wide. Leaves 2–3 ft. long, rich green above, purplish red beneath. Juvenile leaves usually pink striped between veins; intermediate foliage striped white. 'Roseolineata' has pink and white stripes at an angle to midrib.

C. makoyana. PEACOCK PLANT. Zones TS; USDA 10-11. Showy plant to 2–4 ft. high and wide. Leaves have areas of olive green or cream above, pink blotches beneath. Silver featherings on rest of upper surface, corresponding cream-colored areas underneath.

C. zebrina. ZEBRA PLANT. Zones TS; USDA 10-11. Compact plant to 1–3 ft. high, 1–2 ft. wide. Elliptic leaves reach 1–2 ft. long, almost half as wide. Upper surfaces are velvety green with

alternating bars of pale yellow green and olive green extending outward from midrib; undersides are purplish red.

CALCEOLARIA

POCKETBOOK PLANT
Calceolariaceae
Perennials grown as annuals

🗹 **US, MS, LS, CS, TS; USDA 6-11, OR HOUSEPLANT**

◐ ● **PARTIAL TO FULL SHADE; BRIGHT INDIRECT LIGHT**

💧 **REGULAR WATER**

Calceolaria hybrid

Unusual, puffed-up flowers resembling inch-long pocketbooks give these plants their common name. The blooms may be bright yellow, red, or orange and are often marked with spots. Commonly available types are hybrids belonging to the Herbeohybrida group; most reach 9–15 in. high and 6–12 in. wide.

Hailing from the mountains of South America, these are short-lived plants that won't take sustained temperatures higher than 65°F. They can be grown from seed, but most people buy plants in bloom from a florist or greenhouse in winter. Pocketbook plants are largely grown as short-term indoor plants, though they are sometimes bedded out for late winter color in the Coastal South. For best results indoors, place near a north- or east-facing window, away from heating vents or other heat sources. Keep at 50–60°F to prolong the flowering period. The soil should be moist but never soggy; no fertilizing is necessary. When the blooms fade, discard the plant.

CALENDULA OFFICINALIS

CALENDULA,
POT MARIGOLD
Asteraceae
Cool-season annual

US, MS, LS, CS, TS; USDA 6-11

FULL SUN

MODERATE WATER

Calendula officinalis

This Mediterranean native is a popular source of sure, easy color in the cooler months—from late fall through spring in the Lower, Coastal, and Tropical South; from spring to early summer in the Upper and Middle South. Daisylike double blossoms, 2½–4½ in. wide, come not only in the familiar orange and bright yellow, but also in more subtle shades of apricot, cream, and soft yellow. The plant is somewhat branching, reaching 1–2 ft. high, 1–1½ ft. wide. Leaves are long and narrow, with rounded ends; they are aromatic and slightly sticky. Plants attract butterflies but are not browsed by deer. Calendulas are effective for masses of bright, warm color in borders, along drives, or in containers; they make long-lasting cut flowers. In the past, the leaves and flowers went into vegetable stews—hence the common name "pot marigold," a reference to the plant's culinary use as a "pot herb." The vivid petals are still popular today for the tangy flavor they bring to salads and cooked dishes; if simmered with rice, they lend a saffron color to the grain.

CARE

Sow seed in place in the garden or in flats—in late summer or early fall in mild-winter areas, in spring elsewhere. Or buy seedlings at garden centers. Plant adapts well to most soils if drainage is fast. Remove spent flowers to prolong bloom.

Dwarf strains (12–15 in.) include Bon Bon (earliest) and Fiesta (Fiesta Gitana). Taller (1½–2 ft.) are Flashback (orange, peach, apricot, or yellow with red or maroon reverse), Kablouna (pompon centers with looser edges), Pacific Beauty, and Radio (quilled, "cactus"-type blooms).

CALIBRACHOA

Solanaceae
Perennial often grown as annual

US, MS, LS, CS, TS; USDA 6-11

FULL SUN OR LIGHT SHADE

REGULAR WATER

Calibrachoa 'Cabaret Purple'

This cheery summer bloomer looks like a small petunia, to which it is related. It is native to Brazil and Peru, and its garden forms are hybrids. It was once called Million Bells—the name of an early and still-popular series—but now just *Calibrachoa*. Plants have tiny, closely set leaves and a profusion of small, single or double flowers that fall off as they fade; blooms keep coming all season long. Colors include solids, bicolors, and veined patterns in shades of white, yellow, orange, apricot, red, pink, blue, burgundy, lavender, and purple. For hybrids between *Calibrachoa* and *Petunia*, see x *Petchoa*.

There are many excellent calibrachoas series with names like Cabaret, Callie, Colorburst, Can-Can, Million Bells, and Mini Famous. They sometimes differ by color range and pattern, but there is overlap. The heat- and disease-resistant Superbells series, for example, includes about 30 selections in a wide range of colors and habits.

Trailing calibrachoas in all series grow lower (usually 3–7 in. high) and spill out to the sides, while mounding forms can be 8 to 15 in. high, and grow about as wide as high. Intermediates are just that.

Calibrachoas perform superbly in containers but struggle in garden beds that have less than perfect drainage. Consider them perennials only where frosts are nonexistent or light.

CARE

Calibrachoas are generally less hungry and thirsty than petunias grown in the same conditions, but because they are at their best in containers, regular watering and fertilizing are still the rule. (Avoid using water-retention gels.) They do best in slightly acidic soil and quickly decline in alkaline soil. The plants' wiry stems are less subject to breakage than are petunia stems, and tobacco budworms seem uninterested in foliage and flowers.

CALLIANDRA

Mimosaceae
Evergreen and deciduous shrubs

CS, TS; USDA 9-11, EXCEPT AS NOTED, OR GROW IN POTS

FULL SUN, EXCEPT AS NOTED

WATER NEEDS VARY BY SPECIES

Calliandra haematocephala

Grown as landscape plants in the Coastal and Tropical South and in greenhouses elsewhere, these plants sport feathery foliage and blossoms that look like powder puffs. The showy parts of the flowers are actually long, silky stamens. Prune out any dead, damaged, or unwanted growth immediately following bloom.

C. eriophylla. FAIRY DUSTER, FALSE MESQUITE. Deciduous. Native from Southern California east to Texas and south into Baja California. Open growth to 3 ft. tall, 4–5 ft. wide. Leaves finely divided into tiny leaflets. Flower clusters show pink-to-white stamens in fluffy balls to 1½ in. across in late winter or early spring. No watering needed, but flowers and leaves (plant is summer-deciduous) will last longer with some summer water.

C. grandiflora. GIANT FAIRY DUSTER. Evergreen. Native to eastern Mexico and Central America. To 5 ft. tall, 3 ft. wide. Red, 3-in. puffballs in clusters to 15 in. long at branch ends. Attractive, glossy, dark green foliage. Little to moderate water.

C. haematocephala (*C. inaequilatera*). PINK POWDER PUFF, RED POWDER PUFF. Evergreen. Native to Bolivia. Grows fast to 10 ft. or more, with equal spread. Among the most popular large flowering shrubs in central Florida. Its beauty has carried it into areas harsher than those to which it is adapted; it will grow in the Coastal South if given special protection of overhang or warm, sunny wall. In form, it's a natural espalier. Foliage not as feathery as that of *C. tweedii*; leaflets longer, broader, and darker—glossy copper when new, turning to dark metallic green. Big puffs (2–3 in. across) of silky, watermelon-pink stamens are produced in fall and winter. There is a rare white-flowered form. Needs light soil and regular water.

C. tweedii. TRINIDAD FLAME BUSH, BRAZILIAN FLAME BUSH. Evergreen. Zones TS; USDA 10-11. Native from Brazil to Uruguay. Freezes back but recovers in the Coastal South. To 6–8 ft. tall, 5–8 ft. wide, with graceful, picturesque structure. Fernlike leaves, divided into many tiny leaflets, scarcely hide branches. Aside from a rest period in early winter, blooms all year, bearing 2- to 3-in., bright crimson pompons at branch ends. Not fussy about soil. Takes regular to little water. Prune to thin and to retain interesting branch pattern. Often sold as *C. guildingii*.

CALLICARPA

BEAUTYBERRY
Lamiaceae
Deciduous shrubs

US, MS, LS; USDA 6-8, EXCEPT AS NOTED

FULL SUN OR LIGHT SHADE

MODERATE TO REGULAR WATER

Callicarpa americana

Graceful, arching shrubs grown for showy fruit. Small lilac or pink flowers in summer are followed by tight clusters of little, round violet-to-purple fruits that last into winter. Effective in woodland gardens or massed in borders. Bloom and fruit occur on current season's growth, so prune in late winter: Remove a third of oldest stems, or lop whole plant low to ground. Plants may freeze to ground in Upper South, but they come back from roots.

C. americana. AMERICAN BEAUTYBERRY, FRENCH MUL-BERRY. Zones US, MS, LS, CS, TS; USDA 6-11. Native to eastern U.S. To 6 ft. tall, 5 ft. wide. Large, coarse leaves to 6 in. long. Big clusters of magenta fruits. 'Bok Tower' has white fruits; those of 'Welch's Pink' are bright pink.

C. bodinieri. BODINIER BEAU-TYBERRY. Native to China. Grows to 6 ft. or more and nearly as wide, with willowlike leaves that turn pink or orange to purple in fall. 'Profusion' is a heavy bearer.

C. dichotoma. PURPLE BEAU-TYBERRY. Native to China, Korea, Japan. The best, most refined-looking species for the home garden. About 4 ft. tall and slightly wider, with slender branches that sweep the ground. Resembles a smaller, finer-textured *C. bodinieri.* 'Issai' bears abundant purple fruits; 'Early Amethyst' ripens its

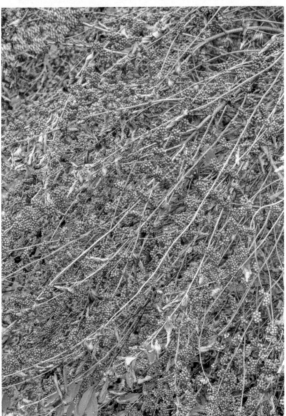

TOP: Callicarpa dichotoma albifructa; BOTTOM: C. americana 'Welch's Pink'

bright purple berries earlier than the species and other selections. *C. d. albifructa* has white fruit.

C. japonica. JAPANESE BEAU-TYBERRY. Native to China, Taiwan, Japan. To 5 ft. tall and wide, with deep reddish purple fall foliage. Becomes open and unkempt without yearly pruning. 'Leuco-carpa' bears white fruits.

CALLIRHOE

WINE CUPS,
POPPY MALLOW
Malvaceae
Perennials

US, MS, LS, CS; USDA 6-9

FULL SUN

LITTLE TO MODERATE WATER

Callirhoe involucrata

Few perennials can match the eye-popping show of wine cups in full bloom. Native to the American Southwest and Midwest, they grow from fleshy roots to become wide-spreading mats of foliage; the leaves are deeply cut, resembling those of some scented geraniums. A profusion of cup-shaped flowers smothers the plant during hot weather. As long as they have good drainage, wine cups will tolerate infertile soil and intense heat. Use them at front of border and on slopes.

C. alcaeoides. Native from Illinois to Nebraska, south to Tennessee and Texas. Whitish (often pink-tinged) flowers to 2½ in. across are held on slender, 5- to 20-in. stems; plant spreads 1–3 ft. wide. 'Logan Calhoun' is an improved selection with sparkling white blossoms; it grows 8–12 in. high, sprawling 3–4 ft. wide.

C. involucrata. Native from Missouri to Wyoming and south to Texas. To 6 in. tall and 2–3 ft. wide. Produces purplish red flow-ers 2 in. across. *C. i. tenuissima,* from the mountains of Mexico, has light purple flowers and more deeply cut foliage than the species.

C. papaver. WOODLAND POPPY MALLOW. From northern Florida to Texas, north to Georgia and Arkansas. Resembles C.

C

C

involucrata but has deep magenta blossoms on stems 5–12 in. long.

CALLISTEMON
BOTTLEBRUSH
Myrtaceae
Evergreen shrubs or trees

🌡 **ZONES VARY BY SPECIES**

☼ **FULL SUN**

💧💧 **MODERATE TO REGULAR WATER**

Callistemon citrinus

Fast-growing plants with colorful flowers carried in dense spikes or round clusters that consist mainly of long, bristlelike stamens—hence the common name "bottlebrush." Attractive to hummingbirds. Flowers are followed by woody capsules that can last for years and may resemble rows of beads pressed into bark.

Some bottlebrushes are naturally dense and compact (making good informal hedges); others are sparse and open (can be pruned up to become small trees). Those with pliant branches can be grown as informal espaliers. Very little routine pruning is needed—just remove any weak or dead branches after bloom or before spring growth. Don't cut into bare wood beyond leaves; if you do, plant may not send out new growth. Generally found in moist ground in their native Australia, bottlebrushes can withstand waterlogged soil. Normally tolerant of saline or alkaline soils but sometimes suffer from chlorosis (yellow leaves with green veins). Often severely damaged at 20°F.

C. citrinus. LEMON BOTTLEBRUSH. Shrub or tree. Zones LS, CS, TS; USDA 8-11. Most commonly grown bottlebrush; most tolerant of heat, cold, and poor soils. Massive shrub to 10–15 ft. tall and wide, but with staking and pruning in youth easily trained into narrowish, round-headed, 20- to 25-ft. tree. Nurseries offer it as a shrub, espalier, or tree. Narrow, 3-in.-long leaves are coppery when new, maturing to vivid green. Bruised leaves smell lemony. Bright red, 6-in.-long brushes appear in waves throughout the year.

Variable plant when grown from seed; look for cutting-grown selections with good flower size and color, such as 'Splendens'. Compared to the species, 'Violaceus' ('Jeffersii'), about 6 ft. tall and 4 ft. wide, has stiffer branches; narrower, shorter leaves; and reddish purple flowers fading to lavender. 'Mauve Mist' is the same but can reach 10 ft.

C. 'Perth Pink'. Shrub. Zones CS, TS; USDA 9-11. Dense, full growth to 6–10 ft. tall and wide, with weeping branches and deep pink flowers to 6 in. long in spring and early summer. New growth is pink.

C. rigidus. STIFF BOTTLEBRUSH. Rigid, sparse shrub or small tree to 20 ft. with 10-ft. spread. Zones LS, CS, TS; USDA 8-11. Sharp-pointed, gray-green (sometimes purplish) leaves to 6 in. long. Spring and summer red flower brushes are 2½–4½ in. long. Produces prominent seed capsules. Least graceful of the bottlebrushes. 'Clemson Hardy' is a compact form (2–3 ft. tall and wide) with bright red flowers; it succeeds in Zones US, MS, LS, CS, TS and has withstood –8°F. Bred in Georgia, 'Scarlet Torch' has a compact form, growing 9 ft. tall and 12 ft. wide.

C. salignus. WHITE BOTTLEBRUSH. Shrub or tree to 20–25 ft. tall, 10–15 ft. wide. Zones TS; USDA 10-11. Dense crown of foliage. Bright pink to copper new growth. Willowlike leaves 2–3 in. long. Pale yellow to cream-colored flowers appear in 1½- to 3-in. clusters in spring, early summer. Train as small shade tree or plant 4–5 ft. apart as hedge.

C. sieberi. ALPINE BOTTLEBRUSH. Zones MS, LS, CS, TS; USDA 7-11. Shrub. To 3–6 ft. tall and wide, with a somewhat upright habit. Small (to 1½-in.-long), dark green leaves densely cover the branches. Cream to yellow flowers in 1½- to 6-in.-long brushes bloom from late spring to midsummer.

C. viminalis. WEEPING BOTTLEBRUSH. Shrub or small tree with pendulous branches. Zones CS, TS; USDA 9-11. Fast growing to 20–30 ft. tall, with 15-ft. spread. Narrow, light green, 6-in.-long leaves. Bright red, 4- to 8-in.-long brushes from late spring into summer; scattered bloom rest of year. Not for windy, dry areas. As a tree, needs staking, thinning to prevent tangled, top-heavy growth. Leaves tend to grow toward ends of long, hanging branches.

'Little John' is a superior dwarf form to 3 ft. tall and wide, with dense growth and blood-red flowers in fall, winter, and spring. 'Captain Cook' is dense, rounded, to 6 ft. tall and wide; good for border, hedge, or screen. 'McCaskillii' has denser habit than others, is more vigorous (to 20 ft. tall), and has better flower color and form.

CALLISTEPHUS CHINENSIS
CHINA ASTER
Asteraceae
Annual

🌡 **US, MS, LS, CS, TS; USDA 6-11**

☼ **FULL SUN**

💧 **REGULAR WATER**

Callistephus chinensis

This summer-blooming Chinese native is a splendid cut flower and an effective bedding plant when well grown and free of disease. Plants range from 8 in. to 3 ft. high, 10–18 in. wide. Some kinds are branching; others (developed mainly for florists) have strong stems and no side shoots. Leaves are deeply toothed or lobed.

Flower forms are classified as peony, pompon, anemone, and ostrich feather. Rays can be quilled, curled, incurved, ribbonlike, or interlaced; some have crested centers. Colors range from white to pastel pink, rose-pink, lavender, lavender-blue, violet, purple, crimson, wine, and scarlet.

CARE

Plant in rich, moist, well-drained soil. After danger of frost is past, sow seed in place, or set out plants started in flats. Keep growth steady; sudden checks in growth are harmful. Subject to aster yellows, a viral disease carried by leafhoppers. Discard infected plants; control leafhoppers. All but wilt-resistant types are subject to aster wilt or stem rot, caused by a parasitic fungus that lives in soil and is transmitted through roots into plants. Overwatering produces an ideal environment for diseases, especially in heavy or poorly drained soil. Never plant in the same location in successive years.

CALLUNA VULGARIS
SCOTCH HEATHER
Ericaceae
Evergreen shrub

🌡 **US; USDA 6**

☼ **FULL SUN**

💧 **REGULAR WATER**

Calluna vulgaris

This, the true Scotch heather, is native to Europe and Asia Minor. It bears tiny, needlelike, dark green leaves and spikes of rosy pink, bell-shaped flowers. Garden types (far more common than the species) range from dwarf ground cover and rock garden sorts only a couple of inches high to plants reaching 3 ft. tall. Blossom colors include white, pale-to-deep pink, lavender, and purple. Most selections flower in mid- to late summer; a few continue on into late fall. Handsome foliage—pale and deeper greens, chartreuse, yellow, gray, or russet—often changes color in winter.

Unfortunately, despite its obvious appeal, Scotch heather is difficult to grow in the South. This attractive plant does best where conditions are neither too hot nor too cold, too dry nor too wet, and it must be grown in strongly acid, sandy or peaty, well-drained soil that is low in nutrients. You can amend the soil with organic matter, but don't apply fertilizer. Avoid cultivating near the plant, as this may damage shallow feeder roots. Mulch thoroughly to keep the soil cool and retain its moisture. Water during summer droughts. To prune, shear off faded flowers and branch tips immediately after bloom (for types blooming into late fall, delay pruning until late winter).

Hundreds of selections are available from specialty nurseries. Try them if you're adventurous, but keep in mind that unless you live in the Upper South or high up in the Appalachians, Scotch heather will probably be short lived in your garden. It is not browsed by deer.

CALOCEDRUS DECURRENS

INCENSE CEDAR
Cupressaceae
Evergreen tree

🌡 US, MS, LS; USDA 6-8

☀ ◐ **FULL SUN OR LIGHT SHADE**

💧 **NO IRRIGATION TO MODERATE WATER**

Calocedrus decurrens

You wouldn't think that a conifer native to Oregon and California would tolerate the heat and humidity of the South. But incense cedar does. It has been grown successfully from one end of the South to the other—from Stillwater, Oklahoma, to Athens, Georgia.

Growing 75–90 ft. tall and only 10–15 ft. wide, this symmetrical tree forms a dense, narrow, pyramidal crown. It features flat sprays of rich green foliage and handsome reddish brown bark. Small yellowish- to reddish-brown cones resembling duckbills ripen in autumn. The foliage produces a pungently sweet fragrance in warm weather, hence the tree's common name.

Although it's slow growing at first, incense cedar may grow 2 ft. per year when established. It takes blazing summer heat and poor soil in stride. Makes an excellent tall screen, windbreak, or specimen for spacious lawns. No pruning required. 'Aureovariegata' has green sprays variably marked with pale yellow. 'Berrima Gold' has soft golden-yellow foliage, turning rich golden orange in winter.

CALTHA PALUSTRIS

MARSH MARIGOLD
Ranunculaceae
Perennial

🌡 US, MS, LS, CS; USDA 6-9

☀ ◐ ● **SUN OR SHADE**

💧 **AMPLE WATER**

◆ **ANY PART CAN CAUSE INFLAMMATION, PAIN IF INGESTED**

Caltha palustris

Native to Eurasia—and from Newfoundland to Alaska, south to North Carolina and Tennessee. Vigorous, lushly foliaged plant, well adapted to life at the edges of pools, ponds, streams, and other moist locations. Given sufficient water, it can also be grown in borders; it looks good with bog irises and moisture-loving ferns. Reaches 2 ft. tall and wide; rounded, 2- to 7-in.-wide, glossy green leaves are heart shaped at the base, give an almost tropical effect. Clusters of cheery yellow flowers to 2 in. across bloom in spring; a double-flowered form is available. Increase by divisions, or sow seed in boggy soil. Not favored by deer.

CALYCANTHUS

Calycanthaceae
Deciduous shrubs

🌡 US, MS, LS, CS; USDA 6-9

☀ ◐ ● **SUN OR SHADE**

💧 **REGULAR WATER**

◆ **SEEDS CAN PRODUCE CONVULSIONS IF INGESTED**

Calycanthus chinensis
'Hartlage Wine'

Deciduous shrubs. Both of these are bulky plants with lush foliage and flowers valued for their fragrance and form.

C. chinensis (*Sinocalycanthus chinensis*). CHINESE SWEETSHRUB. Zones US, MS, LS, CS; USDA 6-9. Coarse-textured deciduous shrubs offer 2½-3 in., nonfragrant flowers resembling the native sweetshrub on steroids. 'Hartlage Wine' offers reddish maroon flowers in mid- to late spring on a plant growing 8-10 ft. high and 6-8 ft. wide. 'Venus' is a hybrid growing 6-8 ft. high and wide with similar flowers, except they are creamy white and appear sporadically from spring into summer. 'Aphrodite' combines a bloom similar to 'Hartlage Wine' with sweet fragrance lacking in others of this group. Grows 6–7 ft. tall and 5–6 ft. wide.

C. floridus. COMMON SWEET-SHRUB, CAROLINA ALLSPICE. Native from Virginia to Florida. Suckering, fast-spreading, stiffly branched plant to 6–10 ft. tall and as wide or wider. Leaves are oval, to 5 in., glossy, dark green above, grayish green beneath; turn yellow in fall. Plant blooms most heavily in April and May, and then sporadically to July. Reddish brown, 2-in.-wide flowers, often with heady strawberry fragrance, are carried at ends of leafy branchlets. Blooms are followed by brownish,

ABOVE: Calycanthus floridus

pear-shaped capsules that are very fragrant when crushed.

Plant in shrub border or around outdoor living space where the flowers' perfume can be appreciated. Aroma varies, so buy when plants are in bloom. 'Michael Lindsay' is dense and compact, with very fragrant blooms. 'Athens' has yellow flowers and an outstanding fragrance reminiscent of cantaloupe.

CALYLOPHUS

SUNDROPS
Onagraceae
Perennials

✎ **US, MS, LS, CS; USDA 6-9, EXCEPT AS NOTED**

☼◐ **FULL SUN OR LIGHT SHADE**

◊◖ **LITTLE TO MODERATE WATER**

Calylophus hartwegii

Found across the Southwest, these showy perennials share the same common name as some of their close relatives (and look-alikes) in the genus *Oenothera*. Bloom over a long season, from spring into late fall, bearing bright yellow, four-petaled flowers that open at sunset and remain open for most of the next day. Plants go dormant in winter and may be sheared just before spring growth begins. They spread by rhizomes and can take over a garden bed if unrestrained by a physical barrier, such as metal edging sunk 6 in. deep into the ground. Good for summer color in rock gardens or on rocky slopes; make nice filler plants in mixed borders. Like lots of heat and excellent drainage.

C. berlandieri (*Oenothera berlandieri*). SQUARE BUD PRIMROSE. Native to Texas, northern Mexico, and the Gulf states. This tough garden perennial grows to 1 ft. tall and 3 ft. wide. The fine-textured foliage gives background to these 1-2 in. flowers in spring and early summer. Great for trailing over a low wall where it enjoys good drainage.

C. drummondianus. To 1½ ft. high, 2 ft. wide, with narrow, tooth-edged, somewhat drooping leaves and inch-wide flowers. This species blooms for a longer period than *C. hartwegii* in spring, but it does not rebloom as well in fall.

C. hartwegii. To 1 ft. high, 2 ft. across, with inch-wide flowers; those of 'Sierra Sundrop' are larger. *C. h. lavandulifolius* has narrow, gray leaves. Excellent in hot, dry locations and when

mixed with desert perennials.

C. serrulatus. US, MS, LS; USDA 6-8. Prairie wildflower found from Saskatchewan to Texas. To 1½ ft. high and wide, with ¾-in. flowers.

C. 'Southern Belle'. LS, MS, CS, TS; USDA 8-11. Complex hybrid to 8–12 in. tall, 18 in. wide. Long-blooming and well-behaved, producing no seeds.

CAMASSIA

CAMASS
Asparagaceae
Perennials from bulbs

✎ **US, MS, LS, CS; USDA 6-9**

☼◐ **FULL SUN OR LIGHT SHADE**

◖ **AMPLE WATER DURING GROWTH AND BLOOM**

Camassia quamash

Northwest natives. Starlike, slender-petaled blossoms are carried on spikes in late spring, early summer; grasslike basal leaves dry quickly after bloom. Plant in consistently moist, fairly heavy soil, where bulbs can remain undisturbed for many years. Set bulbs 4 in. deep, 6 in. apart. To avoid premature sprouting, plant after weather cools in fall. Resistant to deer and rodents.

C. cusickii. Dense clusters of pale blue flowers are borne on stems that grow to 3 ft. tall. A white form is available.

C. leichtlinii. Large, handsome clusters of blue-to-creamy white flowers on stems to 4 ft. tall. 'Sacajawea' has white flowers and white-edged leaves. 'Semiplena' has creamy white semidouble blooms. *C. l. leichtlinii* (*C.* 'Alba') is white with a faint hint of blue. *C. l. suksdorfii* has blue-to-deep blue-violet flowers; its selection 'Blue

Danube' is deep blue.

C. quamash (*C. esculenta*). Loose clusters of blue flowers on 1- to 2-ft. stems. Flowers of 'Orion' are deeper blue. 'Blue Melody' has dark blue flowers and cream-striped foliage.

CAMELLIA

Theaceae
Evergreen shrubs or trees

✎ **US (MILDER PARTS, PROTECTED), MS, LS, CS, TS (SOME); USDA 6-11**

◐ **LIGHT SHADE, EXCEPT AS NOTED**

◖◖ **MODERATE TO REGULAR WATER**

Camellia japonica 'Herme'

The South is the heart of camellia country. Indeed, common camellia (*Camellia japonica*) is Alabama's state flower. Although it seems these beautiful plants must have been born here, in truth they hail from eastern and southern Asia. More than 3,000 named kinds of camellias exist, in a remarkable range of colors, forms, and sizes; they are not usually browsed by deer.

If you live in the Upper or Tropical South and have problems growing camellias, take heart: you can now enjoy hybrids that flourish in the extremes of weather found in both regions. See "Hardy hybrids" (page 213).

The following pages offer a brief discussion of camellias' cultural requirements and describe some lesser-known species, as well as old favorites and new selections. The plant descriptions also include cultural needs unique to individual species and selections.

C. x hiemalis. Formerly considered a separate species,

this group of hybrids involving *C. sasanqua* is noted for bushy, compact growth habit. Often called "dwarf sasanquas"; many are low growing and spreading, although some are tall and upright. Examples include the following (all have 2- to 2½-in. blossoms):

'Bonanza'. Upright, strong grower, 3–10 ft. tall and 3–6 ft. wide. Red flowers of loose peony form.

'Chansonette'. Vigorous, spreading growth to 6 ft. high, 8 ft. wide. Large, bright pink formal double flowers with frilled petals.

'Kanjiro'. Upright plant to 15 ft. tall and 10 ft. wide. Single to semi-double blossoms in rose-pink edged with red.

'Shishi-Gashira'. One of the most useful and ornamental shrubs. Low growing (4 ft. high and 8 ft. wide), with arching branches that in time pile up tier on tier to make a compact, dark green, glossy-leafed plant. Leaves rather small for camellia, giving medium-fine foliage texture. Flowers are rose-red, semidouble, heavily borne over long season— October through March in a good year. Takes considerable sun.

'Showa-No-Sakae'. To at least 8 ft. high, 12 ft. wide. Faster growing, more open than 'Shishi-Gashira'; willowy, arching branches. Semidouble to double flowers of soft pink, occasionally marked with white. Try this as an espalier.

'Showa Supreme'. Very similar to 'Showa-No-Sakae' but has somewhat larger flowers of peony form.

'Sparkling Burgundy'. Upright, slow grower to 5–10 ft. tall and 3–6 ft. wide, with narrow leaves and deep pink peony-form flowers. Very early.

C. japonica. COMMON CAMELLIA. This is the plant most gardeners have in mind when they speak of camellias. Naturally a large shrub or small tree but variable in size, growth rate, and habit. Hundred-year-old plants reach 20 ft. high and equally wide, and even larger specimens exist. However, most gardeners can consider japonicas to be shrubs 6–12 ft. high and wide. Just a few are lower growing.

The following list describes japonica selections that are favorites among Southern gardeners. Included here are a number of old standbys whose beauty belies their age. Some of them are among the oldest camellias still in commerce, having been brought to Europe and the U.S. from China and Japan in the 19th century or even earlier (these venerable camellias are noted by date of introduction in the text).

Those described as "hardy" will survive temperatures as low as 0–5°F. Most camellias get flambéed in the Tropical South, but the following heat-tolerant japonicas perform well as far south as Fort Myers and West Palm Beach in Florida: 'Alba Plena', 'Debutante', 'Gigantea', 'Lady Clare', 'Mathotiana', and 'Professor Charles S. Sargent'. You can even try them in Miami, though you'll have to grow them in pots because of the alkaline soil there.

The list specifies season of bloom as early, midseason, or late. In the Coastal South, early is November and December; midseason is January and February; late is March. In the Lower South, early is December and January; midseason is February and March; late is March and April. In the Middle South, early is February; midseason is March and April; late is April and May. In the Upper South, early is March; midseason is April; late is May. Flower size is also noted for each selection. Very large blooms are over 5 in. wide; large, 4–5 in.; medium-large, 3½–4 in.; medium, 3–3½ in.; small, 2½–3 in.; and miniature, 2½ in. or less.

'Adolphe Audusson' (1877). Midseason. Very large, dark red

HOW TO GROW CAMELLIAS

EXPOSURE In general, camellias grow and bloom better in partial shade, with shelter from hot afternoon sun. This is especially true for young plants, which thrive under the shade of tall trees or when grown on the north side of a house. As they grow larger and their thick canopy of leaves shades and cools their roots, they gradually will accept more sun. Shade provided in winter reduces cold damage in the Upper and Middle South. Shelter them from strong winds, particularly in the Upper and Middle South or near the coast. They do not tolerate salt spray.

PLANTING Plant in well-drained soil rich in organic material. Never plant so trunk base is below soil line, and never let soil cover the base. Spring or fall planting is fine for most areas. Spring is better in the Upper South, where the root system needs time to get established before onset of cold weather. Apply a 2-in.-thick layer of mulch to keep the roots cool and the soil moist; keep mulch a few inches away from the trunk.

WATERING Regular irrigation is critical during the first year. Water thoroughly to moisten the entire root ball; then let the top of the root ball go slightly dry before the next watering. Established plants (over 3 years old, vigorous, and shading their own roots) get by with little supplemental water.

FERTILIZING Feed with an acid-forming azalea or camellia fertilizer in spring, after the flowers have dropped; fertilize again in midsummer if growth seems sluggish or foliage looks sparse and begins to lose its deep green color. Apply at the rate recommended on the label. Don't overdo it, as plants grown in fertile soil need little fertilizer—and never feed plants that are sick or stressed.

PRUNING Prune after blooming has ended. Remove dead or weak wood; thin out growth when it is so dense that flowers have no room to open properly. Shorten lower branches to encourage upright growth; cut back top growth to make lanky shrubs bushier. When pruning, cut just above a scar that marks the end of the previous year's growth (often a slightly thickened, somewhat rough area where bark texture and color change slightly). Making your cuts just above this point usually forces three or four dormant buds into growth.

CAMELLIA PROBLEMS Scorched or yellowed areas in the center of leaves usually indicate sunburn. Burned leaf edges, excessive leaf drop, or corky leaf spots generally point to overfertilizing. Chlorosis (yellow leaves with green veins) results from planting in neutral or alkaline soil; to correct, feed plant with chelated iron and amend soil with sphagnum peat moss and/or garden sulfur to adjust the pH. Poorly drained soil can also cause chlorosis.

Tea scale is a common pest. These pests look like tiny brown or white specks on leaf undersides; sooty mold grows on the honeydew they secrete. Infested leaves turn yellow and drop. To treat tea scale, apply horticultural oil or a systemic insecticide; check with your local County Extension Office for the best choice in your area.

Two fungal diseases are common. Camellia petal blight causes flowers to turn brown rapidly, then drop. Sanitation is the best control: Pick up and destroy all fallen blossoms as well as infected ones still on the plant. Remove and discard any existing mulch, then replace it with a 4- to 5-in. layer of fresh mulch. Camellia leaf gall causes leaves to become distorted, pale, thick, and fleshy; they gradually turn white, then brown, then drop from the plant. The best control is to pick off and destroy affected leaves before they turn white.

Bud drop is a frequent complaint. To some extent, this is natural for camellias (many set more buds than they can open), but it also may be caused by overwatering, summer drought, or sudden freezes.

CAMELLIAS IN CONTAINERS Camellias are outstanding container plants, whether you grow them outdoors on a terrace or indoors in a cool greenhouse. As a general rule, plant gallon-size camellias in 12- to 14-in.-diameter containers; 5-gallon ones in 16- to 18-in. containers. Fill the container with a potting mix containing 50 percent or more organic material. Make sure the container has a generous drainage hole.

C

semidouble flowers, heavily borne on a medium-size, symmetrical, vigorous shrub. Hardy. 'Adolphe Audusson Variegated' is identical, but its blossoms are heavily marbled with white on red.

'Alba Plena' (1792). Early. Brought from China over two centuries ago and still a favorite. Large, white formal double. Slow, bushy growth. Early bloom is a disadvantage in cold or rainy areas; protect blossoms from rain and wind.

'Berenice Boddy'. Midseason. Medium, light pink semidouble blooms with deeper shading. Vigorous, upright growth. One of the hardiest.

'Carter's Sunburst'. Early to late. Large to very large flowers, semidouble to peony form to formal double, in pale pink striped with deeper pink. Medium-size, compact plant.

'C. M. Wilson'. Early to midseason. Sport of 'Elegans' and identical to it except for its pale pink flower color. 'C. M. Wilson Variegated' has white petal markings; many plants sold as 'C. M. Wilson' are actually the variegated form.

'Daikagura' (1891). Early to late. Large, rose-red peony-form blooms on a dense, upright bush. Very long bloom season. 'Daikagura Variegated' is similar but has rose-red blossoms marbled in white.

'Debutante'. Early to midseason. Medium-large, light pink peony-form flowers. Profuse bloomer. Vigorous upright growth. Takes some sun.

'Elegans' ('Chandler'); also sold as 'Francine' ('Chandleri Elegans Pink') (1831). Early to midseason. The founder of a large and growing family of sports. The original plant is slow growing and spreading, bearing large anemone-form blossoms in rose-pink; center petaloids are often marked with white. More frequently grown is 'Elegans Variegated', identical except for white variegation on all petals; it is often known simply as 'Chandleri Elegans'. 'Elegans Supreme' is like 'Elegans' with the addition of deep serrations on petal edges. 'Elegans Champagne' is a white sport of 'Elegans Supreme' with creamy central petaloids. 'Elegans Splendor' has white-margined, pale pink petals with fringed

edges. For other sports in the 'Elegans' family, see 'C. M. Wilson' and 'Shiro Chan'.

'Gigantea'. Midseason. Enormous, semidouble red blooms marbled with white. Vigorous plant.

'Glen 40' ('Coquetii'). Midseason to late. Large, deep red formal double. One of the best red camellia blooms for corsages. Slow, compact, upright growth. Plant is handsome even out of bloom. Hardy; very good container plant.

'Governor Mouton'. Midseason. Upright. Medium, semidouble or loose peony-form flowers are red marked with white. Hardy.

'Guilio Nuccio'. Midseason. Considered by many to be the world's finest camellia. Coral-rose, very large semidouble flowers of unusual depth and substance have inner petals fluted in "rabbit ear" effect. Vigorous, upright growth. Forms with variegated, fringed blossoms are available.

'Herme' ('Jordan's Pride') (1875). Midseason. Medium-large, pink semidouble flowers irregularly bordered in white and streaked with deeper pink. Sometimes bears solid pink blooms on certain branches. Free blooming and dependable.

'Jacks'. Midseason. Medium-large, deep pink, formal double flowers. Compact grower to just 6 ft. tall and half as wide in 10 years.

'Kramer's Supreme'. Midseason. Full peony-form, very large flowers in deep, clear red. Some people can detect a faint fragrance. Compact, upright, unusually vigorous. Takes some sun.

'Kumasaka' (1896). Midseason to late. Medium-large, rose-pink, rose-form double to peony-form flowers. Vigorous, compact, upright growth and remarkably heavy flower production make it a choice landscape plant. Hardy. Takes morning sun.

'La Peppermint'. Early to midseason. Medium, rose-form double flowers are white or palest pink, prominently striped in red. Some blooms may revert to solid red. Bushy, upright grower.

'Lady Clare' ('Akashigita'). Early and midseason. Dense, rounded, vigorous. Large, semidouble deep pink blooms. Hardy.

'Lady Vansittart'. Midseason to late. Moderate growth; upright form. Medium, semidouble white flowers are streaked to varying degrees in shades of rosy red, giving the look of several different flower colors on a single plant. Hardy.

'Magnoliiflora' (1886). Midseason. Medium, pale pink semidouble flowers are borne profusely, make good cut flowers. Medium-size plant with compact yet spreading form. Hardy.

'Mathotiana' (1840s). Midseason to late. Very large rose-form double to formal double blooms in deep crimson, sometimes showing a purplish cast. Vigorous, upright grower. Tolerates cold and stands up well in hot-summer regions.

'Mrs. Charles Cobb'. Midseason to late. Large, deep red semidouble to peony-form flowers. Free blooming. Compact plant with dense foliage; best in warmer areas.

'Nuccio's Cameo'. Early to late. Medium to large, formal double flowers in light pink to coral pink. Bushy, upright grower with a very long bloom season.

'Nuccio's Gem'. Midseason. Medium to large, white, perfectly formed formal double. Strong-growing, full, upright plant.

'Nuccio's Jewel'. Midseason to late. Large flowers in loose to full peony form are white with pink petal edges.

'Nuccio's Pearl'. Midseason. Full formal double, medium blossoms are white with a rim of deep pink outer petals.

'Paulette Goddard'. Midseason. Vigorous and upright. Medium, semidouble or loose peony-form blossoms in deep red. Quite hardy and tough.

'Pink Perfection' ('Otome'). Early to late. Erect to spreading. Small, pale pink formal double flowers. Hardy.

'Prince Eugene Napoleon' ('Pope Pius IX') (1859). Midseason. Cherry-red, medium-large formal double. Medium-size, compact, upright plant.

'Professor Charles S. Sargent' ('Professor Sargent'). Midseason. Compact and upright. Medium-size, dark red anemone-form flowers with ruffled petals in the center. Hardy.

'Purity' (1887). Late. White, medium flowers, rose-form double to formal double, usually

TOP: Camellia japonica 'Elegans Variegated'; C. j. 'Lady Clare'; BOTTOM: C. x hiemalis 'Chansonette'

TOP: Camellia japonica 'Governor Mouton'; *C. x vernalis* 'Yuletide'; *MIDDLE: C. j.* 'Lady Vansittart'; *BOTTOM: C. x vernalis* 'Dawn'; *C. j.* 'Professor Charles S. Sargent'

showing a few stamens. Vigorous, upright plant. Late bloom means it often escapes rain damage.

'Reine des Fleurs'. Midseason, semi-double, deep pink blooms. Reputed to be one of the first camellias planted in the South by famed botanist Andre Michaux at Middleton Place in Charleston, but this is disputed.

'Rev. John C. Drayton'. Late. Moderate grower. Medium, semidouble bright carmine-rose blossoms. Hardy.

'R. L. Wheeler'. Late. Very large, rose-red, semidouble flowers. Hardy.

'Sea Foam'. Late. Large, white formal double flowers. Upright, large plant.

'Shiro Chan'. Early to midseason. A sport of 'C. M. Wilson' with identical habit and flower form. Blossoms may open palest pink, fading to white blushed with pink at petal bases. 'Snow Chan' is a pure white sport.

'Silver Waves'. Early to midseason. Large, white semidouble blooms with wavy petal edges.

'Swan Lake'. Midseason to late. Very large white flowers with formal double to peony form. Vigorous, upright growth.

'Tama-no-ura'. Early to midseason. Small, single flowers are red with a prominent white edge. Vigorous, upright, somewhat open grower.

'Tiffany'. Midseason to late. Very large blossoms in warm pink; rose-form double to loose, irregular semidouble. Vigorous, upright shrub.

'Tom Knudsen'. Early to midseason. Medium to large blooms in dark red with deeper red veining. Formal double to peony-form to rose-form double.

'Ville de Nantes'. Midseason to late. Large semidouble flowers have white-blotched, deep red petals with fringed edges. Bushy, slow-growing plant. 'Lady Kay' is a sport with full peony form.

'Wildfire'. Early to midseason. Medium, orange-red semidouble flowers on a vigorous, upright plant.

C. oleifera. TEA-OIL CAMELLIA. Large shrub or small tree to 20 ft. tall and 12 ft. wide, with glossy, dark green leaves and fragrant, 2-in. white flowers in fall. Specific name *oleifera* means "oil bearing"; oil extracted from the large seeds has been used in China for cooking or as a hair conditioner. Possibly the hardiest of all the camellias.

C. reticulata. NETVEIN CAMELLIA. Some of the biggest and most spectacular camellia flowers occur in this species, and as likely as not they appear on some of the lankiest and least graceful of camellia plants.

Plants differ somewhat according to selection, but generally speaking they are rather gaunt, open shrubs that eventually become trees of considerable size—possibly 35–50 ft. tall. In gardens, consider them 10-ft.-tall shrubs, 8 ft. wide. Leaves are also variable but tend to be dull green, leathery, and strongly net veined.

Culture is similar to that of other camellias, except that these plants seem intolerant of heavy pruning. This, with their natural gawkiness and size, makes them difficult to place in the garden. They are at their best in light shade of old oaks, where they should stand alone with plenty of room to develop. They look good in containers while young but are not handsome there out of bloom. Develop better form and heavier foliage in open ground. These camellias are less hardy than *C. japonica* (not recommended for the Upper or Middle South). In Lower South, grow in containers so you can move them into winter protection, or plant beneath an overhang or near a wall.

Best-known kinds have large (4- to 6-in.) semidouble flowers with deeply fluted and curled inner petals. These inner petals give great depth to the flower. All bloom from late winter to early spring. The following are the best choices for garden use.

'Buddha'. Very large rose-pink flowers; inner petals unusually erect and wavy. Gaunt and open; grows fast.

'Butterfly Wings'. Rose-pink, loose semidouble flower of great size (reported as large as 9 in. across), with broad, wavy petals. Open, rather narrow plant.

'Captain Rawes'. Reddish rose-pink semidouble flowers of large size. Vigorous bushy plant with good foliage. Hardiest of reticulatas.

'Chang's Temple'. True selection bears large, open-centered, deep rose flowers, with notched, fluted center petals. 'Cornelian' is sometimes sold as 'Chang's Temple'.

'Cornelian'. Large, deep, loose peony-form flowers with wavy petals; rosy pink to red, heavily variegated with white. Vigorous plant with big leaves that are usually marked with white. This plant is often sold as 'Chang's Temple' or as 'Lion Head'. (The true 'Lion Head' is not found in American gardens.)

'Crimson Robe'. Very large, bright red semidouble flowers. Firm textured, wavy petals. Vigorous plant of better appearance than most other reticulatas.

'Purple Gown'. Large, purplish red peony-form to formal double flowers. Compact plant with best growth habit and foliage in the group.

'Shot Silk'. Large, loose semidouble flowers of brilliant pink with iridescent finish that sparkles in sunlight. Fast, rather open growth.

'Tali Queen'. Very large, deep reddish pink flowers of loose semidouble form with heavily crinkled petals. Plant form and foliage are very good. This selection is often sold as 'Noble Pearl'; true 'Noble Pearl' is not available in the U.S.

C. sasanqua. SASANQUA CAMELLIA. Though often dismissed as "those other camellias" by Southerners smitten with the huge blooms of *C. japonica*, sasanqua camellias deserve better. True, their flowers are smaller, but the plants offer many advantages over common camellias. They tolerate more sun, more heat, and a wider range of soils, and their looser habit and smaller leaves make them easier to incorporate into a landscape. In form, they vary from upright and treelike to bushy and spreading; heights range from 6 to 15 ft. Glossy, dark green leaves are 1½–3½ in. long, about a third as wide. The plants bloom heavily from late summer through autumn and into winter, depending on the selection, bearing single, semidouble, or double flowers that are sometimes lightly fragrant. Blossoms typically come in pink or white, but there are also some reds. Individual blooms last only a short time, but they're so numerous that the show goes on for months.

Established sasanqua camellias tolerate drought, but those growing in full sun need more water. They make excellent espal-

iers, tall screens, informal hedges, and bonsai specimens, as they accept frequent pruning. Upright selections can be pruned into standards (single trunks). Sasanquas are not as hardy to cold as common camellias; gardeners in the Upper South should plant them in spots protected from winter wind and sun or grow them in cool greenhouses.

'Apple Blossom'. Medium single white flowers blushed with pink, from pink buds. Spreading plant.

'Autumn Moon'. Medium formal double flowers are white. Growth is bushy, upright and narrow, making it a good hedging plant.

'Autumn Sentinel'. Small, double, pale pink blooms are striking against the deep green, narrow leaves. Fast grower with a narrow, slender habit; good as specimen or hedge.

'Bella Rouge'. Red, semidouble flowers on plants 4-5 ft.

TOP: Camellia japonica 'Reine des Fleurs'; BOTTOM: C. j. 'Sea Foam'

tall and wide. Ideal for specimen or hedge.

'Cleopatra'. Large, rose-pink semidouble flowers with narrow, curving petals. Growth is erect, fairly compact. Takes clipping well. Very hardy.

'Hana Jiman'. Large semidouble flowers, white with pink edges. Fast and open growth; good espalier.

'Jean May'. Large double blossoms in shell pink. Compact, upright grower with exceptionally glossy foliage.

'Midnight Lover'. Large, darkest red, semidouble blooms. Vigorous and upright.

'Mine-No-Yuki' ('White Doves'). Large white flowers of full peony form. Spreading, willowy growth; effective espalier.

'Narumi-gata'. Large, cupped, single flowers, white tinged pink.

October Magic series. Bred in Fairhope, Alabama, this group includes sturdy landscape plants that offer a variety of colors and plant forms. 'Bride' blooms white, grows 4-6 ft. tall and wide; 'Dawn' blooms doubled in shades of pale pink, growing into a conical form 4-6 ft. tall and 3-4 ft. wide; 'Inspiration' blooms white with a magenta edge, grows upright 6-8 ft. tall and 4-5 ft. wide; 'Orchid' blooms with a pink blush and grows 3-5 ft. tall and wide; 'Rose' blooms vivid pink and grows remarkably upright at 6-8 ft. tall and 3-4 ft. wide; 'Ruby' blooms doubled and red, growing 4-5 ft. tall and wide; 'Snow' blooms fully doubled white and grows 5-7 ft. tall wide.

'Setsugekka'. Large, white semidouble flowers with fluted petals. Blossoms have considerable substance; cut sprays hold well in water. Upright and rather bushy shrub.

'Tanya'. Small single flowers in deep rose-pink. Tolerates much sun. Low-growing, spreading plant. Good ground cover.

C. sinensis (*Thea sinensis*). TEA PLANT. Dense, rounded shrub is grown in Asia as the commercial source of tea, but in the South it is an ornamental. Reaches 15 ft. tall and wide, with leathery dark green leaves to 5 in. long. Blooms in fall, bearing scented white flowers to 1½ in. wide. Takes well to pruning; can be trimmed into a hedge. 'Blushing Maiden' bears nodding pink flowers; 'Teabreeze' offers fragrant white blooms.

C. x vernalis. A group of sasanqua hybrids noted for later bloom (all flower in late fall and winter), denser growth, shinier foliage, and firmer-textured flowers. Most reach about 9 ft. tall and 6 ft. wide. They take the same care as sasanquas and are often sold as such.

'Dawn'. Small, single to semidouble white flowers blushed pink. Dense, upright shrub of unusual hardiness.

'Egao'. Large, semidouble deep pink flowers that do not shatter easily. Pendulous branches make it good for espalier.

'Hiryu'. Small, deep red, roseform double blooms on a dense, upright plant. 'Hiryu Nishiki' has white markings on flowers.

'Shibori Egao'. Medium, pink, semidouble blooms are heavily splashed with white. Leaves may show yellow splotches. Full and upright.

'Star Above Star'. Medium semidouble flowers in white shading to lavender-pink. Upright and bushy; may reach 10–20 ft. tall and wide.

'Yuletide'. Profusion of small, brilliant red single flowers on a dense, upright, compact plant. Blooms in late December.

HYBRID CAMELLIAS. Several categories of hybrids, described here, have been produced.

Medium-flowered hybrids. The first wave of hybridizing involved *C. japonica* and *C. saluenensis*. The resulting hybrids, most of them medium to large shrubs, are of generally good garden form, with foliage like that of *C. japonica* and abundant flowers. See *C. japonica* for explanations of bloom season and flower-size terminology.

'Coral Delight'. Midseason. Large, coral-pink semidouble flowers form garlands along the branches. Slow grower.

'Crimson Candles'. Early. Rosered blooms open from deep red buds that extend the color show as they mature. Strong-growing, upright, disease-resistant plant.

'Donation'. Midseason. Large semidouble flowers in orchid pink are borne all along stems. Vigorous, upright, compact plant with slightly pendulous branches; blooms young and heavily. Quite resistant to cold and sun. Appreciates a little shade in hot, dry areas. There is a form with variegated flowers.

'E. G. Waterhouse'. Midseason to late. Formal double of excellent form. Light pink, medium flowers heavily produced on vigorous, upright shrub.

'Fragrant Pink'. Midseason. An exception in that it is a cross between *C. j. rusticana* and *C. lutchuensis*. Loose peony-form flowers on spreading bush. Flowers are small, deep pink, very fragrant.

'Freedom Bell'. Midseason. Small to medium, semidouble, bell-shaped blooms of dark red open beneath branches.

'Jury's Yellow'. Early to late. Medium anemone-form blooms with ivory white outer petals, creamy yellow central petaloids. Compact, upright.

'Taylor's Perfection'. Midseason. Profuse show of large, light pink semidouble flowers.

Large-flowered hybrids. A second wave of hybridizing, involving *C. japonica*, *C. reticulata*, and *C. sasanqua* produced plants with more spectacular blossoms than the medium-flowered hybrids. See *C. japonica* for explanations of bloom season and flower-size terminology.

'Dr. Clifford Parks'. Midseason. Very large blossoms in a rich, orange-toned red are semidouble to loose peony form to anemone form. Vigorous, upright plant.

'Flower Girl'. Early to midseason. Large to very large, semidouble to peony-form flowers of bright pink. Vigorous, upright growth. Profuse flowering and small leaves come from its sasanqua parent, big flowers from its *C. reticulata* ancestor.

'Francie L'. Midseason to late. Very large semidouble flowers with wavy petals. Deep rose-pink.

'Frank Houser'. Early to midseason. Very large semidouble to peony form, rose-red flowers. Spreading, open, strong grower. A variegated form is also available.

'Valentine Day'. Midseason to late. Large to very large, salmon-pink formal double flowers. Fast, upright grower.

'Valley Knudsen'. Midseason to late. Large to very large, deep orchid-pink blooms, semidouble to loose peony form. Compact, upright growth.

Hardy hybrids. Dr. William Ackerman of the National Arboretum in Washington, D.C., and Dr. Clifford Parks of the University of North Carolina, Chapel Hill, bred a number of species, notably

the hardy *C. oleifera*, to produce hardy camellias. These hybrids withstand temperatures as low as –15°F with little or no damage, provided they have some shelter from winter sun and wind. They bear 3½- to 4-in. flowers in October and November. Selections include very early-blooming 'Autumn Spirit', with small, bright pink peony-form flowers; 'Snow Flurry' and 'Winter's Snowman', white anemone-form blossoms; 'Winter's Charm' and 'Winter's Interlude', pink peony form; 'Winter's Joy', bright pink semidouble blooms; and 'Winter's Waterlily', white formal double.

'Pink Icicle', with shell-pink peony-form flowers, was selected from *C. japonica* and blooms in early spring. Also selected from *C. japonica* is the April series of hardy camellias, named for the time they typically bloom in the cooler, northern part of their range. Included are 'April Blush', shell-pink semidouble; 'April Dawn', formal double, variegated pink and white; 'April Remembered', cream- to pink-shaded, semidouble; 'April Rose', rose-red formal double; 'April Snow', white rose-form double; and 'April Tryst', bright red anemone form.

CAMPANULA
BELLFLOWER
Campanulaceae
Perennials

🖉 US, MS, LS; USDA 6-8

☼ ◑ **FULL SUN IN COOLER CLIMATES ONLY**

◐ ◑ **MODERATE TO REGULAR WATER**

Campanula persicifolia
'Telham Beauty'

Vast and varied group (nearly 300 species) encompassing trailers,

creeping or tufted miniatures, and erect kinds 1–6 ft. tall. Native throughout the Northern Hemisphere; species described here are perennials mostly from southern Europe, Turkey, the Caucasus, and northern Asia. Flowers are generally bell shaped, but some are star shaped, cup shaped, or round and flat. Usually blue, lavender, violet, purple, or white; some pink.

Uses are as varied as the plants. Gemlike miniatures deserve special settings—close-up situations in rock gardens, niches in dry walls, raised beds, containers. Trailing kinds are ideal for hanging pots or baskets, wall crevices; vigorous, spreading growers serve well as ground covers. Upright growers are valuable in borders, for cutting, occasionally in containers.

In general, campanulas grow better in good, well-drained soil and the cooler climates of the Upper and Middle South. Most species are fairly easy to grow from seed sown in flats in spring or early summer, then transplanted to the garden in fall for bloom the following year; also may be increased by cuttings or divisions. Divide clumps in fall—typically every 3 or 4 years, though some may need yearly division.

C. carpatica. TUSSOCK BELLFLOWER. Forms compact, leafy tufts with branching, spreading stems. About 8 in. tall but may reach 1–1½ ft. Smooth, bright green, wavy, toothed leaves, 1–1½ in. long. Single blue or white flowers to 1–2 in. across are upward facing, bell or cup shaped. Blooms in late spring. Use in rock gardens, borders, edging. Not browsed by deer. 'Blue Clips' ('Blaue Clips') and 'White Clips' (*C. c. alba* 'Weisse Clips') are good dwarf selections that are easily grown from seed; they are sometimes sold as 'Blue Chips' and 'White Chips'. 'China Doll' is a 6-in.-high selection with pale lavender-blue flowers.

C. glomerata. CLUSTERED BELLFLOWER. Upright, with erect side branches to 1–2 ft. Leaves are broad and somewhat hairy, 2–4 in. long; basal leaves are wavy edged, stem leaves toothed. Narrow, bell-shaped, 1-in.-long, blue-violet flowers are tightly clustered at stem tops. Summer bloom. Plant in shaded borders. Seed-grown strains

Superba and Alba are deepest purple and white, respectively. 'Caroline' is lavender. 'Joan Elliott' is deep violet-blue. 'Purple Pixie' has violet-purple flowers on 14-in. stems.

C. lactiflora. MILKY BELL-FLOWER. Erect, branching plant to 3½–5 ft. tall. Oblong, toothed leaves, 2–3 in. long. Broadly bell-shaped to star-shaped, 1-in.-long, white to pale blue flowers in drooping clusters at ends of branches. Summer bloom. Plant in back of borders in sun or partial shade. Endures even dry shade and is long lived. 'Loddon Anna' has pale pink flowers. 'Pouffe' (lavender) and 'White Pouffe' form a 10-in. bloom-covered mound.

C. persicifolia. PEACH-LEAFED BLUEBELL. Graceful, strong-growing plant with bright green foliage. Narrow basal leaves, 4–8 in. long, form a low clump to 1½ ft. wide. Slender, erect, leafy stems rise 2–3 ft. high in summer, in loose spires of open, cup-shaped, inch-wide blossoms of blue, pink, or white. Choice plants for borders. Easy to grow from seed sown in late spring. Longtime favorite 'Telham Beauty' has 3-in. blue flowers. 'La Belle' and 'White Pearl' have double flowers. 'Chettle Charm' has white flowers softly edged with lavender. 'Takion White' and 'Takion Blue' are heavy blooming and compact at 18 in. tall.

C. poscharskyana. SERBIAN BELLFLOWER. Vigorous grower forms a spreading mound to 8 in. high, 2 ft. wide. Mid-green leaves are an elongated heart shape, to 3½ in. long and 3 in. wide. Branching, semiupright flower stems reach 1 ft. long or more, with star-shaped, ½–1-in.-wide flowers in lavender or grayish white. Blooms from spring to late summer. Needs only moderate water; good ground cover for dryish shade. 'Alba' has white flowers. 'Blue Waterfall' ('Camgood') has light blue flowers with white centers. Remove spent flower stems with a gentle tug to prevent reseeding.

CAMPSIS

TRUMPET CREEPER,
TRUMPET VINE

Bignoniaceae

Semievergreen to deciduous vines

✎ **ZONES VARY BY SPECIES**

☼ ◑ **FULL SUN OR PARTIAL SHADE**

◐ ◐ **MODERATE TO REGULAR WATER**

Campsis radicans

Vigorous climbers used for large-scale effects, quick summer screens. All bear radiant, orange-toned blossoms shaped like flaring trumpets, in clusters at branch tips, midsummer to fall. Glossy leaves are divided into 2½-in., ovate leaflets. Stems have aerial rootlets that cling to wood, brick, stucco, and other surfaces. Unless pruned and tied to supporting surface, old plants can become top heavy and pull away. Each dormant season, shorten some branches and thin others. Pinch back shoot tips in summer to keep plants bushy. Plants spread by suckering roots; pull any that appear. If older plants become unmanageable, cut to ground before spring growth begins and train a few strong new stems.

C. grandiflora. CHINESE TRUMPET CREEPER. Zones MS, LS, CS; USDA 7-9. Not as vigorous, large, or hardy as the American native *C. radicans*, but flowers are slightly larger and redder. Each leaf has up to nine leaflets. Grows to 30 ft. under ideal conditions. 'Morning Calm' has peach-colored flowers.

C. radicans. COMMON TRUMPET CREEPER. Zones US, MS, LS, CS; USDA 6-9. Native to eastern U.S. Each leaf has up to 11 leaflets. Flowers are 3-in.-long orange tubes with scarlet lobes flaring to 2 in. wide. Grows fast to 40 ft. or more, bursting with health and vigor. 'Flamenco' features red trumpets with orange centers. 'Atomic Red' flowers are solid deep red. 'Indian Summer' has large blooms in shades of yellow-orange with red centers; it is a more restrained grower than the species. Flowers of 'Judy' are rich golden yellow with a red throat. *C. r. flava* has pure yellow blossoms and somewhat lighter green leaves.

C. x tagliabuana. Zones US, MS, LS, CS; USDA 6-9. Hybrid between above two species. 'Madame Galen', best-known selection, has salmon-red flowers. 'Crimson Trumpet' bears pure red blooms. Those of 'Hot Lips' are a bright reddish orange.

CANNA

Cannaceae

Perennials from rhizomes

✎ **LS, CS, TS; USDA 8-11, OR DIG AND STORE**

☼ **FULL SUN**

◐ ◐◐ **REGULAR TO AMPLE WATER**

Canna 'Phaison'

There's nothing timid about cannas. Native to the southeastern region of the U.S. as well as to subtropical and tropical parts of Central and South America, they loudly proclaim their presence with large, bold leaves and wildly colorful flowers.

In summer and fall, flower stalks (typically 3–6 ft. tall) bear blossoms to 3 in. across, in shades of red, orange, yellow, salmon, coral, pink, and cream; both solids and bicolors are available. Lance-shaped, 1- to 4-ft.-long leaves resemble banana foliage. Green and bronze are the typical leaf colors, but many newer selections feature shockingly bright striped and variegated foliage in all sorts of riotous combinations. Deep-colored foliage typically fades somewhat in hot sun.

Cannas are most effective when planted as masses of a single color against a solid background. They grow best with full sun and high heat, forming lush, spreading colonies. Their leaves combine well with finer-textured foliage, such as that of daylilies (*Hemerocallis*) and lantana. Use taller kinds at the back of borders; compact sorts make good container plants.

C. flaccida. SWAMP CANNA, SOUTHERN MARSH CANNA. Native to swamps and riverbanks from South Carolina to Florida. Grows 4 ft. tall, 3 ft. wide, with green leaves reaching 2 ft. long and 6 in. wide. Bright yellow, 3-in.-wide flowers.

C. hybrids. The vast majority of cannas grown are hybrids grouped under *Canna x generalis*. They feature larger flowers than their parent species and often have strikingly ornate foliage. Most are good subjects for the back of the border. Give them plenty of room, as nearly all spread quickly. Recommended selections include the following.

'Australia'. To 4–5 ft. tall. Glossy, burgundy-black foliage holds color in summer heat. Bright red flowers.

'Black Knight'. To 5–6 ft. tall, with blackish bronze foliage and velvety deep red flowers.

'City of Portland'. To 4 ft. tall. Vigorous, bushy plant. Broad green leaves; showy rosy pink-to-salmon flowers.

'Cleopatra'. To 4 ft. tall. Green leaves and stalks are marked with large purple blotches. Flowers arising from purple tissue are red; those coming from green tissue are yellow. The bicolored foliage tends to revert to plain green; cut out solid green stalks to prevent reversion.

'Constitution'. Grows 5 ft. tall. Narrow, grayish purple leaves with burgundy edges; pale coral-pink flowers. Slower spreader than most cannas.

'Durban'. To 4 ft. tall. Strikingly variegated foliage features yellow veins against a reddish purple background. Large scarlet flowers. Slow spreader.

'Ehemanii' (*C. x ehemanii*). Old-fashioned favorite grows 6–8 ft. tall, with rich green leaves and pendulous flowers in deep rose-pink. Good for back of border.

'Erebus'. Compact grower to 3–4 ft., bred for use in water gardens. Gray-green leaves and salmon-pink flowers.

'Ermine'. To 3 ft. tall. Large, creamy white flowers with a pale yellow center. Gray-green foliage.

'Intrigue'. To 7–8 ft. tall. Narrow, erect, deep burgundy leaves are topped with many small, light salmon blooms.

'Minerva'. To 5 ft. tall. Leaves are striped green and white; large yellow flowers open from red buds.

'Phaison' ('Tropicanna'). To 6 ft. The most shockingly gaudy foliage imaginable—purple leaves striped with yellow and red. Backlit leaves glow as if ablaze; bright orange flowers complete the fiery picture. Very susceptible to canna leaf roller. Feed frequently to keep foliage looking its best.

'President'. To 4 ft. Masses of large scarlet blooms top glossy green foliage.

'Pretoria' ('Bengal Tiger', 'Striata'). To 6 ft. tall. Dramatic-looking foliage features green and yellow stripes and maroon edges; glows brilliantly when backlit. Bright orange flowers.

'Red King Humbert' ('Roi Humbert'). To 4 ft. Reddish bronze foliage; large orange-scarlet to red flowers.

'Tropicanna Gold'. To 4–5 ft. Orange-yellow flowers speckled with dark orange. Leaves striped in green and gold.

'Wyoming'. To 4 ft. Bronzy purple foliage and bright orange blooms.

'Yellow Humbert'. To 5 ft. Green leaves; large bright yellow flowers splashed with spots of crimson.

Low-growing hybrids. Standard-size cannas take up a lot of room—but fortunately, you can find many low-growing hybrids that are better suited to containers and small gardens. 'Striped Beauty' ('Bangkok Yellow'), to 2–3 ft. tall, has striped foliage and flowers; leaves are striped in green and white, and red-throated yellow flowers are marked with white stripes. 'Pink

ABOVE: Canna 'Pretoria'

Sunburst', to 3 ft. tall, has green- and white-striped leaves with a reddish cast; its large flowers are salmon-pink. Cannas in the Futurity series grow 2–3½ ft. tall and come in orange, pink, red, rose (all with burgundy foliage), and yellow (with green leaves). Pfitzer's series are green-leafed plants 2–2½ ft. tall, with coral, crimson, primrose yellow, or salmon-pink flowers. Tropical series plants grow 2½ ft. tall, have green leaves and rose, red, salmon, or white flowers. They're easy to grow from seed, blooming 90 days after sowing. The shortest of all cannas— to just 1½ ft. high—belong to the Seven Dwarfs series; they have green leaves and sport flowers in the full range of typical canna colors.

C. indica. INDIAN SHOT. Native to the tropical Americas; naturalized in the Southeast. To 4 ft. tall, 1½ ft. wide. Green leaves 1½ ft. long, 8 in. wide. Bright red, tubular, 3-in. flowers. The hard, round seeds were used as shot by early colonists.

C. musifolia. BANANA CANNA. Grows 12 ft. tall. Huge canna that resembles a banana tree. Large green leaves—to 2 ft. long and half as wide—have burgundy-red margins and stalks. Small red flowers are sparsely produced. Great as a tropical-looking accent.

C. warscewiczii. Native to Mexico. To 6 ft. tall, 3 ft. wide. Big burgundy leaves, 2 ft. long and 1 ft. wide, on very dark stems. Small, tubular red flowers, attractive to hummingbirds, are carried in spikes held high above the foliage; spent blossoms drop cleanly from the spike. Not susceptible to canna leaf roller.

CARE

Choose a spot with plenty of heat and bright sunshine. Plant rhizomes in spring, after the danger of frost is past. Set them 2–4 in. deep and 1–2 ft. apart. Cannas like lots of moisture (they'll even grow in standing water), but the soil doesn't need to be boggy, just moist. They're heavy feeders and prefer rich soil containing lots of organic matter, such as composted manure and chopped leaves. If you see ragged, stunted foliage and canna leaf roller (see below) is not the problem, the plants are hungry; give them weekly feedings of water-soluble 20-20-20 fertilizer until they perk up. Cut each flower stalk to the ground after it finishes blooming; new stalks will appear and continue to grow into early fall. In the Lower, Coastal, and Tropical South, cannas can overwinter in the ground; elsewhere, lift the rhizomes in fall and store over winter. Divide clumps every 3 or 4 years, making sure each piece of rhizome includes a bud or "eye."

Canna leaf roller is a common pest, mainly attacking hybrids. This caterpillar rolls up the leaves and feeds inside them; infested foliage looks ragged and is full of holes. Sanitation is the best solution. Cut off and destroy infested leaves as soon as you notice them and, in late fall, cut all plants to the ground and destroy all leaves and stems to prevent the pest from overwintering.

Unfortunately, an incurable viral disease has spread rapidly in recent years to infect many cannas worldwide. Plants are not killed outright, but their leaves are seriously disfigured by brown edges and dead areas. Early signs include yellow streaks and tiny, sandlike spots; flowers may also show viral streaking. Immediately dig and destroy infected plants. Buy replacement rhizomes only from sources you trust to have disease-free stock. Or buy plants in leaf, making sure there are no signs of virus on your chosen canna—or any others in the nursery.

CARAMBOLA
CARAMBOLA, STARFRUIT
Oxalidaceae
Evergreen tree

🖊 TS; USDA 10-11

☀ FULL SUN

💧 REGULAR WATER

Carambola

Carambola (known botanically as *Averrhoa carambola*) is a rising star in the world of tropical fruit. It's reliably hardy only in south Florida, but its unique yellow fruits are popular in supermarkets throughout the South: Peeling isn't necessary, and the flavorful slices can be added to fruit salads, floated in bowls of punch, or enjoyed as a dessert.

Native to Sri Lanka and Southeast Asia, carambola is a slow-growing evergreen tree with a short trunk and a broad, rounded canopy, reaching 25–30 ft. tall and wide at maturity. Leaves are arranged spirally on the branches; they are medium green, 6–10 in. long, each with 5 to 11 ovate leaflets. Clusters of fragrant pink-to-lavender flowers appear in several flushes throughout the year; they are followed by oval, pointed, waxy-skinned, juicy yellow fruits, 4–6 in. long, with five prominent longitudinal ribs. Cutting the fruit crosswise produces star-shaped slices. Some compare the flavor to mild citrus, while others call it a blend of pineapple, apple, and citrus. Overall, it may be sweet or rather sour; named selections are usually sweet. Some selections are self-fertile, while others need cross-pollination with another selection to bear fruit.

Carambola is popular as a small shade tree in south Florida. Careful siting is necessary, however, because grass will not grow beneath the dense canopy.

Recommended selections include the following.

'Arkin'. Bright yellow to yellow-orange fruit, 4–5 in. long; firm and very sweet, with few seeds. Keeps well. Self-fertile but bears better with a pollenizer.

'Fwang Tung'. Pale yellow, 5- to 6-in.-long fruit is firm and very sweet, with few seeds. Self-fertile.

'Golden Star'. Originated in Homestead, Florida, in the 1940s. Golden yellow fruit with very waxy skin; 5–6 in. long, crisp and mildly sweet. Self-fertile.

'Lara'. Fruit is 4–5 in. long; dark yellow to orange. Sweet flavor. Self-fertile

'Maher Dwarf'. Hawaiian selection that grows just 2–4 ft. tall in a container. Begins bearing roundish fruit when just 1½ ft. tall. Sweet and crunchy. Self-fertile.

'Sri Kembanqan' ('Sri Kembangan'). Firm, bright yellow-orange, 5- to 6-in.-long fruit with few seeds. Rich, sweet flavor; excellent dessert quality. Needs a pollenizer.

CARE

Although carambola briefly tolerates temperatures as low as 27°F, it really is best planted in frost-free locations. The soil should be well drained and moderately acid (pH 5.5–6.5); chlorosis (yellow leaves with green veins) often occurs in alkaline soil. Fertile soil containing lots of organic matter results in faster growth and more fruit. The tree is quite susceptible to drought, so water it regularly during dry periods, even in winter. Fertilize two or three times a year during periods of active growth with an appropriate fruit-tree fertilizer. Full sun is a must. Pruning is rarely necessary, and pests are seldom serious.

C

CARDOON

Asteraceae
Perennial

📏 **MS, LS, CS; USDA 7-9**

☀️ **FULL SUN**

💧 **REGULAR WATER**

Cardoon

Native to the Mediterranean and related to the artichoke, cardoon (*Cynara cardunculus*) has culinary uses but is principally grown for its striking, unusual foliage and interesting form. It reaches 5 ft. tall and 4 ft. wide, with coarse, spiny, gray-green leaves that look striking in combination with finer-textured plants. In summer, it flaunts purple flowers resembling large thistle blossoms; these can be cut and dried for arrangements. Cardoon naturalizes in the Lower and Coastal South and can become a weed. Not browsed by deer.

Leafstalks are edible. To prepare them for harvest, blanch them by gathering leaves together, tying them up, and wrapping them with paper to exclude light. Do this in late summer or early fall, 4 to 5 weeks before harvesting. To cook, cut the heavy leaf midribs into 3- to 4-in. lengths. Boil until almost tender, then sauté; or boil till tender, and serve with butter or a sauce.

CAREX

SEDGE
Cyperaceae
Perennials

📏 **US, MS, LS, CS; USDA 6-9, EXCEPT AS NOTED**

☀️☀️ **SOME SHADE IN HOTTEST CLIMATES**

💧 **WATER NEEDS VARY BY SPECIES**

Carex comans 'Bronze'

Gardeners may think of the sedges as ornamental grasses, but in fact they belong to an entirely different plant family. Found worldwide, they form clumping tufts of gracefully arching, grasslike foliage. The long, narrow evergreen leaves are often striped or oddly colored. Flowers are generally insignificant. Use sedges in borders, containers, rock gardens, and water gardens. Although they are commonly recommended for moist soils, many will grow in relatively dry soils.

C. buchananii. LEATHER LEAF SEDGE. From New Zealand. Curly-tipped, arching, 2- to 3-ft.-long blades make striking reddish bronze clumps 2–2½ ft. wide. Use with gray foliage or with deep greens. Moderate water.

C. comans. NEW ZEALAND HAIR SEDGE. Dense, fine-textured clumps of narrow, silvery green foliage. Leaves are usually 1 ft. long but may reach 6 ft.; on slopes, they look like flowing water. 'Bronze' is similar but has coppery brown leaves. 'Frosted Curls', sometimes sold as *C. albula*, has silvery foliage with twisted tips and bronze highlights. Moderate water.

C. elata 'Aurea' ('Bowles' Golden'). Selection of a European native. Clump to 2½ ft. high, 1½ ft.

ABOVE: Carex elata 'Aurea'

wide, with leaves that emerge bright yellow in spring and hold some color until late summer. Needs ample moisture; will grow in a water garden.

C. flacca (*C. glauca*). BLUE SEDGE. From Europe. Creeping perennial with blue-gray, grasslike foliage that ranges from 6 in. to 2 ft. tall and wide. Evergreen only in mildest climates. Tolerant of many soils and irrigation schemes. Not invasive; spreads slowly and can be clipped like a lawn. Endures light foot traffic, moderate shade, competition with tree roots. Does best with moderate water.

C. morrowii. Green-leafed Japanese species known for its variegated forms. All take regular water. 'Variegata' is a name given to many selections with white leaf edges. Forms a clump 1 ft. high, 1½ ft. wide, with fairly coarse (½-in.-wide) leaves. 'Fisher's Form' is similar but has creamy yellow leaf margins. Both of these make good edging plants; individual clumps look great among rocks. 'Ice Dance' has more prominent

white leaf borders than 'Variegata' and a spreading habit; it forms a carpet 2–3 ft. wide. Although it increases by rhizomes, it's not invasive. 'Silver Sceptre' has white-edged leaves about ¼ in. wide. It is somewhat spreading but does not cover ground as fast as 'Ice Dance'. Fine-textured, very narrow (⅛-in.) leaves, dark green with a white center, give *C. m. temnolepis* 'Silk Tassel' its delicate, airy look. It spreads about 2 ft. wide.

C. muskingumensis. PALM SEDGE. From North America. The basic species, to 2 ft. tall and spreading widely by rhizomes, has tapered green leaves radiating from lax stems, creating the effect of small, feathery palms. 'Little Midge', to 10 in. high, is miniature in all its parts. Leaves of 'Oehme' are solid green when new, but they quickly develop yellow margins. Regular water.

C. oshimensis. JAPANESE SEDGE. 'Evergold' is a variegated selection of a Japanese native. Clumping growth to 1–2 ft. high, 2–3 ft. wide. Dark green leaves have a broad central band of creamy white. Needs partial to full shade and regular water. 'Everillo' almost radiates light from its lime-green leaves. Grows 1½ ft. tall and wide.

C. pensylvanica. PENNSYL-VANIA SEDGE. Zones US, MS; USDA 6-7. Native from Canada to the Middle South. This is a soft, fine-textured grass for the shade garden standing about 6 in. tall and wide, spreading slowly by rhizomes to make a welcome ground cover under deciduous trees. Commonly associated with oaks. If needed, divide plants to spread more rapidly. Tolerant of moist soil, as well as dry shade. Will take part sun in the cooler zones. Deer resistant.

C. texensis. TEXAS SEDGE, CATLIN SEDGE. Southwestern native. Fine-textured, mat-forming sedge to 4–6 in. high. Medium green, drooping leaves form a wavy carpet dotted by lax flowering stems. Excellent small-scale lawn substitute or ground cover; often used in meadow mixes. Trim to remove seed heads. Needs partial to full shade and regular water.

CARISSA MACROCARPA

NATAL PLUM
Apocynaceae
Evergreen shrub

🌡 **CS, TS; USDA 9-11; OR GROWN IN POTS**

☀️🌤 **BEST IN SUN, TOLERATES SOME SHADE; BRIGHT LIGHT**

💧💧💧 **LITTLE TO REGULAR WATER**

Carissa macrocarpa

One of Florida's most versatile landscape plants, Natal plum is valued for both its ornamental

qualities and its tasty fruit. Vigorous, fast-growing, rounded shrub to 10 ft. tall and wide, with oval, leathery, rich green leaves to 3 in. long. Native to South Africa; prefers the frost-free climes of south Florida but will grow as far north as Orlando with few problems. It blooms throughout the year, bearing star-shaped, five-petaled white flowers that are nearly as fragrant as those of Confederate jasmine (*Trachelospermum jasminoides*) but larger (to 2 in. across). Oval, fleshy red or purple fruits, 1–1½ in. long, follow the flowers; blossoms and fruit at various stages of ripeness often appear together. The fruit has a cranberry-like flavor and can be eaten fresh or used in jelly, sauce, or pie; be sure it is ripe before you harvest it.

Natal plum is easy to grow in most soils. It's one of the very best plants for the beach, as it tolerates salt spray, wind, and sandy soil. Accepts heavy pruning and makes a superior hedge. Sharp spines along its branches discourage trespassers, so it works well as a barrier plant—but don't plant it near walkways, pools, or steps, where the spines might prove hazardous. In bright light, it can be grown as a houseplant. Not browsed by deer.

'Boxwood Beauty'. Exceptionally compact, thornless growth to 2 ft. high and as wide. Has deep green leaves like those of a large-leafed boxwood (*Buxus*). Good for hedging and shaping.

'Fancy'. More upright growth than species, with unusually large fruit.

'Gifford'. Among the best fruit bearers.

'Green Carpet'. Low grower to 1–1½ ft. high, spreading to 4 ft. or wider. Smaller leaves than those of species. Excellent ground cover. 'Emerald Blanket' is similar but slightly lower growing.

'Prostrata'. Vigorous spreader to 2 ft. high; good ground cover. Prune out any upright growth. Can be trained as espalier.

'Ruby Point'. Red-foliaged selection that holds its color well. Grows more upright than species.

'Tomlinson'. Thornless. Compact, slow growth to 2–2½ ft. high and about 3 ft. wide. Good in large container or as a foundation plant.

'Tuttle'. Compact, dense growth to 2–3 ft. high, 3–5 ft. wide. Heavy production of flowers and fruit. Effective as a ground cover.

CARPINUS

HORNBEAM
Betulaceae
Deciduous trees

🌡 **ZONES VARY BY SPECIES**

☀️🌤● **EXPOSURE NEEDS VARY BY SPECIES**

💧 **REGULAR WATER**

Carpinus betulus

These are well-behaved, long-lived, relatively small shade trees; make fine street or lawn trees. Growth rate is slow to moderate. Very hard, tough wood. Dark green, sawtooth-edged leaves color up agreeably in fall in the Upper, Middle, and Lower South, hang on late in season. Fruits (small, hard nutlets in leaflike bracts) are carried in attractive drooping clusters to 5 in. long. Mature trees need little or no pruning.

C. betulus. EUROPEAN HORN-BEAM. Zones US, MS, LS; USDA 6-8. Native from Europe to Iran. Excellent landscape tree to 40 ft. tall. Dense pyramidal form, eventually becoming as broad as tall, with drooping outer branches. Often sheared into a hedge in Europe. Handsome, furrowed gray bark like that of *C. caroliniana*. Leaves seldom marred by insects or disease, 2–5 in. long, turn yellow or dark red in autumn. Best in full sun but tolerates light shade. 'Emerald Avenue' is a vigorous grower with a pyramid shape and good heat tolerance. 'Fastigiata' is the selection commonly sold; tree develops an oval-vase shape with age.

C. caroliniana. IRONWOOD. Zones US, MS, LS, CS; USDA 6-9. Native from Nova Scotia to Minnesota, southward to Texas and Florida. Also known as blue

beech and musclewood in its native range, where it is often found at forest edges or as an understory plant along rivers and streams. Those common names refer to the tree's trunk, which is blue-gray and smooth, with undulations that look like muscles flexing beneath the surface. Grows to 25–30 ft. tall and wide, with round head; can be grown as single- or multitrunked tree. Leaves, 1–3 in. long turn mottled yellow and red in fall; they drop before those of *C. betulus*. Ironwood does well in a range of exposures from full sun to heavy shade. Best in natural gardens. 'Native Flame' has good form and dependable red fall color.

CARROT

Apiaceae
Biennial grown as cool-season annual

🌡 **US, MS, LS, CS, TS; USDA 6-11**

☀️ **FULL SUN**

💧 **REGULAR WATER**

Carrots

Native to Afghanistan, carrots are known botanically as *Daucus carota sativus*. The key to success in growing them is loose, deep soil: Carrots reach smooth perfection only in light soils free of stones and clods. If you have heavy clay or rocky soil, plant in raised beds or choose short-growing kinds. Carrots are a good spring crop and even better for fall; their flavor sweetens as the weather cools. You can leave roots in the ground until a hard freeze, pulling them as desired. In the Coastal and Tropical South, grow them as a winter crop.

For spring harvests, sow seeds about 6 weeks before the last frost. To extend your harvest, make two or three small, consecutive plantings 10 days apart. For a fall crop, sow in midsummer in the Upper and Middle South, in August or September in the Lower South. For winter crops in the Coastal and Tropical South, sow in November or December.

Plant the right selection for your type of soil. Long grocery-store kinds, such as 'Scarlet Nantes' or 'Envy' require loose, sandy soil at least 1 ft. deep. For shallower, heavier soils that contain some clay, try blunt-nosed, half-long selections such as 'Bolero', 'Danvers Half Long', 'Nelson', 'Royal Chantenay',

NOT ALL CARROTS ARE ORANGE. LOOK FOR SELECTIONS LIKE 'PURPLE HAZE', 'RED SAMURAI', 'WHITE SATIN', OR 'YELLOW-STONE' TO ADD UNEXPECTED COLORS TO SALADS AND SLAWS.

'Yaya', and 'Sweet Sunshine' (a yellow carrot). For containers, try miniatures like 'Little Finger' and 'Short 'n Sweet', baby carrots like 'Baby Sweet' and 'Sweet Baby Jane', and round ones like 'Parmex' and 'Thumbelina'.

CARE

Before planting, work into the soil ½ cup of 10-10-10 fertilizer per 10 ft. of row. Cover with no more than ¼ in. of soil. If your soil tends to crust over when dry, cover the seeds with sand, milled peat moss, or potting mix instead of soil. Seeds may take 1 to 3 weeks to germinate. Keep soil evenly moist. When seedlings are 2 in. tall, thin them to 2–4 in. apart. (You can steam these tiny carrots in butter or chop the entire miniature plant, tops and all, for a fresh addition to tossed salads.) Cover root tops with soil to keep them from turning green, which results in bitterness. Most types are ready to harvest 60 to 70 days from sowing.

CARTHAMUS TINCTORIUS

SAFFLOWER, FALSE SAFFRON
Asteraceae
Annual

🌿 **US, MS, LS, CS, TS; USDA 6-11**

☀ **FULL SUN**

💧 **MODERATE WATER**

Carthamnus tinctorius

This thistle relative (probably an Asian native) is ornamental as well as useful: It is grown commercially for the oil extracted from its seeds. To 3 ft. tall, 1–1½ ft. wide, with erect, spiny-leafed stems. In summer, bears orange-yellow flower heads

above leafy bracts; inner bracts are spiny. Durable cut flower, fresh or dried. Dried safflower blossoms have been used for seasoning in place of true saffron, which they somewhat resemble in color and flavor. Sow seeds in place in spring, after danger of frost is past. An ornamental spine-free form is also available.

CARUM CARVI

CARAWAY
Apiaceae
Biennial

🌿 **US, MS, LS; USDA 6-8**

☀ **FULL SUN**

💧 **REGULAR WATER**

Carum carvi

Native to Asia Minor. Caraway is prized for its edible seeds, used in flavoring pickles, vegetables, and breads. In the first year after planting, carrotlike leaves grow from a taproot, forming a mound 1–2 ft. high. In the second spring, umbrellalike clusters of white flowers rise above the foliage and set seed; after the seeds ripen in midsummer, the plant dies.

Start seeds in a garden bed in fall or early spring; be sure soil is well drained. Thin seedlings to 1½ ft. apart. Harvest the seed heads after they have turned brown, then dry them in paper bags until you can shake the seeds loose.

CARYA

HICKORY
Juglandaceae
Deciduous trees

🌿 **US, MS, LS, CS; USDA 6-9**

☀ **FULL SUN**

💧💧 **MODERATE TO REGULAR WATER, EXCEPT AS NOTED**

Carya ovata

These large, grand, picturesque hardwoods combine long life with handsome bark and colorful fall foliage. Many forms of wildlife depend on the nuts for food. Unfortunately, hickories are seldom sold, because long taproots make them hard to transplant. But if hickories grow on your property, by all means conserve them. Leaves divided featherwise into leaflets. Inconspicuous flowers are followed by nuts enclosed in husks that usually break away at maturity. Trees are too large for smaller yards but are attractive where space is available. All develop deep taproots, so they should be planted while young and not moved later.

C. glabra. PIGNUT HICKORY. Native to southern and eastern U.S. Grows to 50–60 ft., sometimes 100 ft., with a canopy nearly as broad. Leaves, 8–10 in. long, with five to nine leaflets, are retained into late fall and turn a beautiful orange, brown, and yellow, even in the Lower South. Smooth bark. Nuts are bitter.

C. illinoensis. See Pecan

C. laciniosa. SHELLBARK HICKORY. Native from New York to Iowa, south to Tennessee and Oklahoma; found in lowlands that are periodically flooded. Similar to *C. ovata* but smaller. Grows slowly to 60–80 ft. tall, 40–60 ft. wide. Leaves usually divided into seven leaflets. Largest of hickory nuts; sweet, hard shelled. Regular to ample water.

C. ovata. SHAGBARK HICKORY. Native to eastern U.S. Typically grows to 60–100 ft. tall and 30–40 ft. wide. Most conspicuous feature is the gray, shaggy bark, with large plates curving out and away from the trunk. The hard-shelled nuts are sweet. Leaves typically have five leaflets; autumn foliage is an attractive bright yellow. Wood is tough and hard.

CARYOPTERIS
BLUEBEARD
Lamiaceae
Deciduous shrubs

🌡 **ZONES US, MS, LS, CS; USDA 6-9**

☼ **FULL SUN**

💧 **MODERATE WATER**

Caryopteris x *clandonensis*
'First Choice'

Cool blue flowers top these upright Asian native shrubs from midsummer to frost. Generally grown as woody-based perennials—if plants don't freeze back in winter, cut them nearly to ground before spring growth flush to ensure a good base for the new season's growth. Bear dense, stalked clusters of small flowers on current season's growth; trim after each wave of bloom to encourage repeat flowering. Provide good drainage, since plants can rot in wet soil. Not browsed by deer.

C. x clandonensis. BLUE MIST. Low-growing mound (to 2 ft. tall and wide) of narrow, 3-in.-long, gray-green leaves. Clusters of small flowers top upper parts of stems. The original selection,

'Arthur Simmonds', is still the hardiest and most reliable; it has bright blue blossoms and gray-green leaves with silvery undersides. 'Heavenly Blue' and 'Sapphire Surf' bear deep blue blossoms; 'Dark Knight', 'Longwood Blue', and 'Sterling Silver' also with deep blue blooms, have silvery foliage. 'Worcester Gold' has yellow leaves and lavender-blue flowers. Leaves of 'Summer Sorbet' are green with yellow edges. 'First Choice' is compact, with profuse dark purple blossoms; it blooms over a longer period than other selections.

C. incana. COMMON BLUEBEARD, BLUE SPIREA. Taller than *C. x clandonensis*, with looser, more open growth to 3–4 ft. tall, 5 ft. wide. Lavender-blue flowers appear in leaf joints. 'Jason' has golden foliage. 'Blue Myth' is noted for deep blue flowers and compact form, growing just 2-3 ft. tall and wide.

CARYOTA
FISHTAIL PALM
Arecaceae
Palms

🌡 **TS; USDA 10-11, OR GROW IN POTS**

☼◐ **SUN OR PART SHADE; BRIGHT INDIRECT LIGHT**

💧 **REGULAR WATER**

⬦ **CRYSTALS IN FRUIT CAN IRRITATE SKIN**

Caryota mitis

Feather palms with huge, finely divided leaves; leaflets flattened and split at tips like fish tails. Tender. Native to Southeast Asia, where they grow in full sun. Not browsed by deer. In pots indoors, place them near a southern or western window. Let the soil

surface go dry to the touch between waterings. Avoid handling fruit with bare hands; invisible crystals inside can cause severe itching and burning.

C. mitis. BURMESE FISHTAIL PALM. Slow grower to 10–40 ft. tall, spreading to 10–20 ft. Basal offshoots eventually form clustered trunks. Light green foliage.

C. ochlandra. CANTON FISHTAIL PALM. May reach 25 ft. tall and spread half as wide. Medium dark green leaves. Hardiest of the caryotas; has survived to 26°F.

C. urens. WINE PALM. Single-stemmed palm to 100 ft. tall and 30 ft. wide in Asia, to 20 ft. tall and 8 ft. wide in Tropical South with careful protection. If temperatures go below 32°F, it's certain to die. Dark green leaves.

CASSIA
Caesalpiniaceae
Evergreen, semievergreen, deciduous trees

🌡 **TS; USDA 10-11**

☼ **FULL SUN**

💧💧💧💧 **WATER NEEDS VARY BY SPECIES**

Cassia fistula

The genus *Cassia* once included many yellow-flowered trees and shrubs now reclassified as *Senna* (see that entry), though some are still sold under their old names. These cassias are showy flowering trees that brighten landscapes in the warmest climates—not just with yellow blossoms but also with pink, cerise, and white ones. Flowering times are approximate, since plants may bloom at any time or bloom intermittently over a long period. Most have long seedpods

that can present a litter problem. Grow in well-drained soil. Plants are best pruned when young (to develop a strong framework) and as needed after flowering is finished. Rarely browsed by deer.

C. fistula. SHOWER OF GOLD, GOLDEN SHOWER. Deciduous or partially evergreen. From India. To 30–40 ft. high and 35 ft. wide, with 2-ft. leaves divided into four to eight pairs of 3- to 6-in.-long leaflets. Summer flowers are bright yellow, in drooping, nearly 2-ft.-long clusters of 50 or more. Prune hard after bloom. Extremely showy. Good drought tolerance.

C. grandis. PINK SHOWER, CORAL SHOWER. Deciduous. From tropical America. Fast growing to 20–50 ft. tall and 30 ft. wide. Abundant coral-pink flowers in 7-in.-long clusters in early spring. Leaves divided into 8 to 20 pairs of 2½-in. leaflets, pink when young. Use for color accent or as shade, street, or park tree. Somewhat drought tolerant but blooms best with regular water.

C. javanica. PINK CASSIA. Deciduous. From Indonesia. To 30–35 ft. high and 25 ft. wide, with irregular habit. Masses of light pink flowers in clusters to 4 in. or longer appear along branches from spring to fall, peaking in early summer. Leaves divided into 5 to 15 pairs of oval, 1- to 2-in.-long leaflets. Useful as color accent or shade, street, or park tree. Good wind tolerance; moderate drought and salt tolerance. Best with moderate water.

C. leptophylla. GOLD MEDALLION TREE. Nearly evergreen. Native to Brazil. Shapeliest and most graceful of the cassias. Grows fast to 20–25 ft. tall, 30 ft. wide, with an open-headed, low-spreading structure; tends to weep. Shape to a single trunk; otherwise, plant becomes very sprawling. Leaves have up to 12 pairs of narrow, 1½- to 2½-in. leaflets; deep yellow flowers are borne in 6- to 8-in. clusters in July and August, with scattered bloom later. Prune hard after bloom. Little to moderate water.

C. x nealiae. RAINBOW SHOWER. Semievergreen to deciduous. A sterile hybrid between *C. fistula* and *C. javanica*, originating in Hawaii. Moderately fast grower to 30–40 ft. high and 35 ft. wide. Dark green foliage. Thrives in any well-drained soil.

Withstands drought well but has only moderate wind tolerance and poor salt tolerance.

Several named selections are available in a range of flower colors from pale yellow through golden yellow to orange and cerise—the "rainbow" of the common name. Some may produce occasional seedpods.

'Lunalilo Yellow'. Flowers open a bright yellow-orange, then age to bright yellow. Late spring to fall bloom.

'Nii Gold'. A sport of 'Wilhelmina Tenney'. Blooms anytime from spring to fall; deep gold buds open to blooms that age to strong yellow.

'Queen's Hospital White'. Flowers open pale yellow, fade rapidly to very light yellow to white. Blooms in spring to late summer.

'Wilhelmina Tenney' produces spectacular blossom clusters from spring to fall. Petal exteriors are deep cerise aging to paler shades; interiors are yellow.

CASTILLEJA

Orobanchaceae
Annuals, biennials, perennials

✏ **US, MS, LS, CS, TS; USDA 6-11**

☼◗ **FULL SUN OR PARTIAL SHADE**

💧 **WATER DURING DRY SEASON**

Castilleja indivisa

Native to the Southeast, the Midwest, and Texas, Indian paintbrushes are among the most difficult wildflowers to get established in garden conditions, but once growing, they are quite tough. Small, inconspicuous flowers appear in spring among showy fan-shaped bracts that range in color from pink and purple to yellow, orange, and flame red. Sow seeds thickly among plants such as grasses or perennials, because during germination these wildflowers may draw nourishment from the roots of other plants.

C. indivisa. INDIAN PAINT-BRUSH, TEXAS. Annual or biennial. Native to southeastern Oklahoma, eastern Texas, and the Coastal Plains. Plant varies from 6 to 16 in. tall, with a width of 6 in. Orange-to-red, 3- to 8-in.-long flower spikes bloom through spring.

C. purpurea. PRAIRIE PAINT-BRUSH, PURPLE PAINTBRUSH. Perennial. Native to the Midwest and Texas. To 9 in. tall, 6 in. wide. Flowers vary widely in color; they may be purple, but are just as often pink, red, or yellow. Also known as lemon paintbrush. Blooms in late spring.

CATALPA

Bignoniaceae
Deciduous trees

✏ **US, MS, LS, CS; USDA 6-9**

☼◗ **FULL SUN OR PARTIAL SHADE**

💧💧 **MODERATE TO REGULAR WATER**

Catalpa bignonioides

Catalpas are among the few truly deciduous trees that can compete in flower and leaf with subtropical species. They bloom in late spring and summer, bearing large, upright clusters of trumpet-shaped, 2-in.-wide flowers in pure white, striped and marked with yellow and soft brown; flowers are held above large, bold, heart-shaped leaves. Long, bean-shaped seed capsules, sometimes called Indian beans, follow the blossoms.

Unusually well adapted to extremes of heat and cold; take any type of soil. Where winds are strong, plant in lee of taller trees or buildings to protect leaves from damage. Some gardeners object to litter of fallen flowers in summer and seed capsules in autumn. Plants need shaping while young; they seldom develop a well-established dominant shoot on their own. Shorten side branches as tree grows. When branching begins at desired height, remove lower branches.

For the tree sometimes called desert catalpa, see *Chilopsis linearis*. Another tree sometimes mistakenly called catalpa is the very similar *Paulownia tomentosa* (empress tree), with lavender flowers. *Paulownia* shows flower buds in winter; catalpa does not.

C. bignonioides. COMMON CATALPA, INDIAN BEAN. Native to southeastern U.S. Grows to 30–50 ft. according to climate or soil, with somewhat smaller spread. Leaves are 5–8 in. long, often in whorls, and give off an odd odor when crushed. Subject to chlorosis (yellow leaves with green veins) in alkaline soil. Yellow leaves of 'Aurea' are showiest in the Upper South. 'Purpurea' has dark purple new growth that later turns green. 'Nana', or umbrella catalpa (usually sold as *C. bungei.*), is a dense globe form usually grafted high on *C. bignonioides*; it grows about 6 ft. high, 5 ft. wide, and never blooms.

C. x erubescens 'Purpurea'. Selection of a hybrid between *C. bignonioides* and *C. ovata*; resembles *C. bignonioides*. Leaves (to 10–16 in. long) and branchlets are deep blackish purple when young, maturing to purplish green in summer.

C. speciosa. NORTHERN CATALPA. Native to central and southern Midwest. Round headed; 40–70 ft. tall, 20–40 ft. wide. Leaves 6–12 in. long. Fewer flowers per cluster than for *C. bignonioides*. Early training and pruning will give tall trunk and umbrella-shaped crown.

CATANANCHE CAERULEA

CUPID'S DART
Asteraceae
Perennial

✏ **US, MS, LS; USDA 6-8**

☼ **FULL SUN**

💧 **MODERATE WATER**

Catananche caerulea

Wispy, free-flowering plant from Europe, good for summer borders and fresh or dried arrangements. Gray-green, grassy leaves form a clump to 1 ft. high and wide. Lavender-blue, 2-in. flower heads, reminiscent of cornflowers (*Centaurea cyanus*) and surrounded by strawlike, shining bracts, appear atop leafless stems to 2 ft. high. Remove faded flowers to prolong bloom. Selections include white 'Alba', cornflower blue 'Blue Giant', and deep blue-violet 'Major'. Plants will flower first year from seed sown in early spring. Rather short lived, but volunteer seedlings usually provide replacements.

CATHARANTHUS ROSEUS

MADAGASCAR PERIWINKLE

Apocynaceae

Perennial usually grown as annual

US, MS, LS, CS, TS; USDA 6-11

FULL SUN OR PARTIAL SHADE

MODERATE WATER

Catharanthus roseus
'Cora Lavender'

Native to Madagascar, India, and tropical Asia, Madagascar periwinkle blooms continuously in hot weather, thriving in both humid and dry heat. Bushy plant grows 1–1½ ft. high and wide, with upright stems clothed in glossy green leaves and adorned with phloxlike, 1½-in. flowers in pure white, pink, rose, or white with a rose or red eye. Bloom goes on all summer, but by autumn the plant gets leggy and flowering is spotty. Survives winter in central and south Florida, where it has escaped cultivation and naturalized. Self-sows readily, especially in sandy or gritty soil.

Recent breeding has produced plants with larger blossoms in a wider range of colors, including vibrant shades of red, lavender, and purple. Flowers of some new types sport overlapping petals, giving them a fuller, more rounded look. Pacifica and Cooler series are compact, 12- to 15-in. plants with large (2-in.) flowers. The Tropicana series features blooms in shades of pink and coral on foot-tall plants. The Stardust series bears orchid, pink, or raspberry-red flowers centered with a white starburst.

Variations in form among Madagascar periwinkles include shorter and more compact types and those with trailing habits. The Little series grows 8–10 in. high; the Carpet series grows 4–8 in. tall, creeping to 1½ ft. wide. Plants in the Mediterranean series grow 5–6 in. high and can spread 2½ ft. wide; they're useful as a seasonal ground cover or in hanging baskets. Blossom colors include apricot, pink, rose, lilac, and white. The disease-resistant Cora series has mounding and trailing forms, many colors, and extra-long bloom; plants grow 14–16 in. tall.

All types bloom the first season from seed sown early indoors or in a greenhouse or cold frame, but most people buy transplants at garden centers. Unfortunately, many of the newer hybrids seem more susceptible than their predecessors to wilt and rot diseases caused by planting in heavy, wet soil. Be sure to plant in loose, fast-draining soil, and take care not to crowd plants.

Madagascar periwinkle was formerly known botanically as *Vinca rosea*, and many people still call it by the name "vinca."

CATTLEYA

Orchidaceae

Epiphytic orchids

TS; USDA 10-11, OR HOUSE PLANTS

LIGHT SHADE; BRIGHT INDIRECT LIGHT

REGULAR WATER

Cattleya skinneri

Native to tropical America. Among the most popular and best-known orchids, with showy flowers that are used for corsages.

Species, selections, and hybrids are too numerous to list here. All have pseudobulbs 1–3 in. thick, bearing leathery leaves and a stem topped with one to four or more flowers. Plants range in size from a few inches tall to 2 ft. or more. Commercial growers offer choices with flowers in many shades of lavender and purple, as well as white-blossomed kinds and semialbas (white blossoms with colored lip). Also available are novelties in yellow, orange, red, green, and bronze; many of these are crosses between cattleyas and other orchids.

Cattleyas are widely grown outdoors year-round in the Tropical South, either in containers or naturalized on trees. Elsewhere, they are indoor plants that can be brought outdoors during warm weather. They grow best in a greenhouse where temperature, humidity, and light can be readily controlled. However, they also can be grown successfully as houseplants if the following needs are satisfied: (1) warm temperatures (55–60°F at night, 65–80°F or higher during the day); (2) relatively high humidity (50 to 60 percent or more); (3) bright indirect light with protection from hot midday sun. Leaves should be light green and erect; if light is too low, they turn dark green and new growth becomes soft.

CAULIFLOWER

Brassicaceae

Biennial grown as cool-season annual

US, MS, LS, CS, TS; USDA 6-11

FULL SUN

REGULAR WATER

Cauliflower

Cauliflower is related to broccoli and cabbage (all members of genus *Brassica*) and has similar cultural needs, but it is less tolerant of heat and harder to grow. Time plantings so plants mature either well before or well after summer heat; early-maturing or heat-tolerant types are your best bets. 'Snow Crown' and 'Early Snowball' (50–60 days from setting out plants until harvest) are popular early cauliflowers. Heat-tolerant kinds include 'Fremont' (62 days), 'Bishop' (65 days), and 'Amazing' (75 days). Romanesco types have cone-shaped heads of lime-green florets with fine flavor. There is also a passel of selections with colored heads: 'Cheddar' (orange, 68 days), 'Graffiti' (purple, 80 days), and 'Panther' (green, 70 days).

CARE

Start with small plants; set them 1½–2 ft. apart in rows spaced 3 ft. apart. Keep plants actively growing, as any check during transplanting or later growth is likely to cause premature setting of undersized heads. At planting, feed with water-soluble 20-20-20 fertilizer; 3 weeks after planting, sprinkle ½ cup of 10-10-10 fertilizer per 10 ft. of row around plants. When heads first appear, tie up the large leaves around them to keep them white. On self-blanching types, leaves curl over heads without assistance. Harvest heads as soon as they reach full size. Most kinds are ready 50 to 100 days after transplanting; overwintering types may take 6 months.

To prevent a buildup of soil-borne pests, plant cauliflower in a different site each year. Club root is a serious fungal pest in acid soils; apply lime, if necessary, to raise the pH to at least 6.5. Floating row covers do a good job of controlling insects such as cabbage loopers, cabbageworms, cutworms, and root maggots. You can also control cutworms and root maggots by ringing the base of the plant with a cardboard collar. *Bacillus thuringiensis* (*Bt*) and spinosad applied according to label directions controls cabbageworms and loopers.

CEANOTHUS

WILD LILAC
Rhamnaceae
Evergreen shrubs

ZONES VARY BY SPECIES

FULL SUN

LITTLE OR NO WATER

Ceanothus delilianus

As a group, these are some of the prettiest flowering shrubs around, with blooms ranging from white through all shades of blue to deep violet. Unfortunately, most fail miserably in the heavy soils and rainy, humid climates of the South. A few notable exceptions are listed below. Give them excellent drainage and full sun. They rarely suffer pest damage.

C. americanus. NEW JERSEY TEA. US, MS, LS; USDA 6-8. Native from Canada south to South Carolina and west to Texas. Compact, rounded shrub 3–4 ft. tall and wide, with slender, upright branches. Oval, pointed, 2- to 3-in.-long, dark green leaves may turn yellow in fall. White, 1- to 2-in.-long flower clusters appear atop the plant in spring and early summer. Colonists reputedly brewed a tea substitute from the leaves during the boycott of British tea prior to the American Revolution.

C. delilianus. FRENCH HYBRID CEANOTHUS. LS, CS, TS; USDA 9-11. Result of a cross between *C. americanus* and a blue-flowered Mexican species; has oval, dark green leaves to 3 in. long and 5-in. clusters of gorgeous blue flowers. 'Gloire de Versailles' grows 10 ft. high and wide, with powder-blue blooms in late summer or fall. 'Henri Desfossé' is similar but more compact at 5-6 ft. high and wide;

violet-blue flowers contrast beautifully with wine-red new stems.

C. pallidus. US, MS, LS; USDA 6-8. Result of a cross between a close relative of *C. americanus* and *C. delilianus*. Grows to form a broad, 2- to 3-ft.-high mound. Shiny, oval to oblong green leaves are 1–2 in. long. Bears dense clusters of pink flowers in summer. 'Marie Simon' bears soft pink blossoms, 'Ceres' lilac-pink blooms. *C. p. plenus* has pink buds that open to double white flowers.

CEDRUS

CEDAR
Pinaceae
Evergreen trees

ZONES VARY BY SPECIES

FULL SUN

MODERATE WATER

Cedrus deodara

These conifers, the true cedars, are stately specimen trees that look best when given plenty of room. Needles are borne in tufted clusters. Cone scales, like those of firs (*Abies*), fall from the tree, leaving a spiky core behind. Male catkins produce prodigious amounts of pollen that may cover you with yellow dust on a windy day. Plant in deep, well-drained soil. All species are deep rooted and drought tolerant once established.

C. atlantica (*C. libani atlantica*). ATLAS CEDAR. Zones US, MS, LS; USDA 6-8. From North Africa. Slow to moderate growth to 60 ft. or more. Open and angular in youth; branches usually get too long and heavy on young trees unless tips are pinched or cut back. Growth naturally less open

with age. Less spreading than other true cedars, but still needs a 30-ft. circle. Needles are bluish green, less than 1 in. long.

Selections include 'Aurea', needles with yellowish tint; 'Fastigiata', upright, with blue-green needles; 'Glauca', silvery blue; 'Glauca Pendula', weeping form with blue needles; 'Pendula', vertically drooping branches. Untrained, spreading, informally branching plants are sold as "rustics." All types stand up well to hot, humid weather.

C. deodara. DEODAR CEDAR. Zones US (some), MS, LS, CS; USDA 6-9. Native to the Himalayas. Fast growing to 80 ft., with 40-ft. spread at ground level; planted in a small lawn, it soon overpowers the area. Lower branches sweep down to ground, then upward. Upper branches openly spaced, graceful. Nodding tip identifies it in skyline. Has a softer, lighter texture than other cedars. To control this tree's spread, cut new growth of side branches halfway back in late spring. Such pruning also makes tree more dense. It can also be pruned to grow as a spreading low or high shrub. Annual pruning in late spring will keep it to the shape you want. This is the best species for hot, humid climates.

Although deodars sold by garden centers are very similar in form, many variations occur in a group of seedlings—from scarecrowlike forms to compact, low shrubs. Needles, to 2 in. long, may be green or have a blue, gray, or yellow cast. Seed-grown 'Shalimar', an extra-hardy selection that has survived to –15°F, has good blue-green color and is the best choice for the Upper South. The following three variations are propagated by cuttings or grafting: 'Aurea', with yellow new foliage turning golden green in summer; 'Descanso Dwarf' ('Compacta'), a slow-growing form reaching 15 ft. in 20 years; and 'Pendula' ('Prostrata'), which grows flat on the ground or will drape over rocks or walls. Other popular low-growing forms include 'Feelin' Blue' (2 ft. high, 6 ft. wide), 'Prostrate Beauty' (2 ft. high, 8 ft. wide), and 'White Imp' (3 ft. high and wide, with white new growth.)

C. libani. CEDAR OF LEBANON. Zones US, MS, LS; USDA 6-8. Native to Asia Minor.

To 80 ft., but slow—to 15 ft. in 15 years. Variable in habit. Usually a dense, narrow pyramid in youth. Spreads picturesquely as it matures to become a majestic skyline tree with long horizontal branches and irregular crown. Needles, less than 1 in. long, are brightest green of any cedar on young trees; on old trees, they are dark gray-green. Rather scarce and expensive because of time it requires to reach marketable size. Routine garden care. No pruning needed. 'Sargentii' grows even more slowly, has a short trunk and crowded, pendulous branches; choice container or rock garden plant. 'Pendula' is a weeping form.

CEIBA PENTANDRA

SILK-COTTON TREE, KAPOK TREE
Malvaceae
Deciduous tree

TS; USDA 10-11

FULL SUN

MODERATE TO REGULAR WATER

Ceiba pentandra

From the tropics of Africa, America, and Southeast Asia. Easily recognized by its huge, spiny, buttressed trunk, this majestic deciduous tree is hardy only in south Florida. Given good soil and moderate to regular moisture, it grows rapidly to 60–70 ft. tall and 15–40 ft. wide. Leaves are medium green, to 6 in. long, each with five to seven leaflets. The tree blooms before leaf-out, bearing cup-shaped, ½-in. flowers in white, pink, or yellow. The flowers are followed by woody seed capsules containing a cottonlike substance—the kapok of commerce (used as a stuffing for pillows and lifejackets).

Silk-cotton tree makes a fine street tree or large shade tree. It needs plenty of room, though: Its trunk can grow to 9 ft. wide, with buttresses extending out to 15 ft. or more.

CELASTRUS
BITTERSWEET
Celastraceae
Deciduous vines

US, MS, LS; USDA 6-8
FULL SUN
REGULAR WATER

Celastrus scandens

Grown principally for clusters of handsome autumn fruit—yellow-to-orange capsules that split open to display brilliant red seeds inside. Birds seem uninterested in the fruit, so the display extends into winter. Branches bearing fruit are much prized for indoor arrangements. To produce fruit, you will need to plant a male and a female plant close to each other.

Bittersweets are vigorous, twining vines with ropelike branches; they need support. They will become a tangled mass of intertwining branches unless pruned constantly. Cut out fruiting branches in winter; pinch out tips of vigorous branches in summer.

C. orbiculatus. ORIENTAL BITTERSWEET. From Japan. To 30–40 ft. Roundish, toothed, medium green leaves to 4 in. Fruit on short side shoots is partially obscured until leaves drop. Foliage may turn an attractive

yellow in fall. A very aggressive grower that has escaped gardens and become a noxious weed that blankets woods.

C. rosthornianus (*C. loeseneri*). LOESENER BITTERSWEET. Native to central and western China. Grows to 20 ft. Dark green, oval leaves to 5 in. long. Heavy crops of fruit. Like *C. orbiculatus* but not as rampant.

C. scandens. AMERICAN BITTERSWEET. Native to eastern U.S. To 20 ft., or even higher if plant has something to grow on. If allowed to climb shrubs or small trees, it can kill them by girdling the stems; still better behaved than *C. orbiculatus*. Very light green, oval, toothed leaves to 4 in. Fruit is borne in scattered, dense clusters that are held above leaves; it looks showy even before foliage falls. 'Autumn Revolution' is self-fertile.

CELERY
Apiaceae
Biennial grown as annual

US, MS, LS, CS, TS; USDA 6-11
FULL SUN
REGULAR TO AMPLE WATER

Celery

Celery (*Apium graveolens dulce*) is native to Europe and Asia and is grown commercially in muck fields in Florida. It's difficult to grow in home gardens, because it needs more moisture and fertilizer than most other vegetables. The keys to success in the South are very rich, organic soil and an unfailing, plentiful water supply. Homegrown celery doesn't taste much different from that sold in markets, so grow it only if you enjoy a challenge.

CARE

Transplants are hard to find, so be prepared to start plants from seed. For a spring crop, sow seeds indoors 10 to 12 weeks before the last frost; then set out young plants 4 weeks before the last frost. For a fall crop, sow in summer, timing so that you can set out transplants 10 to 12 weeks before the first autumn frost. Work lots of composted manure and other organic material into the soil before planting. Space seedlings 7 in. apart in rows 2 ft. apart; plant them so that the crown is level with the soil. Keep soil constantly moist. Side-dress rows every 4 weeks with ½ cup of 10-10-10 fertilizer per 10 ft. of row. To whiten stalks (thought to make them less stringy), place a bottomless milk or orange juice carton over each plant to keep out sunlight, but don't cover the leaves. Available selections include 'Tango Hybrid' (85 days from sowing to harvest), 'Victoria' (85 days), 'Tall Utah 52-70R Improved' (90–100 days), and 'Ventura' (80 days).

CELOSIA
COCKSCOMB
Amaranthaceae
Annuals

US, MS, LS, CS, TS; USDA 6-11
FULL SUN
MODERATE WATER

Celosia argentea (crested form)

Richly colored tropical plants, some with flower clusters in bizarre shapes. In cut arrangements, celosias are attractive with other flowers, but in gardens they are most effective by themselves.

Dry cut blooms for winter bouquets. Sow seed in place in late spring or early -summer, or set out started plants. Plants will bloom by summer.

C. argentea. COCKSCOMB. Two kinds of cockscombs are derived from this species, which has silvery white flowers and narrow leaves to 2 in. or longer. One group, the plume cockscombs (often sold as *C.* 'Plumosa'), has plumy flower clusters. Some of these (sometimes sold as Chinese woolflower or *C.* 'Childsii') have flower clusters that look like tangled masses of yarn. Flowers come in brilliant shades of pink, orange red, gold, crimson. You can get forms that grow 2½–3 ft. high and 1½ ft. wide. Dwarf, more compact selections grow about 1 ft. high and half as wide; they bear heavily branched plumes. In the humid South, plume cockscombs are prone to rot and usually short-lived.

The other celosia group is the crested cockscombs (often sold as *C.* 'Cristata'). These have velvety, fan-shaped flower clusters, often much contorted and fluted. Flowers are yellow, orange, crimson, purple, or red. Tall kinds grow to 3 ft. tall and 1½ ft. wide, dwarf selections to 10 in. high and 6 in. wide. Crested cockscombs perform much better in the South than plume cockscombs.

C. spicata. WHEAT CELOSIA. Plant is covered in small silvery pink and purple spikes; it looks like a tall wild grass with elegant flowers. Ideal for a natural planting or rock garden and good for drying. Reseeds readily. Reaches 3½ ft. high, just 6 in. wide. Selections include 'Flamingo Feather' (soft pink to white), 'Flamingo Purple' (purple spikes and dark reddish green leaves), and 'Pink Candle' (rose-pink spikes).

C

CELTIS
HACKBERRY
Cannabaceae
Deciduous trees

🌿 **US, MS, LS, CS; USDA 6-9**

☀️◐ **FULL SUN OR PARTIAL SHADE**

💧 **MODERATE WATER**

Celtis laevigata

These big, tough, fast-growing shade trees are similar to elms (*Ulmus*) but smaller. All have virtue of deep rooting; old trees in narrow planting strips expand in trunk diameter and nearly fill strips without surface roots or any sign of heaving the sidewalk or curb. Good choice for street or lawn tree, even near buildings or paving. Canopy casts moderate shade in spring and summer; leaves turn yellow in fall. Mature trees have picturesque gray bark with corky warts and ridges. Small, berrylike fruit attracts birds.

Hackberry is exceptionally durable, taking strong winds (stake young trees until well established); dry heat; and dry, alkaline soils. Bare-root plants, especially in larger sizes, sometimes fail to leaf out. Buy in containers or try for small bare-root trees with big root systems. Wholly optids, which look a bit like snowflakes, can be bothersome pests. They suck sap from the leaves and drip sticky honeydew on everything below. Black mold then grows on the honeydew. This doesn't harm the trees, but it makes a mess. Systemic insecticides applied soon after leaf-out provide control.

C. laevigata. SUGARBERRY, SUGAR HACKBERRY. Native to southern Midwest and South. Grows to 60 ft. or taller and equally wide, with rounded crown. Similar to *C. occidentalis* but resistant to witches' broom (ugly clusters of dwarfed twigs). This species is a desirable street or park tree.

C. occidentalis. COMMON HACKBERRY. Native from the Rocky Mountains to the Atlantic, north to Quebec and south to Alabama. Grows to form a rounded crown 50 ft. high or more and nearly as wide. Branches are spreading and sometimes pendulous. Oval, light green leaves are 2–5 in. long, finely toothed on edges. Leafs out fairly late. Withstands urban pollution. Widely used in plains and prairie states, since it endures adverse conditions, including extreme cold, wind, soggy soil. Sometimes disfigured by witches' broom. 'Prairie Pride' has handsome glossy leaves and a uniform habit; it is resistant to witches' broom.

CENTAUREA
Asteraceae
Annuals and perennials

🌿 **ZONES VARY BY SPECIES**

☀️ **FULL SUN**

💧 **MODERATE WATER, EXCEPT AS NOTED**

Centaurea montana 'Amethyst in Snow'

Annual forms of *Centaurea* are grown mainly for cut flowers; perennial kinds are valued principally for their soft, silvery foliage. All are relatively easy to grow. For best performance, add lime to acid soils. In most cases, plan to sow seeds of annuals or set out plants of perennial kinds in spring (or in fall, in mild-winter areas).

ABOVE: Centaurea cyanus

C. americana. BASKET FLOWER. Annual. Zones US, MS, LS, CS, TS; USDA 6-11. Native to central and southwestern U.S. Grows to 5–6 ft. high, 3 ft. wide, with rather rough, oval leaves to 4 in. long. Blooms in summer; flower heads to 4 in. wide are rose-pink, paler toward center. Good in arrangements, fresh or dried.

C. cineraria (*C. gymno-carpa*). DUSTY MILLER. Perennial in Zones LS, CS, TS; USDA 8-11; annual anywhere. (This common name applies to many plants with whitish to silvery white foliage.) From Italy. Compact plant grows to 1 ft. wide, 1 ft. or taller. Velvety white, 3- to 6-in. leaves, mostly in basal clump, are strap shaped, with broad, roundish lobes. Solitary 1-in. flower heads (purple, occasionally yellow) in summer. Trim back after flowering. Attracts bees. Not browsed by deer.

C. cyanus. BACHELOR'S BUTTON, CORNFLOWER. Annual. Zones US, MS, LS, CS, TS; USDA 6-11. Native to northern temperate regions. Grows 1–2½ ft. tall and less than a foot wide; will send out branches if given sufficient space. Narrow, gray-green leaves are 2–3 in. long; spring to midsummer flowers are 1–1½ in. wide, in blue, pink, rose, wine-red, white. Blue forms are traditional favorites for boutonnieres. Bushy, compact 'Jubilee Gem' reaches just 1 ft. high, has deep blue blooms; Polka Dot strain has all the typical cornflower colors on 16-in. plants. 'Black Ball' has dark crimson double flowers on 1½- to 2-ft. stems. Sow seed in late summer or fall.

C. dealbata. PERSIAN CORNFLOWER. Perennial. Zones US, MS, LS; USDA 6-8. Native to the Caucasus. Forms an upright, bushy clump 2–3 ft. tall and about as wide. Deeply cut leaves to 8 in. long are deep green above, silvery beneath. In midsummer, leafy stems bear thistlelike pink blossoms to 1½ in. across; they make long-lasting cut flowers. May require staking, especially if grown in rich soil. 'Steenbergii' is a compact selection just 1–2 ft. tall, with 2-in. blooms in rich carmine-pink.

C. hypoleuca 'John Coutts'. Perennial. Zones US, MS, LS; USDA 6-8. Variety of a species from Asia Minor. Looks something like *C. montana* but has more deeply lobed leaves and deep rose flower heads. Sometimes offered as a selection of *C. dealbata*.

C. macrocephala. GLOBE CENTAUREA. Perennial. Zones US, MS, LS; USDA 6-8. From the Caucasus. Leafy plant with coarse leaves 6–8 in. long; reaches 3–4 ft. tall, 2 ft. wide, with 2-in. clusters of yellow summer flowers tightly enclosed at the base by overlapping papery, shiny brown bracts. Flower heads resemble thistles. Use in fresh or dried arrangements.

C. montana. MOUNTAIN BLUET. Perennial. Zones US, MS, LS; USDA 6-8. Native to the mountains of central Europe. Forms clumps to 1½ ft. tall and wide, with grayish green, broadly lance-shaped, 5- to 7-in.-long leaves. Flowers resembling ragged, 3-in. blue cornflowers top the stems in late spring to midsummer. Divide every other year. This is a cool-season plant and is less vigorous in warmer climates. Regular water. 'Alba' has white blooms. 'Amethyst Dream' has deep purple flowers. The two-toned 'Amethyst in Snow' sports white blooms with a deep purple center. 'Black Spider' has purplish-black flowers, with the outermost petals elongated and incurving.

C. moschata. SWEET SULTAN. Annual. Zones US, MS, LS, CS, TS; USDA 6-11. From Asia Minor. Erect plant, branching at base; grows to 2 ft. tall, 10 in. wide. Imperialis strain reaches 3 ft. high. Deeply toothed green leaves to 4 in. long. Thistlelike, 2-in. flower heads with a musky fragrance bloom from spring to fall—mostly in shades of lilac through rose, but sometimes in white or yellow. Splendid cut flower. Sow seed directly on soil in spring or set out as transplants. Needs lots of heat.

CENTRANTHUS RUBER
VALERIAN, JUPITER'S BEARD
Caprifoliaceae
Perennial

US, MS, LS; USDA 6-8

FULL SUN OR PARTIAL SHADE

LITTLE TO MODERATE WATER

Centranthus ruber

Trouble-free plant from the Mediterranean. Self-sows prolifically, thanks to small dandelionlike parachutes on seeds. Forms a bushy clump to 3 ft. high and wide, with upright stems bearing 4-in.-long bluish green leaves. Dusty crimson or rose-pink flowers about ½ in. long in dense terminal clusters bloom in late spring, early summer. 'Albus' is white.

Valerian puts on a long, showy display in difficult situations: It grows in poor, dry soil and accepts almost any condition except damp shade. Attracts butterflies. Cut off old flowering stems to shape plant, prolong bloom, and prevent self-seeding.

CEPHALANTHUS OCCIDENTALIS
BUTTONBUSH, BUTTON WILLOW
Rubiaceae
Deciduous shrub or tree

US, MS, LS, CS, TS; USDA 6-11

FULL SUN OR PARTIAL SHADE

REGULAR TO AMPLE WATER

FOLIAGE IS TOXIC

Cephalanthus occidentalis

Native to many parts of North America. This open-branched shrub grows 3–15 ft. tall and wide, with bright green, paired or whorled leaves (2–6 in. long) that emerge late in spring. Creamy white, slender-tubed flowers are crowded in rounded, 1- to 1½-in.-wide heads in late summer. Blooms have projecting stigmas that give the flower clusters the appearance of a pincushion or—as one nurseryman put it—"golf balls with antennae." Blossoms attract butterflies. Useful for naturalizing in wet areas. To maintain good form, cut back hard in early spring. The foliage is quite toxic to humans and livestock. 'Sputnik' has large, soft pink flowerheads.

CEPHALOTAXUS
PLUM YEW
Taxaceae
Evergreen shrubs or trees

ZONES VARY BY SPECIES

SUN OR SHADE

MODERATE WATER

Cephalotaxus harringtonii

Still unknown to most Southerners, the plum yews give hope to gardeners in the Lower and Coastal South who love the look of traditional yew (*Taxus*) but whose climates are too hot to grow it. These slow-growing evergreens from Asia have long, bright green needles and, on female plants, produce small green or brown fruits that resemble plums. They accept almost any well-drained soil; do best in partial to full shade but will tolerate sun. And whereas deer will gnaw most *Taxus* species to the ground, they turn up their noses at plum yews.

C. fortunei. FORTUNE'S PLUM YEW. Zones MS, LS, CS; USDA 7-9. Large shrub or small tree to 10–15 ft. tall and wide, with soft, medium green needles up to 3½ in. long. Reddish brown bark peels off in large pieces. 'Prostrate Spreader' is a low-growing, spreading form.

C. harringtonia. JAPANESE PLUM YEW. Zones US, MS, LS, CS; USDA 6-9. Spreading shrub or small tree with bright green, 1- to 2½-in.-long needles. Can grow 10–15 ft. tall and wide, but named selections are smaller and more compact. 'Duke Gardens' grows 3–4 ft. tall and wide and has survived –24°F; 'Fastigiata' ('Stricta') is a broadly columnar form that can reach 10 ft. tall, 6–8 ft. wide. 'Korean Gold' has golden new foliage, columnar habit. 'Prostrata' is the name given to plants propagated from side branches; these do not form a central leader and remain 2–3 ft. tall, spreading somewhat wider. 'Yewtopia' grows into a vase shape just 3–4 ft. tall and wide. Japanese plum yew tolerates much pruning and will resprout even if you cut back into older wood. Makes an excellent substitute for shrub-type junipers (*Juniperus*) and hollies (*Ilex*).

C. sinensis. CHINESE YEW. Zones MS, LS, CS; USDA 7-9. Plant somewhat resembles *C. harringtonia* but with needles that are blackish green above and silvery to bluish green beneath.

CERASTIUM TOMENTOSUM

SNOW-IN-SUMMER
Caryophyllaceae
Perennial

🌿 **US, MS, LS; USDA 6-8**

◐ **LIGHT SHADE**

🌢🌢 **MODERATE TO REGULAR WATER**

Cerastium tomentosum

This vigorous, low-growing European native forms spreading, dense, tufted mats of silvery gray leaves to ¾ in. long. Impressive masses of snowy white, ½- to ¾-in.-wide blossoms appear in early summer. Plant grows 6–8 in. high, spreads 2–3 ft. in a year.

Plant as ground cover on slopes or level ground, as bulb cover, in rock gardens, as edging for paths, and between stepping stones. Particularly attractive against darker-colored backgrounds. Avoid extensive planting in prominent situations, however, since plant is not long lived. Not browsed by deer.

CARE

Tolerates any type of soil as long as the drainage is good; heavy, wet soil or standing water causes root rot. Set divisions or plants 1–1½ ft. apart, or sow seed. Fertilize two or three times a year to speed growth. Shear off faded flowers. Plants may look a bit shabby in winter but revive rapidly in spring. Divide in autumn or early spring.

CERATOSTIGMA

PLUMBAGO
Plumbaginaceae
Evergreen and deciduous shrubs and perennials

🌿 **ZONES VARY BY SPECIES**

☀ ◐ **FULL SUN OR PARTIAL SHADE**

🌢🌢 **MODERATE TO REGULAR WATER**

Ceratostigma plumbaginoides

These durable plants are valued for their clusters of intense blue, phloxlike flowers that bloom in summer to late fall, when cool hues in the garden are most welcome. (For pale blue–flowered Cape plumbago, see *Plumbago auriculata*.) Tolerate inconsistent watering. Not browsed by deer. Shrubby species are usually treated like perennials in colder zones; cut them back after bloom, and mulch heavily.

C. griffithii. BURMESE PLUMBAGO. Evergreen shrub. Zones MS, LS, CS, TS; USDA 7-11. Himalayan native. Resembles *C. willmottianum* but has rounder leaves and more compact, somewhat lower growth (to 2½–3 ft. high and wide). Also blooms somewhat later. Growth often nipped back

by frost. White-blooming selections are available.

C. plumbaginoides. DWARF PLUMBAGO. Perennial. Zones US, MS, LS, CS; USDA 6-9. Native to China. Wiry-stemmed ground cover 6–12 in. high. Bronzy green to dark green, 3-in.-long leaves turn reddish brown with frosts. Most effective in early or midautumn, when blue flowers contrast with red fall foliage. In loose soil and where growing season is long, spreads rapidly by underground stems, eventually covering large areas; plant 1–1½ ft. apart for quick cover.

Dwarf plumbago is semievergreen only in the mildest-winter areas; best to cut back after bloom. Dies back elsewhere; leafs out late in spring. When plants show signs of aging, remove old crowns and replace with rooted stems.

C. willmottianum. CHINESE PLUMBAGO. Deciduous shrub. Zones US, MS, LS, CS; USDA 6-9. Grows as airy mass of wiry stems 2–4 ft. high and wide. Deep green, 2-in.-long leaves are somewhat diamond shaped, with tapering tips; turn yellow or red and drop quickly after frost. 'Palmgold' ('Desert Skies') has golden leaves.

CERATOZAMIA MEXICANA

Zamiaceae
Cycad

🌿 **TS; USDA 10-11**

◐ **PARTIAL SHADE**

🌢🌢 **MODERATE TO REGULAR WATER**

Ceratozamia mexicana

From southern Mexico. Related to sago palm (*Cycas revoluta*) and

similar to it in appearance and very slow growth. Trunk usually 1 ft. high (4–6 ft. in great age) and 1 ft. thick. Leaves are carried in a whorl at top of trunk; they are 3–6 ft. long, divided featherwise into 15 to 20 pairs of foot-long, inch-wide leaflets. Striking in container or protected place in open ground. Protect from frosts. Not browsed by deer.

CERCIDIPHYLLUM JAPONICUM

KATSURA TREE
Cercidiphyllaceae
Deciduous tree

🌿 **US, MS, LS; USDA 6-8**

☀ ◐ **FULL SUN OR LIGHT SHADE**

🌢 **REGULAR WATER**

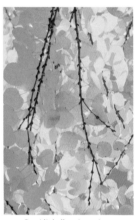

Cercidiphyllum japonicum

In youth, this fine-textured native of China and Japan is upright and pyramidal, but it becomes more rounded with age. It tops out at around 40 ft. At all ages, it has a light, dainty branch and leaf pattern. Brown bark is somewhat shaggy on old trees. Heart-shaped, 2–4-in.-long leaves emerge reddish purple, become bluish green in summer, then turn yellow to apricot in autumn. To enhance fall color, water less frequently in late summer. Foliage of some katsura trees smells like brown sugar on warm autumn days when leaves are falling— and when new growth opens in spring.

Some specimens have a single trunk, but multiple trunks are more usual. 'Rotfuchs' ('Red Fox') leaves are open dark purple. 'Heronswood Globe' is compact but eventually can reach 20 ft.

tall and wide. Weeping forms are particularly elegant; these grow about 25 ft. tall and 15 ft. wide and include 'Amazing Grace', 'Morioka Weeping', and *C. j. pendulum*.

Katsura trees need regular moisture (especially during youth) and shelter from intense sun and drying wind. No serious pest or disease problems. Mature trees need little pruning.

CERCIS
REDBUD
Caesalpiniaceae
Deciduous shrubs or trees

🌿 **ZONES VARY BY SPECIES**

☼ ☀ **FULL SUN OR LIGHT SHADE, EXCEPT AS NOTED**

💧 💧 **WATER NEEDS VARY BY SPECIES**

Cercis canadensis 'Hearts of Gold'

Adaptable and dependable, redbuds include some of our most charming native trees. In early spring, before leaf-out, a profusion of small, sweet pea–shaped, lavender-pink to rosy purple flowers appears on twigs, branches, and even the main trunk. Blossoms are followed by clusters of flat, beanlike pods that persist into winter and give rise to numerous seedlings around the tree. Handsome, broad, rounded or heart-shaped leaves may change to bright yellow in fall, but fall color is inconsistent.

Redbuds make fine lawn trees, look great in groupings, and have their place in shrub borders and even foundation plantings. In winter, the dark, leafless branches form an attractive silhouette, especially effective against a light-colored wall. Larger types make nice small shade trees for patios and courtyards. And you

can't miss when using redbuds in naturalized settings, such as at the edge of a woodland. Do any pruning in the dormant season or (preferably) immediately after bloom.

C. canadensis. EASTERN REDBUD. Zones US, MS, LS, CS; USDA 6-9. Native to eastern U.S. The fastest growing and largest (to 25–35 ft. tall) of the redbuds, and the most apt to take tree form. Round headed but with horizontally tiered branches in age. Leaves are rich green, 3–6 in. long, with pointed tips. Flowers are small (½ in. long), rosy pink or lavender. Needs some winter chill to flower profusely. Regular water.

Eastern redbud is valuable for bridging the color gap between the early-flowering fruit trees (flowering peach, flowering plum) and the crabapples and late-flowering dogwoods and cherries. Effective as a specimen or understory tree, it is also an important early source of pollen and nectar for native pollinators. Available selections include the following.

'Ace of Hearts'. Charming compact selection, about half the size of the species. Flowers are small but borne in profusion.

'Appalachian Red'. Flowers are deep fuchsia pink—not a true red but close to it.

'Flame'. Double pink blooms look quite different from those of other redbuds.

'Floating Clouds'. Striking green and white leaf variegation. Better resistance to leaf burn than 'Silver Cloud'. Thin, willowy, semi-pendant branches.

'Forest Pansy'. Foliage emerges a gaudy purple in spring, then gradually changes to burgundy-toned green as summer heat increases. Rosy purple flowers. Nice color accent; benefits from light afternoon shade in summer.

'Hearts of Gold'. New leaves emerge red and mature to bright golden yellow. Foliage that is shaded may revert to green, but the two-tone effect is striking. Lavender blooms. Grows 20–25 ft. tall and wide.

'Lavender Twist' ('Covey'). Dwarf weeping selection with unusual zigzagging, twisting branches. Lavender flowers; leaves slightly larger than those of the species. Original plant was only 4½ ft. high, 7 ft. wide at 40 years old.

TOP: *Cercis canadensis texensis* 'Texas White'; BOTTOM: *C. canadensis* 'Ruby Falls'

'Merlot'. Purple leaves similar to those of 'Forest Pansy', but thicker, glossier, and more resistant to late-season browning. Dense, semiupright grower to 12–15 ft. tall and wide.

'Pink Heartbreaker'. Weeping form, with lavender-pink flowers.

Improved tiered branching compared with other weeping types.

'Ruby Falls'. Fascinating result of a cross between 'Lavender Twist' and 'Forest Pansy'. Cascading stems hold maroon leaves on a plant just 6–8-ft. tall and 4–6 ft. wide. Blooms are deep lavender.

C

'Rubye Atkinson'. Pure pink flowers.

'Solar Eclipse'. Heart-shaped leaves are lime-green with a dark green margin. New growth is peachy orange. Grows 12 ft. tall and wide.

'Tennessee Pink'. True pink flowers on a plant somewhat smaller than the species.

'The Rising Sun' ('JN2'). Leaves emerge orange to apricot, maturing through shades of golden yellow and lime-green before turning buttery yellow in autumn. Flowers are rosy lavender. Compact grower to about 12 ft. tall.

'Vanilla Twist'. White-flowered weeping selection.

Among the deserving subspecies and forms available are these three:

C. c. alba. A white-flowering form. 'Royal White' is compact, with large, profuse, early blooms.

C. c. mexicana (*C. mexicana*). From many areas of Mexico. Most typical form is single trunked, to 15 ft. with leathery blue-green leaves and pinkish purple flowers. Moderate to regular water.

C. c. texensis. (*C. reniformis*). Zones US, MS, LS, CS; USDA 6-9. Native to Texas, Oklahoma, and Mexico. To 15–25 ft. high and wide. 'Oklahoma' has deep purple buds opening to rosy purple flowers; 'Texas White' bears pure white blossoms. 'Traveller' is a weeping, purple-flowered form to about 5 ft. tall and twice as wide; excellent small specimen tree. All have thick, leathery, dark green leaves and require only moderate water after establishment.

C. chinensis. CHINESE REDBUD. Zones US, MS, LS. Native to China, Japan. Seen mostly as an open shrub or small tree to 10–12 ft. tall, 10 ft. wide. Flower clusters are 3–5 in. long, deep rose, almost rosy purple. Leaves (to 5 in. long) are sometimes glossier and brighter green than those of *C. canadensis*, with a transparent line around the edge. 'Avondale' is a superior form with profuse deep purple flowers. 'Don Egolf' is compact, with bright rosy mauve flowers and good disease resistance; it produces no seedpods. Full sun; regular water.

CESTRUM
Solanaceae
Evergreen shrubs

- ◗ **TS; USDA 10-11, EXCEPT AS NOTED**
- ☼ **PARTIAL SHADE, EXCEPT AS NOTED**
- ◗ **REGULAR WATER**
- ◊ **FRUIT AND SAP ARE POISONOUS IF INGESTED**

Cestrum elegans smithii

These brightly flowered shrubs grow fast in warm, sheltered spots, with an arching, lax growth habit that benefits from consistent pinching and nipping back. May be cut back severely after flowering or fruiting. Clusters of tubular, inch-long flowers are attractive to hummingbirds; the showy fruit that follows can also attract birds. Add organic soil amendments before planting. Feed generously.

C. aurantiacum. ORANGE CESTRUM. CS, TS; USDA 9-11. Native to Guatemala. Rare and handsome. To 8 ft. tall and wide. Brilliant show of clustered orange-yellow flowers in late spring and summer, followed by white berries. Deep green, oval, 4-in. leaves. Good for espalier. May spread by suckers.

C. elegans. RED CESTRUM. Native to Mexico. Shrub or semi-climber to 10 ft. or more in height and spread, with arching branches and deep green, 4-in. leaves. Plant produces masses of purplish red flowers in spring and summer; these are followed by red berries. Good choice for espalier. *C. e. smithii* has pink flowers.

C. fasciculatum. A native of Mexico. Similar to *C. elegans* but larger in all its parts.

C. 'Newellii'. Zones CS, TS; USDA 9-11. May be a hybrid of

C. fasciculatum and *C. elegans*; resembles the former but has bright crimson flowers. Some plants listed as *C.* 'Newellii' may in fact be *C. fasciculatum*.

C. nocturnum. NIGHT-BLOOMING JASMINE. Native to West Indies. To 12 ft. tall and wide, with 4- to 8-in.-long leaves and clusters of creamy white summer flowers followed by white berries. Blossoms powerfully fragrant at night—too much so for some people. 'Orange Peel', a hybrid with another West Indian species, has orange-yellow flowers tipped in yellow. Full sun.

C. parqui. CHILEAN CESTRUM, WILLOW-LEAFED JESSAMINE. Zones LS, CS, TS; USDA 8-11. Native to Chile. To 6–10 ft. tall and wide, with many branches from base. Densely clothed in willowlike, 3- to 6-in.-long leaves. Greenish yellow summer flowers in clusters. Dark, violet-brown berries. Not as attractive as other species in form, flowers, or fruit, but its perfume is potent. Leaves blacken in light frost. Best used where winter appearance is unimportant. In the Lower and Coastal South, protect roots with mulch; treat as perennial.

CHAENOMELES
FLOWERING QUINCE
Rosaceae
Deciduous shrubs

- ◗ **US, MS, LS, CS; USDA 6-9**
- ☼ **FULL SUN**
- ◗◗ **MODERATE TO REGULAR WATER**

Chaenomeles

These are among the first shrubs to bloom each year. As early as January, you can bring a budded stem indoors, place it in water in

a sunny window, and watch it burst into flower. Blossoms are 1½–2½ in. across, single to semidouble or double, in a wide range of colors. Leaves are red tinged when young, then mature to shiny green. Most types are thorny, take pruning well, and make excellent barriers and hedges. Not browsed by deer.

Flowering quince is easy to grow and practically indestructible; its only requirements are sun and well-drained soil. Even if leaf spot (a common disease in humid areas) defoliates the plant by midsummer, the next year's bloom won't be reduced. Prune to shape the plant or reduce its size—either immediately after bloom or during the flowering season (you can use cut branches in bloom for indoor arrangements). Lack of winter chill may lead to sparse bloom in the Coastal South.

Some selections bear small (2- to 4-in.), hard, delightfully fragrant fruits. Although not as tasty as that of common quince (*Cydonia oblonga*; see Quince), the fruit contains lots of pectin, making it good for jelly or preserves. If your flowering quince fails to bear, it probably needs cross-pollination with another selection.

The following list of garden hybrids gives height and flower color. Tall types reach 6 ft. or taller, low types 2–3 ft. Most are broader than tall.

'Apple Blossom'. Tall. White blossoms with pink tones. Good for fruit.

'Cameo'. Low, compact. Double blooms in apricot pink. Good for fruit.

'Contorta'. Low. White to pink; twisted branches. Good as bonsai.

'Dragon's Blood'. Low. Blood-red double blooms.

'Falconnet Charlet'. Tall, thornless. Double salmon-pink flowers.

'Hollandia'. Tall. Large red flowers; reblooms in fall.

'Iwai Nishiki'. Low. Bright red double flowers on a spreading plant (may reach 10 ft. wide).

'Jet Trail'. Low. Pure white.

'Orange Storm'. Low. Large, double, rich orange flowers resemble those of camellia. Thornless and fruitless.

'O Yashima'. Low. Double white.

'Pink Beauty'. Medium tall. Rose-pink flowers.

'Pink Storm'. Low. Double, deep pink, camellialike blooms.

C

TOP: Chaenomeles 'Cameo'; *C.* 'Texas Scarlet'; *MIDDLE: C.* 'Pink Beauty';
BOTTOM: C. 'Snow'; *C.* 'Toyo Nishiki'

Thornless and fruitless.

'Scarlet Storm'. Like 'Pink Storm', but with dark red flowers.

'Snow'. Tall. Large, pure white.

'Texas Scarlet'. Low. Tomato red. Good for fruit.

'Toyo Nishiki'. Tall. Pink, white, pink-and-white, red all on same branch. Good for fruit.

CHAMAECYPARIS
FALSE CYPRESS
Cupressaceae
Evergreen shrubs and trees

- **US, MS, LS; USDA 6-8, EXCEPT AS NOTED**
- **FULL SUN OR PARTIAL SHADE, EXCEPT AS NOTED**
- **REGULAR WATER**

Chamaecyparis obtusa
'Crippsii'

Intensive selection has brought these timber trees down in scale, so most new selections fit well into suburban gardens (some even work as container plants). Dense, richly textured foliage makes them easy to mistake for arborvitae (*Thuja*), but the leaves of false cypress have white lines on the undersides, while those of arborvitae are entirely green. Most false cypresses have two distinct types of leaves: juvenile and mature. Juvenile leaves (short, needlelike, soft but often prickly) appear on young plants and some new growth of larger trees. Mature foliage consists of tiny, scalelike, overlapping leaves. Cones are small and round. All need good drainage and protection from wind.

C. obtusa. HINOKI FALSE CYPRESS. There are dozens of golden, dwarf, and fern-leafed forms of this Japanese native, but a few are the most important

ones in landscaping. 'Crippsii' is a golden-leafed form to 50 ft. high and 25 ft. wide; the strongest yellow color is mainly at the end of foliage sprays. 'Gracilis', slender hinoki cypress, is an upright tree to 20 ft. with nodding branch tips. 'Nana Gracilis' is a miniature of the former, reaching just 4 ft. tall. Bright yellow-foliaged 'Nana Lutea', ideal plant for bonsai, reaches just 1 ft. high and 10 in. wide; it needs protection from full sun.

C. pisifera. SAWARA FALSE CYPRESS. Japanese native to 20–30 ft., rarely seen except in its garden forms. Selections include 'Cyano-Viridis' ('Boulevard'), a slow-growing, dense bush to 6–8 ft. high and wide, with silvery blue-green foliage; 'Filifera', to 8 ft., with drooping, threadlike branchlets; and 'Filifera Aurea', with similar branchlets in yellow.

C. thyoides. WHITE CEDAR. Zones US, MS, LS, CS; USDA 6-9. Eastern U.S. timber tree to 75 ft. tall; columnar form. Found in wet sites in the wild. Garden forms include 'Andelyensis', dense, columnar gray-green shrub to 10 ft., turning bronze in cold weather; and 'Heather Bun', broader than 'Andelyensis', turning intense plum-purple in winter.

CHAMAEDOREA
Arecaceae
Palms

- **TS; USDA 10-11, EXCEPT AS NOTED; OR GROW IN POTS**
- **PARTIAL OR FULL SHADE; BRIGHT INDIRECT LIGHT**
- **REGULAR WATER**

Chamaedorea elegans

Generally small, slow-growing, feather-type palms from the rain forests of Mexico and Central and

South America. Some have single trunks, others clustered trunks; leaves are variable in shape. Perfect for a large container on a shaded patio. If growing indoors, feed monthly during growing season with a balanced liquid fertilizer; cut back on fertilizer and water in winter.

C. cataractarum. CAT PALM, CASCADE PALM. Forms a dense clump to 6 ft. tall, 9 ft. wide. Dark green, arching, feathery leaves to 3 ft. or longer. Does best in a moist, partially shaded location with protection from drying winds. Good as informal hedge, screen, border, or understory plant. Hardy to 24°F.

C. costaricana. If well fed and liberally watered, develops fairly quickly into bamboolike clumps 8–10 ft. tall and wide. Lacy, feathery leaves 3–4 ft. long. Good potted palm.

C. elegans. PARLOR PALM. The best indoor chamaedorea, tolerating crowded roots, poor light. Single stemmed; grows very slowly to an eventual 3–4 ft. tall and nearly as wide. Feathery, lush green leaves to 2 ft. long. Douse the tops of potted plants with water occasionally. Groom by removing old leafstalks. Repot every 2 or 3 years, carefully washing off old soil and replacing it with good potting mix. Plant three or more in a container for most effective display.

C. metallica. METALLIC PALM. To 3 ft. tall and about half as wide. Single stem is topped by erect, broadly oval leaves in the shape of a fishtail. Foliage has a distinctive blue-green sheen. Purple or orange flowers are followed by small black fruits. Excellent in pots.

C. microspadix. HARDY BAMBOO PALM. LS (protected), CS, TS; USDA 8-11. Rather open clumps of slender, upright stems can reach 10 ft. tall. Arching blue-green leaves give plants a feathery look. Tough and adaptable; hardy to 18°F.

C. radicalis. LS (protected), CS, TS; USDA 8-11. This dwarf palm grows just 3–4 ft. tall, and its sprawling, open form makes it a natural choice for planting in groups as a tall ground cover. Takes many years to form a discernible trunk. Best in rich, moist soil. Although it's one of the hardiest in the genus, surviving 10°F with only leaf damage, it benefits

from overhead protection in the Lower South.

C. seifrizii (C. erumpens). BAMBOO PALM. To 4–14 ft. tall, 3–6 ft. wide. Produces a clump of slender, bright green, bamboolike canes bearing deep green leaves. New stems keep forming at the base of the plant, so it never looks sparse. Handsome, fine-textured accent for indoors or out.

C. tenella (C. geonomiformis). Single-trunked palm to 3–4 ft. tall and wide. Dark bluish green leaves to 8 in. long, 2–3 in. wide have a distinctive look: they are undivided except for a deep cleft at the tip.

C. tepejilote. PACAYA PALM. Single trunk ringed with swollen joints like those of bamboo. Moderate growth to 10 ft. or taller and about 8 ft. wide. Velvety green, feathery leaves reach 4 ft. long. Hardy to 28°F.

CHAMAEMELUM NOBILE

ROMAN CHAMOMILE
Asteraceae
Perennial often grown as annual

🌡 **US, MS, LS, CS; USDA 6-9**

☼ ◐ **FULL SUN OR PARTIAL SHADE**

💧 **MODERATE WATER**

Chamaemelum nobile

Soft-textured, spreading mat of bright light green, finely cut, aromatic leaves. Reaches 3–12 in. high. Blooms in summer, sometimes continuing into fall. Blossoms of the most commonly grown form look like small yellow buttons, while those of other types resemble little daisies. Useful between stepping stones or as a low edging along path. 'Treneague'

is a nonflowering selection; 'Flore Pleno' has double daisylike flowers.

Fragrant, sweet chamomile tea comes from the dried flowers of *Matricaria recutita*.

CHAMAEROPS HUMILIS

MEDITERRANEAN FAN PALM
Arecaceae
Palm

🌡 **LS, CS, TS; USDA 8-11; OR GROWN IN POTS**

☼ ◐ **FULL SUN OR PARTIAL SHADE**

💧💧 **MODERATE TO REGULAR WATER**

Chamaerops humilis

From the western Mediterranean. One of the hardiest palms; survives temperatures as low as 10°F. Clumps slowly develop from offshoots, curving to height of 20 ft.; may also reach 20 ft. wide. Growth is extremely slow in northern part of range. Green to bluish green, fan-shaped leaves on leafstalks set with very sharp spines. Use in containers, mass under trees, grow as impenetrable hedge. Tolerates poor soil, strong winds. Deer don't bother with it. 'Vulcano' is compact and shrubby, to about 6 ft. tall and half as wide; its thick leaves are set on nearly spineless stalks. *C. h. argentea* (C. h. cerifera) has silvery blue foliage.

CHASMANTHIUM LATIFOLIUM

RIVER OATS
Poaceae
Perennial grass

🌡 **US, MS, LS, CS; USDA 6-9**

☼ ◐ **FULL SUN OR LIGHT SHADE**

💧 **REGULAR WATER**

Chasmanthium latifolium

Ornamental grass from moist woodlands of eastern U.S. Broad, bamboolike leaves form a 2-ft.-wide clump topped in midsummer by arching, 2- to 5-ft. flowering stems carrying showers of silvery green spikelets that resemble flattened clusters of oats (or flattened armadillos). These turn copper in fall, look good through winter; they dry to a greenish straw color and are attractive in dried arrangements. Clumps widen slowly and are not aggressive. Leaves turn brown in winter, when plants should be cut back almost to ground. Divide clumps when they become crowded and flowering diminishes. Stake if flowering stems sprawl too far. Self-sows extensively and can become invasive. To control spread, remove seed heads before they mature. 'River Mist' has leaves heavily striped in white; developing seed heads are white.

CHAYOTE

Cucurbitaceae
Perennial vine often grown as annual

- CS, TS; USDA 9-11; ANYWHERE AS ANNUAL
- FULL SUN
- REGULAR WATER

Chayote

Known botanically as *Sechium edule*, this native of the tropical Americas belongs to the same family as squash and resembles a squash vine, but its flowers are inconspicuous. Grown for edible fruit: 3–8 in. long, green or yellow green, irregularly oval, grooved, with a large edible seed surrounded by solid flesh. Flavor like that of summer squash. Eat young fruit raw or cooked; boil or bake mature fruit. Large, fleshy tuberous roots can also be eaten—though you cannot, of course, grow the plant as a perennial and consume its roots as well. Also known as mirliton or christophine.

Needs rich soil. Climbs by tendrils. Provide fence or trellis. In areas where fruit is sold in stores, buy in fall and allow to sprout in cupboard; then plant whole fruit edgewise and slanted, with sprouted end at lowest point, narrow end exposed. If shoot is long, cut it back to 1–2 in. Plant two or more vines to ensure pollination. In the Coastal and Tropical South, plant sprouted fruit in ground in late winter; in colder areas, pot in a 5-gallon container and store in a dark, cool spot until frost danger is past. Plant can produce a 20- to 30-ft. vine in first year, reach 40–50 ft. in second. Top dies down in frost. Bloom starts with shorter days in fall; fruit is ripe within a month. A plant can bear 200 or more fruits.

CHELIDONIUM MAJUS

GREATER CELANDINE
Papaveraceae
Perennial or biennial

- US, MS, LS; USDA 6-8
- PARTIAL TO FULL SHADE
- REGULAR WATER
- SAP IS IRRITATING TO THE SKIN

Chelidonium majus

This European native grows 2–3 ft. tall and 10 in. wide, with several erect stems rising from the rootstock. Smooth, bright green leaves, 4–10 in. long, are attractively cut and lobed. Profuse yellow to orange-yellow flowers to 1 in. wide bloom in summer. Self-sows freely and naturalizes (sometimes too well; may become invasive). Double-flowered 'Flore Pleno' also seeds itself freely. Both forms are best in wild gardens. Juice from the stems is said to get rid of warts.

CHELONE

TURTLEHEAD
Plantaginaceae
Perennial

- US, MS, LS; USDA 6-8, EXCEPT AS NOTED
- FULL SUN OR LIGHT SHADE
- AMPLE WATER

Chelone obliqua

Leafy, clump-forming perennials related to penstemon. All are native to the eastern U.S. and grow in damp places in sun or light shade. Frequently used in bog gardens. All bloom in late summer and autumn. Common name comes from the oddly formed flowers—inch-long, puffy, and two-lipped, with a fancied resemblance to a turtle's head. Useful for cut flowers, shade gardens, wild gardens.

C. glabra. WHITE TURTLE-HEAD. Grows 2–3 ft. tall (occasionally much taller), 1½ ft. wide. Medium green leaves to 8 in. long; white or palest pink flowers. 'Black Ace', with white blossoms, typically grows 3–4 ft. tall but can reach 6 ft. Its leaves emerge deep green with an almost black cast, then lighten to green by late summer.

C. lyonii. PINK TURTLEHEAD. Zones US, MS; USDA 6-7. Reaches 3–4 ft. tall, 2 ft. wide. Dark green, 4- to 6-in.-long leaves; rose-pink flowers. 'Hot Lips' has red stems and reddish purple flowers with a spot of white at the base. 'Pink Temptation' grows just 15 in. tall; flowers are dark pink.

C. obliqua. ROSE TURTLE-HEAD. Grows to 2–2½ ft. tall, 1 ft. wide. Dark green leaves to 8 in. long; deep pink blossoms. Latest bloomer among the species listed here.

CHERRY

Rosaceae
Deciduous fruit trees

- ZONES VARY BY TYPE
- FULL SUN
- REGULAR WATER

'Sweetheart' cherries

If George Washington indeed chopped down a cherry tree, it was probably because he was miffed about not getting any fruit. Fruiting cherries, both sweet and sour types, make attractive trees for the home garden, but getting a decent crop is a challenge in the South. For strictly ornamental cherries, see *Prunus*.

Sweet cherries are best grown in the Upper South, preferably in the Appalachian and Blue Ridge Mountains. These are the most common market type, but their high chilling requirement (many hours needed below 45°F) makes them poorly adapted to most of the South. They can't take extreme summer heat or intense winter cold, and freezes and heavy spring rains can damage crop. Trees reach 20–35 ft. tall and broad in some selections.

The worst single problem for sweet cherries grown in the South is bacterial canker. Gardeners should check with their local Cooperative Extension Offices for recommended methods of control.

In the past, many gardeners stayed away from sweet cherries, because the trees are naturally large (to 35 ft. high and wide), and most need cross-pollination, so they have to plant two. But breeding advances have produced many self-fruitful varieties (noted in descriptions) and much smaller sizes.

C

For selections that need pollinators to produce fruit, the second tree must be chosen with care. No combination of these will produce fruit: 'Bing', 'Lambert', 'Royal Ann'. However, the following selections will pollinate any other cherry: 'Angela', 'Black Tartarian', 'Hedelfingen', 'Stella', and 'Van'. Self-fertile types (a lone tree will bear) are noted in the descriptions.

Good selections include the following:

'Angela'. Small, glossy black fruit with excellent flavor. Resists cracking. Midseason to late.

'Bing'. Top quality. Large, dark red, meaty fruit of fine flavor. Midseason.

'Black Tartarian'. Fruit smaller than 'Bing', purplish black, firm and sweet. Early.

'Craig's Crimson'. Medium to large, deep red to black; superb flavor. Naturally dwarf (about two-thirds normal size). Self-fruitful. Midseason.

'Early Ruby'. Dark red, purple-fleshed early cherry that performs well in all sweet cherry areas. 'Black Tartarian', 'Royal Ann', 'Van' are all good pollenizers.

'Hedelfingen'. Medium-large black cherry. Ripens with 'Van', but fruit colors before maturity,

needs early protection from birds. Productive tree begins bearing fruit when young.

'Lambert'. Large, firm black fruit. Flavor more sprightly than 'Bing'. Late.

'Lapins'. Resembles 'Bing' but is self-fruitful. Early to midseason.

'Royal Ann' ('Napoleon'). Large, spreading tree; very productive. Tender, crisp, light yellow fruit with pink blush. Sprightly flavor. Midseason.

'Stella'. Dark fruit like 'Lambert'; ripens a few days later. Self-fertile and good pollenizer for other cherries. 'Compact Stella' is similar, but tree is half the size.

'Sweetheart'. Large, bright red; excellent flavor. Self-fruitful and heavy bearing. Late.

'Van'. Heavy-bearing tree. Shiny black fruit, firmer and slightly smaller than 'Bing'. Ripens slightly earlier than or at the same time as 'Bing'.

'White Gold'. Large, yellow with red blush; fine flavor. Self-fruitful and heavy bearing; resists cracking. Midseason.

The newly introduced German dwarfing rootstocks ('Gisela 5' and 'Gisela 6') now provide gardeners with smaller sweet cherry trees that are easier to manage. Self-fruitful selections now avail-

able on these rootstocks include 'Sandra Rose', 'Barton', and 'Stardust'. Some of these may prove satisfactory in the South.

Sour cherries. Also known as pie cherries. More widely adapted than sweet cherries; succeed along the Atlantic Coast and farther north and south than sweet cherries do. In home gardens and orchards, grow in Upper and Middle South in well-drained soil. Sour cherry trees are smaller than sweet cherry trees—to about 20 ft. tall, with spreading habit. They are self-fertile. There are far fewer types of sour cherries than sweet ones.

'Early Richmond'. Highly recommended. Like 'Montmorency'. Early.

'English Morello'. Dark red, somewhat tart fruit with red juice. Late.

'Kansas Sweet'. Large red fruit is semisweet. Late.

'Meteor'. Fruit like 'Montmorency' but on a smaller tree. Late.

'Montmorency'. Highly recommended. Small, bright red, soft, juicy fruit with a sweet-tart flavor. Midseason to late.

'North Star'. Fruit has red to dark red skin and sour yellow flesh. Susceptible to bacterial canker. Small, very hardy tree. Midseason.

'Surefire'. Bright red skin and flesh; sweet flavor. Late.

HOW TO GROW CHERRIES

PLANTING AND WATERING Plant in deep, well-drained soil, and make sure trees get regular water throughout the growing season. To prevent fruit splitting, cut back on watering as harvest time approaches.

PRUNING AND HARVESTING Fruiting spurs are long lived and do not need to be renewed by pruning. Prune trees only to maintain good structure and shape. Fruit appears in late spring to early summer. Don't pick until the cherries are sweet; they won't ripen further after harvest.

FERTILIZING Standard sweet cherries need no fertilizer if the trees are putting out 6–12 in. of new growth per year. Otherwise, give full-size, fully bearing trees 5 lbs. of 10-10-10 fertilizer in spring, and give young trees ½ lb. per year of age. For dwarf sweet cherries or sour cherries, apply ½ lb. of 10-10-10 fertilizer per inch of trunk diameter.

CHALLENGES Use netting or reflective tape to keep birds from eating the crop. For control of brown rot and blossom blight, apply a copper spray just as leaves fall in autumn, then a fungicide when first blooms appear and weekly during bloom. Resume fungicide program about 2 weeks before harvest or if fruit rot begins to appear. Good sanitation will also help limit disease: Remove any shriveled fruit, and prune out and discard diseased twigs as soon as you see them. Spray horticultural oil during the dormant period to control various pests, including scale insects and mites.

CHESTNUT
Fagaceae
Deciduous trees or shrubs

🌿 **US, MS, LS, CS; USDA 6–9**

☀ **FULL SUN**

💧 **MODERATE WATER**

Chestnuts

Where space allows, these dense, large shade trees bring lush beauty and delicious nuts into the

landscape. They just need to be sited where their litter and rank-smelling pollen won't be too obtrusive. All have handsome dark-to-bright green foliage. Small, creamy white flowers in long (8- to 10-in.), slim catkins make quite a display in summer. The large edible nuts are enclosed in prickly burs. Nuts fall to the ground when ripe. Gather daily, remove from burs, and dry in the sun (in shade in hot climates). Plant two or more trees to ensure cross-pollination and a substantial crop; single trees bear lightly or not at all. Give occasional deep irrigation.

Chestnut blight has made American chestnut (*Castanea dentata*) nearly extinct in its native range, but other species and hybrids that resist the disease are available.

Hybrid chestnuts. Two types of hybrid chestnuts are available. The first group comprises offspring of American and Chinese chestnuts (*C. dentata* and *C. mollissima*), with characteristics intermediate between the two (American chestnut is—or was—a tall, broad timber tree with small but very sweet nuts). Included here are the blight-resistant Dunstan hybrids, 'Alachua', 'Carolina', 'Carpenter', 'Heritage', 'Revival', and 'Willamette'. The second group is made up mostly of crosses between Japanese chestnut (*C. crenata*) and European chestnut (*C. sativa*). Trees usually grow 40–60 ft. tall and wide and do not tolerate alkaline soils. Selections include 'Colossal', 'Nevada' (small-nutted type; proven pollinator for 'Colossal'), 'Schrader', 'Skioka', and 'Sleeping Giant', which produces sweet, large nuts and is blight resistant.

Chinese chestnut. Native to China, Korea; known botanically as *C. mollissima*. To 35–40 ft. tall, with a rounded crown that may spread to 20–25 ft. Leaves 3–7 in. long, with coarsely toothed edges. Most nursery trees are grown from seed, not cuttings; hence, nuts are variable but generally of good quality. Intolerant of alkaline soil. Recommended selections include 'AU-Cropper', 'AU-Homestead', 'AU-Leader', 'Black Beauty', 'Crane', 'Meiling', and 'Nanking'.

Allegheny chinkapin. This eastern U.S. native is known botanically as *C. pumila*. Usually a 6- to 10-ft.-tall shrub, but it can reach 20–25 ft. Leaves are dark green above, fuzzy white underneath, 3–6 in. long, with sharply toothed edges. Nuts are sweet. Good in natural plantings and for attracting wildlife.

CHICORY AND RADICCHIO

Asteraceae
Perennials

US, MS, LS; USDA 6-8

FULL SUN

REGULAR WATER

Radicchio

The wild form of this Mediterranean native, known botanically as *Cichorium intybus*, grows as a perennial roadside weed 2–4 ft. tall in much of the South and is recognized by its pretty sky-blue flowers. Different chicories are grown for three purposes: for salad greens (small-rooted types); for roots to make a coffee substitute (large-rooted types); and for Belgian or French endive ('Witloof' chicory). To grow 'Witloof', sow seeds in spring or early summer; plants will mature by fall. In winter, trim the greens to an inch of stem; then dig the roots, bury them diagonally in moist sand, and set in a dark, cool room until pale, tender new growth has been forced. (For the standard salad green called endive, see Endive.)

Radicchio is the name given to red-leafed chicories grown for salads. 'Indigo', 'Rossa de Verona' ('Rouge de Verone'), 'Red Treviso', and 'Rossana' are good selections. Radicchio makes lettucelike heads that color to a deep rosy red as weather grows cold in fall or winter; its slight bitterness less-ens as color deepens. Best sown in mid- to late summer to mature in cool fall months, though the selection 'Giulio' can be sown in spring to harvest in summer. Sow green-leafed chicory beginning in early spring (and up to early summer where that season is not too hot); in areas with mild winters, you can also plant in mid- to late summer for fall and winter harvest.

Sow both green and red types ¼–½ in. deep; thin seedlings to 6–12 in. apart. Before planting, work into the soil ½ cup of 10-10-10 fertilizer per 10 ft. of row.

CHILOPSIS LINEARIS

DESERT WILLOW, DESERT CATALPA
Bignoniaceae
Deciduous shrub or tree

MS, LS, CS; USDA 7-9

FULL SUN

LITTLE TO MODERATE WATER

Chilopsis linearis

Native to desert washes and streambeds below 5,000 ft. from California to Texas, south into Mexico. Grows 15–30 ft. tall, 10–20 ft. wide; grows fast at first (as much as 3 ft. in a season), then slows. With age, develops shaggy bark and twisting trunks. Narrow, willow-type leaves grow to 2–5 in. long. From spring to fall, produces fragrant, trumpet-shaped blossoms with crimped lobes, resembling those of catalpa or small cattleya orchids; flowers attract hummingbirds. Flower color varies among seedlings; blossoms may be reddish purple, lavender, rose, pink, or white, often marked with purple and gold. Nurseries select for good color, large size, ruffled form. Gallon-size plants can bloom first year. Plant drops leaves early; holds a heavy crop of catalpa-like seedpods through winter and can look messy. Thin growth to enhance picturesque shape. Does best in dry, limy soil. Not for humid, high-rainfall areas. Look for the following recommended selections.

'Art's Seedless'. Large, rose-pink flowers with a darker lower lip. Slender leaves. Sterile flowers produce no seedpods.

'Bubba'. Lavender and purple flowers. To 20 ft. tall.

'Burgundy' ('Burgundy Lace'). Deep purplish red flowers.

'Dark Storm'. Lower lip of flower is deep wine-red, upper one lavender; lips are usually curved inward. Slow grower to 12–15 ft. high and wide.

'Hope'. White flowers with pale yellow throat. Wispy, open growth.

'Lois Adams'. Profuse two-tone blooms in pale lavender and magenta; no seedpods. Compact, upright growth.

'Lucretia Hamilton'. Dark purple flowers in large clusters. To 15–18 ft. high and wide.

'Regal'. Combination of lavender and wine-red like that of 'Dark Storm', but display is better, since blooms are flat faced and open throated.

'Rio Salado'. Large, ruffled, deep burgundy flowers. Vigorous growth.

'Timeless Beauty'. Long season of two-toned lavender and burgundy blooms; no seedpods. To 15–20 ft. high and wide.

'Warren Jones'. Large, ruffled blossoms in pure, unshaded pink with paler throat. Holds its leaves longer; evergreen in Coastal South.

CHIMONANTHUS PRAECOX

WINTERSWEET
Calycanthaceae
Deciduous shrub

US, MS, LS; USDA 6-8

FULL SUN OR PARTIAL SHADE

MODERATE WATER

Chimonanthus praecox

Wintersweet's spicy-scented blossoms appear on leafless branches in winter or early spring and may last for more than a month if not hit by hard frost. Native to China and Japan. Tall, open-structured plant grows slowly to 10–15 ft. high and 6–8 ft. wide, with many basal stems. Blossoms are 1 in. wide, with pale yellow outer sepals and smaller, chocolate-colored inner sepals. Tapered leaves are rough to the touch, medium green, 3–6 in. long and half that wide; turn yellow-green in fall. 'Grandiflorus' has larger (1¾ -in.) blossoms than the basic species, but they are not as fragrant. 'Luteus' has clear yellow flowers.

In the Upper South, plant in a sheltered site to prevent frost damage. In all areas, locate plant where its winter fragrance can be enjoyed, such as near an entrance or path or under a bedroom window. Keep plant lower by cutting back after bloom; shape as a small tree by removing excess basal stems; rejuvenate a leggy plant by trimming to within a foot of the ground in spring. Needs good drainage.

C

C

CHINESE CABBAGE

Brassicaceae
Biennial grown as cool-season annual

🌿 **US, MS, LS, CS, TS; USDA 6-11**

☀️ **FULL SUN**

💧 **REGULAR WATER**

Chinese cabbage

Makes a head somewhat looser than that of usual cabbage; sometimes called celery cabbage. Raw or cooked, it has a more delicate flavor than cabbage. There are three kinds: Michihi types (pe-tsai), with tall, narrow heads; Napa types (wong bok), with short, broad heads; and loose-head varieties (pak choy).

Favorite Michihli selections are 'Greenwich' (50 days to maturity) and open-pollinated Michihl itself. Among Napa varieties, try 'Minuet' (48 days), 'Rubicon' (52 days), and the miniature 'Tenderheart' (50 days). To sample a loose-head type, look for 'Tokyo Bekana' or the purple-leaf type. All are prone to bolt in hot weather if planted in spring; they make a better fall or winter crop. In colder-winter areas, plant seeds in ground in July; in milder climates, plant in August or September.

CARE

Sow seeds thinly in rows 2–2½ ft. apart; thin plants to 1½–2 ft. apart.

To prevent a buildup of soil-borne pests, plant in a different site each year. Club root is a serious fungal pest in acid soils; apply lime, if necessary, to raise the pH to at least 6.5. Floating row covers do a good job of controlling insects such as cabbage loopers, cabbageworms, cut-worms, and root maggots. You can also control cutworms and root maggots by ringing the base of the plant with a cardboard collar. *Bacillus thuringiensis* (Bt) and spinosad applied according to label directions controls cabbageworms and loopers.

CHIONANTHUS

FRINGE TREE
Oleaceae
Deciduous shrubs or trees

🌿 **US, MS, LS, CS; USDA 6-9**

☀️◑ **FULL SUN OR PARTIAL SHADE**

💧💧 **MODERATE TO REGULAR WATER**

Chionanthus virginicus

These spectacular flowering plants get their common name from the narrow, fringelike white petals on flowers that are borne in impressive, ample, lacy clusters. Male and female plants are separate; males have larger flowers. If both plants are present, females produce showy clusters of ½-in., blue-black, olivelike fruit that is favored by birds. Broad leaves turn bright to deep yellow in fall. Give good drainage. Minimal pruning needed. Requires some winter chill.

C. retusus. CHINESE FRINGE TREE. From China. To about 20 ft. tall, not quite as wide spreading as *C. virginicus*. Usually seen as a big, multistemmed shrub but can be trained as a small tree. Leaves 2–4 in. long. Pure white, fragrant blossoms in clusters to 4 in. long appear in late spring or early summer, 2 to 3 weeks before *C. virginicus* comes into flower. A magnificent plant when in bloom, something like a tremendous white lilac (*Syringa*). Handsome gray-brown bark (sometimes golden on young stems) provides winter interest.

C. virginicus. FRINGE TREE, GRANCY GRAYBEARD. Native to southeastern U.S. Leaves and flower clusters often twice as big as those of *C. retusus*; blooms appear a few weeks later. Lightly fragrant, greenish white flowers. Can reach 30 ft. tall, but in gardens usually grows 12–20 ft. high with equal spread. Habit varies from very shrubby and open to more treelike. Grows more slowly in the Upper South, where young plants can be used as shrubs for a number of years. In that zone, it's one of the last deciduous plants to leaf out in spring.

CHIONODOXA

GLORY-OF-THE-SNOW
Asparagaceae
Perennials from bulbs

🌿 **US, MS, LS; USDA 6-8**

☀️◑ **FULL SUN DURING BLOOM, LIGHT SHADE AFTER**

💧 **REGULAR WATER DURING GROWTH AND BLOOM**

Chionodoxa luciliae

Charming little bulbs from alpine meadows of Crete, Cyprus, and Turkey. They are among the first flowers to bloom in spring; each bulb produces a stem to 6 in. high, with six-pointed, starlike blossoms in blue, white, or pink, spaced along upper part. Straight, narrow leaves are a little shorter than flower stem. In fall, plant bulbs in rich, well-drained soil, setting them 2–3 in. deep and 3 in. apart. When bloom quality declines, dig and divide clumps in early fall. Plantings may also increase from self-seeding. Ideal beneath deciduous trees. Resistant to rodents and deer.

C. forbesii. Grows 4–8 in. high, with rich blue, white-centered flowers. 'Blue Giant' is more vigorous, with larger blooms. 'Violet Beauty' is more pink than violet.

C. luciliae. Most commonly grown species; often confused with other species. Stems typically bear one to four 1½-in., violet-blue blooms. 'Gigantea' has larger leaves and larger blossoms; 'Alba' has white flowers larger than those of the species. 'Pink Giant' (*C.* 'Pink Giant') has large pink blooms.

C. sardensis. Inch-wide violet-blue flowers with a very small white eye, carried 4 to 12 to a stem.

X CHITALPA TASHKENTENSIS

Bignoniaceae
Deciduous tree

🌿 **US, MS, LS, CS; USDA 6-9**

☀️ **FULL SUN**

💧💧 **LITTLE TO MODERATE WATER**

X *Chitalpa tashkentensis* 'Pink Dawn'

Fast growing to 20–30 ft. and as wide, this tree combines the larger flowers of its *Catalpa bignonioides* parent with the desert toughness and flower color of *Chilopsis linearis*, its other parent. Leaves are 4–5 in. long, an inch wide. Blooms from late spring to fall, bearing clusters of frilly, trumpet-shaped flowers in pink, white, or lavender. 'Pink Dawn' has pink flowers, 'Morning Cloud' white ones. Like catalpa, unusually tolerant of heat, cold, and various soils; even better suited than catalpa to dry, limy soil. Prone to powdery mildew in areas with high humidity. Litter is not a problem, as flowers dry on tree and no seedpods are formed. Tolerates wind.

CHLOROPHYTUM COMOSUM

SPIDER PLANT
Asparagaceae
Perennial

- **LS, CS, TS; USDA 8-11, OR HOUSEPLANT**
- **PARTIAL SHADE; BRIGHT INDIRECT LIGHT**
- **REGULAR WATER**

Chlorophytum comosum 'Variegatum'

This South African native is evergreen in the Tropical South; light frosts will kill the leaves in the other listed zones, but the roots survive. Forms 1- to 3-ft.-high clumps of soft, curving leaves like long, broad grass blades. Both 'Variegatum' and 'Vittatum' have white-striped leaves. Flowers about ½ in. long, in loose, leafy-tipped spikes held above foliage. Greatest attraction: miniature duplicates of mother plant, complete with root, at end of curved stems (as with offsets of strawberry plants). These can be cut off and potted individually.

Spider plant is a good choice for hanging baskets. To use as a ground cover where it is winter-hardy, set 2 ft. apart in diamond pattern; plants will fill in the area in that same year.

CHOISYA TERNATA

MEXICAN ORANGE
Rutaceae
Evergreen shrub

- **LS, CS; USDA 8-9**
- **LIGHT SHADE IN ZONE TS**
- **MODERATE WATER**

Choisya ternata

This Mexican native grows quickly to 6–8 ft. tall and often slightly wider. Lustrous, rich green leaves are held toward ends of branches; each leaf is divided into a fan of three leaflets to 3 in. long. Fans give shrub a dense, massive look—but with highlights and shadows. Clusters of fragrant white flowers, somewhat like small orange blossoms, open in late winter or early spring and bloom continuously for a couple of months, then intermittently through summer. Appealing to bees. Hardy to 15°F. Sometimes called Mexican mock orange. Foliage of 'Sundance' is yellow when young, gradually turning green. 'Aztec Gold' and 'Aztec Pearl' (*C. x dewitteana*) are more compact at 3–6 ft. tall and have narrower leaves; white flowers open in spring and sometimes again in summer.

CARE

All make attractive informal hedges or screens. During growing season, thin out older branches in plant's center to force leafy new interior growth. Cut freely for decoration when in bloom. Touchy about soil conditions—difficult to grow in alkaline soils or where water is high in salts. Under such conditions, amend soil as for azaleas (*Rhododendron*). Good in large containers. Prone to root rot and crown

rot if drainage is poor. Subject to damage from sucking insects and mites, but not browsed by deer.

CHORISIA

FLOSS SILK TREE
Bombacaceae
Evergreen to briefly deciduous trees

- **TS; USDA 10-11**
- **FULL SUN**
- **MODERATE WATER**

Chorisia speciosa

Native to South America. Heavy trunk is studded with thick spines; it is green in youth, turns gray with age. Leaves divided into 5-in.-long leaflets like fingers of a hand; they drop during autumn flowering or whenever temperatures fall below 27°F. Large, showy flowers somewhat resemble narrow-petaled hibiscus blooms. Fast drainage and controlled watering are keys to success. Water established trees about once a month during the growing season; ease off in late summer to encourage more flowers. Need little pruning except to remove wayward or dead growth.

C. insignis. WHITE FLOSS SILK TREE. To 50 ft. tall and wide. White to pale yellow, 5- to 6-in. flowers. Blooms from fall into winter; stopped by frost.

C. speciosa. Grows 3–5 ft. a year for first few years, then more slowly to an eventual 30–50 ft. tall and wide. Blooms in fall, bearing pink, purplish rose, or burgundy flowers to 4 in. or more across. Grafted selections include 'Los Angeles Beautiful', with wine-red flowers, and 'Majestic Beauty', a thornless selection bearing rich pink blooms.

CHRYSANTHE-MUM

Asteraceae
Perennials and annuals

- **ZONES VARY BY SPECIES**
- **FULL SUN, EXCEPT AS NOTED**
- **REGULAR WATER, EXCEPT AS NOTED**

Florists' chrysanthemum flower form: Decorative

If this entry seems like it has a few friends missing, blame the taxonomists. Many species formerly included under *Chrysanthemum* have been assigned new names and are noted below.

C. balsamita. See *Tanacetum balsamita*

C. coccineum. See *Tanacetum coccineum*

C. frutescens. See *Argyranthemum frutescens*

C. x grandiflorum (*C. x morifolium*). FLORISTS' CHRYSANTHEMUM. Perennial. Zones US, MS, LS, CS; USDA 6-9. The most useful of all autumn-blooming perennials for borders, containers, and cutting—and the most versatile and varied of all chrysanthemum species. Hundreds of selections are available in many flower forms, colors, plant and flower sizes, and growth habits. Colors include white, yellow, red, pink, orange, bronze, purple, and lavender, as well as multicolors. Not browsed by deer.

It's easy to grow florists' chrysanthemums, not so easy to grow prize-winning ones. The latter need more water, feeding, pinching, pruning, grooming, and pest control than most perennials (see care box above). But if you're not planning on competing in the local flower show, choose

TOP ROW: C. 'Apricot' (Single flower form); *SECOND ROW: C.* 'Kelvin Mandarin" (Pompon flower form); *C.* 'Crimson Tide' (Irregular Incarve flower form); *ABOVE: C.* 'Virginia' (Spider flower form); *RIGHT: C.* 'Dorridge King' (Reflex flower form)

from the following old-fashioned florists' chrysanthemums—all longtime border favorites that have survived at old homesites without a gardener in sight. Most have an open, casual look and bloom later than their modern counterparts. Try the following: 'Cathy's Rust', 2–3 ft., rich rusty red; 'Clara Curtis' ('Country Girl'), 2–3 ft., rosy pink; 'Ryan's Pink', 1½–2 ft., soft pink; 'Emperor of China', to 4 ft., silvery rose-pink flowers and red-flushed foliage; 'Hillside Sheffield' ('Sheffield Pink'), 2½ –3 ft., clear pink; 'Mrs. Hathaway', 2½ ft., yellow; 'Single Apricot Korean', 2–3 ft., pale apricot; 'Venus', 2–3 ft., pale pink to white; and 'Virginia's Sunshine', 2 ft., soft yellow flowers as late as November.

Flower forms. Following are flower forms as designated by chrysanthemum hobbyists.

Anemone. One or more rows of rays with large raised center disk or cushion. Center disk may be same color as rays or different.

HOW TO GROW CHRYSANTHEMUMS

PLANTING In the Lower and Coastal South, choose a spot with shade from afternoon sun. Don't plant near large trees or hedges with invasive roots. Set out young plants in early spring. Plant in well-drained garden soil improved with organic matter and a complete fertilizer dug in 2 to 3 weeks before planting.

WATERING Water deeply at intervals determined by your soil structure—frequently in porous soils, less often in heavy soils. Too little water causes woody stems and loss of lower leaves; overwatering causes leaves to yellow, then blacken and drop.

FERTILIZING Feed plants in ground two or three times during the growing season; make last application with low-nitrogen fertilizer not less than 2 weeks before bloom.

CHALLENGES Aphids are the only notable pest in all areas. To avoid them, feed plants with a systemic insecticide/fertilizer combination, or spray with horticultural oil or insecticidal soap.

PINCHING To produce sturdy plants with big flowers, start pinching at planting time by removing plant tip. When lateral shoots form, select one to four shoots for continued growth. Keep pinching all summer, nipping top pair of leaves on every shoot that reaches 5 in. long. (Stop pinching earlier in coldest regions). For huge blooms (on large-flowered sorts), disbud (remove all flower buds except one or two per cluster). Stake plants to keep them upright.

CUTTING BACK Sometimes mums are fooled by cool weather and short days into blooming in spring. After they flower, cut them back to within 8 in. of the ground; they'll bloom again in fall. (However, any mum that blooms prematurely in late summer isn't going to bloom again that year, even if you do cut it back.) After fall bloom, cut plants back to 8 in.; where soils are heavy and likely to remain wet in winter, dig clumps with soil intact and set them on top of the ground in an inconspicuous place. Cover with sand or sawdust, if you wish.

PROPAGATING Take cuttings from early to late spring (up until May for some types), or when shoots are 3–4 in. long. As new shoots develop, you can make additional cuttings of them. Or you can divide older clumps; take divisions from the outside and discard the woody centers.

GROWING IN POTS Pot rooted cuttings any time from February to April, using porous, fibrous, moisture-holding planting mix. Move plants to larger pots as growth requires—don't let them become root bound. Pinch and stake as directed above. Plants need water daily in warm weather, every other day in cool conditions. Feed with liquid fertilizer every 7 to 10 days until buds show color.

Brush. Narrow, rolled rays give brush or soft cactus dahlia effect.

Decorative. Long, broad rays overlap like shingles to form a full flower.

Incurve. Big double flowers with broad rays curving upward and inward.

Irregular incurve. Like above, but with looser, more softly curving rays.

Laciniated. Fully double, with rays fringed and cut at tips in carnation effect.

Pompon. Globular, neat, compact flowers with flat, fluted, or quilled rays. Usually small, they can reach 5 in. if buds are thinned to one or two per cluster.

Quill. Long, narrow, rolled rays; like spider but less droopy.

Reflex. Big double flowers with rays that curl in, out, and sideways, creating a shaggy effect.

Semidouble. Somewhat like single or daisy, but with two, three, or four rows of rays around a yellow center.

Single or daisy. Single row of rays around a yellow center. May be large or small, with broad or narrow rays.

Spider. Long, curling, tubular rays ending in fishhook curved tips.

Spoon. Tubular rays flatten at tip to make little disks, sometimes in colors that contrast with body of flower.

C. leucanthemum. See *Leucanthemum vulgare*

C. maximum. See *Leucanthemum x superbum*

C. pacificum. See *Ajania pacifica*

C. paludosum. See *Leucanthemum paludosum*

C. parthenium. See *Tanacetum parthenium*

C. weyrichii. Perennial. Zones US, MS; USDA 6-7. From Japan. Rock garden plant with finely cut leaves; forms a mat to 1–1½ ft. high and 1 ft. wide. Single, 2-in., white-to-pink daisies with yellow centers appear just above foliage in fall. 'Pink Bomb' has rosy pink rays, 'White Bomb' creamy white ones.

C. zawadskii. Perennial. Zones US, MS, LS, CS; USDA 6-9. To 2–2½ ft. high and wide, with finely cut leaves and 2- to 3-in. daisies over a long season beginning in late summer. 'Clara Curtis' has soft pink flowers; 'Mary Stoker' has blooms of soft yellow touched with apricot.

CHRYSOGONUM VIRGINIANUM
GOLDEN STAR, GREEN AND GOLD
Asteraceae
Perennial

US, MS, LS, CS; USDA 6-9

PARTIAL SHADE

REGULAR WATER

Chrysogonum virginianum

Native to eastern U.S. Useful and attractive native plant for ground cover or foreground planting. Grows 8–10 in. tall and spreads freely by underground rhizomes. Bright green, toothed leaves, 1–3 in. long, make a good background for the bright yellow flower heads. Blossoms have five rays, resemble stars more than daisies. Bloom is heavy in spring and fall, sporadic through summer months. For quick ground cover, plant 1 ft. apart in rich soil high in organic matter. 'Allen Bush' is an excellent selection with dark green leaves. 'Eco Lacquered Spider' has long runners (to 3 ft.) that radiate from the center of the plant like spider legs. 'Pierre' forms compact clumps just 6 in. tall; it blooms over a long period. *C. v. australe* is a more prostrate form with shorter stems. Its flowers aren't as showy as those of the species, and it spreads by above ground stolons or runners (much as strawberry plants do) rather than rhizomes.

CHRYSOPSIS
GOLDEN ASTER
Asteraceae
Perennials

US, MS, LS, CS; USDA 6-9

FULL SUN

MODERATE TO REGULAR WATER

Chrysopsis villosa

These tough, showy, little-known perennials native to the northeastern U.S. deserve wider use. They tolerate heat, drought, humidity, and poor soil and have no serious pests. Daisylike yellow blooms decorate the plants for many weeks in late summer and fall. Give them good drainage and plenty of sun. Dig and divide crowded clumps in early spring. Resist deer.

C. falcata. GROUND GOLD. Grows to about 1 ft. high, 1 ft. wide. Small (¾-in.) flowers appear on branched stems above a rosette of broadly linear leaves to 3½ in. long.

C. mariana. MARYLAND GOLDEN ASTER. Grows to 2 ft. or possibly 3 ft. high, 1½ ft. wide, with large (9-in.) basal leaves, smaller stem leaves, and tight clusters of 1½-in. flowers.

C. villosa. GOLDEN ASTER. Taller than *C. mariana* (to 4–5 ft. tall, 2 ft. wide), with smaller, more scattered flowers. Blooms for a long time; excellent cut flower. Good to combine with ironweed, fall asters, and blue salvia. 'Golden Sunshine' is a compact form to about 3 ft. tall, with large (2-in.) golden flowers.

CIBOTIUM
HAWAIIAN TREE FERN
Cibotiaceae
Tree fern

TS; USDA 10-11; OR GROWN IN POTS

PARTIAL SHADE

REGULAR WATER

Cibotium glaucum

These evergreen ferns are superb for creating tropical effects. A solitary brown trunk—the upper portion of which is thickly covered with silky hairs—supports arching, intricately divided, feathery-looking fronds. Provide reasonably fertile, well-drained soil and shelter from strong winds. Prune to remove old or injured fronds. The two Hawaiian natives listed here are hardy to 30°F; beyond their hardiness range, they can be grown in a large greenhouse or sunroom in bright light.

C. chamissoi. To 6 ft., possibly 20 ft. tall, with crown spreading about 10 ft. wide. Yellow-green fronds.

C. glaucum. Very slow growth to 20 ft. tall, with crown to 15 ft. wide. Leathery, gray-green to bluish fronds with waxy undersides.

C

CINNAMOMUM CAMPHORA
CAMPHOR TREE
Lauraceae
Evergreen tree

🌡 **LS, CS, TS; USDA 8-11**

☀️ ◐ **FULL SUN OR LIGHT SHADE**

◌ ◍ ● **LITTLE TO REGULAR WATER**

Cinnamomum camphora

This Asian native tree grows slowly to 50–60 ft. tall and wide. A heavy trunk and big, upright, spreading limbs give it powerful structure. Beautiful in rain, when trunk looks black. Aromatic, 2½- to 5-in.-long leaves smell like camphor when crushed. New foliage in early spring is pink, red, or bronze; matures to shiny yellow green. Inconspicuous but fragrant yellow flowers bloom profusely in late spring, followed by small blackish fruits.

Though evergreen, camphor tree drops leaves quite heavily in early spring; flowers, fruits, and twigs drop later. Plant where litter will not be a problem. Competitive roots also make this tree a poor choice near garden beds and paved areas; roots may invade sewer and drainage lines as well.

CARE

Camphor tree is subject to verticillium wilt. Symptoms are wilting and dying of twigs, branches, center of tree, or entire tree; wood in twigs or branches shows brownish discoloration. Most susceptible after wet winters or if planted in poorly drained soil. No cure is known, though trees often outgrow the problem. To treat, cut out damaged branches. Apply nitrogen fertilizer and water it in well.

CISSUS RHOMBIFOLIA
GRAPE IVY
Vitaceae
Evergreen vine

🌡 **TS; USDA 10-11; OR HOUSEPLANT**

◐ ● **PARTIAL TO FULL SHADE; BRIGHT LIGHT**

● **REGULAR WATER**

Cissus rhombifolia

Native to South America, grape ivy is one of those long-established, dependable indoor plants that practically everyone grows at one time or another. Handsome dark green leaves have attractive bronze overtones due to reddish hairs on the leaf undersides. Each leaf is divided into three diamond-shaped, 1- to 4-in.-long leaflets with sharply toothed edges; leaves look like miniature grape leaves in overall outline, hence the common name. Tendrils twine around any support provided. Propagate by taking stem cuttings in spring and summer. 'Mandaiana' is more upright and compact than the species, with larger, more substantial leaflets. 'Ellen Danica' is another, compact selection, with darker green, less lustrous leaves than the species; its leaflets are shallowly lobed, like an oak leaf.

Indoors, grape ivy is ideal for hanging baskets. Situate it in bright light but not in direct, hot sun. Let soil go slightly dry between waterings. For best results, feed with a balanced liquid fertilizer monthly; cut back on water and fertilizer in winter. In the Tropical South, you can grow grape ivy outdoors; train it on a wall, pergola, or trellis, or use as ground cover for shaded areas.

CISTUS
ROCKROSE
Cistaceae
Evergreen shrubs

🌡 **LS, CS; USDA 8-9**

☀️ **FULL SUN**

◌ **LITTLE OR NO WATER**

Cistus x *purpureus*

These Mediterranean natives are carefree shrubs that grow well in limy soils and perform beautifully in dry-summer areas such as Southwest Texas, blooming profusely for a month or more in spring or early summer. They need no fertilizer and very little water; if they will be watered, be sure to provide excellent drainage. Periodically prune out a few of the old stems to keep plants looking neat; tip-pinch young plants to make them bushy.

C. ladanifer. CRIMSON-SPOT ROCKROSE. Compact growth to 3–5 ft. high with equal spread. Fragrant leaves to 4 in. long are dark green above, lighter beneath; 3-in.-wide flowers are white with a dark crimson spot at each petal base. Selections include 'Blanche', to 8–12 ft. high, 6–8 ft. wide, with 4-in. white flowers; and 'Frank Birch', to 6–8 ft. tall and wide, also with pure white, 4-in. blossoms. *C. l. petiolatus* 'Bennett's White' grows 4–6 ft. high and wide; 3–4-in. flowers have wavy, crepe paper–textured petals around a large cluster of yellow stamens. *C. l. sulcatus latifolius* is a lower grower (to 2 ft.) but has larger blooms (3–4 in. across). Hybrids include 'Maculatus' (*C.* x *aguilarii* 'Maculatus'), to 6 ft. tall, 4–5 ft. wide, with blooms prominently spotted in maroon.

C. laurifolius. LAUREL ROCKROSE. Stiff, erect growth to 4–6 ft. high and wide. Dark green, 5-in. leaves with pale undersides. White, 2- to 2½-in. flowers, in long-stalked clusters of three or more. Good hedge or background shrub for dry areas.

C. x purpureus. ORCHID ROCKROSE. Compact grower to 4 ft. tall and wide. Leaves 1–2 in. long, dark green above, gray and hairy beneath. Reddish purple, 3-in. flowers with red spot at base of each petal.

C. x skanbergii. Low, broad bush to 3 ft. tall and 8 ft. wide. Gray-green, 2-in. leaves; pure pink, 1-in. flowers in great profusion.

CITRUS
Rutaceae
Evergreen trees and shrubs

🌡 **CS, TS FOR MOST, POSSIBLY LS FOR HARDIER TYPES, EXCEPT AS NOTED; USDA 8-11; OR GROW IN POTS**

☀️ **FULL SUN; BRIGHT LIGHT**

● **REGULAR WATER**

Sweet oranges

Citrus plants offer year-round attractive form and glossy deep green foliage. They also produce fragrant flowers and brightly colored, decorative fruit in season. If you want quality fruit, your choice of plants will largely depend on the amount of winter cold in your area.

Hardiness. Citrus plants of one type or another are grown outdoors year-round in the Tropical South and mildest parts of the Coastal South. Lemons and limes are most sensitive to freezes. Sweet oranges, grapefruit, and most mandarins and their hybrids are intermediate. Kumquats, satsuma mandarins, and cala-mondins are cold resistant, withstanding temperatures in the high teens. Hardy citrus (see page 242) is available to gardeners just beyond the citrus belt.

Other factors affecting a tree's cold tolerance include preconditioning to cold (it will have more endurance if exposed to cold slowly and if first freeze comes late), type of rootstock, and location in garden (planting on the south side of the house is preferred). Prolonged exposure to freezing weather is more damaging than a brief plunge in temperature. All citrus fruit is damaged at several degrees below freezing, so if you live in a freeze-prone area, choose early-ripening types.

Anatomy. Almost all commercially grown citrus trees are grafted, consisting of two parts: scion (upper part of tree producing desirable fruit) and rootstock (lower few inches of trunk and the roots). These are joined at the bud union. Grafted trees begin bearing fruit in just a few years, contrasted with 10 to 15 years for seedling trees. Most kinds produce a single crop in fall or winter, but everbearing types (lemons, limes, calamondins) can produce throughout the year, though they fruit most heavily in spring. Plants don't go completely dormant, but their growth does slow in winter. Citrus fruit ripens only on the tree.

Tree size depends on the category of citrus and on the selection within that category. Standard trees (the norm in Florida, Texas, and along the Gulf Coast) grow full size—typically 20–30 ft. tall and wide. Dwarf trees are grafted onto a rootstock that reduces the size of the tree but not that of the fruit; they are sold through mail-order suppliers (these cannot ship to commercial citrus-producing states) and at some nurseries in Florida.

SWEET ORANGE. Dense globes to about 25 ft. tall. Fruit usually stores on the tree for a few months. The orange blossom is Florida's state flower.

'Cara Cara'. First rosy-fleshed navel, bearing at about same time as 'Washington'. Red flesh in Florida.

'Hamlin'. Nearly seedless juice orange. Matures early, fall into winter. Best in South Texas, Florida.

'Jaffa' ('Shamouti'). Midseason (ripens winter into spring), nearly seedless eating orange from Israel. Grown in South Texas.

'Marrs'. Low-acid fruit with few seeds, ripening fall into winter. Grows well in South Texas.

'Parson Brown'. Early-ripening, small, seedy juice orange. Best in Florida.

'Pineapple'. Leading midseason orange in Florida; also grown in South Texas. Fairly seedy but excellent for juicing. Fruit tends to drop from tree after ripening.

'Republic of Texas'. Early, sweet, cold-hardy selection for Texas. Seedy.

'Valencia'. This is the premier juice orange. Widely adapted, bearing nearly seedless fruit in midwinter and spring. 'Delta' and 'Midknight' are seedless selections ripening a little earlier. If grown in Florida, 'Rhode Red' has more highly colored flesh than 'Valencia'.

'Washington'. Original navel selection from which the other navels developed. Seedless eating orange ripens early, fall into winter. In Texas and Florida, local selections sold simply as "navel" have better flavor.

BLOOD ORANGE. These are characterized by red pigmentation in flesh, juice, and (to a lesser degree) rind. Flavor has raspberry overtones. Need chilly nights during ripening. Main kinds grown are 'Moro', 'Sanguinelli', and 'Tarocco'.

MANDARIN. Small to medium-size trees (10–20 ft. tall and wide) bearing juicy, loose-skinned, and often slightly flattened-looking fruit; most produce in winter. Selections with red-orange peel are usually called tangerines. Many mandarins tend to bear heavily in alternate years.

'Clementine' (Algerian tangerine). Sweet, variably seedy flesh. Ripens early (from fall into winter), holds well on tree. Light crop without a pollenizer. Good for Texas Gulf Coast.

'Dancy'. Small, seedy fruit is traditional Christmas "tangerine"; ripens late fall into winter. Needs high heat; best in Florida. Also grows in hot, dry regions. Alternate bearer.

'Encore'. Ripens very late (spring into summer) and holds on tree until fall. Sweet-tart, seedy fruit. Alternate bearer. Good for South Texas.

'Fremont'. Ripens from late fall into winter; seedy, richly sweet

TOP: 'Valencia' oranges; 'Satsuma' mandarins; *BOTTOM:* 'Ruby' grapefruits

fruit. Alternate bearer. Does well along Upper Gulf Coast.

'Honey'. Seedy, very sweet fruit from winter into spring. Different from 'Murcott' tangor (see "Mandarin hybrids" below), which is marketed as "Honey tangerine." Alternate bearer. Does well in South Texas, Gulf Coast.

'Mediterranean' ('Willow Leaf'). Springtime crop of sweet, aromatic, very juicy fruit gets puffy soon after ripening. Needs high heat. Alternate bearer. Good for South Texas, Gulf Coast.

'Pixie'. Late selection with seedless, mild, sweet fruit. Alternate bearer. Recommended for South Texas.

'Ponkan' (Chinese honey mandarin). Early crop of seedy, very sweet fruit. Alternate bearer. Good for South Texas, Gulf Coast, Florida.

Satsuma. Group of mandarins with mild, sweet fruit that ripens early (beginning in fall). Succeeds in areas too cold for most citrus; mature trees can withstand 15°F. Ripe fruit deteriorates quickly on tree but keeps well in cool storage. Selections include 'Arctic

Frost', 'Brown's Select', 'Dobashi Beni', 'Kimbrough', 'Okitsu Wase', and 'Owari'. Does well in South Texas, Gulf Coast, north Florida. 'Miho' and 'Seto' are large-fruited, good-tasting selections for Texas.

'Seedless Kishu'. Very small, loose skinned, easy to peel; exceptionally rich flavor. Ripens late fall to winter.

'Wilking'. Midseason selection with rich, distinctive flavor. Juicy fruit holds fairly well on tree. Alternate bearer. Recommended for South Texas.

MANDARIN HYBRIDS. These hybrids generally perform best in hot weather. Many were developed in Florida, where they produce outstanding crops.

Tangelo. Hybrid between mandarin and grapefruit. Best with a pollenizer like 'Dancy' or 'Clementine' (both mandarins) or another tangelo. In winter, 'Minneola' bears bright orange-red fruit (often with a noticeable "neck") with rich, tart flavor and some seeds. 'Orlando' produces mild, sweet, fairly seedy fruit about a month earlier than 'Minneola'.

TOP: 'Eureka' lemons; 'Nagami' kumquats; *BOTTOM:* 'Minneola' tangelos

Tangor. Hybrid between mandarin and sweet orange. Especially well adapted to sweet orange–growing areas of Florida. 'Murcott' is an alternate bearer with very sweet, seedy, yellowish orange fruit winter into spring; it's marketed under the name "Honey tangerine." 'Ortanique' has sweet, juicy, variably seedy fruit ripening spring to summer. 'Temple' bears a winter-to-spring crop of sweet-to-tart, seedy fruit; needs high heat and is more cold sensitive than other tangors.

Other mandarin hybrids include the following.

'Ambersweet'. Result of crossing a hybrid of 'Clementine' mandarin and 'Orlando' tangelo with a midseason orange. Juicy fruit, borne fall to winter, is classified as an orange by fresh fruit marketers. Very seedy when grown near another selection.

'Fairchild'. Hybrid of 'Clementine' mandarin and 'Orlando' tangelo. Juicy, sweet fruit in winter. Bigger crop with a pollenizer.

'Fallglo'. Somewhat cold sensitive, like its 'Temple' tangor parent. Juicy, tart, very seedy fruit ripens in fall.

'Lee'. Hybrid between 'Clementine' and an unknown pollen parent. Fairly seedy fruit matures fall to winter. Has best flavor if grown in Florida.

'Nova'. Cross between 'Clementine' mandarin and 'Orlando' tangelo. Juicy, richly sweet fruit fall to winter. Needs a pollenizer.

'Osceola'. Hybrid of 'Clementine' mandarin and 'Orlando' tangelo. Medium-size, seedy fruit ripens in November. Best flavor in Florida. Pollinate with 'Lee' or 'Orlando'.

'Page'. Parents are 'Clementine' mandarin and 'Minneola' tangelo. Many small, juicy, sweet fruits fall into winter. Few seeds, even with a pollenizer to improve fruit set.

'Robinson'. Hybrid between 'Clementine' mandarin and 'Orlando' tangelo. Very sweet fruit in fall. Quite seedy with a pollenizer. Best flavor if grown in Florida.

'Sunburst'. Cross between 'Robinson' and 'Osceola'. Big, sweet red-orange fruit in late fall. Nearly seedless without a pollenizer. Best flavor in Florida.

'Wekiwa' (pink tangelo, 'Lavender Gem'). A cross between a tangelo and a grapefruit; looks like a small grapefruit but is eaten like a mandarin. Juicy, mild, sweet flesh is purplish rose in hot climates. Ripens late fall into winter.

SOUR-ACID MANDARIN. Both of the following bear throughout the year in mild-winter climates; they also fruit well indoors.

Calamondin. A mandarin-kumquat hybrid with fruit like a very small orange but a sweet, edible rind. Juicy, tart flesh has some seeds. Variegated form is especially ornamental.

'Rangpur'. Often called Rangpur lime, though it's not a lime and doesn't taste like one. Fruit looks and peels like a mandarin. Less acid than lemon; a good base for punches and mixed drinks. 'Otaheite' (Tahiti orange) is an acidless form sold as a houseplant.

PUMMELO. Forerunner of the grapefruit, it bears clusters of enormous round to pear-shaped fruits with thick rind and pith. Once peeled, fruit is just slightly bigger than a grapefruit. Different selections range in flavor from sweet to fairly acidic. They need a little less heat than grapefruit and ripen starting in winter in warmest areas. To eat, peel fruit; separate segments and remove membrane surrounding them. Because fruit is so heavy, prune pummelo trees to encourage strong branching.

'Chandler'. Most widely grown selection. Pink flesh; flavorful, moderately juicy, usually seedless.

'Hurado Butan'. A hardy Japanese selection with yellow fruit and firm, yellow-pink interior; good flavor. Seedy.

'Tahitian' ('Sarawak'). Greenish white flesh; moderately acidic flavor with lime overtones.

GRAPEFRUIT. Trees to about 30 ft. tall and wide. Best in Florida and South Texas. Heat zones 12–10.

'Duncan'. Oldest known grapefruit selection in Florida and the one from which all the others developed. Extremely seedy white flesh with better flavor than modern seedless types. Good for juice.

'Flame'. Red flesh similar to that of 'Star Ruby', slight rind blush, and few to no seeds. Now widely planted in Florida.

'Marsh' ('Marsh Seedless'). Main white-fleshed commercial kind. Seedless offspring of 'Duncan'. A pigmented form, 'Pink Marsh' ('Thompson') tends to lose its pink tones as the season progresses.

'Melogold'. Grapefruit-pummelo hybrid. Seedless white flesh is sweeter than fruit of its sister selection 'Oroblanco'; tree tolerates slightly more cold than 'Oroblanco'.

'Oroblanco'. Grapefruit-pummelo hybrid. Fruit containing few to no seeds has a thicker rind and more sweet-tart flavor than 'Melogold'.

'Ray Ruby' and 'Henderson'. Almost identical seedless types that have good rind blush and flesh pigmentation.

'Redblush' ('Ruby', 'Ruby Red'). Seedless, red-tinted flesh. Red internal color fades to pink, then buff by end of season.

'Rio Red'. Seedless type with good rind blush and flesh nearly as red as that of 'Star Ruby'. More dependable producer than 'Star Ruby'.

'Star Ruby'. Seedless selection with the reddest color. Tree is subject to cold damage, erratic bearing, and other growing problems.

LEMON. Low heat requirement; will even produce indoors. Most grow 20–25 ft. tall and wide.

'Bearss'. Selection of a Sicilian lemon grown in Florida; no relation to 'Bearss' lime. Fruit similar to 'Eureka'. Some fruit all year, but main crop comes in fall and winter.

'Eureka'. Familiar lemon sold in grocery stores. Some fruit all

MULTIPLE-SELECTION CITRUS PLANTS

The garden center offerings go by such names as cocktail citrus, salad citrus, and citrus medley. On these plants, which bear more than one kind of fruit, multiple selections (usually two or three) have been budded onto one stem. Such plants save space, but you must continually cut back the vigorous growers (limes, lemons, grapefruit) so the weaker ones (oranges, mandarins) can survive.

HOW TO GROW CITRUS

DRAINAGE Fast drainage is essential. In poorly drained soils or in areas with heavy rainfall or a high water table, plant above soil level in raised beds or on a soil mound. To speed up drainage in average soil and improve water retention in sandy soil, dig in a 4- to 6-in. layer of organic matter (such as garden compost or aged sawdust) to a depth of 1 ft.

WATERING Citrus trees need moist soil, but never standing water. They require moisture all year, but their demand for it is highest during active growth (usually from late winter or early spring through summer), and they must have plenty of water when fruit is developing. Irrigate when top few inches of soil are dry but rest of root zone is still slightly moist. To check soil moisture, simply stick your finger in the soil; or use a moisture meter. When you water be sure to wet the entire root zone (soak the soil to a depth of 2-3 ft.). If in a mulched bed with other plants, maintain at least a foot of bare soil around the trunk of citrus trees, as they are very susceptible to root rot. If the tree is in the lawn, maintain bare soil out to the drip line. Don't mulch citrus.

FERTILIZING In general, use a balanced, relatively low-nitrogen fertilizer, such as 6-6-6, 8-8-8, or 10-10-10. If possible, choose a fertilizer containing slow-release nitrogen. Where soil tests reveal a deficiency in certain minor nutrients, particularly magnesium, zinc, manganese, or iron, make sure the fertilizer contains them. (A popular fruit tree fertilizer in south Florida is 8-4-9-3, the last number representing magnesium.) Be careful not to overfertilize citrus plants growing in alkaline soils. Apply a total of 1 pound of fertilizer per inch of trunk diameter per year, dividing that amount into four equal portions to be applied every 2 months during the 8 months of most active growth. Sprinkle fertilizer over soil surface under entire tree canopy, keeping it 2 in. away from trunk; then water it in. In colder areas, do not fertilize after August.

PESTS AND DISEASES With a few notable exceptions, most problems are minor or can be solved by improving growing conditions. Treat citrus leaf miner, mites, and scale insects with horticultural oil spray or appropriately labeled insecticide; treat greasy spot with sprays of copper fungicide plus oil (and remove fallen leaves to keep the disease from spreading). Copper sprays will also help control scab on grapefruit, mandarins, and mandarin hybrids. Unlike deciduous fruit trees such as apples and peaches, however, citrus trees do not need regular spraying. For more information on problems common in your area and the best controls for them, check with your Cooperative Extension Office or local garden centers.

Several serious problems can affect citrus. Asian citrus psyllid has become the most serious insect pest of citrus (and citrus relatives) worldwide because of its potential to transmit the incurable and deadly disease citrus greening. The pest and/or the disease have spread throughout Florida and many citrus growing areas of the Southeast. Although there is no control for the disease, Asian citrus psyllid can be controlled with frequent oil sprays or appropriately labeled insecticides.

Citrus canker, a highly contagious bacterial disease, has spread throughout much of Florida and areas along the Gulf Coast. The pathogen affects all types of citrus. Leaves develop brown spots with a yellow halo; infected trees usually don't die, but they eventually lose vigor and may stop producing. Their fruit cannot legally be sold fresh, though it can be used for juice. There is no effective chemical control for the disease.

In Florida, millions of citrus trees have died or been removed from commercial groves and home gardens due to citrus greening and citrus canker. To stop the spread of these diseases, federal and state quarantines are in place to restrict the movement of citrus trees, plant parts, and citrus fruit into or out of certain areas. For more information, visit the website *www.saveourcitrus.org* or check with your Cooperative Extension Office for county-specific recommendations.

PRUNING Commercial trees are allowed to carry branches right to ground; production is heaviest on lower branches. Growers prune only to remove twiggy growth and weak branches or, in young plants, to nip back wild growth and balance the plant. They also keep centers open for better spray coverage. You can prune garden trees to shape as desired; espalier is traditional. Lemons are often planted close and pruned as hedges, as are sour oranges. Many citrus plants are thorny, so wear gloves and a long-sleeved shirt when picking fruit or pruning. In freeze-prone areas, don't prune in fall or winter.

CITRUS IN CONTAINERS Use containers at least 1½ ft. in diameter, though calamondin can stay in an 8- to 10-in. pot for years. Plant in light, well-drained soil mix. Daily watering may be necessary in hot weather. Use a slow-release fertilizer to keep nutrients from washing out with each watering.

Potted citrus plants can stay outdoors most or all year in mild-winter climates, but they should be moved to a protected area if a freeze is predicted. In the Upper, Middle, and Lower South, shelter plants in winter. A cool greenhouse is best, but a basement area or garage with good bright light is satisfactory.

CITRUS AS HOUSEPLANTS There is no guarantee of flowering or fruiting indoors, but the plants are still appealing. 'Improved Meyer' and 'Ponderosa' lemons; 'Bearss' lime, kumquats, calamondins, and 'Rangpur' sour-acid mandarin are the most likely to produce good fruit. Locate no more than 6 ft. from a sunny window, away from radiators or other heat sources. Ideal humidity level is 50 percent. Increase air moisture by misting tree; also ring tree with pebble-filled trays of water. Water sparingly in winter.

year in mild climates. Big, vigorous, nearly thornless tree. Prune regularly to maintain tree shape and make fruit easily accessible for harvest.

'Harvey'. Very much like Eureka but more cold hardy.

'Improved Meyer'. Hybrid between lemon and sweet orange or mandarin. More cold tolerant than true lemon. Bears yellow-orange, juicy fruit with few seeds throughout the year. Can grow to 15 ft. tall but is usually considerably shorter.

'Lisbon'. Fruit is similar to 'Eureka' (and is also sold in markets), but tree is bigger, thornier, and more cold tolerant. 'Lisbon Seedless' is the same, but without seeds. These are the best lemons for hot, dry areas. Bear some fruit all year in mild climates. Prune regularly to maintain tree shape and make fruit easily accessible for harvest.

'Ponderosa' ('American Wonder'). Thorny lemon-citron hybrid, naturally dwarf. Seedy, thick-skinned, moderately juicy fruits weighing up to 2 pounds apiece. Some fruit all year. More susceptible to cold than true lemon. Thrives indoors.

'Variegated Pink' ('Pink Lemonade'). Sport of 'Eureka' with green-and-white leaves and green stripes on immature fruit. Light pink flesh doesn't need heat to develop color. Grows to about 8 ft. tall.

LIME. There's a lime for just about every area of the citrus belt warm enough for sweet oranges. Limes outperform lemons in Florida.

Australian finger lime. This Australian native bears oblong fruit filled with tart, cavierlike juice capsules that burst out of the cut rind when fully ripe. Fruit turns blackish and begins to drop as mature. Wiry, small-leafed tree with nasty thorns (wear gloves when picking). Use the capsules to flavor appetizers, drinks, salads and grilled fish.

'Bearss' ('Persian', 'Tahiti'). Commonly grown in Florida. To 15–20 ft. tall and wide (half that size on dwarf rootstock). Thorny

C

and inclined to drop many leaves in winter; quite angular and open when young but forms a dense, round crown when mature. The seedless fruit is almost the size of a lemon; it is green when immature, light yellow when ripe. Main crop comes from winter to late spring, though some fruit ripens all year. Needs less heat for fruiting and tolerates more cold than 'Mexican'.

'Kieffer'. Leaves are used in Thai and Cambodian cooking, as is bumpy, sour fruit. Ripens in spring.

'Mexican' ('Key', West Indian lime, bartender's lime). Very thorny plant to about 15 ft. high and wide, bearing small, rounded, intensely flavored fruit all year. 'Mexican Thornless' is the same, minus the spines. Plants need high heat and are very cold sensitive.

'Palestine Sweet'. Shrubby plant to 15–20 ft. tall and wide, with acidless fruit resembling that of 'Bearss' and used in Middle Eastern, Indian, and Latin American cooking. Ripens fall or winter.

KUMQUAT. Shrubby plants 6–15 ft. or taller (and about as wide as high) bear yellow to reddish orange fruits that look like tiny oranges. Eat whole and unpeeled—spongy rind is sweet, pulp is tangy. Best in areas with warm to hot summers and chilly nights during fall or winter, when fruit is ripening. Hardy to at least 12°F.

'Marumi'. Slightly thorny plant with round fruit. Peel is sweeter than that of 'Nagami', but slightly seedy flesh is more acidic.

'Meiwa'. Round fruit is sweeter, juicier, and less seedy than that of other forms. Considered the best kumquat for eating fresh. Nearly thornless.

'Nagami'. Main commercial type. Oval-shaped, slightly seedy fruit. The hotter the summer, the more abundant and sweeter the fruit. Thornless.

KUMQUAT HYBRIDS. These were the results of early experiments by the citrus industry to produce cold-tolerant kinds of citrus. Fruit has never been a commercial success, but it's good for home gardens. Plants tend to be fairly small even as standards; on dwarfing rootstocks, they reach only 3–6 ft.

Limequat. These hybrids of 'Mexican' lime and kumquat are more cold tolerant and need less heat than their lime parent. Good lime substitutes; edible rind like kumquat parent. Some fruit all year, but main crop comes from fall to spring. 'Eustis' bears fruit shaped like a big olive. 'Tavares' has elongated oval fruit on a more compact, better-looking plant than 'Eustis'.

Orangequat. Most commonly grown is 'Nippon', a cross between 'Meiwa' kumquat and satsuma mandarin. It is cold tolerant and has a fairly low heat requirement. Small, round, deep orange fruit with sweet, spongy rind and slightly acidic flesh. Sweeter than kumquat when eaten whole. Ripens winter and spring, but holds on the tree for months.

Other kumquat hybrids occasionally available include pear-shaped 'Indio' mandarinquat and 'Lemondrop' lemonquat. Both are very attractive trees that load up with fruit.

CITRON. Citron was the first type of citrus cultivated. Plant is small, thorny, irregular in shape; grown for its big, fragrant, unusual fruit. Very sensitive to cold.

'Buddha's Hand'. Fruit is divided into "fingers" that contain all rind and no pulp. Bears some fruit all year round. This plant has absolutely no tolerance for frost.

'Etrog'. Fruit resembles a big, warty-skinned lemon with dry pulp; the peel is sometimes candied. Used in Jewish Feast of the Tabernacles.

HARDY CITRUS. For areas beyond citrus belt. Most are good choices for Lower and Coastal South; some can be grown in chillier areas. Hardiness figures apply to established plants conditioned to cold by the time freezes arrive.

'Changsha' mandarin. Can reach 15–20 ft. high and wide. Fruit is similar to satsuma mandarin but not as tasty. Ripens from fall into winter. Sometimes grown in regions of Texas, Gulf Coast, and Southwest too cold for regular mandarin selections. Hardy to about 5°F.

Citrange. Hybrid between sweet orange and hardy orange. To 15–20 ft. tall and wide. 'Morton' has fruit like slightly tart sweet orange. 'US-119' is newer and sweeter. Ripens late fall. Hardy to 5–10°F.

Hardy orange. See *Poncirus trifoliata*, page 519.

'Thomasville'. Hybrid between citrange and kumquat. Reaches 15 ft. tall and wide. Small, nearly seedless fruit used as lime substitute if picked soon after ripening in fall. Left on tree, may become sweet enough to eat fresh. Hardy to about 0°F.

'Yuzu'. An acidic with highly aromatic, bumpy rind. Both juice and peel are prized in Asian recipes, especially for ponzu sauce. Fruit can be used green to yellow stage. Rangy tree has large thorns and is very hardy (at least into the high teens).

CLADRASTIS KENTUKEA
YELLOW WOOD

Fabaceae
Deciduous tree

🌡 **US, MS, LS; USDA 6-8**

☀ **FULL SUN**

💧 **REGULAR WATER**

Cladrastis kentukea

Native to Kentucky, Tennessee, and North Carolina. Slow-growing tree to 30–50 ft. tall, with broad, rounded head half as wide as tree is high. Leaves are 8–12 in. long, divided into many (usually 7 to 11) oval leaflets resembling those of English walnut (see *Juglans regia*). Foliage is yellowish green when new, turning bright green in summer and brilliant yellow in fall. Bark is gray in maturity; the common name "yellow wood" refers to the color of the freshly cut heartwood.

May not flower until 10 years old and may skip bloom some years, but the late spring display is spectacular when it comes: Clus-

ters of fragrant, wisterialike white flowers to 14 in. long. 'Perkin's Pink' ('Rosea') is a pink-flowering form. Blooms are followed by flat, 3- to 4-in.-long seedpods. Attractive as terrace, patio, or lawn tree even if it never blooms. Deep rooted, so you can grow other plants beneath it. Tolerates alkaline soils; withstands some drought.

CARE

Prune when young to shorten side branches or correct narrow, weak branch crotches susceptible to breakage in storms. Usually low branching; you can remove lower branches entirely when tree is at desired height. Prune in summer, since cuts made in winter or spring bleed profusely.

CLEMATIS

Ranunculaceae
Deciduous and evergreen vines and perennials

🌡 **ZONES VARY BY SPECIES**

☀◐ **ROOTS COOL, TOP IN SUN**

💧 **REGULAR WATER, EXCEPT AS NOTED**

Clematis viticella

The most familiar clematis species are deciduous vines that clamber into trees and over fences and arbors; exceptions include the evergreen *C. armandii* and a few interesting freestanding or sprawling perennials. Flowers are attractive in all kinds, spectacular in many. The clustered true flowers are tiny and inconspicuous; the showy part consists of petal-like sepals that surround them. Blossoms of most are followed by fluffy clusters of seeds with tails, often quite effective in flower arrangements.

Leaves of vining kinds are dark green, usually divided into leaflets; leafstalks twist and curl to hold plant to its support.

C. alpina. ALPINE CLEMATIS. Deciduous vine. Zones US, MS, LS; USDA 6-8. European native. To 8–12 ft., with dangling, 1½- to 3-in.-wide flowers borne singly on long stalks in spring. Flowers may be blue, white, purple, pink, or red, depending on selection; they have four spreading, pointed, petal-like sepals and an inner, smaller cup of modified stamens. 'Pamela Jackman' is lavender-blue. 'Stolwijk Gold' reaches about 6 ft. tall and has blue flowers; its bright yellow foliage matures to chartreuse.

C. armandii. ARMAND CLEMATIS, EVERGREEN CLEMATIS. Zones MS, LS, CS; USDA 7-9. Native to China. Fast-growing vine to 20–35 ft. Leaves divided into three glossy, dark green, 3- to 5-in.-long leaflets; they droop downward, creating a strongly textured look. Creamy white, vanilla-scented, saucer-shaped flowers are 1–2 in. across, are borne in large, branched clusters in spring. Choice selections include 'Apple Blossom' (rosy pink), 'Snowdrift' (pure white), and 'Hendersonii Rubra' (soft pink).

Leaves burn badly at tips in areas where soil or water contains excess salts. Train along substantial frames such as sturdy fence tops or roof gables; or allow to climb tall trees. Makes privacy screen if not allowed to become bare at base. Slow to start but races when established. Needs relentless pruning after flowering to prevent tangling and buildup of dead thatch on inner parts of vine. Keep and tie up stems you want; cut out all others. Frequent pinching will hold foliage to eye level.

C. x cartmanii 'Avalanche'. Evergreen shrubby vine. Zones MS, LS, CS; USDA 7-9. Vigorous hybrid with dark green, deeply cut leaves. Blooms profusely in spring, bearing panicles of 2- to 3-in. white flowers with yellow stamens. Prune after bloom is over.

C. chrysocoma. GOLD WOOL CLEMATIS. Deciduous vine. Zones US, MS, LS, CS; USDA 6-9. Native to western China. Grows to 6–8 ft. or more in height; fairly open grower. Young branches, leaves, and flower stalks covered with yellow down. Clusters of long-stalked, 2-in.-wide, pink-

shaded white blossoms on old wood in spring; later flowers follow from new wood. Will take considerable shade.

C. florida 'Sieboldiana'. Deciduous vine. Zones US, MS, LS; USDA 6-8. Selection of an Asian subspecies. To 8–12 ft. Not as rugged as other clematis vines, but summer flowers are striking: 3–4 in. across, creamy white with a central puff of purple petal-like stamens. *C. f. flore-pleno* 'Plena' is similar but has a creamy to greenish white central puff.

C. heracleifolia davidiana (*C. tubulosa*). Woody-based perennial. Zones US, MS, LS; USDA 6-8. Native to China. To 4 ft. high, 3 ft. wide. Deep green leaves divided into three broad, oval, 3- to 6-in. leaflets. Dense clusters of 1-in.-long, tubular, medium to deep blue, fragrant flowers in summer. Use in perennial or shrub border.

C. integrifolia. Woody-based perennial. Zones US, MS, LS; USDA 6-8. Native to Europe and Asia. To 3 ft. tall, 2 ft. wide, with dark green, undivided, 2- to 4-in.-long leaves and nodding, urn-shaped, 1½-in. blue flowers in summer. Provide twigs for the plant to sprawl over. 'Alba' has white blooms; those of 'Ozawa's Blue' are a rich, true blue. 'Arabella' is blue-mauve. Hybrid 'Rooguchi' is more of a climber, reaching 5–8 ft. tall; its stunning deep purple flowers are up to 2 in. long.

C. lanuginosa. Deciduous vine. Zones US, MS, LS; USDA 6-8. Chinese species best known as a parent of many of the large-flowered hybrids. Its selection 'Candida' has breathtaking 8-in.-wide white blooms on a vigorous but small (6- to 10-ft.) vine. Blooms in spring, again in summer.

C. macropetala. DOWNY CLEMATIS. Deciduous vine. Zones US, MS, LS; USDA 6-8. Native to China, Siberia. Variable in size; may reach 6–10 ft. Lavender to powder-blue flowers to 4 in. across appear in early spring; they look double, resembling a ballerina's tutu. Blooms are followed by bronzy pink seed clusters with silvery tails—very showy. Hybrids 'Blue Bird' (soft blue) and 'Markham Pink' (lavender-pink) are highly recommended.

C. montana. ANEMONE CLEMATIS. Deciduous vine. Zones US, MS, LS, CS; USDA 6-9. Native

TOP: Clematis 'Nellie Moser'; MIDDLE: C. viticella 'Madame Julia Correvon'; C. florida 'Sieboldiana'; BOTTOM: C. integrifolia 'Arabella'

to Himalayas, China. Vigorous grower to 20–30 ft.; give it plenty of room to roam. Massive early spring display of 2- to 2½-in., anemone-like flowers that open white, then turn pink. 'Elizabeth' has pale pink flowers and bronzy foliage that matures to green. *C. m. grandiflora* produces 3-in. white flowers. *C. m. rubens* has crimson new leaves maturing to bronzy green; the fragrant flowers are pink to rose-red. Among its selections are 'Odorata', notable for fragrance; 'Pink Perfection', with large, fragrant blooms; and 'Tetrarose', known for bronze foliage and 3-in., thick-textured floral segments.

C. paniculata. See *C. terniflora*.

C. recta. Perennial. Zones US, MS, LS, CS; USDA 6-9. From central and southern Europe. To 3–6 ft. tall and wide, with dark green, divided leaves and clouds of star-like, inch-wide, white flowers with fragrance of vanilla; blooms from midsummer to early fall. Give support to keep plants from flopping over onto their neighbors. 'Purpurea' and 'Velvet Night' have coppery purple new foliage that gradually fades to green.

C. tangutica. GOLDEN CLEMATIS. Deciduous vine. Zones US, MS, LS, CS; USDA 6-9. Native to Mongolia, northern China.

To 10–15 ft., with finely divided gray-green leaves. Nodding, lantern-shaped, bright yellow flowers, 2–4 in. across, in great profusion from midsummer into fall. Blossoms are followed by handsome, silvery, mop-headed seed clusters.

C. terniflora (*C. dioscoreifolia*). SWEET AUTUMN CLEMATIS. Deciduous vine. Zones US, MS, LS, CS; USDA 6-9. Native to Japan. Tall and vigorous (some would say rampant), producing billowy masses of 1-in.-wide, fragrant, creamy white flowers in late summer, fall. Glossy leaves divided into three to five oval, 1- to 2½-in.-long leaflets. Good privacy screen, arbor cover. Self-sows readily; can become a pest. Often erroneously sold as *C. paniculata*, a little-grown species from New Zealand.

C. texensis. SCARLET CLEMATIS. Deciduous vine. Zones US, MS, LS, CS; USDA 6-9. Native to Texas. Fast growing to 6–10 ft. Dense bluish green foliage; bright scarlet, urn-shaped flowers to 1 in. long from early summer until frost. More tolerant of dry soils than most clematis. Crosses with large-flowered hybrids have produced eye-catching selections such as the vivid pink 'Duchess of Albany', crimson 'Gravetye Beauty', and rich pink 'Princess Diana'.

C. viticella. Deciduous vine. Zones US, MS, LS, CS; USDA 6-9. Native to southern Europe, western Asia. To 12–15 ft. Purple or rose-purple, 2-in. blooms in summer. 'Venosa Violacea' bears 3-4 in.-wide blooms that are rich purple with white bars. 'Madame Julia Correvon' has bright red blooms; vigorous and free-flowering.

Large-flowered hybrid clematis. Zones US, MS, LS, CS; USDA 6-9. Although well over a hundred selections of large-flowered hybrid clematis are being grown today, your local nursery is not likely to offer more than a dozen of the old favorites. Mail-order catalogs remain the best source for collectors seeking the newest. Following is a list of time-honored hybrids, along with some noteworthy newer ones. Most grow 6–10 ft. tall, with saucer-shaped flowers 4–8 in. across, though some may reach 10 in. across. Cut flowers are choice for indoors; float them in a bowl of water. Sear the cut stem ends with a flame to make flowers last longer.

White 'Henryi' is the standard. 'Huldine', 'Hyde Hall', 'Jackmanii Alba', 'Marie Boisselot', and 'Snow Queen' are also excellent choices.

Pink Look for 'Caroline' (pale pink sepals marked with dark pink), 'Comtesse de Bouchard' (bright mauve-pink), 'Dr. Ruppel' (deep pink bands down center of petals), 'Hagley Hybrid' (mauve-pink), 'Kakio' (also known as 'Pink Champagne', with vivid pink sepals and a pale central band), and 'Proteus' (mauve-pink double flowers). Where summers are hot, plant in bright shade to prevent the soft colors from fading.

Red Great choices include vivid magenta 'Ernest Markham', deep red 'Niobe', velvety crimson 'Rouge Cardinal', carmine-red 'Ville de Lyon', and deep maroon 'Warsaw Nike' ('Warszawska Nike').

Purple The classic 'Jackmanii', with velvety, dark purple sepals, remains the most popular; 'Jackmanii Superba' has larger flowers with wider petals. Other fine choices include rich dark purple 'Aotearoa'; deep blue-violet 'Daniel Deronda'; velvety, dark violet 'Gipsy Queen'; rosy purple 'Richard Pennell'; purple-blue 'The President'; and rosy mauve 'Viola'.

Blue Sky blue 'Ramona' is deservedly popular. Other selections include 'General Sikorski' (dark lavender), 'H. F. Young' (periwinkle blue, tinged with mauve), 'Ken Donson' (deep lavender-blue), 'Will Goodwin' (lavender-blue, yellow stamens), and 'William Kennett' (lilac-blue).

Bicolor Choices include 'Asao' (deep rosy pink sepals with a pale pink central bar), 'Barbara Jackman' (lavender with vivid magenta bar), 'Charissima' (cerise-pink with deep pink bar), 'Danielle' ('Vancouver Danielle', violet-blue with carmine bar), 'Kilian Donahue' (opens pink with red bar, then fades to lavender), the ever-popular 'Nelly Moser' (purplish pink with reddish bar), 'Piilu' ('Little Duckling', pastel pink with raspberry bar), 'Prince Philip' (purple blue with magenta bands), and 'Starry Nights' ('Vancouver Starry Nights', 8-in. fuchsia flowers with reddish center bar). In hot-summer areas, plant these selections in bright shade to prevent fading.

Double Fully double, roselike blooms in early summer on old wood are usually followed later by single or semidouble flowers on new wood. Choice selections include silvery blue 'Belle of Woking', lavender-blue 'Blue Light' ('Vanso Blue') and 'Multi Blue', and white 'Duchess of Edinburgh'. 'Josephine' has unusual flowers of mauve-pink with a dark blue central stripe.

CLEOME HASSLERANA

SPIDER FLOWER
Cleomaceae
Annual

🖋 **US, MS, LS, CS, TS; USDA 6-11**

☼ **FULL SUN**

◐ ◑ **MODERATE TO REGULAR WATER**

Cleome hasslerana

Shrubby, branching South American native topped in summer and fall with many open, fluffy clusters of pink or white flowers with extremely long, protruding stamens. Slender seed capsules follow the blossoms. Stems usually have short, strong spines; lower leaves are divided, upper ones undivided. Leaves and stems feel clammy to the touch; they have a strong but not unpleasant smell. Deer resistant. Plant grows 4–6 ft. tall, 4–5 ft. wide; especially vigorous in warm, dry inland areas. Grow in background, as summer hedge, against walls or fences, in large containers; or—since plants self-sow to a fault—naturalize in fringe areas of garden. Flowers and dry seed capsules are useful in arrangements.

Sow seeds in place in spring; they sprout rapidly in warm soil. A number of selections can be grown from seed. In most

TOP: C. integrifolia 'Rooguchi'; *C. texensis* 'Princess Diana'; *BOTTOM: C. viticella* 'Venosa Violacea'

cases color is indicated by the selection's name: 'Cherry Queen', 'Mauve Queen', 'Pink Queen', 'Purple Queen', 'Rose Queen', 'Ruby Queen'. 'Helen Campbell' is snow white. The Sparkler series includes bushy dwarf hybrids to 3–4 ft. tall, in a full range of colors. 'Senorita Rosalita' is a thornless, nonsticky, seedless hybrid that grows 3-5 ft. high and is covered from spring to fall with lavender-pink flowers. It does not get leafless legs like the older selections. 'Senorita Blanca' is the white form.

CLERODENDRUM

GLORYBOWER
Lamiaceae
Evergreen and deciduous shrubs and vines

🌿 **TS, USDA 10-11, EXCEPT AS NOTED**

☼ ◑ ● **EXPOSURE NEEDS VARY BY SPECIES**

💧 **REGULAR WATER**

Clerodendrum bungei

Diverse group of plants grown for big clusters of showy, brightly colored flowers that are fragrant in some species. Bloom comes on current season's growth. Provide support for climbing species. Grow in well-drained soil. Good greenhouse plants in areas that are beyond their hardiness limits. Not browsed by deer.

C. bungei. CASHMERE BOU-QUET. Evergreen shrub. Zones LS, CS, TS; USDA 8-11. Native to China. Plant grows rapidly to 6 ft. tall and wide; spreads rapidly by suckers, eventually forming a thicket if not restrained. Big (to 1-ft.), coarse, broadly oval leaves with toothed edges are dark green above, with rust-colored fuzz beneath.

Leaves release a sickening odor when bruised or crushed. Loose clusters of delightfully fragrant rosy red flowers in summer, sometimes into fall. Plant where its appearance (except during bloom time) is not important. Prune severely in spring and pinch back throughout the growing season to make a compact, 2- to 3-ft. shrub. Partial shade. 'Pink Diamond' is compact with large clusters of pink flowers and creamy white, variegated leaves.

C. myricoides 'Ugandense'. BLUE BUTTERFLY BUSH. Evergreen shrub. Native to tropical Africa. Grows to 10 ft. tall and about half as wide. Glossy, dark green leaves to 4 in. long. Each five-petaled blossom has one violet-blue petal and four pale blue ones; pistil and stamens arch outward and upward. Partial shade.

C. quadriloculare. SHOOT-ING STAR. Evergreen shrub. From the Philippines. To 15 ft. tall, spreading by root suckers. Has an upright habit; can be trained to tree form. Clusters of fragrant pink flowers in fall and spring enhance the deep purple of the leaf undersides. Use as color accent, hedge, screen, or tubbed specimen for the lanai. Protect from harsh winds. Prune to shape. Full sun.

C. speciosissimum (*C. buchananii fallax*). JAVA GLORYBOWER. Evergreen shrub. From Indonesia. Erect growth to 12 ft. tall and 6 ft. wide. Plant produces brilliant scarlet flowers throughout much of the year. Densely hairy, heart-shaped leaves grow to 1 ft. long. Suitable shrub for mass plantings, hedges, or colorful screens; it also makes a good container plant. You can prune to improve appearance and shape as needed. Full sun or partial shade.

C. x speciosum. CLERODEN-DRUM VINE. Evergreen shrubby vine. Hybrid between *C. splendens* and *C. thomsoniae*. A vine of fairly rapid growth to 30 ft. Glossy, oval dark green leaves to 7 in. long. Blooms in winter and spring, bearing clusters of bicolored blooms with a dull pink or red calyx surrounding a short tube in deep crimson shaded with violet. Calyxes hang on. Full sun.

C. splendens. RED CLERODEN-DRUM, FLAMING GLORYBOWER. Evergreen vine. From tropical Africa. Climbs rapidly to 30 ft. Rich green, glossy leaves to 7 in. long. Large clusters of brilliant red

flowers bloom profusely during winter. Protect from strong winds. Best in sun on vertical supports such as a fence or trellis, and can be trained along eaves.

C. thomsoniae (*C. balfouri*). BLEEDING HEART VINE. Evergreen vine. Native to West Africa. Restrained and mannerly growth to no more than 12 ft. Distinctly ribbed, oval, shiny dark green leaves, 4–7 in. long. Blooms from summer to fall, bearing flattish, 5-in. clusters of up to 20 flowers. White calyxes reminiscent of paper lanterns surround scarlet flowers, displaying a striking two-tone contrast. Use it on sheltered patio walls or arbor posts. Grows well in large containers; move it to a frost-free shelter in winter. Partial shade.

C. trichotomum. HARLEQUIN GLORYBOWER. Deciduous shrub.

Zones MS, LS, CS, TS; USDA 7-11. Native to Japan. Reaches 10–15 ft. tall and wide, with many stems growing from base; can also be trained as a small tree. Soft, hairy, oval dark green leaves to 5 in. long. Fragrant blossoms—each a white tube almost twice as long as the prominent, fleshy, scarlet calyx surrounding it—come in late summer. Calyxes hang on and contrast pleasingly with metallic-looking turquoise or blue-green fruit. Give this shrub plenty of room to spread at top; add plants underneath it to hide its legginess. 'Carnival' and 'Variegata' have leaves broadly edged in creamy white. *C. t. fargesii*, from China, is somewhat hardier and smaller; it has smooth leaves and green calyxes that turn pink. Partial shade.

TOP: *Clerodendrum myricoides* 'Ugandense'; BOTTOM: *C. thomsoniae*

CLETHRA

Clethraceae
Deciduous shrubs

- ✎ **ZONES VARY BY SPECIES**
- ☼ **BEST IN PARTIAL SHADE BUT ADAPTABLE**
- ◑ **REGULAR TO AMPLE WATER**

Clethra alnifolia

These attractive shrubs are grown for the small, five-lobed, sweet-scented white or pink flowers that cluster at branch tips in mid- to late summer. Tolerate many soils but do best in moist, organic, slightly acid, well-drained soil. Prefer partial shade but can adapt successfully to less light as well as to full sun, though they need some shade where summers are very hot. Remove some old wood from base annually before spring growth begins. Not browsed by deer.

C. acuminata. CINNAMON CLETHRA. Zones US, MS; USDA 6-7. Native to mountain areas of Virginia, Georgia, and Alabama. Grows to 8–12 ft. (rarely 20 ft.) tall and wide. Habit is open, even gaunt, so that polished-looking bark in various shades of cinnamon, tan, and reddish brown is displayed beautifully. Fragrant white flowers in 3- to 6-in. spires. Oblong, 3- to 6-in.-long leaves are dark green in summer, then turn golden yellow in autumn.

C. alnifolia. SUMMERSWEET, SWEET PEPPERBUSH. Zones US, MS, LS, CS; USDA 6-9. Eastern U.S. native to 4–10 ft. tall and wide, spreading slowly by suckers. Thin, strong branches form a vertical pattern. Tooth-edged, dark green, 3- to 4-in. leaves appear late in spring, turn golden yellow in fall. At bloom time, each branch tip

ABOVE: **Clethra acuminata**

carries several 4- to 6-in.-long spires of tiny, gleaming white flowers with a spicy perfume.

Selections include the following; most grow about as wide as tall.

'Anne Bidwell'. To 4–6 ft., with extra-large flower clusters late in the season.

'Crystalina'. White-flowered, dwarf form to 2-2½ ft. tall.

'Creel's Calico'. To 4 ft.; foliage irregularly variegated in cream.

'Hummingbird'. Reaches 2½–3½ ft. tall and spreads by suckers to form large colonies.

'Pink Spires'. To 4 ft., with deep pink blooms.

'Ruby Spice'. To 6–8 ft.; dark rosy pink blooms. Wonderful for borders, shade plantings. Spreads by suckers to make a broad clump. Tolerates coastal conditions.

'September Beauty'. Late bloomer; reaches 4–6 ft.

'Sixteen Candles'. Similar to 'Hummingbird', but flower spikes are held upright like candles on a birthday cake.

'White Dove'. Compact, profusely blooming dwarf reaching 2–3 ft.

C. barbinervis. JAPANESE CLETHRA. Zones US, MS, LS; USDA 6-8. Slow-growing plant reaches 15–18 ft. tall and about one-half to two-thirds as wide; has attractive, peeling, glossy gray-to-brown bark when mature. Produces drooping, 4- to 6-in. clusters of fragrant, bell-shaped white flowers. Oval, pointed, sharply toothed, dark green leaves turn bright yellow in fall. 'Variegata' has leaves attractively splashed with golden yellow.

CLEYERA JAPONICA

Pentaphylaceae
Evergreen shrub

- ✎ **MS, LS, CS, TS; USDA 7-11**
- ☼ **PARTIAL SHADE**
- ◑ **MODERATE TO REGULAR WATER**

Cleyera japonica

Native to Japan and southeast Asia. Handsome foliage shrub related to camellia. It is quite similar in character to *Ternstroemia gymnanthera*, with which it is often confused. Grows at moderate rate to 15 ft. tall and wide, with graceful, arching branches. New leaves are a beautiful deep brownish red. Mature leaves, 3–6 in. long, are glossy dark green with reddish midrib. Plant produces small clusters of fragrant, creamy white flowers in summer, followed by small, puffy dark red berries that last throughout winter. Flowers and berries are attractive but not showy. Foliage of 'Tricolor' is variegated in yellow and rose.

CLIFTONIA MONOPHYLLA

BUCKWHEAT TREE
Cyrillaceae
Evergreen shrub or tree

MS, LS, CS; USDA 7-9

FULL SUN

REGULAR TO AMPLE WATER

Cliftonia monophylla

Outstanding multitrunked shrub or small tree native to swamps and moist forests of the Southeast. Grows upright to 10–20 ft. tall, half as wide. Leaves are glossy, dark green, leathery, 2–3 in. long. Spreads by suckers to form thickets along streams. Best used in a naturalized area. Clusters of small, fragrant pinkish white flowers bloom in early spring and attract bees and butterflies. Tiny egg-shaped fruits appear in fall. Prefers acid soil with lots of organic matter. 'Berry Pink' is a pink-flowered selection.

CLINTONIA UMBELLULATA

CLINTON LILY
Liliaceae
Perennial

US, MS; USDA 6-7

FULL SHADE

REGULAR WATER

Clintonia umbellulata

This lovely and little-known wildflower, native to the upland forests of the Appalachians, is a veritable gem. It gently spreads across the forest floor to form lush mats of deep green, oblong leaves (to 10 in. long and 3 in. wide) that are every bit as attractive as those of lily-of-the-valley (*Convallaria majalis*). In late spring, rounded clusters of ½-in., fragrant white blossoms (sometimes speckled with purple) appear atop leafless stalks rising 8–18 in. high. Distinctive round, black berries follow the flowers. Plant dies down in winter. Clinton lily needs moist, well-drained, slightly acid soil that contains lots of organic matter. Mulch around it every spring to keep the roots cool and moist. Water during summer drought. Ideal at the foot of tall trees and shrubs in naturalized areas and woodland gardens. Good companions include rhododendron, mountain laurel (*Kalmia*), mayapple (*Podophyllum peltatum*), Christmas fern (*Polystichum acrostichoides*), trillium, and wild ginger (*Asarum*).

CLITORIA

Fabaceae
Perennials, one grown as annual

ZONES VARY BY SPECIES

EXPOSURE NEEDS VARY BY SPECIES

WATER NEEDS VARY BY SPECIES

Clitoria ternatea

This genus includes many and varied species of perennials, vines, and shrubs, but all have the distinctive flowers and foliage of the pea family. Of the two listed here, one is a popular twining vine, the other a native wildflower.

C. mariana. BUTTERFLY PEA, ATLANTIC PIGEON WINGS. Zones US, MS, LS, CS, TS; USDA 6-11. Native to the dry woods, sand hills, and scrub of the eastern U.S. (from New Jersey to Florida), west to Texas and Mexico. Upright and spreading, sometimes twining, thin-stemmed plant that may reach 3 ft. tall. Leaves with three ovate leaflets to 2 in. long; lavender flowers to 2 in. long, 1½ in. wide in early summer. Dies to ground in winter. Best with moderate to regular water and full sun but tolerates some drought and light shade. Good for naturalized areas.

C. ternatea. BLUE PEA VINE. Perennial in Zones TS; USDA 10-11; annual elsewhere. Native to tropical Americas and Asia. A fast-growing, twining vine to 10 ft.; often used to decorate trellises and posts. Blooms continuously in warm weather, bearing deep blue, white-eyed flowers to 2 in. long and 1 in. wide. Leaves consist of five to nine leaflets, each up to 2 in. long. Plant in well-drained soil; give full sun and regular water. Easy to start from seed (soak seed for 3 to 4 hours before sowing). Can bloom as soon as 6 weeks after sowing.

CLIVIA MINIATA

FIRE LILY
Amaryllidaceae
Perennial from tuberous roots

TS; USDA 10-11; OR GROWN IN POTS

PARTIAL TO FULL SHADE; BRIGHT INDIRECT LIGHT

REGULAR WATER

Clivia miniata

Native to South Africa, this evergreen member of the amaryllis family offers both spectacular flowers and handsome foliage. It makes an exceptional and long-lived potted plant for indoors or out. In the Tropical South, where it is hardy, it's also a great addition to the mixed border. Blooms dependably in shade.

Large clusters of brilliant orange, funnel-shaped blossoms are carried atop 2-ft. stalks that rise above dense clumps of strap-shaped dark green leaves to 1½ ft. long; attractive red berries follow the flowers. Blossoms may appear in winter, but bloom mainly comes in spring and lasts for weeks. French and Belgian hybrids have extra-wide leaves and yellow to deep orange-red blooms on thick, rigid stalks. Solomone hybrids have pale to deep yellow flowers. 'Flame' is an exceptionally brilliant orange-red. 'Good Hope' has wide leaves and large clusters of clear yellow flowers.

CARE

Clivias like bright light—but don't expose them to direct, hot sun, which will burn and yellow the foliage. Plants with crowded roots bloom better, so resist the urge to repot or divide. From spring to autumn, fertilize potted plants every other week with a general-purpose liquid houseplant fertilizer; water when the soil surface becomes dry. You can keep potted plants outdoors from spring to fall, but bring them indoors for winter; they are badly damaged by freezing temperatures. Indoors, they do best near an east-facing window. In winter, to encourage bud set, provide cool temperatures (50–60°F), cease feeding, and water once every 4 weeks. Outdoors, set plants 1½–2 ft. apart in fertile, moist, well-drained soil.

CLYTOSTOMA CALLISTEGIOIDES

VIOLET TRUMPET VINE
Bignoniaceae
Evergreen vine

🌿 **CS, TS; USDA 9-11**

☼ ◑ **FULL SUN OR PARTIAL SHADE**

💧💧 **MODERATE TO REGULAR WATER**

Clytostoma callistegioides

Formerly *Bignonia violacea*, *B. speciosa*. Strong-growing vine from Argentina and Brazil will clamber over anything by tendrils; needs support on walls. Leaves are 3–4 in. long, divided into two glossy, dark green leaflets with wavy margins. Extended terminal shoots hang down to create a curtainlike effect. Blooms from late spring to fall, bearing trumpet-shaped blossoms in sprays at ends of shoots; flowers are violet, lavender, or pale purple, 3 in. long and nearly as

wide at the open end. Tops hardy to 20°F, roots to 10°F. Excellent vine for areas of Florida too cold for more tender bignonia relatives such as *Pandorea*. Remove unwanted long runners and spent flower sprays. Prune in late winter to discipline growth.

COBAEA SCANDENS

CUP-AND-SAUCER VINE
Polemoniaceae
Perennial vine usually grown as annual

🌿 **US, MS, LS, CS, TS; USDA 6-11**

☼ **FULL SUN**

💧 **REGULAR WATER**

Cobaea scandens

Native to Mexico. Extremely vigorous growth to 25 ft. in a single season. Bell-shaped, summer-to-fall flowers are first greenish, then violet or rose purple. The common name describes the flower form: a 2-in.-long cup of petals sits in large, saucerlike green calyx. Leaves are divided into two or three pairs of oval, 4-in. leaflets; a curling tendril at the end of each leaf enables the vine to climb rough surfaces without support. 'Alba' has white blooms. 'Key Lime' has pale green flowers. Blossoms of 'Royal Plum' emerge light green, then mature to rich deep purple with a white-streaked throat and chartreuse anthers.

Blooms first year from seed. In the Tropical South and milder parts of the Coastal South, the vine lives from year to year, eventually reaching more than 40 ft. in length and blooming heavily from spring to fall.

The hard-coated seeds may rot if sown outdoors in cool weather. Start indoors in 4-in. pots; notch seeds with a knife and press them edgewise into moistened potting mix, barely covering them. Keep moist but not wet; transplant to warm, sunny location when weather warms up. Protect from wind.

COCCOLOBA

SEA GRAPE
Polygonaceae
Evergreen shrubs or trees

🌿 **TS; USDA 10-11**

☼ **FULL SUN**

💧 **MODERATE WATER**

Coccoloba uvifera

The quintessential seaside plants: tolerant of wind, sand, and salt, though tender to frost. Useful for windbreaks. Thick, often picturesquely twisted trunk and branches. New leaves reddish or coppery, mature ones glossy green with reddish veins. Small white flowers are followed by clusters of greenish fruits that turn purple when ripe; they can be made into jelly. Shape plant by pruning just before new growth emerges. Small plants in containers can be used for bonsai.

C. diversifolia (*C. laurifolia*). PIGEON PLUM. Native to southern Florida and the Caribbean. Can reach 30 ft. high and wide. Similar to *C. uvifera* but with shorter flower clusters, smaller fruits, and 2- to 4-in. oval leaves.

C. uvifera. SEA GRAPE. From the tropical Americas. Can grow to 30 ft. high and wide but is

usually kept much smaller. Nearly round leaves to 8 in. wide. Fragrant flowers in foot-long clusters; fruits ¾ in. wide. Will grow right on the dunes.

COCCULUS

CAROLINA MOONSEED
Menispermaceae
Deciduous and evergreen vines and shrubs

🌿 **ZONES VARY BY SPECIES**

☼ ◑ **FULL SUN OR PARTIAL SHADE**

💧 **REGULAR WATER**

Cocculus carolinus

Woody vines and vinelike shrubs that are easy to grow in moist soil. Flowers are not prominent, but foliage is a lovely glossy green.

C. carolinus. CAROLINA MOONSEED. Woody deciduous or evergreen vine. Zones US, MS, LS, CS; USDA 6-9. Deciduous in Upper and Middle South; evergreen in Lower and Coastal South. Native from Florida to Virginia and west to Texas. Grows rapidly to 10–12 ft., climbing by tendrils; needs support. Oval, pointed, medium green leaves reach 4 in. long. Blooms in spring, with greenish white flowers in 3- to 5-in.-long clusters; blossoms are not as showy as the glossy bright red berries that appear in late summer and fall. Gets its common name from its crescent-shaped seeds. Tolerates most soils, including alkaline ones. Can be weedy and difficult to eradicate.

C. laurifolius. WILD OLIVE. Evergreen shrub. Zones CS, TS; USDA 9-11. Native to the Himalayas. Usually multistemmed, with arching, spreading growth; shiny, leathery oblong leaves to 6 in., with three strongly marked veins running from base to tip. Grows slowly at first, then moderately rapidly to 25 ft. (or more) tall and wide; can be kept smaller by pruning. Long, willowy branches are as easily led and trained as vines; fastened to a trellis, they make an effective screen. Can also be trained as an espalier. Staked and trained as a tree, the plant takes on an umbrella shape.

COCOS NUCIFERA

COCONUT PALM
Arecaceae
Palm

🌿 **TS; USDA 10-11; OR GROWN IN POTS**

☼ **FULL SUN**

💧 **MODERATE WATER**

Cocos nucifera

The coconut palm is both an economically valuable plant and a handsome ornamental, but it is hardy only in south Florida. Can grow to 80 ft. or more but is usually much shorter, with a leaning or curving trunk and a crown of feathery, 20-ft. fronds. Flowers are not notable, but the fruit is the coconut of commerce. Sprouted coconuts are seen fairly often in large pots or tubs; such plants are attractive until they grow too large. Grows best near the shore. Landscape use is limited by the risk that falling coconuts pose to passersby and by a potentially fatal plant disease, lethal yellows. For home gardens, dwarf forms such as 10-ft. 'Nino' are the wisest choice.

CODIAEUM VARIEGATUM PICTUM

CROTON
Euphorbiaceae
Evergreen shrub

🌿 **TS; USDA 10-11; OR HOUSEPLANT**

☼◑ **SOME FORMS TAKE SUN, OTHERS SHADE; BRIGHT LIGHT**

💧💧 **REGULAR TO AMPLE WATER**

Codiaeum variegatum pictum

Native to the tropics. Can reach 6 ft. or more (and as wide) outdoors in Tropical South; indoors, usually seen as single-stemmed plant, 6–24 in. tall. Grown principally for its showy large, leathery, glossy leaves, which may be green, yellow, red, purple, bronze, pink, or almost any combination of these colors. Leaves may be oval, lance shaped, or very narrow; edges may be straight or lobed. Dozens of named forms combine these differing features. Not favored by deer.

CARE
Outdoor exposure depends on the selection. Needs bright light and regular misting indoors; does well in a warm, humid greenhouse, provided you control spider mites, mealybugs, and thrips. Can be brought outdoors at warm times of the year. Repeated contact with croton leaves can cause a skin rash in some people.

COFFEA ARABICA

COFFEE
Rubiaceae
Evergreen shrub

🌿 **TS; USDA 10-11; OR HOUSEPLANT**

◑ **SOME SHADE; BRIGHT INDIRECT LIGHT**

💧 **REGULAR WATER**

Coffea arabica

Native to East Africa. The coffee tree of commerce can be grown as a specimen or in shrub borders in the Tropical South; elsewhere, it's a handsome container plant for patios or large, well-lit rooms. Upright shrub to 15 ft., with evenly spaced tiers of branches clothed in shiny, dark green, oval leaves to 6 in. long. Small (¾-in.), fragrant white flowers are clustered near leaf bases. These are followed by ½-in. fruits—green when they first appear, then turning purple or red. Each fruit contains two seeds—coffee beans. Grow in rich, well-drained soil, and mist frequently. In spring and summer, feed with a complete water-soluble fertilizer every other week. Protect from frosts.

COLCHICUM

MEADOW SAFFRON, AUTUMN CROCUS
Colchicaceae
Perennials from corms

🌿 **US, MS, LS; USDA 6-8; OR GROW IN POTS**

☼ **FULL SUN; BRIGHT INDIRECT LIGHT**

💧 **REGULAR WATER DURING GROWTH AND BLOOM**

⬦ **ALL PARTS ARE POISONOUS IF INGESTED**

Colchicum

This group of delightful Mediterranean natives includes many species. They are sometimes called autumn crocus but are not true crocuses. Shining, brown-skinned, thick-scaled corms send up clusters of long-tubed; flaring; lavender-pink, rose-purple, or white flowers to 4 in. across in late summer or early autumn, whether corms are sitting in a dish on a windowsill or planted in soil. When corms are planted out, broad leaves 6–12 in. long emerge in spring, last for a few months, and then die long before flower cluster rises from ground. Corms are available during a brief dormant period in the summer. Common selections include 'The Giant', single lavender, and 'Waterlily', double violet. Resists rodents and deer.

CARE
Best planted where they need not be disturbed more often than every 3 years or so. Plant corms 3 in. deep and 6–8 in. apart. Cut back on watering during dormancy, but don't let the soil dry out. To plant in bowls, set upright on 1–2 in. of pebbles or in special fiber sold for this purpose, and fill with water to the base of the corms.

COLOCASIA ESCULENTA

ELEPHANT'S EAR, TARO
Araceae
Perennials from tuber

- ✤ **LS, CS, TS; USDA 8-11; OR DIG AND STORE; OR GROW IN POTS**
- ◑ **BEST IN WARM, FILTERED SHADE**
- ◈ **AMPLE WATER**
- ◈ **ALL PARTS MAY CAUSE INDIGESTION IF INGESTED RAW; CONTACT WITH SAP MAY IRRITATE SKIN**

Colocasia esculenta 'Mojito'

Every garden needs its share of bold foliage, and no foliage is bolder than that of elephant's ear. Most Southerners are familiar with the common green-leafed variety of this tropical Asian plant, but many new and exciting forms are making their way to the marketplace. Growing from large tubers, these perennials attain enormous size—some reach 8 ft. or taller—with leathery, heart-shaped leaves that may reach 1½ by 3 ft. Flowers resemble giant callas (*Zantedeschia*) but seldom appear. Some elephant's ears

form a single clump; others spread.

Elephant's ears are effective with tree ferns and other large-leafed tropical plants; they're also good in pots or when massed to create a quick—if temporary—screen. Try combining dark-foliaged selections with yellow- or green-leafed plants. Not browsed by deer.

'Black Coral'. Glossy, deep black leaves with glowing blue veins. Grows 4 ft. high; 3 ft. wide.

'Black Magic'. Spectacular purplish black leaves with purplish red stems. Forms a 5-ft. clump. Great color accent for containers or the back of the border. Hardy to 0°F.

'Diamond Head'. Glossy, chocolate-black leaves are up to 15 inches in. long and ruffled. Forms a 4-ft.-high clump.

'Elena'. Chartreuse leaves with cream-colored veins. Grows 2-4 ft. Spreads.

'Fontanesii.' Purplish black stems rise to 7 ft.; each carries a huge (3-ft.) green leaf with a shiny violet cast. Yellow, papaya-scented flowers to 1 ft. long appear in late summer. Clump forming.

'Maui Gold'. Glossy, lime green leaves form a tight clump to 4 ft. high.

'Mojito'. Bright green leaves marked with dark purple flecks throughout. No two leaves are alike. Forms a 3 ft. clump.

'Illustris'. Charcoal-black, 8-in. leaves with glowing green veins. Grows to 3 ft. tall, 4 ft. wide; spreads slowly in heavy soil, more quickly in loose, rich, wet soil. Good in containers. Hardy to 0°F.

'Nancy's Revenge'. Huge, 25-in.-long, bright green leaves with creamy centers radiating out into the veins. Grows 6 ft. high.

'Puckered Up'. Dark chocolate, rippled, glossy leaves with chocolate stems.

'Ruffles'. Green, 3-ft. leaves with ruffled edges. Forms a 6-ft. clump.

'Thai Giant'. Huge, gray-green leaves are up to 5 ft. long, 4 ft. wide. Large plant can reach 9 ft. high.

'White Lava'. Large glossy green leaves with creamy center radiating out into the veins with a purple spot on each leaf where it attaches to the stalk. 3-ft.-tall clump.

CARE

Choose a planting spot protected from strong wind, which tears leaves. Plant in soil enriched with lots of organic matter, and be sure to provide plenty of moisture (plants thrive in boggy conditions or even standing water). Set tubers about 2 in. deep and 1–1½ ft. apart. Plants grow rapidly in hot, rainy weather, especially when given light applications of fertilizer monthly during growth. Tubers are hardy in the Lower, Coastal, and Tropical South; tops die to the ground with the first frost, then reappear in spring. Elsewhere, dig tubers in fall and store them over winter.

THE STARCHY TUBERS OF ELEPHANT'S EAR ARE A STAPLE FOOD IN POLYNESIA.

LEFT: Colocasia 'Diamond Head'; *RIGHT: C.* 'Maui Gold'

CONOCLINIUM COELESTINUM

WILD AGERATUM, HARDY AGERATUM.
Asteraceae
Perennials

- ✤ **US, MS, LS, CS, TS; USDA 6-11**
- ◐◑ **LIGHT SHADE IN HOTTEST CLIMATES**
- ◈ **REGULAR WATER**

Conoclinium coelestinum

Native to the West Indies, and grows from New Jersey to Missouri, south to Florida and Texas. Reaches 3 ft. tall and 2–3 ft. wide, with freely branching stems set with pairs of toothed, dark green, 4-in. leaves. From summer until frost, bears broad clusters of fluffy blue flowers that exactly resemble those of floss flower (*Ageratum*). Vigorous and freely spreading; invasive in fertile soil. Needs regular water but will not thrive in soggy soil in winter. Attracts bees. Late to appear in spring. Selections include 1½- to 2-ft.-tall 'Album', with pure white flowers; 2-ft. 'Cori', bearing exceptionally clear blue blossoms, later blooming than the species; and compact 'Wayside Form', to just 15 in.

CONRADINA

Lamiaceae
Evergreen shrubs

ZONES VARY BY SPECIES

FULL SUN

LITTLE TO MODERATE WATER

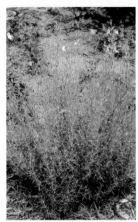
Conradina canescens

Freely branching shrubs that root from trailing branches to make a small-scale ground cover. To 1–1½ ft. high, spreading to 3 ft. or more. Needlelike leaves like those of rosemary (*Rosmarinus*) have a minty scent. Small flowers in spring or early summer. Thrive in lean, sandy soils.

C. canescens. MS, LS, CS; USDA 7-9. SCRUB ROSEMARY, SANDHILL ROSEMARY. Native to sandy coastal plain pinelands of the southeast. Gray-green foliage; pale lavender flowers. Important provider of habitat for endangered beach mouse. Tolerates drought, salt spray. Not browsed by deer. 'Gray Ghost' has gray leaves.

C. verticillata. US, MS, LS; USDA 6-8. CUMBERLAND ROSEMARY. Native to sandy riverbanks of eastern Tennessee and Kentucky. Dark green foliage; lavender-pink blossoms. 'Snowflake' has pure white flowers.

CONSOLIDA AJACIS

LARKSPUR
Ranunculaceae
Annual

US, MS, LS, CS, TS; USDA 6-11

FULL SUN

REGULAR WATER

ALL PARTS, ESPECIALLY SEEDS, ARE POISONOUS IF INGESTED

Consolida ajacis

The colorful spires of larkspur punctuate many a Southerner's garden in spring. Unlike their regal cousins, the delphiniums, these natives of southern Europe flourish in the hot Southern climate. They die after flowering but reseed so readily that they might as well be perennials. The blooms attract butterflies and make superb cut flowers. Larkspurs look great in combination with Shirley poppies (*Papaver rhoeas*).

Plants grow 1–5 ft. tall, about 1 ft. wide. Flowers (double on most types) are up to 1½ in. wide, borne on vertical spikes above deeply cut, almost fernlike leaves; blossom colors include blue, lilac, purple, pink, rose, salmon, and white. Improved strains branch at the base, producing several flower spikes per stalk. Disease-resistant Cannes Mix strain produces sturdy stems of double, tightly packed flowers to 4–5 ft. tall. Great cut flower in a wide range of single and bicolor shades. Giant Imperial strain bears 4- to 5-ft.-tall stalks of double, densely packed blossoms; Regal strain features thick spikes of large flowers similar to delphiniums, grows 4–5 ft. tall. Super Imperial strain produces cone-shaped spikes to 1½ ft. tall.

Heat-tolerant Steeplechase strain, 4–5 ft. tall, bears the largest flowers of all.

Of course, some folks prefer the simpler, "unimproved" larkspurs of their childhoods. Heirloom types include the following.

'Blue Bell'. Soft lilac-blue flowers on 3-ft. spikes. All-America Selections winner in 1934.

'Blue Cloud'. Airy, branching plant producing 3-ft. spikes of deep blue to purple blossoms.

'Earl Grey'. Erect, 3- to 4-ft. spikes of double blooms in a silvery mauve.

'White King'. Double white blossoms on sturdy, 3-ft. stalks. All-America Selections winner in 1937.

CARE

Plant seeds in fall where plants are to grow; sow them on bare soil and barely scratch in (do not mulch over them). For greatest impact, sow in large clusters or sweeps. After flowers fade, allow seeds to drop naturally for a casual look; or collect and store them for fall sowing.

CONVALLARIA MAJALIS

LILY-OF-THE-VALLEY
Asparagaceae
Perennial from rhizome

US, MS, LS; USDA 6-8

PARTIAL TO FULL SHADE

REGULAR WATER

ALL PARTS ARE POISONOUS IF INGESTED

Convallaria majalis

Graceful, creeping, 6- to 8-in.-high ground cover blooms in spring, sending up arching stems that

bear small, nodding, delightfully sweet-scented, waxy white bells along one side. The flowers last only 2 to 3 weeks, but broad, bold, glossy green deciduous leaves are attractive throughout growing season. Bright red berries may appear in autumn; they, like the rest of the plant, are poisonous.

Selections include 'Aureovariegata', with yellow-striped leaves; 'Fortin's Giant', to 12–15 in. high, with extra-large blooms; 'Prolificans', a double-flowered form; and *C. m. rosea*, with light pink blooms. All are charming in woodland gardens; use as carpet between camellias, rhododendrons, pieris, or under deciduous trees or high-branching, not-too-dense evergreens. Best in Upper and Middle South. In Lower South, needs full shade and moist, rich soil that does not dry out. Can become invasive where well adapted.

CARE

Plant clumps or single rhizomes (commonly called pips) in fall before the soil freezes. Give rich soil with ample humus. Set 1½ in. deep; space clumps 1–2 ft. apart, single pips 4–5 in. apart. Spread 1-in. layer of leaf mold, peat moss, or ground bark over bed each year in fall.

Large, prechilled pips are available in December and January and can be potted for bloom indoors in bright light. After bloom, plunge pots in ground in cool, shaded area. When dormant, remove plants from pots and plant in garden; or wash soil off pips, place in clearly labeled plastic bags, and store in vegetable bin of refrigerator until time to repot in December or January.

CONVOLVULUS TRICOLOR

DWARF MORNING GLORY
Convolvulaceae
Annal

🌿 **US, MS, LS, CS, TS; USDA 6-11**

☼ ◑ **BEST IN SUN, TOLERATES SOME SHADE**

💧 **MODERATE WATER**

Convolvulus tricolor 'Red Ensign'

Thanks to its brightly colored, funnel-shaped flowers, this old-fashioned European native is often confused with morning glory (*Ipomoea tricolor*), a twining vine of the tropics. Dwarf morning glory, however, doesn't climb—and its flowers stay open all day, unlike those of its familiar relative. A traditional (if somewhat forgotten) bedding plant, it is excellent for massing, edging, hanging baskets, or containers. Forms a bushy, slightly trailing mound to 12–16 in. high and 2 ft. wide, with narrow, dark green leaves to 1½ in. long. Blooms profusely in summer, covering itself with striking, 1- to 2-in.-wide flowers in royal blue, red, pink, or white, all with a yellow-and-white starburst pattern in the throat. Plants in the Ensign series are compact and free blooming.

CARE

Nick the hard seeds with a knife and soak them in water overnight before sowing. Plant in fall in central and south Florida; elsewhere, plant in spring after the soil has warmed.

CORDIA

Boraginaceae
Evergreen shrubs or trees

🌿 **CS, TS; USDA 9-11**

☼ **FULL SUN**

💧 **WATER NEEDS VARY BY SPECIES**

Cordia boissieri

Members of the forget-me-not family, these are shrubs or trees of tropical or subtropical origin with showy flowers and rough-surfaced, almost sandpapery leaves. Species grown in the U.S. include Southwestern and tropical natives. The two listed here do best in the lower Rio Grande Valley and along the Texas coast from Corpus Christi to Brownsville.

C. boissieri. TEXAS OLIVE, ANACAHUITA. Native to New Mexico, Texas, Mexico. Grayish green, oval leaves to 3 in. long; clusters of white, 2½-in.-wide flowers with yellow throats. Begins flowering in midspring and continues over a long season; may bloom again in autumn. Naturally reaches 8–10 ft. high and 6–8 ft. wide, but can be pruned low (3–5 ft.); can also be trained as small tree. Regular moisture until established; thereafter, give little to moderate water.

C. sebestena. GEIGER TREE. Native to the West Indies. Usually 10–15 ft. (possibly 25 ft.) tall and wide, with dark green leaves 9–12 in. long and half as wide. Brilliant orange-red summer flowers, to 2 in. wide, come in large clusters. Regular water.

CORDYLINE

Asparagaceae
Evergreen palmlike shrubs or trees

🌿 **ZONES VARY BY SPECIES; OR HOUSEPLANT**

☼ ◑ **EXPOSURE NEEDS VARY BY SPECIES; BRIGHT INDIRECT LIGHT**

💧 **WATER NEEDS VARY BY SPECIES**

Cordyline australis 'Royal Star'

These woody plants with swordlike leaves are related to yuccas and agaves, but they have lusher foliage and need more water. Good next to swimming pools. Not browsed by deer. Often sold as *Dracaena*; for true *Dracaena*, see that entry.

C. australis (*Dracaena australis*). GIANT DRACAENA. Zones LS, CS, TS; USDA 8-11. From New Zealand. Hardiest of cordylines, to 15°F. In youth, forms a fountain of 3-ft.-long leaves. Upper leaves are erect; lower ones arch and droop. In maturity, a tree to 20–30 ft. high, 6–12 ft. wide, branching high on trunk, rather stiff looking. Small, fragrant, creamy white flowers appear in long, branched clusters to 3 ft. long in late spring. For a more graceful plant, cut back when young to force multiple trunks. Grows fastest in soil deep enough for big, carrotlike root. Used for tropical effects, with boulders and gravel for desert look, near seashore. Full sun. Moderate to regular water.

Colorful selections include 'Atropurpurea', known as bronze dracaena, with bronzy red leaves; 'Pink Champagne', a more compact plant with narrow leaves edged with white and pink at the base; 'Pink Stripe', bronze with pink margins; 'Red Star', purplish red; 'Southern Splendor', dark green with bright pink margins;

'Sundance', green with a pink midrib; 'Sunrise', dark reddish pink leaves with bright pink margins; and 'Torbay Dazzler', green leaves with cream margins.

C. fruticosa (*C. terminalis*). Zones TS; USDA 10-11. From tropical Southeast Asia. Many named forms with red, pink, yellow, or variegated leaves. White, foot-long flower clusters. Plants are usually started from "logs"—sections of stem that you root. Lay short lengths in mixture of peat moss and sand, covering about one-half their diameter. Keep moist. When shoots grow out and root, cut them off and plant them. Outdoors, it grows 6–8 ft. tall, 3–8 ft. wide in frost-free areas where it receives ample water and soil stays warm; accepts considerable shade. Indoors, it takes ordinary houseplant care; tolerates low light. 'Kiwi', green, pink, white leaves. 'Electra', vivid pink, green, white leaves. 'Dr. Brown', reddish brown wide leaves. 'Ruby', new foliage, pink, darkest to burgundy as it ages, compact habit.

C. hybrids. Zones CS, TS; USDA 9-11. Several cordyline hybrids (parentage not always certain) are extremely colorful plants. Most are shorter than *C. australis*; are clump forming; and have tall clusters of fragrant, white-to-pale lilac flowers in summer. All are great in pots or as an accent. 'Electric Pink' grows 4–5 ft. tall and wide. Narrow, dark maroon leaves are edged in bright pink. 'Festival Grass' forms a fountainlike clump 2–3 ft. high and wide. Glossy, brilliant burgundy leaves are ¾ in. wide and 2–3 ft. long. 'Renegade' forms a tight clump, 2 ft. high and wide with very dark purple, almost black, leaves.

C. stricta. AUSTRALIAN DRACAENA. Zones TS; USDA 10-11. Australian native; hardy to 26°F. Slender, erect stems to 2 ft. long, clustered at base or branching low. Leaves are 2 ft. long, dark green with hint of purple. Fragrant lavender flowers in branched clusters to 2 ft. long, very decorative in spring. To 15 ft. tall and 6 ft. wide but can be kept lower by cutting tall canes to ground; new canes replace them. Long cuttings in ground will root quickly. Fine container plant indoors or out; good in sunrooms or side gardens. Needs some shade. Regular water.

COREOPSIS
Asteraceae
Perennials and annuals

US, MS, LS, CS; USDA 6-9; EXCEPT AS NOTED

FULL SUN, EXCEPT AS NOTED

WATER NEEDS VARY BY SPECIES

Coreopsis 'Jethro Tull'

Easily grown members of sunflower family, yielding a profusion of yellow, orange, maroon, or reddish flowers over a long bloom season. Easy to propagate—annuals from seed sown in place or in pots, perennials from seed or division of root crown. Tend to self-sow; seeds attract birds. Not browsed by deer.

C. auriculata 'Nana'. DWARF-EARED COREOPSIS. Perennial. Selection of a species native to the southeastern U.S. Forms a 5- to 6-in.-high mat of medium green, 2- to 5-in.-long leaves; under ideal conditions, spreads by stolons to form a 2-ft.-wide clump in a year. Bright orange-yellow, 1- to 2½-in.-wide flowers rise well above the foliage; bloom is heaviest in spring, but flowers keep on coming over a long season if you deadhead regularly. Best used in front of taller plants, in borders, or as edging. Moderate water. *C. a.* 'Zamphir' is similar but grows 1-1½ ft. high and wide, with golden yellow, fluted petals.

C. grandiflora. BIGFLOWER COREOPSIS. Perennial. From the central and southeastern U.S. Narrow, dark green leaves with three to five lobes form a foliage clump 1–2 ft. high, spreading to 3 ft. wide. Bright yellow, 2½- to 3-in.-wide flowers bloom all summer on long, slender stems high above foliage. 'Sunburst' has large semidouble flowers; it blooms the first year from seed sown early in spring, then spreads by self-sowing. 'Early Sunrise' is similar but may begin blooming in late spring. 'Flying Saucers' is a nearly sterile selection with flat, single, 2-in. yellow flowers over a long period; 'Sunray' is a dense, compact selection with double and semidouble flowers. 'Corey Yellow' has golden yellow flowers with dark red center, and 'Santa Fe Yellow' is semidouble with golden yellow flowers.

All are tough enough for roadside planting. Moderate water.

C. hybrids. A beguiling array of hybrid coreopsis, both annuals and perennials, have stormed nurseries and garden centers. They offer a wide range of flower colors and varied habits. They bloom from late spring through summer and into fall, and can also be treated as annuals. Most grow about 1½–2 ft. tall and 2½ ft. wide, and look best with moderate water. 'Autumn Blush' bears butter-yellow flowers with red centers. As the weather cools, the flowers blush reddish pink. 'Crème Brûlée' bears abundant, deep yellow blooms on compact plants with good mildew resistance. 'Jethro Tull' grows 18 in. tall and bears golden-yellow flowers with unusual, tubular rays. 'Limerock Ruby' has ruby-red flowers to 1 in. wide. 'Limerock Passion' is similar, but with yellow-centered, lavender-pink flowers. 'Sienna Sunset' has rich salmon-orange blooms and excellent disease resistance. 'Tequila Sunrise' is compact, to 1½ ft. high and 1 ft. wide. Narrow, olive-green leaves are irregularly variegated with cream and yellow, with touches of pinkish red in spring and deeper red in fall. Golden yellow flowers with deep orange-red centers. Members of the Hardy Jewel series are compact perennials, including 'Citrine', bright yellow; 'Ruby Frost', deep red with white edges; 'Garnet', garnet red; and 'Pink Sapphire', bright purplish pink.

Hybrid annual coreopsis include compact 'Little Penny', which grows less than a foot tall and twice as wide and has small copper-red blooms; the mounding (under a foot high) Punch series in bright shades of red, yellow, orange, and red-and-white bicolors; and the Lemon-

TOP: Coreopsis 'Ruby Frost'; *MIDDLE: C. verticillata* 'Moonbeam'; *C.* 'Limerock Passion'; *BOTTOM: C.* 'Sienna Sunset'

ade series, with feathery golden foliage and red, pink, or rose flowers. Many are perennials in mild-winter areas. Most perform best in the optimum conditions of a container garden.

C. lanceolata. LANCE COREOPSIS. Perennial from the central and southern U.S. To 1–2 ft. high, 1–1½ ft. wide. Narrow, somewhat hairy, medium green leaves, mostly in a tuft near plant's base; some leaves on lower stem have a few lobes. Yellow, 1½- to 2-in. flowers on pale green stems

bloom from spring to summer, make excellent cut flowers. When well established, plant persists year after year. Moderate water.

C. rosea. ROSE COREOPSIS. Perennial. Zones US, MS, LS; USDA 6-8. Native from Nova Scotia to Delaware. Fine-textured plant with bright green foliage; grows 1½–2 ft. tall, 1 ft. wide, with 1-in.-wide, yellow-centered pink flowers from summer to fall. 'Heaven's Gate' has fine leaf texture with burgundy flowers. Flower fades in high light to a white flower with a burgundy center. 'Sweet Dreams' has threadlike leaves and masses of big white flowers with a raspberry-colored ring surrounding a golden eye. Shorter lived than other species. Prefers moist soil.

C. tinctoria. CALLIOPSIS, ANNUAL COREOPSIS. Annual. Zones US, MS, LS, CS, TS; USDA 6-11. Native to much of North America. Slender, upright, wiry-stemmed plant 1½–3 ft. tall, 1–1½ ft. wide; much like cosmos in growth habit. Smooth, medium to dark green leaves and smooth stems. Flowers to 1 in. wide, with purple-brown centers; rays are yellow, maroon, bronze, or reddish rays, banded with contrasting colors. Dwarf and double types are also available. Blooms in spring and summer, except where hot, humid weather shortens the show. Sow seed in place in dryish soil and full sun. Little to moderate water.

C. tripteris. TALL COREOPSIS. Perennial. Native to prairies, open woods, and roadsides from Ontario south to Georgia, Mississippi, and Louisiana. To 5–7 ft. tall, 4 ft. wide. Shiny, dark green, three-leafleted leaves. Blooms from midsummer into fall, carrying many 2-in., brown-eyed, butter-yellow flowers on branching stems. Both foliage and flowers are anise scented. Use at the back of a border or in a wildflower or butterfly garden. Prefers moist soil and some shade. 'Lightning Flash' blooms heavier and longer with age; single yellow flower atop yellow foliage.

C. verticillata. THREADLEAF COREOPSIS. Perennial. Native from Maryland to Florida, west to Arkansas. To 2½–3 ft. tall, half as broad; many erect or slightly leaning stems carry many whorls of medium green, finely divided, very narrow leaves. At stem tips are 2-in., bright yellow daisies, freely borne over a long summer and autumn season. One of the most tolerant of drought and neglect. 'Fool's Gold' has variegated foliage with single yellow flower, while 'Golden Gain' has bright yellow flowers on dense clumps of dark green foliage. 'Moonbeam', to 1½–2 ft. tall, has pale yellow blooms; 'Zagreb', to 1 ft., bears golden yellow flowers. Divide in fall or spring every third year to maintain vigor. Little to moderate water.

CORIANDRUM SATIVUM
CILANTRO, CORIANDER
Apiaceae
Annual

🌿 **US, MS, LS, CS, TS; USDA 6-11**

☼ ◐ **LIGHT SHADE IN HOTTEST CLIMATES**

💧 **REGULAR WATER**

Coriandrum sativum

Mediterranean native grows 1–1½ ft. high, 9 in. wide. Delicate, parsleylike foliage; flat clusters of pinkish white flowers in summer. Both fresh leaves and seeds are widely used as seasoning. Leaves (usually called cilantro) are popular in salads, salsa, and many cooked dishes; crush the aromatic seeds (called coriander) for use in sausage, beans, stews, baked goods.

CARE

Cilantro is taprooted and transplants poorly, so start from seed (including coriander seed sold in grocery stores). Sow in fall in Lower, Coastal, and Tropical South. Elsewhere, sow in early spring. Grow in good, well-drained soil. Cilantro grows and flowers extremely quickly ('Delfino', with finely cut leaves, and 'Calypso' are slower to flower). Keep it coming by succession planting every couple of weeks, and trim flower heads as soon as they appear. Or, sow densely in bands 8–12 in. wide and use scissors to shear off leaves (almost to the base of the plant). Plants will regrow. You can also sow in pots.

If you are growing cilantro for seeds only, two or three plants is all you need. To collect seeds, pull up whole plants when seed heads begin to turn gray-brown;

then put the plants headfirst into bags and shake them, or hang them over paper and let the seeds drop.

CORN
Poaceae
Annual

🌿 **US, MS, LS, CS, TS; USDA 6-11**

☼ **FULL SUN**

💧 **REGULAR WATER**

Corn

Nothing beats the taste of sweet corn picked fresh from the garden. Trouble is, corn takes considerable space to produce a decent crop, so it's better suited to large country gardens than to small suburban plots. Another potential drawback is that once sweet corn is picked, its sugar changes to starch nearly as fast as you can run the ears inside to a pot of boiling water. Still, many folks yearn for traditional kinds of sweet corn, such as 'Early Sunglow' (yellow, 62 days from planting to harvest), 'Golden Queen' (yellow, 92 days), 'Merit' (yellow, 80 days), and the all-time favorite 'Silver Queen' (white, 92 days). For information on new hybrids that stay sweet much longer after they're picked, see "Improved sweet corn" (below).

Improved sweet corn. There are two basic classes. The first, called sugary enhanced corn, is about as sweet as or slightly sweeter than regular sweet corn, but the "se" gene slows the conversion of sugar to starch. Among the top sugary enhanced selections are 'Breeder's Choice' (yellow, 73 days), 'Bodacious' (yellow, 75 days), 'Trinity' (bicolor, 70 days), 'Sugar Buns' (yellow, 60

days), and 'Ambrosia' (bicolor, 75 days).

The second class, known as supersweet corn, contains twice as much sugar as regular sweet corn. It's sometimes called "sh2" corn, because the gene responsible for the added sweetness also causes dry kernels to look shrunken. Supersweet corn stays sweet for days after picking, as long as you refrigerate it promptly. Recommended selections include 'How Sweet It Is' (white, 87 days), 'Honey 'N' Pearl' (bicolor, 76 days), 'Early Xtra-Sweet' (yellow, 71 days), 'Illini Xtra-Sweet' (yellow, 85 days), 'Florida Staysweet' (yellow, 87 days), and 'Summer Sweet 7210' (yellow, 78 days).

An increasing number of synergistic (sy) varieties are also sold; they blend sugar-enhanced and supersweet genes. 'Honey Select' and the bicolored 'Frisky' and 'Montauk' selections are examples.

It's perfectly fine to plant sugary enhanced types near regular sweet corn—but don't let supersweet types cross-pollinate with other sweet corn (either regular or sugary enhanced), or the kernels of both will be tough and starchy. Isolate supersweets from other types either by distance (at least 200 ft. away) or by time (stagger plantings so that different types don't tassel at the same time).

Heirloom sweet corn. Unlike hybrid corn, heirloom types are open-pollinated, which means they come true from seed. 'Golden Bantam' (yellow, 78 days) was introduced in 1902 and is still the best choice for small spaces, as its stalks reach only 5–6 ft.; ripened ears must be rushed to the cooking pot to taste sweet. 'Stowell's Evergreen' (white, 98 days), introduced in 1856, remains in the milky stage a long time and is well adapted to the Upper South. 'Country Gentleman' (white, 93 days), introduced in 1891, is a shoepeg corn (with small kernels that are not arranged in rows) with an extended milky stage. 'Texas Honey June' (white, 97 days) has a sweet flavor reminiscent of honey.

Dent corn. Starchy dent corns (named for the dent in the seed's crown) are well adapted to the Southeast and Midwest; many are heirloom types, dating back to the mid-1800s. They are primarily

HOW TO GROW CORN

PLANTING Corn is a warm-weather crop, so don't rush planting in spring: Seeds planted in soil cooler than 65°F will simply rot. Plant at least 2 weeks after the last frost in loose, fertile, well-drained soil. If you plant just a few long, single rows, you won't get much corn, because pollen must be transferred from the tassels (held atop the plants) to the silks (held lower down). A stiff wind can send pollen flying far beyond its mark, so you should always plant in blocks of at least five rows deep.

Before planting, work into the soil 1 cup of 10-10-10 or 10-14-10 fertilizer per 10 ft. of row. Plant seeds 1 in. deep (¾ in. deep for supersweet types), in rows spaced 2–3 ft. apart. Most types are capable of producing two or more ears per stalk. However, rows planted less than 2 ft. apart generally yield one ear per stalk. When seedlings are 6 in. tall, thin them to 1 ft. apart. To extend the harvest, make three or four more plantings at 2-week intervals—or plant early, midseason, and late selections.

WATERING AND FEEDING Regular watering is critical, especially when tassels are being formed. Drought-stressed plants produce puny ears with missing kernels. Corn has a hefty appetite. Fertilize plants when they're 8 in. tall and again when they've reached 18 in.; each time, apply ½ cup of controlled-release 10-14-10 fertilizer per 10 ft. of row.

HARVESTING Check your crop when the ears are plump and the silks have withered; corn is usually ready for harvest 3 weeks after the silks first appear. To test, pull back the husks and try popping a kernel with your thumbnail. It should squirt milky juice; watery juice means that corn isn't ready to eat.

CHALLENGES Corn earworm is the principal insect pest. There is no simple control. Most gardeners expect some ears to show worm damage at the silk ends, and they just cut off those ends. The prevention (it's tedious) goes like this: 3 to 7 days after silks appear, use a medicine dropper to put two drops of mineral oil just inside the tip of each ear. As an alternative, plant selections with tight husks that discourage earworms; these include 'Country Gentleman', 'Hickory King', and 'Texas Honey June'.

used for roasting and for making cornmeal and hominy. 'Blue Clarage' (90 days) features solid blue ears (one ear per stalk) and has a higher sugar content than most dents; in the milky stage, it can be eaten fresh. 'Hickory King' (white, 85 days) produces two ears per stalk and is the best for hominy. Drought-tolerant 'Tennessee Red Cob' (120 days) bears red cobs with white kernels, two ears per stalk. It is excellent for cornmeal, and the cob makes an attractive pipe.

Baby corn. Contrary to popular belief, baby corn isn't a miniature variety. It's just corn harvested very early, when the ears are only a few inches long. The tender ears may be pickled or used fresh in salads or Asian cuisine. Plant seeds 1–2 in. apart; thin seedlings to 4 in. apart. Harvest shortly after the first silks appear, which may be only a few weeks after sowing. 'Bonus' (yellow, 32 days) produces 3-in. ears that are ready to pick when the plant is only 1½ ft. tall.

Ornamental corn. Some kinds of corn are grown for the beauty of their shelled ears rather than for eating. Calico, Indian, Squaw, and Rainbow are some names given to strains with intensely colored kernels—red, brown, blue, gray, black, bright yellow, or mixed colors. 'Indian Summer' has brightly colored, edible kernels. Grow ornamental corn well away from sweet corn; mix of pollen can affect the latter's flavor. For ornamental display, grow like sweet corn, but let ears ripen fully; silks will be withered, husks will turn straw color, and kernels will be firm. Cut ear from plant, including 1½ in. of stalk below ear; pull back husks (leave attached to ears), and dry thoroughly.

Zea mays japonica includes several kinds of corn grown for ornamental foliage. One occasionally sold is 'Gracilis', a dwarf form with bright green leaves striped white.

Popcorn. Grow and harvest just like ornamental corn. When ears are thoroughly dry, rub kernels off cobs, and store in a dry place. White, red, and yellow kinds of popcorn look like other types of corn.

Strawberry popcorn, grown either for its ornamental value or for popping, has stubby, fat, strawberrylike ears packed with red kernels. Don't plant popcorn near sweet corn; pollen of one kind can affect characteristics of another.

CORNUS
DOGWOOD
Cornaceae
Deciduous shrubs and trees, except as noted

🌿 **ZONES VARY BY SPECIES**

☼ ◑ **FULL SUN OR LIGHT SHADE, EXCEPT AS NOTED**

💧 **REGULAR WATER, EXCEPT AS NOTED**

Cornus florida 'Cherokee Chief'

For many Southerners, there's only one dogwood: flowering dogwood (*Cornus florida*), widely considered the region's finest ornamental tree. But many types of dogwood exist, from good-sized, single-trunked trees to small, multistemmed, stoloniferous shrubs; there's even a ground-covering perennial dogwood. Some are spectacular in bloom, others barely noticeable. Some sport dazzling fall foliage; others don't. And even dogwoods lacking showy flowers or foliage have their strong points. Some flaunt colorful bark; others produce attractive fruits that feed birds and other wildlife.

What appear to be flower petals in many dogwoods are in fact bracts—petal-like modified leaves. These surround the inconspicuous true flowers.

C. alba. TATARIAN DOGWOOD. Shrub. Zones US, MS; USDA 6-7. Native to Siberia, northern China, Korea. In cold-winter areas, the bare, blood-red twigs are colorful against the snow. Upright to about 10 ft. high; wide spreading, eventually producing a thicket of many stems. Branches densely clothed with leaves 2½–5 in. long, to 2½ in. wide, deep rich green above, lighter beneath; turn reddish purple in fall. For best color, cut ⅓ of oldest stems to ground each spring. Small, fragrant, creamy white flowers in 1- to 2-in.-wide, flattish clusters in spring. Small whitish fruits.

Selections include the following. In all, new wood is brightest; cut back in spring to force new growth.

'Bud's Yellow'. Bright yellow stems. Disease resistance makes it a good substitute for *C. sericea* 'Flaviramea'.

'Elegantissima' ('Argenteomarginata'). Showy green-and-white leaves on red stems.

'Gouchaltii'. Leaves have yellow borders suffused with pink.

'Ivory Halo'. Compact, to 3–6 ft. tall and wide; red stems hold white-edged green leaves.

'Sibirica'. SIBERIAN DOGWOOD. Smaller and not as wide spreading as species; grows to about 7 ft. high and 5 ft. wide. Gleaming coral-red branches. There is also a variegated form.

'Spaethii'. Leaves edged with gold.

C. alternifolia. PAGODA DOGWOOD. Shrub or small tree. Zones US, MS; USDA 6-7. From eastern North America. Multitrunked, to 20 ft. high and wide. Strong horizontal branching pattern makes attractive winter silhouette. Light green leaves to 5 in. long turn reddish purple in fall. Small clusters of creamy spring flowers are not showy. Small but handsome blue-black fruits follow the flowers. Foliage of 'Argentea' has white markings.

C. angustata 'Elsbry'. EMPRESS OF CHINA DOGWOOD. Evergreen tree. Zones US, MS, LS;

USDA 6-8. Species is native to Japan, Korea, and China. Reaches 15-18 ft. high and up to 15 ft. wide. Masses of large, creamy white flowers late spring into summer followed by translucent red, strawberrylike fruit. Best with protection from afternoon sun.

C. canadensis. BUNCH-BERRY. Perennial. Zones US, MS; USDA 6-7. Native from southern Greenland to northern areas of North America. Ground cover 6–9 in. high, found in the wild under trees by lakes and streams. Creeping rootstocks send up stems topped by whorls of oval or roundish, 1- to 2-in.-long, deep green leaves that turn yellow in fall, die down in winter. In late spring or early summer, plants bear small, compact clusters of tiny flowers surrounded by (usually) four oval, ½- to ¾-in., pure white bracts. Clusters of small, shiny red fruits follow in late summer.

Best performance in full shade in cool mountain climates, in acid soil with generous amounts of organic matter. Set out small plants from pots about 1 ft. apart. Small rooted pieces gathered from the woods may not establish easily. Excellent with rhododendrons, ferns, trilliums, lilies.

C. drummondii. ROUGH-LEAF DOGWOOD. Shrub or small tree. Zones US, MS, LS, CS; USDA 6-9. Native from Texas to Virginia and north to Ontario. To 15–20 ft. tall, spreading to 12 ft. Shrubby and rugged, quite unlike elegant *C. florida*; likely to form a thicket, though it can be trained to make a small tree. Grows quickly. Soft, furry olive-green leaves 1½–3½ in. long hang a little limply from branches. Blooms briefly in early spring, bearing white blossoms (true flowers, not bracts) in clusters to 3 in. across, followed by hard white fruit loved by birds. Planted mostly for its striking orange, red, and purple fall foliage and its adaptability—takes rocky limestone soils, clay, wetlands, drought, full sun or full shade. A beautiful addition to a natural garden; good understory plant in the deep shade of tall trees. 'Lemon Drops' has light yellow flowers.

C. florida. FLOWERING DOGWOOD. Tree. Zones US, MS, LS, CS; USDA 6-9. Native to eastern U.S., from New England to central Florida. Has been called

the most beautiful native tree of North America. Blossom is the state flower of North Carolina and Virginia. May reach 40 ft. high and wide, but 20–30 ft. more common. Low branching, with a fairly horizontal branch pattern, upturned branch tips; makes beautiful winter silhouette. Old trees are broadly pyramidal but rather flat topped. Blooms profusely in midspring before leaves expand, almost covering itself with small flower clusters surrounded by four roundish, inch-wide bracts with notched tips. White is the usual color in the wild, but named selections (see below) also offer bracts in pink shades to nearly red. Only the white-bracted sorts seem to succeed in Florida, however. Oval leaves, 2–6 in. long, 2½ in. wide, are bright green above, lighter beneath; they turn glowing red and crimson before they drop. Clusters of showy, oval, scarlet fruits last into winter or until birds eat them.

Flowering dogwood grows fine in full sun if planted in deep, fertile soil that retains moisture. In shallow, dry, or rocky soil, it often leaf-scorches badly in summer droughts. Succeeds most reliably as an understory tree where it receives light shade; in heavy shade, it will not bloom.

Unfortunately, an anthracnose fungus has been infecting and destroying these trees throughout their range. Dieback symptoms show up first in lower branches and can spread to whole tree. Trees growing at high elevations and in shade are more susceptible. Borers often attack trunks and limbs of stressed trees. Variegated selections generally have more disease problems. *C. florida* has been bred with *C. kousa* to produce more disease-resistant hybrids; see *C. x rutgersensis*.

'Appalachian Joy'. Large white bracts, often more than the normal four. Resists powdery mildew.

'Appalachian Spring'. Large white bracts; attractive foliage. Resists anthracnose and mildew. Fast grower. Upright, symmetrical.

'Cherokee Brave'. Red bracts with white centers. Resists mildew and anthracnose.

'Cherokee Chief'. Deep rosy red bracts, paler at base. Good resistance to anthracnose and mildew.

'Cherokee Daybreak'. Variegated green-and-white leaves turn pink and red in fall. White bracts.

'Cherokee Princess'. Unusually heavy display of large white blooms. Begins blooming while young.

'Cherokee Sunset'. Variegated green-and-yellow leaves turn redish purple in fall. Reddish bracts. Resistant to anthracnose, but susceptible to mildew.

'Cloud 9'. Blooms young and heavily. Tolerates heat and lack of winter chill better than other selections. White bracts are rounded and overlapping.

'Junior Miss'. Deep pink bracts, paler at center. Resists anthracnose.

'Pendula'. Drooping branches give it a weeping look. White bracts.

'Pluribracteata'. Two sets of white bracts (some large, many tiny aborted ones) give appearance of double flowers. Resists anthracnose and mildew.

'Pygmy'. White-flowered dwarf; blooms at 2 ft. tall. Only 12 ft. tall after 20 years.

'Red Pygmy'. Red-flowered dwarf; matures at 7 feet.

'Royal Red'. Big, deep red bracts. Leaves are red when young, turn red again in fall.

'Spring Grove'. Extra-large bracts and very floriferous; often bears two or three flower buds at branch tips. Resists anthracnose.

'Weaver's White'. Large white bracts. Good resistance to anthracnose and mildew.

'Welch's Bay Beauty'. Doubled white bracts, 4-5 in. wide. Tolerant of spot anthracnose.

C. kousa. KOUSA DOGWOOD. Shrub or small tree. Zones US, MS, LS; USDA 6-8. Native to Japan and Korea. Later blooming (late spring or early summer) than other flowering dogwoods. Can be big multistemmed shrub or (with training) small tree to 20 ft. tall and wide (or even larger). Delicate limb structure and spreading, dense horizontal growth habit. Lustrous medium green leaves, 4 in. long, have rusty brown hairs at base of veins on undersurface. Yellow or scarlet fall color. Handsome peeling bark.

Flowers are carried along tops of branches and show above the leaves. Narrow, 2- to 3-in.-long bracts with slender, pointed tips are creamy white, turning pink

along edges. In late summer and fall, red fruits like big raspberries hang below branches. This species is less susceptible to diseases than *C. florida* and has been bred with the latter to produce resistant hybrids; see *C. x rutgersensis*.

C. kousa selections include the following.

'Autumn Rose'. To 20 ft. tall, 25 ft. wide. Leaves are light green when new, pink to red in fall.

C. k. chinensis. CHINESE DOGWOOD. Chinese native to 15–30 ft. tall and wide, with larger leaves and larger bracts than the species.

'Gold Star'. To 12 ft. tall and wide, with yellow-centered green leaves.

'Heart Throb'. Large, deep red to rose-pink flowers over a long period.

'National'. To 25–30 ft. tall, 12–15 ft. wide, with bright red fall color. Blooms earlier than the species.

'Satomi'. ('Satomi Red', 'Rosabella'). Reaches 20 ft. tall and wide. Rose red bracts.

'Summer Stars'. To 25 ft. tall, 18 ft. wide, with vase-shaped form. Lavish bloom; later than the species.

'Wolf Eyes'. Gray-green leaves edged with white. Pinkish red fall color. 'Samaritan' and 'Summer Fun' are other excellent selections with white-variegated leaves.

C. mas. CORNELIAN CHERRY. Shrub or small tree. Zones US, MS, LS; USDA 6-8. Pest-free dogwood native to southern Europe and Asia. Usually an airy, twiggy shrub but can be trained as a small tree, 15–20 ft. high and wide. Tough and adaptable; tolerates most well-drained soils. Provides a progression of color throughout the year. One of earliest dogwoods to bloom, bearing clustered masses of small, soft yellow blossoms on bare twigs in late winter or early spring. Shiny green, oval, 2- to 4-in.-long leaves turn yellow in fall; some forms turn red. Autumn color is enhanced by clusters of bright scarlet, cherry-size fruits that hang on until birds get them. Fruits are edible and are frequently used in making preserves. In winter, flaking bark mottled in gray and tan provides interest. 'Golden Glory' is slightly more upright; produces more bloom. 'Spring Grove' is a generous bloomer with shiny, dark green leaves and no suckers. 'Variegata' features leaves marbled creamy white.

C. officinalis. JAPANESE CORNEL DOGWOOD. Shrub or small tree. Zones US, MS, LS; USDA 6-8. Similar to *C. mas* but blooms slightly earlier and has handsome bark in gray, brown, and orange. Showier in bloom than *C. mas* and a better performer in the Lower South. 'Kintoki' is a heavy-blooming, slightly smaller tree.

C. racemosa. GRAY DOGWOOD. Shrub or small tree. Zones US, MS, LS; USDA 6-8. Native from Minnesota to Maine, south to Nebraska and Georgia. To 10–15 ft. high and wide; will spread even wider, but this can be controlled by removing suckers. Creamy white flowers are held in racemes at branch tips in late spring. Attractive blue-green, 2- to 4-in.-long leaves turn deep purplish red in fall and contrast nicely with white fruits. Adapts to various soils and moisture levels; tolerates air pollution and a good bit of shade.

C. x rutgersensis. STELLAR DOGWOOD. Tree. Zones US, MS, LS.; USDA 6-8 This hybrid between *C. florida* and *C. kousa* has greater disease resistance than *C. florida*. Single-stemmed tree to about 20 ft. tall, 25–30 ft. wide. Bloom time falls between the midspring bloom of *C. florida* and the late spring or early summer bloom of *C. kousa*; bracts are produced with the leaves. 'Stellar Pink' has pink bracts; 'Aurora', 'Galaxy', and 'Ruth Ellen' bear broad white bracts; 'Constellation' and 'Stardust' have narrower white bracts. 'Constellation' has the most upright growth habit; other selections are more rounded. 'Celestial Shadow' has large white bracts and leaves variegated yellow and green. All have brilliant red fall leaves.

C. sanguinea. BLOODTWIG DOGWOOD. Shrub. Zones US, MS; USDA 6-7. Multistemmed growth to 12 ft. high, about 8 ft. wide, with dark green, 1½ to 3-in.-long leaves. Greenish white late-spring flowers in 2-in. clusters are followed by black fruits. Big show comes in fall, with dark blood-red foliage color, and in winter, when purplish to dark red twigs and branches are on display. 'Midwinter Fire' has brilliant orange-red fall color, red fruits. Older stems

turn gray. Cut these to the ground in spring to encourage growth of new red stems.

C. sericea (*C. stolonifera*). Shrub. Zones US, MS; USDA 6-7. Native to moist places, eastern North America and Northern California to Alaska. Another dogwood with brilliant red fall foliage and bright red winter twigs that look striking against a snowy backdrop. Grows rapidly to 7–9 ft. high; spreads to 12 ft. or wider by creeping underground stems and rooting branches. Leaves oval, to 1½–2½ in. long, fresh deep green. Blooms throughout the summer months, bearing small, creamy white flowers in 2-in.-wide clusters among the leaves; blooms are followed by white or bluish fruits. Canker disease can devastate this shrub, causing dieback.

Good space filler in moist ground (good for holding banks); also good planted along property line as a screen. To control spread, use a spade to cut off roots; also trim branches that touch ground. Shade tolerant.

'Alleman's'. To 4–6 ft. tall, with red winter stems.

'Arctic Fire'. Dark red stems on a compact, 3- to 4-ft.-tall plant.

'Arctic Sun'. Yellow stems tipped red; grows 3–4 ft. tall.

'Cardinal'. Cherry-red stems.

'Flaviramea'. YELLOWTWIG DOGWOOD. Yellow twigs and branches. Very susceptible to canker disease.

'Isanti'. Compact growth to 5 ft. tall. Bright red stems.

'Hedgerow's Gold'. Foliage variegated green and gold. Red stems.

'Silver and Gold'. Yellow branches and cream-edged green leaves.

C. 'Venus'. Tree. Zones US, MS, LS, CS; USDA 6-9. A multi-species hybrid that combines large white flowers with disease resistance. More vigorous that *C. kousa*, it grows 14-18 ft. tall and 18-24 ft. wide.

TOP: Cornus florida; BOTTOM: Cornus florida in fall color; C. kousa fruit and leaves in the fall

HOW TO GROW DOGWOODS

EXPOSURE Most take full sun or light shade. Excellent lawn, patio, or understory tree; not recommended for planting near pavement.

SOIL Moist, acid (most), well drained, with lots of organic matter.

WATERING Shallow-rooted tree is susceptible to summer drought. Water deeply during dry spells to prevent scorched leaves, but do not wet foliage.

MULCHING Apply a thick layer of mulch beneath tree to cool soil, conserve moisture. Keep mulch a few inches away from trunk.

PRUNING Seldom necessary except to remove weak or crossed branches; prune immediately after bloom.

CORTADERIA SELLOANA

PAMPAS GRASS
Poaceae
Perennial grass

MS, LS, CS, TS; USDA 7-11, EXCEPT AS NOTED

FULL SUN

ANY AMOUNT OF WATER

Cortaderia selloana

If Southerners know one ornamental grass well, this is it. Thanks to its ease of culture, imposing stature, and exceedingly showy plumes, pampas grass has been showcased throughout the Deep South to the point of cliché. Native to Argentina, it grows very fast in good soil in warm climates—from gallon-size transplant to 8-ft. giant in one season. Established clumps can reach 10–12 ft. tall and wide. Each plant forms a fountain of narrow, cascading, medium green, sawtoothed leaves (be careful—they can cut you). Long stalks bearing 1- to 3-ft., white to chamois or pink flower plumes rise above the foliage in late summer. Plants may be either male or female; females have much showier plumes, but unfortunately, few garden centers sell pampas grass by sex. To ensure that you get a showy specimen, buy a plant in bloom or obtain a division from a known female plant. Or purchase a named selection, like those listed below.

Regular pampas grass doesn't do well in the colder winters of the Upper South and often fails to bloom there, but cold-hardy selections (noted below) solve that problem.

Use pampas grass as a specimen, vertical accent, or tall screen. Especially effective when massed near water. Most are somewhat taller than wide when not in bloom. Not browsed by deer.

'Andes Silver'. To 7 ft. tall in bloom. Cold-hardy selection with silver flower plumes.

'Patagonia'. To 6 ft. tall in bloom. Leaves have a blue-gray cast; flower plumes are silver. Cold hardy.

'Pumila' ('Ivory Feathers'). Smaller than species and a better fit for most home gardens. Gray-green leaves form a clump to 3 ft. tall, 4 ft. wide; white flower plumes increase the height to 6 ft.

'Rosea' ('Rosa Feder'). To 8 ft. tall in bloom. Silvery white plumes with a pink cast.

'Sun Stripe'. Yellow-striped foliage in clumps to 4 ft. tall, 5 ft. wide. White flower plumes rise to 6 ft. high.

'Sunningdale Silver'. Large, sturdy selection that may reach 10 ft. tall and 8 ft. wide in flower. Huge, fluffy, creamy white plumes.

CARE

Pampas grass likes heat, sun, and well-drained soil. It tolerates wind, sand, and salt spray, so it's ideal for growing at the beach. To renew ragged-looking clumps, cut them to within a foot or two of the ground in late winter, using shears or hedge trimmers.

CORYDALIS

Papaveraceae
Perennials

US, MS; USDA 6-7

PARTIAL SHADE

REGULAR WATER

Corydalis lutea

Handsome clumps of dainty, divided leaves like those of bleeding heart (*Dicentra*, to which it is closely related) or maidenhair fern (*Adiantum*). Clusters of small, spurred flowers. Plant in rich, moist soil. Effective in rock crevices, in open woodland, near pool or streamside. Divide clumps or sow seed in spring or fall. Plants self-sow. Summer-flowering species may stop flowering during hottest months; keep soil moist to encourage some continued bloom.

C. 'Blackberry Wine'. Creeping habit, 10–16 in. high and wide. Small, fragrant purple flowers. Will spill over walls. 'Berry Exciting' is similar except has soft yellow foliage and is sterile, so it won't reseed.

C. cheilanthifolius. Hardy Chinese native to 8–10 in. high and wide. Fernlike green foliage; clusters of yellow, ½-in.-long flowers in spring.

C. elata. Native to China. Upright grower to 15 in. high, 2–3 ft. wide. Heat-tolerant species that won't go dormant in summer; the best choice for the South. Cobalt-blue blossoms are carried above attractive, fleshy green leaves from spring through summer. Tantalizing fragrance has been described as a combination of gardenia and coconut.

C. flexuosa. BLUE CORYDALIS. From western China. Typically to 1 ft. high, 8 in. wide, but when conditions are favorable, it rapidly spreads more widely by bulblets on the roots. Finely divided blue-green leaves. Spikelike clusters of blue flowers appear in early spring, often continuing into summer. May go dormant in summer, especially in hot climates, but will reappear the following spring. Selections include gentian-blue 'Blue Panda', pure sky-blue 'China Blue', blue-and-lavender 'Nightshade', and lavender-to-light blue 'Père David'. 'Purple Leaf', the earliest bloomer, has purplish blue flowers and purple-blotched green leaves.

C. heterocarpa. Native to Japan. Makes a 3- by 3-ft. blue-green mound. Rich yellow flowers cover the plant in late winter or early spring and continue to bloom intermittently throughout the growing season.

C. lutea. YELLOW CORYDALIS. Native to southern Europe. Grows to 15 in. tall, 1 ft. wide. Many-stemmed plant with masses of gray-green foliage. Bears golden yellow, ¾-in.-long, short-spurred flowers throughout summer.

C. ophiocarpa. From the Himalayas. To 1½ ft. tall and wide, 3 ft. tall in flower. Gray-green, feathery evergreen foliage. Blooms in spring, bearing cream-colored flowers with dark red tips.

C. solida. FUMEWORT. From northern Europe, Asia. Grows from tubers (sometimes available from bulb catalogs). To 10 in. high and 8 in. wide, with gray-green leaves and erect clusters of up to 20 purplish red, inch-long flowers in spring.

CORYLOPSIS

WINTER HAZEL
Hamamelidaceae
Deciduous shrubs

US, MS, LS; USDA 6-8

FULL SUN OR PARTIAL SHADE

REGULAR WATER

Corylopsis pauciflora

These delightful Asian natives are valued for sweet-scented, bell-shaped, soft yellow flowers that hang in short, chainlike clusters on bare branches in early spring. Foliage that follows is often tinged pink; it later turns bright green. Toothed, nearly round leaves somewhat resemble those of hazelnut (*Corylus*); fall color varies from yellow-green to a good clear yellow. Rather open structure with attractive, delicate branching pattern. Give same soil conditions as you would rhododendrons. Grow in wind-sheltered location in shrub border or at edge of woodland. Not favored by deer.

C. glabrescens. FRAGRANT WINTER HAZEL. Hardiest species. To 8–15 ft. high and wide. Can be trained as a small tree. Flower clusters are 1–1½ in. long.

C. pauciflora. BUTTERCUP WINTER HAZEL. Dainty habit to 4–6 ft. high and wide. Blossom clusters are 1¼ in. long, each containing two or three blooms.

C. sinensis. A variable species. The typical form is a spreading shrub to 15 ft. tall and wide, bearing crowded flower spikes to 2 in. long. Variety *C. s. sinensis* (*C. willmottiae*) has velvety blue-green leaves, hairy leafstalks, and flower clusters to 3 in. long. Its selection 'Spring Purple' has purplish young stems that mature to green. *C. s. calvescens* (*C. platy-petala*) has smooth leaf surfaces and almost hairless leafstalks.

C. spicata. SPIKE WINTER HAZEL. To 8 ft. high, 10 ft. wide. New growth is purple, maturing to bluish green. Each 1- to 2-in.-long flower cluster holds 6 to 12 blossoms. The showiest winter hazel in bloom. 'Golden Spring' has bright yellow new growth, with a touch of red and yellow, turning to chartreuse in midsummer and orange and yellow in fall.

C. 'Winterthur'. US, MS, LS, CS; USDA 6-9. To 12 ft. tall and 15 ft. wide, this hybrid can be grown as a large shrub or small tree if trained. Heat tolerant but looks best in warm regions when it has light shade. Gold fall color.

CORYLUS

FILBERT, HAZELNUT
Betulaceae
Deciduous shrubs and trees

US, MS, LS; USDA 6-8

FULL SUN OR PARTIAL SHADE

REGULAR WATER

Corylus avellana 'Contorta'

Although filberts and hazelnuts are usually thought of as trees

grown for their edible nuts, most listed here are grown for their pleasing ornamental value. Plants have separate female and male flowers; female blossoms are inconspicuous, while male ones, appearing in pendent catkins on bare branches in winter or early spring, are showy. Leaves are roundish to oval, with toothed margins.

C. avellana. EUROPEAN FILBERT. Shrub. European native grows to 10–15 ft. high and wide. Ornamental selections are more widely grown than the species; the following two are popular.

'Contorta'. HARRY LAUDER'S WALKING STICK. Rounded growth to 8–10 ft. tall, 12 ft. wide. Grown for fantastically gnarled and twisted branches and twigs, revealed after its 2- to 2½-in. leaves turn yellow and drop in autumn. Branches are used in flower arrangements. Plants are almost always grafted, so suckers arising from the base below the graft should be removed; they won't have contorted form.

'Fuscorubra' ('Atropurpurea'). Grows to 10–15 ft. high and wide, with 3- to 4-in., reddish purple leaves.

C. maxima. GIANT FILBERT. Shrub or tree. Native to southeastern Europe. One of the species grown for nuts. Suckering shrub to 12–15 ft. high and wide; can be trained as small tree. 'Purpurea', most widely grown ornamental form, has rich dark purple leaves to 6 in. long; male catkins are also heavily tinted

ABOVE: Cosmos bipinnatus

purple. In most areas, leaves fade to green by early summer.

COSMOS

Asteraceae
Perennials and annuals

US, MS, LS, CS, TS; USDA 6-11, EXCEPT AS NOTED

FULL SUN

MODERATE WATER

Cosmos sulphureus

Native to tropical America, mostly Mexico. Showy summer- and fall-blooming plants, open and branching in habit, with bright green, divided leaves and daisylike flowers in many colors and forms (single, double, crested, frilled). Heights vary from 2½ to 8 ft. Use for mass color in borders or background, or as a filler among shrubs. Useful in arrangements if flowers are cut

just after they open and placed immediately in deep, cool water. Sow seed in open ground where plants are to grow; or set out transplants from spring to summer. Plant in not-too-rich soil. Plants self-sow freely and attract birds and butterflies.

C. atrosanguineus. CHOCOLATE COSMOS. Perennial from tuberous roots; often grown as annual. Zones MS, LS, CS, TS; USDA 7-11. Where winters are colder, dig and store as for dahlias. Grows 2–2½ ft. tall, 1½ ft. wide, with coarsely cut foliage. Blooms in late summer and fall, with deep brownish red, nearly 2-in.-wide flowers with a strong perfume of chocolate (or vanilla). Attractive companion for silvery-foliaged plants. Provide well-drained soil. Winter mulch is prudent in all but mildest regions (where plant tends to be rather short lived). 'Choca Mocha' provides nice stands of burgundy flowers that are heat and drought tolerant once established.

C. bipinnatus. COMMON COSMOS. Annual. Heights up to 8 ft., widths to 1½–2½ ft. Blossoms are 3–4 in. wide, with tufted yellow centers and rays in white and shades of pink, rose, lavender, purple, or crimson. Among the many types are 3- to 4-ft.-tall 'Candystripe', with white-and-rose flowers; 'Picotee', to 2½ ft. high, white flowers edged red; 'Cutesy Mix' has mixed colors on a 30- to 36-in. plant; Sensation strain, 3–6 ft. tall, including 'Dazzler' (crimson) and 'Radiance' (rose with red center); 'Double Dutch White' with large white double flowers standing 3-4 ft. tall; 'Rose BonBon' with large double, rosy lavender flowers that stand 4 ft. tall; 'Sea Shells', to 3 ft. tall, grown for quilled ray flowers that look like long, slender cones; and 'Sensation Pinkie Pink' has deep pink flowers on 36- to 48-in.-tall plants. 'Cosimo Collarette' has pink flowers fading to white on a 2-ft.-tall plant. Sonata is a dwarf strain 1½–2 ft. high; 'Sweet Dreams' reaches 3 ft. tall and has pale pink-to-white blossoms with rose centers. Versailles mix, bred for cut flowers, reaches 3½ ft. and bears its blossoms on long, strong stems. 'Sweet Sixteen' with light pink to white flowers with a darker pink edge is also used for cutting.

C

C. sulphureus. YELLOW COSMOS. Annual. To 7 ft. tall, 1½–2½ ft. wide, with yellow-centered, yellow or orange-yellow single flowers. Tends to become weedy looking at end of season. Two 3- to 4-ft.-tall, semidouble-flowering strains are Bright Lights, with 3½-in. flowers in yellow, gold, orange, and orange-red; and Klondike strain, with 2-in. flowers ranging from scarlet-orange to yellow. Dwarf Klondike or Sunny strain is 1½ ft. tall, bears 1½-in. flowers. Foot-tall semidouble bloomers include Ladybird mix, with 2½-in. scarlet, yellow, and orange flowers; and 'Sunny Red', with orange-red blooms. 'Cosmic' series, available in orange, red, and yellow have a branched habit on compact, 12-in. plants; tolerate poor soil, heat, and humidity.

COSTUS
SPIRAL FLAG, GINGER LILY
Costaceae
Perennials

⚡ CS, TS; USDA 9-11

☽ LIGHT SHADE

💧 AMPLE WATER DURING ACTIVE GROWTH

Costus barbatus

Plants in this genus are related to true gingers (*Zingiber*) and other so-called gingers (*Alpinia, Hedychium*), and like them have fleshy rhizomes and stems bearing large leaves. In *Costus*, the leaves are spirally arranged around the stem. Flowers emerge from a tight, conelike cluster of colored bracts at stem ends in summer and fall.

Plants have sprawling, mounding habit. Native to the tropical forest floor, they prefer light shade but can stand full sun if roots are shaded. Use around foundation or near patio or pool; can also be grown in large pots. Plants are dormant in winter and need little water at that time. Provide a winter mulch.

C. barbatus. RED TOWER GINGER. From Costa Rica. To 6–8 ft. tall, 5 ft. wide. Bright green, 5- to 10-in.-long leaves have downy undersides. Flowering cone is 7–13 in. long, with dark red bracts and 1½-in. yellow flowers; lasts for a long time on the plant. Blossoms attract hummingbirds.

C. curvibracteatus. From Central America. To 2 ft. high and 3 ft. wide. Shiny, dark green leaves grow 8–12 in. long. Flowering cone is 2–7 in. long, with 1½-in., reddish orange flowers. Good container plant.

C. cuspidatus (*C. igneus*). FIERY COSTUS. Native to Brazil. Forms a neat clump to 1½–2 ft. high and wide. Deep green, 4- to 7-in.-long leaves with reddish undersides. Unusual, almost cup-shaped, 3-in. orange flowers, often produced in twos or threes at stem ends. Good potted plant; attractive even when out of bloom.

C. speciosus. CREPE GINGER, MALAY GINGER. Native to the East Indies. Clusters of stems grow to 6–8 ft., spreading to 3 ft. Medium green, 5- to 10-in.-long leaves; 5-in.-long flowering cone with green bracts tipped red. Crepe paper–textured white or pink flowers to 4 in. wide emerge from the cone two or three at a time.

C. spiralis. SPIRAL FLAG, SPIRAL GINGER. From South America. Reaches 4–6 ft. tall, 3–4 ft. wide. Glossy, bright green, 8-in. leaves. Flowering cone has orange bracts and pink-to-red, 1½-in. flowers.

COTINUS
SMOKE TREE
Anacardiaceae
Deciduous shrubs or trees

⚡ US, MS, LS; USDA 6-8

☼ FULL SUN

💧 MODERATE WATER

Cotinus coggygria 'Purpureus'

Unusual and colorful shrub-trees creating broad, urn-shaped mass usually as wide as high. Naturally multistemmed but can be trained to a single trunk. Common name derived from dramatic puffs of "smoke" from fading flowers: As the tiny greenish blooms wither, they send out elongated stalks clothed in a profusion of fuzzy, lavender-pink hairs. Plants tolerate poor or rocky soil. In cultivated gardens, give them fast drainage and avoid overly wet conditions. Not browsed by deer.

C. coggygria. SMOKE TREE. Native from southern Europe to central China. Typically 12–15 ft. high and wide, though it may eventually reach 25 ft. The roundish, 1½- to 3-in. leaves are bluish green in the species, but purple-leafed types are more commonly grown. Leaves of 'Nordine' ('Nordine Red') and 'Purpureus' emerge purple and gradually turn green; 'Notcutt's Variety', 'Royal Purple', and 'Velvet Cloak' hold their purple color through most of the summer. Those with purple foliage have richer purple "smoke puffs" than the species. 'Golden Spirit' reaches about 7 ft. high and 6 ft. wide, with leaves that are lime-green in spring and turn golden yellow in summer. 'Pink Champagne' is a green-leafed selection with pinkish tan puffs. Leaves of all types change in fall, taking on colors ranging from yellow to orange-red.

C. 'Grace'. Handsome hybrid between *C. coggygria* and *C. obovatus*. To 15 ft. tall and wide, with blue-green foliage shaded purple. Large deep pink puffs. Orange and purple-red fall foliage.

C. obovatus. AMERICAN SMOKE TREE. From eastern U.S. Small, rounded tree to 20–30 ft. tall and wide; deserves much wider use. Blue-green leaves turn yellow, orange, and reddish purple in fall. Takes alkaline soil; often found growing wild on Edwards Plateau in Texas.

COTONEASTER
Rosaceae
Evergreen, semievergreen, deciduous shrubs

⚡ ZONES VARY BY SPECIES

☼ FULL SUN, EXCEPT AS NOTED

💧 LITTLE TO REGULAR WATER

Cotoneaster lacteus

One positive thing about cotoneasters is that many people call them "cotton-easters," which is always good for a chuckle. But the party ends there. Except for a few species (noted below), cotoneasters typically look pretty dreadful in the Southern landscape. Prostrate types used for ground covers aren't dense enough to discourage weeds and grass. They mainly serve to snag litter. Young plants can look nice, as white or pinkish springtime flowers give rise to abundant orange or red berries in fall and winter. But susceptibility to spider mites, fireblight, and other pests send these Asian natives downhill fast—which is ironic, considering that they're favorites for carpeting banks in front of hotels and shopping malls. Taller, arching types perform much better and are worthwhile additions to the home garden.

C. apiculatus. CRANBERRY COTONEASTER. Deciduous. Zones US, MS; USDA 6-7. Best in cold-winter areas. Dense grower to 3 ft. tall, 6 ft. wide. Small, round, medium-green leaves turn deep red in fall. Clustered fruits are about the size of large cranberries. Can take some shade. Use as bank cover, hedge, background planting. Tolerates alkaline soil.

C. dammeri. BEARBERRY COTONEASTER. Evergreen. Zones US, MS, LS; USDA 6-8. Fast, prostrate growth to 3–6 in. tall, 10 ft. wide. Branches root along ground. Bright, glossy green leaves; bright red fruit. 'Coral Beauty' is 6 in. tall; 'Eichholz', 10–12 in. tall with a scattering of red-orange leaves in fall; 'Lowfast', 1 ft. tall; 'Mooncreeper' grows 8–10 in. high and has large flowers. 'Skogsholmen', ½ ft. tall. All are good ground covers in sun or partial shade and can drape over walls, cascade down slopes. Susceptible to fireblight, lacebugs.

C. franchetii. FRANCHET COTONEASTER. Evergreen. Zones US, MS, LS, CS; USDA 6-9. Arching growth to 10 ft. tall, 6–9 ft. wide. Leaves are grayish green when new, maturing to bright green; undersides are fuzzy. Pink-tinged white flowers in clusters of up to 20 are followed by orange-red berries. Good performer in the Southeast.

C. glaucophyllus. GRAYLEAF COTONEASTER. Evergreen. Zones MS, LS; USDA 7-8. To 6–8 ft. tall and broad, with gracefully arching branches clothed in gray-green foliage. Dense clusters of white flowers are followed by dark red berries. Attractive in shrub beds or as informal hedge. Tolerates alkaline soil.

C. horizontalis. ROCK COTONEASTER. Deciduous. Zones US, MS; USDA 6-7. Can be 2–3 ft. tall, 15 ft. wide, with stiff horizontal branches, many branchlets set in herringbone pattern. Leaves are small, round, bright green; turn orange and red before falling. Out of leaf very briefly. Showy red fruits. Give it room to spread. Fine bank cover or low traffic barrier. 'Variegatus' has leaves edged in white. *C. h. perpusillus* is smaller, more compact than species.

C. lacteus (*C. parneyi*). BRIGHTBEAD COTONEASTER. Evergreen. Zones MS, LS, CS; USDA 7-9. Graceful, arching habit to 8 ft. or taller, 10 ft. or wider, with dark green leaves 2 in. long, clustered white flowers, and a heavy crop of long-lasting red fruit in 2- to 3-in. clusters. Best as informal hedge, screen, or espalier. Can be clipped as formal hedge, but form suffers. Best cotoneaster for the Southeast.

C. salicifolius. WILLOWLEAF COTONEASTER. Evergreen or semievergreen. Zones US, MS; USDA 6-7. Erect, spreading shrub, 15–18 ft. high and wide, with narrow, dark green, 1- to 3½-in.-long leaves and bright red fruits. Graceful screening or background plant. Better known are trailing forms used as ground covers. Compact, small-leafed 'Emerald Carpet' is 12–15 in. tall, spreading to 8 ft. wide; 'Autumn Fire' ('Herbstfeuer') grows to 2–3 ft. tall and 8 ft. wide. 'Repens' is similar; it is sometimes grafted to another cotoneaster species and grown as a weeping tree. Very susceptible to lacebugs.

CRAMBE

Brassicaceae
Perennials

Crambe maritima

Two species of these big, cabbage-like perennials are occasionally seen. Both have large, smooth leaves and much-branched clusters of small, honey-scented white flowers. They appreciate rich, well-drained garden soil and

require considerable space. In the Lower South, provide light afternoon shade.

C. cordifolia. GIANT KALE, HEARTLEAF COLEWORT. From the Caucasus. Forms a 3-ft.-wide mound of branching stems bearing dark green, 1-ft.-wide leaves on long stalks. Flowering stem set with smaller leaves can reach 8 ft. tall. Broad, branching flower cluster, up to 5 ft. wide, somewhat resembles a gargantuan baby's breath (*Gypsophila*). Requires a big garden and leaves a big vacancy when summer flowering is finished; plug in annuals to fill the space. Use in big borders to astonish your friends.

C. maritima. SEA KALE. From coastal northern Europe. To 2 ft. tall and wide, with branched, purplish stems carrying blue-gray leaves up to 1 ft. wide. In early summer, sends up a 1- to 2½-ft.-tall stem with flower clusters to 1½ ft. wide. Leafstalks were once widely used as a cooked (steamed) vegetable. A favorite of Thomas Jefferson at Monticello. Blanch leafstalks as they grow by placing large pots or boxes over them.

CRASPEDIA GLOBOSA

DRUMSTICKS
Asteraceae
Perennial

Craspedia globosa

Odd, attractive, offbeat Australian daisy. Silvery leaves form 8- to 12-in.-wide clumps, send up 2-ft. stalks, each topped by a 1-in.

globe of tiny yellow flowers. Bloom may occur at any time of year. Flowers are useful, fresh or dried, in arrangements.

CRASSULA

Crassulaceae
Succulent perennials

Crassula ovata

This interesting group of succulents, mostly from South Africa, includes many plants with unusual geometric forms. Excellent drainage is a must—be careful not to overwater. Most prefer full sun, but a few tolerate shade. All make excellent houseplants. Gardeners in the Tropical South can use them outdoors in containers, rock gardens, and borders.

C. arborescens. SILVER DOLLAR PLANT. Shrubby, heavy-branched plant is very similar to jade plant (*C. ovata*), but it's smaller, grows more slowly, and has gray-green, red-edged, red-dotted leaves. Star-shaped summer flowers (usually seen only on old plants) are white aging to pink.

C. ovata. JADE PLANT. Top-notch houseplant, large container plant anywhere; an excellent landscaping shrub in the Tropical South. Sometimes sold as *C. portulacea*. Plant has a stout trunk and sturdy limbs; stays small in container. Can reach 9 ft. high, half as wide, but is usually smaller. Leaves are thick, oblong, fleshy pads 1–2 in. long, glossy green, sometimes with red-tinged edges. 'Crosby's Dwarf' is a low, compact grower; variegated kinds are 'Sunset' (yellow-tinged red) and 'Tricolor' (green, white, and pinkish). 'Gollum' and 'Hobbit' have reddish, concave leaf tips. Clusters of pink, star-shaped flowers bloom in profusion, from fall into spring. Good near swimming pools.

C. perfoliata falcata. Grows to 4 ft. high, 2½ ft. wide. Fleshy, gray-green, sickle-shaped, 4-in. leaves are vertically arranged in two rows on stems. Dense clusters of scarlet flowers appear in late-summer.

C. pyramidalis. Interesting oddity grows 3–4 in. high and wide; flat, triangular, 1½- to 5-in.-long leaves are closely packed in four rows to give plant a squarish cross section.

C. schmidtii. Mat-forming, spreading plant to 4 in. tall, 1 ft. wide, with slender, rich green leaves to 1½ in. long. Clusters of small, dark rose or purplish flowers put on a show in winter and spring. Good choice for pots or rock gardens.

C. tetragona. Upright plants with treelike habit, 1–2 ft. high and a little narrower. Narrow, 1-in.-long leaves. Inconspicuous white flowers. Widely used in dish gardens to suggest miniature pine trees.

CRATAEGUS

HAWTHORN
Rosaceae
Deciduous trees

✎ **ZONES VARY BY SPECIES**

☼ **FULL SUN, EXCEPT AS NOTED**

💧 **MODERATE WATER**

Crataegus phaenopyrum

Members of the rose family, these small to medium-size, multi-

trunked trees are well known for their pretty, typically white flower clusters, which appear after leaf-out in spring—in fact, the hawthorn blossom is Missouri's state flower. Showy fruits resembling tiny apples appear in summer and autumn and often hang on into winter. The thorny branches need some pruning to thin out twiggy growth. Hawthorns attract bees and birds but are not usually browsed by deer.

C. crus-galli. COCKSPUR THORN. Zones US, MS; USDA 6-7. Native to eastern U.S. and Canada. Wide-spreading tree to 30 ft. high, 35 ft. across. Stiff thorns to 3 in. long. Smooth, glossy, toothed, 1- to 3-in.-long leaves are dark green, turning orange to red in fall. Dull orange-red fruit. Tough and drought tolerant. Most successful hawthorn for Oklahoma. *C. c. inermis* ('Crusader') is thornless.

C. laevigata. ENGLISH HAWTHORN. Zones US, MS; USDA 6-7. Native to Europe and North Africa. Moderate growth to 18–25 ft. high, 15–20 ft. wide. Best known through its selections. 'Crimson Cloud' ('Superba') has bright red single flowers with white centers, vivid red fruit. Double-flowered forms (which set little fruit) include 'Double White', 'Double Pink', and 'Paul's Scarlet', with clusters of rose to red flowers. All have 2-in. toothed, lobed leaves lacking good fall color. Trees are very prone to leaf spot, which can defoliate them and shorten their life.

C. marshallii. PARSLEY HAWTHORN. Zones US, MS, LS, CS; USDA 6-9. Native to southern U.S. To 10–15 ft. tall and wide, occasionally to 25 ft. Early spring flowers are dainty white with purple-tipped anthers. Finely cut leaves to 1½ in. long resemble parsley, turn red or yellow in fall. Striking cherry-red fruits persist after leaves drop. Tolerates a wide range of soils. Relatively disease free.

C. opaca. MAYHAW. Zones US, MS, LS, CS; USDA 6-9. Native to southeastern U.S. Attractive, large shrub or small tree famous for its fruits—called mayhaws—which are prized for making jelly. Eventually reaches 20–30 ft. tall and wide. Inch-wide flowers; matte green, lobed, 1- to 2½-in.-long leaves with hairy undersides.

Fruits are typically red and ripen in early summer (though in the Lower and Coastal South, bloom may occur as early as January, and fruits may ripen by April or May). In its native range, mayhaw grows in damp ground, but it will tolerate some dryness. If you want to harvest the fruit to make jelly, choose a heavy-yielding selection. The plant is self-fertile, but cross-pollination between two different selections produces heavier crops. Full sun or light shade.

'Big Red'. Red fruit to 1 in. across. Very dependable selection from the Pearl River swamps of Mississippi.

'Elite'. Red fruit to ¾ in. across; all ripen at the same time, rather than over several weeks.

'Golden Farris'. Golden fruit over ½ in. in diameter. Bears heavily and at an early age.

'Goliath'. Dark red fruit almost 1 in. across. Very productive.

'Harrison'. Pink fruit prized for preserves. From Texas and Louisiana.

'Super Spur'. Heavy crop of ¾-in. red fruit; particularly good for jelly.

'Texas Star'. Red to orange-red fruit to almost 1 in. across.

C. phaenopyrum. WASHINGTON HAWTHORN. Zones US, MS, LS; USDA 6-8. Native to southeastern U.S. Moderate growth to 25 ft. tall, 20 ft. across. Graceful, open limb structure. Glossy leaves 2–3 in. long with three to five sharp-pointed lobes (like some maples). In Upper and Middle South, foliage turns beautiful orange, scarlet, or purplish in fall. Broad flower clusters. Shiny red fruit hangs on well into winter. Not successful in the southern Midwest but a choice hawthorn elsewhere. One of the least prone to fireblight but quite susceptible to rust that disfigures fruit and foliage.

C. spathulata. LITTLEHIP HAWTHORN. Zones US, MS, LS, CS; USDA 6-9. Native to southeastern and midwestern U.S. Large shrub or small tree to 15-25 ft. high. Small, bright green leaves are not deeply lobed. Bright red fruit. Tough. Beautiful bark.

C. viridis. GREEN HAWTHORN. Zones US, MS, LS; USDA 6-8. Native to southeastern U.S. Moderate growth to 25–30 ft.; broad, spreading crown. Red fruit. 'Winter King' is vase shaped,

with silvery stems and showy red fruit that lasts all winter; susceptible to rust.

CARE

These trees will grow in any soil as long as it is well drained. Better grown under somewhat austere conditions, since good soil, regular water, and fertilizer all promote succulent new growth that is most susceptible to fireblight. The disease makes entire branches die back quickly; cut out blighted branches well below dead part. The rust stage of cedar-apple rust can be a problem wherever eastern red cedar (*Juniperus virginiana*) grows nearby. Aphids and scale are widespread potential pests.

CRESS, GARDEN

Brassicaceae
Annual

✎ **US, MS, LS, CS, TS; USDA 6-11**

☼ ◑ **FULL SUN OR PARTIAL SHADE**

💧💧 **REGULAR TO AMPLE WATER**

Garden cress

Garden cress is sometimes called pepper grass because of its peppery taste. It comes in broad- and curly-leafed forms. The broad-leafed form is used most often in soups; both kinds are used in sandwiches and salads. The curly-leafed form can also be used as a garnish.

CARE

Easy to grow as long as weather is cool. Sow seeds as early in spring as possible. Plant in rich, moist soil. Make rows 1 ft. apart; thin plants to 3 in. apart (eat thinnings). Cress matures fast; make successive sowings every 2 weeks up to middle of May. Where frosts are mild, sow through fall and winter. Try growing garden cress in shallow pots of soil or planting mix in a sunny kitchen window. It sprouts in a few days, can be harvested (with scissors) in 2 to 3 weeks. Or grow it by sprinkling seeds on pads of wet cheesecloth; keep damp until harvest in 2 weeks.

CRINUM, X AMARCRINUM

Amaryllidaceae
Perennials from bulbs

🌿 **ZONES VARY BY SPECIES; OR GROW IN POTS**

☀️ ◐ **SOME SHADE IN HOTTEST CLIMATES**

💧 💧💧 **REGULAR TO AMPLE WATER**

Crinum 'Bradley'

Among the South's most classic and cherished passalong plants, crinums combine bold, fragrant flowers, imposing foliage, and a bulldog constitution. Seldom seen in newer suburbs, they are now found largely in country gardens, at old home sites, and in cemeteries, where they thrive with little care. Indeed, they tolerate adversity so well that some say no crinum has ever died.

Native to many warm and tropical parts of the world; evergreen in the Tropical South, deciduous elsewhere. Each bulb tapers to an elongated, stemlike neck, from which radiate handsome, long, broad, straplike leaves. Rising from the foliage mass are thick stems to 4 ft. or taller, each bearing a cluster of long-stalked, lilylike flowers in white, pink, rose red, or reddish purple. Most are 4–6 in. long;

many are highly fragrant. Depending on the type, crinums may flower from spring through late summer; in the Tropical South, some bloom year-round. Can be brought indoors in winter. Not browsed by deer.

X Amarcrinum memoriacorsii 'Howardii'. Zones LS, CS, TS; USDA 8-11. Hybrid between *Amaryllis belladonna* and *C. moorei*. More dependable in the south than belladonna lily. Resembles *Crinum* in growth habit and foliage, but its whitethroated, soft pink, very fragrant flowers look more like those of *Amaryllis belladonna*, with narrower funnel shape than blooms of most crinums. Successive stalks emerge and bloom until frost. The plant is evergreen in mild winters.

C. americanum. SOUTHERN SWAMP CRINUM. Zones MS, LS, CS, TS; USDA 7-11. Native to water edges and swamps in the southeastern U.S. and on the Gulf Coast. Fragrant white flowers on 2-ft. stems appear from spring to late fall. Takes deep shade. Spreads by stolons and likes wet soil.

C. asiaticum. GRAND CRINUM, ST. JOHN'S LILY. Zones LS, CS, TS; USDA 8-11. From Southeast Asia. Large (6- to 8-in.-wide), fragrant, spidery-looking white flowers in clusters of up to 50. Foliage does not droop, but is held strait like a big yucca. *C. a. procerum* 'Splendens' has bronze to purple leaves and flowers pink on the backs of the petals. Grows 4–6 ft. tall.

C. bulbispermum. HARDY CRINUM. Zones US, MS, LS, CS, TS; USDA 6-11. Native to South Africa. Deep pink, fragrant flowers. Long, narrow, twisting gray-green leaves tend to lie on the ground. 'Album' has white flowers; seed-grown Jumbo strain has larger flowers in white, pink, or striped.

C. erubescens. Zones LS, CS, TS; USDA 8-11. From South America. To 3 ft. high. Broad, shiny green leaves form a clump that spreads by rhizomes. Makes a large colony and is drought and shade tolerant. Reddish stems bear fragrant, spidery-looking white flowers from midsummer until frost. Good ground cover.

C. hybrids. Zones LS, CS, TS; USDA 8-11, except as noted. Those listed below are some of the many fine choices available.

'Bradley'. Zones MS, LS, CS, TS; USDA 7-11. To 2–3 ft. high. Hybrid of Australian origin. Narrow, arching, glossy green leaves. Very fragrant, waxy, open-faced flowers of deep rosy pink with white centers bloom in summer.

'Bolivia'. To 2½ ft. high and up to 3 ft. wide. Fragrant white flowers with a red stripe down the center of the petals.

'Carnival'. Zones MS, LS, CS, TS; USDA 7-11. Cold-hardy selection with stems to 2½ ft. tall. Flowers in shades of pink and red are marked with white streaks.

'Ellen Bosanquet'. Zones MS, LS, CS, TS; USDA 7-11. Broad, bright green leaves. Fragrant flowers are deep rose, nearly red. An all-time favorite.

'Hannibal's Dwarf'. Zones MS, LS, CS, TS; USDA 7-11. To 1½ ft. high, with strap-shaped, shiny green leaves. Fragrant, deep pink flowers bloom in midsummer, rebloom in early fall. Multiplies quickly to form attractive clumps and could be a ground cover. Shy to flower.

'Infusion'. Zones US, MS, LS, CS; USDA 6-9. An excellent cross of 'Ellen Bosanquet' and 'J.C. Harvey' from Florida. Vigorous plant topped with 3-ft.-high clusters of cherry-red flowers.

'J.C. Harvey'. To 2½ ft. tall. Shiny, ribbed, green leaves. Blooms in summer, bearing reddish pink buds that open to clear pink, headily fragrant flowers with wide-spreading petals. Each flower stalk bears about six blossoms. Spreads rapidly. Great ground cover. Shade tolerant but rarely blooms in shade.

'Milk and Wine'. Creamy white, fragrant flowers with pink stripes; continuous bloom. "Milk and wine" is also a common name for several similar-looking selections and for *C. x herbertii* or *C. x gowennii*. 'Carroll Abbott' has more intense stripes; 'Regina's Disco Lounge' is simply larger.

'Mrs. James Hendry'. Zones MS, LS, CS, TS; USDA 7-11. To 2 ft. high, with rigidly upright, shiny green leaves. Very fragrant white blossoms blushed with pinkish lavender appear in late spring and bloom through mid-summer into fall.

'Peach Blow'. Zones MS, LS, CS, TS; USDA 7-11. Long leaves; pale lavender, spicily fragrant flowers with recurving petals. The classic crinum of the Old South.

'Royal White'. Narrow, semierect leaves. Very large, fragrant white flowers with rose-pink stripes.

'Sangria'. Zones MS, LS, CS, TS; USDA 7-11. Pink flowers borne on dark purple foliage. Grows 4 ft. tall.

'Stars and Stripes'. Compact, with narrow, pleated leaves. Fragrant white flowers with central red stripe reach 2 ft. high. Shy to flower.

'Summer Nocturne'. Zones MS, LS, CS, TS; USDA 7-11. Purple flower spikes topped with 2-ft.-tall, intensely fragrant, pale pink flowers, deepening toward the tips of the petals. Flowers late, in October and November.

'Super Ellen'. Zones US, MS, LS, CS, TS; USDA 6-11. Huge, glossy green leaves are up to 7 ft. long. Cherry-red flowers reach up to 6 ft. high. Takes a few years to bloom after planting.

'Walter Flory'. Zones MS, LS, CS, TS; USDA 7-11. To 4 ft. tall. Lush green foliage. Rich pink, fragrant flowers with a lengthwise burgundy stripe down center of each petal.

'White Emperor'. Large, outfacing, fragrant, white blooms reach up to 3 ft. high.

C. moorei. LONGNECK CRINUM. Zones MS, LS, CS, TS; USDA 7-11. From South Africa. Large (6- to 8-in.-wide) bulbs with stemlike neck to 1 ft. long or more. Long, thin, wavy-edged bright green leaves. Pinkish red, fragrant, bell-shaped blossoms. Prefers light shade in Texas.

C. x powellii. Zones MS, LS, CS, TS; USDA 6-11. Resembles its parent *C. moorei* but has fragrant dark rose flowers. 'Album' is a good pure white form, vigorous enough to serve as a tall ground cover in shade. 'Cecil Houdyshel' (Zones MS, LS, CS, TS; USDA 7-11) has long, tapering leaves and deep rose-red blossoms. 'Eden' has large, clear white flowers. Very cold hardy.

C. scabrum. MILK-AND-WINE LILY, CREOLE LILY. Zones CS, TS; USDA 9-11. From tropical Africa. Usually low-growing but may reach 6 ft. tall under ideal conditions. Sweetly fragrant, 3-in., spidery-looking flowers in pure white with a red stripe lengthwise down middle of each petal. Blooms in midsummer, with some rebloom in early fall.

TOP: *Crinum 'Mrs. James Hendry'; C. 'Stars and Stripes';*
MIDDLE: *C. 'Infusion'; BOTTOM: C. moorei; C. 'Milk and Wine'*

CROCOSMIA
Iridaceae
Perennial from corms

US, MS, LS, CS; USDA 6-9

SOME SHADE IN COASTAL SOUTH

REGULAR WATER DURING GROWTH AND BLOOM

Crocosmia 'Lucifer'

Native to tropical and southern Africa. Formerly called tritonia; related to freesia. Sword-shaped leaves grow in basal clumps; small orange, red, or yellow flowers bloom in summer. Useful for splashes of garden color; good cut flowers.

C. x crocosmiiflora. MONTBRETIA. A favorite for generations, montbretias can still be seen in older gardens, where they have spread freely, bearing orange-crimson, 1½- to 2-in. blossoms on stems 3–4 ft. tall. Leaves are 3 ft. long. Many once-common named forms are making a comeback; colors include yellow, orange, cream, and near-scarlet. Good for naturalizing on slopes or in fringe areas. Spreads quickly when happy.

C. hybrids. Sturdy plants with branching spikes of showy flowers. Some are sold as selections of *C. x crocosmiiflora*.

'Bressingham Beacon'. To 3 ft. tall. Brilliant orange buds open to orange-and-yellow flowers. Purple stems.

'Bright Eyes'. To 20 in. high. Bright orange flowers with red centers. Heavy bloomer.

'Emberglow'. To 2½ ft. high. Burnt orange-red flowers with yellow throat.

'Emily McKenzie'. Grows to 2 ft. tall. Orange with red eye.

'Honey Angels' ('Citronella'). Grows to 2 ft. high: bright yellow flowers.

'Jenny Bloom'. To 2–3 ft. tall. Golden yellow flowers.

'Little Redhead'. Bright red-orange flowers on 20-in.-high stems. Heavy bloomer.

'Lucifer'. To 4 ft. tall. Popular selection with bright red blossoms.

'Star of the East'. To 2½ ft. high. Spreads slowly. Clear orange blooms with burgundy markings and a lighter orange center.

'Venus'. To 2 ft. high. Peachy yellow flowers with maroon-blotched throats. Purple stems.

'Walberton Yellow'. ('Walcroy'). Large, golden yellow flowers with curved petals. Heavy blooming to 2 ft. tall.

CARE

Plant in well-drained, enriched soil; set corms 2 in. deep, 3 in. apart. Where winter temperatures remain above 10°F (–12°C), needs no winter protection. Where lows range from 10°F to –5°F (–12°C to –21°C), provide winter mulch. In colder areas, dig and store over winter. Divide clumps only when vigor, flower quality begin to decline.

CROCUS
Iridaceae
Corms

US, MS, LS; USDA 6-8

FULL SUN OR PARTIAL SHADE

REGULAR WATER DURING GROWTH AND BLOOM

Crocus sativus

For many gardeners, the appearance of crocus signals the end of winter. Native to the Mediterranean region and the Caucasus, these low-growing plants have grasslike leaves, often with a silvery midrib; the foliage appears before, during, or after bloom, depending on the species. Flowers are 1½–3 in. long, with flaring or cup-shaped petals. They're available in a wide range of colors.

Most crocus bloom in late winter or earliest spring. Collectively, the earliest bloomers are known as "snow crocus". Others bloom in fall, the flowers rising from bare earth weeks or days after planting. Mass them for best effect. Lovely in rock gardens, between stepping stones, in containers. Set corms 2–3 in. deep and 3–4 in. apart in light, porous soil. Divide every 3 to 4 years. Don't bother planting crocus if your garden has chipmunks—these rodents will dig up and eat every one. Won't naturalize where winters are warm.

C. ancyrensis. Small golden yellow flowers. Blooms very early.

C. angustifolius. CLOTH OF GOLD CROCUS. Orange-gold, starlike flowers with dark brown center stripe. Starts blooming in January in warmest areas, in March in coldest areas.

C. chrysanthus. Orange-yellow, sweet scented. Hybrids and selections range from white through yellow to blue, often marked with deeper color. Spring bloom. 'Blue Pearl' is palest blue; 'Cream Beauty', pale yellow; 'E. P. Bowles', yellow with purple markings; 'Ladykiller', outside purple edged white, inside white feathered purple; 'Princess Beatrix', blue with yellow center; and 'Snow Bunting', pure white.

C. imperati. Bright lilac inside, buff veined purple outside. Early spring.

C. kotschyanus. Pinkish lavender or lilac flowers in early fall.

C. sativus. SAFFRON CROCUS. Lilac flowers appear in autumn; the orange-red stigma is true saffron. To harvest, pluck stigmas as soon as flowers open, dry them, and store them in vials. Stigmas from a dozen blooms will season a good-size paella or similar dish. To continue good yields of saffron, divide corms as soon as leaves turn brown; replant in fresh or improved soil. Mark planting site so you won't dig up dormant corms

C. sieberi. Delicate lavender-blue flowers with golden throat. One of the earliest bloomers, with flowers appearing in January and February.

C. speciosus. AUTUMN CROCUS. Showy blue-violet flowers in early fall. Lavender and mauve selections available. Fast increase by seed and division. Showiest autumn-flowering crocus.

C. tommasinianus. Slender buds; star-shaped, silvery lavender-blue flowers, sometimes with dark blotch at tips of petals. Very early—January or February in milder areas. Will form clumps in Upper, Middle, and Lower South gardens.

C. vernus. DUTCH CROCUS. Most vigorous and largest flowered crocus, with blooms in shades of white, yellow, lavender, purple; flowers are often penciled or streaked. Blooms in February and March.

CRYPTANTHUS ZONATUS
EARTH STAR
Bromeliaceae
Perennial

TS; USDA 10-11; OR HOUSEPLANT

SOME SHADE; BRIGHT INDIRECT LIGHT

MODERATE WATER

Cryptanthus zonatus

Native to Brazil. Bromeliad grown for showy leaves in spreading, low-growing clusters to 1½ ft. wide, usually less. Leaves are wavy, dark brownish red, banded crosswise with green, brown, or white. Unimportant little white flowers grow among leaves. Pot in equal parts coarse sand, shredded osmunda, and ground bark or peat moss. Makes a fine houseplant; ideal in dish gardens.

C. bivittatus is similar to *C. zonatus* in cultural needs and general appearance, but it has

green leaves striped lengthwise in creamy white. Many other striped and banded species and hybrids are available from specialists.

CRYPTOMERIA JAPONICA
JAPANESE CRYPTOMERIA
Cupressaceae
Evergreen tree

US, MS, LS; USDA 6-8

FULL SUN OR LIGHT SHADE

MODERATE TO REGULAR WATER

Cryptomeria japonica

Graceful conifer, fast growing (3–4 ft. a year) in youth. Eventually skyline tree to 100 ft. tall, 30 ft. wide at base, with straight, columnar trunk, thin red-brown bark peeling in strips. Slightly pendulous branches are clothed with needlelike leaves ½–1 in. long; foliage is soft bright green to bluish green during the growing season, brownish purple in cold weather. Roundish, red-brown cones ¾–1 in. wide. Trees are sometimes planted in groves for Japanese garden effect; they also make a good tall screen. For holiday decorations they are soft and do not shed. Good substitute for Leyland Cypress. Not browsed by deer.

'Benjamin Franklin'. Foliage stays green even with exposure to cold or wind. Salt tolerant.

'Black Dragon'. New spring growth is light green; mature foliage is blackish green. Grows only about 5 ft. high and 7 ft. wide in 10 years.

'Chapel Hill'. Raindrop-shaped tree 5-10 ft. high and 4-8 ft. wide. Upswept branches with blue-green foliage year-round. Coneless.

'Elegans'. PLUME CEDAR, PLUME CRYPTOMERIA. Quite unlike species. Feathery, grayish green, soft-textured foliage turns rich coppery red or purplish in winter. Grows slowly into dense pyramid to 20–60 ft. tall, about 20 ft. wide. Trunks on old trees may lean or curve. For effective display, give it space.

'Globosa Nana'. Dwarf selection with very slow, upright growth to 4 ft. high and wide. Dark green foliage. Boxwood substitute.

'Kitayama'. Narrow, upright, (to 15–18 ft. tall and 8–10 ft. wide), more compact form and better winter color make this an improvement over 'Yoshino'.

'Pygmaea' ('Nana'). DWARF CRYPTOMERIA. Bushy dwarf 1½–2 ft. high, 2½ ft. wide. Dark green leaves, twisted branches.

'Vilmoriniana'. Slow-growing dwarf to 1–2 ft. high and wide. Fluffy, gray-green foliage turns bronze in late fall and winter. Rock garden or container plant.

'Yoshino'. Resembles the species but is smaller (to 30–40 ft. tall and 20 ft. wide), with bluish green foliage that takes on reddish tones in winter.

CUCUMBER
Cucurbitaceae
Annual vine

US, MS, LS, CS, TS; USDA 6-11

FULL SUN

REGULAR WATER

Lemon cucumber

For crisp texture and cool flavor, a freshly harvested homegrown cucumber beats the waxy-coated ones found at the grocery, hands down. And it doesn't take many

HOW TO GROW CUCUMBERS

SHOPPING Catalogs are specific about cucumber pollination requirements. Most cucumbers bear male and female flowers on the same plant, so bees cross-pollinate them easily. Don't get discouraged if flowers don't immediately produce young cucumbers: The male flowers, which don't produce fruit, tend to appear first. Some selections only produce female flowers; when you buy these, a few seeds in the packet will be specially marked to show that they will produce male plants. You must plant at least one of these for every six female plants. Some cucumbers produce seedless fruit without a pollinator, so they are popular both outdoors and in bee-free greenhouses. 'Diva' and 'Sweet Success' are mild tasting and seedless.

PLANTING Cucumbers won't take cold, so plant them at least 2 weeks after the last frost or when the soil and weather are warm. Plant again in midsummer to extend the harvest into fall. Sow seeds at base of support, planting them ½–1 in. deep and 4–6 in. apart. Thin seedlings to 8–12 in. apart. If you prefer to let vines ramble over the ground, sow seeds in small hills spaced 4 ft. apart; sow four to six seeds per hill, and thin to the strongest two or three seedlings.

WATER & FEEDING Apply water in furrows or with drip irrigation–never overhead water (encourages downy mildew). Don't let plants dry out, or fruit will be misshapen and bitter. Before planting, work into the soil ½ cup of 10-10-10 fertilizer per 10 ft. of row (or ¼ cup per hill). One week after bloom begins, sprinkle area around plants with this same amount and water in. Repeat 3 weeks later.

HARVESTING Harvest cucumbers when young and tender. Don't leave any to mature on the vine or the plant will stop producing. Pickling cucumbers should be harvested as soon as they have reached the proper size—tiny for sweet pickles (gherkins), larger for dills or pickle slices.

CHALLENGES Floating row covers will protect young plants from various pests, including cucumber beetles and flea beetles; remove covers when flowering occurs so that bees can pollinate the flowers. Whiteflies are a potential pest late in the season; hose off plants regularly or hang yellow sticky traps. Misshapen fruit is usually due to uneven watering or poor pollination. Bitter flavor (a common problem) results from stress brought on by drought, inconsistent watering, and excessive heat.

---

plants to keep a family supplied for most of summer. Each vigorous, sprawling vine can cover up to 25 sq. ft.; to save space, grow on a trellis or inside wire cages.

If you don't have the room that regular cucumber vines demand, plant smaller bush types that grow short vines, such as 'Fanfare (62 days from sowing to harvest), 'Spacemaster' (60 days), and 'Salad Bush' (57 days). For mild-flavored, "burpless" cucumbers, try 'Sweet Slice' (62 days) or 'Sweet Success' (54 days, doesn't need pollination). Good slicing cucumbers include 'Ashley' (66 days), 'Fanfare' (63 days), 'General Lee' (66 days), and 'Poinsett' (67 days). For pickles, try 'Bush Pickle' (45 days, short vines), 'County Fair' (48 days), and 'Homemade Pickles' (55 days).

Novelty selections include an Asian type called 'Suyo Long' (long, slim, and very mild), Armenian cucumber (actually a long, curving, pale green, ribbed melon with cucumber look and mild cucumber flavor), and English greenhouse cucumber. When well grown, it's the mildest of all cucumbers. Lemon cucumbers are mild, round, and yellow.

CUNNINGHAMIA LANCEOLATA

CHINA FIR
Cupressaceae
Evergreen tree

MS, LS, CS; USDA 7-9

FULL SUN

REGULAR WATER

Cunninghamia lanceolata

This picturesque conifer from China has a heavy trunk; stout, whorled branches; and drooping branchlets. It grows at a moderate rate to 30 ft. tall with 20-ft. spread. Stiff, needlelike, sharp-pointed leaves are 1½–2½ in.

long, green above and whitish beneath. Its brown, 1- to 2-in. cones are interesting but not profuse. Among palest of needled evergreens in spring and summer, China fir turns red-bronze in cold winters. Needs protection from hot, dry wind in summer and cold wind in winter. Becomes less attractive as it ages. Branches with dead needles persist, giving tree an unkempt look. Prune them out. 'Glauca', with striking gray-blue foliage, is more widely grown and hardier than the species. The dwarf 'Little Leo' slowly forms a flattened mound of bright green foliage that turns bronze to purple in winter.

CUPHEA

Lythraceae
Evergreen shrubs or woody perennials

CS, TS; USDA 9-11, ANNUALS ANYWHERE

FULL SUN OR PARTIAL SHADE

REGULAR WATER

Cuphea llavea

These natives of Mexico and Central America provide color throughout warm months; use them in small beds, as formal edging for borders, along paths, in containers. Flowers attract hummingbirds. Pinch tips of shoots for compact growth; severely cut back older plants in late fall or early spring. Reliably perennial only in frost-free areas, but may survive light frosts in Coastal South. Easy to grow from cuttings.

C. cyanea. VIOLET CUPHEA. Can reach 6 ft. in its native Mexico, but usually half that tall and wide in home gardens; as an annual, it grows 1–1½ ft. high. Medium to dark green, ovate leaves 2–3 in. long. Each tubular, ¾- to 1¼-in.-long flower is bright pink with a yellow tip and two earlike violet-blue petals.

C. hyssopifolia. HAWAIIAN HEATHER, MEXICAN HEATHER. To 1–2 ft. tall, about 2½ ft. wide. Flexible, leafy branchlets clothed in very narrow, ½- to ¾-in.-long, medium to dark green leaves. Tiny flowers (scarcely half as long as leaves) in pink, purple, or white. Plants in the Itsy Bitsy Series grow 8 in. high and 6 in. wide, and are excellent rock garden plants. 'Caribbean Sunset', to 2 ft. tall, has orange blooms. 'Riverdene Gold', 1 ft. tall and 2 ft. wide, has golden foliage and deep pink blooms.

C. ignea. CIGAR PLANT. Leafy, compact plant to 1 ft. or taller, as wide as tall. Narrow, dark green leaves, 1–1½ in. long. The flowers explain the "cigar" of the common name: They're tubular, ¾ in. long, bright orange-red with white tip and dark ring at end. Flowers of 'Lutea' are a very soft yellow; those of 'Petite Peach' are a light peach. 'David Verity' has orange-red blooms. 'Starfire' has a pink flower tube and purple petals.

C. llavea. BAT-FACED CUPHEA. To 2–3 ft. tall, 3 ft. wide. Medium green leaves to 3 in. long. Red-and-purple, 1½-in.-long flowers are said to look like a bat's face. Occasionally spreads by seed in gardens. Though cultivated in the desert, it is not drought tolerant—in nature, it grows along stream banks in Mexico. Compact varieties (12–16 in. high, 18 in. wide) include 'Flamenco Rumba', coral red flowers; 'Flamenco Tango', vibrant pink blooms; and 'Totally Tempted', bright red blooms.

C. micropetala. GIANT CIGAR PLANT. To 4 ft. tall, 3–4 ft. wide. Arching stems, each closely set with narrow, 5-in., medium green leaves and topped by a slender, spikelike cluster of 1½-in., bright red flowers tipped with yellow. Deciduous in cold weather.

C. x purpurea. Hybrid to 1–1½ ft. high and wide, good for ground covers and hanging baskets. Red flowers to 1¼ in. long; dark green leaves to 3 in. long. 'Firecracker', bearing dark purple flowers with two earlike bright red petals, thrives in Southern heat and humidity. 'Firefly' bears magenta petals with a white ring in the center and is equally well adapted.

CUPRESSUS

CYPRESS
Cupressaceae
Evergreen trees

🌿 **ZONES VARY BY SPECIES**
☀️ **FULL SUN**
💧 **LITTLE TO MODERATE WATER**

Cupressus arizonica

These conifers have tiny, scalelike leaves, closely set on cordlike branches, and interesting globular, golf ball–size cones made up of shield-shaped scales. For the dry Southwest, choose *C. arizonica* or *C. sempervirens*; these species and their selections thrive in dry, rocky, alkaline soil. In high-rainfall areas, however, they are short lived; *C. lusitanica* is the better choice there. Cypresses are not browsed by deer.

C. arizonica. ARIZONA CYPRESS. Zones MS, LS, CS; USDA 7-9. To 40 ft. tall, spreading to 20 ft. wide; rough, furrowed bark. Seedlings are variable, with foliage varying from green to blue-gray or silvery. *C. a. glabra* (often sold as *C. glabra*) is like the species but has smooth, cherry-red bark. Other forms include 'Blue Ice', forming dense, blue-gray pyramids to at least 20–25 ft. high; 'Blue Pyramid', a dense, blue-gray pyramid to 20–25 ft. tall; 'Carolina Sapphire', to 30 ft., with steely blue-green foliage and broad, symmetrical form; 'Gareei', with silvery blue-green foliage; and 'Pyramidalis', a compact, symmetrical grower. Mass trees for windbreak or screen.

C. lusitanica. MEXICAN CYPRESS. Zones LS, CS; USDA 8-9. Native to northern Florida and Central America. Grows rapidly to 50 ft. tall, 15 ft. wide, with symmetrical, spreading, pendulous branches and beautiful, ferny, blue-green foliage. Use as specimen tree or windbreak. Choose plants grown from cuttings of selected blue clones; these are more uniform and bluer in color than plants grown from seed. Likes fertile, well-drained soil.

C. sempervirens. ITALIAN CYPRESS. Zones MS, LS, CS; USDA 7-9. Native to southern Europe, western Asia. Species has horizontal branches and dark green foliage, but variants are more often sold. 'Stricta' ('Fastigiata'), columnar Italian cypress, and 'Glauca', blue Italian cypress (really blue-green in color), are classic Mediterranean landscape plants; both are dense, narrow trees to 60 ft. high, 5–10 ft. wide at maturity. 'Swane's Golden', another columnar form, has golden yellow new growth. 'Tiny Tower' is a slow, dense grower that reaches only 8 ft. tall, 2 ft. wide after 10 years.

X CUPROCYPARIS LEYLANDII

LEYLAND CYPRESS
Cupressaceae
Evergreen tree

🌿 **US, MS, LS, CS; USDA 6-9**
☀️ **FULL SUN**
💧 **MODERATE TO REGULAR WATER**

X Cuprocyparis leylandii

Hybrid of *Chamaecyparis nootkatensis* and *Cupressus macrocarpa*. Grows very fast (from cuttings to 15–20 ft. in 5 years). Usually reaches 60–70 ft. tall and 8–15 ft. wide in gardens. Widely planted as a quick screen; becoming quite popular as a cut Christmas tree in Lower and Coastal South. Long, slender, upright branches of flattened gray-green foliage sprays give youthful tree a narrow pyramidal form, though it can become open and floppy. Can be pruned into tall (10- to 15-ft.) hedge but will quickly get away from you without regular maintenance. Grows much too large to be planted near the house. Produces small cones composed of scales. Accepts a wide variety of soil and climate conditions; takes strong wind. Susceptibility to canker and root rot diseases has killed thousands in recent years. Bagworms are another serious pest. Popular selections include 'Castlewellan', with golden new growth and narrow, erect habit; 'Emerald Isle', with bright green foliage on plant 20–25 ft. tall and 6–8 ft. wide; 'Gold Rider' also has golden new growth and eventually forms a pyramid 35 ft. high by 15 ft. wide; and 'Naylor's Blue', bearing grayish blue foliage.

CURCUMA

Zingiberaceae
Perennials from rhizomes

🌿 **LS, CS, TS; USDA 8-11**
☀️ **LIGHT SHADE OR MORNING SUN, EXCEPT AS NOTED**
💧 **REGULAR WATER, EXCEPT AS NOTED**

Curcuma alismatifolia

Native to tropical Asia, this group of highly ornamental gingers has both handsome foliage and colorful flowers. Leaves of most are broadly lance shaped, deep green, and attractively pleated. Bloom typically comes in summer, when small blossoms are borne in spikes of colorful bracts; the flower spikes may be

C

hidden beneath the leaves or tower above them.

Most are hardy only in the Coastal and Tropical South, though *C. elata*, *C. longa* 'Bright White', *C. petiolata*, and *C. rubescens* 'Scarlet Fever' will winter over in the Lower South. They make excellent additions to mixed borders. Plant in spring, setting rhizomes 1 in. deep in moist, well-drained, humus-rich soil. Plants die down in winter and need very little water during dormancy.

C. alismatifolia. SIAM TULIP. Grows 2 ft. tall, with foliage like small canna leaves. At bloom time (early summer to early fall), flowering stems are topped by clusters of pink, rose, or white bracts that hide tiny flowers; the inflorescence is shaped a bit like a flaring pinecone. Plant 6 in. apart for lush cover. Each blossom spike lasts for several weeks, then is replaced by others as new plants arise from the rhizome. Spectacular as a bedding plant.

C. elata. GIANT PLUME. The tallest species, growing to 6–7 ft. tall and wide. Among the first gingers to bloom in spring, with large (1- to 2-ft.-long) inflorescences appearing before the leaves. Bracts are greenish near the bottom of the spike, bright pink at the top; yellow flowers bloom along its length. Dramatic cut flower. Performs well in full sun or partial shade.

C. gracillima. Notable for selections with colorful, 4-in.-long inflorescences borne above the foliage. 'Burnt Burgundy' has burgundy-colored flower spikes with darker, burnt-looking streaks on the bracts. 'Candy Cane', sensational in mass plantings, has bracts striped in red and creamy white. Both selections grow to 1½–2 ft. tall, 2 ft. wide.

C. longa 'Bright White' (*C. domestica* 'Bright White'). To 4 ft. tall, 3 ft. wide. Glowing white inflorescence makes an excellent cut flower. The basic species, which bears creamy white flower spikes, is the source of the spice turmeric. Full sun or partial shade.

C. petiolata. HIDDEN LILY, QUEEN LILY. Grows 2–3 ft. high and almost as wide, with very handsome, tropical-looking, 10-in.-long, sheathlike leaves. Rosy purple, 6- to 8-in. bracts are largely hidden by the leaves, which are thin and may burn in hot afternoon sun and tear in strong winds. Cut back to ground in winter; new foliage will sprout from tuberous roots in spring. In the selection 'Emperor' (to 2 ft. tall and wide), the foliage—gray-green leaves edged in creamy white—is the main attraction; the 6-in. flower spikes are white suffused with shades of pale purple.

C. roscoeana. JEWEL OF BURMA. To 3 ft. high and wide. The 8-in.-long inflorescence consists of orange bracts and bright yellow flowers; good for cutting. One of the latest to bloom, at summer's end and in fall.

C. rubescens 'Scarlet Fever'. To 4–6 ft. high, 4 ft. wide. Blood-red stems bear gray-green leaves with a prominent red midrib. Spectacular plant, even without the foot-long flowering spikes, which resemble those of *C. elata*. Does well in full sun or partial shade.

CYATHEA COOPERI
AUSTRALIAN TREE FERN
Cyatheaceae
Tree fern

🗲 TS; USDA 10-11; OR GROW IN POTS

◑ PARTIAL SHADE; BRIGHT LIGHT

💧 REGULAR WATER

Cyathea cooperi

Fastest growing of the fairly hardy tree ferns (to 27°F, but with damage to fronds). To an eventual 20 ft. tall, 12 ft. wide. Starts out as a low, wide clump (can spread from 1 ft. to as much as 6 ft. in a year) before growing upward. Broad, bright green, finely cut fronds. Brownish hairs on leafstalks and leaf undersurfaces can irritate skin; wear long sleeves, hat, and neckcloth when grooming plants. Often sold as *Alsophila australis*, *A. cooperi*, or *Sphaeropteris cooperi*.

CARE

Wet down the fronds and trunk on dry days in summer and autumn. Every spring, cover the base with a few inches of organic fertilizer, such as garden compost or aged cow manure. Prune off old fronds—but not until new ones emerge. Where plant is not hardy, grow in large container and bring indoors to your brightest window for winter. Mist fronds and trunk daily; never let soil dry out. Don't feed with liquid fertilizer; instead, feed monthly with a balanced, controlled-release fertilizer, such as 14-14-14.

CYCAS
CYCADS
Cycadaceae
Evergreens

🗲 ZONES VARY BY SPECIES

◑ PARTIAL SHADE

💧💧 MODERATE TO REGULAR WATER

Cycas revoluta

Neither ferns nor palms, these evergreen plants are primitive, cone-bearing relatives of conifers, excellent for tropical effects. A rosette of dark green, feathery leaves grows from a central point at the top of a single trunk (sometimes several trunks). Eventually as wide as tall. Female plants bear conspicuous, egg-shaped, red-to-orange seeds. Plants can be propagated (best done in spring) either from seed or by separating offsets that sprout near the base.

C. circinalis. QUEEN SAGO. Zones TS; USDA 10-11. Native to Old World tropics. Beautiful specimen plant to 20 ft. tall, 10–20 ft. wide. Graceful, drooping leaves to 8 ft. long atop unbranching trunk. Protect from frost.

C. revoluta. SAGO PALM. Zones CS, TS; USDA 9-11; or indoors. Hardy to 15°F. Native to Japan. In youth, reaches 2–3 ft. tall and wide and has an airy, lacy, fernlike appearance; with age (grows very slowly to 10 ft.), looks more like a palm. Leaves are 2–3 ft. long (larger on very old plants) and divided into many narrow, leathery segments. Tough, tolerant patio plant; good in foundation or entry planting. Leaf spot disease is a problem in high-rainfall areas. Makes an outstanding large houseplant in bright indirect light. Needs only occasional watering (less in winter) and takes many years to outgrow its container.

CYCLAMEN
Primulaceae
Perennials from tubers

🗲 ZONES VARY BY SPECIES

☀ ◑ FULL SUN OR PARTIAL SHADE

💧 REGULAR WATER

Cyclamen persicum 'Winter Ice White'

Native to Europe, Mediterranean region, Asia. Grown for their pretty flowers carried atop attractive clump of roundish to heart-shaped basal leaves that are reddish beneath and often patterned with silver above. Blossoms, 1–3 in. long, resemble shooting stars or butterflies and typically come in white and shades of pink, rose, or red. Most types go through a near-leafless or leafless dormant period at some time during summer.

Large-flowered florists' cyclamen (*C. persicum*) is most often seen as a container-grown gift plant. The other species described here are smaller-flowered, hardier plants better adapted to outdoor culture. Use them in rock gardens, in naturalized clumps under trees, or as carpets under camellias, rhododendrons, and large noninvasive ferns; hardy types also grow well under native oaks. All are good container plants if grown out of direct sun.

When buying any species cyclamen other than *C. persicum*, always check to ascertain that the tubers are commercially grown and not taken from the wild. Look for labels that mention "Holland" or "cultivated."

C. cilicium. Zones US, MS, LS; USDA 6-8. Fragrant, pale pink flowers with purple blotches on 2- to 6-in. stems, fall into winter. Leaves are ½–2½ in. across, heavily mottled with silver. 'Album' has white blossoms.

C. coum. Zones US, MS, LS; USDA 6-8. Deep crimson-rose flowers on 4- to 6-in. stems in winter and early spring. Round, deep green leaves reach 1–2½ in. across. Selections with pink or white flowers are available.

C. hederifolium. Zones US, MS, LS; USDA 6-8. Light green, 2- to 6-in. leaves marbled silver and white. Rose-pink flowers bloom on 3- to 4-in. stems in late summer, early fall. One of the most vigorous and easiest to grow; very reliable in cold-winter climates. Set tubers a foot apart. A white-flowered selection is available.

C. persicum. FLORISTS' CYCLAMEN. Mainly grown indoors. Original species has 2-in., fragrant, deep to pale pink or white blooms borne on 6-in. stems. Selective breeding has resulted in large-flowered florists' cyclamen (the old favorites) and newer, smaller strains; with rare exceptions, fragrance has disappeared. Plants typically have heart- or kidney-shaped, dark green leaves in the 1- to 5½-in. range, most often with silvery mottling. They bear crimson, red, salmon, purple, pink, or white flowers on 6- to 8-in. stems from late fall to spring. Potted plants can be kept from year to

year by withholding water at end of blooming period. Let plants go dormant in summer. Repot in late summer, resume watering, and place in bright light. Make sure top half of tuber is above soil surface.

Dwarf or miniature florists' cyclamens are half- or three-quarter–size replicas of standards. They can bloom in 7 to 8 months from seed. Miniature strains (profuse show of ½-in. flowers on 6- to 8-in. plants) include Miracle and Laser, both with fragrant blossoms.

C. purpurascens. Zones US, MS; USDA 6-7. Distinctly fragrant, crimson flowers on 5- to 6-in. stems, late summer or early fall. Nearly evergreen leaves are 3 in. wide, bright green mottled silvery white.

C. repandum. Zones MS, LS; USDA 7-8. Bright crimson flowers with long, narrow petals on 5- to 6-in. stems in spring. Tooth-edged, ivy-shaped leaves to 5 in. long are rich green marbled silver.

CARE

All cyclamens grow best in fairly rich, porous soil. Loosen soil to a depth of 1 ft. and mix in coarse sand and lots of organic matter. If soil is acid, also work in some lime, as cyclamens prefer a neutral to slightly alkaline pH. Plant tubers of most types 6–10 in. apart, ½ in. deep. (Florists' cyclamen is an exception: Upper half of tuber should protrude above soil level.) Best planting time for tubers is dormant period in summer—except for florists' cyclamen, which is always sold as a potted plant and can be planted out at any time. Top-dress annually with light application of potting soil with complete fertilizer added (being careful not to cover top of florists' cyclamen tubers). Do not cultivate around roots.

Plants grow readily from seed. Small-flowered, hardy species take several years to bloom; older strains of florists' cyclamen need 15 to 18 months to mature and bloom from seed, while newer strains can bloom in as little as 7 months. Grown outdoors in open ground, plants often self-sow. To encourage this, mulch around plants with a thin layer of fine gravel. This provides niches where seeds can lodge—and has the added benefit of improving drainage.

CYLINDROPUNTIA
CHOLLA
Cactaceae
Cacti

🌿 **US, MS, LS, CS, TS; USDA 6-11**

☀️ **FULL SUN**

◌ **LITTLE OR NO WATER, EXCEPT AS NOTED**

Cylindropuntia leptocaulis

Native to the desert Southwest, including Texas, the chollas are garden-worthy plants for anyone trying to minimize water use in a dry landscape. Like their *Opuntia* relatives, they have sections. Unlike the flat *Opuntia*, these are cylindrical, as their name suggests. In a garden they are sculptural and offer showy flowers and fruit. Remarkably cold hardy and drought tolerant.

C. imbricata (*Opuntia imbricata*). CHAIN-LINK CACTUS, WALKING-STICK CHOLLA. Native from Colorado to Mexico. Tree-like cactus with short trunk and branching, cylindrical stems; very slow growing, eventually reaching 3–6 ft. (sometimes as much as 10 ft.) tall. Never plant it near walkways or in gardens where children play; it has many sharp, inch-long spines as well as small, hairlike prickles that are more painful when they stick you (and harder to remove). Magenta, 2- to 3-in. blossoms in early summer; yellow, 1½-in.-long fruits. Very cold hardy.

C. leptocaulis (*Opuntia leptocaulis*). DESERT CHRISTMAS CACTUS, CHRISTMAS CHOLLA, PENCIL CACTUS, TASAJILLO. Native to Texas and desert Southwest. To 2-3 ft. (rarely to 6 ft.) high and equally wide. Joints are 1-12 in. long, ¾ in. thick, and have 1- to 2-in.-long spines. Spring flowers, to ¾ in. across, are green

to yellow. Fleshy fruits about the size and shape of olives mature from green to red, usually around Christmastime and hang on all winter. Very striking cold-hardy species.

CYMBIDIUM
TERRESTRIAL ORCHIDS
Orchidaceae

🌿 **US, MS, LS, CS, TS; USDA 6-11; SUBJECT TO CONDITIONS BELOW**

◑ **PARTIAL SHADE**

💧 **REGULAR WATER**

Cymbidium

Native to high altitudes in Southeast Asia, where rainfall is heavy and nights cool. Very popular because of their relatively easy culture. Except in frost-free areas, grow plants in containers in greenhouse or sunroom, or under overhang or high-branching tree. Long, narrow, grasslike leaves form a sheath around short, stout, oval pseudobulbs. Long-lasting flowers grow on erect or arching spikes and make excellent cut flowers. Standard types usually bloom from February to early May. Bloom season for miniatures starts in September and is usually heaviest from November to January.

Cymbidium growers typically list only hybrids in their catalogs—large-flowered selections with white, pink, yellow, green, or bronze blooms. Most have a yellow throat and dark red markings on lip. Large-flowered forms produce a dozen or more 4½- to 5-in. flowers per stem. Plants reach 2–3 ft. high. Miniature selections, about a quarter the size of large-flowered forms, are popular for their smaller size and free-blooming qualities.

HOW TO GROW CYMBIDIUMS

TEMPERATURES Plants prefer 45–55°F night temperature, rising to as high as 80–90°F during day. They'll stand temperatures as low as 28°F for a short time only, so where there is any danger of harder frosts, take plants inside or protect them with a covering of polyethylene film. Flower spikes are more tender than other plant tissues.

LIGHT For best bloom, give as much light as possible without burning foliage. Plants do well under shade cloth or lath. Leaf color is the guide: Plants with yellow-green leaves generally flower best; dark green foliage means too much shade. Cymbidiums should have shade during the flowering period, though; it prolongs bloom life and keeps flowers from fading.

SOIL Potting soil for cymbidiums should drain fast but retain moisture. Many commercial orchid mixes are available. If the store where you buy your cymbidiums doesn't offer a packaged cymbidium soil mix, here's a good one you can make: 2 parts composted bark, 2 parts peat moss, 1 part builder's sand.

WATERING & FEEDING Keep potting medium moist as new growth develops and matures—usually March to September. In winter, water just enough to keep bulbs from shriveling. On hot summer days, mist foliage early in day. Feed every 10 days to 2 weeks. From January to July, use a complete liquid fertilizer high in nitrogen, such as 30-10-10; from August to December, use a bloom-booster, lower-nitrogen fertilizer, such as 10-30-10.

CYMBOPOGON CITRATUS

LEMON GRASS
Poaceae
Tender perennial

🗡 **TS; USDA 10-11; ANNUAL ANYWHERE**

☀️ **FULL SUN**

💧 **REGULAR WATER**

Cymbopogon citratus

All parts of this plant from India are strongly lemon scented and are widely used as an ingredient in Southeast Asian cooking. Clumps of inch-wide leaves grow 3–4 ft. tall (or more) and 3 ft. wide. The base clump, composed of overlapping leaf bases, is nearly bulbous in appearance. Lemon grass can live over in the mildest-winter regions, but it's safer to pot up a division and keep it indoors or in a greenhouse over winter. Easily planted from divisions.

To harvest lemon grass, cut off the thick, bulbous stems just above the crown (ground level). Only the bottom third of each stalk is used; the bigger the better. Peel off the outer sheath and finely slice or pound the inner stem for salads or cooking. The sharp-edged blades (the upper part of the stems) are too tough to eat.

CYPERUS

Cyperaceae
Perennials

🗡 **ZONES VARY BY SPECIES**

☀️◐● **SUN OR SHADE**

💧 **AMPLE WATER**

Cyperus papyrus

These African natives are sedges—grasslike plants distinguished from true grasses by three-angled, solid stems and very different flowering parts. Valued for striking form, silhouette, shadow pattern.

Most species grow in rich, moist soil or with roots submerged in water. Keep plants groomed by removing dead or broken stems; divide and replant when the clump becomes too large, saving smaller, outside divisions and discarding the overgrown centers. Beyond their hardiness range, pot up divisions and keep them over the winter as houseplants.

C. albostriatus. DWARF UMBRELLA PLANT. Zones LS, CS, TS; USDA 9-11. Resembles *C. involucratus* but tends to be less hardy and shorter (to 20 in.), with broader leaves and lusher, softer appearance. Vigorous, invasive plant; best used in contained space.

C. alternifolius. UMBRELLA PLANT. Zones CS, TS; USDA 9-11. Narrow, firm, spreading leaves arranged like ribs of umbrella at tops of 2- to 4-ft. stems. Flowers in dry, greenish brown clusters. Grows in water or moist soil. Effective near pools, in pots or planters, or in dry streambeds or small rock gardens. Self-sows. Can become weedy and take over a small pool. 'Nanus' ('Gracilis') is a dwarf form to 1½ ft. high.

C. papyrus. PAPYRUS. Zones CS, TS; USDA 9-11. Tall, graceful, dark green stems 6–10 ft. high, topped with clusters of green, threadlike parts to 1½ ft. long (longer than small leaves at base of cluster). Will grow quickly in 2 in. of water in shallow pool, or can be potted and placed on bricks or inverted pot in deeper water. Protect from strong wind. Also grows well in rich, moist soil out of water. Used by flower arrangers.

C. prolifer. DWARF PAPYRUS. Zones CS, TS; USDA 9-11. Flowers and long, thin leaves combine to make filmy brown-and-green clusters on slender stems about 1½ ft. high. Use in Asian-style gardens; sink in pots in water gardens where delicate design of slender, leafless stems will not be lost among larger and coarser plants.

CYRILLA RACEMIFLORA

TITI, LEATHERWOOD
Cyrillaceae
Shrub or small tree

🗡 **MS, LS, CS, TS; USDA 7-11**

☀️◐ **FULL SUN OR PART SHADE**

💧💧💧 **REGULAR TO AMPLE WATER**

Cyrilla racemiflora

Native from Virginia to Florida and to eastern South America and the West Indies. Beautiful flowering shrub or small tree, 10–15 ft. (sometimes 30 ft.) tall, spreading to 15 ft.; semievergreen in Middle and Lower South, evergreen elsewhere. Grows naturally at water edges and in damp, low-lying areas. Noted for its twisted, contorted branches. Narrow, glossy, dark green, 1½- to

4-in.-long leaves; many of the leaves turn orange, rust, or red in fall. Blooms in early summer, bearing fragrant white flowers in dangling, 4- to 6-in.-long sprays. Tan seeds form in late summer and persist into winter. Needs moist, acid soil that is high in organic matter. Tolerates seasonal standing water. Plants sucker in wet soil and form large colonies. 'Graniteville' is a low-growing, spreading selection with smaller leaves.

CYRTANTHUS ELATUS

SCARBOROUGH LILY
Amaryllidaceae
Perennial from bulb

🌿 **CS, TS; USDA 9-11; OR GROW IN POTS**

🔆 **LIGHT SHADE, BRIGHT LIGHT**

💧 **REGULAR WATER DURING GROWTH AND BLOOM**

Cyrtanthus elatus

This South African native looks like a slightly smaller version of the familiar amaryllis (*Hippeastrum*). Good-looking, strap-shaped evergreen leaves grow to 1–2 ft. long. In summer and early autumn, clusters of bright orange-red, funnel-shaped flowers, each 2½–3 in. wide, appear atop 2-ft.-tall stalks. Pink- and white-flowered forms are also available. Will live in the ground year-round in the Coastal and Tropical South; quite tolerant of competition from tree roots. Usually grown in pots, however, since bulbs bloom better when somewhat potbound. Excellent potted plant for the patio or indoors (best with east- or south-facing exposure). Plant in

well-drained potting mix in June or July or just after flowering; set bulbs with tips just below soil surface. During active growth, fertilize monthly with a general-purpose liquid houseplant fertilizer. Water regularly during summer and fall, but let soil go slightly dry between waterings during semidormant period in winter and spring.

CYRTOMIUM

HOLLY FERN
Dryopteridaceae
Fern

🌿 **MS, LS, CS, TS; USDA 7-11; OR GROW IN POTS**

🔆⬤ **PARTIAL OR FULL SHADE**

💧 **REGULAR WATER**

Cyrtomium falcatum

These sturdy, adaptable ferns are so undemanding, they have naturalized in parts of the South. Not browsed by deer.

C. falcatum. Zones MS, LS, CS, TS; USDA 7-11. From Asia, South Africa, Polynesia. Coarse-textured but handsome evergreen fern to at least 1½-2 ft. tall, somewhat wider. Large, leathery, glossy, dark green fronds. Beautiful when used as a solid border or massed with other broad-leafed evergreens beneath the canopies of tall trees. Provide good soil; take care not to plant too deeply. Protect from wind. Can be brought indoors; give bright indirect light. 'Rochfordianum' has fringed leaflets.

C. fortunei. Zones US, MS, LS, CS; USDA 6-9. This evergreen fern from eastern Asia is more cold hardy than the more familiar *C. falcatum* but similar in size and texture.

CYTISUS

BROOM
Papilionaceae
Evergreen and deciduous shrubs

🌿 **US, MS, LS; USDA 6-8**

🔆 **FULL SUN**

💧 **MODERATE WATER**

Cytisus scoparius 'Pomona'

Tough, showy shrubs for dunes, dry hillsides, and other challenging spots. Sweet pea–shaped flowers are often fragrant. Tolerate wind; seashore conditions; and rocky, infertile soil. Prune after bloom to limit size, lessen production of unsightly seedpods. Not browsed by deer.

C. x praecox. WARMINSTER BROOM. Deciduous. Compact growth to 3–5 ft. high and 4–6 ft. wide, with many slender stems. Plant resembles a mounding mass of pale yellow to creamy white flowers in spring. Small leaves drop early. Effective as informal screen or hedge, along drives, paths, garden steps. 'Allgold', slightly taller, has bright yellow flowers; 'Hollandia' has pink ones.

C. scoparius. SCOTCH BROOM. Evergreen. Upright-growing mass of wandlike green stems (often leafless or nearly so) may reach 10 ft. Golden yellow, ¾-in. flowers bloom in spring and early summer. Reseeds readily; can be invasive.

Selections exist that are lower growing, more colorful, and much better behaved than *C. scoparius*. Most of these grow 5–8 ft. tall and wide. Choices include 'Burkwoodii', red blossoms touched with yellow; 'Carla', pink and crimson lined white; 'Dorothy Walpole', rose-pink and crimson;

'Lena', lemon-yellow and red; 'Lilac Time', lilac-pink blooms on a compact plant; 'Lord Lambourne', scarlet and cream; 'Minstead', white flushed deep purple and lilac; 'Moonlight', compact, pale yellow; 'Pomona', orange and apricot; 'St. Mary's', white; 'San Francisco' and 'Stanford', red.

DACTYLICAPNOS SCANDENS

CLIMBING YELLOW BLEEDING HEART
Papaveraceae
Climbing perennial

🌿 **ZONES MS, LS, CS; USDA 7-9**

🔆◐ **FULL SUN, AFTERNOON SHADE IN WARM ZONES**

💧 **REGULAR WATER**

💧 **MAY CAUSE CONTACT DERMATITIS**

Dactylicapnos scandens

Climbing plant reaches to 10 ft., blanketed with bright yellow, inch-long flowers starting in late spring or early summer, then continuing all summer. Yellowish green leaves to 1 ft. long are divided into ovate to lance-shaped leaflets; terminal leaflet reaches out like a tendril. Vigorous, rapid grower but not invasive. Can be grown as an annual. Needs more sun than other bleeding hearts, but it should be protected from hot afternoon sun. 'Athens Yellow' is a selection of the Himalayan species with deeper yellow blooms. Formerly known as *Dicentra scandens*.

DAHLIA

Asteraceae
Perennials from tuberous roots

US, MS, LS; USDA 6-8, EXCEPT AS NOTED

LIGHT AFTERNOON SHADE IN LOWER SOUTH

REGULAR WATER

Dahlia 'Little Beeswings'

Through centuries of hybridizing and selection, dahlias, which originated from Mexico and Guatemala, have become tremendously diversified, available in numerous flower types and flower sizes (from 2 to 12 in. across) and all colors but true blue. Bush and bedding dahlias range from 1 ft. to over 7 ft. tall. The tall bush forms are useful as summer hedges, screens, and fillers among shrubs; lower kinds give mass color in borders and containers. Modern dahlias, with their strong stems, long-lasting blooms that face outward or upward, and substantial, attractive foliage, are striking cut flowers. Leaves are generally divided into many large, deep green leaflets. Some forms have burgundy leaves; a well-known example is 'Bishop of Llandaff'. Not browsed by deer.

Dahlia flower forms. Dahlia flowers are composite (daisy-like) blooms containing many individual flowers called florets. One type of dahlia flower is composed of ray florets (which look like petals) surrounding a central cluster of petal-less disk florets. A second type has ray florets only. The American Dahlia Society has classified dahlias according to the flower forms described below. Blooms range in size from giant (over 10 in.), large (8–10 in.), and medium (6–8 in.) to small (4–6 in.), miniature (2–4 in.), and mignon (under 2 in.).

Anemone form. Single or multiple layers of rays surround tubular disk florets that form a "pincushion" center.

Collarette. One layer of long rays and a second, inner layer of shorter ones that form a "collar" around the center of the flower.

Orchid form. A single layer of rays with inrolled margins for two-thirds or more of their length, giving the flower a pinwheel appearance.

Peony form. Central disk florets are surrounded by two or more rows of rays; innermost rays may be curled or twisted.

Single. One layer of rays arranged in a plane around a central cluster of disk florets.

The following flower forms are composed of ray florets only.

Ball. Flower looks spherical, though it's flattish in profile. Rays have inrolled margins for at least half their length.

Cactus form. Ray margins roll downward; tips are pointed. Straight cactus rays radiate in all directions from center; may be straight or curved downward, margins rolled for over half their length. Incurved cactus rays are similar, but they curve upward. Semicactus flowers have broad-based rays with margins rolled along outer half (portion farthest from center); the rays may be straight or curve upward or downward.

Decorative. Full flowers of two types. Formal decorative has many overlapping layers of symmetrically arranged, fairly flat rays that tend to curve downward. Informal decorative is just as full, but rays are curved, curled, or twisted and are often arranged in a more irregular pattern.

Fimbriated. All rays are split at tips with split portions twisted, giving the flower a fringed look.

Pompon. Similar to ball form, but rays are inrolled along their entire length, giving them a tubular appearance.

Waterlily form. Broad rays curve slightly upward; flower profile is flat to saucer shaped, resembling a waterlily bloom.

Novelty. Any flower form not covered in previous categories.

TOP: Dahlia 'Juanita'; *BOTTOM: D.* 'Bishop of Llandaff'; *D.* 'Blackberry Ripple'

D. imperialis. TREE DAHLIA. Zones LS, CS, TS; USDA 8-11; hardy in MS, but frost there usually kills flower buds before they open. Multistemmed tree grows each year from permanent roots to a possible 10–20 ft. tall, 4–6 ft. wide. Daisylike, 4- to 8-in.-wide lavender flowers with yellow centers bloom at branch ends in late fall. Leaves divided into many leaflets. Frost kills tops completely; cut back to ground afterward. Annual dieback relegates tree

HEAT-TOLERANT DAHLIAS

Dahlias, which are native to higher elevation areas, prefer cooler weather than normally found in much of the South. However, with proper selection and mulching, they can succeed beautifully. Here are some selections that take the heat.

'Bishop of Llandaff' medium, semidouble, red; 3 ft. high with deep purple leaves

'Blackberry Ripple' large, semi-cactus, purple and cream, 3 ft.

'Clair de Lune' small, collarette, yellow with paler collar; 3–4 ft.

'Deuil du Roi Albert' medium, decorative, purple and white; 4–6 ft.

'Edinburgh' small, decorative, white and purple; 2–3 ft.

'Extase' medium, decorative, salmon and apricot; 12–15 in.

'Gallary Cezanne' small, decorative, yellow; 1–2 ft.

'Gallery Monet' small, decorative, white and pink; 1–2 ft.

'Garden Princess' small, cactus and semicactus, yellow, edged red; 1–2 ft.

'Jersey's Beauty' medium, formal decorative, pink; 6–7 ft.

'Juanita'. Small, cactus, ruby-red; 4 ft. high.

'Kidd's Climax' large, formal decorative, cream and pink; 3½ ft.

'Littlebees Wings' mignon, pompon, yellow tipped red; 3 ft.

'Night Queen' miniature, ball, deep wine-red; 3–4 ft.

'Prince Noir' small, semi-cactus, dark burgundy; 5–6 ft.

'Red Riding Hood' miniature, single, red; 1–2 ft.

'Thomas Edison' medium, formal decorative, dark purple; 3½ ft.

'Union Jack' miniature, single, red and white; 2–3 ft.

HOW TO GROW DAHLIAS

PLANTING Most dahlias are started from tuberous roots planted in spring, after danger of frost is past and soil is warm. Several weeks before planting, dig soil to a foot deep and work in organic matter such as compost or ground bark. At planting time, dig about 1-ft.-deep planting holes—1½ ft. wide for larger dahlias (over 4 ft. tall), 9–12 in. wide for smaller types. Space roots of larger selections 4–5 ft. apart, those of smaller ones 1–2 ft. apart.

Mix about ¼ cup of low-nitrogen granular fertilizer or compost into the soil at the bottom of each planting hole, then add 4 in. of soil before placing the root in the center of the hole, its growth bud pointing up. When planting a tall selection, drive a 5- to 6-ft. stake into the hole just off center; place the root horizontally in bottom of hole, 2 in. from the stake and with bud pointing toward it. Cover roots with 3 in. of soil. Water thoroughly. As shoots grow, gradually fill hole with soil.

Dahlias can be started from seed. For tall types, start seeds early indoors; transplant seedlings into garden beds after frost danger is past. For dwarf dahlias, sow seed in place after soil is warm, or buy and plant started seedlings from the nursery. Dwarf dahlias are usually replaced each year, though they can be lifted.

THINNING & PINCHING On tall-growing dahlias, thin out shoots when they're about 6 in. high, leaving only the strongest one or two. When remaining shoots have three sets of leaves, pinch off tops just above the upper set; smaller-flowered dahlias, such as pompons, singles, and dwarfs, need only this first pinching. For the best show of larger-flowered dahlias, pinch again by removing all but terminal flower buds on side shoots.

PLANT CARE After shoots are above ground, start watering regularly to a foot deep; continue throughout active growth. Dahlias planted in enriched soil shouldn't need additional food, but if your soil is light or if roots stayed in the ground the previous year, apply a granular low-nitrogen fertilizer or more compost when the first flower buds show. Mulch to discourage weeds and to eliminate cultivating, which may injure feeder roots.

CUTTING FLOWERS Pick nearly mature flowers in early morning or evening. Immediately place cut stems in 2–3 in. of hot water; let stand in gradually cooling water for several hours or overnight.

LIFTING & STORING In climates where ground freezes in winter, dig and store tuberous roots in fall. In other regions, roots may remain in place as long as drainage is excellent and winter temperatures remain above 20°F. In borderline climates, mulch with 4-in. layer of straw or similar material.

To lift the roots, cut stalks to 4 in. above ground after the tops turn yellow or are frosted. Dig a 2-ft.-wide circle around each plant; carefully pry up clump with spading fork, shake off loose soil, and let the clump dry in sun for several hours. Do not wash them off. From that point, follow either of these methods.

METHOD 1: Divide clumps immediately after digging in fall. Freshly dug roots are easy to cut, and eyes (growth buds) are easy to recognize at this time. To divide, cut the stalks with a sharp knife, leaving 1 in. of stalk attached to each section; make sure each division has an eye, so it will produce a new plant. Dust cut surfaces with sulfur to prevent rot; bury in dry sand, sawdust, peat moss, or perlite and store over winter in a cool (40–45°F), dark, dry place.

METHOD 2: Leave clumps intact until spring. Cover them with dry sand, sawdust, peat moss, or perlite and store in cool, dark, dry place as directed above. With Method 2, roots are less likely to shrivel.

About 2 to 4 weeks before planting in spring, separate intact clumps, as described under Method 1. Then place all roots—whether fall- or spring-divided—in moist sand.

dahlia to tall novelty class; available from specialists. Grow from cuttings taken near stem tops (or from side shoots) in fall; root in containers of moist sand kept in a protected place over winter. Or dig root clump and divide in fall. 'California Angel' has double white blooms.

DANAE RACEMOSA
ALEXANDRIAN LAUREL, POET'S LAUREL
Asparagaceae
Evergreen shrub

✎ **MS, LS, CS; USDA 7-9**

◑ ● **PARTIAL TO FULL SHADE**

💧 **REGULAR WATER**

Danae racemosa

Native to northern Iran and Asia Minor. Rare in gardens, this elegant, pest-free shrub deserves much wider use. It grows 2–4 ft. tall and wide, spreading slowly by underground rhizomes. The glossy green, lance-shaped "leaves" along its arching stems are actually modified stems called cladophylls; they reach 4 in. long. Inconspicuous greenish yellow flowers appear in summer, followed by showy red berries at least ¼ in. across that persist into fall and winter. Cut branches are highly prized by flower arrangers. Newly emerging shoots in spring resemble elongating spears of asparagus, to which the plant is closely related.

Alexandrian laurel makes an elegant addition to the shade border. Give it moist, rich, well-drained soil and shield it from direct sun. Propagate by division in spring. Prune away winter-damaged foliage in early spring. Not browsed by deer.

DANDELION

Asteraceae
Perennial

- US, MS, LS, CS; USDA 6-9
- FULL SUN
- REGULAR WATER

Dandelion

If the sight of bright yellow dandelions dotting your otherwise perfect lawn drives you nuts, blame it on the Pilgrims. It was they who reportedly brought the plant to America from its homeland in northern Europe in the early 1600s. Of course, they had good reasons for doing so. The common dandelion (*Taraxacum officinale*) is among the most nutritious and useful of herbs, with a long history of culinary and medicinal use. Its leaves, which can be boiled or eaten fresh, are high in potassium, iron, and vitamins A, C, B1, and B2. The dried and roasted roots make an acceptable coffee substitute, and the fermented flowers produce dandelion wine and beer. Dandelion tonics are a folk-medicine remedy for liver problems. Beekeepers value dandelions as a rich source of nectar and pollen.

This deep-rooted perennial forms a rosette of sharply toothed leaves 6–12 in. long. Their fancied resemblance to a lion's teeth gives the plant its common name—"dandelion," a corruption of the French *dent de lion* ("lion's tooth"). Blossoms appear from late winter through fall, carried atop hollow stems 4–15 in. high; they're followed by the familiar puffball seed heads that children like to blow on, releasing the seeds to fly hither and yon. Dandelions are usually quickly dispatched by gardeners armed with broadleaf weed killers, but some folks grow the culinary types (selected for larger, thicker leaves) found in specialty seed catalogs. Culinary selections such as 'Pissenlit' and 'Ameliore' give best yield with full sun and fertile, moist, well-drained soil. Pick only young leaves for salads; old ones can be bitter. Culinary dandelions are just as invasive as the common ones, so be sure to remove and dispose of the seed heads before they mature.

DAPHNE

Thymelaeaceae
Evergreen, semievergreen, deciduous shrubs

- ZONES VARY BY SPECIES
- LIGHT SHADE
- MODERATE WATER, EXCEPT AS NOTED
- ALL PARTS, ESPECIALLY FRUITS, ARE POISONOUS IF INGESTED

Daphne odora 'Aureomarginata'

These delightful, well-behaved shrubs merit a place in practically every garden. Having one or more on display earns you instant respect from the gardening cognoscenti. Although some daphnes are easier to grow than others, all require excellent drainage, cool soil (accomplished with mulch and light afternoon shade), occasional watering during summer dry spells, and protection from hot sun and heavy winds. Plants respond well to pruning but rarely need more than an occasional snip to correct their shape—cut back to lateral branches or just above a growth bud. Cut branches can be forced into early bloom indoors in winter. Daphnes are not browsed by deer.

D. burkwoodii. BURKWOOD DAPHNE. Evergreen or semievergreen to deciduous. Zones US, MS, LS; USDA 6-9. Erect, compact growth to 3–4 ft. tall and wide, densely foliaged with narrow, medium green leaves to 1½ in. long. Abundant small clusters of fragrant flowers (white fading to pink) appear at branch ends in late spring and again in late summer. 'Brigg's Moonlight' has pale yellow leaves with a narrow green border; 'Carol Mackie' has gold-edged green leaves. 'Somerset' is larger (to 4 ft. tall and 6 ft. wide) and produces pink flowers. Use all in shrub borders, at woodland edges, as foundation plantings.

D. cneorum. ROSE DAPHNE, GARLAND DAPHNE. Evergreen. Zones US, MS; USDA 6-7. From mountains of central and southern Europe. Matting and spreading; less than 1 ft. high and 3 ft. wide. Good container plant. Trailing branches covered with narrow, 1-in.-long, dark green leaves. Clusters of fragrant, rosy pink flowers appear in spring. Choice rock garden plant. After bloom is through, top-dress with mix of peat moss and sand to keep roots cool and induce additional rooting of trailing stems.

Selections include 'Eximia', lower than the species (to 8 in. high) and with larger flowers; *D. c. pygmaea* 'Alba', 3 in. tall, 1 ft. wide, with white flowers; 'Ruby Glow', with larger, more deeply colored flowers than those of the species and with late-summer rebloom; and 'Variegata', with attractive gold-edged leaves.

D. genkwa. LILAC DAPHNE. Deciduous. Zones US, MS, LS; USDA 6-8. From China. Erect, open growth to 3–4 ft. high and wide. Before leaves expand, clusters of lilac-blue, scentless flowers wreathe branches, making foot-long wands of blossoms. White fruit follows flowers. Oval, medium green, 2-in.-long leaves. Use in rock garden, shrub border. Probably the easiest daphne to grow.

D. mezereum. FEBRUARY DAPHNE. Deciduous. Zones US, MS; USDA 6-7. From Europe, Caucasus, Siberia. Rather gawky, stiff-twigged, erect growth to 4 ft. tall and 3 ft. wide, with thin, roundish, 2- to 3-in.-long leaves in pale green to gray-green. Plant in groups for best appearance. Fragrant, reddish purple flowers in short, stalkless clusters are carried along branches in mid- or late winter before leaf-out and continue into spring. May go dormant in summer. Clustered red fruit follows flowers. *D. m. alba* has white flowers and yellow fruit and is not as rangy as the species.

D. odora. WINTER DAPHNE. Evergreen. Zones MS, LS; USDA 7-8. From China, Japan. So prized for its pervasive floral perfume that it continues to be widely planted despite its unpredictable behavior—it can die despite the most attentive care, or flourish with little attention until you invite all your gardening friends over to admire it, at which point it promptly succumbs without warning, just to show you who's in charge. Very neat, handsome plant, usually to about 4 ft. high and 6 ft. wide. Rather narrow, deep green, 3-in.-long leaves are thick and glossy. Nosegay clusters of charming, intensely fragrant flowers—pink to deep red on outside, with creamy pink throats—appear at branch ends in winter.

The following are among the selections available.

'Leucanthe' is relatively disease resistant, with white-throated pale pink blooms; 'Aureomar-

THE BLOOMS OF MOST *DAPHNES* ARE HIGHLY FRAGRANT. JUST A COUPLE OF CUT SPRAYS CAN PERFUME AN ENTIRE ROOM.

ginata' ('Marginata'), more widely grown than the species, has yellow-edged leaves. 'Mae-jima' has a compact habit with leaves edged cream and yellow and is an improvement over 'Aureomarginata'. *D.o. alba* has white flowers; terminal growth sometimes distorted by fascia-tion (convoluted-looking growths resembling cockscombs).

This species needs much air around its roots, so plant in porous soil (as you would rhodo-dendrons). Always set plant a bit high, so the juncture of roots and stems is 1–2 in. above soil grade. Where soil is heavy and poorly drained, grow in porous, organic soil mixture in raised bed or container. Transplanting is risky, so choose site carefully.

Plant this daphne where it can get at least 3 hours of shade each day around midday. If possible, shade soil around roots with living ground cover. A soil pH of 6.0-7.0 is right for it. Feed right af-ter bloom with complete fertilizer (but not with acid plant food).

DAPHNIPHYLLUM MACROPODUM

YUZURI-HA TREE
Daphniphyllaceae
Evergreen shrub or small tree

🌿 **MS, LS, CS; USDA 7-9**

☀ ◑ **FULL SUN OR LIGHT SHADE**

💧 **MODERATE WATER**

Daphniphyllum macropodum

An under-used beauty native to China, Korea, and Japan. Looks somewhat like a rhododendron in form and foliage. Leaves are 3-8 in. long, shiny dark green with silvery undersides and red petioles extending into the

midvein. The foliage is the main attraction. Make sure you select plants with good red color; seedlings vary. Flowers are not showy; followed by small, blackish blue fruit on female plants. Grows as a rounded shrub or small tree, 10–15 ft. high. Plant in well-drained soil, rich in organic matter.

DARMERA PELTATA

UMBRELLA PLANT, INDIAN RHUBARB
Saxifragaceae
Perennial

🌿 **US, MS; USDA 6-7**

◑ **PARTIAL SHADE**

💧 **AMPLE WATER**

Darmera peltata

Native to mountains of Northern California and Oregon. Large, round clusters of pink flowers appear on bare stalks to 6 ft. tall in spring. Shield-shaped, 1- to 2-ft.-wide leaves appear later on 2- to 6-ft. stalks. Each plant spreads 4–8 ft. wide. Stout rhizomes to 2 in. thick grow in damp ground or even into streams. A spectacular plant for pond, stream, or damp, cool woodland site. 'Nana' is compact, to 2 ft. high.

DASYLIRION

SOTOL
Asparagaceae
Evergreen shrubs

🌿 **ZONES VARY BY SPECIES**

☀ ◑ **FULL SUN OR LIGHT SHADE**

💧 **LITTLE OR NO WATER TO MODERATE WATER**

Dasylirion quadrangulatum

Native to the deserts and mountains of the Southwest and Mexico, these yucca relatives tolerate dry, rocky, alkaline soil and considerable drought, though some irrigation will speed growth. They resemble *Nolina*—but unlike those plants, most sotols have sharp prickles along their leaf margins.

Given plenty of room to spread out, sotols make a bold statement in the garden. Their long, narrow leaves—ranging in color from dark green to blue-green to silvery—can be upright or drooping. The foliage rosette sits atop a woody base that can, with age, form a treelike trunk. Mature plants may bloom in summer, bearing tiny flowers in tight clus-ters on a tall, narrow spike. There are male and female plants; you need one of each to obtain seed.

D. berlandieri. BLUE SOTOL. Zones LS, CS, TS; USDA 8-11. Native to Mexico. Grows 4–6 ft. tall and wide, with slightly arching blue-green leaves to 4 ft. long and 7 in. wide. Male flowers are rust colored; female blossoms are chartreuse. Leaves of 'Delores' curl at the ends. 'Monterrey' features swordlike silvery foliage; 'Zaragoza' sports twisted, strik-ingly blue leaves.

D. leiophyllum. SMOOTH SOTOL. Zones MS, LS, CS, TS; USDA 7-11. Native to West Texas, New Mexico, and northeastern

Mexico. Grows 4–5 ft. tall and wide. Smooth, shiny, green to blue-green leaves are just 1¼ in. wide but over 3 ft. long; margins are lined with stout teeth. Whitish flowers are borne on a spike to 12 ft. or taller. One of the most cold-hardy and drought-tolerant sotols.

D. miquihuanensis. TREE SOTOL. Zones US, MS, LS, CS, TS; USDA 6-11. Large, fast-growing native of the mountains of northeastern Mexico. Over time, grows 8 ft. tall and 6 ft. wide, with a massive trunk and green leaves that reach 4 ft. long and 2 in. wide. Flowers similar to those of *D. texanum*.

D. quadrangulatum (*D. longissimum*). MEXICAN GRASS TREE. Zones MS, LS, CS, TS; USDA 7-11. Native to mountains of northeastern Mexico. Forms a fountainlike clump to about 5 ft. high and wide. Dark green, 3-ft.-long leaves are very narrow—less than 1 in. wide—and unlike leaves of other species, they have smooth margins. Trunk grows slowly, extending the plant's height to at least 15 ft. over time. White to cream-colored flowers appear on a 6-ft. spike.

D. texanum. TEXAS SOTOL. Zones MS, LS, CS, TS; USDA 7-11. Native to Texas Hill Country. Stiff, spiny, sharp-edged green leaves, to 2½–3 ft. long and 1½ in. wide, reflect light prettily as they move in the breeze. Plant grows 3 ft. tall and 4 ft. wide; small whitish flowers appear on a spike that may reach 15 ft. high. More tolerant of cold, moisture, and shade than most other sotols.

D. wheeleri. DESERT SPOON, DESERT SOTOL. Zones MS, LS, CS, TS; USDA 7-11. Native to West Texas, Arizona, and northern Mexico. Forms a near-spherical clump 3–5 ft. high, 4–5 ft. wide. Spiky, fairly stiff, bluish gray leaves to 3 ft. long and less than 1 in. wide. Slowly forms a trunk covered with dried, drooping shag of old leaves (if these are not trimmed off as they fade). Base of each leaf broadens where it joins the trunk to form a long-handled "spoon" prized in dried arrangements. Produces white flowers on a 9- to 15-ft.-tall spike; plants occasionally die after flowering.

CARE

Fast-draining soil is essential. If your soil is heavy, amend it with lots of sand and coarse gravel, or plant in large containers. Spring is the best time for planting. Mulch with gravel rather than organic matter, and keep plants as dry as possible during winter. Promptly remove old, withered leaves at the base for a neater appearance. Pests aren't usually a problem.

DATURA
ANGEL'S TRUMPET
Solanaceae
Annuals and perennials

🌡 **ZONES VARY BY SPECIES**

☼ **FULL SUN**

💧 **REGULAR WATER**

⬦ **ALL PARTS ARE HIGHLY TOXIC IF INGESTED**

Datura inoxia

Together with *Brugmansia*, this genus forms the showy group of plants known as angel's trumpets. Daturas differ from Brugmansias in several ways, however: they are herbaceous rather than shrublike, their flowers are upright rather than pendent, and their seedpods are swollen and spiny rather than beanlike.

D. inoxia. DOWNY ANGEL'S TRUMPET. Perennial. Zones LS, CS, TS; USDA 8-11. Bushy plant native to the southwestern U.S. and Mexico. To 3 ft. tall and wide, with oval, pointed, downy leaves to 10 in. long. Showy, lightly fragrant flowers, 6–8 in. long, may be pink, lavender, or white. Good choice for containers.

D. 'La Fleur Lilac' ('La Fleur Lilas'). Perennial. Dwarf hybrid involving *D. stramonium* that reaches only 3–4 ft. tall and not quite as wide. Serrated, dark green leaves; pale lilac, sweetly fragrant blooms. Small size and compact habit make it ideal for containers.

D. metel. HORN OF PLENTY. Annual. Zones US, MS, LS, CS, TS; USDA 6-11. Native to southern China and India. Grows quickly, reaching 5 ft. tall and 4 ft. wide by late summer. Oval, pointed leaves to 8 in. long; exotic-looking flowers, up to 8 in. long, in white or purple shades. Selections include 'Alba', bearing pure white flowers; 'Aurea', with golden yellow blooms; and 'Belle Blanche, with large leaves and white flowers. 'Cornucopia' features gorgeous double purple-and-white blossoms. This species self-sows aggressively; seedlings are easily transplanted, making it a favorite passalong plant.

CARE

Daturas are easy to grow if given fertile, moist, well-drained soil; full sun; and an occasional feeding with a balanced general-purpose houseplant fertilizer. They're easily propagated from seeds, which burst from seed capsules in late summer. Some species reseed rampantly. Where plants aren't winter hardy, store them in a cool greenhouse or unheated garage during cold months.

DAUCUS CAROTA CAROTA
QUEEN'S ANNE'S LACE
Apiaceae
Biennial

🌡 **US, MS, LS, CS; USDA 6-9**

☼ **FULL SUN**

💧 **MODERATE WATER**

Daucus carota carota

Though we think of it as a Southern wildflower, Queen Anne's lace actually hails from northern Europe and Asia and is a wild form of the carrot (*D. carota sativus*)—but unlike its culinary kin (see Carrot), it forms only a small, inedible root. It compensates for that lack, however, with the lacy, flat-topped white flower clusters that grace fields and meadows in early summer.

Plants grow to about 3 ft. tall. After the flowers fade, old blooms curl up into a cup-shaped clump of seeds resembling a bird's nest. Seeds disperse widely and germinate readily, which explains how the plant has become so widespread. Queen Anne's lace is ideal for naturalized areas and cottage gardens; to add it to your plantings, gently crush a seed cluster in your hand and sprinkle the seeds onto bare soil in late summer. One seed cluster per garden is plenty. Plants thrive in full sun and well-drained soil. Seedlings form tufts of lacy foliage the first year, flower and set seed the second year, then die. Excellent as a cut flower—and if you gather most of the blooms for arrangements, fewer seeds will be formed and spread will be more manageable.

DAVIDIA INVOLUCRATA
DOVE TREE, HANDKERCHIEF TREE
Nyssaceae
Deciduous tree

🌡 **US, MS; USDA 6-7**

☽ **PARTIAL SHADE**

💧 **REGULAR WATER**

Davidia involucrata

Native to China. This is one tree you crow about if it blooms in your garden. In gardens, grows 20–40 ft. tall, 12–25 ft. wide, with pyramidal to rounded crown and strong branching pattern. Has clean look in and out of leaf. Roundish to heart-shaped, 3- to 6-in.-long leaves are vivid green. Comes into bloom in spring; general effect is that of white doves resting among green leaves (or handkerchiefs drying on branches). Small, clustered, red-anthered flowers are carried between two large white or creamy white bracts of unequal size (one 6 in. long, the other about 4 in. long). Trees often take 10 years to come into flower, then may bloom more heavily in alternate years. No fall color. Brown fruit about the size of golf balls hangs on tree well into winter. Susceptibility to stem canker, anthracnose, and powdery mildew makes it challenging to grow in the South.

Plant this tree by itself; it should not compete with other flowering trees. Pleasing in front of dark conifers, where vivid green and white stand out.

DECUMARIA BARBARA
CLIMBING HYDRANGEA, WOOD VAMP
Hydrangeaceae
Deciduous vine

🌡 **US, MS, LS, CS; USDA 6-9**

☽ ● **PARTIAL OR FULL SHADE**

💧 💧💧 **REGULAR TO AMPLE WATER**

Decumaria barbara

Native to wet woodlands and swamps from East Texas to Florida and Virginia. Grows to 30 ft. or more, attaching to walls with aerial rootlets or running loose over the ground. Handsome, oval and pointed, glossy green leaves, 2–4 in. long, 1–2 in. wide. Fragrant, white or yellowish white flowers in dense clusters 2–4 in. across appear in May or June. They're attractive but not showy. Old vines sometimes bear showy, urn-shaped fruit. Leaves turn yellow in fall. Best in moist, shady sites and fertile soil but will also grow in fairly dry woods. Takes some direct sun if kept moist. Of the three vines known as climbing hydrangeas—*Hydrangea anomala* and *Schizophragma hydrangeoides* are the others—this is the only Southern native, and it is the least known.

DELONIX REGIA
ROYAL POINCIANA, FLAMBOYANT
Caesalpiniaceae
Partially or wholly deciduous tree

🗡 **TS; USDA 10-11**

☼ **FULL SUN**

🌢 **REGULAR WATER DURING GROWTH AND BLOOM**

Delonix regia

From Madagascar. "Flamboyant" is the word to describe poinciana. Its large trusses of 4-in., orange-to-scarlet flowers with white markings put on a spectacular display in late spring or early summer. Considered by many the most beautiful of the world's flowering trees. Wide-spreading, umbrella-shaped tree of rapid growth to 30 ft. tall and twice as wide. Fernlike leaves, finely cut into many tiny leaflets, give filtered shade. Blooms are followed by 2-ft.-long black seedpods that hang on bare winter branches. Easy to grow but sensitive to cold.

DELOSPERMA
ICE PLANT
Aizoaceae
Succulent perennials

🗡 **US, MS, LS, CS; USDA 6-9, EXCEPT AS NOTED**

☼ ◖ **LIGHT AFTERNOON SHADE IN HOTTEST CLIMATES**

◖ 🌢 **LITTLE TO MODERATE WATER**

Delosperma cooperi

Along with a few other genera, these low-growing succulents are all known as ice plants. *Delosperma* species, most of which hail from South Africa, are the best ice plants for the South (they do particularly well in the Southwest). They never grow more than a few inches high but spread to form ground-hugging mats ideal for covering a bank or slope. Daisylike flowers (about 2 in. across) appear above the small, succulent leaves, which may be cylindrical or flattened. Need full sun, good drainage, and just enough water to keep them looking fresh. Mulch with gravel to keep base of plant dry. Withhold water in fall to harden off plants for winter.

D. ashtonii. ASHTON'S ICE PLANT. Zones MS, LS, CS; USDA 7-9. Dark lavender-pink flowers with yellow centers bloom over a long period in summer, held on 4- to 6-in.-tall stalks above gray-green leaves that are broader than those of most other species.

D. congestum 'Gold Nugget'. Summer into fall, butter-yellow blossoms emerge from tight clumps of beadlike, dark green leaves. Grows I in. tall, up to 9 in. wide. Foliage turns red in winter.

D. cooperi. PURPLE ICE PLANT. Zones MS, LS, CS; USDA 7-9. Purple flowers appear all summer above light blue-green foliage. To 3–5 in. tall, spreading quickly to 2 ft. across. Hardy to 0°F if protected by snow or mulch.

D. dyeri 'Red Mountain'. Forms a neat carpet 2–4 in. high and 10–20 in. wide. Summer flowers are pinkish red, fading to bronze with creamy white centers. Good ground cover.

D. floribundum 'Starburst'. Glowing lilac-pink blooms, each with a central white eye, appear above shiny, deep green foliage from summer to fall. Grows 4 in. tall, 10–20 in. wide.

D. hybrids. Zones US, MS, LS; USDA 6-8. 'Kelaidis', also called Mesa Verde ice plant, is a vigorous, cold-tolerant hybrid that grows 2 in. high and 1–2 ft. wide, with pale salmon-pink flowers (1½ in. across) from spring until fall. 'John Proffitt', Table Mountain ice plant, is similar but has fuchsia flowers. Both make excellent ground covers.

D. nubigenum. HARDY ICE PLANT. Only 1–2 in. tall, spreading to 3 ft. Cylindrical lime-green leaves turn red in winter. Bright yellow flowers, 1–1½ in. wide, are borne in great profusion in late spring. Excellent ground cover. Very cold hardy, surviving to –10°F. 'Basutoland' is an improved form that reaches 2–4 in. tall.

D. sphalmanthoides. TUFTED ICE PLANT. Tight mat of gray-green foliage grows only ½ in. high and 8 in. wide. Early spring show of pinkish purple flowers.

DELPHINIUM
Ranunculaceae
Perennials, some treated as biennials or annuals

🗡 **ZONES VARY BY SPECIES**

☼ **FULL SUN, EXCEPT AS NOTED**

🌢 **REGULAR WATER, EXCEPT AS NOTED**

Delphiniun elatum

Often associated with the grand borders of England, stately delphiniums are problematic in most of the South. Those fancy hybrids (such as *D. elatum* hybrids) can't take our long, hot, humid summers and seldom last more than a year or two; in fact, they're best treated as annuals. Native species may be less spectacular than the hybrids, but they are reliably perennial, rising up in the garden year after year.

Bloom typically comes from spring to early summer. Cool blue is the classic—and probably the favorite—color, but delphiniums are also available in white, yellow, pink, lavender, purple, and red. Leaves are lobed and fanlike, variously cut and divided. All delphiniums are effective in borders and make good cut flowers; lower-growing types do well in containers. The blossoms attract birds. For annual delphinium (larkspur), see *Consolida ajacis*.

D. belladonna. Zones US, MS; USDA 6-7. To 3–4 ft. tall, 2 ft. wide. Sturdy, bushy plant with deeply cut leaves and short-stemmed, airy flower clusters. Selections include light blue 'Belladonna', dark blue 'Bellamosum', white 'Casa Blanca', and deep turquoise blue 'Cliveden Beauty'. All have 1½- to 2½-in.-wide flowers and are longer lived than tall hybrids listed under *D. elatum*.

D. carolinianum. CAROLINA LARKSPUR. Zones US, MS, LS; USDA 6-8. Native to the Southeast, southern Midwest, Texas. Narrow plant (just 6 in. wide at base) bears erect, 1- to 3-ft. spikes of blue or white flowers. Blooms heavily in spring, then goes dormant in summer. Reseeds readily and tolerates just about any well-drained soil.

D. elatum. CANDLE DELPHINIUM. Zones US; USDA 6, elsewhere as an annual. Siberian species to 3–6 ft. tall and 2 ft. wide, with small dark or dull purple flowers. Along with *D. cheilanthum* and others, it is a parent of modern tall-growing delphinium strains.

Pacific strain hybrids (also called Giant Pacific, Pacific hybrids, and Pacific Coast hybrids) grow to 8 ft. tall. They are available in selected color series; members of these include 'Blue Bird', medium blue; 'Blue Jay', medium to dark blue; 'Galahad', white with white center; 'Percival', white with black center; 'Summer Skies', light blue. Other purple, lavender, pink named selections are sold.

Like Pacific strain but shorter (2–2½ ft. tall) are the Blue Fountains, Blue Springs, and Magic Fountains strains. Even shorter is the Stand Up strain (15–20 in.). These shorter strains seldom require staking.

Centurion is a long-stalked (4–5 ft. tall), large-flowered hybrid strain similar to the Pacific strain. It too will bloom the first year from seed, but it's more reliably perennial. New Millennium hybrids come in a range of heights and colors and were bred for heat tolerance and mildew resistance.

Other strains have flowers in shades of lilac-pink to deep raspberry-rose, clear lilac, lavender, royal purple, and darkest violet.

D. exaltatum. TALL LARKSPUR. Zones US, MS, LS; USDA 6-8. Native to moist woods from Pennsylvania and Ohio south to North Carolina and Alabama. Showy true blue flowers appear on spikes 3–6 ft. tall in summer; plants reach 1–2 ft. wide. Best in light shade but blooms even in full shade. Tolerates drought once established.

D. grandiflorum (*D. chinense*). CHINESE DELPHINIUM, BOUQUET DELPHINIUM. Short-lived perennial treated as biennial or annual. Zones US, MS, LS, CS, TS; USDA 6-11. Native to Siberia and eastern Asia. Bushy, branching, 1 ft. tall or less. Selections include 'Dwarf Blue Mirror', 1 ft., upward-facing, deep blue flowers; and 'Tom Thumb', 8 in. tall, pure gentian-blue flowers.

CARE

Delphiniums are easy to grow from seed. In the Middle, Lower, and Coastal South, sow fresh seed in flats or pots filled with potting soil in July or August; set out transplants in October for bloom in late spring and early summer. In the Upper South, sow seed in March or April, and set out transplants in June or July for first bloom by September (and more bloom the following spring).

Plants need rich, porous soil and regular feeding. Improve poor or heavy soils by working in lots of organic matter. Add lime to strongly acid soils. Work a handful of superphosphate into the soil around the root ball. Be careful not to bury the plant's root crown.

When new stalks appear in spring, remove all but the strongest two or three, tie to stakes, and apply a bloom-booster fertilizer. After blooms fade, cut stalks nearly to the ground, leaving foliage at the bottom. Fertilize again, and you may get a second bloom.

DENDROBIUM

Orchidaceae
Epiphytic orchids

🌿 TS; USDA 10-11; OR HOUSEPLANT

☼ LIGHT SHADE; BRIGHT LIGHT

💧 REGULAR WATER

Dendrobium

This huge genus (it may include as many as 1,400 species and even more hybrids) ranges from Japan and the Himalayas to Australia and the Pacific islands. Many are grown by orchid fanciers in greenhouses (outdoors in southern Florida). Some have thin, canelike pseudobulbs, others short, fat ones. Only a few of the more widely grown are mentioned here.

Culturally, dendrobiums fall into two classes. Intermediate-climate types are evergreen; they need water throughout the year (somewhat less in winter) and temperatures similar to those required by cattleya orchids. Cool growers drop some or all of their leaves during a period of winter dormancy, at which time they need very little water (only enough to keep pseudobulbs from shrinking) and temperatures suitable for green-leafed paphiopedilums.

D. bigibbum phalaenopsis (*D. phalaenopsis*). Intermediate grower. Native to Australia, New Guinea. Blooms throughout the year, with canes up to 3 ft. tall producing arching spikes that carry as many as ten 3-in. purple flowers. The parent of many hybrids.

D. hybrids. A bewildering number of hybrids have been produced in Hawaii and elsewhere, both for ornamental pot plants and for cut flowers and leis. Most are intermediate growers. Buy plants in bloom to get desired flower color and bloom season.

D. kingianum. Cool grower. Native to Australia. Makes large clumps of 2- to 20-in. pseudobulbs topped by 4-in. leaves. In late winter or early spring, erect spikes to 8 in. long carry a few or up to as many as 20 fragrant, inch-wide flowers in pink, white, or red.

D. nobile. Cool grower. Himalayan native. Canes 12–20 in. tall carry two ranks of 2- to 3½-in. leaves; leaves last for about 2 years. Short inflorescences on leafy and leafless canes carry two to four fragrant, 1½-in., white-to-purplish pink flowers with a yellow or white zone around a dark purple eye. Blooms almost any time of year. The parent of many colorful hybrids.

D. speciosum. Cool grower. From Australia. Large masses of pseudobulbs (ranging in height from 4 in.–3 ft.) are topped with leaves that are 1½–10 in. long. Blooms in late winter or early spring. Inflorescences are crowded spikes of fragrant, creamy-to-yellow flowers; they resemble bushy foxtails, can reach 2–2½ ft. long.

CARE

Indoors, dendrobiums need at least 6 hours of good sunlight per day; place them directly in front of a southern window. During active growth and bloom, they need high humidity and frequent watering. Feed monthly with water-soluble 30-10-10 fertilizer. Easier to bloom in a greenhouse than a home.

DENNSTAEDTIA PUNCTILOBULA

HAY-SCENTED FERN
Dennstaedtiaceae
Fern

🌿 US, MS; USDA 6-7

☼ LIGHT SHADE

💧 MODERATE TO REGULAR WATER

Dennstaedtia punctilobula

Native from eastern Canada to the Midsouth. Deciduous fern with finely divided yellow-green fronds to 2 ft. tall arising from creeping rhizomes. Plant spreads quickly to make an attractive ground cover. Crushed fronds smell like freshly cut hay. If given adequate water, thrives even in poor, rocky soil. Can form mats that cover rocks. You may see it growing along the roadside or under rail fences in partly shaded areas.

D

DESCHAMPSIA

HAIR GRASS
Poaceae
Perennial grasses

◢ ZONES VARY BY SPECIES

☼ ◐ FULL SUN OR PARTIAL SHADE

◗ ◗ MODERATE TO REGULAR WATER

Deschampsia cespitosa

Ornamental clumping grasses with narrow, rough leaves obscured by clouds of yellowish flower panicles in late spring or early summer. Use in mass plantings. Best suited to Upper South. Evergreen in warmer part of range, semievergreen in colder part.

D. cespitosa. US, MS, LS; USDA 6-8. TUFTED HAIR GRASS. Native to much of North America, but most forms are imports from Europe. Dark green foliage. Purple-tinged greenish yellow panicles persist into winter. Fountainlike clumps typically 2–3 ft. high in bloom. 'Bronzeschleier' ('Bronzy Veil') has bronzy yellow blooms. Selections with golden yellow flowers include 'Goldgehange', 'Goldschleier', 'Goldstaub'. The leaves of 'Northern Lights' are variegated creamy white and turn pink in winter. *D. c. vivipara*, also known as 'Fairy's Joke', produces plantlets instead of seeds; these droop to the ground and may take root. All of the above forms of *D. cespitosa* take regular water

D. flexuosa. CRINKLED HAIR GRASS. US, MS; USDA 6-7. Glossy, wiry green leaves in tight clumps 1–2 ft. high. Nodding, purple-tinged flowers mature to a yellowish brown color. Succeeds in dry woodland shade, as well as in sunnier or moister situations.

DEUTZIA

Hydrangeaceae
Deciduous shrubs

◢ US, MS, LS; USDA 6-8

☼ ◐ FULL SUN OR LIGHT SHADE

◗ ◗ MODERATE TO REGULAR WATER

Deutzia gracilis 'Nikko'

These shrubs are best used among evergreens, where they can make a show with their small, often fragrant flowers, then blend back in with other greenery later on. Bloom season coincides with that of late spring bulbs such as tulips and Dutch iris. Prune as soon as flowers fade. With low- or medium-growing kinds, cut some of oldest stems to ground every other year. With tall kinds, prune heavily each year after bloom, cutting back wood that has flowered to outward-facing branches. Tough, easy to grow. Not browsed by deer.

D. crenata. Native to Japan. Similar to *D. scabra* but has white flowers. Foliage turns deep purple red in fall. *D. c. nakaiana*, a dwarf form to only 2 ft. tall and 4 ft. wide, has double blossoms.

D. elegantissima. Grows to 6 ft. tall and wide, with pink flowers and dull green, oval, 2- to 3-in.-long leaves. 'Rosealind', to 4–5 ft. tall and wide, has deep rose blooms.

D. gracilis. SLENDER DEUTZIA. Native to Japan. To 2–4 ft. (possibly 6 ft.) tall, 3–4 ft. wide, with many slender, gracefully arching stems. Clusters of snowy white flowers; broadly lance-shaped, bright green, 2½ -in. leaves with finely toothed edges. 'Chardonnay Pearls' has chartreuse foliage. 'Nikko' grows only 1–2 ft. high, spreading to 5 ft. wide; can be used as a ground cover.

D. hybrids. These include 'Pink-a-Boo', an erect grower to 6–8 ft. tall and 6 ft. wide, with large clusters of pink flowers; and 'Magicien' ('Magician'), similar but with dark red blossoms.

D. magnifica. SHOWY DEUTZIA. An open, multi-stemmed shrub that grows 6–10 ft. tall and about 6 ft. wide. Blooms profusely; probably the showiest of the deutzias. Double white blooms.

D. rosea. To 3–4 ft. tall and wide. Short clusters of pinkish flowers with white interiors; broadly lance-shaped, dark green, 1- to 3-in.-long leaves with finely toothed edges. Burgundy fall foliage.

D. scabra. FUZZY DEUTZIA. Native to Japan, China. To 7–10 ft. by 6 ft. Oval, scallop-toothed, 3-in.-long, dull green leaves are roughish to the touch. White or pinkish flowers in narrow, upright clusters. 'Pride of Rochester' has large clusters of small, frilly, double white flowers tinged pink. 'Codsall Pink' ('Godsall Pink') bears double pink blooms. Leaves of 'Variegata' are marked with white.

DIANTHUS

PINK
Caryophyllaceae
Perennials, biennials, and annuals

◢ US, MS, LS, CS; USDA 6-9, EXCEPT AS NOTED

☼ FULL SUN, EXCEPT AS NOTED

◗ ◗ MODERATE TO REGULAR WATER

Dianthus chinensis 'Telstar Picotee'

The pinks include more than 300 species and an extremely large number of hybrids, many with high garden value. Most kinds

form attractive evergreen mats or tufts of grasslike green, gray-green, blue-green, or blue-gray leaves. Single, semidouble, or double flowers in white and shades of pink, rose, red, yellow, and orange; many have rich, spicy fragrance. Main bloom period for most is spring into early summer; some kinds rebloom later in season or keep going into fall if faded flowers are removed. Not browsed by deer.

Among dianthus are appealing border favorites such as cottage pink (*D. plumarius*) and sweet William (*D. barbatus*), highly prized cut flowers such as carnation (*D. caryophyllus*), and rock garden miniatures. Many excellent named selections not mentioned here are available locally.

D. x allwoodii. Perennial. Group of modern pinks derived from crossing *D. plumarius* and *D. caryophyllus*. Plants vary, but most tend to be more compact and more vigorous than their *D. plumarius* parent. They typically grow 10–15 in. high and 2 ft. wide, with gray-green foliage and two 1½- to 2-in. blossoms per stem; they bloom over a long period if deadheaded. One excellent selection is 'Aqua', which bears very fragrant, pure white double flowers on 10- to 12-in. stems. Plants sold as 'Allwoodii Alpinus' are crosses of *D. allwoodii* with dwarf species.

D. arenarius. Perennial. From Europe. Tufted plant to 1½ ft. tall and wide, with narrow, grass green leaves and fringed, inch-wide white flowers sometimes marked with purple or green. Powerfully fragrant; can tolerate some shade. 'Snow Flurries' has pure white flowers.

D. barbatus. SWEET WILLIAM. Vigorous biennial often grown as annual. Zones US, MS, LS, CS, TS; USDA 6-11. From southern Europe. Sturdy stems 10–20 in. high; plants reach 1 ft. wide. Leaves are flat, light to dark green, 1½–3 in. long. Dense clusters of white, pink, rose, red, purplish, or bicolored flowers, about ½ in. across, set among leafy bracts; spicily fragrant. Sow seed in late spring for bloom following year, or set out transplants in fall. Double-flowered and dwarf strains are obtainable from seed.

Amazon series grows 18–36 in. high; heat-tolerant series that blooms into summer.

TOP: *Dianthus gratianopolitanus* 'Firewitch'; BOTTOM: *D. plumarius*

THE GENUS NAME *DIANTHUS*
IS DERIVED FROM THE
GREEK WORDS FOR GOD
(*DIOS*) AND FLOWER (*ANTHOS*).

Dash series plants grow 15–20 in. high, with good heat tolerance; blooms into summer.

Diabunda series plants are just 6-8 in. in height.

'Heart Attack' is early blooming variety with deep reddish black flowers.

Sweet series plants grow 18–36 in. high; bloom into summer.

D. caryophyllus. CARNATION, CLOVE PINK. Perennial. Highly bred Mediterranean species. There are two distinct categories of carnations: florists' and border types. Both have double flowers; bluish green leaves; and branching, leafy stems that often become woody at the base.

Border carnations grow 12–14 in. high and wide; they are bushier and more compact than the florists' type. Flowers 2–2½ in. wide, fragrant, borne in profusion. Effective as shrub border edgings, in mixed flower border, and in containers. Hybrid carnations grown from seed are usually treated as annuals, but they often live over. Hybrid carnations grown from seed are usually treated as annuals but often live over. Among the many selections are bright red 'Cinnamon Red Hots', to 1 ft. high, and the Super Trouper series, 8–10 in. high and available in a wide range of single and multicolored shades. Knight series has strong stems, blooms in 5 months from seed; Bambino strain is a little slower to bloom. There is also a strain simply called Hanging Mixed or Trailing Mixed, with pink- or red-flowered plants that sprawl or hang from pot or window box.

When grown commercially, florists' carnations are raised in greenhouses; gardeners in mild-winter areas can grow them outdoors. Plants may reach 4 ft.; they have fragrant, 3-in.-wide flowers in many colors—white, shades of pink and red, orange, purple, yellow; some are variegated. For large flowers, leave only terminal bloom on each stem, pinching out all other buds down to fifth joint, below which new flowering stems will develop. Stake to prevent sprawling. Start with strong cuttings taken from the most vigorous plants of selected named types. Sturdy plants conceal supports, look quite tidy.

D. chinensis. CHINESE PINK, RAINBOW PINK. Biennial or short-lived perennial; most selections grown as annuals. Zones US, MS, LS, CS, TS; USDA 6-11. From China. Erect, 6–30 in. high and 6–10 in. wide; stems branch only at top. Medium green foliage. Stem leaves narrow, 1–3 in. long, ½ in. wide, hairy on margins. Basal leaves are usually gone by flowering time. Flowers about 1 in. across, rose-lilac with deeper-colored eye; lack fragrance. Modern strains are compact domes (to 1 ft. tall or less) covered with bright flowers in white, pink, red, and all variations and combinations of those colors. Bouquet series plants grow 1½–2 ft. tall and flower in their first year. Diamond series is early flowering and tolerant of heat and cold. Plants in the Diana series form low mounds covered in large blooms. 'Fire Carpet' is a brilliant solid red; 'Snowfire' is white with a red eye. Telstar is an extra-dwarf (6- to 8-in.) strain. Petals are deeply fringed on some, smooth edged on others. Some flowers have intricately marked eyes. Sow directly in ground in spring, in full sun, for summer bloom; or, in mild areas, set out nursery plants in fall for spring bloom. Pick off faded flowers with their bases to prolong bloom. If set out in summer, Telstar will often bloom through the winter in the Lower South.

D. deltoides. MAIDEN PINK. Hardy perennial (even though it blooms in a few weeks from seed). From Europe and Asia. Flowering stems 8–12 in. high with short leaves; forms a loose, dark green mat to 1 ft. wide. Flowers, about ¾ in. across with sharp-toothed petals, are borne at end of forked stems. Colors include white and light or dark rose to purple, spotted with lighter colors. Can tolerate up to a half day of shade. Blooms in summer, sometimes again in fall. Useful, showy ground or bank cover.

Selections include white 'Albus'; 'Arctic Fire', white with red centers; 'Brilliant', reddish pink blooms; and 'Pixie Star', pink with dark pink centers.

D. gratianopolitanus. CHEDDAR PINK. Perennial. Neat, compact mound of blue-gray to gray-green foliage on weak, branching stems. Erect, 9- to 12-in.-tall flowering stems produce 1½-in.-wide, very fragrant, typically pink-to-rose single flowers with toothed petals. Bloom season runs from spring to fall if plants are deadheaded regularly. Effective for ground cover, rock gardens, edging. Performs well in Lower South.

'Bath's Pink'. An old favorite. Blue-green foliage forms a neat mat about 4 in. high and 1 ft. wide, topped by 12- to 15-in. stems bearing single, fringed blossoms in soft pink with a red eye. Blooms profusely in spring, sporadically through summer. Stands up well to summer heat and humidity. Good choice for Lower South.

'Firewitch' ('Feuerhexe'). To 8 in. high, eventually spreading to as wide as 3 ft. Narrow, blue-green leaves; single magenta flowers. Blooms heavily in early spring, sporadically in summer, and heavily again in fall. Heat tolerant and long flowering. Handsome even when out of bloom; foliage is bluer than that of 'Bath's Pink'. Good choice for Lower South.

'Greystone'. Steel-gray leaves. Blooms in early spring, bearing very fragrant, fringed, single white flowers that may be tinged pink in cool weather. To 9 in. high, up to 4 ft. wide. Somewhat like a white-flowered version of 'Bath's Pink'.

'Little Joe'. Forms a clump of deep blue-gray foliage 4–6 in. high and about 6 in. across. Crimson single flowers. Especially effective with rock garden campanulas.

'Mountain Mist'. To 1 ft. high and wide. Attractive silvery blue foliage is topped in early spring by pink, fringed, lightly scented blossoms. Similar to 'Bath's Pink' but needs more cold and thus blooms less profusely in the Lower South. Good-looking foliage plant, even in winter.

'Spotty'. Very narrow leaves form a tight gray-green mat 2–3 in. high. Cerise-rose flowers heavily spotted with white are carried on 6-in. stems.

'Tiny Rubies'. Makes a low mat of gray-green foliage to 3 in. high, spreading to 4 in. high. Small, double, ruby-red flowers produced on 4-in. stems. Ideal for rock gardens and containers.

D. hybrids. Zones US, MS, LS, CS; USDA 6-9. Several new series of long-blooming hybrid dianthus, resembling pinks, have been introduced from England. They include the Star series, derived from alpine dianthus, D. alpinus, which are compact plants under a foot high with dark gray-green foliage and fragrant single and double blooms in a range of single and bicolored shades. The Dessert series includes 'Raspberry Swirl' ('Devon Siskin'), pinkish white flowers with red centers and edges, and 'Cranberry Ice', a pink and red mix.

D. plumarius. COTTAGE PINK. Perennial. Charming, almost legendary European species; cultivated for hundreds of years and used in developing many hybrids. Typically has loosely matted gray-green foliage in a clump to 2 ft. wide. Flowering stems grow 10–18 in. tall, bearing spicily fragrant, 1½- to 2-in., single or double flowers with more or less fringed petals. Colors include rose, pink, and white, some with a dark center. Most highly prized are the old laced pinks, with spicy-scented white flowers in which each petal is outlined in red or pink. Blooms in late spring and summer. Indispensable and much-favored edging for borders or for peony or rose beds. Perfect flowers for small arrangements and old-fashioned bouquets.

Choice selections include 'Dad's Favorite', which bears red-edged double white flowers on 10-in. stems; 'Essex Witch', with semidouble rose-pink flowers on 5-in. stems; 'Itsaul White', with pure white, vanilla-scented single blooms on 8-in. stems; 'Musgrave's Pink', a foot-tall classic that is at least 200 years old and bears intensely fragrant, single white blooms with a green eye; and 'Sweetness', with a mix of darker-centered shades on 4-in. stems.

CARE

All dianthus require well-drained soil. Most tolerate drought. Sow seed of annual or biennial types in flats or directly in garden. Propagate perennial dianthus by cuttings made from tips of growing shoots, by division or layering, or from seed. Perennials are often short lived in Coastal and Tropical South, where they are often treated as annuals. Organic mulches around the base of plants can cause fungal diseases. Use an inorganic material like gravel instead. Carnations and Sweet William are subject to rust and fusarium wilt.

DIASCIA

TWINSPUR
Scrophulariaceae
Perennials and cool-season annuals

🖊 **ZONES VARY BY SPECIES**

☼ ◑ **PARTIAL SHADE IN HOT-TEST CLIMATES**

◖◗ ◗ **MODERATE TO REGULAR WATER**

Diascia 'Little Dancer'

South African natives related to snapdragon (*Antirrhinum*), bearing spikelike clusters of blossoms at stem ends from spring through early summer and often into fall. They go dormant in hot summers. Flowers are coral to purplish pink, about ¾ in. across, with two prominent spurs on the back; these spurs produce oils attractive to pollinating bees. Leaves of most types are medium green, heart shaped, from ¾ in. to 1½ in. long. Not browsed by deer.

Twinspurs are at their best in rock gardens, borders, and containers. With the exceptions noted, all of the species listed here are perennial, though these perennials may die in winter if planted in heavy, wet soil. Shear back after bloom.

D. barberae. Annual. Zones US, MS, LS, CS, TS; USDA 6-11. Mat-forming plant to 10 in. tall, 20 in. wide, with rose-pink blossoms. 'Blackthorn Apricot' bears apricot-colored flowers. 'Ruby Field', to 10 in. high and 2 ft. wide, bears salmon-pink blossoms and has a long bloom season. Selections in the Diamonte series are more compact and full-foliaged, grow about 12 in. high, and come in a range of colors.

D. fetcaniensis. Zones LS, CS; USDA 8-9. To 10 in. high and 20 in. wide, with rose-pink blooms.

D. hybrids. Zones LS, CS; USDA 8-9. More show up every year. Plants in the Flying Colors series have large flowers in shades of red, pink, apricot, and coral; most grow to 6–12 in. high (some grow upright, others are more trailing).

A group of newer hybrids from England (all to 7–10 in. high and 1½ ft. wide) includes coral-pink 'Coral Belle'; 'Little Charmer', pink with dark red eye; soft pink 'Little Dancer'; rosy red 'Red Ace'; and deep pink 'Strawberry Sundae'.

Sundiascia series has shown more heat tolerance than any other series trialed. Upright growers to 15 in. tall and available in 'Blush Pink', 'Orange' and 'Rose Pink'.

Whisper series is a group of annual hybrids. These compact, heat-resistant plants grow 8–10 in. high, spreading to about 2 ft. wide, and bear long-blooming, pansylike flowers. Selections include 'Apricot', 'Cranberry Red', 'Lavender Pink', and 'Salmon Red'.

D. integerrima. Zones LS, CS; USDA 8-9. To 1½ ft. tall, creeping to 3–4 ft. wide. Narrow leaves to 1 in. long; loose spikes of rich purplish pink flowers. 'Coral Canyon' grows 12–15 in. high and 1½ ft. wide, bears salmon-pink blooms.

D. rigescens. Zones MS, LS, CS; USDA 7-9. Sprawling stems form a clump to 1 ft. tall, 2 ft. wide, turn up at ends to display 6- to 8-in. spikes of rich pink flowers. Cut out old stems.

COMBINE PALE CORAL TWINSPUR WITH CORAL CALIBRA-CHOA AND SKY BLUE LOBELIA FOR A GREAT CONTAINER.

DICENTRA

BLEEDING HEART
Papaveraceae
Perennials

- **ZONES VARY BY SPECIES**
- **PARTIAL TO FULL SHADE**
- **REGULAR WATER**

Dicentra eximia

Graceful, fernlike foliage. Leafless stems carry dainty, pendent flowers, usually heart shaped and ½ to 1 in. long, in pink, rose, yellow, or white. Combine handsomely with ferns, hostas, astilbes, epimediums, foam-flowers (*Tiarella*), hellebores. In general, they need rich, light, moist, porous soil. Never let water stand around roots.

D. canadensis. SQUIRREL CORN. Zones US, MS; USDA 6-7. Native from North Carolina to Missouri, Minnesota, and Canada. Reaches just 6–8 in. tall and wide, growing from small tubers resembling ears of corn. White, perfectly heart-shaped flowers in early spring. Foliage dies back after flowering. Locate in ground cover or other area where shallow-growing tubers will not be disturbed. Prefers slightly alkaline soil.

D. eximia. FRINGED BLEED-ING HEART. Zones US, MS, LS, CS; USDA 6-9. Native to north-eastern U.S. Forms tidy clump 1–1½ ft. high and wide. Blue-gray basal leaves are more finely divided than those of *D. formosa*. Big, deep rose-pink flowers with short, rounded spurs bloom from midspring into summer. Cut back for second growth and occasional repeat bloom. Self-sows.

D. formosa. WESTERN BLEED-ING HEART. Zones US, MS, LS, CS;

USDA 6-9. Native to moist woods along Pacific Coast. To 1½ ft. tall, 3 ft. or wider. Blue-green foliage. Blooms in spring, bearing clusters of pendulous pale or deep rose flowers on reddish stems. Spreads freely by rhizomes and seeding, forming large colonies. 'Zestful' is everbloom-ing, with deep rose flowers. *D. f. oregana* grows to 1 ft. tall, has silvery green leaves and cream-colored flowers that are tipped with purple.

D. hybrids. Zones US, MS, LS; USDA 6-8. *D. eximia* and *D. formosa* cross freely to yield hybrids, many of which have been named. The following are among the most commonly cultivated; they grow 1–1½ ft. high and 1½–2 ft. across (eventu-ally spreading more widely) and bloom from spring into summer.

'Bacchanal'. Finely cut gray-green leaves and dark red flowers.

'Bountiful'. Dark blue-green foliage and purplish pink to dusky red flowers.

'Burning Hearts'. Compact with blue-gray foliage. Rose-red flowers lined with white.

'King of Hearts'. Lacy blue-green leaves and big flowers in deep pink.

'Luxuriant'. Medium to dark green leaves and red flowers.

Dicentra scandens. See *Dactylicapnos scandens*.

Dicentra spectabilis. See *Lamprocapnos spectabilis*.

DICHONDRA ARGENTEA

'SILVER FALLS' DICHONDRA
Convolvulaceae
Perennial, everywhere as annual

- **CS, TS; USDA 9-11**
- **FULL SUN OR LIGHT SHADE**
- **REGULAR WATER**

Dichondra argentea 'Silver Falls'

This low-growing foliage plant spreads by rooting surface runners. Grows 2–3 in. high and spreads 4–6 ft. wide. Heart-shaped leaves are covered with silvery down, as are the stems. Eye-catching, shimmering container plant; cascades over the edge of pots or window boxes. Can also be used as a small-scale ground cover. Easy to grow from seed. Use as an annual in cold-winter areas.

THE LONG-LASTING BUDS OF BLUE GINGER ARE NEARLY AS ATTRAC-TIVE AS THE FLOWERS.

DICHORISANDRA THYRSIFLORA

BLUE GINGER
Commelinaceae
Perennial

- **TS; USDA 10-11, OR GROW IN POTS**
- **LIGHT SHADE; BRIGHT INDIRECT LIGHT**
- **AMPLE WATER**

Dichorisandra thyrsiflora

This Brazilian native is not a true ginger but rather a robust and upright-growing relative of wandering Jew (*Tradescantia*). Succulent, unbranched or sparsely branched stems rise from a short, fleshy rhizome and reach 6–8 ft. tall. Deep green, oval, 6- to 12-in.-long, evergreen leaves are spirally arranged around the stem, forming a 3-ft.-wide foliage clump. Deep violet-blue flowers appear in 6-in. spikes at tops of stems throughout the year. Best in moist soil enriched with organic matter. Easy to propagate by cuttings. As a houseplant or in greenhouse, grows 3 ft. tall in an 8-in. pot, taller in a large container. Weeping blue ginger (*D. pendula*) is similar but has drooping clusters of blue flowers.

DICKSONIA

Dicksoniaceae
Tree ferns

- TS; USDA 10-11, OR GROW IN POTS
- PARTIAL TO FULL SHADE
- REGULAR WATER

Dicksonia antarctica

These hardy, slow-growing tree ferns from the Southern Hemisphere are easy to transplant and establish. Arguably the most beautiful of the tree ferns, they produce long, lacy, arching fronds. Caring for them isn't difficult. They need high humidity, so wet down the trunks on dry summer and autumn days. Overhead watering is preferred. Give them moist, well-drained soil rich in humus; shield them from drying winds. Every spring, spread a few inches of organic fertilizer, such as garden compost or composted cow manure, around the base. Don't trim off the old fronds until new ones emerge. Beyond hardiness range, grow in containers.

D. antarctica. TASMANIAN TREE FERN. Native to southeastern Australia, Tasmania. Hardiest of tree ferns; well-established plants tolerate 20°F. Thick, red-brown, fuzzy trunk grows slowly to 15 ft. From top of trunk grow many arching, 3- to 6-ft. fronds; mature fronds are more finely cut than those of Australian tree fern (*Cyathea cooperi*).

D. squarrosa. Native to New Zealand. Slender, dark trunk grows slowly to 20 ft. tall. Flat crown of 8-ft.-long, stiff, leathery fronds. Much less frequently grown than *D. antarctica*.

DICLIPTERA

Acanthaceae
Perennials

- ZONES VARY BY SPECIES
- FULL SUN OR PARTIAL SHADE
- WATER NEEDS VARY BY SPECIES

Dicliptera suberecta

These tender, shrublike perennials offer colorful tubular blossoms from spring to fall. They hold up well in heat, but they must have good drainage. Where stems are not killed to the ground by frost, shear to about 6 in. high in late winter.

D. resupinata. Zones CS, TS; USDA 9-11. Root hardy to about 22°F. Native to washes and rocky slopes from southeastern Arizona and southwestern New Mexico south into Mexico. Open growth to 2 ft. tall, 2–3 ft. wide, with branches sparsely foliaged in elongated, heart-shaped, inch-long, dark green leaves that take on an attractive purplish cast in cool weather. Slender, rosy purple, ¾-in.-long flowers bloom from late spring to fall. Sometimes reseeds but is not invasive. Little or no water.

D. suberecta. HUMMINGBIRD PLANT. Zones LS, CS, TS; USDA 8-11. Native to Uruguay. Woody-based perennial 2 ft. tall, 1½ ft. wide, with grayish green, softly downy leaves 1½–3 in. long and about half as wide. Summertime clusters of bright orange-red, 1½-in.-long flowers attract hummingbirds. Moderate to regular water.

DICTAMNUS ALBUS

GAS PLANT
Rutaceae
Perennial

- US, MS, LS; USDA 6-8
- FULL SUN OR LIGHT SHADE
- MODERATE TO REGULAR WATER
- OIL FROM IMMATURE SEED CAPSULES MAY CAUSE AN ALLERGIC SKIN REACTION

Dictamnus albus

Native from Europe to northern China. Sturdy, long lived, practically immortal in colder climates, needing little care once established. Forms clumps 2½–4 ft. high, 3 ft. wide. In early summer, produces loose spires of blossoms at branch tips; each flower resembles a wild azalea, with narrow petals and prominent greenish stamens. Pink is the basic color, but nurseries offer lilac-purple 'Purpureus' and white 'Albiflorus'. Seedpods that follow can be left in place for fall. Glossy, olive-green leaves with 9 to 11 leaflets, each 1–3 in. long, are handsome throughout growing season. Not browsed by deer.

Plant emits a strong lemony scent when rubbed or brushed against. In warm, humid weather, oils from immature seed capsules may briefly ignite if you hold a match immediately beneath a flower cluster—hence the common name "gas plant" (this "ignition test" does not harm plant).

Effective in borders; good cut flower. Divide infrequently, since divisions are difficult to establish and often take 2 or 3 years to bloom well. Propagate from seed sown in fall or spring; or take root cuttings in spring.

DIEFFENBACHIA

DUMB CANE
Araceae
Perennials

- TS; USDA 10-11; OR HOUSEPLANT
- SUN OR SHADE; BRIGHT INDIRECT LIGHT
- MODERATE WATER
- SAP BURNS MOUTH, MAY PARALYZE VOCAL CORDS

Dieffenbachia amoena

From forests of the tropical Americas. Grown for their striking evergreen foliage—in colors varying from dark green to yellow-green and chartreuse, with variegations in white or pale cream. In the Tropical South, will grow year-round outdoors, either potted or in the ground as accent plants. Elsewhere, grow them indoors. Young plants generally have single stems, while older ones may develop multiple stems. Taller than wide; those listed here are 1½–2 ft. wide. Mature plants bear flowers resembling odd, narrow callas (*Zantedeschia*).

Nomenclature is somewhat confused. Some of the plants described below may be sold as selections of *D. seguine*, a highly variable species quite similar to *D. maculata*.

D. amoena. To 6 ft. or taller. Broad, dark green, 1½-ft.-long leaves with narrow, slanting white stripes on either side of midrib.

D. maculata. Grows to 6 ft. or taller. Broad, oval green leaves reach 10 in. or longer, have greenish white dots and patches. 'Rudolph Roehrs' has pale chartreuse foliage blotched with ivory and edged with green. Foliage of 'Superba' is thicker and slightly more durable than that of species and is more generously marked with creamy dots and patches. Hybrids include 'Camille', with cream leaves edged with green, and 'Paradise,' with cream-colored leaves with small green spots radiating out from the center. 'Tropical Snow' has leaves variegated with cream and white.

CARE

Give container plants fast-draining potting mix, and be sure to let the mix dry to a depth of at least 1 in. before watering. Feed with half-strength general-purpose liquid houseplant fertilizer bimonthly in spring and summer. Underfed, underwatered plants show amazing endurance, recovering from severe wilting when better conditions come. Repotting is necessary when roots begin pushing plant up out of pot. Once repotted, plants usually send out new basal shoots. Sudden change from low to high light level will burn leaves, but you can move houseplants to a sheltered patio or lanai in summer. If plants get leggy, you can cut them back to 6 in. above the soil line; gangly specimens cut back in this way will usually resprout with multiple stems. Or start new plants by air layering or taking stem cuttings; discard the original, overly leggy plant. Spider mites can be a serious pest indoors, causing discolored leaves; treat with insecticidal soap or horticultural oil (take plants outdoors to spray).

DIERVILLA
BUSH HONEYSUCKLE
Caprifoliaceae
Deciduous shrubs

🌱 **US, MS, LS; USDA 6-8**

☼ ◑ **FULL SUN OR PARTIAL SHADE**

💧 **MODERATE WATER**

Diervilla lonicera

This is a small and relatively unknown group of shrubs native to eastern North America. Spreading by suckers, they are suitable for massing or as a ground cover. Oval, pointed leaves make an attractive backdrop for summertime clusters of small yellow flowers that look something like honeysuckle (*Lonicera*) blooms. Tough, hardy, and pest free; cut back in early spring to renew vigor. Not browsed by deer.

D. lonicera. DWARF BUSH HONEYSUCKLE. Native from Canada to North Carolina. Forms a low mound 2–4 ft. tall and wide. Leaves are dark green above, a bit lighter beneath, 2–4 in. long. Sulfur yellow, ½-in.-long flowers appear all summer. 'Copper' produces flushes of copper-colored new foliage throughout the growing season.

D. rivularis. GEORGIA BUSH HONEYSUCKLE. Native from North Carolina and Tennessee south to Georgia and Alabama. Grows 6 ft. tall and wide. Dark green, fuzzy leaves are 2–3 in. long, turn yellow-red in autumn. Clusters of lemon-yellow, inch-long flowers appear in June. 'Summer Stars' is a dwarf selection to 2–3 ft. tall and a bit wider, with profuse trumpetlike flowers in sulfur yellow.

D. sessilifolia. SOUTHERN BUSH HONEYSUCKLE. Same native range as *D. rivularis*. Grows 3–5 ft. high with equal or greater spread. Glossy green leaves to 6 in. long. Sulfur-yellow flowers to ½ in. long appear through much of summer. Selection 'Butterfly' features deep yellow blooms and purple autumn foliage. 'Cool Splash' has leaves broadly edged in white.

DIETES
FORTNIGHT LILY, AFRICAN IRIS
Iridaceae
Perennials from rhizomes

🌱 **LS (PROTECTED), CS, TS; USDA 8-11**

☼ ◑ **FULL SUN OR PARTIAL SHADE**

💧💧 **MODERATE TO REGULAR WATER**

Dietes iridioides

Irislike plants with fans of stiff, narrow, evergreen leaves; form dense, long-lasting clumps. Flowers resembling small Japanese irises consist of three outer and three inner segments; they appear on branched stalks throughout spring, summer, and fall, and sometimes well into winter in mild climates. Bloom bursts seem to occur at 2-week intervals, hence the common name "fortnight lily." Flowers come in solid colors—white, cream, yellow; each of the three outer segments features a small contrasting blotch of orange, yellow, or brown. Each flower lasts only a day, but the supply of flowers on a stem is seemingly endless. Excellent in permanent landscape plantings with pebbles and rocks, shrubs, and other long-lived perennials.

D. bicolor. From South Africa. Stems 2–3 ft. tall. Flowers about 2 in. wide and circular in outline, light yellow with dark brown-to-maroon blotches. Flower stems last only 1 year.

D. hybrids. Both 'Lemon Drops' and 'Orange Drops' are hybrids of *D. bicolor* and resemble it save for flower color. 'Lemon Drops' is ivory with yellow blotches, 'Orange Drops' ivory with orange blotches. As is true for their other parent, *D. iridioides*, these hybrids' flower stems last more than a year; for care see *D. iridioides*. 'Katrina' has improved tolerance to heavy, poorly drained soils and resistance to root and crown diseases.

D. iridioides (*D. vegeta, Moraea iridioides*). From East Africa. Stems to 2½ ft. tall. Waxy white flowers to 3 in. across have yellow-orange blotches and a few orange marks at bases of inner three segments. Three style arms—appendages radiating from flower's center—are usually pale violet. To prolong bloom and prevent self-sowing, break off blossoms individually. Don't cut flower stems (they last for more than a year) until they clearly have stopped producing blooms; then cut back to lower leaf joint near base of stem.

CARE

Plant from containers at any time of year, setting plants 2–3 ft. apart. All types look best with good soil and regular moisture, but once established they perform satisfactorily even in poor soil or with infrequent or erratic watering. Clumps can remain undisturbed for years; when you need to divide, do so in fall or winter.

DIGITALIS

FOXGLOVE
Plantaginaceae
Perennials and biennials

🌿 **US, MS, LS, CS; USDA 6-9**

◐ **LIGHT SHADE**

💧 **REGULAR WATER, EXCEPT AS NOTED**

◊ **ALL PARTS ARE POISONOUS IF INGESTED**

Digitalis purpurea

Mainly from Europe, Mediterranean region. Erect plants 2–8 ft. high form low foliage clumps topped by spikes of tubular flowers shaped like fingertips of a glove; colors include purple, yellow, white, pastels. Blossoms attract hummingbirds. Leaves are typically gray-green and hairy. Common foxglove (*D. purpurea*) is widely grown for height and color display in shaded gardens, but other, less well-known species are deserving subjects for borders, woodland edges, and larger rock gardens. Most tend to be biennials, but some can be coaxed into a second year of bloom if spent flowers are removed before they set seed.

D. ferruginea. RUSTY FOXGLOVE. Biennial or short-lived perennial. To 4 ft. tall, 1½ ft. wide, with stems densely clothed in deeply veined leaves. Long, dense spikes of ¾- to 1¼-in.-long, yellowish flowers netted with rusty red. 'Yellow Herald' and 'Gelber Herold' are common selections similar to the species.

D. grandiflora. YELLOW FOXGLOVE. Biennial or short-lived perennial. To 3 ft. tall, 1½ ft. wide. Toothed leaves wrap around stem. Flowers are 2–3 in. long, yellowish marked with brown. 'John Innes Tetra' is a choice selection to 20 in. tall, with pale yellow flowers richly netted with gold and brown. 'Carillon', to 12–15 in. high, has light yellow flowers. Full sun or light shade.

D. laevigata. Perennial. To 3 ft. high, 1½ ft. wide, with smooth, narrow, dark green leaves and inch-long, creamy yellow flowers speckled with purplish brown.

D. lanata. GRECIAN FOXGLOVE. Biennial or short-lived perennial. To 2 ft. high and 1 ft. wide, with 1¼-in.-long, cream-to-light tan flowers netted with brown.

D. x mertonensis. STRAWBERRY FOXGLOVE. Perennial. Spikes to 2–3 ft. high, bearing attractive coppery rose, 2½-in.-long blooms above a foot-wide clump of furry leaves. Though a hybrid, it comes true from seed. 'Summer King' is compact, with reddish rose blooms.

D. obscura. NARROW-LEAF FOXGLOVE. Woody-based perennial. To 1½ ft. tall, 1 ft. wide, with lance-shaped leaves and spikes of drooping brown-and-yellow bells about 1 in. long. Takes well-drained but not rich soil and occasional deep watering.

D. purpurea. COMMON FOXGLOVE. Biennial or short-lived perennial. Variable, appearing in many garden forms. Bold, erect growth to 4 ft. or taller, with stems rising from clumps of large, rough, woolly light green leaves. Short-stalked stem leaves become smaller toward top of plant; these are the source of digitalis, a much-valued but highly poisonous medicinal drug. Pendulous flowers are 2–3 in. long, purple with darker spots on lower, paler lip. Flowers are borne in one-sided, 1- to 2-ft.-long spikes.

Garden strains include Camelot, which reaches 3½–4 ft. tall in sun or shade and blooms consistently the first and second years in shades of rose, white, lavender, or cream with a speckled throat; 5-ft.-tall Excelsior, with fuller spikes than species and flowers held more horizontally to show off interior spotting; 3-ft. Foxy, which performs as an annual and blooms in 5 months from seed; 4-ft. Gloxiniflora, bearing flowers that are larger and open wider than those of species; 3-ft.-high Peloric Mixed, with topmost flower of each spike open or bowl shaped and 3 in. wide; and Shirley, a tall (6-ft.), robust strain with a full range of colors.

D. thapsi. MULLEIN FOXGLOVE. Perennial. From Spain. To 1 ft. tall and wide, with furry foliage and short spires of drooping purplish pink, 2- to 3-in.-long flowers. Thrives under the same conditions as *D. obscura*. 'Spanish Peaks' is an outstanding selection with raspberry-rose flowers.

CARE

Foxgloves like moist, rich, well-drained soil. Protect the plants from snails and slugs. (Deer leave them alone.) After the first flush of flowers, cut off the main spike; side shoots will develop and bloom late in the season. In the Lower and Coastal South, treat as annuals; set out new transplants in summer and fall for bloom the next spring or summer. In the Upper and Middle South, set out plants or sow seed in spring for bloom the following year. Plants self-sow freely; blooms of volunteers are often white or light colored.

DIMORPHOTHECA

AFRICAN DAISY,
CAPE MARIGOLD
Asteraceae
Annuals

🌿 **US, MS, LS, CS, TS; USDA 6-11**

☀ **FULL SUN**

💧 **MODERATE WATER**

Dimorphotheca sinuata

Cheery, free-blooming South African natives with daisy flowers that close when shaded, during heavy overcast, and at night. Use in broad masses—as ground cover, in borders and parking strips, along rural roadsides, as filler among low shrubs.

Broadcast seed where plants are to grow; sow in early spring (or in late fall or winter, in mildest climates). Do best in light soil. For other plants known as African daisy, see *Arctotis* and *Osteospermum*.

D. barberae. See *Osteospermum barberae*

D. ecklonis. See *Osteospermum ecklonis*

D. fruticosa. See *Osteospermum fruticosum*

D. pluvialis. Branched stems 4–16 in. high. Leaves to 3½ in. long, 1 in. wide, coarsely toothed. Yellow-centered, 1- to 2-in.-wide flower heads with rays that are white above, violet or purple beneath. 'Glistening White', a dwarf form with 4-in.-wide flowers, is especially desirable.

D. sinuata. Best known of annual African daisies. To 4–12 in. high. Narrow, 2- to 3-in.-long leaves with a few teeth or shallow cuts. Flowers 1½ in. wide, with orange-yellow rays that are sometimes deep violet at the base; centers are yellow or dark with flecks of yellow. Hybrids between this species and *D. pluvialis* come in white and shades of yellow and light orange, often with contrasting dark centers.

In north Florida, grow this species as a summer annual. In central and south Florida, it can also be grown as a winter annual, but it's susceptible to soil-borne diseases that make it short lived there. Not bothered by deer.

DIONAEA MUSCIPULA

VENUS'S FLYTRAP

Droseraceae

Insectivorous perennial

🖉 **MS, LS; USDA 7-8; OR HOUSE-PLANT**

☼ **FULL SUN; BRIGHT LIGHT**

💧 💧 **REGULAR TO AMPLE WATER**

Dionaea muscipula

If ever a plant turned the table on insects, Venus's flytrap is the one. Native to the nutrient-starved bogs of the Carolinas, it forms a low rosette of semi-evergreen leaves to 5–6 in. long. At the tip of each leaf are two hinged lobes that form a 1- to 2-in.-long trap, its margins lined with stout bristles and nectar-producing glands. Insects are attracted to the nectar, and when their movement triggers the tiny, sensitive hairs inside the trap, it closes quickly, ensnaring the hapless insect-turned-dinner within the interlocking bristles. The plants use this mechanism to obtain nutrients unavailable in the soil. Tiny white flowers appear in summer. Leaves and traps of the species are green to yellowish green, and traps are often flushed red. Selection 'Akai Ryu' displays bright red stems and carmine-red traps.

Unfortunately, Venus's flytraps are collected from the wild by the thousands each year. Most collected plants die, either at the store or shortly after purchase. To avoid depleting wild populations, buy plants only from reputable nurseries that propagate their own plants by seed, division, or tissue culture.

CARE

These carnivorous curiosities are difficult to cultivate under garden conditions. Outdoors, they need full sun and constantly moist, peaty soil with few nutrients. They should not be fertilized, and the traps should never be fed with meat or anything else. Indoors, they need bright light, moist soil, and very high humidity; a terrarium containing finely milled sphagnum peat moss should do the trick. Plants go semidormant in winter.

DIOON

Zamiaceae

Cycads

🖉 **ZONES VARY BY SPECIES; OR GROW IN POTS**

◑ **PARTIAL SHADE**

💧 **REGULAR WATER**

Dioon

These cycads resemble *Cycas revoluta*, but they are less widely sold, more tender, and even slower growing. Male and female plants are separate. Dioons are excellent choices for tropical effects and as container plants. Native to the American tropics, these living fossils have changed little in 200 million years. Not browsed by deer.

D. edule. VIRGIN PALM. Zones LS, CS, TS; USDA 8-11. Very slow growing. Eventually forms cylindrical trunk 6–10 in. wide, 3 ft. high. Spreading, slightly arching, 3- to 5-ft. leaves are made up of many leaflets that may be toothed at the tips or smooth edged. Foliage on young plants is dusty blue-green and feathery; that on mature plants is deeper green, shiny, more rigid. Established plants tolerate temperatures to -9°C (15°F).

D. spinulosum. Zones TS; USDA 10-11. Slow growth to 12 ft. Leaves reach about 5 ft. long, with up to 100 narrow, spine-toothed, dark green, 6- to 8-in.-long leaflets. Protect plants from frost.

DISANTHUS CERCIDIFOLIUS

Hamamelidaceae

Deciduous shrub

🖉 **US, MS, LS; USDA 6-8**

☼ ◑ **LIGHT SHADE IN HOTTEST CLIMATES**

💧 **REGULAR WATER**

Disanthus cercidifolius

Native to Japan. Slender-branched shrub to 10–12 ft. tall and wide, grown for magnificent fall color. Nearly round, smooth, 2- to 4-in.-wide leaves turn from bluish green to shades of deep red with orange tints at the onset of colder weather. Tiny, purplish fall flowers are mildly fragrant. Provide rich, acid, moist soil and protection from wind. No special pruning needed.

DISPOROPSIS

EVERGREEN SOLOMON'S SEAL

Asparagaceae

Perennials

🖉 **MS, LS, CS; USDA 7-9, EXCEPT AS NOTED**

◑ ● **PARTIAL OR FULL SHADE**

💧 **REGULAR WATER**

Disporopsis pernyi

These remarkably cold-hardy Asian perennials have a year-round presence in the garden, beginning with spring flowers and then growing into welcome clumps of foliage. Cut back in early spring before the flush of new growth to renew the planting.

D. aspersa. This leathery-leaved perennial grows about 15 in. tall and can spread to 3 ft. even in deep shade. White-to-pale yellow flowers with dark freckles have the fragrance of lemons.

D. pernyi. Zones US, MS, LS, CS; USDA 6-9. Upright, 10-in.-tall stems bear flowers in spring from the axils of the glossy leaves, making a row of white bells hanging along the stem.

D. undulata. Low growing to 4–6 in., featuring white, bell-shaped blooms with freckles, followed by purple fruit.

DISPORUM

CHINESE FAIRY BELLS
Colchicaceae
Perennials

✎ **US, MS, LS, CS; USDA 6-9; EXCEPT AS NOTED**

☼ ● **PARTIAL OR FULL SHADE**

💧 **REGULAR WATER**

Disporum cantoniense

Native to both Asia and the South, these shade-loving perennials are worthy but relatively unknown additions to the woodland garden. In spring, colorful, bamboolike shoots emerge from rhizomes in shades of white, pink, purple-pink, or green. Shiny leaves are lance shaped. Fragrant spring flowers are bell shaped and dangle at the ends of the arching stems. Flowers are followed by purplish black berries. Plant in moist soil, rich in organic matter. Although many are evergreen, a cutback in early spring assures attractive new growth.

D. cantoniense. CHINESE FAIRY BELLS. Zones US, MS, LS, CS, TS; USDA 6-11. From China, Southeast Asia, and the Himalayas. The plant forms an upright clump 3 ft. tall and 3 ft. wide and dies to the ground in cold weather. Flowers can be white or purple.

D. longistylum. Almost exclusively grown as one of the following selections. 'Green Giant' has white flowers and grows 4–6 ft. tall. 'Night Heron' has creamy white flowers born against dark purple spring foliage that fades to blackish green. Grows 2½–4 ft. tall.

D. sessile. JAPANESE FAIRY BELL. Zones US, MS, LS; USDA 6-8. 'Awa-no-tsuki' makes a show all season with creamy yellow leaves edged in green, growing 12–15 in. tall. 'Variegatum' has green and white striations on each leaf, reaching 9–12 in tall.

D. uniflorum (*D. flavens*). This handsome fairy bell from Korea has soft yellow blooms on stalks that reach 2½ ft. tall and 2 ft. wide.

DISTICTIS

Bignoniaceae
Evergreen vines

✎ **ZONES VARY BY SPECIES**

☼ ☽ **FULL SUN OR PARTIAL SHADE**

💧 **REGULAR WATER**

Distictis buccinatoria

These Mexican natives are spectacular vines for milder climates, reaching heights of 20–30 ft. Glossy leaves consist of two leaflets with a central, three-part tendril that plants use for climbing. All bear long-lasting, trumpet-shaped flowers. Plant in good, well-drained soil; provide sturdy support, since growth is dense and heavy. Prune in winter to thin stems, control size. Not browsed by deer.

D. buccinatoria (*Bignonia cherere, Phaedranthus buccinatorius*). BLOOD-RED TRUMPET VINE. Zones CS, TS; USDA 9-11. Oblong to oval leaflets 2–4 in. long. Clusters of 4-in.-long, yellow-throated flowers in orange-red fading to bluish red; blossoms stand out well from vine. Blooms in bursts throughout year when weather warms. Give protected site in hottest climates.

D. laxiflora (*D. lactiflora, D. cinerea*). VANILLA TRUMPET VINE. Zones TS; USDA 10-11. More restrained than most trumpet vines and requires less pruning. Oblong, 2½-in.-long leaflets. Vanilla-scented, 3½-in.-long trumpets appear in generous clusters throughout warmer months, sometimes giving 8 months of bloom; they are violet at first, fading to lavender and white.

D. 'Rivers'. ROYAL TRUMPET VINE. Zones TS; USDA 10-11. Plants sold under this name are nearly a match for *D. buccinatoria* in vigor and foliage and have flowers of about the same size; blossoms are mauve to purple with a yellow-to-orange throat. Sometimes labeled *D. riversii*.

DISTYLIUM

ISU TREE, WINTER HAZEL
Hamamelidaceae
Evergreen shrubs

✎ **US, MS, LS, CS; USDA 6-9**

☼ ☽ **FULL SUN OR PARTIAL SHADE**

○○💧💧 **LITTLE TO REGULAR WATER**

Distylium

Hardy, little-known members of witch hazel family with lovely layered, arching branches and small clusters of late-winter to early-spring flowers in leaf axils followed by small, nutlet-like fruit. Maintains green color throughout winter. Adaptable but grows best in well-drained soil rich in organic matter. Responds well to hard pruning.

D. hybrids. Several excellent hybrids have been developed from the species listed below. All have reddish maroon flowers in late winter. 'Blue Cascade' has bronzy red new growth maturing to blue-green; cascading to 3 ft. high by 4 ft. wide. 'Emerald Heights' produces bright green new growth darkening to dark blackish green; grows 5-6 ft. high and wide. 'Vintage Jade' is spreading and wonderfully layered to 2 ft. high and 5 ft. wide in 5 years; shiny, dark green foliage.

D. myrcoides. BLUE ISU TREE. From China. Spreading, arching shrub with narrow, blue-green leaves 3–3½ in. long and ¾–1 in. wide. Grows 4–5 ft. high by 8 ft. wide. Pretty, but not especially showy, clusters of red flowers. Cut branches good for arrangements.

D. racemosum. ISU TREE. From Japan. Spreading, eventually becoming an upright shrub to 15 ft. high. Reddish purple flowers in early spring; fairly showy. Oval, shiny, dark green leaves; 1½ in. long. Best in moist, acid soils.

DODECATHEON MEADIA

SHOOTING STAR
Primulaceae
Perennial

✎ **US, MS, LS; USDA 6-8**

☽ **PARTIAL SHADE**

💧 **REGULAR WATER DURING GROWTH AND BLOOM**

Dodecatheon meadia

Native to the eastern U.S. Light green, oblong leaves to 10 in. long form a basal rosette nearly a foot across. In early to midspring, leafless stalks rise to 16 in. high, topped by many-flowered clusters of ½- to ¾-in.-long blossoms in white to occasionally pink or purple with quite prominent, downward-pointing yellow stamens. Swept-back petals give blooms the look of small comets or shooting stars. Dies back completely at onset of hot weather. Prefers rich, loose, well-drained soil. Excellent in woodland gardens.

DOLICHOS LABLAB

HYACINTH BEAN
Papilionaceae
Perennial vine also grown as annual

- LS, CS, TS; USDA 8-11
- FULL SUN
- REGULAR WATER
- SEEDS TOXIC IN LARGE QUANTITIES

Dolichos lablab

Probably from Asia. Fast-growing, twining vine to 10 ft. Leaves are made up of three broad, oval leaflets to 3–6 in. long. Fragrant, sweet pea–shaped, purple or white flowers appear in late summer or autumn, borne in loose clusters on long stems that stand out from foliage. Blossoms are followed by velvety, beanlike pods to 2½ in. long, in a stunning

ABOVE: Dolichos lablab

shade of bright magenta-purple. Grow like string beans for quick, dense screening. Provide trellis or other support. Needs good drainage.

DORONICUM ORIENTALE

LEOPARD'S BANE
Asteraceae
Perennial

- US, MS, LS; USDA 6-8
- PARTIAL SHADE
- REGULAR WATER

Doronicum orientale 'Little Leo'

Summer is the season for most yellow daisies, but this European native bears its profuse showy flowers in mid- to late spring. Golden yellow, 1- to 2-in.-wide blossoms are borne singly on 2-ft. stems. Good cut flower. Dark green, 2½- to 5-in.-long leaves are rounded to heart shaped, with toothed edges; clumps may spread to a width of 3 ft. Selections may be of hybrid origin. 'Finesse' has larger flowers (to 3 in.) on sturdy stems; excellent for cutting. 'Little Leo' is compact, growing just 12–15 in. high and wide. 'Magnificum' is a compact grower to about 20 in. tall.

Dies back by midsummer, so best used in a strictly spring-flowering scheme or where summer annuals can fill the gap. Combine with white, purple, or lavender tulips and blue violas or forget-me-nots (*Myosotis*); use in front of purple lilacs (*Syringa*) or with hellebores at edge of woodland or shade border. Mark location before plant dies back so you don't accidentally disturb it. Provide some moisture during dormancy. Divide clumps every 2 or 3 years in early autumn; young plants bloom best.

DRACAENA

Asparagaceae
Evergreen palmlike shrubs and trees

- TS; USDA 10-11; OR HOUSE PLANTS
- FULL SUN OR PARTIAL SHADE; BRIGHT INDIRECT LIGHT
- MODERATE WATER

Dracaena marginata 'Tricolor'

About 40 species of tropical trees and shrubs. Although they're hardy outdoors in the Tropical South, most people grow them indoors. Some species and selections display graceful, fountainlike forms with broad, curved, ribbonlike leaves that may be striped with chartreuse or white; others bear stiff, sword-like foliage.

D. australis. See *Cordyline australis*

D. deremensis. Native to tropical Africa. Most commonly sold selection is 'Warneckii': erect, slow growing to 15 ft. tall, 3–4 ft. wide, with 2-ft.-long, 2-in.-wide leaves in rich green striped white and gray. 'Bausei' has green leaves with a white center stripe; 'Longii' has a broader white center stripe; 'Janet Craig' has broad, dark green leaves. Compact forms of 'Janet Craig' and 'Warneckii' are also available.

D. draco. DRAGON TREE. Native to Canary Islands. Stout trunk with upward-reaching or spreading branches topped by clusters of heavy, sword-shaped, 2-ft.-long leaves. Grows slowly to 20 ft. high and wide. Makes odd but interesting silhouette. Clusters of greenish white flowers form at branch ends. After blossoms drop, stemmy clusters remain; trim them off to keep plant neat.

D. fragrans. CORN PLANT. Native to West Africa. Upright and slow growing, eventually reaching 20 ft. high and 5 ft. wide. Heavy, ribbonlike, blue-green leaves grow to 3 ft. long and 4 in. wide. (Typical plant in 8-in. container will bear leaves about 1½ ft. long.) 'Massangeana' has broad yellow stripe in center of each leaf. Other selections with striped foliage are 'Lindenii' and 'Victoriae'.

D. marginata. MADAGASCAR DRAGON TREE. Very easy to grow and one of the most popular species. To 12 ft. tall and 5–6 ft. wide. Slender, erect, smooth gray stems are topped by crowns of narrow, leathery leaves to 2 ft. long, ½ in. wide; stems carry chevron markings where old leaves have fallen. Leaves are deep glossy green with a narrow margin of purplish red. If plant grows too tall, cut off crown and reroot it. New crowns will appear on old stem. 'Tricolor' ('Candy Cane') adds a narrow gold stripe to the green and red of the species.

D. sanderiana. RIBBON PLANT. Native to West Africa. Neat and upright, to a possible 6–10 ft. tall, 2 ft. wide; somewhat resembles a young corn plant. Strap-shaped, 9-in.-long leaves striped with white. Unrooted trunk sections of a green-leafed selection are marketed in gift shops as "lucky bamboo." If their bases are placed in several inches of water, they'll quickly root and sprout foliage. Add a small amount of half-strength general-purpose liquid houseplant fertilizer to the water every couple of months. Change water if it becomes cloudy.

CARE

Dracaenas are popular houseplants because they look good even if neglected or grown in low light. Let soil dry to a depth of ½ in. between waterings; overwatering results in leaves that are yellowed or spotted with brown. In spring and summer, feed twice monthly with a general-purpose liquid houseplant fertilizer; don't feed at all in fall and winter. If stems get leggy, cut them back to just above a node; new shoots will sprout. Watch out for spider mites. Outdoors, all but *D. draco* need protection from sweeping winds. For other plants often called dracaena, see *Cordyline*.

DRACOPIS AMPLEXICAULIS

CLASPING CONEFLOWER
Asteraceae
Annual

🌡️ **US, MS, LS, CS, TS; USDA 6-11**

☼ ◐ **FULL SUN OR PARTIAL SHADE**

◌ ◔ ◓ ◕ **LITTLE TO AMPLE WATER**

Dracopis amplexicaulis

Native from Kansas to Texas and Georgia; closely related to coneflowers (*Echinacea*, *Rudbeckia*) and Mexican hat (*Ratibida columnifera*). Slender stems reach 2–3 ft. tall; oval, pointed, medium green leaves clasp the stems. Blooms in late spring, bearing flowers to 2 in. across with a dark brown or purple central cone and yellow rays that are sometimes flushed orange or brown at the base. Tolerates a wide range of soils, including wet, heavy, poorly drained ones. Use in wildflower meadows or naturalized areas; also good in mixed herbaceous borders. Attracts butterflies. No significant pests. Sow seed directly into the garden after last spring frost. Will self-seed.

DROSERA

SUNDEW
Droceraceae
Insectivorous perennials

🌡️ **US, MS, LS, CS, TS; USDA 6-11; OR INDOORS**

☼ **FULL SUN; BRIGHT LIGHT**

◔ ◕ **REGULAR TO AMPLE WATER**

Drosera

These bizarre plants inhabit bogs in many parts of the world. Leaves vary from narrow and arching to almost round, but all are covered with small hairs that hold drops of sticky liquid. These hairs trap and digest the insects that land on them, providing nutrients not found in the soil where it grows. All species bear small, five-petaled flowers.

Care for sundews as you would Venus's flytrap (*Dionaea muscipula*); the two can be grown indoors and make good companions for a terrarium. Outdoors, they thrive in full sun and constantly moist, peaty soil. Be sure to purchase only nursery-propagated plants that are grown from seed, division, or tissue culture; buying wild-collected plants depletes native populations.

D. brevifolia. DWARF SUNDEW. Native from Virginia south to Florida and west to East Texas. Small, low-growing plant, forming a rosette only 1–2 in. across. Spoon-shaped, ½-in.-long leaves are covered with red hairs. White or pink blossoms about ½ in. wide appear atop 3- to 6-in.-tall stems in summer.

D. capillaris. PINK SUNDEW. Same native range as *D. brevifolia*. Forms a tight rosette of short-stemmed, rounded, reddish leaves, each ½–1 in. long. Pink, ¼-in.-wide flowers bloom in summer on stems 2–16 in. tall.

D. filiformis. THREADLEAF SUNDEW. Native to the Coastal Plains from South Carolina to Florida, west to Louisiana. Reddish, threadlike, 4- to 10-in.-long leaves grow upright, unfurling like the fiddlehead of a fern. Blooms in spring, bearing lavender, ⅝-in.-wide blossoms on stems 3–9 in. tall.

D. rotundifolia. ROUND-LEAFED SUNDEW. Native to bogs throughout North America. Grows 1–3 in. wide, with rounded, ½-in. leaves on thin stems; leaves turn from green to bright red in sun. White to pink flowers, ¼ in. wide, on stems reaching 2–12 in. tall; blooms from summer to early fall. One of the easier sundews to grow.

DRYOPTERIS

WOOD FERN
Dryopteridaceae
Ferns

🌡️ **ZONES VARY BY SPECIES**

◐ ● **PARTIAL TO FULL SHADE**

◔ **REGULAR WATER, EXCEPT AS NOTED**

Dryopteris filix-mas

The more than 100 species in this genus are found in many parts of the world, though only a few are generally offered by garden centers. Use them in shade or woodland gardens, where their fronds contrast nicely with the bolder foliage of other perennials, especially such large-leafed plants as hosta and hydrangea. They prefer rich soil with adequate organic material and moisture—but as a rule they are rather forgiving, making them good choices for beginning gardeners. Some species tolerate drought and less-than-ideal soil. They are seldom bothered by deer or other pests.

D. affinis. SCALY MALE FERN. Semievergreen. Zones US, MS, LS; USDA 6-8. Native to Europe and southwestern Asia. To 3–5 ft. high and wide. Finely cut fronds are chartreuse green with light brown scales when they unfold, dark green later. 'Cristata' ('Cristata The King') is more compact, with 3-ft., arching fronds with crested tips. 'Crispa Gracilis' is an evergreen dwarf form to only 6–12 in. high and wide.

D. carthusiana (*D. spinulosa*). SPINULOSE WOOD FERN, TOOTHED WOOD FERN, SHIELD FERN. Evergreen. Zones US, MS, LS; USDA 6-8. A native of Europe, Asia, and North America. Clumps reach 1 ft. across. Coarsely cut yellowish green fronds to 6–18 in. tall, half as wide, have shaggy black scales on frond stem and lower part of midrib. Tolerates bog conditions.

D. celsa. LOG FERN. Semievergreen. Zones US, MS, LS, CS; USDA 6-9. Native to moist woods and bogs in eastern U.S.; often found growing on rotting logs in the wild, hence the common name. Upright habit to 3–4 ft. high, 1½–2½ ft. wide. Deeply cut, glossy, deep green fronds with darker stems and midribs.

D. complexa 'Robust'. Semievergreen. Zones US, MS, LS, CS; USDA 6-9. Sometimes sold as *D. filix-mas* 'Undulata Robusta', this hybrid has 3- to 4-ft.-long, dark green fronds that are deeply divided, with undulating edges. Vigorous and easy to grow.

D. dilatata. BROAD BUCKLER FERN. Evergreen. Zones US, MS, LS, CS; USDA 6-9. Native to many areas in Northern and Southern Hemispheres. Grows to 1–2 ft. tall, possibly much taller; spreads a little wider than it is high. Finely cut, dark green, widely spreading

FOR A SHADY LOCATION, COMBINE MALE FERN WITH *GERANIUM MACRORRHIZUM* AND CORSICAN HELLEBORE (*HELLEBORUS ARGUTIFOLIUS*).

fronds. 'Jimmy Dyce' has blue-green, upright fronds.

D. erythrosora. AUTUMN FERN. Evergreen. Zones US, MS, LS, CS; USDA 6-9. Native to China and Japan. Erect growth in tuft to 2 ft. tall, 1½ ft. wide. One of the few ferns with seasonal color variation. Expanding fronds in spring are an attractive blend of copper, pink, and yellow; they turn green in summer, then rusty brown in autumn. Bright red spore cases are produced on leaf undersides in fall; they become a handsome winter feature. Takes some drought. 'Brilliance' has especially bright coppery red new growth.

D. filix-mas. MALE FERN. Evergreen, sometimes becoming deciduous. Zones US, MS, LS, CS; USDA 6-9. Native to much of Northern Hemisphere. Grows 2–5 ft. tall and wide, with finely cut medium green fronds to 1 ft. wide. 'Linearis Polydactyla' has very narrow leaf divisions with spreading, fingerlike tips.

D. goldiana. GOLDIE'S WOOD FERN, GIANT WOOD FERN. Evergreen in milder climates, deciduous in colder-winter areas. Zones US, MS, LS; USDA 6-8. Native to North America. Robust grower to 4 ft. tall, half as wide, with arching, light green fronds to 1½ ft. wide.

D. marginalis. MARGINAL SHIELD FERN, LEATHER WOOD FERN. Evergreen. Zones US, MS, LS; USDA 6-8. From eastern North America. Grows 2–4 ft. tall and wide. Finely cut, dark blue-green fronds. Takes some drought.

D. wallichiana. WALLICH'S WOOD FERN. Evergreen. Zones US, MS, LS; USDA 6-8. Native to India, China. Stately fern 3–5 ft. high, not quite as wide. Fronds have scaly brown stems, turn from bright golden green to dark green with maturity.

DURANTA

Verbenaceae
Evergreen shrubs

✎	**TS; USDA 10-11; OR GROW IN POTS**
☼	**FULL SUN**
◉	**REGULAR WATER**
◈	**D. ERECTA BERRIES ARE POISONOUS IF INGESTED**

Duranta erecta 'Sweet Memories'

These tender flowering shrubs feature glossy green leaves arranged in pairs or whorls along stems. Attractive blue or white flowers in clusters attract butterflies in summer, are followed by bunches of berrylike

yellow fruit. Plants marketed as *D. stenostachya* are often actually *D. erecta*; distinguishing characteristics are described below. Use as quick, tall screen. Thrive in heat. Need continual thinning and pruning to stay under control. Good container plants.

D. erecta (*D. repens*, *D. plumieri*). SKY FLOWER, GOLDEN DEWDROP, PIGEON BERRY. Native to southern Florida, West Indies, Mexico to Brazil. Fast growing to 10–25 ft. tall, 6–10 ft. wide. Tends to form multistemmed clumps; branches often drooping and vinelike. Stems may or may not have sharp spines. Oval to roundish leaves are 1–2 in. long, rounded or pointed at tip. Tubular violet-blue flowers flare to less than ½ in. wide; they are followed by waxy yellow berries in clusters 1–6 in. long. 'Alba' has white flowers. 'Cuban Gold' ('Goldii') has leaves in shades of lime-green and gold. 'Sweet Memory' is thornless, with flower petals edged in white. 'Geisha Girl' ('Sapphire Swirl') and 'Sapphire Showers' also have purple flowers edged with white. 'Golden Edge' has brilliant gold leaves with a streak of dark green down the center; often grown as an annual in areas where it isn't

ABOVE: *Duranta erecta* 'Sheena's Gold'

hardy. 'Sheena's Gold' is the revese—green leaves with golden centers. The golden-leafed 'Aurea' is a drought-tolerant dwarf form reaching only 2 ft. high.

D. stenostachya. BRAZILIAN SKY FLOWER. Native to Brazil. Not as hardy as *D. erecta*; seems to require more heat. Makes neater, more compact shrub than *D. erecta*, growing to about 4–6 ft. tall, 3–5 ft. wide (under ideal conditions, 15 ft. high). Stems do not have spines. Leaves are larger (3–8 in. long) than those of *D. erecta* and taper to a long, slender point. Lavender-blue flowers are also somewhat larger; fruit clusters grow to 1 ft. long.

DYPSIS LUTESCENS

ARECA PALM, BUTTERFLY PALM
Arecaceae
Palm

✏ **TS; USDA 10-11; OR HOUSEPLANT**

☀ ☽ ● **SUN OR SHADE; BRIGHT LIGHT**

💧 **REGULAR WATER**

Dypsis lutescens

Formerly known as *Chrysalido-carpus lutescens*. From Madagascar. Clumping feather palm grows slowly to 10–15 ft. or even taller, spreading to at least 8 ft. wide. Graceful plant with smooth trunks and yellowish green leaves. Can take dense shade; intolerant of salt. Used in foundation plantings and as a patio plant in the Tropical South. Tricky to maintain indoors. Prone to spider mites as a houseplant.

ECHEVERIA

HEN AND CHICKS
Crassulaceae
Succulent perennials

✏ **ZONES VARY BY SPECIES**

☀ ☽ **FULL SUN OR PARTIAL SHADE, EXCEPT AS NOTED**

💧 **MODERATE WATER, EXCEPT AS NOTED**

Echeveria secunda glauca

Mexican natives that form rosettes of fleshy leaves, often marked or overlaid with deeper colors. "Baby" plants (offsets) form around the "mother" plant, hence, the common name. (For other plants called "hen and chicks," see *Sempervivum*.) Bell-shaped, nodding flowers, usually pink, red, or yellow, in long, slender, sometimes branched clusters. Good in rock gardens. Some make good houseplants if sited in a south- or west-facing window; they benefit from being moved outdoors to a lightly shaded spot during the warm months. Feed houseplants monthly with a general-purpose liquid houseplant fertilizer diluted to half-strength; reduce feeding and watering in winter.

E. agavoides Zones TS; USDA 10-11. Stiff, fleshy, smooth, sharp-pointed leaves are bright green, marked with deep reddish brown at tips and edges. Rosettes reach 6–8 in. across; flower stalks to 1½ ft. bear small red-and-yellow blooms in spring to early

summer. 'Lipstick' has bright green leaves with a crisp red edge. 'Maria' grows up to 12 in. wide and has green leaves edged and tipped with red.

E. crenulata. Zones TS; USDA 10-11. Short, thick stems hold foliage rosettes to 1½ ft. across. Pale green or white-powdered leaves to 1 ft. long, 6 in. wide, with purplish red, crimped edges. Blooms from early summer until winter; flower stalk rises to 3 ft., topped by clusters of a few yellow-and-red blossoms. Shelter from hottest sun; water freely in warm weather. Makes a striking container plant, indoors or out.

E. elegans. Zones CS, TS; USDA 9-11. Tight grayish white rosettes to 4 in. across, spreading freely by offsets. Pink flowers tipped in yellow, in clusters to 8 in. long, bloom from late winter to early spring. Useful for pattern planting, edging, containers. May burn in hot summer sun.

E. hybrids. Zones CS, TS; USDA 9-11. Often grown as house-plants. Generally have large, loose rosettes of big leaves on branched or unbranched stems; leaves are crimped, waved, or wattled, sometimes heavily shaded with red, bronze, or pur-ple. They include 'Afterglow', with powdery, pinkish lavender leaves edged with brighter pink edges; 'Arlie Wright', with large, open rosettes of wavy-edged pinkish leaves; 'Black Prince', which grows only 3 in. wide and has dark reddish purple leaves; 'Blue Curls', with frilly-edged, blue-green leaves that pick up pink tones in cool weather; 'Cameo', with big, blue-gray leaves, each centered with a large, raised lump in the same color; 'Domingo', with powder-blue leaves; 'Lola', which has silvery pink-to-mauve leaves and is about 4 in. wide; and 'Perle von Nürnberg', which features pearly lavender-blue foliage. 'Doris Taylor' is a smaller selection with short, close-set leaves densely covered with short white hairs.

E. imbricata. Zones CS, TS; USDA 9-11. Saucer-shaped gray-green rosettes reach to 4–6 in. across. Clusters of bell-shaped red-orange flowers bloom from late spring to early summer. Spreads freely by offsets.

E. runyonii. Zones LS, CS, TS; USDA 8-11. Blunt-tipped gray-green leaves form an open

rosette to 5 in. across. Showy spikes of coral blossoms from late spring to early summer. Likes the dry, chalky, rocky soils of the Southwest. 'Topsy Turvy' features blue-gray, upwardly curving, V-shaped leaves.

E. secunda. Zones TS; USDA 10-11. Gray-green or blue-green rosettes to 4 in. across; spreads freely by offsets. Egg-shaped red flowers with a yellow interior bloom in late spring or early summer. *E. s. glauca* (*E. glauca*) has blue-green leaves faintly edged in purple red.

E. setosa. Zones TS; USDA 10-11. Very tender species forms dense rosettes to 4 in. wide; leaves are dark green, densely covered in stiff white hairs. Urn-shaped red flowers tipped in yellow appear in late spring or summer. Good choice for rock gardens, shallow containers; makes an excellent houseplant.

ECHINACEA

CONEFLOWER
Asteraceae
Perennials

✏ **ZONES VARY BY SPECIES**

☀ **FULL SUN**

💧💧 **MODERATE TO REGULAR WATER**

Echinacea 'Sunrise'

These sun-loving perennials form large clumps of long-stemmed, very showy flowers with drooping to horizontal rays and a beehive-like central cone. Bloom over a long period in summer and may continue sporadically until frost; deadheading prolongs bloom. May start blooming in spring in mild-winter climates. If left in place, the bristly seed heads hang

E

TOP: Echinacea 'Flame Thrower'; BOTTOM: E. purpurea

on into winter; finches like the seeds. To make coneflowers last, be sure to plant where drainage is good. Plants should be well established going into winter, preferably planted in spring.

Use on outskirts of garden or in wide borders with other robust perennials such as Shasta daisy (*Leucanthemum* x *superbum*), sunflower (*Helianthus*), Michaelmas daisy (*Symphyotrichum novi-belgii*). Seldom bothered by deer.

E. angustifolia. NARROW-LEAF CONEFLOWER. Zones US, MS, LS; USDA 6-8. Native to central U.S. Prairie wildflower to 3–4 ft. high, 2 ft. wide. Flowers to 2 in. wide, with pink-to-rosy purple rays drooping from a purple-brown cone. Narrow, bristly leaves to 6 in. long.

E. hybrids. Zones US, MS, LS, CS; USDA 6-9. Complex crosses have produced hybrid coneflowers that are popular for their vigor and extended color range. Plants in the Big Sky series grow 2–3 ft. high and 2 ft. wide; choices include butter-yellow 'Sunrise', bright orange 'Sunset', and reddish orange 'Sundown' ('Evan Saul'). 'Cheyenne Spirit' first-year flowering, heavily blooming, drought tolerant, grows to 2 ft. 'Adam Saul' ('Crazy Pink') is one of the heaviest bloomers, topping out at only 2 ft. tall and wide. 'Flame Thrower' grows 2½-3 ft. tall and has bright yellow petals flushed with orange near the cone. Heavy bloomer. 'Green Envy', 2–3 ft. high, has fragrant, lime-green blooms that pick up magenta-purple near the cone

as they age. The green cone also fades to purple. 'Hot Papaya' is doubled with a pompon rather than a cone and blooms in mango-red. 'Mango Meadow-brite' grows 2–3 ft. high and wide; orange-yellow petals surround orange-brown centers. 'Orange Meadowbrite' ('Art's Pride') grows about the same size, bears reddish orange flowers. 'Pixie Meadowbrite' grows only about 1½ ft. tall and a bit wider, with pink, nondrooping petals surrounding a yellow-brown center. The Sombrero series grows to 2 ft. and has bold colors on early-blooming, heat-tolerant plants. 'Tomato Soup' has bright red flowers up to 6 in. wide on 2-ft.-high plants. 'Tiki Torch' has bright orange-to-rose blooms on a 2- to 2½-ft.-tall plant.

E. paradoxa. YELLOW CONEFLOWER. Zones US, MS, LS; USDA 6-8. Native to the Ozarks. To 2–3 ft. high, 2 ft. wide. Drooping, yellow to orange-yellow rays surround a brown cone; flowers are about 2 in. wide. Smooth, lance-shaped leaves to 8 in. long. Hybrids involving this and *E. purpurea* have produced many new colors.

E. purpurea. PURPLE CONE-FLOWER. Zones US, MS, LS, CS; USDA 6-9. Native to central and eastern North America. Coarse, stiff plant to 4–5 ft. tall, about 2 ft. wide, with bristly, oblong leaves 3–8 in. long. Blossoms reach 2–3 in. wide, with drooping rosy purple rays and an orange-brown central cone.

Many fine selections are available. 'Coconut Lime' has a double flower, with a single row of large white petals surrounding a tuft of smaller light green petals around the cone. Grows to 2–3 ft. high. 'Doubledecker' ('Doppelganger'), another 2-footer, has something extra: a second set of pink petals emerging from the top of the cone. 'Fragrant Angel' grows 2–2½ ft. high with sweetly scented white flowers. 'Kim's Knee High' grows 1½–2 ft. high and has clear pink flowers. 'Magnus' grows 3–4 ft. tall and has deep purplish pink, orange-centered flowers to 7 in. wide. 'Pink Poodle' produces fully double pink flowers that resemble zinnias. 'Rubinstern' ('Ruby Star') grows 2–3 ft. high with carmine-red, nondroop-ing rays. Both 'White Lustre' (2½ ft. high) and 'White Swan' (1½–2 ft. high) have white rays and

orange-yellow cones. 'PowWow Wildberry' grows 1½ -2 ft. tall with pink-purple flowers that bloom heavily the first year.

E. tennesseensis. TENNESSEE CONEFLOWER. Zones US, MS, LS; USDA 6-8. From the southeastern U.S. Similar to *E. purpurea*, but rays are horizontal rather than drooping, and cone is greenish pink. Stems to 1½ ft. tall. Forms a low, casual mound. This beautiful coneflower is rare and endangered in the wild but is being propagated under permit. Available from a few wildflower nurseries.

CARE

Coneflowers generally do not need staking. They perform well in summer heat and tolerate drought. Clumps spread slowly, become crowded after 3 or 4 years. Fleshy rootstocks can be difficult to separate; divide carefully, making sure that each division has a shoot and roots. Plantings can also be increased by taking root cuttings, seeding, or transplanting self-sown seedlings.

ECHINOCEREUS
HEDGEHOG CACTUS
Cactaceae
Cacti

🌡 **ZONES VARY BY SPECIES**

☀ **FULL SUN**

◯ 💧 **LITTLE TO MODERATE WATER**

Echinocereus reichenbachii

Nearly 50 species of hedgehog cactus are native to the Southwest, including Texas, New Mexico, and Mexico. Some grow at fairly high elevations, where they survive freezing temperatures. All have cylindrical, ribbed stems in clumps; showy flowers in spring to early summer; and fleshy fruit that is edible in some species. Blooms come in red, yellow, purple, pink, or white and have many rows of petals; they typically close at night. Plant in masses for best effect. Excellent choices for dry-land gardens. Give them maximum sun and gritty, well-drained soil.

E. berlandieri. Zones LS, CS, TS; USDA 8-11. Stems 1 in. thick, 1 ft. long; forms a clump 2 ft. wide. Purplish pink, 3-in. flowers with darker throat. Good candidate for a hanging basket.

E. engelmannii. Zones MS, LS, CS, TS; USDA 7-11. Clumps 1–2 ft. tall, 3 ft. wide, with 3- to 4-in.-thick stems. Lavender to deep purplish red flowers are 2–3 in. wide. Inch-long red fruits are edible.

E. enneacanthus. STRAW-BERRY CACTUS. Zones CS, TS; USDA 9-11. Stems 1½–4 in. thick, 2½ ft. long. Forms colonies 3 ft. wide. New stems start at or just above the ground and grow sideways, then upright. Goblet-shaped, purplish red, 2- to 3-in. flowers remain open at night. The inch-long, greenish to brownish purple fruit is edible and taste like strawberries.

E. reichenbachii. CREAM LACE CACTUS. Zones US, MS, LS, CS, TS; USDA 6-11. Each stem is 2 in. thick, 6 in. tall. Plant may have a single stem or as many as a dozen. Large (4-in.) flowers vary from pink to magenta. White, lacy-looking spines.

E. triglochidiatus. CLARET CUP. Zones US, MS, LS, CS; USDA 6-9. Dense clump, up to 3 ft. wide, sometimes with hundreds of 2- to 3-in.-diameter stems to a foot tall. Flowers are 3½ in. wide, orange to red; inch-long fruits (not edible) are pink to red.

E. viridiflorus. Zones US, MS, LS, CS, TS; USDA 6-11. Stems grow to 2 in. thick, 1 ft. long, forming a clump to 2 ft. wide. Slender, 1-in. flowers are yellowish green with a lemon scent; remain nearly closed day and night.

ECHINOPS
GLOBE THISTLE
Asteraceae
Perennial

🌿 **US, MS, LS, CS; USDA 6-9**

☼ **FULL SUN**

💧 **MODERATE WATER**

Echinops

Well-behaved, decorative thistle relative for the perennial border. Rugged-looking, erect, rigidly branched plant 2–4 ft. tall and 2 ft. wide, with coarse, prickly, deeply cut gray-green leaves to 1 ft. long. Distinctive flower heads are spherical, about the size of golf balls; they look like pincushions stuck full of tubular, metallic blue pins. Bloom mid-summer to late fall.

Plants may be offered as *E. bannaticus*, *.E. exaltatus*, *E. humilis*, *E. ritro*, or possibly *E. sphaerocephalus*. Whatever name you encounter, you're likely to get a plant closely resembling the general description above. 'Arctic Glow' and 'Star Frost' have white flowers on 3–4-ft.-tall plants. 'Blue Globe' ('Blue Glow') has intense blue flowers on 4-ft.-tall plants. 'Taplow Blue' has bright blue blossoms on 3- to 4-ft. stems. 'Veitch's Blue' has darker blue flowers on a plant 2½ –3 ft. high.

CARE

Grow from divisions in spring or fall, or sow seed in flats or open ground in spring. Provide average, well-drained soil and moderate water. Clump can be left in place, undivided, for many years. Flowers are good for dried arrangements; cut them before they open, and dry them upside down.

EDGEWORTHIA CHRYSANTHA
PAPER BUSH
Thymelaeaceae
Deciduous shrub

🌿 **MS, LS, CS; USDA 7-9**

☼ ◑ **FULL SUN OR LIGHT SHADE**

💧 **REGULAR WATER**

Edgeworthia chrysantha

Native to China, this daphne relative is becoming a winter-blooming shrub. Grows 6–12 ft. tall and wide, with pliable stems produced freely from the base; dark blue-green, 3- to 4-in.-long leaves are clustered at branch tips. Flower buds covered with silky white hairs emerge in late summer; they resemble white blossoms, so after leaves drop in fall, the plant looks like it's already in bloom. Clusters of fragrant, tubular flowers that are white on the outside and yellow inside finally open in late winter. Selections include 'Akebono' ('Red Dragon'), red-orange blooms, not as vigorous as yellow forms, 5 ft. tall and wide in 10 years; 'Gold Rush', yellow blooms, 6 ft. tall and wide; 'Hawkridge Selection', yellow flowers, 4 ft. tall and wide, good for small gardens; 'Nanjing Gold', yellow flowers, 8-inch leaves, 8 ft. tall and wide; and 'Snow Cream', yellow flowers, very vigorous, 12 ft. tall and wide.

Paper bush is a vigorous pest-free shrub that prefers light shade and moist, fertile, well-drained soil containing plenty of organic matter. Water during summer droughts. Little pruning required. Easy to root from cuttings and to force cut branches into early bloom indoors. Not browsed by deer.

EGGPLANT
Solanaceae
Annual

🌿 **US, MS, LS, CS, TS; USDA 6-11**

☼ **FULL SUN**

💧 **REGULAR WATER**

Eggplant

Few vegetable plants are more beautiful than this Southeast Asian native, known botanically as *Solanum melongena*. Although most people associate eggplant with big purple fruit, the common name comes from a small type with white fruit that does indeed resemble a swan's egg.

The plant grows to a shrubby 2–3 ft. high and wide, with large, lobed leaves that are green with a purplish tinge. Drooping violet flowers shaped like those of potato (a close relative) are 1½ in. across. The glossy-skinned fruit may be blackish purple, purple, pink, green, orange-red, white, or bicolored. Fruit is generally oval or rounded and may reach 1 ft. long, depending on type; those that are long and slender are often called Japanese or Ichiban eggplants. An eggplant or two adds striking color to vegetable gardens; single plants make good container subjects.

If you enjoy eating tiny whole eggplants, allow the plants to grow and produce naturally. If you want large fruit, pinch out some terminal growth and some blossoms; three to six big fruits per plant will result. Pick fruit when it develops color but before it loses shine. To harvest, use a knife or hand pruners to cut fruit from the plant, leaving an inch or so of stem on each fruit. Flea beetles are a problem on young plants. Grow plants under row covers until big enough to tolerate leaf damage. Control aphids and whiteflies with horticultural oil. Recommended selections include the following.

'Black Beauty'. Rounded black-purple fruit to 8 in. long; 74 days from transplant to harvest.

'Blue Marble'. Gorgeous, rounded fruit 7–8 in. wide, deep violet with white tops; 62 days.

'Cloud Nine'. Pure white, oblong fruit; best when harvested at 7 in. long; 75 days.

'Dusky'. Early, 6- to 7-in., glossy black, oval fruit; 58 days.

'Gretel'. Miniature, 3- to 4-in.-long, thin, white fruit born in clusters. 55 days.

'Hansel'. Miniature, 3- to 10-in.-long, thin, deep purple fruit born in clusters; 55 days.

'Ichiban Hybrid'. Japanese type. Slender, dark purple fruit may reach 10 in. long. Purple foliage; 61 days.

'Louisiana Long Green'. Light green, zucchini-shaped fruit to 7 in. long. Southern heirloom; 100 days.

'Neon'. Deep pink, semicylindrical fruit. Ready to pick when 5–6 in. long; 73 days.

'Pingtung Long'. Japanese type. Slender, pinkish purple fruit up to 1 ft. long. Heavy producer; 50 days.

'Purple Rain'. Egg-shaped fruit to 6 in. long, in a beautiful shade of purple; 66 days.

'Rosa Bianca'. Italian heirloom noted for delicious flavor. Elongated, egg-shaped, 4- to 5-in.-long fruit in creamy white with lavender striping; 75 days.

'White Beauty'. Oval, white fruit, 7–8 in. across. Very productive in hot, humid areas; 70 to 74 days.

CARE

Plants are quite sensitive to cold, so don't set out in spring until daytime temperatures are in the 70s—about 2 to 6 weeks after the last frost. Plant in loose, fertile, slightly acid, and well-drained soil. To maintain healthy growth, keep soil evenly moist. In Florida and along the Gulf Coast, you can grow plants from seed started indoors 8 to 10 weeks before the last frost. Elsewhere, it's easier to buy transplants. Space transplants 2–3 ft. apart in rows spaced 2–2½ ft. apart. At planting time, feed with liquid 20-20-20 fertilizer.

Every 4 to 6 weeks, sprinkle 1 cup of 10-10-10 fertilizer per 10 ft. of row around plants. Stake plants to keep fruit off the ground and to keep branches from breaking under the weight of a heavy crop. Control weeds. Eggplant grows rapidly in warm weather and, if cared for properly, will produce over a long season.

EICHHORNIA CRASSIPES

WATER HYACINTH
Pontederiaceae
Aquatic plant

✓ LS, CS, TS; USDA 8-11; ANNUAL IN COLDER CLIMATES

☼ FULL SUN

💧 GROW ORNAMENTAL PODS OR CONTAINERS

Eichhornia crassipes

Native to tropical America. Feathery roots; inflated stems set with floating, nearly circular leaves ½–5 in. wide. Showy, 2-in. flowers, carried many to a spike, are lilac-blue; upper petals have a yellow spot in center. Needs warmth to flower profusely. Where it is winter hardy, it can become an extremely serious, ineradicable pest; do not turn it loose in natural bodies of water.

ELAEAGNUS

Elaeagnaceae
Deciduous and evergreen shrubs and trees

✓ ZONES VARY BY SPECIES

☼ ◐ FULL SUN OR PARTIAL SHADE

◌ ◌ ● LITTLE TO REGULAR WATER

Elaeagnus pungens 'Maculata'

These useful screening plants grow fast when young, becoming dense, full, firm, and tough—and they do it with little upkeep. However, birds spread the seeds and they can be weedy. All tolerate seashore conditions, heat, and wind. Established plants will tolerate considerable drought. Resistant to damage by deer.

Evergreen kinds serve a prime role as screening plants and are also useful as natural espaliers, clipped hedges, and high bank covers. Their foliage is distinguished by silvery (sometimes brown) dots on leaves; these reflect sunlight, giving the plants their distinctive sparkle. Both evergreen and deciduous sorts bear insignificant but usually fragrant flowers that are followed by decorative fruit (typically red with silvery flecks).

E. angustifolia. RUSSIAN OLIVE. Deciduous tree. Zones US, MS; USDA 6-7. Native from Europe to Asia. To 20 ft. high and wide, but can be clipped as medium-height hedge. Angular trunk and branches (sometimes thorny) are covered by shredding dark brown bark that is picturesque in winter. Bark contrasts with narrow, willowlike, silvery gray leaves to 2 in. long. Small, very fragrant greenish yellow flowers in early summer are followed by berry-

like fruit resembling miniature olives. Can take almost any kind of punishment, including hot summers, bitterly cold winters, drought, poor soil. Doesn't do as well in mild winters or very humid summers. Good background plant, barrier.

E. ebbingei. Evergreen shrub. Zones MS, LS, CS; USDA 7-9. Hybrid derived from *E. pungens.* More upright (to 10–12 ft. high and wide) than its parent, with thornless branches. Leaves are 2–4 in. long; they are silvery on both sides when young, later dark green above and silvery beneath. Tiny, fragrant, silvery flowers in fall. Red fruit makes good jelly. 'Gilt Edge' has striking yellow leaf margins.

E. multiflora. CHERRY ELAEAGNUS. Deciduous shrub. Zones US, MS; USDA 6-7. From China and Japan. To 6–10 ft. high and wide. Leaves are 1½–2½ in. long, silvery green above, silvery brown below. Small, fragrant spring flowers followed by bright orange-red, 1-in.-long berries on 1-in. stalks; fruit is edible but tart, loved by birds. 'Variegata' has leaves variegated with gold, yellow, and cream; its berries are red.

E. pungens. THORNY ELAEAGNUS, SILVERBERRY. Evergreen shrub. Zones US, MS, LS, CS; USDA 6-9. From Japan. To 6–15 ft. tall and wide, with rather rigid, sprawling, angular habit. Long, naked shoots, some of them 5–6 ft. long, tend to skyrocket off in all directions, creating a Medusa-like appearance. Fortunately, these shoots can be pruned away (flower arrangers prize them) to give the shrub a neater look; it also can be sheared into a nice hedge. Grayish green, wavy-edged, 1- to 3-in.-long leaves have rusty dots that give them a brown tint; spiny branches are also covered with rusty dots. Shrub has an overall olive drab color. Small, fragrant, cream-colored blossoms appear in fall; the oval, ½-in.-long berries that follow are red with silvery dust. Tough container plant in reflected heat and wind. The variegated forms listed below are more widespread than the species and have a brighter, lighter, and often startling look in the landscape; they are less hardy than the species, however, and may suffer damage in the Upper South. Be sure to cut out growth that reverts to green. Effective barrier plantings—growth is dense and twiggy, and spininess is a help, yet plants are not aggressively spiny. Will reseed.

'Fruitlandii'. Large, silvery leaves.

'Maculata'. GOLDEN ELAEAGNUS. Leaves have gold blotch in center.

'Marginata'. SILVER-EDGE ELAEAGNUS. Silvery white leaf margins.

'Variegata'. YELLOW-EDGE ELAEAGNUS. Leaf edges yellowish white.

E. umbellata. AUTUMN OLIVE. Deciduous shrub. Zones US, MS, LS; USDA 6-8. From Himalayas, China, Japan. Spiny-branched plant to 12–18 ft. high and wide, with an open, spreading shape. Elliptical, 2- to 4-in.-long leaves are bright green above, silvery green beneath. Small, silvery white, very fragrant flowers appear in mid- to late spring, followed by great quantities of tiny silvery berries that turn red as they ripen in fall. Fruit is tasty when fully ripe and can be eaten fresh or made into jam. Birds adore it and spread the seed, so be aware that this plant can be very weedy. Tolerates drought and poor soil. 'Titan' is upright and compact, to about 12 ft. tall and 6 ft. wide. Selections chosen for high-quality fruit include 'Brilliant Rose', 'Charlie's Golden', 'Delightful', and 'Jewel'. Plant is considered invasive in the Upper South.

VARIEGATED LEAVES GIVE EVEN LARGE SHRUBS A LIGHT, SPARKLING LOOK.

ELEUTHERO-COCCUS SIEBOLDIANUS

FIVELEAF ARALIA
Araliaceae
Deciduous shrub

🌿 **US, MS, LS; USDA 6-8**

☼ ☽ ● **SUN OR SHADE**

◌ ◍ ● ●● **ANY AMOUNT OF WATER**

Eleutherococcus sieboldianus 'Variegatus'

Native to China, Japan. Grows 8–10 ft. tall and wide; erect, eventually arching stems have short thorns below each leaf. Bright green leaves have five to seven 1- to 2½-in.-long leaflets arranged like fingers on a hand. Small, inconspicuous white flowers are borne in clusters; these are very occasionally followed by clusters of small black berries. This plant's virtues are its somewhat tropical appearance, adaptability (takes rich or poor soil, any exposure, any amount of irrigation), and high tolerance for difficult conditions, including air pollution. 'Variegatus', a 6- to 8-ft. shrub with white-bordered leaflets, is more widely grown than the species. Formerly known as *Acanthopanax sieboldianus*.

ENDIVE

Asteraceae
Biennial or annual

🌿 **US, MS, LS, CS, TS; USDA 6-11**

☼ **FULL SUN**

● **REGULAR WATER**

Endive

Mediterranean native known botanically as *Cichorium endivia*. This species includes curly (also called frisée), as well as broad-leafed endive (escarole), both of which form rosettes of leaves. Tolerates more heat than lettuce and grows faster in cold weather. Matures in 90 to 95 days from seed. 'Green Curled', 'Keystone', 'Rhodos', and 'Salad King' are standard curly endives. 'Broad-Leaved Batavian', 'Full Heart Batavian', and 'Full Heart NR65' are good full-leafed selections. Belgian and French endives are the blanched sprouts of a kind of chicory; see Chicory.

CARE

For a spring crop, sow seeds 2 to 4 weeks before the last frost; for a fall crop, set out transplants in late summer. Space plants 1½ ft. apart in rows 2 ft. apart. Water and fertilize as directed for lettuce (see Lettuce). To harvest, remove the outer leaves; the inner ones keep growing. Or cut the entire plant at the base when the heads are full and leafy. As warm weather approaches, leaves may develop a bitter taste; for a milder flavor, blanch the head before harvest by pulling up the large outer leaves and tying them at the top (but not when they're wet). After a week, the head should be ready to pick. In fall, harvest before the first hard frost.

ENKIANTHUS

Ericaceae
Deciduous shrubs

🌿 **US, MS; USDA 6-7**

☼ ☽ **FULL SUN OR PARTIAL SHADE**

● ●● **REGULAR TO AMPLE WATER**

Enkianthus campanulatus

Native to Japan. Upright stems with tiers of nearly horizontal branches; plants are narrow in youth, broader in age, but always attractive. Leaves are grouped or crowded near branch ends, turn orange or red in autumn. Clusters of nodding, bell-shaped flowers bloom in spring. Like rhododendrons, these shrubs require moist, well-drained acid soil enriched with plenty of organic matter such as peat moss or ground bark. Prune only to remove dead or broken branches. Plant in location where silhouette, flowers, and fall color can be enjoyed close up. Deer don't care for these plants.

E. campanulatus. REDVEIN ENKIANTHUS. Slow-growing shrub to 10–20 ft. tall and half as wide. Bluish green, 1½- to 3-in.-long leaves turn brilliant red in fall. In late spring, pendulous clusters of yellow-green, red-veined, ½-in.-long bells hang below leaves. 'Red Bells' has red flowers and notably deep red fall color. 'Showy Lantern' produces an abundant display of cherry-red blooms and has orange and red fall color. *E. c. albiflorus* bears white blooms; *E. c. palibinii* bears deep red blossoms. *E. c. sikokianus* has deep red flowers streaked with pink and yellow; autumn leaves are orange and red.

E. cernuus. Seldom over 10 ft. tall and wide, with bright green,

E

1- to 2-in.-long leaves. White flowers. Better known than the species is the variety *E. c. rubens*, which has translucent deep red flowers in late spring.

E. perulatus. WHITE ENKIANTHUS. To 6–8 ft. high and wide. Roundish, medium green, 1- to 2-in.-long leaves; exceptionally good scarlet fall color. Small white flowers open in early spring before leaves emerge.

ENSETE VENTRICOSUM

ABYSSINIAN BANANA
Musaceae
Perennial

▨ **LS, CS, TS; USDA 8-11; OR GROW IN POTS**

☼ ◐ **FULL SUN OR PART SHADE**

⬤ **REGULAR WATER**

Ensete ventricosum 'Maurelii'

African native grown for its lush, tropical-looking foliage. For fruit-bearing banana trees, see Banana. Fast growing to 15–20 ft. high, 10–15 ft. wide. Dark green leaves with stout midribs grow out in arching form from a single vertical stem; each leaf is 10–20 ft. long, 2–4 ft. wide. 'Maurelii' has dark red leafstalks and leaves tinged with red on upper surface, especially along edges. 'Red Stripe' has green leaves with a red midrib. Bloom typically occurs 2 to 5 years after planting, when inconspicuous flowers form within a cylinder of bronzy red bracts at end of stem. Plant dies to roots after flowering; it's possible to grow new plants from the shoots that will sprout from the crown but easier simply to discard the old plant and replace it with a new one from the

nursery. Unlike fruiting bananas, Abyssinian banana doesn't form suckers.

Leaves are easily shredded by wind, so plant in a wind-sheltered location. Evergreen only in the Tropical South. Root-hardy in Coastal and Lower South and survives temperatures down to 10°F if mulched heavily in late fall and kept dry. Attractive near swimming pools. Good container subject to grow outdoors in summer, move indoors or into a greenhouse over winter.

EPIMEDIUM

Berberidaceae
Perennials

▨ **US, MS, LS; USDA 6-8**

◐ ⬤ **PARTIAL TO FULL SHADE**

⬤ **MODERATE WATER**

Epimedium pinnatum

Low-growing plants that spread by creeping underground stems. Thin, wiry leafstalks hold leathery leaves divided into heart-shaped leaflets 3–4 in. long. Foliage is bronzy pink in spring, green in summer, bronzy in fall. Even in deciduous types, leaves last late into the year. In spring, plants produce loose spikes of small, waxy flowers like tiny columbines (*Aquilegia*) in pink, red, red-orange, creamy yellow, or white. The flowers have four petals, which may be spurred or hooded, and eight sepals—four inner ones resembling petals and four (usually small) outer ones.

Use as ground cover under trees or among rhododendrons, azaleas, camellias; outstanding choice for dry shade. Compete well with surface-rooted trees. Prefer partial shade but tolerate

heavy shade. Foliage and flowers are long lasting in arrangements. Cut back foliage of semievergreen and deciduous types in late winter before bloom. Divide large clumps in spring or fall by severing tough roots with a sharp spade. Adaptable to containers. Not browsed by deer.

E. alpinum. ALPINE EPIMEDIUM. Evergreen. From southern Europe. Spreads fast; grows 6–9 in. high. Flowers to 1½ in. across, with red inner sepals and yellow petals.

E. 'Amber Queen'. Grows 2 ft. tall and wide in bloom with bright yellow flowers accented in orange-red.

E. x cantabrigiense. Semievergreen. To 8–12 in. high, with olive-tinted foliage and ½-in. yellow-and-red flowers.

E. 'Cherry Blossom'. Vivid pink flowers hover at 18 in. over a 3 ft. wide mass of green foliage.

E. 'Domino'. Growing 2 ft. tall and 3 ft. wide. Each white flower has a burgundy center, echoing the maroon stem and mottling on the leaves.

E. grandiflorum. BISHOP'S HAT, LONGSPUR EPIMEDIUM. Deciduous. From China, Korea, Japan. About 1 ft. high. Flowers 1–2 in. across, shaped like a bishop's miter; they have red outer sepals, pale violet inner sepals, white petals with long spurs. Selections have white, pinkish, or violet flowers. 'Rose Queen', bearing crimson flowers with white-tipped spurs, is outstanding. 'White Queen', with silvery white blooms, is another good selection.

E. x perralchicum. Evergreen hybrid between *E. perral-derianum* and *E. pinnatum colchicum*. Grows 16 in. high; bears ¾-in., yellow flowers. Yellow blooms of 'Frohnleiten' (leaves marked with brown in frosty weather) and yellow-and-bronze ones of 'Wisley' are 1 in. across.

E. perralderianum. From North Africa. To 1 ft. tall, with shiny evergreen leaves and ¾-in., bright yellow flowers.

E. pinnatum. Nearly evergreen. From northern Africa. To 12–15 in. high. Flowers are ⅔ in. across and have bright yellow inner sepals and short red spurs. *E. p. colchicum* (often sold as *E. p. elegans*) is larger, has showier flowers.

E. 'Pretty in Pink'. Peaks at 18 in. with raspberry flowers and

spreads to a 3-ft.-wide mound of red-green, mottled, heart-shaped leaves.

E. x rubrum. RED EPIMEDIUM. Semievergreen. A hybrid of *E. alpinum* and *E. grandiflorum*. To 1 ft. high. Flowers, to 1 in. across, are borne in showy clusters, have bright crimson inner sepals, white or pale yellow slipperlike petals, upward-curving spurs. Among the best selections offered by specialty nurseries are rosy 'Pink Queen'; white 'Snow Queen'; and 'Sweetheart', with large, sturdy leaves and pinkish flowers sporting creamy white spurs.

E. x versicolor. YELLOW EPIMEDIUM. Semievergreen. Several hybrids of *E. grandiflorum* and *E. pinnatum* bear this name. Best-known selection is vigorous 'Sulphureum', a 12- to 20-in. plant with clusters of light yellow, ¾-in.-wide flowers and leaves marked with brownish red.

E. x warleyense. Evergreen. To 1½ ft. high. Light green foliage; clusters of coppery orange-red, ½-in. flowers. Also known as *E. 'Ellen Wilmott'*. 'Orangekönigin' spreads more slowly and has flowers in a softer shade of orange.

E. x youngianum. Deciduous. Hybrid derived from *E. grandiflorum*; grows to 8–10 in. high, bears ¾-in.-wide flowers in palest

EPIMEDIUMS MAKE EXCELLENT GROUND COVERS FOR DRY AREAS IN PARTIAL OR FULL SHADE.

pink. Leaves often have wavy margins. The most common selection sold is 'Niveum', with pure white blossoms; 'Yenomoto' is similar but bears larger flowers.

EPIPHYLLUM

ORCHID CACTUS
Cactaceae
Cacti

🌿 TS; USDA 10-11; OR HOUSEPLANT

☼ BEST UNDER LATH IN SUMMER OR UNDER TREES; BRIGHT FILTERED LIGHT

💧💧 REGULAR WATER IN SUMMER, LITTLE IN WINTER

Epiphyllum 'Space Rocket'

Growers use the name "epiphyllum" to refer to a wide range of plants—*Epiphyllum* itself and a number of crosses with related plants. All are tropical (not desert) cacti, and most grow on tree branches as epiphytes, like some orchids. Grow epiphyllums indoors or in lathhouse or in shade outdoors. They require rich, quick-draining soil with plenty of sand and leaf mold, peat moss, or ground bark. Cuttings are easy to root in spring or summer. Let the base of the cutting dry for a day or two before potting it up. Overwatering and poor drainage cause bud drop.

In winter, epiphyllums need protection from frost. Most have arching (to 2-ft.-high), trailing stems and look best in hanging pots or baskets. Stems are long, flat, smooth, quite spineless, and usually notched along edges. Spring flowers range from medium size to very large (up to 10 in. across); colors include white, cream, yellow, pink, rose, lavender, scarlet, and orange.

Many selections have blends of two or more colors. Feed with low-nitrogen fertilizer before and after bloom.

EPIPREMNUM AUREUM

POTHOS, DEVIL'S IVY
Araceae
Evergreen vine

🌿 TS; USDA 10-11; OR HOUSEPLANT

☼ ☼ ● SUN OR SHADE; BRIGHT INDIRECT LIGHT

💧 REGULAR WATER

Epipremnum aureum

If you can't grow pothos, you may as well give up gardening. This philodendron relative from the Solomon Islands is one of the toughest houseplants around, tolerating low light, infrequent watering, and near-total neglect. Oval, leathery, 2- to 4-in.-long leaves are dark green splashed or marbled with cream or yellow. Indoors, pothos is commonly used as a trailing vine for decorating tabletops, window boxes, and plant stands; it never stops growing and eventually follows you from one room to another. Outdoors in the Tropical South, it becomes a big, tropical-looking vine with deeply cut, really large (2- to 2½-ft.-long) leaves. It is capable of climbing the tallest trees. Popular 'Marble Queen' displays white foliage flecked with cream and green. 'Neon' is lime-green.

CARE

Pothos tolerates shade but shows better color when grown in sun. Allow the soil to become fairly dry between waterings. Feed every other week in spring and

summer and monthly in fall and winter with a general-purpose liquid houseplant fertilizer. Mist occasionally for best appearance. Do not expose plants to temperatures below 50°F. Easily propagated by cuttings (best taken in summer). Mealybugs can be a problem; wipe them off with a cotton swab dipped in alcohol.

EPISCIA

FLAME VIOLET
Gesneriaceae
Perennials

🌿 TS; USDA 10-11; OR HOUSE-PLANTS

● FULL SHADE; BRIGHT INDIRECT LIGHT

💧💧 AMPLE WATER

Episcia

Related to African violets (*Saintpaulia*), these low-growing natives of tropical America are popular chiefly for their striking foliage: oval, velvety, beautifully colored leaves to 2–5 in. long, 1–3 in. wide. They bloom sporadically throughout the year, bearing tubular, 2-in.-long flowers in shades of red, pink, orange, yellow, lavender, or white. Plants spread by runners that form new plants at their tips, a trait that makes them excellent candidates for hanging baskets or strawberry pots.

Many different selections are available, including the following.

'Alice's Aussie'. Foliage in shimmering pink and chocolate-brown. Orange-red flowers.

'Chocolate Soldier'. Chocolate-brown leaves with silver veins. Orange-red blooms.

'Kee Wee'. Chocolate-brown leaves prominently veined in deep pink. Orange-red flowers.

'Metallica'. Olive-green leaves with red edges. Bright red flowers.

'Pink Brocade'. Leaves marked in white and brown, with pink edges. Flowers are red-orange.

'Pink Panther'. Chocolate-brown leaves with central pattern of lime-green. Fuchsia-pink blooms.

'Silver Sheen'. Crinkled leaves are silver and green, with coppery margins. Deep red flowers.

CARE

Flame violets are among the most cold-sensitive plants in this book. They sulk when the temperature drops to 60°F and die if it dips much below 50°F. Yet they don't like temperatures much above 80°F either. You can take potted plants outdoors to a lightly shaded spot when the temperature is just right, but most people grow them as houseplants. Indoors, they need morning sun to retain their foliage color and compact form, but hot midday or afternoon sun will burn their leaves. You can grow them under fluorescent lights left on at least 12 hours a day. Let the soil go slightly dry between waterings. Use room-temperature water—never cold water. Feed every other week in spring and summer and monthly during fall and winter with a general-purpose liquid houseplant fertilizer diluted to half-strength. Check plants periodically for mealybugs; if you see them, wipe them off with a cotton swab dipped in alcohol.

E

EQUISETUM HYEMALE

HORSETAIL
Equisetaceae
Perennial

🖋 **US, MS, LS, CS, TS; USDA 6-11**

☼ ◐ **FULL SUN OR PARTIAL SHADE**

💧 **LOCATE IN MARSHY AREA OR POND**

Equisetum hyemale

Rushlike survivor of Carboniferous Age in Europe, North America. There are several species, but *E. hyemale* is most common. Slender, hollow, 4-ft. stems are bright green, showing a ring of black and ash-gray at each joint. Spores are borne in conelike spikes at stem ends. Miniature *E. scirpoides* is similar but only 6–8 in. high. The common name "horsetail" refers to the bushy look produced by the many whorls of slender, jointed, green stems that radiate out from joints of main stems on some of the other species.

Although horsetail is effective in some garden situations, especially near water, use it with caution: It is extremely invasive and difficult to get rid of. Best confined to containers without drainage holes. In open ground, use paving or steel edging sunk in ground to confine roots.

ERAGROSTIS

LOVE GRASS
Poaceae
Perennial grasses

🖋 **ZONES VARY BY SPECIES**

☼ ◐ **FULL SUN TO PARTIAL SHADE**

◐ 💧 **LITTLE TO MODERATE WATER**

Eragrostis spectabilis

Of about 250 species native to many temperate and tropical regions of the world, only a few are cultivated in gardens. These tough, carefree perennials form graceful clumps of fine-textured foliage. Airy floral plumes look like clouds floating above the leaves. Use love grasses as textural accents in containers or as bank or ground covers. They are drought tolerant and need excellent drainage; they thrive in sandy soils. Reseed readily and can be invasive. Not browsed by deer.

E. curvula. WEEPING LOVE GRASS. Zones US, MS, LS, CS, TS; USDA 6-11. From southern Africa and India. Billowing mass of slender, dark green, hairlike leaves reaches 3 ft. tall and wide. Purple-black flower plumes appear in summer, increasing plant height to 4 ft. Foliage turns bronzy red after frost. Evergreen in Florida. Excellent massed; controls erosion.

E. elliottii. ELLIOTT'S LOVE GRASS. Zones US, MS, LS, CS, TS; USDA 6-11. From Puerto Rico, Virgin Islands, and southeastern U.S. Narrow, powder-blue leaves form a clump 3 ft. high and wide. Airy, tan flower plumes are held above the leaves in spring and persist into fall. Makes a dramatic specimen plant. 'Wind Dancer' features white blooms in summer.

E. spectabilis. PURPLE LOVE GRASS. Zones US, MS, LS, CS; USDA 6-9. Native from Maine to Minnesota, south to Florida, Arizona, and Mexico. Light green, narrow leaves form a compact clump to almost 1½ ft. tall and wide. In late summer, plants are covered by wispy clouds of rosy purple blooms that increase the clump's height to 2 ft. Leaves reddish in fall, when flowers have faded to soft brown. Combines well with gray-leafed plants.

E. trichodes. SAND LOVE GRASS. Zones US, MS, LS, CS; USDA 6-9. Native from Illinois to Colorado and Texas. Narrow, bright green leaves grow in an upright clump to 1½–2 ft. tall and wide; they turn buff to russet in fall. Delicate bronze to purplish blooms double the plant's height in late summer and last through winter.

ERANTHEMUM PULCHELLUM

BLUE SAGE
Acanthaceae
Evergreen shrub

🖋 **TS; USDA 10-11, OR GROW IN POTS**

◐ **PARTIAL SHADE**

💧 **REGULAR WATER**

Eranthemum pulchellum

Native to India, blue sage is a large, tender shrub that's prized in central and south Florida and the Rio Grande Valley for its showy flowers of celestial blue. It grows fairly quickly into an open, upright plant about 4–5 ft. high and half as wide. Deep green, prominently veined leaves reach 8 in. long. In winter, spikes of intensely blue, ¾- to 1½-in.-wide blossoms,

attractive to butterflies, appear along the branches and at their tips. Blue sage prefers sandy, well-drained soil of moderate fertility; it does not tolerate salt spray. If frost kills branches, cut shrub to the ground; new growth will emerge with the advent of warm weather.

ERANTHIS HYEMALIS

WINTER ACONITE
Ranunculaceae
Perennial from tuber

🖋 **US, MS; USDA 6-7**

☼ ◐ **FULL SUN DURING BLOOM, PART SHADE DURING REST OF YEAR**

💧 **REGULAR WATER DURING GROWTH AND BLOOM**

Eranthis hyemalis

Native to Europe, Asia. Charming plant that reaches 2–8 in. high, blooming in late winter or early spring. Single yellow flowers resembling buttercups are about 1½ in. wide, with five to nine petal-like sepals; each bloom sits on a single, deeply lobed, bright green leaf that looks like a ruff. Immediately after the flowers bloom, round basal leaves divided into narrow lobes emerge; all traces of the plant have vanished by the time summer arrives. The species *E. cilicica* is similar but blooms later, bears slightly larger flowers, and has bronze-tinted new leaves. Not browsed by deer.

CARE

Plant tubers in late summer; if they look dry or shriveled, plump them up in wet sand before planting. Plant 3 in. deep and 4 in. apart in moist, porous soil.

Reduce water in summer but don't let soil dry out completely. Divide clumps infrequently; when doing so, separate into small clumps rather than single tubers.

EREMURUS
FOXTAIL LILY,
DESERT CANDLE
Asphodelaceae
Perennials from tuberous roots

US, MS, LS; USDA 6-8

FULL SUN

REGULAR WATER DURING GROWTH AND BLOOM

Eremurus x *isabellinus*

Native to western and central Asia, these imposing lily relatives have spirelike flowering stems that look great in bulb catalogs. Unfortunately, they're difficult to grow well in most of the South. They need long, cold winters, which we seldom have—and they require absolutely perfect drainage. When these conditions are met, however, the results are spectacular. Not browsed by deer.

Flower spikes stand 3–9 ft. tall. Spaced closely along the upper third to half of the spike are bell-shaped, ¼- to 1-in.-wide flowers in white, yellow, pink, or orange. Rosettes of strap-shaped basal leaves appear in early spring, then wither after summer bloom. Magnificent in large borders against a background of dark green foliage, wall, or solid fence. Dramatic in arrangements; cut when lowest flowers on spike have opened.

E. himalaicus. To 6–7 ft. tall, with white flowers. Leaves to 1½ ft. long.

E. x. isabellinus. Likely best known in this group are Shelford hybrids, 4–5 ft. tall, with blossoms in mixed colors (white, yellow, pink, orange). 'Cleopatra' is a 3- to 6-ft.-tall, orange-and-red selection of the Ruiter hybrids, a Dutch strain featuring bright, clear flower colors.

E. robustus. To 6–9 ft. tall, with pink flowers lightly veined in brown. Dense basal rosettes of leaves to 2 ft. long.

E. stenophyllus. To 3–5 ft. tall, with bright yellow flowers aging to orange-brown. Leaves to 1 ft. long.

CARE

Handle the thick, brittle roots carefully; they tend to rot when bruised or broken. Plant them in rich, fast-draining soil, setting crown just below surface in Lower South, 4–6 in. deep in Upper and Middle South. Space roots 2–4 ft. apart. When leaves die down, mark spot; don't disturb roots. Don't let soil dry out completely during dormancy. Provide winter mulch in Upper South. Stake tall flower spikes.

ERICA
HEATH
Ericaceae
Evergreen shrubs

ZONES VARY BY SPECIES

PARTIAL SHADE IN SUMMER

REGULAR WATER

Erica carnea 'Springwood Pink'

Usually associated with the Scottish highlands, heaths are delightful little shrubs. They combine fine-textured, short, needlelike leaves with masses of showy flowers in winter, spring, or summer; blooms may be shaped like tiny bells, urns, or tubes. Flower color ranges from white to pink through lavender to red; foliage colors include bright green, gray-green, yellow, orange, and bronze. Heaths are most effective when massed on berms and banks or used as a ground cover. Deer don't browse them.

E. carnea. SPRING HEATH. Zones US, MS; USDA 6-7. From central and southern Europe. Forms a cushionlike mound to 6–10 in. high, 12–20 in. wide. Foliage is green, yellow, orange, or bronze, depending on selection. In winter or early spring, single or double flowers appear in 2- to 4-in. spikes; bees like them. Among the hundreds of named selections are 'Ruby Glow', with dark green leaves and ruby-red flowers; 'Springwood Pink', bright green foliage and pink blossoms; 'Springwood White', light green leaves, white blooms; 'Winter Beauty' ('King George'), dark green leaves and deep pink flowers.

E. darleyensis. DARLEY HEATH. Zones US, MS, LS; USDA 6-8. Hybrid involving *E. carnea* and *E. erigena*. Has performed reasonably well in the Southeast. Larger and more shrublike than *E. carnea*; forms an attractive low mound that is broader than tall. Blooms late winter to early spring. 'Darley Dale', 1 ft. tall and 2 ft. wide, has medium green leaves and shell-pink flowers that darken to rosy purple. 'George Rendall' reaches 1 ft. tall, 2 ft. wide, has bluish green foliage and purple blooms. 'Ghost Hills', to 2 ft. tall and 2½ ft. wide, has bright green, white-tipped leaves and pink flowers. 'Silberschmelze' ('Molten Silver'), to about 1 ft. tall and 2½–3 ft. wide, has medium green leaves and white blossoms.

E. tetralix. CROSS-LEAFED HEATH. Zones US; USDA 6. From western Europe. Grows 1–2 ft. high and about half as wide. Very cold hardy. Blooms midsummer to fall. Selections include 'Afternoon', with gray-green foliage and lilac-pink flowers; 'Alba Mollis', silvery gray foliage and white blooms; and 'Ken Underwood', gray-green leaves and deep salmon flowers; 'Swedish Yellow', yellow-green foliage and pale pink blooms.

CARE

Heaths do better in the South than their cousins the heathers (*Calluna*), but that doesn't mean they're easy to grow. They require a sunny spot but need light afternoon shade during the hottest days of summer. The soil should be loose, acidic, and well drained, with plenty of organic matter. Sandy soil amended with sphagnum peat moss or compost is ideal; heavy clay usually proves fatal. Do not fertilize. Shear or cut off faded flower spikes in spring, but don't cut back into leafless wood—if you do, new foliage may not sprout. The most dependable heath for the South is *E. darleyensis*.

ERIGERON
FLEABANE
Asteraceae
Perennials

ZONES VARY BY SPECIES

FULL SUN OR LIGHT SHADE

MODERATE WATER

Erigeron pulchellus

Free-blooming plants with daisy-like flowers, the fleabanes are similar to closely related Michaelmas daisy (*Aster novi-belgii*), except that flower heads have threadlike rays in two or more rows rather than broader rays in a single row. White, pink, lavender, or violet flowers, usually with yellow centers, bloom from early summer into fall. Give sandy soil. Cut back after flowering to prolong bloom.

E. karvinskianus. MEXICAN DAISY, SANTA BARBARA DAISY. Zones US, MS, LS; USDA 6-8. Native to Mexico. Graceful, trailing plant 10–20 in. high, 3 ft. wide. Leaves 1 in. long, often toothed at tips. Dainty, ¾-in.-wide flowers with numerous white or pinkish rays. Use as ground cover in garden beds or large containers, in rock gardens, in hanging baskets, on dry walls. Naturalizes easily. 'Moerheimii' is somewhat more compact than species, with lavender-tinted flowers. 'Profusion' has white flowers that age to pink.

E. 'Prosperity'. Zones US, MS, LS, CS; USDA 6-9. Compact hybrid with lance-shaped leaves in a rosette to 1½ ft. Clusters of lavender blue, semidouble, 1½-in.-wide flowers are borne on stems to about 1½ ft. tall. Does particularly well in the South; takes heat, humidity, and considerable drought.

E. pulchellus. ROBIN'S PLANTAIN. Zones US, MS, LS; USDA 6-8. Native from Maine to Minnesota, south to Georgia and East Texas. Crinkled, 5-in.-long leaves grow in flat, ground-hugging rosettes that reach 1½ ft. across. Erect stems about 2 ft. tall carry flowers to 1½ in. wide, in blue, pink, or sometimes white. Spreads slowly.

ERIOBOTRYA

LOQUAT
Rosaceae
Evergreen trees or shrubs

🖋 **ZONES VARY BY SPECIES**

☼ ☼ **FULL SUN OR PARTIAL SHADE**

◌ ◐ ● **LITTLE TO REGULAR WATER**

Eriobotrya japonica

You know you're in the Deep South when you start seeing loquats. Native to China, these handsome evergreens feature large, glossy, prominently veined foliage. Use them for tall screens or as large container subjects; beautiful when espaliered against a fence or wall. Both of the species listed here produce fruit enjoyed by birds, but

only that of *E. japonica* is eaten by people. Loquats thrive in fertile, well-drained soil. They accept heavy pruning. Subject to fireblight, especially if given too much fertilizer. Not bothered by deer.

E. deflexa. BRONZE LOQUAT. Zones CS, TS; USDA 9-11. Shrubby but easily trained into small tree form. Leaves are slightly smaller, shinier, and more pointed than those of *E. japonica*, but not as leathery or deeply veined. They emerge bright copper and hold that color for a long time before turning green. Attractive spring show of creamy white flowers in garlands to 4–5 in. long. Good for espaliers (not on hot wall), patio planting, or containers. Fast growing to 15–20 ft. tall and 10–15 ft. wide.

E. japonica. LOQUAT. Zones LS, CS, TS; USDA 8-11. Tree is hardy to 7°F, but fruit often injured by low temperatures. Grows 15–30 ft. tall, equally broad in sun, slimmer in shade. Leathery, crisp leaves, stoutly veined and netted, 6–12 in. long, 2–4 in. wide; they are glossy deep green above and show rust-colored wool beneath. New branches are woolly; small, dull white flowers, fragrant but not showy, in woolly, 3- to 6-in. clusters in fall. Orange-to-yellow, 1- to 2-in.-long fruit ripens in winter or spring. Sweet, aromatic, tangy flesh; seeds (usually big) in center. The leaves of 'Variegata' have cream-colored margins.

Most trees sold are seedlings; they are good ornamental plants with unpredictable fruit quality. If you definitely want fruit, look for a grafted selection. 'Big Jim' bears large, midseason fruit with yellow flesh and rich, juicy texture. Early-ripening 'Champagne' has yellow-skinned, white-fleshed, juicy, tart fruit. Midseason 'Gold Nugget' has sweeter, orange fruit. Early 'MacBeth' has exceptionally large fruit with yellow skin, creamy flesh. 'Premiere' has fruit with yellow-orange skin, white flesh, and good flavor born midseason on a compact tree. 'Thales' is a late, yellow-fleshed selection.

CARE

Plant in well-drained soil. In dry climates, it will thrive with no irrigation once established, but it does better in youth with regular moisture. Mulch over root zone. Prune to shape; if you like the fruit, thin branches somewhat to

let light into tree's interior. If tree sets fruit heavily, remove some while it's small to increase the size of remaining fruit and to prevent limb breakage. Fireblight is a danger. If leaves and stems blacken from top downward, prune back 1 ft. or more into healthy wood. Use as lawn tree; train as espalier on fence or trellis but not in reflected heat. Good in container for several years.

ERYNGIUM

SEA HOLLY
Apiaceae
Perennials

🖋 **US, MS, LS; USDA 6-8, EXCEPT AS NOTED**

☼ **FULL SUN**

● **MODERATE WATER, LESS IN WINTER**

Eryngium alpinum

Most are erect, stiff-branched, thistlelike plants that bloom in summer, putting on a show of striking oval, steel-blue or amethyst flower heads surrounded by spiny blue bracts. They make long-lasting cut flowers and dry well for winter arrangements. Plants are sparsely clothed in deeply cut dark green leaves with spiny-toothed edges; upper leaves and stems are sometimes blue.

Another group of sea hollies has long, narrow, spiny-edged leaves that are quite similar to those of yucca. One of these, *E. yuccifolium*, is native to the U.S.

Use sea hollies in borders or fringe areas, in deep, well-drained, sandy or gritty soils that are low in fertility. They are taprooted and difficult to divide, so propagate by root cuttings or by sowing seed in place (thin

seedlings to 1 ft. apart). Plants often self-sow. Resist deer.

E. alpinum. ALPINE SEA HOLLY. From southeastern Europe. To 2½ ft. high, 1½ ft. wide, with steel-blue, 2-in. flower heads and large, deeply cut blue bracts. Upper leaves and stems are tinged with soft blue to steel-blue. 'Blue Star' is a choice selection.

E. amethystinum. AMETHYST SEA HOLLY. From Italy and the Balkans. To 2½ ft. tall, 1½ ft. wide. Silvery blue stems; rich blue, inch-wide flower heads surrounded by silvery blue, 2-in. bracts.

E. giganteum. MISS WILLMOTT'S GHOST. From the Caucasus and Iran. Biennial to short-lived perennial. To 3–4 ft. or taller, 2½ ft. wide. Oval or heart-shaped, medium green leaves to 6 in. long. Three-lobed stem leaves. In late summer, bears blue or pale green, conical flower heads surrounded by silvery, 2½–4-in. bracts; the plant dies after flowering ends. Reseeds well. Provide fertile soil, regular water. 'Silver Ghost' is shorter (2 ft.) with larger blooms.

E. planum. FALSE SEA HOLLY. From southeastern Europe to central Asia. To 3 ft. high, 1½ ft. wide. Leathery evergreen leaves; freely borne light blue flower heads to ¾ in. across, surrounded by narrow blue-green bracts. 'Blue Glitter' is a heavy producer of glittering, steel-blue flowers.

E. 'Saphhire Blue'. One of the best sea hollies, with intense, steely blue flowers. Upper leaves and stems also infused with blue. Grows 2½ ft. high and 1½ ft. wide.

E. variifolium. MOROCCAN SEA HOLLY. US, MS, LS, CS; USDA 6-9. From Morocco. Grows to 16 in. tall and 10 in. wide, with inch-wide, rounded, blue-gray flower heads and bluish white bracts. Thistlelike evergreen leaves are heavily veined with white.

E. yuccifolium. RATTLESNAKE MASTER. US, MS, LS, CS; USDA 6-9. Native to eastern and central U.S. Long (to 3-ft.), narrow, spiny-edged leaves in a basal rosette to 2 ft. wide. Erect stems to 3–4 ft. branch toward top and carry 1½-in.-wide white flowers without significant bracts.

ERYSIMUM

WALLFLOWER

Brassicaceae

Perennials and biennials, some grown as annuals

✒ **ZONES VARY BY SPECIES**

☼ ☼ **FULL SUN OR LIGHT SHADE**

◊ ◌ ◌◌ **WATER NEEDS VARY BY SPECIES**

Erysimum 'Pastel Patchwork'

They may be called wallflowers, but for early-season bloom, these biennials and perennials are belles of the ball. All have the clustered, four-petaled flowers typical of the plants in the brassica (mustard) family, but their habits and uses differ widely. In the South, usually grown as cool-season annuals.

E. cheiri. ENGLISH WALL-FLOWER. Perennial in Zones US, MS; USDA 6-7, but usually grown as a biennial or an annual. From southern Europe. Branching, woody-based plants to 1–2½ ft. high, 1–1½ ft. wide, with narrow, bright green leaves and broad clusters of showy, sweet-scented flowers in spring. Blossoms are yellow, cream, orange, red, brown, or burgundy, sometimes shaded or veined with contrasting color. Sow seeds in spring for bloom the following year (some strains flower the first year if seeded early); or set out plants in fall or earliest spring. May self-sow. Regular water. Charity series includes dwarf plants (12–14 in. tall and not quite as wide) that don't need winter chill to induce flowering; set out in spring for fall bloom. Selections include soft yellow 'Charity Cream', golden yellow 'Charity Yellow', and dusty rose 'Charity Rose'.

E. hybrids. Perennials. Zones US, MS, LS, CS; USDA 6-9. Many

excellent choices available. Most popular is 'Bowles Mauve', 3 ft. high and 4–6 ft. wide, with narrow gray-green leaves held on erect stems, each topped by a 1½-ft.-long, narrow, spikelike cluster of mauve flowers. Often begins blooming in midwinter, continuing until hot weather begins in May. Often short-lived. 'Compact Bowles Mauve' is about half the size. 'Lemon Zest' grows 8–12 in. high and wide, with pale to lemon-yellow blooms in early spring. 'Moonlight' has bright yellow flowers that open from red buds. 'Sweet Sorbet' has lilac-pink flowers on a 14–18-in. plant. 'Wenlock Beauty' grows 2 ft. high and wide, with spring-time flowers varying from buff to purple in a single spike. All these hybrids take moderate water.

E. kotschyanum. Short-lived perennial in Zones US, MS, and LS, often treated as an annual; USDA 6-8. Light green leaves form 6-in. mats from which rise scented, deep yellow flowers on 2-in. stems in spring. Moderate water. Use in rock garden or with other small perennials between paving stones. If plants hump up, cut out central portions, transplant them, and press original plants flat again. Divide clumps in fall.

E. linifolium 'Variegatum'. VARIEGATED WALLFLOWER. Zones MS, LS, CS; USDA 7-9. Shrubby growth to 2 ft. high, 2–3 ft. wide. Prized for its narrow, 3½-in.-long leaves, which are gray-green and edged in creamy white. Mauve flowers about ½ in. across appear from spring to fall. Moderate water.

E. x marshallii (*E.* x *allionii*). SIBERIAN WALLFLOWER. Perennial, often grown as biennial or annual. Zones US, MS, LS, CS; USDA 7-9. Branching plants 1–1½ ft. high and somewhat wider are covered in spring with fragrant flowers in rich orange or yellow. In mild-winter climates, sow seeds in fall; elsewhere, sow in spring for well-established plants by fall. Full sun, moderate water. 'Golden Bedder' has golden yellow flowers.

ERYTHRINA

CORAL TREE

Papilionaceae

Deciduous or nearly evergreen trees and shrubs, some grown as perennials

✒ **TS, EXCEPT AS NOTED; USDA 10-11**

☼ **FULL SUN**

◌ **MODERATE WATER**

◊ **SEEDS ARE POISONOUS IF INGESTED**

Erythrina crista-galli

These thorny trees and shrubs are prized for their brilliant flowers, in colors ranging from pink through red, orange, and yellow that attract hummingbirds and butterflies. The flat, beanlike pods that follow contain poisonous seeds. Leaves have three leaflets and usually drop in fall or winter. *E.* x *bidwillii*, *E. crista-galli*, and *E. herbacea* are hardy outside the Tropical South. Not browsed by deer.

E. acanthocarpa. TAMBOOKIE THORN. Deciduous shrub. Native to South Africa. To 3 ft. tall (rarely 6 ft.); as wide as tall. Roundish blue-green leaflets to 1½ in. long. Spring flower spikes are 7 in. long, 6 in. wide, with scarlet, yellow-tipped flowers. Thorny plant grows from large, thick tuberlike root. Don't plant it near pavement, which can be lifted by root.

E. americana. MEXICAN CORAL TREE. Deciduous tree. Native to Mexico; used as street tree in Mexico City. Grows to 25 ft. tall and wide. Resembles *E. coralloides* in both habit and flowers. Leaves are gray-green.

E. x. bidwillii. Deciduous shrub. Zones LS, CS, TS; USDA 8-11. To 8 ft., sometimes treelike to 20 ft. or more, wide spreading.

Hybrid of *E. crista-galli* and *E. herbacea*. Leaves to 8 in. long. Pure red, 2-ft.-long flower clusters on long, willowy stalks from spring until winter; main show in summer, when display is spectacular. Cut back flowering wood when flowers are spent. Very thorny, so plant away from paths and prune with long-handled shears.

E. coralloides. NAKED CORAL TREE. Deciduous tree. Native to Mexico. To 30 ft. high and as wide, but easily contained by pruning. Fiery red blossoms like fat candles or pinecones bloom at the tips of naked, twisted, black-thorned branches in spring. At end of flowering season, 8- to 10-in. leaves develop; these give shade in summer, then turn yellow in late fall before dropping. Bizarre branch structure when tree is out of leaf is almost as valuable as spring flower display. Sometimes sold as *E. poianthes*.

E. crista-galli. CRY-BABY TREE, COCKSPUR CORAL TREE. Deciduous shrub or small tree 15–20 ft. high and wide in nearly frostless areas; perennial to 4 ft. in colder areas. Zones LS, CS, TS; USDA 8-11. From eastern South America. Leathery leaves 1 ft. long. First flowers form after leaves come in spring—at each branch tip is a big, loose, spikelike cluster of velvety, birdlike blossoms in warm pink to wine-red (plants vary). Teardrops of nectar that drip from flowers explain common name "cry-baby tree." There can be as many as three flowering periods, spring through fall. Cut back old flower stems and dead branch ends after each bloom.

E. falcata. BRAZILIAN CORAL TREE. Nearly evergreen tree. Native to Brazil and Peru. Grows upright to 30–40 ft. high. Must be in ground several years before it flowers (may take 10 to 12 years). Leaves similar to those of *E. crista-galli*. Rich deep red (occasionally orange-red), sickle-shaped flowers in hanging, spikelike clusters at branch ends in late winter, early spring. Some leaves fall at flowering time.

E. herbacea. CORAL BEAN, CHEROKEE BEAN. Perennial to 6 ft. high in Middle and Lower South; deciduous shrub or small tree to 15 ft. tall in Coastal and Tropical South. Zones MS, LS, CS, TS; USDA 7-11. Grows taller than wide. Bright red, 2-in. blooms appear in 8- to 12-in. spikes from spring until frost. Red seeds that follow the flowers are attractive but extremely poisonous.

E. humeana. NATAL CORAL TREE. Deciduous shrub or tree (sometimes almost evergreen). Native to South Africa. May reach 30 ft. tall and wide but begins to bear bright orange-red flowers when 3 ft. high. Blooms continuously from late summer to late fall, with flowers in long-stalked clusters at branch ends well above foliage (unlike many other types). Dark green leaves. 'Raja' is shrubbier, has leaflets with long, pointed "tails."

E. variegata. VARIEGATED CORAL TREE. Deciduous tree. Native to Africa, Asia, Polynesia. To 20–30 ft. tall or much taller, with spreading form. Thick, prickly trunk and branches. Rich green leaves have 3- to 8-in. leaflets. Profuse display of coral-red flowers in late winter, early spring. Forms are available with white flowers and variegated leaves.

ERYTHRONIUM

Liliaceae
Perennials from bulbs

- **ZONES VARY BY SPECIES**
- **LIGHT SHADE**
- **REGULAR WATER DURING GROWTH AND BLOOM**

Erythrinum americanum

Spring-blooming plants with dainty, nodding, lily-shaped flowers to 1–1½ in. across, on stems usually 1 ft. high or less. All have two (rarely three) broad, tongue-shaped, basal leaves that are mottled in many species. All need some subfreezing temperatures. Plant in groups under trees, in rock gardens,

beside pools or streams. Set out bulbs in fall, 2–3 in. deep, 4–5 in. apart, in rich, porous soil; plant bulbs as soon as you receive them, and don't let them dry out. May take a few years after planting to begin blooming. Difficult to transplant once established, because bulbs work their way deep into the soil. Not eaten by rodents or deer.

E. albidum. WHITE TROUT LILY. Zones US, MS, LS; USDA 6-8. Native from Minnesota to Ontario and south to Texas. White flowers flushed yellow at the base come on stems 6–12 in. tall. Blooms later in spring than most other species. Leaves are soft green, sometimes mottled with silver or brown. Spreads slowly to form colonies.

E. americanum. TROUT LILY. Zones US, MS, LS; USDA 6-8. Native from Minnesota to Nova Scotia and south to Florida. Shiny green leaves mottled brown and purple. Blooms in late spring, at about the same time as *E. albidum*; 3- to 6-in. stems bear pale yellow blossoms sometimes flushed with purple.

E. dens-canis. DOG-TOOTH VIOLET. Zones US, MS, LS; USDA 6-8. European species. Leaves mottled with reddish brown; 6-in. stems bear purple or rose flowers. Specialists can supply named forms with white, pink, rose, and violet blossoms. 'Rose Queen' has deep pink blooms.

E. 'Pagoda'. Zones US, MS, LS, CS; USDA 6-9. Probable cross between *E. tuolumnense* and *E. californicum* 'White Beauty'. Vigorous grower, with deep green leaves heavily mottled in bronze. In spring, 6- to 14-in.-tall stems hold up to 10 bright yellow flowers with rusty central rings.

E. revolutum. PINK FAWN LILY. Zones US, MS, LS; USDA 6-8. Western native quite similar to *E. californicum*, but with larger foliage and flowers. Flower stems up to 16 in. hold pink blossoms marked yellow in the center. 'Pink Beauty' has deep pink flowers without yellow center. 'White Beauty', with large white, red-centered flowers, is often sold under this species but is now thought to be a variety of *E. californicum*.

ESCALLONIA

Escalloniaceae
Evergreen shrubs

- **LS, CS, TS; USDA 8-11**
- **PARTIAL SHADE IN HOTTEST CLIMATES**
- **REGULAR WATER**

Escallonia rubra 'Crimson Spire'

Native to South America, principally Chile. These fast-growing plants look good year-round in a border or as a screen. They have handsome, glossy leaves; foliage of some exudes a resinous fragrance. Clusters of small (to 1 in.) flowers appear in summer and fall (nearly year-round in mild climates). Plants may freeze badly at 10°F to 15°F (–12°C to –9°C) but will recover quickly. They stand up to coastal conditions and high winds and grow in most soils, except those that are highly alkaline. Prune taller types by removing one-third of old wood each year after bloom, cutting to the base; or shape into multitrunked trees. Tip-pinch smaller kinds to keep them compact. They can be sheared as formal hedges, but this may sacrifice some bloom. Not browsed by deer.

E. x exoniensis. This cross between *E. rubra* and another Chilean species is a strong, erect grower to 12–20 ft. tall and nearly as wide. Leaves are deep green above, lighter beneath. Loose clusters of white or pale pink flowers appear at the branch tips. 'Frades' is more compact, with a prolific show of pure pink-to-rose flowers.

E. rubra. Upright, variable, compact shrub grows to 6–15 ft. tall and wide. Leaves are smooth,

very glossy dark green. Flowers are red or crimson, in 1- to 3-in. clusters. Much used as a screen or hedge, especially near the coast. 'Crimson Spire' is an upright grower with large, bright crimson flowers. *E. r. macrantha* is similar, but with rose-red flowers and a more sprawling shape.

ESCHSCHOLZIA

CALIFORNICA
CALIFORNIA POPPY
Papaveraceae
Perennial usually grown as annual

- **US, MS, LS, CS, TS; USDA 6-11**
- **FULL SUN**
- **LITTLE TO REGULAR WATER**

Eschscholzia californica

Native to California, Oregon. It is the state flower of California. Free branching from base, with slender, 8- to 24-in.-long stems and blue-green, finely divided leaves. Individual plants grow about 6 in. wide. Single, satiny-petaled flowers about 2 in. wide; color varies from pale yellow to deep orange. Flowers close at night and on overcast days. In mild climates, it blooms from spring to summer, reseeds freely.

California poppy is not the best choice for important beds viewed close up—unless you trim off dead flowers regularly, plants go to seed and all parts turn straw colored. It can't be surpassed, however, for naturalizing on sunny hillsides, along drives, or in dry fields, vacant lots, parking strips, or country gardens.

There are dozens of garden forms of California poppy, and new ones appear on the market regularly. The flowers come in shades of yellow, pink, rose, flame orange, red, reddish purple, and creamy white. Some have petals streaked or bordered in contrasting colors; they may be single, semidouble, double, fluted, or frilled. All tend to revert to the basic orange or yellow form when they reseed.

Sow seeds in fall where plants are to grow; seedlings don't transplant well. Broadcast on cultivated, well-drained soil; if rain is absent, water to keep ground moist until seeds germinate. For large-scale sowing, use 3 to 4 pounds of seeds per acre. Birds are attracted to the seeds, so keep an eye out. Drought tolerant, but looks better and blooms longer with more water.

ETLINGERA ELATIOR
TORCH GINGER
Zingiberaceae
Perennial

- TS; USDA 10-11; OR GROW IN POTS
- LIGHT SHADE
- REGULAR WATER

Etlingera elatior

From Indonesia. One of the most imposing and spectacular of the flowering gingers, with large clumps of leafy stalks that rise as high as 15 ft. Rich green, lance-shaped leaves are up to 2 ft. long, 6 in. wide. In summer, flower stems grow to 4 ft. tall, each topped by a spectacular, pyramidal inflorescence consisting of clustered, waxy pinkish bracts and a red corolla. Easy to grow in rich, acid soil; ideal location is in the light shade

of tall trees. Propagate by division in spring. Very tender to cold. Choice container plant.

EUCALYPTUS
Myrtaceae
Evergreen trees and shrubs

- ZONES VARY BY SPECIES
- FULL SUN
- LITTLE WATER, EXCEPT AS NOTED

Eucalyptus cinerea

Prized for their beautiful foliage, these fast-growing plants are also famously drought tolerant. Most are native to Australia. Lack of cold hardiness limits their use in the South. Sudden freezes or hard winters may kill fairly large trees to the ground or kill them outright. For this reason, some Southerners grow them as annuals or herbaceous perennials for summer color. Still, some species are surprisingly hardy; they are listed here. None is bothered by deer.

Outside of prime eucalyptus territory, you may wish to try your hand at growing the plants if you enjoy experimenting. Plants are easily started from seed; most grow very rapidly, perhaps as much as 10–15 in. in 1 year. Some are large trees with great skyline value; some are medium to large shrubs or multitrunked trees. Most bear small white or cream flowers that are conspicuous only in masses, while others have colorful, showy blooms. Some have leaves of unusual form, highly valued in floral arrangements. Nearly all have foliage that is aromatic when crushed. Most have two different kinds of leaves; those on young plants or new growth differ markedly from mature foliage.

The sizes listed for trees below apply to plants grown in the Coastal and Tropical South; plants grown elsewhere are unlikely to reach such heights. Hardiness figures are not absolute. In addition to air temperature, you must take into account the plant's age (generally, the older the hardier), its condition, and the timing of the frost (24°F following several light frosts is not as dangerous as the same low temperature following warm autumn and winter weather). Consider any eucalyptus a risk; occasional deep or prolonged freezes can kill even large trees. If you are committed to growing eucalyptus, don't hasten to remove apparently dead trees; although their appearance may be damaged, they could resprout from trunk or main branches.

E. cinerea. SILVER DOLLAR TREE. Zones LS, CS, TS; USDA 8-11; grow as annual in Upper South and Middle South. Hardy to 10–12°F. Small to medium tree of irregular habit; grows 20–50 ft. tall and nearly as wide. Grown for attractive juvenile foliage, which is popular in floral arrangements; paired, gray-green to blue-green, nearly round, 1- to 2-in.-long leaves. Mature leaves are green, narrow, up to 4½ in. long. Unimportant small white flowers. Cut back often to maintain a good supply of young foliage. Recovers from freezes if base of trunk is heavily mulched.

E. gunnii. CIDER GUM. Zones MS (protected), LS, CS, TS; USDA 7-11. Hardy to 5–10°F. Dense form; upright, medium to tall tree—to 30–70 ft. tall, 18–40 ft. wide. One of the fastest-growing eucalyptus. Silvery blue-green, oval to roundish young foliage; dark green, narrowly oval, 3- to 5-in.-long mature leaves. Small, creamy white flowers.

E. neglecta. OMEO GUM. Zones MS, LS, CS, TS; USDA 7-11. Hardy to 0°F. Shrubby, fast-growing, small to medium tree to 20 ft. tall and 12 ft. wide (or larger). Handsome round, blue-green, paired juvenile leaves to about 2 in. long; excellent for cutting. Mature leaves are more oval in shape; they retain the attractive color of the juvenile foliage. Good-looking brown, peeling bark. Unimportant white flowers.

E. pauciflora niphophila (*E. niphophila*). SNOW GUM.

Zones MS, LS, CS, TS; USDA 7-11. Hardy to near 0°F. Small, picturesque tree to 20 ft. tall, with wide-spreading, open habit. Oval, pointed young leaves are gray-green, to 2–3 in. long. Lance-shaped, silvery blue adult leaves reach 4 in. long. Smooth, peeling white bark on trunk contrasts handsomely with red branches.

E. torelliana. CADAGA. Zones TS; USDA 10-11. Hardy to 28–30°F. Straight-trunked tree with rounded or spreading form; grows fast to 45–60 ft. tall. Juvenile leaves are 2–4 in. long, broadly oval; mature leaves are dark green, 3–6 in. long, narrower and more pointed. Profuse display of showy white flowers. Regular water. Often grown in south Florida.

EUCHARIS AMAZONICA
EUCHARIST LILY, AMAZON LILY
Amaryllidaceae
Perennial from bulb

- TS; USDA 10-11; OR HOUSEPLANT
- FULL SHADE; BRIGHT FILTERED LIGHT
- REGULAR WATER DURING GROWTH AND BLOOM

Eucharis grandiflora

Formerly known as *E. grandiflora*. Native to the Andes of Colombia and Peru, this evergreen plant combines handsome, glossy, deep green foliage with showy, sweet-smelling flowers. It forms a cluster of short-stemmed, broadly oval leaves with pointed tips; leaves are about 1 ft. long, and foliage mass reaches 1½–2 ft. high and wide. In late winter or early spring, a leafless stalk rises above the leaves, carrying up to six nodding white flowers that look something like daffodils. Older plants may stay in bloom for 6 weeks. 'Christine' is more compact than the species.

CARE

Eucharist lily is very tender and can be grown in the ground only in south Florida and south Texas, where it should be sited in full shade. Even there, it does better in a pot, as plants bloom more heavily when pot bound; plant four or five bulbs in a 6-in. pot. Indoors, mist frequently (leaves but not flowers) and give bright filtered light. Let the soil go slightly dry between waterings. Gradually reduce watering in fall and winter, but don't let plants dry out completely. Feed with a general-purpose liquid houseplant fertilizer—every other week in spring and summer, once a month in fall. In winter, cease fertilizing; this encourages formation of flower buds. When new leaves appear, resume regular watering and fertilizing schedule. Check foliage frequently for scale, which is a common pest; treat with horticultural oil.

EUCOMIS
PINEAPPLE LILY
Asparagaceae
Perennials from bulbs

🌱 **MS, LS, CS, TS; USDA 7-11; OR DIG AND STORE**

☼ ◐ **FULL SUN OR LIGHT SHADE; BRIGHT LIGHT**

💧 **REGULAR WATER DURING GROWTH AND BLOOM**

Eucomis comosa
'Sparkling Burgundy'

It's easy to see how these unusual plants from southern Africa got their common name—the summertime spikes of tiny, closely packed, star-shaped blossoms are topped with leaflike bracts resembling those of a pineapple. They make striking cut flowers. Purplish seed capsules follow the flowers, keeping the show going even longer. Leaves are coarse and straplike, emerging from large bulbs to form a basal rosette. Plants go dormant in winter. Not browsed by deer.

E. bicolor. Spikes to 2 ft. tall; green flowers with purple-edged petals. Attractive, wavy-edged light green leaves to 1 ft. long, 3–4 in. wide.

E. comosa. Thick spikes 2–3 ft. tall are set with greenish white flowers tinged pink or purple. Stems are spotted purple at the base. Light green leaves grow to 2 ft. long and are less wavy than those of *E. bicolor*. 'Sparkling Burgundy' grows to 1½–2 ft. tall. Foliage emerges deep burgundy, then slowly fades to olive-green as weather warms. Flower spikes to 20 in. tall are set with creamy white blossoms tinged pink and purple. Flowers are followed by a new crop of burgundy leaves.

E. 'Dark Star'. Dark purple foliage gives the plant its name. Flowers are pink up to 10 in. tall.

E. Mini Tuft series. Growing just 10 in. tall and 15 in. wide, these pineapple lilies bloom in shades of soft to vivid pink.

E. 'Oakhurst'. This glossy, burgundy foliage crowned with a cluster of pink flowers makes it a drama plant.

E. 'Twinkle Stars'. Two-foot tall spikes of dark purple buds open into light purple flowers atop 16-in. clumps of green leaves.

CARE

Plant bulbs 5 in. deep and 8 in. apart in well-drained, humus-rich soil in fall—or start plants from seed in spring. Bulbs are hardy to about 5°F; where temperatures dip lower, mulch plantings heavily in late fall, or dig and store bulbs over winter. Divide clumps when they become crowded (every 5 or 6 years). Pineapple lilies can also be grown as houseplants beside a bright (south- or west-facing) window; while they are actively growing, give plenty of water and feed monthly with a general-purpose liquid houseplant fertilizer.

EUCOMMIA ULMOIDES
HARDY RUBBER TREE
Eucommiaceae
Deciduous tree

🌱 **US, MS; USDA 6-8**

☼ **FULL SUN**

💧💧 **MODERATE TO REGULAR WATER**

Eucommia ulmoides

From central China. Rubber can be made from this tree's sap, but the process isn't economically feasible—instead, the plant is grown for its ornamental qualities. Attractive rounded habit; can reach 40–60 ft. tall, with equal or greater spread. Leaves resemble those of elm (*Ulmus*) but are glossier and more leathery. When a leaf is slowly torn in two, sap from the veins congeals into threads of rubber, holding the two halves together. Tolerates a wide variety of soils but requires good drainage. Not troubled by pests. 'Emerald Point' has a more upright, narrow, oval habit and smaller leaves. Useful street tree.

EUGENIA (SYZGIUM)
Myrtaceae
Evergreen shrubs or trees

🌱 **ZONES VARY BY SPECIES**

☼ ◐ **FULL SUN OR PARTIAL SHADE**

💧 **REGULAR WATER**

Eugenia myrtifolia

Grown for attractive foliage, white flowers, edible "cherries." Perform best in a moist atmosphere, with rich, well-drained soil and a sheltered location.

E. aggregata. CHERRY OF THE RIO GRANDE. Zones TS; USDA 10-11. Native to Brazil. To 15 ft. tall and 10 ft. wide, with bark peeling in thin layers. Narrow, elliptical, glossy, dark green leaves to 3 in. long. Showy flowers to about 1 in. across. Oval fruit to 1 in. long ripens from orange-red to deep purplish red, is said to taste like cherries. Eat fresh or use for jams, jellies.

E. myrtifolia. AUSTRALIAN BUSH CHERRY. Zones CS, TS; USDA 9-11. Although known to grow into a 15-ft.-tall, multi-trunked shrub, it is often used as a privacy screen or a topiary plant, trimmed into playful spirals and pompons. New growth emerges bronze and remains showy against the older green foliage. Flowers are creamy white puff balls in spring, and they are followed by red berries.

E. uniflora. SURINAM CHERRY, PITANGA. Zones CS, TS; USDA 9-11. From the tropical Americas. Very slow, open growth to about 15–25 ft. tall and 10–15 ft. wide, though it's commonly seen at 6–8 ft. tall with equal spread. Glossy, copper-tinged green leaves reach 2 in. long, deepen in color to purplish or red in cold weather. Fragrant, showy, ½-in.-wide flowers with prominent stamens. Roundish, inch-wide fruit ripens from yellow to orange to deep red; it is edible when fully ripe. Fruit of seedlings ranges from quite sweet and cherrylike to very sour. 'Lolita' has sweet, black fruit that is far superior in flavor to that of seedlings; it's good for jams, jellies. Grafted selections are sometimes available. Good screen. Can be sheared into a hedge, but by doing so you'll sacrifice fruit.

EUONYMUS
Celastraceae
Evergreen and deciduous shrubs and vines

🖊 **ZONES VARY BY SPECIES**

☀ ◐ ● **EXPOSURE NEEDS VARY BY SPECIES**

◌ ◑ **MODERATE TO REGULAR WATER**

Euonymus alatus

Maybe the reason so many people mistakenly call euonymus "anonymous plants" is that they can be hard to recognize—the evergreen and deciduous kinds look nothing alike. The colorful seed capsules common to both provide the only obvious hint that they're related. Deciduous types are valued for their brilliant fall leaf color or showy fruit. Evergreen types—which include some of the most cold-hardy, broad-leafed evergreens—are employed as hedges, screens, and foundation plants. Foliage is quite variable in shape, but leaves of most are pointed-oval to lance-shaped. Most species tolerate either sun or shade, but deciduous types need sun for

good fall color. Scale is a likely problem on any euonymus; treat with horticultural oil.

E. alatus. WINGED EUONYMUS, BURNING BUSH. Deciduous shrub. Zones US, MS, LS; USDA 6-8. Native of China and Japan. Though nursery tags may indicate a much smaller plant, the species can reach 15–20 ft. high and wide. This plant is quite dense, twiggy, and flat topped, with horizontal branching; if lower limbs are removed, it makes an attractive, vase-shaped, small tree. Young twigs have flat, corky wings; these disappear on older growth. Fruit is smaller and less profuse than that of *E. europaeus*, but fall color is impressive: The dark green, 3-in.-long leaves turn flaming red (or pink, in shade). Best autumn color comes in Upper and Middle South. 'Compactus', a smaller plant (grows 6–10 ft. high and wide) with smaller corky wings, isn't quite as hardy. 'Little Moses' is smaller still, just 2½–3 ft. high and slightly wider, with particularly long-lasting fall color. 'FireBall' is compact to 5–7 ft. high, with bright red fall color. 'Rudy Haag' is a dense grower to just 4–5 ft. tall and wide, with rose-to-red fall color.

Species *E. alatus* and its selections take sun or shade. Group them as a screen, or plant them singly against dark evergreen plants for the greatest color impact. Compact selections make excellent unclipped hedges or foundation plants. Note that birds spread the seeds all over, and *E. alatus* is considered an invasive pest in parts of the Upper and Middle South.

E. americanus. HEART'S-A-BUSTIN', STRAWBERRY BUSH. Deciduous shrub. Zones US, MS, LS, CS; USDA 6-9. Native to eastern and southern U.S. Many-stemmed, suckering, well-behaved shrub that deserves wider use. To 6 ft. tall and broad, with green stems clothed in medium green, 3-in.-long leaves that turn pale yellowish pink in fall. Showy scarlet fruit about ¾ in. wide opens in September and October to reveal purple interiors and bright orange seeds. Stems hold their green color all winter. Tolerates much shade; use in woodland plantings.

E. europaeus. SPINDLE TREE. Deciduous shrub or tree. Zone US, MS; USDA 6-7. From Europe

and western Asia. Eventually grows as tall as 30 ft.; narrow when young, becoming rounded with age. Dark green leaves to 3 in. long; fall color varies from yellowish green to yellow to red. Profuse, ¾-in.-wide fruit is the ornamental feature: four-chambered, pink-to-red capsules that open to reveal bright orange seeds. Very prone to scale. 'Aldenham' ('Aldenhamensis') bears large pink capsules on long stems; 'Red Cascade' has rosy red capsules. Full sun or partial shade.

E. fortunei. WINTERCREEPER EUONYMUS. Evergreen vine or shrub. Zones US, MS, LS, CS; USDA 6-9. Native to China. One of the best broad-leafed evergreens where temperatures drop below 0°F. Trails or climbs by rootlets. Use prostrate forms to control erosion. Rich dark green, 1- to 2½-in.-long leaves with scallop-toothed edges; round white or pinkish fruit just ¼ in. wide. Mature growth is shrubby and bears fruit; cuttings taken from this shrubby wood produce upright plants. Sun or shade.

The selections of *E. fortunei*, several of which are listed here, are better known than the species itself. Many garden centers still sell them as forms of *E. radicans*, which was once thought to be the species but is now considered to be a botanical variety (see *E. f. radicans*). Use restraint when considering the variegated forms; gaudy foliage can be overpowering.

'Blondy'. Neat, mounding growth to about 2 ft. high, 3 ft. wide; golden yellow leaves have irregular green edges.

'Canadale Gold'. Compact growth to 4 ft. high, 3–3Í ft. wide, with light green, yellow-edged leaves.

'Coloratus'. PURPLE-LEAF WINTER CREEPER. To 2 ft. high, 6–8 ft. wide. Same sprawling growth habit as *E. f. radicans* but makes a more even ground cover. Leaves turn dark purple in fall and winter.

'Emerald Gaiety'. To 4–5 ft. high, 3 ft. wide. Dense-growing, erect shrub with deep green leaves edged in white.

'Emerald 'n Gold'. Similar to 'Emerald Gaiety', but with gold-edged leaves.

'Golden Prince'. To 4 ft. high and wide. New growth tipped

gold. Older leaves turn green. Extremely hardy; good hedge plant.

'Green Lane'. To 3–4 ft. high, 4–5 ft. wide, with erect branches, deep green foliage, orange fruit in fall.

'Ivory Jade'. Resembles 'Green Lane' but has creamy white leaf margins that show pink tints in cold weather.

'Minimus'. DWARF WINTER CREEPER. Tiny green leaves (¼ in.) spaced close together make a fine-textured ground cover or a trailing plant in a container.

'Moonshadow'. To 3 ft. high, 5 ft. wide. Bright yellow leaves with dark green margins.

'Sunspot'. To 3–6 ft. high and wide; dark green leaves have a central bright yellow spot.

E. f. radicans. COMMON WINTER CREEPER. Zones US, MS, LS; USDA 6-8. A tough, hardy, trailing or vining shrub with dark green, thick-textured, 1-in.-long leaves. Given no support, it's a sprawling, foot-high ground cover. Roots as it spreads. Given a masonry wall to cover, it does the job completely. Sun or shade.

E. japonicus. JAPANESE EUONYMUS. Evergreen shrub. Zones MS, LS, CS; USDA 7-9. Japanese native grows upright to 8–10 ft. tall and 6 ft. wide, but it's usually held lower by pruning or shearing. Older shrubs are attractive trained as trees, pruned and shaped to show their curving trunks and umbrella-shaped tops. Can be grouped to form a hedge or screen. Very glossy, leathery leaves are deep green, 1–2½ in. long, oval to roundish.

The species and its selections are very tolerant of heat, unfavorable soil, and seacoast conditions, but they're pest prone and susceptible to scale, thrips, and spider mites. Plants are notorious for powdery mildew; place in full-sun location with good air circulation to avoid it.

Variegated forms are most popular; they are among the few shrubs that keep variegation in full sun in hot-summer climates. Their garish foliage is hard to work into the landscape, however, and often becomes an eyesore. Some confusion exists in plant labeling of variegated types.

'Aureomarginatus'. GOLDEN EUONYMUS. To 5–10 ft. tall and 3–5 ft. wide. Gaudy, bright golden foliage nearly glows in the dark. Extremely popular; extremely overplanted. Often reverts to solid green.

'Chollipo'. Narrow, erect plant to 12 ft. tall, half as wide. Green leaves bordered with white. Dense grower; good for topiary.

'Grandifolius'. To 6–8 ft. tall, 4–6 ft. wide. Plants sold under this name have shiny, dark green leaves that are larger than those of the species. Compact, well branched; good for shearing into pyramids, globes.

'Green Spire'. Columnar, to 6–8 ft. tall and only 1–2 ft. wide. Lustrous, dark green leaves. Excellent as a narrow hedge.

'Microphyllus' (E. j. microphyllus). BOX-LEAF EUONYMUS. Compact and small leafed, 1–2 ft. tall and half as wide. Formal looking; usually trimmed as low hedge. Similar in form are 'Microphyllus Butterscotch' ('Microphyllus Aureovariegatus'),

with yellow-variegated leaves, and 'Microphyllus Variegatus' ('Microphyllus Albovariegatus'), with leaves splashed in white.

'Ovatus Aureus' ('Aureovariegatus'). GOLDSPOT EUONYMUS. To 10 ft. tall, 6 ft. wide. Leaves have brilliant yellow blotches, green edges.

'Silver King'. To 6 ft. tall and about half as wide. Green leaves with silvery white edges.

'Silver Princess'. Like 'Microphyllus Variegatus' but larger (to 3 ft. tall, 2 ft. wide), with larger leaves.

'Silver Queen'. Similar to 'Silver King', but green leaves are edged in creamy white.

E. kiautschovicus. SPREADING EUONYMUS. Evergreen shrub. Zones US, MS, LS; USDA 6-8. From China. To 8 ft. high and as wide or wider, with some low branches trailing on the ground and rooting. Light green, relatively thin-textured leaves to 3 in. long;

NATIVE PERENNIALS LIKE JOE-PYE WEED ARE NOT WEEDY AT ALL.

ABOVE: Euonymus americanus

profuse tiny, greenish cream flowers in late summer. Bees and flies swarm the plant when it is in bloom, so it is not a good choice for planting near porches, terraces, or walkways. Flowers are followed by conspicuous pink to reddish fruit with red seeds. Two hybrids make good hedges: 'DuPont', a 4- to 6-ft.-high plant with large, dark green leaves; and 'Manhattan', an upright grower to 6–8 ft., with dark, glossy leaves. Scale is a serious problem on all forms. Full sun or partial shade.

EUPATORIUM
Asteraceae
Perennials

🌡 **US, MS, LS, CS; USDA 6-9, EXCEPT AS NOTED**

☀ ◐ **LIGHT SHADE IN HOTTEST CLIMATES**

○ ◗ ◗ ◖◗ **WATER NEEDS VARY BY SPECIES**

Eupatorium purpureum

These are generally large plants with big domes of small flower heads that are rich in nectar and pollen. Blossoms attract butterflies. Most of the species described here are native to meadows of the eastern and central U.S.; popular in perennial borders and naturalistic meadow plantings.

E. cannabinum. HEMP AGRIMONY. Native to Europe. Grows 5–6 ft. tall, 4 ft. wide, with opposite pairs of deeply cut, 5-in.-long leaves and broad clusters of fluffy white, pink, or purple flowers in the summer. 'Album' produces white flowers; 'Plenum', pinkish purple blooms. Ample water.

E. dubium 'Little Joe'. DWARF JOE-PYE WEED. From eastern U.S. To 4 ft. tall and about

as wide. Large domes (to 10 in. across) of small lavender flowers are held above whorls of deep green foliage in late summer and fall. 'Baby Joe' is even smaller, at 2–2½ ft. high and wide. Moderate water.

E. greggii. GREGG'S MIST FLOWER. Native to Arizona, Texas. Weak-stemmed plant to 1½–2½ ft. tall, 2–3 ft. wide, with clusters of fluffy lavender flowers similar in form to those of floss flower (*Ageratum*). Blooms from spring to fall. Lacy, divided, light green leaves are somewhat hairy and usually sparse. Excellent for attracting butterflies. Native to dry, hot, rocky places but prefers some shade in low desert. Drought tolerant but looks best with occasional water. 'Boothill', first found near Tombstone, Arizona, is a choice form.

E. maculatum. SPOTTED JOE-PYE WEED. Similar to *E. purpureum* but smaller (to 6 ft. tall, 3 ft. wide at most), with green stems speckled or blotched in purple. Flat-topped clusters of pink, purple, or white flowers bloom from midsummer to early fall. Commonly sold is 'Gateway', to 5 ft. tall, with dusky purplish rose flowers at the tops of purplish stems. Give ample water, rich soil.

E. perfoliatum BONESET. Grows to 3–5 ft. tall and 2–3 ft. wide. Long (8-in.), narrow, medium green leaves are joined at their bases, so that the stem seems to grow through the leaves. Blooms from late summer to fall, with fluffy white flowers in flat-topped clusters. Attractive in meadow restoration, but poisonous to cattle and thus considered a nuisance by ranchers. Best with regular to ample water but takes considerable drought. In the past, it was thought to have medicinal value, helping to knit broken bones (hence the common name).

E. purpureum. JOE-PYE WEED. Often sold as *E. fistulosum*. Native to damp meadows in the eastern U.S., this imposing plant deserves wider use. Clumps of hollow stems reach 3–9 ft. tall and 1–3 ft. wide. Whorls of medium green, strongly toothed leaves to 1 ft. long; leaves have a vanilla scent when bruised. Dusty rose flowers, which are attractive to butterflies, appear in large, dome-shaped clusters in late summer or early fall. 'Carin' grows 5–7 ft. tall, has dark purple stems topped by silvery pink flowers. 'Little Red' is smaller to 4 ft. high and has pinkish purple flowers. Ample water.

E. rugosum. WHITE SNAKE-ROOT. Zones US, MS, LS; USDA 6-8. To 4 ft. tall, 2 ft. wide. Stems and lance-shaped, gray-green leaves to 5 in. long are heavily marked with deep brownish red; 'Chocolate' has especially dark color. Fluffy white flowers in late summer and early fall. Give rich soil, ample water.

EUPHORBIA

Euphorbiaceae
Annuals, biennials, perennials, and evergreen and deciduous shrubs or trees

✎ **ZONES VARY BY SPECIES**

☼ ☽ ● **EXPOSURE NEEDS VARY BY SPECIES**

◐ ◑ **MODERATE TO REGULAR WATER, EXCEPT AS NOTED**

◊ **SAP IS IRRITATING TO SKIN OR POISONOUS WHEN INGESTED IN MANY SPECIES**

Euphorbia amygdaloides
'Helena's Blush'

Large genus of about 2,000 species. What is called a "flower" is technically a cyathium, which consists of fused bracts that form a cup around the much-reduced true flowers. Cyathia may appear singly or in clusters. In some cases, as with poinsettia (*E. pulcherrima*), additional bracts below provide most of the color. Fruit is usually a dry capsule that releases seeds explosively, shooting them up to several feet away. Many euphorbias are succulents; these often mimic cacti in appearance and are as diverse in form and size. Only a few succulent types are listed here, but specialists in cacti and succulents can supply scores of species and selections.

All euphorbias have milky white sap that is irritating on contact or toxic if ingested (degree of irritation or toxicity varies, depending on species). Before using cut flowers in arrangements, dip stems in boiling water or hold in a flame for a few seconds to prevent bleeding sap.

Give these plants well-drained soil. Deer don't care for them.

E. amygdaloides. WOOD SPURGE. Perennial. Zones US, MS, LS, CS; USDA 6-9. From Europe and Turkey. To 3 ft. tall, 1 ft. wide, with reddish green stems. Evergreen, 1- to 3-in.-long, dark green leaves have red undersides that turn darker red in winter. Greenish yellow flowers in clusters to 8 in. long at stem ends in late winter to early spring. Best in sun but tolerates some shade. 'Purpurea' has heavily purple-tinted foliage, bright green inflorescences.

E. a. robbiae. MRS. ROBB'S BONNET. Zones US, MS, LS, CS; USDA 6-9. Shorter than the species, usually under 1 ft. high. Pale, lime-green flower clusters. Spreads slowly but surely from underground rhizomes. Can thrive in sun (but not hottest afternoon sun) and in deep shade. Regular to little water.

E. biglandulosa. See *E. rigida*

E. characias. Perennial. Zones US, MS, LS, CS; USDA 6-9. Mediterranean native. Upright stems crowded with narrow, blue-green leaves form a dome-shaped bush 4 ft. high and wide. Chartreuse or lime-green flowers in dense, round-to-cylindrical clusters appear in late winter, early spring. Color holds with only slight fading until seeds ripen; then stalks turn yellow and should be cut out at base, since new shoots have already made growth for next year's flowers. 'Glacier Blue' grows just over a foot high and has blue-green leaves edged in cream. 'Humpty Dumpty' is a shorter (to 2½-ft.-high), vigorous selection. *E. c. wulfenii* (*E. veneta*), a commonly grown form, has broader clusters of yellow flowers. All are fairly drought resistant and perform best in full sun.

E. cotinifolia. CARIBBEAN COPPER PLANT. Shrub or tree. Zones TS; USDA 10-11. From tropical America. Usually grown as an annual to add colorful foliage to a summer border, though it can become a small tree to 18 ft. tall if grown in a warm, frost-free spot. Long-stalked leaves to 4 in. long, 3 in. wide, usually borne in threes, are similar to those of smoke tree (*Cotinus*); 'Atropurpurea', the form most commonly grown, has wine-red leaves. Loose flower clusters have small white bracts, are not showy. Likes full sun, heat, good drainage; can't take frost.

E. dulcis 'Chameleon'. Perennial. Zones US, MS, LS, CS; USDA 6-9. Forms a mound to 2 ft. high and wide. New spring growth is burgundy, maturing to dark bronzy green. Greenish yellow flower heads with a purplish tint appear at stem ends in early summer. Leaves and bracts turn rich purple in fall. Spreads by self-sowing; comes true from seed. Full sun. Tolerates dry soil.

E. epithymoides. See *E. polychroma*

E. griffithii. Perennial. Zones US, MS, LS, CS; USDA 6-9. Erect-stemmed Himalayan native to 3 ft. tall and wide; spreads by creeping roots but is not aggressive. Narrow leaves are medium green, tinged with red when they emerge. Reddish orange-to-red bracts in early summer; those of 'Fireglow' are vivid orange-red. Dies back in winter. Full sun or light shade.

E. hypericifolia. Perennial in Zones TS; USDA 10-11. Annual anywhere. Delicate, airy mounds to 12–18 in. high and nearly as wide. Small white flowers look like snowflakes interspersed with the sparse, olive-green foliage. Plant resembles baby's breath (*Gypsophila paniculata*). Blooms year-round in mild winter areas, spring to fall elsewhere. Excellent in pots and hanging baskets. 'Diamond Frost' and 'Euphoric White' are popular and dependable. 'Breathless Blush' has leaves and flowers flushed in deep pink. Full sun to partial shade.

E. lathyris. MOLE PLANT, GOPHER PLANT. Biennial. Zones US, MS, LS, CS; USDA 6-9. From Europe, northwest Africa. Legend claims that it repels gophers and moles. Stems have poisonous, caustic, milky juice; keep away from skin and especially eyes, as painful burns can result. Juice could conceivably bother a gopher or mole enough to make it beat a hasty retreat. Single-

Euphorbia IS A HIGHLY VARIABLE GENUS, WITH MANY SPECIES THAT LOOK NOTHING LIKE EACH OTHER.

stemmed plant to 5 ft. tall and 1 ft. wide. Stem is densely set with large leaves growing at right angles to the stem and to each other (forming four longitudinal rows along stem). In second summer, produces short-lived cluster of unspectacular yellow flowers at top of stem. Flowers soon go to seed, after which the plant dies. Start from seed; plant will keep going by self-sowing. Sun or shade. Little to regular water.

E. marginata. SNOW-ON-THE-MOUNTAIN. Annual. Zones US, MS, LS, CS, TS; USDA 6-11. From central North America. To 2 ft. high, 1 ft. wide. Oval, light green leaves; upper ones are striped and margined white, sometimes even solid white. Summer flowers are variegated in green and white. Good for contrast with bright-colored dahlias, scarlet sage (*Salvia splendens*), zinnias, or with dark-colored plume celosia. Sow seeds in place in spring, in sun or partial shade. Thin to only a few inches apart, since plants are somewhat rangy.

E. milii. CROWN OF THORNS. Woody shrub; evergreen but sparsely leafed. Zones CS, TS; USDA 9-11; or indoor, greenhouse, or summer potted plant. Some frost damage below 28°F. From Madagascar. To 1–4 ft. high, 1½ ft.

TOP: *E. tirucalli* 'Sticks on Fire'; *E. milii*; MIDDLE: *Euphorbia pulcherrima* 'Marblestar'; BOTTOM: *E. hypericifolia* 'Diamond Frost'; *E cotinifolia*

wide. Stems armed with long, sharp thorns. Roundish, thin, light green leaves are usually found only near branch ends. Clustered pairs of bright red bracts put on a show all year. Many selections and hybrids, varying in form, size, and bract color (red, white, yellow, orange, pink). Thai Giant hybrids feature much larger flowers in red, pink, yellow, and sometimes multicolor. 'Red Jillian', for example, has 2-in. red flowers with accents of bright green. Train on small frame or trellis against a sheltered wall; or grow in container. Salt tolerance makes it an ideal choice for seaside plantings. Grow in porous but not rocky soil, in full sun or light shade. Indoors, give bright light, regular water (less in winter); feed with half-strength general-purpose liquid houseplant fertilizer once a week in spring and summer.

E. myrsinites. SPURGE. Perennial. Zones US, MS, LS, CS; USDA 6-9. Native from southern Europe to central Asia. To 6 in. high, 1 ft. wide. Evergreen plant with stems that trail outward from central crown, then rise toward tips. Stiff, roundish, blue-gray leaves set closely in spirals around stems. Flattish clusters of chartreuse-to-yellow flowers top stem ends in late winter, early spring. Cut out old stems as they turn yellow. Withstands cold, heat, and aridity but is short lived in warm-winter areas. Use in sunny rock garden with succulents and gray-leafed plants.

E. polychroma. CUSHION SPURGE. Perennial. Zones US, MS, LS, CS; USDA 6-9. From Europe. Neatly rounded hemisphere to 1 ft. high, 2 ft. wide, with deep green leaves symmetrically arranged on closely set, hairy stems. From midspring to midsummer, plant is covered with rounded clusters of bright yellow flowers surrounded by whorls of yellow-green bracts. Effect is of a gold mound suffused with green. Displays good fall color (yellow to orange or red) before going dormant. 'Bonfire' has leaves that emerge green but mature to red and hold their color all summer. 'Lacy' has white-variegated leaves. Use in rock gardens, perennial borders. Needs some afternoon shade in Lower and Coastal South. Short lived but reseeds.

E. pulcherrima. POINSETTIA. Evergreen, semievergreen, or deciduous shrub. Zones CS (protected), TS; USDA 9-11 or indoors. Native to Mexico. Leggy plant to 10 ft. or taller, 6 ft. wide. Coarse leaves grow on stiffly upright canes. Showy part of plant consists of petal-like bracts; true flowers in center are yellowish and inconspicuous. Red single form is the most familiar; less well known are double-bracted red sorts and forms with white, yellowish, pink, or marbled bracts. 'Winter Rose' has unched, curled bracts that resemble rose blooms and come in several colors; make excellent cut flowers. Plants bloom only when they experience long nights—in winter and into spring. To get potted plants to bloom, starting in October, put them in a closet (no light at all) each night for 14 hours, then move them into light in the morning for a maximum of 10 hours. Continue this procedure for 10 weeks; you can have poinsettia blossoms by Christmas. Bracts of paler kinds often last until later in spring. Milky sap is not poisonous; most people find it either completely harmless or at most mildly irritating to skin or stomach.

Useful garden plant in well-drained soil and full sun. Where adapted outdoors, needs no special care. Grow as informal hedge in the Tropical South; in the Coastal South, plant against sunny wall, in sheltered corner, under south-facing eaves. Plants grown outdoors in the Coastal South are likely to die down in winter. Thin branches in summer to produce larger bracts; or prune them back at 2-month intervals for bushy growth (but often smaller bracts). To improve red color, feed every 2 weeks with high-nitrogen fertilizer, starting when color begins to show.

Unlike their predecessors, modern poinsettia selections retain their foliage well into spring if given reasonable light. To care for holiday gift plants, keep them in a cool, well-lit room until after the last frost. Avoid sudden temperature changes; keep soil moist, but don't let water stand in pot saucer. When frost danger is past, cut back stems to two buds and set plants out in garden; or keep them in containers in a sunny spot on the patio. Potted plant will probably grow too tall for indoor use the next winter but may survive winter if well sheltered. Start new plants by making late-summer cuttings of stems with four or five eyes (joints).

E. rigida. Perennial. Zones LS, CS, TS; USDA 8-11. Mediterranean native forms a 3- to 5-ft.-wide clump of stems that angle outward, then rise up to 2 ft. high. Fleshy, gray-green leaves to 1½ in. long are narrow and pointed, their bases set tightly against stems. Broad, domed flower clusters in late winter or early spring are chartreuse-yellow, fading to pinkish. After seeds ripen, stems die back and should be removed; new stems take their place. Reseeds in mildest-winter areas, but not enough to become a pest. Showy display plant in borders, rock gardens, containers. Full sun. Tolerates drought.

E. robbiae. See *E. amygdaloides robbiae*

E. tirucalli. MILKBUSH, PENCIL CACTUS, PENCIL TREE. Succulent tree or shrub. Zones TS; USDA 10-11; or indoors. From tropical eastern Africa. Grown for striking pattern of silhouette or shadow. Fast growing to possible 30 ft. tall and 6 ft. wide, usually much smaller. Single or multiple trunks support tangle of light green, pencil-thick, succulent branches with tiny leaves present only on actively growing tips. Flowers are unimportant. 'Sticks on Fire' has pale pink to fiery salmon-pink stems; new growth has the most intense color in bright light. Both species and selections are very tolerant of seacoast conditions. Full sun. Keep milky sap away from eyes, as it can cause severe damage. As houseplant, thrives in driest atmosphere; needs plenty of light, well-drained potting mix, routine watering and fertilizing.

E. veneta, E. wulfenii. See *E. characias*

EURYBIA DIVARICATA

WHITE WOOD ASTER
Asteraceae
Perennial

🌿 **US, MS, LS; USDA 6-8**

◐ ● **PARTIAL TO FULL SHADE**

◔ ● **MODERATE TO REGULAR WATER**

Eurybia divaricata

Native to eastern North America. Grows 1–2½ ft. tall and wide, with a strong horizontal branching pattern and a generous show of ½-in. flowers in white aging to pink. Thrives in shade. Attracts butterflies. Blooms in late summer to fall. Not browsed by deer. Formerly known as *Aster divaricatus*.

EURYOPS PECTINATUS

BUSH DAISY, GRAY-LEAFED EURYOPS
Asteraceae
Evergreen shrub

🌿 **CS, TS; USDA 9-11; ANYWHERE AS ANNUAL**

☼ **FULL SUN**

◔ ◑ ● **LITTLE TO REGULAR WATER**

Euryops pectinatus 'Munchkin'

Native to South Africa, this tender shrub combines handsome foliage with showy, daisylike blooms. It's easy to grow and quite long blooming, making it a natural choice for low-maintenance gardens; it is also good for the back of the border, in containers, or as a low screen. Grows 3–6 ft. high and wide, with gray-green, deeply cut leaves about 2 in. long. Bright yellow, 1½- to 2-in.-wide daisies on 6-in. stems appear nearly continuously in warm weather, though blooming may slow during the dog days of summer. 'Viridis' is identical to the species but has deep green leaves. 'Munchkin' tops out at 3 ft. tall and 4 ft. wide.

Bush daisy thrives in almost any well-drained soil and tolerates buffeting ocean winds. It's winter hardy in the Coastal and Tropical South; in colder areas, grow it as an annual. Pick off old blooms to maintain neat appearance and extend the blooming season; shear lightly to control size.

EVOLVULUS GLOMERATUS

Convolvulaceae
Perennial usually grown as annual

🌿 **TS; USDA 10-11; ANYWHERE AS ANNUAL**

☼ ◐ **FULL SUN OR LIGHT SHADE**

◔ ● **MODERATE TO REGULAR WATER**

Evolvulus glomeratus

Native to Brazil. Small, trailing morning glory relative with stems to 20 in. long and oval leaves ⅓ - 1¼ in. long. Half-inch-wide blue flowers bloom in summer; they close in the evening and on dark, cloudy days. Plants most widely offered are labeled 'Blue Daze', 'Hawaiian Blue Eyes', or *E. g. grandiflorus*; or they may simply bear the common name 'blue daze.' 'Blue My Mind' is a dwarf to a foot high and 2 ft. wide. These plants vary somewhat: Foliage may be green or gray, blossoms bright blue or powder blue. Stems of all root where they touch the ground, and cuttings root very easily in water or moist soil. Use in hanging baskets, beds, borders.

EXACUM AFFINE

PERSIAN VIOLET
Gentianaceae
Annual or short-lived perennial grown as annual houseplant

◑ **BRIGHT INDIRECT LIGHT**

◔ ◑ **REGULAR TO AMPLE WATER**

Exacum affine

This is the little potted flower you see in the grocery store that looks so pretty you'd swear it was fake. Despite the common name, it comes not from Persia but from Socotra, an island off the Horn of Africa. Sweet-scented, star-shaped blue flowers with yellow stamens are held above inch-long, egg-shaped leaves. A white-flowered form is also available.

CARE

Persian violet is not a long-lived plant: you can keep it for 6 to 8 weeks at best, after which you should throw it away. To get the best and longest show, give it bright light (but not hot sun) and pick off faded blooms regularly. Allow the soil surface to become dry to the touch before watering; overwatering will cause the plant to collapse. Make sure the pot drains freely. Thrives in high humidity, such as near the sink or shower. Don't bother to fertilize—the plant won't last long enough to make it worthwhile. Just enjoy the brief beauty it brings indoors at any time of the year.

F

EXOCHORDA

PEARL BUSH
Rosaceae
Deciduous shrubs

🌿 **US, MS, LS; USDA 6-8**

☀️ **FULL SUN**

💧💧 **MODERATE TO REGULAR WATER**

Exochorda x *macrantha* 'The Bride'

From China. Loose, spikelike clusters of 1½- to 2-in.-wide white flowers open from a profusion of buds resembling pearls. Flowering spans several weeks in early spring, at about the same time the roundish, 1½- to 2-in.-long leaves expand.

These shrubs are showy during spring but undistinguished at other times of year, so choose your site accordingly. Prefer well-drained, acid soil but will grow in neutral or alkaline soil; will take considerable neglect. Pest free. Not browsed by deer. Flowers are formed on previous year's growth, so prune after bloom.

E. giraldii. Resembles the widely grown species *E. racemosa* but is somewhat smaller, with slightly smaller flowers and red tints in leaf veins and flower stalks.

E. x macrantha. Hybrid between *E. racemosa* and another species. The only selection available, 'The Bride', is a compact shrub to about 4 ft. tall and wide. Very showy bloom. 'Blizzard' and 'Niagara' (Snow Day Surprise) have larger flowers.

E. racemosa. COMMON PEARL BUSH. Loose, open, slender; grows to 10–15 ft. tall and wide, possibly larger. In small gardens, remove lower branches to make small, upright, airy, multistemmed tree. Often found in older gardens in the Middle and Lower South. Reseeds readily, and seedlings are often shared.

FAGUS

BEECH
Fagaceae
Deciduous trees

🌿 **ZONES VARY BY SPECIES**

☀️◐ **FULL SUN OR LIGHT SHADE**

💧💧 **MODERATE TO REGULAR WATER**

Fagus grandifolia

Beeches are grand trees, capable of growing 90 ft. tall and 60 ft. wide after many years. Their majestic outlines range from rounded to broadly pyramidal, with wide, sweeping lower branches that sometimes touch the ground; some selections weep attractively. Handsome, smooth gray bark contrasts nicely with glossy, dark green foliage. In autumn, leaves turn yellow with green veins, then golden or reddish brown, then fade to tan; these buff-colored leaves hang on through most of winter and are quite beautiful in the winter landscape. A layered, lacy branching pattern and long, pointed leaf buds add to the attractive winter silhouette. Small nuts enclosed in spiny husks attract squirrels, blue jays, and other wildlife.

Beeches aren't the easiest trees to work into a home landscape. They are too large for smaller lots; their thick network of surface roots and the heavy shade they cast make it almost impossible to grow a lawn or other plants beneath them. However, they work well at the edge of a woodland or in naturalized areas. Fancy-leafed or weeping forms of European beech (*F. sylvatica*) are good as specimens or accents.

F. crenata. JAPANESE BEECH. Zones US, MS; USDA 6-7. From Japan. Leaves scallop edged, somewhat smaller than those of other beeches. Reddish brown fall color. Likes some shade, especially when young.

F. grandifolia. AMERICAN BEECH. Zones US, MS, LS, CS; USDA 6-9. A stately tree and a principal component of the vast hardwood forests that once covered much of the eastern U.S. Tolerates shade and makes a good understory tree when young. More tolerant of summer heat than the other two species described here; can be grown farther south. Cigar-shaped buds. Toothed, 3- to 6-in.-long leaves turn golden bronze in fall, then to a beautiful parchment tan. They stay on the tree throughout winter. Handsome silvery gray bark. Allow plenty of room for this tree.

F. sylvatica. EUROPEAN BEECH. Zones US, MS; USDA 6-7. Native from central Europe to the Caucasus. Lustrous green leaves to 4 in. long turn russet and bronzy in autumn. Many selections, including the following.

'Asplenifolia' (*F. s. heterophylla* 'Asplenifolia'). FERNLEAF BEECH. Large, robust, spreading tree with delicate-looking foliage—narrow leaves, deeply cut or lobed nearly to the midrib.

'Black Swan'. Upright tree to about 25 ft. tall and 12 ft. wide, with strongly weeping side branches. Leaves are shiny black-purple.

'Dawyck' ('Fastigiata'). DAWYCK BEECH. Narrow, upright tree; just 8 ft. wide with 35 ft. tall. Broader in great age but still narrower than the species.

'Dawyck Gold'. Columnar tree to 60 ft. tall, 20 ft. wide. New leaves emerge yellow, mature to light green, and turn yellow again in autumn.

'Dawyck Purple'. Columnar, to 70 ft. tall, 15 ft. wide, with purple foliage.

'Laciniata'. CUTLEAF BEECH. Narrow, deeply cut green leaves.

'Pendula'. WEEPING BEECH. Irregular, spreading form with green leaves and long, weeping branches that reach to the ground and can root where they touch. Without staking to establish vertical trunk, it will grow wide rather than high.

'Purpurea Pendula'. WEEPING COPPER BEECH. Purple-leafed weeping form matures to 10 ft. tall and wide. Splendid container plant.

'Riversii'. COPPER BEECH, PURPLE BEECH. The most widely sold of the purple-leaved types. Grows 50–60 ft. tall and 35–45 ft. wide. Deep reddish or purple leaves hold color all summer.

'Rohan Obelisk' ('Red Obelisk'). Columnar growth to 15–40 ft. high and 3–10 ft. wide. Dark purple-red foliage. Some leaves are deeply cut, others are smooth-edged.

'Rohanii'. Wavy-edged leaves open dark purple and gradually mature to green. Fall color is reddish to purplish brown.

'Tricolor'. TRICOLOR BEECH. Grows slowly to 24–40 ft., usually less. Green leaves are marked white and edged pink. Foliage burns in hot sun or dry winds. Choice container plant.

'Zlatia'. GOLDEN BEECH. Leaves are yellow when new, then age to yellow-green. Subject to sunburn. Good container plant.

CARE

Beeches like deep, fertile, loose, soil that is neutral to slightly acid. Never park cars or heavy vehicles under a large beech, as this crushes sensitive feeder roots and results in the tree's slow demise. Woolly beech aphids on the undersides of the leaves sometimes cause the foliage to pucker, turn blotchy, and drop, but they are seldom a serious problem.

FALLOPIA

Polygonaceae
Deciduous vines

US, MS, LS, CS; USDA 6-9

EXPOSURE NEEDS VARY BY SPECIES

LITTLE TO REGULAR WATER

Fallopia baldschuanica

Formerly listed as *Polygonum*, the two plants described offer showy flowers. Both merit vigilance, as they spread by rhizomes and can be highly invasive and difficult to eradicate. Don't plant them in unmanaged areas.

F. baldschuanica (*Polygonum aubertii*). SILVER LACE VINE. This extremely vigorous vine from Asia can cover a large space in a short time. It typically puts on 10–15 ft. of new growth in a single season and can fully drape an arbor, fence, or gazebo in short order. Glossy, dark green leaves are arrowhead shaped, 1½–2 in. long. A frothy mass of fragrant, creamy white flowers, sometimes tinged with pink, smothers the plant in summer and fall. Prune silver lace vine severely to keep it in bounds; you can cut it to the ground in winter and it will resprout in spring and bloom in summer. Adaptable to most well-drained soils; tolerates drought. Full sun.

F. japonica (*Polygonum cuspidatum, Reynoutria japonica*). JAPANESE KNOTWEED. From eastern Asia. Tough, vigorous plant with wiry, reddish brown stems that form large clumps to 4–8 ft. tall. Pale green leaves are nearly heart shaped, to 5 in. long. Showy clusters of greenish white flowers appear in leaf axils in late summer and fall. Spreads rampantly by underground runners and is particularly hard to control: Shoots have been known to push up through asphalt. Good choice for bank cover or erosion control in difficult areas where little else will grow. Full sun or partial shade. 'Crimson Beauty' bears fiery red flowers on 7- to 8-ft. stems from late summer through fall; it is known to some Southerners by the name "kiss-me-at-the-gate." It's better behaved than the species, forming clumps that are not invasive. *F. j. compacta* 'Variegata' is less invasive than the species, but if in doubt, treat it like mint and keep it in a container.

FALLUGIA PARADOXA

APACHE PLUME
Rosaceae
Semievergreen shrub

US, MS, LS, CS, TS; USDA 6-11

FULL SUN

NO WATERING NEEDED

Fallugia paradoxa

Native to mountains of medium and high deserts of California, west to Edwards Plateau and Trans-Pecos regions of Texas, and northern Mexico. Grows 4–6 ft. tall, 5 ft. wide, with straw-colored branches and flaky bark. Small, lobed leaves are deep green on top, rusty beneath; carried in clusters. Flowers resembling single white roses just 1½ in. wide bloom in spring, summer. Large, showy clusters of feathery seed heads follow, creating a soft haze through which you can see the shrub's rigid branch pattern; they are greenish at first, then later turn pink or take on a reddish tinge. Needs gritty, well-drained soil. Pruning usually not needed.

Reseeds freely, which makes it good for naturalized areas but a problem in formal beds. Not for areas with high rainfall, heavy soil. Deer resistant.

FARFUGIUM JAPONICUM

LEOPARD PLANT
Asteraceae
Perennial

MS, LS, CS, TS; USDA 7-11, EXCEPT AS NOTED; OR HOUSEPLANT

SOME SHADE; BRIGHT INDIRECT LIGHT

AMPLE WATER

Farfugium japonicum 'Aureomaculatum'

From China and Japan. Glossy, bright green, 6- to 12-in.-wide leaves on long (1- to 2-ft.) leaf-stalks form a clump to about 2 ft. tall and wide; leaves are kidney shaped, scalloped, or shallowly lobed. From fall into winter, flower stems rise 1½ to 2 ft. tall, each carrying several yellow 1½- to 2-in. daisies. The species is not as popular or widely grown as its selections, which include the following. Formerly known as *Ligularia tussilaginea*.

'Argenteum'. Somewhat smaller leaves than the species, in deep green marbled with gray green and white.

'Aureomaculatum'. Zones US, MS, LS, CS, TS; USDA 6-11. Thick, leathery leaves are heavily, evenly speckled with yellow.

'Crispatum'. Thick, ruffle-edged, gray-green leaves; sometimes called pie crust ligularia.

'Gigantea' (*F. j. giganteum*). Thick, glossy leaves up to 15 in. across.

'Kagami Jishi'. Combines the ruffled edges of 'Crispatum' with the yellow-spotted foliage of 'Aureomaculatum'.

'Last Dance'. Hybrid with another Japanese species. Leaves are more angular and scalloped than those of others listed here.

CARE

All are choice container plants for shady beds or entryways. Tops hardy to 20°F. Plants die back to roots at 0°F but put on new growth in spring. Control snails and slugs. Can be grown indoors if placed near a window with bright light.

X FATSHEDERA LIZEI

Araliaceae
Evergreen shrub, vine, or ground cover

MS, LS, CS, TS; USDA 7-11

PARTIAL TO FULL SHADE

REGULAR WATER

x *Fatshedra lizei* 'Lemon & Lime'

Hybrid between Japanese fatsia (*Fatsia japonica*) and English ivy (*Hedera helix*), with characteristics of both parents. Highly polished, 4- to 10-in.-wide leaves with three to five pointed lobes look like giant ivy leaves; plant also sends out long, trailing or climbing stems like ivy, though without aerial holdfasts. This hybrid inherited shrubbiness from its Japanese parent, though its habit is more irregular and sprawling. Leaves of 'Lemon & Lime' ('Annemieke') are splashed with yellow; those of 'Variegata' are bordered in white.

Leaves are injured at 15°F, dies to the ground at 0°F, but grows back. Seems to suffer more from late frosts than from winter cold. Give it protection from hot, drying winds. Watch out for slugs and snails. This plant tends to grow in a straight line, but it can be shaped if you work at it. Pinch tip growth to force branching. Two or three times a year, guide and tie stems before they become brittle. If plant gets away from you, cut it back to ground; it will regrow quickly. If you use it as ground cover, cut back vertical growth every 2 or 3 weeks during growing season. Grown as vine or espalier, plants are heavy, so give them strong support. Even a well-grown vine is leafless at base. Deer reistant.

FATSIA JAPONICA

JAPANESE FATSIA
Araliaceae
Evergreen shrub

🌡 **LS, CS, TS; USDA 8-11; OR HOUSEPLANT**

◐ ● **PARTIAL TO FULL SHADE; BRIGHT LIGHT**

💧 **REGULAR WATER**

Fatsia japonica

From Korea, Japan. Tropical-looking, sparsely branched shrub with long-stalked, big, glossy dark green, deeply lobed, fanlike leaves to 16 in. wide. Moderate growth to 5–8 ft. high and wide (rarely more). Many roundish clusters of small, creamy white flowers in fall and winter; these are followed by clusters of small, shiny black berries.

A natural landscaping choice where bold pattern is wanted. Most effective when thinned to show some branch structure. Provides year-round good looks for shaded entryway or patio. 'Moseri' has a compact habit; 'Variegata' has leaves edged golden yellow to creamy white. 'Spider's Web' has new leaves edged and heavily speckled in white, fading to green as they mature.

Grows in nearly all soils except soggy ones. Adapted to containers. If leaves are chronically yellow, add iron to soil. During prolonged dry spells, wash occasionally with hose to clean leaves and to lessen insect attack. Control slugs and snails. Established plants sucker freely; keep suckers or remove them with spade. Rejuvenate spindly plants by cutting back hard in early spring. Plants that set fruit often self-sow.

In areas where Japanese fatsia isn't winter hardy, it's a popular indoor plant. It does best with lots of morning sun—but not hot afternoon sun. Allow the soil surface to go dry between waterings, but don't let the plant wilt; reduce watering somewhat in winter. Feed every other week in spring and summer and monthly in fall and winter with a general-

JAPANESE FATSIA IS ELEGANT BUT TOUGH, EASILY TOLERATING COASTAL CONDITIONS AND AIR POLLUTION.

purpose liquid houseplant fertilizer. Spider mites are common pests; use insecticidal soap or horticultural oil to control them.

FEIJOA SELLOWIANA

PINEAPPLE GUAVA
Myrtaceae
Evergreen shrub or tree

🌡 **LS, CS, TS; USDA 8-11**

☀ **FULL SUN**

💧 **REGULAR WATER**

Feijoa sellowiana

South American native. Hardiest of so-called subtropical fruits. Normally a large multistemmed plant; reaches 18–25 ft. with equal spread if not pruned or killed back by frosts. Can take almost any amount of training or pruning to shape as espalier, screen, hedge, or small tree (late spring is the best time to prune). Oval, 2- to 3-in.-long leaves are glossy green above, silvery white beneath. Blooms in spring, bearing unusual inch-wide flowers with big central tufts of red stamens and four fleshy white petals tinged purplish on inside; blossoms attract bees and birds. Flowers are edible and can be added to fruit salads or used for jams and jellies. Plant is drought tolerant, but give it regular water for best fruiting.

Fruit ripens 4 to 5½ months after flowering in the Tropical South, 5 to 7 months after bloom in Lower and Coastal South. Oval, grayish green, 1- to 4-in.-long fruit has soft, sweet to bland pulp with flavor that is somewhat like pineapple. The best way to harvest is to wait until first fruit drops, then spread a tarp underneath

and give the tree a shake. Repeat every few days. Fruit is sometimes sold in markets.

Improved selections 'Apollo', 'Coolidge', 'Mammoth', 'Nazemetz', and 'Trask' are self-fruitful, although cross-pollination will produce a better crop. Single plants of seedlings or other named selections may need cross-pollination.

FESTUCA GLAUCA

BLUE FESCUE
Poaceae
Perennial grasses

🌡 **US, MS, LS, CS; USDA 6-9, EXCEPT AS NOTED**

☀ ◐ **BEST IN SUN, TOLERATE SOME SHADE**

💧💧 **MODERATE TO REGULAR WATER**

Festuca glauca 'Elijah Blue'

From Europe. Ornamental grass grows to 1 ft. high, 10 in. wide. Dense tufts of extremely fine leaves; color varies from blue-gray to silvery gray. Summer flowers in upright spikes. Tolerates drought and thrives with good drainage and air circulation. Use as edging or ground cover. Effective in rock gardens, between stepping stones, in containers. 'Elijah Blue' forms an 8-in.-high foliage clump in intense silver-blue; it is one of the tougher, longer-lived selections. 'Siskiyou Blue', to 1–2 ft. high, has luminous blue leaves. 'Golden Toupee' grows about 8 in. high, with fine-textured chartreuse foliage; does best in light shade.

FICUS

Moraceae

Evergreen and deciduous trees, shrubs, vines

🌿 **TS; USDA 10-11, EXCEPT AS NOTED**

☀ ◑ ● **EXPOSURE NEEDS VARY BY SPECIES**

💧 **REGULAR WATER**

Ficus benjamina 'Variegata'

The average gardener would never expect to find the commercial edible fig, small-leafed climbing fig, and potted rubber tree under one common heading—but they are classed together because they bear small or large figs (inedible in most species). Ornamental types are discussed here; for sorts grown for tasty fruit, see Fig.

Many ornamental species make good houseplants. Generally, they thrive on rich, steadily moist (not wet) soil; frequent light feedings; and bright, indirect light.

F. auriculata. Briefly deciduous shrub or small tree. Native to India. To 25 ft. high and wide. Sandpapery textured, unusually large leaves—broadly oval to round, about 15 in. across. New growth is mahogany-red, turning to rich green. Large figs are borne in clusters on trunk and framework branches. Can be shaped into a small tree or espaliered. Beautiful in large container; good near swimming pools. Grow in wind-protected, sunny location.

F. benjamina. WEEPING FIG. Evergreen tree. Makes good houseplant. From India and Malaysia. Grows to 30 ft. tall, with greater spread. Good shade or specimen tree for larger gardens or parks, since it requires space for its invasive surface root sys-tem. Used in large containers as entryway or patio tree; also good as screen, espalier, or clipped hedge. Leathery, 5-in.-long, shiny green leaves densely clothe drooping branches. New plants are easy to start from semihard-wood cuttings taken between late spring and early summer. Give a frost-free, wind-protected location in sun or shade.

One of the most popular indoor plants for a place in bright light. Sudden leaf shedding is a common problem, often resulting from plant's being moved to a new location. If shedding begins shortly after a move, be patient; leaves usually grow back. Leaves that fall off while green usually indicate insufficient water; try to keep soil evenly moist. If fallen leaves are yellow, overwatering may be to blame. If shedding is accompanied by a sweet smell and sticky leaves, look for scale insects and control with horticultural oil as needed. Don't site weeping figs in drafty areas or near stoves or heat registers.

For an indoor tree that is similar in size and habit to *F. benjamina* but doesn't drop its foliage, try *F. binnendijkii* 'Alii'. It can tolerate lower light better than *F. benjamina*.

As an indoor plant, weeping fig typically grows slowly to 8–10 ft. tall, not quite as wide. These are among the most popular selections.

'Exotica'. Like the species but has wavy-edged leaves with long, twisted tips. Often sold simply as *F. benjamina*.

'Indigo'. Open, weeping habit. Thick, glossy leaves are a very dark green when young, maturing to blue-black. Some leaves may be slightly variegated with lighter tones. Quite shade tolerant.

'Midnight'. Compact and bushy, with very thick leaves. Foliage is such a deep green that it looks almost blue-black.

'Monique'. Upright habit. Elliptical, shiny, bright green leaves with ruffled edges. Very resistant to leaf drop.

'Starlight'. Bushy grower. Leaves are variegated—some almost solidly—in creamy white.

'Too Little'. Dwarf form that may reach only 3–4 ft. high after many years; densely foliaged with tiny, slightly curled leaves. Ideal for bonsai.

F. binnendijkii (*F. maclel-landii*). Evergreen tree. Grows well indoors. Similar to *F. benjamina* but easier to grow indoors, less likely to shed leaves. Dark green, stiff, willowlike leaves reach 7 in. long, less than 1 in. wide. Outdoors, grow in sun or partial shade. Indoors, select a perma-nent position with good light and no drafts. Let soil go dry between waterings, then soak thoroughly—but don't leave plant standing in water. Dust or rinse leaves with water occasionally. Feed with a general-purpose liquid house-plant fertilizer once in spring and once in fall, more often if plant is in very bright light. Pest problems are rare. If scale or mealybugs appear, spray the former with horticultural oil; wipe off the latter with a cotton swab dipped in alcohol. 'Amstel King' is similar to the species but has thicker, wider, glossier leaves; when plant is actively growing, leaf tips may be pink or red.

F. deltoidea. MISTLETOE FIG. Evergreen shrub. Makes good houseplant. Native to Southeast Asia. Grows very slowly to 8–10 ft. high, about half as wide. Interest-ing open, twisted branch pattern. Thick, dark green, roundish, 2-in. leaves are sparsely stippled with tan specks on upper surface and a few black dots underneath. Attractive, small, greenish to yellow fruit borne continuously. As outdoor plant, most often grown in container on patio. Part shade.

F. elastica. RUBBER PLANT. Evergreen shrub or tree. Makes good houseplant. Native to India and Malaysia. Familiar plant found in almost every florists' shop. It can become a 40-ft. tree in the Tropical South; often seen as a small tree or shrub in shaded "tunnel" garden entrances in cooler part of range. Comes back quickly if killed to ground by frost. Narrow, leathery, dark green leaves are 8–12 in. long. New leaves unfold from rosy pink sheaths that soon wither and drop. Partial or full shade.

One of the most foolproof indoor plants; can take less light than most big houseplants. If potted plant becomes too tall and leggy, you can cut off the top and select a side branch to form a new main shoot. Or get a new plant by air layering the top section; when roots form, cut branch section with attached roots and pot it up. The following are among the best selections.

'Abidjan' ('Burgundy'). West African selection made from 'Decora'. New growth, leaf

ABOVE: Ficus 'Too Little'

sheaths, and leaf midribs are red. On plants grown in bright light, older leaves are dark maroon.

'Asahi'. Selection from Japan. Similar to 'Doescheri' but with slightly smaller leaves and more extensive creamy yellow variegation.

'Decora' ('Belgica'). The common rubber plant sold for indoor use is usually this selection. Superior to the species because of its broader, glossier leaves. Foliage is bronzy when young.

'Doescheri'. Leaves are marbled in green and gray-green, with green margins, creamy yellow midribs, and pink leafstalks.

'Rubra'. New leaves are reddish and retain a red edge as rest of leaf turns green.

'Schrijveriana'. Broad leaves are variegated in green, gray-green, creamy yellow, and white. Leafstalks are red.

'Variegata'. Long, narrow leaves variegated in yellow and green. Variegation is interesting when leaves are viewed close up in container—but as an outdoor tree, plant has a sickly look.

F. lyrata. FIDDLELEAF FIG. Evergreen tree or shrub. Makes good houseplant. Native to tropical Africa. Dramatic structural form with prominently veined, fiddle-shaped, huge leaves (to 15 in. long, 10 in. wide) in glossy dark green. In protected outdoor position, can grow to 20 ft. high and as wide, with trunks 6 in. thick. Good near swimming pools. To increase branching, pinch back when plant is young. Full sun or light shade. Highly effective as a houseplant; give bright light. Compact selections 'Bambino' and 'Little Fiddle' have smaller leaves more tightly spaced on the stems, but they still have the potential to be large plants indoors.

F. microcarpa. INDIAN LAUREL FIG, CHINESE BANYAN. Evergreen tree. Native from Malay peninsula to Borneo. Grows at a moderate rate to 25–30 ft. high, 35–40 ft. wide. Beautiful weeping form, with long, drooping branches thickly clothed with blunt-tipped, 2- to 4-in.-long leaves. Light rose-to-chartreuse new leaves, produced almost continuously, give pleasing two-tone effect. Plants sold as *F. m. nitida* (a name with no botanical standing) may have the same weeping form as the species

or may have upright-growing branches.

Prune at any time of year to shape as desired. Remove lower branches to reveal slim, light gray trunk. Responds well to shearing into formal hedge as low as 5 ft. Where pest free, makes a highly satisfactory tree or tub plant. Unfortunately, subject to thrips damage in some areas; these pests are hard to control, since they quickly curl new leaves (thus protecting themselves from sprays). Afflicted leaves show stippling, then drop. Full sun. 'Green Gem' has thicker, darker green leaves and is apparently unaffected by thrips.

F. pumila. CREEPING FIG. Evergreen vine. Zones LS, CS, TS; USDA 8-11; or houseplant. Native to China, Japan, Australia. Has a most unfiglike habit; it is one of the few plants that attaches itself securely to wood, masonry, or even metal in barnacle fashion. Because it is grown on walls and thus protected, it is found in colder climates more often than any other evergreen fig. Grows in sun or shade; not for hot south or west wall. Indoors, provide consistently moist soil and a location in bright filtered or indirect light.

Looks innocent enough in youth, making a delicate tracery of tiny, heart-shaped leaves. Neat little juvenile foliage ultimately develops into big (2- to 4-in.-long), leathery leaves borne on stubby branches that bear large, oblong fruits. In time, stems will envelop a three- or four-story building so completely that it becomes necessary to keep them trimmed away from windows. It's safe to use on masonry house walls, but not wooden ones. Remove fruiting stems from time to time as they form. Roots are invasive. 'Minima' has shorter, narrower leaves than the species. Small, lobed leaves of *F. p. quercifolia* look like miniature oak leaves. 'Variegata' has standard-size leaves with creamy white markings.

F. religiosa. PEEPUL, BO-TREE. Briefly deciduous tree. Native from India to Southeast Asia. May reach 40 ft. high and wide after 25 years or more. Foliage is quite open and delicate, revealing structure of tree at all times. Bark is warm, rich brown. Pale green leaves are thin textured and rather crisp, 4 to 7 in. long, round-

ish in shape but with a long, tail-like point. They move easily in even the slightest breeze, giving the foliage mass a fluttering look. Leaves drop completely in late spring or early summer—a frightening experience for the gardener who has bought an "evergreen" fig. Full sun.

F. retusa. See *F. microcarpa*

F. roxburghii. See *F. auriculata*

F. rubiginosa. RUSTYLEAF FIG. Evergreen tree. Native to Australia. A single- or multitrunked, densely foliaged tree to 20–50 ft. tall, with broad crown 30–50 ft. wide. Leaves about 5 in. long, deep green above, generally rust colored and woolly beneath. Plant may develop hanging aerial roots characteristic of many of the evergreen figs that grow in tropical and semitropical environments. Full sun. A small-leafed form has been sold as *F. microphylla*. 'Australis' is virtually identical to the species but may vary in having leaf undersides with a less pronounced rust color. 'Variegata', with leaves mottled green and cream, is sometimes sold as a houseplant.

FIG

Moraceae
Deciduous fruit tree

✏ **MS, LS, CS, TS; USDA 7-11; OR GROW IN POTS**

☀ **FULL SUN**

💧 **REGULAR WATER**

'Papa John' figs

A traditional favorite fruit tree of the Deep South, edible fig (*Ficus carica*) is a low-branching plant with multiple trunks; it grows fairly rapidly to 15–30 ft. tall and

spreads at least as wide. In the Middle South, it may freeze back to the ground during cold winters and act like a big shrub. It's easy to grow in a large container and can also be trained as an espalier. Heavy, gray-barked, smooth trunks (gnarled in really old trees) are picturesque in silhouette. Bright green, rough-textured leaves with three to five lobes are 4–9 in. long and nearly as wide. Casts dense shade. Winter framework, tropical-looking foliage, strong trunk and branch pattern make fig a top-notch ornamental tree, especially near a patio where it can be illuminated from beneath. Protect container plants in winter. Fruit drop is a problem immediately above deck or paving.

The type of figs generally grown in the South do not require pollination. Some will even bear two crops. Depending on the selection, the first crop comes in June or July on last year's wood; the second and more important one comes in July to October from current summer's wood. Keep fruit picked as it ripens; protect from birds if you can. In late fall, pick off any remaining ripe figs and clean up fallen fruit. Types differ in climate adaptability; most need prolonged high temperatures to bear good fruit, while some thrive in cooler conditions. Selections are noted below. Those with "everbearing" in their name will produce a good crop even if damaged by cold the previous winter.

In general, the darker colored figs usually have greater shelf life. The lighter ones may have fantastic flavor, but may lose quality more quickly.

'Alma'. Very sweet, medium-size fig with golden brown skin and amber-to-tan flesh.

'Brown Turkey'. Adaptable to most fig climates; widely grown in Southeast. Small and cold hardy; good garden tree. Fruit has purplish brown skin, pinkish amber flesh; good for fresh eating.

'Celeste' ('Blue Celeste', 'Celestial'). The most widely grown fig in the Southeast. Cold-hardy plant. Bronzy, violet-tinged skin, pinkish amber flesh; good for fresh eating.

'Conadria'. Choice thin-skinned white fig blushed violet; white-to-red flesh, fine flavor. Takes intense heat without splitting.

FIG | 315

TIME TO PICK A FIG

Plant several selections of figs to enjoy a range of flavors for months. Eat them fresh, or use them in preserves, jellies, desserts, and salads.

'Green Ischia'
Light green outside, strawberry-red inside; late season; so sweet that they taste like jam

'Italian Black'
Black outside, red inside; midseason; an exceptionally beautiful fig; great for preserves

'LSU Purple'
Purple outside, white/yellow inside; midseason; firm; mildly sweet flavor; great grilled

'Celeste'
Brown/violet outside, light red inside; midseason; a classic Southern fig; sweet like candy

'Brown Turkey'
Brown/yellow outside, light red inside; late season; a classic Southern fig; sweet, sugary taste

'Papa John'
Purple outside, white/red inside; midseason; sweet, rich flavor; great for preserves

'Alma'
Light brown/yellow outside, amber inside; late season; honey flavor; a Texas A&M selection

'O'Rourke'
Brownish purple/green outside, light red inside; early season (first fig of summer); sugary sweet

'White Marseilles'
Green/yellow outside, white/yellow inside; midseason; mild flavor; introduced by Jefferson

F

'Genoa' ('White Genoa'). Greenish yellow to white skin; strawberry to yellow flesh.

'Green Ischia'. Light green to yellowish green skin, red flesh. Light and refreshing; good fresh or dried. Plant has low upright, spreading form.

'Italian Black'. Jet black fruit with red pulp. Produces two crops a year.

'Italian Everbearing'. Resembles 'Brown Turkey' but bears somewhat larger fruit with reddish brown skin. Good fresh or dried.

'Kadota' ('White Kadota', 'Florentine'). Tough-skinned yellowish green fruit with rich, sweet, amber-to-yellow flesh. Excellent for canning. Strong grower; needs little pruning. If pruned severely, will bear later, with fewer, larger fruits.

'Lemon' ('Blanche'). Medium-large green figs distinctively shaped without a slender neck. Also known as 'Marseilles'.

'LSU Everbearing'. Medium-large figs with yellow-green skin and sweet, white-to-amber

flesh. Produces fruit from July through fall.

'LSU Purple'. Dark purple skin with whitish, amber flesh with flecks of pink. Good flavor when fully ripe. Vigorous, upright, spreading tree.

'O'Rourke'. Medium-size fruit with bronze-violet tinted skin like 'Celeste'. Amber flesh with light pink overtones.

'Papa John'. Medium-size fruit with dark purple skin and strawberry flesh. Great flavor, cold hardy, strong tree, good producer.

'Peter's Honey' ('Rutara'). Fruit has greenish yellow skin, amber flesh. Very sweet.

'Texas Everbearing'. Medium to large fig with brownish yellow skin, pinkish amber flesh.

'White Adriatic'. Medium to large, sweet white figs with yellowish green skin, strawberry pink flesh. Very drought tolerant.

'White Marseilles'. Greenish yellow, thin skin with translucent white flesh. This is sweet and reliable.

CARE

Not particular about soil. In the Middle South, plant figs near a south wall—or train them against one—to benefit from reflected heat. Cut back tops hard at planting. As tree grows, prune lightly each winter: Cut out dead wood, crossing branches, and low-hanging branches that interfere with traffic. Pinch back runaway shoots at any time. Avoid deep cultivation, which may damage surface roots. Do not use high-nitrogen fertilizers; they stimulate growth at expense of fruit. If burrowing animals are a problem, plant trees in ample wire baskets. Figs are not usually browsed by deer.

TOP: 'Green Ischia' figs; 'Brown Turkey' figs; *BOTTOM:* 'Celeste' figs

FILIPENDULA

Rosaceae
Perennials

US, MS, LS; USDA 6-8

PARTIAL SHADE, EXCEPT AS NOTED

REGULAR TO AMPLE WATER, EXCEPT AS NOTED

Filipendula rubra

These lush plants bear plumes of tiny flowers above large, coarsely divided leaves. Most species prefer moist to constantly damp soil. Use in borders, in naturalistic landscapes, beside ponds.

F. purpurea. JAPANESE MEADOWSWEET. From Japan. Pink, 3- to 4-ft.-tall plumes rise above maplelike, 5- to 7-in. leaves in clumps to 2 ft. across. 'Alba' (*F. p. albiflora*) has white plumes to 2 ft. tall. 'Elegans' is compact at 1½–2 ft. tall; its white plumes have red stamens.

F. rubra. QUEEN OF THE PRAIRIE. Native to eastern U.S. Given plenty of moisture and rich soil, can reach 8 ft. high in bloom and about half as wide. Bears pink plumes. 'Venusta' has purplish pink flowers and is a little shorter, to 4–6 ft. high.

F. ulmaria. MEADOWSWEET, QUEEN OF THE MEADOW. From Europe, western Asia. To 4–6 ft. high and 2 ft. wide, with 10-in., creamy white plumes. 'Flore Pleno', just 3 ft. tall, has dense plumes of double white flowers; 'Variegata' is similar, but with gold-speckled leaves. 'Aurea' is grown not for flowers but for bright golden leaves; protect from sun.

F. vulgaris (*F. hexapetala*). DROPWORT. Native to Europe and northern and central Asia. White plumes on 3-ft. stems rise above 10-in., fernlike leaves with

1-in. leaflets; mounds reach 1½ ft. wide. Double-flowered 'Multiplex' ('Flore Pleno') has heavier-looking plumes. Needs less water than the other species; also prefers full sun in the Upper and Middle South. Thrives in alkaline soils.

FIRMIANA SIMPLEX

CHINESE PARASOL TREE
Malvaceae
Deciduous tree

🌱 **MS, LS, CS, TS; USDA 7-11**

☀ ◐ **FULL SUN OR PARTIAL SHADE**

💧 **REGULAR WATER**

Firmiana simplex

This fast-growing native of China and Japan reaches 35–40 ft. tall and half as wide, with unique light gray-green bark. Trunk often is unbranched for 4–5 ft. before dividing into three or more slender, upright, slightly spreading stems that carry lobed, tropical-looking, 1-ft. leaves. Each stem looks as if it could be cut off and carried away as a parasol. Large, loose, upright clusters of greenish white flowers appear at branch ends in early summer. Interesting fruit resembles two opened green pea pods with seeds on margins. Tree goes leafless for a long period in winter—an unusual trait for a tropical-looking tree.

Tolerates all soil types. Does well in courtyards protected from wind. Useful near swimming pools. Large trees are hard to transplant because of deep taproot. Prolific self-seeder; can be a pest.

FITTONIA VERSCHAFFELTII

NERVE PLANT
Acanthaceae
Perennial

🌱 **TS; USDA 10-11; OR HOUSEPLANT**

● **SHADE; BRIGHT INDIRECT LIGHT**

💧 **REGULAR WATER**

Fittonia verschaffeltii

Native to Peru, this evergreen plant gets its common name from the network of rosy red veins that decorate its dark green, 4-in.-long, oval or elliptical leaves. It grows about 4 in. tall and produces long, cascading stems that can spread widely. Bracts containing small flowers appear sporadically, but they detract from the plant's appearance and should be pinched off. Several forms are available. *F. v. argyroneura* has silvery white veins on leaves that are somewhat narrower and paler green than those of the species. *F. v. pearcei* has bright pink veins.

CARE
Nerve plant does well in hanging baskets, in terrariums, or as a tabletop houseplant. Indoors, place it near a window where it receives bright light but no direct sun. Keep the soil evenly moist; the plant wilts dramatically if it dries out, and though it recovers quickly if watered promptly, the foliage will be left with unattractive brown spots. Feed every other week in spring and summer and once a month in fall and winter with a general-purpose liquid houseplant fertilizer diluted to half strength. Frequent misting is beneficial. Stem cuttings taken in summer root easily. Watch out for mealybugs; wipe them

off with a cotton swab dipped in alcohol. Outdoors, plant in rich, well-drained soil and keep moist. Do not expose plants to temperatures lower than 55°F.

FOENICULUM VULGARE

COMMON FENNEL
Apiaceae
Perennial, sometimes treated as annual

🌱 **ZONES VARY BY SPECIES**

☀ **FULL SUN**

💧 **MODERATE WATER**

Foeniculum vulgare

Two forms of this Mediterranean native are commonly grown. One is a perennial, popular for its licorice-flavored seeds and young leaves; the other is grown as an annual for its edible leaf bases.

The plain species is a perennial (Zones US, MS, LS, CS; USDA 6-9) reaching 3–5 ft. tall, about 1½ ft. wide, with finely cut yellow-green leaves and flat clusters of yellow flowers. Looks much like dill (*Anethum graveolens*) but is coarser in texture. Sow in light, well-drained soil; thin seedlings to 1 ft. apart. Use seeds of either type to flavor baked goods; use leaves as a garnish for salads, fish. New stems grow in spring from the perennial root. Bronze fennel ('Purpurascens', 'Smokey') grows to 6 ft. tall and has bronzy purple foliage; it is handsome enough to be grown as an ornamental. Fennel self-sows abundantly, unless you remove the flower heads.

F. v. azoricum, called Florence fennel or finocchio, is grown as a summer annual in Zones US, MS, LS, CS, TS; USDA 6-11. Lower growing than the species (to 2 ft.),

with larger, thicker leafstalk bases that are used as a vegetable to be eaten cooked or raw. Remove flower buds before they open to encourage larger bulbs. 'Orion' forms especially thick, flavorful bulbs.

Don't reach for the bug killer if you see large, black-and-green caterpillars munching on your fennel plants. These are the larvae of beautiful swallowtail butterflies—so let them have a plant or two. Fennel blossoms' pollen and nectar also feed many beneficial insects, such as lacewings, ladybugs, hover flies, and soldier beetles.

FORSYTHIA

Oleaceae
Deciduous shrubs

🌱 **US, MS, LS; USDA 6-8, EXCEPT AS NOTED**

☀ **FULL SUN, EXCEPT AS NOTED**

💧💧 **MODERATE TO REGULAR WATER**

Forsythia

Though it's originally from China and Korea, this harbinger of spring has adorned Southern gardens for so long that folks assume it's native. At garden centers, it's often the top-selling flowering deciduous shrub because it's inexpensive, easy to grow, and dependably colorful. From late winter to early spring, countless yellow, ¾- to 1½-in. flowers smother the arching, leafless branches. During the rest of the growing season, the medium green foliage blends well with that of other shrubs. Fall color is inconsistent, but leaves may turn purplish or burgundy.

Forsythia can be used as a clipped hedge, an informal

F

ABOVE: Forsythia x intermedia

ABOVE: Fothergilla gardenii

screen, a bank cover, or part of a shrub border. It thrives in most well-drained soils. Somewhat resistant to damage by deer. Rejuvenate after bloom by cutting a third of the oldest canes to the ground in late spring; also remove dead wood and old, woody branches. Prune to preserve graceful, fountain-like form; do not shear into balls or boxes. Cut branches are easy to root—just stick them into moist soil.

F. 'Arnold Dwarf'. Grows 1½–3 ft. high, to 6 ft. wide. Flowers are sparse and not especially attractive, but plant is a useful, fast-growing ground cover.

F. x intermedia. BORDER FORSYTHIA. The most widely grown forsythias are in this hybrid group. Most grow 7–10 ft. tall and have arching branches; smaller selections are also included in the following list.

'Beatrix Farrand'. Upright to 10 ft. tall, 7 ft. wide. Branches thickly set with 2- to 2½-in.-wide flowers in deep yellow marked with orange.

'Fiesta'. Grows 3–4 ft. tall and a little wider. Deep yellow flowers are followed by green-and-yellow variegated leaves that hold their color all summer long.

'Golden Times'. To 6–8 ft. tall and wide. Variegated selection with yellowish green leaves edged in gold; extremely attractive, especially when grown in light shade. Remove any branches that revert to green. Soft yellow flowers.

'Gold Tide' ('Courtasol'). Compact growth to 20 in. tall by 4 ft. wide; profuse bright yellow flowers.

'Goldzauber' ('Gold Charm'). Erect to 6–8 ft. high and not quite as wide, with large flowers in deep yellow.

'Karl Sax'. Resembles 'Beatrix Farrand' but is lower growing, neater, more graceful.

'Lynwood Variety' ('Lynwood Gold'). Stiffly upright to 7 ft., with 4- to 6-ft. spread. Profuse tawny yellow blooms survive spring storms.

'Magical Gold'. Upright grower to 5 ft. high, 4 ft. wide, with large golden-yellow blooms.

'Spectabilis'. Dense, upright, vigorous shrub to 9 ft. tall and 6 ft. wide. Deep yellow blossoms.

'Spring Glory'. To about 6 ft. tall and wide, with a profuse show of pale yellow flowers.

F. ovata. KOREAN FORSYTHIA. Zones US, MS; USDA 6-7. To 4–6 ft., with wider spread. Heavy crop of bright yellow blossoms appears early in the season. Flower buds are hardy to -20°F. 'Tetragold' is lower growing (3–5 ft. high and wide) and has deep yellow blooms.

F. suspensa. WEEPING FORSYTHIA. Dense, upright growth habit to 8–10 ft. tall, 6–8 ft. wide. Drooping, vinelike branches root where they touch damp soil. Golden yellow flowers. Useful large-scale bank cover. Can be trained as vine; if you support main branches, branchlets will cascade. *F. s. fortunei* is somewhat more upright, more available in garden centers.

F. viridissima. GREENSTEM FORSYTHIA. Stiff-looking shrub to 6–10 ft. high and wide with deep green foliage, olive-green stems, greenish yellow flowers. 'Bronxensis' is a slow-growing dwarf to 1–1½ ft. tall and 2–4 ft. wide; good for shrub borders or ground cover. *F. v. koreana* (*F. koreana*), to 8 ft., has larger, brighter yellow flowers and attractive purplish fall foliage. Its selection 'Kumsom' has striking silver-veined leaves and purple branches; grows just 6 ft. tall and 5 ft. wide.

FOTHERGILLA

Hamamelidaceae
Deciduous shrubs

US, MS, LS; USDA 6-8

PARTIAL SHADE IN LOWER SOUTH

REGULAR WATER

Fothergilla gardenii

Native to southeastern U.S. Grown mainly for fall foliage color, but spring bloom is pretty: Small, honey-scented white flowers in 1- to 2-in., brushlike clusters on zigzagging stems. Blossoms may appear before or with leaves. Perform best in moist, well-drained, acid soil.

F. gardenii. DWARF FOTHERGILLA. Typically 2–3 ft. high (though it can grow considerably taller) and as wide or wider, with 1- to 2½-in.-long, dark green leaves. Foliage turns intense yellow to orange to scarlet in autumn, often with all three colors in the same leaf. 'Blue Mist' has blue-green foliage that turns yellow in fall. 'Suzanne' is choice, with reliably compact growth and showy orange-red fall color.

F. major. LARGE FOTHER-GILLA. Erect shrub to 9 ft. tall and 6 ft. wide, with roundish, 2- to 4-in.-long leaves turning yellow to orange to purplish red in autumn. 'Mount Airy' (F. x intermedia) is smaller (3–5 ft. high and wide), with abundant bloom, good dark green leaf color, and consistently superb fall color in yellow, orange, and scarlet. 'Blue Shadow' (F. x intermedia) grows 3-4 ft. tall and wide with powder-blue foliage.

FRAGARIA HYBRIDS

ORNAMENTAL STRAWBERRY
Rosaceae
Perennials

✎ **US, MS, LS, CS; USDA 6-9**

☀ ◑ **AFTERNOON SHADE IN COASTAL SOUTH**

💧 **REGULAR WATER**

Fragaria 'Pink Panda'

The genus *Fragaria* includes all types of strawberry plants; for those types grown strictly for their edible fruit, see Strawberry. The hybrids described here are crosses of wild strawberry with *Potentilla*. They spread widely by trailing runners to form a mat of rich green, glossy leaves. Leaves are made up of three oval,

tooth-edged leaflets 1–1½ in. long; colorful, inch-wide flowers contrast beautifully with the foliage. Fruits are few and far between—edible but not tasty. Pretty in borders, rock gardens, as edging; excellent in planters, window boxes, and hanging baskets. Grow in sandy or other well-drained soil. 'Lipstick' reaches 6–8 in. high, has rosy red flowers. 'Pink Panda' grows 4–6 in. tall and bears showy bright pink flowers from spring to fall.

FRANKLINIA ALATAMAHA

FRANKLIN TREE
Theaceae
Deciduous tree

✎ **US, MS, LS; USDA 6-8**

☀ ◑ **FULL SUN OR PART SHADE**

💧 **REGULAR WATER**

Franklinia alatamaha

This legendary tree, native to the banks of Georgia's Alatamaha River, mysteriously disappeared from the wild shortly after it was discovered there in 1770 by famed botanist John Bartram. All plants in commerce today can be traced to the ones he collected. Open, airy form; may reach 30 ft. but more typically grows 10–20 ft. high. Tree tends to be fairly slender when grown with a single trunk; when grown as a multitrunked plant, it is broad spreading. Attractive dark gray bark has faint white vertical striping. Shiny, dark green leaves are spoon-shaped to oblong and pointed, 4–6 in. long; they turn orange and red in fall and hang on for a long time before dropping. Fragrant, white, 3-in.-wide, five-petaled flowers

centered with clusters of yellow stamens open from round white buds from July to early October, sometimes coinciding with fall foliage color in the Upper South. Blossoms somewhat resemble single camellias—not surprising, since *Franklinia* and *Camellia* belong to the same family. Flowers are followed by small, woody capsules that are split into ten segments, each containing five seeds. Highly decorative lawn or accent tree. Especially nice for contrast in azalea or rhododendron plantings.

CARE

Provide moist, rich, light, acid soil. Good drainage is critical. Not the easiest plant to grow. Susceptible to phytophthora root rot, a fatal soil-borne disease, in heavy, wet soils during hot weather. Grows well in light shade but has best bloom and fall color in full sun. Easy to grow from seed, blooming in 6 to 7 years.

FRAXINUS

ASH
Oleaceae
Deciduous and evergreen trees

✎ **ZONES VARY BY SPECIES**

☀ **FULL SUN**

◌◔💧 **WATER NEEDS VARY BY SPECIES**

Fraxinus americana
'Autumn Purple'

Fairly fast-growing trees, most of which tolerate hot summers, cold winters, and many kinds of soil, including alkaline sorts. Chiefly used as street, shade, and lawn trees. In most cases, leaves are divided into leaflets. Male and female flowers (generally

inconspicuous, in clusters) grow on separate trees in some species, on the same tree in others. In the latter case, flowers are often followed by clusters of single-seeded, winged fruit, often in such abundance that they can be a litter problem. When flowers are on separate trees, you'll get fruit on a female tree only if a male tree grows nearby.

Ashes are prone to borers, and in 2002, a particularly destructive type was found to have made its way to the U.S. from Asia. The emerald ash borer (EAB) is a ½-in.-long, dark metallic green beetle in the adult stage; the larvae, which can reach 1¼ in. long, feast beneath the tree's bark and cut off the supply of water and nutrients to the branches above. Most of an infected tree's canopy will die within 2 years. Adults can fly up to ½ mile from tree to tree, and the pests are also believed to be spread by ash firewood being shipped from one area to another. EAB has been found in Georgia, Kentucky, Maryland, Missouri, North Carolina, Tennessee, Virginia, and West Virginia. There is no effective treatment so far. Contact your local Cooperative Exension Office for more information.

F. americana. WHITE ASH. Deciduous. Zones US, MS, LS, CS; USDA 6-9. From eastern U.S. Reaches 80 ft. or more, with straight trunk and oval-shaped crown to 50 ft. wide. Leaves 8–15 in. long, with five to nine oval, 2- to 6-in.-long leaflets; dark green above, paler beneath. Foliage turns purplish in fall. Male and female flowers on separate trees, but plants sold are generally seedlings, so you don't know what you're getting. If you end up with both male and female trees, you will get a heavy crop of seed; both litter and seedlings can be problems. Give this tree regular water.

Seedless selections include 'Autumn Applause' and 'Autumn Purple', both with exceptionally good, long-lasting purple fall color; 'Champaign County', a dense grower with pale yellow fall color; 'Greenspire', narrow, upright habit, deep orange fall color; 'Rosehill', with bronzy red fall color; 'Royal Purple', upright grower with purple autumn leaves; and 'Skyline', an upright oval with brown and purple fall color.

F. berlandierana. MEXICAN ASH. Deciduous. Zones MS, LS, CS, TS; USDA 7-11. From southern Texas and northeastern Mexico; often found along stream banks. Grows very fast when young, eventually reaching 30–40 ft. tall, with a symmetrical, dense crown (to about 25 ft. across) that provides good shade. Glossy green leaves are made up of three to five leaflets to 4 in. long. Moderate water.

F. cuspidata. FRAGRANT ASH. Deciduous. Zones MS, LS, CS, TS; USDA 7-11. From Texas, Southwest, Mexico. Bushy shrub or small tree, 10–15 ft. tall and broad, sometimes 20½ ft. Leaves are divided into seven 2½-in.-long leaflets; turn yellow in fall. Long panicles of white, vanilla-scented flowers cover the tree in mid- or late spring, making a very showy display against a dark background. Tolerant of drought and alkaline soil. Grows fast if watered regularly.

F. greggii. LITTLELEAF ASH, GREGG ASH. Evergreen. Zones MS, LS, CS, TS; USDA 7-11. Native from Arizona to Texas. To 25 ft. tall and 20 ft. wide, with leaves divided into three to seven ¾-in., leathery, bright green leaflets. Useful desert tree. Little water.

F. ornus. FLOWERING ASH, MANNA ASH. Deciduous. Zones US, MS; USDA 6-7; best in Upper South. From southern Europe and Asia Minor. To 30–40 ft., with rounded crown 20–30 ft. wide. Luxuriant foliage mass: 8- to 10-in.-long leaves divided into 7 to 11 oval, medium green, 2-in.-long leaflets with toothed edges. Foliage turns to soft shades of lavender and yellow in fall. In spring, displays quantities of fluffy, branched, 3- to 5-in.-long clusters of showy, fragrant, white to greenish white blossoms. Moderate water.

F. pennsylvanica. GREEN ASH. Deciduous. Zones US, MS, LS, CS; USDA 6-9. Native to eastern U.S. To 50–60 ft. tall, with irregular oval crown 25–30 ft. across. Gray-brown bark; dense, twiggy structure. Bright green leaves 10–12 in. long, divided into five to nine rather narrow, 4- to 6-in.-long leaflets. Inconsistent yellow fall color. For assured fall color, plant a named selection. Male and female flowers on separate trees. Takes wet soil and severe cold, but foliage burns in hot, dry winds. Regular water.

Seedless kinds include 'Emerald', a round-headed tree with glossy, deep green leaves and yellow fall color; 'Georgia Gem', with large, bright green leaves and good heat tolerance; 'Marshall's Seedless', a male form with lustrous, deep green foliage and good yellow fall color; 'Summit', upright habit, good golden yellow fall color; and 'Urbanite', pyramidal shape and bronze fall color.

F. texensis. TEXAS ASH. Deciduous. Zones MS, LS, CS; USDA 7-9. From Oklahoma and Texas. Round-headed tree to 35–50 ft. tall and wide, fairly fast growing. Leaves have five dark green, 3-in.-long leaflets, which may turn shades of gold, orange, maroon in fall. Particularly suited to rocky limestone soils, but well adapted to regular garden watering and average soil. Usually long lived. Very drought tolerant.

F. velutina. ARIZONA ASH. Deciduous. Zones US, MS, LS, CS; USDA 6-9. Southeastern native. Takes hot, dry conditions and cold to about –10°F. To 30 ft. (possibly 50 ft.) tall. Pyramidal when young; spreading 30–40 ft. wide when mature, with a more open shape. Gray-green leaves are divided into three to five narrow to oval, 3-in.-long leaflets; turn bright yellow in fall. Male and female flowers on separate trees. Regular water.

'Rio Grande' ('Fan-Tex') is most commonly grown in Texas. Its leaflets are larger and darker green than those of the species; they resist wind burn.

FREESIA

Iridaceae
Corms

⚜ **CS, TS; USDA 9-11; OR INDOORS**

☼ ◑ **FULL SUN OR PARTIAL SHADE; BRIGHT LIGHT**

💧 **REGULAR WATER DURING GROWTH AND BLOOM**

Freesia hybrid

South African natives prized for the rich perfume of flowers. In spring, wiry, 1- to 1½-ft. stems bear spikes of tubular flowers that reach 2 in. long and flare to 2 in. wide. Each stem bends at nearly a right angle just beneath the lowest bud. Narrow, sword-shaped leaves to 1 ft. tall grow in iris-like fans. Hardy to 20°F.

The old-fashioned favorite *F. lactea* (*F. alba*) has white blooms with a powerfully sweet scent, but more commonly available today are hybrids (Dutch and Tecolote hybrids represent the majority of those sold) with single or double blossoms in yellow, orange, red, pink, lavender, purple, blue, and white. You can buy mixed-color assortments as well as named varieties in specific colors.

CARE

Plant in fall, setting corms 2 in. deep (pointed end up) and 2 in. apart in well-drained soil. Plants go dormant after bloom and need no irrigation until growth resumes in fall. In areas with high summer rainfall, it's best to dig them when foliage yellows and store the corms until it's time to replant in early fall. Freesias will self-sow if faded flowers are not removed; volunteers tend to revert to cream marked with purple and yellow. In Upper, Middle, and Lower South, plant

2 in. deep, 2 in. apart in pots and grow indoors in a sunny window. Keep room temperature as cool as possible at night. Freesias are easily grown from seed sown in July or August; they will often bloom the following spring. Flowering potted freesias grown from chilled and stored corms are available throughout the year.

FRITILLARIA

FRITILLARY
Liliaceae
Perennials from bulbs

⚜ **US, MS, LS; USDA 6-8**

☼ ◑ **FULL SUN OR LIGHT SHADE**

💧 **REGULAR WATER DURING GROWTH AND BLOOM**

Fritillaria meleagris

If you demand a quick return on your investment, these are not the bulbs for you. They usually take their time to settle in before putting on their impressive show—and they may rest for a year after blooming, too. In spring, unbranched stems ranging from 6 in. to 3 ft. high are topped by bell-shaped, nodding flowers, often odd looking and unusually colored and mottled. Use in woodland gardens, rock gardens, or borders. Deer reisistant

F. imperialis. CROWN IMPERIAL. Native to Europe. Stout stalk to 3 ft. tall, clothed with broad, glossy leaves and crowned by circle of large (2- to 3-in.-long) bells in red, orange, or yellow; a tuft of leaves tops the flowers. Bulb and plant have musky odor that some people find offensive.

F. meleagris. CHECKERED LILY, SNAKESHEAD. Native to damp meadows in Europe,

Asia; does best in moist soil and tolerates occasional flooding. One to three showy, 2-in. bells top each 1- to 1½-ft. stem; blossoms are checkered and veined with reddish brown and purple. Lance-shaped leaves are 3–6 in. long. There is a white-blossomed form.

F. michailovskyi. From Turkey. To 6 in. high. Each stem bears one to six 1- to 1½-in. bells that are purplish brown at base, bright yellow toward tip.

F. pallidiflora. From northern China, Siberia. Each 2- to 3-ft. stem carries one to six 1¼-in. bells in pale yellow tinted with green.

F. persica 'Adiyaman'. Selection of a species from western Asia. Stems 2–3 ft. tall carry up to 30 deep plum-purple, inch-long flowers on upper half. Foliage is gray-green. Plant is hardy and easy to grow, but emerging stems need protection from late frosts. 'Ivory Bells' is similar, but with greenish white blooms.

F. verticillata. Native to central Asia. Stems 1–2 ft. tall bear one to six flowers in white or yellow speckled with green or purple. Upper leaves have a tendril-like tip.

CARE

In fall, plant bulbs in porous soil with ample humus. Set smaller bulbs 3–4 in. deep and 6 in. apart; set largest ones (*F. imperialis*) 4–5 in. deep, 8–12 in. apart. All appreciate some winter chill and tend to perform poorly where summers are hot and dry. Reduce watering as foliage dies back in summer. Clumps seldom need dividing.

FUCHSIA

Onagraceae
Tender shrubs, many treated as annuals

⬤ **ZONES VARY BY SPECIES**

◑ **PARTIAL SHADE**

⬤ **REGULAR WATER**

Fuchsia magellanica molinae

Native to wet, mountainous areas mainly in the tropical Americas, these colorful shrubs have a hard time in most parts of the South. While they do fine in the Upper South and higher elevations of the Appalachian and Blue Ridge Mountains, most suffer in the hot summers elsewhere in our region.

F. x hybrida. HYBRID FUCHSIA. Zone US; USDA 6 (if overwintered indoors); or grow as annual. The vast majority of fuchsias sold in garden centers fall into this group. Hundreds of selections offer a wide array of color combinations. Sepals (top parts that flare back) are always white, pink, or red. Corolla (inside

part of flower) may be almost any color in the range of white, blue, violet, purple, pink, red, and shades approaching orange. Plant form varies widely, from erect shrubs 3–6 ft. high to trailing types grown for hanging baskets. You can also buy fuchsias trained as espaliers and standards (single-trunked tree form). Hummingbirds find the flowers irresistible.

The following hybrid fuchsias are among the most heat-tolerant. 'Gartenmeister Bonstedt' grows 2 ft. tall and wide, with reddish bronze leaves and drooping clusters of intense orange-red, long-tubed flowers. The Angel Earrings series includes upright, semitrailing, and trailing plants with showy flowers in various combinations and white; sizes vary in height from 15 to 20 in. and in width from 20 to 40 in.

Hybrid fuchsias need porous, water-retentive soil containing plenty of organic matter; those in hanging baskets require frequent watering. Give sun in the morning and shade in the afternoon; protect from any wind. To keep blooms coming, feed every other week during growing season with water-soluble 20-20-20 fertilizer. Blooming decreases during hot weather. To overwinter indoors, cut back severely; then place beside a sunny window. Watch out for whiteflies—spray the leaf undersides from time to time with insecticidal soap or horticultural oil just to make sure these pests don't take up residence.

F. magellanica. HARDY FUCHSIA. Zones MS, LS; USDA 7-8. A tender shrub that dies down to the ground each winter, then resprouts in spring. Native to Chile and Argentina. Grows 3 ft. tall and wide. Blooms profusely in summer, bearing drooping, 1½-in.-long, red-and-purple flowers. Plant in rich, well-drained soil; mulch heavily in late fall. 'Riccartonii' (F. 'Riccartonii') is an especially cold-hardy form. *F. m. gracilis* 'Aurea' has golden leaves that make a striking contrast with the flowers. *F. m. molinae* has pale lavender-pink flowers.

GAILLARDIA

BLANKET FLOWER
Asteraceae
Perennials, one grown as annual

⬤ **US, MS, LS, CS, TS; USDA 6-11**

☀ **FULL SUN**

◐⬤ **LITTLE TO MODERATE WATER**

Gaillardia x *grandiflora*

Native to the South and Midwest, these easygoing summer bloomers feature daisylike flowers in warm colors—yellow, orange, and red. They thrive on neglect, so put away the watering can and fertilizer. They love heat, have no serious pests, and are not fussy about soil (though they must have good drainage). Easy to grow from seed; excellent cut flowers; deer resistant. Well-adapted to the beach.

G. aristata. BLANKET FLOWER. Perennial. This parent of the hybrid G. x *grandiflora* has been replaced to a large degree by its offspring, but the wild form is still much used in prairie restoration and wildflower mixes. Grows 2–2½ ft. tall and 2 ft. across, with flower heads up to 4 in. wide. Colors range from yellow to red; most familiar form is red with a jagged yellow border on the ray flowers.

G. x grandiflora. Perennial. Offspring of G. *pulchella* and G. *aristata*. Grows to 2–4 ft. high, 1½ ft. wide. Somewhat rough, gray-green foliage; single or

ABOVE: Fuchsia 'Gartenmeister Bonstedt'

double flowers to 3–4 in. across. Much variation in flower color; range includes various warm shades of red and yellow with orange or maroon bands. Exceptionally long bloom period for a perennial—from early summer until frost. Plants flower first year from seed. Can be short lived in hottest, most humid areas.

Many strains and selections are available, including dwarf kinds and types with extra-large blossoms. 'Baby Cole' grows just 6–8 in. tall, with yellow-tipped red flowers. Foot-tall choices include 'Arizona Apricot' (golden yellow flowers with soft apricot center), 'Arizona Red Shades' (deep red petals with yellow tips), 'Goblin' (red-orange flowers with bright yellow tips), and 'Goblin Yellow' (solid yellow). 'Mesa Yellow' is a uniform grower to 16–18 in. tall, with a profusion of solid yellow flowers. Commotion series offer brightly colored flowers with striking, fluted petals. Grow 18–24 in. tall. Among 2½-ft.-tall choices are deep red 'Burgundy'; pure orange 'Tokajer'; 'Painter's Palette', a seed strain with blooms in burgundy, clear yellow, rosy red with golden tips, and other red-and-gold combinations; and 'Torchlight', with yellow flowers bordered in red. 'Yellow Queen' has clear yellow blossoms with a golden eye and may reach 3 ft. tall.

G. pulchella. INDIAN BLANKET. Short-lived perennial usually treated as an annual. To 1½–2 ft. high, 1 ft. wide, with soft, hairy leaves and long, whiplike stems carrying 2-in. flowers in red, yellow, gold. Easy to grow; sow seeds in warm soil after danger of frost is past. 'Red Plume' and 'Yellow Plume' are double flowered, with 2-in. blossoms on uniform 12- to 14-in. plants. 'Dazzler Mix' reaches 20 in. high, with double flowers in cream, pink, rose, and orange. Plants in the Galya series are vigorous and free-blooming; available in single, double, and trumpet-petaled blooms in the full color range.

GALANTHUS

SNOWDROP
Amaryllidaceae
Perennials from bulbs

🌿 **US, MS, LS; USDA 6-8**

☼ ◐ **FULL SUN DURING BLOOM, LIGHT SHADE AFTER**

💧 **REGULAR WATER**

☠ **BULBS ARE POISONOUS IF INGESTED**

Galium nivalis

Natives of Europe and Asia Minor; perform best in cold-winter climates. Closely related to and often confused with *Leucojum* (snowflake), these harbingers of spring are among the first bulbs to bloom as winter ends. Nodding, bell-shaped white flowers are borne one per stalk; inner flower segments are infused or marked with green, while larger outer segments are pure white. Plants have two or three strap-shaped basal leaves. Effective in rock gardens or under flowering shrubs, naturalized in woodland settings, or grown in pots. Not eaten by deer or rodents.

Plant in autumn, setting bulbs 3–4 in. deep and 3 in. apart in moist soil with ample humus. Bulbs prefer year-round moisture. Do not divide often; when division is necessary, do the job when the foliage begins to yellow, right after bloom.

G. 'Atkinsii'. Stems to 8 in. high bear slender, 1½-in.-long blooms. Each inner flower segment has a heart-shaped green mark at the tip. Narrow leaves to 4 in. long.

G. elwesii. GIANT SNOWDROP. Foot-high stems carry 1½-in. flowers; inner segments are heavily infused with green. Blooms a little earlier in spring

and is better adapted to mild-winter climates than *G. nivalis*.

G. 'Hippolyta'. Stems to 8 in. tall carry double blooms in a bowl shape; inner petals are green with white edges.

G. nivalis. COMMON SNOWDROP. More delicate version of *G. elwesii*. Stems 6–9 in. high bear inch-long flowers, their inner segments marked at tips with a green crescent. 'Flore Pleno' has double blooms. 'Magnet' has extra-long arching flower stalks. 'White Dream' has leaves striped in white.

G. 'S. Arnott' ('Sam Arnott'). To 8 in. high. Rounded blossoms to 1½ in. long have an inverted V-shaped green mark at the tip of each inner flower segment. Leaves 3–6 in. long.

GALAX URCEOLATA

WANDFLOWER
Diapensiaceae
Perennial

🌿 **US, MS, LS; USDA 6-8**

◐ ● **PARTIAL TO FULL SHADE**

💧 **REGULAR WATER**

Galax urceolata

Native to mountain woodlands from Virginia to Georgia. Often used as a ground cover, although it spreads slowly. The plant's real distinction comes from its evergreen foliage, which is much used in indoor arrangements. The shiny, heart-shaped leaves grow in basal tufts that reach 6–9 in. high; they turn bronzy in fall unless the plant is grown in deep shade. In early summer, flower stems rise to 2½ ft., bearing foxtails of small white flowers at their tips.

Grow in acid soil with plenty of organic material—preferably mulch of leaf mold. Locate under plants that appreciate the same conditions: dogwood (*Cornus*), rhododendron, azalea, *Pieris*. Space 1 ft. apart.

GALIUM ODORATUM

SWEET WOODRUFF
Rubiaceae
Perennial

🌿 **US, MS, LS; USDA 6-8**

◐ ● **PARTIAL TO FULL SHADE**

💧💧 **REGULAR TO AMPLE WATER**

Galium odoratum

Attractive, low-spreading perennial that brings to mind deep-shaded woods. Slender, square stems 6–12 in. high are encircled every inch or so by whorls of six to eight aromatic, bristle-tipped leaves. Clusters of tiny white flowers show above foliage in late spring and summer. Leaves and stems give off a fragrant, haylike odor when dried; they are used to make May wine.

In the shade garden, sweet woodruff is best used as ground cover or edging. Will spread rapidly in rich soil with abundant moisture; can become a pest if allowed to grow unchecked. Self-sows freely. Increase by division in fall or spring. Give full shade in Lower South. Rarely browsed by deer.

GALPHIMIA GLAUCA

SHOWER-OF-GOLD, THRYALLIS
Malpighiaceae
Evergreen shrub

⬗ **CS, TS; USDA 9-11; OR GROW IN POTS**

☀ **FULL SUN**

💧 **MODERATE WATER**

Galphimia glauca

Native to Mexico and Guatemala. Tropical evergreen shrub, 4–6 ft. tall and wide; grows outdoors only in the Coastal and Tropical South. Handsome, 2-in., oblong, gray-green leaves; showy, ¾-in., bright yellow flowers in branched clusters, summer and fall. Fertilize from spring through fall. Prune out crowded branches to keep shape open. Brittle stems break easily, so don't plant where people will brush against the foliage. In cooler climates, grow in a pot that you can bring indoors for winter. Deer leave it alone. Formerly known as *Thryallis glauca*.

GALTONIA CANDICANS

SUMMER HYACINTH
Asparagaceae
Perennial from bulb

⬗ **MS, LS, CS, TS; USDA 7-11**

☀☽ **LIGHT SHADE IN TROPICAL SOUTH**

💧 **REGULAR WATER DURING GROWTH AND BLOOM**

Galtonia candicans

If you're looking for a way to add punch to your summer border, this bold, little-known bulb from South Africa may be the answer. Stout, 4-ft. spikes of nodding, sweet-scented white flowers rise above clumps of strap-shaped, 2- to 3-ft.-long leaves. The summer show is so grand that a half-dozen bulbs can dominate a border. Hardy to about 10°F. Where winters are colder, dig bulbs in fall and store over winter as you would gladiolus—though summer hyacinth does bloom best when left undisturbed. Plant bulbs 6 in. deep and 1 ft. apart in moist, well-drained soil that contains lots of organic matter.

GARDENIA

Rubiaceae
Evergreen shrubs

⬗ **ZONES VARY BY SPECIES**

☀☽ **FULL SUN OR PARTIAL SHADE**

💧 **REGULAR WATER**

Gardenia jasminoides 'Veitchii'

No plant expresses the grace of the South better than gardenia. Intensely fragrant white blossoms contrast beautifully with shiny, leathery, dark green leaves. Double forms are a classic choice for corsages.

Gardenias are lovely in flower borders and also do well in large pots on decks and patios; gardeners in cold-winter areas can grow them in cool greenhouses.

G. jasminoides. COMMON GARDENIA, CAPE JASMINE. Zones LS, CS, TS; USDA 8-11, except as noted. Native to China, Taiwan, Japan. Glossy, bright green leaves and usually double white flowers to 3 in. across. Most are hardy to about 10°F; they will survive 0°F but are likely to die back to roots.

The many selections are useful in containers or raised beds, as hedges, espaliers, low screens, or single plants.

'Aimee' ('First Love'). Somewhat larger shrub than 'August Beauty', with larger double flowers. Spring bloom.

'August Beauty'. Grows 4–6 ft. high and 3–4 ft. wide. Blooms heavily midspring into fall. Large double flowers.

'Chuck Hayes'. Extra-hardy type, possibly as hardy as 'Kleim's Hardy'. To 4 ft. high and wide. Double flowers in summer, heavy rebloom in fall.

'Crown Jewel'. Selected from a cross between 'Kleim's Hardy'

and 'Chuck Hayes'. Grows 2–2½ ft. tall and 4 ft. wide, with fully double blooms over a long period. One of the hardiest selections listed here, surviving -10°F.

'Golden Magic'. Reaches 3 ft. tall, 2 ft. wide in 2 to 3 years, eventually larger. Extra-full flowers open white, gradually age to deep golden yellow. Blooms from spring through summer, peaking in midspring.

'Grif's Select'. Compact, 3–4 ft. tall and wide; profuse single flowers in late spring and early summer, red seed capsules in fall. Hardy to about 5°F.

'Jubilation'. Compact grower to 3–4 ft. tall and wide. Very fragrant blooms are produced heavily in spring and again in fall.

'Kimura Shikazaki' ('Four Seasons'). Compact plant 2–3 ft. tall. Flowers similar to those of 'Veitchii', but slightly less fragrant. Extremely long bloom season—spring to fall.

'Kleim's Hardy'. For cold-winter areas; hardy to 0°F. To 2–3 ft. high and wide. Single flowers in summer. Grow in a wind-protected site.

'Miami Supreme'. Grows to 10 ft. tall and wide, with large double flowers (4–6 in. wide) in spring, periodic flowering through summer. Fast grower. Most popular selection for South Florida.

'Mystery'. Best-known selection. Bears 4- to 5-in. double flowers from mid- to late spring or longer. Tends to be rangy and needs pruning to keep it neat. Can reach 6–8 ft. high and wide.

'Pinwheel'. An interesting variation on the gardenia theme. Each petal is rolled at the base and flares at the tip, giving the flowers the appearance of a pinwheel. Intensely fragrant. Grows 4 ft. tall and wide, with good repeat bloom from late spring well into fall. Reportedly hardy to -10°F.

'Radicans' ('Prostrata'). Grows 6–12 in. tall and spreads to 2–3 ft., with small leaves; inch-wide double flowers bloom in summer. Good for small-scale ground cover or pots. Not as cold hardy as the species; not well suited to Middle South. 'Radicans Variegata' ('Prostrata Variegata') has gray-green leaves with white markings.

'Shooting Star'. Upright grower to 6–8 ft. tall and wide, with large leaves and single flowers in late spring and early summer. Hardy to 0°F.

G

'Veitchii'. Compact, reliable grower to 3½–4½ ft. tall and 6 ft. wide. Blooms prolifically from midspring into fall (and sometimes even during warm winters), bearing fully double 1- to 1½-in. flowers.

'White Gem'. At just 1–2 ft. tall and wide, this selection is useful for edgings, containers, or raised beds, where the fragrance of its single, creamy white summer flowers can be appreciated.

G. thunbergia. STARRY GARDENIA. Zones TS; USDA 10-11. Native to South Africa, this winter bloomer is much less common than G. jasminoides, because it is less cold hardy and not as showy. Sometimes grown as an ornamental in south Florida. Primary use is as a rootstock to impart nematode resistance and increased vigor to G. jasminoides. Reaches 15 ft. tall and wide. Dark green leaves to 6 in. long; single, 3- to 4-in., white- to cream-colored flowers with a long tube and typically eight overlapping, petal-like lobes.

CARE

Provide fast-draining but moisture-retentive, acidic soil containing lots of organic matter. Plant gardenias high (like azaleas and rhododendrons) and don't let them be crowded by other plants or competing roots. To suppress weeds, mulch plants instead of cultivating around them. Feed every 3 to 4 weeks during the growing season with acid fertilizer, fish emulsion, or blood meal. Prune to remove straggly branches and faded flowers. Control whiteflies, aphids, and other sucking insects with light horticultural oil. Magnesium deficiency can result in yellow leaves with green veins; treat by dissolving one tablespoon of Epsom salt in a gallon of water and soaking the root zone (best done in early spring). Though you can grow gardenia as a houseplant, doing so can be pure torture: Mealybugs, mites, and whiteflies love it.

GARLIC

Liliaceae
Perennial from bulb

🌿 **US, MS, LS, CS, TS; USDA 6-11**

☀️ **FULL SUN**

💧 **REGULAR WATER**

Garlic

Classified botanically as *Allium sativum*; not known in the wild. For ornamental relatives, see *Allium*. Seed stores and some mail-order seed houses sell disease-free mother bulbs ("sets") for planting—and some gardeners have had good luck planting bulbs from grocery stores. In mild-winter areas, plant in fall for early summer harvest; where winters are cold, plant in early spring. Break up bulbs into cloves and select largest ones. Plant in rich, well-drained soil, setting cloves pointed end up, 1 in. deep, 3–6 in. apart, in rows 15 in. apart. Harvest when leafy tops fall over; lift out with garden fork rather than pulling. Air-dry bulbs, cut off most of tops and roots, and store in cool, well-ventilated place out of sunlight. Giant or elephant garlic (*A. scorodoprasum*) has unusually large (fist-size) bulbs and mild flavor. Grow as for regular garlic, but space 8–12 in. apart. Harvest when first leaves turn yellow.

GAULTHERIA PROCUMBENS

WINTERGREEN, CHECKERBERRY
Ericaceae
Evergreen ground cover

🌿 **US, MS; USDA 6-7**

◐ **LIGHT SHADE**

💧 **REGULAR WATER**

Gaultheria procumbens

Native to eastern North America, this handsome, low-growing shrub is the source of oil of wintergreen. Creeping stems send up erect stems to 6 in. high, with oval, 2-in.-long, glossy dark green leaves clustered near their tips. Foliage emits a strong wintergreen odor when bruised, turns reddish in winter. Small, pinkish white summer flowers are followed by scarlet berries. Ideal as ground cover for a partly shaded rock garden or a woodland garden. Space plants 1 ft. apart in acid, well-drained soil containing plenty of organic matter; wintergreen will not survive in clay soil. It performs best in the Upper South and higher elevations of the Appalachian and Blue Ridge Mountains. 'Very Berry' is more compact than the species and bears a very heavy crop of berries.

GAURA LINDHEIMERI

Onagraceae
Perennial

🌿 **US, MS, LS, CS; USDA 6-9**

☀️ **FULL SUN**

💧 **MODERATE WATER**

Gaura lindheimeri 'Siskiyou Pink'

Native to Texas and Louisiana. Airy plant growing to 2¼–4 ft. high, 2–3 ft. wide. Stalkless leaves to 1½–3½ in. long grow directly on stems. Long bloom period (often from late spring into fall). Pink buds closely set on branching spikes open just a few at a time; blossoms are about 1 in. long, white aging to rose. Used widely in most of the South. Performs best in the Southwest, where it is a profusely blooming, long-lived perennial. Taproot makes it very drought tolerant.

Selected forms include the following.

'Corrie's Gold'. To 2½–3 ft. tall and wide. Leaves edged with gold.

'Crimson Butterflies'. Grows only 1½ ft. high and a little wider, with smaller, more closely spaced leaves and dark pink blossoms. Good in containers.

'Dauphin'. Rigidly upright to 4–6 ft. tall, not quite as wide. Dark pink buds open to pink flowers that quickly turn white.

'Passionate Blush'. Upright and compact, to 1–2 ft. high and wide, with red stems and pink flowers.

'Passionate Rainbow'. Compact grower to 2–2½ ft. high, half as wide. Leaves are thinly edged in white; flowers are rose-pink.

'Pink Cloud'. Upright plant to 2½ ft. high and 2 ft. wide. Profuse bright pink blooms.

'Pink Fountain'. To 2–3 ft. high, with an especially dense mass of soft pink flowers.

'Rosyjane'. Low, well-branched plant to 2 ft. high and wide. White flowers are edged with bright pink.

'Siskiyou Pink'. Reaches 2–2½ ft. tall and a little wider. Deep maroon buds open to rose-pink flowers. Leaves are mottled with rich maroon.

'Sparkle White'. Compact grower to 1–2 ft. high and 1–1½ ft. wide. Soft pink buds open to pure white flowers. Uniform growth and heavy bloom.

'Whirling Butterflies'. To 3 ft. tall and wide. White flowers are slightly larger than those of the species.

CARE

Plant prefers lean, unfertilized soil; planting in rich soil results in legginess and sparse bloom. Faded flowers drop cleanly from stems, but seed-bearing spikes should be cut to improve appearance, prevent overly enthusiastic self-sowing, and prolong bloom. Needs good drainage. Clumps never need dividing; for additional plants, allow some of the volunteer seedlings to grow.

GAZANIA
GAZANIA DAISY
Asteraceae
Perennials, some grown as annuals

US, MS, LS, CS, TS; USDA 6-11

EXPOSURE NEEDS VARY BY SPECIES

MODERATE TO REGULAR WATER

Gazania 'Tiger Eye'

Native to South Africa. The daisy flowers put on a dazzling display of color during peak bloom in late spring and early summer and they continue to bloom intermittently throughout the year. Gazanias grow well in almost any well-drained soil. Feed once in spring with slow-acting fertilizer. Divide plants every 3 to 4 years.

G. hybrids. The two basic types are clumping and trailing; both take full sun. Clumping gazanias (complex hybrids involving a number of species) form a mound of evergreen leaves—dark green above, gray and woolly beneath, often lobed. Flowers are 3–4 in. wide, on 6- to 10-in.-long stems; they open on sunny days, close at night and in cloudy weather. Available in single colors or in a mixture (as plants or seeds) in different hues. Available colors include yellow, orange, white, or rosy pink, with reddish purple petal undersides and (often) dark blossom centers.

Seed grown kinds include 'Carnival', with silver leaves and flowers in many colors; 'Chansonette', an early bloomer with round, medium-size blossoms on compact plants; and 'Daybreak', with low-growing, spreading plants bearing flowers in orange, bronze, yellow, yellow striped with red, and mixed colors. 'Harlequin' has eyed and banded blooms in many colors. 'Mini-Star' is compact and floriferous. 'New Day' has large blooms in the full color range; shorter flower stems give plants a compact, beefy look. 'Sunbather' is compact and heat tolerant, with large (nearly 6-in.-wide) flowers in golden orange, yellow, bronzy orange, and creamy white; blooms are semidouble, so they don't close completely, regardless of light levels. 'Sundance' produces especially large (to 5-in.-wide) striped and banded flowers; 'Sunshine Giants' produce big, multicolored flowers and gray leaves.

Selections of special merit are 'Aztec' (cream with maroon stripes), 'Aztec Queen' (multicolored), 'Burgundy', 'Christopher Lloyd' (bright pink with a yellow eye encircled by green), 'Copper King', and 'Fiesta Red'. All are best used in small-scale plantings, though the last is sturdy enough for large areas. 'Moonglow' is a double-flowered bright yellow of unusual vigor; its blossoms, unlike most, stay open even on overcast, dull days. 'Tiger Eye' has golden-orange blooms and green leaves edged with cream.

Trailing gazanias (derived from *G. rigens leucolaena*) grow about as tall as clumping ones but spread rapidly by long, trailing stems. Foliage is a handsome silvery gray; flowers are yellow, white, orange, or bronze. Larger-flowered kinds are 'Sunburst' (orange with black eye) and 'Sunglow' (yellow). 'Sunrise Yellow', also in larger-flowered group, has black-eyed yellow blooms; leaves are green. Hybrid trailing plants are superior to older kinds in length of bloom and resistance to dieback. Use trailing gazanias on banks; or grow them at the top of a wall and allow them to trail over. Attractive in hanging baskets.

GELSEMIUM
JESSAMINE
Gelsemiaceae
EVERGREEN VINES

MS, LS, CS; USDA 7-9

FULL SUN OR PARTIAL SHADE

WATER NEEDS VARY BY SPECIES

ALL PARTS ARE POISONOUS IF INGESTED

Gelsemium sempervirens

These fast-growing, twining vines are beloved for their showy yellow flowers. They'll quickly cover a lamppost, trellis, or arbor, but their thin, twining stems won't damage the support. May be semievergreen in the Middle South. Deer usually leave them alone.

G. rankinii. SWAMP JESSAMINE. Native to swamps from North Carolina to Florida and Louisiana. To 20 ft. Foliage is similar to that of *G. sempervirens*. Bright yellow, scentless, inch-wide

DON'T FEED CAROLINA JESSAMINE TOO HEAVILY, OR YOU'LL GET LOTS OF LEAVES AND FEW FLOWERS.

flowers bloom in both spring and fall, and they bloom sporadically in fall and winter in the Lower and Coastal South. Prefers regular to ample water; tolerates boggy soil.

G. sempervirens. CAROLINA JESSAMINE, YELLOW JESSAMINE. One of the South's most popular native vines and the state flower of South Carolina. Grows quickly to 20 ft. or more. Pairs of light green, shiny, 1- to 4-in.-long leaves clothe long, streamerlike branches. Fragrant, tubular, 1½-in.-long flowers bloom in late winter and early spring. 'Pride of Augusta' has double flowers. 'Pale Yellow' has large blooms in creamy yellow. 'Margarita' tolerates more cold than the species and has slightly larger flowers. 'Lemon Drop' forms a spreading mound rather than a climbing vine; snip off long runners to keep it low.

Prefers fertile soil but adapts to almost any well-drained soil. Needs regular water in youth but is very drought tolerant once established. Blooms better in sun but tolerates partial shade. Often seen scrambling companionably through tree branches in the wild. In gardens, it's a favorite choice for climbing over mailboxes; also excellent for training above doorways and bay windows, along fences and walls. May be used as a ground cover on banks; keep trimmed to 3 ft. high. Sometimes gets too heavy on top and bare around the base; if this happens, cut back severely after bloom.

GENISTA

BROOM, WOADWAXEN
Papilionaceae
Deciduous and evergreen shrubs

🌡️ **ZONES VARY BY SPECIES**

☀️ **FULL SUN**

💧 **LITTLE TO MODERATE WATER**

Genista x spachiana

These twiggy, low-growing shrubs make fine bank or ground covers and are a welcome addition to the rock garden. Good drainage is essential for their survival; they grow well in sandy or gravelly, infertile soils. Showy, sweet pea–shaped yellow flowers appear in spring. Leaves are often small and short lived; green branches give deciduous sorts an evergreen look.

G. lydia. Zones US, MS, LS; USDA 6-8. Evergreen; nearly leafless. Grows to 2 ft. tall and 3 ft. wide; makes a good ground cover. Profuse show of blossoms at tips of shoots in late spring. Sets few seeds.

G. pilosa. Zones US, MS; USDA 6-7. SILKYLEAF WOADWAXEN. Deciduous. Fairly fast-growing prostrate shrub, ultimately to 1–1½ ft. tall with 7-ft. spread. Intricately branched gray-green twigs; roundish, ¼- to 1-in.-long leaves. Blooms in spring. 'Vancouver Gold' is a good selection.

G. tinctoria. Zones US, MS; USDA 6-7. DYER'S GREENWEED, WOADWAXEN. Deciduous. To 6 ft. tall and wide, with undivided

leaves to 2 in. long. Upright flower spikes in late spring or early summer. 'Royal Gold' is a compact selection 2 ft. tall and wide.

GENTIANA

GENTIAN
Gentianaceae
Perennials

🌡️ **ZONES VARY BY SPECIES**

◐ **PARTIAL SHADE**

💧💧 **WATER NEEDS VARY BY SPECIES**

Gentiana asclepiadea

Offering some of the richest blues in the garden, these delightful, refined plants are considered by many to be difficult customers—and some of the rock-garden types are indeed pretty finicky. All of the species listed here, however, are easy to grow if planted in moist, acid soil enriched with plenty of organic matter. Most are best suited to the Upper and Middle South and the higher elevations of the Appalachians, Blue Ridge Mountains, and Ozarks, but some can also be grown as far south as Mississippi and Alabama. Do not disturb plants once they're established.

G. andrewsii. BOTTLE GENTIAN. Zones US, MS; USDA 6-7. A legendary wildflower of the eastern U.S. To 2 ft. tall and less than half as wide, with erect, unbranched stems set with paired, dark green, 2- to 3-in.-long leaves. Clusters of 2-in.-long, deep blue flowers appear atop the plant in autumn. Blossoms never open completely, so they have a distinctive bottle shape. Often the last wildflower to bloom in fall. Does well in soil that is constantly

moist or even boggy; perfect along the edge of a stream or pond. A white-flowering form is available.

G. asclepiadea. WILLOW GENTIAN. Zones US, MS, LS; USDA 6-8. Native to Europe and western Asia. Forms a clump of arching stems to 2 ft. tall, 1½ ft. wide. Dark green, 2- to 3-in.-long leaves. Blooms in late summer and early fall, with deep blue blossoms appearing singly or in twos or threes in joints of upper leaves; flowers are 1½ in. wide and open into a star shape. Give regular water and well-drained soil. 'Rosea' has pink blooms.

G. clausa. CLOSED GENTIAN. Zones US, MS; USDA 6-8. Native to eastern U.S. Very similar to *G. andrewsii*, but the flowers are slightly larger and have white showing around the edges of the petals. Give same conditions as *G. andrewsii.*

G. saponaria. SOAPWORT GENTIAN, HARVESTBELLS. Zones US, MS, LS, CS; USDA 6-9. Native to eastern and southern U.S. Slender, erect stems to 2 ft. tall, with medium green, broadly lance-shaped leaves to 3½ in. long. Clusters of light blue, closed, cigar-shaped flowers to 1½ in. long appear in fall. Does well with regular to ample water; best in moist, rich, well-drained soil but tolerates boggy conditions.

G. septemfida. SUMMER GENTIAN. Zones US, MS, LS, CS; USDA 6-9. From Caucasus, Turkey, and Iran to central Asia. Arching or sprawling stems 9–18 in. long form a spreading mass about 8 in. high, 1 ft. wide. Medium green, oval leaves to 1½ in. long. Clusters of 2-in., dark blue flowers in late summer. Easy to grow if given regular water and rich, well-drained soil. Good choice in rock gardens; tolerates a bit more sun than other species listed. *G. s. lagodechiana*, the form commonly sold, is similar but has more widely spaced flowers.

GERANIUM

CRANESBILL
Geraniaceae
Perennials

🌡️ **US, MS, LS; USDA 6-8**

☀️ ◐ **AFTERNOON SHADE**

💧 **REGULAR WATER**

Geranium 'Rozanne'

The common indoor/outdoor plant that most people know as geranium is, botanically, *Pelargonium*. Considered here are true geraniums, which are hardy plants. Many types bloom over a fairly long period, bearing flowers that are attractive, though not as showy as those of *Pelargonium*. Carried singly or in clusters of two or three, flowers have five overlapping petals that look alike. (*Pelargonium* blossoms also have five petals, but two point in one direction, the other three in the opposite direction.) Colors include rose, blue, and purple; a few are pure pink or white. The beaklike fruit that follows the flowers accounts for the common name "cranesbill." Leaves are roundish or kidney shaped, with lobed or deeply cut edges; plants may be upright or trailing. Good in perennial borders; some are useful as small-scale ground covers.

All of the species listed here appreciate afternoon shade and moist, well-drained soil. Clumps of most types can be left in place for many years before they decline due to crowding; at that point, divide clumps in early spring. Increase plantings by transplanting rooted portions from a clump's edge. Most types bloom heavily in spring and early summer, then go dormant when the weather gets hot in July and August. Resist browsing deer.

G. 'Ann Folkard'. Mounding, billowing plant (1½ ft. high, to 5 ft. wide) with chartreuse leaves that age to light green. Saucer-shaped, 1½-in.-wide blossoms are rich magenta purple suffused with pink and blue, centered and veined in black. Blooms from June through August. Effective planted at edge of patio and sprawling onto it.

G. 'Anne Thomson'. Similar to G. 'Ann Folkard' but more compact (1½ ft. high, 3 ft. wide) and with greater heat tolerance.

G. 'Brookside'. Hybrid developed from G. pratense. To 2½ ft. tall and wide, with deeply serrated leaves. Covered in late spring with rich blue, bowl-shaped flowers to 2 in. across. Somewhat similar to G. 'Johnson's Blue' but easier to grow.

G. x cantabrigiense. Excellent ground cover, 6–8 in. high, spreading slowly but widely. Dark green leaves 1½–2½ in. wide, deeply cut with multiple lobes. 'Cambridge' has bright bluish pink flowers, ¾–1 in. wide. The blooms of 'Bioko-vo' and 'St. Ola' are white blushed pale pink and slightly larger.

G. cinereum. From the Pyrenees. Grows to 6 in. tall, much wider, with deeply cut, soft gray-green leaves. Inch-wide pink flowers with darker veining appear in late spring and summer. 'Ballerina' has lilac-pink flowers with purple veining; blooms over a long summer season. 'Laurence Flatman' has slightly larger flowers of a deeper color. 'Purple Pillow' has bright purple flowers with dark purple veins. Variety G. c. subcaulescens (G. subcaulescens) has darker green leaves and deep purplish red flowers with black centers.

G. dalmaticum. From the Balkans. Low (4–5-in.) carpeting plant with glossy, 1½-in., finely cut leaves and soft pink, inch-wide flowers in spring. Leaves turn orange and red in fall. Spreads slowly to make a 2-ft.-wide mat; useful in rock gardens.

G. endressii. From southern Europe to southwest Asia. Bushy plant to 1–1½ ft. tall, spreading to 2 ft. across. Leaves are 2–3 in. wide, deeply cut into five lobes. Rose-pink flowers to about 1 in. across.

G. himalayense (G. grandiflo-rum). Wiry, branching stems form a clump to 1–2 ft. high, spreading wider. Roundish, long-stalked, five-lobed leaves to 1¾ in. across.

Clustered, 1½- to 2-in.-wide flowers are lilac with purple veins and a red-purple eye. 'Graveteye' is a dependable selection; 'Baby Blue' has larger light blue flowers. 'Plenum' ('Birch Double') is less vigorous, with double flowers in light lavender.

G. 'Johnson's Blue'. Hybrid resembling its G. himalayense parent, but with more finely divided leaves and blue-violet, 2-in.-wide flowers.

G. macrorrhizum. From southern Europe. To 8–10 in. high, spreading by underground rootstocks and fleshy rhizomes that root on soil surface. Inch-wide magenta flowers in spring; fragrant, five- to seven-lobed, 4- to 8-in.-wide leaves that take on attractive tints in autumn. Good ground cover for small areas, though it can overwhelm delicate smaller plants. Selections include deep reddish purple 'Bevan's Variety'; pink 'Spessart'; 'Ingwersen's Variety', with soft bluish pink blossoms over a long season; and 'Album', bearing white flowers with pink sepals and stamens. Flowers of 'White-Ness' are pure white.

G. maculatum. WILD GERANIUM, WILD CRANESBILL. Native to eastern North America; the only commonly cultivated native cranesbill. To 1½ ft. high, 2 ft. wide, deeply divided leaves and an abundance of lilac-pink, 1- to 1½-in.-wide flowers in spring. 'Album' has white blooms. Leaves of 'Elizabeth Ann' and 'Espresso' are dark chocolate-brown.

G. x magnificum. Vigorous sterile hybrid that spreads steadi-ly, forming broad clumps 2–2½ ft. high and wide. Rounded, quilted, 3-in. leaves are divided into broad segments; take on red and orange tones in fall. Profuse 2-in. violet blossoms heavily veined in deep purple appear in late spring and summer. 'Rosemoor' is a choice selection with darkly veined, blue-violet flowers produced over an extended period.

G. x oxonianum. Among the best selections is 'Claridge Druce', which forms a vigorous clump 2–3 ft. tall, 3 ft. wide. Rounded, 3- to 4-in. leaves are deeply cut into broad, toothed lobes. Funnel-shaped, broad-petaled, 1½- to 1¾-in., cool pink flowers with purplish veins bloom late spring to summer. Good large-scale ground cover but can over-whelm adjacent plants. Self-sows

TOP: Geranium 'Johnson's Blue'; G. 'Ann Folkard'; BOTTOM: G. x magnificum 'Rosemoor'; G. x cantabrigiense 'Biokovo'

profusely; seedlings resemble parent, but blossoms often have narrower petals. 'Wargrave Pink' is similar in habit but a little less vigorous, with glossy, warm pink blossoms that resemble those of G. endressii.

G. phaeum. MOURNING WIDOW, DUSKY CRANESBILL. Shade-loving native of southern and central European mountains. Grows to 2 ft. high, 1½ ft. wide. Leaves are basal, 3–4 in. across, shallowly cut into seven to nine tooth-edged lobes, often with brown markings. Bears clusters of dusky purple or maroon, ¾- to 1-in. blossoms in May and June. 'Album' has blooms of pure white. 'Lily Lovell' has purplish maroon blooms with a white eye. Leaves of 'Margaret Wilson' are heavily streaked with creamy yellow; flowers are light purple. 'Samobor' has maroon flowers and leaves heavily marked with maroon.

G. platypetalum. From Turkey and the Caucasus. Clump 1½ ft. high and wide with rounded, quilted, 4- to 8-in.-wide leaves, shallowly cut into seven to nine scalloped lobes. Saucer-shaped,

1½- to 1¾-in. flowers with notched petals are deep violet blue with paler center and dark veins. Late spring bloomer.

G. pratense. MEADOW CRANESBILL. Native from Ireland to Siberia and Japan. Forms a clump 1½–2 ft. tall, 2–3 ft. wide. Hairy, 3- to 6-in. leaves on upright stalks are deeply cut into seven narrow, pointed, divided lobes. Flowers about 1 in. wide, typically blue with reddish veins. Self-sows profusely; cut to ground when flowers fade to prevent seedlings and encourage rebloom. 'Black Beauty' has dark purple leaves and light blue blooms. 'Midnight Reiter' has plum-colored foliage; the flowers are lavender-blue. 'Mrs. Kendall Clark' has pale blue flowers with lighter veins. 'Plenum Violaceum' ('Flore Pleno') has fully double, deep violet-blue blossoms. 'Striatum' has white blossoms irregularly splashed, streaked, or spotted with violet-blue.

G. 'Rozanne'. This naturally occurring hybrid between G. himalayense and G. wallichi-anum 'Buxton's Variety' is popular and easy to grow. Plants reach 1½–2 ft. high and spread a little wider, forming a lush mound of deeply lobed, dark green leaves. Foliage takes on attractive red tones in the fall. Stunning flowers, to 2½ in. wide, are rich violet-blue with darker veins and a large white eye. Blooms summer into fall.

G. sanguineum. BLOODY CRANESBILL. Native from western Europe to the Caucasus and Turkey. Grows 1½ ft. high, with trailing stems spreading to 2 ft. Roundish, 1- to 2½-in.-wide, dark green leaves with five to seven lobes; turn blood red in fall. Deep purple to almost crimson flowers, 1½ in. wide, bloom from late spring well into summer. 'Album' is somewhat taller than the species and has white flowers. Other 1- to 1½-ft. selections include 'John Elsley', pink with deeper pink veins; 'Max Frei', reddish purple; 'New Hampshire', deep purple; and 'Vision', reddish purple. 'Elke' (G. 'Elke') grows 10 in. tall and 3 ft. wide, with bright pink, red-veined flowers; petals are edged in white.

The variety G. s. striatum (G. s. 'Prostratum', G. lancastriense) is a dwarf form—lower and more compact and an excellent choice for rock garden or foreground. It has light pink flowers heavily veined with red (its seedlings may vary somewhat).

G. sylvaticum. Native from Ireland to Siberia, south to Turkey. To 2½ ft. tall and wide. Leaves are deeply lobed and toothed; inch-wide flowers range in color from bluish to reddish purple.

G. wallichianum. Native to the Himalayas. Grows to 1 ft. tall and 3 ft. wide, with marbled, wrinkled, tooth-edged leaves. Lilac, 1- to 1½-in. flowers with a white eye. 'Buxton's Variety' has pure blue flowers with a large white eye and striking black stamens.

GERBERA JAMESONII
GERBERA DAISY, TRANSVAAL DAISY
Asteraceae
Perennial in coastal and tropical south; annual elsewhere

🗡 **CS, TS; USDA 9-11; ANNUAL ELSEWHERE, EXCEPT AS NOTED**

☼ ◐ **FULL SUN OR PARTIAL SHADE**

💧 **REGULAR WATER**

Gerbera jamesonii 'Revolution Orange'

For stunning, vibrant color, it's hard to beat this South African native. Slim yet sturdy stems, up to 1½ ft. tall, emerge from clumps of tongue-shaped, lobed leaves. The 4- to 5-in. daisies, borne one to a stem, fairly glow in colors of red, orange, coral, pink, yellow, and cream. The basic form features a single ring of petal-like rays surrounding a prominent central disk. Hybrid forms may display two rows of long rays or an outer ring of long rays and an inner ring of short, tufted ones; or they may be fully double with a fluffy look.

Many strains are available, including types with dark centers and dwarfs just 6 in. tall. Where gerberas are perennial, they can bloom at almost any time of year, unless frost kills them to the ground. In this case, they'll sprout from underground stems in spring and begin blooming shortly afterward.

Outside the Coastal and Tropical South, they're traditionally treated as annuals. Plants in the Jaguar (8–10 in. tall) and Royal (10–14 in. tall) series are early, dependable bloomers.

The strains below have proven hardy into the Middle and Lower

South as well; USDA 7-11. Wolfpack Country, bred at North Carolina State University, will bloom continuously from spring until frost. Hybrids in the Drakensberg Daisy series produce many medium-size blooms in the full color range on stems 8–10 in. tall; vigorous, long-blooming, and tolerant of humidity. Top performers in the Garvinea series are light orange 'Orangina' and deep orange 'Jilly'. Keep them well-watered in full sun. For part sun and containers, try the large-flowered Patio series.

CARE
Gerberas need excellent drainage; if your soil drains poorly, plant in raised beds. Space about 2 ft. apart, with root crowns at least ½ in. above soil level. Feed monthly with a balanced liquid fertilizer. Pick off old, yellow leaves. Water deeply and let soil become nearly dry before watering again. Divide (in late winter) only when clump is crowded and flowering declines. When cutting flowers for arrangements, slit the bottom inch of stem before placing in water.

Most people start with transplants, but you can also grow gerberas from seed. Seed must be fresh to germinate well. Sow in moist potting soil; keep air temperature at about 70°F. Water carefully. Seed may take several weeks to sprout. Seedlings flower in 4 to 6 months.

Powdery mildew can be a problem when humidity is high and temperatures are moderate. Crowded plantings and shade makes the problem even worse. The best defense is to start with disease-free plants and to choose the newer, more disease-resistant selections. If a chemical control is needed, consult your local Cooperative Extension Office for a recommendation.

GEUM
AVENS
Rosaceae
Perennials

🗡 **US, MS; USDA 6-7**

☼ ◐ **FULL SUN OR PARTIAL SHADE**

💧 **REGULAR WATER, EXCEPT AS NOTED**

Geum chiloense 'Lady Stratheden'

This group of plants combines handsome foliage with showy flowers. Double, semidouble, or single blossoms in red, orange, pink, or yellow appear throughout the summer if plants are deadheaded regularly; they make good cut flowers. Leaves of most are divided into many leaflets, often with scalloped or toothed margins. Geums are not suited to extended summer heat. They'll grow in the Middle South, but they prefer the Upper South and higher elevations of the Appalachians, Blue Ridge Mountains, and Ozarks. Soil should be consistently moist and, except for G. rivale, well drained. Start from seed sown in early spring, or set out transplants. Divide established plants in fall or spring. Deer resistant.

G. 'Alabama Slammer'. This hybrid forms a clump of light green leaves 14 in. high and 10 in. wide. Ruffled, single or semidouble flowers up to 1¼ in. wide are multicolored: golden yellow marked with red and orange. Stems and calyxes are deep burgundy.

G. chiloense. CHILEAN AVENS. Best-known species. Native to Chile. Mounding foliage clumps to 15 in. high, 2 ft. wide. Leafy, branched, flowering stems reach about 2 ft. high, topped by 1- to

1½-in.-wide flowers. Dozens of hybrids and selections are available. Look for semidouble orange 'Dolly North', semi-double orange-scarlet 'Fire Opal', double yellow 'Lady Stratheden', double scarlet 'Mrs. J. Bradshaw', semidouble soft yellow 'Prinses Juliana' ('Princess Juliana'), and double tangerine 'Starker's Magnificum'. 'Totally Tangerine' is heavy blooming, with single, warm orange flowers on a plant 2½ ft. high and 1½ ft. wide.

G. coccineum. Native to the Balkans, Asia Minor. To 12–20 in. tall and wide, with coarsely divided foliage and brick-red, 1½-in. flowers. Two selections to 1 ft. tall and wide are 'Borisii', with orange-red flowers, and 'Werner Arends', with bright orange blooms. 'Red Wings', to 28 in. tall and wide, has semidouble scarlet flowers.

G. rivale. WATER AVENS, INDIAN CHOCOLATE. Native to North America and Eurasia. Grows to 1 ft. tall and wide, bearing slightly nodding, ivory to pink, ¾-in. flowers. Needs a cool site with boggy soil. Boiled roots of plant yield a liquid that tastes faintly like chocolate. 'Leonard's Variety' has double coppery rose flowers. Hybrid 'Lionel Cox' has creamy apricot blooms with wavy petals.

G. triflorum. PRAIRIE SMOKE. Native to the prairies and mountains of North America. Foot-wide, leafy mound produces stems to 20 in. tall, each bearing clusters of nodding maroon flowers to 1½ in. wide. Entire plant is often furry. Seeds have long, upright, feathery gray "tails" resembling wisps of smoke.

GILLENIA TRIFOLIATA

BOWMAN'S ROOT, INDIAN PHYSIC
Rosaceae
Perennial

US, MS, LS; USDA 6-8

PARTIAL SHADE

REGULAR WATER

Gillenia trifoliata

This charming woodland wild-flower is native from southern Ontario south to Georgia and Alabama. Grows 2–3 ft. tall and 2 ft. wide, with reddish stems and bronzy green, 2- to 4-in.-long leaves divided into three narrow, toothed leaflets; foliage turns yellow, orange, and red in fall. Panicles of starlike, white or pinkish, 1½-in.-wide flowers seem to float above the leaves in late spring and early summer. Red sepals remain after the petals drop. Bark from the thick root has many uses in traditional medicine. 'Pink Profusion' has flowers of light pink. Plant thrives in moist, well-drained soil loaded with organic matter; a good companion for hostas, ferns, foamflower (*Tiarella*), false solomon's seal (*Polygonatum*), and blue phlox. Will self-sow if not deadheaded. Resists deer. Formerly known as *Porteranthus trifoliatus*.

GINKGO BILOBA

MAIDENHAIR TREE
Ginkgoaceae
Deciduous tree

US, MS, LS, CS; USDA 6-9

FULL SUN

MODERATE TO REGULAR WATER

Ginkgo biloba

Ancient survivor from prehistoric times (200 million years ago), when it grew worldwide; now native only to two small areas in China. Related to conifers but differs in having broad (1- to 4-in.-wide), fan-shaped leaves rather than needlelike foliage. In shape and veining, leaves resemble leaflets of maidenhair fern, hence the tree's common name. Attractive in any season—especially in fall, when the leathery light green leaves suddenly turn gold (they practically glow when backlit by the sun). Leaves hang on for a time, then drop quickly and cleanly to make a golden carpet where they fall.

Can grow to 70–80 ft. tall, but most mature trees are 50–60 ft. May be gawky in youth, but becomes graceful and well proportioned with age—narrow to spreading or even umbrella shaped. Typical width is no more than one-half to two-thirds height. Usually grows slowly, about 1 ft. a year, but under ideal conditions can grow up to 3 ft. a year. Seeds are considered a delicacy in China and Japan, and an extract made from ginkgo is said to improve brain function, especially memory, by increasing blood flow. Not favored by browsing deer.

Use as street tree or lawn tree. Plant only male trees (grafted or grown from cuttings of male plants); female trees produce messy, fleshy, ill-smelling fruit in quantity. Named selections listed below are male.

'Autumn Gold'. Upright to 50 ft., eventually rather broad and spreading to about 30 ft.

'Fairmount'. Fast-growing, pyramidal form similar to 'Princeton Sentry'. To 60 ft. tall, 30 ft. wide.

'Golden Colonnade'. Strong, upright grower to 45 ft. high and 25 ft. wide. Uniform, narrowly oval habit makes it a good choice for street plantings.

'Jade Butterflies'. Vase-shaped, shrubby form growing only about 10 ft. tall in 10 years. Dark green leaves have a deep V-shape cut in the center of the leaf, giving the impression of a butterfly.

'Pendula' (Pendula Group). These slow-growing plants are usually grafted, with branches that grow horizontally, then weep, for an umbrella shape. Eventually reaches 12 ft. tall and wide.

'Princeton Sentry'. Erect to 60 ft. high; 25-ft. spread at base, tapering toward top.

'Saratoga'. Similar to 'Autumn Gold', with a distinct central leader. To 40 ft. tall, 30 ft. wide.

'Shangri-La'. Pyramidal shape; to 45 ft. tall, 25 ft. wide.

'The President' ('Presidential Gold'). Full, dense growth even in youth; reaches 45 ft. high and 35 ft. Mature trees are broadly pyramidal.

'Windover Gold'. Resembles 'Shangri-La' in habit and size.

'Woodstock' ('Emperor'). Strong central leader gives this variety a uniform oval to broadly pyramidal crown. Grows 50 ft. tall and 35 ft. wide.

CARE

Plant in deep, loose, well-drained soil. Be sure nursery plants are not root bound. Young growth may be brittle, but wood becomes strong with age. In general, ginkgos are not bothered by insects or diseases, and they're very tolerant of air pollution, heat, and acid or alkaline conditions. Water young trees regularly until they reach about 15 ft. tall, then let rainfall take over. On young trees, cut back any awkward branches and vertical shoots growing parallel to central leader. Older trees need minimal pruning; just remove weak, broken, or dead branches.

G

GLADIOLUS
Iridaceae
Perennials from corms

MS, LS, CS, TS; USDA 7-9, EXCEPT AS NOTED; OR DIG AND STORE

☼ **FULL SUN**

◐ **REGULAR WATER DURING GROWTH AND BLOOM**

Gladiolus communis byzantinus

These old-fashioned favorites are prized for their tubular, often flaring or ruffled blossoms borne in unbranched or branching, usually one-sided spikes in an extremely wide color range. All have sword-shaped leaves. Bloom from spring to fall, depending on kind and time of planting. Superb cut flowers. Good in borders or beds behind mounding plants that cover lower parts of stems, or in large containers with low annuals at base.

Baby gladiolus. Flaring, 2½- to 3¼-in. flowers in short, loose spikes on 1½-ft. stems. Flowers are white, pink, red, or lilac; they may be solid or blotched with contrasting color. When left in the ground, will form large clumps in border or among shrubs. Plant in fall or early spring for late spring bloom.

G. communis byzantinus (*G. byzantinus*). Zones US, MS, LS, CS; USDA 6-9. HARDY GLADIOLUS, BYZANTINE GLADIOLUS. Mainly maroon, sometimes reddish or coppery, 1- to 3-in. flowers in groups of 6 to 12 on 2- to 3-ft. stems. Narrower leaves than garden gladiolus. Plant in early spring for summer bloom. An old Southern favorite. They can be left in the ground.

G. murielae (*Acidanthera bicolor*). ABYSSINIAN SWORD LILY. Native to Africa. Stems grow 2–3 ft. tall, bearing 2 to 10 fragrant, creamy white flowers marked chocolate-brown on lower segments. Each blossom is 2–3 in. wide and 4–5 in. long. Excellent cut flowers. Plant in spring for bloom in late summer and fall.

Primulinus and butterfly hybrids. These summer bloomers derive in part from an African species with hooded (rather than funnel-shaped), primrose-yellow flowers. Named selections grow 3–4 ft. tall, each spike carrying up to 18 widely spaced, somewhat hooded blossoms in a wide range of colors. Plants multiply quickly. 'Atom' (sometimes sold as 'Atomic') has brilliant red flowers with a white picotee edge. Blooms of 'Mirella' are reddish orange. Coldhardy 'Carolina Primrose' blooms are soft yellow with a red-striped throat. 'Boone' is also extra hardy; it has apricot flowers with a yellow throat marked with red.

Group known as butterfly gladiolus has 2- to 3-ft. stems bearing more closely spaced flowers; distinct throat markings or blotches of contrasting color give butterfly appearance. Plant in early spring.

Summer-flowering grandiflora hybrids. GARDEN GLADIOLUS. These complex hybrids are the best-known gladiolus, with the widest color range—white, cream, buff, yellow, orange, apricot, salmon, red shades, rose, lavender, purple, smoky shades, even green shades. Individual blooms may be as large as 8 in. across. Stems are 4–5 ft. tall.

The newer types of garden gladiolus grow to about 5 ft. tall, have sturdier spikes bearing from 12 to 14 open flowers at one time. They are better garden plants than older types and stand upright without staking. Another group, called miniature gladiolus, grows 3 ft. tall, with spikes of 15 to 20 flowers, each 2½–3 in. wide; useful in garden beds and for cutting.

High-crowned corms, 1½–2 in. wide, are more productive than older, larger corms (2 in. wide or more). After soil has warmed in spring, plant at 1- to 2-week intervals for 4 to 6 weeks for progression of bloom. Corms bloom 65 to 100 days after planting. Mix plenty of organic compost into the soil before planting. When plants have five leaves, apply complete bulb fertilizer 6 in. from plants and water it in thoroughly. For cut flowers, cut spikes when lowest buds begin to open, leaving a minimum of four leaves on plants to build up corms. If thrips cause whitish streaking on leaves, spray foliage with insecticidal soap or horticultural oil.

CARE

Plant in rich, well-drained soil. Set corms about four times deeper than their height (plant somewhat shallower in heavy soils). Space big corms 6 in. apart, smaller ones 4 in. apart. Corms can generally be left in the ground from year to year in Middle, Lower, and Coastal South. In the Upper South, dig soon after first frost in autumn. Dry corms on a flat surface in a dark, dry area for 2 to 3 weeks; then store over winter in a single layer in flats or ventilated trays in a cool place (40–50°F). In the Tropical South, refrigerate corms for a month before planting, then treat as annuals and discard after plant has finished blooming.

GLEDITSIA TRIACANTHOS

HONEY LOCUST
Caesalpiniaceae
Deciduous tree

🌱 **US, MS, LS; USDA 6-8**

☼ **FULL SUN**

◐● **MODERATE TO REGULAR WATER**

Gleditsia triacanthos inermis 'Sunburst'

Native to central and eastern North America. Fast growing, especially when young, with upright trunk and spreading,

arching branches. To 35–70 ft. tall and 25–35 ft. wide. Bright green, fernlike leaves to 10 in. long are divided into many oval, ¾- to 1½-in.-long leaflets. Late to leaf out; leaves turn golden yellow and drop early in fall. Inconspicuous flowers are followed by broad, 1- to 1½-ft.-long pods filled with sweetish pulp and hard, roundish seeds.

Foliage casts filtered shade, allowing growth of lawn or other plants beneath. Small leaflets dry up and filter into grass, decreasing raking chores, but pods make a mess in autumn. Trunks and branches of the species are formidably thorny. Honey locusts listed here, however, are selections of *G. t. inermis*, thornless honey locust, with no thorns and few or no pods.

These trees are not good in narrow area between curb and sidewalk, since roots of old plants will heave paving. Stake until good, basic branch pattern is established. Tolerant of acid or alkaline conditions, salt, drought, cold, heat, wind. Prune out any wayward or crossing branches. Susceptible to many pests, several of which are prevalent in humid-summer regions: mimosa webworm (chews leaves), pod gall midge (deforms foliage), honey locust borer (attacks limbs and trunks). Resist deer, however.

Popular garden selections include the following.

'Halka'. Fast growing; forms sturdy trunk early. Strong horizontal branching pattern; oval shape. To 40–50 ft.

'Imperial'. Spreading, symmetrical tree to about 35 ft. More densely foliaged than other forms; gives heavier shade.

'Moraine'. Best-known selection. Fast-growing (to 50 ft. high), spreading tree with branches angled upward, then outward. Yellow fall color. Subject to wind breakage. Has greater resistance to webworms than do some of the newer selections.

'Rubylace'. Deep red new growth, fading to bronzed green by mid-summer. Subject to wind breakage, webworm attack.

'Shademaster'. More upright and faster growing than 'Moraine' —to 24 ft. tall, 16 ft. wide in 6 years; eventually to 35 ft. tall, 25 ft. wide.

'Skyline'. Pyramidal and symmetrical, growing to 45 ft. tall. Bright golden fall color.

'Sunburst'. Golden yellow new leaves are showy against deep green background. Summer color is better in Upper and Middle South. Defoliates early in response to temperature changes, drought. Prone to wind breakage. Very susceptible to foliage pests. To 40 ft. tall.

'Trueshade'. To 40 ft. tall, with rounded form. Light green foliage.

GLOBBA

DANCING GIRL GINGER
Zingiberaceae
Perennials

🌱 **CS, TS; USDA 9-11; OR GROW IN POTS**

☼ **PARTIAL SHADE; BRIGHT INDIRECT LIGHT**

● **REGULAR WATER DURING GROWING SEASON**

Globba marantina

These small, delicate-flowered members of the ginger family are native to Southeast Asia. They grow upright to 1–3 ft. tall; leaves are lustrous green sheaths, and graceful, spidery flowers bloom in summer or fall among long, arching sprays of brightly colored bracts. Bulbils are often found inside the bracts and if planted promptly will produce new plants. Space 1½ ft. apart. Easy to grow if fertilized and kept moist during the growing season and fed with a balanced controlled-release fertilizer in early spring and again in midsummer. In cold-winter areas, bring indoors before frost; mist to provide humidity if necessary, and stop watering during the winter to give plant a period of dormancy. Resume watering gradually in spring. Most make good cut flowers.

G. globulifera. PURPLE GLOBE GINGER. Has short panicles of purple bracts and yellow flowers.

G. marantina. YELLOW DANCING GIRLS. Produces 3-in. panicles of light green-yellow bracts and yellow flowers with red spots.

G. winitii. Has 6-in. panicles of rosy purple bracts and bright yellow flowers. Particularly delicate and long blooming. 'Mauve Dancing Girl' has lavender-purple bracts and golden yellow flowers; panicles may reach 8–10 in. long. Foliage of 'Red Leaf' has maroon undersides. 'White Dragon' has pure white bracts and small yellow flowers.

GLORIOSA SUPERBA

GLORY LILY, CLIMBING LILY
Colchicaceae
Perennial from tuber

🌱 **CS, TS; USDA 9-11; OR DIG AND STORE; OR GROW IN POTS**

☼◑ **LIGHT SHADE IN HOTTEST CLIMATES**

● **REGULAR WATER DURING GROWTH AND BLOOM**

☠ **ALL PARTS ARE HIGHLY POISONOUS IF INGESTED**

Gloriosa superba

This lily relative is native to tropical Africa and Asia. A tendril at the tip of each tapering, lance-shaped, 5- to 7-in. leaf wraps around any handy support, helping plant climb to 6 ft. In summer, top part of plant bears flashy 4-in. blossoms, each with six recurved, wavy-edged segments. 'Citrina' has bright yellow flowers tinted or striped with purplish red. Blooms of 'Lutea' are solid yellow.

G

'Rothschildiana', the most popular selection, has brilliant red flowers with yellow bases and margins.

CARE

Glory lily can survive outdoors in frost-free areas, but even there is best grown in pots or sharply drained soil. For appearance of permanent planting, sink containers into garden bed. Choose pots at least 8 in. in diameter; fill with rich, loose soil mix. Set in tubers horizontally, one to a container, about 4 in. deep. Start indoors or in greenhouse in winter; set out after frosts. Give climbing stems support from trellis, wires, string, or even loose-growing shrubs. Feed with a balanced liquid fertilizer every 3 weeks. Withhold water and fertilizer when leaves begin to yellow and die back in fall. Sever dead stems and move pots to dry, cool spot for winter. In late winter, knock tubers out of containers; repot in fresh soil mix. Or dig tubers from pots in fall, and store.

GLOXINIA SYLVATICA

BOLIVIAN SUNSET
Gesneriaceae
Perennial from rhizome

🌱 **LS, CS, TS; USDA 8-11; OR HOUSEPLANT**

◐ **PARTIAL SHADE; BRIGHT INDIRECT LIGHT**

💧 **MODERATE WATER**

Gloxinia sylvatica

Hailing from Bolivia and Peru, this tender beauty is usually grown as a houseplant—though it is hardy enough to grow outdoors in the Coastal and Tropical South. A single stem rises to 1–2 ft., clothed in narrow, pointed, dark green leaves to 6 in. long. From late summer into winter, slender stems rise from the upper leaf joints, bearing tubular, nodding flowers about 1 in. long. Blossoms are orange-red with a golden interior and seem to glow from within. For other plants often called gloxinia, see *Sinningia*.

CARE

Indoors, plant in regular potting mix and water only when soil is dry to the touch. Feed monthly with half-strength general-purpose liquid houseplant fertilizer during active growth. After bloom, stop fertilizing and reduce watering until spring. Outdoors, grow in fairly moist, humus-rich soil in dappled shade or morning sun.

GOMPHRENA

GLOBE AMARANTH
Amaranthaceae
Annuals and perennials grown as annuals

🌱 **US, MS, LS, CS, TS; USDA 6-11**

☀️◐ **FULL SUN OR PARTIAL SHADE**

💧 **MODERATE WATER**

Gomphrena 'Fireworks'

Stiffly branching plants to 1–2 ft. tall, 1 ft. wide, covered in summer and fall with rounded, papery, cloverlike flower heads ¾–1 in. wide. These are easy to dry, retaining color and shape for winter arrangements. Narrow, oval leaves are 2–4 in. long. Drought tolerant and easy to grow; rarely bothered by pests, including deer. It's easy to harvest seeds from the faded flowers and save them for planting next year; start indoors or sow in place after soil has warmed in spring.

LEFT: Gomphrena 'QIS'; *RIGHT: G. globosa*

G. 'Fireworks'. Annual. Vigorous, fast-growing plant to 4 ft. high and nearly as wide. Strong stems are topped by 1-in. pom-pon blooms. Each hot pink petal is delicately tipped in yellow.

G. globosa. Annual. From Central America. White, pink, lavender, or purple flower heads on 1- to 2-ft. stems. Plants in the QIS series can reach 30 in. tall, with large flowers in the full range of colors. 'Strawberry Fields' has hot red, ½-in. blossoms on 2-ft. stems. Plants in the Audray series grow at least that tall, with flowers in a range of colors including bicolor rose (pink with white tip). The Las Vegas series (16–20 in. tall) works well in borders or containers; available in pink, purple, and white. Dwarf selections for use as edging or bedding plants include 9-in. 'Buddy' (purple) and 'Cissy' (white). All types can be planted closely in large containers for a long-lasting living bouquet.

G. haageana. Perennial treated as annual. From southern U.S., Mexico. Heads of tightly clustered, bright orange bracts resembling inch-wide pinecones are borne on 2-ft. stems. Tiny yellow flowers peek from the bracts. Often sold as 'Haageana Aurea' or orange gomphrena.

G. 'Pink Zazzle'. Annual. Oversized bright pink flowers reach 3 in. wide on a plant 12-16 in. tall.

GONIOLIMON TATARICUM

GERMAN STATICE
Plumbaginaceae
Perennial

🌱 **US, MS, LS, CS, TS; USDA 6-11**

☀️ **FULL SUN**

💧 **MODERATE WATER**

Goniolimon tataricum

From southern Russia, Caucasus. Dense clumps of dark green, narrowly oval leaves grow from a woody rootstock. In summer, leafless flower stalks rise to 1½ ft., forking repeatedly to form a broad, domed cluster to 1½ ft. wide. Tiny flowers are light purplish to white and make good fillers in fresh bouquets. Entire inflorescence can also be dried for winter arrangements. Plant withstands both cold and heat; also highly salt tolerant. Best where summers are hot and dry. To avoid fungal problems, provide well-drained soil and good air circulation.

GONIOPHLEBIUM SUBAURICULATUM 'KNIGHTII'

LACY PINE FERN
Polypodiaceae
Ferns

🌿 **TS; USDA 10-11; OR GROW AS HOUSEPLANT**

◐● **PARTIAL TO FULL SHADE; BRIGHT INDIRECT LIGHT**

💧 **REGULAR WATER**

Goniophlebium subauriculatum

Formerly known as *Polypodium subauriculatum* 'Knightiae'. Native to tropical Asia. Gracefully drooping, fringe-edged fronds to 3 ft. or longer. Spectacular when well grown. Needs high humidity; mist frequently if growing indoors. Outdoor plants shed old fronds in spring, then quickly produce new ones.

GORDONIA LASIANTHUS

LOBLOLLY BAY
Theaceae
Evergreen tree

🌿 **MS, LS, CS; USDA 7-9**

☀◑ **FULL SUN OR LIGHT SHADE**

💧💧 **REGULAR TO AMPLE WATER**

Gordonia lasianthus

Native to wet soils ("loblollies") of the Coastal Plain from Virginia to Louisiana. Narrow, erect, rather open-structured tree to 30–40 ft. tall and half as wide, with shiny, oval leaves 4–6 in. long. Attractive flowers up to 2½ in. wide bloom from midspring to midautumn; they look something like single white camellias and are enhanced by a big central brush of yellow stamens. Although wild trees grow in bogs, those in garden conditions need good drainage. They are sometimes transplanted from the wild (with the owner's permission, of course), but these transplants are quite difficult to grow. Easier to grow are container-grown plants from garden centers, but these too are finicky.

　　x *Gordlinia grandiflora* 'Sweet Tea'. This selection of a rare cross between *Gordonia* and *Franklinia* has resulted in a semievergreen tree that features 5-in. white flowers from mid- to late summer. Grows 20-30 ft. tall in a sunny to slightly shaded bed with good garden soil and even moisture.

GOSSYPIUM TOMENTOSUM

COTTON
Malvaceae
Annual

🌿 **US, MS, LS, CS, TS; USDA 6-11**

☀ **FULL SUN**

💧 **REGULAR WATER**

Gossypium tomentosum

No plant is more cloaked in Southern history and culture than cotton. Among the world's oldest cultivated plants, it was used for cloth making in Mexico as early as 5,000 B.C. Upland cotton, the type grown in the South, is native to Central America and the West Indies. First grown in the American colonies in 1607, it flourished in the South's warm, humid climate—and with Eli Whitney's invention of the cotton gin in 1793, the industry got a dramatic boost, as the new machine removed seeds from the fibers 50 times faster than a person could by hand.

　　Cotton is a shrubby plant 4–6 ft. tall, about half as wide. It belongs to the mallow family, a fact clearly evidenced by its foliage and flowers. Coarse, dark green leaves are usually palmately lobed; attractive summer flowers to 3 in. long are white or yellowish, fading to pinkish purple. Blossoms are followed by prominent, sharp-edged seed capsules or "bolls" filled with seeds and cotton. White cotton is the cotton of commerce, but there are also other colors, including brown, green, yellow, and pink. Heirloom types, such as those noted below, are still grown and spun.

　　Cotton makes an interesting and historically relevant addition to the garden—and the fluffy bolls never fail to fascinate children. Include a few plants in your vegetable beds; they also make fine additions to a cottage planting. Plants thrive in hottest sites with regular water and well-drained soil. Cut branches of mature cotton are excellent for use in flower arrangements. Two favorite heirloom kinds are 'Erlene's Green', a green cotton from East Texas that turns yellowish green after the fibers are spun and washed, and 'Nankeen', a short-fiber brown cotton that grows well in poor, dry soil and has a long bloom cycle that lasts into fall. 'Sea Island Brown' has longer fibers than other brown cottons, and 'Red Foliate White' is an ornamental form with red stems and leaves, rose-pink flowers, and white cotton bolls.

GOURD

Cucurbitaceae
Annual vines

🌿 **US, MS, LS, CS, TS; USDA 6-11**

☀ **FULL SUN**

💧 **REGULAR WATER**

Gourd

Many plants bear gourds. One of the most commonly planted is *Cucurbita pepo ovifera*, a yellow-flowered vine that produces small ornamental gourds in various shapes and sizes, in both solid colors and stripes; many of the little gourds you see in stores likely come from this plant. *Luffa cylindrica* (*L. aegyptiaca*), called loofah, dishcloth gourd, or vegetable sponge gourd, is another yellow-flowered plant; it bears cylindrical, 1- to 2-ft.-long fruit with a fibrous interior that, when dried, may be used as a sponge or cloth for scrubbing or bathing. *Lagenaria siceraria* (*L. vulgaris*), white-flowered gourd, produces fruit from 3 in. to 3 ft. long, in round, crooknecked, coiled, bottle, dumbbell, or spoon shapes. Dipper gourds and birdhouse gourds are favorites from this species.

CARE

All gourd vines grow fast and will reach 10-15 ft. Sow seeds when ground is warm; start indoors if growing season is short. In order to develop fruit by frost, gourds need all the summer heat they can get. If you plan to use the gourds for ornamental purposes, give vines the support of wire or a trellis to hold ripening fruit off ground. Set out transplants or thin seedlings to 2 ft. apart. You can harvest gourds when tendrils next to their stems are dead, but it's best to leave them on the vine as long as possible—until the gourds turn yellow or brown. They can even stay on the vine through frosts, but a heavy frost can discolor them. Cut each gourd with some stem attached so you can hang it up to dry slowly in a cool, airy spot. When thoroughly dry, preserve with coating of paste wax, lacquer, or shellac.

HOW TO MAKE A LOOFAH SPONGE

Harvest the loofah gourds in late summer or fall. Those picked earlier will make softer sponges than ones picked later. Cure the gourds in a dry, warm location until the skin turns brown and papery. Slice off the ends and peel off the skin. Shake out the seeds and store them for planting next year. Soak the fibrous "sponges" in a solution consisting of 1 part bleach and 3 parts water for several hours to brighten their color, then soak for several hours in pure water to remove the bleach. Finally, air-dry the sponges and store in a mesh bag until you're ready to use them.

GRAPE

Vitaceae
Deciduous vines

✎ **ZONES VARY BY SPECIES**
☼ **FULL SUN**
💧 **MODERATE WATER**

See chart on following pages

Concord grapes

Grapes are among the few ornamental vines with bold, textured foliage; colorful, edible fruit; and a dominant trunk and branch pattern for winter interest. A single grapevine can produce enough new growth every year to arch over a walk, roof an arbor, form a leafy wall, or provide an umbrella of shade over a deck or terrace.

For good-quality fruit, choose a type that fits your climate, train it carefully, and prune it regularly.

There are several basic types of grapes. **European grapes** (*Vitis vinifera*) have tight skin, a high heat requirement, and cold tolerance to about 0°F. These are the market table grapes, such as 'Thompson Seedless'. The classic wine grapes, such as 'Cabernet', 'Chardonnay', and 'Pinot Noir', are also European in origin. Production of European wine grapes is well established in Texas, Virginia, Maryland, Missouri, and North Carolina.

American grapes are derived from *V. labrusca*, with some influence from other American native species and also often from *V. vinifera*. These are slipskin grapes of the 'Concord' type, which have a moderate summer heat requirement and tolerate temperatures well below 0°F. American grapes are used mainly for jelly, in unfermented grape juice, and as soft-drink flavoring;

some wine, usually sweet, is also made from them. Most will not thrive in the Lower and Coastal South; there the grape of choice is the **muscadine** (*V. rotundifolia*), which bears large fruit in small clusters. Most muscadine selections are self-fertile, while others (females) require cross-pollination. (All other types of grapes are self-pollinating.)

Pierce's disease, caused by a bacterium spread by the sharpshooter insect, is lethal to European grapes and severely limits their cultivation in Florida and the Coastal South. They should not be planted south of a line that runs roughly from Raleigh, North Carolina, west through Atlanta, Birmingham, and Greenwood, Mississippi, to Shreveport, Louisiana, to Dallas-Fort Worth. In Texas, Pierce's disease affects only the state's southeastern corner. Most muscadine grapes and some American grapes resist Pierce's disease.

European and American grapes may also suffer from the fungal diseases black rot, which causes fruit to rot on the vine, and downy mildew, resulting in cottony white patches on the leaf undersides and shoot dieback. Control both by applying a fixed-copper fungicide. Muscadines can have problems with fruit rots but are less susceptible to a number of diseases affecting European and American grapes.

In some areas, a regular spraying program may be necessary to protect vines and fruit from insects and/or diseases.

Vines need regular applications of fertilizer to remain productive. Specific recommendations vary slightly among different parts of the South, so contact your Cooperative Extension Office to see whether additional nutrients are needed in your area. In general, however, you can begin fertilizing after the newly planted vines have been settled by a drenching rain. Before growth begins, apply ¼ cup of 10-5-10 fertilizer around each plant, keeping the fertilizer at least 6 in. away from the vine. Repeat every six weeks until mid-July. Two-year-old vines need double that amount of fertilizer applied at the same six-week intervals and for the same duration. For mature vines, apply 2½ pounds of 10-5-10 fertilizer per plant in March. If

growth is poor, an additional pound of the same fertilizer can be applied in May.

Once established, grapevines grow rampantly. If all you want is a leafy cover for an arbor or a sitting area, you need only train a strong vine up and over its support and thin out tangled growth each year. But most people plant grapes for fruit, even if they want shade as well. For good fruit production, you will need to follow more careful pruning procedures (see illustrations on facing page).

Grapes are produced in late summer and fall on stems that develop from 1-year-old wood—stems that formed the previous season. These stems have smooth bark; older ones have rough, shaggy bark. The purpose of pruning is to limit the amount of potential fruiting wood, ensuring that the plant doesn't produce too much fruit and that the fruit it does bear is of good quality.

The two most widely used methods are spur pruning and cane pruning; see chart for recommended pruning method for each selection. Either technique can be used for training grapes on arbors. Whichever method you choose, the initial steps—planting and creating a framework—are the same. Pruning should be done in winter or earliest spring, before the buds swell. (See facing page for planting details.)

MUSCADINE GRAPES ARE SOMETIMES CALLED BULLACE OR SOUTHERN FOX GRAPES.

GRAPE PLANTING AND TRAINING

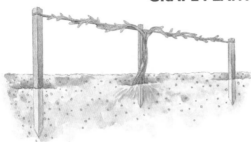

SINGLE-WIRE TRELLIS A single-wire trellis for grapes is easy to build and maintain, and it makes harvesting simple. Set stout posts in the ground 15–20 ft. apart (farther apart for more vigorous grapes, such as muscadines) so that their tops are 5 ft. above the ground. String sturdy galvanized wire across the top posts. Some gardeners may wish to add a second wire at the 2½-ft. level.

PLANTING Plant grapevine next to support stake at same depth as it grew in the nursery pot. Cut the stem back to two buds.

FIRST SPRING Let the vine grow without pruning. The more leaves, the better the root development. Select the strongest shoot and tie it loosely to a stake.

FIRST SUMMER When shoot reaches wire, remove top 4 inches. This forces lateral buds to produce shoots that will form the vine's lateral arms. Train the arms to the wire. Remove all other branches growing from the trunk.

SECOND SUMMER Continue training arms along wire. Prune off ends of arms when they reach halfway to the adjacent support post. To prevent girdling, remove any tendrils that wrap around arms.

SECOND WINTER Prune all shoots growing from arms to four buds. Remove any shoots growing from trunk beneath the arms.

THIRD SUMMER Allow vine to grow and fruit freely.

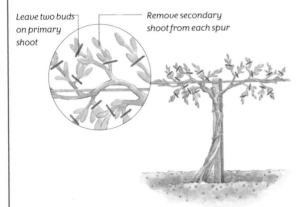

Leave two buds on primary shoot

Remove secondary shoot from each spur

SPUR PRUNING FROM THIRD WINTER This type of pruning is done for all muscadine and some American grapes. Remove weak side shoots from the arms. Leave the strongest shoots (spurs) spaced 6–10 in. apart, and cut each to two buds. Each spur will produce two fruit-bearing shoots during next growing season. During next winter and every winter thereafter, remove the secondary shoot on each spur and cut the primary shoot to two buds. Those buds will develop into stems that bear fruit the following summer.

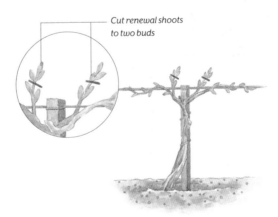

Cut renewal shoots to two buds

CANE PRUNING FROM THIRD WINTER This type of pruning is done for all European and most American grapes. Cut back each arm to 12 buds; these will produce shoots and fruit the following summer. Then select two strong lateral shoots at the trunk just above or below the arms and cut each to two buds. These renewal shoots will grow canes that will eventually replace the existing arms. Every winter thereafter, remove the previous year's arms. Select the two strongest canes from the renewal shoots and tie each to the wire as shown; prune each of these canes to 12 buds.

GRAPES

VARIETY	ZONES	SEASON	PRUNING METHODS	COMMENTS
AMERICAN AND AMERICAN HYBRID SELECTIONS				
'Buffalo'	US, MS, LS; USDA 6-8	Early	Cane	Seeded black table and juice grape with spicy flavor; performs well; may bloom again after late frost and bear a crop
'Canadice'	US, MS; USDA 6-7	Early	Spur	Seedless red grape; very heavy bearing; cane pruning often recommended, but should be spur pruned, possibly thinned, to prevent overcropping
'Concord'	US, MS, LS; USDA 6-8	Midseason	Cane	Oldest cultivated American grape and the one most commonly used for juice, jelly; seeded dark blue fruit
'Daytona'	LS, CS; USDA 8-9	Midseason	Cane or Spur	High-quality seeded pink grape introduced by the University of Florida; good for juice, wine, jelly, fresh eating; resistant to Pierce's disease; American hybrid
'Delaware'	US, MS, LS; USDA 6-8	Early midseason	Cane	Seeded reddish fruit, small but sweet; good selection for wine, juice, and jelly; American hybrid
'Foxy Lottie'	LS, CS; USDA 8-9	Early	Cane or Spur	Medium, seeded, deep purple grape produced in small to medium clusters; good for eating fresh, juice, or jelly
'Fredonia'	US, MS, LS; USDA 6-8	Early midseason	Cane	Large, seeded, deep bluish purple grape produced in small clusters; good for juice, fresh eating
'Golden Muscat'	US, MS, LS; USDA 6-8	Late	Spur	Very large, seeded, yellowish green fruit with citrusy flavor; not a true muscat; good for fresh eating, juice, jelly; American hybrid
'Himrod'	US, MS; USDA 6-7	Very early	Cane	Firm, seedless white grape with spicy flavor; for fresh eating, raisins; very vigorous; well suited to arbors
'Interlaken'	US, MS; USDA 6-7	Very early	Cane or Spur	Like 'Himrod' but sweeter, less vigorous, and more productive; ripens a week earlier
'Lakemount'	US, MS; USDA 6-7	Early midseason	Cane or Spur	Seedless white table grape with higher acid content than 'Himrod' or 'Interlaken'; keeps well in cold storage
'Niagara'	US, MS, LS; USDA 6-8	Midseason	Cane	Seedless green-to-pale yellow grape; good for juice, jelly, fresh eating; vigorous and productive
'Reliance'	US, MS, LS; USDA 6-8	Early midseason	Spur	Seedless red grape for fresh eating, juice; may be ready to eat before it colors up; reliably heavy bearer, very cold hardy; resistant to black rot, downy mildew
'Steuben'	US, MS; USDA 6-7	Midseason	Cane	Seeded blue grape with spicy flavor for fresh eating, juice; very productive; good resistance to black rot, downy mildew
'Suwanee'	MS, LS, CS; USDA 7-9	Early	Cane	Seeded white grape developed by the University of Florida; good-flavored fruit for fresh eating and wine; resistant to Pierce's disease; American hybrid
'Swenson Red'	US, MS; USDA 6-7	Early	Spur	Red or reddish blue grape with excellent strawberrylike flavor, small seeds; clusters may have distinctive dumbbell shape; vines may take a few years to develop full vigor and yield
'Vanessa'	US, MS; USDA 6-7	Early	Cane	Seedless red grape stands up to rain; vines tend to have excess vigor
'Venus'	US, MS, LS; USDA 6-8	Early	Cane	Large, seedless blue grape; flavor can be very good, aromatic; for fresh eating, juice, jelly; good fall leaf color; resistant to black rot, downy mildew
EUROPEAN SELECTIONS				
'Centennial'	US, MS, LS; USDA 6-8	Late midseason	Cane	Big clusters of elongated, firm white grapes for fresh eating, raisins; among the largest of the seedless grapes
'Flame'	US, MS, LS, CS; USDA 6-8	Early	Cane	Seedless red grape with excellent flavor; takes heat and humidity well

VARIETY	ZONES	SEASON	PRUNING METHODS	COMMENTS
'Thompson Seedless'	US, MS, LS; USDA 6-8	Late midseason	Cane	Big bunches of small, sweet, mild-flavored, greenish amber grapes for fresh eating, raisins, wine; the most common type sold in grocery stores

MUSCADINE SELECTIONS

VARIETY	ZONES	SEASON	PRUNING METHODS	COMMENTS
'Alachua'	MS, LS, CS; USDA 7-9	Early to midseason	Spur	Small, deep purple table or juice grape with very good flavor; self-fertile
'Black Beauty'	MS, LS, CS; USDA 7-9	Midseason to late	Spur	Large purple grape with excellent flavor; great for fresh eating; very vigorous and productive
'Carlos'	MS, LS, CS; USDA 7-9	Midseason	Spur	Large clusters of small bronze fruit; heavy producer; best bronze muscadine for making wine; self-fertile
'Cowart'	MS, LS, CS; USDA 7-9	Early to midseason	Spur	Large blue-black table and juice grape; self-fertile
'Fry'	MS, LS, CS; USDA 7-9	Midseason to late	Spur	Very large clusters of big bronze fruit with excellent flavor; needs pollenizer; quite vigorous and productive, but susceptible to black rot; best for fresh eating; developed in Georgia
'Golden Isles'	MS, LS, CS; USDA 7-9	Midseason	Spur	Bronze grape for table, wine, juice; self-fertile
'Higgins'	MS, LS, CS; USDA 7-9	Midseason to late	Spur	Medium to large clusters of huge pinkish to reddish bronze fruit; needs pollenizer; cold hardy and very productive; good for fresh eating but poor for wine; great type for roadside sales; developed by the Georgia Experiment Station
'Hunt'	MS, LS, CS; USDA 7-9	Early to midseason	Spur	Large bunches of medium to large black fruit; good yield; sweet and flavorful; ripens uniformly; needs pollenizer; all-purpose grape for wine, juice, jelly
'Ison'	MS, LS, CS; USDA 7-9	Early midseason	Spur	Medium to large purple fruit with excellent flavor; good for fresh eating; self-fertile; good pollenizer; productive
'Jumbo'	MS, LS, CS; USDA 7-9	Midseason to late	Spur	Huge black fruit; vigorous vines; heavy producer; needs pollenizer
'Magnolia'	LS, CS; USDA 8-9	Midseason	Spur	Medium clusters of bronzy, medium to large, sweet fruit; excellent quality; self-fertile; vigorous, prolific grower; superb for wine; does better in Lower South
'Noble'	MS, LS, CS; USDA 7-9	Early to midseason	Spur	Large clusters of small to medium, bluish black fruit of good quality; good disease resistance; quite vigorous and productive; self-fertile; excellent for wine, juice, and jelly; selection developed in North Carolina
'Scuppernong'	MS, LS, CS; USDA 7-9	Midseason	Spur	The classic muscadine, and the one most Southerners know and love; bronze, speckled grape with distinctive aroma and flavor; needs pollenizer; good for fresh eating, wine
'Southland'	MS, LS, CS; USDA 7-9	Midseason	Spur	Medium to large, sweet purple-black fruit; good quality; self-fertile; pest and disease resistant; excellent for fresh eating, jams, jellies; better in Lower and Coastal South
'Sterling'	MS, LS, CS; USDA 7-9	Midseason	Spur	Medium-size bronze fruit; excellent for juice
'Supreme'	MS, LS, CS; USDA 7-9	Midseason to late	Spur	Large purple grape with excellent flavor; good for fresh eating; productive
'Triumph'	MS, LS, CS; USDA 7-9	Early midseason	Spur	Reliably heavy crop of bronze to nearly yellow grapes with pineapple flavor; thin-skinned; for juice, fresh eating, wine; self-fertile; good pollenizer for other selections
'Welder'	MS, LS, CS; USDA 7-9	Midseason	Spur	Medium-size bronze fruit; great quality; vigorous and productive; good for fresh eating and jelly; superb for wine; tolerates partial shade; good for garden and commercial plantings; disease resistant; self-fertile; excellent pollinizer

HOW TO GROW GRAPES

SOIL Deep, fertile, well-drained, sandy loam is ideal, but plants adapt to many soil types.

AIR CIRCULATION Free movement of air around plants is important. If you're on hilly terrain, it's better to plant on a slope than in a low-lying basin, where trapped air increases danger from frost and disease.

PRUNING High-quality crop depends on initial training and dormant-season pruning (see page 335).

HARVESTING Cut bunches from vines of American and European grapes in late summer or fall, when grapes are sweet and fully colored. Muscadines are harvested by removing individual ripe fruit from clusters or harvesting entire clusters with some selections.

TOP: Assorted muscadines; BOTTOM: 'Scuppernong'; 'Lakemont'

GRAPTOPHYL-LUM PICTUM
CARICATURE PLANT
Acanthaceae
Evergreen shrub

TS; OR INDOORS

LIGHT SHADE; BRIGHT FILTERED LIGHT

REGULAR WATER

Graptophyllum pictum

This frost-tender native of New Guinea is prized for its fancy marbled foliage. Reaching 6–8 ft. tall and wide, it features handsome, glossy, deep green leaves about 6 in. long and half as broad. Distinctive cream-colored marbling decorates each leaf along the midrib. In summer, purplish red, tubular, 1½-in.-long flowers are borne in short clusters. 'Alba Variegata' has leaves heavily and irregularly edged with cream. "Aurea Marginada' is similar but with golden edges. 'Chocolate' offers leaves mottled burgundy-green and bronze, with pinkish cream marbling and deep pink midribs. 'El Dorado' has medium green leaves with wide, irregular margins of golden yellows. 'Tricolor' has bright green leaves with white marbling and pink midribs. In frostless locations, may be used as a landscape plant in light shade; the broad, colorful leaves make a good contrast to ferns.

CARE

Plant in well-drained soil containing lots of organic matter. Elsewhere, grow in pots that are brought indoors to a bright location during late fall and winter, or grow as houseplants year-round. Keep soil evenly moist and make sure potting mix drains well. Prune lightly or pinch out growing tips to promote bushy growth. Propagate by cuttings. Susceptible to nematodes in Florida.

GREVILLEA
Proteaceae
Evergreen shrubs and trees

ZONES VARY BY SPECIES

EXPOSURE NEEDS VARY BY SPECIES

WATER NEEDS VARY BY SPECIES

Grevillea 'Noelii'

Native to Australia. Many species and hybrids. Plants vary in size and appearance but generally have fine-textured foliage and long, slender, curved flowers, usually in dense clusters. Provide good drainage. Like other members of the protea family, grevilleas are sensitive to high levels of phosphorus in the soil, so feed lightly and avoid fertilizers with high phosphorus content. Intolerant of salt. Seldom browsed by deer.

G. banksii. BANKS GREVILLEA. Shrub or small tree. Zone TS; USDA 10-11. Often sold as *G. banksii forsteri*. To 9–20 ft. tall and 9–12 ft. wide. Leaves 4–10 in. long, deeply cut into narrow lobes. Erect, 3- to 6-in.-long clusters of dark red flowers appear sporadically all year; bloom is heaviest in late spring. Showy used singly against a high wall, near an entryway, or grouped with other big shrubs. Freezes at 24°F but tolerates wind. Full sun. Little to regular water.

G. 'Canberra Gem'. Shrub. Zone LS, CS, TS; USDA 8-11. Open, graceful growth to 8 ft. tall, 12 ft.

wide. Bright green, needlelike, 1-in. leaves. Clusters of red flowers in spring (and intermittently at other times). Full sun or partial shade. Moderate water.

G. 'Noellii'. Shrub. Zones, LS, CS, TS; USDA 8-11. To 4 ft. tall, 4–5 ft. wide. Densely clad with narrow, inch-long, glossy medium green leaves. Clusters of pink-and-white flowers bloom in spring. Takes light shearing well; good as formal or informal hedge. Full sun or partial shade. Moderate water.

G. robusta. SILK OAK. Tree. Zones CS, TS; USDA 9-11. Fast growing to 75 ft. (rarely to 100 ft.) tall. Symmetrical, pyramidal when young. Old trees are broad topped (40–50 ft. wide), usually with a few heavy horizontal limbs; picturesque against skyline but too large for most home gardens. Fernlike leaves are golden green to deep green above, silvery beneath. Heavy leaf fall in spring, sporadic leaf drop throughout the rest of year. Large clusters of bright golden orange flowers in early spring. Wood is brittle, easily damaged in high wind. Young trees are damaged at 24°F; older ones are hardy to 16°F. Use for quick, tall screen, or clip as tall hedge. Full sun. Grows in poor, heavy soils if not overwatered; can take regular water in fast-draining soils.

G. rosmariniifolia. ROSE-MARY GREVILLEA. Shrub. Zones LS, CS, TS; USDA 8-11. To 6 ft. tall, nearly as broad. Narrow, 1½-in.-long leaves are dark green on top, silvery beneath; look a bit like those of rosemary (*Rosmarinus*). Red-and-cream flower clusters (rarely pink or white) in fall and winter; scattered bloom in other seasons. Use as clipped or informal hedge in dryish places. Impervious to heat and aridity. A dwarf form, 3 ft. high and 6 ft. wide, bears pink-and-cream flowers in waves throughout the year, most heavily in spring and fall. 'Scarlet Sprite', another dwarf, is similar but bears blooms in bright red and cream. Full sun or partial shade. Little water.

GUAVA
Myrtaceae
Evergreen shrubs or trees

🗡 **ZONES VARY BY SPECIES**

☼ ◑ **FULL SUN OR PARTIAL SHADE**

💧 **REGULAR WATER**

Common guava

Native to tropical America, guavas (botanical name *Psidium*) are prized for their tasty fruit. They are resilient plants, easy to grow along the Gulf Coast and in South Texas and Florida; in fact, they have escaped cultivation and become invasive in some areas of Florida. (For pineapple guava, see *Feijoa*.)

Common or tropical guava. Zone TS; USDA 10-11. Native to southern Mexico and Central America; known botanically as *P. guajava*. Grows into a small tree to 20 ft. tall, with branches close to the ground and a spreading crown to 20 ft. wide. Smooth, reddish brown or mottled green bark peels off in flakes. Dull green, leathery, prominently veined, oblong leaves are 3–7 in. long, 1–2 in. wide. Lightly fragrant white flowers to 1 in. across are borne singly or in clusters; heaviest bloom comes in spring, but flowers appear year-round in southern parts of Florida and Texas. Blossoms quickly shed petals, leaving tufts of white stamens tipped with pale yellow anthers.

Fruit generally ripens in summer and fall, but some selections ripen fruit nearly year-round. Each guava weighs up to a pound and may be round, oval, or pear-shaped. Skin is usually yellow; flesh may be white, yellow, pink, or red and often contains small seeds (fully edible in most selections). Fruit is rich in potassium, vitamin A, and vitamin C—in fact, the fruit of some selections has five times the vitamin C of an orange. Trees are self-fruitful but bear more heavily if cross-pollinated with another selection. Fruit ripens better on the tree but can be picked green and ripened at room temperature; when ready to eat, it emits a sweet, pungent odor and is soft to the touch.

Recommended selections include these five:

'Patillo'. Medium to large, round fruit. Yellow skin and medium pink flesh with small seeds. Agreeable flavor good for cooking.

'Red Indian'. Large, round fruit. Yellow skin with pink blush; sweet red flesh, high in sugar and vitamin C.

'Ruby x Supreme'. 'Homestead'. Hybrid with small to medium-size, roundish fruit. Greenish yellow skin, pinkish orange flesh. Sweet, delicious flavor. Particularly high in vitamin C.

'Sweet White Indonesian'. Large, round fruit with pale yellow skin and juicy, sweet, delicious white flesh. Very productive.

'White Seedless'. Small to medium-size, roundish fruit. Seedless white flesh with excellent flavor.

Common guava tolerates most soils but grows best in those with a pH between 5 and 7. Withstands temporary flooding and seasonal drought, but not salt. Responds well to fertilizer: Feed monthly during the growing season with 8-4-8 fertilizer, following package directions. For good fruit production in areas with limestone soils, applications of iron chelate or iron sulfate may be necessary. Common pests in Florida include nematode, guava whitefly, Caribbean fruit fly, and guava moth. Consult your local Cooperative Extension Office for best methods of control. Young trees may be killed by frost, but older trees are hardy to about 29°F; if frozen to the ground, they usually resprout and bear fruit within 2 years.

Strawberry guava. Zones CS, TS; USDA 9-11. From Brazil; known botanically as *P. cattleianum* (*P. littorale*). Large shrub or small tree to 15 ft. tall and wide, with smooth, attractive reddish to golden brown bark. Oval, shiny, dark green leaves are 2–4 in. long and 1–2 in. wide. Solitary, sweetly fragrant white flowers to 1 in. across appear in spring; these are followed in summer by edible purple or yellow fruit about the size and shape of a golf ball. Flesh is white, with a sweet-tart, resinous flavor. Strawberry guava has become a serious pest in Florida because it reproduces freely by seeds and root suckers and tolerates a wide range of growing conditions. More cold hardy than common guava.

GYMNOCLADUS DIOICA
KENTUCKY COFFEE TREE
Caesalpiniaceae
Deciduous tree

🗡 **US, MS, LS; USDA 6-9**

☼ **FULL SUN**

💧 **REGULAR WATER**

☣ **LEAVES, SEEDS, AND PODS ARE POISONOUS**

Gymnocladus dioica

Native to eastern U.S. Grows very fast as a sapling but slows once it hits 8–10 ft. Give it plenty of room, since it will ultimately reach 60–100 ft. tall and 45–50 ft. wide. Provides year-round interest, featuring attractive foliage as well as striking branch structure. Leaves are 1½–3 ft. long, divided into many 1- to 3-in. leaflets; they are pinkish when emerging late in spring, deep bluish green by summer. In leaf, the tree casts light shade. Fall color usually not effective, but foliage sometimes turns bright yellow. The relatively few, heavy, contorted branches and stout twigs make the bare tree picturesque in winter.

Male and female plants are separate. Narrow, creamy to greenish white flower panicles at ends of branches in spring are up to 1 ft. long (and fragrant) on female trees, to 4 in. long on males. Blossoms on female trees are followed by flat, 6- to 10-in.-long, reddish brown pods containing hard black seeds. Pods persist through winter. Early settlers roasted the seeds to make a coffee substitute, hence the tree's common name. (Roasting neutralizes the seeds' toxicity.) Grows best in moist, rich, deep soil but adapts to poor soil, drought, city conditions. Can take much heat and cold. Needs minimal pruning.

Three male—and therefore seedless—kinds are sometimes offered at garden centers; all have potential for use as street trees. 'Espresso' grows to 50 ft. tall, 30 ft. wide, has an attractive spreading form and vase shape. 'Prairie Titan' may reach 60–70 ft. tall, 30–40 ft wide; it has particularly good-looking foliage. 'J.C. McDaniel' ('Stately Manor') grows in a narrow and upright form, to 50 ft. tall and only 20 ft. wide; good street tree.

GYNURA
VELVET PLANT
Asteraceae
Evergreen perennials or small shrubs

- 🖊 **ZONES VARY BY SPECIES; OR INDOORS OR ANNUALS**
- ☼ ☼ **EXPOSURE NEEDS VARY BY SPECIES; BRIGHT LIGHT**
- 💧 **REGULAR WATER**

Gynura aurantiaca

These natives of the Old World tropics offer strikingly colorful foliage. Usually grown as houseplants, they also make interesting additions to borders. Thrive in fertile, well-drained soil outdoors.

G. aurantiaca. PURPLE VELVET PLANT. CS, TS; USDA 9-11. Native to Indonesia. Upright in youth, clambering when mature. Grows 4–5 ft. tall in south Florida but is shorter elsewhere; may spread twice as wide as tall. Deeply toothed leaves, to 8 in. long and 4 in. wide, are heavily cloaked with velvety purple hairs, as are the stems. Leaves emerge bright purple, then mature to deep green. Sometimes blooms in late summer, bearing ¾-in., yellowish orange flowers that take on purple tones with age. 'Purple Passion' has smaller leaves and is distinctly trailing; excellent for use in hanging baskets.

Outdoors, purple velvet plant grows best in light shade. Indoors, give it bright light from a south- or west-facing window. Let the soil surface become dry to the touch before watering; then water thoroughly. Feed every other week in spring and summer and monthly in fall and winter with a general-purpose liquid houseplant fertilizer. Watch out for mealybugs and dispatch them by dabbing them with a cotton swab dipped in alcohol. Propagate by stem cuttings taken in spring and summer. Cut back old, woody plants to produce fresh, colorful foliage.

G. bicolor. OKINAWAY SPINACH. LS, CS, TS; USDA 8-11. Native to the Moluccas in east Indonesia. Forms a leafy mass to 1–2 ft. tall, 2–3 ft. wide. Coarse, deeply toothed, nearly hairless leaves reach 6 in. long and half as wide; they are chocolate-purple with prominent green veins on their upper surface, rich purple beneath. Edible leaves are popular in Taiwan. Showy orange-yellow blossoms to ½ in. across are borne on slender, erect stems; they attract butterflies and emit a sweet, pungent odor that some people do not enjoy. Good in combination with finer-textured plants. Outdoors, plant in full sun or partial shade. Indoor culture is same as for *G. aurantiaca*.

GYPSOPHILA
Caryophyllaceae
Annuals and perennials

- 🖊 **ZONES VARY BY SPECIES**
- ☼ **FULL SUN**
- 💧 **MODERATE WATER**

Gypsophila paniculata

Slender-stemmed, much-branched plants are upright or spreading, ranging from 3 in. to 4 ft. tall. Bloom profusely in summer, covering themselves in clusters of tiny single or double flowers in white, pink, or rose. Leaves (sparse when plants are in bloom) are typically blue green. Use for airy look in borders and bouquets and for contrast with large-flowered, coarse-textured plants. Dwarf kinds are ideal for rock gardens, for trailing from pockets in walls or over tops of dry rock walls.

G. cerastioides. Perennial. Zones US, MS, LS; USDA 6-8. Native to the Himalayas. Gray leaves may be spoon shaped or pointed-oval; they form a mat to 3 in. high and twice as broad. Clustered flowers, ½ in. across, vary from pink-veined white to pure pink. Use in rock gardens or between stepping stones.

G. elegans. Annual. Zones US, MS, LS, CS, TS; USDA 6-11. Native to Asia Minor, the Caucasus, southern Ukraine. Upright grower to 1½ ft. high and wide. Lance-shaped, rather fleshy leaves to 3 in. long. Profuse single white flowers to ½ in. wide or wider; pink and rose forms are also available. Plants live only 5 to 6 weeks; for continuous bloom, sow seed in open ground every 3 to 4 weeks from late spring into summer. Sow in fall and winter in the Tropical South. Excellent cut flower.

G. paniculata. BABY'S BREATH. Perennial. Zones US, MS, LS, CS; USDA 6-9. Native to central Asia, central and eastern Europe. This is the classic filler in bouquets. To 3 ft. or taller and as broad. Slender, sharp-pointed leaves 2½–4 in. long. Single, very tiny white flowers (about 1⁄16 in. across), hundreds in a spray. 'Bristol Fairy' is an improved, more billowy form to 4 ft. high, covered with double blossoms ¼ in. wide. Florists' favorite is 'Perfekta' ('Perfecta'), which bears even larger flowers (to about ½ in. wide). Dwarf, double-flowered forms include white-blossomed 'Compacta Plena', 1½ ft. high, and pink 'Viette's Dwarf', 12–15 in. high.

CARE

Add lime to strongly acid soils before planting. Perennial kinds are not always easy to transplant (especially *G. paniculata*, which has deep, carrot-like roots). If possible, do not disturb them often. Protect roots from gophers; protect tender new growth from snails and slugs. To encourage repeat bloom on perennial sorts, cut back flowering stems before seed clusters form. Perennial species are usually short lived in the Coastal and Tropical South; treat as annuals there.

FOR USE IN DRIED ARRANGEMENTS, HANG BABY'S BREATH IN A COOL, DARK, AIRY PLACE FOR ABOUT A WEEK.

H

HABRANTHUS

RAIN LILY
Amaryllidaceae
Perennials from bulbs

- ✓ **MS, LS, CS, TS; USDA 7-11, OR GROW IN POTS**
- ☼ ◑ **FULL SUN OR LIGHT SHADE**
- ● **REGULAR WATER DURING GROWTH AND BLOOM**

Habranthus tubispathus texanus

Native from Texas to Argentina, these bulbous plants sprout and bloom almost immediately following a summer rain (thus their common name). Their trumpet- to funnel-shaped blossoms closely resemble those of their relatives, *Zephyranthes*. Plant bulbs in spring or summer in well-drained soil, spacing them 3 in. apart, with tips at soil level. Plant in sweeps for best effect. Good plants for the front of borders, in rock gardens, or in naturalized areas. In areas where ground freezes in winter, grow in pots. Best with winter moisture and dry summers with occasional downpours.

H. brachyandrus. Blooms from early summer to fall. Lavender-pink, 3-in.-long flowers with shades of blackish purple at petal bases are borne one per stem.

H. x floryi. Hybrid between *H. brachyandrus* and *H. robustus.* 'Purple Base' is the selection usually offered; it has blue-green foliage and 2- to 3-in.-long, rosy pink flowers with crimson-purple

throats atop 15-in. stems. Blooms intermittently all summer.

H. robustus. Blooms midsummer to fall. Flowers— sometimes borne two to each 9-in. stem—are 3 in. long, light pink with green throats and deeper pink veining. 'Russell Manning' is an especially floriferous, large-flowered selection that multiplies quickly.

H. tubispathus (*H. andersonii*). Summer bloomer with 1½-in.-long flowers in yellow veined with red. Stems and leaves about 6 in. high. 'Cupreus' is coppery orange; *H. t. texanus*, known as Texas copper lily, has bronzy yellow flowers.

HAKONECHLOA MACRA

JAPANESE FOREST GRASS, HAKONE GRASS
Poaceae
Perennial grass

- ✓ **US, MS; USDA 6-7**
- ◑ ● **PARTIAL TO FULL SHADE**
- ● **REGULAR WATER**

Hakonechloa macra 'Aureola'

This choice perennial from Japan is one of the few ornamental grasses that thrive in shade. Clumps of narrow, gracefully arching leaves grow 1–3 ft. tall; they spread somewhat wider by underground runners but advance slowly and are not invasive. Delicate sprays of flowers among the leaves in mid- to late summer are attractive but not showy. Whole plant turns an attractive buff color in winter. Good candidate for rock gardens, patio containers. The species has solid green leaves that turn coppery orange in fall, but most gardeners plant types with

variegated leaves to bring summer color to shade gardens. Try them in combination with evergreens with dark green foliage, such as rhododendron, camellia, Japanese black pine (*Pinus thunbergii*), or green-leafed Japanese aucuba. Plant in spring in rich, moist, well-drained soil. Does not like drought or root competition. Deer resistant.

'Albovariegata' ('Albo Striata'). To 3 ft. high, with leaves striped lengthwise in green and white.

'All Gold'. Forms a 1½ ft.-high mound of bright golden leaves.

'Aureola'. Most popular selection. To 1½ ft. high. Green leaves have longitudinal yellow stripes; in deep shade, the yellow turns to chartreuse. Foliage is sometimes suffused with pink in cool weather. Looks nice next to blue-leafed hostas.

'Nicolas'. A green-leafed dwarf selection (just 10 in. high) selected for its dependable fall color. Leaves turn brilliant red, orange, and chartreuse when weather cools. Great in containers.

HALESIA

SILVER BELL
Styracaceae
Deciduous trees

- ✓ **US, MS, LS; USDA 6-8, EXCEPT AS NOTED**
- ☼ ◑ **FULL SUN OR PARTIAL SHADE**
- ● **REGULAR WATER**

Halesia diptera

These elegant and underappreciated trees are native to the Southeast. Bell-shaped white flowers appear in spring, usually just before the leaves emerge. Medium green foliage turns yellow in fall. Pretty in woodland

gardens. Good substitute for dogwood (*Cornus*) where dogwoods will not grow. Grow best in rich, well-drained, acid soil. Buy container-grown plants, as balled-and-burlapped ones do not transplant easily.

H. carolina (*H. tetraptera*). CAROLINA SILVER BELL. Moderate growth to 30–40 ft. tall, 20–35 ft. wide. Clusters of snow white, ½-in. flowers in midspring hang along length of graceful branches. Oval, finely toothed, 2- to 5-in.-long leaves. Four-winged brown fruit hangs on almost all winter. Train to a single trunk when young, or it will grow as a large shrub. Flowers show off to best advantage when you can look up into tree. 'James Laubach' has leaves heavily splashed in gold.

Plants in the Vestita Group, sometimes offered as *H. c. vestita*, top out at about 30 ft. tall and 20 ft. wide, with larger flowers than those of the species. 'Rosea' has light pink flowers.

H. diptera. TWO-WINGED SILVER BELL. Zones US, MS, LS, CS; USDA 6-9. To 20–30 ft. tall and wide, usually multitrunked. Oval leaves, pointed at the tip. Flowers resemble that of *H. carolina*, but they are more deeply lobed and bloom a week or two later, just after leaves emerge. Fruit is similar to that of *H. carolina* but has two rather than four wings. *H. d. magniflora*, the showiest silver bell, has larger flowers and is a more profuse bloomer.

H. monticola. MOUNTAIN SILVER BELL. Similar to and sometimes listed as *H. carolina.* Monticola Group. Plants are larger, eventually to 60–80 ft. tall and at least half as wide. Leaves are also bigger (3–6 in. long), but tree casts only moderate shade. Flowers and fruit are also somewhat larger.

HAMAMELIS

WITCH HAZEL

Hamamelidaceae

Deciduous shrubs or trees

🌡 **US, MS, LS; USDA 6-8, EXCEPT AS NOTED**

☀ ◐ **FULL SUN OR PARTIAL SHADE**

💧 **REGULAR WATER**

Hamamelis mollis

Medium-size to large shrubs, sometimes treelike, usually spreading with angular or zigzag branches. Valued for bright fall foliage and nodding clusters of interesting yellow to red blooms that typically appear in winter. Flowers consist of many narrow, crumpled petals and are said to resemble shredded coconut, eyelashes, or spiders. Most witch hazels are fragrant and bloom over a long period. They appreciate rich, organic soil. Prune only to guide growth, remove suckers, or obtain flowering stems for scented bouquets. In some types, old leaves hang on into winter, obscuring flowers; it may be necessary to strip them by hand.

H. x intermedia. Group of winter-blooming hybrids between *H. mollis* and *H. japonica*. Big shrubs (12–15 ft. high and wide). Often grafted; remove any growth originating from below graft. The following selections are among the best.

'Angelly'. Pale yellow flowers; yellow fall foliage.

'Aphrodite'. Orange-yellow flowers; leaves turn red in fall.

'Arnold Promise'. The best yellow-flowered selection, with bright yellow blossoms. Yellow, orange, and red fall foliage.

'Barmstedt Gold'. Golden yellow flowers; leaves turn yellow in autumn.

'Birgit'. Dark red flowers; yellow, orange, and red fall foliage.

'Carmine Red'. Light red flowers; red-orange fall foliage.

'Diane'. Dark red flowers aging to orange-red. Red-purple fall foliage.

'Hiltingbury'. Coppery red flowers; orange-yellow fall color.

'Jelena' ('Copper Beauty', 'Orange Beauty'). Coppery orange flowers. Fall foliage in orange, red, and scarlet.

'Magic Fire' ('Feuerzauber', 'Fire Charm'). Flowers in coppery orange blended with red. Fiery red fall foliage.

'Moonlight'. Pale yellow blooms marked red at base; yellow fall foliage.

'Pallida'. Luminous light yellow blossoms; yellow fall foliage.

'Primavera'. Broad-petaled, light yellow flowers. Yellow-orange autumn foliage.

'Ruby Glow'. Coppery red flowers; bright red fall foliage.

'Sunburst'. Heavy clusters of radiant yellow, unscented flowers. Yellow fall foliage.

H. japonica. JAPANESE WITCH HAZEL. From Japan. Much like *H. x intermedia*, though perhaps somewhat more erect and treelike (to 12–20 ft. tall and broad). Broadly oval, medium to dark green leaves are 2–4 in. long. Fairly small, lightly scented yellow flowers in late winter or earliest spring. Chief draw is fall foliage in shades of red, purple, and yellow. *H. j. flavopurpurascens* has yellow-orange flowers, purple at the base, and reddish yellow fall foliage. For the plant sometimes offered as *H. j.* 'Superba', see *H. mollis* 'Rochester'.

H. mollis. CHINESE WITCH HAZEL. From China. Moderately slow-growing shrub to 8–10 ft. tall and wide (may reach twice that size after many years). Roundish, 3½- to 6-in.-long leaves are dark green and rough above, gray and felted beneath, turning a good pure yellow in fall. Sweetly fragrant, 1½-in.-wide, rich golden yellow flowers with red-brown sepals bloom on bare stems in winter. Flowering branches excellent for cutting. Selections include 'Coombe Wood', a very heavy bloomer with especially fine fragrance, 'Early Bright', earliest to bloom, and 'Wisley Supreme', with large, pale yellow blooms that are red at the base. 'Rochester' (sometimes listed as *H. japonica* 'Superba') is a probable hybrid with *H. vernalis*; it offers an early show of coppery orange flowers with a strong spicy scent.

H. vernalis. OZARK WITCH HAZEL. Native to central and southern U.S. Multistemmed shrub 6–10 ft. tall, spreading wider. Small, fragrant yellow to orange flowers from winter to spring. Medium to dark green, 2- to 5-in.-long leaves turn bright yellow in fall and hold for several weeks in favorable weather. 'Autumn Embers' has orange blossoms and brilliant red-purple fall foliage. 'Lombarts' Weeping' is a 5- to 6-ft. tree with drooping branches. 'Sandra' has unremarkable yellow spring flowers but bears reddish purple new growth and brilliant red fall foliage.

H. virginiana. COMMON WITCH HAZEL. Zones US, MS, LS, CS; USDA 6-9. Native to eastern North America. Sometimes reaches 25 ft. tall but usually grows 10–15 ft. high and wide. Open, spreading, rather straggling habit. Moderately slow growing. Bark is the source of the liniment witch hazel. Roundish leaves are similar to those of *H. mollis*, but they are

A-WITCHING WE WILL GO

Witchhazels get their common name for their pliant stems, which were used in colonial times as 'witching rods' or 'divining rods' to find water.

ABOVE: Hamamelis 'x intermedia 'Diane'

not gray and felted beneath; turn yellow to orange in fall. Small, fragrant, golden yellow blossoms appear in fall but tend to be lost in colored foliage. 'Green Thumb' has new leaves heavily marked with greenish yellow. 'Harvest Moon' blooms after leaves have fallen; the large flowers are closely packed on bare stems. 'Little Suzie' is compact at just 4 ft. high and wide; excellent in a large container or mixed border.

HAMELIA PATENS

FIREBUSH
Rubiaceae
Evergreen shrub or tree

- CS, TS; USDA 9-11
- FULL SUN
- REGULAR TO AMPLE WATER

Hamelia patens

From southern Florida south to Central and South America. This relative of gardenia and coffee grows 9–10 ft. tall (possibly much taller), 5–6 ft. wide, with whorls of oval, gray-green, 6-in. leaves. Leafstalks and flower stems are red. Clusters of ¾-in., tubular, orange to bright red blooms form at branch tips all summer long; thanks to their shape and color, plant is also known as firecracker shrub. Blooms attract butterflies and hummingbirds. Flowers are followed by small, dark red, purple, or black fruit much relished by birds. Likes lots of moisture but needs good drainage. Tolerant of salt, lime. 'Calusa' is dense and uniform, with darker red leaves and brighter red-orange flowers than the species.

HATIORA GAERTNERI

EASTER CACTUS
Cactaceae
Cactus

- TS; OR HOUSEPLANT
- PARTIAL SHADE; BRIGHT LIGHT
- REGULAR WATER

Hatiora gaertneri

Native to Brazil. For culture and description, see *Schlumbergera*. Much like *S. buckleyi* but initially more upright, then semipendent to 6 in. high, 1 ft. wide (*S. buckleyi* is completely pendent). Leaves have hair-like bristles on the tips. Blooms in spring, often again in late summer or early fall. There are many selections, with blossoms in various shades of white, pink and red. Good houseplant; bring outdoors during warm times of year, if desired. Suffers in hot sun. Keep plants cool and moist when in bloom to extend flowering season. 'Sirus' has white flowers. Formerly known as *Rhipsalidopsis gaertneri*.

HAWORTHIA

Asphodelaceae
Succulent perennials

- ZONES TS; USDA 10-11; OR INDOORS
- PARTIAL SHADE; BRIGHT INDIRECT LIGHT
- LITTLE TO MODERATE WATER

Haworthia fasciata

Small, rosette-forming succulents from South Africa. Many types produce offsets to form dense, spreading colonies. Fleshy leaves may be slender and rough textured or pillowlike and smooth; some have small white bumps or ridges. Tiny flowers are held on long, whiplike stems from spring to late fall; these may be clipped off as they fade to keep plants tidy.

Haworthias are well suited to containers, and their small size and tolerance of low humidity make them good houseplants. In pots or in the ground, provide sandy, fast-draining soil that is allowed to dry out between waterings. Protect from frost and hot sun. Acclimate nursery plants to the garden gradually, or the leaves may sunburn. Numerous species and hybrids make these variable plants popular with collectors.

H. attenuata. Similar to *H. fasciata*, but inner leaf surface is dotted with white bumps.

H. cymbiformis. To 3 in. high, looking something like a small, chubby artichoke. Wedge-shaped leaves have light and dark green markings.

H. fasciata. ZEBRA PLANT. To 6 in. high. Rigid, dark green leaves up to 3 in. long are slender and triangular; each leaf is smooth on the inner surface and banded with raised white horizontal

ridges on the outside. Give just enough sun to make outer leaves blush red-orange.

HEDERA

IVY
Araliaceae
Evergreen vines

- ZONES VARY BY SPECIES
- SHADE IN LS, CS, TS; USDA 8-11
- MODERATE TO REGULAR WATER

Hedera helix 'Glacier'

Ivy is appreciated by some gardeners for its ability to cover quickly, reviled by others for its invasive tendencies. Spreads horizontally over the ground; also climbs on walls, fences, trellises. Sometimes a single planting does both: Wall ivy spreads to become a surrounding ground cover, or vice versa. Climbs almost any vertical surface by aerial rootlets—a factor to consider in planting against surfaces that must be painted. A chain-link fence planted with ivy soon becomes a wall of foliage. As a ground cover, it holds the soil, discouraging erosion and slippage on slopes. Roots grow deep and fill soil densely; branches root as they grow, further knitting soil.

Thick, leathery leaves are usually lobed. Mature plants will eventually develop stiff branches that bear round clusters of small greenish flowers followed by black berries. These branches have unlobed leaves; cuttings taken from them will also have unlobed leaves and will produce shrubby rather than vining plants. Such shrubs taken from variegated Algerian ivy (*H. algeriensis*

'Gloire de Marengo') are known by the name "ghost ivy". Plain green *H. helix* 'Arborescens' is another selection of this shrubby type.

Plant ivy in spring or fall. Standard spacing is 1½–2 ft. apart. Amend soil (to depth of 8–12 in. if possible) with organic matter such as ground bark or peat moss. Before planting, thoroughly moisten soil; also make sure transplants' roots are moist.

Most ivy ground covers should be trimmed around edges two or three times a year (use hedge shears or a sharp spade). Fence and wall plantings likewise need shearing or trimming two or three times a year. When ground cover builds up higher than you want, mow it with a rugged rotary power mower or cut it back with hedge shears. Do this in spring so ensuing growth will quickly cover bald look.

Many trees and shrubs can grow compatibly in ivy ground cover, but small, soft, or fragile plants will be smothered. Ivy ground covers can be a haven for slugs and snails and can also harbor rodents, especially if the ivy is never cut back.

H. algeriensis (*H. canariensis*). ALGERIAN IVY. Zones MS, LS, CS, TS; USDA 7-11. Shiny, rich green leaves 5–8 in. wide, with three to five shallow lobes. Leaves are more widely spaced along stems than those of *H. helix*. Coarse-looking plant; aggressive grower. 'Gloire de Marengo' ('Variegata') has dark leaves marbled with gray-green and irregularly margined in creamy white; it does not take extreme heat. 'Ravensholst' is vigorous, with dark green leaves sometimes tinged purple in winter.

H. colchica. PERSIAN IVY. Zones US, MS, LS, CS, TS; USDA 6-11. Oval to heart-shaped leaves are largest among all ivies: 3–7 in. wide, to 10 in. long. 'Dentata' has slightly toothed leaves; 'Dentata Variegata' is marbled with deep green, gray-green, and creamy white. 'Sulphur Heart' ('Paddy's Pride') has central gold variegation.

H. helix. ENGLISH IVY. Zones US, MS, LS, CS, TS; USDA 6-11. Not as vigorous as *H. algeriensis*, this ubiquitous species features three-to five-lobed leaves that are dull green with paler veins and reach 2–4 in. long and wide. Tremen-

dous genetic variation has given rise to a dizzying assortment of foliage shapes, sizes, and colors. Ivy fanciers classify the hundreds of selections according to leaf shape, and also by type if unusual. Leaf-shape categories are bird's foot (leaves have long, prominent main lobe), curly (undulated, frilled, or curly leaves), fan (broad leaves with small lobes of roughly equal size), heart-shaped, and ivy (traditional five-lobed leaves). Plants are also grouped as miniature (very small leaves), variegated, or arborescent (shrublike plants with unlobed leaves propagated from mature ivies). Oddity types have unusual growth patterns, odd leaf forms, or both.

English ivies have many uses besides their usual role as ground covers. They are excellent in pots and hanging baskets, trained into intricate patterns on walls, or grown on wire frames to create topiaries. Arborescent forms make superb additions to foundation plantings and shade gardens. Some arborescent ivies are short and mounding, others more upright. All are drought tolerant and carefree—good substitutes for euonymus and cherry laurel (*Prunus laurocerasus*). Resistant to damage by deer. Recommended selections include the following.

'Baltica' (*H. h. baltica*). Ivy type. Dark green leaves with whitish veins. Very cold hardy.

'California'. Curly type. Dense grower with dark green leaves.

'California Fan'. Fan type. Broad, light green leaves with frilly edges. Perhaps the most beautiful fan ivy.

'Conglomerata'. Oddity type. Upright grower with stiff stems and closely set, curly dark green leaves.

'Deltoidea' (*H. hibernica* 'Deltoidea'). Heart-shaped type. Dark green leaves. Also known by the name "sweetheart ivy".

'Fluffy Ruffles'. Curly type. Ruffly, nearly circular, medium green leaves resemble pompons.

'Glacier'. Ivy type, variegated. Leaves are patched in blue-green and gray-green and edged in white.

'Gold Dust'. Ivy type, variegated. Green leaves with bright gold specks and blotches.

'Goldheart' ('Oro di Bogliasco'). Heart-shaped type,

variegated. Irregular gold splash in center of dark green leaf.

'Manda's Crested'. Curly type. Light green leaves with long, curly lobes.

'Needlepoint'. Bird's-foot type. Slim, graceful, medium green leaves. Very popular.

'Ritterkreuz'. Bird's-foot type. Dark green, five-lobed leaves with lighter midrib.

'Shamrock'. Bird's-foot type, miniature. Dark green leaves with lighter veins have three nearly round lobes, with the outer two overlapping the middle one. Named for the Shamrock Hotel in Houston.

'Spetchley' ('Gnome'). Bird's-foot type, miniature. Leaves are only ¼–½ in. long, turn from dark green to bronze-purple in winter.

'Thorndale' ('Sub-Zero'). Ivy type. Large, dark green leaves with veins that turn light green to white in winter. Very cold hardy.

HEDYCHIUM
GINGER LILY
Zingiberaceae
Perennials

✄ ZONES VARY BY SPECIES

☼ ◐ FULL SUN OR LIGHT SHADE

💧 AMPLE WATER

Hedychium 'Kinkaku'

Native to India and tropical Asia, these old Southern favorites combine handsome foliage with showy, often deliciously fragrant flowers. Rich green, alternate leaves ascend stems growing from stout rhizomes. In late summer or early fall, blossoms in dense spikes open from cones of overlapping bracts at the ends of stalks. Plants are evergreen in the Tropical South, deciduous

elsewhere. Use them in borders or grow in containers. Southern specialty growers offer dozens of species and selections in heights from 2–9 ft., in colors ranging from white and cream through pink to red—and a host of yellow, orange, and salmon shades.

H. coccineum. RED GINGER LILY. Zones LS, CS, TS; USDA 8-11. To 6–9 ft. tall, with leaves to 20 in. long and 2 in. wide. Particularly showy, bearing orange-scarlet flowers with prominent red stamens on blossom spikes to 10 in. long. 'Disney' has bluish gray foliage and reddish stems and leaf undersides. 'Slim's Orange' is dwarf, to just 3 ft. tall.

H. coronarium. COMMON GINGER LILY, BUTTERFLY GINGER. Zones MS, LS, CS, TS; USDA 7-11. To 3–7 ft. high, with leaves 8–24 in. long and 2–5 in. wide. White flowers in 6- to 12-in.-long clusters are especially fragrant; good cut flowers.

H. flavum. GOLDEN BUTTERFLY GINGER. Zones LS, CS, TS; USDA 8-11. Old Southern favorite. To 5–7 ft. tall, with oblong leaves 4–20 in. long and 1–4 in. wide. Dense, 6-in. spikes of particularly fragrant, rich yellow-orange flowers with orange spots on the tips.

H. gardnerianum. KAHILI GINGER. Zones LS, CS, TS; USDA 8-11. To 8 ft. high, with leaves 8–18 in. long, 4–6 in. wide. Pure yellow flowers with dark orange stamens are borne in 1½-ft.-long spikes. 'Compactum' grows about 4 ft. tall.

H. greenii. Zones LS, CS, TS; USDA 8-11. To 3–5 ft. tall. Leaves 8–10 in. long, 2 in. wide are held on red stems; orange-red flowers in 5-in. spikes.

H. hasseltii. Zones LS, CS, TS; USDA 8-11. Small plant (to just 2 ft.), with broadly lance-shaped leaves to 1½ ft. long. Spidery-looking white flowers in slender spikes. Seedpods split to reveal pretty red seeds.

H. hybrids. Zones MS (lower half), LS, CS, TS; USDA 7-11. These hybrids feature excellent foliage and blossoms; all are worth trying. Leaves are typically large, lance shaped, and rich green.

'Anne Bishop'. Choice plant to 5 ft. tall, with large spikes of rich golden orange flowers that fade to golden yellow. Very fragrant.

'Daniel Weeks'. Among the longest-blooming ginger lilies, with stems to 4 ft. tall, carrying yellow flowers with a darker gold throat. Grows quickly, making a clump 3–4 ft. wide in its second year. Honeysuckle fragrance.

'Doctor Moy'. Handsome foliage speckled with white. Stalks to 3 ft. tall bear peachy orange blooms with a darker orange throat. Fragrant.

'Elizabeth'. Among the most impressive of the ginger lilies, with towering 9-ft.-tall stems carrying huge reddish orange flowers. Honeysuckle fragrance.

'Flaming Torch'. Robust grower to 7 ft. tall, with foot-long spikes of orange flowers; may bloom once in midsummer and again in fall.

'Golden Butterfly'. Stems 6 ft. tall are topped with bright orange flowers with red stamens.

'Kinkaku'. To 6 ft. tall, with large, pale peach flowers.

'Luna Moth'. Compact growth to 3–4 ft. tall, with large, fragrant, white flowers.

'Moy Giant'. To 7 ft. tall, featuring large clusters of pale yellow blossoms with a darker yellow throat. Very fragrant.

'Palani'. Strong grower to 8 ft. tall, with bright orange blooms.

'Pink V'. Grows 5–7 ft. tall, with lightly scented, creamy apricot flowers and red stamens. Citrus fragrance.

'Pradhan'. To 7 ft. Creamy white blooms with peach-tinged yellow throats and pink stamens.

'Tara'. To 6 ft. tall, with gray-green leaves and bottlebrush spikes of bright orange blooms.

'Vanilla Ice'. To 3 ft. tall, with bright green leaves heavily striped and speckled in creamy white. Flowers are peachy pink. Remove any larger, nonvariegated shoots promptly. Very fragrant.

CARE

Ginger lilies need moist, well-drained soil that contains lots of organic matter. Cutting back old stems after the flowers fade encourages new growth. Propagate by division in late fall or early spring.

HELENIUM AUTUMNALE

SNEEZEWEED, HELEN'S FLOWER
Asteraceae
Perennial

US, MS, LS, CS; USDA 6-9

FULL SUN

REGULAR WATER

ALL PARTS ARE POISONOUS IF INGESTED

Helenium 'Double Trouble'

This native perennial should be one of our more popular summer and fall flowers—but when folks hear the common name "sneezeweed" they assume that the plant causes hay fever and grows invasively. In fact, it does neither. Numerous leafy stems yield great sheaves of daisylike, typically dark-centered blossoms with yellow, orange, red, or coppery rays (folded back, in many types). Although sneezeweeds are usually listed as selections of *H. autumnale*, most are hybrids. Resist deer.

The following sneezeweeds are widely available. Tall types reach 4–5 ft. and need staking so are best suited to back of the border. Compact types reach about 3 ft. tall and look great in mixed borders. Both sizes combine well with ornamental grasses.

'Baudirektor Linne'. Tall. Velvety red blooms with a brown center.

'Butterpat'. Tall. Light yellow blossoms with a deeper yellow center.

'Coppelia'. Compact grower. Warm coppery orange petals surround a brown cone.

'Crimson Beauty'. Compact. Dusky deep red, brown-centered flowers.

'Cymbal Star' ('Zimbelstern'). Tall. Gold touched with bronze; brown centers.

'Double Trouble'. This compact grower is the first selection with double flowers. Frilly, bright yellow petals; gold center.

'Mardi Gras'. Compact. Yellow petals heavily splashed with red; deep brown centers.

Mariachi series. Compact, upright, and disease resistant. Available in orange-red ('Salsa'), orange with yellow center ('Fuego'), and deep red with ruffled edges ('Siesta').

'Moerheim Beauty'. Compact. Coppery red petals; brown centers.

'Sahin's Early Flowerer'. Compact. Bright orange-red petals are splashed with yellow, most heavily near the tips; centers are chocolate-brown. Heavy bloom over a long period.

'September Gold'. Compact. Bright yellow, brown-centered blooms.

'Sunball' ('Kugelsonne'). Tall. Lemon-yellow petals, chartreuse centers.

'Wyndley'. Compact grower. Butter-yellow petals around a yellow-brown central disk.

CARE

Trim off faded blooms to encourage more flowers; be sparing with fertilizer. Divide clumps every 2 or 3 years. Sneezeweeds tolerate drought but look better with regular moisture; they must have good drainage, though. Space plants 2 ft. apart. Taller types may need staking.

> ## DON'T SNEEZE AT SNEEZEWEED
>
> Despite its common name, sneezeweed is not responsible for sneezing or the sniffles.

HELIANTHUS

SUNFLOWER
Asteraceae
Annuals and perennials

ZONES VARY BY SPECIES

FULL SUN

REGULAR TO AMPLE WATER, EXCEPT AS NOTED

Helianthus annuus

These sturdy plants are grown for their familiar, colorful blooms; most are prime subjects for cut flowers. Plants are tough and widely adapted. Perennial kinds spread rapidly and may become invasive. Tall kinds are not for tidy gardens; may need staking. All bloom in summer and fall.

H. angustifolius. SWAMP SUNFLOWER. Perennial. Zones US, MS, LS, CS; USDA 6-9. Native to eastern U.S. Grows 5–12 ft. tall, 3–4 ft. wide. Bears narrow, 6-in. leaves and sheaves of bright yellow, 2- to 3-in. daisies with dark brown centers. Likes ample moisture but adapts to ordinary garden conditions. Sometimes confused with *H. salicifolius* but blooms 2 weeks later. Spreads rapidly by rhizomes. Very showy. 'Gold Lace' has the bright yellow flowers of the basic species, but it tops out at 5–6 ft. tall and spreads less vigorously. 'Mellow Yellow' has pale yellow blossoms.

H. annuus. COMMON SUNFLOWER. Annual. Zones US, MS, LS, CS, TS; USDA 6-11. The wild ancestor of today's familiar sunflowers is a coarse, hairy plant with 2- to 3-in.-wide flowers, native to much of the central U.S. and southward to Central America. It is the state flower of Kansas and the only plant native to the contiguous 48 states to have become an important agri-

SOW A LITTLE SUNSHINE

Let sunflowers bring a splash of vibrant color to your garden and table.

'Lemon Queen'

'Ring of Fire'

'Moulin Rouge'

'Van Gogh'

'Pro Cut BiColor'

'Pro Cut Orange'

'The Joker'

'Maya'

cultural commodity. It has been bred to produce giant plants as well as a host of smaller (but still significant) selections for garden decoration and cut flowers. For children, annual sunflowers are easy to grow and bring a sense of great accomplishment. Sow seeds in spring where plants are to grow. Large-flowered kinds need rich, moist soil. People eat the roasted seeds; birds enjoy the raw ones in fall and winter.

Best known among the giant forms are 'Mammoth Russian', 'Russian Giant', and 'Sunzilla'. They grow 10 ft. (possibly 15 ft.) tall and 2 ft. wide, typically producing a single huge head (sometimes over a foot across) consisting of a circle of short yellow rays with a brown central cushion of seeds. 'Kong' is similarly towering; 'Sunspot' carries 10-in.-wide flower heads on 2-ft.-high plants. 'Maya' produces multiple 4–5 in. blooms of golden yellow and lots of seeds for goldfinches.

Sunflowers for cutting come on compact, branching plants and bear 4- to 8-in.-wide blooms in a rich variety of colors. They fall into two basic categories: pollen-bearing types and pollenless ones. Kinds with pollen include 'Del Sol', early-blooming, yellow, 5 ft. tall; 'Indian Blanket', red with yellow tips, 4–5 ft. tall; 'Italian White', creamy yellow to near white, 5 ft. tall; 'Lemon Eclair', light yellow, 4–6 ft. tall; 'Moonshadow', pale yellow to cream, 4 ft. tall; 'Ring of Fire', petals dark red at base and golden yellow at tips, 5–6 ft. tall; and 'Soraya', 5–6 ft. tall, with heavy production of rich orange flowers. 'Teddy Bear', only 1½ ft. tall, has fully double, 6-in.-wide flowers that look like pompons.

Kinds without pollen, classified as *H.* x *hybridus*, have the advantage of not shedding on tabletops. Many have a branching growth pattern, producing several flowers on each plant. Look for Large Flowered Mix, yellow, red, and bronze, 6–10 ft. tall; 'Bright Bandolier', yellow-and-mahogany bicolor, 5–7 ft. tall, branching; 'Cinnamon Sun', cinnamon-bronze, 4–7 ft. tall; 'Moulin Rouge', burgundy, 5–6 ft., branching; 'Peach Passion', peachy yellow, 4 ft. tall, branching; Pro Cut series, 4 ft. tall, single stem; 'Prado Red', deep garnet, 3½–4 ft. tall, branching; 'Straw-

berry Blonde', red with yellow tips, 6–7 ft. tall, branching; 'The Joker', burgundy with yellow tips, 5–6 ft. tall, single stalk; 'Valentine', light yellow, 4–5 ft. tall, branching; and 'Velvet Queen', combination of bronze, burgundy, chestnut red, and mahogany, 6–8 ft. tall, branching.

H. atrorubens. DARK-EYED SUNFLOWER. Perennial. Zones US, MS, LS; USDA 6-8. Native to southeastern U.S. Grows 5–6 ft. tall, not quite as wide, with coarse, bristly foliage and 2-in. yellow flower heads centered in dark purple. 'Monarch' has semidouble flowers somewhat resembling the quilled flowers of a cactus-form dahlia.

H. 'Lemon Queen'. Perennial. Zones US, MS, LS, CS; USDA 6-9. Selected from a hybrid of two species native to the U.S., this stately plant grows 6–8 ft. tall, 2–3 ft. wide. Numerous pale yellow, brown-centered, 2-in. flowers appear in late summer. Perfect for back of casual border or in combination with large ornamental grasses. Takes moist or dry soil. Does not require staking, provided soil is not too rich and plants are not overfertilized.

H. maximilianii. MAXIMILIAN SUNFLOWER. Perennial. Zones US, MS, LS; USDA 6-8. Native to central and southwestern U.S. Clumps of 10-ft. stems clothed in narrow, 8- to 10-in. leaves and topped with narrow spires of 3-in. yellow flowers. Spreads to 3 ft. wide.

H. microcephalus. SMALL-HEAD SUNFLOWER. Perennial. Zones US, MS, LS, CS; USDA 6-9. Native from New Jersey to Florida. To 3–6 ft. tall, 2–3 ft. wide. Lance-shaped to ovate 3- to 4-in.-long leaves. Clear yellow, 1- to 1½-in. flowers.

H. x *multiflorus.* Perennial. Zones US, MS, LS; USDA 6-9. Hybrid between *H. annuus* and a perennial species. To 5 ft. high, 2½–3 ft. wide, with thin, toothed, 3- to 8-in.-long leaves and numerous 3-in.-wide flower heads with yellow centers. Excellent for cutting. Flowers of 'Capenoch Star' are single, lemon-yellow with a large central brown disk. Recommended double-flowered types include bright yellow 'Flore Pleno', golden yellow 'Loddon Gold', and golden yellow 'Sunshine Daydream' (with numerous small blooms that resemble dahlias).

H. salicifolius. WILLOWLEAF SUNFLOWER. Perennial. Zones US, MS, LS, CS; USDA 6-9. Native to the central U.S. Grows 6–8 ft. tall and 3 ft. wide, with narrow, gracefully drooping leaves to 8 in. long. Stems are topped by profuse 2-in. yellow flowers with purplish brown centers. Looks somewhat like *H. angustifolius* but leaves are narrower. 'First Light' is compact at 3–4 ft. tall and wide, and 'Low Down' is smaller still, growing 1–1½ ft. tall and 2 ft. wide.

H. tuberosus. JERUSALEM ARTICHOKE. Perennial. Zones US, MS, LS, CS; USDA 6-9. From eastern and central North America. Also grown as a commercial crop; tubers are edible and sold in markets under the name 'sunchokes'. Grows 6–10 ft. tall, 3 ft. wide, with bright yellow flower heads. Oval leaves 8 in. long. Spreads readily and can become a pest. Best to harvest tubers every year and save out two or three for replanting. If controlled, makes a good, quick temporary screen or hedge.

HELICHRYSUM
Asteraceae
Annuals and perennials

✎ **ZONES VARY BY SPECIES**

☼ **FULL SUN**

💧 **MODERATE WATER**

Helichrysum petiolare

Best known are the annual strawflowers (*H. bracteatum* and *H. subulifolium*) used in fresh and dried arrangements. Others, though less familiar, are choice plants for landscape use. Seldom bothered by deer.

H. bracteatum (*Xerochrysum bracteatum*). STRAWFLOWER. Annual. Zones US, MS, LS, CS, TS;

USDA 6-11. From Australia. To 2–3 ft. tall, 1 ft. wide, with straplike, 2- to 5-in.-long, medium green leaves. Blooms from summer until frost, bearing many papery, 2½-in. flowers that look like prickly pompons. Colors include yellow, orange, red, pink, and white. Known as "everlasting" because its blossoms last indefinitely when dried. Sow in place in late spring or earliest summer (at same time as zinnias). Dwarf forms are also available.

For shrubby perennial forms (such as 'Cockatoo', 'Dargan Hill Monarch', 'Diamond Head') previously included with annual strawflower, see *Bracteantha bracteata*.

H. italicum (*H. angustifolium*). CURRY PLANT. Woody-based perennial in Zones LS, CS, TS; USDA 8-11; can be grown as annual elsewhere. From southern Europe. Spreading, branching plant to 2 ft. high, about as broad, with crowded, narrow, nearly white leaves to 1½ in. long. Leaves emit a strong fragrance of curry powder when bruised or pinched; though they are not used in curry, a few can add a pleasant aroma to a salad or meat dish. Bright yellow, ½-in. flower heads appear in clusters 2 in. across, midsummer to autumn.

H. petiolare. LICORICE PLANT. Perennial in Zones CS, TS; USDA 9-11; can be grown as annual elsewhere. From South Africa. Woody-based plant to 1½–3 ft. high, with trailing stems to 4 ft. long. White, woolly, inch-long leaves; insignificant flowers. Licorice aroma sometimes noticeable—in hot, still weather, for example, or when leaves are dry. 'Licorice Splash' has variegated, yellow-green foliage; 'Limelight' has luminous light chartreuse leaves; and 'Variegatum' has foliage with white markings. All kinds are useful for their trailing branches, which thread through mixed plantings or mix with other plants in large pots or hanging baskets. For the so-called dwarf form, see *Plecostachys serpyllifolia*.

H. subulifolium (*Schoenia filifolia*). YELLOW STAR. Annual. Zones US, MS, LS, CS, TS; USDA 6-11. From western Australia. Mound-shaped plant to 20 in. tall, 10–12 in. wide, with glossy, green, 5-in. leaves and bright, shining, orange-yellow summer flowers 1½ in. wide. Excellent for fresh or dried arrangements.

HELICONIA

LOBSTER CLAW, FALSE
BIRD-OF-PARADISE
Heliconiaceae
Perennials

TS; USDA 10-11; OR GROW IN POTS

FULL SUN OR LIGHT SHADE

AMPLE WATER

Heliconia rostrata

Few plants combine the colorful and bizarre as well as these natives of tropical Central and South America and the southwest Pacific. Members of this large group feature big clusters of showy bracts containing small, true flowers. In some, the clusters look like lobster claws; in others, they remind you of bird-of-paradise (*Strelitzia*) blossoms. Bract colors include red, orange, yellow, pink, lavender, and green. Plants form sizable clumps of large leaves and range in size from 3-ft.-tall patio plants (excellent in containers) to giants reaching upwards of 15 ft. Clumps expand with age, so provide sufficient room. Potted plants can bloom any time; those in the ground flower in spring and summer. Deer don't seem to care for them.

Heliconias are excellent cut flowers. To extend the bloom's life, cut off the bottom ½ in. of the stem; then submerge the flowers and foliage in tepid water for an hour prior to display.

H. angusta. To 4–10 ft. tall, with leaves to 3 ft. long. Erect flower clusters to 2½ ft. long. Yellow or orange to vermilion or scarlet bracts; white or yellow-tipped green flowers.

H. bihai. To 6–15 ft. tall, with 2- to 6-ft.-long leaves. Erect blossom clusters 1½–3½ ft. long. Reddish orange bracts with green margins; white to pale green flowers.

H. caribaea. WILD PLANTAIN. To 12–20 ft. tall, with 5 ft.-long leaves and erect flower clusters to 1½ ft. Bracts are red or yellow, often marked with contrasting colors; flowers are white with green tips.

H. latispatha. Can reach 10 ft. tall, with leaves to 5 ft. long. Erect flower clusters to 1½ ft. tall, with spirally set orange, red, or yellow bracts and green-tipped yellow flowers.

H. pendula. To 8 ft. tall; 2- to 3-ft.-long leaves. Pendulous, 2-ft. inflorescence with spirally arranged red bracts, white flowers. Sometimes sold as *H. collinsiana.*

H. psittacorum. PARROT HELICONIA. Highly variable species; more vigorous than other heliconias. Grows 4–8 ft. tall, with leaves to 20 in. long, blossom clusters to 7 in. long. Bracts spread upward at a 45° angle. They vary in color; may be red, sometimes shading to cream or orange, and are often multicolored. Flowers are yellow, orange, or red, usually tipped in dark green or white. Many named selections are available.

H. rostrata. To 4–6 ft. tall, with 2- to 4-ft.-long leaves. Hanging inflorescences to 1–2 ft. long contain red bracts shading to yellow at the tip; flowers are greenish yellow.

H. schiedeana. Grows to 6–10 ft. tall, with leaves to 5 ft. long. Upright, 1½-ft.-long blossom clusters feature red or orange-red, spiraling bracts that enclose yellow-green flowers. 'Fire and Ice' is compact, at 4–5 ft. high; more cold hardy than the species.

H. stricta. Variable growth to 2–12 ft. tall. Dark green, maroon-stalked leaves to 5 ft. long. Upright, foot-tall flower stalks hold green, white-tipped flowers in red or orange bracts with green tips and yellow edges. 'Dwarf Jamaican' grows 1½–3 ft. tall, with peachy red bracts. 'Firebird', to 4 ft. tall, has brilliant red bracts. 'Sharonii', to 3–5 ft., has orange and yellow bracts.

CARE

Heliconias grow best with rich soil, heavy feeding, and plenty of water. They prefer acid soil; chlorosis (yellow leaves with green veins) is common in alkaline soil. During periods of active growth, give plants plenty of water and feed frequently with a balanced liquid fertilizer. Stems that have flowered should be cut away to make room for new growth. Reduce watering in cool weather. Frost will kill plants to the ground, but they will resprout from rhizomes if the cold spell is short. Where winters are cold for long periods, take potted plants indoors until spring. Smaller types can be easily stored in a garage without water or light; they will turn brown but will green up when taken outdoors once winter is over.

HELICTOTRICHON SEMPERVIRENS

BLUE OAT GRASS
Poaceae
Perennial grass

US, MS, LS; USDA 6-8

FULL SUN

LITTLE TO REGULAR WATER

Helictrichon sempervirens

Native to western Mediterranean region. Resembles a giant blue fescue (*Festuca glauca*) but is more graceful, with bright blue-gray, narrow leaves forming a fountainlike clump 2–3 ft. high and wide. In spring, stems to 2 ft. or taller rise above foliage, bearing wispy, straw-colored flower clusters. Grows best in rich, well-drained soil. Dry soil gives the best foliage color. Attractive in borders or with boulders in rock garden. Pull out occasional withered leaves. Evergreen in mild-winter climates; semiever-green in colder areas. Rust-resistant 'Sapphire' has bluer, slightly broader leaves than species. Deer resistant.

HELIOPSIS HELIANTHOIDES

FALSE SUNFLOWER
Asteraceae
Perennial

US, MS, LS, CS; USDA 6-9

FULL SUN OR LIGHT SHADE

MODERATE TO REGULAR WATER

Heliopsis helianthoides
'Golden Plume'

This tough, easy-to-grow, long-flowering plant deserves much wider use in gardens. Native from Ontario to the midwestern and southern U.S., it resembles the annual sunflower *Helianthus annuus*. Forms clumps to 5 ft. high and half as wide, with 6-in., rough-textured, medium green leaves. Bright yellow to orange-yellow flowers, 3 in. wide, appear from June until frost. Good, long-lasting cut flower. Tolerates drought and is seldom bothered by pests or deer. Selections are sometimes offered as varieties of *H. h. scabra*. The following are some of the best selections.

'Ballerina' ('Spitzentänzerin'). Compact plant to 3 ft. tall, 2 ft. wide. Early bloomer with semi-double yellow flowers.

'Bressingham Doubloon'. Sturdy plant to 4–5 ft. tall, 2–4 ft. wide, with semidouble yellow blooms.

'Gold Greenheart' ('Goldgrün-herz'). Double golden flowers with unusual green centers. To 3 ft. tall, 2 ft. wide.

'Golden Plume' ('Goldgefie-der'). Double yellow flowers on

a plant reaching 3 ft. tall and 2 ft. wide.

'Hohlspiegel'. Deep orange-yellow blooms with concave centers. To 4 ft. tall, 2 ft. wide.

'Karat'. Large single flowers in bright yellow. Grows to 3½ ft. tall and 2 ft. wide.

'Loraine Sunshine'. A conversation piece. White leaves with green veins; single yellow blooms. Compact plant grows just 2½ ft. tall and 1½ ft. wide.

'Summer Nights'. Golden yellow, single flowers on dark red stems. Plant grows 3–4 ft. tall and 2 ft. wide.

'Summer Sun' ('Sommersonne'). Yellow blooms—some single, some semidouble. To 3 ft. tall, 2 ft. wide.

HELIOTROPIUM

Boraginaceae

Perennial usually treated as annual

- ☀ **TS; USDA 10-11; ANYWHERE AS ANNUAL**
- ☽ **AFTERNOON SHADE**
- ☵ **REGULAR WATER, EXCEPT AS NOTED**
- ☦ **ALL PARTS ARE POISONOUS IF INGESTED**

Heliotropium arborescens

Grown mainly for their fragrant summer flowers, which are individually tiny but borne in striking clusters 3–4 in. across. Attract both butterflies and hummingbirds. Although most often treated as annuals, they can be grown as short-lived perennials in the Tropical South. Plants can be massed in flower beds; they also look great in window boxes and planters. Provide well-drained soil.

H. amplexicaule 'Azure Skies'. Perennial in MS, LS, CS, TS; USDA 7-11. Selection of a South American species. Grows 1 ft. tall, spreading up to 1½ ft. across. Narrow, deep green, crinkly leaves make a nice backdrop for the lavender blooms. Very heat and drought tolerant.

H. arborescens. COMMON HELIOTROPE. This old-fashioned favorite from Peru is prized for its showy, vanilla-scented flowers. Plants grow 1–1½ ft. tall and wide. Dark green leaves have an overall purplish cast; they are 1–3 in. long, crinkled, and hairy, with sunken veins. Recommended selections include white 'Alba', deep purple 'Black Beauty', and deep violet-blue 'Marine', with blossom clusters up to 10 in. across. The Regal Hybrids sport rose and lavender flowers on the same plant. Hybrid 'Simply Scentsational' grows 2½ ft. tall and 1 ft. tall; its softly fragrant, pale lavender blooms have white centers and golden yellow throats.

In Southern gardens, common heliotrope grows best with morning sun and afternoon shade. Pinch young plants to encourage bushy growth. If growing as a perennial, prune back hard in early spring. Be sure to keep watered during dry spells.

COMMON HELIOTROPE IS SO FRAGRANT, IT'S GROWN FOR PERFUME PRODUCTION IN PARTS OF EUROPE.

HELLEBORUS

HELLEBORE

Ranunculaceae

Perennials

- ☀ **ZONES VARY BY SPECIES**
- ☽ ● **FULL OR PARTIAL SHADE**
- ☵☵ **WATER NEEDS VARY BY SPECIES**
- ☦ **ALL PARTS ARE POISONOUS IF INGESTED**

Helleborus x *hybridus*

Distinctive, long-lived plants that add color to the garden for several months in winter and spring, hellebores are also appreciated for their attractive foliage. Each leaf consists of a long leafstalk ending in large, leathery leaflets grouped together like fingers on an outstretched hand.

All hellebores form tight clumps of many growing points, but species differ in their manner of growth. Some have stems that rise from the ground, with leaves all along their length; stems produce flowers at their tip in their second year, then die to the ground as new stems emerge to replace them. In other species, leaves are not carried on tall stems but arise directly from growing points at ground level; separate (typically leafless) flower stems spring from the same points.

Flowers are usually cup or bell shaped (those of *H. niger* are saucer shaped), either outward facing or drooping; they consist of a ring of petal-like sepals ranging in color from white and green through pink and red to deep purple (rarely yellow). Flowers of all hellebores persist beyond the bloom periods listed below, gradually turning green. Blossoms

are attractive in arrangements: After you cut them, slice the bottom inch of the stems lengthwise or seal cut ends by searing over a flame or immersing in boiling water for a few seconds. Then place in cold water. Or simply float flowers in a bowl of water.

Mass hellebores under high-branching trees, on north or east side of walls, or in beds. They are not damaged by deer or rodents.

In addition to the following, a half-dozen or more other species are sometimes available. Species here have leafy stems unless otherwise noted.

H. argutifolius (*H. corsicus*). CORSICAN HELLEBORE. Zones MS, LS; USDA 7-8. From Corsica, Sardinia. Erect or sprawling, to 2–3 ft. tall and wide. Substantial enough to use as a small shrub. Blue-green, 6- to 9-in. leaves divided into three sharply toothed leaflets. Leafy stems carry clusters of 2-in., pale green flowers from winter into spring. More sun tolerant than other hellebores. Two compact selections with white-marbled leaves are 'Janet Starnes' (with a touch of pink in new foliage) and 'Pacific Frost'. 'Silver Lace' has blue-gray foliage overlaid with a silver lace pattern. Moderate water.

H. x ballardiae. Zones US, MS, LS; USDA 6-8. This cross between *H. niger* and *H. lividus* grows to 1–1½ ft. high and 2 ft. wide, with 2½-in.-wide outward-facing blooms on deep red stems. 'Cinnamon Snow' has dark green leaves and white flowers with warm rose and cinnamon tones. 'HGC Pink Frost' has gray-green leaves with silvery veins; its flowers combine pale pink and rose.

H. x ericsmithii. Zones US, MS, LS; USDA 6-8. Hybrid of complex parentage. Grows 1–1½ ft. high and 1½ ft. wide, with dark green, pale-veined leaves and large sprays of pale pink or white flowers, each up to 4 in. across. Blooms face out, not down. Examples include choice 'Ivory Prince' and 'Pink Beauty'. 'Monte Cristo' is a heavy bloomer with blue-gray leaves and cream-colored flowers with a peachy rose blush. Regular water.

H. foetidus. BEAR'S-FOOT HELLEBORE. Zones US, MS, LS; USDA 6-9. From western and central Europe. To 2½ ft. high and wide, the stems clothed with dark green leaves divided into seven to ten narrow, leathery leaflets to 8 in. long. Blooms from winter to spring, bearing clusters of inch-wide light green flowers with purplish red edges. Plant parts are malodorous if crushed or bruised (don't smell bad otherwise). Self-sows freely where adapted. Moderate water. 'Green Giant' is bigger than the basic species, forming a 2½-ft. clump of green foliage that is topped at bloom time with 1-ft.-tall clusters of green bells. 'Piccadilly' has whitish green blossoms and dark green leaves tinged with reddish purple. 'Pontarlier' has toothed green leaves and large clusters of light green, long-lasting flowers. Wester Flisk strain has stems, flower stems, and leafstalks infused with purplish red, with the color extending into leaf bases.

H. x hybridus. Zones US, MS, LS, CS; USDA 6-9. Leaves have no obvious stems. These hybrid

plants generally resemble principal parent _H. orientalis_, but flower color range has been extended and superior parents selected for seed production. Some are sold under the breeder's name, such as Ballard's Group, which has flowers in several colors. Others are sold as color strains, such as Piccadilly Farm (chartreuse, dark purple, variegated, pink, and white), Sunshine selections (white, pink, yellow, or red flowers), Royal Heritage strain (pink, purple, maroon, or white blooms over vigorous foliage), and Winter Queen mix (white, pink, maroon, or spotted flowers). Others are grouped according to form, such as the Winter Jewels group, which has double flowers in many colors. The Spring Promise series includes uniform growers that bloom from a young age, with single and double flowers in a wide variety of colors; 'Rebecca', with single, dark plum blooms, is

particularly striking. 'Walberton's Rosemary', a vigorous grower resulting from a cross between _H. x hybridus_ and _H. niger_, is a heavy producer of outward-facing, rosy pink flowers that age to a darker salmon-pink; prefers a bit more sun than others listed here. All take moderate to regular water.

H. lividus. MAJORCAN HELLEBORE. Zones MS, LS, CS; USDA 7-9. From Majorca. To 1½ ft. high and twice as wide. Leaves resemble those of _H. argutifolius_ but lack noticeable teeth and have purplish undersides and a network of pale veins above. Winter-to-spring flowers are 1¼–2 in. wide, pale green washed with pinkish purple; carried in clusters of up to ten. 'Pink Marble' has pink flowers on rosy red stems. Leaves of 'White Marble' have pronounced silvery white veins. Moderate water.

H. niger. CHRISTMAS ROSE. Zones US, MS, LS; USDA 6-8. From Europe. Leaves have no obvious stems. Elegant plant to 1 ft. tall, 1½ ft. wide, blooming from December into spring. Lustrous dark green leaves are divided into seven to nine lobes with a few large teeth; they seem to rise directly from the soil. White, 2-in. flowers appear singly or in groups of two or three on a stout stem about the same height as the foliage clump. Blooms turn pinkish with age. 'HCG Jacob' is compact at 6–8 in. tall, with lots of early flowers that open white and fade to pink in cooler regions, greenish white in warmer areas. 'HGC Josef Lemper' is vigorous and upright, with light green leaves and an early and long bloom period. 'White Magic' and 'Potter's Wheel' are large-flowered selections. 'Nell Lewis' is a vigorous strain from North Carolina. All need more shade than other hellebores. Provide alkaline soil and regular water. Plants of _H. orientalis_ are often mislabeled Christmas rose.

H. orientalis. LENTEN ROSE. Zones US, MS, LS; USDA 6-8. From Greece, Turkey, Caucasus. Leaves have no obvious stems. Much like _H. niger_ in growth but more tolerant of warm-winter climates. Basal leaves with 5 to 11 sharply toothed leaflets; branched flow-

ering stems to 1 ft. tall, with leaf-like bracts at branching points. Blooms in late winter and spring; flowers are 2–4 in. wide, in colors including white, pink, purplish, cream, and greenish, often spotted with deep purple. Easier to transplant than other hellebores. A widely variable plant, but all forms are attractive. Encourage self-sowing and keep the colors you like. Hybridizes freely with many other species; many nursery plants may be hybrids. Regular water.

H. x sternii. Zones US, MS, LS; USDA 6-8. Hybrid between _H. argutifolius_ and _H. lividus_, with bluish green foliage netted with white or cream. Greenish, 1- to 2-in. flowers suffused with pink bloom from winter to spring. Variable from seed. 'Silver Dollar' has large, heavily silvered leaves and comes true from seed. Moderate water.

H. viridis. GREEN HELLEBORE. Zones US, MS, LS; USDA 6-8. To 1½ ft. tall and wide. Graceful bright green leaves are divided into 7 to 11 leaflets; leafy stems bear 1- to 2-in.-wide flowers in pure green to yellowish green, sometimes with purple on inside. Blooms from winter through late spring. _H. v. occidentalis_ has smaller blossoms and larger leaves. Regular water.

CARE

Plant in good, well-drained soil amended with plenty of organic matter. Plants prefer soil that is somewhat alkaline but will also grow well in neutral to slightly acid conditions (_H. niger_ is an exception; it must have alkaline soil). Feed once or twice a year. Don't disturb hellebores once planted; they resent moving and may take 2 or more years to re-establish. If well sited, however, they may self-sow, and young seedlings can be transplanted in early spring. Offspring may not resemble the parent exactly, but all are attractive. Remove spent flowers when they become unattractive. For _H. argutifolius_ and _H. foetidus_, cut flowering stems back to ground level after blooms fade. Black spot is a common fungal disease of _H. x hybridus_ that can be minimized by removing all foliage in winter before the flowers push up. Do not compost these leaves, as they will spread the spores.

TOP: Helleborus niger; BOTTOM: H. x hybridus Ballard's Group; H. argutifolius

HEMEROCALLIS

DAYLILY
Hemerocallidaceae
Perennials from tuberous roots

🖊 **US, MS, LS, CS, TS; USDA 6-11, EXCEPT AS NOTED**

☼ ◑ **PARTIAL SHADE IN HOTTEST CLIMATES**

💧 **REGULAR WATER**

Hemerocallis citrina

When talk turns to surefire perennials for the South, it doesn't take long for the word "daylily" to come up. Few plants offer so many flowers in so many colors for so little care. Tuberous, somewhat fleshy roots give rise to large clumps of arching, sword-shaped leaves that may be evergreen, semievergreen, or deciduous, depending on selection.

Clusters of flowers resembling lilies appear at the ends of generally leafless, wandlike stems that rise well above the foliage. Each daylily flower stays open for only one day, hence the name daylily (the genus name comes from the Greek words for "day" and "beauty"). Most daylilies bloom once a year, producing numerous flowers over a 3- to 6-week period. Other types may bloom again later in the summer and are called rebloomers.

Mass daylilies in solid sweeps, or mix them into herbaceous borders. Plant them on banks and roadsides, or group them near pools and streams. Dwarf types are excellent in rock gardens and containers or as low edging. Because the individual blooms close each evening, daylilies are not great cut flowers. But if you cut stems with well-developed buds, these will open on successive days, though each blossom is slightly smaller than the previous one.

Set out bare-root or container-grown plants anytime the ground isn't frozen. Preferred times for planting are spring or fall. If deer are plentiful in your area, be warned—deer love most daylilies.

H. altissima. TALL DAYLILY. Deciduous. From China. To 5–6 ft. tall, 3 ft. wide. Blooms in late summer and early autumn; the pale yellow, 4-in. flowers give off a light perfume at night. 'Statuesque', with 5-ft. stems, blooms in mid- to late summer.

H. citrina. CITRON DAYLILY. US, MS, LS, CS; USDA 6-9. Deciduous. From China. To 3–4 ft. high, 1½–2 ft. wide. Blooms in midsummer, bearing fragrant, narrow-petaled, soft lemon-yellow flowers to 3 in. across that open in early evening and last until noon the next day. Leaves are longer and narrower than those of most daylilies.

H. fulva. TAWNY DAYLILY, COMMON ORANGE DAYLILY. Deciduous. From China or Japan. To 3–5 ft. high and 4 ft. wide; quickly spreads into colonies. Leaves are 2 ft. or longer. Tawny, orange-red, 3- to 5-in., unscented flowers in summer. A tough, persistent plant suitable for holding banks; rarely sold but commonly seen in old gardens and along roadsides. Double-flowered 'Kwanso' and 'Flore Pleno' are sometimes seen in the same locales.

H. hybrids. Deciduous, evergreen, and semievergreen. Standard-size hybrids generally grow 2½–4 ft. tall, 2–3 ft. wide; some selections reach 6 ft. high. Dwarf types grow just 1–2 ft. tall and wide. Flowers of standard kinds are 4–8 in. across, those of dwarfs 1½–3½ in. wide. Some have broad petals, others narrow, spidery ones; many have ruffled petal edges. Colors range far beyond the basic yellow, orange, and rusty red to pink, vermilion, buff, apricot, plum or lilac purple, cream, and near-white, often with contrasting eyes or midrib stripes that yield a bicolor effect. Many are sprinkled with tiny iridescent dots known as diamond dust. Selections with semidouble and double flowers are available. Tetraploid types have unusually heavy-textured petals.

Bloom usually begins in mid- to late spring, with early,

TOP: Hemerocallis fulva; MIDDLE: H. lilioasphodelus; H. 'Condilla'; BOTTOM: H. 'Pardon Me'

CHOOSE YOUR DAYLILY

APRICOT

Elizabeth Salter—melon peach-pink, 5½-in. blooms, 22 in. tall
Ruffled Apricot—apricot, 7-in. blooms, 28 in. tall

DARK, BLACK

Derrick Cane—black, 5-in. blooms, 34 in. tall
Jungle Beauty—black, 5½-in. blooms, 30 in. tall
Midnight Magic—black-red, 5½-in. blooms, 28 in. tall

GOLD

Condilla—bright gold, double, 4½-in. blooms, 20 in. tall
Fooled Me—bright gold with a red eye, 5½-in. blooms, 24 in. tall
Mary's Gold—tall, bright gold, 6½-in. blooms, 34 in. tall
Star Struck—bright gold, 5-in. blooms, 26 in. tall

LAVENDER/PURPLE

Bela Lugosi—deep purple, 6-in. blooms, 33 in. tall
Indian Giver—deep purple, 4½-in. blooms, 20 in. tall
Lavender Vista—lavender, 5-in. blooms, 22 in. tall
Little Grapette—grape-purple, 2-in. blooms, 12-18 in. tall

NEAR WHITE

Joan Senior—one of the whitest, 6-in. blooms, 25 in. tall
Lullaby Baby—near white-pink blush, 3½-in. blooms, 18–24 in. tall
Moonlit Masquerade—cream with a purple eyezone, 5½-in. blooms, 26 in. tall

ORANGE

Lady Lucille—bright, deep orange, 6-in. blooms, 24 in. tall
Mauna Loa—bright orange, 5-in. blooms, 22 in. tall
Orange Velvet—the color of orange sherbet, 6½-in. blooms, 24 in. tall
Orange Vols—deep orange, 6½-in. blooms, 24 in. tall

PINK

Barbara Mitchell—medium pink, 6-in. blooms, 20 in. tall
Persian Market—rose-pink, 7-in. blooms, 27 in. tall
Strawberry Candy—strawberry-pink with a rose eye, 4¼-in. blooms, 26 in. tall

RED

Chicago Apache—scarlet-red, 5-in. blooms, 27 in. tall
Pardon Me—burgundy-red, 3-in. blooms, 14 in. tall
Red Volunteer—red, 7-in. blooms, 30 in. tall
Spiderman—red with yellow throat, 7-in. blooms, 24 in. tall

SOME OF THE BEST REBLOOMERS

Apricot Sparkles—soft apricot, 4-in. blooms, 18 in. tall
Bitsy—yellow, 1½-in. blooms, 18 in. tall
Buttered Popcorn—butter-yellow, 6-in. blooms, 32 in. tall
Dublin Elaine—light pink, double, 5½-in. blooms, 32 in. tall
Earlybird Cardinal—watermelon-red, 4-in. blooms, 21 in. tall
Frankly Scarlet—scarlet red, 4-in. blooms, 24 in. tall
Happy Returns—bright yellow, 3½-in. blooms, 18 in. tall
Infinity—coral-peach, double, 5½-in. blooms, 30 in. tall
Janice Brown—light pink with rose eye, 4¼-in. blooms, 21 in. tall
Miss Amelia—very pale yellow, 3½-in. blooms, 30 in. tall
Plum Perfect—plum-purple, 3½-in. blooms, 24 in. tall
Stella de Oro—bright gold, 3-in. blooms, 12 in. tall
Yellow Bouquet—light yellow, double, 3-in. blooms, 18 in. tall

YELLOW

Autumn Minaret—yellow, 4-in. blooms, 66 in. tall
Hyperion—fragrant, light yellow, 5-in. blooms, 36 in. tall
Mary Todd—bright yellow, 6-in. blooms, 22 in. tall

midseason and late bloomers available. The warmer the climate the earlier the season starts. By planting all three types, you can extend the bloom period for up to two months. Reblooming types may put on a second or even third display in late summer to midautumn. These include 2-ft.-high dwarf selections such as bright yellow 'Happy Returns', bright gold 'Stella de Oro', and burgundy 'Pardon Me'.

New hybrids appear in such numbers that no book can keep up. To get the ones you want, visit daylily specialists, buy plants in bloom at your local nursery, or study catalogs.

H. lilioasphodelus (*H. flava*). LEMON DAYLILY. Deciduous. From China. Reaches 3 ft. high and wide, with 2-ft.-long leaves and 4-in., fragrant, pure yellow flowers in mid- to late spring. Newer hybrids may be showier, but this species is still cherished for its delightful perfume and early bloom time.

H. minor. GRASS-LEAF DAYLILY. Deciduous. Zones US, MS, LS, CS; USDA 6-9. From eastern Asia. To 2 ft. high and wide, with narrow (¼-in.-wide) leaves. Blooms for a relatively short time in late spring or early summer, when fragrant, bright golden yellow, 4-in. flowers are held just above the foliage.

CARE

Daylilies adapt to almost any soil type, but for best results give them well-drained soil amended with organic matter. Provide regular moisture from spring through autumn. In spring, apply a complete organic fertilizer (5-3-3, 3-4-5, or similar) to soil around established plants. Follow label directions; be sure to keep fertilizer off foliage. Do not fertilize newly planted daylilies. When clumps become crowded (usually after 3 to 6 years), dig and divide them in fall or early spring.

Though otherwise pest free, daylilies are now threatened by a potentially serious disease, daylily rust (*Puccinia hemerocallidis*), which is primarily a problem for growers in the Lower South and warmer. First identified in Georgia in 2000, this rapidly spreading fungus causes yellow to orange streaks and pustules to form on the leaves. The fungus is killed by cold weather, so its impact

has been negligible in areas that receive freezing temperatures. To control, pick off and burn all infected leaves; then spray at regular intervals with a recommended product according to label directions. Consult with your local Cooperative Extension Office for product recommendations.

HEPATICA

LIVERWORT
Ranunculaceae
Perennials

🗡 **US, MS, LS, CS; USDA 6-9**

◑ ● **PARTIAL TO FULL SHADE**

💧 **REGULAR WATER**

Hepatica americana

Diminutive woodland plants (just 6–9 in. high and 6 in. wide) with evergreen or nearly evergreen leaves and charming blooms. Plants resemble smaller sorts of anemones and were formerly considered to be anemones. In herbal medicine, they have been used to treat disorders of the liver, hence the common name. Plants bloom in early spring, bearing flowers with numerous narrow, petal-like sepals arranged around a central mass of yellow stamens. Each bloom rises on its own stalk above the clump of last year's foliage. A new crop of leaves follows bloom.

These are choice plants for woodland gardens and shaded rock gardens. Though little known in North America except among wildflower fanciers, they are popular with plant collectors in Japan, where many selections are cultivated.

H. acutiloba. SHARPLOBE HEPATICA. Native to eastern and

central North America. Leathery, 4-in. leaves are divided into three sharp-pointed lobes. Flowers are lilac and white, ½–1 in. across, on stems to 9 in. high.

H. americana. LIVERWORT. Native to eastern and central North America. Leathery, 4-in. leaves with three rounded lobes. Flowering stems are usually 6 in. high. Flowers are ½–1 in. wide, typically light blue but sometimes pink or white.

H. nobilis (*H. triloba*). Native to Europe. Very similar to *H. americana*. Flowers are usually bluish purple but may be white or pink.

HEPTACODIUM MICONIOIDES

SEVEN SONS FLOWER
Caprifoliaceae
Deciduous shrub or tree

✎ US, MS, LS; USDA 6-8

☼ ◑ FULL SUN OR LIGHT SHADE

💧 REGULAR WATER

Heptacodium miconioides

From China. Handsome fountain-shaped shrub to 15–20 ft. tall, 8–10 ft. wide. Large, narrowly heart-shaped leaves are shiny green, deeply veined. Fragrant, creamy white flowers in 6-in.-long clusters at branch ends open over a long bloom season in late summer and fall. Blooms are succeeded by even showier masses of small fruit with bright purplish red calyxes. Common name derives from the number of flowers in each of the clusters forming part of the larger inflorescence. Picturesque even in winter, when bark is on show: Thin, pale tan strips peel away to reveal dark brown bark beneath.

Not fussy about soil; not bothered by pests or diseases. Can be trained as a single- or multitrunked tree.

HESPERALOE

Asparagaceae
Perennials

✎ MS, LS, CS, TS; USDA 7-11, EXCEPT AS NOTED

☼ ◑ FULL SUN OR LIGHT SHADE

◊ 💧 LITTLE TO MODERATE WATER

Hesperaloe parviflora

Clumps of narrow, evergreen leaves with threadlike fringe along edges give rise to tall, branching inflorescences set with many tubular flowers that attact hummingbirds. Foliage clumps resemble yucca or coarse grass. Plants require little maintenance aside from removal of spent flower clusters. Established plants can get by with little summer water and aren't fussy about soil as long as it is well drained.

H. campanulata. From northern Mexico. Bright green leaves form tight clumps of rosettes to 3 ft. high and wide. In summer, stems to 9 ft. tall bear bell-shaped, light pink flowers about 1 in. across.

H. funifera. From northern Mexico. Clumps to 6 ft. tall, 6–8 ft. wide. Stems to 15 ft. high bear inch-wide, greenish white flowers in late spring or early summer.

H. nocturna. From northern Mexico. Foliage clump 5 ft. tall, 6 ft. wide. In late spring and early summer, blossom spikes, to 12 ft. high, bear many 1-in., night-blooming, slightly fragrant, greenish lavender flowers.

H. parviflora. RED YUCCA. Zones US, MS, LS, CS, TS; USDA 6-11. From Texas and New Mexico. Foliage clumps 3–4 ft. tall and wide produce 5-ft. stalks carrying many rose-red to bright red, 1¼-in. flowers from late spring through midsummer, sometimes into early fall. Especially heat tolerant, thriving even in reflected heat. Excellent container plant. A form with creamy yellow flowers is available.

HESPERANTHA COCCINEA

CRIMSON FLAG
Iridaceae
Perennial from rhizome

✎ LS, CS; USDA 8-9; OR GROW IN POTS

☼ ◑ FULL SUN OR LIGHT SHADE

💧💧 REGULAR TO AMPLE WATER

Hesperantha coccinea

Virtually evergreen South African native that resembles a small gladiolus. Forms a foot-wide clump of upright, swordlike leaves to 16 in. long. Clusters of 4 to 14 star-shaped flowers to 1½ in. across are carried on slender, 1½- to 2-ft.-tall stems in late summer and fall; may also bloom late winter and spring in Coastal and Tropical South. The species has crimson flowers, but several color variants with larger flowers are available. Look for white 'Alba', watermelon-red 'Oregon Sunset', soft pink 'Jennifer' and Mrs. Hegarty', deep salmon-pink 'Sunrise', and pale pink 'Viscountess Byng'. 'Major' is a strong grower, with large (to 2½-in.) shiny red blooms. All make excellent cut flowers. Good in containers and in meadow plantings. Formerly known as *Schizostylis coccinea*.

CARE

Plant in spring, in humusy, well-drained soil that stays moist. Set rhizomes ½–1 in. deep, 1 ft. apart. Water generously from planting until autumn flowering ends, then sparingly until growth resumes in spring. If clumps become crowded, divide them in early spring; each division should have at least five shoots.

HESPERIS MATRONALIS

DAME'S ROCKET, SWEET ROCKET
Brassicaceae
Perennial or biennial

✎ US, MS, LS, CS, TS; USDA 6-11

☼ ◑ FULL SUN OR LIGHT SHADE

💧 REGULAR WATER

Hesperis matronalis

An old-fashioned favorite for Southern cottage gardens. Freely branched plant grows to 3 ft. tall and as broad, with 4-in., toothed leaves and rounded clusters of ½-in., four-petaled lavender to purple blooms. Flowers resemble those of stock (*Matthiola*) and are fragrant at night. Plant grows readily from seed and often self-sows. Old, woody plants should be replaced by young seedlings. White- and double-flowered forms exist but are rare. Seldom damaged by browsing deer.

H

HEUCHERA
CORAL BELLS, ALUM ROOT
Saxifragaceae
Perennials

- US, MS, LS; USDA 6-8
- LIGHT SHADE OR MORNING SUN
- MODERATE TO REGULAR WATER

Heuchera **'Delta Dawn'**

Few plants in recent years have seen as many new introductions with such dazzling new colors as *Heuchera*. These refined, well-behaved plants offer both attractive bell-shaped blossoms and handsome evergreen foliage. Slender, wiry, 1- to 2½-ft. stems bear loose clusters of nodding flowers that are typically no more than ⅛ in. across. These dainty blooms, which often lack petals, make an interesting and long-lasting addition to arrangements; they also attract hummingbirds and other pollinators. Colors include carmine, crimson, red, coral, rose, pink, greenish, pale yellow, and white. Most bloom in spring and late summer, and some continue into fall. Leaves are roundish, with scalloped or ruffled edges; colors run the gamut from yellow and orange to red, purple, and brown. Most recent introductions are grown more for fancy foliage than for flowers.

Use *Heuchera* in combination with other perennials in mixed borders; try them in rock gardens and in sweeping masses. Selections with light-colored foliage can brighten a shady spot. All excel in containers, actually growing better than in the ground in most cases.

H. x brizoides. Diverse group of hybrids between *H. sanguinea* and other species. To 1–2½ ft. tall, 1–1½ ft. wide, with spring or summer bloom. 'Lipstick' has dark red flowers; its green leaves are heavily mottled with silver. A seed-grown strain called Bressingham Hybrids offers flowers in white and shades of pink and red. Other seed-grown types include 'Firefly' ('Leucht-käfer'), with fragrant bells in fiery scarlet; 'Freedom', profuse rosy pink blooms; 'Ruby Bells', red flowers; and 'Bressingham White', long-blooming white. Cutting-grown types include 'June Bride', large pure white blossoms; 'Snow Angel', deep reddish pink flowers above white-variegated foliage.

H. hybrids. The following selections have been selected for their marvelously colored and sometimes ruffled foliage. Some have as a parent *H. americana*, a species from the central U.S. with marbled and veined leaves up to 4½ in. across. Many newer hybrids involve *H. villosa*, a large-leafed native to the mid-Southern U.S. and thus quite tolerant of heat and humidity. Both form mounds of foliage 8–12 in. high and 12–16 in. wide. Tiny summer flowers are held on thin stalks to 2–3 ft. high and are white to cream unless otherwise noted.

'Beaujolais'. Dark purple to maroon leaves.

'Blackout'. Compact mound of glossy, nearly black foliage. Striking.

'Brownies'. Large, chocolate-brown leaves.

'Caramel'. Leaves emerge dusky red and mature through apricot tones to golden yellow. Highly recommended.

'Citronelle'. Leaves are chartreuse to bright lemon-yellow. Vigorous grower once established.

'Crimson Curls'. Deep red, ruffled leaves, fading to gray-green in summer.

'Delta Dawn'. Large roundish leaves with golden-green edges and red centers.

'Electric Lime'. Large lime-green leaves with red veining.

'Georgia Peach'. Leaves emerge peachy orange and age through red tones to rosy purple; dark veins and a silvery sheen. Heat tolerant and vigorous.

'Mocha'. Vigorous grower. Leaves are chocolate-brown above, deep purple beneath; turn nearly black in sun.

TOP: Heuchera 'Obsidian'; *H.* 'Citronelle'; *MIDDLE: H.* 'Georgia Peach'; *BOTTOM: H.* 'Peach Flambe'; *H.* 'Spellbound'

'Obsidian'. Foliage deepest burgundy, nearly black, with glossy sheen. Dependable.

'Peach Flambe'. Bright peach-colored leaves turn plum in winter. Heat tolerant.

'Pinot Gris'. Leaves emerge ginger with a silver overlay, aging to rose tones; undersides are deep purple.

'Pinot Noir'. New growth is black-purple, developing a strong silvery overlay and black veins as it matures.

'Pistache'. Lime-green to chartreuse foliage. Fresh-looking all season.

'Southern Comfort'. Very large (9-in.) leaves are peachy orange when new, taking on copper and amber tones as they age. Vigorous and heat tolerant. Highly recommended for the South.

'Spellbound'. Vigorous grower with lightly ruffled, silvery leaves with purple highlights.

'Tiramisu'. Leaves emerge chartreuse with a large central area of red, which fades as the season progresses. In fall, center turns burgundy while edges re-main chartreuse. Late blooming.

H. micrantha. Native to California, Washington, Oregon, Idaho. Adapts easily to garden conditions. Long-stalked, roundish, gray-green, 1- to 3-in.-wide leaves are toothed and lobed, hairy on both sides. Late-spring to early-summer flowers are whitish or greenish, about ⅛ in. long, carried in loose clusters on leafy, 2- to 3-ft. stems. Hybrid forms developed from *H. micran-tha* are more adaptable than the species. 'Ruffles' has green leaves that are deeply lobed and ruffled around the edges. 'Palace Purple' has maplelike, rich brownish or purplish leaves that retain their color year-round if given adequate sunlight

H. sanguinea. CORAL BELLS. Native to New Mexico and Arizona. Round, 1- to 2-in. leaves with scalloped edges form neat foliage tufts. From spring into summer, slender, wiry, 1- to 2-ft. stems bear open clusters of nodding, bell-shaped, bright red or coral-pink flowers. Selections include 'Carmen' (deep brick-red flowers), 'Chatterbox' (rosy coral), 'Gaiety' (coral-pink), and 'White Cloud' (pure white). These selections display red flowers above variegated foliage: 'Cherry Splash' (white and gold variega-

tion), 'Snowstorm' (bright white), and 'Frosty' (silvery). All of these require perfect drainage.

H. villosa. HAIRY ALUM ROOT. Native from Virginia to Georgia and Tennessee, with high tolerance for heat and humidity. Both foliage and flowers are softly hairy. Tooth-edged green leaves to 5 in. across have triangular lobes, form a mound 1½–2 ft. high and wide. White to pinkish blos-soms on stems to 3 ft. tall appear late in the season, near the end of summer. 'Autumn Bride' has green leaves and white flowers. 'Purpurea' features deep purple foliage and white blossoms.

CARE

These plants require well-drained soil containing lots of organic matter, such as compost. Divide clumps every 2 to 3 years in spring or fall. Replant vigorous rooted divisions; discard older, woody portions. Can also be started from dust-like seed sown in spring. Watch out for mealy-bugs, which sometimes infest plants near the base and even on the roots; control with regular applications of insecticidal soap. Black vine weevils can cause much damage; look for notched leaf edges in summer and C-shaped white grubs below the soil line in fall and winter. These grubs chew through the base of the plant (detached crowns can be rerooted in fresh soil). Scalding water poured over the grubs is a good organic control. Rust may occur; remove and dispose of infected leaves.

BOTH THE LEAVES AND FLOWERS OF *HEUCHERA* LAST A LONG TIME IN A VASE.

X HEUCHERELLA

Saxifragaceae
Perennials

| 🖊 US, MS, LS; USDA 6-8 |
| ◑ LIGHT SHADE |
| 💧 REGULAR WATER |

X *Heucherella* 'Stoplight'

These hybrids combine the flowering habit of coral bells (*Heuchera*) with the heart-shaped leaves of foamflower (*Tiarella cordifolia*). Most produce foliage clumps 4–5 in. high and about 1 ft. wide; good in shaded rock gardens or as woodland ground cover. Newer, trailing forms look great in hanging baskets or spilling over the edge of a pot; they are more tolerant of heat and humidity. Most bloom in late spring or early summer, with a possible second bloom in fall. Unless otherwise noted, all types described here produce plumes of small pink flowers.

All require well-drained, humus-rich soil; they'll quickly fail in clay soil.

X *H.* 'Alabama Sunrise.' Vigorous grower with deeply cut foliage resembling a maple leaf. New growth is gold with red veins, aging to green with red veins in summer and to orange-pink in fall. Tiny white flowers.

X *H.* 'Gold Zebra'. Bright yellow, deeply cut leaves are boldly marked with dark red. Stands up well to high heat and humidity.

X *H.* 'Gunsmoke'. Silver-veiled, maple-shaped leaves have purple-red undertones on the new growth, maturing to silver with dark veins.

X *H.* 'Stoplight'. Large red-centered yellow leaves change to lime-green with red centers in summer. Airy white flowers are produced in spring.

X *H.* 'Strike it Rich Gold'. Burgundy-veined lime-green foliage turns golden yellow with age. Cream to white flowers

X *H.* 'Sweet Tea'. Large star-shaped leaves are cinnamon-brown surrounded by orange, tea-colored borders. Very popular Southern selection.

X *H.* 'Tapestry'. Dark-centered blue-green leaves change to green with dark centers in fall and winter.

X *H.* 'Twilight'. Velvety, dark-veined, charcoal-gray leaves are symmetrically arranged on this low grower. Lacy white flowers in late spring. Quite sun tolerant.

X *H.* 'Yellowstone Falls'. Chartreuse to lime foliage with splotches of deep crimson. Vigorous grower with trailing stems up to 3 ft. long.

ABOVE: Heucherella 'Sweet Tea'

hairy leaf
(villosa)
American

...green shrubs,
...als

...PECIES

...PT AS NOTED

...EXCEPT AS

...sinensis
'Reggae Breeze'

Among the showiest flowering plants in Southern gardens, hibiscus typically bear funnel-shaped blossoms—sometimes as big as dinner plates and often with prominent stamens. The many species offer an astonishing range of flower colors, and most bloom over a long season. Flowers attract butterflies and hummingbirds. Whiteflies and aphids are common pests; insecticidal soap is a good control for both.

H. acetosella (*H. eetveldeanus*). REDLEAF HIBISCUS. Evergreen shrubby perennial. Zones TS; USDA 10-11; or grow in pots. From central and eastern Africa. Reaches 5 ft. tall and 3 ft. wide. Cultivated more for its foliage than its dark-centered red or yellow flowers. Leaves are up to 1 ft. across; they may be lobed (somewhat like a maple leaf) or unlobed. Color varies from green to deep purplish red. 'Haight Ashbury' leaves are heavily splashed with pink. 'Red Shield' has deep red foliage.

H. coccineus. TEXAS STAR. Shrubby perennial. Zones US, MS, LS, CS, TS; USDA 6-11. Native to coastal swamps of Florida and Georgia. Moderately fast-growing bush to 6 ft. tall and 3 ft. wide, with handsome glossy foliage; very showy scarlet flowers, 3 in. wide, bloom from June to

October. Palmate leaves with three to seven lobes look much like those of Japanese maple (*Acer palmatum*). Use as an accent or at the back of a perennial border. Does well in either wet or well-drained soil. 'Lone Star' has blooms of pure white.

H. militaris. HALBERD-LEAFED ROSE-MALLOW. Shrubby perennial. Zones US, MS, LS, CS, TS; USDA 6-11. Native to marshes and wet woods from Pennsylvania to Minnesota, south to Florida and Texas. If grown in moist soil, quickly attains 8 ft. tall, 3 ft. wide. Dagger-shaped dark green leaves to 6 in. long; pinkish white, 4- to 6-in. flowers from May to October. Tolerates partial shade; takes heavy soils with poor drainage.

H. moscheutos. HARDY HIBISCUS, COMMON ROSE-MALLOW. Perennial. Zones US, MS, LS, CS, TS; USDA 6-11. Native to the southern U.S., and an old Southern favorite. Largest flowers of all hibiscus, some to 1 ft. across, on a plant 6–8 ft. tall and 3 ft. wide. Bloom starts in June, continues until fall. Oval, toothed leaves to 8 in. long are deep green above, whitish beneath. Plants die down in winter. Feed at 6- to 8-week intervals during growing season. Protect from wind.

Seed-grown strains often flower the first year if sown indoors and planted out early; these plants are bushier and more uniform than the species. Southern Belle strain grows 4 ft. tall; Cordials series plants are 3½ ft. tall; Vintage series reach 2½–3 ft. tall; Disco Belle, Frisbee, Luna, and Rio Carnival strains are 2–2½ ft. tall. Flowers are 8–12 in. wide, come in red, pink, rose, or white, often with a red eye.

The many cutting-grown selections and hybrids include the following. Unless otherwise noted, all reach about 4 ft. high.

'Anne Arundel'. Blooms to 9 in. across, in clear pink with a red eye.

'Blue River II'. Pure white flowers to 10 in. across. Foliage may have a bluish cast.

'Cranberry Crush'. Heavy producer of 7- to 8-in.-wide, cranberry-red to deep scarlet flowers that appear along the length of the stems. Foliage is deep green with purple overtones.

'Fantasia'. To 2–3 ft. high, with rosy pink, 9-in. flowers with a rosy red center.

'Fireball'. To 4 ft. tall, with 10-in., bright red flowers.

'George Riegel'. Pink, ruffly, 10-in. blooms with a red eye.

'Lady Baltimore'. Glowing pink, 6- to 8-in.-wide flowers with a large red center.

'Lord Baltimore'. Deep red, 10-in. blossoms over an exceptionally long period.

'Raspberry Rose'. Large plant, to 7 ft. tall and 10 ft. wide, with a profusion of bright raspberry-red blooms to 10 in. across.

'Royal Gems'. Grows 3–4 ft. tall, with bright pink flowers to 12 in. across. Oval, pointed, incurving leaves are an attractive dusky purple. Cold hardy.

'Summer Storm'. Light pink blooms with a red eye can reach 10 in. across. Grows 5 ft. tall and a little wider. Foliage is deep purple to chocolate-brown, striking in contrast to the flowers.

'The Clown'. Light pink flowers with red eye; 6–8 in. across.

'Turn of the Century'. Red-centered blooms with bicolor petals of pink and white range from 5–10 in. wide.

H. mutabilis. CONFEDERATE ROSE. Deciduous shrub. Zones LS, CS, TS; USDA 8-11. From China. Shrubby or treelike in the Coastal and Tropical South, 15 ft. tall, 8 ft. wide; acts more like a perennial in the Lower South, growing flowering branches from woody base or short trunk. Broad, oval leaves have three to five lobes. In late summer and fall, flowers open from buds that resemble cotton bolls. Blooms are 4–6 in. wide, opening white or pink often and changing to deep red by the next day. 'Rubrum' has red flowers. 'Flore Pleno' has double, rosy pink flowers.

H. rosa-sinensis. CHINESE HIBISCUS, TROPICAL HIBISCUS. Evergreen shrub. Zones CS, TS; USDA 9-11; provide overhead protection where winter lows frequently drop below 30°F. Where temperatures go much lower, grow in containers and shelter indoors over winter; or grow as annual, setting out fresh plants each spring. Also makes a good houseplant that can be brought outdoors during the warm season.

A longtime favorite of Southern gardeners, this is one of the showiest flowering shrubs. Reaches 30 ft. tall and 15–20 ft. wide in its native tropical Asia,

but seldom grows over 15 ft. tall in the U.S. Glossy foliage varies somewhat in size and texture, depending on selection. Growth habit may be dense and dwarfish or loose and open. Flowers are single or double, 4–8 in. wide. Colors range from white through pink to red, from yellow and apricot to orange. Individual flowers usually last only a day or two, but the plant blooms continuously in spring and fall; may slow in summer, as high temperatures can cause bud drop. Aphids may also cause bud drop; use horticultural oil or insecticidal soap to control them.

Requires acid soil and excellent drainage; if necessary, improve soil or set plants in raised beds or containers. Fertilize monthly (potted plants twice monthly) with a general-purpose liquid fertilizer April to September, then stop fertilizing and let growth harden. For good branch structure, prune poorly shaped young plants when you set them out in spring. To keep a mature plant growing vigorously, prune out about a third of old wood in early spring. Pinching out tips of stems in spring and summer increases flower production. These are some of the selections available:

'All Aglow'. Tall (10- to 15-ft.) plant has large single flowers with broad, gold-blotched orange petals, pink halo around a white throat.

'Baja Breeze'. Compact and symmetrical at 2–3 ft. high and wide; good in large containers. Rich red flowers with darker red center.

'Bridal Veil'. Large, pure white, single flowers last 3 or 4 days. Grows 10–15 ft. tall.

'Bride'. Very large, single, palest blush to white flowers. Slow to moderate growth to open-branched 4 ft.

'Brilliant' ('San Diego Red'). Bright red single flowers in profusion. Tall, vigorous, compact, to 15 ft. Hardy.

'Butterfly'. Small, single, bright yellow flowers. Slow, upright growth to 7 ft.

'Cajun Blue'. Pale lavender-gray flowers with a white eye. Open grower to 4–6 ft. tall.

'Chiffon Breeze'. Pale yellow flowers with a white eye. Grows 2–3 ft. high and wide; elegant choice for containers.

'Cool Wind'. White to softest pink flowers with a bright red eye. Compact grower, reaching just 2–3 ft. high and wide.

'Crown of Bohemia'. Double gold flowers; petals fade to carmine-orange toward base. Moderate or fast growth to 5 ft. Bushy, upright. Hardy.

'Diamond Head'. Large, double flowers in deepest red (nearly black-red). Compact growth to 5 ft.

'Ecstasy'. Large, bright red, single flowers with striking white variegation. Upright growth to 4 ft.

'Fiesta'. Large, single flowers in bright orange centered with a red-edged white eye; petal edges are ruffled. Strong, erect growth to 6–7 ft.

'Full Moon' ('Mrs. James E. Hendry'). Double, pure yellow flowers. Moderately vigorous growth to a compact 6 ft.

'Golden Dust'. Bright orange, single flowers with yellow-orange centers. Compact, thick-foliaged plant to 4 ft. tall.

'Hula Girl'. Large, single flowers in canary yellow with a deep red eye. Compact growth to 6 ft. Flowers stay open several days.

'Itsy Bitsy Peach', 'Itsy Bitsy Pink', and 'Itsy Bitsy Red'. Tall (10- to 15-ft.) plants with small leaves and small single flowers.

'Kate Sessions'. Large single flowers with broad petals; red with a gold tinge on petal undersides. Moderate growth to 10 ft. tall. Upright and open habit.

'Kona'. Ruffled, double pink flowers. Vigorous, upright, bushy growth to 15–20 ft. Prune regularly. 'Kona Improved' produces fuller flowers in a richer pink.

'Kona Princess'. Small, double pink flowers on a 6- to 7-ft. shrub.

'Morning Glory'. Single, blush-pink flowers changing to warmer pink with white petal tips. Grows 8–10 ft. tall.

'Moy Grande'. Compact grower to 5 ft. tall. Single, brilliant rosy red flowers are huge, to more than 1 ft. across.

'Peppermint Flare'. Grows 4 ft. tall and wide. Blooms to 10 in. across are white to palest pink, with a red eye and pronounced red flecks.

'Powder Puff'. Double flowers of creamy white; during cool weather, take on a pink tinge. Grows 8–10 ft. tall.

'President'. Large single blossoms, intense red shading to deep pink in throat. Upright, compact, 6–7 ft. tall.

'Red Dragon' ('Celia'). Small to medium, double, dark red flowers. Upright, compact, 6–8 ft. tall.

'Reggae Breeze'. Golden blooms centered with a pink starburst and burgundy throat. At 2–3 ft. high and wide, a good choice for large pots.

'Ross Estey'. Heavy-textured, very large single blooms with broad, overlapping petals of pink shading to coral-orange toward tips; last 2 or 3 days on bush. Vigorous. To 8 ft. Very large, ruffled leaves in polished dark green.

'The Path'. Large, ruffled, single flowers in bright yellow shading to orange and bright fuchsia-pink in the center. Grows 6–8 ft. high.

'Vulcan'. Yellow buds open to large single flowers in red with yellow on the petal backs. Blossoms often last for more than a day. Compact grower to 4–6 ft. high.

'White Wings'. Profuse, narrow-petaled, single white flowers with small red eye. Vigorous, open, upright to 20 ft.; prune to control legginess. A compact form with smaller flowers is available.

H. schizopetalus. FRINGED HIBISCUS, CORAL HIBISCUS. Evergreen shrub in Zone TS; USDA 10-11; annual elsewhere. From tropical east Africa. To 9–15 ft. tall, 6–12 ft. wide, with weeping habit. Blooms almost all year, bearing white, pink, red, or yellow blossoms with fringed petals and an unusually long column of stamens that resembles a bottle-brush. Plants are sometimes kept small and grown in hanging baskets.

H. syriacus. ROSE OF SHARON, SHRUB ALTHAEA. Deciduous shrub or small tree. Zones US, MS, LS, CS, TS; USDA 6-11. This old Southern favorite has come full circle. Native to Korea and India (not Syria, despite the name), it was one of Grandma's standby plants for colorful summer blooms. But most nurseries sold unnamed seedlings only by color. When showier trees like crepe myrtle gained favor, rose of Sharon fell by the wayside. Improved, named selections now offer better blooms over a longer period, more colors, fewer seeds, and nicer forms.

Plant grows upright and compact when young, spreading and opening with age to 10–12 ft. tall

TOP: Hibiscus syriacus 'Blue Chiffon'; H. coccineus; MIDDLE: H. moscheutos 'Lady Baltimore'; BOTTOM: H. m. 'Blue River II'; H. mutabilis

and 6 ft. wide; easily trained to a single trunk or espaliered against a wall. Leaves to 4 in. long, with three coarsely toothed lobes, emerge somewhat late in spring and drop in fall with little color. Flowers resembling those of hollyhock (*Alcea*) appear in summer. Blossoms are single, semidouble, or double, 2½–3 in. across, often with a contrasting purplish throat. Though single forms are more attractive than doubles, most produce more seeds (and hence, more seedlings) than doubles.

Self-sown seedlings can be weedy. New sterile selections are seedless.

Easy to grow in almost any well-drained soil. Tolerates heat and drought. Prune in winter, as blooms form on new growth. Japanese beetles that eat flowers and leaves can be serious pests. Control by hand-picking the beetles or spraying plant with neem oil, a natural pesticide. Deer resistant.

Recommended selections include the following:

'Ardens'. Double lilac-purple flowers with darker center. Few seeds.

'Blue Bird'. Single, blue flowers with small red eye. Considered the best blue form for many years, this selection has now been surpassed by newer introductions.

'Blushing Bride'. Double, bright pink blossoms. Few seeds.

'Boule de Feu'. Double, deep violet-pink flowers. Few seeds.

'Freedom'. Double flowers in deep mauve-pink. Larger flowers than most doubles. Strong grower with handsome foliage. Few seeds.

'Jeanne d'Arc'. Double flowers of pure white. Few seeds.

'Pink Giant'. Large rose-pink blooms with a red eye and yellow stamens.

'Red Heart'. Single white flowers with a red eye. Strong grower.

Plants in the Chiffon series have soft-colored flowers with a ruffled center that gives them the look of anemones. Satin series plants are robust growers with blooms in rich shades of blue, light pink, rose-pink, and violet, all with a dark red center.

The U.S. National Arboretum has introduced selections developed by famed plant breeder Don Egolf. These plants are triploids; the extra set of chromosomes results in large blossoms with strong, heavy-textured petals. Because plants produce little seed, flowers appear over a long period. Choices include 'Aphrodite', bearing single, rose-pink flowers with a deep red eye; 'Diana' (the most popular of this group), with single, pure white blossoms; 'Helene', single, white flowers with a deep red eye; 'Minerva', single, ruffled, lavender blooms with a reddish purple eye.

HIPPEASTRUM
AMARYLLIS
Amaryllidaceae
Perennials from bulbs

🌿 **LS, CS, TS; USDA 8-11, EXCEPT AS NOTED; OR GROW IN POTS**

☀ ◑ **FULL SUN OR LIGHT SHADE; BRIGHT LIGHT**

💧 **REGULAR WATER DURING GROWTH AND BLOOM**

Hippeastrum

Native to the tropics and subtropics. Many species are useful in hybridizing, but only hybrids are generally available; these are often sold as giant amaryllis or Royal Dutch amaryllis (though many are grown in South Africa or elsewhere). Named selections come in reds, pinks, white, salmon, near-orange; some are variously marked and striped. Two to several flowers, often 8–9 in. across, form on stout, 2-ft. stems. Where plants are grown outdoors, flowers bloom in spring; indoors, they bloom just a few weeks after planting. Favorites include Picotee (white with a thin red edge), 'Samba' (red with white edges and central streaks), 'Red Lion' (scarlet), and 'White Christmas' (pure white).

Newer forms include double-flowered selections in several colors (some with red picotee edges); look for 'Aphrodite' (white, with petals lined and edged in pink), 'Ballerina' (rose-pink), 'Blossom Peacock' (white, with pink splashes and red edges), 'Double Dragon' (deep red), 'Elvas' (white, centrally splashed in red), and 'Stars 'n Stripes' (red, with white stripes and streaks). Miniatures sport 3- to 5-in. flowers topping 12- to 15-in. stems; among the best are 'Scarlet Baby' and

rich red 'Pamela'. An unusual evergreen species, *H. papilio*, has 5-in., greenish white flowers heavily patterned with dark red. Hardy hybrid 'San Antonio Rose' (Zones MS, LS, CS, TS; USDA 7–11) is a compact grower to 15 in. high; it has reddish veins on the leaf undersides and single flowers in bright rosy red. 'Charisma', another hardy hybrid, grows about 2 ft. tall, with 10-in.-wide flowers; its red-edged petals are white, heavily splashed with deep red.

H. x *johnsonii*, Saint Joseph's lily, is an early hybrid popular in old gardens in the South. Its 5-in.-wide trumpet flowers are scarlet with white stripes and emerge in clusters of 4 to 6 atop 2-ft. stems; mature bulbs may produce 4 stems and 24 blooms. Tough and resilient, it blooms well in sun or light shade. *H. reginae*, Mexican lily, another heirloom type, has satiny, bright red trumpets with white stars in the throats. Flowers appear in clusters of two, three, or four on 1-ft. stems in summer.

CARE

Where hardy in the ground, amaryllis bulbs can be planted outdoors. In fall, set bulbs 1 ft. apart in organically enriched, well-drained soil; keep bulb necks even with soil surface. They will bloom, and then grow foliage through summer. Water as needed, and feed with timed release fertilizer granules. The foliage will wither with frost; otherwise, some leaves will remain. Divide infrequently.

All types can be grown in pots. Plant from November to February in good potting mix. Allow 1-2 in. between bulb and edge of pot. Set upper half of bulb above the soil surface. Water well, and keep in a sunny spot. Growth begins almost immediately. Stake flower stalks if they are apt to fall over. When flowers fade, cut the entire stalk, but keep the leaves.

Either plant potted bulbs outdoors after danger of frost has passed (see above) or maintain them in the pot in full sun to partial shade. Fertilize with time release granules and water regularly. Let the leaves grow and nourish the bulb. Potted amaryllis need to go dormant in late summer or early fall, about 8-10 weeks before you want them to grow again. Bloom requires another

6-8 weeks. To induce dormancy, stop watering and place them where they can stay dry and cool, about 55°F. When buds begin to emerge, repot if needed, and bring bulbs into a warm, sunny spot to resume watering.

HORSERADISH
Brassicaceae
Perennial

🌿 **US, MS, LS, CS; USDA 6-9**

☀ **FULL SUN; AFTERNOON SHADE**

💧 **REGULAR WATER**

Horseradish

Botanically known as *Armoracia rusticana*. Native to southeastern Europe. Large (to about 3-ft.), coarse, weedy-looking plant grown for its large white roots. Does best in rich, moist, acid, well-drained soils. Grow it in some sunny, out-of-the-way corner. In late winter or early spring, set in a hole 6–8 in. deep so that top of root is even with soil surface. Fill hole with soil and then mound 3–5 in. of soil over the top. One plant should provide enough horseradish for a family of four. For multiple plants, space 2½–3 ft. apart. Keep soil slightly moist during summer months; drought results in bitter roots.

Through fall, winter, and spring, harvest pieces of horseradish roots from the outside of the root clump as you need them—that way you'll have your horseradish fresh and tangy. Scrub and peel the roots, cutting away any dark parts; then grate them. Good ventilation is a must. Mix with vinegar, sweet cream, or sour cream—or simply sprinkle directly onto food. Roots can also be stored in plastic bags in the refrigerator for up to 3 months.

St. Jude Children's
Research Hospital
ALSAC · Danny Thomas, Founder
Finding cures. Saving children.

stjude.org

midnight rose
Raspberry Ice } Purple
Frosted Violet

Stainless Steel - total Silver @ return

Nebulous marble - green silver purple

Christie - small - caramel
Georgia Peach

Plum royal

golden Zebra - Henschedller

autumn leaves

Electra + golden / lime + red veins all seasons

Peach Flambe
Sashay
Geisha Fan
Ginger Ale

Terra Nova
Crisp - Apple
Blackberry
Peach

Solar eclipse
Amber Waves
Snow angel - flounces red
   Plum pudding
Ermine curls
rayon

   tapestry - heuchella
   Yellowstone falls - trailing
Spellbound - Terra Nova

Littbentis 'sweet tart'
Dolce 'Cinnamon curls'
   Holly Wood
Leute Veit
   Sunspot - heuchella

   Dolce "Key Lime Pie"
   Amethyst mist
   Marmalade
   lime marmalade
Blackberry Ice

HOSTA
PLANTAIN LILY
Asparagaceae
Perennials

🌿 **US, MS, LS; USDA 6-8, EXCEPT AS NOTED**

◐ ● **PARTIAL OR FULL SHADE**

💧 **REGULAR WATER**

Hosta 'Antioch'

The most popular of all plants for shade, hostas are prized for their marvelous foliage. The thin spikes of lavender or white, trumpet-shaped flowers that appear for several weeks in summer are a bonus, and they are a favorite among hummingbirds. There's a tremendous variety in leaf size, shape, and color; to fully appreciate the diversity, you'll need to consult a specialist's catalog or visit a well-stocked garden center. All hostas are native to eastern Asia.

Leaves may be heart shaped, lance shaped, oval, or nearly round, carried at the ends of leafstalks that rise from the ground and radiate from a central point. Leaves overlap to form symmetrical, almost shingled foliage mounds ranging in size from dwarf (as small as 3–4 in.) to giant (as big as 5 ft.). Leaf texture may be smooth, deeply veined, quilted, or puckery; surface may be glossy or dull; edges may be smooth or wavy. Colors range from light to dark green to chartreuse, bright gold, gray, and blue. There are also combinations of colors, including variegations with white, cream, or yellow.

All hostas go dormant in winter, collapsing to almost nothing. All are splendid companions for ferns and for plants with fernlike foliage, such as bleeding heart (*Dicentra* and *Lamprocapnos*). They're also good in containers. In the ground, hostas last for years; clumps expand in size and shade out weeds. They are generally shade lovers, though some will tolerate dappled or morning sun if well watered. Plants grown in more sun will be more compact and produce more flowers. Unfortunately, hostas are a favorite dessert for deer and voles.

New selections are legion. To be sure you're getting the one you want, buy the plant in full leaf or deal with a reputable mail-order firm. Species and selections listed below are just a few of the many available.

H. fortunei. FORTUNE'S PLANTAIN LILY. May be an ancient hybrid affiliated with *H. sieboldiana*. Variable plant known for its many selections in a wide range of foliage colors. Plants grow to 1–1½ ft. high, up to 3 ft. wide, with oval, foot-long leaves, lilac flowers. Young leaves of *H. f. albopicta* are yellow with uneven green border; the yellow fades to a greenish shade by summer. *H. f. aureomarginata* has distinctly round, deep olive-green leaves irregularly rimmed in yellow. *H. f. hyacinthina* has large, gray-green leaves edged with a fine white line.

H. hybrids. The following list includes some of the best, most widely grown hostas.

'Albomarginata'. Grows 2–3 ft. high and 3–4 ft. wide. Leaves have an irregular yellow border that fades to white; late bloom.

'Antioch'. To 1½ ft. tall, 3 ft. wide. Broad, green leaves with wide, creamy white margins. Lavender flowers are held well above foliage mound.

'Blue Angel'. Heavily veined, blue-green leaves 16 in. long, nearly as wide. White flowers over a long bloom period. Enormous mound to 3–4 ft. tall and 4 ft. wide.

'Blue Mouse Ears'. Charming miniature to just 6–8 in. high and 12 in. wide. Thick, slightly cupped, heart-shaped leaves are blue-green. Lavender flowers held just above the foliage. Lovely in containers.

'Blue Wedgwood'. To 2 ft. high, 1 ft. wide. Wavy-edged, strongly veined, heart-shaped leaves in 1½-ft. mound. Pale lavender flowers bloom early.

'Chartreuse Wiggles'. Dwarf (6–8 in. high, 10 in. wide), with lance-shaped, wavy-edged, chartreuse-gold leaves. Lavender flowers bloom late.

'Earth Angel'. Sport of 'Blue Angel', with similar size and appearance, except each leaf has wide, creamy yellow margins that age to creamy white.

'First Frost'. Sport of 'Halcyon' grows 16 in. high and 3 ft. wide. Heart-shaped, blue-green leaves are heavily edged in creamy yellow, aging to white. Light lavender flowers appear on 2-ft.-tall stalks in midsummer.

'Fragrant Bouquet'. Vigorous mounding growth to 20 in. tall and 3 ft. wide, with roundish, apple-green leaves widely edged in creamy yellow. Large (to 3 in. long), highly fragrant, lavender-blushed white flowers are held on 3-ft.-tall scapes.

'Francee'. To 1½–2 ft. tall, 3 ft. wide. Broadly heart-shaped leaves to 6 in. long with striking white edges. Lavender flowers bloom late. Sun tolerant.

'Frances Williams'. Forms a mound to 2½–3 ft. tall and 3 ft. wide. Round, puckered, blue-green leaves have a bold, irregular yellow edge. Pale lavender flowers bloom early.

'Ginko Craig'. To 1–1½ ft. tall and wide. Elongated, frosty green leaves with silver margins. Abundant lavender flowers.

'Gold Edger'. To 10–12 in. high, 1½ ft. wide. Heart-shaped, 3-in. leaves in chartreuse gold. Masses of lavender blossoms. One of the most sun tolerant; in fact, it needs some sun for best color.

'Golden Tiara'. To 1 ft. tall, 1½ ft. wide. Heart-shaped leaves are 4 in. long, light green with gold edge. Purple flowers. Sun tolerant.

'Gold Standard'. To 2 ft. tall, 3 ft. wide. Heart-shaped, bright golden leaves with a green margin. Pale lavender flowers. Sun tolerant.

'Great Expectations'. To 2 ft. tall, 2½ ft. wide. Leaves sport a creamy yellow center surrounded by a wide blue-green edge. White flowers.

'Guacamole'. Grows 1½–2 ft. tall and 4–5 ft. wide. Distinctly veined leaves are apple-green, shading to blue-green along the edges. White flowers are very fragrant.

'Hadspen Blue'. Low grower (to 1 ft. tall, spreading to 1½ ft.) with slightly wavy, broadly oval, slug-resistant blue leaves. Many lavender flowers.

'Halcyon'. To 1½ ft. tall, 3 ft. wide. Heart-shaped, heavy-textured, blue-gray leaves. Short spikes of rich lilac-blue flowers.

'Honeybells'. To 2½ ft. high, 4 ft. wide. Wavy-edged, yellow-green leaves; lightly scented pale lilac flowers.

'June'. Low grower to just 1 ft. high and 2½ ft. wide. Slender, heart-shaped leaves are heavy textured. Each golden leaf has wide, streaked margins of sage-green, shading to blue-green at the edges. Fragrant white blooms.

'Krossa Regal'. Big, leathery, frosty blue leaves arch up and out, making a vase-shaped clump to 3 ft. tall and wide. Slug-resistant foliage. Blooms late, with lavender flower spikes that can reach 5–6 ft. high.

'Liberty'. This sport of 'Sagae' grows in an upright vase shape to about 2 ft. tall and 3 ft. wide. Thick, heart-shaped leaves are blue-green, with very wide margins in yellow. As the season progresses, the blue-green turns greener, and the yellow fades to white. Pale lavender flowers on 3½-ft.-tall scapes bloom in midsummer.

'Paradigm'. Thick, corrugated, rounded leaves are gold, with a wide margin of dark blue-green. Grows 22 in. high and 3–3½ ft. wide. Light lavender blooms appear in early summer.

'Patriot'. To 15 in. tall, 3 ft. wide. Resembles 'Francee', but leaves have a wider white border. Lavender blooms.

'Paul's Glory'. Forms a sturdy clump to 1½–2 ft. high and 4½ ft. wide. Heart-shaped leaves are chartreuse, with a dark green margin. The center slowly ages to gold (white in more sun). Lavender flowers in midsummer.

'Piedmont Gold'. To 2 ft. high, 3 ft. wide. Broadly heart-shaped, heavily veined, slightly wavy-edged, 7-in. leaves of glowing chartreuse gold. White flowers. Sun tolerant.

'Praying Hands'. Unusual upright form sets this one apart. Narrow, folded leaves are held erect on upright stems for an overall vase shape with a height of 14–18 in.; clumps may reach 2 ft. across. Dark green leaves have thin edging of creamy yellow. Plenty of lavender flowers appear in late summer.

'Rainforest Sunrise'. Forms a mound about 1 ft. tall and 1½–2 ft.

wide, with rounded, corrugated, cupped foliage. Each golden leaf is bordered in deep green. Pale lavender flowers appear in early summer.

'Regal Splendor'. Sport of 'Krossa Regal'. Grows 2½ ft. tall and nearly 6 ft. wide. Huge blue-green leaves are frosty blue, with a creamy yellow margin. Lavender flowers in midsummer.

'Royal Standard'. To 2 ft. high, 3–4 ft. wide. Glossy, light green leaves, elongated and undulated. Fragrant, white flowers. Sun tolerant.

'Sagae'. Vase-shaped plant to 2½ ft. tall and 4–5½ ft. wide. Large, heart-shaped, heavily ribbed leaves are blue-green with an irregular creamy white edge. Showy pale lavender flowers. Sun tolerant and resistant to slug damage.

'Shade Fanfare'. To 1–1½ ft. high, 1½ ft. wide. Leaves are pointed ovals to 7 in. long, green to gold with creamy white margin. Lavender flowers. Very sun tolerant.

'So Sweet'. Upright grower to 1½ ft. high and 2–3 ft. wide. Glossy, deep green, heart-shaped leaves have irregular white margins. Fragrant white flowers. Takes considerable sun.

'Stained Glass'. To 1½ ft. tall and 3–4 ft. wide. Shiny, golden leaves have a 2-in.-wide margin of dark green. Vigorous and sun tolerant, with very fragrant, pale lavender flowers.

'Striptease'. Sport of 'Gold Standard' and similar in size and leaf shape, but with wider dark green margins on the golden leaves. A narrow white strip separates the green from the golden areas. Pale lavender flowers show up in midsummer.

'Sum and Substance'. To 3 ft. high, 5 ft. wide. Textured, shiny yellow leaves to 20 in. long. Slug-resistant foliage. Lavender flowers. Very sun tolerant.

'Sun Power'. To 2 ft. high, 3 ft. wide. Ruffled, twisted leaves are chartreuse to golden; retain their color all season. Lavender flowers on 3-ft. stalks. Takes morning sun.

'Touch of Class'. Vigorous grower to 1 ft. high, 1½ ft. wide. Thick, quilted, blue leaves are

marked with a large central flame of gold. Lavender flowers.

'True Blue'. Sturdy, mounding growth to 2½ ft. tall and a little wider. Slightly wavy, heavily corrugated leaves are blue-green. White flowers may show a distinctive lavender stripe.

'Wide Brim'. Oval, pointed, dark green leaves are widely edged in creamy white to pale yellow. Forms a mound about 1½ ft. high and 3 ft. wide. Pale lavender flowers top the plant in mid- to late summer.

H. plantaginea. FRAGRANT PLANTAIN LILY. Zones US, MS, LS, CS; USDA 6-9. Glossy, bright green leaves to 10 in. long, broadly oval with parallel veins and quilted surface. Foliage mound 2 ft. high, 3 ft. wide. Noticeably fragrant, large white flowers bloom late. Heat tolerant. Performs better than other species in Coastal South. 'Aphrodite' (*H.* 'Aphrodite') is double flowered.

H. sieboldiana. SIEBOLD PLANTAIN LILY. To 2½–3 ft. tall, 4 ft. wide. Blue-green, broadly heart-shaped leaves, 10–15 in. long, heavily veined and puckered. Many slender, pale lilac flower spikes nestle close to foliage mound early in season. Foliage dies back early. *H. s. elegans* has especially handsome blue-gray leaves that are slug resistant.

H. sieboldii 'Kabitan'. To 8 in. tall, 10 in. wide. Wavy, lance-shaped leaves to 5 in. long, chartreuse to yellow with thin green margins. White flowers.

H. undulata. WAVY-LEAFED PLANTAIN LILY. Wavy-edged, narrowly oval leaves, 6–8 in. long, in a mound 1½ ft. tall and wide. Typical leaf is green with a creamy white center stripe. Foliage is used in arrangements. Pale lavender flowers. *H. u. albomarginata* has creamy white margins on leaves. *H. u. erromena* is solid green.

H. ventricosa. BLUE PLANTAIN LILY. To 2 ft. tall, 3 ft. wide. Named for its violet-blue blooms. Leaves are glossy deep green, broadly heart shaped, prominently veined, to 8 in. long. Leaves of *H. v. aureomaculata* are yellowish green with a green border. In 'Aureomarginata' (*H.* 'Aureomarginata'), each leaf is green edged with creamy white.

TOP: Hosta 'Sum and Substance'; *MIDDLE: H.* 'Golden Tiara'; *H.* 'Aphrodite'; *ABOVE: H.* 'Halcyon' (blue) *and H.* 'Gold Edger' (yellow)

CARE

Provide good, organically enriched soil with regular feeding during the growing season. A blanket of mulch or low-growing ground cover around plants will prevent mud from splattering leaves. Slugs and snails can ravage hosta foliage; where these pests are a problem, protect plants or choose slug-resistant selections (those with heavily textured or waxy leaves are your best bets). Deer also enjoy hosta.

HOUSTONIA CAERULEA

BLUETS, QUAKER LADIES
Rubiaceae
Perennial

🌿 **US, MS, LS, CS; USDA 6-9**

◑ **LIGHT SHADE**

💧 **REGULAR WATER**

Houstonia caerulea

Creeping perennial that forms low (2- to 3-in.), widely spreading mounds of tiny oval leaves. Flowers appear singly on 2- to 2½-in. stalks in late spring. The ½-in.-wide, four-lobed flowers are pale blue (sometimes white) with a yellow eye. Although small, they are profuse enough to create a charming effect. Use in woodland gardens, around stepping stones, or as carpet for large potted shrubs like camellia or aucuba. Needs acid soil. In the wild, thrives among mosses in light shade under tall oak trees. Will also grow in sparse lawns. Formerly known as *Hedyotis caerulea*.

HOUTTUYNIA CORDATA

Saururaceae
Perennial

🌿 **US, MS, LS, CS, TS; USDA 6-11**

☼◑● **SUN OR SHADE**

💧💧 **REGULAR TO AMPLE WATER**

Houttuynia cordata 'Chameleon'

From China, Japan. Spreading, underground stems send up a 9-in.-high blanket of foliage—heart-shaped green leaves to 3 in. long that look very much like those of English ivy (*Hedera helix*). Foliage emits a pungent scent when crushed, reminiscent of orange peel. Inconspicuous clusters of white-bracted flowers like tiny dogwood (*Cornus*) blossoms. Unusual ground cover that disappears completely in winter, even in mild climates. Most commonly grown form is showy 'Chameleon' ('Tricolor', 'Variegata'), with green leaves splashed in cream, pink, yellow, and red; colors are most intense in sun. Attractive in containers.

Can spread aggressively in wet ground and will even thrive with roots in water. For ground cover, plant 1½–2 ft. apart; curb growth with wood, concrete, or metal barrier extending 8–12 in. into the soil. The plant can also spread by seed. Once you bring it into your garden, it may well be with you forever.

HOWEA

Arecaceae
Palms

🌿 **TS; USDA 10-11; OR HOUSE PLANTS**

◑ **PARTIAL SHADE; BRIGHT INDIRECT LIGHT**

💧 **REGULAR WATER**

Howea forsteriana

These slow-growing feather palms are native to Lord Howe Island in the South Pacific. They are the kentia palms of florists and are usually sold under the name *Kentia*. With age, leaves drop to show clean, green trunk ringed with leaf scars. When using these palms outdoors, plant them beneath another tree to provide cold protection (they are very sensitive to frost) and to shield them from strong winds. Give them well-drained soil high in organic matter. They do not tolerate salt.

Howeas are ideal potted plants—the classic parlor palms. To minimize problems with spider mites, keep the fronds clean and free of dust. Feed with quarter-strength general-purpose houseplant fertilizer monthly from spring through fall.

H. belmoreana. SENTRY PALM. Less common than *H. forsteriana*; also smaller and more compact (to 25 ft. tall, 15 ft. wide), with overarching fronds 6–7 ft. long. Withstands some neglect—capricious watering, drafts, dust.

H. forsteriana. PARADISE PALM, FORSTER'S SENTRY PALM. Faster growing than *H. belmoreana*, to 60 ft. tall and 20 ft. wide. Fronds reach 9 ft. long, have long, drooping leaflets.

HOYA

WAX FLOWER, WAX PLANT
Apocynaceae
Perennials

🌿 **TS; USDA 10-11; OR HOUSE PLANTS**

◑● **PARTIAL TO FULL SHADE; BRIGHT LIGHT**

💧 **REGULAR WATER**

Hoya carnosa

Tropical plants with thick, waxy evergreen leaves and tight clusters of small, waxy flowers that appear in leaf joints during summer. These plants prefer rich, loose, well-drained soil. When grown as container plants, they bloom best when pot bound. Do not prune out the short stalks that bear flowers, because new flower clusters will develop on them. Feed with a quarter-strength general-purpose liquid houseplant fertilizer monthly from spring through fall. Specialists list dozens of available species and hybrids, with growth habit varying from vining to shrubby.

H. carnosa. WAX FLOWER, WAX PLANT. From India, Burma, southern China. Vining plant grows to 10–20 ft., with green, oval, rigid, 2- to 4-in.-long leaves. Big, round, convex clusters of ½-in., creamy white blossoms, each centered with a five-pointed pink star. Flowers are fragrant, especially at night. Red young leaves give extra color. Attractive trained on a pillar or trellis. Indoors, traditionally trained on wire in a sunny window.

'Variegata' has leaves edged in white suffused with pink; it is not as vigorous or hardy as the plain species. 'Exotica' shows yellow-and-pink variegation. 'Krinkle Kurl' has crinkly leaves closely spaced on short stems; it is often sold as 'Compacta' or as Hindu-rope plant.

H. lanceolata bella. House or greenhouse plant. Native from Himalayas to Burma. Shrubby growth to 1½–3 ft. high and wide, with fleshy green leaves to 1½ in. long and sweetly aromatic clusters of ½-in., purple-centered, white flowers. Slender, upright branches droop as they grow older. Best used in hanging basket.

H. wayetii. Often sold as *H. kentiana*. Native to the Philippines. Vining stems are set with fleshy green leaves to 3½ in. long and just ¾ in. wide; new leaves and leaf edges redden in bright light. Clusters of ½-in., maroon flowers have a sweet, butterscotch perfume and produce lots of sticky nectar. Best used in a hanging basket. 'Variegata' has leaves heavily variegated in white and pink.

HUMATA TYERMANNII

RABBIT'S FOOT FERN
Davalliaceae
Fern

- **CS, TS; USDA 9-11; OR HOUSEPLANT**
- **PARTIAL SHADE; BRIGHT, INDIRECT LIGHT**
- **REGULAR WATER**

Humata tyermannii

Native to China. This small fern has furry, creeping rhizomes that look something like rabbit's feet. Fronds 8–10 in. long, very finely cut, rising at intervals from the rhizome. Like squirrel's foot fern (*Davallia trichomanoides*) in appearance and uses, but slower growing. Can be used as ground cover where it is cold hardy.

HUMULUS

HOP
Cannabaceae
Perennial vines

- **US, MS, LS; USDA 6-9**
- **FULL SUN**
- **REGULAR WATER**

Humulus lupulus

These fast-growing, twining vines are attractive for summer screening on trellises or arbors—and one species yields the hops used in beer. Leaves to 6 in. long are deeply lobed and toothed. Bloom in late summer. Male plants produce flower panicles; females bear blossoms in greenish spikes resembling pinecones. Squarish, hairy stems are set with deeply lobed, toothed leaves to 6 in. long. Stems twine vertically; to get horizontal growth, twine stem tips by hand. Cut stems to ground after frost turns them brown; regrowth comes the following spring.

H. japonicus. JAPANESE HOP. From eastern Asia. To 20–30 ft. Bears ¾-in. female flower spikes. Dark green leaves have five to seven lobes; foliage of 'Variegatus' is marked with white. Sow seeds in place in spring.

H. lupulus. COMMON HOP. From many northern temperate regions of the world. This species produces the traditional flavoring for beer. The hops—female flowers—are soft, flaky, 1- to 2-in., light green cones of bracts and blossoms with a fresh, piny fragrance. Bright green leaves have three to five lobes. Tender top shoots can be cooked as a vegetable. Plants sold in nurseries are typically female; no pollenizer needed. May be offered as pot-

ted plants or as dormant roots. The roots should be planted in rich soil in early spring; set just below soil surface with thick end up. Many selections are available, including 'Aureus', which has attractive chartreuse foliage.

HYACINTHOIDES

BLUEBELL, WOOD HYACINTH
Asparagaceae
Perennials from bulbs

- **ZONES VARY BY SPECIES**
- **FILTERED SUN OR LIGHT SHADE**
- **REGULAR WATER DURING GROWTH AND BLOOM**
- **BULBS MAY CAUSE AN ALLERGIC SKIN REACTION**

Hyacinthoides hispanica

These spring-blooming bulbs were once classed in the genus *Scilla* and are still popularly known by that name; some bulb dealers continue to list them as such. They resemble hyacinths but are taller, with looser flower clusters and fewer, narrower leaves. Spanish bluebell (*H. hispanica*) is the preferred choice for most Southern gardens. English bluebell (*H. non-scripta*) definitely prefers colder winters and moderate to cool summers. When grown near each other, the two species sometimes hybridize, producing intermediate forms.

H. hispanica. SPANISH BLUE-BELL. Zones US, MS, LS, CS; USDA 6-9. From Spain, North Africa. Prolific and vigorous, with inch-wide, strap-shaped leaves and sturdy, 20-in. stems bearing 12 or more nodding, unscented bells about ¾ in. long. Blue is the most popular color, 'Excelsior' (deep blue) the most popular selection.

There are also white, pink, and rose forms. Leaves can look a trifle ratty before dying back.

H. non-scripta. ENGLISH BLUEBELL, WOOD HYACINTH. Best in Zones US, MS; USDA 6-7. From western Europe. Fragrant, blue flowers are narrower and smaller than those of *H. hispanica*, on 1-ft. stems that nod at the tip and carry their flowers on only one side. Leaves are also narrower—only about ½ in. wide. 'Alba' is white flowered; 'Rosea' has pink blooms.

CARE

Plant bulbs in fall, setting them 3 in. deep in mild climates, as deep as 6 in. where winters are severe. Space about 6 in. apart. Propensity for reseeding makes these good subjects for naturalizing; lovely in informal drifts among tall shrubs, under deciduous trees, among low-growing perennials. Need regular moisture from planting time until foliage dies and at least some moisture in summer. Divide infrequently; when division is needed, do it in late spring or early summer, when the leaves yellow. Plants thrive in pots, and flowers are good for cutting. Bulbs can cause allergic reactions on contact. Not favored by browsing deer.

COMMON HYACINTH IS ONE OF THE EASIEST BULBS TO FORCE INTO EARLY BLOOM INDOORS.

HYACINTHUS ORIENTALIS

COMMON HYACINTH
Asparagaceae
Perennial from bulbs

- 🌿 **ZONES VARY BY SPECIES**
- ☀️ ◑ **FULL SUN OR PARTIAL SHADE**
- 💧 **REGULAR WATER DURING GROWTH AND BLOOM**
- ◈ **BULBS MAY CAUSE AN ALLERGIC SKIN REACTION**

Hyacinthus orientalis

Together with tulips and daffodils, hyacinths are considered the "major bulbs" of spring. They feature glorious, thick spikes of fragrant, bell-shaped flowers that rise from a clump of narrow, bright green leaves. Plants grow 1 ft. tall, with straplike leaves that may be erect or somewhat arching. Blossom spikes are tightly packed with flowers in white, pale blue, or purple-blue. Hyacinths are at their best when massed or grouped; if set out in rows, they tend to look too stiff and formal. Try massing a single color beneath a flowering tree or in a border. Two basic forms are the Dutch and the Roman or French Roman.

Dutch hyacinth, derived from *H. orientalis* by breeding and selection, has large, dense spikes of waxy, bell-like flowers in white, cream, buff, and shades of blue, purple, pink, red, and salmon. Size of flower spike is directly related to size of bulb. Biggest bulbs are desirable for exhibition plants or for potting; next largest size is satisfactory for bedding outside. Small bulbs give smaller, looser clusters with more widely spaced flowers. These are sometimes called miniature hyacinths.

As perennials, Dutch hyacinth is best adapted to the Upper and Middle South, but it can be grown as an annual anywhere.

Roman or French Roman hyacinth (*H. o. albulus*) has white, pink, or light blue flowers loosely carried on slender stems, usually several stems to a bulb. Earlier to bloom than Dutch hyacinth; also needs little or no winter chill, making it better adapted to the Lower, Coastal, and Tropical South (where it will grow as a perennial under favorable conditions).

CARE

Plant from October to December. Set larger Dutch hyacinth bulbs 6 in. deep, 5 in. apart; set smaller ones and Roman hyacinth bulbs 4 in. deep, 4–5 in. apart. The bulbs have invisible barbs on the surface that can cause your skin to itch; after handling them, wash hands before touching your face or eyes. If you are growing hyacinths as perennials, fertilize just as blossoms fade; then remove spent spikes and continue to water regularly until foliage yellows. Flowers typically are smaller in succeeding years, but they keep the same color and fragrance.

Choice container plants. Pot in porous mix with bulb tip near surface. Then cover containers with thick mulch of sawdust, wood shavings, or peat moss to keep bulbs cool, moist, and shaded until roots are well formed; when tips of shoots show, remove mulch and place pots in full light. You can also grow hyacinths in water in a special hyacinth glass, the bottom filled with pebbles and water. Keep in dark, cool place until rooted; give light when top growth appears, then place in a sunny window when leaves have turned uniformly green.

HYDRANGEA

Hydrangeaceae
Deciduous shrubs and vines

- 🌿 **ZONES VARY BY SPECIES**
- ◑ **MORNING SUN, LIGHT AFTERNOON SHADE, EXCEPT AS NOTED**
- 💧 **REGULAR WATER**

Hydrangea quercifolia
'Snowflake'

Hydrangeas have exploded in popularity in recent years, thanks to their spectacular, long-lasting flowers in blue, purple, pink, red, or white. Close inspection reveals that each flower cluster is composed of tiny, fertile, seed-producing flowers on the inside, and large, showy, sterile flowers on the outside. 'Mopheads' feature large, rounded or conical clusters of sterile flowers that hide the fertile flowers inside. 'Lacecaps' display flattened clusters of fertile flowers ringed by showy sterile flowers. Fertile and sterile flowers may be two different colors depending on soil.

These plants are famed for the ability of their flowers to change colors due to soil conditions, but this only occurs in three of the listed species—*H. aspera*, *H. macrophylla*, and *H. serrata*—and for selections with flowers of blue, purple, pink, or red. Strongly acid soil (pH 5.5 and lower) produces the bluest colors; alkaline soil (pH 7.1 and above) produces pink and red flowers; and slightly acid to neutral soil (pH 6.5 to 7) produces a mix of blue, pink, and purple flowers. Soil pH does not affect white blooms in these species. It also doesn't cause the color change in species like *H. paniculata* and *H. quercifolia*; their blooms typically change

from white to rose as they age.

To acidify the soil, sprinkle aluminum sulfate or garden sulfur around your hydrangea, and water it in. To make the soil alkaline, do the same with lime. Don't expect overnight change. The change could take a year and require repeated applications.

H. anomala petiolaris. CLIMBING HYDRANGEA. Deciduous vine. Zones US, MS, LS; USDA 6-8. Native to Russia, Korea, and Japan. Truly one of the world's most beautiful vines, considering its flowers, foliage, and structure. Can climb to 60 ft. or more using clinging aerial rootlets. Green, 2- to 4-in., heart-shaped leaves turn soft yellow in fall. Mature vine develops a picturesque, woody scaffold of short branches held out from the support. Flat lacecap clusters of white flowers 6–10 in wide appear from late spring into summer. Some vines may take 10 years to start blooming. Needs little pruning.

H. arborescens. SMOOTH HYDRANGEA. Deciduous shrub. Zones US, MS, LS, CS; USDA 6-9. Native from New York to Iowa, south to Florida and Louisiana. Not much to look at in the wild; offers small clusters of creamy white, mostly fertile flowers in May or June. Named selections, listed below, are far superior. Prune in late winter. Severe pruning produces much larger blooms, but fewer of them. Can take full sun.

'Annabelle'. Classic all-time favorite, famous for huge, rounded clusters of sterile, white flowers up to a foot across over a long period. Grows about 4 ft. tall and wide.

'Bella Anna'. Often called 'the pink 'Annabelle',' although flower clusters are smaller. Rosy pink blooms held upright on sturdy stems. Grows 3–4 ft. tall and wide.

'Incrediball' ('Abetwo'). Offspring of 'Annabelle' with even larger clusters of white blooms.

'White Dome'. Dome-shaped clusters of sterile flowers to 10 in. across. Grows 5 ft. tall and wide.

H. aspera. Deciduous shrub. MS, LS; USDA 7-8. From eastern Asia. Imposing shrub to 10–12 in. tall, spreading nearly as wide. Dark green, velvety leaves to 10 in. long, 4 in. wide. Rather flat, 10-in. lacecap flower clusters contain purplish white to pink fertile flowers surrounded by 1-in. white, pink, or purple sterile blooms. Prune in late winter. Happier on the West Coast than in the South. Not a hydrangea for the beginner. 'Plum Passion' has dramatic purple foliage and insignificant flowers.

H. macrophylla. FRENCH HYDRANGEA, BIGLEAF HYDRANGEA. Deciduous shrub. Zones US, MS, LS, CS; USDA 6-9. From Japan, not France (many early selections originated in France). The South's most popular hydrangea. Symmetrical, rounded shape; grows 3–8 ft. tall and wide. Thick, shiny, coarsely toothed leaves to 8 in. long. Blooms first appear in May or June. Does not like drought; usually the first plant in your yard to wilt in summer.

Hundreds of named selections exist. Those listed below represent our top picks. Some bloom once a year for several weeks on the previous year's growth. Others bloom repeatedly on both old and new growth, as long as plant is kept actively growing in summer through frequent watering. Flowers for most can be either blue or pink, depending on soil pH.

ABOVE: Hydrangea macrophylla 'Endless Summer'

'All Summer Beauty'. Mophead. Repeat bloomer. Grows 4–5 ft. tall and wide. Dependable.

'Ami Pasquier'. Mophead. Once bloomer. Maintains deep-pink color in all but the most acidic soils, where it turns purple. Grows 4–5 ft. tall and wide.

'Ayesha'. Mophead. Once bloomer. Large clusters of uniquely cupped petals look like little buttons. Glossy foliage. Grows 6 ft. tall and wide.

'Big Daddy'. Mophead. Repeat bloomer. Gigantic blooms up to 14 in. across. Glossy foliage. Grows 5–6 ft. tall and wide.

'Blue Wave'. Lacecap. Once bloomer. Old, reliable choice. Glossy foliage. Grows 6 ft. tall and wide.

'Blushing Bride'. Mophead. Repeat bloomer. Blooms emerge white, turn blush pink, then finish deep rose. Grows 4 ft. tall and wide.

Cityline series. Mopheads. Compact, sturdy-stemmed plants that need no pruning. Variety of colors. Mildew resistant. Grows 3 ft. tall and wide.

'Dooley'. Mophead. Once bloomer. Cold hardy selection named for Vince Dooley, legendary football coach of the University of Georgia Bulldogs. Flower buds cold hardy to single digits. Grows 6 ft. tall and wide.

'Endless Summer'. Mophead. Repeat bloomer. The selection that turned the hydrangea world on its head, thanks to repeat blooms and clever marketing. Grows 4 ft. tall and wide.

Forever & Ever series. Mopheads and lacecaps. Repeat bloomers. Similar to 'Endless Summer' Series, but with larger flower clusters and larger individual florets. Blue, pink, white, red, and bicolor plants. Grow 4 ft. tall and wide.

'Fuji Waterfall'. Lacecap. Once bloomer. Double, white, sterile flowers on long stems appear to dance above the flower heads. A showstopper. Grows 3–4 ft. tall and wide.

'Générale Vicomtesse de Vibraye'. Mophead. Once bloomer. Like 'Dooley,' flower buds very cold hardy. Great for cut flowers. Grows 7 ft. tall and wide.

'Lanarth White'. Lacecap. Once bloomer. Compact, very dependable. Grows 3–4 ft. tall and wide. White, sterile flowers.

'Madame Emile Mouillère'. Mophead. Usually blooms once, but may repeat. Widely considered the best white mophead. Grows 6 ft. tall and wide.

'Merritt's Supreme'. Mophead. Once bloomer. Keeps deep pink color in all but most acid soils, where it turns royal purple. Grows 3–4 ft. tall and wide.

'Mini Penny'. Mophead. Repeat bloomer. Compact-growing seedling of 'Pennymac'. Grows 3–4 ft. tall and wide. Good in containers.

'Nikko Blue.' Mophead. Once bloomer. Cold-hardy flower buds continue the popularity of this dependable old favorite. Grows 5 ft. tall and wide.

'Penny Mac'. Mophead. Repeat bloomer great for cut flowers. Named for Penny McHenry, founder of the American Hydrangea Society. Grows 6 ft. tall and wide.

'Pia'. Mophead. Once bloomer. Charming dwarf great for containers. Pink or purple flowers. Grows 3 ft. tall and wide.

'Twist-n-Shout'. Lacecap. Repeat bloomer. Red to burgundy fall foliage. Grows 3–5 ft. tall and wide.

H. paniculata. PANICLE HYDRANGEA. Deciduous shrub or small tree. Zones US, MS, LS, CS; USDA 6-9. Native to Japan and China. Upright, spreading growth to 10–20 ft. tall and wide, sometimes larger. Recent breeding efforts have resulted in smaller plants, more manageable in the garden. Medium to dark green leaves, oval and pointed, 3–6 in. long, turn light yellow in fall. Flowers begin as elongated clusters of greenish white buds in early summer, opening to 4- to 8-in.-long cones of white, sterile flowers hiding fertile flowers within. Blooms age to a tawny pink, making a show that lasts for months. This is the toughest, most adaptable species listed here. Can take full sun. Prune in late winter. The plain species is seldom grown in favor of the following recommended selections.

'Grandiflora'. PEE GEE HYDRANGEA. An old favorite, sometimes called "the crepe myrtle of the North" for its cold hardiness and summer blooms. Coarse-textured plant can be trained into a 25-ft. tree or maintained as a shrub. Huge, rounded flower clusters to 1½ ft. long.

'Limelight'. White, upright blooms sometime age to deep pink. Grows 6–10 ft. tall. Extremely popular and deservedly so.

'Little Lime'. Dwarf version of 'Limelight', growing 3–5 ft. tall.

'Pink Diamond'. Pink buds open to cream-colored flowers that gradually darken to rosy red. To 10 ft. tall.

'Pinky-Winky'. Flower heads emerge white in summer and elongate. Blooms turn pink with age, creating a bicolor effect. To 8 ft.

'Tardiva'. Late-blooming form with conical flowers that appear in August and September. To 10 ft.

'White Diamonds'. Compact grower to 5–6 ft. tall and wide. Upright flower clusters to 8 in. long open white, then age to light green.

H. quercifolia. OAKLEAF HYDRANGEA. Zones US, MS, LS, CS; USDA 6-9. Native to the Southeastern U.S. The state wildflower of Alabama. Broad, rounded shrub to 6 ft. tall, 8 ft. wide. Handsome, deeply lobed, 8-in.-long leaves resembling those of oaks turn scarlet and crimson in fall. Elongated clusters of white flowers appear in late spring and

A HOST OF HYDRANGEAS

Hydrangea serrata 'Bluebird'

H. macrophylla 'Twist-n-Shout'

H. m. 'Mini Penny'

H. m. 'Blushing Bride'

H. m. 'Nikko Blue'

H. m. 'Big Daddy'

H. m. 'Fuji Waterfall'

early summer and age to rose. Prune in early summer. Favorite selections include:

'Alice'. Large flower clusters up to 14 in. long. Grows 12 ft. tall and wide.

'Harmony'. Huge, heavy clusters up to 12 in. long of mostly sterile flowers weigh down the branches. To 10 ft. tall.

'Jetstream'. Dense, compact grower (5–6 ft. tall, 4–5 ft. wide), with strong stems. Heavy bloomer; good orange-red fall color.

'Pee Wee'. Dwarf form with leaves and blooms about half the size of the species. Grows 3–4 ft. tall, 6 ft. wide.

'Sike's Dwarf'. Dwarf form growing 2 ft. tall, 4 ft. wide.

'Snowflake'. All-time favorite discovered by Alabama nurseryman Eddie Aldridge. Nodding blooms up to 15 in. long. As blooms age, new white florets emerge atop older ones that have turned dusty rose, creating a double-flowered, bicolored effect. Grows 10 ft. tall and wide.

'Snow Queen'. Showy clusters up to 8 in. long stand upright atop the shrub. Grows 6 ft. tall and wide. Superior selection.

H. serrata. MOUNTAIN HYDRANGEA. Deciduous shrub. Zones US, MS, LS; USDA 6-8. Native to Japan and China. Resembles *H. macrophylla* but is more compact and graceful, with smaller leaves. Also blooms earlier. Grows 3–6 ft. tall and wide. Many selections develop burgundy fall foliage. Prune in early summer.

'Akishino-temari'. Mophead. Compact shrub to 3 ft. tall and wide. May rebloom in fall.

'Beni-gaku'. Lacecap. Once bloomer. Flowers open white and age to red. Handsome, deep green foliage. Grows 4 ft. tall and wide.

'Blue Billow'. Lacecap. Dependable once bloomer with cold hardy flower buds. Grows 4 ft. tall, 6 ft. wide. One of the deepest blues when grown in acid soil.

'Bluebird'. Lacecap. Flowers off and on through summer. Leaves turn coppery red in fall. Grows 3–4 ft. tall and wide.

'Blue Deckle'. Lacecap. Like 'Bluebird,' blooms off and on all summer. Red fall foliage. Grows 4 ft. tall and wide.

'Kurohime'. Lacecap. Once bloomer. New stems are deep

purple. Grows 4 ft. tall and wide.

'Preziosa' (*H. macrophylla* 'Preziosa', *H.* 'Preziosa'). Mophead. Once bloomer. Compact growth to 3–4 ft. tall and wide, with dark maroon stems. Cold hardy.

'Purple Tiers' ('Miyama yae Murasaki'). Lacecap. Once bloomer. Layers of double, sterile flowers, purple in acid soil, are quite beautiful. Grows 4 ft. tall and wide.

'Woodlander'. Lacecap. Once bloomer. Green leaves age to dusky purple. Grows 4 ft. tall and wide.

CARE

Moist, well-drained, fertile soil is best. Prune hydrangeas that bloom on new growth in late winter. Prune those that bloom on last year's growth as this year's blooms start to fade. Prune repeat bloomers anytime. Keep in mind that most hydrangeas need little pruning other than removing dead wood in spring.

HYDRASTIS CANADENSIS

GOLDEN SEAL
Ranunculaceae
Perennial

* US, MS, LS; USDA 6-8
* PARTIAL OR FULL SHADE
* REGULAR WATER

Hydrastis canadensis

Native to the eastern U.S., this handsome plant offers bold, luxuriant foliage for woodland and shade gardens. It grows from a thick yellow rootstock, sending up two deeply lobed, maplelike, 8-in.-long leaves that are held 10–12 in. above the ground. In spring, a foot-tall stalk appears,

topped by a solitary, short-lived white flower to ½ in. across. The blossom is followed in summer by a large, showy red berry that resembles a raspberry, though it isn't edible.

Golden seal accepts ordinary garden soil but prefers moist soil containing plenty of organic matter. Because the root contains berberine, an antibacterial agent used in herbal medicine, the plant is threatened in the wild due to overcollection. Fortunately, it is easily propagated by seed, and in time specialty nurseries will be able to meet the demands of herbalists and native plant enthusiasts alike.

HYLOCEREUS UNDATUS

NIGHT-BLOOMING CEREUS, QUEEN OF THE NIGHT
Cactaceae
Cactus

* TS; USDA 10-11; OR GROW IN POTS
* FULL SUN OR LIGHT SHADE; BRIGHT INDIRECT LIGHT
* LITTLE TO REGULAR WATER

Hylocereus undatus

A plant that is often passed along from friend to friend, parent to child. Of unknown origin, but it is widely grown and naturalized in the tropical Americas. Deep green, three-ribbed, 2-in.-wide stems with short, dark spines grow quickly to 15 ft. (possibly to 30 ft.), attaching themselves to a tree trunk, wall, or house by means of strong aerial roots. Without a support, the stems create a large, freestanding mound with a beautiful snaking pattern. Grown primarily for its

waxy, fragrant, nocturnal white flowers, which are up to 1 ft. long. Individual flowers last just one night, but plant may bloom all summer. May also produce showy, 4-in.-long red fruit, which is edible and even deliciously sweet. Tolerates salt spray.

CARE

Easy to grow outdoors in well-drained soil in Tropical South. Elsewhere, grow in container and bring indoors in winter; keep humidity high and night temperature above 55°F. Fertilize monthly in spring and summer with balanced liquid fertilizer diluted to half-strength. Can survive drought but does best if watered regularly until flowering starts, then sparingly through the summer to encourage flowering.

HYMENOCALLIS

SPIDER LILY, PERUVIAN DAFFODIL
Amaryllidaceae
Perennials from bulbs

* ZONES VARY BY SPECIES; OR DIG AND STORE DECIDUOUS TYPES; OR GROW IN POTS
* FULL SUN OR PARTIAL SHADE
* REGULAR WATER DURING GROWTH AND BLOOM, EXCEPT AS NOTED
* BULBS ARE POISONOUS IF INGESTED

Hymenocallis coronaria

Stems rising from leafy clumps bear very fragrant flowers in summer; blooms resemble daffodils in having a center cup, but cup is surrounded by six slender, spidery segments. Deciduous species maintain foliage throughout summer if watered, then die back in fall.

Plant in rich, well-drained soil—in late fall or early winter in frostless areas, after frosts in other areas. Set bulbs with tips 1 in. below surface; space 1 ft. apart. Deciduous sorts can be dug after foliage has yellowed (do not cut off fleshy roots), dried in an inverted position, and stored in open trays in a cool, dark, dry place. These are pest-free plants; deer, squirrels, and voles won't eat them.

H. caroliniana. SOUTHERN SPIDER LILY. Deciduous. Zones US, MS, LS, CS; USDA 6-9. Native to swampy woodlands of Georgia, Indiana, and Louisiana. Each bulb produces as many as 12 deep green leaves 1½ ft. long, ½ ft. wide. White flowers to 5 in. across appear in spring and summer, in clusters of two to seven. Multiplies rapidly.

H. coronaria. SHOALS SPIDER LILY, CAHABA LILY. Deciduous. Zones MS, LS; USDA 7-8. Rare species found in a few rocky shoals of rivers in Alabama, Georgia, and South Carolina. Straplike leaves up to 3 ft. long rise above water from bulbs anchored in soil between rocks. Groups of six to nine fragrant white flowers with yellowish centers, to 2 in. across, appear atop 3-ft. stalks from mid-May to early June. Each flower lasts one day. Species endangered by degradation of habitat due to sedimentation; do not collect plants from the wild.

H. eulae (*H. galvestonensis*). Deciduous. Zones MS, LS, CS, TS; USDA 7-11. Native to Texas and Louisiana. Blue-green foliage appears in late winter, disappears in spring. Flower stems to 20 in. high emerge in midsummer, bearing clusters of six to nine white flowers, each about 5 in. across.

H. x festalis (*Ismene x festalis*). Deciduous. Zones LS, CS, TS; USDA 8-11. A hybrid of two Peruvian species. Mid-green leaves can reach 3 ft. long. Erect stems hold clusters of 2–5 fragrant white flowers, each up to 6 in. across. 'Zwanenburg' has larger, fuller flowers with scalloped cups.

H. latifolia (*H. keyensis*). CAYMAN ISLANDS, SPIDER LILY. Evergreen. Zone TS; USDA 10-11. Native to southern Florida and the West Indies. Clusters of 10 to 16 white flowers, each consisting of a 3-in. cup outlined by spidery segments to 5 in. long.

H. liriosme. TEXAS SPIDER LILY. Deciduous. Zones MS, LS, CS, TS; USDA 7-11. Native from Alabama to Texas. White, exceedingly fragrant flowers to 8 in. across are held in clusters of 8 to 10. Likes wet soil.

H. maximiliani. MAXIMILIAN'S SPIDER LILY. Deciduous. Zones MS, LS, CS, TS; USDA 7-11. From Mexico. Dense clump of slender, glossy green leaves. Each stem bears a cluster of several 6-in., spidery, white flowers in early summer.

H. narcissiflora (*Ismene calathina*). BASKET FLOWER, PERUVIAN DAFFODIL. Deciduous. Zones LS, CS, TS; USDA 8-11. Leaves 1½–2 ft. long, 1–2 in. wide. White, green-striped flowers to 4 in. across are held in clusters of two to five. 'Advance', a hybrid with *H. x festalis*, has pure white flowers, faintly lined with yellowish green in the throat.

H. 'Sulphur Queen'. Deciduous. Zones LS, CS, TS; USDA 8-11. Primroselike yellow flowers, to 6 in. across, with light yellow, green-striped throats; up to six per cluster. Sweetly fragrant. Leaves are much like those of *H. narcissiflora*.

H. 'Tropical Giant'. Deciduous. Zones MS, LS, CS, TS; USDA 7-11. Reliable old garden hybrid often found on abandoned properties in the South. Excellent foliage plant, its glossy green leaves forming an impressive clump in the boggy conditions it prefers. Blooms in midsummer, bearing small-cupped, white flowers to 6 in. across on 2- to 3-ft. stems. Good in containers.

HYPERICUM
ST. JOHNSWORT
Hypericaceae
Evergreen, semievergreen, and deciduous shrubs or perennials

🖊 **ZONES VARY BY SPECIES**

☼ ◐ **PARTIAL SHADE IN LOWER AND COASTAL SOUTH**

◌◌ **MODERATE TO REGULAR WATER, EXCEPT AS NOTED**

Hypericum patulum 'Hidcote'

Large group of shrubs and perennials bearing yellow flowers that resemble single roses with a prominent sunburst of stamens in center. Open, cup-shaped, five-petaled blooms range in color from creamy yellow to gold; flowers may be solitary or in clusters. Neat leaves vary in form and color. Plants are useful for summer flower color and fresh green foliage. Various kinds are used for mass plantings, ground covers, informal hedges, borders. Most types resist deer damage. Perform especially well in mild, moist areas.

H. beanii (*H. patulum henryi*). Evergreen shrub or perennial; more perennial-like in Upper South. Zones US, MS; USDA 6-7. From China. To 4 ft. tall and slightly wider, with light green, oblong leaves on graceful, willowy branches. Flowers brilliant golden yellow, 2 in. across, midsummer into fall. Good for low, untrimmed hedge, mass planting. Shabby in winter.

H. buckleyi. BLUE RIDGE ST. JOHNSWORT. Deciduous shrub. Zones US, MS, LS; USDA 6-8. Native to mountains from North Carolina to Georgia. Spreading plant to 1 ft. high; space plants 2 ft. apart for ground cover. Rich green leaves to 1 in. long, rounded at tip. Golden yellow flowers to

1 in. wide bloom in summer. 'Appalachian Sun' is compact at 10 in. high and 18 in. wide.

H. calycinum. AARON'S BEARD, CREEPING ST. JOHNSWORT. Evergreen to semievergreen shrub; tops often killed in cold winters but come back in spring. Zones US, MS, LS, CS; USDA 6-9. From Bulgaria, Turkey. To 1 ft. high, spreading by vigorous underground stems. Short-stalked leaves to 4 in. long are medium green in sun, yellow-green in shade. Bright yellow, 3-in.-wide flowers bloom all summer. A tough, dense ground cover that competes successfully with tree roots, takes poor soil. Fast growing; will control erosion on hillsides. May be invasive unless confined. Plant from flats or as rooted stems 1½ ft. apart. Clip or mow tops every 2 or 3 years during dormant season.

H. frondosum. BLUELEAF ST. JOHNSWORT. Deciduous shrub; evergreen in mildest areas. Zones US, MS, LS; USDA 6-9. Native to southeastern U.S. Grows 1–3 ft. tall, with mounding form. Blue-green leaves set off clusters of 1½-in., bright yellow flowers that bloom from midsummer to early autumn. 'Sunburst' forms a tight mound to 3 ft. tall and wide.

H. 'Hidcote' (*H. patulum* 'Hidcote'). Evergreen to semievergreen shrub. Zones US, MS, LS; USDA 6-8. To 4 ft. tall and 5 ft. wide. Leaves 2–3 in. long. Yellow flowers, 2½–3 in. wide, bloom all summer.

H. x moserianum. GOLD FLOWER. Evergreen subshrub or perennial. Zones US, MS, LS; USDA 6-8. Mounding plant with arching, reddish stems; reaches 2–3 ft. tall and wide. Leaves are 2 in. long, with blue-green undersides. Blooms in summer and possibly into fall, with golden yellow, 2½-in. flowers borne singly or in clusters of up to five. Cut back in early spring. 'Tricolor' has gray-green leaves edged in pink and white.

H. patulum 'Sungold'. Semievergreen shrub. Zones US, MS, LS; USDA 6-8. Selection of a species from China. Twiggy, rounded growth to 1½–2 ft. tall, 2–3 ft. wide. Oval, pointed 2-in.-long leaves. Golden yellow, 2- to 3-in.-wide flowers bloom in summer. Sometimes sold as *H. kouytchense*.

H. prolificum. SHRUBBY ST. JOHNSWORT. Deciduous shrub. Zones US, MS, LS; USDA 6-8. Native from New Jersey to

H

Georgia. Slow, dense grower to 1–4 ft. high and wide. Narrow, shiny, dark green leaves grow 1–3 in. long. Bears 1-in., yellow blossoms late spring to late summer. Attractive in masses.

H. reductum. ATLANTIC ST. JOHNSWORT. Evergreen shrub. Zones MS, LS, CS; USDA 7-9. Native to sandy, scrubby sites from North Carolina to Florida and Alabama. Forms a mat to 1–1½ ft. high, 2–4 ft. wide. Aromatic, needlelike green leaves turn bronzy in winter. Small (to ⅔-in.-wide) yellow flowers bloom in early summer. Once established, needs no supplemental watering.

HYPOESTES PHYLLOSTACHYA

POLKA-DOT PLANT, FRECKLE FACE
Acanthaceae
Tender perennial treated as annual

US, MS, LS, CS, TS; USDA 6-11; OR HOUSEPLANT

FULL SUN OR LIGHT SHADE; BRIGHT LIGHT

REGULAR WATER

Hypoestes phyllostachya

Formerly known as *H. sanguinolenta*. Grown for its pink-and-white-spotted green leaves, this 1- to 2-ft.-high and 1-ft.-wide South African plant is popular as a bedding plant or houseplant. Pair it with green-leafed plants such as baby's tears (*Soleirolia soleirolii*) or small ferns. Plants bloom very rarely. 'Splash' has larger spots. 'Confetti' has more, smaller freckles.

CARE

Tip-pinch to keep plant bushy. Growth can be cut to within an inch or so of the soil in early spring

to renew. Tend to become woody and need replacement every few years. For indoor use, plant in loose, peaty mixture in pots or planters. Feed every two weeks with half-strength general-purpose liquid houseplant fertilizer.

HYPOXIS

STAR GRASS
Hypoxidaceae
Perennial

ZONES VARY BY SPECIES

FULL SUN OR LIGHT SHADE

MODERATE TO REGULAR WATER

Hypoxis hirsuta

Pretty woodland plants with narrow to lance-shaped green leaves and small, star-shaped flowers. Need light, well-drained soil; well suited to rock gardens. Plants spread into wide colonies over time, but they're not invasive; dig up offsets to obtain new plants.

H. decumbens. GIANT STAR GRASS. Zones US, MS, LS, CS, TS; USDA 6-11. Native to Mexico. Dense mound of light green, grassy leaves to 8 in. tall, sprawling at least twice as wide. Bright yellow, 1-in. flowers in spring, summer, and fall.

H. hirsuta. YELLOW STAR GRASS. Zones US, MS, LS, CS; USDA 6-9. Native from Maine to Florida and west to Texas. Usually found in dryish, open woodlands, growing in sandy or stony soil. Grassy, somewhat hairy, foot-long leaves rise from a short rhizome. In spring and early summer, a foot-tall stem carries one to seven bright yellow, starlike, inch-wide flowers. A second bloom may follow later.

HYSSOPUS OFFICINALIS

HYSSOP
Lamiaceae
Perennial

US, MS, LS, CS; USDA 6-8

FULL SUN OR LIGHT SHADE

MODERATE TO REGULAR WATER

Hyssopus officinalis

This compact southern European herb grows 2 ft. high, 3 ft. wide, with narrow, glossy, dark green leaves on woody-based stems. Foliage has a pungent scent and a peppery taste; sometimes used in cooking. Profusion of dark blue flower spikes appears throughout summer and into autumn; not a dramatic show but pleasing. 'Rosea' has pink blooms; selections with white and lavender blooms also exist.

CARE

Start from seed sown in early spring or stem cuttings in late spring or early summer. Once established, it may self-sow. Takes some drought but will thrive with regular moisture if drainage is good. Tolerates trimming as a low hedge or as border for a knot garden.

I

IBERIS

CANDYTUFT
Brassicaceae
Perennials and annuals

ZONES VARY BY SPECIES

FULL SUN

REGULAR WATER

Iberis sempervirens

Free-blooming plants from southern and western Europe with clusters of white, lavender, lilac, pink, rose, purple, carmine, or crimson flowers. Perennial candytufts bloom in spring; can be used as winter annuals in Coastal and Tropical South. Annual species bloom in spring and summer; they are most floriferous when nights are cool. Use all types for borders, cutting; use perennials for edging, rock gardens, small-scale ground covers, containers. Deer resistant.

I. 'Absolutely Amethyst'. Perennial. Zones US, MS, LS, CS; USDA 6-9. This foot-high, spreading plant grows like evergreen candytuft but is pinkish purple.

I. amara. HYACINTH-FLOWERED CANDYTUFT, ROCKET CANDYTUFT. Annual. Zones US, MS, LS, CS, TS; USDA 6-11. To 12–15 in. high and 6 in. wide. Fragrant white flowers in tight, round clusters that elongate into hyacinthlike spikes. Narrow, slightly fuzzy leaves.

I. gibraltarica. Perennial. Zones MS, LS, CS; USDA 7-9. Like

I. sempervirens but is less hardy to cold and bears flatter clusters of light pinkish or purplish flowers, sometimes white near center.

I. 'Masterpiece'. Perennial. Zones LS, CS; USDA 8-9. Upright and spreading, to 10–12 in. high and 24 in. wide. Produces 3-in., white flower clusters; light pink buds give a subtle bicolor effect.

I. sempervirens. EVERGREEN CANDYTUFT. Perennial. Zones US, MS, CS; USDA 6-9. Grows 8 in. to 1 ft. or even 1½ ft. high, spreading about as wide. Narrow, shiny, dark green leaves look good all year. Pure white flower clusters carried on stems long enough to cut for bouquets.

Several lower-growing, more compact types are available. Look for 'Alexander's White', 6 in. tall, with fine-textured foliage; 'Little Gem', 4–6 in. tall; and 'Purity', a wide-spreading selection 6–12 in. high. 'Snowflake', 6–10 in. tall, spreading to 1½–3 ft., has broader, more leathery leaves than the species; it also has larger flowers in larger clusters on shorter stems. It is extremely showy in spring and continues sporadic bloom through summer and fall. 'Snowmantle' is similarly vigorous but slightly more compact. 'Snow White' grows into a 12- by 24-in. mound. Early-flowering 'Tahoe' is an upright grower to 10–12 in. high and wide.

I. umbellata. GLOBE CANDYTUFT. Annual. Zones US, MS, LS, CS, TS; USDA 6-11. Bushy plant to 12–15 in. high, 9 in. wide. Lance-shaped leaves to 3½ in. long; flowers in pink, rose, carmine, crimson, salmon, lilac, and white. The Candy Cane series is vigorous and uniform. Dwarf strains Dwarf Fairy and Magic Carpet grow 6 in. tall.

CARE

All types need well-drained soil. In early spring (or in fall in mild climates), sow seed of annuals in place or in flats; set transplants 6–9 in. apart. Plant perennials in spring or fall. After they bloom, shear lightly to stimulate new growth.

ILEX
HOLLY
Aquifoliaceae
Evergreen and deciduous shrubs and trees

ZONES VARY BY SPECIES

FULL SUN OR PARTIAL SHADE

REGULAR WATER, EXCEPT AS NOTED

BERRIES CAUSE GASTRIC UPSET

Ilex cornuta 'Berries Jubilee'

Few plants are as dependable, versatile, and popular as hollies. More than 400 species and countless hybrids exist. Although a number of deciduous kinds have spectacular winter berries, Southerners generally prefer evergreen types that feature handsome foliage year-round and showy fruit as a bonus. In size, hollies range from foot-high mounds to trees 40–50 ft. tall. Smaller, shrublike plants are useful as foundation plantings and low hedges. Large evergreen hollies make attractive tall screens and informal hedges, and they're also good in corner plantings or as single specimens in a spacious lawn. Small-leafed types can be sheared into formal hedges or used for topiary.

Nearly all holly plants are either male or female, and as a rule both sexes must be present for female plants to set fruit. The selections described here are female unless otherwise noted. A few set fruit without a pollenizer; these are noted too.

I. x altaclerensis. ALTACLARA HOLLY. Evergreen shrub or tree. Zones US, MS, LS; USDA 6-8. Hybrid between *I. aquifolium* and a species from western Europe. Large, vigorous plant naturally reaches 60 ft. tall and 40 ft. wide, but it can be trained into a large shrub or small tree to 15–20 ft. high, 10–12 ft. wide. Adapts to most soils, tolerates wind.

'Camelliifolia'. Lustrous, nearly spineless, dark green leaves up to 5 in. long. Large berries are dark red.

'James G. Esson'. Dark green, undulating, spiny leaves are a bit smaller than those of 'Camelliifolia'. Glossy red berries.

'Wilsonii'. Spiny, glossy, bright green leaves up to 5 in. long. Heavy crop of bright red berries. Makes a nice espalier, screen, or formal clipped hedge. Not as cold hardy as other selections.

I. aquifolium. ENGLISH HOLLY. Evergreen shrub or tree. Zones US, MS; USDA 6-7. Native to Europe, this is the holly of song, legend, and Christmas wreaths. It's a slow-growing plant that can eventually reach 40 ft. tall and 25 ft. wide, though it is usually much smaller in the South. Leaves are 2–4 in. long, highly variable in color, shape, and spininess. Some selections bear fruit without pollination, but the berries so produced are usually small and drop quickly. Deer resistant.

English holly is arguably the most ornamental holly, but it's not easy to grow in most of the South. Dislikes high humidity coupled with high temperatures; does not do well with poor drainage, extreme cold, dry winter winds. *I.* 'Nellie R. Stevens' is a better choice for achieving a similar effect. Selections of English holly include the following.

'Argentea Marginata'. Dark green leaves with whitish margins.

'Aurea Marginata'. Dark green leaves edged in bright yellow.

'Balkans'. Upright grower with smooth, dark green leaves; most cold hardy of the English hollies. Both male and female forms are available.

'Brilliant' (*I.* 'Brilliant'). Hybrid resulting from a cross with a Chinese species. Compact, dense, pyramidal growth to 10–20 ft. tall and wide. Dependably sets abundant fruit without a pollenizer.

'Ciliata Major'. Vigorous female form with bronzy green, flat leaves on which the spines point toward the tip.

'Gold Coast'. Grows slowly to just 4–6 ft. tall and wide. Dark green leaves are heavily edged in bright golden yellow. Male form; produces no berries.

'San Gabriel'. Female form with glossy, spiny leaves. Bright red fruit is produced without a pollenizer.

'Silver Queen'. Vigorous and upright, to 12–24 ft. tall and 10–12 ft. wide, with dark green leaves edged in white. New growth tinged pink. No fruit.

'Sparkler'. Strong, upright growth to about 12 ft. tall, 8 ft. wide. Heavy crop of glistening red berries at an early age.

'Teufel's Zero' ('Zero'). Upright grower with long, slender, weeping branches. Dark red berries ripen early. Cold hardy.

I. x aquipernyi. Evergreen shrub or tree. Zones US, MS, LS; USDA 6-8. Hybrid between *I. aquifolium* and *I. pernyi*. Dense, conical plant to 20 ft. tall (or taller), 12 ft. wide. Deep green, spiny leaves to 1½ in. long; red berries. Deer resistant.

'Aquipern'. Male form used as a pollenizer.

'Carolina Sentinel'. Narrow, columnar form. Very deep green leaves; bright red berries. A good choice for screening in narrow spaces.

'Patricia Varner'. Broad, upright form with dark green foliage and heavy crops of large berries. Fast grower.

'San Jose'. Dense, pyramidal form; reaches 15 ft. tall, 10 ft. wide. Glossy leaves and plenty of bright red berries. Sets fruit without a pollenizer.

I. x attenuata. Evergreen tree. Zones US, MS, LS, CS; USDA 6-9. Hybrid between *I. opaca* and *I. cassine*. To 12–30 ft. tall and about half as wide, with dense foliage and a conical or pyramidal habit. Light green leaves are sparsely toothed, to 3 in. long. Dark red berries. Fast growing; a popular choice for screening. Selections include these four:

'East Palatka'. Discovered near East Palatka, Florida, in 1927. Abundant bright red berries. More open and less hardy than 'Foster #2'. Young leaves have few spines; mature leaves are often spineless.

'Foster #2'. The most popular and ornamental of several hybrids known by the name Foster holly. Narrow, conical form. Small, narrow leaves with short spines. Plentiful red berries.

'Hume #2'. Glossy, rounded, nearly spineless leaves. Shiny red berries. Can reach 35 ft. tall.

'Savannah'. Very popular selection prized for fast growth and tremendous crops of bright red berries. Narrow, upright growth to 35 ft. tall and 8 ft. wide. Leaves have short spines and look more like traditional holly foliage than do leaves of other *I.* x *attenuata* selections. Tolerates limy soil.

I. cassine. DAHOON. Large evergreen shrub or small tree. Zones MS, LS, CS, TS; USDA 7-11. Native to swamps and moist lowlands from North Carolina to Florida and Louisiana. Dense, upright habit to 20–30 ft. tall, 8–15 ft. wide. Leathery, medium green leaves, 2–4 in. long, toothed only at tips. Heavy crops of small berries in red to reddish orange (sometimes nearly yellow). Grows naturally in wet, acid soils;

tolerates mild alkalinity and has some salt tolerance. Regular to ample water.

I. cornuta. CHINESE HOLLY. Evergreen shrub or small tree. Zones US, MS, LS, CS; USDA 6-9. From China and Korea. Very tolerant of heat, drought, alkaline soil. Dense or open form to 10 ft. or more. Leaves typically glossy, leathery, nearly rectangular, 1½–4 in. long, with sharp pines at four corners and at tip. Very large, bright red, long-lasting berries. Selections rather than species usually grown; fruit set, leaf form, and spininess vary. The following selections set fruit without pollination. Deer resistant.

'Berries Jubilee'. Dome-shaped plant to 6–10 ft., with large leaves and heavy crop of large, bright

red berries. Leaves are larger, spinier than those of 'Burfordii'.

'Burfordii'. BURFORD HOLLY. To 20 ft. tall and wide. Leaves nearly spineless, cupped downward. Sets a heavy crop of red fruit (much prized by mockingbirds and cedar waxwings) without a pollenizer. Useful as espalier. Discovered in Atlanta's Westview Cemetery around 1900; hard to find in nurseries nowadays.

'Carissa'. Dwarf to 3–4 ft. high and 4–6 ft. wide at maturity. Dense grower with small leaves; good for low hedge. No berries. Sometimes reverts to 'Rotunda', the plant from which it was developed.

'Dazzler'. Compact, upright growth. Glossy leaves have a few stout spines along wavy margins. Loaded with rich red berries.

'D'Or'. Quite similar to 'Burfordii' but has bright yellow berries.

'Dwarf Burford' ('Burfordii Nana'). Like 'Burfordii' but is somewhat smaller, to about 8 ft. tall and wide. Densely covered with small (1½-in.), light green, nearly spineless leaves. Dark red berries.

'Needlepoint'. NEEDLEPOINT HOLLY. Dense, upright, a little larger than 'Dwarf Burford'. Dark, narrow, green leaves with a single spine at tip; large crops of red berries.

'Rotunda'. DWARF CHINESE HOLLY. Compact grower to 3–4 ft. tall and 6–8 ft. wide at maturity. Usually does not produce berries. A few stout spines and rolled leaf margins between spines make the medium light green leaves nearly rectangular.

'Willowleaf'. WILLOWLEAF HOLLY. Dense spreader to 15 ft. high and wide; makes a good screen. Oblong, dark green leaves have smooth margins and a single spine at the tip. Heavy crop of blood-red berries.

I. crenata. JAPANESE HOLLY. Evergreen shrub. Zones US, MS, LS; USDA 6-8. From Russia, Japan, Korea. The backbone of many a foundation planting because it's an attractive plant that's hard to kill. Looks more like boxwood (*Buxus*) than holly. Dense, erect, usually 3–4 ft. high, sometimes to 10 ft. Narrow, fine-toothed, dark green leaves, ½–¾ in. long; black berries. Extremely hardy and useful where winter cold

limits choice of tender evergreens for hedges, edgings. Selections include the following.

'Beehive'. Dense, compact mound to 3–4 ft. tall, 5–6 ft. wide.

'Compacta'. Rounded shrub to 6 ft. tall. Dense habit. Many different plants are sold under this name.

'Convexa'. Compact, rounded shrub to 4–6 ft. high, spreading wider. Leaves are roundish, cupped downward at the edges. Use clipped or unclipped. Many different plants are sold under this name.

'Dwarf Pagoda'. Exceptionally dense, slow-growing plant—to 1 ft. high and wide in 8 years. Leaves are tiny.

'Fine Line'. Upright pyramid to 10–15 ft. tall, 4–8 ft. wide. Glossy, dark green leaves have a yellow-green, translucent edge. Red fruit.

'Glory'. Male (fruitless) selection. Small, dense, round form; grows 5 ft. tall, 8 ft. wide. Extremely hardy.

'Golden Gem'. Male (fruitless) selection with bright golden leaves (best color when grown in full sun). Grows 1½–2 ft. tall and wide.

'Helleri'. Dwarf selection to 1 ft. high, 2 ft. wide; larger after many years, to 4 ft. tall and 5 ft. wide. Very sensitive to poor drainage. Brittle branches.

'Jersey Pinnacle'. Compact, dense, erect. To eventual 8 ft. tall, 2 ft. wide.

'Piccolo'. Slowly forms a tidy, dense, dark green mound 1 ft. high and wide.

'Sky Pencil'. Narrow, columnar plant to 6–8 ft. tall and 2 ft. wide. Striking in containers.

'Soft Touch'. Grows 2 ft. tall, 3 ft. wide. Unlike other selections, it has soft, flexible branches.

I. decidua. POSSUMHAW. Deciduous tree. Zones US, MS, LS, CS; USDA 6-9. Native to the Southeast. To 6–10 ft., possibly to 20 ft. Pale gray stems; shiny dark green leaves to 3 in. long. Orange to red berries last into winter or spring. 'Warren's Red', eventually 15–20 ft. tall, bears a heavy crop of large red berries. 'Byers Golden' is a yellow-fruited selection. 'Council Fire' is lower growing, sports orange-red berries. For fruit production, these need a male pollenizer such as 'Red Escort' or any male selection of *I. opaca*, such as 'Jersey Knight'.

TOP: Ilex decidua branches; BOTTOM: I. aquifolium 'Silver Queen'; I. opaca 'Canary'

I. 'Doctor Kassab'. Evergreen shrub or tree. Zones US, MS, LS, CS; USDA 6-9. Hybrid between *I. cornuta* and *I. pernyi*. To 15–20 ft. high and 12–15 ft. wide, with broad, pyramidal form. Beautiful foliage: lustrous dark green, oval, pointed leaves with toothed edges, to 2 in. long. Plenty of bright red berries. Quite cold hardy, surviving –10°F.

I. 'Emily Bruner'. Evergreen shrub or tree. Zones MS, LS, CS; USDA 7-9. Chance hybrid between *I. cornuta* 'Burfordii' and *I. latifolia*. Dense, pyramidal grower to 12–20 ft. tall, 10–15 ft. wide. Handsome dark green leaves to 4–5 in. long, with prominently toothed edges. Large red berries. Use male selection *I.* 'James Swann' as pollenizer.

I. glabra. INKBERRY. Evergreen shrub. Zones US, MS, LS, CS; USDA 6-9. Native to eastern North America. To 10 ft. tall and wide, with thick, spineless, dark green leaves to 2 in. long (leaves turn olive-green in winter). Berries are black. More widely sold than the species is dwarf form 'Compacta'; it reaches 4 ft. high and wide but can be sheared to make a 2-ft. hedge. 'Densa', 'Nigra', 'Nordic', and 'Shamrock' are other dwarf forms. Grows in sun or partial shade; prefers acid soil. Tolerates wet soil and salt spray. Deer resistant.

I. latifolia. LUSTERLEAF HOLLY. Evergreen tree. Zones MS, LS, CS; USDA 7-9. Native to China, Japan. Slow-growing, stout-branched plant to 20–25 ft. tall, 15 ft. wide. Leaves are 6–8 in. long (largest of all hollies), dull dark green, leathery, fine toothed. Big clusters of large, dull red berries. In youth, resembles Southern magnolia (*Magnolia grandifolia*).

I. 'Lydia Morris'. Evergreen shrub or small tree. Zones US, MS, LS, CS; USDA 6-9. Hybrid between *I. cornuta* 'Burfordii' and *I. pernyi*. Dense, pyramidal habit; reaches 20–25 ft. tall, 15 ft. wide. Very spiny, 1½- to 3-in.-long, lustrous blackish green leaves are held close to stems. Cardinal red berries. Use male selection *I.* 'John Morris' as pollenizer. Deer resistant.

I. 'Mary Nell'. Evergreen shrub or small tree. Zones US, MS, LS, CS; USDA 6-9. Complex hybrid involving *I. cornuta* 'Burfordii', *I. latifolia*, and a selection of *I. pernyi*. To 25–30 ft. tall, 15 ft. wide, with pyramidal habit. Very shiny, spiny dark green leaves to 4 in. long; great quantities of bright red berries. Popular in the Southeast.

I. x meserveae. MESERVE HOLLY. Evergreen shrub. Zones US, MS; USDA 6-7. Apparently the most cold hardy of hollies with the true holly look. Most plants in this category are hybrids between *I. aquifolium* and *I. rugosa*, a cold-tolerant species from northern Japan; they are dense, bushy shrubs 6–7 ft. tall and wide, with purple stems and spiny, glossy, blue-green leaves. Among red-berried female selections are 'Blue Girl' and 'Blue Princess'; male pollenizers include 'Blue Boy' and 'Blue Prince'. 'Golden Girl' has yellow berries. Red-fruited 'China Girl' and male pollenizer 'China Boy', both to 10 ft. tall, are crosses of *I. cornuta* and *I. rugosa*. They are slightly hardier and tolerate more summer heat than the Blue series. 'Ebony Magic' reaches at least 8–12 ft. tall, 6–8 ft. wide, with upright, pyramidal form. Blackish purple stems and spiny-edged, shiny, dark green leaves to 1–2 in. long; big orange-red berries last through spring. Use 'Ebony Male' as pollenizer.

I. 'Nellie R. Stevens'. Evergreen shrub or small tree. Zones US, MS, LS, CS; USDA 6-9. Hybrid between *I. aquifolium* and *I. cornuta*. The South's most popular large holly. Dense, fast-growing, conical plant to 15–20 ft. tall, 10 ft. wide. Leathery, glossy, dark green leaves are sparsely toothed and reach 3 in. long. Sets fruit without a pollenizer but produces more berries if pollinated by a male selection of *I. cornuta*. A favorite for foundation and corner plantings as well as for tall screens. Probably the best all-around holly for the South.

I. 'Oakland'. Evergreen shrub. Zones US, MS, LS. CS; USDA 6-9. Hybrid of complex parentage. Dense, pyramidal plant to 15–20 ft. high and 12–15 ft. wide. Closely spaced, bright green leaves have the look of an elongated oak leaf with spines. Red berries appear without the need for a pollenizer. Makes a fine specimen or large hedge. Good resistance to diseases and pests.

I. opaca. AMERICAN HOLLY. Evergreen tree. Zones US, MS, LS, CS; USDA 6-9. Native to eastern U.S. Slowly grows to 40–50 ft.

TOP: Ilex pedunculosa BOTTOM: I. verticillata 'Winter Red'

tall, 20–40 ft. wide; densely pyramidal when young, then becomes open, irregular, and picturesque with age. Spiny green leaves reach 2–4 in. long, may be glossy or dull; show some bronzing in winter. Red berries. Site in a wind-protected spot. Subject to many pests, with leaf miner being perhaps the most troublesome; to control, pick off and destroy all affected leaves in spring. If this is impractical, spray with an insecticide registered for use on holly (check with your local Cooperative Extension Office). Rarely bothered by deer. Hundreds of selections exist, offering great variety. The following are some of the better and more widely available forms.

'Canary'. Large crops of buttercup-yellow berries. Light olive-green leaves have small spines and do not discolor in winter.

'Dan Fenton'. Forms a compact pyramid to 20 ft. tall and 15 ft. wide. Large, dark green leaves have a squarish appearance. Lustrous red berries.

'Jersey Knight'. Slow-growing male selection with shiny, dark green leaves. Selected to pollinate 'Jersey Princess'.

'Jersey Princess'. Lustrous, very dark green leaves hold color throughout winter. Abundant red berries. Very cold hardy. Excellent performer in the Southeast.

'Maryland Dwarf' ('Maryland Spreader'). Unusual prostrate form grows slowly to 3 ft. high,

6–10 ft. wide. Large, glossy, deep green leaves; red berries.

'Merry Christmas'. Fast-growing, densely branched tree. Glossy, deep green leaves have short spines. Profuse bright red berries.

'Miss Helen'. Dense, conical tree with leathery, dark green leaves. Plenty of egg-shaped, dark red berries are produced if a male pollenizer such as 'Jersey Knight' is nearby.

I. pedunculosa. LONGSTALK HOLLY. Evergreen shrub or small tree. Zones US, MS; USDA 6-7. Exceptionally cold hardy for a broad-leafed evergreen. From China, Japan. Grows to 15 ft. or taller; awkward shape when young. Narrow, smooth-edged leaves 1–3 in. long, half as wide. Bright red, ¼-in. berries dangle on 1- to 1½-in.-long stalks in fall.

I. pernyi. PERNY HOLLY. Evergreen tree. Zones US, MS, LS; USDA 6-8. Native to China. Slow growth to 20–30 ft. tall, 10 ft. wide. Glossy, 1- to 2-in.-long leaves, square at base, one to three spines on each side; closely packed against branchlets. Red berries set tightly against stems.

I. 'Red Beauty'. Evergreen shrub. Zones US, MS, LS, CS; USDA 6-9. Hybrid between *I.* x *meserveae* and *I. pernyi.* Forms a dense pyramid 7–10 ft. tall and 4–5 ft. wide, with dark green, spiny leaves and bright red berries. Sets fruit without a pollenizer but puts on a better show near a male variety of *I.* x *meserveae.*

I. 'Robin'. Evergreen shrub or small tree. Zones US, MS, LS, CS; USDA 6-9. Seedling of *I.* 'Mary Nell'. Beautiful, spiny leaves to 3 in. long emerge maroon, then mature to dark green. Abundant red berries. Similar in form and cold hardiness to *I.* 'Nellie R. Stevens' but may grow somewhat larger.

I. 'Sparkleberry'. Deciduous shrub. Zones US, MS, LS, CS; USDA 6-9. Female selection of hybrid between *I. verticillata* and *I. serrata*, released by the U.S. National Arboretum. 'Harvest Red' and 'Bonfire' (pollinated by 'Ruritam Chief') are even better. Grows to 6 ft. high and wide; old specimens may reach 12 ft. Toothed-edged, dark green leaves to 4 in. long drop in early winter. Sets copious amounts of large, bright red fruit that persists through winter; pollinate with male 'Apollo'. Tolerates wet soils.

I. verticillata. WINTERBERRY. Deciduous shrub. Zones US, MS, LS, CS; USDA 6-9. Native to swamps of eastern North America. Unlike most hollies, this one thrives in boggy soils, but it will succeed in any moist, acid, organic soil. Species and most selections grow 6–10 ft. tall and wide, eventually forming clumps by suckering. Dark green, oval leaves to 3 in. long may turn yellow in autumn. Female plants bear enormous crops of bright red berries that ripen in early fall and last all winter (if the birds don't eat them). Plant one male plant for every six females. Selections include the following. Deer resistant.

'Afterglow'. Orange to orange-red berries on a slow-growing, compact, globe-shaped plant.

'Cacapon'. Compact and upright, with glossy, crinkled leaves. Particularly long-lasting berries. Does very well in the Southeast.

'Jim Dandy'. Male form used to pollinate 'Afterglow', 'Cacapon', 'Red Sprite', and 'Shaver'. Grows 3–6 ft. tall, 4–8 ft. wide.

'Red Sprite'. Dwarf form grows to 3–5 ft. high and wide. Large bright red berries—the largest fruit of the dwarf winterberries.

'Shaver'. Slow-growing plant with large orange-red berries.

'Southern Gentleman'. Male form used to pollinate 'Cacapon', 'Shaver', 'Winter Red'.

'Winter Gold'. Resembles 'Winter Red', but with lighter green leaves and pinkish or golden orange berries. Use male selection 'Southern Gentleman' as pollenizer.

'Winter Red'. Large, rounded form; profuse bright red berries that retain their color into February. Lustrous, good-looking leaves. Considered by many to be the best winterberry. Use male selection 'Southern Gentleman' as pollenizer.

I. vomitoria. YAUPON. Evergreen shrub or small tree. Zones MS, LS, CS, TS; USDA 7-11. Native to the South. Grows in almost any soil—acid or alkaline, wet or dry, rich or poor. Good plant for the beach. Tolerates salt spray. Grows to 15–20 ft. tall, with narrow, inch-long, shallowly toothed, dark green leaves. Can be grown as standard or sheared into columnar form; good topiary plant. Tiny scarlet berries are borne in profusion. Resists damage by deer. Popular selections include the following.

'Bordeaux'. To 3–4 ft. high and wide, with lustrous green leaves that turn wine-red in winter.

'Gold Top'. Golden new growth. Red fruit.

'Katherine'. Bears a heavy crop of golden yellow fruit.

'Nana'. DWARF YAUPON. Low shrub. Compact grower to 1½ ft. high and twice as wide. Refined, attractive. Inconspicuous berries.

'Pendula'. Weeping branches look best when plant is trained as standard.

'Pride of Houston'. Upright, freely branching. Use as screen or hedge. Bears an abundant crop of berries.

'Stokes' ('Stokes Dwarf', 'Schillings Dwarf'). Male form. Compact plant with tiny, dark green leaves closely set on branches. Smaller than 'Nana'.

'Scarlet's Peak'. Female form. Narrow, upright grower to 20 ft. tall and just 3 ft. wide. Dark green leaves and plenty of red berries. Does not splay open with time like the male 'Will Fleming'.

CARE

Most hollies prefer rich, moist, slightly acid, well-drained soil, though there are some exceptions (these are noted). All appreciate a layer of mulch to discourage weeds and keep the soil cool and moist. Though hollies will grow in sun or light shade, you'll get denser growth and heavier berry production in full sun. Diseases and insects are seldom serious; scale and leaf miner are the most common pests.

Evergreen hollies accept pruning quite well. Prune in winter to shape, control size, and harvest berry-laden branches for holiday arrangements. Also remove dead, broken, or crossing branches. Hollies that have grown too large or have become misshapen can be restored by severely shortening main branches; new growth will sprout from branch stubs and quickly fill in.

ILLICIUM

ANISE TREE
Schisandraceae
Evergreen shrubs or trees

◾ **MS, LS, CS; USDA 7-9, EXCEPT AS NOTED**

◑ ● **PARTIAL OR FULL SHADE, EXCEPT AS NOTED**

💧 **AMPLE WATER, EXCEPT AS NOTED**

◆ **ALL PARTS OF *I. ANISATUM* ARE POISONOUS IF INGESTED**

Illicium mexicanum

Little-used but attractive clan of shrubs or small trees noted for both foliage and flowers. Thick, leathery, glossy leaves are anise-scented when crushed; spring flowers have many petal-like segments and are reminiscent of small magnolia blossoms. Fruit that follows are small, one-sided pods arranged in a ring. The star anise of Chinese cookery is the fruit of the tropical tree *I. verum*, apparently not grown in North America. All like rich soil with abundant organic material. Big, bold foliage gives the impression of rhododendrons. Good understory plants for woodland gardens; also useful for screening. Seldom need pruning. Unappealing to deer.

I. anisatum. JAPANESE ANISE. Native to Japan, South Korea, Taiwan. To 6–10 ft. (possibly 15 ft.) tall, 6–8 ft. wide; conical growth habit. Oval to lance-shaped, blunt-tipped, glossy leaves to 5 in. long, 2 in. wide are held perpendicular to the stems. Inch-wide, scentless flowers on short, nodding stalks cluster in leaf axils; they open yellowish green, then fade to creamy white. Much planted in Buddhist cemeteries; cut branches are used to decorate graves. Highly fragrant wood is used for incense.

I. floridanum. FLORIDA ANISE. Zones US, MS, LS, CS; USDA 6-9. Native Florida to Louisiana. Reaches 6–10 ft. or taller, equally wide. Pointed oval leaves 6 in. long and 2 in. wide, with prominent midribs. Waxy, nodding, maroon flowers 1–2 in. across on 1½- to 2-in.-long stalks; most people find scent unpleasant. *I. f. album* is white flowered. 'Halley's Comet' is more compact, with larger, redder flowers than the species; often blooms into fall. 'Variegatum' has maroon-purple flowers with subtle green-on-green leaf variegation. Each leaf of vigorous 'Pink Frost' is edged in cream; entire leaf turns pink in fall. 'Shady Lady' has leaves edged in white; its flowers are soft pink. 'Woodland Ruby' is a hybrid with ruby-pink, 2-in. flowers shaped like starfish; flowering period extends through summer.

I. mexicanum. MEXICAN ANISE. Shrub. Native to northern Mexico. Grows 4–8 ft. tall and nearly as wide, with narrowly oval, pointed, medium-green leaves held on red stems. Fragrant, reddish pink flowers to 2 in. across are produced mainly in spring, with some repeat bloom through summer. 'Aztec Fire' has larger flowers held on longer stems and thus further out from the foliage, making for a showier plant in bloom.

I. parviflorum. YELLOW ANISE. Zones US, MS, LS, CS; USDA 6-9. Native to Florida. Grows 15–20 ft. tall, 10–15 ft. wide, with 4-in., oblong, olive-green leaves and ½-in. yellow-green flowers. Can form small colonies by suckering. More tolerant of sun and dry soil than other anise trees, but equally at home in damp shade. 'Florida Sunshine' is vigorous and compact, reaching 6–8 ft. tall and 4–6 ft. wide; its leaves are chartreuse to golden, shading to bright yellow with cooler weather.

IMPATIENS
IMPATIENS, SULTANA, BALSAM
Balsaminaceae
Perennials and annuals

✎ **US, MS, LS, CS, TS; USDA 6-11, EXCEPT AS NOTED**

☀◑ ● **EXPOSURE NEEDS VARY BY SPECIES**

◖◗ ◖◗ **REGULAR TO AMPLE WATER**

Impatiens walleriana

Of the hundreds of species, only the following are usually seen in gardens. Most of these are annuals or tender perennials treated as annuals; all are valuable for long bloom period (most flower in summer, and a few continue into fall). When lightly touched, ripe seed capsules burst open and scatter seeds.

I. balfourii. Annual. From the Himalayas. To 20 in. high and broad, with 4- to 5-in. leaves and loose clusters of inch-wide, pink-tinted white flowers. Seldom planted but often pops up unannounced. It can become a pest by reseeding, but it is attractive in shady, informal plantings.

I. balsamina. BALSAM. Annual. From Southeast Asia. Erect, branching plant reaches 8–30 in. high and 6–8 in. wide. Sharp-pointed, 1½- to 6-in.-long leaves with deeply toothed edges. Large, spurred flowers are borne among leaves along main stem, branches; they may be solid colored or variegated, in white or shades of pink, rose, lilac, or red. Compact, double camellia–flowered forms are most frequently grown. Sow seeds in flats or pots in early spring; after frost danger is past, set out young plants (or purchased transplants) in full sun (light shade in hottest climates).

IMPATIENS DOWNY MILDEW

In 2011, a devastating fungal disease began showing up on *I. balsamina*, *I. capensis*, and *I. walleriana* and its hybrids. By 2012, impatiens downy mildew had made its way into commercial nurseries across the U.S. Early symptoms include yellowing and downward curving of infected leaves, soon followed by white, downlike fungal growth on the leaf undersides. Infected plants quickly die, and there is no effective treatment. Avoid overhead watering, as this quickly spreads the disease. Destroy infected plants immediately. New Guinea hybrids are immune.

ABOVE: Impatiens SunPatiens

I. capensis. JEWEL WEED. Annual. Native to damp, shady sites in Canada and the northern U.S. Grows 2–5 ft. tall, 2 ft. wide. Smooth, tooth-edged, green leaves to 3½ in. long. Spurred, 1-in. orange-yellow flowers with reddish brown splotches; blooms in summer, fall. Partial or full shade. Juice from crushed stems is used to treat dermatitis caused by poison ivy, poison oak.

I. New Guinea hybrids. Perennials in Zone TS; USDA 10-11; annuals anywhere. A varied group of striking plants developed from a number of species native to New Guinea, especially *I. hawkeri*. Plants can be upright or spreading; most are 1–2 ft. tall and as wide or wider. Leaves are typically large, often variegated with cream or red. Flowers usually large (2½ in. wide) though not profuse, held well above foliage; colors include lavender, purple, pink, red, orange, and white. Once considered primarily potted plants, they also perform well as bedding plants; provide ample fertilizer and give somewhat more sun than you would *I. walleriana*.

Popular strains include 'Celebration' (with 3-in. flowers),

'Paradise', 'Sunshine', and 'Pure Beauty'. Most New Guinea hybrids are cutting-grown plants, but 'Spectra' ('Firelake') and 'Java' strains can be grown from seed. 'Spectra' offers a mix of flower colors and has leaves variegated with cream or white; bronze-leafed 'Java' is available in single or mixed colors. 'Tango', also seed grown, has bright orange blooms and bronze-green foliage.

SunPatiens strain is the result of a cross between New Guinea hybrids and a wild species. These are long-lived, free-blooming plants that can take full sun in all but the hottest areas. Flower colors range from pinks and reds through coral and orange and white. Three form-based series are offered: Compact (upright and bushy, to 2–3 ft. tall and wide); Spreading (mounding growth to 2½–3½ ft. tall and 3 ft. wide); and Vigorous (vase-shaped, 3–4 ft. tall and 3 ft. wide).

I. omeiana. HARDY IMPATIENS. Perennial in Zones US, MS, LS, CS; USDA 6-9. From mountainous areas of China. To 1–1½ ft. high, spreading by runners. Primarily grown for its attractive leaves that grow to 1½ in. long and are velvety dark green with a whitish stripe down the center. Blooms in early fall, bearing small yellow to apricot flowers that resemble little goldfish. Partial or full shade.

I. repens. YELLOW IMPATIENS. Perennial in Zone TS; USDA 10-11, usually grown as annual. From India, Sri Lanka. To 8 in. high, 1 ft. wide, with thick reddish stems and kidney-shaped, 1-in., green leaves. Hooded, clear yellow, 1½-in. flowers from summer to fall. Good choice for hanging baskets. Partial shade.

I. sodenii. POOR MAN'S RHODODENDRON. Perennial in Zone TS; USDA 10-11; indoor/outdoor plant elsewhere. From eastern tropical Africa. To 4–8 ft. tall, 10 ft. wide, with woody-based stems clothed in whorls of 8-in.-long, glossy, dark green leaves. Produces many 2½-in., slender-spurred flowers in lilac, pale lavender, or pinkish shades. Tolerates seacoast conditions. Frosts kill it to ground, but it regrows in spring. Blooms in partial or deep shade; takes sun in cool-summer areas. 'Flash' has white blooms streaked with bright rose-pink. 'Madonna' has pure white flowers.

I. walleriana. IMPATIENS, SULTANA. Perennial in Zone TS; USDA 10-11, annual anywhere. The South's most popular flowers for partial or full shade; will take full sun if watered frequently almost daily. Rapid, vigorous growth; tall types reach 2 ft. high, dwarf kinds 6–12 in. high. Narrow, glossy, dark green, 1- to 3-in.-long leaves on juicy pale green stems. Flowers 1–2 in. wide, in all colors but yellow and true blue. All types are useful for many months of bright color. Grow plants from seed or cuttings, or buy them in cell packs or pots. Space taller types 1 ft. apart, dwarfs 6 in. apart. If plants overgrow, cut them back to 6 in. above ground—it's a tonic. New growth emerges in a few days, and flowers cover it in 2 weeks. Plants often reseed in moist ground.

At any given moment, there are dozens of excellent strains on the market; many are just nuanced versions of the others. Following are some of the more popular.

Accent. To 10 in. high, in numerous individual colors or a mix.

Blitz. To 16 in. high, with 2-in. flowers in mixed or single colors.

Dazzler. To 11 in. high, in all colors plus a star pattern.

Super Elfin. To 8–10 in. high. Comes in an exceptionally wide range of individual colors and blends of harmonizing hues. One example is 'Blue Pearl', with flowers in an unusual bluish lilac shade.

Swirl. To 10–12 in. high. Pastel shades with picotee edges of deeper color.

Many novelty strains and selections are available. They include 'Firefly', dwarf series to 6–8 in. high, with ½-in. flowers in the full range of impatiens colors; 'Confection', 10–12 in., producing a high percentage of double and semidouble flowers from seed; and 'Victorian Rose', 10–12 in., with frilly, rose-pink, semidouble flowers. Other double impatiens with flowers resembling rosebuds include cutting-grown 'Fiesta', 'Rockapulco', and 'Tioga' strains. The double-flowered types are best used as potted plants, located where flower detail can be observed close up.

IMPERATA CYLINDRICA 'RUBRA' ('RED BARON')

JAPANESE BLOOD GRASS
Poaceae
Perennial grass

🌱 **US, MS, LS, CS; USDA 6-9**

☀️ ◐ **FULL SUN OR PARTIAL SHADE**

💧 **REGULAR WATER**

Imperata cylindrica 'Rubra'

Elegant clumps of bright red, nearly vertical grass blades give this Japanese native grass both textural and visual punch. Erect stem forms a clump 1–2 ft. tall, 1 ft. wide. Striking in borders,

especially where sun can shine through blades. Completely dormant in winter. Spreads slowly by underground runners. Rarely, if ever, flowers. Good for textural contrasts; mixes well with perennials that have yellow-green or blue-green foliage. Best in rich, well-drained soil. Waste no time in removing and destroying any reversions to the plain green-leafed form called cogon grass, which is extremely invasive and has spread throughout Alabama, Florida, and Mississippi.

INCARVILLEA

Bignoniaceae
Perennials

🌱 **ZONES VARY BY SPECIES**

☀️ ◐ **LIGHT SHADE IN HOTTEST CLIMATES**

💧 **REGULAR WATER**

Incarvillea delavayi

Native to the Himalayas and China, these plants have showy trumpet-shaped flowers similar to those of their trumpet vine relatives (*Bignonia*, *Campsis*, and the like). Flowers are large for the size of the plant. Many species are coming into cultivation, but only the following two have reached North American gardens in any numbers. Leaves are 2–8 in. long, divided featherwise into leaflets. Plants are deep rooted and need reasonably deep soil and excellent drainage. In Upper South, mulch plants after the soil has frozen (to prevent ground from heaving). Protect from slugs and snails.

I. arguta. HIMALAYAN GLOXINIA. Zones LS, CS; USDA 8-9. Can be treated as annual in colder areas, since it will bloom first year from seed if started in

earliest spring. Grows erect to 5 ft. tall and 3 ft. wide, or sprawls to 3 ft. tall and 5 ft. wide; somewhat shrubby at base. Leaves divided into 4 to 12 leaflets, each up to 2 in. long. Blooms in spring and summer; inflorescences have 5 to 20 pink or white, 1½-in.-long flowers. Effective leaning over walls or spilling down slopes. Self-sows but not a pest.

I. delavayi. HARDY GLOXINIA. Zones US, MS; USDA 6-7. To 2 ft. high, 1 ft. wide. Like *I. arguta*, has divided leaves and trumpet-shaped flowers—but in other respects, it is entirely different. Grows from a carrot-shaped perennial root and forms a rosette of foot-long leaves, each divided into many leaflets. The foot-tall flower stalk is topped by 2–12 flowers that are 3 in. long and wide, rosy purple outside, yellow and purple within. Blooms in late spring, early summer. Division is difficult. 'Bee's Pink' has mauve-pink blooms; those of 'Snowtop' are white.

INDIGOFERA

INDIGO BUSH
Papillionaceae
Deciduous shrubs

🌱 **US, MS, LS, CS; USDA 6-9**

☀️ ◐ **FULL SUN TO PARTIAL SHADE**

💧💧 **MODERATE TO REGULAR WATER**

Indigofera kirilowii

Native to northern China, Korea, Japan. Woody-stemmed plants with finely divided, almost ferny foliage and dense clusters of tiny, sweet pea–shaped flowers in spring and summer. Plants can be killed to the ground in a hard winter, but they recover quickly from the roots and bloom on new wood. Even in mild-winter areas, they are more compact and attractive when cut back hard in late dormant season. Provide good drainage. Very heat and drought tolerant. Nearly indestructible.

I. decora. CHINESE INDIGO. To 1–2½ ft. tall and 3 ft. wide, with arching branches. Narrow, somewhat drooping blossom clusters to 8 in. long hold as many as 40 white blooms suffused with pink. Spreads steadily by suckers to form a patch. Makes good ground cover under trees.

I. heterantha. HIMALAYAN INDIGO. To 4–8 ft. high and wide, with arching branches. Purplish pink flowers in upright clusters 6–8 in. long.

I. kirilowii. KIRILOW INDIGO. To 2½–3 ft. tall, 3 ft. wide, with upright shoots and erect, 5-in. clusters of rose-pink flowers. *A. k. alba* has white blooms.

I. 'Rose Carpet' (*I. pseudotinctoria* 'Rose Carpet'). Dense, low-growing plant to 1 ft. tall and 4 ft. wide. Rose-pink blooms appear over a long period from mid- to late summer.

INULA
Asteraceae
Perennials

⚊ US, MS, LS; USDA 6-8

☼ ☽ EXPOSURE NEEDS VARY BY SPECIES

💧💧💧 WATER NEEDS VARY BY SPECIES

Inula magnifica

Large group of plants native to Europe and Asia grown for their showy, daisylike, yellow flowers. Imposing and erect, they have large basal leaves and progressively smaller leaves higher up on the stems. Medium green, oval, pointed leaves are often hairy or downy. Good for open, casual gardens or against a dark-colored background. Soil should be well drained. Deer resistant.

I. helenium. ELECAMPANE. Robust plant to 6 ft. tall, 3 ft. wide, with basal leaves 1½–2 ft. long. Blooms in summer, bearing single or clustered, bright yellow flowers to 3 in. across. Widely naturalized in the U.S. Root is used medicinally for respiratory complaints. Full sun or partial shade. Regular water.

I. magnifica. SUNRAY FLOWER. About the same size as *I. helenium* but with broader, rougher leaves. Clusters of up to 20 deep yellow, 6-in. flowers appear in late summer. Good plant for the back of the border. Excellent cut flower. Full sun. Regular to ample water; will grow in boggy soil.

IOCHROMA
Solanaceae
Evergreen vining shrubs

⚊ ZONES CS, TS; USDA 9-11

☼ ☽ FULL SUN OR PARTIAL SHADE

💧 REGULAR WATER

Iochroma cyaneum 'Royal Queen Purple'

From the forests of Central and South America. These fast-growing, vining shrubs have drooping, tubular or trumpet-shaped flowers in clusters of up to 20 near ends of branches. Blooms from early spring through fall—or year-round in frost-free areas. Leaves 5–8 in. long, 1½–3 in. wide. Fruit is pulpy berries.

Lax growth is best staked up, espaliered, or draped over a fence or wall. Prune selectively to maintain size and shape—and to keep the flowers coming. Avoid pruning in late fall or when cold weather approaches. Hard pruning delays bloom. Protect from hard frosts. Cucumber beetles love to eat the leaves.

In addition to the following, specialists offer a number of other species and hybrids.

I. cyaneum. Grows to 8 ft. or more, with dull dark green leaves. Stems and new shoots are covered with soft, grayish down. Narrow trumpets are 2–3 in. long. Blossom color of seedlings varies from blues through violets and deep reds to purplish rose and pink. All have a metallic sheen. Buy plants in bloom to get the color you want, or select named varieties. 'Indigo' is glossy violet-blue; 'Peachy Keen' has peachy red flowers; 'Royal Blue' is a lighter, more brilliant blue; 'Royal Queen Purple' has bright purple blooms; and 'Sky King' is a pure light blue.

I. fuchsioides. To 10 ft. or more, with glossy, bright green leaves. Brilliant orange-scarlet, tubular flowers with yellow throats look like fuchsia flowers.

IPHEION UNIFLORUM
SPRING STAR FLOWER
Iliaceae
Perennial from bulb

⚊ US, MS, LS, CS; USDA 6-9

☼ ☽ FULL SUN OR PARTIAL SHADE

💧 REGULAR WATER DURING GROWTH AND BLOOM

Ipheion uniflorum 'Wisley Blue'

Spring-blooming Argentine native with wildflower charm. Each bulb produces several slender stems, each bearing a single half-inch blossom with six overlapping petals. Usual color is light blue, but variants include white *I. u. album* and 'White Star', pink 'Charlotte Bishop', deep violet 'Froyle Mill', bright blue 'Rolf Fiedler', and medium blue 'Wisley Blue'. All have narrow, nearly flat, bluish green leaves that smell like onions when bruised. Use in borders or under deciduous shrubs; or naturalize in woodland areas or among low grasses. Not bothered by rodents or deer.

CARE

In fall, set bulbs 2 in. deep and 2 in. apart. Prefers dry conditions during summer dormancy but will accept water if drainage is good. Divide infrequently—plantings become more attractive over the years as bulbs multiply and reseed. They'll grow, multiply, and live happily in a low, wide container for several years.

IPOMOEA
MORNING GLORY
Convolvulaceae
Perennial and annual vines

⚊ ZONES VARY BY SPECIES

☼ FULL SUN

💧💧 MODERATE TO REGULAR WATER

Ipomoea tricolor 'Wedding Bells'

In this genus, ornamentals and edibles abound, from edible sweet potatoes (see Sweet Potato) to trellis-climbing morning glories and the sweet potato vines that fill out container plantings so well. Native to tropical and subtropical regions of the world.

Most have hard seeds; to encourage faster sprouting, nick

TOP: *Ipomoea alba*; BOTTOM: *I. tricolor* 'Heavenly Blue'; *I. quamoclit*

the coating or soak overnight in water before planting. For annual display, sow seeds in place after frost danger is past; or, for an earlier start, sow seeds indoors, then set out plants 6–8 in. apart. Use morning glory vines on fence or trellis or as ground cover. Or grow in containers; provide stakes or a wire cylinder for support, or let plant cascade. For cut flowers, pick stems with buds in various stages of development and place in deep vase; buds open on consecutive days.

I. alba. MOONFLOWER, MOON VINE. Perennial in TS; USDA 10-11; annual elsewhere. Fast growing (20–30 ft. in a season), providing quick shade for arbor, trellis, or fence. Luxuriantly clothed in heart-shaped leaves to 8 in. long, closely spaced on stems. Blooms from early summer until fall, showing off fragrant, 6-in., funnel-shaped white blossoms after sundown and into the night (flowers also

open on cloudy or dark days).

I. batatas. SWEET POTATO VINE. Perennial from tuberous roots. Zones LS, CS, TS; USDA 8-11, or indoor/outdoor plant. Annual in US, MS; USDA 6-7. For the edible sort, see Sweet Potato; the following fancy-leafed forms are grown for ornament. Trailing in habit, they have leaves that vary in size from 2–4 in. long, range in shape from heart shaped to deeply lobed. 'Ace of Spades' has purple-black, perfectly heart-shaped leaves; those of 'Blackie' are similar in color but are deeply lobed. 'Margarita' has golden green foliage. 'Pink Frost' ('Tricolor') has green foliage with white and pink variegation. 'Lady Fingers' has medium green leaves divided into long, fingerlike lobes; veins and leafstalks are burgundy-red. Sweet Caroline series features deeply toothed leaves available in green, bright lime-green, dark burgundy, red, and bronze (rust color). Plants in the Illusion series have dense,

deeply dissected foliage in light green or purple. All of these selections look great in window boxes and hanging baskets but can overrun less vigorous companion plants. Feeding by golden tortoise beetle can riddle the leaves with holes. 'Margarita' is particularly susceptible.

I. indica. BLUE DAWN FLOWER. Perennial. Zones CS, TS; USDA 9-11. Vigorous, rapid growth to 15–30 ft. Dark green, 2½- to 7-in, heart-shaped or three-lobed leaves. Clusters of 3- to 4-in., funnel-shaped flowers from spring into fall; blooms open bright blue, then fade to pinkish purple by day's end. Use to cover large bank, wall, or unsightly fence or other structure. Blooms in 1 year from seed; can also be grown from cuttings, divisions, and layering of established plants.

I. lindheimeri. LINDEHEIMER MORNING GLORY. Perennial. Zones LS, CS, TS; USDA 8-11. Native from Texas to New Mexico and Mexico. Deeply cleft leaves; fragrant blue flowers to 3½ in. long from spring until fall. Trailing habit, but not invasive. Well suited to dry, chalky soils.

I. lobata (*Mina lobata*). FIRECRACKER VINE, SPANISH FLAG. Perennial. Zones TS; USDA 10-11; grown as annual elsewhere. Grows quickly to 10–15 ft. Dark green, deeply lobed leaves are 4 in. long. Bloom begins in late summer and continues until frost; flower spikes to 6 in. long are held above the foliage and carry tubular, ½- to ¾-in. blossoms on just one side. Blooms start out red, then fade to orange, yellow, and finally white; 'Citronella' features lemon-yellow flowers that age to cream and white. Blossoms attract hummingbirds; also make good cut flowers. Plant in fertile, well-drained soil, and provide a post, trellis, or fence for support. Don't overdo the fertilizer or you'll get mostly leaves and few flowers.

I. x multifida. CARDINAL CLIMBER. Annual. To 15 ft. Broad leaves to 4½ in. wide, each divided into 7 to 15 sharp-pointed segments to ½ in. wide. Crimson flowers with a white eye bloom in summer.

I. nil. MORNING GLORY. Annual. Summer bloomer resembling *I. tricolor*, but with leaves that are often shallowly three-lobed (leaves of *I. tricolor* are unlobed). The large-flowered

(to 6-in.-wide) Imperial Japanese strain belongs to this species; other selections include rosy red 'Scarlett O'Hara', odd pinkish tan 'Chocolate', and mixed-color Early Call strain. Flowers of 'Tie Dye' are white with bold stripes and splashes of blue or pink.

I. pes-caprae. BEACH MORNING GLORY, RAILROAD VINE. Evergreen perennial. Zones CS, TS; USDA 9-11. Native to Florida. Sprawling vine grows to great length, rooting at leaf joints as it runs. Medium green leaves are fleshy, 1½–4 in. long, notched at the tip, and nearly round to kidney shaped. Pink summer flowers to 2 in. wide. Useful as a ground cover on sandy saltwater beaches.

I. purpurea. COMMON MORNING GLORY. Perennial in TS; USDA 10-11; annual elsewhere. Like *I. tricolor* but generally has smaller leaves and flowers. Blooms in summer. Rapid growth to 30–40 ft. Medium green leaves are broadly oval and pointed, three lobed or unlobed. First flowers appear a few weeks after sowing seed; then vine quickly covers itself in 5-in.-wide purple, blue, white, and pink blooms with pale throats, especially showy because of their many colors. Water and fertilize sparingly during summer to encourage flowers. Reseeds and returns in spring; watch that it doesn't escape and become a nuisance. 'Grandpa Otts' and 'President Tyler' are deep purple with a rosy red, star-shaped overlay and white throat; 'Milky Way' is pure white with a maroon star. 'Crimson Rambler' has bright red, white-throated blooms.

I. quamoclit. CYPRESS VINE. Annual. To 20 ft., with 2½- to 4-in.-long, dark green leaves finely divided into slender threads. Summer flowers are scarlet (rarely white), 1½-in.-long tubes that flare at mouth into a five-pointed star.

I. tricolor. MORNING GLORY. Annual. Vigorous growth to 10–15 ft., with large, heart-shaped leaves in light to medium green. Showy, funnel-shaped to bell-like flowers are single or double, in solid colors of blue, lavender, pink, red, or white, often with throats in contrasting colors; some are bicolored or striped. Most types open only in morning, fade in afternoon. Bloom from summer until frost. Among the most popular selections is 'Heavenly Blue', to 15 ft., bearing 4- to 5-in., pure sky-blue flowers with yellow throat. 'Wedding Bells' is similar, but with rosy-purple blooms. 'Flying Saucers' has 4- to 5-in. white blossoms variably streaked with purplish blue. Dwarf strain with white markings on the leaves (known as Spice Islands or simply as Variegated) grows only 9 in. high and spills to 1 ft. across; flower colors include red, pink, blue, and bicolors.

IPOMOPSIS RUBRA

STANDING CYPRESS
Polemoniaceae
Biennial or short-lived perennial

- **US, MS, LS, CS; USDA 6-9**
- **FULL SUN OR PARTIAL SHADE**
- **MODERATE TO REGULAR WATER**

Ipomopsis rubra

Native to the South. To 6 ft. tall, 1 ft. wide. Tubular flowers are red outside, yellow marked with red inside. Erect, unbranched stems are clothed in finely divided dark green leaves. Startling in appearance, best massed; individual plants are narrow. Sow seed in spring or early summer for bloom the following summer. Difficult to transplant once established. Adapts to almost any well-drained soil. Attracts hummingbirds.

IRESINE HERBSTII

BLOODLEAF
Amaranthaceae
Perennial

- **TS; USDA 10-11, OR GROW IN POTS**
- **FULL SUN; BRIGHT LIGHT**
- **REGULAR WATER**

Iresine herbstii 'Blazin' Rose'

This tender, upright plant is grown for its vibrant leaf colors; flowers are inconspicuous and may be pinched out. From Brazil. Grows 1–3 ft. high and wide, or even larger under ideal conditions. Leaves are 1–3 in. long, oval to round, usually notched at tip. Leaf colors run from purple to red, bronze, and green, with light or yellowish midrib and veins. Stems may be green, purple, or red. 'Blazin Rose' and 'Brilliantissima' are red-leafed varieties. 'Purple Lady' is purple.

Performs best in rich, well-drained soil. Pinch tips of young plants to encourage bushiness. Good in containers. Beyond hardiness range, bring indoors for winter, treat as annual, or grow as houseplant next to a south-facing window. Easy to propagate from cuttings taken in fall and grown for spring and summer display.

IRIS

Iridaceae
Perennials from bulbs and rhizomes

- **ZONES VARY BY SPECIES OR TYPE**
- **EXPOSURE NEEDS VARY BY SPECIES**
- **WATER NEEDS VARY BY SPECIES**
- **TOXIC KINDS NOTED IN ENTRIES**

Siberian iris 'Caesar's Brother'

A large and remarkably diverse group of 200 to 300 species, varying in flower color and form, cultural needs, and blooming periods (although the majority flower in spring or early summer). Leaves are swordlike or grasslike. Flowers (fragrant, in many kinds) are showy and complex in structure. The three inner segments (the standards) are petals; they are usually erect or arching but, in some kinds, may flare to horizontal. The three outer segments (the falls) are petal-like sepals; they are held at various angles, from nearly horizontal to drooping.

Irises grow from bulbs or rhizomes. In floral detail, there are three categories: bearded (each fall bears an adornment resembling a small, fuzzy caterpillar), beardless (each fall is smooth), and crested (each fall bears a comblike ridge instead of a full beard).

Described here are the irises most available in the South. Tall bearded irises (and other bearded classes) are the most widely sold; many new hybrids are cataloged every year. Specialty growers abound. A smaller number offer various beardless classes and some species. Retail nurseries carry bulbous irises for fall planting. Deer don't usually bother irises.

BULBOUS IRISES. Irises that grow from bulbs have beardless flowers. Bulbs go dormant in summer and can be lifted and stored until planting time in fall.

Dutch and Spanish irises. Zones US, MS, LS; USDA 6-8. The species that parented this group come from Spain, Portugal, Sicily, and northern Africa. (Dutch irises acquired their name because the hybrid group was developed by Dutch bulb growers.) Flowers are borne atop slender stems that rise from rushlike foliage. Standards are narrow and upright; oval to circular falls project downward. Colors include white, mauve, blue, purple, brown, orange, yellow, as well as bicolor combinations—usually with a yellow blotch on falls. Dutch iris flowers reach 3–4 in. across, on stems 1½–2 ft. tall; these are the irises sold by florists. Bloom is early spring in warm-winter regions, late spring in colder ones. Spanish irises are similar but have smaller flowers that bloom about two weeks later.

Plant bulbs in autumn, setting them 4 in. deep, 3–4 in. apart; give full sun. Bulbs are hardy to about –10°F; in Upper South, apply a mulch in winter. Give regular water during growth and bloom. Bulbs can be left in the ground for several years where summers are dry; elsewhere, they should be lifted. After bloom, let foliage ripen before digging; store bulbs in a cool, dry place for no more than two months before replanting. Dutch and Spanish irises are good in containers; plant five bulbs in a 5- to 6-in. pot.

Reticulata irises. Zones US, MS, LS; USDA 6-8. The netted outer covering on the bulbs gives the group its name. These are classic rock garden and container plants, with flowers like small Dutch irises appearing on 6- to 8-in. stems in early spring. Narrow, blue-green leaves appear after bloom. Available species include *I. reticulata*, with 2- to 3-in. violet-scented flowers (purple, in the usual forms), and *I. danfordiae*, with bright yellow blooms. Pale blue–flowered species *I. histrio* and large-flowered, blue-and-yellow *I. histrioides* may be carried by some specialists. Far more common are named hybrids such as 'Cantab' (pale blue with orange markings), 'Harmony' (sky-blue marked yellow), 'J. S. Dijt' (reddish purple), 'Katherine Hodgkin' (light greenish blue marked with white,

TOP: **Bearded Iris 'Savannah Sunset'; Tall Bearded Iris 'Rare Quality';**
MIDDLE: Various tall bearded irises; *BOTTOM:* Tall Bearded Iris 'Magic
Rainment'; **Bearded Iris 'Wonderful World'**

yellow, and violet), 'Natascha' (palest blue flowers marked yellow), and 'Pixie' (deep blue marked gold and white).

Bulbs are hardy to about –10°F and need some subfreezing winter temperatures to thrive. Plant in autumn, in well-drained soil in a sunny location; set bulbs 3–4 in. deep and 3–4 in. apart. Need regular moisture from fall through spring. Soil should be kept dry during summer dormant period; in rainy climates, lift bulbs in summer or grow in pots so you can control moisture. Divide only when vigor and flower quality deteriorate. Watch for slugs and snails.

RHIZOMATOUS IRISES.
Irises that grow from rhizomes (thickened, modified stems) may have bearded, beardless, or crested flowers; among this group are the most widely grown types. Leaves are swordlike, overlapping each other to form flat fans of foliage.

Clumps become overcrowded after 3 or 4 years, and quantity and quality of bloom decrease. Lift and divide crowded clumps at best planting time for your area. Save large rhizomes with healthy leaves; discard old and leafless ones from clump's center. Break rhizomes apart or use a sharp knife to separate. Trim leaves, roots to about 6 in.; let cut ends heal for several hours to a day before replanting. If replanting in the same soil, amend it with organic matter.

Bearded irises. Zones US, MS, LS, CS; USDA 6-9. The most widely grown irises fall into the bearded group. More than a century of breeding has produced a vast array of beautiful hybrids. All have upright standards and flaring to pendent falls that have characteristic epaulette-like beards. Tall bearded irises are the most familiar of these, but they represent just one subdivision of the entire group. Eating any part of these causes gastric upset, and plants have poisoned livestock. In addition, some people get contact dermatitis from handling the rhizomes.

Dwarf and median bearded irises. These irises generally have flowers shaped like those of the familiar tall beardeds, but flower size, plant size, and stature are smaller. Median iris is a collective term for the categories standard dwarf, intermediate and border bearded, and miniature tall bearded.

Miniature dwarf bearded irises. Grow to 8 in. tall; flowers large for size of plant. Earliest to bloom of bearded irises (about six weeks before main show of tall beardeds). Hardy, need winter chill. Plants multiply quickly. Shallow root systems need regular moisture and periodic feeding.

Standard dwarf bearded irises. Grow 8–15 in. tall. Flowers and plants are larger than miniature dwarfs. Profuse bloom. Perform best with some winter chill.

Intermediate bearded irises. Grow 15–28 in. tall, bear flowers 3–5 in. across. Flower later than dwarfs but one to three weeks before tall bearded irises. Most are hybrids between standard dwarfs and tall bearded selections and resemble larger standard dwarfs rather than border beardeds. Some give second bloom in fall.

Border bearded irises. Grow 15–28 in. tall—proportionately smaller versions of tall beardeds in the same wide range of colors and patterns. Bloom period is same as for tall bearded.

Miniature tall bearded irises. Grow 15–28 in. high and flower at the same time as tall beardeds. Their small flowers (2–3 in. wide), narrower foliage, and pencil-thin stems give them appearance of tall bearded irises reduced in every proportion. Good for cutting and arrangements—hence their original name, "table irises."

Tall bearded irises. Among choicest perennials for borders, massing, and cutting. Easy to grow. Midspring flowers come on branching stems 2½–4 ft. high. All colors but pure red and green; patterns of two colors or more and blends produce infinite variety. Countless named selections are available. Modern hybrids often have elaborately ruffled, fringed flowers. Available variegated-foliage selections include 'Pallida Variegata' (often cataloged as 'Zebra'), with green leaves striped with cream; and 'Argentea', producing green leaves with white stripes. Both bear smallish blue-lavender flowers on stems to 2 ft. high.

Remontant (reblooming) tall bearded irises flower in spring, again in mid- to late summer or fall, depending on selection and climate. Plants need fertilizer, regular moisture for best performance. Specialists' catalogs offer

HOW TO GROW BEARDED IRISES

SOIL Bearded irises need good drainage. They'll grow in soils from sandy to claylike—but in clay soils, plant in raised beds or on ridges to assure good drainage, avoid rhizome rot.

PLANTING Plant in September or October, in full sun or light shade. Space rhizomes 1–2 ft. apart; set with tops barely beneath soil surface, spreading roots well. Growth proceeds from the leafy end of rhizome, so point that end in direction you want growth initially to occur. For a quick show, plant three rhizomes 1 ft. apart—two with growing ends pointing outward, the third aimed to grow into the space between them. On slopes, set rhizomes with growing end facing uphill. If weather turns hot, shade newly planted rhizomes to prevent sunscald and possible rot.

WATER Water newly planted rhizomes well to settle soil and start growth. Thereafter, water judiciously until new growth shows plants have rooted; then water regularly until fall rains or frosts arrive. From the time growth starts in late winter or early spring, water regularly until about 6 weeks after flowers fade; buds for next year's flowers form during postbloom period. During the summer, plants require less water. In heavy soil, it may be sufficient to water plants every other week; in lighter soils, try watering weekly.

FERTILIZER For best performance, feed plants with commercial bulb fertilizer as growth begins in spring, then again after bloom has finished.

CHALLENGES In cool, moist springs, leaf spot may disfigure foliage; use appropriate fungicide at first sign of infection. Remove old and dry leaves in fall.

increasing numbers of remontant tall beardeds.

BEARDLESS IRISES. Flowers in this group all have smooth, "beardless" falls but otherwise differ considerably in appearance from one type or species to another. Rhizomes have fibrous roots (unlike fleshy roots of bearded types); most prefer or demand more moisture than bearded irises. Many can perform well in crowded clumps but will eventually need division when performance declines. Timing varies; dig and replant quickly, keeping roots moist until planted. The following four hybrid groups contain the most widely sold beardless irises.

Japanese irises. Zones US, MS, LS, CS; USDA 6-9. Derived solely from *I. ensata* (formerly *I. kaempferi*), these irises feature sumptuous blossoms 4–12 in. across on slender stems to 4 ft. high. Flower shape is essentially flat. "Single" types have three broad falls and much-reduced standards, giving triangular flower outline; "double" blossoms have standards marked like the falls and about the same size and shape, resulting in circular flower outline. Colors are purple, violet, pink, rose, red,

white—often veined or edged in contrasting shade. Plants have graceful, narrow, upright leaves with distinct raised midribs. Use in moist borders, at edge of pools or streams, or even in boxes or pots plunged halfway to rim in pond or pool during growing season.

Plants need much moisture during growing, flowering period. Both soil and water should be neutral to acid. If soil or water is alkaline, apply aluminum sulfate or iron sulfate (1 ounce to 2 gallons water) several times during growing season. Plant rhizomes in fall or spring, 2 in. deep and 1½ ft. apart; or plant up to three per 12-in. container. Full sun. Divide about every 3 years, in early fall.

Louisiana irises. Zones US, MS, LS, CS; USDA 6-9. Approximately four species from the lower Mississippi region and Gulf Coast compose this group of so-called swamp irises. Graceful, flattish blossoms on stems 2–5 ft. tall, carried above and among leaves that are long, narrow, and unribbed. The range of flower colors and patterns is extensive—nearly the equal of tall beardeds. Zigzag

iris (*I. brevicaulis*, sometimes listed as *I. foliosa*) has blue flowers with flaring segments carried on zigzag stems among the foliage. Copper iris (*I. fulva*) has coppery to rusty red (rarely yellow) blossoms with narrow, drooping segments. *I. giganticaerulea* is indeed a "giant blue" (sometimes white) with upright standards and flaring falls; stems to 4 ft. or more, with proportionally large leaves. *I. hexagona* also comes in blue shades with upright standards and flaring falls. *I. x nelsonii*, a natural hybrid population derived from *I. fulva* and *I. giganticaerulea*, resembles the *I. fulva* parent in flower shape and color (but also includes purple and brown tones) and approaches the *I. giganticaerulea* parent in size.

Plants thrive in well-watered, rich garden soil as well as at pond margins; soil and water should be neutral to acid. Locate in light afternoon shade. Plant in late summer; set rhizomes 1 in. deep, 1½–2 ft. apart. Mulch for winter where ground freezes. Divide every 3 to 4 years, in late summer or early fall.

Siberian irises. Zones US, MS, LS; USDA 6-8. The most widely sold members of this group are named hybrids derived from *I. sibirica* and *I. sanguinea* (formerly *I. orientalis*)—species native to Europe, Asia. Clumps of narrow, almost grasslike leaves (deciduous in winter) bear slender stems to 4 ft. high (depending on selection), each bearing two to five blossoms with upright standards and flaring to drooping falls. Colors include white and shades of blue, lavender, purple, wine, pink, and light yellow.

Give plants partial or dappled shade, neutral to acid soil. Plant in spring or fall; set rhizomes 1–2 in. deep, 1–2 ft. apart. Water liberally from onset of growth until several weeks after bloom. Divide infrequently—when clumps show hollow centers—in late spring or fall.

Spuria irises. Zones US, MS, LS, CS; USDA 6-9. In flower form, spurias resemble Dutch irises. Older members of this group had primarily yellow or white-and-yellow blossoms; *I. orientalis* (*I. ochroleuca*) has naturalized in many parts of the South, its 3- to 5-ft. stems bearing white flowers with yellow blotches on the falls. Dwarf *I. graminea* bears narrow-petaled, fragrant blue-and-maroon

blossoms on foot-high stems. Modern hybrids show a great color range: blue, lavender, gray, orchid, tan, bronze, brown, purple, earthy red, and near black—often with a prominent yellow spot on the falls. Flowers are held closely against 3- to 6-ft. stems, rising above handsome clumps of narrow, dark green leaves. Flowering starts during latter part of tall bearded bloom and continues for several weeks beyond.

Plant rhizomes in late summer or early fall, in rich, neutral to slightly alkaline soil; set them 1 in. deep, 1½–2 ft. apart. Plants grow well in full sun but will also take light shade for part of the day. They need ample moisture from onset of growth through bloom period but little moisture during summer. Divide clumps (not an easy task) infrequently; do the job in late summer or early fall.

SPECIES IRISES.

I. albicans. YEMEN IRIS, WHITE FLAG. Zones US, MS, LS; USDA 6-8. Sterile hybrid originating in the Middle East, where it was often planted in Muslim graveyards. Popular passalong plant in the South, usually seen in older gardens and cemeteries. Sword-shaped leaves to 1½ ft.; white flowers with yellow-and-white beards in very early spring. Easy to grow, needing only good drainage and a spot in full sun or light shade. Moderate to regular water; established plants take drought and neglect.

I. domestica (*Belamcanda chinensis*). BLACKBERRY LILY. Zones US, MS, LS, CS; USDA 6-9. Native to East Asia. Forms clumps of sword-shaped leaves in fanlike sheaves from slowly creeping rhizomes. Flowers are yellowish orange dotted with red; they appear on 3- to 4-ft.-high zigzag stems in summer. Each blossom lasts only a day, but new ones keep opening for weeks. As blooms fade, rounded seed capsules develop; they split open to expose shiny black seeds that look like blackberries (hence the plant's common name). Cut seed-bearing stems for unique dried arrangements. Effective in clumps in border. 'Freckle Face' grows to 12–15 in. high; has slightly larger flowers with distinct red spots. 'Hello Yellow' is a dwarf form (2 ft. high) with unspotted yellow flowers. Plant rhizomes in porous soil, 1 in. deep and 1 ft.

apart. Full sun or partial shade. Give regular water during growth and bloom.

I. foetidissima. GLADWIN IRIS. Zones US, MS, LS, CS; USDA 6-9. Native to Europe. Glossy evergreen leaves to 2 ft. make handsome foliage clumps. Stems 1½–2 ft. tall bear subtly attractive flowers in blue-gray and dull tan; specialists may offer color variants in soft yellow and lavender-blue, as well as a form with white-variegated leaves. Real attraction is large seed capsules that open in fall to show numerous round, orange-scarlet seeds; the cut stems with seed capsules are attractive in arrangements. Grow in partial to

full shade. Likes moist soil, but established plants tolerate drought. Mulch in fall in Upper South. Ingestion causes gastric upset.

I. laevigata. RABBIT-EAR IRIS. Zones US, MS, LS, CS; USDA 6-9. Native to China, Korea, Japan. Smooth, glossy leaves reach 1½–2½ ft. long, to 1 in. wide. Flower stems grow to about the same height, bearing violet-blue blossoms with upright standards and drooping falls enlivened with yellow central stripes. Bloom period comes after that of tall bearded irises. Named color variants include kinds with white, magenta, and patterned purple-and-white blooms. 'Variegata' sports crested

flowers in light blue and leaves with longitudinal white stripes. There are also selections whose standards mimic falls in shape, pattern, and carriage, producing the effect of a double blossom. This is a true bog plant, growing best in constantly moist, acid soil—even in shallow water. Full sun.

I. x norrisii (x *Pardancanda norrisii*). CANDY LILY. Zones US, MS, LS, CS, TS; USDA 6-11. Group of sun-loving garden hybrids resulting from a cross between *Belamcanda* (blackberry lily) and *Pardanthopsis*, an iris relative. To 3 ft. tall, 2 ft. wide. Foliage fans are like those of iris. From midsummer to fall, plants produce six-segmented, 3- to 4-in.-wide flowers in a great range of colors, including yellow, blue, red, purple, pink, white, orange, and bicolors. Each bloom lasts only a day, but new flowers keep the show going. Good cut flowers. Plants are short lived, often blooming themselves to death, but they do self-sow. Grow from seed; in areas where the growing season is long, early sowing results in flowers the first year. Provide regular water and good drainage. Drought tolerant. Dazzler strain offers a variety of colors but on a dwarf plant, growing only 16 in. tall.

I. prismatica. SLENDER BLUE FLAG. Zones US, MS, LS, CS; USDA 6-9. Native to eastern North America. Foliage and flowers suggest a small Siberian iris. Typical form grows about 1 ft. high, bearing dainty purple-and-white blossoms on branching, sinuous stems. A pure white form exists. Give plants full sun and moist (but not boggy), acid soil. Rhizomes spread widely, forming loose colonies rather than tight clumps.

I. pseudacorus. YELLOW FLAG. Zones US, MS, LS, CS; USDA 6-9. Native to Europe but now found worldwide in temperate regions; seeds float, aiding plant's dispersal. Impressive foliage plant; under best conditions, upright leaves may reach 5 ft. tall. Flower stems grow 4–7 ft. (depending on culture), bear bright yellow flowers 3–4 in. across. Selected forms offer ivory and lighter yellow flowers, double flowers, variegated foliage, and plants with shorter and taller leaves. Plant in sun to light shade. Needs acid soil and more than average moisture; thrives in shallow water and can become invasive where running

water disperses seeds. Ingestion of leaves or rhizomes causes gastric upset. Handling plants causes skin irritations in some people.

Several hybrids are excellent foliage plants with distinctive blossoms. All prefer ample water (but not pond conditions), sun to light shade. 'Holden Clough' perhaps has *I. foetidissima* as its other parent. Flowers, 3–4 in. across, are soft tan heavily netted with maroon veins. Stems grow to 4 ft.; leaves reach 4–5 ft., but tips arch over. Two of its seedlings are similar but larger. 'Phil Edinger' grows to 4½ ft. with arching foliage; 4- to 5-in. flowers are brass colored, heavily veined in brown. 'Roy Davidson' is similar, but flowers are dark yellow with fine brown veining and maroon thumbprint on falls.

I. setosa. NORTHERN BLUE FLAG. Zones US, MS, LS; USDA 6-8. Native to Siberia (extending to Kamchatka), Alaska, eastern Canada, and New England. Leaves are a slightly grayed green, ½–1 in. wide; plants vary from less than 1 ft. to about 2 ft. high, with flower stems taller than leaves. Blooms in late spring and summer, bearing typically blue-purple to red-purple flowers with broadly rounded falls, standards reduced to mere bristles. *I. s. nasuensis* is larger in all parts than species, reaches about 3 ft. high. Garden culture as for Siberian irises: moist, well-drained, neutral to acid soil; partial or dappled shade. Will grow where buffeted by salt-laden ocean spray. Plant in late summer, early fall.

I. unguicularis (*I. stylosa*). ALGERIAN IRIS, WINTER IRIS. Zones MS, LS, CS; USDA 7-9. Native to Greece, the Near East, northern Africa. Dense clump of narrow, dark green leaves. Depending on selection and mildness of winter, flowers appear from November to March. Typical form has violet-tinted blue blossoms elevated on 6- to 9-in. tubes that serve as stems. Named selections vary in flower color (lighter and darker lavender, orchid-pink, white) and in coarseness and length of foliage. Plants require neutral to acid soil, heat, and scant water during summer (but will take moderate water if soil is very well drained). In the Middle South, grow against sunny wall or house foundation to increase summer heat and to lessen winter cold. Divide overcrowded clumps in early fall (mild regions)

TOP: Iris domestica; BOTTOM: Reticulata iris; *I. tectorum* 'Alba'

I

or in late winter after flowering (colder regions). Slugs and snails are attracted to the flowers.

I. versicolor. BLUE FLAG. Zones US, MS, LS, CS; USDA 6-9. Widely distributed North American species, found in bogs and swamps from Mississippi Valley to eastern Canada. Grows 1½–4 ft. tall; narrow leaves are thicker in the center but not ribbed. Shorter-growing forms have upright leaves, but foliage of taller types may recurve gracefully. The typical wild flowers are a light violet-blue, but lighter and darker forms exist. 'Kermesina' is wine-red. 'Mysterious Monique' is deep violet, almost black. 'Raspberry Slurp' is white with raspberry veins. 'Rosea' is pink. Like *I. pseudacorus*, this species thrives in sun to light shade, in moist, acid soil or shallow water.

Specialty growers offer hybrids between *I. versicolor* and other species. Violet-flowered 'Gerald Darby', a hybrid with *I. virginica*, has striking wine-red stems. Violet-flowered 'Black Gamecock', a hybrid with *I. x fulvala*, has dark purple blooms.

I. virginica. SOUTHERN BLUE FLAG. Zones US, MS, LS, CS; USDA 6-9. Native to Eastern seaboard, from Virginia south and west to Mississippi River and Gulf Coast. Similar to *I. versicolor* in form and flower; distinguishing floral feature is longer standards. Flower colors include light to dark blue, wine-red, pink, lavender, and white. A plant sold as 'Giant Blue' is distinctly larger in all parts, approaching *I. pseudacorus* in size. Plant in moist, acid soil or grow in shallow water. In deep ponds, plant in large pots barely submerged beneath the surface. Full sun or light shade.

CRESTED IRISES. Though these are botanically placed with beardless irises, they represent a transition between beardless and bearded: Each fall bears a narrow, comblike crest where a beard would be in bearded sorts. Slugs and snails are especially attracted to foliage and flowers.

I. cristata. CRESTED IRIS. Zones US, MS, LS, CS; USDA 6-9. Native to South except for Florida, Louisiana, and Texas. Leaves 4–6 in. long, ½ in. wide; slender greenish rhizomes spread freely. White, lavender, or light blue flowers with golden crests. 'Powder Blue Giant' can reach 8 in. tall; its light blue flowers are almost 3 in. across.

Give light shade, organically enriched soil, regular water. Divide just after bloom or in fall after leaves die down.

I. tectorum. ROOF IRIS. Zones US, MS, LS, CS; USDA 6-9. Native to Japan, where it is planted on cottage roofs. Foliage fans to 1 ft. tall look like those of bearded irises, but light green leaves are ribbed and glossy. Foliage looks good all summer. Flowers suggest an informal bearded iris with fringed petals and crests in place of beards. Blooms are violet-blue with white crests; standards are upright at first, opening to horizontal as flower matures. 'Alba' has white petals with yellow-throated crests. 'Wolong' forms tight clumps; flowers are lavender with a white crest surrounded by dark purple flecks.

Provide organically enriched soil, light shade, and regular water. Good companion for hostas. Short lived in regions where summers are hot and dry. 'Paltec', a hybrid of *I. tectorum* with a bearded iris, will grow with bearded irises; it reaches about 1 ft. high, with lavender flowers suggesting a bearded iris with beards superimposed on crests.

ISATIS TINCTORIA
DYER'S WOAD
Brassicaceae
Short-lived perennial or biennial

🌿 **US, MS, LS, CS; USDA 6-9**

☀️ **FULL SUN**

💧💧 **MODERATE TO REGULAR WATER**

Isatis tinctoria

Known since pre-Christian times as a source for deep blue dye (it is extracted from the foliage), this

plant was probably imported into the U.S. by European colonists in the late 17th century. It quickly spread by seed and is now considered a weed in many dry Western states. In the South, however, it's less likely to become weedy and makes a fine addition to a mixed herbaceous border. Bluish green, 8-in.-long basal leaves grow in clumps from a thick taproot. Flowers usually come in April and May of the second year, when the plant sends up 2- to 4-ft.-tall stems tightly clasped by lance-shaped, blue-green leaves with white midveins; blossom stalks branch off near the stem tops, bearing large (up to 1-ft.-wide) clusters of small, bright yellow blooms. Deep purplish black seedpods form after the flowers fade. Plant in well-drained soil; space 1½ ft. apart. Rarely bothered by pests or diseases.

ITEA VIRGINICA
VIRGINIA SWEETSPIRE
Iteaceae
Deciduous shrubs

🌿 **US, MS, LS, CS; USDA 6-9**

☀️ **FULL SUN**

💧 **REGULAR WATER**

Itea virginica

A colorful deciduous shrub native to eastern U.S. Grows to 3–10 ft. tall. Where well adapted, spreads by suckers to form large patches. Narrow, oval, 4-in.-long, dark green leaves turn purplish or bright red in fall, hang on the plant for a long time—possibly all winter. Fragrant, creamy white summer flowers in erect clusters to 6 in. long. 'Henry's Garnet', a superior selection, grows 3–4 ft. tall, 4–6 ft. wide, has

brilliant purplish red fall foliage. 'Little Henry' is a more compact selection, reaching just 2 ft. high. 'Longspire' has flower clusters to 7 in. long. 'Sarah Eve' has pink-tinged blossoms. 'Saturnalia' features autumn foliage of orange, purple, and wine-red. Little pruning required. Deer resistant.

IXIA
AFRICAN CORN LILY
Iridaceae
Perennials from corms

🌿 **LS, CS, TS; USDA 8-11; OR DIG AND STORE**

☀️ **FULL SUN**

💧 **REGULAR WATER DURING GROWTH AND BLOOM**

Ixia

Clump of narrow, almost grasslike leaves sends up wiry, 18- to 20-in. stems topped by short spikes of 2-in. flowers in late spring. Each six-petaled blossom opens out nearly flat in full sun but remains cup shaped or closed on overcast days. Colors include cream, yellow, red, orange, and pink, typically with dark centers. Most ixias sold are hybrids of the South African species *I. maculata*. They aren't usually browsed by deer.

CARE

Grow ixias in well-drained soil. They prefer slightly alkaline conditions, so add lime to acid soil at planting time. Space corms about 3 in. apart. Where winter temperatures typically remain above 20°F, plant in early fall and set corms 2 in. deep; where lows dip to 10°F, plant in late fall, set corms 4 in. deep, and cover the planting with mulch. In areas where winter temperatures fall below 10°F, delay planting until spring (set corms

Let soil go dry when foliage yellows after bloom. Where corms won't be subject to rainfall or irrigation during dormant period, they can be left undisturbed until the planting becomes crowded or flowering declines. When this occurs, dig corms in summer and store as for gladiolus until recommended planting time in your area. Where corms will receive summer moisture, dig and store them after foliage dies back; or treat as annuals. Potted corms (planted close together and about 1 in. deep) can be stored in pots of dry soil.

IXIOLIRION TATARICUM

Ixioliriaceae
Perennial from bulb

🌿 **US, MS, LS, CS; USDA 6-9**

☀️ **FULL SUN**

💧 **MODERATE WATER DURING GROWTH AND BLOOM**

Ixiolirion tataricum

Native to central Asia. Wiry, 12- to 16-in. stems rise from a clump of narrow, gray-green leaves, bearing loose clusters of 1½-in. flowers in late spring. Each blue-violet blossom has six narrow petals marked with a darker central line. Foliage dies down in summer, not to reappear until the following spring. Bulbs tolerate moderate summer moisture but don't need any.

Plant in fall, setting bulbs 3 in. deep, 3 in. apart. Bulbs can remain in place for many years—though good drainage is essential to prevent rotting. Dig and divide clumps in fall when they become crowded.

IXORA

Rubiaceae
Evergreen shrubs

🌿 **CS, TS; USDA 9-11; OR GROW IN POTS**

☀️ ◐ **FULL SUN OR LIGHT SHADE**

💧 **REGULAR WATER**

Ixora casei

Large group of tropical evergreen shrubs with handsome foliage, showy clusters of flowers. They take salt air and prefer fertile, well-drained, acid soil; plants suffer from chlorosis (yellow leaves with green veins) in alkaline soil. Subject to a host of insects and diseases; difficult to keep healthy without constant vigilance. Not usually browsed by deer.

I. casei (*I. duffii*). MALAY IXORA. Native to Caroline Islands. To 3–10 ft. tall, 5 ft. wide. Slender, oblong leaves are somewhat leathery, 6–12 in. long, 2½ in. wide. Large flower clusters, sometimes up to 10 in. across; blossoms open deep red, then fade to crimson. 'Super King' is an excellent, long-blooming selection (sometimes sold as *I. coccinea*).

I. coccinea. FLAME OF THE WOODS, JUNGLE FLAME. Native to India. Most commonly grown ixora, with many selections featuring blossoms in shades of red, orange, pink, yellow. Grows 7–8 ft. high and 6 ft. wide but is usually kept smaller by occasional tip pinching or pruning. Whorled leaves are glossy and leathery, 2–4 in. long and about half as wide. Flowers are 2 in. long and appear in large, dense clusters at branch tips throughout the warm months of the year. Dies back after a freeze but recovers. Favorite decorative hedge in Florida. Great plant for the beach where hardy.

J

JACARANDA MIMOSIFOLIA

Bignoniaceae
Deciduous or semievergreen tree

🌿 **TS; USDA 10-11**

☀️ **FULL SUN**

💧 **MODERATE WATER**

Jacaranda mimosifolia

Native to Brazil, Bolivia, and Argentina, this is surely one of the world's prettiest flowering trees. Quickly grows to 45–60 ft. tall and 25–40 ft. wide, with rounded, spreading form. Large, bright green, much-divided leaves up to 20 in. long are soft and fernlike, resembling those of mimosa (*Albizia julibrissin*), hence the species name *mimosifolia*. Leaves drop in late winter. New leaves may emerge quickly or branches may remain bare until tree comes into bloom, usually in mid- to late spring. Tubular, 2-in.-long, blue or lavender-blue blossoms with white throats appear in many 8-in.-long clusters. Flat, mahogany-colored seedpods look great in arrangements but are messy on the ground. 'Alba', a white-flowered selection, is sometimes offered; it has lusher foliage and sparser blooms. 'Bonsai Blue' grows 6 ft. tall with deep purple blooms.

Jacaranda is fairly hardy after it matures a bit; young plants are injured below 25°F but often come back from a hard freeze to make multistemmed, bushy plants. Prefers sandy, well-drained, moderately fertile soil. Not salt tolerant—often fails to flower in the path of ocean winds. Makes a nice lawn, shade, or street tree. Stake young plants and prune out wayward branches to produce a single, sturdy trunk. Once established, needs little pruning.

JASMINUM

JASMINE
Oleaceae
Evergreen, semievergreen, deciduous shrubs and vines

🌿 **ZONES VARY BY SPECIES**

☀️ ◐ **FULL SUN OR LIGHT SHADE**

💧💧 **MODERATE TO REGULAR WATER**

Jasminum polyanthum

Think of fragrant plants, and jasmine is one of the first to come to mind. Yet not all jasmines are fragrant; and despite its common name, the intensely sweet Confederate jasmine is not a true jasmine at all, but a member of the genus *Trachelospermum*.

Growth habits of jasmines range from vining to vining-shrubby to decidedly shrubby. True vining types climb by twining stems. Vining shrubs do not twine, but rather put out long, slender, lax stems that must be tied into place if the plants are to function as vines. Otherwise, they'll flop over to make green haystacks of foliage. To grow these plants as shrubs, shorten any shoots that become too long. Only one of the species listed here, *J. parkeri*, is a true shrub; its dwarf size suits it to rock gardens. Most resist deer.

J. angulare. SOUTH AFRICAN JASMINE. Evergreen vining shrub.

Zones CS, TS; USDA 9-11. From South Africa. Vigorous grower with stems 10–20 ft. long. Rich green leaves are divided into three leaflets. White summer flowers over 1 in. wide are borne in groups of three; some folks detect a subtly sweet scent, others no fragrance at all.

J. floridum. SHOWY JASMINE. Evergreen or semievergreen vining shrub. Zones LS, CS, TS; USDA 8-11. From China. To 5 ft. high. Dark green leaves divided into three (rarely five) small (½- to 1½-in.-long) leaflets. Clusters of golden yellow, ½- to ¾-in., scentless flowers bloom primarily from spring into fall.

J. gracillimum. PINWHEEL JASMINE. Evergreen vining shrub. Zones TS; USDA 10-11. From Borneo. Similar to *J. multiflorum* but with darker green leaves.

J. humile. ITALIAN JASMINE. Evergreen vining shrub. Zones LS, CS, TS; USDA 8-11. From the Mideast, Myanmar, and China. Erect, willowy shoots reach 20 ft., arch to make 10-ft. mound. Light green leaves with three to seven 2-in.-long leaflets. Clusters of ½-in., fragrant bright yellow flowers all summer. Can be clipped into a hedge. 'Revolutum' has larger flowers (to 1 in. wide) and larger, darker green leaves than the species.

J. laurifolium nitidum (*J. nitidum*). SHINING JASMINE, ANGELWING JASMINE. Evergreen or semievergreen vine. Zones TS; USDA 10-11. From Admiralty Islands in the southwest Pacific. Requires long, warm growing season to bloom satisfactorily. Not reliably hardy below 25°F. Moderate growth to 10–20 ft. Undivided, glossy, green leaves to 2 in. long. Very fragrant flowers shaped like 1-in. pinwheels open from purplish buds in late spring and summer. Flowers are white inside, purplish outside, borne in clusters of three. Can be used as ground cover or container plant. Often sold as *J. magnificum*.

J. leratii. PRIVET-LEAFED JASMINE. Evergreen vine. Zones TS; USDA 10-11. From New Caledonia. To 15 ft., with glossy, dark green leaves to 2 in. long that resemble those of privet (*Ligustrum*). Slightly fragrant white flowers in spring.

J. magnificum. See *J. laurifolium nitidum*

J. mesnyi. PRIMROSE JASMINE. Evergreen vining shrub. Zones

LS, CS, TS; USDA 8-11. From China. Willowy, arching branches 6–10 ft. long. Dark green leaves with three lance-shaped, 2- to 3-in. leaflets. Bright lemon-yellow, unscented flowers to 2 in. across are semidouble or double, produced singly rather than in clusters. Main bloom in winter or spring; may flower sporadically at other times. Needs space. Best tied up at desired height and permitted to spill down in waterfall fashion. Use to cover pergola, bank, or large wall; or clip as 3-ft.-high hedge. In any form, may need occasional severe pruning to avoid brush-pile look.

J. multiflorum. DOWNY JASMINE. Evergreen vining shrub. Zones CS, TS; USDA 9-11. From India. Leaves (to 2 in. long) and stems have a downy coating, producing an overall gray-green effect. Clustered white flowers in early spring; not strongly scented.

J. nudiflorum. WINTER JASMINE. Deciduous vining shrub. Zones US, MS, LS, CS; USDA 6-9. From China. If unsupported, reaches 4 ft. or higher and 7 ft. wide; if trained on a trellis or wall, can grow to 15 ft. Slender, willowy green stems stand out in winter landscape. Unscented, bright yellow, 1-in. flowers appear in winter or early spring, before handsome, glossy green, three-leafleted leaves unfurl. Good bank cover; spreads by rooting where stems touch soil. Attractive planted at the top of retaining walls, with branches cascading over side. Can also be trained like *J. mesnyi* (tie plant at desired height and let branches spill down like a waterfall).

J. officinale. COMMON WHITE JASMINE, POET'S JASMINE. Semievergreen or deciduous vine. Zones LS, CS, TS; USDA 8-11. From Himalayas, Caucasus. To 30 ft. Very fragrant white flowers to 1 in. across; blooms throughout summer and into fall. Rich green leaves have five to nine leaflets, each to 2½ in. long.

J. o. affine (*J. grandiflorum*). SPANISH JASMINE. Zones CS, TS; USDA 9-11. Main difference from basic species is size—this form climbs only to 15 ft. but bears larger (1½-in.) blooms.

J. parkeri. DWARF JASMINE. Evergreen shrub. Zones LS, CS, TS; USDA 8-11. From India. Dwarf, twiggy, tufted shrub to 1 ft. high, 1½–2 ft. wide. Bright green, ½- to

1-in.-long leaves with three to five tiny leaflets. Small, scentless, yellow flowers borne profusely in spring. Good choice in rock garden or as container plant.

J. polyanthum. PINK JASMINE. Evergreen vine. Zones LS, CS, TS; USDA 8-11. From China. Fast-climbing, strong-growing vine to 20 ft. Bright to dark green leaves are slightly paler on undersides, have five to seven 1- to 3-in.-long leaflets. Highly fragrant, ¾-in. blossoms are white inside, rose colored outside, borne in dense clusters. Blooms in late winter and spring; sporadic flowers rest of year. Can be used as ground cover; sometimes grown in large containers or hanging baskets. 'Variegatum' has leaves with pale yellow margins.

J. primulinum. See *J. mesnyi*

J. sambac. ARABIAN JASMINE. Evergreen vining shrub. Zones CS, TS; USDA 9-11. Thought to be native to tropical Asia. To 6–10 ft. Undivided glossy green leaves to 3 in. long. Blooms in summer, bearing clusters of powerfully fragrant, ¾- to 1-in., white flowers. 'Grand Duke of Tuscany' has double blooms. 'Maid of Orleans' has single blossoms and a compact, shrubby form; it is well suited to containers. In Asia, leaves of this species are used in jasmine tea.

J. simplicifolium australiense (*J. volubile*). WAX JASMINE. Evergreen shrub or vine. Zones LS, CS, TS; USDA 8-11. Native to Australia. To 10–15 ft., with glossy, undivided, dark green leaves about 2 in. long. Small, fragrant, white flowers appear intermittently throughout the year. Adapted to sandy and salty soil.

J. x stephanense. Evergreen to deciduous vine. Zones MS, LS, CS, TS; USDA 7-11. To 15–20 ft., with dull green foliage. Evergreen in Tropical South, semievergreen to deciduous elsewhere. Leaves may be undivided and about 2 in. long or divided into five 2-in.-long leaflets. Pale pink, ¾-in., fragrant flowers, carried in clusters of five or more, appear in late spring and summer.

CARE

Jasmines grow more rapidly in fertile, well-drained soil and bloom more profusely in sunny sites, but all adapt quite well to less-than-perfect conditions. When plants become tangled

or untidy, cut them back heavily just before spring growth begins. Pinch and prune as needed throughout the year to control growth.

JATROPHA
Euphorbiaceae
Evergreen and deciduous shrubs and trees

🌡 **TS; USDA 10-11; OR GROW IN POTS**

◐ **LIGHT SHADE; BRIGHT LIGHT**

◌◌ **MODERATE TO REGULAR WATER**

◆ **VARIOUS PLANT PARTS ARE EXTREMELY POISONOUS IF INGESTED**

Jatropha integerrima

Large group of tropical and subtropical plants related to poinsettia (*Euphorbia pulcherrima*), with milky latex or clear juice in the stems. The most commonly grown species are popular for their large, deeply lobed, typically heart-shaped leaves, which provide tropical effects in the garden.

J. curcas. PHYSIC NUT. Evergreen shrub or small tree. Native to the tropical Americas. Reaches 8–15 ft. tall and wide. Easy to grow; cuttings from mature stems are sometimes set out in the ground, watered, and left to make a hedge. Deep green leaves are heart shaped, to 1 ft. long and 7 in. wide, on 4- to 6-in. stalks. Inconspicuous yellowish green flowers appear in spring. Oval, 1½-in.-long nuts contain poisonous seeds. Oil from seeds being evaluated as source for biodiesel. Leaves and stems of this species are also poisonous.

J. integerrima. PEREGRINA. Evergreen shrub or small tree.

Native to Cuba and the West Indies. Can reach 20 ft. tall, 15 ft. wide, but usually attains just half that size in gardens. Grow as a multitrunked shrub or prune into tree shape. Good in a container or as a patio tree. Glossy, pointed leaves to 5 in. long emerge bronzy red, then age to dark green with brownish undersides. Bright scarlet to coral flowers about an inch across bloom in clusters at branch tips most of the year; they attract hummingbirds and butterflies. Berries and sap are poisonous. 'Compacta' grows about half as large as the species.

J. multifida. CORAL PLANT. Evergreen shrub or small tree. From Mexico, Brazil, West Indies. To 20 ft. tall, 12 ft. wide. Leaves 1 ft. across, white on undersides; almost circular but deeply divided into 7 to 11 narrow lobes. Scarlet, ¼-in. flowers on red stems bloom in summer; they are followed by oval fruit to 1 in. long. All plant parts are poisonous.

J. podagrica. GOUT PLANT. Deciduous shrub. From Central America, West Indies. Grows to 1½–5 ft. tall, about 1 ft. wide. Named for its swollen, gouty-looking trunk. Three- to five-lobed leaves reach 10 in. across, have white undersides. Coral-red flowers about ½ in. wide appear from winter through summer. Berries and sap are poisonous.

CARE

Need gritty, very well-drained soil with added humus; not salt tolerant. Resist deer. Indoors, site in bright light, but don't expose to direct hot sun. In spring and summer, water moderately and feed monthly with a general-purpose liquid houseplant fertilizer. Leave plants unwatered in fall and winter.

JEFFERSONIA DIPHYLLA

TWINLEAF
Berberidaceae
Perennial

- **US, MS; USDA 6-7**
- **PARTIAL TO FULL SHADE**
- **REGULAR WATER**

Jeffersonia diphylla

Native from Maryland and Virginia south to Georgia and Alabama. Named for Thomas Jefferson. Pretty, cup-shaped, white flowers, an inch across, appear briefly in spring among new leaves. At bloom time, plant is no more than 8 in. high; once flowers fade, leaves develop into handsome mounds 1½ ft. high and about half as wide. Foliage is unusual: Each 5- to 6-in.-wide leaf looks like a shield split into two parts. Leaves emerge purplish gray, then mature to light green.

Grow in rich, preferably limy soil amended with organic matter. Lovely in a woodland garden with ferns, primroses (*Primula*), trilliums, and bloodroot (*Sanguinaria canadensis*). Cover dormant plants with a humus-rich mulch. Keep soil evenly moist; watch out for slugs and snails. Buy nursery propagated plants. Do not transplant from wild.

JICAMA

Fabaceae
Annual vine

- **CS, TS; USDA 9-11**
- **FULL SUN**
- **AMPLE WATER**
- **SEEDS ARE POISONOUS IF INGESTED**

Jicama

Known botanically as *Pachyrhizus erosus*, this tropical American native is grown for its edible root, which resembles a large brown turnip and tastes something like a water chestnut. Twining or scrambling vines (to 14 ft. high) are attractive, with luxuriant deep green foliage and pretty flower clusters. Leaves have three leaflets, each the size of a hand; upright spikes of sweet pea–shaped purple or violet blossoms appear in late summer. Flowers should be pinched out to encourage maximum root production, but you can allow seed for next year's crop to form on one or two plants. Needs a long, warm growing season and rich soil. Train on a trellis or grow on the ground as a trailing mound. Sow seeds after danger of frost is past, 1–1½ in. deep and 6–12 in. apart, in rows 3–4 ft. apart. Feed once or twice in early or midsummer with a high-nitrogen fertilizer. The edible roots will form as days begin to grow shorter; harvest them before the first frost. Each vine produces a single 1- to 6-pound taproot. Peel off the rough brown skin and eat the white flesh raw or cooked. Best suited to south Texas and south Florida.

JUGLANS

WALNUT
Juglandaceae
Deciduous trees

- **ZONES VARY BY SPECIES**
- **FULL SUN**
- **REGULAR WATER, EXCEPT AS NOTED**

Juglans nigra

Large, spreading trees suitable for big properties. All produce oval or round, edible nuts in fleshy husks. Nuts of native species have a wild flavor; those of English walnut (*J. regia*) are the ones sold commercially. These trees have shallow, competitive root systems (a chemical released by the roots, fallen leaves, and nuts of black walnut trees can kill other plants), and their pollen can cause an allergic reaction. They tend to be out of leaf for a long time and can be messy when in leaf. Worth growing if you like the nuts or need large trees that thrive in adverse conditions.

J. cinerea. BUTTERNUT. Zones US, MS; USDA 6-7. Native from New Brunswick to Georgia, west to Arkansas and North Dakota. To 50–60 ft. (even 100 ft.) tall, with broad, spreading canopy 40–50 ft. across. Resembles *J. nigra* but is smaller, with 11 to 19 leaflets per leaf and fewer nuts, which are oval or elongated rather than round. Flavor is good, but shells are thick and hard to crack. Tolerates alkaline soil.

J. microcarpa. RIVER WALNUT. Zones US, MS, LS, CS; USDA 6-9. Native to Oklahoma, Texas, New Mexico, and northwest Mexico. Grows to about 20 ft. (rarely 30 ft.) tall and wide; often multistemmed and more shrubby than treelike. Dark green leaves have 15 to 23 leaflets, each about 3 in. long. Small (¾-in.) nuts are mostly eaten by wildlife. Thrives in dry, rocky, limy soil.

J. nigra. BLACK WALNUT. Zones US, MS, LS, CS; USDA 6-9. Native from Massachusetts to Florida, west to Texas and Minnesota. A huge tree that can reach 150 ft. high, though it's usually closer to 50–75 ft. tall and wide in gardens. High-branched, oval- to round-headed habit. Furrowed, blackish brown bark. Leaves have 11 to 23 dark green leaflets, each 2½–5 in. long. Nuts are 1–1½ in. across, with a rich, distinctive flavor and very thick, hard shells (some types, such as 'Thomas Myers' and 'Surprise', are easier to crack than others). Wood is highly prized for furniture, cabinets.

J. regia. ENGLISH WALNUT, PERSIAN WALNUT, CARPATHIAN WALNUT. Zones US, MS, LS, CS; USDA 6-9. Native to southwest Asia, southeastern Europe. To 60 ft. high, with equal spread. Fast growing, especially when young. Trunk and heavy, horizontal or upward-angled branches are covered with smooth, gray bark. Leaves are medium to dark green, with five to seven (occa-

THE UNGRATEFUL DEAD

Some plants don't appreciate being sited under or even near a black walnut tree, and for good reason: It may mean a different kind of "black death" for them. To limit competition from other plants for sunlight, water, and nutrients, black walnuts (*Juglans nigra*) release a toxin called juglone into the soil. Susceptible plants are stunted or killed. To avoid this sinister plague, choose plants that tolerate juglone, or plant susceptible ones far from the root zones of these trees. Sure-to-expire plants include tomato, potato, eggplant, cucumber, pepper, azalea, cotoneaster, and rhododendron. Juglone-tolerant plants include chrysanthemum, crocus, maple, red cedar, and viburnum.

sionally more) 3- to 6-in.-long leaflets. Roundish nuts to 2 in. long, with ridged shells and sweet, rich flavor. Husks open in fall, dropping nuts to the ground; to hasten drop, knock nuts from tree. Gather fallen nuts immediately, remove any adhering husks, and dry in a single layer in airy shade until kernels are brittle (crack a nut open to test); then store.

JUJUBE
Rhamnaceae
Deciduous small tree

🌿 **US, MS, LS, CS; USDA 6-9**

☼ **BEST IN SUN, TOLERATES SOME SHADE**

💧 **MODERATE WATER**

Jujube

Native to temperate regions of Asia and known botanically as *Ziziphus jujuba*. Slow to moderate growth to 15–20 ft. (possibly 30 ft.) tall and 10–15 ft. wide. Spiny, gnarled, somewhat pendulous branches. Glossy, bright green, 1- to 2-in.-long leaves with three prominent veins; good yellow fall color. Clusters of small yellowish flowers appear in late spring or summer.

Round to oval fruit with a central pit matures in fall; it can be eaten fresh from the tree or dried. Harvest the fruit for fresh eating when it begins to turn from yellow-green to reddish brown; it has a crisp texture and tastes like a sweet apple. If allowed to turn completely brown and become mushy, fruit is better for drying. The dried fruit looks and tastes like dates. The two most common cultivated selections are 'Lang', with 1½- to 2-in., elongated fruit, and 'Li', bearing 2-in., round fruit with a very small

pit. 'Lang' needs 'Li' as pollenizer; 'Li' is more productive with 'Lang' nearby, though it will produce some fruit if planted alone.

Jujube is a decorative tree but a tough one, too. It withstands drought and heat; it takes saline and alkaline soils (but grows better in good garden soil). Thrives in lawns, though suckering from roots can be a problem in moist soil. Prune in winter to shape, encourage weeping habit, or reduce size.

JUNCUS
RUSH
Juncaceae
Perennials

🌿 **US, MS, LS, CS; USDA 6-9, EXCEPT AS NOTED**

☼ ◐ **FULL SUN OR LIGHT SHADE**

💧 **AMPLE WATER**

Juncus patens 'Carman's Gray'

Rushes somewhat resemble grasses, with leaflike, cylindrical stems and tiny, inconspicuous flowers clustered near stem tips. Some have a rigid, upright habit; stems of others are twisted into spirals. Specialists usually suggest planting them with grasses or aquatic plants at the edge of a pond or stream, in water, or among stones and pebbles.

J. effusus. SOFT RUSH. Native to many temperate regions of the world. To 2½ ft. high and wide. Medium green stems are erect, arching somewhat toward tips. Stems turn brown with frost. *J. e spiralis* and its selections 'Twister' and 'Unicorn' have corkscrew foliage.

J. inflexus. HARD RUSH. Native to many parts of the world. Upright, blue-gray stems form a clump to 2½ ft. tall, 2 ft. wide.

'Afro' grows to 1–1½ ft. tall and 2 ft. wide; with coiled stems. 'Lovesick Blues' forms a striking 3-ft. mound of steely blue stems.

J. patens. CALIFORNIA GRAY RUSH. Zones MS, LS, CS; USDA 7-9. Native to California and Oregon. To 2 ft. high and wide, with stiffly upright green or gray-green stems. Tolerates more heat and drought than *J. effusus* but thrives best in moist soil or even shallow water. Gray-green 'Carman's Gray' and blue-gray 'Elk Blue' are good selections.

JUNIPERUS
JUNIPER
Cupressaceae
Evergreen shrubs and trees

🌿 **ZONES VARY BY SPECIES**

☼ **FULL SUN**

💧💧💧 **LITTLE TO REGULAR WATER; SEE CARE BOX BELOW**

Juniperus rigida conferta

People plant junipers for two main reasons. First, they're tough—they tolerate drought and almost any soil, and they're hard to kill. Second, they come in many forms—ground covers, shrubs, columns, or trees—and their needlelike foliage may be green, gold, gray, or various shades of blue. That's the good.

On the down side, junipers seem to be the number one choice for landscaping hotels, office buildings, shopping malls, gas stations, and highway medians. Using lots of them can give your yard a distinctly commercial look. But if you don't mind your home resembling a galleria, feel free.

Ground covers. This group includes low, spreading plants from a few inches to a few feet high. It takes a planting several years to fill in completely, so for the first few years, mulch between plants to keep down weeds. You'll see how important this is if you ever have to reach into prickly juniper foliage to pull weeds.

Shrub types. These plants usually grow wider than tall and range from about 2 ft. to more than 10 ft. tall. Shapes include mounding, gracefully spreading, weeping, and weirdly twisted.

Columnar types. These upright growers have dense, pyramidal to conical shapes and are often used as vertical accents. (Planting them on the corners of your house, though, can make it look like King Arthur's castle.) They grow from about 6–25 ft. tall.

Tree types. These picturesque plants love chalky soil. Spread by birds, they dot the Southern countryside. Single trees become stately. Groups make handsome windbreaks and allees and are classic plants for lining a long driveway.

In many cases, junipers are best known by their selections. Pure species are seldom seen.

J. ashei. OZARK WHITE CEDAR, ASHE JUNIPER. Tree. Zones US, MS, LS, CS; USDA 6-9. Native to south-central U.S. and northern Mexico. Common juniper of Texas Hill Country. Irregular or spherical crown to 20 ft. tall and wide. Trunk often divides near the base. Gray-green foliage. Shredding gray bark. Female plants bear blue, ¼- to ½-inch berries with a waxy sheen. Likes dry, chalky soil. Immune to cedar-apple rust. Pollen of male plants can trigger allergies.

J. chinensis. CHINESE JUNIPER. Zones US, MS, LS, CS; USDA 6-9. Native to northeast Asia.

'Blue Point'. Columnar. Broad column to 12 ft. tall by 8 ft. wide. Dense, blue-green foliage.

'Hetzii' (*J. chinensis* 'Hetzii'). HETZ CHINESE JUNIPER. Shrub. Inverted pyramid to 15 ft. tall and wide. Blue-gray foliage. Branches spread outward and upward at 45° angle.

'Kaizuka' ('Torulosa'). HOLLY-WOOD JUNIPER. Shrub. Irregular, upright to 20 ft. tall by 10 ft. wide. Rich, green foliage with soft texture. Branches have outlandish, twisted appearance. Give it plenty of room. Good in large containers. Tolerates salt spray. 'Variegated Kaizuka' ('Kaizuka Variegata') has foliage splashed with creamy white.

'Robusta Green'. Columnar. Irregular column to 12–18 ft. tall by 5–7 ft. wide. Brilliant, green, dense foliage.

'San Jose'. Ground cover. Prostrate, dense, and spreading to 2 ft. tall by 6 ft. or more wide. Dark green foliage. Heavy trunked; slow growing.

'Spartan'. Columnar. Pyramidal to columnar to 20 ft. tall by 3–4 ft. wide. Rich green, dense foliage. Fast-growing, very handsome plant.

J. c. sargentii. SARGENT CHINESE JUNIPER. Ground cover. Zones US, MS, LS, CS; USDA 6-9. Ground hugging, spreading to 2 ft. tall by 10 ft. wide. Feathery, gray-green or green foliage. Classic bonsai plant. Selections include blue-green 'Glauca' and bright green 'Viridis'.

J. davurica 'Parsonii'. Ground cover. Zones US, MS, LS, CS; USDA 6-9. Native to Asia, Siberia, and possibly Japan. Spreading to 1 ft. tall by 8 ft. or more wide. Rich sprays of dark green needles on slender branches. One of the best junipers for the Southeast.

J. horizontalis. CREEPING JUNIPER. Zones US, MS, LS, CS; USDA 6-9 unless noted. Native to Canada and northern U.S.

'Bar Harbor'. Ground cover. Ground-hugging, creeping to 1 ft. tall by 8 ft. or more wide.

Fast growing. Feathery, blue-gray foliage turns purple in winter. Tolerates salt spray.

'Icee Blue'. Ground cover. Creeping, very flat to 4 in. tall by 6–8 ft. wide. A marked improvement over 'Wiltonii'; intense silvery and denser foliage.

'Plumosa'. ANDORRA CREEPING JUNIPER. Ground cover. Creeping to 1 ft. tall by 10 ft. wide. Plumy foliage is gray-green in summer, plum-purple in winter. Flat branches with upright branchlets.

'Prince of Wales'. Ground cover. Creeping to 8 in. tall by 8–10 ft. wide. Medium green foliage turns purplish in fall.

'Wiltonii'. BLUE RUG CREEPING JUNIPER. Ground cover. Very flat, creeping to 4 in. tall by 8–10 ft. wide. Silver blue foliage. Long, trailing branches set with short, dense branchlets. Like 'Bar Harbor' but tighter; rarely shows limbs.

'Yukon Belle'. Zones US, MS, LS; USDA 6-8. Ground cover. Creeping to 6 in. tall by 6–8 ft. wide. Silvery blue foliage. Extremely cold hardy.

J. x pfitzeriana (*J. chinensis* 'Pfitzeriana'). PFITZER JUNIPER. Zones US, MS, LS, CS; USDA 6-9. Native to northeast Asia.

'Armstrong'. Shrub. Upright, dense to 4 ft. tall by 5 ft. wide. Lacy, medium green foliage.

'Gold Coast'. Shrub. Compact to 3 ft. tall by 5 ft. wide. Soft, lacy, golden yellow foliage.

'Mint Julep'. Shrub. Vase shaped to 4–6 ft. tall by 6 ft. wide. Mint green foliage. Arching branches. Very attractive.

'Pfitzeriana Aurea'. Shrub. Arching to 3–4 ft. tall by 8–10 ft. wide. Greenish gray foliage; current seasons growth golden yellow.

'Pfitzeriana Glauca'. Shrub. Arching to 5–6 ft. tall by 10–15 ft. wide. Silvery blue foliage.

'Wilhelm Pfitzer' ('Pfitzeriana'). Shrub. Arching to 5–6 ft. tall by 15–20 ft. wide. Feathery, gray-green, sharp-needled foliage.

J. procumbens. JAPANESE GARDEN JUNIPER. Ground cover. Zones US, MS, LS, CS; USDA 6-9. Native to Japan. To 2 ft. tall by 12–20 ft. wide. Feathery yet substantial blue-green foliage on strong branches.

'Nana'. Ground cover. To 1 ft. tall by 6–8 ft. wide. Curved branches spreading in all directions. Shorter needles and slower growth than species. Can be

ABOVE: Juniperus virginiana

staked into picturesque shrub. Good in containers.

J. rigida conferta (*J. conferta*). SHORE JUNIPER. Ground cover. Zones US, MS, LS, CS; USDA 6-9. Native to coastal Japan. Prostrate, creeping to 1 ft. tall by 10 ft. wide. Bright, soft green needles. Excellent for seashore. Takes sandy soil and salt spray. 'Blue Pacific' is denser, bluer, and more heat tolerant. 'Emerald Sea' is bright green.

J. sabina. SAVIN JUNIPER. Zones US, MS; USDA 6-7. Native to central and southern Europe to central Asia.

'Broadmoor'. Ground cover. Dense, mounding, and spreading to 2–3 ft. tall by 10 ft. wide. Soft, bright green foliage.

'Buffalo'. Ground cover. To 8–12 in. tall by 8 ft. wide. Soft, feathery, bright green foliage.

'Tamariscifolia'. Ground cover. Symmetrically spreading to 1 ft. tall by 10–12 ft. wide. Dense, blue-green foliage. Widely used.

J. scopulorum. ROCKY MOUNTAIN JUNIPER. Zones US, MS; USDA 6-7. Native to western North America.

'Blue Arrow'. Columnar. Very narrow to 12–15 ft. tall by 2 ft. wide. Tight, bright blue foliage.

'Blue Creeper'. Ground cover. Spreading to 2 ft. tall by 6–8 ft. wide. Bright blue-green foliage.

'Blue Heaven'. Columnar. Neatly pyramidal to 20 ft. high by 6 ft. wide. Foliage remains bright blue all year.

'Gray Gleam'. Columnar. Symmetrical to 15 ft. tall by 5–7 ft. wide. Silver-gray foliage. Slow grower. Tidy, formal-looking plant.

'Pathfinder'. Columnar. Upright pyramid to 25 ft. tall by 12 ft. wide. Blue-gray foliage; looser than 'Gray Gleam'.

'Skyrocket'. Columnar. Narrow spire to 10–15 ft. tall by 1–2 ft. wide. Blue-gray foliage. Good vertical accent.

'Tolleson's Blue Weeping'. Shrub. Weeping to 20 ft. tall by 10 ft. wide.

'Witchita Blue'. Columnar. Broad pyramid to 18 ft. tall by 6 ft. wide. Bright blue foliage; very striking.

J. squamata. SINGLESEED JUNIPER. Zones US, MS; USDA 6-7. Native to western China.

'Blue Star'. Shrub. Mounding to 3 ft. tall by 5 ft. wide. Squat, dense plant with silvery blue, sharp-pointed needles.

'Chinese Silver'. Shrub. Dense pyramid to 7 ft. tall by 4 ft. wide. Foliage is shiny blue. Red, peeling bark.

'Holger'. Shrub. Dense, spreading to 3–5 ft. tall and wide. Yellow new growth matures to blue-green.

J. virginiana. EASTERN RED CEDAR. Tree. Zones US, MS, LS, CS; USDA 6-9. Native to eastern North America. Conical to broadly pyramidal to 40–50 ft. tall to 15–30 ft. wide. Picturesque tree with dark green foliage that turns bronze in cold weather. Tolerates drought, poor soil; thrives in limy soil. Many selections sold. Aromatic foliage and wood. Female trees adorned with thousands of bright blue fruit.

'Canaertii'. Tree. Upright pyramid to 20 ft. tall. Dark green foliage sets huge amount of blue fruit.

'Emerald Sentinal'. Tree. Upright pyramid to 15–25 ft. tall by 5–8 ft. wide. Dark green foliage. Useful hedge or screen.

J. v. siliciola. SOUTHERN RED CEDAR. Native to southern-most U.S. Zones MS, LS, CS, TS; USDA 7-9. Tree. Cone-shaped to 30 ft. tall by 20 ft. wide. Very similar to the above species, though often more open and wide-spreading. Grows in sand. Frequently planted in rows and used as windbreak. Tolerates seaside conditions.

CARE

Junipers take about any kind of soil as long as it is well drained. Wet soil causes root rot and death. Full sun is the rule. Very little trimming is needed if you choose a plant of the right size and shape to fill the allotted space. Deer seldom browse junipers, but the plants are subject to various pests and diseases. Among the most common are bagworms (foliage is stripped), spider mites (yellowing or browning needles with fine webbing present), cedar-apple rust (orange, jellylike galls in foliage), and tip blight (branch tips turn brown in spring).

JUSTICIA
Acanthaceae
Perennials and evergreen shrubs

✎ **ZONES VARY BY SPECIES**

☼ ☽ ● **EXPOSURE NEEDS VARY BY SPECIES**

◌ ◑ ● ● **WATER NEEDS VARY BY SPECIES**

Justicia carnea

These New World natives are grown chiefly for their tubular, tightly clustered flowers—or, in the case of *J. brandegeeana*, for showy spikes of bracts. Blossoms of all species attract hummingbirds. Leaves are paired, opposite each other on the stems.

J. americana. AMERICAN WATER WILLOW. Perennial. Zones US, MS, LS, CS, TS; USDA 6-11. Aquatic species native to eastern half of U.S. Upright, 15-in. stems are clothed in willowlike deep green leaves with a white midrib. Small, white to pale violet flowers with splashy purple markings appear atop stems from early summer into fall. Spreads by creeping rhizomes to form large colonies. Plant at edge of pond for a natural look; grows best in shallow water or very moist soil. Full sun.

J. aurea. YELLOW JUSTICIA, BRAZILIAN PLUME. Evergreen shrub. Zones CS, TS; USDA 9-11. From Mexico and Central America. To 6–10 ft. tall and 6–8 ft. wide, with dark green leaves to 1 ft. long, half as wide. Blooms in summer; bright yellow blossom clusters reach up to 1 ft. long and look something like ginger flowers. Remove faded flowers to prolong bloom period; cut whole plant back hard in spring. Watch for snails. Best in partial shade. Moderate water.

J. brandegeeana (*Beloperone guttata*). SHRIMP PLANT. Evergreen shrub. Zones CS, TS; USDA 9-11; elsewhere as annual or indoor/outdoor plant. Native to Mexico. To 3–4 ft. high and wide. Apple-green, oval to elliptic leaves to 2½ in. long. Tubular white flowers spotted with purple are enclosed in overlapping coppery bronze bracts to form compact, drooping, jointed-looking spikes 3 in. long (eventually lengthening to 6–7 in.). Spike formation somewhat resembles a large shrimp. Blooms mainly from spring to fall, sporadically rest of year. 'Chartreuse' has chartreuse yellow bracts that sunburn more easily than the coppery kind.

Good in pots and for close-up planting near terraces, patios, entryways. To shape, pinch young plants continuously until compact mound of foliage is obtained, then let bloom. To encourage bushiness, cut back stems when bracts turn black. Leaves often drop in cold weather or if soil is too wet or dry. Give moderate water (less in winter) and feed with a balanced liquid fertilizer monthly during active growth. Takes full sun, but bracts and foliage fade unless plant is grown in partial shade. Give at least half-day shade in hottest climates.

J. carnea. BRAZILIAN PLUME FLOWER. Evergreen shrub. Zones CS, TS; USDA 9-11; elsewhere as annual or indoor/outdoor plant. From South America. Erect, soft-wooded shrub to 4–6 ft. high, 2½–3 ft. wide. Medium green, prominently veined leaves to 10 in. long. Dense, 6-in.-long clusters of pink to crimson, tubular, 2-in. flowers from midsummer to fall. Hybrids between this and other species may have yellow, orange, apricot, or white blooms. 'Huntington Form' is a more compact plant (3–4 ft. high) with deeper pink flowers and leaves that are bronze colored on lower surfaces. Cut back plants in early spring to encourage strong new growth. Upper portions of branches freeze at 29°F. Give partial or full shade, rich soil, regular to ample water.

J. leonardii. ORANGE JUSTICIA. Evergreen shrub. Zones CS, TS; USDA 9-11. Exotic-looking Mexican native reaching 3 ft. tall and wide, with gray-green stems and velvety dark green leaves to

K

6 in. long. Small clusters of reddish orange, 1½-in. flowers appear at branch tips and along stems off and on through warm months. Full sun. Little water.

J. runyonii. RUNYON'S WATER WILLOW. Perennial. Zones CS, TS; USDA 9-11. From Texas and northern Mexico. Rare. To 2-3 ft. tall, with stems sparsely clothed in soft, narrow leaves that may turn from green to deep maroon when temperatures drop. Small purple flowers with white markings are held above foliage in fall. Cut back hard in winter. Full sun. Needs regular water.

J. spicigera. MEXICAN HONEYSUCKLE. Evergreen shrub. Zones CS, TS; USDA 9-11. From Mexico and Central America. To 3 ft. high, 4 ft. wide, with light green, smooth or velvety leaves. Few-flowered clusters of 1½-in. orange or orange-red flowers appear nearly year-round, peaking in spring and fall. Full sun or partial shade. Little to regular water.

KADSURA JAPONICA

JAPANESE KADSURA
Schisandraceae
Evergreen vine

- MS, LS, CS, TS; USDA 7-11
- PARTIAL TO FULL SHADE
- REGULAR WATER

Kadsura japonica 'Fukurin'

This elegant twining vine from Japan and Korea is seldom seen in Southern gardens, but discriminating gardeners may wish to track it down. It reaches 12-15 ft. and does so in well-behaved fashion—it won't strangle nearby trees or shrubs. Handsome, glossy, dark green leaves are oval and pointed, 2-4 in. long and 1-2 in. wide. Small, yellowish white flowers bloom from summer to autumn; these are followed by pretty red berries to 1¼ in. across on female plants. Vines of both sexes must be present for fruit to be produced. Needs fertile, well-drained soil. Easy to propagate from cuttings. 'Alba' has white fruit. 'Chirimen' has leaves marbled with creamy white; 'Fukurin' offers striking foliage edged in cream and yellow.

KAEMPFERIA

PEACOCK GINGER
Zingiberaceae
Perennials

- LS, CS, TS; USDA 8-11; OR GROW IN POTS
- FULL SHADE; BRIGHT INDIRECT LIGHT
- AMPLE WATER DURING GROWING SEASON

Kaempferia pulchra

Native to tropical Asia, these small, shade-loving plants grow outdoors only in humid, very warm climates. Flowers (sometimes fragrant) resemble small orchids or African violets (*Saintpaulia*) but have just three petals, one of which is a deeply lobed "lip." Foliage is usually more decorative than the flowers; leaves of many species have iridescent veining and feathery zoning, giving them the look of a peacock's tail. Leaves of most species lie horizontally, making a low (1- to 6-in.-tall), strikingly textured ground cover during the growing season. In winter, foliage dies back and plant becomes dormant. Reduce watering in fall; stop watering altogether in winter; resume watering in spring. Plants grow easily in moist soil with lots of organic matter. Some spread by rhizomes. Tuberous types can be divided.

In the Upper, Middle, and Lower South, grow in containers and overwinter indoors. Keep nighttime temperature above 60°F. During growing season, air and soil must be moist and daytime temperatures high; plants will thrive in temperatures over 90°F.

K. galanga. Rounded, shiny, green leaves to 6 in. long. Fragrant white flowers with purple spots on lip bloom in spikes of up to 12 in. Plant is tuberous and spreads to about 1 ft. wide.

K. gilbertii. VARIEGATED PEACOCK GINGER. Narrow, pointed, bright green leaves, 4-7 in. long and 1-2 in. wide, with white margins and stripes, gray undersides. White flowers with violet lip bloom from late spring into summer. Reaches 9 in. wide and spreads by rhizomes.

K. pulchra. PEACOCK GINGER. Broad, oval leaves to 7 in. long are dark green and bronze, marked with silvery veining; undersides are pale green. Lilac flowers with a white eye bloom from summer to early fall. Plant grows about 1 ft. wide, spreading by rhizomes. *K. p. mansonii* has iridescent leaves that are deeply veined, nearly pleated looking; it is about 2 in. taller than the species and blooms continuously from spring to fall. 'Silver Spot' and 'Bronze' produce variegated foliage.

K. roscoeana. PEACOCK LILY. Similar to *K. pulchra*, but leaf undersides are reddish and flowers are white. Spreads by rhizomes.

K. rotunda. ASIAN CROCUS. Narrow leaves to 1 ft. long are carried erect, making this a much taller plant than other species. Leaves are purplish beneath and show a featherlike pattern of dark and pale green on top surface. Fragrant white flowers with purple lip bloom before leaves appear. Tuberous plant to 1½ ft. wide. 'Raven' has more pronounced coloration on the upper sides of leaves. 'Silver Diamonds' is a beauty.

KALANCHOE

Crassulaceae
Succulent perennials

- TS; USDA 10-11; OR HOUSEPLANT
- FULL SUN OR PARTIAL SHADE; BRIGHT LIGHT
- MODERATE TO REGULAR WATER

Kalanchoe blossfeldiana

From Old World tropics. Kalanchoes have fleshy, typically green leaves and bell-shaped flowers; they are used principally as houseplants but can be grown outdoors year-round where winters are mild and frost free. Site indoor plants in a south-facing window and let them go fairly dry between waterings. Feed with a general-purpose liquid houseplant fertilizer monthly from spring until fall. Reduce watering in winter, but don't let soil dry out so much that leaves wither.

K. beharensis. FELT PLANT. Very narrow plant; grows to 4-5 ft. (possibly even 10 ft.) tall, just 1-2 ft. wide. Stems are typically unbranched, carrying thick, triangular to lance-shaped leaves—usually six to eight pairs of them—at the tips. Leaves are 4-8 in. long and half as wide, strikingly waved and crimped at the edges and covered with a dense, feltlike coating of white to brown hairs. Flowers are unimportant. Hybrids between this and other species differ in leaf size, color, and degree of felting and scalloping. Impressive in big rock gardens and raised beds.

K. blossfeldiana. KALANCHOE. To 1½ ft. tall and wide. Shiny, dark green, smooth-edged or slightly lobed leaves thinly bordered in red; 2½ in. long, 1-1½-in. wide. Small, bright red flowers come in big clusters held above the leaves. Hybrids and named selections come in regular or dwarf (6-in.) sizes and in different flower colors, including yellow, orange, salmon, and red. Blooms in winter and early spring. Popular houseplant for the winter holidays (often sold in supermarkets then) but can be kept for years.

K. daigremontiana. MOTHER-OF-THOUSANDS, MATERNITY PLANT. Upright, single-stemmed plant 1½–3 ft. tall, 1 ft. wide. Leaves to 6–8 in. long, 1½ in. wide (or wider), in gray-green spotted with red. Leaf edges are notched; young plants sprout in the notches and can be removed and planted. Clusters of small, drooping, grayish purple flowers in winter.

K. fedtschenkoi. SOUTH AMERICAN AIR PLANT. Popular ground cover in south Florida. To 1–2 ft. tall, 10–12 in. wide, with smooth, scalloped, blue-green leaves 1–2 in. long. Clusters of pendent reddish flowers in summer. Prostrate stems root where they touch soil. Often erroneously called gray sedum.

K. luciae. FLAPJACK PLANT, PADDLE PLANT. From southeastern Africa. Colorful, sculptural plant grows 1–1½ ft. high and wide, spreading by offsets. Short, thick trunk holds fleshy, broadly oval leaves to 8 in. long and 6–8 in. wide. Leaves are gray-green, with margins that turn bright red in full sun. In winter or early spring, a single stem rises 2–3 ft. high and bears clusters of ½–¾-in.-long, tubular, dark yellow flowers with a pleasing fragrance. Provide protection from slugs and snails, which can permanently disfigure leaves. 'Fantastic' (also sold as K. thyrsiflora 'Fantastic') has gray-green leaves striped with cream variegation, and shading red at the margins.

K. pinnata. AIR PLANT. To 2–3 ft. tall and wide. First leaves to form are undivided and scallop edged. Later ones divided into three to five leaflets. These are also scalloped. Produces many plantlets in notches of scallops. Leaves can be removed and pinned to curtain, where they will produce plantlets until they dry up. Greenish white to reddish flowers in clusters to 3 in. long; not particularly attractive. Likes moisture.

K. tomentosa. PANDA PLANT. Branching plant eventually reaches 3 ft. high, 8 in. wide. Leaves 2 in. long, with dense, feltlike coating of white hairs. Leaf tips and shallow notches in leaves are strongly marked dark brown. Yellowish green flowers in spring.

K. uniflora. Trailing plant 6 in. high, 2 ft. wide; good in hanging pots. Thick, 1-in.-long leaves have a few scallops near rounded tips. Inch-long summer flowers; color ranges from red to purple.

KALE AND COLLARDS

Brassicaceae
Biennials grown as cool-season annuals

🌡 **US, MS, LS, CS, TS; USDA 6-11**

☀🌗 **FULL SUN OR LIGHT SHADE**

💧 **REGULAR WATER**

'Toscano' kale

These knee-high, cool-season cabbage relatives are grown for their leaves, which can be steamed, stir-fried, sautéed, or added to soups. Both are high in vitamins A and C and calcium. Hardy to 5°F (–15°C), these vegetables are winter staples. Kale grows 14–30 in. high, and collards average 2–3 ft. high.

Curly-leafed kales (such as red-veined, purple-tinged 'Redbor' and blue-green 'Winterbor') form compact clusters of tightly curled leaves. 'Toscano' ('Lacinato') is a noncurly green kale also known as "dinosaur kale" and considered by many to be the best tasting. 'Red Russian' is a noncurly red kale whose leaves are gray-green with purple veins. Flowering kale is similar to flowering cabbage, with brightly

ABOVE: 'Champion' collard greens

colored, decorative foliage; it too is edible and is sometimes sold in markets under the name "salad savoy." Collard greens come from large, smooth-leafed plants that do not form a head. Collard selections include 'Champion', 'Flash', 'Georgia', and 'Vates'.

CARE

Sow seeds in place, and thin to 1½–3 ft. apart; or set out transplants at the same spacing. Planted in early spring or late summer, collards and kale will yield edible leaves in fall, winter, and spring. Late-summer planting is preferable for the Lower, Coastal, and Tropical South; plant in either season for the Upper and Middle South.

Harvest leaves by removing them from the outside of clusters, or harvest entire plant. Light frost sweetens flavor. Plants suffer far fewer pest and disease problems than most other crops in the cabbage family.

KALIMERIS

Asteraceae
Perennials

🌡 **US, MS, LS, CS; USDA 6-9**

☀🌗 **FULL SUN OR LIGHT SHADE**

💧 **REGULAR WATER**

Kalimeris incisa

An underused group of flowering perennials from eastern Asia. Easy to grow and colorful over a long season from summer into fall. Flowers resemble asters. Thrive in heat and humidity. Shear to encourage rebloom.

K. incisa. JAPANESE ASTER. Mound-forming perennial 1–1½ ft. high and about as wide. Light blue, daisylike flowers with yellow centers are 1 in. across. Oblong, bright green leaves are 3–4 in. long. 'Blue Star' has brighter blue petals. 'Edo Murasaki' has darker purple petals.

K. integrifolia 'Daisy Mae'. Clear white, 1-in. blooms with greenish yellow centers. Grows 2 ft. high and wide.

K. pinnatifida. FALSE ASTER. Perennial similar to *Boltonia asteroides*. White, 1-in. flowers resembling small chrysanthemums are borne by the hundreds all summer, forming a cloud over the foliage. Blossoms may be tinged pink or blue, have creamy yellow centers. The oval, pointed leaves are rich green. A basal rosette is formed by 3-in.-long leaves that are heavily serrated. Leaves on upper stems are only 1 in. long and usually have smooth edges. Grows to 2–4 ft. tall, 2 ft. wide; spreads slowly.

KALMIA

Ericaceae
Evergreen shrubs

✀ **ZONES VARY BY SPECIES**

◑ **PARTIAL SHADE**

● **REGULAR WATER**

◊ **LEAVES AND FLOWER NECTAR ARE POISONOUS IF INGESTED**

Kalmia latifolia 'Keepsake'

Elegant shrubs related to rhododendron, with showy flower clusters. Each long flower stalk bears a small bud resembling a fluted turban; buds open to chalice-shaped blooms with \five starlike points. Plants share rhododendron's need for moist air and rich, well-drained, acid soil. Tolerate shade but bloom much better in part sun (provided soil does not dry out). Challenging for most people to grow.

K. angustifolia. SHEEP LAUREL, LAMBKILL. Zones US; USDA 6. Native to high elevations in eastern states from Georgia to Virginia. Ground cover or shrub, to 1–3 ft. (rarely 5 ft.) tall and 5 ft. wide. Spreads by self-layering (branches root where they touch the ground). Dark green leaves are leathery, oblong to pointed-oval, to 2½ in. long. Rose-pink to purplish crimson flowers, ½ in. across, bloom in clusters in early summer. 'Candida' has white flowers, 'Rubra' dark purple blossoms.

K. latifolia. MOUNTAIN LAUREL. Zones US, MS, LS, CS; USDA 6-9. Native to eastern North America from Canada to Florida, west across the Appalachians into states drained by the Ohio and Mississippi river systems. Southern forms of plant grow better in the Lower and Coastal South; those from more northerly seed sources grow better in the Upper and Middle South. Success also depends on plant source. Named selections are unlikely to perform well in all zones listed.

Slow growing to 6–8 ft. or taller, with equal spread. Glossy, leathery, oval leaves are 3–5 in. long, dark green above, yellowish green beneath. Blooms in late spring; typically bears 1-in.-wide, light pink flowers opening from darker pink buds, but blossoms often have subtly different color in their throats and may have contrasting stamens. Flowers held in clusters to 5 in. across.

Dozens of named selections are available. Here are examples by color.

Those with flowers marked in contrasting colors include 'Freckles', white with spots and splashes of purplish red; and 'Bullseye', which has cream-colored blossoms with white and purple-red markings in throat, white edge, and broad, purple-red band around the inside—new foliage is reddish. 'Keepsake' has burgundy blooms with a thin white edge.

Red-budded selections include 'Firecracker', 'Nathan Hale', and 'Olympic Fire', which all have pink flowers; and 'Sarah', with reddish pink flowers. 'Pristine' is a white-flowered selection; 'Snowdrift' is white with faint red markings.

Dwarf selections (to 3 ft. in 10 years) include 'Elf', with pink buds opening to white flowers; 'Minuet', light pink buds opening to white flowers with a maroon ring inside; and 'Tinkerbell', whose pink buds open to deep pink flowers.

KALOPANAX SEPTEMLOBUS

CASTOR ARALIA, TREE ARALIA
Araliaceae
Deciduous tree

✀ **US, MS; USDA 6-7**

☼ **FULL SUN**

● **REGULAR WATER**

Kalopanax septemlobus

Native to eastern Asia. Unusual in being the only cold-hardy large tree in its family. Also notable for the tropical look conferred by big (7- to 10-in.) leaves with five to seven lobes. On young trees, leaves may exceed 1 ft. in width. Tree is open and gaunt in youth but eventually develops an attractive, rounded habit; reaches 40–60 ft. tall and equally wide, with a spiny trunk and relatively few coarse, spiny branches. With age, spines eventually disappear from trunk and larger branches. Tiny white flowers appear in flattish, 1- to 2-ft. clusters at branch ends in summer. Tiny black fruit follows the blossoms; it is quickly consumed by birds. Seeds dropped by birds can sprout in fields and wet areas.

KERRIA JAPONICA

JAPANESE KERRIA
Rosaceae
Deciduous shrub

✀ **US, MS, LS, CS; USDA 6-9**

◑ **LIGHT SHADE**

●● **MODERATE TO REGULAR WATER**

Kerria japonica 'Shannon'

Though it hails from China and Japan, this shrub has become a true Southern passalong plant, often seen gracing older cottage and country gardens. Grows 3–6 ft. tall and somewhat wider, with an open, rounded habit. Bright green, 2- to 4-in.-long, tooth-edged leaves are oval and pointed, with prominent veining; they emerge early in spring and may turn soft lemon-yellow in fall. Showy yellow flowers are single or double, 1¼–2 in. across; they appear mainly in spring but continue sporadically throughout the summer. Flowers are solitary and resemble small roses—in fact, Japanese kerria is sometimes mistakenly called "the yellow rose of Texas." In winter, the leafless bright green stems lend welcome color to the garden.

Give Japanese kerria room to display its naturally arching form. Use it in mixed borders and in combination with spring-blooming shrubs and bulbs; also striking when massed. Best sited in some shade, as the flowers tend to fade in hot sun. Cut branches are easy to force into early bloom indoors. Flowers dry easily—just cut branches in full flower, place them in a vase of water, and let the stems gradually absorb the water. Selections include the following.

'Albiflora'. Sometimes called white kerria, but single flowers are actually pale, creamy yellow with bright yellow stamens. Grows 3–5 ft. tall and a bit wider.

'Geisha'. Leaves variably flecked with white and yellow. Double yellow flowers. Grows 4–6 ft. tall, 6–8 ft. wide.

'Golden Guinea'. Single golden yellow flowers are especially large—to 1½ in. across. Plants reach 3–5 ft. tall and 6–8 ft. wide.

'Kin Kan'. Like the species but has soft yellow stems with thin, vertical green stripes.

'Picta' ('Variegata'). Gray-green leaves are attractively edged in white. Single bright yellow flowers are gaudy. Prune out any branches with leaves that revert to solid green. Grows 3–4 ft. tall, 5–6 ft. wide.

'Pleniflora'. Most popular form. Spreads more quickly than other types. Double golden blooms resemble tiny pompons. Upright grower; tends to be lanky. To 6–8 ft. tall and wide.

'Shannon'. Early bloomer, with large, deep yellow single flowers. Grows 5–6 ft. tall and a little wider.

CARE

Grows well in almost any reasonably well-drained soil. Plants form colonies from spreading roots. Propagation by division is easy: Use a sharp spade to separate a stem or two from the base of the mother plant in late winter. Or propagate by taking cuttings in summer. Prune heavily after bloom, cutting to the ground older stems that have bloomed. Also remove dead wood and spindly growth.

KIRENGESHOMA PALMATA
YELLOW WAXBELLS
Hydrangeaceae
Perennial

🌿 **US, MS, LS; USDA 6-8**

◑ **PARTIAL SHADE**

💧 **REGULAR WATER**

Kirengeshoma palmata

A perennial of great elegance, yellow waxbells grows 2–4 ft. tall, 2–2½ ft. wide, with dark purplish stems carrying deeply lobed and toothed leaves. Pale yellow flower clusters appear in joints of upper leaves and at tops of stalks in late summer and early autumn. Blossoms are drooping and narrowly bell shaped, 1½ in. long. Lovely in partially shaded border or woodland garden. Needs ample organic matter in soil. Native to Japan and Korea.

TRY YELLOW WAXBELLS AS THE CENTER- PIECE OF A MOSTLY GREEN WOODLAND GARDEN.

KIWI
Actinidiaceae
Deciduous vines

🌿 **ZONES VARY BY SPECIES**

◐ **EXPOSURE NEEDS VARY BY SPECIES**

💧 **REGULAR WATER**

'Hayward' kiwis

These East Asian twining vines are remarkably vigorous and beautiful, producing fruit whose flavor is a combination of melon, strawberry, and banana. Fuzzy-skinned kiwifruit (the type sold in markets) has a delicious piquancy; the other kinds are sweeter. Unless you have a self-fruitful selection, you will need to grow a male plant nearby to pollinate the female (fruit-bearing) plant. Supply sturdy supports, such as a trellis, an arbor, or a patio overhead. You can also train kiwi vines to cover walls and fences; guide and tie vines to the support as necessary.

For an ornamental kiwi grown for its beautiful variegated foliage, see *Actinidia kolomikta*.

Fuzzy-skinned kiwi (*Actinidia deliciosa* or *A. chinensis*). MS, LS, CS; USDA 7-9. Generally grows best in the Lower and Coastal South, where temperatures do not drop below 10°F. Long, warm summers are needed to ripen the fruit. Give it full sun or partial shade. Note that a vine can take up to five years from planting to flower or set fruit. Sometimes called Chinese gooseberry vine, it twines to 30 ft. if not curbed. Roundish, 5- to 8-in.-long leaves are rich dark green above, velvety white below. New growth often has rich red fuzz. Spring flowers are 1–1½ in. wide, opening cream colored and fading to buff. Fuzzy,

brown-skinned, green-fleshed fruit is the size and roughly the shape of an egg. 'Hayward' is the most common fruiting selection. To pollinate it, use 'Chico Male', 'Matua', 'Tomuri', or plants simply sold as "male." 'Vincent' and 'Elmwood' need little winter chill and are good choices for warmest-winter climates; use 'Chico Male' as its pollenizer. Male hardy kiwi selections (see below) can also supply pollen for female fuzzy-skinned kiwis.

Hardy kiwi (*A. arguta*). US, MS, LS; USDA 6-8. Much like fuzzy-skinned kiwi vine in appearance but has smaller leaves (which are smooth and fuzzless), flowers, and fruit. The 1- to 1¼-in.-long, fuzzless fruit can be eaten skin and all. Best in partial shade in most of the South. Green-fruited female selections 'Ananasnaja' ('Anna'), 'Hood River', and 'Jumbo', need a male plant (may be sold simply as "male") for pollen. 'Issai', also with green fruit, is self-fruitful. Female 'Ken's Red' is a hybrid with red fruit; it needs a pollenizer.

CARE

These vines prefer good, well-drained soil and regular applications of nitrogen fertilizer. Plants are sensitive to salt burn in alkaline soils. In fall, harvest fruit while it is firm and let it ripen off the tree; fruit left on the vine too long will spoil or be eaten by birds. Start harvesting when the first fruit just starts to soften or when fuzzy kiwis turn from greenish brown to fully brown.

During dormant season, prune for form and fruit production. Cut back to one or two main trunks and remove closely parallel or crossing branches. Fruit is borne on shoots from year-old or older wood; cut out shoots that have fruited for three years and shorten younger shoots, leaving three to seven buds beyond previous summer's fruit. In summer, shorten overlong shoots and unwind any shoots twining around main branches. Because male pollenizer's sole purpose is flower production, you can prune it back drastically after bloom.

KNAUTIA

Caprifoliaceae
Perennials

- US, MS, LS; USDA 6-8
- FULL SUN
- REGULAR WATER

Knautia macedonica 'Mars Midget'

These mid-height perennials are covered with pincushion flowers in summer. Basal leaves are barely lobed, but those on upper stems are deeply divided. Undemanding meadow plants, they are at home in cottage gardens, wild gardens, perennial borders, and roadside plantings. Cut flowers are good for fresh or dried arrangements. Resist deer.

K. arvensis. BLUE BUTTONS. From Europe, the Caucasus, and the Mediterranean region. To 1–5 ft. tall, 1½ ft. wide. Blue, 1½-in. flower heads in summer.

K. macedonica. From central Europe. To 1½–3 ft. high and as wide. Deep purplish red flower heads bloom from early summer through fall. Reseeds manageably. 'Mars Midget', to 16 in. high, is more upright and has crimson flowers. Melton Pastels grow 1½–3 ft. or higher, 1½ ft. wide, with flower heads in tones of blue, mauve, pink, rose, salmon-pink, and crimson from late spring to fall. 'Red Cherry' grows almost 3 ft. high and has reddish purple flowers. 'Thunder and Lightning' combines burgundy blooms with green leaves edged in white.

KNIPHOFIA

RED-HOT POKER, TORCH LILY
Asphodelaceae
Perennials

- US, MS, LS, CS; USDA 6-9
- FULL SUN OR PARTIAL SHADE
- MODERATE TO REGULAR WATER

Kniphofia hybrid

Dense clumps of grasslike, finely toothed foliage send up bare stems topped by nodding, tubular flowers in tight, overlapping clusters. Flowering stems look like glowing pokers or torches, hence the common names. Blossoms open from bottom to top over the course of several days, changing color as they mature. Increasing numbers of species—mostly from South Africa—are now grown in gardens and hybridized. The old 3-ft.-high forms of *K. uvaria* in shades of coral-orange and yellow have given way to kinds with blooms ranging from coral-red through every conceivable shade of orange, peach, and yellow to near-white and light green, on plants varying in size from 1½-ft. dwarfs to 6-ft. giants. The flowers attract hummingbirds. Resist deer.

K. caulescens. Blue-green leaves (purple at base) are 3–4 ft. long, 2–3 in. wide; they are produced in rosettes on short, branching, woody stems like trunks. Stalks 2 ft. tall bear heads of coral-red to terra-cotta buds that open to pale yellow flowers. Blooms from mid-summer into fall.

K. citrina. Smallish species with narrow, dark bluish green leaves and globular flower heads in various yellow shades on 2- to 2½-ft.-tall stems. Summer to fall

bloom. 'Lime Select' has bright lime-green buds that open chartreuse and fade to cream.

K. hybrids. Although they involve several species, these hybrids generally share the narrow leaves and summer bloom season of *K. uvaria*. A distinct departure is 'Christmas Cheer', a hybrid of the vigorous species *K. rooperi*. New strains are available as seed (be aware that seedlings will vary in color and quality).

'Alcazar'. Dark, bronzy stems to 3½ ft., with brick-red flowers that age to pinkish orange.

'Bees' Sunset'. Stems to 3 ft. high, with glowing yellow-orange buds opening light yellow.

'Border Ballet'. Buds are a soft, dusty coral-pink opening to cream blooms. Stems reach 4–4½ ft.

'Bressingham Comet'. Stems to 2 ft. high; flower clusters are orange with a yellow base.

'Christmas Cheer'. Brilliant orange buds open to deep gold flowers on 4- to 5-ft. stems. Blooms fall through late spring in mild-winter areas, fall until frost elsewhere. Give it room; leaves (to 5 ft. long and 2 in. wide) become lax and collapse on the ground, smothering any plants in their way. Clump increases rapidly to 6–8 ft. or more across. Divide in early summer.

Echo series. A group of strong, repeat-blooming selections with mango-orange, deep orange to red and orange fading to white blooms. Gray-green leaves reach 2 ft. high topped with flower stalks to 3 ft. high.

Flamenco Mix. Seed-grown strain that blooms in early fall in its first year, in summer in subsequent years. Flower colors range from coral through orange and yellow to creamy white. Stems to 2½ ft. tall.

Glow series. Similar to Popsicle series. Flowers in shades of orange stand 20 in. tall. Repeat blooming.

'Gold Mine'. Glowing orange-yellow buds opening golden amber on 3- to 3½-ft. stems.

'Little Maid'. Thin, grassy leaves and narrow flower stems to 2 ft. tall. Creamy white blossoms open from buds in buff-tinted pale yellow.

'Malibu Yellow'. Stems 5–6 ft. tall bear 8- to 10-in.-long heads of lime-green buds that open primrose yellow.

'Peaches and Cream'. Stems about 4 ft. high bear peach-colored buds opening to cream blossoms.

'Percy's Pride'. To 4 ft. tall, with green-tinted yellow buds opening cream.

Popsicle series. Grassy foliage to 1 ft. high topped with bright flowers in a range of yellow, orange, coral, and cream colors on stems reaching 1½ ft. high. Excellent repeat bloomers.

K. uvaria. Leaves to 1 in. wide, 2 ft. long. Oblong flower heads on stems 3–3½ ft. tall. Coral-red buds open to orange or deep yellow blossoms in summer (in fall, in cold-winter climates). Most selections sold under this name are actually hybrids.

CARE

Red-hot pokers require adequate moisture when blooms are forming and will fail to flower if conditions are too dry then. In summer, they'll tolerate even marshy conditions—but for winter survival, well-drained soil is essential. Most of these plants flower in summer, but some start in late spring and repeat throughout the growing season. Where winter temperatures drop to 0°F or below, tie foliage over clumps in fall to protect growing points (or at least leave all foliage in place over winter). In milder climates, cut or pull out any ratty-looking leaves in fall; new leaves will replace them by spring. Crowns increase slowly, forming clumps 2–3 ft. wide (or wider) at base; you will get the best show if clumps are left in place for several years. Increase plantings by division in spring, except for types still blooming then; for these, wait until summer to divide. Protect from slugs and snails. Not heavily browsed by deer.

TOP ROW: K. 'Creamsicle'; *K.* 'Papaya Popsicle'; *SECOND ROW: K.* 'Pineapple Popsicle'; *K.* 'Fire Glow'; *THIRD ROW: K.* 'Redhot Popsicle'; *K. uvaria; BOTTOM ROW: K.* 'Mango Popsicle'; *K.* 'Lemon Popsicle'

KOELREUTERIA

Sapindaceae
Deciduous trees

✎ **ZONES VARY BY SPECIES**

☼ **FULL SUN**

◌◔ **MODERATE TO REGULAR WATER**

Koelreuteria paniculata 'September'

Native to Asia, these small trees are admired for large, loose clusters of yellow flowers followed by fat, papery fruit capsules resembling little Japanese lanterns. Capsules are used in both fresh and dried arrangements. Good patio, lawn, or street trees. Very adaptable to different soils as long as drainage is fairly good. Self-sown seedlings can be invasive.

K. bipinnata (*K. integrifoliola*). CHINESE FLAME TREE. MS, LS, CS; USDA 7-9. To 20–40 ft. tall and not quite as wide, eventually flat topped. Deep green leaves 1–2 ft. long, divided into 7 to 12 oval leaflets; turn yellow for a short time before dropping in fall. Blooms in mid- to late summer; flower clusters are like those of *K. paniculata*, but 2-in. capsules are more colorful, in shades of orange, red, or salmon. Capsules come quickly after flowers and persist into fall. Prodigious number of seedlings.

K. elegans (*K. formosana*). FLAMEGOLD. Zones CS, TS; USDA 9-11. Round-headed tree 20–30 ft. tall and equally broad. Dark green leaves about 1½ ft. long, with 9 to 16 leaflets. Bright yellow fall flowers in tall, erect clusters are followed by especially showy clusters of long-lasting, puffy, orange-red to salmon fruit. Fall foliage is yellow but not consistent; show is often poor.

K. paniculata. GOLDENRAIN TREE. Zones US, MS, LS, CS, USDA 6-9. To 20–35 ft. tall, 25–40 ft. wide. Open branching, giving slight shade. Leaves to 15 in. long, with 7 to 15 oval, toothed or lobed leaflets, each 1–3 in. long. New leaves are purplish, maturing to bright green in summer; may turn yellow to gold in fall. Very showy, 8- to 14-in.-long flower clusters in early to midsummer. Fruit capsules are red when young, maturing to buff and brown shades; last well into autumn. Tree takes cold, heat, drought, wind. Prune to shape; can be gawky without pruning. 'Coral Sun' is a nonflowering selection with coral new growth that matures to green, contrasting with coral stems. 'Fastigiata' is 25 ft. tall, 3 ft. wide. 'Golden Candle' grows 35 ft. tall, 3–4 ft. wide. 'Rose Lantern' has seedpods flushed with pink. 'September' blooms a month after the species.

KOHLRABI

Brassicaceae
Biennial grown as a cool-season annual

✎ **US, MS, LS, CS, TS; USDA 6-11**

☼ **FULL SUN**

◌ **REGULAR WATER**

'Kolibri' kohlrabi

Resembling a tennis ball sprouting kale leaves, kohlrabi looks odd but tastes great. Leaves and leafstalks

but most gardeners grow it for the enlarged, bulblike part that forms just above the soil surface. Probably native to Europe's west coast. Plants go from seed to harvest in 50 to 60 days; the quality declines if harvest is delayed.

Standard selections are 'Early White Vienna' and 'Early Purple Vienna'—similar in size and flavor, differing only in skin color. They're ready when globes are 2–3 in. in diameter. Other white selections include 'Triumph' and early-maturing 'Grand Duke'. 'Kolibri' is a popular purple-skinned variety with 4–6-in. globes. 'Superschmelz', 'Kossack', and 'Gigante' all reach 8–10 in. in diameter.

Harvest bulbous part when 2–3 in. wide. Peel, slice, and serve raw; or steam or sauté slices or chunks. Steam young leaves and leafstalks.

CARE

Plants are very fast growing, ready to harvest in 50 to 60 days from seed. Sow seed in rich soil about 2 weeks after average date of last frost. Before planting, work ½ cup of 10-10-10 fertilizer per 10 ft. of row into soil. Follow first planting with successive sowings 2 weeks apart. In areas with warm winters, plant again in late fall and early winter. Sow seed ½ in. deep, in rows spaced 1½ ft. apart; thin seedlings to 4–6 in. apart. Cabbageworms are the primary pests. For controls, see Cabbage.

KOLKWITZIA AMABILIS

BEAUTY BUSH
Caprifoliaceae
Deciduous shrub

🗡 US, MS, LS; USDA 6-8

◑ FULL SUN OR PARTIAL SHADE

💧 REGULAR WATER

Kolkwitzia amabilis

This fountainlike central Chinese native grows quickly to 10–12 ft. tall and wide. In partial shade, it has an arching form; in full sun, it's denser and shorter. Mid- to late spring is its best season, when beauty bush is covered with clusters of 1-in.-long, yellow-throated pink flowers. Gray-green leaves to 3 in. long sometimes turn reddish in fall. Blooms heavily in mid- to late spring, bearing clusters of 1-in.-long, yellow-throated pink flowers. Blossoms are followed by conspicuous pinkish brown, bristly fruit that prolongs color display. Brown, flaky bark gradually peels from stems during winter. An old Southern favorite. 'Pink Cloud' is a particularly floriferous selection, bearing masses of pink blossoms.

Adapts to many soils and climates. Blooms on wood formed the previous year. Thin out oldest stems after blossoms have faded; or, to enjoy the fruit, wait until early spring to prune, then do so lightly. Tends to get leggy with age; plant can be renewed by cutting the oldest, woodiest stems to ground after bloom.

KOSTELETZKYA VIRGINICA

SEASHORE MALLOW
Malvaceae
Perennial

🗡 US, MS, LS, CS; USDA 6-9

☀ FULL SUN

💧💧 REGULAR TO AMPLE WATER

Kosteletzkya virginica

Native to the coastal marshes of the Southeast, this upright, free-flowering mallow deserves much wider use in gardens. Breaking dormancy in late spring, it sends up thick stems in a cluster that may reach 5 ft. tall and 2 ft. wide. Foliage is light green and fuzzy; lower leaves on stems are 6 in. long, with three to five lobes, while upper ones are smaller, either triangular or arrow shaped. Hundreds of pink, 2-in.-wide flowers resembling those of hibiscus smother the plant from midsummer to fall. Seashore mallow thrives in swampy soil and even standing water but adapts to regular garden soil as well. 'Immaculate' features large white blooms. 'Ace Basin' has rich pink blooms.

L

LABURNUM

GOLDENCHAIN TREE
Papilionaceae
Deciduous trees or shrubs

🗡 US, MS; USDA 6-7

◑ AFTERNOON SHADE

💧💧 MODERATE TO REGULAR WATER

💧 ALL PARTS, ESPECIALLY SEEDPODS, ARE HIGHLY POISONOUS IF INGESTED

Laburnum x *watereri*

Native to central and southern Europe, these are among the garden's prettiest flowering trees. They grow upright and are typically pruned to a single trunk but can be shrubby if allowed to keep basal suckers and low branches. Olive-green bark is a trademark; bright green leaves are divided into three leaflets (like clover leaves). Beautiful in bloom in mid- to late spring, when hanging clusters of bright yellow, fragrant flowers appear. Flexible branches make them easy to espalier; they can be trained on narrow arches to form spectacular flowering tunnels. They're also good as single specimens, in foundation plantings, and in groupings.

Plants need good drainage; will tolerate alkaline soil. Susceptibility to insects and disease can make them rather short lived. They don't do well in extended summer heat, so protect them from hot afternoon sun. Prune after bloom. Removing seedpods promptly may increase the next year's bloom.

L. alpina. SCOTCH LABURNUM. To 30–35 ft. tall, 20–25 ft. wide. Flower clusters are 10–15 in. long. 'Pendulum' has weeping branches.

L. anagyroides. COMMON GOLDENCHAIN. Bushy, spreading plant grows to 20–30 ft. tall and 15–20 ft. wide. Flower clusters 6–10 in. long. 'Pendulum' is a weeping form.

L. x watereri. Hybrid between species above. To 15–30 ft. tall, 10–20 ft. wide, with flower clusters 10–20 in. long. 'Sunspire' ('Columnaris') grows to 20 ft. tall and 10 ft. wide. 'Vossii', with 20-in. blossom clusters, is the showiest, most widely grown selection.

LAGERSTROEMIA

CREPE MYRTLE
Lythraceae
Deciduous shrubs and trees

✐ **US, MS, LS, CS; USDA 6-9, EXCEPT AS NOTED**

☼ **FULL SUN**

◐ ◐ **MODERATE TO REGULAR WATER**

See chart beginning on page 397.

Lagerstroemia 'Pink Velour'

Crepe myrtle is the premier flowering tree of the South for good reason. It combines glorious, long-lasting summer blooms in a rainbow of colors with handsome bark, sculptural form, and brilliant fall foliage. It loves the heat, grows quickly, tolerates drought, and accepts almost any well-drained soil. Plus, improved selections resist disease, insects, and even deer.

Most crepe myrtles planted today are selections of *L. indica* or hybrids between this species and *L. faurei.* New selections pop up all the time. One thing we've learned over the past two decades is that the mature size of many selections, particularly those named for tribes of Native Americans, such as 'Natchez,' grow bigger than first advertised. When planted in small yards or near the house, they may quickly outgrow their welcome, resulting in a winter-spring pruning ritual known as "crepe murder," in which innocent trees are chopped back into ugly, knuckled trunks. (See "Don't Commit Crepe Murder" on p. 399.)

Fortunately, many smaller selections don't get too big and need little, if any, pruning. Mature size is so important that our revised chart (pages 397–399) now groups popular selections into **dwarf** (2–5 ft. tall), **short** (6–10 ft. tall) **medium** (11–20 ft. tall), and **tall** (21–50 ft.) categories. Use dwarf kinds in containers, mixed borders, and masses. Use short types in containers, shrub borders, or near the house. Use medium types as small shade trees, street trees, or for screening. Give tall types lots of room and don't plant near the house. One 'Natchez' is plenty for a 900-square-ft. lawn.

Consider these four factors before buying a crepe myrtle.

- What color are the flowers?
- How big will it grow?
- Is the yard sunny enough? (The more sun, the more flowers.)
- Is it cold-hardy enough? (important if you live in the Upper South, USDA 6)

L. faurei. JAPANESE CREPE MYRTLE. Upright tree to 25–50 ft. tall with arching branches. Native to Japan. Seldom grown in the South. Main contribution has been imparting mildew resistance and showy, flaking, cinnamon-brown bark to hybrids. Light green leaves to 4 in. long and 2 in. wide turn yellow in fall. Small, white flowers in 4-in. clusters appear in early summer. 'Fantasy' grows quickly to 50 ft. 'Kiowa' grows 30 ft.

L. indica. CREPE MYRTLE. This species was first introduced into the U.S. from China in the early 1800s by famed botanist Andre Michaux in Charleston, South Carolina. Grows to 25 ft. tall and wide. Dark green, oval leaves, about 2-in. long, turn bright orange or red in the fall. Showy, 6–12-in. clusters of crinkly pink, red, lavender, or purple flowers in summer. Smooth gray or light brown bark peels off to reveal polished inner bark. Older selections plagued by powdery mildew are not listed here.

L. speciosa. QUEEN'S CREPE MYRTLE. Zone TS; USDA 10-11. This is the showiest and least cold-hardy of the crepe myrtles, forming a rounded tree 40–50 ft. tall. Magnificent clusters of pink, lavender, or purple flowers up to 3 in. across weigh down the branches in summer. Large leaves, 8–12 in. long and 4 in. wide, turn red in fall. Smooth, mottled, exfoliating bark. Native to Old World tropics.

CARE

Crepe myrtles bloom on new growth and should be pruned in late winter or early spring. Dwarf and short types need only minor, cosmetic pruning. On medium and tall types, prune to a tree form. Remove suckers at the base, twiggy growth, crossing branches, and branches growing toward the center of the plant. Also gradually remove side branches on main trunks up to a height of 4–5 ft. The tree should be open enough that a bird could fly through unimpeded. This exposes the handsome bark and also improves air circulation, making leaf diseases such as mildew and leaf spot less likely. Pruning off spent flower clusters (if you can reach them) in summer results in a second flush of blooms. If your soil is sandy or poor, give newly-planted crepe myrtles a drink of liquid fertilizer every 2 weeks in summer. After its first year in the ground, crepe myrtle needs no fertilizing.

ABOVE: Lagerstroemia 'Cherry Dazzle'

A CREPE MYRTLE SAMPLER

'Catawba'
Medium (12–15 ft.)

'Dynamite'
Medium (15–20 ft.)

'Miami'
Tall (18–25 ft.)

'Osage'
Medium (15–20 ft.)

'Yuma'
Medium (12–15 ft.)

CREPE MYRTLES

NAME	FORM/HEIGHT	FLOWER COLOR	FALL FOLIAGE	MILDEW RESISTANCE	COMMENTS
DWARF CREPE MYRTLES					
'Chickasaw'	Dense mound, 3–4 ft. tall and wide	Lavender-pink	Bronze-red	Very good	Slow grower; great in container
'Pocomoke'	Mounding, 2–3 ft. high, 3–4 ft. wide	Rosy pink	Bronzy red	High	Great in containers; no pruning needed; heavy bloomer; cold hardy
Razzle Dazzle series	Mounding, 3–4 ft. high and wide	See comments.	Burgundy	Good	Begins blooming a little later than most crepe myrtles, usually in July; selections include 'Cherry Dazzle' (our favorite), cherry-red blooms; 'Diamond Dazzle,' white blooms; and 'Sweetheart Dazzle,' bubble-gum-pink
'Tightwad Red'	Tight mound, 3–4 ft. tall and wide	Deep red	Burgundy	High	Small leaves emerge wine-red in spring, changing to deep green in summer; sterile—no seedpods; cold hardy
'Victor'	Compact, 3–5 ft. tall and wide	Deep red	Orange-yellow	Good	Cold hardy
SHORT CREPE MYRTLES					
'Acoma'	Arching-spreading, 6–10 ft. tall and wide	White	Reddish purple	High	Handsome, light gray bark; repeat bloomer; cold hardy; our favorite white
'Delta Jazz'	Upright, 6–10 ft. tall, 4–5 ft. wide	Pink	Burgundy	Good	Dark burgundy leaves are main attraction; not a heavy bloomer
Early Bird series	Upright, 5–8 ft. high, 3–4 ft. wide	White, lavender, or purple	Burgundy-red	Good	Blooms earlier than most crepe myrtles, as early as Mother's Day; reblooms over summer, offering over 100 days of blooms; great in containers
'Hopi'	Spreading, bushy. 7–10 ft. tall and wide	Medium pink	Orange-red	High	Handsome, gray-brown bark; repeat bloomer; cold hardy
Magic series	Rounded, bushy, 6–10 ft. tall and wide	See comments.	Light yellow	Good	Selections include 'Coral Magic' (coral-pink blooms), 'Plum Magic' (fuchsia-pink), and 'Purple Magic' (purple); new growth emerges reddish and then changes to deep green
'Red Rooster'	Upright, 8–10 ft. tall, 5 ft. wide	Bright red	Red	Good	New foliage emerges maroon-red; cold hardy
'Siren Red'	Rounded, 8–10 ft. tall and wide	Dark red	Yellow	High	New foliage emerges wine-red and then changes to dark green
'Velma's Royal Delight'	Bushy, 4–6 ft. tall and wide	Rich, magenta-purple	Yellow-orange	Good	Gorgeous flowers; handsome bark; cold hardy
'White Chocolate'	8–10 ft. tall and wide	White	Orange and yellow	Good	Beautiful in the landscape; leaves emerge maroon, then change to burgundy-green
'Zuni'	Vase-shaped, spreading, 6–10 ft. tall and wide	Medium lavender	Orange-red	High	Graceful form, long bloomer, handsome bark, cold hardy; our favorite lavender

CREPE MYRTLES (continued)

NAME	FORM/HEIGHT	FLOWER COLOR	FALL FOLIAGE	MILDEW RESISTANCE	COMMENTS
MEDIUM CREPE MYRTLES					
Black Diamond series	Upright, spreading, 10–12 ft. tall, 8 ft. wide	See comments.	Deep purple	Good	These new trademarked plants are the same as the Ebony series developed by the USDA; they're noted for striking, blackish purple foliage and contrasting flowers of red, pink, and white; selections include 'Best Red' ('Ebony Flame'), 'Blush' ('Ebony Glow'), 'Crimson Red' ('Ebony Fire'), and 'Pure White' ('Ebony & Ivory')
'Burgundy Cotton'	Upright to 12 ft. tall, 6–7 ft. wide	White	Burgundy	Good	Burgundy flower buds; leaves emerge wine-red and then change to burgundy-green; fast grower
'Catawba'	Upright, 12–15 ft. tall, 8–10 ft. wide	Deep purple	Orange-red	Good	Cold hardy; our favorite purple
'Comanche'	Upright, spreading, 12–15 ft. tall and wide	Coral-pink	Orange-red	High	Handsome tan to sandalwood bark; cold hardy
'Dynamite'	Upright, 15–20 ft. tall, 10 ft. wide	Cherry-red	Orange-red	Good	Flowers may develop white flecking if they open on cool, overcast days; nearly seedless; new growth is crimson, changing to green; cold hardy
'Lipan'	Upright, spreading, 15–20 ft. tall and wide	Medium lavender	Orange	High	Beautiful white to beige bark; cold hardy
'Near East'	Open, vase-shaped, 10–15 ft. tall and wide	Soft pink	Yellow	Fair to good	Beautiful blooms; not very cold hardy; not for Middle or Upper South
'Osage'	Open, arching to pendulous, 15–20 ft. tall and wide	Clear, light pink	Red	High	Outstanding, chestnut-brown bark; heavy and long bloomer
'Pink Velour'	Upright to vase-shaped, 10–12 ft. tall and wide	Neon pink	Yellow	Good	Very showy blooms; leaves emerge wine-red and then change to burgundy-green; nearly seedless
'Red Rocket'	Upright to 15–20 ft. tall, 15 ft. wide	Cherry-red	Orange-red	Good	Huge flower clusters; flowers opening on cool, overcast days may show white flecking; new growth is red and then changes to deep green; cold hardy; our favorite red
'Regal Red'	Upright to rounded, 15–20 ft. tall and wide	Vivid, deep red	Red-orange	Good	Heavy bloomer; handsome bark; cold hardy
'Rhapsody in Pink'	Upright to rounded, 12–15 ft. tall and wide	Soft pink	Yellow-orange	Good	Seedless; leaves emerge purple and hold color through summer; flower clusters rebloom
'Sioux'	Upright to 15–20 ft. tall, 15 ft. wide	Bright pink	Red	High	Heavy and long bloomer; smooth, light-brown bark; susceptible to leaf spot in high rainfall areas
'Tonto'	Rounded, 10–12 ft. tall and wide	Red	Maroon	High	Handsome, cream-colored to gray bark

NAME	FORM/HEIGHT	FLOWER COLOR	FALL FOLIAGE	MILDEW RESISTANCE	COMMENTS
'Tuscarora'	Vase-shaped, 15–20 ft. tall and wide	Deep coral-pink	Orange-red	High	Handsome, mottled, light brown bark
'Yuma'	Upright, vase-shaped, 12–15 ft. tall and wide	Medium lavender	Yellow-orange	Good	Beautiful blooms; handsome, light gray bark; cold hardy

TALL CREPE MYRTLES

NAME	FORM/HEIGHT	FLOWER COLOR	FALL FOLIAGE	MILDEW RESISTANCE	COMMENTS
'Arapaho'	Upright, vase-shaped, 18–25 ft. tall and wide	Intense red	Maroon	High	Handsome, tan bark; fast grower; cold hardy
'Basham's Party Pink'	Upright, spreading, to 50 ft. tall and wide	Lavender-pink	Orange-red	Good	Very popular in south Texas; not very cold hardy; not recommended for Upper and Middle South
'Biloxi'	Upright, vase-shaped, to 35 ft. tall, 15 ft. wide	Light pink	Yellow-orange to red	High	Fast grower; beautiful, chestnut-brown bark; cold hardy
'Miami'	Upright, spreading, 18–25 ft. tall and wide	Deep pink	Orange-red	High	Outstanding, chestnut-brown bark; cold hardy; our favorite pink
'Muskogee'	Broad, spreading, to 30 ft. tall and wide	Light lavender	Orange-red	High	Handsome, light gray-brown bark; long bloomer; cold hardy
'Natchez'	Upright, arching, to 35 ft. tall and wide	White	Orange-red	High	Spectacular, cinnamon-brown bark; fast grower; long bloomer; most widely planted crepe myrtle in the South
'Tuskegee'	Broad, spreading, 18–25 ft. tall and wide	Dark rose-pink	Orange-red	High	Mottled, light tan bark; long bloomer
'William Toovey'	Upright, spreading, 18–25 ft. tall and wide	Watermelon-red	Orange-red	Good	Often sold as 'Watermelon Red'; first named crepe myrtle selection

DON'T COMMIT "CREPE MURDER"

Crepe myrtle trunks are too pretty to cut into ugly stubs, just because your neighbors do. This ruins the natural form and encourages the growth of spindly, whiplike branches that are too weak to hold up the flowers. To reduce a crepe myrtle's height, use hand pruners or loppers to shorten the topmost branches by 2–3 ft. in late winter, always cutting back to a side branch or bud. For branches more than 2 in. thick, always cut back to the crotch or trunk. Don't leave big, ugly stubs.

ABOVE: A mature crepe myrtle in full glory.

LAMIUM
DEAD NETTLE
Lamiaceae
Perennials sometimes used as annuals

🌡 **US, MS, LS; USDA 6-8**

◐ ● **PARTIAL TO FULL SHADE**

💧 **REGULAR WATER**

Lamium maculatum 'Orchid Frost'

Native from Europe to western Asia. Heart-shaped, tooth-edged leaves, often marked with white or silver, are borne in opposite pairs; clustered flowers come in pink, white, yellow, lavender. Vigorous growers that thrive in shade; *L. maculatum* is used as a ground cover.

L. galeobdolon (*Lamiastrum galeobdolon*). YELLOW ARCHANGEL. Grows upright to 2 ft., spreading slowly to form tight clumps. Yellow flowers are inconspicuous. Best-known selection is 'Hermann's Pride', with leaves evenly streaked and spotted with white.

L. maculatum. SPOTTED DEAD NETTLE. Running or trailing plant used as a ground cover or in hanging baskets. To 6 in. tall, spreading 2–3 ft. wide, with grayish green leaves marked in silver. The species is very vigorous (even weedy) and is not planted as often as its selections. All of these nicely light up shady areas of the garden. Groom periodically to remove old, shabby growth.

'Anne Greenaway'. Lavender flowers. Unusual leaves have gold edges and a central silver streak surrounded by olive-green.

'Beacon Silver'. Pink flowers and green-edged, silvery gray leaves.

'Beedham's White'. White blooms and yellow to chartreuse leaves with a white stripe in the center.

'Chequers'. Pink flowers and green leaves with a central white stripe.

'Orchid Frost'. Pink blossoms; silver leaves edged in bluish green.

'Pink Pewter'. Pink blooms and silvery leaves edged in greenish gray.

'White Nancy'. Like 'Beacon Silver' but with white flowers.

LAMPROCAPNOS SPECTABILIS
COMMON BLEEDING HEART
Papaveraceae
Perennial

🌡 **US, MS, LS, CS; USDA 6-9**

◐ ● **PARTIAL TO FULL SHADE**

💧 **REGULAR WATER**

Lamprocapnos spectabilis 'Gold Heart'

Formerly known as *Dicentra spectabilis*. Native to Japan; old garden favorite. To 2-3 feet high, 3 feet wide; stems are set with soft green leaves. Blooms in spring, bearing big flowers on one side of arching stems–rose-pink, pendulous, heart-shaped, with protruding white inner petals. 'Gold Heart' has bright golden leaves that hold their color into summer. 'Alba' ('Pantaloons') is a pure white form. 'Valentine' has bright-red flower with white inner petals.

Plants usually die down to the ground by midsummer. To keep the gap from showing, plant next to perennials that hold their foliage all summer. Not browsed by deer.

LEFT: Lamium maculatum 'White Nancy'

LANTANA
Verbenaceae
Evergreen shrubs

🌡 **LS, CS, TS; USDA 8-11, EXCEPT AS NOTED; GROWN AS ANNUALS IN US, MS; USDA 6-7**

☀ **FULL SUN**

💧 **MODERATE WATER, EXCEPT AS NOTED**

◆ **FRUIT IS POISONOUS IF INGESTED**

Lantana 'Spreading Sunset'

Few plants supply as much long-lasting, dependable color as these tough-as-nails tropical American natives. Tiny flowers in tight clusters that resemble miniature nosegays appear continuously in warm weather. Foliage gives off a pungent odor when brushed against or crushed. Small fruit usually follows the flowers, maturing from green to bluish black; some selections are fruitless. Lantanas thrive in hot, dry weather and tolerate just about any well-drained soil, growing well even near the beach. They're a magnet for butterflies. Plant them in masses, let them cascade over a wall, or display them in window boxes, hanging baskets, or planters. Deer don't usually care for lantana species, but they may browse hybrid types.

L. camara. COMMON LANTANA. The most popular species in the South, and one of two used in hybridizing (the other is *L. montevidensis*). Coarse, upright plant to 6 ft. tall and wide. Rough-textured, dark green leaves are oval and pointed, to 4 in. long. Yellow, orange, or red flowers in 1- to 2-in. clusters.

L. horrida. TEXAS LANTANA. Native to southern Texas and Mexico. Prickly, coarse shrub, to

3 ft. (rarely 6 ft.) tall and wide. Broadly oval leaves to 3 in. long have pointed tips and coarsely toothed edges. Spreads by shoots that root where they touch the ground. Good ground cover on very dry sites in full sun. Flowers open yellow, age to orange.

L. montevidensis. TRAILING LANTANA. Along with *L. camara*, this species is used extensively in breeding. A little hardier than *L. camara*, it's a ground cover to about 2 ft. high, with branches trailing to 3 ft. or even 6 ft. Dark green, inch-long leaves have coarsely toothed edges; sometimes tinged red or purplish, especially in winter. Rosy lilac flowers in 1- to 1½-in.-wide clusters. 'Lavender Swirl' is a larger form that produces white, lavender, and white-and-lavender flower clusters. 'Sunny Daze' has leaves attractively edged in creamy yellow and grows more slowly than the species. 'White Lightnin' looks similar but has pure white flowers; it too is a slow grower.

L. selections and hybrids. In this list, some of the selections are forms of *L. camara* or hybrids between those forms; others are hybrids resulting from crosses between *L. camara* and *L. montevidensis*. Lantanas are considered invasive in some areas. Gardeners there should plant fruitless or nearly fruitless selections (noted).

Bandana series. Plants have compact growth to 2–2½ ft. high and wide. Large flowers open yellow and turn orange, pink, or cherry-red.

'Chapel Hill Yellow'. To 1½ ft. by 2–3 ft. Golden yellow. Hardy.

'Christine'. To 6 ft. by 5 ft. Cerise-pink. Can be trained into a small patio tree.

'Confetti'. To 2–3 ft. by 6–8 ft. Blossoms in a mix of yellow, pink, and purple.

'Dallas Red'. To 3–4 ft. by 3–5 ft. Deep red. Nearly fruitless.

'Gold Mound'. To 3 ft. by 3–5 ft. Golden yellow. Fruitless.

'Gold Rush'. To 1½–2 ft. by 4–6 ft. Rich golden yellow.

'Ham and Eggs'. To 2 ft. by 4 ft. Pink with creamy yellow center. Fruitless.

'Irene'. To 3 ft. by 4 ft. Compact. Clusters feature magenta and lemon-yellow flowers.

Landmark series. Dense, mounding plants to 1½ ft. tall, 2 ft. wide, in colors of orange, gold, white, peach, pink, and rose.

Neat, uniform growth; great in borders.

'Lemon Swirl'. Slow growing to 2 ft. tall, 3 ft. wide. Bright yellow band around each leaf; yellow flowers. Fruitless.

Lucky series. Compact. Bloom early. Good for containers.

'Miss Huff'. To 3–5 ft. by 10 ft. Orange and pink. Hardier than other lantanas, surviving –3°F. Nearly fruitless.

'New Gold'. To 2–3 ft. by 6–8 ft. Golden yellow. Fruitless.

Patriot series. Plants range from 12–15 in. high and wide to 4–5 ft. tall and wide, depending on selection. Flowers in single shade and different combinations of yellow, pink, purple, orange, and red. Nearly fruitless.

'Pinkie'. To 1 ft. by 3 ft. Pink and cream. Fruitless.

'Radiation'. To 3–5 ft. high and wide. Rich orange-red.

'Silver Mound'. To 2 ft. tall and wide. Cream blossoms with golden yellow centers.

'Spreading Sunset'. To 2–3 ft. by 6–8 ft. Vivid orange-red.

'Spreading Sunshine'. To 2–3 ft. by 6–8 ft. Bright yellow.

'Star Landing'. To 2 ft. by 6–8 ft. Yellow and orange to red and orange. Hardy and fruitless.

'Sunburst'. To 2–3 ft. by 6–8 ft. Bright golden yellow.

'Sunny Side Up'. To 1½ ft. by 3 ft. Open yellow changing to white with yellow center.

'Tangerine'. To 2–3 ft. by 6–8 ft. Burnt orange.

L. trifolia. LAVENDER POPCORN. Zone TS; USDA 10-11. Somewhat rangy, sparsely branched shrub to 3–5 ft. tall and half as wide. Medium green leaves to 5 in. long, whorled around branches in groups of three. Dense clusters of pink, lavender, or purple blossoms appear in conjunction with showy spikes of lavender-purple fruit that resembles that of beautyberry (*Callicarpa*).

CARE

Lantanas are treated as annuals in most of the Upper and Middle South, as perennials elsewhere. Where they overwinter, prune back hard in early spring to remove dead wood and encourage vigorous new growth. Unpruned plants may become large, woody shrubs. Feed and water lightly, as too much fertilizer and water will reduce bloom.

LARIX
LARCH
Pinaceae
Deciduous trees

⚐ ZONES VARY BY SPECIES

☀ FULL SUN

💧 REGULAR WATER

Larix kaempferi

These conifers form slender pyramids with horizontal branches and drooping branchlets. Needles are ½–1½ in. long, in soft, fluffy tufts. Woody, roundish, ½- to 1½-in.-long cones are scattered all along branchlets. Notable for color in spring and fall and for winter silhouette. In spring, trees show off tufts of pale green new needles, bright purple-red new cones. In fall, needles turn brilliant yellow and orange before dropping. Winter interest is enhanced by the many cones, which turn brown with age and hang on to create a polka-dot pattern against the sky. Best in regions with cold winters. Not particular about soil. Plant with dark evergreen conifers as background or near water for reflection. Larches attract birds.

L. decidua. EUROPEAN LARCH. Zone US; USDA 6. From mountains of Europe. Moderate to fast growth to 30–60 ft. tall, 10–25 ft. wide. Summer foliage is grass-green. Branches of 'Pendula' arch out and down, with branchlets hanging nearly straight down.

L. kaempferi. JAPANESE LARCH. Zones US, MS; USDA 6-7. Native to Japan. Fast growing to 60 ft. or taller, 20–30 ft. wide, but can be dwarfed in containers. Summer foliage is a soft bluish green. 'Pendula' has long, weeping branches.

LARREA TRIDENTATA
CREOSOTE BUSH
Zygophyllaceae
Evergreen shrub

⚐ MS, LS, CS, TS; USDA 7-11

☀ FULL SUN

💧 LITTLE TO MODERATE WATER

Larrea tridentata

One of the most common native shrubs in Texas and northern Mexico. Grows 4–8 ft. tall and about as wide, with many upright branches. Straggly and open in shallow, dry soil; with more constant moisture, becomes attractive and densely foliaged, with rounded, spreading form. Leathery, yellow-green to dark green leaves divided into two ⅜-in.-long crescents. Gummy secretion makes leaves look varnished and yields distinctive creosote odor, especially noticeable after rain. Small yellow flowers bloom off and on all year, followed by small, roundish fruit covered with shiny white or rusty hairs.

This plant does not need fertilizer, but one or two doses of balanced liquid fertilizer during the course of the growing season will produce shiny, dark green leaves. Use as wind or privacy screen, foundation shrub, or small tree. Long taproot makes it very drought tolerant but also makes established plants difficult to transplant. Needs well-drained soil. Not a good choice for high-rainfall, high-humidity areas. Sometimes sold as *L. divaricata*.

LATHYRUS

SWEET PEA
Papilionaceae
Annuals and perennials

⚂ **ZONES VARY BY SPECIES**

☼ **FULL SUN**

◐◑● **WATER NEEDS VARY BY SPECIES**

Lathyrus odoratus

Few flowers are better suited to the cottage garden than beloved, old-fashioned sweet peas. Despite the name, not all are fragrant. But all have the classic pea-family bloom—one large, upright, roundish petal (called the banner or standard), two narrow side petals (the wings), and two lower petals that form a boat-shaped structure (the keel).

L. latifolius. EVERLASTING PEA. Perennial. Zones US, MS, LS; USDA 6-8. Native to Europe. Strong-growing vine to 9 ft., with blue-green foliage. Plants usually bear unscented flowers in mixed colors (reddish purple, white, pink); single colors may be sold. Blooms all summer if not allowed to go to seed. Grows with little care, tolerates drought (best with moderate water). May escape and become naturalized, even weedy. Use as bank cover, as trailer over rocks, on trellis or fence.

L. odoratus. SWEET PEA. Annual. Zones US, MS, LS, CS, TS; USDA 6-11. Native to the Mediterranean region. Blooms in winter, spring, or summer, bearing many spikelike clusters of crisp-looking flowers with a clean, sweet perfume. Blossoms come in single and mixed colors. Mixes include deep rose, blue, purple, scarlet, white, cream, salmon, bicolors. Vining types grow to 5 ft. or more;

bush kinds grow anywhere from 8 in. to 3 ft. tall. Sweet peas make magnificent cut flowers in quantity. Seeds are poisonous.

To hasten germination, soak seeds for a few hours before planting. Sow seeds 1 in. deep and 1–2 in. apart. When seedlings are 4–5 in. high, thin to at least 6 in. apart. Pinch out tops to encourage strong side branches. Where climate prevents early planting or soil is too wet to work, start three or four seeds in each small peat pot, indoors or in a protected place, and set out when weather has settled. Plant peat pots 1 ft. apart, thinning each to one strong plant. This method is ideal for bush types. Protect young seedlings from birds, and control slugs and snails. Never let vines lack for water; soak heavily. To prolong bloom, cut flowers at least every other day and remove all seedpods. Regular monthly feeding with a general-purpose fertilizer will keep vines vigorous and productive.

For vining sweet peas, provide trellis, strings, or wire before planting. Seedlings need support as soon as tendrils form. A freestanding trellis running north and south is best. When planting against fence or wall, keep supports away from wall to ensure good air circulation.

The following entries describe vine-type sweet peas (heirloom types first, then in groups by time of bloom) and bush types.

Heirloom selections. Not as large and showy as modern hybrids, these old spring-blooming favorites (some dating back hundreds of years) are notable for powerful fragrance.

'America'. Crimson to scarlet with white stripes.

'Annie Gilroy'. Bright cerise standard with lighter wings.

'Blanche Ferry'. Carmine-rose standard, pink wings. Similar to 'Painted Lady' but with more intense color.

'Cupani'. Deep blue standard, purple wings. More vigorous than 'Matucana'.

'Flora Norton'. Blossoms in bright, clear blue.

'Indigo King'. Purplish maroon standard, blue wings. Very prolific.

'Matucana'. Same coloring as 'Cupani'. This and 'Cupani' are very close to the original wild *L. odoratus*.

Old Spice Mix. A mixture of eight old-fashioned selections with flowers in white and in shades of pink, red, and purple.

'Painted Lady'. Dates from the 18th century; bears small rose-and-white flowers.

Early flowering. Includes Early Spencer Mix. The name "Spencer" once described a type of frilled flower (with wavy petals) that is now characteristic of almost all selections. Others of note are Chiffon Elegance Mix (earliest bloomers) and 'Zinfandel' (very fragrant claret-burgundy blooms).

The value of early-flowering types is that they will bloom in mid-winter when days are short; try them in the Coastal and Tropical South. (Spring-flowering types will not bloom until days have lengthened to 15 hours or more.) Sow seeds in late October and November for blooms in late winter and spring. If you want to force sweet peas in a greenhouse,

use selections from this group. They are not heat resistant. Generally sold in mixtures of several colors.

Spring flowering. Includes heat-resistant Cuthbertson Type, Cuthbertson's Floribunda, Floribunda-Zvolanek strain and Perfume Delight Mix. Both mixtures and single-color named selections are available in seed packets. Wide color range: pink, lavender, purple, white, cream, rose, salmon, cerise, carmine, red, blue. Royal or Royal Family are somewhat larger flowered, more heat resistant than the others. Plant between October and early January.

Bush type. The so-called bush-type sweet peas are strong vines with predetermined growth heights. Unlike vining kinds, these stop their upward growth at anywhere from 8 in. to 3 ft. high. Some kinds are completely self-supporting; others need support of a few sticks or pieces of

TOP: Lathyrus odoratus Early Spencer Mix (Early Flowering); 'Zinfandel' (Early Flowering); BOTTOM: Perfume Delight Mix (Spring Flowering); Chiffon Elegance Mix (Spring Flowering)

brush (similar to what you would provide for many perennials). Suitable for all regions. Flowers come in full range of colors. Most are early or spring blooming, as noted on the seed packet; follow planting dates given for early- or spring-flowering vining types.

Bijou Mix. To 1 ft. Available in single or mixed colors; four or five flowers appear on each 5- to 7-in. stem. Self-supporting plants are spectacular in borders, beds, window boxes, containers. Not as heat resistant or as long stemmed as 'Knee-Hi'; performs better in containers.

Cupid Mix. To 4–6 in. by 1 ft. Trails on ground or hangs from containers.

Jet Set Mix. Bushy plants grow 2–3 ft. tall; need some support.

Knee-Hi Mix. To 2½ ft.; need some support. Large, long-stemmed blooms are carried five or six to the stem. Has all the virtues and color range of Cuthbertson's Floribunda, but on bush-type plants. Good for mass display in beds, borders. Growth will exceed 2½ ft. where planting bed joins a fence or wall; keep in the open for uniform height.

Little Sweethearts Mix are rounded bushes to about 8 in. tall; they need no support, bloom over a long season.

Snoopea Mix (12–15 in.) and Supersnoop Mix (2 ft.) need no support.

TIPS FOR STARTING SWEET PEAS

In less-than-perfect soil, prepare ground for sweet peas like this. Dig a trench 1–1½ ft. deep. Mix 1 part peat moss or other soil conditioner to 2 parts soil. As you mix, add in a complete fertilizer according to label directions. Backfill trench with mix; plant seeds in it.

LAURUS NOBILIS

BAY
Lauraceae
Evergreen shrub or tree

🗡 **LS, CS, TS; USDA 8-11; OR GROW IN POTS**

☼ ◐ **FULL SUN OR PARTIAL SHADE**

💧 **MODERATE WATER**

Laurus nobilis

This Mediterranean native grows slowly to 12–40 ft. tall and wide. Natural habit is compact and broad based—often that of a multistemmed, gradually tapering cone. Leathery, aromatic leaves are the traditional bay leaves of cookery—oval, 2–4 in. long, dark green. Clusters of small yellow flowers are followed by ½- to 1-in.-long, black or dark purple berries. Dense habit makes it a good large background shrub, screen, or small tree. Takes well to clipping into standards, hedges, or topiary shapes such as globes and cones. A classic formal container plant and longtime favorite in the South. 'Little Ragu' has narrow, golden-green leaves and grows 5–8 ft. tall. 'Saratoga' has broader leaves and a more treelike habit.

CARE

Not fussy about soil but needs good drainage. Tends to sucker heavily. In the Upper and Middle South, grow in a container and move to greenhouse or cool, well-lighted room when temperatures reach about 20°F; water sparingly until spring.

LAVANDULA

LAVENDER
Lamiaceae
Evergreen shrubs

🗡 **ZONES VARY BY SPECIES**

☼ **FULL SUN**

💧 **MODERATE WATER**

Lavandula angustifolia

Native to the Mediterranean region, lavender is prized for its showy, fragrant, lavender or purple flowers. The blossom spikes of some species are used for perfume, aromatic oil, soap, sachets, medicine, and flavoring. Narrow, aromatic, blue-green or gray-green foliage is a hallmark.

Unfortunately, the South's hot, humid climate and heavy soils don't suit most lavenders at all. English lavender (*L. angustifolia*), considered by many the most desirable species, is also the most problematic in Southern gardens. Poor drainage, wet winters, and high humidity often lead to rot and quick demise. Success depends on planting in gravelly, fast-draining soil that contains few nutrients. Do not fertilize. To reduce humidity around plants, mulch with gravel. To keep plants neat and compact, shear back by one-third to one-half every year just after bloom. If they become woody and open in the center, remove a few of the oldest branches; take out more when new growth comes.

To dry flowers for sachets and potpourri, cut the spikes or strip blossoms from stems just as they show color; dry in a cool, shady place. Dried flowers can also be used to add a fresh scent to water or soap. Dried spikes make fragrant wreaths, swags, and wands. To flavor ice

cream, pastries, and salads, use fresh flowers of *L. angustifolia* and *L. intermedia* selections; other species contain toxic chemicals that should not be ingested.

Because lavenders have been cultivated for centuries and tend to interbreed, many selections and hybrids have arisen. Names are often confused, so some of the names that follow may not agree with those you see on nursery labels. Be aware that only cutting-grown plants are uniform; seed-grown strains vary in color and growth habit. Deer do not care for lavender.

L. angustifolia (*L. officinalis, L. vera*). ENGLISH LAVENDER. Zones US, MS, LS; USDA 6-8. This is the sweetly fragrant lavender used for perfume and sachets. Common name notwithstanding, it is native to southern Europe. It's the hardiest, most widely planted species. Most selections are low growing, forming mounds of foliage from 8 in. to 2 ft. high and wide. Narrow, smooth-edged, gray-green or silvery gray leaves to 2 in. long. Unbranched flower stems rise 4–12 in. above foliage, topped with 1- to 4-in.-long spikes of flowers in white, pink, lavender-blue, or various shades of purple. Blooms mainly from early to mid-summer, but some selections repeat in late summer or fall. Named selections include the following.

'Alba'. To 1½–2 ft. high and wide. Pure white flowers, gray-green foliage.

'Blue Cushion'. To 1½ ft. tall, 2 ft. wide. Profuse bright violet-blue flowers above medium green foliage.

'Compacta'. To 1½ ft. high and wide; good dwarf hedge plant. Light violet flowers; gray-green leaves.

'Dwarf Blue' ('Nana'). Slow growing to 1 ft. high, 16 in. wide. Stiff lavender-blue flower spikes in midsummer; gray foliage. Ideal for rock garden or edging. Somewhat hardier than most other English lavenders.

'Ellagance Purple'. To 1 ft. tall and wide. Generous bloom of purple flowers. Gray-green foliage.

'England'. To 1 ft. high, 15 in. wide. Light violet-blue flowers; downy, silvery foliage.

'Gray Lady'. To 2 ft. tall and wide. Lavender-blue flowers; gray foliage.

TOP: Lavandula 'Phenomenal'; MIDDLE: L. angustifolia 'Thumbelina Leigh';
L. stoechas 'Bella White'; BOTTOM: L. s. 'Hazel'

'Hidcote'. The original had deep violet flowers and medium green leaves on a plant 1½–2 ft. tall. The plants sold under this name today are frequently grown from seed; they may bear gray foliage and/or vary in size from the original. 'Hidcote Blue' (with deep blue flowers) and 'Hidcote Superior' (compact, uniform, 16 in. high and 18 in. wide) are popular selections.

'Irene Doyle'. To 1½–2 ft. high and wide, with gray-green leaves. Light violet flowers bloom in early summer and give a repeat performance in late summer.

'Lady' ('Cambridge Lady', 'Lavender Lady'). Seed-grown strain that blooms in 3 months from spring-sown seed. Gray-green foliage. Very short spikes of lavender-blue flowers on a plant 1–1½ ft. high and wide; some variation in flower color and growth habit.

'Martha Roderick'. Compact growth to 1½–2 ft. high and wide. Dense gray foliage. Bright violet-blue blossoms in great abundance from late spring to early summer.

'Melissa'. Dense, compact grower to 1½ ft. high and wide. Good pink flower color, fading to white in hottest sun. Gray-green leaves.

'Munstead'. The original is 1½ ft. tall, 2 ft. wide, with bright lavender-blue flowers and medium green foliage. Long bloomer; makes a good low hedge. Quite variable when grown from seed.

'Nana Alba'. White-flowered version of 'Dwarf Blue'.

'Premier'. To 2 ft. high, 2½ ft. wide. Long-stemmed, airy, dark purple to violet blooms. Good cut flower.

'Rosea' ('Jean Davis'). To 1½–2 ft. high and wide. Pale lilac-pink flowers; gray-green foliage.

'Sharon Roberts'. Semiopen growth a little over 2 ft. high and to 2 ft. wide. Profuse show of bright violet-blue flowers begins in late spring, often repeats in fall. Medium green to gray-green foliage.

'Thumbelina Leigh'. Very compact mound of medium green leaves to just 6 in. high and 12 in. wide. Bright violet-blue flowers rise 6 in. above foliage.

L. dentata. FRENCH LAVENDER, TOOTHED LAVENDER. Zones LS, CS; USDA 8-9. To 3–4 ft. tall, 4–6 ft. wide. Narrow green or gray-green leaves are 1½ in. long, ½ in. wide, with square-toothed edges. Purple flowers in short, rounded spikes, each topped with a pair of flaglike bracts that look like rabbit ears. Long spring-into-summer flowering period; almost year-round in mild-winter areas. Takes humidity better than L. angustifolia. Should be treated as a tender perennial in Upper and Middle South; pot up and bring indoors for winter. 'Linda Ligon' has smaller leaves with irregular creamy white variegation. L. d. candicans ('French Gray') has grayer, somewhat larger leaves than the species, with dense grayish white down on young foliage.

L. x ginginsii 'Goodwin Creek Grey'. Zones MS, LS, CS; USDA 7-9. Most likely a hybrid between L. lanata and L. dentata. This densely foliaged plant grows to 2½–3 ft. high and 3–4 ft. wide, with silvery leaves that are toothed at tips. Deep violet-blue flowers from spring to late fall; virtually year-round in mild-winter climates. More tolerant of heat and humidity.

L. x intermedia. LAVANDIN, HEDGE LAVENDER. Zones US, MS, LS; USDA 6-8. This group of sterile hybrids between parents L. angustifolia and L. latifolia is distinguished from English lavender by larger growth and by branching stems topped with interrupted flower spikes; blooms from mid- to late summer. Long used in the perfume and soap industries, lavandins are vigorous, fragrant plants, almost as hardy as L. angustifolia and more tolerant of warm, humid summers. They include the following selections.

'Abrialii'. Once the mainstay of the French lavender oil industry. Grows to 2½ ft. high, 3 ft. wide, with gray-green foliage. Dark violet-blue blossoms in narrow, conical, 3½- to 5-in.-long spikes are excellent for drying.

'Alba' ('White Spikes'). To 2½ ft. high and wide, with silvery leaves. Spikes of white blossoms and sage green calyxes are 1½–2 in. long, bloom from early summer through fall. Becomes woody with age.

'Dutch'. To 3 ft. tall and 2–2½ ft. wide, with gray foliage. Few-branched stems topped with narrow, conical, 2- to 3-in. spikes of flowers in deep blue-violet. Most common selection in U.S.

'Fred Boutin'. To 3–4 ft. tall and wide. Dense, silvery gray foliage topped in early to midsummer with 1½- to 3-in.-long spikes of violet-blue blossoms on un-branched stems.

'Grey Hedge'. To 3 ft. or more in height and width. Dense foliage in a very silvery gray; profuse lavender-blue flowers on few-branched stems. Makes an excellent rounded or square-sheared hedge; set plants 2 ft. apart.

'Grosso'. Widely planted commercial selection in France and Italy; possibly the most fragrant lavandin of all. Compact growth to 2½ ft. high and wide. Silvery foliage; large (to 3½-in.-long), conical spikes of violet-blue flowers with darker calyxes. Often gives repeat bloom in late summer. Excellent flower for drying.

'Hidcote Giant'. To 2½ ft. high and 3 ft. wide, with gray-green foliage. Stout stems topped by fat spikes of vivid violet-blue flowers.

'Phenomenal'. To 3 ft. high and wide. Very fragrant, violet-blue flowers held high atop aromatic silvery green foliage. Seedling of 'Grosso'. Very disease resistant and well adapted to warm, humid climates. Has performed well as far south as Florida. Good drainage is essential.

'Provence'. Though it is often described as a traditional perfume lavandin, this selection does not produce the kind of oil that is used in perfumery. Grows to 2 ft. high, 3 ft. wide, with fragrant, light violet flower spikes that dry well. Good hedge plant.

'Thumbelina Leigh'. Compact mound of green leaves, 6 in. high and 12 in. wide. Bright violet-blue flowers.

L. latifolia (L. spica). SPIKE LAVENDER, BROADLEAF LAVENDER. Zones US, MS, LS; USDA 6-8. Compact growth to 3 ft. tall and 1½–2 ft. wide, with gray-green leaves to 3 in. long, ¼ in. wide; resembles L. angustifolia. Slender, widely branching flower stems support interrupted spikes 1½–4 in. long; blossoms range from soft mauve to bright violet-blue, with woolly gray calyxes tipped in violet. Blooms in late summer.

L. stoechas. SPANISH LAVENDER. Zones MS, LS, CS; USDA 7-9. Includes several subspecies, all stocky plants 1½–3 ft. tall and wide, with narrow gray or gray-green, ½- to 1-in.-long leaves. Small flowers are typically blackish maroon, borne on short, fat, 2-in. spikes topped by two to four

flaglike bracts resembling rabbit ears; bracts come in assorted shades of purple and pink. Blossoms open first in four vertical rows, evenly spaced around the spike; then rest of spike fills in with flowers. Blooms from spring into summer; often repeats if sheared. Flower stem length varies from 1½ in. to 8 in. or more. Very drought resistant. Takes heat and humidity better than other species but is not as fragrant; best choice for Lower and Coastal South. Seeds profusely; can be invasive; bracts come in white and assorted shades of purple and pink. Named forms include the following.

'Anouk'. Compact to 2 ft. high and over 6 ft. wide. Purple spikes topped with wavy, lighter colored bracts. Hardy.

'Bella White'. Dense growth to about 2 ft. tall, 20 in. wide, with gray-green leaves. Pure white flowers held on short, sturdy stems appear in spring and fall.

'Hazel'. To 2½ ft. high, 2 ft. wide. Dense, sturdy mound of gray-green foliage is topped by darkest purple flowers and bright violet bracts. Heavy bloom in spring, modest autumn rebloom.

'Kew Red'. Grows 3–4 ft. tall and wide, with aromatic gray-green foliage. Reddish violet flowers have pink bracts, peak in spring and fall but bloom nearly all year in mild climates.

'Otto Quast'. To 2 ft. high or a bit more, 2½–3½ ft. wide. Flower stems 2–3 in. long, with maroon blossoms and red-purple bracts. Medium green to gray-green leaves. Plants sold under this name are usually grown from seed and are often shorter than the plant just described, with shorter flower stalks.

Ruffles series. These grow 2 ft. high and wide and flower about 2 weeks earlier than other Spanish lavenders. All the following are variations on the pink to lavender-pink theme: 'Blueberry Ruffles', 'Boysenberry Ruffles', 'Mulberry Ruffles', and 'Sugarberry Ruffles'.

'Willow Vale'. Vigorous, upright, to 1½ ft. tall and wide. Wispy gray-green leaves; deep blue-violet flowers and bluish purple bracts. Short (1- to 2-in.) flower stems.

'Wings of Night'. Heavy bloomer resembles 'Otto Quast' but has a broader habit.

'Winter Bee'. About 2 ft. high, with equal or greater spread. Gray-green foliage. Dark purple flowers and lavender bracts appear in early spring, about 3 weeks earlier than those of other Spanish lavenders. Blooms are long lasting.

L. s. pedunculata. Zones MS, LS, CS; USDA 7-9. Taller than other forms, with longer flower stems. Green or gray-green foliage. Its selection 'Atlas' grows 2½–3 ft. tall, about as wide, with 7- to 14-in. flower stalks and vibrant red-violet bracts.

LAVATERA
TREE MALLOW
Malvaceae
Annuals and evergreen shrubs

🖊 **ZONES VARY BY SPECIES**

☀ **FULL SUN**

💧 **REGULAR WATER**

Lavatera trimestris 'Ruby Regis'

Offering colorful single flowers throughout the summer, these easy-to-grow plants resemble their cousins, the hollyhocks (*Alcea*). Use them in the back of the border, in combination with other annuals and perennials.

L. thuringiaca. Evergreen shrub. Zones US, MS, LS; USDA 6-8. Native to central and southeastern Europe. Flowers are purplish pink, 3 in. across, nearly everblooming (except in colder-winter zones). 'Barnsley' has lighter pink flowers with deep pink centers. 'Red Rum' grows about 4–5 ft. tall and 3–4 ft. wide, with deep pink flowers held on burgundy stems.

L. trimestris. ANNUAL MALLOW. Annual. Zones US, MS, LS, CS, TS; USDA 6-11. Mediter-

ranean native reaches 3–6 ft. tall and wide from spring-sown seed. Satiny flowers to 4 in. wide. Species is seldom seen in gardens; more commonly grown are named selections with blossoms in white, pink, or rosy carmine. Bloom extends from midsummer until frost if spent flowers are removed to halt seed production. Thin seedlings to allow each plant ample room to spread. Makes a colorful, fast-growing summer hedge or background planting. In mild-winter regions, can also be sown in autumn for winter-to-spring bloom. Compact (2- to 3-ft.) selections include white 'Mont Blanc', rose-pink 'Mont Rose', and bright pink 'Silver Cup'. 'Ruby Regis', to 2 ft. high and wide, has 3½-in. flowers of deep rose veined in a deeper shade. 'Loveliness' has similar blossoms but grows 3–4 ft. tall and wide.

LEEK
Liliaceae
Biennial grown as cool-season annual

🖊 **US, MS, LS, CS, TS; USDA 6-11**

◐ ☀ **PARTIAL SHADE IN HOTTEST CLIMATES**

💧 **REGULAR WATER**

Leek

Botanically speaking, the leek is *Allium porrum*, an onion relative. Unlike onions, though, leeks don't form distinct bulbs. Plants grow 2–3 ft. tall; edible, mild-flavored stem resembles long, fat, green onion. Leeks need very rich soil. Plant them to grow and mature in cool weather. In most areas, late summer to early fall planting is best. Sow seed or set out transplants. 'Arkansas' (108 days) and the heirloom 'American Flag'

L

(120 days) are proven selections. Leeks are quite cold hardy and can overwinter in ground; in fact, cold temperatures improve flavor. When plants have considerable top growth, mound up soil around fat, round stems to blanch them white. Harvest when stem bases are 1–2½ in. in diameter. Offsets may be detached and replanted. If leeks bloom, small bulbils may appear in flower clusters; plant these for later harvest. Leeks are free of many of the pests and diseases that attack onions.

LEONOTIS
LION'S TAIL, LION'S EAR
Lamiaceae
Annuals and tender shrubs

🌿 **ZONES VARY BY SPECIES**

☀️ **FULL SUN**

💧 **LITTLE OR NO WATER**

Leonotis leonurus

These showy members of the mint family include both annuals and tender shrubs. Most are native to South Africa. Fuzzy, square stems carry opposite pairs of narrow, pointed, toothed, 2- to 5-in.-long leaves. Bloom comes from summer through fall, when dense, ball-shaped, whorled flower clusters to 4 in. across appear at regular intervals up and down the stems. Each cluster is composed of deep orange, tubular, 2-in. flowers that are covered with fine hairs. The plants attract butterflies and hummingbirds; deer don't seem to care for them.

L. leonurus. LION'S TAIL. Zones LS, CS, TS; USDA 8-11. Semi-evergreen shrub, often grown as a tender perennial. One of the

ABOVE: Leonotis leonurus

first South African plants brought back to Europe for cultivation. Grows 4–6 ft. tall and wide. Tolerates drought and salt spray. Needs good drainage; be careful not to overwater. Tends to get leggy and bare at the stem bases; to curb this tendency, prune back fairly hard in spring. Hardy in warmer parts of Lower South but loses its leaves after a frost. 'Snow Tiger' has white flowers.

L. menthifolia. MINT-LEAFED LION'S TAIL. Zones LS, CS, TS; USDA 8-11. Evergreen shrub, often grown as a tender perennial. To 3–5 ft. tall and wide. Resembles *L. leonurus* but is smaller and doesn't lose its foliage near the base. 'Savannah Sunset' has tall spikes of bright orange flowers.

L. nepetifolia. ANNUAL LION'S TAIL. Annual. Zones US, MS, LS, CS, TS; USDA 6-11. Upright, gangly plant for the back of the border; may reach 8 ft. tall and 5 ft. wide in a single season. Rounded, spiny flower clusters are hummingbird magnets. Re-seeds readily and has naturalized in warm-climate areas throughout the world, where it rapidly colonizes disturbed areas. *L. n. nepetifolia* 'Staircase' is like *L. nepetifolia* but with larger leaves and flowers.

LESPEDEZA THUNBERGII
SHRUB BUSH CLOVER
Papilionaceae
Deciduous perennial or shrub

🌿 **US, MS, LS; USDA 6-8**

☀️ **FULL SUN**

💧 **LITTLE TO MODERATE WATER**

Lespedeza thunbergii

Late-summer flowers from a shrub are rare—but this one fills the void. It forms a spreading, fountain-shaped mass 6 ft. tall and 10 ft. wide, with arching branches clothed in blue-green leaves composed of three leaflets. Drooping, 6-in. clusters of showy, sweet pea–shaped flowers appear in late summer

and fall. Tolerates hot, dry conditions and infertile soil. Good drainage is a must. Cut plant to within a few inches of the ground in late winter; it will regrow rapidly and bear multitudes of blooms on the new growth. Recommended selections include white-flowered 'Avalanche', with cascading habit; purple-and-white 'Edo-Shibori'; rosy purple 'Gibraltar'; pink 'Pink Fountain', with cascading habit; beautifly white variegated and magenta-blooming 'Spilt Milk'; and white-blossomed 'White Fountain', with weeping form.

LETTUCE
Asteraceae
Cool-season annual

🌿 **US, MS, LS, CS, TS; USDA 6-11**

☀️◐ **PARTIAL SHADE IN COASTAL AND TROPICAL SOUTH**

💧 **REGULAR WATER**

Butterhead lettuce
'Merveille des Quatre Saisons'

Classified botanically as *Lactuca sativa*. A short browse through a seed catalog, seed display rack, or selection of nursery seedlings will reveal enough variety to keep your salad bowl crisp and colorful throughout the growing season. There are four principal types of lettuce: crisphead, butterhead or Boston, loose-leaf, and romaine.

Crisphead is most exasperating for home gardeners to produce. Heads form best with monthly average temperatures of 55–60°F. Best selections include 'Great Lakes', 'Nevada', and 'Summertime'. 'Rosy' is a small crisphead with reddish burgundy leaves.

Butterhead or Boston type has a loose head with green, smooth outer leaves and yellow inner leaves. Good choices include 'Bibb' ('Limestone'), 'Buttercrunch', and 'Tom Thumb'. 'Mignonette' ('Manoa') stands heat without bolting to seed. 'Tennis Ball' is an heirloom Boston type with small, loose heads. 'Key Lime' is another heirloom that is larger than most butterheads and resists bolting.

Loose-leaf lettuce makes a rosette rather than a head. It stands heat better than other types. Choice selections are 'Black-seeded Simpson', 'Green Ice', and 'Oak Leaf' (all with green leaves); 'Salad Bowl' (with deeply cut green leaves); and 'Prizehead' and 'Ruby' (red-tinged leaves). 'Slo-Bolt' has ruffled green leaves and resists bolting.

Romaine lettuce has an erect, cylindrical head of smooth leaves; outer leaves are green, inner ones yellowish. Stands heat moderately well. Try heat-resistant 'Jericho', 'Medallion', 'Olga', or 'Parris Island'.

Lettuces with bronzy to pinkish red leaves add color to a salad. 'Freckles', 'Merveille des Quatre Saisons', and 'Perella Red' are butterheads; 'Lollo Rosso', 'Red Oak Leaf', 'Red Sails', and 'Ruby' are loose-leaf selections; 'Rouge d'Hiver' and 'Sierra' are romaines.

Various loose-leaf and romaine lettuces are typically included in mesclun mixes—mixtures of fast-growing, tender salad greens (usually some mild and some tangy) that may include mustards, arugula, cress, chicory, radicchio, and/or mizuna.

CARE

All lettuces need loose, well-drained soil. Sow in open ground; barely cover seeds. Loose-leaf lettuce can be grown as close as 4 in. apart; thin all other types to 1 ft. apart. Grow mesclun in blocks 4 in. wide, and don't thin.

For prolonged harvest, sow at 2-week intervals. In Upper South, begin sowing seed for all types after frost, as soon as soil is workable. In the Coastal and Tropical South, plant in fall or winter for harvest in winter and early spring.

Feed plants lightly and frequently. Control snails, slugs, earwigs. Harvest when heads or leaves are of good size; once

---

HARVESTING LOOSE-LEAF LETTUCE

With loose-leaf lettuce you get three opportunities to harvest over a long period. Use the thinnings for salads; clip off just the outer leaves as you need them; finally, when bloom stalks just begin to grow, pull up whole plants.

---

lettuce reaches maturity, it rapidly goes to seed, becoming quite bitter. Snip off young leaves of mesclun mix for salads.

LEUCANTHEMUM
Asteraceae
Perennials and annuals

✎ **ZONES VARY BY SPECIES**

☀ **FULL SUN, EXCEPT AS NOTED**

💧 **REGULAR WATER**

Leucanthemum x *superbum*

Three species of these popular flowers were formerly listed under *Chrysanthemum*.

L. paludosum (*Chrysanthemum paludosum, Mauranthemum paludosum*). SWAMP CHRYSANTHEMUM. Annual, sometimes living over for a second bloom season. Zones US, MS, LS, CS, TS; USDA 6-11. In summer, this western Mediterranean native bears white daisies 1–1½ in. wide on 8- to 10-in. stems above dark green, deeply toothed leaves. Flowers look like miniature Shasta daisies.

L. x superbum (*Chrysanthemum maximum, C.* x *superbum,*

L. maximum). SHASTA DAISY. Perennial. Zones US, MS, LS, CS; USDA 6-9. Summer and fall bloomer. Original 2- to 4-ft.-tall Shasta daisy, with coarse, leathery leaves and gold-centered, white flower heads 2–4 in. across, has been largely superseded by types with larger, better-formed, longer-blooming flowers. These are available in single, double, quilled, and shaggy-flowered forms. All are white, but two show a touch of yellow. Some bloom from May to October. Shasta daisies are splendid in borders and cut arrangements.

Some of the selections available in garden centers include: 'Esther Read', most popular double white, long bloom; 'Marconi', large, frilly double; 'Aglaya', similar to 'Marconi', long blooming season; 'Wirral Supreme', double white with short white central petals; 'Alaska', big, old-fashioned single; 'Horace Read', 4-in.-wide dahlialike flower; 'Majestic', large, yellow-centered, single flower; 'Thomas Killin' ('T. E. Killin'), 6-in.-wide (largest), yellow-centered, double flower. 'Becky', a tall single selection with sturdy stems, is a popular Southern passalong plant known by several names, including 'July daisy,' 'Ryan's daisy,' and 'Becky's daisy.' 'Cobham's Gold' has distinctive flowers in a yellow-tinted, off-white shade. 'Canarybird', another yellow-toned selection, is a dwarf with attractive dark green foliage. Most popular selections for cut flowers are 'Esther Read', 'Majestic', 'Aglaya', and 'Thomas Killin'.

Shasta daisies are easy to grow from seed. Catalogs offer many strains, including Diener's Strain (double) and Roggli Super Giant (single). 'Marconi' (double), also available in seed, nearly always blooms double. 'Silver Princess' ('Little Princess', 'Little Miss Muffet') is a 12- to 15-in. dwarf single. 'Snow Lady' (single), an All-America winner, 10–12 in. tall, begins to bloom in 5 months from seed, then blooms nearly continuously.

Set out divisions of Shasta daisies in fall or early spring; set out container-grown plants any time. These plants thrive in fairly rich, moist, well-drained soil. Prefer sun but do well in partial shade in Lower and Coastal South; double-flowered kinds

---

hold up better in very light shade in all zones. Divide clumps every 2 or 3 years in early spring (or in fall in Lower and Coastal South). Shasta daisies are generally easy to grow but have a few problems. Gall disease causes the crown to split into many weak, poorly rooted growing points that soon die. Dig out and dispose of afflicted plants; don't replant Shasta daisies in the same spot.

L. vulgare (*Chrysanthemum leucanthemum*). OX-EYE DAISY, COMMON DAISY. Perennial. Zones US, MS, LS, CS; USDA 6-9. European native naturalized in many places. To 2 ft. high, 1 ft. wide, with bright green foliage and yellow-centered, 1- to 2-in. daisies from late spring through fall. 'May Queen' begins blooming in early spring. Spreads by rhizomes and seeds.

LEUCOJUM
SNOWFLAKE
Amaryllidaceae
Perennials from bulbs

✎ **ZONES VARY BY SPECIES**

☀◐ **FULL SUN DURING BLOOM; LIGHT SHADE AFTER**

💧 **REGULAR WATER DURING GROWTH AND BLOOM**

Leucojum aestivum

Native to Europe. Easy-to-grow perennial with dark green, strap-shaped leaves and nodding, bell-shaped, white flowers with segments tipped green. Naturalize under deciduous trees, in shrub borders or orchards, or on cool slopes. Plant bulbs in fall, setting them 4 in. deep and 3 in. apart. Do not disturb until really crowded; then dig, divide, and replant after foliage dies down. Not eaten by rodents.

L. aestivum. SUMMER SNOW-FLAKE. Zones US, MS, LS, CS; USDA 6-9. One of the classic passalong bulbs of the South, shared by gardeners for centuries. Often seen in cemeteries and on old home sites. Named "summer snowflake" by gardeners in northern Europe, where it blooms in early summer and has been cultivated since 1594. Leaves are 1–1½ ft. long; stems grow 1½ ft. tall, each carrying three to five 1-in. flowers. 'Gravetye Giant' is a bit taller and larger flowered than the species; it has as many as nine flowers per stem.

Summer snowflake doesn't need much winter chill to bloom well; it even blooms dependably as far south as central Florida. In the Coastal South, flowers come from late fall through winter; elsewhere, expect bloom in late winter and early spring, with early daffodils.

L. vernum. SPRING SNOW-FLAKE. Zones US, MS, LS; USDA 6-8. Much less common than *L. aestivum* and less tolerant of mild winters. Leaves are 9 in. long. In earliest spring, each foot-long stem bears a single large white flower (occasionally two per stem).

LEUCOPHYLLUM

TEXAS RANGER, SILVERLEAF
Scrophulariaceae
Evergreen shrubs

✎ **LS, CS, TS; USDA 8-11**

☼ **FULL SUN**

◌ ◕ **LITTLE TO MODERATE WATER**

Leucophyllum langmaniae

Native to the Southwest and northern Mexico, these compact, slow-growing shrubs are highly useful and attractive in dry

ABOVE: Leucophyllum frutescens

gardens. Most have silvery foliage and a good show of ½- to 1-in.-wide flowers with an open bell shape. Flowering may occur at varying times of the year, often after summer showers. In fact, they can bloom in response to increased humidity, flowering a few days before rain and earning them the nickname "barometer bush". Need very good drainage. Tolerate heat, wind, and alkaline soil. Resist damage from browsing deer. Use as informal or clipped hedges, massed as tall ground cover, or in mixed dry-country gardens. Unless formally hedged, plants require little pruning. Old, leggy plants can be rejuvenated by cutting close to the ground.

L. candidum. VIOLET SILVERLEAF. To 5 ft. high and wide, with small (½-in.), silvery leaves and deep purple flowers. 'Silver Cloud' is a heavy bloomer with very white foliage. 'Thunder Cloud' is smaller than the species (to 3–4 ft. high and wide) and has deeper purple, more closely spaced blossoms.

L. frutescens. TEXAS RANGER, TEXAS SAGE, CENIZO. To 6–8 ft. tall and wide, with gray foliage and light purple flowers. 'Green Cloud' has bright green foliage and dark rose or magenta flowers; it may be deciduous in coldest winters. 'White Cloud' has gray foliage and white flowers. 'Compacta', with gray foliage and pink flowers, grows 5 ft. high and wide.

L. laevigatum. CHIHUAHUAN SAGE. Open, angular growth to 4 ft. tall, 5 ft. wide. Tiny, dark green leaves; profuse lavender flowers.

L. langmaniae. Dense grower to 5 ft. high and wide, with bright green leaves and lavender flowers. 'Lynn's Legacy' ('Lynn's Everblooming') flowers profusely over a long period in summer.

L. pruinosum. Open growth habit to 6 ft. tall and wide, with silvery foliage. Purple flowers have a strong fragrance of grape bubble gum.

L. 'Rain Cloud'. Hybrid derived from *L. frutescens*. Erect growth to 6 ft. tall, 3–4 ft. wide. Small, silvery leaves; violet-blue flowers.

L. revolutum. Slow growth to about 4 ft. tall, 4–5 ft. wide, with light green, somewhat succulent foliage. Bears purple flowers that appear in fall, later than for other leucophyllums. 'Houdini' has larger, showier blossoms than the species.

L. zygophyllum. To 3 ft. tall and wide, with gray-green, cupped leaves and light blue flowers. 'Cimarron' is a dense grower with bluish purple flowers tightly packed along stems; leaves have a distinctly cupped shape.

LEUCOTHOE

Ericaceae
Evergreen and deciduous shrubs

✎ **US, MS, LS; USDA 6-8**

☼◕ ● **PARTIAL TO FULL SHADE**

◔ ◔ **WATER NEEDS VARY BY SPECIES**

⬥ **LEAVES AND NECTAR ARE POISONOUS IF INGESTED**

Leucothoe axillaris 'Curly Red'

These arching shrubs have leathery leaves and clusters of small, urn-shaped white flowers reminiscent of lily-of-the-valley (*Convallaria*). They need acid, well-drained, woodsy, deep soil; do best in woodland gardens. Best used in masses, since they are not especially attractive individually. Bronze-tinted winter foliage is a bonus. Not easy to grow; short lived in most gardens.

L. axillaris. COASTAL LEUCOTHOE. Evergreen. Native to southeastern U.S. Spreading, arching growth to 2–4 ft. tall, 3–6 ft. wide. Leathery leaves to 4 in. long are bronzy when new. Flower clusters, 1–3 in. long, droop along stems in spring. Regular water. 'Curly Red' features puckered leaves that emerge red and purple, turn dark green in summer, and change to burgundy in fall.

L. fontanesiana. DROOPING LEUCOTHOE. Evergreen. Native to southeastern U.S. Slow grower to 2–6 ft. high and wide; branches arch gracefully. Leathery, 3- to 6-in.-long leaves turn bronzy purple in fall (bronzy green in deep shade). Spreads from underground stems. Blooms in spring, bearing drooping clusters of slightly fragrant flowers. 'Rainbow' grows 3–4 ft. high, has leaves marked yellow, green, and pink. 'Lovita' is also smaller than the species (2 ft. tall, 4 ft. wide), with smaller, darker green leaves that turn mahogany red in winter. 'Scarletta' is similar in size to 'Lovita'; its leaves are brilliant red on expanding, deep green in summer, and deep red in late fall and winter.

The species and its selections take regular water. You can control the plants' height to make a 1½-ft. ground cover in shade; just cut older, taller stems to ground. Blooming branches make decorative cut flowers. Where summers are hot and humid, various leaf spot diseases can cause serious disfiguration or defoliation.

L. racemosa. SWEETBELLS. Deciduous. Zones US, MS, LS, CS; USDA 6-9. Native to southeastern U.S. Grows 3–8 ft. tall and wide, with 3-in. leaves that turn red before dropping from their red stems in autumn. Flowers in one-sided, 3-in. clusters at ends of branches in late spring or early summer. Suckers to form colonies. A pink-flowering form is available. Moderate water.

LEVISTICUM OFFICINALE

LOVAGE
Apiaceae
Perennial

🌿 **US, MS, LS; USDA 6-8**

☼ ◑ **FULL SUN TO PART SHADE**

💧 **REGULAR WATER**

Levisticum officinale

From the eastern Mediterranean region. Ornamental herb with divided, glossy, deep green leaves to 2½ ft. long. Hollow stems rise from the foliage clumps in

summer, crowned by sprays of flat-topped, greenish yellow flower clusters. Flowering plants may reach 6 ft. tall under ideal conditions, but more usual size is 3 ft. high and wide. Plant has a history of culinary uses: Seeds are valued for their celery flavor, leaves are added to salads and soups. Grow from seeds sown in place in fall; or start seeds in containers and transplant into garden in spring. You can also divide an established clump in early spring. Volunteer seedlings are another source of extra plants.

LEYMUS ARENARIUS

BLUE LYME GRASS
Poaceae
Perennial grass

🌿 **US, MS, LS, CS, TS; USDA 6-11**

☼ ◑ **FULL SUN OR LIGHT SHADE**

💧 💧 **LITTLE TO MODERATE WATER**

Leymus arenarius 'Blue Dune'

Formerly known as *Elymus arenarius* 'Glaucus', this Eurasian dune grass is the bluest ornamental grass of all. It is stunning as a 2- to 3-ft.-tall specimen in a flower border or when massed and used as a ground cover. Flowers are inconspicuous. Given moist, fertile soil, it spreads aggressively by rhizomes and can be invasive; better behaved in dry soils and heavy clay. Tolerates heat, drought, deer, sandy soil, and salt spray. Good plant for the beach or in containers. Mow or cut back in late winter to stimulate fresh new blue growth. 'Findhorn' is a compact selection. 'Blue Dune' has especially bright blue foliage.

LIATRIS

BLAZING STAR, GAYFEATHER
Asteraceae
Perennials

🌿 **US, MS, LS, CS; USDA 6-9**

☼ **FULL SUN**

💧 💧 💧 **LITTLE TO REGULAR WATER**

Liatris spicata

These showy plants native to the southern and central U.S. are butterfly magnets. Basal tufts of narrow, grassy leaves grow from thick, often tuberous rootstocks. In summer or early fall, the tufts lengthen into tall stems densely set with slender leaves and topped by a narrow plume of small, fluffy purple (sometimes white) flower heads. Flowers of most species are unusual in opening from top of spike downward. Choice cut flowers; deer resistant.

These plants endure heat, cold, drought, and poor soil. Fertilizing will give you larger flower spikes, but it also results in taller plants that need staking. Best used in mixed perennial borders, although the rosy purple color calls for careful placing to avoid color clashes.

L. ligulistylis. MEADOW BLAZING STAR. Grows 3–5 ft. tall and 1½ ft. wide, with reddish purple flowers that open from dark red buds.

L. microcephala. DWARF BLAZING STAR. Only 1–2 ft. tall and up to 1 ft. across, with rosy purple flowers. Try this small blazing star in rock gardens or as a ground cover in hot, dry areas.

L. mucronata. BOTTLE-BRUSH BLAZING STAR. To 3 ft. tall and 1 ft. wide. Rosy purple spikes. Tolerates dry, limy soils, providing drainage is good. Goldfinches eat the seeds.

L. pycnostachya. KANSAS BLAZING STAR. To 3–5 ft. tall, 1–2 ft. wide, with bright purple flowers. Likes some moisture but tolerates drought.

L. scariosa. PRAIRIE BLAZING STAR. To 2–3 ft. high, 1½ ft. wide. Reddish purple flowers. Differs from most other blazing stars in that its blossoms open nearly all at once; also prefers somewhat drier soil than most. 'September Glory' is taller than the species (to 4–5 ft.); 'White Spire' is similar but has white flowers.

L. spicata. SPIKE BLAZING STAR. To 5 ft. tall and 1½ ft. wide, with light purple blossoms tightly clustered in dense spikes. Lower-growing selections include white-flowered 'Alba' (3–4 ft. tall); 'Floristan White' (2–3 ft.), with profuse white blossom spikes that are good for cutting; 'Kobold' (2–2½ ft., needs no staking), with deeper purple blooms than the species; and 'Silvertips' (2½–3 ft.), bearing lavender flowers with a silvery finish.

L. squarrosa. SCALY BLAZING STAR. To 2–3 ft. tall and 1 ft. wide. Bears branched spikes of large, red-purple flowers, with the top flower cluster larger than the lower ones.

LIGULARIA

GOLDEN RAY
Asteraceae
Perennials

🌿 **US, MS, LS; USDA 6-8**

◑ ● **PARTIAL TO FULL SHADE**

💧💧 **AMPLE MOISTURE**

Ligularia dentata

These stately perennials from China and Japan form 3-ft.-wide clumps of large leaves topped by daisy-type flowers in yellow to orange. All need rich soil, plenty of moisture, and some shade; they do not tolerate low humidity or hot afternoon sun. Good around pools, along streambeds, in bog gardens. Control slugs and snails. Clumps can remain undisturbed for years; if more plants are needed, divide clumps in early spring.

L. dentata. Grown primarily for big, attractive leaves (to more than a foot across), roundish with a heart-shaped base. In mid-summer to early fall, sends up 3- to 5-ft. stems holding large, branching heads of orange-yellow, 4-in.-wide daisies. 'Othello' and 'Desdemona' have deep purple leafstalks, veins, and leaf undersides; upper surfaces of leaves are green. 'Midnight Lady' has dark, bronzy purple leaves.

L. 'Gregynog Gold'. Clump of 14-in.-wide, heart-shaped, tooth-edged leaves sends up stems to 6 ft. tall. In late summer and fall, stems bear conical clusters of 4-in. yellow flowers.

L. 'Osiris Café Noir'. Grows 20 in. high and nearly as wide. Purple-black new growth progressively lightens through bronze to green. Leathery leaves have serrated margins. Yellow flowers appear on 20-in. stems in mid- to late summer.

L. przewalskii. LEOPARD PLANT. Deeply lobed and cut leaves grow to 1 ft. wide. Dark purplish blossom stalks rise to about 6 ft. and are loaded with dense, narrow spires of ¾-in., yellow flowers in summer. 'Dragon's Breath' is more compact to 30 in. high and 24 in. wide.

L. stenocephala. Especially stunning flower spikes. Usually represented by its selection 'The Rocket', which forms a large clump of foot-wide, irregularly toothed leaves topped by tall (up to 5-ft.), narrow, dark-stemmed spires bearing many 1½-in., yellow daisies in summer.

L. wilsoniana. GIANT GROUNDSEL. Bears kidney-shaped leaves that reach 20 in. wide. Stems grow to 6 ft. tall, carry spikes of inch-wide yellow daisies in summer.

LIGUSTRUM
PRIVET
Oleaceae
Evergreen, semievergreen, deciduous shrubs and trees

⚡ **ZONES VARY BY SPECIES**

☀ ◐ **FULL SUN OR PARTIAL SHADE, EXCEPT AS NOTED**

💧 **REGULAR WATER**

◊ **LEAVES AND FRUIT CAUSE GASTRIC DISTRESS IF INGESTED**

Ligustrum japonicum 'Texanum'

Although one species makes a fine landscape tree, privets are first and foremost hedge plants. They take well to shearing and can be clipped into almost any shape. In spring or early summer, all bear abundant clusters of showy, white to creamy white flowers that are highly fragrant. Some people don't care for the cloyingly sweet scent—and the pollen may cause allergic reactions. Bees and wasps also swarm to the flowers. Clipped hedges produce fewer flowers, as shearing removes most of the flower buds. Blossoms are followed by small, berrylike, blue-black fruit. Birds eat them and distribute the seeds everywhere—with the result that seedlings come up everywhere, too. Since most privets will grow well in any kind of soil, vigilance is required to keep them from taking over. Most make good container subjects. They are resistant to browsing deer.

L. japonicum. JAPANESE PRIVET. Evergreen shrub. Zones MS, LS, CS, TS; USDA 7-11. From northern China, Korea, Japan. Dense, compact growth to 10–12 ft. tall, 8 ft. wide, but can be kept smaller by trimming. Roundish oval leaves are 2–4 in. long, dark to medium green and glossy above, distinctly paler to almost whitish beneath. They have a thick, slightly spongy feel. Excellent plant for hedges or screens or for shaping into small trees. In caliche soil or where Texas root rot prevails, grow it in containers. Often confused with its selection 'Texanum'.

'Howardi'. Garish, two-tone shrub: leaves are yellow when new, aging to green. Both colors are usually present at once.

'Jack Frost'. Dark green leaves edged with creamy white.

'Recurvifolium'. Leaves are wavy edged, twisted at the tip, and slightly smaller than those of the species. Somewhat open grower.

'Rotundifolium'. ROUNDLEAF JAPANESE PRIVET. Grows 4–5 ft. high; has nearly round leaves to 2½ in. long. Partial shade.

'Silver Star'. Grows 6–8 ft. high. Deep green leaves have gray-green mottling and startling creamy white edges. Provides a good contrast to solid deep green foliage.

'Texanum'. Similar to the species but grows a little smaller (to 8–10 ft, tall, 4–6 ft. wide), with somewhat denser, lusher foliage. Useful as windbreak. Often sold as *L. texanum*.

'Variegatum'. Leaves have creamy white margins and blotches.

L. lucidum. GLOSSY PRIVET. Evergreen tree. Zones LS, CS, TS; USDA 8-11. Native to China, Korea, Japan. Makes a round-headed tree that eventually reaches 35–40 ft. high and wide. Can be kept lower as a big shrub or may form multitrunked tree. Glossy, 4- to 6-in.-long leaves are tapered and pointed, dark to medium green on both sides. They feel leathery but lack the slightly spongy feel of *L. japonicum* leaves. Flowers in especially large, feathery clusters are followed by a profusion of fruit. Fine lawn tree. Can grow in narrow areas; good street tree if not planted near pavement or where fruit will drop on cars (see disadvantages noted below). Performs well in large containers. Or set 10 ft. apart for tall privacy screen. Useful as windbreak.

Before planting this tree, carefully weigh the advantages against the disadvantages. Eventual fruit crop is immense; never plant where fruit will fall on cars, walks, or other paved areas (they stain).

Fallen seeds (and those dropped by birds) sprout profusely in ground cover and will need pulling. Fruiting clusters are bare and unattractive after fruit drop.

L. ovalifolium. CALIFORNIA PRIVET. Semievergreen shrub. Zones US, MS, LS; USDA 6-8. Native to Japan. Dark green, oval, 2½-in.-long leaves. Grows rapidly to 15 ft. but can be kept to any height; reaches 10 ft. wide. For use as hedge, set plants 9–12 in. apart; clip early and frequently for low, dense branching. Be prepared for regular maintenance; you may need to shear every 3 weeks in hot, wet weather. Well-fed, well-watered plants hold their leaves the longest.

This species is a good choice for a fast-growing hedge or screen, but be aware of disadvantages: The plant has greedy roots, its seedlings come up everywhere; and once established, it is hard to eradicate.

'Aureum'. YELLOW-EDGE CALIFORNIA PRIVET, GOLDEN PRIVET. Leaves have broad yellow edges. Often sold as 'Variegatum'.

L. sinense. CHINESE PRIVET. Evergreen shrub. Zones MS, LS, CS, TS; USDA 7-11. From China. To 10–15 ft. tall and wide. Avoid planting the plain species, which has become a horrible weed in the Southeast, conquering woodlands and stream banks. It tolerates just about any conditions and is known to pop up through cracks in the pavement. Hard to kill but worth the effort required to annihilate it. The following three selections are better behaved.

'Pendulum'. WEEPING CHINESE PRIVET. To 10 ft. high and wide, with billowing, cascading branches that create a soft, cloudlike appearance. Branches occasionally revert to upright form; cut these out to maintain pleasing shape.

'Sunshine'. Sterile selection with bright golden foliage. Grows 3–4 ft. tall and wide. Good for low hedge. Also good in containers.

'Variegatum'. VARIEGATED CHINESE PRIVET. Grows quickly to 6 ft. tall and wide. One of the better-looking variegated plants, popular for its handsome matte green leaves with creamy white margins. Useful for brightening dull areas of the garden. Cut out any branches with leaves that revert to solid green.

L. 'Suwannee River'. Evergreen shrub. Zones MS, LS, CS, TS; USDA 7-11. Reported to be a hybrid between *L. japonicum* 'Rotundifolium' and *L. lucidum*. Slow-growing, compact plant reaches 1½ ft. tall in 3 years, eventually grows 4–5 ft. high and wide. Leathery, somewhat twisted dark green leaves; no fruit. Use as low hedge, as foundation planting, in containers.

L. 'Vicaryi'. VICARY GOLDEN PRIVET. Deciduous shrub. Zones US, MS, LS, CS; USDA 6-11. This one has yellow leaves; color is strongest on plants in full sun. To 4–6 ft. (possibly 12 ft.) high and 8–10 ft. wide. Best planted alone; color does not develop well under hedge shearing.

LILIUM

LILY
Liliaceae
Perennials from bulbs

✎ **US, MS, LS, CS; USDA 6-9, EXCEPT AS NOTED**

☀ ◐ **ROOTS COOL, TOPS IN SUN OR FILTERED LIGHT, EXCEPT AS NOTED**

💧 **REGULAR WATER, EXCEPT AS NOTED**

Lilium 'Stargazer'

The most stately and varied of bulbous plants, offering large, colorful, and often fragrant blooms equally effective in the garden or vase. For many years, only the species—the same plants growing wild in parts of Asia, Europe, and North America—were available, and many of these were difficult and unpredictable. Around 1925, however, lily growers began a significant breeding program. They bred new hybrids, strains, and selections that were healthier,

hardier, and easier to grow than the original species. Today, hybrids and strains are typically the best garden lilies, but it is still possible to get some desirable species.

Although the official classification of lilies lists eight divisions of hybrids and a ninth division of species, the following listings describe the lilies commonly available to Southern gardeners. Advances in breeding are producing lilies with forms, colors, and parentage hitherto considered unlikely, if not impossible. Consult specialists' catalogs to learn about these wonders, which are reaching the market faster than books can deal with them.

Asiatic hybrids. Bred from primarily Chinese species, these are easy to grow, reliable lilies for the average garden. Flowers are 6–8 in. long—upward facing in some types, horizontally held or drooping in others. Stems are strong, erect, and short (1½ ft.) to moderate (4½ ft.) in height. Colors range from white through yellow and orange to pink and red. Many have dark spots or contrasting "halos." They are early to bloom (early summer). Examples are 'Brunello', bright orange; 'Dizzy', white with crimson bands along the center of each petal; 'Fata Morgana', double yellow; 'Forever Susan', striking orange with large burgundy blotch; 'Grand Cru', bright yellow with maroon spots near the center; 'Hotline', white with hot pink edges on each petal; 'Landini', dark burgundy with purple tint; 'Lollipop', white with bright pink tips; 'Mona Lisa', dark pink fading to pale pink at the edge of the petals; 'Navona', pure white; 'Netty's Pride', almost black centers turning to deep purple then white toward the tips of the petals; and 'Vermeer', medium pink with white blotch.

LA hybrids. Zones US, MS, LS; USDA 6-8. These lilies are the result of crosses between Easter lilies (*L. longiflorum*) and Asiatic hybrids (*L. asiaticum*), producing garden lilies that bloom early at 2–4 ft. with up-facing, trumpet-shaped blooms that are fragrant and lasting flowers, either cut or in the garden. 'Golden Stone' has bright yellow flowers with red-brown freckles; 'Royal

TOP: L. 'Muscadet'; *L. auratum*; *MIDDLE: L.* 'Casa Blanca'; *BOTTOM: L. speciosum; L. lancifolium*

HOW TO GROW LILIES

PREPARATION Plant bulbs in spring or fall as soon as possible after you get them. If you must wait, keep them in a very cool place until you plant. Don't buy bulbs with dry, withered scales; they won't rehydrate, and their appearance may indicate that the growing tip inside is dead. Before planting bulbs, remove any injured scales and then let the bulbs callous in a cool place for a few hours before planting. If bulbs are dry, place them in moist sand or peat moss until scales get plump and new roots begin to sprout.

PLANTING Choose a spot that gets full sun. Locating lilies among low-growing plants is a good way to keep their roots shaded. Lilies need soil containing ample organic matter. If you want to plant in heavy clay or very sandy soil, add material such as compost, leaf mold, or composted ground bark. Spread a 3- to 4-in. layer of such material over the soil surface; broadcast a complete fertilizer (follow directions for preplanting application) on top of it, then thoroughly till both into the soil to a depth of at least 1 ft. For each bulb, dig a generous planting hole (8–12 in. deeper than height of the bulb). Place enough soil at bottom of hole to bring it up to proper level for bulb (see below). Set bulb with its roots spread; fill hole with soil, firming it around bulb to eliminate air pockets. If your area is infested with gophers, you may have to plant each bulb in a 6-in.-square wire basket made of ½-in. hardware cloth. (The depth of the basket will depend on the planting depth.) Planting depths vary according to size and rooting habit of bulb. Lilies have stem roots above the bulb, so it is important to plant deeply. General rule is to cover smaller bulbs with 2–3 in. of soil, medium bulbs with 3–4 in., and larger bulbs with 4–6 in. (but never cover *L. candidum* bulbs with more than 1 in. of soil). Planting depth can be quite flexible, since lily bulbs have contractile roots that draw them down to the proper depth. Ideal spacing for lily bulbs is 1 ft. apart, but you can plant as close as 6 in. for densely massed effect. After planting, mulch with 2–3 in. of organic material to conserve moisture, keep soil cool, and reduce weed growth.

WATERING Lilies need constant moisture; keep soil moist to about 6 in. deep. Reduce watering somewhat after tops turn yellow in fall, but never allow roots to dry out completely. (*L. candidum* is an exception to this rule.) Soaking is preferable to overhead watering, which may help to spread disease spores. If you use drip irrigation, keep the emitter 8 in. from the stem. Irrigate in the morning so leaves have time to dry before disease can set in.

FEEDING When plants reach 6 in. tall in spring, apply a complete controlled-release bulb fertilizer. Feed the bulbs annually by feeding the soil with 2–3 in. of compost on top.

WEEDING Pull weeds by hand; hoeing may injure roots. Avoid pre-emergent weed suppressants; they can also suppress lily root growth.

POST-BLOOM CARE Deadhead lilies after bloom, and return the energy back to the bulb that would have gone to the seeds. Wait until the stems and leaves turn yellow before you cut plants back. If clumps become too crowded, dig up, divide, and transplant them in spring or fall. If you're very careful, you can lift lily clumps at any time, even in bloom.

CHALLENGES Viral or mosaic disease is a problem. No cure exists. To avoid it, buy healthy bulbs from reliable sources. Dig and destroy any lilies that show mottling in leaves or seriously stunted growth. Control aphids, which spread the infection. Don't plant tiger lilies with other lilies, since they can carry the virus without showing it. Control botrytis blight, a fungal disease that causes reddish brown spots on leaves and blooms, by quickly removing and destroying diseased tissue and keeping lily foliage dry. Fungicides can also be effective. Where rabbits and deer are plentiful, lilies can be damaged. Spray repellent on beds as the lilies emerge from the soil.

Sunset' is brilliant with an orange center and pink tips on the petals; 'Samur' has medium pink flowers.

OT hybrids. When Japan's Oriental lilies were crossed with China's Trumpet lilies, gardeners gained exciting new garden lilies called Orienpets or OT hybrids. They have strong stems, are more heat tolerant, and require less winter cold. The fragrance is sweet but light, and the colors range from cream through yellow to pink. 'Conca d'Or' has lemon petals with pale edges and grows 4–5 ft., 'Miss Freya' is maroon-red and 6–7 ft., and 'Scheherazade' is rose-red with cream-yellow edges, growing up to 10 ft. tall. 'Triumphator' 3–4 ft. tall; pink white flowers.

Oriental hybrids. The most exotic of the hybrids bred from mainly Japanese species. Bloom from midsummer to early fall, with big (to 9-in.), fragrant flowers of white or pink, often spotted with gold and shaded or banded with red. Most are tall, with nodding flowers, but a few are dwarf and have upward-facing blooms. Examples are 'Casa Blanca', pure white; 'Le Reve', soft pink with a few maroon freckles toward the center; 'Muscadet', white with pink freckles and pink center lines; 'Salmon Star', pink flushed with salmon toward the center and base of each petal, 2–3 ft. high; and 'Stargazer', rose-red with white margins.

Trumpet lily hybrids (*Aurelian* hybrids). Zones MS, LS, CS; USDA 7-9. Derived from Asiatic species such as *L. henryi* and *L. regale* (but not *L. auratum* or *L. speciosum*). Midsummer bloomers with trumpet- or bowl-shaped, 6–8 in. flowers are usually heavily scented. Blossoms range from white and cream through yellow and pink, many with green, brown, or purple shading on their outer surfaces. Plants are typically 3–6 ft. tall; each stem carries 6 to 15 flowers. Examples include the Golden Splendor strain, deep gold with maroon striping on petal backs; the Pink Perfection strain; and 'African Queen', apricot-orange with brown streaks.

Species and variants.

L. auratum. GOLD-BAND LILY. Zones US, MS, LS; USDA 6-8. Native to Japan. Sweetly fragrant white flowers to 5 in. long appear atop 4- to 6-ft. stems in summer. Petals feature reddish purple spots and a gold band along the midrib.

L. candidum. MADONNA LILY. Native to the Balkans and eastern Mediterranean. Cultivated since 3000 BC and named by Greek poet Virgil. Pure white, fragrant, 4-in. blooms on 3- to 4-ft. stems in late spring, early summer. Unlike most lilies, it dies down soon after bloom, then makes new growth in fall; no summer water is needed. Plant while dormant in August. Choose a sunny location and set top of bulb only 1–2 in. deep (Madonna lilies do not have stem roots). Bulb quickly makes a foliage rosette that lives over winter, lengthens to become a blooming stem in spring. This species is subject to diseases that shorten its life. Seed grown. Does well in alkaline soil.

L. catesbaei. SOUTHERN RED LILY, PINE LILY. Zones LS, CS; USDA 8-9. Native to moist sites from southeastern Virginia to Florida, Mississippi, and Louisiana. Blooms in late summer, early fall; each purple, 2- to 2½-ft.-tall stem bears a solitary 5-in.-long, 5- to 6-in.-wide, red flower marked with purple spots and a patch of yellow near each petal base. Partial shade. Although native to bogs, it thrives in regular garden moisture.

L. formosanum. FORMOSA LILY. Zones MS, LS, CS, TS; USDA 7-11. Native to Taiwan. An often-overlooked, easy-to-grow species that is worthy of wider use. Showy, fragrant flowers are narrow, pendent trumpets 8–12 in. long, appearing atop 5- to 7-ft. stems in late summer. Blooms are white, with a pinkish purple midrib on each petal back; stems are dark purple toward the base. Foliage is narrow, grasslike, and attractive; upright seedpods give rise to many seedlings that often bloom within their first year. 'Little Snow' grows 3 ft. high. A delightful variant, *L. formosanum pricei*, reaches just 10 in. high and bears 6-in.-long white trumpets with plum-colored midribs. It blooms a month earlier than the species. Both are among the better lilies for the Coastal and Tropical South; bloom reliably throughout Florida.

Formosa lily is often confused with a similar but lower-growing lily that also grows well in the South, *L. philippinense*. The resulting hybrids, called Philippine lilies, retain the look and growth habit of *L. formosanum* but are more floriferous.

L. hansonii. HANSON LILY. Native to Japan, Korea. Grows 2–4 ft. tall, producing fragrant, nodding, yellow-orange summer blooms. Leaves grow in whorls around stems. Prefers light shade and slightly moist soil with lots of organic content. Slow to establish. Extremely virus resistant.

L. henryi. HENRY'S LILY. Zones US, MS, LS; USDA 6-8. From China. Slender stems reach 8–9 ft., each bearing 10 to 20 bright orange, 6-in.-long flowers with sharply recurved petals. Mid-summer bloom. Best in light shade. Long-term perennial.

L. lancifolium (*L. tigrinum*). TIGER LILY. Zones US, MS, LS, CS, TS; USDA 6-11. Native to China, Japan, Korea. Summer-blooming old Southern favorite to 4 ft. or taller, with pendulous, 7-in.-long orange flowers spotted in black. Very easy to grow. 'Flore Pleno' is a double. 'Splendens' bears large flower clusters. Newer tiger lilies are available in white, cream, yellow, pink, and red (all with the typical black spots).

L. longiflorum. EASTER LILY. Zones US, MS, LS, CS, TS; USDA 6-11. Native to Japan and Taiwan. Short stems bear very fragrant, trumpet-shaped, white blossoms to 7 in. long. Usually purchased in bloom at Easter. Set out in garden after flowers fade—but don't plant forced Easter lilies near other lilies, as they may transmit a virus. Stems will ripen and die down. Plant may rebloom in fall; in 1 or 2 years, it may flower in midsummer, its normal bloom

time. Selections include 'Ace' (1½ ft. tall), 'Croft' (1 ft.), 'Estate' (to 3 ft.), and 'Nellie White' (2–2½ ft.; very popular). Hybridization has yielded colorful offspring, as well as white, such as the dark pink 'Faith' and 'White Heaven', both growing 2–3 ft. tall. Does very well throughout Florida.

L. martagon. TURK'S CAP LILY. Zones US, MS, LS; USDA 6-8. Native from Europe to Mongolia. Purplish pink, recurved, pendent, 7-in.-long flowers bloom in early summer on 3- to 5-ft. stems. This old favorite is slow to establish, but it's long lived and eventually forms big clumps. 'Arabian Night' is red and orange. 'Sunny Morning' is yellow-orange with deeper orange markings. These are among the most shade tolerant of lilies.

L. pumilum. CORAL LILY. Native to northern China, Mongolia, Siberia. Early summer bloomer to 1–1½ ft. high, with up to 20 fragrant red, recurved, 3-in.-long blossoms per stem. 'Yellow Bunting' has yellow flowers.

L. regale. REGAL LILY. From western China. Popular and easy to grow. To 6 ft., with fragrant, trumpet-shaped, 6-in.-long, white flowers in early to midsummer.

L. speciosum. SHOWY LILY. Native to China, Japan, Taiwan. Grows 2½–5 ft. tall. Wide, fragrant, 7-in.-long flowers with broad, deeply recurved segments bloom in late summer; they are white, heavily suffused with rose-pink and sprinkled with raised crimson dots. Named forms are available, including pure white *L. s. album* and red *L. s. rubrum*. 'Uchida' is the most popular selection; it has white-edged pink blooms with deep pink speckles and red anthers. Does best in light shade (or at least afternoon shade); needs rich soil with plenty of leaf mold.

L. superbum. SWAMP LILY. Zones US, MS, LS; USDA 6-8. Native to the eastern U.S. Reaches 6–9 ft. tall, producing nodding orange, Turk's cap flowers whose petals turn red-orange at the tips with maturity. In the wild, it prefers moist meadows or woodlands but does fine in regularly watered gardens.

LIMONIUM
Plumbaginaceae
Perennials and annuals

✎ ZONES VARY BY SPECIES

☼ FULL SUN

💧 MODERATE WATER

Limonium sinuatum

Large, leathery, green basal leaves contrast with airy clusters of tiny, delicate flowers on nearly leafless, many-branched stems. The flowers consist of two parts: an outer, papery envelope (the calyx) and an inner part (the corolla). Calyx and corolla are often of different colors. Flowers are good for cutting and keep their color when dried. Plants tolerate heat and many kinds of soil but need good drainage. They often self-sow. For spring and summer bloom of annual kinds, sow indoors and move to garden when weather warms up. Or sow outdoors in early spring for later bloom. Resistant to deer.

L. platyphyllum. SEA LAVENDER. Perennial. Zones US, MS, LS, CS; USDA 6-9. Native to central

> ## STATICE SYMBOLS
>
> Cut sprays of statice for fresh bouquets after most flowers in each cluster have opened. For dried arrangements, cut after blossoms are open but before sun has faded them. With a rubber band, join several bunches together by the stem bases; hang them upside down in a dry spot out of bright sun until flowers are dry.

and southeastern Europe. Vigorous plant to 2½ ft. tall, covered in a 3-ft.-wide cloud of flowers in summer. Calyx is white, corolla bluish; pure white and pink kinds exist. Smooth-edged leaves to 10 in. long.

L. sinuatum. STATICE. Annual. Zones US, MS, LS, CS, TS; USDA 6-11. Mediterranean native widely grown for use as a cut flower in both fresh and dried arrangements. To 1½ ft. tall and 1 ft. wide, with basal leaves lobed nearly to midrib. Flower stems are distinctly "winged," with flattish extensions on their sides. Calyx is blue, lavender, or rose; corolla is white. Improved strains come in rose, yellow, apricot, orange, peach, light blue, deep blue, purple, and white. Plant in fall in Coastal and Tropical South.

LINARIA
TOADFLAX
Plantaginaceae
Annuals and perennials

✎ US, MS, LS, CS; USDA 6-9

☼ ◗ FULL SUN OR LIGHT SHADE

💧 MODERATE WATER

Linaria 'Enchantment'

Brightly colored flowers resemble small, spurred snapdragons (*Antirrhinum majus*). Easy to grow; thrive in light or sandy soil. Look best when planted in masses, as individual plants are rather wispy. Toadflaxes are not usually browsed by deer.

L. hybrids. Annuals. The Fantasy series produces compact plants to 1 ft. high, 6–8 in. wide, with very narrow, bluish green leaves. Clusters of ½- to 1-in. flowers appear in spring and summer, come in blue with yellow throat, magenta, pink, yellow, and white. 'Enchantment' has very fragrant magenta-and-gold flowers on plants to 16 in. high.

L. maroccana. BABY SNAP-DRAGON, TOADFLAX. Annual. From Morocco. To 1½–2 ft. high, 6 in. wide. Light green, narrow leaves to 1½ in. long. Summer flowers to ½ in. long, in rose, pink, mauve, chamois, blue, violet, purple, or a red-and-gold combination; all are blotched with a different shade on the lip. Spur is longer than flower. Fairy Bouquet strain is only 9 in. tall and has larger flowers in pastel colors. Northern Lights strain features shades of red, orange, and yellow, as well as bicolors.

Seed baby snapdragon in quantity for a show. It performs best during cool weather. Where winters are cold, sow in early spring after danger of frost is past, then again in late summer; in mild-winter areas, sow in late summer for fall bloom, then again in autumn for winter flowers.

L. purpurea. PURPLE TOAD-FLAX. Perennial. From southern Europe. Narrow, bushy, erect plant to 2–4 ft. tall, 10 in. wide. Blue-green, very narrow leaves; violet-blue, ½-in. summer flowers. 'Canon Went' is a pink form. Short lived in hot, humid regions, but volunteer seedlings ensure a continuing supply.

L. reticulata. Annual. From Portugal and North Africa. To 2–4 ft. tall, 10 in. wide, with very narrow, bluish green leaves and showers of small purple-and-orange flowers in late spring and summer. 'Flamenco' (1–1½ ft. high) has yellow flowers with a conspicuous maroon blotch. 'Flaming Passion' (16 in. high, 8 in. wide) has red flowers with yellow centers.

L. vulgaris. COMMON TOADFLAX, BUTTER-AND-EGGS. Perennial. From Europe and Asia; naturalized in North America. Stiffly erect habit to 1–3 ft. high, 1 ft. wide. Narrow, pale green leaves to 2½ in. long; pale yellow blossoms to 1¾ in. wide from spring into fall. Invasive, weedy plant; unleash it in a cottage garden, where you are more likely to appreciate its propensity to spread by rhizomes and self-sow.

LINDERA
SPICEBUSH
Lauraceae
Deciduous shrubs or trees

🌿 **ZONES VARY BY SPECIES**

☀️ ◑ **FULL SUN OR PART SHADE**

💧 **REGULAR WATER**

Lindera obtusiloba

Spicebushes are grown principally for the beauty of their fall foliage; early spring clusters of small, greenish yellow flowers on leafless shoots are attractive but not conspicuous. On female plants, fruit will follow the blossoms if a male plant is nearby. Best used at woodland edge or as space fillers. Need good drainage; tolerate some drought. The common name

IN FALL, THE LEAVES OF JAPANESE SPICEBUSH TURN AN EXTREMELY BRIGHT SHADE OF YELLOW.

refers to the spicy odor of the crushed leaves.

L. benzoin. SPICEBUSH. US, MS, LS, CS; USDA 6-9. Native to woodlands of eastern U.S. Reaches 6–12 ft. tall and broad. Light green leaves are 3–5 in. long, half as wide. Yellow fall color and plant form are best in full sun; if plants are grown in shade, foliage color isn't as intense and habit is loose and open. Fruit (noticeable after leaf fall) is bright red, up to ½ in. long. Host plant for the spicebush swallowtail butterfly.

L. obtusiloba. JAPANESE SPICEBUSH. US, MS; USDA 6-7. Native to Japan, China, Korea. To 10–20 ft. tall, not quite as wide. Leaves are 5 in. long, 4 in. wide, occasionally lobed near the tip to give a mitten shape. Fall color is an exceptionally brilliant yellow that develops even in shade and holds for 2 weeks or more. Small (¼-in.-wide) red fruit eventually turns black.

LINDHEIMERA TEXANA
TEXAS YELLOW STAR, STAR DAISY
Asteraceae
Annual

🌿 **US, MS, LS, CS, TS; USDA 6-11**

☀️ **FULL SUN**

💧 **LITTLE WATER**

Lindheimera texana

This rugged Texas native forms a basal rosette of coarse, tapered leaves that reach 2–3 in. long. Thick, hairy stems rise 1–2 ft. tall and are topped by star-shaped, yellow flowers to 1½ in. across. Blooms profusely from March through May, providing early

color for wildflower gardens. Spent petals drop cleanly. Does best in dryish, sandy or rocky soil. Space plants about 1 ft. apart.

LINUM
FLAX
Linaceae
Perennials and annuals

🌿 **ZONES VARY BY SPECIES**

☀️ **FULL SUN**

💧 **MODERATE WATER**

Linum perenne

Plants with erect, branching stems and narrow leaves produce an abundance of shallow-cupped, five-petaled flowers over a long bloom period. Each bloom lasts only a day, but others keep coming. The flax of commerce—*L. usitatissimum*—is grown for its fiber and seeds, which yield linseed oil.

Use in borders; some naturalize freely in uncultivated areas. Do best in light, well-drained soil. Most perennial kinds live only 3 or 4 years and should be replaced regularly. Easy to grow from seed; perennials also can be propagated from cuttings. Difficult to divide.

L. flavum. GOLDEN FLAX. Perennial. Zones US, MS, LS, CS; USDA 6-9. From central and southern Europe. To 12–15 in. high, 1 ft. wide, with somewhat woody base. Grooved branches, green leaves. Branched clusters of golden yellow, inch-wide flowers bloom in spring and summer. 'Compactum' is just 6 in. high and wide.

L. grandiflorum. FLOWER-ING FLAX. Annual. Zones US, MS, LS, CS, TS; USDA 6-11. From North Africa. To 1½–2½ ft. tall and 6–12 in. wide, with narrow, gray-green leaves. Summer flowers are rose-pink, 1–1½ in. wide. Sow seed thickly in place in early spring or (in mild-winter climates) in fall. Self-sows without becoming a pest and is often included in wild-flower mixes. Two selections are far more common than the species: 'Rubrum', scarlet flax, with bright red flowers; and 'Bright Eyes', bearing white flowers with a brownish red eye.

L. narbonense. Perennial. Zones US, MS, LS; USDA 6-8. Wiry-stemmed Mediterranean native to 2 ft. tall, 1½ ft. wide. Narrow, blue-green leaves. Open clusters of 1¾-in., azure-blue flowers with white eye; blooms in late spring and early summer. 'Six Hills' has rich sky-blue blossoms.

L. perenne. PERENNIAL BLUE FLAX. Perennial. Zones US, MS, LS; USDA 6-8. Native from Europe to central Asia. Most vigorous blue-flowered flax, to 2 ft. tall, 1½ ft. wide. Narrow, blue-green leaves; stems are usually leafless on lower part. Blooms profusely in late spring and summer, producing branching clusters of light blue flowers that close in shade or late in the day. Self-sows freely.

LIQUIDAMBAR

SWEET GUM

Hamamelidaceae

Deciduous trees

  ZONES VARY BY SPECIES

☼ FULL SUN

◗◗ MODERATE TO REGULAR WATER

Liquidambar styraciflua

People often are of two minds when it comes to sweet gums: They praise them for their

ravishing fall color but curse them for their copious gum balls. Distinguished by their maplelike leaves, they're upright, conical trees that spread with age. Inconspicuous flowers are followed by spiny seed balls that are a boon for fans of dried arrangements but a bane for those who like to walk barefoot. Seedless selections are becoming available, however, so the best of both worlds could be in sight.

Provide fertile, well-drained, slightly acid to neutral soil; alkaline soil often causes chlorosis (yellow leaves with green veins), and the problem can be hard to correct. Prune young trees to develop a strong central leader. Mature trees need little pruning.

Given ample room, sweet gums make fine street and shade trees, though their surface roots can be a problem in lawns or in the narrow space between sidewalk and curb. Fall foliage is brilliant in the Upper and Middle South, less so in the Lower, Coastal, and Tropical South. Young plants are somewhat resistant to browsing deer.

L. formosana. CHINESE SWEET GUM. Zones US, MS, LS, CS; USDA 6-9. Native to China. To 40–60 ft. tall, 25 ft. wide. Free-form outline; sometimes pyramidal, especially when young. Three- to five-lobed leaves are 3–4½ in. across, violet-red when expanding, deep green at maturity. Fall color ranges from red in northern part of range to yellow-beige farther south. Leaves drop late, usually in early winter. 'Afterglow' has lavender-purple new growth, rosy red fall color.

L. orientalis. ORIENTAL SWEET GUM. Zones MS, LS, CS; USDA 7-9. Native to Turkey. To 20–30 ft. tall and wide. Leaves 2–3 in. wide, deeply five lobed, each lobe again lobed to give a lacy effect. Leafs out early after short dormant period. Fall color varies from deep gold and bright red in cooler areas to dull brown-purple farther south.

L. styraciflua. AMERICAN SWEET GUM. Zones US, MS, LS, CS; USDA 6-9. Native to eastern U.S., and by far the most commonly planted sweet gum. To about 60 ft. tall in gardens; much taller in the wild. Narrow and erect in youth, with lower limbs eventually spreading to 20–25 ft. Tolerates damp soil.

Good-looking all year. Branching pattern, furrowed bark, and corky wings on twigs all provide winter interest, as do hanging seedpods—½-in., spiky spheres reminiscent of tiny medieval maces. On mature trees, seedpods are profuse enough to cause a litter problem (especially on lawns, where they interfere with mowing).

Five- to seven-lobed, 3- to 7-in.-wide leaves are deep green in spring and summer, turning to purple, yellow, or red in fall. Seedling trees usually give good fall color, though color varies widely. To get desired and uniform color, purchase named selections, preferably while they are in fall color. Good selections include the following.

'Burgundy'. Deep purple-red fall color. Foliage hangs on late into winter—or even into early spring if storms are not heavy.

'Cherokee'. Produces very few or no seedpods. Fall color is burgundy-red (yellow on trees grown in shade).

'Festival'. Narrow, columnar. Light green foliage turns a combination of yellow, peach, pink, orange, and red in fall.

'Golden Treasure'. Deep green leaves bordered in gold. In fall, gold rim lightens to pale yellow, then white; green center turns burgundy.

'Gumball'. Dense, rounded, shrubby habit rarely over 6 ft. on its own. When grafted as a standard tree, forms a neat round-topped tree, 10–12 ft. high and wide. Burgundy-red in fall.

'Palo Alto'. Orange-red to bright red fall color.

'Rotundiloba'. Leaves have rounded rather than sharp-pointed lobes. Sets no seedpods. Fall color is yellow, red, burgundy, and purple. Weak-wooded and subject to storm damage.

'Silver King'. Leaves are edged in creamy white; may be flushed with rosy tones in late summer and fall.

'Slender Silhouette'. Grows 60 ft. tall, 8 ft. wide; orange to burgundy fall color.

'Variegata'. Green leaves with yellow streaks and splotches. In fall, the yellow variegation turns pink; green part of leaf becomes red.

LIRIODENDRON TULIPIFERA

TULIP POPLAR

Magnoliaceae

Deciduous tree

  US, MS, LS, CS; USDA 6-9

☼ FULL SUN

◗ REGULAR WATER

Liriodendron tulipifera

The tallest native hardwood in the United States, tulip poplar can grow upwards of 150 feet in the wild. Despite its common name, it's not a poplar, but belongs to the Magnolia family. "Tulip" comes from the large, tulip-shaped flowers borne high in the branches in late spring and early summer. They're greenish yellow with an orange base and usually don't appear until the tree is 10–12 years old.

Tulip poplar is easily recognizable for its distinctive, pyramidal shape and 4-lobed foliage. A fast grower, this tree ascends straight as an arrow and features smooth, gray, shallowly furrowed bark. It tends to drop its lower branches as it grows, so eventually the lowest branches may be high above the ground. Bright green leaves turn bright yellow in fall. In winter, conspicuous seed cones high in the branches make identification easy. It's the state tree of Tennessee.

Because of its size, this species may not be suitable for smaller yards. It also tends to drop twigs and small branches throughout the year. Don't park cars beneath it, because aphids feeding on the leaves drip sticky honeydew.

Tulip poplar thrives in deep, moist, well-drained soil that's slightly acid to neutral. It's not a good choice for dry soil, as it responds to summer droughts by dropping yellowed leaves prematurely. It's not a good street tree either, as rising heat from hot pavement may scorch the leaves. Prune in winter.

'Aureomarginatum' ('Majestic Beauty'). Grows 40–60 ft. tall and 15–20 ft. wide with leaves edged in yellow.

'Emerald City.' Grows 55–60 ft. tall and 25 ft. wide with glossy leaves.

'Fastigiatum' ('Arnold'). Narrow, upright form grows 50–60 ft. tall and 15–20 ft. wide. Great as a tall screen or vertical accent. Blooms 2–3 years after planting.

'Little Volunteer.' Good choice for smaller gardens; grows only 30–40 ft. tall. Discovered in Tennessee.

'Tennessee Gold.' Striking gold leaves with splash of green in center. Propagated from a branch mutation by nurseryman Don Shadow. Should grow 60–70 ft. tall.

LIRIOPE

MONKEY GRASS, LILY TURF
Asparagaceae
Perennials

🗡 **US, MS, LS, CS, TS; USDA 6-11, EXCEPT AS NOTED**

◐ ● **PARTIAL TO FULL SHADE, EXCEPT AS NOTED**

💧 **REGULAR WATER**

Liriope muscari 'Mark Anthony'

Forming tufts of grasslike leaves, these popular, tough-as-nails ground covers from Asia are known by a number of names—but to most Southerners, they're plain old monkey grass. One species grows in clumps; the other spreads aggressively. Summer flowers, often quite showy, appear atop the foliage

in spikes or branching clusters and come in lavender, blue, pink, purple, or white.

In addition to their use as a ground cover, these plants make excellent edgings for walks and planting beds. They're good beneath large trees, as they tolerate the shallow soil between surface roots. They also make nice additions to containers and mixed plantings. They generally prefer filtered sun to full shade, although some selections do well in full sun. Good drainage is important; regular fertilizing isn't necessary. To get more plants, divide in early spring, using a sharp spade to cut through the clumps. Deer don't usually eat the foliage.

Liriope's close cousin, *Ophiopogon japonicus*, is also called monkey grass. It has many of the same uses but is less cold hardy. See page 460.

L. muscari. BIG BLUE LIRIOPE, BIG BLUE LILY TURF. Forms large clumps 1–2 ft. tall and eventually a bit wider—but does not spread by underground stems. Loose growth habit, with arching, typically dark green leaves to 2 ft. or longer, ½–¾ in. wide. Dense, spike-like, 6- to 8-in. blossom clusters reminiscent of grape hyacinth (*Muscari*) appear on 5- to 12-in. stems. Blooms are held above the foliage on young plants, partly hidden by leaves on older ones. Round, shiny black fruit follows flowers.

'Big Blue'. Stiffly arching plant to 12–15 in. high. Narrow leaves, dark violet flowers. Does well even in dry shade.

'Cleopatra'. To 15 in. tall, with slightly twisted leaves. Very showy dark purple flowers.

'Evergreen Giant'. Zones CS, TS; USDA 9-11. To 2 ft. tall, with straplike leaves and lavender flowers. Evergreen plant, best used as edging or border.

'John Burch'. To 12–15 in. high. Broad, yellow-green leaves with wide green edging. Heavy flower spikes like lavender cockscombs stand well above the foliage. Performs best in full sun.

'Lilac Beauty'. Grows 12–15 in. tall. Pale violet flowers.

'Majestic' (*M. exiliflora*). To 15–18 in. high. Somewhat open clumps. Blooms heavily, bearing large (up to 10-in.-long) clusters of dark violet blossoms resembling cockscombs; flowers are held

above the leaves. 'Royal Purple' and 'Webster Wideleaf' are similar.

'Mark Anthony'. To 16 in. high. New growth variegated golden yellow and green, turning white and as it matures. Pinkish lavender blooms.

'Monroe White'. To 12–15 in. high, with broad leaves and large white flower spikes that stand well above the foliage. Fruit is purple. Prefers more shade than most types.

'Pee Dee Ingot'. Grows 10–12 in. tall. Yellow young growth matures to gold or chartreuse. Lavender blooms.

'Samantha'. Grows 12–15 in. tall. Narrow leaves; pink blooms.

'Silvery Sunproof'. Open, strong growth to 12–15 in. high. Medium green foliage has gold stripes that age to white; whole leaf is whiter in sun, yellower or greener in shade. Lilac flowers are held well above foliage. One of the best for full sun and for flowers.

'Variegata'. To 10–15 in. high. Forms loose, soft clumps. Leaves are green with yellow edges when new, then turn solid dark green in second season. Violet flowers are held well above the leaves. May be sold as *Ophiopogon jaburan* 'Variegatus'.

L. spicata. CREEPING LIRIOPE, CREEPING LILY TURF. Dense ground cover that spreads widely by underground stems; can be invasive. Grows 8–9 in. high. Deep green, grasslike leaves are only ¼ in. wide. Foliage is not as upright as that of *L. muscari*. Pale lilac to white flowers appear in spikelike clusters barely taller than the leaves. Set plants 1 ft. apart for quick cover. For best effect, mow yearly in early spring, before new growth emerges. 'Silver Dragon' has a somewhat sparser habit, leaves striped in silvery white, and pale purple flowers held on short spikes. Fine ground cover for shade; slower growing than species.

MANICURING MONKEY GRASS

Though liriope is evergreen in most of the South, its leaves look pretty ragged by late winter. Neaten it up by mowing plants or clipping all foliage back close to the ground in early spring, before new growth appears. Don't be late with this grooming, though—if you mow after new leaves emerge, those leaves will have unattractive cut tips the entire year.

LIVISTONA

Arecaceae
Palms

🗡 **CS, TS; USDA 9-11, EXCEPT AS NOTED**

☼ **FULL SUN**

💧 **REGULAR WATER, EXCEPT AS NOTED**

Livistona decipiens

These slow-growing fan palms somewhat resemble *Washingtonia* but generally have shorter, darker, shinier leaves. They are generally hardy to about 22°F. All make good potted plants.

L. australis. AUSTRALIAN FAN PALM. From coastal forest of eastern Australia. To 40–50 ft. tall, 15 ft. wide. Trunk is clean and slender, marked with interesting-looking leaf scars. Dark green, 3- to 5-ft.-wide leaves.

L. chinensis. CHINESE FAN PALM, CHINESE FOUNTAIN PALM. Zones LS, CS, TS; USDA 8-11. From Japan, Taiwan. Very slow growing; eventually reaches 40 ft. tall, 15 ft. wide. Roundish, bright green, 3- to 6-ft.-wide leaves droop strongly at outer edges. Hardy to about 15°F.

L. decipiens. WEEPING FAN PALM. From northeastern Australia. To 30–40 ft. tall and 15 ft. wide in 20 years. Stiff, open head of leaves that are green on top, bluish beneath, 2–5 ft. across; leaves are carried on long, spiny stems.

L. mariae. BRONZE FAN PALM. From hot, dry, interior Australia. To 10–15 ft. tall and 15 ft. wide after many years (ultimately may reach 80 or even 100 ft. tall, 25 ft. wide). Leaves 3–4 ft. wide. Young plants and those grown in containers have attractive reddish leaves and leaf stems. Little to moderate water.

LOBELIA

Campanulaceae
Perennials and annuals

| 🌿 ZONES VARY BY SPECIES |
| 🌤 ☀ PARTIAL TO FULL SUN |
| 💧 💦 REGULAR TO AMPLE WATER |
| ◆ MOST CONTAIN POISONOUS ALKALOIDS |

Lobelia x *speciosa* 'Monet Moment'

All are grown for their tubular, lipped flowers, which resemble those of honeysuckle (*Lonicera*) or salvia. Annual kinds are low plants for edgings or hanging baskets; perennial sorts are larger, vertical-growing plants with flowering stalks that rise above the foliage clumps.

L. cardinalis. CARDINAL FLOWER. Perennial. Zones US, MS, LS, CS; USDA 6-9. Native to eastern U.S. and to a few sites in mountains of the Southwest. Erect, single-stemmed plant to 2–4 ft. high, 1 ft. wide. Sawtooth-edged leaves are set directly on the stems. Spikes of flame-red, inch-long flowers in summer. A bog plant in nature, it needs rich soil and ample moisture throughout the growing season. 'Queen Victoria' grows 4–5 ft. tall, with purple-red foliage and scarlet flowers. 'St. Elmo's Fire' ('Elmfeuer') grows 3 ft. tall, with bronze foliage, scarlet flower

spikes. 'Summit Snow' is a white-flowering form.

L. erinus. EDGING LOBELIA. Annual. Zones US, MS, LS, CS, TS; USDA 6-11. From South Africa. Popular and dependable edging plant to 3–6 in. high. Compact forms reach 5–9 in. wide; trailing types spread to 1½ ft. Leafy, branching stems with green or bronzy green foliage. Blooms from spring to frost, bearing ¼-in.-wide flowers in light blue to violet (sometimes pink, reddish purple, or white) with white or yellowish throats. Lives over winter in mild climates. In the Lower, Coastal and Tropical South, grow it as a winter-to-spring annual. If started from seed sown in pots, takes about 2 months to reach planting-out size. Give rich soil, regular water. Self-sows where adapted.

Compact types include 'Cambridge Blue', with green leaves and flowers in a soft pure blue; and 'Crystal Palace', with rich deep blue blossoms and bronzy green leaves. Newer strains include the heat-tolerant Magadi series, in mounding (12 by 10 in.) and trailing (10 by 12 in.) forms, in several shades of purple, blue, and white. Also heat tolerant is the Laguna series in various shades of blue, purple, lavender, and white. Trailing, green-foliaged kinds include the Cascade series, with carmine-red, violet-blue, blue, pink, or white blooms, and 'Sapphire', with bright blue flowers. Trailers are well suited to hanging baskets, wall plantings. They also make a graceful under-planting in containers, where the stems, loaded with flowers, can spill over the edges.

L. siphilitica. BLUE CARDINAL FLOWER. Perennial. Zones US, MS, LS; USDA 6-8. Native to eastern U.S. Leafy plant to 2–3 ft. tall, 1 ft. wide. Blue summer flowers. Give ample water. 'Alba' has white blossoms.

L. x speciosa. (L. x gerardii). Perennial. Zones US, MS, LS, CS; USDA 6-9. Group of hybrids of uncertain ancestry. Can reach 5 ft. tall, 1 ft. wide; many combine red leaves and red flowers. Provide rich soil. Compliment series, to 2½ ft. high, has dark green leaves; blossoms may be scarlet, deep red, or blue-purple. Fan series grows 2 ft. high, 16 in. wide; comes in blue, burgundy, red, rose, salmon, and scarlet. 'Grape

Knee-Hi', 2 ft. high, is a sturdy plant with rich purple blooms. 'Cotton Candy', named for its bright pink blossoms, grows ½ ft. tall. 'Monet Moment', to 3 ft. tall, bears big clusters of rich rose-pink blossoms. 'Ruby Queen' reaches 3 ft. high and has ruby-red blooms; 'Ruby Slippers' grows to 3–4 ft. tall, with spikes of velvety, ruby-red flowers and foliage that may take on purple tones.

LOBULARIA MARITIMA

SWEET ALYSSUM
Brassicaceae
Annual

| 🌿 US, MS, LS, CS; USDA 6-9 |
| ☀ 🌤 BEST IN SUN, TOLERATES LIGHT SHADE |
| 💧 REGULAR WATER |

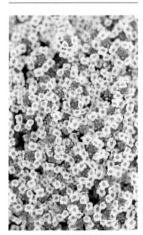

Lobularia maritima
'Snow Princess'

These easy-to-grow mounds of white, pink, or purple, honey-scented flowers work well in containers or casual landscaping situations. Useful for carpeting, edging, bulb cover; temporary filler in rock garden or perennial border; between flagstones; in window boxes. Plants are low and branching, trailing to 1 ft. high and wide, with narrow or lance-shaped leaves ½–2 in. long. Crowded clusters of tiny, four-petaled white flowers attract bees. Native to the Mediterranean. In most areas, blooms from spring to frost. In the Coastal and Tropical South, it may go dormant during hottest period, but flowering will resume when weather cools. Seeds are sometimes included in wildflower

mixes or erosion-control mixes for bare or disturbed earth.

Garden selections are better known than the species. These self-sow too, but seedlings tend to revert to taller, looser growth and bear smaller, paler blossoms than the parent. 'Carpet of Snow' (2–4 in. tall) is a good compact white. 'Rosie O'Day' (2–4 in.) has lavender-pink blooms. 'Snow Crystals' (10 in. high, trailing) and the Clear Crystal series (mounded 10 in. high, 14 in. wide; in white, rose, pink, lavender, peach, lemonade, and violet) are tetraploids whose genetics give them extra vigor and heat resistance. The Stream series grows 8–12 in. high, is heat tolerant, and comes in shades of purple, lavender and white. An increasing number of strains combine many colors in each seed packet. 'Snow Princess', a hybrid, is a trailing white selection that grows 6 in. high. Because it's sterile, it keeps on blooming—even through hot summers as far south as Miami.

CARE

Sweet alyssum is a dependable, easy-to-grow annual that takes almost any soil and blooms from seed in six weeks. If you shear plants back and fertilize by half about four weeks after they come into bloom, new growth will make another crop of flowers, and plants won't become rangy.

LONICERA

HONEYSUCKLE
Caprifoliaceae
Evergreen, semievergreen, deciduous
shrubs and vines

✓ ZONES VARY BY SPECIES

**☼ ☽ FULL SUN OR PARTIAL
SHADE, EXCEPT AS NOTED**

**◐ ◑ MODERATE TO REGULAR
WATER**

Lonicera japonica 'Halliana'

Most honeysuckles are valued
for their clustered or paired,
often fragrant flowers. Blossoms
are tubular in form. Some have
two flaring, unequal lips; others
are trumpets or straight tubes,
sometimes flaring at the mouth
into five equal lobes. Flowers
attract hummingbirds, and the
red or purple berries that follow
provide food for many other
kinds of birds. Blossoms typically
deepen in color after opening,
so clusters contain both pale
and darker blooms. Vining
species climb by twining and
need staking until they are tall
enough to reach a trellis or other
support. As they grow, they may
need to be tied to the support
here and there to distribute the
branches well.

Provide good drainage.
Honeysuckles typically need
some thinning; ideal time for the
job is after bloom. Cut old, straggling honeysuckles to the ground
before spring growth begins;
they will regrow rapidly. Generally free of serious pests, though
aphids sometimes infest them.

L. x brownii. SCARLET TRUM-
PET HONEYSUCKLE. Deciduous
vine. Zones US, MS; USDA 6-7.
Represented in nurseries by its
superior selection 'Dropmore
Scarlet', which climbs to 9–10 ft.
Unscented, bright red flowers

that look like trumpets bloom
from late spring or early summer
until frost. Pairs of triangular blue-
green leaves to about 3 in. long
appear to be joined at the bases.

L. fragrantissima. WINTER
HONEYSUCKLE. Deciduous
shrub, semievergreen in Lower
South. Zones US, MS, LS; USDA
6-8. From China. Longtime
favorite of Southern gardeners,
with arching, rather stiff growth
to 8 ft. tall and at least as wide.
Oval, 1- to 3-in.-long leaves are
dull dark green above, blue-green
beneath. Creamy white, ½-in.-
long, two-lipped flowers bloom in
late winter, early spring; they are
sweetly fragrant but not showy.
Berrylike red fruit. Can be used as
a clipped hedge or a background
plant; bring budded branches
indoors to bloom.

L. x heckrottii. GOLD FLAME
HONEYSUCKLE. Deciduous vine
or small shrub, semievergreen in
Lower and Coastal South. Zones
US, MS, LS; USDA 6-8. Vigorous
grower to 12–15 ft., with oval,
2-in., blue-green leaves. Blooms
profusely from spring to frost.
Clusters of coral-pink buds open
to 1½-in.-long, two-lipped, slightly
fragrant flowers that are bright
coral-pink outside, rich yellow
within. Train as espalier or on wire
along eaves.

L. japonica. JAPANESE
HONEYSUCKLE. Evergreen to
semievergreen vine. Zones US,
MS, LS, CS, TS; USDA 6-11. From
eastern Asia. Beloved for its
fragrant spring flowers, which
yield drops of sweet nectar for
children's tongues, but reviled for
its invasive nature—if unchecked,
it tangles its way through woodlands and throttles small trees.

Deep green, oval leaves to 3 in.
long are held on reddish brown
stems. Two-lipped, 1½-in.-long
blossoms age from white to
yellow; they are followed by small
black berries. Birds eat the berries
and spread seeds everywhere.
Grows very quickly, especially in
the Southeast, and can twine its
way to 30 ft.

Several selections are cultivated. 'Halliana', the most widely
available, resembles the species
and is every bit as weedy. It is
sometimes used as a bank and
ground cover in the Southwest,
where it is somewhat less aggressive. 'Aureoreticulata' features
green leaves netted with yellow.
'Purpurea' offers purple-tinged

green foliage and flowers that
are purple-red on the outside,
white inside.

Although Japanese honey-
suckle does a great job of hiding
chain link fences, it is seldom
appropriate for home gardens. *L.
x heckrottii* and *L. periclymenum*
are just as pretty and far better
behaved.

L. nitida. BOX HONEYSUCKLE.
Evergreen shrub, deciduous in
Upper South. Zones MS, LS, CS;
USDA 7-9. Native to southwestern
China. To 4–6 ft. tall, with densely
leafy branches. Tiny (½-in.), oval,
dark green leaves. Attractive
bronze to plum-colored winter
foliage. Late spring or early summer flowers are straight tubes—
fragrant, creamy white, ½ in. long.
Translucent blue-purple berries.
Grows fast and tends to get un-

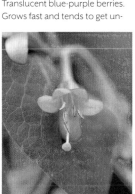

tidy but is easily pruned as hedge
or single plant. Takes salt spray.
'Baggesen's Gold' has golden
foliage in sun. 'Lemon Beauty',
to 4–6 ft. tall and wide, has dark
green leaves edged in shades of
lemon and chartreuse. 'Red Tips',
to 4–6 ft. tall and wide, has deep
raspberry-red new growth that
ages to dark green with red-tinted
tips and edges. 'Silver Beauty',
3–4 ft. tall and wide (possibly
up to 6 ft.), has bright silver leaf
margins.

L. periclymenum. WOOD-
BINE HONEYSUCKLE. Deciduous
vine, semievergreen in Lower
South. Zones US, MS, LS; USDA
6-8. Native to Europe and the
Mediterranean region. Grows 10–
20 ft. tall; resembles *L. japonica*
but is less rampant. Whorls of
2-in.-long, fragrant, two-lipped

TOP: *Lonicera x brownii* 'Dropmore Scarlet'; *L. sempervirens*;
BOTTOM: *L. x heckrottii*

flowers in summer, fall. Blooms of 'Serotina' are purple outside, yellow inside. 'Berries Jubilee' has yellow flowers followed by a profusion of red berries. Heavy-blooming 'Belgica' is less vining, more bushy than most, with purple-flushed white flowers fading to yellow; flowers and red fruit come in large clusters. 'Graham Thomas' has white blossoms that age to copper-tinted yellow. 'Peaches and Cream' is a vibrant, two-tone flower that provides lots of fragrance. 'Scentsation' produces showy yellow flowers that bloom from mid-spring to late summer.

L. pileata. PRIVET HONEY-SUCKLE. Evergreen to semievergreen shrub. Zones US, MS, LS; USDA 6-8. Native to China. Low, spreading plant to 3 ft. tall, with stiff, horizontal branches. Dark green, 1½-in. leaves resemble those of privet (*Ligustrum*). Small, fragrant, tubular white flowers in late spring; translucent violet-purple berries. 'Moss Green' is a low-growing to 2 ft. high and 3 ft. wide. Good bank cover with low-growing euonymus or barberries (*Berberis*). Does well at the seashore. Give part or full shade in Lower South.

L. sempervirens. TRUMPET HONEYSUCKLE. Deciduous twining vine, semievergreen in Coastal South. Zones US, MS, LS, CS; USDA 6-9. Old-time favorite, native to eastern and southern U.S.; can climb 10–20 ft. tall but is shrubby if not given support. From late spring into summer, bears showy, unscented, orange-yellow to scarlet flowers in whorls at branch ends. The trumpet-shaped, 1½- to 2-in.-long blooms are followed by scarlet berries. Oval, 1½- to 3-in.-long leaves are medium green above, bluish green beneath. 'Cedar Lane' (known by the name "coral honeysuckle" in Florida) is a vigorous selection with deep red flowers. 'Alabama Crimson' also has dark red blossoms; 'Magnifica' bears big scarlet flowers marked yellow inside. 'Major Wheeler' is a generous bloomer with good mildew resistance. *L. s. sulphurea* (*L. s.* 'Flava') produces yellow flowers in late spring. 'John Clayton' is more retrained (6–12 ft. high) and known for its prolific bloom of yellow flowers and abundant berries.

LOROPETALUM CHINENSE

CHINESE FRINGE, CHINESE WITCH HAZEL
Hamamelidaceae
Evergreen shrub

🌿 **MS, LS, CS; USDA 7-9**

☀️ ◐ **PARTIAL TO FULL SUN**

💧💧 **MODERATE TO REGULAR WATER**

Loropetalum chinense 'Purple Diamond'

Native to China and Japan. Large, rounded, evergreen shrub to 8–15 ft. tall and wide. Neat, compact habit, with tiers of arching or drooping branches. Roundish, light green leaves are 1–2 in. long; creamy white flowers consisting of four narrow, twisted, inch-long petals appear in clusters at the end of branch tips in late winter and early spring. Sporadic flowering may occur in fall. *L. c. rubrum* has pink flowers and purple-bronze foliage. Good in corner and understory plantings, as a screen, sheared formal hedge, in mixed shrub borders, as a single specimen or espalier. You can also prune away lower branches to make a nice small tree. Deer resistant.

Recently introduced burgundy-leafed, pink-flowered selections of *L. c. rubrum* have taken garden centers by storm; they now share center stage with blue rug junipers (*Juniperus horizontalis* 'Wiltonii') and golden euonymus. To the untrained eye, most are identical and interchangeable. Use them judiciously—too much burgundy is not a good thing.

Selections include the following.

'Burgundy'. Reddish purple new foliage matures to purple-green. Very fast grower; young plants grow flat like cotoneasters the first year, then quickly shoot upward. Deep pink flowers. Grows 10 ft. tall and wide.

'Carolina Moonlight'. Olive-green foliage and white flowers. Compact, 3–4 ft. tall and 4–5 ft. wide.

'Emerald Snow'. Lime-green foliage and white flowers. Compact, 3–4 ft. tall and wide.

'Ever Red'. Darkest burgundy foliage. Bright red flowers. Grows 6 ft. tall and wide.

'Fire Dance'. Ruby-red new leaves mature to reddish purple. Deep pink flowers. Grows 8–10 ft. tall and wide.

'Purple Diamond'. Rich, deep purple leaves all year. Magenta-pink flowers. Grows 4–5 ft. tall and wide.

'Purple Pixie'. Purple foliage on a weeping, spreading plant 1–2 ft. high and 4–5 ft. wide. Pink flowers. Useful ground cover or purple accent in pots, hanging baskets, and window boxes. May drop leaves in cold winters.

'Razzleberri'. Originally named 'Blush'. Leaves emerge bronze-red and age to olive-green. Fuchsia-pink flowers. Grows 10 ft. tall and wide.

'Ruby'. Compact grower to just 4–5 ft. tall and wide. Deep red leaves; bright pink flowers.

'Sizzling Pink'. Similar to 'Burgundy' but with a growth habit that is more horizontal. Grows 4–6 ft. tall and wide.

'Suzanne'. Compact, rounded shrub to 3–4 ft. tall and wide. Small, rounded, reddish maroon leaves. Pink flowers.

'Zhuzhou' ('Zhuzhou Fuchsia'). Upright, fast-growing plant with deep pink flowers. Narrow, elliptical leaves are nearly black. Grows 15 ft. tall and wide. Good selection as a small tree to shape.

CARE

This tough, pest-free plant tolerates heat and drought. Give it acid or neutral, well-drained soil; tends to suffer from chlorosis (yellow leaves with green veins) in alkaline soil. Once established, it grows fast; a transplant from a 1-gallon can will easily grow to 6 ft. in three years.

LUDISIA DISCOLOR

JEWEL ORCHID
Orchidaceae
Terrestrial orchid

🌿 **TS; USDA 10-11; OR HOUSEPLANT**

◐ **BRIGHT INDIRECT LIGHT**

💧 **REGULAR WATER**

Ludisia discolor

If you think all orchids are hard to grow indoors, you haven't tried this one. Native to the forest floors of Indonesia and Malaysia, jewel orchid is prized more for its foliage than for its flowers. The handsome bronze leaves, up to 3 in. long and 1 in. wide, are streaked with parallel red veins. Creeping stems send up leafy rosettes, each of which produces a foot-tall spike of tiny white flowers in winter.

Jewel orchid is best sited in a north- or east-facing window. Shield it from direct midday or afternoon sunlight. Provide well-drained potting soil. Feed every three weeks with a general-purpose liquid houseplant fertilizer diluted to half-strength. Remove flower stalk after blossoms fade. Cut stems are easy to root in water. Outdoors, plant in well-drained soil in a warm, protected spot.

LUNARIA ANNUA

MONEY PLANT, HONESTY

Brassicaceae

Biennial

▧ **US, MS, LS, CS; USDA 6-9**

☼ ◑ **AFTERNOON SHADE IN HOTTEST CLIMATES**

◌◔● **LITTLE TO REGULAR WATER**

Lunaria annua

Native to Europe. Old-fashioned garden plant grown for the translucent, 1¼-in.-wide circles that hang onto flower stalks; these "coins" are all that remains of the ripened seedpods after the outer coverings have dropped with the seeds. Reaches 1½–3 ft. high, 1 ft. wide, with coarse, heart-shaped, tooth-edged leaves. Showy spring flowers resemble wild mustard blooms but are purple or white and larger in size. Plant in an out-of-the-way spot in poor soil, or use in a mixed flower bed where the shining pods can be admired before they are picked for dried arrangements. Tough and persistent; can reseed and become weedy.

LUPINUS

LUPINE

Papilionaceae

Annuals and perennials

▧ **ZONES VARY BY SPECIES**

☼ **FULL SUN**

◌◔● **WATER NEEDS VARY BY SPECIES**

Lupinus havardii

There are hundreds of lupine species, many of them native to the southwestern U.S.; they're found in a wide range of habitats, from alpine rocks to beach sand. Leaves are divided into many leaflets (like fingers of a hand). Sweet pea–shaped flowers are borne in dense spikes at stem ends. Most lupines take poor soil, but hybrids prefer rich, slightly acidic, well-drained soil.

L. hartwegii. Annual. Zones US, MS, LS, CS, TS; USDA 6-11. Native to Mexico. Grows 1½–3 ft. tall, with flowers in shades of blue, white, and pink. Easy to grow from seed sown in place in spring for summer bloom. Moderate water.

L. havardii, L. subcarnosus, L. texensis. BLUEBONNET. Annuals. Zones MS, LS, CS; USDA 7-9. All require poor, dry soil to survive; with regular flower border pampering, these Texas roadside flowers rot. For small areas, set out plants in fall to flower the following April. For meadows, scatter treated seeds (see "Help in the Nick of Time," at right) onto moist ground in September and lightly rake the soil surface; keep soil moist only until seeds germinate. Replant or resow each fall for several years; seed from current year's flowers does not germinate reliably to produce next spring's floral display. Adequate fall and winter rains are necessary to produce spectacular spring show.

L. havardii, Big Bend bluebonnet, is the tallest bluebonnet, reaching 3–4 ft. high; its flowers are very deep blue. *L. subcarnosus,* the state flower of Texas, grows to 1 ft. tall, has sky-blue flowers with a tinge of white. *L. texensis,* Texas bluebonnet, to 1 ft. tall, has dark blue flowers with a white eye that turns red after pollen is no longer viable, signaling bees not to visit plant.

L. hybrids. Perennials often treated as annuals. Zone US; USDA 6. To 4–5 ft. tall, 2 ft. wide. These English-bred hybrid groups are descended from plants native to western America. Their dislike of summer heat and humidity makes them hard to grow in the South, even in the Upper South. Plant them in fall, be grateful for the flowers they produce the following year—and don't expect more than that. Self-sown seedlings won't resemble parents. Regular water.

Russell hybrids—the classic lupines—bloom during late spring or early summer, bearing tall flower spikes in white, cream, yellow, pink, red, orange, blue, purple, or bicolors. Little Lulu and Minarette are small strains—to 1½ ft. high and wide. All Russell hybrids tend to be short lived. They are prone to powdery mildew, so provide good air circulation. Grow from seed or buy nursery plants.

New Generation hybrids have all the merits of the Russell hybrids (from which they were developed), but they are sturdier (needing no staking) and mildew resistant. They also come in a wider range of brighter, more intense colors, including interesting bicolors such as yellow-and-orange combinations. Bloom period is longer, too. Sold as seedling plants.

L. perennis. WILD LUPINE. Perennial. Zones US, MS, LS, CS;

USDA 6-9. Native to eastern U.S. To 2 ft. high, with purple flowers in late spring or early summer. Regular water.

> ## HELP IN THE NICK OF TIME
>
> Lupine seeds are hard coated and often slow to sprout. They will germinate faster if you soak them in hot water or scratch or nick the seed coats with a file before planting.

LYCHEE

Sapindaceae

Evergreen tree

▧ **TS; USDA 10-11**

☼ **FULL SUN**

● **REGULAR WATER**

Lychees

Native to China and known botanically as *Litchi chinensis,* this is a round-topped tree with smooth, gray bark. Grows slowly to 20–40 ft. tall and wide. Leaves consist of three to nine leathery, 3- to 6-in.-long, oval, pointed leaflets that emerge coppery red, then turn dark green.

Inconspicuous flowers in late spring give rise to tasty, walnut-size fruit (variously known as lychees, litchis, or litchi nuts); it is ripe when the leathery rind covering it turns red (in summer and fall). The translucent, white flesh surrounding the central pit is sweet, juicy, and delicious. The fruit must ripen fully on the tree; after harvest, it can be frozen, dried, or stored fresh for up to 5 weeks in the refrigerator (if stored at room temperature, it will deteriorate within 3 days). The most widely grown selections are 'Brewster' (large fruit and seeds, midseason) and 'Mauritius' (medium-size fruit, small seeds, early), although specialty nurseries offer many others.

CARE

Best grown in a frost-free site, although mature trees may withstand temperatures as low as 25°F for several hours. Provide acid, well-drained soil containing plenty of organic matter; mulch thoroughly with pine straw or ground bark after planting. Keep soil constantly moist during periods of active growth. Young trees need little fertilizer, but you should apply chelated iron and garden sulfur if planting in alkaline soil. Lychees do not tolerate salt spray.

LYCHNIS

Caryophyllaceae
Perennials

✀ US, MS, LS; USDA 6-8

☼ ◑ FULL SUN OR LIGHT SHADE

◍ ◍ WATER NEEDS VARY BY SPECIES

Lychnis coronaria

Hardy, old-fashioned garden flowers, all very tolerant of adverse soils. The different kinds vary in appearance, but all offer eye-catching colors in summer. Plants are generally short lived and need to be replaced every few years.

L. alpina. ALPINE CAMPION. From Europe and northeastern North America. Mounding, tufted plant, with narrow, dark green leaves forming a rosette to 6–8 in. tall and wide. In summer, dense clusters of rosy purple flowers rise above the foliage. 'Alba' has white flowers; 'Rosea' bears soft pink blooms. Good edging or rock garden plant. Regular water.

L. arkwrightii. ARKWRIGHT CAMPION. Hybrid of *L. chalcedonica* and *L. haageana*. To 1½ ft. tall, 1 ft. wide, with brown-tinted dark green leaves. Clusters of 1½-in., orange-scarlet flowers. Remove faded blossoms for repeat

bloom. 'Vesuvius' is taller (to 2 ft.), with large orange-red flowers; 'Orange Gnome' ('Orange Zwerg'), sporting bright orange flowers, grows only 5–7 in. tall and wide. Regular water.

L. chalcedonica. MALTESE CROSS. Native to Russia. Loose, open growth to 2–3 ft. high and 1 ft. wide, with hairy leaves and stems. Dense terminal clusters of scarlet, ½-in. flowers with deeply cut petals. Effective in large borders with white-blossomed or gray-foliaged plants. 'Alba' is a white-flowered form. Regular water.

L. coronata. ORANGE CATCHFLY. From Korea and northeast China. Grows 1½–3 ft. tall, 2 ft. wide. Upright stems carry deep green, oval, pointed leaves 2–3 in. long. Flowers in a lovely shade of salmon-pink to apricot-orange are 2–2½ in. wide, held singly or in clusters of three or more. Each petal has frilled edges; a deep central notch; and a long, slender "tooth" along one side. 'Orange Sherbet' has light orange blooms on a compact plant 1 ft. high and wide. Easy to grow from seed, blooming in the first year. Pinch young plants to induce bushiness. Moderate to regular water.

L. coronaria. ROSE CAMPION. From southeastern Europe. Grows to 1½–2½ ft. tall, with attractive white, silky foliage and magenta to crimson flowers that are a little less than an inch across. Effective massed. 'Alba' has white flowers; 'Angel's Blush' bears white blossoms with a deep pink eye. 'Gardeners' World' has double red flowers. Species and selections all self-sow freely if faded flowers are not removed. Moderate water.

L. x haageana. ORANGE CAMPION. Red, orange, salmon, or white flowers carried in clusters of two or three throughout summer. Stems clothed in green leaves reach 1½–2 ft. high; plant grows 1 ft. wide. Dies down shortly after bloom. Mulch to protect against extreme heat or cold. Though a hybrid, it comes fairly true from seed. Regular water. 'Molten Lava' has vivid, orange-red blooms.

L. viscaria. GERMAN CATCH-FLY. From Eurasia. Compact, low, evergreen clumps of grasslike leaves to 5 in. long. Pinkish purple, ½-in. flowers on 1½- to 2-ft. stalks.

'Alba' has white blooms. Foot-high 'Splendens' bears magenta blossoms; 'Splendens Plena' ('Flore Pleno') is similar but has double flowers. Two deep red bloomers are 1½-ft. 'Zulu' and 8-in. *L. v. atropurpurea*. 'Molten Lava' has vivid, orange-red blooms. Moderate to regular water.

LYCIANTHUS RANTONNETII

BLUE POTATO BUSH
Solanaceae
Evergreen shrub

✀ CS, TS; USDA 9-11

☼ ◑ FULL SUN TO PARTIAL SHADE

◍ REGULAR WATER

⬦ ALL PARTS ARE POISONOUS IF INGESTED

Lycianthus rantonnetii 'Variegatum'

From Paraguay and Argentina. As a shrub, it grows to 8–12 ft. tall and 6–10 ft. wide. But it can be staked into a tree form or, with support, grown as a vine to 12–15 ft. or more. Can also be allowed to sprawl as a ground cover. Leaves are bright green, oval; violet-blue, ½- to 1½-in. flowers throughout warm weather, often nearly year-round. Informal, fast growing, not easy to use in tailored landscapes; prune hard to keep it neat. In severe cold, leaf drop is heavy and branch tips may die back. Not browsed by deer. 'Royal Robe' is more compact (to 6–8 ft. high and wide), bears darker purple flowers over a longer season. 'Variegatum' has green leaves edged in white. Formerly known as *Solanum rantonnetii*.

LYCORIS

SPIDER LILY, SURPRISE LILY
Amaryllidaceae
Perennials from bulbs

✀ ZONES VARY BY SPECIES; OR GROW IN POTS

☼ FULL SUN, EXCEPT AS NOTED

◍ REGULAR WATER DURING GROWTH AND BLOOM

Lycoris squamigera

Frequently spotted on old homesites and in cemeteries, most are native to China or Japan. Narrow, strap-shaped leaves appear in spring (or in fall, in mild-winter regions); they remain green until some point in summer, then die down completely. Leafless flower stalks emerge after the foliage disappears. In late summer or early fall, each stalk bears a cluster of blooms with narrow, pointed, petal-like segments and—in some species—projecting, spidery-looking stamens. Blossoms may be funnel shaped or have segments splayed outward or reflexed.

L. aurea. GOLDEN SPIDER LILY, HURRICANE LILY. Zones CS, TS; USDA 9-11; or indoor/outdoor potted plant. Bright yellow blooms to 3–4 in. long.

L. chinensis. YELLOW SPIDER LILY. Zones MS, LS, CS; USDA 7-9. From China and Korea. To 2½ ft. tall, with flat-topped clusters of golden yellow, 3-in. blossoms.

L. x haywardii. Zones MS, LS; USDA 7-8. To 20 in. high. Magenta-pink flowers resemble those of *L. squamigera*, but petals are more deeply divided. Easy to grow.

L. incarnata. Zones US, MS, LS, CS, TS; USDA 6-11. To 20 in. high, with clusters of fragrant, 3-in. flowers that open white and then turn salmon to rose colored;

each petal has a darker stripe running lengthwise down the center.

L. longituba. WHITE SPIDER LILY. Zones MS, LS, CS; USDA 7-9. To 2½ ft. tall, bearing pure white, long-tubed (at least 2-in.) flowers.

L. radiata. SPIDER LILY, HURRICANE LILY. Zones MS, LS, CS; USDA 7-9. The best-known spider lily, and the easiest to grow. Coral-red, 3- to 4-in. flowers with a golden sheen are borne on 1½-ft. stems. 'Alba', known as white spider lily, has white blossoms. 'Fire Engine' has ruffled, red flowers on blackish stems. 'Fireworks' has double, red flowers. Species and selections take light shade. In the Upper South, protect with mulch in winter.

L. sanguinea. Zones US, MS, LS, CS; USDA 6-9. To 2 ft. tall, with 2- to 2½-in., bright red to orange-red flowers.

L. sprengeri. Zones US, MS, LS, CS; USDA 6-9. Rose-pink flowers with striking blue tips. Grows about 12 in. tall.

L. squamigera. MAGIC LILY, SURPRISE LILY, NAKED LADY. Zones US, MS, LS, CS; USDA 6-9. Clusters of funnel-shaped, 3-in., fragrant, pink or rosy lilac flowers on 2-ft. stems. Hardiest species, old favorite.

CARE

Plant in late summer, setting bulbs in well-drained soil about 1 ft. apart. Keep tops of bulb necks at or just above soil surface—except in coldest part of range, where tops of necks should be just under surface. Water regularly while plants are growing and again when flower stalks emerge. Disturb clumps (after bloom) only when you want to move them or divide them to increase a planting. Beyond hardiness range, grow spider lilies in containers, and overwinter them indoors.

LYONIA LUCIDA
FETTERBUSH
Ericaceae
Evergreen shrub

⬩ **MS, LS, CS; USDA 7-9**

◑ ● **PARTIAL TO FULL SHADE**

💧 **REGULAR WATER**

Lyonia lucida

Native to moist woodlands from Virginia to Florida, west to Louisiana. Open, arching, suckering shrub to 3–5 ft. high and wide. Glossy, bright green leaves to 3 in. long are broadly oval and pointed, reminiscent of *Leucothoe* foliage. Clusters of pale pink, urn-shaped, ¼-in. flowers emerge from leaf axils all along the stems in spring. Rather finicky—requires well-drained, acid soil and will not tolerate drought. Best used in a woodland garden or naturalized area. 'Morris Minor' is a compact, small-leafed selection.

THE FLOWERS OF FETTERBUSH HAVE A SWEET SMELL REMINISCENT OF HONEY.

LYSIMACHIA
Primulaceae
Perennials

⬩ **US, MS, LS; USDA 6-8, EXCEPT AS NOTED**

☼ ◑ **FULL SUN OR PARTIAL SHADE, EXCEPT AS NOTED**

💧💧 **MODERATE TO REGULAR WATER**

Lysimachia nummularia 'Aurea'

Most of these perennials are vigorous spreaders with a penchant for conquering new territory, especially in moist, fertile soil. Keep them under surveillance to ensure they don't invade choicer plantings. Blossoms are yellow or white and appear in summer, except as noted.

L. barystachys. Native to eastern Russia and Asia. To 2 ft. high, 1½ ft. wide, with narrow, green leaves to 3 in. long. Small white flowers come in foot-long spikes that start out horizontal and gradually turn upright.

L. ciliata. FRINGED LOOSE-STRIFE. Zones US, MS, LS, CS; USDA 6-9. Native to northeastern U.S. Erect clump to 4 ft. tall, 2 ft. wide, with narrow, green leaves to 6 in. long. Nodding, 1-in., yellow flowers with red-brown centers appear singly or in loose clusters in upper leaf joints. 'Firecracker' is similar but has reddish leaves.

L. clethroides. GOOSENECK LOOSESTRIFE. Native to China, Korea, Japan. To 3 ft. tall, quickly spreading as wide or wider. Erect stems with pointed, olive-green leaves to 5 in. long. Flower spikes densely packed with tiny white blossoms are 6–8 in. long, arched like a goose's neck. Extremely aggressive spreader; plant only in confined beds. 'Geisha' has leaves edged in creamy yellow.

L. congestiflora. GOLDEN GLOBES. Zones MS, LS, CS; USDA 7-9. Native to China. Mat-forming plant grows to 4 in. high and 1 ft. or wider. Oval, green leaves to 2 in. long; upturned yellow flowers, ½ in. across, in leafy terminal clusters. Blooms from spring to summer. Good in a rock garden or as ground cover in naturalized areas. 'Eco Dark Satin' has yellow blooms with red centers. 'Outback Sunset' has red-tinged leaves with yellow variegation and yellow flowers with red centers. 'Persian Chocolate' has brownish purple leaves.

L. ephemerum. Native to southwestern Europe. Leathery, gray-green leaves to 6 in. long form a neat clump to 3 ft. tall and 1 ft. wide. Slender clusters of white, ½-in.-wide, long-lasting flowers. Not invasive.

L. nummularia. CREEPING JENNY, MONEYWORT. Native to Europe; naturalized in eastern North America. Grows 4–8 in. high and spreads to 2 ft. or more, rooting as it goes. Forms an attractive mat of roundish, light green, 1-in. leaves. Yellow flowers about 1 in. across appear singly in leaf joints. Best use is in corners or containers where it need not be restrained. Also good in rock garden or as casual ground cover. Will spill from wall, hanging basket. 'Aurea' has bright yellow leaves that combine especially well with dark-foliaged plants such as black mondo grass (*Ophiopogon planiscapus* 'Nigrescens'); it requires a shady location.

L. punctata. YELLOW LOOSE-STRIFE. Native to central Europe, Asia Minor. To 3 ft. tall, spreading to 2 ft. or more by underground stems. Narrow, green leaves to 3 in. long are borne in whorls on erect stems; inch-wide yellow flowers, also in whorls, appear on top third of stems. Looks nice in masses or mixed borders. 'Alexander' has leaves with gold edges that fade to cream as the weather warms; it grows less vigorously than the basic species and reaches about 2 ft. tall. 'Golden Alexander', to 2 ft. high and wide, has yellow-edged leaves.

M

MACFADYENA UNGUIS-CATI

CAT'S CLAW, YELLOW TRUMPET VINE

Bignoniaceae

Semievergreen vine

🌿 LS, CS, TS; USDA 8-11

☼☽ **FULL SUN OR PARTIAL SHADE**

💧 **MODERATE WATER**

Macfadyena unguis-cati

Vigorous vine native from Mexico and West Indies to Uruguay. It climbs high (to 25–40 ft.) and fast by hooked, clawlike, forked tendrils. Leaves divided into two oval, glossy, green leaflets to 2 in. long. Blooms in early spring, bearing yellow trumpets to 2 in. long. Vigorous; puts down roots where stems touch ground. Clings to any support—stone, wood, tree trunk. Good for covering chain-link fence. Tends to produce leaves and flowers at stem ends; after bloom, prune hard to stimulate new growth lower down. Loses all of its leaves in cold winters. May be invasive in the Coastal and Tropical South.

MACLEAYA

PLUME POPPY

Papaveraceae

Perennials

🌿 US, MS, LS; USDA 6-8

☼☽ **FULL SUN OR LIGHT SHADE**

💧 **REGULAR WATER**

Macleaya cordata

These tall perennials from China and Japan are sometimes still listed as *Bocconia*, a name properly belonging to their shrubby tropical relatives. The two species described below resemble each other. Both have creeping rhizomes; tall, erect stems; large, deeply lobed leaves much like those of edible fig (*Ficus carica*); and small flowers in large, branching clusters. These plants have a tropical look, and their value lies in size and structure rather than flower color. Can be invasive if not controlled; plant among shrubs rather than amid delicate perennials. Resist deer.

M. cordata. PLUME POPPY. To 7–8 ft. tall, with 3-ft.-wide clumps of grayish green, 10-in. leaves and clouds of tiny white to beige flowers. Considered somewhat less invasive than *M. microcarpa*.

M. microcarpa. Resembles *M. cordata* but has pinkish beige flowers. Flowers of 'Kelway's Coral Plume' are more decidedly pink.

MACLURA POMIFERA

OSAGE ORANGE, BOIS D'ARC

Moraceae

Deciduous tree

🌿 US, MS, LS, CS; USDA 6-9

☼ **FULL SUN**

◐💧💧 **LITTLE OR NO WATER TO REGULAR WATER**

Maclura pomifera

An old Southern favorite, native from Arkansas to Oklahoma and Texas. Fast growth to 60 ft. tall and 40 ft. wide (though often smaller), with spreading, open habit. Orange-brown, fissured bark. Wood is very hard, orange in color, and highly resistant to rot. Glossy, medium green leaves are oval and pointed, to 5 in. long. Young branches are thorny, mature ones less so. If a male tree is present, female trees may bear inedible, 4-in.-wide fruit that resembles bumpy, yellow-green oranges and is prized for holiday decorations.

Withstands heat, cold, wind, and almost any kind of soil—acid or alkaline, wet or dry, fertile or terrible. Easy to transplant; easy to propagate by seed or cuttings. Makes a good windbreak or informal screen and is often planted in hedgerows. If people will be walking or sitting beneath the tree, always plant a male selection: A heavy, hard fruit falling from a high branch can knock a person silly. Two thornless male selections are worth seeking out. 'White Shield' features beautiful, lustrous, dark green leaves and grows especially rapidly, up to 5 ft. per year. 'Wichita' forms an upright, spreading tree with a dense canopy.

MAGNOLIA

Magnoliaceae

Deciduous and evergreen trees and shrubs

🌿 **ZONES VARY BY SPECIES**

☼☽ **FULL SUN OR PARTIAL SHADE**

💧 **REGULAR WATER**

Magnolia stellata

This large group of magnificent flowering trees includes species native to the South as well as many imported from Asia. They range in size from shrubby to enormous. Some are evergreen, while most are deciduous. Showy flowers appear in late winter, spring, or summer. Colors include white, pink, rose, red, purple, yellow, and coral. Many are powerfully fragrant. New selections and hybrids arrive every year. You'll find many at local nurseries, but mail-order nurseries have a wider selection.

EVERGREEN MAGNOLIAS. Our iconic Southern magnolia (*M. grandiflora*) is the first one of this type that comes to mind. The state flower of Mississippi and Louisiana, it combines huge, fragrant, white blossoms with large, glossy leaves. Few trees can match its year-round beauty, but it does have drawbacks. Unnamed seedlings often take 10 years or more after planting to start blooming. Dense shade and shallow roots make it impossible to grow grass beneath the canopy, and the roots often lift and crack pavement if the tree is planted between sidewalk and curb. Leaves drop 365 days a year. And since this native tree grows as wide as 40 ft., it takes up a lot of space.

A smaller Southern native, sweet bay (*M. virginiana*) is easier to fit into most gardens. Though mostly deciduous in the Upper and Middle South, it's evergreen in the Lower and Coastal South and more cold hardy than *M. grandiflora*.

New entries to this group are plants previously listed under the genus *Michelia*. These trees and shrubs hail from China and the Himalayas and are generally less cold hardy than other evergreen magnolias. They're renowned for their profuse, wonderfully fragrant flowers, which are borne among their leaves as opposed to the ends of the branches.

M. champaca (*Michelia champaca*). CHAMPACA. Shrub or tree. Zones CS, TS; USDA 9-11. To 10–20 ft. tall and broad. Glossy, bright green, 10-in. leaves. Orange-yellow, 3-in. flowers with up to 20 segments are borne intermittently throughout the year, most often in winter and summer; their perfume is legendary. 'Alba' (*M. alba*) has white flowers.

M. doltsopa (*Michelia doltsopa*). Tree. Zones CS, TS; USDA 9-11. To 90 ft. tall in its native Himalayas; closer to 40 ft. tall in the South. Varies from bushy (nearly as wide as high) to narrow and upright (about half as broad as tall). Choose plants for desired form, then prune to shape. Thin-textured, leathery, dark green leaves 3–8 in. long, 1–3 in. wide. In winter, furry brown buds open to blossoms ranging from cream colored to white, with a slight green tinge at the base; they are 5–7 in. across, with 12 to 16 segments, each 1 in. wide.

M. figo (*Michelia figo*). BANANA SHRUB. Shrub. Zones LS, CS, TS; USDA 8-11. Slow growing to 6–8 ft. tall (possibly to 15 ft.) and about two-thirds as wide. Densely clothed with glossy, leathery leaves. Plant blooms most heavily in spring but produces scattered flowers throughout summer. Blossoms are 1½ in. wide, creamy yellow with a thin, brownish purple border on each segment. Notable feature is the powerful, fruity fragrance, like that of ripe bananas; the perfume is strongest in a warm, wind-free spot. Choice plant for entry or patio. 'Port Wine' has rose to maroon flowers.

M. x foggii (*Michelia x foggi*). Shrub. Zones CS, TS; USDA 9-11. Group of hybrids between *M. figo* and *M. doltsopa*. 'Allspice' grows 15–18 ft. tall, 6–8 ft. wide,

with glossy, dark green foliage; from spring to summer bears fruity-scented, 1½-in., light yellow flowers bordered in maroon. 'Jack Fogg', about 18 ft. tall and 6–8 ft. wide, has fragrant spring flowers of white, with each segment bordered in purplish pink.

M. grandiflora. SOUTHERN MAGNOLIA. US, MS, LS, CS; USDA 6-9. Classic Southern tree. Pure white blooms, aging to buff; large (8–10 in. across), powerfully fragrant. Species and its selections bloom throughout. Useful street or lawn tree, big container plant, or wall or espalier plant. Named seedlings vary greatly in size, shape, and blooming. Grafted named plants usually bloom at younger age. Grows to 80 ft. tall and 60 ft. wide. Can grow as a multitrunked tree. Glossy, leathery leaves. Attracts birds. Twig borers can be a cosmetic problem, causing branch tips to die and fall off.

'Alta'. Compact, columnar to 20 ft. tall and 9 ft. wide in 10 years, eventually almost twice that. Slow growing, good for small spaces, as screen, or on streets. Glossy, green leaves with rusty undersides.

'Bracken's Brown Beauty'. Pyramidal to 35 ft. tall and 15 ft. wide. Hardier than most other selections. Flowers are smaller than species but still showy. Compact, full shape. Lustrous, dark green leaves are rusty brown underneath. A top selection.

'D. D. Blanchard'. A handsome pyramidal selection to 50 ft. tall or more and 25–35 ft. wide. Lustrous dark green leaves are orange-toned brown on undersides.

'Edith Bogue'. A shapely, vigorous tree, 35 ft. tall and 20 ft. wide, and one of the hardiest selections of *M. grandiflora*; has withstood –24°F. Excellent for the Upper South but not a top choice elsewhere. Keep it out of strong winds. Young plants are slower to come into heavy bloom than some other selections.

'Little Gem'. Slow growing to 20–25 ft. tall and 10–15 ft. wide. Small (5- to 6-in.-wide) flowers from spring through late summer (fewer blooms form during midsummer heat). Narrow form makes it good in a container, as an espalier, or in a confined area. Blooms at very young age. Half-size leaves are dark green above, rusty beneath. Reportedly

less hardy than the species. Quite susceptible to twig borers.

'Majestic Beauty'. Very large flowers (to 1 ft. across). Vigorous, dense-branching street or shade tree of broadly pyramidal form grows to 35–50 ft. tall and 20 ft. wide. Leaves are exceptionally long, broad, and heavy. Most luxuriant of the Southern magnolias.

'St. Mary'. Usually grows to 20 ft. tall; much larger in old age. A heavy producer of 8- to 10-in. flowers on small tree. Fine where standard-size magnolia would grow too large and too fast. Left

alone, it will form a big, dense bush. Staked and pruned, it makes a small tree. Good plant for containers and espalier.

'Teddy Bear'. Compact, upright to 16–20 ft. tall and 10–12 ft. high. Good for small spaces or as screen. Glossy green leaves with rusty undersides.

'Timeless Beauty'. A natural hybrid between *M. grandiflora* and *M. virginiana*. Creamy white, fragrant flowers to 10 in. wide. Blooms in spring and summer. Extremely dense crown, to 15–20 ft. tall and 20–25 ft. wide, with spreading branches.

TOP: *Magnolia grandiflora*; *M. x soulangiana*; MIDDLE: *M. x loebneri* 'Merrill'; *M. figo*; BOTTOM: *M. virginiana*; *M. stellata* 'Centennial'

M. virginiana. SWEET BAY. US, MS, LS, CS; USDA 6-9. Creamy white, fragrant, nearly globular blossoms are 2–3 in. wide. Late spring to late summer. Prefers moist, acid soil. Grows in swamps in eastern U.S. Deciduous shrub in the upper South; semievergreen to evergreen elsewhere. Multi-stemmed. Grows 10–20 ft tall and 2 ft. wide but can reach upwards of 40 ft. tall. Leaves bright green above, nearly white beneath. Twigs and branches are bright green.

'Henry Hicks' is narrow and upright, 40–50 ft. tall and 15–25 ft. wide. Stays evergreen into the upper South.

'Moonglow' ('Jim Wilson') is a bit hardier and more upright (35–40 ft. tall, 15–18 ft. wide) than the species, with glossy, dark green leaves. Grows fast and starts blooming young.

M. v. australis. SOUTHERN SWEET BAY. MS, LS, CS, TS; USDA 7-11. White, lemon-scented blossoms, 2–4 in. wide. Late spring to summer. Single trunked with upright, open habit; glossy green, silver-backed leaves. Grows to 45–50 ft. tall and 15–20 ft. wide. Evergreen to deciduous. Gets much larger in woodland setting, sometimes to 80 ft. tall.

'Green Shadow' is an oval, hardy selection to 30 ft. high and half as wide. Remains evergreen into the Upper South.

'Sweet Thing' is dwarf and compact to 12 ft. high and about half as wide. Can be grown as a hedge or screen.

'Tensaw' is compact, upright, growing to 10–20 ft. tall and half as wide with smaller leaves.

DECIDUOUS MAGNOLIAS. This class runs the gamut from those grown for tulip- or lily-shaped spring flowers (*M. acuminata subcordata*, *M. denudata*, *M. lilifora*, *M. x soulangiana*) to those with star-shaped spring flowers (*M. x loebneri*, *M. stellata*) to those grown principally for their large, imposing leaves (*M. acuminata*, *M. macrophylla*, *M. tripetela*). All are hardy, adaptable, and easy to grow. They range in size from large shrubs to big shade trees.

A drawback to spring bloomers in the South is that some, principally *M. denudata*, *M. stellata*, and *M. x soulangiana*, bloom so early during mild winters that late freezes brown and kill the flowers. When shopping for selections of these species, choose those that bloom later in spring. We've

noted in the descriptions the ones that do. *M. acumina*, *M. macrophylla*, and *M. tripetala* are native to the South.

M. acuminata. CUCUMBER TREE. US, MS, LS; USDA 6-8. Grows 60–80 ft. tall and 30 ft. wide. Greenish yellow flowers to 3½ in. wide; not conspicuous. Appear after leaves in late spring, summer. Handsome reddish seed capsules with red seeds. Dense shade or lawn tree. Dislikes hot, dry winds. 'Brenda' bears deep yellow blooms on a compact, rounded tree, 12 ft. tall and wide. 'Koban Dori' is a smaller selection, to 15–20 ft. tall, with canary-yellow flowers. *M. a. subcordata* is shrubbier (25–35 ft. tall by 20–30 ft. wide) with larger, showier blooms with mild lemony scent. Blossoms appear as leaves expand. *M.a.s.* 'Miss Honeybee' has larger, pale yellow flowers.

M. denudata (*M. heptapeta*). YULAN MAGNOLIA. US, MS, LS, CS; USDA 6-9. Fragrant white flowers, sometimes tinged purple at base. Blossoms are erect; somewhat tulip shaped, 5–6 in. long, spreading to 6–7 in. Early bloom on base branches; often a few flowers appear in summer. Good cut flower. Tends toward irregular form; good against dark background or open sky in informal garden or at woodland edge. Grows 35 ft. tall and 30 ft. wide. 'Gere' blooms late, avoiding frosts. 'Double Diamond' has more petals than species.

M. liliflora (*M. quinquepeta*). LILY MAGNOLIA. US, MS, LS; USDA 6-8. Tulip-shaped flowers 3–5 in. wide are white on the inside, purplish outside. Blooms over long spring, summer season. Grows 12 ft. tall and 15 ft. wide. Good for shrub border; strong vertical effect in big flower border. Spreads slowly by suckering. Leaves 4–6 in. long. Blooms of 'Gracilis', 'Nigra', and 'O'Neill' are dark purplish red outside, pink inside.

M. Kosar-De Vos hybrids (Little Girl series). US, MS, LS; USDA 6-8. Hybrids between *M. liliiflora* 'Nigra' and *M. stellata* 'Rosea'; bred to bloom later than *M. stellata*, thus avoiding frost damage. Star-shaped flowers range from deep to pale purple (sometimes with pink or white interior), depending on selection. Trees bloom in spring before leaf-out; sporadic rebloom in sum-

mer. Erect, shrubby growers to 12 ft. tall and 15 ft. wide. Selections bear girls' names such as 'Ann' (deep purple-pink), 'Betty' (rose-pink), 'Jane' (red-purple, white inside), and 'Susan' (purplish red). Use in shrub-border or singly in lawn. Excellent performers.

M. x loebneri. LOEBNER MAGNOLIA. US, MS, LS; USDA 6-8. Hybrids between *M. kobus* and *M. stellata* that grow slowly to 12–15 ft. tall (can reach 50 ft. tall) and wide. Narrow, strap-shaped flower segments similar to those of *M. stellata*, but generally fewer and somewhat longer and wider. Blooms 4–6 in. wide appear before leaves in midspring. Some selections are fragrant. 'Ballerina', white with faint pink blush, and taller, pure white 'Spring Snow' are both fragrant. Very lightly scented are 'Leonard Messel', with pink blooms from darker buds, and 'Merrill' ('Dr. Merrill'), a vigorous, free-flowering, white-blossomed form. Use in lawn, shrub border, at woodland edge.

M. macrophylla. BIGLEAF MAGNOLIA. US, MS, LS, CS; USDA 6-9. Fragrant white flowers to 16 in. across in late spring and early summer, after leaf-out. Showy tree with leaves 1–3 ft. long and 9–12 in. wide. Grows slowly to 30–50 ft. tall and 20–30 ft. wide. Needs to stand alone. Be sure to give it some shade. Old Southern favorite. *M. m. ashei* is a shrubbier version of bigleaf magnolia, forming a 10- to 20-ft.-tall by 15-ft.-wide, multistemmed plant. Creamy white flowers may be spotted with red. Valuable for its tropical effect where space is limited. Very hardy.

M. sieboldii. OYAMA MAGNOLIA. US, MS; USDA 6-7. Grows 6–15 ft. tall and wide; good choice for small gardens. Leaves are 3–6 in. long. Blooms from late spring through late summer. Flower buds resembling white Japanese lanterns open into cup-shaped, 4-in.-wide, fragrant, white blossoms centered with crimson stamens; bright pink seedpods follow. Nice planted on a hill, where you can look up into the nodding flowers. Best in partial shade. 'Colossus' has larger, semidouble to double blooms. 'Harold Epstein' has semidouble flowers, which are sometimes fully double in late summer to fall. 'Michiko Renge' bears semidouble flowers.

ABOVE: Magnolia x soulangiana

M

M. x soulangiana. SAUCER MAGNOLIA, TULIP TREE. US, MS, LS, CS; USDA 6-9. White to pink or purplish red, fragrant flowers variable in form and size (5–10 in. wide). Blooms from late winter into spring, both before leaves emerge and as they open. Grows to 25 ft. tall and wide. Good lawn plant; good anchor plant in big container plantings. Medium green, rather coarse-looking leaves 4–6 in. long or longer. Seedlings highly variable; look for named selections (especially later-blooming ones for frost-prone regions).

'Alba Superba' ('Alba'). Purple-suffused buds open to large, nearly pure white flowers. Early blooming. Rather more upright and slightly taller than most selections.

'Alexandrina'. Blooms are deep purplish pink outside, white inside, to 10 in. across. Subject to bloom damage in late freezes. Large, rather heavy leaves.

'Black Tulip'. Bears large, goblet-shaped blooms of deep wine-red. Slender, upright grower (30 ft. tall, 15 ft. wide). Excellent for small gardens. In mild climates, can be grown in containers when young. Can be pruned as a hedge.

'Brozzonii'. White blossoms very slightly flushed purplish rose at base; 8 in. across. Late. One of the most handsome white-flowered magnolias. Vigorous tree.

'Lennei'. Bears very large, globlet-shaped blossoms that are deep purple outside, white inside. Spreading, vigorous plant. Late bloom helps it escape frosts. 'Lennei Alba' (*M. lennei* 'Alba') is similar but with earlier, pure white, slightly smaller blooms.

'Lilliputian'. Grows to just 18 ft. tall and 10–15 ft. wide. Good where a smaller magnolia is called for. Flowers are pink outside, white inside, somewhat smaller than those of other selections. Late blooming.

'Rustica Rubra'. Bears large, 8-in.-wide, cup-shaped, deep reddish purple flowers. Blooms somewhat past midseason. Big (6-in.) dark rose seedpods. Vigorous grower for large areas. More treelike than many selections.

M. stellata. STAR MAGNOLIA. US, MS, LS; USDA 6-8. White flowers to 3 in. across, with 12–18 narrow, strap-shaped segments. Profuse bloom comes very early—late winter to early spring,

before leafout. Some selections are fragrant.

Slow growing, shrubby to 10 ft. tall and 20 ft. wide. Use for borders, entryway gardens, edge of woods. Plant this early bloomer where you can see flowers from indoors. Quite hardy, but flowers often nipped by frost in colder part of range. Fine texture in twig, leaf. Fair yellow-and-brown fall leaf color.

'Centennial'. Bears white blossoms faintly marked pink, 5 in. across, with 40–50 segments. It's like an improved 'Water Lily'.

'Dawn'. Has white flowers with 25 or more segments, each with a longitudinal pink stripe.

'Jane Platt'. Grows a little bigger than the species (12–15 ft. tall by 10–12 ft. wide) and has rich pink, 4- to 5-in. blossoms with 40–50 segments.

'Rosea'. PINK STAR MAGNOLIA. Has pink buds; flowers open pink-flushed white, age to plain white. Various plants are sold under this name.

'Royal Star'. Grows quickly to 18–20 ft. tall and 15 ft. wide, with fragrant white blooms with 25–30 segments. It blooms 2 weeks later than species.

'Rubra'. Bears rosy pink blooms to 5 in. across and is more treelike in form than other selections.

'Water Lily'. Has pink buds opening to very fragrant white blossoms to 5 in. across, with 40–50 segments. Blooms later and is faster growing than most star magnolias.

M. tripetela. UMBRELLA MAGNOLIA. US, MS, LS; USDA 6-8. Greenish white blossoms are up to 10 in. across with purple stamens and heavy fragrance. Grows 10–35 ft. tall and 15–20 ft. wide. Huge leaves cluster at the ends on the branches. Vigorous and unkempt, with open and irregular crown; difficult to site in the garden. Large red seedpods.

NEW COLOR MAGNOLIAS. As if the blooms of older deciduous magnolias weren't spectacular enough, breeders have been working hard to create even more dazzling forms with amazing new colors—yellow, coral, salmon, red, and blackish purple. Doing so usually demands complex crosses of multiple species, such as *M. acuminata*, *M. liliflora*, *M. sprengeri*, as well as their selections.

HOW TO GROW MAGNOLIAS

LOCATION For any magnolia, pick planting site carefully. Virtually all types are hard to move once established, and many grow quite large. Southern magnolia (*M. grandiflora*) is good for planting at the beach, though not on dunes. Sweet bay (*M. virginiana*) tolerates wet soil. The species and selections listed here are adapted to a wide range of growing conditions and are easy for most gardeners to grow.

Magnolias never look their best when crowded, and they may be severely damaged by digging around their roots. Larger deciduous sorts are most attractive standing alone against a background that will display their flowers at bloom time and show off their strongly patterned, usually gray limbs and big, fuzzy flower buds in winter. Small deciduous magnolias show up well in large flower or shrub borders and make choice ornaments in Asian-style gardens. Most magnolias are excellent lawn trees; try to provide a good-size grass-free area around the trunk, and don't plant under the tree.

SOIL The best soil for magnolias is fairly rich, well drained, and neutral to slightly acid; if necessary, add generous amounts of organic matter when planting. They will grow in somewhat alkaline soil but may develop chlorosis (yellow leaves with green veins).

PLANTING Balled-and-burlapped plants are available in late winter and early spring; container plants are sold all year. Do not set plants lower than their original soil level. Stake single-trunked or very heavy plants to prevent them from being rocked by wind, which will tear the thick, fleshy, sensitive roots. To avoid damaging the roots, set stakes in planting hole before placing tree. Prevent soil compaction around root zone by keeping foot traffic to a minimum. Prune only when absolutely necessary.

MULCHING At least in the early years, keep a cooling mulch over the root area.

WATERING Irrigate deeply and thoroughly, but don't waterlog the soil or the tree will drown. Only *M. virginiana* can take constantly wet soil.

FERTILIZING Treat chlorosis with iron chelates. Feed trees if new growth is scanty or weak, or if you see significant dieback despite adequate watering and drainage. Use a controlled-release product; magnolias are very susceptible to salt damage from overfertilizing, resulting in burned leaf edges.

PRUNING Prune as little as possible. For deciduous magnolias, best time is after bloom; for evergreen kinds, do the job before the spring growth flush. Best method is to remove the entire twig or limb right to its base. Cuts on deciduous kinds are often slow to heal, so prune these only when necessary to correct plant's shape, eliminate or cut back wayward branches, or remove lower limbs from trunk as tree gains height.

CHALLENGES Magnolias seldom have pest or disease problems. Twig borers and ambrosia beetles have caused serious cosmetic damage in certain areas. Consult your local Cooperative Extension Office for control options.

'Ambrosia'. US, MS, LS, CS; USDA 6-9. Multicolored flowers are yellow with green shading and washed with pink. Grows 15-20 ft. tall.

'Athene'. US, MS, LS, CS; USDA 6-8. Large (8–10 in.) cup-and-saucer-shaped blooms; rosy purple at base, shading to pale pink, with ivory white interior. Richly fragrant. Grows 18–25 ft. tall and

wide. Moderate to fast growth. Flowers well when young.

'Black Beauty'. US, MS, LS, CS; USDA 6-9. Tulip-shaped flowers are dark purple outside, white inside. Blooms in late spring, escaping frost damage. Grows 15–25 ft. tall and 15 ft. wide.

'Butterflies'. US, MS, LS, CS; USDA 6-9. Produces many 4- to 5-in., light yellow flowers with red stamens.

Blooms in midspring, before leaves emerge. Upright and pyramidal when young; later spreading. Grows 20 ft. tall and 15 ft. wide. Leaves 8 in. long, medium to dark green, sparsely hairy. Very hardy.

'Coral Lake'. US, MS, LS, CS; USDA 6-9. Large (7 in. across), unique blossoms in a blend of coral-pink tones shading into vertical yellow stripes. Blooms late but before leaves expand. Grows 20–25 ft. tall and 8–10 ft. wide. Very upright growth habit.

'Daphne'. US, MS, LS, CS; USDA 6-9. Long-lasting, deep yellow blooms held above the foliage. Reportedly one of the best yellow magnolias. Upright tree 10–20 ft. tall.

'Daybreak'. US, MS, LS, CS; USDA 6-9. Huge (8–10 in.), very fragrant, bright rose-pink flowers. Blooms in late spring, escaping frost damage. Narrow form to 18 ft. tall and 4 ft. wide; useful in small lots, side yards.

'Elizabeth'. US, MS, LS; USDA 6-8. Fragrant, soft yellow flowers, 6–7 in. wide. Color is paler in mild-winter areas. Blossoms appear before or with the leaves. Grows to at least 40 ft. tall and 20 ft. wide as single-trunked tree or multitrunked shrub-tree. Hardy.

'Flamingo'. US, MS, LS, CS; USDA 6-9. Coral-pink blossoms, up to 10–12 in. wide. Pyramidal tree, 18–20 ft. tall, 8 ft. wide.

'Galaxy'. US, MS, LS, CS; USDA 6-9. Abundant bright red-purple, slightly fragrant, goblet-shaped blossoms to 10 in. across. Blooms in midspring, before leaves emerge but usually after last frost. Fast-growing, broadly conical tree to 40 ft. tall and 25 ft. wide.

'Genie'. US, MS, LS, CS; USDA 6-9. Blackish red buds open to dark maroon blossoms; curled edges are lighter magenta, 10 in. wide. Flowers appear before leaves, repeat in summer and are lightly fragrant. Grows 10–13 tall and 5 ft. wide.

'Golden Gift'. US, MS, LS, CS; USDA 6-9. Deep yellow, 2- to 5-in.-wide blooms produced over a long period in spring. Grows 8–15 ft. tall and 5–10 ft. wide.

'Rose Marie'. US, MS, LS; USDA 6-8. Large (9-in.-wide), deep pink blossoms with lighter interior; appear after the leaves. Light lemony fragrance. Grows 8–10 ft. tall and 8 ft. wide.

'Royal Splendor'. US, MS, LS, CS; USDA 6-9. Long season of reddish pink blooms with lighter pink interior. Grows 15–20 ft. tall, half as wide.

'Sunspire'. US, MS, LS, CS; USDA 6-9. Medium yellow blooms appear before the leaves but later in the season; long-lasting. Narrow, columnar tree, 15–20 ft. tall, half as wide.

'Vulcan'. US, MS, LS, CS; USDA 6-9. Showy, ruby-red blossoms to 10–12 in. across. Flowers borne in tree's younger years may be smaller and paler than those on older trees. Blooms in spring, before leaf-out. Open form when young, becoming more rounded with age. Grows 25 ft. tall and wide.

'Woodsman'. US, MS, LS, CS; USDA 6-9. Multicolored blossoms in blended shades of yellow, green, and pink appear after leaves. Grows 25–30 ft. tall and 20 ft. wide.

'Yellow Bird'. US, MS, LS, CS; USDA 6-9. Deepest yellow color of the yellow hybrids. Slight green tinge at base of erect, 3-in.-long flower segments. Blooms for 2–3 weeks in early to midspring, as leaves emerge. Upright and pyramidal when young, broadly oval when mature. Grows 40 ft. tall and 20 ft. wide. Furrowed bark.

MAHONIA
Berberidaceae
Evergreen shrubs

✎ ZONES VARY BY SPECIES

☼ ◐ ● EXPOSURE NEEDS VARY BY SPECIES

◔ ◕ WATER NEEDS VARY BY SPECIES

Mahonia aquifolium

These useful and easy-to-grow plants remind many people of holly (*Ilex*), though they're closely related to barberry (*Berberis*). Handsome, typically spiny leaves are divided into leaflets. Showy yellow flowers are borne in dense, rounded or spikelike clusters in late winter or spring. Blooms are followed by berrylike blue, blue-black, or red fruit that attracts birds. Prune to reduce size or lankiness, cutting selected stems to the ground or to a node. Avoid planting too close to walkways and sitting areas, where prickly foliage might snag passersby. Generally pest free and seldom browsed by deer. Provide well-drained soil.

M. aquifolium. OREGON GRAPE HOLLY. Zones US, MS, LS; USDA 6-8. Native from British Columbia to Northern California. Erect growth to 6 ft. or taller; spreads by underground stems to 5 ft. wide. Leaves 4–10 in. long, with five to nine very spiny-toothed, oval, 1- to 2½-in. leaflets that are glossy green in some forms, dull green in others. Young growth is ruddy or bronzy; scattered mature red leaves. Purplish or bronzy leaves in winter, especially in Upper South or where plants are grown in full sun. Spring flowers in 2- to 3-in. clusters along stems; edible blue-black fruit with a powdery coating (makes good jelly).

'Compactum' grows 2–3 ft. tall and wide and spreads freely to make broad colonies. New leaves glossy, light to coppery green; mature leaves matte, medium green. 'King's Ransom' is an upright grower to 5–6 ft. tall and 4–5 ft. wide; dark bluish green leaves turn red-purple in winter. 'Orange Flame', 2 ft. tall and 3 ft. wide, has bronzy orange new growth and glossy green mature leaves that turn wine red in winter.

Oregon grape holly can take any exposure, though it does best with some shade in the Lower South and wind protection in the Upper South. Use in masses as foundation planting, in woodland garden, as low screen or garden barrier. Control height and form by pruning; if woody stems jut out, cut them down to ground (new growth fills in quickly). Unlike other mahonias, this one needs acid soil; develops chlorosis (yellow leaves with green veins) in alkaline soil. Regular water.

M. eurybracteata 'Soft Caress'. Zones MS, LS, CS; USDA 7-9. Grows 3 ft. tall and 3½ ft. wide with soft textured, narrow, bamboo-like foliage. Thornless. Bright yellow flowers in winter, followed by dark blue berries. Great texture for containers, Asian gardens, and as specimen. Best in part to full shade. Regular water.

M. fortunei. CHINESE MAHONIA. Zones LS, CS; USDA 8-9. Native to China. Grows to 6 ft. high, 3 ft. wide; stems bear 10-in., matte green leaves with 7 to 13 spiny-toothed leaflets. Undersurface of leaves is yellowish green, with heavily netted veins. Flowers in short clusters in late summer to early fall; purple-black berries seldom develop. Plant has an unusual stiff charm and is grown for form and foliage, not fruit. Full sun to light shade. Moderate water.

M. gracilis. MEXICAN BARBERRY. Zones MS, LS, CS; USDA 7-9. Native to Mexico. To 3 ft. high, 4 ft. wide. Glossy leaves have 5 to 13 overlapping leaflets, each about 1½ in. long. Foliage is most colorful in full sun: leaves are lime-green when new, darker green in summer, and a lively mix of reds, oranges, yellows, and light green in winter. Bright yellow, very fragrant blossoms in winter. Blue fruit with a powdery sheen. Tolerates extreme heat and poor soils, even hard-packed clay. Needs little or no supplemental water.

M. japonica Bealei Group (*M. bealei*). LEATHERLEAF MAHONIA. Zones US, MS, LS, CS; USDA 6-9. Native to China. Grows 10–12 ft. high and 10 ft. wide, with strong pattern of vertical stems, horizontal foliage. Leaves over 1 ft. long, divided into 7 to 15 broad, leathery leaflets to 5 in. long; leaflets grayish or bluish green above, olive-green below, with spiny-toothed edges. Very fragrant flowers in erect, 3- to 6-in.-long, spikelike clusters at branch ends in earliest spring. Blue berries with a powdery sheen. Distinguished plant against stone, brick, wood, glass. Takes sun in Upper and Middle South; best in part shade elsewhere. Plant in rich soil with ample organic material. Regular water.

M. oiwakensis lomariifolia (*M. lomariifolia.*) BURMESE MAHONIA. Zones LS, CS; USDA 8-9. Native to China. Showy plant to 6–12 ft. high and 6 ft. wide, with erect stems that branch only slightly. Young plants often have

TOP: *Mahonia japonica* Bealei Group; *M. aquifolium* 'Orange Flame';
BOTTOM: *M. eurybracteata* 'Soft Caress' in planter

a single, vertical, unbranched stem; with age, plants send up more near-vertical branches from near base. Clustered near ends of these branches are horizontally held leaves to 2 ft. long. In outline, leaves look like stiff, crinkly, barbed ferns; each has as many as 47 thick, spiny, glossy, green leaflets arranged symmetrically along both sides of central stem. Flowers in winter or earliest spring grow in foot-long, erect clusters at branch tips, just above uppermost cluster of leaves. Blue fruit has a powdery sheen. Prune stems at varying heights to induce branching. Needs shade at least in afternoon to keep deep green color. Regular water.

M. x media. Zones MS, LS, CS; USDA 7-9. Hybrids between *M. lomariifolia* and *M. japonica.*

Plants bear upright clusters of fragrant flowers in late fall and winter; generally resemble *M. oiwakensis lomariifolia* and require the same conditions. 'Arthur Menzies' grows to 15 ft. high and half as wide. 'Buckland' and 'Charity' grow to 15 ft. high, 12 ft. wide; 'Faith' reaches 6–10 ft. high and 6 ft. wide; 'Hope' and 'Lionel Fortescue' grow to 6 ft. high and wide; 'Underway' and 'Winter Sun' reach 4–5 ft. high and as wide.

M. swaseyi. TEXAS MAHO-NIA. Zones MS, LS, CS, TS; USDA 7-11. Native to Texas and Mexico. Spiny growth to 3–5 ft. tall, 5 ft. wide. Leaves are rosy when young, light green in summer, reddish purple in fall and winter. Fragrant yellow spring flowers; bright red berries. Good barrier plant; can be sheared but looks most attractive when allowed to take its natural shape. Best in full sun; tolerates much heat. Provide well-drained soil. Needs little or no supplemental water.

M. trifoliolata (*Berberis trifoliolata*). AGARITA, TEXAS CUR-RANT. Zones MS, LS, CS; USDA 7-9. Native to Arizona, southern New Mexico, Texas. To 8 ft. tall, 6 ft. wide. Stiff, upright branches hold leathery, blue-green to gray-green leaves to 3 in. long, each consisting of three spiny-tipped leaflets. Fragrant yellow flowers in spring. Red berries ripen in summer; they make good jelly; also favored by wildlife. Needs good drainage and full sun. Tolerates heat and drought, thriving on little or no supplemental water.

MAIANTHEMUM

Asparagaceae
Perennials

✎ **US, MS, LS; USDA 6-8**

☼ **LIGHT SHADE**

💧 **REGULAR WATER**

Maianthemum racemosa

These perennials spread by creeping rhizomes to form dense colonies. Need rich, loose, moist, slightly acid soil. Good for naturalizing in wild garden; commonly seen in moist woods and roadside ditches. The fruit is favored by wildlife. Formerly called *Smilacina.*

M. racemosum. FALSE SOLO-MON'S SEAL, FALSE SPIKENARD. Native to woods throughout much of North America. Grows 1–3 ft. tall. Each arching stalk has several 3- to 6-in.-long leaves with hairy undersides; foliage is medium green, turning golden yellow in autumn. In spring, stalks are topped by fluffy, conical clusters of small, fragrant, creamy white flowers. Red autumn berries have purple spots. Resembles true Solomon's seal (*Polygonatum*).

M. stellatum. STARFLOWER, STARRY SOLOMON'S SEAL. Native to Virginia, north to Newfoundland and west to Kansas and California. Grows 1–2 ½ ft. tall. Stems erect or somewhat spreading. Light green, 6-in. leaves are folded lengthwise, or channeled, and clasp the stem. Creamy white spring flowers smaller than those of *M. racemosa.* Berries are green with black stripes, maturing to deep red or dark blue.

MALUS

FLOWERING CRABAPPLE
Rosaceae
Deciduous trees

✎ **ZONES VARY BY SELECTION**

☼ **FULL SUN**

💧 **MODERATE TO REGULAR WATER**

Malus 'Candied Apple'

From North America, Europe, Asia. These beloved ornamental trees have much to offer, including spectacular springtime flowers, ornamental (and occasionally edible) fruit, and adaptability to a wide range of soil types and growing conditions. More than 600 kinds are cultivated, and a new selection seems to appear every few days.

Trees range in height from 6–40 ft., but most reach about 25 ft. high. Oval, pointed leaves may be solid deep green, burgundy tinged, or even purple; fall color is seldom rousing, but some types do turn yellow or even orange. Profuse single, semidouble, or double blossoms in white, pink, or red appear in spring, usually before the leaves unfurl; they sometimes have a sweet, musky fragrance. Small red, orange, or yellow apples (size varies from ¾ to 2 in. wide) ripen from midsummer into autumn and can be quite showy. In some types, the fruit persists well into winter and supplies food for robins, mockingbirds, cardinals, cedar waxwings, blue jays, and many other birds.

Among the most popular crabapple selections grown for fruit (used for jelly making and pickling) are 'Transcendent', with 2-in., red-cheeked yellow apples that ripen in summer; 'Centennial', with 1½-in., scarlet-and-yellow fruit; and 'Dolgo', with 1½-in. crimson fruit. The red-fruited 'Maypole' is a newer columnar dwarf crabapple. Other crabapples are prized for cider, including 'Virginia Crab' ('Hewe's Crab'), 'Geneva', and 'Giant Russian'. For information about general care, see Apple.

SPECIES CRABAPPLES.

M. angustifolia. SOUTHERN WILD CRABAPPLE. MS, LS, CS; USDA 7-9. Rounded tree 25–30 ft. tall by 25 ft. wide. Red buds open to single, very fragrant pink flowers that fade to white. Aromatic, yellowish green fruit to 1½ in. across. Susceptible to fireblight, rust, and scab. Attractive in natural settings.

M. coronaria. WILD SWEET CRABAPPLE. US, MS; USDA 6-7. Broad, spreading tree to 30 ft. tall by 35 ft. wide. Pink buds open into single flowers in pure white or pink-tinged white. Large, yellowish green fruit. Blooms late. Susceptible to rust and scab.

M. floribunda. JAPANESE FLOWERING CRABAPPLE. US, MS, LS; USDA 6-8. Broad, dense tree to 15–25 ft. tall and wide. Deep pink buds open to incredibly profuse, single, fragrant, white flowers. Small fruit is red, blushed yellow; does not last long. Moderate disease resistance.

M. hupehensis. TEA CRABAPPLE. US, MS, LS; USDA 6-8. Grows 15–25 ft. tall and wide. Deep pink buds open to single, white, fragrant flowers. Small, greenish yellow to red fruit; not showy. Picturesque form, with branches angled from

short trunk. Moderate disease resistance.

M. sargentii. SARGENT CRABAPPLE. US. MS. LS; USDA 6-8. Broad, densely branched tree to 10 ft. tall by 20 ft. wide. Profuse show of small, single, white, fragrant flowers. Tiny, red, long-lasting fruit. Good disease resistance. 'Candymint' has pink flowers with petals outlined in pink. 'Rosea', a pink-flowered form, may be more disease prone than the species.

M. x sieboldii zumi (*M. zumi* 'Calocarpa'). US, MS, LS; USDA 6-8. Densely branched, rounded tree to 15 ft. tall and wide. Fragrant, single open pale pink then fade to white. Small, glossy, bright red, long lasting fruit. Moderate susceptibility to fireblight. Usually resistant to scab.

HYBRID CRABAPPLES.

'Adams'. US, MS, LS; USDA 6-8. Dense, round-headed tree to 20 ft. tall and wide. Red buds open to single pink flowers. Dull red, small, long-lasting fruit. Orange fall foliage. Low chill; good disease resistance.

'Adirondack'. US, MS, LS; USDA 6-8. Columnar tree to 12 ft. tall by 6 ft. wide. Red buds open to large, red-tinged, single, waxy white flowers. Red to orange-red fruit. Formal in appearance. High disease resistance.

'Brandywine'. US, MS, LS; USDA 6-8. Vigorous, shapely tree to 15–20 ft. tall and wide. Double, rose-pink flowers are fragrant. Yellowish green fruit. Leaves have reddish cast. Fair disease resistance.

'Callaway'. US, MS, LS; USDA 6-8. Attractive, round-headed tree to 15–25 ft. tall by 15–20 ft. wide. Pink buds open to single, white flowers. Deep red, large, long-lasting fruit. Low chill requirement; good choice for mild winter areas. High disease resistance.

'Candied Apple'. US, MS, LS; USDA 6-8. Weeping tree to 10–15 ft. tall by 20 ft. wide. Reddish buds open to single blossoms with deep pink outer petals, whitish inner petals edged in pink. Bright red, small fruit persists all winter. Good disease resistance.

'Centurion'. US, MS, LS; USDA 6-8. Oval tree to 25 ft. tall by 15–20 ft. wide. Reddish buds open to single red flowers. Shiny, deep red, long-lasting fruit. Blooms young. High disease resistance.

HOW TO GROW CRABAPPLES

PLANTING You can set out trees from nursery pots anytime, though spring and fall are preferred. Plant bare-root trees in late winter or early spring. For best growth and flowering, plants need at least 600 hours at 45°F or lower. Crabapples make fine lawn trees (protect trunks from damage from weed eaters and lawn mowers, which creates an entry point for diseases), informal screens, and espaliers. Small-fruited selections also make good street or patio trees, as fruit not consumed by birds will wither on the tree without causing a mess.

SOIL Prefer good, well-drained, deep soils but will grow in rocky or gravelly ones, can succeed even in clay, and tolerate acid to slightly alkaline conditions.

PRUNING Prune in winter to build a good framework, remove any suckers, and correct shape. Also remove watersprouts (unbranched shoots that grow straight up from main limbs). Crabapple trees can be trained as espaliers.

CHALLENGES Fireblight, scab, powdery mildew, and cedar-apple rust can be serious problems for crabapples. Prevention is the best control for all of these diseases—grow resistant selections (disease resistance is noted in descriptions). Unless you are fond of frequent spraying, avoid these disease-prone selections: 'Almey', 'Bechtel' (*M. ioensis* 'Plena'), 'Eleyi', 'Hopa', 'Prarie Rose', 'Radiant', 'Red Silver', 'Royal Ruby', and 'Royalty'.

Many insects feast on crabapples (the same ones that feed on apples), including aphids, Japanese beetles, tent caterpillars, and borers. But these pests are minor compared with several potentially serious diseases mentioned above.

ABOVE: Malus 'Strawberry Parfait'

'Coralburst'. Compact, rounded tree to 15 ft. tall and wide. Coral-pink buds open to double rose flowers. Susceptible

to scab, resists rust and fire blight.
'Donald Wyman'. US, MS, LS, CS; USDA 6-9. Broad tree to 20 ft. tall by 25 ft. wide. Pink to

red buds open to single white flowers. Small, shiny, bright red, long-lasting fruit. Lustrous foliage. Good disease resistance. An outstanding selection.

'Harvest Gold'. US, MS; USDA 6-7. Vigorous, narrow tree to 30 ft. tall by 15 ft. wide. Pink buds open to single white flowers. Showy, yellow fruit hangs on until spring. Blooms late. High disease resistance.

'Indian Summer'. US, MS, LS; USDA 6-8. Rounded tree to 15–20 ft. tall and wide. Single, rose-red flowers. Bright red, long-lasting fruit. Good orange-red fall color. High disease resistance.

'Jewelberry'. US, MS, LS; USDA 6-8. Dwarfish, dense tree to 8 ft. tall by 12 ft. wide. Pink buds open to single white flowers. Small, shiny red, long-lasting fruit. Blooms young. Good disease resistance.

'Liset'. US, MS, LS; USDA 6-8. Roundish, dense tree to 15–20 ft. tall and wide. Crimson buds open to deep red-to-crimson, single flowers. Dark red to maroon fruit holds well on the tree. Deep purplish green leaves. Fair disease resistance.

'Louisa'. US, MS, LS; USDA 6-8. Broad, weeping tree to 15 ft. tall and wide. Profuse, single, rose-pink flowers. Small, golden orange fruit. Excellent, graceful weeper. Glossy, dark green foliage. Good disease resistance.

'Molten Lava'. US, MS, LS; USDA 6-8. Spreading, weeping tree to 12 ft. tall by 15 ft. wide. Deep red buds open to single white flowers. Small, red-orange, long-lasting fruit. Bark is yellow; looks especially attractive against snow in winter. Good disease resistance.

'Narragansett'. US, MS, LS; USDA 6-8. Broad, round-headed tree to 15 ft. tall and wide. Red buds open to single white flowers with a faint touch of pink. Small, bright red, showy fruit. High disease resistance.

'Pink Princess'. US, MS, LS; USDA 6-8. Low, broad tree to 15 ft. tall by 12 ft. wide. Single, rose-pink flowers. Small, deep red, long-lasting fruit. Reddish green foliage. Good disease resistance.

'Prairifire'. US, MS, LS; USDA 6-8. Round-headed tree to 20 ft. tall and wide. Red buds open to single, deep pinkish red flowers.

Small, dark red, long-lasting fruit. Leaves emerge reddish maroon, turn dark green. High disease resistance.

'Profusion'. US, MS, LS; USDA 6-8. Upright, spreading tree to 20 ft. tall and wide. Deep pink buds open to single, deep purplish pink flowers. Dark red, long-lasting fruit. Foliage is purple when young, matures to bronzy green. Good disease resistance.

'Red Jade'. US, MS; USDA 6-7. Irregular, weeping tree to 15 ft. tall and wide. Small, single, white flowers. Profuse, bright red fruit holds well into fall. Fair disease resistance.

'Red Jewel'. US, MS, LS; USDA 6-8. Small, rounded tree to 15 ft. tall by 12 ft. wide. Large, single, white flowers. Small, bright red, long-lasting fruit. Susceptible to scab, resists rust and fireblight.

'Robinson'. US, MS, LS; USDA 6-8. Dense, upright, vase-shaped tree to 25 ft. tall by 15 ft. wide. Deep red buds open to single, deep pink flowers. Dark red fruit. Copper-tinged foliage. High disease resistance.

'Royal Raindrops'. US, MS, LS; USDA 6-8. Upright, spreading tree to 20 ft. tall and 15 ft. wide. Single, bright, rose-colored flowers. Long-stemmed, red fruit. Purple, cutleaf foliage has excellent disease resistance.

'Show Time'. US, MS, LS; USDA 6-8. Broadly oval to rounded tree to 22 ft. tall and 20 ft. wide. Abundant, single, pinkish red flowers. Bright red fruit. Purple-bronze to bronzy green leaves. Susceptible to scab, otherwise good disease resistance.

'Strawberry Parfait'. US, MS, LS; USDA 6-8. Open, vase-shaped tree to 20 ft. tall by 25 ft. wide. Red buds open to profuse, single pink flowers, edged in red. Fruit is yellow blushed red. High disease resistance.

'Sugar Tyme'. US, MS, LS; USDA 6-8. Upright, oval tree to 18 ft. tall by 15 ft. wide. Delicate, light pink buds open to fragrant, single, white flowers. Abundant, red, long-lasting fruit. High disease resistance.

'Thunderchild'. US, MS, LS; USDA 6-8. Erect, oval tree to 20 ft. tall by 18 ft. wide. Single, rose-pink flowers. Dark red fruit. Purple foliage. Good disease resistance.

MALVA
MALLOW
Malvaceae
Perennials or biennials

🗡 **US, MS, LS; USDA 6-8**

☼ **FULL SUN**

💧 **REGULAR WATER**

Malva moschata

From Europe; naturalized in U.S. These plants are related to and somewhat resemble hollyhock (*Alcea*), but they are bushier, with smaller, roundish to heart-shaped leaves. They are easy to grow from seed and usually bloom the first year. Need good drainage, average soil. Use in perennial borders or for a quick tall edging. Not long lived.

M. alcea. Perennial. To 4 ft. tall, 2 ft. wide; upper leaves deeply divided. Saucer-shaped, pink flowers to 2 in. wide appear from late spring to fall. Subject to root rot in hot, wet weather. The most widely available variety is *M. a. fastigiata*; it is narrower than the species. Resists deer.

M. moschata. MUSK MAL-LOW. Perennial. Erect, branching plant to 3 ft. tall, 2 ft. wide. Finely cut leaves; pink or white flowers to 1 in. wide or somewhat wider, summer to fall. Entire plant emits a mildly musky odor if brushed against or bruised. Named selections are more frequently grown than the species. 'Rosea' has pink blossoms; 'Alba' is shorter than the species (to 2 ft. tall) and bears white flowers.

M. sylvestris. FRENCH HOL-LYHOCK. Perennial or biennial. Easy-to-grow plant with erect, bushy growth to 2–4 ft. tall, 2 ft. wide. Flowers are 2 in. across and appear throughout summer, often right up until frost. Reseeds; often seen in older gardens

of the Lower South. Common selection 'Zebrina' (often sold as *M. zebrina*) has blossoms in pale lavender-pink with pronounced deep purple veining. 'Marina' bears light blue blossoms; 'Mauritiana' has deep lavender-pink, often semidouble flowers with dark purple veining. Resists deer.

MALVAVISCUS ARBOREUS DRUMMONDII

TURK'S CAP, TURK'S TURBAN
Malvaceae
Perennial

🗡 **LS, CS; USDA 8-9**

◐ ● **PARTIAL TO FULL SHADE**

◌ ◍ ● **LITTLE TO REGULAR WATER**

Malvaviscus arboreus drummondii

Native from Florida west to Texas and Mexico. Spindly, shrubby perennial with semiwoody stems. Blooms from early summer right through fall, bearing nodding, bright red, twisted-looking, 1- to 1½-in.-long blossoms with long, prominent stamens similar to those of hibiscus. May reach 9 ft. tall if soil is fertile and growing season long and warm, but usually grows 3–5 ft. high and almost as wide. Dies back to the ground in winter. Long-stalked yellow-green leaves are coarse textured, heart shaped, 2–3 in. wide. Blooms attract humming-birds. Small, rounded, applelike fruit follows the flowers, changing from white to red as it ripens. Tough, easy plant; tolerates alkaline and rocky soils and drought. Not usually browsed by deer. 'Big Momma' has coral-red blooms. 'Pam Puryear' has pink to coral-pink blooms.

MANDEVILLA

Apocynaceae
Evergreen and deciduous vines
or vining shrubs

🌿 **ZONES VARY BY SPECIES; OR GROW IN POTS**

☼◐ **FULL SUN OR PARTIAL SHADE**

💧 **REGULAR WATER**

Mandevilla 'Alice du Pont'

Widely grown for showy flowers, the genus *Mandevilla* includes plants formerly called *Dipladenia*. They thrive in warm, humid weather and bloom continuously from late spring to frost in most areas of the South. They are generally hardy outdoors in the Coastal and Tropical South; elsewhere, they can be overwintered indoors or treated as annuals. Blossoms consist of five broad lobes that flare out from a tubular throat; except as noted, they are unscented. Plants climb by twining. Use them to cover arbors, trellises, and fences. Excellent container plants. Plant in fertile, well-drained soil. Provide protection from hottest afternoon sun. Feed with a balanced, water-soluble fertilizer every 2 to 3 weeks throughout the growing season. Growth may need thinning from time to time. Watch for spider mites.

M. boliviensis. Evergreen. Zone TS; USDA 10-11. Native to Ecuador and Bolivia. Grows to 12 ft. as a vine; reaches 3 ft. tall and 5 ft. wide as a sprawling shrub. Glossy, oval, pointed leaves to 4 in. long; 2½-in.-wide white flowers with golden-yellow throats.

M. hybrids. Evergreen. Zone TS; may grow as root-hardy perennials in Zone CS; USDA 9. The hybrid mandevillas described

here are sometimes sold as selections of *M.x amabilis* or *M.x amoena*. Plants grow to 15–20 ft., with glossy, dark green, oval leaves 3–8 in. long. Most widely grown is 'Alice du Pont', with clusters of glowing pink, 2- to 4-in. flowers appearing among the leaves; even very small plants in 4-in. pots will bloom. 'Moonlight Parfait' is a vigorous grower; pink buds open to large white blossoms with a double-petaled pink center. 'Summer Snow' ('Monte', 'Flora Snow') bears blush-pink blossoms that eventually fade to white. 'White Delight' has pale pink buds opening to white blooms with a light yellow throat. 'Ruby Star' is a slightly more compact plant with narrower-lobed, 3-in.-wide flowers; blossoms open deep pink, then mature to magenta with a touch of yellow deep in the throat. 'Rita Marie Green' ('Pink Parfait') has long-lasting, hot pink, double flowers; 'Tango Twirl' offers upright clusters of light pink, double blooms. The Sun Parasol series blooms at a young age and is available in shades of red, pink, and white. Plant all hybrids in rich soil and provide a frame, trellis, or stake for support. Pinch tips of young plants to induce bushiness.

M. laxa (*M. suaveolens*). CHILEAN JASMINE. Deciduous; evergreen in frost-free areas. Zones CS, TS; USDA 9-11. Native to Chile and Argentina. Grows to 15 ft. or more, with heart-shaped, 2- to 6-in.-long leaves. Clustered flowers are white, 1½–2 in. across, with a powerful perfume like that of gardenia. Requires less heat to bloom than other mandevillas. Provide rich soil. If plant becomes badly tangled, cut to ground in winter; it will resprout and bloom on new growth. Roots are hardy to about 5°F.

M. sanderi (*Dipladenia splendens*). BRAZILLIAN JASMINE. Evergreen. Zone TS; USDA 10-11; may grow as root-hardy perennial in Zone CS; USDA 9. Native to southeastern Brazil. Compact, shrubby plant to 2 ft. tall, 3 ft. wide; eventually starts to twine (to 15–20 ft. tall with support), but you can keep it bushy by pinching climbing shoots. Deep green leaves are 4–8 in. long, tinged with bronze when new. Flowers are 3–4 in. wide, rose-pink with yellow throats; color fades as

blossoms age. 'Red Riding Hood', with deep cherry-red flowers; white-blossomed 'Faire Lady' ('My Fair Lady'); and scarlet 'Scarlet Pimpernel' are lower growing and shrubbier than the species (to 6–8 ft. as climbers) and superb in hanging baskets. Similar in form is 'Strawberry Lemonade', with deep pink, yellow-throated flowers; its leaves are beautifully variegated in mint-green, cream, and white, with pink flushes when young.

MANGO

Anacardiaceae
Evergreen tree

🌿 **TS; USDA 10-11; OR GROW IN POTS**

☼ **FULL SUN**

💧 **MODERATE WATER**

◊ **SAP AND JUICE FROM FRUIT CAUSE SKIN RASH IN SOME PEOPLE**

Mangoes

Tropical Asian native known botanically as *Mangifera indica*. Now cultivated in warm-weather regions around the globe. One of the easiest fruit trees to grow—but since it won't take frost, its cultivation in the South is limited to south Florida and South Texas. Trees range in size from 50-ft. giants with a 30-ft. spread to 6- to 10-ft. specimens better suited to the average backyard. Handsome, large (8- to 16-in.-long) leaves are often coppery red or purple when new, later turning dark green. Tree size is heavily dependent on selection and pruning. Almost all trees will get over 40 ft. without pruning, but some can be kept at 8–12 ft. with selective annual pruning. Larger selections can be kept at 15–20 ft. with pruning.

Mangoes are usually self-fruitful. Long clusters of yellow to reddish flowers appear at branch ends from spring into summer; these are followed by fleshy fruit that typically weighs from ¾ to 1 pound, though it can tip the scales at as much as 4 pounds. Most mangoes are more flavorful if allowed to ripen on the tree; they're usually ready to harvest 4 to 5 months after bloom. The trees can be incredibly productive—a 6-ft. tree can bear up to 60 pounds of fruit per year. Mangoes can be grown in containers, but it is much more difficult than if the trees are planted in the ground. Trees bloom best when they go through a dry season and are exposed to cooler temperatures. South Florida's winter is ideal because it is typically dry with moderate cold. Trees bloom about 30 days after being exposed to temperatures in the 40s.

Mangoes typically have green to reddish or yellowish skin, a large seed, and very juicy pale yellow to deep orange flesh that tastes somewhat like a peach with flowery or perfumy overtones—but there's incredible diversity in size, shape, color, and flavor. Most groceries stock 'Tommy Atkins', a selection that is to mangoes what 'Red Delicious' is to apples; it looks pretty and ships well, but taste and texture are not exceptional. Choices offering better flavor and texture include the following.

'Angie'. Selected in Florida. Yellow, reddish orange-blushed fruit weighs almost a pound and has sweet apricot flavor. Semidwarf tree, easily maintained below 8 ft. tall; excellent disease resistance.

'Cogshall'. Selected in Florida. Yellow-orange, red-blushed, aromatic, elongated oval fruit weighs up to 1 pound, has yellow flesh with rich, spicy flavor. Small, disease-resistant, very productive tree, easily kept pruned to about 8 ft. tall and wide.

'Duncan'. Selected in Florida. Bright yellow, oblong fruit topping 1 pound with smooth, excellent-tasting, yellow flesh. Heavy-producing, disease-resistant tree easily maintained at 12 ft. tall.

'Fairchild'. From Panama. Oblong, yellow, ½-pound fruit with sweet, fiberless, deep orange flesh. Handsome, disease-resistant tree can be kept at 8 ft. tall and wide. Heavy producer.

M

'Graham'. From Trinidad. Oval yellow fruit to about ½ pound, with sweet, fiberless, deep orange flesh. Compact tree; easily kept to 8 ft. tall and wide with pruning. Usually has multiple blooms.

'Keitt'. Selected in Florida. Oval fruit is very large, weighing up to 4 pounds. Yellowish green skin flushed reddish orange; firm yellow flesh has a resinous sweetness, few fibers. Bears late in the season, producing into fall. Dense-foliaged, disease-resistant tree to 15 ft. tall and as wide.

'Mallika'. From India. Bright yellow, potato-shaped fruit weighs about 1 pound; fiberless, deep orange flesh has complex, honey-like flavor. For best flavor, harvest fruit before fully ripe and let stand at room temperature for a week or two. Keep trees pruned to 8–10 ft. tall and wide.

'Manilita'. From Mexico. Pastel red, elongated fruit weighs about ½ pound and has sweet-flavored yellow flesh. Dwarf, disease-resistant tree easily maintained at 8 ft. tall. Good for containers.

'Nam Doc Mai'. From Thailand. Greenish to yellow, sometimes lightly blushed red, slender fruit weighs up to a pound and has fine-flavored, juicy, sweet, fiberless yellow flesh. Often used green. Small tree, easily maintained below 8 ft. tall, has good disease resistance.

'Neelum'. From India. Cashew-shaped, yellow fruit weighs about ½ pound or more and has intensely flavored, aromatic, orange-yellow, fiberless flesh. Best picked green and ripened off tree at room temperature. Small tree, easily maintained at 8 ft. tall, with good disease resistance.

'Rosigold'. Selected in Florida. Earlier than most mangoes—fruit may be ripe in March. Cylindrical fruit to Î pound is bright yellow with red highlights; has fiberless, juicy, deep orange flesh with rich, sweet flavor. Small tree can be pruned to 8 ft. tall and wide.

CARE

Mangoes will grow in most well-drained soils. Water only to get them established; after that, they'll get by on rainfall. (However, trees grown in containers will need regular watering.) Spread ¼ pound of 8-3-9 fertilizer per inch of trunk diameter evenly at the drip line twice a year and water it in well. Be careful not to apply too much nitrogen, as this will force vegetative growth rather than bloom. Foliar sprays of minor elements are recommended. Spraying for pests is seldom necessary, though scale, anthracnose, and powdery mildew cause occasional problems; for controls, consult your Cooperative Extension Service.

MARANTA
Marantaceae
Perennials

- **ZONE TS; USDA 10-11; OR HOUSEPLANT**
- **PARTIAL SHADE; BRIGHT INDIRECT LIGHT**
- **AMPLE WATER DURING SUMMER**

Maranta leuconeura

Genus of about 20 species from tropical Central and South America. Densely spreading clumps of stems hold attractive leaves typically marked with colorful, interesting patterns.

M. arundinacea. ARROWROOT. Slender branches grow 6 ft. tall, with small white flowers and tropical-looking dark green leaves to 10 in. long. Spreads by rhizomes, which are the source of the arrowroot starch used as a thickening agent for sauces, puddings, and fruit pie fillings. *M. a.* 'Variegata' has dark green leaves variegated with light green and yellowish green. A form with reddish purple leaves is sometimes offered.

M. leuconeura. PRAYER PLANT. Satiny dark green leaves with light green and brownish black markings, silver or red veins. Spreads by rhizomes to make a striking ground cover in tropical gardens; soil must be rich and fast draining, air very warm and humid. The 5-in.-long leaves lie flat during the day, then fold toward the center of the plant at night—hence the common name "prayer plant." Flowers are insignificant. *M. l. erythroneura* has red veins; *M. l. kerchoveana*, known as rabbit's foot, has light green leaves with dark blotches (like animal tracks) on either side of the midrib.

CARE

Indoors, locate out of direct light. Keep soil moist during the growing season, and use a humidifier to keep moisture in the air; maintain night temperatures above 55°F. Indoors or out, feed monthly during summer with a general-purpose liquid houseplant fertilizer.

MARRUBIUM VULGARE
HOREHOUND
Lamiaceae
Perennial

- **US, MS, LS, CS; USDA 6-9**
- **FULL SUN**
- **LITTLE TO MODERATE WATER**

Marrubium vulgare

Native to Mediterranean region and western Asia; naturalized throughout Europe and the Americas. Coarse, upright plant to 1–3 ft. tall, 1–1½ ft. wide, with wrinkled, woolly, aromatic, gray-green leaves to 2 in. long. Blooms in second year from seed, bearing rounded whorls of white flowers (similar to those of mint) on foot-long, branching stems in summer. As a garden plant, it is invasive and rather weedy looking, but it makes a serviceable edging in a garden of gray-leafed plants. Used for medicinal purposes and in candy. Foliage lasts well in bouquets. Requires little water but will take more if drainage is good; otherwise not fussy about soil. Give protection from cold and wind.

MASCAGNIA
ORCHID VINE
Malpighiaceae
Deciduous vines

- **ZONES VARY BY SPECIES**
- **FULL SUN**
- **MODERATE WATER**

Mascagnia macroptera

Vines of Mexican origin that bloom during the hottest time of year. Bright green leaves in opposite pairs look like those of honeysuckle (*Lonicera*). Clusters of five-petaled, 1-in. blooms centered with ten stamens; petals are shaped like Ping-Pong paddles. Oddly winged seedpods look something like butterflies and are sometimes used in dried arrangements.

M. lilacina. LAVENDER ORCHID VINE. Zones CS, TS; USDA 9-11. To 15–20 ft., with 1½-in. leaves and lilac flowers that are followed by inch-wide seedpods. Plant is hardy to 15–18°F; leaves drop off at 22°F.

M. macroptera. YELLOW ORCHID VINE. Zone LS, CS, TS; USDA 8-11. To 15 ft., with 3-in. leaves. Abundant, bright yellow flowers are followed by conspicuous, 2-in., yellow-green seedpods. Hardy to 10°F but may die back to the ground.

MATRICARIA RECUTITA

FALSE CHAMOMILE
Asteraceae
Annual

🌱 **US, MS, LS, CS; USDA 6-9**

☀️ **FULL SUN**

💧 **MODERATE WATER**

Matricaria recutita

Formerly known as *M. chamomilla*. Native to Europe, western Asia; naturalized in North America. Aromatic plant grows to 2 ft. tall and 1½ ft. wide, with finely cut, almost fernlike foliage. White-and-yellow daisy-type flowers to 1 in. wide bloom in summer. Grows easily in ordinary soil; sow seed in late winter or spring. Valued for its herbal use: dried flowers are used in making the familiar, fragrant chamomile tea.

M. 'White Stars' is often sold as a selection of *Tanacetum parthenium*; it has an extended row of white outer petals. Chamomile sold as a walk-on ground cover is *Chamaemelum nobile (Anthemis nobilis)*.

MATTEUCCIA STRUTHIOPTERIS

OSTRICH FERN
Onocleaceae
Fern

🌱 **US, MS; USDA 6-7**

🌗 **LIGHT SHADE**

💧💧 **REGULAR TO AMPLE WATER**

Matteuccia struthiopteris

Native to northern parts of North America, Europe, Asia. Tolerates extreme cold but cannot take long, hot, dry summers. Good choice for the Upper South and mountainous regions where summer nights cool off and there is ample moisture. Forms a clump that looks like a shuttlecock—narrow at the base, spreading out at the top. Can reach 6 ft. tall and 3 ft. wide in rich, moist soil; spreads by underground rhizomes. Attractive in woodland garden or growing beside a pond or stream. The unfolding young fronds (fiddleheads) are edible and can be served as a cooked vegetable.

MATTHIOLA

STOCK
Brassicaceae
Biennials grown as cool-season annuals

🌱 **US, MS, LS, CS, TS; USDA 6-11**

☀️🌗 **FULL SUN OR LIGHT SHADE**

💧 **REGULAR WATER**

Matthiola incana

This genus from the mustard family contains many plants grown for their scented blooms.

M. incana. STOCK. Old-fashioned plants native to the Mediterranean region, well suited to the cottage garden. All have long, narrow, gray-green leaves and masses of delightfully scented flowers in erect, spike-like clusters.

Valued for fragrance, cut flowers. Oblong leaves to 4 in. long. Single or double, inch-wide flowers with spicy-sweet scent. Colors include white, pink, red, purple, lavender, blue, yellow, cream. Blues and reds are purple toned; yellows tend toward cream.

Many strains are available (most of them hybrids), ranging from under 1 ft. to as tall as 3 ft., from 10 to 16 in. wide. Taller selections are best for cutting.

Need light, fertile soil and good drainage. Like pansies and violas, stocks bloom in cool weather. In the Upper South, choose early bloomers, and plant in earliest spring to get flowers before hot weather comes. Elsewhere, set out plants in fall for bloom in winter or early spring. Stocks take moderate frost but will not set flower buds if nights are too chilly, so late planting delays bloom until spring. In areas with heavy winter rainfall, plant in raised beds to ensure good drainage and prevent root rot.

M. longipetala bicornis. EVENING SCENTED STOCK. To 1 ft. or a little taller, 9 in. wide, with lance-shaped leaves to 3½ in. long. Small purplish flowers are not showy but emit a powerful fragrance at night.

MAZUS REPTANS

Phrymaceae
Perennials

🌱 **US, MS, LS; USDA 6-8**

☀️🌗● **EXPOSURE NEEDS VARY BY ZONE (SEE TEXT)**

💧 **REGULAR WATER**

Mazus reptans

Himalayan native growing to 2 in. high, spreading 1 ft. or wider by slender stems that creep and root along the ground. Small, sparsely toothed, rather narrow leaves are bright green. Spring and early-summer flowers are ¾ in. across, purplish blue with white and yellow markings; they appear in clusters of two to five. In shape, the blossoms resemble those of monkey flower (*Mimulus*). Use in a rock garden, as a small-scale ground cover, or as a filler between pavers (it takes heavy foot traffic in this last role). Needs rich soil. Evergreen in mild-winter climates; in colder areas, freezes to ground but usually recovers quickly in spring if protected over winter by snow cover or light mulch. Give full sun or partial shade in Upper and Middle South, partial to full shade in Lower South. A white-blossomed form is available, sold by some nurseries as *M. reptans* 'Albus' and by others as *M. japonicus* 'Albiflorus'.

MECARDONIA

Plantaginaceae
Perennial used as annual

ZONES CS, TS; USDA 9-10

FULL SUN

MODERATE WATER

Mecardonia

This low-growing plant blankets a bed or cascades over the edge of a container. It grows 2–6 in. tall and 12–18 in. wide. Small, grass-green leaves are topped with clear yellow blooms (¼–⅝ in. wide) all season. No deadheading is needed. Heat and drought tolerant. In areas where blackened by frost, a quick cutback will make way for the plant to rebound, acting like a root-hardy perennial in the Lower South. Best known through its hybrids. 'GoldDust' performs better in the landscape due to more of a mounding habit than trailing. Reaches 2–4 in. in height. 'Goldflake' performs in much of the same way but flowers later than 'GoldDust'. 'Magic Carpet' has a slightly larger flower and shows a true trailing habit in a container, reaching 4–6 in. tall.

MELALEUCA VIRIDIFLORA RUBRIFLORA

PAPERBARK TREE
Myrtaceae
Evergreen tree

CS, TS; USDA 9-11

FULL SUN

LITTLE TO REGULAR WATER

Melaleuca viridiflora rubriflora

What could possibly be wrong with a tree that looks attractive, is simple to grow, tolerates just about any soil, accepts salt spray, and suffers no serious pests or diseases? In the case of paperbark tree, just about everything.

Imported from Australia (and also known as cajeput tree), it quickly found favor among south Florida gardeners as an interesting choice for a lawn, shade, or street tree. Then intrepid land speculators decided to spread seeds of the thirsty tree throughout the south Florida swamplands to help drain them. Seedlings, which will grow on dry land or with their roots submerged, quickly invaded the wetlands to form impenetrable stands, virtually eliminating native vegetation. Hundreds of thousands of acres of the Florida Everglades have fallen victim.

Trees can reach 50–80 ft. tall and 30–50 ft. wide, with pendulous young branches. Thick, spongy, light brown to whitish bark peels off in sheets. Stiff, narrowly oval, shiny pale green leaves reach 2–4 in. long; spikes of yellowish white flowers resembling bottlebrushes crowd branch tips in summer and fall. Cylindrical or squarish, woody seed capsules contain many seeds.

Although paperbark tree can be a fine ornamental in the appropriate setting, its devastating impact on native ecosystems marks it as a tree that should never be planted. In fact, the state of Florida legally prohibits planting, growing, and selling it. It is included in this book as a warning, not a recommendation.

There is, however, one good, safe use for paperbark tree—cut and ground up, it makes an attractive, long-lasting, commercially available mulch that is a fine substitute for cypress mulch. Using this mulch helps reduce the cutting of cypresses, which are a vital component of many swampland ecosystems.

ABOVE: *Melampodium divaricatum*

MELAMPODIUM

Asteraceae
Annuals and perennials

ZONES VARY BY SPECIES

FULL SUN, EXCEPT AS NOTED

MODERATE WATER

Melampodium leucanthum

These tough, drought-tolerant plants produce masses of small daisies over a long period. Provide well-drained soil.

M. cinereum. HOARY BLACKFOOT. Perennial. Zones LS, CS; USDA 8-9. Native to limestone soils of Arkansas, Colorado, and Texas. To 4–12 in. tall and wide. Similar to *M. leucanthum* but not as hardy; blooms from spring.

M. divaricatum. STAR DAISY, BUTTER DAISY. Annual. Zones US, MS, LS, CS, TS; USDA 6-11. From Portugal and Spain. To 1–3 ft. tall and half as wide, with narrow, dark green leaves and deep yellow daisies throughout summer and into fall (no deadheading required). Start seeds indoors for earliest bloom; or sow in ground after soil has warmed. Plants will also self-sow. 'Medallion' grows to 3 ft. tall and often becomes leggy by midsummer. 'Melanie' and 'Million Gold' are a lower-growing selection (1 ft. high) that blooms prolifically. Dense-growing 'Showstar' is also more compact than the species (to 1½-2 ft. tall), with showier blooms; 'Derby' is similar, but it's a little shorter and more compact still. 'Casino Light Yellow' averages 12 in. tall and is a compact, heavy bloomer both in ground and in containers, but it can split in late summer. 'Lemon Delight' is less vigorous and more compact than 'Casino Light Yellow' with bright yellow flowers. All tolerate heat and humidity, perform well in full sun or light shade. Perfect for the front of a border or container.

M. leucanthum. BLACKFOOT DAISY. Perennial. Zones US, MS, LS, CS, TS; USDA 6-11. From Arizona, New Mexico, Texas, Mexico. Wiry stems set with narrow, gray leaves form a clump to 1 ft. tall and wide. In spring, summer, and (in mild climates) sporadically in winter, the foliage clump is topped by clouds of inch-wide, honey-scented white daisies with yellow centers. Deer resistant.

MELIA AZEDARACH

CHINABERRY
Meliaceae
Deciduous tree

✀ MS, LS, CS, TS; USDA 7-11

☼ FULL SUN

◉ MODERATE WATER

⬥ FRUIT IS POISONOUS TO MAMMALS IF INGESTED

Melia azedarach

Native to China, northern India. To 30–50 ft. high and wide, with irregular habit. Shiny, rich green, 1- to 3-ft.-long leaves are cut into many toothed, narrow or oval leaflets 1–2 in. long. Blooms in spring or early summer, bearing loose clusters of lilac flowers that are fragrant in the evening. Blossoms are followed by hard, berrylike yellow fruit about ½ in. wide. Tough plant; tolerates heat, wind, poor alkaline soil, drought. In areas with year-round moisture, tends to self-sow and become a pest (birds eat the fruit and spread seedlings all over creation).

'Umbraculiformis'. TEXAS UMBRELLA TREE is less picturesque than the species. It reaches 25–30 ft. high, with a dense, dome-shaped crown and drooping leaves. Grows true from seed. 'Jade Snowflake' is a variegated form that is heavily mottled with green and white.

MELINIS

NATAL RUBY GRASS
Poaceae
Perennial grasses

✀ TS; USDA 10-11 ANYWHERE AS ANNUALS

☼ FULL SUN

◉◉ MODERATE TO REGULAR WATER

Melinis nerviglumis

These tropical African grasses are just the ticket if you want lots of show in a sweltering site. They're easy to grow, adapt to any well-drained soil, tolerate drought once established, and are impervious to heat. Bloom in summer, when nodding, pinkish, 3- to 4-in.-long plumes rise above the clumps of slender, arching, blue-green leaves. Excellent complements to agaves, yuccas, and salvias. Great in drifts; also make good container subjects. Though short lived, they're easy to start from seed and are often grown as annuals. They reseed rampantly. Formerly known as *Rhynchelytrum*.

M. nerviglumis. RUBY GRASS. To 2–2½ ft. tall, up to 1½ ft. wide. Coral-pink plumes appear in June and fade to silvery pink by September. 'Pink Crystals' has bright ruby plumes.

M. repens. NATAL GRASS. Similar to above but shorter (to just 1–2 ft. tall). Billowy clouds of soft pink plumes fade to cream and tan.

MELISSA OFFICINALIS

LEMON BALM, SWEET BALM
Lamiaceae
Perennial

✀ US, MS, LS, CS; USDA 6-9

☼☼ FULL SUN OR PARTIAL SHADE

◉ REGULAR WATER

Melissa officinalis

From southern Europe. A single plant grows to about 2 ft. tall, 1½ ft. wide—but plants self-sow and spread rapidly, sometimes becoming pests. Leaves are used fresh in cold drinks, fruit cups, salads, fish dishes; dried leaves give lemon perfume to sachets, potpourris. Likes rich soil. Shear occasionally to keep compact. Lemon-scented, heavily veined foliage is light green in the species. Check catalogs to find 'Aurea' and 'All Gold', 'Variegata', intensely fragrant 'Citronella', and the hardier and more intense 'Quedlinburger Niederliegende'.

MELON

Cucurbitaceae
Annuals

✀ US, MS, LS, CS, TS; USDA 6-11

☼ FULL SUN

◉ REGULAR WATER

Cantaloupe

Nothing says "summer" better than a sweet, juicy melon—and the South's long, warm growing season gives melons the time they need to develop their sweetest flavor. Known botanically as *Cucumis melo*, they probably originated in India. This entry covers cantaloupes (with orange flesh) and honeydews (with green flesh) and includes a list of selections recommended for the South. For information on watermelons, see Watermelon.

Recommended cantaloupe selections for the South include 'Ambrosia' (86 days to maturity), 'Athena' (75 days), 'Burpee Hybrid' (82 days), 'Delicious 51' (77 days), 'Edisto 47' (86 days), 'Hale's Best' (86 days), 'Park's Whopper' (77 days), 'Sarah's Choice' (76 days), 'Saticoy' (90 days), 'Super 45' (80 days), and 'Sweet & Early' (75 days). Recommended honeydews include 'Earli-Dew Hybrid' (80 days), 'Honeymoon Hybrid' (90 days), 'Jenny Lind' (80 days), and 'Sweet Delight' (82 days).

CARE

Melons should be planted after all danger of frost is past, and only in warm soil; seeds will rot in cold soil. Before planting, work ½ cup of 10-10-10 fertilizer per 10 ft. of row into the soil. Melons are usually planted in hills spaced 3–4 ft. apart. Sow four to six seeds per hill, planting them ½–1 in. deep; thin seedlings to the most vigorous one or two per hill. To space out the harvest, make two or three plantings 2 weeks apart; or plant selections with different maturity dates.

When vines begin to run, apply ¼ cup of 10-10-10 fertilizer per 10 ft. of row (or per hill) and water it in. Keep the soil moist throughout the growing season, but reduce watering as harvest approaches (too much water during the week or so before harvest can make the fruit less sweet).

Poor fruit set or misshapen fruit may be caused by poor pollination. Remove deformed melons from the vine to allow normal fruit to form. Some melons may shrivel instead of developing fully; this is a normal process by which the vine sheds fruit it cannot support.

It takes some practice to be able to tell when melons are ready to harvest. Fruit picked too early will not ripen further. To test cantaloupes, sniff the stem end for characteristic aroma, look for pronounced netting of the skin and a change in color from green or yellow to tan, and check for a crack between stem and fruit. This is called the "full slip" stage and is the ideal time to harvest; "partial slip" is also common. To test honeydews, look for a slightly soft or springy blossom end and a change in skin color from green to ivory or greenish white, depending on the selection. Typically these melons do not have a "full slip" stage.

Sometimes diseases such as bacterial wild, powdery mildew, downy mildew, and gummy stem blight will plague melons. You can avoid problems by planting disease-resistant selections that resist one or more infections. Try 'Athena', 'Edisto 47', 'Hale's Best', 'Honeymoon Hybrid', and 'Sarah's Choice'. It's also best not to wet the foliage when you water to avoid spreading or incubating fungal diseases.

MENTHA
MINT
Lamiaceae
Perennials

- **US, MS, LS, CS; USDA 6-9, EXCEPT AS NOTED**
- **FULL SUN OR PARTIAL SHADE**
- **REGULAR WATER**

Mentha spicata

These Mediterranean natives spread rapidly by underground stems and can be quite invasive; to keep them in bounds, grow them in pots or boxes. Tough and unfussy, they grow almost anywhere but perform best in light, moist, medium-rich soil. Not favored by deer. Plants disappear in winter in colder part of range. Replant about every 3 years; propagate by division or runners.

M. x gracilis. GOLDEN APPLE MINT. Zones MS, LS, CS; USDA 7-9. Grows to 2 ft. tall. Smooth, deep green, 1½- to 3-in.-long leaves with yellow variegation have a spicy apple fragrance and flavor. Produces inconspicuous flowers. Use them for flavoring foods. Foliage is excellent in mixed bouquets.

M.x piperita. PEPPERMINT. Grows to about 3 ft. tall. Strongly scented, tooth-edged leaves to 3 in. long, dark green often tinged with purple. Small purplish flowers come in 1- to 3-in. spikes. Leaves are good for flavoring tea.

M.x p. citrata. ORANGE MINT, BERGAMOT MINT. Grows to about 2 ft. high and produces small lavender flowers and broad, 2-in.-long leaves with a slight orange flavor. Orange mint is used in potpourris and for flavoring foods.

M. pulegium. PENNYROYAL. Zones MS, LS, CS; USDA 7-9. Creeping plant 4–16 in. high, with inch-wide, bright green, nearly round leaves. Small lavender flowers in tight, short whorls. Strong mint fragrance and flavor. Poisonous if consumed in large quantities but safe as a flavoring. Needs a cool, moist site.

M. requienii. CORSICAN MINT. Creeping, mat-forming mint reaches only ½ in. high. Tiny, round, bright green leaves give it a mossy appearance; leaves release a delightful minty or sagelike fragrance when bruised. Can be used as an aromatic filler between stepping stones (but won't take heavy foot traffic). Bears tiny, tubular, light purple flowers.

M. spicata. SPEARMINT. Grows to 1–3 ft. high. Dark green, toothed leaves are slightly smaller than those of *M.x piperita*. Leafy spikes of flowers in pale lilac, pale blue, or white. Clip leaves and use them fresh from the garden or dry them and use to add flavor to foods, cold drinks, or jelly.

M. suaveolens. APPLE MINT. Zones MS, LS, CS; USDA 7-9. Stiff stems reach to 1½–3 ft. tall, bearing rounded, somewhat hairy, gray-green leaves 1–4 in. long. Produces purplish white flowers in 2- to 3-in. spikes. Aromatic foliage combines the fragrances of apple and mint. 'Variegata', pineapple mint, has white-marked leaves with a faint pineapple scent.

MERTENSIA VIRGINICA
VIRGINIA BLUEBELLS
Boraginaceae
Perennial

- **US, MS, LS; USDA 6-8**
- **PARTIAL TO FULL SHADE**
- **REGULAR WATER**

Mertensia virginica

Like a larger version of forget-me-not (*Myosotis*), these charming plants are native to woodlands in the eastern U.S. Plants emerge and flower early, then go dormant soon after ripening seeds, usually before midsummer. Bluish green, broadly oval leaves form loose clumps to 1½ ft. wide; from these clumps rise leafy, 1½- to 2-ft.-high stems bearing open clusters of nodding, 1-in. flowers. Buds usually range from pink to lavender, but they open to blue bells, sometimes with a pinkish cast. Virginia bluebells are good companions with naturalized daffodils (*Narcissus*) or with ferns, trillium, and bleeding heart (*Lamprocapnos*) in woodland gardens.

CARE

Provide moist soil rich in organic matter. Use summer annuals to fill void after plants die back. Clumps can be left in place indefinitely; they will slowly spread. To get more plants, use volunteer seedlings or dig and divide clumps in early autumn.

METASEQUOIA GLYPTOSTRO-BOIDES

DAWN REDWOOD
Cupressaceae
Deciduous tree

🌿 US, MS, LS, CS; USDA 6-9

☀️ FULL SUN

💧 REGULAR WATER

Metasequoia glyptostroboides

Thought to have been extinct for thousands of years, this plant was found growing in a few isolated sites in its native China during the 1940s. It is a pyramidal tree with small cones and soft, pale green needles that turn light orange-brown in autumn, then drop to reveal an attractive winter silhouette. Branchlets tend to turn upward. Young trees have reddish bark; older ones have darker, fissured bark and rugged, fluted trunk bases. Grows very fast when young—sometimes as much as 4–6 ft. a year. Give it room. Reaches about 90 ft. tall and 20 ft. wide at the age of 40 or so (trees haven't been in cultivation long enough to determine the maximum garden size). Looks like bald cypress (*Taxodium distichum*), another deciduous conifer. 'Ogon' has yellow foliage; 'Raven' is more vigorous, pyramidal, symmetrical, and resistant to diseases.

Grows best in good, well-drained soil with steady moisture. Not a good lawn tree due to protruding surface roots on older trees. Not suited to arid regions or seacoast, since dry heat and salty ocean winds will burn foliage.

MICROBIOTA DECUSSATA

SIBERIAN CARPET CYPRESS
Cupressaceae
Evergreen shrub

🌿 US, MS; USDA 6-7

☀️◐ FULL SUN OR PARTIAL SHADE

💧💧 MODERATE TO REGULAR WATER

Microbiota decussata

Native to Siberian mountains and hardy to any amount of cold, this neat, sprawling shrub resembles a trailing arborvitae (*Thuja*). Grows 1½ ft. tall, 7–8 ft. wide, with many plumy, horizontal or trailing branches closely set with scalelike leaves. Foliage is green in summer, turning purplish or reddish brown in winter. More shade tolerant than junipers (*Juniperus*). Needs excellent drainage. 'Fuzz Ball' has softer-textured new growth and more open habit to 3 ft. high and 4 ft. wide. Use as a bank cover.

MILIUM EFFUSUM 'AUREUM'

BOWLES' GOLDEN GRASS
Poaceae
Perennial grass

🌿 US, MS, LS; USDA 6-8

◐ LIGHT SHADE

💧💧💧 REGULAR TO AMPLE WATER

Milium effusum 'Aureum'

This cool-season grass is native to eastern North America and Eurasia. Its colorful selection 'Aureum' forms a clump to 2 ft. high and wide. Bright greenish gold leaves first grow erect, then take on arching, weeping form. Foliage is brightest in spring, turns light green by summer. In spring or late summer, it has delicate sprays of tiny golden flowers.

Effective for a spot of color in a woodland garden or shaded rock garden. Does best where summers are cool or mild; in hotter regions, plant goes partially dormant in summer. Seedlings usually have yellow foliage, though color may vary.

MILLETTIA RETICULATA

EVERGREEN WISTERIA
Papilionaceae
Evergreen or deciduous vine

🌿 LS, CS, TS; USDA 8-11

☀️ FULL SUN

💧 REGULAR WATER

Millettia reticulata

From China. Vigorous, twining vine with leaves like those of wisteria: shiny, leathery, divided into many leaflets. In fall, bears tight clusters of dark purple-red flowers with odor of cedar and camphor; unlike those of true wisteria, they stand atop the foliage. Usually described as reaching 15 ft., but—like wisteria—can attain great size. Grows extremely fast; once established, can overwhelm trees if permitted to climb into them. Best used as cover for large arbor, pergola, or chain-link fence. Evergreen in the Tropical South, deciduous elsewhere.

M. taiwanensis is a newer introduction, similar in appearance but more cold hardy and less vigorous, increasing its range into the Middle South.

M

MIMULUS X HYBRIDUS

MONKEY FLOWER
Scrophulariaceae
Perennial grown as cool-season annual

🌢 **US, MS, LS, CS, TS; USDA 6-11**

◐ **LIGHT SHADE**

💧 **REGULAR WATER**

Mimulus x hybridus

This uncommon annual gets its common name from its colorful, velvety flowers, which people with overactive imaginations liken to grinning monkey faces. Smooth, succulent, medium green leaves form mounds about 1 ft. high and wide. Two-lipped, funnel-shaped blooms, 2–2½ in. long, range in color from cream to rose, orange, yellow, and scarlet, usually with brownish maroon spots. Magic Mix series features largely unspotted flowers in warm, vibrant colors. Monkey flower is among the better annuals for shade; use it in borders, hanging baskets, or window boxes. *Mimulus alatus* 'Curious Orange' is a good performer, reaching 18 in. tall with bright orange flowers.

CARE

This plant keels over in high temperatures, so in most places it's best used as a cool-weather annual. Sow seeds in fall for winter and spring bloom; or set out plants in early spring (or in winter in Florida and South Texas). Provide rich soil and feed with a balanced water-soluble fertilizer every 2 weeks. Pull up plants when heat causes them to decline.

MIRABILIS

FOUR O'CLOCK
Nyctaginaceae
Perennials (grown as annuals in Upper South)

🌢 **US, MS, LS, CS, TS; USDA 7-11**

☼ **FULL SUN**

◌ **LITTLE WATER, EXCEPT AS NOTED**

◈ **SEEDS AND ROOTS ARE POISONOUS IF INGESTED**

Mirabilis jalapa

Fragrant, trumpet-shaped summer flowers open in late afternoon, hence the common name "four o'clock." Frosts kill these bushy plants to the ground, but in mild-winter areas they'll resprout from large, tuberous roots the following spring. Sow seeds in fall or spring; plants also self-sow freely. Treat as annuals in the Upper South.

M. jalapa. FOUR O'CLOCK, MARVEL OF PERU. From Peru. Erect, many-branched shrub forms a mounding clump 3–4 ft. high and wide. Deep green, oval, 2- to 6-in.-long leaves; sweet-scented, 1- to 2-in. flowers in white, red, yellow, magenta, and many intermediate shades. The hard black seeds are often exchanged by gardeners seeking particular flower colors. 'Broken Colors' bears streaked and freckled blossoms of raspberry-red, orange, lemon-yellow, and white, all on a single plant. 'Limelight' has bright green foliage topped with magenta flowers. 'Salmon Sunset' is soft orange with a pink star, and the Marbles series features color variegation in the blooms. 'Baywatch' is a giant, reaching 6–9 ft. tall, with large blooms in palest yellow. Regular water.

M. longiflora. SWEET FOUR O'CLOCK. Native to western Texas, Arizona, and Mexico. Grows 3 ft. tall and wide. Medium green, oval, pointed leaves are about 2 in. long. Blossoms are very slender, 4- to 6-in.-long tubes that flare open at the end; they are white flushed with rose or violet and have prominent magenta stamens. The fragrance is particularly sweet, excellent for the night garden.

M. multiflora. DESERT FOUR O'CLOCK. Native to the southwestern U.S. Forms a bushy mound 1–3 ft. high and 3–5 ft. wide. Gray-green, roundish to heart-shaped leaves to 3 in. long. Rose-pink or magenta, 2-in.-long flowers have a musky, sweet scent.

MISCANTHUS

SILVER GRASS
Poaceae
Perennial grasses

🌢 **US, MS, LS, CS; USDA 6-9**

☼☼ **FULL SUN OR PARTIAL SHADE, EXCEPT AS NOTED**

💧💧 **MODERATE TO REGULAR WATER**

Miscanthus 'Adagio'

Among the showiest and liveliest-looking of ornamental grasses, these are clump-forming plants that range from very large kinds to dwarf types good for small gardens and containers. Attractive flower panicles appear atop tall stalks; they open as tassels and gradually expand into silvery to pinkish or bronze plumes that usually last well into winter. Leaves are broad or narrow, always graceful; they may be solid colored, striped lengthwise, or banded crosswise.

In fall and winter, foliage of most species turns shades of yellow, orange, or reddish brown; it looks especially showy against snow or a background of dark evergreens. Stunning accent plants in large pots. Best planted in spring. Deer resistant.

M. x giganteus. GIANT SILVER GRASS. Impressive upright grass to 10–14 ft. tall, 8–10 ft. wide; self-supporting on stems to 2 in. thick. Arching, drooping leaves to 3 ft. long, 1½ in. wide, dark green with white midrib. Flower plumes to 1 ft. long rise 1–2 ft. above foliage during very late summer to fall; they emerge tan, open silver. Leaves turn purplish green in fall, then drop to leave tall, bare stalks over winter. Good summer screen or hedge; provides tropical effect. Takes seacoast conditions. Give partial shade in the Coastal South.

M. 'Purpurascens'. FLAME GRASS. Best in Upper and Middle South, where summers are not so long and hot. Upright clump 3–4 ft. high and wide, with green leaves to ½ in. wide. Silvery flower plumes 5–6 ft. tall. Foliage turns orange-red in fall, then fades to reddish brown. Can be short lived.

M. sinensis. JAPANESE SILVER GRASS. Native to Japan, Korea, China. Variable in size and foliage. Blooms in late summer or fall. Flowers are usually held well above foliage clumps; they may be cut for fresh or dried arrangements. Many selections are obtainable, and new ones arrive on the market every year. Here are some of the choicest.

'Adagio'. Very narrow, green leaves form a clump 2–3 ft. high and wide. Pink plumes rise to 4–5 ft. Better flower production than similar 'Yaku Jima'. Yellow fall foliage. Good container plant.

'Dixieland'. Compact grower to 3–4 ft. tall and wide. Green leaves edged with prominent white stripes.

'Goldfeder' ('Gold Feather'). Clump grows 4–5 ft. high and wide, with -in.-wide leaves edged light golden yellow. Silvery pink flower plumes on lax stems to 7 ft. tall. Stems tend to flop, but do so gracefully; can be staked to keep upright.

'Gracillimus'. MAIDEN GRASS. Narrow, dark green leaves with silver midrib; graceful clump to 4–5 ft. high, 6–8 ft. wide. Stems

5–6 ft. tall bear coppery plumes that mature to cream. Tends to flop; divide in spring every year or two to keep compact. Bright orange fall foliage. Self-sows profusely and can become a pest.

'Gracillimus Nanus'. DWARF MAIDEN GRASS. Growing only 3-4 ft. tall, it could be the answer for smaller gardens, containers, or compact compositions.

'Graziella'. Narrow leaves form a clump 4–5 ft. tall, 5–8 ft. wide. Silvery "ostrich" plumes rise to 6–7 ft. Coppery red and orange fall foliage. More refined and upright than 'Gracillimus'.

'Kirk Alexander'. Clump to 3–4 ft. tall and wide, with green leaves horizontally banded in greenish yellow. Pinkish copper plumes on stems to 5 ft. tall. More compact than the comparable 'Zebrinus'.

'Malepartus'. Dark green leaves are broader than those of species, in a clump 3 ft. high and wide. Flower plumes on 6- to 7-ft. stalks open rose-pink, fade to silvery white, finish tan. Orange fall foliage.

'Morning Light'. Sport of 'Gracillimus', with narrow band of white on leaf margins; less vigorous and more compact than

'Gracillimus'. Grows to 3–4 ft. high and wide; coppery flower plumes reach 5–6 ft. tall. Where the growing season is long, dig and divide clumps yearly to keep plants compact. Seedlings have leaves like those of 'Gracillimus'—deep green with silvery midrib. Good choice for heat and humidity.

'Sarabande'. Resembles 'Gracillimus' but is finer textured over all, with narrower leaves that are held more erect.

'Strictus'. PORCUPINE GRASS. Narrow, erect clump 4–6 ft. tall, 3–4 ft. wide. Spiky, ½-in.-wide leaves are banded horizontally with creamy yellow, suggesting porcupine quills. Golden plumes on 5- to 7-ft.-tall stems. Tends to flop with weight of blooms; should be staked.

'Variegatus'. A fountain of silver. Graceful, weeping clump 3–4 ft. high and wide, with -in. green leaves edged and striped in white. Spikes 5–6 ft. tall, tend to flop, especially on older plants; need staking. Divide every year or two. Give partial shade in Coastal South.

'Yaku Jima'. Compact, fine-leafed selection similar in form

to 'Adagio'. Tan flower plumes; reddish brown fall foliage.

'Zebrinus'. ZEBRA GRASS. Like 'Strictus' but lax and broadly arching; certain to flop in bloom unless staked. Most plants sold under this name are 'Strictus'.

M. s. condensatus 'Cabaret'. Boldest variegated miscanthus. Big, upright clump 6–7 ft. tall, 4–5 ft. across; wide (to 1¼-in.), ribbonlike leaves with a broad white center stripe and green edges. Pink-suffused stems to 8–9 ft. bear coppery pink plumes that age to cream.

M. s. c. 'Cosmopolitan'. Similar in growth and bloom to 'Cabaret', but foliage has the reverse pattern: leaves have a green center (with a white midrib) and white margins.

M. transmorrisonensis. EVERGREEN MISCANTHUS. Native to Taiwan. Forms a compact clump 2½–3½ ft. high and 3–4 ft. wide, with leaves 2–3 ft. long, ½ in. wide. Foliage remains green into early winter (and is evergreen in mildest-winter areas). Slender, silvery flower plumes on stems 5–7 ft. tall.

Plant begins blooming in spring in Coastal South; cutting stems nearly to ground when plumes begin to fade will produce a second bloom flush—sometimes even a third one. Cutting back stems also keeps clump looking fresh. Where winters are cold, bloom time comes in mid- to late summer. Plumes age to tan and drop their seeds before winter, leaving bare stems. Makes a good large-scale ground cover if given regular moisture and yearly mowing.

CARE

Cut back old foliage nearly to the ground before new leaves sprout in early spring; in climates with a long growing season, you can cut back again in midsummer to keep compact and to freshen foliage. Some selections collapse at bloom time unless given support of four or five narrow stakes inserted inconspicuously at edge of clump, concealed by foliage; wind twine or wire around stakes and clump at two levels. Divide in early spring every 2 or 3 years to limit clump size and prevent decline in vigor. Variegated types and thin-leafed species don't do well in central and southern Florida.

MITCHELLA REPENS
PARTRIDGEBERRY, TWINBERRY
Rubiaceae
Perennial

⬤ **US, MS, LS, CS; USDA 6-9**

◐ **PARTIAL TO FULL SHADE**

◖◖ **REGULAR TO AMPLE WATER**

Mitchella repens

Attractive small, creeping evergreen plant native to much of eastern North America. Roundish leaves are less than 1 in. long, borne in pairs along trailing, somewhat woody stems that root where they touch the ground. Paired, small white flowers appear in late spring or early summer; these are followed by bright red berries less than ¼ in. across. Small-scale ground cover best seen near eye level, such as on a shady bank or above a wall. Ideal for a woodland garden among shade-loving native plants such as ferns, mosses, may apple (*Podophyllum peltatum*), and galax. Provide steady moisture and acid soil containing plenty of leaf mold or other organic material.

ABOVE: Miscanthus sinensis 'Dixieland'

M

MOLINIA CAERULEA

MOOR GRASS
Poaceae
Perennial grasses

🌾 **US, MS, LS; USDA 6-8**

☼:◐ **FULL SUN OR PARTIAL SHADE**

💧💧 **REGULAR TO AMPLE WATER**

Molinia caerulea

Native to moist places from the British Isles to Siberia, south to the Caucasus and Turkey; resents dry, alkaline conditions. Long lived but slow growing, taking several years to reach full size. Erect, narrow, light green leaves form a neat, dense clump. In summer, spikelike clusters of yellowish to purplish flowers rise above clump; they age to tan and last well into fall. Wispy flowers give clump a see-through quality. Good cut flowers. In late fall, both leaves and flower clusters detach from plant's base, leaving nothing visible above ground. Set out new plantings in spring. There are two forms of moor grass, each with several selections. They bloom better in the Upper and Middle South.

M. c. arundinacea. TALL MOOR GRASS. Broader, gray-green leaves form a clump 2–3 ft. high and wide. Flowering stems are 5–8 ft. tall; they arch to the ground when wet, then straighten up as they dry. Give this one space so you can enjoy its form and motion in the wind. Among its forms are old favorite 'Karl Foerster', still one of the best; it has arching, 2½-ft.-long leaves and semierect flower stalks to 7 ft. tall. 'Skyracer' has erect, 3-ft.-tall leaves and 7- to 8-ft. stems bearing yellow flowers

that sparkle with morning dew. The arching, 6-ft.-tall stems of 'Transparent' have a translucent section between highest leaf and beginning of flower spike; plant bears tiny, airy blossoms and has bright orange-yellow fall foliage. 'Windspiel' ('Windplay') has wiry, vertical, 7- to 8-ft.-tall stems that sway with the slightest breeze.

M. c. caerulea. PURPLE MOOR GRASS. Produces a leafy clump 1–2 ft. high and wide; flower stalks are 2–3 ft. tall. 'Moorflamme' ('Moor Flame') has airy, purple-tinged flower heads held 2 ft. above the foliage, good red-orange autumn foliage color. 'Variegata' has leaves broadly edged in creamy white; yellowish flower stems arch out in all directions, giving a perfect fountain effect.

MOLUCCELLA LAEVIS

BELLS-OF-IRELAND, SHELL FLOWER
Lamiaceae
Cool-season annual

🌾 **US, MS, LS, CS, TS; USDA 6-11**

☼ **FULL SUN**

💧 **REGULAR WATER**

Moluccella laevis

Though its common name implies Irish origin, this plant is in fact native to the Mideast. To 2–3 ft. high, 10 in. wide. Flowers are carried almost from base in whorls of six. Showy part of flower is its large, apple-green, shell- or bell-shaped calyx, very veiny and crisp textured; small white tube of united petals in center is inconspicuous. Blossom spikes are quite attractive and long lasting in either fresh or dried

arrangements; be sure to remove the leaves, which are not especially good looking. Deer don't usually bother it.

CARE

Not an easy plant to grow in the South, as it dislikes hot, humid weather. Sow seeds in an empty planting bed in loose, fertile, well-drained soil in fall. Do not cover them with soil—they need light to germinate. Sow where you want plants to grow, as seedlings do not transplant well. In most areas, seedlings appear in spring. For long flower spikes, fertilize with a balanced water-soluble fertilizer every 2 weeks. In Florida and South Texas, seeds will germinate in fall (refrigerate them for a week before sowing), and the plant can be grown as a winter annual.

MONARDA

Lamiaceae
Perennials

🌾 **US, MS, LS; USDA 6-8**

☼:◐ **FULL SUN OR PARTIAL SHADE**

💧💧 **REGULAR TO AMPLE WATER**

Monarda didyma 'Violet Queen'

Native to eastern North America. Bushy, leafy clumps to 2–4 ft. high spread rapidly; can be invasive. Dark green leaves grow 4–6 in. long, have strong, pleasant odor like a blend of mint and basil. In summer, upright stems are topped by tight clusters of long-tubed flowers much visited by hummingbirds. Plant 10 in. apart. Divide every 3 or 4 years. Not long lived. Prone to mildew and other leaf diseases in dry, humid weather. Deer resistant.

M. bradburyana. EASTERN BEE BALM. Native perennial blooming white to pink to purple in late spring. Drought and disease tolerant.

M. didyma. BEE BALM, OSWEGO TEA. An old Southern favorite. Basic species has scarlet flowers surrounded by reddish bracts. Numerous garden selections and hybrids provide a choice of flower color, plant size, and disease resistance. If spent flowers are removed, all selections bloom over a period of 2 months or more. Don't let soil dry out.

Shorter selections include 'Petite Delight', 1–1½ ft. tall, lavender-rose, some disease resistance; 'Fireball', 2 ft. tall, red; and 'Grand Parade', just over 1 ft. tall, lavender-purple flowers.

Standard-sized selections are 'Adam', 3–4 ft. tall, scarlet; 'Cambridge Scarlet', 3–4 ft. tall, red; 'Croftway Pink', 3–4 ft. tall, pink; 'Dark Ponticum', 3 ft., violet-purple; 'Gardenview Scarlet', 3½–4 ft. tall, red, good disease resistance; 'Granite Pink', 2–4 ft. tall, purplish pink; 'Jacob Cline', 3 ft. tall, deep rosy red, good disease resistance; 'Mahogany', 3–4 ft. tall, dark red; 'Marshall's Delight', 2½–4 ft. tall, purplish pink, good disease resistance; 'Raspberry Wine', 3–4 ft. tall, purplish red, good disease resistance; 'Snow White', over 4 ft. tall, white; and 'Violet Queen', 3–4 ft. tall, purple, good disease resistance.

M. fistulosa. BERGAMOT. Lavender to light pink flowers encircled by whitish bracts are less showy than those of *M. didyma*. Best suited to wild gardens. This is not the source of the oil of bergamot used to flavor Earl Grey tea; that comes from the fruit of a type of citrus. Look for 'Claire Grace', 3 ft. tall, soft lavender; and 'Peter's Purple', 3–4 ft. tall, lavender-purple flowers. Both are highly mildew resistant.

M. punctata. SPOTTED HORSEMINT, DOTTED MINT. Usually smaller than the other species listed here. Blooms in midsummer, bearing two or more whorled clusters of purple-spotted yellow or pink blossoms per stem. Good plant for wildflower meadows and naturalized areas.

MONSTERA

Araceae
Evergreen vines

⚡ TS; USDA 10-11; OR HOUSEPLANT

☼ FILTERED SUNLIGHT; BRIGHT LIGHT

💧 REGULAR WATER

Monstera deliciosa

Tropical American natives related to philodendrons and resembling them in the glossiness and texture of their foliage. Most have cut and perforated leaves. Need rich soil. They can be grown outdoors only in the Tropical South. Indoors, direct sun in winter and bright reflected light the rest of the year are ideal; in dim light, leaves will be small and widely spaced on long, droopy stalks. If a tall potted plant gets bare at the base, replant it in a larger container along with a younger, lower plant to fill in; or cut it back and let it regrow from new shoots. Plants benefit from frequent misting.

M. deliciosa. SPLIT-LEAF PHILODENDRON, CUT-LEAF PHILODENDRON. To 30–60 ft. if planted in open bed outdoors or in greenhouse. Protect from frost (recovers fairly quickly from frost damage, though). Long, cordlike roots hang from stems and root when they reach soil; they also help support plant on trees or on moss logs. Young foliage is uncut; mature leaves are heavy, leathery, dark green, deeply cut, and perforated. Big plants may bear flowers like those of calla (*Zantedeschia*), with a thick, 10-in.-long spike surrounded by a boatlike white bract. If heat, light, and humidity are high, spike may ripen into edible fruit said to combine flavors of banana and pineapple. Eat only when fully ripe (green, caplike rind will knock off easily, exposing sticky fruit kernels); fruit can be painfully caustic before that stage. Allow plenty of room when growing this species as a houseplant; it may reach 15 ft. Often sold as *Philodendron pertusum*.

M. obliqua (*M. friedrichsthalii*). SWISS CHEESE PLANT. Plant can reach 25 ft. outdoors but is more commonly used as indoor plant. Smaller, thinner-textured leaves than those of *M. deliciosa*, with wavy rather than deeply cut edges. Common name comes from oval holes on either side of leaf midrib.

MORELLA

Myricaceae
Evergreen and semievergreen or deciduous shrubs or trees

⚡ ZONES VARY BY SPECIES

☼ FULL SUN

💧 WATER NEEDS VARY BY SPECIES

Morella cerifera

These North American native plants may not be spectacular, but they are tough and adaptable and have no serious pests. Excellent as informal screens, as foundation plantings, and in naturalized areas; *M. cerifera* is attractive enough to serve as a specimen tree. Good plants for coastal gardens—tolerate wind, sandy soil, salt spray. Foliage is pleasantly aromatic, especially when bruised. Although neither of the two species described here is showy in flower, female plants bear great quantities of subtly attractive autumn fruit that is favored by birds. These plants are not usually browsed by deer. Formerly called *Myrica*.

M. cerifera. WAX MYRTLE. Evergreen shrub or small tree. Zones MS, LS, CS, TS; USDA 7-11. Native to southeastern U.S. Grows quickly to at least 15–20 ft. tall and wide. Glossy, olive-green leaves are narrowly oval and pointed, to 3½ in. long. Small, grayish white fruit, borne in dense clusters, is heavily coated with a wax valued in candle making. Tolerates dry or wet soil, but best with moderate to regular water, especially when newly planted. 'Luray' is a compact selection reaching just 4 ft. tall and wide. *M. c. pumila* is a dwarf, suckering form that grows to only 3 ft. tall but spreads widely. 'Fairfax' is a compact, mounding plant, growing 6–8 ft. tall.

M. pensylvanica. BAYBERRY. Deciduous to semievergreen shrub. Zones US, MS; USDA 6-7. Native to coastal eastern North America. Dense and compact, to 9 ft. tall and 5–12 ft. wide. Narrowish, glossy, green leaves to about 4 in. long. Roundish fruit is covered with fragrant white wax—the bayberry wax used for candles. Regular water.

MORUS

MULBERRY
Moraceae
Deciduous trees

⚡ ZONES VARY BY SPECIES

☼ FULL SUN

💧 REGULAR WATER

Morus alba

Deciduous trees with leaves of variable size and shape, often on the same tree. Yellow fall color ranges from subdued to bright. Fruit resembles miniature blackberries and is eagerly gobbled by birds.

M. alba. WHITE MULBERRY, SILKWORM MULBERRY. Zones US, MS, LS, CS; USDA 6-9. Native to China, where its leaves are used as food for silkworms. Brought by European settlers to Jamestown, Virginia, where it escaped cultivation and quickly spread across the U.S., becoming a quite bothersome weed. Grows very fast, as much as 3 ft. per year. Takes rocky, alkaline soil; withstands just about any conditions, including heat, wind, salt spray, air pollution, and drought (but grows faster with regular water). Eventually reaches 30–50 ft. tall and wide. Leaves are 6 in. long, often lobed; flowers are inconspicuous.

Male trees produce prodigious amounts of pollen, which can be a problem for allergy sufferers. In summer, female trees bear sweet, insipid white, pink, or purple fruit that stains pavement where it falls—and birds flock to the fruit, gorge themselves, and then proceed to sully any deck, car, driveway, or passerby unlucky enough to be below. Seedlings come up everywhere, and surface roots make it difficult to garden beneath the tree. 'Pendula' ('Teas Weeping'), is a low-growing, strongly weeping form, but a fruit producer. Fruitless (male) forms are better for home gardens, though they do produce pollen. Selections include 'Chaparral' (weeping), 'Fruitless', 'Kingan', and 'Stribling' ("Mapleleaf").

M. bombycis 'Unryu' (*M. australis* 'Unryu'). CONTORTED MULBERRY. Zones US, MS, LS, CS; USDA 6-8. To 25 ft. tall and wide, with twisted, contorted branches useful in dried floral arrangements or for winter silhouette. Fast growth means that branches may be cut freely with no harm to the tree. Dark green, broadly oval, 6- to 7-in.-long leaves.

M. rubra. RED MULBERRY. Zones US, MS, LS; USDA 6-8. Native to eastern and central U.S. Well-behaved tree that resembles *M. alba* but is less weedy and produces less pollen and less fruit. Fruit—red when immature, ripening to black—is somewhat larger than that of *M. alba* and has a better flavor. Does best in rich soil. 'Illinois Everbearing' is a hybrid between this species and *M. alba*; its fruit ripens throughout summer.

MUHLENBERGIA

MUHLY GRASS
Poaceae
Perennial grasses

◈ **MS, LS, CS, TS; USDA 7-11, EXCEPT AS NOTED**

☼◑ **FULL SUN OR LIGHT SHADE**

◊◖◗ **LITTLE OR NO WATER TO REGULAR WATER**

Muhlenbergia capillaris

Showy and easy to grow, these native U.S. grasses combine handsome, slender leaves with eye-catching flower plumes that typically appear in late summer and fall. Foliage is semievergreen to evergreen in mild-winter areas, deciduous elsewhere. Plants tolerate heat and drought, but they look better and grow larger if given supplemental water. Good drainage is a must. Most are well adapted to Texas and the Southwest but will also succeed in many other areas, including Florida. Cut plants nearly to the ground in late winter to encourage fresh new growth.

M. capillaris. PINK MUHLY, HAIRY AWN MUHLY. Native to eastern U.S. Looks much like *M. filipes* but is taller and blooms earlier. Dark green foliage forms a mound to 3–4 ft. tall and at least as wide. Very showy flower plumes, like puffs of rosy red smoke, rise 2 ft. above the foliage in early fall. 'Regal Mist' ('Lenca') sports deep rosy pink flowers. 'White Cloud' is a 4-ft.-tall-and-wide white cloud in autumn. 'Pink Flamingo' is a hybrid between *M. capillaris* and *M. lindheimeri*, growing upright to 3–5 ft. tall with showy, 12-inch pink plumes.

M. dumosa. BAMBOO MUHLY. Zones MS, LS, CS; USDA 7-9. Native to Arizona, Mexico. To 3–6 ft. high and wide. Resembles bamboo, with slender, pendulous, woody stems set with narrow, bright green leaves up to 3 in. long. Inconspicuous flower clusters in spring. Endures heat, cold, and limy soil.

M. emersleyi. BULL GRASS. Native to Arizona, New Mexico, Texas. Gray-green leaves form a mound 1½–3 ft. tall, 3–4 ft. wide. From summer into fall, reddish or purplish flower spikes rise 2–3 ft. above the foliage; they fade to cream with age.

M. filipes. GULF MUHLY, SWEET GRASS. Native to the Southeast. Considered by some to be a variety of *M. capillaris*, this plant is shorter and blooms a little later in the year. Narrow, dark green leaves form mounds 2–3 ft. tall and wide. Rosy purple, wispy plumes rise an additional 2 ft. in mid- to late fall. Young leaves are used by the Gullah people of South Carolina to make traditional baskets. Called sweet grass because of its pleasant fragrance, which some liken to the scent of freshly mown hay.

M. lindheimeri. LINDHEIMER'S MUHLY. Native to Texas, Mexico. Clump of soft, arching, blue-green leaves grows to 5 ft. tall and wide, with amber flower spikes rising 2 ft. above foliage in autumn. Blooms of the species fade to gray; those of 'Amber Glow' turn yellow in fall. Tolerates moist conditions as well as dry, rocky, chalky soil.

M. rigens. DEER GRASS. Zones US, MS, LS, CS: USDA 6-9. Native from California to Texas and south into Mexico. Bright green leaves form a dense, tight clump to 4 ft. high and wide. Slender yellow or purplish flower spikes rise 2 ft. above the leaves in autumn; they are erect at first, then leaning. Good vertical accent.

M. rigida. PURPLE MUHLY. Native to Texas, New Mexico. Green clump to 2 ft. high and wide, producing 3-ft. spikes of brownish purple flowers in late summer and fall. Blossoms of 'Nashville' are an attractive true purple.

MURRAYA PANICULATA

ORANGE JESSAMINE
Rutaceae
Evergreen shrub

◈ **TS; USDA 10-11**

◑ **FILTERED SUNLIGHT**

◗ **REGULAR WATER**

Murraya paniculata

Native to Southeast Asia. An open, fast-growing shrub related to citrus that reaches 6–15 ft. tall and wide. Good as hedge, filler, or foundation plant. Sometimes grown as small single- or multi-trunked tree. Has graceful, pendulous branches with glossy, dark green leaves divided into three to nine oval, 1- to 2-in. leaflets. Blooms in late summer and fall (sometimes in spring). The white, bell-shaped blossoms have a wonderful jasmine fragrance. On mature plants, small red fruit follows flowers. Blooms attract bees. Reseeds and may become weedy.

A dwarf variety is usually sold as *M. exotica*. It is slower growing, more upright, and more compact than the species, reaching 6 ft. tall, 4 ft. wide. Its leaves are a lighter shade of green and have smaller, stiffer leaflets; bloom is usually less profuse.

CARE

Needs rich soil, frequent feeding. Subject to the same pests as citrus; also susceptible to nematodes.

MUSA

BANANA
Musaceae
Perennials

◈ **CS, TS; USDA 9-11, EXCEPT AS NOTED; OR GROW IN POTS**

☼◑ **FULL SUN OR PARTIAL SHADE**

◗ **AMPLE WATER**

Musa acuminata 'Siam Ruby'

For information on fruiting types, see Banana. The ornamental bananas described here include tall, medium-size, and dwarf plants; some of the tall sorts are the size of trees. All types are fast growing; all have soft, thickish stalks (called pseudostems) and spread by suckers or underground roots to form clumps that are often as wide as or wider than the plant is tall. Spectacular-looking long, typically broad leaves are easily tattered by strong winds, so choose protected planting sites. Will usually regrow from roots if cut down by frost; in frost-prone areas, locate plants where their absence won't be conspicuous. Give rich soil; feed heavily. Can be grown in containers and overwintered indoors (cut tops off tall plants). No water or fertilizer needed until moved outdoors after last spring frost. To overwinter plants in the ground in northern parts of hardiness range, mulch heavily in early winter.

M. acuminata. From Southeast Asia. Many selections available. Plants are grown for fruit in warmest gardens, but they also make handsome ornamentals there as well as in cooler areas. Some have especially attractive foliage. Leaves of 6- to 10-ft.-tall 'Zebrina' ('Roja', 'Rojo', 'Sumatra',

'Sumatrana') are green with maroon stripes; the plant produces tiny, inedible, dark maroon fruit. 'Siam Ruby' boasts rusty red foliage with lime-green flecks, growing 8 ft. tall under ideal conditions. 'Bordelon' has red striped leaves backed with red, one of the hardiest of the group, surviving into the Lower South.

M. balbisiana 'Thai Black'. Zones LS, CS, TS; USDA 8–11. This black-stemmed banana impresses with fast growth that can reach 18 ft. tall, sending up new shoots to increase the clump annually. Named for the black midribs coming from the pseudostem. Needs good drainage in winter.

M. basjoo. JAPANESE BANANA. Zones US, MS, LS, CS, TS; USDA 6–11. From China. The hardiest of the banana clan. To 15 ft. tall, with narrow, green leaves about 8 ft. long. Terminal spikes of yellow flowers may be followed by small, unpalatable fruit.

M. itinerans xishuang-bannaensis. Zones MS, LS, CS, TS; USDA 7–11. From China. This cold-hardy giant has been known

to overwinter as far north as Louisville, Kentucky. Growing 40 ft. tall in warm zones and half that in cool climates, 'Mekong Giant' develops pink-purple pseudostems. The plant spreads rapidly by underground rhizomes. Flowers are red and yellow; grows in either sun or shade. Ornamental fruit.

M. ornata. FLOWERING BANANA. Grows to 9 ft. tall, with blue-green leaves 4–6 ft. long and 1–1½ ft. wide; each leaf has a red-purple midrib on the underside. Erect blossom stalks carry pale pink or pale purple bracts tipped with yellow; these are used as cut flowers. Small fruit (to 3 in. long) is decorative but inedible. 'African Red' has red bracts and yellow fruit. 'Bronze' features light green leaves and pink-tinged stems; it bears orange-bronze inflorescences. 'Milky Way' has white bracts and white fruit; 'Royal Purple' bears bluish purple bracts.

M. x paradisiaca. This hybrid of *M. acuminata* and *M. balbisiana* provides the most common ornamental and some selections

of fruiting bananas. Clumps grow to 20 ft. tall and half as wide, with leaves to 9 ft. long. Flower stalks are pendent, bearing large, showy, powdery purple bracts; fruit (usually seedy and inedible) follows in warm and frost-free areas such as south Florida or sheltered courtyards during mild winters in the Coastal South. For information about growing edible fruit, see Bananas.

M. velutina. PINK BANANA. Zones LS, CS, TS; USDA 8–11. From India. Grows to 5–7 ft. tall, with 3-ft.-long leaves that are green above, bronzy beneath. Upright pink bracts; orange flowers; and small, velvety pink bananas that are seedy and inedible but highly decorative.

MUSCARI
GRAPE HYACINTH
Asparagaceae
Perennials from bulbs

🖊 **US, MS, LS; USDA 6–8**

☼◐ **FULL SUN OR LIGHT SHADE**

💧 **REGULAR WATER DURING GROWTH AND BLOOM**

Muscari armeniacum 'Valerie Finnis'

Native to the Mediterranean and southwestern Asia. Clumps of grassy, fleshy leaves appear in fall and live through cold and snow. Spikes of small, typically urn-shaped blue or white flowers (fragrant, in some species) bloom in early spring. Deer and rodent resistant.

M. armeniacum. ARMENIAN GRAPE HYACINTH. Bright blue, slightly fragrant flowers on 8-in. stems rise above a clump of floppy foliage. 'Blue Spike' has double blue flowers in a tight

cluster at top of spike. 'Early Giant' blooms somewhat earlier than the species, has darker blue flowers edged in white. 'Cantab', with light blue blossoms, grows lower than the species and has neater foliage and a later bloom time. 'Christmas Pearl' is also earlier and is easy to force without much chilling. 'Valerie Finnis' has lightly fragrant, powder-blue flowers tightly packed onto 6- to 8-in.-tall stems in a roughly spiral pattern. Spreads more slowly than other types.

M. aucheri. Stems to 8 in. tall. Flowers on lower part of spike are bright blue; those on upper part are paler blue.

M. azureum. Blossom spikes are between those of hyacinth and grape hyacinth in appearance. Stalks to 8 in. high bear tight clusters of fragrant, sky-blue flowers that have a bell shape (rather than the usual urn shape).

M. botryoides. An old-time favorite. Medium blue, lightly scented flowers on stems to 1 ft. tall. 'Album' has white flowers.

M. comosum. FRINGE HYACINTH, TASSEL HYACINTH. Bears loose clusters of unusual, tattered-looking flowers on 1- to 1½-ft. stems. Blossoms are greenish brown on lower part of spike, bluish purple on upper part. 'Plumosum', feathered or plume hyacinth, produces violet-blue to reddish purple flowers that look like shredded coconut.

M. latifolium. Possibly the showiest of the grape hyacinths. Each bulb produces just one leaf and a flowering stem to 6 in. tall. Flowers on lower part of spike are deepest violet, those on upper part vivid indigo blue.

M. neglectum. STARCH HYACINTH. Stems about 6 in. tall. Lower part of bloom spike holds tightly crowded, very dark blue blossoms edged in white, while upper part is set with pale blue blooms. Flowers are said to smell like laundry starch.

CARE

Plant in early fall, setting bulbs about 2 in. deep and 3 in. apart in well-drained soil. Plant in masses or drifts under flowering trees or shrubs; use in edgings and rock gardens; grow in containers. Very long lived. Dig and divide when clumps become crowded. Plants

ABOVE: Musa basjoo at Montrose Gardens, Hillsborough, North Carolina

self-sow under favorable conditions. Naturalized grape hyacinths are often seen blooming in old cemeteries.

MUSELLA LASIOCARPA

CHINESE YELLOW BANANA
Musaceae
Perennial

🌗 **MS, LS, CS, TS; USDA 7-11**

☀️◐ **FULL SUN OR PARTIAL SHADE**

💧 **REGULAR WATER**

Musella lasiocarpa

Unusual ornamental banana from Yunnan Province in China. Very cold hardy, surviving temperatures into the teens. A single thick pseudostem, broad at the base and tapering toward the tip, grows 5–6 ft. tall and is topped with dark green, 3- to 4-ft.-long leaves. Prized by plant collectors for the exotic, waxy inflorescence that emerges at the plant's top and resembles a golden, 8-in.-wide artichoke; it can last all summer. Clusters of small true flowers peek out between the bracts. After flowering, the original pseudostem dies, but suckers sprout from the base. Best enjoyed as an oddity. During the course of flowering, it may drop its foliage and look like a big yellow starfish sitting atop a stump, but it can still stop traffic.

MUSTARD

Brassicaceae
Cool-season annual

🌗 **US, MS, LS, CS, TS; USDA 6-11**

☀️ **FULL SUN**

💧 **REGULAR WATER**

'Green Wave' mustard

Eating mustard greens in spring and fall is a time-honored Southern tradition. Loaded with Vitamins A and C, the nutritious greens reach full size just 4 to 6 weeks after sowing.

Two types of mustard are widely grown. Curly-leafed mustard has leaves with crinkled edges; they take some time to clean, as grit tends to collect in the crinkles. Smooth-leafed mustard (also called tendergreen mustard or mustard spinach) has smooth, dark green leaves. It matures earlier than the curly-leafed type and is more tolerant of warm, dry weather. Use young leaves of either as a salad green; older leaves can be cooked like spinach.

For spring harvests, sow seed 2 to 4 weeks before the expected last frost. A single spring planting will produce until plants bolt (go to seed) after the onset of warm weather. To extend the harvest, make a second planting 2 to 3 weeks after the first. For fall harvests, sow in late summer or early fall. A light frost will sweeten the greens' flavor.

Recommended curly-leafed selections include 'Green Wave' (heat tolerant; slow to bolt; 45 days), 'Old Fashioned Ragged Edge' (Southern heirloom with excellent flavor; early to bolt; 42 days), and 'Southern Giant Curled' (large, bright green leaves; slow to bolt; 45 days). Recommended smooth-leafed mus-

tards include 'Florida Broadleaf' (very large leaves; slow to bolt; 47 days), 'Red Giant' (beautiful reddish purple leaves; slow to bolt; 43 days), 'Savannah' (large, deep green leaves; mild flavor; very early; slow to bolt; 20 days), and 'Tatsoi' (pretty, dark green rosettes, mild flavor, cold hardy; 43 days).

From an ornamental perspective, mustard is one of the greens used in winter flower gardens. Selections with especially attractive foliage include 'Garnet Giant' (deep purple, rounded leaves), 'Golden Streak' (bright green with lacy foliage), 'Green Wave', 'Mizuna Purple' (purple stem with serrated foliage), 'Mizuna Red Streak' (fringed purple and green leaves), 'Red Giant', 'Red Mizuna' (lobed leaf with green and red foliage), 'Ruby Streak' (lacy thread-shaped leaves from green to maroon), 'Scarlet Frill' (lacy scarlet leaves), 'Spicy Green' (frilly green leaves), and 'Wasabina' (extremely wavy lime-green leaves).

CARE

Mustard is one of the easiest vegetables to grow. You can start from transplants, but direct seeding is easier. Before planting, work into the soil either ¼ cup of 10-10-10 fertilizer per 10 ft. of row or a 2-in. layer of compost. Sow seeds thinly in rows spaced 2 ft. apart—or broadcast the seeds over a wide bed. Cover with ½ in. of soil. Thin seedlings to 4–8 in. apart (thinnings can be eaten cooked as a vegetable or fresh in salads). Keep the soil evenly moist throughout the growing season. Three to four weeks after planting, sprinkle 10-10-10 fertilizer around base of plants at the rate of ¼ cup per 10 ft. of row; water it in. To harvest, break off outer leaves when they are 4–5 in. long; let inner ones continue to grow. Once the plants flower, the leaves will develop a strong, peppery flavor.

ABOVE: 'Red Giant' mustard in a mixed container planting

MYOSOTIS

FORGET-ME-NOT

Boraginaceae

Perennials, biennials, and cool-season annuals

✀ **US, MS, LS; USDA 6-8**

◖ **PARTIAL SHADE**

💧 **REGULAR WATER**

Myosotis sylvatica

The species described feature exquisite, typically blue springtime flowers, tiny but profuse. Grow easily and densely as ground covers. Do best in cool, moist areas, as in woodland gardens, at pond edges, along stream banks. Not usually browsed by deer.

M. palustris 'Southern Blues'. Perennial. This forget-me-not tolerates more heat than most. It spreads like a ground cover without taking over, and blooms from spring into summer. Grows best in moist garden soil or on the edge of a pond.

M. scorpioides. Perennial. Native to Europe, Asia, North America. This species is similar in most respects to *M. sylvatica*, but it grows a little lower, blooms even longer, and has roots that live over from year to year. Flowers are about ¼ in. wide; they come in blue, white, or pink, usually with a yellow or white eye. Shiny, oblong, bright green leaves. Plant spreads by creeping roots.

M. sylvatica. Annual or biennial. Native to Europe. To 6–12 in. high, 2 ft. wide. Soft, hairy foliage; basal leaves reach 4 in. long, while those set higher on stems are ½–2 in. long. Pure blue flowers with a white eye are ⅛ in. wide, set loosely along top portions of stems. Blooms and seeds profusely for a long season, beginning in late winter or early spring.

Self-sows and will persist for years unless weeded out. Often sold as *M. alpestris*. Improved selections include 'Bluesylva' and 'Rosylva'.

MYRTUS COMMUNIS

MYRTLE

Myrtaceae

Evergreen shrub

✀ **LS, CS, TS; USDA 8-11**

☀◖ **FULL SUN OR PARTIAL SHADE**

◍💧 **LITTLE TO MODERATE WATER**

Myrtus communis

Native to the Mediterranean, this venerable shrub has never quite made its mark in the South. It's a bulky, dense, rounded plant with fine-textured foliage: glossy, bright green, oval, pointed leaves to 2 in. long, pleasantly aromatic when brushed or bruised. Typically reaches 5–6 ft. high and 4–5 ft. wide (though old plants may reach 15 ft. high, 20 ft. wide). White, sweet-scented, -in. flowers with many stamens bloom in summer; they are followed by small, bluish black berries. Good for a foundation planting or informal hedge or screen; requires little or no pruning. Also takes well to shearing into a formal hedge or topiary; can be pruned like a small tree to reveal attractive branches. Best in fertile, well-drained soil. Fairly common in Florida but does not tolerate salt spray. Not usually bothered by deer.

Named selections vary in foliage character and overall size. 'Variegata' fits the basic description but has white-edged leaves. 'Boetica' is especially upright, with thick, twisted branches and larger, darker leaves. 'Buxifolia'

has small leaves like those of boxwood (*Buxus*). Dwarf forms include 'Compacta', a small-leafed selection popular for edgings and low formal hedges; 'Compacta Variegata', similar but with white-margined foliage; and 'Microphylla', with tiny, closely set leaves.

N

NANDINA DOMESTICA

NANDINA, HEAVENLY BAMBOO

Berberidaceae

Evergreen or semievergreen to deciduous shrub

✀ **US, MS, LS, CS; USDA 6-9**

☀◖● **SUN OR SHADE; COLORS BETTER IN SUN**

💧💧 **MODERATE TO REGULAR WATER**

Nandina domestica

From China and Japan, nandina is a true survivor. Old plants are often seen growing in cemeteries, overgrown gardens, on abandoned homesites, where they fruit and flower for decades with absolutely no care. Nandina takes sun or shade, tolerates drought (although well-drained soil is essential), and has no serious pests. Semievergreen or deciduous in the Upper South; leaves drop at 10°F and stems are damaged at 5°F, but plants usually recover quickly.

Nandina belongs to the barberry family but is reminiscent of bamboo in its lightly branched, canelike stems and delicate,

fine-textured foliage. Remarkably upright, its growth is slow to moderate, reaching 6–8 ft. tall and 3 ft. wide. It spreads slowly by stolons to form large clumps. Can be divided in fall, winter, or spring. Leaves are intricately divided into many 1- to 2-in., pointed, oval leaflets, creating a lacy pattern. Foliage expands pinkish and bronzy red, then turns to soft light green. It picks up purple and bronze tints in fall and often turns fiery crimson in winter, especially in sun and with some frost. Pinkish white or creamy white blossoms in loose, erect, 6- to 12-in. clusters at branch ends in late spring or early summer. If plants are grouped, shiny red berries follow the flowers; single plants seldom fruit as heavily. Berries supply winter food for birds; clusters cut for holiday decorations last a long time. Birds will also spread the seeds, so plants may appear where you didn't plant them. Resistant to damage by deer. Good for screening, containers, and planting in narrow beds. Nandina will not scratch cars or people. Selections include the following.

'Blush Pink' ('AKA'). To 2 ft. tall and wide. Foliage emerges bright pink in spring, turns red in fall and winter. No berries.

'Compacta'. To 4–5 ft. tall, 3 ft. wide. Very lacy looking, with more canes and narrower, more numerous leaflets than the species.

'Fire Power'. To 2 ft. tall and wide. Red-tinged summer foliage turns bright red in winter.

'Flirt' ('Murasaki'). To 1–2 ft. tall and 1½–2 ft. wide. New growth is bright red fading to dark red and green. Hardy to -10°F (-23°C).

'Gulf Stream'. Slow-growing, dense mound to 3–3½ ft. tall, 1½ ft. wide, with blue-green summer foliage and good red winter color. Does not sucker. No berries.

'Harbour Dwarf'. To 2–3 ft. tall. Rather than forming a discrete clump, it spreads by rhizomes to make a good ground cover. Foliage has orange-red to bronzy red winter color.

'Moyers Red'. Standard-size plant with broad leaflets. Brilliant red winter color in regions that get frost. Flowers are pinker than those of the species, and berries ripen a month or two earlier.

'Nana' ('Nana Purpurea', 'Atropurpurea Nana'). To 2 ft. tall,

N

ABOVE: Nandina domestica leucocarpa 'Alba'

2–3 ft. wide. Coarse foliage is purplish green in summer, purplish red to bright red in winter. Leaves typically show cupping, curling, and color streaks. Much overused—and out of place in most gardens. A nice gas station plant. Not known to flower or fruit.

'Obsession' ('Seika'). To 3–4 ft. tall and 3–4 ft. wide. Hardy to -10°F. Red new growth.

'Plum Passion'. Grows to 4–5 ft. tall and 3 ft. wide. Narrow leaves are deep purplish red when young, deep green during summer, and reddish purple in winter.

'Sienna Sunrise'. Slow grower to 3–4 ft. tall, 2½ ft. wide. Foliage is fiery red when new; it matures to medium green by summer, then picks up red highlights again in winter.

'Woods Dwarf'. Slow, dense grower to 1½ ft. high and wide.

Foliage turns crimson-orange to scarlet in winter.

N. d. leucocarpa ('Alba'). Similar to the species in size and shape, but berries of this selection are creamy yellow and the light green foliage lacks the typical reddish bronze tinge.

CARE

Nandina grows best in rich soil with regular water, but its roots can even compete with tree roots in dry shade. In alkaline soil, leaves may appear yellow with green veins due to iron deficiency. To reduce height, use hand pruners, never hedge shears. Maintain a natural look by pruning each stalk to a different height, cutting back to a tuft of foliage. Renew neglected clumps by cutting one-third of the main stalks to the ground each year for three years.

NARCISSUS
DAFFODIL, NARCISSUS, JONQUIL
Amaryllidaceae
Perennials from bulbs

- US, MS, LS, CS (NORTHERN THIRD); USDA 6-9, EXCEPT AS NOTED
- FULL SUN OR PARTIAL SHADE
- REGULAR WATER DURING GROWTH AND BLOOM

Narcissus 'Barrett Browning'

Native to Western Europe primarily, these are arguably the finest and most valuable spring bulbs for the South. They are long lived, increasing naturally from year to year; they stand up to cold and heat; they have many garden uses; and they offer a fascinating array of flower forms, sizes, and colors. Given minimal care at planting, all thrive with virtually no further attention. They do not require summer watering (although they'll accept it) and need only infrequent division. Finally, rodents and deer won't eat them.

Flowering commences in winter in the Lower and Coastal South, in early spring elsewhere. The basic colors are shades of yellow and white, but you'll also find orange, salmon, peach, apricot, pink, green, and even red.

Gardeners tend to use the names "daffodil," "narcissus," and "jonquil" interchangeably. Technically, "daffodil" is the common name for the genus *Narcissus* in all forms, whereas "jonquil" denotes one type of narcissus, *N. jonquilla* and its hybrids. Jonquils have smaller, fragrant, clustered blooms and cylindrical leaves with pointed tips, reminiscent of quills. If you stick to calling them all "narcissus," you can't go wrong.

All have the same basic flower structure. Each bloom has a perianth (six outer petal-like segments) that surrounds (and is held at right angles to) a central corona (also called the trumpet or cup, depending on its length).

Most types reach 1–1½ ft. tall. Flowers usually face the sun; be sure to keep this in mind when choosing a planting spot. Use narcissus under high-branching trees and flowering shrubs, among ground cover plantings, in woodland and rock gardens, or in borders, but be sure they are not on the north side of taller plants that would shade them. They need sunlight to bloom year after year. Plant them in naturalistic, sweeping drifts. Grow them in containers. They make fine cut flowers, but it is best to pick them, breaking the stem at the base by hand, rather than with clippers. Give them a vase of their own; freshly cut stems release a substance that causes other cut flowers to wilt.

Following are the generally recognized divisions of daffodils and recommended selections in each division. While there are many more selections than space allows, these are certainly proven growers in Southern gardens. Some old favorites are no longer in production, but some new ones are ready to take their places in a spring garden.

Trumpet daffodils. The trumpet is as long as or longer than the perianth segments; one flower per stem. The best known is yellow 'King Alfred', a classic type no longer in the market. Buying 'King Alfred' usually means planting 'Carlton', 'Dutch Master', or 'Golden Harvest' (susceptible to basal rot). Newer 'Arctic Gold', 'Dutch Master', 'Marieke', and 'Primeur' are superior yellows. The best pure white selection is 'Mount Hood'. Bicolors with white segments and a yellow trumpet include 'Bravoure', 'Holland Sensation', and 'Las Vegas'. 'Spellbinder' features yellow segments and a yellow-tipped white trumpet. 'Pay Day' and 'Pistachio' have a halo of white at the base of the trumpet but are otherwise yellow. For the earliest daffodils, plant 'Rijnveld's Early Sensation'.

Large-cupped daffodils. The cup is shorter than the perianth segments but always more than one-third their length;

one flower per stem. Solid yellow selections include 'Carlton' (the second most numerous daffodil), 'Gigantic Star', and 'Saint Keverne' (a great choice for the Lower South). Solid whites include 'Misty Glen', 'Stainless', and 'White Plume'. Selections with white segments and a colored cup include 'Accent' (salmon-pink cup), 'Bella Vista' (red-orange cup), 'Garden Club of America' (coral-rimmed yellow cup), 'Ice Follies' (yellow cup), 'Pink Charm' (pink cup), 'Roulette' (yellow-orange cup), and 'Salome' (apricot-yellow cup that fades to salmon). Those with yellow segments and a colored cup include 'By George' (peachy pink cup), 'Ceylon' (red-orange cup), 'Fortissimo' (orange cup), and 'Monal' (orange-red cup). 'Altun Ha' has yellow segments and a cup that turns white.

Small-cupped daffodils. The cup is no more than one-third the length of the perianth segments; one flower per stem. Selections include 'Angel' (white segments and white cup with green eye), 'Audubon' (white segments and pale yellow cup banded with pink), and 'Barrett Browning' (white segments and orange-red cup).

Double daffodils. Doubling of the cup, perianth segments, or both; one or more flowers per stem. Flower looks more like a peony than a typical daffodil. Examples are 'Cheerfulness' (white with yellow flecks), 'Golden Smiles' (golden yellow), 'My Story' (white segments with pink), 'Erlicheer' (white segments with yellow), and 'Tahiti' (soft yellow with red segments).

Triandrus hybrids. Cup at least two-thirds the length of perianth segments; several nodding flowers per stem. Diminutive 'Hawera' has four to six lemon-yellow flowers per stem; it is good for naturalizing and will spread by seed. 'Petrel' is pure white, 3–5 flowers per stem, and excellent fragrance. Old favorite 'Thalia' offers 2–3 elegant, pure-white, fragrant flowers per stem.

'Katie Heath' is white with pink cup; 'Ginter's Gem' is glowing yellow with orange at the base of the cup.

Cyclamineus hybrids. Early bloomers with one flower per stem. Perianth segments strongly swept back. Popular selections include 'February Gold' (solid yellow), 'Jack Snipe' (white segments, yellow cup), 'Jetfire' (yellow segments, red-orange cup), 'Rapture' (classic form, solid yellow), 'Surfside' (white segments, pale yellow cup turns white), and 'Wisley' (white segments, yellow cup).

Jonquilla hybrids. These are some of the best for the South, because they are native to the southern Mediterranean and accustomed to hot summers. Each stem bears one to five small, very fragrant flowers; leaves are dark green and very narrow. Choices include 'Baby Moon' (bright yellow); 'Intrigue' (lemon-yellow segments, yellow cup fading to white); 'Pipit' (yellow segments, white cup); and 'Quail', 'Sun Disc' (the latest bloomer), 'Sweetness', and 'Baby Boomer' (all solid yellow). For color diversity, choose 'Blushing Lady' (yellow segments, pink cup), 'Beautiful Eyes' (white segments, orange cup), 'Pappy George' (yellow segments, orange cup), 'Sailboat' (white segments, pale yellow cup), and 'Sweet Smiles' (white segments, pink cup).

Tazetta and Tazetta hybrids. These are perennials in Lower and Coastal South gardens because they have little requirement for cold weather to bloom and they can be easily forced into bloom by gardeners at any latitude.

Early-blooming types bearing clusters of 3 to 20 flowers on each stout stem; many have a musky-sweet fragrance that can be overpowering indoors. The most heat-tolerant group, they do well in central Florida; hardy only to about 10°F. 'Avalanche' ('Seventeen Sisters') produces clusters of 15 to 20 blossoms with white segments and a yellow cup. 'Aspasia' is a lovely heirloom with white segments and yellow cup. 'Falconet' and 'Martinette' feature yellow segments and a red-orange cup. 'Geranium' and 'Cragford' have creamy white segments and an orange cup; 'Minnow' has a pale yellow cup and pale yellow segments that fade to cream.

This division also includes the popular paperwhite group of narcissus that are commonly forced into early bloom indoors. Plant them in bowls of pebbles or soil and give them cool temperatures (50–60°F) and bright light. 'Grand Soleil d'Or' has golden yellow segments and an orange cup, 'Wintersun' has white segments and a soft yellow cup, and pure white 'Ziva' has the strong fragrance and easy-to-force nature of the classic paperwhite. 'Inbal' has all the quality of 'Ziva' but with a more delicate fragrance and flatter cup.

Poeticus daffodils. Fragrant flowers with white perianth segments and a short, disk-shaped cup with a green or yellow center and a red rim; one blossom per stem. 'Actaea' has the largest flowers (up to 4 in. across) and is the best known. 'Angel Eyes' is another good choice. These daffodils with a red-rimmed cup are sometimes given the name "pheasant's eye," but this term is correctly applied to the heirloom *Narcissus poeticus recurvus*.

Split-corona hybrids. Cup is split for at least one-third its length into two or more segments. 'Cassata' (white perianth segments, yellow cup), 'Curly Lace' (all golden yellow with a ruffled cup), 'Exotic Mystery' (all greenish yellow), 'Mary Gay Lirette' (white segments, peachy pink cup), and 'Smiling Twin' (white segments, pale yellow cup) are some of the more readily available selections in this small but growing class.

Heirloom daffodils. These old favorites often can be seen blooming at old homesites and graveyards and along roadsides throughout the South.

N. bulbocodium. HOOP PETTICOAT DAFFODIL. Grows to 6 in. tall. Small, upward-facing flowers are mostly trumpet shaped, with very narrow, pointed perianth segments. Deep and pale yellow selections are available. Spreads by seed; good choice for naturalizing.

***N.* 'Butter and Eggs'** ('Golden Phoenix', 'Aurantius Plenus'). Double yellow flowers. An old Southern favorite similar to *N. pseudonarcissus* 'Telemonius Plenus', but flowers open dependably throughout climate range and are softer in color, without streaks. Grows 16–18 in. tall.

HOW TO GROW DAFFODILS

EXPOSURE Narcissus do best in full sun, though they'll tolerate the dappled shade beneath high-branching deciduous trees. They won't bloom well in shade so be careful to plant them where they are not on the north side of trees, shrubs, or even a building.

SOIL They are not fussy about soil as long as it is loose and well drained. To improve drainage in heavy soils, deeply dig in plenty of organic matter prior to planting.

PLANTING Set bulbs about 2 to 3 times as deep as they are tall—a minimum of 5–6 in. deep for large bulbs and 3–5 in. deep for smaller ones. Space bulbs approximately 3 times their width apart.

WATERING Water newly planted bulbs thoroughly. In many regions, fall and winter are wet or snowy enough to provide moisture. Keep plantings well watered in spring if precipitation fails; continue until foliage begins to yellow. Daffodils don't need summer moisture.

DIVIDING Clumps need dividing only when bloom quantity and/or quality declines. Wait until the leaves die back, then dig the clumps and replant.

FORCING For early bloom indoors, set bulbs close together in a pot with their tips level with the soil surface. Place the pot in a well-drained trench or a cold frame, and cover with 6–8 in. of sand, chopped leaves, or pine straw. They should be well rooted in 2 weeks if kept at 50-60°F. However, more chilling is needed. Early bulbs need 8 weeks at 35°F or below; later bloomers need as much as 16 weeks. Then move the pot to a greenhouse or well-lit, cool room, and watch for blooms. Keep well watered.

An easy alternative is to plant bulbs in a pot as above and cover with mulch to keep them cool. When they start growing, bring them indoors. After the blooms fade and the last frost is past, transfer the bulbs to your garden. Paperwhite narcissus can be forced into winter bloom with no chilling.

SUREFIRE DAFFODILS FOR THE SOUTH

These daffodils bloom dependably in most areas and increase with little care: 'Barrett Browning', 'Carlton', 'Ceylon', 'February Gold', 'Geranium', 'Hawera', 'Ice Follies', 'Jack Snipe', 'Jetfire', 'Minnow', *Narcissus odorus*, 'Quail', 'Saint Keverne', 'Salome', 'Tête-à-tête', and 'Thalia'. In general, the early-blooming ones perform best in the South.

N. jonquilla. JONQUIL. Semi-cylindrical, erect to spreading, rushlike leaves. Clusters of early, very fragrant, golden yellow flowers with short cups. To 1 ft. tall. Much like 'Baby Moon'.

N. medioluteus. TWIN SISTERS. Grows to 14 in. tall, bearing two flowers per stem; white segments, small yellow cup. Very late; last daffodil of the season.

N. odorus. CAMPERNELLE JONQUIL. A sweet-scented, old-fashioned favorite. Often found in older gardens and cemeteries in Texas, Louisiana, and Arkansas. Grows to 1 ft. tall. Early in the season bears golden yellow, bell-like cups with recurved round segments; two to four flowers per stem. Rushlike leaves. Tolerates heavy clay and limy soils. 'Plenus' has double flowers.

N. poeticus recurvus. PHEASANT'S EYE. Old favorite. To 1 ft. tall. Small yellow cup with green central "eye" and red rim; pure white, reflexed segments.

N. pseudonarcissus. LENT LILY. One of the oldest daffodils—in cultivation since 1200 A.D. Grows to 12–14 in. tall. Long yellow cup; twisted yellow perianth segments that are swept forward, giving the blossoms a dog-eared look. Blooms early. 'Telemonius Plenus' (considered by many to be identical to 'Van Sion') has double yellow flowers with green streaks. Flowers of this selection often fail to open properly in the warm, humid springs of the Lower and Coastal South.

Other daffodil selections. This category contains all types that don't fit the other divisions. 'Tête-à-Tête' (the most numerous daffodil) and 'Jumblie' (both yellow) have flowers like those of the *Cyclamineus* hybrids, but they are dwarf plants that reach a height of only 6 in.

CARE

Plant bulbs as soon as they are available in fall. They should feel solid and heavy and be free of discoloration. "Double-nose" bulbs will give you the most and largest flowers the first season after planting. For planting depth and spacing, see "How To Grow Daffodils" on page 447.

After the blossoms fade, let the leaves mature and yellow naturally—if you cut the foliage before it yellows, subsequent flowering may be reduced or eliminated. Lift and divide clumps when flowers get smaller and fewer. To make this job easier, dig clumps just after the foliage withers so you can tell where the bulbs are. Separate the bulbs and replant them in freshly amended soil.

Like other plants, narcissus bulbs need food. Bonemeal used to be the recommended fertilizer, but no more: It lacks the nitrogen that promotes healthy foliage. Special bulb fertilizers are much better; look for a 10-10-20 or 9-9-6 formulation with controlled-release nitrogen. Mix fertilizer into the soil at planting time. In subsequent years, sprinkle bulb fertilizer over the bulb bed each fall (when roots develop) at the rate specified on the bag, then scratch or water it in. Many gardeners are finding that the old-fashioned method of using compost at planting time and again in fall as a topdressing supplies the nutrients that bulbs need.

The most serious pest is the narcissus bulb fly. An adult fly resembles a small bumblebee. The female lays eggs on leaves and on necks of bulbs; when eggs hatch, young grubs eat their way into bulbs. Check bulbs before planting, and destroy any grubs. Planting at the recommended depth will reduce infestations.

TOP ROW: N. 'Red Devon'; N. 'Tahiti'; SECOND ROW: Mixed display at Moss Mountain Farm; THIRD ROW: N. 'Fortissimo'; N. 'February Gold'; BOTTOM ROW: N. 'Tête-à-tête'; N. 'Ice Follies'

NASSELLA TENUISSIMA

MEXICAN FEATHER GRASS,
TEXAS NEEDLE GRASS
Poaceae
Perennial grass

✂ MS, LS, CS, TS; USDA 7-11

☼ FULL SUN

◊ LITTLE OR NO WATER

Nassella tenuissiuma

Native to Texas and Mexico,
this is one of the finest-textured,
softest-looking ornamental
grasses. Threadlike, bright green
leaves form a clump to 2 ft. tall,
2–3 ft. wide. In summer, produces
very thin flowering stems that
arch outward and downward,
ending in a cloud of silvery green
inflorescences that age to a light
straw color and remain attractive
into winter. Especially effective
when massed toward the front
of a border, on slopes, and
beside walkways or pools. It will
self-sow, but only enough to
provide seedlings to transplant
into desired locations. Deer
resistant. This plant was formerly
known as *Stipa tenuissima*.

NELUMBO

LOTUS
Nelumbonaceae
Aquatic plants

✂ US, MS, LS, CS, TS; USDA 6-11

**☼ ☽ FULL SUN OR PARTIAL
SHADE**

**◊◊ LOCATE IN PONDS, WATER
GARDENS**

Nelumbo nucifera
'Alba Grandiflora'

Huge, round leaves attached at
their centers to leafstalks rise
above the water. Large, fragrant
summer flowers form above or
below leaves. Ornamental, woody
fruit is perforated like a saltshaker
and looks attractive in dried
arrangements. Do not introduce
into natural bodies of water, as
plants can quickly cover the
surface.

If you buy started plants in
containers, put them in a pond,
positioned so soil in pots is
8–10 in. below surface of water. If
you acquire roots, plant them in
spring, setting them horizontally
and about 4 in. deep in a 1- to
1½-ft.-deep container of fairly
rich soil; then place container
at the recommended depth in
pond, as described above for
started plants. Do not let roots
freeze; where freezes are possible,
cover the pond or fill it deeper
with water. Beware of introducing lotus plants or roots into
earth-bottomed ponds 3–4 ft. or
shallower; plants will eventually fill
in pond, and rhizomes are difficult
to remove. Lotus also spreads via
floating seeds.

N. lutea. AMERICAN LOTUS.
Native to North America. Similar
to *N. nucifera* but somewhat
smaller in leaf and flower. Flowers
are pale yellow.

N. nucifera (*Nelumbium
nelumbo*). INDIAN or CHINESE

LOTUS. Native to Asia, Australia.
Round leaves to 2 ft. or wider are
carried 3–6 ft. above the water's
surface. Pink, 4- to 10-in.-wide
flowers are borne singly on stems.
Both the tubers and the seeds
are esteemed in Chinese cookery,
and entire plant has great religious
significance for Buddhists: It represents the human soul rising from
the mud and aspiring to light and
purity. White, rose-colored, and
double-blossomed selections
exist. 'Speciosum' is the classic,
single, light pink lotus of Oriental
art. 'Alba Grandiflora' bears
large, very fragrant, white flowers.
'Empress' has single white blooms
with deep pink edges. Dwarf forms
(1–2 ft. tall) suitable for tubs and
small ponds include 'Tulip' ('Shiro-
kunshi'), single white; and 'Momo
Botan', with double blooms in
deep rose, fading to white.

NEMESIA

Scrophulariaceae
Annuals

✂ US, MS, LS, CS, TS; USDA 6-11

**☼ ☽ FULL SUN OR PARTIAL
SHADE**

◊ REGULAR WATER

Nemesia strumosa

These colorful South African
natives—represented in nurseries
by *N. caerulea*, *N. strumosa*, and
N. versicolor—love cool weather,
although the *N. caerulea* hybrids
show promise for more heat
tolerance. Growing to 24 in. high
and trailing to 18 in. wide, depending on the species, nemesias need
well-drained soil. Use them as
bedding or rock garden plants, in
hanging baskets, or as a cover for
beds of bulbs. Set out transplants
if available, or sow seeds directly

into the garden in late summer or
early fall for color going into
winter. In Coastal and Tropical
South gardens where winter is
mild, they will bloom in winter. In
Lower South gardens they endure
winter to bloom again when the
weather is warm. In Upper and
Middle South gardens they can
be planted in late winter or early
spring for color until summer heat
overtakes them. It is helpful to
place them where they will receive
some shade as deciduous trees
sprout leaves. Remove faded
flowers to prolong their bloom.

Despite their preference for
cool weather, the many hybrids
withstand temperatures as high
as 95°F. Growing about 1 ft. high
and wide are 'Innocence Compact', with yellow-centered white
flowers, and 'Innocence Compact
Pink', with pink blooms. The Poetry
series (12–14 in. high), Aromatica
series (12–14 in. high), Serengeti series (18 in. tall), and Sunsatia series
(6–12 in. high) all come in a range
of colors. Particularly heat-tolerant
'Bluebird' has blue-violet blossoms
centered with yellow. The Nessie
series has shown excellent heat
tolerance, standing at 15 in. tall
and blooming in vibrant shades
of red, purple, and yellow. Well-
established plantings of the species and hybrids are hardy to 15°F.

NEMOPHILA

Boraginaceae
Cool-season annuals

✂ US, MS, LS, CS, TS; USDA 6-11

**☼ ☽ FULL SUN OR PARTIAL
SHADE**

◊ REGULAR WATER

Nemophila menziesii

These cool-weather annuals grow
6–12 in. high and trail to 1 ft. wide,

with saucer-shaped flowers to 1 in. across in spring. Pale green, hairy, ferny leaves give plants a delicate appearance. Often used as bulb cover. Sow seed in place in fall; plants will bloom in winter in the Coastal and Tropical South, in spring in the Upper, Middle, and Lower South.

N. maculata. FIVE-SPOT NEMOPHILA. Native to California. Flowers are white, marked with fine purple lines and dots; a large purple dot appears at the tip of each of the five lobes.

N. menziesii. BABY BLUE EYES. From California, southern Oregon. Plant blooms freely, bearing sky-blue blossoms with a white or near-white center. 'Snowstorm' has white flowers dotted with black. 'Pennie Black' bears blackish purple flowers rimmed in white.

NEOMARICA
Iridaceae
Perennials

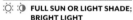

🌡 **CS, TS; USDA 9-11; OR GROW IN POTS**

☼ ◑ **FULL SUN OR LIGHT SHADE; BRIGHT LIGHT**

💧 **REGULAR WATER**

Neomarica caerulea

Like iris, these old favorites produce fans of lance-shaped leaves that arise from rhizomes. Foliage and flowering stems grow to about the same height. Flowers are intricate, with three large, rounded outer segments around three smaller, curled inner segments banded in contrasting colors. Each flower lasts only a day, but others follow over an extended period. Indoors, give bright light but protect from hot sun. During active growth, feed

monthly with a balanced fertilizer; let soil go fairly dry between soakings. In winter, stop feeding and give little water.

N. caerulea. BRAZILIAN WALKING IRIS. From Brazil. To 5–5½ ft. tall, 2–3 ft. wide, with stiffly erect leaves. As plant grows, lower leaves fan out to the side. Branching flower stems carry a succession of 3- to 4-in. blue blossoms, their centers intricately banded in yellow, white, and brown. Blooms in early summer. Offsets are produced at flowering points on the stems; they detach easily for additional plants.

N. gracilis. WALKING IRIS. Native from Mexico to Brazil. To 2–2½ ft. tall, 1–1½ ft. wide. Blooms in late spring and summer; flower stems resemble the leaves so closely that blossoms appear to emerge directly from the foliage. Flowers are 2½ in. wide, with white outer segments and inner ones in a combination of blue, brown, and yellow. As flowers fade, the blossom stalk bends downward and produces plantlets that take root—hence the common name.

N. longifolia. YELLOW WALKING IRIS. From Brazil. Upright growth to 2 ft. tall, 1–1½ ft. wide. Blooms all summer, bearing 2-in. yellow flowers banded with brown. "Walks" the same way *N. gracilis* does.

NEOREGELIA
Bromeliaceae
Perennials

🌡 **TS; USDA 10-11; OR HOUSE-PLANTS**

◑ **LIGHT SHADE; BRIGHT INDIRECT LIGHT**

◐◑💧💧 **SEE TEXT FOR WATERING INSTRUCTIONS**

Neoregelia carolinae 'Flandria'

Native to South America, these bromeliads consist of rosettes of leathery, often strikingly banded or marbled leaves. Inconspicuous flowers appear in a cup at the center of the rosette; the cup turns red when the plant is ready to bloom. In the rain forest, this central cup serves to collect rain, which quickly evaporates. For neoregelias grown outdoors, you can keep the cup filled with water from spring to fall. For indoor plants, though, be sure to let the cup dry completely before refilling—otherwise, the water can become stagnant and the plant may rot.

Give loose, fast-draining soil, and let it go dry to the touch between waterings. From spring through summer, feed monthly with a general-purpose liquid houseplant fertilizer diluted to half-strength; to apply, sprinkle the liquid over the entire plant.

N. carolinae. BLUSHING BROMELIAD. To 1 ft. tall, 2½ ft. wide. Many medium green, shiny leaves about 1 ft. long, 1½ in. wide. 'Tricolor' is identical but sports lengthwise white stripes on its leaves. 'Flandria' has leaves edged in white.

N. spectabilis. PAINTED FINGERNAIL PLANT. To 1½ ft. tall, 3 ft. wide. Leaves are about 1 ft. long, 2 in. wide, olive-green with bright red tips. Foliage takes on a bronzy color in strong light.

NEPETA
Lamiaceae
Perennials

🌡 **ZONES VARY BY SPECIES**

☼ ◑ **FULL SUN OR PARTIAL SHADE**

💧💧 **MODERATE TO REGULAR WATER**

Nepeta racemosa

Vigorous, spreading members of the mint family, with aromatic foliage. With the exception of catnip (*N. cataria*), these plants are valuable for their spikes of two-lipped blue or blue-violet (or sometimes pink, white, or yellow) flowers. As soon as blossoms fade, shear plants back by half, or cut faded flower stems to the ground to encourage rebloom. (Most species seed freely and can become invasive if spent flowers are not removed.) Plants make attractive, informal low hedges or edgings. Deer don't usually eat them.

In winter or early spring, cut out last year's growth to make way for new stems. At that time, you can also divide clumps for increase, though it's easy to start new plants from cuttings (take them before flower buds form). When buying named selections, be sure to obtain cutting-grown plants; seedlings vary in flower color and habit. Flowering is spotty in the Tropical South. Provide good drainage.

N. 'Blue Dragon'. Zones US, MS, LS, CS; USDA 6-9. Named for the dragonlike appearance of individual flowers, this bright blue-violet selection grows upright, unlike others, reaching 2½ ft. tall and wide.

N. cataria. CATNIP. Zones US, MS, LS; USDA 6-8. From the Mediterranean and western Asia. To

2–3 ft. high and wide, with downy, heart-shaped, tooth-edged gray-green leaves. Spikes of small (¼- to ½-in.) whitish or pinkish flowers in late spring, early summer. Not very ornamental but worthy of a place in the herb garden. Grows easily in light soil and self-sows readily. Common name refers to stimulant effect on cats. Their susceptibility to the herb varies, though: Some felines fall into a rapturous frenzy, rolling wildly on the plant, but others ignore it. If necessary, protect crown of plant with an inverted wire basket; stems will grow through. The same tactic also helps preserve potted plants grown outdoors and brought indoors occasionally for cats to enjoy. You can also sprinkle dried leaves over your cat's food or use them to stuff cloth toys. Some people use catnip to flavor tea. 'Citriodora' has lemon-scented foliage.

N. 'Dropmore'. Zones US, MS, LS, CS; USDA 6-9. Grows to 1½ ft. high and 3 ft. wide, can bloom from late spring to fall with lavender-blue flowers.

N. x faassenii. CATMINT. Zones US, MS, LS; USDA 6-8. Sterile hybrid of *N. racemosa* and a European species; often sold as *N. mussinii*. Soft, silvery gray-green, spreading mound grows to 1 ft. high, 1½–2 ft. wide. Scallop-edged, heart-shaped leaves to 1 in. long. Attractive to some cats, who enjoy nibbling on and rolling in plantings; insert short, blunt-tipped sticks in the ground among the leaves to discourage cats and prevent destruction. Loose, lax spikes of ½-in. lavender-blue flowers in late spring, early summer. Set plants 1–1½ ft. apart for ground cover. 'Limelight' grows only 10 in. tall and 2 ft. wide, the lime-green foliage makes an energetic backdrop for the blue-lavender flowers. Less robust than other selections. 'Kit Cat' (Zones US, MS; USDA 6-7) is shorter, reaching 15 in. with blue-purple flowers on gray-green foliage. 'Select Blue' has darker flowers than the species; 'Snowflake' has pure white blooms. 'Cats Meow' forms a dense, rounded mound with sky-blue flowers.

N. grandiflora. GIANT CAT-MINT. Zones US, MS, LS, CS; USDA 6-9. Native to Europe, Caucasus. Open clump to 2½–4 ft. tall, 3–5 ft. wide. Gray-green, hairless or sparsely hairy, scallop-edged, egg-shaped leaves to 4 in. long. Violet-blue, ¾-in. flowers in late spring, early summer. 'Bramdean' has lavender-blue blossoms with purple calyxes; 'Dawn to Dusk' has lilac-pink blooms, smoky violet calyxes. 'Wild Cat' has purplish red calyxes. Calyxes of all these selections persist after flowers have faded.

N. nervosa. Zones US, MS, LS, CS; USDA 6-9. Native to Kashmir. Grows to 1–2 ft. tall but may spread into a mound 1–2 ft. wide. Bright green, conspicuously veined, tooth-edged leaves are lance shaped, 2–4 in. long. Brilliant violet-blue (rarely yellow), ½-in. flowers bloom from midsummer to early fall. Afternoon shade is helpful. 'Blue Carpet' and 'Pink Cat' grow to 1 ft.

N. 'Purple Haze'. Zones US, MS, LS, CS; USDA 6-9. At only 10 in. tall, this vigorous selection grows into a mound 4 ft. across. The showy flowers are held in spikes.

N. racemosa (*N. mussinii*). PERSIAN CATMINT. Zones US, MS, LS; USDA 6-8. Native to the Caucasus, Turkey, Iran. Sprawling plant grows from 6 in. to 1 ft. tall and about 2 ft. or more wide. Roundish, scallop-edged, ½- to 1¼-in.-long leaves range in color from medium green to gray-green; they are covered with fine hairs. The typical form produces ⅓-in.-long lavender flowers for a short period in mid-summer; may rebloom if sheared. Reseeds wildly. Inferior to its hybrid *N. x faassenii*, but there are several worthwhile selections that are more compact than the species and bloom over a longer period. 'Blue Ice' has dense, gray-green foliage and pale blue flowers that fade to near-white. 'Superba' has a dense, matlike habit and gray-green leaves that are smaller than those of the species; it bears lavender-blue blossoms from spring through fall. Violet-blue flowers of 'Walker's Low' grows 2–3 ft. tall and has vivid lavender-blue flowers.

N. sibirica (*N. macrantha*). SIBERIAN CATNIP. Zones US, MS, LS; USDA 6-8. Native to Siberia. Sturdy, upright habit to 2–3 ft. tall and 1½–2 ft. wide. Dark green, oblong to lance-shaped, 3-in.-long leaves are softly hairy beneath. Spikes of large (1½-in.) violet-blue blossoms appear for about a month, beginning in early summer. 'Souvenir d'André Chaudron' ('Blue Beauty') is similar but grows only 1½ ft. high and blooms for a longer period, with season extending into late summer.

N. 'Six Hills Giant'. Zones US, MS, LS; USDA 6-8. Possibly a hybrid of *N. x faassenii* and similar to it—but grows taller (reaches 2½–3 ft. high and as wide), has greener foliage, and bears deeper blue flowers. More tolerant of damp climates than other nepetas.

NEPHROLEPIS
SWORD FERN
Lomariopsidaceae
Ferns

🌿 TS; USDA 10-11; OR HOUSEPLANT

☼ SOME SHADE; BRIGHT INDIRECT LIGHT

💧 REGULAR WATER

Nephrolepis cordifolia

Tough and easy to grow, these are the most widely used of all ferns. Where winters are cold, they're popular houseplants, benefiting from well-drained soil, frequent misting, and monthly applications of a general-purpose liquid houseplant fertilizer from spring through fall. In frost-free areas, they make splendid ground covers for shady areas. Not usually browsed by deer.

N. biserrata. GIANT SWORD FERN. Native to the tropical Marquesas islands, this species is known primarily for the selection 'Macho'. Arching fronds grow 3–4 ft. long and 6–7 in. wide, making a plant 5–6 ft. wide. Bright shade or morning sun is ideal. Often grown as a summer annual. Container plants fill their pots quickly; daily watering is necessary.

N. cordifolia. SOUTHERN SWORD FERN. Native to many tropical regions of the world. To 2–3 ft. tall, 5 ft. wide. Tufts of bright green, narrow (2-in.-wide), upright fronds with closely spaced, finely toothed leaflets. Roots often have small, roundish tubers. Plant spreads by thin, fuzzy runners and can be invasive. Will not take hard frosts but is otherwise adaptable, tolerating poor soil and erratic watering. Good in narrow, shaded beds; can thrive in full sun with adequate water. Good in pots and hanging baskets. Often sold as *N. exaltata*. 'Lemon Buttons' grows to 1 ft. tall and wide with short, rounded leaflets, making the frond only an inch wide. It's named for its scent, not its color.

N. exaltata. SWORD FERN. Like *N. cordifolia*, this is a tropical species, but it grows larger (to 7 ft. high and as wide) and has broader fronds (to 6 in. wide). Most common are named selections grown as houseplants. Best known is 'Bostoniensis', Boston fern. Growing about 3 ft. high, it is the classic parlor fern, with spreading, arching habit and graceful, eventually drooping fronds broader than

---

OVERWINTERING YOUR BOSTON FERN

There seems to be an unwritten law in the South that any house with a spacious front porch is required to display two or more Boston ferns in pots or hanging baskets. When cold weather arrives, many folks simply let the plants die, then start over with new ones the following spring. But if you can't bear the thought of your fern's demise, take heart: You can help it survive the winter. In fall, use sharp scissors to cut back all side fronds to the rim of the pot, leaving the top growth about 10 in. high. Place the pot indoors next to your brightest window, and keep the soil fairly moist. By spring, your plant should be bushy again and ready for its return to the porch.

those of the species. Among the many forms with more finely cut and feathery fronds are 'Fluffy Ruffles', 'Rooseveltii', and 'Whitmanii'. 'Rita's Gold' has 18- to 24-in. fronds of bright lime-green, demanding shade but giving the illusion of light wherever it is grows.

N. obliterata. From northwestern Australia. Grows to 3–4½ ft. high and wide. Similar to *N. cordifolia* but has darker green, somewhat narrower fronds. Used mainly as a houseplant. Habit is stiffer and more erect than that of *N. exaltata* 'Bostoniensis', and plant is more tolerant of low humidity and both high and low light conditions. Selections include 'Kimberly Queen' and 'Western Queen'. 'Medusa' grows about half the size of the species, with compact fronds that tend to curve, creating the illusion of tangled hair.

NERINE

Amaryllidaceae
Perennials from bulbs

🗡 **LS, CS, TS; USDA 8-11; OR GROW IN POTS**

☼ ◐ **PARTIAL SHADE IN HOTTEST CLIMATES**

💧 **REGULAR WATER DURING GROWTH AND BLOOM**

Nerine bowdenii

South African relatives of spider lily (*Lycoris*), which they closely resemble. Most have strap-shaped leaves to about 1 ft. long; these usually die back well before bloom time in late summer or early autumn, then reappear later in the year (typically around bloom time or shortly afterward). Some types are essentially evergreen. All have attractive, broad,

funnel- or trumpet-shaped flowers carried in clusters atop leafless stems; each blossom has six spreading segments, recurved at their tips.

Withhold summer water for species that experience summer dormancy, but keep watering the essentially evergreen kinds. These plants can be grown in pots in areas beyond their hardiness range or where soil cannot be kept dry for summer-dormant types.

N. bowdenii. Lightly scented flowers to 3 in. long that are soft pink marked with deeper pink, in clusters of 8 to 12 on 2-ft. stems. Forms with taller stems and larger flower clusters are available in deeper pink, crimson, and red. One example is 'Pink Triumph', with large blossoms in dark pink. Goes dormant in summer.

N. filifolia. Essentially evergreen or nearly so, since new leaves—narrow, grassy, and reaching 6–8 in. long—are produced as old ones fade. Inch-wide, rose-red flowers with narrow, crinkled segments are carried in clusters of 8 to 12 on each 1-ft. stem. Plant spreads rapidly. Mulch in late fall in Lower South.

N. masoniorum. Virtually evergreen species like *N. filifolia*, but it bears its flowers in clusters of 4 to 12 on 9-in. stems. Mulch in late fall in Lower South.

N. sarniensis. GUERNSEY LILY. Large clusters of 1½-in., iridescent crimson flowers with prominent stamens, borne on stalks to 2 ft. tall. Pink, orange, scarlet, and pure white selections are available. *N. s. curvifolia fothergillii* has scarlet flowers overlaid with shimmering gold. Goes dormant in summer.

NERIUM OLEANDER

OLEANDER
Apocynaceae
Evergreen shrub

🗡 **LS, CS, TS; USDA 8-11; OR GROW IN POTS**

☼ **FULL SUN**

◐ 💧 **LITTLE TO REGULAR WATER**

⬥ **ALL PARTS ARE POISONOUS IF INGESTED. DON'T BURN PRUNINGS; SMOKE CAN CAUSE SEVERE IRRITATION**

Nerium oleander 'Petite Pink'

Selections of this species are superb landscape plants wherever they are winter hardy. These Mediterranean natives are tough as nails and combine spectacular flowers with handsome foliage. Growing quickly to 3–20 ft. tall and 4–12 ft. wide (depending on the selection), they naturally form billowing shrubs but are easy to train into single-trunked trees. They make outstanding windbreaks and tall screens and also do well in containers. Narrow, 4- to 12-in.-long leaves are dark green, leathery, and attractive in all seasons. Clusters of single or double, sometimes fragrant flowers in red, pink, salmon, yellow, or white appear at branch tips from spring to fall, depending on the climate.

All parts of oleander plants are poisonous; deer don't browse them. Keep prunings and dead leaves away from hay or animal feed, and don't use branches for fires or barbecue skewers. Smoke from burning oleander branches can cause severe irritation to mucous membranes.

Dozens of named selections exist, some of which are described below. They typically

grow about half as wide as tall. For the plant called yellow oleander, see *Thevetia*.

'Algiers'. Single dark red flowers. To 10–12 ft. tall.

'Calypso'. Cold tolerant and vigorous with single red flowers. Grows 10–18 ft. tall.

'Casablanca'. Profuse show of single white flowers. To 4–6 ft. tall.

'Franklin D. Roosevelt'. Single deep salmon flowers with yellow throat. Very hardy. To 10 ft. tall.

'Hardy Pink'. Single salmon-pink flowers. Probably the hardiest oleander, tolerating temperatures into the low teens without damage. Reaches 10 ft. tall.

'Isle of Capri'. Single light yellow blossoms. To 5–7 ft. tall.

'Lane Taylor Sealy'. Single, fragrant, light salmon blooms with a yellow throat. To 8 ft. tall.

'Little Red'. Single dark red flowers. Hardier than most. Compact grower to 3–4 ft. tall.

'Mathilde Ferrier'. Cold-tolerant, double yellow bloom, grows to 8 ft. tall.

'Morocco'. Single white blooms. To 5–7 ft. tall and wide.

'Mrs. George Roeding' ('Carneum Plenum'). Double, fragrant, salmon-pink flowers; fine-textured foliage. Slightly weeping form. Grows to about 6 ft. tall.

'Petite Pink'. Single shell-pink blooms. To 3–4 ft. tall.

'Petite Salmon'. Single salmon-pink flowers. To 3–4 ft. tall.

'Ruby Lace'. Single, large ruby-red blossoms. Grows to 8 ft. tall.

'Sister Agnes' ('Soeur Agnès'). Single white flowers. Vigorous grower reaches 15–20 ft. tall.

'Sue Hawley Oakes'. Creamy yellow flowers with a yellow throat. Grows to 8 ft. tall.

'Sugarland' ('Hardy Red'). Single red flowers. More cold tolerant than most. Reaches 10 ft. tall.

CARE

Few plants are as adaptable to challenging growing conditions as oleanders. They are ubiquitous along Southern coasts, because they tolerate wind, salt spray, and sandy soil. Once established, they need little water; they'll also grow in poorly drained soil, be it acid or alkaline. Their only limitation is susceptibility to cold. Most selections will weather brief periods of 10°F or a bit colder, but they may be killed to the ground. They will, however, usually resprout the following spring and bloom at the usual time. Older, established plants are hardier than young ones. In the Upper and Middle South, grow oleanders in containers and bring them indoors for the winter.

Regular pruning isn't necessary, but if you need to shape the plant or reduce its size, do so immediately after flowering. Avoid pruning within three months of the first expected fall frost. To renew old, unattractive, leggy plants, lop them nearly to the ground before new growth begins in spring.

Oleanders are usually pest free, but infestations of bright orange oleander caterpillars can defoliate entire plants; the damage typically isn't fatal. A new scourge called oleander leaf scorch has recently appeared in Texas. Caused by a bacterium spread by a sucking insect, this disease causes leaves to turn brown, then drop; eventually, the plant succumbs. Quickly remove and dispose of infected plants.

NEVIUSIA ALABAMENSIS

ALABAMA SNOW-WREATH
Rosaceae
Deciduous shrub

🗡 **US, MS, LS; USDA 6-8**

☼ ◑ **FULL SUN OR PARTIAL SHADE**

💧💧 **REGULAR TO AMPLE WATER**

Neviusia alabamensis

Native to Alabama. Ornamental multistemmed shrub 3–6 ft. tall and wide, with arching, delicate branches and clouds of feathery white flowers in spring. Grows rather slowly. Medium green,

pointed, oval leaves to 3 in. long. Unusual, showy flowers: spreading, inch-wide bunches of white stamens, without petals. Easy to grow if given well-drained soil and plenty of water during summer.

NICOTIANA

Solanaceae
Perennials usually grown as annuals

🗡 **US, MS, LS, CS, TS; USDA 6-11**

☼ ◑ **FULL SUN OR PARTIAL SHADE**

💧 **REGULAR WATER**

⬦ **ALL PARTS ARE EXTREMELY POISONOUS IF INGESTED**

Nicotiana x *sanderae*
'Perfume Deep Purple'

Tender perennials from South America. All are grown as annuals, but they may live over in the Coastal and Tropical South. Upright-growing plants with soft, oval, often quite large leaves; both foliage and stems are slightly sticky. Flowers—very fragrant in some species—are tubular, typically flaring at the mouth into five pointed lobes; they appear near tops of branching stems in summer. They usually open at night or on cloudy days, though some kinds open during the day. Some nicotianas reseed readily.

N. alata. FLOWERING TOBACCO. Wild species (for which seed is available) grows 2–4 ft. tall (possibly to 6 ft. under ideal conditions), 1 ft. wide. Leaves to 10 in. long. Bears large, intensely fragrant, white flowers that open toward evening. Selection and hybridization with other species have produced many garden strains that stay open day and night and come in colors, includ-

ing white, pink shades, red, and lime-green, but their perfume is not as strong as that of the "unimproved" species. If scent (especially during evening) is important to you, plant 3-ft.-high 'Grandiflora'.

N. langsdorffii. To 5 ft. tall, 1½ ft. wide. Leaves to 10 in. long. Branching stems are hung with drooping sprays of bell-shaped, bright green flowers about 2 in. long. Unusual blossom color blends well with blues, yellows in flower border. No noticeable scent.

N. x sanderae. Many of the newer hybrids, such as the Perfume series (to 20 in. high), have nice fragrance. 'Perfume Deep Purple' has been a standout. Domino strain grows to 12–15 in. high and has upward-facing flowers that take heat and sun better than taller kinds. Nicki strain is taller, to 15–18 in. The older Sensation strain is taller still (to 4 ft.) and looks more at home in informal mixed borders than as a bedding plant. 'Avalon Bright Pink' is very compact, rarely exceeding 15 in. high, 1 ft. wide. Inch-long leaves are virtually hidden by a profusion of star-shaped, 1½-in. flowers in bright pink. Quite heat tolerant; good in containers. The Starmaker series, growing 10–12 in. tall, is led by 'Lime/Purple Bi-color'.

N. sylvestris. FLOWERING TOBACCO. To 5 ft. tall, 2 ft. wide, with leaves that can reach 1–2 ft. long. Intensely fragrant, 3½-in.-long, tubular white flowers are borne in tiers atop a statuesque plant. Striking in a night garden. 'Only the Lonely' shows great flower power and heat tolerance from mid-spring into summer.

NIEREMBERGIA

CUP FLOWER
Solanaceae
Perennials often grown as annuals

🗡 **US, MS, LS, CS, TS; USDA 6-11**

☼ ◑ **LIGHT SHADE IN HOTTEST CLIMATES**

💧 **REGULAR WATER**

Nierembergia linariifolia
'Augusta Blue Skies'

These plants bear tubular flowers that flare into saucerlike or bell-like cups. The species listed here grow as a spreading mound or a ground-covering mat. All are covered with blooms during summer. Can be grown as perennials in the Lower South, cool-weather annuals in the Coastal and Tropical South, summer annuals elsewhere.

N. gracilis. Native to the Argenine desert, this species and its primary selection, 'Starry Eyes', endure hot summer, either arid or humid, growing into a mound 10 in. tall and 18 in. wide. Plant in sun, with good drainage. After the lavender-centered white bells fade, shear for more flowers. Perennial in the Lower South, (USDA 8) and warmer.

N. linariifolia (*N. caerulea*, *N. hippomanica*). DWARF CUP FLOWER. To 6–12 in. high and wide. Much-branched, mounding plant with very small, stiff leaves. Flowers are blue to violet. Trimming back plant after bloom to induce new growth seems to lengthen its life. 'Augusta Blue Skies' is a compact hybrid with lavender-blue flowers and improved heat tolerance. Plants may surprise you and overwinter in the Middle South, (USDA 7) and warmer.

N

N. repens. WHITE CUP. Bright green foliage forms a mat to 4–6 in. high, 2 ft. wide. White blossoms. For best performance, don't crowd it with more aggressive plants. Not as heat tolerant as *N. linariifolia*. However, plants can overwinter in the Middle South, (USDA 7) and warmer.

N. scoparia. TALL CUP FLOWER. Growing 1–2 ft. tall, favorites include 'Purple Robe' and the white 'Mont Blanc', usually sold as *N. hippomanica*. Plants may overwinter in the Middle South, (USDA 7) and warmer, so cut back, but don't pull them out at summer's end.

Summer Splash series. Grows 10–12 in. tall and 1–2 ft. wide in both white and blue. Tolerant of heat and humidity.

NIGELLA DAMASCENA

LOVE-IN-A-MIST
Ranunculaceae
Annual

🌿 **US, MS, LS, CS, TS; USDA 6-11**

☼ ☽ **FULL SUN OR PARTIAL SHADE**

💧 **REGULAR WATER**

Nigella damascena

An old-fashioned Mediterranean favorite to 1–1½ ft. high, 10 in. wide. All leaves, even those that form under the collar beneath each flower, are finely cut into threadlike divisions. Blue, white, or rose-colored blooms, 1–1½ in. across, are borne singly at branch ends in spring. Curious papery-textured, horned seed capsules lend an airy effect to bouquets and mixed borders and look decorative in dried arrangements. 'Miss Jekyll', to

1½ ft. tall, has semidouble cornflower-blue blossoms. Persian Jewels, to 15 in. tall, is a superior strain in a mix of colors.

'African Bride' is a selection of the similar *N. papillosa*. It has flat, white petals with prominent blackish purple stamens. The black seedpods are useful in dried arrangements. Reaches 3 ft. high and about 1 ft. wide.

CARE

Love-in-a-mist comes into bloom quickly in spring, dries up in summer heat. Start from seed in spring, as soon as ground is workable and frost danger is past; can be sown in autumn in mild-winter areas. Sow seeds where plants are to grow, since the long taproot makes transplanting unsatisfactory. Self-sows freely.

NOLINA

Asparagaceae
Perennials

🌿 **ZONES VARY BY SPECIES**

☼ **FULL SUN**

💧 **LITTLE OR NO WATER TO MODERATE WATER**

Nolina nelsonii

Yucca and agave relatives with tough, narrow, grassy leaves, typically carried atop a thick trunk. Mature plants bear flowers; the blossoms are tiny, but they're usually borne on tall stalks that make for a good show. Good for dry areas; tolerate poor, alkaline soil. Not suited to areas with high rainfall and high humidity.

N. erumpens. BEAR GRASS. Zones MS, LS, CS, TS; USDA 7-11. Native to Mexico and western Texas. Sharp-edged, thick leaves to 3 ft. long form a mound 3–4 ft.

tall, 6 ft. wide. Showy spikes of creamy white flowers flushed with rose-pink rise several feet above the foliage, spring into summer.

N. lindheimeriana. DEVIL'S SHOESTRING. Zones MS, LS, CS, TS; USDA 7-11. Native to Texas. Wiry, narrow, 2- to 3-ft.-long leaves; foliage mounds reach 6 ft. across. Wands of white flowers rise to 3–4 ft. in late spring.

N. longifolia. MEXICAN GRASS TREE. Zones CS, TS; USDA 9-11. Native to central Mexico. In youth, forms a fountain (to about 6 ft. wide) of grasslike, 3-ft.-long, 1-in.-wide leaves. In time, the foliage fountain is carried atop a 6- to 10-ft. trunk, sometimes with a few branches. White flowers come in late spring, on stalks up to 6 ft. tall.

N. nelsonii. NELSON'S BLUE BEAR GRASS TREE. Zones MS, LS, CS, TS; USDA 7-11. Slow-growing plant native to the deserts of northern Mexico. Forms a foliage rosette 3–5 ft. tall and twice as wide; narrow (1- to 1½-in.-wide), finely tooth-edged leaves are gray-green and flexible when young, silvery blue-gray and stiff when mature. In time, foliage is carried atop a 5- to 12-ft. trunk. Dead leaves hang onto the trunk; remove them for a neater look. Blooms in summer, bearing creamy blossoms on a 7- to 10-ft. spike. Dramatic and sculptural.

N. texana. SACAHUISTA, BASKET GRASS. Zones MS, LS, CS; USDA 7-9. Native to Texas, the Southwest, and Mexico. Very grasslike foliage forms a mound 1½–2 ft. tall and twice as wide. Stalks of creamy white blossoms are 1–1½ft. tall; they don't rise above the leaves. Blooms from spring into summer. Especially hardy.

NYMPHAEA

WATER LILY
Nymphaeaceae
Aquatic plants

🌿 **US, MS, LS, CS, TS; USDA 6-11**

☼ **FULL SUN**

💧 **LOCATE IN PONDS, WATER GARDENS**

Nymphaea alba

These aquatic perennials grow with their roots in submerged soil and their long-stalked leaves floating on the surface. Floating leaves are rounded, with deep notch at one side where leafstalk is attached. Showy flowers either float on surface or stand above it on stiff stalks. There are hardy and tropical kinds. Hardy types come in white, yellow, copper, pink, and red. Tropical types add blue and purple to the color range, as well as an unusual greenish blue. Some tropicals in the white-pink-red color range are night bloomers; all others close at night. Many are fragrant.

Hardy kinds. These are easiest for beginners. Plant them from February to October in mild-winter areas, from April to July in cold-winter regions. Set 6-in.-long pieces of rhizome on soil at pool bottom or in boxes (not redwood ones, since these can discolor the water), placing rhizome in a nearly horizontal position with its bud end up. In either case, top of soil should be 8–12 in. below surface of water. Feed at planting time and monthly thereafter, using a controlled-release product. Groom plants by removing spent leaves and blossoms. They usually bloom throughout warm weather and go dormant in fall, reappearing in spring. In very cold areas, protect plants by covering the pond or by adding more water to it.

Tropical kinds. These begin to grow and bloom later in summer but last longer, often until the first frost. Buy started tropical plants and set them at the same depth as hardy rhizomes. Tropical types go dormant but do not survive really low winter temperatures. Their best chance of long-term survival is in regions where orange trees grow. Where winters are colder, store dormant tubers in damp sand indoors over winter, or buy new plants each year.

NYSSA SYLVATICA

BLACK GUM, SOUR GUM, TUPELO
Nyssaceae
Deciduous tree

🌱 **US, MS, LS, CS; USDA 6-9**

☼ ◐ **FULL SUN OR PARTIAL SHADE**

💧💧 **MODERATE TO REGULAR WATER**

Nyssa sylvatica

Native to the eastern U.S., this is one of our finest large trees for fall color—and one of the first to color up in autumn, with leaves turning yellow, orange, burgundy, crimson, or bright scarlet before they drop. Display is best in the Upper and Middle South, where foliage turns color all at once; in the Lower and Coastal South, individual leaves tend to color and drop over a period of weeks, diminishing the show.

Grows at a slow to moderate rate, reaching 30–60 ft. tall, 20–30 ft. wide; pyramidal when young, rounded or flat-topped when mature. Horizontal

branches and rugged, nearly black bark create a dramatic picture against the winter sky. Plants are usually entirely male or entirely female, but some are a little of both. Flowers of all are inconspicuous. If pollinated by a nearby male, females bear bluish black fruit resembling small olives that ripens in late summer and autumn. Birds relish them, but fruit drop can make a mess on decks and driveways. Lustrous dark green leaves are oval and pointed, 3–6 in. long.

Because cuttings are hard to root and seedlings tend to grow slowly, relatively few named selections exist. Two choices, both with red fall color, are fast-growing: 'Forum', with conical form, and the weeping selection 'Autumn Cascade'. 'Red Rage' ('Hayman Red') offers glossy foliage, great fall color, and resistance to leaf spot. 'Zydeco Twist' features contorted stems and leaves for accent in the garden.

Two other American species, native to Southern swamps, are best appreciated in their natural settings. *N. aquatica*, water tupelo, is similar to *N. sylvatica* but has larger leaves and fruit and a trunk that is swollen at the base. *N. ogeche*, Ogeechee tupelo, is smaller (to 30–40 ft. high) and has only negligible fall color. Its edible, ¾-in., reddish fruit is pickled to make "Ogeechee limes."

CARE

Black gum prefers moist, acid, well-drained soil containing lots of organic matter, but it takes poorly drained clay soil. It doesn't tolerate pollution, though, so it's not a good choice for city gardens. Superb shade or lawn tree; excellent for naturalized areas. Select a permanent location, as taproot makes it difficult to move later on. Trees that are cut down seem to produce suckers forever.

O

OCIMUM BASILICUM

BASIL
Lamiaceae
Annual or tender perennial

🌱 **US, MS, LS, CS, TS; USDA 6-11**

☼ **FULL SUN**

💧 **REGULAR WATER**

'Sweet Basil'

Native to tropical and subtropical Asia, basil is an annual herb so simple to grow that even first-time gardeners can plant it with confidence. It thrives in hot, humid weather and grows well throughout the South from spring until frost. Deer don't like it.

The normally 2-ft.-tall, bushy plant produces spikes of small white or pinkish flowers, but it's prized for its shiny green leaves—oval, 1–2 in. long, with a clovelike fragrance and spicy-sweet flavor that make them indispensable in the kitchen. However, there are endless variations of the theme, including forms with purple or variegated foliage; dwarf globe or columnar habits; giant or tiny leaves; and white, pink, and purple flowers. Flavors cover a wide range, including anise, cinnamon, clove, coriander, lemon, and lime.

Fresh basil leaves are a must for summer salads, especially with tomatoes. In fact, it is critical for pesto, Italian, Indian, and Southwestern cuisine. Used

fresh or dried, its leaves lend a pleasant, mildly sweet flavor to sauces and cooked dishes of all sorts. The most flavorful leaves are from younger stems that have not yet borne flowers. And don't overlook basil as a cut flower. Both green- and purple-leaved stems give a bouquet of zinnias the scent of summer.

There are too many selections to list them all here, but the following is a sampling of what's available.

Big leaves. 'Italian Large Leaf', 'Large Green', 'Mammoth Sweet', 'Napoletano', and 'Rapper' have especially big leaves; use them as wraps for appetizers or in place of lettuce on a sandwich.

Compact plants. Try 'Aristotle', 'Boxwood', 'Finissimo Verde a Palla', 'Genovese Compact', 'Greek' ('Spicy Globe'), 'Green Ball' (no blooms), 'Magical Michael', 'Marseillais Dwarf', 'Pluto', and 'Red Ball' (purple with green edges), any of which make small-leafed globes of basil flavor. 'Genovese Compact' has full-size leaves and remains 16–18 in. tall.

Columnar plants. Try 'Greek Columnar' (24–36 in. tall, 9 in. wide) and 'Pesto Perpetuo' (up to 48 in., does not flower).

Flavored leaves. Because basil comes in so many flavors, taste a leaf, if possible, before you buy. Most of the selections describe their flavors: 'Cinnamon', 'Clove', 'Cuban' (spicy), 'Holy' (Thai cuisine), 'Lemon', 'Licorice', 'Lime', 'Mrs. Burns' Lemon', 'Sweet Dani' (intense lemon, larger leaves), or 'Sweet Thai Basil' (flavor of anise and cloves).

Perennial types. Grow these outdoors in virtually frost-free climates or indoors: 'Magic Mountain' (3 ft.) or 'Pesto Perpetua' (to 4 ft., with light green leaves that have creamy variegation). 'African Blue' (to 5 ft. tall) has showy blooms almost like purple salvia, and the bloom spikes do not seem to compromise the growth of the plant.

Best for pesto. Start with a Genovese type such as 'Aroma 1' or 'Aroma 2', 'Emily' (compact form), 'Genovese', 'Nufar', 'Profumo', or 'Superbo'; or use a standard selection such as 'Sweet Basil'.

Purple foliage. These *O. b. purpurascens* selections can be touchy to grow, but they are beautiful and much used in Asian cooking: 'Amethyst' (Genovese type), 'Purple Ruffles', 'Red Lettuce Leaved', 'Red Osmin' (an improved 'Dark Opal'), and 'Red Rubin'.

Disease tolerant. Look for 'Aroma 1', 'Aroma 2', 'Habana', 'Harlekin' (green and purple), 'Nufar', and 'Red Ball' (purple with green edges).

Ornamental. 'Chistmas' has

TOP: Ocimum basilicum purpurascens 'Red Rubin'; *MIDDLE: O. b.* 'African Blue'; *O. b.* 'Italian Large Leaf'; *BOTTOM: O. b.* 'Genovese Compact'

glossy, medium leaves, purple flowers, and fruity taste. 'Siam Queen', to 2 ft. tall, is a licorice-flavored basil that's good for Thai and Vietnamese dishes; produces showy purple flowers. 'Magical Michael' forms a neat mound to 1½ ft. tall and wide and has both culinary and ornamental value. Dwarf sweet basils form dense, compact plants under 1 ft. tall; they're good for edging and also do well in containers. Recommended selections include 'Finissimo Verde a Palla', 'Minette', 'Pluto', and 'Spicy Globe'.

CARE

Sow seeds of any basil in early spring indoors, or sow seeds or set out nursery plants after all danger of frost has passed and the soil has warmed, about the time you plant tomatoes. Choose a spot with well-drained soil, 6-8 hours of sunlight per day. Plant seeds ¼ in. deep. When seedlings are 2–3 in. tall, thin them to 1½–2 ft. apart. Alternatively, space transplants about 10–12 in. apart. Use a generous amount of compost in the soil at planting time, and, if needed, use a timed-release fertilizer as directed on the label.

Where the growing season is long, these annual plants complete their lifecycles by flowering and setting seeds. This also means that plants stop growing flavorful leaves. Postpone the inevitable by pinching out bloom spikes when they form. You can also cut plants back by a third, even if you don't have time to make pesto. Pruning more severely cuts into older stems that will not sprout as readily. Feed plants lightly with compost tea or a similar liquid product to spur new leafy growth. Two branches will grow wherever a single branch is cut. Plants will produce new leaves until it begins to bloom again.

Because flowering is associated with high temperatures, Southern gardeners should mulch plants to help keep the soil cool. Gardeners in the warmest areas of the South may find that basil will actually grow better with a little afternoon shade. If your season is long, replant in late summer for a second crop. Growth will continue until temperatures drop below 50°F. Basil will be blackened by the slightest frost, so when the first freeze is

forecast, it is time to process your basil, whether you make pesto for the freezer or dry it for winter use.

Basil is susceptible to fusarium wilt, which causes plants to collapse in a day. Defeat it by growing tolerant selections and never plant basil in the same bed more than once every 4 years. Alternatively, plant in containers.

ODONTONEMA

FIRESPIKES
Acanthaceae
Evergreen shrubs

✎ **CS, TS; USDA 9-11; OR GROW AS ANNUALS OR IN POTS**

☼ **FULL SUN**

💧 **REGULAR WATER**

Odontonema tubaeforme

These Central American natives are some of autumn's showiest plants, especially in the Tropical South, where they appreciate a little afternoon shade. Hummingbirds and butterflies frequent the blossoms. If given moderately fertile, well-drained soil, they need little care. They are very tender to cold—stems and leaves blacken with the first touch of frost. However, they often come back from the roots in the Coastal and Tropical South; elsewhere, treat them as annuals or overwinter indoors. Easily propagated from stem cuttings of mature new growth.

O. callistachyum. PURPLE FIRESPIKE. Grows as much as 8 ft. tall, featuring 10- to 12-in. spikes of purple blooms.

O. tubaeforme (*O. strictum*). FIRESPIKE. Forms a multistemmed mound to 6 ft. tall and about half as wide, with shiny, deep green leaves that are oval, pointed, and up to 6 in. long. Stunning, foot-long spikes of small, tubular, fiery red flowers crown the foliage for weeks, beginning in late summer and continuing through the fall.

OENOTHERA

EVENING PRIMROSE,
SUNDROPS
Onagraceae
Perennials, annuals, or biennials

🌿 **ZONES VARY BY SPECIES**

☼◑ **FULL SUN OR PARTIAL SHADE, EXCEPT AS NOTED**

◐◐ **LITTLE TO MODERATE WATER, EXCEPT AS NOTED**

Oenothera fruticosa

Valued for showy, four-petaled, silky flowers in bright yellow, pink, or white. Some types display their blossoms during the day, but others open in late afternoon and close the following morning. Flowers of some are fragrant. Plants succeed in tough, rough places. Resist deer.

O. biennis. EVENING PRIMROSE. Annual or biennial. Zones US, MS, LS, CS; USDA 6-9. Variable in size, ranging from 1 ft. to 4 ft. or even as much as 6 ft. tall. Best grown in meadows, as it is usually weedy, reseeds, and can be invasive. Fragrant yellow blossoms open in the evening; they are yellow at first, then fade to gold. Japanese beetles are particularly fond of this species.

O. drummondii. BEACH EVENING PRIMROSE. Perennial. Zones LS, CS, TS; USDA 8-11. Native to the Coastal South and Mexico. Evening-blooming plant that forms a foliage mat 5 in. high and 4 ft. wide; prostrate stems root along the ground, forming offset plants. Narrow, dark green leaves to 2½ in. long. Yellow, 2½-in. flowers rise

on individual stems 6–8 in. above foliage. Blooms most heavily in spring, sporadically throughout the rest of the year. Endures heat and drought but does better with occasional water.

O. fruticosa. SUNDROPS. Perennial or biennial. Zones US, MS, LS, CS; USDA 6-9. Native to eastern U.S. Erect growth to 2 ft. high and wide. Branching reddish stems are set with medium green, lance-shaped leaves to 4½ in. long; leaves turn dull red with frost. From late spring through summer, bears clusters of 1- to 2-in.-wide, deep yellow flowers that open in daytime. 'Fireworks' ('Fyrverkeri') has red flower buds and leaves tinted purplish brown. *O. f. g.* (*O. tetragona*) has light yellow flowers and red stems; its leaves (red-tinted when young) are broader than those of the species. Foliage of *O. f. glauca* 'Summer Solstice' ('Sonnenwende') turns bright red in summer, darkens to burgundy in fall.

O. 'Lemon Drop'. Perennial. Zones US, MS, LS, CS; USDA 6-9. This showy hybrid blooms yellow in the daytime through hot, dry summers, growing 8–12 in. tall and wide. Use on the front edge of a flower bed, in a mixed container, or as a blooming ground cover.

O. longifolia 'Lemon Sunset'. Perennial. Zones US, MS, LS, CS; USDA 6-9. Grows 2–4 ft. tall and 1–3 ft. wide. Fragrant, 4-in. flowers in summer, opening soft yellow in the evening and fading to coral the next day. Can spread underground to form a clump. Tolerates heat and drought.

O. macrocarpa (*O. missouriensis*). OZARK SUNDROPS. Perennial. Zones US, MS, LS; USDA 6-8. Native to south-central U.S. To 6 in. tall and 2 ft. wide, with narrow, medium green, lance-shaped leaves to 3 in. long. Late spring to early fall, bears pure yellow, 4-in. flowers that remain open all day. Large winged seedpods follow the flowers. Good in rock gardens. Give partial shade in hottest climates. *O. m. incana* 'Silver Blade' has silvery blue leaves.

O. speciosa. SHOWY EVENING PRIMROSE. Perennial. Zones US, MS, LS, CS, TS; USDA 6-11. Native to southwestern U.S. and Mexico. An old favorite in the South. To 1 ft. high and 3 ft. or more wide, spreading quickly by rhizomes. Forms rosettes of

medium green, narrow, 1- to 3-in.-long leaves. Fragrant, 2-in. flowers are white to pinkish, aging to pink; despite plant's common name, they open during the day. Blooms from spring or early summer into fall, then stems die back. Good ground cover for dry slopes or parking strips but is aggressive and invasive. Selections include pure white form 'Alba', light pink 'Rosea', pink 'Siskiyou', and 'Woodside White' (white blossoms with a chartreuse eye).

OKRA

Malvaceae

🌿 **US, MS, LS, CS, TS; USDA 6-11**

☼ **FULL SUN**

💧 **REGULAR WATER**

Okra

Vegetable gardeners can't claim to be truly Southern unless they've grown okra. Native to tropical Asia, this vegetable (known botanically as *Abelmoschus esculentus*) arrived aboard slave ships from Africa in the 1600s and quickly became a regional staple. It's a large, erect, bushy plant to 6 ft. or taller, with big, bold, deeply lobed leaves. The edible seedpods are produced in leaf joints and can be pickled, fried in batter, or used in stews, gumbos, and soups.

Okra loves hot weather, so don't plant it until the soil has warmed to at least 75°F. To speed germination, soak the hard seeds in water overnight before planting; use only those that are swollen. Work ½ cup of 10-10-10 fertilizer per 10 ft. of row into the soil. Sow seeds ½–1 in. deep and about 2 in. apart in rows 3–4 ft.

apart. When seedlings reach 2 in. tall, thin them to 6–12 in. apart. After the first pods set, apply ¼ cup of 10-10-10 fertilizer per 10 ft. of row; repeat three to four weeks later.

Allow 48 to 60 days from planting to harvest. Developing pods grow quickly, as much as an inch per day in hot weather; begin harvesting them when they are 2–4 in. long, and be sure to pick every couple of days (plants stop producing if pods are left to mature fully). Pods longer than 4 in. are typically too tough to eat. Use a sharp knife or pruners to remove the pods from the stems—and wear gloves, since okra pods are usually prickly.

For small gardens, try a dwarf form that reaches only 3–4 ft. tall, such as 'Annie Oakley II' (48 days), 'Baby Bubba' (53 days), 'Cajun Delight' (50 days), or 'Lee' (50 days). Despite their smaller size, these are heavy producers. 'Clemson Spineless' (56 days), the old standby, grows 5–6 ft. tall; its pods lack prickles.

Some selections have pods that remain tender even when they reach large size. 'Burgundy' (49 days) features maroon-red pods (green when cooked) that stay tender to 8 in. long. 'Burmese' (58 days) an heirloom from Burma, produces pods when only 18 in. tall amid oversize foliage and continues until frost. 'Cow Horn' (55 days), a Southern heirloom, grows 7–8 ft. tall and produces tender pods 10 in. long. 'Hill Country Red' (64 days) is a Texas heirloom. Red stems yield red-tipped pods still tender at 6 in. 'Jade' (55 days) grows to 4½ ft. tall, bears tender pods to 6 in. long.

OLIVE

Oleaceae
Evergreen trees

LS, CS; USDA 8-9

FULL SUN

LITTLE TO MODERATE WATER; DROUGHT TOLERANT

Olives

Olives (*Olea europaea*) come from the Mediterranean region. They thrive in areas with hot, dry summers, but also perform adequately in coastal areas. Willowlike foliage is a soft gray-green, and smooth gray trunks and branches become gnarled and picturesque in age. Trees grow slowly, typically to 25–30 ft. tall and as wide; however, young ones put on height (if not substance) fairly fast. They usually tolerate temperatures down to 15°F (-9°C). Growers from Texas to the Carolinas have planted groves of olives for oil production. Homeowners can grow them as well, both for oil or eating. Unlike other tree fruits that ripen and are ready to eat, olives require a curing process of soaking in brine or lye to remove the bitterness. Then they are rinsed and marinated in jars before they are ready to eat.

O. e. 'Arbequina'. This Spanish selection is a good choice for the home gardener interested in either fruit or oil. Growing 12–15 ft., it is more cold tolerant than most, surviving down to 10°F but needs warm summers to bear fruit. It is self-fertile, so only one tree is needed.

O. e. 'Manzanillo'. Originating in Spain, this olive is widely planted for canned black olives, but it is suitable for oil as well. It is self-fertile.

O. e. 'Mission'. This U.S. selection is self-fertile, grows to about 20 ft. and can be used for oil or cured for the table.

CARE

A suitable climate is the most important factor in success with olives. Unlike most fruit trees, olives don't set flower buds in fall. Instead, they only set buds following exposure to cool nights (35–50°F) and warm days (80°F) during winter.

Olive trees look best when grown in deep, rich soil, but they will also grow in shallow, alkaline, or stony soil.

Choose a sunny location with good drainage. Set plants, and water well. Cut off the tip of young trees at 2½ ft. to make them branch. Remove basal sprouts as the tree grows if a single-trunked tree is desired. Fertilize in spring and midsummer with a slow-release product containing at least 10 percent nitrogen plus micronutrients. They get by on little water but produce better crops with a deep soaking every two weeks.

Olives ripen and drop late in the year. They can stain paving and harm lawns if not removed.

OMPHALODES VERNA

BLUE-EYED MARY
Boraginaceae
Perennial

US, MS, LS; USDA 6-8

PARTIAL SHADE

REGULAR WATER

Omphalodes verna

Native to the mountains of Europe. Attractive, creeping perennial, nice for ground cover in shaded rock garden or woodland planting; evergreen in mild-winter areas. Medium green leaves are oval, pointed, 2–4 in. long; form a mat about 3 in. high, spreading to 3 ft. or more. Half-inch-wide spring flowers are an intense pure blue with a tiny white eye. Tolerates drought but looks better with regular water.

ONCIDIUM

Orchidaceae
Epiphytic orchids

TS; USDA 10-11; OR GROW IN POTS

PARTIAL SHADE; BRIGHT INDIRECT LIGHT

REGULAR WATER

Oncidium ornithorhynchum

Orchids native from Florida and Mexico through South America. The several hundred species and countless hybrids range from tiny plants just 1 in. tall to giants with branching flower spikes to 6 ft. or more, bearing dozens of blooms. Most produce long spikes of yellow or brown-and-yellow flowers; a few come in white or rose. Some (including the plants described here) have compressed pseudobulbs, while others are almost without pseudobulbs; some have just one or two large leaves, others cylindrical, pencil-like leaves. Plants typically produce a few large blossoms or many small ones, but some have numerous large flowers and a few bear their blooms singly. In many, flowers have a large, flaring lip reminiscent of a flamenco dancer's skirt; these are sometimes called dancing ladies. Blossoms of some are scented.

As outdoor plants, oncidiums are usually grown on tree trunks or in pots on the patio; indoor plants can be brought outdoors during warm weather. Take same houseplant culture as cattleya, page 221.

O. crispum. Pseudobulbs 4 in. high are topped by 8-in. leaves. In fall, produces a branching, 3-ft.-tall spike carrying many 4-in. flowers in chestnut brown spotted with yellow. Each bloom has a brown lip with a large bright yellow spot.

O. ornithorhynchum. Pseudobulbs 2½ in. tall are topped by leaves to 1 ft. long. In summer, many branching, 8- to 12-in.-tall spikes carry a cloud of inch-wide pink or purplish pink flowers with yellow markings.

Sharry Baby. A series of powerfully fragrant hybrids with 4-in.-high pseudobulbs topped by 8-in. leaves. Spikes to 2–3 ft. long bear many inch-wide blossoms in summer and fall; some liken the flowers' perfume to chocolate, others to vanilla. 'Sweet Fragrance' has reddish purple blossoms with a white lip.

ONION

Alliaceae
Biennial grown as annual

US, MS, LS, CS, TS; USDA 6-11

FULL SUN

REGULAR WATER

Onions

People who love onions (*Allium cepa*) may be used to weeping for joy—but tears don't have to be part of the affair. "Sweet" onions contain little pyruvate, the chemical that causes tears and hot flavor. Unfortunately, these types don't keep as well as their stronger-tasting brethren, so choosing the right onion depends on your needs.

In addition to flavor and shelf life, onions vary in size, shape, and color. More important, different types form bulbs in response to varying day lengths. If you choose a type inappropriate for your area, it may go to seed before bulbing up, form small bulbs, or not form bulbs at all.

Short-day selections need 10 to 12 hours of daylight and are well adapted to most areas of the South. These tend to be sweet, but they are poor keepers. They typically begin to form bulbs in spring. Examples are 'Burgundy', 'Crystal White Wax', 'Granex 33' ('Vidalia'), 'Southern Belle', 'Georgia Sweet' (Yellow grapex), 'Texas Grano 502', 'Texas Grano 1015' ('1015 Supersweet'), and 'Yellow Bermuda'.

Intermediate-day onions, requiring 12 to 14 hours of daylight, also grow well in the South. They have a stronger flavor than short-day types and keep longer. Examples include 'Candy Hybrid', 'Stockton Sweet Red', and 'Super Star Hybrid'. They usually form bulbs in summer.

Long-day onions, which need 14 to 16 hours of sunlight, keep the best. They form bulbs in summer. They're suited only to the Upper South and parts north. Examples include 'Ebenezer', 'Sweet Spanish', 'Walla Walla', and 'Yellow Globe'.

Bunching onions do not form large bulbs but have slightly swollen white stalks. Depending on where you're from, you may know them as green onions, scallions, or spring onions. They can be planted in fall or spring. 'Evergreen White Bunching' is a favorite selection. Egyptian walking onion (*A. cepa proliferum*) gets its name from the bulbils that cluster near the tops of the leaves; the foliage bends to the ground, and the bulbils take root. Shallots and potato onions (*A. cepa aggregatum*) are smaller, milder-flavored regular onions; see Shallots.

Cipollini onions are very small bulbing onions that are listed as in their own class in catalogs. They are flattish, 2- to 3-in.-diameter, sweet, long-day onions that come in red, yellow, or white.

CARE

You can grow onions from seeds, sets (small bulbs), or transplants. Sets and transplants are quicker and easier for beginners; starting from seed gives a larger crop for a smaller investment and offers a wider choice of selections.

In the Lower, Coastal, and Tropical South, onions grow well from seeds sown in fall. Sets and transplants can be planted from late fall throughout the winter. In the Upper and Middle South, sow seeds outdoors six to eight weeks before the last frost in spring; plant sets and transplants four weeks before the last frost.

Soil should be loose, fertile, and well drained. Space sets and transplants 4–5 in. apart (closer if you want to harvest some early as green onions). When planting sets, push them just under the soil surface, so the point of the bulb remains visible; when planting transplants, trim foliage back by about half after planting. Sow seeds ¼ in. deep in rows spaced 15–18 in. apart. Thin seedlings to 4–5 in. apart; thinnings can be eaten as green onions or transplanted.

To produce large bulbs, onions need moist soil and repeated applications of fertilizer. Scratch in ¼ cup of 10-10-10 fertilizer per 10 ft. of row before planting. Sprinkle this same amount around plants four to six weeks later and again when bulbs begin to form; water it in. Carefully eliminate weeds, being sure you don't damage the onion bulbs or their shallow roots. When most of the tops have begun to yellow and fall over, dig the bulbs, leaving the tops on; spread them out (tops and all) in a dry, dark place for 10 to 14 days to cure. When tops and necks are completely dry, pull off the tops and brush dirt from the bulbs. Store in a dark, cool, airy place; use mesh or cloth bags, not plastic ones.

ONOCLEA SENSIBILIS
SENSITIVE FERN
Onocleaceae
Fern

🌿 **US, MS, LS, CS; USDA 6-9**

☀◐◑● **SUN OR SHADE**

💧 **REGULAR TO AMPLE WATER**

Onoclea sensibilis

Native to the eastern U.S. This bold-textured, easy-to-grow fern got its name because it turns brown with the very first kiss of frost in fall. It produces two types of fronds. The sterile ones are large (2–4 ft. long) and lance-shaped to triangular; the fertile ones are smaller, holding erect clusters of beadlike leaflets that turn brown at maturity. Fronds grow from creeping rhizomes that spread quickly in moist, fertile soil. Plant is a good choice for rain garden, pond, and streamside plantings and naturalized areas. Be sure plants grown in sun are kept well watered. Dies to the ground in winter.

OPHIOPOGON
Asparagaceae
Perennials

🌿 **MS, LS, CS, TS; USDA 7-11**

◐● **PARTIAL TO FULL SHADE**

💧💧 **MODERATE TO REGULAR WATER**

Ophiopogon planiscapus 'Nigrescens'

It's hard to imagine more serviceable ground covers for shade than these Asian natives. Though slightly less cold hardy than their *Liriope* cousins (see page 416), they're just as carefree, needing little more than well-drained soil and shelter from hot sun. Deer don't generally bother them. Plant them in large sweeps in areas where you don't want to mow or under large trees where grass won't grow. They also do well in containers. Use them for their lush evergreen foliage; the summer flowers, borne on short spikes, are largely hidden by the leaves.

It's easy to obtain more plants by division. Use a sharp spade to divide clumps in early spring; or use a knife to divide clumps sold in flats or cell-packs at garden centers. To get divisions of mondo grass (*O. japonicus*, *O. planiscapus* 'Nigrescens') off to a fast start, trim the roots back by half before replanting. This encourages rapid root growth.

ALL HAIL THE VIDALIA!

The Vidalia onion, often touted as "the world's sweetest onion," got its start as a Bermuda onion imported into South Texas in 1898. Breeders worked to produce a sweet onion that matured early and enjoyed the Southern heat. In 1952, their hard work paid off with the introduction of 'Granex 33', a somewhat flattened-looking yellow onion with a sweet, mild flavor. Before long, the new onion made its way to Toombs County in Georgia, where the favorable climate and low-sulfur soil produced an especially sweet flavor. The state of Georgia built a farmer's market in the town of Vidalia and began promoting "Vidalia onions." Today, this crop enjoys legal protection—no onion grown outside the official 20-county production area in Georgia can be called a "Vidalia." But Texans don't mind—they'll tell you their 'Texas Grano 1015' ('1015 Supersweet') is even sweeter.

O. intermedius 'Argenteo-marginatus'. AZTEC GRASS. Forms foot-tall clumps with a cascading look and spreads widely and aggressively. Thin, dark green leaves with yellowish white margins grow 1½ ft. long, ½ in. wide; white flowers are followed by bright blue fruit. Sometimes sold as *Liriope muscari* 'Variegata', but that plant has violet blooms.

O. jaburan. GIANT LILY TURF. Sometimes sold as *Liriope gigantea*. Grows 2–3 ft. tall, 1½ ft. wide, with dark green leaves to 1½–3 ft. long, ½ in. wide. Clump forming; does not spread. Nodding clusters of small white flowers are followed by showy fruit in metallic violet blue (attractive in arrangements). 'Vittatus' (sometimes sold as *Liriope muscari* 'Variegata') has leaves edged in creamy white.

O. japonicus. MONDO GRASS, MONKEY GRASS. Dark green, grasslike leaves grow 8–12 in. long, ⅛ in. wide. Forms dense, 6- to 8-in.-tall clumps that steadily spread by underground stems to form an evergreen mat at least 1 ft. across. Short spikes of lilac flowers are followed by metallic blue fruit. Makes an excellent shade-tolerant lawn that never needs mowing, though it takes several years to fill in. Great for filling cracks between pavers and stepping stones. A number of dwarf selections spread much more slowly than the species; these include 'Gyoku Ryu' (1–2 in. tall), 'Kyoto Dwarf' (2–4 in.), and 'Nana' (3 in.). 'Little Tabby' (also sold as *O. planiscapus* 'Little Tabby') and 'Shiroshima Ryu' (also sold as *O. japonicus* 'Variegatus') have green-and-white striped leaves and grow 4–6 in. tall.

O. planiscapus 'Nigrescens' ('Arabicus'). BLACK MONDO GRASS. Nearly black, grasslike leaves grow to 14 in. long, ⅛–¼ in. wide. New leaves are green, but they soon darken. Spreads slowly, forming tufts to 8 in. high; clumps can reach 1 ft. across, but they don't form a thick carpet. Flowers are white or (sometimes) light pink. Looks great in mixed containers; striking when combined with yellow or chartreuse foliage, such as yellow creeping Jenny (*Lysimachia nummularia* 'Aurea').

OPUNTIA
Cactaceae
Cacti

- ▨ **ZONES VARY BY SPECIES**
- ☼ **FULL SUN**
- ◌ **LITTLE OR NO WATER, EXCEPT AS NOTED**

Opuntia

Some of the species described here originate in the desert Southwest and Mexico; others are native to those areas and/or to other parts of the western U.S., the Great Plains, Canada, and Florida. Many kinds, with varied appearance. Most species fall into one of two sorts: those having flat, broad joints (pads) or those having cylindrical joints. Members of the first group are often called prickly pear; those in the second group are frequently known as cholla and now placed in the genus *Cylindropuntia*. Pods that break off and fall to the ground root quickly and hasten the plant's spread. Hardiness is variable, but all require excellent drainage. Flowers are generally large and showy. The fruit is a berry, often edible.

O. cacanapa 'Ellisiana'. ELLISIANA SPINELESS PRICKLY PEAR. Zones MS, LS, CS, TS; USDA 7-11. This spineless prickly pear grows 3 ft. tall and 6 ft. wide in as few as five years. Yellow flowers in August result in showy red fruit in the fall.

O. ficus-indica. PRICKLY PEAR. Zones CS, TS; USDA 9-11. From Mexico. Big, shrubby or treelike cactus to 15 ft. tall, 10 ft. wide, with woody trunks and smooth, flat, green joints with clusters of bristles; few or no spines. Bears yellow to orange,

3- to 5-in.-wide flowers in late spring, early summer. Blossoms are followed by roundish, 2- to 3½-in.-long fruit that ripens from yellow to red; these are the prickly pears used in Mexican cooking you may see sold in grocery stores as *nopales*. Handle them carefully; the bristles break off easily and irritate the skin. Wear rubber gloves when peeling the fruit, or impale it on a fork and carefully strip off skin, avoiding bristly areas. This species is very drought tolerant, but in the hottest regions it will need regular moisture for best fruit.

O. humifusa. HARDY PRICKLY PEAR. Zones US, MS, LS, CS, TS; USDA 6-11. An old Southern favorite, native from Canada south to Florida and eastern Texas. Spreading clump grows to 12 in. or less in height, with few-spined, 3- to 6-in.-long pads. Bears yellow, 3- to 4-in.-wide flowers in early summer; 2-in.-long fruit, purple when ripe. Tolerates moister soil than most cacti. Very cold hardy. Good choice for the beach; dry, sunny banks; or containers.

O. lindheimeri. TEXAS PRICKLY PEAR. Zones MS, LS, CS, TS; USDA 7-11. Native to southern Texas. Large, clumping cactus with pads that grow to 1 ft. long and carry 1- to 2-in. spines. Typically 4–6 ft. tall, but it can reach 12 ft. high and spread even wider. Flowers are yellow, orange, or red, blooming 3–4 in. wide in late spring or early summer, followed by 2- to 3-in., red-purple fruit.

O. microdasys. BUNNY EARS. Zones CS, TS; USDA 9-11; or houseplant. Native to northern and central Mexico. Grows fast to 2 ft. high, 4–5 ft. wide (much smaller in pots). Flat, thin, nearly round, velvety green pads reach 6 in. wide; they are set with neatly spaced tufts of short golden bristles, giving a polka-dot effect. 'Albispina' has white bristles. Small, round new pads grow atop larger old ones, giving the plant a silhouette reminiscent of an animal's head. A great favorite with children.

Indoors, site in bright light. In spring through fall, let soil become dry between soakings; every two to three months, apply a general-purpose liquid houseplant fertilizer diluted to half-strength. In winter, water sparingly and stop fertilizing.

O. phaeacantha. Zones MS, LS, CS, TS; USDA 7-11. Native from northern Texas to California. Low, spreading clump (2–3 ft.), with 4- to 6-in. pads and thick, 2-in. spines. Yellow flowers usually with orange-red centers, 2–3 in. across, in spring or summer; inch-long red fruit.

ORIGANUM
OREGANO, MARJORAM
Lamiaceae
Perennials sometimes grown as annuals

- ▨ **ZONES VARY BY SPECIES**
- ☼ **FULL SUN**
- ◌◖ **LITTLE TO MODERATE WATER**

Origanum majorana

Mint relatives with tight clusters of small flowers. Each blossom has a collar of bracts—large, colorful, and quite decorative in some species—that can overlap to give the look of a small pinecone. These can be cut and dried as the first flowers open for use in arrangements and wreaths. Blossoms are especially attractive to bees and butterflies. Most oreganos have pleasantly aromatic foliage. Though several kinds are valued for cooking, others are chiefly ornamentals, used as ground covers or to cascade over rocks, retaining walls, and the edges of hanging baskets. Some are hardy and evergreen; others are tender and killed by frost. None is seriously damaged by browsing deer.

All types of *Origanum* look good in the garden. But for kitchen use, the following are best. Sweet marjoram (*O. marjorana*) has a sweet, spicy flavor; it can even be used to make tea.

Italian marjoram (*O.* x *majoricum*) has a more complex, slightly less sweet flavor, while pot marjoram (*O. onites*) has a savory, thyme-like taste.

Flavor of the plain oregano (*O. vulgare*) is variable; choose a selected form with an aroma and flavor you like. Biblical hyssop (*O. syriacum*) and Greek oregano (*O. v. hirtum*) are pungent and spicy-hot.

O. dictamnus. DITTANY OF CRETE, HOP MARJORAM. Zones MS, LS, CS; USDA 7-9. Native to Crete. Aromatic herb to 8 in. high, 1½–2 ft. wide, with slender, arching stems to 1 ft. long. Thick, roundish, woolly white leaves to ¾ in. long. Pink to purplish flowers emerge from rose-tinted, light green bracts; blooms summer to fall. Primarily ornamental, it shows up best when planted individually in rock garden or in hanging basket.

O. laevigatum. Zones US, MS, LS, CS; USDA 6-9. Native to Turkey, Cyprus. A sprawling, ornamental oregano with grayish green leaves about 1¼ in. long; reaches 2 ft. tall in bloom. It spreads by rhizomes and arching stems that root at the joints to form a dense clump 2–3 ft. wide. Branching, airy clusters of 1-in., tubular pink or purple flowers and small purplish bracts appear from late spring to fall. Useful on a bank or as a ground cover. 'Herrenhausen' has larger bracts and more compact heads of lilac-pink flowers. 'Hopleys', probably a hybrid with *O. vulgare*, blooms from mid- to late summer, bearing denser heads of purplish pink flowers and purplish bracts; it self-sows freely, producing seedlings with variable foliage and flower color. Both 'Herrenhausen' and 'Hopleys' have purple leaves in cool weather. 'Pilgrim' has gray-green leaves that set apart the lavender flowers with dark purple calyxes.

O. majorana. SWEET MARJORAM, KNOTTED MARJORAM. Zones CS, TS; USDA 9-11. Native to the Mediterranean and Turkey. To 1–2 ft. tall and wide. Oval, gray-green leaves to 1 in. long. In summer, inconspicuous white flowers emerge from clusters of knotlike heads at top of plant. Keep blossoms cut off and plant trimmed to encourage fresh growth. Fresh or dried leaves are used for seasoning meats, scrambled eggs, salads, vinegars, casseroles, and tomato dishes. Often grown in pots indoors on sunny windowsill in cold-winter areas. Leaves of 'White Anniversary' have a distinct cream margin.

O. x **majoricum.** ITALIAN MARJORAM, SICILIAN MARJORAM. Zones US, MS, LS, CS; USDA 6-9. Similar to *O. majorana* but with wider, greener leaves. Some gourmet cooks consider this the best marjoram for seasoning.

O. microphyllum. Zones MS, LS, CS; USDA 7-9. Native to Crete. Grows to 10 in. high and 1 ft. wide, with domelike form. Reddish branches bear tiny gray-green leaves to ¼ in. long. Clusters of small, pale pink to purple flowers bloom in summer. Thrives in dry rock crevices.

O. 'Norton Gold'. Zones US, MS, LS, CS; USDA 6-9. Hybrid ornamental to 1–1½ ft. high, 2 ft. wide. Forms a dense mat of small, rounded leaves that are bright green when new, aging to a darker shade. Profuse lavender-pink flowers with rosy bracts in summer. Best with moderate water.

O. onites. POT MARJORAM, RHIGANI. Zones US, MS, LS, CS; USDA 6-9. Eastern Mediterranean native. To 2 ft. tall and wide, with bright green, inch-long leaves and 2-in.-wide, flattish heads of white or purplish flowers in late summer. Sometimes called Cretan oregano. Has a strong, musky fragrance.

O. rotundifolium. Zones US, MS, LS, CS; USDA 6-9. Native to Turkey, Armenia, and Georgia. Dense, suckering plant grows to 8 in. high and 1 ft. wide, bearing numerous wiry stems set with pairs of blue-green leaves that have a rounded heart shape. Blooms throughout summer, bearing spikes of small, pale pink blossoms and green, 2- to 3-in.-long bracts like those of hop (*Humulus*) at stem ends (bracts almost obscure the flowers). 'Kent Beauty' is a hybrid with *O. scabrum* and has a more compact habit (4 in. high, 8 in. wide). It bears conspicuously mauve-toned pink blossoms and deep rose bracts in the summer. It's a charming, easy-to-grow addition to garden beds, window boxes, and pots.

O. syriacum. BIBLICAL HYSSOP, SYRIAN MARJORAM. Zones CS, TS; USDA 9-11. From Syria, Turkey, Cyprus. With its strong, sweet, pungent flavor, this plant is a favorite herb for flavoring Middle Eastern dishes. To 1½ ft. tall and wide. Soft, gray-green leaves to 1½ in. long. Blooms in late spring and early summer, with pale pink, ¼-in. flowers in branching, 2- to 3-in. clusters.

O. vulgare. OREGANO, WILD MARJORAM. Zones US, MS, LS, CS; USDA 6-9. Native to most of Europe and temperate Asia. Upright growth to 2½ ft. tall, 2–3 ft. wide. Oval, dark green leaves to 1½ in. long and ¾ in. wide; white or purplish pink blossoms from midsummer to early fall. Fresh or dried leaves are used in many dishes, especially Spanish and Italian ones.

Most wild forms have scentless leaves and are useless for cooking; be sure to choose a selected form with a good aroma and a flavor that you like. For best flavor, keep this plant trimmed to prevent flowering—but let some clumps bloom for bees and butterflies to enjoy.

'Aureum' has pinkish flowers and foliage that is bright golden in spring (if the plant gets morning sun), green by late summer and fall; 'Thumble's Variety' is similar but has white blossoms. 'Aureum Crispum' has curly golden leaves. 'Compactum' ('Humile') is a wide-spreading plant just a few inches tall, suitable for a ground cover or a filler between paving stones; it seldom flowers, but leaves turn purple in winter. 'Country Cream' (with white flowers) and 'Polyphant' (lilac-pink blooms, also sold as 'White Anniversary') are compact growers to 4–6 in. and have leaves with a distinct creamy white edge; they are often confused in commerce (and both are sometimes sold as 'Variegatum'). 'Roseum' has bright rose-pink flowers, green leaves.

O. v. hirtum (*O. heracleoticum*). GREEK OREGANO. Native to Greece, Turkey, the Aegean islands. Like the species, but with broader, slightly fuzzy, gray-green leaves. Spicy and pungent; considered by many to have the best true oregano flavor.

CARE

Oreganos aren't fussy about soil as long as it is well drained. They'll tolerate light shade, but most do better in full sun (culinary types need full sun to develop best flavor). In milder areas, many species become woody and less productive with age; to restore vigor, cut the previous year's stems to the ground in winter or early spring. You can start plants from seed, but because oreganos cross-pollinate freely, you may not get the plant you want. It's a better bet to purchase potted plants whose identities are certain.

To keep plants producing, cut sprigs often. For a large harvest for drying, wait until just before plants bloom and cut the stems above the lowest set of leaves; new foliage will sprout, and you can cut again in late summer. Don't harvest within a month before the first expected frost, however, as the plants need time to re-establish themselves before cold weather. Strip leaves from stems after they dry.

ORNITHOGALUM

Asparagaceae
Perennials from bulbs

🌡 **ZONES VARY BY SPECIES; OR HOUSEPLANTS**

☼◐ **FULL SUN OR PARTIAL SHADE; BRIGHT LIGHT**

💧 **REGULAR WATER, EXCEPT AS NOTED**

⬥ **ALL PARTS, ESPECIALLY BULBS, ARE POISONOUS IF INGESTED**

Ornithogalum dubium

Clusters of typically star-shaped flowers appear in spring; *O. dubium* may start blooming in late winter. Leaves vary from narrow to broad and tend to droop. In areas where they are hardy, ornithogalums can fill many different roles. Set them in open woodlands, wild gardens, or rock gardens, where many kinds will naturalize; plant them in containers or mass them in borders. Where winters are too cold for in-ground growing, plant the bulbs in pots and force them into early bloom indoors or in a greenhouse. Deer and rodents don't eat them.

O. arabicum. STAR OF BETHLEHEM. Zones LS, CS, TS; USDA 8-11. From the eastern Mediterranean. Stems to 2 ft. tall carry clusters of 2-in., waxy-looking white flowers, each centered with a shiny, beadlike black eye. Bluish green, strap-shaped, inch-wide leaves may reach same length as stems, but they're usually floppy. Requires a dry dormant period from midsummer through winter, so best grown in pots. Water from spring through early summer, then let foliage dry out. Store indoors over winter.

O. dubium. Zones LS, CS, TS; USDA 8-11. From South Africa. Stems 8–12 in. high bear blooms resembling those of *O. arabicum*, but petals surrounding the beady black eye come in shades of yellow to orange. Dark green to yellowish green, lance-shaped leaves are about 4 in. long, nearly prostrate. Same cultural requirements as *O. arabicum*.

O. longibracteatum. PREGNANT ONION, FALSE SEA ONION. Zones CS, TS; USDA 9-11. From South Africa. Grown for bulb and foliage rather than its tall wands of small green-and-white flowers. To 3 ft. tall in leaf; flowers increase height to 5 ft. Long, drooping, strap-shaped, light green leaves. Gray-green, smooth-skinned bulb is 3–4 in. wide and grows on top of, not in, the soil. Bulblets form under skin and grow quite large before they drop out and root. Hardy to 25°F. Moderate water.

O. magnum. STAR OF BETHLEHEM. Zones US, MS, LS; USDA 6-8. Native to the Caucasus Mountains, these bulbs are not shy. Growing 1–2 ft. tall in early summer, it looks like a white camassia. It may reseed modestly, but not enough to become a problem. Tall foliage disappears soon after flowering.

O. nutans. NODDING STAR OF BETHLEHEM. Zones US, MS, LS, CS; USDA 6-9. From the eastern Mediterranean. To 1½-2 ft. tall. Starlike to nearly bell-shaped, 1¼-in. flowers are white striped with green on the outside; they have pronounced central clusters

of stamens. Up to 15 blooms are spaced along upper part of each stalk. Narrow, floppy, bright green leaves. Spreads rapidly and may become weedy. Sometimes called silver bells.

O. oligophyllum (*O. balansae*). Zones US, MS, LS; USDA 6-8. From the eastern Mediterranean. Stems grow 3–5 in. high, bearing thick clusters of white, green-centered, 1¼-in. blossoms with bright yellow stamens and a faint green stripe on the outside of each petal. Medium green leaves to 6 in. long. This species naturalizes but is not an aggressive spreader.

O. thyrsoides. CHINCHERINCHEE. Zone LS, CS, TS; USDA 8-11. Native to South Africa. Flowering stems grow 1½-2 ft. high produce elongated clusters of 2-in., white flowers often with centers tinted green or cream. Upright, bright green leaves grow 1 ft. long, 2 in. wide and usually start to die back while the plants are in bloom. They make excellent cut flowers. Moderate water.

O. umbellatum. STAR OF BETHLEHEM. Zones US, MS, LS, CS; USDA 6-9. Native to the eastern Mediterranean. Erect stems to 1 ft. tall produce clusters of inch-wide, white flowers striped green on the outside. Semierect, grassy-looking leaves are about as long as the flower stems. Cut flowers last well but close at night. Once this species is established, it may naturalize and become weedy.

CARE

Plant bulbs in early fall in well-drained soil amended with plenty of organic matter, setting them 3 in. deep and 3–4 in. apart. Provide regular moisture during growth and bloom. Dig and divide plantings of all species only when plant vigor and bloom quality decline. Indoors, grow in bright light but protect from hottest summer sun. Let soil dry slightly between thorough soakings, and feed every two weeks with a general-purpose liquid houseplant fertilizer. After flowering has ended and leaves begin to yellow, withhold water and fertilizer; don't resume watering and feeding until new growth appears in fall.

ORTHOSIPHON
Lamiaceae
Herbaceous shrubs

🌿 **CS, TS; USDA 9-11**

☼ **FULL SUN**

🌢🌢 **REGULAR TO AMPLE WATER**

Orthosiphon aristatus

These Old World plants are valued for their striking flowers and medicinal use. They bloom nonstop in warm weather.

O. aristatus. CAT'S WHISKERS. Native to tropical and subtropical regions from India to Australia, this tender perennial gets its common name from the long white stamens that protrude from its white or pale blue flowers. In frost-free areas, the plant can grow to 5 ft. tall and 3 ft. wide; in cold-winter areas, where it's treated as an annual and must be replanted each spring, it reaches only half that size. Purple stems hold deep green, shiny, toothed leaves that are 1–3 in. long. Upright clusters of many flowers appear continuously in warm weather and attract bees, butterflies, and hummingbirds. Requires fertile, well-drained soil that is not allowed to dry out; it will not tolerate frost. Makes an excellent addition to the mixed border, never failing to elicit comment, questions, and admiration. Also good grown in containers.

O. labiatus 'Lilac Splash'. PINK SURPRISE BUSH, SHELL BUSH. Native to southern Africa, the spikes of this woody shrub lack the "whiskers" that are the hallmark of *O. aristatus*. However, it is similar in that it blooms from spring to frost, if there is one, and hummingbirds and butterflies can't get enough of it.

OSMANTHUS
Oleaceae
Evergreen shrubs

🌿 **ZONES VARY BY SPECIES**

☼:☼ **FULL SUN OR PARTIAL SHADE, EXCEPT AS NOTED**

🌢🌢🌢 **LITTLE TO REGULAR WATER**

Osmanthus heterophyllus 'Variegatus'

This versatile group of easy-to-grow, broad-leafed evergreens combines handsome foliage with fragrant—though inconspicuous—flowers (white, in most cases). Most are large shrubs that can eventually reach the size of a small tree. Use them as tall screens, hedges, or foundation plantings. They tolerate many soils (including heavy clay), accept heavy pruning, and do well with little moisture or regular garden watering. Somewhat resistant to damage by browsing deer.

O. americanus. DEVILWOOD. Zones US, MS, LS, CS; USDA 6-9. Native to Mexico, and from North Carolina to Florida and Mississippi. Grows rather slowly to 15–25 ft. tall and 15–20 ft. wide, though it may eventually become much larger. Neat, upright, oval form. Handsome, leathery, shiny olive-green foliage: smooth-margined leaves to 7 in. long, 2½ in. wide. Creamy flowers in spring; dark blue, ½-in. fruit in early fall. Very cold hardy. Tolerates wet soil.

O. x burkwoodii. Zones US, MS, LS; USDA 6-8. Hybrid between *O. delavayi* and *O. decorus*. Slow growing to 6–10 ft. tall, 8–12 ft. wide. Densely clothed in 1- to 2-in., glossy, bright green, tooth-edged leaves. Spring bloom. Useful as a hedge.

O. delavayi. DELAVAY OSMANTHUS. Zones MS, LS, CS; USDA 7-9. From China. Slow-growing, graceful plant with arching branches; reaches 4–6 ft. tall, 6–8 ft. wide. Dark green, oval, tooth-edged leaves to 1 in. long. Blooms profusely in spring, bearing clusters of four to eight blossoms (blooms are ½ in. wide—the largest of any osmanthus). Attractive all year. Good choice for foundation plantings, massing. Handsome on retaining walls where branches can hang down. Does best in partial shade.

O. x fortunei. FORTUNE'S OSMANTHUS. Zones MS, LS, CS; USDA 7-9. Hybrid between *O. heterophyllus* and *O. fragrans*. Slow, dense growth to an eventual 15–20 ft. tall, 6–8 ft. wide; usually seen at about 6 ft. tall. Oval, 4-in.-long leaves resemble those of holly (*Ilex*). Extremely fragrant flowers in autumn. Selection 'San Jose' bears flowers ranging in color from cream to orange. 'Fruitlandii' is a slightly more cold hardy, compact form with cream-colored flowers.

O. fragrans. SWEET OLIVE, TEA OLIVE. Zones LS, CS, TS; USDA 8-11. Native to China, Japan, Himalayas. Long a favorite of Southern gardeners. Broad, dense, compact. Grows at a moderate rate to 15 ft. tall, 8–10 ft. wide (though older plants may reach 30 ft. tall, 12–15 ft. wide). Oval, glossy, medium green leaves to 4 in. long, toothed or smooth edged. Flowers are powerfully fragrant, with a scent like that of ripe apricots. Bloom is heaviest in spring, but plants flower sporadically throughout year. Can be pruned to upright growth where space is limited; can be trained as a small tree, hedge, screen, background, espalier, or container plant. Pinch out growing tips of young plants to induce bushiness. Give afternoon shade. 'Butter Yellow' produces lots of butter-yellow flowers. 'Fudingzhu' is an outstanding form, more cold hardy and not as large as the species, and it blooms for a much longer time with large, showy clusters of blooms. 'Orange Supreme' is a well-shaped plant with bright orange blossoms. *O. f. aurantiacus* has narrower, less glossy leaves than the species; its crop of wonder-fully fragrant orange flowers is concentrated in early fall.

O. heterophyllus. HOLLY OSMANTHUS. Zones US, MS, LS, CS; USDA 6-9. From Japan. Grows to 8–10 ft. (possibly 20 ft.)

tall and slightly wider, with 2½-in., spiny-edged, glossy, green leaves. Resembles English holly (*Ilex aquifolium*), but leaves are opposite one another on stems rather than alternate. Fragrant white flowers in late fall and winter are followed by berrylike, blue-black fruit. Useful as hedge.

'Goshiki'. Erect growth to 3½ ft. tall, 5 ft. wide. New leaves have pinkish orange markings; in mature foliage, the variegations are creamy yellow (on a deep green background). Few flowers.

'Gulftide'. Dense grower to 8–10 ft. tall and 10 ft. wide (may eventually reach 20 ft. high), with deep green, very glossy foliage. More cold hardy than the species. Probably the most popular selection.

'Purpureus'. Same growth habit as species. Leaves are dark purple when new, maturing to purple-toned deep green.

'Rotundifolius'. Slow growing to 5 ft. tall and wide. Small, roundish leaves are lightly spined.

'Variegatus'. Slow growing to an eventual 8–10 ft. tall and wide, with densely set leaves edged in creamy white. Useful for lighting up shady areas. A bit less cold tolerant than the species.

OSMUNDA
Osmundaceae
Ferns

🖊 **ZONES VARY BY SPECIES**

☀ ◑ ● **EXPOSURE NEEDS VARY BY SPECIES**

💧 **AMPLE WATER**

Osmunda regalis

Three species of graceful, imposing deciduous ferns useful in naturalistic plantings. All like

plenty of moisture but can survive with less, responding with smaller, less vigorous growth. Rhizomes have heavy growth of matted brown roots—the source of the osmunda fiber used for potting orchids.

O. cinnamomea. CINNAMON FERN. US, MS, LS, CS; USDA 6-9. To 5 ft. tall, 2 ft. wide. Plant has erect, sterile fronds that arch out toward top. Fertile fronds are also erect but are narrower and much shorter, turning cinnamon-brown as spores ripen. Unfolding young fronds (fiddleheads) are edible; they are usually served as a cooked vegetable, steamed and lightly buttered. Fronds turn showy yellow to orange in fall. Full or light shade.

O. claytoniana. INTERRUPTED FERN. Zones US, MS, LS; USDA 6-8. Grows as tall as 5 ft., more typically to 3 ft. tall, 2 ft. wide. Shorter in dryish soils. Each frond is "interrupted" in the middle by several short, brown, spore-bearing segments. Full or light shade.

O. regalis. ROYAL FERN. US, MS, LS, CS; USDA 6-9. Large fern (to 6 ft. tall, 3 ft. wide) with twice-cut fronds, each leaflet quite large. Coarser in texture than most ferns. Tips of fronds have modified segments that somewhat resemble flower buds; these produce the spores. One of the better ferns for fall color; fronds may turn bright yellow. 'Cristata' has crested fronds; 'Purpurascens' has purplish red new growth and stems that remain purple throughout the season. Likes light shade, but will thrive in sun in wet soil, even in mud. Especially attractive beside streams or ponds.

OSTEOSPERMUM
AFRICAN DAISY
Asteraceae
Perennials

🖊 **CS, TS; USDA 9-11; ANYWHERE AS ANNUALS**

☀ **FULL SUN**

💧💧 ● **MODERATE TO REGULAR WATER**

Osteospermum hybrid

Native to South Africa, these woody perennials are closely related to *Dimorphotheca* and often sold as such. Mounded or trailing in habit, they bear a profusion of daisylike flowers during mild weather; flowering decreases or halts altogether during long, hot stretches. Tend to be short lived in the South. Used as winter annuals in Florida. Narrow, oval leaves are 2–4 in. long. Flowers of most open only in sunlight.

Tolerate heat and drought but look better with moderate water. Give loose, fertile soil; good drainage is a must. Pinch out growing tips of young plants to induce bushiness; cut back old, sprawling branches to young side growth in late summer to midautumn. Mass along driveways and paths; or use in borders, rock gardens, containers. Types that spread by rooting stems are good on slopes. Not usually browsed by deer.

O. ecklonis. To 2–5 ft. tall, 2–4 ft. wide. Long stems bear 3-in. flowers centered in dark blue, with rays that are white above, lavender-blue beneath. Blooms in spring.

O. fruticosum. TRAILING AFRICAN DAISY. To 6–12 in. tall, spreading rapidly by trailing, rooting stems; will cover a 2- to 4-ft.-wide circle in a year. Deep lilac buds open to 2-in.-wide flowers with a dark purple center; rays are lilac above (fading nearly to white by second day), deeper lilac beneath. Blooms during the cool weather of spring, autumn, and (in mild-winter areas) winter. Essentially dormant in summer. Requires well-drained soil. Does well near the ocean. Use as ground cover or bank cover; if it gets too tall or weedy, mow or cut back in midsummer. Also a good choice planted at the top of a wall or in a hanging basket.

'Burgundy' has purple blooms at 19–20 in. tall.

'Nairobi Purple' ('African Queen') bloom at 18–20 in. tall.

'Silver Sparkler' has green leaves edged in creamy white; blossoms have a dark blue eye and rays that are silvery white above, pale blue beneath.

'Voltage' begins blooming bright yellow in late winter-early spring and keeps going as long as other osteospermums. Only 10–16 in. tall, it spreads to 2 ft. or more.

'White Lightning' has a pure white flower with yellow center and bronze yellow back petals, beginning in early spring and growing into an 18-in mound.

'Whirlygig' ('Pinwheel') bears unusual white-and-blue flowers with rays that are white on upper surface, blue on back; each ray is pinched in the middle to reveal its blue underside, giving it the look of a spoon with a blue handle and a white bowl.

O. hybrids. These hybrids are an ever-increasing group of plants in an amazing array of colors.

3D series is all about the prominent tuft at the center of the flower, rather than the traditional tidy button. Colors are in shades from white to pink, and into purple. Flowers stay open on cloudy days.

Akila series are excellent selections grown from seeds, especially 'Akila White'. Plants are 16–20 in. tall.

Crescendo series is a vigorous series, available in shades of yellows and pinks. Even at 12–18 in. tall, it can overflow a large container, remaining in bloom from early spring until midsummer. It will tolerate the heat but stop blooming.

Flower Power series has outstanding diversity of color, as well as plant and flower forms. In addition to the white, pink,

purple, yellow, and bronze color palette, there are compact plants, taller plants, traditional flower forms and slender-petaled spider flowers.

'Gold Sparkler' has similar flowers, but its leaves are yellowish green with golden yellow margins.

Passion Mix features compact growth to 1–1½ ft. high and about as wide, with 2- to 2½-in. flowers in a variety of colors (pink, rose, purple, white), all with sky-blue centers. Blooms throughout the year, more heavily in spring and fall. Blossoms stay open in low light better than those of many non-hybrid selections.

Serenity series brings a wide color range, including offerings that have subtlety of pastel washes, as well as vibrant color, to compact mounded plants growing 10–14 in. tall and wide.

Side Show series offers dense, full, heavy blooming plants.

OSTRYA
HOP HORNBEAM
Betulaceae
Deciduous trees

🗡 **US, MS, LS, CS; USDA 6-9**

☼◐ **FULL SUN OR LIGHT SHADE**

💧💧 **MODERATE TO REGULAR WATER**

Ostrya carpinifolia

Slow-growing, small to medium-size trees (seldom more than 40 ft. high and wide), hop hornbeams get their common name from the female flowers and fruit, which are enclosed in bractlike husks that form 1½- to 2½-in. clusters resembling those of hop (*Humulus*). Oval, pointed, 4- to 5-in.-long leaves

turn from dark green to yellow in fall. Inch-long male catkins are attractive in winter. Wood is hard, heavy, and dense. Grow best in well-drained, slightly acid soil; perform well in city plantings.

Hop hornbeams are attractive trees, but they're little used because of their slow growth—a fault to nurseryfolk, perhaps, but a possible advantage from the gardener's point of view.

O. carpinifolia. EUROPEAN HOP HORNBEAM. Scarcely differs from the more common American species, *O. virginiana*.

O. virginiana. AMERICAN HOP HORNBEAM. Native to eastern North America, where it is typically planted as an understory or street tree.

OXALIS
Oxalidaceae
Perennials

🗡 **ZONES VARY BY SPECIES**

☼◐ **FULL SUN OR LIGHT SHADE**

💧 **REGULAR WATER**

Oxalis acetosella

Leaves typically divided into three leaflets, giving them the look of clover leaves. Flowers may be pink, white, rose, or yellow. Good in borders or pots. Resist deer.

O. acetosella. WOOD SORREL, SHAMROCK. Zones US, MS, LS, CS; USDA 6-9. From many northern temperate regions of the world. To 5 in. high, spreading widely by rhizomes. Typical clover-type leaves with three heart-shaped leaflets. Blooms in late spring, bearing ¾-in.-wide, white flowers with purple to pink veins; blossoms rise just above the foliage. Can be somewhat invasive in its favored woodland conditions (moist, rich

soil and partial shade). See also Shamrock.

O. adenophylla. Zones US, MS, LS, CS; USDA 6-9. Native to South America. Dense, compact, leafy tuft to 4 in. high, 6 in. wide. Each leaf has 9 to 22 crinkly, gray-green leaflets. In late spring, 4- to 6-in. stalks bear 1-in., bell-shaped flowers in lilac-pink with deeper veins. Good rock garden plant or companion to bulbs such as species tulips or smaller kinds of narcissus, either in pots or in the ground. Needs good drainage. Plant tubers in fall, setting 1 in. deep, 3–5 in. apart.

O. articulata crassipes (*O. crassipes*). PINK WOOD SORREL. Zones MS, LS, CS, TS; USDA 7-11. Probably from South America. Similar to but slightly less hardy than the species *O. articulata rubra*. Like that species, it often becomes a weed in lawns in the Lower and Coastal South and is highly susceptible to rust. Selection 'Alba' has white flowers; 'Rosea' naturally has pink flowers.

O. a. rubra (*O. rubra*). OXALIS, WOOD SORREL. Zones US, MS, LS, CS, TS; USDA 6-11. Native of Brazil and Argentina. Forms low mounds, 6–12 in. tall and wide. Cloverlike leaves with three notched leaflets. Showy flowers in pink, rose, or lavender with darker veins, late winter or early spring. Pretty as ground cover or in rock garden or front of border. In fertile, moist soil in the Lower and Coastal South, it may spread and become hard to eradicate. Very susceptible to rust.

O. brasiliensis. Zones CS, TS; USDA 9-11. Native to Brazil. To 6 in. high and wide, with purplish leaves to 1 in. long. Blooms in spring and summer, bearing inch-wide reddish purple flowers with a yellow throat. Plant bulbs in fall, setting them 1 in. deep, 3–5 in. apart. Best used in pots.

O. depressa. Zones MS, LS, CS, TS; USDA 7-10. Native to South Africa. Cloverlike leaves remain tidy at 4 in. tall. Rose-pink flowers open in a spiral to reveal a yellow throat. Best grown in a pot to contain its spread in warm zones.

O. purpurea. Zones MS, LS, CS, TS; USDA 7-11. Native to South Africa. Grows to 4 in. tall and 6 in. wide; dark green leaves have large (up to 1½-in.-wide) leaflets. Bears 1- to 2-in., rose-red flowers over a long period in fall and winter.

Spreads by bulbs and rhizome-like roots but is not aggressive or weedy. Plant bulbs in fall, setting them 1 in. deep, 3–5 in. apart. Improved kinds, sold under the name 'Grand Duchess', have larger flowers in rose-pink; and there are also 'Grand Duchess White' and 'Grand Duchess Lavender'.

O. tetraphylla. GOOD LUCK PLANT. Zones MS, LS, CS, TS; USDA 7-11. From Mexico. Forms a clump to 6–10 in. high and wide. Medium green leaves to 3 in. across have four leaflets instead of the usual three, each one banded purple toward the base. In 'Iron Cross', the purple markings are more extensive splotches that form a cross shape. Both species and selection are usually grown as foliage plants, but they bear attractive clusters of 1-in., reddish flowers with greenish yellow throats in spring and summer. Plant bulbs in fall—1 in. deep, 3–5 in. apart.

O. triangularis (*O. regnellii*). Zones MS, LS, CS, TS; USDA 7-11. Native to South America. To 8–10 in. high, 1 ft. wide. Grows from rhizomes. Green leaves 1–3 in. across; tiny white blossoms in spring and summer. *O. t. papilionacea* (*O. r. atropurpurea*), called purple shamrock, features large, velvety purple leaves and pinkish lilac blossoms. Tolerates drought. Great garden plant.

O. versicolor. CANDY CANE SORREL. Zones MS, LS, CS, TS; USDA 7-11. Native to South Africa. To 3–6 in. high and 8 in. wide. Medium green leaves have deeply notched leaflets smaller than ½ in. wide. Funnel-shaped flowers are white, over 1 in. wide, with a crimson margin on the petal backs; buds also show striping. Plant bulbs in fall for spring flowers (set them 1 in. deep, 3–5 in. apart); bloom lasts for months.

OXYDENDRUM ARBOREUM

SOURWOOD, SORREL TREE
Ericaceae
Deciduous tree

🌿 **US, MS, LS, CS; USDA 6-9**

☀️◐ **FULL SUN OR LIGHT SHADE**

💧 **REGULAR WATER**

Oxydendrum arboreum

Native from Pennsylvania and Ohio south to Florida, Mississippi, and Louisiana. Beautiful flowering tree that offers year-round interest. Very slow growth (often less than 1 ft. a year) to 25–30 ft. tall and wide, though 50 ft. is possible. Pyramidal shape with slender trunk, rounded top, slightly pendulous branches; handsome winter silhouette.

Narrow, 5- to 8-in.-long leaves somewhat resemble peach leaves; they are bronze tinted in early spring, rich green in summer, orange and scarlet to blackish purple in autumn. Bark of new stems is bright red. Blooms in summer, bearing fragrant, bell-shaped, creamy white flowers in 10-in.-long, drooping clusters at branch tips. Flowers are used to make a prized honey. In fall, when foliage is brilliantly colored, branching clusters of greenish seed capsules extend outward and downward like fingers; capsules turn light silver-gray, hang on late into winter.

'Chameleon' is a bit more upright and offers reliably brilliant fall colors, including lime-green, yellow, rosy red, and purple. 'Mt. Charm' is symmetrical and gives a bright show of autumn color a little earlier than the species.

CARE

Grow in well-drained, acid soil. Tolerates some drought but not urban pollution. Will grow in partial shade, but for best bloom and fall color plant in full sun. Excellent specimen, patio, or lawn tree (remove grass from beneath canopy and mulch well). Also good in naturalized areas or in large containers. Large trees are difficult to transplant. Best planted from a container.

P

PACHYPODIUM LAMEREI

MADAGASCAR PALM
Apocynaceae
Succulent shrub

🌿 **CS, TS; USDA 9-11; OR HOUSEPLANT**

☀️◐ **FULL SUN OR PARTIAL SHADE; BRIGHT LIGHT**

💧 **REGULAR WATER; SEE TEXT**

Pachypodium lamerei

Native to Madagascar. Not a palm, though it looks something like one. Attractive, easy-to-grow shrub with impressive silhouette: spiny, succulent, unbranched trunk topped with a circle of strap-shaped leaves to 1 ft. long and 1–4 in. wide. Usually seen at 2–4 ft. high and 2 ft. wide, though it can grow to 18 ft. tall and 8 ft. wide under ideal conditions. Large, old plants may bloom in summer, bearing fragrant, saucer-shaped white flowers to 4 in. across; smaller, younger plants seldom bloom. May take up to 10 years or more to fully mature.

Madagascar palm can be grown outdoors year-round in mild-winter areas. Elsewhere, it can be raised in a container (use a clay pot, not a plastic one) and summered outside or grown exclusively as a houseplant. Indoors, place it in maximum light before a south- or west-facing window. In spring and summer, let the soil go dry between waterings, and fertilize at every other watering with a general-purpose liquid houseplant fertilizer diluted to half-strength. Good drainage is critical. Leaves usually drop in winter (though specimens grown in south Florida and houseplants may hold their foliage). Whether grown indoors or out, the plant requires no water or fertilizer in fall and winter; resume watering and feeding when new growth begins.

PACHYSANDRA

PACHYSANDRA, SPURGE
Buxaceae
Perennials

🌿 **ZONES VARY BY SPECIES**

◐● **PARTIAL TO FULL SHADE**

💧 **REGULAR WATER**

Pachysandra terminalis

Spreading slowly but surely from underground runners, these low-growing evergreen perennials are invaluable ground covers for shady places. They are hardy to cold and well able to compete with tree roots. Compact growth and clean, attractive foliage are their chief virtues. Small spring flowers aren't showy when viewed casually, but they're attractive at close range.

For best growth, give well-drained soil amended with plenty

of organic matter. Set 6 in. apart for reasonably quick cover; apply a mulch, and keep soil moist until plants are established. Give them light to full shade; too much sun causes foliage to turn yellow. Deer don't usually bother pachysandra.

P. procumbens. ALLEGHENY PACHYSANDRA, ALLEGHENY SPURGE. Zones US, MS, LS, CS; USDA 6-9. From the southeastern U.S. Not as widely available or as quick to spread as *P. terminalis.* Grows 6–12 in. high, with grayish green leaves (2–4 in. long, 2–3 in. wide) clustered near stem tips; leaves are often mottled with gray or brown. Fragrant white or pinkish flowers. Prefers neutral soil.

P. terminalis. JAPANESE PACHYSANDRA, JAPANESE SPURGE. Zones US, MS, LS; USDA 6-8. Native to Japan and northern China. Grows to 8–12 in. high. Shiny, leathery, dark green leaves, clustered at ends of stems, are 2–4 in. long and ½–1½ in. wide; upper half of leaf has shallowly toothed edges. White flowers are borne in 1- to 2-in. spikes. Popular selections include 'Green Carpet', shorter and denser in growth than the species, with shinier, deeper green leaves; 'Green Sheen', glossy leaves and more heat tolerant; 'Silver Edge' ('Variegata'), with creamy-edged foliage; and fast-spreading 'Cut Leaf', with deeply dissected leaves.

Japanese pachysandra can stand very heavy shade and is widely used under trees; it is also an excellent filler for those difficult spots where lawn grass won't grow. Luxuriant-looking, top-choice ground cover for shade in the Upper and Middle South. In the Lower South, it sulks during long, dry summers. Prefers slightly acid soil. Seldom bothered by pests, but a leaf blight can cause serious damage if it gets out of hand; control with fungicides and, if possible, by limiting overhead watering.

PACHYSTACHYS
Acanthaceae
Evergreen shrubs

- ✎ CS, TS; USDA 9-11; OR GROW IN POTS
- ☀◑ EXPOSURE NEEDS VARY BY SPECIES
- ◔◑ WATER NEEDS VARY BY SPECIES

Pachystachys lutea

Large-foliaged plants with showy terminal blossom spikes that attract hummingbirds. Stems are soft wooded, more herbaceous than shrubby. Similar to *Justicia,* another member of the same family.

P. coccinea. CARDINAL'S GUARD. Native to the West Indies and South America. Lanky-looking plant to 5 ft. or taller, 2–3 ft. wide; for a tidier look, cut back established plants in late winter. Oval, prominently veined leaves to 8 in. long. Summertime flower spikes reach about 6 in. long, with green bracts and tubular, 2-in.-long blossoms in blazing scarlet. Give light shade, well-drained soil, regular water.

P. lutea. YELLOW SHRIMP PLANT, LOLLIPOP PLANT. Native to Peru. To 3–6 ft. tall, 1½–2½ ft. wide, with narrow, dark green leaves to 5 in. long. Pinch tips during growing season, and cut plant back in winter to reduce lankiness. Blooms constantly in warm weather, bearing 3- to 6-in.-long spikes of neatly overlapping golden yellow bracts; flowers are slender white tubes that emerge from between the bracts. Good for massing and in mixed borders. Give full sun or light shade, moderate water.

PACKERA
Paeoniaceae
Perennials and annuals

- ✎ ZONES VARY BY SPECIES
- ☀◑ FULL SUN OR PARTIAL SHADE
- ◔◑ REGULAR TO AMPLE WATER

Packera aurea

These carefree plants provide bright yellow daisies in spring. Both spread readily by seed; remove spent blooms to prevent spread. Don't allow soil to dry out.

P. aurea. GOLDEN GROUND-SEL. Zones US, MS, LS; USDA 6-9. Native to eastern North America. To 2 ft. high, 6 in. wide. Clump of bright green, toothed leaves is topped in spring by flat clusters of deep yellow, ½- to 1-in.-wide daisies. Good bog garden plant. Formerly known as *Senecio aureus.*

P. glabella. BUTTERWEED. Zones US, MS, LS, CS, TS; USDA 6-11. Native to the southeastern U.S. Fast-growing, prolifically self-seeding, easy-to-grow plant that makes a bright swath of yellow in wet soils from very early spring to the beginning of summer. Medium green, broadly toothed leaves to 10 in. long form a basal rosette, from which rises a 1- to 3-ft.-tall stem topped by clusters of golden yellow, inch-wide, daisylike flowers. Formerly known as *Senecio glabellus.*

PAEONIA
PEONY
Paeoniaceae
Perennials and deciduous shrubs

- ✎ US, MS, LS; USDA 6-8
- ☀◑ AFTERNOON SHADE IN HOTTEST CLIMATES
- ◔ REGULAR WATER

Paeonia 'Sea Shell'

True royalty among garden plants, peonies feature blossoms that can take your breath away. Most types flourish in areas with long, cold winters, leading folks to the mistaken conclusion that they're not suitable for the South. But while it's true that peonies do generally perform best in the Upper and Middle South, quite a few tolerate the mild winters and hot summers of the Lower South, blooming as far south as Jackson, Mississippi; Montgomery, Alabama; and Columbus, Georgia.

The two basic types are herbaceous peonies, which die to the ground in late fall, and tree peonies (really shrubs), which form woody trunks. Both are from Chinese species: herbaceous peonies are chiefly from *P. lactiflora,* tree types from *P. suffruticosa.* Most garden peonies are hybrids.

Peonies dominate many a flower border in late spring—they're great companions for iris, old roses, poppies (*Papaver*), dianthus, and early daylilies (*Hemerocallis*). Remember that they grow to a good size over time and may get too big for a small border. When the site is properly prepared and plants are carefully selected and given proper care, all are extremely long lived, bringing beauty to your garden for as long as you live.

Herbaceous peonies. Perennials. Need varying degrees

P

of winter chill to bloom well. Established plants need no dividing and resent disturbance. If you must transplant them, move them during their dormancy in fall. Transplants may take a year or two to begin blooming again.

Plants grow 3–4 ft. tall and wide. Large, deep green, attractively divided leaves are an effective background for the spectacular spring or early summer flowers and look good throughout the summer. Depending on the selection, blossoms can be anywhere from 2 in. to 10 in. across; colors range from pure white through cream and rose to red. Many have a perfume reminiscent of old-fashioned roses.

Herbaceous peonies are classified by flower form. Depending on which expert you consult, there are anywhere from three to eight categories; here, we'll list four.

Single peonies have one row of broad petals surrounding a central cluster of yellow stamens.

Semidouble types are similar, but with an additional row or two of broad central petals.

Double types have very full flowers bursting with broad petals; stamens are absent or inconspicuous.

Japanese peonies have a single row of petals surrounding a central mass of thin, petal-like segments called staminodes.

In the South, early-blooming peonies tend to outperform those that flower late—but all the selections listed below are proven performers in our region. If you have room for only one peony, choose 'Festiva Maxima' (double white flowers with red flecks), a Southern heirloom plant that blooms dependably throughout our region. Other recommended selections include the following.

'Belle Center'. Early semidouble. Deep, mahogany-red blossoms with yellow stamens. To 30 in.

'Belvidere Princess'. Mid to late semidouble. Lightly fragrant, soft pink. To 28 in.

'Big Ben'. Early double. Fragrant, dark red blooms. To 38 in. tall and wide.

'Do Tell'. Midseason Japanese type. Pink outer petals surround rose-pink and red staminodes. To 34 in.

'Edulis Superba'. Very early double. Fragrant, rose-pink blos-

soms. Very floriferous; good cut flower. To 36 in.

'Elsa Sass'. Late double. Large, very fragrant white flowers with creamy yellow centers. Strong stems make it excellent for cut flowers. Vigorous grower. To 26 in.

'Félix Crousse'. Late double. Fragrant, ruby-red blossoms. Very floriferous; superb cut flower. To 34 in.

'Festiva Maxima'. Early double. Fragrant, pure white flowers flecked with red. Very floriferous. Long-lived, dependable bloomer, even in the Lower South. To 34 in.

'Kansas'. Midseason double. Long-lasting, red blossoms on strong, upright stems. Very reliable bloomer. To 36 in.

'Karl Rosenfield'. Midseason double. Mildly fragrant, velvety crimson flowers. Floriferous; great cut flower. To 36 in.

'Kelway's Glorious'. Midseason double. Huge, very fragrant, white flowers with creamy centers. Strong stems; very floriferous. To 34 in.

'Krinkled White'. Early, single. White with yellow stamens. To 32 in. Good cut flower.

'Lake of Silver'. Midseason double. Pink that fades to silver on edge. To 34 in. Heat tolerant.

'Magenta Gem'. Midseason semidouble. Strong pink. To 24 in. tall and 36 in. wide.

'Minnie Shaylor'. Midseason semidouble. Light pink blossoms fade to pure white. Blooms over a long period. To 36 in.

'Monsieur Jules Elie'. Midseason double. Giant-size, moderately fragrant blossoms in light pink shading to deeper rose. Good cut flower. To 36 in.

'Mrs. Franklin D. Roosevelt'. Midseason double. Fragrant blossoms with shell-pink outer petals surrounding a peach-colored center. Floriferous; excellent cut flower. Vigorous grower to 34 in.

'Nippon Beauty'. Late Japanese type. Deep garnet blooms with gold-tipped staminodes. Floriferous and vigorous. To 38 in.

'Philippe Rivoire'. Midseason double. Fragrant, deep crimson blossoms. Good cut flower. To 30 in.

'Sarah Bernhardt'. Midseason double. Fragrant, rose-pink blossoms with silver-edged petals. Very reliable. Excellent cut flower. To 34 in.

'Scarlett O'Hara'. Early, single red flowers with bright yellow sta-

TOP ROW: Tree Peony; *SECOND ROW: P.* 'Bartzella'; *P. obovata* 'Alba'; *THIRD ROW: P.* 'Belle Center'; *BOTTOM ROW: P.* 'Festiva Maxima'; *P. suffruticosa* 'Shintenchi'

P

HOW TO GROW PEONIES

Because peony plants live for decades, they should be considered a permanent addition to your landscape, not unlike planting a tree. Proper planting will ensure flowers for years to come.

TIMING Herbaceous peonies are best planted in fall or earliest spring, as bare-root plants consisting of compact rhizomes with thick, fleshy roots and several "eyes" (growth buds). Tree peonies, nearly all of which are grafted onto herbaceous peony roots, may also be purchased bare-root and planted in fall or spring. However, many growers offer container-grown tree peonies that can be set out at any time the ground isn't frozen.

EXPOSURE Choose a site in full sun, or light afternoon shade in the Lower South.

SOIL Choose a sunny, well-drained spot free from competing roots of nearby trees and shrubs. For each rhizome, dig an area 1½–2 ft. wide, loosening and turning the soil to a depth of at least 1 ft. Work in copious amounts of organic matter—such as garden compost, composted manure, or chopped leaves—to which you've added a cup of super-phosphate.

PLANTING Position herbaceous peony roots so that the eyes are exactly 1 in. below the soil surface; deeper planting may reduce flowering. Make sure each rhizome has at least three eyes; rhizomes with fewer eyes take a long time to bloom. Set tree peonies so that the graft line is 3–4 in. below the soil surface (the object is to get the shrubby top to root on its own). Mulch peonies in spring to cool the roots and retain soil moisture. Plants usually don't bloom the first year, so be patient.

FERTILIZING Peonies should bloom every year after their first season if fertilized twice annually. Feed plants with a low-nitrogen fertilizer, such as 5-10-10. Spread about ½ cup around mature plants in spring when the shoots are beginning to emerge. Reduce the amount to ¼ cup around new, young plants. Repeat in fall. Alternatively, top dress with an inch of compost in spring before mulching; repeat in fall.

PROBLEMS The good news is that deer seldom browse peonies. However, a fungal disease called botrytis sometimes appears during cool, damp weather. Flower buds blacken and fail to develop, and stems wilt and collapse. To prevent the problem, make sure there's adequate air circulation around the plants, and clean up the garden in autumn, disposing of all fallen peony leaves and old mulch. As new growth emerges in spring, spread fresh mulch, and spray it with a copper fungicide.

STAKING As buds begin to enlarge and grow top heavy, support stems with subtle wire stakes or branches left over from pruning. Stick them into the soil to support the heavy blooms, especially during spring rains.

CUTTING To gather peony flowers for bouquets, cut them just as the buds begin to open. Leave at least three leaves behind on every stem you cut, and don't remove more than half the blooms from any clump. This preserves sufficient leaf surface to build up food reserves for the following year. Promptly removing spent flowers before they set seed also aids future flowering.

WHY DIDN'T MY PEONY PUT ON A SHOW? Poor flowering has many possible causes, including these: The plant is too young (wait awhile); planting depth is too deep or too shallow (lift during dormant season and plant at proper depth); flower buds were killed by a late freeze (wait until next year); location is too shady (move to a sunnier spot during dormancy); weather was too hot too soon (plant early-flowering types); plant has nutrient deficiency (apply fertilizer); clump has been moved or divided too often (leave it alone).

mens. To 36 in. tall. Heat tolerant.

'Sea Shell'. Midseason single. Lightly fragrant, pink blossoms. Excellent cut flower. To 3 ft.

'Shirley Temple'. Very early double. Very fragrant, pale pink blossoms age to blush white. Floriferous and vigorous. To 34 in.

Three species are also recommended for the South. *P. tenuifolia*, called fernleaf peony, hails from southeastern Europe. It reaches 1½–2½ ft. high and wide and has dark green, exceedingly finely cut leaves. Deep red, single flowers on short stems seem to be sitting on the foliage. From Asia come *P. obovata* and *P. japonica*, both only 1½–2 ft. high and wide. *P. obovata* has deep green foliage that is pale gray-green and slightly hairy beneath. It produces cup-shaped, single white to purplish red blossoms with yellow stamens; the seed heads that follow split open to reveal red receptacles holding metallic blue seeds. *P. japonica* is similar but with hairier leaf undersides and yellow-centered white flowers that appear a little earlier than those of *P. obovata*.

Tree peonies. Deciduous shrubs. Slow growth to 3–5 ft. tall and eventually as wide, with handsome, blue-green to bronzy green, divided leaves. Single to double, typically very large flowers (to 10–12 in.) appear in spring. These peonies seldom show their full potential until they have spent several years in your garden, but the spectacular results are worth the wait. Small, recently grafted, packaged plants are sometimes available, usually sold only by color (red, pink, white, yellow, purple). These are a good buy if you are patient—they'll take two or three years longer to reach flowering size than older, container-grown or field-grown plants costing much more.

Catalogs offer named selections of Japanese origin in white and shades of pink, red, and purple; blossoms are generally semidouble. More recent and more expensive are orange, yellow, and copper-colored hybrids resulting from crosses of *P. suffruticosa* with *P. delavayi* and *P. lutea*; these bear semidouble blooms that face outward and upward.

Tree peonies require less winter chill than herbaceous peonies. The large flowers are

fragile and should be sheltered from strong winds. Prune only to remove faded flowers and any dead wood.

Itoh peonies. Itoh, or intersectional peonies, are crosses between herbaceous peonies and tree peonies. They behave like herbaceous peonies by going dormant with no stem visible in winter. However, the foliage is recognizable as that of a tree peony. Best of all, they put on a show for as long as six weeks as new buds open and replace the faded blooms. Flowers are huge, like their tree peony parent, but do not need staking. Look for yellow 'Bartzella', in addition to others in shades of pink and coral.

PANDANUS UTILIS

SCREWPINE
Pandanaceae
Evergreen tree

🌿 **TS; USDA 10-11; OR GROW IN POTS**

☼ **FULL SUN; DIRECT OR BRIGHT FILTERED LIGHT**

💧 **REGULAR WATER**

Pandanus utilis

Native to Africa and Pacific islands, including Madagascar, Réunion, and Mauritius. Palmlike, round-headed tree 20–30 ft. high, 20–40 ft. wide. Striking appearance; sends down aerial roots and bears spirals of stiff, spiny, 3-ft.-long leaves at the ends of stubby branches. Female plants develop large fruit that resembles pineapples.

Screwpine can be grown outdoors only in south Florida. It has good wind and salt tolerance and thrives in any well-drained soil, even beach sand. Excellent shade or windbreak tree for the beach garden. Produces litter; needs maintenance to remove old leaves.

Outside of south Florida, grow this tree in pots. Young plants make picturesque container subjects; bring them indoors during winter, and maintain night temperatures above 55°F. They need high humidity (mist frequently), direct or bright filtered light, and ample water (less in winter). Fertilize frequently with a general-purpose liquid houseplant fertilizer during the growing season.

PANDOREA

Bignoniaceae
Evergreen vines

✎ **ZONES VARY BY SPECIES**

◐ **PARTIAL SHADE**

◊ ◊ **WATER NEEDS VARY BY SPECIES**

Pandorea jasminoides 'Variegata'

Twining vines noted for clusters of trumpet-shaped flowers and for rich green, glossy, divided leaves; the foliage is so attractive that the plants look lovely even when out of bloom. Perform best in good, organically enriched soil. Blooms are borne on previous year's growth. Prune to shape or thin vines after flowering.

P. jasminoides. BOWER VINE. LS, CS, TS; USDA 8-11. Native to Australia. Fast growth to about 20–30 ft. Each leaf has five to seven oval, 1- to 2-in.-long leaflets with pointed tips. Typically unscented flowers are white with pink throats, 1½–2 in. long; bloom from late spring to early fall. 'Alba' and the stronger-growing 'Lady

Di' have pure white flowers; 'Rosea' produces soft pink blooms with nearly red throats. 'Rosea Superba' and a selection known simply as 'Deep Pink Form' are fragrant. There is a form with variegated leaves. Plant in lee of prevailing wind. May die to ground in winter in Lower South, but then grows back. Regular water.

P. pandorana. WONGA-WONGA VINE. Zones CS, TS; USDA 9-11. Native to Australia, Pacific islands. More vigorous than *P. jasminoides*, covering twice the space; give it plenty of room. Leaves are divided into 8 to 17 leaflets that are 1–3 in. long and somewhat narrower than those of *P. jasminoides*. Small (to ¾-in.-long), unscented spring flowers are typically creamy white, often spotted brownish purple in the throat. 'Golden Showers' has golden yellow blossoms. Moderate water.

FOR A PORTABLE SCREEN, GROW BOWER VINE ON A TRELLIS IN A LARGE POT.

PANICUM

SWITCH GRASS, PANIC GRASS
Poaceae
Perennial grasses

✎ **US, MS, LS, CS; USDA 6-9**

☼ ◑ **FULL SUN OR LIGHT SHADE**

◊ ◊ ◊ ◊ **ANY AMOUNT OF WATER**

Panicum virgatum 'Hänse Herms'

These bold ornamental grasses native to many parts of the U.S. can satisfy gardeners wishing to feature native plants, as well as those who simply want pretty plants. Their self-supporting, upright growth is best in full sun. Like other ornamental grasses, these stand through the winter months with dormant leaves and plumes and provide seeds for feeding birds. Cut back to the ground in late winter or early spring. Divide in spring before growth begins every three to four years or as needed. Deer resistant.

P. amarum. BITTER PANIC GRASS. Native to sand dunes in all coastal Southern states, where it can be used to stabilize dunes. Extremely drought tolerant. 'Dewey Blue' is a powder-blue selection that grows 3–4 ft. tall, spreading only 2–3 ft. It is clump forming, but may slowly enlarge over time.

P. bulbosum. BULBOUS PANIC GRASS. Native to the arid Southwest, including Texas, but adapted to gardens throughout the South. This grass forms a clump that produces upright plumes to 4 ft. However, it has a sparse, wispy appearance lacking in many ornamental grasses.

P. virgatum. SWITCH GRASS. Although a major component of the tall-grass prairies of the

Great Plains, this grass is found throughout the Southern states. Upright, 2- to 4-ft.-wide clump of narrow, deep green or gray-green leaves grows 3–5 ft. tall; it is topped in summer by slender flower clusters that increase the plant's height to 4–7 ft. The loose, airy sprays of tiny pinkish blossoms gradually age to white; foliage turns yellow or red in fall, then slowly fades to beige. Flowers and leaves persist all winter, making for an attractive silhouette in the cold-season garden. Switch grass tolerates many soils, wet or dry. Use in masses, sweeps, or mixed borders, or as an accent. Selections include the following.

'Cheyenne Sky'. Typically blue-green foliage turns deep red in early summer. Late in the season purple plumes rise above the foliage. Compact plants grow 3 ft. tall.

'Cloud Nine'. Metallic blue foliage turns gold in autumn. Billowing clouds of reddish brown flowers. Reaches 6 ft. tall in bloom. Best selection for Florida.

'Dallas Blues'. Powder-blue foliage fades to attractive rust and tan tones. Large, layered clusters of reddish purple flowers. Plant reaches height of 5 ft. in bloom.

'Hänse Herms'. Delicate, light green leaves turn bright red by early fall, then deepen to burgundy. To 4–5 ft. tall in bloom.

'Heavy Metal'. Silvery blue, sturdy leaves turn bright yellow in fall. To 4–5 ft. in bloom.

'Northwind'. Strongly vertical, olive-green foliage turns yellow in autumn. Narrow, erect flower plumes increase plant height to 5 ft.

'Prairie Sky'. Strongly vertical, 4-6 ft. Foliage is powder-blue, turning yellow in fall. Flowers are dark red in midsummer and mature to beige.

'Ruby Ribbons'. Zones US, MS, LS; USDA 6-8. Upright to 4 ft. tall with blue-gray foliage that turns burgundy as summer progresses. Flowers appear in late summer and hold into winter.

'Shenandoah'. Foliage emerges blue-green, turns maroon-red by midsummer to early fall. Airy red flower clusters. To 3–4 ft. tall in bloom.

'Squaw'. Upright, green foliage to 3½ ft. The tan flowers appear in late summer and hold remarkably well through winter. Sterile; no seedlings to weed.

PAPAVER

POPPY
Papaveraceae
Perennials and cool-season annuals

✎ **ZONES VARY BY SPECIES**

☼ **FULL SUN**

◐◑ **MODERATE TO REGULAR WATER**

Papaver rhoeas

Poppies provide bright spring and summer color for borders and cutting. Give ordinary, well-drained soil; feed lightly until established. Perennial species tend to be short lived. When using poppies as cut flowers, sear cut stem ends in a flame before placing them in water.

P. atlanticum. MOROCCAN POPPY. Perennial. Zones US, MS, LS; USDA 6-8. Native to Morocco. Grows to 1½–2 ft. tall, with downy, gray-green leaves in a basal rosette to 6 in. across. Flowers are soft orange to red, 2–4 in. across, opening in late spring and early summer. 'Flore Pleno' is soft orange, doubled, and grows 2 ft. tall. Sow seed in fall. To prolong bloom period, remove spent flowers.

P. commutatum 'Lady Bird'. Annual. Zones US, MS, LS, CS, TS; USDA 6-11. Selection of a species native to Greece, Turkey, the Caucasus, Iran. To 1½ ft. tall and nearly as wide. Downy, coarsely lobed, medium green leaves to 6 in. long. Blooms profusely for several weeks in midsummer, producing 3-in., bright red flowers with a black blotch in the middle of each petal; flower stems are softly hairy. Sow in late winter or early spring; or set out plants in midspring. In Tropical South, sow in winter.

P. nudicaule. ICELAND POPPY. Short-lived perennial in Zones US,

MS; USDA 6-7. Grown as annual in most places. Native to subarctic regions. Blue-green, coarsely hairy, divided leaves make basal rosettes 6 in. wide. Hairy, 1- to 2-ft. stalks bear cup-shaped, slightly fragrant flowers to 3 in. across, in yellow, orange, salmon, rose, pink, cream, white. For winter or spring bloom, sow seed or set out transplants in fall. To prolong flowering, pick flowers freely. Deer don't seem to care for Iceland poppies.

Champagne Bubbles series (to 1 ft.) and wind-resistant Wonderland series (to 10 in.) are widely grown strains. Oregon Rainbow series (to 15–20 in.) produces large (to 8-in.-wide) blooms in pastel colors, including bicolors and picotees, but in the South many buds fail to open.

P. orientale. ORIENTAL POPPY. Perennial. Zones US, MS; USDA 6-7. Native to the Caucasus, northeastern Turkey, northern Iran. Needs winter chill for best performance. In mild-winter areas, flowers tend to form without stalks, so they are partly or completely hidden among the leaves. Height is variable; some types are just 16 in. tall, others reach 4 ft. Plants spread by offsets to 2 ft. or more. These are among the leafiest of poppies, forming bushy clumps of hairy, medium green, coarsely cut leaves to 1 ft. long. Blooms are 4–6 in. across; deeply crinkled petals often have a black blotch at the base. Many named varieties are sold, offering single or double flowers in orange, scarlet, red, pink, salmon, or white.

A great many named selections are sold; they bloom in late spring and early summer, then go dormant in midsummer. In all types, new leafy growth appears in fall, lasts over winter, and develops rapidly in spring.

Set sprawling perennials such as *Symphyotrichum*, *Gypsophila*, or *Perouskia* nearby to cover bare areas after poppies die down. Plant dormant roots in early spring with tops 3 in. deep; set container-grown plants flush with soil line in fall. Give well-drained soil and make sure air circulation is good. Divide crowded clumps in August, after foliage has died down.

P. rhoeas. FLANDERS FIELD, CORN, or SHIRLEY POPPY. Annual. Zones US, MS, LS, CS, TS; USDA 6-11. Native to Eurasia,

North Africa. Slender, branching, hairy-stemmed plant to 3 ft. tall, 1 ft. wide, with short, irregularly divided leaves. Resembling its original or wild form with single scarlet flowers and black petal bases, 'American Legion' or 'Flanders Field' poppies are recognized as the flowers that grew on the disturbed soil of WWI battlefields and graveyards and are often grown in remembrance. The Shirley group was selected in, and named for, the English parish of Shirley. Single- or double-flowered forms are 2 in. or wider, in white, pink, red, orange, salmon, scarlet, lilac, soft blue, bicolors. 'Angels' Choir Mixed' offers double flowers on 2- to 2½-ft. stems. 'Falling in Love' from 1–1½ ft. tall has double flowers in white to red and shades of pink and coral in between. 'Bridal White' is pure white; Mother of Pearl group includes pastel shades such as

grayish pink to soft orange, white, and picotee blooms.

Mix seed with an equal amount of fine sand, and broadcast it in fall where plants are to grow. For cut flowers, pick when buds first show color. Remove seed capsules (old flower bases) weekly to prolong the bloom season. Prolific self-sower. Not usually browsed by deer.

P. somniferum (*P. paeoniflorum*). OPIUM POPPY, BREADSEED POPPY. Annual. Zones US, MS, LS, CS, TS; USDA 6-11. Believed to have originated in southeastern Europe and western Asia. To 4 ft. tall, 1 ft. wide. Virtually hairless, gray-green leaves have jagged edges. Late-spring flowers are 4–5 in. across, in white, pink, red, purple, deep plum; sometimes single, usually double. Some of the double forms have fringed petals. Blooms are followed by large, decorative seed

TOP: Papaver nudicaule; BOTTOM: P. orientale 'Lauren's Lilac'; P. somniferum 'Single Black'

capsules used in dried arrangements. Opium is derived from the green capsules; ripe pods yield large quantities of the poppy seed used in baking. Shake pods over a tray to collect the seeds. Because of its narcotic properties, this species is not as widely offered as many other types—but since the flowers are exceedingly beautiful, the seed is often shared among gardeners. Sow in late fall; barely cover seed with soil.

PAPAYA

Caricaceae
Perennials

🌿 **TS; USDA 10-11**

☼ **FULL SUN**

💧 **REGULAR WATER; SEE TEXT**

Papayas

It may look like a tree, but papaya (*Carica papaya*) is actually a big perennial with a hollow stem. Native to the lowland regions of the tropical Americas, it forms an erect, unbranched trunk 6–20 ft. tall, with a palmlike, 3- to 6-ft.-wide head of foliage. Leafstalks about 2 ft. long carry deeply lobed leaves to 2 ft. across. Plants flower and fruit simultaneously throughout the year. Plants can either be male, female, or hermaphroditic. Only female and hermaphroditic plants will set viable fruit, so plant several seeds and discard the male plants. Male flowers are yellowish and held on stalks; female flowers are larger, white or cream colored, and sprout directly from the trunk. Plants usually begin blooming 6 to 12 months after germination.

Two types of papaya are grown in the South—Hawaiian and Mexican. Hawaiian types (the kinds found in grocery stores) bear oblong, pear-shaped, or rounded fruit that typically weighs 1 to 2 pounds and has orange, red, or pinkish flesh. The fruit of Mexican types weighs up to 10 pounds and has yellow, orange, or pink flesh. Though you can pick papayas slightly green and let them ripen at room temperature (do not chill unripe fruit), they'll have the sweetest flavor if allowed to ripen on the tree. Harvest when the fruit feels slightly soft and its skin is almost completely yellow. Avoid touching the stem's milky sap, which can cause dermatitis. Selections include these eight.

'Mexican Yellow'. Mexican type. Yellow-fleshed fruit up to 10 pounds.

'Rainbow'. Hawaiian. Pear-shaped, 1- to 2-pound fruit is similar to 'Solo'. Genetically modified to resist ringspot.

'Solo'. Hawaiian type. Pear-shaped to rounded fruit has reddish orange flesh, weighs 1 to 2 pounds. Plant may be either female or hermaphroditic.

'Sunrise'. Hawaiian type. Pear-shaped, 1- to 2-pound fruit with reddish orange flesh. Bears fruit when only 3 ft. tall.

'Tainung No. 1'. Hawaiian type developed in Taiwan. Roundish, red-fleshed fruit weighs about 2 pounds. Good keeper. Tolerates ringspot.

'Tainung No. 2'. Hawaiian type developed in Taiwan. More productive than 'Tainung No. 1'; fruit is similar but slightly smaller and has reddish orange flesh. Tolerates ringspot.

'Tainung No. 3'. Hawaiian type developed in Taiwan. Smaller plant than the preceding two but produces the largest fruit—up to 3 pounds. Fruit is roundish to oblong; flesh is yellowish orange. Tolerates ringspot.

'Waimanalo'. Hawaiian type. Rounded, 1- to 2-pound fruit. Orange-yellow flesh. Bears fruit when only 3 ft. tall.

CARE

Papayas are easily started from the soft black seeds found inside the fruit; just be sure that the seeds are fresh. Germination takes two to five weeks. Sow the seeds in pots indoors in winter, then set out plants in the garden in spring. Plant in full sun and fertile, well-drained soil. These plants detest even light frosts so they are best grown in south Florida and the Rio Grande Valley of Texas. In other areas, they make attractive houseplants or container plants but do not bear fruit. Give young plants lots of water from spring to fall and little to none during the winter. Shield from strong wind. Papayas are short lived, and young trees produce better fruit than older ones, so it's a good idea always to keep a few plants coming along.

Major pests are fruit flies and nematodes. Consult your local Cooperative Extension Service for controls. Papaya ringspot virus, for which there is no chemical control, can be a serious disease. The virus is spread by aphids, and symptoms include sunken green rings on the leaves, bumpy fruit, and poor fruit production. Hawaiian selections are particularly susceptible. A few selections, however, do tolerate the disease, and 'Rainbow' resists it.

PAPHIOPEDILUM

TROPICAL LADY'S SLIPPER
Orchidaceae
Terrestrial orchids

🌿 **INDOOR OR GREENHOUSE PLANTS, EXCEPT AS NOTED**

☼ **PARTIAL SHADE; BRIGHT INDIRECT LIGHT**

💧 **REGULAR WATER**

Paphiopedilum 'Lord Derby'

Sometimes sold as *Cypripedium*, these terrestrial orchids are native to tropical regions of Asia. Although usually grown in a greenhouse, they grow well as houseplants and will bloom annually with proper care. The group also includes large-flowered hybrids grown commercially for cut flowers. The perky blooms often shine as if lacquered. They are usually carried one to a stem but may appear in clusters of two or more, and each has a distinctive pouch. Colors include white, yellow, green with white stripes, pure green, or a combination of background colors and markings in tan, mahogany, brown, maroon, green, and white.

Leaves are graceful and arching. Green-leafed types usually flower in winter, mottled-leafed kinds in summer. Most of the plants obtained from orchid dealers are hybrids.

A noteworthy species is *P. insigne*. Among the hardiest of the green-leafed types, it withstands brief exposure to 28°F and can remain outdoors year-round in south Florida and South Texas. Lacquered-looking flowers on stiff, brown, hairy stems appear at any time from October to March. Sepals and petals are a combination of green and white, with brown spots and stripes; pouch is reddish brown.

CARE

In general, mottled-leafed forms do best with temperatures of 55–60°F at night, 65–80°F during the day. Plain-leafed forms require temperatures of 50–55°F at night, 60–75°F during the day. Lady's slipper lacks pseudobulbs in which to store moisture, so the roots must never be allowed to go completely dry (water freely in spring and summer, less in fall and winter). For a good potting medium, choose one that drains well and retains moisture; many good orchid mixes are available. Don't plant in oversize pots, as these orchids thrive when crowded. The hardiest kinds can be grown in pots indoors in indirect, fairly bright light (they flourish in less light than most orchids require). Tropical lady's slippers never go dormant; keep them at their preferred temperatures in steadily moist soil year-round.

P

P

PARKINSONIA ACULEATA

JERUSALEM THORN,
MEXICAN PALO VERDE

Caesalpiniaceae

Deciduous tree

LS, CS, TS; USDA 8-11

FULL SUN

LITTLE TO REGULAR WATER

Parkinsonia aculeata

Native to southwestern U.S.
and Mexico. Rapid growth at
first, then slowing; eventually
reaches 15–30 ft. high and wide.
Yellow-green bark, spiny twigs,
picturesque form. Sparse foliage;
leaves 6–9 in. long, with many
tiny leaflets that quickly fall in
drought or cold. Numerous
yellow flowers in loose, 3- to
7-in.-long clusters. Blooms over
a long season in spring, intermittently throughout the rest
of the year. Flowers are followed
by 2- to 6-in.-long seedpods
that mature in summer.

A good choice for water-
conserving gardens, since it
grows in dry soil; also performs
well in moist soil as long as drainage is good. Tolerates alkaline
soil. Requires minimal care once
established. Stake young trees,
and train for high or low branching. As a shade tree, it filters sun
rather than blocking it. Thorns
and sparse foliage rule it out for
tailored gardens, and litter drop
can be a problem. Flowering
branches are attractive in arrangements. Hardy to 18°F.

PARROTIA PERSICA

PERSIAN PARROTIA

Hamamelidaceae

Deciduous tree or shrub

US, MS, LS; USDA 6-8

FULL SUN OR LIGHT SHADE

**MODERATE TO REGULAR
WATER**

Parrotia persica

Native to the Caucasus and
northern Iran. A choice, colorful
tree with good looks in all seasons.
Grows slowly to 15–35 ft. tall and
wide; naturally multistemmed but
can be trained to a single trunk.
Young trees are fairly upright; older
ones have a wide-spreading,
rounded form. Oval leaves 3–6 in.
long have noticeably wavy margins.
Choice, colorful tree, attractive in
all seasons. Most dramatic display
comes in autumn: Leaves usually
turn golden yellow, then orange or
rosy pink, and finally scarlet.
Smooth, gray bark flakes off to
reveal white patches and looks
especially showy when on display
in winter. Dense clusters of tiny
flowers with red stamens and
woolly brown bracts appear in late
winter or early spring before leaves
open; they give the plant an overall
reddish haze. New foliage unfurls
reddish purple, matures to a
lustrous dark green. Prefers slightly
acid soil but tolerates alkaline soil.
Plant is pest resistant. 'Biltmore' is a
large, round form, 'Pendula' is a
weeping form that grows 10–12 ft.
tall and 12–15 ft. wide, although
some sold as 'Pendula' are not
weeping, but spreading. 'Persian
Spire' (25 ft. tall and 10 ft. wide with
purple edges on green leaves),
and 'Vanessa' (about 30 ft. tall and
half as wide) grow into a dense,
upright plant.

PARSNIP

Apiaceae

Biennial grown as annual

US, MS, LS; USDA 6-8

FULL SUN

REGULAR WATER

Parsnips

If growing okra marks you as
Southern, growing parsnips
probably signals that you're
from the North. Known botanically as *Pastinaca sativa*, this
carrot relative from Siberia and
Europe is among the most cold
hardy of vegetables. It's grown
for its delicately sweet, creamy
white to yellowish root, most
often used in stews.

To develop long roots,
parsnips need well-prepared,
loose, deep soil (roots of some
selections grow to 15 in. long).
Sow seeds in late summer or
fall, planting them ½–¼ in. deep
in rows spaced 2 ft. apart. Thin
seedlings to 3 in. apart. Leave
plants in the ground over winter,
as cold weather sweetens the
roots. Harvest in spring; twist
off the leaves to keep moisture
in the roots. Parsnips left in the
ground will continue to grow
and become tough and woody.
Interplanting them with onions
or garlic is said to help keep pests
away. Avoid planting parsnips
near carrots, as the two will compete for nutrients. 'Hollow Crown'
is a time-tested selection (1820s)
that is still popular today.

PARTHENOCISSUS

Vitaceae

Deciduous vines

ZONES VARY BY SPECIES

SUN OR SHADE

MODERATE WATER

Parthenocissus tricuspidata

Valued for handsome foliage—
green in summer, reliably turning
to superb orange or red shades
in fall. Blossoms are insignificant;
more noticeable are clusters of
small blue-black fruit that forms
in late summer or fall and hangs
on into winter if not consumed
by birds. Vines typically cling to
walls by suction disks at ends of
tendrils. All but the fairly restrained
P. henryana are said to grow to
50–60 ft., but they are really
limited only by the size of the
support.

These vines thrive in organically enriched soil. Think twice
before letting them attach to
shingles, clapboard, or mortared
brick or stone. At repainting time,
the clinging tendrils are hard
to remove, and the stems can
creep under siding. They also
hasten deterioration of wood and
mortar. When vines reach desired
size, prune each dormant season
to restrain spread and—for those
trained on buildings—to keep
them away from doors, windows,
and eaves. Cut out any wayward
branches; likewise cut out any
that have pulled away from their
support, since disks will not reat-
tach. Trim as needed during the
growing season.

P. henryana. SILVER-VEIN
CREEPER. Zones US, MS, LS; USDA
6-8. Native to China. Grows to
20 ft.; less aggressive growth than
the other species listed here.
Leaves have five leaflets to 2 in.

long; they open purplish, then turn an attractive dark bronzy green with pronounced silver veining and purple undersides. Color is best in partial or full shade; in strong light, leaves fade to plain green. Foliage turns rich red in autumn. This vine clings to walls, but it needs some support to get started. Also a good choice for spilling over walls or as a small-scale ground cover.

P. quinquefolia. VIRGINIA CREEPER. Zones US, MS, LS, CS; USDA 6-9. Native to eastern U.S. Big, vigorous vine that clings or runs over ground, fences, trellises, arbors, trees. Looser growth than *P. tricuspidata*; has a see-through quality. Leaves divided into five 6-in. leaflets with saw-toothed edges. Foliage is bronze-tinted when new, matures to semiglossy dark green, turns crimson and burgundy in early fall. Good ground cover on slopes; can control erosion. In a home garden, however, it can be a terror as it spreads by roots and seeds at lightning speed. 'Engelmannii' is a denser, smaller-leafed selection; 'Star Showers' has white-splashed leaves that in fall first take on pink tones, then turn red.

P. tricuspidata. BOSTON IVY. Zones US, MS, LS; USDA 6-8. Native to China, Japan. Semievergreen in mild-winter areas. Foliage color is similar to that of *P. quinquefolia* in spring and summer but covers a broader spectrum in fall, varying from orange to wine-red. Leaves are glossy, to 8 in. wide, variable in shape; usually three lobed or divided into three leaflets. Clings tightly, grows fast to make a dense, uniform wall cover. This is the "ivy" of the Ivy League; covers brick or stone in areas where English ivy (*Hedera helix*) freezes. Grows best on walls with northern or eastern exposure. 'Green Showers' has large (10-in.) leaves that turn burgundy in fall. 'Lowii' and 'Veitchii' produce half-size leaves on less rampant vines. The foliage of 'Fenway Park' is lime-green (gold in sun). 'Calico Cat' has mottled, tri-color foliage of white and pink on a green background with burgundy stems.

PASSIFLORA

PASSION VINE
Passifloraceae
Evergreen, semievergreen, deciduous vines

✏️ **ZONES VARY BY SPECIES**

☀️ ◐ **FULL SUN OR PARTIAL SHADE**

💧💧 **MODERATE TO REGULAR WATER**

Passiflora caerulea

You'd be hard pressed to find flowers more exotically beautiful than those of a passion vine. To many, the flower parts symbolize the passion of Christ—the circle of whiskerlike filaments represents the crown of thorns; the three pistils, the nails; the five stamens, the five wounds; the five petals and five sepals, the ten steadfast apostles—hence the name passionflower.

With the exception of the Southern native, *P. incarnata*, all the passion vines listed here are native to South America. All have rich green leaves, will tolerate most well-drained soils, and can climb by tendrils to 20–30 ft. in a rather short time. Flowers are often fragrant and usually appear during warm weather. Many species produce edible fruit; for the species cultivated specifically for their fruit, see Passion Fruit.

P. x belotii (*P. x alatocaerulea*). Evergreen or semievergreen. Zones LS, CS, TS; USDA 8-11; or indoors. Hybrid between *P. caerulea* and *P. alata*, a species not described here. Among the best-known, most widely planted passion vines—and probably the least subject to caterpillar damage. Three-lobed leaves are 3 in. long; fragrant, pink-and-white flowers are 4 in. wide, with deep blue or purple crowns. No fruit.

Excellent for indoors.

P. caerulea. BLUE CROWN PASSION FLOWER. Evergreen or semievergreen. Zones LS, CS, TS; USDA 8-11; dies to the ground in the Lower South but comes back if roots are mulched in late fall. Leaves to 4 in. long, with three to nine lobes. Flowers to 4 in. wide, with a stunning combination of rose-pink and white sepals and petals and a purple crown. Egg-shaped, bright orange, 2½-in. fruit is edible but not very tasty. 'Constance Elliott' has pure white blooms.

P. coccinea. RED PASSION FLOWER. Evergreen or semievergreen. Zones CS, TS; USDA 9-11. Bright scarlet, 3- to 5-in.-wide flowers with white, purple, and yellow crowns. Blooms on new growth, so any pruning should be done early in the season. Oblong leaves to 5 in. long and 2½ in. wide. Mottled orange or yellow, 2-in.-long fruit is quite tasty. Not a good houseplant.

P. incarnata. MAYPOP. Deciduous. Zones US, MS, LS, CS, TS; USDA 6-11. Native to southeastern U.S. This old Southern favorite is the hardiest of the passion vines, surviving temperatures as low as –10°F. Dies to the ground in winter in most areas. Three-lobed leaves are 4–6 in. wide. Blooms profusely, bearing fragrant, 3-in. flowers in pale lavender with showy crowns banded in purple and pink. Egg-shaped, yellow, 2-in. fruit is edible and pleasantly sweet, although not exactly luscious. Spreads vigorously from seeds and underground roots and can become an attractive pest. Pull shoots where they are unwanted. 'Alba' has pure white flowers.

P. vitifolia. GRAPE LEAF PASSION FLOWER. Evergreen. Zones TS; USDA 10-11; or indoors. Dazzling bright red flowers to 3 in. wide. Deep green, three-lobed leaves resemble those of grapevines. Very free flowering; widely considered the best red passion flower. A good choice for beginners. Good for indoors.

P. hybrids. These have complex pedigrees, but they offer a remarkable variety of color, vigor, and hardiness.

'Amethyst'. Evergreen. Zone TS; USDA 10-11. Profuse show of 4-in.-wide, lavender flowers with deep violet crowns. No fragrance; small, orange, edible fruit. Very

similar to 'Lavender Lady', but less cold tolerant.

'Blue Eyed Susan'. Evergreen. Zones CS, TS; USDA 9-11. Big, 4-in. blue flowers bloom continuously on a 20- to 30-ft. vine.

'Coral Glow'. Evergreen. Zones CS, TS; USDA 9-11. Pendent, coral-pink flowers up to 4 in. across have very short crowns. Broad, three-lobed, lustrous leaves to 6 in. wide. Unlike most passion vines, blooms most heavily in winter. More heat tolerant than other red-flowered selections. Grows 10–15 ft. No fruit.

'Elizabeth'. Evergreen. Zones CS, TS; USDA 9-11. Spectacular fragrant flowers up to 5 in. across, in a combination of mauve and deep purple. Crown contains dozens of long, crinkled, purple-and-white filaments. Sweet, edible purple fruit.

'Incense'. Deciduous. Zones US, MS, LS, CS; USDA 6-11. Dies back to ground in cold weather but will survive –8°F. Fragrant flowers are 5 in. wide, royal purple, with wavy purple crowns. Egg-shaped, 2-in., olive-green to yellow-green fruit has fragrant, tasty pulp. Vigorous to 30 ft.

'Inspiration'. Deciduous. Zones MS, LS, CS, TS; USDA 7-11. A sibling to 'Incense', 'Inspiration' has deep purple blooms on vine growing 10–15 ft.

'Jeanette'. Evergreen. Zones LS, CS, TS; USDA 8-11. Very free flowering. Large mauve-and-white blossoms with deep purple, curly crowns. No fruit.

'Lady Margaret'. Evergreen. Zones CS, TS; USDA 9-11. Red flowers with a white center set this passion vine apart. Less vigorous, growing 6–12 ft.

'La Lucchese'. Evergreen. Zone TS; USDA 10-11. Big, 4-in., light purple flowers repeat all season on a moderate-size vine.

'Lavender Lady'. Evergreen. Zones CS, TS; USDA 9-11. Fragrant, blue-purple blooms on a 15–20 ft. vine. In frost-free zones, 'Lavender Lady' blooms year-round, but heaviest in spring and fall. In areas with killing frosts, flowering is from midsummer into fall. Often confused with 'Amethyst' but doesn't produce edible fruit.

'Monika Fischer'. Evergreen. Zones CS, TS; USDA 9-11. Light purple sepals and petals back the frilly white-banded blue fringe of these showy flowers. Repeat blooming.

P

'Pura Vida'. Evergreen. Zone TS; USDA 10-11. Very free flowering. Fragrant, 4-in.-wide, lavender-blue flowers with deep blue crowns. No fruit. Good for indoors.

'White Wedding'. Evergreen. Zones CS, TS; USDA 9-11. Pure white, 4-in.-wide flowers on a 10–15 ft. vine. Fragrant.

CARE

Train passion vines on trellises, arbors, or walls. They tend to be rampant, so be prepared to prune and thin unwanted growth. Chemicals in the leaves forestall attack by most insects—but *Passiflora* foliage attracts and is the favorite food (host) for caterpillars of several butterflies, including the Julia longwing, zebra longwing, and Gulf fritillary. Many passion vines are quite tender to cold and suitable for outdoor culture only in the Coastal and Tropical South. If growing where the plant is marginally hardy, be sure the soil is well drained. You can grow them as houseplants, but this requires a very sunny window, a sizable support, and frequent misting. Feed indoor plants with a general-purpose liquid houseplant fertilizer weekly from spring through fall.

PASSION FRUIT
Passifloraceae
Evergreen or semievergreen vine

TS; USDA 10-11

FULL SUN

REGULAR WATER; SEE TEXT

Passion fruit

Passion fruit is prized for the exotic, citrus-like flavor of its orange pulp. Use the fruit for juice; or cut it in half and eat it from the skin, seeds and all, with a spoon. Most of the commercially produced passion fruit in the U.S. comes from California and Hawaii, but three types are grown in Florida: purple passion fruit (*Passiflora edulis*), yellow passion fruit (*P. edulis flavicarpa*), and giant granadilla (*P. quadrangularis*). Purple passion fruit is hardy as far north as Tampa; the others are restricted to south Florida.

Purple passion fruit has light yellow-green, tooth-edged leaves with three lobes. White, 2- to 3-in. flowers with white-and-purple crowns bloom in warm weather; rounded or egg-shaped, dark purple fruit to 2 in. long follows in spring and early summer. The plant is self-pollinating. Due to its susceptibility to nematodes, purple passion fruit grown in south Florida must be grafted onto rootstocks of yellow passion fruit or other resistant species.

Yellow passion fruit has leaves and flowers similar to those of purple passion fruit, but its fruit is deep yellow and slightly longer.

Giant granadilla has four-sided stems set with oval leaves to 10 in. long, 6 in. wide. From midsummer to fall, bears fragrant, 5-in., pink to brick-red flowers with prominent bluish purple crowns banded with pink, purple, and white. Oblong, golden fruit is ready for harvest two to three months later; each one may weigh a pound or more. Both yellow passion fruit and giant granadilla need cross-pollination from another passion vine.

CARE

Grow passion fruit in well-drained soil, in a spot protected from wind. All types are easy to start from seed sown in flats or pots (be sure seed is fresh). Germination takes 10 to 20 days. From early spring until fall, feed lightly at four- to six-week intervals with a balanced low-nitrogen fertilizer (such as 6-6-6 or 8-8-8) that contains micronutrients. Train plants on a trellis, fence, or wall. Harvest purple and yellow passion fruits when fruit turns color and drops to the ground; giant granadilla is ready to pick when it turns deep golden. Prune vines in late winter when they're not actively growing, removing dead and weak wood. Withhold water during winter. Plants are naturally short lived, generally lasting only three to five years.

PATRINIA
Caprifoliaceae
Perennials

US, MS, LS; USDA 6-8

EXPOSURE NEEDS VARY BY SPECIES

REGULAR WATER

Patrinia scabiosifolia

Native to eastern Asia, these easy-to-grow, long-blooming perennials have yet to be discovered by many gardeners. The plants form mounds of deeply cut or lobed leaves that are typically medium green, up to 6 in. long. Nearly leafless blossom stalks rise from the foliage from mid- to late summer; these carry flat-topped clusters of tiny yellow or white flowers that attract butterflies and make a nice addition to both fresh and dried bouquets. Excellent in perennial borders. All appreciate rich, well-drained soil. Fanciers of daylilies (*Hemerocallis*) should avoid patrinias, however, as they are alternate hosts of daylily rust.

P. gibbosa. GREATER PATRINIA. Compact, clump-forming plant to 1–1½ ft. tall and about 1 ft. wide, with coarsely toothed leaves and loose clusters of tiny yellow flowers. Full sun or partial shade.

P. scabiosifolia. PATRINIA, GOLDEN LACE. The showiest and most popular species. Grows 5–6 ft. tall and 2 ft. wide; may require staking. Finely divided leaves. Sparsely foliaged stalks and open clusters of lemon-yellow flowers give plant a see-through quality that makes it useful for either the front or back of the border. Looks nice in combination with asters, ironweed (*Vernonia*), Joe-pye weed (*Eupa-torium purpureum*), and 'Indigo Spires' salvia. 'Nagoya' grows only 2–3 ft. tall. Full sun.

P. triloba. Grows 1–1½ ft. tall and spreads slowly to make a small-scale ground cover. Glossy, deep green leaves are 2–4 in. long and deeply divided into three to five lobes. Bears fragrant yellow flowers. Grows best in light shade.

P. villosa. WHITE PATRINIA. To 2–3 ft. tall, 2 ft. wide, with leaves that may or may not be divided. Showers of white blossoms over a long period. Spreads steadily but is not invasive. Full sun.

PAULOWNIA TOMENTOSA
EMPRESS (PRINCESS) TREE
Paulowniaceae
Deciduous tree

US, MS, LS, CS; USDA 6-9

FULL SUN OR PARTIAL SHADE

MODERATE TO REGULAR WATER

Paulownia tomentosa

Native to China. Somewhat similar to catalpa in growth habit and leaves. Fast growth to 40–50 ft., with nearly equal spread. Can grow 8–10 ft. a year in youth. Often touted as "miracle shade tree" in advertising supplements. Heavy trunk and heavy, nearly horizontal branches. Foliage gives tropical effect: Light green, roughly heart-shaped leaves are 5–12 in. long, 4–7 in. wide. No significant fall color. Brown flower buds the size of small olives form in fall and persist through winter; they open before leaf-out in early spring, unfurling into 6- to 12-in.-long clusters of trumpet-shaped, 2-in.-long, fragrant flowers of lilac blue with darker spotting and yellow stripes on inside. Flowers are followed by 1½- to 2-in. seed capsules shaped like tops; these remain on tree with flower buds. Does not bloom well where winters are very cold (buds freeze) or very mild (buds may drop off). Where it does bloom, numerous seedlings quickly invade disturbed areas such as highway banks, mining sites, and construction areas.

Performs best in deep, moist, well-drained soil, though it will grow in many soils—and even in cracks in the pavement. Tolerates air pollution. Protect from strong winds. Plant where falling flowers and leaves are not objectionable. Not a tree to garden under because of dense shade, surface roots. If tree is cut back annually or every other year, it will grow as billowy foliage mass with giant-size leaves up to 2 ft. long; however, such pruning will reduce or eliminate flower production.

The wood is lightweight but strong, highly prized in Japan for making bowls, pots, spoons, furniture, and sandals. A mature tree commands a high market price. Unfortunately, this has led to "tree rustling" in the South. A happy tree owner retires at night, only to discover a stump the next morning.

PAVONIA

Malvaceae
Shrubs

🗹 **LS, CS, TS; USDA 8-11**

☼ ◑ **FULL SUN OR PARTIAL SHADE**

◌ **LITTLE WATER, EXCEPT AS NOTED**

Pavonia multiflora

Native to North and South America, this group includes both hardy and tender shrubs. All are grown chiefly for their attractive, mallowlike flowers in shades of pink and purple.

P. cymbalaria. ARGENTINE MALLOW. Low, spreading shrub to about 8 in. tall, 2½–3 ft. wide. Gray-green leaves to 1 in. long and ¾ in. wide; pink, dark-centered, 2½-in. flowers over a long period in summer.

P. hastata. SPEARLEAF PAVONIA. Gangly, hardy shrub to 3–5 ft. tall and 2–3 ft. wide. Narrow, evergreen leaves; pink, dark-centered flowers up to 3–4 in. across from spring to fall. Self-seeds readily and can become a pest. Responds well to shearing.

P. lasiopetala. ROCK ROSE. Most popular species. Native to the dry, rugged limestone soils of Texas; nearly evergreen except in coldest parts of range, where it dies back to the roots each winter. Bears many showy, 2-in.-wide, rose-pink flowers from June to first frost. Light green leaves are slightly lobed, coarsely toothed, to 1½ in. long and wide. The plant naturally grows as a spindly, open-structured bush to 5 ft. tall and almost as wide, but it can be cut back in winter for a neater appearance. Useful for dry, shady areas. Tends to be short lived but self-seeds freely; let a few seedlings survive each year to replace the original plant.

P. multiflora. BRAZILIAN CANDLES. Tender evergreen shrub grows to 6 ft. tall and 3 ft. wide. Deep green, lobed leaves to 10 in. long. Spidery, bright red bracts enclose tubular purple flowers (they never fully open) with protruding blue stamens. Needs regular water.

PAWPAW

Annonaceae
Deciduous tree

🗹 **US, MS, LS, CS; USDA 6-9**

☼ ◑ **FULL SUN OR PARTIAL SHADE**

💧 **REGULAR WATER**

Pawpaws

Native to eastern North America, the pawpaw (*Asimina triloba*), sometimes called Indian banana, is a hardy member of a family of tropical fruits that includes cherimoya (*Annona cherimola*). The tree grows to 30 ft.; it generally spreads as wide as tall when grown alone, but you'll often see thickets of narrow, erect plants that arise from suckering. Large, tropical-looking, medium green leaves are oval, somewhat drooping, 4–10 in. long; they turn bright yellow in fall. Purplish or brownish (sometimes green) flowers with three prominent petals are large but not showy. Fruit is roughly oval, 3–5 in. long, yellowish green ripening to brown. Soft, custardlike flesh has a flavor between that of banana and mango and contains numerous large brown seeds.

Pawpaw is a pest-resistant plant and needs no spraying. It fruits well in sun or shade but grows better if given light shade in its early years. The only major drawback is the perishability of the fruit, which won't keep for more than a week unless frozen. If possible, purchase grafted plants of named selections such as 'Allegheny', 'KSU Atwood', 'Mango', 'Mitchell', 'NC-1', 'Overleese', 'Potomac', 'Prolific', 'Rappahannock', 'Shenandoah', 'Sunflower', 'Susquehanna', 'Taylor', and 'Wabash'. Plant two or more selections for cross-pollination.

Dwarf pawpaw (*A. parviflora*) resembles *A. triloba* but is smaller in all respects. It grows 6–8 ft. tall and 4–6 ft. wide, bearing small, brownish purple to greenish purple flowers in early spring. Fruit is ½–2 in. long. Often found in dry woods. Better used for naturalizing than for fruit.

PAXISTIMA CANBYI

CANBY'S MOUNTAIN LOVER
Celastraceae
Evergreen shrub

🗹 **US, MS; USDA 6-7**

☼ ◑ **FULL SUN OR PARTIAL SHADE**

💧 **REGULAR WATER**

Paxistima canbyi

Native to mountains of Virginia and West Virginia. Slowly forms a mat 9–12 in. tall and 3–5 ft. wide. Leathery leaves, ¼–1 in. long, ¼ in. wide, are shiny and dark green, turning bronzy in fall and winter. Good as edging and ground cover. Best in well-drained soil. Tolerates alkaline soil.

PAXISTIMA CANBYI | 475

PEA

Papilionaceae
Cool-season annual

US, MS, LS, CS, TS; USDA 6-11

FULL SUN

REGULAR WATER

Snow pea

In the South, you can't simply say "peas" and be done with it. You might be talking about black-eyed peas, cowpeas, purple hulls, or crowder peas—all of which are lumped into the category of Southern peas (see Southern Pea). Or you might mean garden peas, sometimes called green peas, *Pisum sativum*, the subject of the following discussion.

Though native to southern Europe, garden peas are often called English peas to distinguish them from Southern peas. They come in three basic types: shelling, snow, and snap peas. Shelling peas form large, sweet peas inside tough pods that are not good for eating. Recommended selections include 'Mr. Big' (60 days from sowing to harvest), 'Maestro' (60 days), 'Green Arrow' (70 days), 'Premium' (51 days), 'Sabre' (62 days), and Wando (68 days). Snow peas, popular in Asian cooking, feature edible pods as well as peas. 'Dwarf White Sugar' (50 days), 'Estancia' (55 days), 'Oregon Giant' (60 days), and 'Oregon Sugar Pod II' (60 days) are good bush or short vine types. 'Snowbird' (58 days) grows 16–18 in. 'Snow Wind' (70 days) has few leaves on its upper stems, putting most of its energy into producing peas. Snap peas combine the best qualities of shelling and snow peas. You can eat the immature pods; eat pods whole with peas inside, as you would string beans (the most popular way); or wait for the peas to mature, and harvest them for shelling. Try 'Mammoth Melting Sugar' (68 days), 'Masterpiece' (24-60 days), 'Sugar Ann' (52 days), 'Sugar Daddy' (68 days), 'Sugar Heart' (75–80 days), 'Super Sugar Snap' (64 days), 'Sugar Sprint' (62 days), and the semileafless 'Sugar Lace II' (68 days).

CARE

All peas are easy to grow when conditions are right. They need coolness and moisture at planting time. In the Upper South, plant shelling and snow peas as soon as the ground can be worked in spring. Snap peas like slightly warmer soil, so plant them two weeks later. In the Middle and Lower South, plant all types in late summer for a fall crop (snap peas are especially good for this, as they take some heat) and late winter for a spring crop. In the Coastal and Tropical South, plant around late December. Successive plantings made several days apart will extend the harvest.

Grow peas in slightly acid to slightly alkaline soil that retains moisture but drains well. If you have the space and don't mind the bother, grow tall vining peas on trellises, strings, or chicken wire; they climb by tendrils to 6 ft. or more and bear heavily. Bush types are better for small gardens; they require no support, though they can be grown on short trellises for easy picking. Soak seeds in water overnight before planting. Sow 2 in. deep in sandy soil, ½–1 in. deep in heavy soil. Leave 2 ft. between rows for bush types, 5 ft. for tall vines. Water thoroughly after planting; then don't water again until seedlings sprout. Thin seedlings to 2–4 in. apart. Plants need little fertilizer, but if soil is very sandy, give one application of a complete fertilizer (such as 5-10-5) about six weeks after planting. Don't wet the foliage when watering; wet leaves encourage mildew.

When peas reach harvesting size, pick all the pods that are ready; if seeds are allowed to ripen, the plants will stop producing. Harvest shelling peas when the pods swell to an almost cylindrical shape but before they lose their bright green color. Harvest snow peas when the pods are 2–3 in. long, before the seeds begin to swell. Vines are brittle; steady them with one hand while picking with the other, or use small clippers or scissors. Refrigerate peas without washing them; then rinse and use them as soon as possible.

PEACH AND NECTARINE

Rosaceae
Deciduous fruit trees

ZONES VARY BY SPECIES

FULL SUN

REGULAR WATER DURING FRUIT DEVELOPMENT

See chart on next pages

'Redhaven' peaches

Which came first—the peach or the nectarine? At first glance, the nectarine (*Prunus persica nucipersica*) looks like a peach (*P. persica*) that has lost its fuzz. Recent evidence suggests, however, that the nectarine evolved first. No matter—peaches and nectarines, while native to Asia, do just fine throughout the South. In most areas, crops ripen between May and September, depending on the selection. A standard-size fruiting peach or nectarine grows rapidly to 15 ft. high and wide, though properly pruned trees are usually kept to a height of 10–12 ft. They start bearing at three to four years old and reach peak production at six to eight years of age. Genetic dwarf trees, most of which grow to 5–6 ft. tall and produce medium-size fruit, are good for containers and small gardens. With a few exceptions (see comments in chart), most peaches and nectarines are self-pollinating. For ornamental peaches grown for their flowers, see *Prunus*.

If you're considering planting a peach or nectarine, keep several things in mind. First, these are not low-maintenance plants. They require good drainage, heavier pruning than other fruit trees, and regular spraying if you expect to get fruit. Second, it is essential to consider the chill hours a particular selection needs in order to bloom and set fruit (see chart). Once a tree's chill requirement has been satisfied, the onset of mild weather will bring it into bloom within several weeks. A subsequent sudden freeze may doom the crop. Therefore, growers in the Upper, Middle, and Lower South are safer planting selections that require at least 750 chill hours and bloom later in spring. On the other hand, growers in Florida and along the Gulf and South Atlantic Coasts, where winters are mild, need to plant low-chill selections that require less than 650 hours of winter chill. Third, remember that cold air is heavier than warm air, so it collects in low spots. Air temperatures of 28°F and lower can kill peach and nectarine flowers. Plant these trees on slopes and hilltops to avoid frost pockets. A mere 10 ft. of elevation can mean the difference between saving and losing a crop.

PEACHES AND NECTARINES

NAME	ZONES	FRUIT	COMMENTS
PEACHES			
'Belle of Georgia'	US, MS, LS; USDA 6-8	Large; freestone; skin is creamy white blushed red; flesh is white; fine flavor; midseason	Vigorous tree; heavy bearer; old favorite; Originated in Georgia in 1810; bruises easily; needs 850 hours of winter chill; not a good keeper
'Bonanza II'	CS; USDA 9	Large; freestone; attractive red-and-yellow skin; deep yellow to orange flesh; good flavor; midseason	Genetic dwarf; showy flowers; improvements on 'Bonanza', the original dwarf selection for home gardens. Needs just 400 chill hours
'Carolina Belle'	US, MS, LS; USDA 6-8	Large; freestone; white skin blushed red; rich flavor; midseason	Thought to be an improved form of 'Belle of Georgia' but bears earlier in season; needs 750 hours of winter chill
'Challenger'	US, MS, LS; USDA 6-8	Small; freestone; yellow flesh; early-midseason	Needs 1,050 chill hours; excellent flavor; consistent producer; disease resistant; seldom damaged by late frost
'Contender'	US, MS, LS; USDA 6-8	Large; freestone with good-quality yellow flesh; resists browning; blooms late, so fruit often survives late freezes	Consistent producer; needs 1,050 hours of winter chill; introduced by North Carolina State University
'Cresthaven'	US, MS, LS; USDA 6-8	Medium to large; freestone; golden skin with red blush; yellow flesh; high-quality, firm fruit; midseason to late	Blooms late; fruit holds well on tree; good fresh, frozen, or canned; needs 850 hours of winter chill
'Halehaven'	US, MS, LS; USDA 6-8	Medium to large; freestone; highly colored yellow fruit is firm, very sweet; midseason	Flower and leaf buds are winter hardy; fruit is good fresh or canned; needs 900 chill hours
'Harvester'	US, MS, LS; USDA 6-8	Medium-size; freestone; yellow fruit of excellent quality; early	Good producer, but needs four or five years to produce heavy crops; needs 750 chill hours
'Indian Cling'	US, MS, LS; USDA 6-8	Large; clingstone; dark crimson skin and flesh; midseason	Old-fashioned, disease-resistant peach; heavy, dependable bearer; needs 800 chill hours
'Intrepid'	US, MS, LS; USDA 6-8	Large; freestone; yellow flesh; early-midseason	Needs 1,050 chill hours; excellent flavor; heavy bearer; fruit may need thinning for better quality crop; seldom damaged by late frost
'La Felicina'	LS, CS; USDA 8-9	Medium-size; freestone; yellow fruit of high quality; early midseason	Originated in Louisiana; needs only 550 hours of winter chill; disease resistant
'Madison'	US, MS, LS; USDA 6-8	Medium-size; freestone; golden yellow skin blushed bright red; firm, golden flesh; very good flavor; midseason	Seedling of 'Redhaven' from Virginia; good frost tolerance during bloom period; heavy bearer; needs 850 chill hours
'Ranger'	US, MS, LS; USDA 6-8	Medium to large; freestone; red-blushed fruit with firm, yellow, good-tasting flesh	Vigorous, productive tree; requires 900 hours of winter chill; good for areas with late spring frosts; can or freeze the fruit
'Redhaven'	US, MS, LS; USDA 6-8	Medium-size; semifreestone; yellow skin blushed bright red; firm yellow flesh; good flavor; early	Among best of early peaches; productive; thin out fruit; colors up early, so test for ripeness; good fresh; freezes well; needs 950 hours of winter chill
'Redskin'	US, MS, LS; USDA 6-8	Large; freestone; yellow skin with good red coloring; yellow flesh; high quality; midseason	Showy flowers; fruit is good for eating fresh, canning, or freezing; needs 750 chill hours

P

PEACHES AND NECTARINES (continued)

NAME	ZONES	FRUIT	COMMENTS
'Reliance'	US, MS; USDA 6-8	Medium to large; freestone; yellow skin blushed dull medium red; yellow flesh can be fairly soft; fair flavor; midseason	Very hardy; has produced crops after temperatures of –25°F; showy flowers; needs heavy thinning; needs 950 hours of winter chill
'Rio Grande'	CS; USDA 9	Medium to large; freestone; red-blushed yellow skin; firm yellow flesh with mild flavor; early	Low-chill selection from Florida; productive; showy flowers; fruit has irregular surface and varies in size; needs just 450 chill hours
'Southern Rose'	CS; USDA 9	Medium-size; freestone; yellow skin with red blush; yellow flesh; fair flavor; midseason	Genetic dwarf; requires only 300 hours of winter chill; 'Southern Flame' and 'Southern Sweet' are two other selections available in the series
'Surecrop'	US, MS; USDA 6-7	Medium-size; semifreestone; yellow flesh; late bloomer; fruit often survives spring freezes	Cold hardy; needs 1,000 hours of winter chill
'Texstar'	CS; USDA 9	Semifreestone; red-blushed yellow skin; yellow flesh; early	Needs 500 hours of winter chill
'Tropic Beauty'	TS; USDA 10-11	Large; semiclingstone; round, firm fruit with yellow flesh; midseason	Needs only 150 hours of winter chill
'Tropic Snow'	TS; USDA 10-11	Medium-size; freestone; red skin; white flesh; superb flavor; early	Best low-chill white peach; needs only 200 chill hours
'White County'	US, MS, LS; USDA 6-8	Large. Freestone; white flesh; midseason	Very sweet flavor; needs 800 chill hours; disease resistant

NECTARINES

NAME	ZONES	FRUIT	COMMENTS
'Fantasia'	CS; USDA 9	Large; freestone; bright yellow-and-red skin; firm yellow flesh; midseason	Vigorous; showy flowers; needs 650 hours of winter chill
'Karla Rose'	LS, CS; USDA 8-9	Medium-size; freestone; red skin; white flesh	Needs 750 hours of winter chill; good choice for cooler parts of the Gulf Coast region and for areas farther north
'Redgold'	US, MS, LS; USDA 6-8	Large; freestone; deep red skin; golden yellow flesh; good flavor; midseason	Vigorous, productive; excellent flavor; has fair disease resistance; requires 850 hours of winter chill
'Southern Belle'	MS, LS, CS; USDA 7-9	Large; freestone; yellow skin with red blush; yellow flesh; good flavor; early	Genetic dwarf; needs only 300 chill hours
'Summer Beauty'	US, MS, LS; USDA 6-8	Medium-large; semifreestone; yellow flesh; good flavor	Needs 800 chill hours; bears larger crops when pollinated by another selection
'Sunglo'	US, MS, LS; USDA 6-8	Large; semifreestone; red-and-yellow skin; firm, sweet, deep yellow flesh of high quality	Developed in California; requires 850 hours of winter chill; very sweet
'Sunraycer'	CS, TS; USDA 9-11	Large; semifreestone; beautiful red-and-yellow fruit with good flavor; midseason	Needs only 250 hours of winter chill; good choice for central Florida

HOW TO GROW PEACHES AND NECTARINES

SELECTIONS Most selections need 600 to 900 hours of winter chill (45°F or lower). Low-chill selections are the best bet for mild-winter regions. The peach and nectarine selections listed in the chart are the most widely available and recommended. Nematodes are a problem for peaches and nectarines. In Florida, trees must be budded onto nematode-resistant rootstocks such as 'Flordaguard', 'Nemaguard', and 'Okinawa'. For information on those likely to perform best in your area, check with your Cooperative Extension Service or a local nursery.

PLANTING Although you can buy peach and nectarine trees in containers, most people purchase and plant them as dormant bare-root plants in late winter. Soak the roots in water for 24 hours before planting.

TRAINING If you buy a bare-root tree that is an unbranched "whip," cut it back to 24–28 in. high. New branches will form below the cut. Select three of these branches to become main limbs, making sure they are evenly spaced and between 18 and 32 in. above the ground. Remove all other branches. During the first winter, cut back these main branches by a third, to an outward-facing lateral branch or bud; this encourages a spreading growth habit. Repeat this procedure during the second and third winters.

ANNUAL PRUNING More pruning is needed than for other fruit trees, because they produce fruit on 1-year-old branches. Prune in winter to remove overcrowded branches, suckers from the base, and watersprouts (unbranched shoots that grow straight up from main branches). Prune to open up the center of the tree so that sunlight can reach all of the leaves. Genetic dwarfs need much less pruning than standard trees. Severe annual pruning not only renews fruiting wood—it encourages fruiting throughout the tree rather than at the ends of sagging branches that can easily break.

FRUIT THINNING Even with good pruning, peaches and nectarines form too much fruit. When fruit is 1 in. wide, thin it out so remaining fruit is at least 6 in. apart.

DISEASE CONTROL Peaches and nectarines are plagued by a host of diseases and insects. If you're philosophically opposed to spraying, you may want to reconsider growing them. Among the most serious ailments these trees suffer are peach leaf curl, brown rot, and peach scab. Peach leaf curl causes emerging leaves to thicken, pucker, and fall by midsummer. Brown rot causes fruit to rot on the tree. Peach scab covers the fruit with small, circular, greenish to black spots. To control these diseases, practice good sanitation, getting rid of diseased parts to avoid reinfection the next year. Also give two dormant-season sprayings of fixed copper or lime sulfur; spray once after autumn leaf drop, then again in spring just before leaf-out. Spraying with *Bacillus subtilis*, a biological fungicide, during the growing season can control many diseases as well.

Peach tree borer is the most serious insect pest, causing defoliation, dieback, and even death. It tends to attack trees stressed by wounds or poor growing conditions. Jellylike material exuding from holes near the base of the trunk is the first indication of the insect's presence. To control borers, insert a wire into the holes to kill the wormlike larvae or spray the trunk with an appropriate pesticide (consult your Cooperative Extension Service for advice).

ABOVE: 'Indian Cling' peach; *TOP RIGHT:* 'Sunglow' nectarine; *BOTTOM RIGHT:* 'Fantasia' nectarine

PEANUT
Papilionaceae
Annual

US, MS, LS, CS, TS; USDA 6-11

FULL SUN

REGULAR WATER

Peanuts

The peanut originated in South America and bears best where summers are long and warm. It is tender to frost but worth growing even in the Upper South. Plants resemble bush sweet peas (*Lathyrus*), 10–20 in. tall. After the bright yellow flowers fade, a "peg" (shootlike structure) develops at each flower's base and grows down into soil; peanuts develop underground. For best performance, give fertile, well-drained soil; sandy or other light-textured soil is ideal for penetration by pegs.

The four basic classes of peanuts are Virginia (roasting); Runner types (peanut butter, boiling), with two large seeds per pod; Spanish (candy, peanut butter), with two or three small seeds per pod; and Valencia (roasting or boiling), with three to six small seeds per pod. Buy seeds (unroasted peanuts) from mail-order suppliers.

CARE

Plant just as soon as soil has warmed in spring, setting seeds (with shells removed but skins intact) 1½–2 in. deep. Sow seeds of Virginia and Runner peanuts 6–8 in. apart; sow Spanish and Valencia peanuts 4–6 in. apart. Fertilize at planting time. Within 110 to 120 days after planting, foliage yellows and plants are ready to dig; loosen soil, then pull up plants. Let peanuts dry on vines in a warm, airy, shaded place for two to three weeks; then strip them from plants.

PEAR, ASIAN

Rosaceae
Deciduous fruit trees

US, MS, LS; USDA 6-8, EXCEPT AS NOTED

FULL SUN

REGULAR WATER

'Shinko' Asian pear

These pears are descendants of two Asian species: *Pyrus pyrifolia* (*P. serotina*) and *P. ussuriensis*. Unlike the more familiar European pears, they have crisp, firm flesh. Asian pears of Japanese origin are roundish in shape and are often called "apple pears" (even though they are not hybrids between apples and pears, as some folks mistakenly believe); those of Chinese origin have a traditional pear shape.

Trees grow 25–30 ft. tall and wide but are easily kept to half that size by pruning. They thrive in the same general growing conditions as European pears but typically have a lower winter chill requirement (from as low as 500 chill hours upward to 850). This would seem to indicate suitability for cooler areas of South Texas, the Gulf and South Atlantic Coasts, and northern Florida—but because most Asian pears are susceptible to fireblight (a devastating disease in warm, humid areas), growing them in the Deep South is problematic. Spraying with a copper fungicide at bud break and again a week later may help. The following selections will keep for months if stored in the refrigerator, preferably in plastic freezer bags.

'Hosui'. Excellent golden brown, russeted, medium to large fruit. Juicy, crisp, very sweet flesh. Ripens from late July to mid-August. Stores for three months. Pollinate with 'Shinko' or 'Korean Giant'.

'Korean Giant' ('Dan Bae'). Olive-green, russeted, very large fruit (can weigh up to a pound). Very juicy, sweet, and crisp. Ripens later than other selections—in mid- to late September. Stores for up six months. Resists fireblight. Pollinate with 'Hosui'.

'Shinko'. Large, brownish green fruit with some russeting. Crisp texture and sweet flavor. Ripens early to mid-August. Stores for four to five months. Resists fireblight. Pollinate with 'Hosui' or 'Korean Giant'.

CARE

To produce heavy crops, Asian pears need cross-pollination with another selection that flowers at the same time; European pears are not reliable pollenizers, because their bloom periods do not always overlap. When fruit approaches the size of a quarter coin, thin it to one pear per fruiting spur. Unlike European kinds, Asian pears should be left to ripen on the tree before picking. They're excellent combined with other fruits and vegetables in salads. Store in refrigerator or cool, dark place.

PEAR, EUROPEAN

Rosaceae
Deciduous fruit trees

ZONES VARY BY SPECIES

FULL SUN

REGULAR WATER

See chart on next pages

'Moonglow' pear

Most pears sold in markets and grown in gardens are derived from *Pyrus communis*, a European species. Some selections are of pure European stock; these are noted for their soft, juicy, sweet flesh and are good for fresh eating. Others are European hybrids; they share many of the qualities of purely European pears but tolerate more heat and need less winter chill. A few, classified as "hard pears," are hybrids of European and Asian species; these have coarse or gritty flesh and are usually used for canning or baking.

Trees are generally pyramidal in form, with strongly vertical branching, and grow 30–40 ft. tall (or taller) and 15–25 ft. wide. Pears on dwarfing understocks are good for small gardens; they range from one-half to three-

HOW TO GROW EUROPEAN PEARS

PLANTING European pears are long lived and among the easiest of fruit trees to grow. They adapt to most soils, even poorly drained ones. They don't bloom quite as early as peaches, so late frosts don't damage them as often. Nevertheless, it's a good idea to plant them on slopes or higher ground to avoid low-lying frost pockets. Plant dormant trees in fall, winter, or early spring. Soak the roots of bare-root trees in water overnight before planting. Dig a hole wide enough to spread the roots easily, and set the tree at the same depth it had been growing previously.

TRAINING AND PRUNING For both bare-root trees and those transplanted from containers, prune to promote strong, spreading branches. To help a young "whip" develop a strong framework of branches, cut back the trunk to 28–30 in. tall at planting time. New shoots will sprout below the cut. Select three to five shoots below the cut to become the main branches. Allow the strongest shoot to grow upward. This helps lower branches to develop wider, stronger angles with the trunk. The upward growing leader can be cut again after 2 or 3 ft. of growth to produce additional side branches (scaffolds) during the first year. After a year or two of growth, a spiral of four to six branches should provide strong branches on all sides of the tree. Thereafter, prune in winter to remove crowded, crossing, or inward-growing branches. Also promptly remove suckers growing from the base. Open up the tree's center so that sunlight can reach all of the branches.

POLLINATION Some selections are said to be self-pollinating, but they normally need cross-pollination for good fruit set; plant two or more selections.

WINTER CHILL Pears need at least 600 hours of winter chill (45°F or lower), and most do better with 900 hours. In the Coastal South, choose a low-chill selection such as 'Baldwin', 'Hood', 'Pineapple', or 'Warren'. Note: These are all hard, cooking pears, not dessert pears.

HARVESTING Fruit may be ripened on the tree, but shelf life will be reduced. If picked firm but still somewhat green, pears are easily ripened off the tree. If a pear is ready to harvest, the stem will snap free from the branch when you lift the fruit so that it is horizontal. If stem remains connected, check again in a few days.

CHALLENGES Fireblight can be a serious problem for pears; in areas prone to the disease, the best strategy is to plant resistant selections. Fireblight causes entire branches to die back quickly. As soon as you see blackened growth (usually with the tip arched over and pointing down), cut it back to a growth bud or stem with green, healthy tissue, disinfecting pruning tools after each cut. To avoid profuse new growth, with resultant risk of fireblight, do not prune heavily in any one dormant season; also fertilize sparingly. Spraying trees with a copper fungicide at bud break and again a week later may prevent the disease. Spraying with *Bacillus subtilis*, a biological control, during bloom has also proven effective. Dormant oil sprays will control various other pests.

EUROPEAN PEARS

NAME	ZONES	FRUIT	COMMENTS
'Anjou' ('d'Anjou', 'Buerre d'Anjou')	US, MS; USDA 6-7	Medium to large fruit may be round or have a short neck; yellow to russeted yellow skin; fine flavor; late	Upright, vigorous tree; tie down limbs for more consistent bearing; susceptible to fireblight; 'Red d'Anjou' is a red-skinned form
'Ayers'	MS, LS, CS; USDA 7-9	Small to medium size; yellow flushed with red; excellent for fresh eating; midseason	Needs a pollinizer; 'Moonglow' is a good choice; resists fireblight; one of the best for Lower and Coastal South; requires little winter chill
'Baldwin'	LS, CS; USDA 8-9	Medium to large oblong fruit, light green and russeted; good fresh or canned; late	Moderately resistant to fireblight and leaf spot; requires little winter chill; good selection for Lower and Coastal South
'Bartlett'	US, MS; USDA 6-7	Medium to large, with short but definite neck; thin skinned, yellow or slightly blushed, very sweet and tender; midseason	Standard summer pear of fruit markets; use any selection listed here except 'Seckel' to pollinate; tree does not have the best form, is susceptible to fireblight; nevertheless a good choice for home gardens; 'Sensation Red Bartlett' is bright red over most of the skin, less vigorous than 'Bartlett'
'Bosc' ('Buerre Bosc', 'Golden Russet')	US, MS; USDA 6-7	Medium to large, quite long necked, interesting and attractive in form; heavy russeting on green or yellow skin; fine flavor; firm, juicy flesh; holds shape when cooked; midseason	Large, upright, vigorous tree; needs pruning in youth; highly susceptible to fireblight
'Clapp Favorite'	US, MS; USDA 6-7	Resembles 'Bartlett'; soft, sweet flesh; early	Productive, shapely tree; attractive foliage; highly prone to fireblight
'Flordahome'	LS, CS; USDA 8-9	Small to medium, light green fruit with short pear shape; juicy flesh; early	Resistant to fireblight; requires little winter chill; pollinate with 'Hood'; tends to overbear; thin well
'Harrow Delight'	US, MS; USDA 6-7	Resembles 'Bartlett' but is smaller; smooth texture, very good flavor; early	Cold-hardy selection developed in Canada; excellent resistance to fireblight
'Harvest Queen'	US, MS, LS; USDA 6-8	Medium to large pear with red-flushed yellow skin; similar to its parent	Can be pollinated by most selections, but not 'Bartlett' and its strains; resists fireblight; hardy
'Honeysweet'	US, MS, LS; USDA 6-8	Medium size; yellow-green skin with red blush; sweet flesh; midseason	Moderately resistant to fireblight
'Hood'	LS, CS; USDA 8-9	Large yellow-green fruit with typical pear shape; a little later than 'Flordahome'	Vigorous tree; resistant to fireblight; needs very little winter chill; pollinate with 'Flordahome'
'Kieffer'	US, MS, LS, CS; USDA 6-9	Medium to large, oval; greenish yellow skin blushed red; gritty texture; fair flavor; best used for canning, baking; late	European-Asian pear hybrid; low-chill selection; good for hot and cold climates; most widely grown hybrid pear in the South; quite resistant to fireblight
'Louisiana Beauty'	MS, LS, CS; USDA 7-9	Yellow-green skin; sweet, crisp, tender flesh; great for fresh eating; midseason	Consistent bearer; low winter-chill requirement; very resistant to fireblight; an excellent selection for Louisiana and the Gulf Coast
'Magness'	US, MS, LS; USDA 6-8	Medium to large, russeted fruit; sweet, juicy, and aromatic; midseason	Does not produce good pollen; pollinate with two other selections for good fruit set
'Maxine'	US, MS, LS, CS; USDA 6-9	Large, yellow, smooth-textured fruit; good for eating fresh and canning; midseason	Moderately resistant to fireblight

EUROPEAN PEARS *(continued)*

NAME	ZONES	FRUIT	COMMENTS
'Moonglow'	US, MS, LS, CS; USDA 6-9	Somewhat like 'Bartlett' in looks; juicy, soft fruit with good flavor; ripens 2 weeks before 'Bartlett'	Upright, vigorous tree; very heavy bearer; moderately resistant to fireblight
'Orient'	US, MS, LS, CS; USDA 6-9	Large, bell-shaped fruit with russeting on yellow skin; firm, juicy, and somewhat sweet; good for canning, baking; late	European-Asian hybrid; heavy producer; highly resistant to fireblight; needs only 150 hours of winter chill; good choice for north-central Florida
'Pineapple'	LS, CS; USDA 8-9	Yellow fruit with red blush and pineapple flavor; good for preserves; course texture; early	European-Asian hybrid; self-pollinating; good resistance to fireblight; needs only 150 hours of winter chill; good choice for north-central Florida
'Seckel' ('Sugar')	US, MS, LS; USDA 6-8	Quite small, aromatic fruit with roundish to pear shape; yellow-brown skin; very sweet, granular flesh; a favorite for home gardens; good for preserves; early to mid-season	Highly productive; moderately resistant to fireblight; self-fruitful but bears more heavily with pollinizer (any except 'Bartlett' and its strains will do)
'Sensation Red Bartlett'	US, MS; USDA 6-7	Medium to large, similar to Bartlett but neck more tapering	Bright red over most of skin, less vigorous than 'Bartlett'
'Starking Delicious'	US, MS; USDA 6-7	Medium-size fruit; excellent quality	Moderately vigorous; tends to perform best in areas that receive 1,000 hours of chilling or more
'Tyson'	US, MS, LS, CS; USDA 6-9	Medium-size yellow fruit with spicy-sweet flavor; great for fresh eating; early to midseason	Resists fireblight
'Warren'	MS, LS, CS; USDA 7-9	Medium to large fruit with teardrop shape; pale green skin, often with a red blush; buttery, juicy flesh with excellent flavor; good keeper; late	Discovered in Mississippi; cold-hardy, heavy-bearing tree with low chill requirement; resistant to fireblight

ABOVE: 'Seckel' pear; *RIGHT:* Bartlett pear; *FAR RIGHT TOP:* Honeysweet pear; *FAR RIGHT BOTTOM:* 'Bosc' pear

fourths the size of standard trees. Dwarf pears have not performed particularly well in the South, but gardeners may wish to try them. All types have leathery, glossy, bright green leaves and bear handsome clusters of white flowers in early spring. Pears also make excellent espaliers. For ornamental pears grown for flowers and foliage, see *Pyrus*.

Thinning the fruit isn't usually necessary. Harvest season is July through October, depending on the selection. Fruit doesn't ripen properly on the tree, so pick when it is full size but unripe (firm and green), then store in a cool, dark place until ripe.

PECAN

Juglandaceae
Deciduous tree

☀ US, MS, LS, CS; USDA 6-9

☼ FULL SUN

💧 REGULAR WATER

Pecans

Native to the southern and central U.S. While commercial production of pecans (*Carya illinoensis*) is largely limited to the Lower and Coastal South, hardy selections do quite well in the Upper and Middle South. Graceful, shapely tree to 70 ft. tall and equally wide. Its upright, spreading limbs make it a good shade tree, but most residential lots aren't big enough for more than one. Prone to toppling during hurricanes—a consideration if you live near the coast. Foliage like that of English walnut (*Juglans regia*) but prettier, with more (11 to 17) leaflets that are narrower and longer (4–7 in.); foliage has a finer-textured look

HOW TO GROW PECAN TREES

PLANTING Pecan trees need well-drained soil. Set out bare-root trees in winter. Dig a planting hole deep enough to accommodate the long taproot; position the bud union above soil level. Firm soil around roots, then water thoroughly.

WATERING Don't let soil dry out.

FERTILIZING Properly fertilize pecan trees in mid- to late February. Without proper fertilization, pecan trees are more likely to have alternate bearing years as well as an early nut drop. (Early nut drop is also caused by drought conditions.) A soil test will help to determine the soil pH and nutrient levels. Nutrients are most readily available at a soil pH of 6 to 6.5. In the absence of a soil test, broadcast 4 pounds of a complete fertilizer, such as 10-10-10, for each inch of trunk diameter (measured at 4½ ft. above soil level). Do not place fertilizer in holes, but broadcast fertilizer evenly beneath the canopy of the tree. Pecan trees also require zinc for proper growth and development, as well as good nut production. Zinc deficiency causes a disorder known as rosette. Symptoms of rosette include bronzing and mottling of leaves; early defoliation; dead twigs at the top of the tree; abnormally small nuts; small, yellowish leaves; and short, thin leaves on older branches with rosettes (clusters) of small yellowish green leaves at the tips. In general, 3 to 5 pounds of zinc sulfate can be applied to large trees each year to maintain proper zinc levels. Alternatively, pecan tree fertilizer containing zinc can be applied. Many pecan fertilizers are available as 10-10-10 with 2% zinc. Apply at the same rate mentioned above for 10-10-10.

HARVESTING Harvest when nuts fall in autumn; you can shake or beat the branches to hasten drop. Remove husks right away. Leave the nuts in a dry, moderately warm place for several days until pecans are crisp. Store them in sealed containers or freezer bags.

CHALLENGES Prevent pecan rosette (abnormal clumps of twigs caused by zinc deficiency) by spraying zinc sulfate on expanding leaves in spring. Because pecan trees are prone to aphid infestations (and resulting sticky honeydew droppings), don't plant a tree where it will overarch a parking area or patio. Instead, plant in a place (such as near a lawn) where honeydew droppings won't be a problem. Although there is treatment, pecan trees grow so large that you would need a professional arborist with spray gear to reach infested areas.

and casts less shade. Inconspicuous flowers are followed by nuts enclosed in husks. In autumn, husks split and mature nuts drop. To harvest, gather fallen nuts and remove any husks right away; then dry and store the nuts.

Papershell pecans have thin shells and are easy to harvest, making them good choices for home gardens. They need a 210-day growing season to ripen. 'Choctaw', 'Desirable', 'Jackson', 'Stuart', and 'Houma' resist scab (a common fungal disease) and are suitable for the Southeast. Western papershells, recommended for drier areas of West Texas, include 'Caddo', 'Pawnee', 'Shoshoni', and 'Wichita'. Hardy northern types include the prevalent 'Major', as well as 'Colby', 'Norton', and 'Peruque'. Most selections need a pollenizer (consult a local nursery about the best combination for your area).

PEDILANTHUS TITHYMALOIDES SMALLII

DEVIL'S BACKBONE
Euphorbiaceae
Evergreen shrub

☀ TS; USDA 10-11; OR HOUSEPLANT

☀☼ FULL SUN OR PARTIAL SHADE; BRIGHT INDIRECT LIGHT

💧 MODERATE WATER

⬦ MILKY SAP CAN CAUSE STOMACH UPSET

Pedilanthus tithymaloides smallii
'Variegatus'

Native to the Caribbean, this bizarre plant is passed from gardener to gardener as a curiosity. It grows 3 ft. tall and about half as wide, featuring succulent, zigzagging stems set with 3- to 6-in.-long, medium green, diamond-shaped leaves. If growing conditions are good, it may produce small red flowers in summer. Commonly grown on windowsills, where it thrives in bright indirect light. Fertilize houseplants monthly from spring through summer with a general-purpose liquid houseplant fertilizer; let soil go fairly dry between thorough waterings and provide excellent drainage. Ease up on watering in winter. Easy to propagate by cuttings. 'Variegatus', the most popular form, has leaves variegated with pink and creamy white.

PELARGONIUM

GERANIUM
Geraniaceae
Shrubby perennials

🌡 **CS, TS; USDA 9-11; AS ANNUALS ANYWHERE; OR GROW IN POTS**

☼◑ **SOME SHADE IN HOTTEST CLIMATES; BRIGHT SUNNY WINDOW**

💧💧 **MODERATE TO REGULAR WATER**

Pelargonium graveolens

The common name "geranium" is widely used for members of the genus *Pelargonium*—but botanically speaking, it is not really accurate. Pelargoniums are woody-based perennials (most of them native to South Africa) that endure light frosts but not hard freezes and have slightly asymmetrical flowers in clusters. True geraniums, on the other hand, belong to the genus *Geranium*—annuals and perennials (some woody based) native mainly to the Northern Hemisphere, bearing symmetrical flowers either singly or in clusters.

P. cordifolium. HEARTLEAF GERANIUM. Rounded plant to 4 ft. tall and wide, with 2½-in., dull green, toothed and lobed leaves. Loose clusters of reddish purple, 1-in. flowers. Good for borders.

P. x domesticum. LADY WASHINGTON GERANIUM, MARTHA WASHINGTON GERANIUM. Erect or somewhat spreading, to 3 ft. tall and wide. Rangier than *P. x hortorum*. Heart-shaped to kidney-shaped leaves are dark green, 2–4 in. wide, with crinkled margins and unequal sharp teeth. Loose, rounded clusters of large (2-in. or wider), showy flowers; colors include white and many shades of pink, red, lavender, purple, with brilliant blotches and markings of darker colors. Can be planted in beds if pruned hard after flowering to prevent lanky, rangy growth. First-class potted plant. Some selections are used in hanging baskets. Most suffer during extended high temperatures, but the hybrid Grandirosa series is surprisingly heat tolerant.

P. x hortorum. COMMON GERANIUM, GARDEN GERANIUM. Succulent stemmed; grows to 3 ft. or more high and wide. In mild climates, older plants grown in the open become woody. Round or kidney-shaped leaves are velvety and hairy, soft to the touch, aromatic, edges indistinctly lobed and scallop toothed; most selections show a zone of deeper color just inside edge of leaf, though some have plain green foliage. Flowers are single or double; they are flatter and smaller than those of *P. domesticum*, but clusters bear many more blossoms. Many selections are sold, in white and shades of pink, rose, red, orange, and violet; flowers are usually solid colored.

Tough, attractive geraniums for outdoor bedding can be grown from seed; will flower the first summer. Available strains include Americana (bright green foliage, compact); Eclipse (dark green foliage, compact); Elite (quick to reach blooming stage, compact, needs no pinching); Maverick (open habit with many flowering stems); Multibloom (compact, early blooming); and Orbit (distinct leaf zoning; broad, rounded flower clusters). 'Orange Appeal', a seed-grown selection, has blooms in pure bright orange.

TOP: Pelargonium fragrans 'Nutmeg'; *P. peltatum; BOTTOM: P.* 'Mrs. Pollock'

There are also dwarf, cactus-flowered, and other novelty types.

Fancy-leafed or color-leafed selections have zones, borders, or splashes of brown, gold, red, white, and green in various combinations. Some also have highly attractive flowers. 'Golden Ears', 1 ft. high and wide, has small, deeply cut, almost star-shaped leaves of deep bronzy red with a wide border of chartreuse; flowers are bright coral. 'Vancouver Centennial' is very similar if not identical. 'Mrs. Pollock' has green leaves with a red zone and a creamy yellow margin; it bears vermilion blooms.

Common geraniums sometimes stop blooming during extended periods of high summer heat—a condition known as "heat check." (They'll resume blooming when cooler weather arrives.) To avoid this condition, give plants light afternoon shade; or grow heat-tolerant types, such as the Americana, Eclipse, Maverick, or Orbit series.

P. peltatum. IVY GERANIUM. To 1½ ft. tall, trailing to 3 ft. wide. Rather succulent, 2- to 3-in.-wide, glossy, bright green leaves with pointed lobes resemble foliage of ivy (*Hedera*). Spectacular summer show of single or double, inch-wide flowers in rounded clusters of five to ten; colors include white, pink, rose, red, salmon, and lavender. Upper petals may be blotched or striped. Many named selections are available. Most types cannot tolerate extended heat and are grown as summer annuals only in the Upper and Middle South (though they perform well as winter annuals in the Coastal and Tropical South). However, heat-tolerant Blizzard and Cascade and Summer Showers series perform well throughout summer in much of the Lower South, as well as farther north. Focus series is compact with dark leaves for dense baskets. Use ivy geraniums in hanging baskets, window boxes, and tall planters.

P. hybrids. Crossing zonal geraniums and ivy geraniums has produced garden hardy selections. Double Take series has semidouble flowers that are slow to shatter. Calliope and Caliente series are a geranium lover's answer to Southern summer heat. Place them where they get all-day sun in the Upper and Middle

South, but afternoon shade in the Lower and Coastal South.

Scented geraniums. Many aromatic species, hybrids, and selections are available. Most grow 1–3 ft. tall, spreading as wide as high. Foliage scent is the main draw; clusters of small, typically white or rosy flowers are secondary in appeal. Leaves vary in shape from nearly round to finely cut and almost ferny; they range in size from minute to 4 in. across. Plants' common names usually refer to the fragrance of their leaves: almond geranium (*P. quercifolium*), apple geranium (*P. odoratissimum*), lime geranium (*P. nervosum*), nutmeg geranium (*P. fragrans* 'Nutmeg'), peppermint geranium (*P. tomentosum*). There are several rose geraniums, including *P. capitatum*, *P. graveolens*, and *P.* 'Lady Plymouth'. Various types offer lemon fragrance, including *P. crispum* and *P. c.* 'Prince Rupert'. All scented geraniums are good for herb gardens, edgings, front of borders, window boxes, hanging baskets; peppermint geranium makes a good ground cover in frost-free gardens. Use fresh leaves of all types for flavoring jelly and iced drinks; use dried leaves in sachets and potpourri.

CARE

Plant in any good, fast-draining soil. Amend poor soil with plenty of organic matter. Geraniums growing in good garden soil need little fertilizer; those in light, sandy soil should receive two or three feedings during active growth. Remove faded flowers regularly to encourage new bloom. Pinch growing tips of young, small plants to force side branches. All geraniums do well in pots; they bloom best when somewhat potbound. Common pests include aphids, whiteflies, and spider mites. Tobacco budworm may be a problem in some areas; affected flowers look tattered or fail to open at all. Most pests easily controlled by spraying with neem oil or spinosad.

PELLAEA
CLIFF-BRAKE
Pteridaceae
Ferns

🗡 **ZONES VARY BY SPECIES; OR HOUSEPLANT**

🔅 **FILTERED SUNLIGHT; BRIGHT INDIRECT LIGHT**

💧 **WATER NEEDS VARY BY SPECIES**

Pellaea rotundifolia

The appeal of these small plants lies in subtle beauty, not overwhelming show. They sport charmingly detailed foliage, with thin-stemmed leaves divided into numerous narrow to rounded leaflets. Where hardy (down to 24°F), they make nice rock garden plants and ground cover, but they are most popular as houseplants. Indoors, give them good light but protect from midday sun; feed monthly with a general-purpose liquid houseplant fertilizer diluted to half-strength.

P. mucronata. BIRD'S FOOT FERN. Zones US, MS, LS, CS, TS; USDA 6–11. Native from California to Texas. To 6–12 in. high and wide, with gray-green, airy-looking fronds and narrow leaflets arranged in groups of three. Little water. Good tucked into rock walls.

P. rotundifolia. BUTTON FERN. Zones CS, TS; USDA 9–11. Native to Australia, New Zealand. Neat little plant grows to 1 ft. high and 2 ft. wide, with spreading fronds divided into nearly round, evenly spaced leaflets. Pretty fern for contrast with finer-textured ferns or to show off in pots, baskets, or raised beds. Good ground cover. Regular water.

P. viridis. GREEN CLIFF-BRAKE. Zones CS, TS; USDA 9–11. Native to Africa. Grows to 1 ft. high and about as wide, with fronds consisting of fresh green, oval- to lance-shaped leaflets. Good as ground cover, in rock garden, in containers. Regular water.

PELTOPHORUM PTEROCARPUM
YELLOW POINCIANA
Caesalpiniaceae
Evergreen tree

🗡 **TS; USDA 10-11**

🔆 **FULL SUN**

💧 **REGULAR WATER**

Peltophorum pterocarpum

Native to Australia and Malaysia, this fast-growing, highly ornamental tree is popular in south Florida. It reaches 50 ft. tall and 25–30 ft. wide and features large, feathery leaves that resemble those of mimosa (*Albizia julibrissin*). Handsome smooth, gray bark. Erect flower spikes, 1–1½ ft. long, carry fragrant, 1½-in. yellow flowers over a long period in summer. Flowers give rise to flattened, winged, wine-red seedpods up to 4 in. long.

CARE

Yellow poinciana is easy to grow; tolerates most well-drained soils and has no serious pests. It naturally forms a multitrunked, wide-spreading tree but is easily pruned to a single trunk. Good choice for a lawn, shade, or street tree. Roots can lift pavement, so allow 8–10 ft. between tree and sidewalk or other paved area.

PENNISETUM
FOUNTAIN GRASS
Poaceae
Annual and perennial grasses

🗡 **ZONES VARY BY SPECIES**

🔅🔆 **FULL SUN OR PARTIAL SHADE, EXCEPT AS NOTED**

💧 **MODERATE TO REGULAR WATER, EXCEPT AS NOTED**

Pennisetum setaceum

Growing in graceful, fountainlike mounds, these are among the most foolproof grasses for the South. They have long, narrow leaves and arching stems that bear furry, foxtail-like plumes. Bloom begins in summer and often extends into fall. Excellent in containers, in mixed borders, as dramatic sweeps, and for bank covers. Cut back perennial types to within a few inches of the ground in late winter for fresh new growth in spring. Resist deer.

P. x advena 'Fireworks'. FIREWORKS FOUNTAIN GRASS. Perennial in Zones CS, TS; USDA 9-11; annual elsewhere. Showy, 2-ft.-tall mound of upright foliage is bright pink with a burgundy stripe down the center. With soft burgundy, arching plumes, it reaches 2½ ft.

P. alopecuroides. CHINESE PENNISETUM. Perennial. Zones US, MS, LS, CS; USDA 6-9. From eastern Asia. To 5 ft. high and wide. Clump of bright green foliage is topped by silvery pink, tan, or whitish flower plumes. Bright green leaves turn yellow in fall, then brown in winter. Recommended selections include 'Cassian's Choice' ('Cassian'), with light brown plumes and golden, red-tinted fall foliage to 3 ft. high and wide; 'Foxtrot', with tall tan plumes reaching 5 ft. tall; 'Hameln', with wide,

P

silvery plumes at 2–2½ ft. tall and wide; 'Little Bunny', with pinkish plumes at only 1 ft. tall and wide; and 'Moudry', with striking black plumes at 3 ft. high and wide. The species and its selections all can self-sow in moist conditions; 'Moudry' is an especially heavy self-seeder.

P. glaucum 'Purple Majesty'. PURPLE MAJESTY ORNAMENTAL MILLET. Perennial in Zones CS, TS; USDA 9-11; annual elsewhere. Developed from a species from Asia and Africa that has long been cultivated for its edible seeds. To 3–5 ft. tall and 2–3 ft. wide, with spear-shaped leaves to 3 ft. long, 2 in. wide. Foliage is rich purple, darkest in full sun. Stiff, cylindrical flower spikes to 20 in. long appear atop foliage in midsummer. Cut the flower spikes before they mature, and use them in dried arrangements; or leave them to mature on the plant, where they'll attract birds. Easy to start from seed. Best in full sun, with regular water.

P. macrostachyum 'Burgundy Giant'. Perennial in Zones CS, TS; USDA 9-11; annual elsewhere. Variant of a species from the East Indies. This bold, tropical-looking, very tender grass resembles a reddish purple corn plant. Grows 4–5 ft. tall and 2 ft. across, with foot-long leaves that are broader than those of most other fountain grasses (nearly 1½ in. wide). Foliage is held on strong, upright burgundy stems. Red-purple flower plumes up to 1 ft. long appear on nodding stems above the foliage in mid-summer; fade to cream in fall. Needs full sun, regular water. Not to be confused with purple fountain grass (P. setaceum 'Rubrum'), a shorter, more graceful plant.

P. orientale. ORIENTAL FOUNTAIN GRASS. Perennial. Zones US, MS, LS, CS; USDA 6-9. From central and western Asia. To 2 ft. high, 2½ ft. wide, with pinkish plumes standing above a mound of green to gray-green foliage. Plumes mature to light brown; foliage turns straw colored in winter. Seldom self-sows. Recommended selections include 3-ft.-tall 'Karley Rose', with an upright form with dark green foliage and deep pink plumes, and 'Tall Tails', a very heat-tolerant 6-footer with tan plumes that does well in Florida.

P. purpureum. ELEPHANT GRASS. Perennial in Zones LS, CS, TS; USDA 8-11; annual in the Middle and Upper South. Native to Africa. Give it sunlight and moderate moisture and it thrives. The species will reseed in frost-free areas and can be invasive, growing to 15 ft. tall. However, cultivated forms are a more manageable choice, being shorter and unlikely to reseed. 'Prince' and 'Princess' have purple leaves, growing 5–6 ft. tall and 2–3 ft. tall, respectively. 'Vertigo' is also purple and intermediate, growing 3–4 ft. tall. All are heat tolerant and keep their color in sun.

P. setaceum. FOUNTAIN GRASS. Perennial in Zones CS, TS; USDA 9-11; annual elsewhere. From tropical Africa, southwestern Asia, Arabian Peninsula. Dense, rounded, medium green foliage clump to 4 ft. high and wide. Coppery pink or purplish plumes are held within the clump or just above it. Tolerates drought once established. Particularly prone to self-sowing. Less likely to set seed is its selection 'Rubrum', purple fountain grass, with reddish purple leaves and showy rose-colored plumes; it's among the most popular of ornamental grasses, outstanding in containers and mixed borders. 'Sky Rocket' has white and green variegated foliage, white plumes blushed with pink.

P. villosum. FEATHERTOP. Perennial in Zones LS, CS, TS; USDA 8-11; annual elsewhere. From Africa. Thin, cascading, medium green leaves form a mound to 3 ft. tall and wide. Foliage is topped in summer by soft, feathery, creamy white plumes that look great in fresh or dried arrangements. Easy to start from seed. Will self-sow. Best in full sun, with regular water. 'Cream Falls' is a heavily blooming selection.

PENSTEMON

PENSTEMON, BEARD TONGUE
Plantaginaceae
Perennials

🖊 **ZONES VARY BY SPECIES**

◐ **AFTERNOON SHADE, EXCEPT AS NOTED**

💧💧 **MODERATE TO REGULAR WATER, EXCEPT AS NOTED**

Penstemon 'Pensham Laura'

Penstemons are beloved for their colorful flowers, but in most areas of the South, they can be problematic to grow. Of the more than 250 species, the majority are native to the West, ranging from Canada to Mexico—and they prefer dry air, cool night temperatures, and excellent drainage, which doesn't sound much like Dixie. Fortunately, there are native Southern species that thrive here naturally; and the hybrids and selections presented here also accept Southern conditions.

Most species have narrow, pointed leaves. Narrow, tubular or bell-shaped flowers are typically ¾–1½ in. long and are held in erect clusters. Bright reds and blues are the common colors, but you'll also find blooms in shades of soft pink through salmon and peach to deep rose, lilac, dark purple, white, and yellow. Blossoms attract hummingbirds. Plants are generally short lived (three to four years). All need fast-draining soil.

P. australis. Zones MS, LS, CS; USDA 7-9. Native from southeastern Virginia to Florida and west to Mississippi. Grows to 3 ft. tall, 1½ ft. wide. Creamy white flowers marked with shades of reddish purple bloom in summer.

P. baccharifolius. ROCK PENSTEMON. Zones LS, CS, TS; USDA 8-11. Native to southern Texas. Woody-based growth to 1½ ft. high and wide. Small, broad, glossy, dark green leaves with toothed edges have a thick, leathery feel. Coral-pink, inch-long flowers bloom all summer long. Grows on limestone; prefers dry conditions.

P. barbatus. BEARDLIP PENSTEMON. Zones US, MS, LS; USDA 6-8. Native to mountain regions from Colorado and Utah south to Mexico; needs some winter chill for best performance. Open, somewhat sprawling plant to 3 ft. tall, 1½ ft. wide. Inch-wide red flowers bloom in tall, loose spikes from midsummer to early fall. Selections include bright pink 'Elfin Pink', with 1-ft. flower spikes; coral-pink 'Rose Elf', with 2-ft. spikes and some rebloom later in fall; and lemon-yellow 'Schooley's Yellow', to 2 ft. tall.

P. canescens. PINK BEARD TONGUE. Zones US, MS, LS; USDA 6-8. Native to dry slopes and woods of the Appalachian Mountains. Green leaves (often densely covered with gray hairs) form a clump 1–3 ft. high, 1–1½ ft. wide. Blooms in late spring and early summer, when upright, hairy-gray stems hold pale to dark violet flowers to 1½ in. long.

P. cardinalis. CARDINAL PENSTEMON. Zones US, MS, LS, CS; USDA 6-9. Native to New Mexico. Good for borders; takes irrigation well and also tolerates some drought. To 2–3 ft. tall, 1½–2 ft. wide, with thick, dark green leaves. Spikes of brilliant red, 1-in. flowers bloom in summer.

P. cobaea. WILD FOXGLOVE. Zones US, MS, LS, CS; USDA 6-9. Native from Nebraska to Texas. To 1–2 ft. tall, 1–1½ ft. wide. Blooms in mid- to late spring, bearing showy clusters of large (2-in.), foxglove-like blossoms in white or lavender with deeper-colored throat markings. Leathery, glossy, green leaves form a basal rosette. Takes little to regular water; tolerates limy soil and clay.

P. digitalis. SMOOTH PENSTEMON. Zones US, MS, LS; USDA 6-8. Native to eastern and central U.S. To 5 ft. tall, 3 ft. wide. Medium green leaves to 7 in. long; flowers to 1½ in. long in white or pink shades, often with faint purple lines. Spring to early summer bloom. 'Husker Red', 2½–3 ft. tall, has maroon leaves and pink-tinted white flowers; 'Pocahontas', 2 ft. tall with lavender-pink

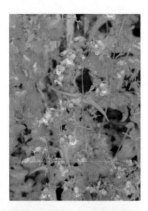

TOP: *Penstemon barbatus; P. tenuis; MIDDLE: P.* 'Dark Towers';
BOTTOM: P. 'Watermelon Taffy'; *P.* 'Cha Cha Pink'

flowers; and 'Precious Gem', standing 3 ft. tall with medium pink flowers.

P. dissectus. FEATHERLEAF PENSTEMON. Zones US, MS, LS, CS; USDA 6-9. Native to sandstone outcrops in Georgia's coastal plain. To 2 ft. high, 1½ ft. wide. Finely cut leaves; stiff stems topped with inch-long purple flowers in late spring, early summer.

P. havardii. HAVARD PENSTEMON. Zones MS, LS, CS, TS; USDA 7-11. Native to Texas. In spring, several upright, 2- to 4-ft. stems clad in rounded, light green leaves rise from a low foliage rosette to about 2 ft. wide. Scarlet, 2-in.-long

flowers bloom from late spring until June. Tolerates a wide range of soils, including limestone and clay. Cut back after bloom.

P. multiflorus. WHITE BEARD-TONGUE. Zones LS, CS, TS; USDA 8-11. Native to Alabama, Georgia, and Florida, this vigorous species can be quite drought tolerant, although intolerant of wet soil. Normal, well-drained garden soil in partial shade is best. White flowers from spring to early summer. 'Lilac Beauty' has a touch of color.

P. x mexicali. Zones US, MS, LS, CS; USDA 6-9. Summer blooming. Growing 1–2 ft. tall,

'Red Rocks' has cherry-pink flowers with white throats. The Carillo series, including 'Carillo Red', grow only 8–10 in. tall with tubular flowers sporting white throats. Both are hummingbird magnets.

P. smallii. SMALL'S PENSTEMON. Zones US, MS, LS; USDA 6-8. Native to North Carolina and Tennessee. Grows 1–3 ft. tall and 1–2 ft. wide. Pink-purple or lavender flowers, 1 in. long, in late spring. Tolerates moist woodland soils as well as dry soils.

P. tenuis. GULF COAST PENSTEMON. Zones MS, LS, CS; USDA 7-9. This native of the wet prairies of Louisiana, Texas, and Arkansas blooms heavily in spring, bearing ¾-in. pink or purple flowers. To 2 ft. tall and wide, with large medium green leaves. Tolerates wet soils and partially shaded areas. Self-sows to produce plenty of new plants.

P. hybrids.

Cha Cha series. Zones US, MS, LS; USDA 6-8. Bushy plants in a variety of colors grow 20 in. tall and wide. Heavy bloom in summer.

'Dark Towers'. Zones US, MS, LS; USDA 6-8. Compared to *P. digitalis* 'Husker Red', 'Dark Towers' is bigger and stronger, with pink-purple flowers that create a harmonious combination with the dark foliage. Grows 2½-3 ft. tall.

Pensham series. Zones MS, LS, CS; USDA 7-9. Perennial but suitable for use as an annual in zones cooler than recommended. With blooms in late spring and early summer reaching 2–2½ ft. tall, the plant is best in full sun, transitioning to afternoon shade in warmer zones. Although there are many, 'Pensham Laura' is a favorite.

Polaris series. Zones MS, LS, CS; USDA 7-9. Growing 1½–2 ft. tall in full sun to partial shade, the Polaris series blooms in late spring into summer. Colors include Purple, Rose, and Red, all with cheery white throats.

'Prairie Dusk'. Zones US, MS, LS; USDA 6-8. At 1½–2 ft. tall, 'Prairie Dusk' resembles a summer-blooming purple foxglove. Plant it with yellow flowers and foliage to make the purple sing. Full sun.

'Prairie Twilight'. Zones US, MS, LS, CS; USDA 6-9. Hybrid growing 1½–2½ ft. tall with lavender-pink flowers tipped in white. It is a more colorful version of *P. smallii*. Blooms from late spring into

early summer atop burgundy stems and green foliage. Needs well-drained soil. Cut back after bloom.

'Purple Tiger'. Zones MS, LS, CS, TS; USDA 7-11. Large purple bells with white centers on 2-ft. spires.

'Red Riding Hood'. Zones US, MS, LS; USDA 6-8. Growing 2–2½ ft. tall, the red, 1-in. flowers are a long-standing, summer show-off.

Taffy series. Zones US, MS, LS; USDA 6-8. Long-blooming, upright plants that branch at the base. Grows 18–24 in. tall and wide. No deadheading needed.

PENTAS LANCEOLATA

PENTAS, EGYPTIAN STAR CLUSTERS
Rubiaceae
Perennial usually grown as annual; or houseplant

🗡 **US, MS, LS, CS, TS; USDA 6-11; OR INDOORS**

☼ **FULL SUN; BRIGHT LIGHT**

💧 **REGULAR WATER**

Pentas lanceolata

It's hard to beat this tropical African native for continuous, eye-catching color. Spreading, multistemmed plants reach 2–3 ft. tall and wide, thickly foliaged in deep green, lance-shaped leaves to 6 in. long. During warm weather, 4-in.-wide clusters of red, pink, lavender, or white starlike flowers appear above the leaves. The blooms attract a host of butterflies and hummingbirds; cut flowers can last for two weeks.

The hybrid Butterfly series, to 12–20 in. tall and a little wider, is a better performer, offering larger flowers on denser-foliaged,

P

rounder plants. The Graffiti series features compact plants growing 12–18 in. The Kaleidoscope series stands 12–22 in. with large flower clusters. The New Look series offers compact plants to only 12–15 in. tall and wide. The Starla series grows 12–22 in. and has proven to be extremely drought tolerant. 'Stars and Stripes' is about 12–24 in. tall and combines showy red flowers with green-and-white variegated foliage.

CARE

Thrives in fertile soil with good drainage; will not tolerate drought. Feed monthly in summer with water-soluble 20-20-20 fertilizer; remove spent flowers to encourage more blooms. Pentas can be grown as a perennial in the Coastal and Tropical South; prune it heavily each year (before spring growth begins) to keep it compact and encourage flowering. It can also be used as a houseplant: Set in bright west- or south-facing window, keep soil moist (barely moist in winter), and feed monthly from spring through fall with a general-purpose liquid houseplant fertilizer.

PEPEROMIA

Piperaceae
Perennials

TS; USDA 10-11; OR HOUSEPLANT

BRIGHT LIGHT

MODERATE WATER

Peperomia caperata

Native to Central and South America, these perennials belong to the same family as *Piper nigrum*—the source of black pepper. Small and compact,

they rarely exceed 1 ft. in height and are grown for their highly ornamental foliage. Some are trailing, others upright; most feature stout, fleshy stems and leaves. Tiny flowers are borne on erect, cordlike spikes, usually in late summer.

P. argyreia (*P. sandersii*). WATERMELON PEPEROMIA. To 6–12 in. tall, not quite as wide. Rounded to oval leaves to 5 in. long and 4 in. wide; they are shiny green above and pale green beneath, with silver blotches between the veins. Leaves are held on short red stems. Green flowers appear on spikes 2–3 in. tall.

P. caperata. EMERALD RIPPLE PEPEROMIA. Compact plant to 6 in. tall and wide. Short, pinkish red stems hold tufts of heart-shaped, rich green, waxy leaves to 2 in. long. White flowers are borne on 2- to 3-in.-tall spikes.

P. obtusifolia. BABY RUBBER PLANT. Bushy plant to 6–12 in. tall and wide, noted for its smooth, glossy, deep green foliage. Leaves reach 4 in. long and 2½ in. wide, rounded to oval, notched at the tip. The leaves of 'Variegata' have wide, irregular margins of creamy white.

CARE

Peperomias are very tender to cold, with 55°F being the minimum temperature they'll tolerate. Outdoors, place in light shade. Indoors, place in a bright window, but protect from hot afternoon sun, which will burn the leaves. Excellent drainage is essential, so make sure pots have adequate drainage holes. Let the soil go nearly dry between thorough waterings; feed twice a month with a general-purpose liquid houseplant fertilizer diluted to half-strength. Reduce watering and feeding in winter. Propagate by division or by taking leaf or stem cuttings in spring or summer. Frequent repotting isn't necessary—peperomias prefer to be slightly pot bound.

PEPPER

Solanaceae
Annual

US, MS, LS, CS, TS; USDA 6-11

FULL SUN, EXCEPT AS NOTED

REGULAR WATER

'Habanero' peppers

Among the treasures Christopher Columbus brought back from the New World was a bushy plant whose fiery fruit tasted to him like black pepper. This fruit became wildly popular in Spain—and before long, people were calling them "peppers," though in fact they're not related to the source of black pepper, *Piper nigrum* (a vining plant native to India). Most New World peppers are varieties and selections of *Capsicum annuum*. The Tabasco pepper derives from *C. frutescens*.

Attractive, shrubby plants range from less than a foot high to 4 ft. tall, depending on selection; some are attractive enough to be used as ornamentals. Edible peppers are divided into two basic categories, sweet and hot, according to the amount of capsaicin (the substance that causes the heat) they contain. One way to measure a pepper's heat level is by Scoville units (SU), which were developed through extensive taste tests. Sweet bell peppers, for example, are rated at 0 SU and can easily be eaten whole—but do the same with a volcanic 'Habanero' (rated at up to 600,000 SU) or 'Bhut Jolokia' (1 million SU), and your hair will catch fire.

Sweet peppers are ready to pick when they have reached good size (like those you see in markets). Pimientos should be picked only when red-ripe, but

you can pick other sweet types green or ripe (red, yellow, orange, or purple, depending on the selection). The flavor typically sweetens as the fruit ripens. Pick hot peppers when they are fully ripe. Possible pests include aphids, whiteflies, cutworms, hornworms, stinkbugs, and Colorado potato beetles.

Sweet peppers

These peppers are mild in flavor, even when they ripen and change color. The group includes bell peppers, commonly used for stuffing and salads. Outstanding selections are 'California Wonder' (75 days from planting to harvest), 'Big Bertha' (72 days), 'Corno di Toro' (70–80 days), 'Cubanelle' (70–80 days), 'Gypsy' (60 days), and 'Peto Wonder' (75 days); all change from green to red as they mature (red fruit is very high in vitamin C). You can also buy selections that ripen to yellow ('Early Sunsation', 70 days), orange ('Valencia', 70 days, or 'Orange Blaze', 65–75 days), purple ('Purple Beauty', 70 days), and even brown ('Choco Hybrid', 70 days). These hybrids are bred for high yield and disease resistance.

Many other sweet peppers are popular. Banana peppers (65–75 days), shaped like the namesake fruit, are heavy bearers, with fruit ripening from green through yellow and orange to red; use them for frying and in salads. Bell-shaped pimientos (75–85 days) are very sweet—perfect for salads, cooking, and canning. Sweet cherry peppers are good for pickling. Long, cylindrical Italian peppers, such as 'Giant Marconi' (63 days), are great for grilling and roasting. Let them turn red before picking.

Hot peppers

Hot peppers range from pea-size firebombs to fingerlike types reaching 6–7 in. long. All are pungent, ranging from mildly hot Italian pepperoncini (73 days; 500 to 800 SU) to the aforementioned, nearly incandescent 'Habanero' (85–95 days; up to 600,000 SU). 'Anaheim' (74 days; 800–1,400 SU) is a mildly spicy pepper used for making canned green chiles. 'Cajun Belle' is mildly spicy but also sweet (61 days; 100–1,000 SU). Mexican cooking employs a wide variety of hot peppers, including 'Pasilla Bajio' (75 days; 100–250

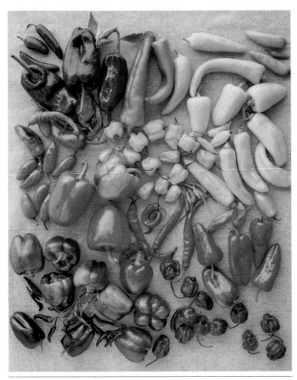

ABOVE: Assorted peppers

HOW TO GROW PEPPERS

CLIMATE Peppers need a long, warm growing season. As soon as weather warms up in spring and nighttime temperatures remain consistently above 55°F, set out transplants 1½–2 ft. apart.

WATER Keep soil moist, particularly during flowering and fruiting.

FERTILIZER Apply a balanced liquid fertilizer once or twice after plants become established, but before blossoms set. Too much fertilizer produces lots of leaves but few fruit.

HARVEST Snip the stem with pruning shears or scissors. Be careful when handling hot peppers, as oils on the outside of the fruit can irritate the skin and burn the eyes.

SU), 'Ancho' (dried red form of the fresh green 'Poblano', 75–80 days; 1,200–3,000 SU), 'Holy Molé' (85–110 days, 700 SU), 'Jalapeño' (73 days; 2,500–5,000 SU), and 'Serrano' (75 days; 5,000–15,000 SU). 'Long Red Cayenne' (70 days; 30,000–50,000 SU) is used both for cooking and for decoration; often dried for use in wreaths and arrangements. 'Tabasco' (80 days; 30,000–50,000 SU) is a foundation for hot sauces (as are 'Habanero' and 'Jalapeño'). Thai cuisine also uses very hot peppers; one example is 'Thai Dragon' (70 days; 35,000–45,000 SU). Indian food is not shy either with 'Bhut Jolokia' (100–120 days; 1 million SU).

Ornamental peppers

These small, bushy plants, usually 10–15 in. tall and wide, are often used for bedding and in pots. Rounded or conical, ½- to 2-in.-long fruit may be yellow, red, orange, or purple. Showy enough to take the place of flowers, they're typically quite hot and seldom used for cooking.

An exceptional plant with both ornamental and culinary uses is chili pequin (*Capsicum annuum glabrisculum*). Native to Texas, Mexico, and Central America, it forms a mounding shrub 2–5 ft. tall and wide and bears small white flowers continuously from spring to fall. Jewel-like, rounded fruit, about ½ in. in diameter and orange-red when ripe, decorates the plant in summer and fall, lending welcome color to the lightly shaded areas it favors. Fruit is quite hot (30,000–50,000 SU) and is widely used in salsas, sauces, soups, and vinegars.

PERICALLIS X HYBRIDUS

CINERARIA
Paeoniaceae
Annual

🌿 **US, MS, LS, CS, TS; USDA 6-11**

◑ **PARTIAL TO FULL SHADE**

💧 **REGULAR WATER**

Pericallis x hybridus

Most common are large-flowered dwarf kinds, usually sold as Multiflora Nana or Hybrida Grandiflora. These are compact growers (to 12–15 in. high and wide) bearing broad clusters of 3- to 5-in. daisies; colors range from white through pink and purplish red to blue and purple, often with contrasting eyes or bands. You'll usually find plants for sale in garden centers and supermarkets between Valentine's Day and Easter. Give them moist, cool, loose, rich soil. Once they finish blooming, throw them away. Formerly known as *Senecio x hybridus*.

PERILLA FRUTESCENS

PERILLA, WILD BASIL, SHISO
Lamiaceae
Annual

🌿 **US, MS, LS, CS, TS; USDA 6-11**

☀ ◑ **FULL SUN OR LIGHT SHADE**

💧 **REGULAR WATER**

Perilla frutescens

This longtime Southern favorite is native from the Himalayas to eastern Asia. It's a sturdy, leafy, warm-weather plant that grows quickly to 2–3 ft. tall, 1 ft. wide. Leaves are broadly oval, pointed, and deeply toothed, reaching about 5 in. long. The kinds most commonly seen have bronzy or purple leaves resembling those of purple-foliaged forms of basil (*Ocimum basilicum*). Extremely easy to grow. Self-sows freely, winding up in all sorts of unlikely places. Tiny white flowers appear in spikes to 6 in. long; seedheads of dead plants are prominent in winter.

Perilla makes an attractive addition to summer borders, and various parts of the plant are also edible. Use leaves as a vegetable or flavoring (they taste something like mint, something like cinnamon); fry the long, thin clusters of flower buds in tempura batter, and serve as a vegetable. In Asia, the seeds are pressed for oil. Plants marketed as 'Magilla' perilla are, in fact, coleus (*Solenostemon*).

P

PEROVSKIA ATRIPLICIFOLIA

RUSSIAN SAGE

Lamiaceae

Shrubby perennial

🌿 **US, MS, LS, CS; USDA 6-9**

☼ **FULL SUN**

◐ ◑ **LITTLE TO MODERATE WATER**

Perovskia atriplicifolia

Neither Russian nor a sage, this clumping perennial combines handsome foliage with colorful summer flowers. Mature plants stand 3–4 ft. tall and wide, with graceful, upright, whitish stems holding finely cut, aromatic, gray-green leaves. Sprays of small, lavender-blue flowers appear continuously from late spring through summer, forming a soft haze above the foliage. 'Blue Spire' has deep violet-blue blossoms; 'Filagran' sports silvery foliage and a distinctive upright form. 'Longin' is more upright than the species, reaching 3–4 ft. tall. 'Lacy Blue' and 'Little Spire' grow only 2 ft. tall.

Russian sage can be used in the garden in many ways. Its cool-colored flowers and foliage combine well with reds, oranges, and yellows; its fine-textured foliage is a good foil for plants with coarser leaves, such as coneflower (*Echinacea*), black-eyed Susans (*Rudbeckia*), iris, aster, and sedum. Mass plantings are very effective.

CARE

Even though it is scarcely bothered by pests (not even deer have much interest in it) and withstands heat, drought, and infertile soils, Russian sage is difficult for some Southerners to grow. The most common problem is heavy, poorly drained soil. If you have clay, try planting in raised beds and mixing gravel with the soil. Water infrequently, and don't fertilize or crowd plants. Instead of pruning in fall, wait until new growth begins in spring, then cut old stems nearly to the ground.

PERSEA

Lauraceae

Evergreen trees and shrubs

🌿 **ZONES VARY BY SPECIES**

☼ ◑ **EXPOSURE NEEDS VARY BY SPECIES**

◐ ◑ ◑ ◑ **WATER NEEDS VARY BY SPECIES**

Persea borbonia

Group of about 150 species of trees and large shrubs grown chiefly for their handsome evergreen foliage. Related to avocado (*Persea americana*) and camphor tree (*Cinnamomum*). None is very common, but all are well worth seeking out.

P. borbonia. RED BAY. Tree. Zones MS, LS, CS; USDA 7-9. Native to swamps from Delaware to Florida. Grows 20–40 ft. tall and 20 ft. wide, with a dense crown of aromatic, shiny, dark green leaves to 6 in. long and 2 in. wide. Often multitrunked and shrubby. Creamy flowers in May or June are inconspicuous. Small, dark blue to black fruit appears in early fall, borne on attractive red stalks. Needs regular to ample water; tolerates very wet soil and salt spray. Full sun or light shade.

P. humilis. SILK BAY. Shrub or small tree. Zones LS, CS, TS; USDA 8-10. Native to Florida scrub. Handsome plant to 10 ft. tall, 6–10 ft. wide. Leaves are shiny green above and covered with silky, chestnut brown hairs beneath; they grow 1–3 in. long and ½–1¼ in. wide. When crushed, foliage smells like that of culinary bay (*Laurus nobilis*). Small, yellowish spring flowers are followed by small purplish black fruit in fall. Very drought tolerant; needs good drainage and full sun.

P. thunbergii. JAPANESE PERSEA. Zones LS, CS, TS; USDA 8-11. Tree. Native to Japan, China, Korea. Fast grower to 60–80 ft. tall, 40–60 ft. wide. Thick, glossy leaves are deep green above, paler beneath, to 6 in. long and 2½ in. wide. Tiny, yellowish spring flowers; blackish purple fruit in summer. A nice lawn, shade, or street tree. Provide regular water and full sun.

PERSICARIA

KNOTWEED

Polygonaceae

Perennials

🌿 **ZONES VARY BY SPECIES**

☼ ◑ **FULL SUN OR PARTIAL SHADE**

◑ **REGULAR WATER, EXCEPT AS NOTED**

Persicaria bistorta 'Superba'

Sturdy plants with jointed stems and small white or pink flowers. Some kinds tend to get out of hand and need to be controlled.

P. affinis. HIMALAYAN KNOTWEED. Zones US, MS, LS; USDA 6-8. Himalayan native. Spreading plant to 1 ft. high, 2 ft. or more wide. Deep green, lance-shaped, finely tooth-edged leaves are mostly basal; they grow 2–4½ in. long, turn bronze in winter. Dense, erect, 2- to 3-in. spikes of bright rosy red flowers bloom in summer, early fall. Informal border or ground cover. 'Darjeeling Red' forms 3-in.-high foliage mats, has 10-in. spikes of deep pink flowers that age to red; its foliage turns red in fall. 'Dimity' sports pale pink flowers and larger leaves than the species.

P. alpina (*P. polymorpha*) ALPINE KNOTWEED. Zones US, MS, LS, CS; USDA 6-9. Native to China, Japan. To 4–6 ft. tall, 4 ft. wide. Forms a bushy clump of rough-textured, lance-shaped, dark green leaves to 8 in. long. In summer, sturdy stems are topped by big, fluffy, creamy white flower plumes reminiscent of astilbe. Not invasive. Tolerates heat and humidity.

P. amplexicaulis. MOUNTAIN FLEECE. Zones US, MS; USDA 6-7. Himalayan native. Forms a big clump—to 4 ft. tall and wide when plants are in flower. Medium green leaves are pointed ovals up to 10 in. long. Blooms profusely from midsummer to fall, bearing narrow, 4-in. blossom spikes similar to those of lavender (*Lavandula*) but in a wider range of colors—pink, purple, red, white. 'Firetail' has bright scarlet flowers.

P. bistorta. BISTORT. Zones US, MS; USDA 6-7. Native to Eurasia. Makes a clump to 2½ ft. tall, 3 ft. wide, with broadly oval, medium green, 4- to 12-in.-long leaves. Tight, 2- to 3-in. spikes of pale pink or white flowers bloom from late spring until well into summer. 'Superba' is a good pink selection.

P. capitata. PINK KNOTWEED. Perennial in Zones US, MS, LS, CS; USDA 6-9; annual elsewhere. Himalayan native. Tough, trailing ground cover grows 3–6 in. high, spreading indefinitely both by rooting stems and by self-seeding. Oval, 1½-in.-long leaves are dark green when new, take on pinkish overtones when mature. Leaves of all ages have a bronzy cast that deepens in cooler weather; they discolor and die below 28°F. Stems and small, round flower heads are pink. Blooms almost all year in mild climates. Best in confined spots (where it won't be able to spread) or in uncultivated areas. No watering needed.

P. microcephala. FLEECE FLOWER. Perennial. Zones US, MS, LS, CS; USDA 6-9. 'Red Dragon' is the poster child of the species and a striking addition to a sun-to-part shade bed. Dark burgundy foliage is the reason to grow it, although it does have small white flowers in late summer. It does not spread underground, remaining in a clump unless a stem bends over and puts down roots. Well-behaved to 3 ft. tall.

P. vacciniifolia. CREEPING FLEECE FLOWER. Zones US, MS, LS; USDA 6-8. Himalayan native. Prostrate plant forms a foliage mat to 3 in. high, trailing to 2 ft. or wider. Slender, branching, reddish stems are clothed in oval, ½-in.-long, shiny green leaves that turn red in fall. In late summer, 6- to 9-in. flower stalks bear dense, upright, foxtail-like, 2- to 3-in. spikes of rose-pink blossoms. Excellent as a bank cover or for draping over a boulder in a large rock garden.

P. virginiana. VIRGINIA KNOTWEED. Zones US, MS, LS; USDA 6-8. Native to eastern North America, eastern Asia. To 2–4 ft. tall, spreading indefinitely by creeping rhizomes. Oval green leaves 3–10 in. long; insignificant flowers. The species is rarely found in gardens. More commonly seen is 'Painter's Palette', valued for its flashy foliage: Leaves are marbled in green, pale gray-green, and ivory, with a ragged chocolate-maroon V in the center. On new growth, the ivory patches are closer to yellow, and the central V-shaped mark has a pink cast.

PERSIMMON

Ebenaceae
Deciduous fruit trees

🗡 **ZONES VARY BY SPECIES**

☼ **FULL SUN**

💧 **WATER NEEDS VARY BY SPECIES**

'Fuyu' persimmon

Two types of fruiting persimmons are grown in the South. The native American species is a bigger, more cold-tolerant tree than its Asian counterpart, but the Asian type bears larger fruit. Neither species is fussy about soil, as long as it is well drained. For the ornamental Texas persimmon, see *Diospyros texana*.

American persimmon (*Diospyros virginiana*) is native from Connecticut to Kansas and southward to Texas and Florida. Grows well in Zones US, MS, LS, CS; USDA 6-9. Can grow to 35–60 ft. tall, 20–35 ft. wide. As a landscape tree, it is not as ornamental as the Asian species and is probably best used in woodland gardens. Attractive gray-brown bark is fissured in a checkered pattern. Glossy, green, broadly oval leaves to 6 in. long turn yellow, pink, or reddish purple in fall. Round, 1- to 2-in.-wide fruit is yellow to orange (often blushed red); very astringent until soft-ripe, then very sweet. On wild species, fruit ripens in early fall after frost; some selections do not require much winter chill. Both male and female trees are usually needed to get fruit. 'Meader' is self-fruitful; its fruit is seedless if not pollinated. 'Early Golden' has more flavorful fruit; it needs cross-pollination for best crop. Trees usually need pruning only to remove broken or dead

branches. Does best with regular moisture but will also perform well with moderate water.

Japanese or Oriental persimmon (*Diospyros kaki*) grows and fruits best in Zones MS, LS, CS; USDA 7-9. It reaches 30 ft. tall (or more) and at least as wide. Has a handsome branch pattern and is one of the best fruit trees for ornamental use; makes a good small shade tree and is suitable for espalier. Leaves are leathery ovals 6–7 in. long—light green when new, maturing to dark green. They turn vivid yellow, orange, or red in fall (even in mild climates). After leaves drop, brilliant orange-scarlet, 2- to 3½-in. fruit brightens the tree for weeks and persists until winter unless harvested. Without pollination, sets seedless fruit; pollinated trees often produce more abundant crops.

Prune trees when they are young to establish a good framework; thereafter, prune only to remove dead wood, shape the tree, or open up a too-dense interior. Remove any suckers that shoot up from below the graft line. Rootstock sprouts that emerge from the soil some distance from the trunk must also be removed.

Fruit drop is a common problem in young trees. To avoid it, water regularly and feed once in late winter or early spring; too little or inconsistent moisture causes fruit drop, as does overfertilizing (too much fertilizer also causes excessive growth). Excessive fruit drop can also be reduced by providing a pollenizer (such as 'Gailey'), but fruit will be seedy.

Some Japanese persimmon selections are astringent until soft-ripe—at which stage they become very sweet. To save the crop from birds, pick fruit when fully colored but still hard, then let it ripen off the tree. Astringent types must be eaten when the flesh is mushy and puddinglike. Nonastringent types are hard (like apples) when ripe, with a mildly sweet flavor; they can be eaten hard, but their flavor improves when they are allowed to soften slightly off the tree.

'Chocolate'. Astringent. Medium-size, acorn-shaped fruit. When pollinated, has seeded flesh with dark streaks; when unpollinated, has seedless

yellow-orange flesh. Fruit from pollinated trees has best flavor. Must be soft to eat.

'Fuyu'. Nonastringent. Firm fleshed; about the size of a baseball but flattened like a tomato. Similar but larger is 'Gosho', widely offered as 'Giant Fuyu'.

'Fuyu Imoto'. Nonastringent. Square-shaped fruit. Excellent quality. Ripens lightly later than 'Fuyu'.

'Gailey'. Astringent. Roundish to conical fruit. Bears many male flowers and is often used as a pollenizer.

'Hachiya'. Astringent. Big, slightly pointed fruit. Very shapely tree for ornamental use.

'Izu'. Nonastringent. Medium-size, round fruit borne on a tree about half the standard size. Ripens early.

'Matsumoto Wase Fuyu'. Non-astringent. An early-ripening form of 'Fuyu'. Thin fruit to prevent limb breakage.

'Tamopan'. Astringent. Large, acorn-shaped fruit.

PETASITES JAPONICUS

JAPANESE COLTSFOOT, FUKI
Asteraceae
Perennial

🗡 **US, MS, LS, CS; USDA 6-9**

◐ ● **PARTIAL TO FULL SHADE**

💧 **AMPLE WATER**

Petasites japonicus

Giant perennial for constantly moist locales near ponds, streams. Creeping rhizomes give rise to big (2½-ft.-wide), round leaves on edible, 3-ft.-long stalks that are used by the Japanese as a vegetable (called fuki). Short, thick spikes of fragrant white daisies appear in early spring before the leaves emerge. Locate this plant with care; it has thick, invasive rhizomes and can be difficult to eradicate. *P. j. giganteus* has leaves to 4 ft. wide on 5-ft. stalks. Its selection 'Variegatus', with 3- to 4-ft. stalks, has 2- to 3-ft.-wide leaves with bold white markings.

X PETCHOA
Solanaceae
Perennial grown as annual

US, MS, CS, TS; USDA 6-11

FULL SUN OR LIGHT SHADE

REGULAR WATER

x Petchoa

This intergeneric hybrid was created by crossing *Petunia* with *Calibrachoa*; the resulting plants possess the best traits of each parent. Like *Calibrachoa*, they are well branched, producing many flowering stems (no pinching needed), and their spent blooms drop off cleanly and don't stick to the foliage. Like *Petunia*, they produce large flowers (2 in. across) and are easy to grow. Plants are very fast growing and withstand heat, wind, and rain better than either parent. Nearly covered in flowers from late spring until frost, they reach about 1 ft. high and 2 ft. wide, with a semitrailing habit that makes them ideal for containers and hanging baskets. Good for planting out in beds in mild climates.

The SuperCal series includes flowers in blue, cherry-red, bright rose-pink, light pink, and purple. Blooms of 'Terracotta' are yellow-orange, beautifully suffused with shades of amber and pink.

'Vanilla Blush' has soft pink flowers with a yellow throat; 'Velvet' has deep burgundy blooms, with a nearly black throat.

Plants grow best in well-drained, light soil; they will tolerate alkaline and even somewhat salty soil conditions. Best with consistent moisture but will take brief periods of drought. Weekly applications of a balanced fertilizer will keep the flowers coming.

PETREA VOLUBILIS
QUEEN'S WREATH
Verbenaceae
Evergreen vine

TS; USDA 10-11

FULL SUN

REGULAR WATER

Petrea volubilis

Woody vine native to Mexico, Central America, and the West Indies. Twines to 20–40 ft. but can easily be kept smaller. Elliptical, deep green leaves to 8 in. long have a sandpapery surface. Stunning floral display several times a year during warm weather: pendent, foot-long clusters of star-shaped, blue-purple, 1½-in.-wide blossoms. Blue calyxes hang on after the petals drop. 'Albiflora' has white flowers. People describe it as a "tropical wisteria", but only for its looks. It is neither invasive nor destructive.

Beautiful plant trained on arbor or pergola, along eaves, on a high wall. Grow in organically enriched, well-drained soil. Provide support for climbing stems. Prune and thin growth as needed in winter. Wind resistant. Frost sensitive.

PETROSELINUM CRISPUM
PARSLEY
Apiaceae
Biennial grown as annual

US, MS, LS, CS, TS; USDA 6-11

AFTERNOON SHADE

REGULAR WATER

Petroselinum crispum

This popular and ubiquitous herb is native to southern Europe. Two kinds are grown, both with finely cut dark green foliage: curly-leafed and Italian flat-leafed. Leaves of both are used as a seasoning (both fresh and dried), and fresh sprigs and minced leaves are classic garnishes. Curly-leafed parsley is more often grown for its good looks; it makes a lush, deep green, 6- to 12-in.-high border or edging and also looks great when combined with other plants in containers. Italian flat-leafed parsley grows 2–3 ft. tall and is considered more flavorful.

CARE
Buy plants at garden centers or sow seeds directly in the garden—in spring in the Upper South, in fall or spring elsewhere. To speed germination, soak seeds in warm water for 24 hours before planting. (Even after soaking, they may not sprout for several weeks; according to an old story, they must first go to the devil and back.) Thin seedlings to 1–1½ ft. apart for flat-leafed parsley, 6–8 in. apart for curly-leafed parsley—or space plants at these distances. Pick fresh leaves as needed, or dry them on a wire rack. Where plants are left to overwinter, they'll flower at the beginning of their second year, then set seed

and die. Most gardeners simply set out new plants each year.

Be merciful if you spot large caterpillars with black, green, and yellow stripes munching on the leaves; these are the larvae of the stunning black swallowtail butterfly.

PETUNIA X HYBRIDA
Solanaceae
Perennial grown as annual

US, MS, LS, CS, TS; USDA 6-11

FULL SUN

MODERATE TO REGULAR WATER

Petunia

Perhaps no flowers have seen such dramatic improvement in their suitability to Southern gardens in recent decades as petunias. They've long been mainstays in borders and containers because of their profuse blooming and incredible range of colors. But they just didn't stick around long enough to suit us. Our hot, humid climate meant their flowers often melted and entire plants died by midsummer.

Petunias used to be divided into two groups—*Grandiflora* (large flowers on a bouquet-shaped plant) and *Floribunda* (medium-size flowers on a compact, mounding plant). Neither group liked our weather and pretty much became superfluous. While you can still get improved, large-flowered specialty petunias in a wild assortment of colors and patterns (as well as generic petunias sold by color in big box stores), by and large gardeners have turned to a new

TOP: Petunia 'Supertunia Sangria Gharm'; *P.* 'Supertunia Vista Bubblegum'; *MIDDLE: Mixed Supertunias; BOTTOM: P.* 'Tidal Wave Silver'; *P. violacea*

category of hybrids that we like to call Landscape petunias.

Landscape petunias have slightly smaller flowers than their predecessors, but lots more of them for a much longer time. Whether mounding or trailing, they're dense and full. Their biggest advantage is that they tolerate our Southern climate. In most places in the South, they'll bloom continuously from spring until fall and don't need deadheading. Plant them in masses or grow them in containers.

Four of our favorite groups of Landscape petunias are described below. Two are grown from seed and two from cuttings. Cutting-grown plants are said to be more uniform and reliable. However, since seed mixes are refined and improved each year, average consumers likely won't notice any difference.

Wave petunias. Seed grown. Wave petunias blazed the trail for better performing petunias with the introduction of the landmark Purple Wave petunia in 1995. It hugged the ground at only 5–7 in. tall and spread up to 48 in., making it possible to create a ground cover of petunias. It's now included among other colors in the Wave Classic series. Other Wave series include Shock Wave (7–10 in. tall, 36-in. spread, dazzling colors), Easy Wave (6–12 in. tall, 30- to 36-in. spread), and Tidal Wave (mounding plants 16–22 in. tall, 30 to 48 in. wide). Tidal Wave Silver is an exceptional performer in the South and may survive a mild winter to show up the following year.

Supertunia petunias. Cutting grown. Supertunias are vigorous, mounding, dense plants that fill the garden with flowers. They grow 16–24 in. tall and 18–24 in. wide. Our favorite is 'Supertunia Vista Bubblegum'. It's a gardening superstar; its bubblegum-pink flowers can probably be seen from space.

Surfinia petunias. Cutting grown. Surfinias are very low-growing, trailing plants. They grow only 3–6 in. tall but can spread up to 4 ft. Blooms don't form just on the ends of stems, but all along the stems, so you end up with a mat of solid color.

Picobella petunias. Seed grown. These dwarf plants sport abundant 1–2 in. blossoms on small, mounding plants that grow 10–12 in. tall and wide. Great in smaller garden and in containers.

Species petunias. All modern petunias have as their ancestors the following two species. Violet petunia (*P. violacea*, also listed as *P. integrifolia*) hails from South America. This trailing plant boasts multitudes of rosy purple, 1-in. flowers with dark throats. It blooms nonstop from spring to fall and is outstanding in window boxes, pots, hanging baskets, and planters. It's very heat tolerant and usually winter hardy from the Lower South down. The selection 'Laura Bush' grows 18–24 in. tall and its flowers are twice as big. White petunia (*P. axillaris*) sports fragrant, 2-in. flowers of white to blush pink. Native to the U.S., it self-sows readily and sometimes naturalizes in fields and country gardens.

CARE

Petunias thrive in sun and rich, well-drained soil. Space them 8–18 in. apart, depending on plant size. Feed large-flowered kinds monthly during the growing season with a bloom booster liquid fertilizer. Hungry landscape petunias—referred to by growers as the teenage boys of the plant world—do best when given controlled-release fertilizer at planting time in addition to weekly applications of liquid fertilizer. Cut back leggy plants to force new growth and blooms.

In Florida, grow petunias as winter annuals. Plant them in fall, enjoy their flowers through the cool months into spring, and then replace them with summer flowers that take the Florida heat.

Just a few pests bother petunias, including slugs, snails, and tobacco budworms. Botrytis gray mold can mar the blossoms and foliage during cool, wet weather.

PHACELIA

Boraginaceae
Annuals and biennials

ZONES VARY BY SPECIES

EXPOSURE NEEDS VARY BY SPECIES

REGULAR WATER

Phacelia bipinnatifida

Large genus of flowering plants native mostly to western U.S. and Mexico. One of the species listed here is native to the Texas prairie; the other is a wildflower from shady, moist areas of the Southeast.

P. bipinnatifida. SCORPION WEED, FERNLEAF PHACELIA. Biennial. Zones US, MS, LS; USDA 6-8. Native from West Virginia and Illinois to Arkansas and Georgia. Deeply divided, dark green leaves to 4 in. long and wide. Overwinters as an attractive low foliage mound to 1 ft. wide; in late spring, flower stalks to 2 ft. tall bear sprays of white-eyed lavender-blue blossoms. Showy as a mass planting. Dies after flowering; self-sows reliably. Grow in partial or full shade, in soil with lots of organic matter.

P. congesta. BLUE CURLS. Annual or biennial. Zones US, MS, LS, CS, TS; USDA 6-11. Native to Texas and New Mexico. Grows 3 ft. tall, 1½ ft. wide. Deeply cut, bright green, soft leaves to 4 in. long, 1½ in. wide. Blooms throughout spring; buds form on a curled spike, which uncoils as the buds open into blue-purple flowers. Easy to grow from seed. For a long bloom period, be sure to water during dry spells. Full sun.

PHAIUS

Orchidaceae
Terrestrial orchids

🌿 **CS, TS; USDA 9-11; OR HOUSE-PLANTS**

◑ **LIGHT SHADE; BRIGHT LIGHT**

💧 **REGULAR WATER**

Phaius tankervilleae

These orchids owe their popularity to their attractive foliage, striking flowers, and ease of cultivation. Large, broad, rich green leaves somewhat resemble those of cast-iron plant (*Aspidistra*); they are marked with prominent parallel veins. Erect flower spikes to 3 ft. tall arise from the bases of large, thick pseudobulbs. In the Coastal and Tropical South, *Phaius* species are perennials; elsewhere, they're quite easy to grow as houseplants.

P. flavus. From India, Thailand, Malaysia, and Indonesia. Leaves to 2 ft. long are attractively marked with yellow blotches and spots. In spring, blossom spikes carry many fragrant, 3-in.-wide flowers in sulphur yellow with a reddish brown band on the lip. 'Punctata' has yellow-spotted foliage.

P. tankervilleae. NUN'S ORCHID. Native to China, India, Sri Lanka, Southeast Asia, and Australia. May well be the easiest of all orchids to grow. Handsome, oblong to oval and pointed leaves 2–3 ft. long. Fragrant, 2- to 3-in.-wide blooms appear from late winter into spring; they are dusty rose inside and creamy white outside, with a rosy purple lip.

CARE Although they'll take full sun for short periods, these orchids prefer light shade. Those grown indoors will bloom just fine if placed next to a bright window (they will, however, need protection from hot, direct sun). Give them fertile, well-drained soil that contains plenty of organic matter. From winter through the end of summer, keep the soil evenly moist (use room-temperature water); then let it go slightly dry for three to four weeks in fall. From spring through summer, feed every other week with water-soluble 20-20-20 fertilizer diluted to half-strength. Be careful with the leaves, which break easily. Plants are easy to divide. Scale can be a serious pest, especially on indoor plants; control it by spraying with horticultural oil.

PHALAENOPSIS

MOTH ORCHID
Orchidaceae
Epiphytic orchids

🌿 **TS; USDA 10-11; OR HOUSE-PLANTS**

◑ **FILTERED SUN; BRIGHT INDIRECT LIGHT**

💧 **REGULAR WATER**

Phalaenopsis

These are tropical orchids with thick, broad, leathery leaves and no pseudobulbs. Leaves are rather flat, to 1 ft. long. From spring to fall, plants bear long (to 3-ft.) sprays of 3- to 6-in.-wide flowers in white, cream, pale yellow, or light lavender-pink; some are spotted or barred or have lips in a contrasting color. Many lovely hybrids are sold. Very popular orchid commercially.

If you've never grown orchids before, moth orchids are good ones to start with. They are usually greenhouse plants, since they need fairly high humidity and warmer growing conditions than most orchids (minimum of 60–65°F at night, 70–85°F during the day). In the house, a good location is near a bathroom or kitchen window with light coming through a gauze or other sheer curtain (foliage burns easily in direct sun). Some smaller-flowered new hybrids give promise of being easier to grow, tolerating somewhat lower night temperatures. Give moth orchids same potting medium as cattleya. When cutting flowers, cut back to just above one of the tiny bracts on the stem; secondary sprays may form. To promote stronger new growth, many growers prefer to cut out the entire stem after blossoms fade.

PHALARIS ARUNDINACEA PICTA

RIBBON GRASS
Poaceae
Perennial grass

🌿 **US, MS, LS, CS; USDA 6-9**

☼ ◑ **FULL SUN OR PARTIAL SHADE**

💧 **REGULAR WATER**

Phalaris arundinacea picta

This tough, tenacious grass from North America and Eurasia is an old Southern favorite; it forms a 2- to 3-ft.-high clump that spreads aggressively—and indefinitely—by underground runners. Deep green leaves with longitudinal white stripes turn buff colored in autumn; airy white flower clusters age to pale brown. To keep this plant in bounds, grow it in large containers or use same control methods as for running kinds of bamboo (see Bamboo). Less invasive selections are 'Woods Dwarf' ('Dwarf's Garters'), which grows about half as tall as the species and has brighter white stripes; and 'Feesey' ('Strawberries and Cream'), to 1½–2 ft. tall, with white stripes that usually take on pink tints during cool weather.

PHILADELPHUS

MOCK ORANGE
Hydrangeaceae
Deciduous, semievergreen, evergreen shrubs

🌿 **ZONES VARY BY SPECIES**

☀️◐ **PARTIAL SHADE IN HOTTEST CLIMATES**

💧💧 **MODERATE TO REGULAR WATER**

Philadelphus coronarius

Grown for white or cream-colored, usually fragrant flowers that bloom in late spring or early summer. Blossoms are four petaled, typically 1–2 in. wide; they range from single to fully double and may be borne singly or in clusters, depending on species. Mock oranges are generally large and vigorous, with fountainlike form. Oval, 2- to 4-in.-long leaves (typically medium green in color) are arranged in pairs along the stems.

Prune every year just after bloom, cutting out oldest wood and surplus shoots at base. To rejuvenate, cut to the ground after bloom. Taller types are striking planted in lawns and as background and corner plantings; smaller kinds can be planted near foundations or used as low screens or informal hedges. Buy plants in bloom to check for best fragrance. Not fussy about soil type but must have good drainage.

P. coronarius. SWEET MOCK ORANGE, ENGLISH DOGWOOD. Deciduous. Zones US, MS, LS, CS; USDA 6-9. Native to southern Europe, Caucasus. Strong-growing old favorite to 10–12 ft. tall and wide. Clusters of fragrant, 1½-in. flowers. 'Aureus', to 8 ft. high, has bright golden foliage that turns yellow-green in summer.

P. hybrids. Deciduous. Zones US, MS, LS; USDA 6-8. A group of showy selections, often with intense fragrance. Sometimes sold as selections *P. x lemoinei* or *P. x virginalis*.

'Avalanche'. Grows 5–6 ft. high and wide with single, 1-inch, white blooms.

'Belle Etoile'. Grows to 5 ft. tall and 8 ft. wide with fringed, purple-centered, single flowers to 2½ in. across. Very popular.

'Buckley's Quill'. Dense, compact grower to 4–5 ft. tall and wide with clusters of 1-in.-wide, double flowers. Petals are narrow and pointed.

'Enchantment'. Grows 5–6 ft. high and wide with double, 1-in., white blooms.

'Glacier'. Grows 3–4 ft. tall and about as wide, with 1½-in., double, white blossoms.

'Mont Blanc'. Grows 5–6 ft. high and wide with single, 1-in., white blooms.

'Natchez'. Grows to 8–10 ft. high and wide, is one of showiest selections of all, with profuse, unscented, single white blooms up to 2 in. across.

'Silberregen' ('Silver Showers'). Arching to 6 ft. high and wide with 2-in., single, white flowers.

'Virginal'. Grows 6–8 ft. high and wide with 2-in., double, white blossoms.

P. mexicanus. EVERGREEN MOCK ORANGE. Zones CS, TS; USDA 9-11. From Mexico. Vining shrub has long, supple stems clothed with evergreen leaves. Creamy white, highly fragrant, 1½-in. flowers in small clusters may bloom sporadically throughout year. Can be kept to 6 ft. high and wide as a freestanding shrub. It is best used, however, as a vine or bank cover; can climb 15–20 ft. if given support.

P. texensis. TEXAS MOCK ORANGE. Semievergreen. Zones LS, CS; USDA 8-9. Texas native to 3 ft. tall and wide. Small, shiny, dark green leaves. Fragrant spring flowers are 1–3 in. across. Grows in virtually any well-drained soil—limestone, clay, sand, or loam.

PHILODENDRON

Araceae
Evergreen vines and shrubs

🌿 **ZONES VARY BY SPECIES; OR HOUSEPLANTS**

☀️◐● **EXPOSURE NEEDS VARY BY TYPE; BRIGHT INDIRECT LIGHT**

💧 **REGULAR WATER**

Philodendron 'Xanadu'

From the tropical Americas. Fast-growing plants that are nearly indestructible—can be grown well even by those who manage to kill everything else. Plants are favored for attractive, leathery, usually glossy leaves. In good conditions, old plants may bloom; flowers resemble those of calla (*Zantedeschia*), with a boatlike bract surrounding a club-shaped structure. Bracts are usually greenish, white, or reddish. Browsing deer don't seem to care for these plants.

Philodendrons fall into two main classes.

Arborescent; relatively hardy. These are large, shrub-size plants with big leaves and sturdy, self-supporting trunks. They can be grown indoors but need much more space than most houseplants. They grow outdoors in the Coastal and Tropical South (USDA 9-11). As landscape plants, they do best in sun (some shade at midday where light is intense) but can take considerable shade. Use them for tropical effects or as massive silhouettes against walls or glass. Excellent in large containers; very effective near swimming pools.

Vining and self-heading; tender. This class includes tender plants of two different habits. They can grow outdoors only in the Tropical South (USDA 10-11),

where they require partial or full shade; elsewhere, they are houseplants. Many kinds are sold, with many different leaf shapes and sizes. Self-heading types form short, broad plants with leaves radiating out from a central point. Vining types do not really climb and must be tied to or leaned against a support until they eventually shape themselves to it. The support can be almost anything, but certain water-absorbent columns (sections of tree fern stem, wire and sphagnum "totem poles," slabs of bark) serve especially well, since they can be kept moist.

The following list indicates the class of each species and selection. Note that one popular "philodendron"—the so-called split-leaf philodendron—belongs to another genus, *Monstera*.

P. bipinnatifidum (*P. selloum*). Arborescent. Treelike shrub to 6–15 ft. high and wide, typically with a single upright trunk that leans with age. Deeply cut leaves to 3 ft. long, on equally long stalks. 'Hope' is a compact shrub to 4 ft. high and wide and is reported to be hardier than the species.

P. domesticum. Vining. Often sold as *P.* 'Hastatum'. Grows to 10–20 ft. high, with arrow-shaped, bright green leaves to 2 ft. long and 1 ft. wide.

P. erubescens. Vining. Often sold as *P.* 'Hastatum'. To 10–20 ft. high, with foot-long, arrow-shaped, deep green leaves with coppery undersides. Subject to leaf spot in overly warm, moist conditions. A number of selections and hybrids are available; they are more resistant to leaf spot and tend to be more compact. Some, possibly hybrids, have much red in new foliage and in leafstalks. 'Royal Queen' has bright red new growth; mature leaves are dark green heavily tinged with red. 'Emerald Queen' is a choice deep green form. 'Pink Princess' has shiny black to deep burgundy leaves splashed and speckled with white and pink. Best color in bright light.

P. 'Hastatum'. See *P. domesticum, P. erubescens*

P. hybrids. 'Lynette' is self-heading to 1 ft. high, 2 ft. wide. Makes a tight cluster of foot-long, broadish, bright green leaves that are strongly patterned by deeply sunken veins. Good tabletop plant. 'Xanadu' is self-heading and grows 3 ft. high and 5 ft. wide with large, drooping, glossy, green, deeply lobed leaves. 'Autumn' is self-heading, grows 2 ft. high and wide with colorful leaves that emerge coppery red then go through shades of red, orange, and yellow before maturing to shiny green. 'Cobra' is a climber with oval leaves variegated and spotted with white.

P. martianum. Self-heading. To 2 ft. tall, 3–4 ft. wide. Leathery, lance-shaped, dark green leaves grow to 1½ ft. long and 6–8 in. wide; each leaf has a broad midrib and a swollen-looking, spongy, deeply channeled leafstalk to 15 in. long. Makes a nice coarse-leafed ground cover.

P. melanochrysum. BLACK-GOLD PHILODENDRON. Vining. To 10–20 ft. high, with velvety, lance-shaped greenish black leaves to 3 ft. long, 1 ft. wide. Midribs and lateral veins are pale green. The new leaves are heart shaped and have a coppery tinge.

P. scandens. HEART-LEAF PHILODENDRON. Vining. Among the most common philodendrons. Can reach 50 ft. Deep green, heart-shaped leaves; juvenile leaves are 4–6 in. long, while mature ones can grow to 1 ft. long. *P. s. micans* has velvety young leaves; mature leaves are smooth. *P. s. oxycardium* (often sold as *P. oxycardium* or *P. cordatum*) has glossy leaves throughout its life. Juvenile forms of both are most popular; they are grown on tree trunks, in hanging baskets and window boxes, as houseplants. Indoors, train them on string or wire for a variety of decorative effects; or grow on moisture-retentive columns.

P. wendlandii. Self-heading. To 1 ft. high, 2 ft. wide. Compact clusters of 12 or more deep green, foot-long, broadly lance-shaped leaves on short, broad stalks. Indoors, this species is useful where a tough, compact foliage plant is needed.

P. williamsii. Arborescent. Arrow-shaped, glossy, deep green leaves to 2½ ft. long and 1 ft. wide. Leafstalks almost as long as leaves.

CARE

Whether grown in containers or open ground, all philodendrons need rich, loose, well-drained soil. Feed lightly and frequently for good growth and color. Clean dust from leaves of indoor plants. Most philodendrons—especially those grown in containers—tend to drop their lower leaves, leaving a bare stem. Once a plant gets gangly and overgrown, the best course is often simply to discard it and replace it with a new plant. However, you can also cut the plant back to short stub, then let it regrow; or you can air-layer the leafy top, then plant the layer once it roots (and discard the parent). Some philodendrons send down aerial roots. Push these into soil or cut them off (removing them won't hurt plant).

PHLEBODIUM AUREUM

GOLDEN POLYPODY FERN, HARE'S FOOT FERN
Polypodiaceae
Ferns

📋 **TS; USDA 10-11; OR HOUSE-PLANTS**

◐● **PARTIAL TO FULL SHADE; BRIGHT INDIRECT LIGHT**

💧 **REGULAR WATER**

Phlebodium aureum

Native from Florida south to Argentina. To 2½ ft. high and 5 ft. wide, with heavy, brown, creeping rhizomes. Coarse, blue-green fronds drop if hit by frost, but plants recover fast. 'Mandaianum', sometimes called crisped blue fern or lettuce fern, has frilled and wavy frond edges. Both it and the species are showy. Formerly known as *Polypodium aureum*.

PHLOMIS

Lamiaceae
Perennials and evergreen shrubs

📋 **ZONES VARY BY SPECIES**

☀ **FULL SUN, EXCEPT AS NOTED**

💧🌢 **LITTLE TO MODERATE WATER**

Phlomis fruticosa

Mediterranean natives related to sage (*Salvia*). Erect stems are set with widely spaced whorls of hooded, two-lipped flowers in yellow, purple, or lilac. Moisture-conserving, thick, typically furry or hairy leaves are lance shaped to oval, set opposite each other on stems. Not particular about soil but must have good drainage. Not usually damaged by browsing deer. Cut flowers are striking in arrangements.

P. 'Edward Bowles' ('Grande Verde'). Shrub. Zones MS, LS, CS, TS; USDA 7-11. Grows to 3–4 ft. tall, 5–6 ft. wide. Hybrid between *P. fruticosa* and *P. russeliana*. Resembles a bulkier *P. fruticosa* and has broader leaves (to 6 in. long, 3 in. wide) and larger, pure yellow flowers. Often sold as *P. fruticosa* and takes the same care.

P. fruticosa. JERUSALEM SAGE. Shrub. Zones MS, LS, CS, TS; USDA 7-11. To 4 ft. tall and wide, with woolly, gray-green leaves to 6–8 in. long, 1¼ in. wide. Deep golden yellow, 1-in. flowers in ball-shaped whorls along upper half of stems. Cut plants back by half in fall to keep them compact. With watering, will produce several waves of bloom in spring and summer if cut back lightly after each flowering. Can tolerate light shade for part of day. 'Miss Grace' ('Compact Grey') reaches 3 ft. high and as much as twice as wide with soft gray-green leaves and bright yellow flowers.

P. lanata. WOOLY JERUSALEM SAGE. Shrub. Zones LS, CS, TS; USDA 8-11. Dense, compact plant to 2½ ft. tall, 4–6 ft. wide. Woolly, wrinkled, sage-green leaves to about 1 in. long. Stems and leaf undersides have brownish scales. Whorls of deep yellow, 1-in. flowers bloom from spring to fall if faded stems are cut out.

P. purpurea. PURPLE JERUSALEM SAGE. Shrub. Zones CS, TS; USDA 9-11. Rather lax habit to 4–6 ft. high and wide. Lance-shaped leaves to 4 in. long are gray-green and sparsely hairy above, white and woolly beneath; new shoots are also white and woolly. Purplish pink flowers bloom mainly in late spring, but scattered blossoms appear all year long where winters are mild. After each flowering, cut plant back by one-third to keep it neat and compact.

P. russeliana. TURKISH SAGE. Perennial. Zones US, MS, LS, CS; USDA 8-9. Spreads by rhizomes to make a low clump of furry, olive-green foliage. Leaves are large (to 8 in. long, 6 in. wide) and heart shaped. Creates an effective weed-suppressing ground cover. Sends up 2- to 3-ft.-tall stems bearing flowers in soft yellow fading to cream. The main bloom period comes in early summer, but some flowers are produced later as well. Flower spikes are attractive even after blooms fade; they dry out and remain upright throughout winter. Tolerates partial shade.

PHLOX

Polemoniaceae
Perennials and annuals

◢ ZONES VARY BY SPECIES

☼ ◐ **FULL SUN OR LIGHT SHADE, EXCEPT AS NOTED**

💧 **REGULAR WATER, EXCEPT AS NOTED**

Phlox paniculata 'John Fanick'

Mostly from North America, the many types show wide variation in form, but all have showy flower clusters. Tall kinds are excellent border plants; dwarf ones are mainstays of the rock garden. Unless otherwise noted, grow in ordinary garden soil and provide regular moisture. Two common problems affect phlox: red spider mites (attack almost all species) and powdery mildew (*P. paniculata* is especially susceptible). Horticultural oil or insecticidal soap controls the first; planting resistant selections solves the second.

P. x arendsii. Zones US, MS, LS, CS; USDA 6-9. Hybrid between *P. divaricata* and *P. paniculata*. To 1½ ft. high, not quite as wide, with 1-in.-wide blossoms in clusters to 6 in. across, early summer. Cut off faded flowers for later rebloom. Selections include reddish purple 'Anja'; lavender 'Hilda'; and 'Suzanne', bearing white blooms with a red eye. Mildew-resistant 'Eyecatcher' bears light pink flowers with darker reddish centers. 'Miss Jill' (white with a small pink eye) and 'Miss Mary' (dark red) are part of the mildew-resistant Spring Pearl series. 'Ping Pong' is a mildew-resistant selection with soft rose flowers, reddish green leaves, and reddish stems.

P. bifida. SAND PHLOX. Zones US, MS, LS; USDA 6-8. From the central U.S. Clumps to 8–10 in. tall, 6–8 in. wide, with narrow, light green leaves. Blooms spring through early summer, bearing profuse, ½-in., lavender to white flowers with deeply notched petals. 'Betty Blake' has dark, lavender-blue blooms. Likes full sun and excellent drainage; tolerates drought.

P. buckleyi. Zones US, MS, LS; USDA 6-8. Native to Virginia and West Virginia. Trailing stems, set with willowlike evergreen leaves to 5 in. long, form a clump to 6 in. tall, 2 ft. wide. Upright stems to 1½ ft. high hold clusters of rosy purple flowers in late spring and summer. Makes a good ground cover.

P. carolina 'Miss Lingard'. US, MS, LS, CS; USDA 6-9. Popular selection of a species native to the central and eastern U.S. Grows about 3 ft. high and half as wide, with pure white, highly fragrant blooms in early summer. Heat tolerant and mildew resistant. Excellent cut flowers.

P. divaricata. BLUE PHLOX. Zones US, MS, LS, CS; USDA 6-9. Native to eastern North America. To 1 ft. high, 2 ft. wide, with creeping underground shoots. Slender stems are clothed in oblong, 1½- to 2-in.-long leaves. Blooms in spring, bearing open clusters of ¾- to 1½-in.-wide, somewhat fragrant blossoms; color varies from pale blue (sometimes with pinkish tones) to white. Flowers of 'Dirigo Ice' are palest blue. 'Blue Moon' has deep violet-blue blooms; flowers of 'Louisiana Purple' are an intense blue-purple. 'Montrose Tricolor' has lavender-blue blossoms and leaves variegated in pink, white, and green. *P. d. laphamii* 'Chattahoochee' has pale lavender-blue blooms with a purple eye. All are good in rock gardens or as bulb covers. Grow in good, deep soil. Light shade.

P. drummondii. ANNUAL PHLOX, DRUMMOND PHLOX. Zones US, MS, LS, CS, TS; USDA 6-11. Native to Texas. To 6–18 in. high, 10–12 in. wide, with erect, leafy stems more or less covered with rather sticky hairs. Lance-shaped to oval, nearly stalkless leaves are 1–3 in. long. Profuse blossoms in tight clusters at tops of stems. Comes in bright and pastel colors (no blue or orange), some with contrasting eye. Tall strains (about 1½ ft. high) in mixed colors include Finest and Ford-

TOP: Phlox paniculata 'Laura'; P. subulata; MIDDLE: P. divaricata 'Louisiana Purple'; BOTTOM: P. p. 'Robert Poore'; P. p. 'David'

hook Finest. Hybrid Intensia series stands up to heat and humidity and blooms in shades of pink, magenta, lavender, and white on 12-in. plants. Dwarf (6- to 8-in.) strains include Beauty and Globe, both with roundish flowers; and starry-blossomed Petticoat and Twinkle Star. Bloom period lasts from early summer until frost if faded flowers are removed. Plant in fall. Grow in light, rich soil well amended with organic matter. Full sun.

P. glaberrima triflora. SMOOTH PHLOX. Zones US, MS, LS, CS; USDA 6-9. From the eastern U.S. Grows to 1½–2 ft. tall, 1–1½ft. wide, with smooth, narrow, 3-in.-long leaves. Lavender-pink flowers in late spring. This species is mildew free. 'Triple Play' has pink flowers with a dark eye and leaves variegated white.

P. maculata. MEADOW PHLOX, THICK-LEAF PHLOX. Zones US, MS, LS; USDA 6-8. Native to

P

eastern North America. To 3–4 ft. tall, 1½ ft. wide, with thick, narrow, pointed leaves 2–4 in. long. Early summer flowers about ¾-in. wide in 15-in.-long clusters; colors range from white (often with a colored eye) through pink shades to magenta. Shiny, mildew-resistant foliage. Selections include 'Alpha', rose-pink; 'Delta', white with pink eye; 'Natascha', pink and white bicolor; 'Omega', white with purplish pink eye; and 'Rosalinde', deep rose-pink. 'Flower Power' has tall, airy, dark stalks of white flowers blushed pink with a small pink eye.

***P.* 'Minnie Pearl'.** Zones US, MS, LS, CS. USDA 6-9. A naturally occurring hybrid found in Mississippi. To 12 in. high and twice as wide. Early-blooming, large, bright white flowers. Mildew resistant.

P. nivalis. TRAILING PHLOX. Zones US, MS, LS; USDA 6-8. Native to central U.S. Trailing plant to 4–6 in. high, 1 ft. wide. Forms a loose mat of narrow, inch-long leaves. Pink or white, 1-in. flowers in fairly large clusters, late spring or early summer. Excellent in rock gardens; needs good drainage. 'Camla' is a good pale salmon-pink selection. 'Snowdrift' has pure white blooms.

P. latifolia (*P. ovata*). MOUNTAIN PHLOX. Zones US, MS, LS; USDA 6-8. From the eastern U.S. To 15–20 in. tall, 1 ft. wide, with smooth, green, oval, mildew-free leaves to 6 in. long. Deep pink flowers in late spring.

P. paniculata. SUMMER PHLOX. Zones US, MS, LS, CS; USDA 6-9. From eastern North America. To 3–5 ft. tall, 2 ft. wide, with narrow, 2- to 5-in.-long leaves tapering to a slender point. Fragrant, 1-in. flowers in large, dome-shaped clusters throughout summer. Colors include white and shades of lavender, pink, rose, and red; blooms of some selections have a contrasting eye. Plants do not come true from seed—most seedlings tend toward an uncertain purplish pink, though some may be attractive.

Summer phlox thrives in full sun. After setting out young plants, pinch stem tips to induce branching. Mulch to keep roots cool. Divide every few years, replanting young shoots from outside of clump.

Very susceptible to mildew at end of bloom season. To minimize the problem, provide good air circulation: Don't crowd plants, and thin mature plants to leave only six to eight stems. Plant mildew-resistant selections 'Blue Paradise', deep violet-blue; white-flowered 'David' and 'Mt. Fuji' ('Fujiyama'); 'Delta Snow', white with purple eye; 'Eva Cullum', pink with red eye; 'Franz Schubert', lilac-pink; 'John Fanick', light pink with darker throat; 'Laura', purple with white eye; 'Nicky', deep magenta; compact (12–15 in. high) 'Pina Colada', white; 'Robert Poore', violet-pink; and 'Shortwood', bright pink with darker center. The free-blooming, disease-resistant Volcano series comes in a full range of flower colors, some with darker or contrasting centers. 'Becky Towe' has leaves edged with light gold and dark-centered, red flowers. 'Lord Clayton' has dark purple new leaves with green veins that age to bronzy purple-green; pinkish red flowers.

***P. pilosa* 'Forest Frost'.** US, MS, LS; USDA 6-8. A Mississippi selection of prarie phlox, an Eastern North American native. To 18 in. high and 2 ft. wide. Star-shaped, pure white, fragrant flowers. Small, needlelike green leaves. Beautiful planted in drifts.

P. stolonifera. CREEPING PHLOX. Zones US, MS, LS; USDA 6-8. Old favorite from eastern North America. Creeping, mounding plant to 6–8 in. high, 1 ft. wide, with narrow evergreen leaves to 1½ in. long. Profuse springtime show of 1-in. lavender flowers. Selections include lavender-blue 'Blue Ridge', white 'Bruce's White', deep lavender 'Sherwood Purple' and lavender-pink 'Weesie Smith'. Light shade.

P. subulata. MOSS PINK. Zones US, MS, LS; USDA 6-8. From eastern U.S. Forms a mat to 6 in. high, 1½ ft. or wider, with creeping stems clothed in ½-in., needlelike evergreen to semievergreen leaves. Blooms in late spring or early summer, bearing ¾-in. flowers in colors including white, pale to deep shades of pink, and lavender-blue. Makes sheets of brilliant color in rock gardens. Plant in loose, not-too-rich soil; give moderate water. After flowering, cut back halfway. Specialists offer two dozen or more selections of this old Southern favorite; many are actually selections of other low-growing species, or hybrids between those species and *P. subulata*. 'Tamaongalei' ('Candy Stripe') has rose-pink blossoms edged in white; it is somewhat drought tolerant and has good fall rebloom.

PHOENIX

DATE PALM
Arecaceae
Palms

CS (MILDER PARTS), TS; USDA 9-11

FULL SUN, EXCEPT AS NOTED

REGULAR WATER

Phoenix dactylifera

These feather palms are mostly large trees, though the following list includes two that grow less than 20 ft. tall. Trunks are patterned with bases of old leafstalks. Small, yellowish flowers in large, hanging sprays. On female trees, blossoms are followed by clusters of dates—but only if the tree has been in the ground for at least several years and if a male tree is nearby. Dates of *P. dactylifera* and *P. sylvestris* are used commercially; those of other species don't have as much edible flesh. Date palms hybridize freely, so buy these trees from a reliable nursery that knows the seed or plant source. Deer seldom bother date palms.

P. canariensis. CANARY ISLAND DATE PALM. Hardy to 20°F; slow to develop new head of foliage after damage from hard frosts. Canary Island native. Big, heavy-trunked palm to 60 ft. tall, with a great many bright green to deep green, gracefully arching fronds that form a crown to 50 ft. wide. Grows slowly until it forms a trunk, then speeds up a little. Young plants do well in pots for many years, looking something like pineapples. Best planted in parks, along wide streets, or in other large spaces; not for small city lots. Takes seacoast conditions.

P. dactylifera. DATE PALM. Leaves killed at 20°F, but plants have survived 4°F. Native to the Mideast. Classic palm of desert oases. Slender-trunked tree to 80 ft., with a crown 20–40 ft. wide; gray-green, waxy leaves have stiff, sharp-pointed leaflets. Sends up suckers from base; its natural habit is a clump of several trunks. Bears the dates you find in markets; principal selection is 'Deglet Noor'. Too large and stiff for most home gardens. Does well at seaside.

P. loureirii (*P. humilis*). Hardy to 20°F. Native from India to China. Resembles a smaller, slimmer, more refined *P. canariensis*. Slow grower to 10–18 ft. tall and wide, with dark green leaves. Thrives in containers.

P. reclinata. SENEGAL DATE PALM. Damaged below 25°F. Native to tropical Africa. To 20–30 ft. high and wide. Produces offshoots, forming picturesque clumps with several curving trunks; if you want a single-trunked tree, remove offshoots. Fertilize for fast growth. Good seaside plant.

P. roebelenii. PYGMY DATE PALM. Foliage browns at around 26°F but recovers rapidly in spring. From Laos. Small, slow-growing, single-trunked palm to 6–10 ft. high. Fine-textured, curving leaves form a dense crown 6–8 ft. across. Good in groves or as a potted plant. Full sun or partial shade.

P. rupicola. CLIFF DATE PALM. Hardy to 26°F. Native to India. As stately as *P. canariensis*, but it has a slender trunk and is a much smaller tree, reaching only 25 ft. high, 15–20 ft. wide. Lower leaves droop gracefully.

P. sylvestris. SILVER DATE PALM. Hardy to 22°F. Native to India. Beautiful single-trunked palm to 30 ft. tall, 20–25 ft. wide. Tapering trunk is wide at base, narrow at top. Dense, rounded crown of gray-green leaves. Fruit is used commercially for making date sugar.

PHORADENDRON SEROTINUM

AMERICAN MISTLETOE
Loranthaceae
Evergreen shrub

✎ US, MS, LS, CS, TS; USDA 6-11

☼ ◑ FULL SUN TO LIGHT SHADE

◉ REGULAR WATER

Phoradendron serotinum

Native from New Jersey to Florida, west to southern Illinois and Texas. The deep green boughs of mistletoe are familiar sights in the South in winter, when they festoon the leafless branches of deciduous trees. Growing 1–3 ft. tall and wide, this plant begins its life as a seed dropped by a bird onto the branch of a host tree. The seed quickly sprouts rootlike structures which penetrate the bark and tap into the flow of water and nutrients. Leathery, oval leaves, about 1 in. long, line mistletoe's crowded, forked branches. Small whitish flowers appear in late spring to early summer and are followed by clusters of single-seeded white berries. Although commonly thought to be highly poisonous, the berries are only moderately toxic; one would have to consume a large quantity to become seriously ill. In ancient times, people associated the berries with fertility; this may explain the custom of kissing under the mistletoe.

Mistletoe infests more than 100 species of hardwood trees; oaks, particularly water oak (*Quercus nigra*), are its favorite hosts. Others include hickory and pecan (*Carya*), honey locust (*Gleditsia triacanthos*), apple, hawthorn (*Crataegus*), and linden (*Tilia*). In most cases, the host tree is not seriously harmed. Pruning mistletoe removes it only temporarily; it will grow back from the point of attachment. For permanent removal, the infested branch must be removed at least 1 ft. below the point of attachment. But since this process may disfigure the tree—and reinfestation from nearby trees is likely— it's usually best to leave the tree alone. Mistletoe is the state flower of Oklahoma.

PHORMIUM

NEW ZEALAND FLAX
Hemerocallidaceae
Perennial

✎ LS, CS, TS; USDA 8-11; OR GROW IN POTS

☼ ◑ FULL SUN OR PARTIAL SHADE

◌ ◔ ◉ LITTLE TO REGULAR WATER

Phormium 'Jubilee'

From New Zealand, these dramatic plants have many swordlike evergreen leaves that grow in a fan pattern; they're good massed or used as focal points. Many variegated selections provide year-round color in perennial and shrub borders, on hillsides, in seaside plantings, near swimming pools. Cool weather intensifies foliage colors. On established plants, branched clusters of tubular flowers appear in late spring or early summer, rising to twice the height of the foliage clump in some kinds. Hummingbirds love the flowers.

Rugged New Zealand flax, *P. tenax*, and its selections are sturdy and fast growing. While most phormiums dislike humid summers and cold winters, New Zealand flax accepts the Southern climate. It takes almost any soil and tolerates drought and coastal conditions; good drainage, however, is essential to success. Grow in containers wherever soil doesn't freeze in winter.

More finicky than *P. tenax* are forms of *P. cookianium* and the spectacular hybrids between these two species. They require a bit more water; in hot areas, their arching leaves need afternoon shade to prevent burning.

All phormiums are harmed by temperatures below 20°F. In cold-winter areas, you can grow smaller sorts indoors or move larger containers to shelter when deep cold threatens.

Nursery plants in containers are deceptively small; when you plant, allow enough room to accommodate a mature specimen. Cut out flower stalks when blossoms wither. As leaves age, colors fade; cut out older (outer) ones as close to base as possible to maintain best appearance. On variegated sorts, watch for reversions to solid green or bronze; remove reverted crowns down to root level before they take over the clump. Clumps can remain in place indefinitely. To increase plantings, take individual crowns from clump edges; or divide large clumps (not an easy job).

P. cookianum (*P. colen-soi*). MOUNTAIN FLAX. Leaves arch gracefully, drooping at the tips; they grow 4–5 ft. long, 2½–3 in. wide. Mature clumps are 4–5 ft. tall, spreading to 8–10 ft. or more. 'Black Adder' grows 3–4 ft. tall and wide, with glossy, deep burgundy-black leaves. 'Flamingo' grows just 1–2 ft. high and wide, with leaves in shades of orange, rose, light green, and yellow. *P. c. hookeri* 'Cream Delight' has leaves with a broad, creamy yellow central stripe and narrow green margins edged in dark red. *P. c. h.* 'Tricolor' has green leaves margined in cream and red; foliage is flushed with rose in cool weather.

P. hybrids. These crosses between *P. cookianum* and *P. tenax* were selected for distinctive leaf color. Leaves are 1½–2 in. wide unless otherwise noted. These are a few you'll find in the South.

'Jubilee'. To 3 ft. tall and wide with green leaves edged with bright cherry-red and completely red underneath.

'Sundowner'. Erect growth to 5–7 ft. tall and wide, with leaves to 3 in. wide. Olive or bronzy green foliage has stripes of pinkish red (aging to cream) at or near edges and a fine red edge; leaf undersides are grayish green.

'Yellow Wave'. To 4–5 ft. tall, 5–7 ft. wide, with 2¼-in.-wide leaves in chartreuse with lime-green margins. Leaves can burn in hot sun.

P. tenax. NEW ZEALAND FLAX. Large, bold plant with bronzy green leaves to 9 ft. long and 5 in. wide; rigid and mainly upright, curving mainly (if at all) near tips. Mature clumps are about as wide as or a little wider than high. Note that bronze-leafed selections take on a deeper color in full sun.

'Atropurpureum', 'Bronze', 'Purpureum', 'Rubrum'. These names are used interchangeably in the trade for plants with purplish or brownish red foliage that grow 6–8 ft. tall and wide. Usually grown from seed and somewhat variable; if you want a particular color, make sure you see the actual plant before buying.

'Atropurpureum Compactum' ('Monrovia Red'). To 5 ft. tall and wide, with burgundy-bronze foliage. Uniform; propagated by tissue culture.

'Bronze Baby'. To 3 ft. tall and wide, with 1½-in.-wide leaves. Foliage is deep reddish brown aging to deep bronze; narrow orange leaf edges and midrib (on underside) glow in sunlight.

'Chocolate'. To 4–5 ft. high and wide. Rich brown leaves have reddish undertones.

'Dusky Chief'. Dense clump to 6 ft. high and wide. Wine-red leaves are 2–3 in. wide and have coral edges that glow when backlit.

'Jack Spratt'. To 1½ ft. high and wide, with ½-in.-wide, twisting, reddish brown leaves. 'Thumbelina' is similar but a little darker.

'Morticia'. To 3–4 ft. high and wide, with stiff, 1½-in.-wide, purple-black leaves.

'Pink Stripe' ('Pink Edge'). To 4–5 ft. high and wide. Gray-green foliage has a purplish tinge. Each leaf has a bright pink margin that is broader at base, gradually narrowing to almost nothing at tip.

'Tiny Tiger' ('Aurea Nana'). Miniature of 'Variegatum', reaching barely 1 ft. high and wide. Leaves are flushed pink in cool weather. 'Tony Tiger' is a 2-ft. version.

P

'Tom Thumb'. Upright clump to 2–3 ft. high and wide. Green, wavy-edged, ½-in.-wide leaves have red-bronze margins.

'Variegatum'. To 6–8 ft. tall and wide, with ¾-in.-wide, grayish green leaves that have creamy yellow stripes along edges.

'Veitchianum' ('Radiance'). To 5–6 ft. tall, 7 ft. wide. Green leaves have a central yellow stripe and lime-green margins with a thin orange edge.

'Wings of Gold'. Resembles 'Variegatum' but reaches just 2–3 ft. high and wide. Ideal for containers.

PHOTINIA

Rosaceae
Evergreen and deciduous shrubs and trees

- 🌿 ZONES VARY BY SPECIES
- ☀️ FULL SUN, EXCEPT AS NOTED
- 💧💧 MODERATE TO REGULAR WATER

Photinia x fraseri

Prized for their bright, coppery red new foliage, these large, handsome plants are mainly used for screening and hedges, although they can be pruned into single-trunk small trees. But consider their inherent problems before adding them to your garden. They produce flattened clusters of malodorous, white flowers in spring; the flowers are followed in fall by red or black berries that birds eat and distribute seedlings everywhere. In most of the South, they're subject to serious, disfiguring diseases. Evergreen species are injured or killed by prolonged periods of temperatures below 10°F.

P. x fraseri. FRASER PHO-TINIA. REDTIP. Evergreen shrub or small tree. Zones US, MS, LS, CS; USDA 6-9. A hybrid between Japanese photinia (*P. glabra*) and Chinese photinia (*P. serratifolia*), this makes up about 95% of the photinias planted in the South. The original Fraser photinia, named 'Birmingham,' was born at Fraser Nursery in Birmingham, Alabama, around 1940. Because of the shrub's fast growth to 10–15 ft. tall and its bright-red new foliage to 5 in. long, it quickly became a mainstay in gardens, parks, and commercial plantings. Unfortunately, the red growth is severely susceptible to *Entomosporium* leaf spot in the humid Southeast. Shearing the plant into hedges to produce more red foliage just leads to more leaf spot that eventually defoliates and kills it. Fireblight and mildew attack Fraser photinia too. Arid parts of Texas are about the only places it's worth growing. 'Red Robin,' a supposedly leaf spot-resistant selection popular in Britain, has not lived up to that billing here. Does not produce berries.

P. glabra. JAPANESE PHO-TINIA. Evergreen shrub from Japan. Zones MS, LS, CS; USDA 7-9. Broad, dense growth to 6–10 ft. tall and wide. Glossy leaves to 3 in. long emerge bright red and then change to dark green. Red berries age to black. Seldom sold in nurseries. Main claim to infamy is that, as one of the parents of Fraser photinia, it contributed the genes responsible for susceptibility to leaf spot.

P. serratifolia. CHINESE PHOTINIA. Evergreen shrub or small tree. Zones US, MS, LS, CS; USDA 6-9. Broad, dense-growing Chinese native becomes an upright to rounded plant 20–30 ft. tall and wide. Large leaves to 8 in. long have serrated edges when young that become smoother with age. New bronze foliage isn't as showy as that of the above two species but compensates with large, showy clusters of bright red berries that last through the winter—until birds eat them and disperse the seeds. Tough plant that grows in sun or shade and in any soil except wet. Not susceptible to leaf spot but can get fireblight and mildew.

P. villosa. ORIENTAL PHO-TINIA. Deciduous shrub or small tree. Zones US, MS; USDA 6-7.

From China, Korea, Japan. Uncommon plant deserves wider use where fireblight isn't a problem. Dark green leaves, 1½–3 in. long, turn bright red, orange, and yellow in fall. Bright red berries ripen in fall and persist into winter. Grows 10–15 ft. tall, not as wide, and is usually vase shaped and multitrunked.

PHYGELIUS

CAPE FUCHSIA
Scrophulariaceae
Perennials

- 🌿 US, MS, LS, CS; USDA 6-9
- ☀️◐ FULL SUN OR LIGHT SHADE
- 💧 REGULAR WATER

Phygelius 'Croftway Coral Princess'

While true fuchsias sulk in hot Southern summers, these South African natives like the weather just fine. They die to the ground in winter in the Upper and Middle South but remain shrubby in the Lower South. Plants grow 3–4 ft. high, spreading about as wide by underground stems or rooting prostrate branches. From summer into fall, plants bear tubular, curved flowers resembling fuchsias in loosely branched clusters. After bloom, cut out old flower stalks to neaten plants. In the Upper South, mulch heavily in late fall. Species can be started from seed, but named selections should be grown from cuttings or by layering bottom branches.

P. aequalis. Pyramidal clusters of dusty rose flowers. 'Yellow Trumpet' has pale yellow blooms.

P. Croftway series. British hybrids bred for compact growth and long blooming period.

P. capensis. More open and sprawling than *P. aequalis*, with loose clusters of orange to red flowers.

P. x rectus. Hybrids between *P. aequalis* and *P. capensis*. 'African Queen' has deep salmon-orange flowers with a yellow throat; 'Devil's Tears', scarlet with yellow throat; 'Moonraker', solid pale yellow; 'Salmon Leap', orange; 'Tommy Knockers', peach with yellow throat; 'Winchester Fanfare', deep rose with yellow throat. 'Pink Elf' bears pink flowers on a smaller plant than the usual (2 ft. high, 3 ft. wide). 'Sunshine' has dark red flowers atop golden yellow foliage.

PHYSALIS ALKEKENGI

CHINESE LANTERN PLANT
Solanaceae
Perennial often grown as annual

- 🌿 US, MS, LS, CS; USDA 6-9
- ☀️◐ FULL SUN OR LIGHT SHADE
- 💧 REGULAR WATER

Physalis alkekengi

From Europe, Asia. Grown for the flowers' decorative, papery, 2-in. calyxes, which look like lanterns and mature to a striking orange-red in late summer and fall. Plant grows 1½–3 ft. high and wide, with angular branches and light green, oval, 2- to 3-in.-long leaves. Small white flowers appear in leaf joints in summer; these are followed by inedible berries, each enclosed in a colorful, inflated husk. Dry, leafless stalks hung with these "lanterns" make choice winter arrangements.

Sow seeds in light soil in spring. Plant is clump forming, spreading widely by long, creeping, whitish underground stems; can become invasive. Increase established plantings by digging and dividing the roots. *P. a. franchetii* 'Zwerg' is a dwarf selection just 8 in. high; it makes a good potted plant.

A *Physalis* species that produces edible fruit within a papery husk is *P. ixocarpa*; see Tomatillo.

PHYSOCARPUS OPULIFOLIUS

COMMON NINEBARK
Rosaceae
Deciduous shrub

⚑ US, MS, LS; USDA 6-8

☼ ● SUN OR SHADE

◐ ● MODERATE TO REGULAR WATER

Physocarpus opulifolius
'Diabolo'

Native to eastern and central North America. The common name refers to the plant's peeling bark, which strips off to reveal several layers. Graceful, arching growth to 9 ft. tall, 10 ft. wide; looks something like a larger version of spiraea, to which it is closely related. Medium green leaves to 3 in. long are broadly oval, with lobed edges. Rounded clusters of many tiny white or pinkish blossoms appear in spring or early summer. Prune as needed after bloom; rejuvenate by cutting old stems to the ground.

Selections are more attractive than the species. 'Diabolo', to 9–12 ft. tall and wide, has intense reddish purple leaves (foliage color can tend toward dark green in very hot summers or when plant is grown in partial shade). 'Luteus' is about the same size, with leaves that are yellow when

plant is grown in sunlight, yellow-green in shade. 'Center Glow' reaches 6–8 ft. tall and wide, with leaves that emerge greenish gold and mature to burgundy. Similarly sized 'Coppertina' has coppery orange foliage. Compact selections to 4–6 ft. tall and broad include 'Dart's Gold', similar to 'Luteus' but brighter; 'Lady in Red', with purplish red foliage; 'Little Devil' ('Donna May'), growing 3–4 ft. with small burgundy leaves; 'Nanus', with small, shallowly lobed, dark green leaves; 'Nugget', with leaves that unfold golden yellow, gradually mature to lime-green, and then turn gold again in fall; and 'Summer Wine', with dark purple leaves.

PHYSOSTEGIA

OBEDIENT PLANT, FALSE DRAGONHEAD
Lamiaceae
Perennial

⚑ US, MS, LS, CS; USDA 6-9

☼ ◐ FULL SUN OR PARTIAL SHADE

● REGULAR WATER

Physostegia virginiana 'Alba'

These North America native plants have many fine qualities—but common name notwithstanding, obedience isn't one of them: Most are notoriously invasive when growing in moist, fertile soil. Keep that in mind when choosing a site, and don't let them spread into wild areas. Slender, upright stems carry medium green, oblong, 3- to 5-in. leaves with toothed edges and pointed tips. Dense spikes of funnel-shaped, 1-in. flowers in pink, rose, white, or lavender top the stems. Blossoms resemble

snapdragons (hence the name "false dragonhead") and remain in place if pushed or twisted out of position (hence "obedient plant"). Long-lasting cut flowers.

Spiky form makes these plants useful in composing borders. Combine with summer phlox (*Phlox paniculata*), asters, patrinia, Japanese anemone (*Anemone hybrida*), false aster (*Boltonia*). Tall bloom stalks may need staking. Cut to ground after bloom; divide every two years to keep plants in bounds.

P. angustifolia. Native to Texas, Illinois, Mississippi. Grows 2–6 ft. tall, 2–3 ft. wide; tallest in swampy conditions, where plant forms thick colonies. Pink-purple flowers on 4- to 6-in. spikes in spring and summer.

P. pulchella. Native to eastern Texas. Grows to 2 ft. tall (taller if kept moist), 1½ ft. wide. Bears spikes of rosy purple flowers in spring and summer.

P. virginiana. Native to the eastern U.S. To 4 ft. or taller, 2 ft. wide. Flowers are borne on 10-in. spikes from mid- or late summer into autumn. Rose-pink 'Bouquet Rose' grows 3 ft. tall. 'Miss Manners' has pure white blooms and forms a neat clump 2–2½ ft. high; it spreads to 3 ft. or a little wider rather than running aggressively. 'Pink Manners' is similar but has pink flowers and grows to 3 ft. tall. Selections to about 2 ft. tall include white 'Summer Snow'; bluish pink 'Variegata', with white-edged leaves; and rose-pink 'Vivid'. 'Crystal Peak' has sturdy stems of white flowers reaching 12–15 in. high.

PICEA

SPRUCE
Pinaceae
Evergreen trees

⚑ US, MS; USDA 6-7, EXCEPT AS NOTED

☼ ◐ FULL SUN OR LIGHT SHADE

◐ ● MODERATE TO REGULAR WATER, EXCEPT AS NOTED

Picea pungens

Like firs, spruces are pyramidal and have stiff needles, with branches arranged in neat tiers. But unlike firs, they have pendent cones, and their needles are attached to branches by small pegs that remain after needles drop. Most spruces are tall timber trees that lose their lower branches fairly early in life as they head upward; their canopies thin out noticeably as they age. Many species have dwarf forms useful as foundation plantings, for rock gardens, in containers. Not favored by deer.

P. abies. NORWAY SPRUCE. Native to northern Europe. Fast growth to 60 ft. tall, 20 ft. wide. Stiff, deep green, attractive pyramid in youth; ragged in age, as branchlets droop and oldest branchlets (those nearest trunk) die back. Extremely hardy and wind resistant; valued for windbreaks. Tolerates heat and humidity better than most spruces. Following are two of the more common dwarf forms, of which there are many.

'Nidiformis'. BIRD'S NEST SPRUCE. Dense growth to 3–5 ft. tall (ultimately to 10 ft.), 4–6 ft. wide. Individual plants vary in form. Some are flat topped; in others, the semierect main branches curve outward, leaving a shallow depression at the plant's top that gives it the look of a bird's nest.

'Pendula'. Grows naturally as a ground cover about 1½ ft. high, 10 ft. wide. Looks attractive cascading downward from rocks or walls. Can be staked to desired height and grown as a short, weeping tree.

P. glauca. WHITE SPRUCE. Native to Canada and northern U.S. Narrowly cone-shaped tree grows 60–70 ft. tall, 10–12 ft. wide. Dense when young, with pendulous twigs and silvery green foliage. Crushed needles have an unpleasant odor. The following two types are widely grown.

P. g. albertiana 'Conica'. DWARF ALBERTA SPRUCE, DWARF WHITE SPRUCE. Compact, pyramidal tree, slowly reaching 6–8 ft. tall, 4–5 ft. wide in 35 years. Short, soft needles are bright grass-green when new, gray-green when mature. Needs shelter from drying winds (whether hot or cold) and from strong reflected sunlight. Popular container plant. 'Tiny Tower' grows only 4–6 ft. tall.

P. g. densata. BLACK HILLS SPRUCE. Slow-growing, dense pyramid; can reach 20 ft. tall, 10–12 ft. wide in 35 years.

P. omorika. SERBIAN SPRUCE. Native to southeastern Europe. Narrow, conical, slow-growing tree to 50–60 ft. tall, 6–10 ft. wide. Shiny, dark green needles with silvery undersides. Retains branches to the ground for many years. Considered by some to be the most attractive spruce; one of the best for hot, humid climates. 'Nana' is a dwarf to 3–4 ft. tall and wide (possibly to 10 ft. high), with short, closely packed needles.

P. orientalis. ORIENTAL SPRUCE. Native to the Caucasus, Asia Minor. Dense, compact, cone-shaped tree with very short needles; grows slowly to 50–60 ft. high, 20 ft. wide. Can tolerate poor soils if they are well drained, but may suffer leaf burn in very cold, dry winds. Among the many available selections are 'Aurea' and 'Aureospicata', with chartreuse new growth that matures to deep green; and 'Skylands', with creamy gold leaves year-round.

P. pungens. COLORADO BLUE SPRUCE. Zones US, MS, LS; USDA 6-8 (cooler parts). Native to the Rocky Mountains, from Colorado and Wyoming to New Mexico.

TOP: Picea glauca albertiana 'Conica'; *BOTTOM: P. abies; P. pungens* 'Hoopsii'

The many blue-needled forms have made this the most popular spruce for home gardens; it does well in dry soil. Stiff, dense, horizontal branches form a narrow to broad pyramid with a very formal look. Grows at a slow to moderate rate; in the wild, it can reach 100 ft. tall, 25–35 ft. across, but typically grows 30–60 ft. tall, 10–20 ft. wide in gardens. Will grow in the Lower South but definitely prefers the shorter summers and longer winters farther north. Foliage of seedlings varies in color from dark green through blue-green shades to steely blue. The following selections have consistent blue color.

'Fat Albert'. Broad, formal-looking tree to 10–15 ft. tall, 10–12 ft. wide. Good as living Christmas tree. Handsome blue foliage.

'Foxtail'. Vigorous, heat-tolerant selection that has performed well in cooler parts of the Lower South. Grows faster than the species, with upright, symmetrical habit. Young plants are bushy, with bluish, twisted needles.

'Glauca Pendula' ('Pendula'). WEEPING BLUE SPRUCE. This gray-blue plant with weeping branchlets can be grown as ground cover; it can also be trained to a small, weeping tree by staking at desired height when

young. 'The Blues' is similar but even more strongly weeping.

'Hoopsii'. Beautiful plant with striking blue color. Fast growing; conical shape. Many consider this the finest selection.

'Moerheimii'. Rich blue color but more open habit than others with longer needles.

'Montgomery'. Slow-growing dwarf forms a broad, silver-blue mound to 3–5 ft. high, 3 ft. wide.

'Thompsen'. Similar to 'Hoopsii' in color, but needles are twice as thick. Vigorous, symmetrical habit.

CARE

Check spruces for aphids in late winter; if the pests are present, take prompt control measures to avoid spring defoliation. Other common pests are bagworms, spruce budworms, pine needle scale, and spider mites.

Prune only to shape. If a branch grows too long, cut it back to a well-placed side branch. For slower growth and denser form, trim part of each year's growth to force side branches. When planting larger spruces, don't place them too close to buildings, fences, or walks; they need space.

PIERIS

Ericaceae
Evergreen shrubs

🖉 **ZONES VARY BY SPECIES**

☼ **FILTERED SUN OR PARTIAL SHADE**

💧 **REGULAR WATER**

◊ **LEAVES AND NECTAR ARE POISONOUS IF INGESTED**

Pieris japonica 'Variegata'

Elegant in foliage and form the year around, these plants make good companions for rhododendron and azalea, to which they are related. They have whorls of leathery, narrowly oval, glossy leaves in medium to dark green. Most plants form flower buds by autumn; these resemble strings of tiny beads in greenish pink, red, or white and provide a subtle decorative feature during winter. Clusters of small, urn-shaped, typically white flowers open from late winter to midspring. New spring growth is often brightly colored (pink to red or bronze). Splendid in containers, in woodland and Japanese gardens, in entryways where year-round quality is essential. Deer resistant.

P. floribunda. MOUNTAIN PIERIS. Zone US; USDA 6. Native to southeastern U.S. Compact, rounded shrub to 6 ft. tall, 10 ft. wide. Differs from the other species—new growth is pale green, mature leaves dull dark green, 1½–3 in. long. Blossoms in upright clusters. Cold hardy. Tolerates sun and low humidity better than the others but does not thrive in hot, humid regions.

P. japonica. JAPANESE ANDROMEDA, LILY-OF-THE-VALLEY SHRUB. Zones US, MS, LS; USDA 6-8. Upright, dense, tiered growth to 9–10 ft. high and wide. Leaves are 3 in. long, bronzy pink to red when new. Drooping clusters of white, pink, or nearly red flowers; flower buds are often dark red.

'Bert Chandler'. Salmon-pink new foliage ages to cream, then white, then matures to pale green. White flowers. Grows 5 ft. tall and wide.

'Cavatine'. To 2–3 ft. high and wide, with red new growth. Creamy white flowers. Choice dwarf form.

'Christmas Cheer'. Early bloomer with bicolor flowers in white and deep rose-red; flower stalks are rose-red. Grows to 5 ft. tall and wide.

'Compacta'. Grows 4–6 ft. high and wide. Heavy bloomer.

'Dorothy Wyckoff'. White flowers open from deep red buds. Grows to 5 ft. tall and wide.

'Grayswood'. Grows 4–5 ft. tall and wide. Abundant white flowers. Bronze-green new growth.

'Karenoma'. Compact grower to 3–6 ft. high and wide, with upright red flower clusters.

'Mountain Fire'. Fiery red new growth. White flowers. Grows 4–8 ft. tall.

'Prelude'. To 2–3 ft. high and wide; pink new growth. White blooms.

'Purity'. To 3–4 ft. high and wide. Late bloomer with unusually large white flowers.

'Pygmaea'. Tiny dwarf to 1 ft. high and wide, with very few flowers and narrow leaves to 1 in. long.

'Spring Snow'. Similar to 'Karenoma'.

'Temple Bells'. Compact, tiered habit; slow grower to 3–5 ft. high and wide. A bit less cold tolerant than the species. Ivory flowers.

'Valley Fire'. Brilliant red new growth. White flowers. Grows 6–10 ft. tall and wide.

'Valley Rose'. Light pink flowers. Grows to 3–5 ft. tall and wide.

'Valley Valentine'. To 5–7 ft. tall and wide. Deep red buds and flowers.

'Variegata'. Slow growing to 6 ft. high and wide. Creamy white leaf variegation; the white markings are tinged pink in spring. Prune out any green-leafed shoots. White flowers. Sun tolerant.

'White Cascade'. Extremely heavy show of pure white blooms. Grows 4–6 ft. tall and wide.

CARE

Same cultural requirements as rhododendron and azalea. Need acid, well-drained but moisture-retentive soil; do not thrive in hot, dry conditions. Choose a planting location sheltered from wind, where plants will get high shade or dappled sunlight at least during the warmest afternoon hours. Prune by removing spent flowers. Thin older specimens by taking out whole branches; or limb them up to reveal attractive, peeling bark.

PILEA
Urticaceae
Annuals and perennials

🌡 TS; USDA 10-11; OR HOUSEPLANT

◐ ● PARTIAL TO FULL SHADE; BRIGHT INDIRECT LIGHT

💧 REGULAR WATER

Pilea cadierei

Plants in this large group are grown for their colorful, often interestingly patterned and textured leaves; flowers of most are inconspicuous. Many are popular houseplants—but where hardy, they also make nice outdoor potted plants or even ground covers for shady areas. Outdoors, they'll grow in moist soil in dappled morning sun to full shade.

P. cadierei. ALUMINUM PLANT. Perennial. Native to Vietnam. Prominent silver markings on the oval, quilted-looking dark green leaves explain the common name. Leaves are 3 in. long; plant grows erect to 12–15 in. tall, 6–9 in. wide. Pinch periodically to induce bushiness. Dwarf 'Minima' is less than half the size of the species.

P. involucrata. FRIENDSHIP PLANT. Perennial. Native to Central and South America. Grows just 1 in. tall, spreading to 1 ft. wide. Broadly oval, tooth-edged, heavily quilted leaves to 1½ in. long are bronzy green above, purplish beneath. Pinch periodically to induce bushiness. 'Moon Valley' is more upright, to 1 ft. tall and wide, with larger green leaves featuring prominent bronze veins.

P. microphylla. ARTILLERY PLANT. Annual or short-lived perennial. From Florida, Mexico, West Indies, South America. Trailing, succulent stems form a mound to 1 ft. tall and somewhat

wider. Bright green oval, tiny leaves (¼–½ in. long) are crowded along the wandering stems. Tiny flowers eject pollen forcefully, hence the common name. Outdoors, can spread widely and become a pest. 'Variegata' has leaves variegated with white, pink, and green.

P. nummulariifolia. CREEPING CHARLIE. Perennial. Native to West Indies and Panama, south to northern South America. Fast-growing, trailing plant to 6 in. tall and 2 ft. wide; perfect for hanging baskets. Roots at the nodes and spreads to make a good ground cover where hardy. Rounded light green leaves to about 1̂ in. wide are deeply quilted, with prominent veins and scalloped edges.

CARE

Indoors, they like bright, indirect light and high humidity. Make sure soil is well drained, and let it go somewhat dry between thorough soakings. Feed every other week in spring and summer and once a month in fall and winter with liquid houseplant fertilizer. Mealybugs are common pests; dispatch them by dabbing with a cotton swab dipped in alcohol.

PIMPINELLA ANISUM
ANISE
Apiaceae
Annual

🌡 US, MS, LS, CS, TS; USDA 6-11

☀ FULL SUN

💧 REGULAR WATER

Pimpinella anisum

Mediterranean native to 2 ft. tall, 1½ ft. wide. First growth produces a clump of bright green, roundish to heart-shaped, tooth-edged leaves. Foliage clumps send up stems set with feathery leaves; in summer, stems bear umbrellalike clusters of tiny white flowers at their tips. Use fresh leaves in salads; use seeds for flavoring baked goods, confections.

CARE

Grow in light, well-drained soil. Plants are fairly wispy and look better when grouped. They develop taproots and do not transplant easily once they pass the seedling stage. Not usually browsed by deer.

Intolerance for heat and humidity makes this herb difficult to grow in much of the South. In the Upper and Middle South (USDA 6-7), sow seeds ½ in. deep in the garden after the last spring frost—or get a head start by sowing seeds indoors in peat pots four weeks before the last frost, then planting outdoors once the weather has warmed. Plants take about four months to mature. In the Lower, Coastal, and Tropical South (USDA 8-11) sow seeds in the garden in autumn; plants will grow through the winter and flower in spring. Seed production in these areas is iffy.

PINEAPPLE

Bromeliaceae
Perennial

🌿 **TS; USDA 10-11; OR GROW IN POTS**

☼ **FULL SUN FOR FRUIT; BRIGHT LIGHT**

💧 **REGULAR WATER**

Pineapple

Native to South America, this familiar bromeliad is known botanically as *Ananas comosus*. Reaches 2–3 ft. tall, 1½–2 ft. wide,

with a short, thick stem topped by a rosette of long (1½- to 6-ft.), narrow, dark green leaves with saw-toothed edges. At bloom time, the stem lengthens and produces a head of small red or purple flowers, which eventually develops into the pineapple fruit. Fruit is typically borne one per stem.

To grow pineapple, cut the leafy top from a market pineapple (cut about an inch below the leaves). Root in water or fast-draining but moisture-retentive potting mix. When roots have formed, move pineapple to an 8-in. pot of rich soil. Plant will overwinter only in the Tropical South (USDA 10-11); elsewhere, grow it as a full-time houseplant or move it indoors in winter. Water when soil goes dry; feed every three or four weeks with a general-purpose liquid houseplant fertilizer. If you're lucky, fruit will form in about two years, but it will be much smaller than a typical market pineapple.

'Variegatus', with pink, white, and olive-green leaves, is sometimes sold as a houseplant; it can take reduced light, since it is grown for foliage rather than fruit. It will fruit outside, however.

PINUS

PINE
Pinaceae
Evergreen trees, rarely shrubs

🌿 **ZONES VARY BY SPECIES**

☼ **FULL SUN**

💧 **LITTLE TO REGULAR WATER, EXCEPT AS NOTED**

Pinus taeda

It's hard to escape pines if you live in the South. And few of us would

want to. The native longleaf pine (*Pinus palustris*) is just as iconic to the region as is the live oak (*Quercus virginiana*). As a group, these conifers are much better adapted to our soils and climate than firs (*Abies*) and spruces (*Picea*). They tolerate heat, humidity, drought, clay, and sand. Many become tall, graceful shade trees, providing filtered light to gardens below and "whisper" as the wind blows through the needles. Others featuring weeping, creeping, or dwarf forms make excellent garden accents.

Differences in cone size and shape offer one way to tell these trees apart; another identifying characteristic is the number of needles in a bundle (pines bear their needles in clusters, or "bundles," on the branches). Most species carry their long, slender needles in groups of two, three, or five. Those with two needles tend to tolerate unfavorable soil and climate better than three-needle species, and three-needle pines more so than five-needle ones.

Young trees tend to be pyramidal, while older ones are more open or round topped. Seeds of all pines attract birds; some species produce the pine nuts enjoyed by people and sold commercially.

P. bungeana. LACEBARK PINE. Zones US, MS; USDA 6-7. Hardy to -20°F. From northern and central China. Grows 50–75 ft. tall, 20–35 ft. wide. Slow growing. Starts out pyramidal to rounded, then becomes more open, spreading, and picturesque. Often multi-trunked, sometimes shrubby. Smooth, dull gray bark flakes off to reveal creamy white patches. Bright green needles in groups of three are 2–4 in. long. Cones are up to 2½ in. long and yellowish brown. Limbs are brittle, can break under heavy ice or snow load. 'Great Wall' is a dense, pyramidal form.

P. cembroides. MEXICAN PINYON PINE. Zones US, MS, LS; USDA 6-8. From Arizona to Baja, California, and northern Mexico. Grows slowly to 10–20 ft. tall, nearly as wide. Rather rangy in youth; in older trees stout, spreading branches form a round-topped head. Dark green needles in groups of two or three are 1–2 in. long. Cones are 1–2 in.

long, rounded, and yellowish or reddish brown. Very drought tolerant and adapted to poor, rocky, limy soils. Good choice for drier areas of Texas and Oklahoma. Cones contain edible seeds (pine nuts).

P. clausa. SAND PINE. Zones LS, CS, TS; USDA 8-11. From the Gulf Coast and coastal areas of Florida. Grows moderately to 30–40 ft. tall and 15–20 ft. wide. Slender and upright with an irregular crown. Dark green needles in groups of two are 2–3½ in. long. Cones are 2–3 in. long; ovoid-conic. Good in sandy soils along the coast.

P. echinata. SHORTLEAF PINE. Zones US, MS, LS, CS; USDA 6-9. From dry, upland soils of Georgia, Oklahoma, and Texas. Fast growing to 50–80 ft. tall and 30–45 ft. wide. Open, pyramidal habit when mature, with sinuous branches. Dark, bluish green needles in groups of two or three and 3–5 in. long. Pale brown cones are 1½–2½ in. long; ovoid-oblong. Important timber species. Adaptable but deep rooted and difficult to move once established. Good lawn tree. Resistant to most insects and diseases that affect other pines.

P. eldarica (*P. brutia eldarica*). AFGHAN PINE. Zones US, MS, LS, CS; USDA 6-9. From southern Russia, Afghanistan, and Pakistan. Grows fast to 30–80 ft. tall, 15–30 ft. wide. Dense, erect habit, somewhat rounded with age. Dark green needles in groups of two reach 5–6½ in. long. Cones are oval to oblong, 3 in. long, reddish brown. Thrives in heat, wind, and poor soil. Well adapted to the Southwest. Often grown there for Christmas trees.

P. elliotti. SLASH PINE. Zones LS, CS, TS; USDA 8-11. From the Coastal Plain from South Carolina to Florida and west to eastern Louisiana. Fast growing, possibly to 80 ft. high and 35 ft. wide. Dense, rounded crown. Dark green, stiff needles in groups of two or three are up to 1 ft. long. Shiny brown cones to 3½–6 in. long. Usually planted for quick shade or erosion control. Adapted to acid-soil areas of east Texas. *P. e. densa* thrives in southern Florida.

P. glabra. SPRUCE PINE. Zones LS, CS; USDA 8-9. From South Carolina to Louisiana. Grows to 40–60 ft. high and 30 ft. wide.

P

HOW TO GROW PINES

DRAINAGE Well-drained soil is crucial to a pine's good health. In nature, many pines grow on rocky slopes or sandy barrens, where drainage is very fast. Symptoms of excessive moisture are yellowing needles (seen first in older growth) and a generally unhealthy appearance. Most pines are quite drought tolerant; exceptions are noted in the descriptions.

MULCHING Pines benefit from a thick layer of mulch to protect their shallow roots. Spread 2–3 in. of organic mulch beneath trees, but keep it 6 in. away from the trunk. Pine straw gives the most natural look.

FEEDING Pines need little if any fertilizer; heavy feeding encourages too rapid, rank growth.

PRUNING All pines can be shaped, and often improved, by some pruning. The best time to prune is in spring, when new growth emerges. Cut the "candles" (upright shoots of new growth) to promote bushiness or limit the plant's size. Cutting back partway will promote bushiness and allow some overall increase in size; cutting out candles entirely will limit size without distorting the natural shape. This kind of careful pruning can even allow you to maintain pines as screens or hedges. You can remove unwanted limbs to accent a pine's branching pattern—but before you cut out a branch, remember that a new one won't sprout to take its place. Avoid cutting back branches to bare stubs, as those will not produce new foliage. In time, lower limbs of most pines will die naturally; when this happens, cut them off.

CHALLENGES Pines are vulnerable to air pollution, which causes abnormal needle drop and poor growth and may even kill the tree. Numerous pests can attack pines, including aphids, spider mites, pine tip moths, pine sawflies, spittlebugs, and scale. A healthy tree can usually cope; those weakened by drought, air pollution, compacted soil, or cut roots are at greater risk. Most five-needle pines are susceptible to white pine blister rust, a disease that can kill the tree. Pine bark beetles have devastated stands of loblolly (*P. taeda*), slash (*P. elliottii*), and shortleaf (*P. echinata*) pines in the Southeast: Needles turn brown, trunks ooze sap, and trees die. Trees stressed by environmental conditions are most susceptible. Infested trees cannot be saved; promptly removing and burning them is the best control. Your Cooperative Extension Service can also offer advice concerning each species' adaptability to your area and any local environmental or pest problems. Pines are not usually browsed by deer.

TOP: Pinus strobus 'Louie'; BOTTOM: P. mugo mugo; P. thunbergii

Horizontal branching at the top of trunk with a rounded crown. Branches low, casting heavy shade. Difficult to grow grass under. Dark green, twisted needles in groups of two are 2–3½ in. long. Buff-colored cones to 2–2½ in. long; ovoid. Likes fertile, moist, acid soil but tolerates heavy clay. Widely planted in Lower South (USDA 8) east of the Mississippi River.

P. mugo. MUGO PINE, SWISS MOUNTAIN PINE. Zones US, MS; USDA 6-7. From the mountains of central and southern Europe. This slow-growing, extremely variable species can reach 75 ft. tall, but smaller forms offered in nurseries and garden centers tend to be

shrubby and symmetrical. Dark green needles to 3 in. long are held in groups of two, crowded on the branches. Cones to 2½ in. long are tawny to dark brown. Durable and adaptable. Moderate to regular water.

Look for named selections to ensure uniformity in size and shape. All look best if left to grow naturally; choose plants with a pleasingly rounded form rather than trying to shape them later through pruning.

'Big Tuna' is dense and upright, to 10 ft. tall and 6–8 ft. wide. 'Gnom' forms a tight globe just 2½ ft. high and wide after 10 years. The popular dwarf 'Mops' forms

a dense mound to 2–3 ft. high and wide; needles take on a golden cast in winter. 'Slow-mound' is dense and slow growing to 1–2 ft. high and wide in 10 years. 'Tannenbaum' grows slowly into a dense Christmas-tree shape about 10 ft. tall and 6 ft. wide. The Pumilio Group includes several compact selections. Selections with golden needles are also available.

P. mugo mugo, dwarf mugo pine, is widely offered. It is low growing, usually topping out at 4–8 ft. tall and up to twice as wide. Excellent performer but quite variable in habit.

P. palustris. LONGLEAF PINE. Zones MS, LS, CS, TS; USDA 7-11. From Virginia to Florida and west to Mississippi, southeastern coast. Slow growing for 5–10 years, then fast to 55–80 ft. tall and 25–30 ft.

wide. Young plants look like fountains of grass. With age, gaunt, sparse branches ascend to form an open, oblong head. Dark green needles in groups of three are 1½ ft. long in youth (called grass stage) and replaced by 9-in. needles when mature. Cones are 6–10 in. long and dull brown. Prefers deep soils (grows on sandy ridges in its native range). The classic, graceful pine of the South.

P. parviflora. JAPANESE WHITE PINE. Zones US, MS; USDA 6-7. From Japan and Taiwan. Slow to moderate grower to 20–50 ft. tall and wide or larger. In youth, a dense pyramid; with age, wide spreading and flat topped. Needles are 1½–2½ in. long, bluish green, and held in groups of five. Reddish brown cones are 2–3 in. long. Widely used and popular as bonsai subject, container tree. 'Bergman' has thin, blue-green needles and an upright habit; grows 6 ft. tall, 4 ft. wide, in 10 years. 'Glauca Brevifolia' has short, blue-green needles and persistent dark cones; upright and broad, it grows to an eventual 40 ft. tall and wide. Many other blue-gray and dwarf forms are available. Regular water.

P. strobus. WHITE PINE, EASTERN WHITE PINE. Zones US, MS; USDA 6-7. From Newfoundland to Manitoba, south to Georgia and west to Illinois and Iowa. Slow in seedling stage, then fast to 50–80 ft. tall (or taller), 20–40 ft. wide. Forms a symmetrical pyramid, with horizontal branches in regular whorls. Becomes broad, open, and irregular with age. Fine-textured, handsome tree. Blue-green needles are soft, 3–5½ in. long, held in groups of five. Light brown cones reach 3–8 in. long. Intolerant of strong winds. Needs regular water and excellent drainage. Popular Christmas tree. 'Contorta' has twisted branches and needles. 'Angel Falls' and 'Pendula' have weeping, trailing branches. 'Niagara Falls' is also weeping, but with a very broad, cascading habit. 'Blue Shag' is a blue-needled form. 'Louie' has bright-yellow needles in fall.

Plants in the Nana group are broad shrubs, growing slowly to 3–7 ft. tall, 6–12 ft. wide. Useful in rock gardens or containers, though plants sold under this name have been known to grow into small trees.

P. sylvestris. SCOTCH PINE. Zones US, MS; USDA 6-7. From northern Europe, western Asia, northeastern Siberia. Grows fast at first, then moderately to 30–70 ft. (possibly to 100 ft.) tall and 25–30 ft. wide. Forms a narrow, well-branched pyramid when young. With age, becomes irregular, open, and picturesque, with drooping branches. Stiff, 1½- to 3-in.-long, blue-green needles often turn yellow-green in winter. Cones to 2 in. long are gray to reddish brown. Popular as a Christmas tree and in gardens. Showy red bark, sparse foliage in maturity. Deer and wind resistant. Needs regular water in hottest areas, moderate water elsewhere.

Plants in the Aurea group take on bright golden tones in winter. 'French Blue' keeps its blue color throughout the cold months. Handsome and dense 'Fastigiata' grows slowly to 20–30 ft. tall and just 4–6 ft. wide. 'Inverleith', to 40–60 ft. tall and 20–25 ft. wide, sports needles tipped in creamy white. Dwarf forms include rounded 'Beuvronensis', blue-green 'Glauca Nana', and relatively fast-growing 'Watereri'. 'Hillside Creeper' is well named; it grows to 2 ft. high and 8 ft. wide in 10 years and makes an interesting ground cover.

P. taeda. LOBLOLLY PINE. Zones US, MS, LS, CS; USDA 6-9. From southern New Jersey to Florida, east Texas, and Oklahoma. Fast growing to 50–90 ft. tall and 30–40 ft. wide. Loose, cone shape in youth; as it matures, loses lower branches to become a rather opened crowned tree. Dark yellowish green needles are 6–10 in. long and grouped in threes (rarely twos). Rust-brown, oval to narrowly conical cones are 3–6 in. long in clusters of two to five. Tough tree; withstands poor soils. Useful in Lower South (USDA 8) for quick screening and shade. Adapted to acid soils of east Texas. Widely planted for pulp lumber. Provides light shade; good to garden under. Old favorite in the South.

P. thunbergii. JAPANESE BLACK PINE. Zones US, MS, LS; USDA 6-8. From Japan. Grows at a moderate rate to 20–40 ft. tall and 15–20 ft. wide. Spreading branches form a broad, conical tree; irregular and spreading in age, often with a leaning trunk. Bright green needles are stiff, 3–4½ in. long, held in groups of two; new growth (candles) nearly white. Brown cones grow to about 3 in. long. Handsome tree that can be sheared as a Christmas tree or pruned as a cascade or giant bonsai. Regular water in hottest areas. Very salt tolerant but subject to nematodes. 'Majestic Beauty' has good form and tolerates smog and salt. Dwarf 'Thunderhead' (6 ft. tall, 5 ft. wide in 10 years) has dark foliage and white candles that are eye-catching in spring.

P. virginiana. VIRGINIA PINE, SCRUB PINE. Zones US, MS, LS; USDA 6-8. From New York to Georgia and Alabama. Slow growing to 45–55 ft. tall and 30–40 ft. wide. Broad, open, sparsely branched habit with wide, stiff top. Yellow-green to dark green, twisted needles are 1¼–4 in. long and grouped in twos. Persistant, 3-in.-long, conical to ovoid cones in clusters of two to four. Seldom used as an ornamental but valuable in clay or poor soils. Popular cut Christmas tree in the Lower South (USDA 8). Adapts to most well-drained soils.

P. wallichiana. HIMALAYAN WHITE PINE. Zones US, MS; USDA 6-7. From the Himalayas. Slow to moderate growth to 30–50 ft. tall, 15–30 ft. wide; much larger in the wild. Broad and conical, it often retains branches to the ground even in age. Gracefully drooping, soft-looking, blue-green needles 6–8 in. long are held in groups of five. Cones are 6–10 in. long and light brown. Good form and color make this a fine choice for featured pine in a big lawn or garden. 'Nana' is dense and upright, to about 3 ft. high and wide after 10 years. 'Zebrina' has needles banded in yellow, giving the plant an overall glow.

PISTACIA

PISTACHE
Anacardiaceae
Large semievergreen to deciduous trees, shrubs

🌡 **ZONES VARY BY SPECIES**

☼ ◑ **EXPOSURE NEEDS VARY BY SPECIES**

◊ ◑ ● **WATER NEEDS VARY BY SPECIES**

Pistacia chinensis

Though the nut-bearing *Pistacia vera* is the best-known pistachio, the two ornamental species described here (*P. chinensis* and *P. texana*) are far more useful in most of the South. Leaves are divided into leaflets; flowers are insignificant. Trees may be either male or female; if a male is nearby, females bear clusters of tiny fruit in fall. Young trees tend to be irregular in form and benefit from early training and pruning.

P. chinensis. CHINESE PISTACHE. Deciduous tree. US, MS, LS, CS; USDA 6-9. Native to China. Fast becoming a favorite lawn, shade, and street tree in the South due to its quick growth, ease of care, adaptability, and outstanding and dependable fall color. Develops an oval to rounded shape, 30–35 ft. tall and wide. Foot-long leaves consist of 10 to 12 leaflets, 2–4 in. long, that change from lustrous dark green to brilliant scarlet, orange, and yellow in fall. Female tree bears small fruit that ripens from red to robin's-egg blue in October.

Plant in full sun for best growth and fall color. Tolerates almost any well-drained soil. Quite drought tolerant and pest-resistant. Also tolerates pollution, making it a good choice for urban settings. Its filtered shade allows grass to grow beneath it.

P. texana. TEXAS PISTACHIO. Large, semievergreen to deciduous shrub or small multitrunked tree. Zones LS, CS, TS; USDA 8-11. Native to Texas. Grows 20–30 ft. tall, rarely to 40 ft.; eventually a bit wider than tall. Makes a feathery screen or, if cut back annually when young to promote dense habit, a fine-textured hedge. Female plants bear attractive red berries. Leaves have 7 to 21 oval, pointed leaflets; they have a reddish cast when new, then mature to glossy dark green. Foliage persists late into winter (plant is semievergreen where temperatures stay above 15°F). Does well with moderate water but grows faster with regular water. Thrives in regular garden soil but is well adapted to a range of conditions, including limestone and caliche, provided drainage is good. Partial shade or full sun.

P. vera. PISTACHIO, PISTACHIO NUT. Deciduous tree. Zone LS; USDA 8. From Iran. Broad, bushy tree to 30 ft. tall and at least as wide. Gray-green leaves have three to five roundish, 2- to 4-in.-long leaflets. Reddish, wrinkled fruit in heavy clusters. Needs low humidity; chilly winters; and long, hot, dry summers to perform well. This limits pistachio production in the South to parts of West Texas. To get nuts, include a male tree in your planting; 'Peters' is the most widely planted male selection. 'Kerman' is the principal fruiting (female) type.

When planting, avoid rough handling; budded tops are easily broken away from rootstock. Pistachios are inclined to spread and droop; stake them and train branches to good framework of four or five limbs beginning at 4 ft. above ground. Established trees need little watering. Full sun.

PISTIA STRATIOTES
WATER LETTUCE
Araceae
Aquatic perennial, usually treated as annual

- 🍃 **LS, CS, TS; USDA 8-11**
- ☼ ◑ **FULL SUN OR LIGHT SHADE**
- 💧 **LOCATE IN PONDS, WATER GARDENS**

Pistia stratiotes

Native to tropical regions. Attractive plant that resembles a floating, grayish green, loose-leaf lettuce; each foliage rosette grows to about 4 in. high and wide. The trailing roots provide a refuge for small fish. Inconspicuous flowers. Reproduces rapidly by offsets and seeds and is now considered a serious pest in many lakes, rivers, and coastal waters of Florida, Georgia, South Carolina, Mississippi, and Texas. Can survive temperatures as low as 15°F. Be careful not to let it escape into the wild.

PITTOSPORUM
Pittosporaceae
Evergreen shrubs or small trees

- 🍃 **ZONES VARY BY SPECIES**
- ☼ ◑ **FULL SUN OR PARTIAL SHADE**
- 💧💧 **MODERATE TO REGULAR WATER**

Pittosporum tobira
'Wheeler's Dwarf'

These plants are valued primarily for their foliage and form, though they also bear clusters of small, bell-shaped, sweetly fragrant flowers in early spring, followed by fairly conspicuous fruit the size of large peas. They are basic, dependable plants with pleasing outlines when allowed to branch naturally. Prune periodically to enhance form, thinning out weak branches and wayward shoots. They make good clipped hedges. Excellent for screens, windbreaks. Susceptible to aphids and scale; sooty mold on leaves is a sign of infestation. Ripe fruit (yellowish or orange) splits open to reveal sticky seeds; fallen fruit can be a nuisance on lawns and paving.

P. heterophyllum. CHINESE PITTOSPORUM. Zones MS, LS, CS; USDA 7-9. From China. Hardier than Japanese pittosporum. Glossy, green leaves are 1–1½ in. long and usually diamond shaped. Small, white, fragrant flowers fade to yellow. Usually grows 6–10 ft. tall and wide but can form a small tree up to 15 ft. if left unpruned. Tough plant. Useful as hedge or background. 'Variegatus' has small leaves edged with creamy white. Smaller growing and less hardy than species. 'Winter Frost' is similar if not identical.

P. tobira. JAPANESE PITTOSPORUM. Zones LS, CS, TS; USDA 8-11. From Japan. Dense, rounded shrub, eventually reaching 10–15 ft. tall and wide if not restricted by pruning. Lower limbs can be removed from older plants to make small trees. Whorls of leathery, narrowly elliptical, shiny, dark green leaves to 5 in. long. Creamy white flowers, borne at branch tips, smell like orange blossoms. Very tolerant of seacoast conditions. One of the few plants that will thrive on dunes. 'Variegatum', whitespot Japanese pittosporum, grows 5–10 ft. high and wide, with gray-green leaves edged in white; 'Turner's Variegated Dwarf' has the same leaf color but reaches only 2–3 ft. high and wide. 'Cream de Mint' forms a compact mound 2–2½ ft. high and wide, with mint-green leaves that are edged in creamy white. 'Mojo' grows 3 ft. high and wide with dense variegated foliage. 'Wheeler's Dwarf' grows 3–4 ft. high and a little wider; it is not as hardy as the species (may die at 10°F), but it (and other dwarf types) can be moved indoors where winters are cold (site in bright light and water sparingly while indoors).

PLATANUS
SYCAMORE, PLANE TREE
Platanaceae
Deciduous trees

- 🍃 **ZONES VARY BY SPECIES**
- ☼ **FULL SUN**
- 💧 **REGULAR WATER**

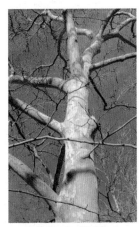

Platanus occidentalis

All are large, with heavy trunk (or trunks) and sculptural branch pattern. Older bark sheds in irregular patches to reveal creamy, smooth new bark beneath. Big, rough-surfaced, bright green leaves (to 10 in. across) have three to five lobes, resemble maple (*Acer*) leaves. Fall foliage color is yellowish to brown, not striking. Ball-shaped brown seed clusters, usually on threadlike stalks, hang on the bare branches through winter; these are prized for winter arrangements. Plane trees do best in rich, deep, moist, well-drained soil. All are subject to anthracnose, which causes early leaf drop and twig dieback. Rake up and dispose of dead leaves, since fungus spores can overwinter on them.

P. hispanica (*P.* x *acerifolia*) LONDON PLANE TREE. Zones US, MS, LS; USDA 6-8. Hybrid between *P. occidentalis* and *P. orientalis*. Grows 30–40 ft. tall in 20 years; it may reach 70–100 ft. tall, 65–80 ft. wide in gardens. Smooth, cream-colored upper trunk and limbs. Handsome in winter. Tolerates many soils, city smog, soot, dust, reflected heat. Susceptible to powdery mildew. Good avenue, street tree. Can fit smaller spaces when pollarded to create a low, dense canopy. 'Columbia' and 'Liberty' are resistant to both anthracnose and powdery mildew and somewhat resistant to cankerstain disease, which can kill branches or the entire tree. 'Exclamation' ('Morton Circle') is an upright, pyramidal grower to 50 ft. tall, 30 ft. wide; resists anthracnose. 'Bloodgood' resists anthracnose; 'Yarwood' is mildew resistant.

P. mexicana. MEXICAN SYCAMORE. Zones LS, CS, TS; USDA 8-11. Native to northeastern Mexico. To 60 ft. tall, not quite as wide. Five-lobed, smooth-edged leaves are about 8 in. wide, with felty white undersides. Well adapted to dry, rocky, alkaline soils of the Southwest.

P. occidentalis. AMERICAN SYCAMORE, AMERICAN PLANE TREE. Zones US, MS, LS, CS; USDA 6-9. Very hardy. Native to the South and north to Maine and Minnesota. Similar to *P.* x *acerifolia* but has whiter new bark and a longer leafless period. Tree is spectacular viewed against blue sky in winter. Irregular habit, contorted branches. Occasionally grows with multiple or leaning trunks; good climbing tree. In the wild, populations naturally follow streams. Old trees sometimes reach 100 ft. or more in height and spread. Because of its size

and habit of dropping bark, seedballs, and leaves year-round, it's not a good choice for small properties.

PLATYCERIUM
STAGHORN FERN
Polypodiaceae
Ferns

🌡 **TS; USDA 10-11, EXCEPT AS NOTED**

◑ **PARTIAL SHADE**

💧 **REGULAR WATER**

Platycerium bifurcatum

Native to tropical regions, where they grow on trees; gardeners grow them on slabs of bark or tree fern stem, occasionally in hanging baskets or attached to trees. They do best with regular moisture, though they can dry out briefly without suffering damage.

These ferns have two kinds of fronds. Sterile ones are pale green in color, aging to tan and brown; they support the plant and accumulate organic matter to help feed it. Fertile fronds vary in color from gray-green to deep green; they are forked, resembling spreading antlers held either erect or pendent. For plants growing on slabs, be sure to water behind the sterile frond that attaches it to the slab.

P. bifurcatum. STAGHORN FERN. Zones CS, TS; USDA 9-11. From Australia and New Guinea. Most common type and easiest to grow. Clustered, gray-green fertile fronds to 3 ft. long. Makes numerous offsets, which can be used in propagation.

P. hillii. ELK'S-HORN FERN. From Australia. Similar to *P. bifurcatum*. Kidney-shaped

sterile fronds grow like plaques behind the fertile fronds, which fan out almost horizontally; they resemble deep green fingers to 3 ft. long, with forked tips.

P. superbum. GIANT STAGHORN FERN. From Australia. Grayish green fertile fronds may reach 6 ft. long. Both fertile and sterile fronds are forked; fertile ones are broad but divided somewhat like moose antlers. Protect plants from frosts. Sensitive to overwatering.

PLATYCODON GRANDIFLORUS
BALLOON FLOWER
Campanulaceae
Perennial

🌡 **US, MS, LS, CS; USDA 6-9**

☼ ◑ **FULL SUN TO LIGHT SHADE**

💧 **REGULAR WATER**

Platycodon grandiflorus

Attractive, easy-to-grow, pest-free plant from Siberia, Japan, and northern China. To 3 ft. tall and 2 ft. wide. Inflated, balloonlike buds are carried on slender stalks at the ends of upright stems clad in broadly oval, 1- to 3-in. leaves. Buds open into 2-in., star-shaped, blue-violet flowers with purple veins. Bloom begins in early summer and will continue for two months or more if spent blossoms (but not entire stems) are removed. Double-flowered types are available, as well as pink- and white-flowered types.

Blooms of 'Shell Pink' and 'Mother of Pearl' are soft pink. 'Astra Pink' has soft pink flowers and grows 6–12 in high. 'Astra Blue' is very dwarf to only 4 in. tall with small blue flowers. 'Fairy Snow' has clear white flowers on

a 6- to 10-in.-tall plant. 'Hakone Blue' bears double, bright blue flowers on stems reaching 18–24 in. tall. 'Komachi' bears clear blue blossoms that maintain their balloon shape, never opening fully. 'Mariesii', a dwarf to only 1–1½ ft., also bears rich blue blossoms. 'Misato Purple' has deep purple flowers and grows just 8 in. tall. 'Sentimental Blue' has upward-facing blue flowers and grows 6–12 in. tall.

Plant is deep rooted and takes two or three years to get well established. Dies back completely in fall, and new growth appears quite late in spring; mark position to avoid digging up fleshy roots. If you do unearth a root, replant it—or the pieces—right away. Protect roots from gophers and voles by planting in buried wire cages.

BALLOON FLOWER IN BORDERS

With its round buds, graceful star-shaped blossoms, and long bloom season, balloon flower is a nice choice for a summer border. Companion plants in shades of pink, yellow, deep to light blue, and white make for a lovely color combination; try astilbe, various kinds of yarrow (*Achillea*), phlox, coral bells (*Heuchera*), and mallow (*Malva*). Lush foliage plants such as hosta are good partners, too.

PLECTRANTHUS

Lamiaceae

Perennials and evergreen shrubs; often grown as annuals

🌡 **TS; USDA 10-11; OR HOUSE-PLANTS, EXCEPT AS NOTED**

◐ **PARTIAL SHADE, EXCEPT AS NOTED; BRIGHT INDIRECT LIGHT**

💧 **REGULAR WATER**

Plectranthus argentatus

Close relatives of coleus; native to many tropical regions of the world. They have square stems, opposite pairs of fleshy, tooth-edged or scalloped leaves, and whorls of tubular, two-lipped blossoms. Some are highly aromatic, used as seasonings or home remedies. Others are grown for their attractive foliage, yet others for their striking floral displays. Some are good bedding plants for summer color; some make dense, weed-suppressing ground covers for frost-protected areas. Several are trailing plants that drape gracefully from hanging baskets or wall pots. All are superb in containers, either alone or in combination with other plants.

P. argentatus and *P. fruticosus* are the shrubbiest of the species listed here, but the others get somewhat woody at the base after a year or more. Pinch all types to induce branching; discard old plants when they become leggy or too woody, and start new ones.

P. amboinicus (*Coleus amboinicus*). CUBAN OREGANO, SPANISH THYME, INDIAN MINT. From Africa. Summer-blooming trailer to 1 ft. high, 3 ft. wide, with white, lilac-pink, or light purple flowers in 6-in. spikes. Velvety, ovate, gray-green leaves are 3 in.

long, with broadly toothed edges. Popular in Cuban cooking, with a fragrance that falls midway between oregano and thyme but has a sweet note not present in either. Leaves of 'Variegatus' are bordered in cream, with the very edge often tinged bright pink; excellent flavor. 'Well-Sweep Wedgwood', with extra-sweet flavor, has Wedgwood blue flowers and leaves in chartreuse and gray-green with a dark green margin.

P. argentatus. SILVER SPUR-FLOWER. From Australia. Erect to spreading plant to 3 ft. tall, 6 ft. or wider. Densely hairy, scallop-edged, oval leaves to 7 in. long are silvery gray-green, with a light purplish flush on growing tips and stems. Pink-tinged white flowers in foot-long spikes in late summer, fall. Best in at least half-day direct sun; will take hot afternoon sun if adequately watered. 'Silver Shield' is more compact to 24–30 in. tall, has bluish white flowers, and leaves with a silvery sheen.

P. ciliatus. From southern Africa. Handsome, burgundy-stemmed trailer to 6–12 in. high, 3–5 ft. wide. Excellent dense ground cover. Blooms in late summer and fall, with white or purplish flowers in 8- to 12-in. spikes. Oval leaves to 3½ in. long, with finely toothed edges and pointed tips; leaves have deep green upper surfaces, burgundy undersides and veins. 'Old Gold' leaves are yellow or chartreuse

above, burgundy beneath; new leaves are flushed with burgundy. 'Tricolor' is similar, but tops of leaves also have dark green splotches. Both selections have white blooms. 'Lemon Twist' has leaves edged yellow with lemony fragrance.

P. cylindraceus. VICK'S PLANT, MENTHOLATO. Zones CS, TS; USDA 9-11. From Africa. Mounding growth to 1½–3 ft. high, 2–4 ft. wide. Sometimes blooms, bearing blue or lavender flowers in dense, narrow, pointed spikes 12–15 in. long (there may be a pair of shorter spikes near base). Velvety, triangular, gray-green leaves 1½–3 in. long, with three to five broad teeth on each side of leaf. Foliage smells like a combination of camphor and menthol and is used medicinally in Mexico.

P. ecklonii. Zones LS, CS, TS; USDA 8-11. From south Africa. Tender, multistemmed shrub growing 4–6 ft. tall. Very showy blue-purple flower spikes, 6–12 in. tall, top plant in fall. Pink- and white-flowering forms exist. Cut back to 10 in. in winter.

P. forsteri. From Australia, Fiji, New Caledonia. To 10 in. high, 3 ft. wide; stems actually grow 3 ft. tall, but they arch over from weight of foliage. Tip-pinch early to induce branching; repeat to keep compact. Medium green, ovate, irregularly toothed leaves to 4 in. long. White or pale mauve flowers in 6- to 8-in. spikes are produced intermittently throughout the

ABOVE: Plectranthus ecklonii

year. Leaves of 'Marginatus' (*P. coleoides* 'Marginata') are irregularly edged in creamy white. 'Green and Gold' has lime-green leaves with a neat gold margin.

P. madagascariensis. MINTLEAF. From southern Africa. Vigorous trailer reaches 1 ft. high; spreads 3–4 ft. wide initially, eventually much wider by rooting at leaf joints. Medium green leaves to 2 in. long are hairy, roundish, scallop edged; they smell like mint when crushed. Lavender-blue or white flower spikes in late spring, early summer. 'Variegated Mintleaf', the most commonly grown form, has irregular white leaf margins. Good ground cover to brighten shady areas. Often mistakenly sold as *Iboza*, another genus in the same family.

P. 'Mona Lavender'. Hybrid developed in South Africa. Multistemmed plant to 2–3 ft. tall and wide, with deep purple stems holding glossy, deep green, coarsely toothed leaves with purple-bronze veins and undersides. Leaves reach 2 in. long, 1 in. wide. Lavender-blue flowers with darker flecks, borne in 6-in. spikes, appear continuously in warm weather. Great as a bedding plant or grown in containers.

P. oertendahlii. MOSAIC SWEDISH IVY, ROYAL CHARLIE, CANDLE PLANT. From South Africa. Easy-care specimen for hanging basket or pot; most often grown as houseplant. To 8–12 in. high, with branches trailing to 1½–2 ft. long. Roundish, irregularly toothed, velvety dark green leaves up to 2½ in. long, with purple undersides and intricate network of silver veins. In autumn, white or light blue flowers bloom in loose, 8- to 12-in.-long spikes. Foliage of 'Uvongo' is more heavily netted with silver than that of the species; leaves of 'Variegatus' are irregularly edged in creamy white.

P. saccatus. From South Africa. Woody-based plant to 1½–3 ft. high and wide. Green, almost canelike stems are set with fragrant, nearly triangular, bright green leaves with prominently toothed edges. Large blue to lilac (sometimes white) flowers bloom in midsummer.

P. verticillatus. SWEDISH IVY, CREEPING CHARLIE. From southern Africa. Typically grown in hanging basket or pot in the house or outdoors; also makes a good ground cover in a warm, protected spot. To 4–8 in. high, 4–6 ft. wide, with trailing branches. Waxy, shiny, dark green, scallop-edged leaves are roundish, up to 1½ in. across. White or pale purplish blossoms in 8-in. spikes bloom intermittently all year. To grow as a ground cover, plant cuttings 1–2 ft. apart for quick coverage. 'Marmoratus' produces leaves irregularly marked with ivory.

CARE

Easy to grow. Stems take root wherever they touch the ground, and cuttings root quickly in soil or water. Remove flower spikes after they fade. Site houseplants in a bright window, but protect from hottest sun; keep moist, and apply a general-purpose liquid houseplant fertilizer monthly in spring and summer. Stop fertilizing and reduce watering in fall and winter.

PLUM

Rosaceae
Deciduous fruit trees

ZONES VARY BY SELECTION

FULL SUN

MODERATE TO REGULAR WATER

SEE CHART PAGE 512

'Stanley' plums

Like their cherry, peach, and apricot relatives, these are stone fruits belonging to the genus *Prunus*; for flowering plums, see page 524. Three categories of edible plums are grown in the diverse climates of North America: European, Japanese, and native species. Plants bloom in late winter or early spring.

Harvest season is from June into September, depending on type and selection.

The two most widely grown groups in the South are European plums (*P. domestica*) and Japanese plums (*P. salicina*). Prunes are European plum selections with a high sugar content, a trait that allows them to be sun dried without fermenting at the pit.

Plums come in many colors—both inside and out. The skin may be yellow, red, purple, green, blue, or almost black; the flesh may be yellow, red, orange, or green. Japanese plums are the largest and juiciest of the lot, with a pleasant blend of acid and sugar; they are typically eaten fresh. European kinds are firmer fleshed and can be eaten fresh or cooked; prune types are used for drying or canning, but they can also be eaten out of hand if you like the very sweet flavor.

European plums live longer than Japanese types, and they are more cold hardy and bloom later, making them less susceptible to late freezes. Japanese types need less winter chill and tolerate heat and humidity better, making them good choices for the Lower and Coastal South (USDA 8-9)—but greater susceptibility to diseases and insects makes them short lived in most areas. Plant disease-resistant selections, if possible.

Most European and Japanese types are grafted onto a rootstock. Standard trees grow about 15–20 ft. high and wide, but with pruning are easily kept to 10–15 ft. high and wide. There are no truly dwarfing plum rootstocks; semidwarf trees are only slightly smaller than standards.

Native species include wild plum (*P. americana*), Chickasaw plum (*P. angustifolia*), and Mexican plum (*P. mexicana*). These tough, hardy trees are easy to grow; their fruit is used to make jelly and preserves.

TOP: 'AU-Producer' plums; *MIDDLE ROW:* 'Ozark Premier' plums; 'Explorer' plums; *BOTTOM:* 'Red Heart' plums

PLUMS

NAME	ZONES	FRUIT	COMMENTS
EUROPEAN TYPES			
'Damson'	US, MS, LS; USDA 6-8	Small; purple or blue-black skin; green flesh; very tart flavor; late	Old favorite; fruit makes fine jam and jelly; strains of this selection are sold as 'French Damson', 'Shropshire'
'Earliblue'	MS, LS; USDA 7-8	Medium; blue skin; tender green-yellow flesh; early	Light to moderate producer; slow to begin bearing
'Green Gage'	US, MS, LS; USDA 6-8	Small to medium; greenish yellow skin; amber flesh; good flavor; midseason	Very old selection; still a favorite for eating fresh, cooking, canning, or jam; selected strain sold as 'Jefferson'
'Stanley'	US, MS, LS; USDA 6-8	Large; purplish black skin; yellow flesh; sweet and juicy; midseason	Good prune plum; good for canning; old Southern favorite; tends to overbear; best if fruit is thinned
JAPANESE TYPES			
'AU-Cherry'	US, MS, LS, CS; USDA 6-9	Small; red skin and flesh; good flavor; midseason	Good disease resistance; Auburn University introduction
'AU-Producer'	US, MS, LS, CS; USDA 6-9	Small to medium; dark red skin; red flesh; good quality; midseason	Good disease resistance; good yields; Auburn University introduction
'AU-Roadside'	US, MS, LS, CS; USDA 6-9	Medium to large; red skin and flesh; very good quality; midseason	Good disease resistance; Auburn University introduction
'AU-Rosa'	US, MS, LS, CS; USDA 6-9	Small to medium; dark red skin; yellow flesh of excellent quality; midseason, a few days after 'Santa Rosa'	Good disease resistance; Auburn University introduction; fruits lightly some years
'AU-Rubrum'	US, MS, LS, CS; USDA 6-9	Medium to large; maroon skin; red flesh; excellent flavor; midseason	Very disease resistant; Auburn University introduction
'Black Ruby'	US, MS, LS, CS; USDA 6-9	Medium; purple-black skin; sweet yellow flesh; midseason to late	Developed by USDA in Byron, Georgia
'Byron Gold'	US, MS, LS; USDA 6-8	Medium to large; yellow skin, sometimes blushed red; yellow flesh with mild to slightly tart flavor; aromatic; midseason to late	Excellent quality; disease resistant; developed by USDA in Byron, Georgia
'Crimson'	US, MS, LS; USDA 6-8	Small; crimson skin and flesh; excellent flavor and texture; early to midseason	Productive tree; excellent fruit set; good for eating fresh and for jams, jellies; disease resistant
'Early Golden'	US, MS, LS; USDA 6-8	Medium; yellow skin with red blush; golden flesh; good flavor; early	Poor quality if not heavily thinned
'Explorer'	US, MS, LS; USDA 6-8	Large; reddish to black skin; sweet, juicy, yellow flesh; midseason	Developed at the Georgia Agricultural Experiment Station
'Gulfbeauty'	CS, TS; USDA 9-10	Small; darkish red skin; yellow flesh; sweet; early	Low-chill, disease-resistant selection from the University of Florida; others in Gulf series include later ripening 'Gulfblaze' and 'Gulfrose'

PLUMS (continued)

NAME	ZONES	FRUIT	COMMENTS
'Homeside'	US, MS, LS, CS; USDA 6-9	Medium to large; orange to light red skin; orange flesh; very good texture; excellent flavor; early	Tree is quite vigorous and spreading
'Methley'	US, MS, LS, CS; USDA 6-9	Medium; reddish purple skin; dark red flesh; sweet, mild flavor; early	Bud-hardy, with early bloom; self-pollinating; good pollenizer
'Morris'	US, MS, LS; USDA 6-8	Large; purple skin; deep red flesh; good, sweet flavor; midseason	Productive, reliable, disease resistant; Texas A&M introduction
'Ozark Premier'	US, MS, LS; USDA 6-8	Very large; red to purple skin; juicy yellow flesh; very good flavor; late midseason	Vigorous, productive; good for eating fresh, canning, cooking, jelly; can be short lived
'Red Heart'	US, MS, LS, CS; USDA 6-9	Medium to large; dark red fruit of good quality, but with rather tough skin; late midseason	One of the best pollenizers for other Japanese selections; vigorous, productive; fruit holds well
'Robusto'	US, MS, LS; USDA 6-8	Medium; bright red skin; red flesh; midseason	Vigorous and productive; blossoms often escape damage from late-spring frosts
'Rubysweet'	US, MS, LS; USDA 6-8	Medium; red skin; orange-red flesh; sweet and juicy	Disease resistant; developed by the USDA in Byron, Georgia
'Shiro'	US, MS, LS; USDA 6-8	Medium to large; flavorful fruit with yellow skin and flesh; early to midseason	Heavy producer; fruit is good for eating fresh or cooking
'Wade'	MS, LS, CS; USDA 7-9	Large; dark red skin; juicy, sweet, yellow flesh streaked red; flattish shape; very early	Low winter-chill requirement; good choice for Florida, Coastal South

HOW TO GROW PLUMS

LOCATION Choose a spot with full sun and where fallen fruit won't be a problem. Plants tolerate many soil types but do best in fertile, well-drained soil. Most Japanese plums require 500 to 900 hours at 45°F or lower; European plums demand 700 to 1,000 hours of chill. Choose warm microclimates to avoid damage to blossoms from spring frost.

POLLINATION Most European plums don't require a pollenizer, though they set fruit better when grown near other European selections. Japanese plums produce better crops when cross-pollinated, so plant two Japanese selections.

WATERING Provide consistent moisture for good fruit production.

FERTILIZING In March, broadcast 10-10-10 fertilizer in a circle around the tree, starting 6 in. from the trunk and continuing out to 3 ft. Apply 1 cup of fertilizer for each year of the tree's age, up to a maximum of 12 cups. Water in thoroughly. For young trees apply a second application of ½–1 cup in July. For bearing trees, apply 1–2 cups after harvest.

PRUNING Japanese selections require heavy annual pruning to ensure fruit set and healthy growth throughout the tree. Train young trees to a vase shape. After selecting framework branches, cut back to lateral branches. If tree tends to grow upright, cut to outside branches; if it is spreading, cut to inside branches. Prune to avoid formation of V-shaped crotches. On types that produce excessive upright growth, shorten shoots to outside branchlets. Mature European plum trees require limited pruning, mainly to thin out annual shoot growth. Do any pruning of plum trees in late winter, before bloom.

FRUIT THINNING Japanese selections bear very heavily, producing lots of small fruit. If the entire crop were allowed to ripen, its weight might damage the tree—so thin fruit to 4–6 in. apart as soon as it is large enough to be seen. European plums usually don't need thinning.

CHALLENGES Certain insects and diseases plague most plums. Black knot (black, warty growths caused by a fungus) is a common problem. To control it, prune off infected branches, cutting at least 4 in. below signs of disease. Or plant resistant selections 'Damson', 'Methley', 'Shiro', and 'Stanley'. Peach tree borer may also cause trouble; see Peach and Nectarine for controls.

The more humid the climate, the more troublesome are plum curculio (a weevil that infests the fruit) and the diseases bacterial canker (which causes open wounds on trunk and branches) and brown rot. Dormant season sprays of horticultural oil and lime sulfur (applied as separate applications) help reduce several pest problems, including insects, mites, and diseases. AU hybrid plums, developed by Auburn University in Alabama and the low-chill Gulf series from the University of Florida, have good resistance to disease; several of these are listed in the chart.

Most plum trees will not succeed in areas where nematodes are prevalent, though rootstocks 'Nemaguard' and 'Guardian' are resistant to root-knot nematodes. 'Guardian' also resists bacterial canker.

PLUMBAGO

Plumbaginaceae

Evergreen or semievergreen shrubs

◼ **ZONES VARY BY SPECIES**

☼ ◑ **FULL SUN OR LIGHT SHADE**

◊ ◐ ● **LITTLE TO REGULAR WATER**

Plumbago auriculata

Sprawling plants that bloom over a long season, bearing phloxlike clusters of blue or white flowers at branch ends. Prune these shrubs back hard in late winter to control their growth and keep them compact. For other plants that are called plumbago, see *Ceratostigma*.

P. auriculata. CAPE PLUMBAGO. Evergreen or semievergreen. Zones CS, TS; USDA 9-11. Native to South Africa. Makes a mounding shrub to 6 ft. tall, 8–10 ft. wide; or, if tied to a support, grows as a vine to 12 ft. or more. Oblong, 1- to 2-in., light to medium green leaves. Inch-wide flowers. In seedling plants, blossom color varies from white through pure light blue to sky-blue; best way to get good blue color is to buy cutting-grown selections such as 'Royal Cape' or 'Imperial Blue'. 'Alba' and 'White Cape' are white-flowering forms. Blooms from spring through summer—or nearly all year in warm, frost-free locations.

Evergreen where frosts are absent or light; heavy frost can burn new growth and blacken leaves, but recovery is fast. Prune out any damaged parts when frost danger is past. Not fussy about soil type but must have good drainage. Good cover for bank, fence, wall; good background and filler plant. Does very well in pots. Tolerates light salt spray. Not browsed by deer.

P. indica. SCARLET LEADWORT. Evergreen. Zones LS, CS, TS; USDA 8-11. From Asia. Thin-stemmed plant to 6 ft. high, 3 ft. wide, with smooth, oval, medium to deep green leaves to 4 in. long. Blooms from winter to spring, bearing long-tubed, deep rose-pink to red flowers in clusters to 1 ft. long.

P. scandens. DOCTORBUSH. Evergreen. Zones CS, TS; USDA 9-11. Native from Florida to Arizona, south to Central America. To 4 ft. or more high and wide. Oblong leaves to 4 in. long are deep red when new, maturing to medium green; nearly all foliage turns red in late fall and winter. Blooms year-round (with a short break during hottest part of summer), bearing typically white (sometimes blue-tinged) flowers nearly 1 in. wide. Particularly striking when white blooms appear in combination with red leaves. With this species, hard pruning both controls size and encourages the growth of colorful new foliage. Accepts most soils. Can get powdery mildew in late summer but doesn't seem to be greatly harmed by it. Attractive ground cover. 'Summer Snow' has pure white blooms.

PLUMERIA BLOOMS ARE STRUNG TOGETHER TO MAKE HAWAIIAN LEIS.

PLUMERIA

FRANGIPANI

Apocynaceae

Deciduous shrubs or trees

◼ **TS; USDA 10-11; OR GROW IN POTS**

☼ ◑ **FULL SUN OR PARTIAL SHADE IN HOTTEST CLIMATES**

◐ ● **MODERATE TO REGULAR WATER**

⬦ **SAP IS POISONOUS AND MAY CAUSE SKIN RASH**

Plumeria 'Carmen'

Native to the American Tropics, plumerias are fabulous additions to the home garden, whether grown in containers or, where winter hardy, the ground. The source of flowers for Hawaiian leis, they range in size from compact shrubs rarely exceeding 4 ft. in height to small, rounded trees that reach 30 ft. Showy clusters of flowers up to 6 in. across appear atop large, leathery, oblong leaves for months on end. The waxy, five-petaled blooms may be star shaped, saucer shaped, or pinwheel shaped. They exhibit a dizzying range of colors and patterns. Most are highly fragrant. Propagation is easy by seeds or tip cuttings. Named selections represent the species *Plumeria obtusa*, *Plumeria rubra*, or hybrids of the two. Here are some of our favorites:

'Aztec Gold'. Buttercup-yellow shading to white at petal edges.

'Candy Stripe'. Vibrant blooms suffused with white and pink; petals are marked with bright yellow on upper surfaces, striped red and white beneath. 'Smith's Candystripe' is similar but more fragrant.

'Carmen'. Pink and white with yellow center and red band on the reverse.

'Celadine' ('Hawaiian Yellow'). Yellow with white petal margins. Especially sturdy plant.

'Cerise'. Bright magenta, star-shaped blossoms.

'Daisy Wilcox'. Extra-large blossoms with yellow centers and pale pink petals aging to white.

'Dean Conklin'. Salmon with orange center.

'Dwarf Singapore Pink'. Palest pink, darker at the edges with yellow center. Dwarf plant.

'Guillot Sunset'. Pink-and-white bicolor with orange center.

'Intense Rainbow'. Yellow blending to pink.

'Kauka Wilder'. Combination of reds and yellows gives blossoms an overall rich orange color. Very sweet fragrance.

'Kimo'. First orange plumeria. Starts orange-yellow changing to apricot-orange with red bands on front and back.

'Mary Moragne'. Rose-pink and white with orange veins.

'Pink Parfait'. Large reddish pink blooms.

'Scott Pratt'. Dark, velvety red with fine purple-black veins and darker bands on the reverse.

CARE

Plumerias thrive in either acid or alkaline soil that contains lots of organic matter. Good drainage is a must. They have big appetites while actively growing, so feed regularly during this time with a bloom-booster fertilizer that's relatively high in phosphorus and low in nitrogen, with added iron and magnesium. Let the soil go dry between thorough waterings. Established plants in the ground require very little water. Plumerias enjoy hot weather but also tolerate brief frosts. Can be left outdoors for winter only in the Tropical South. Fortunately, they do great in containers—but they can quickly become rootbound. When you see roots protruding from the drainage hole, remove the plant, prune off roots that tightly encircle the root ball, and replant in a larger pot.

Few insects and diseases affect plumerias. The most common, a fungus called plumeria rust, causes orange pustules on the undersides of leaves. Leaves then develop black blotches and drop prematurely. Control rust by promptly removing and throwing away any diseased leaves. Then spray healthy foliage with neem oil.

Almost all plumerias go through an annual dormant period lasting one to several months in which they drop their leaves. Though this is a resting phase not related to temperature, gardeners outside of the Tropical South can easily make it coincide with winter. When nights start to cool in fall, stop watering. Leaves will turn yellow and drop. Move plumerias into a cool room or garage. No water or light is needed until you take them out in spring.

PODOCARPUS

Podocarpaceae
Evergreen shrubs or trees

🌡 **ZONES VARY BY SPECIES**

☀ ◑ **FULL SUN OR PARTIAL SHADE**

💧 **REGULAR WATER**

Podocarpus macrophyllus

Versatile plants grown for their good-looking foliage and interesting form. They are adaptable to many climates and have many uses. Make good screens and background plants. Foliage generally resembles that of related yews (*Taxus*), but leaves of the better-known species are longer, broader, and lighter in color. If a male plant is growing nearby, female plants bear fruit after many years, producing small, fleshy fruit rather than cones. Grow well (if slowly) in most soils but may develop chlorosis (yellow leaves with green veins) where soil is alkaline. Tolerate salt spray and resist pests. Not browsed by deer.

P. elongatus. For plants sold under this name, see *P. gracilior*

P. gracilior. FERN PINE. Tree, often grown as an espalier. Zone TS; USDA 10-11. From eastern Africa. To 20–60 ft. tall, 10–20 ft. wide. Among the cleanest, most pest-free trees for street, lawn, patio, garden; good as big shrub, as hedge, in container.

Method of propagation determines growth habit. If grown from seed, plants are upright even when young (and stay that way); these plants are usually sold as *P. gracilior*. In youth, they have branches set somewhat sparsely with glossy, dark green leaves 2–4 in. long, ½ in. wide. With age, they produce 1- to 2-in., soft grayish green to bluish green leaves that are more closely spaced on branches. Stake seedling plants until a strong trunk develops.

If grown from cuttings or grafts of a mature tree, plants have the smaller, more closely set leaves just described, but they have very limber branches and are often reluctant to make strong vertical growth. These more willowy plants, suitable for espalier, hanging pots, or growing as vines along fences, are often sold as *P. elongatus*. Given staking and tying, *P. elongatus* types eventually become upright trees, though their foliage mass persists in drooping for some time. An exception is *P.* 'Icee Blue', which has striking blue-gray foliage and shrubby, upright growth to 25 ft. tall and wide.

P. macrophyllus. SOUTHERN YEW. Shrub or tree. Zones LS, CS, TS; USDA 8-11. Native to eastern China, Japan. Generally narrow and upright; to 15–50 ft. tall, 6–15 ft. wide. Bright green leaves 4 in. long, ½ in. wide. Good as a street or lawn tree, screen, or large shrub; limber enough to espalier. Easily pruned as clipped hedge or topiary. Does well in containers. Very heat tolerant.

P. m. 'Maki'. SHRUBBY YEW PINE. Slower growing and smaller than the species, reaching just 8–15 ft. tall, 2–4 ft. wide. Dense and upright, with leaves to 3 in. long, ¼ in. wide. A choice shrub; one of the best container plants for outdoor or indoor use. Excellent as a hedge.

P. nagi (*Nageia nagi*). BROAD-LEAF PODOCARPUS. Tree. Zones CS, TS; USDA 9-11. From Japan, where it reaches 80–90 ft. tall.

In the South, more commonly seen at 15–20 ft. tall, 6–8 ft. wide. Pendulous branchlets; leathery, smooth, dark green, sharp-pointed leaves to 1–3 in. long, ½–1½ in. wide. Grows upright in youth without staking; plant in groves for slender sapling effect. Makes a decorative foliage pattern against wood or masonry background. Excellent tall screen, hedge, accent or container plant.

PODOPHYLLUM

MAY APPLE
Berberidaceae
Perennials

🌡 **US, MS, LS; USDA 6-8**

◑ ● **PARTIAL TO FULL SHADE**

💧 💧💧 **REGULAR TO AMPLE WATER**

❂ **ALL PARTS (EXCEPT RIPE FRUIT) ARE POISONOUS IF INGESTED**

Podophyllum peltatum

Odd-looking yet striking plants, these herbaceous barberry (*Berberis*) relatives grow from thick underground rhizomes that send up stalks crowned with large, shield-shaped, deeply lobed leaves. Shoots with a single leaf are barren; those with two leaves bear a single, 2-in.-wide flower (set between the leaves) in mid- to late spring. Blossoms are followed by juicy, 2-in. berries; these are edible when fully ripe (poisonous until that stage) but can have a powerful laxative effect. Make attractive, slowly spreading deciduous ground covers for shady areas with rich, moist, woodsy soil.

P. hexandrum. HIMALAYAN MAYAPPLE. From Himalayas, western China. To 1–1½ ft. tall and wide. Dark green, brown-mottled

leaves to 10 in. wide are divided into three or five lobes; each lobe is further divided. White or pink flowers are followed by bright red berries.

P. peltatum. MAYAPPLE, WILD MANDRAKE. From eastern North America. To 1–1½ ft. high, 1 ft. wide. New growth pushing up through leaf litter is one of the earliest signs of spring in woodlands. Foliage is bronze when new; mature leaves are shiny dark green, to 1 ft. wide, divided into five to nine lobes. White flowers are followed by bright yellow berries. Spreads fairly fast in its preferred rich, moist soil. Dies back completely in late summer. 'Kaleidoscope', of hybrid origin, has octagonal leaves dramatically marked with creamy silver and bronze.

P. pleianthum (*Dysoma pleiantha*). CHINESE MAYAPPLE. From central and southeastern China and Taiwan. To 1½–2 ft. high, ½–1½ ft. wide. Large (12–16 in. wide), glossy green, umbrella-like leaves divided into shallow lobes. Clusters of unusual-smelling, bell-shaped, maroon flowers appear in spring but are mostly concealed by the leaves. Yellow or red fruit follows blossoms. Looks good until the first frost in fall.

P. versipelle. CHINESE MAYAPPLE. From China. Large, glossy, green, lobed leaves are up to 18 in. wide and can reach up to 3 ft. high. Clusters of deep maroon, meaty-smelling flowers are followed by bright red, berry-like fruit. Stays attractive until the first frost. 'Spotty Dotty' is lower growing, has light green leaves marked with chocolate-brown spots.

PODRANEA RICASOLIANA

PINK TRUMPET VINE
Bignoniaceae
Evergreen vine

⚡ CS, TS; USDA 9-11; OR GROW IN POTS

☼ ◐ FULL SUN OR PARTIAL SHADE

◐ MODERATE TO REGULAR WATER

Podranea ricasoliana

Native to South Africa. Sprawling growth to 20 ft.; must be fastened to its support. Glossy, dark green leaves consist of two to five opposite pairs of 2-in. leaflets plus one terminal leaflet. Blooms in spring or summer, when tips of new growth produce loose clusters of 2- to 3-in.-wide, red-veined pink flowers shaped like open trumpets. Grows slowly when young, then speeds up as it matures. Likes heat, good drainage. Planting in sterilized, fertile soil is recommended in Florida, since this plant is very subject to nematode damage there.

Use pink trumpet vine on posts, arbors, trellises, walls, trunks of high-branching trees. It also does well in large pots. Thin out any tangling growth in winter. Light frosts may cause leaves to drop; heavier frosts may kill vine to the ground, but regrowth is almost certain as long as soil doesn't freeze.

POLEMONIUM

JACOB'S LADDER
Polemoniaceae
Perennials

⚡ US, MS, LS; USDA 6-8

◐ ● PARTIAL TO FULL SHADE

◐ REGULAR WATER

Polemonium caeruleum

These shade-loving perennials form lush rosettes of finely divided, ferny, typically light to medium green foliage; clusters of bell-shaped flowers appear in spring or early summer. Good under trees. Lovely in combination with bellflower (*Campanula*), bleeding heart (*Laprocapnos*), ferns, hellebore, hosta, lilies. Grow from seed or from divisions made after bloom or in spring; give well-drained soil. The following species and hybrids are among those most commonly available in nurseries.

P. caeruleum. JACOB'S LADDER. Native to Europe and Asia. Fairly upright-growing plant to 1–3 ft. high, 1–1½ ft. wide. Lavender-blue, pendulous, inch-wide flowers. 'Brise d'Anjou', with each leaflet neatly outlined in white, is one of the most striking variegated-foliage plants.

P. reptans. CREEPING JACOB'S LADDER. Native from New Hampshire to Georgia, west to Minnesota, Oklahoma, and Alabama. Weak-stemmed plant to 1–1½ ft. high, 1 ft. wide; light blue, ¾-in. flowers. Better known than the species is heavy-blooming 'Blue Pearl'; it grows 10 in. high, 1½ ft. wide and bears bright blue blossoms. 'Firmament' grows to 20 in. high, 1 ft. wide, with bright blue flowers. 'Stairway To Heaven' has leaves edged in white and light blue flowers. 'Touch of Class'

is similar but is a little more vigorous. Good in shaded borders and rock gardens.

POLIANTHES TUBEROSA

TUBEROSE
Agavaceae
Perennial from rhizome

⚡ MS, LS, CS, TS; USDA 7-11; OR GROW IN POTS

☼ FULL SUN

◐ REGULAR WATER DURING GROWTH AND BLOOM

Polianthes tuberosa

Native to Mexico; longtime favorite in Southern gardens. Noted for powerful, heady fragrance. Blooms in late summer or fall, with glistening white, tubular, 2½-in.-long flowers loosely arranged in spikelike clusters on stems to 3 ft. tall. Long, narrow, grasslike basal leaves. Double-flowered selection 'The Pearl' is most widely available; it's a good garden plant but not as long lasting a cut flower as the single type. 'Mexican Single' is a more dependable bloomer in the Lower, Coastal, and Tropical South. 'Marginata' has white-edged leaves.

P. howardii, another Mexican native, grows in alkaline soil and has red-and-green blooms that attract hummingbirds. Hybrids between it and other species are good choices for the Southwest. They include *P.* x *bundrantii* 'Opal Eyes', which has 2½-ft.-high spikes of violet flowers in midsummer.

CARE

To bloom year after year, tuberoses require a warm season of at least four months before flowering.

Start indoors, or plant outside after soil is warm. Set rhizomes 2 in. deep, 4–6 in. apart. If soil or water is alkaline, apply acid fertilizer when growth begins. Where winter temperatures remain above 20°F, rhizomes may stay in ground all year; divide clumps about every four years. Even in those mild areas, however, most gardeners dig and store them over winter. Dig plants in fall after leaves have yellowed; cut off dead foliage. Allow rhizomes to dry for two weeks, then store them in a cool (40–50°F), dry place. Tuberoses can also be grown in pots and moved to a protected area during cold weather.

POLYGALA FRUTICOSA

SWEET PEA SHRUB
Polygalaceae
Evergreen shrub

⚡ CS, TS; USDA 9-11

☼ ◐ FULL SUN OR LIGHT SHADE

◐ REGULAR WATER

Polygala fruticosa 'Petite Butterfly'

South African native grown for colorful, asymmetrical flowers that look somewhat like sweet peas (*Lathyrus*). Dense growth to 2–3 ft. high and wide. Inch-long, rounded leaves are gray-green. Purplish pink, sweet pea–shaped blooms are about 1 in. across, with a pale pink central crest. Blooms almost year-round in mildest areas, spring to fall elsewhere. Plant in well-drained soil. Excellent near coast. Good cut flower. 'Petite Butterfly' is the selection most often found in nurseries.

POLYGONATUM

SOLOMON'S SEAL
Asparagaceae
Perennials

US, MS, LS; USDA 6-8, EXCEPT AS NOTED

PARTIAL TO FULL SHADE

REGULAR WATER, EXCEPT AS NOTED

Polygonatum biflorum

Slowly spreading rhizomes send up arching stems clothed in broadly oval leaves arranged in nearly horizontal planes. Where leaves join stems, pairs or clusters of small, bell-shaped greenish white flowers appear in spring, hanging beneath the stems on threadlike stalks. Small blue-black berries may follow flowers. Leaves and stems turn bright yellow in fall before plant dies to the ground. Attractive for form and flowers in woodland garden; good with astilbe, ferns, hellebore, hosta, wild ginger (*Asarum*). Grow in loose, woodsy soil. Can remain in place for years; to increase your plantings, dig rhizomes from clump edges in early spring, and replant. Good in containers. For false Solomon's Seal, see *Smilacina*.

P. biflorum. SOLOMON'S SEAL. Zones US, MS, LS, CS; USDA 6-9. Native to eastern North America. To 1–3 ft. tall, 2 ft. wide, with bright green leaves to 4 in. long and flowers usually in pairs or threes. A form sometimes sold as *P. commutatum* or *P. canaliculatum* is much more vigorous, growing 3–7 ft. tall, 3–4 ft. wide. It has leaves to 7 in. long and flowers in groups of two to ten.

P. falcatum 'Wedding Bells'. US, MS, LS, CS; USDA 6-9. From Korea. Arching stems to 2 ft. tall clothed in dangling white flowers tipped with green.

P. humile. DWARF SOLOMON'S SEAL. Native to eastern Europe, western Asia. Dwarf species to just 4–6 in. tall, spreading to 20 in. wide. Erect, upright stems carry dark green, 1½- to 3-in.-long leaves. In spring, diminutive white flowers are produced singly or in pairs along the length of the stems. 'Tom Thumb' grows only 6 in. high.

P. odoratum. FRAGRANT SOLOMON'S SEAL. Native to Europe, Asia. To 1½–3½ ft. tall, 2 ft. wide, with bright green, 4- to 6-in. leaves. Flowers are fragrant, usually borne in pairs but sometimes borne singly. Drought tolerant; does well in dry shade. The leaves of 'Byakko' are marked with white near the red stems. 'Double Stuff' has red stems and wide white margins on the leaves. 'Fireworks' has leaves splashed and striped with white. *P. o. pluriflorum* 'Variegatum' has white-edged leaves; its stems are dark red until fully mature.

POLYPODIUM

POLYPODY FERN
Polypodiaceae
Ferns

ZONES VARY BY SPECIES; OR HOUSEPLANTS

PARTIAL TO FULL SHADE; BRIGHT INDIRECT LIGHT

MODERATE TO REGULAR WATER

P. polypodioides

Widespread and quite variable group. Types described here are often grown on tree branches, logs, large rocks, and in moss. Good for woodland gardens.

P. polypodioides RESURRECTION FERN. Zones US, MS, LS, CS, TS; USDA 6-11. Native from Delaware to southern Illinois, south to Florida, Texas, and Central and South America. An old Southern favorite that grows about 1 ft. high and spreads widely by slender, creeping rhizomes. Often found on massive limbs of live oaks. Fronds are deeply cut and leathery, with scaly undersides; they reach 7 in. long, 2 in. wide. Fronds curl up and "play dead" in dry weather but quickly come back to life when it rains (hence the plant's common name).

P. vulgare. COMMON POLYPODY. Zones US, MS, LS; USDA 6-8. Native to Europe and Asia. Found in woodlands, among rocks, or on trees in areas with high rainfall. Grows 1 ft. high, with indefinite spread. Medium green fronds are held erect. Thrives in acidic or alkaline soil with moderate water. Highly variable; many named forms with crested or dissected leaves are available. 'Uulong Island' grows 6 in. tall and spreads slowly; a form found in Korea but well-suited to Southern gardens.

POLYSCIAS

Araliaceae
Evergreen shrubs or trees

TS; USDA 10-11; OR HOUSEPLANTS

FULL SUN OR PARTIAL SHADE; BRIGHT INDIRECT LIGHT

MODERATE TO REGULAR WATER

Polyscias fruticosa

Like many other aralia relatives, these natives of Polynesia (except as noted) are grown for their handsomely divided leaves; flowers are unimportant and seldom produced outside the tropics. Plants appreciate warmth, humidity, and good drainage. Outdoors, they need protection from frost and mites. Often grown as hedges in south Florida. As houseplants, they are considered fussy: they need fresh, fairly still air (they cannot tolerate drafts), good light but no direct sun, and enough water but not too much. Overwatering and mite damage are the two main causes of failure. Misting is useful, along with light feeding. If plants are doing well, don't move them. They will grow slowly, maintaining their shapeliness for years.

P. balfouriana. DINNER PLATE ARALIA. To 15 ft. tall, 4–8 ft. wide. The species has green foliage, but more commonly sold is its selection 'Marginata', with white-edged leaflets. 'Pennockii' has white to pale green leaflets with irregular green spots.

P. crispatum. GERANIUM-LEAF ARALIA, CHICKEN GIZZARD ARALIA. From Brazil. To 12 ft. high and half as wide. Green leaves are crinkled and irregularly indented.

P. fruticosa. MING ARALIA. Grows 6–10 ft. tall, 4–6 ft. wide. Leaves finely divided and redivided into a multitude of narrow, toothed segments. 'Elegans' is a small selection with extremely dense foliage.

P. guilfoylei 'Victoriae'. Grows to 15 ft. tall, 4–6 ft. wide. Has white-edged leaflets that are deeply slashed and cut.

POLYSTICHUM

Dryopteridaceae
Ferns

- ◪ **ZONES VARY BY SPECIES**
- ◑ ● **PARTIAL TO FULL SHADE**
- ◊ **REGULAR WATER, EXCEPT AS NOTED**

Polystichum polyblepharum

Hardy, symmetrical plants with medium-size, evergreen (except on *P. braunii*) fronds. Among the most useful and widely planted ferns, they combine well with other plants and are easy to grow. Do best in rich, organic, well-drained soil. Use in shady beds, along house walls, in mixed woodland plantings.

P. acrostichoides. CHRISTMAS FERN. Zones US, MS, LS, CS; USDA 6-9. Native to eastern North America. Grows to 1–1½ ft. tall, about 3 ft. wide, with dark green leaves that make a fine contrast to snow or to the brown of dead leaves during the winter holiday season. The easiest evergreen fern to grow in the Upper, Middle, and Lower South. Stiff fronds stay upright until pushed over by heavy snow or hard frost.

P. aculeatum. PRICKLY SHIELD FERN, HARD SHIELD FERN. Zones US, MS, LS; USDA 6-8. Native to Europe. Grows 2–4 ft. tall, 3 ft. wide. Glossy, firm, fairly upright, once- or twice-cut fronds; final segments are tipped by soft prickles. Pale green young fronds make an attractive show against the dark green mature ones.

P. braunii. BRAUN'S HOLLY FERN. Zones US, MS, LS; USDA 6-8. Semievergreen to deciduous. Native to northern latitudes of North America and Asia. Grows 1–3 ft. tall and wide, with twice-divided fronds. Silvery green new growth.

P. makinoi. MAKINO'S HOLLY FERN. US, MS, LS; USDA 6-8 Native to China and Japan. Grows 2 ft. high and wide, with glossy, olive-green fronds. Formal looking.

P. munitum. WESTERN SWORD FERN. Zones US, MS, LS; USDA 6-8. Native to western North America. To 2–4 ft. high and wide, with leathery, shiny, dark green fronds that emerge erect, then spread at the top to give plant a wide vase shape. Old plants may have 75 to 100 fronds. Once established, needs little water.

P. neolobatum. LONG-EARED HOLLY FERN, ASIAN SABER FERN. Zones US, MS, LS, CS; USDA 6-9. Native to Asia. Upright, arching growth to 2 ft. high and a bit wider, with shiny, dark green fronds that have pale green undersides. Upper leaflets closest to midrib on each frond are enlarged and a bit rounded, like little "ears."

P. polyblepharum. TASSEL FERN, JAPANESE LACE FERN. Zones US, MS, LS, CS; USDA 6-9. Native to Asia. Handsome, dense, lacy plant to 2–3 ft. tall, 3 ft. wide. Resembles *P. setiferum* but is taller, darker green, and somewhat coarser; shiny fronds are a little more upright (to 2 ft. high).

P. setiferum. SOFT SHIELD FERN. Zones US, MS, LS; USDA 6-8. Native to Europe. Finely cut fronds give effect of dark green lace, spread out in flattened vase shape. Many forms, 2–4½ ft. tall and wide. 'Proliferum' makes plantlets on midribs of older fronds; these can be detached and planted. Other fancy selections are sometimes sold under the name "English fern."

P. tsussimense. KOREAN ROCK FERN. Zones US, MS, LS, CS; USDA 6-9. From Asia. Forms a neat, dainty clump 12–15 in. high and wide. Erect, leathery, dark green fronds are held on dark stems. Use at front of shaded borders, among rocks, in pots. Established plants can take short periods of dryness.

POMEGRANATE

Lythraceae
Deciduous shrub or tree

- ◪ **MS, LS, CS, TS; USDA 6-10, EXCEPT AS NOTED**
- ◌ **FULL SUN**
- ◊ **MODERATE WATER ONCE ESTABLISHED**

Pomegranate

Native to Iran and northern India, the pomegranate has been cultivated since the times of the ancient Egyptians and grows throughout the Mediterranean region. Spurred by the healthful effects of its fruit and juice (which is also used to flavor the cocktail syrup grenadine), Southerners are now getting in on the act. Pomegranate prefers growing in areas with hot, dry summers and cool winters. However, new selections with increased cold hardiness and adaptability encourage more people outside the ideal range to grow them. (For ornamental selections grown just for flowers, see *Punica granatum*.)

Pomegranate forms a rounded, small tree or large shrub about 15–20 ft. tall and wide, although most growers prune them to half this size. Showy red or orange flowers appear at the branch tips in spring and develop into 5-in.-wide fruit with a leathery skin and a prominent tubular calyx at the blossom end. No cross-pollination is necessary for fruit production, although it will produce larger crops.

Each fruit contains hundreds of sacs of seedy, sweet-tart, juicy pulp. Harvest fruit when it reaches full color. Fruit left on the plant is likely to split and rot, especially during rainy weather. Fruit can be stored in the refrigerator for up to seven months. To eat fresh, cut into quarters or eighths and pull back the rind (starting from the ends) to expose the juicy sacs; eat them, seeds and all. To remove juice for drinking fresh or use in jams, jellies, and sauces, cut in half and ream with a juicer. Or roll the fruit firmly on a hard surface and then cut a hole in the stem end and squeeze out the juice.

Recommended selections include:

'Ambrosia'. Bears huge fruit up to three times larger than that of 'Wonderful', with pale pink skin and purple pulp.

'Angel Red'. Considered by many the top selection. Heavy crops of bright-red fruit that is extra juicy with soft, chewable seeds.

'Granada'. Red fruit with pink pulp ripens in August, a month ahead of 'Wonderful.' Juice is less tart.

'Kashmir'. Zones LS, CS, TS; USDA 8-11. Pinkish red fruit has red seeds with intense flavor that's great for juice.

'Russian 18'. Zones US, MS, LS, CS, TS; USDA 6-11. Cold-hardy selection from Russia. Medium to large, bright-red fruit with excellent, sweet-tart taste.

'Salavatski'. Zones US, MS, LS, CS, TS; USDA 6-11. Cold-hardy selection from Russia. Large red fruit with sweet flavor.

'Sweet'. Medium to large, very sweet fruit with pink skin and pulp. Seeds hardly noticeable. Very productive.

'Utah Sweet'. Zones US, MS, LS, CS, TS; USDA 6-11. Very sweet fruit with soft seeds and pink pulp and skin.

'White'. Whitish pink skin with white, transparent pulp. Very sweet and juicy.

'Wonderful'. Zones LS, CS, TS; USDA 8-11. The old standby. Large, purple-red fruit with tangy flavor. Reliable producer.

CARE

Choose a container-grown selection that is cold hardy in your area. Soil can be acid or alkaline, but good drainage is a must. Thoroughly water new plants at planting, and repeat every few days for the first two to three weeks. Then gradually water less often until you're depending only on rain. Feed with a slow-release fruit tree fertilizer once in spring and summer.

Pomegranate is best maintained as a large shrub. Prune as you would for its cousin, the crepe myrtle (*Lagerstromia sp.*). Select three to five shoots to become the main trunks, and remove all others at the ground. In late winter, open up the plant by pruning away twiggy growth, dead branches, and any branches growing inward toward the center. Shorten main trunks to 10 ft. to make harvesting easier. In the Upper South, plant against a south or west wall for extra cold protection. Pomegranate isn't well-suited to Florida.

PONCIRUS TRIFOLIATA

HARDY ORANGE, TRIFOLIATE ORANGE
Rutaceae
Deciduous shrub or small tree

🌿 **US, MS, LS, CS; USDA 6-9**

☼ **FULL SUN**

🌢🌢 **MODERATE TO REGULAR WATER**

Poncirus trifoliata 'Flying Dragon'

Native to China and Korea, this is the hardiest member of the citrus family, tolerating temperatures as low as –20°F. It is also a formidable barrier plant: stout, needle-sharp spines, 1–2 in. long, arm the length of its glossy green stems. Anyone planning to penetrate a hedge of hardy orange should line up blood donors first.

Dense, low-branched plant reaches 20 ft. tall and 12 ft. wide. Takes pruning and shearing into hedges very well; also good as espalier. Used as a dwarfing rootstock for many types of citrus. Glossy, dark green, 2½-in.-long

leaves are composed of three oblong leaflets; foliage turns yellow or yellow-green in autumn. Fragrant, 1- to 2-in.-wide white blossoms appear in spring. Sticky, aromatic (but inedible) fruit follows the flowers; it is green at first, ripening to yellowish orange in fall. Seeds from fallen fruit sprout prolifically. Easy to grow in just about any well-drained soil. 'Flying Dragon', to about one-third the size of the species, is a rather bizarre dwarf selection with twisted branches and curving, clawlike thorns.

PONTEDERIA CORDATA

PICKEREL WEED
Pontederiaceae
Aquatic perennial

🌿 **US, MS, LS, CS, TS; USDA 6-10**

☼ ◐ **FULL SUN OR LIGHT SHADE**

🌢 **LOCATE IN PONDS, WATER GARDENS**

Pontederia cordata

From eastern North America. To 3–4 ft. high, 2–2½ ft. wide. Long-stalked, glossy, green leaves stand well above surface of water; they are heart shaped, to 10 in. long, 6 in. wide. From late spring to fall, bears short spikes of blue, pink, or white flowers. Blooms attract bees and butterflies; dragonflies use the flower spikes as landing pads. Good companion to water lilies (*Nymphaea*); plant in pots of rich soil placed in 1 ft. of water. Gives an informal garden pool the look of a wild pond. To use in natural ponds, set plants at shoreline—underwater, directly in the soil. Dormant in winter.

POPULUS

POPLAR, COTTONWOOD, ASPEN
Salicaceae
Deciduous trees

🌿 **ZONES VARY BY SPECIES**

☼ **FULL SUN**

🌢🌢 **MODERATE TO REGULAR WATER**

Populus tremuloides

Poplars may be popular out West, but in the South they're problematic. They're messy, pest and disease prone, weak wooded, and short lived. Their aggressive surface roots crowd out other plants, invade water lines, and crack pavement. Cut or disturb the roots, and they'll sucker profusely. If your yard already has a poplar, leave it or remove it, but don't ever plant one unless you live in West Texas. (This warning does not apply to tulip poplar [*Liriodendron tulipifera*], which belongs to a different genus and makes a fine shade tree.)

Some poplars are beautiful or distinctive enough that people buy them despite their liabilities. Several have good fall color. Leaves of most poplars are roughly triangular, sometimes toothed or lobed. Pendulous catkins appear before spring leaf-out; those on male trees are denser textured. Female trees later bear masses of cottony seeds that blow about and become a nuisance; for that reason, male (seedless) selections are offered in garden centers. Deer don't usually browse poplars.

P. alba. WHITE POPLAR. Zones US, MS, LS; USDA 6-8. Native to Europe, Asia. Broad, widespreading tree to 40–60 ft. tall and wide. Leaves are dark green above,

white and woolly beneath, 2–5 in. long, usually with three to five lobes. A "lively" tree even in light breezes, with flickering white and green highlights. Poor fall color. Tolerates a wide range of soils. Suckers profusely. A seedless selection, *P. a. pyramidalis*, called Bolleana poplar (and often sold as *P. bolleana*), forms a narrow column; it has a white trunk like that of birch (*Betula*).

P. deltoides. EASTERN COTTONWOOD. Zones US, MS, LS, CS; USDA 6-9. Native from Quebec to Florida and Texas. Grows very fast in moist soils, quickly reaching 30 ft. tall; eventually reaches 75–100 ft. tall, up to 70 ft. wide. Provides fast shade and tolerates wet sites, drought, salt spray, acid and alkaline soils, and winter cold, but not good in gardens because of its huge size, short life, and tendency to break up in storms.

P. fremontii. WESTERN COTTONWOOD, FREMONT COTTONWOOD. Zones US, MS, LS, CS, TS; USDA 6-11. From California and Arizona. The cottonwood of desert water holes and watercourses. To 40–60 ft. or taller, about 30 ft. wide, with 2- to 4-in.-wide, thick, coarsely toothed, glossy, yellow-green leaves that turn bright lemon-yellow in fall. Does well in West Texas. 'Nevada' is a male selection. *P. f. wislizenii*, Rio Grande cottonwood, is similar but has slightly larger leaves. It is well adapted to arid regions; its native range is from southern Colorado to northern Mexico.

P. nigra 'Italica'. LOMBARDY POPLAR. Zones US, MS, LS, CS; USDA 6-9. Male selection of a European species. Lovely columnar tree to 40–100 ft. tall, 15–30 ft. wide, with upward-reaching branches. Bright green, 4-in. leaves turn a beautiful golden yellow in autumn. However, it's subject to a canker disease that will soon kill it. Upright English oak (*Quercus robur* 'Fastigiata'), a more permanent tree, is a good substitute.

P. tremuloides. QUAKING ASPEN. Zones US, MS; USDA 6-7. Widely distributed in North America; native to northern latitudes and mountains. Takes poor soil; generally performs poorly or grows slowly at low elevations. To 40–50 ft. tall, 20–30 ft. wide; often grows with several trunks or in a clump. Smooth, pale gray-green to whitish bark. Dainty, round,

2- to 4-in., light green leaves flutter and quake with even the slightest movement of air. Brilliant golden yellow autumn foliage. Apt to suffer from sudden dieback or borers. 'Prairie Gold', to 40 ft. tall and 15 ft. wide, was bred to tolerate lowland conditions and resist disease.

PORTULACA

Portulacaceae
Annuals

⚐ **US, MS, LS, CS, TS; USDA 6-11**

☼ **FULL SUN**

◔◕ **MODERATE TO REGULAR WATER**

Portulaca grandiflora

Low-growing, fleshy plants. One is called a weed but can be used in cooking and salads. The others are grown for their brilliant flowers, on display from late spring until frost; generally, the blossoms open fully in bright light and close by midafternoon in hot weather. The various plants described here thrive in high temperatures and intense sunlight. Not fussy about soil. Bright-flowered types are attractive in rock gardens, parking strips, hanging baskets, or as edgings and bank covers; they don't require deadheading to prolong bloom.

P. grandiflora. MOSS ROSE, PORTULACA. From South America. To 6 in. high, 1½ ft. across. Trailing, branching, reddish stems are set with narrow, cylindrical, pointed leaves to 1 in. long. Inch-wide, lustrous-petaled flowers shaped like tiny roses, in white and many bright and pastel shades of red, cerise, rose-pink, orange, yellow. Available as single

colors or mixes, in either single- or double-flowered strains. Magic Carpet, Cupcake, Margarita, Afternoon Delight, and Sundance strains stay open longer in the afternoon. Happy Trails is a low, spreading strain that reaches 6-9 in. tall and twice as wide. The Sundial strain also resists closing and has larger (2-in.), double blossoms. Sunseeker strain also resists closing and has larger (2-in.), double blossoms. All self-sow, but they often fail to come true from seed.

P. oleracea. PURSLANE. Unimproved form is thought to have originated in India; it's an edible weed with tiny yellow flowers and plump, oval leaves to 1¼ in. long. Warm weather and moisture encourage its growth. Control by hoeing or pulling before it goes to seed; don't let pulled plants lie about, since they can reroot or ripen seed. Improved forms offer larger, showy flowers in colors of red, orange, yellow, pink, and white.

POTATO

Solanaceae
Perennial treated as annual

⚐ **US, MS, LS, CS, TS; USDA 6-11**

☼ **FULL SUN**

◔ **REGULAR WATER**

⚘ **GREEN SKIN AND RAW SHOOTS ARE POISONOUS IF INGESTED**

'Yukon Gold' potatoes

Native to the Andes and a cool-weather crop, the potato (*Solanum tuberosum*) may not seem particularly well suited to growing in the South. But by employing proper techniques and choosing the right selections, you can make the venerable spud

HOW TO GROW POTATOES

SEED Potatoes aren't started from true seed, but from either certified, disease-free minitubers or seed potatoes (potatoes cut into pieces with two eyes to each piece). Plant early enough so that they'll mature before it gets hot. Don't use potatoes bought at grocery stores, as they're treated with a growth inhibitor to prevent sprouting.

SOIL Loose, acid (pH 5-6), fast-draining soil containing lots of organic matter is critical. If your soil doesn't meet this description, plant in raised beds or large containers to which you've added the proper soil. You can also grow potatoes in mulch. Just plant the minitubers or seed potatoes about an inch below the soil surface and cover with 12–18 in. of hay, straw, or pine needles. Clean, easy-to-harvest tubers will form in the mulch.

PLANTING In the garden, place minitubers or seed potatoes 10–12 in. apart and 4 in. deep in furrows spaced 24 in. apart. (The cut sides of seed potatoes should face down.) Cover with 2 in. of soil. As the tops grow, gradually add soil or mulch until you've "hilled-up" a mound 4 in. above the soil surface. Tubers will form on the soil surface or just below it. Be sure that sunlight can't reach them or they will turn green and toxic due to a chemical called solanine.

FERTILIZING Potato plants are heavy feeders. At planting time, mix into the soil a complete vegetable garden fertilizer containing nitrogen, phosphorus, and potassium at the rate specified on the label. You'll find few fertilizers formulated for just potatoes, but it's OK to use one labeled for tomatoes.

WATERING Keep the soil uniformly moist during growth. Stop watering when the leaves turn from yellow to brown and die down.

HARVESTING Dig "new potatoes" when the plants begin blooming. Dig mature potatoes when the plants die down. Dig potatoes to be stored two to three weeks after the plants have died. Avoid piercing or cutting the tubers. Spread harvested potatoes on dry ground for several hours until the soil dries and flakes off. Don't wash potatoes until just prior to use or they will rot. Store the tubers in a dark, cool place.

PESTS The most common pest for potatoes in home gardens is the Colorado potato beetle. Adult beetles are striped yellow and black, while the larvae are red. Both eat potato plants. Most synthetic insecticides don't work. The best control is to locate clusters of yellow-orange eggs on the undersides of leaves and destroy them before they hatch. Or use natural controls, such as neem oil or spinosad. Floating row covers also work. To avoid a buildup of harmful insects and diseases, don't plant potatoes in the same spot year after year.

your best bud. Like its cousin, the tomato, it produces a lot of food per plant. Two pounds of seed potatoes can produce 50 pounds of potatoes. The tasty, fat-free tubers are an excellent source of Vitamin C, potassium, and fiber.

The large, thick-skinned russet-type potato may be the most popular in supermarkets, but it doesn't do well in the South due to its long growing season. Potatoes that mature more quickly in cooler weather, such as 'Yukon Gold,' are a better bet. And you don't have to stick to white potatoes anymore. You can grow novelty potatoes with skins and flesh of blue, purple, red, pink, or yellow. Shapes vary from round to cylindrical or fingerlike (the latter are called fingerlings). Most selections take at least three months to mature. Plant in either very early spring or, in the Tropical South, fall and winter.

Recommended selections include:

'All Blue.' Blue skin and flesh, round to oblong. Matures in 110 days. Moist, good flavor, great for potato salad. Excellent keeper.

'Caribe.' Blue skin, white flesh, oblong. 70–80 days. A little dry, good for baking. Good keeper.

'Cranberry Red.' Red skin, pink flesh, round. 90–100 days. Moist, creamy, good for baking. Excellent keeper.

'Irish Cobber.' Yellow-brown skin, white flesh, round to oblong. 65–85 days. Great flavor, excellent for mashed potatoes and baking. Heirloom.

'Kennebec.' Yellow skin, white flesh, round. 85–90 days. Great flavor for baking or frying. Excellent keeper.

'Red LaSoda.' Red skin, white flesh, oval. 80–100 days. Highly adaptable and productive. No. 1 potato for north Florida. Good baked or fried. Excellent keeper.

'Red Pontiac.' Red skin, white flesh, oval. 80–100 days. Does well in heavy soil. Good all-around potato. Good keeper.

'Sebago.' Light brown skin, white flesh, round to oblong. Great flavor and creamy texture. Popular in Florida. Good all-around potato.

'Yukon Gold.' Gold skin, yellow flesh, round to oblong. 70–80 days. Very popular for its delicious, rich, buttery flavor. Great all-around potato. Not a long keeper.

POTENTILLA
CINQUEFOIL
Rosaceae
Perennials and deciduous shrubs

✎ ZONES VARY BY SPECIES

☼ ◑ PARTIAL SHADE IN HOTTEST CLIMATES

💧 MODERATE WATER

Potentilla fruticosa
'Pink Beauty'

Hardy plants useful for ground covers and borders, with bright green or gray-green leaves divided into small leaflets. Small, roselike, typically single flowers come in white; cream; and soft to bright shades of pink, red, yellow, and orange. Cinquefoils typically prefer cool nights and cool soils. Deer don't usually bother them.

Evergreen Perennials

These include creeping plants used as ground covers as well as sturdy, clumping types for rock gardens or perennial borders. Leaves are divided fanwise into leaflets and are reminiscent of strawberry foliage; flowers are generally about 1 in. wide.

P. atrosanguinea. RUBY CINQUEFOIL. Zones US, MS, LS; USDA 6-8. Sprawling, mounding Himalayan native to 1½ ft. high, 2 ft. wide, with furry, three-leafleted, 2- to 3-in.-long leaves and red blossoms in summer. A parent of superior hybrids such as 1- to 2-ft. 'Flamenco', bearing blood red flowers with a dark center; 1½-ft. 'Gibson's Scarlet', bright red with dark center; and 'William Rollison', semidouble bright orange with yellow center.

P. nepalensis. NEPAL CINQUEFOIL. Zones US, MS, LS, CS; USDA 6-9. From the Himalayas. To 1–2 ft. high, 2 ft.

wide. Leaves are 3–4 in. long, divided into five roundish leaflets; branching clusters of purplish red blossoms in summer. Selections are superior to the species for borders, cut flowers. 'Melton Fire', 12–15 in. high, bears bright red blooms marked with yellow and blending to a deep red center. 'Miss Willmott', 10–12 in. high, has salmon-pink flowers. 'Ron Mc-Beath' bears carmine blooms with distinctly heart-shaped petals.

P. neumanniana 'Nana'. DWARF SPRING CINQUEFOIL. Zones US, MS, LS; USDA 6-8. Dainty-looking yet tough and persistent creeping ground cover. Grows quickly to 3–6 in. high and about 1 ft. wide. Bright green leaves divided into five leaflets; butter yellow, ¼-in. flowers in spring and summer. Takes more water than other cinquefoils but also tolerates heat and drought. May turn brown in cold winters. Foliage blankets the ground completely yet is permeable enough to be a good bulb cover. Good lawn substitute for no-traffic areas; mow annually before spring growth begins. Subject to a disfiguring rust in some areas.

P. recta 'Warrenii'. WARREN'S SULFUR CINQUEFOIL. Zones US, MS, LS; USDA 6-8. Selection of a European species. Grows 2 ft. tall, 1½ ft. wide, with 4-in. leaves divided into five to seven leaflets. Profuse show of bright yellow flowers in late spring. Tolerates a wide range of soils.

P. x tonguei. STAGHORN CINQUEFOIL. Zones US, MS, LS; USDA 6-8. Hybrid between *P. nepalensis* and another species. Creeping plant to just 4 in. tall, with foot-long stems and 2-in. leaves divided into three to five leaflets. Blooms in late spring or summer, bearing ½-in.-wide apricot flowers with a red center.

Deciduous Shrubs

The shrubby potentillas, most often sold as named forms of bush cinquefoil (*P. fruticosa*), are native to northern latitudes everywhere. They perform well in Zones US, MS; USDA 6-7. All have leaves divided into three to seven leaflets; some are distinctly green on top, gray beneath, while others look more gray-green all over. All bloom cheerfully from late spring to early fall.

Fairly trouble free. Best in well-drained soil with moderate water, but tolerate poor soils, limestone, drought, heat. Selections with red or orange tinting should be grown in light shade, since they tend to fade quickly in hot sun. After bloom period ends, cut out older stems from time to time to make room for new growth. Here are some of the selections found in garden centers.

'Abbotswood'. To 3 ft. high and wide, with dark blue-green leaves, 2-in. white flowers.

'Elizabeth'. Grows 3 ft. high, 3½ ft. wide, with bright yellow blooms.

'Goldfinger'. Dense-foliaged, dark green plant to 3 ft. tall, 4 ft. wide, with golden yellow, 1½-in. blooms.

'Gold Star'. To 2 ft. tall, 2½ ft. wide, with large, deep green leaves and 2-in. bright yellow flowers.

'Jackman's Variety'. To 4 ft. tall and 5 ft. wide, with 1½-in., bright yellow blossoms.

'Katherine Dykes'. Can reach 5 ft. but usually stays much lower; spreads at least as wide as high. Pale yellow, 1-in. flowers.

'Klondike'. Dense grower to 2 ft. high and wide; 1½- to 2-in. yellow blossoms.

'Mount Everest'. Bushy, upright grower to 4 ft. high and wide; 1½-in. pure white blooms.

'Pink Beauty'. To 3 ft. high and wide, with profuse clear pink blooms.

'Primrose Beauty'. Silvery gray-green foliage on a plant 2–3 ft. high and wide. Pale yellow, 1½-in. flowers.

'Princess'. To 2 ft. high, 3–4 ft. wide. Soft pink flowers.

'Red Ace'. To 2 ft. high, 3–4 ft. wide. Flowers are 1½ in. wide, bright red with yellow center and yellow petal backs. Blooms fade to yellow as they age (fading is rapid in hot summer weather or poor growing conditions).

'Sunset'. To 2–2½ ft. tall, 3 ft. wide, with bright green foliage, 1½-in. yellow flowers shaded orange.

'Sutter's Gold'. To 1 ft. high, spreading to 3 ft. Clear yellow flowers about 1 in. across.

'Tangerine'. To 2½ ft. high and wide, with bright yellow-orange, 1½-in. blooms.

P

PRATIA PEDUNCULATA

BLUE STAR CREEPER
Campanulaceae
Perennial

🌿 **US, MS, LS, CS; USDA 6-9**

◐ **PARTIAL SHADE**

💧 **REGULAR WATER**

Pratia pedunculata

Native to Australia, this dainty creeper is excellent for growing between stepping stones, filling in niches in rock walls, or forming a prostrate ground cover. It produces an inch-tall mat of tiny (½-in.-long), oval leaves. Equally tiny light blue flowers appear atop the foliage in spring. Can take light foot traffic. Provide moist, well-drained soil. Feed lightly once a month from spring until fall. 'Alba' has white blooms. 'County Park' has deep blue flowers. Formerly known as *Laurentia fluviatilis* or *Isotoma fluviatilis*.

PRIMULA

PRIMROSE
Primulaceae
Perennials, most grown as
cool-season annuals

🌿 **ZONES VARY BY SPECIES**

◐ **LIGHT SHADE**

💧 **REGULAR WATER, EXCEPT AS
NOTED**

Primula auricula

Primroses form tufts of foliage, above which rise flowering stems carrying showy, circular, five-petaled blossoms in late winter and spring. The blooms may come on individual stems, in clusters at stem ends, or in tiered clusters like candelabra up the stem.

Most primroses are native to the Himalayas and cool regions of southeast Asia and Europe, so they thrive with a combination of moist, rich soil and cool, humid air. Few areas in the South supply these conditions. While most primroses listed below will grow as perennials in the zones indicated, many of them are best treated as cool-weather annuals.

P. auricula. AURICULA. Zones US, MS, LS; USDA 6-8. To 6–8 in. high, with broad, leathery gray-green leaves to 5 in. long forming rosettes to 1 ft. wide. Blooms in early spring, bearing clusters of fragrant, yellow- or white-eyed flowers in colors including orange, pink, rose, red, purple, blue, white, cream, and brownish. Usually grown in pots.

P. elatior. OXLIP. Zones US, MS, LS; USDA 6-8. Leaves to 8 in. long, hairy on undersides, form foliage clumps to 10 in. wide. Sulfur-yellow spring blossoms appear in many-flowered clusters on 8- to 12-in. stems.

ABOVE: Primula x polyantha

P. japonica. JAPANESE PRIMROSE. Zones US, MS, LS; USDA 6-8. From Japan. Stout, 2½-ft. stems bear whorls of up to five yellow-eyed purple flowers. Leaves are 6–9 in. long, 3 in. wide; clumps grow about 1½ ft. wide. Among the best selections are 'Alba' (white), 'Apple Blossom' (pale pink with a red eye), 'Miller's Crimson' (red), and 'Postford White' (white with red eye). Ample water; will even grow in shallow water.

P. juliae hybrids. JULIANA PRIMROSE. Zones US, MS, LS; USDA 6-8. Rounded, scallop-edged, bright green leaves to 2½ in. long form a 10-in.-wide rosette. In early spring, flowers are borne singly or in clusters on 3- to 4-in. stalks; colors include white, blue, yellow, orange, red, pink, purple. Excellent for edging, woodland, rock gardens. Best with regular water but will accept drier soil than most primroses.

P. malacoides. FAIRY PRIMROSE, BABY PRIMROSE. Usually grown as annual (indoor potted plant). Foot-wide evergreen rosettes of soft, pale green, long-stalked leaves, oval with lobed and cut edges, 1½–3 in. long. White, pink, rose, red, or lavender blooms in lacy whorls along upright, 8- to 15-in. stems. Good under high-branching trees, with spring bulbs, in flower beds. Tolerates light frost. Available from greenhouses in late winter and early spring.

P. obconica. Usually grown as annual (indoor potted plant). White, pink, salmon, lavender, or reddish purple flowers, 1½–2 in. wide, in broad clusters on 1-ft. stems. Plants reach 1 ft. wide. Evergreen, roundish, hairy leaves

on long stems. Hairs on stems (except those of Freedom strain) may irritate skin. Available from greenhouses in late winter and early spring.

P. x polyantha. POLYANTHUS PRIMROSE. Zones US, MS; USDA 6-7, usually grown as an annual. Often called English primrose. Foliage clumps to 9 in. wide; the 8-in.-long, green leaves resemble romaine lettuce. Bloom season runs from winter to early or midspring; 1- to 2-in.-wide flowers in many brilliant colors come in large, full clusters on 1-ft.-tall stems. Miniature Polyanthus types have smaller flowers on shorter stalks. Choose from the many large-flowered strains, like Crescendo and Pacific Giant, or look for novelties such as the Gold Lace group, with gold-edged, yellow-centered, deep mahogany petals; 'Zebra Blue' with lovely blue-and-white striped petals; 'Penumbra', similar, with silver-edged petals; and 'Guinevere', with bronzy foliage and soft pink, yellow-eyed blooms. All good for massing, bulb companions, or pots.

P. sieboldii. ASIATIC PRIMROSE. Zones US, MS, LS; USDA 6-8. Grows 1 ft. high and wide, with oval, light green, deeply lobed and toothed leaves. Produces white, pink, or purple, white-eyed flowers, each 1½ in. wide, in clusters of 2 to 15 in early spring. Many named selections in deep or light colors; flowers of some have fringed petals. Leaves of all types usually die back shortly after flowering.

P. veris. COWSLIP. Zones US, MS, LS; USDA 6-8. Leaves to 8 in. long, slightly hairy on undersides, form a clump to 10 in. wide. Large clusters of fragrant, bright yellow (sometimes red or apricot) flowers are held on 8- to 12-in. stems. Blossoms of 'Sunset Shades' feature yellow throats and petals in a blend of orange to deep red.

P. vulgaris. ENGLISH PRIMROSE, PRIMROSE. Zones US, MS, LS; USDA 6-8. Tufts of leaves much like those of *P. polyantha*; clumps grow about 1 ft. wide. Spring flowers are typically borne singly on 8-in. stalks, though some garden strains have two or three blossoms per stalk; colors include white, yellow, red, blue, bronze, brown, and wine. Single series like Danova, sweet-scented Primera, and large-flowered Supreme are ubiquitous, but doubles and rose-flowered series like Belarina and Rosanna are gaining popularity. Hybrids called the Kennedy Irish Primroses include 'Drumcliff', with flowers that emerge light lavender changing to white with a yellow eye, and 'Innisfree' with yellow-eyed red flowers atop bronzy purple foliage. Use as edging, in woodland garden.

PROSOPIS GLANDULOSA

MESQUITE, HONEY MESQUITE
Mimosaceae
Deciduous tree

🌱 **MS, LS, CS; USDA 7-9 (DRY AREAS)**

☼ **FULL SUN**

◊ **LITTLE TO NO WATER**

Prosopis glandulosa

Native to Mexico and a common sight on dry grasslands and hills of West, Southwest, and Central Texas. Seeds believed to have

entered Texas in the stomachs of cattle driven across the Rio Grande. The plant quickly spread and is now considered a nuisance by ranchers, because its greedy, wide-spreading roots compete with pasture grasses for water.

Mesquite's gnarled, sculptural trunks and wispy, light green foliage make it a picturesque lawn tree. Its light shade allows grass to grow right up to the trunk. Reaches 30 ft. tall and about as wide. Deep taproot makes it nearly impossible to transplant. Does not need watering. Tolerates lawn irrigation better if soil is sandy. Little pruning is needed; just cut out dead or broken limbs. Thorniness is variable. Some selections have branches set with very long, sharp, almost needlelike thorns, but thornless selections, such as cutting-grown 'Maverick', are available.

Many prize mesquite for its wood, which is used in flavoring smoked and grilled meats. But its long seedpods, which change from red to mottled purple and tan as they dry, do just as good a job.

Two other forms of mesquite are found in Texas—screw bean (*P. pubescens*) and Arizona mesquite (*P. velutina*). Both are smaller and shrubbier than *P. glandulosa*. Screw bean is named for its spirally twisted pods, which are popular in dried arrangements. All three species hybridize freely, making exact identification of individual plants difficult.

PRUNELLA

SELF-HEAL, HEAL-ALL
Lamiaceae
Perennials

🌱 **US, MS, LS; USDA 6-8**

☼ ◐ **FULL SUN OR LIGHT SHADE**

◊ **REGULAR WATER**

Prunella 'Summer Daze'

Native to Europe, these creeping perennials spread by surface and underground runners to form low, dense foliage mats. Upright spikes of hooded flowers rise above the leaves in summer. Though names are much confused, all species are tough, tolerant, and deep rooted. They are useful for small-scale ground covers and can endure the occasional footstep; set 1 ft. apart. Choose location carefully, though: These plants are too invasive to risk near choice, delicate rock garden plants. After bloom, shear off spent flower spikes to keep the planting neat and prevent seed formation.

P. grandiflora. Leaves to 4 in. long; stems to 1½ ft. tall, bearing spikes of 1- to 1½-in., purple blossoms. Varieties include 'Blue Loveliness', 'Freelander Blue' (compact grower with violet-blue blooms over a long period), 'Pink Loveliness', 'Purple Loveliness' (lilac-purple touched with white), and 'White Loveliness'. Hybrid 'Summer Daze' is compact, at 10 in. high and wide, with rich pink flowers.

P. vulgaris. This is the common species. Smaller in all its parts than *P. grandiflora*, with leaves to 2 in. long, 1-ft. stems, and purple or pink flowers just ⅓ in. long. *P. v. incisa* has deeply cut leaves.

PRUNUS

Rosaceae
Evergreen and deciduous shrubs and trees

🌱 **ZONES VARY BY SPECIES**

☼ **FULL SUN, EXCEPT AS NOTED**

◊◊ **MODERATE TO REGULAR WATER, EXCEPT AS NOTED**

Prunus x *yedoensis*

Discussed here are the ornamental members of the genus *Prunus*. Fruit trees belonging to *Prunus*—collectively called the stone fruits—can be found under their common names. See Almond, Apricot, Cherry, Peach and Nectarine, and Plum.

Ornamentals are divided into two classes: evergreen and deciduous. Evergreens are used chiefly as shade trees, street trees, hedges, and screens. Deciduous flowering trees and shrubs, closely related to the fruit trees mentioned above, are valued for their floral display as well as for attractive form and for foliage shape and texture. Many of these also bear edible fruit, attractive to wildlife or used to make jams and jelly.

DECIDUOUS TYPES
Flowering cherry.
Zones vary by type. Cultural needs of all are identical. They require full sun and fast-draining, well-aerated soil; if your soil is substandard, plant in raised beds. Prune only to remove awkward or crossing branches; pinch back the occasional overly ambitious shoot to force branching. You can cut during bloom time and use branches in arrangements. Trees bloom in early to midspring, depending on type.

All are good to garden under. Use them as their growth habit indicates: Large, spreading kinds make good shade trees, while smaller ones are indispensable in Japanese gardens. Foliage may sustain damage from insect pests. Plants growing in heavy soil are sometimes subject to root rot (for which there is no cure); an afflicted tree will usually bloom, then send out new leaves that suddenly collapse.

P. 'Accolade'. Zones US, MS; USDA 6-7. Small tree with spreading branches, twiggy growth pattern. Very vigorous. To 25 ft. tall and wide. Semidouble, blush-pink, 1½ in. wide in large drooping clusters; open from rose-pink buds. Early. Hybrid between *P. sargentii* and *P. x subhirtella*.

P. campanulata, TAIWAN FLOWERING CHERRY. Zones MS, LS, CS; USDA 7-9. Graceful, slender, upright-growing small tree; densely branched. To 20–25 ft. high and wide. Single, bell shaped, dropping, ¾ in. wide, in clusters of two to five. Striking shade of bright purplish pink. Very early. Red fruit about ½ in. long. Good choice for Coastal South.

P. 'Dream Catcher'. Zones US, MS; USDA 6-7. Upright, vase-shaped. Dark green leaves turn yellow-orange in fall. To 25 ft. tall and 15 ft. wide. Single pink. Early; about a week after parent *P.* 'Okame'. Good resistance to pests and diseases.

P. 'First Lady'. Zones US, MS, LS, CS; USDA 6-9. Very upright, almost columnar. To 25 ft. tall and 15 ft. wide. Single, dark rose-pink. Very early. Hybrid between 'Okame' and *P. campanulata*.

P. 'Hally Jolivette'. Zones US, MS, LS; USDA 6-8. Dense, shrubby. Slow to 6–8 ft. high and wide; eventually reaches twice that size. Double white blooms open from pink buds. Early; relatively long bloom, lasting several weeks. Can be used in shrub borders. Hybrid between *P. x subirtella* and *P. x yedoensis*.

P. incisa. FUJI CHERRY. Zone US; USDA 6. Large shrub to small tree, growing 15–20 ft. tall and wide, blooming pale pink before midspring. 'Kojo-no-mai' ('Little Twist') is smaller than the species, growing up to 6 ft. tall and 3 ft. wide with twisted branches.

P. 'Okame'. Zones US, MS, LS, CS; USDA 6-9. Upright, oval habit. Fast growing. Dark green, fine-textured foliage. Good yellow-orange to orange-red fall color. To 25 ft. by 20 ft. Single, carmine-pink, 1 in. wide. Very early. Blooms well even in Coastal South. Hybrid between *P. campanulata* and *P. incisa*.

P. 'Royal Burgundy'. Zones US, MS, LS; USDA 6-8. Remarkable for its red foliage to complement pink flowers. Upright branches that grow into a rounded tree 30 ft. tall and 20 ft. wide. Midseason.

P. sargentii. SARGENT'S CHERRY. Zones US, MS; USDA 6-7. Upright, spreading branches form rounded crown. Good orange-red fall color. To 40–60 ft. tall and wide. Single, blush-pink flowers in clusters of two to four. Midseason. 'Columnaris' is narrower and more erect than species, though more vase-shaped than columnar. *P. sargentii* 'Pink Flair' is compact; upright with a narrow vase shape. Good orange-red fall color. To 25 ft. tall and 15 ft. wide. Single, pink flowers. Midseason.

P. serrulata. Known through its many selections.

'Amanogawa'. JAPANESE FLOWERING CHERRY. Zones US, MS, LS; USDA 6-8. Columnar in youth, becoming vase shaped with age. To 20–25 ft. tall, 4–8 ft. wide. Semidouble, light pink with deep pink petal margins; 1 in. wide. Early midseason.

'Kanzan' ('Kwanzan', 'Sekiyama'). Zones US, MS, LS; USDA 6-8. Stiffly upright branches form a narrow, inverted cone that spreads with age. Orange fall foliage. To 30 ft. by 20 ft. Large (2½ in. wide), double, deep rosy pink, in pendent clusters. Blossoms appear before or with red young leaves. Midseason. Tolerates heat and humidity well.

'Shirofugen'. Zones US, MS, LS; USDA 6-8. Wide horizontal branching. To 25 ft. high and wide. Long-stalked double blooms 2 in. wide, in pink fading to white. Flowers appear at same time as coppery red new leaves. Latest to bloom among *P. serrulata* selections.

'Shirotae' ('Mt. Fuji'). Zones US, MS, LS; USDA 6-8. Strong horizontal branching. To 20 ft. by 25 ft. Semidouble, to 2 in. wide. Pink in bud; white when fully open, aging to purplish pink. Early.

'Shogetsu'. Zones US, MS, LS; USDA 6-8. Spreading growth,

arching branches. To 15 ft. by 25 ft. Semidouble and fully double, to 2 in. wide. Pale pink, often with white center. Late.

P. 'Snow Goose'. Zones US, MS, LS; USDA 6-8. Erect; narrow at first, eventually becoming broader. To 20 ft. tall and wide. Single white. Early.

P. x subhirtella. Known for its popular selections.

'Autumnalis'. Zones US, MS, LS; USDA 6-8. Loose-branching, bushy tree with flattened crown. To 25–30 ft. high and wide. Double white or pinkish white, ½ in. wide. Often blooms during mild autumn or winter weather as well as in early spring.

'Rosea'. Zones US, MS, LS; USDA 6-8. Widespreading; horizontally branching. To 20–25 ft. by 30 ft. Single pink blossoms open from nearly red buds. Profuse, very early bloom.

P. x yedoensis. YOSHINO FLOWERING CHERRY. Zones US, MS, LS; USDA 6-8. Horizontal branches; graceful, open pattern. Fast growing. Leaves may turn orange or red in fall. To 40 ft. by 30 ft. Single light pink to nearly white, to 1½ in. wide. Early. This is the cherry planted around the Tidal Basin in Washington, D.C. Tolerates heat and humidity.

'Akebono' (sometimes called 'Daybreak'). Zones US, MS, LS; USDA 6-8. Horizontal branches; graceful, open pattern. Fast growing. Leaves may turn orange or red in fall. To 25 ft. high and wide. Flowers pinker than those of *P. x yedoensis*.

Weeping Flowering Cherry
P. 'Pink Snow Showers'. Zones US, MS, LS; USDA 6-8. Weeping. To 25 ft. tall and 20–25 ft. wide. Single pink blooms. Early.

P. 'Snow Fountains' ('White Fountain'). Zones US, MS, LS; USDA 6-8. Slightly curving trunk; weeping branches reach the ground. Sold as a small tree or trunkless ground cover. To 12–15 ft. tall and wide as a tree; 1 ft. by 10–15 ft. as a ground cover. Single white. Early.

P. x subhirtella 'Pendula'. WEEPING HIGAN CHERRY. Zones US, MS, LS; USDA 6-8. Usually sold grafted at 5–6 ft. high on upright-growing understock. Graceful branches hang down, often to ground. To 15–25 ft. high and wide. Profuse show of ½-in., pale pink, single flowers. Trees

TOP: Prunus serrulata 'Kanzan'; P. mume; BOTTOM: P. 'Okame'; P. x blireana

P

grown on own roots are rare but more graceful than those grown from grafts. Early.

P. x subhirtella 'Pendula Plena Rosea' ('Yae-shidare-higan'). DOUBLE WEEPING CHERRY. Zones US, MS, LS; USDA 6-8. Double rose-pink. Midseason.

Flowering peach. Zones US, MS, LS, CS; USDA 6-9. Most are more widely adapted than fruiting peach but otherwise identical in size, growth habit, cultural needs, and potential problems. Place trees where they will be striking when in bloom yet fairly unobtrusive out of bloom. Bloom period runs from late winter to early spring. The following selections are strictly "flowering" in that the 2- to 2½-in. blooms are showy and fruit is either absent or inferior. In areas with late frosts, choose late bloomers; early bloomers are best in areas with early springs.

'Bonfire'. Dwarf form to only 5–6 ft. tall, 7 ft. wide. Red leaves; double pink flowers. Midseason.

'Early Double Pink'. Very early.

'Early Double Red'. Deep purplish red or rose-red. Very early. Brilliant color is beautiful but likely to clash with other pinks and reds.

'Early Double White'. Blooms with 'Early Double Pink'.

'Helen Borchers'. Semidouble, clear-pink flowers. Late.

'Late Double Red'. Later than 'Early Double Red' by three to four weeks.

'Peppermint Stick'. Double flowers striped red and white; may also bear all-white and all-red flowers on same branch. Midseason.

'Weeping Double Pink'. Smaller than other flowering peaches, with weeping branches. Requires careful staking and tying to develop main stem of suitable height. Midseason.

'Weeping Double Red'. Like 'Weeping Double Pink', but with deep rose-red flowers. Midseason.

'Weeping Double White'. White version of weeping forms listed above.

'White Icicle'. Double white flowers. Late.

Flowering plum. Zones vary by type. Flowers appear before leaves, from late winter to early spring. Less particular

about soil than flowering cherries, nectarines, and peaches but will fail if soil is waterlogged for long periods. If soil is boggy, plant in raised beds. Little pruning is needed. Potential pests include aphids, borers, scale, tent caterpillars. Possible diseases include canker and leaf spot. The most ornamental flowering plums are described below. Note that purple-foliaged types have a dominating color that makes them difficult to work into a landscape successfully—so use them sparingly (and never plant them in front of red brick). For more flowering plums, see listings for *P. americana, P. angustifolia, P. x cistena, P. maritima,* and *P. mexicana.*

Prunus x blireana. US, MS, LS; USDA 6-8. Graceful form. New leaves reddish purple; turn greenish bronze by summer. To 25 ft. by 20 ft. Double, fragrant pink to rose flowers to 1¼ in. wide. Little or no fruit. Hybrid of *P. cerasifera* 'Pissardii' and *P. mume.*

P. cerasifera. MYROBALAN, CHERRY PLUM. US, MS, LS; USDA 6-8. Most often used as rootstock for various stone fruits. Dark green leaves. To 30 ft. high and wide. Pure white flowers to 1 in. wide. Red, 1- to 1¼-in-wide fruit is sweet but bland. Self-sows freely; some seedlings bear yellow fruit. Purple- and red-leafed selections are more popular than species.

'Allred'. US, MS, LS; USDA 6-8. Upright, slightly spreading. Red leaves. To 20 ft. by 12–15 ft. Single, white flowers. Red, 1½-in., tart fruit good for preserves, jelly.

'Crimson Pointe'. US, MS, LS; USDA 6-8. Grows like an exclamation point, 20–25 ft. tall and 5–6 ft. wide. White flowers in early spring. Dark red foliage. Small ornamental fruit.

'Krauter Vesuvius'. US, MS, LS; USDA 6-8. Upright, oval form. Darkest foliage (blackish purple) of any flowering plum. To 18 ft. by 12 ft. Single, light pink flowers. Little or no fruit.

'Mt. St. Helens'. US, MS, LS; USDA 6-8. Upright, spreading, with rounded crown. A sport of *P. c.* 'Newport' but more robust, with larger leaves of a richer purple color. Faster growing than 'Newport' to 20 ft. high and wide. Fragrant, single, white to pale pink flowers. Will bear a little fruit.

'Newport'. US, MS, LS; USDA 6-8. Upright and spreading, with

ABOVE: Prunus laurocerasus

rounded crown. Foliage is dark all summer, attractively reddish in autumn. To 15–20 ft. by 20 ft. Fragrant, single, white to pale pink flowers. Will bear a little fruit.

'Pissardii' ('Atropurpurea'). PURPLE-LEAF PLUM. US, MS, LS; USDA 6-8. Rounded habit. Leaves are coppery red when new, later deepen to dark purple; turn red in autumn. Fast to 25–35 ft. high and wide. Single, white flowers. Heavy crop of red, 1- to 1½-in. fruit.

'Thundercloud'. US, MS, LS; USDA 6-8. Rounded in habit (more so than *P. c.* 'Pissardii'). Dark coppery leaves. To 20 ft. high and wide. Fragrant, single, light pink to white flowers. Sometimes sets good crop of 1-in. red fruit.

Japanese flowering apricot (P. mume). Zones US, MS, LS, CS; USDA 6-9. Tree from China, Korea. Not a true apricot. Longer lived, tougher, and more trouble free than many other flowering fruit trees. Eventually develops into a gnarled-looking, picturesque tree to 20 ft. tall and wide. Broadly oval, pointed leaves to 4½ in. long; profuse, inch-wide

winter blossoms with a clean, spicy perfume. In the Lower and Coastal South (USDA 8-9), sudden freezes following warm spells will kill just-opened blossoms. New ones seem to replace the frosted ones. Fruit is small and inedible.

'Beni-chidori'. Bushy and upright, to 8 ft. tall and wide, with dark pink flowers.

'Bonita'. Semidouble, rose-red blooms.

'Dawn'. Large, ruffled double, pink flowers.

'Matsubara Red'. Double, deep red flowers.

'Peggy Clarke'. Double flowers in deep rose, with extremely long stamens and red calyxes.

'Pendula'. Weeping branches hold semidouble, rich pink blossoms.

'Rosemary Clarke'. Double, white flowers with red calyxes. Very early.

'W. B. Clarke'. Double, pale pink flowers; weeping form. Effective large bonsai or container plant. Bloom and form make it the center of attention in a winter garden.

ADDITIONAL DECIDUOUS SPECIES

P. americana. WILD PLUM, GOOSE PLUM. Shrub or small tree. Zones US, MS, LS; USDA 6-8. Native from Manitoba to Massachusetts, south to Utah, New Mexico, and Georgia. Tough, hardy plant grows to 15–20 ft. high and 10–15 ft. wide, spreading to form thickets. Blooms profusely before the dark green leaves emerge, bearing clusters of white, inch-wide blossoms. Yellow to red, 1-in. fruit is sour but good for jelly.

P. angustifolia. CHICKASAW PLUM. Large shrub. Zones US, MS, LS, CS; USDA 6-9. Native from New Jersey to Missouri, south to Florida and Texas. Grows to 12–16 ft. tall and wide, forming a somewhat thorny, shiny, dark green thicket; spreads by root suckers. Clouds of ½-in. white blossoms in early spring; ¾-in. red or yellow fruit is prized by wildlife. Likes sandy soils; takes sun or partial shade.

P. x cistena. PURPLE-LEAF SAND CHERRY, DWARF RED-LEAF PLUM. Shrub. Zones US, MS; USDA 6-7. Dainty, multibranched hybrid to 6–10 ft. high. Can be trained as single-stemmed tree; good for small patios. Bears white to light pink flowers as leaves emerge, then covers itself in red-purple foliage. May offer a summer crop of small blackish purple fruit.

P. glandulosa. DWARF FLOWERING ALMOND. Shrub. Zones US, MS, LS; USDA 6-8. Native to China and Japan. An old Southern favorite. To 4–6 ft. high, with clumps of upright, spreading branches and light green, willow-like, 4-in. leaves. In early spring, before leaf-out, the slender stems are transformed into wands of blossoms. Double-flowered 'Alba Plena' (white) and 'Sinensis', sometimes sold as 'Rosea Plena' (pink), are commonly sold; both have fluffy, 1- to 1¾-in. blooms. A rare single-blossomed type known in some areas as Easter cherry is the only one that fruits. Prune heavily during or after flowering to promote new growth for next year's bloom. Suckers freely. Fireblight can be a problem.

P. maritima. BEACH PLUM. Shrub. Zones US, MS; USDA 6-7. Native to Atlantic coast from Maine to Virginia. Suckering shrub to 6 ft. or taller, spreading to form large colonies. Dull green leaves grow 1½–3 in. long, half as wide. White, ½-in. flowers in spring are followed by ½- to 2-in., dark red or purple fruit that is highly valued for preserves. Tolerates strong winds and salt spray.

P. mexicana. MEXICAN PLUM. Tree. Zones US, MS, LS, CS; USDA 6-9. Native from Kentucky to Texas and northeast Mexico. Beautiful native plum with delicate, spreading form and handsome, peeling bark. Usually single trunked; grows 15–25 ft. (occasionally to 35 ft.) tall, not quite as wide. Yellow-green, oval, pointed leaves to 4 in. long turn orange in autumn. Not a sucker-ing species. Very fragrant, ½-in. white blossoms (fading to pink) bloom in early spring; purplish red fruit, good for jellies and preserves, follows in late summer. Foliage turns orange before dropping in fall. Tolerates drought but grows fast with regular water; takes many soils, including limestone and sand, but must have good drainage. Full sun or partial shade.

P. serotina. BLACK CHERRY, WILD CHERRY. Large tree. Zones US, MS, LS, CS; USDA 6-9. Native from Canada to Florida and Texas. Fast growing to 50–60 ft. tall, 30 ft. wide; possibly much taller. Leaves to 5 in. long, oval and pointed; dark green above, light green below. Yellow to red fall foliage. Fragrant white spring flowers in drooping clusters; red to purple-black, bittersweet cherries, used in jellies and wines. Wood is prized for furniture. Tolerates many soils, but not extremely wet or very dry sites. Not good for planting near the house; dropping fruit is messy, and nests of eastern tent caterpillars in branches are unsightly in spring. One of the larval hosts of Eastern tiger swallowtail butterfly. Seeds prodigiously.

P. tomentosa. NANKING CHERRY. Shrub. Zones US, MS; USDA 6-7. From Tibet, China. Extremely tough and cold hardy. To 6–8 ft. tall, 10 ft. wide. Small, fragrant white flowers open from pinkish buds in spring; ½-in. scarlet fruit follows.

P. triloba 'Multiplex'. DOUBLE FLOWERING PLUM, FLOWERING ALMOND. Small tree or large treelike shrub. Zones US, MS; USDA 6-7. From China. Slow to 8–10 ft. (possibly to 15 ft.) tall, with equal spread. The rather broad leaves are 1–2½ in. long. Double, pink flowers about 1 in. wide appear in early spring before leaf-out. A white form is sometimes available.

P. virginiana. CHOKECHER-RY. Shrub or small tree. Zones US, MS; USDA 6-7. Native from Newfoundland to Saskatchewan, south to Kansas, east to North Carolina. To 20–30 ft. high, 18–25 ft. wide, with suckering habit. Oval, pointed leaves are 2–4 in. long; they are dark green above, grayish green beneath. In late spring, small, very fragrant white flowers appear in slender, 3- to 6-in. clusters among the leaves; these are followed by astringent, dark red to black fruit to ½ in. wide. 'Canada Red' ('Shubert') has leaves that open green, turn red as they mature.

EVERGREEN SPECIES

The following evergreen species are all large shrubs or small trees.

P. caroliniana. CAROLINA CHERRY LAUREL. Zones US, MS, LS, CS; USDA 6-9. Native from North Carolina to Texas. As an upright shrub, it can be well branched from the base and used as clipped hedge or tall screen to 20 ft. high; can also be sheared into formal shapes. Trained as a tree, it is a broad-topped plant reaching 35–40 ft. high and nearly as wide; looks attractive with multiple trunks. Densely foliaged in glossy, green, smooth-edged, 2- to 4-in.-long leaves. Small, creamy white flowers in 1-in. spikes appear in late winter or spring, followed by black fruit to ½ in. wide. Flower and fruit litter can be a problem in paved areas. Produces lots of seedlings. Very tolerant of heat, wind, drought. 'Bright 'n Tight' and 'Compacta' are denser than the species, reach only 8–10 ft. tall and 6–8 ft. wide, and take well to pruning.

P. laurocerasus. CHERRY LAUREL. Zones US, MS, LS; USDA 6-8. Hardy to 5°F; selections listed below are hardier. Native from southeastern Europe to Iran. To 20 ft. tall and wide, though generally seen as a lower clipped hedge. Leathery, glossy, dark green leaves are 3–7 in. long, 1½–2 in. wide. Blooms in summer, bearing 3- to 5-in. spikes of creamy white flowers that are often hidden by leaves. Small purple to black fruit appears in late summer and fall.

Where adapted, a fast-growing, greedy plant that's difficult to garden under or around. Regular water and nutrients will speed growth and keep top dense. Needs reasonably good drainage. Give partial shade in hottest areas. Tolerates salt spray. Stands heavy shearing but with consider-able mutilation of leaves; best pruned by one cut at a time, using hand pruners, to remove overlong twigs just above a leaf. Leaf spot can be a serious prob-lem in the Lower South.

The compact selections listed below are good garden plants, better behaved than the species.

'Etna'. Grows 6–8 ft. tall and wide. Compact growth; takes well to shearing. Coppery new leaves.

'Mount Vernon'. Very slowly forms a dense mound to about 2 ft. high and 5 ft. wide. Though very dwarf, it has full-size leaves like those of the species. Can be used as ground cover.

'Otto Luyken'. To 4 ft. tall, 5–6 ft. wide. Deep green, glossy leaves 2–4 in. long.

'Schipkaensis'. SCHIPKA LAU-REL. Usually 4–5 ft. high (possibly 10 ft. tall), 7 ft. wide. Narrow leaves are 2–4½ in. long.

'Zabeliana'. ZABEL LAUREL. Narrow, 2- to 4½-in.-long leaves; branches angle upward and outward from plant base. Eventu-ally reaches 6 ft., with equal or greater spread. More tolerant of full sun than species. Versatile plant; good for low screen, big foundation plant, bank cover (with branches pegged down), espalier.

P. lusitanica. PORTUGAL LAUREL. Zones MS, LS, CS; USDA 6-9. Native to Spain, Por-tugal. Densely branched shrub 10–20 ft. high and wide; or multi-trunked, spreading tree to at least 30 ft. tall and wide. Trained to a single trunk, it is used as formal street tree. Glossy, dark green leaves to 5 in. long, 2 in. wide. Small, creamy white flowers in 5- to 10-in. spikes in spring and early summer, fol-lowed by clusters of tiny bright red to dark purple fruit. Slower growing than P. laurocerasus and more tolerant of heat, sun, and wind. Drought tolerant.

P

PSEUDERANTHE-MUM

Acanthaceae
Evergreen shrubs

- 🌡 **TS; USDA 10-11; OR GROW IN POTS**
- ◐ **PARTIAL SHADE; BRIGHT LIGHT**
- 💧 **REGULAR WATER**

Pseuderanthemum carruthersii 'Variegatum'

Group of about 60 species from tropical woodlands in many parts of the world. Of the two discussed here, one is grown for its colorful leaves, the other for its showy flowers. Plants thrive in fertile, well-drained soil free from nematodes. In areas where they aren't hardy, they make excellent container plants for deck, porch, or greenhouse. If you grow them in pots, give bright light (with protection from hot afternoon sun); let soil dry out somewhat between soakings, and feed monthly during active growth with a general-purpose liquid houseplant fertilizer.

P. carruthersii. From Polynesia. Upright, open-growing plant to 3–5 ft. tall, 1–2½ ft. wide. Shiny, blackish purple leaves, sometimes spotted with pink, yellow, green, or white, are 4–6 in. long, broadly oval, and pointed. Tubular, inch-long white flowers appear occasionally in summer. Dark foliage is perfect for contrast with yellow or orange flowers or yellow or chartreuse leaves. Pinch back in youth to encourage bushiness. 'Variegatum' ('Tricolor') has bronzy purple leaves heavily marked with pink and creamy yellow; flowers are pink.

P. laxiflorum 'Shooting Stars'. SHOOTING STARS, AMETHYST STARS. Probably a selection of a Polynesian species. Upright and spreading, to 3–4 ft. tall, 2–3 ft. wide. Bright green, narrowly oval, pointed leaves to 3 in. long are good looking, but the inch-long, star-shaped purple blossoms provide the real show: They bloom profusely and almost continuously in warm weather and are attractive to hummingbirds.

PSEUDOCYDONIA SINENSIS

CHINESE QUINCE
Rosaceae
Deciduous shrub or small tree

- 🌡 **US, MS, LS; USDA 6-8**
- ☼ **FULL SUN**
- 💧 **REGULAR WATER**

Pseudocydonia sinensis

Seldom seen, curious tree, usually 15–20 ft. high (sometimes taller) and about as wide. Trunk is very attractive, with bark that flakes off to reveal shades of brown, green, and gray. Trunks on old trees are often fluted. Roundish oval, dark green leaves to 4½ in. long turn yellow and red in fall. Spring bloom produces a scattering of flowers rather than a show—the pale pink, 1- to 1½-in. blossoms are borne singly at ends of year-old twigs. Blossoms are followed by extraordinary fruit: fragrant, yellow, egg-shaped quinces to 7 in. long, weighing over a pound apiece. The fruit can be made into jam. Very susceptible to fireblight in warm, humid areas; control by pruning out damaged wood. Needs acid soil and good drainage.

PSEUDOGYNOXYS CHENOPODIOI-DES

MEXICAN FLAME VINE
Paeoniaceae
Evergreen or deciduous vine

- 🌡 **CS, TS; USDA 9-11**
- ☼ ◐ **FULL SUN OR LIGHT SHADE**
- 💧 **REGULAR WATER**

Pseudogynoxys chenopodioides

Native from Mexico to Honduras. Twines to 8–10 ft. Light green, rather fleshy leaves are 1–4 in. long, ½–1 in. wide, coarsely toothed. Large clusters of ¾- to 1-in., startling orange-red blooms with golden centers appear at branch ends; 'São Paulo' is deeper orange, almost brick-red. Plants bloom all year where winters are mild. Provide light soil Full sun or light shade. Use on trellis or column, let cascade over bank or wall, or plant in hanging basket. Formerly known as *Senecio confusus*. We wish it still was—the new botanical name is nearly impossible to pronounce.

PSEUDOLARIX AMABILIS

GOLDEN LARCH
Pinaceae
Deciduous tree

- 🌡 **US, MS; USDA 6-7**
- ☼ **FULL SUN**
- 💧 **REGULAR WATER**

Pseudolarix amabilis

Where space permits, golden larch becomes a specimen tree of great character. This Chinese native grows very slowly into a 40–70-ft. pyramid, nearly as broad as tall at the base. Foliage has a feathery look; needles are clustered in tufts except near pendulous branch ends, where they are single. Needles open light green, mature to bluish green, then turn a magnificent golden yellow very briefly in autumn before dropping. Cones and bare branches present an interesting pattern in winter. Needs shelter from cold winds. Best in deep, rich, well-drained, acid soil; performance is better in colder part of range.

PSEUDOTSUGA MENZIESII

DOUGLAS FIR
Pinaceae
Evergreen tree

🌿 US, MS; USDA 6-7

☀️ FULL SUN; TAKES PART SHADE IN YOUTH

💧 MODERATE TO REGULAR WATER

Pseudotsuga menziesii

Popular as a living or cut Christmas tree. It reaches 70–200 ft. tall in Western forests; in gardens it is more likely to grow 40–80 ft. tall and 12–20 ft. wide. Trees are cone shaped and foliaged to the ground when young, but lose lower limbs as they age. Soft, densely set, green or blue-green needles to 1½ in. long radiate in all directions from the branches; they give off a lemon scent when crushed. Pointed, wine-red buds form at branch tips in winter, then open to apple green new growth in spring. Reddish brown, oval cones are about 3 in. long, with three-pronged bracts. Unlike upright cones of true firs (*Abies*), these hang down.

Native from Alaska through Northern California, eastward into the Rocky Mountains, and southward into northern Mexico. In the Upper South (USDA 6), tree is fast growing, dark green, with slightly drooping branchlets. Rocky Mountain form, *P. m. glauca*, is blue-green and slower growing, more cold tolerant, more compact, and stiffer than the species. Compact, weeping, and other forms are grown mostly in arboretums and botanical gardens. All tolerate wind; will grow in most soils except boggy ones. Deer don't browse them.

PTELEA TRIFOLIATA

HOP TREE
Rutaceae
Deciduous shrub or small tree

🌿 US, MS, LS, CS; USDA 6-9

☀️ FULL SUN OR PARTIAL SHADE

💧 MODERATE TO REGULAR WATER

Ptelea trifoliata

Native to the eastern U.S. Gets its name from its late-summer fruit, once used as a substitute for hops. Bushy plant grows slowly to 15–20 ft. tall and wide. Dark green, 2½- to 5-in.-long leaves are divided into three oval, pointed leaflets; they turn yellow in fall. Greenish white flowers appear in late spring; they aren't showy, but the fruit that follows is conspicuous—roundish and flattened, to 1 in. across, pale green aging to brown. Easy to grow, very adaptable, and free from serious pests, hop tree is a good candidate for a woodland garden, naturalized area, or even a shrub border. Stems and leaves emit a strong citrus odor when bruised. Leaves of 'Aurea' emerge bright yellow in spring, then fade to lime-green by late summer.

PTERIDIUM AQUILINUM

BRACKEN
Dennstaedtiaceae
Fern

🌿 US, MS, LS, CS, TS; USDA 6-11

☀️ FULL SUN OR PARTIAL SHADE

💧 LITTLE TO REGULAR WATER

☠️ FRONDS ARE POISONOUS IF INGESTED

Pteridium aquilinum

Found all over the world, bracken is represented by various subspecies that differ in minor details. Coarse, much-divided fronds rise directly from deep, running rootstocks; plant grows from as low as 2 ft. high to as tall as 7 ft. under good conditions. Occurs naturally in many places and can be tolerated in untamed gardens, but beware of planting it: deep rootstocks can make it a tough, invasive weed. Do not gather fronds to cook as fiddleheads, since they contain a slow poison. Deer avoid these ferns.

PTERIS

BRAKE
Pteridaceae
Ferns

🌿 LS, CS, TS; USDA 8-11; OR HOUSEPLANTS

☀️ PARTIAL TO FULL SHADE; BRIGHT LIGHT

💧 REGULAR WATER

Pteris cretica albolineata

Small evergreen ferns of subtropical origin. They are mostly used as houseplants, but the ones listed here will also grow outdoors. Indoors, they should be sited in bright light but shielded from hot sun; an east-facing window is ideal. They benefit from frequent misting. Provide good drainage; keep the soil evenly moist. Fertilize every 2 weeks during spring and summer and once monthly in fall and winter with a general-purpose liquid houseplant fertilizer.

P. cretica. CRETAN BRAKE. To ½ ft. high, 2 ft. wide, with comparatively few long, narrow leaflets. Numerous selections exist; some have forked or crested fronds, others are variegated. *P. c. albolineata* ('Albolineata') has a broad white band down the center of each leaflet. 'Mayi' is similar but with crested tips. Light green 'Wimsettii' has fronds that are forked at the tip on mature plants; it is so dense and frilly that it does not even look like a fern.

P. quadriaurita. Reaches 2–4 ft. tall and wide. Rather coarsely divided fronds. Not as easy to grow as other species, but worth the effort for unusual coloring of varieties *P. q. argyraea* (*P. argyraea*), with green fronds heavily marked white, and 'Tricolor', with fronds marked white, green, and red. Protect from frost watch for slugs and snails.

P. tremula. AUSTRALIAN BRAKE. To 5 ft. tall and 3 ft. wide. Extremely graceful fronds on slender, upright stalks. Good landscape fern with excellent silhouette. Fast growing but tends to be rather short lived.

PTEROSTYRAX

Styracaceae
Deciduous trees

🗡 **US, MS, LS; USDA 6-8**

☼ **FULL SUN**

💧 **REGULAR WATER**

Pterostyrax hispida

Once classified with eastern American silver bell (*Halesia*), to which they are related, these trees make handsome, interesting garden specimens. White flower clusters appear in late spring or early summer. Slim petals show from behind alternate leaves; plant where you can look up into them—on a bank beside a path, above a bench, in a raised bed. These are choice plants for the woodland edge or as a focal point in a large shrub border. Established trees need little pruning.

P. corymbosa. Native to Japan. Similar to *P. hispida*, but a little smaller in stature and leaf, and less widely grown. Flower clusters are slightly broader, and individual blooms are more bell-shaped with protruding stamens. Fruit is downy, not furry, and winged, not ribbed.

P. hispida. EPAULETTE TREE. Native to Japan and China. Single- or multitrunked tree to 20–30 ft. (possibly 40 ft.) tall and equally wide. Oval to oblong leaves are light green above, gray-green beneath. Creamy white, lightly

fragrant flowers with fringed petal edges appear in drooping clusters to 9 in. long, 3 in. wide, giving bloom puffs an airy look. Pendent clusters of small, furry gray fruit hang on well into winter, are attractive on bare branches.

PTYCHOSPERMA

Arecaceae
Palms

🗡 **TS; USDA 10-11; OR GROW IN POTS**

☽ **LIGHT SHADE**

💧 **REGULAR WATER**

Ptychosperma macarthurii

Native to Australia and the South Pacific. Small feather palms with slender, ringed trunks and well-defined crown shafts (the smooth, usually green upper portion of the trunk, formed by overlapping bases of newer leaves). Frond segments are toothed at the tip. Small, fragrant flowers come in 1- to 2-ft.-long clusters in summer; these are followed by bright red fruit. Grow in well-drained soil.

P. elegans. ALEXANDER PALM, SEAFROTHIA PALM. From Australia. Erect, single-trunked palm to 25 ft. tall, 15 ft. wide. Fronds to 8 ft. long.

P. macarthurii. MACARTHUR PALM. Native to New Guinea. To 10–25 ft. tall, 12–15 ft. wide, with several clustered trunks. Fronds to 6½ ft. long. Good large understory plant. Often grown in containers.

PUERARIA MONTANA LOBATA

KUDZU
Papilionaceae
Deciduous vine or ground cover

🗡 **MS, LS, CS, TS; USDA 7-11**

☼ **FULL SUN**

💧 **REGULAR WATER**

Pueraria montana lobata

Native to Japan but now known as "the vine that ate the South," kudzu has covered millions of acres since it was introduced in 1876. Smothers arbors, telephone poles, houses, and fields—and any plant in its path—at the rate of up to 1 ft. per day. Thrives under almost any conditions. Medium green, 3- to 6-in.-long leaves are broadly oval, with three leaflets. Leaves and stems are somewhat hairy and coarse. Fragrant red-purple flowers in clusters 8–12 in. long, July through September. Too invasive for garden use unless you're hiding from the government and need something to cover your tracks. Its good points: tubers and leaves are edible, and you can make a tasty jelly from the flowers. Civil War buffs will be delighted to know there is now a variegated form with white-splotched leaves called 'Sherman's Ghost'.

PULMONARIA

LUNGWORT
Boraginaceae
Perennials

🗡 **US, MS, LS; USDA 6-8**

☽● **PARTIAL TO FULL SHADE**

💧 **REGULAR WATER**

Pulmonaria 'Mrs. Moon'

Low-growing shade lovers with quiet charm. In many kinds, foliage is attractively dappled with gray or silver. The long-stalked leaves are mostly in basal clumps, though there are a few on the flower stalks. Plants bloom in spring (just before leaves appear or as they emerge), bearing drooping clusters of funnel-shaped, typically blue or purplish flowers. After flowering finishes, more leaves arise from the base of the clump. If plants are well watered, foliage will remain ornamental through the growing season. All have creeping roots and can be used as small-scale ground covers or edgings for beds or woodland paths. Look good beneath spring-flowering trees, in combination with ferns, azaleas, rhododendrons, blue scillas, pink tulips. Need moist, well-drained, organically enriched soil. Clumps may become crowded after a few years; divide them in early fall.

P. angustifolia. COWSLIP LUNGWORT. Native to Europe. To 8–12 in. high, 1½ ft. wide, with narrowish dark green leaves and bright blue flowers that open from pink buds. 'Azurea' (*P. a. azurea*) has sky-blue blossoms.

P. hybrids. Most are usually about a foot high and twice as wide.

'Dark Vadar'. To 8–12 in. high, 1½ ft. wide. Thick, dark green leaves with large silver pots. Blue, purple or pink flowers.

'Janet Fisk'. Leaves that are silvery almost all over. Pink flowers aging to blue.

'Lewis Palmer' ('Highdown'). Early blooming with deep blue blossoms; spotted leaves.

'Mrs. Moon'. An old favorite with large silvery leaves. Pink flowers age to blue.

'Pierre's Pure Pink'. Shiny, spotted leaves and pink blossoms.

'Raspberry Splash'. Stiffly upright, narrow green leaves spotted with silver. Bright raspberry purple flowers open from burgundy buds.

'Roy Davidson'. Resembles *P. longifolia* 'Bertram Anderson' but has slightly wider leaves and flowers that open pink before deepening to blue.

'Silver Bouquet'. To 6 in. high, 2 ft. wide. Beautiful, lance-shaped silver leaves. Flowers change from pink to blue as they mature.

'Sissinghurst White'. Leaves spotted white. Large white flowers.

'Smoky Blue'. Bears blue flowers atop deep green, white-spotted leaves.

'Trevi Fountain'. Long, silver-spotted leaves give rise to abundant cobalt blue flowers.

P. longifolia. Native to the British Isles, western Europe. To 8–12 in. high, 1½ ft. wide. Slender leaves to 20 in. long are deep green spotted with silver. Blooms a little later than other species; flowers are purplish blue. 'Bertram Anderson' has deep blue blossoms.

P. rubra. RED LUNGWORT. Hairy, unspotted, light green leaves to 2 ft. long, 5 in. wide; clumps can reach 3 ft. across. Blooms very early in spring, sending up flowering stems to 16 in. tall; blossoms are typically red, but there are also selections with blue or white blooms. The following reach 1 ft. high: 'Bowles Red', with deep red to rosy coral flowers and leaves spotted in lime-green; 'David Ward', brick-red blossoms and white-edged leaves; and 'Redstart', bearing blossoms in an interesting shade between salmon and brick-red.

P. saccharata. BETHLEHEM SAGE. To 1–1½ ft. high, 2 ft. wide, with broadly oval, pointed leaves in medium green spotted with silver. Blue flowers open from pink buds.

PULSATILLA VULGARIS

PASQUE FLOWER
Ranunculaceae
Perennial

US, MS, LS; USDA 6-8

☀ **FULL SUN**

💧 **REGULAR WATER**

Pulsatilla vulgaris

This central European native starts as a foot-wide rosette of finely cut leaves covered with silky hairs; smaller leaves clothe the short flowering stems. In early spring, each stem is topped by a single cup-shaped, erect or nodding blossom with silky hairs on the outside and a mass of yellow stamens within. Colors range from white through pink shades to purple or red. The fluffy seed clusters are almost as showy as the flowers; each seed is topped by a long, twisting, feathery appendage. Plants grow from a woody root, reach 5–6 in. high in bloom, rise to about 1½ ft. high by the time seeds appear. 'Pinwheel White' and 'Alba' have white flowers; 'Rubra' and 'Red Clock' have red blooms. Best in cool conditions with well-drained soil. May go dormant in summer.

PUMPKIN

Cucurbitaceae
Annual

US, MS, LS, CS, TS; USDA 6-11

☀ **FULL SUN**

💧 **REGULAR WATER**

'Small Sugar' pumpkin

Thought to have originated in South America; related to squash, gourd, melon. Fruit varies greatly in size, depending on selection.

One of the best for a jumbo Halloween pumpkin is 'Atlantic Giant' (which can weigh upwards of 500 pounds!). A great choice for pies is 'Small Sugar', a smaller pumpkin with finer-grained, sweeter flesh. 'Jack Be Little' and 'Wee-B-Little' are miniature (3- to 4-in.) types used for decoration. Novelties with white skin and orange flesh include miniature 'Baby Boo' and 8- to 10-in. 'Lumina'. Seeds of all are edible, but the easiest to eat are those of hull-less selections like 'Trick or Treat'.

CARE

Pumpkins are available in vining and bush types. Both need lots of room: A single vine can cover 500 sq. ft., and even bush sorts can spread over 20 sq. ft. Where the growing season is short, start plants indoors and use floating row covers early in the season. In most areas, sow seeds outdoors in late spring after soil has warmed; plant in rich soil. For vining pumpkins, sow five or six seeds 1 in. deep in hills 6–8 ft.

TOP: 'Big Mac'; *BOTTOM:* 'Lumina' pumpkin; 'Wee-B-Little'

P

apart; thin seedlings to two per hill. Plant bush pumpkins in rows spaced 3 ft. apart; plant seeds 1 in. deep in clusters of three or four, spacing clusters 2 ft. apart along the row. Thin seedlings to one or two plants per cluster.

Before planting, work ¼ cup of 10-10-10 fertilizer into each hill. Then feed periodically with a balanced water-soluble fertilizer. Water during rainless periods, but keep foliage dry to prevent leaf diseases. Plants do not do well in high heat and humidity. In late summer, slide wooden shingles under fruit to protect it from wet soil and rot. Pumpkins are ready to harvest about 90 to 120 days after sowing, when the shell has hardened. Pick after first frost kills the plant. Use a sharp knife or hand pruners to harvest fruit, leaving 1–2 in. of stem. Subject to same pests and diseases as squash.

GROW A GIANT PUMPKIN

Plant 'Atlantic Giant' seeds in spring as soon as soil warms. Grow one plant per hill, spacing hills 40 ft. apart. (Yes, we do mean 40 ft.—one hill and plant could cover most of a small garden!) As plant develops, cut off all but one main stem; after fruits have formed, remove all but one fruit. Along the length of the stem, mound a 4-in.-wide hill of soil every 2 ft.; roots will form there. Feed every few weeks. Keep soil moist, but don't overdo it—too much water causes pumpkins to split. To avoid damaging the stem, don't move pumpkins until harvest. Good luck!

PUNICA GRANATUM

ORNAMENTAL POMEGRANATE
Lythraceae
Deciduous shrub or tree

MS, LS, CS, TS; USDA 7-11

FULL SUN

MODERATE TO REGULAR WATER

Punica granatum 'Nana'

Native from Iran to the Himalayas. For fruiting types, see Pomegranate. Plants described here either fail to fruit at all or bear red fruit that is more decorative than tasty. Good landscape plants. Use taller types as foundation plants, in shrub borders, as tall hedges or small trees; lower-growing kinds are excellent for edgings, in containers. All bear showy single or double summer flowers with ruffled petals surrounding a central cluster of stamens. Narrow leaves are bronzy when new, maturing to glossy bright green or golden green; they turn brilliant yellow in fall except where winters are very mild. Take many soil types, including alkaline soil. In the Middle South, plant against south or west wall. In late dormant season, prune as needed to shape. On shrubby types, remove oldest stems occasionally to encourage strong new growth. Resistant to damage by deer.

'Chico'. DWARF CARNATION-FLOWERED POMEGRANATE. Compact shrub to 3 ft. high and wide. Easily kept to 1½ ft. high with occasional pruning. Double orange-red flowers. No fruit.

'Legrellei' ('California Sunset'). To 8–10 ft. high and wide. Creamy white double flowers heavily striped coral-red. No fruit.

'Nana'. DWARF POMEGRANATE. Dense grower to 3 ft. high, 6 ft. wide. Blooms when a foot tall or less. Orange-red single flowers followed by small fruit. Nearly evergreen in mild winters.

'Nochi Shibari'. Grows to 8–10 ft. high and wide. Bears double dark red flowers. No fruit.

'Orange Blossom Special'. Dwarf, 2–3 ft. high and wide. Bright orange flowers. Great for pots. No fruit.

'Toyosho'. To 8–10 ft. high and wide. Double light apricot flowers. May produce small fruit.

PYCNANTHEMUM INCANUM

MOUNTAIN MINT
Lamiaceae
Perennial

US, MS, LS; USDA 6-8

FULL SUN OR PARTIAL SHADE

LITTLE TO MODERATE WATER

Pycnanthemum incanum

Native to the eastern U.S. This is one of those subtly attractive plants you see growing by the roadside—and then ask yourself, "I wonder what that is?" Grows 2–3 ft. tall and 3–4 ft. wide, with multiple upright stems. Dense clusters of silvery white flowers resembling those of bee balm (*Monarda didyma*) appear atop the stems by midsummer. Blooms are often spotted with green and pale pink. The silvery coloring extends down from the flowers to include the top 6–12 in. of the stems and leaves. Foliage has a pleasant minty fragrance; flowers attract bees and butterflies. Carefree plant for sun or dappled shade, moist

or dry soils. Good candidate for meadows, naturalized areas, woodland edges, even mixed borders.

PYRACANTHA

FIRETHORN
Rosaceae
Evergreen shrubs

ZONES VARY BY SPECIES

FULL SUN

MODERATE WATER

Pyracantha

Grown for bright fruit, evergreen foliage (may be semievergreen in cold climates), versatility in the landscape, ease of culture. All grow fast and vigorously, varying in habit from upright to sprawling. All have glossy green, 1- to 4-in.-long, ½- to 1-in.-wide leaves that are generally oval or rounded at ends; all bear flowers and fruit on spurs along wood of last year's growth. Small, spring blooms are dull creamy white, carried in flattish clusters; they're effective thanks to their profusion. Nearly all species have needlelike thorns—thus, the common name, firethorn.

The real glory of firethorns is in their thick clusters of pea-size, orange-red berries, which light up the garden for months. Selections with red, orange, or yellow berries are available; if color is important to you, buy plants when they are in fruit. Depending on selection, berries color up from late summer to mid-autumn; some types hang on until late winter, when they are cleared out by birds, storms, or decay. Dislodge old, withered or rotted berries with a jet of water or an old broom.

As shrubs and ground covers, firethorns look better and fruit more heavily if allowed to follow their natural growth habit. Prune only to check wayward branches. Plants can also be espaliered or sheared as hedges (though shearing comes at the expense of much fruit). Firethorns tolerate most soils but should not be overwatered. Two serious problems are fireblight (which can kill the plant) and scab (which causes defoliation and sooty-looking fruit); for best success, choose disease-resistant selections.

P. angustifolia 'Yukon Belle'. Zones US, MS, LS, CS; USDA 6-9. Selection of a Chinese native. To 8–10 ft. tall, 6–8 ft. wide. Bright orange berries. Quite cold hardy.

P. coccinea. SCARLET FIRETHORN. Zones US, MS, LS, CS; USDA 6-9 . From the eastern Mediterranean. Rounded growth to 8–10 ft. high (20 ft. trained against wall). Red-orange fruit. Best known for its cold-hardy selections, which include the following.

'Chadwickii'. Compact to 6 ft. high and spreading a few feet wider. Abundant orange-red berries.

'Red Cushion'. Spreading to 4 ft, high; 6 ft wide.

'Rutgers'. To 3 ft. high, 5 ft. wide, with orange berries. Good disease resistance.

P. crenatoserrata (*P. fortuneana, P. yunnanensis*). CHINESE FIRETHORN. Zones MS, LS, CS; USDA 7-9. From China. Vase-shaped plant to 15 ft. tall, 10 ft. wide. Limber branches make it a good choice for espalier. Orange to coral berries last through winter.

'Graberi'. More upright than the species, with huge clusters of dark red fruit.

P. hybrids. This category includes some of the most desirable firethorns. Plants vary in size, habit, and cold hardiness.

'Apache'. Zones US, MS, LS, CS; USDA 6-9. To 5 ft. high and 6 ft. wide. Large bright red berries last well into winter. Resistant to fireblight and scab.

'Fiery Cascade'. Zones US, MS, LS, CS; USDA 6-9. To 8 ft. tall, 9 ft. wide; berries turn from orange to red. Good disease resistance.

'Gold Rush'. Zones MS, LS, CS; USDA 7-9. To 10 ft, high and wide. Orange-yellow fruit. Resistant to scab.

'Mohave'. MOHAVE PYRACANTHA. Zones US, MS, LS, CS; USDA 6-9. To 12 ft. tall and wide. Heavy producer of big orange-red fruit that colors in late summer and lasts well into winter. Resistant to fireblight and scab.

'Navaho'. NAVAHO PYRACANTHA. Zones US, MS, LS, CS; USDA 6-9. To 6 ft. high, 8 ft. wide. Orange-red berries. Resistant to fireblight and scab.

'Red Elf'. Zones MS, LS, CS; USDA 7-9. Densely branched plant to 2 ft. high and wide—good in containers. Long-lasting bright red fruit.

'Ruby Mound'. Zones MS, LS, CS; USDA 7-9. Among the most graceful of ground cover firethorns. Long, arching, drooping branches make broad mounds 2½ ft. high, spreading to about 10 ft. Bright red fruit.

'Silver Lining'. Zones MS, LS, CS; USDA 7-9. Grows to 3 ft. high and wide. Green leaves with white edges. In winter, leaves turn purple with pinkish-white edges. Few berries.

'Teton'. TETON PYRACANTHA. Zones US, MS, LS, CS; USDA 6-9. Very cold hardy. Columnar growth to 12 ft. tall, 4 ft. wide. Golden yellow fruit.

'Tiny Tim'. Zones US, MS, LS, CS; USDA 6-9. Compact, small-leafed plant to 3 ft. high. Few or no thorns. Red berries. Informal low hedge, barrier, tub plant.

P. koidzumii. FORMOSA FIRETHORN. Zones LS, CS; USDA 8-9. Unruly grower to 8–12 ft. tall and wide. Selections are better known than the species and include the following.

'Santa Cruz' ('Santa Cruz Prostrata'). Low-growing, spreading plant, branching from base. To 6 ft. tall but easily kept below 3 ft. by pinching out the occasional upright branch. Red fruit. Plant 4–5 ft. apart for ground or bank cover. Very resistant to scab.

'Victory'. Vigorous growth to 10 ft. tall, 8 ft. wide. Dark red berries color late in the year but hold on well. Resistant to scab.

PYROSTEGIA VENUSTA

FLAME VINE
Bignoniaceae
Evergreen vine

🌡 **CS, TS; USDA 9-11**

☼ ◑ **FULL SUN OR PARTIAL SHADE**

💧 **MODERATE WATER**

Pyrostegia venusta

Flame vine is as brilliant as it sounds, with branch-end clusters of tubular, 3-in., orange flowers lighting up this 20–40-ft. evergreen vine during winter; in warmest gardens, bloom starts in fall and continues into spring. Native to South America. Climbs rapidly by tendrils, twining along fences and eaves and over pergolas and arbors, ultimately spilling off retaining walls and covering banks. Leaves consist of two or three oval, 2-in. leaflets; paired leaflets have a tendril between them rather than a third leaflet. Plants growing in Florida sometimes form slender, foot-long fruit capsules. In central Florida, this is the most popular vine for covering fences and other structures.

Tolerates many soils. Revels in heat; in cooler climates, plant along a south- or west-facing wall. Prune in spring or summer, after bloom has finished. Formerly known as *P. ignea*, *Bignonia venusta*.

PYRUS CALLERYANA

CALLERY PEAR
Rosaceae
Deciduous tree

🌡 **US, MS, LS, CS; USDA 6-9**

☼ **FULL SUN**

💧 **MODERATE TO REGULAR WATER**

Pyrus calleryana

"How can something start off so good and end up so bad?" is a question that aptly sums up the life of this ornamental pear in the South. Native to China, it rocketed to overwhelming popularity since its flagship selection, 'Bradford,' appeared in the 1960s. It combines spectacular spring flowers and fall foliage with a tidy, formal shape and tolerance for heat, drought, compacted soil, and polluted air. Unfortunately, it wasn't until callery pears festooned practically every highway median, shopping mall parking lot, and suburban front yard that its serious flaws became apparent.

Growing 50 ft. tall and nearly as wide with a pyramidal to rounded shape, callery pear is both weedy and savagely thorny. Blooms have a fishy odor. "Tuna on a trunk" is a good way to describe the situation. When thornless selections like those listed below cross-pollinate, they produce hundreds of mostly thorny seedlings that form impenetrable thickets. Indeed, this tree is now considered an invasive weed in many states. Most selections are prone to fireblight, a disease that blackens leaves and branch tips. 'Capital,' 'Redspire,' and 'White House' are very susceptible; do not plant them.

'Aristocrat.' One of three recommended substitutes for 'Bradford' (see below). Grows to 40 ft. tall, 25 ft. wide with a shape reminiscent of red maple (*Acer rubrum*). Well-spaced branches are more horizontal and less prone to storm damage than those of 'Bradford'. However, it doesn't flower as profusely, and its yellow-orange fall foliage is less showy. Somewhat susceptible to fireblight.

'Bradford.' BRADFORD PEAR. Fast-growing, easy to transplant, tough, adaptable, and disease-resistant. Showy spring flowers and spectacular glossy red fall foliage. Unfortunately, it lacks a central leader; main limbs fan out from a small area on the trunk, making it extremely prone to splitting in storms. Can grow 50 ft. tall and 40 ft. wide in 20 years, but seldom survives that long. Should no longer be planted.

'Chanticleer' ('Cleveland Select,' 'Select,' 'Stone Hill'). Best substitute for 'Bradford.' Grows 40 ft. tall, 20 ft. wide with a narrowly pyramidal shape. Not susceptible to fireblight or storm damage. Heavy bloomer with yellow-orange to purple fall foliage.

'Trinity.' Round-headed tree to 30 ft. tall and wide. Resists fireblight. Not prone to wind damage. Showy orange-red fall color.

QUERCUS
OAK
Fagaceae
Deciduous and evergreen trees

✎ **ZONES VARY BY SPECIES**

☼ **FULL SUN**

💧 **REGULAR WATER, EXCEPT AS NOTED**

Quercus alba

Any search for sturdy, long-lived, trouble-free shade and street trees should start with the oaks. Of the more than 600 species worldwide, many are native to the South. They thrive in such a wide range of habitats, it's hard to find a place where one or more species won't grow. Some are evergreen. Deciduous species often display terrific fall color. Massive trunks and limbs, handsome bark, and picturesque winter silhouettes are the norm. Acorns, however, are their most distinguishing feature. These nuts held by cuplike caps provide vital sustenance for a host of wildlife, including deer, wild turkeys, wood ducks, quail, squirrels, and rabbits. Those produced by species in the white oak group (*Q. alba*, *Q. bicolor*, *Q. macrocarpa*, *Q. montana*, and others) mature in one year and can be eaten by humans. Those in the red and black oak group (*Q. coccinea*, *Q. palustris*, *Q. rubra*, *Q. velutina*, and others) mature in two years and are too bitter with tannin to be palatable. Leaves of the first group have rounded lobes; leaves of the latter have pointed lobes.

BEST OAKS FOR THE SOUTH

Here are our choices for the best oaks to plant or conserve in Southern gardens.

Q. acutissima. SAWTOOTH OAK. Deciduous. Zones US, MS, LS, CS; USDA 6-9. Native to China, Korea, Japan. Moderate to fast growth to 35–45 ft. tall and wide, usually with open, spreading habit. Deeply furrowed bark. Bristle-toothed, shiny dark green leaves are 3½–7½ in. long, a third as wide; they look like chestnut (*Castanea*) leaves. Foliage is yellowish on expanding, yellow to yellowish brown in fall; it may hang on late into winter. Fairly tolerant of various soils, though it prefers well-drained acid soil. Stands up well to heat and humidity. No serious problems. Good shade, lawn, or street tree. Should not be planted near unmanaged or natural areas, as its abundant seedlings crowd out native oaks, and its acorns are less nutritious for wildlife.

Q. alba. WHITE OAK. Deciduous. Zones US, MS, LS, CS; USDA 6-9. Native from Maine to Florida, west to Minnesota and Texas. Slow to moderate growth to 50–80 ft., taller in the wild. Pyramidal when young; in maturity, a majestic round-headed tree with massive limbs, often broader than tall. Leaves are 4–8 in. long, dark green above, lighter beneath, with deep, rounded lobes. Light gray to brown bark is attractively ridged and furrowed, beautiful in early morning or late afternoon sun. Folklore has it that when the emerging leaves are as big as a mouse's ear, it is time to plant corn. Fall color varies from russet red to wine-red. Best in rich, deep, moist, preferably acid soil. One of the handsomest oaks, useful for timber, flooring, and barrel making but not widely planted because of its ultimate size and slow growth. Where it occurs naturally, however, it is among the most cherished of trees; it is the oak associated with treaty signings and other historic events.

Q. bicolor. SWAMP WHITE OAK. Deciduous. Zones US, MS, LS; USDA 6-8. Native from Quebec to Georgia, west to Michigan and Arkansas. Slow to moderate growth to 50–60 ft.,

ABOVE: Pyrus calleryana

rarely taller, with equal or greater spread. Shallowly lobed or scalloped leaves are 3–7 in. long, a little more than half as wide, shiny dark green above, silvery white beneath. Fall color usually yellow, sometimes reddish purple. Bark of trunk and branches flakes off in scales. Needs acid soil. Native to wet sites but tolerates drought.

Q. buckleyi. TEXAS RED OAK. Deciduous. Zones US, MS, LS, CS; USDA 6-9. Native to Texas. To 15–30 ft. with nearly equal spread; makes either a low-branching, multitrunked small tree or a multistemmed shrubby clump. Yellow-green leaves, to 4 in. long, are deeply cut into five to seven sharp-pointed lobes; turn maroon and scarlet in fall. Gray-brown bark is smooth in youth, develops narrow ridges and shallow fissures with age. Adapts to various soils; tolerates drought.

Q. coccinea. SCARLET OAK. Deciduous. Zones US, MS, LS, CS; USDA 6-9. Native from Maine to Florida, west to Minnesota and Missouri. In deep, rich, acidic soil, grows at a moderate to rapid rate, reaching a possible 60–80 ft. tall, 40–60 ft. wide. High, light, open-branching habit. Bright green leaves are 3–6 in. long, a little more than half as wide, with deeply cut, pointed lobes. Foliage turns scarlet where fall nights are chilly. Scaly gray-brown bark. Deep roots. Good street or lawn tree. Fine to garden under.

Q. falcata. SOUTHERN RED OAK, SPANISH OAK. Deciduous. Zones US, MS, LS, CS; USDA 6-9. Native from Virginia to Florida, westward to southern Illinois and Arkansas. Moderate growth to 70–80 ft., eventually with rounded crown as wide or wider than tree is tall. Dark green leaves 5–9 in. long, sometimes longer, with sharp-pointed lobes varying in number from three to nine. Fall color not usually significant. Dark gray bark has deep, narrow furrows. Best in acidic soils, but tolerates relatively poor and dry soils. The related cherrybark oak (*Quercus falcata pagodifolia*) grows on occasionally flooded sites.

Q. fusiformis. TEXAS LIVE OAK. Evergreen. Zones MS, LS, CS; USDA 7-9. Often compared to live oak (*Q. virginiana*), as it is evergreen, similar in size and form, and a regional icon. However, it has a distinct natural range from northern Mexico into Oklahoma, so it is more cold hardy than *Q. virginiana*. Tolerant of high heat as well, it is drought tolerant, growing 20–50 ft. tall and 25–40 ft. wide. Grows in well-drained, alkaline to slightly acid soil. It can form thickets when roots send up new sprouts, resulting in the classic oasis in a sunny field of bluebonnets.

Q. glauca. BLUE JAPANESE OAK, EVERGREEN OAK. Evergreen. Zones LS, CS; USDA 8-9. Native to Japan, China, Taiwan. Moderately slow growth to 20–30 ft. (rarely 40 ft.) tall and about half that wide; upright, oval form. Foliage grows in a dense mass, making this tree an excellent choice for a screen. Leathery, wavy-margined leaves to 5½ in. long, 2½ in. wide; dark green above, silky gray beneath. New leaves are especially handsome, often bronzy or purplish green. Smooth bark. Prefers well-drained, fertile, slightly acid soil but tolerates heavy clay.

Q. glaucoides (*Q. laceyi*). LACEY OAK. Zones MS, LS, CS; USDA 7-9. Evergreen. Native to the Texas Hill Country and central and southern Mexico. Rounded form to 20–25 ft. tall, 20–30 ft. wide. Bluish green leaves to 6 in. long, half as wide, smooth edged or very subtly toothed; new growth is pinkish. Textured gray bark. Tolerates heat, drought, alkaline soil. Moderate water.

Q. gravesii. CHISOS RED OAK. Deciduous. Zones US, MS, LS, CS; USDA 6-8. Texas native to 40 ft. tall, 35 ft. wide. Lobed leaves are smaller and less deeply indented than those of *Q. texana*. Dark green leaves; blackish bark. Foliage often turns bright yellow and red in fall. Tolerates drought and limy soils.

Q. hemisphaerica. DARLINGTON OAK, LAUREL OAK. Zones MS, LS, CS, TS; USDA 7-11. Evergreen in Coastal and Tropical South, deciduous elsewhere. Native to sandy uplands on the Coastal Plains and piedmont from southern Virginia to Florida, eastward to East Texas and southeast Arkansas. To 50 ft. or more in height, somewhat less in spread. Narrowly oval, smooth-edged, leathery leaves are shiny dark green, 1–4 in. long, 1½–1¼ in. wide. Adapts to acid or alkaline conditions. *Q. laurifolia*, also called laurel oak or diamondleaf oak, is similar but needs acid soil and is native to floodplains. Both are useful street trees, being taller and less spreading than *Q. virginiana*.

Q. lyrata. OVERCUP OAK. Deciduous. Zones US, MS, LS, CS; USDA 6-9. Native to wetlands of central and southern U. S. from Delaware, east to southern Illinois and south to northern Florida and southeastern Texas. To 40–60 ft. high and wide with broad, rounded crown. Deep green leaves, 6–10 in. long and 4 in. wide, have five to nine rounded lobes and soft white undersides; turn yellow-brown, or sometimes orange to red, in fall. Burred cap covers most of the acorn. Prefers moist, acid soil. Good for wet areas. Tolerates flooding.

Q. macrocarpa. BUR OAK, MOSSY CUP OAK. Deciduous. Zones US, MS, LS; USDA 6-8. Native from Nova Scotia to Pennsylvania, westward to Manitoba and Texas. Rugged-looking tree growing slowly to 60–80 ft. high and at least as wide. Deeply furrowed dark gray bark. Leaves are glossy green above, whitish beneath, 4–10 in. long and half as wide, broad at tip, tapered at base. Yellowish fall color. Large acorns form in mossy cups. Similar to *Q. bicolor* but faster growing, more tolerant of adverse conditions. Needs lots of room. Acid or alkaline soil.

Q. michauxii. SWAMP CHESTNUT OAK. Deciduous. Zones US, MS, LS, CS; USDA 6-9. Native to moist areas, mostly in the coastal plains from New Jersey south to northern Florida, west to eastern Texas and north into the central Midwest. To 50–80 ft. tall and 30–50 ft. wide with a narrow, rounded crown. Shiny, dark green leaves, up to 11 inches long, are broad at the tip, narrow at the base, with large rounded teeth, wavy edges, and soft gray undersides; turn dark red in fall. Perfers moist, acid soil. Good for wet areas. Tolerates flooding.

Q. montana (*Q. prinus*). CHESTNUT OAK, BASKET OAK. Deciduous. Zones US, MS, LS; USDA 6-8. Native from southern parts of Maine and Ontario southward to South Carolina and Alabama. Moderate growth to an eventual dense, rounded form, 60–70 ft. tall, 50 ft. wide. Large, edible acorns are prized by wildlife. Bark often quite dark, even nearly black, becoming deeply furrowed with age. Unlobed leaves with coarse, rounded teeth are 4–6 in. long, 1½–3½ in. wide; in fall, they change from deep yellowish green to yellow or orange. This tree needs acid soil; it tolerates poor, dry, rocky soil but looks better and grows faster with good soil and adequate water. Does not tolerate poor drainage.

Q. muehlenbergii. CHINKAPIN OAK. Deciduous. Zones US, MS, LS, CS; USDA 6-9. Native from New England west to Minnesota and Texas. Moderate growth during early years, slowing with age. Reaches 80 ft. or more in the wild, with an even greater spread; usually smaller in cultivation, and slender until middle-aged. Leaves are 6½ in. long and 3 in. wide, with coarse, sawtoothed margins; dark glossy green above, silvery beneath. Fall color varies from yellow brown to rust brown. Scaly gray bark. Grows in a wide range of soils, including clay and dry, rocky limestone.

Q. myrsinifolia. JAPANESE LIVE OAK. Evergreen. Zones MS, LS, CS; USDA 7-9. Native to Japan, China. To 20–30 ft. tall and nearly as wide; usually round headed in age. Narrow, glossy, dark green leaves 2½–4 in. long, toothed toward tip; purplish when new. Smooth dark gray bark. Grows well in almost all soils. Unlike most oaks, it is graceful rather than sturdy; typically identified as an oak by its acorns. No serious problems. Most cold-hardy evergreen oak that is commonly cultivated.

Q. nigra. WATER OAK. Deciduous. Zones US, MS, LS, CS; USDA 6-9. Native to lowland stream banks throughout southeastern U.S. Moderate to fast growth to 50–80 ft. tall and not quite as wide, with conical or rounded canopy. Dark green, slightly 3-lobed leaves 1½–4 in. long, broader toward the tip; turn yellow to brown in fall, hang on late. Dark gray bark is smooth in youth, rougher with age. Limbs subject to breakage by wind, snow, ice. Tolerates many types of soil, but not alkaline soil. Provide moist to wet conditions. Used as shade and street tree. A favorite host for mistletoe (*Phoradendron serotinum*).

Q. palustris. PIN OAK. Deciduous. Zones US, MS, LS; USDA 6-8. Native from Massachusetts to Delaware, westward to Wisconsin and Arkansas. Moderate to fairly rapid growth to 50–80 ft. tall, 25–40 ft. wide. Slender and pyramidal when young, open and round headed at maturity. Smooth brownish gray bark becomes shallowly ridged with age. Lower branches tend to droop almost to the ground; if the lowest whorl is cut away, branches above will adopt same habit. Only when fairly tall will it have good clearance beneath lowest branches. Glossy, dark green leaves, 3–6 in. long and nearly as wide, are deeply cut into bristle-pointed lobes. In fall, leaves turn red and then russet-red; may hang on in winter. Needs plenty of water; tolerates poorly drained soils. Widely used as a lawn and street tree. Needs acid soil. 'Green Pillar' is columnar to 50 ft. tall by 15 ft. wide and has very glossy, dark green leaves.

Q. phellos. WILLOW OAK. Deciduous. Zones US, MS, LS, CS; USDA 6-9. Native from New York to Florida, westward to Missouri and Texas. Fast to moderate growth to 50–90 ft. tall, 30–50 ft. wide. Superior lawn or street tree. Oval to rounded form with upswept branches. Smooth gray bark becomes shallowly ridged in age. Smooth-edged leaves are bright rich green, 2½–5 in. long, ⅓–1 in. wide; they look more like willow (*Salix*) leaves than oak leaves. Foliage turns yellowish or russet-red before falling. Most delicate foliage pattern of all oaks. No serious problems. Tolerates poor drainage. Needs acid soil. 'Hightower' is pyramidal, has shiny, dark green leaves, and resists mites. 'Shiraz' is also pyramid shaped; leaves turn red in fall.

Q. polymorpha. MONTER-REY OAK, MEXICAN WHITE OAK. Evergreen, semievergreen. Zones MS, LS, CS, TS; USDA 7-10. Native to Mexico and southernmost Texas; however, it is a reliable landscape plant for Hill Country and Dallas landscapes. In the cooler zones, it will lose its leaves like a deciduous oak. Resistant to oak wilt. Drought tolerant. Leaves are 3–5 in. long. Grows relatively fast, reaching 45 ft. tall and 35 ft. wide at maturity.

Q. rhisophylla. LOQUAT-LEAFED OAK. Evergreen. Zones MS, LS, CS, TS; USDA 7-10. Native to Mexico, this large-leaved oak

is a good heat- and drought-tolerant choice. Grows 40 ft. tall and wide.

Q. robur. ENGLISH OAK. Deciduous. Zones US, MS, LS; USDA 6-8. Native to Europe, northern Africa, western Asia. Moderate growth rate; reaches 90 ft. tall in the wild, but in gardens typically grows 40–60 ft. tall, 30 ft. wide. Rather short trunk and very wide, open head in maturity. Grayish black, deeply furrowed bark. Dark green leaves grow 3–4½ in. long and half as wide, with rounded lobes; they hold until late fall, then drop without much color change. Takes acid or alkaline soil.

Q. r. fastigiata, upright English oak, is narrow and columnar (much like Lombardy poplar, *Populus nigra* 'Italica') when young, then branches out to a broad, pyramidal form at maturity. Both *Q. r. fastigiata* and the species are prone to mildew. Selections in the Fastigiata Group include 'Regal Prince', which is similar in height but slightly wider. It is a cross between *Q. r. fastigiata* and an oak from the southeastern U.S.; it's adaptable and resistant to mildew.

Other mildew-resistant selections include 'Crimson Spire', a columnar form to 45 ft. tall and only 15 ft. wide, with red fall color; 'Rose Hill', with particularly attractive glossy foliage; and 'Skyrocket', an excellent performer with the same form as 'Crimson Spire' but with yellow-brown fall foliage. 'Concordia' grows about 25 ft. tall and wide, with golden foliage. 'Kindred Spirit', a hybrid between columnar English oak and *Q. bicolor*, grows 35 ft. tall, 6 ft. wide, with good disease resistance and tolerance to wet soil and drought.

Q. rubra. RED OAK, NORTH-ERN RED OAK. Deciduous. Zones US, MS, LS; USDA 6-8. Native from Nova Scotia to Pennsylvania, westward to Minnesota and Iowa. Fast growth to 60–75 ft. tall, 50 ft. wide in gardens (over 100 ft. tall in wild) with broad, spreading branches and round-topped crown. With maturity, bark becomes quite dark and fissured. Dark green leaves to 5–8 in. long, 3–5 in. wide, with sharp-pointed lobes. New leaves and leafstalks are red in spring, turning bright red to russet red in fall. Smooth gray bark. Prefers moist,

TOP: Quercus virginiana; BOTTOM: Q. coccinea; Q. stellata

fertile soils. Stake young plants. High-branching habit and reasonably open shade make it a good tree for big lawns, parks, broad avenues. Deep roots make it good to garden under. Usually fairly trouble free. Needs acid soil.

Q. shumardii. SHUMARD RED OAK. Deciduous. Zones US, MS, LS, CS; USDA 6-9. Native from Kansas to southern Michigan, southward to North Carolina and Florida, westward to Texas. Similar to *Q. coccinea* but slightly less cold hardy. Smooth gray bark. Dark green leaves turn yellow to red in autumn. Tolerates drought and a wide range of soils, including both acid and alkaline types. 'Panache' has dark green leaves that turn orange-red in fall. 'Prominence' is dense with up-sweeping branches and red fall color.

Q. stellata. POST OAK. Deciduous. Zones US, MS, LS, CS; USDA 6-9. Native from Florida to Massachusetts, west to Kansas and Texas. Slow growing to 40–50 ft. tall and wide (may reach 100 ft.

tall). Forms dense, round canopy and stout, picturesque branches. Leathery, dark green leaves are large (to 8 in. long), with straplike lobes that give them a cruciform appearance. Fall color is not usually bright—it varies from yellow to brown—but leaves hang from branches through winter. Distinctive gray bark with scales, ridges, furrows, cracks. Tolerates dry, rocky, and sandy soils; takes acid or alkaline soil.

Q. texana (*Q. nuttallii*). NUT-TALL OAK. Deciduous. Zones US, MS, LS, CS; USDA 6-9. Native to bottomland hardwood forest from east Texas to Alabama. This species has shot to the top of many a landscaper's list from relative obscurity just 10 years ago. It combines fast growth, pleasing form, tolerance of many soils, and bright red fall color. Grows to 70 feet tall with a symmetrical, rounded form. Glossy green leaves, 4–9 in. long, have 5 to 9 deeply cut lobes. Unlike most oaks, will grow in poorly drained, compacted clay and seasonally flooded areas.

'Charisma'. To 50–60 ft. tall, with open branching habit. New foliage emerges maroon to chocolate colored before changing to deep green in summer. Good red fall color.

'Highpoint'. To 60–70 ft. tall, with dominant central leader. Leaves emerge bronzy red, turn green in summer, and then change to bright yellow and red in fall.

'Sangria'. Grows 60–70 ft. tall, with dominant central leader. New foliage emerges deep burgundy, changes to dark green in summer and yellow-orange in fall.

Q. virginiana. LIVE OAK. Evergreen. Zones LS, CS, TS; USDA 8-11. Native from Virginia to Florida, westward to Texas. Signature tree of the South. Moderate growth to 40–80 ft. tall, with spreading, heavy-limbed crown up to twice as wide. Very long lived; with age, bark becomes very dark and checked. Smooth-edged, quite narrow leaves, 1½–5 in. long, shiny dark green above, whitish beneath. Old leaves are all shed in spring before new growth emerges. Tree is often draped with Spanish moss (*Tillandsia usneoides*). Thrives on moisture and does best in deep, rich soil, though it tolerates most soils, including alkaline ones. Also tolerates salt spray; makes an excellent tree for the beach when planted in groups back from the dunes. Widely used as street tree in native range. Needs lots of space. 'Boardwalk' is pyramidal in shape, as is densely foliaged 'Cathedral'. 'Highrise' is columnar to upright oval in form and ideal for streets or limited spaces.

CARE

Nothing is more important to success in growing oaks than choosing a species well adapted to your local soil and climate. For example, some oaks tolerate the salt air along the coast; most don't. A common mistake is planting acid-loving oaks, such as pin oak (*Q. palustris*) and red oak (*Q. rubra*) in alkaline soil. Trees quickly develop chlorosis (yellow leaves with green veins) and eventually die. Good oaks for alkaline soil include Texas red oak (*Q. buckleyi*), Texas live oak (*Q. fusiformis*), Chinkapin oak (*Q. muhlenbergii*), Monterrey oak, (*Q. polymorpha*) Nuttall oak (*Q. texana*), Shumard red oak

(*Q. shumardii*), and post oak (*Q. stellata*). Those that tolerate wet or poorly drained sites include *Q. hemisphaerica*, *Q. laurifolia*, *Q. lyrata*, *Q. falcata pagodifolia*, and *Q. michauxii*.

Plant oaks where you expect them to stay. Large, established oaks are very sensitive to disturbance or compaction of the soil. Don't park vehicles under the canopies of oaks. Don't pave beneath them. Don't pile or spread soil there. Don't cut roots.

Many insects and diseases attack oaks, but damage is seldom serious. Infestations of the large red-and-blue spotted gypsy moth caterpillars in the Upper South can defoliate entire trees. Wrapping trunks with single bands of duct tape smeared with a gummy paste called Tanglefoot provides control. The most serious disease, a fungus called oak wilt, has killed many trees in Texas. Spread by beetles attracted to wounds in the bark, it causes trees to defoliate and die. Methods of prevention include limiting any pruning to before February 1 or after June 30 and quickly painting fresh wounds with wound dressing or latex paint.

QUINCE
Rosaceae
Deciduous shrub

🌡 US, MS, LS, CS; USDA 6-9

☀ FULL SUN

💧 MODERATE WATER

'Pineapple' quince

Fruiting quince is a multistemmed shrub to 15–20 ft. tall and wide. White or blush pink flowers bloom in midspring; these are followed in autumn by fragrant,

yellow, round to pear-shaped or oblong fruit traditionally used in the South for jelly and preserves. Fruit reaches 3½–4½ in. long and remains as hard as a golf ball even after ripening. Native to Asia. For flowering quince, see *Chaenomeles*. Discussed here is the closely related *Cydonia oblonga*, a native of western Asia grown for fruit rather than flowers (it is often confused with flowering quince).

Quince is easy to grow in a sunny spot with slightly acid, well-drained soil; once established, it is incredibly tenacious and nearly impossible to kill, deliberately or otherwise. Named selections are usually available only through mail-order catalogs. Some selections need a pollenizer; planting at least two different ones ensures cross-pollination and larger crops.

'Aromatnaya'. Round; sweet yellow flesh that tastes like pineapple. This selection can be thinly sliced and eaten fresh.

'Cooke's Jumbo'. Pear-shaped fruit with white flesh. Very large; can weigh more than a pound.

'Crimea'. Large, round, yellow-fleshed selection with citrus, pineapple flavor. Can be thinly sliced and eaten fresh.

'Orange'. Medium-size, rounded fruit with orange-yellow flesh.

'Pineapple'. Large, roundish, golden yellow fruit. White flesh has a pineapple flavor.

'Portugal'. Oblong fruit with pinkish flesh that turns red when cooked. Ripens early.

'Smyrna'. Large, round to oblong fruit with lemon-yellow skin and white flesh. Good flavor.

QUISQUALIS INDICA
RANGOON CREEPER
Combretaceae
Deciduous vine

🌡 TS; USDA 10-11

☀◑ FULL SUN OR PARTIAL SHADE

💧 REGULAR WATER

Quisqualis indica

This plant had early botanists scratching their heads for some time. Translated from the Latin, its name means "Who?" and "What?" The confusion stems from the fact that the plant is shrubby in youth, then becomes a scrambling vine. Its flowers also change color with age.

Native to Burma, Malaysia, New Guinea, and the Philippines. In south Florida and South Texas, where it is hardy, it climbs to an eventual 30 ft.; elsewhere, it may reach half this size in a season. Rich green, oval, pointed leaves with prominent veins grow to 5 in. long; new growth is covered with brownish fuzz. Fragrant, long-tubed flowers up to 3 in. long are borne at stem ends during summer. Blossoms are white at first, then change to pink and, finally, to red. Rangoon creeper is easy to grow and tolerates most soils. Prune to shape after flowering.

R

RADERMACHERA SINICA

CHINA DOLL
Bignoniaceae
Evergreen tree

✎ **TS; USDA 10-11; OR HOUSEPLANT**

☼ ◑ **FULL SUN OR PARTIAL SHADE; BRIGHT LIGHT**

💧 **REGULAR WATER**

Radermachera sinica

This beautiful native of China is most often grown as a houseplant, but when planted outdoors in South Texas or central or southern Florida, it grows quickly into a small, graceful tree about 25 ft. tall and 10–12 ft. wide. Prized for its handsome, glossy, rich green leaves, which are divided into many 2-in. leaflets. Hardy to about 20°F. Airy, layered branches and symmetrical, upright form are reminiscent of chinaberry (*Melia*). Mature plants bloom in summer, bearing at their branch tips clusters of powerfully fragrant, 3-in. blossoms in pure white to sulphur-yellow. The flowers open at night and drop from the branches the next day. 'Crystal Doll' is a slower-growing selection with striking yellow-and-green variegated leaves.

Indoors, place in a very bright window (but be sure to protect from hottest afternoon sun). Insufficient light results in leggy growth. Provide evenly moist, well-drained soil; do not let soil dry out, or plant will drop leaves. Fertilize every other week in spring and summer and once a month in fall and winter with a general-purpose liquid house-plant fertilizer. Spider mites and aphids are frequent pests; control them with insecticidal soap or horticultural oil. Plants grown outdoors have fewer problems; they thrive in fertile, well-drained soil.

RADISH

Brassicaceae
Cool-season annual

✎ **US, MS, LS, CS, TS; USDA 6-11**

☼ ◑ **LIGHT SHADE IN HOTTEST CLIMATES**

💧 **REGULAR WATER**

'Cherry Belle' radishes

Colorful and crunchy, the radish is a fast-maturing, easy-to-grow vegetable that prefers cool weather. It is also surprisingly varied. The edible roots may be short and rounded or long and slender; flavor may be sweet, mild, or hot; and colors include red, pink, rose, lavender, purple, black, and white.

Radishes are divided into spring, summer, and winter types.

Spring radishes mature in just three to four weeks from seed. Their crisp texture and mildly pungent flavor result from growing in cool weather. Begin planting two to six weeks before the last frost, and continue until four weeks after it; quality declines with warm weather in late spring. You can also plant them for a fall crop by sowing seed in early fall, four to six weeks before the first frost. And in the Coastal and Tropical South (USDA 9-11), radishes can be grown in winter. Recommended selections include 'Burpee White' (25 days from sowing to harvest; round white roots), 'Cherry Belle' (22 days; round red), 'Cherriette' (24 days; round red), 'Easter Egg II' (25 days; oval roots in mix of lavender, pink, rose, red, white), 'Long Scarlet' (25 days; long, narrow red), and 'Sparkler White Tip' (24 days; round red-and-white).

Summer radishes tolerate heat better than spring types. Plant for harvest in spring, early summer, or fall. The group includes 'French Breakfast' (23 days; oblong red roots with white tip) and 'White Icicle' (25 days; long, slender white roots).

Winter radishes, which require 50 to 60 days to mature, are larger and firmer than spring and summer radishes. Some are rounded; others, including the oriental daikon types, are long and carrot shaped. Roots are crisp and mildly pungent and keep well in storage. They require cool weather at the end of their growing season, so plant them as a fall crop (or as a winter crop in the Coastal and Tropical South). Sow seeds at least four weeks before the first fall frost. If you plant them in spring, they may flower before forming roots. Selections include 'April Cross' (60 days; white daikon type), 'Miyashige' (50 days; white daikon type), 'Red Flame' (24 days; sweet, long, narrow, white-tipped), 'Red Meat' (50 days; pink flesh, green skin), 'Round Black Spanish' (55 days; round, black roots with white flesh), and 'Summer Cross' (50 days; white daikon type). There are also novelties like 'Misato Rose Flesh' (60 days), which is green outside and pink inside; 'Watermelon (55 days; green skin that fades to white and bright red interior); and 'China Rose' (55 days; red outside and white inside).

CARE

Like other root crops, radishes need soft, loose soil. If your soil is heavy clay, till in plenty of organic matter or plant in raised beds. Sow spring and summer radishes ½ in. deep in rows spaced 6–12 in. apart. Sow winter radishes ¾ in. deep; space rows 18–20 in. apart. Thin plants soon after they emerge, leaving 2–3 in. between spring and summer radishes and 6 in. between winter radishes. When first true leaves emerge, apply ¼ cup of 10-10-10 fertilizer per 10 ft. of row. Keep soil evenly moist; excessive or uneven moisture may cause radishes to split or become tough and hot in flavor. Floating row covers placed over developing plants will protect them against flea beetles (which eat the foliage) and root maggots (which eat the roots).

Harvest spring and summer radishes as soon as they reach ¾–1½ in. in diameter. ('White Icicle' pushes up out of the ground when it is ready.) Leaving them in longer than this can result in hot-tasting, woody roots. Winter radishes can stay in the ground longer, especially in cool weather. Daikon types can grow 1–1½ ft. long with no loss in quality.

RANUNCULUS

Ranunculaceae
Perennials

✎ **ZONES VARY BY SPECIES**

☼ ◑ ● **EXPOSURE NEEDS VARY BY SPECIES**

💧 **REGULAR WATER**

Ranunculus asiaticus

This very large genus comprises about 250 species of widely differing habit and appearance, but the three listed here are the ones most commonly grown in gardens. Not browsed by deer.

R. asiaticus. PERSIAN BUTTERCUP. Zones LS, CS, TS; USDA 8-11 (see below). Native to Asia Minor. Tuberous-rooted plant to 1½–2 ft. tall and wide, with fresh green, almost fernlike leaves. Blooms profusely in spring, when each flowering stalk bears one to four 3- to 5-in.-wide, semidouble to fully double blossoms that some say resemble small peony blooms. Flowers come in white, cream, and many shades of yellow, orange, red, and pink. Popular Tecolote Giant strain is available in single colors, mixed colors, and picotees. Bloomingdale strain offers the same range of colors on dwarf plants 8–10 in. high. All types are good in the ground or in pots.

Tuberous roots are hardy to 10°F. In the Coastal and Tropical South (USDA 9-11), plant in fall for bloom in winter, early spring; treat plants as annuals there. Beyond hardiness range, plant in spring as soon as ground is workable; or start roots indoors four to six weeks before the usual last-frost date. Nurseries sell tuberous roots of various sizes; all produce equally large blossoms, but bigger roots yield a greater number of flowers.

Grow in full sun, in organically enriched, very well-drained soil (if necessary, plant in raised beds). Set roots with prongs down, 2 in. deep (1 in. deep in heavier soils) and 6–8 in. apart. Water thoroughly, then withhold water until leaves emerge. Birds are fond of ranunculus shoots, so protect sprouting plants with netting or wire. Or start plants in pots or flats, then set them in the garden when they're 4–6 in. tall—too mature to appeal to birds. (You can also start with nursery-grown seedlings.) Remove faded flowers to encourage more bloom.

When flowering tapers off and leaves start to yellow, stop watering the plants and allow the foliage to die back. Where tuberous roots are hardy in the ground, they can be left undisturbed—as long as soil can be kept dry during summer. Some gardeners dig plants when foliage turns yellow; cut off the tops; let roots dry for a week or two; and store them in a cool, dry place until planting time. But because roots don't store that well, most people find it simpler to discard the plants and set out new roots when the time comes.

R. ficaria. LESSER CELANDINE. Zones US, MS, LS, CS; USDA 6-9. From Europe and Eastern Asia. Aggressive, weedy perennial spreading by bulblets on stems and underground tubers. Forms a dense mat of heart-shaped, 1- to 2-in.-wide, shiny, dark green leaves, mounding to 3–4 in. tall. Bright yellow, buttercup-like flowers rise above the foliage in spring. Dies back in late summer. Has become a rampant weed in some areas. Less aggressive selections include 'Brazen Hussy', with purple-black leaves; 'Collarette', with heart-shaped leaves marked with silver; and 'Randall's White', with cream-yellow flowers and leaves marked with silver.

R. repens pleniflorus. CREEPING BUTTERCUP. Zones US, MS, LS, CS; USDA 6-9. From Eurasia; naturalized in North America. Vigorous plant with thick, fibrous roots and runners that root at the joints. Forms a lush, glossy, green mat to 1 ft. high, 6 ft. wide; leaves are roundish, deeply cut into three tooth-edged, 2-in.-long leaflets. Fully double, 1-in., button-shaped, bright yellow flowers are held above foliage on 1- to 2-ft. stems in spring. Can be invasive in constantly moist soil. Attractive deciduous ground cover for full sun to deep shade. Basic species is single flowered and just as aggressive as *R. r. pleniflorus.*

RASPBERRY
Rosaceae
Deciduous shrubs

✎ **US, MS; USDA 6-7, EXCEPT AS NOTED**

☼ **FULL SUN**

💧 **REGULAR WATER**

Raspberries

Savoring a mouthful of sweet, juicy raspberries is one of life's heady experiences. Several different species are found in Southern gardens. Red and yellow raspberries are derived

HOW TO GROW RASPBERRIES

PLANTING Raspberries prefer deep, slightly acid, moist but well-drained soil that contains plenty of organic matter. Choose a sunny, slightly sloping site with good air movement; avoid low-lying frost pockets. Do not plant where tomatoes, potatoes, eggplants, or peppers have been recently grown, as this increases the danger of soil-borne wilt disease. Also, remove any nearby wild raspberry or blackberry plants, which may harbor viral diseases. Don't accept divisions of raspberry plants from friends: They often have diseases that reduce production. Instead, buy certified disease-free plants from nurseries.

Plant bare-root plants during the dormant season (soak the roots in water overnight before planting). Set red and yellow raspberries and Mysore types 2½–3 ft. apart, in rows spaced 6–10 ft. apart; plant black and purple raspberries in slightly raised mounds 2–3 ft. apart, in rows 6–8 ft. apart. Cut back all canes to 6 in. at this time. Mulch plantings to discourage weeds and keep soil moist.

WATERING & FEEDING Give plants extra water during blooming and fruiting. Feed by sprinkling a handful of 10-10-10 fertilizer around each plant in spring and watering it in.

PRUNING & TRAINING Red, yellow, and Mysore raspberries are produced on erect plants with long, straight canes; they can be grown as freestanding shrubs and staked, but they are tidier and easier to manage if trained on a trellis or confined to a hedgerow (pairs of parallel wires strung at 3 ft. and 5 ft. above ground along either side of a row of plants).

Summer-bearing raspberries should produce three to five canes in the first year. Tie these to a trellis or confine them to a hedgerow. Dig or pull out any canes that grow more than 1 ft. away from trellis or outside of hedgerow. In late dormant season, cut the canes on trellis to 5–5½ ft. high, those in hedgerow to 4 ft. When growth recommences, new canes will appear all around the parent plant and between rows. After the original canes bear fruit, cut them to the ground. Then select the best 5 to 12 new canes and train these (they will bear the following summer); cut remaining new canes to ground.

Everbearing red and yellow raspberries fruit in the first autumn on the top third of cane, then again in the second summer on the lower two-thirds of cane. Cut off the upper portion of the cane after first harvest; cut out the cane entirely after the second harvest. As an alternative, you can follow the example of growers who cut everbearing canes to the ground yearly in fall after fruiting has finished (wait until late dormant season in the Upper South). You'll sacrifice one of the annual crops but get an extended harvest from late summer into fall, since the energy that would have gone into a summer crop is available for a bang-up fall harvest. Use a power mower in a large berry patch.

Canes of Mysore raspberries should be pruned heavily in late fall of the first year. This forces new growth that will produce berries the following year, from late winter to late spring. After canes have fruited, cut them to the ground.

Black and purple raspberries are produced on clump-forming plants with arching canes. No support is needed. In the first summer, force branching by cutting back new canes of black selections to 2 ft., those of purple kinds to 2½ ft. If you prefer trellising, cut black selections to 2–2½ ft., purple ones to 2½–3 ft. In late dormant season, remove all weak or broken canes. Leave six to eight canes in a hill or spaced 6–8 in. apart in a row. Shorten side branches to 8–10 in. for black raspberries, to 12–14 in. for purple types. The side branches will bear fruit in summer. After harvest, cut to the ground all canes that have fruited and cut back all new canes as described for first summer's growth.

CHALLENGES To control insects and fungal diseases on all raspberries, spray with lime sulfur during dormancy and again as leaf buds begin to open.

TOP: 'Allen' black raspberries; BOTTOM: 'Heritage' raspberries; 'Fallgold' raspberries

RASPBERRIES THAT TAKE THE HEAT

Though most raspberries dislike hot summers and need extended winter cold, there are some that take heat and thrive with little or no chill. 'Heritage' and 'Autumn Bliss' grow well in the Lower South (USDA 8). In the Coastal South (USDA 9), try 'Dorman Red' or 'Redwing'. In the Tropical South (USDA 10-11), plant Mysore raspberry (*R. niveus*), which has fruit that is black when ripe but is grown like red or yellow raspberry. Gardeners in the Tropical South can also grow everbearing raspberries such as 'Autumn Bliss' and 'Heritage' as annuals: Plant in spring and harvest in fall.

from *Rubus idaeus*, native to North America, Europe, and Asia. Black raspberries are selections of *R. occidentalis*, a North American species. Purple raspberries are hybrids between red and black types. Gardeners in the Tropical South grow Mysore raspberry (*R. niveus*), which, unlike other species, needs no winter chill to flower and fruit. For species grown as ornamentals, see *Rubus*.

Raspberries grow from shallow perennial roots that produce thorny biennial stems called canes. The canes of summer-bearing types grow to full size in the first year, then bear fruit the following summer. Red and yellow raspberries known as everbearing (or fall-bearing) produce two crops on the same canes—one in fall of the first year, the second in summer of the next year. In either case, the canes die after fruiting in the second year. New canes sprout to replace the old. Mysore raspberries bloom and fruit throughout the year, but the best crop comes from February to June.

Most raspberries generally have a high winter-chill requirement (more than 1,000 hours below 45°F per year), a demand not often met in the South. Without sufficient chill, bloom and fruit are poor. In addition, most raspberries don't like high summer heat. Thus, the most dependable areas for growing raspberries are the Upper and Middle South (USDA 6-7). For exceptions, see "Raspberries That Take the Heat," at left.

Red and yellow raspberries. Red selections are the most common; yellow types are mutations of red raspberries.

'Anne'. US, MS, LS; USDA 6-8. Everbearing. Large, sweet, yellow berries have unique flavor of apricots.

'Autumn Bliss'. Zones US, MS, LS; USDA 6-8. Everbearing. Very large red berries with fine flavor. Resists root rot.

'Dorman Red'. Zones US, MS, LS, CS; USDA 6-9. Summer-bearing. Large, firm, red fruit ripens late. Widely adapted selection with low winter-chill requirement. Vigorous, black-berrylike habit; must be trellised.

'Fallgold'. Everbearing. Large yellow fruit with good flavor. Very productive; very cold hardy.

'Goldie'. Everbearing. A sport of 'Heritage'. Produces deep yellow, high-quality fruit.

'Heritage'. Zones US, MS, LS; USDA 6-8. Everbearing. Firm, tasty red berries. Very popular selection.

'Indian Summer'. Everbearing. Small crops of large, tasty, red berries. Fall crop is often larger.

'Killarney'. Summer-bearing. Medium-size, firm red fruit with sweet-tart flavor. Good all-purpose raspberry that can be harvested over a long period. Vigorous, hardy.

'Kiwigold'. Everbearing. Yellow sport of 'Heritage' with excellent flavor. Vigorous and erect.

'Newburgh'. Summer-bearing. Large red berries. Late-ripening selection. Takes heavy soil fairly well.

'Polka'. Zones US, MS, LS; USDA 6-8. Everbearing. Very productive; nearly thornless. Excellent flavor. Heat tolerant.

'Redwing'. Zones US, MS, LS, CS; USDA 6-9. Everbearing. Larger, softer, and earlier than 'Heritage'. Heat tolerant.

'Reveille'. Summer-bearing. Very large, choice, bright red berries. Early. Vigorous, upright, and productive.

'Ruby'. Everbearing. Very large, mild-flavored red berries.

'Southland'. Everbearing. Medium-size, juicy, red fruit with excellent flavor. Early. Vigorous and hardy.

'Summit'. Everbearing. Large red berries with good flavor. Very productive. Resistant to root rot.

Black and purple raspberries. Black selections have blue-black fruit that is firmer and seedier than the fruit of red and yellow types, with a more pronounced flavor. Purple raspberries are crosses between black and red kinds.

'Allen'. Zones US, MS, LS; USDA 6-8. Large, glossy black fruit. Very sweet. Disease-resistant.

'Black Hawk'. Large, glossy, black berries. Sweet to mildly acid. Vigorous and productive.

'Brandywine'. Large purple berries. Tart flavor; good for jams and jellies. Ripens late.

'Cumberland'. Large black berries. Old, heavy-bearing selection.

'Jewel'. Large black berries. Vigorous, disease-resistant plant.

'Royalty'. Dusty purple, very large berries with excellent flavor. Vigorous and very productive.

RATIBIDA

Asteraceae
Perennials

🌿 **US, MS, LS, CS; USDA 6-9**

☀️ **FULL SUN**

💧 **REGULAR WATER**

Ratibida columnifera

Stiffly erect, branched, roughly hairy plants with deeply cut leaves. Flower heads like those of black-eyed Susan (*Rudbeckia hirta*) but have fewer ray flowers and a taller, more prominent central cone. Plant with other easy-care perennials.

R. columnifera. MEXICAN HAT. From the Great Plains. To 2½ ft. tall, 1 ft. wide. Flowers have drooping, yellow or brownish purple rays and a tall, columnar brown cone; look like sombreros.

R. pinnata. PRAIRIE or YELLOW CONEFLOWER. Native to central North America. To 4 ft. tall, 1½ ft. wide, with yellow rays and a nearly globular brown cone.

THE LARGE FLOWER BRACTS OF TRAVELER'S TREE RESEMBLE THOSE OF ITS COUSIN, BIRD OF PARADISE.

RAVENALA MADAGASCARIENSIS

TRAVELER'S TREE, TRAVELER'S PALM
Strelitziaceae
Evergreen tree

🌿 **TS; USDA 10-11; OR GROW IN POTS**

☀️ **FULL SUN**

💧 **REGULAR WATER**

Ravenala madagascariensis

Native to Madagascar. Upright clump to 30–40 ft. tall, 25–30 ft. wide, with numerous large leaves held in the shape of a gigantic fan atop an unbranched trunk. Foliage resembles that of banana (*Musa*). Spectacular accent in the garden or displayed against a large building. Protect from strong winds, which will shred the leaves. Small plants have some shade tolerance, can be used as potted specimens.

REHMANNIA ELATA

CHINESE FOXGLOVE
Plantaginaceae
Perennial

🌿 **MS, LS, CS, TS; USDA 7-11**

◐ **PARTIAL SHADE**

💧 **REGULAR WATER**

Rehmannia elata

Native to China. To 3 ft. tall, 1½–2 ft. wide. Clump of coarse, deeply toothed leaves (evergreen in mild-winter climates) sends up stalks loosely set with tubular, 3-in.-long flowers that look something like big, gaping foxgloves (*Digitalis*). Common form bears rosy purple blossoms with a yellow throat dotted in red; there is also a fine white form with cream throat (this one must be grown from cuttings or divisions). Where winters are mild, blooms from midspring well into fall; in colder climates, bloom comes in summer. Long lasting as a cut flower. Provide rich soil. Easy to grow from seed, root cuttings, divisions. Spreads quickly in moist, fertile soil and can be invasive.

RHAPHIOLEPIS

Rosaceae
Evergreen shrubs

🌿 **LS, CS, TS; USDA 8-11**

☀️◐ **FULL SUN OR LIGHT SHADE**

💧 **LITTLE TO REGULAR WATER**

Rhaphiolepis indica 'Dancer'

These dependable shrubs are among the best plants for the beach (they tolerate wind and salt spray), but they have many other uses as well. Their glossy, leathery leaves and compact form make them good subjects for foundation plantings, berms, low hedges, and containers. They bloom profusely from fall or midwinter until late spring, with flowers ranging in color from white through pink to nearly red. Berrylike dark blue fruit (not especially showy) follows the blossoms. Emerging leaves are tinged bronze and red.

Most stay low. The taller kinds seldom reach more than 5–6 ft., and pruning can keep them at 3 ft. almost indefinitely. For bushy, compact plants, pinch back branch tips at least once yearly, after flowering. Tolerate drought; need good drainage. Plants growing in partial shade are less compact and have fewer flowers than those growing in full sun.

R. x delacourii. Pink-flowered hybrid of *R. indica* and *R. umbellata*. To 6 ft. tall, 8 ft. wide. Small pink flowers in upright clusters. Leaves are 1¼–2¾ in. long. 'Georgia Petite' grows 2½ ft. high, 3½ ft. wide, with pink buds opening to white flowers; 'Snowcap' grows 4 ft. tall and wide. Pink buds open to pale pink flowers that fade to white; foliage turns burgundy-red in winter.

R. indica. INDIAN HAWTHORN. Native to China. To 4–5 ft. high, 5–6 ft. wide, with 1½- to 3-in.-long pointed leaves and ½-in. flowers in white tinged with pink. The species is seldom seen in gardens, but its selections are widely grown and sold. They differ mainly in flower color and in plant size and form; there is variation even within a selection. Flower color is especially inconsistent: In warmer climates and exposures, blossoms are usually lighter, and in general blooms are paler in fall than in spring. In high-rainfall, high-humidity areas such as Florida and the Gulf Coast, the same fungal leaf spot disease that defoliates photinia can ravage this species. In these regions, choose resistant selections such as 'Eskimo', 'Indian Princess', 'Olivia', 'Rosalinda', 'Snow Pink', and 'Snow White'; avoid susceptible ones like 'Enchantress', 'Fascination', 'Harbinger of Spring', 'Heather', 'Spring Rapture', 'Springtime', and 'White Enchantress'.

Selections include the following.

'Ballerina'. To 2 ft. tall, 4 ft. wide. Deep rosy pink flowers. Leaves take on a reddish tinge in winter.

'Clara'. To 3–5 ft. tall and wide. White flowers. Red new growth.

'Dancer'. Reaches 4 ft. tall, 5 ft. wide. Pure pink flowers.

'Enchantress' ('Pinkie'). To 3 ft. tall, 5 ft. wide, with rose-pink blooms. 'White Enchantress' has white blossoms.

'Eskimo'. To 6 ft. tall, 8 ft. wide. Highly resistant to leaf spot; hardy to 5°F.

'Indian Princess'. Up to 3 ft. high, 5 ft. wide. Light pink flowers. Resists leaf spot.

'Jack Evans'. To 4–5 ft. high, 4 ft. wide. Bright pink flowers. Leaves sometimes have a purplish tinge.

'Olivia'. To 4 ft. high, 2 ft. wide. Pure white flowers. Resistant to leaf spot.

'Rosalinda'. To 12–14 ft. high, 10 ft. wide. Pink flowers. Vigorous, can be trained to a small tree. Good disease resistance.

'Snow Pink'. Compact grower to 3 ft. high and wide. Pink flowers. Resists leaf spot.

'Snow White'. To 3–4 ft. high, 5 ft. wide. White flowers. Spreading habit. Resistant to leaf spot.

'Spring Rapture'. To 3–4 ft. high and wide. Rose-red blossoms.

'Spring Sonata'. To 4–5 ft. tall and wide. White flowers appear two to three weeks later than those of other selections.

'Springtime'. Vigorous, upright; 4–6 ft. tall and wide. Deep pink flowers.

R. 'Majestic Beauty'. Larger in every detail than the others. Can be trained as a single- or multitrunked tree to 20–25 ft. tall, 8–10 ft. wide; as a shrub, easily kept at 10–12 ft. tall, 6–8 ft. wide. Fragrant light pink flowers in clusters to 10 in. wide. Leaves are 4 in. long. Thought to be a hybrid between *Rhaphiolepis* and loquat (*Eriobotrya*).

R. umbellata. YEDDO HAWTHORN. Native to Japan, Korea. Vigorous grower to 4–6 ft. (sometimes to 10 ft.) high and wide. Distinguished from *R. indica* by its leathery dark green, 1- to 3-in.-long, roundish leaves. White, about ¾-in.-wide flowers. Thick and bushy in full sun. 'Minor' ('Gulf Green') is a compact, slow-growing form to 3–4 ft. high and wide.

RHAPIDOPHYL-LUM HYSTRIX

NEEDLE PALM
Arecaceae
Palm

✂ **US, MS, LS, CS, TS; USDA 6-11**

☀ ● **SUN OR SHADE**

💧💧 💧💧 **MODERATE TO AMPLE WATER**

Rhapidophyllum hystrix

Perhaps the hardiest palm in the world, taking temperatures well below 0°F; has reportedly survived winters as far north as Massachusetts. Native to the Coastal Plains from South Carolina to Florida and Mississippi. Shrubby and very slow growing, eventually reaching 6–8 ft. tall and wide; does not have a distinct trunk. The common name refers to the sharp black needles that protect the plant's crown and seeds. Dramatic-looking leaf fans are carried at the ends of smooth stems—they are lustrous dark green, to 3 ft. across, deeply cut into 6 to 12 segments.

Needle palm tolerates a wide range of soils and resists damage by browsing deer. Makes a good accent or understory plant. It's hard to find in garden centers and is usually purchased by mail. Buy only nursery-propagated plants, not those collected from the wild.

RHAPIS

LADY PALM
Arecaceae
Palms

✂ **CS, TS; USDA 9-11, EXCEPT AS NOTED; OR HOUSEPLANTS**

☽ **SOME SHADE; BRIGHT INDIRECT LIGHT**

💧 **REGULAR WATER**

Rhapis excelsa

These choice, slow-growing fan palms are beautiful, extremely versatile, and easy to grow. Cultivated in China since the 17th century, they achieved star status in Japan, where the samurai collected multitudes of prized forms. The two species described here, both hardy to 18°F, feature large, deep green leaves on sturdy canes like those of bamboo. In the Tropical and Coastal South, they may be grown outdoors in the shade, where they make excellent additions to foundation and understory plantings. Perfect for a large container in a Florida room. Elsewhere, they're wonderful, low-maintenance houseplants and patio plants (bring them indoors during cold weather). Because they take many years to reach a large size, lady palms command a premium price.

R. excelsa. LADY PALM. The only ornamental palms to have named selections in both green-leafed and variegated forms. Coarse, dark brown fiber covers the canes. Well adapted to summer heat.

Divided into three classes by size; most grow about as wide as tall. Standard forms grow to 14 ft. high; dwarf types to 5–8 ft.; mini-dwarfs to 4 ft. tall after 30 to 40 years. Selections include the following.

'Daruma'. Dwarf. Upright form. Resembles a small version of a standard lady palm.

'Gyokuho'. Mini-dwarf. Small, oval leaves and short, bushy habit. Grows only a few inches per year.

'Heiseinishiki'. Dwarf. Leaves are heavily variegated with broad, creamy yellow stripes.

'Koban'. Dwarf. Most popular selection. Full, spreading plant with large, wide leaves.

'Kodaruma'. Mini-dwarf. The shortest of all *R. excelsa* selections, often wider than tall. Good subject for bonsai.

'Tenzan'. Dwarf. Tallest of the dwarfs. Large, drooping leaves and slender canes.

'Zuikonishiki'. Dwarf. Leaves are elegantly striped in white and green.

R. humilis. SLENDER LADY PALM. The tallest of lady palms, sometimes exceeding 18 ft. high—but it grows only 3 ft. wide. Common name refers to slender canes. Large leaves are divided into many narrow segments. Despite its common name, all plants are male and must be propagated asexually.

▶ **CARE**

These palms do best with light shade and fertile, well-drained soil. Outdoors, site in the shadow of the house or the shade of tall trees. Indoors, place in bright indirect light and let soil go dry between waterings (but when you do water, soak the entire root system). Feed monthly from spring through fall with a general-purpose liquid houseplant fertilizer diluted to quarter-strength. Yellowing leaves are typically a sign that more fertilizer is needed. Regular repotting isn't necessary, as lady palms prefer to be slightly rootbound. To get more plants, divide in spring or early summer.

RHODODENDRON

Ericaceae
Evergreen and deciduous shrubs

✎ **FOR ZONES, SEE BELOW**

☼ **FILTERED SUNLIGHT, EXCEPT AS NOTED**

💧💧 **REGULAR TO AMPLE WATER**

⬦ **LEAVES ARE POISONOUS IF INGESTED**

Rhododendron 'Herbert'
(Gable hybrid azalea)

Rhododendrons and azaleas are among the South's favorite shrubs. Many people think of them as entirely different plants, but they both belong to the genus *Rhododendron*, which comprises more than 800 species and 10,000 named selections. Even to the untrained eye, one difference between the two groups is obvious: Rhododendrons generally have much larger leaves. From a technical standpoint, rhododendron flowers are bell shaped and have ten or more stamens, while azalea blooms are typically funnel shaped and have five stamens.

By making their choices carefully, gardeners in almost every part of the South can enjoy some of these plants, even if that means growing them in containers. Rhododendrons generally do better in the Upper and Middle South (USDA 6-7), though a number of selections thrive in the Lower South (USDA 8).

These include 'A. Bedford', 'Album Elegans', 'Anah Kruschke', 'Belle Heller', 'Caroline', 'Cheer', 'Chionoides', 'Cynthia', 'Fastuosum Flore Pleno', 'Ginny Gee', 'Holden', 'Jean Marie de Montague', 'Lee's Dark Purple', 'Nova Zembla', 'PJM', 'Purple Splendour', 'Scintillation', 'Trude Webster', 'Vulcan', 'Yaku Prince'. In addition, the following extend the range of rhododendrons into the Coastal South (USDA 9): 'Anna Rose Whitney', 'English Roseum', 'Janet Blair', 'Roseum Elegans', and the Southgate series (see by color below).

RHODODENDRON HYBRIDS AND SPECIES

Dozens of recommended rhododendrons are organized by color and described in the lists that follow. Hybrids are listed first, then species. Many are available at garden centers; you'll have to order others by mail. All are evergreen unless otherwise noted. While much attention is on hybrids, rhododendron species have plenty to offer, especially in woodland gardens and naturalized areas. Four of the species listed are native to the Southeast.

In the listing below, the typical height for each is given; most grow at least as wide as tall. Bloom times given are approximate and vary with weather and location. In the descriptions, "very early" corresponds to late winter, "early" to early spring, "midseason" to midspring, "late" to late spring, and "very late" to early summer.

WHITE

'Album Elegans'. To 6 ft. Flowers open pale mauve and fade to white. Vigorous, open form. Late. Heat tolerant.

'Belle Heller'. To 5 ft. Pure white with gold blotch. Midseason. Takes sun and heat.

'Boule de Neige'. To 5 ft. Rounded plant with bright green leaves and snowball-like clusters of white flowers. Midseason.

'Catawbiense Album'. To 6 ft. Pink buds; white flowers with greenish blotch. Midseason to late. Takes cold and heat.

'Chionoides'. To 4 ft.; dense, compact, rounded form. White flowers with light yellow spotting. Late midseason. Takes sun and heat.

'Cunningham's White'. To 4 ft. An old-timer bearing blooms in white with greenish yellow blotch. Late midseason.

'Dora Amateis'. To 3 ft. Compact, rather small-foliaged plant; good for foreground. Profuse bloomer with green-spotted white flowers. Spicy fragrance. Early midseason.

'Gomer Waterer'. To 5 ft. Pink buds open to white flowers with yellowish green blotch. Late midseason. Old-timer. Tolerates sun; endures heat and drought better than most.

'Loder's White'. Shapely growth to 5 ft. Tall trusses of white flowers with faint yellow throat and light pink picotee edge; blooms turn pure white as they age. Midseason. Blooms freely even when young. Best white for most regions. Heat tolerant.

'Sappho'. To 6 ft. Easy to grow; gangly without pruning. Use at back of border. White blossoms with a dark purple eye. Midseason. Heat tolerant.

'Southgate Divine'. To 5 ft. Light pink buds open to white blooms with purple flecks. Heat tolerant.

'Southgate Grace'. To 4–6 ft. Deep pink buds open to the lightest pink to white blooms. Heat tolerant.

PINK

'Anna Rose Whitney'. To 6 ft., with excellent foliage. Big trusses of blossoms in rich, deep pink. Late midseason. Heat tolerant.

'Antoon Van Welie'. To 6 ft. Tall trusses of carmine-pink blooms. Late midseason.

'Autumn Gold'. To 5 ft. Well-branched plant with rather upright growth. Salmon blossoms in flat-topped trusses; blooms from an early age. Very late.

'Bow Bells'. Forms a 3-ft. mound. Rounded leaves; bronzy new growth. Loose clusters of bright pink, cup-shaped flowers open from deeper pink buds. Early midseason.

'Caroline'. To 6 ft. Lightly fragrant flowers in orchid-pink. Light green, twisted leaves. Midseason to late. Heat tolerant.

'Cheer'. Mound-shaped, glossy-leafed plant to 4 ft. Pink flowers. Early. Heat tolerant.

'English Roseum' ('Roseum Pink'). Erect habit to 6 ft. Lavender-pink blooms. Midseason. Tough and undemanding. Heat tolerant.

'Furnivall's Daughter'. To 5 ft. Tall trusses of bright pink flowers with cherry-red blotch. Midseason.

'Ginny Gee.' Striking 2-ft. dwarf with small leaves, dense growth. Small pink bells are dotted inside and out with white. Profuse bloom in early midseason. Heat tolerant.

'Janet Blair'. To 5 ft.; vigorous and spreading. Large, ruffled flowers blend pastel pink, cream, white, and gold; rounded trusses. Midseason to late. Heat tolerant.

'Molly Ann'. To 3 ft. Compact grower with roundish leaves. Rose-pink flowers in upright trusses. Early midseason. Heat tolerant.

'Mrs. Furnivall'. To 4 ft. Compact-growing plant. Tight, round trusses of light pink flowers with deep red blotch. Late midseason.

'Pink Pearl'. To 6 ft.; open and rangy if not pruned. Tall trusses of rose-pink flowers. Midseason. Grows and blooms dependably.

'PJM'. Dense, bushy plant to 4 ft. Exceptional purplish pink flowers; profuse bloom. Flowers early, when foliage still has its mahogany winter color. Takes heat as well as cold. Can be sheared into a hedge.

'President Lincoln'. To 6 ft. Lilac-toned lavender-pink with bronze blotch. Midseason to late.

'Roseum Elegans'. To 6 ft. Olive-green foliage. Lilac-pink flowers. Midseason to late. Tolerates both heat and cold. Very tough.

'Scintillation'. To 5 ft. Compact plant covered in lustrous dark green leaves. Blossoms come in rounded trusses; they open pastel pink with brownish pink markings in throat. Midseason. Heat tolerant.

'Southgate Brandi'. To 4 ft. Deep pink buds open to pink, ruffled blooms. Heat tolerant.

'Southgate Breezy'. To 5 ft. Medium pink buds open to light pink to white blooms with medium maroon blotch. Heat tolerant.

'Trude Webster'. To 5 ft. Strong-growing plant with large leaves. Huge trusses of pure pink flowers in midseason. One of the best pinks. Heat tolerant.

YELLOW

'Patty Bee'. To 1½ ft. Small plant, well clothed with small (1-in.-wide) leaves that turn dark red in winter. Loose trusses of lemon-yellow flowers cover even young plants. Early midseason.

'Unique'. To 4 ft.; outstanding neat, rounded, compact habit. Bright pink buds open to tight, rounded trusses of creamy pale yellow blossoms. Early midseason. Heat tolerant.

'Virginia Richards'. Upright, compact habit to 4 ft. Flowers open unspotted pink, then turn yellow with a dark red blotch. Big, deep green, strongly veined leaves. Early to midseason.

RED

'America'. To 5 ft. Dark red. Late. Heat tolerant.

'Cynthia'. To 6 ft. Rosy crimson blooms with blackish markings. Midseason. Old favorite for background. Heat tolerant.

'Elizabeth'. To 3 ft. One of the most popular low-growing red rhododendrons, very widely planted. Attractive foliage sets off large, bright red, waxy, trumpet-shaped flowers that are carried in clusters of three to six at branch ends and in upper leaf joints. Blooms very young. Early midseason; often reblooms in early fall. Very susceptible to fertilizer burn, salts in water or soil.

'Holden'. To 4 ft. Compact plant. Rose-red flowers marked with deeper red. Midseason. Heat tolerant.

'Jean Marie de Montague'. To 5 ft., with brilliant scarlet flowers and attractive foliage. Midseason. Heat tolerant.

'Johnny Bender'. To 4–5 ft. Glossy, dark green leaves set off blood-red flowers. Midseason.

'Kluis Sensation'. Compact grower to 5 ft. Small, tight trusses of dark red, faintly spotted flowers. Midseason.

'Lem's Stormcloud'. To 5 ft. Large, erect trusses of bright red flowers; blossoms flare out flat when fully open. Late midseason.

'Leo'. To 5 ft., well clothed in large, dark green leaves. Rounded to dome-shaped trusses packed with rich cranberry-red blooms. Midseason to late.

'Lord Roberts'. To 5 ft. Handsome, dark green foliage and rounded trusses of red flowers spotted in black. Midseason. Plants grown in sun are more compact, bloom more profusely.

'Mars'. To 4 ft. Dark red. Late midseason. Handsome form, foliage, flowers.

'Nova Zembla'. To 5 ft. Bears profuse red flowers in midseason. Takes heat.

'Scarlet Wonder'. Outstanding, compact dwarf to 2 ft. Shiny, quilted-looking foliage forms backdrop for many bright scarlet blossoms. Midseason.

'Trilby'. To 5 ft. Deep burgundy flowers with black markings. Matte green leaves; red stems. Midseason.

'Vulcan'. To 5 ft. Bright, brick-red flowers. Late midseason. New leaves often grow past flower buds, partially hiding them. Heat tolerant.

LAVENDER TO PURPLE & BLUE

'A. Bedford'. To 6 ft. Large trusses of lavender-blue blooms with darker flare. Late. Heat tolerant.

'Anah Kruschke'. To 6 ft. Lavender-blue to reddish purple. Good foliage and is very tolerant of heat and sun. Can be sensitive to root rot in warm, wet soils. Midseason to late. Heat tolerant.

'Ben Mosley'. Compact grower to 6 ft. tall, 8 ft. wide. Pinkish purple flowers with reddish purple blotch. Midseason.

'Blue Diamond'. To 3 ft.; compact, erect. Small leaves. Small lavender-blue flowers cover plant in early midseason. Takes considerable sun.

'Blue Ensign'. To 4 ft.; compact, well-branched, rounded growth. Leaves tend to spot. Lilac-blue flowers have a striking dark blotch. Midseason. Tolerates sun and heat.

'Blue Peter'. To 4–5 ft. Broad, sprawling growth; needs regular pruning. Large trusses of lavender-blue flowers with purple blotch. Midseason. Tolerates heat and sun.

'Catawbiense Boursault'. Like 'Catawbiense Album' (white) but with pinkish lavender flowers. Takes cold and heat.

'Fastuosum Flore Pleno'. Open, rounded habit to 6 ft. Lavender-blue double flowers marked with gold blotch. Flower center is filled with small, lavender, petal-like structures. Midseason. Dependable old-timer. Tolerates heat and sun.

'Lee's Dark Purple'. To 6 ft. Dark purple blossoms with greenish blotch. Wavy-edged, dark green leaves. Early midseason.

TOP: Rhododendron 'Nova Zembla'; *R. catawbiense; MIDDLE: R.* 'Blue Ensign'; *BOTTOM: R.* 'Scintillation'; *R.* 'Ben Mosley'

R

RHODODENDRONS IN CLAY OR ALKALINE SOIL?

They don't like it. Planting in raised beds that are 1–2 ft. above the original soil level is the simplest way to give these plants the conditions they need. Liberally mix organic material into top foot of native soil, then fill bed above it with a mixture of 50 percent organic material, 30 percent soil, 20 percent builder's sand. This mixture will hold air and moisture while allowing excess water to drain.

'Marchioness of Lansdowne'. Spreading, open growth to 5–6 ft. Rosy violet flowers with a dark blotch and white stamens. Midseason to late.

'Purple Splendour'. To 5 ft. Informal habit. Ruffled-looking, deep purple blossoms with black-purple blotch. Late midseason. Tolerates sun and heat.

'Ramapo'. Dense, spreading growth to 2 ft. in sun, taller in shade. New growth is dusty blue-green, maturing to dark green. Pinkish violet flowers cover plant in early midseason. Useful rock garden or low border plant.

'Sapphire'. To 2½ ft. Twiggy, rounded, and dense, with tiny, narrow, gray-green leaves. Small, azalealike, light blue flowers. Early midseason.

'Southgate Radiance'. To 5 ft. Deep lavender buds open to light purple blooms. Heat tolerant.

'Van Nes Sensation'. To 5 ft. Strong grower. Large trusses of pale lilac flowers. Midseason.

R. carolinianum. CAROLINA RHODODENDRON. Zones US, MS, LS; USDA 6-8. Native to mountains of the Carolinas and Tennessee. To 3–6 ft. tall and as broad or broader, with tight clusters of pink flowers in midseason. Leaves turn purplish in cold winters. 'Carolina Gold' is an upright grower with yellowish white blossoms. 'White Perfection' has light pink buds that open to white flowers; it is more compact than the basic species (to 4 ft. high and wide) and bears younger and more profusely.

R. catawbiense. CATAWBA RHODODENDRON. Zones US, MS, LS; USDA 6-8. Native to mountains from West Virginia to Alabama. To 15 ft. tall and wide, eventually much larger. Lavender (or sometimes reddish purple) flowers in midseason. An ancestor of many heat-tolerant

selections.

R. maximum. ROSEBAY RHODODENDRON. Zones US, MS; USDA 6-7. Native from New England to Georgia and Alabama; the state flower of West Virginia. Large, handsome, densely foliaged shrub or small tree with open habit. Usually 10–15 ft. tall, but may reach 30 ft. Striking, satiny, dark green leaves to 4–10 in. long. Small clusters of many rose or purplish pink, 1½-in. flowers with white centers and green freckles. Tolerates full shade. Late to very late.

R. minus. PIEDMONT RHODODENDRON. Zones US, MS, LS, CS; USDA 6-9. Heat-tolerant native rhododendron. An upright grower to 4 ft. (eventually 6 ft.) tall, it has round clusters (up to 4 in. across) of spotted or flecked, rose-pink blossoms with distinctive dark anthers. Shiny, oblong leaves to just 3 in. long. Endangered species; be careful to buy only nursery-propagated plants. Midseason. *R. m. minus.* Native to Alabama, northwest Florida, Georgia, North Carolina, South Carolina, and Tennessee. Selections include 'Red Hills

Strain' (lavender), 'Southern Cerise' (dark pink, compact), and 'Mockingbird Hill' (lavender-pink, upright mound). *R. m. chapmanii,* Chapman's rhododendron, is found in the pine woods of northwest Florida.

R. mucronulatum. KOREAN RHODODENDRON. Zones US, MS. USDA 6-7. From China, Mongolia, Korea, Japan. Deciduous, azalealike rhododendron. Open, thin growth to 5 ft.; very early bloom makes up for bare, leggy branches. Small clusters of bright purple flowers. Form 'Cornell Pink' also available.

R. yakushimanum. Zones US, MS; USDA 6-7. From Japan. Forms a tight mound to 1-4 ft. high. New growth has a soft-as-down coating of white hairs; older leaves are glossy, dark green above, brown and felted beneath. Clear, pink, bell-like flowers age to white. Late midseason. Selections include 'Ken Janeck', a large (to 4-ft.) form with intense pink flowers, and smaller-growing 'Yaku Angel', with pink-tinged buds opening to pure white flowers. There are also a number of hybrids that perform as well in cold climates as they do in milder ones. Among them are 'Mardi Gras', 'Yaku Sunrise', 'Yaku Prince' and 'Yaku Princess'. The four hybrids just mentioned all have blooms in white or pink-tinged white.

KINDS OF AZALEAS

Azaleas are divided into evergreen and deciduous categories. The following describes evergreen hybrids first, then deciduous hybrids and species.

COLLECTOR'S ITEMS

The Vireya rhododendrons, from the tropics of Southeast Asia, manage nicely in frost-free and nearly frostless zones. They are also fine container plants (even indoors), so they can be grown in colder zones if brought inside for the winter. They need an especially fast-draining potting mix (many species are epiphytes in the wild); a combination of equal parts peat moss, ground bark, and perlite works well. Typically, plants flower on and off throughout the year rather than in one blooming season. They bear waxy-textured blossoms in exciting shades of yellow, gold, orange, vermilion, salmon, and pink, plus cream, white, and bicolors. Species, named hybrids, and unnamed seedlings are offered by some specialty growers.

Among the best ones you are likely to find are *R. aurigeranum* (a hybrid of *R. brookeanum,* commonly listed as *R. b. gracile*), *R. javanicum, R. konori, R. laetum, R. lochiae, R. macgregoriae,* and the hybrids 'George Budgen' (orange-yellow), 'Ne Plus Ultra' (a red-flowering hybrid between *R. laetum* and *R. zoelleri*), and 'Taylori' (pink).

EVERGREEN AZALEA HYBRIDS

Evergreen azaleas fall into more than a dozen groups, though an increasing number of hybrids have such mixed parentage that they don't fit conveniently into any category. The following list includes some of the most popular groups. Except as noted, bloom season is late winter or spring. Plants grown in greenhouses can be forced for winter bloom. Size varies considerably, but most of these slow-growing plants reach 2–5 ft. high and at least as wide.

Aromi hybrids. Zones LS, CS; USDA 8-9. Like their better-known deciduous counterparts, the evergreen Aromi hybrids were bred for warm climates. They include 'Amelia Rose', purplish red blooms in classic rose form; 'Hallie', purplish pink and double; and 'Micheale Lux', purplish pink with purplish red blotch.

Belgian Indica hybrids. Zone TS; USDA 10-11. These hybrids were originally developed for greenhouse forcing. Where winter lows don't dip below 20°F, many of them serve well as landscape plants. They are profuse bloomers with lush, thick foliage and typically semidouble or double, 2- to 3-in. blossoms. Among the most widely sold are 'Albert and Elizabeth', white with pink edges; 'California Sunset', salmon-pink with white border; 'Chimes', dark red; 'Mardi Gras', salmon with white border; 'Mission Bells', red semidouble; 'Mme Alfred Sanders', cherry-red; 'Orange Sanders', salmon-orange; 'Orchidiflora', orchid-pink; 'Paul Schame', salmon. Three choices with pendent growth are 'Red Poppy', deep purple 'Violetta', and orange-red 'William Van Orange'; all are suitable for hanging baskets.

Beltsville hybrids. Zones US, MS, LS, CS; USDA 6-9. Similar to the Glenn Dale hybrids. 'Guy Yerkes' has pink flowers. Selection 'H. H. Hume' has single white blossoms with a yellowish throat; 'Polar Bear' is an exceptionally hardy white.

Bloom-A-Thon hybrids. Zones MS, LS, CS; USDA 7-9. Bred in Seneca, South Carolina, by Bob Head. Bloom in spring, summer, and fall in shades of 'Lavender' (3 ½-4 ½ ft. tall), 'White' (shortest; 2 ½-3 ft. tall), 'Red' (3-4 ft. tall), and 'Pink Double' (3-4 ft. tall).

R

Promise to bloom for 6 weeks in spring and another 12 to 16 weeks in summer and fall.

Carla hybrids. Zones MS, LS, CS; USDA 7-9. Bred at North Carolina State and Louisiana State universities by Dr. R. J. Stadtherr for resistance to *Phytophthora*. These midseason bloomers include deep rose-pink 'Adelaide Pope', semidouble 'Carror', double light pink 'Elaine', deep rose-red 'Emily', deep rose-pink 'Sunglow', and bright red 'Wolf-pack Red'.

Encore hybrids. Zones LS, CS; USDA 8-9. Bred by Buddy Lee of Franklinton, Louisiana, and introduced by Flowerwood Nursery in Mobile, these azaleas bloom most heavily in both fall and then again in spring. Unlike other azaleas, they can take full sun. They include soft purple 'Autumn Amethyst', deep pink 'Autumn Cheer', salmon-pink 'Autumn Coral', orange-red 'Autumn Embers', vivid pink 'Autumn Rouge', and purple 'Autumn Royalty'.

Gable hybrids. Zones US, MS, LS; USDA 6-8. Bred in Pennsylvania to produce cold-hardy azaleas of Kurume type. In the Upper South, they may lose some leaves during winter. Bloom heavily in midseason. Frequently sold pink selections include 'Caroline Gable', 'Louise Gable' (semidouble), 'Pioneer', and 'Rosebud' (double). Among purple choices are 'Herbert' and 'Purple Splendor'. 'Rose Greeley' has white blossoms. 'Stewartstonian' is orange-red.

Girard hybrids. Zones US, MS, LS; USDA 6-8. Handsome-foliaged plants bred for extra cold hardiness; originated from Gable crosses. Selections include 'Girard's Crimson', with bright crimson-red blooms and maroon fall foliage; 'Girard's Fuchsia', reddish purple flowers; 'Girard's Hot Shot', with orange-red blossoms as well as orange-red fall and winter foliage; 'Girard's National Beauty', rose-pink blooms; and 'Girard's Roberta', double pink, 3-in. blooms; and 'Girard's Rose', deep rose blooms.

Glenn Dale hybrids. Zones US, MS, LS, CS; USDA 6-9. Bred by Benjamin Y. Morrison at the National Arboretum. Developed primarily for hardiness, though they do drop some leaves in cold winters. Some are tall and rangy, others low and compact.

Growth rate varies from slow to rapid. Some have small leaves like Kurume hybrids; others have large leaves. Some familiar selections include orange 'Anchorite'; pale pink 'Aphrodite'; orange-red 'Buccaneer', 'Copperman', and 'Fashion'; white 'Everest' and 'Glacier'; 'Geisha', white with red stripes; 'Martha Hitchcock', magenta-crimson with a white center; and 'Treasure', white edged with a hint of pink.

Harris hybrids. Zones MS, LS, CS; USDA 7-9. Bred in Lawrenceville, Georgia, by James Harris beginning in 1970. His azaleas include 'Coronado Red', clear red; 'Midnight Flare', dark red; 'Pink Cascade'; and 'Fascination', pink center with red border. More recently, his work on repeat bloom has been marketed in the Bloom N' Again series, marked by bright colors.

Holly Springs hybrids. Zones MS, LS, CS; USDA 7-9. Bred in Holly Springs, Mississippi, by Pete Vines between 1977 and the early 90s. Of the dozens released, favorites include 'Astronaut', white with light green blush and occasional red streak, and 'Irish Cream', white with yellow-green blotch.

Kaempferi hybrids. Zones US, MS, LS; USDA 6-8. From *R. kaempferi*, the torch azalea, a cold-hardy plant with orange-red flowers. These are hardier than Kurume hybrids (to –15°F), with a taller, more open habit. Nearly leafless below 0°F. Profuse bloom. Available choices are salmon-rose 'Fedora'; 'Holland', a late-season bloomer with large red flowers; and orange-red 'John Cairns'.

Kurume hybrids. Zones US, MS, LS; USDA 6-8. Compact, twiggy plants densely clothed in small, glossy leaves. Small flowers are borne in incredible profusion. Plants have mounded or tiered form, look handsome even out of bloom. Widely used in foundation plantings—to the point of cliché. Of the many available selections, these are among the most widely sold: pink 'Coral Bells', crimson 'Hexe', bright red 'Hershey's Red' and 'Hino-crimson', cerise-red 'Hino-degiri', orange-red 'Sherwood Red', and white 'Snow'.

North Tisbury hybrids. Zones US, MS, LS; USDA 6-8. Most of these hybrids reflect the characteristics of a common

prostrate-growing ancestor, *R. nakaharai*. Their dwarf, spreading habit and very late bloom (into midsummer) make them naturals for hanging baskets and ground covers. Some of the best selections are 'Alexander', with red-orange flowers and bronze fall foliage; pink-blossomed 'Pink Cascade'; and 'Red Fountain', with dark red-orange blooms that appear around the Fourth of July.

Pericat hybrids. Zones US, MS, LS; USDA 6-8. These were originally developed for greenhouse forcing but are about as hardy as Kurume hybrids and look much the same, though flowers tend to be somewhat larger. Selections include rose-pink 'Hampton Beauty', light pink 'Mme Pericat', blush pink 'Sweetheart Supreme', and rose pink 'Twenty Grand'.

ReBloom hybrids. Zones MS, LS, CS; USDA 7-9. A second line of repeat-blooming azaleas from Bob Head, these have a good color range from pastels into more vivid hues, blooming again in summer as well as fall. They include 'Blush Elegance', pink, 18–24 in.; 'Cherry Pink Prestige', double pink, 12–18 in.; 'Coral Amazement', triple-petaled vivid coral, 24–30 in.; 'Firebrick Fame', red-orange, 24–30 in.; 'Fuchsia Extravagance', violet-purple, 18–24 in.; 'Pink Adoration', pink, 24–30 in.; 'Purple Spectacular', purple, 18–24 in.; and 'White Nobility', white, 30–36 in.

Robin Hill hybrids. Zones MS, LS, CS; USDA 7-9. A large group with typically large flowers bred in the 1950s and 60s by Robert Gartrell of Wycoff, New Jersey, ironic due to their popularity among gardeners in the Lower and Coastal South. Most are 3-4 ft. tall and wide; some are shorter or taller. Known to bloom for two to three months—in fall as well as spring. There are so many good ones (several with "Robin Hill" in their names) that it's difficult to single out only a few. Try 'Betty Ann Voss', pink; 'Conversation Piece', pink with light center; 'Dorothy Rees', white; 'Nancy of Robin Hill', pink with red blotch; 'Robin Hill Gillie', red-orange; 'Hilda Niblett', with blossoms in a combination of light pink, deep pink, and white; and 'Watchet', ruffled light pink. The newest is 'Freddy'. A popular white sport of 'Watchet', it was found and

introduced by Margie Jenkins of Amite, Louisiana.

Satsuki hybrids. Zones MS, LS, CS; USDA 7-9. Includes azaleas referred to as Gumpo and Macrantha hybrids. Hardy to 5°F. Low-growing plants; some make nice ground covers. They bloom late, bearing large flowers. Popular selections include white 'Gumpo'; rose-pink 'Gumpo Pink', tight-growing mounds of late-spring color. However, due to their compact form, they can be plagued by rhizoctonia, a blight that is usually fatal. Other excellent choices include 'Aikoku', orange; 'Amagasa', deep pink to coral-red; 'Johga', white to light pink with dark pink blotch; 'Gyokushin' white with fuchsia blotch; 'Momo no Haru', purple-lavender; 'Chinzan', warm pink; and 'Wakebisu', salmon-pink.

Southern Indica hybrids. Zones MS, LS, CS; USDA 7-9. Selected from Belgian Indica hybrids for vigor and sun tolerance. Most take temperatures of 10–20°F, but some are damaged even at the upper end of that range. They generally grow faster, more vigorously, and taller than other kinds of evergreen azaleas. They range from 4 to 12 ft. tall and almost as wide, depending on the selection, age, and culture. Flowers are large, usually 2–3 in. across. Used for massing and as specimens—as shrubs, standards, espaliers. Popular choices include 'Brilliant', carmine-red; 'Duc de Rohan', salmon-pink; 'Fielder's White'; 'Formosa', brilliant rose-purple; 'George Lindley Taber', light pink; 'Imperial Princess', rich pink; 'Imperial Queen', double pink; 'Iveryana', white with orchid streaks; 'Judge Solomon', clear pink; 'Mrs. G. G. Gerbing', white; 'Orange Pride', bright orange; 'President Claeys', orange-red; 'Pride of Dorking', brilliant red; 'Pride of Mobile', deep rose-pink; 'Red Formosa', reddish purple; and 'Southern Charm', watermelon-pink. A selection grown largely for foliage is 'Little John' (CS; USDA 9), a dense, rounded, 6-ft. bush with burgundy leaves; its red flowers are borne only sparsely.

Other azaleas of note. These popular azaleas (all about 3–5 ft. high and wide) belong to other categories. 'Delaware Valley White' is a cold-hardy Mucronatum hybrid; 'Elsie Lee' is a lovely semidouble lavender Shammarello hybrid. Two double white selections are 'Hardy Gardenia', a Linwood hybrid, and 'Helen Curtis', a Shammarello hybrid. 'Marian Lee' is a white-and-purple Back Acres hybrid. 'Palestrina' is a Vuykiana hybrid featuring large white flowers with a yellow blotch. Spider azalea (*Rhododendron stenopetalum* 'Linearifolium') is unique, combining long, narrow leaves with spidery, lavender pink flowers.

DECIDUOUS AZALEA HYBRIDS AND SPECIES

Few shrubs can equal deciduous azaleas for showiness and range of color, and this has fueled the development of many excellent hybrids over the years. They offer the yellow, gold, peach, orange, and flaming red colors that are missing or rare among evergreen azaleas—and fall foliage is often brilliant orange-red to maroon. Flowers of some are highly fragrant. Deciduous species (typically with blossoms 1–1½ in. across) are listed after the hybrids below. Many of these species are native to the South and are less fussy about soil and watering than evergreen types; they need a good amount of sun, however, and won't bloom well in full shade.

Aromi hybrids. Zones US, MS, LS, CS; USDA 6-9. Bred by Dr. Eugene Aromi of Mobile, Alabama, who wanted azaleas of Knap Hill–Exbury type that would tolerate long, hot summers. Crossing Exburys with Southern native species *R. austrinum*, *R. canescens*, *R. oblongifolium*, and *R. viscosum* produced azaleas with large trusses of striking, almost incandescent blooms. All are very heat tolerant. They are upright growers to 12–15 ft. (though they may reach only half that height in the Upper South; USDA 6). Most have fragrant flowers. Selections include 'Aromi Sunny Side Up', golden yellow with a darker, egg yolk–yellow blotch; 'Aromi Sunrise', orange-red buds opening to light orange blossoms with a deep orange center; 'Canary Isles', large yellow flowers with petals tipped in orange; 'Carousel', pale pink with prominent gold blotch; 'Centerpiece', white with yellow blotch; 'High Tide', flowers tipped in pink with yellow blotch; 'King's Trumpeter', dark red buds open to yellow-flushed red flowers; 'Radiant

Red', fragrant dark red flowers; 'Spring Fanfare', coral buds open medium yellow; 'Clearcreek', yellow with darker yellow blotch. Midseason.

Choptank River hybrids. Zones US, MS, LS; USDA 6-8. Natural hybrids of *R. atlanticum* and *R. periclymenoides* found near the Choptank River in Maryland by Mr. and Mrs. Julian Hill. Grow 3–6 ft. tall. Fragrant flowers in midseason. Selections include: 'C-1', white, spreads by rooting stems; 'Choptank River Belle', white flushed with pink; 'Choptank Rose', rose-and-white blooms with golden blotch; 'Choptank Yellow', yellow with golden blotch; and 'Nacoochee', white and pale pink.

Confederate series hybrids. Zones US, MS, LS, CS; USDA 6-9. Similar to Aromi hybrids. Bred for heat tolerance by Bob Schwindt, Tom Dodd, Jr., and Tom Dodd III of Semmes, Alabama. Crossing the Knap Hill–Exbury hybrid 'Hotspur Yellow' with *R. austrinum* produced (among others) the following, all with fragrant blossoms: 'Admiral Semmes', large yellow flowers with a deep yellow blotch; 'Colonel Mosby', frilly salmon-pink blooms with a yellow flare; 'Stonewall Jackson', golden orange; 'J.E.B. Stuart', rose-pink with yellow blotch. Midseason.

Ghent hybrids. Zones US, MS; USDA 6-7. Upright growers, variable in height. Flowers are generally 1½–2¼ in. wide. Colors include shades of yellow, orange, umber, red, and pink. Two double-flowered selections are soft pink 'Corneille' and light yellow 'Narcissiflora'. Midseason.

Knap Hill–Exbury hybrids. Zones US, MS, some in LS; USDA 6-7, some in 8. These extraordinary hybrids come from crosses made in England, first at Knap Hill, then at Lionel de Rothschild's estate at Exbury. Plants are spreading to upright, reaching 4–6 ft. tall. Midseason to late bloom. Huge trusses of large (3- to 5-in.-wide) flowers stand atop the foliage; blossoms are sometimes ruffled or fragrant. Colors include white,

TOP: Rhododendron 'Girard's Rose'; 'George Lindley Taber' (Southern Indica hybrid azalea); *MIDDLE:* 'Stewartstonian' (Gable hybrid azalea); *BOTTOM: R. austrinum; R. stenopetalum* 'Linearifolium'

TOP: Rhododendron prunifolium; R. alabamense; BOTTOM: 'Formosa'
(Southern Indica hybrid azalea)

NATIVE WILD HONEYSUCKLES

The South is home to almost all of the deciduous azaleas indigenous to North America. Many are intensely fragrant (hence their common name, wild honeysuckle); their leaves may have brilliant fall colors. Purchase only nursery-propagated plants, and plant them in small groves or drifts in filtered light below native trees. Native wild honeysuckles include *Rhododendron alabamense,* *R. arborescens, R. atlanticum, R. austrinum, R. bakeri, R. calendulaceum, R. canescens, R. colemanii, R. flammeum, R. oblongifolium, R. periclymenoides, R. prinophyllum, R. prunifolium, R. serrulatum, R. vaseyi,* and *R. viscosum.*

pink, orange, yellow, salmon, and red, often with contrasting blotches. Among the best are pink 'Cannon's Double'; orange 'Gibraltar' and 'Hotspur Orange'; double deep pink 'Homebush'; yellow 'Hotspur Yellow'; golden tangerine 'Klondyke'; and 'Oxydol', white with yellow markings. 'Gibraltar' and 'Hotspur Yellow' accept the heat of the Lower South (USDA 8); most of the others do not.

Mollis hybrids. Zones US, MS; USDA 6-7. Hybrids of *R. molle* and *R. japonicum.* Upright growth to 4–5 ft. Flowers 2½–4 in. wide, in clusters of 7 to 13. Colors range from chrome yellow through bright red. Very heavy bloom in midseason. Leaves have a light skunky fragrance when new, but they turn a lovely yellow to orange in autumn. Blooms of 'Hamlet' are yellowish pink with a reddish orange blotch; 'Koster's Brilliant Red' has bright orange-red flowers; 'Radiant' is deep red.

Viscosum hybrids. Zones US, MS; USDA 6-7. Hybrids of Mollis azaleas and *R. viscosum.* Size varies from 3–8 ft. Flowers have colors of Mollis types but wonderful clove fragrance of *R. viscosum.* Late.

R. alabamense. ALABAMA AZALEA. Zones US, MS, LS; USDA 6–8. Native to Alabama and Georgia. Grows 5–6 ft. tall and spreads by suckering to form colonies. Highly fragrant white flowers, usually blotched with yellow. Early.

R. arborescens. SWEET AZALEA. Zones US, MS, LS; USDA 6–8. Native to mountains from Pennsylvania to Alabama. Erect, open shrub to 8 ft. (possibly 20 ft.) tall. Fragrant white to pale pink, 1½- to 2-in. flowers appear late, after leaves have expanded. 'White Lightning', which may be a hybrid, has intensely fragrant, white flowers touched with yellow. Hybrid 'Lady Barbara' has pink flowers and scarlet and gold fall color.

R. atlanticum. COAST AZALEA. Zones US, MS, LS, CS; USDA 6-9. Native from Delaware to South Carolina. Suckering shrub to 3–6 ft. tall. Fragrant, somewhat sticky, white to pink flowers bloom early, before or as leaves expand. 'Yellow Delight' has soft yellow blooms.

R. austrinum. FLORIDA FLAME AZALEA. Zones MS, LS, CS; USDA 7-9. Native to northern and western Florida and southern parts of Georgia, Alabama, Mississippi. To 8–10 ft. tall, with fragrant flowers that may be pale yellow, gold, cream, pink, orange, or red in color. One of the easiest native azaleas to grow. Tolerates heat, humidity, drought. Early bloom. 'Alba' has white blooms touched with yellow. 'Harrison's Red' has rosy red to coral blooms. 'Lisa Gold' bears bright golden yellow flowers. 'Millie Mac' has reddish orange buds opening to bright yellow flowers edged in white; 'My Mary' bears pure yellow blooms; 'Pretty One' has salmon-red flowers blotched yellow.

R. bakeri. CUMBERLAND AZALEA. Zones US, MS; USDA 6-7. Native to mountains of Kentucky, Virginia, Tennessee, Georgia, Alabama. Grows 3–8 ft. tall. Flowers about 1¾ in. wide; typically red, sometimes yellow or orange. Late midseason. Does not like long, hot summers. Flowers of 'Camp's Red' are a strong red in the mountains, a lighter red at lower elevations. Blossoms of 'Sunlight' blend deep orange-red and gold; its leaves turn bright plum-red in fall.

R. calendulaceum. FLAME AZALEA. Zones US, MS; USDA 6-7. Native to mountain regions from southern Pennsylvania to Georgia. Grows to 4–8 ft. or taller. Clusters of 2-in.-wide flowers in yellow, red, orange, or scarlet. Late. A very important parent of many hybrid deciduous azaleas. Dislikes extended summer heat and drought. 'Cherokee' bears soft apricot blossoms with red stamens; 'Currahee' has striped red-and-yellow buds that open to orange blooms bordered with rosy pink. 'Soquee River' produces big trusses of orange, red, and yellow blooms. Several hybrids are also available. 'Chattooga' has ruffled pink flowers with a yellow blotch. 'Keowee Sunset' bears rose-pink flowers with a yellow blotch. 'Tangerine Delight' has bright orange blooms.

R. canescens. PIEDMONT AZALEA. Zones US, MS, LS, CS; USDA 6-9. Native from North Carolina to Texas. Large (to 10-ft.), suckering shrub with fragrant white to pink or rose flowers. Early. Sun or shade. 'Varnadoe's Phlox Pink' has bright pink blooms.

R. colemanii. RED HILLS AZALEA. Zones US, MS, LS, CS;

R

USDA 6-9. Native to southern Alabama and Georgia, this recent discovery is already making its way into gardens. Desirable for its late-spring bloom in remarkably variable colors of white, pink, or yellow. To 12 ft.

R. flammeum. OCONEE AZALEA. Zones US, MS, LS; USDA 6-8. Native to South Carolina, Georgia. Fairly compact to 6 ft., with clusters of 1¾-in. flowers in midseason. Colors range from red and pink to yellow or orange. Resembles *R. calendulaceum* but is more tolerant of heat and drought. 'Magenta Rose Flame' has bright magenta-pink flowers with a yellow flare.

R. oblongifolium. TEXAS AZALEA. Zones US, MS, LS; USDA 6-8. Native to East Texas, Oklahoma, and Arkansas. To 6 ft. tall. Small (½- to 1-in.), slightly fragrant white flowers appear in midseason, after leaves emerge. Tolerates drought better than most other deciduous azalea species.

R. periclymenoides (*R. nudiflorum*). PINXTERBLOOM AZALEA. Zones US, MS, LS; USDA 6-8. Native from Massachusetts to Ohio and North Carolina. Suckering shrub grows 2–3 ft. high, sometimes much taller. Pale pink to deep pink, fragrant, 1½-in. flowers appear in midseason, as leaves expand. 'Paxton's Blue' has showy lavender-blue flowers.

R. prinophyllum. ROSESHELL AZALEA. Zones US, MS, LS; USDA 6-8. Native from southern Quebec to Virginia, west to Missouri and Oklahoma. To 4–8 ft. tall, occasionally much taller; bright pink (sometimes white), 1½-in. flowers with strong clove fragrance. Blooms in midseason, before or as leaves emerge. 'Marie Hoffman' has clear pink blossoms.

R. prunifolium. PLUMLEAF AZALEA. Zones US, MS, LS; USDA 6-8. Native to Georgia and Alabama. To 10 ft., with orange-red to bright red, 1½- to 1¾-in. flowers. This is the signature plant of Callaway Gardens in Pine Mountain, Georgia. One of the latest azaleas, blooming in July and August. 'Apricot Glow' has orange flowers, 'Pine Prunifolium' bright red ones. Hybrid 'Summer Lyric' bears pink blossoms with a yellow throat.

R. schlippenbachii. ROYAL AZALEA. Zones US, MS; USDA 6-7. Native to Korea and Manchuria.

HOW TO CARE FOR RHODODENDRONS & AZALEAS

LIGHT & EXPOSURE The sun tolerance of azaleas and rhododendrons varies by species and selection. In general, most types prefer the partial sun or filtered shade beneath tall trees. The east and north sides of the house are better locations than the west and south. Too much sun bleaches or burns the leaves; too little results in lanky plants that don't bloom. They can take more sun in the Upper and Middle South (USDA 6-7), but full sun will be too much for them in the Lower, Coastal, and Tropical South (USDA 8-11). Shield them from strong winds. Choose species and selections well adapted to your climate.

SOIL Rhododendrons and azaleas have much the same basic requirements for soil. They need acid, well-drained, organically enriched soil (use composted cow manure, ground bark, chopped leaves, or compost) that should neither get too dry nor remain soggy. Planting in heavy clay is a no-no; root rot often ensues, indicated by yellowing, wilting foliage and collapse of the plant. Planting in limy, alkaline soil is another mistake; lack of iron quickly results in chlorosis (yellow leaves with green veins). Alkaline soil has not, however, discouraged azalea lovers in Texas and Oklahoma. The recommended practice there is to build raised beds 15–18 in. deep and fill them with a half-and-half mixture of finely milled bark and coarse sphagnum peat moss (be sure to mix the two thoroughly with water before filling the beds). Irrigating with alkaline water will slowly raise the pH; to keep it in the desired range of 5.0–6.0, prepare a mixture of 3 parts garden sulfur to 1 part iron sulfate, then apply it at the rate of 1 pound per 100 sq. ft. of garden bed. This should lower the pH by one point.

PLANTING & WATERING Plant azaleas and rhododendrons with the top of the root ball slightly above soil level. Never allow the soil to dry out or become too soggy.

Because they absorb water through their foliage, wet both the leaves and entire root zone when you water. Overhead watering with sprinklers works well, but to prevent fungal diseases do this in morning so that leaves dry by afternoon. Avoid drip irrigation—it doesn't wet the root system uniformly.

FERTILIZER AND MULCH Plants growing in fertile, acid soil need only infrequent fertilizing. In spring, just after the blooms fade, apply a mulch and fertilize with a controlled-release, acid-forming fertilizer such as cottonseed meal or commercial azalea/camellia food. Do not mulch in fall; this will hold heat in the soil and delay the onset of dormancy, increasing the chances of winter damage. And don't fertilize before bloom—you'll encourage leafy growth at the wrong time. If chlorosis (yellow leaves with green veins) sets in, apply garden sulfur or iron sulfate. Don't cultivate around these plants, as they have shallow roots.

PRUNING Pruning rhododendrons is simple—just follow these general guidelines. Tip-pinch young plants to make them bushy; prune older, leggy plants to restore shape by cutting back to a side branch, leaf whorl, or cluster of dormant buds. Do any extensive pruning in late winter or early spring. Pruning at this time will sacrifice some flower buds, but the plant's energies will be diverted to latent growth buds, which will then be ready to push out their new growth early in the growing season. You can do some shaping while plants are in bloom; use cut branches in arrangements. To prevent seed formation, which can reduce next year's bloom, clip or break off spent flower trusses, taking care not to damage growth buds at base of each truss.

Evergreen azaleas are dense, usually shapely plants; cutting back the occasional wayward branch restores symmetry. To keep bushes compact, tip-pinch frequently, starting after flowering ends and continuing until mid-June. Prune rebloomers after spring bloom ends. Prune deciduous azaleas while they are dormant and leafless. You don't have to prune azaleas as carefully as you do rhododendrons—the leaves are fairly evenly spaced along the branches, with a bud at base of each leaf, so new growth will sprout from almost anywhere you cut (in either bare or leafy wood).

PESTS Insects and diseases seldom bother healthy, vigorous plants. However, rhododendrons growing in heavy clay often fall victim to *Phytophthora*, a deadly soil-borne fungus that causes dieback. Azaleas growing in full sun are often plagued by sucking insects called lace bugs.

Densely branched shrub to 6–8 ft. Leaves in whorls of five at tips of branches. Blooms in early midseason as leaves are expanding, producing large (2- to 4-in.), highly fragrant, pure light pink flowers in clusters of three to six. A white form is also available. Good fall color: yellow, orange, scarlet, crimson. Protect from full sun.

R. serrulatum. SWEET AZALEA, SOUTHERN SWAMP AZALEA. Zones US, MS, LS, CS; USDA 6-9. Native from Georgia and Florida to Louisiana. Tall shrub (to 12–20 ft.) with reddish branches. Extremely fragrant white flowers, sometimes tinged cream, pale pink, or pale violet, bloom among new foliage. Small (to 3-in.-long), distinctly toothed leaves. Blooms very late—from July into September.

R. vaseyi. PINKSHELL AZALEA. Zones US, MS, LS; USDA 6-8.

Native to mountains of North Carolina. Upright plant with irregular, spreading form. To 10–15 ft. Blooms before leaf-out, bearing light pink, 1½- to 2-in. flowers in clusters of five to eight. Midseason. 'Pinkerbell' has deep pink blossoms, 'White Find' fragrant white blooms with a greenish yellow blotch.

R. viscosum. SWAMP AZALEA. Zones US, MS, LS, CS; USDA 6-9. Native to damp or wet ground,

ABOVE: Rhododendron calendulaceum

Maine to Alabama. To 5–8 ft. tall. Flowers are white (sometimes pink), 2 in. long, sticky on the outside, with a powerful clove scent. Blooms late, often in June. Hybrids include 'Jolie Madame', fragrant, rosy pink flowers with a gold blotch; 'Lemon Drop', peach buds opening to lemon-scented, pale yellow blooms; and 'Peaches and Cream', yellowish white flowers with a purplish pink margin and yellow blotch.

R. yedoense poukhanense. KOREAN AZALEA. Zones US, MS, LS; USDA 6-8. Native to southern and central Korea. To 3–6 ft. tall. Lightly fragrant, lavender to rosy purple, 2-in.-wide flowers. Early. Sometimes reblooms in fall. Dark green leaves turn orange-red in fall. Remains evergreen in mild-winter areas. Foliage turns orange to red in fall. A parent to many modern evergreen azaleas.

RHODOPHIALA BIFIDA

OXBLOOD LILY
Amaryllidaceae
Perennial from bulb

📏 **MS, LS, CS, TS; USDA 7-11**

☀ **FULL SUN**

💧 **REGULAR WATER DURING GROWTH AND BLOOM**

Rhodophiala bifida

Native to Argentina, this tough-as-nails amaryllis relative was

introduced into the Texas Hill Country by German settlers in the 1850s. Narrow, foot-long leaves emerge in fall, persist through winter and spring, and then die down. In August or September, following a rain, clusters of blood-red, 2-in.-long flowers appear atop leafless foot-tall stalks.

Set bulbs out in spring, planting them 4 in. deep, 1½ ft. apart. The plant multiplies naturally in just about any well-drained soil. It likes moisture during winter and spring but needs no water in summer. An old Southern favorite and a popular passalong plant. 'Hill Country Red' is a clone of the old Texas heirloom strain.

RHODOTYPOS SCANDENS

BLACK JETBEAD
Rosaceae
Deciduous shrub

📏 **US, MS, LS; USDA 6-8**

☀ ◑ **FULL SUN OR LIGHT SHADE**

💧💧 **MODERATE TO REGULAR WATER**

☠ **FRUIT IS POISONOUS IF INGESTED**

Rhodotypos scandens

Native to Japan and China. Trouble-free shrub for light shade or tough soil conditions, with interesting, showy flowers and fruit. Grows moderately fast to 6 ft. tall and wide (often much more in the wild), with spreading branches that leaf out early in spring. Leaves are bright green, oval, prominently veined and toothed, to about 4 in. long and 2 in. wide. Single white flowers, 2 in. across, appear in late spring

and early summer, followed by pea-size, jet black, shiny berries, four per cluster, in fall and persisting through winter. Fruit is quite toxic.

Thin out overcrowded mature plants by cutting back old branches to base after flowering.

RHUBARB

Polygonaceae
Perennial

📏 **US, MS; USDA 6-7, EXCEPT AS NOTED**

☀ **FULL SUN**

💧 **REGULAR WATER**

☠ **LEAVES ARE POISONOUS IF INGESTED; USE LEAF STEMS ONLY**

Rhubarb

Just as many Northerners have never tried black-eyed peas, many Southerners have never partaken of rhubarb (*Rheum* x *cultorum*). There are a couple of good reasons for this. First, the plant grows best where winters are long and cold—a condition met only in the Upper South (USDA 6) and high elevations of the Middle South (USDA 7). Second, most garden centers here don't carry rhubarb, so Southerners usually have to start with divisions ordered through the mail.

Rhubarb bears big, crinkled leaves borne on thick, typically reddish stalks. Leaves are toxic if eaten, but the stalks have a delicious, sweet-tart flavor and are used for sauces, pies, and preserves (strawberry-rhubarb pie is a real treat). Flowers are insignificant, held in spikelike clusters. Preferred selections include 'Canada Red', 'Cherry

Red', 'Crimson Red', 'MacDonald', 'Strawberry', and 'Valentine', all producing red stalks; and 'Victoria', which produces green stalks.

CARE

Plant divisions (each containing at least one bud) in late winter or early spring. Loosen the soil to a depth of 1 ft. and work in lots of organic matter. Set the divisions 1–2 in. deep and 3–4 ft. apart. After the plants come up, sprinkle ⅛ cup of 10-10-10 fertilizer around each plant and water it in. Keep plants well watered and mulch them to keep the soil cool.

Let plants grow for two full seasons before you begin harvesting stalks. After that, harvest stalks for four to five weeks in spring; older, huskier plants can be harvested for up to eight weeks. To harvest stalks, grasp them near the base of the plant and pull sideways and then outward; do not cut stalks, as this leaves a stub that will decay. Never remove all the leaves from a single plant; stop harvesting when slender stalks appear. After the final harvest, feed and water freely. Cut out any blossom stalks that appear.

In the Lower South (USDA 8), treat rhubarb as an annual. Set out divisions in fall for winter-to-spring harvest. 'Victoria' is the recommended selection for this treatment.

RHUS
SUMAC
Anacardiaceae
Evergreen and deciduous shrubs and trees

- ✎ **ZONES VARY BY SPECIES**
- ☼ **FULL SUN, EXCEPT AS NOTED**
- ◌◐ **LITTLE TO MODERATE WATER**

Rhus typhina

Though gardeners frequently dismiss them as weeds, sumacs can make fine ornamentals. Most display brilliant fall color and (on female plants) showy clusters of berries that attract birds. All species thrive in almost any well-drained soil and tolerate drought with ease. On the down side, most sumacs sucker freely—especially if their roots have been disturbed by cultivation—and they can be quite invasive. They are best used in naturalized areas.

R. aromatica. FRAGRANT SUMAC. Deciduous shrub. Zones US, MS, LS, CS; USDA 6-9. Native to eastern North America. Fast-growing plant to 3–5 ft. tall, sprawling 5 ft. or wider. Three-leafleted leaves to 3 in. long are fragrant when brushed against or crushed. Foliage turns red in fall. Tiny yellowish flowers in spring; small red fruit. Coarse bank cover, ground cover for poor or dry soils. 'Gro-Low' grows 2–3 ft. high, 6–8 ft. wide. 'Green Globe' is dense and rounded, to 6 ft. high and wide.

R. copallinum. SHINING SUMAC. Deciduous shrub or small tree. Zones US, MS, LS, CS, TS; USDA 6-11. Native to the eastern U.S. Grows quite fast to 10–25 ft. tall, becoming very broad as it matures, with a picturesque flat top. Highly ornamental—but unsuitable for small gardens, as it produces suckers and self-sows freely, forming large colonies. Shiny, dark green leaves are divided featherwise into 9 to 21 leaflets. Fall color varies from rich crimson, red-purple, or scarlet. Bears showy chartreuse flower spikes in summer, followed by clusters of crimson fruit that persists into winter. Particularly well adapted to dry, poor, rocky soils. *R. c. latifolia* 'Morton', prairie flame shining sumac, has larger leaves that turn brilliant red in fall; a lower (5–7 ft.), more compact habit; and doesn't produce fruit.

R. glabra. SMOOTH SUMAC. Deciduous shrub or tree. Zones US, MS, LS, CS; USDA 6-9. Native to much of North America. Upright grower to 10 ft., sometimes treelike to 20 ft. Spreads widely by suckers; in the wild, forms large patches. Looks much like *R. typhina* and has the same garden uses, but usually grows lower and does not have velvety branches. Leaves divided into 11 to 23 tooth-edged, rather narrow, 2- to 5-in.-long leaflets that are deep green above, whitish beneath; foliage turns scarlet in fall. Inconspicuous flowers in early summer are followed by showy clusters of scarlet fruit that remains on the bare branches well into winter. Leaves of 'Laciniata' are deeply cut and slashed, giving the plant an almost fernlike appearance. It may be a hybrid.

R. trilobata. SQUAWBUSH, SKUNKBUSH. Deciduous shrub. Zones US, MS, LS; USDA 6-8. Native from Illinois westward to Texas and California, north to Washington. Similar in most details to *R. aromatica*, but most people find the scent of the bruised leaves unpleasant. Clumping habit makes it a natural low hedge. Brilliant yellow to red fall color.

R. typhina. STAGHORN SUMAC. Deciduous shrub or tree. Zones US, MS, LS; USDA 6-8. Native to eastern North America. Upright to 15 ft. (sometimes 30 ft.) tall, spreading much wider by suckers. Very similar to *R. glabra*, but the branches have a velvety coat of short brown hairs—much like antlers of a deer "in velvet." Leaves are divided into 11 to 31 toothed leaflets, to 5 in. long; they are deep green above, grayish beneath, turn yellow-orange to rich red in fall. About 4- to 8-in.-long

clusters of tiny greenish blooms show in early summer, followed by clusters of fuzzy crimson fruit that hangs on all winter, gradually turning brown. 'Dissecta' ('Laciniata'), known as cutleaf staghorn sumac, is a female selection with deeply cut leaflets; it grows 10–12 ft. tall. 'Tiger Eyes', to 6 ft. tall and wide, has deeply cut golden leaves with pink leafstalks; foliage turns orange and scarlet in autumn. It does not spread aggressively.

R. virens. EVERGREEN SUMAC. Evergreen shrub. Zones LS, CS, TS; USDA 8-11. Native to southeastern Arizona, New Mexico, Texas, Mexico. Generally makes a mounding clump about 6 ft. tall and wide, with lowest branches close to or touching ground, but can reach 12 ft. high and wide. Relatively slow growing. New leaves are often reddish; mature leaves (to 6 in. long, with five to nine leaflets) are glistening dark green, with purple winter tints. Honey-scented white flowers in late summer attract bees and butterflies and are followed by plump, fuzzy clusters of red fruit. Highly tolerant of dry, rocky, or chalky soils. Sun or light shade.

R

RICINUS COMMUNIS

CASTOR BEAN
Euphorbiaceae
Tender shrub usually grown as annual

CS, TS; USDA 9-11

FULL SUN

REGULAR WATER

SEEDS (OR BEANS) ARE POISONOUS IF INGESTED

Ricinus communis

Long a fixture in old Southern gardens, this bold, striking plant from Africa and Asia remains a source of dread for children with digestive problems: Mothers still prescribe a spoonful of foul-tasting castor oil, pressed from the plant's seeds, to "clean you out." Enemies of the former Soviet Union had even more to fear. Ricin, a poison extracted from the seeds, was used by the KGB to dispatch selected targets (it is deadlier than cyanide). Fortunately, castor oil doesn't contain ricin—but ingesting just one of the beautifully marbled beans can cause serious illness, so do not plant this shrub where small children play.

Soak seeds in water overnight before planting in warm soil. Castor bean can provide a tall screen or accent in a hurry; it grows 6–15 ft. tall and half as wide in a single season. The plant overwinters in the Coastal and Tropical South and can become woody and treelike there. Large, coarsely lobed leaves are 1–3 ft. across on young, vigorous plants, smaller on older plants. Small white flowers are borne on foot-high stalks in summer; they're unimpressive but are followed by attractive, prickly seedpods. Selections

include 'Carmencita', with deep purple leaves and leafstalks and coral-red seedpods; 'Dwarf Red Spire', a lower grower (to 6 ft.) with red leaves and seedpods; 'Sanguineus', with blood-red leaves and stems; and 'Zanzibarensis', sporting huge green leaves with white veins.

ROBINIA

LOCUST
Papilionaceae
Deciduous trees and shrubs

US, MS, LS, CS; USDA 6-9

FULL SUN

LITTLE TO REGULAR WATER

BARK, LEAVES, AND SEEDS ARE POISONOUS IF INGESTED

Robinia x ambigua

Fairly fast-growing plants, well adapted to hot, dry regions. Leaves are divided like feathers into many roundish leaflets. Clusters of white or pink, sweet pea–shaped flowers bloom from midspring to early summer, followed by beanlike pods about 4 in. long. Locust trees tolerate poor soil and can get by on little or no water, but they do have some drawbacks: Wood is brittle, roots are aggressive, and plants often spread by suckers.

R. x ambigua. Tree. Hybrid between *R. pseudoacacia* and *R. viscosa*, a seldom-grown pink-flowering locust. The following are the best-known selections.

'Decaisneana'. To 40–50 ft. tall, 20 ft. wide. Flowers are like those of *R. pseudoacacia*, but color is pale pink.

'Idahoensis'. IDAHO LOCUST. Shapely tree 25–40 ft. tall and 15–30 ft. wide. Reddish bronze new growth and bright rose-pink

ABOVE: Robinia pseudoacacia 'Lace Lady'

flowers in 8-in. clusters make it one of the showiest locusts. Bears no seedpods. Thrives under arid conditions; good choice for western parts of Texas and Oklahoma.

R. hispida. ROSE ACACIA, BRISTLY LOCUST. Shrub. Native from Virginia and Kentucky to Georgia and Alabama. Small, showy shrub that will form colonies from root suckers. Extremely invasive in good soil. Grows to 7 ft. (sometimes 10 ft.) tall, 8 ft. wide. Bristly stems; blue-green leaves to 10 in. long, with 7 to 15 leaflets. Rose or pale purplish pink flowers in dangling, 4-in. clusters in late spring. Tolerates dry, poor soils. Use on dry banks, in naturalized settings.

R. x margaretta. Tree. Hybrid between *R. hispida* and *R. pseudoacacia*. Grows at a moderate rate into an open, rounded tree 15–30 ft. high and wide. Bristly stems; leaves to 8 in. long, with up to 19 leaflets. Fragrant, ½-in. pink flowers hang in clusters to

7 in. long. 'Flowering Globe' reaches 18 ft. tall and wide, with 8- to 10-in. clusters of dark pink flowers. 'Pink Cascade' ('Casque Rouge') reaches 15 ft. tall and wide, has purplish pink flowers and pinkish new growth.

R. pseudoacacia. BLACK LOCUST. Tree. Native to eastern and central U.S. Fast growth up to 40–75 ft. tall, 30–60 ft. wide, with rather sparse, open branching habit. Deeply furrowed brown bark. Thorny branches. Leaves divided into 7 to 19 leaflets, each 1–2 in. long. White, fragrant, ½- to ¾-in.-long flowers are held in dense, pendent clusters 4–8 in. long.

Black locust is little valued in its native territory, but it is a favorite in Europe. Rot-resistant wood is sought after for fence posts. Bees make delicious honey from the nectar of its flowers. The tree manufactures its own fertilizer through nitrogen-fixing root nodule bacteria and can colonize the poorest soil. Given some pruning and training in its early years, it can be a truly handsome flowering tree, but locust borer limits its usefulness in many regions; locust leaf miner is also a damaging pest, especially in the Upper and Middle South.

Often used as street tree, but not good in space between sidewalk and curb or under power lines. Wood is extremely hard; suckers are difficult to prune out where not wanted.

Recommended selections include the following.

'Frisia'. To 50 ft. tall, 25 ft. wide. New growth is nearly orange; mature leaves are yellow, turning greener in summer heat. Thorns and young wood are red.

'Lace Lady' ('Twisty Baby'). Dwarf to 8–10 ft. tall and 12–15 ft. wide. Picturesquely twisted branches; few flowers.

'Pyramidalis' ('Fastigiata'). Narrow, columnar, to 50 ft. tall, 10 ft. wide.

'Tortuosa'. Slow grower to 50 ft. tall, 30 ft. wide, with twisted branches. Few flowers.

'Umbraculifera'. Dense and round headed, to 20 ft. tall and wide. Usually grafted 6–8 ft. high on another locust to create a living green lollipop. Very few flowers.

R. 'Purple Robe'. Tree. Hybrid of uncertain parentage often sold as *R. pseudoacacia* 'Purple Robe'. Resembles *R.* x *ambigua* 'Idahoensis' but has darker, purple-pink flowers, reddish bronze new growth; blooms 2 weeks earlier and over a longer period. Suckers from the rootstock spread and reseed heavily.

R. viscosa. CLAMMY LOCUST. Tree. To 40 ft. tall, 20 ft. wide. Rare. Native to eastern U.S., from North Carolina to Alabama. Leaves are divided into 12 to 24 leaflets. Deep pink flowers in 3-in. clusters appear in late spring. Common name refers to sticky glands on the stems, leafstalks, and seedpods.

RODGERSIA
Saxifragaceae
Perennials

🗡 **US, MS, LS; USDA 6-8, EXCEPT AS NOTED**

◑ **PARTIAL SHADE**

💧 **AMPLE WATER**

Rodgersia pinnata

Native to China, Japan. Large plants with imposing leaves and clustered tiny flowers in plumes somewhat like those of astilbe; bloom in early to midsummer. Primary feature is handsome foliage, which often takes on bronze tones in late summer. Plants spread by thick rhizomes, need rich soil. The various species hybridize freely. Dormant in winter; provide winter mulch in cold climates. Showy in moist woodland or bog gardens.

R. aesculifolia. FINGERLEAF RODGERSIA. To 6 ft. tall, 3 ft. wide. Leaves are divided like fingers of a hand into five to seven toothedged, 10-in. leaflets; they are similar to those of horsechestnut (*Aesculus*). Shaggy brown hairs on flower stalks, leaf stems, major leaf veins. White flowers.

R. pinnata. FEATHERLEAF RODGERSIA. Zones US, MS; USDA 6-7. To 4 ft. tall, 2½ ft. wide. Leaves have five to nine 8-in. leaflets. Red flowers. 'Chocolate Wing' foliage is chocolate, bronze, and dark green, with red flowers; 'Fireworks' foliage has red-tinged edges, pink-red flowers; 'Superba' has bronze-tinted foliage that gives rise to bright pink flowers.

R. podophylla. To 5 ft. tall, 6 ft. wide. Coppery green leaves divided into five 10-in.-long leaflets. Creamy flowers. 'Rotlaub' has burgundy and green, cupped leaves.

R. sambucifolia. To 3 ft. high and wide. Leaves have up to 11 leaflets. Flat-topped clusters of white or pink flowers.

ROHDEA JAPONICA
LILY OF CHINA, SACRED LILY
Asparagaceae
Perennial

🗡 **MS, LS, CS, TS; USDA 7-11**

◑ **PARTIAL OR LIGHT SHADE**

💧💧 **MODERATE TO REGULAR WATER**

Rohdea japonica

Native to Japan and China. Useful, low-maintenance plant for massing in a shade garden. Thick, arching or erect tufts of evergreen, leathery leaves, each to 2 ft. long, 2–3 in. wide. Pale yellow flowers bloom on small spikes in early spring; they're barely noticeable amid the foliage but are followed by showy red berries. Grows slowly. Space plants about 1 ft. apart. Withstands neglect and is not fussy about soils. Combines well with ferns, hostas, hellebores. Several selections with leaves variegated in cream or white are available, including whitestreaked 'Gunjaku'; white-edged 'Miyako No Jo' and 'Chirimen Boshi'; 'Mure Suzume', with white streaking that intensifies toward leaf edges; and 'Suncrest', with a raised white area running down the center of each leaf. 'Nobori Ryu' has crinkled green leaves with raised ridges down the center.

ROSA
ROSE
Rosaceae
Deciduous and evergreen shrubs and vines

🗡 **US, MS, LS, CS, TS; USDA 6-11, EXCEPT AS NOTED**

☀◑ **FULL SUN TO PART SUN**

💧 **REGULAR WATER, EXCEPT AS NOTED**

'Olympiad' hybrid tea rose

The South's love affair with roses continues to evolve. We prize them for their intoxicating fragrance and the myriad shapes, sizes, and colors of their blossoms. But the ways we use them in our gardens have changed. Gone are the days of lining out scores of roses with name tags at the foot of each one like grave markers in a cemetery. What people want now are roses that solve problems, perform functions, combine well with other plants, and don't demand round-the-clock attention.

Fortunately, the sheer variety of roses allows for many possibilities. Climbing roses can frame a doorway, drape an arbor or pergola, and embellish a fence or wall. Compact roses like floribundas do great in containers. Reblooming shrub and ground cover roses catch the eye on banks or in sweeps. Old garden roses lend grace, perfume, and color to cottage-style gardens and mixed borders. Hybrid tea and grandiflora roses are tops for formal cutting gardens edged with clipped evergreen shrubs.

CLIMATE CONSIDERATIONS

Most roses grow very well throughout the South, but where you live does affect their performance.

Best flowering is in spring and fall, extending to winter in the Tropical South. If you get a lot of rain, roses have more disease problems like black spot and mildew. Low-rainfall areas see less disease, but you'll have to water regularly during the growing season. Hot summer weather can cause roses to go dormant and quit flowering. In areas with cool, wet springs, roses with lots of petals tend to "ball," opening poorly or not at all. Some roses aren't winter hardy in the Upper South (USDA 6).

BUYING PLANTS

Mail-order catalogs and/or websites offer the widest choice of roses. They're practically the only way to shop when looking for lesser-known kinds. You'll also find roses for sale in local nurseries and garden centers, home centers, and even supermarkets.

Container-grown roses. Potted roses are available at retail stores from spring through fall and year-round in the Coastal and Tropical South (USDA 9-11). Their big advantage is that you can plant them anytime during the growing season. The best time to plant, however, is from mid- to late spring, when the plants are blooming, the largest selection is available, and you can set them out before the summer heat arrives.

Choose plants with healthy new growth. A large container is better than a small one, because it's less likely to have had its roots cut back to fit it in the pot when it was planted. Avoid plants with roots protruding through the bottom of the pot, as pot-bound plants may not grow well in your garden. Don't buy plants left over from last year, unless you get a sizeable discount.

Bare-root roses. During late winter and early spring, nurseries and stores may offer bare-root roses. These are dormant plants with no soil around the roots. Instead, the roots are usually packed in moist organic matter and wrapped in plastic or other material. This is what you'll receive from mail-order nurseries. It doesn't harm the plants to be dug, transported, and sold this way. In fact, bare-root roses adapt to native soil more quickly and are usually less expensive.

Bare-root plants are graded 1,

1½, or 2, number 1 being the best. Suppliers usually offer only grade 1 plants, which have thick, green canes and a big cluster of sturdy, fibrous roots. Don't buy plants with dried-out, shriveled canes or roots or roses beginning to leaf out.

Buy bare-root roses as soon as they appear for sale, rather than when they are marked down as "bargains." Beware of packaged bare-root roses displayed indoors on store shelves. The indoor warmth may cause the roots to dry out. If they dry, they die.

Budded vs. own-root roses. Many old roses, species roses and their hybrids, and virtually all miniature and shrub roses are propagated from cuttings and grown on their own roots. However, about 50 percent of modern roses begin as a bud grafted onto an understock—a completely different type of rose whose root system thrives in a wide range of soils and climates. In Florida, for example, modern roses should be budded onto nematode-resistant rootstocks of *Rosa* x *fortuniana*.

Both budded and own-root roses grow well and produce fine flowers. Budded plants are often huskier at the time of purchase, but both kinds will be the same size within a year or two. Still, the current trend is to grow new selections on their own roots whenever possible. Own-root roses have one big advantage: If the plant is killed to the ground by cold (or mowed down by a texting teenager), it will regrow from the roots and be the same rose. Regrowth from the roots of a budded plant, in contrast, will come from the understock rose, whose flowers won't look anything like those of the rose you bought. So if you don't like the knobby center that often forms with grafted roses, or if you are tired of pruning off rootstock suckers, try own-root roses.

MODERN ROSES

Most of the thousands of roses for sale are modern roses—ones introduced after 1867, the year the first hybrid tea rose was developed. For more than 100 years after that, breeders raced to produce the most perfect hybrid teas, grandifloras, and floribundas, the flowering "modern" rose bushes that form the core of

many public and residential rose gardens. However, in the past few years, landscape roses, particularly the lax and leafy shrub roses, have become almost as popular.

The list at right includes a host of excellent modern roses grouped by type and color. Refer to the information below to learn about the ancestry and growing characteristics of the different types of modern roses.

Hybrid tea roses. These are the classic, aristocratic roses, with long, stylish, pointed buds that spiral open to large blossoms with high centers. Typically, hybrid teas carry one blossom at the end of each flowering stem. They bloom profusely in spring, then continue to produce blossoms—either in

flushes or continuously—until frosty weather. Their strong, long stems make them ideal for cutting and bringing indoors.

Hybrid tea bushes tend to have an upright, narrow, almost stiff look. They grow 2–6 ft. tall, depending on selection and climate. Group three or more together to create a generous, bushy look. Consider planting low-growing perennials beneath them or a low hedge in front of them to hide their bare ankles (bases of canes are usually sparsely foliaged). Hybrid teas need good growing conditions and more care than some other types, but for many gardeners, their spectacular blooms are worth the extra effort.

TOP: 'Belinda's Dream' shrub rose; 'Mutabilis' China rose; *BOTTOM:* 'Double Pink Knock Out' shrub rose

GREAT ROSES FOR SOUTHERN GARDENS

The following modern roses are among the best choices for Southern gardens. (AARS) identifies winners of the All-America Rose Selections award, and (f) indicates roses with dependably powerful fragrance. Selections marked with * are designated "No Spray Roses" through testing done by the University of Tennessee Cooperative Extension. Selections marked + are Earth-Kind roses, proven to have superior pest tolerance and outstanding landscape performance through years of research by Texas AgriLife Extension Service.

Shrubs

Red: Benjamin Britten (f), Carefree Spirit (AARS), Double Knock Out*, Golden Eye*, Hansa*, Home Run*, Knock Out (AARS)*+, My Hero*, Oso Easy Cherry Pie, Tess of the d'Urbervilles (f)
Pink: Ballerina, Belinda's Dream+, Caldwell Pink+, Blushing Knock Out, Bonica (AARS), Carefree Beauty+, Carefree Delight (AARS), Carefree Wonder (AARS), Gertrude Jekyll (f), Good N' Plenty*, Heritage (f), Island Dancer*, My Girl*, Palmengarten Frankfurt*, Pink Home Run*, Pink Knock Out*, Pink Meidiland, Sunrise Sunset, Wisley (f)
Orange/warm blend: All the Rage*, Coral Cove, Lady Elsie May (AARS)*, Oso Easy Paprika, Watercolors
Yellow: Baby Love, Carefree Sunshine*, Charlotte, Graham Thomas (f), Happenstance (f), Jude the Obscure (f), Lemon Splash, Molineux (f), Oso Easy Honey Bun, Sunny Knock Out, Teasing Georgia (f)*, Yellow Brick Road*, Yellow Submarine*
White: Macy's Pride*, Sally Holmes, Sea Foam+, Snowdrift*, White Meidiland
Lavender/mauve/purple: Midnight Blue (f), Outta the Blue (f), Rhapsody in Blue (f), Wildberry Breeze (f)*

Ground Covers

Red: Candy Oh!, Fire Meidiland, Red Drift, Red Flower Carpet, Red Meidiland, Red Ribbons, Ralph's Creeper, Scarlet Flower Carpet, Scarlet Meidiland
Pink: Appleblossom Flower Carpet, Coral Flower Carpet, Peach Drift, Pink Drift, Pink Flower Carpet, Roseberry Blanket, Sweet Drift, 'Farmer's Dream'
Orange/coral: Electric Blanket
Yellow: Happy Chappy, Sunrise Vigorosa, Yellow Flower Carpet
White: Icy Drift, White Flower Carpet, White Meidiland

Climbers

Red: All Ablaze, Altissimo, Blaze Improved, Crimson Sky, Don Juan (f), Dortmund, Dublin Bay, Fourth of July (AARS), Red Cascade, Valentine's Day
Pink: Blossomtime, Candy Land, Cl. Cécile Brünner, Clair Matin, Climbing Pinkie+, Eden, Jeanne Lajoie, New Dawn+, Nozomi, Parade, Pearly Gates, Peggy Martin, Rhonda
Orange/warm blend: America (AARS) (f), Buff Beauty (f), Compassion (f), Handel, Jacob's Robe, Joseph's Coat, Polka (f), Royal Sunset (f)
Yellow: Autumn Sunset (f), Garden Sun, Golden Gate, Golden Showers (AARS), Royal Gold (f), Scent from Above (f), Sky's the Limit
White: City of York, Cl. Iceberg, Prosperity (f), White Dawn (f)
Purple: Cl. Angel Face, Night Owl, Purple Splash, Veilchenblau

Hybrid Teas

Red: Chrysler Imperial (f), Firefighter (f), Ingrid Bergman, In the Mood, Kentucky Derby, Lasting Love (f), Mayor John Land (f), Mister Lincoln (AARS) (f), Olympiad (AARS), Opening Night (AARS), Red Masterpiece (f), Veterans' Honor
Pink: Aromatherapy (f), Beverly (f), Bewitched (AARS) (f), Brigadoon, Dainty Bess, Elle (AARS) (f), Falling in Love, Gemini (AARS), Grand Dame (f), First Prize (AARS) (f), Memorial Day (AARS) (f), New Zealand (f), Perfume Delight (AARS) (f), Pink Promise (AARS) (f), Secret (AARS) (f), Sheer Bliss (AARS) (f), The McCartney Rose (f), Tiffany (AARS) (f)
Orange/warm blend: Brandy (AARS), Cary Grant (f), Chicago Peace, Dolly Parton (f), Double Delight (AARS) (f), Fragrant Cloud (f), Just Joey (f), Marilyn Monroe, Over the Moon, Perfect Moment (AARS), Rio Samba (AARS), Sunset Celebration (AARS), Sunstruck, Touch of Class (AARS), Tropicana (AARS) (f), Tahitian Sunset (AARS)
Yellow: Celebrity, Elina, Graceland, Henry Fonda, Mellow Yellow, Midas Touch (AARS), Orogold (AARS), Peace (AARS), St. Patrick (AARS), Summer Love
White: Garden Party (AARS), Full Sail, Honor (AARS), John F. Kennedy, Moonstone, Pascali (AARS) (f), Pope John Paul II (f), Pristine, Sugar Moon (f)
Lavender/mauve: Barbra Streisand (f), Fragrant Plum (f), Neptune (f), Paradise (AARS), Stainless Steel (f)

Grandifloras

Red: Cherry Parfait (AARS), Crimson Bouquet (AARS), Dick Clark (AARS), Love (AARS), Ole (f), Rock & Roll (f)
Pink, blends: Fame! (AARS), Queen Elizabeth (AARS), Tournament of Roses (AARS)
Orange/warm blend: Caribbean (AARS), Dream Come True (AARS), Octoberfest
Yellow: Ch-Ching (f), Gold Medal, Strike It Rich (AARS) (f)
White: White Lightnin' (AARS) (f)
Lavender/mauve: Fragrant Plum (f), Lagerfeld (f), Melody Perfume (f), Wild Blue Yonder (AARS) (f)

Floribundas

Red: Black Forest, Drop Dead Red, Europeana (AARS), Impatient (AARS), Lavaglut (Lava Flow), Sarabande (AARS), Scentimental (AARS) (f), Showbiz (AARS), Topsy Turvy, Trumpeter
Pink: Betty Prior, Brilliant Pink Iceberg, Easy Does It (AARS), Else Poulsen+, Gene Boerner (AARS), Sexy Rexy, Our Lady of Guadalupe
Orange/warm blend: Amber Queen (AARS), Apricot Nectar (AARS) (f), Betty Boop (AARS), Chihuly, Cinco de Mayo (AARS), Colorific, Day Breaker (AARS), George Burns, Hot Cocoa (AARS), Livin' Easy (AARS), Mardi Gras (AARS), Marmalade Skies (AARS), Playboy, Pumpkin Patch, Rainbow Sorbet (AARS)
Yellow: Easy Going, Julia Child (AARS) (f), Shockwave, Sun Flare (AARS), Sunsprite (f), Walking on Sunshine (AARS)
White: French Lace (AARS), Iceberg, Moondance (AARS)
Lavender/mauve: Angel Face (AARS) (f), Burgundy Iceberg, Distant Drums, Ebb Tide (f), Intrigue (AARS) (f)

Polyanthas

Red: Wing Ding
Pink: Cécile Brünner+, China Doll, La Marne+, Marie Daley+(f), The Fairy+
Orange/warm blend: Margo Koster, Perle d'Or+

Miniatures

Red: Gypsy Sunblaze, Red Sunblaze, Ruby Ruby, Starina, Warm & Fuzzy
Pink: Baby Boomer, Be My Baby, Child's Play (AARS), Coffee Bean, Cupcake, Daddy's Little Girl, Minnie Pearl
Orange/warm blend: All A'Twitter, Jean Kenneally, Little Artist, Magic Carrousel, Mandarin Sunblaze, Rainbow's End, Smoke Rings
Yellow: Hopscotch, Lemon Drop, Rise 'n' Shine (Golden Sunblaze), Sequoia Gold, Sunbeam, Texas, Tiddly Winks
White: Gourmet Popcorn, Snowbride, Starla
Lavender/mauve: Ruby Pendant, Winsome

Grandiflora, floribunda, and polyantha roses. These are the workhorses of rose gardens, noted for producing large quantities of flowers from spring through fall. Many have hybrid tea ancestry, evident in the long stems and/or elegant shape of the flowers. Unlike the hybrid teas, however, they produce clusters of blossoms rather than a single flower at the end of each stem; this makes them excellent for providing masses of color.

Grandifloras are about the same size as full-size hybrid teas and work well at the back of a flower bed or as barrier plants. Floribundas are smaller than hybrid teas—both in flower size and in height; use them for informal hedges, for low flower borders, or as container plants. 'Iceberg', one of the best-selling roses ever, is a floribunda.

Polyanthas produce small blossoms in large sprays; they are compact bushes, generally not much more than 2 ft. high. The first polyanthas appeared in the late 19th century. Two of the early polyanthas are now classics. 'Cécile Brünner' (the shrub dates from 1889, while the climbing form goes back to 1894) has light pink flowers of perfect hybrid tea form. 'The Fairy' (from 1932) is a rose covered with masses of 1-in. pink flowers.

Climbing roses. These are simply rose bushes that produce long, strong canes that will grow upright against a wall or arbor. They do not climb by twining or attachment but must be trained through or tied to their support. There are two types of modern climbing roses: large-flowered climbers and climbing mutations of bush roses, such as 'Cl. Iceberg' and 'Cl. Cécile Brünner'. Large-flowered climbers generally produce the most blooms, but the climbing mutations have the exquisite flowers of their famous parents.

Left to their own devices, many climbers make attractive arching shrubs or even ground covers. For more climbers, including some very large ones,

see the species roses section beginning on page 559.

Shrub roses. Planting roses for general landscape use is not a new idea; some fine shrub roses date to the early 20th century. Today, however, rose breeders are developing new roses for use purely as flowering shrubs. The emphasis is on plants that bloom prolifically over a long season and have abundant disease-resistant foliage. Modern shrub roses need little or no pruning to remain shapely. Because they bloom almost continuously, they pair well with perennials in borders.

Recognizing public loyalty to brand-name products, some rose breeders have created trademarked brands to which new selections can be added. Most of these are called shrub roses or landscape roses.

The Meidiland roses from Meilland, a French firm, were the first in this category to attract significant interest. The trademarked Meidiland series (including 'Pink Meidiland' and 'White Meidiland') are mostly somewhat billowy shrubs. They also created the Romantica roses described below under "New Classic Roses".

Flower Carpet is a series of ground cover roses bred by noted German rosarian Werner Noack for easy care and a long season of prolific bloom. Oso Easy is another series of compact landscape roses available in a variety of colors, some with good fragrance.

Trademarked brands also include new colors for classic old selections such as 'Burgundy Iceberg' and 'Double Red Simplicity'. Even popular newer selections like 'Home Run' have been expanded into series with shrubs like 'Pink Home Run'.

But of all the trademarked roses, none has been as popular as Knock Out roses, developed by Wisconsin rose breeder William Radler. Since the introduction of the original 'Knock Out' in 2000, it has become one of the most popular roses sold. Known for its disease resistance and free-blooming character, this bright red rose is now a common sight in gardens and landscapes across the country. Recently, additional colors and flower forms, including shades of pink and yellow, have been added to the Knock Out series. Unfortunately, the

TOP: 'Heritage' David Austin shrub rose; 'Graham Thomas' David Austin shrub rose; *MIDDLE:* 'Peggy Martin' climbing rose; *BOTTOM:* 'Veilchenblau' climbing rose; 'New Dawn' hybrid tea rose

Knock Outs have also proven very susceptible to rose rosette (see page 557), a devastating virus spread by mites, which could limit its usefulness. Many other roses are susceptible too (see "challenges" on page 557).

Shrub roses vary widely in growth habit and flower color; loose categories are listed below. Some shrub roses make tidy small climbers. For more shrub-rose choices, check the section on species roses on page 559.

Hybrid musk roses. The hybrid musks are large (6- to 8-ft.) shrubs or small climbers that perform well in dappled or partial shade or in sun. Most are nearly everblooming, with fragrant, clustered flowers in white, yellow, buff, pink shades, and red. Popular selections include buff apricot 'Buff Beauty', coral 'Cornelia', pink 'Felicia', pink 'Kathleen' (with single flowers reminiscent of apple blossoms), salmon 'Penelope', and red 'Will Scarlet'.

New Classic roses. The David Austin English roses were created by crossing various old roses (albas, centifolias, gallicas) with modern roses in order to combine the forms and fragrances of old roses with the colors and repeat flowering of modern hybrids. The group is extremely varied and includes low shrubs as well as plants that are determined to be climbers regardless of pruning. Popular selections include 'Abraham Darby', an upright to

TEN SWEET ROSES

For those who love fragrant roses most of all, here are ten of our favorites: 'Blanc Double de Coubert', white rugosa; 'Blush Noisette', light pink Noisette; 'Chrysler Imperial', deep red hybrid tea; 'Double Delight', creamy white and dark pink hybrid tea; 'Fragrant Cloud', coral-red hybrid tea; 'Gertrude Jekyll', deep pink English rose; 'Mme Hardy', white damask; 'Madame Isaac Pereire', magenta-red Bourbon; 'Mr. Lincoln', dark red hybrid tea; 'Sombreuil', creamy white tea.

climbing plant with flowers in a blend of pink, yellow, and apricot; 'Charles Austin', a bushy grower with apricot blossoms; 'Fair Bianca', spreading plant with creamy white blooms; 'Gertrude Jekyll', tall, upright grower bearing deep pink flowers; 'Graham Thomas', tall bush with rich yellow blooms; 'Heritage', fragrant and nearly thornless with soft pink flowers; and 'Othello', featuring dusky dark red blooms on a tall bush or climber.

Romantica roses, most of which are named for well-known figures in European arts and letters (such as 'Yves Piaget'), are more recent introductions with old rose character.

Ground cover roses. These low-growing plants, around 2–2½ ft. high, spread to at least 3½ ft. wide (some reach 6 ft. or wider). Vigor, disease resistance, and a profusion of bloom from late spring until frost are the hallmarks of this category. Ground cover roses are perfect for covering slopes, creating low barriers to foot traffic on level ground, and growing in pots.

The most commonly available ground cover roses are those in the Flower Carpet series, available in red, scarlet, pink, apple blossom, coral, yellow, and white. Several of the trademarked Meidiland roses, such as 'White Meidiland', are sufficiently low growing to be used as ground covers. More recently, their Drift series ('Coral Drift', 'Peach Drift', 'Sweet Drift', and so on) continue the practice with 2-ft. plants that combine the best traits of ground cover roses and miniature roses.

'Sea Foam', a shrub rose, makes a fine ground cover about 3 ft. high and 6 ft. wide, and some miniature roses have a pretty, sprawling habit. Several of the species roses and some of the climbing roses make good ground covers as well.

Miniature roses. These plants are perfect replicas of modern hybrid teas and floribundas, but plant size is reduced to about 1–1½ ft. tall (grown in the ground) with flowers and foliage in the same reduced proportion. Derived in part from *R. chinensis minima*, they come in all the modern hybrid tea colors. Plants are everblooming. Grow them outdoors in containers, window boxes, or as border and bedding

plants. To grow them indoors, pot in rich soil in 6-in. (or larger) containers and locate in a cool, bright window. Miniatures are hardier than hybrid teas but may still need winter protection in the Upper South (USDA 6). They also require a good amount of care. The shallow roots demand regular water, regular feeding, and mulching; powdery mildew, black spot, and spider mites are common problems. On the plus side, nearly all are own-root, cutting-grown plants.

OLD ROSES

Old roses belong to the various rose classes that existed prior to 1867 (even though some in these classes were introduced as late as the early 20th century). These roses fall into two categories. The old European roses comprise albas, centifolias, damasks, gallicas, and moss roses—the oldest hybrid groups derived from species native to Europe and western Asia. Most flower only in spring; many are hardy throughout the South with little or no winter protection. The second group contains classes derived entirely or in part from east Asian roses: Chinas, Bourbons, damask perpetuals, hybrid perpetuals, Noisettes, and teas. The original China and tea roses were brought to Europe from eastern Asia; 19th-century hybridizers greatly increased their numbers and also developed the other classes from crosses with European roses. Repeat flowering is a characteristic of these classes; hardiness varies, but nearly all need winter protection in cold-winter areas.

Alba roses. Developed from *R. alba*, the White Rose of York; associated with England's Wars of the Roses. Spring flowers range from single to very double, white to delicate pink. Upright plants are vigorous and long lived, with green wood and handsome, disease-tolerant, gray-green foliage. Garden forms include white 'Alba Semiplena' and these in shades of pink: 'Celestial', 'Félicité Parmentier', 'Great Maiden's Blush', and 'Königin von Dänemark'.

Centifolia roses. The roses often portrayed by Dutch painters; developed from *R. centifolia*, the cabbage rose. Open-structured plants have prickly stems that can reach 6 ft. tall but

arch with the weight of the blossoms. Intensely fragrant spring flowers typically are packed with petals, often with large outer petals that cradle a multitude of smaller petals within. Colors include white and pink shades. 'Paul Ricault' produces silken, deep pink flowers on an upright plant; 'Rose des Peintres' is a typical rich pink cabbage rose; 'Tour de Malakoff' is a tall, rangy plant with peonylike blossoms of pink fading to grayish mauve. Dwarf forms (to 3 ft. or less) are 'Petite de Hollande', 'Pompon de Bourgogne', and 'Rose de Meaux'.

Damask roses. Originating with *R. damascena*. Plants reach 6 ft. or taller, typically with long, arching, thorny canes and light green or grayish green, downy leaves. The summer damasks flower only in spring; forms of these are cultivated to make attar of roses (used in the perfume industry). Available selections include blush-pink 'Celsiana'; white 'Mme Hardy'; 'Leda', white with crimson markings; and 'Versicolor'('York and Lancaster'), with petals that may be pink, white, or a blend of pink and white. The autumn damask rose, *R. d.* 'Semperflorens' (*R. d. bifera*), flowers more than once in a year; slender buds open to loosely double, clear pink blossoms. This is the Rose of Castille of the Spanish missions.

Gallica roses. Cultivated forms of *R. gallica*, also known as French Rose. Fragrant spring flowers range in color from pink through red to maroon and purple shades. Plants reach 3–4 ft. tall, with upright to arching canes bearing prickles (but few thorns) and dark green, often rough-textured leaves. Grown on their own roots, these plants will spread into clumps from creeping rootstocks. Historic 'Officinalis', known as the Apothecary Rose, is presumed to be the Red Rose of Lancaster from Wars of the Roses; it is a dense, medium-size plant with semidouble cherry-red flowers. A mutation, 'Versicolor'—known as 'Rosa Mundi'—has pink petals boldly striped and stippled red. Other gallicas include 'Belle de Crécy', pink aging to violet; 'Cardinal de Richelieu', slate purple; 'Charles de Mills', crimson to purple; and 'Tuscany', dark crimson with gold stamens.

HOW TO GROW ROSES

SITE Plant where your roses will receive at least six hours of sunshine daily. If summer heat is intense, find a spot that receives filtered sunlight during the hottest afternoon hours. Soil for roses should drain reasonably well; if the soil in your chosen spot does not, the best alternative is to plant in raised beds. Don't locate roses too close to trees or large shrubs; their roots will steal the water and nutrients intended for your roses. Choose a spot where there is good air circulation—it helps discourage foliage diseases—but avoid windy locations. High winds can wreck the flowers and increase transpiration from the leaves, making frequent watering necessary.

SPACING Generous distance between plants aids air circulation, which reduces the incidence of mildew, black spot, and other foliage diseases. Exact spacing depends on the growth habit of the roses and on your climate. The colder the winter and the shorter the growing season, the smaller the bushes will be. But some selections are naturally small, others tall and massive—and those relative size differences will hold in any climate.

SOIL PREP Dig it deeply, incorporating organic matter such as aged bark or compost to help aerate dense clay soils and improve moisture retention in sandy soils. If you are planting new roses in a spot where existing bushes have been growing for five or more years, be sure to add plenty of rich organic material, as the soil is most likely quite spent. After planting, apply a complete, slow-release fertilizer.

PLANTING Healthy, ready-to-plant, bare-root roses should have plump, fresh-looking canes and roots. Before planting, immerse the entire plant in water for up to two days to be certain that all canes and roots are plumped up. After planting, some gardeners mound mulch over the bud union (the knob from which the canes grow) and around the canes to conserve moisture, then gradually and carefully remove the mulch when the leaves begin to expand.

If you're planting a budded plant (whether container grown or bare-root), set the plant in the hole so that the bud union is just above or right at soil level. In the Upper South and Middle South (USDA 6-7), some gardeners set the bud union 1–2 in. beneath the soil surface for increased protection from cold, but since this usually results in fewer canes, many gardeners in these cold-winter zones keep to the standard guideline (bud union just above soil level) and give their roses plenty of winter protection.

WATERING With the exception of some old garden roses and species roses that thrive on little water once they are established, roses need watering at all times during the growing season. Inadequate water inhibits growth and bloom.

Water deeply enough to moisten the entire root system (16–18 in. deep). How often you need to water depends on the soil type and weather. Big, well-established plants need more total water than newly set plants, but you will need to water new plants more frequently until they are established.

Soaking the soil is a simple way to water individual rose plants. If you have a drip-irrigation system, you will be able to water many plants at one time. Overhead sprinkling freshens foliage and helps remove dust; it can also wash away aphids, spider mites, and the spores of powdery mildew and other fungal leaf diseases. On the other hand, overhead sprinkling encourages blackspot, rust, and other diseases, washes off sprays that were applied to control pests and diseases, and may leave mineral deposits on foliage if water is hard. If you use an overhead sprinkler, do it early in the day to allow foliage time to dry off during daylight hours; leaves that stay wet for several hours are more likely to develop blackspot and other foliage diseases.

MULCHING Each spring, spread a 2- to 3-in.-thick layer of fresh mulch around your roses. If using aged bark, which breaks down

slowly, you may only need to replenish an inch or two each year. Mulching conserves moisture and deters weed growth. It also helps keep soil cool—a benefit in all but the coolest-summer climates.

FEEDING Nutrient needs vary depending on rose type and your soil's natural fertility. Many old roses, shrub roses, and species roses do not need regular fertilizer if growth is satisfactory. But for many repeat-flowering modern roses, regular fertilizing is needed to produce the most gratifying results.

In the Coastal and Tropical South (USDA 9-11), give established roses their initial feeding with a complete fertilizer in February; elsewhere, give the first feeding just as growth begins. Thereafter, time fertilizer applications to bloom periods. For roses that flower repeatedly throughout the growing season, fertilize after each blooming cycle has ended, when new growth is just beginning. For roses that bloom only in spring, one additional feeding just after flowering ends will encourage vigorous new growth and plenty of blooms next year.

Stop feeding in late summer or fall, at least six weeks before the first expected hard frost. In mild-winter zones experiencing virtually no subfreezing weather, you may continue fertilizing until mid-October for a crop of late-fall flowers.

Dry fertilizer, applied to the soil, is most frequently used. A variation on this type is controlled-release fertilizer; follow directions on the package for the amount and frequency of applications. Liquid fertilizers are useful in smaller gardens. Most liquid types can also be sprayed on rose leaves, which absorb some nutrients immediately. If you are looking for an organic fertilizer for roses, try alfalfa meal, cottonseed meal, and kelp meal. Avoid fertilizers with high levels of phosphorous, which can lock up micronutrients needed for healthy growth.

GROOMING Remove spent flowers during the growing season by cutting back to an outward-facing bud or a five-leaflet leaf.

CLEANUP Start each year by removing plant debris and old mulch from around your plants, as this may harbor overwintering insect eggs and disease spores.

INVITE BENEFICIALS Allies in the battle against rose pests include ladybugs, lacewings, beetles, flies, spiders, birds, and wasps. You can buy predators such as ladybugs at nurseries and release them in your garden; encourage them to stay awhile by setting out plants that attract them, such as dill, fennel, and yarrow. Avoid using broad-spectrum pesticides, which kill beneficial insects. For more information about pest management, see pages 715–721.

CHALLENGES Roses require certain controls during the growing season. Principal rose pests are aphids, spider mites, and, in some areas, Japanese beetles, rose midges, and thrips. If you don't want to rely on natural predators, start controlling aphids and spider mites when they first appear in spring, and repeat as needed until they are gone or their numbers are severely reduced. Natural controls include insecticidal soap, neem oil, spinosad, or horticultural oils. Synthetic insecticides, including systemics, are also available to control Japanese beetles, soil-born rose midge larvae, and many other pests. Thrips do their damage inside flower buds, disfiguring petals so badly that buds may not open—and if they do, flowers look discolored or appear scorched at the edges. Chili thrips are a relatively new pest to the Coastal and Tropical South (USDA 9-11) and distort buds and leaves and even mottle canes. Treat thrips with systemic insecticides according to label directions.

Blackspot and powdery mildew are the most common foliage diseases. First line of defense is thorough cleanup of all dead leaves and other debris during the dormant season; this is simplest right after you have pruned plants. Then, before new growth begins,

spray plants and soil with a dormant-season spray of horticultural oil or lime sulfur. This will destroy many disease organisms (as well as insect eggs) that might live over winter to reinfect plants in spring. Natural disease controls include the bacteria *Bacillus subtilis*, azadirachtin (Neem), and sodium bicarbonate/oil combinations (you can make your own by combining 2 tsp. baking soda and 2 tsp. of fine-grade horticultural oil in 1 gallon of water). To be effective, natural controls must be used early and often, before diseases become established. Synthetic fungicides are also available. The best way to prevent black spot and powdery mildew is by choosing resistant roses. See "Great Roses for Southern Gardens" on page 553.

Rose rosette is a newer disease causing havoc on roses throughout the South. The virus is principally spread by eriophyid mites so tiny they literally blow into gardens on the wind. When they feed on a rose, they transmit the virus. A healthy plant starts producing Medusalike bunches of bright-red new shoots. The shoots bloom, but the flowers look distorted. As rose rosette spreads through the plant, the rose gradually dies back until it dies completely. Because rose rosette is caused by a virus, it eventually spreads internally to every part of the plant. You may be able to save a rose by promptly removing the bright red shoot clusters before they are more than 6 in. long by cutting to healthy green wood below them. But once a rose gets full-blown rose rosette, turn out the lights. You must pull up the rose, roots and all, bag it, and throw it out with the trash. Spraying will not work. You can work to prevent the infection by removing invasive multiflora rose if it has naturalized in your area. In addition, prune your roses before spring growth begins. The mite

TOP: 'Ballerina' shrub rose; *Rosa banksiae;* 'Climbing Pinkie' climbing rose; *BOTTOM:* 'Souvenir de la Malmaison' Bourbon rose

only lays eggs in the top 6 in. of a plant. If you prune that off and burn it before growth begins, you will greatly reduce the chance of infection.

Chlorosis—evidenced by leaves turning light green to yellow while veins remain dark green—is not a disease but a symptom, usually of iron deficiency. This occurs in strongly alkaline soil. Adding iron chelate to the soil corrects chlorosis most quickly; iron sulfate is also effective, but slower to act. Chlorosis can also be caused by overwatering, heat, or drought stress.

Leaves that show irregular yellow or cream patterning indicate the presence of a mosaic virus. Some plants show symptoms consistently, others just occasionally. Although plants may appear to grow with vigor, the virus does impair overall strength and productivity, and it can make foliage unsightly. Fortunately, it is not transferred from plant to plant by insects or by pruning; it is transmitted in propagation—from infected rootstock or bud wood. Commercial rose producers are diligently working to eliminate virus-infected stock. If you have an infected plant that is growing poorly or is unattractive, remove it from the garden.

For local help with pests and diseases, consider joining the American Rose Society (ars.org). Its consulting rosarians advise member gardeners on rose problems at no cost.

Moss roses. Two old rose classes—centifolia and damask—include variant types that feature mosslike, balsam-scented glands covering unopened buds, flower stems, and sometimes even leaflets. The "moss" of centifolias is soft to the touch; that of damasks is stiffer and pricklier. Flowers are white, pink, or red, often intensely fragrant. 'Centifolia Muscosa' ('Muscosa') and 'Communis' are typical pink centifolias with moss added; 'White Bath' is 'Centifolia Muscosa' in white. Other available selections are pale pink to white 'Comtesse de Murinais', deep pink 'Gloire des Mousseux', salmon-pink 'Mme Louis Lévêque', dark red 'Nuits de Young', and dark red to purple 'William Lobb'. Repeat-flowering mosses include creamy pink 'Alfred de Dalmas', apricot 'Gabriel Noyelle', red 'Henri Martin', and bright pink 'Salet'.

China roses. The first two China roses to reach Europe (around 1800) were cultivated forms of *R. chinensis* that had been selected and maintained by Chinese horticulturists. Flowers were pink or red, less than 3 in. across, borne in small clusters on 2- to 4-ft.-high plants. 'Old Blush' ('Parson's Pink China'), one of the original two, is still sold. Other available selections include 'Archduke Charles', with pink blossoms aging to crimson; red 'Cramoisi Supérieur' ('Agrippina'); white 'Ducher'; crimson 'Louis Philippe'; and 'Mutabilis', with flowers that open soft yellow-buff and age to pink, then crimson. Also sold is the bizarre-looking Green Rose, *R. c. viridiflora*, with blossoms resembling clusters of bright green leaves. China rose ancestry is the primary source of repeat flowering in roses developed in the late 19th and early 20th centuries.

Bourbon roses. The original Bourbon rose was a hybrid between *R. chinensis* and the autumn damask rose (*R. damascena* 'Semperflorens'). Later developments were shrubs, semiclimbers, and climbers with flowers in white, pink shades, and red, mostly quite fragrant. Best known today are 'La Reine Victoria', 'Mme Ernst Calvat', 'Mme Pierre Oger', 'Souvenir de la Malmaison' (all pink); and 'Zéphirine Drouhin' and the supremely fragrant 'Madame Isaac Pereire' (both magenta-red).

A famous Bourbon-China hybrid, 'Gloire des Rosomanes' gained widespread distribution as a rootstock (called "Ragged Robin") in commercial production. Occasionally it is offered as a hedge rose; growth is upright to fountainlike, with coarse foliage and semidouble cherry-red flowers throughout the growing season.

Damask perpetuals. This was the first distinct hybrid group to emerge, beginning around 1800, combining the China roses with old European rose types. Ancestries vary, but all appear to include China roses and the autumn damask rose (*R. damascena* 'Semperflorens'); generally they were known as Portland roses after the first representative, 'Duchess of Portland'. All are fairly short, bushy, repeat-flowering plants with centifolia- and gallica-like flowers. Among those sold are 'Comte de Chambord', cool pink; 'Duchess of Portland', crimson; 'Jacques Cartier', bright pink; and 'Rose du Roi', crimson with purple shadings.

Hybrid perpetuals. In the 19th and early 20th centuries, before hybrid teas dominated the catalogs, these were *the* garden roses. They are big, vigorous, and hardy to about –30°F with minimal winter protection. Plants need more water and fertilizer than hybrid teas to produce repeated bursts of bloom. Prune high, thin out oldest canes, and arch over remaining canes to encourage many blooms. Flowers are full, often large (to 6–7 in. wide), and strongly fragrant; buds usually are shorter and plumper than those of hybrid teas. Colors range from white through pink shades to red and maroon. Selections still sold include white 'Frau Karl Druschki'; cherry-red 'Général Jacqueminot'; rose-pink 'Mrs. John Laing'; deep pink, peonylike 'Paul Neyron'; and carmine-red 'Ulrich Brünner Fils'.

Noisette roses. In Charleston, South Carolina, in the early 1800s, the union of a China rose and the musk rose (*R. moschata*) produced the first Noisette rose: 'Champneys' Pink Cluster', a shrubby, repeat-flowering climber with small pink flowers in medium-size clusters. Crossed with itself and China roses, it led to a race of similar fragrant roses in white, pink shades, and red; crossed with tea roses, it yielded

the large-flowered, climbing tea-Noisettes. Small-flowered Noisettes include white 'Aimée Vibert-Scandens', light pink 'Blush Noisette', and cherry-red 'Fellenberg'. Among tea-Noisettes are yellow 'Alister Stella Gray' and 'Maréchal Niel'; orange 'Crépuscule'; white 'Lamarque' and 'Mme Alfred Carrière'; and buff-apricot 'Rêve d'Or'. Not reliably hardy in the Upper and Middle South (USDA 6-7).

Tea roses. This race of elegant, virtually everblooming, relatively tender roses does best in the Lower, Coastal, and Tropical South (USDA 8-11). Plants are long lived, building on old wood and disliking heavy pruning. Flowers are in pastel shades—white, soft cream, light yellow, apricot, buff, pink, and rosy red; flower character varies, but many resemble hybrid teas. In crosses with hybrid perpetuals, tea roses were parents of the first hybrid teas. Available selections include 'Duchesse de Brabant', warm pink, tuliplike; 'Lady Hillingdon', saffron; 'Maman Cochet', creamy rose-pink; 'Marie van Houtte', soft yellow and pink; 'Mlle Franziska Krüger', pink and cream to orange; 'Monsieur Tillier', warm dark pink with gold and rosy red; 'Mrs. B. R. Cant', silvery pink; 'Sombreuil', creamy white; and 'White Maman Cochet', creamy white shaded pink. The cross of a tea rose and the tea ancestor *R. gigantea* produced 'Belle

Portugaise' ('Belle of Portugal'), a rampant climber bearing large pale pink blossoms in spring.

SPECIES ROSES AND THEIR HYBRIDS

Species roses are the original wild roses from which all other roses descend. Among the following species and their hybrids are excellent shrub roses, climbing roses, and roses that will help control erosion on slopes. Some are extremely vigorous and cold hardy.

R. banksiae. LADY BANKS'S ROSE. Evergreen climber. Zones MS, LS, CS, TS; USDA 7-11. From China. An old-time favorite. Vigorous grower to 20 ft. or more. Aphid resistant, almost immune to disease. Stems have almost no prickles; glossy, leathery leaves have three to five leaflets to 2½ in. long. Large clusters of small yellow or white flowers bloom in spring. Good for covering banks, ground, fence, or arbor. The two forms sold are 'Lutea', with scentless, double yellow flowers, and *R. b. banksiae* ('Alba Plena' or 'White Banksia'), with violet-scented, double white flowers. The fragrant 'Fortuniana' (*R. fortuniana*) is sometimes sold as the double white banksia; it differs in having thorny canes, larger leaves, and larger flowers that come individually rather than in clusters.

R. bracteata. MACARTNEY ROSE. Evergreen climbing shrub with large, creamy white single

R

MAKING THE CUT

Early pruning each year contributes to the health, productivity, and longevity of roses. The basic objective is to promote strong growth that will bear good flowers.

1. Prune conservatively. Never chop down a vigorous 6-ft. bush to 1½-ft. stubs unless you want only a few huge blooms for exhibition.

2. Prune at the right time. The best pruning time for most roses is at the end of the dormant season, when growth buds begin to swell. The exact time varies according to locality but is usually sometime between mid-January (in mild climates) and early April (in colder ones). Where late frosts are common, be sure not to prune too early—the resulting new growth will be vulnerable to freezes.

3. Use sharp pruners; remove the right branches. Prune out wood that is dead, wood that has no healthy growth coming from it, branches that cross through the plant's center or rub against larger canes, branches that make a bush appear lopsided, as well as any unproductive old canes that strong new ones have replaced during the past season. Removing any foliage that remains on the plant will reduce the incidence of disease later. Then cut back the previous season's growth by one-third to one-half, making cuts above outward-facing buds (except for very spreading selections, in which some cuts to inside buds will promote more height without producing many crossing branches). The ideal result is a V-shaped bush with a relatively open center.

4. Remove suckers. If any suckers (growth produced from the understock of a budded plant) are present, completely remove them. Dig down to where the suckers grow from the understock and pull them off with a downward motion; this removes growth buds that would otherwise produce additional suckers in subsequent years. Let the wound air-dry before you replace soil around it.

Be certain you are removing a sucker rather than a new cane growing from the bud union. Suckers usually are easy to distinguish from desired canes; differences can be seen in foliage size, shape, and color, as well as in size of thorns and habit of growth. If in doubt, let the presumed sucker grow until you can establish its difference from a cane; its flowers will be noticeably different. A flowerless, climbing cane from a bush rose is almost certainly a sucker.

5. Match pruning to the roses you grow. Prune hybrid teas and grandifloras according to the guidelines above.

Floribunda, polyantha & shrub roses. On shrub roses, follow the guidelines above, but cut back the previous season's growth by only one-fourth to one-third, and leave as many strong new canes and stems as the plant produced. On polyanthas and floribundas, remove one-third to one-half of the previous year's foliage.

Old roses & species roses. For kinds that bloom only once, prune after they have flowered in spring. Prune repeat-blooming types at the end of the dormant season. Most need only a light annual pruning—provided you've allowed these typically vigorous roses sufficient space. Remove any dead or weak canes; then prune the tip of each remaining cane. If the center of the plant is dense and over-crowded, completely remove a few old, woody canes. The roses in this group that produce long, arching canes (many of the hybrid perpetuals, for example) can be pruned the same way as climbers.

Climbing roses. Leave all climbers unpruned for the first two or three years after planting, but do train the canes, even in the first season. Spread them so that they are as horizontal as possible, which will stimulate the production of flowering branches. A fan shape works best.

Prune climbing roses that bloom only in spring just after they finish flowering, removing old canes that show no signs of strong new growth. For climbers that bloom off and on in other seasons as well as in spring, prune at the same time you'd prune bush roses in your locality. Remove the oldest unproductive canes and any weak, twiggy growth; cut back the lateral branches on the remaining canes to two or three buds.

---

blossoms. Zones LS, CS, TS; USDA 8-11. From southeastern China; naturalized in the Southeast. Its celebrated offspring is 'Mermaid', an evergreen or semievergreen climber hardy in the Coastal and Tropical South. Vigorous (to 30 ft.) and thorny, it has glossy, leathery, dark green leaves and many single, creamy yellow, lightly fragrant flowers to 5 in. across. Bloom comes in spring, summer, fall, and intermittently through winter. Tough and disease resistant; thrives in sun or partial shade. Plant 8 ft. apart for quick ground cover; or use to climb walls (will need tying), run along fences, or climb trees. Forms dense thickets and can be invasive.

R. eglanteria. See R. rubiginosa

R. foetida (R. lutea). AUSTRIAN BRIER. Deciduous shrub. Zones US, MS, LS; USDA 6-8. From central and western Asia. Slender, prickly, erect or arching green stems to 5–10 ft. long. Dark green, smooth or slightly hairy leaves are especially susceptible to black spot and may drop in early fall. Single bright yellow, 2- to 3-in. flowers with an odd scent bloom in mid- to late spring. This species and its well-known selection 'Bicolor', often called Austrian Copper, are the source of orange and yellow color in modern roses. 'Bicolor' is a 4- to 5-ft. shrub with brilliant coppery red flowers, their petals backed in yellow. Its form 'Persiana', called Persian Yellow, has fully double yellow blooms.

Species and selections do best in warm, fairly dry, well-drained soil and in full sun. Prune only to remove dead wood.

R. glauca. REDLEAF ROSE. Deciduous shrub. Zones US, MS, LS; USDA 6-8. From mountains of central and southern Europe. Foliage, not blossoms, is the main feature of this rose: The 6-ft. plant is clothed in leaves that combine gray-green and coppery purple. Small, single, pink flowers bloom in spring; they are followed by small, oval hips that turn red in autumn.

R. x harisonii. HARISON'S YELLOW ROSE. Deciduous shrub. Zones US, MS, LS; USDA 6-8. Hybrid between R. foetida and R. pimpinellifolia. Very old rose that was taken westward to Texas by pioneers. Vigorous, disease free, cold hardy, and drought tolerant, with fine-textured foliage on thickets of thorny stems to 6–8 ft. tall. Profuse show of semidouble, fragrant, bright yellow flowers in late spring, with occasional rebloom in fall. Blackish red, showy hips. Useful deciduous landscape shrub; also called the Yellow Rose of Texas.

R. hugonis. See R. xanthina hugonis

R. laevigata. CHEROKEE ROSE. Evergreen climber. Zones MS, LS, CS, TS; USDA 7-11. Native to Southeast Asia but highly naturalized in the southern U.S.; the state flower of Georgia. Green stems to 10 ft. long hold sharp, hooked thorns and lacquered-looking, dark green leaves, each with three leaflets. Single white flowers to 3½ in. wide appear only in spring. Crossed with a tea rose, this species produced 'Anemone', a mostly spring-flowering climber bearing single, soft silvery pink flowers reminiscent of Japanese anemone. 'Ramona' is a magenta-pink variation.

R. moschata. MUSK ROSE. Deciduous shrub. Zones US, MS, LS, CS, TS; USDA 6-11. Probably from western Asia; an old Southern favorite. Vigorous, arching plant to 10 ft. high and wide, densely clothed in matte, medium green leaves that turn butter-yellow in late fall. Clusters of ivory-white, single flowers with a delicious, somewhat honeylike perfume appear in late spring and bloom through the summer. R. m. plena has double blossoms,

TOP: 'Old Blush' China rose; *R. laevigata; BOTTOM:* 'Peace' hybrid tea rose

though their effect is lessened because the inner petals wither before the outer ones.

R. moyesii. Deciduous shrub. Zones US, MS, LS; USDA 6-8. From western China. Large, loose shrub to 10 ft. high, 8 ft. wide; best as background plant or featured shrub-tree specimen. Spring bloom is a glorious display of bright red single flowers to 2½ in. across, carried singly or in groups of two. A second show comes in fall, when the large, bottle-shaped hips ripen to brilliant scarlet. 'Geranium', a hybrid, is a somewhat shorter, more compact selection with red flowers in clusters of up to five. 'Sealing Wax', also a hybrid, offers pink flowers, also on a smaller and more compact bush.

R. multiflora. JAPANESE ROSE. Deciduous shrub. Zones US, MS, LS, CS; USDA 6-9. From Japan. Arching growth on dense, vigorous plant to 8–10 ft. tall and wide. Susceptible to mildew, spider mites. Profuse clusters of small white flowers (like blackberry blossoms) in mid- to late spring; sweet fragrance akin to that of honeysuckle (*Lonicera*). Heavy fall crop of ¼-in. red hips, much loved by birds. One of the most widely used rootstocks in commercial rose production.

R. multiflora is promoted as a hedge, but this has been disastrous. Profuse volunteer seedlings can put it in the "pest" category. It has become so invasive in some areas that it has been declared a noxious weed, and people have been forbidden to sell or plant it. A number of distinctive climbing roses, however, are noninvasive hybrids of this species. Known as multiflora ramblers, they include several well-known "blue ramblers": 'Bleu Magenta', with crimson-purple blooms fading to grayish violet; 'Rose-Marie Viaud', crimson purple aging to violet and lilac; 'Veilchenblau', maroon-purple turning grayish lilac with age; and 'Violette', with maroon-purple blooms that turn grayish plum.

R. m. platyphylla, also known as 'Seven Sisters', is an heirloom rose often seen in old Southern gardens. It is not invasive and sports larger flowers than species, in shades of deep reddish purple to palest mauve.

R. roxburghii. CHESTNUT ROSE. Deciduous shrub. Zones US, MS, LS, CS; USDA 6-9. Native to western China. Spreading plant with prickly, 8- to 10-ft.-long stems and peeling gray bark. Light green, ferny, very fine-textured foliage is tipped in bronze and gold when new. Immune to mildew and blackspot. Buds and hips are spiny, like chestnut burrs. Unscented, soft rose-pink, typically double flowers appear in mid- to late spring. Normally a big shrub for screen or border, but if stems are pegged down, it makes a good bank cover, useful in preventing erosion.

R. rubiginosa (*R. eglanteria*). SWEET BRIAR ROSE, EGLANTINE. Deciduous shrub or climber. Zones US, MS, LS; USDA 6-8. From Europe, western Asia, North Africa. Vigorous grower to 8–12 ft. tall, 6–8 ft. wide. Prickly stems bear dark green leaves that smell like green apples, especially after a rain. Pink, 1½-in., single flowers appear singly or in clusters in late spring. Red-orange hips. Used as hedge, barrier, or screen; can be held to 3–4 ft. Plant 3–4 ft. apart and prune annually in early spring. Good hybrid forms are 'Lady Penzance' and 'Lord Penzance'.

R. rugosa. RUGOSA ROSE. Deciduous shrub. Zones US, MS, LS, CS; USDA 6-9. From northern China, Siberia, Korea, Japan. Vigorous, hardy shrub with prickly stems. To 3–8 ft. tall and wide. Bright, glossy, green leaves have distinctive heavy veining that gives them a crinkled look. Wonderfully fragrant flowers are 3–4 in. across and range from single to double and from pure white and creamy yellow through pink to deep purplish red. Blooms spring, summer, early fall. Bright red, tomato-shaped fruit, an inch or more across, is seedy but edible, sometimes used in preserves.

All rugosas are extremely tough, withstanding hard freezes, wind, drought, and salt spray. They make fine hedges; plants grown on their own roots make sizable colonies and help prevent erosion. Foliage remains free of diseases and insects, except possibly aphids. Among the most widely sold rugosas and rugosa hybrids are 'Blanc Double de Coubert', double white; 'Frau Dagmar Hartopp' ('Fru Dagmar Hastrup'), single pink; 'Hansa', double purplish red; and 'Will Alderman', double pink. Four

WINTER PROTECTION

Where winter temperatures regularly drop below 10°F, thaw, and freeze again, some cold protection will help modern roses. Prolonged low temperatures can also kill exposed canes, and winter winds can fatally desiccate them. Apply a thick layer of mulch that covers the graft, if there is one. On windy sites, bundle canes together in a wire mesh cage filled with fallen leaves.

unusual rugosa hybrids are cherry-red 'F. J. Grootendorst', crimson-red 'Grootendorst Supreme', 'Pink Grooten-dorst', and 'White Grootendorst'; their semidouble to double flowers with deeply fringed petals resemble carnations (*Dianthus*) more than roses.

R. spinosissima (*R. pimpinellifolia*) SCOTCH ROSE, BURNET ROSE. Deciduous shrub. Zones US, MS, LS; USDA 6-8. From western Europe east to Korea. Spreading shrub to 3–4 ft. tall; initially as wide as high, then spreading wider by suckers. Upright, spiny, bristly stems are closely set with small, ferny leaves. Handsome bank cover in good soil; helps prevent erosion. White to pink, 1½- to 2-in. spring flowers; dark brown to blackish hips. Its form 'Altaica', with larger leaves and garlands of 3-in. white flowers, can reach 6 ft. high. Several hybrids are noteworthy. 'Stanwell Perpetual' bears blush pink double blooms from spring to fall on a mounding, twiggy plant with small gray-green leaves. 'Frühlingsmorgen' is the best known of several German hybrids; it's a tall, arching plant that bears large, single yellow flowers edged in cherry-pink and centered with maroon stamens. 'Golden Wings', to 6 ft., blooms throughout the growing season; its 4-in., single blossoms have light yellow petals and red stamens.

R. wichuraiana. MEMORIAL ROSE. Evergreen or partially evergreen vine. Zones US, MS, LS, CS; USDA 6-9. From Japan, Korea, eastern China. Trailing stems grow 10–12 ft. long in one season, root in contact with moist soil. Leaves 2–4 in. long, with five to nine smooth, shiny, ¼- to 1-in. leaflets. Midsummer flowers are white, to 2 in. across, in clusters of six to ten. Good ground cover, even in relatively poor soil. Wichuraiana ramblers, produced in the first 20 years of the 20th century, are hybrids between the species and various garden roses. Pink 'Dorothy Perkins' and red 'Excelsa' produce lavish spring displays of small blooms that obscure the often-mildewed leaves. Larger, shapelier flowers and glossy, healthier leaves are found in creamy white 'Albéric Barbier', coral-pink 'François Juranville', light yellow 'Gardenia', coppery salmon 'Paul Transon', and white 'Sander's White Rambler'.

R. xanthina hugonis (*R. hugonis*). FATHER HUGO'S ROSE, GOLDEN ROSE OF CHINA. Deciduous shrub. Zones US, MS, LS; USDA 6-8. From northern China. Dense growth to 8 ft. tall, 5 ft. wide. Arching or straight stems with bristles near base. Handsome, deep green, 1- to 4-in.-long leaves; each has 5 to 11 leaflets. Blooms profusely in mid- to late spring, when branches become garlands of 2-in.-wide, bright yellow, faintly fragrant flowers. Good in borders, for screen or barrier plantings, against a fence, trained fanwise on a trellis. Takes high, filtered afternoon shade. Prune oldest wood to ground each year to shape the plant and get maximum bloom.

ROSMARINUS OFFICINALIS
ROSEMARY
Lamiaceae
Evergreen shrub

US (SOME), MS (SOME), LS, CS, TS; USDA 6-11; OR GROW IN POTS

FULL SUN

LITTLE TO MODERATE WATER

Rosmarinus officinalis 'Tuscan Blue'

Rosmarinus means "dew of the sea," reflecting the plant's native habitat on seaside cliffs in the Mediterranean region. Tough and versatile, rosemary grows most luxuriantly just above the tide line, braving wind and salt spray—but it will thrive inland, even enduring blistering sun and poor alkaline soil, if given moderate water and infrequent light feeding.

The many forms of rosemary vary in habit from stiff, erect types through rounded shrubs and squat, dense tufts to rock-hugging creepers. Height ranges from as low as 1 ft. to as tall as 6 ft. or more. Plants are thickly clothed in narrow, typically 1- to 1½-in.-long, resinous, aromatic leaves that are usually glossy dark green above, grayish white beneath. Small clusters of ¼- to ½-in. blossoms in various shades of blue (rarely pink or white) bloom through winter and spring; bloom occasionally repeats in fall. Leaves are widely used as a seasoning. Flowers also are edible; add them to salads or use as a garnish. Blossoms attract birds, butterflies, and bees and are the source of excellent honey. Deer leave rosemary alone.

Use taller types of rosemary as clipped or informal hedges or in dry borders with native and gray-leafed plants. Lower kinds are good ground or bank covers, useful in erosion control. Set container-grown plants or rooted cuttings 2 ft. apart for moderately quick cover. Foliage of most types has culinary uses, but flavor and fragrance vary; the best have a mildly pungent flavor and a complex aroma with sweet as well as resinous notes. Rosemary is also an ingredient in medicines, cosmetics, potpourri, and moth repellents.

Rosemary plants sold without names are frequently seedlings, which lack the uniformity of cutting-grown, named selections. Unfortunately, selection names are often confused, and many have synonyms; but named plants are still a better bet than nameless ones.

'Albus' ('Albiflorus'). Semi-upright grower, eventually reaching 6 ft. tall and wide. White flowers veined in pale lavender. Hardy to 0°F.

'Arp'. One of the hardiest selections, taking temperatures as low as –10°F. Discovered in Arp, Texas. Open grower to 4 ft. tall and wide; best with frequent pruning. Dark green foliage has a grayish tinge. Bright, medium blue flowers.

'Barbecue'. Grows 5 ft. tall, 2–3 ft. wide, has excellent fragrance for cooking; blue flowers.

'Blue Boy'. Young plant makes a dense, symmetrical mound 8–12 in. high, 14–18 in. across, reminiscent of a dwarf spruce (*Picea*). Leaves are just ½ in. long; flowers are light blue. Plant creeps with age, but habit becomes irregular; shear to maintain domed appearance. Good in rock gardens, pots. Pleasant fragrance and flavor. Tender.

'Blue Spires'. Strong vertical grower, to 5–6 ft. tall and as wide or wider with age; can be pruned for narrower form. Deep blue flowers. Superb landscape plant; makes tight sheared hedge. Excellent for seasoning.

'Chef's Choice'. Compact, mounding to 12–18 in. tall and 12 in. wide. Selected for higher oil content and spicy flavor. Hardy to –10°F.

'Hill's Hardy'. Compact, bushy plant grows semiupright to 5 ft. high and wide. Stiff foliage. Light blue flowers; repeat bloom in fall. Pleasant, light fragrance. Discovered by the late Madalene Hill of Round Top, Texas. Hardy to –10°F.

'Huntington Carpet' ('Huntington Blue'). To 1½ ft. high; spreads quickly yet maintains a dense center. Pale blue flowers. Best selection for ground or bank cover.

'Irene' ('Renzel's', 'Renzel's Irene'). Vigorous spreader that covers 2–3 ft. or more per year, mounding to 1–1½ ft. high. Deep lavender-blue flowers. Reputedly one of the most cold-hardy prostrate selections.

COOKING WITH ROSEMARY

You can use any selection of rosemary for cooking. But upright kinds with broader leaves contain more aromatic oil. 'Tuscan Blue' is a favorite of many chefs; its leaves are wider than average and very aromatic; flowers are dark blue. 'Blue Spires', with clear blue flowers, is good for flavoring grilled meats and roasted potatoes. 'Spice Islands', normally sold in the herb section at nurseries, is another good choice; it bears dark blue flowers. 'Barbecue' has flavorful, aromatic leaves and clear blue flowers; stiff branch clippings (scrape off lower leaves) are sometimes used as skewers for grilling kebabs.

'Lockwood de Forest' ('Santa Barbara', 'Lockwoodii', 'Forestii'). Resembles 'Prostratus' but mounds up to 2½ ft. or more; has lighter, brighter green foliage and bluer flowers.

'Majorca Pink'. Initially erect to 2–4 ft. tall and 1½–2 ft. wide; eventually twists into picturesque shape under the weight of its heavy seed crop, flopping to 3–4 ft. wide. Lilac-pink flowers. Slightly fruity fragrance.

'Prostratus'. To 2 ft. tall, with 4- to 8-ft. spread. Will trail straight down over wall or edge of raised bed to make a green curtain. Pale lavender-blue flowers come in waves from fall into spring. With age, tends to mound up and become woody and bare in center (except at seashore, where it remains lush throughout). Effective in hanging containers. Tender.

'Salem'. Dependable old selection with dense, erect growth to 3 ft. high and wide; lavender-blue flowers. Fairly cold hardy.

'Spice Islands'. Upright growth reaches 6–8 ft., making this a good screen or background. Large blue flowers, good fragrance. Once grown for commercial seasoning production.

'Tuscan Blue'. Vita Sackville-West's original, brought to England from Tuscany, had relatively broad (to ¼-in.-wide), 1- to 1½-in.-long leaves, deep violet-blue flowers, and upright habit to 6–7 ft. tall and 1½–2 ft. wide. A plant long sold as 'Tuscan Blue' in the U.S. fits this general description but has light blue flowers; with age, it becomes woody and bare at the base. Some nurseries sell 'Blue Spires' under this name.

CARE

Good drainage is essential; lighten heavy soils with plenty of organic matter. Heavy feeding and too much water result in rank growth, subsequent woodiness. Control growth by frequent tip-pinching when plants are small. Prune older plants frequently but lightly; cut to side branch or shear. If plants become woody and bare in center, cut back selected branches by half so plant will fill in with new growth (be sure to cut into leafy wood; plants will not regrow from bare wood). Or discard plant and start over with a new one. Branches root wherever they touch the ground; creeping types will spread indefinitely,

forming extensive colonies. To get new plants, root tip cuttings or dig and replant layered branches.

Cold hardiness varies considerably, depending on selection. In general, upright types are hardier, while prostrate ones (native to Majorca and Corsica) are more tender, suffering damage at 20°F or even higher. In the Upper and Middle South, choose the hardiest types and shelter them from winter winds. Note that even the hardiest types can succumb to cold if they have wet feet. Beyond hardiness range, grow rosemary in pots and winter indoors on a sunny windowsill; or treat as an annual.

ROYSTONEA
ROYAL PALM
Arecaceae
Palms

| ✎ **TS; USDA 10-11** |
| ☼ **FULL SUN** |
| ◗ **REGULAR WATER** |

Roystonea regia

Stately, symmetrical, fast-growing feather palms. Tall, smooth, gray trunk is marked with rings and topped by a green crown shaft formed by the overlapping frond bases. Hardy to 28°F. Do best in moist, well-drained soil. If grown in alkaline soil, they are subject to a disfiguring disease ced frizzle top, caused by a deficiency of manganese or potassium. To prevent this, feed regularly with an 8-4-12 palm fertilizer containing manganese. Have good wind and salt resistance. Resist damage by browsing deer. Can be used as street or avenue trees, to frame

large buildings, in groups with other palms. Look especially majestic planted in rows.

R. oleracea. CARIBBEAN ROYAL PALM. Native to the Caribbean and South America. May reach over 100 ft. tall, 35 ft. wide. Green fronds grow as long as 20 ft.; they are usually semiupright or spreading.

R. regia. CUBAN ROYAL PALM. Native to Cuba. To 50–75 ft. high, 30 ft. wide. Trunk is swollen at base, tapering toward top, sometimes swollen toward middle. Bright green, 10- to 20-ft.-long fronds arch gracefully in all directions. Segments stand out from midrib at many angles.

The Florida royal palm, formerly *R. elata,* is identical.

RUBUS
BRAMBLE
Rosaceae
Evergreen and deciduous shrubs

| ✎ **ZONES VARY BY SPECIES** |
| ☼ ◖ **EXPOSURE NEEDS VARY BY SPECIES** |
| ◗ ◖ **MODERATE TO REGULAR WATER** |

Rubus odoratus

Though best known for blackberry and raspberry (see separate entries), the brambles include many ornamental plants, most of them thornless. Those listed here differ from blackberry and raspberry not only in their lack of prickles but also in having perennial rather than biennial stems. Spring flowers are followed by small, edible berries that attract birds. Need good drainage; spread widely by rhizomes. Plant ground cover types about 2 ft. apart. Deer seldom bother these plants.

R. odoratus. FLOWERING RASPBERRY. Zones US, MS; USDA 6-7. Deciduous. Native to northeastern U.S. and Appalachians. Loose, rambling shrub to 5–8 ft. tall and wide. Handsome, rich green, maplelike leaves grow 5–10 in. long, with three to five lobes. Clusters of showy, rosy purple, 1- to 2-in.-wide flowers appear in early summer; these are followed by mealy reddish berries (edible but tasteless) that ripen in July or August. Good for woodland gardens, naturalized areas. Grow in moist, organically enriched soil and filtered shade.

R. rolfei (*R. pentalobus, R. calycinoides*). CREEPING BRAMBLE, CREEPING RASPBERRY. Evergreen. Zones US, MS, LS; USDA 6-8. Native to mountains of Taiwan. Thickly foliaged stems spread at a moderate rate to form a dense carpet to 1 ft. high. Rounded, 1- to ½-in. leaves have three to five broad, ruffled-edged lobes; upper surfaces are lustrous dark green and rough textured, undersides are grayish white and felted. Small white flowers resemble those of strawberry; tasty berries are salmon colored. Full sun or light shade. 'Emerald Carpet' is a commonly sold selection with superior foliage.

R. rosifolius. ROSELEAF RASPBERRY. Evergreen. Zones US, MS, LS; USDA 6-8. Native to Asia and Australia. Rambling shrub to 6 ft. tall; spreads to form large thickets. Dark green, corrugated-looking leaves, 4–6 in. long, have three to seven leaflets and resemble rose foliage. Single, inch-wide white flowers bloom in early summer and again in fall; tasteless red berries ripen in summer and late fall. 'Coronarius' is a spectacular 4- to 5-ft.-tall selection with double white, 4-in.-wide blossoms that strongly resemble old roses; they appear from March through June on last year's growth, from August through September on the current year's growth. Blooms at an early age; produces no berries. Tolerates most soils and prefers light shade. Sometimes listed as *R. coronarius.*

ABOVE: Rubus rolfei

RUDBECKIA
CONEFLOWER
Asteraceae
Perennials and biennials

✎ **US, MS, LS, CS; USDA 6-9, EXCEPT AS NOTED**

☼ **FULL SUN**

♦♦ **MODERATE TO REGULAR WATER**

Rudbeckia fulgida

The showy garden rudbeckias that brighten summer and fall borders are descended from wild plants native mainly to the eastern U.S. All are tough and easy to grow. Blossoms have yellow or orange rays and a raised central cone. Choice cut flowers; cutting also encourages rebloom late in season. Divide perennials when crowded, usually every few years.

R. auriculatus. EARED BLACK-EYED SUSAN. Perennial. Zones MS, LS, CS, TS; USDA 7-10. Native to moist areas of southeastern Alabama and nearby Georgia and Florida. Grows 6 ft. high. Golden yellow flowers are 2 to 3 in. wide. Often needs staking. Takes alkaline soils.

R. fulgida. YELLOW CONEFLOWER. Perennial. Initially 3 ft. tall, 2 ft. wide; after a few years, spreads by rhizomes to form a larger clump. Branching stems; broadly lance-shaped, 5-in.-long, hairy, dark green leaves. Yellow, 2- to 2½-in.-wide flowers with a black to brown central cone bloom in summer. Selections are more often grown than the species. Among the most popular is *R. f. sullivantii* 'Goldsturm', bearing 3-in., black-eyed yellow flowers on 2- to 2½-ft. stems. Some nurseries offer the taller, more variable seed-grown Goldsturm strain. 'Early Bird Gold' has an especially long bloom season, running spring to fall.

R. f. speciosa (*R. speciosa*), to 2½ ft. high and 2 ft. wide, is native from New Jersey to Alabama and Georgia; it has bright orange-yellow petals surrounding a black cone. Its selection 'Viette's Little Suzy' is a dwarf to about 14 in. high and wide, with dark-eyed yellow blooms.

R. hirta. BLACK-EYED SUSAN, GLORIOSA DAISY. Biennial or short-lived perennial; often grown as annual because it blooms the first summer from seed sown in early spring. Zones US, MS, LS, CS, TS; USDA 6-11. To 3–4 ft. tall, 1½ ft. wide, with upright, branching habit. Stems and lance-shaped leaves to 4 in. long are rough and hairy. Daisylike, 2- to 4-in.-wide flowers have orange-yellow rays and a prominent purplish black cone. Not usually browsed by deer. 'Indian Summer' produces 6- to 9-in., single to semidouble flowers in golden yellow. 'Irish Eyes' ('Green Eyes') has 2- to 3-in., golden yellow flowers with a light green central cone that ages to brown. 'Prairie Sun' has golden petals with light yellow tips surrounding a pale green cone. 'Denver Daisy' bears large (6–8 in.) yellow flowers with a dark cone and a large burgundy eye. It is a heavy bloomer that reaches 22–26 in. tall. 'Cherokee Sunset' has semidouble to double flowers (3–4½ in.) in a range of yellow, orange, red, bronze, and mahogany. It grows 2–3 ft. tall.

For front of border, try lower-growing selections 'Goldilocks' (double flowers) and 'Toto', both 8–10 in. high; Becky Mix (12–15 in.); 'Sonora' (15 in.); 'Tiger Eye' (16–24 in. high and wide, with unusually profuse bloom), and 'Marmalade' (2 ft.).

R. laciniata. CUTLEAF CONEFLOWER. Perennial. The species grows 10 ft. tall, 4 ft. wide; it has light green, deeply lobed leaves to 4 in. long and blooms from summer to fall, bearing 2- to 3½-in.-wide flowers with drooping yellow rays and a green cone. Very heat tolerant. More widely grown in gardens are the following three selections. 'Golden Glow' ('Hortensia'), to 6–7 ft. tall, is an old favorite that bears bright yellow double flowers 2–3½ in. wide. Good summer screen or tall plant for back of borders. Does not seed, but spreads rapidly (sometimes aggressively) by underground stems. 'Goldquelle', with double blooms in lemon-yellow, is a less aggressive form growing 3 ft. tall, 1½ ft. wide. 'Autumn Sun' ('Herbstonne', often listed as the similar native *R. nitida*) grows to 6 ft. tall, 2 ft. wide; bears single, 4- to 5-in.-wide flowers with yellow rays and a bright green cone that ages to yellow.

R. maxima. GREAT CONEFLOWER. Perennial. Large (to 5-in.) bluish gray leaves form a mound to 2–3 ft. tall and wide. In midsummer, 5- to 6-ft. stems bear flowers to 3 in. across, with a prominent brown central cone and drooping yellow rays. 'Golda Emanis' combines golden foliage that fades to chartreuse as it blooms, producing golden, daisy-like blooms on 7 ft. tall stalks.

R. triloba. BROWN-EYED SUSAN. Biennial or perennial. To about 4 ft. tall and as wide, with stiff, much-branched stems and 5-in.-long leaves, some deeply lobed. Blossoms to 3 in. wide, with yellow-orange rays and dark brown-purple centers. Can be weedy looking. 'Prairie Glow' has large, bicolored, yellow and orange-red blooms that make great cut flowers.

ABOVE: Rudbeckie hirta 'Denver Daisy'

RUELLIA

Acanthaceae
Evergreen shrubs and shrubby perennials

US, MS, LS, CS, TS; USDA 6-11, EXCEPT AS NOTED

FULL SUN OR LIGHT SHADE

MODERATE TO REGULAR WATER

Ruellia tweediana

Thanks to their pretty blooms and easy culture, ruellias have come into their own in recent years. Though most common in Texas, they're quickly making inroads into the rest of the South, especially among gardeners who want lots of bloom with little fuss. The flowers resemble small, thin-textured petunias. These plants resist damage by browsing deer.

R. elegans 'Ragin' Cajun'. Perennial. LS, CS, TS; USDA 8-11. The species is native from Brazil to Chile. Grows to 4 ft. tall and 8 ft. wide and is covered with scarlet flowers from late spring through frost. Needs little to moderate water after it's established. Grow as annual in Upper and Middle South (USDA 6-7).

R. humilis. WILD PETUNIA. Shrubby perennial. Native to central U.S. Grows 1–2 ft. tall and wide, with oval to lance-shaped leaves 1½–4 in. long. Bears 2-in.-long bluish flowers from early summer into fall. 'Blue Shade' is a low-growing (6- to 10-in.), wide-spreading form with lavender-blue flowers; roots by creeping stems. Selection is popular in Central Texas as a ground cover for light shade.

R. macrantha. PINK WILD PETUNIA. Shrub. Zones CS, TS; USDA 9-11. Native to Brazil. To 3 ft. high and wide, with oval, dark green leaves to 6 in. long. Clusters of rose-pink, 3- to 4-in. flowers with deeper pink veining. Blooms in late fall in most areas, through winter in the Tropical South. Best grown as a container plant and given shelter during frosty weather.

R. malacosperma. MEXICAN PETUNIA. Shrubby perennial native to Mexico. Often confused with *R. tweediana*, but its leaves are a bit shorter and wider. Tough plant that takes dry or wet soil. Grows 3 ft. tall, 1 ft. wide, with lavender flowers in summer. 'Alba' (sometimes sold as White Flower Form) produces hundreds of pure white blooms from June through September.

R. tweediana (*R. brittoniana*). WILLOWLEAF MEXICAN PETUNIA. Zones LS, CS, TS; USDA 8-11. Shrubby perennial. Mexican native naturalized in many areas of the southern and southwestern U.S. To 3 ft. high; initially 1–1½ ft. wide, but can be invasive and should be contained (by an edging, for example). Narrow, dark green leaves to 3 in. long, ¾ in. wide; 2-in.-long, lavender-blue flowers throughout warm times of year. 'Chi-Chi' bears soft pink blossoms. 'Katie' is a non-invasive dwarf (10- to 12-in.-tall) selection. Other dwarfs include 'Colobe Pink', pink flowers; 'Strawberries and Cream', lavender blossoms and white-speckled leaves; and 'White Katie', similar to 'Katie' but with white blooms. 'Purple Showers' is sterile and produces no seed but spreads aggressively by roots. Large, deep purple flowers form on 2- to 3-ft.-tall plants.

RUMOHRA ADIANTIFORMIS

LEATHERLEAF FERN
Polypodiaceae
Fern

CS, TS; USDA 9-11

FULL SUN OR PARTIAL SHADE

MODERATE TO REGULAR WATER

Rumohra adiantiformis

From many tropical and subtropical areas of the Southern Hemisphere. To 3 ft. high and wide, spreading wider by rhizomes. Deep glossy green, triangular, finely cut fronds are firm textured, last well in arrangements. Easy to grow in rich, well-drained soil. Hardy to 24°F. Often sold as *Aspidium capense*.

GROW LEATHER-LEAF FERN IN A CUTTING GARDEN AS A HANDY FILLER FOR BOUQUETS.

RUSCUS

BUTCHER'S BROOM
Asparagaceae
Evergreen shrubs

MS, LS, CS; USDA 7-9

BEST IN SHADE, TOLERATE SOME SUN

LITTLE TO REGULAR WATER

Ruscus aculeatus

Native to Mediterranean region. Unusual leafless plants with some value as small-scale ground cover, curiosity, or source of material for dried arrangements. These old favorites are usually not sold by garden centers, but rather passed around by gardeners. Flattened, leaflike branches do the work of leaves and bear tiny greenish white flowers in centers of upper surfaces. If male and female plants are present, or if you have a plant with male and female flowers, bright red (sometimes yellow) fruit follows the flowers. Plants spread widely by rhizomes. Tolerate competition from tree roots. Subject to chlorosis (yellow leaves with green veins) in alkaline soil.

R. aculeatus. To 1–4 ft. tall, with branched stems. Spine-tipped "leaves" are 1–3 in. long, one-third as wide, leathery dull dark green. Fruit is ½ in. across. 'Wheeler's Variety' is a self-fruiting form.

R. hypoglossum. To 1½ ft., with unbranched stems. "Leaves" to 4 in. long, 1½ in. wide, glossy green, not spine tipped. Fruit is ¼–½ in. across. Spreads faster than *R. aculeatus*. Superior as small-scale ground cover.

RUSSELIA
Plantaginaceae
Shrubby perennials

🗡 **CS, TS; USDA 9-11, OR HOUSE-PLANTS**

☀ ◑ **FULL SUN OR PART SHADE; BRIGHT LIGHT**

🌢 🌢 **MODERATE TO REGULAR WATER**

Russelia equisetiformis

Group of about 50 plants native to Cuba, Mexico, and Central America. Prized for colorful flowers produced nearly continuously in warm weather. The two species listed below are the most common; both look great billowing over the top of a retaining wall, massed on a slope, or used in raised planters and hanging baskets. Provide well-drained soil. Propagate by taking cuttings, layering branches that touch the ground, or dividing. Can be grown indoors in a sunny window. During active growth, water moderately and feed monthly with a general-purpose liquid houseplant fertilizer; then reduce water and fertilizer in winter.

R. equisetiformis. FIRE-CRACKER PLANT. Suckering shrub to 3–4 ft. tall and wide, with cascading, wiry, nearly leafless bright green stems. Blooms all summer, with side branches bearing a profusion of tubular bright red flowers resembling 1¼-in.-long firecrackers. Hardy to about 24°F; comes back quickly if cut down by mild frost. A yellow-flowered form is available.

R. sarmentosa. CORAL PLANT. Often confused with *R. equisetiformis*, but stems are leafy and floral display is even showier. Grows about 4 ft. tall and 6 ft. wide. Abundant clusters of small bright red flowers nearly hide the oval, 3-in.-long leaves. Not as hardy as *R. equisetiformis*.

RUTA GRAVEOLENS
RUE, HERB-OF-GRACE
Rutaceae
Perennial

🗡 **US, MS, LS, CS; USDA 6-9**

☀ **FULL SUN**

🌢 🌢 **MODERATE TO REGULAR WATER**

Ruta graveolens

To 2–3 ft. high and wide, with aromatic, fernlike, blue-green leaves. Small, greenish yellow flowers are followed by decorative brown seed capsules. Sow seeds in flats; transplant to 1 ft. apart. Needs good garden soil; add lime to strongly acid soil. Cut back in early spring to encourage bushiness. Seed clusters can be dried for use in wreaths or swags. 'Blue Beauty' and 'Jackman's Blue' are dense, compact selections with fine blue-gray color; 'Blue Mound' and 'Curly Girl' are even more compact.

Rue owes its status as an herb to history and legend rather than to any medicinal or culinary use. It was once thought to ward off disease, guard against poisons, and aid eyesight. It was also used to make brushes for sprinkling holy water. The sap causes dermatitis in some people.

SABAL
PALMETTO
Arecaceae
Palms

🗡 **ZONES VARY BY SPECIES**

☀ ◑ **FULL SUN OR PARTIAL SHADE**

🌢 **MODERATE WATER**

Sabal palmetto

Sterling group of cold-hardy fan palms, unsurpassed for their versatility, adaptability, and ease of culture. They tolerate almost any soil and thrive in sun or light shade; they'll even take salt spray. Some have trunks, while others do not; all grow rather slowly. Tree types make excellent street, lawn, and shade trees; shrubby sorts are useful in understory plantings and naturalized areas. Mature plants bear large clusters of tiny flowers among the leaves, typically in summer.

S. causiarum. PUERTO RICAN HAT PALM. Zones CS, TS; USDA 9-11. Native to Puerto Rico. Young leaves are collected and woven into hats, hence the plant's common name. This is a stout, columnar tree that grows to 60 ft. tall and about 12 ft. wide. Distinguished from other species by its smooth, massive gray trunk, which can reach 4 ft. in diameter. Leaves to 6 ft. long, divided into 50 to 60 segments. Unlike other palmettos, this one drops its dead leaves quickly, and the bases of old leaves shed from the trunk. Hardy to 16°F.

S. domingensis. HISPANIOLAN PALMETTO. Zones LS, CS, TS; USDA 8-11. From the Caribbean. Ultimately reaches 80 ft. or taller, 20 ft. wide, with immense green fans 9 ft. across. Hardy to 10°F.

S. etonia. SCRUB PALM. Zones MS, LS, CS, TS; USDA 7-11. Shrubby palm native to the dry, sandy Florida scrub. Usually trunkless; grows to 6 ft. tall, 8 ft. wide. Resembles *S. minor*, but leaves are smaller, with more and thinner segments. Hardy to 0°F.

S. louisiana (*S.* 'Louisiana'). Zones MS, LS, CS, TS; USDA 7-11. Form resembles that of *S. palmetto*, but plants grow slowly to only 12 ft. tall. Blooms in late spring and early summer. It produces fragrant flowers. Sometimes offered as *S. minor* 'Louisiana'.

S. mexicana (*S. texana*). TEXAS PALMETTO, OAXACA PALMETTO. Zones CS, TS; USDA 9-11. Native from Texas to Guatemala. Leaf stems hang on trunk in early life, then drop to show attractive, slender trunk. Grows 30–50 ft. high, 12 ft. wide. Established trees are hard to transplant. Hardy to 18°F.

S. minor. DWARF PALMETTO. Zones MS, LS, CS, TS; USDA 7-11. Shrubby palm native to the forest understory, scrublands, and alluvial floodplains of the Southeast. Slow growing to 6 ft. tall, 10 ft. wide. Usually trunkless; older specimens have a short, thick trunk. Blue-green, fan-shaped leaves to 3 ft. long; old leaves fold at base, hang down like closed umbrellas. Tolerates wet or dry soils and salt spray. One of the hardiest palms. Seedlings collected in McCurtain County, Oklahoma, have survived temperatures of –24°F.

S. palmetto. CABBAGE PALMETTO. Zones LS, CS, TS; USDA 8-11. Native to the hammocks, marshes, and Coastal Plains of the Southeast, from North Carolina to Florida. Grows slowly to 90 ft., with a dense, globular, 12- to 18-ft.-wide head formed by leaves 5–8 ft. across. Together with live oak (*Quercus virginiana*), cabbage palm helps define the urban character of Charleston, Savannah, and other coastal cities of the Old South. Excellent street or lawn tree; best tree for the beach. Tolerates wind, salt spray, and sand; can be planted right on dunes. Very easy to transplant. Huge, dormant specimens are often stacked up like cordwood, then trucked to new locations and plopped like telephone poles into deep, narrow holes. Hardy to 10°F.

S. uresana. SONORAN PALMETTO. Zones LS, CS, TS; USDA 8-11. Highly ornamental, surprisingly hardy Mexican species, deserving of a spot in more gardens. Straight-trunked tree grows to about 40 ft. tall and reaches 10 ft. across. Impressive leaves to 6 ft. long, in a striking silvery blue. Hardy to 10°F.

SACCHARUM

PLUME GRASS, SUGAR CANE
Poaceae
Perennial grasses

✎ ZONES VARY BY SPECIES

☼ FULL SUN, EXCEPT AS NOTED

💧 REGULAR WATER, EXCEPT AS NOTED

Saccharum officinarum

These very large grasses include the species known as sugar cane. They are spectacular in the garden—but be sure to give them plenty of room. Use in masses, group as tall screens, or plant as specimens and accents where you want a dramatic vertical element in the garden. Easy to grow in moist, well-drained, fertile soil. No serious pests.

S. arundinaceum. HARDY SUGAR CANE. Zones US, MS, LS, CS, TS; USDA 6-11. Native to China, India, and Southeast Asia. Its pulp has been used in the making of paper. The grass forms a huge clump—up to 10 ft. tall (in bloom) and quite nearly as wide. Long, narrow, gray-green leaves have

white midribs. Blooms in early autumn, holding its upright flower plumes well above the foliage; plumes emerge purplish pink, then fade to silver by late fall. 'Purple People Greeter' has leaves edged in amber-purple.

S. brevibarbe contortum (*S. contortum*). BENT-AWN PLUME GRASS. Zones US, MS, LS, CS; USDA 6-9. Native to the eastern U.S., from Delaware south to Florida and Texas. Forms a 3- to 4-ft.-tall, narrowly upright clump of slender, bluish green leaves that turn purple, bronze, and red in fall and hold their color in winter. Erect, reddish to purple-brown plumes rise 2–4 ft. above the foliage in late summer and fall. Self-sows. Full sun or light shade. Formerly listed as *Erianthus contortus*.

S. officinarum. SUGAR CANE. Zones CS, TS; USDA 9-11. Probably native to India and Southeast Asia. This giant grass has been grown for centuries—the sweet juice contained in its thick canes is the commercial source of sugar. Only recently, however, has it been more broadly appreciated for its ornamental potential. Forms an imposing clump (eventually expands to 6–8 ft. wide) of upright, long, slender, green to bluish green leaves; clump can reach 15 ft. tall, growing 8–10 ft. in just one year. Fluffy, whitish, nodding flower plumes are slender and arching, appear in early fall (though they are rarely seen in nontropical areas). Hardy to 20°F. Tolerates wet soils. In most gardens, it's treated as an annual and used as a vertical accent; sometimes grown as an edible novelty or a substitute for bamboo. Selections with colored canes and leaves are becoming available and popular; one of these is 'Pele's Smoke', featuring showy, bronze-purple leaves with pink midribs growing from dusky purple canes.

S. ravennae. RAVENNA GRASS. Zones US, MS, LS, CS, TS; USDA 6-11. Native to southern Europe. The slender, gray-green leaves form a dense, 4- to 6-ft.-wide and 6-ft.-tall fountain that bears giant plumes of silvery gray flowers in late summer. Mature plants may produce 40 plumes—each 15 ft. high—that cast a spectacular silhouette when backlit by the sun. Similar to pampas grass (*Cortaderia*) but less sym-

metrical and much hardier; good substitute for pampas grass in the Upper South (USDA 6). Vigorous grower. Does well in average to poor soils but must have good drainage. Little to moderate water once established. Formerly listed as *Erianthus ravennae*.

SAGINA SUBULATA

IRISH MOSS, SCOTCH MOSS
Caryophyllaceae
Perennial

✎ US, MS, LS; USDA 6-8

☼ ◑ FULL SUN OR PARTIAL SHADE

💧 REGULAR WATER

Sagina subulata

Of two different prostrate plants of similar appearance, *Sagina subulata* is the more common. The other is *Arenaria verna*, usually called *A. v. caespitosa*. Both of these European natives make dense, compact, mosslike masses of slender leaves on slender stems. But *A. verna* has tiny white flowers in few-flowered clusters, while *S. subulata* bears flowers singly and differs in other details. In common usage, however, green forms of the two plants are called Irish moss, and golden green forms (*A. v.* 'Aurea' and *S. s.* 'Aurea') are called Scotch moss.

Both *Sagina* and *Arenaria* are grown primarily as ground covers for limited areas; they're also useful for filling gaps between paving blocks. They won't grow well under conditions that suit true mosses. They need good soil, good drainage, and occasional feeding with controlled-release fertilizer. They take some foot

traffic and tend to hump up over time; control this by occasionally cutting out narrow strips, then pressing or rolling lightly. Set out plants 6 in. apart for fast cover. Control snails, slugs, and cutworms. Can tend to 'melt away' during long stretches of hot, humid weather.

SAINTPAULIA

AFRICAN VIOLET
Gesneriaceae
Perennials grown as houseplants

◑ FILTERED MORNING SUN; BRIGHT INDIRECT LIGHT

💧 WATERING IS AN ART; SEE BELOW

Saintpaulia

If you would dismiss African violets as "grandma plants," you might want to consider whether your grandma ever flew in space. African violets have. Among the most popular of flowering houseplants, they bloom nearly continuously if given proper care. Most are hybrids derived from several species native to east Africa. They form clumps of velvety green leaves that may be roundish or pointed. Some grow big enough to command a 6-inch pot. Dwarf kinds can fit in a teacup.

The variation in flower shape, size, and color is amazing. Flowers may be single, semidouble, or double; some have fringed or ruffled petals. Colors include blue, purple, lavender, red, pink, magenta, burgundy, crimson, white, bicolors, and even green. Recommended series include Artist's Palette, Island, myViolet, Rhapsodie, US State, and Victorian Charm. The EverFloris series resulted from seeds that spent six years in space, courtesy of the space shuttle. When the seeds returned and were planted, several exciting mutations became apparent. Plants grow 50 percent bigger than normal. More important, they display clusters of 20 blooms rather than the usual 5–7, and blooming is continuous.

CARE

To bloom well, African violets need 16 hours of bright, filtered light (no direct sun except in winter) and 8 hours of complete darkness. A plant that is leggy, stretches, and never blooms isn't getting enough light. Light can be natural or provided by grow lights. The soil should be moist and well drained. Using a potting soil formulated for African violets is your best bet.

Watering from the bottom is better than watering from the top. To do this, set the pot in a saucer filled with water as long as it takes the soil to become fully moist, and then dump the remaining water from the saucer. Or use a self-watering African violet pot that essentially does the job for you. Don't use soft, filtered water. Let tap water stand overnight before using it to let the chlorine evaporate and the water assume room temperature.

Mix in a bloom-booster fertilizer formulated for African violets, such as 14-12-14, each time you water. These plants like high humidity; provide this by setting the pot atop a pebble-lined saucer filled with water. Keep air temperatures around 70°F. Pick off spent flowers and old leaves.

SALIX
WILLOW
Salicaceae
Deciduous trees and shrubs

🗡 **US, MS, LS; USDA 6-8, EXCEPT AS NOTED**

☼ **FULL SUN, EXCEPT AS NOTED**

💧 **REGULAR TO AMPLE WATER**

Salix alba

It's easy to see what people like about willows. They're fast growing and tolerate just about any type of soil. They're also the easiest of trees and shrubs to propagate: Just take cuttings at any time of year and stick them into moist soil. On the other hand, they are weak-wooded, short-lived trees, and their shallow, greedy roots make them hard to garden under and can invade water lines. Most are attacked by a host of pests (tent caterpillars, aphids, borers, spider mites) and diseases. Weeping willows do best near lakes and streams, although they can, with training, make satisfactory shade trees. Shrubby willows are grown chiefly for their showy catkins (this group is known as "pussy willows") or colorful twigs, or to control erosion on riverbanks. Branches of pussy willows can be cut in bud in late winter and brought indoors to bloom. Willow species hybridize freely, resulting in much confusion of names in the nursery trade.

S. alba. WHITE WILLOW. Tree. Native to Europe, North Africa. Upright to 75–100 ft. tall, 50–100 ft. wide. Yellowish brown bark. Narrow, 1½- to 4-in., bright green leaves are silvery beneath, may turn golden in fall. The following forms are valued for colorful twigs.

TOP: *Salix babylonica*; BOTTOM: *S. discolor*; *S. matsudana* 'Tortuosa'

S. a. 'Tristis'. GOLDEN WEEPING WILLOW. Pendulous form, to 50–70 ft. tall and wide (or wider). Young stems are bright yellow. Among the most attractive of weeping willows; may be sold as *S. alba* 'Niobe', *S. babylonica* 'Aurea', or *S. vitellina* 'Pendula'.

S. a. vitellina. Upright, with brilliant yellow twigs in winter. Can grow to tree size, but cutting back gives best color display: Lop to 1 ft. high yearly, just before spring growth begins. Stems may grow 8 ft. in a season. 'Britzensis' and 'Yelverton' have red or orange-red winter stems.

S. babylonica. WEEPING WILLOW. Tree. From China. To 30–50 ft. tall and wide (or wider). Longer (3- to 6-in.) leaves, more pronounced weeping habit than *S. a.* 'Tristis'. Greenish or brown branchlets. This is a popular lawn tree, but keep its size in mind; planting anywhere near

the house or a driveway, walk, or patio is usually a mistake. Be sure to give it moist soil, as it quickly becomes disconsolate and ratty looking in dry soil. 'Crispa' ('Annularis'), ringleaf or cork-screw willow, has leaves curled into rings or circles; it is somewhat narrower than the species.

S. caprea. GOAT WILLOW, FLORIST WILLOW. Shrub or tree. Native from Europe to northeastern Asia. Grows to 15–25 ft. tall, 12–15 ft. wide. Broad, 3- to 6-in.-long leaves are dark green above, gray and hairy beneath. Before leaf-out, male plants produce fat, woolly, pinkish gray catkins about 1 in. long. Can be kept to shrub size by cutting to ground every few years. 'Kilmarnock' (a male plant) and 'Weeping Sally' (its female counterpart) are two selections that will naturally sprawl on the ground; they are more effective grafted or staked to form small weeping trees 6–8 ft. tall, 6 ft. wide.

S. discolor. PUSSY WILLOW. Shrub or tree. Native to eastern U.S.; an old favorite in the South. To 15–25 ft. tall, 12–15 ft. wide. Slender, red-brown stems; bright green, 2- to 4-in. leaves with bluish undersides. Catkins of male plants are main draw—soft, silky, pearl gray, to 1½ in. long.

S. gracilistyla. ROSE-GOLD PUSSY WILLOW. Shrub. Zones US, MS; USDA 6-7. To 6–10 ft. tall, 12 ft. wide. Narrowly oval, 2- to 4-in.-long leaves are gray-green above, bluish green beneath. Male plants produce plump, gray, furry, 1½-in.-long catkins with numerous stamens sporting rose-and-gold anthers. Cut branches for arrangements to curb plant's size. Every three or four years, cut plant back to short stubs; you'll get very vigorous shoots with large catkins. 'Melanostachys' has black catkins with red anthers.

S. matsudana (S. babylonica pekinensis). HANKOW WILLOW. Tree. Upright, pyramidal growth to 40–50 ft. tall, 30–40 ft. wide. Bright green, narrow, 2- to 4-in.-long leaves. Can thrive on less water than most willows.

'Navajo'. GLOBE NAVAJO WILLOW. Large, spreading, round-topped tree to 70 ft. tall and wide.

'Tortuosa'. CORKSCREW WILLOW. To 30 ft. tall, 20 ft. wide; branches fantastically twisted into upright, spiraling patterns. Valued for winter silhouette and cut branches for arrangements.

'Umbraculifera'. GLOBE WILLOW. To 35 ft. high and wide. Umbrella-shaped crown with upright branches, drooping branchlets.

S.nigra. BLACK WILLOW. Tree. Zones US, MS, LS, CS; USDA 6-9. Native to central and eastern North America, where it is common along streamsides and riverbanks. To 30–60 ft. tall, 30 ft. wide. Narrow, finely toothed leaves to 7 in. long are shiny dark green above, light green beneath. Tree bark is scaly, furrowed, and dark brown to black. The soft wood is used for making baskets and wicker furniture. Tolerates flooding; often used for wetland reclamation. Will take full sun but does best in partial shade.

SALPIGLOSSIS SINUATA
PAINTED TONGUE
Solanaceae
Cool-season annual

🌿 **US, MS, LS, CS, TS; USDA 6-11**
☀️ **FULL SUN**
💧 **REGULAR WATER**

Salpiglossis sinuata

Native to South America. Upright, open habit to 2–3 ft. tall, 1 ft. wide. Stems and narrow, 4-in.-long leaves are sticky. Flowers are 2–2½ in. wide; resemble petunias in shape but offer more unusual colors—mahogany-red, reddish orange, yellow, purple, deep blue, and pink shades, marbled and penciled with contrasting colors. Plants bloom most heavily in late spring and early summer. Good background plant for border; handsome cut flower. 'Kew Blue' is an excellent blue with a deep purple throat. Bolero (to 2 ft. tall), Stained Glass (18 in.), and Royale (12–16 in.) are compact strains.

CARE

Seeds are rather difficult to start, especially when sown directly in garden. A better way to start them is to plant in potting mix in peat pots, several seeds to a pot. Keep pots in a warm, protected location; thin seedlings to one per pot. In most areas, plant seeds in late winter, then set out young plants once they're well established and all danger of frost is past. In Florida and South Texas, sow seeds in early fall and grow plants for winter and spring bloom. Performs best in rich soil. Stake tall types. Tip-pinch growing plants to induce branching.

SALVIA
SAGE
Lamiaceae
Evergreen and deciduous shrubs, perennials, and biennials (some grown as annuals)

🌿 **ZONES VARY BY SPECIES**
☀️ **FULL SUN, EXCEPT AS NOTED**
💧 **REGULAR WATER, EXCEPT AS NOTED**

Salvia farinacea 'Evolution'

Planting sages proves a wise move for many a Southern gardener. *Salvia* is the largest genus of the mint family, including as many as 900 species from around the world. Some serve as annual bedding plants, others are border perennials, and still others are shrubs, culinary herbs, or ground covers. Where winters are cold, tender perennials and shrubs are grown as annuals. Where plants are marginally hardy, well-drained soil can be key to their winter survival.

All sages have square stems and whorls of two-lipped flowers, either neatly spaced along the flower stalks or so tightly crowded that they look like one dense spike; some species have branched inflorescences. Flower colors range from white and yellow through salmon and pink to scarlet, red, lavender, blue, and darkest purple. A few sages have fragrant blossoms; many have aromatic foliage. They attract hummingbirds, bees, and butterflies.

S. 'Amistad'. Perennial. Zones LS, CS, TS; USDA 8-11. Possible hybrid between *S. guaranitica* and a species from Mexico. Bushy grower to 3–5 ft. high and wide, with bright green, slightly puckered leaves. Begins blooming when young, producing lots of

upright stems set with large, rich purple flowers held in very dark—almost black—calyxes. Cut back hard in spring to maintain shape.

S. 'Anthony Parker'. Evergreen shrub. Zones LS, CS, TS; USDA 8-11. Hybrid between *S. leucantha* and *S. elegans*. To 5 ft. high and wide. Leaves are similar to those of *S. elegans*. Wands of blossoms appear at stem ends throughout the year where winters are mild; in colder climates, they come from spring to frost. The flowers are like those of *S. leucantha*, but the color is an intense dark violet-blue.

S. argentea. SILVER SAGE. Biennial or short-lived perennial. Zones US, MS, LS; USDA 6-8. From southern Europe, northwestern Africa. Soft, scallop-edged, silky-haired, gray-green leaves grow 6–10 in. long, form a low foliage rosette to 2 ft. wide. In summer, many-branched, 3- to 4-ft. flowering stems bear 1¼-in.-long, hooded white flowers (sometimes tinged pink or yellow) with silvery calyxes. Cut to ground when flowers fade. Handsome focal point for front of border. Protect from slugs, snails.

S. azurea grandiflora (S. pitcheri). PRAIRIE SAGE, PITCHER SAGE. Shrubby perennial. Zones US, MS, LS, CS; USDA 6-9. Native from Colorado and Texas east to Michigan and Georgia. Slender, vertical, usually unbranched stems to 5 ft. form a 2- to 3-ft.-wide clump. Plant is lax; needs support. Smooth or hairy, medium green to deep green, narrow leaves to 4 in. long. Pure azure-blue flowers with white-blotched lower lip on spikes to 1 ft. long; blooms summer to frost. Tolerates heat and humidity.

S. blepharophylla. EYELASH SAGE. Shrubby perennial. Zones MS, LS, CS, TS; USDA 7-11. From northeastern Mexico. To 1½–2 ft. tall, spreading indefinitely by creeping rhizomes. Thin, hairy, purplish stems; oval, glossy, dark green leaves to 1½ in. long, edged with fine hairs resembling eyelashes. Blooms nearly all year in mild-winter climates, from spring to frost elsewhere; inch-long scarlet flowers are carried on stems that lengthen to about 1 ft. as season goes on. If confined, makes a good ground cover in partial shade. 'Diablo' is more upright, and its vivid red flowers have two upright anthers

S

that could be said to look like horns. 'Painted Lady' grows 1 ft. high and 4 ft. wide, bearing vivid red flowers that sport a velvety hood; it remains evergreen where temperatures stay above 20°F.

S. chamaedryoides. GERMANDER SAGE. Perennial. Zones MS, LS, CS, TS; USDA 8-11. From eastern Mexico. Rounded plant to 1–2 ft. tall, spreading to 2–3 ft. or more by underground runners. Silvery, ¾-in.-long leaves; brilliant true blue, 1-in. flowers on stems to 8 in. long. Heaviest bloom comes in late spring and fall, with intermittent flowering during rest of growing season. Deadhead to encourage rebloom. Elegant front-of-border plant. Drought tolerant but blooms longer and better with more water.

S. coccinea. TEXAS SAGE. Perennial in Zones CS, TS; USDA 9-11; annual anywhere. From Mexico. Bushy, upright grower to 2–3 ft. tall, 2½ ft. wide. Dark green, hairy, oval to heart-shaped leaves to 2½ in. long. In summer, slender stems to 1 ft. long carry many ¾- to 1-in. flowers with broad lower lip. Colors range from bright red through orange-red to pink and white, including many bicolors. Widely used as bedding plant, border filler. Stems are brittle; shelter from wind. Deadhead to encourage rebloom.

If plant lives over, cut back to 4–6 in. when new spring growth begins, then fertilize. By end of second season, plant will be woody and in decline. Reseeds copiously. Good seed-grown selections include salmon-pink 'Brenthurst' ('Lady in Pink'); 'Coral Nymph', near white with coral lip; and white 'Snow Nymph' ('White Nymph'). 'Lady in Red', with scarlet blooms, is a compact plant (to about 16 in.), excellent in the foreground of a colorful border. 'Summer Jewel Pink' (soft pink) and 'Summer Jewel Red' (scarlet) are compact, uniform growers to 20 in. tall; early and long bloom season and good resistance to heat, drought, and wind.

S. 'Costa Rica Blue' (S. guaranitica 'Costa Rica Blue'). Evergreen shrub. Zones LS, CS, TS; USDA 8-11. Possible hybrid between S. guaranitica and S. mexicana. Grows 6–7 ft. tall and wide; can be kept lower by cutting back to 1 ft. in early spring. Broadly oval to heart-shaped,

hairy, shiny bright green leaves to 5 in. long. Brilliant true blue, 1- to 1½-in. flowers on 1- to 1½-ft. stems. Blooms from the end of summer until frost (through spring in mildest climates). Needs support, shelter from wind and cold. 'Omaha Gold' is a sport with leaves irregularly edged in yellowish green.

S. darcyi. DARCY SAGE. Perennial. Zones US, MS, LS, CS, TS; USDA 6-11. From northeastern Mexico. Upright growth to 3–4 ft. tall; spreads by rhizomes to 3–7 ft. wide. Softly hairy, triangular, light green leaves are sticky and have a pleasant, fruity aroma. Widely spaced whorls of 1½-in. coral-red blossoms on unbranched stems from early summer to late fall. Stems are 6–12 in. high, sometimes as high as 2 ft. They are brittle; shelter from wind. Protect from slugs and snails. Dies back to the ground in winter. Tolerates partial shade.

S. elegans. PINEAPPLE SAGE. Perennial. Zones LS, CS, TS; USDA 8-11. Native to southern Mexico, Guatemala. In the wild, this species is variable in habit, bloom time, and leaf fragrance. The most commonly grown form, 'Scarlet Pineapple', grows upright to 3–4 ft. high and wide, with branching, brittle stems; in part shade, growth is lush and needs support. Densely hairy, bright green leaves to 4 in. long, broadly oval with pointed tip. Foliage has fragrance of ripe pineapple; use it in cool drinks, fruit salads. Slender, 1½-in., bright red flowers in loose clusters of 8 to 12 are carried on 6- to 8-in. stems. In mild-winter areas, blooms from late fall through spring; elsewhere, flowers come from late summer into fall.

'Sonoran Red' is more compact than the species (to 2 ft. tall and wide) and hardier to cold. 'Golden Delicious' grows just 1–2 ft. high, with bright yellow foliage that makes for an eye-catching contrast with the fire-engine red flowers; long bloom period. 'Honey Melon' grows about 2 ft. high and spreads rapidly to form a dense ground cover; it has small, rounded leaves that smell something like ripe honeydew melon; blooms from early summer through fall if faded flowers are sheared off. 'Golden Delicious' has bright yellow leaves and red flowers.

TOP: Salvia splendens; BOTTOM: S. madrensis

S. farinacea. MEALYCUP SAGE. Zones LS, CS, TS; USDA 8-11. Grown as an annual where it is not winter hardy. Native to southern New Mexico, Texas, Mexico. Upright growth to 3–4 ft. tall, half as wide. Narrowly lance-shaped leaves to 3 in. long are smooth above, woolly white below. Tall, densely packed spikes of ¾- to 1-in. flowers on stems 6–12 in. long, late spring to frost. Blossom color varies from deep violet-blue to white; cuplike calyxes are covered with white hairs that often have a blue or violet tinge.

Many strains and selections are sold for bedding and container use; typically have heavier bloom, better branching, more compact than species. 'Augusta Duelberg' grows into a mound 3 ft. high and wide, with a profusion of pure white blooms; 'Henry Duelberg' is similar, but with blue flowers. Cathedral series grows 12–18 in. tall, with heavy production of flowers in purple, lavender, deep blue, sky-blue, and white. 'Evolution', 20 in. high and 14 in. wide, has 9-in. lilac flower spikes. 'Rhea', 14–16 in. high and 12 in. wide, has deep blue flowers, bluish calyxes; starts blooming earlier in spring. 'Saga Blue' grows just 10 in. high and wide, with blue flowers. Sallyfun series, to 30 in. high, blooms heavily; available in shades of blue through white. 'Strata', to 12–18 in. high and wide, has blue flowers and large, woolly, silvery white calyxes. 'Texas Violet', 3–4 ft. high and about half as wide, has deep violet-blue flowers on white calyxes. 'Victoria', with upright growth to 18–20 in. high, has violet-blue flowers and calyxes; 'Victoria White' is a white form.

S. greggii. AUTUMN SAGE. Evergreen or deciduous shrub. Zones MS, LS, CS, TS; USDA 7-11. Native to southwestern Texas, north-central Mexico. Rounded plant, branching from base; typically grows 1–4 ft. high and wide. Slender, hairy stems are closely set with glossy green, ¾- to 1¼-in.-long leaves that vary in shape from rounded to linear. Blooms throughout summer and fall, bearing ¼- to 1-in. flowers on 3- to 6-in. stems, in colors ranging from deep purplish red through true red to various rose and pink shades to white. To keep plants tidy and free blooming, prune and remove dead flower

stems frequently. Before new spring growth begins, shorten and shape plants, removing dead wood. Good low hedge. Replace plants every 4 or 5 years, when they become woody and unproductive. Drought tolerant but does best with moderate water. Grows best in the Southwest. Give full sun for best flower production.

A few of the best selections are 'Icing Sugar', a compact grower with lavender-pink flowers; 'Lipstick', with rosy pink, white-throated flowers over a long period; 'Pink Preference', with deep reddish pink flowers; and 'Teresa', with soft pink flowers whose lower lip is white with pink stripes. Sally G. series plants are dense and bushy, with large flowers in bright pink, fuchsia, magenta, red, or white. Selections sold as S. greggii with flowers in shades of orange, orange-red, or yellow actually belong with S. x jamensis.

S. guaranitica (S. ambigens). ANISE-SCENTED SAGE. Shrubby perennial. Zones MS, LS, CS, TS; USDA 7-11. From South America. Upright, branching plant to 4–5 ft. high and nearly as wide. Spreads by short underground runners; roots form tubers resembling small sausages. Narrowly heart-shaped, sparsely hairy, mint-green leaves to 5 in. long. Blooms from early summer to frost. Most common form bears 2-in., cobalt-blue blossoms, carried several to each foot-long stem; calyxes are bright green, turning purplish on sunny side. Needs support. Gets woody by season's end—but that wood dies during winter and must be cut back to ground. Elegant container plant. Can be demolished by Mexican giant whitefly. Tolerates partial shade, especially in hottest climates. 'Argentine Skies' has light blue flowers. 'Black and Blue' produces deep blue blossoms with dark purplish blue calyxes. 'Van Remsen' can reach 7 ft. tall, with cobalt-blue flowers.

S. 'Indigo Spires'. Shrubby perennial. Zones LS, CS, TS; USDA 8-11. Anywhere as annual. Can build up to a sprawling 6–7 ft. by 10 ft. but is easily kept to 3–4 ft. high, 2–3 ft. wide with support and selective pruning. Soft, silky, oval to oblong leaves (to 6 in. long near base of plant, shorter higher up) have a grayish sheen

above, are white and woolly beneath. Narrow, twisted spikes of closely spaced, ½-in., violet-blue flowers can reach 3 ft. or longer. Blooms from early summer to frost (almost all year in mildest climates). Indigo calyxes are colorful long after blossoms fall. Excellent cut flowers. Top growth damaged by frost. Full sun or partial shade.

S. x jamensis. JAMÉ SAGE. Evergreen shrub. Zones LS, CS, TS; USDA 8-11. Plants sold under this name are hybrids involving S. greggii, S. microphylla, an unknown yellow-flowering species, and possibly other sages; they are found wild in Mexico. Habit varies from upright to horizontal, but plants are usually under 3 ft. high, with fairly open branching; stems often root where they touch soil. Glossy green, oval to elliptical, toothed leaves ¾–1¼ in. long. Stems 3–6 in. long bear ½- to ¾-in. flowers in many colors: violet, wine-red, orange-red, hot pink, coral, salmon, yellow, white, and bicolors. Best in moderate climates without extreme temperature swings. Give afternoon shade, as plants burn in full sun. Drought-tolerant but perform best with moderate water.

Excellent selections include 'Cienega de Oro' (creamy yellow flowers), 'Golden Girl' (butter yellow blooms), and 'Sierra de San Antonio' (light peach blooms with pastel yellow lips); all grow 1½–2 ft. high, 2–3 ft. wide. 'San Isidro Moon' has an open, horizontal habit to 2 ft. high, 2–4 ft. wide; it bears two-tone flowers in peach shades. 'California Sunset' grows about 3 ft. high and wide; its gorgeous flowers blend shades of coral. Selections often sold as forms of S. greggii include soft orange-red 'Coral' and pale yellow 'Moonlight'.

S. koyamae. JAPANESE YELLOW SAGE. Perennial. Zones US, MS, LS, CS, TS; USDA 6-11. From Japan. Loose-growing ground cover to about 1 ft. tall, with lax stems up to 2 ft. long. Very attractive, heart-shaped, yellow-green leaves to 6 in. long, 5 in. wide. Whorls of pale yellow flowers on 6- to 12-in. spikes in summer and fall. Does best in a shady spot, in rich, moisture-retentive, well-drained soil; looks great weaving among other shade-loving plants.

S. leucantha. MEXICAN BUSH SAGE. Evergreen shrub. Zones LS, CS, TS; USDA 8-11. From central

and eastern Mexico. Vigorous, upright, velvety plant 3–4 ft. tall, 3–6 ft. or more wide; sprawls in bloom. Lance-shaped to linear, 5- to 6-in.-long leaves are dark grayish green above, whitish below. Stems to 1 ft. long bear whorls of ¾- to 1¼-in. white flowers with purple calyxes. Bloom period runs from fall through spring in the Tropical South, throughout the fall elsewhere. To limit plant size and renew flowering stems, cut back close to ground before spring growth begins or at end of bloom cycle; where growing season is especially long, cut back again in early to midsummer. Also limit watering to every two or three weeks and remove blossoms as soon as they fade. 'Eder' has leaves with creamy white edges. 'Midnight' ('Purple Velvet'), considered by many to be the best-looking form, has purple flowers and calyxes. Dwarf form 'Santa Barbara' reaches only 3 ft. high and 3–5 ft. wide.

S. lyrata. LYRE-LEAF SAGE. Perennial. Zones US, MS, LS, CS, TS; USDA 6-11. Woodland and roadside wildflower native to the Southeast. To 1–2 ft. high, spreading widely by rhizomes and seeds. Features rosettes of 3-in., lyre-shaped leaves with reddish purple markings. Spikes of little lavender-blue flowers in winter and spring are showy in masses. Takes sun or shade. Prefers drier, well-drained soils; good for hillsides. 'Purple Volcano' ('Purple Knockout') has burgundy foliage and white flowers.

S. 'Madeline'. Perennial. Zones US, MS, LS; USDA 6-8. Upright, bushy growth to 2½ ft. high, 1½–2 ft. wide. Mass of deep green, 7-in.-long leaves is topped in summer by tall spikes of bicolored flowers: bright violet-blue with a white lip delicately edged in violet. Cut back by half after bloom to encourage rebloom.

S. madrensis. FORSYTHIA SAGE. Perennial. Zones MS, LS, CS, TS; USDA 7-11. From west-central Mexico. Strong grower, building up to 5–8 ft. tall and wide. Spreads by rhizomes to make a broad thicket (but stems are easily pulled out). Square stems are very thick—to 2 in. on a side at base. Bright green, rough-textured leaves with an elongated heart shape reach 6 in. long at bottom of plant, become smaller toward top. Butter-yellow,

1-in. flowers on 1- to 2-ft. stems; good for cutting. Blooms from fall until frost (through spring in the Tropical South). Top growth damaged by frost. Plant in light shade or afternoon shade in moist, well-drained soil. Propagate by division or cuttings. Cold-hardy selection 'Dunham', from the garden of Rachel Dunham in Cary, North Carolina, has survived −9°F. 'Red Neck Girl' has deep reddish purple stems.

S. mexicana. MEXICAN SAGE. Shrubby perennial. Zones LS, CS, TS; USDA 8-11. From central Mexico. Robust, erect growth to 10 ft. or taller, 3–5 ft. wide. Leaves to 6 in. long, typically elongated oval or heart shaped; they may be medium green and smooth above, fuzzy beneath, or gray to gray-green and densely hairy on both sides. Pleasant pine fragrance. Tightly spaced whorls of flowers on 12- to 20-in.-long stems; blossoms are dark blue or violet with green or reddish purple calyxes. Blooms from early fall through spring in mild-winter climates; stops with hard frost elsewhere. Protect from wind. To keep compact, remove flower stems and shape plant as blooms are fading. Tolerates some shade; good under high-branching trees.

Best with moderate water; more frequent watering produces excessive, brittle growth. 'Limelight' grows 6 ft. tall, 3 ft. wide, with a striking combination of chartreuse calyxes and blue flowers. 'Tula' is larger growing, with even brighter chartreuse calyxes.

S. microphylla. BABY SAGE. Evergreen shrub. Zones MS, LS, CS, TS; USDA 7-11. Native from southeastern Arizona through southern Mexico, with many local variant forms. Full sun or partial shade. Moderate water.

'Belize Form', to 5 ft. tall and 8 ft. wide, is long blooming but somewhat tender, with bright green leaves and brilliant red flowers. 'Berzerkeley', 2 ft. tall and 3–4 ft. wide, bears glowing pinkish red blossoms. ' Hot Lips' is upright, to 1½–2 ft. high, with striking flowers that vary from fire engine red to white to red-and-white bicolors throughout the growing season. 'San Carlos Festival', 2–3 ft. tall, 4–6 ft. wide, is a nonstop bloomer bearing raspberry-pink flowers. Hybrids with *S. greggii* include vigorous 'Maraschino', 3–4 ft. high, 6 ft. wide, with bright cherry-red flowers; and purplish pink 'Plum Wine', 3–4 ft. high and 2½–3½ ft. wide.

S. m. microphylla (*S. grahamii*) is a tough, dense, wiry-looking plant to 3–4 ft. tall and 3–6 ft. wide. Triangular to oval, tooth-edged leaves are dark green, ½–1 in. long. Rosy red, 1-in. flowers have small, hooded upper lip, three-lobed lower lip. Blooms most heavily in late spring and fall, sporadically at other times of year. *S. m. neurepia* grows 3–5 ft. tall and wide. It is a more open-branched plant than *S. m. microphylla*, with yellowish green leaves and a very long show of brilliant red flowers.

S. miniata. BELIZE SAGE. Evergreen shrub treated as tender perennial or annual in all but the Tropical South. Zone TS; USDA 10-11. Native to moist regions of Mexico and Belize. Tropical-looking plant to about 3 ft. tall and wide, with arching stems carrying toothed, glossy, dark green leaves that reach 5 in. long, 2 in. across. Small bright red flowers held in dark bracts bloom year-round in the Tropical South, from spring until frost in colder climates. Good container plant. Best in partial shade.

S. nemorosa. VIOLET SAGE. Perennial. Zones US, MS. LS; USDA 6-8. From eastern Europe, eastward to central Asia. To 1½–3 ft. tall, spreading 2–3 ft. wide by rhizomes. Forms a tight foliage rosette from which rise erect, branching flower stems. Wrinkled, dull green, finely toothed leaves are oval or lance shaped. Lower leaves are stalked, to 4 in. long; upper ones are smaller, virtually stalkless, and clasp flower stem. Sprawls if not supported. Stems 3–6 in. long hold ¼- to ½-in. flowers in violet, purple, pink, or white, with persistent violet, purple, or green bracts. Blooms for several weeks in late spring and early summer; may rebloom if deadheaded. The following selections are recommended.

'Burgundy Candles', to 28 in. tall, has attractive burgundy stems and bracts; flowers are rich blue. Heat and drought-tolerant Lyrical series, 22–24 in. tall, offers a profuse show of blooms in blue tones, rose, and white; 'Lyrical Silvertone' has deep blue flowers with petals edged in silver. Growing about 1½ ft. high are 'Caradonna', with dark purple stems and violet blossoms; 'Lubecca', with grayish green leaves and violet flowers with reddish purple bracts; and 'Ostfriesland' ('East Friesland'), with intense violet-blue flowers, pink to purple bracts. Sallyrosa series grows 16 in. high and is a heavy bloomer (pink, violet, and blue); heat and drought tolerant. There are also several compact selections, including 'Marcus', with intensely violet flowers on plants just 12 in. high and 18 in. wide. Sensation series is about the same size; pink-flowered 'Sensation Rose' is among the most popular.

S. officinalis. COMMON SAGE. Shrubby perennial. Zones US, MS, LS; USDA 6-8. Short lived in the Lower South. Grow as annual anywhere. From the Mediterranean region. The traditional culinary and medicinal sage. To 1–3 ft. tall, 1–2½ ft. wide; stems often root where they touch soil. Aromatic, oval to oblong, wrinkled, 2- to 3-in. leaves are gray-green above, white and hairy beneath. Branching, 8- to 12-in. stems bear loose, spikelike clusters of ½-in. flowers in late spring, summer. Usual color is lavender-blue, but violet, red-violet, pink, and white forms exist. Delay

TOP: Salvia microphylla 'Hot Lips'; *S. officinalis* 'Tricolor';
MIDDLE: S. leucantha 'Santa Barbara'; *S. elegans* 'Golden Delicious';
BOTTOM: S. splendens 'Salsa Salmon'; *S. mexicana* 'Limelight'

S

pruning until new leaves begin to unfurl, then cut just above fresh growth; cutting into bare wood usually causes dieback. Replace plants when they become woody or leggy (about every 3 or 4 years). Subject to root rot where drainage is less than perfect. Give afternoon shade in hottest climates.

'Berggarten' ('Mountain Garden') is a compact grower to just 16 in. high, with denser growth, rounder leaves, and fewer flowers than species; may be longer lived. 'Compacta' ('Nana', 'Minimus') is a half-size (or even smaller) version of the species, with narrower, closer-set leaves. 'Holt's Mammoth' has large leaves (4–5 in. long), used in making condiments. 'Icterina' has gray-green leaves with golden border; does not bloom. 'Purpurascens' ('Red Sage') has leaves flushed with red-violet when new, slowly maturing to gray-green. 'Tricolor' has gray-green leaves with irregular cream border; new foliage is flushed with purplish pink. 'Silver Sabre' has similarly variegated leaves on a denser, lower-growing plant; excellent for containers.

S. pratensis. MEADOW SAGE. Perennial. Zones US, MS, LS, CS; USDA 6-9. Native to Europe, Morocco. To 3 ft. tall, 1 ft. wide, with broadly oval, pointed, dark green basal leaves to 8 in. long. Spikes of small lavender-blue blooms (less than 1 in. long) on branching, foot-tall stems put on a very showy (but short) springtime display. Needs a warm, well-drained site. Reseeds.

S. 'Purple Majesty'. Shrubby perennial. Zones LS, CS, TS; USDA 8-11. To 3 ft. tall, 4 ft. wide. Hybrid of *S. guaranitica*, with leaves of a yellower green; brilliant royal purple flowers with violet-black calyxes. Blooms from summer until frost in most of the Coastal South, nearly all year in the Tropical South (where it is evergreen).

S. regla. ROYAL SAGE. Evergreen or deciduous shrub. Zones MS, LS, CS, TS; USDA 7-11. Native to western Texas, central Mexico. Upright stems to 4–6 ft. high; these arch and branch out to form an almost equally wide mass. Scalloped, puckered, fan-shaped leaves (drawn out to sharp points in some forms) are 1 in. across. Orange-scarlet, 1-in. flowers with flaring calyxes appear in short clusters at branch ends; calyxes persist for several weeks after flowers drop. Profuse bloom from fall until frost (through early spring—though less profusely—in the Tropical South). Prune this plant (if ever) only when it is growing strongly in summer; winter-pruned plants recover slowly, may even die. Loses leaves at 28°F. Excellent nectar source for hummingbirds. 'Huntington' has larger flowers, spreading habit (4–5 ft. tall, to 6 ft. wide). 'Jame', to 4–6 ft. tall and wide, has larger leaves and 3-in. persimmon orange blooms. 'Royal' is an upright grower to 4 ft. high and wide, with bright orange flowers and calyxes.

S. reptans. Perennial. Zones US, MS, LS, CS, TS; USDA 6-11. From the high mountains of Mexico. Light green, almost needlelike leaves on thin stems form a dense mound to 2 ft. high and 3 ft. wide; masses of light blue, ½-in. flowers held in dark calyxes bloom from late spring through fall. Plant disappears in winter. Although native to dry, gravelly washes, it thrives in the humid Southeast. Hardy to 20°F. A West Texas form discovered in the Trans-Pecos region is more upright, to 3 ft. high and about 2 ft. wide. 'Blue Willow' has bright blue flowers.

S. splendens. SCARLET SAGE. Perennial in TS; USDA 10-11; grown as annual elsewhere. Native to Brazil. The traditional bright scarlet bedding sage now comes in a range of colors, from vivid true red through salmon and pink to purple shades. White forms are also available. Plants vary in size from compact 1-ft. dwarfs to 3- to 4-ft. kinds. Leaves are bright green, heart shaped, 2–4 in. long. Blooms from late spring or summer through fall (all year in the Tropical South); 4- to 12-in. stems bear 2-in. flowers that emerge from 1-in. calyxes of same color. Can be ravaged by Mexican giant whitefly. Give afternoon shade in hottest climates.

Seed-grown strains include Fizz, just 8–12 in. high, with dense flower spikes in several single colors and white; Firecracker, to 1 ft. high and wide, in many single colors and bicolors; Sizzler, about the same size, a heat-tolerant early bloomer with bicolored flowers in a wide color range; Salsa, 12–14 in. tall, in purple, scarlet, burgundy, rose, and salmon, including a bicolored white and scarlet; Amore, heat-tolerant, 14-in.-tall plants with flowers in reds and purples; and Picante, 14–16 in. tall, blooms early and heavily in colors similar to those of Salsa. 'Van Houttei' is a vigorous old cutting-grown selection to 3 ft. tall, 4 ft. wide (even larger in mild-winter climates); it bears maroon flowers with an orange-scarlet tinge from early fall through spring where temperatures remain above 28°F. Similar to 'Van Houttei' are 'Louie's Orange Delight' (with orange-toned red blooms and bracts) and 'Paul' (with reddish purple flowers and bracts).

S. x superba. Perennial. Zones US, MS, LS; USDA 6-8. Form generally available is 'Superba', but many plants sold under this name are seedlings or selections of *S. x sylvestris* or *S. nemorosa*. The real *S. x superba* forms a tight foliage clump that spreads 2–3 ft. by rhizomes and sends up erect, much-branched, 3-ft.-tall flowering stems. Smooth, scallop-edged green leaves are lance shaped; basal ones are stalked and 3–4 in. long, upper ones stalkless and smaller. At bloom time, top 6–8 in. of stems bear clusters of ½-in., violet-blue flowers with reddish purple bracts that persist long after flowers fall. (Bracts on most seedlings are green, sometimes with a purple tinge.) Blooms midsummer to fall if deadheaded. Blooming plant will sprawl 5–6 ft. wide unless staked. 'Adora Blue' grows just 14 in. high and wide.

S. x sylvestris. Perennial. Zones US, MS, LS; USDA 6-8. Like its parent *S. nemorosa* but more compact, with stems that are less leafy. Oblong to lance-shaped, medium green, scalloped leaves are wrinkled, softly hairy, to 3 in. long. Typically unbranched or few-branched flowering stems to 6–8 in. long, set with pinkish violet, ½-in. blossoms. Blooms summer through fall if faded flowers are removed. 'Blauhügel' ('Blue Hill'), to 2 ft., has medium blue flowers. 'Blue Queen', just 1–1½ ft. high, has deep blue flowers. 'Mainacht' ('May Night'), 2–2½ ft., bears ¾-in. indigo flowers with green bracts (purplish at base), begins blooming in midspring. 'Rosakönigen' ('Rose Queen'), 1½–2 ft. high, has purplish pink flowers and crimson bracts. About the same size is 'Schneehügel' ('Snow Hill'), with pure white blossoms with green bracts. 'Viola Klose' grows 18 in. high, with lavender-blue flowers.

S. texana. BLUE TEXAS SAGE. Perennial. Zones US, MS, LS, CS; USDA 6-9. From Central and West Texas. Well-branched, bushy plant to 15 in. tall and about half as wide. Densely hairy stems; narrow, tapering, 2-in.-long leaves, also hairy, toothed along the upper margins. Produces spikes of inch-long flowers in purplish blue with a white throat that appear in spring. Tolerates alkaline soil. Moderate water.

S. uliginosa. BOG SAGE. Perennial. Zones US, MS, LS, CS, TS; USDA 6-11. From moist lowlands in South America. Upright, dense; to 4–6 ft. tall, 3–4 ft. wide, spreading aggressively by rhizomes. Smooth green leaves are lance shaped, toothed; they reach 3½ in. long near plant's base, decrease in size toward top. Branched inflorescence with 5- to 6-in. stems carries whorls of ½-in., intense sky-blue flowers with white throat, wide lower lip. The flower color is heavenly; the scent of the leaves when touched is not. Plant produces blooms from summer through fall. To restrain its spread, give only moderate water or confine roots by planting it in 15-gallon nursery can sunk in ground to its rim.

S. verticillata. WHORLED CLARY. Perennial. Zones US, MS, LS; USDA 6-8. From central Europe, western Asia. Foliage clump to 2½ ft. wide sends up branching, 2½- to 3-ft.-tall flower stems. Wavy-margined, medium green, softly hairy leaves to 5–6 in. long; shape varies from oval to elliptical or oblong. Basal leaves often divided into one or two pairs of smaller leaflets. Widely spaced whorls of 20 to 40 buds open to violet or lavender-blue flowers nearly ½ in. long, with purple-tinged, persistent calyxes. Blooms in summer; may rebloom if deadheaded. Protect from slugs, snails. 'Alba' has pure white flowers and calyxes. Vigorous 'Endless Love' is 2 ft. tall, 3 ft. wide, with large leaves; its lavender-purple flowers appear over a long period. 'Purple Rain' is 1–2 ft. high, with profuse, showy, deep purple blossoms and calyxes.

CARE

Give sages good air circulation to deter mildew and other fungal diseases. Most require good drainage, especially in winter; waterlogged plants rarely make it through hard freezes. If soil is heavy, work in plenty of organic matter and apply a thick mulch of well-rotted compost. When it comes to watering, "deep" is the operative word. Most of the plants discussed here need regular (or in some cases, moderate) water during dry spells. Plants described as drought tolerant require a deep soaking at least once a month during the heat of summer to retain their foliage and prolong their bloom period.

Remove spent blossoms to encourage continued bloom. Most sages resent severe pruning except in late winter or early spring, when weather is cool and vigorous new growth is emerging from the plant base. To shape during the growing season, either tip-pinch shoots or cut them back by no more than one-third (keeping most of the leaves on each stem). Give lax varieties inconspicuous support by letting them grow through a cylinder of green-painted wire mesh.

In many sages, aromatic compounds in the foliage repel pests—but this is not true for all species. Some are damaged by slugs and snails; in warmer climates, Mexican giant whiteflies can demolish plants. Aphids may be a problem. Deer may nibble flowers, but they usually don't browse plants heavily. Sages are generally easy to propagate from cuttings or seeds; you can also propagate perennial kinds by dividing the roots or taking cuttings.

SAMBUCUS
ELDERBERRY
Adoxaceae
Deciduous shrubs

🌡 **ZONES VARY BY SPECIES**

☀ ◑ **FULL SUN OR LIGHT SHADE**

💧 **REGULAR WATER**

❂ **LEAVES AND RAW FRUIT OF SOME TYPES CAN CAUSE GASTRIC DISTRESS**

Sambucus nigra
'Aureomarginata'

Grow these large, airy shrubs for their white spring flowers and colorful summer berries. In big gardens, they make effective summer screens or windbreaks. To keep shrubby types dense, prune hard in dormant season, removing older stems and heading back last year's growth to a few inches. Overgrown plants can be cut to the ground. Types that grow into trees need early training to single or multiple trunks.

The various elder species have bright to dark green leaves and near-black, blue, or red berries. Fruit of red-berried species and of *S. nigra caerulea* can cause gastric upset if consumed in large quantities. (Red-fruited forms of black- and blue-berried species are not poisonous.)

S. canadensis (*S. nigra canadensis*). AMERICAN ELDER-BERRY. Shrub. Zones US, MS, LS, CS; USDA 6-9. Native to central and eastern North America. Spreading, suckering shrub to 12 ft. tall and wide. Almost tropical-looking light green leaves, each with seven 2- to 6-in.-long leaflets. Blooms in early summer, bearing flat, creamy white flower clusters to 10 in. wide; these are followed by tasty purple-black berries. The ripe fruit is good in

pies, jams, jellies; both flowers and fruit are used for wine. Strictly fruiting selections include 'Adams', 'Johns', the larger-fruited (and later) 'York', and many more; plant any two for cross-pollination. 'Aurea' has golden green foliage (golden in full sun) and red berries.

S. nigra. BLACK ELDER, EUROPEAN ELDER. Shrub or tree. Zones US, MS; USDA 6-7. Native to Europe, North Africa, and Asia. Shrubby, upright growth to 20–30 ft. tall and wide. Each leaf is up to 10 in. long and divided into many oval, pointed leaflets. Scented white flowers come in flat-topped, 5- to 8-in.-wide clusters in late spring or early summer. Purple-black berries are less than ½ in. across; for maximum fruit production, plant two different selections. 'Aurea', 10–20 ft. tall and broad, has yellow new growth maturing to yellow-green. Selections such as 'Black Beauty' and 'Black Lace' have foliage that emerges blackish-purple, but then fades to purple-green in hot weather.

Several selections grow 6–8 ft. tall and wide: 'Aureomarginata', green leaves edged in yellow; 'Laciniata', very finely cut green foliage; and white-fruited 'Marginata' ('Albovariegata', 'Variegata'), green leaves bordered in creamy white.

THE HOLLOWED-OUT STEMS OF AMERICAN ELDERBERRY WERE ONCE POPULAR FOR MAKING MUSICAL PIPES.

Two smaller selections (4–5 ft. tall and wide) are 'Madonna', bearing green leaves that are variegated in light green to chartreuse when young and in cream, yellow, or gray-green when mature; and 'Pulverulenta', with leaves that unfold white, then mature to green splashed and striped with white.

SANGUINARIA CANADENSIS
BLOODROOT
Papaveraceae
Perennial

🌡 **US, MS, LS; USDA 6-8**

◑ ● **PARTIAL TO FULL SHADE**

💧 💧 **REGULAR TO AMPLE WATER**

Sanguinaria canadensis

Native to North America. This low-growing member of the poppy family gets its common name from the orange-red juice that seeps from cut roots and stems. Deeply lobed, gray-green leaves reach 6–12 in. across. Blooms in spring, bearing lovely (but ephemeral) white or pink-tinged, 1½- to 2-in. flowers carried singly on 8-in. stalks. Spreads slowly by rhizomes; good choice for damp, shaded rock gardens or woodland plantings. Combines well with ferns. Mulch in spring. *S. c. multiplex* 'Plena' has longer-lasting, fully double flowers.

SANGUISORBA

BURNET

Rosaceae

Perennials

✏ **ZONES VARY BY SPECIES**

☼ ◑ **LIGHT SHADE IN HOTTEST CLIMATES**

💧 **REGULAR WATER**

Sanguisorba obtusa

These plants grow from creeping rhizomes. Leaves are divided featherwise into toothed, oval or roundish leaflets. Small flowers carried in dense, feathery spikes much like small bottle-brush (*Callistemon*) blossoms.

S. canadensis. AMERICAN BURNET, CANADIAN BURNET. Zones US, MS, LS; USDA 6-8. Native to eastern North America. To 3–6 ft. tall, 3 ft. wide, with bright green foliage and 8-in. spikes of white flowers in late autumn. Dies to the ground in winter even in mild climates.

S. minor. GARDEN BURNET, SALAD BURNET. Zones US, MS, LS, CS, TS; USDA 6-11. Native to Europe, western Asia. Can reach 1½ ft. high and wide but is usually kept clipped to a few inches to maintain a fresh supply of new foliage. Leaves have a mild cucumber flavor and are used in salads, soups, cool drinks. Can be used as an edging for border or herb garden. If not sheared too low, bears roundish, inch-long clusters of red flowers from late spring to midsummer. Self-sows prolifically if allowed to go to seed. Evergreen in all but the Upper South.

S. obtusa. JAPANESE BURNET. Zones US, MS, LS, CS; USDA 6-9. Native to Japan. To 4 ft. tall, 2 ft. wide, with grayish green leaves and pink flower spikes 4 in. tall in summer. Evergreen in all but the coldest winters.

S. officinalis. GREATER BURNET. Zones US, MS, LS, CS; USDA 6-9. Native to northern regions of Europe, Asia, and North America. Grows 3–4 ft. tall and about half as wide. Basal leaves can reach 20 in. long; leaves on upright, reddish stems are smaller. Young leaves are tasty in soups and salads. Dark reddish-purple flowers are held well above the foliage mass in summer; may need staking. Remove spent blooms to prevent rampant self-seeding. 'Red Thunder' has ruby-red flowers on stiff stems.

SANSEVIERIA

Asparagaceae

Perennials

✏ **TS; USDA 10-11, EXCEPT AS NOTED; OR HOUSEPLANTS**

☼ ◑ **SUN OR LIGHT SHADE; BRIGHT LIGHT**

💧 **MODERATE WATER**

Sansevieria trifasciata 'Laurentii'

Group of approximately 60 species native to Africa and India. Admired for their stiff, attractive leaves, which grow from rhizomes. Very popular as houseplants; can also be grown outdoors in mild-winter areas. Outdoors, they accept sun or light shade and just about any well-drained soil, tolerating drought and even salt spray. Indoors, they do best in bright light but will accept dim light. Allow soil to go dry between soakings. For best growth, feed monthly in spring and summer with a general-purpose liquid houseplant fertilizer diluted to half-strength. Easy to root from leaf cuttings. Mature, pot-bound plants may occasionally bear spikelike clusters of fragrant flowers in spring or summer.

S. cylindrica. SPEAR SANSEVIERIA. Forms a rosette of three or four rigidly upright, unusual-looking leaves, each 2–4 ft. long and only about 1 in. wide; they are cylindrical, in dark green with lighter green horizontal bands. White or pinkish, 1½-in.-long flowers.

S. parva. KENYA HYACINTH. Zones CS, TS; USDA 9-11. Rosette of 6 to 12 narrow leaves that grow upward, then arch outward; each leaf is 8–16 in. long and ½–1 in. wide. Leaves are medium green with dark green horizontal bands; flowers are pinkish white. Hardy to 25°F.

S. trifasciata. SNAKE PLANT, MOTHER-IN-LAW'S TONGUE, BOWSTRING HEMP. The original brown-thumb houseplant, supremely tolerant of neglect. If you kill this one, better give up gardening and turn to macramé. Dark green leaves with gray-green horizontal bands can reach 4 ft. tall, 2 in. wide; they are rigidly upright or slightly spreading at the top. Tiny greenish white flowers.

Few plants boast such colorful common names. The first one listed refers to the banded or mottled foliage, resembling the skin of some snakes; the second name comes from the long leaves, which are sharp and always fully extended. The third comes from the tough leaf fibers, which were used for bowstrings. Selections include the following.

'Bantel's Sensation'. Narrow, upright, dark green leaves heavily marked with irregular vertical stripes of creamy white.

'Black Star'. Short, broad leaves are dark green with a golden yellow rim.

'Golden Flame'. Leaves are somewhat broader than those of species. Each golden leaf has a central green stripe.

'Hahnii'. BIRD'S-NEST SANSEVIERIA. Dwarf to just 1 ft. tall, forming a vase-shaped rosette of short, broad, dark green leaves with horizontal silver bands. Good tabletop houseplant. 'Golden Hahnii' has leaves widely edged in creamy yellow.

'Laurentii'. GOLDBAND SANSEVIERIA. Similar to the species, but leaves have golden yellow margins. The most popular snake plant.

'Moonshine'. Broad leaves are silvery green, with faint horizontal markings and a thin edge of dark green.

'Robusta'. Like the species, but leaves are shorter and nearly twice as wide.

'Silver Hahnii'. Same shape and size as 'Hahnii', but leaves are silvery gray-green with faint horizontal dark green bands.

'Silver Queen'. New leaves are silvery gray-green, edged with a thin dark green margin; older leaves turn solid dark green.

'Twist'. Spiraling, twisted leaves have yellow horizontal stripes and broad, bright yellow margins. Grows about 14 in. tall.

SANTOLINA

Asteraceae

Evergreen shrubs

✏ **US, MS, LS, CS; USDA 6-9**

☼ **FULL SUN**

◐ ◒ **LITTLE OR NO WATER TO MODERATE WATER**

Santolina chamaecyparissus 'Pretty Carol'

These Mediterranean natives are notable for their attractive foliage, profuse summer show of small, round, buttonlike flower heads, and stout constitutions. All are aromatic if bruised. Unpruned plants tend to become sparse and woody in the center. Cut back yearly, before spring growth begins; you can simply trim as needed around the edges (as if giving the plant a haircut) or cut the whole plant back to a few inches high. After blossoms fade, shear or clip off flowering shoots. Remove and replace plants if they become too woody. In coldest part of range, plants may die to the ground, but they should grow back from roots. Good as ground covers, bank covers, edgings for walks or borders, low informal or sheared hedges. Grow in any well-drained soil. Not usually browsed by deer.

S. chamaecyparissus. LAVENDER COTTON. To 2 ft. tall, 3 ft. wide. Brittle, woody stems are densely clothed with rough, finely divided, whitish gray leaves. Bright yellow flower heads. Smaller versions of the species include 'Nana', to 1 ft. tall and 2–3 ft. wide; and 'Pretty Carol', to 16 in. high and wide. 'Lemon Queen', to 2 ft. tall and wide, has creamy yellow flowers.

S. pinnata. Grows to 2–2½ ft. tall, 3 ft. wide; narrow, tooth-edged, dark green leaves, cream-colored flowers. S. p. neapolitana grows to 12–15 in. tall and has silvery foliage and bright yellow flowers.

S. rosmarinifolia. GREEN SANTOLINA. To 2 ft. tall, 3 ft. wide, with narrow, green leaves like those of rosemary (Rosmarinus). Leaves may have tiny teeth or none at all. Bright yellow flowers. 'Morning Mist' is similar but more compact; tolerates wet conditions better than species. 'Lemon Fizz', to 1½ ft. tall and 2 ft. wide, has golden leaves and creamy yellow flowers.

SANVITALIA PROCUMBENS

CREEPING ZINNIA
Asteraceae
Annual

US, MS, LS, CS, TS; USDA 6-11

FULL SUN

MODERATE TO REGULAR WATER

Sanvitalia procumbens 'Sunbini'

This bright-blossomed and heat-resistant Mexican native is not really a zinnia, but it looks enough like one to fool most people. Grows only 4–6 in. high but spreads or trails to 1½ ft. or wider. Leaves are like miniature (to 2-in.-long) zinnia leaves. Flowers are nearly 1 in. wide, with vivid yellow or orange rays around a dark purple-brown center. Blooms from midsummer until frost. The Tsavo strain has single or double yellow flowers. Popular selections include 'Mandarin Orange', 'Sprite Orange', and double-flowered 'Gold Braid'. 'Sunbini' is a mounding selection with yellow blooms.

Needs good drainage. Sow seeds or set out nursery transplants in spring (creeping zinnia resents transplanting, so sow where plants are to grow). Use in borders or edgings, as annual cover for slope or bank; or plant in hanging baskets or pots.

SAPINDUS

SOAPBERRY
Sapindaceae
Deciduous and evergreen trees

ZONES VARY BY SPECIES

FULL SUN

LITTLE TO MODERATE WATER

Sapindus saponaria drummondii

Group of about 12 species of deciduous or evergreen trees and shrubs from tropical and subtropical parts of the world; the two described here are both U.S. natives. All of these plants are tough and easy to grow. Saponin, a substance contained in the berries, lathers when mixed with water—hence the common name.

S. marginatus. FLORIDA SOAPBERRY. Evergreen. Zones LS, CS; USDA 8-9. Native to the South Atlantic coast, from South Carolina to Florida. Grows 40 ft. tall and 30 ft. wide. Bright green leaves to 14 in. long, each with 7 to 13 lance-shaped leaflets; turn golden in fall. Clusters of small white flowers in spring.

S. saponaria drummondii (*S. drummondii*). WESTERN SOAPBERRY. Deciduous. Zones US, MS, LS, CS; USDA 6-9. Native to southwestern U.S. and Mexico. Attractive round-headed, spreading tree to 25–30 ft. tall and eventually as wide, with yellowish green, 10- to 15-in.-long leaves divided into many leaflets. In early summer, tiny yellowish white flowers bloom in 8- to 10-in.-long clusters; these are followed by beadlike, ½-in., orange-yellow fruit that turns black by winter. Fall foliage is a lovely orange-yellow. Makes a good shade or street tree, thanks to its tolerance for adverse conditions: poor, dry, rocky, alkaline soil; polluted air; wind; occasional drought. Fruit drop and self-sown seedlings can cause problems. 'Narrow Leaf' has narrower leaves than the species.

SAPONARIA

Caryophyllaceae
Perennials

ZONES VARY BY SPECIES

FULL SUN

MODERATE TO REGULAR WATER

Saponaria officinalis 'Rosea Plena'

These European natives are generally low, spreading plants that are useful as ground covers or in rock gardens. Best in lean, very well-drained soil.

S. x lempergii. GIANT-FLOWERED SOAPWORT. Handsome blue-green leaves to ½ in. long form a mat 8 in. tall, 1½ ft. wide. Large clusters of bright pink, inch-wide flowers virtually smother the foliage for weeks in midsummer. 'Max Frei' has soft pink blooms.

S. ocymoides. ROCK SOAPWORT. Zones US, MS, LS; USDA 6-8. Trailing habit to 1 ft. high and 3 ft. across. Dark green, oval, ½-in.-long leaves. In spring, plants are covered with ¼-in. pink flowers in loose bunches shaped much like those of phlox. Looks especially nice cascading over a wall. Selections include white 'Alba' and deep pink 'Rubra Compacta'.

S. officinalis. SOAPWORT, BOUNCING BET. Zones US, MS, LS, CS; USDA 6-9. Grows to 2 ft. tall, spreading wider by underground runners. Can be invasive in rich, moist soil. Dark green, oval, pointed leaves to 4 in. long; loose clusters of inch-wide red, pink, or white flowers in midsummer. When crushed in water, roots produce a sudsy, detergent-like lather. This is one tough plant; before the days of herbicides, it could be seen growing in the cinders along railroad rights-of-way. The selection 'Rosea Plena', with double light pink flowers, is the common garden form. 'Rubra Plena' has crimson blooms that turn paler as they age.

S. x olivana. CUSHION SOAPWORT. Zones US, MS, LS; USDA 6-8. Tiny, dark green leaves form a compact cushion spreading to 2–4 in. tall, 8 in. wide. In early summer, the foliage mound is covered with short-stemmed pink blooms to ¾ in. across.

SARCOCOCCA

SWEET BOX
Buxaceae
Evergreen shrubs

US, MS, LS, CS; USDA 6-9, EXCEPT AS NOTED

PARTIAL TO FULL SHADE

MODERATE TO REGULAR WATER

Sarcococca confusa

Native to the Himalayas, China. Grown for handsome, waxy, dark green leaves and tiny, powerfully fragrant, white blossoms that come in late winter or early spring, hidden in the foliage. Small, berrylike fruit follows the flowers. Useful in shaded areas—under overhangs, in entryways, beneath low-branching evergreen trees. Plants maintain slow, orderly growth and polished appearance in deepest shade. Grow best in organically enriched soil; very tough and drought-tolerant once established. Scale insects are the only pests. Deer leave it alone.

S. confusa. Quite similar to the species S. *ruscifolia* and generally sold as such. S. *ruscifolia*, however, produces red fruit, while that of S. *confusa* is black.

S. hookeriana. This rhizomatous species is known mainly for the following two outstanding variants, both of which bear glossy, blue-black fruit. *S. h. humilis* (S. *humilis*) is low growing, seldom more than 1½ ft. high, and spreads to 8 ft. or more by underground runners. Branches are thickly set with pointed leaves 1–3 in. long, ½–¾ in. wide. Good ground cover. *S. h. digyna* is taller, to 5 ft. high and 6 ft. wide, with longer, narrower leaves. Its selection 'Purple Stem' has dark purple-pink young shoots and pink-tinged flowers.

S. ruscifolia. FRAGRANT SARCOCOCCA. LS, CS; USDA 8-9. Slow growth to 4–6 ft. high, 3–7 ft. wide. If grown against a wall, it will form a natural espalier, with branches fanning out to create patterns. Oval to elliptical leaves to 2 in. long, densely set on branches. Red fruit.

SARRACENIA

PITCHER PLANT
Sarraceniaceae
Carnivorous perennials

US, MS, LS, CS; USDA 6-9

FULL SUN

AMPLE WATER

Sarracenia leucophylla

Famed for having insects for dinner, pitcher plants can also make excellent garden plants. Ten or so species inhabit bogs from Maryland south to Florida. They are found where soils are constantly moist but only briefly flooded, and where periodic wildfires remove encroaching trees and shrubs, providing full sun. The soil in such sites is usually nutrient starved and acidic, lacking nitrogen and other elements. Pitcher plants compensate by obtaining these nutrients from the creatures they consume, including insects, spiders, and the occasional small frog.

Growing from fleshy roots, plants form whorls of hollow, modified leaves—the "pitchers" of the common name—that both carry out photosynthesis and trap insects. Attracted by nectar, victims fall into pools of digestive fluid at the bottom of the pitchers. Depending on the species, the pitchers range from a few

inches to over 3 ft. tall; they may be upright and shaped like tubes or trumpets, or they may look like jugs and lie on the ground. Some have "lids" above the opening, giving the plant a hooded appearance. Colors include green, yellow-green, burgundy, and bright red, and some pitchers also sport dramatic red veining—apparently a ploy to attract more prey. Showy, solitary spring blossoms in red, pink, or yellow, typically 2–3 in. across, rise on stalks alongside or above the pitchers. Most species and a number of interesting hybrids resulting from complex crosses are available from mail-order specialists.

S. alata. PALE PITCHER PLANT. Native to the Gulf Coast from Alabama west to Texas. Upright, trumpet-shaped, green- to yellow-green pitchers to 2½ ft. tall; lid is held nearly erect. Pale yellow flowers in early spring. Some variants have reddish bronze pitchers; those of 'Black Tube' are deep purplish red.

S. x catesbyi. CATESBY'S PITCHER PLANT. Naturally occurring hybrid of S. *flava* and S. *purpurea*. Found along the Coastal Plains from Virginia to South Carolina. Upright brick-red pitchers to 15 in. tall; brick-red flowers in late spring.

S. 'Dixie Lace'. Complex hybrid. Butterscotch-yellow pitchers with dramatic red veining grow 1½ ft. tall and are held at a 45° angle. Showy maroon-red flowers.

S. flava. YELLOW PITCHER PLANT. Native to Coastal Plains from Virginia to Florida. Erect pitchers to 3 ft. or taller, in yellowish green with striking crimson veining. Pendulous bright yellow flowers to 4 in. across appear on tall stalks. The showiest pitcher plant in bloom.

S. 'Flies Demise'. Complex hybrid. Upright, hooded pitchers to 10 in. tall are dusty orange with dramatic red veining near the top. Maroon flowers.

S. 'Judith Hindle'. Complex hybrid. Upright pitchers to 3 ft. tall are brilliant ruby-maroon, with ruffled lids veined in ruby and pink. Maroon flowers.

S. 'Ladies in Waiting'. Complex hybrid. Vigorous plant with upright pitchers to 2 ft. tall; they are bright red with white speckles on the upper part, fading to bright green near the base. Fluted lids. Showy maroon-red flowers.

S. leucophylla. WHITE PITCHER PLANT. Native to southern Georgia, southern Alabama, southern Mississippi, Florida Panhandle. Considered by many to be the most beautiful species—and it catches more insects than any other. Upright pitchers to nearly 3½ ft. tall sport open lids. Pitchers are green on the lower half; the upper half and lid are white laced with reddish purple veins. Large (to 4-in.-wide) purplish red flowers. 'Schnell's White' has white, green-veined pitchers and pure yellow flowers. 'Tarnok' has a bizarre, beautifully contorted double flower.

S. Little Bug series. Complex hybrids selected for compact habit and prolific production of pitchers. Easy and adaptable. 'Doodle Bug' has arching, 8-in.-tall pitchers marked in red and white. 'Lady Bug' is a strong grower, with stout, red-spotted pitchers to about 6 in. tall. 'Love Bug' has a rounded, red hood that flares outward. 'Red Bug' has upright, dark red, fuzzy pitchers to 8 in. tall.

S. minor. HOODED PITCHER PLANT. Native to Coastal Plains from North Carolina to Florida. Unusual pitchers to 1 ft. tall resemble the hooded robes of monks, with the lid forming a domed canopy over the mouth; they are green with coppery red shading on the upper quarter. Yellow flowers.

S. oreophila. GREEN PITCHER PLANT. Very rare species; native to northeastern Alabama and mountainous juncture of Georgia and the Carolinas. Upright light green pitchers with red veining grow 2½ ft. tall. Yellowish green flowers bloom in late spring.

S. psittacina. PARROT PITCHER PLANT. Native to Coastal Plains from south Georgia to Mississippi. Jug-shaped, red-veined green pitchers to 8 in. long lie on the ground and form a rosette; their interiors are lined with needlelike hairs. Small, sweet-smelling, purplish red blooms appear over a long period. In the plant's native grassy swamps, periodic flooding allows this one to feed on tadpoles and small fish.

S. purpurea. PURPLE PITCHER PLANT. Native to bogs of the eastern U.S. and Canada. A variable and widespread species. Jug-shaped pitchers to 1 ft. long lie on the ground; they may be green with red veining or solid maroon or red. Flower colors include purple, red, pink, and purplish red.

S. rubra. SWEET PITCHER PLANT. A highly variable species divided into five subspecies; found in the Carolinas, Florida, and Alabama. Upright, trumpet-like pitchers with open lids range from 10 in. to 2 ft. tall; they may be green with red veining or solid red. Bright red to dark red flowers, sometimes fragrant.

CARE

Pitcher plants need a dormant period in winter, so they're not suited to indoors or the Tropical South. They grow best in sunny bogs. To create a bog garden, dig out a large depression about 1½ ft. deep, line it with a plastic pond liner, then fill it with a mixture of 2 parts sphagnum peat moss, 1 part perlite, and 1 part builder's sand. Keep the soil constantly moist but not flooded. Do not fertilize, and never feed meat to pitcher plants. Propagate them by seed or division.

SASSAFRAS ALBIDUM

SASSAFRAS
Lauraceae
Deciduous tree

🌡 **US, MS, LS; USDA 6-8**

☀☀ **FULL SUN OR PARTIAL SHADE**

💧 **REGULAR WATER**

Sassafras albidum

Native to eastern U.S. Grows fast to 20–25 ft. high, then more slowly to reach an eventual 50–60 ft. Often shrubby in youth; with maturity, it becomes dense

ABOVE: Sassafras albidum in fall color

and pyramidal, to 40 ft. across, with heavy trunk and rather short branches. Interesting winter silhouette. Dark reddish brown, furrowed bark. Leaves 3–7 in. long, 2–4 in. wide; they may be oval, mitten shaped, or lobed on both sides. Excellent fall color—shades of yellow, orange, scarlet, and purple. Yellow flowers aren't usually showy, but clusters outline the bare branches in early spring. Male and female flowers are borne on separate trees; when the two sexes are grown near each other, the female tree bears dark blue, ½-in. berries on bright red stalks.

Sassafras is a pleasantly aromatic tree; the bark of roots is sometimes used for making tea, which has a flavor like that of root beer. The tree's volatile oil contains safrole, which is carcinogenic in animals, but extracts sold in markets for making sassafras tea are safrole free.

Performs best in well-drained, nonalkaline soil; won't take prolonged drought. Hard to transplant. Tends to produce suckers, especially if roots are cut during cultivation. No noteworthy diseases, but Japanese beetles can be a serious problem in the Upper and Middle South. Deer don't seem to care for the taste of sassafras.

SATUREJA

Lamiaceae
Annuals and perennials

🌡 **ZONES VARY BY SPECIES**

☀ **FULL SUN**

💧💧 **WATER NEEDS VARY BY SPECIES**

Satureja montana

These aromatic plants serve many culinary purposes. They're used to flavor sauces, vinegars, stews, soups, meat stuffings, and vegetables. Summer savory has a mild, delicate flavor; winter savory has a strong, pungent taste and retains its intensity when dried. Both are favored by honeybees but ignored by deer.

S. hortensis. SUMMER SAVORY. Annual. Zones US, MS, LS, CS, TS; USDA 6-11. From southeastern Europe. Upright to 1½ ft., with loose, open habit. Aromatic, rather narrow leaves to 1½ in. long; use fresh or dried as a seasoning. Whorls of tiny, delicate, pinkish white to rose flowers in summer. Grow in light, well-drained, organically enriched soil. Sow seeds in place; thin to 1–1½ ft. apart. Good potted plant. Regular water. 'Midget' is bushy and uniform, with a high oil content.

S. montana. WINTER SAVORY. Shrubby perennial. Zones US, MS, LS, CS; USDA 6-9. From southern Europe. To 15 in. high, 2 ft. wide. Stiff, narrow to roundish leaves to 1 in. long. Use leaves fresh or dried; clip at start of flowering season for drying. Blooms profusely in summer, bearing whorls of small white to lilac flowers that attract bees. Use in rock garden, as dwarf clipped hedge in herb garden (space plants 1½ ft. apart). Grow in light, well-drained soil. Prune as needed to keep compact. Moderate water.

SAXIFRAGA STOLONIFERA

STRAWBERRY GERANIUM, STRAWBERRY BEGONIA
Saxifragaceae
Perennial

🌡 **MS, LS, CS; USDA 7-9; OR HOUSEPLANT**

☀● **PARTIAL TO FULL SHADE; BRIGHT INDIRECT LIGHT**

💧 **REGULAR WATER**

Saxifraga stolonifera

Native to Asia, this pretty, old-timey plant is neither strawberry, geranium, nor begonia. It forms rosettes of nearly round, silver-veined leaves to 4 in. across; leaves are olive-green above, purplish underneath. Spreads like strawberries do, by sending out threadlike runners with baby plants attached. Clusters of white or pink, dovelike, inch-long flowers appear on 1- to 2-ft. spikes in late summer and fall.

Several colorful selections are available. 'Harvest Moon' has sulphur yellow to golden foliage and pink flowers. 'Kinki Purple' and 'Maroon Beauty' are vigorous spreaders with white flowers; their silver-veined leaves are dark green above, deep purple beneath. 'Tricolor' ('Magic Carpet') is hardier than the species, with white flowers and cupped leaves of rich green with white-and-pink edging above, raspberry-red beneath.

CARE

Where hardy, this plant grows beautifully outdoors—as a ground cover or in rock gardens, strawberry pots, hanging baskets. Give it a mostly shady spot and moist, well-drained soil containing lots of organic matter. Indoors, it makes a nice houseplant for pots and hanging baskets. Give it morning sun or day-long bright indirect light, and allow soil to dry only slightly before watering. Feed monthly with a general-purpose liquid houseplant fertilizer; stop feeding and reduce watering slightly in fall and winter.

SCABIOSA
PINCUSHION FLOWER
Dipsacaceae
Annuals and perennials

🌢 **US, MS, LS, CS, TS; USDA 6-11, EXCEPT AS NOTED**

☼ **FULL SUN, EXCEPT AS NOTED**

🌢🌢 **MODERATE TO REGULAR WATER**

Scabiosa columbaria 'Butterfly Blue'

Resembling a pincushion full of pins, each *Scabiosa* flower has stamens that protrude well beyond the curved surface of the flower head. Bloom begins in midsummer, continues until frost if flowers are deadheaded or cut regularly. Good in mixed or mass plantings. Excellent cut flowers. Not usually browsed by deer.

S. atropurpurea. PINCUSHION FLOWER, MOURNING BRIDE. Annual. May also be sold as *S. grandiflora.* From southern Europe. To 2½–3 ft. tall, 1 ft. wide. Oblong, coarsely toothed leaves. Many carry flowers to 2 in. or more wide, in colors ranging from blackish purple to salmon-pink, rose, white. Tall Double Mixed strain, 'Black Knight', and 'Salmon Queen' reach 3 ft. tall; Dwarf Double Mixed grows to 1½ ft. high.

S. caucasica. PINCUSHION FLOWER. Perennial. Zones US, MS, LS; USDA 6-8. From the Caucasus,

Turkey, Iran. To 1½–2½ ft. high, 1–2 ft. wide. Leaves vary from finely cut to uncut. Flowers 2½–3 in. across, in blue to bluish lavender or white, depending on selection. Needs partial shade in hottest climates. Many selections are sold. 'Fama' has branching stalks carrying blue, 3-in. flowers with broad rays; 'Fama White' has white flowers. The Perfecta series bears white, blue, and lavender-blue flowers with fringed rays. House's Hybrids contains a mixture of blue shades and white.

S. columbaria. Perennial. From Europe, Africa, Asia. To 2 ft. high and wide, with finely cut, gray-green leaves. Flowers to 3 in., in lavender-blue, pink, or white; bloom almost all year in the Tropical South. Hybrids 'Butterfly Blue' (deep lavender-blue) and 'Pink Mist' (bright pink) are choice.

SCAEVOLA
Goodeniaceae
Perennials

🌢 **CS, TS; USDA 9-11; ANYWHERE AS ANNUALS**

☼ **FULL SUN**

🌢🌢 **MODERATE TO REGULAR WATER**

Scaevola aemula 'New Wonder'

Notable for fan-shaped blossoms, with all the segments on one side. Named for the Roman hero Mutius Scaevola, who burned off one of his hands to prove his bravery. Plants are evergreen in the Coastal and Tropical South and nearly everblooming as well. In colder regions, where they are often grown as annuals, they bloom from late spring until frost and are useful as ground covers and in hanging baskets, window boxes, and containers. Good

drainage is a must. Not favored by browsing deer.

S. aemula. FAN FLOWER. This Australian native gets its common name from the shape of its flowers—they do indeed resemble little fans, with all the petals on one side. Some forms are prostrate, others upright to 2½ ft.; fleshy stems of some spread to 3 ft. wide, while those of others trail or sprawl to twice that width. Bright green, 1½- to 2-in.-long leaves; lavender-blue, 1½-in. flowers all along the leafy branches.

Selections feature blue, lavender-blue, purple, pink, or white blossoms. Popular 'Blue Wonder' and 'New Wonder' are lavender-blue; 'Whirlwind White' and 'White Charm' have snowy white blooms. Flowers of 'Zig Zag' sport blue and white stripes.

S. albida. From Australia. Flowers are smaller and stems less fleshy than those of *S. aemula.* Forms a mat 4–6 in. high, eventually spreading to 3–5 ft. across. 'Mauve Clusters' has ½-in.-wide flowers in lilac-tinged mauve; often grown as a long-lived ground cover (space plants 2 ft. apart). 'Alba' is similar but with white flowers.

SCHEFFLERA
Araliaceae
Evergreen shrubs or trees

🌢 **TS; USDA 10-11, EXCEPT AS NOTED; OR HOUSEPLANTS**

☼ ☼ **SOME SHADE IN HOTTEST CLIMATES; BRIGHT INDIRECT LIGHT**

🌢 **REGULAR WATER**

Schefflera arboricola 'Variegata'

The hallmark of these fast-growing plants is their exotic leaves, which are divided into leaflets

that spread out like the fingers of a hand. In most of the South, they are popular houseplants. They prefer bright light but need protection from direct sun, which may burn leaves. Give good drainage; let the soil go fairly dry between soakings. Feed once a month with a general-purpose liquid houseplant fertilizer; stop feeding and reduce watering in fall and winter. Watch for mealybugs, red spider mites, aphids, and scale; apply insecticidal soap or horticultural oil to control these pests. Dust-free, well-humidified plants suffer the fewest problems, so frequent misting is a good idea.

Outdoors, plant scheffleras in fertile, well-drained soil, either in the ground or in large pots. In central and south Florida, they grow into small trees. Bold texture makes them useful accents for patios and Florida rooms. Summer flowers (showy in some species) are followed by tiny dark fruit; houseplants are unlikely to bloom.

S. actinophylla. QUEENS-LAND UMBRELLA TREE, OCTOPUS TREE, SCHEFFLERA. Zone TS; USDA 10-11. Native to Australia. Fast growth to 20–40 ft. tall and eventually as wide. The "umbrella" of the common name comes from the foliage form: The long-stalked, glossy-green leaves are divided into 7 to 16 large (1-ft.-long) leaflets that radiate outward like ribs of an umbrella. Foliage grows in tiers. "Octopus" refers to showy flower heads: Narrow, raylike structures to 3 ft. long, set all along their length with little blossoms, radiate from a central point. Flowers age from greenish yellow to pink to dark red. Good for tropical effects, silhouette, contrast with fern-type foliage plants. Cut out tips occasionally to keep plant from becoming leggy. Cut back overgrown plants nearly to ground level; they will grow back with a better form.

S. arboricola. DWARF SCHEFFLERA. Native to Taiwan. To 20 ft. tall with equal or greater spread, but easily kept smaller with pruning. The dark green leaves are much smaller than those of *S. actinophylla,* with 3-in. leaflets that broaden toward rounded tips. If plants are set into the ground with stems at an angle, they'll continue to grow at that angle—which can give attractive multistemmed effects. Yellowish flowers are clustered in flattened, foot-wide spheres; they turn bronze with age. Over all, this species produces a denser, darker, less treelike effect than *S. actinophylla*. Less prone to pests than *S. actinophylla*—a far better houseplant. Selections with gold-variegated leaves are popular. Look for 'Gold Capella', 'Trinette' ('Trinetta'), and 'Variegata'. Low light causes variegation to fade.

S. delavayi. Zones LS, CS, TS; USDA 8-11. Native to southeastern China and Vietnam. Hardiest by far of the species listed here, surviving temperatures as low as 8°F without protection. Grows slowly to 6–15 ft. tall and about half as wide. Large leaves (to 3 ft. across) are divided into 5–7 leaflets; dark green above and felted creamy gray beneath. Produces 3-ft.-long sprays of tiny white in fall.

S. elegantissima. FALSE ARALIA. Native to New Caledonia. Airy and elegant. As a juvenile, it is a houseplant; when mature, it's a garden plant to 25 ft. tall and wide. Leaves are divided like fans into leaflets with notched edges. Young plants are unbranched, with narrow (1-in.), lacy-looking leaflets to 9 in. long; foliage is shiny dark green above, reddish beneath. The plant branches as it matures, and leaflets grow slightly longer, broaden to 3 in., and become less glossy. Greenish yellow flowers in clusters to 1 ft. long. Be warned that false aralia bears a striking resemblance to marijuana, so be prepared to explain its presence in your garden to local authorities and nosy neighbors.

S. pueckleri. Native to southern Asia. Resembles *S. actinophylla* but is a denser plant that branches from the base. May be trained to single trunk. Leaves to nearly 2 ft. wide are divided into seven to nine stalked, glossy, bright green leaflets, each to 7 in. long, 2½ in. wide. Flowers are greenish, borne on shorter, fewer "rays" than those of *S. actinophylla*.

SCHIZACHYRIUM SCOPARIUM

LITTLE BLUESTEM
Poaceae
Perennial grass

🌿 US, MS, LS, CS; USDA 6-9

☀️ FULL SUN

💧 MODERATE TO LITTLE WATER

Schizachyrium scoparium

Native to much of North America; an important grass in the native tall-grass prairie. Formerly known as *Andropogon scoparius*. Clump-forming grass 2–4 ft. tall, 1–2 ft. wide, with narrow leaves that may be erect or arching. Late-summer flowers are inconspicuous but age to an attractive silvery shade. Leaf color varies from bright green to distinctly bluish in summer, from light brown to dark red in fall and winter. Types that are bluer in summer take on the deeper cold-weather colors: Blue-green leaves of 'Blaze' turn a strong red in fall, while 'The Blues' and 'Prairie Blues' have striking light blue leaves that turn burgundy-red.

All are heat-loving, pest-free plants that look especially nice in meadow plantings. Plant in almost any well-drained soil, though rich, fertile soils are not to its liking.

SCHIZOPHRAGMA HYDRANGEOIDES

JAPANESE HYDRANGEA VINE
Hydrangeaceae
Deciduous vine

🌿 US, MS, LS; USDA 6-8

◐ PARTIAL SHADE

💧 REGULAR WATER

Schizophragma hydrangeoides

Native to Korea, Japan. Resembling climbing hydrangea (*Hydrangea anomala petiolaris*), vine climbs to 30 ft. or more by holdfasts. Pointed, tooth-edged, dark green leaves are 3–5 in. long. Blooms in summer, producing flat, 8- to 10-in.-wide clusters of white flowers. Like the bloom clusters of lace-cap hydrangeas, these feature tiny fertile flowers surrounded by a ring of sterile ones—but the sterile blossoms of this plant have only a single "petal." Use to climb shaded walls or trees. Needs good, well-drained growth. Prune only errant growth. 'Moonlight' has blue-green foliage with a silvery cast. Leaves of 'Silver Slipper' are silvery green with white margins. 'Roseum' bears pink flowers.

SCHLUMBERGERA

Cactaceae
Cacti

🌿 TS; USDA 10-11; OR GROW IN POTS

◐ PARTIAL SHADE; BRIGHT INDIRECT LIGHT

💧 MODERATE TO REGULAR WATER

Schlumbergera truncata

In the wild, these cacti live on trees, as epiphytic orchids do. In the home, they are dependable, easy, long-lived houseplants. Plants are often confused with *Zygocactus*. The many kinds differ principally in flower color.

S. x buckleyi. CHRISTMAS CACTUS. May be labeled *S. bridgesii*. Old favorite to 2 ft. high, 3 ft. wide. Arching, drooping, bright green branches of flattened, scallop-edged, smooth, spineless, 1½-in. joints. Can bear hundreds of many-petaled, long-tubed, 3-in.-long, rosy purplish red flowers at Christmastime. For late December bloom, give plant cool night temperatures (50–55°F), and about 14 hours of darkness per day during November.

S. truncata. THANKSGIVING CACTUS. Native to Brazil. To 1 ft. high and wide. Bright green, 1- to 2-in., toothed joints; two large teeth at tip of last joint on each branch. Short-tubed, 3-in.-long, scarlet flowers with spreading, pointed petals from late fall through winter. Tends to bloom earlier than *S. x buckleyi*, though bloom periods may overlap. Many selections are sold, with blooms in white, pink, salmon, orange, and yellow.

CARE

Plant in well-drained soil. Feed with liquid fertilizer every 7-10 days during active growth and bloom.

Keep soil moist from time flower buds appear to after blooms finish. Then let soil go somewhat dry between waterings. Like poinsettias, Christmas and Thanksgiving cacti need long nights and short days to initiate flowering—at least 14 hours of complete darkness per day.

SCIADOPITYS VERTICILLATA

UMBRELLA PINE
Sciadopityaceae
Evergreen tree

🌿 **US, MS, LS; USDA 6-8**

☼ ◐ **FULL SUN OR PARTIAL SHADE**

💧 **REGULAR WATER**

Sciadopitys verticillata

In its native Japan, this tree reaches 100–120 ft. tall, but in Southern gardens it is not likely to exceed 25–40 ft. tall, 25–30 ft. wide. Very slow grower. In youth, it is symmetrical, dense, and rather narrow; with age, it is more open, and limbs tend to droop. Small, scalelike leaves are scattered along branches and bunched at branch ends. Glossy, dark green needles grow in whorls of 20 to 30 at branch and twig ends, radiating out like spokes of an umbrella; they are flattened, firm, fleshy, 3–6 in. long. Woody, 3- to 5-in. cones may appear on older trees.

Choice decorative tree for open ground or containers. Plant in rich, well-drained, neutral or slightly acid soil. Watch for mites in hot, dry weather. Boughs are beautiful and long lasting in arrangements.

SCILLA

SQUILL, BLUEBELL
Asparagaceae
Perennials from bulbs

🌿 **US, MS, LS; USDA 6-8, EXCEPT AS NOTED**

☼ ◐ **FULL SUN DURING BLOOM, PARTIAL SHADE AFTER**

💧 **REGULAR WATER DURING GROWTH AND BLOOM**

⚠ **ALL PARTS ARE POISONOUS IF INGESTED**

Scilla peruviana

The three hardier species are native to cold-winter regions of Europe and Asia and need some winter chill. Gardeners in cold-winter climates know them as harbingers of spring; the earliest ones come into flower with winter aconite (*Eranthis*) and snowdrop (*Galanthus*). Less hardy to cold is Peruvian scilla (*S. peruviana*); despite its name, it is native to the Mediterranean region. All squills have bell-shaped or starlike flowers borne on leafless stems that rise from clumps of strap-shaped leaves.

Cold-hardy species look best when naturalized; grow them in small patches or larger drifts. *S. peruviana* is most attractive in clumps along pathways, at edges of mixed plantings, in pots. Deer seem to avoid all species.

S. bifolia. Each 8-in. stem carries three to eight star-shaped, inch-wide flowers in turquoise-blue. White, pale purplish pink, and violet-blue selections are available. Each bulb produces only two leaves.

S. peruviana. PERUVIAN SCILLA. Zones LS, CS; USDA 8-9. Grows best with protection from frost. Large bulb produces numerous floppy leaves which appear in autumn and last through winter. In late spring, 10- to 12-in. stems

appear, each topped with dome-shaped cluster of 50 or more starlike flowers. Most forms have bluish purple blooms, but there is a white form.

S. siberica. SIBERIAN SQUILL. Does best in Upper and Middle South. Each 3- to 6-in. stem bears several flowers shaped like flaring bells. Typical color is intense medium blue, but there are selections in white and light to dark shades of violet-blue, often with darker stripes. 'Spring Beauty' has brilliant violet-blue blooms that are larger than those of the species.

CARE

Plant all types in fall, in well-drained, organically enriched soil. Set bulbs of cold-hardy species 2–3 in. deep, 4 in. apart; set those of *S. peruviana* 3–4 in. deep, 6 in. apart. Reduce watering when foliage yellows after bloom. Hardy kinds will tolerate less moisture during summer dormancy, but don't let soil dry out completely. *S. peruviana* will accept summer moisture but doesn't need any. Divide clumps (during dormancy) when vigor and bloom quality decline.

SCINDAPSUS PICTUS

SATIN POTHOS
Araceae
Evergreen vine

🌿 **TS; USDA 10-11; OR HOUSEPLANT**

◐ **DAPPLED SHADE; BRIGHT INDIRECT LIGHT**

💧 **REGULAR WATER**

⚠ **ALL PLANT PARTS ARE POISONOUS IF INGESTED**

Scindapsus pictus

Resembles more familiar green-and-yellow pothos (*Epipremnum*

aureum; also sold as *Scindapsus aureus*) but has dark green leaves with gray-green mottling. Leaves are also thinner in texture and usually somewhat larger (to 6 in., compared with the 2- to 4-in. leaves of pot-grown pothos). Flowers are insignificant. All plant parts are poisonous, and the sap can cause a skin rash. The most frequently grown selection is 'Argyraeus', with silky-sheened leaves carrying almost silvery markings that are more prominent and larger than those of the species.

Satin pothos is fussier than pothos: needs perfect drainage, high humidity, and good light but no direct sun. Water as soon as soil becomes dry to the touch; feed every other week with a general-purpose liquid fertilizer. In winter, reduce watering and cease fertilizing.

SCOPARIA DULCIS 'ILLUMINA LEMON MIST IMPROVED'

Plantaginaceae
Annual

🌿 **US, MS; USDA 6-7; HARDY LS, CS, TS; USDA 8-11**

☼ **FULL SUN**

💧 **REGULAR WATER**

Scoparia dulcis 'Illumina Lemon Mist Improved'

Forms a soft-looking, airy mound about 1 ft. high and 1½–2 ft. wide; thin, branching stems are set with tiny, lance-shaped, medium green leaves. From spring through fall, whole plant is covered in small, bright yellow, star-shaped blooms with a refreshing sweet-licorice fragrance. Good choice for mixed container plantings, hanging baskets, and window boxes; also suited for use as a small-scale ground cover or path edging. Heat and drought tolerant.

SCUTELLARIA

SKULLCAP
Lamiaceae
Perennials and annuals

🌿 **ZONES VARY BY SPECIES**

☼ ☽ **FULL SUN OR LIGHT SHADE**

🌢 🌢 **REGULAR TO MODERATE WATER**

Scutellaria wrightii

These clump-forming plants are mint relatives, with the family's typical square stems and paired leaves. Long, tubular flowers flare out into two lips, the upper one narrow and hooded, the lower one broad; in many species, the lower lip is marked in white. The species listed here are easy to grow in light, gravelly, well-drained soil; tolerate drought and alkaline soil.

S. drummondii. DRUMMOND SKULLCAP. Annual. Native to Texas, New Mexico, Oklahoma, Florida, Louisiana, Arizona, and Mexico. Upright, branching plant forms a mound 1 ft. tall and wide. Oval, gray-green leaves to 1 in. long; lavender spring flowers about ½ in. across.

S. ocmulgee. OCMULGEE SKULLCAP. Perennial. Zones MS, LS, TS; USDA 7-10. Native to Georgia and South Carolina. Upright grower to 2 ft. tall and 3 ft. wide, with fuzzy, gray-green leaves to 3 in. long. Midsummer blooms are lavender-blue. Rare in nature and in commerce.

Listed as a threatened species in Georgia.

S. resinosa. RESINOUS SKULLCAP, PRAIRIE SKULLCAP. Perennial. Zones MS, LS, TS; USDA 7-10. Native from Kansas and Colorado south to Texas and Arizona. Mounding plant 6–8 in. tall, 1 ft. wide, with roundish, resinous, grayish green leaves less than ½ in. long. One-sided, elongated clusters of 1-in., blue-violet flowers are produced in late spring. Deadhead to encourage intermittent bloom through autumn. 'Smoky Hills' grows 10–12 in. high and 12–15 in. wide; flowers are deep purplish blue.

S. suffrutescens. PINK SKULLCAP. Perennial. Zones MS, LS, CS; USDA 7-9. From Mexico. Forms a dense mound to 1 ft. tall, 1½ ft. wide, with oval, bright green leaves just ½ in. long. Deep rosy pink flowers to 1 in. long bloom from late spring until frost. 'Texas Rose' is a superior selection.

S. 'Violet Cloud'. Perennial. Zones US, MS, LS; USDA 6-8. Sterile hybrid resulting from a cross between S. *resinosa* and S. *suffrutescens*. Forms a low mound about 8 in. high and 12 in. wide, with profuse deep violet blooms from late spring through fall.

S. wrightii. SHRUBBY SKULLCAP. Perennial. Zones LS, CS, TS; USDA 8-11. Native to Texas and Oklahoma. Mounding plant 6–10 in. high and a bit wider, with small, rounded, green leaves. Deep violet-blue, ½- to 1-in.-long flowers have prominent white anthers that give them a striped appearance. Blooms heavily in June, then off and on until frost. Good for massing and rock gardens. Evergreen in mild-winter areas.

SEDUM

SEDUM, STONECROP
Crassulaceae
Succulent perennials

🌿 **US, MS, LS; USDA 6-8, EXCEPT AS NOTED**

☼ ☽ **FULL SUN OR PARTIAL SHADE, EXCEPT AS NOTED**

🌢 🌢 **LITTLE TO MODERATE WATER, EXCEPT AS NOTED**

Sedum x *rubrotinctum*

Mostly ground cover-scale succulents that grow nicely in the spaces between rocks (thus, "stonecrop"), sedums are native to many parts of the world. Some are quite hardy to cold, others fairly tender; some are tiny and trailing, others much larger and upright. Fleshy leaves are evergreen (unless otherwise noted) but highly variable in size, shape, and color. Typically small, star-shaped flowers, sometimes brightly colored, are usually borne in fairly large clusters.

Smaller sedums are useful in rock gardens, as ground or bank covers, in small areas where unusual texture is needed. Some are prized by collectors of succulents, who grow them in pots, dish gardens, or miniature gardens. Larger types are good in borders or containers. Most sedums are easy to propagate by stem cuttings; even detached leaves will root and form new plants. Soft and easily crushed, they will not take foot traffic, but they are otherwise tough, low-maintenance plants. Low-growing types often escape damage by browsing deer.

S. acre. GOLDMOSS SEDUM. Zones US, MS, LS, CS; USDA 6-9. Native to Europe, North Africa, Turkey. To 2–5 in. high, with upright branchlets rising from trailing, rooting stems. Light green leaves only ¼ in. long; clustered yellow flowers in spring. This old favorite is extremely hardy but can get out of bounds and become a weed. Use as ground cover (set plants 1–1½ ft. apart), between stepping stones, or in chinks of dry walls.

S. album. WHITE SEDUM. From Europe, Siberia, western Asia, North Africa. Creeping plant to 2–6 in. high, with ½-in.-long, light to medium green, sometimes red-tinted leaves. White or pinkish summer flowers. Plant 1–1½ ft. apart for ground cover. This species will root from the smallest fragment, so beware of planting it near choice, delicate rock garden plants. 'Coral Carpet' has new growth that emerges salmon-orange, matures to bright green, and turns reddish-bronze in winter. Pale pink flowers.

S. anglicum. ENGLISH STONECROP. Zones US, MS, LS, CS; USDA 6-9. From western Europe. Low, spreading plant 2–4 in. high. Dark green leaves are tiny, to just ⅛ in. long. Pinkish or white flowers appear in spring. For ground cover, set plants 9–12 in. apart.

S. 'Autumn Joy'. See S. Herbstfreude group.

S. brevifolium. Zones US, MS, LS, CS; USDA 6-9. Native to the Mediterranean region. Grows just 2–3 in. high, slowly spreading to 1 ft. wide. Gray-white, red-flushed leaves are tiny (less than ⅛ in. long), tightly packed on stems. Pinkish or white summer flowers. Needs acid soil and good drainage. Best in rock gardens or with larger succulents in containers, miniature gardens. Requires perfect drainage. Sunburns in hot, dry places.

S. cauticola. Zones US, MS, LS, CS; USDA 6-9. Native to Japan. Slowly forms a mound 4–6 in. high, 1–1½ ft. wide. Blue-gray, slightly toothed, 1-in. leaves. Clusters of rose-red flowers top stems in late summer or early fall. Dies to ground in winter.

S. confusum. MEXICAN STONECROP. Zones MS, LS, CS; USDA 7-9. Native to Mexico. Spreading, branching plant grows 6–18 in. high and wide. Shiny, dark green, ¾- to 1½-in.-long leaves tend to cluster in rosettes toward branch ends. Dense clusters of yellow flowers in spring. Makes a good ground cover but is sometimes plagued by dieback in wet

soils, hot weather; it looks best during cooler weather. Use in borders or containers, as edging. A similar, smaller plant with light green leaves is the closely related *S. kimnachii.*

S. dasyphyllum. Zones US, MS, LS, CS; USDA 6-9. Native to the Mediterranean region. Forms a low (1½- to 4½-in.-high) mat that spreads to 1 ft. or wider. Gray-green, ⅛- to ¼-in. leaves are densely packed on stems. Blooms in summer, bearing white flowers with pink streaks. Pink-blossomed 'Riffense' has silver-gray leaves that are especially plump and succulent. Partial shade.

S. dendroideum. TREE SEDUM. Zones CS, TS; USDA 9-11. Native to Mexico. Branching plant to 3 ft. tall and wide. Rounded leaves to 2 in. long are yellow-green, often bronze tinted. Deep yellow flowers in spring and summer. For the plant sometimes sold as *S. d. praealtum,* see *S. praealtum.*

S. erythrostictum 'Frosty Morn'. Zones US, MS, LS, CS; USDA 6-9. Resembles S. 'Autumn Joy', but the light blue-green leaves are boldly outlined in creamy white. Blooms in late summer, bearing large clusters of flowers that are white in hot climates, pale pink in cooler ones. Dies down in winter. Excellent for rock gardens, edgings.

S. forsterianum. Zones US, MS, LS, CS; USDA 6-9. From western Europe, British Isles. To 8 in. high, 10 in. wide, with rounded rosettes of blue-green, needlelike leaves and yellow flowers. Tolerates heat, humidity, and poor soils. 'Oracle' is a top selection.

S. Herbstfreude group. Zones US, MS, LS, CS; USDA 6-9. Hybrids of *S. telephium* and *S. spectabile.* To 1–2 ft. tall, 2 ft. wide, with green leaves to 2–3 in. long and about as wide. Rounded clusters of blossoms are pink when they open in late summer or autumn, age later to coppery pink and finally to rust. Good cut flowers. All die down in winter.

'Autumn Charm' ('Lajos'). White-edged leaves on 16-in. plants; light pink flowers.

'Autumn Delight' ('Beka'). Golden green leaves with darker edges on 18- to 24-in. plants; dusty pink flowers.

'Autumn Fire'. Green leaves and dusty pink flowers on 18- to 24-in. plants.

'Autumn Joy' ('Herbstfreude'). Green leaves. Rounded clusters of blossoms are pink when they open in late summer or autumn, later age to coppery pink and finally to rust.

'Elsie's Gold'. Golden green leaves with cream edges; shell-pink flowers.

'Frosted Fire'. Resembles 'Autumn Fire' but with leaves edged in creamy yellow.

'Mini Joy'. Similar to 'Autumn Joy' but a few inches shorter and with salmon-pink flowers.

S. kamtschaticum. Native to Korea, Japan. Variable species to 4–12 in. high, 2 ft. wide, with trailing stems set with thick, somewhat triangular, 1- to 1½-in., medium green leaves, toothed on the upper third. Summer flowers open yellow, age to red. Useful in colder climates as a rock garden plant or small-space ground cover (set plants 1 ft. apart). 'Sweet and Sour' has leaves that emerge nearly white, then age to green with a yellow edge. 'Variegatum' has cream-edged leaves. *S. k. ellacombianum* (sometimes sold as *S. ellacombianum*) is a shorter plant (4–6 in. high) with more compact growth, unbranched stems, and brighter green leaves. *S. k. floriferum* (sometimes sold as *S. floriferum*) is a more profuse bloomer with smaller flowers in a lighter yellow; its selection 'Weihenstephaner Gold' has abundant golden yellow blossoms that turn orange with age.

S. lineare. Zones US, MS, LS, CS; USDA 6-9. Native to China, Japan. To 4 in. high. Trailing, rooting stems to 1 ft. long are closely set with narrow, inch-long, light green leaves. Loads of yellow flowers in late spring, early summer. For ground cover, set plants 1–1½ ft. apart. 'Sea Urchin' has long, narrow, light green leaves; spreads to 3 ft. wide. 'Variegatum', with white-edged leaves, is often grown in containers.

S. makinoi. Zones US, MS, LS, CS; USDA 6-9. Native to Japan. Prostrate or trailing plant with small, plump leaves and yellow flowers. 'Ogon' has rounded, golden leaves. 'Limelight' has

TOP ROW: Sedum rupestre 'Angelina'; S. spathulifolium 'Cape Blanco'; SECOND ROW: S. foresterianum 'Oracle'; THIRD ROW: S. spurium 'Voodoo'; S. telephium; BOTTOM ROW: S. 'Autumn Joy'

MEET THE SUCCULENTS

Plants in this diverse group have fleshy leaves, stems, or roots that store water to help them withstand periods of drought. Most come from warm, frost-free regions of the world such as Mexico, South Africa, and Madagascar. They do not necessarily have spines, nor do they require desert conditions; in fact, many will not thrive in extreme summer heat or deserts, even in shade. Most are frost tender and can't stand prolonged wet conditions, but a few thrive in colder, rainier climates; among these are *Sempervivum* (from Europe) and many sedums, which grow on sunny, rocky slopes and ledges.

Cacti are technically succulents, but their needlelike spines and desert growing conditions put them in a category of their own.

Succulents are grown everywhere as houseplants; many are useful and decorative as landscaping plants, either in open ground or in containers. When well grown and well groomed, they are attractive all year, in bloom or out.

A few words of caution to growers of succulents—variety of forms, colors, textures offers many possibilities for handsome combinations, but be sure you don't end up with a jumbled medley. Don't use too many kinds in one planting; mass a few species instead of putting in one of each. You can combine succulents with other types of plants, but be sure they like the same growing conditions.

Ground Covers Many succulents make good ground covers, though none withstands foot traffic. Smaller kinds are useful between stepping stones or for creating patterns in small gardens. Others are sturdy and quick growing enough for erosion control on large banks. Most of these are easily started from stem or leaf cuttings, and a stock can quickly be grown from a few plants. See *Echeveria*, Ice Plants, *Sedum*, *Senecio*.

Containers Most succulents grow well in containers filled with fast-draining potting mix. Combine sizes, shapes, and colors in pots with plenty of drainage holes.

Garden Accents Larger succulents have great decorative value,

making architectural focal points in the garden. See *Agave*, *Aloe*, *Crassula*, *Echeveria*, *Kalanchoe*. Some smaller succulents are primarily collectors' items, grown for odd form or flowers. See smaller species of *Aloe*, *Crassula*, *Echeveria*, *Euphorbia*, *Stapelia*.

Colorful Leaves or Blooms Many succulents have colorful leaves, from bright green to soft gray and shades of pink, purple, red, and yellow—often with contrasting hues on a single plant or single leaf. Among those with particularly showy flowers are *Aloe*, some species of *Crassula* and *Sedum*, *Hoya*, *Delosperma*, and *Kalanchoe*.

How to Grow Succulents

EXPOSURE Light shade is best for most succulents, though most will tolerate full sun. Introduce nursery-grown succulents to sunny locations gradually or their leaves may sunburn.

SOIL Fast-draining. Amend garden soil with pumice, decomposed granite, or coarse sand—or plant in cactus mix purchased from your local nursery.

WATERING Although most succulents are drought-tolerant, prolonged periods without water may cause their leaves to lose color, shrivel, or drop. The amount of water needed depends on heat, humidity, and rainfall. Give plants just enough water to keep them plump and attractive. When siting them near plants that need more water, position succulents atop small mounds of amended soil so that water drains away from their roots.

GROOMING Most succulents need little tending other than removal of spent flower stalks and dead leaves.

FEEDING One light feeding at the start of the growing season should be enough for plants in open ground. For more vigorous growth (and for potted plants), feed several times during the growing season at half the recommended dose. Larger and later-blooming succulents may benefit from additional fertilizing.

---

lime-green leaves. 'Salsa Verde' has deep green leaves. All thrive in shade in rocky soil with regular water.

S. 'Matrona'. Zones US, MS, LS, CS; USDA 6-9. To 2–2½ ft. high and 12–18 in. wide, with rose-edged, gray-green leaves that age to grayish brown (retaining the pink edge); large heads of pink flowers appear on red stems.

S. morganianum. DONKEY TAIL, BURRO TAIL. Zone TS; USDA 10-11; or houseplant. From Mexico. Produces long, trailing stems that reach 3–4 ft. in 6 to 8 years. Thick, ¾-in.-long, light gray-green leaves overlap each other along stems to form braided-looking "tails" less than 1 in. thick. Pink to deep red flowers may appear from spring to summer but are only rarely seen. Similar relatives include *S. burrito* (*S.* 'Burro'), with fatter (1-in.-thick) tails composed of densely packed, ½-in. leaves; and giant donkey tail (sometimes sold as *S. orpetii*), with somewhat shorter, thicker tails.

Because of their long stems, all of these are best grown in a hanging basket or wall pot; or try them spilling from the top of a wall or in a rock garden. Provide rich, fast-draining soil (such as a half-and-half mixture of sand and potting soil). Protect from wind and give partial shade. Indoors, site in a south-facing window. Allow soil to become quite dry between thorough waterings, and feed in spring and summer with a general-purpose liquid houseplant fertilizer diluted to half-strength. Reduce watering and cease feeding in winter.

S. oxypetalum. Zones CS, TS; USDA 9-11. Native to Mexico. To 3 ft. tall (usually much less) and 1½ ft. wide. Even when tiny, the plant has the look of a gnarled tree. Narrow, 1- to 1½-in.-long, olive-green leaves; dull red, aromatic summer flowers. Evergreen or semievergreen in mildest areas; deciduous elsewhere. Handsome container plant.

S. praealtum. Zones MS, LS, CS, TS; USDA 7-11. Native to Mexico. Similar to *S. dendroideum* (and sometimes sold as *S. d. praealtum*) but has a wider spread and is less treelike (to 5 ft. high and wide), with greener leaves and lighter yellow flowers. Blooms in spring and summer.

S. x rubrotinctum. PORK AND BEANS. Zones CS, TS; USDA 9-11. Thought to be native to Mexico. Sometimes sold as *S. guatemalense*. Sprawling, leaning, 6- to 8-in. stems are set with ¾-in. leaves that look like jelly beans; they are green with reddish brown tips, often entirely bronze-red in sun. Leaves detach easily and root readily. Yellow spring flowers. Grow in rock garden, in pots, or as a small-space ground cover (set plants 8–10 in. apart). Leaves of 'Aurora' are bright pink.

S. rupestre (*S. reflexum*). Zones US, MS, LS, CS; USDA 6-9. Native to Europe. Spreading, creeping plant to 4 in. high, 1–2 ft. wide. Narrow, light blue-gray

leaves to 1 in. long are closely set on stems; yellow summer flowers. Spreads freely; plant 9–12 in. apart for ground cover. 'Angelina' is an excellent golden-leaved form. 'Blue Spruce' has needlelike foliage.

S. sediforme (*S. altissimum*). Zones US, MS, LS, CS, TS; USDA 6-11. Mediterranean native. This spreading, creeping plant grows 4–6 in. high, 8–12 in. wide. Narrow, light blue-gray leaves to 1½ in. long are closely set on stems. Small greenish white to light yellow flowers in summer. Use in rock garden, for blue-green effect in pattern planting, or as small-space ground cover (set plants 1 ft. apart).

S. sieboldii. Zones US, MS, LS, CS; USDA 6-9. Native to Japan. Low-growing plant just 4 in. high, 8–12 in. wide, with spreading, trailing, unbranched stems to 8–9 in. long. Blue-gray leaves with red edges are carried in threes; they are nearly round, stalkless, toothed along upper half. Plant turns coppery red in fall, dies to ground in winter. Each stem bears a broad, dense, flat cluster of dusty pink flowers in autumn. Leaves of 'Variegatum' have yellowish white markings. Species and selection are beautiful in rock gardens, hanging baskets. Light shade.

S. spathulifolium. Zones US, MS, LS, CS; USDA 6-9. Native from California's Coast Ranges and Sierra Nevada north to British Columbia. Spoon-shaped, ½- to 1-in., blue-green leaves tinged with reddish purple are packed into rosettes on short, trailing stems; mounds reach 4 in. high. Light yellow flowers bloom in spring and summer. Use as ground cover (set plants 1–1½ ft. apart), in rock garden. Very drought tolerant. 'Cape Blanco' is a selected form with silvery white leaves. 'Purpureum' has deep purple foliage.

S. spectabile. SHOWY SEDUM. Zones US, MS, LS, CS; USDA 6-9. Native to China, Korea. Long a favorite in Southern gardens. To 1½ ft. tall and wide, with upright or slightly spreading stems thickly clothed in blue-green, roundish, 3-in. leaves. Dense, 6-in.-wide, dome-shaped flower clusters appear atop stems in late summer and fall; they open pink, mature to dark brown seed heads that put on a long-lasting show. Dies to ground in winter. Full sun. Moderate to regular water. 'Brilliant' has deep rose-red blossoms; its sport 'Neon' has bubble-gum-pink flowers in thicker, more rounded clusters. Other selections include 'Carmen', soft rose; 'Indian Chief', coppery red; 'Meteor', carmine-red; and 'Ruby Jewel', deep maroon.

'Class Act', a hybrid between 'Brilliant' and *S. telephium*, reaches 2½ ft. tall and wide, with thick green leaves and pink flowers that age to dark purplish red. 'Mr Goodbud', another hybrid with the same parents, grows just 16 in. tall and 20 in. wide, with deep blue-green leaves and purple-pink flowers; its short stature and strong stems make it less likely to flop over. 'Birthday Party', a hybrid between 'Neon' and *S. telephium*, is compact at just 7 in. tall, 20 in. wide, with leaves tinted purplish brown; its large flower heads bear deep rose-pink blooms. Those same parents also produced the vigorous 'Chocolate Drop',

about 8 in. tall and 14 in. wide, with red-brown leaves and dusky rose-pink blooms.

S. spurium. TWO-ROW SEDUM. Zones US, MS, LS, CS; USDA 6-9. From the Caucasus. Low-growing plant with trailing stems and dark green or bronze-tinted leaves just an inch or so long; spreads to 2 ft. or wider. In summer, pink flowers appear in dense clusters at ends of 4- to 5-in. stems. For rock garden, pattern planting, ground cover. 'Dragon's Blood' ('Schorbuser Blut') bears purplish bronze leaves, dark red blooms. Red-leafed selections include 'Red Carpet' (with red blossoms) and 'Fuldaglut' (with rosy pink flowers). 'John Creech' has small, scalloped green leaves and pink blossoms. Leaves of 'Tricolor' are variegated in green, creamy white, and pink; flowers are pink. 'Voodoo' has reddish leaves and red flowers.

S. telephium. LIVE-FOREVER SEDUM. Zones US, MS, LS, CS; USDA 6-9. Native from Europe eastward to Japan. Old favorite. To 2 ft. high, 1–2 ft. wide. Resembles *S. spectabile* but has gray-green, somewhat narrower leaves. Long-lasting floral display begins in late summer and fall; blossom clusters open purplish pink, age to brownish maroon. Plant dies to ground in winter. Plant in full sun (stems tend to flop in shaded sites). Moderate to regular water.

Desert series. Compact and vigorous. 'Desert Black' (very dark purple leaves, rose-pink flowers) and 'Desert Blonde' (blue-green leaves, creamy yellow flowers) reach about 8 in. tall and 11 in. wide. 'Desert Red' (blue-green leaves, deep pink flowers) is just 6 in. high, 11. in. wide.

'Möhrchen'. Grows 2 ft. high, 1½ ft. wide, with purple new growth and rosy pink flowers.

'Picolette'. To 15 in. high and wide; bronze-red foliage, pink flowers.

'Postman's Pride'. To 2 ft. high and wide, with small, deep purple leaves and pinkish red flowers that mature to burgundy.

'Purple Emperor'. Grows 18 in. high and wide, with dark purple foliage and dusty pink blooms.

'Red Cauli'. To 15 in. high and wide. Purple-tinted, gray-green leaves; red flowers.

'Strawberries and Cream'. To 1 ft. high, 1½ ft. wide. Purple-tinted

green leaves; green-centered white flowers.

'Xenox'. Grows 14 in. high and 18 in. wide, with mauve-green foliage that matures to burgundy-purple. Pink flowers.

'Yellow Xenox'. Grows 16 in. high, 20 in. wide, with dark foliage and yellow flowers.

S. ternatum. MOUNTAIN SEDUM. Native to moist, open woodlands in eastern U.S. Spreads by creeping stems to form large, low (3- to 6-in.-tall) mats of pretty foliage. The small, roundish, ½- to 1-in.-long leaves grow in whorls of three; they are pale green when new, aging to dark green. Blooms profusely in late spring and early summer, when ½-in. white flowers with purple-red stamens open along the stems. Thrives in moist soil with plenty of organic matter. Partial to full shade. 'Larinem Park' is compact and choice.

S. tetractinum. CHINESE SEDUM. Zones US, MS, LS; USDA 6-8. From China. Cascading stems, loaded with flat, nearly round leaves ½–¾ in. across, form a clump 2–3 in. tall and 1–2 ft. wide. Leaves are bright glossy green, often with reddish margins; turn a rich reddish bronze in fall. In early summer, clusters of bright yellow flowers just above the foliage. 'Coral Reef' has rounded, rich green leaves that turn reddish bronze in winter.

S. 'Vera Jameson'. Zones US, MS, LS, CS; USDA 6-9. This popular hybrid grows 8–12 in. high and 1½ ft. wide, with spreading purple stems clothed in pinkish purple leaves. Rose-pink flowers in late summer and fall. Dies to ground in winter.

SELAGINELLA

Selaginellaceae
Perennials

🗡 **MS, LS, CS, TS; USDA 7-9, EXCEPT AS NOTED**

◑ ● **PARTIAL TO FULL SHADE**

💧 **REGULAR WATER**

Selaginella kraussiana

Evergreen or semievergreen ground covers—mosslike, beautiful, and easy to grow in

ABOVE: Selaginella braunii

humid, moist shade and slightly acid soils with lots of organic matter. Some of the many species form erect tufts of green often mistaken for ferns, but most spread very low to the ground, the sprawling stems rooting as they grow.

S. braunii. ARBORVITAE FERN. From China. Easy-to-grow, erect plant to 1½ ft. high, spreading widely. Lower stems are undivided; upper, much-branched stems carry lacy dark green leaves.

S. kraussiana. CLUB MOSS, TRAILING SPIKEMOSS. Native to tropical and southern Africa. Creeping, trailing habit; grows 1 in. tall and spreads widely by rooting stems. Bright green leaves. Useful for hanging baskets. 'Aurea' has bright golden green foliage; 'Brownii' is especially dwarf, forming a 2-in.-tall cushion on the soil. 'Variegata' has bright green foliage splashed with cream.

S. lepidophylla. RESURRECTION PLANT. Native from Arizona and Texas southward to Peru. To 3 in. high, 6 in. wide; branched to base. Dense tufts of dark green leaves. Gets its common name from the fact that it curls into a ball when dry but opens flat when soaked in water.

S. pallescens. DWARF CEDAR FERN. Native to North and Central America. To 6 in. high, 1 ft. wide; branched nearly to base. Leaves are light yellow-green above, white beneath.

S. stauntoniana. STAUNTON'S SPIKEMOSS. From China. Slowly spreading habit to at least 12 in. wide, with many 8-in.-tall stems rising from rhizomes. Good in dryish woodland gardens.

S. uncinata. PEACOCK MOSS. From China. Creeping, trailing habit; 1–2 in. tall, spreading to 2 ft. across by rooting stems. In filtered light, leaves are bright metallic blue-green.

SEMPERVIVUM
HOUSELEEK
Crassulaceae
Succulent perennials

✎ **US, MS, LS, CS; USDA 6-9**

☼ ◐ **FULL SUN TO LIGHT SHADE**

◊ ◉ **LITTLE TO MODERATE WATER**

Sempervivum hybrid

Native to mountains of Europe. Form tightly packed rosettes of fleshy, evergreen leaves; spread by little offsets that cluster around parent rosette. Clustered, star-shaped summer flowers in white, yellowish, pink, red, or greenish; pretty in detail but not showy. Blooming rosettes die after setting seed, but offsets (easily detached and replanted) carry on. There are many species; all are good in rock gardens, pots, even in pockets in boulders or pieces of porous rock. Need excellent drainage. Water only to prevent shriveling.

S. arachnoideum. COBWEB HOUSELEEK. Gray-green rosettes of many leaves are joined by fine hairs for a cobweb-covered look. Larger rosettes (to 2 in. wide) are surrounded by a host of smaller ones. Spreads slowly to make a dense mat to 1 ft. or wider. Bright red flowers on 4- to 6-in. stems. 'Cebennense' has cobwebby green leaves with burgundy tips. Leaves of 'Rubrum' are flushed with red in spring.

S. hybrids. Most selections sold fall into this category. All form crowded rosettes that vary mainly in color and leaf shape. 'Oddity' is the most widely sold, with burgundy-tipped green tubular leaves; grows 8 in. high, 12 in. wide. 'Black' has deep maroon leaves with contrasting green new growth. 'Carmen' has

large rosettes of green leaves tipped in red. Leaves of 'Krebs' are chocolatey green; those of 'Rubikon Improved' are red.

S. tectorum. HEN AND CHICKENS. Gray-green, 2- to 5-in.-wide rosettes spread quickly to form clumps to 2 ft. or wider. Leaves have red-brown, bristly tips. Red or reddish blossoms are borne on stems to 2 ft. tall. An old-time passalong plant.

SENECIO
Asteraceae
Annuals, perennials, and evergreen or deciduous vines

✎ **ZONES VARY BY SPECIES**

☼ ◐ **EXPOSURE NEEDS VARY BY SPECIES**

◊ ◉ ◉ **WATER NEEDS VARY BY SPECIES**

Senecio cineraria

Daisy relatives that range from garden cineraria and dusty miller to vines, shrubs, perennials, succulents, even a few weeds. Succulents are often sold as *Kleinia*, an earlier name.

S. cineraria. DUSTY MILLER. Shrubby perennial in Zones MS, LS, CS; USDA 7-9. Annual in the Upper South. To 2–2½ ft. tall and wide. Woolly white leaves cut into many blunt-tipped lobes; clustered heads of yellow or creamy yellow flowers in summer. Gets leggy unless sheared occasionally. Full sun. Needs good drainage, little to moderate water. Striking in night garden. Deer don't seem to care for it. 'Silver Dust' grows 10 in. high and wide, with deeply cut, velvety, silvery green leaves.

S. macroglossus. KENYA IVY, NATAL IVY, WAX VINE. Evergreen vine in the Tropical South; houseplant anywhere. From

Africa. Twining or trailing vine to 6½ ft., with thin, succulent stems and thick, 2- to 3-in.-wide, waxy or rubbery leaves shaped like ivy leaves, with three, five, or seven shallow lobes. Tiny yellow daisies in summer. Leaves of 'Variegatus' are boldly splashed with creamy white. Give part shade and moderate water. As houseplant, grow in sunny window and water only when soil is dry. Feed monthly with a general-purpose liquid houseplant fertilizer; in winter, stop fertilizing and reduce water.

S. viravira (*S. leucostachys*). DUSTY MILLER. Shrubby perennial. Zones MS, LS; USDA 7-8. Native to Argentina. To 4 ft. tall and wide, with sprawling habit. Leaves like those of *S. cineraria* but more strikingly white, more finely cut into much narrower, pointed segments. Creamy white summer flowers are not showy. In full sun, it is brilliantly white and densely leafy; in part shade, it is looser and more sparsely foliaged, with larger, greener leaves. Tip-pinch young plants to keep them compact. Moderate water.

S

SENNA

Caesalpiniaceae
Perennials and evergreen and
deciduous shrubs

🌡 **ZONES VARY BY SPECIES**

☼ ◐ **FULL SUN OR LIGHT SHADE**

💧💧 **MODERATE TO REGULAR
WATER, EXCEPT AS NOTED**

Senna bicapsularis

Previously included in *Cassia* and
still often sold as such, these
species have been reclassified as
Senna. Grown for their lavish
show of yellow, five-petaled
flowers that look something like
those of potentilla. Blossoms are
followed by seedpods that may
create litter; to reduce pod
production, prune lightly after
bloom. Rangy, rank growers
should also be cut back
periodically to encourage more
compact growth. Good for
screens, massing, background
plantings. Prefer well-drained soil.

S. alata. CANDLESTICK
SENNA. Evergreen shrub. Zones
CS, TS; USDA 9-11. Native to many
tropical regions of the world. May
reach 30 ft. tall and half as wide,
but more likely to be 6–10 ft. tall
and 3–4 ft. wide in gardens. Bright
green leaves divided into 14 to 28
oblong leaflets, each 2½ in. long.
Golden yellow, inch-wide flowers
in big, spikelike clusters appear
from fall into winter. Prune hard
after bloom.

S. artemisioides. FEATHERY
CASSIA. Evergreen shrub. Zones
LS, CS, TS; USDA 8-11. Native to
Australia. To 3–5 ft. tall and wide,
with attractive light, airy structure.
Gray leaves divided into six to
eight needlelike, 1-in.-long leaflets.
Bears bright yellow, ¾-in. flowers
in clusters of five to eight in winter
and spring, with bloom often

continuing into summer. Heavy
seed production. Very drought
tolerant but looks better with
moderate to regular water.

S. bicapsularis. CHRISTMAS
SENNA. Evergreen shrub. Zones
LS, CS, TS; USDA 8-11. Native
to tropical Central and South
America. Recovers after being
killed to ground by frost. To 10 ft.
tall and wide. Bright green leaves
with six to ten roundish, rather
thick leaflets, each to ¾ in. long.
Bright yellow, ½-in.-wide flowers in spikelike clusters from
midautumn to midwinter or until
cut down by frost. Prune severely
after flowering. Resembles
S. pendula glabrata, which can be
quite invasive; buy from a trusted
source to be sure you are getting
the true *S. bicapsularis*.

S. corymbosa. FLOWERY
SENNA. Evergreen shrub. Zones
LS, CS, TS, USDA 8-11. Native to
South America. Rangy growth to
10 ft. tall, 10–12 ft. wide. Dark green
leaves with six narrow, oblong,
1- to 2-in. leaflets. Rounded
clusters of 1½-in. bright yellow
flowers, spring to fall. Self-sowing
can be a problem.

S. lindheimeriana. VELVET-
LEAF SENNA. Perennial. Zones
LS, CS, TS; USDA 8-11. Native to
Texas, Arizona, Mexico. Usually
slender and upright to 2–3 ft. tall,
but may reach 6 ft. tall, 2 ft. wide.
Velvety gray leaves are divided
into 8 to 16 narrowly oval, pointed
leaflets, each 1–2 in. long. Rich
yellow, 1½-in.-wide flowers in late
summer and fall. Grows well in
caliche soils. Not a good choice
for high-rainfall areas or heavily
watered gardens; it will rot if soil
is too wet.

S. marilandica. WILD SENNA,
MARYLAND SENNA. Perennial.
Zones US, MS, LS, CS; USDA 6-9.
Native from Pennsylvania to
Florida, west to Iowa, Kansas, and
Texas. Slender and usually unbranched; grows 4–6 ft. tall, 2–3 ft.
wide. Feathery bright green leaves
are divided into 8 to 16 oval,
inch-long leaflets. Tall clusters of
brownish yellow flowers top the
stems in summer. Dies to ground
in winter.

S. splendida. GOLDEN WON-
DER SENNA. Evergreen shrub.
Zones CS, TS; USDA 9-11. Native
to Brazil. To 9–12 ft. high and 6–10
ft. wide, with bright green leaves
divided into four oval, pointed
leaflets to 3 in. long. Deep golden
yellow, 1½-in.-wide flowers come

in loose clusters at branch ends
from autumn into winter. This
common name has been applied
to a number of sennas of varying
growth habits; other "golden
wonder sennas" have bright yellow flowers and are strongly horizontal in branch pattern, growing
5–8 ft. high and spreading to
12 ft. wide. All sennas known by
this name produce many seeds
and should be severely pruned
after flowering.

S. wislizeni. CANYON SENNA.
Deciduous shrub. Zones LS, CS,
TS; USDA 8-11. Native to West
Texas, New Mexico, Arizona, and
Mexico. To 5–8 ft. tall and 5–10 ft.
wide. Attractive upright branches
hold small green leaves divided
into four to six leaflets, each 1¼
in. long. Clusters of bright yellow,
inch-wide flowers appear all summer. Little water.

SERENOA REPENS

SAW PALMETTO
Arecaceae
Palm

🌡 **LS, CS, TS; USDA 8-11**

☼ ◐ **FULL SUN OR PARTIAL
SHADE**

💧💧 **MODERATE TO REGULAR
WATER**

Serenoa repens

Native to the Coastal Plains from
South Carolina to Florida, and
west to Texas. This charming and
trouble-free fan palm grows into
a clump only 4–7 ft. tall and wide.
It adapts to a wide range of
habitats, from sand dunes and
dry scrub to moist woods and
wetlands. The short trunk may be
entirely underground or run
parallel to the ground. Green to
bluish green, palmate leaves are
2–3 ft. across, held on saw-

toothed leaf stems to 2 ft. long;
teeth are quite sharp, so take care
when handling, and site away
from areas where children play.
Clusters of small white flowers
give rise to berries that age from
yellowish green to blue-black. An
extract from the berries is used to
treat enlarged prostate in men.

Saw palmetto looks good in
foundation plantings, in naturalized areas, or massed under tall
trees. Plant in its permanent location, as established plants don't
transplant well. Hardy to 15°F. A
form with attractive silvery foliage
is popular and widely available;
blue-leafed forms are sometimes
available.

SESBANIA

Papilionaceae
Deciduous shrubs and trees

🌡 **CS, TS; USDA 9-11, EXCEPT AS
NOTED**

☼ **FULL SUN**

💧 **REGULAR WATER**

⚠ **SEEDS ARE POISONOUS IF
INGESTED**

Sesbania punicea

Fast-growing but short-lived
plants with broad, open canopies
of feathery foliage. Pretty,
pendent clusters of summer
flowers, reminiscent of wisteria,
are followed by beanlike
seedpods that dry and then rattle
in the wind. Need well-drained
soil. Somewhat drought tolerant.

S. drummondii. RATTLE-
BUSH. Shrub. Zones LS, CS, TS;
USDA 8-11. Native from Florida
to Arkansas and Texas. To 20 ft.
tall, 15 ft. wide; usually smaller
in colder part of range, where
branches often die back. Leaves
to 8 in. long, with 10 to 25 pairs of

oblong, 1-in. leaflets. Small (½-in.) flowers are yellow, sometimes marked with red; 2-in.-long seedpods.

S. grandiflora. SCARLET WISTERIA TREE. Tree. Native to tropical Asia; almost evergreen in warmest parts of the South. To 30–40 ft. tall, 15–20 ft. wide, with foot-long leaves made up of 10 to 30 pairs of 1- to 2-in. leaflets. Pendent clusters of sweet pea–shaped blossoms to 4 in. long, in rusty red, pink, or white. Pods can reach over 1 ft. long.

S. punicea. RATTLEBOX. Shrub. Native to North America; naturalized in the Coastal South. Sometimes sold as *Daubentonia*. Usually grows to 6 ft. tall, though it can reach up to 12 ft.; 5–8 ft. wide. Self-seeds, forming colonies (sometimes rather rangy looking) with broad, flat crowns of delicate foliage. Leaves are variable in length, with 6 to 20 pairs of ½- to 1-in. leaflets. Small vermilion flowers in 4-in. clusters appear over an especially long season, from early summer into early fall. Seedpods are 3–4 in. long.

SETARIA PALMIFOLIA

PALM GRASS
Poaceae
Perennial

🌿 **CS, TS; USDA 9-11; OR GROW IN POTS**

☀️ ◐ **FULL SUN OR LIGHT SHADE**

💧 **REGULAR WATER**

Setaria palmifolia 'Variegata'

To most people, this native of India doesn't look like a grass at all—its deeply pleated, swordlike leaves, 1–3 ft. long and 2–5 in. wide, more closely resemble the foliage of cast-iron plant (*Aspidistra*) or the expanding young fronds of a palm. The leaves arch gracefully from a central crown to form a large mound. In south Florida, clumps can grow 8–10 ft. tall and wide; where frosts occur (but the ground doesn't freeze), they reach about 3 ft. tall and wide. Cylindrical greenish flower spikes appear above the foliage in summer but are not particularly showy. Leaves of 'Rubra' have purplish midribs; 'Variegata' features white-edged foliage, burgundy stems, and reddish flower spikes.

In the garden, the coarse foliage of palm grass is an excellent foil for smaller or thinner leaves. The plant makes a fine container subject and also looks good as an understory plant in woodland gardens. Tolerates drought but looks better with regular moisture. Be careful where you plant it; palm grass self-sows aggressively and can become a pest.

SHALLOT

Liliaceae
Perennial often grown as annual

🌿 **US, MS, LS, CS, TS; USDA 6-11**

☀️ **FULL SUN**

💧 **REGULAR WATER**

Shallots

Closely related to onion and, like it, a member of the genus *Allium*. Thought to have originated in western or central Asia. The bulb is divided into cloves that grow on a common base; it is prized in cooking for its distinctive flavor, a combination of mild onion and pungent garlic. Young green shoots are also edible. Dutch shallots have golden brown skin and white cloves; red shallots have coppery skin, purple cloves.

CARE

In the Lower, Coastal, and Tropical South, you can plant shallots in fall to harvest green tops through winter and early spring, bulbs in late spring and summer. In the Upper and Middle South, plant them in early spring for green shoots in summer, bulbs in autumn.

Shallots are usually grown from cloves (sections of bulbs). You can purchase these from a seed company or simply buy shallots in the grocery store and separate them into cloves. Plant cloves pointed end up, 4–8 in. apart; cover with ½ in. of soil. You'll have green shoots in about 60 days, new bulbs in 90 to 120 days. Some seed companies sell seeds of selections such as 'Bonilla', 'Matador', and 'Prima'; plant 12 seeds per foot. Nurseries with stocks of herbs may sell growing plants. Feed regularly, especially early in the growing season, with a balanced liquid fertilizer. Keep soil moist during growth, but withhold water for a couple of weeks before harvest. Bulbs will be ready to harvest in about 100 days.

When bulbs are mature, shoots turn yellow and die. To harvest, pull up clumps and separate the bulbs; before using them, let dry for about a month in a cool, dry place. If stored properly, shallots will keep for up to eight months.

SHORTIA GALACIFOLIA

OCONEE BELLS
Diapensiaceae
Perennial

🌿 **US, MS; USDA 6-7**

◐ ● **PARTIAL TO FULL SHADE**

💧 💧💧 **REGULAR TO AMPLE WATER**

Shortia galacifolia

This elegant little plant hails from the mountains of Georgia, Tennessee, and North and South Carolina; it is difficult to grow outside of its small native range. Forms a foot-wide clump of evergreen, round or oval, glossy green, 1- to 3-in.-long leaves with scalloped edges. Each of the many 4- to 6-in.-high stems is topped in spring with a single bloom—a nodding, 1-inch-wide white bell with toothed edges. Spreads slowly by underground stems. Intolerant of extended summer heat. Needs acid, organically enriched soil. Grow with azaleas and rhododendrons.

SIDALCEA
CHECKERBLOOM,
MINIATURE HOLLYHOCK
Malvaceae
Perennials

🌿 **US, MS; USDA 6-7**

☀️ **FULL SUN**

💧 **REGULAR WATER, EXCEPT AS NOTED**

Sidalcea 'Elsie Heugh'

All are grown for clusters of five-petaled flowers like little hollyhocks (*Alcea*). Plants described here range from erect to sprawling; leaves are typically dark green, roundish to kidney-shaped, about 3 in. across. Basal leaves are shallowly lobed, stem leaves more deeply cut. Provide good drainage. Divide clumps every few years in spring or fall.

S. candida. Native to High Plains. To 2–3 ft. high, spreading by rhizomes to 1½ ft. wide. Unbranched stems bear bluish green leaves to 8 in. across. Crowded spikes of white, 1-in. flowers in midsummer.

S. hybrids. Most sidalceas grown in gardens are hybrids involving *S. candida*, *S. malviflora*, and *S. oregana* (a species native to much of the western U.S.). They form clumps to about 2 ft. wide and bear 1½- to 2-in. flowers; bloom all summer if deadheaded. Popular choices include 3-ft. 'Elsie Heugh', with fringed pale pink flowers; 2½-ft. 'Loveliness' (shell-pink); 2- to 3-ft. 'Party Girl' (deep pink); 3-ft. 'Rosanna' (deep purplish pink); and 3-ft. 'William Smith' (salmon-tinted, deep rose-pink). 'Little Princess' is compact at just 11–15 in. tall and about as wide; its profuse flowers are soft pink.

S. malviflora. CHECK-

ERBLOOM. Native to Oregon, California, Baja California. May grow erect to 2 ft. high and wide; or may sprawl and spread more widely by rooting at the nodes. Pink or purplish pink, 2-in. flowers in early spring. Moderate water.

SILENE
Caryophyllaceae
Perennials

🌿 **ZONES VARY BY SPECIES**

☀️ **FULL SUN OR PARTIAL SHADE, EXCEPT AS NOTED**

💧 **WATER NEEDS VARY BY SPECIES**

Silene virginica

The plants listed here are North American wildflowers with showy white, pink, or bright red blossoms. Some grow upright; others form low mats. Excellent for use in naturalized areas, in woodland and rock gardens, and at the front of the border. Provide fertile, well-drained soil.

S. caroliniana. WILD PINK. Zones US, MS, LS, CS; USDA 6-9. Native from Florida to New Hampshire, west to Missouri. Low-growing (4- to 8-in.-tall) mound to 1 ft. across. Bluish green leaves to 5 in. long; clusters of upward-facing, inch-wide, white to deep pink flowers with notched petals in late spring, early summer. Best in sandy or gravelly soil. Little to moderate water. 'Short and Sweet' has deep pink blooms.

S. laciniata. MEXICAN CATCHFLY. Zones US, MS, LS, CS; USDA 6-9. Native to mountains of Mexico, New Mexico, and California. Somewhat sprawling, 2- to 3-ft. stems carry leaves 1–5 in. long. Blooms in summer, bearing showy, bright red, inch-wide flow-

ers with deeply fringed petals. Likes full sun and lean soil. Little to moderate water. 'Jack Flash' produces brilliant orange-red flowers over a long period.

S. polypetala. FRINGED CAMPION. Zones US, MS, LS; USDA 6-8. Native to the southern Appalachians. Rare and endangered; be careful to buy only nursery-propagated plants. Dark green, spoon-shaped leaves to 4 in. long form a mat to 1½ ft. across, 4–6 in. high. Blooms in late spring, bearing lovely soft pink flowers to 1½ in. across; petal tips are deeply fringed, the fringes fading to white with age. Lovely plant for a woodland garden; needs partial shade and moist, well-drained soil loaded with organic matter. 'Longwood', a hybrid with *S. caroliniana*, has fringed, deep pink flowers and forms an evergreen mound to 8 in. high.

S. regia. ROYAL CATCHFLY. Zones US, MS, LS, CS; USDA 6-9. Native to eastern U.S. To 3–4 ft. high, 1½–2 ft. wide. Slender, often reclining stems carry thick, lance-shaped leaves to 5 in. long. Small clusters of 2-in.-wide scarlet blossoms appear in summer. The common name "catchfly" comes from the sticky calyxes—they can trap small insects. Best in partial shade. Little to moderate water. 'Prairie Fire' is vigorous and free-blooming.

S. virginica. FIRE PINK. Zones US, MS, LS; USDA 6-8. Native to eastern and central U.S. Narrow, lance-shaped leaves to 4 in. long in a clump 1–2 ft. tall and 1 ft. wide. Clusters of inch-wide crimson flowers with deeply notched petals in late spring or early summer. Regular water.

SILPHIUM
Asteraceae
Perennials

🌿 **US, MS, LS, CS; USDA 6-9, EXCEPT AS NOTED**

☀️ **FULL SUN OR LIGHT SHADE**

💧 **MODERATE TO REGULAR WATER, EXCEPT AS NOTED**

Silphium perfoliatum

Native to the Midwestern prairies as well as the scrublands of the Southeast, these tough, pest-free, underappreciated perennials feature tall spikes of showy, sunflower-like blooms in mid- to late summer. Broken stems exude a gummy sap that smells like pine or turpentine—hence the common name "rosinweed." Erect stalks holding loose, branching clusters of blooms rise from a clump of large basal leaves; stalk leaves are smaller. In most species, the foliage is rough and hairy. Plants tolerate wet or dry conditions, grow particularly well in heavy soil. Easily started from seed or grown from young transplants. Good additions to wildflower meadows, naturalized areas, and (if staked) the back of the border. Resist deer.

S. dentatum. STARRY ROSINWEED. To 6 ft. tall, 2–3 ft. wide. Dark green, shallowly toothed leaves reach 1 ft. long. Star-shaped light yellow flowers with greenish yellow centers reach 4 in. across.

S. laciniatum. COMPASS PLANT. Common name refers to the basal leaves' tendency to orient themselves on a north-south axis. Foliage is green with pink veins; deeply cut basal leaves reach 1½ ft. long, form a clump 2 ft. across. Blossom stalks rise 6–9 ft. high, carrying showy yellow flowers up to 5 in. across.

S. perfoliatum. CUP PLANT.

Paired basal leaves are fused at the squarish stems, forming a "cup" that catches water; birds and butterflies will stop by for a sip. Dark green, nearly hairless, coarsely toothed leaves reach 14 in. long, may be triangular or pointed-oval; plant grows about 3 ft. wide. Stalks rising 4–8 ft. bear bright yellow, daisylike flowers up to 3 in. wide. Grows naturally in moist soils; provide regular water.

S. terebinthinaceum. PRAIRIE DOCK. Light green, spade-shaped basal leaves with coarsely toothed edges can reach 2 ft. long. Almost leafless flower stalks range from 3–10 ft. tall, may be red or green; blossoms are bright yellow, 2–3 in. wide. Plants reach 4–6 ft. wide. Once the stout taproot is established, prairie dock tolerates considerable drought.

SINNINGIA

Gesneriaceae
Perennials

🖊 **ZONES VARY BY SPECIES**

☼ ◐ **FULL SUN OR LIGHT SHADE; BRIGHT INDIRECT LIGHT**

◊ ◖ ◕ ◕ **WATER NEEDS VARY BY SPECIES**

Sinningia speciosa

This group includes a number of perennials, mostly native to tropical forests of South America. All are grown for their colorful, showy, solitary or clustered flowers in the shape of tubes, trumpets, or bells. These plants require well-drained soil.

S. hybrids. Zones LS, CS, TS; USDA 8-11. Breeding work in recent years has produced a number of deciduous hybrids of complex parentage. Flowering stems of most are held well above foliage clumps. Examples include deep pink 'Arkansas Bells' (3 ft. tall and wide), light yellow 'Bananas Foster' (2 ft. tall and wide), mauve-pink 'Carolyn' (3 ft. tall, 2 ft. wide), peachy pink 'Georgia Peach' (15 in. tall, 1 ft. wide), and pink 'Pink Pockets' (just 10 in. tall, 2 ft. wide). All take moderate water.

S. sellovii. Zones LS, CS, TS; USDA 8-11. From Argentina. Upright stems are set with thick, light green, sandpapery leaves. Erect or nearly horizontal flower spikes are 2½–4 ft. long, each set with 100 or more small hanging flowers that resemble fuzzy orange or orange-red goldfish. Yellow and red forms are available. Beloved by hummingbirds. With age, develops a large tuber that tends to push above ground. Mulch any exposed part of the tuber well to protect it from temperatures below 25°F. Give this plant plenty of room. Little to moderate water.

S. speciosa (*Gloxinia speciosa*). GLOXINIA. Indoor plant. Native to Brazil. Squat, full-foliaged plant to 1 ft. high and wide. Broad, oval leaves reach 6 in. or longer, look like quilted green velvet. Blooms in summer, producing showy, velvety-sheened, ruffled bells up to 4 in. wide in a cluster near top of plant. Colors include white, red, pink, blue, and light to dark shades of purple. Some flowers have dark dots or blotches, others contrasting bands at edges. 'Carangola' is white with a deep blue-purple interior.

Gloxinias need constant warmth and are most often grown in a greenhouse or as houseplants, though they can be taken outdoors in warm weather. Tubers are usually available in winter or spring. For each tuber, choose a container big enough to leave 2 in. between all sides of tuber and container edges. Fill with a mix of equal parts peat moss, perlite, and leaf mold or compost; set tuber ½ in. deep. Place in a warm spot (about 72°F during day, no cooler than 65°F at night) with plenty of bright light but no direct sun. Water sparingly until first leaves appear, then increase watering as roots and leaves grow. Apply water to soil only, or pour it into a saucer to be absorbed through pot's drainage holes (pour off any water left unabsorbed after an hour). Feed with a general-purpose liquid houseplant fertilizer diluted to half-strength; start feeding when leaves emerge, then feed every two weeks until flowers fade. After bloom has finished, gradually dry off plants. When leaves have died down completely, move container to dark place where temperatures remain around 60°F. Mist soil just enough to keep tubers from shriveling. When tubers show signs of resuming growth in midwinter, repot in fresh soil mix. If roots have filled container, move tuber to a larger pot.

S. tubiflora. HARDY GLOXINIA. Zones LS, CS, TS; USDA 8-11. From Argentina, Paraguay, Uruguay. As its common name suggests, this is a hardy perennial in much of the South. Growing from tubers, it forms 1- to 2-ft.-wide clumps of velvety green leaves to 5 in. long, 1½ in. wide. Fragrant, tubular white flowers, 2–3 in. long, appear on spikes to 2 ft. tall throughout the summer. Needs moderate water and fertile, very well-drained soil. Excellent in a rock garden or large container.

SISYRINCHIUM

Iridaceae
Perennials

🖊 **ZONES VARY BY SPECIES**

☼ ◐ **FULL SUN OR LIGHT SHADE**

◊ ◖ ◕ ◕ **WATER NEEDS VARY BY SPECIES**

Sisyrinchium angustifolium

Iris relatives with narrow, grasslike leaves and small, six-segmented flowers that open in sunshine. The blossoms are pretty up close but not showy from a distance. Best suited for informal gardens or naturalizing; small types are good in rock gardens. Easy to start from seed; will self-sow. Not usually browsed by deer.

S. angustifolium. COMMON BLUE-EYED GRASS. Zones US, MS, LS, CS, TS; USDA 6-11. Native to North America. Grows 6–18 in. tall, 6 in. wide, with dark green leaves and clusters of ½-in. blue blossoms in summer. 'Lucerne' is 8–10 in. tall and bears large, bright blue flowers over a long period; 'Mrs. Spivey', with pure white blooms, may reach 2½ ft. tall. 'Suwanee', which may be a hybrid, is a compact grower to about 8 in. tall; vigorous and adaptable, with a profusion of sky-blue flowers. Moderate to regular water.

S. atlanticum. ATLANTIC BLUE-EYED GRASS. Zones US, MS, LS; USDA 6-8. Native to eastern U.S. Violet-blue flowers with yellow centers are carried on slender, wiry, branched stems that range in height from 4 in. to 2½ ft. tall. Plants reach 6–8 in. wide. Pale grayish green leaves. Blooms from late spring into early summer. Regular water.

S. striatum. ARGENTINE YELLOW-EYED GRASS. Zones MS, LS, CS; USDA 7-9. Native to Chile, Argentina. To 3 ft. tall, 1 ft. wide, with attractive gray-green leaves. In spring, produces spikelike clusters of many ½-in. flowers in pale yellow streaked with brown; blooms well into summer if old flower clusters are removed (if you don't remove them, you may have hordes of unwanted seedlings the next year). Leaves of 'Aunt May' ('Variegatum') are striped with creamy yellow. Moderate water.

S. tinctorium. MEXICAN YELLOW-EYED GRASS. Zones US, MS, LS, CS; USDA 6-9. From Mexico and South America. To 1 ft. high and wide. Narrow, blue-green leaves; light yellow, ¾-in. flowers from early spring into summer. 'Puerto Yellow' has bright yellow blossoms. Moderate to regular water.

S

SKIMMIA JAPONICA

JAPANESE SKIMMIA
Rutaceae
Evergreen shrub

☀ **US, MS; USDA 6-7**

◐ ● **PARTIAL TO FULL SHADE**

💧 **REGULAR WATER**

Skimmia japonica

Handsome shrub from Japan and China. Compact, slow grower to 2–5 ft. or taller, 3–6 ft. wide. Glossy, rich green leaves are oval and pointed, to 3–4 in. long and 1 in. wide, most often clustered toward the twig ends. In spring, 2- to 3-in. clusters of tiny, fragrant white flowers open from pinkish buds held well above foliage. Flowers are larger and more fragrant on male plants. If a male plant is present, female plants produce bright red fruit resembling holly (*Ilex*) berries in fall and winter; these are attractive enough to make planting both sexes worth the effort. Plants tend to be sold as simply "male" and "female" rather than by selection name. A form with ivory-white berries is available. *S. j. reevesiana* (sometimes sold as *S. reevesiana*) is looser and more open in habit, growing slowly to 1½–3 ft. high, 2–3 ft. wide; it is self-fertile, producing dull red berries.

Good under windows, beside shaded walks, flanking entryways, in containers. Prefers moist, highly organic, acid soils; must have good drainage. Mites are the main pests; they give foliage a sunburned look. Thrips may also attack. Shield from cold, sweeping winds.

SMILAX

GREENBRIER, CATBRIER
Liliaceae
Evergreen, semievergreen, deciduous vines

☀ **MS, LS, CS; USDA 7-9**

☀ ☀ **FULL SUN OR PARTIAL SHADE, EXCEPT AS NOTED**

💧 💧 **LITTLE TO REGULAR WATER**

Smilax smallii

Native to the Americas, this is a large group of tough, moderately fast-growing, evergreen to deciduous vines that grow from rhizomes or large tubers. Some species are valuable ornamentals, others flat-out weeds; some are viciously thorny, others nearly thornless. All climb by tendrils. Greenish or yellowish flowers in spring or early summer are small and insignificant, but the berries that follow are often showy and are relished by birds. Because many species look similar, this is a difficult group to sort out; the common names can be as tangled as the vines.

S. bona-nox. SAW GREEN-BRIER, CATBRIER, BULLBRIER. Semievergreen to deciduous. May scramble to 20 ft., but usually forms large thickets close to the ground. The prickly, squarish green stems are set with glossy green, 2- to 5-in.-long leaves shaped like fiddles or arrowheads; leaves may have lighter green blotches. Blue-black berries. Best use for this weedy plant is as wildlife cover. Partial shade.

S. glauca. CAT GREENBRIER, SAWBRIER. Deciduous. To 8–12 ft., with thin stems armed with short prickles. Oval to kidney-shaped green leaves with silvery undersides reach 6 in. long, turn orange-red in fall. Blue-black berries. Worth leaving in a naturalized

area to attract birds.

S. pumila. DWARF SMILAX, WILD SARSAPARILLA. Evergreen in the southern part of its range, deciduous farther north. Low-growing vine trails to 10 ft., with oval to lance-shaped, glossy, green leaves to 4 in. long. Thornless, fuzzy stems. Clustered, showy berries change from golden to red in fall. Can be used as a casual ground cover. Best in sandy soil and partial to full shade.

S. rotundifolia. COMMON GREENBRIER, HORSE BRIER. Deciduous. Vigorous, high-climbing (to 20-ft.) scrambler with thorny, squarish stems. Green leaves with lighter green markings are round to heart shaped, up to 6 in. long. Blue-black berries. Grows from a huge tuber. Good choice for a wildlife garden.

S. smallii. JACKSON VINE, LANCELEAF GREENBRIER. Evergreen. The most important ornamental species, this old favorite, named for Stonewall Jackson, is prized for its glossy, deep green foliage; leaves and stems are popular for holiday decorations, as they retain their color long after cutting. The plant climbs to 10 ft.; it's a favorite for training over doorways, windows, and arbors in the Lower South. Stems near the plant's base are thorny, but thinner stems higher up are essentially thornless. Oval, pointed leaves are 6 in. long. Clustered berries are large and colorful, maturing from green through red to blackish blue. Jackson vine is usually started from enormous tubers dug from the wild but can be easily started from seed.

S. walteri. CORAL GREEN-BRIER. Deciduous. Thin-stemmed species to a possible 20 ft.; noted for bright orange-red berries. Leathery, rounded to oval, bright green leaves to 5 in. long; they turn orange-red in fall. Stems near the plant's base are prickly, but upper stems are thornless. Tolerates wet soil and just about any exposure. Good for bringing fall color to naturalized areas.

SOLANDRA MAXIMA

CUP-OF-GOLD VINE, CHALICE VINE
Solanaceae
Evergreen vine

☀ **TS; USDA 10-11**

☀ **FULL SUN**

💧 **REGULAR WATER**

☇ **ALL PLANT PARTS ARE POISONOUS**

Solandra maxima

Native from Mexico to Venezuela and Colombia. Fast-growing, sprawling, rampant vine to 40 ft.; must be tied to its support. Heavy stems bear highly polished, broadly oval, rich green leaves to 6 in. long. Inflated-looking buds open to big (6- to 8-in.), leathery, bowl-shaped, five-lobed flowers that release a coconut fragrance at night; blooms are golden yellow, with a red-brown stripe running down the inside of each lobe. Main bloom period is summer, but scattered flowering can occur at any time. Use on big walls and pergolas, along eaves, as bank cover. Spectacular along fence near swimming pool. Can be trimmed back to make a rough hedge.

CARE

Give good, well-drained soil for best growth. Provide shade for roots in hottest climates. Light frost blackens the leaves, but plants usually recover to produce new growth. Cut back long, vigorous shoots to induce branching and more flowers. To make it easy to see inside the big flowers, encourage growth low on plant by tip-pinching. Pruning is best done in late winter or early spring. Often sold as *S. guttata*.

SOLANUM

Solanaceae

Evergreen, semievergreen, and deciduous shrubs and vines

ZONES VARY BY SPECIES

FULL SUN OR PARTIAL SHADE

MODERATE TO REGULAR WATER, EXCEPT AS NOTED

MANY SPECIES ARE POISONOUS IF INGESTED; MOST ARE SUSPECT

Solanum crisipum 'Glasnevin'

In addition to eggplant and potato (described under those names), *Solanum* includes a number of ornamental plants. All have small, star-shaped, five-petaled blue or white flowers with reproductive parts that form a pointed yellow structure in the blossom's center. A few of the species described here produce decorative fruit.

S. crispum. Evergreen vine. Zones CS, TS; USDA 9-11. From Chile, Peru. Modest (even shrubby) climber to 12 ft., with ovate to lance-shaped, soft green, often wavy-edged leaves to 5 in. long. In summer, bears 4-in. clusters of fragrant, lilac-blue flowers with yellow centers. Small, inedible yellowish fruit. Must be fastened to its support; well suited to trellises, walls, posts. May lose leaves in hard frost. Selection 'Glasnevin' has deeper blue flowers in larger clusters.

S. jasminoides (*S. laxum*). POTATO VINE. Evergreen or semievergreen vine. Zones LS, CS, TS; USDA 8-11. From Brazil. Twines rapidly to 30 ft. Purplish-tinged, arrow-shaped, 1½- to 3-in.-long leaves. Bluish white, 1-in. flowers are carried on threadlike stalks in clusters of up to 12; bloom is almost continuous all year, heavi-

est in spring. Grown for flowers or to provide light overhead shade. Cut back severely at any time to prevent tangling, promote vigorous new growth. Control rampant runners that grow along ground. 'Album' bears pure white flowers; 'Variegatum' has leaves edged with creamy yellow.

S. pseudocapsicum. JERUSALEM CHERRY. Evergreen shrub. Zones CS, TS; USDA 9-11; annual or indoor/outdoor plant anywhere. From Madeira; widely naturalized in tropics and subtropics. To 3-4 ft. high and wide (about half that size if grown as an annual). Shiny, deep green, smooth, elliptical leaves to 4 in. long. White, ½-in. summer flowers are followed in autumn by a fine show of scarlet (rarely yellow), ½-in. fruit that looks like cherry tomatoes but is poisonous. In mildest-winter areas, plant bears flowers and fruit (and self-sows) year-round. More popular than taller kinds are the many dwarf strains, which grow to 1 ft. high and bear larger fruit (to 1 in. across). Leaves and developing fruit of 'Variegatum' are striped in green and white; fruit matures to orange.

S. seaforthianum. BRAZILIAN NIGHTSHADE. Evergreen or semievergreen vine. Zone TS; USDA 10-11. Slender-stemmed plant to 15 ft.; must be fastened to its support. Oval, 4- to 8-in.-long, medium green leaves are either undivided or quite deeply cleft into three or more lobes. Clusters of violet-blue, 1-in.-wide flowers bloom in summer. Pea-size red fruit is enjoyed by birds but should not be eaten by people.

S. wendlandii. COSTA RICAN NIGHTSHADE. Deciduous vine. Zone TS; USDA 10-11. From Costa Rica. To 15-20 ft., climbing by twining stems and hooked spines. Glossy, green, ovate or (sometimes) lobed leaves 4-10 in. long are corrugated in texture. Foliage forms a lush backdrop for dense, domed clusters of lavender-blue, 2½-in. summer flowers. Somewhat reminiscent of bougainvillea. Let it clamber into tall trees, cover a pergola, decorate eaves of large house. Loses leaves in low temperatures, even without frost; slow to leaf out in spring.

S. wrightii (*S. macranthum*). BLUE POTATO TREE. Evergreen shrub. Zone TS; USDA 10-11. From Brazil. Grows quickly to 6-15 ft. tall

and wide; can be kept smaller by tip-pinching or pruned up into a small tree. Prickly, irregularly lobed leaves to 15 in. long. Fragrant flowers 2-2½ in. across open purple and age through shades of lavender to white; blooms intermittently from spring to fall. Needs rich soil. Good for a tropical effect.

SOLEIROLIA SOLEIROLII

BABY'S TEARS

Urticaceae

Perennial

CS, TS; USDA 9-11; OR HOUSEPLANT

PARTIAL TO FULL SHADE; BRIGHT INDIRECT LIGHT

REGULAR TO AMPLE WATER

Soleirolia soleirolii

You practically have to accept on faith that baby's tears has leaves, because even from a short distance they're almost too tiny to see. Native to the Mediterranean region, this tender perennial grows 2-4 in. high, spreading indefinitely by creeping stems to form a lush green mat. Gardeners in the Coastal and Tropical South can grow it outside in a moist, shady spot—but most people treat it as a favored houseplant. Indoors, give it bright indirect light; be sure to shield it from hot sun. Keep the soil evenly moist, but water a bit less in winter. Feed every other week in spring and summer and monthly in fall and winter with a general-purpose liquid houseplant fertilizer diluted to half-strength. Makes an excellent tabletop or windowsill houseplant and also does well in terrariums. Easily propagated by

division or cuttings. Selections with golden green and silver leaves are sometimes offered. Formerly known as *Helxine soleirolii*.

SOLENOSTEMON SCUTELLARIODES

COLEUS

Lamiaceae

Perennials usually grown as annuals

TS; USDA 10-11; ANYWHERE AS ANNUAL; OR HOUSEPLANT

SOME FORMS TAKE SUN, OTHERS SHADE; BRIGHT INDIRECT LIGHT

REGULAR TO AMPLE WATER

Solenostemon scutellarioides 'Dipt in Wine'

Coleus hybrids were all the rage when they were first introduced into Europe from Java in the 1700s—and their popularity has remained high. The dizzying array of electrifying colors and foliage shapes enthralled the Victorians, and more than 100 years later, these seed-grown, shade-loving plants are still the most widely sold types. Useful for adding color to beds, in window boxes, and in pots used indoors or out. They need constantly moist, fertile, well-drained soil and should be fed every other week from spring to fall with a general-purpose, water-soluble fertilizer. Pinch out flower spikes as soon as they appear (they are not attractive, and, if allowed to develop, they'll cause plants to look leggy and untidy).

Don't plant too early in spring—all coleus hate the cold. They're winter-hardy only in south Florida and south Texas. (Cuttings root quickly in water, though, so gardeners in cold-winter areas can save prized

TOP: Solenostemon scutellariodes 'Alligator Tears'; *S. s.* 'Royal Glissade'; *MIDDLE: S. s.* 'Keystone Kopper'; *BOTTOM: S. s.* 'Henna'; *S. s.* 'Lime Time'

range from tiny-leafed ground-cover types to large-foliaged sorts with the size and form of small shrubs. They also bloom sparsely, which is good since the flowers aren't pretty. The following listing describes just a few of the hundreds of selections; you will find them in mail-order nursery catalogs and, increasingly, in garden and home centers. With the exception of their light requirements, care for them as you would for seed-grown coleus. They grow about as wide as tall, except as noted.

'Alabama Sunset'. Large cranberry-pink leaves with gold centers. Grows to 3–4 ft., with shrublike form.

'Alligator Tears'. Green, spear-shaped leaves with light yellow centers. Grows 2 ft. tall. Part of the ColorBlaze series.

'Aurora'. Broad, luminescent leaves of cream, pink, and green with soft pink undersides. To 2 ft.

'Big Red Judy'. Large, brick-red leaves with serrated edges. Upright growth to 4 ft. tall.

'Buttercream'. Strongly ruffled leaves of soft cream edged in medium green. A little over 2 ft. tall.

'Dipt in Wine'. Crimson leaves edged with lime-green. Grows 2 ft. tall. Part of the ColorBlaze series.

'Ducksfoot Red'. Trailing type with small maroon leaves that resemble a duck's foot. To 2 ft. tall and a little wider. 'Ducksfoot Yellow' is similar in size and form.

'Electric Lime'. Bright lime-green leaves prominently veined with chartreuse. To 20 in. tall, spreading a bit wider.

'Gay's Delight'. Chartreuse to yellow, slightly cupped leaves sport dramatic dark purple veins. Upright grower to 2 ft.

'Henna'. Foliage is splashed with chartreuse and coppery red. Each deeply toothed leaf curls to show its burgundy underside. Bushy growth to 20 in. high.

'India Frills'. Tough, sprawling ground cover type to 1 ft. tall and 2 ft. wide. Small, deeply cut leaves in soft red with sharply contrasting yellow and green edges.

'Inky Fingers'. Rounded, deeply lobed, bright green leaves with dark purple centers. To 2 ft. tall, 1½ ft. wide.

'Keystone Kopper'. Coppery-orange leaves. Grows 2 ft. tall. Part of the ColorBlaze series.

'Kiwi Fern'. Low-growing form with deeply cut burgundy leaves edged in gold and green. May reach 1½ ft.

'Lime Time'. Bright chartreuse foliage resembles that of 'Wasabi'. Grows 2 ft. tall. Part of the Color-Blaze series.

'Mardi Gras'. Bushy plant with foliage splashed in red, green, and yellow. To 1½ ft.

'Orange King'. Exquisite selection features broad, orange-tinged golden leaves with reddish purple undersides and purple stems. To 2 ft. tall and 1½ ft. wide.

'Plum Parfait'. Pointed, serrated leaves in rich purple with wide pink margin and a thin, chartreuse edge. To 3 ft. tall. Part of SuperSun series.

'Redhead'. Large, uniform, serrated leaves are bright true red. Upright grower to 2 ft. tall and wide.

'Royal Glissade'. Raspberry-purple leaves dusted with yellow-green. Grows 2 ft. tall. Part of the ColorBlaze series.

'Saturn'. Maroon leaves with contrasting edges and centers of guacamole green. To 1½ ft. tall.

'Sedona'. Rusty-orange leaves with hints of burgundy. To 2 ft. tall. Part of the ColorBlaze series.

'The Line'. Narrow, pointed leaves in soft yellow with a prominent purple midvein. To 1½ ft. tall.

'Trusty Rusty'. Deeply scalloped leaves are coppery red with a golden yellow edge with a beaded look. To 2 ft. tall.

'Vino'. Large, velvety, burgundy leaves with serrated margins of bright lime-green; with more sun, the foliage darkens to nearly black. Upright grower to 30 in. tall.

'Wasabi'. Bright chartreuse leaves with lobed edges hold their color beautifully even in full sun. Vigorous, upright grower to about 2 ft. tall.

selections from year to year.) Large-leafed strains such as Giant Exhibition (12–15 in. tall and wide) and Kong (18–22 in. tall and wide) have leaves 3–8 in. long. Dwarf strains, such as Fairway, Carefree, and Wizard, grow 8–12 in. tall and wide, with 1- to 1½-in. leaves.

Types that tolerate more sun, collectively referred to as "sun coleus," are popular and versatile. As their name implies, these plants (which are propagated by cuttings rather than from seed) thrive in sun or light shade. They're tougher, larger, more vigorous, and tidier than seed-grown types, and they offer an incredible array of growth habits, colors, and leaf shapes. They

SOLIDAGO

GOLDENROD
Asteraceae
Perennials

**US, MS, LS, CS; USDA 6-9,
EXCEPT AS NOTED**

FULL SUN OR LIGHT SHADE

**MODERATE WATER, EXCEPT AS
NOTED**

Solidago canadensis

These North American natives are
not as widely grown as they
deserve, largely due to the
mistaken belief that their pollen
causes hay fever (in fact, other
plants are responsible). Although a
few of the hundred-plus species
are weeds in many regions, many
are choice garden plants. All have
leafy stems rising from tough,
woody, spreading rootstocks; all
bear small yellow flowers in large,
branching, typically one-sided
clusters from mid- or late summer
into fall. Good cut flowers. These
are tough plants that thrive in
not-too-rich soil. Use in borders
with black-eyed Susan (*Rudbeckia
hirta*) or Michaelmas daisy (*Aster
novi-belgii*), or naturalize in
meadows. Butterflies are attracted
to goldenrod flowers, and birds
enjoy the seeds.

S. altissima (*S. canadensis
scabra*). TALL GOLDENROD. The
state flower of Kentucky, this is
a stiff, erect, much-branched
plant to 3–7 ft. tall, 1½ ft. wide.
Every part of it is bristly. Bears
large, branched, pyramidal flower
heads. Clumping growth.

S. caesia. BLUE-STEMMED
GOLDENROD, WREATH GOLD-
ENROD. Grows 1½–3 ft. tall, with
arching, downy, blue-green stems
loaded with blooms. Clumping
growth.

S. canadensis. CANADA
GOLDENROD. Stands 3–5 ft. tall,

3 ft. wide. Large, showy flower
panicles, densely packed with
blossoms. Robust and vigorous,
spreading widely by underground runners; can be invasive.

S. hybrids. The following are
among the best garden selections. All form slowly spreading,
manageable clumps.

'Cloth of Gold'. To 1½ ft. tall,
1 ft. wide, with a long bloom season beginning in midsummer.

'Crown of Rays'. To 2–3 ft. tall,
1–2 ft. wide. Stiff and erect, with
flattish flower clusters.

'Golden Baby' (Goldkind'). To
2 ft. high, 1½ ft. wide, with plumelike flower clusters.

'Goldenmosa'. To 2½–3 ft. tall,
1½ ft. wide, with very large flower
clusters reminiscent of florist's
mimosa (*Acacia baileyana*).

'Gold Spangles'. To 2–2½ ft.
high, 1–1½ ft. wide. Leaves are
splashed with gold and green.
Showy plumes of fragrant bright
yellow flowers. A bit of a spreader; divide every two to three years
to keep in bounds.

'Laurin'. Vigorous dwarf selection to 1–1½ ft. high and about as
wide. Looks refined.

'Little Lemon' ('Dansolitlem').
Upright, dense dwarf to just 14
in. high, 18 in. wide. Soft yellow
flowers.

S. nemoralis. GRAY GOLDEN-
ROD. Tidy-looking plant ranging
from 6 in. to 2 ft. tall and wide.
Soft, gray-green basal leaves;
curved flower plumes in rich yellow. Blooms over a longer period
than most species. Likes dryish
soil. Short lived; best treated as
a biennial. Deadhead to prevent
prolific self-seeding.

S. odora. SWEET GOLDEN-
ROD. Tall grower to 6½ ft. high,
3 ft. wide. Unbranched stems
are set with anise-scented leaves.
Large, long-lasting flower heads.
Particularly tolerant of poor, dry
soils. Clumping growth.

S. rigida. STIFF GOLDENROD.
To 1½–2½ ft. wide, with stems
2–5 ft. high. Dense golden
blossom heads. Very adaptable to garden conditions; takes
average or rich soil, much or little
moisture. Moderately vigorous
spreader.

S. rugosa. ROUGH-LEAFED
GOLDENROD. Hairy-stemmed
plant to 5 ft. tall, 3 ft. wide, with
arching, widely branching stems.
'Fireworks' makes a more compact clump (3 ft. tall, 2 ft. wide).
Clumping.

S. sempervirens. SEASIDE
GOLDENROD. Stately clumping
species to 8 ft. tall, 1½ ft. wide.
Tolerates dry soil, heat, salt, wind.
May topple in rich soil. Spoon-
shaped basal leaves.

S. shortii. 'Solar Cascade'.
Grows 2–2½ ft. tall and 2 ft. wide,
with gracefully arching stems.
Good ground cover. Clumping
growth.

S. speciosa. SHOWY GOLD-
ENROD. Upright growth to 2–4 ft.
tall and wide, with erect, densely
packed flower heads. Very showy.
Clumping.

**S. sphacelata 'Golden
Fleece'.** Stands just 1½–2 ft. high
when in bloom. Low foliage
mound makes it a good ground
cover; if you set plants 15 in. apart,
spreading growth will give you a
solid mat in just a year.

X SOLIDASTER
LUTEUS

Asteraceae
Perennial

US, MS, LS, CS; USDA 6-9

FULL SUN

MODERATE WATER

X Solidaster luteus 'Lemore'

Probable bigeneric hybrid
between an obscure aster and
Solidago canadensis. Grows erect
to 2–3 ft. tall and 1–2 ft. wide, with
sturdy stems holding medium
green, lance-shaped leaves to
6 in. long. In late summer or early
autumn, sprays of ½-in., daisylike
yellow flowers (wonderful for
cutting) appear atop the foliage.
Fairly trouble free in well-drained
soil, though it can get mildew.
An excellent companion for
fall-blooming asters, perennial
salvias, and ironweed (*Vernonia*

noveboracensis). 'Lemore'
features larger blooms in creamy
yellow. Formerly known as
Solidago x *luteus*.

SOPHORA

Papilionaceae
Evergreen and deciduous trees and
shrubs

ZONES VARY BY SPECIES

**FULL SUN OR PARTIAL
SHADE**

MODERATE WATER

**SEEDS OF *S. AFFINIS* AND
S. SECUNDIFLORA ARE
POISONOUS IF INGESTED**

Sophora secundiflora

Attractive flowering plants with
showy, drooping clusters of
sweet pea–shaped blossoms that
are followed by interesting-
looking seedpods. Leaves are
divided into many leaflets. Be
sure to provide good drainage.

S. affinis. EVE'S NECKLACE.
Small deciduous tree. Zones MS,
LS, CS; USDA 7-9. Native to the
Southwest. Fast growth to 15–20
ft. (rarely 30 ft.) tall, with a round
canopy to about 15 ft. across. Lustrous, dark green, 3- to 10-in.-long
leaves with 13 to 19 leaflets, each
1½ in. long. Blooms in late spring,
bearing rosy pink to white, lightly
scented flowers in pendent, 4- to
6-in. clusters. Lovely, slender,
twisted black seedpods grow
3–6 in. long and look like strings
of beads; they hang on through
fall and winter. Tolerates thin, dry,
limy soils.

S. davidii. DAVID'S MOUN-
TAIN LAUREL. Deciduous shrub.
Zones US, MS, LS, CS; USDA 6-9.
From China. Bushy, rounded
plant to 8–12 ft. tall and a little
wider. Gray-green, 3½-in. leaves
divided into 13 to 19 oval leaflets,

each under ½ in. long. In late spring or early summer, produces 6-in.-long clusters of small, white, fragrant flowers marked with purplish blue. Long (to 2-in.), narrow pods are constricted between the two to four seeds held inside.

S. secundiflora (*Calia secundiflora*). TEXAS MOUNTAIN LAUREL, MESCAL BEAN. Evergreen shrub or tree. Zones LS, CS; USDA 8-9. Shrubby, but can be trained into 25-ft. tree with short, slender trunk or multiple trunks, narrow crown, upright branches. To 15–20 ft. wide. Leaves are 4–6 in. long, divided into 7 to 11 oval, glossy, dark green leaflets, each up to 2 in. long. Violet-blue flowers in drooping, 4- to 8-in. clusters reminiscent of wisteria smell like grape juice; midwinter to early spring bloom. Silvery gray, woody, 1- to 8-in.-long seedpods open when ripe to show poisonous, bright red, ½-in. seeds. If possible, remove pods before they mature. Thrives in heat and alkaline soil with good drainage. Choice small tree for street, lawn, courtyard. Old-time favorite in Southwestern gardens, though its floral display may be eliminated or sharply reduced if late freezes hit when the plants are in bud. 'Alba' is a white-flowered form. 'Silver Peso' has silvery foliage.

SORBARIA
FALSE SPIREA
Rosaceae
Deciduous shrubs

🌡 **US, MS; USDA 6-7**

☀ ◑ **FULL SUN OR LIGHT SHADE**

💧 **REGULAR WATER**

Sorbaria sorbifolia

These good-size shrubs bloom from mid- to late summer,

producing big, plumelike clusters of tiny white or creamy flowers at branch ends. Flowers mature into brown seed clusters, so cut off faded blossoms unless you like the look of brown plumes. Green, ferny-looking leaves are finely divided into many narrow, toothed leaflets. Use in large shrub borders or at edge of woodland, near water; effect is almost tropical. Spread by suckering and will cover large areas if not curbed.

S. sorbifolia. URAL FALSE SPIREA. Native to eastern Asia. To 3–8 ft. tall, 10 ft. wide. Leaves 6–12 in. long; flower plumes to 1 ft. long. 'Sem' is compact, at 3–4 ft. tall and wide, with foliage that emerges bright pinkish red in spring, fading through chartreuse shades to green in summer and coppery bronze in autumn.

S. tomentosa angustifolia (*S. aitchisonii*). KASHMIR FALSE SPIREA. Native to Afghanistan, Pakistan. To 10 ft. tall and wide. Leaves to 1½ ft. long; flower plumes to 16 in. long.

SORBUS
MOUNTAIN ASH
Rosaceae
Deciduous trees and shrubs

🌡 **ZONES VARY BY SPECIES**

☀ ◑ **FULL SUN OR LIGHT SHADE**

💧💧 **MODERATE TO REGULAR WATER**

Sorbus aucuparia

These mountain natives are valued for their showy flowers and even showier fruit. Blossoms are grouped in broad, flat clusters that are scattered over the foliage canopy in spring; they develop into hanging clusters of small,

berrylike fruit that colors up in late summer or early fall. Most species have red or orange-red fruit, but white, pink, and golden forms are occasionally available. Birds feed on the fruit, but usually not until after leaves have fallen. Foliage is typically finely cut and somewhat fernlike, though some less widely planted species have undivided leaves.

Mountain ashes need some winter chill, and their dislike of extended summer heat makes them poor choices for most of the South. Where adapted, they are good small garden trees or street trees, though fruit can make a mess on paved surfaces. Provide good, well-drained soil. Like other members of the rose family, they are subject to fireblight. Borers and cankers are problems for plants under stress.

S. alnifolia. KOREAN MOUNTAIN ASH. Tree. Zones US, MS, LS; USDA 6-8. From China, Korea, Japan. Dense growth to 40–50 ft. tall, 20–30 ft. wide. The specific name *alnifolia* refers to the leaves, which are undivided (like those of alder, *Alnus*); they are 2–4 in. long, toothed, dark green, turning yellow to orange in fall. Reddish pink to orange-red fruit. Grayish bark is mottled with white. Tolerates heat, drought, and humidity better than other mountain ashes. Takes acid or alkaline soils and is less susceptible than its kin to borers.

S. americana. AMERICAN MOUNTAIN ASH. Tree or shrub. Zone US; USDA 6. From eastern North America. Grows 10–30 ft. tall and wide. Dark green leaves with paler undersides are 10 in. long and consist of 11 to 17 leaflets; turn yellow in fall. Orange-red fruit. This species is very hardy and tolerates damp soil, but it is not the choicest of mountain ashes. Attractive in its native mountainous environment. 'Red Cascade' grows just 18 ft. tall and 8 ft. wide, with an attractive oval crown.

S. aucuparia. EUROPEAN MOUNTAIN ASH. Tree. Zones US, MS; USDA 6-7. Native from Europe to western Asia and Siberia; naturalized in North America. To 20–40 ft. tall (or taller), 15–25 ft. wide. Sharply rising branches form a dense, oval to round crown. Leaves are 5–9 in. long, with 9 to 15 leaflets; they are dull green above, gray-green below, turning tawny yellow to reddish

in autumn. Orange-red fruit. 'Cardinal Royal' has especially large bright red berries. 'Black Hawk' and 'Fastigiata' are slightly narrower, upright forms.

SORREL, GARDEN
Polygonaceae
Perennial often grown as annual

🌡 **US, MS, LS, CS, TS; USDA 6-11**

☀ **FULL SUN**

💧 **REGULAR WATER**

'Blood Veined' common sorrel

Two similar species are grown for their edible leaves, which can be used raw in salads or cooked in soups, sauces, egg dishes. Flavor is like that of a sharp, sprightly spinach, but sorrel is more heat tolerant and produces throughout the growing season. Common sorrel (*Rumex acetosa*) is the larger plant (to 3 ft. tall), with leaves to 6 in. long, many shaped like elongated arrowheads. It is native to northern climates. French sorrel (*R. scutatus*) is a more sprawling plant, to 1½ ft. high, with shorter, broader leaves and a milder, more lemony flavor than *R. acetosa*. Native to Europe, western Asia, and North Africa.

CARE

Grow sorrel in reasonably good soil. Sow seeds in early spring; thin seedlings to 8 in. apart. Or set out transplants at any time, spacing them 8 in. apart. Pick tender leaves when they are big enough to use; cut out flowering stems to encourage leaf production. Replace (or dig and divide) plants after 3 or 4 years.

SOUTHERN PEA

Papilionaceae
Annual

US, MS, LS, CS, TS; USDA 6-11

FULL SUN

REGULAR WATER

Purple hull Southern peas

Long a staple of Southern cuisine, Southern peas grow somewhat like ordinary green peas ("garden" or "English" peas), but their pods look more like lumpy string beans. Unlike green peas, Southern peas thrive in the long, hot summers of the South, where they are ready for harvest about 65 days after sowing.

"Southern pea" is a collective term; there are many different types. Field peas (also called cowpeas) are planted primarily for animal feed and for loosening and improving the soil. Some, however, do make good table peas. For example, 'Red Ripper' is very popular in Texas because it tolerates very hot, dry summers and bears as many as 18 tasty peas per pod. Drought-tolerant 'Whippoorwill' will grow in almost any soil.

The best-known Southern pea is the black-eyed pea, named for the dark spot on the notch of its tan or white seeds. Ironically, it grows better in the West than in the South—but if you want to try it, plant the selections 'Queen Anne' or 'California Blackeye #5'.

By far the largest group is crowder peas, named for the

blocky, square-edged seeds that "crowd" into the pod. Crowders do a great job of fixing atmospheric nitrogen, thereby enriching the soil, and they are very productive. Recommended selections include 'Calico', 'Colossus', 'Mississippi Silver', and 'Peking Black'.

Two other types of Southern peas, purple hulls and cream peas, are quite popular. The pods of purple hulls turn purple at maturity. Folks like them because they're highly productive and make a dark, flavorful "pot liquor" (the liquid left in the cooking pot). Favorite selections include 'Mississippi Pinkeye', and 'Pinkeye Purple Hull'. Cream peas are named for their white or cream-colored seeds. Try 'Zipper Cream' (its pods have a "zipper" for easy shelling), 'Lady Cream', 'Mississippi Cream', 'Texas Cream 40', and 'White Acre'.

CARE

All Southern peas tolerate drought and poor soil, need little fertilizer, and fend off pests. If nematodes plague your soil, plant resistant selections such as 'Mississippi Cream' and 'Mississippi Pinkeye'. All types need warm soil to germinate. Sow seeds for summer crops about 2 weeks after your last spring frost. For fall crops, sow in early July. To speed germination, soak seeds overnight before planting.

Sow in rows 2 ft. apart, planting seeds 1 in. deep in clay soils and 2 in. deep in sandy soils. When seedlings have reached 3 in. tall, thin them to 6–12 in. apart. Don't feed with nitrogen fertilizer or you'll get all leaves and no peas. Peas are almost ready for picking when the green pods start to change color; purple hulls turn purple, other types turn tan or yellow. Pick when they're halfway turned. Shell and cook the peas right away or freeze them for later. Frozen fresh peas keep up to a year. Or let the peas dry in the pod until they rattle, then shell and store them in a bag or jar.

SPATHIPHYLLUM

PEACE LILY
Araceae
Perennials

TS; USDA 10-11; OR HOUSE-PLANTS

SOME SHADE; LOW TO BRIGHT INDIRECT LIGHT

REGULAR TO AMPLE WATER

Spathiphyllum

From the tropics, mainly in the Americas. The various types range from dwarf forms a few inches high to 8-footers; foliage color varies from light to dark green. Leaves are carried on slender stalks that rise directly from the soil; they are generally large for the plant size, oval or elliptical, narrowed to a point. Flowers—fragrant in some species and selections—resemble those of calla (*Zantedeschia*) or anthurium, consisting of a leaflike white or greenish white bract surrounding a central club-shaped structure of closely set, tiny flowers. Outdoors, use as border plants or accents, for ground cover, in containers on shaded lanai or patio. Provide rich soil, wind protection. Deer aren't fond of them.

Peace lilies are among the few flowering plants that grow and bloom readily indoors; they're also among the best at absorbing indoor air pollutants. Grow them in loose, fibrous potting mix and feed monthly with diluted liquid fertilizer. Mist frequently, and wipe leaves with a damp cloth occasionally to keep them dust free. If plants refuse to bloom, move them to a brighter spot, but avoid hot, direct sun. Good choices include *S. wallisii* 'Clevelandii', to 2 ft. high, 20 in. wide; *S.* 'Mauna Loa', 3½ ft. high, 2 ft. wide; and *S.* 'Sensation', 4–6 ft. tall, 3 ft. wide.

SPATHODEA CAMPANULATA

AFRICAN TULIP TREE
Bignoniaceae
Evergreen tree

TS; USDA 10-11

FULL SUN

MODERATE WATER

Spathodea campanulata

From tropical Africa. Very showy, fast-growing tree to 40–75 ft. tall, 20–50 ft. wide. Glossy, deep green leaves to 1½ ft. long, divided featherwise into 9 to 19 oblong to ovate leaflets. Clusters of spectacular, tulip-shaped, 4-in. flowers in scarlet, blood red, or yellowish orange appear at branch ends. Blooms mainly in spring and summer, but flowers may appear in any season. Give good drainage and a warm site. This tree grows rapidly and blooms young, but it can be devastated by frosts. Best suited to south Florida.

S

SPHAGNETICOLA TRILOBATA

Asteraceae
Perennial

🌿 **CS (WARMER PARTS), TS; USDA 9-11**

☼ ☼ **FULL SUN OR LIGHT SHADE**

💧 **REGULAR WATER**

Sphagneticola trilobata

Native to Central and South America. Trailing evergreen plant to 1½–2 ft. high, spreading to 6 ft. or more by stems that root where they touch damp earth. Fleshy, glossy, dark green leaves to 4 in. long, half as wide, with a few coarse teeth or shallow lobes toward tips. Inch-wide flowers resembling tiny yellow zinnias or marigolds (*Tagetes*) bloom almost year-round. Spreads fast; easily propagated by lifting rooted pieces or placing tip cuttings in moist soil. Best in sandy, fast-draining soils but takes heavier soils if drainage is good. If killed to ground by frost, it makes a fast comeback. Tolerates high heat, seaside conditions. Can take lower light but blooms more sparsely in shady conditions. Good for erosion control on slopes: Plant 1½ ft. apart, feed lightly. Shear close to ground if planting mounds up or becomes stemmy. Can become invasive. Formerly known as *Wedelia trilobata*.

SPIGELIA MARILANDICA

INDIAN PINK
Loganiaceae
Perennial

🌿 **US, MS, LS, CS; USDA 6-9**

☼ **LIGHT SHADE**

💧 **REGULAR WATER**

⬧ **ALL PARTS ARE POISONOUS IF INGESTED**

Spigelia marilandica

This charming woodland plant is among the showiest and easiest Southern wildflowers. Grows 1–2 ft. high, with stiff, erect stems bearing pairs of glossy, green, 4-in., broadly lance-shaped leaves. Clusters of 2-in., trumpet-like flowers; blossoms are red on the outside and yellow inside, facing upward to show a yellow five-pointed star at the mouth. Early summer bloom; attracts hummingbirds. Easy to grow if given light shade and moist, acid soil. With enough moisture, will tolerate much sun. Tolerates dry soil in shade. 'Little Redhead' grows just 15 in. tall.

SPINACH

Amaranthaceae, Aizoaceae, Basellaceae
Annuals and perennials

🌿 **ZONES VARY BY SPECIES**

☼ **FULL SUN**

💧 **REGULAR WATER**

True spinach

One of the three plants described here is true spinach (*Spinacia*); the other two are warm-season vegetables used as substitutes for the real thing, which needs cool weather to succeed. All are grown for their edible leaves, used raw or cooked. All do best in rich, well-drained soil.

True spinach. This is the cool-season annual *Spinacia oleracea*, a member of the amaranth family (*Amaranthaceae*). It probably originated in southwestern Asia. All zones. Spinach matures slowly during fall, winter, and spring; long days of late spring and heat of summer make it bolt (go to seed) quickly. For a spring harvest, sow seeds in earliest spring. Choose heat-tolerant selections that are slow to bolt, such as 'Avon' (44 days from seed to harvest), 'Bloomsdale Long Standing' (48 days), 'Crocodile Hybrid' (46 days), 'Indian Summer' (39 days), 'Space' (39 days), or 'Tyee' (38 days). For fall and winter harvests, sow seeds four to eight weeks before the first expected fall frost. Plants will survive freezing temperatures and can be harvested through the winter. Look for disease-resistant, cold-hardy selections, such as 'Bloomsdale Long Standing', 'Dixie Market' (45 days), 'Melody' (42 days), 'Python' (35 days), 'Racoon' (36 days), and 'Winter Bloomsdale' (47 days). Sow seeds thinly in rows

spaced 1½ ft. apart, or scatter them over a wide bed; cover with ½ in. of soil. Thin seedlings to 4–6 in. apart. There are two ways to harvest. You can pinch off only the large outer leaves when they are 3–6 in. long, allowing the plant to produce new foliage from its center. Or you can cut the entire plant at soil level when it reaches 4–6 in. wide.

New Zealand spinach. Native to New Zealand and Australia, *Tetragonia tetragonioides* belongs to *Aizoaceae*, a family of succulent plants. It is an evergreen perennial in the Coastal and Tropical South but goes dormant after a frost. Elsewhere it can be grown as a summer annual.

Sow seeds in early spring after danger of frost is past; thin established seedlings to 1–1½ ft. apart. Plants reach maturity about 50 days after sowing; they are 1–2 ft. tall, with spreading form. Harvest greens by plucking off top few inches of tender stems and attached leaves; a month later, new shoots will have grown up for another harvest. New Zealand spinach tolerates heat and drought but also thrives in cool, damp conditions.

Malabar spinach. *Basella alba* is a native of India; it belongs to the family *Basellaceae*. Perennial vine in the Tropical South; grown as an annual elsewhere. It needs night temperatures above 58°F and will not survive frost. There is an especially attractive red-stemmed form.

Sow seeds in early summer; thin established seedlings to 1 ft. apart. When young plants are about 1 ft. high, train them on wires or a trellis. At 2 ft. high, pinch out a few inches of stem tip (harvesting any young, tender leaves) to encourage the plants to branch and form more stems. Vine grows about 4 ft. tall. As leaves reach full, succulent size (about 4 in. long; 50 to 60 days after sowing), pick them individually. They are bigger and thicker than leaves of true spinach, so you'll need fewer per serving.

SPIRAEA

SPIREA
Rosaceae
Deciduous shrubs

🌡 **ZONES VARY BY SPECIES**

☀ ◐ **FULL SUN OR LIGHT SHADE**

💧 💧 **REGULAR TO MODERATE WATER**

Spiraea japonica 'Little Princess'

Unless your garden sits in a cave or the middle of the ocean, you probably have room for a spirea. They are a varied lot, offering a number of sizes, forms, and flowering seasons—but they can be broken down into two basic groups according to bloom time. Spring bloomers feature clusters of white flowers cascading down from arching branches; summer bloomers are compact and shrubby, with pink, red, or white flowers clustered at the branch ends. Both types look more effective when massed in sweeps and borders than when used singly. White-flowered spireas look better against a dark background. The cut branches of spring-flowering types are great for forcing into bloom for indoor arrangements.

All spireas are tough and easy to grow; with few exceptions, they are not fussy about soil. Deer don't favor them.

S. cantoniensis 'Flore Pleno' ('Lanceata'). DOUBLE REEVES SPIREA. Zones US, MS, LS, CS; USDA 6-9. From China, Japan. To 5–6 ft. tall, 10 ft. wide, with arching branches. Double white flowers wreathe the leafy branches in late spring to early summer. Lance-shaped, blue-green leaves to 2½ in. long; they drop late, show no fall color. Plant is nearly evergreen in mildest climates. Prune as for spring bloomers.

S. japonica. JAPANESE SPIREA. Zones US, MS, LS; USDA 6-8. Native to Japan, China. Upright and shrubby to 4–6 ft. tall and wide, with flat, 8-in.-wide clusters of pink flowers carried above oval, toothed, 1- to 4-in.-long green leaves. Best known through its selections, which are typically lower than the species and bloom between summer and fall. They include plants formerly classified as hybrids of *S.* x *bumalda*, itself now considered merely a selection.

'Albiflora'. To 2 ft. tall, 3 ft. wide. Pale green leaves; white flowers.

'Anthony Waterer'. To 3–5 ft. tall and wide. Carmine-pink blossoms. Leaves are reddish purple when new, maturing to bright green.

'Bumalda'. To 3 ft. high and wide. Dark pink flowers; bronzy new growth.

'Candlelight'. To 2–3 ft. high and wide. Butter-yellow foliage; pink blooms.

'Coccinea'. To 2–3 ft. tall and wide. Maroon-tinged foliage; red flowers.

'Dart's Red'. To 2 ft. high and wide. A compact sport of 'Anthony Waterer', with redder flowers.

'Firelight'. To 2–3 ft. high, 4 ft. wide. Leaves emerge reddish orange and retain their color into summer, then turn fiery red in fall. Pink flowers.

'Golden Elf'. Dwarf to 6–9 in. high, 1–2 ft. wide. Golden leaves usually hold their color into autumn. Tiny pink blossoms.

'Goldflame'. To 2½ ft. high and wide. Bronze new growth matures to yellowish green, turns dark reddish orange in fall. Red flowers.

'Limemound'. To 3 ft. tall, 6 ft. wide. Lemon-yellow new leaves mature to lime-green, then turn orange-red in fall. Light pink flowers.

'Little Bonnie'. To 2–3 ft. tall, 3 ft. wide. Blue-green foliage. Lavender-pink blooms over a long period.

'Little Princess'. To 3 ft. tall, 6 ft. wide. Rose-pink blossoms.

'Magic Carpet'. To 1½–2½ ft. tall, slightly wider. Reddish bronze new leaves turn chartreuse to yellow as they mature. Pink flowers.

'Nana' ('Alpina'). ALPINE SPIREA. To 2 ft. tall, 5 ft. wide. Pink flowers. Good red fall foliage in some years.

'Neon Flash'. To 3–4 ft. tall, 4–5 ft. wide. Purple-tinted foliage; bright rose-pink flowers.

'Shirobana'. To 2–3 ft. high and wide. Red buds open to bicolored blossoms in white and deep pink.

S. nipponica 'Snowmound'. Zones US, MS, LS; USDA 6-8. From Japan. Compact, spreading plant to 2–3 ft. tall, 3–5 ft. wide. Profusion of white flowers in late spring or early summer. Ovate to roundish, dark green leaves to 1¼ in. long; little autumn color. Prune as for spring bloomers.

S. prunifolia. BRIDAL WREATH SPIREA. Zones US, MS, LS; USDA 6-8. From China, Taiwan. Graceful, arching branches on a suckering, clump-forming plant to 6–7 ft. tall and wide. In early to midspring, bare branches are lined with small, double white flowers resembling tiny roses. Small dark green leaves turn bright shades of red, orange, and yellow in autumn. An old Southern favorite.

S. thunbergii. BABY'S BREATH SPIREA. Zones US, MS, LS; USDA 6-8. From China, Japan. Showy, billowy, graceful species 3–6 ft. or taller, 6 ft. wide, with many slender, arching branches. Round clusters of small white flowers appear all along the bare branches in early spring. Blue-green, extremely narrow leaves to 1½ in. long turn soft reddish brown in fall. An old-time favorite in the South, with several outstanding selections. 'Fujino Pink' has dark pink buds that open to light pink flowers. 'Mount Fuji' bears the typical white blooms, but its leaves (some of them twisted and curled) are green striped with white. White-flowered 'Ogon' has soft yellow foliage.

S. trilobata 'Swan Lake'. Zones US, MS, LS; USDA 6-8. Selection of a species from Siberia and northern China. Like a small version of *S. prunifolia*. Grows 3–4 ft. tall and wide, with a massive show of tiny white flowers in mid- to late spring. Leaves are just 1 in. long, often three lobed. 'Fairy Queen' is similar but more compact, seldom exceeding 3 ft.

S. x **vanhouttei.** VAN HOUTTE SPIREA. Zones US, MS, LS; USDA 6-8. Hybrid between *S. cantoniensis* and *S. trilobata*. The classic spring-blooming spirea for Southern gardens. Arching branches form a fountain to about 6 ft. high by 8 ft. or wider.

Leafy branches are covered with circular, flattened clusters of white blossoms in mid- to late spring. Dark green, diamond-shaped leaves to 1½ in. long may turn purplish in fall.

CARE

Prune spring bloomers yearly in late spring after flowering, cutting one-third of the oldest branches to the ground. Prune summer bloomers in winter or earliest spring, before new growth begins; they generally need less pruning than spring bloomers. If you remove spent flower clusters in summer, plants will produce a second (but less lavish) bloom.

SPIRANTHES CERNUA ODORATA

NODDING LADIES' TRESSES
Orchidaceae
Terrestrial orchid

🌡 **US, MS, LS, CS; USDA 6-9**

☀ ◐ **FULL SUN OR PARTIAL SHADE**

💧 💧 **REGULAR TO AMPLE WATER**

Spiranthes cernua odorata

Native to swamps of southeastern U.S. Forms low rosettes of dark green, 2- to 10-in.-long leaves; spreads slowly by underground rhizomes to form small colonies. In late summer and early fall, gorgeous, 1- to 2-ft.-tall spikes appear atop the foliage, with small, bell-shaped, white flowers arranged spirally up and down their length. Blooms are very fragrant, like a blend of vanilla and jasmine. Easy to grow in constantly moist soil that is highly enriched with organic matter. Excellent addition to bog or streamside garden; lovely at the edge of a pond. 'Chadd's Ford' is vigorous, with large, very fragrant blooms.

SPOROBOLUS

DROPSEED
Poaceae
Perennial grasses

US, MS, LS, CS; USDA 6-9

FULL SUN

LITTLE TO MODERATE WATER

Sporobolus heterolepis

Don't let the graceful appearance and fine texture of these clumping grasses fool you—they're as tough as they come. Deep rooted and drought tolerant; excellent for massing in hot, dry areas and effective in meadow gardens, mixed borders, naturalized areas, rock gardens, even by swimming pools. Plumelike flower heads appear in summer or fall; after they fade, tiny seeds drop to the ground, hence the common name.

S. airoides. ALKALI SACATON, ALKALI DROPSEED. Native from Arkansas and Missouri northwest to Washington and south to Mexico. Foliage clump grows 3 ft. high and wide; leaves are grayish green during growing season, yellow in fall, beige in winter. In summer or fall, showy, erect or arching flower plumes increase plant height to 5 ft.; plumes are pinkish, eventually fading to pale straw color. Takes a wide range of soils; good for alkaline conditions. Noninvasive.

S. heterolepis. PRAIRIE DROP-SEED. Native to the Midwest, High Plains, and much of the eastern U.S. Emerald-green, hairlike leaves form a billowing mass to 15 in. tall and 1½ ft. wide. Foliage turns golden to orange in fall, then fades to light bronze in winter. Slender-stemmed panicles of flowers rise to 3 ft. tall, soaring above the foliage in late summer. Blossoms are pink to light brown and smell faintly of coriander. The seeds are highly nutritious and were ground into flour by Plains Indians. Plant tolerates almost any soil but likes it on the dry side. It can be started from seed but is rather slow to establish. Unlike many other grasses, this one doesn't self-sow extravagantly, so volunteer seedlings are seldom a problem.

S. wrightii. GIANT SACATON. Native to sandy open areas and hillsides in southwestern Canada and the southwestern U.S. Narrow, arching, blue-green leaves grow quickly to form a clump 3–4 ft. tall and wide. Feathery, golden yellow seed heads nearly double the plant's height in late summer to early fall; good in dried arrangements. Evergreen in all but the coldest climates. Quite drought tolerant but looks best with occasional deep watering. Noninvasive.

SPREKELIA FORMOSISSIMA

AZTEC LILY, JACOBEAN LILY, ST. JAMES LILY
Amaryllidaceae
Perennial from bulb

LS (PROTECTED), CS, TS; USDA 8-11; OR DIG AND STORE; OR GROW IN POTS

FULL SUN

REGULAR WATER DURING GROWTH AND BLOOM

Sprekelia formosissima

Mexican native often sold as *Amaryllis formosissima*. Foliage looks like that of daffodil (*Narcissus*), but each 1-ft.-tall stem is topped with a dark red, 6-in.-wide bloom resembling an orchid, with three erect upper segments and three drooping lower ones that are united at their bases (near the flower's center) to form a tube. Bloom comes primarily in spring, with a second bloom in fall. In mild climates, foliage may be evergreen and plant may bloom several times a year if you can give it a dry period after flowering, then resume regular watering to trigger a new growth cycle. Not damaged by deer or rodents.

CARE

Where bulbs are hardy, plant them in fall, setting them 3–4 in. deep and 8 in. apart in good, well-drained soil. Look most effective in groups. Display increases if plants are left undisturbed for several years. Where winters are cold, set out bulbs in spring, lift plants in fall when foliage yellows, and store in a cool, dark, dry place over winter (leave dry tops on). Or grow in pots as directed for amaryllis (*Hippeastrum*); repot every three or four years.

SQUASH

Cucurbitaceae
Annual

US, MS, LS, CS, TS; USDA 6-11

FULL SUN

REGULAR WATER

Summer squash

Few vegetables give you as big a return on your investment of time and energy as squash. There are two main forms, both derived from various species native to the Americas. Summer squash is harvested all summer long, while still soft skinned and immature. It's served steamed, sautéed, or fried. Winter squash is harvested in late summer and fall after it has matured and developed a tough skin; it stores very well and is used for baking, stuffing, and pies. A special kind of winter squash, called spaghetti squash, can substitute for pasta; its nutty-tasting flesh consists of long, spaghetti-like strands.

Each individual squash plant produces both male and female flowers, with the female flowers forming fruit after bees transfer pollen from male blossoms. The first flowers are typically male, so if your vine doesn't start fruiting right away, be patient. The blossoms and developing fruit at the base of female flowers are eaten as delicacies.

Summer squash yields prodigious crops from just a few plants and continues to bear for many weeks. The three most popular types are yellow (both straightneck and crookneck), zucchini, and pattypan (also called scallop). Plant immediately after the last spring frost, then again three weeks later for an extended harvest. Summer squash is usually planted in hills (mounds) spaced 3–4 ft. apart. For better pollination and fruiting, plant two rows of hills side by side instead of one long row. Vines are large (up to 5 ft. at maturity) and need plenty of room; if space is limited, plant bush types such as 'Peter Pan' and 'Sweet Zuke'.

Sow five to seven seeds per hill, planting them 1 in. deep. Thin seedlings to the strongest two plants per hill. Four weeks after planting, fertilize each hill with ¼ cup of 10-10-10 fertilizer. Fruit reaches harvest size quickly, usually within five to seven days after the flowers open. Pick yellow squash when they're 4–6 in. long, zucchini when 6–8 in. long, and pattypans when 3–5 in. wide. Don't allow fruit to reach full maturity on the vines, as this may halt production.

Good yellow straightneck selections include 'Early Prolific Straightneck' (48 days from sowing to harvest), 'Seneca Prolific' (50 days), and 'Park's Super Creamy' (55 days). For yellow crookneck, try 'Yellow Crookneck' (58 days), 'Early Golden Summer'

HOW TO GROW SQUASH

LOCATION Choose a spot with full sun and good air circulation. Most selections need plenty of room. Plant squash in a different place each year to avoid a buildup of pests.

SOIL Provide fertile, well-drained soil containing plenty of organic matter, such as composted manure, chopped leaves, or garden compost. If your soil is strongly acid (pH 5.5 or lower), add lime.

WATERING Water often enough to keep soil moist and prevent the plants from wilting, especially when fruit is forming.

PESTS The most serious pest is squash vine borer, a large white caterpillar that tunnels through stems, causing vines to wilt and die. Squash bugs are another possible pest; they suck plant juices, causing stems to blacken and wilt. To control both, plant under floating row covers until plants begin blooming, then remove row covers and spray with neem oil. Squash bugs lay yellowish to brown egg clusters on the undersides of leaves; look for these and destroy them.

DISEASES The most common disease affecting squash is powdery mildew on the foliage; to discourage it, plant in full sun, maintain good air circulation around plants, avoid wetting the foliage, and remove infected leaves as soon as you see them. Neem oil and antitranspirants can also be effective.

(53 days), and 'Sunglo' (40 days). Recommended zucchini selections include 'Embassy' (45 days), 'Costata' (50 days), 'Black Beauty' (50 days), 'Gold Rush' (45 days), and 'Burpee Hybrid' (50 days). Among the best pattypans are 'Sunburst' (52 days), 'Scallopini' (50 days), and 'White Pattypan' (60 days). Novelties include 'Eight Ball' (40 days), a round zucchini; 'Bush Baby' (49 days), miniature zucchini; 'Golden Egg' (41 days), a golden, egg-shaped zucchini; 'Magda' (50 days), a white-fleshed, nutty-tasting squash shaped like a thick zucchini to 4 in. long; and 'Kuta' (48 days), a light green squash that can be eaten like summer squash at 6 in. long or allowed to mature into a 1-ft. winter squash.

Winter squash typically needs more room than summer squash. Plant smaller types, such as acorn, buttercup, butternut, and spaghetti squash, in hills spaced 4–5 ft. apart. These produce fruit weighing 2 to 5 pounds. Large types, such as banana and Hubbard, bear fruit weighing 12 to 15 pounds or more; they require 5–7 ft. between hills and 6–10 ft. between rows. Planting and care are the same as for summer squash. Fruit is ready to harvest when you can't pierce the skin with your thumbnail. Cut the squash from the vine, leaving 1–2 in. of stem attached;

store in a cool, dry place.

Recommended winter squash selections include acorn types 'Table Ace' (70 days), 'Jersey Golden' (70 days), and 'Cream of the Crop' (85 days); buttercup type 'Sweet Mama' (85 days); butternut types 'Waltham Butternut' (105 days), 'Pilgrim' (85 days), and 'Nicklow's Delight' (78 days); spaghetti types 'Tivoli' (98 days) and 'Pasta Hybrid' (85 days); banana type 'Pink Banana Jumbo' (120 days); and Hubbard type 'Blue Hubbard' (100 days). 'Green Striped Cushaw' (110 days) is a light green, creamy-striped squash with light yellow flesh; the fruit is bulb-shaped with a curved neck and can reach 40 pounds.

STACHYS

Lamiaceae
Perennials

🖋 **US, MS, LS; USDA 6-8, EXCEPT AS NOTED**

☀ ◗ **FULL SUN OR LIGHT SHADE**

💧 **MODERATE WATER**

Stachys byzantina

These mint-family members have the typical square stems and leaves in opposite pairs; foliage ranges from rough textured to furry. Most of the species described here have short-stalked or stalkless leaves. Spikelike clusters of small, usually two-lipped flowers bloom in late spring and summer; blossoms are attractive to bees. All are fairly unfussy about soil type, needing only good drainage. Green-leafed species need some shade where summers are hot. Clumps often die out in center; divide and replant outer sections. Deer usually leave these plants alone.

S. albotomentosa. HIDALGO. Native to Mexico. To 2½ ft. tall, sprawling to 5–6 ft. wide. Green, heavily veined leaves have a felty texture and an elongated heart shape. Stems and leaf undersides are woolly. Flowers are peach to salmon-pink when they open, then age to brick-red. Sometimes listed as *S. coccinea* 'Hidalgo'.

S. byzantina (*S. lanata*). LAMB'S EARS. Native to the Caucasus, Iran. To 1½ ft. high, spreading freely by surface runners. Dense, ground-hugging rosettes of soft, thick, rather tongue-shaped, woolly white leaves to 4–6 in. long. Blossom stalks 1–1½ ft. high bear small purplish flowers; many gardeners feel that these flowering stems detract from the foliage and so cut them

off or pull them out. Continued rains can mash plants down and make them mushy, and frost can damage foliage, but recovery is usually strong.

'Silver Carpet' does not produce flower spikes and is somewhat less vigorous than the species. 'Big Ears' ('Countess Helen von Stein') has larger leaves. Flowers of 'Cotton Boll' are like little balls of fluff spaced along the stem. Furry leaves of 'Primrose Heron' are yellow when new, maturing to chartreuse, then gray-green.

Use all forms for contrast with dark green foliage and with leaves of different shapes, such as those of strawberry or some sedums. Good edging for paths, flower beds. Excellent ground cover in high, open shade, such as under tall oaks; space plants 2 ft. apart.

S. coccinea. SCARLET BETONY. Native to southern Texas, New Mexico, Arizona. Forms a clump to 1½ ft. high and wide, with wrinkled, heavily veined, medium green foliage. Leaves are elongated ovals to 3 in. long. Bears short spikes of scarlet flowers. 'Hot Spot Coral' has coral-red flowers. For the form sometimes sold as 'Hidalgo', see *S. albotomentosa*.

S. macrantha. BIG BETONY. Native to the Caucasus, Turkey, Iran. Dense foliage clump to 1 ft. high and wide, with long-stalked, heart-shaped, scallop-edged, dark green leaves to 3 in. across; they are wrinkled and roughly hairy. Showy purplish pink blossoms are held on 1½- to 2-ft.-tall stems. 'Robusta' and 'Superba' offer larger flowers; 'Alba' has white blooms.

S. officinalis. BETONY. Similar to *S. macrantha*, but leaves are elongated (to 5 in. long) and may be hairy or nearly smooth. The purplish or dark red flowers are densely packed into short spikes atop leafy stems. Little grown except by herb fanciers, but white-blooming 'Alba' and pink-blooming 'Rosea Superba' are attractive 2-ft. plants for perennial border or woodland edge. 'Hummelo' is choice, with profuse rosy purple blooms on a compact, uniform plant.

S

STACHYTARPHETA

PORTERWEED

Verbenaceae

Perennials often grown as annuals

- TS; USDA 10-11
- EXPOSURE NEEDS VARY BY SPECIES
- REGULAR WATER

Stachytarpheta mutabilis 'Coral'

Group of shrubby perennials native to New and Old World tropics and treasured for their flowers. Bloom continuously in warm weather, with long, whiplike spikes bearing clusters of small, showy blossoms that attract butterflies and hummingbirds. Effective in naturalized areas, in mixed herbaceous borders, and when massed. Plants self-sow readily and can be weedy.

S. jamaicensis. BLUE PORTERWEED. Native to south Florida, where it is widely sold and planted. Mounding plant to 1–2 ft. tall and wide, with dull green, coarsely toothed, pointed-oval leaves to 3 in. long. Slender flower spikes resembling a rat's tail rise at least a foot above the foliage. Blue, ¼-in. flowers appear singly or in clusters, starting at bottom of spike and proceeding upward. Individual flowers last just a day. Best in partial shade.

S. mutabilis. PINK PORTER-WEED. Native to South America. Shrubby, sprawling growth to 7 ft. tall and wide. Fuzzy, light green leaves to 4 in. long are oval and pointed. Thick flower spikes rise a foot above the foliage, bearing clusters of ½-in. pink flowers that last for several days. 'Coral' is very showy, flaunting masses of coral-pink blossoms. Full sun.

S. urticifolia. NETTLELEAF VERVAIN. Native to Asia. Similar to and often confused with *S. jamaicensis*, but leaves are darker green and noticeably quilted on upper surface. Flowers are also slightly smaller and darker blue and have white centers. Upright, shrubby growth to 5 ft. high, not quite as wide. Individual flowers last for only a day. Full sun.

STACHYURUS PRAECOX

Stachyuraceae

Deciduous shrub

- US, MS, LS; USDA 6-8
- FULL SUN OR LIGHT SHADE
- REGULAR WATER

Stachyurus praecox

Native to Japan. Slow grower to 10 ft. tall and about as wide, with slender, polished-looking, chestnut-brown branches. Pendulous, 3- to 4-in.-long flower stalks, each carrying 12 to 20 buds, hang like strings of pearls from branches in fall and winter. In late winter, buds open into bell-shaped, pale yellow or greenish yellow flowers, ⅓ in. wide. Greenish yellow, berrylike fruit follows in late summer. Bright green, toothed leaves are 3–7 in. long and oval, tapering to sharp tip; foliage is often somewhat sparse. Rosy red and yellowish fall color is pleasant but not spectacular. Provide moist, acid, well-drained soil.

STAPELIA

STARFISH FLOWER, CARRION FLOWER

Asclepiadaceae

Succulent perennials

- CS (WARMER PARTS), TS; USDA 9-11; BEST IN POTS
- FULL SUN
- MODERATE WATER

Stapelia gigantea

From Africa. Plants resemble cacti, with clumps of four-sided, spineless stems. Summer flowers are large, fleshy, shaped like five-pointed stars; they usually have an elaborate, circular, fleshy disk in the center. Blossoms of most smell like carrion to attract insect pollinators, but odor is not usually pervasive enough to be offensive. They need a cool, dry rest period in winter. Best managed in pots; allow to dry somewhat between soakings. Tolerate extreme heat.

S. gigantea. Grow this plant as a remarkable novelty. Stems grow about 9 in. tall, bearing wrinkled, fringy-edged, brown-purple flowers marked in creamy white or yellow; each bloom reaches 10–16 in. wide. Protect plants where frosts can occur.

S. scitula. Resembles *S. gigan-tea*, but grows just 3 in. tall, with dark red blooms up to 1 in. across. Perfect size for a windowsill plant.

STEPHANOTIS FLORIBUNDA

MADAGASCAR JASMINE

Asclepiadaceae

Evergreen vine

- TS; USDA 10-11; OR HOUSEPLANT
- ROOTS COOL, TOPS IN FIL-TERED SUN; BRIGHT LIGHT
- REGULAR WATER

Stephanotis floribunda

Native to Madagascar. Twines to 15–30 ft. Waxy, glossy green, oval leaves to 4 in. long. Valued for the intense fragrance of its funnel-shaped, 1- to 2-in.-long, waxy white blossoms. Borne in open clusters, the flowers are a favorite for bridal bouquets and are also used in leis. Blooms from June until summer's end. Provide support; train on trellis or fence or along eaves. Give good drainage.

CARE

As houseplant, will bloom if given ample light; better suited to greenhouse. Feed liberally from spring through fall with a general-purpose liquid house-plant fertilizer. Watch for scale and mealybugs; both pests can be dispatched with a cotton swab dipped in alcohol. Give indoor plants a rest period by letting them dry out in winter. Can be brought outdoors during warm times of year.

STERNBERGIA LUTEA

Amaryllidaceae
Perennial from bulb

- US, MS, LS; USDA 6-8; OR GROW IN POTS
- FULL SUN
- REGULAR WATER DURING GROWTH AND BLOOM

Sternbergia lutea

Native to the western Mediterranean region and central Asia, these bulbs bear golden yellow flowers that provide a pleasant autumn surprise in borders, rock gardens, and along paths. In early fall, the 1½-in. blooms appear singly on 6- to 9-in. stems; they are chalice shaped at first, then open out to a star. Narrow, 6- to 12-in.-long leaves appear in fall along with the flowers; they remain green all winter, then die to the ground in spring. Unappetizing to deer and rodents.

CARE

Plant bulbs as soon as they become available in garden centers (usually in August and September). Set them 4 in. deep and about 6 in. apart in well-drained soil. Where winter temperatures drop to 20°F or lower, cover them with a thick layer of mulch. Try to keep planting bed dry in summer when bulbs are dormant. After planting, the bulbs often take two or three years to settle in and begin blooming well. Divide clumps only when vigor and flowering decline.

If you can't keep the planting area dry during summer dormancy, grow sternbergia in pots and move them to a dry spot in summer. They bloom better when pot-bound, so don't be in a hurry to repot. Also, don't fret if these temperamental bulbs fail to bloom in any one year, as they are sensitive to annual variations in the weather. There's nothing the gardener can do about this but sigh.

STEVIA REBAUDIANA

PARAGUAYAN SWEET HERB, HONEYLEAF, STEVIA
Asteraceae
Perennial

- TS; USDA 10-11; OR GROW IN POTS
- FULL SUN
- REGULAR WATER

Stevia rebaudiana

Native to Paraguay, Colombia, Venezuela, and Brazil. For growers of this herb, life is sweet indeed: Extracts from the leaves contain a noncaloric compound called stevioside, a substance that is 100 to 300 times sweeter than sugar. Because stevia does not cause tooth decay and has a negligible effect on blood sugar, it has become a popular sweetener.

Stevia is a shrubby plant to 1½ ft. tall and about 1 ft. wide, with toothed, oblong to lance-shaped, papery-textured leaves to about 2 in. long. Clusters of small white flowers with purple throats appear in summer atop wandlike stems.

CARE

Start with plants purchased at a garden center or from a mail-order nursery. Choose a site with full sun and moist, fertile, well-drained soil. Stevia does equally well in the ground or in pots, but it will not tolerate frost. Propagate by cuttings taken in summer. Wait until late fall to harvest leaves, as cool temperatures and short days intensify the sweetness. Cut stems near the base of the plant and place them on a net or screen to dry. When stems and leaves have dried completely, strip and crush the leaves. Foliage retains its bright green color even when dry.

STEWARTIA

Theaceae
Deciduous shrubs or trees

- ZONES VARY BY SPECIES
- LIGHT SHADE
- REGULAR WATER

Stewartia monadelpha

These slow-growing plants are all-season performers that show off fresh green leaves in spring, white flowers resembling single camellias in summer, and colorful foliage in fall. Winter reveals a distinctive pattern of bare branches and smooth bark that flakes off in varying degrees, depending on species. All grow best in well-drained, acid soil with lots of organic matter. Good in woodland gardens and as foreground specimens against a backdrop of larger, darker-leafed trees.

S. malacodendron. SILKY STEWARTIA. Shrub or small tree. Zones MS, LS, CS; USDA 7-9. Native to the Southeast. Heat-tolerant plant to 10–15 ft. tall and wide. Young shoots and leaf undersides are downy textured. Leaves grow 2–4 in. long; flowers are 3½ in. wide and feature purple stamens with blue anthers. Bark is not as showy as that of other species.

S. monadelpha. TALL STEWARTIA. Tree. Zones US, MS, LS; USDA 6-8. From Korea, Japan. To 25 ft. tall, 20 ft. wide, with slender, upward-angled branches. Leaves are 1½–3 in. long; brilliant red in fall. Flowers to 1½ in. wide. Smooth, cinnamon-brown bark. Heat tolerant and easy to grow.

S. ovata. MOUNTAIN CAMELLIA. Shrub or small tree. Zones US, MS, LS; USDA 6-8. From the Southeast. To 10–15 ft. tall and wide. Leaves grow 2–5 in. long, turn orange to scarlet in fall; 3-in.-wide flowers have frilled petals. Bark is not as handsome as that of other species. *S. o. grandiflora* has 4-in. flowers with lavender anthers; it will bloom even as a young plant.

S. pseudocamellia. JAPANESE STEWARTIA. Tree. Zones US, MS; USDA 6-7. Native to Japan and Korea. Forms a pyramid that may reach 30–40 ft. tall, 20–25 ft. wide after many years. Leaves to 2½–3 in. long; bronze to purple fall color. Cup-shaped flowers 2½ in. wide have orange anthers. Very showy bark: It flakes off to reveal a patchwork of green, gray, brown, rust, terra-cotta, and cream. Two good selections are 'Ballet', with flowers nearly 4 in. wide, and 'Milk and Honey', an especially profuse bloomer with brighter-colored bark. Members of Koreana Group (*S. koreana*, *S. pseudocamellia koreana*) have orange to red-orange fall color and 3-in.-wide flowers that open out flatter than those of the species. All of these need cool, moist soil. They suffer badly from leaf scorch if planted in hot, dry areas.

STIPA
FEATHER GRASS
Poaceae
Perennial grasses

- US, MS, LS, CS; USDA 6-9
- FULL SUN
- WATER NEEDS VARY BY SPECIES

Stipa gigantea

These clump-forming grasses produce large, open, airy inflorescences that can add lightness and motion to the garden. The genus has undergone much revision by botanists, and some of its former members are now known by other names; for one example, see *Nassella tenuissima*, the highly ornamental Mexican feather grass. Deer don't seem to care for these grasses.

S. gigantea. GIANT FEATHER GRASS. From Spain, Portugal, Morocco. Narrow, arching, evergreen leaves in a clump to 2–3 ft. tall and slightly wider. Open, airy sheaves of yellowish flowers bloom in summer, forming a broad, shimmering cloud that rises 6 ft. tall and as wide or slightly wider. Little to moderate water.

S. ramosissima (*Austrostipa ramosissima*). PILLAR OF SMOKE. From Australia. To 6–7 ft. tall, 3 ft. wide. The erect column of evergreen foliage and blossoms does somewhat resemble a pillar of smoke. Flowering is almost continuous; the airy, light tan inflorescences make up half (or a little more) of the plant's total height. Regular water.

STOKESIA LAEVIS
STOKESIA, STOKES' ASTER
Asteraceae
Perennial

- US, MS, LS, CS; USDA 6-9
- FULL SUN
- REGULAR WATER

Stokesia laevis 'Purple Parasols'

Native to the Southeast. Rugged and very adaptable; one of the best perennials for Florida. Semievergreen in the Upper South, evergreen elsewhere. Grows 1½–2 ft. high, 1½ ft. wide, with stiff, erect, much-branched stems. Smooth, firm-textured, medium green leaves are 2–8 in. long, sometimes toothed at the base. Blooms from May to September. Leafy, curved, finely toothed bracts surround the tight flower buds, which open to 3- to 4-in.-wide, asterlike blossoms in blue, purple, white, or yellow. Each flower consists of a central button of small florets surrounded by a ring of larger rays. Choices include these favorite selections, all of which grow a little taller than wide.

'Blue Danube'. Large flowers in medium blue. Grows 12–15 in. tall.

'Bluestone'. Heavy bloomer with medium blue blossoms. To 10 in. tall.

'Honeysong Purple'. Bright purple flowers on a 12- to 15-in.-tall plant.

'Mary Gregory'. Striking lemon-yellow blooms on a 1½-ft.-tall plant.

'Peachie's Pick'. Rich blue flowers come a bit later than those of other selections; long bloom period. Grows 1–1½ ft. tall.

'Purple Parasols'. Flowers change from powder-blue through purple to magenta with age. To 1½ ft. tall.

'Silver Moon'. Pure white flowers. Grows to 1½ ft. tall.

'Wyoming'. Deep purple blooms. To 1½ ft. tall.

ABOVE: Stokesia laevis 'Silver Moon'

STRAWBERRY
Rosaceae
Perennial

- ZONES VARY BY SELECTION
- FULL SUN
- REGULAR WATER, EXCEPT AS NOTED

Strawberries

Strawberries of one type or another can be grown pretty much throughout the South. Known botanically as *Fragaria x ananassa*, they are easily accommodated in most any garden. Plants have toothed, roundish, medium green leaves and white flowers. They grow 6–8 in. tall and spread by long runners to about 1 ft. across. For descriptions of ornamental strawberries, see *Fragaria*.

Strawberries are grouped into three main categories. June-bearing types produce one crop per year in late spring or early summer; they are generally the highest quality, most dependable strawberries Southerners can grow. Everbearing types (a rather misleading term in the South) bear one crop in late spring or early summer and a second, smaller crop in fall. With a few exceptions, they're better performers in the Upper and Middle South than they are farther south, where long, hot summers do them in. Day-neutral strawberries (so-called because day length doesn't determine when they fruit) are similar to everbearing types in that they bear both spring and fall crops—but they produce more fruit in fall over a longer period, and the fruit quality is better. Everbearing and day-neutral types produce few runners and are great for small gardens.

STRAWBERRIES

SELECTION	ZONES	DESCRIPTION	RESISTANCE
JUNE-BEARING TYPES			
'Allstar'	US, MS, LS, CS; USDA 6-9	Large, tasty, light red berries; consistent producer; great all-around performer	Resists most diseases; susceptible to anthracnose
'Apollo'	US, MS, LS, CS; USDA 6-9	Big crop of large, tasty berries; reliable; fairly late	Disease resistant
'Camarosa'	US, MS, LS, CS; USDA 6-9	Huge, conical berries of excellent quality; needs little winter chill; not very cold hardy; introduced in California, now popular in Florida	Susceptible to powdery mildew
'Chandler'	US, MS, LS, CS, TS; USDA 6-11	Very large, bright red berries with good flavor; does well in all areas	Resists most diseases; susceptible to anthracnose
'Earliglow'	US, MS, LS; USDA 6-8	Firm, deep red fruit with an excellent sweet flavor	Disease resistant
'Rosa Linda'	CS, TS; USDA 9-11	Early good-size crop of large, bright red, aromatic fruit with good flavor; needs little winter chill; popular in Florida	Resists most diseases and pests
'Strawberry Festival'	CS, TS; USDA 9-11	Bright red, medium to large, conical fruit that is sweet and fragrant; long stems make harvest easy	Resists most diseases
'Surecrop'	US, MS, LS; USDA 6-8	Large crop of medium to large berries with excellent flavor; very productive; tolerates drought and poor soil	Resists most diseases
'Sweet Charlie'	CS, TS; USDA 9-11	Large, very sweet, orange-red berries; needs little winter chill; does well in Florida	Resists anthracnose; susceptible to botrytis (gray mold)
'Tennessee Beauty'	US, MS, LS; USDA 6-8	Late crop of dark red, medium to large berries with slightly tart flavor; vigorous and productive	Resists most diseases; susceptible to red stele
EVER-BEARING TYPES			
'Ozark Beauty'	US, MS, LS; USDA 6-8	Large, long-necked fruit with mild, sweet flavor; produces many runners; very cold hardy	Resists most diseases
'Quinault'	US, MS, LS; USDA 6-8	Large, attractive berries are tasty buy rather soft	Resists most diseases; susceptible to botrytis (gray mold)
DAY-NEUTRAL TYPES			
'Albion'	US, MS, LS; USDA 6-8	Long, conical, firm fruit with excellent flavor	Disease resistant
'Aromas'	US, MS, LS, CS; USDA 6-9	Excellent vigor; produces large, sweet, high-quality berries; developed in California; popular in Florida	Resists mites and mildew
'Seascape'	US, MS, LS; USDA 6-8	Heavy producer of large, sweet fruit	Disease resistant
'Tristar'	US, MS, LS; USDA 6-8	Large berries with excellent flavor; bears well the first year; widely adapted	Disease resistant
'Tristan'	US, MS, LS; USDA 6-8	Noted for deep-pink flowers; almond-shaped fruit is so-so	Susceptible to botrytis (gray mold)

How many strawberries should you plant? For a small harvest, grow a dozen or so plants in a sunny patch in a flower or vegetable garden, or put them in containers on the patio. For a big crop, set out as many plants as you can handle, spacing them 14–18 in. apart in rows 2–2½ ft. apart. Strawberries reproduce

HOW TO GROW STRAWBERRIES

LOCATION Choose an open, sunny area with little root competition. Avoid low spots, where frosts might damage flowers in spring. Don't plant where tomatoes, potatoes, peppers, or eggplants have previously grown, as the soil may harbor wilt disease.

SOIL Plant in well-drained, fertile, slightly acid soil (pH 6–6.5). If your soil is alkaline, plant in raised beds or containers such as strawberry pots.

PLANTING Planting time often depends on when plants are available from local garden centers. In the Coastal and Tropical South, set out June-bearing sorts in October for a spring crop; elsewhere, plant in early spring for a harvest the following year. Set out everbearing and day-neutral plants in spring for summer and fall berries. (In the Coastal and Tropical South, day-neutrals may be available for fall planting; everbearing types aren't recommended there.) Pinch off the first set of blooms to increase plant vigor. Mulching around plants deters weeds, conserves soil moisture, and keeps berries clean. Where winter temperatures dip below 20°F, a winter mulch is a necessity. Cover with a 4- to 6-in. layer of straw or other light, weed-free, organic material. When weather warms in spring, rake the mulch between plants.

WATERING Plants need constant moisture during bearing season. Water in early morning so that foliage can dry out before nightfall. Drip irrigation is ideal, because it keeps foliage dry and reduces disease problems.

FERTILIZING Feed twice a year – once when spring growth begins, then again after the spring crop is harvested. Don't overfertilize, or you'll get mostly leaves and few berries.

THINNING AND RENEWING Crowding leads to diseases and small crops of poor fruit. If planting gets too dense, remove runners as needed. Get rid of older "mother" plants every few years and keep the "daughter" plants (offsets).

Strawberries grown as perennials benefit greatly from annual renovation. After harvest, use a lawn mower set at 2½ in. to cut off the foliage without injuring the crowns. Rake up and dispose of the foliage. Water and fertilize to encourage new growth. Some home gardeners follow the example of commercial growers, who treat strawberries as annuals. Plants are set out in summer or fall with the ground between them covered with black plastic. They're not allowed to make offsets. After harvest, the plants are yanked out and new ones put in. This results in healthier plants, fewer weeds, and bigger berries. June-bearing 'Chandler' is especially well adapted to this technique, but almost any selection can be grown this way.

PESTS AND DISEASES Strawberry plants are subject to many diseases: fruit rots such as anthracnose and botrytis (gray mold); leaf diseases (leaf spot, leaf scorch, leaf blight); crown diseases (anthracnose, Southern blight); and root diseases (verticillium wilt, red stele, black root rot). Powdery mildew can be a problem. Anthracnose is of particular concern in Florida. Strawberry weevils, aphids, mites, slugs, thrips, leafrollers, and nematodes are potential pests. To reduce problems, purchase only certified disease-free, disease-resistant plants; also remove and destroy diseased foliage and fruit. Replace plants with new ones as they begin to decline, usually after 3 years; or start a whole new bed with new plants every few years.

by making new plants (offsets) on the ends of runners, although some make few or no offsets. To get bigger berries (but smaller yields), pinch off all runners. For heavy crops of smaller berries, let runners and offsets fill in the space between rows.

Strawberries are sensitive to local conditions, so a selection that does well in one area may perform poorly in another. Consult with local experts (nursery personnel, Cooperative Extension agents) about the best selections for your garden.

STRELITZIA
BIRD OF PARADISE
Strelitziaceae
Perennials

- ✎ **ZONES VARY BY SPECIES**
- ☼ ◐ **LIGHT SHADE IN HOTTEST CLIMATES**
- 💧 **REGULAR WATER**

Strelitzia reginae

From South Africa. Evergreen plants with long-stalked, leathery leaves. Remarkable blossoms are produced intermittently throughout year; they are long lasting on plant and as cut flowers. Good for poolside; plants produce no litter and withstand some splashing. Resist deer damage. Hardy to about 28°F.

S. nicolai. GIANT BIRD OF PARADISE. Zone TS; USDA 10-11. Clumping, treelike plant to 30 ft. tall and wide. Grown mainly for its dramatic foliage, similar to that of banana (*Musa*): gray-green, 5- to 10-ft.-long leaves arranged fanwise on erect or curving trunks. Flowers are larger than those of *S. reginae* but not as colorful. Floral envelope is purplish gray;

flower is white with dark blue "tongue." Feed young plants frequently until they reach full dramatic size; then give little or no fertilizer. The goal is to achieve and maintain maximum size without lush growth and need for dividing. Cut off dead leaves and thin out any surplus growth.

S. reginae. BIRD OF PARADISE. Zones CS (protected), TS; USDA 9-11. This old favorite is grown for its spectacular flowers, which bear a startling resemblance to the heads of crested tropical birds. Blooms combining orange, blue, and white are borne on long, stiff stems. Flowering is best in cooler seasons (though blooms appear year-round). This species is trunkless, growing 5–6 ft. high and about as wide; blue-green leaves are 1½ ft. long. Benefits greatly from frequent, heavy feeding. Divide infrequently, since large, crowded clumps bloom best. Good in containers. Recovers slowly from frost damage.

STREPTOCARPUS
CAPE PRIMROSE
Gesneriaceae
Perennials

- ✎ **TS; USDA 10-11; OR HOUSEPLANTS**
- ◐ **PARTIAL SHADE; BRIGHT INDIRECT LIGHT**
- 💧💧 **REGULAR TO AMPLE WATER**

Streptocarpus

These tender plants are related to gloxinia (*Sinningia*) and African violet (*Saintpaulia*) and look something like a cross between the two. They have fleshy, sometimes velvety leaves, and their trumpet-shaped flowers appear over a long season; some kinds flower intermittently all year.

Several species are of interest to fanciers, but the most widely available cape primroses are large-flowered hybrids, which form a 2-ft.-wide clump of long, narrow leaves. Foot-tall stems carry 1½- to 2-in. flowers in white, blue, pink, rose, red, purple, often with blotches in a contrasting color. Plants in the subgenus *Streptocarpella* are similar, but leaves are held in stemless rosettes rather than on erect stems.

CARE

All types are typically grown in containers in rich potting mix; repot annually in spring. In frost-free areas, grow outdoors in partial shade. Indoors, grow in bright light but with protection from hot sun. When in growth, water liberally but allow potting mix to dry between soakings. Apply a high-potash fertilizer every other week. In winter, cut back on fertilizer and keep plants barely moist. Remove spent flowers and stems.

STROBILANTHES DYERANUS

PERSIAN SHIELD
Acanthaceae
Tender shrub

LS (PROTECTED), CS, TS; USDA 9-11; OR GROW IN POTS

PARTIAL SHADE

REGULAR WATER

Strobilanthus dyeranus

Native to Burma. Beautiful foliage plant for warm, humid gardens. Grows to 4 ft. tall and 3 ft. wide; soft stemmed and more like a perennial than a shrub. Broadly oval, pointed leaves are 6–8 in. long, somewhat puckered, dark green but richly variegated with

purple and iridescent silver-blue tints. Leaf undersides are bright purple. Pale violet, tubular flowers come in summer in 1½-in. spikes; less showy than foliage.

CARE

Needs rich soil and regular watering. Tip-pinching creates bushier plants, but they often become straggly with age; replace or start over from cuttings. Feed potted plants once a month during growing season with a balanced liquid fertilizer. May survive freezing in Lower South if mulched heavily in late fall; or grow in container, move to shelter over winter. Can also be overwintered indoors in a sunny window.

STYLOPHORUM DIPHYLLUM

CELANDINE POPPY, WOOD POPPY
Papaveraceae
Perennial

US, MS, LS, CS; USDA 6-9

PARTIAL TO FULL SHADE

REGULAR WATER

Stylophorum diphyllum

Native to eastern U.S. Forms a 1- to 2-ft.-wide basal rosette of downy, gray-green, 8- to 12-in.-long leaves that are deeply lobed into five or seven scallop-edged segments. Golden yellow, quite showy flowers are 1–2 in. wide; they appear singly or in loose, few-flowered clusters on branched stems 1–2 ft. tall. Resembles greater celandine (*Chelidonium majus*) but is shorter and blooms in spring rather than summer. Easy to grow in acid or alkaline soil; reseeds and forms colonies if soil is rich

and moist. Stems leak yellow sap when cut. Excellent in woodland gardens as companion to blue phlox, foamflower (*Tiarella*), Virginia bluebells (*Mertensia pulmonarioides*), and mayapple (*Podophyllum*).

STYPHNOLOBIUM JAPONICUM

JAPANESE PAGODA TREE, CHINESE SCHOLAR TREE
Fabaceae
Deciduous tree

US, MS, LS; USDA 6-7

FULL SUN OR PARTIAL SHADE

MODERATE WATER

Styphnolobium japonicum

Native to eastern Asia. Spreading growth to 50–75 ft. high and wide. Young wood is smooth, dark gray-green. Old branches and trunk gradually take on rugged look of oak. Dark green, 6- to 10-in. leaves are divided into 7 to 17 oval leaflets, each 1–2 in. long; undistinguished yellow fall color. Small, yellowish white flowers are carried in branched, foot-long sprays in summer. Pods 2–3½ in. long are narrowed between big seeds for a bead necklace effect. Dropping seeds can be messy and stain pavement. Takes heat, drought, city conditions. 'Regent' is an exceptionally vigorous, uniform grower; 'Princeton Upright' is similar but more erect. 'Pendulum', to 15–25 ft. high and wide, has weeping branches. Spreading forms are good shade trees, though stains from flowers and pods may be a problem on paved surfaces and parked cars. Formerly known as *Sophora japonica*.

STYRAX

SNOWBELL
Styracaceae
Deciduous trees and shrubs

ZONES VARY BY SPECIES

FULL SUN OR PARTIAL SHADE, EXCEPT AS NOTED

REGULAR WATER

Styrax japonicus 'Pink Chimes'

Neat, well-behaved flowering trees of modest size for patios or lawns; make a nice contrast in front of larger, darker-leafed trees. The species described below put on a spring or early summer show of white, bell-shaped flowers in hanging clusters. Leaves of most are oval and pointed. Easy to garden under, since roots are deep and nonaggressive. Provide good, well-drained, acid soil, except as noted.

S. americanus. AMERICAN SNOWBELL. Zones US, MS, LS, CS, TS; USDA 6-9. Native from Florida to Virginia, west to Missouri, Arkansas, and Louisiana. Round-topped shrub, 6–9 ft. tall and not quite as wide, with zigzagging stems carrying bright green leaves to 3½ in. long. Fragrant, ¾-in. flowers, solitary or in clusters of four. Some tolerance of poor drainage. Performs better in light shade.

S. grandifolius. BIGLEAF SNOWBELL. Zones MS, LS, CS; USDA 7-9. Native from Virginia to Florida. To 12 ft. tall and 6 ft. wide, but often smaller. Dark green leaves up to 7 in. long. Fragrant, ½- to 1-in. flowers in 8-in.-long, drooping clusters. Best in light shade and cool, moist soil.

S. japonicus. JAPANESE SNOWBELL, JAPANESE SNOW-DROP TREE. Zones US, MS, LS; USDA 6-8. To 30 ft. tall and 25 ft. wide, with slender, graceful trunk; branches often strongly horizontal, giving tree a broad, flat top. Scallop-edged leaves to 3 in. long turn from dark green to red or yellow in fall. Faintly fragrant, white, ¾-in. flowers hang in small clusters on short side branches. Leaves angle upward from branches while flowers hang down, giving the effect of parallel green and white tiers. Prune to control shape; tends to be shrubby unless lower side branches are suppressed. Splendid tree to look up into; plant it in raised beds near outdoor entertainment areas, or on a high bank above a path. 'Carillon' is a shrubby selection with weeping branches; 'Pink Chimes', also shrubby, has a more upright form and bears pink flowers. 'Marley's Pink Parasol' grows only 6–8 ft. tall and 4 ft. wide in a weeping form with distinctive foliage that is big, dark, and glossy compared to the species. Look for a heavy bloom of pink flowers followed by pale yellow fall color.

S. obassia. FRAGRANT SNOWBELL. Zones US, MS, LS; USDA 6-8. Grows to 20–30 ft. tall, about two-thirds as wide. Oval to round, deep green leaves to 3–8 in. long. Where frosts come very late, leaves may color yellow in autumn. Foliage may partly obscure highly fragrant, 1-in. flowers carried in drooping, 6- to 8-in. clusters at branch ends. Blooms earlier in spring than *S. japonicus*. Newly planted trees often take a few years to start blooming. Good against background of evergreens, or for height and contrast above border of rhododendrons and azaleas.

SUTERA CORDATA

BACOPA
Scrophulariaceae
Perennial

🌡 **TS; USDA 10-11; ANYWHERE AS ANNUAL**

☀ ◐ **AFTERNOON SHADE IN HOTTEST CLIMATES**

💧 **REGULAR WATER**

Sutera cordata

From moist regions of South Africa. Wiry-stemmed creeper with green, roughly heart-shaped, toothed leaves less than 1 in. long. Blooms profusely from late spring to frost (though in much of the South it gives out once the dog days of summer arrive), producing small, five-petaled, golden-throated flowers. Fine in pots, hanging baskets, or as a small-scale ground cover. If used at the front of a border, plant in masses for greater impact. Perhaps best employed as a cool-season annual for spring or fall, or as a winter annual in Florida. Hardy to 28°F.

Original selection (sold as 'Snowflake') has ¼-in. white flowers and grows 1–2 in. high, spreading 1–2 ft. in a growing season; eventually covers 3–4 ft. in mild climates. 'Giant Snowflake' is more vigorous, reaching 6–8 in. high, 3–4 ft. wide in a season; its white flowers are ½ in. wide. 'Snowstorm' resembles 'Giant Snowflake' but blooms more profusely and has greater heat tolerance. 'Snowstorm Blue' and 'Snowstorm Pink' are also available. 'Olympic Gold' has leaves splotched with yellow but is otherwise identical to 'Snowstorm' (to which it sometimes reverts).

CARE

Needs good drainage and air circulation, fertile soil, and regular feeding. Don't allow it to dry out; if it wilts, it probably won't recover. Pinch branch tips to keep plant shapely. If a thick layer of dead stems builds up under foliage, remove dead material and cut plant back to leave 5- to 6-in.-long branches with leafy growth.

SWEET POTATO

Convolvulaceae
Perennial grown as annual

🌡 **US, MS, LS; USDA 6-8**

☀ **FULL SUN**

💧 **REGULAR WATER**

Sweet potatoes

Southerners and sweet potatoes are a match made in heaven. We love the tasty flesh; sweet potatoes love our long, hot summers. In fact, about 40 percent of the nation's sweet potato crop is grown in North Carolina. Unlike true potatoes (that hail from the Andes) or yams (from Africa and Asia), these thickened roots of tropical vines are native to the Caribbean region, most likely the Yucatan Peninsula. They are fat-free and high in fiber and vitamins A, C, and E. Sweet potato's botanical name is *Ipomoea batatas*; see *Ipomoea* for ornamental types.

More than 400 selections of sweet potato are grown; many heirlooms are still popular. Skin colors range from buff to pink to dark red. Flesh may be orange, yellow, white, pink, red, or purple. The following are just a few of the most popular selections.

'Beauregard'. Ready for harvest in 90–95 days. Rose skin, orange flesh. High yields. Stores well. Originated in Louisiana.

'Bonita'. 90–100 days. Tan to light pink skin, white flesh. High sugar content. Nematode resistant. Originated in Louisiana.

'Carolina Ruby'. 115 days. Ruby to purple-red skin, orange flesh. High yields. Heirloom.

'Centennial'. 80–90 days. Red skin; deep orange, soft flesh. Very high yields. Widely planted.

'Covington'. 105–115 days. Rose skin, orange flesh. High yields. Nematode resistant. Originated in North Carolina.

'Evangeline'. 100–110 days. Rose skin, deep orange flesh. Very sweet and moist. Nematode resistant. Originated in Louisiana.

'Jewel'. 120–135 days. Copper skin, orange flesh. High yields. Nematode resistant. Originated in North Carolina.

'O' Henry'. 90 days. Creamy white skin, white flesh. High yields. More disease resistant than most other white sweet potatoes.

'Porto Rico'. 110 days. Pink skin, orange flesh. Average yields. Bush type; good for small gardens.

'Topaz'. 90 days. Copper-orange skin, orange flesh. Good yields. Nematode resistant.

'Vardaman'. 100 days. Yellow-orange skin, deep orange flesh. Delicious flavor. Bush type; good for small gardens. Originated in Mississippi.

'White Delight'. 100–110 days. Purplish pink skin, white flesh. Good yields; good keeper. Nematode resistant. Originated in Georgia.

CARE

Sweet potatoes grow best in well-drained, acid soil (pH 5.8–6.2); sandy loam is ideal. Vining types can spread to 20 ft. and need plenty of room. Bush types are compact, spreading just 3–5 ft., and are better for small gardens.

Start with certified disease-free "slips" (rooted cuttings) obtained from a local or mail-order nursery. If Southern root-knot nematodes are a problem in your area, choose resistant selections. Plant in late spring when the soil has warmed to 70°F. Before planting, mark off rows (3 ft. apart) and dig shallow ditches between them. Pile excavated soil onto rows to form planting ridges; this ensures good drainage. Work in a controlled-release, low-nitrogen fertilizer such as cottonseed meal or composted manure; too much nitrogen produces lots of leaves and small roots. Set slips into ridges so that only stem tips and leaves show aboveground. Space plants 1 ft. apart. Cover plants with row covers to keep out insect pests. To prevent a buildup of disease organisms in the soil, don't grow sweet potatoes in the same location two years in a row.

Harvest before first frost; if tops are killed by sudden frost, harvest immediately. Dig carefully to avoid cutting or bruising roots. Flavor improves in storage (starch is converted to sugar). Let roots dry in the sun until soil can be brushed off; then cure by storing 10 to 14 days in a warm (about 85°F), humid place. Store in a cool, dry environment (not below 55°F).

SWISS CHARD

Chenopodiaceae
Biennial grown as annual

/ US, MS, LS, CS, TS; USDA 6-11

☼ ◐ FULL SUN TO PART SUN

◉ REGULAR WATER

Swiss chard 'Bright Lights'

A form of beet (*Beta vulgaris*) grown for its tasty leaves and stalks, this is one of the easiest vegetables for the home garden. It probably originated in the Mediterranean. New leaves grow up from the center of plants, continue for months, and seldom bolt (go to seed). They're delicious eaten fresh in salads or steamed.

'Fordhook Giant', a heavy-yielding selection with white stalks and crinkled green leaves,

is the standard Swiss chard. For something more colorful, try 'Rhubarb' or 'Vulcan'; both sport blood-red stalks. 'Bright Lights', with stalks of yellow, orange, pink, purple, white, and red, is as good an ornamental as it is a vegetable. 'Peppermint' has pink-and-white striped stems.

CARE

All Swiss chards take about 60 days from sowing to harvest. For a summer crop, sow the big, crinkly, tan seeds ½ to ¾ in. deep at any time from early spring to early summer. For a fall crop, sow in early August. For a winter crop in the Coastal and Tropical South, sow in October. Sow about six seeds per foot in rows 1½–2 ft. apart. Thin seedlings to 1 ft. apart. Apply a complete fertilizer after plants are established. About two months after sowing (when plants are generally 1–1½ ft. tall), you can begin to harvest leaves from the base by cutting or breaking them off.

SYAGRUS ROMANZOFFIANA

QUEEN PALM
Arecaceae
Palm

/ CS (PROTECTED), TS; USDA 9-11

☼ FULL SUN

◉ REGULAR WATER

Syagrus romanzoffiana

This South American palm (sometimes sold under its former name, *Cocos plumosa*) grows 40–50 ft. tall, 20–25 ft. wide, with an arrow-straight trunk. A common lawn and street tree throughout south Florida, though it is weak wooded and prone to

breaking or toppling in storms. Arching, feathery, glossy, green fronds are 10–15 ft. long. White summer flowers come in drooping spikes to 3 ft. long; these are followed in winter by copious quantities of decorative (though messy) yellow-orange fruit. Prefers slightly acid, well-drained soil. If grown in alkaline soil, subject to a disfiguring disease called frizzle top, caused by a deficiency of manganese or potassium. To prevent it, feed regularly with 8-4-12 palm fertilizer containing manganese. Hardy to about 26°F. A hardier form, usually listed as 'Silver Queen', is a robust grower with a thicker trunk and denser canopy; reports indicate hardiness to 15°F. Formerly known as *Arecastrum romanzoffianum*.

SYMPHORICAR-POS

SNOWBERRY, CORALBERRY
Caprifoliaceae
Deciduous shrubs

/ US, MS; USDA 6-7

☼ ◐ ● EXPOSURE NEEDS VARY BY SPECIES

◊ ◖ LITTLE TO MODERATE WATER

Symphoricarpos albus

North American natives. The various plants described here are upright or arching, typically 2–6 ft. high and wide, often spreading by root suckers. Most are best used as informal hedges or as wild thickets for erosion control on steep banks. Clusters of small pink or white flowers in spring or early summer. Attractive round, berrylike fruit remains on stems after leaves drop in autumn; looks nice in winter arrange-

ments, attracts birds. Plants are not usually damaged by browsing deer.

S. albus (*S. racemosus*). COMMON SNOWBERRY. Native from California to Alaska, east to Montana. Roundish, dull green, ¾- to 2-in.-long leaves (to 4 in. and often lobed on sucker shoots). Pink flowers are followed by white fruit from late summer to winter. Produces most fruit in full sun but takes shade. Not a first-rate shrub but useful for its tolerance of poor soil, lower light, general neglect.

S. x chenaultii. Hybrid between *S. orbiculatus* and a species from Mexico. Bears inch-long, blue-green leaves, greenish white flowers, and red fruit lightly spotted with white. Can take full sun in cooler climates; needs partial or full shade in hot areas. 'Hancock' is a foot-high dwarf valued as woodland ground or bank cover.

S. x doorenbosii. This hybrid was developed from *S. orbiculatus*, *S. x chenaultii*, and a selection of *S. albus*. Rounded habit to about 5 ft. high, spreading at least as wide by runners. Broadly oval, pointed leaves to 1½ in. long are dark green above, lighter green beneath. Greenish white flowers are followed by clusters of ½-in., pink-tinged white fruit. Sun or shade. 'Magic Berry' is a compact, spreading plant with rosy pink fruit; 'Mother of Pearl' has a somewhat drooping habit and pink-cheeked white fruit. Stiffly upright 'White Hedge' bears white fruit in clusters that are held mainly above the foliage.

S. orbiculatus (*S. vulgaris*). CORALBERRY, INDIAN CURRANT. From eastern U.S. Resembles *S. albus* but bears white or pink-tinged flowers followed by small purplish red fruit. Fruit is bright and plentiful enough to provide a good fall-into-winter show. Full sun. 'Foliis Variegatis' ('Variegatus') has leaves edged in creamy white.

SYMPHYOTRI-CHUM

ASTER
Asteraceae
Perennials

🌿 **US, MS, LS; USDA 6-8**

☀️ **FULL SUN, EXCEPT AS NOTED**

💧 **REGULAR WATER**

Symphyotrichum oblongifolium
'Fanny'

Recent castoffs from the genus *Aster*, these familiar garden perennials have an unfamiliar name. These are the New World asters, and they now have their own genus. Gardeners rely upon them for their clouds of blue, purple, pink, and white blooms in the autumn garden.

S. cordifolium (*A. cordifolius*). BLUE WOOD ASTER. Native to eastern North America. To 6 ft. tall, 3 ft. wide, with loose, branching clusters of inch-wide lavender flowers. Sun or light shade. 'Little Carlow', to 2 ft. high, bears a profusion of violet-blue flowers.

S. ericoides (*A. ericoides*). HEATH ASTER. Native to eastern North America. To 3 ft. tall and 1 ft. wide, with narrow leaves and strong horizontal branching. Profuse ½-in. blooms in white, pink, or blue. Plants sold as *S. e.* 'Monte Cassino' may actually belong to *S. pringlei*.

S. laeve (*A. laevis*). SMOOTH ASTER. Native to eastern North America. Grows to 3½ ft. tall, 1½ ft. wide, with smooth, mildew-free foliage and clustered 1-in. flower heads of deep purplish blue. 'Bluebird' is a superior selection to 4–5 ft. tall.

S. lateriflorum (*A. lateriflorus*). CALICO ASTER. North American native. Species grows to 4 ft. tall, 1 ft. wide. Garden selections are shorter (to 2 ft.), with profuse branching, tiny leaves and a haze of ½-in., purplish pink flowers. Foliage turns a coppery purplish red in early fall. 'Prince' has blackish purple stems and leaves; its blooms are white with a red center. 'Lady in Black' is a bolder version of 'Prince', with the same dark foliage and masses of tiny, red-centered white flowers; it grows 3–4 ft. tall. 'Coombe Fishacre' is a hybrid developed from *S. lateriflorum*; it produces tiny pink flowers with red centers on a plant to 2–3 ft. tall.

S. novae-angliae (*A. novae-angliae*). NEW ENGLAND ASTER. Native from Vermont to Alabama, west to North Dakota, Wyoming, and New Mexico. Stout-stemmed plant to 3–5 ft. tall and nearly as wide, with hairy leaves to 5 in. long. Flowers are 2 in. wide; they are violet-blue in the basic form, with selections in other blue shades, white, pink, nearly red, and deep purple. All are very tolerant of wet soils and will reseed. Two longtime favorite selections are good garden plants: 'Alma Potschke' produces salmon-pink, single blooms on 3-ft. stems from late summer to early fall; 'Harrington's Pink' produces clear pink single flowers over a long autumn season on 3- to 4-ft. stems. Another good selection is 'Purple Dome', which reaches just 1½ ft. tall and has brilliant purple blooms.

S. novi-belgii (*A. novi-belgii*). NEW YORK ASTER, MICHAELMAS DAISY. Native to eastern North America. To 4 ft. tall and 3 ft. wide, with full clusters of bright blue-violet flowers. Similar to *S. novae-angliae* but with smooth leaves. Hundreds of selections are available, varying in height from less than a foot to over 4 ft.; flower colors include white, cream, blue, lavender, purple, rose, and pink. Among the many choices are 'Persian Rose' (rose-pink) and semidouble 'Professor Anton Kippenburg' (lavender-blue), both under 1 ft. high and 1½ ft. wide. Robust 'Climax' bears large sprays of single medium blue blossoms on stems to 6 ft. high.

S. oblongifolium (*A. oblongifolium*). AROMATIC ASTER. From the central U.S. Grows 2 ft. tall and wide, with light blue-violet, 1-in. flowers that last into late fall, unperturbed by heavy frosts. Pale green leaves are aromatic when crushed. Prefers a dry, open site; tolerates harsh conditions, including heat, cold, poor or alkaline soil, and strong winds. Selection 'October Skies' produces rich sky-blue flowers; 'Raydon's Favorite' bears bluish purple ones. 'Fanny', growing 3–4 ft. tall, has grayish green leaves and masses of bright purple blossoms. 'Raydon's Birthday Pink' grows upright up to 3 ft. tall.

S. patens (*A. patens*). LATE PURPLE ASTER. From the eastern and southeastern U.S. To 3 ft. tall, 1½–2 ft. wide. Prolific show of bright violet-blue, 1-in. flowers. Tolerates drought and partial shade.

S. pilosum pringlei (*A. pilosus pringlei, A. pringlei*). HAIRY ASTER. Eastern U.S. native known in cultivation through its selection 'Monte Cassino', a familiar florists' cut flower. Grows to 5 ft. tall and 1½ ft. wide; tall, narrow stems have many short side branches set with starry, white, ¾-in. flowers. This plant is often sold as *S. ericoides* 'Monte Cassino'.

SYMPHYTUM OFFICINALE

COMFREY
Boraginaceae
Perennial

🌿 **US, MS, LS, CS; USDA 6-9**

☀️🌓 **PARTIAL SHADE IN HOTTEST CLIMATES**

💧 **REGULAR WATER**

⚠️ **LEAVES CAN BE HARMFUL IF INGESTED**

Symphytum officinale

From Eurasia. Deep-rooted plant forms a clump to 3–4 ft. high, 2 ft. wide. Furry leaves are set with stiff hairs. Basal leaves grow to 8 in. or longer; upper leaves are smaller. Small (½-in.-long), unshowy flowers are usually dull rose in color but sometimes white, cream, or purple. In frost-free climates, plant remains leafy through winter; elsewhere, it dies to the ground in fall.

Comfrey has a long history as a folk remedy. The leaves can be dried and brewed to make a medicinal tea, though this use is no longer recommended (leaves have been found to contain potentially carcinogenic substances). Herb enthusiasts claim that the plant adds minerals to compost, but think hard before establishing it in your garden: it spreads freely from roots and is difficult to eradicate.

SYMPLOCARPUS FOETIDUS

SKUNK CABBAGE, EASTERN SKUNK CABBAGE
Araceae
Perennial

🌿 **US, MS; USDA 6-7**

🌓⚫ **LIGHT TO FULL SHADE**

💧💧 **AMPLE WATER**

Symplocarpus foetidus

Native to freshwater wetlands of eastern North America from Canada south to Tennessee and North Carolina. A truly fascinating plant featuring large, glossy, green leaves reminiscent of hostas, it forms long-lived colonies along streams and creeks in the shade of tall hardwoods.

Its common name comes from the pungent odor briefly released by unusual flowers in early spring to attract pollinating insects. Inconspicuous flowers are held inside a modified leaf with an opening in the side, called a spathe. This hoodlike spathe, reddish maroon, often with yellow streaks, is remarkable for its ability to generate internal heat, averaging 30 degrees higher than the surrounding air temperature, which it uses to melt any snow or ice covering it. After pollination, the flowers give rise to wine-red fruit clusters that drop seeds in late summer.

Leaves emerge in spring from a large bud next to the spathe. The bud elongates into the shape of a spear and then handsome, bright-green leaves unfold in a spiraling pattern to form a rosette. Held on long stems, the oblong leaves may eventually grow 3 ft. long. Foliage begins to decay in summer and usually disappears by August.

CARE

Skunk cabbage needs consistently moist soil. Established plants are virtually impossible to dig from the wild due to massive networks of contractile roots that actually pull the plants deeply into mucky soil. Order skunk cabbage from specialty nurseries instead. Virtually no insects or animals eat it.

SYMPLOCOS PANICULATA
SAPPHIREBERRY
Symplocaceae
Deciduous shrub

🌿 **US, MS, LS; USDA 6-8**

☼ **FULL SUN**

💧 **REGULAR WATER**

Symplocos paniculata

To 10–20 ft. tall; wider than tall in maturity. Can be trained as a low-branching or multitrunked

small tree. Dark green leaves to 3½ in. long and half as wide. In late spring or early summer, 2- to 3-in. clusters of small, fragrant, white flowers bloom on previous year's wood—but the main draw is the autumn show of sapphire-blue, ⅓-in. fruit that garlands the branches. Berries are much appreciated by birds. Single plants set little or no fruit, so it's best to plant groups of seedlings; groups of cutting-grown plants from the same parent will not produce well. Some growers always sell plants in groups of three seedlings to ensure fruiting. Use for screening or as a feature in a large shrub border.

SYNGONIUM
ARROWHEAD VINE
Araceae
Evergreen vines

🌿 **TS; USDA 10-11; OR HOUSE-PLANTS**

☼ **PARTIAL SHADE; BRIGHT INDIRECT LIGHT**

💧 **REGULAR WATER**

Syngonium podophyllum

Outdoors in the Tropical South, these vines trail over the ground or loop around palm trees, their stems wrist thick and their leaves huge, green, and multifingered. They are hardly recognizable compared to the juvenile forms, which are common houseplants. Young leaves have an arrowhead shape and range in color from solid green to shades of green with white, pink, or yellow markings that usually fade on adult leaves. Grow fast in moderately moist soil with lots of organic matter; reduce watering in winter. Indoors, maintain a minimum temperature of 60°F,

place in bright indirect light, and mist to keep leaves looking lush. Feed with a general-purpose liquid houseplant fertilizer monthly, spring through fall. For a compact, clumping plant that keeps producing young leaves, pinch stem tips and cut back runaway vining stems.

In the following entries, leaf descriptions apply to juvenile leaves.

S. podophyllum. Native from Mexico to Panama. Dark green, glossy leaves, 6–12 in. long, on slender, 1- to 2-ft.-long leafstalks. Many selections are available, including 'Emerald Gem', quilted green leaves with a varnished luster; 'Maya Red' (*S.* 'Maya Red'), pink young leaves; and 'White Butterfly', green-and-white marbled leaves on stout stems.

S. wendlandii. Native to Costa Rica. Velvety, thin-textured, green leaves, 4–8 in. long, with silver-gray veins. 'Neon Robusta' is an upright grower with pink leaves.

SYRINGA
LILAC
Oleaceae
Deciduous shrubs, rarely trees

🌿 **ZONES VARY BY SPECIES**

☼ **LIGHT SHADE IN HOTTEST CLIMATES**

💧 **REGULAR WATER**

Syringa vulgaris 'Sensation'

If there is one shrub Northerners wish they could bring with them to the South, this is it. No plant is more cherished than lilac for big, flamboyant, fragrant flowers. Most popular are the common lilac (*S. vulgaris*) and its scads of selections, but many other

species and hybrids merit attention. Most are medium-size to large shrubs with no particular appeal when out of bloom. Leaves are typically oval and pointed or rounded, with smooth edges. Floral show (always after leaf-out) comes from numerous small flowers packed into dense clusters shaped like pyramids or cones. Depending on where you live, flowering may occur anywhere from earliest spring to early summer—that is, if flowering occurs. Like the Green Bay Packers, most lilacs are used to long, cold winters, and without that chill they are likely to perform poorly. This disappoints folks who are looking for the same spectacle in Atlanta that they enjoyed in Bangor. Some types, however, such as *S.* x *laciniata* and others described here, bloom well with only light winter chill and put on a good show even in the Lower South. Most lilacs won't bloom in the Coastal South—and certainly not in the Tropical South.

S. x chinensis. CHINESE LILAC. Zones US, MS; USDA 6-7. Hybrid between *S. vulgaris* and *S.* x *persica*. To 15 ft. high and wide, usually much less. More graceful than *S. vulgaris*, with finer-textured leaves to 3 in. long. Profuse, open clusters of fragrant, rosy purple flowers. Does well in mild-winter, hot-summer climates. 'Alba' has white blossoms. 'Lilac Sunday' is a vigorous, disease-resistant selection with light purple blossoms.

S. x hyacinthiflora. Zone US; USDA 6. Group of fragrant hybrids between *S. vulgaris* and *S. oblata*, a Chinese species. Resemble *S. vulgaris* but generally bloom 7 to 10 days earlier; unreliable bloom in most of the South. 'Asessippi' (lavender) and 'Mount Baker' (white) are earliest. Other selections include 'Alice Eastwood' (double magenta), 'Blue Hyacinth' (lavender), 'Clarke's Giant' (lavender; larger flowers than others), 'Esther Staley' (magenta), 'Excel' (light lavender), 'Gertrude Leslie' (double white), 'Maiden's Blush' (pink; excellent performer), 'Pocahontas' (purple), and 'Purple Heart' (purple).

A group of complex hybrids developed by the U.S. National Arboretum include uniform, heavy-blooming, disease-tolerant plants, some of which thrive in

S

the Middle South (USDA 7). Look for 'Betsy Ross', to 10 ft. tall, 13 ft. wide, with large white flowers; 'Declaration', to 8 ft. tall and wide, with reddish purple flowers; and 'Old Glory', to 12 ft. tall and wide, with bluish-purple flowers.

S. x laciniata. CUTLEAF LILAC. Zones US, MS, LS, CS; USDA 6-9. Open-structured plant to 8 ft. tall, 10 ft. wide. Leaves to 2½ in. long, divided nearly to midrib into three to nine segments; good rich green color. Many small clusters of fragrant, lilac-colored blooms. Highly mildew resistant. Blooms well even in Lower and Coastal South.

S. meyeri. MEYER LILAC. Zones US, MS, LS; USDA 6-8, except as noted. From northern China and Japan. Compact, rounded shrub to 5–6 ft. tall and 4 ft. wide, with oval leaves to 1¼ in. long. Fragrant, lavender-pink blooms appear in 3-in.-long clusters. Resists mildew. Best-known variety 'Palibin' is slow growing, with dense, twiggy growth to 3–5 ft. tall and wide. It blooms

when only 1 ft. high; a profusion of reddish purple buds open to fragrant, single bright pink flowers in 5-in. clusters.

Several popular hybrids resulted from crosses involving *S. m.* 'Paliban'. 'Josée' (US, MS; USDA 6-7) grows 6 ft. tall, 5 ft. wide, with small, fragrant, lavender-pink blooms produced in spring and then occasionally throughout the growing season, often with a second flush of bloom in fall. 'Bloomerang' (US, MS, LS, CS; USDA 6-9) is another reblooming lilac; it grows just 3–4 ft. high and wide, with a profusion of light purple or reddish purple flowers in spring and late summer or fall. 'Tinkerbelle' (US, MS; USDA 6-7), a dense, upright grower to 5–6 ft. tall and wide, has fine-textured foliage and spicy-scented pink flowers; makes a nice specimen shrub or informal hedge.

S. x persica. PERSIAN LILAC. Zones US, MS; USDA 6-7. Graceful, loose form to 6 ft. high and wide; leaves 2½ in. long. Many clusters of fragrant, pale violet flowers ap-

pear all along arching branches. 'Alba' has white flowers.

S. x prestoniae. PRESTON LILAC. Zones US, MS; USDA 6-7. Group of extra-hardy hybrids developed in Canada. To 12 ft. tall and wide. Flowers come on new growth at the end of the lilac season, after *S. vulgaris* has finished. Bulky, dense plants resemble *S. vulgaris*, but individual flowers are smaller and are not as fragrant. One of the best is 'James MacFarlane', a pink-blooming selection that blooms well as far south as Atlanta.

S. pubescens microphylla 'Superba' (*S. microphylla* 'Superba'). Zones US, MS, LS; USDA 6-8. Selection of a lilac native to China. Compact grower to 7 ft. tall, twice as wide. Mildew-resistant leaves to 2 in. long, with bronze fall color. Deep red buds open to fragrant, single bright pink flowers. May rebloom in early autumn. Heat tolerant.

S. pubescens patula 'Miss Kim' (*S. patula* 'Miss Kim'). Zones US, MS, LS; USDA 6-8. Selection of a lilac from northern China and Korea. Dense, twiggy, rounded; eventually to 8–9 ft. high and wide, but stays small for many years. Sometimes grafted high to make a standard tree. Purple buds open to very fragrant ice-blue flowers. Leaves are 2–4½ in. long; may turn burgundy in fall. Heat tolerant.

S. reticulata. JAPANESE TREE LILAC. Zones US, MS, LS; USDA 6-7. From Japan. To 30 ft. tall, 20 ft. wide; can be grown as large shrub or easily trained as single-stemmed tree. Smooth, glossy, red-brown bark. Leaves to 5 in. long. Blooms on new growth late in the lilac season, bearing white, musky-scented flowers in showy clusters to 1 ft. long. This is the most problem-free lilac. It makes a good lawn tree, street tree, or informal screen. 'Ivory Silk' is a compact grower to 20 ft. tall, with cream-colored flowers borne in profusion even at a young age. 'Snowdance' is slightly smaller, with large panicles of white blooms. 'Signature', to 25 ft. high, has rounded clusters of white flowers.

S. vulgaris. COMMON LILAC. Zones US, MS, LS (some); USDA 6-9. From eastern Europe. Can eventually reach 20 ft. tall, with nearly equal spread. Suckers strongly. Prune out suckers on

grafted plants (no need to do so on own-root plants). Dark green leaves to 5 in. long. Blooms in midspring, bearing pinkish or bluish lavender flowers in clusters to 10 in. long or longer ('Alba' has pure white flowers). Fragrance is legendary; lilac fanciers swear that the species and its older selections are more fragrant than newer types. Make excellent cut flowers.

Selections, often called French hybrids, number in the hundreds. They generally flower a little later than the species and have larger clusters of single or double flowers in a wide range of colors. Singles are often as showy as doubles, sometimes more so. All of these lilacs require 2 to 5 years to settle down and produce flowers of full size and true color. Here are just a few of the many choice selections: 'Andenken an Ludwig Späth' (reddish purple to dark purple), 'Charles Joly' (double dark purplish red), 'Katherine Havemeyer' (lavender-pink), 'Madame Lemoine' (double white), 'Miss Ellen Willmott' (double white), 'President Grevy' (double medium blue), 'President Lincoln' (Wedgwood blue), 'President Poincaré' (double two-tone purple), 'Sensation' (deep purple to wine-red with white picotee edge), and 'William Robinson' (double lilac-pink).

Other hybrids include 'Krasavitsa Moskvy' ('Beauty of Moscow'), with large clusters of pink buds opening into white double flowers; 'Nadezhda' ('Hope'), with deep purple buds opening into lilac-blue double flowers; and 'Primrose', with pale yellow blooms.

Descanso hybrids, developed to accept mild winters, perform well in the Lower and Coastal South. Best known is 'Lavender Lady'; others include 'Blue Boy', 'Blue Skies', 'Chiffon' (lavender), 'Forrest K. Smith' (light lavender), 'Sylvan Beauty' (rose-lavender), and 'White Angel' ('Angel White').

CARE

Provide well-drained, neutral to slightly alkaline soil. If your soil is strongly acid, dig in lime before planting. These plants typically bloom on wood formed the previous year, so prune just after flowers fade. (Until plants are established, just pinch back any overlong stems.) Remove spent

TOP: Syringa vulgaris 'Lavender Lady'; *S.* 'Josée'; *BOTTOM: S. v.* 'White Angel'

blossom clusters, cutting back to a pair of leaves; growth buds at that point will make flowering stems for next year. Renovate old, overgrown plants by cutting a few of the oldest stems to the ground each year. For the few types that bloom on new growth, prune in late winter, before new growth starts. Major insect and disease problems include borers, scale, and powdery mildew.

T

TABEBUIA
TRUMPET TREE
Bignoniaceae
Deciduous, evergreen, semievergreen trees

TS; USDA 10-11

FULL SUN OR LIGHT SHADE

REGULAR WATER

Tabebuia chrysotricha

Native to the tropical Americas. Showy, trumpet-shaped flowers are borne in rounded clusters that become larger and more profuse as trees mature. Leaves are typically green; may be simple (undivided) or divided into as many as seven leaflets arranged like fingers of hand. Number of leaflets is often variable within a species.

These trees tend to be gangly or irregular when young; benefit from training in early years. Need well-drained soil; respond well to regular fertilizing. All are useful as color accents and as stand-alone flowering trees for display. Larger types are excellent as street or park plantings; smaller species make beautiful patio trees or container plants.

T. caraiba. TRUMPET TREE. Semievergreen. Grows 15–25 ft. high and 10–15 ft. wide, with a dense, usually asymmetrical crown. Silvery leaves are divided into narrow leaflets. In late winter, just after leaf drop, the tree is covered with 2- to 3-in.-long golden yellow flowers.

T. chrysotricha. GOLDEN TRUMPET TREE. Briefly deciduous. To 25–50 ft. high and wide. Young twigs, leaf undersides covered with tawny fuzz. Golden yellow flowers are 3–4 in. long, often with maroon stripes in throat. Blooms most heavily in spring, when tree loses leaves for brief period. May also bloom lightly at other times, when in leaf.

T. heterophylla. PINK TRUMPET TREE. Evergreen to semievergreen. Slender habit to 40 ft. high, 20 ft. wide; sometimes grown as a large shrub. Flowers 2–3 in. long, in colors ranging from pinkish purple through pink shades to white. Blossoms appear abundantly in spring but may also be seen occasionally throughout the rest of the year.

T. impetiginosa. PINK IPE. Semievergreen. Slow to 25–50 ft. high and wide. In late winter or spring, bears 2- to 3-in. flowers in white to light pink and purple. May rebloom in late summer or fall. Does not bloom as a young tree.

TAGETES
MARIGOLD
Asteraceae
Annuals and perennials

ZONES VARY BY SPECIES

FULL SUN

REGULAR WATER, EXCEPT AS NOTED

Tagetes patula 'Queen Sophia'

In the 1940s and 50s, annual marigolds were America's favorite bedding plants, prized for their extended show of yellow, orange, or maroon flowers. Marigolds are the traditional flowers used in Day of the Dead celebrations. Their popularity in the South has since declined, as many newer annuals that offer more colors and better performance have come on the scene. French and African marigolds, however, are still appreciated for their mass displays in late summer and fall, when other annuals are finished blooming. And the perennial species listed here remain excellent garden plants.

Native to Mexico, Central America, marigolds are free-branching plants ranging from 6 in. to 6 ft. tall. Leaves are finely divided and are usually strongly scented. Easy to grow in well-drained soil. Annuals will bloom from early summer to frost if old flowers are picked off. Handsome, long-lasting cut flowers; strong aroma from leaves, stems, and blossoms permeates a room.

T. erecta. AFRICAN MARIGOLD. Annual. Zones US, MS, LS, CS, TS; USDA 6-11. Original strains were single-flowered plants to 3–4 ft. tall, 2 ft. wide. Modern strains are more varied; most have fully double flowers. They range from dwarf Antigua (10–12 in.); Guys and Dolls, Inca, and Inca II series (12–14 in.) through Galore, Lady, and Perfection (16–20 in.); and Climax (2½–3 ft.). 'Moonsong Deep Orange', 12–15 in. tall, has deep orange, fully double blooms. 'Flagstaff' grows quickly to 4 ft. tall and is loaded with fiery orange, fully double flowers to 3 in. across. Novelty tall strains include Odorless (2½ ft.). Sweet Cream has creamy white flowers on 16-in. stems. Hybrid 'Snowball' has large (3-in.) white flowers on stems to 2 ft. tall. Triploid hybrids, crosses between *T. erecta* and *T. patula*, have exceptional vigor and bear profuse 2-in. flowers over a long bloom season; they are generally shorter than other *T. erecta* strains. Examples are Zenith series (12–15 in. high) and Nugget series (10–12 in. high).

Avoid overhead sprinkling on taller kinds; stems will sag and even break under weight of water. To make tall types stand as firmly as possible (perhaps stoutly enough to do without staking), dig planting hole extra deep, strip any leaves off lower 1–3 in. of stem, and plant with stripped portion below soil line.

T. filifolia. IRISH LACE. Annual. Zones US, MS, LS, CS, TS; USDA 6-11. Forms a mound of bright green, finely divided foliage to 6 in. high and wide; resembles an unusually fluffy, rounded fern. Used primarily as an edging plant for its foliage effect, but tiny white flowers are attractive.

T. lemmonii. COPPER CANYON DAISY. Shrubby perennial. Zones LS, CS, TS; USDA 8-11. Grows 3–6 ft. tall and wide. Finely divided, 2- to 4-in.-long leaves are strongly fragrant when brushed against or rubbed—they smell like a blend of marigold, mint, and lemon. Golden yellow flowers with orange cones are carried at branch ends late summer through fall; may bloom sporadically at other times. Cut back before new spring growth begins. Damaged by frost in open situations; cut back to remove damaged growth or to correct shape. Tends to be short lived. Moderate to regular water. 'Gold Medal' grows just 1–2 ft. tall and wide.

T. lucida. MEXICAN MINT MARIGOLD, MEXICAN TARRAGON. Perennial in Zones LS, CS, TS; USDA 8-11; often grown as an annual in all zones. To 3 ft.

high and wide, typically with unbranched stems. Narrow, uncut, smooth, dark green leaves have strong scent and flavor of tarragon or licorice (stems and roots are similarly fragrant). Yellow flowers, produced in fall and spring, are a nice surprise. Moderate to regular water.

T. patula. FRENCH MARIGOLD. Annual. Zones US, MS, LS, CS, TS; USDA 6-11. Most selections grow 6 in. to 1½ ft. high and wide, in flower colors from yellow to rich maroon-brown. Blossoms may be fully double or single; many are strongly bicolored. Excellent for edging are dwarf, very double strains such as Little Hero (6–8 in.), Janie (8 in.), Bonanza (10 in.), and Hero (10–12 in.), all with 2-in. flowers in a range of colors from yellow through orange to red and brownish red. Aurora and Sophia strains have flowers that are larger (to 2½ in. wide) but not as double. 'Harlequin', to 2–3 ft. tall and wide, has 3-in.-wide flowers boldly striped in red and yellow.

T. tenuifolia (T. signata). SIGNET MARIGOLD. Annual. Zones US, MS, LS, CS, TS; USDA 6-11. Infrequently grown species. Flowers are small (just 1 in. wide) and single, but bloom is incredibly profuse. Finely cut foliage. Gem strain offers golden yellow, lemon-yellow, and tangerine-orange blossoms on 10- to 12-in.-tall plants.

CARE

Annual marigolds are among the easiest flowers to grow from seed. Large, easy-to-handle seeds sprout in a few days in warm soil. For earlier bloom, buy nursery plants. Watch out for snails and slugs, which often devour young plants. Spider mites often attack during hot, dry weather.

TALINUM
Portulacaceae
Perennials often grown as annuals

- ✎ **CS, TS; USDA 9-11**
- ☼ **FULL SUN**
- 💧 **MODERATE WATER**

Talinum paniculatum 'Variegatum'

These easy-to-grow perennials are prized for their attractive, delicate flowers. They're not particular about soil, but they do require good drainage.

T. calycinum (*Phemeranthus calycinus*). FAME FLOWER. Native from Missouri and Arkansas south to Mexico. In the wild, forms large colonies in rocky soils. Very narrow, succulent leaves to 2 in. long form basal foliage clumps to 1 ft. wide. Open clusters of pink to red, five-petaled flowers appear atop 8-in.-tall leafless stems. Flowers open in morning, close by midafternoon. Perfect for a rock garden.

T. paniculatum. JEWELS-OF-OPAR. Tender perennial, native from southern U.S. to Central America. A true Southern passalong plant, rarely purchased at garden centers but frequently showing up as an unannounced but welcome guest in gardens. Forms a low, 1- to 2-ft.-wide rosette of oval, pointed, bright green leaves to 3 in. long. In summer, thin stalks to 2 ft. tall carry large clusters of tiny pink flowers; these are followed by beadlike yellow seedpods that mature to a rich burgundy-red. Good in containers or at the front of the border. Reseeds readily. 'Limon' has chartreuse foliage. 'Variegatum' has grayish green leaves with white margins.

TAMARIX
TAMARISK
Tamaricaceae
Deciduous shrubs or trees

- ✎ **ZONES VARY BY SPECIES**
- ☼ **FULL SUN**
- 💧 **LITTLE OR NO WATER TO MODERATE WATER**

Tamarix parviflora

Native to Europe and Asia. These large shrubs or small trees are useful in areas where wind, salt, and poor soil are challenges, as in coastal gardens. Their only demands are sun and good drainage. Tiny, scalelike, light green or bluish leaves are held on airy, arching, reddish branches; in spring or summer, narrow plumes of small pink or rose blooms appear at branch ends. Prune regularly to maintain graceful effect. Locate where plant won't be prominent while out of leaf. These plants have become pests in the arid Southwest, where their greedy roots compete with those of native plants for water. *T. gallica* is abundant along stream banks in western Oklahoma and Texas. There is much confusion in labeling of tamarisks in nurseries and among botanists.

T. gallica. FRENCH TAMARISK. Zones US, MS, LS, CS; USDA 6-9. Variable in size, but typically 15–20 ft. tall and wide. Reddish brown to dark purple bark and blue-green foliage. Blooms in summer, mostly on new season's growth, so prune in late winter; flowers are white to pink, in 2-in.-long clusters. Thrives in sandy, alkaline soil. Tolerates drought and salt spray. Good plant for beach areas. Excellent drainage is essential.

T. parviflora. SMALL-FLOWERED TAMARISK. Zones US, MS, LS; USDA 6-8. To 12–15 ft. tall, not as wide. Pink blossoms in late spring. Blooms on old wood; prune right after bloom.

T. ramosissima (T. pentandra). SALT CEDAR. Zones US, MS, LS; USDA 6-8. Grows 10–15 ft. tall, usually not as wide. Bears rosy pink flowers in spring or early summer. Blooms on new wood; prune in late dormant season. This species not only tolerates salty soil, it also secretes salt through glands in its leaves. Selection 'Cheyenne Red' has deeper pink blooms than the species; 'Pink Cascade' has wispy stems and feathery plumes of pink blooms; 'Rosea' bears rich pink flowers later in summer; 'Summer Glow' has bright pink flowers and blue-tinged foliage.

TANACETUM
Asteraceae
Perennials

- ✎ **ZONES VARY BY SPECIES**
- ☼ **FULL SUN**
- 💧 **MODERATE TO REGULAR WATER**

Tanacetum vulgare

Most species have finely divided leaves (often highly aromatic) and clusters of daisylike flower heads that attract butterflies. Some have gray to nearly white foliage. Resist deer.

T. balsamita (*Chrysanthemum balsamita*). COSTMARY. Zones US, MS, LS, CS; USDA 6-9. Native from Europe to central Asia. Weedy, rhizomatous plant grown for its sweet-scented foliage (used in salads and sachets) rather than its tiny daisies. Leggy stems reach 3 ft. high; if these are cut back, the gray-green, finely scallop-margined basal leaves can make a nice edging for an herb garden. Divide clumps and reset divisions in late summer or fall.

T. coccineum (*Chrysanthemum coccineum, Pyrethrum roseum*). PYRETHRUM, PAINTED DAISY. Zones US, MS, LS; USDA 6-8. Native to Iran and the Caucasus. Bushy plant to 2–3 ft. high, 1½ ft. wide, with very finely divided bright green leaves. Bears long-stemmed single daisies in pink, red, or white in spring; if cut back, may bloom again in late summer. Also available in double- and anemone-flowered forms. Excellent for cutting, borders. Divide clumps or sow seeds in spring. Double forms may not come true from seed; they may revert to single flowers.

T. densum amani. PARTRIDGE FEATHER. Zones US, MS, LS, CS; USDA 6-9. Native to Turkey. Sometimes sold as *Chrysanthemum haradjanii*. Low-growing (6- to 8-in.-high) plant, spreading slowly to make a mat about 1½ ft. wide. Leaves are finely cut, silvery white, featherlike in appearance. Small yellow flower heads appear a few inches above foliage in late spring. Use in rock garden or as small-scale ground cover in bright, sunny area with good drainage. Can withstand some dry spells when established. One of the whitest-looking plants.

T. parthenium (*Chrysanthemum parthenium*). Zones US, MS, LS, CS; USDA 6-9. FEVERFEW. Native to southern Europe and the Caucasus. Compact, leafy, aggressive plant that spreads by volunteer seedlings. Leaves have a strong peppery scent that some people find offensive. Attracts beneficial insects. Selections are 1–3 ft. high. 'Golden Ball' has bright yellow flower heads and no rays; 'Silver Ball' is fully double, with only the white rays showing. In 'Aureum' (commonly sold in flats as 'Golden Feather'), chartreuse foliage is the main attraction. To propagate, divide the clumps in spring; or sow seeds in spring for bloom by midsummer.

T. vulgare. TANSY. Zones US, MS, LS, CS; USDA 6-9. Native to Europe. Coarse, rather weedy garden plant to 3 ft. tall, 2 ft. wide, with finely divided, bright green, aromatic (some say smelly) leaves.

Small, buttonlike yellow flowers appear in late summer. Thin clumps yearly to keep in bounds. This plant is no longer used medicinally, though it is still grown in herb gardens. 'Isla Gold' has bright golden leaves. *T. v. crispum*, fern-leaf tansy, grows 2½ ft. tall; it has finely cut foliage and is more decorative than the species.

TAXODIUM
Cupressaceae
Deciduous trees

⚲ **US, MS, LS, CS; USDA 6-9**

☀ ◐ **FULL SUN TO PART SUN**

💧 💧 **REGULAR TO AMPLE WATER**

Taxodium distichum

Deciduous conifers of great size with shaggy, cinnamon-colored bark and graceful sprays of short, narrow, flat, needlelike leaves. Female flowers are followed by round, fragrant cones about 1 in. across. All are very tough, tolerant trees. Need acid soil. Both of the following species are native to the southeastern U.S.

T. ascendens. POND CYPRESS. Somewhat narrower, more erect than *T. distichum*; trunk not as strongly buttressed. Awl-shaped leaves stand erect on branchlets; those of *T. distichum* are spirally arranged. Can grow 70–80 ft. tall, 20 ft. wide. Leafs out late in spring. In the wild, found on higher ground around ponds, but will grow in standing water, as *T. distichum* does. 'Nutans' is widely grown; it has somewhat pendent branchlets. 'Prairie Sentinel' is very narrow, reaching only about 10 ft. wide.

T. distichum. BALD CYPRESS. From southeastern U.S. Can grow into 100-ft.-tall, broad-topped

tree in the wild, but young and middle-aged garden trees are pyramidal to 50–70 ft. high, 20–30 ft. wide. Feathery foliage sprays with narrow, ½-in.-long leaves in a pale, delicate, yellow-tinged green. Foliage turns orange-toned brown before dropping. Interesting winter silhouette.

When growing in moist or wet soil, develops knobby growths (called knees) around the base. Bagworms may be troublesome in some years, but otherwise this tree is not much bothered by pests or diseases. Requires only corrective pruning to remove dead wood and unwanted branches. An outstanding tree for stream bank or edge of lake or pond. 'Cascade Falls' is a strongly weeping form usually grafted onto understock trunk; can eventually reach 20 ft. high and wide. 'Green Whisper' has very soft-textured, bright green foliage. 'Peve Minaret' is dwarf, forming a dense pyramid just 6 ft. tall and 2–3 ft. wide after 10 years. 'Shawnee Brave' grows into a dense, narrow pyramid just 15–20 ft. wide.

TAXUS
YEW
Taxaceae
Evergreen shrubs or trees

⚲ **US, MS; USDA 6-7, EXCEPT AS NOTED**

☀ ◐ **SUN OR SHADE, EXCEPT AS NOTED**

💧 💧 **MODERATE TO REGULAR WATER**

☘ **FRUIT (SEEDS) AND FOLIAGE ARE POISONOUS IF INGESTED**

Taxus baccata

Yews are to Northern gardens what hollies are to Southern ones—nearly indispensable

evergreen plants suited to a multitude of uses. Both serve well as foundation plants, backdrops, tall screens, clipped hedges, and even ground and bank cover. Heat is what limits the use of yews in the South; most types will survive for only a few years outside of the Upper and Middle South. Plum yew (*Cephalotaxus*) is a good heat-tolerant substitute. Where they grow well, yews are tough plants. They are long lived and can be safely moved even when large. Because yews sprout foliage even from bare wood, they adapt very well to pruning and shearing. They tolerate just about any well-drained soil, and pests are few. Be warned, though: if deer are plentiful where you live, don't bother planting yews, as they'll be quickly devoured. Although they are conifers, yews do not bear cones. Instead, female plants produce juicy, scarlet, berrylike fruit among the dark green needles.

T. baccata. ENGLISH YEW. Tree or shrub. From Europe, North Africa, western Asia. To 25–40 ft. or taller, 15–25 ft. wide, with broad, low crown. Needles ½–1½ in. long, dark green and glossy above, pale beneath; spirally arranged. Far more common than the species are garden selections, including the following.

'Adpressa'. Usually sold as *T. brevifolia*. Wide-spreading, dense shrub to 4–5 ft. high, 6–8 ft. wide. Female.

'Aurea'. Broad pyramid to 25 ft. tall, 12 ft. wide after many years. New foliage is golden yellow from spring to fall, then turns green. Female.

'Fastigiata' ('Stricta'). IRISH YEW. Dark green column to 15–30 ft. tall, 3–10 ft. wide. Has larger needles and more crowded, upright branches than the species. Branches tend to spread near top, especially in snowy regions or where moisture is plentiful. Branches can be tied together with wire. Plants that outgrow their space can be reduced by heading back and thinning; old wood sprouts freely. Golden-leafed forms are available. 'Fastigiata Aureomarginata' is a male selection with yellow-edged green leaves.

'Repandens'. SPREADING ENGLISH YEW. Long, horizontal,

spreading branches make 2- to 4-ft.-high ground cover; extend to 8–10 ft. after many years. Useful low foundation plant. Will arch over wall. Female.

T. cuspidata. JAPANESE YEW. Tree or shrub. In its native Japan, reaches 50 ft. tall; in North America, usually seen as a compact, pyramidal tree to 10–25 ft. (possibly taller), half as wide. Can be kept lower by pinching new growth. Fruits heavily. Needles ½–1 in. long, dark green above, tinged yellowish beneath; usually arranged in two rows along twigs to make a flat or V-shaped spray. The following selections are commonly sold.

'Bright Gold'. Shrubby, upright dwarf to just 3 ft. tall and wide after 10 years; eventually twice that size. Leaves are broadly edged in golden yellow in spring, turning more green in summer. Tolerates full sun better than most; color is best in sunny sites. Male.

'Capitata'. PYRAMIDAL YEW. Upright grower to 40 ft. tall, about half as wide. Female.

'Emerald Spreader'. Flat-topped form to 2½ ft. high, 8–10 ft. wide. Dense growth. Good ground cover for large areas. Female.

'Nana'. Often sold as *T. brevifolia*. Very slow growing—just 1–4 in. a year. Can reach 3 ft. tall, 6 ft. wide in 20 years. Serves as a good low barrier or foundation plant for many years. Female; heavy fruiter.

T. floridana. FLORIDA YEW. Zones LS, CS; USDA 8-9. Extremely rare tree found only on the banks of the Apalachicola River in northern Florida. Bushy evergreen shrub to 15 ft. tall, spreading a bit wider. Flat, inch-long needles are arranged in two ranks on stems. Female plants bear red berries in fall. Prefers shade and slightly acid soil. Do not disturb wild populations of this endangered plant.

T. x media. Shrubs. Hybrids between *T. baccata* and *T. cuspidata*; intermediate between the two in color and texture. Of the dozens of selections available, the following (all with dark green foliage) are among the most widely offered.

'Brownii'. Compact, rounded plant to 6–8 ft. tall, 8–10 ft. wide. Good dense hedge. Male.

'Densiformis'. Dense, flat-topped; grows 2–3 ft. tall, 4–6 ft. across. Female.

'Hatfieldii'. Broad column or pyramid. Reaches 12 ft. tall, 10 ft. wide after 20 years. Male.

'Hicksii'. Upright-growing selection to 10–12 ft. tall, 3–4 ft. wide; slightly broader at center than at top or bottom, widening with age. Good hedge, foundation plant. Male and female forms are sold.

'Kelseyi'. Upright, dense grower to 15 ft. tall, 10 ft. wide. Very dark green needles. Female; heavy fruiter.

'Wardii'. Wide-spreading, flat-topped shrub to 6 ft. tall, 15 ft. wide. Female.

TECOMA

Bignoniaceae
Evergreen shrubs, trees, vines

🌱 **ZONES VARY BY SPECIES**

☼ ☼ **FULL SUN OR LIGHT SHADE**

💧 **MODERATE WATER, EXCEPT AS NOTED**

Tecoma stans

This heat-loving group includes several showy shrubs, one of which can be grown as a vine and another as a tree. All feature 2-in.-long, trumpet-shaped flowers in the yellow-orange-red range and leaves divided featherwise into many leaflets. Excellent for attracting butterflies and hummingbirds. Easy to grow in well-drained soil. Take drought but look best with periodic soakings. Remove faded flowers to prolong bloom and lessen production of seedpods. Resist damage from browsing deer.

T. x alata. ORANGE BELLS. Shrub. Zones LS, CS, TS; USDA 8-11. Grows to 8 ft. tall, 4–5 ft. wide, with bright green foliage and orange flowers throughout warm weather. Tolerates light frost; may die to ground in a hard freeze but recovers quickly in warm weather. Some consider 'Orange Jubilee' to be a selection of this plant; others identify it as a hybrid between *T. capensis* and *T. stans*.

T. capensis (*Tecomaria capensis*). CAPE HONEYSUCKLE. Shrub or vine. Zones CS, TS; USDA 9-11. From South Africa. If tied to a support, can scramble to 15–30 ft.; with hard pruning, makes an upright shrub 6–8 ft. tall, 4–5 ft. wide. Shiny dark green leaflets give it a fine-textured look. Brilliant orange-red flowers in compact clusters appear from fall into spring. Takes wind, salt air. Use as espalier, bank cover (good on hot, steep slopes), coarse barrier hedge. Little water. 'Aurea' has lighter green foliage and yellow flowers; somewhat less vigorous than the species. 'Buff Gold' has golden orange blooms.

T. garrocha. ARGENTINE TECOMA. Shrub. Zones LS, CS, TS; USDA 8-11. From Argentina. To 10 ft. tall and wide. Clusters of salmon to orange blossoms throughout warm weather. Reacts to freezes like *T. x alata*.

T. stans (*Stenolobium stans*). YELLOW BELLS, YELLOW TRUMPET FLOWER, YELLOW ELDER, ESPERANZA. Shrub or tree. Zones CS, TS; USDA 9-11. Native from southern U.S. to Guatemala. In Tropical South, can be trained as a tree. Usually a large shrub in the Coastal South. Wood may die back in hard freezes, but new growth comes on quickly. Can reach 25 ft. tall, 10–20 ft. wide. Large clusters of lightly fragrant, bright yellow flowers from late spring to early winter. Good for boundary planting, big shrub border, screening. Needs heat, deep soil, fairly heavy feeding.

'Gold Star' is a profuse, early bloomer sometimes used as an annual in cold-winter areas. It grows about 3 ft. tall and wide in its first season and may reach 8 ft. tall and wide if not cut back or frozen. Has extra-large blooms that come earlier in the season. 'Sierra Apricot', a hybrid with *T. x alata*, has apricot-colored flowers on a compact, bushy plant just 3 ft. tall and 4–5 ft. wide.

T. s. angustata. Zones LS, CS, TS; USDA 8-11. Native from Arizona to Texas and adjoining Mexico. To 4–10 ft. tall, 3–8 ft. wide. Narrow leaflets. Blooms from midspring to late fall. Needs less water and fertilizer than the species. Hardy to 10°F.

TERNSTROEMIA GYMNANTHERA

JAPANESE CLEYERA
Pentaphylacaceae
Evergreen shrub

🌱 **MS, LS, CS, TS; USDA 7-11**

☼ ☼ **SUN OR LIGHT SHADE**

💧 **REGULAR WATER**

Ternstroemia gymnanthera
'Variegata'

Large, slow-growing, carefree shrub to 10 ft. tall, 6 ft. wide (easily kept smaller through pruning). Good substitute for the overused and disease-prone Fraser photinia (*Photinia x fraseri*). Often confused with true Japanese cleyera (*Cleyera japonica*), page 246.

Glossy, leathery, rounded oval to narrowly oval leaves are 1½–3 in. long, borne on red leafstalks; they are bronzy red when new, maturing to deep green, bronzy green, or purplish red depending on season, exposure, and the particular plant. Red tints are deeper in cold weather. Summer flowers are ½ in. wide, creamy yellow, fragrant but not showy. Fruit resembles little red-orange holly berries.

Grow in moist, well-drained, acid soil. Tip-pinch to encourage compact growth. Use as basic landscaping shrub, informal hedge, foundation plant, poolside plant. Good companion for camellias (to which it is related), azaleas, nandina, pieris, ferns. Cut foliage keeps well.

Several interesting selections are available. 'Bigfoot' has large, glossy, light green leaves and a notably upright habit; it grows quickly to 12–14 ft. tall and only 5–6 ft. wide. 'Bronze Beauty' has bronze new growth and reddish bronze fall color. 'Burnished Gold' produces bright golden new growth that gradually fades to bronzy green. 'LeAnn' has glossy, orange-red new growth that matures to deep green. 'Variegata' has dark green leaves with a creamy yellow edge that turns pink in winter.

TETRADIUM DANIELLII

KOREAN EVODIA
Rutaceae
Deciduous tree

🌿 **US, MS, LS; USDA 6-8**

☼ **FULL SUN**

◐◑ **MODERATE TO REGULAR WATER**

Tetradium daniellii

From northern China and Korea. Distantly related to citrus, but the shiny, dark green leaves are more reminiscent of walnut (*Juglans*): 12–16 in. long, each with five opposite pairs of 2- to 5-in.-long, pointed-oval leaflets plus a single leaflet at the end. Quickly grows to 30–50 ft. tall and wide. Foliage is handsome throughout summer and early fall; in autumn, it may turn yellow or simply drop from the branches while still green. Blooms in early summer, bearing showy, 4- to 6-in.-long, rather flat clusters of small white flowers that are very popular with bees. Fruit is small but eye catching because of its numbers; it ages from red to black. Although the plant was

introduced nearly a century ago, it remains little known, despite its good looks, soil tolerance, and freedom from pests. Casts light shade, making it a good specimen tree for a lawn. Formerly known as *Evodia daniellii*.

TETRANEURIS

Asteraceae
Perennials

🌿 **US, MS, LS, CS; USDA 6-9**

☼ **FULL SUN**

◊◑ **LITTLE TO MODERATE WATER**

Tetraneuris acaulis

Taprooted plants with narrow, grassy, aromatic leaves that form small, evergreen foliage tufts about 8 in. high, 1 ft. wide. Somewhat reminiscent of thrift (*Armeria*). Blooms during warm months (nearly all year in mild-winter climates). Yellow daisies to 1½ in. wide have rays with notched edges; blossoms are usually carried singly on stems. Give well-drained soil. Cut off faded flower spikes to neaten plants and prolong bloom. Tolerant of heat, cold, drought. With some moisture, will reseed. Attractive in containers.

T. acaulis. ANGELITA DAISY. Native to plains from Canada to Texas. Golden yellow flowers on stems to 1 ft. high.

T. scaposa. CLUSTERED GOLDFLOWER. Native from Colorado to Kansas, south to New Mexico, Texas. Leaves are sometimes lobed. Bright yellow flowers on 16-in. stems; rays may have red-brown veins on undersides.

TETRAPANAX PAPYRIFERA

RICE PAPER PLANT
Araliaceae
Evergreen shrub

🌿 **LS, CS, TS; USDA 8-11**

☼ ◐ **AFTERNOON SHADE IN HOTTEST CLIMATES**

◐ **REGULAR WATER**

Tetrapanax papyrifera

From China. Fast growing to 10–15 ft. tall and wide; often multitrunked. Big, bold, long-stalked leaves are 1–2 ft. wide, deeply lobed, gray-green above, white and felted beneath, carried in clusters at ends of stems. Fuzz on new growth can irritate eyes or skin. Tan trunks often curve or lean. Big, branched clusters of creamy white flowers on furry tan stems appear in winter. Flowers are followed by small, round, black fruit.

Young plants sunburn easily; older ones adapt. Easy to grow. Seems to suffer only from high winds, which break or tatter leaves, and from frost—foliage is severely damaged at 22°F (however, it recovers fast and often puts up suckers to form thickets). Digging around roots stimulates sucker formation; suckers may arise 20 ft. from parent plant. Use this old Southern favorite for silhouette against walls, on patios; combines well with other sturdy, bold-leafed plants for a tropical effect. Name comes from the thick pith of the stems, which is used to make Chinese rice paper.

TEUCRIUM

GERMANDER
Lamiaceae
Shrubby perennials

🌿 **US, MS, LS, CS; USDA 6-9**

☼ **FULL SUN, EXCEPT AS NOTED**

◐ **MODERATE WATER, EXCEPT AS NOTED**

Teucrium chamaedrys

Most germanders are from the Mediterranean, though one listed here (*T. canadense*) is native to eastern North America. All have aromatic evergreen foliage and whorls of little flowers. These are tough plants that endure poor, rocky soils; most can't stand wet or poorly drained soils but will tolerate regular watering where drainage is good. Not usually browsed by deer.

T. canadense. AMERICAN GERMANDER, WOOD SAGE. From prairies and meadows of eastern North America. Erect grower to 3 ft. tall, 6 in. wide, usually with a single stem. Spreads by creeping rhizomes to form colonies. Narrowly oval, pointed, dark green leaves are large for a germander—up to 4 in. long. Rosy pink flowers appear on 8- to 12-in.-tall spikes in mid- to late summer. Full sun or partial shade. Regular to ample water.

T. chamaedrys. GERMANDER. To 1 ft. tall and 2 ft. wide, with many upright, woody-based stems densely clothed in toothed, dark green, ¾-in.-long leaves. Red-purple or white summer flowers in loose spikes (white-flowered form is looser). Attracts bees. Use as edging, foreground, low clipped hedge, or small-scale ground cover. Shear back once or twice a year to keep neat and force side branching.

'Nanum' ('Prostratum') is 4–6 in. high, spreading to 3 ft. or more; good substitute for dwarf English boxwood in formal parterres.

T. fruticans. BUSH GERMANDER, TUTTI-FRUTTI. Loose, silvery-stemmed plant to 4–8 ft. tall and wide (or wider). Gray-green, ¼-in.-long leaves have silvery white undersides, giving plant an overall silvery gray appearance. Blooms almost year-round, bearing lavender-blue flower spikes at branch ends. Thin and cut back before spring growth begins. 'Azureum' has deeper blue flowers than the species; 'Compactum', also with dark blue blooms, grows just 3 ft. high and wide.

T. marum. CAT THYME. To 1½ ft. high and wide. Upright, densely clustered stems are closely set with tiny gray-green leaves. Blooms profusely in summer, when stems are covered with many deep pink or purplish flowers in 2-in. spikes. Attracts cats, like catnip (*Nepeta cataria*).

THALICTRUM

MEADOW RUE
Ranunculaceae
Perennials

🌿 **ZONES VARY BY SPECIES**

◑ **LIGHT SHADE**

💧 **REGULAR WATER**

Thalictrum aquilegiifolium

Foliage clumps resemble those of columbine (*Aquilegia*). Plants typically bloom in late spring or summer, sending up sparsely leafed stems topped by puffs of small flowers, each consisting of four sepals and a prominent cluster of stamens. Superb for airy effect; offer a pleasing contrast

to sturdier perennials. Delicate tracery of leaves and flowers is particularly effective against dark green background. Foliage is good in arrangements. Most meadow rues need some winter chill; all thrive in dappled sunlight at woodland edges. Protect from wind. Divide clumps every 4 or 5 years. Deer resistant.

T. aquilegiifolium. COLUMBINE MEADOW RUE. Zones US, MS, LS; USDA 6-8. From Europe, northern Asia. To 2–3 ft. tall, 1 ft. wide, with bluish green foliage. Earliest of the meadow rues to bloom: Clouds of fluffy stamens (the white or greenish sepals drop off) appear for a couple of weeks in mid- to late spring. Rosy lilac is the usual color, but white and purple selections are available. If left in place, spent flowers are followed by attractive, long-lasting seed heads. Heat tolerant. 'Thundercloud' is a vigorous, heavy-blooming variety with deep rose-purple stamens. 'Album' has white stamens; those of 'Purpureum' are pinkish purple.

T. 'Black Stockings'. Zones US, MS, LS, CS; USDA 6-9. Hybrid of uncertain parentage. Resembles *T. rochebrunianum*, but with sturdy black stems.

T. delavayi (*T. dipterocarpum*). CHINESE MEADOW RUE. Zones US, MS, LS; USDA 6-8. From western China. To 3–4 ft. (even 6 ft.) tall, 1½–2 ft. wide, with thin, dark purple stems that need support. Green foliage. Violet to lavender sepals, yellow stamens. 'Album' has white sepals. 'Hewitt's Double' sports double lilac-colored flowers (one row of sepals, another of modified stamens that resemble petals); bloom continues for two months or longer. Heat tolerant.

T. flavum. YELLOW MEADOW RUE. Zones US, MS, LS, CS; USDA 6-9. Native from Europe to the Caucasus and Siberia. Heat-tolerant, green-foliaged species to 3–5 ft. tall, 1½–2 ft. wide; stems need staking. Blooms in summer, bearing flowers like those of *T. aquilegiifolium*, but in lemon-yellow. Leaves of 'Illuminator' emerge yellow-green, then turn bright green. *T. f. glaucum* (*T. speciosissimum*), called dusty meadow rue, has blue-green leaves and stems; its selection 'True Blue' is an improved, sturdier plant.

T. kiusianum. DWARF MEADOW RUE. Zones US, MS, LS; USDA

6-8. From Japan. Bluish green leaves; plant spreads to form mats of tidy rosettes, each to 6 in. high and wide. Light purple, ½-in. blooms rise just above the foliage in late spring or early summer. Excellent in rock gardens or along paths.

T. rochebrunianum. Zones US, MS, LS, CS; USDA 6-9. From Japan. To 4–6 ft. tall, 1½–2 ft. wide, with sturdy stems that don't need staking. Flowers consist of white or lavender sepals and pale yellow stamens. 'Lavender Mist', with violet sepals, is a superior selection.

THELYPTERIS

Thelypteridaceae
Ferns

🌿 **ZONES VARY BY SPECIES**

◑● **PARTIAL TO FULL SHADE, EXCEPT AS NOTED**

💧💧 **REGULAR TO AMPLE WATER**

Thelypteris noveboracensis

Among the easier ferns to grow. Deciduous in most areas, they thrive in moist, organic soil but will tolerate some drought if soil is rich. They take more sun than most ferns, provided moisture is plentiful. Effective in masses or combined with plants having coarser leaves. All spread by rhizomes to form colonies.

T. hexagonoptera (*Phegopteris hexagonoptera*). BROAD BEECH FERN. Zones US, MS, LS; USDA 6-8. From eastern North America. Medium green, triangular fronds to 1½–2 ft. long and wide. Fronds are once divided, each division deeply toothed.

T. kunthii. SOUTHERN SHIELD FERN, WOOD FERN. Zones US, MS, LS, CS; USDA 6-9. Native from

the southeastern U.S. to South America; an old-time Southern favorite. Triangular fronds to 3 ft. (sometimes 5 ft.) long, with leaflets widely spaced along the stem; the light green color contrasts well with dark green–foliaged plants. Spreads quickly to form a tall, soft, pretty mass. Takes poor soils and moderate sun. Brown winter fronds are quite attractive, but cut them back before new spring growth begins.

T. noveboracensis (*Parathelypteris novae-boracensis*). NEW YORK FERN. Zones US, MS, LS; USDA 6-8. Native from Newfoundland to Georgia, Alabama, and Tennessee. Pale green, 1- to 2-ft.-long fronds are once divided, with the segments deeply lobed. A vigorous colonizer, it can be used as a ground cover in shade—or even in full sun if kept moist.

T. palustris. MARSH FERN. Zones US, MS, LS; USDA 6-8. From Europe, Asia. The bluish green fronds, which occur singly or in tufts, are of two kinds: sterile and fertile. Sterile fronds are 6–24 in. long and half as wide, tapered at both ends, once divided, with segments deeply lobed. Fertile fronds are 1–3 ft. long, sturdier and stiffer than the sterile ones. Spreads rapidly.

T. torresiana (*Macrothelypteris torresiana*). MARIANA MAIDEN FERN. Zones MS, LS, CS, TS; USDA 7-11. Native to tropical and subtropical Africa and Asia; has naturalized in much of the South. Light green, arching, triangular fronds to 3½ ft. long are thrice divided, for a lacy, delicate look. 'Eco Maiden Lace' is a vigorous, cold-hardy selection that can reach 5 ft. tall.

THERMOPSIS

BUSH PEA, FALSE LUPINE
Papilionaceae
Perennials

- 🌿 **ZONES VARY BY SPECIES**
- ☀️ ◐ **FULL SUN OR LIGHT SHADE**
- 💧💧 **MODERATE TO REGULAR WATER**

Thermopsis villosa

These easy-to-grow perennials resemble lupines (*Lupinus*). Silvery leaves are divided into leaflets that spread like fingers on a hand; erect, spikelike clusters of sweet pea–shaped yellow flowers appear in spring. Because of their tendency to spread by underground rhizomes, they are best in informal or wild gardens. Need little care. Somewhat drought tolerant.

T. chinensis. CHINESE BUSH PEA. Zones US, MS, LS; USDA 6-8. Native to China. Grows 2 ft. high, 1½ ft. wide, with 8-in. flower spikes.

T. villosa (*T. caroliniana*). CAROLINA BUSH PEA. Zones US, MS, LS; USDA 6-8. Native to the Carolinas and Georgia. To 3–4 ft. tall, 2 ft. wide, with 10-in. flower clusters. More heat tolerant than *T. chinensis*.

THEVETIA

Apocynaceae
Evergreen shrubs or trees

- 🌿 **ZONES VARY BY SPECIES**
- ☀️ **FULL SUN**
- 💧 **REGULAR WATER**
- ◊ **ALL PARTS ARE POISONOUS IF INGESTED**

Thevetia thevetioides

Fast-growing plants with narrow, glossy, deep green leaves and clusters of showy, funnel-shaped flowers at branch ends. Thrive in heat; sensitive to frost.

T. peruviana. YELLOW OLEANDER, LUCKY NUT. Zones LS, CS, TS; USDA 8-11. From the tropical Americas. In frostless areas, it can be trained as a tree to 20–30 ft. tall and wide. Where frosts are light or rare, it's an 8-ft. (or larger) shrub; makes a good hedge, screen, or background plant. Leaves 3–6 in. long, with edges rolled under. Fragrant, 2- to 3-in., yellow to apricot flowers bloom from early summer into fall (all year where winters are warm). Small (1-in.), squat, four-angled fruit is red at first, then ages to black. Provide good drainage, wind protection. In colder part of range, mound sand 6–12 in. deep around base of stem in late autumn. Dies back in freezes but recovers quickly; new growth will bloom same year.

T. thevetioides. GIANT THEVETIA. Zone TS; USDA 10-11. From Mexico. Open growth to 12 ft. or more tall and wide. Leaves are darker green than those of *T. peruviana*; they resemble oleander (*Nerium*) leaves but are corrugated and have heavily veined undersides. Large clusters of brilliant yellow, 4-in. flowers bloom from late spring through

fall; these are followed by 2½-in.-wide fruit that ripens from green to black. Makes an attractive patio tree, but fruit can be a litter problem.

THUJA

ARBORVITAE
Cupressaceae
Evergreen trees or shrubs

- 🌿 **ZONES VARY BY SPECIES**
- ☀️ ◐ **PARTIAL SHADE IN HOTTEST CLIMATES**
- 💧💧 **MODERATE TO REGULAR WATER**

Thuja

Neat, symmetrical plants often mistakenly trimmed into odd geometrical forms—globes, cones, cylinders. Juvenile foliage is feathery, with small, needlelike leaves; mature foliage is scalelike, carried in flat sprays. Foliage in better-known selections is often yellow-green or bright golden yellow. Small (½- to ¾-in.-long) cones are green or bluish green, turning to brownish. Although arborvitaes will take both damp and fairly dry soils, they grow best in well-drained soil. Bagworms and spider mites are common pests on all species.

T. occidentalis. AMERICAN ARBORVITAE. Zones US, MS; USDA 6-7. Native to eastern U.S. Upright, open growth to 30–60 ft. tall, 10–15 ft. wide, with branches that tend to turn up at ends. Bright green to yellowish green leaf sprays. Foliage turns brown in severe cold. Needs moist air to look its best. Basic species is seldom seen, but smaller garden selections are common. Among these, the taller ones make good informal or clipped screens, while lower kinds are often used

around foundations, along walks or walls, as hedges. Be sure to check on the ultimate height of selections used for foundation plantings; plants are too often seen wedged under an overhang at the corner of a house. Also keep in mind that deer find them very tasty. The following are some good choices.

'Brandon'. Fast growth to 12–15 ft. tall, 6–8 ft. wide. Useful as screen.

'Degroot's Spire'. Narrow column with spirally arranged branchlets for a full look. Grows slowly to 15–20 ft. tall, 4–5 ft. wide.

'Golden Globe'. Dense, rounded growth to 3–5 ft. tall and wide. Bright golden yellow foliage contrasts beautifully with deep green or blue-green evergreens. Does not sunburn even in full sun.

'Hetz Midget'. Globe-shaped plant with rich green foliage. Not likely to exceed 3–4 ft. tall and wide.

'Nigra'. Dense, dark green cone to 20–30 ft. tall, 4–5 ft. wide.

'North Pole'. Narrow, upright column to 10–15 ft. tall, 5–7 ft. wide, with dense, dark green foliage.

'Polar Gold'. Narrow cone grows 12–15 ft. tall, 4–6 ft. wide, with dense, fine-textured golden foliage. Resists winter burn.

'Rheingold'. Cone-shaped, slow-growing, bright golden plant with a mixture of scale and needle foliage. Even very old plants seldom exceed 6 ft. tall and wide.

'Smaragd' ('Emerald', 'Emerald Green'). Neat, dense-growing, narrow cone to 10–15 ft. tall, 3–4 ft. wide. Holds its color throughout winter.

'Techny'. Compact, broad-based pyramid to 15–20 ft. tall, 10–12 ft. wide. Dark green, soft-looking foliage resists winter burn.

'Woodwardii'. Widely grown, dense, globe-shaped shrub with rich green color. May attain considerable size with age but stays small over a reasonably long period; to 4 ft. high and wide in 10 years.

'Yellow Ribbon'. To 8–10 ft. tall, 2–3 ft. wide, with bright yellow foliage throughout the year.

T. platycladus orientalis (*Thuja orientalis*). ORIENTAL ARBORVITAE. Zones US, MS, LS, CS, TS; USDA 6-11. Native to northern China, Manchuria, Korea. Species

T

(to 25 ft. tall, 15 ft. wide) is rarely grown; nurseries offer more attractive, shrubbier selections. Widely used around foundations, by doorways or gates, in formal rows. Less hardy to cold than *T. occidentalis* but tolerates heat (grows all the way to Key West). Has survived well in nematode-infested soils. Give good drainage; protect from reflected heat of light-colored walls or pavement.

'Aurea Nana'. DWARF GOLDEN ARBORVITAE, BERCKMAN'S GOLDEN ARBORVITAE. Golden-foliaged, compact globe. Usually 3 ft. tall and 2 ft. wide but can grow as high as 5 ft. Sometimes sold as *T. o.* 'Berckmanii'.

'Bakeri'. Compact, cone shaped, bright green. To 5–8 ft. high, 4 ft. wide.

'Blue Cone'. Dense, upright, conical; good blue-green color. To 8 ft. tall, 4 ft. wide.

'Bonita' ('Bonita Upright', 'Bonita Erecta'). Rounded, full, dense cone to 3 ft. tall, 2 ft. wide. Dark green with slight golden tinting at branch tips.

'Fruitlandii'. FRUITLAND ARBORVITAE. Compact, upright, cone shaped, with deep green foliage.

'Minima Glauca'. DWARF BLUE ARBORVITAE. To 3–4 ft. tall and wide. Blue-green foliage.

'Raffles'. Resembles 'Aurea Nana' but is smaller, with denser growth and brighter color.

'Westmount'. To 3 ft. tall, 2 ft. wide. Green foliage has yellow tips throughout the growing season.

T. plicata. WESTERN RED CEDAR. Zones US, MS; USDA 6–7. Native from coastal Northern California north to Alaska and inland to Montana. One of the West's most beautiful and imposing native trees. Can reach 200 ft. tall in the temperate rain forests of coastal Washington. Does surprisingly well in the lower Midwest and Upper and Middle South if planted in moist, fertile, well-drained soil; it can grow at least 2–3 ft. per year. Makes a magnificent lawn tree, but give it plenty of room—in gardens, it may reach 75 ft. tall and 25 ft. wide. Selections include the following.

'Atrovirens'. Narrow pyramid to 70 ft. tall, 25 ft. wide, with gracefully drooping limbs.

'Clemson Select'. Good tolerance of heat and cold. To

25–30 ft. tall, 8–10 ft. wide. Bright green foliage; new growth has creamy highlights.

'Fastigiata'. Narrow, erect growth to 80–90 ft. tall, 20–25 ft. wide. Very dense foliage; fine for tall screen.

'Green Giant'. Hybrid between *T. plicata* and *T. standishii*, a Japanese species. Can grow 3–5 ft. a year, ultimately reaching 30–50 ft. tall, 10–20 ft. wide. Shear as a tall hedge or use as a tall screen. Good substitute for Leyland cypress.

'Hillieri'. Irregularly shaped, dense plant to 6–10 ft. high and wide, eventually larger.

'Spring Grove'. To 8–10 ft. high in five years; ultimately reaches 40–60 ft. tall, 10–15 ft. wide. Can be sheared as a hedge.

'Stoneham Gold'. Dense, slow-growing dwarf to 6 ft. tall, 2 ft. wide. Orange-yellow new growth.

'Zebrina'. Slow grower; same size as species. Foliage is banded in green and golden yellow. Often sold as 'Aurea', a less commonly seen selection with green foliage tinted golden.

THUNBERGIA
Acanthaceae
Perennial vines and shrubs, some grown as annuals

🌿 **TS; USDA 10-11, EXCEPT AS NOTED**

☼ ◑ **PARTIAL SHADE IN HOTTEST CLIMATES**

💧 **REGULAR WATER**

Thunbergia grandiflora

Tropical, typically twining plants noted for showy flowers. Some grow fast enough to bloom the first season and can be treated as annuals. Those grown as perennials are evergreen in the

Tropical South. Provide rich, well-drained soil. Good greenhouse plants.

T. alata. BLACK-EYED SUSAN VINE. Perennial vine grown as annual. May live over in Zones CS, TS; USDA 9-11. From Africa. To 10 ft., with triangular, 3-in., medium green leaves. Blooms all summer long; tubular flowers flare out to 1 in. wide, come in orange, yellow, or white, all with purple-black throat. Start seed indoors; set plants out in good soil in a sunny spot as soon as weather warms. Display in hanging basket or window box, use as ground cover, or train on strings or low trellis.

T. battiscombei. BLUE CLOCK VINE. Vining shrub. From Africa. Unless given support, it forms a mound 4–6 ft. high, 6–8 ft. wide. Scrambling stems bear broadly oval, glossy, bright green leaves to 7 in. long. Fuzzy greenish white buds appear in leaf joints; from spring into fall, these open to 2- to 3-in.-long, yellow-throated flowers in an intense blue-purple. Top dies back in cold weather, but roots are hardy to 20°F.

T. erecta. KING'S MANTLE. Vining shrub to 6 ft. tall and wide. Native to Africa. Erect, sometimes twining, with dark green, ovate to oblong leaves to 3 in. long. Velvety dark blue, 3-in.-long flowers with orange or cream throats resemble those of gloxinia (*Sinningia*); they appear in joints of upper leaves throughout summer and fall. 'Alba' is a white-flowered form.

T. fragrans. SWEET CLOCK VINE, WHITE LADY. Perennial vine. Native to India. Woody, twining stems reach 8–10 ft. high, set with notched, oval green leaves to 3 in. long. Lightly scented summer flowers to 3 in. across appear singly or in clusters; white is the usual color, but blossoms may be blue, lavender, or even yellow. Prune this vine regularly, or it may get away from you.

T. grandiflora. SKY FLOWER. Perennial vine. From India. Vigorous growth to 20 ft. or more, with 8-in., heart-shaped, medium to dark green leaves. Slightly drooping clusters of tubular, flaring, sky-blue flowers to 3 in. across appear from late summer through fall. Use on arbor, large trellis, or wire fence; casts dense shade. 'Alba' has white flowers.

T. gregorii. ORANGE CLOCK VINE. Perennial vine; grow as

summer annual outside Tropical South. Native to Africa. Showy and easy to grow; twines to 6 ft. high or sprawls over ground to cover a 12-ft. circle. Gray-green, triangular, tooth-edged leaves to 3 in. long. Tubular, flaring, bright orange, 3-in. flowers are borne singly on 4-in. stems. Blooms nearly all year long in the Tropical South, in summer elsewhere. Set plants 3–4 ft. apart to cover a wire fence, about 6 ft. apart as ground cover. Plant above a wall and let stems cascade down; or grow in hanging baskets.

T. mysorensis. INDIAN CLOCK VINE. Perennial vine. From India. Climbs to 15–35 ft., with narrow, elliptical, dark green leaves up to 6 in. long. Spectacular, pendent, 1- to 1½-ft.-long clusters of gaping, 2-in.-long flowers that are red on the outside, yellow within. Blooms much of the year, most heavily in spring. Train on pergola, arbor, or other overhead structure to permit flowers to dangle. Protect from frost.

THYMOPHYLLA TENUILOBA
DAHLBERG DAISY, GOLDEN FLEECE
Asteraceae
Perennial, usually grown as annual

🌿 **CS, TS; USDA 9-11**

☼ **FULL SUN**

💧 **MODERATE WATER**

Thymophylla tenuiloba

This heat-loving plant is native from Texas to Florida and Mexico. Mounding growth to 1 ft. high, 1½ ft. wide. Divided, threadlike leaves make a dark green background for flowers that look like tiny golden marguerites

(*Anthemis*). Use for mass display or pockets of color. Blooms from early summer to fall. In warm-winter areas, can be planted in fall for winter-to-spring bloom. Quick and easy to start from seed planted in flats or sown in place. Not particular about soil type but must have good drainage. When plants become ragged with age, pull them out.

THYMUS

THYME
Lamiaceae
Shrubby perennials

✿ **ZONES VARY BY SPECIES**

☼ ◐ **LIGHT SHADE IN HOTTEST CLIMATES**

💧 **MODERATE WATER**

Thymus citriodorus

Diminutive Mediterranean members of the mint family with tiny, usually heavily scented leaves and masses of little flowers in whorls. Well suited to herb garden, rock garden; prostrate, mat-forming types make good small-space ground covers. Attractive to bees but not to deer. Provide light, well-drained soil. Shear or cut back established plants to keep them compact. Easy to propagate from cuttings taken in early summer. Botanical names are constantly undergoing revision.

T. camphoratus. CAMPHOR THYME. Zones US, MS, LS, CS, TS; USDA 6-11. To 1½ ft. high and wide, with narrow, gray-green leaves that smell like camphor. Blooms in late spring, early summer; flower clusters consist of woolly, rosy purplish bracts and tiny white flowers.

T. citriodorus. LEMON THYME. Zones US, MS, LS, CS; USDA 6-9. Long considered to be a hybrid (and listed as *C. x citriodorus*), this may be simply a highly variable species with erect or spreading growth to 1 ft. high, 2 ft. wide. Ovate to lance-shaped, medium green leaves have a lemon fragrance. Pale lilac flowers in summer. Leaves of 'Argenteus' are splashed with silver, those of 'Aureus' with gold. 'Doone Valley', with yellow-spotted leaves, reaches only 5 in. high. 'Goldstream' has yellow-variegated leaves. 'Lemon Frost' has white flowers on a 3- to 6-in.-high plant. 'Lime' has lime-green foliage. 'Silver Queen' (*T.* 'Silver Queen'), to 1 ft. high, 1½ ft. wide, has leaves edged in silvery white.

T. herba-barona. CARAWAY-SCENTED THYME. Zones US, MS, LS, CS; USDA 6-9. Fast growing to 2–4 in. high, 2 ft. or more wide; stems root as they spread. Forms a dense mat of wiry stems set with widely spaced, dark green, ovate to lance-shaped leaves with caraway fragrance. Clusters of rose-pink flowers in midsummer.

T. polytrichus britannicus (*T. praecox arcticus*). CREEPING THYME. Zones US, MS, LS, CS; USDA 6-9. Variable subspecies to 3 in. high, 3 ft. wide. Round leaves range from glossy green to soft gray and may be variegated or have golden highlights. Flowers come in various shades of pink and white. Soft and fragrant underfoot. Leaves can be used as seasoning and in potpourris. Pink-flowering selections include 'Coccineum', 'Creeping Pink', and 'Reiter'. White-flowered selections are sometimes available.

T. pseudolanuginosus. WOOLLY THYME. Zones US, MS, LS; USDA 6-8. Forms a flat to undulating mat 2–3 in. high, 3 ft. wide. Stems are densely clothed with elliptical, woolly gray leaves. Blooms seldom and sparsely; when it does, produces pinkish flowers in leaf joints in midsummer. Becomes slightly rangy in winter. Use in rock crevices, between stepping stones, spilling over bank or raised bed, covering small patches of ground. 'Hall's Woolly' is a profuse bloomer.

T. pulegioides. MOTHER-OF-THYME. Zones US, MS, LS; USDA 6-8. Fast grower to 1 ft. high and wide, with shiny, green, oval, lemon-scented leaves. Pinkish-purple

TOP: Thymus pulegioides; T. vulgaris; BOTTOM: T. citriodorus 'Variegata'

LOOKING FOR A GOOD THYME?

You can't go wrong with one of our favorites, lemon thyme (*Thymus citriodorus*). Not only does it have a lemony fragrance, but it's also highly ornamental. Some forms have green leaves edged in gold; others in silver.

flowers in summer. 'Archer's Gold' has golden yellow foliage. 'Aureus' green leaves with bright yellow variegation. Leaves of 'Bertram Anderson' are bright green in summer, turning bright gold with red tips in fall and winter.

T. serpyllum. CREEPING THYME, WILD THYME. Zones US, MS, LS, CS; USDA 6-9. Grows slowly to form a 6- to 12-in.-wide mat 1–3 in. high. Thin stems are closely set with tiny, rounded, blue-green leaves with variable scent. Deep pink flowers appear in summer. 'Elfin' ('Minus') has miniscule, tightly packed leaves and is a shy bloomer. 'Pink Chintz' is loaded with salmon-pink flowers from early to midsummer.

T. vulgaris. COMMON THYME. Zones US, MS, LS, CS; USDA 6-9. Variable plant to 1 ft. high, 2 ft. wide, with gray-green, narrow to oval leaves. White to lilac flowers in late spring, early summer. Low edging for flower, vegetable, or herb garden. Good container plant. Use leaves fresh or dried for seasoning fish, shellfish, poultry stuffing, soups, vegetables. 'Argenteus', called silver thyme, has leaves variegated with silver. 'Orange Balsam' has narrow, orange-scented leaves.

TIARELLA

FOAMFLOWER
Saxifragaceae
Perennials

US, MS, LS, CS; USDA 6-9

PARTIAL TO FULL SHADE

REGULAR WATER

Tiarella 'Pink Skyrocket'

Clump-forming plants to about 1½ ft. tall (in bloom) and 1½–2 ft. wide; spread by rhizomes (and by aboveground runners, in the case of *T. cordifolia*). Leaves arise directly from rhizomes; they are evergreen but may change color in autumn. Selections with year-round colorful foliage are popular; look for new introductions in addition to those described below. Narrow, erect flower stems carry many small white or pink flowers. Useful in shady rock gardens; make pretty ground covers but will not bear foot traffic. Deer resistant.

T. cordifolia. FOAMFLOWER. Rapid spreader from eastern North America. Light green, lobed, 4-in. leaves show red and yellow fall color. Creamy white flowers on foot-tall stalks. Leaves of 'Eco Red Heart' have dark red centers and veins; those of 'Oakleaf' are deeply lobed. Both selections have pink blossoms.

T. selections and hybrids. Many of the choicest foamflowers are of uncertain origin.

'Butterfly Wings'. Light green leaves have centers heavily splashed with purplish black. Light pink flowers.

'Crow Feather'. Deeply cut, bright green leaves with dark veins. Leaves color up well in winter in shades of pink, red, and darkest purple. Light pink flowers.

'Cygnet'. Star-shaped leaves with purple markings along the veins. White flowers open from pink buds.

'Happy Trails'. Round-lobed leaves are medium green with deep brown veins. Trailing habit; nice choice for spilling over container edges. Short white flowers.

'Mint Chocolate'. Deeply lobed leaves have a central zone of deep brownish purple. Pinkish white flowers.

'Neon Lights'. Large, deeply cut leaves are bright green with a burgundy central zone. Pale pink flowers.

'Ninja'. Deeply cut leaves are marbled with blackish purple, turning almost entirely purple in winter. Pinkish white blooms.

'Pink Skyrocket'. Deeply cut green leaves have deep red veins. Profuse show of large pink flowers.

'Skeleton Key'. Very deeply cut leaves with deep purple midrib. White blossoms.

'Spring Symphony'. Green leaves with a central black blotch; pink flowers. Tolerates heat and humidity.

'Sugar and Spice'. Glossy, bright green leaves are deeply cut and heavily marked with maroon. White flowers open from pink buds.

T. wherryi. From southeastern U.S. Like *T. cordifolia* but lacks aboveground runners, is slower to spread. Flower clusters are somewhat more slender, often tinged pink. 'Heronswood Mist' has leaves heavily marbled and blotched with creamy white; pink stems hold light pink flowers.

TIBOUCHINA

Melastomataceae
Evergreen shrubs and trees

TS; USDA 10-11; OR GROW IN POTS

PARTIAL SHADE IN HOTTEST CLIMATES

REGULAR WATER

Tibouchina urvilleana

Brazilian natives with deeply veined, oval, pointed leaves and big, showy, five-petaled flowers in various shades of purple. Bloom is intermittent over a long period. These plants prefer rich, well-drained, slightly acid soil; a thick layer of mulch helps keep the roots cool. They have a tendency to legginess and should be pruned lightly after every bloom cycle, somewhat more heavily in spring; resprout quickly after heavy pruning. Pinch tips of young plants to encourage bushiness. Somewhat resistant to deer damage.

T. granulosa. PURPLE GLORY TREE. Tree. To 40 ft. in its native setting, but more likely to reach 20 ft. tall and at least as wide in gardens. Broad, spreading habit. Glossy, dark green, 5- to 8-in.-long leaves with fuzzy undersides.

Deep rose to violet flowers are 2 in. across, held in clusters up to 1 ft. long. 'Gibraltar' is dwarf, to just 1½ ft. tall and wide, with leaves edged in creamy white; excellent in containers.

T. heteromalla (*T. grandifolia*). SILVERLEAFED PRINCESS FLOWER. Shrub. To 4–6 ft. tall, 6–8 ft. wide, with very large (to 9-in.-long), fuzzy, silvery green leaves. Inch-wide violet flowers are held above the foliage in upright, 8- to 16-in.-tall spikes.

T. urvilleana. PRINCESS FLOWER. Shrub. Open growth to 5–18 ft. high, 3–10 ft. wide. Branch tips, buds, and new growth are shaded with velvety hairs in orange and bronze red. Velvety, 3- to 6-in.-long, rich green leaves are often edged red; older leaves add attractive touches of red, orange, or yellow, especially in winter. Clusters of brilliant royal purple, 3- to 5-in.-wide flowers. Protect from strong winds. 'Athens Blue' is a more compact selection, with tightly branching habit. Leaves of 'Variegata' are broadly and irregularly edged in creamy yellow.

TILIA

LINDEN
Malvaceae
Deciduous trees

ZONES VARY BY SPECIES

FULL SUN

REGULAR WATER

Tilia cordata

Stately, attractive, densely foliaged trees that grow at a moderate rate. All have irregularly heart-shaped leaves and small, fragrant, yellowish white flowers in drooping clusters in late spring, early summer. Flowers develop into nutlets, each with an attached papery bract. Best in deep, rich, moist soil. In cold-winter areas, fall color varies from negligible to a good yellow. Young trees need shaping, older ones only corrective pruning. Aphids can cause honeydew, which drips disagreeably and encourages sooty mold.

T. americana. AMERICAN LINDEN, BASSWOOD. Zones US, MS, LS, CS; USDA 6-9. Native to eastern North America. To 40–60 ft. tall, 20–25 ft. wide. Straight-trunked tree with a narrow crown. Dull, dark green leaves to 4–6 in. long, nearly as wide. Not at its best in city conditions. 'Redmond' is a pyramidal form with glossy foliage.

T. cordata. LITTLE-LEAF LINDEN. Zones US, MS; USDA 6-7. Native to Europe. Dense pyramid to 30–50 ft. tall, 15–30 ft. wide. Leaves 1½–3 in. long and as wide (or wider), dark green above, silvery beneath. Excellent lawn or street tree for the Midwest and Upper and Middle South. Given room to develop its crown, it can be a fine patio shade tree (but expect bees in flowering season). Can be sheared into hedges. Very tolerant of city conditions. Selected forms include 'Chancellor', fast-growing 'Glenleven', dense 'Greenspire', heavy-blooming 'June Bride', and 'Olympic'. 'Summer Sprite' is compact, at just 20 ft. tall and 15 ft. wide.

T. x euchlora. CRIMEAN LINDEN. Zones US, MS; USDA 6-7. Hybrid derived from *T. cordata*. To 25–35 ft. (perhaps eventually to 50 ft.) tall, almost as wide. Slightly pendulous branches. Rich green, glossy leaves have paler undersides, reach 2–4 in. long and wide. Casts more open shade than *T. cordata*.

T. tomentosa. SILVER LINDEN. Zones US, MS, LS; USDA 6-8. From Europe, western Asia. To 40–50 ft. tall, 20–30 ft. wide. Leaves are 3–5 in. long and wide, light green above, silvery beneath; they turn and ripple in the slightest breeze. Good yellow fall color. Takes more heat and drought than most other species and isn't as messy. 'Sterling' has silvery young leaves and an especially handsome winter silhouette.

TILLANDSIA

Bromeliaceae
Perennials

- 🗓 **TS; USDA 10-11, EXCEPT AS NOTED; OR HOUSEPLANTS**
- ☼ ● **EXPOSURE NEEDS VARY BY SPECIES**
- ◐ ● **WATER NEEDS VARY BY SPECIES**

Tillandsia usneoides

This large family of bromeliads is commonly found throughout Texas, Mexico, and Central and South America. Most are epiphytes (tree dwellers) that depend on rain, dew, and fog for moisture. A few grow in soil. Plants vary greatly in size and appearance. Leaves may be wide, narrow (even hairlike), or sword shaped; they may be twisted or curled. Those with green leaves generally need regular water and filtered light; types with gray-green to bluish foliage need less water and tolerate more sun. Often seen mounted on plaques of wood that are hung on walls, indoors or out; also look good in containers filled with loose, fast-draining potting mix. Let the mix go dry between waterings.

T. caput-medusae. From Mexico and Central America. Mass of curling, channeled, gray-green leaves to 1 ft. long resembles the head of Medusa. Blooms in late spring, producing a foot-long spike with red bracts and blue flowers. Prefers bright filtered light.

T. cyanea. From Ecuador. Rosette of bright green, arching, 1-ft. leaves produces a showy flower cluster in spring or autumn: a flattened plume of deep red or pink bracts, from which violet-blue flowers emerge one or two at a time over a long season.

T. ionantha. From Mexico and Nicaragua. Rosettes of 2-in.-long leaves covered with silvery gray fuzz. Small, tubular spring flowers are violet; at bloom time, center of rosette turns red. Tough and undemanding plant.

T. juncea. Native from southern Florida to northern South America. Forms a rosette of upright, very narrow, 12- to 16-in.-long leaves in olive-green tinged with copper. Short, erect inflorescence appears in summer, consists of bright red bracts and bluish purple petals.

T. latifolia. From Ecuador and Peru. Bayonet-shaped gray-green leaves to 8 in. long. Blossom spike reaches 15 in. tall, with yellow-orange bracts and flowers ranging in color from fuchsia to blue. Spring bloom.

T. recurvata. BALL MOSS. Zones LS, CS, TS; USDA 8-11. From southern U.S. and South America. Ball-like clusters of gray-green leaves to 6 in. across grow on the branches; blue-violet flowers bloom in summer.

T. usneoides. SPANISH MOSS. Zones LS, CS, TS; USDA 8-11. Native from Florida and Texas south to Argentina. Drapes itself on live oaks (*Quercus virginiana*), cypresses (*Taxodium*), and telephone lines, hanging as long as 15 ft.; a live oak draped with Spanish moss is a classic image of the South. Greenish gray stems and leaves are wiry, threadlike. Has no roots. Inconspicuous green flowers in late spring or fall. Thrives in shade and high humidity; very sensitive to air pollution.

TITHONIA ROTUNDIFOLIA

MEXICAN SUNFLOWER
Asteraceae
Perennial grown as annual

- 🗓 **US, MS, LS, CS, TS; USDA 6-11**
- ☼ **FULL SUN**
- ● **REGULAR WATER**

Tithonia rotundifolia 'Torch'

Native from Mexico to Central America. Husky, rather coarse plant with velvety green leaves, spectacular gaudy flowers. Grows rapidly to 6 ft. tall, 4 ft. wide. Blooms from summer to frost, bearing 3- to 4-in.-wide blossoms with orange-scarlet rays and tufted yellow centers. Use taller selections for temporary screens or hedges. All have hollow stems, so cut carefully for bouquets to avoid bending stalks. Sow seed in place in spring, in well-drained soil that's not too rich. Tolerates intense heat and some drought; attractive to butterflies and hummingbirds. Will self-sow.

Available choices on the smaller side include 2- to 2½-ft.-tall Arcadian Blend, with gold, orange, and yellow flowers; 2½-ft. 'Fiesta del Sol', bearing 2- to 3-in. orange flowers earlier in the season than other selections. Taller selections (to 4 ft.) are 'Aztec Sun', bearing apricot-gold blooms; bushy 'Goldfinger', with deep orange flowers; and 'Torch', another bushy grower bearing orange-red to vivid red blooms. 'Yellow Torch' yellow flowers.

T

TOLMIEA MENZIESII

PIGGYBACK PLANT

Saxifragaceae

Perennial

✎ TS; USDA 10-11; OR HOUSEPLANT

◐ ● PARTIAL TO FULL SHADE; BRIGHT INDIRECT LIGHT

◗ ◗◗ REGULAR TO AMPLE WATER

Tolmiea menziesii

Native to the Coast Ranges from California to Alaska, this plant gets its common name from the little plantlets that appear atop its hairy leaves once they've matured. Attractive, triangular to heart-shaped, shallowly lobed leaves of variable size (to 5 in. long) are borne on leafstalks that also vary in length. Leaves are solid medium green. Tiny, rather inconspicuous reddish brown flowers are held atop 1- to 2-ft.-tall stems. Flowers are small and inconspicuous. 'Taff's Gold' has foliage irregularly mottled in yellow to chartreuse.

Where it's winter hardy, piggy-back plant makes a nice, spreading, foot-tall ground cover for moist shade; plantlets formed at the junction of leafstalks and leaf blades root where they touch soil. Most people, however, grow it as a houseplant, usually in a hanging basket.

▶ CARE

Outdoors, grow in cool, moist, rich soil. Indoors, give bright indirect light (no hot sun). Let the soil surface go dry to the touch between waterings. Fertilize every other week in spring and summer and monthly in fall and winter with a general-purpose liquid houseplant fertilizer. Easy to propagate: Just detach a leaf carrying a plantlet and place on

top of moist potting mix so that the juncture between stem and leaf is in contact with soil. Pins or a U-shaped wire will help keep the leaf in position. Keep the soil evenly moist. The leaf will gradually die, but the plantlet will root.

TOMATILLO

Solanaceae

Annual

✎ US, MS, LS, CS, TS; USDA 6-11

◌̇ FULL SUN

◗ REGULAR WATER

Tomatillos

From Mexico. Easy-to-grow, summer-fruiting tomato relative known botanically as *Physalis ixocarpa*. Bushy, sprawling growth to 4 ft. high and at least as wide. Fruit swells to fill—and eventually split—the loose, papery husk (calyx) that surrounds it. When fully ripe, fruit is yellow to purple, about 2 in. wide, and very sweet, but it is usually picked when green and tart and used in sauces and other dishes.

▶ CARE

Sow seeds directly in fertile soil four to six weeks after last frost, when soil has warmed; in moist, warm soil, seeds will germinate in five days. Thin seedlings to 10 in. apart. Or start plants indoors and set out in the garden; plant deep, as for tomatoes. Tomatillos can be trained to a trellis like tomatoes but are usually left to sprawl. Once fruiting begins, cut back on water but don't let plants become drought stressed. Harvest fruit when walnut size (or smaller, if it seems fully developed) and deep green. Don't remove the papery husk until you are ready to use the fruit.

TOMATO

Solanaceae

Perennial grown as annual

✎ US, MS, LS, CS, TS; USDA 6-10

◌̇ FULL SUN

◗ REGULAR WATER

'Sweet Baby Girl' tomatoes

There are two kinds of gardeners in the South—those who have grown tomatoes and those who will grow them. No other crop produces so much for so many for so little expense. Just about everyone swears by his or her own favorite method of growing tomatoes. If yours works, stick with it—but if you're a beginner or dissatisfied with the results you've achieved thus far, the following information should help.

First, choose selections adapted to your area. Those listed on the following pages perform well in most of the South. Fine-tune these recommendations by checking with local garden centers and your Cooperative Extension Service. Next, decide whether you want big tomatoes for slicing, meaty ones for canning and sauce, or small ones for popping into your mouth.

Factor into the equation when you expect to plant and how long you want to wait for harvest. It's hard to go wrong with midseason types; they ripen fruit anywhere from 60 to 75 days after transplants are set out. But if it's midsummer and you're trying to squeeze in a fall crop before frost, you'll need to plant an early tomato that ripens in 50 to 60 days. Late tomatoes that ripen in 80 to 95 days are best planted in spring.

Also consider how much fruit you want and how much space

you can devote to your plants. Tomato plants (*Solanum lycopersicum*, native to the Andes) are classified as either determinate or indeterminate. Determinate tomatoes are bushy and ripen all of their fruit over several weeks; they need less space and support than indeterminate types. Indeterminate tomatoes are vinelike and ripen their fruit over a period of months; they give more total fruit but need more space and support.

TOMATO SELECTIONS

The following lists offer just a sampling of the incredible number of different tomatoes you can buy as seeds or started plants.

Main crop or midseason tomatoes. 'Atkinson', 'Better Boy', 'Big Boy', 'Celebrity', 'Creole', 'Floramerica', 'Rutgers', and 'Supersonic' are among the most widely grown.

Early tomatoes. When you want the first tomato on the block or aim to get a fall crop in just under the wire, try 'Burpee's Early Pick', 'Early Girl', 'First Lady', 'Fourth of July', 'Park's Early Challenge'. 'Quick Pick', and 'Stupice'.

Late tomatoes. These generally taste better than early types, because plants have more time to develop flavor. 'Abraham Lincoln', 'Arkansas Traveler', 'Homestead 24', 'Mule Team', and 'Tropic' are delicious examples.

Heat-tolerant tomatoes. Tomato plants often fail to set fruit once daytime temperatures rise above 95°F and night temperatures exceed 78°F. Those that bear up under the heat include midseason 'Atkinson', 'Creole', 'Heatwave', 'Homestead', 'Neptune', 'Ozark Pink', 'Pink Girl', 'Sioux', 'Solar Set', 'Sun Chaser', 'Sun Leaper', and 'Sunmaster'; paste tomato 'Viva Italia'; cherry tomato 'Sun Gold'; and heirloom 'Arkansas Traveler'.

Large-fruited tomatoes. These grow to full size where the growing season is warm and long. Fruit can weigh several pounds. 'Beefsteak', 'Beefmaster', 'Big Boy', 'Brandywine', 'German Johnson', 'Mortgage Lifter', and 'Watermelon Beefsteak' are typical. 'Burpee Supersteak' can produce 2-pound fruit; 'Goliath' weighs in at 3 pounds; 'Giant Belgium' has tipped the scales at 5 pounds; and 'Delicious' has produced a tomato weighing 7 pounds, 12 ounces for Gordon Graham of Edmond, Oklahoma.

Small-fruited tomatoes. Plants bear large clusters of round, oblong, or pear-shaped fruit that ranges from grape size to cherry size. Grape types include 'Cupid', 'Ildi', 'Juliet', 'Rosalita', and 'Summer Sweet'. Among standard cherry types are 'Black Cherry', 'Blush', 'Gardener's Delight', 'Jolly', 'Mexico Midget', 'Pink Bumble Bee', 'Purple Bumble Bee', 'Sun Gold', 'Supersweet 100', 'Sweet 100', 'Sweet Baby Girl', and 'Sweet Million'. 'Yellow Pear' and 'Red Pear' are pear-shaped novelties. Small-fruited types that grow on dwarf plants suitable for pots or hanging baskets include 'Cherry Falls', 'Florida Basket', 'Florida Petite', 'Micro-Tom', 'Patio', 'Red Robin', 'Small Fry', and 'Tiny Tim'.

Paste tomatoes. These bear prodigious quantities of meaty, oval fruit. Often called plum tomatoes, they're favorites for canning, sauces, and tomato paste. Look for 'La Roma', 'Plum Dandy', 'Roma', 'Super San Marzano', and 'Viva Italia'.

Novelty tomatoes. Among these are selections of various colors: yellow ('Lemon Boy', 'Mountain Gold', 'Yellow Brandywine'), orange ('Orange Banana', 'Orange Queen', 'Sun Gold'), white ('New Snowball', 'White Beauty'), green ('Evergreen'), deep reddish brown ('Black Prince'), purple ('Cherokee Purple', 'Black Krim', 'Paul Robeson'), and even striped ('Green Zebra', 'Mr. Stripey', 'Tigerella'). 'Caro Rich' is very high in vitamin A and beta carotene. 'Health Kick' contains 50% more of the antioxidant lycopene than other tomatoes. Tomatoes in the Indigo series were bred for high levels of the antioxidant anthocyanin, which gives them a deep purple, eggplant-like color. 'Long Keeper' stays fresh in storage (at 60–70°F) for three months. 'Red Stuffer' and 'Yellow Stuffer' produce large, hollow fruit that resembles bell peppers.

Heirloom tomatoes. Varying in size, appearance, and growth habit, these represent old types lovingly maintained by tomato growers all over the country. 'Brandywine', thought to have been developed by the Pennsylvania Amish, is considered

HOW TO GROW TOMATOES

WHEN TO PLANT You can plant tomatoes in spring for summer crops, in summer for fall crops, and (if you live in the Tropical South [USDA 10-11]) in fall for winter crops. Just remember that tomatoes can't take frost and don't like cold soil.

SEEDS OR TRANSPLANTS? Most people start with purchased transplants, but the choice of selections is often limited. To grow heirloom or novelty types, you'll probably be starting from seed. About five to seven weeks before you plan to set out plants, sow seeds in flats or pots filled with light, seed-starting soil mix (available at garden centers); cover seeds with ½ in. of mix. Place containers in a warm, sunny spot with a temperature of at least 65–70°F; keep the soil moist. When seedlings are 2 in. tall, transplant them to individual 3- or 4-in. pots. If you opt to buy transplants, look for sturdy plants that haven't begun flowering or fruiting.

SITE AND SOIL Plant in a sunny site. Good soil is crucial for great tomatoes. Plants like fertile, moist, well-drained soil loaded with organic matter. Work in lots of composted manure, garden compost, or chopped leaves before planting. The soil should be slightly acid to neutral (pH 6.5–7.0). If the pH drops below 6.5, add lime to prevent blossom-end rot (a sunken brown or black spot on the end of the tomato opposite the stem). In Florida, where nematodes are prevalent, gardeners should consider treating their soil with a soil sterilant before planting, even if they're planting nematode-resistant selections. has shown resistance to root-knot nematodes.

PLANTING Don't worry if tomato plants get a bit leggy before you plant. Because of the way they are planted, this can actually be an advantage. (Grafted plants are an exception; see below.) Most folks use either the hole-planting or trench-planting method. With the first, you use a shovel or posthole digger to dig a fairly deep hole, fill the bottom of the hole with a few inches of compost, place the plant vertically in the hole, then fill in with soil so that only the top pair of leaves shows above ground level. With the second, you dig a trench about 4 in. deep and 15 in. long, place the plant horizontally in the trench, bend the top end of the plant upward, and then fill in the trench so that, again, only the top pair of leaves shows. Both methods accomplish the same thing: They encourage the plant to form roots all along the buried stem, producing a larger, more vigorous, and more drought-tolerant plant. Grafted tomato plants are an exception: Prepare a single hole as described above for each plant, but plant with the graft line well above the soil level (at the same level as in the purchased container).

After planting, give each plant a drink of liquid 20-20-20 fertilizer. Mulch plants generously to keep soil evenly moist and discourage weeds.

SPACING Space staked plants 1–2 ft. apart and caged plants 3 ft. apart. Allow 3 ft. between rows.

TRAINING Tomato plants, particularly indeterminate types, tend to sprawl along the ground—but if you allow this, you'll end up with fruit that's rotten or half-eaten by insects. Instead, stake or cage your plants. To stake, drive a sturdy, 6-ft. stake (at least 1 by 1 in.) into the ground a foot away from the plant. Use soft ties to secure the plant to the stake as it grows. You'll need to prune staked plants to one or two main stems to make them manageable. To cage, grow each plant inside a cylinder made from iron reinforcing wire (6-in. mesh). Use iron reinforcing bars on opposite sides to anchor the cage to the ground. As the vine grows, poke protruding branches back inside the cage. No pruning is required.

WATERING Water regularly and deeply, since tomatoes are deep-rooted plants—but avoid overhead irrigation, which wets leaves and encourages diseases. To prevent splitting, reduce watering slightly as fruit ripens.

FERTILIZING After the first fruit has set, sprinkle ¼ cup of 10-10-10 fertilizer per 10 ft. of row around plants, and water in well. Repeat every four weeks.

HARVESTING Harvest when fruit is fully colored and juicy. When frost is predicted, harvest all fruit, even if it is green. Store in a dry place away from direct sunlight at 60–70°F. Unripe tomatoes that have formed a corky ring where the fruit joins the stem will ripen slowly indoors.

PESTS AND DISEASES Hornworms (large green caterpillars with diagonal white stripes) are major pests. Handpick them or spray in early evening with *Bt* (*Bacillus thuringiensis*). Other pests include whiteflies (spray with horticultural oil) and nematodes (sterilize soil and plant resistant selections).

Tomatoes are also prone to a host of diseases. Early blight (also called alternaria blight) shows up on leaves as dark spots with concentric rings and on fruit as sunken lesions with the same ring pattern. Spraying with copper fungicide is an effective control. If plants are growing strongly, then suddenly wilt and die, the cause is probably verticillium wilt, fusarium wilt, or both. Pull up and discard wilted plants. Plant in a different location each year.

You can minimize fussing, cussing, and spraying by planting selections that resist one or more problems. Keys to resistance to look for on seed packets, on plant labels, or in catalog descriptions include V (verticillium wilt), F (fusarium wilt), FF or F2 (fusarium wilt races 1 and 2), T (tobacco mosaic virus), N (nematodes), A (early or alternaria blight), S (septoria leaf spot), and St or L (stemphylium gray leaf spot). For example, a plant labeled VFFNT resists verticillium wilt, two races of fusarium, nematodes, and tobacco mosaic virus.

Some tomato problems—leaf roll, blossom-end rot, cracked fruit—are caused by growing conditions. These can usually be prevented or corrected by maintaining uniform soil moisture and proper pH.

COLORFUL CHOICES

You can enjoy tomatoes in a virtual crayon box of bold colors. Different hues offer distinctive flavors, so try the whole spectrum.

ORANGES
Try this one:
'Persimmon' for slicing
Others we love:
'Sun Gold,' 'Flamme,' 'Kellogg's Breakfast,' and 'Orange Strawberry'

YELLOWS
Try this one:
'Yellow Plum' for sauces
Others we love:
'Taxi,' 'Yellow Pear,' 'Pineapple,' 'Ildi,' and 'Lemon Boy'

PINKS
Try this one:
'Rose de Berne' for slicing
Others we love:
'Watermelon Beefsteak,' 'Rosalita,' and 'Arkansas Traveler'

WHITES
Try this one:
'Great White' for slicing
Others we love:
'White Queen,' 'White Beauty,' 'Italian Ice,' and 'Snow White'

GREENS
Try this one:
'Cherokee Green' for slicing
Others we love:
'Green Zebra,' 'Green Grape,' 'Evergreen,' and 'Green Giant'

PURPLES
Try this one:
'Black Cherry' for snacking
Others we love:
'Black Plum,' 'Black Krim,' 'Southern Night,' and 'Cherokee Purple'

by many to be the best-tasting tomato of all. Unfortunately, it doesn't like our Southern summers. Better bets for the South include 'Arkansas Traveler', 'Black Krim', 'Cherokee Purple', 'Eva Purple Ball', 'German Johnson', 'Giant Belgium', 'Kellogg's Breakfast', 'Mule Team', 'Mortgage Lifter', 'Pineapple', 'Pink Berkeley Tie Dye', and 'Virginia Sweets' .

Determinate tomatoes. Examples of these bushy types include 'Amelia', 'BHN 602', 'Celebrity', 'Floramerica', 'Health Kick', 'Heatwave', 'La Roma', 'Long Keeper', 'Patio', 'Rutgers', 'Sunmaster', and 'Viva Italia'.

Indeterminate tomatoes. 'Arkansas Traveler', 'Atkinson', 'Beefmaster', 'Better Boy', 'Big Boy', 'Creole', 'Delicious', 'Early Girl', 'First Lady', 'German Johnson', 'Juliet', 'Mortgage Lifter', 'Park's Whopper CR Improved', 'Supersonic', and 'Sweet Million' are just a few of the plants in the vinelike category.

Grafted tomatoes. These plants are made by attaching the top part of the desired selection (the scion) to an extra vigorous rootstock chosen for its resistance to pests and soil-borne diseases. This results in increased uptake of water and nutrients, better resistance to environmental stresses, and bigger harvests of high-quality fruit. Grafting has long been used on woody plants (such as roses and fruit trees), but it seems to work just as well for herbaceous plants like tomatoes, eggplants, and cucumbers. A major benefit here is that it allows Southerners to grow certain heirloom types that otherwise struggle in our climate.

TORENIA FOURNIERI

WISHBONE FLOWER
Linderniaceae
Annual

🌿 **US, MS, LS, CS, TS; USDA 6-11**

◐ **PARTIAL SHADE**

💧 **REGULAR WATER**

Torenia fournieri

This increasingly popular, care-free annual from tropical Asia deserves much wider use. Due to its shade tolearance and array of colors, it is often used as a complement to impatiens. However, new strains take a good bit of sun and also thrive in heat and drought. Grows to 1 ft. high and wide. Blooms from spring to frost; the flowers look like miniature gloxinias (*Sinningia*), with stamens arranged in a wishbone shape. Species has pale lavender blossoms with deeper purple markings and bright yellow throat; a white-flowered form is also sold. Use as edging or in pots and window boxes.

Summer Wave hybrids are the top performers in the South; their spreading habit makes them a good choice for hanging baskets. The Moon series comes in a range of blue, purple, and pink shades, as well as yellow and white, with contrasting markings. Plants sprawl nicely and grow 6–10 in. high. Duchess strain prefers more shade, is more compact (6–8 in. tall and wide), and offers blooms in light blue, dark blue, blue with white, pink, and burgundy. Kauai series grows 8 in. tall and wide, with blooms in blue, burgundy, magenta, rose-pink, and white with lemon-yellow markings; needs more shade than others.

CARE

Sow seeds in pots and transplant to garden after frost danger is past; or buy nursery plants. Plant in fertile, well-drained soil. Keep roots cool with a mulch. Prefers light shade in the hot afternoon. Deadheading not necessary. No serious pests.

TRACHELOSPER-MUM

STAR JASMINE
Apocynaceae
Evergreen shrubs or vines

🌿 **MS, LS, CS, TS; USDA 7-11**

☀ ◐ **FULL SUN OR PARTIAL SHADE**

💧💧 **MODERATE TO REGULAR WATER**

Trachelospermum jasminoides

These old favorites are among the most versatile and useful of plants, serving as ground covers, trailers, or climbers. They bear delightfully fragrant, pinwheel-shaped blossoms in spring and early summer. Plant in well-drained soil; for lush growth, fertilize once before spring growth begins, again after flowering. Prune back as needed to shape. Cut stems exude a milky sap.

T. asiaticum. ASIAN STAR JASMINE. From Japan, Korea. Excellent, tough, fast-growing ground cover. Hardier than *T. jasminoides*, with smaller, darker, duller green leaves; flowers are also smaller, in creamy yellow or yellowish white. Several selections are grown for their attractive foliage. 'Ogon-ni-shiki' is dramatic, with orange and red new growth that ages to deep green splashed with gold. 'Snow N Summer' and 'Tricolor' have leaves that emerge pink, then age to white, then to deep green with white splashes. 'Summer Sunset' has new leaves of orange and red that slowly turn creamy white with a wide irregular edge of green.

T. jasminoides. CONFEDER-ATE JASMINE, STAR JASMINE. From China. Given support, a twining vine to 20–30 ft.; without support and with some tip-pinching, a spreading shrub or ground cover to 1½–2 ft. tall, 4–5 ft. wide. Oval leaves to 3 in. long are glossy, light green when new, mature to lustrous dark green. Profusion of white, inch-wide flowers in small clusters on short side branches. Attractive to bees. If grown as a shrubby plant, it is good in raised beds or entry gardens, for edging a walk or drive, as extension of lawn, spilling over walls, as ground cover under trees and shrubs. Set plants 5 ft. apart for ground cover. As a vine, good for training on a wall, pergola, trellis, or over a doorway. 'Madison' is a bit more compact, with a longer bloom period, sweeter scent, and improved cold hardiness. Leaves of 'Variegatum' are bordered and blotched in white.

TRACHYCARPUS FORTUNEI

WINDMILL PALM
Arecaceae
Palm

🌿 **LS, CS, TS; USDA 8-11; OR HOUSEPLANT**

☀ ◐ **FULL SUN OR LIGHT SHADE; BRIGHT LIGHT**

💧💧 **MODERATE TO REGULAR WATER**

Trachycarpus fortunei

From China. Medium-size, care-free, very hardy fan palm (to 10°F or lower). Moderate to fast growth to 30 ft. high, 10 ft. wide. Trunk is usually thicker at top than at bottom and is covered with dense, blackish fiber; as trunk elongates, fiber falls off its lower portion. Toothed, 1½-ft. stalks carry 3-ft.-wide leaves. Cut off old leaves when they droop and turn yellow. Tolerates some drought and exposure to salt. May look untidy in high winds. Young plants can be grown indoors in good light; plant them outdoors when they become too big. Cold-hardy selections such as 'Charlotte' and the slightly larger, more vigorous 'Nainital' have survived 5°F with little damage.

T. wagnerianus (*T. fortunei wagnerianus*) is similar to *T. fortunei* but is hardier and slower growing, with smaller, stiffer, more circular leaves.

TRACHYMENE COERULEA

BLUE LACE FLOWER
Apiaceae
Cool-season annual

🌿 **US, MS, LS, CS, TS; USDA 6-11**

☀ **FULL SUN**

💧 **REGULAR WATER**

Trachymene coerulea

From Australia. Upright plant to 2 ft. tall, 10 in. wide, with finely divided leaves and numerous small lavender-blue flowers in 2- to 3-in.-wide, flat-topped clusters. Blossoms have a lacy look, make good cut flowers. Grow in light, rich, well-drained soil. Sow seeds in place, as taproot makes transplanting difficult. Does not perform well in heat. Sow in fall for winter and spring bloom.

TRADESCANTIA

Commelinaceae

Perennials

ZONES VARY BY SPECIES

EXPOSURE NEEDS VARY BY SPECIES

WATER NEEDS VARY BY SPECIES

Tradescantia pallida 'Purpurea'

Most are virtually indestructible plants with long, trailing stems. Usually seen in pots or hanging baskets, but can be used as ground covers—though the most vigorous, rambling types can be invasive. On variegated forms, pinch out any growth that reverts to solid green. Deer don't normally browse these plants. Types grown as houseplants should be given bright, indirect light and kept fairly moist; feed them with a general-purpose liquid houseplant fertilizer twice a month from spring through fall, once a month in winter.

T. x andersoniana. See *T. virginiana*

T. fluminensis. GREEN WANDERING JEW. Zones CS, TS; USDA 9-11; or houseplant. From South America. Rapid grower to 2 in. high, with indefinite spread. Succulent stems have swollen joints where dark green, oval or oblong, 2½-in.-long leaves are attached. Tiny, unshowy, white flowers. Easy to grow. Excellent for window boxes and dish gardens. If plants are overgrown, renovate by cutting back severely; or discard them and start new plants with fresh tip growth. Stems will live a long time in water, rooting quickly and easily. Partial to full shade; regular to ample water. Variegated forms include 'Albovittata', leaves finely and evenly streaked with white;

'Aurea', bright yellow-green foliage; 'Laekenensis', leaves banded in white and pale lavender; and 'Variegata', yellow- or white-striped foliage.

T. pallida 'Purpurea' (*Setcreasea pallida* 'Purple Heart'). PURPLE HEART. Zones MS, LS, CS, TS; USDA 7-11; or houseplant. From Mexico. Creeping plant to 1–1½ ft. high, 1 ft. wide; stems tend to flop. Pointed, rather narrowly oval leaves are deep purple, three-petaled, pink flowers in summer. Cuttings root quickly.

Generally unattractive in winter. Frost may kill tops, but recovery is fast in warm weather. Use as ground cover, for bedding, in pots. Full sun or light shade. Moderate water. Pinch back after bloom. *T. p.* 'Variegata' sports dazzling purple, cream, and pink stripes; not quite as cold hardy. 'Blue Sue' has blue-green foliage with a purple margin.

T. spathacea. MOSES-IN-THE-CRADLE, OYSTER PLANT. From Mexico, Central America. Zones CS, TS; USDA 9-11; or houseplant. Grows 2 ft. tall and 1 ft. wide. Each plant has a dozen or so broad, sword-shaped, rather erect leaves that are dark green above, deep purple beneath. Small, three-petaled, white blooms are interesting rather than beautiful, crowded into boat-shaped bracts borne down among leaves. Most often used as a ground cover or a potted plant. Tough plant; takes heat, low humidity, sun or shade. Best with regular moisture but withstands inconsistent watering. Try to keep water out of leaf joints when watering. There is also a dwarf form. 'Vittata' has leaves striped in red and yellowish green.

T. virginiana. SPIDERWORT. Zones US, MS, LS, CS; USDA 6-9. From the eastern U.S., but long a favorite in Southern gardens. Clump-forming border plant to 1½ ft. high and wide. Long, grassy-looking, deep green, erect or arching leaves. Three-petaled flowers last for only a day, but buds come in large clusters, and plants are seldom out of bloom in summer. May self-sow and become somewhat invasive. Divide clumps when crowded. Sun or shade; regular to ample water. Named garden selections offer flowers in white, blue shades, lavender, purple, shades of pink from pale to near-red; these plants are often sold as *T. x andersoniana*

or as members of the Andersonia Group. 'Sweet Kate' has yellow foliage, striking in contrast with the purplish blue flowers. 'Concord Grape' has grape, purple flowers. 'Little Doll' has lavender flowers; compact habit.

T. zebrina (*Zebrina pendula*). WANDERING JEW. Zones LS, CS, TS; USDA 8-11; or houseplant. From southern Mexico. Similar to *T. fluminensis* but more cold hardy; bears pinkish or bluish flowers. Most widely grown are forms with colorful leaves, including 'Quadricolor', purplish green leaves with longitudinal bands of silver, pink, and red; and 'Purpusii', dark red or greenish red foliage. Attractive ground covers for shady, frost-free sites. Partial to full shade. Regular water.

TRIADICA SEBIFERA

CHINESE TALLOW, POPCORN TREE

Euphorbiaceae

Deciduous tree

LS, CS, TS; USDA 8-11

FULL SUN

MODERATE TO REGULAR WATER

MILKY SAP IS POISONOUS IF INGESTED

Triadica sebifera

Native to China and Japan. Fast-growing tree to 40 ft. tall, 30 ft. wide, with a rounded or conical crown. Its names come from its unusual seeds: The Chinese once extracted wax from the seed capsules to make soap and candles, and the ripened, whitish seeds resemble popcorn. Decorating wreaths with this "popcorn" is a popular tradition

in Charleston and other Southeastern cities. The tree has long been prized in the South for its spectacular scarlet, orange, burgundy, and yellow fall display; it's one of the few trees with brilliant fall color in the Deep South. In the northern end of the Lower South, young trees may be killed to the ground in winter, and branches of established trees may be frozen back several feet.

Medium green leaves to 3 in. long and wide are rounded, tapering to a slender point; they flutter in the slightest breeze. Tree has an airy look and casts moderate shade, making it a good choice for lawns and terraces. Blooms in summer; flowers are yellowish green, stringlike catkins 2–4 in. long. The seed capsules that follow open by October, revealing the white, waxy seeds.

Chinese tallow tolerates almost any soil. Seedlings can easily grow 5 ft. tall the first year. Unfortunately, almost every seed produced germinates somewhere; the tree has spread so prolifically in Florida and along the South Atlantic coast that in those areas it is considered a noxious weed. Formerly known as *Sapium sebiferum*.

TRICYRTIS

TOAD LILY

Liliaceae

Perennials

US, MS, LS, CS; USDA 6-9

PARTIAL TO FULL SHADE, EXCEPT AS NOTED

REGULAR TO AMPLE WATER

Tricyrtis 'Lightning Strike'

Woodland plants that resemble false Solomon's seal (*Smilacina*) in foliage. Interesting, heavily spotted, inch-long flowers appear at leaf joints and in terminal clusters in late summer and fall. They are complex in structure, somewhat orchidlike: Each blossom has three petals and three sepals, with a column of decorative stamens and styles rising from the center. Need soil enriched with plenty of organic matter. Excellent companions to ferns, foamflower (*Tiarella*), and hostas. Unfortunately (like hostas), they are a favorite snack for voles.

T. formosana (*T. stolonifera*). From Taiwan. To 2½ ft. tall. Spreads by aboveground runners to form a clump 1½ ft. or wider, but is not invasive. More erect than *T. hirta*, with flowers mostly in terminal clusters. Leaves are green, mottled with deeper green; brown or maroon buds open to white to pale lilac flowers spotted with purple. 'Autumn Glow' has green leaves with a wide yellow border; flowers are purple. 'Gates of Heaven' has bright golden foliage and purple flowers. Late-blooming 'Variegata' has lavender blossoms and gold-edged leaves. For the plant sold as *T. f.* 'Amethystina', see *T. lasiocarpa*.

T. hirta. From Japan. To 3 ft. tall, 2 ft. wide; it lacks runners. Arching stems bear pale green, softly hairy foliage. White to pale lilac blossoms are peppered with purple; they appear in leaf joints all along the stems. The following are somewhat shorter than the species: 'Miyazaki' bears pink to white flowers with crimson spots; 'Miyazaki Gold' is similar but has gold-edged leaves. Possible hybrid 'White Towers' (1–2½ ft. tall) has pure white blossoms with purple stamens.

T. hybrids. Specialty nurseries offer many interesting hybrids, including the following. 'Dark Beauty' ('Purple Beauty'), to 4 ft. tall, 1 ft. wide, has large leaves and purple-and-white spotted flowers. 'Empress', to 2 ft. high and 1 ft. wide, bears large, spidery-petaled blossoms in white heavily spotted with purple. 'Tojen', to 3 ft. high and 2 ft. wide, has large flowers that are lavender-purple at the tips, fading to white in the center. 'Blue Wonder' has blue and deep purple speckles on creamy-white petals. 'Lightning Strike', to 2 ft. tall and wide, has pale lavender blooms with purple speckles; its leaves are heavily streaked with gold.

T. lasiocarpa. From Taiwan. Formerly sold as *T. formosana* 'Amethystina'. Upright grower to 3 ft. tall and wide; dark stems are set with large (to 12 in. long), glossy, green leaves speckled with purple. From midsummer to early fall, stems are topped by branched sprays of inch-long, white-throated flowers marked with blue and purple. Needs more sun than other toad lilies; thrives in part sun to light shade.

T. macropoda. From China. Upright growth to 2 ft. high, 16 in. wide. Rounded gray leaves are unspotted. Profuse show of white flowers with purple spots and backward-pointing petals. 'Tricolor' has gray leaves striped with pink and white.

TRILLIUM
WAKE ROBIN
Melanthiaceae
Perennials

✎ **US, MS, LS; USDA 6-8, EXCEPT AS NOTED**

◐ ● **PARTIAL TO FULL SHADE**

💧 **REGULAR WATER**

Trillium grandiflorum

If you asked folks to name their favorite wildflowers, these charming woodland plants would rank high on many lists. They bloom in early spring and need some winter chill. Each stem is topped with a whorl of three leaves; from center of these rises a single flower with three petals. Plant the thick, deep-growing, fleshy rhizomes in a shady, woodsy site. Left undisturbed, they will gradually increase. Plants die to the ground in mid- to late summer. In addition to species listed below, many others are

offered by specialists in native plants. Browsing deer often pass trilliums by.

T. catesbaei. CATESBY TRILLIUM. From the southeastern U.S. Resembles *T. grandiflorum* but has pink flowers.

T. cuneatum. SWEET BETSY. Native to Southeast. Reaches 1½ ft. high, 1 ft. wide, with gray-mottled leaves and a banana-scented flower.

T. decipiens. CHATAHOOCHEE TRILLIUM. Zones MS, LS, CS; USDA 7-9. From Alabama, Georgia, and Florida. To 6–18 in. high, 4 in. wide. Mottled green leaves with pale centers, to 7 in. long. Greenish flowers, sometimes with purplish tints. Takes limy soils.

T. erectum. PURPLE TRILLIUM. From eastern North America. Grows to 2 ft. high, 1 ft. wide, with 7-in. leaves and 2-in., erect, brownish purple flowers. Sometimes known by the name "stinking Benjamin" due to the odd odor of its flowers. *T. e. albiflorum* has white or pale pink flowers.

T. grandiflorum. WHITE TRILLIUM. From eastern North America. The showiest trillium. To 1½ ft. tall, 1 ft. wide, with stout stems and 2½- to 6-in.-long leaves. Nearly stalkless flowers are nodding, to 3 in. across, white aging to rose. Several choice double-flowered forms are available, including 'Flore Pleno' and 'Snowbunting'.

T. luteum. YELLOW TRILLIUM. Native primarily to the Southeast and midsouth. Grows 12–15 in. high and wide, with 6-in.-long, medium green leaves mottled with pale green. Canary-yellow flowers, with petals up to 3½ in. long, are held upright; their fragrance is lemony and sweet.

T. recurvatum. PRAIRIE TRILLIUM, BLOODY BUTCHER. Native to eastern U.S. To 15 in. high, 1 ft. wide. Leaves to 3 in. long, spotted in reddish purple; purple-brown flowers.

T. sessile. TOADSHADE. From northeastern U.S. Grows 1 ft. high, 8 in. wide, with purple-spotted, 5-in.-long leaves and dark purplish red flowers.

T. underwoodii. UNDERWOOD'S TRILLIUM. Zones US, MS, LS, CS; USDA 6-9. Native to southeast U.S. To 8 in. tall, not quite as wide. Dark purple flowers contrast nicely with the beautiful foliage: 2- to 4-in.-long leaves

mottled in light and dark green, with an irregular silver streak running down the center.

T. undulatum. PAINTED TRILLIUM. Zones US, MS; USDA 6-7. From eastern U.S. To 1½ ft. high, 6 in. wide, with 6-in. leaves and upright, somewhat nodding, 1½-in. white flowers marked reddish purple near petal bases. Not easy to grow; needs cool conditions and acid soil.

TRITELEIA
Liliaceae
Perennials from corms

✎ **US, MS, LS, CS; USDA 6-9**

☀ **FULL SUN**

○ **NO IRRIGATION NEEDED**

Triteleia ixioides

Many are native to the West Coast, where they bloom in sunny fields and meadows in spring and early summer, but they also adapt to Midwestern prairies and the Texas Hill Country. Plants sport a few grasslike leaves topped by a cluster of funnel-shaped or tubular, ½- to 2-in.-long blossoms; they die to the ground after blooming. Great choice for rock gardens and dry meadows. Good cut flowers. Many *Triteleia* species were previously listed as *Brodiaea*.

T. hyacinthina (*Brodiaea hyacinthina*, *B. lactea*). WHITE TRITELEIA. Heirloom plant; introduced in 1835. Stems 1–2 ft. high bear clusters of 10 to 40 bowl-shaped, ½-in., purple-tinged white flowers with green veins.

T. ixioides (*Brodiaea ixioides*, *B. lutea*). PRETTY FACE, GOLDEN TRITELEIA. Flower stalk to 2 ft.; inch-long, golden yellow flowers with purple-black midrib and veins. 'Starlight' has soft yellow buds that open to creamy white, star-shaped flowers.

T. laxa (Brodiaea laxa). GRASS NUT, ITHURIEL'S SPEAR. Stalks to 2 ft. tall are topped with trumpet-shaped, ¾- to 1½-in.-long purple-blue flowers. 'Königin Fabiola' ('Queen Fabiola') sports large, upward-facing dark blue flowers. 'Rudy' (T. 'Rudy') has white flowers with a bold violet stripe down the center of each petal. 'White Sweep' has pure white blooms.

CARE

These plants grow naturally in heavy adobe soil in areas that are rainy in winter and early spring, then dry the rest of the year. If you can't provide a long dry period, be sure to plant in sandy or gritty soil. Set corms 2–3 in. deep and 2–4 in. apart.

TROLLIUS
GLOBEFLOWER
Ranunculaceae
Perennials

🌿 **US, MS; USDA 6-7**

☼ ◑ **FULL SUN OR PARTIAL SHADE**

💧💧 **REGULAR TO AMPLE WATER**

Trollius x cultorum 'Lemon Queen'

Lush-looking meadow plants that form clumps of finely cut, shiny dark green leaves topped by 2- to 3-ft.-tall stems bearing yellow to orange flowers typically shaped like globes or rounded cups. Excellent cut flowers.

T. chinensis. CHINESE GLOBE-FLOWER. From China, Siberia. To 3 ft. tall, 1½ ft. wide. Light orange-yellow, 2-in. flowers with open

bowl shape; summer bloom. 'Golden Queen' has semidouble, golden yellow blooms with a deep orange center.

T. x cultorum. Group of hybrids between T. europaeus and two Asian species. Plants grow to 2–3 ft. tall and resemble T. europaeus in most details. Bloom comes at some time from spring into summer, depending on hybrid. Choices include primrose yellow 'Alabaster', creamy yellow 'Cheddar', and golden orange 'Orange Princess'. Compact growers (1–2 ft.) include pale orange-yellow 'Earliest of All', lemon-yellow 'Lemon Queen', and creamy yellow 'New Moon'.

T. europaeus. COMMON GLOBEFLOWER. From Europe, the Caucasus, and North America. To 1½–2 ft. tall, ½ ft. wide. Globular, lemon-yellow or orange flowers, 1–2 in. across, in spring. Somewhat more tolerant of dry soil than other species.

CARE

Remove faded flowers to prolong bloom period. Cannot take drought or extreme heat; constantly damp area near a pond or stream is an ideal planting site. If you are growing globeflowers in a regular garden bed, liberally amend soil with organic matter and keep well watered. Divide clumps only when they thin out in center.

TROPAEOLUM MAJUS
NASTURTIUM
Tropaeolaceae
Cool-season annual

🌿 **US, MS, LS, CS, TS; USDA 6-11**

☼ ◑ **FULL SUN OR LIGHT SHADE**

💧 **REGULAR WATER**

Tropaeolum majus

Few flowers capture the carefree feeling of a cottage garden better than nasturtiums, whether they're climbing a wire fence, spilling from a window box, or tumbling over rocks. These easy-to-grow plants fall into in two main groups. Mounding types are bushy; they grow to 15 in. tall and stay put. Climbing types trail over the ground or use coiling leafstalks to climb as high as 6 ft. Both sport distinctive, long-stemmed, rounded leaves with prominent veins and a fresh bright green color. Broad, showy blossoms (to 2½ in. across) have a pleasant fragrance and come in many colors, including orange, yellow, maroon, red, and creamy white; you can get mixed or single colors in seed packs. Both single- and double-flowered forms are available. Young leaves, flowers, and unripe seedpods add a peppery flavor to salads.

Popular selections include Alaska series (mounding type with variegated leaves speckled in cream and flowers in yellow, coral, or dark red); 'Empress of India' (mounding, with blue-green leaves and dark scarlet blossoms); 'Moonlight' (climbing, with pale yellow blooms); Out of Africa series (climbing, with cream-variegated leaves and red, yellow, peach, or cream flowers); 'Red Wonder' (mounding, with

dark red flowers and olive-green leaves); 'Vesuvius' (mounding, with blue-green leaves and salmon blooms); and Whirlybird Mix (mounding, with yellow, orange, rose, and red blooms).

CARE

Nasturtiums need well-drained, preferably sandy soil. They give out in hot weather, so grow them as a cool-season annual in a hanging basket or as a flowering ground cover. To speed germination, soak the large seeds in water overnight before planting. In the Upper, Middle, and Lower South, plant immediately after the last spring frost for spring and early summer flowers. In the Coastal and Tropical South, sow in fall for autumn and winter blooms. Fertilize sparingly or you'll get all leaves and no flowers.

TSUGA
HEMLOCK
Pinaceae
Evergreen trees

🌿 **ZONES VARY BY SPECIES**

☼ ◑ **FULL SUN OR PARTIAL SHADE, EXCEPT AS NOTED**

💧 **REGULAR WATER**

Tsuga canadensis

These are mostly big trees with horizontal to drooping branches and an unusually graceful appearance. Needlelike leaves are banded with white beneath, flattened and narrowed at the base to form distinct, short stalks. Small, oval, medium brown cones hang down from branches. Bark is deeply furrowed, cinnamon colored to brown.

All hemlocks need some winter chill; all are shallow rooted.

They do best in acid soil and high summer humidity, with protection from hot sun and wind. Hemlocks take well to heavy pruning and make excellent clipped hedges and screens. Subject to browsing deer.

T. canadensis. CANADIAN HEMLOCK. Zones US, MS; USDA 6-7. Native from Nova Scotia to Minnesota, southward along mountain ranges to Alabama and Georgia. Dense, pyramidal tree grows 40–70 ft. or taller, half as wide. Tends to be multitrunked. Outer branchlets droop gracefully. Dark green, about ½-in.-long needles are mostly arranged in opposite rows on branchlets. Fine specimen tree, tall screen, or clipped hedge. 'Cole's Prostrate' is 1 ft. tall (usually less) and spreads to 3 ft. or more. 'Gentsch White', to 2 ft. high and 1½ ft. wide, has white-tipped new growth. 'Jeddeloh' spreads to 3–4 ft. tall and 4–6 ft. wide, with a bird's nest–like depression in the center. 'Moon Frost' is rounded, 3 ft. high and wide, with white new growth that blushes pink in winter. 'Pendula', Sargent weeping hemlock, grows slowly to 10–15 ft. tall and twice as wide, with pendulous branches; with careful pruning, it can easily be kept to handsome, 2- to 3-ft., cascading mound suitable for a large rock garden. Many other dwarf, weeping, and variegated selections are sold.

T. caroliniana. CAROLINA HEMLOCK. Zones US, MS; USDA 6-7. Native to mountains in the southeastern U.S. Resembles *T. canadensis* but is somewhat slower growing, a little stiffer in habit, and darker green in color. Longer needles are arranged all around the twigs instead of in opposite rows.

CARE

Easily damaged by salt and drought. Subject to various pests and diseases, but damage is not always serious if plants are well grown. A woolly adelgid (a type of aphid) is causing the decline and even death of many hemlocks in the Southern Appalachians. Check with your local Cooperative Extension Service for best treatment practices in your area.

A HEMLOCK TO DIE FOR

Relax, native-plant fans. When the ancient Greeks used poison hemlock to execute Socrates, it had nothing to do with one of our beloved native conifers. Rather, they used an extract from a perennial called 'hemlock' (*Conium maculatum*) that looks a lot like Queen Anne's lace.

TULBAGHIA VIOLACEA
SOCIETY GARLIC
Alliaceae
Perennial from rhizomes

🌿 MS, LS, CS, TS; USDA 7-11

☀️ FULL SUN

💧 REGULAR WATER

Tulbaghia violacea

From South Africa. Bluish green, very narrow leaves form a dense evergreen clump. In spring and summer, 1- to 2-ft. stems are topped by clusters of 8 to 20 small, trumpet-shaped, pinkish lavender flowers. Leaves and flower stems have an onion or garlic odor if cut or crushed; leaves can be used in cooking. Makes a nice edging for vegetable beds; good cut flower. Suffers frost damage at 20–25°F but recovers quickly. Deer don't browse these plants. 'Variegata' has a creamy stripe down the middle of each leaf; in 'Silver Lace', leaves are edged in white. Foliage of 'Tricolor' has white edges with a pinkish cast that intensifies in cool weather.

CARE

Start plants from containers or divisions in early spring or early fall. Give well-drained, organically enriched soil. Divide clumps to increase plantings; set divisions 1½ ft. apart.

TULIPA
TULIP
Liliaceae
Perennials from bulbs

🌿 US, MS (USDA 6-7); TREAT MOST AS ANNUALS IN LS, CS, TS (USDA 8-10)

☀️🌓 FULL SUN DURING BLOOM, PART SHADE IN AFTERNOON IN HOT CLIMATES

💧 REGULAR WATER DURING GROWTH AND BLOOM

Tulipa 'Flaming Parrot'

No other spring bulb matches the tulip for sheer spectacle. Tulips come in just about every color; their imposing flowers atop strong stems form the backbone of many a spring garden display. If you've only tried the big-flowered sorts, though, you're missing out on a lot. Many kinds are available, from the tall and stately to the dainty and whimsical—and even to the decidedly bizarre. In fact, many of the smaller, lesser-known species perform better in the South than their aristocratic cousins.

Large-flowered tulips, such as the Darwin hybrids, are ideal for sweeps and borders; mass at least 50 of a single color for impact. Plant them behind low, spring-blooming perennials such as candytuft (*Iberis*) or pinks (*Dianthus*), or with annuals such as forget-me-nots (*Myosotis*), sweet alyssum (*Lobularia*), or pansies and violas (*Viola*). Plant smaller,

---

lower-growing species in rock gardens, raised beds, and alongside paths. Tulips are superb container plants; especially lovely in this role are the more unusual kinds, such as the Double Early, Parrot, and Rembrandt types.

Tulips have been classified into many divisions, defined mainly by flower type. For the convenience of gardeners, we have arranged the divisions into additional groupings; the first three are by bloom season, while the fourth contains species and their hybrids. For most divisions, we've also included "best bets"—selections that perform especially well in the South.

EARLY TULIPS

Single Early tulips. Single flowers on 10- to 16-in. stems. Colors include white, yellow, salmon, pink, red, dark purple. Popular for forcing and growing indoors in pots. Best bets include 'Apricot Beauty' (soft salmon-pink), 'Bestseller' (blended salmon-pink and orange tones), 'Christmas Marvel' (cherry-red), 'Flair' (yellow heavily marked with red), and 'Mickey Mouse' (golden yellow marked with red flames).

Double Early tulips. Peony-like double flowers, often measuring 4 in. across, on 6- to 12-in. stems. Same color range as Single Early tulips. Effective massed in borders. In rainy areas, mulch around plants or surround with ground cover to keep mud from splashing the short-stemmed flowers. Look for 'Monsella' (yellow with red streaks), 'Montreau' (soft yellow blushed with rose), and 'Monte Carlo' (bright yellow, good perennializer).

MIDSEASON TULIPS

Triumph tulips. Single flowers on sturdy stems to 20 in. tall. Wide range of solid colors, including red, white, yellow, and bicolors. Try 'Annie Schilder' (coral and orange blend), 'Gavota' (burgundy with yellow edge), 'Hibernia' (white), 'Passionale' (purple), and 'Princess Irene' (orange with purple flame).

Darwin hybrids. Spectacular group with brightly colored flowers on 24- to 28-in. stems. Most are in scarlet-orange to red range; some have contrasting eyes or penciling. Some reach 7 in. across. Pink, yellow, and white selections exist. Best bets include 'Banja

TOP ROW: Tulipa 'Maureen' (Single late); *T.* 'Annie Schilder' (Triumph); *SECOND ROW: T.* 'Passionale' (Triumph); *T.* 'Hocus Pocus' (Single late); *THIRD ROW: T.* 'Green Star' (Lily-flowered); *T. whittallii; BOTTOM ROW: T. clusiana* 'Tinka'; *T. clusiana* 'Lady Jane'

Luka' (golden yellow marked with red), 'Come-Back' (blood red), 'Daydream' (apricot orange), 'Golden Apeldoorn' (golden yellow), 'Golden Parade' (pale buttercup yellow), 'Ivory Floradale' (ivory-white), 'Jewel of Spring' (soft yellow with thin red margins), 'Parade' (bright red), 'Pink Impression' (soft pink marked with deep rose), 'Red Impression' (red), and 'Silverstream' (creamy yellow sometimes streaked with red and white).

LATE TULIPS

Single Late tulips. Graceful plants with large, oval or egg-shaped blooms on 1½- to 3-ft. stems. Clear, beautiful colors: white, yellow, orange, pink, red, mauve, lilac, purple, maroon. May have contrasting margins. Includes old Darwin and Cottage groups. Good choices are 'Hocus Pocus' (butter-yellow with pink flame), 'Maureen' (white), 'Queen of Night' (blackish maroon), and 'Temple of Beauty' (salmon-rose).

Lily-flowered tulips. Graceful, lilylike flowers with recurved, pointed segments; come in white and shades of yellow, pink, red, and magenta, often with contrasting markings. Stems 20–26 in. high. Look for the unusual green-and-white 'Green Star' and the elegant 'White Triumphator' (ivory-white).

Fringed tulips. Flowers have finely fringed edges. Colors include white, yellow, pink, red, and violet; fringing is often in a different color than rest of flower. Stems 16–24 in. high. Recommended are 'Burgundy Lace' (wine red), 'Fringed Elegance' (yellow), and 'Honeymoon' (white).

Viridiflora tulips. Flowers edged in green or colored in blends of green with other hues—white, yellow, rose, red, buff. Stems 10–20 in. high. Try 'China Town' (soft pink and green), 'Spring Green' (white and soft green), and 'Yellow Spring Green' (pale yellow and apple-green).

Rembrandt tulips. Streaks and variegation on the original Rembrandts were caused by a transmittable virus; these infected bulbs can no longer be imported and should not be planted. Tulips now sold as Rembrandts have "flame" patterning of genetic, not viral, origin. New types in other divisions have a similar appearance.

Parrot tulips. Large, long, deeply fringed, and ruffled flowers atop 16- to 20-in. stems are striped, feathered, and flamed in various colors, including green. They once had weak, floppy stems, but modern types are stouter. Best bets include 'Blue Parrot' (deep violet), 'Flaming Parrot' (yellow and red), and 'Orange Favorite' (deep orange).

Double Late tulips. Often called peony-flowered tulips, these have very large (to 5-in.-wide), heavy-textured double blossoms on 14- to 20-in. stems. Colors include orange, rose, red to purple shades, yellow, and white. Recommendations include 'Angelique' (pink and white), 'Mount Tacoma' (white), 'Orange Princess' (orange marked with purple), and 'Uncle Tom' (deep maroon).

SPECIES TULIPS

Kaufmanniana tulips. Often called waterlily tulip, *T. kaufmanniana* is a very early bloomer with 3-in., creamy yellow flowers (marked red on petal backs) with dark yellow centers; the flowers open flat in sun. Stems reach 6–8 in. high. Hybrids come in various colors, usually with flower centers in a contrasting color; many have mottled leaves like Greigii tulips. 'Ancilla' is a good example.

Fosteriana tulips. Early-blooming *T. fosteriana* has very large flowers—to 8 in. wide. The red blossoms appear atop relatively short (8- to 10-in.) stems, which makes them look even larger. Hybrids include selections with flowers in red, orange, yellow, pink, and white. The 16-in.-high 'Red Emperor' ('Mme Lefeber') has fiery red flowers. 'Purissima' ('White Emperor') has large, pure white petals on 12- to 18-in. stems.

Greigii tulips. Midseason-blooming *T. greigii* has big (6-in.) flowers borne on 10-in. stems; leaves are heavily spotted and streaked with brown. Hybrids have flowers in white, pink, orange, red; many feature several colors in a single blossom. 'Fire of Love' has bright red blooms; green leaves are heavily streaked with maroon and cream. 'Red Riding Hood' has scarlet flowers; its leaves are streaked with brown.

Other species. Sold mainly by bulb specialists. Most are

T

HOW TO GROW TULIPS

SHOPPING Buy tulips as soon as you see them offered in garden centers. Choose the biggest bulbs you can find; bigger bulbs produce bigger flowers. Look for firm, fat bulbs; avoid those that are soft, shriveled, or moldy. Reputable mail-order sources are another option; they are likely to offer far more choices than your local garden center.

CHILLING Nearly all hybrid tulips and most species types need an extended period of winter chill to bloom well. Gardeners in the Lower, Coastal, and Tropical South (USDA 8–10), where winters are short and mild, can refrigerate bulbs for 8 to 10 weeks prior to planting in fall (don't put them near ripening fruit or in the freezer). Bloom comes at some time from March to May, depending on type.

Even in cold-winter regions, most hybrid tulips are not a long-term investment. The bulbs form offsets that take a few years to reach blooming size, but as these mature, they draw energy from the mother bulb. (Darwin hybrids are an exception; they are slow to form offsets). The result is a gradual decline in flowering. For this reason, most hybrid tulips are best treated as annuals or short-lived perennials.

EXPOSURE Tulips need sunshine at least while in bloom; they will lean toward the source of light if planting area is partly shaded. It's fine to plant under deciduous trees if the trees won't leaf out until after the tulips have bloomed and their leaves have begun to turn yellow.

SOIL Rich, sandy soil is ideal, though tulips will grow in any good, fast-draining soil. They perform poorly if planted in soil where other tulips were recently growing; choose a new site or dig out soil to the requisite planting depth and replace it with fresh soil from elsewhere in the garden.

PLANTING Set bulbs three times as deep as they are wide (a little shallower in heavy soils). Space 4–8 in. apart, depending on eventual size of plant. Where winter temperatures regularly dip below 32°F, plant in October or November, after soil has cooled. In warmer regions, plant in December or January.

WATER In areas with warm, wet summer soil, bulbs of hybrids are prone to rot and shouldn't be counted on for more than a year or two. A number of species tulips however, perform quite well under these conditions. In general, it's a good idea to avoid watering while they're dormant.

DIVIDING If tulips do persist from year to year, they will eventually need separating. Dig and divide clumps in late summer; replant at the best time for your climate. Species tulips can be left undisturbed for many years.

PROBLEMS Squirrels, chipmunks, and gophers like tulips as much as you do, but for a different reason. To keep these pesky rodents from gobbling up your bulbs, coat them before planting with sticky rodent repellants (found at most garden centers) or plant the bulbs inside baskets made from ¼-in. wire mesh. Protect from slugs and snails. Aphids are another possible pest.

from western and central Asia. Simpler looking than large hybrid tulips, with a wildflower charm. Generally best in rock gardens or wild gardens, where plantings can remain undisturbed for many years; plant 4 in. apart. Also good in pots. Most are reliably perennial. Species that will persist from

year to year in mild-winter areas are noted.

T. acuminata. Flowers have long, twisted, spidery segments of red and yellow on 1½-ft.-tall stems. Late.

T. bakeri. Similar to and often listed as *T. saxatilis*. Lilac to purple flowers with a yellow base open

to a wide, flat star; they are borne in clusters of three or four on stems to 1 ft. high. 'Lilac Wonder', to 6–7 in. high, has rosy purple flowers with a large, circular lemon-yellow base. Midseason. Good in mild-winter areas.

T. batalinii. Soft yellow flowers on 6- to 10-in. stems. Very narrow leaves. 'Red Jewel' has scarlet-red blossoms; 'Yellow Jewel' has lemon-yellow blossoms tinged with rose. Midseason.

T. clusiana. LADY or CANDY TULIP. Slender flowers on 9-in. stems are white, with outer petals marked in rosy red. Midseason bloom; good permanent tulips in mild-winter areas. 'Cynthia' is chartreuse, with outer petals heavily marked in red. 'Lady Jane' is white, with pink outer petals. 'Tinka' is creamy yellow; outer petals are rich red. Blossoms of 6-in.-high *T. c. chrysantha* are star shaped when fully open; they have yellow inner petals and rose-carmine outer ones. *T. c. stellata* (to 12 in. tall) is also star shaped when fully open; inner petals are creamy white, outer ones brushed in rich pink. Good in mild-winter areas.

T. eichleri. Foot-tall stems bear shining scarlet flowers with jet black centers outlined in yellow. Early.

T. humilis (*T. pulchella*). One to three pale pink or purplish pink flowers with a yellow center atop each 4- to 6-in. stem. Early. 'Violacea' has deep violet flowers, usually with a yellow base. 'Little Beauty' (*T. hageri* 'Little Beauty') has reddish-pink flowers with a bluish base outlined in white.

T. praestans. Up to six orange-red flowers on each 2-ft. stem. Midseason. 'Fusilier' is an improved selection growing 10–14 in. high. Blooms of 'Shogun' (10–12 in. high) are a yellow-and-orange blend with subtle red streaks.

T. saxatilis. Fragrant, yellow-based pale lilac flowers open nearly flat, are carried one to three to each 1-ft. stem. Early. Good choice for areas with mild winters.

T. sylvestris. Yellow, 2-in. flowers, one or two to each 1-ft. stem. Late. Good in mild-winter areas.

T. tarda (*T. dasystemon*). Each 3- to 5-in. stem has three to six upward-facing, starlike flowers

with golden centers, white-tipped segments. Early. Good in mild-winter areas.

T. turkestanica. Fragrant, creamy white flowers with yellow centers. Borne on 6- to 8-in.-high stems, as many as 12 per bulb. Early to midseason.

T. whittallii. Star-shaped blooms in clusters of up to 4 combine shades of orange and yellow; center is nearly black. Grows 8–12 in. high. Early to midseason. Good in mild-winter areas.

TURNIP AND RUTABAGA

Brassicaceae
Biennials grown as cool-season annuals

🌿 US, MS, LS, CS, TS; USDA 6-11

☀ FULL SUN

💧 REGULAR WATER

Turnip

These European natives are cabbage relatives and, like cabbage, belong to the genus *Brassica*. Although turnips are best known in other parts of the country for their roots, in the South their leaves are also enjoyed as a green vegetable and some selections are grown for leaves only. Turnip roots come in various colors (white, white topped with purple, creamy yellow) and shapes (globe, flattened globe). Rutabaga is a tasty turnip relative with large yellowish roots; its leaves are palatable only when very young (they turn coarse as they mature). Turnip roots are quick growing and should be harvested and used as soon as big enough to eat; rutabaga is a late-maturing crop that stores well in the ground. Flavor of rutabaga improves with light frost. Roots of both turnip and rutabaga are milder flavored if soil is kept moist; they become more pungent under drier conditions.

For a quick crop of greens only, try 'Seven Top' (45 days). For both turnip greens and tasty roots, plant 'Purple-Top White Globe' (50–60 days), 'Royal Crown' (45–55 days), or 'White Lady' (35–45 days). A widely recommended rutabaga is 'American Purple Top' (90 days).

CARE

Grow both in rich, loose, moist, well-drained soil. In the Upper and Middle South (USDA 6 and 7), plant in early spring for early summer harvest, or in summer for fall harvest. Elsewhere, plant in August to October for fall and winter crops. Feed with a liquid fertilizer after seedlings are up, then again monthly. Sow seeds ½ in. deep, 1 in. apart. Thin turnips to 2–6 in. apart if growing for roots, 1–4 in. apart for greens. Thin rutabagas to 5–8 in. apart; they need ample space for roots to reach full weight of 3 to 5 pounds. Turnip roots grow fast and should be harvested and used as soon as they are big enough to eat, usually 40–70 days after sowing. Rutabaga roots are ready to harvest in 90 to 120 days; they store well in the ground, and flavor improves with light frost. Cabbage root maggot is a pest of turnip (it is less likely to infest rutabaga); see Cabbage for control.

ULMUS
ELM
Ulmaceae
Deciduous or semievergreen trees

✂ **US, MS, LS, CS; USDA 6-9, EXCEPT AS NOTED**

☼ **FULL SUN**

💧 **REGULAR WATER, EXCEPT AS NOTED**

Ulmus parvifolia

Once highly prized shade trees, elms have fallen on hard times. Dutch elm disease (spread by a bark beetle) has killed millions of American elms throughout North America and can attack most other elm species. Many of the larger elms are appealing fare for various beetles, leafhoppers, aphids, and scale, making them time consuming to care for, messy, or both. Elms have other problems not related to pests. They have aggressive, shallow root systems, so you'll have trouble growing other plants beneath them. Many types produce suckers; branch crotches are often narrow, splitting easily in storms. Still, elms are widely planted, valued for their fast growth, moderate shade, and environmental toughness. Researchers continue to devote much effort to finding disease-resistant selections. All elms are fairly soil tolerant, have handsome oval leaves.

U. alata. WINGED ELM. Deciduous. Native to the South-

east. To 20–40 ft. tall, not quite as wide. Open, airy canopy. Leaves 1–2½ in. long, finely toothed, dark green turning pale yellow in fall. Common name derives from corky outgrowths ("wings") on twigs and young branches. Degree of winging varies among seedlings—the wings stand out on some, while on others they're almost nonexistent. Your best bet is to get a cutting-grown tree from a parent with good bark characteristics. Small red spring flowers are followed by small reddish seeds. 'Lace Parasol' is a weeping form (to 8 ft. tall, 12 ft. wide after 45 years).

U. americana. AMERICAN ELM. Deciduous. Native to eastern North America. This majestic tree once graced lawns and streets throughout its range, but its ranks have been decimated by Dutch elm disease. Grows fast to 100 ft. tall, with equal or greater spread. Prized for its high, arching branches, which create a beautiful, symmetrical canopy. Dark green, tooth-edged, pointed-oval leaves are 3–6 in. long and rough to the touch; they turn yellow in fall, with the intensity of the color varying from tree to tree. Small red flowers in early spring. Easily transplanted. Tolerates wet, alkaline, and saline soils.

A long search for American elms resistant to Dutch elm disease has culminated in a number of improved selections. Probable hybrid 'Jefferson' has dark green leaves that emerge earlier and are retained later. 'New Harmony' is broadly V-shaped, often with gracefully drooping branch tips. 'Valley Forge' grows into a dense, broad, upright vase shape; it is considered the most disease-resistant selection. Moderately resistant 'Princeton' forms a broad umbrella.

U. crassifolia. CEDAR ELM. Deciduous; semievergreen in extreme South Texas. Native from Texas to Mississippi and northern Mexico. Fairly fast growth to 50–75 ft. tall and 40–60 ft. wide. Stiff, shiny, dark green leaves to 2 in. long, rough to the touch; they turn burnt yellow or gold in autumn. Twigs and branches (like those of *U. alata*) have corky wings. Tiny flowers in late summer. Well adapted to alkaline soils. Little to moderate water.

U. parvifolia. CHINESE ELM, LACEBARK ELM. Semievergreen or

deciduous, depending on winter temperature and particular selection. The best elm for home gardens and an excellent shade or lawn tree. Fast growth to 40–60 ft. tall, 25–40 ft. wide. Extremely variable in form, but generally rounded, with long, arching, pendulous branchlets. On older trees, bark flakes off in patches, creating a beautifully mottled combination of gray, green, orange, and brown. Leathery dark green leaves are ¾ to 2½ in. long, broadly oval and pointed, evenly toothed; may turn yellow to reddish orange in fall. Tiny red flowers from late summer to autumn. Resistant to Dutch elm disease, elm leaf beetle, and Japanese beetle. Drought tolerant.

Forms that hold their leaves are often sold as 'Sempervirens', but that is not a valid name. Two more or less evergreen selections popular in the Coastal South (USDA 9) are 'Drake' and 'True Green'; they are not as cold hardy as others and are not recommended for the Upper or Middle South (USDA 6-7). Selections with particularly showy exfoliating bark include 'Allee', a vase-shaped tree to 70 ft. tall, 60 ft. wide; 'Athena', a lower, wide-spreading tree to 40 ft. tall, 55 ft. wide; 'Bosque', oval tree with strong central leader, 40–50 ft. tall and wide; 'Burgundy', a rounded tree

CHINESE ELM GROWS QUICKLY, RESISTS MOST PESTS AND DIS- EASES, AND TOLERATES DROUGHT.

to 18 ft. tall, 20 ft. wide after eight years, with burgundy fall color; 'Everclear', columnar, 40 ft. tall, 15 ft. wide; and 'Milliken', an oval to rounded tree to 50 ft. high, 40 ft. wide. Numerous dwarf and compact selections, such as 'Hokkaido', are popular for bonsai.

A word of caution: A vastly inferior species, *U. pumila*, Siberian elm, is sometimes sold as Chinese elm.

UNGNADIA SPECIOSA

MEXICAN BUCKEYE
Sapindaceae
Deciduous shrub or small tree

MS, LS, CS; USDA 7-9

FULL SUN OR PARTIAL SHADE

LITTLE TO REGULAR WATER

SEEDS ARE POISONOUS IF INGESTED

Ungnadia speciosa

Native to Texas, New Mexico, and northern Mexico. Shrub or small, multitrunked tree, usually 12–15 ft. (occasionally 30 ft.) tall and not quite as wide as high. Easy-to-grow plant with appealing flowers, interesting seedpods, and lush foliage. Clusters of showy, fragrant blossoms with purplish pink petals and red anthers appear in early spring, before or with the new leaves. Flowers are followed in fall by leathery dark brown, buckeyelike seed capsules that split and drop black, shiny, ½-in. seeds. Dark green, 5- to 12-in.-long leaves with three to seven leaflets turn golden yellow in fall. Tolerates a wide range of soils, including dry, limy ones.

UVULARIA

MERRYBELLS, BELLWORT
Colchicaceae
Perennials

US, MS, LS; USDA 6-8

PARTIAL TO FULL SHADE

REGULAR WATER

Uvularia grandiflora

Delightful wildflowers native to eastern and central North America. Grown for their handsome foliage and bell-shaped yellow blooms. Easy to grow in shady places with rich, moist, acid soil. Plants grow about 1 ft. wide and spread by rhizomes to form colonies; propagate by division. Good companions to hostas and ferns.

U. grandiflora. BIG MERRYBELLS. To 2½ ft. tall. Upright, leafy stems, somewhat reminiscent of Solomon's seal (*Polygonatum*), hold downward-pointing, medium green, narrowly oval and pointed leaves to 5 in. long. In spring, bright yellow, 2-in.-long, narrowly bell-shaped flowers with twisted petals hang from upper leaf axils.

U. perfoliata. WOOD MERRYBELLS. To 2 ft. tall, with narrow, oval, pointed blue-green leaves to 4 in. long. Leaf bases encircle the stems. Pale yellow bells are 1½ in. long.

U. sessilifolia. LITTLE MERRYBELLS. Dainty, charming plant to 1½ ft. tall. Wiry stems carry stalkless, lance-shaped leaves to 3 in. long. Nodding yellow flowers to 1½ in. long appear at stem ends in spring. 'Cobblewood Gold' has gold-edged green leaves; 'Variegata' has foliage edged in white.

VACCINIUM

Ericaceae
Evergreen and deciduous shrubs

ZONES VARY BY SPECIES

EXPOSURE NEEDS VARY BY SPECIES

WATER NEEDS VARY BY SPECIES

Vaccinium macrocarpon

Excellent ornamental shrubs with clusters of small, bell-shaped spring flowers and colorful, edible fruit that attracts birds. Species described here are shrubs—ranging from ground covers to the height of a small tree—that are grown for decorative, landscaping use; see Blueberry for relatives grown primarily for their edible fruit. All require rich, organic, acid soil. Good for woodland gardens.

V. arboreum. SPARKLEBERRY, FARKLEBERRY. Evergreen or deciduous, depending on winter cold. Zones MS, LS, CS; USDA 7-9. Native to the South and to southeastern and eastern Texas. Spreading plant to 10–25 ft. tall and about as wide, with shiny, dark green leaves to 2 in. long; leaves turn rich red and crimson in fall and persist through most of the winter. Fragrant white flowers; unpalatable, ¼-in. black berries. Older shrubs have beautiful, exfoliating cinnamon-brown to gray-orange bark. Full sun or partial shade. Needs only moderate water.

V. ashei. See Blueberry

V. corymbosum. See Blueberry

V. crassifolium. CREEPING BLUEBERRY. Evergreen. Zones MS, LS; USDA 7-8. Native from southeast Virginia to South Carolina. Sprawling ground cover to 6 in. tall and 6 ft. across, with leathery, dark green leaves just ½ in. long. Rosy red flowers in late spring; sweet, black berries to ½ in. across. 'Bloodstone' has reddish new and mature leaves, red stems in winter. 'Wells Delight' is particularly broad spreading and disease tolerant. Full sun or partial shade; regular water.

V. darrowii. DARROW'S BLUEBERRY. Evergreen. Zones LS, CS; USDA 8-9. Native to Florida, Georgia, Alabama. Grows to 2 ft. tall in the wild, but can reach 5 ft. tall and 3 ft. wide in garden conditions. Very small blue-green leaves; pinkish new growth. White flowers are followed by small, sweet, black berries with a bluish bloom. Two named selections are 'John Blue' and 'Sebring'. Full sun; little to regular water.

V. elliottii. ELLIOTT'S BLUEBERRY. Deciduous. Zones US, MS, LS, CS; USDA 6-9. Native from Florida to Virginia, west to Arkansas and Louisiana. Clump-forming, straggly shrub of variable size; grows from 6 to 13 ft. tall and about 6 ft. wide. Shiny, thin-textured green leaves to 1½ in. long. Pink to white flowers often appear before leaf-out; dark purple-blue or black berries are less than ½ in. wide. Full sun or partial shade; moderate to regular water.

V. macrocarpon. CRANBERRY. Evergreen. Zones US, MS; USDA 6-7. Native from Newfoundland to Minnesota, south to North Carolina. Creeping plant 2–6 in. high, spreading indefinitely by rooting stems. Narrow, ¾-in.-long leaves are dark green in summer, turning coppery or purplish red in winter. Tiny pinkish flowers are followed by tart red fruit to ¾ in. across in autumn. Commercial producers grow cranberries in bogs—beds that can be flooded to control weeds and pests, provide winter protection, and make harvesting easier. Gardeners can use cranberry as an attractive small-scale ground cover in full sun, with regular to ample water.

V. myrsinites. GROUND BLUEBERRY. Evergreen. Zones MS, LS, CS, TS; USDA 7-11. Native from

Virginia to Florida and Louisiana. To 2 ft. tall, more sprawling than erect. White to pink flowers; tiny blue-black or black berries. Full sun; moderate to ample water.

V. stamineum. DEERBERRY. Deciduous. Zones US, MS, LS, CS; USDA 6-9. Native to eastern North America. Open, airy growth to a possible 10–15 ft. high and wide, although many mature specimens are half that size or even smaller. Twisted trunks and branches; peeling, reddish brown bark. Oval leaves to 3 in. long are green above, whitish underneath; they turn red and orange in autumn. Clustered white flowers have prominent yellow stamens and flaring petals. Purplish berries less than ½ in. across are edible but not always sweet. Full sun or partial shade; moderate to regular water.

VELTHEMIA BRACTEATA
Asparagaceae
Perennial from bulb

- 🌿 **CS, TS; USDA 9-11; OR INDOORS**
- ◐ **PARTIAL SHADE; BRIGHT INDIRECT LIGHT**
- 💧 **REGULAR WATER DURING GROWTH AND BLOOM**

Velthemia bracteata

Handsome foliage is reason enough to grow this South African native. Each bulb produces a fountainlike rosette of wavy-edged, glossy, green leaves to 1 ft. long, 3 in. wide. In winter or early spring, brown-mottled flower stems to about 1 ft. high are topped by elongated clusters of tubular, drooping, pinkish purple flowers with petals tipped in green. Leaves turn yellow and die back in

late spring; new growth resumes in fall. Most plants sold as *V. capensis* are actually *V. bracteata*; the true *V. capensis* has nonglossy, blue-green leaves and green-tipped, pale pink flowers. It is also not as hardy and prefers full sun.

CARE
In frostless areas, it can be grown in the ground, but even there it is usually grown in pots. For each bulb, use a pot large enough to allow about 3 in. between all sides of bulb and container edges. Plant in fall, in fast-draining soil; set top of bulb neck just above soil surface. Fertilize every two weeks throughout the growing season. Keep soil dry during summer dormancy. Can remain outdoors where temperatures stay above 25°F; where light frosts are possible, give overhead protection.

VERBASCUM
MULLEIN
Scrophulariaceae
Biennials and perennials

- 🌿 **US, MS, LS; USDA 6-8, EXCEPT AS NOTED**
- ☀ **FULL SUN**
- 💧 **MODERATE WATER**

Verbascum 'Cotswold Queen'

Large group of rosette-forming, summer-blooming plants that send up spikes closely set with nearly flat, five-petaled, circular flowers about an inch across. Both foliage and stems are often covered in woolly hairs. Taller mulleins make striking vertical accents. All mulleins self-sow freely—and some are downright weedy, such as the attractive roadside wildflower *V. thapsus*.

Perennial species are short lived in hot, humid climates.

V. blattaria. MOTH MULLEIN. Biennial. Zones US, MS, LS, CS; USDA 6-9. Native from Europe to central Asia. To 2–4 ft. tall, 1–1½ ft. wide, with smooth-textured, dark green, cut or toothed leaves to 10 in. long. Pale yellow or white flowers have purple centers. A pink-flowered form has rose-pink flowers that open from red buds.

V. bombyciferum 'Arctic Summer' ('Polarsommer'). Biennial. Selection of a species native to Turkey. To 6 ft. tall, 2 ft. wide, with furry, gray-green leaves to 1½ ft. long. Yellow flowers on powdery white stems.

V. chaixii. CHAIX MULLEIN. Perennial. From Europe. To 3 ft. tall and 2 ft. wide, with hairy, green leaves to 6 in. long. Red-eyed, pale yellow flowers in narrow, often branching spikes. 'Album' and 'Wedding Candles' have white flowers with purple centers. 'Sixteen Candles' has bright yellow blooms with violet centers.

V. hybrids. Many hybrids are obtainable, either as blends or in single colors. Most must be grown from seed.

'Banana Custard'. Biennial. To 5–6 ft. tall, 2 ft. wide. Bright yellow flowers.

'Clementine'. Perennial. To 5 ft. tall, 2 ft. wide, with peacy apricot-to-orange flowers centered with violet-purple.

'Copper Rose'. Perennial. To 4–6 ft. tall, 2 ft. wide, with blossoms in buff, apricot, rose, or tan. Blooms the first year from seed sown in late winter or earliest spring.

Cotswold hybrids. Perennials. These resemble *V. phoeniceum* but come in white, cream, yellow, pink, and purple. Named selections are sometimes offered, including creamy yellow 'Gainsborough' and bright pink 'Pink Domino'.

'Helen Johnson'. Perennial. To 3–4 ft. tall, 2 ft. wide. Apricot flowers with purple centers; large, silvery green leaves. To propagate this sterile hybrid, take root cuttings in early spring.

'Jackie'. Short-lived perennial. To 1½–2 ft. high, 1½ ft. wide. Purple-eyed blossoms are a soft orange, similar to the color of cantaloupe flesh. To propagate this sterile hybrid, take root cuttings in early spring.

'Sierra Sunset'. Perennial.

Rosettes 8 in. high and 14–18 in. wide produce flower stalks 1½ ft. high that hold large blossoms in shades of melon and salmon, with rose accents.

'Southern Charm'. Perennial. To 2–3 ft. high, 1½–2 ft. wide. Seed strain in mixed colors, including cream, buff, lavender, rose.

V. olympicum. OLYMPIC MULLEIN. Perennial. From Greece. To 5 ft. high, 3 ft. wide, with soft, downy white leaves to over 2 ft. long. Bright yellow flowers are very showy; many flowering stems.

V. phoeniceum. PURPLE MULLEIN. Perennial. To 2–4 ft. high, 1½ ft. wide. Dark green leaves to 6 in. long are smooth on top, hairy beneath. Slender spikes of purple flowers. 'Flush of White' has snow-white blooms; those of 'Violetta' are deep violet.

CARE
Grow in well-drained soil that is not too rich; fertile, acidic soil makes plants grow so tall that they may need staking. Cut off spent flowers to encourage a second round of blooming. Leave spikes of biennial species in place if you want plants to spread by reseeding.

VERBENA
Verbenaceae
Perennials, some grown as annuals

- 🌿 **ZONES VARY BY SPECIES**
- ☀ **FULL SUN**
- 💧 **MODERATE WATER, EXCEPT AS NOTED**

Verbena bipinnatifidea

This large group includes some of the garden's most colorful, useful, and easy-to-grow plants. Most bear clusters of small, five-petaled, tubular blossoms from late spring until frost. Low verbenas make good ground covers and edging plants; they're also great in hanging baskets and containers or tumbling over rock walls. Use taller types in borders. Most thrive in heat and tolerate drought. Provide good air circulation and well-drained soil. Not favored by deer.

V. bipinnatifida. DAKOTA VERBENA. Perennial. Zones US, MS, LS; USDA 6-8. Native from Great Plains to Mexico. Grows 8–15 in. high, 1½ ft. wide or wider, with blue flowers and finely divided leaves. Spreads by self-sowing in most areas.

V. bonariensis. Perennial in Zones MS, LS, CS, TS; USDA 7-11; annual in Upper South (USDA 6). Native to South America but naturalized in the southeastern U.S. Airy, branching stems to 3–6 ft. carry purple flowers. Leaves are mostly in a basal clump to 1½ ft. high and 1½–3 ft. wide. This plant has a see-through quality that makes it suited for foreground or back of border. Self-sows freely. 'Lollipop' is a smaller, more compact plant 24 in. wide.

V. canadensis. ROSE VERBENA. Perennial in Zones US, MS, LS, CS; USDA 6-9, but usually treated as annual. Native from Virginia to Florida, west to Colorado and Mexico. To 1½ ft. high, 1½–3 ft. wide, with rosy purple flowers. There is a compact (6-in.-high) form suitable for rock gardens; white- and pink-flowering forms are also offered. 'Greystone Daphne', to 6–8 in. tall and up to 1½ ft. wide, has dark green leaves and lavender-pink flowers; it thrives in Southern gardens. When growing the species or its selections as perennials, provide good winter drainage; in the Upper South, cover with light winter mulch.

V. gooddingii. Short-lived perennial. Zones LS, CS, TS; USDA 8-11. Native to the Southwest. Grows to 1½ ft. high, spreading to about 3 ft. wide. Oval, deeply cut leaves. Pinkish lavender flowers at ends of short spikes. Will bloom first summer from seed sown in spring. Can reseed where moisture is adequate. Tolerates dry heat.

V. x hybrida. GARDEN VERBENA. Short-lived perennial grown as annual. Zones US, MS, LS, CS, TS; USDA 6-11.

Much-branched plant to 6–12 in. high, spreading 1½–3 ft. wide. Oblong, 2- to 4-in., bright green or gray-green leaves with toothed margins. Flowers come in flat, compact clusters to 3 in. wide; colors include white, pink, bright red, purple, blue, and combinations. Superior strains include Romance (to 6 in. tall), Novalis (to 8 in.), and Showtime (to 10 in.). All are colorful but prone to insect damage, particularly by thrips.

V. hybrids. Perennials. Zones MS, LS, CS, TS; USDA 7-11. Grow as annuals where not hardy. Group of mostly low-growing, wide-spreading plants that love hot, dry weather and bloom all summer.

'Batesville Rose'. To 1–2 ft. high, 3 ft. wide. Vivid magenta flowers. Found in a road ditch in Batesville, Texas.

'Blue Princess'. To 1 ft. high, 2–3 ft. wide. Fragrant lavender-blue blossoms; mildew-resistant leaves.

'Homestead Purple'. To 1 ft. high, 4 ft. wide. Rich, deep purple blooms; mildew-resistant foliage. Thrives in the South. Discovered on old Georgia homestead.

'Hot Lips'. To 6–10 in. high, 2–3 ft. wide. Bright red-violet flower heads, with each tiny blossom shading to a darker color toward the center.

'Mystic'. To 6–10 in. high, 2–3 ft. wide. Light lavender-blue flowers.

'Pinwheel Princess'. To 1–2 ft. high, 2–3 ft. wide. Sport of 'Blue Princess'. Lightly scented blossoms are striped in lavender and white; they look like little pinwheels.

'Sissinghurst'. To 8 in. high, 3–4 ft. wide. Coral-pink flowers.

'Texas Appleblossom'. To 6 in. high, 2–3 ft. wide. Flowers open cotton candy pink, then gradually fade to white.

'Tie Dye'. To 6 in. high, 2–3 ft. wide. Resembles 'Pinwheel Princess', but stripes are lavender, pink, and white.

V. peruviana. Perennial in Zones CS, TS; USDA 9-11, but usually treated as an annual everywhere. Native to South America. Spreads rapidly, forming a flat mat to 2 ft. wide. Small, closely set leaves; flat-topped clusters of scarlet-and-white flowers on stems to 3 in. tall cover the foliage. *V. p.* 'Alba' has pure white flowers. Hybrids feature blossoms in white, pink, or red; they spread

TOP: Verbena bonariensis; BOTTOM: V. Tapien Lilac; V. 'Sissinghurst'

more slowly than the species and have slightly larger leaves and stouter stems.

V. rigida. Perennial in Zones MS, LS, CS; USDA 7-9, or grow as annual anywhere. Native to South America but naturalized in Southeast. To 1–2 ft. high, spreading to 3–4 ft. wide. Rough, strongly toothed, dark green leaves to 2–4 in. long. Lilac to purple-blue flowers in cylindrical clusters on tall, stiff stems. Blooms in four months from seed. 'Polaris', a dense grower to 2 ft. high, 1 ft. wide, has pale porcelain-blue flowers.

V. Superbena hybrids. Perennials in Zones LS, CS, TS; USDA 8-11, and grown as annuals in cooler zones. Heat and disease tolerant. Superbena hybrids have large flowers that make large

clusters. Growing 6–12 in. tall and trailing up to 48 in. wide, they are available in selections called 'Burgundy', 'Coral Red', 'Dark Blue', 'Large Lilac Blue', 'Pink Parfait', 'Pink Shades', 'Purple', 'Royale Chambray', 'Royale Iced Cherry', 'Royale Peachy Keen', 'Royale Plum Wine', 'Royale Silverdust', 'Royale Whitecap', and 'Violet Ice'.

V. Tapien hybrids. Perennials in Zones CS, TS; USDA 9-11, annuals anywhere. Prostrate plants to 4 in. high, 1–1½ ft. wide, with finely cut, dark green leaves. Wide range of colors, including pink, lavender, pale blue, deep purple, red. Resistant to mildew. Regular water.

V. Temari hybrids. Perennials in Zones CS, TS; USDA 9-11, annuals anywhere. Low, spreading plants to 3 in. high, 2½–3 ft. wide.

Broad, dark green leaves. Burgundy, bright pink, coral-pink, soft apricot and cream blend, lilac, violet, blue, red, or white flowers. Regular water.

V. tenera 'Sissinghurst' (*Glandularia tenera* 'Sissinghurst'). Perennial in Zones MS, LS, CS, TS; USDA 7-11, annual anywhere. Low grower to about 3 in. high and 3–4 ft. wide, with deeply cut, dark green foliage and a profuse show of fragrant, coral-pink flowers. Loves heat.

V. tenuisecta. MOSS VERBENA. Short-lived perennial in Zones MS, LS, CS, TS (USDA 7-11), annual in Upper South (USDA 6). Native to South America but naturalized in the Lower South. To 8–12 in. high, with finely cut leaves. Rose-violet to pink flowers. Short lived. Selections include white 'Alba', lavender-pink 'Edith', violet 'Michelle', violet-blue 'Imagination', and bright purple 'Decked Out'.

VERNICIA FORDII

TUNG-OIL TREE
Euphorbiaceae
Deciduous tree

🌱 **LS, CS, TS; USDA 8-11**

☀️ 🌤️ **FULL SUN OR PARTIAL SHADE**

💧 **REGULAR WATER**

⬧ **ALL PARTS ARE POISONOUS IF INGESTED**

Vernicia fordii

This plant gets its common name from the oil in its seeds, which is used as a drying agent in paints and varnishes—and was also used to lubricate jet engines in World War II. Native to central Asia, the tree grows quickly to 15–20 ft. tall and wide, with broadly rounded

form. Dark green leaves to 6 in. across turn orange and red in fall. Small, tubular, pinkish white flowers with darker markings appear in early spring. These are followed in autumn by large (2- to 3-in.-wide) nuts that change from green to reddish to brownish black as they mature. All plant parts are toxic, but the nuts are especially poisonous; they can be lethal if eaten.

Tung-oil tree self-sows prolifically and is naturalized throughout much of the Lower and Coastal South. It is seldom grown as an ornamental, since the nuts make a mess when they fall. Formerly known as *Aleurites fordii*.

VERNONIA NOVEBORACENSIS

IRONWEED
Asteraceae
Perennial

🌱 **US, MS, LS, CS; USDA 6-9**

☀️ 🌤️ **FULL SUN OR LIGHT SHADE**

💧💧💧 **MODERATE TO AMPLE WATER**

Vernonia noveboracensis

Native from Massachusetts to Mississippi and Georgia. This meadow plant is a handsome choice for the back of a border or for a contrasting color scheme with goldenrod (*Solidago*) and black-eyed Susan (*Rudbeckia hirta*). Clumps of leafy stems to 6–8 ft. tall, 2 ft. wide are topped in late summer by broad, flat clusters of fluffy, bright purple, ½-in. flower heads. These should be clipped off before they develop into the rust-colored seed clusters that give the plant its name (unless you want plants

to naturalize). Grows in wet or fairly dry soils and needs no coddling. Resists deer. 'Albiflora' has white flowers.

V. gigantea (*V. altissima*) is a similar species, somewhat taller and with longer leaves. Its selection 'Purple Pillar' produces 10-ft.-tall stalks topped with large clusters of clear purple flowers in midsummer. 'Jonesboro Giant' can reach 12 ft. tall; very strong stems resist toppling under the weight of the large flower clusters.

VERONICA

SPEEDWELL
Plantaginaceae
Perennials

🌱 **US, MS, LS; USDA 6-8**

☀️ **FULL SUN, EXCEPT AS NOTED**

💧💧💧 **WATER NEEDS VARY BY SPECIES**

Veronica spicata 'Red Fox'

Handsome plants ranging from less than an inch tall to 2 ft. in height. Masses of small (¼- to ½-in.-wide) flowers in white, rose, pink, or pale to deep blue make an effective display. Use in borders and rock gardens. Flowers attract butterflies. Prostrate kinds are good between stepping stones, as bulb covers. Named selections are not easily assigned to a species; authorities differ.

V. austriaca teucrium 'Crater Lake Blue'. Selection of a species native to Europe. To 12–15 in. high and wide, with tooth-edged, 1½-in.-long leaves. Short spikes of intensely blue flowers in midsummer. Regular water.

V. gentianoides. GENTIAN SPEEDWELL. From the Caucasus. Creeping rootstock forms a

dense mat to 1–2 ft. high and wide. Oblong, glossy, dark green, 2- to 3-in.-long leaves. In spring, foliage is topped by leafy stems carrying 10-in. spikes of ice-blue flowers with darker veining. 'Alba' has white blooms. 'Variegata' has leaves marked with white. Regular water.

V. hybrids. The following are among the best selections. Regular water, except as noted.

'Blue Reflection'. Forms a gray-green foliage mat to 3–4 in. high and 1–1½ ft. wide, covered with blue flowers in midspring. Little to moderate water.

'Goodness Grows'. Bushy growth to 1 ft. tall and wide, with medium green, lance-shaped leaves. Violet-blue blossoms over long bloom period—from late spring to frost, if old flowers are removed.

'Hocus Pocus'. Compact, bushy growth to 1½ ft. high, 1 ft. wide, with tall, branching spikes of blue-violet flowers. Early to midsummer bloom. Good in containers.

'Sunny Border Blue'. Compact, clump-forming plant to 1½–2 ft. tall, 1 ft. wide, with crinkled, dark green leaves. Spires of dark violet-blue flowers appear in late spring or early summer; deadheading prolongs the show until frost.

'Waterperry Blue'. Low, trailing plant to 4–6 in. high and 1½ ft. or more wide; roots as it spreads. Small, rounded, bronze-tinted leaves. Loose clusters of pale blue flowers veined in deeper blue; main bloom in spring, with sporadic flowering throughout summer and fall.

V. pectinata. WOOLLY SPEEDWELL. Western Mediterranean native. Forms prostrate mat of foliage to 3 in. high and 1 ft. wide; spreads by creeping stems that root at joints. Small grayish leaves have scalloped or deeply cut edges. Profuse spring or early summer show of deep blue flowers with white centers; blossoms are borne on 5- to 6-in. spikes among the leaves. Little to moderate water.

V. prostrata. PROSTRATE SPEEDWELL. From Europe. Stems are hairy and tufted. Some are prostrate and form a 1- to 1½-ft.-wide foliage mat; others grow erect to 8 in. high and are topped by short clusters of pale blue flowers in late spring or early summer. 'Alba' has white flowers. 'Heavenly Blue' is almost entirely prostrate, with flower stems reaching 6 in. high. 'Mrs. Holt' has pale pink flowers. 'Aztec Gold' and 'Trehane' have golden yellow leaves, bright blue flowers. Little to moderate water.

V. repens. CREEPING SPEED-WELL. Mediterranean native. Flat mat to ½ in. high, 1 ft. or wider. Small, shiny green leaves clothe the prostrate stems, give plant a mossy look. Clusters of tiny lavender to white flowers in spring. 'Sunshine' is grown mainly for its greenish gold foliage; the tiny purple flowers are secondary. Tolerates some shade. Little to moderate water.

V. spicata. SPIKE SPEEDWELL. From Europe, Asia. Rounded, 1½- to 2-ft.-wide clump sends up 2-ft.-tall stems clothed in pointed oval, glossy, green leaves and topped in summer with spikes of bright blue flowers. Long bloom season if faded flowers are removed. 'Blue Charm', to 2 ft. tall, bears lavender-blue blossoms. 'Glory' ('Royal Candles') is an exceptionally long-blooming, 1½-ft.-high selection with blue-purple flowers. 'Icicle', to 15–18 in. high, has white flower spikes. 'Red Fox' ('Rotfuchs'), to 15 in. tall and wide, has deep rosy red blooms. 'Tickled Pink', 12–18 in. high and wide, has pink flowers. Regular water.

V. s. incana. SILVER SPEED-WELL. Furry, silvery white foliage forms a 1- to 1½-ft.-wide mat. Blooms in summer, producing deep blue blossoms on stems to about 1 ft. high. Little to moderate water. 'Nana', reaching just 6 in., bears violet-blue blossoms.

TOP: Veronica spicata 'Glory'; BOTTOM: V. prostrata; V. gentianoides

V. umbrosa 'Georgia Blue'. From Georgia (in Europe). Forms a 6- to 8-in.-high mat that spreads to several feet wide; small, dark green leaves turn bronze in cool weather. Profuse, white-eyed, cobalt-blue flowers in spring, with a few flowers appearing throughout summer and fall. Regular water.

VERONICASTRUM VIRGINICUM

CULVER'S ROOT
Plantaginaceae
Perennial

🌿 **US, MS, LS; USDA 6-8**

☼ ◑ **FULL SUN OR LIGHT SHADE**

💧 **REGULAR WATER**

Veronicastrum virginicum

From eastern U.S. Erect grower to 5–7 ft. tall, 1½ ft. wide; resembles a very tall *Veronica*. Stems are clothed with whorls of toothed, 6-in., lance-shaped, dark green leaves. Stems branch in the upper portions and are topped by slender, spikelike clusters (to 9 in. long) of tiny pale blue or white flowers. Useful plant for background in large borders. Makes a striking pattern against dark background, such as tall hedge or woodland edge, but too much shade makes it floppy. Likes fertile, well-drained, slightly acid soil. Selections with flowers in specific colors, most of which are somewhat smaller than the species, include white 'Album', reddish purple 'Apollo', soft pink 'Fascination', light lavender 'Lavendelturm', and rosy pink 'Pink Glow'. 'Adoration' (*V.* 'Adoration') is upright and shapely, with lavender-pink flowers.

VIBURNUM

Adoxaceae
Deciduous, evergreen, semievergreen shrubs or trees

🌿 **ZONES VARY BY SPECIES**

☼ ◑ **FULL SUN OR PARTIAL SHADE, EXCEPT AS NOTED**

💧 **REGULAR WATER, EXCEPT AS NOTED**

Viburnum plicatum tomentosum 'Mariesii'

Large, diverse group of plants with generally oval, often handsome leaves and clusters of typically white, sometimes fragrant flowers that attract butterflies. Blossoms are usually followed by single-seeded, often brilliantly colored fruit much appreciated by birds. Many viburnums are grown for their flower display, a few for their showy fruit. In general, heaviest fruit set occurs when several different named selections of seedlings that bloom at the same time are planted together. Many evergreen types are valuable as foliage plants. Several species (noted below) can be grown as small trees. Viburnums are somewhat resistant to deer damage.

V. acerifolium. MAPLE LEAF VIBURNUM. Deciduous. Zones US, MS, LS; USDA 6-8. Native throughout the Southeastern states in its hardiness zones, this colony-forming shrub grows 4–6 ft. tall and equally wide in a decade. Ideally in a naturalistic planting scheme and tolerant of shade, it offers late-spring flowers in flat clusters of greenish white. Fruit begins red and turns purple and black, set against fall colors of pink, red, and even dark purple.

V. x bodnantense. BODNANT VIBURNUM. Deciduous. Zones

US, MS, LS; USDA 6-8. To 10 ft. (or more) tall, 6 ft. wide. Dark green, 1½- to 4-in.-long leaves are deeply veined, turn dark scarlet in fall. Loose clusters of very fragrant, deep pink flowers age to paler pink; blooms in winter, but buds often freeze. Red fruit is not showy. Best known is 'Dawn' ('Pink Dawn').

V. x burkwoodii. BURKWOOD VIBURNUM. Deciduous in cold areas, nearly evergreen elsewhere. Zones US, MS, LS; USDA 6-8. To 6–12 ft. tall, 4–8 ft. wide. Glossy leaves to 3½ in. long are dark green above, white and hairy beneath; turn purplish red in cold weather. Dense, 4-in. clusters of pink buds open to very fragrant white flowers in late winter or early spring. Blue-black fruit is not showy. Early growth is straggly, but mature plants are dense. Can be espaliered.

'Anne Russell' is compact and rounded at 6–7 ft. high and wide; good red-purple fall color. 'Chenaultii', to 10 ft. tall, 8 ft. wide, is dense, slightly later blooming, and more deciduous in mild climates than the species. 'Conoy' tends to be evergreen, with dense growth to 5 ft. high and wide; slightly fragrant flowers are followed by long-lasting red berries. 'Mohawk', to 7 ft. tall, 5 ft. wide, has red buds that are showy long before they open into white flowers; orange-red fall color. 'Park Farm Hybrid', 8–10 ft. high and wide, sports glossy, narrow leaves and large, long-lasting flowers that open from deep pink buds.

V. x carlcephalum. FRAGRANT SNOWBALL. Deciduous. Zones US, MS, LS; USDA 6-8. To 6–10 ft. tall and wide. Dull, grayish green, 2- to 3½-in.-long leaves are downy beneath; turn reddish purple in autumn. Long-lasting, waxy, sweetly perfumed spring flowers in dense, 4- to 5-in. clusters. No fruit. As showy as *V. opulus* 'Roseum' but has the bonus of fragrance. 'Cayuga' is a compact grower to 5 ft. tall and wide.

V. carlesii. KOREAN SPICE VIBURNUM. Deciduous. Zones US, MS, LS; USDA 6-8. Native to Korea, Japan. Old Southern favorite. Loose, open habit to 4–8 ft. tall and wide. Leaves like those of *V. x carlcephalum*; inconsistent reddish fall color. Pink buds in 2- to 3-in. clusters open to sweetly fragrant white flowers in spring. Blue-black fruit is not showy. Does best with part shade during hottest months. 'Compactum' grows slowly to just 3–4 ft. tall and wide. 'Aurora' is a bit larger at 4–5 ft. tall and wide (possibly to 8 ft. in ideal conditions); its dark red buds open to large pink flowers that slowly fade to white, and it shows good red fall color. Flowers of 'Spice Girl' have a spicy-sweet perfume.

V. davidii. DAVID VIBURNUM. Evergreen. Zones US, MS, LS; USDA 6-8. Native to China. This species undoubtedly has the most handsome foliage of all viburnums: glossy, dark green, deeply veined leaves 3–6 in. long. Forms a compact mound to 3–4 ft. high and wide. White spring flowers aren't especially showy, but the display of metallic turquoise-blue fruit that follows is definitely eye catching. Unfortunately, David viburnum seldom sets fruit unless growing conditions are perfect and several genetically distinct plants (not "sibling" seedlings, but individuals from different parents) are grouped together for cross-pollination. It's better suited to the mild climate of the Pacific Northwest than the extremes of the South. Here, it requires very well-drained, moist, acid soil and afternoon shade.

V. dentatum. ARROWWOOD. Deciduous. Zones US, MS, LS, CS; USDA 6-9. Native from New Brunswick to Minnesota, south to Georgia. To 6–10 ft. or taller, equally wide. Cream-colored flowers in late spring are followed by blue-black fruit. Dark green, oval to rounded, 4-in. leaves turn yellow, orange, or deep red in fall. Plants tolerate heat, cold, and alkaline soil. Use as screen or tall hedge. 'Cardinal' has reliable brilliant red fall color. 'Blue Muffin' is a compact selection reaching only 5–7 ft. high and 4 ft. wide with intense blue fruit.

V. dilatatum. LINDEN VIBURNUM. Deciduous. Zones US, MS, LS; USDA 6-8. From China,

Japan. Grows to 8–10 ft. tall and not quite as wide. Nearly round, 2- to 5-in. gray-green leaves; inconsistent rusty red fall color. Tiny, creamy white, somewhat unpleasant-smelling flowers in 5-in. clusters, late spring or early summer. Showy bright red fruit ripens in early fall, hangs on into winter. Outstanding named selections include the following.

'Asian Beauty'. To 8–10 ft. tall, 6–8 ft. wide. Profuse show of cherry-red fruit that stays in place for a long time.

'Cardinal Candy'. To 4–5 ft. high and wide. Extra-hardy selection; has survived –25°F. Bright red fruit. Leaves turn bronze and burgundy in fall.

'Catskill'. Compact growth to 5–8 ft. tall, 8–10 ft. wide, with smaller leaves than species. Dark red fruit. Fall color is a combination of yellow, orange, and red.

'Erie'. Rounded habit to 6 ft. tall, 10 ft. wide. Red fruit. Leaves turn yellow, orange, and red in autumn. Highly disease resistant.

'Iroquois'. To 9 ft. tall, 12 ft. wide. Selected for heavy production of larger, darker red fruit. Orange-red to maroon fall foliage.

'Michael Dodge'. Compact and rounded growth to just 5–6 ft. tall and wide. Bright yellow fruit stands out beautifully against the scarlet fall foliage.

V. hybrids. Zones US, MS, LS; USDA 6-8. These spring-blooming viburnums all have complex ancestries.

'Chesapeake'. Semievergreen. To 8 ft. tall, 10 ft. wide, with glossy, wavy-edged, 3½-in. dark green leaves. Two-inch clusters of fragrant white flowers open from pink buds; dull red fruit matures to black.

'Chippewa'. Semievergreen to deciduous. To 8–9 ft. tall, 9 ft. wide. Dense plant with glossy, dark green leaves that turn maroon and red in fall. Big show of creamy white flowers; glossy, deep red fruit. Cold hardy.

'Eskimo'. Semievergreen. Dense, compact habit to 5 ft. tall and wide. Shiny, dark green leaves to 4 in. long. Unscented flowers in 3- to 4-in., snowball-like clusters; dull red fruit ages to black.

'Huron'. Semievergreen to deciduous. Dense grower to 8–9 ft. tall, 9–10 ft. wide. Glossy, dark green leaves with good fall color in rich red and maroon tones. Flowers virtually cover the plant

TOP: V. davidii; BOTTOM: V. plicatum 'Mariesii'

at bloom time. Dark red fruit. Cold hardy.

V. japonicum. JAPANESE VIBURNUM. Evergreen. Zones LS, CS, TS; USDA 8-10. From Japan. Grows 10–15 ft. tall, 8–12 ft. wide; can be trained as a small tree. Leathery, glossy, dark green leaves to 6 in. long. Sparse spring show of fragrant flowers in 4-in. clusters. Red fruit is likewise sparse—but very attractive. Best with some shade.

V. x juddii. JUDD VIBURNUM. Deciduous. Zones US, MS, LS; USDA 6-8. To 4–8 ft. tall, 6–10 ft. wide. Bushier, more spreading, and more heat-tolerant than V. carlesii but similar to it in other respects, including fragrance.

V. luzonicum. LUZON VIBURNUM. Evergreen; deciduous in cooler zones. Zones MS, LS, CS; USDA 7-9. Native to Taiwan and the Philippines, this large shrub or small tree is a gift to gardeners in the Lower South wanting fall color. Even where evergreen, the foliage turns red and persists. Grows to 20 ft. tall and 15 ft. wide. Flat clusters of white flowers are followed by sparse red fruits.

V. macrocephalum. CHINESE SNOWBALL. Deciduous in coldest areas, nearly evergreen elsewhere. Zones US, MS, LS, CS; USDA 6-9. Rounded habit to 12–20 ft. tall and wide. Dull green, oval to oblong, 2- to 4-in.-long leaves. Spectacular big, rounded, 6- to 8-in. flower clusters bloom in spring (or any time during warm weather); they are composed of sterile flowers that start out lime-green, change to white. No fruit. Can be espaliered.

V. nudum 'Winterthur'. WINTERTHUR SMOOTH WITHERROD. Deciduous. Zones US, MS, LS, CS; USDA 6-9. Native to Southern states, this shrub grows 6–10 ft. tall and wide. The sheen on the dark green leaves gives the fall foliage more impact as it turns red. The flat-topped, creamy white flower clusters in early summer are followed by fruit that progresses through pinks and reds on its journey from green to black. Tolerates occasionally wet soil but grows in average garden soil as well.

V. odoratissimum awabuki. AWABUKI VIBURNUM. Evergreen. Zones MS, LS, CS; USDA 7-9. Native to Taiwan and Japan, growing to 12 ft. tall with upright form. Foliage is glossy and dark green, the

perfect setting for early-summer white flower cluster followed by red fruit that turns black. 'Chindo' has large, red, pendant fruit clusters.

V. opulus. EUROPEAN CRANBERRY BUSH. Deciduous. Zones US, MS, LS; USDA 6-8. From Europe, North Africa, central Asia. To 8–15 ft. tall and wide, with arching branches. Lobed, maplelike dark green leaves to 2–4 in. long and as wide or wider. Fall foliage color may be yellow, bright red, or reddish purple. Blooms in spring; flower heads have a lace-cap look, with a 2- to 4-in. cluster of small fertile blossoms ringed with larger sterile blossoms. Large, showy red fruit persists from fall into winter. Takes moist to boggy soils. Control aphids. Selections include the following.

'Aureum'. Golden yellow foliage. Give some shade to prevent sunburn.

'Compactum'. To 4–5 ft. high and wide.

'Nanum'. To 2 ft. high and wide. Needs no trimming as low, informal hedge. Cannot take poorly drained, wet soils. No flowers or fruit.

'Roseum' ('Sterile'). COMMON SNOWBALL. Resembles the species but has snowball-like flower clusters 2–2½ in. across, composed entirely of sterile flowers (so bears no fruit). Aphids are especially troublesome.

'Xanthocarpum'. Rounded growth to 6–8 ft. tall and wide, with glossy, apple-green foliage. Showy yellow fruit matures to translucent golden yellow.

V. plicatum plicatum. JAPANESE SNOWBALL. Deciduous. Zones US, MS, LS; USDA 6-8. From China, Japan. To 8–15 ft. tall and wide. Horizontal branching pattern gives plant a tiered look, especially when in bloom; flower clusters are held above the branches, while leaves hang down. Strongly veined, 3- to 6-in.-long, dull, dark green leaves turn purplish red in autumn. Showy, 3-in., snowball-like clusters of sterile flowers look like those of V. opulus 'Roseum', but this plant is less bothered by aphids. Mid-spring bloom. No fruit. Tolerates occasionally wet soils. 'Newport' is compact and dense, to 5 ft. tall and wide. 'Popcorn', 5–8 ft. tall and nearly as wide, is an early bloomer with a profusion of small, rounded flower clusters.

TOP: Viburnum opulus; MIDDLE: Viburnum macrocephalum; BOTTOM: V. dentatum; V. carlesii

V. plicatum tomentosum. DOUBLEFILE VIBURNUM. Deciduous. Zones US, MS, LS; USDA 6-8. This truly beautiful viburnum is native to China and Japan. It resembles V. plicatum plicatum, but

midspring flower display consists of small fertile flowers in flat, 2- to 4-in. clusters edged with 1- to 1½-in. sterile flowers in lace-cap effect. Fruit is red aging to black; it is showy, if not always profuse.

Needs good drainage and moist soil. Excessive summer heat and drought often result in leaf scorch. Selections include the following.

'Cascade'. To 10 ft. tall, 12 ft. wide. Wide-spreading branches bear large, sterile flowers.

'Copper Ridges'. To 10 ft. tall and wide. Heavily textured leaves emerge with copper highlights, then age to deep green in summer before turning shades of maroon and wine-red in fall. Profuse flowers and fruit.

'Mariesii'. Grows to 10 ft. tall and 12 ft. wide. Has large flower clusters, large, sterile flowers.

'Pink Beauty'. To 9 ft. tall, 12 ft. wide, with white flowers that age to pink.

'Shasta'. Horizontal habit (to 12 ft. tall, 15 ft. wide), with large, sterile flowers. Considered by many to be the finest selection.

'Shoshoni'. To 5 ft. tall, 8 ft. wide.

'Summer Snowflake'. Reaches 5–8 ft. tall and wide. Blooms from spring to autumn.

V. x pragense. PRAGUE VIBURNUM. Evergreen. Zones US, MS, LS; USDA 6-8. Fast-growing, rounded plant to 10 ft. tall and broad. Shiny, dark green, 2- to 4-in.-long leaves. Faintly fragrant white flowers in 3- to 6-in. clusters open from pink buds in early spring.

V. prunifolium. BLACK HAW. Deciduous. Zones US, MS, LS, CS; USDA 6-9. Native from Michigan and Connecticut south to Texas and Florida. Upright to 15 ft., spreading as wide. Can be trained as a small tree. Common name comes from dark fruit and from plant's resemblance to hawthorn (*Crataegus*). Oval, finely toothed leaves to 3 in. long turn purplish to reddish purple in fall. Many clusters of creamy white flowers in spring; edible blue-black fruit in fall and winter. Use as dense screen or barrier, attractive specimen shrub. Best in full sun. Tolerates drought. 'Ovation' grows slowly to form a compact, upright column to 10 ft. tall, 6 ft. wide; leaves emerge pink, aging to bright celery-green and finally to rich burgundy in autumn.

V. x rhytidophylloides. Zones US, MS, LS; USDA 6-8. These are hybrids between *V. rhytidophyllum* and *V. lantana*, a deciduous species from Europe and Asia Minor. Among the best

is 'Allegheny', a dense, rounded plant 6–8 ft. tall and broad; it is evergreen in most winters. Leaves resemble those of *V. rhytidophyllum* but are broader and less wrinkled. Flowers and fruit are also similar. 'Willowwood' resembles 'Allegheny' but has a more arching habit.

V. rhytidophyllum. LEATHERLEAF VIBURNUM. Evergreen. Zones US, MS, LS; USDA 6-8. From central and western China. Upright grower to 8–15 ft. tall, 6–12 ft. wide. Narrow, 4- to 10-in.-long leaves are deep green and wrinkled above, fuzzy beneath. Yellowish white spring flowers come in 4- to 8-in. clusters; scarlet fruit ages to black. Leaves droop in cold weather, and plant looks tattered where cold winds blow. Tolerates deep shade. Some find this plant striking; others consider it coarse.

V. rufidulum. RUSTY BLACK HAW. Deciduous. Zones US, MS, LS, CS; USDA 6-9. Native from Texas to Florida and north to Virginia. Large shrub or small tree growing 12–20 ft. tall and spreading a little wider. Blossoms come in 5-in.-wide clusters in late spring; they're followed by handsome dark blue berries. Oval, 2- to 4-in., glossy, dark green leaves; young shoots, leafstalks, and leaf undersides are covered with rust-colored hairs. Fall foliage color ranges from orange and yellow through red and purple shades. Vigorous grower 'Emerald Charm' ('Morton') is slightly more upright.

V. setigerum. TEA VIBURNUM. Deciduous. Zones US, MS, LS; USDA 6-8. From China. To 8–12 ft. tall, 6–8 ft. wide. Multistemmed, rather erect; often bare at base (plant lower-growing shrubs around it for concealment). Leaves were once used for making tea; they are 3–6 in. long, dark green or blue-green turning to purplish in fall. Spring flowers in 1- to 2-in. clusters are not striking, but heavy production of scarlet fruit makes this the showiest of fruiting viburnums. 'Aurantiacum' has orange fruit.

V. suspensum. SANDANKWA VIBURNUM. Evergreen. Zones CS, TS; USDA 9-11. From Japan. To 8–10 ft. tall and broad. Leathery, 2- to 4-in.-long leaves are glossy, deep green above, paler beneath. Blooms in early spring, bearing flowers in loose, 2- to 4-in. clusters; some people find the

scent objectionable. Red fruit ages to black, is not long lasting. Serviceable screen or hedge; very popular in Florida. Watch for thrips, spider mites, aphids. Little to moderate water.

V. tinus. LAURUSTINUS. Evergreen. Zones CS, TS; USDA 9-10, except as noted. Mediterranean native. To 6–12 ft. tall, half as wide. Leathery, dark green, 2- to 3-in.-long leaves with edges slightly rolled under. Wine-red new stems. Blooms in winter; tight clusters of pink buds open to lightly fragrant white flowers. Bright metallic blue fruit lasts through summer. Dense foliage right to ground makes it good for screens, hedges, clipped topiary shapes. Can be trained as a small tree. Susceptible to mildew, mites. Selections include the following.

'Bewley's Variegated'. Upright grower to 3–5 ft. tall and wide. Deep green leaves edged in creamy white.

'Lucidum'. SHINING LAURUSTINUS. Zone TS; USDA 10-11. Less hardy than the species, with larger leaves. Less prone to mildew.

'Spring Bouquet' ('Compactum'). Upright to 4–6 ft. high and wide; good for hedges. Leaves are deeper green, slightly smaller than those of the species.

V. trilobum (*V. opulus americanum*). AMERICAN CRANBERRY BUSH. Deciduous. Zones US, MS; USDA 6-7. Native to Canada, northern U.S. To 15 ft. tall, 12 ft. wide. Leaves look much like those of *V. opulus*; they emerge reddish tinged, mature to dark green, turn yellow to red-purple in fall. Blooms midspring, bearing lacecap flowers to 4 in. across. Fruit is similar to that of *V. opulus* but is used for preserves and jellies. Less susceptible to aphid damage than *V. opulus*. 'Wentworth' has larger berries and bright red fall foliage. 'Compactum' is a smaller form, to 6 ft. high and wide.

V. wrightii. WRIGHT VIBURNUM. Deciduous. Zones US, MS, LS; USDA 6-8. From Japan. Similar to *V. dilatatum* except for its larger leaves, which may turn a good red in fall. Useful tall hedge.

CARE

V. davidii needs acid soil, but the other viburnums are very soil tolerant, accepting even heavy or limy soils. Many have a wide range

of climate adaptability. Where summers are long and hot, most evergreen viburnums look better with some shade. Prune to prevent legginess; some evergreen kinds can be sheared. Nematodes can be a problem, and aphids, thrips, spider mites, scale, and root weevil are potential pests in many areas, but plants are not usually seriously troubled by them. Powdery mildew sometimes afflicts viburnums, but don't treat it with sulfur sprays, which will damage the leaves.

VIGNA CARACALLA

SNAIL VINE
Papilionaceae
Perennial vine sometimes grown as annual

🌿 **TS; USDA 10-11; OR GROW IN POTS**

☼ **FULL SUN**

💧 **REGULAR WATER**

Vigna caracalla

Tropical American native that generally resembles pole bean in form and foliage. The spring-to-summer flowers are different, though: fragrant, cream to pale purple, with lilac or purple markings and twisted keel petals that are coiled like a snail shell—odd and pretty. Twines rapidly to 10–20 ft.; good summer screen or bank cover. A favorite of Thomas Jefferson at Monticello. Evergreen in Tropical South; in colder regions, treat as annual or bring indoors for winter. Sometimes sold as *Phaseolus gigantea*. Formerly known as *Phaseolus Caracalla*.

VINCA

PERIWINKLE
Apocynaceae
Perennials

ZONES VARY BY SPECIES

PARTIAL TO FULL SHADE

MODERATE TO REGULAR WATER

Vinca minor 'La Grave'

With trailing, arching stems that root where they touch soil, these plants are useful as ground and bank covers. Shiny, dark green, oval to oblong leaves. Lavender-blue, five-petaled, pinwheel-shaped flowers appear in leaf joints in early spring. Plant the larger species and its selections 2–2½ ft. apart, dwarf kinds 1½ ft. apart. When plantings mound up or are layered with old stems, shear or mow before new spring growth begins. Very soil tolerant. Compete successfully with surface tree roots. Deer don't care for periwinkles.

V. major. GREATER PERIWINKLE. Zones MS, LS, CS; USDA 7-9. The larger, more aggressive species. Leaves to 3 in. long, purple flowers to 2 in. across; mounds to 1–2 ft. high. Spreads rapidly and can be extremely invasive in sheltered, shady areas. 'Variegata', probably as common as the green form, has leaves strongly edged in white.

V. minor. COMMON PERIWINKLE, DWARF PERIWINKLE. Zones US, MS, LS, CS; USDA 6-9. Miniature version of *V. major*, with ¾- to 1¾-in.-long leaves, flowers to 1 in. wide, and a height of just 4–6 in. More restrained, less likely to invade adjacent plantings. 'Atropurpurea', deep purple flowers, small leaves; 'Illumination', bright gold leaves edge in green, blue

flowers; 'La Grave' ('Bowles' Variety'), deeper blue flowers, larger leaves; 'Ralph Shugert', white-edged leaves, blue flowers, repeat autumn bloom; and 'Sterling Silver', blue flowers, white-edged leaves speckled with pale green. White-flowered versions include *V. m. alba* and its smaller-growing, heavier-blooming selection 'Gertrude Jekyll' ('Miss Jekyll').

VIOLA

VIOLA, VIOLET, PANSY
Violaceae
Perennials, some grown as annuals

ZONES VARY BY SPECIES

EXPOSURE NEEDS VARY BY SPECIES

REGULAR WATER

Viola x *wittrockiana* 'Pandora's Box'

Botanically speaking, violas, pansies, and almost all violets are perennials belonging to the genus *Viola*. However, violas and pansies are usually treated as annuals, invaluable for fall, winter, and spring bloom in mild-winter areas, for spring-through-early-summer color in colder climates. Typically used for mass color in borders and edgings, as covers for spring-flowering bulbs, and in containers. Violets are more often used as woodland or rock garden plants.

Violas and pansies take sun or partial shade, though pansies will bloom longer into spring if given afternoon shade. Violets grow in part or full shade, but most are natives of deciduous forests and bloom best with at least some sun during the flowering season. Violas are tougher than pansies, more tolerant of both heat and cold.

TOP: Viola wittrockiana 'Freefall Purple & White'; *BOTTOM: V. cornuta* 'Penny Clear Yellow' *and V. w.* 'Matrix Yellow Blotch'

Almost all violets have two kinds of flowers: normal, conspicuous ones that are held above the foliage and may be pollinated and set seed, and short-stemmed, inconspicuous cleistogamous (Greek for "closed mouth") flowers that set seed without pollination and produce copious offspring identical to the parent. Many violets also spread by aboveground runners. Some reproduce so freely they can crowd out other small plants.

Violas and pansies have such complex ancestries that many botanists are unwilling to assign them to species, preferring to list them by selection name. However, we believe it will avoid confusion if we retain these plants under their former names, invalid though they now may be.

V. affinis (V. sororia affinis). LECONTE VIOLET. Zones US, MS, LS; USDA 6-8. Native from New England south to Georgia and Alabama, west to Wisconsin. To 3 in. tall, spreading wider, with small, triangular, wavy-toothed leaves. Dark-veined violet flowers, white at petal bases and centered with a lighter eye, open above the foliage in spring.

V. blanda. SWEET WHITE VIOLET. Zones US, MS, LS; USDA 6-8. From eastern North America. To 2–3 in. high, spreading indefinitely by runners. Fragrant white flowers with purple veining have sharply reflexed petals. Likes moist soil with lots of organic material.

V. cornuta. VIOLA. Perennials grown as cool-season annuals. Zones US, MS, LS, CS, TS; USDA 6-11. Native to Spain. To 6–8 in. high and 8 in. wide, with smooth, wavy-edged leaves. Purple, pansylike, slender-spurred flowers about 1½ in. across. Modern strains and selections are complex hybrids with larger, shorter-spurred flowers; they come in solid colors (purple, blue, yellow, apricot, ruby-red, white) or with elaborate markings ("faces"). Plants in the Sorbet and Penny series are top performers in the South; Gem and Jewel series do very well too.

V. cucullata (V. obliqua). MARSH BLUE VIOLET. Zones US, MS, LS; USDA 6-8. From eastern and central North America. To 6 in. high, 10 in. wide. Toothed, heart-shaped leaves to 4 in. across. Blue, ¾-in.-wide flowers are held well above the leaves in early spring. Good ground cover; no runners, but self-sows liberally and can become a pest. Thrives in moist and wet soils. 'Alba' has white flowers. The violet often

sold as 'White Czar'—white with yellow throat veined in black—is a selection of this species; the name, however, correctly belongs to an old variety of V. odorata.

V. odorata. SWEET VIOLET. Zones US, MS, LS; USDA 6-8. The violet of song and story. To 8 in. high, 1½ ft. wide. Probably native to Europe. Dark green, heart-shaped, 2½-in.-long leaves with toothed margins. Fragrant, short-spurred flowers to ¾ in. wide or wider in deep violet, bluish rose, or white. Selections include 'Alba' (white), 'Rosina' (pink), 'Royal Elk' (violet), and 'Royal Robe' (deep violet). For better spring display, remove runners and shear rank growth in late fall, then apply a complete fertilizer in earliest spring.

V. pedata. BIRD'S-FOOT VIOLET. Zones US, MS, LS; USDA 6-8. From eastern North America. So named because its finely divided leaves resemble a bird's foot. Forms a clump to 2 in. high, 4 in. wide; does not spread by runners. Blooms early spring to early summer; 4-in. stems bear inch-wide, typically two-tone violet-blue flowers with darker veining. Not as easy to grow as other violets; likes excellent drainage, filtered sun or high shade, and acidic soil.

V. sororia. DOORYARD VIOLET. Zones US, MS, LS, CS; USDA 6-9. From eastern and central North America. To 4–6 in. high, 8 in. wide; does not spread by runners but self-sows freely. Roughly heart-shaped leaves to 5 in. wide vary from densely hairy to almost smooth. Good ground cover under woodland shrubs. Nearly scentless, ½- to ¾-in. flowers in spring to early summer are held close to leaves; colors range from white to red-violet to blue-violet. Most commonly seen are the following smooth-leafed selections (all come true from seed): 'Albiflora', pure white with yellow in throat; 'Freckles', white liberally spotted with blue; 'Priceana' (popularly known as Confederate violet), white with blue-violet veining in throat.

V. tricolor. JOHNNY-JUMP-UP. Perennial grown as cool-season annual. Zones US, MS, LS, CS, TS; USDA 6-11. From Europe, Asia. Spring bloomer 6–12 in. tall and broad; spreads widely by profuse self-sowing. Oval, deeply lobed leaves to 1¼ in. long. Pert, ½- to

ABOVE: Viola sororia 'Priceana'

¾-in., velvety purple-and-yellow or blue-and-yellow flowers are the original wild pansies. Same planting and care as pansy. Crosses with closely related small-flowered species have produced forms with flowers in violet, blue, white, yellow, lavender, mauve, apricot, orange, red—with or without markings ("faces"). Flowers of 'Molly Sanderson' (V. 'Molly Sanderson') are very dark purple—almost black.

V. walteri. WALTER'S VIOLET. Zones US, MS, LS, CS; USDA 6-9. Native from South Carolina to Florida and west to Texas, Ohio. To 6–8 in. tall, wide spreading, with mottled, dark green foliage, often tinged purple beneath. Stems root where they touch the ground, producing new plants. In spring, bears blue-violet flowers with dark veins and white petal bases, paler eye. 'Silver Gem' has silvery foliage.

V. x wittrockiana. PANSY. Perennial grown as cool-season annual. Zones US, MS, LS, CS, TS; USDA 6-11. To 6–10 in. high, 9–12 in. wide. Many strains with 2- to 4-in. flowers in white, blue, mahogany-red, rose, yellow, apricot, purple; also bicolors. Most have dark blotches on the lower three petals; such flowers are often said to resemble faces. Shiny green leaves are oval to nearly heart shaped, slightly lobed, 1½ in. or longer.

Series are almost too numerous to mention; here are just a few. Heat-tolerant Antique Shades boasts a mix of jewel-toned flowers to 3 in. across. Crystal Bowl is a compact grower, with a profusion of small flowers

in vivid, clear colors without faces. Heat- and cold-tolerant Majestic Giants II sports large blooms, to 4 in. across, in the full color range, including many bicolors. Strong-growing Matrix freely produces large blooms in a wide color range, with and without faces. The floriferous 'Pandora's Box' has blooms in rose, pink, orange, and yellow. Plants in the heavy-blooming Panola series, also available in the full range of colors and faces, produce medium-size, thick-petaled flowers that resist damage from rain and snow.

A group of recently developed trailing pansies grow quickly to 6–8 in. tall and 24–30 in. wide; they work beautifully as ground covers or spilling from hanging baskets and window boxes. Look for the vigorous, long-blooming Cool Wave series in yellow, blue, purple, white, and bicolors. Freefall series features rich, saturated colors. WonderFall series is similar but also offers red and pink flowers.

CARE

In the Upper South (USDA 6), set out nursery plants of pansies and violas in spring for summer bloom; elsewhere, plant in autumn for winter-to-spring (or longer) bloom. Or start from seed: In the Upper South (USDA 6), sow in mid- to late summer and overwinter seedlings in cold frame until spring; or sow indoors in winter, plant in spring. Elsewhere, sow in mid- to late summer, plant out in fall. To prolong bloom, pick flowers (with some foliage) regularly and remove faded blooms before they set seed. In hot areas, plants get ragged by mid- to late spring and should be removed.

VITEX

CHASTE TREE
Lamiaceae
Deciduous and evergreen shrubs or trees

🌿 **US, MS, LS, CS; USDA 6-9, EXCEPT AS NOTED**

☀️ **FULL SUN**

💧 **MODERATE TO REGULAR WATER**

Vitex agnus-castus

Given the paucity of blue-flowered summer-blooming trees and shrubs, it's a wonder more people aren't planting chaste trees. These drought-tolerant, pest-free plants combine striking blue or purple, tubular summer blossoms with handsome leaves shaped like an open hand. They grow in almost any well-drained soil, will take coastal conditions, and are not usually browsed by deer. The common name derives from the belief in medieval times that an extract from their fruit would curb the libido.

V. agnus-castus. LILAC CHASTE TREE. Deciduous shrub or small tree. Native to southern Europe, central Asia. In most areas, grows fast to make a multitrunked tree with a broad, spreading habit—about 15–20 ft. high and wide. In the Upper South, growth is slower and mature size is 8–10 ft. high and wide. Aromatic leaves are divided into five to seven narrowly oval, pointed leaflets that are grayish green above, green beneath; each leaflet is 2–6 in. long. No real fall color.

Small, lightly fragrant, lilac to dark blue flowers in 6- to 12-in. spikes appear at branch ends and leaf joints in summer. Blooms come on new growth, so prune in late winter, removing twiggy growth and crowded branches. If you remove spent flowers before seeds form, plant will send out a second flush of blooms.

Unnamed seedlings vary in showiness of flowers, so buy a plant in bloom to see what you're getting. Or choose one of the following superior named selections. For blue or violet flowers, look for 'Abbeville Blue', with very showy deep blue spikes; 'Montrose Purple', a strong grower with rich violet flowers; and 'Shoal Creek', with blue-violet blossoms on spikes up to 1½ ft. long. Pink-flowered choices include 'Fletcher Pink', a fast grower with lavender-pink flowers, and 'Rosea', with mauve-pink blooms. White-flowered selections include 'Alba', with particularly large flower spikes, and fast-growing 'Silver Spire'. *V. a. latifolia* has shorter, broader leaves and is said to be tougher and more cold hardy.

V. negundo. CHINESE CHASTE TREE. Deciduous shrub or small tree. Native to southeast Africa, eastern Asia. Similar to *V. agnus-castus* but a little larger and more cold hardy. The 5- to 8-in. flower spikes aren't as showy. *V. n. heterophylla* has delicate-looking, finely lobed leaflets.

V. trifolia. Evergreen shrub or small shrubby tree. Zones CS, TS; USDA 9-11. Native to Asia and Australia. Fast growth to 12–20 ft. high and wide. Leaves are sometimes simple but are usually divided into three 4-in.-long leaflets with felted gray undersides. Lavender-blue flowers with a white spot on the lip open in summer on 4- to 10-in.-long spikes. Makes a fine-textured hedge; clip regularly. 'Purpurea', sometimes called Arabian lilac, is the most widely sold selection; leaf undersides are dusky purple. 'Variegata' has white-variegated foliage; cut out shoots that revert to plain green.

VRIESEA

Bromeliaceae
Perennials

🌿 **TS; USDA 10-11; OR HOUSEPLANTS**

◐ **PARTIAL SHADE; BRIGHT INDIRECT LIGHT**

💧 **REGULAR WATER**

Vriesea hieroglyphica

Native to high elevations in Mexico, Central and South America, and the West Indies. *Vrieseas* combine spectacular, long-lasting flower spikes with the most handsome foliage of any bromeliad. Rosettes of long, leathery leaves may be banded, mottled, or plain. Spear-shaped flower spikes rising from the plant's center may hold their color for months. There are dozens of vrieseas from which to choose, offering a wide range of colors, shapes, and sizes. Hybridization has produced many plants of complex parentage.

V. carinata. LOBSTER CLAW. Pale green foliage in a small rosette—just 8 in. high and wide. Colorful inflorescence with red bracts and green-tipped yellow flowers increases plant height to 1 ft.

V. fosteriana. Rosette to 2½ ft. tall, 3 ft. wide. Yellowish to deep green leaves sport crosswise bands of purple or maroon. Yellow inflorescence increases height to 5 ft. 'Red Chestnut' has light green to whitish leaves with red and maroon bands; 'Vista' produces white foliage with reddish brown markings.

V. gigantea 'Nova'. Rosette to 2½ ft. high, 3–4 ft. wide. Bluish green leaves have light green markings that fade to near-white as the plant ages. Spike to 1½ ft. tall

holds yellow-and-white flowers in green bracts.

V. hieroglyphica. Rosette to 3 ft. tall and wide. Leaves are yellowish green with pronounced cross-banding; bands are dark green on upper surface of leaf, dark purplish brown on underside. Greenish flower spike to 2½ ft. tall holds yellow flowers in greenish yellow bracts.

V. imperialis. GIANT VRIESEA. Light green leaves with reddish purple undersides form a rosette to 5 ft. high and wide. Inflorescence features red bracts and yellow or white flowers; it increases plant height dramatically—to 10–15 ft.

V. splendens. FLAMING SWORD. Rosettes to 3 ft. tall, 1 ft. wide. Bluish green leaves sport blackish purple cross-banding. Flower stalk resembles a 1½- to 2-ft.-long feather of bright red bracts from which small yellow flowers emerge.

CARE

Vrieseas are epiphytes, naturally growing in the crotches of trees. In the Tropical South (USDA 10-11), you can grow them that way, too—just wrap the plant's base in coarse sphagnum moss and secure it to a tree branch. Mist the moss daily. Elsewhere, grow these bromeliads as potted plants you take in for the winter. Plant in loose, fast-draining potting mix; let the mix go slightly dry between waterings, and mist plants frequently. You can fill the central cup with water occasionally during the warmer months, but do not keep it continuously filled or the plant may rot. Feed with a general-purpose liquid houseplant fertilizer diluted to half-strength once a month in spring and summer; don't feed in fall and winter. Indoors or out, place vrieseas where they'll get good light but not hot, direct sun.

WASHINGTONIA

Arecaceae
Palms

CS, TS; USDA 9-11

☀ **FULL SUN**

◐ ◑ ● **LITTLE TO REGULAR WATER**

Washingtonia 'Filibusta'

These fast-growing fan palms are too tall for most suburban gardens; they are best suited to large properties, avenues, parkways. The two species often hybridize if growing near each other. Widely grown in Florida.

W. 'Filibusta'. A fast-growing hybrid between the two species listed here; intermediate between them in size and appearance. Said to be at least as hardy as *W. filifera*; more tolerant of humidity.

W. filifera. DESERT FAN PALM. From California, Arizona. Hardy to 18°F. To 60 ft. tall, 20 ft. wide, with thicker trunk than *W. robusta*. Long-stalked, 3- to 6-ft., light green leaves stand well apart in open crown. As leaves mature, they bend down to form a "skirt" of thatch.

W. robusta. THREAD PALM, MEXICAN FAN PALM. From Mexico. Hardy to 20°F. To 100 ft. tall (though more like 60–80 ft. in Southern gardens), 10 ft. wide; trunk is slightly curved or bent, slimmer than that of *W. filifera*. Head of bright green foliage is more compact; leafstalks are shorter, with a red streak on the undersides. Good plant for the beach.

WATERMELON

Cucurbitaceae
Annual

US, MS, LS, CS, TS; USDA 6-11

☀ **FULL SUN**

● **REGULAR WATER, ESPECIALLY WHEN PLANTS ARE YOUNG**

Watermelons

One of the South's favorite late-summer treats. World records for size of melons have been held by families in Arkansas and Tennessee. Needs a long growing season, more heat than most other melons, and more space than other vine crops—about 8 ft. by 8 ft. for each hill (circle of seed). Other than that, culture is as described under Melon. Unlike other melons, watermelon does not grow sweeter after harvest—it must be picked ripe. Three tests for ripeness: thumping the melon produces a "thunk"; underside has turned from white to pale yellow; and and the closest tendril has browned.

Large selections such as 'Ali Baba', 'Carolina Cross #183', 'Charleston Gray', 'Congo', 'Crimson Sweet', 'Dixie Queen', and 'Fairfax' may need as many as 85 to 95 days of hot, sunny weather to mature. If your summers are shorter, choose a smaller, earlier-ripening "icebox" type that will produce in 70 to 75 days, such as 'Minilee', 'Sugar Baby', or yellow-skinned 'Golden Crown'. 'New Queen' is an icebox type with orange flesh. Seed companies also offer yellow-fleshed kinds ('Golden Honey', 'Yellow Doll'), seedless types ('Crimson Trio', 'Queen of Hearts'), and heirlooms ('Moon and Stars', 'Georgia Rattlesnake', 'Orange Tendersweet', 'White Sugar Lump'). Dwarf-fruited types are also available.

WEDELIA TEXANA

TEXAS CREEPING OX-EYE
Asteraceae
Evergreen or deciduous shrub

MS, LS, CS, TS; USDA 7-11

☀ ◐ **FULL SUN OR PARTIAL SHADE**

◐ ◑ **MODERATE TO LITTLE WATER**

Wedelia texana

Native to southern Texas, Mexico, and Central America. Upright, mounding shrub grows 1½–3 ft. high and 2½ ft. wide, with gray-green, rough-textured, narrow leaves to 3 in. long. From spring into fall, plant is covered by 1- to 1½-in.-wide, golden orange flowers held well above the foliage. Flowers attract butterflies; seeds attract goldfinches. Evergreen in warmer parts of its range. In colder areas, it may die to the ground in winter and return in spring; When grown in part shade, plants are less upright and have fewer blooms. Long-lived and very heat tolerant. Grows in almost any well-drained soil. Once established, needs little if any supplemental irrigation. If it looks ragged, cut back by half in midsummer to rejuvenate. Will reseed if spent blooms are not sheared. Sometimes sold as *W. acapulcensis hispida*. Formerly known as *Zexmenia hispida*.

WEIGELA

Caprifoliaceae
Deciduous shrubs

US, MS, LS; USDA 6-8

☀ ◐ **FULL SUN OR LIGHT SHADE**

● **REGULAR WATER**

Weigela florida 'Versicolor'

Few shrubs have seen such dramatic improvements in the past decade as weigelas. What were previously dismissed as ho-hum, one-season wonders have magically morphed into delightful forms that offer colorful foliage, a variety of flower colors, compact growth, and repeat blooming. Profuse display of inch-long, funnel-shaped flowers occurs in spring. Use these Asian natives in mixed borders or in sweeps.

W. florida. Fast growth to 6–10 ft. tall, 9–12 ft. wide, with branches often arching to the ground. Leaves 2–4½ in. long. Pink to rose-red flowers. The following three selections grow about 6 ft. high and wide: 'Bristol Snowflake', white flowers opening from pinkish buds; 'Java Red', red-tinted foliage, red buds opening to deep pink flowers; 'Pink Princess', lilac-pink flowers. 'Wine and Roses' ('Alexandra'), to 5 ft. tall and wide, has deep purple new leaves highlighted by bright pink flowers; foliage matures to purplish green, then turns blackish purple in autumn. 'Midnight Wine' is similar but dwarf, to just 2 ft. tall and wide. 'My Monet', just 12–18 in. tall and wide, has pink flowers and variegated leaves combining pink, cream, and green. The flowers of 'Versicolor' open white and then age to pink and red.

W. hybrids. These are hybrids involving *W. florida*, the early-flowering species *W. praecox*, and other species.

'Briant Rubidor'. A sport of 'Bristol Ruby' with yellow foliage. To 6 ft. high and wide.

'Bristol Ruby'. To 6–7 ft. tall and nearly as wide, with ruby-red flowers. Some repeat bloom in midsummer and fall.

'Candida'. To 5 ft. tall and wide; white flowers that are tinged with green.

'Carnaval'. Dense growth to 3–5 ft. tall and wide, with flowers in white and shades of pink and red; may rebloom in mid-to late summer.

'Dark Horse'. Compact grower to just 2–3 ft. tall and wide. Dark purple leaves keep their color all season and contrast nicely with the profuse pink blooms.

'Florida Variegata'. Compact growth to 4–6 ft. tall and wide, with leaves edged in creamy yellow to white. Deep rosy red flowers. 'Nana Variegata' is 3 ft. tall and wide.

'French Lace'. Mid-green leaves have wide, irregular yellow margins; good orange to red fall color. Flowers are scarlet-red. To 6 ft. tall, 4 ft. wide.

'Lucifer'. Compact growth to 3–5 ft. high and wide. Dark green leaves and extra-large deep red flowers.

'Minuet'. Dwarf selection to 3 ft. tall, 5 ft. wide. Purplish leaves. Flowers blend red, purple, and yellow.

'Newport Red'. To 6 ft. tall and wide, with bright red flowers. Young stems are bright green in winter.

'Red Prince'. To 5–6 ft. tall and wide, with red flowers, some summer rebloom.

Sonic Bloom series. Heavy bloom in spring, with repeated flushes of flowers until frost. Available in lipstick-red, hot pink, and pink-flushed white. Compact growth to 4–5 ft. tall and wide.

CARE

Provide moderately fertile, well-drained soil for best growth. Larger selections can become rangy with time if not pruned. After flowering, cut back stems that bloomed to side shoots that didn't bloom. Cut some of the oldest, woodiest stems to the ground; vigorous new growth will quickly replace them. Compact selections need only occasional pruning. Spring-blooming types will flower again the following spring. Repeat bloomers will flower again that same year in summer.

WISTERIA

Papilionaceae
Deciduous Vines

🌿 **US, MS, LS, CS; USDA 6-9**

☼ **FULL SUN**

◐ ◖ **LITTLE TO MODERATE WATER**

Wisteria floribunda

Twining, woody vines of great size, long life, and exceptional beauty in flower. So adaptable they can be grown as trees, shrubs, or vines. All have large, bright green leaves divided into many leaflets; spectacular clusters of blue, violet, pinkish, or white blossoms and velvety, pealike pods to about 6 in. long. Fall color in subdued shades of yellow. To get off to a good start, buy a cutting-grown, budded, or grafted wisteria; unnamed seedlings may not bloom for many years. If you start with budded or grafted plants, keep suckers removed for the first few years, or they may take over. Do not allow aggressive Asian species to grow on trees or escape into ornamental areas, as they will quickly smother the landscape. Also be wary of growing them near the house, as their muscular stems can tear apart structures. Wisterias resist damage by browsing deer.

W. brachybotrys. SILKY WISTERIA. Native to Japan. Silky-haired, 8- to 14-in.-long leaves divided into 9 to 13 leaflets. White, very large, long-stalked, highly fragrant flowers in short (4- to 6-in.) clusters that open all at once during leaf-out. Older

ABOVE: Wisteria sinensis

plants (especially in tree form) have remarkably profuse bloom. 'Shiro Kapitan' ('Alba') is the most commonly sold form; it bears pure white (sometimes double) flowers with yellow markings. 'Murasaki Kapitan' ('Violacea'), bears blue-violet flowers with white markings. 'Okayama' has faintly scented deep mauve blossoms.

W. floribunda. JAPANESE WISTERIA. From Japan. Leaves are 12–16 in. long, divided into 15 to 19 leaflets. Very fragrant, 1½-ft. clusters of violet or violet-blue flowers appear during leaf-out. Clusters open gradually, starting from the base; this prolongs bloom season but makes for a less spectacular burst of color than that provided by *W. sinensis*. Many selections are sold in white; pink; and shades of blue, purple, and lavender, usually marked with yellow and white. 'Macrobotrys' ('Longissima', 'Multijuga') has long (1½- to 4-ft.) clusters of violet flowers. 'Longissima Alba' bears 2-ft. clusters of white blossoms; 'Ivory Tower' is similar. 'Rosea' has lavender-pink blooms; 'Violacea Plena' sports very full clusters of double, deep violet-blue flowers. 'Texas Purple' blooms at an early age.

W. frutescens. AMERICAN WISTERIA. Native from Virginia to Florida and Texas. Leaves 7–12 in. long, divided into 9 to 15 leaflets. Later blooming and less vigorous than *W. floribunda* and *W. sinensis*, with thinner stems; not destructive. Mildly fragrant, pale lilac flowers with yellow blotch appear in dense, 4- to 6-in.-long clusters in late spring after leaf-out; blossoms look like grape clusters. 'Amethyst Falls' has vivid lilac-blue flowers. White-flowered 'Nivea' blooms earlier than the species.

W. macrostachya. KENTUCKY WISTERIA. Native from Illinois to Texas. A good choice for smaller gardens. Like *W. frutescens*, blooms among new leaves in late spring, after the Asian species bloom. Mildly fragrant flowers are light blue to violet or blue-purple, in 8- to 12-in.-long, fragrant, pendulous clusters. Shiny leaves usually divided into nine leaflets, each to 3 in. long. The 4-in. pods are smooth,

W

sometimes twisted. Less vigorous and better behaved than Asian species. Not destructive. 'Clara Mack' has white flowers. 'Bayou Two o' Clock' has blue-violet flowers held in long, pointed racemes. 'Pondside Blue' bears pale blue-violet blossoms.

W. sinensis. CHINESE WISTERIA. Native to China. Leaves are 10–12 in. long, divided into 7 to 13 leaflets. Violet-blue, fragrant flowers appear before leaf-out; they come in shorter clusters (to 1 ft.) than those of *W. floribunda* but make quite a show by opening all at once, nearly all along the cluster. 'Alba' has white flowers. 'Cooke's Special' is a grafted form with blue-purple flowers to 20 in. long. Blue-violet 'Caroline', probably a hybrid, blooms early and is highly fragrant.

CARE

Plants are not fussy about soil but need good drainage; in alkaline soil, watch for chlorosis (yellow leaves with green veins) and treat with iron chelates or iron sulfate. Pruning and training are important for control of size and shape and for bloom production. Let newly planted wisteria grow to establish framework you desire, either single trunked or multitrunked. Remove stems that interfere with desired framework and pinch back side stems and long streamers. For single-trunked form, rub off buds that develop on trunk. For multiple trunks, select as many vigorous stems as you wish and let them develop; if plant has only one stem, pinch it back to encourage others to develop. The main stem will become a good-sized trunk, and the weight of a mature vine is considerable. Support structures should be sturdy and durable.

Tree wisterias can be bought already trained; or you can train your own. Remove all but one main stem and stake this one securely. Tie stem to stake at frequent intervals, using plastic tape to prevent girdling. When plant has reached height at which you wish head to form, pinch or prune out tip to force branching. Shorten branches to beef them up. Pinch back long streamers and rub off all buds that form below head.

In general, wisterias do not need fertilizer. Prune blooming plants every winter: Cut back or thin out side shoots from main or structural stems, and shorten back to two or three buds the flower-producing spurs that grow from these shoots. It's easy to recognize fat flower buds on these spurs.

In summer, cut back long streamers before they tangle up in main body of vine; save those you want to use to extend height or length of vine and tie them to support—eaves, wall, trellis, arbor. If old plants grow rampantly but fail to bloom, withhold all nitrogen fertilizers for an entire growing season (buds for the next season's bloom are started in early summer). If that fails to produce bloom the next year, you can try pruning roots in spring—after you're sure no flowers will be produced—by cutting vertically with a spade into plant's root zone.

WOODSIA OBTUSA

BLUNT-LOBED WOODSIA, COMMON WOODSIA
Woodsiaceae
Fern

🌿 **US, MS, LS, CS; USDA 6-9**

☀️ ◑ **FULL SUN OR LIGHT SHADE**

💧 **REGULAR WATER**

Woodsia obtusa

Native from Quebec to Florida. Small deciduous fern to 2 ft. tall, 1½ ft. wide. Fronds 12–15 in. long, 4 in. wide, bright green in shade, gray-green in sun. May be once cut into deeply lobed segments or twice cut. Fronds produced throughout growing season. Likes well-drained soil that is neutral or even slightly alkaline. Use in woodland or rock garden.

WOODWARDIA

CHAIN FERN
Blechnaceae
Ferns

🌿 **US, MS, LS, CS; USDA 6-9**

◑ **PART SHADE**

💧 **AMPLE WATER**

Woodwardia virginica

Medium to large, upright, usually coarse-textured, deciduous ferns with rich green fronds. Common name comes from the chainlike pattern of spore cases beneath frond segments. Shade beneath canopy of tall trees is an ideal site. Deer aren't fond of these ferns.

W. areolata. NETTED CHAIN FERN. Native to eastern, southeastern U.S. To 2 ft. high and wider than tall, with deeply lobed fronds, the lobes finely toothed. Spore-bearing fronds are narrower. Can take considerable sun if roots are kept wet.

W. virginica. VIRGINIA CHAIN FERN. Native to eastern, southern U.S. To 1–2 ft. tall, 1 ft. wide, with twice-cut fronds that are bronzy green when they emerge. Likes wet soil and can even grow with roots submerged.

XANTHOSOMA

ELEPHANT'S EAR
Araceae
Perennials

🌿 **LS, CS, TS; USDA 8-11; OR GROW AS HOUSEPLANTS**

☀️ **FILTERED SUNLIGHT; BRIGHT INDIRECT LIGHT**

💧💧 **REGULAR TO AMPLE WATER**

Xanthosoma 'Lime Zinger'

Tropical plants related to *Alocasia* and *Colocasia*. Stemless plants grow to 6 ft. tall and wide and produce big, arrow-shaped leaves on long stalks. Bloom intermittently throughout the year. Flowers are more curious than attractive, resembling those of calla (*Zantedeschia*), with a central spike surrounded by a usually greenish or yellowish bract. These plants need moist, rich, well-drained soil for best performance. Protect from hard frosts. Indoors, grow in large pots and apply a balanced liquid fertilizer every two to three weeks during active growth; reduce watering and feeding in winter.

X. 'Lime Zinger'. Probable hybrid, but parentage is uncertain. Sometimes sold as *X. aurea*. Grows quickly to 3–4 ft. tall, with chartreuse to lime-green, arrow-shaped leaves that can reach 1½ ft. long.

X. sagittifolium. ARROWLEAF ELEPHANT'S EAR. Dark green, 3-ft.-long leaves on 3-ft. stalks. Greenish white, 7- to 9-in.-long bracts. 'Lanceolatum' has lance-shaped blackish green leaves. Leaves and leafstalks of 'Yellow Leaf' have a golden cast.

X. violaceum. BLUE TARO. Grows from edible, pink-fleshed tubers. Dark green leaves to 2 ft. long have paler undersides, purplish veins and margins, powdery appearance. Purple, 2½-ft. leafstalks have a heavy, waxy, bluish or grayish coating. Yellowish white bracts to 1 ft. long.

XANTHORHIZA SIMPLICISSIMA

YELLOWROOT
Ranunculaceae
Deciduous shrub

US, MS, LS, CS; USDA 6-9

FULL SUN OR PARTIAL SHADE

REGULAR WATER

Xanthorhiza simplicissima

This species from the eastern U.S. is the only one in its genus. Grows naturally in moist woodlands and along streambanks, reaching 1–3 ft. high and 5 ft. wide; can spread more widely by suckers. Attractive leaves to 10 in. long comprise three to five oval, pointed leaflets with irregularly toothed edges. Foliage emerges bronzy purple in spring, matures to bright green in summer, then takes on yellow and finally red-purple tones in autumn. In spring, just as leaves emerge, look for hanging, 4-in.-long clusters of tiny brownish purple flowers. Common name refers to bright yellow roots, which were used by Native Americans to make a dye.

Good ground cover beneath trees and shrubs but can overwhelm smaller plants; a root barrier may be needed to keep it in

its place. Excellent for transitional areas between sun and shade and between wet and dry.

Grows in most soils and is not bothered by pests or diseases. Prune lightly to maintain attractive shape; or cut back hard in early spring if plants become ragged. Easy to propagate by division in spring.

YUCCA

Asparagaceae
Evergreen perennials, shrubs, trees

ZONES VARY BY SPECIES; OR GROW AS HOUSEPLANTS

FULL SUN; BRIGHT LIGHT

WATER NEEDS VARY BY SPECIES

Yucca gloriosa 'Bright Star'

Yuccas grow over much of North America; hardiness depends on species. All have tough, sword-shaped leaves and large clusters of white or whitish, rounded to bell-shaped flowers. Some are stemless, while others reach tree size. Best in well-drained soil.

Taller kinds make striking silhouettes, and even stemless species provide important vertical effects when in bloom. Some have stiff, sharp-pointed leaves; keep these away from walks, terraces, and other well-traveled areas. Yuccas are not usually browsed by deer.

Young plants of some species can be used as indoor plants; they withstand the dry indoor atmosphere and will grow well near hot, sunny windows. Give

moderate water; feed monthly during growth with a balanced liquid fertilizer. Buy 1-gallon size or smaller; set out in ground when plants become too large for indoors. Successful indoors are *Y. aloifolia* (but beware of sharp-pointed leaves), *Y. elephantipes*, *Y. filamentosa*, *Y. gloriosa*, and *Y. recurvifolia*.

Y. aloifolia. SPANISH BAYONET, SPANISH DAGGER. Zones MS, LS, CS, TS; USDA 7-11. Native to the South. Slow growth to 10 ft. by 5 ft. or larger; trunk may be single or branched, sometimes sprawling in picturesque effect. Stems densely clothed in dark green, sharp-pointed leaves to 2½ ft. long and 2 in. wide. White flowers (sometimes tinged purple) to 4 in. across, in dense, erect clusters to 2 ft. tall in summer. Moderate water. 'Variegata' has green foliage edged in yellowish white.

Y. baccata. BANANA YUCCA. Zones US, MS, LS, CS, TS; USDA 6-11. Native to the Southwest. Slow growth to 3 ft. high, 5 ft. wide. Foliage clump may have no stem or a short, prostrate one. Thick, stiff leaves to 2 ft. long, 2 in. wide have fibers along the edges. Large, fleshy flowers in late spring are red-brown outside, white inside, in dense, 2-ft.-long clusters. Fleshy, edible, bananalike fruit to 6 in. long. Little water. 'Compactum' is somewhat smaller than the species.

Y. elata. SOAPTREE YUCCA. Zones US, MS, LS, CS, TS; USDA 6-11. Native to the Southwest, northern Mexico. Slow growth to 6–20 ft. tall, 8–10 ft. wide, with single or branched trunk. Leaves to 4 ft. long, ½ in. wide. Tall spikes of white flowers in summer. Little water.

Y. elephantipes (*Y. gigantea*). GIANT YUCCA. Zones CS, TS; USDA 9-11. Native to Mexico. Fast growing (to 2 ft. per year), eventually 15–30 ft. tall, 8 ft. wide, usually with several trunks. Leaves 4 ft. long, 3 in. wide, dark rich green. Striking silhouette alone or combined with other big-scale foliage plants; out of scale in smaller gardens. Large spikes of creamy white flowers in spring. Does best in good, well-drained soil with regular water. A variegated form has pale green leaves with broad cream-colored stripes.

Y. filamentosa. ADAM'S NEEDLE. Zones US, MS, LS, CS, TS; USDA 6-11. Native to the Southeast. Stemless plant to 2½ ft. tall,

5 ft. wide. Stiff, dark green leaves 2½ ft. long, 1 in. wide, with long, loose fibers at edges. Blooms in late spring and summer, with lightly fragrant, yellowish white flowers, 2–3 in. wide, carried in tall, narrow clusters to 4–7 ft. or taller. Looks similar to *Y. flaccida* and *Y. smalliana*. One of the most cold hardy and widely planted yuccas. Moderate water. 'Bright Edge' has leaves edged in yellow; 'Color Guard' and 'Garland's Gold' have creamy gold leaves widely edged in green. 'Variegata' has green leaves edged with white.

Y. flaccida. Zones US, MS, LS, CS, TS; USDA 6-11. Native to the Southeast. Stemless. Differs from *Y. filamentosa* in having less rigid leaves, straight fibers on leaf edges, and somewhat shorter flower clusters. Moderate water. 'Golden Sword' has yellow leaves edged in dark green. 'Ivory' has out-facing rather than drooping flowers.

Y. glauca. SOAPWEED. Zones US, MS, LS, CS; USDA 6-9. Native to central and southwestern U.S. To 3–4 ft. high and wide or larger, with short or prostrate trunk. Stiff, narrow, 1- to 2½-ft.-long leaves form a clump 3–4 ft. wide. Leaves are grayish green, edged with a hairline of white and a few thin threads. White summer flowers bloom on a spike 4–5 ft. tall. Moderate water.

Y. gloriosa. MOUND-LILY YUCCA, SPANISH DAGGER, SOFT-TIP YUCCA. Zones MS, LS, CS, TS; USDA 7-11. Native to the Southeast. Much like *Y. aloifolia*; generally multitrunked to 10 ft. tall and 8 ft. wide. Plant is usually stemless in youth. Leaf points are soft and will not penetrate skin. Summer bloom. Good green color blends well with tropical-looking, lush plants. Needs moderate water; too much moisture may produce black areas on leaf margins. Leaves of 'Variegata' are edged in creamy white. 'Bright Star' is a slow-growing dwarf form (to 2 ft. tall, 5 ft. wide) with broad margins of golden yellow.

Y. pallida. PALE-LEAF YUCCA. Zones MS, LS, CS, TS; USDA 7-11. Native to Texas. To 1½ ft. tall, 2½ ft. wide. Compact rosette of 1- to 2-ft.-long, pale blue-green leaves with thin yellow or brownish margins and a spine at the tip. Branched spikes to 7 ft. high hold many pale green to creamy white flowers in spring. Little to moderate water.

TOP: Yucca filamentosa 'Bright Edge'; *MIDDLE: Y. gloriosa; Y. f.* 'Variegata'; *BOTTOM: Y. recurvifolia* 'Banana Split'

Y. recurvifolia. CURVE-LEAF YUCCA, SOFT-LEAF YUCCA. Zones MS, LS, CS, TS; USDA 7-11. Native to the Southeast. The botanical name of this plant is a bit of a moving target: You may find it listed as above or as *Y. gloriosa recurvifolia, Y. g. tristis,* or *Y. pendula.* Whatever its name, it forms a single trunk to 6–10 ft. tall; it is unbranched in younger plants but may be lightly branched in age. Reaches 6–8 ft. wide; spreads by offsets to form large groups. Beautiful blue-gray leaves are 2–3 ft. long, 2 in. wide, sharply bent downward; leaf tips are spined but bend to the touch (they aren't dangerously sharp). Less stiff and metallic looking than most yuccas. Loose, open, 3- to 5-ft.-tall clusters of large white flowers in late spring or early summer. Easy to grow in all garden conditions; give moderate water. 'Banana Split' has golden yellow leaves edged in gray-green.

Y. rostrata. BLUE BEARD YUCCA. Zones US, MS, LS, CS, TS; USDA 6-11. Native to Mexico, extreme southwestern Texas. To 12 ft. tall, 9 ft. wide. The most notable feature is the trunk: up to 8 in. thick, covered with soft gray fuzz (fibers remaining from old leaf bases). Needle-pointed blue-green leaves to 2 ft. long, ½ in. wide. Blooms in autumn, bearing 2-ft. clusters of white flowers on a 2-ft. stalk. Little to moderate water. 'Sapphire Skies' has narrow, flexible, powder-blue leaves; just 4 ft. tall after 10 years.

Y. rupicola. TWISTED-LEAF YUCCA. Zones MS, LS, CS, TS; USDA 7-11. Clump-forming Texas native to 3 ft. high and wide. Sharp-pointed, green leaves reach 2 ft. long; they are straight when young, then twist with age. In spring, stalks to 3–8 ft. tall bear bell-shaped, creamy white flowers with a yellow-green tinge. Little to moderate water.

Y. smalliana (*Y. filamentosa smalliana*). ADAM'S NEEDLE, BEAR'S GRASS. Zones US, MS, LS, CS, TS; USDA 6-11. Native to southeastern and south-central U.S. Like *Y. filamentosa* but has narrower, flatter leaves and smaller flowers. Moderate water.

Y. thompsoniana. THOMPSON'S YUCCA. Zones US, MS, LS, CS, TS; USDA 6-11. Native to Texas. Tree to 6–10 ft. tall, 5 ft. wide. Trunk (sometimes branched) is topped with an asymmetrical rosette of narrow, foot-long blue-green leaves; old brown leaves hang from its sides. Blooms in late spring, when white to cream flowers with green-tinged petal bases appear on a 4- to 5-ft. spike. Moderate water.

Y. torreyi. TORREY YUCCA. Zones LS, CS, TS; USDA 8-11. Native from New Mexico and Texas into Mexico. Eventually forms a tree to 15 ft. tall, 9 ft. wide. Begins as a rosette of rigid, sharp-tipped, blue-green leaves on short trunks that slowly elongate. White flowers are borne in late spring on a 4-ft. spike. Needs very little water but tolerates wetter conditions.

Y. treculeana. GIANT SPANISH DAGGER. Zones MS, LS, CS, TS; USDA 7-11. Native to Texas and Mexico. Single-trunked or branching tree to 25 ft. tall, 12 ft. wide, topped with symmetrical rosettes of sharp-pointed, thick, stiff, dark green to blue-green leaves to 2½–4 ft. long. White or purple-tinged white flowers bloom on a 3-ft. spike in late winter or early spring. Little to moderate water.

Z

ZAMIA
Zamiaceae
Cycads

- **CS, TS; USDA 9-11; OR GROW AS HOUSEPLANTS**
- **PARTIAL SHADE; BRIGHT LIGHT**
- **REGULAR WATER**

Zamia furfuracea

Of 100 or so species, only the following two are generally seen. They are slow growing and costly, but with good care will last for many years, both indoors and out. Short trunks (may be completely or partially beneath soil level) are usually marked with scars from old leaf bases. Trunks are topped with circular crowns of leaves that resemble stiff fern fronds or small palm fronds.

Z. furfuracea. CARDBOARD PALM. From southeastern coastal Mexico. To 3 ft. high, 6 ft. wide. Short, sometimes subterranean stem. Fronds to 3 ft. long, usually much less; have as many as 12 pairs (usually fewer) of extremely stiff, leathery, dark green segments to 4½ in. long, 1½ in. wide. Segments may have a few teeth toward the tip. Best in a fairly sunny spot, but with protection from hottest midday sun.

Z. pumila. COONTIE. From Florida, Cuba, West Indies. To 4 ft. high, 6 ft. wide. Short trunk is largely below soil level. Fronds to 3 ft. long, with as many as 30 pairs of dark green segments to 5 in. long, 1¼ in. wide. Good seaside plant; tolerates salt spray.

CARE

Outdoors, plant in organically enriched, fast-draining soil. Grown as houseplants, they need bright light (with protection from hottest sun), occasional misting, and monthly feeding in spring and summer with a general-purpose liquid houseplant fertilizer. Water when soil becomes dry to the touch; reduce watering in winter.

ZAMIOCULCAS ZAMIIFOLIA

ZZ PLANT, ZANZIBAR GEM
Araceae
Evergreen perennial

🌱 CS, TS; USDA 9-11; OR GROW AS HOUSEPLANTS

◐ ● PARTIAL TO FULL SHADE; BRIGHT INDIRECT LIGHT

💧 REGULAR WATER

Zamioculcas zamiifolia

From eastern Africa. This stemless plant sends up 3-ft.-long, bulbous-based leaves directly from a large potato-like rhizome. The leaves comprise six to eight pairs of very glossy, deep green leaflets, each to 6 in. long. Mature plants may flower, producing near the base a green, hoodlike spathe surrounding a single spike-like spadix that holds many tiny cream-colored flowers. Has the look of a cycad, such as *Zamia*, but is actually related to *Philodendron* and peace lily

(*Spathiphyllum*). It is supremely tolerant of low light and infrequent watering, making it an ideal houseplant.

CARE

Indoors or out, it is usually grown in containers. Give well-drained soil. Water regularly, but let the soil dry out between soakings. Don't let plant stand in water or it will quickly rot (yellow leaves are an indicator of too much water). Feed with a diluted liquid fertilizer during summer. Bring indoors when temperatures dip below 60°F; water sparingly in winter.

ZANTEDESCHIA

CALLA
Araceae
Rhizomes

🌱 LS, CS, TS; USDA 9-11; OR DIG AND STORE; OR GROW IN POTS

☀ ◐ FULL SUN OR PARTIAL SHADE

💧 REGULAR WATER DURING GROWTH AND BLOOM

Zantedeschia 'Edge of Night'

Native to South Africa. Basal clumps of long-stalked, shiny, rich green, arrow- or lance-shaped leaves, sometimes spotted white. Flower bract (spathe) surrounds central spike (spadix) that is tightly covered with tiny true flowers. Deer usually leave callas alone.

Z. aethiopica. COMMON CALLA. To 2–4 ft. tall. Forms a large clump of unspotted deep green leaves that are 1½ ft. long, 10 in. wide. Pure white or creamy white, 8-in.-long spathes on 3-ft. stems appear mostly in spring and early summer. 'Green Goddess' is a robust selection with large spathes that are white at the base, green toward the tip.

'Hercules' is larger than species, with big spathes that open flat and curve backward; leaves are spotted with white. 'White Giant' is aptly named, with flowers that may reach 6–7 ft. tall; leaves are thick, leathery, and spotted with white. Dwarf 'Childsiana' grows just 1 ft. tall. 'Pink Mist' grows 1–2 ft. tall, with palest pink flowers with a darker pink eye.

Z. albomaculata. SPOTTED CALLA. Grows to 2 ft. high, with bright green, white-spotted leaves 1–1½ ft. long, 10 in. wide. Creamy yellow or white, 4- to 5-in.-long spathes have a purplish crimson blotch at base. Blooms from early spring into summer.

Z. hybrids. Plants are usually about the size of *Z. albomaculata* and bloom in late spring and summer. Leaves are typically spotted, though some selections have solid green leaves. Spathe colors include cream, buff, orange, pink shades, lavender, purple. "Captain Murano' has hot pink spathes with an orange base. Spathes of 'Edge of Night' are darkest purple. 'Picasso' blends yellow and purple.

Z. rehmanii. RED or PINK CALLA. To 1½–2 ft., with narrow, lance-shaped, unspotted green leaves to 1 ft. long, 2½ in. wide. Pink or rosy pink spathes to 5 in. long in midspring. 'Alba' has white spathes. 'Superba' has dark pink spathes.

CARE

Common calla (*Z. aethiopica*) is basically evergreen but goes partly dormant even in the Tropical South. It will thrive in almost any moist, even boggy soil all year. It cannot withstand storage and so should be grown as a container plant where winter temperatures fall below 10°F.

The other callas described here die to the ground yearly in fall and reappear in spring. They need slightly acid soil and regular water during growth and bloom, followed by a resting period in which, ideally, water is withheld. In rainy climates, rhizomes will tolerate moisture if soil is well drained. Store potted rhizomes dry in their containers. Beyond their hardiness range, rhizomes of deciduous species can be dug and stored over winter, then replanted in spring.

Where callas are hardy, plant all types in fall, setting rhizomes of

Z. aethiopica 4–6 in. deep, those of other species 2 in. deep. Space rhizomes 8–12 in. apart. Leave undisturbed until overcrowding causes a decline in vigor and bloom quality. Elsewhere, plant rhizomes in spring and lift them in fall.

ZELKOVA SERRATA

SAWLEAF ZELKOVA
Ulmaceae
Deciduous tree

🌱 US, MS, LS; USDA 6-8

☀ FULL SUN

💧 💧 MODERATE TO REGULAR WATER

Zelkova serrata

East Asian relative of elm (*Ulmus*). Good shade and street tree; sometimes used as a substitute for American elm (*U. americana*). Grows at moderate to fast rate to 60 ft. or higher, equally wide. Silhouette ranges from vase shaped to quite spreading. Has smooth gray bark. Narrowly oval, sawtoothed, 2- to 3½-in.-long leaves are dark green and similar to those of elm but rougher in texture. Fall color varies from yellow to dark red to orange-red. Excellent shade, lawn, or street tree. Takes wide range of soils. Fairly tolerant of drought, wind. You may need to train and prune young trees to establish a good framework; thin out crowded ascending branches.

Recommended selections include the following. 'City Sprite' is semidwarf, to just 24 ft. tall, 18 ft. wide; leaves are bright green. Cold-hardy, fast-growing 'Green Vase' has a narrow vase shape to 60–80 ft. tall and 40–50 ft. wide;

Z

leaves are pale green in summer, orange-bronze in fall. 'Musashino' is columnar, to 45 ft. tall and just 15 ft. wide; good choice for planting on narrow city streets. 'Ogon' grows 40 ft. tall, 25 ft. wide and boasts bright yellow spring leaves that turn yellow-green in summer; amber stems add color year-round. Vigorous 'Village Green', to 40 ft. tall and wide, has dense foliage and good rust-red fall color.

ZEPHYRANTHES
RAIN LILY, ZEPHYR FLOWER, FAIRY LILY
Amaryllidaceae
Perennials from bulbs

🌿 **MS, LS, CS, TS; USDA 7-11, EXCEPT AS NOTED; OR GROW IN POTS**

☼ **FULL SUN, EXCEPT AS NOTED**

💧 **REGULAR WATER DURING GROWTH AND BLOOM**

Zephyranthes carinata

Clumps of grassy, 1- to 1½-ft.-long leaves give rise to slender, hollow stems, each bearing a single funnel-shaped flower with six segments. Flowers of some kinds resemble lilies; those of other types look like crocuses. In the wild, flowers bloom after a rain (hence the common name "rain lily"), and they may appear in the garden after a good soaking. These are old-timey passalong plants. Deer don't bother with them.

Need little care. Pretty in rock garden or foreground of border. Excellent pot plant for patio or greenhouse. Plant in early summer; set bulbs 1-2 in. deep, 3 in. apart. In the Upper South, mulch hardier species heavily over winter. Container plants bloom better when somewhat pot-bound.

Z. atamasca. ATAMASCO LILY. Semievergreen. Native to the Southeast. Blooms in midspring, with pink-striped buds opening to fragrant, crocuslike, pure white flowers to 3 in. long. Florida native *Z. a. treatiae* (Zones CS, TS; USDA 9-11), has grasslike leaves and pure white, crocuslike flowers that open from red buds; blooms two to four weeks before the species.

Z. candida. WHITE RAIN LILY. Evergreen. From Argentina and Uruguay. Glossy, crocuslike flowers are 2 in. long, pure white outside, tinged with rose inside, borne on stems as long as the leaves. Blooms in late summer, early fall.

Z. carinata. PINK RAIN LILY. Deciduous. From Central America. Lilylike, rose-pink, 4-in.-wide flowers bloom on 8-in. stems in summer. Blossoms open out flat at midday, close by afternoon.

Z. citrina. YELLOW RAIN LILY. Deciduous. From tropical South America. About the same size as *Z. candida* and blooms at the same time, but the fragrant blossoms are deep yellow.

Z. drummondii. GIANT PRAIRIE LILY. Deciduous. Zones LS, CS, TS; USDA 8-11. Native to the Texas Hill Country and Mexico. Large (4-in.), fragrant, lilylike, pure white flowers open in the evening. Blooms most heavily in early spring, then sporadically through late summer, fall. 'San Carlos Form' and 'Fedora' are Mexican selections.

Z. flavissima. Deciduous. From Brazil and Argentina. Resembles *Z. citrina*, but with brighter green leaves and canary-yellow flowers. May remain evergreen with sufficient summer water.

Z. hybrids. Deciduous. Most widely offered is 'Ajax' (a cross between *Z. candida* and *Z. citrina*), a free-flowering plant with light yellow blossoms. Other hybrids available from mail-order specialists include 'Alamo', with deep rose-pink flowers flushed yellow; 'Apricot Queen', yellow blossoms stained pink; 'Batik', apricot flowers centered in yellow; 'Big Dude', large white flowers blushed pink at the tips; 'Heart Throb', dark pink flowers with a white eye; 'Krakatau', bright red-orange with a yellow center; 'Prairie Sunset', large light yellow blooms suffused with pink; 'Ruth Page', rich pink blooms; and 'Tenexico Apricot', rich apricot flowers that turn pale pink on their second day of bloom.

Z. macrosiphon. Evergreen in warmer part of range. From Mexico. Similar to *Z. grandiflora* but produces smaller (nearly 3-in.), rich pink flowers, comes into flower a little earlier, and continues blooming over a longer period. Full sun or partial shade.

Z. reginae. Deciduous. From Mexico. Bears 2½-in., crocuslike yellow flowers in midsummer; blossoms open bright yellow, then fade to cream on the second day. Originally sold as 'Valles Yellow'.

ZINGIBER
GINGER
Zingiberaceae
Perennials from rhizomes

🌿 **LS, CS, TS; USDA 8-11**

◑ **PARTIAL SHADE**

💧💧 **REGULAR TO AMPLE WATER**

Zingiber officinale

Growing gingers is a snap. Plants thrive in Southern heat and humidity, spreading slowly but widely by rhizomes. Most folks' knowledge of this genus begins and ends with one species, *Z. officinale*, the source of culinary ginger—but there are also dozens of highly ornamental species, of which a small sampling is presented here.

Z. citriodorum 'Chiang Mai Princess'. Selection of a species from Thailand. To 3-4 ft. tall, with glossy, green leaves. Large (8-in.) flowering cone with sharp-pointed bracts starts out dark green, turns blood-red. Blooms appear 1-1½ ft. above the ground. Sweet citrus fragrance. Good cut flower.

Z. malaysianum. BLACK GINGER, MIDNIGHT GINGER. From Malaysia. To 2-3 ft. high. Grown primarily for dark purplish brown foliage, borne on dark stems. Ground-level flowers open yellow, then age to pink.

Z. mioga. MIOGA GINGER. Native to China. To 2 ft. high, with dark green leaves. Small yellow flowers with white edges are borne at ground level. Commonly cultivated in Japan for edible shoots in spring, flower buds in summer or fall. In hot climates, goes dormant in summer. Highly attractive foliage of 'Dancing Crane' is green, with white streaks reminiscent of lightning bolts running vertically through each leaf. This selection spreads slowly and is noninvasive; it looks great massed in a shade garden.

Z. niveum 'Milky Way'. Selection of a species from Thailand. Grows 2½-3 ft. high, with light green foliage. The ground-level, 4- to 6-in. flowering cones are white to pale pink, with yellow flowers.

Z. officinale. COMMON GINGER. Native to Southeast Asia. This is the ginger used in cooking. Stems 2-4 ft. tall, with narrow, glossy, bright green leaves to 1 ft. long. Summer flowers (rarely seen) are yellowish green, with purple lip marked yellow; not especially showy. Buy roots (fresh, not dried) at the grocery store in early spring; cut into 1- to 2-in.-long sections with well-developed growth buds. Let cut ends dry before planting. Allow several months for roots to reach some size, then harvest at any time.

Z. rubens. BENGAL GINGER. From India. To 4 ft. tall. Green foliage. Bright red flowering cones about 1½ in. across bloom at ground level or even partially below the soil. Each scale of the cone produces a single inch-wide red flower with a cream lip marked in red; blossoms emerge one after the other, over the course of several weeks.

Z. spectabile. BEEHIVE GINGER. From Malaysia. To 6 ft. tall. Deep green, slender-pointed leaves to 1-1½ ft. long, with long, slender, pointed tips. Stem about 3 ft. tall bears a showy, foot-long inflorescence; overlapping bracts are yellow, aging to scarlet, and flowers are yellowish with black tips. Good cut flower.

Z. zerumbet. PINE CONE GINGER, SHAMPOO GINGER. Native to India and Malaysia. To 6 ft. tall. Dark green leaves to 1 ft. long and 3 in. wide (broader than those of

Z. officinale). Inflorescence is a 3- to 5-in. green cone that appears on a separate, short stalk in late summer, then turns brilliant red for 2 to 3 weeks. Small yellow flowers open between the bracts. 'Darcyi' has cream-striped leaves. Good cut flower.

CARE

Plant in rich, moist, well-drained soil, placing rhizomes just below the soil surface. Propagate by division in early spring. Plants go dormant in winter, and rhizomes may rot in cold, wet soil. You can grow gingers in pots and move them to shelter in winter; feed once a month during active growth with a general-purpose liquid fertilizer.

ZINNIA

Asteraceae
Annuals and perennials

✔ US, MS, LS, CS, TS; USDA 6-11, **EXCEPT AS NOTED**

☼ **FULL SUN**

💧 **REGULAR WATER, EXCEPT AS NOTED**

Zinnia 'Giant Dahlia Flowered Violet'

Longtime favorites for colorful, round flowers, typically in summer and early fall. Butterflies love them. These are hot-weather plants that don't gain from being planted early; they stand still until weather warms up. Subject to mildew in humid places, if given overhead water, and when autumn brings longer nights, more dew and shade. Moderately resistant to damage by browsing deer. Sow seeds where plants are to grow (or set out nursery plants) from late spring to early summer. Give good garden soil, feed generously. Most garden

zinnias belong to *Z. elegans.*

Z. acerosa. DESERT ZINNIA. Perennial. Zones MS, LS, CS; USDA 7-9. From southern Arizona, Texas, Mexico. To 6–10 in. high, 2 ft. wide, with hairy, needlelike, ¾-in.-long leaves. Flowers are 1½ in. wide, with fairly large, creamy white rays veined in green on underside. Blooms sporadically from spring through fall, whenever moisture is present; goes dormant during extended periods of drought.

Z. angustifolia. NARROW-LEAF ZINNIA. One of the best annuals for the South; does not get mildew. Compact growth to 16 in. high and wide, with very narrow leaves to 2½ in. long. Orange, 1-in. flowers; each ray has a paler stripe. Blooms in six weeks from seed, continues late into fall. 'Classic' grows to 1 ft. high and 2 ft. wide, has 1½-in. flowers. 'Crystal White', 8–10 in. high and 1 ft. wide, bears 1-in. single flowers in pure white. The Star series, also to 1 by 2 ft., has 2-in. blooms in orange, golden yellow, and white

Z. elegans. COMMON ZINNIA. Annual. From Mexico. Sold in strains ranging from less than a foot high and wide to 4 ft. tall, half as wide. Oval to lance-shaped leaves to 5 in. long; summer flowers from less than 1 in. to as much as 5–7 in. across. Forms include full double, cactus flowered (with quilled rays), and crested (cushionlike center surrounded by rows of broad rays); the many colors available include white, pink, salmon, rose, red, yellow, orange, lavender, and purple. 'Envy' is a novelty type with lime-green flowers.

Among smaller strains (to about 1 ft.) for edging or foreground are Dasher, very quick to bloom; bushy Dreamland; and large-flowered Magellan and Peter Pan. Mildew-resistant Small World grows just 6 in. tall. All have 3-in. blooms.

Intermediate types include 18-in.-tall Candy Cane, with white or gold flowers heavily speckled with pink, rose, and cherry; 18- to 20-in. Sunbow, with fully double, 1½-in. flowers; 1½- to 2 ft.-tall Lilliput mix, with 2-in. pompons in red, pink, yellow, lavender, and white; 2-ft.-tall Candy Stripe Mix, with 4-in. white flowers striped with pink, rose, or red; 2- to 2½-ft. Sun hybrids, with 5-in. flowers; 2½- to 3-ft. Ruffles hybrids, 3½-in. blos-

TOP: Zinnia elegans 'Zowie! Yellow Flame'; Z. e. 'Magellan Salmon'; BOTTOM: Z. marylandica 'Zahara Starlight Rose'; Z. e. 'Benary's Giant Lime'

soms with ruffled rays; and 3-ft. Giant Cactus-flowered Mix, with 4- to 5-in. semidouble blooms.

Tall plants for cutting and back-of-border planting include 4-ft. Benary's Giants (also sold as Park's Picks, Blue Point) and 3-ft., double-blossomed Dahlia-Flowered Mix; both have 4- to 5-in. blooms. 'Big Red Hybrid', to 3 ft., has bright red, 5- to 6-in. flowers. State Fair Mix, also to 3 ft. tall, has 5- to 6-in. double flowers in red, orange, purple, yellow, and pink. 'Zowie! Yellow Flame' is a bicolored selection with rose centers and yellow tips; 24- to 36-in. tall.

Z. grandiflora. ROCKY MOUNTAIN ZINNIA. Perennial in Zones CS, TS; USDA 9-11; annual elsewhere. Native to Rocky Mountains, south into Mexico. To 1 ft. high and wide. Bright green leaves to 1 in. long, ⅛ in. wide. Spring-into-fall flowers are 1½ in. wide, bright yellow with orange eye. Survives with no supplemental moisture but needs regular water to bloom satisfactorily.

Z. haageana. ORANGE ZINNIA. Annual. From southeastern U.S., Mexico. To 2 ft. tall, 1 ft. wide.

Narrow, 3-in. leaves. Persian Carpet (1 ft. tall) and Old Mexico (16 in. tall) have double blossoms in yellow, orange, and mahogany-red, with all three colors usually mixed in the same flower. Long summer bloom season.

Z. marylandica. Annual. These mildew-resistant selections originated with a cross between Z. angustifolia and Z. elegans. Plants grow 1–1½ ft. high and wide, with 2½-to 3½-in. flower heads. Pinwheel series has large single flowers in red, orange, and yellow. Profusion series includes single cherry, orange, and white flowers. Large-flowered Zahara series includes an ever-expanding range of colors; 'Zahara Starlight Rose' is a favorite, with double white flowers centrally marked in deep rose.

Z. peruviana. PERUVIAN ZINNIA. Annual. Native from southern U.S. to Argentina. Grows to 3 ft. tall and as wide; leaves to 3 in. long, 1¼ in. wide. In summer, bears profuse, 1½-in. flowers in brick-red or soft gold. Blossoms dry well for arrangements, either in a vase or on the plant. Also called Bonita zinnia or Z. pauciflora.

This front yard in Arlington, Virginia, feels like an intimate room.
Design: Tom Mannion

A PRACTICAL GUIDE TO GARDENING

PREPARE GOOD SOIL

Healthy garden soil supports plant roots and gives them access to nutrients, water, and air. It's fast draining yet moisture retentive, neither too dense nor too loose. Most roots grow in its upper layer (topsoil), which is especially biologically active—home to earthworms, microbes, and other beneficial organisms.

In the topsoil, earthworms improve drainage and aeration as they tunnel, while their castings add nutrients. And organic matter such as ground bark and vegetable matter decomposes, creating a soft, dark substance called humus. Below the topsoil is the subsoil. Although it contains plant nutrients, it's not as hospitable to roots as the topsoil. Improving your topsoil can have the most beneficial effect on plant health. To achieve healthy top soil, treat your planting beds with organic amendments, or grow cover crops to add organic material to the soil and loosen it. Organic gardeners prefer natural fertilizers (page 659), which provide a more sustained release of nutrients and encourage beneficial soil-dwelling organisms.

CHECK SOIL TEXTURE

All soils contain mineral particles formed by the natural breakdown of rock (as well as varying amounts of organic matter, air, and water). The size and shape of these particles determine the soil's texture, whether clay, sandy, or loam.

What To Do
• Thoroughly wet a patch of soil; let it dry out for a day.
• Pick up a handful of soil, and squeeze it firmly in your fist.
  • It is predominantly clay if it forms a tight ball and feels slippery.
  • It's sandy if it feels gritty, doesn't hold its shape, and crumbles when you open your hand.
  • It's loam if it is slightly crumbly but still holds a loose ball.
• Amend the soil as needed (see page 655).

CHECK SOIL DRAINAGE

Poor drainage causes water to remain in the pore spaces, so air—necessary to roots and beneficial soil-dwelling organisms—is unable to enter the soil. Soil texture and a low-lying location can contribute to poor drainage, as can running heavy machinery over the soil and walking on planting areas. The best way to improve soil drainage is to work in large amounts of organic matter. You can also regrade the area so that excess water drains off. Or create raised beds above the problem soil and fill them with good soil.

CHECK SOIL pH

Soil pH is a measure of how soil ranges from acid through neutral to alkaline. A pH of 5 to 7.2 is ideal for most plants. Soil with a pH of 7 is neutral—neither acid nor alkaline. A pH below 7 indicates acidity, while one above 7 indicates alkalinity. If the

1. Sandy (light) soils. Their big particles have large pore spaces between them that allow water and nutrients to drain away freely. Plants growing in sandy soil need water and feeding more often.
2. Loam. It contains mineral particles of various sizes, organic matter, and enough air for healthy root growth. It drains well but doesn't dry out—or lose nutrients—too fast.
3. Clay (heavy) soils. Their tiny particles pack together, helping them to hold the greatest volume of nutrients in soluble form. But they're sticky when wet, hard when dry, and slow to drain.

pH is extreme in either direction, key nutrients are chemically "tied up" in the soil and not available to plant roots.

- **ACID SOIL.** Acid soil typically occurs throughout the Southeast and East Texas—regions with heavy rainfall and soils high in organic matter, although limestone deposits form some pockets of alkaline soil. Most plants thrive in mildly acid soil, but highly acid soils can be inhospitable.
- **ALKALINE SOIL.** Found in Texas and Oklahoma where rainfall is relatively light and other spots as well, this soil is high in calcium carbonate. Many plants grow well in moderately alkaline soil. Others, including camellias and azaleas, do not.
- **SALTY SOILS.** Usually found near the seashore, salty soils also can result from the overuse of fertilizers and fresh manures. Salty soil pulls water from plant roots, making it difficult for plants to take up enough moisture or nutrients. Symptoms include scorched and yellowed leaves or browned and withered leaf margins.

What To Do

- **TEST THE SOIL.** If you're not sure whether your soil is acid or alkaline, or if you suspect your soil is deficient in some nutrients, check it using a simple test kit from the nursery. For a more precise reading, have the test done at a laboratory. (Check online under soil-test labs.)
- **ADJUST pH.** Acid soil: Raise pH by adding lime. Alkaline soil: Lower soil pH by adding sulfur. For salty soil, add organic matter and flood the soil periodically to wash away the salts.

CHOOSE A SOIL AMENDMENT

BUY THE BEST TYPE FOR YOUR SOIL (your nursery can help you). The amendments listed below are typically sold at nurseries in 1- or 2-cubic-ft. bags, and in bulk at building suppliers. You'll need a cubic yard of organic material to cover 100 square feet of planting bed to a depth of about 3 inches.

OTHER OPTIONS: Make your own compost (see page 657). Or grow cover crops; they're natural soil enrichers.

COMPOST. Made from grass clippings, chopped leaves, and other garden trimmings, it's easy to produce, it's good

ELEMENTS THAT WILL HELP SAVE RESOURCES

1. HEALTHY SOIL. Fast draining and filled with plenty of organic matter (which earthworms love), good soil is essential for growing flowers, edibles, and other kinds of plants.

2. POLLINATOR PLANTS. Flowers that attract bees, butterflies, and hummingbirds are a gardener's best friends (see page 713). As the pollinators feed on nectar, they move pollen from one plant to another, ensuring healthy crops of veggies, fruits, and more.

3. WATER SAVERS. The smartest gardens use water wisely. Keep water features small, and make sure they recirculate. Use drip-irrigation systems and soaker hoses to apply water to plant roots and reduce water loss due to runoff and evaporation.

4. MULCH. Material that covers soil surfaces and allows air and water through, mulch helps hold moisture in the soil and prevents most weed seedlings from catching hold. Take care not to pile it against plants' bases, as too much moisture can cause rot. Organic mulch is sold by the cubic yard. Determine how many square feet you need to cover (multiply the area's length by its width); then use the guidelines below. Apply 1–2 inches.

- **PINE STRAW.** Good around fruits, vegetables, and acid-loving trees and shrubs. Buy at your local garden center or rake from your yard.
- **GROUND PINE BARK.** An all-purpose mulch; mini size looks best.
- **DECOMPOSED GRANITE (DG).** Firms quickly and doesn't blow away. Best around ornamentals.
- **SHREDDED HARDWOOD BARK.** Slow to decompose; stays in place.

for your garden, and it lightens the load at landfills.

MANURE. Containing more plant nutrients than some other amendments, manures can also contain high concentrations of soluble salts, which can harm plant roots, so never use fresh manure. Use only manure that has been composted for a year and does not come from animals grazed on pastures treated with herbicides, as these chemicals pass through the animals unaltered and can kill your plants. Composted cow manure contains a good balance of nutrients, is widely available in bags at your local garden center, and does not smell bad.

WOOD PRODUCTS. Ground bark is useful in clay soils; it helps separate fine clay particles. But it can take nitrogen from the soil as it decomposes (add nitrogen along with it for best plant growth). Some wood products, such as soil conditioner, can be purchased already fortified with nitrogen; check the labels to be sure. Never use fresh wood chips.

SPHAGNUM PEAT MOSS. It helps acidify the soil, but there are concerns over the damage that may result from the overmining of some peat bogs. A coir fiber by-product of the coconut fiber industry is similar in texture; it's sold in bales, bricks, and discs that expand when soaked in water to make 5 to 10 quarts of fluffy material. Coir fiber won't help acidify the soil the way peat does.

AMEND THE SOIL

DAMPEN the soil thoroughly, and allow it to dry for a few days before you dig. Don't try to work soil that's too wet or too dry.

DIG to a depth of about 10 in. Break up dirt clods and remove any stones or debris as you go. In small areas, use a spading fork; for larger beds, try a rotary tiller.

ADD fertilizer now as well. Spread it over the soil, using the amount indicated on the label. Then work it into the topsoil where it will have the greatest benefit.

MIX with a spading fork or tiller, incorporating the amendments evenly into the soil.

LEVEL the bed with a rake, breaking up any remaining clods of earth.

WATER well; let the improved soil settle for at least a few days before planting.

Improving your soil has great benefits for your plants.

GATHER THE RIGHT TOOLS

These five are the most useful for working the soil.

ROUND-POINT SHOVEL Loosens soil, transfers soil to a pile or wheelbarrow, and digs planting holes.

GARDEN SPADE Prepares soil for planting and digs narrow, straight-sided trenches.

SPADING FORK Great for loosening and turning soil, working with manure, and turning compost.

SOIL RAKE Breaks up clods of dirt, levels the soil, tamps seedbeds to make them firm, and works amendments into the top few inches of a planting bed.

TROWEL Plants and cultivates. Also scoops fertilizers and amendments from bags.

HOW TO MAKE COMPOST

Composting is a natural process that converts raw organic materials into a valuable soil conditioner. In addition to being good for your garden, composting lightens the load at the landfill, as you recycle garden and kitchen debris at home rather than consign it to the dump.

A pile of leaves, branches, and other garden trimmings will eventually decompose in a process called slow, or cold, composting. With hot composting—which occurs when you create optimum conditions for the organisms responsible for decay by giving them the right mixture of air, water, and carbon- and nitrogen-rich nutrients—the pile heats up quickly and delivers finished compost in just a few months.

You can make compost in a freestanding pile or use an enclosure, such as those shown below. Regardless of the methods, the fundamentals of composting are the same.

GATHER AND PREPARE INGREDIENTS. You'll need approximately twice as much (by volume) brown matter as green matter. Brown matter (dry leaves, hay, sawdust, wood chips, woody prunings) is high in carbon.

Green matter (grass clippings, fruit and vegetable scraps, coffee grounds) is high in nitrogen. Avoid badly diseased or insect-infested plants, meat, bones, weeds with seeds, and perennial weeds that might survive composting. Shred or chop large, rough materials into smaller pieces to speed the composting process.

BUILD THE PILE. Put down a 4- to 8-in. layer of brown material, then add a layer of green material, about 2–4 in. deep (layers of grass clippings should be only 2 in. deep). Add another layer of brown material, and sprinkle the pile with water. Mix these first three layers with a spading fork. Continue adding layers, watering, and mixing.

TURN THE PILE. In just a few days, the pile should heat up dramatically. In time, it will decompose on its own, but hurry things along by turning the pile to introduce more oxygen. Using a spading fork or pitchfork, restack the pile, redistributing it so that the materials originally on the outside are moved to the pile's center, where they'll be exposed to higher heat. If necessary, add water; the pile should be as moist as a wrung-out sponge.

Recycle plant clippings and debris by composting them and adding them to soil.

Adding an occasional shovelful of aged manure or finished compost gives the pile a dose of extra nutrients and microbes and speeds decomposition. Turn the pile weekly, if possible, until it is no longer generating internal heat and most of the materials have decomposed.

COMPOSTERS

WIRE CYLINDER. Bend a length of wire into a cylinder about 3 or 4 ft. tall and 4 ft. in diameter. Secure the wire to a framework or support it with stakes. To turn the pile, lift the cylinder and move it to one side, then fork the materials back into it.

THREE-BIN SYSTEMS. The left bin holds new green and brown material; the center one contains partly decomposed material; the right bin holds nearly finished or finished compost. Turn the material in each bin weekly, moving decomposed material to the right.

MANUFACTURED COMPOSTERS. They include this static compost bin in which compost sits without turning. (Occasional aerating with a spading fork is helpful.) Add new materials at the top, and remove the finished compost through a door at the base.

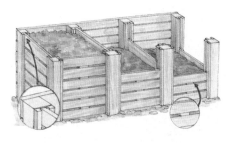

FERTILIZE FLAWLESSLY

Actively growing plants need a steady supply of nutrients. Many nutrients are present in soil, water, and air, but gardeners need to provide others. Most likely to need feeding are vegetables, flowers, lawns, container plants, and fruit trees. Here's how to pick the right product.

ABOVE: The quality of your soil and what you're growing determine how often you need to fertilize.

RIGHT: Timed-release fertilizer feeds plants over a longer period of time as the outside coating wears away.

WHAT'S IN THE BAG

MACRONUTRIENTS. These elements—nitrogen, potassium, and phosphorus—are needed by plants in large amounts.

NITROGEN (N) helps synthesize proteins, chlorophyll, and enzymes. Nitrogen is the nutrient most likely to be inadequate in garden soils. Too much can make plants too leafy (often at the expense of flowers and fruit) and prone to attack by sucking insects. Applied too late, it promotes new growth that's vulnerable to frost damage.

PHOSPHORUS (P) promotes flowering and fruiting, strong root growth, and the transfer of energy within the plant. Phosphorus deficiency is rare, and an overdose can interfere with a plant's absorption of other essential elements.

POTASSIUM (K) helps regulate the synthesis of proteins and starches that make sturdy plants. It also helps increase resistance to diseases, heat, and cold. Too much potassium interferes with the absorption of calcium and magnesium, making plants grow poorly.

SECONDARY NUTRIENTS. Plants need these in about the same amounts as they do the macronutrients. But they're less likely to be deficient in most soils. Calcium (Ca) plays a fundamental role in cell formation and growth, and most roots require some calcium right at the growing tips. Magnesium (Mg) forms the core of the chlorophyll molecules in the cells of green leaves. Sulfur (S) acts with nitrogen in the manufacture of protoplasm for plant cells.

MICRONUTRIENTS. Also known as trace elements, micronutrients are required in very small quantities (excess amounts can be toxic). Among them are zinc (Zn) and manganese (Mn)—both thought to function as catalysts for utilizing other nutrients—and iron (Fe), essential for chlorophyll formation. Some plants, particularly vegetables such as Swiss chard, need boron (B), an element often lacking in alkaline soils.

TYPES OF FERTILIZER

SIMPLE VS. COMPLETE. Complete fertilizers contain nitrogen (N), phosphorus (P), and potassium (K). Some may also include secondary and/or micronutrients. Simple fertilizers supply just one macronutrient. Most familiar are the nitrogen-only types—ammonium sulfate (21-0-0)—and phosphorus-only superphosphate (0-20-0). Incomplete fertilizers fall between simple and complete; an example is 0-10-10, providing phosphorus and potassium but no nitrogen.

GENERAL PURPOSE. Fertilizers labeled "general purpose" or "all purpose" contain equal or nearly equal amounts of the macronutrients N, P, and K (a 10-10-10 formula, for example). They are intended to meet most plants' needs throughout the growing season.

SPECIAL PURPOSE. These formulas are designed to meet specific needs. High-nitrogen blends (such as 29-3-4), for instance, help keep lawns green and growing quickly. Higher-phosphorus mixes (6-10-4, for example) are intended to promote flowering and fruiting. Other packaged fertilizers are formulated for particular types of plants. Those designed for acid lovers, such as camellias and rhododendrons, are especially useful, as are fertilizers for citrus.

INORGANIC (CHEMICAL) fertilizers are made from synthetic substances with precisely formulated amounts of specific nutrients, primarily nitrogen, phosphorus, and potassium. These can be formulated for fast or slow release.

ORGANIC (NATURAL) fertilizers are made from the remains or by-products of living or once-living organisms. Manure, fish emulsion, bonemeal, cottonseed meal, and kelp meal are all examples of organic fertilizers that can be used alone or in various combinations to produce complete fertilizers. Most release their nutrients more slowly than inorganics (but some, like blood meal, release quickly). Organics also usually have slightly lower proportions of nutrients than most inorganic fertilizers. They make up for this by adding organic matter to the soil.

SIGNS OF NUTRIENT DEFICIENCIES

Your local nursery can often recommend a foliar spray to solve the immediate problem and a fertilizer supplement for long-term care.

COMMON SYMPTOMS	DEFICIENCY
Leaves are yellow and smaller than normal. On some plants they may turn red or purple. Overall growth is stunted or dwarfed.	Nitrogen
Small leaves, with edges scorched, purplish, or blue-green in color. May fall early. Overall growth is reduced and weakened. Flower and fruit production diminished. Rare.	Phosphorus
Leaf tips and edges become yellow and scorched looking, with brownish purple spotting underneath.	Potassium
Leaves turn dark from the base outward and die. Tomatoes and related vegetables may rot on the blossom end.	Calcium
Leaves yellow between the veins, which remain green or slightly yellow. Growth is weak. Usually occurs in alkaline soils.	Iron
Leaf centers turn reddish or yellow. Dead spots appear between veins. Usually occurs in very acid soils.	Magnesium
Upper leaves yellow in center, between veins, with no sign of red. New fronds on palms curl and yellow. Usually occurs in alkaline soils.	Manganese
Veins grow lighter in color than the leaf tissue in between. Usually occurs in soils with low organic matter.	Sulfur

---

BY THE NUMBERS

Every fertilizer label states the percentage by weight of the three macronutrients used in mineral form, in alphabetical order: nitrogen (N), phosphorus (P), and potassium (K). So a fertilizer labeled 10-8-6 contains 10 percent nitrogen, 8 percent phosphorus, and 6 percent potassium. The label also tells you the source of each nutrient and lists any micronutrients present.

NITROGEN may be included in a fertilizer in nitrate form. If so, it will be water soluble and fast acting, especially in cool soils, but is easily leached (requiring frequent replenishment) and can pollute surface and groundwater if used to excess. Nitrogen in the form of ammonium is from organic sources (such as blood meal) and IBDU (isobutylidene diurea, a synthetic organic fertilizer). These are released more slowly and last longer in the soil.

PHOSPHORUS is expressed on product labels as phosphate, P_2O_5 and listed as "available phosphoric acid."

POTASSIUM is expressed as potash, K_2O, and may be described in various ways, including "water-soluble potash."

Phosphorus and potassium do not move readily through the soil in solution and must be applied near plant roots to do the most good.

HOW TO APPLY

Spread dry fertilizers (powders, granules, or pellets) on the ground or dig them into the soil. Controlled-release types may be beadlike granules, spikes, or tablets. Dig granules into soil at planting time or scratch them into the soil surface. Use a mallet to pound spikes into the ground; dig holes for tablets.

Liquid fertilizers are sold as crystals, granules, or liquid concentrates that you mix with water and apply with a hose or spray bottle. The spray types, known as "foliar feeds," deliver instant supplies of specific nutrients. To avoid burning leaves, follow label directions.

NATURAL FERTILIZERS FROM COVER CROPS

Cover crops are legumes that improve garden soil. Legumes such as clover, ryegrass, and vetch also add nitrogen to the soil, thanks to their association with nitrogen-fixing bacteria that "fix" nitrogen in nodules in the legume's roots. Sow cover crops in fall in prepared soil, in rows 1 foot apart and about 3 inches deep. In spring, before flowers set seed, cut or mow the crop down and till it into the soil. Allow a couple of days, till again. Rake smooth, and plant. When the plants decompose, the nitrogen is released back into the soil.

WATER WISELY

Plants can't survive without water. But too much or too little causes problems that you might mistakenly blame on diseases or insects. More plants have been killed by improper watering than just about anything else. The basic problem is, of course, that no two plants have exactly the same water requirements. So you can't put your irrigation system on automatic pilot and give all your plants the optimum amount at once. Follow these tips for wise watering.

KNOW YOUR SOIL

Soil types differ in how much water they hold and how long they hold it. Sand holds little water and dries out quickly. Clay holds lots of water and dries out slowly. Loam reacts somewhere in between. If necessary, add organic matter to new planting areas to improve soil texture and help hold moisture better.

PLANT IN ZONES

There's no magic rule of watering that covers all plants. Our advice is to learn as much as you can about the water needs of individual plants (see plant encyclopedia); then group together plants based on those needs. For example, put impatiens, cardinal flower (*Lobelia cardinalis*), astilbe, and other moisture-loving plants in one spot. Then plant ones that prefer dry soil, such as junipers, sedums, and yuccas elsewhere.

CHECK YOUR WATERING SYSTEM

If you have automatic sprinklers, don't think you can set them and forget about them. Keep a close eye out for leaks or malfunctioning heads. Adjust sprinklers to minimize overspray. After all, you don't want to water the street. Also set separate spray patterns for lawns and other plants. A heavily mulched planting bed will need much less water than your lawn.

Lawns and planting beds need different amounts of water, so plan accordingly.

TOOLS OF THE TRADE

Tools for applying water range from simple handheld sprayers to hose-end sprinklers to more complex underground rigid-pipe and drip systems. The equipment appropriate for your garden depends on how often you need to water, the size of your garden, and how much gear you want to buy.

HOSES. These come in lengths up to 100 feet and with standard diameters from ⅜ to 1 inch. A ⅝-inch size is best for all-around use. Keep in mind that as hose length increases, water pressure decreases, so the longer the hose, the larger diameter you should consider.

PORTABLE HOSE-END SPRINKLERS. These include stationary models that resemble salt shakers or rings; oscillating, rotating, and impulse sprinklers; and "walking" types that slowly roll through the area to be irrigated. When selecting a sprinkler, look for one with a coverage pattern that most closely matches the area to be irrigated (the shape and size of the space the sprinkler covers should be listed on the package).

SOAKER HOSES. These long tubes made of perforated or porous plastic or rubber, with hose fittings at one or both ends, deliver water slowly. When you attach a soaker to a regular hose and turn on the system, water seeps or sprinkles from the soaker along its entire length. Water wide beds by snaking soakers back and forth around the plants, or trees and shrubs by coiling the soaker hose over the outermost edges of the root zone. You'll probably need to leave soakers on longer than you would sprinklers. To determine timing, check water penetration with a trowel or screwdriver.

IN-GROUND SPRINKLER SYSTEMS. These offer some advantages over hose-end options. They free you from moving hoses and can operate even if you're away from home. Newer sprinklers produce less runoff and overspray and distribute water more evenly.

It's a good idea to hire a professional to plan and install the system, which entails much physical labor. For such a system to work properly, it must be well designed, with as few sprinklers as possible to achieve head-to-head coverage, and sprinkler heads positioned to prevent overspray onto paved areas.

DRIP IRRIGATION. Drip or low-volume irrigation delivers water at low pressure and volume (in gallons per hour) to specific areas or individual plants. Water penetration is slow, its depth regulated by the length of time the system is on. The tubing with inline emitters, shown at bottom, encircles a citrus. U-stakes hold the line in place. Components of a drip system include:

- DRIP EMITTERS. These release water directly to the soil and waste virtually no water.
- MINI-SPRINKLERS. Available in many different styles, which vary primarily in output (gallons per hour) or in the watering pattern. Mini-sprayers and mini-sprinklers, which spray water into the air, deliver less water than ordinary sprinklers do.
- CONTROLLERS. Technology can help you to water more efficiently. Rain sensors override automatic controllers after significant rainfall. Newer controllers are easy to adjust seasonally, and some can be connected to moisture sensors or weather stations. They can reduce waste and do a better job of watering than most gardeners can.

Oscillating Sprinkler

Soaker Hoses

In-ground Sprinklers

Drip Irrigation

Heavily mulched beds conserve moisture. A gravel path soaks up rain instead of letting it run off. Limiting the size of the lawn and letting the grass grow a little taller also cuts down on irrigation needs.

DIFFERENT PLANTS, DIFFERENT NEEDS

Use these guidelines to determine the best ways to water your plants.

LAWN
- Hose-end sprinklers with built-in timers can work well for a small lawn.
- In-ground sprinklers connected to a controller (some newer ones connect to weather stations) will water more precisely.

ANNUALS AND PERENNIALS
- Overhead watering may cause flowers to droop or spotting on petals; certain species are more subject to disease if watered from above.
- In-ground sprinklers with pop-up risers work in extensive flower beds. Risers should be tall enough that foliage doesn't block spray.
- Choose drip-emitter lines for beds with closely spaced plants. Use individual emitters for widely spaced plants.

GROUND COVERS
- Use in-ground sprinklers; select stationary heads for plantings more than a foot tall and low-precipitation-rate heads for ground covers (including lawns) on a slope.
- Drip emitters are suitable for shrubby ground covers.

- Drip mini-sprayers work well for mass plantings of small plants.

ROSES
- Soaker hoses are easy to use on level ground.
- Use in-ground sprinklers with flat-head sprayers run early in the day to keep leaves dry to prevent disease.
- Drip irrigation with emitter line works well with closely spaced bushes. Or use individual emitters for each bush.

TREES AND SHRUBS
- Use basins around trunks to direct water to the roots and avoid runoff.
- Soaker hoses can handle deep-watering of established trees.
- Low-volume systems with emitters or microsprinklers are most efficient, especially on sloping ground.

VEGETABLES
- Hand-water in basins and furrows.
- Use soaker hoses on flat ground.
- Install a low-volume system with emitter line for closely spaced plants, individual emitters for widely spaced vegetables.

HARVEST THE RAIN

Like pennies from heaven, rainwater is a gift. Don't let it run off your roof and down the storm drain. Save it for a non-rainy day.

INSTALL A RAIN BARREL. All the water that hits your roof and is channeled through the downspouts can be saved to water your plants. Simply cut your downspout to the height of your barrel and divert water into it. For ease of watering, elevate your rain barrel so when the hose is connected to the bottom, gravity helps the water flow from the spout. Place containers nearby to keep them within reach, or plant around your barrel. To keep mosquitos at bay, choose a barrel that is sealed around the downspout. For more water, install barrels at each downspout, connect several rain barrels together, or go for a larger cistern.

HANG A RAIN CHAIN. This simple, time-honored gardening trick guides rain down from the roof into a large pot or planting bed. It can be as basic as a heavy gauge metal chain you pick up from the hardware store or as elaborate as hand-forged piece of art.

PLANT A RAIN GARDEN. A rain garden is a depression in the landscape where runoff can collect. It's filled with plants, so don't picture a giant mud hole. Water that collects there will slowly soak back into the landscape over a 24- to 36-hour period. Check with your local nursery for plants best suited for your area that don't mind being inundated with water for brief periods.

GO PERMEABLE. Paths and patios that are paved with gravel, spaced flagstones, or porous concrete are the best choices for water-conserving gardens. They allow rainwater to pass through them and into the soil, watering plants and preventing runoff that can clog storm drains and pollute nearby lakes, streams, and coastal areas.

HOW TO WATER JUST RIGHT

Like toddlers, plants will let you know when they're unhappy. Here are some common ways plants tell you they're not getting the right amount of water.

TOO LITTLE
- Wilting throughout the day
- Leaf scorch on the edges of leaves
- Leaves that curl or drop prematurely
- Leaves that lose their bright green color
- Flowers that drop prematurely
- Fruit that shrivels and drops before maturing
- A lawn that shows footprints 10 minutes after you've walked across it

TOO MUCH
- Wilting in bright sunlight
- Yellowing leaves
- Leaves that drop while green
- Sudden collapse of plant
- Rotting roots
- Malodorous soil
- Edema (blisters that form on leaves)

LEFT: A rain barrel and rain chain divert rainwater from downspouts.

ABOVE: Bluestone pavers rimmed by dark green mondo grass form a striking pattern and let water permeate the ground.

PLANTING 101

There are several ways to get your garden started. Seeds are an economical choice but require a bit of patience. Transplants are ready to go in the ground as soon as you get home from the nursery. Trees and shrubs can be purchased in nursery pots, as bare-root plants, or balled and burlapped. No matter which way you go, follow our planting techniques to get your garden growing.

Seeds: Make furrows, following package instructions for depth. Sow seeds evenly, spacing as package directs. Cover with soil, and water gently.

Transplants: Water plant, then gently remove transplant from cell pack or plastic container. For peat pots, remove the top edge of pot before planting. See plant tag for proper spacing.

SEED

WORKS FOR: Annual flowers, herbs, and vegetables; some perennials.
LOOK FOR: Fresh seeds. The packets should be dated for the current year.

How to Sow

Seeds of many plants are easy to sow directly in the ground. You just scatter small ones over prepared soil, or plant larger ones atop low soil mounds or in furrows as shown in photo at left.

Others, especially for warm-season annual vegetables, get off to a better start when sown in containers and transplanted to garden beds later in the season. The information given on the seed packet will help you decide when to plant.

Sow most annual flowers and vegetables four to eight weeks before it's time to transplant them outdoors.

To start seed indoors:
STEP 1: Fill small pots or cell packs to just below the rim with light, porous seed-starting mix. Moisten the mix; let drain.

STEP 2: Sow seeds following guidelines on seed packet, and cover seeds with the recommended amount of mix. Moisten lightly.

STEP 3: When seeds germinate, move the container to a warm area with bright light. As they grow, thin out the weakest seedlings. About 10 days before planting outside, "harden off" the seedlings by setting them outdoors for a few hours each day to get them acclimated.

SEEDLINGS AND TRANSPLANTS

STEP 1: Loosen Roots. With your fingers or a pencil, lightly separate the roots so they can grow out into the soil. If there is a pad of coiled roots at the bottom of the rootball, pull it off.

STEP 2: Plant. Place each plant in its hole so the top of the rootball is even with the soil surface. Firm the soil around plant roots. If transplants come in a peat pot, remove the top edges of the pot before planting.

STEP 3: Water. Water each plant with a gentle flow that won't disturb soil or roots.

NURSERY CONTAINERS

WORKS FOR: Most shrubs and trees; perennials, ground covers, some annuals.

LOOK FOR: Healthy foliage and strong shoots. Avoid leggy or root-bound plants (with roots protruding above the container's soil level or growing through the drainage holes).

Water the plant before removing it from its container. Tap sharply on the bottom and sides to loosen the rootball. The plant should slide out easily. With fiber or pulp pots, tear the pot away from the rootball, taking care not to damage the roots.

How to Plant

STEP 1: Dig a hole about three times as wide and 1 inch less than the height of the container. Remove the plant from the container; spread the roots out over the soil. The root ball should be 1 to 2 in. above the surrounding soil.

STEP 2: Backfill with the unamended soil you dug from the hole, adding the soil in stages and firming it around the roots with your hands as you work.

STEP 3: Make a berm of soil to form a watering basin. Irrigate gently. Spread a layer of mulch on top of the root ball, but take care not to mound it up against the trunk.

BARE ROOT

WORKS FOR: Perennial vegetables such as Jerusalem artichoke and asparagus; deciduous cane berries, strawberries, fruit trees, roses, and some ornamental trees.

LOOK FOR: Bare-root plants with strong stems and fresh-looking, well-formed roots. Avoid any with slimy roots or dry, withered ones. Bare-root plants are sold in late winter and early spring by retail nurseries and mail-order companies. They cost only 40 to 70 percent as much as the same selections purchased in containers later in the year. Plant them as soon as possible after purchase, after first soaking the roots in water overnight.

How to Plant

STEP 1: Dig a hole that is about the same depth as the plant's roots and twice as wide as it is deep. Make a firm cone of soil in the hole; spread the roots over the cone, positioning the plant at the same depth as (or slightly higher than) it was in the growing field. Use a shovel handle or yardstick to check the depth.

STEP 2: Hold the plant upright as you firm the soil around its roots. When the process is almost complete, add water. If the plant settles below the level of the soil, pump it up and down while the soil is saturated to raise it to the proper level.

STEP 3: Finish filling the hole with soil, then water again. Take care not to overwater while the plant is dormant. When the growing season begins, make a ridge of soil around the planting site to form a watering basin. Water when the top 2 in. of soil are dry.

BALLED AND BURLAPPED

WORKS FOR: Woody plants whose root systems won't survive bare-root transplanting, especially very large shade trees and evergreens.

LOOK FOR: Healthy foliage and an even branching structure. The covering should be intact and the roots unexposed; the rootball should feel firm and moist.

Balled-and-burlapped plants are dug from the field with a ball of soil around their roots; the ball is then wrapped in burlap and tied with twine. When moving the plant, support the bottom of the root ball. A broken root ball can kill the plant.

How to Plant

STEP 1: Measure the root ball from top to bottom. The planting hole should be a bit more shallow, so that the top of the rootball will be about 2 in. above the surrounding soil. Adjust the hole to the proper depth; then set in the hole.

STEP 2: Untie the covering. If it's burlap, it will eventually rot, so just spread it out to uncover about half the rootball. If it's synthetic material, remove it entirely. Fill the hole with soil to within 4 in. of the top. Water gently.

STEP 3: Continue to fill the hole, firming the soil as you go. Make a berm of soil to form a watering basin; then water the plant. Cover with mulch. As it becomes established, keep the plant moist but not soggy. Most trees do not need staking for the first year. Tall palms are an exception, as they have small root balls.

CONTAINERS 101

Growing plants in containers lets you enjoy a garden even when space is limited. Use containers to turn a tiny balcony or patio into a leafy haven, to experiment with new plant combinations, or to try plants that are borderline hardy in your area. Many plants grow better in containers than they do in the ground!

THE BASICS

CHOOSE THE CONTAINER. It should have at least one drainage hole to prevent root rot. Before planting, submerge terra-cotta pots in clean water and let them soak thoroughly. Sterilize used containers by scrubbing with a solution of 1 part household bleach to 9 parts hot water. Cover the drain hole with a coffee filter or a small piece of fine wire screen to keep soil from washing out.

CHOOSE THE POTTING MIX. The potting mix should contain organic materials such as ground bark or compost, plus mineral matter like perlite, pumice, or sand. Fertilizers and wetting agents may also be included.

PLANT. Fill pot partway with potting soil; press to firm, then set plants on top. For best effect, plant singly or in groups of three or five. Finish adding potting soil, firming as you go; water.

WATER. Container plants need water more often than those grown in the ground. In hot or windy weather, some may need watering several times a day. Test the mix with your finger: if it is dry beneath the surface, it's time to water (unless you're growing succulents and cacti). To moisten the entire soil mass and prevent any potentially harmful salts from accumulating in the mix, apply water over the entire soil surface until it flows from the pot's drainage holes.

FERTILIZE. For most plants, apply a liquid fertilizer every two weeks during the growing season, or mix controlled-release-type granules into the soil. Succulents and grasses need feeding less often.

RECIPE FOR SUCCESS

You can't go wrong filling your containers with one type of plant, but to take your pots to the next level, you need three components: a thriller, a filler, and a spiller.

THE THRILLER: Consider this the focal point. Usually the tallest element in your pot, it provides vertical interest and drama. You can choose any tall plant for your thriller. Ornamental grasses work well, or consider a small evergreen shrub or tree, which will anchor your container throughout the year, allowing you to swap out only your fillers and spillers throughout the season. *Thriller below*–purple fountain grass.

THE FILLER: Here's your chance to use your favorite colors and textures. Try annuals and foliage plants. Remember, foliage can carry the show when flowers fade. *Filler below*–'Bandana Red' lantana.

THE SPILLER: Bring on the romance with trailing plants that drape nicely over the edges and soften the look of the container. *Spiller below*–'Margarita' sweet potato vine.

thriller

filler

spiller

EASY DOES IT

Perfect for the beginning gardener, forgiving succulents survive both drought and heat and practically take care of themselves. Water thoroughly once a week, and let soil dry out between waterings. Try stacking two pots together to get the height you need with plants that are low growing. Choose glazed pots, because they retain water longer, meaning less work for you.

1. 'FLAPJACKS' KALANCHOE
2. 'COPPERTONE' SEDUM
3. 'PERLE VON NURNBERG' ECHEVERIA
4. 'BLUE' SENECIO
5. 'RED STEM' PORTULACARIA
6. 'ZORRO' ECHEVERIA
7. 'BLACK KNIGHT' ECHEVERIA
8. 'VIOLET QUEEN' ECHEVERIA

GROW A SALAD BOWL

The rich colors, textures, and flavors of homegrown lettuce beat anything you'll find at the grocery store. Look for transplants at the garden center or start your own from seed.

STEP 1: Choose a large, low bowl with drainage holes; this one is 12 inches in diameter. Fill it with a good-quality, soilless potting mix.
STEP 2: Use transplants for a quick and easy harvest. This bowl contains three (4-inch) transplants of mixed lettuces.
STEP 3: Keep plants evenly moist. Harvest the outer leaves to keep new lettuce coming back.

Collards in galvanized wash tub

TASTEFUL CHOICES

Containers aren't limited to flowers and foliage. Lots of vegetables do well in pots too. Plant collards, mustard, and lettuce in the spring and again in fall. Cherry tomatoes, eggplant, and peppers work well for summer harvest. Make sure your containers are generously sized for the plants you choose. Look for 18- to 24-in.-diameter pots to allow room for roots to spread. Use a trellis or other support for plants that are heavy with fruit. Keep in mind that containers can dry out quickly, so check them daily during the summer. If the top inch of soil has dried, water thoroughly.

PLANT YOUR WALLS

Transform any bare vertical spot into a lush living wall with this simple and smart planting system. The basic unit (available at kinsmangarden.com) consists of a frame measuring 14 inches tall and wide by 5 inches deep. It's lined with a coco-fiber mat with planting holes cut into the sides and front. Hang four together to form a large square like the one shown here. Plant as you would a strawberry jar, starting at the bottom and adding soil and plants as you go. Gently water by hand from the top, allowing it to reach all the way to the bottom. Water when plants wilt or soil feels dry. Use a quality potting soil such as Fafard. Each unit comes with metal J-hooks for hanging. To prevent moisture damage, insert spacers (such as plastic bottle caps) at each bottom corner if hanging on wooden siding.

1. NERVE PLANT
2. IVY
3. SPIDER PLANT
4. PINK ARROWHEAD VINE
5. VARIEGATED DRACAENA
6. 'NEON' POTHOS
7. FERN

GARDEN UNDER GLASS

No time to dig in the dirt? Bring the outdoors in with a terrarium. It takes three easy steps.

STEP 1: Choose a glass container with an opening wide enough for your hand to fit through. Add an inch or two of finely washed gravel. Top with a thin layer of activated aquarium carbon. (You can find both at the pet store.) Next add moistened potting soil.

STEP 2: Add plants. Good choices include ferns, succulents, mosses, miniature moth orchids, African violets, and kalanchoes. Start with the smallest plants available. Be sure not to over-water, because your container will not have a drainage hole. Use a turkey baster to apply just the right amount.

STEP 3: Place in diffused light with a cork pad underneath to protect surfaces from condensation

1. MINIATURE MOTH ORCHID
2. SILVER RIBBON FERN
3. RIPPLE PEPEROMIA
4. TABLE FERN
5. MOSS

ADD SOME WOW WITH WINDOW BOXES

These miniature gardens give your home loads of charm with minimal upkeep. Treat them as you would any other container, and follow these tips for sure-fire success.

- **Don't place window boxes up against the house.** Leave at least ½ inch between the window box and the side of the house for water to drip through. This is especially important for houses with wood siding.
- **Make sure the filled window boxes won't be too heavy** for the support brackets that hold them to the house. You can significantly reduce weight by using fiberglass window boxes and filling them with potting mix, not soil.
- **Plant according to the season.** For cool weather, plant calibrachoa, lobelia, bacopa, twinspur, snapdragons, violas, nasturtiums, and flowering kale. For warm weather, switch to lantana, verbena, begonias, angelonia, impatiens, coleus, sweet potato vine, fan flower, narrowleaf zinnia, and Wave petunia.
- **Don't forget to water.** Plants in window boxes dry out faster than those planted in the ground. Fertilize every two weeks with a water-soluble fertilizer. Or incorporate a granular slow-release fertilizer into the potting mix before planting. Make sure the boxes have drainage holes.

This vivid coral wall demands a strong counterpoint. Blue is the opposite of orange on the color wheel, so Panola pansy, delphinium, and lobelia in shades of blue are complementary choices. White common geranium and 'Diamond Frost' euphorbia pick up the white of the window trim, while coral twinspur echoes the house.

Don't be afraid to pack a lot of plants into one large window box for maximum impact. This one contains six: 'Aaron' white caladium, 'Key Lime Pie' heuchera, 'White Nancy' spotted dead nettle, holly fern, ivy, and light pink periwinkle.

Follow the thriller, filler, spiller formula. Here Japanese iris is the thriller. White snapdragon, violet African daisy, red common geranium, and white petunia are fillers. Pink and red ivy geraniums, dark red calibrachoa, and purple verbena are spillers.

PRUNE LIKE A PRO

Pruning is important to maintain the health of your plants, direct growth, remove undesirable growth, increase the quality of flowers and fruit, and ensure safety. The best time to prune varies with the plant (see "Pruning Primer," opposite). However, dead wood should be removed right away.

Proper pruning keeps plants looking their best. In most cases, you should try to preserve the natural form of the plant, because this saves you work, and it looks better. The exception is if you're shaping plants for specific purposes such as creating espaliers or hedges. So before you pull out your clippers, keep these six basic reasons for pruning in mind.

- To remove unwanted growth, such as dead, broken, or wayward branches
- To stimulate new growth
- To rejuvenate an overgrown or neglected plant
- To train a plant into a specific shape
- To control size
- To remove seed heads and spent flowers.

MAKING THE CUT

Each time you make a pruning cut, you stop the growth in one direction and encourage it to begin in another, because growth continues in buds and branches left behind. Follow these techniques for best results.

THINNING. Plants that have become too densely branched should be thinned to allow air and sunlight to reach the inner branches, leaves, and stems. Most of the cuts you make when pruning should be thinning cuts. Such cuts direct growth, eliminate competing or old stems, reduce overall size, and open up a plant's structure.

MAKING SMALL CUTS. This is the simplest type of pruning. Using your thumb and forefinger or a pair of hand shears, nip off the tips of new growth, removing the terminal bud. This stops the shoot from growing longer and stimulates branching. Pinching is used primarily on annuals and perennials to make them more bushy and to encourage the production of more flowers.

SHORTENING. This technique stimulates the growth of lateral buds just below the cut. For maintenance pruning of most woody plants, shortening is less desirable than thinning. Continual shortening ruins the natural shape. It is useful when your goal is to induce vigorous growth beneath a cut, force branching at a particular point on a branch or stem to train young fruit trees, fill a hole in the tree's crown, increase bloom production in roses, or rejuvenate neglected shrubs.

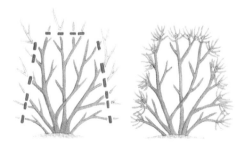

SHEARING. An indiscriminate form of pruning, shearing does not involve careful, precise cutting just above a growing point. Instead, you simply clip a plant's outer foliage to create an even surface as in hedges or topiaries.

PRUNING PRIMER

When you prune is very important. Prune flowering trees and shrubs at the wrong time and you'll cut off the flower buds. Then they won't bloom. So before you cut anything, know whether it blooms and when. Prune spring-flowering trees and shrubs just after they finish blooming. Prune summer bloomers in late winter, before they begin the current season's growth.

What about trees and shrubs that don't bloom? With a few exceptions (noted below), late winter is a good time. Prune deciduous trees when the leaves have dropped, so you can easily see what needs to be removed.

AZALEA (EVERGREEN):

BEST TIME TO PRUNE: Immediately after flowering stops in spring; definitely by mid-June.

COMMENTS: Use hand pruners, not hedge trimmers. Cut back to a leaf or another branch.

BEAUTYBERRY:

BEST TIME TO PRUNE: Winter or early spring.

COMMENTS: Cut back hard. Blooms and fruits on new growth.

BUTTERFLY BUSH:

BEST TIME TO PRUNE: Winter or early spring.

COMMENTS: Same care as for beautyberry.

BLACKBERRY:

BEST TIME TO PRUNE: Spring.

COMMENTS: Cut off at the ground all canes that fruited last year. They're dead. New fruiting canes will replace them.

BLUEBERRY:

BEST TIMES TO PRUNE: Winter or late spring after flowering.

COMMENTS: Remove dead branches. If fruit set is heavy, use hand pruners to remove some fruiting branches now and leave remainder well spaced. Remaining berries will be larger and sweeter.

BOXWOOD:

BEST TIME TO PRUNE: Spring and summer.

COMMENTS: Can shear them into formal hedges if you want. Otherwise, use hand pruners to open up the plants and remove some inner branches, so the plants aren't solid blobs. Improved air circulation reduces disease.

CHASTE TREE (VITEX):

BEST TIME TO PRUNE: Late winter and

Prune grape vines in winter.

again in summer after first bloom.

COMMENTS: Chaste tree produces lots of twigs and needs regular pruning to keep from looking like a mess. Clean out the interior growth in winter, leaving the main trunks looking like a well-trained crepe myrtle. If you prune off the faded flowers in summer, you'll usually get a second bloom.

COMMON CAMELLIA:

BEST TIME TO PRUNE: Late spring and early summer.

COMMENTS: To reduce size, use hand pruners to cut back branches to a leaf or bud.

CREPE MYRTLE:

BEST TIME TO PRUNE: Late winter and early spring.

COMMENTS: DO NOT CHOP IT DOWN INTO THICK, UGLY STUMPS! Simply remove suckers at the base, crossing or rubbing branches, and branches growing inward toward the center of the plant.

TOOLS OF THE TRADE

From clippers to loppers, choosing the right tool is the key to a job well done.

HEDGE SHEARS

Best for: Shearing coarse-leaved hedges, such as ligustrum, holly, cleyera, bougainvillea, or photinia

LIGHT HEDGE SHEARS

Best for: Trimming fine-leaved hedges, such as boxwood, lavender, rosemary, podocarpus, or loropetalum

PROFESSIONAL SCISSORS

Best for: Snipping herbs such as basil, thyme, and rosemary

HAND PRUNER

Best for: Cutting branches and stems throughout your garden; good all-purpose pruner

LONG STRAIGHT SNIP

Best for: Clipping flowers (from roses to zinnias) for arrangements

LOPPER

Best for: Pruning branches no larger than 1.5 inches in diameter

---

DOGWOOD:

BEST TIME TO PRUNE: Late spring after flowering.

COMMENTS: Hardly ever needs pruning.

ELAEAGNUS:

BEST TIME TO PRUNE: Any time.

COMMENTS: Can reach up to 15 ft. tall, shear top to control height, or shape into a hedge.

FIG:

BEST TIME TO PRUNE: Spring.

COMMENTS: Often damaged by cold winters. Wait until new growth starts in spring, then prune off all dead branches above it.

FLOWERING QUINCE:

BEST TIME TO PRUNE: Late spring after flowering.

COMMENTS: Watch out for thorns.

FORSYTHIA:

BEST TIME TO PRUNE: Late spring after flowering.

COMMENTS: If you have an old, overgrown plant, renew it by cutting to the ground one-third of the oldest, woodiest trunks. Do this for 3 straight years. New, vigorous growth will emerge rapidly.

FRUIT TREES:

BEST TIME TO PRUNE: Winter or late spring after flowering.

COMMENTS: Remove dead, rubbing, or crossing branches; also branches growing inward toward center of trees. Open up center of trees for better air and light penetration. Thinning fruiting branches results in bigger, juicier fruit on the remaining branches.

GARDENIA:

BEST TIME TO PRUNE: Summer after flowers turn yellow and drop.

COMMENTS: Some gardenias, such as 'Mystery' (an older selection), bloom on growth made the previous year. Pruning in fall will remove flower buds and greatly reduce flowering next year. Other types, including 'August Beauty,' 'Kimura Shikazaki,' and 'Miami Supreme,' bloom on both previous year's growth and new growth. This means that fall pruning will reduce the spring bloom, but new spring growth will produce flowers in summer.

GRAPE:

BEST TIME TO PRUNE: Winter.

COMMENTS: See illustrations, page 671.

HOLLY (EVERGREEN):

BEST TIME TO PRUNE: Any time except late summer.

COMMENTS: Prune in December, and use the berries in arrangements.

HYDRANGEA 'ANNABELLE':

BEST TIME TO PRUNE: Winter.

COMMENTS: Blooms on new growth. Severe pruning results in larger but fewer blooms.

HYDRANGEA FRENCH TYPES (BLUE OR PINK FLOWERS):

BEST TIME TO PRUNE: For once-blooming types such as 'Nikko Blue,' prune in summer after blooms fade. Finish by mid-July. For rebloomers such as 'Endless Summer,' prune in winter, spring, or summer.

COMMENTS: Prune as little as possible, primarily removing dead and spindly growth.

HYDRANGEA 'LIMELIGHT':

BEST TIME TO PRUNE: Winter or early spring.

COMMENTS: Treat same as 'Annabelle.' Prune 'Peegee' and 'Tardiva' this way too.

HYDRANGEA, OAKLEAF:

BEST TIME TO PRUNE: Summer after flowers turn rose.

COMMENTS: Seldom needs pruning.

INDIAN HAWTHORN:

BEST TIME TO PRUNE: Late spring or summer after flowering.

COMMENTS: Doesn't need much pruning. Prune or pinch new growth to control it.

JUNIPER:

BEST TIME TO PRUNE: Any time.

COMMENTS: Cut back to a wispy little shoot of foliage that parallels the original branch.

'KNOCKOUT' ROSE:

BEST TIME TO PRUNE: Winter, spring, summer.

COMMENTS: 'Knockout' gets 4 ft. tall and wide over time, so cut it back as far as you want in winter or early spring, but don't cut below the graft union (notch on the trunk where the top meets the rootstock). Trim off old flowers throughout the summer to keep the shrub neat and bring on more blooms.

LEYLAND CYPRESS:

BEST TIME TO PRUNE: Winter, spring, summer.

COMMENTS: Will get gigantic if you let it go. To control height, use pole pruners to prune out tops, cutting back to the next branch lower down.

LILAC:

BEST TIME TO PRUNE: Late spring or early summer after flowering.

COMMENTS: Renew old bushes using same technique as for forsythia.

LOROPETALUM:

BEST TIME TO PRUNE: Late spring after flowering.

COMMENTS: You can shear this shrub into formal hedge; let if form its natural, mounding shape; or remove lower branches to make a single-trunked small tree.

MAGNOLIA, SAUCER:

BEST TIME TO PRUNE: Late spring after flowering.

COMMENTS: Needs very little pruning.

MAGNOLIA, SOUTHERN:

BEST TIME TO PRUNE: Summer or winter.

COMMENTS: Shorten branches by using hand pruners or loppers to cut them back to another branch. Cut foliage for Christmas decorations.

MOCKORANGE:

BEST TIME TO PRUNE: Late spring after flowering.

COMMENTS: Renew old bushes using same technique as for forsythia.

NANDINA:

BEST TIME TO PRUNE: Spring or summer.

COMMENTS: Renew old bushes using same technique as for forsythia.

OLEANDER:

BEST TIME TO PRUNE: Summer after flowering.

COMMENTS: Cut back last year's

branches by half. Renew old bushes using same technique as for forsythia.

PHOTINIA (REDTIP):

BEST TIME TO PRUNE: See recommendations for elaeagnus.

PITTOSPORUM:

BEST TIME TO PRUNE: Just about any time.

COMMENTS: Needs little pruning.

POMEGRANATE:

BEST TIME TO PRUNE: Summer after flowering.

COMMENTS: Prune to produce well-spaced branches that don't cross or rub.

PRIVET:

BEST TIME TO PRUNE: See recommendations for elaeagnus.

PYRACANTHA:

BEST TIME TO PRUNE: Summer.

COMMENTS: Keep this baby pruned or it'll eat your house. Prune back to a crotch or another branch. Don't leave stubs—they die. Wear leather gloves to protect hands from thorns.

RHODODENDRON:

BEST TIME TO PRUNE: Late spring or early summer after flowering.

COMMENTS: Shorten branches by cutting back to another branch.

ROSEMARY:

BEST TIME TO PRUNE: Spring or summer.

COMMENTS: Shorten branches to control growth.

ROSE-OF-SHARON:

BEST TIME TO PRUNE: Winter or early spring.

COMMENTS: Remove dead, spindly, crossing, and rubbing branches.

SPIREA, SPRING-BLOOMING:

BEST TIME TO PRUNE: Late spring after blooming.

COMMENTS: Renew old shrubs using same technique as for forsythia.

SPIREA, SUMMER-BLOOMING:

BEST TIME TO PRUNE: Winter and early spring.

COMMENTS: Shorten branches to 4–5 buds.

VIBURNUM:

BEST TIME TO PRUNE: Late spring or summer.

COMMENTS: Remove spindly, crossing, or rubbing branches. Renew old bushes using same technique as for forsythia.

WISTERIA:

BEST TIME TO PRUNE: Late winter and summer.

COMMENTS: For best bloom, cut back spurlike side shoots that grow from main canes to 5–6 buds in late winter. Pinch out tips of runners throughout the summer to control growth. Remove basal suckers whenever they appear.

Oakleaf Hydrangea

Forsythia

'Lavender Lady' Lilac

Flowering Quince

A GUIDE TO GROWING
ANNUALS

The quickest way to bring seasonal color to the garden, annuals germinate, grow, flower, set seed, and die in less than a year. Use them to accent pots at your front door, bridge the gap between perennial bloom cycles, or to decorate a special place in your garden.

CHOOSE

When selecting flowers for your yard, look for nursery-grown plants that are relatively small, with healthy foliage and few flowers.

WATER

Annuals need to be watered thoroughly after planting. Thereafter, keep the soil moist but not soggy. Water young plants more often in warm weather.

FEED

Mixing a complete fertilizer into the soil before planting will generally supply annuals with nutrients sufficient for at least half the growing season. Supplement with a water-soluble bloom-booster fertilizer after bloom begins—about every two weeks throughout the growing season.

DEADHEAD

As their flowers fade, annuals focus their energy into ripening seeds. If you regularly deadhead a plant, it will usually bear more flowers in a continued effort to produce seed. It also keeps the garden tidy. To do the job, just pinch or cut off individual, spent flowers or shear the flower heads with pruning or hedge shears, being careful not to remove any more than one-third of the plant.

SEASONAL ALL-STARS

Annuals are either cool-season or warm-season growers. Some tender perennials, such as geraniums, are grown as annuals where winters are cold. And a few cold-hardy perennials, such as hollyhocks, are grown as annuals because older plants don't perform as well as young ones. The selection at the garden center will reflect the time of year you are planting.

COOL-SEASON ANNUALS These develop their roots and foliage in fall and early spring; they can withstand fairly heavy frosts. Plant in fall for winter and early-spring bloom. Or plant in late winter or very early spring for spring bloom. Cool-season annuals include calendula, foxglove, forget-me-not, larkspur, pansy, sweet William, Shirley poppy, stock, sweet peas, viola, snapdragon, and ornamental cabbage and kale.

WARM-SEASON ANNUALS These grow best during the warm months between late spring and fall, and cannot withstand low temperatures. Set them out after all danger of frost has passed but before summer heat sets in. Warm-season annuals include angelonia, begonia, coleus, lantana, calibrachoa, cosmos, globe amaranth, impatiens, lobelia, marigold, petunia, spider flower, sunflower, sweet alyssum, and zinnia.

ANNUALS THAT SEED THEMSELVES

Some annuals drop seeds as they mature. Then if the weather and soil in your garden are just right, new plants will reappear the next year. You may be fooled into thinking that they are perennials, but these annuals re-establish themselves from seed as nature intended. The offspring may be different heights and colors from the original, but such surprises are part of the fun of gardening.

Bachelor's button	Impatiens	Money plant
Bluebonnet	Indian paintbrush	Poppy
Calliopsis	Larkspur	Spider flower
Cosmos	Madagascar periwinkle	Sunflower
Crested cockscomb	Marigold	Sweet pea
Globe amaranth	Melampodium	Zinnia

TRIED-AND-TRUE ANNUALS FOR THE SOUTH

ANGELONIA
WHY WE LOVE IT: This warm-season annual resembles a snapdragon but can take the heat of summer, tolerates drought, and is resistant to deer. Choose from shades of pink, purple, blue, and white. See page 151 for growing information.
USES: Plant in the back of the border to add height. Add trailing types to window boxes. Some selections are also fragrant.

CLEOME
WHY WE LOVE IT: Easy to start from seed in the spring, Cleome, also known as spider flower, sports balls of blooms with spiderlike legs. Choose from lavender, pink, and white blooms.
USES: This annual grows up to 6 feet tall and readily reseeds, so plant it in the back of the border for blooms summer through fall. However, 'Senorita Rosalita' grows 2–4 ft. tall and doesn't seed. See page 244 for growing information.

'DRAGON WING' BEGONIA
WHY WE LOVE IT: These begonias are loaded with bright blooms that will give a splash of color to shady spots late spring through fall. See page 182 for growing information.

USES: Its crimson, pink, or white blooms make a striking thriller in containers and hanging baskets. Or plant them en masse for a bright border.

LANTANA
WHY WE LOVE IT: Great for beginning gardeners and people who don't have time to baby their plants, lantana is a fuss-free bloomer all summer long. Flowers come in just about every shade but blue. Butterfly magnet. See page 400 for growing information.
USES: Try it in hanging baskets, cascading over walls, or massing in large sweeps.

PETUNIA
WHY WE LOVE IT: Blooms blanket the garden from spring through frost. New hybrid petunias are better suited to the South's heat and humidity than the old-fashioned types. Try the Wave series for rambling spreaders (up to 4 ft. wide). Plant Supertunias for a more compact habit (up to 2 ft. wide). Neither needs deadheading. Surfinia series spreads up to 4 ft., are more tolerant of rain and heat, but benefit from deadheading. See page 492 for growing information.
USES: Petunias work great as ground covers or as spillers in hanging baskets

and window boxes. Pair them with coleus for a striking mix.

SUN COLEUS
WHY WE LOVE IT: Bold foliage comes in every color of the rainbow. While other annuals fade, coleus remains vibrant in the garden from spring through fall. See page 591 for growing information.
USES: Plant a solid sweep in a border or mix and match colors in containers.

VIOLA
WHY WE LOVE IT: Prolific bloomers from fall through early summer, violas don't need deadheading like pansies do. See page 641 for growing information.
USES: Plant them en masse in your flower border or plant them in containers for a bright, long-lasting display.

ZINNIA
WHY WE LOVE IT: It's one of the fastest and easiest flowers to grow from seed and provides a bounty of cut flowers from spring through frost. See page 651 for growing information.
USES: Plant them in a flower border or mix them in your vegetable garden to kick up the color and attract bees.

'Dragon Wing' begonia

Angelonia

Cleome

Coleus

A GUIDE TO GROWING
PERENNIALS

Year after year, you can rely on perennials to bring color, fragrance, and texture to your garden. Herbaceous types, such as hosta, die to the ground when each growing season ends, then reappear the next season. Other perennials, such as coral bells, go through winter as low tufts of leaves. Evergreen types persist almost unchanged throughout winter.

CHOOSE

Nurseries and garden centers sell perennials in containers that range from 4-in. to 1-gallon pots. Big plants give immediate impact but cost much more.

PLANT

DIG a hole as deep as and 1 to 2 inches wider than your plant's container. Then water the plant.
REMOVE the plant from its pot, and if the roots are matted, gently loosen them.
PLACE the plant in its hole—the top of the root ball should be even with the soil surface. Fill in around it with soil, and water thoroughly again.

Black-eyed Susans

WATER

Routine watering during growth and bloom will satisfy most perennials. (Some prefer drier soil; others demand lots of moisture. Consult Plant Encyclopedia for each.) Young plants need more frequent watering while getting established.

FEED

Give established perennials a complete fertilizer once annually in spring. Spreading organic matter such as composted manure around them helps too.

DIVIDE

In fall, dig and divide overgrown perennials to rejuvenate them and get more plants.
CUT into the soil 6–12 in. beyond the plant's perimeter with a shovel or spading fork; then dig under the roots to lift the clump out of the ground.
TEASE some soil from the root ball. For fiborous-rooted perennials, such as daylilies, hose off as much soil as possible. Note the natural dividing points between stems and root sections.
PULL or cut apart the clump using clippers or a sharp-bladed shovel. Divide clumps into good-size sections.
TRIM any damaged roots, stems, or leaves. Replant the divisions.

DEADHEAD

Clip spent flowers throughout the bloom season to keep plants tidy and blooming. Some perennials, such as *Echinacea*, have especially attractive seed heads; many gardeners prefer to leave their seed heads in place through winter to provide food for seed-eating birds. Cut back in fall or winter. Remove old, dead, and fallen foliage, flowers, and stems.

TRIED-AND-TRUE PERENNIALS FOR THE SOUTH

'AUTUMN JOY' SEDUM

WHY WE LOVE IT: Very heat and drought tolerant. In fall, blooms slowly turn from a rich pink to a coppery red as they dry on the stem. See page 581 for growing information.

USES: Place it in borders or to mark a focal point or path.

BLACK-EYED SUSAN

WHY WE LOVE IT: Easy to grow and carefree, black-eyed Susan can't be beat for mid- to late-summer blooms. See page 563 for growing information.

USES: Plant them where they can freely reseed and multiply.

BUTTERFLY WEED

WHY WE LOVE IT: Not only do you get to enjoy clusters of bright orange flowers, but as the name implies, butterflies will flock to your garden as well. See page 168 for growing information.

USES: Combine with other butterfly favorites near a window so you can enjoy the view inside and out. Or add to a meadow garden.

DAYLILY

WHY WE LOVE IT: Tough as nails, daylilies thrive in the heat of summer and offer a wide range of colors. See page 351 for growing information.

USES: Plant them in a mixed border, along the driveway, or in large sweeps.

DIANTHUS

WHY WE LOVE IT: Cheerful, fragrant blooms perfume the garden in spring and early summer. See page 279 for growing information.

USES: The evergreen foliage makes dianthus a pretty addition to borders and beds even when it's not in bloom.

GINGER LILY

WHY WE LOVE IT: In addition to its sweet honeysuckle scent, ginger lily sports handsome sword-shaped foliage. See page 344 for growing information.

USES: Plant them in pots to add tropical flair around a pool or patio. Or plant at the edge of a pond or stream, as they like wet soil.

HOSTA

WHY WE LOVE IT: Beautiful foliage in all shapes and sizes wakes up shady spots in the garden. Colors from blue to chartreuse to variegated. See page 359 for growing information.

USES: Plant them with small- or narrow-leafed plants for a pretty pairing. Use their wide leaves to hide the foliage of fading daffodils in your garden.

LENTEN ROSE

WHY WE LOVE IT: When it comes to beautiful blooms in the dead of winter, no other perennial can touch Lenten roses. See page 350 for growing information.

USES: Plant groupings under the shade of tall-growing trees or use them as a shady ground cover. Don't forget to snip a few to brighten a winter day indoors.

OLD-FASHIONED CHRYSANTHEMUM

WHY WE LOVE IT: These dependable bloomers steal the show in a fall border. See page 235 for growing information.

USES: Drop the nursery container in a decorative pot for color by the front door, or give them room to roam in a border.

PURPLE CONEFLOWER

WHY WE LOVE IT: These flowers thrive in the heat of summer and attract birds, butterflies, and bees. Despite its name, purple coneflower comes in a range of colors including, yellow, orange, pink, and red. See page 292 for growing information.

USES: Plant as accents or in wide swaths. Cut them for a charming bouquet or centerpiece.

SUMMER PHLOX

WHY WE LOVE IT: Tall stems hold clusters of fragrant flowers in a multitude of colors that put on a show from early summer until frost. See page 497 for growing information.

USES: Place them in the back of the border for months of show-stopping color.

TALL BEARDED IRIS

WHY WE LOVE IT: It's one of the choicest perennials for a cutting garden. Fragrant irises bloom in spring, but reblooming types will flower again in mid- to late summer. See page 377 for growing information.

USES: Mass in borders, so you'll have plenty for cutting and arranging indoors.

Dianthus

Purple Coneflower

Old-fashioned Mums

A GUIDE TO GROWING
BULBS

They may flower for only a few weeks each year, but multiplied by scores of blossoms over a lifetime, bulbs make the garden rich with flowers. Specialized roots or stem bases store nutrients and energy for the plants' growth, and they can send up new plants year after year (depending on type).

Some bulbs (daffodil, for example) thrive in most of the South; others have a more restricted range. Outside their preferred climate zones, grow bulbs in pots, or dig up and store them for winter. Bulbs graded "large" generally yield more flowers, but for mass planting, buy midsize specimens. Choose plump, firm bulbs that feel heavy; avoid those that are soft, squishy, or shriveled.

PREP

Work a complete bulb fertilizer into the entire bed or mix a tablespoon of fertilizer into the bottom of individual holes; add 2 inches of compost over that.

PLANT

Place the bulb in the hole. For depth and spacing for specific bulbs, check the entries in the encyclopedia.

WATER

Water bulbs while they're growing actively. After the foliage dies back, they need no watering.

GROOM

Don't cut back foliage until it yellows and withers, or bulbs may not bloom the next year.

TRIED-AND-TRUE BULBS FOR THE SOUTH

DAFFODIL
WHY WE LOVE IT: Daffodils come back year after year, and rodents won't eat them. See page 446 for growing information.
USES: These blooms aren't fussy. Plant a few in a pot, go for a bold swath in the border, or let them naturalize in a field.

SPIDER LILY
WHY WE LOVE IT: Easy to grow, spider lilies are the ultimate garden legacy, as they can last for generations. In late summer, tall spikes of flowers with long stamens that resemble spider legs appear seemingly overnight. See page 421 for growing information.
USES: Plant in beds or large naturalized areas, where they can pop up at will.

CRINUMS
WHY WE LOVE IT: A relative of amaryllis, this tough-as-nails bulb blooms from spring to fall, usually after a rain. When one flower fades, snap it off, and new buds will keep opening up. See page 263 for growing information.
USES: Plant them where you won't need to move them. Once established, bulbs can weigh 20 pounds or more!

TIGER LILY
WHY WE LOVE IT: An old favorite that's easy to grow, tiger lily sports orange flowers with black spots. See page 413 for growing information.
USES: They top out around 4 feet, so plant them in the back of the border.

SPANISH BLUEBELL
WHY WE LOVE IT: This easy-to-grow bulb spreads steadily into glorious sweeps of white, pink, or blue. See page 362 for growing information.
USES: Plant in a large sweep to maximize their impact.

GRAPE HYACINTH
WHY WE LOVE IT: Flower spikes resemble small clusters of grapes and give off a sweet scent. Grape hyacinths are the best, most dependable source of true, deep blue in the Southern bulb world. See page 443 for growing information.
USES: These bulbs are at home in formal beds and country gardens alike. They mix well with daffodils, and also work great in pots.

'Saint Keverne' *daffodil*

'Valerie Finnis' *grape hyacinth*

THE FIVE BULB TYPES

TRUE BULB

An underground stem base containing an embryonic plant surrounded by scales. A basal plate at the bottom of the bulb holds the scales together and produces roots. Most true bulbs have a protective papery outer skin. Lilies do not, so they are more susceptible to drying and damage; handle them with care. To divide, simply separate offsets from the mother bulb.

True bulbs include allium, amaryllis, hyacinth, spider lily, lily, daffodil, grape hyacinth, crinum, snowdrops, tulips, and snowflakes.

RHIZOME

A thickened stem growing partially or entirely below ground. Its roots grow directly from the underside. The primary growing point is at one end of the rhizome, and additional growing points form along the sides. To divide, cut into sections that have visible growing points.

Rhizomes include agapanthus, calla lily, canna, some iris, lily-of-the-valley, tuberose, society garlic, and oxalis.

TUBEROUS ROOTS

Unlike the other four bulb types, these are true roots, thickened to store nutrients. Fibrous roots for the uptake of water and nutrients develop from its sides and tip. Tuberous roots grow in a cluster, with the swollen portions radiating out from a central point. The growth buds are at the bases of old stems rather than on the roots themselves. To divide, cut the root cluster apart so each division contains both roots and part of a stem base with one or more growth buds.

Tuberous roots include alstroemeria, clivia, dahlia, daylily, liatris, and ginger lily.

TUBER

Swollen underground stem bases that lack a corm's distinct organization. There is no basal plate, so roots can grow from all sides. Instead of just one or a few growing points, a tuber has multiple growth points scattered over its surface. Some tubers, such as begonia, are perennials that increase in size each year. Others are annual. As

Planting daffodils

new tubers grow, the old ones disintegrate. To divide either kind of tuber, cut it into sections, making sure each has one or more growing points.

Tubers include anemone, caladium, elephant's ear, cyclamen, and tuberous begonia.

CORM

A swollen underground stem base composed of solid tissue rather than scales. Roots grow from a basal plate at the corm's bottom, and the growth point is at the top. Each corm lasts a year. As it shrinks away, a new corm and, in many species, small cormels form on top of it. To divide, separate healthy new corms and any cormels from the old corms (cormels may take as long as two to three years to reach flowering size).

Corms include crocosmia, crocus, freesia, gladiolus, and triteleia.

A GUIDE TO GROWING
LAWNS

Lawns have taken a lot of heat lately—and not just from the sun. Environmentalists argue that lawns need too much water, fertilizer, and pesticides. However, with good management practices and the right choice of grass, none of these problems need exist. For example, in the South's high-rainfall areas, a drought-tolerant grass such as Zoysia needs little watering. In low-rainfall areas, a large lawn may be a mistake. Before you decide whether to have a big lawn, small lawn, or none at all, let's discuss the benefits of lawns.

Zoysia grass interplanted between coquina stone in this Florida driveway reduces the heat and glare that a long expanse of concrete would produce in the hot sun.

BENEFITS OF LAWNS

1. AESTHETICS. A lush, green lawn is beautiful. In garden design, it supplies vital, "negative" space around which all other plantings are organized. Without some empty, negative space, the yard looks like a jungle. With it, your garden now has a frame or a stage.

2. COMFORT. Ever walked barefoot across a bluegrass lawn in summer? It felt good, didn't it? A picnic on the lawn is so much better than a picnic on the mulch. The comfort doesn't stop there. In summer, grass plants act as tiny natural air conditioners. As they transpire moisture, they cool the air. That's why suburbs with lawns are often 8 to 10 degrees cooler on a hot day than the concrete and asphalt cities they surround.

3. RECREATION. A nice lawn in the front or back yard provides the perfect place to toss a football, jump through a sprinkler, throw a party, or garden without getting muddy. Where would you prefer your kids play? The street? The sewage treatment plant? Your cactus, yucca, and agave collection? Or the lawn?

4. WATER QUALITY. Despite what you've probably been told, a properly maintained lawn does a great job of filtering nutrients such as nitrogen and phosphorus before they pollute streams, lakes, rivers, and groundwater. Lawns also control erosion. After a heavy rain, compare the color of the water running down the gutter from an empty lot to that coming from a healthy lawn, and you'll see the difference.

5. AIR QUALITY. Grass is a plant, just like a tree. It releases oxygen and absorbs carbon dioxide, a greenhouse gas. Grass absorbs other air pollutants as well. It also traps dust particles. Dust storms don't start in places covered by grass.

6. EASE OF MAINTENANCE. The biggest lie in gardening today is that lawn care is too much work. What baloney! The amount of work it takes to maintain a lawn pales beside what it takes to maintain the same size vegetable garden or mixed flower border. With a lawn, all you basically have to do is water and mow. And mowing is good aerobic exercise.

CHOOSE THE RIGHT GRASS
WARM-SEASON LAWN GRASSES

BAHIAGRASS *(Paspalum notatum).* Zones CS, TS; USDA 8-11. Perennial. From Brazil. Tough, rather coarse grass used for lawns in Florida. Green blades turn brown with the first frost. Needs full sun. Tolerates drought and takes heavy wear. Tall seed heads are produced continuously from May through November, so frequent mowing is needed to keep lawn looking

A soft carpet of lawn offers a prime spot for gathering and having a little friendly competition.

tidy. Mow at 3-4 in. Establish from seed or sod. Prefers acid soil; does not tolerate shade or salt spray. 'Argentina' produces fewer seed heads, has a wider blade, and is dark green. However, it is susceptible to cold. 'Pensacola' is finer textured, more cold tolerant (LS, CS, TS, USDA 8-11), and is used more than any other Bahia selection.

BERMUDAGRASS, COMMON (*Cynodon dactylon*). Zones MS, LS, CS, TS; USDA 7-11. Perennial. Choose common Bermuda for a good lower-maintenance lawn in large areas in full sun. It needs feeding in spring and summer, and frequent mowing to remove seed spikes. Plant from hulled seed, plugs, or sod. Originally intended for pasture, it develops deep, underground rhizomes that can be difficult to eradicate in garden beds. However, this can be an advantage on roadsides, high-traffic areas, or similar tough situations.

BERMUDAGRASS, IMPROVED (*Cynodon dactylon*). Zones MS, LS, CS, TS; USDA 7-11. Perennial. These Bermuda selections grow thicker and darker green than common Bermuda. They make a dense, dark green turf, requiring moderate maintenance, so they are good choices for lawns and utility areas. Available as seed, sod, or plugs. Commercially packaged blends of 3 or more selections offer a more adaptable turf.
- 'Mohawk'. Medium-fine texture. Mow at ½ to 1½ in.
- 'Princess 77'. Medium-fine texture, dense, drought tolerant. Mow at ¼ in. to 3 in.
- 'Riviera'. Medium-fine texture, drought tolerant. Mow at ½ in. to 2 in.
- 'Yukon'. Low growing and dense, with fine texture. Drought tolerant. Available as seed or sod. Mow at ½ to 1½ in.
- 'Yuma'. Low, dense grower. Tolerates heat and drought. Mowing height ½ to 1½ in.

BERMUDAGRASS, HYBRID (*Cynodon dactylon* x *Cynodon transvaalensis*). Zones MS, LS, CS, TS; USDA 7-11, except as noted. Often utilized for golf greens, sports fields, and lawns, hybrid Bermudagrass is established from sod or sprigs. It requires frequent fertilizing, watering, and dethatching. Some selections tolerate mowing as low as ⅛ in. A reel mower must be used for a quality cut below 1 inch. Closely mowed lawns sometimes needing to be clipped every two days; taller ones every 3 to 5 days. However, those who have the time and energy can enjoy an amazing lawn.
- 'Celebration'. Zones LS, CS, TS; USDA 8-11. Blue-green color with better shade tolerance than 'Tifway.' Very vigorous, prone to thatch. Mowing height ½ to 1½ in.
- 'Floratex'. Keeps green color well into fall; greens up early in spring. Needs less water and fertilizer than most other hybrid Bermudas, but produces numerous seed heads. Mow at ½ to 1¼ in.
- 'Tifdwarf'. Extremely low and dense; takes very close mowing. Slower to establish than others—but also slower to spread where it's not wanted. Mow at 3⁄16 to 7⁄16 in.
- 'TifGrand'. Zones LS, CS, TS; USDA 8-11. Similar to 'Tifway' with improved shade tolerance.
- 'Tifway'. Low growing and fine textured, with stiff dark green blades. Dense, wear-resistant. Not shade tolerant. Mow at ½ to 1¼ in. The most common hybrid Bermudagrass for lawns.

BUFFALOGRASS (*Buchloe dactyloides*). Zones US, MS, LS, CS, TS; USDA 6-11. Perennial. Native from central Montana south to Arizona, this grass makes a relatively low-maintenance lawn that takes hard wear and looks fairly good with very little water during dry periods. Green from late spring to the first hard frosts; then straw colored through winter. Not well adapted to areas with regular rainfall. Buffalograss is at its best when allowed to grow tall but needs mowing three times a year to form a good thick turf. Cut it short (to about 1 in.) in late winter or very early spring; then cut it to 2 in. in mid-June and again to 2 in. in early fall. Between mowings, let it grow to 4–6 in.

Sodded lawns look best, but seed and plugs are less expensive. Sow seed at the rate of 2 lbs. per 1,000 sq. ft. In absence of rain, soak soil occasionally to a depth of 1 ft. while grass is getting started. Slow to sprout and fill in. Plant 4-in.-wide plugs 3–4 ft. apart in prepared soil in spring; cover should be complete in two seasons. Once established, buffalograss spreads rapidly by surface runners. Selections include:

- 'Bison'. Very cold hardy. Produces seed heads. Summer color and thickness not as good as '609' or 'Prairie'. Available as seed.
- 'Prairie'. Spreads more aggressively than '609', but summer color is not quite as good. Produces a thick turf without seed heads. Available as sod or plugs.
- '609'. Lovely blue-green summer color. Makes a thick lawn with no seed heads. Available as sod or plugs.
- 'Shadow Turf'. Dense-growing hybrid developed for shade and cold tolerance. Available as plugs.
- 'Stampede'. Dense-growing semidwarf to about 4 in. high. Attractive green color. Available only as sod.
- 'Tech Turf'. Dense hybrid with good green color and high density; keeps out weeds effectively. Tolerates some shade. Available as plugs.
- 'Texoka'. Produces lots of seed heads. Inferior quality for home-lawn use; much better suited to roadsides and industrial parks. An old selection, available as seed.
- 'Topgun'. Superior to 'Bison' in appearance and thickness. Produces seed heads. Available as seed.

CARPETGRASS (*Axonopus affinis*). Zones CS, TS; USDA 9-11. Perennial. This is a lawn grass of last resort, grown chiefly in areas of Florida where wet, acid soil makes it difficult to grow other grasses. Does not tolerate drought, alkaline soil, or salt spray. Produces numerous tall, unsightly seed heads. Needs mowing every 10 to 14 days to 1–2 in. to stay attractive. Susceptible to nematodes and brown patch. Turns brown with first cold spell in fall and greens up slowly in spring. Start from seeds or sprigs. Feed each spring with a complete controlled-release fertilizer, such as 16-4-8.

CENTIPEDEGRASS (*Eremochloa ophiuroides*). Zones LS, CS; USDA 8-9. Perennial. Native to southern and central China, centipedegrass is sometimes known by the name "poor man's grass," thanks to its ease of establishment and the minimal attention required to keep it going. It thrives in areas with poor, acidic, infertile soil; annual rainfall greater than 40 in.; and mild winter temperatures. A popular lawn grass in the Lower and Coastal South, it's probably the most widely used grass in the Florida Panhandle. People sometimes confuse it with St. Augustinegrass (*Stenotaphrum secundatum*), but centipede-grass has narrower leaves, is a lighter green in color, and takes longer to green up in spring. It is also more cold hardy and less prone to diseases and insects.

Improved selections are available only as sod or plugs. Cold-hardy types include 'Oklawn'; 'Tennessee Hardy'; and 'Tifblair', which may be hard to find; and the more widely available 'AU Centennial'. This last selection was released by Auburn University in 1983; it is lower growing and denser than other choices, with shorter seed heads. It is also more cold hardy and tolerates neutral to slightly alkaline soil.

This is one grass you won't spend endless weekends fertilizing. In fact, too much fertilizer will kill it. Apply controlled-release 15-0-15 centipedegrass fertilizer just once per year, in spring or summer, at the rate specified on the package. Do not fertilize until after your last spring frost. Note that centipede-grass is naturally apple-green; extra nitrogen won't deepen the color. Maintain soil pH between 5.0 and 6.0.

Seed at the rate of ¼ to ½ pound per 1,000 sq. ft. Seed takes 2 to 3 weeks to germinate. Centipedegrass can start from plugs or sprigs; also available as sod. Mow at 1–2 in.; if left unmowed, it will reach no more than 3 in., but it will look unkempt when it seeds. Centipedegrass is fairly tolerant of drought and shade, but it doesn't stand up to salt spray or heavy wear.

This versatile lawn works as a kid's play space as well as an entertaining area.

SEASHORE PASPALUM (*Paspalum vaginatum*). Zones LS, CS, TS; USDA 8-11. Perennial. Native to sandy soils along the coast from North Carolina to Texas. Compared to Bermudagrass, it needs less water and fertilizer, but requires full sun. Finer textured and more cold hardy than Bahiagrass (*P. notatum*). Spreads by stolons and rhizomes. Establish from seed, sod, or sprigs. Tolerates salt spray better than any other lawn grass and is used for lawns and fairways along the coast, making it possible to irrigate from brackish water sources. It does not tolerate shade. Withstands drought once established, but be sure to water sod or sprigs thoroughly for 3 weeks after planting, until roots are well settled.

'Aloha' is deep green, tolerates mowing under ½ in., and grows into a solid lawn faster than others. 'Sea Isle 2000', released by the University of Georgia, is similar in texture to hybrid Bermudagrass (*Cynodon dactylon*), but it doesn't go dormant and turn brown until temperature reaches 28°F. Unlike other selections, fine-textured 'Sea Spray' is best established by seeding, either as a lawn or a golf green. 'Sea Dwarf' is the finest textured selection, bright green, and tolerates cutting heights less than ½ in. Most selections can be mowed from 1 to 2 in.

ST. AUGUSTINEGRASS (*Stenotaphrum secundatum*). Zones LS, CS, TS; USDA 8-11. Perennial. Native to the Gulf Coast and other tropical and subtropical regions, St. Augustine is a coarse-textured grass, spreading rapidly by surface runners that root at the nodes. In warm, rainy weather, runners can completely hide a sidewalk in a few weeks. It turns brown in winter but never goes completely dormant, and it greens up early in spring. It can be difficult to mow, especially when tall and wet, and it's not very tolerant of drought or severe cold. On the plus side, it establishes rapidly, recovers quickly from wear, and accepts more shade than other warm-season lawn grasses. It also grows in almost any soil and tolerates salt spray and occasional inundation, making it the best choice for beach areas. A variegated form is sometimes offered; it's an interesting subject for hanging baskets.

St. Augustinegrass is very popular in Florida, South Texas, and along the Gulf and South Atlantic coasts. It can be started from sod or plugs. Mow standard selections at 2½–4 in. tall; mow semidwarf selections at 1½–2 in. tall. Chinch bugs, which suck the juices from leaf blades, can be a major pest. The best defense is to plant a resistant selection (as noted in the following list) and to use a slow-release fertilizer. Selections include the following.

- 'Bitterblue'. Standard type, blue-green. This is the most shade-tolerant selection.
- 'Captiva'. Semidwarf, dark green. Fine-textured, slow-growing selection with moderate shade tolerance. Resistant to chinch bugs.
- 'Delmar'. Semidwarf, dark green. Fine-textured, cold-hardy selection with good shade tolerance.
- 'Floralawn'. Standard type, dark green. Very coarse textured. Not particularly tolerant of shade or cold, but resists chinch bugs.
- 'Floratam'. Similar to 'Floralawn', but susceptible to chinch bugs.
- 'Jade'. Semidwarf, dark green. Very fine textured. Cold-hardy selection with good shade tolerance. Resistant to chinch bugs.
- 'Palmetto'. Semidwarf, dark green. Quite cold hardy. Good shade and drought tolerance.
- 'Raleigh'. Standard type, medium green. Very cold-hardy selection with good shade tolerance.
- 'Sapphire'. Semidwarf, blue-green. Folded leaf blades give this variety a fine-textured appearance. Fast-growing. Cold-hardy; good shade tolerance.
- 'Seville'. Semidwarf, dark green. Fine textured. Cold-hardy selection with excellent shade tolerance. Some resistance to chinch bugs.

ZOYSIAGRASS HYBRIDS (*Zoysia japonica x Zoysia tenuifolia*). Perennial. Among the South's most popular lawn grasses. These tough Asian natives resist pests, tolerate drought, and take much wear. Green in summer, straw colored in winter. Started from sod or plugs. Spread more slowly and are more expensive than other warm-season grasses. Form a dense carpet of turf that chokes out weeds. Mow at 2 in.

- 'Cashmere'. Zones LS, CS, TS; USDA 8–11. Dark green, fine, dense turf; similar to 'Emerald' but softer and not as cold hardy.
- 'Emerald'. Zones MS, LS, CS, TS; USDA 7–11. Perennial. Dense, fine-textured, medium green grass; turns a beautiful beige in winter. Prone to thatch build-up. Somewhat prickly to bare feet.

ZOYSIA, JAPANESE GRASS (*Zoysia japonica*). Zones US, MS, LS, CS, TS; USDA 6-11. Perennial. Several selections: 'Meyer' ('Z-52'), called Meyer Zoysia, is coarser than Z. 'Emerald' and quite cold hardy; it's the preferred selection for the Upper South. Turns brown earliest in winter, turns green latest in spring. 'Belaire' is medium green, particularly cold hardy, coarser textured than 'Meyer', and faster to establish. 'El Toro' resembles 'Meyer' but has a faster establishment rate, better color in cool season, and less thatch buildup. 'Empire' is dense and soft, with good blue-green color; does well in many soils as long as it gets full sun.

ZOYSIA, KOREAN GRASS (*Z. tenuifolia*). Zones CS, TS; USDA 9-11. Perennial. The finest-textured Zoysiagrass but also the least cold hardy. Makes a beautiful grassy meadow or gives mossy effect in areas impossible to mow or water often. Can develop excessive thatch.

ZOYSIA, MANILA GRASS (*Z. matrella*). Zones LS, CS, TS; USDA 8-11. Perennial. Resembles Bermudagrass (*Cynodon dactylon*) in color, texture. Holds color a little better than 'Meyer' Zoysia but is not as cold hardy. Susceptible to nematodes. 'Diamond' is fine textured, with good tolerance of shade and salt; does best when mown low (½ in.).

COOL-SEASON LAWN GRASSES

BLUEGRASS, KENTUCKY (*Poa pratensis*). Zones US, MS; USDA 6-7. Perennial. Rich blue-green lawn grass best adapted to Upper South and southern Midwest. Forms the most lush and beautiful of lawns—an utter delight to stroll upon in bare feet. Unfortunately, it demands much maintenance, including regular watering and fertilizing. Susceptible to disease during warm, humid weather. Mow at 2 in. high in spring and fall, at 3 in. in summer. If seeding, use a seed blend of 3–5 selections. Many selections are available as seed or sod, including the following.

- 'Adelphi'. Darkest green, medium texture; good disease resistance.

Paths don't have to be made of brick or stone. A wide swath of grass makes a pretty alternative.

- 'Bonnieblue'. Medium dark green, medium texture; establishes quickly.
- 'Glade'. Dark green, fine texture, dense; tolerates shade better than most.
- 'Majestic'. Dark green, medium texture; establishes fast.
- 'Midnight'. Dark, blue-green. Fine texture. Dwarf habit and good disease resistance.
- 'Parade'. Medium green, fine texture; good disease resistance.
- 'Touchdown'. Medium dark green, fine texture; tolerates shade well.
- 'Victa'. Dark green, medium texture; establishes fast.

FESCUE, FINE (*Festuca spp.*). Zones US, MS; USDA 6-7. Perennials. From Europe. Finer leaf texture than tall fescue. Includes red fescue (*F. rubra*), chewings fescue (*F. rubra ssp. commutata*), and hard fescue (*F. longifolia*). Numerous selections available. Spreads by rhizomes. Poor heat tolerance, often going dormant and turning brown during hot summer conditions. Principal use is in cool-season blends with Kentucky bluegrass or other lawn grasses to add shade tolerance. Leaf blades vary in color from blue-green to dark green. Pink seed heads. Not fussy about soil. Tolerates shade better than most grasses but doesn't take heavy traffic. It's a light feeder, too, so fertilize once in September with a controlled-release fertilizer such as 20-5-10. Seed new lawns at 3 to 5 pounds per 1,000 sq. ft. Mow at 1½–2½ in.

FESCUE, TALL (*Festuca arundinacea*). Zones US, MS; USDA 6-7. Perennial. This clumping, tall-growing grass is native to Europe and northern Asia. In the Upper and Middle South, it is a popular substitute for Kentucky bluegrass and perennial ryegrass in lawns, as it stands up better to heat, wear, and compacted soil. It should not be used as a pasture grass; it is toxic to horses, sheep, cattle, and goats.

People living in the "transition zone" (the lower part of the Middle South and upper part of the Lower South) often grow tall fescue for its green winter color. To keep it attractive in this area, give it afternoon shade, lots of summertime water, and yearly overseeding. Irrigate only when the grass shows signs of thirst (wilting or rolling leaves); then water deeply, wetting the soil to a depth of 3–4 in. Seed new lawns heavily, at the rate of 8 pounds per 1,000 sq. ft., using a mix of several different selections. Fertilize once in September and again in March or April with a controlled-release, high-nitrogen fertilizer, such as 30-3-8 or 27-3-6. To keep the lawn thick, overseed every fall at the rate of 4 pounds per 1,000 sq. ft. The typical mowing height is about 2–3 in., though dwarf types such as 'Bonsai' and 'Duster' can be mowed at 1–2 in. high. Avoid 'Kentucky 31' in favor of a turf-type tall fescue.

RYEGRASS, ANNUAL (*Lolium multiflorum*). Zones US, MS, LS, CS, TS; USDA 6-11. Annual. Taller and coarser than perennial ryegrass. Sets seed and dies at onset of hot weather. Used for temporary lawns at new homesites and for erosion control on banks and roadsides. Primary use is for overseeding warm-season grasses in fall to produce deep green lawns in winter. To overseed, cut existing lawn short (about 1 in.) in early fall, then sow annual ryegrass at rate of 10 pounds per 1,000 sq. ft.

RYEGRASS, PERENNIAL (*Lolium perenne*). Zones US; USDA 6. Perennial. Finer in texture than annual ryegrass (*L. multiflorum*) and deep, glossy green. Disadvantages are clumping tendency and tough flower and seed stems that lie down under mower blades. However, improved selections do produce a uniform lawn of fine appearance. These include 'Derby', 'Loretta', 'Manhattan' and 'Pennfine'. 'Manhattan II', 'Palmer' and 'Prelude' have improved disease resistance. Planting a mix gives better results. Sow 8 to 10 pounds per 1,000 sq. ft. Mow at 1½–2 in., higher in summer. Use for overseeding warm-season grasses in fall to produce deep green lawns in winter. Perennial ryegrass is finer in texture than annual ryegrass and dies when the weather gets hot.

PLANT

Before planting a lawn, till the soil to a depth of about 8 inches and spread it with a 3- to 4-inch layer of organic matter. Also apply a lawn fertilizer. Till again; then rake the area smooth, water it thoroughly, and let the soil settle for a few days. If this sounds like a lot of work (it is), hire a lawn or landscape company to do it.

How to Seed

Seed is the cheapest way to start a lawn. It is also the slowest. Seed cool-weather grasses in fall; seed warm-weather grasses in spring.

• After preparing the area, scatter seeds. A mechanical spreader helps sow seeds evenly.

• Lightly rake seeds into the soil.

• Spread a ½-inch layer of mulch such as compost over the area. Roll with an empty roller to press seeds into soil. Water thoroughly. Keep the seedbed moist until the seeds sprout.

A flat of 70 plugs is enough to cover 30 square feet.

PLUGS. These are small-rooted plants used for warm-season spreading grasses such as buffalo and Zoysia. Plant them in spring, following the supplier's directions. Water often until roots take hold.

SPRIGS. These pieces of grass stem and root are used to plant warm-season grasses; they give faster coverage than seeds. Plant in spring, setting sprigs 2–3 in. deep at 4-in. intervals, in rows 6–12 in. apart. One end of each sprig should barely poke out of the ground.

How to Sod

Sod is the most expensive way to start a lawn, but it gives instant coverage with almost no weed problems. Select grasses adapted to your area.

• After preparing the site, moisten the soil. Unroll the strips and lay them out with their ends staggered, pressing the edges together firmly.

• Use a knife to trim sod so it fits snugly around paving or plants.

• Press roots into the soil, using a roller half-filled with water. Water lawn once daily (more in hot weather) for six weeks.

WATER AND FEED

To encourage deep rooting and conserve water, water established lawns deeply but infrequently. One watering of 60 minutes is better than 3 waterings of 20 minutes each. Water in the cool morning, so that less water evaporates and grass blades dry quickly. Blades that stay wet too long are prone to disease. In mild climates, once or twice a week should be adequate during warm weather; in hotter regions, you'll need to water more often. Contact your local water department or Cooperative Extension Office for specific lawn-watering guidelines for your area.

SPRINKLER SYSTEMS. In-ground sprinkler systems are certainly more convenient than hauling hoses. On the other hand, they're expensive, use more water, and need regular maintenance to keep in good working order. Adjust sprinklers so they don't overshoot onto paving. To improve water penetration and reduce runoff, aerate and dethatch your lawn once a year.

FEED REGULARLY. Most lawns are heavy feeders, requiring regular applications of controlled-release high-nitrogen fertilizer. Give cool-season lawns two applications of fertilizer, one in spring and another in fall. Fertilize most warm-season lawns several times from late spring into late summer. (Centipede is an exception. Feed it once in spring using fertilizer formulated for Centipede.) Apply dry fertilizers using a spreader; overlap the spreader's wheel marks so swaths just touch as you pass over. Check the packages for recommended application rates. If you cut back on watering because of drought, hold back on fertilizer as well.

MOW

CUT THE GRASS AT ITS HIGHEST RECOMMENDED HEIGHT. Never take more than a third of the blade off each time. If you do, the loss of food-producing leaf blade temporarily halts root growth. Less vigorous roots mean a thinner lawn and more weeds. If possible, use a mulching mower that chops cut grass into tiny bits and returns them to the lawn. This adds both nutrients and organic matter. Lawns mowed this way need much less fertilizer.

USE A SHARP BLADE. A dull blade leaves the grass ragged and brown on the tips. A sharp blade cuts fast and clean, leaving the grass healthy.

DETHATCH

Warm-season grasses like Bermuda grass and Zoysia tend to build up a spongy layer of thatch (dead leaves and stems) on the surface over time. This can block the penetration of water and nutrients and increase disease problems. Dethatch your lawn once a year in late winter before it greens up by mowing it at 1 in.

A GUIDE TO GROWING
HERBS

An "herb" is any plant used for seasoning, medicine, or fragrance.
The world of herbs includes tall, willowy plants such as dill, and fine-textured
creepers such as thyme; annuals and biennials grown for their leaves and seeds;
perennials such as chives; and shrubs such as rosemary. Use them to
spice up your landscape as well as your recipes.

HERB BASICS

SITE. Choose a spot that receives six to eight hours of full sun each day—ideally near the kitchen, so you can snip herbs easily while cooking. Or, if space is limited, grow some in containers.

SOIL. Herbs cannot tolerate soggy roots, so well-drained soil is a necessity.

WATER. After planting, water herbs regularly while they get established. Basil, chives, mint, and parsley prefer evenly moist soil, while most like oregano and rosemary like it on the drier side.

FERTILIZER. Plant with a timed-release, granular fertilizer, such as 14-14-14. In midsummer, use a low-nitrogen, organic fertilizer such as 3-4-4. Herbs aren't heavy feeders, so don't overdo it.

MAINTENANCE. Trim herbs often to keep them from flowering. When they bloom, their flavor diminishes, and growth of tasty new foliage slows. Chives are an exception. Enjoy their showy blooms!

TRIED-AND-TRUE HERBS FOR THE SOUTH

We love these herbs because they're attractive, easy to grow, and excellent choices for beginners. They'll reward you with great flavor and make a nice addition to the garden.

BAY (*Laurus nobilis*)
USES: Add to soups and stews for flavor. Shrub or tree. See page 403.
GREEK OREGANO (*Origanum vulgare hirtum*)
USES: Add to pasta sauces, vinaigrette, and Mediterranean dishes. Perennial. See page 460.
GOLDEN VARIEGATED LEMON THYME (*Thymus x citriodorus* 'Aureus')
USES: Lemon flavor brightens poultry, fish, and vegetable dishes. Shrubby perennial. See page 616.

COMMON SAGE (*Salvia officinalis*)
USES: Popular for poultry dishes and stuffings. Perennial. See page 568.
FLAT-LEAF PARSLEY (*Petroselinum crispum*)
USES: Adds delicate flavor to vegetable dishes, marinades, and poultry. Biennial. See page 492.
'TUSCAN BLUE' ROSEMARY (*Rosemary officinalis* 'Tuscan Blue')
USES: Mediterranean favorite used to flavor bread, soups, vegetables, and meat. Shrubby perennial. See page 561.

SPANISH LAVENDER (*Lavandula stoechas*)
USES: Adds delicate floral notes to ice cream, lemonade, and tea; an ingredient in herbes de Provence. Perennial. See page 395.
'AFRICAN BLUE' BASIL (*Ocimum x* 'African Blue')
USES: Makes great pesto. Annual. See page 455.
'GREEK COLUMNAR' BASIL (*Ocimum basilicum*)
USES: Great for seasoning Italian and Asian dishes. Annual. See page 455.

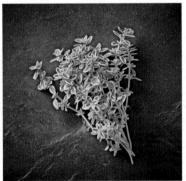

TOP: 'African Blue' Basil, Golden Variegated Lemon Thyme, Greek Oregano; *MIDDLE:* 'Greek Columnar' Basil, Flat-Leaf Parsley, Common Sage; *BOTTOM:* Bay, Rosemary

HOW MANY PLANTS?

For a basic starter herb garden, use this list as a guideline, adjusting the number to reflect your preferences. If you love to cook with basil, set out six plants to start with; then add more several weeks later to extend the harvest season.

Basil: 4 to 6 plants
Chives: 3 to 4 plants
Cilantro: 2 to 3 plants
Oregano: 2 plants
Parsley: 1 to 3 plants
Rosemary: 1 to 2 plants
Sage: 1 to 2 plants
Sweet marjoram: 2 to 3 plants
Thyme: 3 to 4 plants

DRYING HERBS

HARVEST. Snip herbs just as the first flower buds begin to open, when the oils in the leaves are most concentrated. In the morning after the dew has evaporated is the best time.

HANG THEM. For large-leaved herbs, such as basil and sage, or herbs with woody stems such as rosemary, snip off leafy stems, tie the cut ends together with twine. Hang bundled herbs upside down in a warm, dry place (away from direct sun) with good air circulation. When the leaves are crisp and crumble readily, strip them from the stems, and store them whole in airtight jars.

SPREAD THEM OUT. For fine-leaved herbs such as oregano, remove the leaves from the stems and dry them on a clean window screen in a warm, dry place.

HERBS FOR TEA

You won't find most of these at your grocery store, so pull out your trowel and plant your own. These herbs grow well in pots or in the ground as long as they have well-drained soil and full sun. Keep watered until they are established. Harvest to brew your own tea.

ANISE HYSSOP (*Agastache foeniculum*). Try both the licorice-flavored blooms and leaves of 'Golden Jubilee' (to 3 ft. tall).

BEE BALM (*Monarda didyma*). Its mildly citrus-flavored pink, red, and pure white blossoms are striking in a mug or cup.

CHAMOMILE (*Matricaria recutita*). Snip the fragrant, mellow blossoms of this 2-ft.-tall plant to use fresh or dried.

LAVENDER (*Lavandula angustifolia*). Although it's compact, silvery 'Thumbelina Leigh' English lavender produces plenty of blossoms for steeping.

LEMON BALM (*Melissa officinalis*). In the same family as mint but not as invasive. Has a strong citrus flavor.

LEMON VERBENA (*Aloysia triphylla*). Intensely flavored and highly fragrant.

NUTMEG GERANIUM (*Pelargonium* x *fragrans* 'Nutmeg'). Aromatic leaves taste and smell like nutmeg.

From back to front: chamomile, lemon verbena, lavender, and bee balm

A GUIDE TO GROWING
NATIVE PLANTS

Just because a plant is native doesn't make it better. A wise gardener
chooses the right plant for the right spot.

*Pink muhly grass (Muhlenbergia capillaris)
and chalk maple (Acer leucoderme)*

Some people tell you that you should plant only native plants
in your garden. They say native plants are inherently more
adaptable and easier to grow than plants imported from
elsewhere. And they'll insist that native plants are better for
wildlife and the local ecosystem than exotic ones.

No offense, but these statements are wrong, because
they're too absolute. Let's discuss.

**1. "NATIVE PLANTS ARE EASIER TO GROW THAN NON-
NATIVE ONES."** This depends on where exactly the plants are
native. A plant native to Texas won't necessarily grow in
Florida. A plant native to the North Carolina coast isn't
guaranteed to thrive in the North Carolina mountains. In fact,
numerous native plants are quite finicky, inhabiting small areas
that supply very specific growing conditions. Planting them in
your garden amounts to a death sentence.

On the other hand, many exotic plants are actually easier for
Southerners to grow than natives. Azaleas are a good example.
Most people find evergreen azaleas imported from Asia much
easier to grow than our native deciduous azaleas.

2. "NATIVE PLANTS ARE BETTER FOR WILDLIFE." Try telling
that to a mockingbird gulping down a pyracantha berry or a
hummingbird sipping nectar from as Asiatic lily. Granted, lots
of plants imported from abroad have become invasive plagues
that choke out native vegetation—kudzu, Chinese privet,
paperbark tree, water hyacinth, bamboo, and purple
loosestrife come to mind—but native plants such as silver
maple, box elder, Virginia creeper, prickly pear, poison ivy, and
sumac can be thugs too.

So if you like native plants, choose those that do well in your
area. The plant descriptions in this book will help. However,
don't be afraid of an exotic plant if it's easy to grow, fills a need,
and doesn't take over the world. Your garden will be more
interesting for it.

A GUIDE TO GROWING
PALMS

Most palms are tropical or subtropical; a few are surprisingly hardy, thriving in towns like Birmingham, Atlanta, and Norfolk. These trees offer great opportunity for imaginative planting; in nature, they grow not only in solid stands but also with other plants, notably broad-leafed evergreen trees and shrubs. They are effective near swimming pools, where they give the impression of a tropical garden. Most palms are not heavily browsed by deer. Where not winter-hardy, grow in pots.

HOW TO GROW

EXPOSURE. Most young palms prefer shade, and all tolerate it; this fact makes them good house or patio plants when they are small. As they grow, they can be moved into full sun or partial shade, depending on the species.

GROWTH RATE. Palm species vary, but keeping plants in pots usually slows down the faster-growing kinds. If temperatures are 60°F or higher, fertilize potted palms often; also wash them off frequently to provide some humidity and clean the foliage. Washing also dislodges insects, which (indoors, at any rate) are protected from their natural enemies and can increase extremely rapidly.

TRANSPLANTING. Most palms, even big ones, transplant easily in late spring or early summer. All tropical palms do their growing during warm times of year. Since new roots form from the base of the trunk, the root ball need not be large; a new root system will form and produce lush new growth. When transplanting large palms, contractors usually tie leaves together over the center "bud" or heart, then secure the leaf mass to a length of 2-by-4 tied to the trunk.

PLANTING. To pot a palm, supply good potting soil, adequate drainage, and not too big a container. As with all potted plants, pot or repot a palm in a container just slightly larger than the one in which it is already growing.

In the garden, planting holes for palms should generally be the same depth as and 1–2 ft. wider than the root ball, and you can use unamended native soil for backfill. If you are planting in very poor, alkaline, or clay soil, however, some experts suggest a different procedure. For a 5-gal.-size palm, dig a 3-ft.-wide hole that is 8 in. deeper than root ball. Place 1–2 cu. ft. of well-rotted manure, nitrogen-fortified sawdust, or other organic amendment in the hole, then mix in a handful or two of blood meal and top with a 6-in. layer of soil. Set in the palm, and fill in around it with a mixture of half native soil and half nitrogen-fortified sawdust, ground bark, or peat moss.

WATERING AND CLEANING. Water newly planted palms faithfully until established. See individual entries for recommendations on long-term water needs. Rain rinses the foliage and, in areas with sandy or salty soil, leaches out accumulated salts. Palms growing in dry or dusty areas or beyond the reach of rain or dew should be hosed off periodically; this helps control populations of spider mites and sucking insects that find refuge in the long leaf stems. Beach plantings should also be washed off occasionally to keep salt from accumulating on the leaves.

Coconut palms (Cocos nucifera).

FERTILIZING. Use a fertilizer specially formulated for palms with an analysis of around 8-4-12 that contains micronutrients such as manganese and magnesium. Lack of manganese often leads to distorted foliage, a condition known as "frizzle top."

PRUNING. Feather palms and many fan palms look neater when old leaves are removed after they have turned brown. Make neat cuts close to trunk, leaving leaf bases. Some palms shed old leaf bases on their own. Others, including *Syagrus* and *Chamaedorea*, may hold old bases. You can remove them by slicing them off at the very bottom of base (be careful not to cut into trunk).

Many palm admirers say that dead leaves of *Washingtonia* should remain on the tree, the thatch being part of the palm's character. If you agree but prefer a neater look, you can cut lower fronds uniformly close to trunk but leave leaf bases, which present a rather attractive lattice surface.

COLD HARDINESS. Most palms are frost sensitive, although some are quite tolerant. Frost becomes more damaging to them as it extends its stay and is repeated. A light frost that lasts for half an hour may not harm plants at all, but if the same degree of frost persists for 4 hours, it may injure some palms, kill others. Hardiness is also a matter of plant size; larger palms may survive severe frosts without harm, while smaller ones perish. If you are planting a palm where it is marginally hardy, use a plant that is as large as you can find or afford. At its least serious, frost damage consists simply of burned leaf edges—but frost may affect whole leaves, parts of trunk, or crown. Damage to the crown is usually fatal (though some trees have recovered from it).

LARGE PALMS

Archontophoenix, Brahea, Cocos nucifera, Jubaea chilensis, Livistona sp., Phoenix canariensis, P. dactylifera, P. loureirii, P. rupicola, Ptychosperma elegans, Roystonea, Sabal causiarum, S. palmetto, S. uresana, Syagrus romanzoffianum, Washingtonia sp.

SMALL TO MEDIUM-SIZE PALMS

FOR FROST-FREE GARDENS *Archontophoenix, Caryota, Chamaedorea, Chamaerops humilis, Chrysalidocarpus lutescens, Howea.*

TOLERATE LIGHT, BRIEF FROST *Acoelorrhaphe wrightii, Brahea armata, B. dulcis, Butia capitata, Chamaedorea, Chamaerops humilis, Livistona, Phoenix canariensis, P. dactylifera, P. loureirii, P. roebelenii, Ptychosperma macarthurii.*

HARDIEST PALMS

Brahea armata, Chamaerops humilis, Jubaea chilensis, Livistona chinensis, Rhapidophyllum hystrix, Rhapis sp., Sabal causiarum, S. etonia, S. mexicana, S. minor, S. palmetto, S. texensis, Serenoa repens, Trachycarpus fortunei, Washingtonia. Refer to individual entry to determine the cold tolerance of each.

SALT-TOLERANT PALMS

Butia capitata, Chamaerops humilis, Cocos nucifera, Phoenix canariensis, P. dactylifera, P. reclinata, Roystonea sp., Sabal sp., Washingtonia robusta.

PALMS FOR HOT, DRY CLIMATES

Brahea armata, Butia capitata, Chamaerops humilis, Jubaea chilensis, Livistona chinensis, L. mariae, Nannorrhops ritchiana, Phoenix canariensis, P. dactylifera, P. loureirii, P. sylvestris, Sabal mexicana, S. minor, Washingtonia sp.

PALMS TO GROW UNDER OVERHANGS OR INDOORS

Rhapis sp., Chamaedorea sp., Howea sp., and *Phoenix roebelenii* may spend decades in pots indoors. Others that later may reach great size—*Archontophoenix sp., Caryota mitis, C. ochlandra, C. urens, Chamaerops sp., Livistona sp., Phoenix reclinata, Washingtonia sp.*—make charming temporary indoor plants but eventually must be moved. Indoor palms should occasionally be brought outdoors into mild light.

UNDERSTORY PALMS

Young palms, especially slow growers such as *Livistona chinensis* and *Chamaerops humilis*, stay low for 5 to 10 years and can be used effectively as plantings under tall trees. *Sabal texensis* takes many years to reach its ultimate height of 15 ft. Or choose among these shrubby palms that rarely exceed 6 ft. tall: *Chamaedorea radicalis, Rhapidophyllum histrix, Sabal etonia, S. minor, Serenoa repens.*

PALMS FOR LIGHTING

All palms are good subjects for creating nighttime drama. Light them from behind or below; or direct floodlights to silhouette them against light-colored walls.

Parlor palm
(*Chamaedorea elegans*)

A GUIDE TO GROWING
TREES

The backbone of the garden, trees provide shade and year-round beauty with foliage, bark, branches, and sometimes flowers and fruit. The difference between a tree and a large shrub is sometimes blurred, but trees are typically tall plants with one dominant trunk and a leafy crown.

CHOOSE THE RIGHT TREE

As your garden's largest living element, trees have an enormous impact on your landscape and, sometimes, your wallet. Spring and fall are great times to plant, but knowing what you want before you go to the nursery will save you time and maybe even some yard work. That innocent-looking specimen in the nursery pot could reach 80 ft. at maturity or drop leaves faster than a teenager can text. Are you after a tree with showstopping flowers, pretty fall foliage, or sculptural form? Follow our tips, and you can't go wrong.

EVERGREEN OR DECIDUOUS.
Deciduous trees start their growth with a burst of new leaves in early spring, then remain in leaf through summer. In autumn, the foliage often changes color before dropping to reveal bare limbs. The tree then goes dormant for winter. Evergreen trees include both broad-leaved types and conifers, (though there are a few deciduous conifers). Both kinds serve well as screens and windbreaks. Broad-leaved evergreens may drop some leaves, but there's always enough foliage on the branches to give the tree a well-clothed look.

LANDSCAPE FUNCTION. If you need shade, choose a deciduous tree with a wide canopy that blocks the sun in summer, then allows sun into the house after its leaves drop in fall. To add privacy to your home or garden, choose relatively tall, dense trees. For a specimen tree to serve as a garden focal point, search for interesting foliage or a striking display of blossoms or berries.

ADAPTABILITY. Select trees that will grow well in your climate and soil, with the amount of water they'll receive naturally or that you can easily provide. Keep the tree's ultimate size in mind; an overly large one could eventually crowd structures and other plants and might eventually need to be removed.

MESSY OR NEAT. Trees that produce litter from falling leaves, flowers, or fruit shouldn't be planted beside a patio or near a pool or pond. They are better candidates for natural areas where litter can remain where it falls. In areas with high winds, avoid trees with weak or brittle wood. They can be hazardous.

SILHOUETTES. Consider a tree's mature shape, which may not be obvious when you buy a small sapling at the nursery (see illustrations below). Spreading trees, such as fruit trees, tend to branch low to the ground and aren't good candidates for the middle of a lawn. Rounded, spreading trees, such as live oaks and sugar maples, need lots of space to extend their branches. Columnar or conical trees, such as eastern red cedar and Arizona cypress, work well in closer quarters.

LONGEVITY. Some trees can be planted for future generations to enjoy, while others grow and decline quickly. Trees that are planted for screening or shade should be long lived, but for specimen planting, shorter-lived kinds may be an excellent choice. Plant the latter only where removal will be relatively easy and won't compromise your landscape. If a flowering tree dies after 20 years, you can easily replace it.

Columnar	Oval	Pyramidal	Rounded	Spreading	Weeping

PLANT

Many deciduous trees (including fruit trees) are sold bare-root during the dormant season, from late fall through early spring. Deciduous trees may also be sold balled and burlapped from early fall into the following spring, or in containers throughout the year. For instructions on planting balled-and-burlapped or container-grown trees, see page 665.

What To Do

· Soak roots in water for at least four hours before planting.
· Dig a hole as deep and twice as wide as the root mass; form a firm cone of soil to set the plant on.
· Backfill with soil (for extremely heavy clay or sandy soils, mix compost into the backfill), and water to settle in.
· Mulch around the plant to insulate roots and conserve water.

STAKE

A young tree develops a sturdier trunk if it grows unsupported and can sway with the wind. But there are times when staking is necessary: when a tree is planted in a very windy location, when the main trunk is too weak to stand upright on its own, or when the crown (the tree's top) is very large in proportion to the trunk.

What To Do

· Sink two stakes into the ground, one on each side of the root ball. Determine where to attach the ties. Support the trunk with two fingers, starting 3 ft. above the soil surface, and move your fingers upward. Stop at the place where your support keeps the tree upright. Attach the ties 6 in. above this point.
· Use soft ties that have broad, smooth surfaces, such as canvas or UV-degradable fabric (available at garden centers). Allow enough slack so the trunk can move 2 in. in every direction. Do not use wire or wire-filled hose, which can girdle the bark. Remove the stakes and ties from six months to a year after planting.

TEND

WATER. All trees, even drought-tolerant kinds, need regular watering during the first several years after planting, until their roots have grown deep enough to carry them through dry periods. Once established, many kinds require only infrequent irrigation.

FEED. Fertilize in spring for a few years after planting by spreading tree fertilizer at the rate recommended on the bag atop the soil from the trunk out to the edge of the tree's canopy. Once a tree is well settled in, though, it may grow satisfactorily with no further feeding—unless its new growth is weak, sparse, or unusually pale. In fact, fertilizing a tree that continues to put out healthy, vigorous new growth is a waste of time and fertilizer.

PRUNE

Young trees often need selective pruning of suckers or spindly lower branches to guide new growth and to establish a strong structure. On mature trees, prune to maintain shape, to open up the canopy, or to remove dead or crossing branches. Always cut back to the trunk, or to another branch.

To avoid ripping the bark, shorten the branch to a stub before cutting it off just outside the branch collar.

What To Do

· About a foot from the branch base, make a cut from the underside, approximately a third of the way through (1).
· About an inch farther out on the branch, cut through the top until the branch splits cleanly between the two cuts (2).
· Make final cut as shown; avoid cutting the branch collar (3).
For more information on pruing trees and shrubs, see page 671.

EIGHT TRIED-AND-TRUE TREES FOR THE SOUTH

CREPE MYRTLE (*Lagerstroemia sp.*)

WHY WE LOVE IT: Few trees can match its combination of spectacular summer flowers, colorful autumn foliage, and handsome trunks that stand out in the winter.

USES: Planted together, they make a large deciduous hedge or screen. A single tree can create a distinctive focal point, while a pair framing a front door greets visitors with a warm Southern welcome. See page 395.

EASTERN REDBUD (*Cercis canadensis*)

WHY WE LOVE IT: This is one of the toughest trees around. It tolerates heat, cold, and drought. Pretty flowers ranging from lavender-pink to rose-purple to white smother the branches in spring.

USES: Plant this small tree as a focal point in the garden or near the house, or as an understory beneath larger trees. See page 227.

FLOWERING DOGWOOD (*Cornus florida*)

WHY WE LOVE IT: Midspring blooms cover branches and seem to float in midair. Foliage turns crimson in fall, and in winter flowering dogwood supplies birds with clusters of red berries.

USES: Plant around shaded patios or as an understory tree in a natural area. See page 227.

JAPANESE MAPLE (*Acer palmatum*)

WHY WE LOVE IT: Green, burgundy, or red leaves turn blazing yellow, orange, or scarlet in late fall.

WHAT TO CONSIDER: Dozens of available selections mean there is a Japanese maple to fit nearly every situation. Trees can be weeping or upright and range from 3 to 25 ft. tall. See page 127.

LIVE OAK (*Quercus virginiana*)

WHY WE LOVE IT: No tree evokes the region's timeless grace and beauty better than a massive live oak draped in Spanish moss.

USES: Prized for its evergreen foliage and colossal wide-spread limbs, it's the perfect shade tree for suburbs, city streets, and country lanes. If properly cared for, it can last for centuries. See page 535.

RED MAPLE (*Acer rubrum*)

WHY WE LOVE IT: Silvery bark and yellow-to-red fall foliage make red maple a handsome addition to your garden. Try 'October Glory' for its scarlet fall foliage. See page 129.

SUGAR MAPLE (*Acer saccharum*)

WHY WE LOVE IT: Brilliant autumn foliage ranges from yellow and orange to deep red and scarlet. See page 129.

YOSHINO FLOWERING CHERRY (*Prunus x yedoensis*)

WHY WE LOVE IT: White to blush-pink flowers smother leafless branches in spring. Tree grows quickly to 30 ft. tall and wide. When planted on both sides of a residential street, forms a breathtaking canopy over the road. See page 523.

Yoshino flowering cherry

Eastern redbud

Crepe myrtle

Dogwood

FOUR SEASONS OF INTEREST

To prolong the show, choose trees that peak in different seasons, with flowers, foliage, and beautiful bark.

SPRING. Flowering trees bedeck themselves with blooms to announce that winter is finally over. Choose saucer magnolia (*Magnolia* x *soulangeana*), Eastern redbud (*Cercis canadensis*), 'Okame' cherry (*Prunus* 'Okame'), flowering dogwood (*Cornus florida*), and Yoshino flowering cherry (*Prunus* x *yedoensis*) for plentiful blooms on leafless branches.

SUMMER. When the temperature rises, these trees add color or fragrance to the landscape, beckoning you out of the air-conditioning and into the garden. Available in all sizes and colors, there's a crepe myrtle (*Lagerstroemia sp.*) to fit every yard. These summer stalwarts thrive in heat and tolerate drought. Chaste tree (*Vitex agnus-castus*) covers itself in blue flowers, a cool and unusual palette for a tree. Southern magnolia (*Magnolia grandiflora*) fills the garden with fragrance when it blooms in May and June.

FALL. As the temperatures cool, many deciduous trees are ready for a change in wardrobe. Green leaves give way to fiery golds, oranges, and reds that glow in the sunlight. Good choices for fall color include red maple (*Acer rubrum*), yellow to scarlet; ginkgo (*Ginkgo biloba*), golden yellow; American beech (*Fagus grandifolia*), golden bronze; flowering dogwood (*Cornus florida*), crimson; Japanese maple (*Acer palmatum*), yellow, orange, or scarlet—varies with selection.

WINTER. Conifers and broadleaf evergreens lend structure to the garden this time of year. But don't overlook deciduous trees in winter. Once they shed their leaves, their striking bark and sculptural form become apparent. Choose coral bark maple (*Acer palmatum* 'Sango Kaku') for vibrant red-coral twigs and branches, paperbark maple (*A. griseum*) for cinnamon-colored exfoliating bark, crepe myrtles for sculptural trunks that make a fine silhouette against a backdrop of evergreens, and Chinese elm (*Ulmus parvifolia*) for mottled bark of gray, green, orange, and brown.

Gingko

Chaste tree

Japanese maple

Southern magnolia

CREPE MURDER

Don't commit crepe murder! Just because your neighbors are doing it doesn't make it okay. Cutting big crepe myrtles into fenceposts produces wild, weak growth and ruins their form. The satin-smooth bark and sinewy trunks make a statement in the winter garden. But amputated, knuckled, and disfigured branches mar the tree's outline, just when it should be an asset.

Crepe myrtles do need pruning, but if done correctly, the pruning goes unnoticed. Think of it as training. By enhancing the natural habit of the tree, you guide your crepe myrtle into a form that is both handsome and easy to maintain. For a beautiful tree in every season, follow these pruning tips.

- Prune in late winter. February is ideal.
- Remove suckers at the base, crossing or rubbing branches, and branches growing inward toward the center of the tree.
- As the tree grows, gradually remove all side branches up to a height of 5 ft. or so.
- Cut back to another branch, or to the branch collar (a swollen area where the branch joins the trunk). Never leave stubs.
- Try to remove unwanted branches before they get thicker than a pencil.
- It's okay but unnecessary to cut off old seed heads. Leaving them on won't affect blooming next year.
- Don't round off or "hat-rack" your tree by cutting back all its branches to the same height. This ruins the natural form.

WHAT IF IT'S TOO LATE?

If you've been committing crepe murder, you and your tree can be reformed. Cut your crepe myrtle back to near the ground in winter, and start all over. Although this may seem drastic, you can have a new tree in only two or three years, because the established root system will support rapid growth. When new shoots appear, select the ones that are strong and well placed to become the new trunks. Remove all others.

LANDSCAPING AND REMODELING AROUND TREES

The time to protect mature trees on your property from damage during a house remodel—if you decide to save them—is before construction starts. Otherwise, you could end up paying many thousands of dollars to replace trees that are injured or killed by heavy machinery or other mishaps.

When roots are compacted by heavy equipment or severed by trenching, as shown in the illustrations below, chances are you won't see the damage immediately. But injured roots are often unable to take up water, air, or nutrients, and this results in the decline and eventual death of the tree, even years later. Mature oaks are especially sensitive to root disturbance. Disease organisms or pest infestations that enter unhealed wounds can also, in time, kill the tree.

Avoid building within the drip linear root zone of a large, established tree. Allow at least 1 foot of space between the trunk and the structure for every inch of trunk diameter measured at 54 in. above soil level.

Learn where any new underground lines will go and, if possible, reroute them away from trees. If it's not possible for contractors to work outside the root zone, up to one-third of a healthy tree's roots can be removed without severely harming the tree.

If heavy equipment must be moved over the root zone, cover the area from the trunk out to the drip line with a 12-in.-thick layer of wood chips; then top the mulch with interlocking sheet-metal plates or plywood sheets to minimize soil compaction.

Make sure your contractor knows your wishes regarding your trees and will convey them to workers; the best way to do that is to spell them out in the remodeling contract.

TROUBLE SPOTS

THE CANOPY
BROKEN OR CUT BRANCHES. Large branch stubs created by storm damage or improper pruning, such as "topping," seldom heal over. Weak new growth follows.

THE TRUNK Injuries. Heavy equipment can gouge the trunk, exposing the tree to disease and insect pests.

THE ROOTS Most roots are within the top 24 inches of soil and can extend beyond the drip line. They're susceptible to damage shown below.

PROTECTIVE MEASURES

THE CANOPY. If low branches need removal to make way for heavy equipment, hire an arborist to do it. Instead of topping, cut selected branches back to lower branches.

THE TRUNK. If you need to work close to the trunk, prop hay bales against it to protect the bark. Use rope to tie thinner, flexible branches up and out of the way of trucks and machinery.

THE ROOTS. Put a fence around the tree as far outside the drip line as possible. Lay plastic tarps to keep out contaminants.

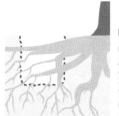
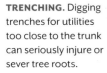

TRENCHING. Digging trenches for utilities too close to the trunk can seriously injure or sever tree roots.

SOLID PAVING. Non-porous paving under the canopy can prevent water and air from reaching roots.

GRADE CHANGE. Even 2 in. of fill dirt, if it does not have good drainage, can smother roots.

SOIL CONTAMINATION. Spilling wet concrete, paint, or solvents within the root zone can poison the tree.

COMPACTION. Heavy equipment or pallets of pavers can squash a tree's shallow surface roots.

A GUIDE TO GROWING
VEGETABLES

Produce that's bursting with flavor at the peak of ripeness is reason enough
to start your own vegetable garden. Till up a plot in the backyard or start small
with a few pots on the deck. Either way, you'll have the beginnings of the
ultimate veggie plate right outside your door.

PLANT

If you're new to vegetable gardening, start small. An area of just 200 sq. ft. can provide a substantial harvest. Before planting, prepare the soil to promote faster growth and a larger harvest. Follow the steps on page 664 for preparing your planting bed. If you want to go even smaller, plant a few vegetables in large pots. See "Vegetable Containers" on page 698 for growing tips.

Either way, you can start vegetables by planting seeds directly into the soil, or by setting out transplants that you have started yourself or purchased at the garden center. For more on sowing seeds and on starting and setting out transplants, see page 664.

EXPOSURE. Vegetables grow best with at least six hours of full sun a day. Leafy vegetables like lettuce need less sun than fruiting ones like peppers. Locate the garden away from trees and large shrubs that create shade and root competition.

SITE. Good drainage is also a must. On sites with too little slope, the soil may stay soggy, and seeds and plant roots will rot. On a slope that is too steep, runoff will wash seeds away. A gentle slope with easily crumbled soil, little erosion, and no standing water is ideal. If you don't have the ideal site, you can terrace a slope or build raised beds in an area that doesn't drain well.

ROWS. Separated by paths, rows give you access to the plants and let you easily till or hoe the soil. This layout works well for tall-growing plants, such as corn, and for those that need support, such as tomatoes and pole beans.

HILLS. Grouped in a cluster, but not necessarily on a mound. This method is useful for sprawling plants such as most types of melons and winter squash.

WIDE BEDS. Determine the ideal bed width by the length of your reach; you should be able to reach comfortably to the center of the bed from either side. For most people, that means a bed width of 4 to 5 ft. Wide beds are good for broadcasting seeds of beets, carrots, spinach, mustard, turnips, and lettuce.

TEND

WATER. Provide a steady supply of moisture from planting until harvest. Until transplants are well established, they will need frequent watering—enough to keep the soil moist but not

A kitchen garden lined with 'Wintergreen' boxwood contains peppers, 'Bright Lights' chard, basil, and mini pumpkins.

soggy. Rows or beds of seeds and young seedlings likewise need steady moisture. As transplants and seedlings grow, and their roots reach deeper, you can water less often—but when you do, be sure to moisten the entire root zone thoroughly. To water, use sprinklers, the hose, or a drip system (see pages 660-663).

MULCH. An organic mulch such as pine straw or ground bark cools the soil, conserves moisture, and suppresses weed growth; it also improves the soil structure as it decomposes, making the top 2 in. looser and more crumbly (apply when warm weather arrives). A mulch of plastic sheeting, on the other hand, helps warm the soil quickly and also blocks out weeds. It is especially helpful for heat-loving crops such as melons and eggplant. It's not very attractive, however.

FEED. There are plenty of fertilizers on the market to give your veggies a boost. Look for organic choices, such as composted manure, fish emulsion, and specially-blended brands for specific plants at your local nursery. Or choose a premium-quality slow-release granular fertilizer specially formulated for vegetables, and work it into the soil before planting. It will last for two to four months. For vegetables that have a long growing season or are heavy feeders, such as tomatoes, you may want to reapply organic or granular fertilizer or use a water-soluble fertilizer to supplement.

ROTATE. It's important to move crops to different beds from season to season. This prevents the buildup of diseases and insects specific to certain kinds of vegetables in any one part of the garden.

Vegetables need a sunny spot with well-drained soil.

VEGETABLE CONTAINERS

Many vegetables do well in containers. Follow these tips to get the biggest harvest.

CHOOSE THE RIGHT POT. Just like in the ground, vegetables in pots need room to grow. Vegetables don't like soggy feet, so make sure there are plenty of drainage holes in the bottom of your pot. For tomatoes, you want to be able to plant them deep, so choose a tall container that is at least 24 in. in diameter. Broccoli, eggplants, and greens will be happy in 18-in.-diameter pots or half whiskey barrels. When in doubt, go for the bigger container. Leafy veggies love containers.

SOIL. Never use garden soil or topsoil in your containers. These are heavy, compact easily, and don't drain well. Instead, opt for a good-quality potting soil. Look for bags that include a small amount of fertilizer so that you don't have to feed your plants right away. Some mixes also include wetting agents, which allow organic matter to absorb water easily and evenly, saving you time on watering.

WATER. Keep in mind that pots tend to dry out more quickly than plants in the ground. Check the soil often. Stick your finger about an inch down into the soil. If it feels dry, it's time to water. You may need to water daily in the summertime. Thoroughly wet soil, and keep the hose running until you see water run out of the bottom of the pot.

SUPPORT. Provide climbing plants such as cucumbers and pole beans a trellis to climb on, or plant bushing types in your pots. Tomatoes and eggplants will need stakes to support heavy fruit.

Keep watering in mind when planning your garden. This one is set up in a rectangular pattern, so one oscillating sprinkler covers it all.

ROOTS TO ROAST

Root crops such as carrots and turnips are classic side dishes for fall roasts—also for dropping into stews and casseroles. Below are five favorites. All need rich, deep soil to thrive; raised beds like the 4- by 8-ft. one pictured are ideal. Line the bottom with chicken wire to keep out gophers; fill with fast-draining planting mix. Plant the crops in rows (see encyclopedia listings for spacing).

RUTABAGA. A tasty turnip relative with large yellowish roots; its leaves are palatable only when young. Roast and serve with meat, or mash with potatoes.

TURNIP. Best known for roots, which come in various colors, including creamy yellow, and white with a purplish top. Foliage is also edible. Harvest and use as soon as they are big enough to eat (when flavor is sweetest). Roast and serve with meat, or mash with potatoes.

BEET. Grow for its edible roots and leafy tops, which, when young and tender, are tasty when sautéed. 'Bull's Blood' has glossy, red-bronze leaves; 'Chioggia' (sliced, the beet shows rings of red and white) and yellow-rooted selections are also available.

PARSNIP. Related to carrot, parsnip has long, creamy white to yellowish roots that taste delicately sweet. Needs frost to develop its flavor. Roast or use in stews; or pan roast with apples, carrots, and pork.

CARROT. Orange types are most familiar, but selections are available with yellow, white, or purple roots. Long market kinds such as 12-inch 'Envy' need a foot of loose soil to grow well. If you can give them only a few inches, grow half-long Nantes types or miniatures such as 'Short 'n Sweet'.

Cucumbers

Lettuce

Collards

Eggplants

Peppers

Snow Peas

Tomatoes

Okra

Pole Beans

WARM-WEATHER VEGETABLES

These favorites include tomatoes, cucumbers, eggplants, okra, and peppers. They thrive in summer and can be set out when the soil warms and all chances of frost have passed. See chart for more choices and what to plant in your zone.

TOMATOES

WHY WE LOVE THEM: Whether you like yours fried green or sliced on a sandwich, a fresh-picked tomato warmed from the sun is hard to beat. Tomatoes are highly productive and offer many different colors, shapes, sizes, flavors, and uses.
SECRETS TO SUCCESS: Keep soil consistently moist to prevent fruit from cracking or developing blossom-end rot.
HOW TO HARVEST: Pick them green or wait for them to ripen on the vine. A ripe tomato will fall into your hand with a gentle tug.

OKRA

WHY WE LOVE IT: This Southern staple thrives in long, hot summers and bears pods from July until frost. Great fried or used in stews, soups, and gumbo.
SECRETS TO SUCCESS: Keep the soil moist but be careful not to overwater, because plants will produce more foliage than pods. Don't sow seed until soil is warm.
HOW TO HARVEST: Cut pods when they are about 3 in. long (any longer, and they can be tough).

HOT AND SWEET PEPPERS

WHY WE LOVE THEM: Whether you're after a mild bell or a hot habañero that packs a punch, peppers thrive in Southern gardens and come in a range of colors and flavors.
SECRETS TO SUCCESS: Sometimes peppers stop producing when the weather gets too hot. Keep them watered and mulched, and they will produce again when the weather cools a bit.
HOW TO HARVEST: You can harvest peppers as soon as they reach a usable size, but for the most flavor (sweet or hot) allow them to ripen on the plant. Wear gloves when picking hot peppers and don't rub your eyes.

YELLOW SQUASH AND ZUCCHINI

WHY WE LOVE THEM: These fast-growing summer squash are some of the most productive vegetables in the garden.

SECRETS TO SUCCESS: All summer squash is susceptible to squash vine borers. Use a sharp knife to cut into the center of a wilted stem and kill the large, white borer inside. Mound moist soil over the cut area and keep it watered. New roots will grow along the stem.
HOW TO HARVEST: Summer squash will quickly reach harvest size in three to seven days after the flowers open, so keep an eye on them. Pick yellow squash when it's 4 to 6 in. long, zucchini when it's 6 to 8 in. long.

POLE BEANS

WHY WE LOVE THEM: Great for beginners, pole beans need little maintenance and yield a big harvest.
SECRETS TO SUCCESS: Sow seeds directly into the garden because they don't transplant easily. Pick beans regularly so plants will continue producing.
HOW TO HARVEST: Pick most pole beans when they are 4 to 6 in. long.

CUCUMBERS

WHY WE LOVE THEM: Their refreshing taste is just right for hot summer days.
SECRETS TO SUCCESS: Bitter cucumbers are the result of uneven watering. Keep the soil evenly moist. Seedy cucumbers have been left on the vine too long.
HOW TO HARVEST: You can begin to harvest when cucumbers are about 3 in. long.

EGGPLANTS

WHY WE LOVE THEM: You'll find this culinary globetrotter in many different cuisines, from Mediterranean to Indian. Eggplants come in a range of colors, from violet to chartreuse to fuchsia, as well as a range of shapes and sizes.
SECRETS TO SUCCESS: Eggplants are very sensitive to cold temperatures. Don't set out transplants until the soil warms. To maintain steady growth, keep the soil evenly moist and well mulched.
HOW TO HARVEST: To avoid bitterness and seediness that come with overmaturity, harvest when eggplants reach two-thirds their maximum size. Use shears to cut the fruit from the plant, leaving an inch or so of stem on the fruit.

SWEET POTATOES

WHY WE LOVE THEM: Sweet potatoes thrive in our long, hot summers. They're fat free, high in vitamins and fiber, come in many different kinds, and are the key ingredient to sweet potato pie.
SECRETS TO SUCCESS: Sweet potatoes need acid, well-drained soil and plenty of

room for the vines to spread. Don't plant until the soil has warmed to at least 70°F.
HOW TO HARVEST: Harvest before the first frost. Dig carefully to avoid damaging roots. Let roots dry in the sun until soil can be brushed off. Flavor improves in storage.

COOL-WEATHER VEGETABLES

These veggies take advantage of the pleasant temperatures and low humidity of early spring and fall. The combination of warm days and cool nights makes root crops such as carrots and beets crisp and sweet. Leafy greens such as mustard and kale become sweeter with a touch of frost. See chart for more choices and what to plant in your zone.

LETTUCE

WHY WE LOVE IT: Planting your own salad garden means more variety than you can find at the grocery store. And lettuce is easy.
SECRETS TO SUCCESS: Lettuce can take a light frost, but hard frosts can turn it to mush. Some selections are more cold tolerant, and some take heat better than others. Plant accordingly.
HOW TO HARVEST: Pick outside leaves first on loose-leaf types. Cut entire head for butterhead and Romaine.

SNOW PEAS

WHY WE LOVE THEM: You can pop these sweet, crunchy, edible pods straight from the vine into your mouth.
SECRETS TO SUCCESS: Plant early, as soon as the soil temperature reaches 45°F. Provide peas with a trellis to climb for easy harvest without bending down.
HOW TO HARVEST: Pick pods when they are 1½ to 2 in. long. They will be tough if you let them get bigger.

COLLARDS

WHY WE LOVE THEM: Every Southerner worth his salt knows these bring fortune for the year to come if eaten on New Year's Day. Grow your own for a dose of good luck in spring and fall.
SECRETS TO SUCCESS: Choose a fertilizer high in nitrogen to promote lots of leaves. Keep the soil pH about 6.5. Add lime if soil is too acidic.
HOW TO HARVEST: Use a small knife or clippers to cut the entire plant about 4 in. from the ground; the plant will send up new leaves from the remaining stem. You can also pop off single leaves by hand, starting from the bottom.

WHEN TO PLANT YOUR CROPS

The edibles listed in the chart below and on the following pages include plants that can be grown during various seasons. For almost all of these vegetables, the fruit is the edible part. Planting times are listed by frost date. To determine your date of the last frost in your area, consult your local Cooperative Extension Service, or do an online search, "zipcode last frost" and look for the NOAA (National Weather Service) website.

SPRING & SUMMER CROPS

IF THE AVERAGE DATE OF THE LAST FROST IN YOUR AREA IS...	JANUARY 30	FEBRUARY 8	FEBRUARY 18	FEBRUARY 28	
...THEN THE BEST TIMES TO PLANT ARE...					
Beans, lima	Feb. 10-Apr. 15	Feb. 20-May 1	Mar. 1-May 1	Mar. 15-June 1	
Beans, snap	Feb. 1-Apr. 1	Feb. 10-May 1	Feb. 20-May 15	Mar. 1-May 15	
Beets	Jan. 1-Mar. 15	Jan. 10-Mar. 15	Jan. 20-Apr. 1	Feb. 1-Apr. 15	
Broccoli*	Jan. 1-30	Jan. 10-Feb. 5	Jan. 25-Feb. 15	Jeb. 1-Mar. 1	
Brussels sprouts*					
Cabbage*	Dec. 15-Jan. 30	Dec. 25-Feb. 5	Jan. 10-Feb. 15	Jan. 15-Feb. 25	
Cabbage, Chinese*	Dec. 15-Jan. 30	Dec. 25-Feb. 5	Jan. 10-Feb. 15	Jan. 15-Feb. 25	
Carrots	Dec. 20-Mar. 1	Dec. 25-Mar. 1	Jan. 10-Mar. 1	Jan. 15-Mar. 1	
Cauliflower*	Jan. 1-30	Jan. 10-Feb. 10	Jan. 25-Feb. 25	Feb. 1-28	
Chard, Swiss	Jan. 1-Apr. 1	Jan. 10-Apr. 1	Jan. 20-Apr. 15	Feb. 1-May 1	
Collards & Kale	Dec. 15-Jan. 30	Dec. 20-Feb. 5	Jan. 10-Feb. 15	Jan. 15-Feb. 25	
Corn, sweet	Feb. 1-May 15	Feb. 10-June 1	Feb. 20-June 1	Mar. 1-June 1	
Cucumbers	Feb. 15-Mar. 15	Feb. 20-Apr. 1	Mar. 5-Apr. 15	Mar. 10-Apr. 15	
Eggplant	Feb. 10-Mar. 15	Feb. 20-Mar. 30	Mar. 5-Apr. 1	Mar. 10-Apr. 10	
Leeks	Jan. 1-Feb. 1	Jan. 1-Feb. 1	Jan. 10-Feb. 1	Jan. 15-Feb. 15	
Lettuce, head*	Dec. 20-Feb. 1	Jan. 1-Feb. 1	Jan. 10-Feb. 1	Jan. 15-Feb. 15	
Lettuce, leaf	Dec. 20-Feb. 10	Jan. 1-Mar. 1	Jan. 10-Mar. 5	Jan. 15-Mar. 10	

* Started from transplants

Swiss Chard

Carrots

Broccoli

	MARCH 10	MARCH 20	MARCH 30	APRIL 10	APRIL 20	APRIL 30	MAY 10
	Mar. 20-June 1	Apr. 1-June 15	Apr. 15-June 20	Apr. 25-June 30	May 5-June 20	May 15- June 15	May 25-June 15
	Mar. 15- May 15	Mar. 25-May 25	Apr. 1-June 1	Apr. 15-June 30	Apr. 25-June 30	May 1-June 30	May 15-June 30
	Feb. 10-May 1	Feb. 20-May 15	Mar. 1-June 1	Mar. 10-June 1	Mar. 20-June 1	Apr. 1-June 15	Apr. 10-June 15
	Feb. 10-Mar. 10	Feb. 10-Mar. 15	Mar. 1-20	Mar. 15-Apr. 15	Mar. 25-Apr. 20	Apr. 1-30	Apr. 10-June 1
	Feb. 10-28	Feb. 20-Mar. 15	Mar. 1-20	Mar. 15-Apr. 15	Mar. 25-Apr. 20	Apr. 1-30	Apr. 10-June 1
	Jan. 30-Mar. 10	Feb. 5-Mar. 15	Feb. 15-Mar. 20	Mar. 1-Apr. 1	Mar. 10-Apr. 1	Mar. 20-Apr. 10	Apr. 1-May 15
	Jan. 30-Mar. 10	Feb. 5-Mar. 1	Feb. 15-Mar. 10	Mar. 1-Apr. 1	Mar. 10-Apr. 1	Mar. 20-Apr. 10	Apr. 1-May 15
	Jan. 30-Mar. 15	Feb. 5-Mar. 20	Feb. 20-Apr. 10	Mar. 1-Apr. 20	Mar. 5-May 15	Mar. 20-June 1	Mar. 30-June 15
	Feb. 10-Mar. 10	Feb. 20-Mar. 20	Mar. 1-30	Mar. 10-Apr. 10	Mar. 20-Apr. 20	Mar. 30-Apr. 30	Apr. 10-May 10
	Feb. 15-May 15	Feb. 20-May 1	Mar. 1-May 25	Mar. 10-June 15	Mar. 20-June 15	Mar. 30-June 15	Apr. 10-June 15
	Jan. 30-Mar. 10	Feb. 1-Mar. 1	Feb. 15-Mar. 10	Mar. 1-30	Mar. 10-30	Mar. 15-Apr. 10	Apr. 1-May 15
	Mar. 10-June 1	Mar. 20-July 15	Mar. 30-July 15	Apr. 10-July 15	Apr. 20-July 15	Apr. 30-July 15	May 10-July 1
	Mar. 25-Apr. 25	Apr. 1-May 1	Apr. 15-May 15	Apr. 20-June 1	May 1-June 15	May 15- June 15	May 25-June 15
	Mar. 25-Apr. 25	Apr. 1-30	Apr. 15-May 15	Apr. 25-May 25	May 5-June 5	May 15-June 15	May 25-June 15
	Feb. 1-20	Feb. 1-Mar. 1	Feb. 15-Mar. 15	Mar. 1-Apr. 1	Mar. 15-Apr. 15	Apr. 1-May 1	Apr. 15-May 15
	Feb. 1-20	Feb. 5-Mar. 10	Feb. 20-Mar. 20	Mar. 1-30	Mar. 5-Apr. 10	Mar. 20-Apr. 20	Apr. 1-30
	Feb. 1-Mar. 25	Feb. 5-Apr. 1	Feb. 20-Apr. 10	Mar. 1-Apr. 20	Mar. 5-Apr. 30	Mar. 20-May 15	Apr. 1-May 30

SPRING & SUMMER CROPS (CONTINUED)

IF THE AVERAGE DATE OF THE LAST FROST IN YOUR AREA IS...	JANUARY 30	FEBRUARY 8	FEBRUARY 18	FEBRUARY 28	
...THEN THE BEST TIMES TO PLANT ARE...					
Melons	Feb. 10-Mar. 15	Feb. 20-Mar. 30	Mar. 5-Apr. 1	Mar. 10-Apr. 10	
Mustard	Jan. 1-Feb. 5	Jan. 10-Feb. 15	Jan. 20-Feb. 25	Feb. 1-Mar. 5	
Okra	Feb. 5-Apr. 1	Feb. 15-Apr. 15	Feb. 25-June 1	Mar. 5-June 1	
Onion sets	Jan. 1-15	Jan. 1-15	Jan. 1-15	Jan. 1-Feb. 1	
Peas, English	Dec. 5-Feb. 15	Dec. 10-Mar. 1	Dec. 25-Mar. 1	Jan. 1-Mar. 1	
Peas, Southern	Feb. 15-May 1	Feb. 15-May 15	Mar. 1-June 15	Mar. 10-June 20	
Peppers*	Feb. 10-Mar. 15	Feb. 20-Mar. 30	Mar. 5-Apr. 1	Mar. 10-Apr. 10	
Potatoes, Irish	Jan. 1-Feb. 15	Jan. 1-Feb. 15	Jan. 15-Mar. 1	Jan. 15-Mar. 1	
Potatoes, sweet	Feb. 20-May 15	Mar. 1-May 15	Mar. 10-June 1	Mar. 20-June 15	
Pumpkins	Feb. 15-Mar. 15	Feb. 20-Mar. 30	Mar. 5-Apr. 30	Mar. 10-July 1	
Radishes (spring)	Dec. 20-Feb. 28	Dec. 25-Mar. 5	Jan. 10-Mar. 20	Jan. 15-Mar. 25	
Rutabagas	Dec. 5-Jan. 30	Dec. 10-Feb. 8	Dec. 25-Feb. 18	Jan. 1-Mar. 1	
Spinach	Dec. 20-Feb. 15	Dec. 25-Feb. 15	Jan. 10-Mar. 1	Jan. 15-Mar. 1	
Spinach, Malabar	Feb. 1-Aug. 30	Feb. 10-Aug. 30	Feb. 20-Aug. 30	Mar. 1-Aug. 30	
Spinach, New Zealand	Feb. 1-Apr. 15	Feb. 15-Apr. 15	Mar. 1-Apr. 15	Mar. 15-May 15	
Squash, summer	Feb. 1-Apr. 15	Feb. 10-Apr. 15	Feb. 20-Apr. 15	Mar. 1-May 15	
Squash, winter	Feb. 15-May 30	Feb. 20-Mar. 30	Mar. 5-July 1	Mar. 10-July 1	
Tomatoes*	Feb. 1-Apr. 1	Feb. 10-Apr. 10	Feb. 20-Apr. 20	Mar. 1-May 1	
Turnips	Jan. 1-Feb. 15	Jan. 10-Feb. 20	Jan. 20-Mar. 1	Feb. 1-Mar. 10	

* Started from transplants

	MARCH 10	MARCH 20	MARCH 30	APRIL 10	APRIL 20	APRIL 30	MAY 10
	Mar. 25-Apr. 25	Apr. 1-30	Apr. 15-May 15	Apr. 25-May 25	May 5-June 5	May 15- June 15	May 25-June 15
	Feb. 15-Mar. 15	Feb. 20-Mar. 25	Mar. 1-Apr. 5	Mar. 10-Apr. 15	Mar. 20-Apr. 30	Mar. 30-May 5	Apr. 10-May 15
	Mar. 15-July 15	Apr. 1-July 15	Apr. 10-July 15	Apr. 20-June 15	May 1-30	May 10-30	May 20-June 10
	Jan. 15-Feb. 15	Feb. 20-Mar. 10	Mar. 1-15	Mar. 10-30	Mar. 20-Apr. 10	Apr. 1-30	Apr. 10-30
	Jan. 15-Mar. 15	Jan. 25-Mar. 15	Feb. 5-Mar. 20	Feb. 15-Mar. 20	Mar. 1-Apr. 10	Mar. 5-May 1	Mar. 15-May 15
	Mar. 15-July 1	Apr. 1-July 1	Apr. 15-July 1	Apr. 15-July 1	Apr. 25-July 15	May 10-June 1	
	Mar. 25-Apr. 25	Apr. 1-30	Apr. 15-May 15	Apr. 25-May 15	May 5-June 5	May 15-June 15	May 25-June 15
	Feb. 1-Mar. 1	Feb. 10-Mar. 15	Feb. 20-Mar. 20	Mar. 10-Apr. 1	Mar. 15-Apr. 10	Mar. 20-May 10	Apr. 1-June 1
	Apr. 1-July 1	Apr. 10-June 1	Apr. 25-June 1	Apr. 30-June 1	May 10-June 10	May 20-June 10	June 1-15
	Mar. 25-July 1	Apr. 1-30	Apr. 15-May 15	Apr. 25-May 25	May 5-May 25	May 15-May 25	May 15-25
	Feb. 1-Apr. 10	Feb. 5-Apr. 15	Feb. 20-Apr. 30	Feb. 28-May 5	Mar. 10-May 15	Mar. 20-May 30	Mar. 25-June 5
	Jan. 15-Mar. 1	Jan. 25-Mar. 1	Jan. 30-Mar. 1	Feb. 15-Mar. 1	Feb. 20-Mar. 10	Mar. 5-June 1	Mar. 15-June 1
	Feb. 1-Mar. 10	Feb. 5-Mar. 15	Feb. 20-Mar. 20	Feb. 28-Apr. 1	Mar. 5-Apr. 1	Mar. 20-Apr. 15	Mar. 25-June 15
	Mar. 15-Aug. 30	Mar. 25-July 30	Apr. 1-July 30	Apr. 15-July 30	Apr. 25-July 30	May 1-July 30	May 15-July 30
	Mar. 20-May 15	Apr. 1-May 15	Apr. 10-June 1	Apr. 20-June 1	May 1-June 15	May 1-June 15	May 10-June 15
	Mar. 10-May 1	Mar. 20-May 15	Apr. 1-June 1	Apr. 10-June 1	Apr. 20-June 15	May 1-30	May 10-June 10
	Mar. 25-July 1	Mar. 20-Apr. 30	Apr. 1-May 15	Apr. 10-May 25	Apr. 20-May 25	May 1-May 25	May 10-May 25
	Mar. 10-May 10	Mar. 20-May 20	Apr. 1-June 1	Apr. 10-June 1	Apr. 20-June 10	May 1-June 15	May 10-June 15
	Feb. 15-Mar. 25						

FALL & WINTER CROPS

IF THE AVERAGE DATE OF THE FIRST FROST IN YOUR AREA IS...	SEPT. 30	OCT. 10	OCT. 20	OCT. 30	
...THEN THE BEST TIMES TO PLANT ARE...					
Asparagus*		Nov. 1-Mar. 30	Nov. 1-Mar. 30	Nov. 15-Mar. 15	
Beans, lima	June 1-15	June 1-15	June 15-30	July 1-30	
Beets	July 1-30	July 5-Aug. 15	July 15-Aug. 30	July 25-Sept. 1	
Broccoli*	June 1-30	June 15-July 15	July 1-30	July 1-Aug. 15	
Brussels sprouts*	July 1-25	July 5-30	July 15-Aug. 15	July 25-Aug. 20	
Cabbage*	June 25-Aug. 5	July 5-Aug. 15	July 5-Aug. 25	July 25-Sept. 5	
Cabbage, Chinese*	June 25-Aug. 5	July 5-Aug. 15	July 5-Aug. 25	July 25-Sept. 5	
Carrots	June 5-July 10	June 10-July 20	June 25-July 30	July 5-Aug. 10	
Cauliflower*	July 25-Aug. 5	Aug. 1-15	Aug. 15-25	Aug. 20-Sept. 5	
Chard, Swiss	June 10-July 10	June 20-July 20	July 1-30	July 10-Aug. 5	
Collards & Kale	July 10-Aug. 5	July 15-Aug. 15	Aug. 1-30	Aug. 5-Sept. 5	
Cucumbers	July 1-25	July 10-30	July 25-Aug. 15	Aug. 1-20	
Lettuce, leaf	June 25-Aug. 15	July 1-Aug. 22	July 15-Sept. 5	July 25-Sept. 10	
Mustard	July 10-Aug. 20	July 15-Aug. 25	Aug. 1-Sept. 10	Aug. 5-Sept. 15	
Onion sets				Sept. 1-15	
Peas, English	July 10-25	July 15-30	Aug. 1-15	Aug. 1-15	
Potatoes, Irish		June 10-July 15	June 25-Aug. 1	July 5-Aug. 5	
Pumpkins		June 10-July 10	June 25-July 25	July 1-30	
Radishes, summer	July 25-Aug. 20	Aug. 1-30	Aug. 15-Sept. 10	Aug. 20-Sept. 15	
Radishes, winter	Aug. 1-Sept. 5	Aug. 10-Sept. 10	Aug. 20-Sept. 25	Aug. 30-Oct. 1	
Rutabagas	July 1-15	July 1-30	July 1-30	July 1-30	
Squash, winter	---	June 10-July 10	June 25-July 25	July 1-30	
Tomatoes*	June 5-25	June 10-July 5	June 25-July 25	July 1-30	
Turnips	June 25-Aug. 20	July 10-Aug. 25	July 15-Sept. 10	July 25-Sept. 20	

* Started from transplants

	NOV. 10	NOV. 20	NOV. 30	DEC. 10	DEC. 20
	Nov. 30-Mar. 1	Dec. 1-30			
	July 1-Aug. 15	July 15-Sept. 1	Aug. 1-Sept. 15	Sept. 1-30	Sept. 1-30
	Aug. 10-Sept. 20	Aug. 5-Sept. 15	Aug. 15-Sept. 25	Aug. 25-Oct. 10	Sept. 5-Oct. 15
	Aug. 1-30	Aug. 1-Sept. 15	Aug. 1-Oct. 1	Aug. 1-Nov. 1	Sept. 1-Nov. 1
	Aug. 5-Sept. 5	Aug. 5-Sept. 10	Aug. 20-Sept. 20	Sept. 1-Oct. 1	Sept. 10-Oct. 10
	Aug. 5-Sept. 20	Aug. 15-Sept. 25	Aug. 20-Oct. 1	Sept. 5-Oct. 15	Sept. 10-Oct. 20
	Aug. 5-Sept. 20	Aug. 15-Sept. 25	Aug. 20-Oct. 1	Sept. 5-Oct. 15	Sept. 10-Oct. 20
	July 15-Aug. 20	Aug. 5-Oct. 1	Aug. 15-Oct. 10	Aug. 25-Oct. 25	Sept. 5-Nov. 1
	Sept. 1-15	Sept. 10-25	Sept. 20-30	Oct. 1-15	Oct. 10-25
	July 25-Aug. 20	Aug. 1-30	Aug. 5-Sept. 5	Aug. 20-Sept. 20	Sept. 1-30
	Aug. 10-Sept. 10	Aug. 25-Sept. 25	Sept. 1-30	Sept. 15-Oct. 15	Sept. 25-Oct. 25
	Aug. 15-30	Aug. 20-Sept. 10	Aug. 30-Sept. 20	Sept. 10-Sept. 30	Sept. 20-Oct. 10
	Aug. 5-Sept. 25	Aug. 15-Sept. 30	Aug. 20-Sept. 30	Sept. 1-Nov. 30	Sept. 1-Nov. 30
	Aug. 20-Oct. 1	Aug. 30-Sept. 30	Sept. 5-Oct. 15	Sept. 20-Nov. 1	Sept. 25-Nov. 5
	Sept. 15-30	Sept. 25-Oct. 10	Oct. 1-15	Oct. 15-30	Oct. 25-Nov. 5
	Aug. 15-30	Aug. 25-Sept. 10	Sept. 5-20	Sept. 15-30	Sept. 25-Oct. 10
	July 15-Aug. 20	July 25-Aug. 25	Aug. 1-Sept. 5	Aug. 15-Sept. 20	Aug. 20-Sept. 25
	July 15-Aug. 15	July 25-Aug. 20	Aug. 1-30	Aug. 15-Sept. 10	Aug. 20-Sept. 20
	Sept. 1-Oct. 1	Sept. 10-Oct. 10	Sept. 20-Oct. 15	Oct. 1-Nov. 1	Oct. 10-Nov. 5
	Sept. 10-Oct. 15	Sept. 20-Oct. 25	Sept. 25-Nov. 1	Oct. 10-Nov. 15	Oct. 15-Nov. 20
	July 1-Aug. 31	Aug. 1-30	Aug. 1-Sept. 15	Aug. 15-Sept. 15	Aug. 15-Sept. 15
	July 15-Aug. 15	July 25-Aug. 20	Aug. 1-30	Aug. 15-Sept. 10	Aug. 20-Sept. 20
	July 15-Aug. 5	July 25-Aug. 15	Aug. 1-20	Aug. 15-Sept. 5	Aug. 20-Sept. 10
	Aug. 5-Oct. 1	Aug. 15-Oct. 10	Aug. 20-Oct. 15	Sept. 5-Nov. 1	Sept. 10-Nov. 5

Red Cabbage

Radish

Purple Mustard

WHAT IS AN HEIRLOOM SEED?

When you hear the word "heirloom," you might think of your grandmother's silver. In gardening the treasures are no less valuable. Heirloom vegetables and fruits are grown from open-pollinated seeds that have been collected and passed down from generation to generation. Unlike hybrids, which took hold after World War II or the often-controversial GMOs you'll find today, heirloom seeds will remain true to type year after year and are often prized for superior flavor. One of the country's most influential seed savers, Thomas Jefferson, viewed this practice as good insurance. He traded seeds with his neighbors and friends, knowing that if he lost his seeds or killed his plants, he could always find replacements.

Why should you care? Many hybrids today, especially food crops, are patented selections owned by multinational corporations. These companies set the price and availability and can tinker with the seeds' genetics any way they choose.

Open-pollinated varieties aren't owned by anyone or patented. The only way they can disappear is if people stop growing them in favor of the hybrids. Here are a few of our favorites.

WARM-WEATHER HEIRLOOMS

- **'RED NOODLE' BEANS**—Also called yardlong beans, these Asia natives are fun to grow because of their size (more than 20 in. long). Beans turn green when cooked.
- **'AUNT HETTIE'S RED' OKRA**—a burgundy-podded heirloom from Tennessee, featuring beautiful red stalks and leaves.
- **'MORTGAGE LIFTER' TOMATO**—hailing from West Virginia, this heat- and disease-resistant tomato from the 1930s bears tomatoes weighing up to 4 pounds (1-2 pounds is average).

- **'BLACK BEAUTY' ZUCCHINI**—a native of Italy, the plant has an open growth habit, which makes it easy to see zucchini and harvest before they get too big.
- **'LOUISIANA LONG GREEN' EGGPLANT**—as the name implies, this is a Louisiana native. It's a prolific producer of long, light-green skinned fruit.

COLD-WEATHER HEIRLOOMS

- **'GEORGIA SOUTHERN' COLLARD**—a heat-tolerant collard that dates back to 1880, green with big, dark-green leaves and a mild flavor.

- **'LACINATO' KALE**—Grown by Jefferson at Monticello, this kale originates from 18th-century Italy. Crinkled leaves add texture to the garden. Also called "dinosaur kale."
- **'CALABRESE' BROCCOLI**—brought to the U.S. by Italian immigrants in the late 19th century, this broccoli is tolerant of light frost and produces lots of side shoots.
- **'SPOTTED ALEPPO' LETTUCE**—a Romaine lettuce introduced in the 18th century, its red spotted leaves make a pretty addition to salads as well as vegetable gardens.

SWAPPING SEEDS

Don't worry if you don't know someone willing to part with seeds. There are several good mail-order sources for heirloom selections.

BAKER CREEK HEIRLOOM SEEDS
rareseeds.com
BURPEE
burpee.com
D. LANDRETH SEED COMPANY
landrethseeds.com
MONTICELLO
monticelloshop.org
PARK SEED
parkseed.com
SEED SAVERS EXCHANGE
seedsavers.org
SEEDS OF CHANGE
seedsofchange.com
SOUTHERN EXPOSURE SEED EXCHANGE
southernexposure.com
SOW TRUE SEED
sowtrueseed.com

Sea kale was a Jefferson favorite at Monticello. Special clay pots are used to cover and blanch the vegetables as he would have done.

A GUIDE TO GROWING
FRUIT

Why should you grow your own fruit? First, store-bought fruit is often picked, shipped, and sold before it's fully ripened. Second, stores generally stock selections that look pretty but are not necessarily the best tasting. Finally, some fruit, such as blueberries and figs, makes outstanding ornamental plants in the landscape. Choose some of our favorites, and enjoy the fruits of your labor.

PLANT

The best times to plant fruit in the ground is when it's dormant in fall or early spring. However, potted plants can be set out almost anytime, provided they receive sufficient water.

EXPOSURE. Fruit enjoys full sun. Sunlight promotes more flowers, which means more fruit. Sun also encourages sugar production, resulting in sweeter fruit. Choose a spot that gets at least 6 hours of direct sunlight a day. The more sun, the better.

SITE. Good drainage is essential for almost all fruit. Be aware what soil is best for what you are planting. Blueberries, for example, need highly acid soil, while figs, grapes, and apples are more adaptable. See the plant encyclopedia for each plant.

TEND

WATER. Water newly planted trees and bushes deeply until they have time to establish their root systems. Fruit with a high water content such as blueberries and blackberries need consistent watering to produce juicy fruit.

FEED. Choose fertilizers that are especially formulated for your particular plant, and follow label instructions. Slow-release, organic fertilizers are preferred.

MULCH. A thick layer of organic mulch will help retain water and keep weeds down. For trees and bushes, never pile mulch against the trunks.

CRITTER CONTROL. Animals love fruit as much as we do. Birds are especially attracted to berries. Hang reflective tape near your berries or cover plants with nylon netting. Deter deer with 6- to 8-ft. fencing, motion-activated sprinklers, or commercial deer repellent. For more tips on derailing four-legged gluttons, turn to page 716.

OUR TOP PICKS

APPLES

WHY WE LOVE THEM: Crisp apples grow well throughout most of the South and are quite productive. Many heirloom types, like 'Arkansas Black' and 'Grimes Golden' originate in the South.

SECRETS TO SUCCESS: Self-pollinating selections, such as 'Golden Delicious' and 'Grimes Golden', will bear fruit without having another apple tree around. But most selections need cross-pollination with a different selection to bear fruit. If you are short on space, buy a multiselection tree, which will have up to 5 different types grafted onto a single trunk and rootstock. This will also ensure pollination within a single tree. You can buy three different sizes: standard (matures at 20 to 25 ft. tall and wide), semidwarf (10 to 20 ft.), and dwarf (5 to 8 ft.). Dwarf and semidwarf are good choices for most people; they take up less room and bear fruit at a young age. Also, if you're not into climbing 20 ft. in the air to pick apples, stay away from the standards.

HOW TO HARVEST: Firmly grasp fruit and twist off of stem.

MUSCADINES

WHY WE LOVE THEM: These grapes are native to the South. Adapted to heat and humidity, they thrive in the Coastal, Lower, and Middle South, as well as protected areas of the Upper South.

SECRETS TO SUCCESS: Fertilize with a balanced fertilizer, such as 10-10-10, in late winter or early spring. A reduced-rate application of calcium nitrate after harvest in early fall may also prove beneficial. Most selections of muscadines are "self-fruitful" meaning you need only one vine to have fruit—a great option for small spaces. Good self-fruitful choices include 'Noble' and 'Dixie Red'. Other muscadines, such as

'Arkansas Black' *Apples*

'Black Beauty' *Muscadine*

'Kiowa' Blackberries

Strawberries

'Fuyu' Oriental Persimmon

'Darlene', 'Pam', 'Janet', 'Black Beauty', and 'Fry', need to be planted near self-fruitful selections to cross-pollinate and bear fruit.

HOW TO HARVEST: Simply pluck fruit from the vine.

'IMPROVED MEYER' LEMON

WHY WE LOVE IT: A hybrid between lemon and a Mandarin orange, its glossy green leaves and sweet scented blooms makes this an attractive tree to place in a pot on the patio. And the fruit is tasty.

SECRETS TO SUCCESS: Citrus plants are heavy feeders. Fertilize with a product made especially for citrus in late winter, late spring, and fall. Follow recommendations on the label. In the Tropical and mildest parts of the Coastal South, you can plant in the ground in a sunny spot with well-drained soil. Elsewhere, plant in a container that's at least 18 in. in diameter. Bring pots indoors, or overwinter in a garage or other covered area that gets bright light. If you grow indoors, keep plants away from radiators or other heat sources.

HOW TO HARVEST: For sweetest flavor, wait until your Meyer lemons have ripened completely. Twist fruit from tree.

FIGS

WHY WE LOVE THEM: With their tropical-looking leaves and stout trunks, fig trees make picturesque additions to the yard. Even better, they require very little attention.

SECRETS TO SUCCESS: Figs are self-pollinating, so you need only one to get fruit. Most selections bear a small crop of fruit in June or July and a larger one August to October. If you live in the Upper South, grow fig trees in containers and bring them indoors for winter. In the Middle South, fig trees may die to the ground following cold winters, but will then resprout. They are fully hardy in the Lower, Coastal, and Tropical South.

HOW TO HARVEST: A ripe fig should feel soft like a ripe peach but not mushy. Pull up on it, and the fruit should come off easily in your hand.

STRAWBERRIES

WHY WE LOVE THEM: These sweet, juicy berries can grow in the ground or in a container, so you don't need a lot of space.

SECRETS TO SUCCESS: Whether you choose June-bearing (produce one crop a year in late spring or early summer) or everbearing (produce fewer runners but set fruit over a longer period), plants need about 1 in. of water per week in the growing season, more when bearing fruit.

HOW TO HARVEST: Size doesn't determine when to harvest. Pick berries when they are plump, firm, and fully red—even if they are small.

BLUEBERRIES

WHY WE LOVE THEM: In addition to the fruit, these handsome shrubs sport dainty, white flowers in early spring, followed by leaves that turn orange and scarlet in fall.

SECRETS TO SUCCESS: Rabbiteye and Southern highbush selections do well in the Middle, Lower, and Coastal South. Choose Northern highbush selections in the Upper and Middle South. You'll need two or more selections for optimal pollination and lots of fruit.

HOW TO HARVEST: Blueberries don't ripen all at once. You'll see green, pink, and blue all on the same bush. If there's a hint of pink on the berry, that means it's not ripe yet. Be patient, and don't pick until they are fully blue.

BLACKBERRIES

WHY WE LOVE THEM: Great straight off the vine or baked into a blackberry cobbler.

SECRETS TO SUCCESS: Apply lime sulfur spray in late winter to control pests. Train them against a wall or fence to make harvesting easy. If you don't want to bother with training, choose self-supporting, upright selections, such as 'Arapaho' and 'Navaho'. These two selections are also thornless, a bonus when you want to harvest without the pain of getting stuck.

HOW TO HARVEST: When ripe, berries will pull away from the plant easily. Look for a dull black color. If berries are red or purple, they aren't ready yet.

ORIENTAL PERSIMMONS

WHY WE LOVE THEM: Unlike their American cousins (*Diospyros virginiana*), which are sour before they are soft and ripe, Oriental persimmons (*D. kaki*) are sweet from the start and bear bigger fruit.

SECRETS TO SUCCESS: Prune young trees in spring to open up the center and provide well-spaced branches aiming outward. Pruning is seldom needed after that.

HOW TO HARVEST: Use sharp clippers to snip fruit from the branches. Don't harvest fruit when it's green. Once it starts to show color, you can harvest, and fruit will ripen on its own.

A GUIDE TO GROWING
VINES

Whether draping an arbor, twining through a trellis, or clambering over a wall,
vines soften structures and add a sense of romance to the garden.

CHOOSE

Vines may be deciduous, semievergreen, evergreen, or annual.
Some provide greenery alone, others bear decorative fruit or
booms. A vine's weight at maturity and its method of attachment will determine the kind of support needed. Once you
have a good idea of what you're looking for, choose wisely.

PLANT AND TEND

Most vines are sold in containers; some deciduous kinds, such
as roses, are available as bare-root plants (see page 665 for
planting guidelines). Many are happy in containers, or you can
plant them in the ground and train them on an arbor, or simply
let them ramble for a fast-growing ground cover.

BLOOMING BEAUTIES

These vines not only reward you with foliage, but they're also
loaded with flowers.

CAROLINA JESSAMINE (*Gelsemium sempervirens*)
This low-maintenance vine offers evergreen foliage, outstanding
flowers, and sweet fragrance. What more could you ask? It
makes itself at home on fences, trellises, and mailboxes. Or you
can let it loose to form a bushy ground cover. Zones MS, LS, CS;
USDA 7-9.

CHINESE TRUMPET CREEPER (*Campsis grandiflora*)
Tough and heat tolerant, Chinese trumpet creeper is not as
vigorous as its native relative, common trumpet creeper
(*C. radicans*). More reserved in nature, it actually makes the
better garden guest, with big trumpet-shaped flowers in
shades of orange, red, and peach from summer until fall.
Under ideal conditions, it will grow to about 30 ft. in length—
perfect for covering an arbor or softening a stark privacy fence.
Zones US, MS, LS, CS; USDA 6-9.

CLEMATIS (*Clematis sp.*)
Depending on species, clematis can be deciduous or
evergreen. They offer blossoms of blue, purple, red, pink, or
white. Grow them on a fence, on a trellis, or in a container.
Jackman clematis (*C. x jackmanii*), an old-fashioned hybrid,
blooms so heavily that it's hard to even see the leaves. All
clematis like cool roots, so mulch them heavily. Zones vary by
species; see plant encyclopedia for specifics.

CROSSVINE (*Bignonia capreolata*)
Choose this rapid climber if you want to shade an arbor
quickly. Trumpet-shaped flowers will smother the vine in
spring, attracting hummingbirds and butterflies. Crossvine is

*The showy orange trumpets of Chinese trumpet
creeper are magnets for hummingbirds.*

evergreen in most of the South but may drop its leaves in cooler part of the Upper South. Zones US (milder parts), MS, LS, CS; USDA 6-9.

CONFEDERATE JASMINE (*Trachelospermum jasminoides*)
This vigorous, evergreen vine bears extremely fragrant, white flowers in spring or early summer. Train on a trellis, arbor, or gazebo. Zones LS, CS, TS; USDA 8-11

TRUMPET HONEYSUCKLE (*Lonicera sempervirens*)
Showy flowers in late spring and summer attract hummingbirds. This semievergreen vine retains some of its leaves in the Lower and Coastal South, but will drop leaves when the temperature cools in the rest of the South. A good vine to cloak arbors and trellises. Zones US, MS, LS, CS; USDA 6-9.

ENGLISH IVY (*Hedera helix*)
Though it's tempting to plant English ivy to climb a wall, be aware that it can be aggressive and damage brick, wood, and concrete. Instead, use it as a fast-growing ground cover, a leafy camouflage for a chain-link fence, and to spill from the edges of containers. Or make it the star of the container and train it as a topiary. Zones US, MS, LS, CS; USDA 6-9.

CREEPING FIG (*Ficus pumila*)
Heart-shaped leaves cling by aerial roots (gluelike disks) that won't harm brick walls. Don't use it on wooden structures, because it will trap moisture and also make it difficult to paint. Zones LS, CS, TS; USDA 8-11.

JACKSON VINE (*Smilax smallii*)
Dark green, glossy, evergreen leaves climb with tendrils. It gets its common name from the fact that during the Civil War, ladies in Alabama used it to decorate tables when Stonewall Jackson came to town. Today, many of the older homes in Huntsville and Birmingham use it to frame the front door. It is difficult to find transplants, but easy to start from seed. Zones MS, LS, CS; USDA 7-9

Carolina Jessamine

FIVE VINES TO AVOID

They may charm you with their pretty blooms, colorful berries, or brilliant fall foliage, but beware! These vines will take over your yard or tear down a trellis.

JAPANESE WISTERIA (*Wisteria floribunda*) OR CHINESE WISTERIA (*W. sinensis*)
Asian wisterias spread by seed, runners, and suckers. They'll grow as tall as whatever they're growing on. So if they get loose in your yard, watch out. The only way to kill one is to cut through the trunk near the ground and paint the cut end with herbicide according to label directions. Fortunately, there is a nice, friendly, native wisteria you can plant — American wisteria (*W. frutescens*). Unlike its cousins, it's well-behaved and doesn't destroy things. Look for a selection called 'Amethyst Falls' at the garden center.

ORIENTAL BITTERSWEET (*Celastrus orbiculatus*)
Unlike our relatively tame native American bittersweet (*Celastrus scandens*), Oriental bittersweet is more bitter than sweet. Birds eat the seeds and spread them everywhere. Suckers from the roots shoot up yards from the original plant. Its thick, sinewy branches throttle small trees and climb as far as they can reach. If you buy a bittersweet wreath for the holidays, seal it inside a plastic trash bag when you're through with it, and put it out with the trash. To kill an Oriental bittersweet growing in your yard, treat it as recommended for wisteria.

PORCELAIN BERRY (*Ampelopsis brevipedunculata*)
No plant has prettier berries than porcelain berry. They start out yellow, progress to pale lilac, then deep magenta, and finally end up bright blue. Often all four colors are present in the same cluster. As with bittersweet, birds love the berries of this ornamental grape from Asia. They gobble them all, poop out the seeds, and every seed germinates. With its thin, pliable stems, porcelain berry doesn't crush structures or plants, but it grows like kudzu and will take over your garden in a heartbeat.

JAPANESE HONEYSUCKLE (*Lonicera japonica*)
Few childhood memories are as sweet as the scent of honeysuckle blooms or the single drop of nectar stolen from each flower. Japanese honeysuckle would be a treasure if only it would stay put. But it won't. This fast-growing, twining vine spreads by berries eaten by birds and by suckers. It turns woodlands into impenetrable thickets. In high-rainfall areas like the Southeast, it's nearly impossible to eradicate.

VIRGINIA CREEPER (*Parthenocissus quinquefolia*)
Our native Virginia creeper doesn't twine, but uses small, rootlike tendrils to climb straight up anything—bark, steel, concrete, chain-link fences, PVC. Anything. And it grows fast. Again, birds love the berries, which cause seedlings to sprout everywhere; runners tunnel below the soil and come up 20 ft. away; and the vines get on everything. Virginia creeper's one redeeming virtue is its brilliant red fall foliage. But try to resist its costly charms.

ATTRACT BUTTERFLIES, BIRDS, AND BEES

Times are tough—and getting tougher—for birds, butterflies, and bees. As wildlands are paved over in favor of housing and shopping developments and the roads that lead to them, wildlife habitats grow smaller and smaller. The good news is that making your garden attractive to wildlife isn't that hard. Like us, they have four basic needs: food, water, shelter, and a place to raise their young.

BUTTERFLIES

A shallow dish filled with moist sand offers them a place to drink. Butterflies also love to bask in the sun, so add a few flat rocks so they can rest between flights. Choose flowers that provide a lot of nectar such as salvias, firebush (*Hamelia patens*), pentas, zinnias, lantana, butterfly weed, porterweed, summer phlox (*Phlox paniculata*), and butterfly bush. Add host plants for caterpillars to feed on, such as passion vine, milkweed, and parsley.

BIRDS

Set out feeders and birdhouses in places secure from predators. Add plants that provide good nesting areas, such as large shrubs and small trees. Evergreen shrubs with berries will supply food and shelter in the winter months. Offer fresh water for drinking and bathing. To keep birdbaths mosquito free, use mosquito dunks or install a fountain (mosquitos won't lay eggs in running water).

BEES

Bees are vital for pollinating crops. Attract them by planting flowers that produce lots of nectar and pollen. Try asters, cosmos, clover, salvia, and sunflowers. Like birds and butterflies, bees also appreciate a source of water.

One of the biggest challenges many bees face is finding suitable nesting sites. Honeybees nest in colonies—hives tended by professionals or backyard beekeepers. But the majority of our native bees (honeybees are a European import) are solitary, raising their young alone. Having no hive to defend, they're not aggressive and rarely sting. While most do not produce honey, all are efficient pollinators.

About 70 percent of native bees are ground nesters. A small patch of bare earth in a sunny spot—as little as 1 square foot—is all they need. The remainder are wood nesters; they'll occupy holes in trees or move into bee houses. Or you can make nesting blocks for them. Pick up a piece of untreated wood at the hardware store, and drill a grid of small holes in it. The female bees will lay their eggs in the holes, and then seal them; their offspring will emerge and start the cycle over again.

Attract bees to your garden with a bee house surrounded by plants they love, such as sunflowers, yarrow, and beebalm.

ELEMENTS OF A WILDLIFE GARDEN

FLOWERS. Include a wide range of plants that provide nectar for butterflies, beneficial insects, and hummingbirds. Also plant species whose foliage feeds butterfly larvae. Let plants go to seed to furnish food for songbirds. Add shrubs and trees that produce berries.

TALL TREES. These provide shelter, food (seeds or fruit), and nesting places. They also protect the garden from strong winds.

VINES. Flowering vines provide shelter, nesting sites, and nectar. Many also bear berries and foliage that are sources of food for both birds and butterfly larvae.

SHELTERS. Arrange rocks for butterflies to light on. Hang nesting boxes for birds; locate them away from activity around feeders and face them away from prevailing winds. Consider butterfly and bee houses too.

WATER FEATURES. Birds are especially drawn to splashing water of a small stream or fountain but also appreciate a birdbath. Locate your water feature 10 to 20 feet away from shrubs as a safety zone from hidden predators.

TOP LEFT: Butterflies are the prettiest pollinators in the garden.

TOP RIGHT: Birds appreciate a place to cool off and have a drink. Shallow water is important.

MIDDLE: Painting your birdhouses is an easy way to add year-round color to your garden, along with shelter for the birds.

BOTTOM LEFT: No feeder is squirrel proof, so try a hot birdseed, such as Cole's Hot Meats and Cole's Blazing Hot Blend made with habañero oil. The birds don't mind the taste, but it will put those pesky squirrels on the hot seat!

BOTTOM RIGHT: Limit your use of chemical pesticides around flowering plants to protect the bees.

PEST PROBLEM SOLVER

A healthy garden hosts abundant life, including insects and wildlife.
Most of these share the garden without causing problems. Many are welcome visitors,
performing vital functions such as pollinating plants; feeding on undesirable insects;
and helping to break down plant matter, building soils and recycling nutrients.
But some are pests that feed on and injure plants.

Approach pests with Integrated Pest Management (IPM), a philosophy whose primary aim is prevention. IPM uses biological, cultural, and physical controls to help avoid serious insect, disease, and other pest problems and to reduce pests' effects to tolerable levels. Chemical controls using pesticides are employed only as a last resort.

IPM begins with good cultural practices. Choose plants that are adapted to your climate and garden conditions. Buy selections that are resistant to diseases or unpalatable to pests. Prepare planting beds well, and periodically amend the soil with organic matter to improve conditions for root growth. Water and fertilize appropriately to promote healthy plants. Check plants frequently to spot problems before they get out of hand. Healthy plants are less prone to pests.

PHYSICAL CONTROLS

Physical controls include actions that directly kill, deter, or capture pests.

HANDPICK to destroy snails, caterpillars, insect egg masses, and other pests that you find among the plants. Take care to leave the lady beetle larvae and other beneficial insects that are sometimes mistaken as pests.

PRUNE and destroy branches, canes, and other plant tissues that show evidence of actively developing pests, such as borers, scales, aphids, and any plant diseases.

SPRAY plants with a strong jet of water to dislodge or kill small insects such as aphids, thrips, and spider mites.

BARRIERS deter pests. These may range from a high, continuous fence around an entire garden to deter deer to row covers protecting a bed of plants from insects.

REPEL pests by bordering target plants with herbs such as dill, tansy, and thyme.

ROTATE the location of plants in your garden from season to season. This is particularly helpful for reducing plant diseases and root-feeding insects.

TRAP to capture and monitor pests. Look during the day under pots or trap boards, and scrape any snails or slugs into a bucket of soapy water. Yellow sticky cards can capture flying insects such as whiteflies and aphids. Damp newspaper or other cover can concentrate slugs and earwigs that seek daytime shelter. Adults of some moths can be captured with pheromone traps that include as a lure the chemicals used by the female moth to attract a mate. Such traps are particularly useful in helping you know when to spray for fruit insects, such as codling moth in apples.

BIOLOGICAL CONTROLS

Every garden has a homegrown army of pest controls—predators, parasites, and beneficial pathogens that feed on garden pests. To help increase beneficial populations, avoid using persistent pesticides and grow a diversity of plants. Many of these beneficials can be encouraged by planting flowers that provide nectar and pollen. Birds, toads, and garter snakes all prey on insects.

Spiders all feed on insects and can provide tremendous benefits in plant protection. Other insects, such as parasitic wasps and tachinid flies, lay eggs onto or inside of pests; as the larvae develop, they kill the pest.

Parasitic nematodes are microscopic roundworms that kill insects through introducing a bacterium into their body. Nematodes (which generally must be mail-ordered and applied) can help control pests that spend part of their lives in the soil, such as white grubs, root weevils, and cutworms.

SYNTHETIC PESTICIDES

Many of the older synthetic insecticides have been removed from the market due to environmental contamination and concerns about their effects on animals and human health. They have been replaced with pesticides of natural origin (see page 726) and with new classes of synthetic pesticides, such as neonicotinoids and pyrethroids (bifenthrin, permethrin, cyfluthrin, and esfenvalerate).

While natural pesticides degrade quickly, synthetic insecticides kill insects that contact or eat sprayed foliage for days or weeks after their application. They are more toxic to beneficial insect pollinators, predators, and parasites, and some cause problems due to contamination of surface waters.

Some synthetic pesticides applied to the soil are absorbed by roots and moved systemically throughout the plant. Pesticides formulated as baits (combined with an attractant) can be particularly selective in their effects.

Never "blanket-spray" your garden with synthetic pesticides as a preventative measure according to a pre-set schedule or before you see any pests. Such routine spraying inevitably leads to resistant pests. It also eliminates pedatory insects that keep pests under control. No garden is bug free. Don't aim for one.

STORAGE AND DISPOSAL OF PESTICIDES

Store pesticides where they can be locked away from children and pets and separate from food. Buy only the amount that you need, and never mix more pesticide solution than you need. Never pour pesticides down the sink, the toilet, or a storm drain, as this will pollute surface waters. The only legal way to dispose of pesticides is to take them to your local household hazardous waste facility. Only completely empty home-use pesticide containers may be disposed of in the trash. Contact your city or county public works department or your local waste disposal company for information.

NATURAL PESTICIDES

Natural pesticides are products whose active ingredients originate in a plant, animal, or mineral, or whose action results from a biological process. "Natural" does not mean harmless; some natural products can still harm people, pets, or plants if they are used incorrectly, and most of them will kill beneficial insects along with the pests.

When using any pesticide, read the label carefully and follow the manufacturer's directions exactly. The label will clearly state the plants and pests for which the control can be used.

BACILLUS THURINGIENSIS (Bt) is a naturally occurring bacterium. Several strains exist; each targets different kinds of insects. The most common, *Bt kurstaki*, controls leaf-feeding caterpillars.

DIATOMACEOUS EARTH (DE) is a powdery substance made from the skeletons of microscopic marine organisms. It damages the protective coats of invertebrate pests such as ants, slugs, and snails, but must be kept dry to be effective. Use the horticultural product, not the one intended for swimming pool filters. Wear a mask during application.

FOOD-GRADE OILS AND EXTRACTS are commercial versions of homemade repellents and pesticides that gardeners have relied on for centuries. Active ingredients include citrus peels, garlic, and hot pepper.

HORTICULTURAL OILS are typically highly refined petroleum oils. Botanical oils are derived from plants, such as citrus peels or seeds of neem or soybean. Oils act on contact by smothering aphids, mites, whiteflies, scales, and other insects. Do not apply oils when plants are under drought stress and temperatures are high.

INSECTICIDAL SOAP is made from potassium salts of fatty acids from plants and animals. Soaps work on contact against aphids, mealybugs, mites, scales, thrips, and whiteflies. Hard water inactivates the soap, so mix the concentrate with soft water, distilled water, or rainwater. Avoid using dish detergents.

NEEM OIL (AZADIRACHTIN) is from the tropical neem tree (*Azadirachta indica*). Effective against aphids, beetles, caterpillars, mealybugs, mites, thrips, whiteflies, and powdery mildew.

PYRETHRINS are derived from the dried flowers of *Tanacetum cinera-riifolium*. Lethal to many pests. They break down quickly in sunlight; apply after sundown.

SPINOSAD is made from the extracts of a soil microbe, *Saccharopolyspora spinosa*. It controls caterpillars, thrips, and some beetles and sawflies. Although relatively selective, it kills some beneficial species.

SULFUR is dusted or sprayed over plants to control mites and psyllids as well as some plant diseases. Do not use in conjunction with horticultural oils or when air temperature is above 85°F (29°C).

PLANT PESTS

	PEST	MANAGEMENT
	Ants Most ants don't damage plants, but some species protect sap-sucking insects—such as aphids, mealybugs, soft scales, and whiteflies—for the honeydew they produce. Sooty mold may develop from honeydew.	Place sticky barriers around tree and shrub trunks; prune off branches that touch the ground. Insecticide baits can eliminate colonies but are deliberately slow acting so ants will carry the insecticide to their underground colony. Which ant baits are effective varies depending on the ant species and situation. Insecticide treatments are usually short lived.
	Aphids Soft-bodied, rounded insects that range from pin- to match-head size. May be black, white, pink, or pale green. They cluster on new growth, sucking plant juices. Some kinds transmit viral diseases. Aphids remove sap, causing wilted, discolored, and/or stunted leaves. Sooty mold may develop from honeydew.	Don't overfertilize or overwater; aphids thrive on succulent growth. Use floating row covers and reflective mulch to prevent infestation of small plants. Encourage beneficials. Hose aphids off with a blast of water. Spray with insecticidal soap, horticultural oil (overwintering eggs), or pyrethrins. Many synthetic pesticides are effective but usually not necessary.
	Borers Larvae of beetles or moths; tunnel into branches, trunk, or roots of woody plants. Attracted to weakened, injured, or stressed plants, restricting water and nutrient flow, killing, deforming, or weakening branches or limbs.	Encourage healthy plant growth. Avoid wounding susceptible species. Prune out infested limbs before beetles emerge as adults. Preventive sprays of pyrethroids may control egg-laying adults but not borers inside plants. Systemics can be effective against some types (check product label).
	Caterpillars (including tobacco budworms, hornworms, cabbageworms) Soft-bodied crawling insects, often striped or spotted. Chew leaves or tunnel through buds and blossoms.	Handpick, especially at dusk or in early morning. Spray with *Bacillus thuringiensis* (*Bt*), pyrethrins, or spinosad. Synthetics are also effective.
	Cucumber Beetles Oval-shaped, greenish yellow beetles with black spots or stripes. They eat all parts of cucumbers, squash, and melons. Spotted beetles also feed on roses. The beetles transmit bacterial wilt, which attacks cucumbers, and other diseases. Underground larvae may damage roots.	Handpick and destroy. Vacuum beetles from plants; dispose of bag. Use floating row cover before plants become infested. Encourage birds, soldier beetles, and tachinid flies. Apply parasitic nematodes to moist soil, spray plants with pyrethrins or appropriately labeled synthetics.
	Cutworms Dull brownish, hairless caterpillars that live in the soil and cut off stems of seedlings at ground level. Some kinds climb into plants and eat leaves.	Clear and till beds to destroy cutworms. Use protective collars or spread diatomaceous earth around stems of young seedlings. Handpick at night when the cutworms are active. Release parasitic nematodes or use *Bacillus thuringiensis* (*Bt*) or appropriately labeled synthetics (e.g., pyrethroids).
	Earwigs These familiar pests aren't all bad—they also prey on aphids and other insects. They feed on tender new growth of many plants, especially flowers and vegetables.	Keep the garden clean, removing hiding places such as weedy areas and dead foliage. Trap and drown them in a low-sided can with ½ inch of tuna fish oil or vegetable oil with a drop of bacon grease. Set traps of rolled newspaper, corrugated cardboard, or hose pieces, and dispose of earwigs in soapy water or sealed bags.

PLANT PESTS

	PEST	MANAGEMENT
	Flea Beetles	
	Very small, shiny, oval beetles that jump like fleas. May be blue-black, brown, or bronze. Adult beetles riddle leaves with small holes. They feed on many vegetable crops and seedlings, especially cabbage and potato-family plants. Vigorous older plants usually survive.	Remove dead or damaged leaves and plants. Till the soil in fall. Plant in uninfested soil. Use floating row covers. Spray with neem. Spread diatomaceous earth. Use pyrethroids and other appropriately labeled synthetics.
	Grasshoppers	
	Also called locusts. Adults are 1–2 in. long and may be brown, green, or yellow. Newly hatched nymphs resemble adults, but are wingless and smaller and feed voraciously. During their periodic outbreaks, they can cause severe damage, defoliating most plants.	Difficult. Handpick. Use floating row covers. If grass-hoppers migrating in are expected to be or have been a problem in previous years, try the biological control *Nosema locustae*. The grasshopper's mobility restricts effectiveness of most insecticides.
	Leaf Miners	
	A catchall term for certain moth, beetle, and fly larvae that tunnel within plant leaves, leaving a nearly transparent trail on the surface. Damage is mostly cosmetic, although yield of some crops may be reduced.	Plant vegetables under floating row covers. Remove debris, where pupae overwinter, and till the soil. Pick off and destroy infested leaves; use yellow sticky traps to catch adults. Spray with neem or spinosad to discourage adults from laying eggs; once the larvae are inside the leaves, most sprays are not effective. Systemics may be effective.
	Mealybugs	
	Have an oval body with overlapping soft plates and a white, cottony covering. They move around slowly. They suck plant juices, causing stunting. Sooty mold may develop from honeydew (see page 733). In warm climates, they target a wide range of plants, but azaleas, hibiscus, and citrus trees of all kinds are prime targets.	Control ants (see page 719), which nurture mealybugs. Encourage or release beneficials. Dab pests with a cotton swab dipped in rubbing alcohol. Horticultural oils, insecticidal soap, pyrethrins, neem, and appropriately labeled synthetics are also effective.
	Mites	
	Tiny spider relatives found on leaf undersides. Webbing is often present where they live. Mites suck plant juices; the damaged leaf surface is pale and stippled, and the leaves often turn brown, dry out, and die. Drought-stressed plants are prime targets.	To check plants for mites, hold a piece of white paper under the affected foliage and briskly tap it. The pepper-like pests will drop onto the paper. Don't let plants dry out. Mist foliage undersides frequently with water. Release predatory mites, which feed on the harmful mites. Spray with insecticidal soap, horticultural oil, neem, or sulfur.
	Pill Bugs and Sowbugs	
	Soil-dwelling crustaceans. When disturbed, pillbugs roll up into balls about the size of a large pea; sowbugs are usually gray and don't roll up. Both pests eat decaying vegetation (which they help break down into humus), very young seedlings, the skins of melons and cucumbers, and berries.	Limit moisture and decaying matter. Water early in the day so the soil dries by evening, and use drip or furrow irrigation instead of sprinklers. Use raised beds or planting boxes. Apply pyrethroids. Spread diatomaceous earth.
	Root Weevils	
	Many species of long-snouted, hard-shelled insects, including the troublesome black vine weevils and (in lawns) billbugs. Adult black vine weevils feed on leaves, flowers, and bark of rhododendron, grape, and other plants; larvae consume roots. Billbugs target lawns. Larvae eat grass roots, leaving small circles of yellowish turf.	Keep planting beds free of debris, especially around plants' crowns, where adults overwinter. To help prevent billbug infestation, improve soil drainage or replace grass with plants that thrive in damp soil. Trap adult weevils in late May with sticky traps or by shaking plants in the evening and gathering fallen insects. Control larvae with parasitic nematodes.

PLANT PESTS

	PEST	MANAGEMENT
Scales		
	Classified as "armored" (hard) or soft. In spring or summer, young scales ("crawlers") emerge. Adult scale insects have a waxy, scalelike covering. As scales suck out plant juices, yellow spots appear on foliage, and leaves may drop off. If the infestation is left unchecked, the whole plant turns sickly and stunted.	Difficult to control. Encourage lady beetles and parasitic wasps that kill scales. Control ants (see page 719), which often protect soft scales. Horticultural oil and insecticidal soap will help control them, as will systemic products appropriately labeled synthetics.
Snails and Slugs		
	Night-feeding mollusks. Snails have shells; slugs do not. Both feast on the seedlings and leaves of many plants. They hide by day, though they may be active on gray or rainy days.	Minimize garden clutter and keep organic litter and mulch back from plants during wet weather. Trap and dispose of pests. Wrap copper strip barriers around raised beds and tree trunks. Spread diatomaceous earth around plants. Set out shallow containers filled with beer to drown the pests. Use bait containing iron phosphate. (Baits containing metaldehyde are a hazard to pets.)
Thrips		
	Tiny, elongated insects that suck plant tissue. In heavy infestations, both flowers and leaves are discolored and fail to open normally. Leaves may take on a silvery or tan cast. Greenhouse thrips feed in a group and leave small black droppings on leaves.	Use row covers before plants become infested. Clip off and destroy infected plant parts. Encourage beneficials. Spray with insecticidal soap, horticultural oil, pyrethrins, spinosad, neem, or appropriately labeled synthetics, including systemics.
Whiteflies		
	Adults are tiny white pests that fly up in a cloud when disturbed. The nymphs and adults suck plant juices from leaf undersides. Foliage may show yellow stippling, curl, and turn brown. Some kinds transmit plant virus diseases.	Use floating row covers before plants are infested. For greenhouse infestations, release *Encarsia formosa*, a predatory wasp, or use sticky yellow traps. Spray leaves with strong jets of water, insecticidal soap, oils, or neem.

BENEFICIAL INSECTS

Encourage beneficial insects by planting nectar-rich flowers. Visit anbp.org for sources of beneficial insects.

ASSASSIN BUGS. Slim ½ to ¾-in.-long insects; may be red, black, brown, or gray. They feed on a wide variety of pests.
DAMSEL BUGS. Dull gray or brown, ½-in.-long, very slender insects with long, narrow heads. Nymphs resemble the adults but are smaller and have no wings. Both nymphs and adults feed on aphids, leafhoppers, and small worms.
GROUND BEETLES. Shiny black, ½ to 1-in.-long insects. The smaller species eat other insects, caterpillars, cutworms, and grubs; some larger species prey on slugs and snails and their eggs.
LACEWINGS. The adults are 1-inch-long flying insects that feed only on nectar, pollen, and honeydew; but the larvae, which resemble ½-in.-long alligators, devour aphids, leafhoppers, and thrips, as well as mites. Larvae are commercially available.
LADY BEETLES. Adults and their larvae (which look like ¼-in.-long alligators) feed on aphids, mealybugs, and insect eggs. You can buy the aphid-eating convergent lady beetle, but these must be released repeatedly and most soon fly away. Freeing them in large numbers at night after first wetting foliage may encourage them to stay a while.
TRICHOGRAMMA WASPS. These very tiny parasitoid wasps attack the eggs of caterpillar pests. Commercially available species are adapted for gardens or for fruit trees. Because they are short lived, repeated releases may be needed.

Assassin bug

Damsel bug

THE SINISTER SIX

Gardeners everywhere should be on the lookout. The following varmints are headed your way and considered extremely hungry. They're evil, persistent, and insatiable. These pests have no respect for the plants of others. To them, every flower and leaf is just another morsel waiting to be plundered. These marauders call themselves The Sinister Six. They must be stopped. Study the following profiles and be ready when one of these critters strikes your garden.

ARMADILLO

138-

WANTED

- Aliases: "Road Rat," "Highway Hash," "Bypass Burger"
- Size: 8 to 17 lbs
- Distinguishing Marks: Looks like a big, armored rat with claws
- Last Seen: Laying waste to your entire yard
- Method of Operation: Operates mostly at night. Often found in rigor mortis by the side of the interstate
- Control: Trap and relocate. Or build a highway through your yard.
- Last Heard Saying: "I was in this road first. That truck will just have to stop."

GROUNDHOG

Aliases: "Punxsutawney Phil," "Bryson City Bubba" **Size:** 4 to 14 pounds

Distinguishing marks: Squat, fat, short-legged marmot with grizzled brown or yellowish brown fur; face shows no trace of thought

Last seen: Being temporarily blinded by television camera lights on the morning of February 2

Methods of operation: Operates during the day; loves to raid vegetable gardens, especially patches of corn

Control: Trap repeat offender, and relocate to Iowa, or surround garden with a wire fence that is at least 3 ft. tall and buried 1 ft. in the ground

Last heard saying: "I think I'll run for Congress."

EASTERN COTTONTAIL RABBIT

Aliases: "Peter," "Thumper," "Stew" **Size:** 2 to 4 pounds

Distinguishing marks: White tail, brown or gray coat, large ears

Last seen: Vigorously pruning your brand-new transplants

Methods of operation: Usually sneaks into the garden in early morning and late afternoon; gorges himself on young vegetable plants, especially bean and lettuce seedlings; in winter, chews the bark off the bases of young fruit trees

Control: Surround garden with chicken wire that's anchored to the ground and at least 2 ft. high. Wrap trunks of young fruit trees with wire mesh or plastic tree guards. Develop your family's taste for rabbit

Last heard saying: "Here comes Peter Cottontail, scarfing down your beans and kale"

GRAY SQUIRREL

Aliases: "Precious," "Muffler" **Size:** 1 to 3 pounds

Distinguishing marks: Gray coat, bushy tail

Last seen: Digging up your transplants and leaving them atop the ground to die

Methods of operation: Disarms you with cuteness, then robs every fruit from your fruit tree, gobbles every seed from your bird feeder, and cuts down your azaleas to make a nest; in fall, buries mass quantities of acorns and promptly forgets where they are

Control: Try a hungry cat, a handy trap, or a tactical nuclear weapon.

Last heard saying: "Now, where in the heck did I bury that tactical nuclear weapon?"

WHITE TAILED DEER

Aliases: "Bambi," "Trophy," "Sausage" **Size:** 150 to 300 pounds

Distinguishing marks: White tail, reddish brown coat in summer, grayish brown in winter; a buck has antlers, a doe has dependents

Last seen: Looking like a politician caught in the headlights

Methods of operation: Feeds mainly at night, dining on a wide array of vegetable and ornamental plants; favorites include corn, rhododendron, yew, daylily, and hosta

Control: Place sign that reads: "Hunting Season Opens Today" in yard. Spray plants with a commercial deer repellent. Or enclose garden with an 8-ft.-tall electrified fence.

Last heard saying: "Oh, honey, look at the people; look at the people!"

PINE VOLE

Aliases: "Ninja Vermin" **Size:** 1 ounce

Distinguishing marks: Looks like a cross between a mouse and a hamster with auburn fur, short tail, and small ears

Last seen: Chewing off your prized hosta

Methods of operation: Burrows around the base of plants, eating stems, seeds, and bulbs; sometimes uses mole tunnels to fool people into thinking the mole is the culprit

Control: Remove mulch from around plants; dig a 6-in.-deep trench around planting bed, and line it with wire mesh. Plant perennials in half soil and half gravel. Hire a hungry weasel.

Last heard saying: "A mole did it!"

PREVENT DISEASES

The Integrated Pest Management (IPM) approach applies to diseases as well as pests. IPM aims to maintain a productive garden with minimal use of synthetic controls.

All plant diseases are caused by three kinds of organisms: fungus, bacteria, and viruses. Any of the three may be responsible for leaf, stem, and flower diseases, but the vast majority of soilborne diseases are caused by fungus. Note that often what appears to be a disease is actually a result of cultural problems, such as nutrient deficiency, sunscald, or soil compaction.

Because many diseases cannot be eradicated once their symptoms are apparent, prevention is important. If diseases do appear in your garden, immediately remove infected annuals and vegetables to keep the problem from spreading. On larger plants, including perennials, remove diseased flowers, leaves, and, if possible, branches.

NATURAL PRODUCTS

Natural disease controls include baking soda, which helps to control powdery mildew; biofungicides (such as *Bacillus subtilis*), copper compounds, copper soaps, garlic solutions, neem oil, potassium bicarbonate, and sulfur (do not use this in conjunction with horticultural oil sprays or when the outdoor temperature is above 85°F/29°C). The package will clearly state the plants and diseases for which the product should be used if the substance is not subject to registration.

SYNTHETIC PRODUCTS

The most common synthetic fungicides include chlorothalonil and myclobutanil, both labeled for some edibles, and the systemics tebuconazole and triforine. Be sure to read all manufacturer's instructions before applying any synthetic fungicide to your garden. Make sure the plant to be sprayed and the disease to be treated are on the label.

PLANT DISEASES

	DISEASE	PREVENTION & CONTROL
	Black Spot Caused by *Diplocarpon rosae*, a fungus that overwinters on rose canes and fallen leaves, black spot is the bane of rose lovers. It thrives in warm, moist environments. Spores spread to other plant parts through splashing rain or overhead watering.	Plant resistant rose selections such as 'Bonica', 'Carefree Beauty', 'Carefree Wonder', 'Dr. W. Van Fleet', 'Flower Carpet', 'Lady Banks's Rose', and 'Mrs. B. R. Cant'. Give roses lots of sun and air circulation. Avoid overhead watering, and rake up any fallen leaves. At the first appearance, spray leaves thoroughly with *Bacillus subtilis*, neem oil, or wettable or liquid sulfur.
	Damping Off Various soil fungus that cause seeds to rot in the soil before they sprout or cause seedlings to collapse at or near the soil surface. Most common in poorly drained or too-wet soils.	Improve drainage and reduce watering. Treat seeds, potting soil, or seedlings with a biological fungicide or buy pretreated seeds. Avoid planting in too-cold soils. Use sterilized medium and containers. Provide good air circulation. Thin crowded seedlings. Discard infected seedlings and starting medium.
	Early Blight This fungus, *Alternaria solani*, attacks tomatoes, eggplant, and potatoes. Small dark brown to black spots with concentric rings form on the oldest, lowest leaves first and move up. Leaves turn yellow, wither, and die.	Plant resistant tomatoes. Use certified disease-free seed potatoes. Avoid wetting foliage when watering. Throw away all plant debris—do not compost.

PLANT DISEASES

	DISEASE	PREVENTION & CONTROL
	Fireblight Bacterial disease that affects members of the rose family, including apple, cotoneaster, crabapple, hawthorn, pear, pyracantha, and quince. Shoots (and sometimes entire plants) blacken, appear scorched, and die suddenly. Appears in moist weather, especially early spring. Spread by insects, splashing water.	Plant resistant selections. Using disinfected pruners, remove and discard diseased branches, cutting 6–8 in. below blighted tissue. Spray at 3- to 5-day intervals during the bloom season with copper fungicides.
	Powdery Mildew Fungal disease that causes a white, powdery coating on leaves, stems, buds, and fruit. New growth and blossoms may be stunted. Most powdery mildews thrive in humid air, but the spores—unlike those of other fungus—need dry surfaces.	Plant resistant selections. Give plants sufficient light and air circulation. Spray with jets of water early in the day. Spray with biofungicide *Bacillus subtilis*, baking soda mixtures, neem, horticultural oils, sulfur, or copper soap fungicide. Apply an antitranspirant. Several synthetic fungicides are labeled for powdery mildew.
	Root Rots and Water Molds Fungal diseases active in warm soils, but can lie dormant in cool conditions. Plants wilt, and their leaves discolor, become stunted, and drop prematurely. Branches or even the entire plant may die.	Plant resistant selections. Remove and destroy dead plants or branches. Improve drainage or plant in raised beds. Do not overwater. Also inspect roots at the nursery so you don't purchase root rot-infected plants. There are also fungicides that will control some root rot organisms.
	Rust Various fungal diseases, many plant specific, that cause orange pustules to form on undersides of leaves. Upper surfaces may be spotted with yellow; eventually the whole leaf may discolor, then drop.	Plant resistant selections. Remove and destroy infected leaves or badly infected plants. Provide good air circulation. In winter, clean up all debris. Avoid overhead watering. Spray with a garlic-based or copper soap fungicide, *Bacillus subtilis*, or an appropriately labeled synthetic fungicide.
	Sooty Mold Fungus that grows on honeydew produced by sap-sucking insects. The fungus itself does not injure plants but can block sun from the leaves, which may then turn yellow and drop prematurely.	Wash or wipe the fungus from leaves. Prune to open canopy. Control honeydew-excreting insects (see page 728), such as aphids, scales, and whiteflies, by spraying with horticultural oil or insecticidal soap.
	Verticillium and Fusarium Wilts A long-lived, soilborne fungus that plugs the water-conducting tissues in crops such as tomatoes and strawberries, and in woody plants. One side of the plant may wilt and die. Leaves, then branches, turn yellow or brown, then die. Small plants may be destroyed in one season; mature trees may survive longer.	Plant resistant selections. Dig up and destroy infected crops, and prune out dead branches. Give deep but infrequent irrigation. Rotate crops, or grow in containers or raised beds filled with sterile soil. Soil solarization may destroy the fungus (see page 727).
	Viruses Often transmitted by insects and mites, viruses often cause mottled leaves and stunted or deformed flowers and growth. Some viruses are non-lethal; others kill plants. Once a virus infects a plant, it cannot be removed.	When growing vegetables, choose disease-resistant selections. For other plants buy from a reputable grower and inspect plants closely for signs of virus. Many weeds carry viruses, so keep them in check, and clear debris regularly. Spray plants periodically with insecticidal soap or horticultural oil to control insects and mites. Remove and destroy infected plants.

CONTROL WEEDS

Weeds are plants that grow where gardeners don't want them. They rob desirable plants of water, nutrients, and sunlight; they may also harbor insects and diseases. Some spread so aggressively that they jump garden fences to invade natural areas. Others might be weedy in one region but well-behaved garden plants elsewhere.

Oriental bittersweet—beautiful to look at, but a terror in the landscape.

Annual weeds grow shoots and leaves, flower, set seed, and die within a year. Most are summer annuals, germinating in spring or summer and dying by fall. Winter annual weeds begin growth in fall or early winter, then set seed in early spring while the weather is still cool. Biennial weeds produce a cluster or rosette of leaves in their first year of growth, and in the following year, they flower, set seed, and die.

Both annuals and biennials reproduce by seed. Most perennial weeds, which live for several years, also reproduce by seed, but weedy plants such as giant reed (*Arundo donax*) do not produce any viable seed. Once they mature, however, they produce large deep root crowns or taproots, or structures that allow them to spread, including stolons, rhizomes, bulbs, tubers, or even creeping roots. These structures make control of perennials more difficult.

NONCHEMICAL CONTROLS

It is rarely possible to eradicate weeds entirely, but you can substantially reduce infestations.

HAND PULL OR HOE. For perennial weeds that have passed the seedling stage, it's usually necessary to dig out their roots, or the weeds can resprout from fragments left behind. You'll probably need to repeat the process several times to manage perennial weeds. Don't leave pulled or hoed-out weeds on bare ground, particularly when it is moist, as they can take root again. Toss leafy annual or biennial types that do not yet have flowers or seeds into the compost pile, along with the top growth of perennial weeds (before seeding). But roots of perennials, such as dandelions, should go into the trash, as should any weeds that have set seed.

ROTOTILL. Use this technique for annual and biennial weeds in larger areas intended for future gardens. The soil must be fairly dry and then be allowed to completely dry out to prevent plants from resprouting. This method knocks down weeds and mixes them into the soil, where they decay to form humus. Perennial weeds, however, usually sprout again, and some kinds even grow more abundantly after tilling.

MOW. Use a rotary mower or string trimmer for seasonal annual weed control in larger areas. Both tools cut the weeds. String trimmers leave the severed tops behind, while mowers grind them up as they cut them.

SMOTHER. Cover weeds in areas earmarked for future planting. After mowing or cutting off the top growth, put down a layer of heavy cardboard, newspapers (at least three dozen sheets thick), or black plastic. Overlap the material so weeds can't grow through the cracks. Anchor the covering with a layer of bark chips or other organic mulch. Leave these smothering materials in place for at least a full growing season. Allow a year or more for tough or perennial weeds.

PRESPROUT. Use this method in parts of the garden plagued by weeds if you're planning to plant vegetables, perennial beds, or a new lawn there. Add needed amendments, till the soil, water it, and then wait a week or two for weed seeds to germinate. When they're only a few inches high, scrape them away or hand-weed them out. Then sow or transplant your vegetables, flowers, or lawn, disturbing the soil as little as possible to avoid bringing more weed seeds to the surface.

SOLARIZE. Use the sun to bake the soil's weed seeds as well as harmful fungus, bacteria, and some nematodes. The process (see box, far right) is carried out in summer. Daytime temperatures above 80°F (27°C) are ideal.

APPLY A HOMEMADE SPRAY. Organic gardeners have myriad herbicide recipes that use ingredients straight from the kitchen or medicine chest. One effective formula consists of 1 tablespoon of dishwashing liquid and ¼ cup of salt mixed with 1 quart of vinegar. You can also spray unwanted plants with isopropyl (rubbing) alcohol. A solution of 2 tablespoons per quart of water works for most weeds. For tougher ones, you may need to increase the amount of alcohol.

Regardless of the ingredients, apply the potion with a spray bottle and coat the plants thoroughly. Do the job on a hot, sunny, wind-free day, when herbicides are most effective.

MULCH. Once you've destroyed weeds, take steps to prevent their reappearance. Mulch bare soil to deter weed growth.

CHEMICAL CONTROLS

Herbicides are classified according to what stage of weed growth they affect, as well as by how they damage weeds.

SYNTHETIC HERBICIDES. These are manufactured compounds that do not normally occur in nature.

Synthetic herbicides are not recommended for food gardens. In home ornamental gardens, use them only when all other methods have failed. Beyond the potential risks they may pose to health and the environment, many of these chemicals can damage desirable plants if they drift through the air or run off in irrigation or rainwater. Some herbicides persist in the soil for long periods, injuring later plantings.

If you use herbicides, always make sure the product is safe for the desirable plants growing in and near the areas to be treated. Also keep in mind that you can be held responsible for any damage to neighboring properties resulting from herbicide use.

PRE-EMERGENCE HERBICIDES. These inhibit the growth of germinating weed seeds and very young seedlings. They do not affect established plants. To be effective, they must be applied before the seeds sprout. Some pre-emergence products are formulated to kill germinating weeds in lawns. These may be sold as "weeds-and-feeds." Such dual-purpose products should not be treated solely as fertilizers and reapplied whenever the lawn needs feeding. For that purpose, use a regular lawn fertilizer. Some pre-emergence products must be watered into the soil, while others are incorporated into it. Some may also harm seeds you sow later in the season.

POSTEMERGENCE HERBICIDES. These act on growing weeds rather than on germinating seeds. Chemicals that are translocated like glyphosate must be absorbed by the plant

HOW TO SOLARIZE

CULTIVATE THE SOIL. Clear it of weeds, debris, and large clods of earth. Make a bed at least 2 ft. wide, as narrower beds make it difficult to build up enough heat to have much effect.

RAKE THE BED LEVEL. Carve a small ditch around the perimeter. Soak the soil to a depth of 1 ft.

COVER WITH 1- TO 4-MIL CLEAR PLASTIC. Use UV-resistant plastic if it's available, as it won't break down during solarization. Stretch the plastic tightly so that it is in contact with the soil. Bury the edges in the perimeter ditch. An optional second layer of plastic increases heat and makes solarization more effective. Use soda cans as spacers between the two sheets.

LEAVE THE PLASTIC IN PLACE. Allow four to six weeks (eight weeks for persistent weeds) to pass, then remove it. Don't leave it down longer than eight weeks, or soil structure may suffer. You can now plant. After planting, avoid cultivating more than the upper 2 in. of soil, as weed seeds at deeper levels may still be viable.

through its leaves or stems; this kills the plant by interfering with specific biochemical pathways. Contact herbicides kill only the plant parts they touch—regrowth can still occur from underground reproductive parts or unsprayed buds. Some postemergence herbicides, such as glyphosate, will damage or kill any plant they touch, while others may be specific for grasses or broad-leafed plants. Use them very carefully around desirable plants; application timing is critical.

NATURAL HERBICIDES

These are products whose active ingredients originate in a plant or mineral.

CORN GLUTEN MEAL. Pre-emergence. Most often used to control weeds, especially crabgrass in lawns, but is also effective in garden beds. Also acts as a fertilizer. Relatively expensive. May take multiple applications over several years for full effectiveness.

HERBICIDAL SOAPS. Postemergence. Contact herbicides that degrade quickly. Made from selected fatty acids (as are insecticidal soaps), they kill top growth of young, actively growing weeds and are most effective on annual weeds.

VINEGAR. Postemergence. Many organic-gardening catalogs sell vinegar-based herbicides, usually with soap and/or lemon juice added for extra sticking and penetrating power.

COMMON GARDEN WEEDS

	WEED	MANAGEMENT
	Annual Bluegrass (*Poa annua*)	
	Winter annual. Forms a bright light green tuft of softly textured grass. Troublesome in lawns, flower borders, and winter vegetable crops. Dies after setting seed in spring.	Pull or dig when the plants are young. Appropriately labeled pre-emergence herbicides are effective when applied to turf in fall. The best control is maintaining a thick, healthy lawn that leaves no room for this weed to sprout.
	Chickweed (*Stellaria media*)	
	Winter annual. A low-growing succulent found in lawns and gardens, chickweed grows most vigorously in the cool weather of fall, winter, and spring, then sets seed and dies when hot weather arrives.	If just a few chickweed plants appear, pulling them when they are young is easy. Use a preemergence herbicide in fall. Postemergence herbicides will kill sprouted plant. The best control is a thick, healthy lawn that leaves no room for weeds.
	Chinese privet (*Ligustrum sinense*)	
	This ornamental shrub, brought to the South from Europe in the late 1800s, spread like wildfire after birds discovered the berries. Growing 15 ft. tall and wide, Chinese privet forms a dense thicket of leaves and shoots. It thrives in sun or shade, wet soil or dry.	Prune it regularly to keep it from flowering and producing seed. Pull or dig young seedlings. Repeatedly cut established shrubs to the ground. To get rid of Chinese privet, spray entire plant with a nonselective translocated herbicide containing triclopyr or glyphosphate.
	Common Purslane (*Portulaca oleracea*)	
	A low-growing annual weed with fleshy stems and leaves and small yellow flowers. It thrives in moist conditions but can survive considerable drought. The seeds germinate in late spring.	Though common purslane is easy to pull or hoe, pieces of stem reroot readily, so be sure to remove them from the garden. Spot-treat with a postemergence herbicide.
	Crabgrass (*Digitaria species*)	
	A shallow-rooted annual weed that grows in spring and summer, thriving in hot, moist areas. As the plant grows, it branches out at the base; stems can root where they touch the soil. Its favorite spot is a sparse, stressed lawn that is mowed too short.	Keep lawn thick and healthy. Mow at 2 inches or higher. Apply a pre-emergence herbicide in early spring.
	Dandelion (*Taraxacum officinale*)	
	Low-growing perennial with dark green, lobed leaves; a deep taproot; and bright yellow flowers. It reproduces both by seed and by any root fragment left in the soil. Grows in gaps in the lawn.	Pull young plants before they flower, or take out the entire taproot of older plants to prevent regrowth. A healthy, vigorous lawn can outcompete this weed. Mow grass at 2 inches or more. Appropriately labeled pre-emergence and postemergence herbicides are effective.
	Dollar weed (*Hydrocotyle*)	
	Also known as pennywort, this weed gets its name from rounded leaves that resemble dollars or pennies. Given moist soil and a bit of shade, it can invade the lawn in no time. Plus it tolerates close mowing. Very hard to control once established.	Avoid overwatering the lawn. Apply a pre-emergence herbicide containing isoxaben on Bahia grass, Bermuda grass, centipede grass, St. Augustine, and Zoysia lawns only. Pull or dig isolated plants. Treat infested lawns with a selective postemergence herbicide or weed-and-feed labeled for your type of grass.

COMMON GARDEN WEEDS

	WEED	MANAGEMENT
	**Japanese honeysuckle** (*Lonicera japonica*) Sweet scented flowers and nectar aside, this ornamental vine is one of the worst weeds in the South. Shortly after its arrival from Asia, it escaped into the wild and quickly covered forests with impenetrable thickets, smothered shrubs, and strangled small trees. Berries ripen in fall and are spread by birds.	Pull, dig, or hoe seedlings as soon as you notice them. Remove vines before they climb trees. To kill established vines, spray with glyphosphate. Or cut the vine near ground level and paint the cut surface with triclopyr in late summer.
	**Kudzu** (*Pueraria lobata*) Many consider this perennial vine to be the world's fastest growing plant. It can grow up to a foot in a single day and quickly swallow trees, homes, and anything else in its path. It spreads from seeds and trailing stems that root at the leaf joints.	Spray foliage with gyphosphate when vines are actively growing in summer. Or cut the stem near ground level and paint the cut surface with triclopyr.
	**Nutsedges, yellow and purple** (*Cyperus*) Also called nut grass, nutsedges favor moist, poorly drained soil and can invade the lawn and garden. Yellow nutsedge (*Cyperus esculentus*), shown at left, grows 6–30 in. tall. Purple nutsedge (*C. rotundus*) grows 1–2 ft. tall. Both reproduce by seed and underground stems (rhizomes) and "nutlets" (tubers), which allow them to spread rapidly.	Remove nutsedges when they are young—fewer than 5 leaves or less than 6 in. tall before they can produce nutlets. To suppress them in beds, cover area with several layers of landscape fabric, and top with bark or pine-straw. Leave cover in place for one growing season. For postemergence chemical control of young plants, apply a selective herbicide containing imazaquin, or spot-treat with glyphosphate. These will not affect any nutlets that have become detached from the plant, however.
	**Oxalis** (*Oxalis articulata crassipes*) An aggressive perennial that spreads quickly by seed. Small yellow flowers develop into long seed capsules that can propel seeds as far as 6 ft.	Dig out small plants before—or as soon as—they flower. Soil solarization may also help. Appropriately labeled pre-emergence and postemergence herbicides are effective in beds and turf.
	**Quackgrass** (*Elymus repens repens*) This perennial weed can reach 3 ft. tall and produces an extensive underground network of long, slender, branching, yellowish white rhizomes that can spread laterally 3–5 ft.	Because it reproduces readily from even small pieces of rhizome left in the soil, quackgrass is difficult to eliminate. Before planting, thoroughly dig the area and remove all visible pieces of rhizome. Spray postemergence herbicides labeled for grassy weeds. Spot-treat with glyphosate.
	**Spotted Spurge** (*Euphorbia maculata*) This aggressive annual makes many seeds that may germinate immediately, producing several generations in one summer. Cut or broken stems exude a milky juice.	Hoe or pull out plants early in the season, before they bloom and set seed. Mulch to prevent seeds already in the soil from germinating. Spot-treat with herbicidal soap when plants are young. Appropriately labeled pre-emergence and postemergence herbicides are effective in beds and turf.
	**Thistle** (*Crisium*) A number of thistles invade gardens. Canada thistle (*Crisium arvense*), shown at left, is a tough perennial that grows from deep, wide-spreading horizontal roots. Bull thistle (*C. vulgare*) is a biennial that produces a rosette of deeply lobed and toothed leaves in the first year, then flowers the second. Musk thistle (*C. nutans*) is a biennial or winter annual with deep green, spiny leaves and stems that can grow up to 6 ft. tall and support dark rose or white flowers.	Hoe or dig thistles before they set seed, removing as much of the root system as possible. Use a selective herbicide for broad-leafed weeds. Or use a nonselective herbicide containing glyphosphate. The best time to spray depends on the type of thistle, so check herbicide label. Repeated treatment may be necessary.

GROW GUIDE

SPRING
checklist

March
ASSESS YOUR AZALEAS

As this Southern classic comes into bloom, mark the color of each plant, if you haven't already planted them by color. For maximum impact, group azaleas in masses of one hue or in layers of different shades. It's okay to move them while they are blooming. But if you wait until they finish, they can be rearranged, pruned, and shaped for a better show next year.

FEED YOUR LAWN

Fertilize warm-season lawns, such as Zoysia, Bermuda, and St. Augustine, after they turn green.

SHAPE UP SHRUBS

Prune spiraeas, forsythias, flowering quince, and azaleas once they have finished blooming. If you wait until summer to cut them back, you will remove next year's blooms.

ROOT A BOXWOOD CUTTING

It's easy to get more boxwoods without spending a dime. Cut off a twig about 6 inches long. Strip off the two or three lowest pairs of leaves. Dust the cut end with rooting powder. Stick the cutting into a pot of moist potting soil, and place it in shade. It should root within one month.

DIVIDE PERENNIALS

Crowded bloomers, such as Shasta daisies, chrysanthemums, and black-eyed Susans, should be divided and replanted now. If you have room, space them out in your beds. If not, pass some along to a neighbor or fellow gardener.

April
PLANT TOMATOES

Choose large containers, or plant them in a sunny spot in the garden. Tomatoes prefer moist, well-drained soil with lots of organic matter. Before planting, remove the lower leaves of your tomato plants with clippers or sharp scissors. Bury the stem up to the first two leaflets on the plant. It will develop roots along the entire buried portion of the stem.

GROW VINES

Moonflowers, morning glories, and hyacinth beans are pretty additions to the garden. Wait until the soil has warmed to sow seeds. Soak seeds overnight in water to soften the seed coat and help speed up germination.

PLANT HERBS

Culinary herbs are easy to grow. Once the frost period has passed, you can safely plant. Be sure to plant enough of the ones you frequently use. Keep this in mind: It generally takes twice as many fresh herbs as it does dried ones to equal the same amount of flavor in cooking.

CUT THE GRASS

It's time to start cutting warm-season turf, such as Bermuda, St. Augustine, and centipede. Be careful not to scalp your lawn. Adjust the blade height on your mower so that you remove only about the top third of the grass blades each time you cut the lawn. During periods of fast growth, try to mow your lawn at least once a week.

ATTRACT BEES

Don't be afraid! Bees are a gardener's friend because they help pollinate. Plant some flowers near your tomatoes and squash to lure them.

May
SOUTHERN MAGNOLIA
{MAGNOLIA GRANDIFLORA}

Fragrant flowers and glossy evergreen leaves make this Southern native a must for gardeners. Magnolias bloom best and grow fuller in a sunny spot. They prefer rich, well-drained soil but tolerate a range of conditions. Use as specimens, or plant several as a large screen. Look for named selections when buying, and water regularly to transition them into your yard.
Note: They're messy and drop leaves.

SOUTHERN MAGNOLIA SELECTIONS
'Brackens Brown Beauty', 'Claudia Wannamaker', 'Little Gem' (good for small spaces), 'Edith Bogue' (cold hardy), 'Alta', 'Teddy Bear', 'Baby Grand'

TRY HYDRANGEAS

Plant different types for gorgeous garden blooms. Our native oakleaf hydrangea (*Hydrangea quercifolia*) offers the earliest blooms in snowy white. The summer blooms of French hydrangeas (*H. macrophylla*) respond to the soil pH. Blue flowers are produced in acid soil (pH 5.5 and lower), and pink flowers are produced in alkaline soil (pH 7 and higher).

TRIM YOUR HEDGES

Boxwoods will benefit from a little pruning now. Shear them into formal hedges, if you like, or use hand pruners to open up the plants and remove some inner branches. This improves air circulation and reduces disease.

SET OUT ANNUALS

It's time to finish planting your summer annuals, such as petunias, marigolds, salvia, and impatiens. If the plants are in pots or trays, make sure the roots are not so matted that they can't expand into the soil easily. If they are, gently pull the roots apart.

SUMMER
checklist

June
BLACK-EYED SUSAN
{RUDBECKIA HIRTA}

Among the South's most beautiful native wildflowers, these bright yellow blooms will cheer up any border. Various selections offer new and different color combos. They can be biennials or short-lived perennials. Plant seeds or transplants in sunny spots with average, well-drained, slightly moist soil. Black-eyed Susans make great cut flowers and will attract butterflies, plus deer tend to avoid them.

BLACK-EYED SUSAN SELECTIONS
'Irish Eyes' (green centers), 'Denver Daisy', 'Indian Summer'

GROW CALADIUMS

For easy, dependable color in shade, caladiums can't be beat. The leaves come in a variety of colors and shapes and pair well with impatiens, silver ribbon fern, asparagus fern, Korean rock fern, and variegated creeping fig.

MULCH NEW PLANTINGS

Apply extra shredded bark or pine straw mulch around newly planted trees and shrubs. This will reduce water loss and heat stress on the new roots.

GIVE BIRDS A BREAK

Relocate birdbaths to a shady spot to slow evaporation and keep water from becoming hot. Place it near a small tree or large shrub to give birds shelter too.

WATER PLANTS

Pay attention to hanging baskets and containers because they dry out more quickly with the higher temperatures. Irrigate plants at dawn and dusk to reduce water loss from evaporation. As you make additions to your garden, you will need to water them more than established areas.

PLANT A PERENNIAL

Purple coneflower (*Echinacea purpurea*) will bloom year after year in your garden. Try 'Ruby Star', 'Magnus', and 'Bravado' for shades of purple. 'White Swan' and 'White Lustre' offer elegant snowy blooms.

August
ROSE OF SHARON
{HIBISCUS SYRIACUS}

Rose of Sharon, or althaea, is a deciduous shrub that loves hot weather. It will bloom in sun or part shade. Newer selections in the Satin, Chiffon, and Lil' Kim series offer plants in different sizes, colors, and flower forms. Use them in the back of the border or as a bright informal hedge. They are attractive to butterflies and hummingbirds.

ROSE OF SHARON SELECTIONS
'Lavender Chiffon', 'Blue Chiffon', 'Azurri Satin', 'Ruffled Satin', 'Blue Satin', 'Rose Satin', 'Lil' Kim Violet'

July
PLANT A PATRIOTIC MIX

Try this red, white, and blue container in full sun. Keep in mind that planters dry out fast in the summer; retain moisture by adding several handfuls of compost or peat to the potting mix.

1. Red zinnia **2.** Shasta daisy **3.** 'Techno Blue' lobelia **4.** 'Watermelon' sun coleus **5.** 'New Wonder' fanflower **6.** 'Supercascade White' petunia

CUT BACK ANNUALS

Trim leggy plants now so they will be full in the fall. Cut back impatiens, coleus, begonias, narrow-leaf zinnias, and salvias by one-third. Water and then fertilize with a slow-release, granular product.

PINCH HERBS

Frequently pinch or trim basil, oregano, fennel, rosemary, and thyme to keep them in full summer production. Place a container or two on your porch, patio, or deck for easy access when you are grilling.

ADJUST YOUR MOWER BLADE

Raise the cutting height of your lawn mower by 1 to 1.5 inches to help your grass survive drought and heat. Tall turf shades the soil, slows evaporation, and reduces weed growth.

ROSARIAN MUST-HAVE

If you ever try to tackle a rosebush without gloves, you'll come away looking like you tried to bathe with your cat. Rose gauntlet gloves offer plenty of forearm and hand protection without being stiff. You can also use them for picking blackberries or taming other prickly plants.

FALL
checklist

September

BUY MUMS

You'll find every shape and color at nurseries this month. Plant them in fall beds or containers. Be sure to keep mums watered well. Look for tightly budded plants with just a hint of color for a longer show. If you're adding them to a fall border, mulch to protect roots as they become established. For a pretty cottage garden look, try loosely growing, old-fashioned types like 'Hillside Sheffield' and 'Single Apricot Korean'.

AMERICAN BEAUTYBERRY
{CALLICARPA AMERICANA}

This native, deciduous shrub starts to show off now with purple berries and leaves that turn a pale yellow. After the foliage has fallen, the berries (which birds love) are especially showy, hugging the arching stems. Plant American beautyberry solo or en masse in full sun to light shade. Prune in winter. In the Upper South, plants may freeze to the ground in cold weather but will come back.

AMERICAN BEAUTYBERRY SELECTIONS
'Welch's Pink' (pink berries), 'Bok Tower' (white berries)

EASE UP ON WATERING

As temperatures begin to cool, plants need less water. Adjust your watering schedule for lawns and borders. Pay close attention to containers, as they can become waterlogged.

PLANT TREES AND SHRUBS

Planting in autumn allows them time to grow roots and transition into the garden.

CELEBRATE THE AUTUMN EQUINOX

September 23 marks the end of summer and the beginning of fall. A new garden season lies ahead, one with cooler weather and fewer bugs. Now is the time to begin setting out fall annuals and vegetables, creating container gardens, buying bulbs, and planting shrubs and trees. This is one of the best times to garden in the South, so be sure to get outside, dig in the dirt, and enjoy the days ahead.

October

AMP UP YOUR POTS

Don't let your pumpkins steal all the glory. Combine the season's hottest hues in a vibrant mix of annuals, perennials, and shrubs.

1. 'Snapshot Orange' snapdragon **2.** 'Sparkling Burgundy' heuchera **3.** 'Penny Clear Yellow' viola **4.** 'Purple Pixie' loropetalum **5.** 'Miracle' heuchera

OVERSEED WARM-SEASON GRASSES

For a green lawn during the upcoming winter months, overseed centipede or Bermuda with annual ryegrass. Water lightly to help seeds germinate.

PLANT ANNUALS

Remove spent summer annuals, and replace them with pansies or other cool-weather annuals. For a good start, add a balanced slow-release fertilizer and compost to the bed before planting.

DON'T BRING IN THE BUGS

Before houseplants that have summered outside come indoors, make sure bugs aren't hitchhiking on the foliage. Fill a spray bottle with water, and add three or four drops of dish-washing liquid.

November

THINK AHEAD FOR SPRING

Buy and plant tulip bulbs now for bright blossoms in spring. Reliable selections include 'Apricot Beauty' (salmon) and 'Monte Carlo' (yellow), which bloom early in the season. 'Ivory Floradale' (white) and 'Golden Oxford' (yellow) are good midseason selections. 'Maureen' (white) and 'Temple of Beauty' (salmon) bloom later. If planting in a pot, nestle bulbs closely together for a full show. In beds, follow spacing on package.

SHOP FOR SASANQUAS

For the best selection, look for sasanqua camellias (*Camellia sasanqua*) at the garden center now. These fall-blooming shrubs will put on a show through winter. Suited to all areas except the Tropical South, sasanquas love summer heat and can take full sun or light shade. They're not quite as cold hardy as common camellias. In the Upper South, plant so they're sheltered from winter wind.

START A COMPOST PILE

Cleaning up the garden will yield plenty of fallen leaves and plant debris for compost. In an out-of-the-way corner of the garden, mix green and dry materials with a shovelful of soil and an optional handful of fertilizer (any kind except a weed-and-feed product). Sprinkle with water weekly if there is no rain. You'll have compost by spring, sooner if you turn the pile.

GROW GUIDE

WINTER
checklist

December
YAUPON HOLLY
{ILEX VOMITORIA}

Yaupon holly is a native evergreen that is drought tolerant and versatile—use it as a screen or foundation shrub. Female plants have small, bright red berries that persist through fall and winter and provide food for birds. Use 'Pride of Houston' for 6- to 10-foot hedges with berries. 'Scarlet's Peak' is a columnar form that is excellent as an accent. 'Nana' (male) can be utilized as a low hedge in formal gardens.

OTHER FAVORITES FOR A HOLLY, JOLLY CHRISTMAS
'Nellie R. Stevens', 'Dwarf Burford', 'Stokes Dwarf'

ATTRACT BIRDS

Cardinals, chickadees, titmice, and finches will flock to feeders this time of year. White proso millet, Nyjer seeds, and sunflower seeds will appeal to a wide range of birds. Hang feeders at least 5 feet off the ground and 10 feet away from vegetation and structures to deter predators. Water for drinking and bathing is also appreciated, with running water being the best.

MULCH SHRUBS

Azaleas, boxwoods, hollies, and camellias will appreciate extra protection during winter. After the first frost, add a 2-inch-thick layer of finely shredded pine bark mulch or pine straw around the base of shrubs.

TRY A LIVE CHRISTMAS TREE

Decorate it for the holidays, and transplant into your yard later. For best results, locate the tree in a cool room away from heating ducts. Keep it watered, and don't leave it in the house for any longer than a week.

January
LOOK AT YOUR FLOWERBEDS

Are they being shaded by nearby evergreens? Simply cutting a few branches can let more light onto your beds. If your containers of flowers are not blooming, move them to a new spot that receives more sun.

PERK UP VIOLAS

The happy blooms of these plants can get a little weary with cold weather. Jump to their rescue by removing spent blossoms and trimming leggy, discolored foliage with scissors. (Deadhead regularly to encourage prolific blooms.) Water your plants well, and let them drain. Then use a liquid fertilizer such as Schultz All Purpose Liquid Plant Food 10-15-10.

BUY CAMELLIAS

The best time to purchase common camellias (*Camellia japonica*) is when they are in bloom. Early-flowering selections include 'Lady Clare', 'Debutante', and 'Professor Charles S. Sargent'. Try 'Kramer's Supreme', 'Nuccio's Pearl', 'Pink Perfection', and 'Swan Lake' for midseason blooms. For late-blooming shrubs, try 'Purity' and 'Governor Mouton'.

FLOWERING QUINCE
{CHAENOMELES SP.}

This reliable shrub is one of the earliest blooms of winter. It prefers a sunny location and well-drained soil. Plant several as an informal hedge or one as a specimen. Bloom colors can be white, pink, red, or orange.

FLOWERING QUINCE SELECTIONS
'Toyo-Nishiki', 'Scarlet Storm', 'Cameo'

February

FORCE BRANCHES INTO BLOOM

When forsythia, quince, star magnolia, and saucer magnolia buds show a touch of color, they are easy to force into bloom indoors. Cut branches, taking care not to destroy the natural shape of the plant. They should be in full bloom several days after you place them in a vase of water indoors.

PRUNE TREES

Except for maples and birches, now is a good time. If limbs are more than an inch in diameter, use this method: Make the first cut on the underside of the limb 6 inches away from the trunk. Cut about half the thickness of the branch. At the top of the limb, cut it off halfway between the underside cut and the trunk. Cut the stub within ½ inch of the trunk.

HOW TO PICK A DAFFODIL

Don't cut the stem, says Brent Heath of Brent and Becky's Bulbs in Gloucester, Virginia. The bloom will last longer in water if you use your thumb and finger to snap off the stem at the base so it has a white bottom.

FIND YOUR ZONE

■ Upper South
USDA ZONE 6

■ Middle South
USDA ZONE 7

■ Lower South
USDA ZONE 8

■ Coastal South
USDA ZONE 9

■ Tropical South
USDA ZONE 10-11

BELIEVE IT OR NOT, CUT THE GRASS!

A dry winter day is a good time to mow a dormant, warm-season lawn. This grooms the lawn and removes fallen leaves and pine needles. It also allows you to inspect your yard for winter weeds. Control them by spraying when the weather warms in spring.

TRIM LIRIOPE

Now is a great time to groom your liriope and mondo grass before new leaves emerge. Cut small plantings by hand; for larger ones, use a lawn mower with the blade set 2 ½ to 3 inches high, or use a string trimmer. Be careful not to cut the foliage too short, or you may damage this season's new leaves.

SOLVING THE MYSTERY OF BOTANICAL NAMES

Although Southerners feel comfortable with common names, botanical names are often intimidating. So why do we need botanical names at all? For a very good reason— common names for plants vary from region to region and even from town to town. One plant may live under several common names. Or a single common name may refer to several plants that don't look anything alike.

ARE COMMON NAMES PRECISE?

A common name may refer to several different plants. A good example of this is the plant commonly known as "dusty miller." This name actually applies to four similar plants that have silvery foliage—*Senecio viravira*, *Senecio cineraria*, *Centaurea cineraria*, and *Artemisia stellerana*.

Rudbeckia hirta

Thunbergia alata

Only the first of these plants is frequently sold at garden centers.

And some plants that share a common name aren't the least bit similar. "Black-eyed Susan" applies to a golden-flowered perennial (*Rudbeckia hirta*), as well as to a vine that is usually planted and grown as a summer annual (*Thunbergia alata*). "Texas sage" is a shrub with silvery leaves and purple flowers (Leucophyllum frutescens) and also a perennial with purple-blue flowers (*Salvia texana*).

Having multiple common names for the same plant also causes confusion. For instance, if you call a shrub with brilliant-red autumn foliage "burning bush" and someone else knows it as "winged euonymus," you may not realize that you're both talking about the same plant—in this case, *Euonymus alatus*.

So there are practical reasons for using botanical names. They provide the most accurate means we have for identifying a plant. And they're still the best way to ensure that the plants you buy are ones you really want.

KEEP AN EYE OUT FOR CLUES

Botanical names, once you break them down, reveal important clues to the natures of plants. The first word of a botanical name is the genus, which tells you the group of plants to which this one belongs. The second word is the species name, which is usually descriptive and easy to decipher once you know how to look for clues.

Descriptive words used often in species names are listed at right. When you know the meanings of these words, many plant names become easy to understand and can help you identify plants. For example, the species name for twinleaf (*Jeffersonia diphylla*) combines *di* (double or two) with *phylla* (leaves) to mean "two leaves."

The easiest botanical names to remember are those directly translated into common names. For instance, big-leaf magnolia (*Magnolia macrophylla*) does have huge leaves. And *macro* means large, *phylla* means leaves.

Some botanical names are so much like English words that they offer immediate clues to that plant's appearance. We can easily gather the meaning of words like *compacta*, *contorta*, *canadensis*, *deliciosa*, *fragrans*, and *micro*.

A GUIDE TO BOTANICAL NAMES

COLOR OF FLOWERS OR FOLIAGE

alba—white
argentea—silvery
aurantiaca—orange
aurea—golden
azurea—azure, sky blue
caerulea—dark blue
caesia—blue-gray
candida—pure white, shiny
cana—ashy gray, hoary
cereus—waxy
citrina—yellow
coccinea—scarlet
concolor—one color
cruenta—bloody
discolor—two colors, separate colors
glauca—blue-gray, blue-green
incana—gray, hoary
lutea—yellow
pallida—pale
purpurea—purple
ruber, rubra—red, ruddy
rufa—ruddy
viridis, virens—green

FORM OF LEAF (FOLIA—LEAVES OR FOLIAGE)

acerifolia—maplelike
angustifolia—narrow
aquifolia—spiny
buxifolia—boxwoodlike
ilicifolia—hollylike
laurifolia—laurel-like
parvifolia—small
populifolia—poplarlike
salicifolia—willowlike

Lavandula angustifolia 'Hidcote'

SHAPE OF PLANT

adpressa—pressing against, hugging
alta—tall
arborea—treelike
capitata—headlike
compacta—compact, dense
conferta—crowded, pressed together
contorta—twisted
decumbens—lying down
depressa—pressed down
elegans—elegant, slender, willowy
fastigiata—branches erect and close together
humifusa—sprawling on the ground
humilis—low, small, humble
impressa—impressed upon
nana—dwarf
procumbens—trailing
prostrata—prostrate
pumila—dwarf, small
pusilla—puny, insignificant
repens—creeping
reptans—creeping
scandens—climbing

WHERE IT CAME FROM

A number of suffixes are added to place names to specify the habitat where the plant was discovered or the place where it is usually found.

africana—of Africa
alpina—from the mountains
australis—southern
borealis—northern
campestris—of the field or plains
canadensis—of Canada
canariensis—of the Canary Islands
capensis—of the Cape of Good Hope area
caroliniana—of the Carolinas
chinensis—of China
hispanica—of Spain
hortensis—of gardens
indica—of India
insularis—of the island
japonica—of Japan
montana—of the mountains
riparia—of riverbanks
saxatilis—inhabiting rocks
texana—of Texas
virginiana—of Virginia

PLANT PARTS

dendron—tree
flora, florum, flori, florus—flowers
phyllus, phylla—leaf or leaves

Cestrum elegans

Zephyranthes grandiflora

Elaeagnus pungens

Ligustrum japonicum

Passiflora caerulea

Rosa rugosa

PLANT PECULIARITIES

armata—armed
baccata—berried, berrylike
barbata—barbed or bearded
campanulata—bell or cup shaped
ciliaris—fringed
cordata—heart shaped
cornuta—horned
crassa—thick, fleshy
decurrens—running down the stem
densi—dense
diversi—varying
edulis—edible
florida—free flowering
fruticosa—shrubby
fulgens—shiny
gracilis—slender, thin, small
grandi—large, showy
-ifer, -ifera—bearing or having;
    e.g., stoloniferus, having stolons

imperialis—showy
laciniata—fringed or with torn edges
laevigata—smooth
lobata—lobed
longa—long
macro—large
maculata—spotted
micro—small
mollis—soft, soft-haired
mucronata—pointed
nutans—nodding, swaying
obtusa—blunt or flattened
officinalis—medicinal
-oides—like or resembling;
    e.g., jasminoides, like a jasmine
patens—open, spreading growth
pinnata—constructed like a feather
platy—broad
plena—double, full
plumosa—feathery
praecox—precocious, early
pungens—piercing
radicans—rooting,
    especially along the stem
reticulata—net-veined
retusa—notched at blunt apex
rugosa—wrinkled, rough
saccharata—sweet, sugary
sagittalis—arrowlike
scabra—rough feeling
scoparia—broomlike

Gardenia jasminoides

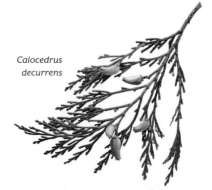
Calocedrus decurrens

Hydrangea macrophylla

GENERAL INDEX

PLANT INDEX

CREDITS

Photographs and illustrations are listed sequentially either in horizontal or vertical order. For additional clarification, the following position indicators may be used: Left (L), Center (C), Right (R), Top (T), Middle (M), Bottom (B), Upper (U).

William D. Adams: 510RC1, 510R; AgStock Images, Inc./Bill Barksdale: 483L; Sari Akene (Photos Lamontagne)/ Garden Picture Library/ Photolibrary: 231L, 495RC; Masao Akiyama/ Sebun Photo: 53L4; Jean Allsopp/ Southern Living: 399RC, 411RC2; courtesy of Ames True Temper: 656R1, 656R2, 656R3, 656R4; Peter Anderson/Getty Images: 418RC2; Ralph Anderson/Southern Living: Front inset 2, Front inset 3, Front inset 4, Front inset 6, Front inset 7, Back inset 1, 2, 5, 6, 12-13, 16-17, 20, 21, 23, 25, 27, 41L4, 42L5, 49L1, 51L1, 53R4, 56R2, 56R3, 60L4, 63L2, 67R4, 71L1, 77R3, 78L2, 84L3, 86R3, 87R4, 88L4, 92R1, 100L2, 100R4, 101R1, 108R1, 115L5, 118R3, 119R1, 126RC, 128L1, 128L2, 128L3, 130L, 132L, 135RC, 136L, 139RC, 141R, 142R, 146RC2, 150L, 151R, 153LC, 153RC, 160L, 179LC, 182RC, 183L, 183LC, 186RC, 187R, 194LC, 195LC, 197LC, 202L, 205L, 207R, 210LC, 211L1, 211L2, 211L3, 211LC2, 212L2, 215L, 227RC1, 229L1, 229LC1, 229L3, 229LC2, 230LC, 234LC, 243RC2, 243RC3, 244L1, 244L2, 253RC3, 260R, 285L, 288L2, 290RC2, 292L2, 292R, 295RC, 308L3, 314RC, 315 (all), 316L1, 316L2, 321L, 325RC, 330L1, 332LC, 332RC, 332R1, 344RC, 350L2, 353LC, 357R2, 360L3, 363RC, 364L, 365 (all), 370L1, 370LC, 371LC1, 375LC, 378 (all), 380LC, 385LC, 394RC, 395RC, 396 (all), 406L, 406LC, 411R2, 416L, 419LC, 421L, 421R, 424R2, 431L, 434R, 435LC, 438R, 442R, 445RC, 446L, 446RC, 448L1, 448LC2, 448L4, 449L, 451RC, 483LC, 487LC1, 492LC, 497L, 497RC3, 499L, 521L, 530R, 542L1, 542L2, 542L3, 542LC2, 545RC1, 545R1, 545RC2, 545RC3, 545R2, 546L1, 551R, 552R, 554L1, 554L2, 557RC2, 561LC, 568RC1, 580R, 581L, 584RC, 586L, 586RC, 587L, 592L3, 593L, 595RC, 614LC, 618R, 624 (all), 630LC1, 630L2, 630LC3, 630L4, 630LC4, 634R, 635RC1, 641RC1, 641RC2, 645RC, 646R, 651L, 660, 663L, 667R1, 667R2, 669R1, 669BL1, 669BR2, 672 (all), 676, 677R2, 678R1, 679, 681, 682, 684, 686, 687 (all), 697, 703R, 707R1, 707R3, 710L1, 712, 714R1, 714L2, 714L3, 728LC1, 729R1, 729R2, 730R1, 730C3, 730R2, 731L1, 731L2, 732L, 733LC1, 735L1, 735R2; Cedric Angeles: 122L; courtesy of Annie's Annuals & Perennials: 213LC, 245L, 259LC, 275RC, 283LC, 297L, 328R, 375R, 470R;

Antagain/Getty Images: 728R1, 729L3; Nicholas Appleby/Garden World Images: 519L; Anne Green-Armytage/Getty Images: 193RC, 279L; Arco Images GmbH/ Photolibrary: 433L, 464RC; Scott Atkinson: 91L2; Lee Avison: 134LC; courtesy of Debra Lee Baldwin: 186LC; Jan Baldwin/Photolibrary: 169RC; courtesy of Ball Horticultural Company: 146RC1, 343R, 345LC; Noel Barnhurst: 83L3; Beanstock Images/Getty Images: 222R; Bill Beatty/Visuals Unlimited: 717L1, 726L3; courtesy of Benary: 582L2; Pernilla Bergdahl/ Getty Images: 261RC, 303LC, 607L; Pernilla Bergdahl;plusphoto/a. collectionRF/Getty: 400R; Laura Berman/Visuals Unlimited, Inc./ Getty Images: 588R; Ugurhan Betin/Getty Images: 510RC3; Gerry Bishop/Visuals Unlimited, Inc.: 562RC; Sue Bishop/Getty Images: 522L; BIOS (W. Lapinski)/ Peter Arnold, Inc.: 63R3; Black Diamond Images/Flickr: 361RC; Anthony Blake/Photolibrary: 223LC; John Block/Getty Images: 180LC; Richard Bloom/Getty Images: 393L4; Christina Bollen/ Getty Images: 329LC, 393LC3; Bon Appetit/Alamy: 699B1; Mark Bolton/Age fotostock/Photolibrary: 610LC; Mark Bolton/ Garden Picture Library/Photolibrary: 625RC; Mark Bolton/Getty Images: 55L3, 59L3, 136LC, 198LC, 294RC, 295R, 324R, 375RC, 469RC, 524RC, 582L4, 597L, 602LC2, 615L, 703L; Botanic Images, Inc./ Garden World Images: 233LC; John W Bova/Getty Images: 368LC; Marion Brenner: 42R3, 49R4, 52R4, 61L3, 65R2, 67L5, 71L4, 72R4, 73L4, 73R5, 89L5, 97L3, 98R4, 100L1, 106R5, 109L2, 109R2, 115L2, 117R1, 117R2, 118L3, 119L4, 119R3, 293LC, 300RC; Kathleen Norris Brenzel: 84L4; Rob D. Brodman/Sunset: 182L, 458R, 463R, 469L, 519LC, 577RC, 591RC, 602R, 685R; Lynne Brotchie/Getty Images: 343LC, 521RC, 579R; Deni Brown/Getty Images: 81R1, 270LC; Ruth Brown/Getty Images: 475LC; courtesy of Gene Burch: 239RC1; John Burgoyne (illustration): 729C, 734L; John Burke/Getty Images: 534RC1; Burpee Seed Company (Courtesy): 548R; Chris Burrows/GardenPictureLibrary/Photolibrary: 280L2, 539L, 642RC; Chris Burrows/Getty Images: 131LC, 143L2, 198L2, 252L, 286R, 327R1,

341L, 492L, 637RC; Andrew Butler: 424RC1, 648L1; Ralph S. Byther: 722L2; Scott Calhoun: 408L; Rosemary Calvert/Getty Images: 54R2; Robbie Caponetto/ Southern Living: 8, 35, 133L, 152R, 191RC, 223RC, 261LC, 330RC, 456LC, 546LC, 608RC, 669L1, 698L, 708, 714L1; Rob Cardillo: 167L, 191LC, 225RC, 242RC, 271RC, 286RC, 311RC, 316R, 318R, 319LC, 349RC, 361LC, 374RC, 390L, 390R, 394LC, 414LC, 440LC, 474RC, 483R, 489R, 501L, 578RC, 600LC, 643L; James Carrier: 70R1, 71R4, 91R2; Brian Carter/Getty Images: 351RC3, 514L, 589L; Nigel Cattlin/ Visuals Unlimited, Inc./Getty Images: 718L7, 723L3; David Q. Cavagnaro: 48L2, 59R1, 64L1, 78L3, 78R1, 82L6, 83R1, 84L1, 85L1, 90L1, 93L2, 95R1, 102L1, 106L1, 199L, 240LC, 249L, 251RC, 283L, 296LC, 362RC, 538L1, 538LC, 550LC, 577R, 650L, 726L6, 727L5; David Q. Cavagnaro/Getty Images: 101R4, 110R1, 165LC, 203LC, 229R, 538L2, 577L; Jess Chamberlain/Sunset: 298L; Van Chaplin/Southern Living: 11, 14, 24, 26, 29, 55R2, 70L2, 102R1, 103L1, 109L4, 120L, 167R, 171LC, 172L, 183L2, 190L, 199LC, 205LC1, 212L1, 220L, 243R, 258R, 263L, 272RC1, 272R, 280L1, 284RC, 287R, 291LC, 297LC, 302L, 317R, 318L, 346 (all), 360L1, 371LC2, 373RC, 395L, 400RC, 411L, 420LC, 423R, 424R1, 424RC2, 424R3, 425L, 443L, 448L3, 448LC4, 457RC, 470RC1, 479R, 492R, 509LC, 523L2, 546L2, 554L3, 554LC2, 557L, 557R, 560LC, 573R, 578LC, 605LC, 608L, 622RC, 644LC, 645, 648LC, 663R, 664L2, 673R, 675LC1, 700L2, 700C3, 714R2, 728RC1, 730C2; Jennifer Cheung: 321LC; Gary Clark: 43L1; Lucy Claxton/Getty Images: 293R, 402RC2; Willard Clay/Getty Images: 514RC; Gerald & Buff Corsi/Getty Images: 428RC; Paul Costello: 145R; Crandall & Crandall: 92L3, 99R1, 113L4; Rosalind Creasy: 83R4; John D. Cunningham/Visuals Unlimited: 727L2; Claire Curran: 40L4, 48R1, 49R3, 51R3, 53L3, 54L3, 56L2, 56L4, 57L1, 57R2, 60L5, 60R5, 63L4, 64L2, 67R5, 77L4, 77R4, 85R2, 88R2, 89L4, 89R1, 91R3, 93R1, 94L1, 94R3, 94R4, 97L4, 98L3, 111L4, 111L5, 112L2, 112R3, 113R1, 114L1, 114L2, 115L1, 736L1, 736L2; Claire Curran/Sunset: 141RC; Robin Bachtler Cushman: 53R1, 57R4, 68R5, 85L5, 480LC, 482RC, 488R2, 529RC3, 536LC,

622LC; DAJ/Getty Images: 286L, 81R4; Darcy Daniels: 293RC Julie Dansereau/Getty Images: 351RC2; Jennifer Davick: 489L Jennifer Davick/Southern Living: 517RC; Davies and Starr/Getty Images: 691(only); Michael Davis/ Garden Picture Library/Photolibrary: 218LC; Michael Davis/ Getty Images: 110R4,165L,179RC1,3 51L,582LC2,593RC; Francoise Davis/ Garden World Images: 198R; Todd Davis: 58L3, 69L3, 69L4, 72R1, 97R2; DEA /A.CROCI/ Getty Images: 648L2; DEA/C. DANI/Getty Images: 131RC, 317LC, 465RC, 536L, 580RC; DEA/C. DANI-I.JESKE/Getty Images: 291L, 456R; DEA / C.DELU/Getty Images: 605RC; DEA / C. SAPPA/ Getty Images: 450RC; De Agostini Picture Library/Getty Images: 239R, 489RC, 565LC; DEA/ RANDOM/Getty Images: 76R3, 224L, 434LC2; DEA PICTURE LIBRARY/Getty Images: 309R, 649R; DEA/S.MONTANARI/Getty images: 49L3, 75R2, 76L2, 267LC; Paul Debois/Getty Images: 402RC1; Gilles Delacroix/Garden World Images: 191R, 328LC, 409LC, 423LC, 430R, 498RC; Danita Delimont/Getty Images: 206L, 420R, 608R, 613LC Shelley Dennis/Getty Images: 609LC; Alan & Linda Detrick: 42L3, 66L1, 79L5, 101L4, 101R2, 104R1, 108R2, 109L1, 112L4, 114R5, 117L1, 119L1, 119L2, 644R; William B. Dewey: 40R2, 51L4, 87R; Frédéric Didillon/ Bios/Photolibrary: 217RC Frédéric Didillon/ Mise au Point: 99L1, 196R; Diez O/Photolibrary: 134R; Greg Dimijian/Getty Images: 472L; David Dixon/Getty: 188LC, 331R; Mike Dirr: 126L, 134L, 137L, 148R, 247L, 248R, 251L, 267RC, 270R, 273R, 276R, 287RC, 306L, 309RC, 317L, 318RC, 332L, 338RC, 388L, 401RC, 418R, 422LC, 437R, 441LC, 453L, 475R, 490LC, 575LC, 609L; Christine M. Douglas/Getty Images: 485R, 596L, 644RC, 646LC; Ray Dove/Getty Images: 587R; Jacqui Dracup/Garden World Images: 620L; Carole Drake/Getty Images: 508RC; Ken Druse: 58R1; Nicole Duplaix/Getty Images: 248RC; Wally Eberhart: 166L; Dana Edmunds/Getty Images: 441L; Chris Ellenbogen: 159 (All); Clyde Elmore: 726L5 Thomas E. Eltzroth: 722L1,723L2, 83L1,84R5; David England/Getty Images: 50L1; courtesy of Emerisa

Nursery: 234R; **Craig Engle:** 96R2 **Marc Epstein/Getty Images:** 586R, 516LC; **Ron Erwin/Getty Images:** 633RC; **esolla/Getty Images:** 58R2 **Ron Evans/Getty Images:** 47L1, 56R4, 271LC, 323LC, 487L1, 550RC, 616L; **Tina Evans:** 52L4, 59R3, 74R2, 85R5, 103R2; **Derek Fell:** 60R1, 60R3, 63L1, 63R4, 70R4, 86L5, 91R5, 92L2, 94R5, 96R5, 97R3, 99L3, 103R5, 113L3, 116R3; **William E. Ferguson:** 719L2; **FhF Green-media/Getty Images:** 281LC; **Victoria Firmston/Getty Images:** 127L, 482LC; **Guenter Fischer/Getty:** 189R, 234RC, 249RC; **Dennis Flaherty/Getty Images:** 616RC; **FLETCHER & BAYLIS/Getty Images:** 331RC; **Neil Fletcher/Getty Images:** 119L3; **W K Fletcher/Getty Images:** 237RC; **flower-photos/Alamy:** 368RC; **f.Olby/Getty Images:** 699B2; **Giorgio Fochesato/Getty Images:** 163R; **Roger Foley:** Back inset 3, 22, 30, 31, 32-33, 45L4, 91R4, 100L3, 130L2, 144L, 195RC1, 198RC, 199RC1, 199RC2, 205LC2, 216RC, 219LC, 250L1, 250L2, 250LC, 330L2, 342RC, 348L, 351R, 357RC2, 357RC3, 376L2, 428L2, 493L1, 493LC1, 493L2, 497R1, 534R, 552RC2, 568RC2, 571LC2, 571LC3, 571L2, 591R, 592L1, 592LC1, 592L2, 592LC2, 600L, 629RC, 630L1, 630LC2, 630L3, 652, 662, 673L, 675R, 680, 689, 690, 698R, 710L2; **Food Collection/Photolibrary:** 262R; **Ryann Ford:** 282RC; **Federica Fortunat/Getty Images:** 513RC; **fotolinchen/Getty Images:** 143L1, 222L, 515LC; **Fresh Food Images/Photolibrary:** 324LC; **Jill Fromer/Getty Images:** 472RC; **Doug Fulton/Getty Images:** 384LC; **Andrew Furlong/Getty Images:** 733R2; **Michael P Gadomski/Getty Images:** 163LC, 208L1, 257RC1, 527L, 617RC; **Tim Gainey/Alamy:** 226RC; **Paroli Galperti/Cubo Images/Photolibrary:** 194L, 530LC; **GAP Photos/Getty Images:** 619RC1; **Gentl and Hyers/Getty Images:** 467RC1; **Karl Gercens III:** 593R, 633L; **Adam Gibbs:** 42R1; **Fiona Gilsenan:** 60R4, 106R1, 108L2; **Susan M. Glascock:** 727L1; **Laurey W. Glenn/Southern Living:** 99R2, 154LC, 188RC, 224RC, 251LC, 666L, 668L2; **Richard Goerg/Getty Images:** 621LC; **David Goldberg:** 42L1, 49R1, 91L3, 92R4, 116L1, 727L3; **David T. Gomez/iStockPhoto.com:** 384RC; **Alexandra Grablewski/Getty Images:** 334LC; **John Granen:** 347RC; **Gilbert S Grant/Getty Images:** 247RC, 504LC; **Harold E. Greer:** 93R2; **Gregory MD/Getty Images:** 58R3; **James A. Guilliam/Getty Images:** 536LC; **Steven A. Gunther:** 136LC, 164RC, 225LC, 565L, 607LC, 607RC; **Bob Gurr/Getty Images:** 567RC2; **Melina Hammer/Southern Living:** 480L; **Paul Hammond:** 95L3; **William Harlow/Getty Images:** 632LC; **Jerry Harpur/Harpur Garden Images:** 221LC; **Marcus**

Harpur/Harpur Garden Images: 271L, 405R, 628L, 637R; **Chris Harris/Garden World Images:** 634L; **Jessie M. Harris:** 68L1; **Lynne Harrison:** 110L2; **Sunniva Harte/Getty Images:** 231RC, 237LC, 246L, 487L3, 528R; **Kennan Harvey/Southern Living:** 542LC1; **Martin Harvey/Getty Images:** 286LC; **Steffen Hauser/botanikfoto/Alamy:** 437LC; **Steffen Hauser/Garden World Images:** 320RC, 421RC, 625L, 637L2; **Carolyn Hebbard/Getty Images:** 235R; **Francois De Heel/Getty Images:** 288RC, 625R; **Francois De Heel/Photolibrary:** 317RC; **Jim Henkens:** 587LC; **C. Andrew Henley/Getty Images:** 643RC; **Michael Hieber/Getty Images:** 594LC; **Claire Higgins/Getty Images:** 482R1; **High Country Gardens:** 404L2; **David Hillegas:** 51L3, 639RC2, 728L1; **Walter H. Hodge/Peter Arnold, Inc.:** 87R1; **Neil Holmes/Getty Images:** 350LC, 418L, 450R, 484RC2, 567R, 638L1; **Gary Holscher Photography:** 479RC1; **Saxon Holt:** 41L3, 46L2, 50L3, 51R2, 55R1, 62R2, 68R3, 70L3, 72L1, 72L5, 76R2, 84L5, 90L2, 90R3, 90R5, 107L2, 111L2, 111R3, 112R4, 114R3, 117R5, 128LC1, 236L2, 236LC1, 236LC2; **Saxon Holt/Photo-Botanic:** 138RC, 149R, 228RC, 238R, 258LC, 296L, 311LC, 362LC, 377RC, 437L, 437RC, 448LC1, 454LC, 491LC, 612RC, 629LC; **Horticultural Art- Fred Michel/Getty Images:** 647L; **Horticultural Photography:** 510RC2; **Jody Horton:** 671; **Lisa Hubbard/Getty Images:** 615R; **Laura Dunkin-Hubby/Sunset:** 174L, 214LC, 221L, 428R, 490L; **Martin Hughes-Jones/Alamy:** 636RC; **Mary-Gray Hunter:** 41R3, 53R2, 61L2, 80R2, 81L4, 82L4, 88R4, 99R4, 107L3, 113R2; **Jacqui Hurst/Getty Images:** 299L; **Roger Hyam/Getty Images:** 502RC; **Anne Hyde/Getty Images:** 467R2; **I am happy taking photographs/Getty Images:** 150RC; **IMAGEMORE Co, Ltd./Getty Images:** 304RC; **Image Source/Getty Images:** 74L3; **Sian Irvine/Getty Images:** 340LC, 362LC; **iStock:** Front main, 51R5, 100R1, 139R, 164L, 166R, 181L, 192 (all), 218R, 219RC, 226R, 244LC, 249LC, 259LC, 260RC, 261R, 270RC, 276L, 278LC, 288L1, 298RC, 305L, 331L, 340RC, 343L, 366RC, 366R, 376L1, 388R, 392LC, 404L1, 438L, 439L, 441RC, 455RC, 456L1, 456L2, 458L, 492RC, 539LC, 565RC, 567RC1, 610L1, 636L, 661R1, 688L, 700R3, 732R2, 733R3, 736R2, 737R1, 737L3, 738C1, 738R1, 739LC1; **Gail Jankus/Getty Images:** 151L, 366LC, 466RC; **Jon Jensen Photography:** 394R; **Cary Jobe/Southern Living:** 449LC; **Johner Images/Getty Images:** 619RC; **Adam Jones/Getty Images:** 493R; **Andrea Jones/Garden Exposures Photo Library:** 574L, 579RC, 588L, 594R, 604RC, 606RC, 650RC; **Andrea Jones/Garden Picture Library/**

Photolibrary: 171L, 175RC, 205R, 370L2; **Chris L Jones/Garden Picture Library/Photolibrary:** 399L; **Christopher Lavis-Jones/Garden World Images:** 418RC1; **JTB Photo/Photolibrary:** 163L; **Kallista Images/Getty Images:** 433R; **Raj Kamal/Getty Images:** 405RC; **Dency Kane:** 68R6, 236L3; **Lynn Keddie/Getty Images:** 381LC, 409RC; **Dorling Kindersley/Getty Images:** 86R4, 88R1, 137R, 140RC, 154L, 457L, 458RC, 496LC, 527LC; **Susanne Kischnick/Alamy:** 474L; **Sachiko Kono/a.collectionRF/Getty Images:** 358LC; **Ernst Kucklich:** 151RC, 204L, 255RC, 259L, 298R, 310LC, 329RC, 342L, 345R, 348RC, 403RC, 463LC, 505R, 516L, 523LC1, 523LC2, 549LC; **Michel Lefèvre/Bios/Photolibrary:** 612R; **Leonie Lambert/Getty Images:** 225R, 526R; **Georgianna Lane/Garden Photo World/Photolibrary:** 610L2; **Angelina Lax/Getty Images:** 530RC; **Martin Leigh/Getty Images:** 467R1; **Randall Levensaler/Getty Images:** 95L2; **Pia Liikala/Getty Images:** 576LC; **Adam Lister/Getty Images:** 80R4; **Janet Loughrey:** 64R1, 70R3, 86R1, 106L2; **Andrew de Lory/Getty Images:** 74L4; **Diane Macdonald/Getty Images:** 513L; **Paul Madden/Getty Images:** 627LC; **Samuel R. Maglione/Getty Images:** 436R; **Horst Mahr/Getty Images:** 258L, 644L; **Gerald Majumdar/Getty Images:** 389R; **Allan Mandell:** 115R2; **George & Judy Manna/Getty Images:** 324RC; **MAP/Arnaud Descat/Garden World Images:** 91R1, 101R3, 105L3, 106L4, 471RC; **MAP/Nathalie Pasquel/Garden World Images:** 602LC1; **MAP/ Nicole et Patrick Mioulane/ Garden World Images:** 238L, 515L, 528LC; **Joseph A. Marcus, Lady Bird Johnson Wildflower Center:** 408LC; **Steve W. Marley:** 82R3, 83L2; **John Martin/Alamy:** 393LC4 **John Martin/Garden World Images:** 341LC; **Sylvia Martin/Southern Living:** 411R1, 411RC3; **Nakano Masahiro/amanaimages-RF/Getty images:** 357R1; **Anthony-Masterson/Getty images:** 595L; **Matthew Benson Foto:** 34; **Beth Maynor:** 75L4, 76L4; **Joshua McCullough/Getty images:** 88L3, 193R, 217R, 253R, 275L, 287L, 303R, 333LC, 377L, 442L, 462RC, 484L, 505RC1, 507LC, 508LC, 516RC, 518L, 563RC, 600RC, 605R, 612LC, 703C; **Joshua McCullough/Phyto-Photo:** 149L, 235RC, 276RC, 301RC, 312RC, 319RC, 323L, 358R, 380L1, 431RC, 444L, 445LC, 494RC, 500R, 574LC, 598LC; **Jim McCausland/Sunset:** 353RC; **J.R. McCausland:** 465R, 609RC; **Pam McLean/Getty Images:** 95R3; **Jane McCreary:** 657BL, 657BC, 657BR; **Niall McDiarmid/Alamy:** 548LC; **David McDonald/PhotoGarden, Inc.:** 40L2, 42L2, 50L2, 53L5, 63R1, 64L4, 64R3, 66R1, 66R4, 67L2, 67R2,

67R3, 68R1, 78L1, 79L2, 79L3, 80R1, 80R5, 86R5, 110L4; **Joe McDonald/Getty Images:** 352R; **Jack McDowell:** 82R4; **Ian McKinnell/Getty Images:** 734C2; **Fiona McLeod/Getty Images:** 160R; **Matt Meadows/Getty Images:** 528RC; **Bree Mercer/Getty Images:** 566R; **Art Meripol/Southern Living:** 448L2; **Alison Miksch/Southern Living:** 709R1; **Emily Minton/Southern Living:** 193LC; **MarkMirror/Shutterstock:** 639RC1; **Mizuki/a.collectionRF/Getty Images:** 124L; **MNS Photo/Alamy:** 434LC1, 61L; **Terrence Moore:** 615RC; **Lai Morris/Getty Images:** 475RC; **Maria Mosolova/Getty Images:** 50R1, 58L1, 119R4, 203L, 204RC, 363L, 497RC1, 497RC2, 407LC, 429RC, 454LC, 461R, 494L, 497R2, 560L2; **Moelyn Photos/Getty Images:** 467RC3; **courtesy of Monrovia:** 571LC1; **Arthur Mount:** 696 (all); **courtesy of Mountain Valley Growers, Inc.:** 332R2; **MsEli/Getty Images:** 529RC1; **Veena Nair/Getty Images:** 485RC; **Natural Sciences, Philadelphia/VIREO:** 86L2; **Nature's Inc/Getty Images:** 414RC; **Darlyne A. Murawski/Getty Images:** 265LC, 596LC; **Masahiro Nakano/ a. collectionRF images:** 53L2, 231LC; **Nature's Images/Getty Images:** 140LC, 487LC2; **Kimberly Navabpour/Sunset:** 130R, 144RC, 151LC, 166RC, 174RC, 201L, 242R, 268R, 413R, 453LC, 536R, 568RC, 651RC1, 685L, 699T; **Ngoc Minh Ngo/Getty Images:** 594L; **Clive Nichols/GAP Photos/Getty Images:** 320R; **Clive Nichols/Garden Picture Library/Photolibrary:** 637LC; **Helen Norman:** 306RC, 338L1, 338L2, 389RC, 444RC, 668L1, 700R1, 709R2, 710L3, 735C1; **John O'Hagan/Southern Living:** 246LC, 422RC, 440RC, 598RC; **George Olson/Sunset:** 661R3; **TOSHIAKIONO/a.collectionRF/Getty Images:** 93L1, 626RC; **courtesy of Pacific Plug and Liner:** 174LC, 226L, 301LC; **Panoramic Images/Getty Images:** 297RC, 361L; **Jerry Pavia:** 49L4, 54L1, 54L2, 54L4, 59L4, 59R4, 60L2, 62L4, 63L3, 74R1, 75R3, 79R3, 83R2, 84L2, 87L2, 96L2, 96L3, 97L1, 98R3, 106L3, 107R4, 113R4, 116R4, 117L2, 142L, 147L, 208RC, 217L, 218RC, 222LC, 247R, 262L, 279LC, 303L, 326L, 326LC, 368L, 391RC, 393RC, 409L, 409R, 427LC, 433LC, 440L, 452RC, 472LC, 485LC, 504L, 507RC, 518RC, 529LC, 540RC, 562LC, 590R, 614R, 622L; **Jerry Pavia/Getty Images:** 54R4, 80L1, 101L2, 109R4, 133LC, 147RC, 161L, 216LC, 283R, 351RC1, 387RC, 406RC; **Joann Pavia:** 118R2; **Greg Pease/Getty Images:** 532RC; **Pamela K Peirce:** 61R1, 718L3, 723L1, 726L1, 726L2, 726L4, 727L6, 727L4; **David E. Perry:** 143R; **Linda Lamb Peters/Sunset:** 125LC, 147LC, 170LC, 206R, 224LC, 230RC, 235LC, 238RC, 254LC, 274LC, 287LC, 302R, 312L, 312R, 327RC1, 338R, 368R,

ISBN-13: 978-0-8487-4298-0
ISBN-10: 0-8487-4298-2
Library of Congress Control Number: 2014918096

Printed in the United States of America
First Printing 2015

Oxmoor House

Editorial Director: Leah McLaughlin
Creative Director: Felicity Keane
Art Director: Christopher Rhoads
Executive Photo Director: Iain Bagwell
Photo Editor: Kellie Lindsey
Managing Editor: Elizabeth Tyler Austin
Assistant Managing Editor: Jeanne de Lathouder

The New Southern Living® Garden Book

Garden Editors: Steve Bender, Gene Bussell
Editor: Susan Hernandez Ray
Project Editor: Emily Chappell Connolly
Designer: Allison Sperando Potter
Editorial Assistant: April Smitherman
Senior Production Managers: Greg Amason, Sue Chodakiewicz
Photographers: Robbie Caponetto, Laurey W. Glenn, Hector Sanchez
Photo Editor: Paden Reich
Assistant Photo Editor: Kate Phillips Robertson
Production Manager: Mary Elizabeth McGinn Davis
Assistant Production Manager: Rachel Ellis
Photo Administrative Assistant: Courtney Authement

Time Home Entertainment Inc.

Publisher: Margot Schupf
Vice President, Finance: Vandana Patel
Executive Director, Marketing Services: Carol Pittard
Publishing Director: Megan Pearlman
Assistant General Counsel: Simone Procas

Contributors:

Managing Editor: Linda Askey
Senior Editors: Lance Walheim, Tom Wilhite
Writer: Dawn Cannon
Associate Garden Editor: Rebecca Reed
Photographers: Ralph Anderson, Lee Anderson
Assistant Production Manager: Christy Coleman
Designer: Cathy Robbins
Copy Editor: Rebecca Benton Henderson
Proofreader: Barry Wise Smith
Project Editor: Megan Thompson Brown
Photo Editor: Stacy Allen, Karen Williams
Fellows: Kylie Dazzo, Nicole Fisher, Anna Maria Jacob, Amy Pinney, Anna Ramia

Special Consultants:

Allan Armitage
Tony Avent
Richard Bir
Mark Chamblee
Arnold Caylor
Dave Creech
Micahel Dirr
Janet Egger
Jenks Farmer
Greg Gran
Stephen F. Austin
Robert D. Hartman
Brent and Becky Heath
Dan Heims
Hayes Jackson
Noris Ledesma
Roger Lewis, Jr.
David W. Marshall
Bob McCartney
Bert McCarty
James D. McCreight
Tom MacCubbin
Dean Norton
Ken Oakes
David Parks
Jerry Parsons
Arlie Powell
Jason Powell
Robert Saunders
Judith Knot Tyler
Chris Van Cleave
Maarten van der Giessen
Mark Viette
Jeff Wasielewski, M.S.
Jenny Wegley
Todd C. Wehner
Dennis J. Werner
Paul Westervelt
Brian Williams

Bringing a modern twist to
an old tradition, this bottle
tree is crafted from iron.